Oxford Textbook of

Anaesthesia

Oxford Textbooks in Anaesthesia

Oxford Textbook of Anaesthesia
Edited by Jonathan G. Hardman, Philip M. Hopkins, and Michel M. R. F Struys

Oxford Textbook of Anaesthesia for the Elderly Patient
Edited by Chris Dodds, Chandra M. Kumar, and Bernadette Th. Veering

Oxford Textbook of Anaesthesia for Oral and Maxillofacial Surgery
Edited by Ian Shaw, Chandra M. Kumar, and Chris Dodds

Oxford Textbook of Cardiothoracic Anaesthesia
Edited by R. Peter Alston, Paul S. Myles, and Marco Ranucci

Oxford Textbook of Obstetric Anaesthesia
Edited by Vicki Clark, Marc Van de Velde, and Roshan Fernando

Oxford Textbook of Transplant Anaesthesia and Critical Care
Edited by Ernesto A. Pretto, Jr, Gianni Biancofiore, Andre De Wolf, John R. Klinck, Claus Niemann, Andrew Watts, and Peter D. Slinger

Principles and Practice of Regional Anaesthesia, Fourth Edition
Edited by Graeme McLeod, Colin McCartney, and Tony Wildsmith

Free personal online access for 12 months

Individual purchasers of this book are also entitled to free personal access to the online edition for 12 months on *Oxford Medicine Online* (www.oxfordmedicine.com). Please refer to the access token card in Volume 1 for instructions on token redemption and access.

Online ancillary materials, where available, are noted at the end of the respective chapters in this book. Additionally, *Oxford Medicine Online* allows you to print, save, cite, email, and share content; download high-resolution figures as Microsoft PowerPoint slides; save often-used books, chapters, or searches; annotate; and quickly jump to other chapters or related material on a mobile-optimized platform.

We encourage you to take advantage of these features. If you are interested in ongoing access after the 12-month gift period, please consider an individual subscription or consult with your librarian.

VOLUME 2

Oxford Textbook of
Anaesthesia

Edited by

Jonathan G. Hardman

Professor and Head, Anaesthetics & Critical Care, School of Medicine, University of Nottingham
Consultant Anaesthetist, Nottingham University Hospitals NHS Trust, Nottingham, UK

Philip M. Hopkins

Professor of Anaesthesia, University of Leeds
Honorary Consultant Anaesthetist, Leeds Teaching Hospitals NHS Trust, St James's University Hospital, Leeds, UK

Michel M. R. F. Struys

Professor and Chair, Department of Anesthesiology, University of Groningen, University Medical Center Groningen, Groningen, The Netherlands
Professor in Anaesthesia, Ghent University, Gent, Belgium

Great Clarendon Street, Oxford, OX2 6DP,
United Kingdom

Oxford University Press is a department of the University of Oxford. It furthers the University's objective of excellence in research, scholarship, and education by publishing worldwide. Oxford is a registered trade mark of Oxford University Press in the UK and in certain other countries

First Edition Published in 2017

Impression: 1

Published in the United States of America by Oxford University Press
198 Madison Avenue, New York, NY 10016, United States of America

British Library Cataloguing in Publication Data
Data available

Library of Congress Control Number: 2016952559

Set ISBN 978-0-19-964204-5
Volume 1 978-0-19-870847-6
Volume 2 978-0-19-870848-3
Only available as part of a set

Printed in Great Britain by
Bell & Bain Ltd., Glasgow

To my Mother, who inspired my work but will never read it; to my Father, who made all my achievements possible; and to my loving wife and three daughters, who mean the world to me.

J.H.

To Carmel, for ignoring what I said when I completed my last book and for being my rock.

P.H.

To Dominique, Olivier, Mathieu, Thibault, and Louis for their never-ending support.

M.S.

Foreword

While one could be forgiven for thinking that the era of a single, comprehensive anaesthetic textbook has been superseded by the need for a series of individual specialist texts, this is certainly not the case for the vast majority of anaesthetists, who tend to be generalists with a special interest. During training, anaesthetists are exposed to all the major surgical subspecialties, together with intensive care medicine and pain management, but also need to acquire skill and versatility to treat patients in a variety of non-theatre environments. On the one hand, these two volumes are a comprehensive 'bible' of all that the anaesthetic trainee needs to know to pass their general and specialist anaesthetic examinations and complete their higher training. On the other, they provide a single reference for everything that one is likely to encounter as a specialist, who, in all but the most specialist hospitals, will normally provide anaesthesia for a variety of surgical specialities, together perhaps with one or two special interests. The real issue for the general clinical anaesthetist is their acute, on-call commitment, when they may be asked to work outside their normal comfort zone, particularly in the non-teaching hospital environment. Having access to a comprehensive and up-to-date text book is a vital reference point, which many will find invaluable during their clinical practice. This book is therefore something which, having been one's bedrock during training, will provide an invaluable reference point in one's subsequent clinical practice.

Written by clinicians for clinicians, arranged in two volumes along familiar lines, and with contributions from eminent anaesthesiologists from around the world, this *Oxford Textbook of Anaesthesia* sets out both the evidence base and current practice in anaesthesia from first principles. It not only covers those areas that traditionally are part of a basic science and clinically orientated textbook of this nature, but also includes a number of new and innovative areas which are increasingly important and yet, apart from reading individual journal articles, are not available in a collated form for the clinician to read and understand.

Volume one focuses on applied basic science in anaesthesia together with evidence-based medicine and the practice and management of anaesthesia, the latter comprising a collection of chapters of major relevance to modern anaesthetic practice. Each chapter is well set out using colour to highlight text alongside excellent diagrams, illustrations and photographs. The chapter on central nervous system physiology in anaesthetic practice is an example of up to date knowledge on theories of consciousness, sleep and memory and their implications for anaesthesia. This volume concludes with two excellent and relevant chapters on post-surgical analgesia and acute pain management.

The second volume centres on clinical practice, beginning with up to date anaesthetic techniques and including two additional chapters on conscious sedation and blood conservation and transfusion. Regional anaesthesia of the upper and lower limbs, extensively illustrated by the use of ultrasound images is followed by chapters on the conduct of anaesthesia for each surgical specialty. These are a key part of any comprehensive textbook written either for those in training, or for the general anaesthetist confronted with occasional problems outside a specialist unit and needing to have an up to date understanding of current practice. The chapter on cardiac anaesthesia is an excellent example of such a sub-speciality overview, after which one would need to resort to specialist textbooks. The same is true of neuroanaesthesia, neuroradiology and intensive care.

By contrast, there is a comprehensive section on paediatric anaesthesia, which gives excellent guidance to the occasional paediatric anaesthetist as well as the trainee and certainly cautions that children are certainly not just small adults! The chapter on ethics, consent, and safeguarding in paediatric anaesthesia is particularly opportune. Chapters on pre-hospital care and military anaesthesia also significantly enhance the breadth and depth of the whole book. Again by contrast, the final section on critical care is simply limited to four important areas for the general anaesthetist, thus avoiding trying to recreate a comprehensive textbook on intensive care medicine within a general text.

In this new and innovative *Oxford Textbook of Anaesthesia*, the authors, under the close direction of the three editors, have produced an outstanding text, relevant to both trainees and established clinicians alike. The extensive use of illustrations, photographs and diagrams makes the text easy to read and dividing it up into small relevant sections, allows the reader to rapidly access the necessary information. Written by experts in their individual fields and yet with an acute awareness of their readers' needs, I am sure that this textbook will become one of the key anaesthetic texts in the United Kingdom, in Europe and further afield.

Sir Peter Simpson
MD FRCA FRCP FRCS (Hon) FCARCSI (Hon)
Past President, Royal College of Anaesthetists
Past President, European Society of Anaesthesiology

Preface

The *Oxford Textbook* series represents the pre-eminent authority on medical practice worldwide. In creating this, the first edition of the *Oxford Textbook of Anaesthesia*, a unique opportunity was presented: to craft a major scholarly work detailing the evidence base and current practice in anaesthesia from the ground up. Not being shackled to previous contents lists or existing editors, we have designed this textbook from the many years of learning and the ongoing scientific endeavour that underpin our specialty. While we are each experienced researchers, authors, and book and journal editors, foremost we are practising anaesthetists who are passionate about providing the very best clinical care to our patients: we hope that this is reflected in this book.

This two-volume, comprehensive work has been written by leading experts as the definitive resource for anaesthetists. It covers all aspects of anaesthesia, including those aspects of intensive care and pain medicine that are core knowledge for the general anaesthetist. While it focuses on the clinical aspects of anaesthesia, it also covers the underpinning sciences, the understanding of which is required for a logical, effective, and evidence-based approach to practice.

In aspiring to match the quality of other titles in the *Oxford Textbook* series, our chapter authors have been invited as representing the very pinnacle of practice, learning, and prestige in their discipline. Contributors have been drawn from across the globe, although we have concentrated our invitations in the United Kingdom, Europe, and Commonwealth countries in order to maintain a necessary degree of standardization of the context of practice and consistency of content. The contributing authors are all experts in the relevant field, either through appropriate research, extensive clinical experience in the specialist area, other demonstrable relevant scholarly activity, or a combination of these. However, where they present their own preferred approach to clinical management of a specific condition or surgical procedure it must be recognized that other techniques may be equally valid in the hands of an anaesthetist with the relevant experience and expertise.

Today's anaesthetists need to access trustworthy up-to-date information while on the move. In response to this, the *Oxford Textbook of Anaesthesia* will publish both in print and online on *Oxford Medicine Online* where it can be accessed via smartphones and other devices. The online version will be updated annually to reflect major changes in clinical practice. The print edition of the *Oxford Textbook of Anaesthesia* comes with a year's access to the online version. By activating your unique access code, you can print, save, cite, email, and share content; download high-resolution figures as Microsoft PowerPoint slides; and save often-used chapters, or searches, all on a mobile-optimized platform. By closely linking the printed book to the online edition and by pursuing this integration between major textbook and portable device, we hope to re-invigorate the usability and popularity of the 'tome of anaesthesia', rendering it indispensable to anaesthetists of all grades and subspecialty interest.

We see this book as being essential for all anaesthetists who require a comprehensive text covering all aspects of anaesthesia. With its focus on UK, European, and Commonwealth practice, it brings a fresh insight and coverage of our specialty. We very much hope that you find the *Oxford Textbook of Anaesthesia* brings benefit to your working lives and to the treatment your patients receive.

Producing this edition has been a mammoth task, coordinating the efforts of over 160 authors from all corners of the world. We thank all those who have contributed to this project.

January 2017

J. G. Hardman
P. M. Hopkins
M. M. R. F. Struys

Acknowledgements

From conception to completion this book has taken more than six years. The scale of the project and the current pressures on clinicians and academics have meant that we have been entirely dependent on the goodwill, patience, and dedication of our colleagues who have authored the chapters—we are extremely grateful to them all. We particularly want to thank Tony Wilkes, Neil Morton, Peter Mahoney, and Neil Soni for providing additional assistance as co-editors of specialist sections. We would also like to thank all at Oxford University Press who have made this book possible.

Brief contents

Contents

Abbreviations

3D	three-dimensional
5-HT	5-hydroxytryptamine (serotonin)
AAA	abdominal aortic aneurysm
AAGA	accidental awareness during general anaesthesia
AAGBI	Association of Anaesthetists of Great Britain and Ireland
ACC	American College of Cardiology
ACE	angiotensin-converting enzyme
ACEI	angiotensin-converting enzyme inhibitor
ADE	adverse drug event
ADH	antidiuretic hormone
ADP	adenosine diphosphate
AER	auditory-evoked response
AF	atrial fibrillation
AHA	American Heart Association
AHVR	acute hypoxic ventilatory response
AIMS	anaesthetic information management system
AKI	acute kidney injury
ALF	airway lining fluid
ALS	advanced life support
ANTS	anaesthetists' non-technical skills
APC	antigen-presenting cell
aPTT	activated partial thromboplastin time
ARDS	acute respiratory distress syndrome
ASA	American Society of Anesthesiologists
ASM	airway smooth muscle
ATP	adenosine triphosphate
AVP	arginine vasopressin
BBB	blood–brain barrier
BIS™	Bispectral Index™
BNP	B-type natriuretic peptide
BP	blood pressure
BSA	body surface area
CA	carbonic anhydrase
CABG	coronary artery bypass graft
CAD	coronary artery disease
cAMP	cyclic adenosine monophosphate
CBF	cerebral blood flow
CCA	closed-circuit anaesthesia
CCI	corrected count increment
CD	cluster of differentiation
CEA	carotid endarterectomy
CICO	can't intubate, can't oxygenate
CLAB	central line-associated bacteraemia
CNS	central nervous system
CO	cardiac output *or* carbon monoxide
COPD	chronic obstructive pulmonary disease
CPAP	continuous positive airway pressure
CPB	cardiopulmonary bypass
CPG	central pattern generator
CPNB	continuous peripheral nerve block
CPR	cardiopulmonary resuscitation
CPSP	chronic postsurgical pain
CRH	corticotrophin-releasing hormone
CRP	C-reactive protein
CSA	continuous spinal anaesthesia
CSE	combined spinal–epidural
CSF	cerebrospinal fluid
CSHT	context-sensitive half-time
CT	computed tomography
cTn	cardiac troponin
CVC	central venous catheterization
CVP	central venous pressure
CVS	cardiovascular system
CYP	cytochrome P450
DBP	diastolic blood pressure
DBS	double-burst stimulation
DIC	disseminated intravascular coagulation
DMN	default mode network
DPG	diphosphoglycerate
DRG	dorsal respiratory group
DSE	dobutamine stress echocardiography
DVT	deep vein thrombosis
EBA	European Board of Anaesthesiology
ECF	extracellular fluid
ECG	electrocardiogram/electrocardiography
EEG	electroencephalogram/electroencephalography
EMG	electromyogram/electromyography
EPR	electronic patient record
ERP	event-related potential
ESA	European Society of Anaesthesiology
ESC	European Society of Cardiology
*F*A	alveolar gas concentration
*F*a	arterial gas concentration
FDA	Food and Drug Administration
FE_{Na}	fractional urinary sodium excretion

FEV_1	forced expiratory volume in one second
FFT	fast Fourier transformation
*F*I	inspired gas concentration
$F_{I_{O_2}}$	fraction of inspired oxygen
fMRI	functional magnetic resonance imaging
FRC	functional residual capacity
FSH	follicle-stimulating hormone
FVC	forced vital capacity
GA	general anaesthesia
GABA	γ-aminobutyric acid
GDFT	goal-directed fluid therapy
GDHT	goal-directed haemodynamic therapy
GFR	glomerular filtration rate
GH	growth hormone
GHRH	growth hormone-releasing hormone
GI	gastrointestinal
GICU	general intensive care unit
GMC	General Medical Council
GMP	guanosine monophosphate
GP	glycoprotein
GPCR	G protein-coupled receptors
HbA_1	glycosylated haemoglobin
HbCO	carboxyhaemoglobin
HbF	fetal haemoglobin
HbF	haemoglobin
HbO_2	oxyhaemoglobin
HCT	haematocrit
HHb	deoxyhaemoglobin
HLA	human leucocyte antigen
HNA	human neutrophil antigen
HPA	hypothalamic–pituitary–adrenal *or* human platelet antigen
HPV	hypoxic pulmonary vasoconstriction
HR	hazard ratio
HRQL	health-related quality of life
HRV	heart rate variability
HTA	health technology assessment
HTR	haemolytic transfusion reaction
I:E	inspiratory:expiratory
IASP	International Association for the Study of Pain
ICF	intracellular fluid
ICP	intracranial pressure
ICU	intensive care unit
IGF	insulin-like growth factor
IGL	ideal gas law
IHCA	in-hospital cardiac arrest
IL	interleukin
IMP	investigational medicinal product
INR	international normalized ratio
IOM	Institute of Medicine
IOP	input–output principle
ISO	International Organization for Standardization
K_d	equilibrium dissociation constant
LAST	local anaesthetic systemic toxicity
LC	locus coeruleus
LED	light-emitting diode
LGIC	ligand-gated ion channel
LH	luteinizing hormone
LMA	laryngeal mask airway
LV	left ventricular
MAC	minimum alveolar concentration
MAP	mean arterial pressure
MET	metabolic equivalent
MetHB	methaemoglobin
MHC	major histocompatibility complex
MHRA	Medicines and Healthcare products Regulatory Agency
MI	myocardial infarction
MLAC	minimum local analgesic concentration
MPS	myocardial perfusion scintigraphy
MSCT	multislice computed tomography
MV	minute ventilation
nAChR	nicotinic acetylcholine receptor
NADH	nicotinamide adenine dinucleotide, reduced form
NDNMBA	non-depolarizing neuromuscular blocking agent
NEFA	non-esterified fatty acid
NIAA	National Institute of Academic Anaesthesia
NIBP	non-invasive blood pressure
NIOSH	National Institute of Occupational Safety and Health
NK	natural killer
NMB	neuromuscular block
NMBA	neuromuscular blocking agent
NMDA	*N*-methyl-D-aspartate
NNH	number-needed-to harm
NNT	number-needed-to-treat
NSAID	non-steroidal anti-inflammatory drug
NSQIP	National Surgical Quality Improvement Program
NSRI	Noxious Stimulus Response Index
NT-proBNP	N-terminal pro-B-type natriuretic peptide
NWMA	new wall motion abnormality
OLV	one-lung ventilation
OR	odds ratio
Pa_{CO_2}	arterial carbon dioxide tension
PACU	post-anaesthesia care unit
PAF	platelet-activating factor
Pa_{O_2}	arterial oxygen tension
PBPK	physiologically based pharmacokinetic
PCA	patient-controlled analgesia
PCC	posterior cingulate cortex
PCEA	patient-controlled epidural analgesia
PCI	percutaneous coronary intervention
P_{CO_2}	partial pressure of carbon dioxide
PD	pharmacodynamic
PDE	phosphodiesterase
PE	pulmonary embolism
PEEP	positive end-expiratory pressure
PEFR	peak expiratory flow rate
PET	positron emission tomography
PICC	peripherally inserted central catheter
PK	pharmacokinetic
pK_a	negative decadic logarithm of the acid dissociation constant
PMI	perioperative myocardial infarction
PMS	patient-maintained sedation
P_{O_2}	partial pressure of oxygen
POCD	postoperative cognitive dysfunction
POISE	PeriOperative ISchemic Evaluation

POMS	Postoperative Morbidity Survey
PONV	postoperative nausea and vomiting
PPG	pulse plethysmography
ppm	parts per million
PRBC	packed red blood cell
PRD	pupillary reflex dilation
PRIS	propofol infusion syndrome
PRR	pattern recognition receptor
PTC	post-tetanic count
PVC	polyvinyl chloride
PVR	pulmonary vascular resistance
QEEG	quantitative electroencephalogram
RA	regional anaesthesia
RBC	red blood cell
rCBF	regional cerebral blood flow
RCoA	Royal College of Anaesthetists
RCT	randomized controlled trial
RE	Response Entropy
RM	recruitment manoeuvre
ROSC	return of spontaneous circulation
RR	relative risk
RV	residual volume
Sa_{O_2}	arterial oxygen saturation
SBP	systolic blood pressure
SD	standard deviation
SDL	self-directed learning
SE	State Entropy
SEM	standard error of the mean
SHM	simple harmonic motion
SID	strong ion difference
SNP	single-nucleotide polymorphism
SP	surfactant protein
SPECT	single-photon emission computed tomography
SSI	surgical site infection
SSRI	selective serotonin reuptake inhibitor
TAP	transversus abdominis plane
TBW	total body water
TCI	target-controlled infusion
TCR	T-cell receptor
TIVA	total intravenous anaesthesia
TLC	total lung capacity
TLR	Toll-like receptor
TMN	tuberomammillary nucleus
TNS	transient neurological symptoms
TOE	transoesophageal echocardiography
TOF	train-of-four
TRALI	transfusion-related acute lung injury
TRIM	transfusion-related immunomodulation
TRP	transient receptor potential
TSH	thyroid-stimulating hormone
TTP	thrombotic thrombocytopenic purpura
TTX	tetrodotoxin
$\dot{V}/\dot{Q}$	ventilation/perfusion
VAS	visual analogue scale
VATS	video-assisted thoracic surgery
VC	vital capacity
V_c	central volume of distribution
V_d	volume of distribution
V_{dss}	volume of distribution at steady state
VLPO	ventrolateral preoptic nucleus
VT	tidal volume
VTE	venous thromboembolism
WDR	wide dynamic range
WFSA	World Federation of Anaesthesiologists
WHO	World Health Organization

Part editors

Professor Jonathan G. Hardman, Anaesthetics & Critical Care, School of Medicine, University of Nottingham; Consultant Anaesthetist, Nottingham University Hospital NHS Trust, Nottingham, UK
Parts 1, 3, 4, 6, 10, and 13

Professor Philip M. Hopkins, University of Leeds; Honorary Consultant Anaesthetist, Leeds Teaching Hospitals NHS Trust, St James's University Hospital, Leeds, UK
Parts 5, 8, 9, and 12, and assisted with Part 6

Colonel Peter F. Mahoney, Emeritus Defence Professor Anaesthesia, Royal Centre for Defence Medicine, Birmingham, UK
Part 11

Dr Neil S. Morton, Consultant in Paediatric Anaesthesia and Pain Management, Royal Hospital for Sick Children, Glasgow, UK
Part 10

Dr Neil Soni, Consultant in Intensive Care and Anaesthesia, Chelsea and Westminster Hospital, London, UK
Part 13

Professor Michel M. R. F. Struys, Department of Anesthesiology, University of Groningen, University Medical Center Groningen, Groningen, The Netherlands; Ghent University, Gent, Belgium
Parts 2, 7, and 11

Professor Antony R. Wilkes, Consultant in Medical Devices, Edinburgh, UK
Part 3 and assisted with Part 6

Contributors

Anthony Absalom, Department of Anesthesiology, University Medical Center Groningen, University of Groningen, Groningen, The Netherlands

Ram Adapa, Cambridge University Hospitals NHS Foundation Trust, and University of Cambridge, Cambridge, UK

Dominic Aldington, Department of Anaesthetics, Royal Hampshire County Hospital, Winchester, UK

Peter D. G. Alexander, University Hospital of South Manchester, and University of Manchester, Manchester, UK

Brian J. Anderson, Department of Anaesthesiology, University of Auckland, Auckland, New Zealand

Takashi Asai, Department of Anesthesiology, Dokkyo Medical University Koshigaya Hospital, Koshigaya City, Saitama, Japan

Simon Ash, Department of Anesthesia, Memorial University Newfoundland, St. John's, NL, Canada

Christophe Aveline, Private Hospital Sevigne, Department of Anaesthesia and Intensive Care, Cesson Sevigne, France

Sanjay Bajaj, Khoo Teck Puat Hospital, Singapore

Katy Beard, Morriston Hospital, Cwmrhydyceirw, Swansea, UK

Mark Bellamy, Intensive Care Unit, St James's University Hospital, Leeds, UK

Andrew Berrill, Department of Anaesthesia, Leeds General Infirmary, Leeds, UK

Paul Bhalla, Royal National Orthopaedic Hospital, Stanmore, UK

Valérie Billard, Gustave Roussy Cancer Center, Département of Anesthésia & Surgical Intensive Care, Villejuif, France

Julian Bion, University of Birmingham, University Department of Intensive Care Medicine, Birmingham, UK

Peter Biro, Institute of Anesthesiology, University Hospital Zurich, Zurich, Switzerland

Andrew R. Bodenham, Department of Anaesthesia and ICM, Leeds General Infirmary, Leeds, UK

Francis Bonnet, Université Pierre & Marie Curie Paris VI, Assistance Publique Hôpitaux de Paris, Paris, France

Adrian Bosenberg, Department of Anesthesiology, Seattle Children's Hospital, University of Washington, Seattle, WA, USA

G. Boukes Eindhoven, University Medical Center Groningen, University of Groningen, Groningen, The Netherlands

Sebastian Brandt, Department of Anaesthesiology and Intensive Care Medicine, University Medical Center Schleswig-Holstein, Campus Lübeck, Lübeck, Germany

Donal J. Buggy, Mater University Hospital, School of Medicine, University College Dublin, Dublin, Ireland

Maxime Cannesson, Department of Anesthesiology and Perioperative Medicine, David Geffen School of Medicine at UCLA, Los Angeles, California, USA

Maurizio Cecconi, Anaesthesia and Intensive Care, St George's University Hospitals Foundation Trust, London, UK

Chi Wai Cheung, Department of Anaesthesiology, The University of Hong Kong, Hong Kong, China

Andrew J. Clarkin, Intensive Care Unit, Aberdeen Royal Infirmary, Aberdeen, UK

Malachy O. Columb, University Hospital of South Manchester, Wythenshawe, Manchester, UK

Lesley A. Colvin, Department of Anaesthesia, Critical Care & Pain Medicine, University of Edinburgh, Western General Hospital, Edinburgh, UK

Alistair Cranston, Department of Anaesthesia, Birmingham Children's Hospital NHS Trust, Birmingham, UK

Nicholas Crombie, Queen Elizabeth Hospital Birmingham, UK; Midlands Air Ambulance, DCAE Cosford, Albrighton, UK

Steven Cruickshank, Department of Anaesthesia and Critical Care, Royal Victoria Infirmary, Newcastle upon Tyne, UK

Andrew Davidson, Department of Anaesthesia, Royal Children's Hospital, Parkville, VIC, Australia

Joost T. M. de Wolf, previously at University Medical Center Groningen, Groningen, The Netherlands

Bert Dercksen, University Medical Centre Groningen, Department of Anesthesiology/HEMS 'Lifeliner 4', Groningen, The Netherlands

Chris Dodds, James Cook University Hospital, Middlesbrough, UK (retired)

Natalie Drury, Consultant in Anaesthesia, St James's University Hospital, Leeds, UK

Douglas Eleveld, Department of Anesthesiology, University Medical Center Groningen, University of Groningen, Groningen, The Netherlands

Mfonobong Essiet, Department of Anesthesiology & Perioperative Care, University of California, Irvine, CA, USA

Marie T. Fallon, University of Edinburgh, Edinburgh, UK

Peter A. Farling, Department of Anaesthetics, Royal Victoria Hospital, Belfast, UK

William J. Fawcett, Department of Anaesthesia, Royal Surrey County Hospital NHS Foundation Trust, Guildford; University of Surrey, Guildford, UK

Laura Flutter, Queen Elizabeth Hospital, Birmingham, UK

Christopher Frerk, Department of Anaesthesia & Critical Care, Northampton General Hospital, Northampton, UK

Michael Fries, Department of Anesthesiology, University Hospital RWTH Aachen, Aachen, Germany

Thomas Fuchs-Buder, Université de Lorraine, Faculté de Médicine, Département d'Anesthésie-Réanimation, Nancy, France

Helen F. Galley, University of Aberdeen, School of Medicine, Medical Sciences and Nutrition, Aberdeen, UK

Hartmut Gehring, University Medical Center Schleswig-Holstein, Campus Lübeck, Department of Anesthesiology and Intensive Care Medicine, Lübeck, Germany

Marc E. Gentili, Department of Anaesthesia and Intensive Care, Centre Hospitalier Privé Saint-Grégoire, Saint-Grégoire, France

Steven J. Gill, Department of Intensive Care Medicine, Nottingham University Hospitals NHS Trust, Nottingham, UK

Ronnie Glavin, Scottish Centre for Clinical Simulation and Human Factors, Forth Valley Royal Hospital, Larbert, Falkirk, UK

Joanna K. Gordon, The Leeds Teaching Hospitals NHS Trust, Leeds, UK

Erin A. Gottlieb, Texas Children's Hospital-Baylor College of Medicine, Division of Pediatric Cardiovascular Anesthesiology, TX, USA

J. K. Götz Wietasch, Department of Anaesthesiology, University Medical Center Groningen, University of Groningen, Groningen, The Netherlands

Pawan Gupta, Leeds Teaching Hospitals, Leeds, UK

Robert G. Hahn, Södertälje Hospital, Södertälje, Sweden

George M. Hall, Department of Anaesthesia and Intensive Care Medicine, St George's Hospital Medical School, London, UK

Mark Hamilton, St George's Hospital, London, UK

Tom G. Hansen, Department of Anaesthesia & Intensive Care – Paediatric Section, Odense University Hospital, and Department of Clinical Research, University of Southern Denmark, Odense, Denmark

Jonathan G. Hardman, Anaesthetics & Critical Care, School of Medicine, University of Nottingham; Nottingham University Hospital NHS Trust, Nottingham, UK

Jan F. A. Hendrickx, OLV Hospital, Department of Anesthesiology/CCM, Aalst, Belgium

Herman G. D. Hendriks, University Medical Center Groningen, Department of Anesthesiology, Groningen, The Netherlands

Stefan De Hert, Department of Anesthesiology, Ghent University Hospital, Ghent University, Ghent, Belgium

W. Hiu Lam, Department of Anaesthesia, Plymouth Hospitals NHS Trust, Plymouth, UK; Health Education England (South West), UK

Kwok M. Ho, Department of Intensive Care Medicine, Royal Perth Hospital, School of Population Health, University of Western Australia, School of Veterinary & Life Sciences, Murdoch University, Perth, WA, Australia

Philip M. Hopkins, University of Leeds & Honorary Consultant Anaesthetist, Leeds Teaching Hospitals NHS Trust, St James's University Hospital, Leeds, UK

Simon Howell, Leeds Institute of Biomedical and Clinical Sciences, University of Leeds, Leeds, UK

Jennifer M. Hunter, University of Liverpool, Liverpool, UK

Michael G. Irwin, Department of Anaesthesiology, University of Hong Kong, Queen Mary Hospital and HKU Shenzhen Hospital, Hong Kong, China

Jan Jakobsson, Institution for Clinical Science, Karolinsak Institutet, Department of Anaesthesia, Danderyds Hospital, Stockholm, Sweden

Michael F. M. James, Department of Anaesthesia, University of Cape Town, Cape Town, Western Cape, South Africa

Robert Jan Stolker, Department of Anesthesiology, Erasmus University Medical Center, Rotterdam, The Netherlands

Ian A. Jenkins, Wales and West Acute Transport for Children, Southwest Paediatric Intensive Care Unit, Bristol Royal Hospital for Children, Bristol, UK

Will Jones, Leeds Teaching Hospitals NHS Trust, Leeds, UK

Cor J. Kalkman, Division of Anesthesiology, Intensive Care & Emergency Medicine, University Medical Centre Utrecht, Utrecht, The Netherlands

Hanane El Kenz, Blood Bank Department, CHU-Brugmann, Université Libre de Bruxelles, Blood Bank Department, Hôpital Universitaire Des Enfants Reine Fabiola (HUDERF), Université Libre de Bruxelles, Brussels, Belgium

Emrys Kirkman, CBR Division, Dstl Porton Down, Salisbury, UK

Markus Klimek, Department of Anesthesiology, Erasmus University Medical Center, Rotterdam, The Netherlands

Johannes (Hans) T. A. Knape, Division of Anaesthesiology, Intensive Care & Emergency Medicine, University Medical Centre Utrecht, Utrecht, The Netherlands

Andreas Koster, Institute of Anaesthesiology, Heart and Diabetes Centre NRW, Bad Oeynhausen, Germany

Chandra M. Kumar, Khoo Teck Puat Hospital, Singapore

David G. Lambert, Department of Cardiovascular Sciences, Division of Anaesthesia, Critical Care and Pain Management, University of Leicester, Leicester Royal Infirmary, Leicester, UK

Felix van Lier, Department of Anesthesiology, Erasmus University Medical Center, Rotterdam, The Netherlands

Philippe Van der Linden, Department of Anesthesiology, CHU Brugmann, Department of Anesthesiology, Hôpital Universitaire des Enfants Reine Fabiola (HUDERF), Université Libre de Bruxelles, Brussels, Belgium

Francisco A. Lobo, Anesthesiology Department, Division of Neuroanesthesia, Hospital Geral de Santo António, Centro Hospitalar do Porto, Porto, Portugal

Stephan A. Loer, Department of Anaesthesiology, VU University Medical Center Amsterdam, Amsterdam, The Netherlands

Martin Luginbühl, Department of Anesthesia and Pain Medicine, University of Bern, Spital Tiefenau, Bern, Switzerland

Andrew B. Lumb, Department of Anaesthetics, School of Medicine, University of Leeds, Leeds, UK

Alan J. R. Macfarlane, Department of Anaesthesia, Glasgow Royal Infirmary, Honorary Clinical Senior Lecturer, Anaesthesia, Pain and Critical Care Medicine, University of Glasgow, Glasgow, UK

Anthony P. Madden, Past President, Society for Computing and Technology in Anaesthesia, Retired Consultant Anaesthetist, Southmead Hospital, Bristol, UK

Patrick Magee, Bath Anaesthetic Group, Bath, UK

Peter F. Mahoney, Royal Centre for Defence Medicine, Birmingham, UK

Bruno Marciniak, Clinique d anesthésie réanimation de l hôpital Jeanne de Flandre, CHRU, Lille, France

Gernot Marx, Klinik für operative Intensivmedizin und Intermediate Care, University Hospital Aachen, Aachen, Germany

Colin J. L. McCartney, University of Ottawa, The Ottawa Hospital, Ottawa, ON, Canada

Jillian McFadzean, Royal Hospital for Sick Children, Edinburgh, UK

Alistair G. McKenzie, Department of Anaesthesia, Critical Care & Pain Medicine, Royal Infirmary of Edinburgh, Edinburgh, UK

Christoph Melzer-Gartzke, Department of Anaesthesiology and Intensive Care Medicine, Charité Universitätsmedizin Berlin, Campus Virchow-Klinikum, Berlin, Germany

Simon J. Mercer, Royal Navy, Surgeon Commander, Defence Medical Services, Aintree University, NHS Foundation Trust, Liverpool; Centre for Simulation and Patient Safety, NHS North West, Liverpool, UK

Alan F. Merry, University of Auckland, Auckland City Hospital, Auckland, New Zealand

Gary H. Mills, Sheffield Teaching Hospitals NHS Foundation Trust, University of Sheffield, Sheffield, UK

Gary Minto, Plymouth University Peninsula School of Medicine, Consultant, Derriford Hospital, Plymouth, UK

Simon J. Mitchell, Department of Anaesthesiology, University of Auckland, Consultant Anaesthetist, Auckland City Hospital, Auckland, New Zealand

Ann Merete Møller, Research Unit, Department of Anaesthesiology, Herlev Hospital, Copenhagen; Cochrane Anaesthesia, Critical Care and Emergency Medicine Group, Copenhagen, Denmark

Anthony Moores, Anaesthetic Department, Royal Hospital for Children, Glasgow, UK

Iain Moppett, Anaesthesia & Critical Care, School of Medicine, University of Nottingham, UK

Margareta Mure, Karolinska Institutet and Department of Anesthesiology and Intensive Care, Karolinska University Hospital Solna, Stockholm, Sweden

Michael H. Nathanson, Nottingham University Hospitals NHS Trust, UK

Grainne Nicholson, Department of Anaesthesia, St George's University of London, UK

Jerry P. Nolan, Royal United Hospital, Bath, UK

Giles Nordmann, Academic Department of Military Anaesthesia, Royal Centre for Defence Medicine, Birmingham, UK

Suzanne Odeberg-Wernerman, Karolinska Institutet and Department of Anaesthesiology and Intensive Care Medicine, Karolinska University Hospital Huddinge, Stockholm, Sweden

Klaus T. Olkkola, Department of Anaesthesiology, Intensive Care and Pain Medicine, University of Helsinki and Helsinki University Hospital, Helsinki, Finland

Erik Olofsen, Department of Anesthesiology, Leiden University Medical Center, Leiden, The Netherlands

Sandip K. Pal, Department of Anaesthesia, Broomfield Hospital, Regional Centre for Plastic Surgery and Burns, Chelmsford, UK

David Pegg, Anaesthetic Department, Leeds General Infirmary, Leeds, UK

Tom Pettigrew, Queen Elizabeth University Hospital, Glasgow, UK

Michael A.E. Ramsay, Baylor University Medical Center, Dallas, TX, USA

Komal Ray, St James's University Hospital, Leeds, UK

J. Robert Sneyd, Plymouth University Peninsula Schools of Medicine and Dentistry, Plymouth, UK

Andrew Roscoe, Department of Anaesthesia, Papworth Hospital, Cambridge, UK

David A. Rowney, Royal Hospital for Sick Children, Edinburgh, UK

Thomas W. L. Scheeren, Department of Anaesthesiology, University Medical Center Groningen, University of Groningen, Groningen, The Netherlands

Uwe Schirmer, Institute for Anaesthesiology, Heart and Diabetes Centre NRW, Bad Oeynhausen, Germany

Lothar A. Schwarte, Department of Anaesthesiology, VUmc University Medical Center, Amsterdam, The Netherlands

John Sear, University of Oxford, Oxford, UK

Alex Sell, Royal National Orthopaedic Hospital, Stanmore, UK

Frédérique S. Servin, APHP, HUPNVS - Hôpital Bichat, Département d'anesthésie et de reanimation, Paris, France

Kulraj S. Sidhu, Department of Anesthesiology & Perioperative Care, University of California, Irvine, CA, USA

Peter Slinger, Department of Anesthesia, University of Toronto, Toronto, ON, Canada

Charlotte Small, Department of Anaesthetics and Critical Care, Queen Elizabeth Hospital Birmingham, Birmingham, UK

Andrew Smith, Royal Lancaster Infirmary, Lancaster, UK

Karen Smyth, Wing Commander, Royal Air Force; Consultant in Cardiothoracic Anaesthesia and Intensive Care Medicine, UK

Claudia Spies, Department of Anaesthesiology and Intensive Care Medicine, Charité - Universitätsmedizin Berlin, Campus Charité Mitte and Campus Virchow-Klinikum, Berlin, Germany

Sven Staender, Department of Anaesthesia & Intensive Care Medicine, Regional Hospital, Maennedorf, Zurich, Switzerland and Paracelsus Medical University, Salzburg, Austria

Stephen Stayer, Baylor College of Medicine, Texas Children's Hospital, Houston, TX, USA

Luzius A. Steiner, Anesthesiology, University Hospital Basel, Basel, Switzerland

Michael Sury, Department of Anaesthesia, Great Ormond Street Hospital NHS Trust, London, UK

Nicholas T. Tarmey, Academic Department of Critical Care, Queen Alexandra Hospital, Portsmouth, UK

Dafydd Thomas, Cardiac Intensive Care Unit, Morriston Hospital, Cwmrhydyceirw, Swansea, UK

Jonathan P. Thompson, Anaesthesia, Critical Care & Pain Management, University of Leicester, and University Hospitals of Leicester NHS Trust, UK

Andrew Toner, Department of Anaesthesia and Pain Medicine, Royal Perth Hospital, WA, Australia

Mark Tooley, Medical Physics and Bioengineering, Royal United Hospitals NHS Foundation Trust, Bath, UK

Simon Turner, Critical Care Air Support Team, Tactical Medical Wing, Royal Air Force, UK

Eveline L. A. van Dorp, Leiden University Medical Center, Leiden, The Netherlands

Anurag Vats, The Leeds Teaching Hospitals NHS Trust and University of Leeds, Leeds, UK

Bernadette Veering, Leiden University Medical Center, Department of Anesthesiology, Leiden, The Netherlands

Marc Van De Velde, Department of Anesthesiology, Department of Cardiovascular Sciences, KU Leuven and UZ Leuven, Leuven, Belgium

Hugo E. M. Vereecke, University Medical Center Groningen, University of Groningen, Groningen, The Netherlands

Jaap Vuyk, Department of Anesthesiology, Leiden University Medical Center, Leiden, The Netherlands

Alyson Walker, Department of Anaesthesia, Royal Hospital for Children, Glasgow, UK

Sarah Watts, Medical & Trauma Sciences, CBR Division, DSTL, Porton Down, Salisbury, UK

Nigel R. Webster, University of Aberdeen, UK

Robert Wheeler, Department of Clinical Law, University Hospital Southampton, Southampton, UK

Stuart White, Royal Sussex County Hospital, Eastern Road, Brighton, UK

Antony R. Wilkes, Consultant in Medical Devices, Edinburgh, UK

John Williams, MRC-ARUK Centre of Excellence for Musculoskeletal Ageing Research, School of Medicine, University of Nottingham, Royal Derby Hospital, Derby, Derbyshire, UK

Heather M. Wilson, University of Aberdeen, School of Medicine, Medical Sciences and Nutrition, Aberdeen, UK

Niall Wilton, Department of Paediatric Anaesthesia and Operating Rooms, Starship Children's Hospital, Auckland, New Zealand

Andre De Wolf, Department of Anesthesiology, Feinberg School of Medicine, Northwestern University, Chicago, IL, USA

Gordon T. C. Wong, Department of Anaesthesiology, University of Hong Kong, Hong Kong, China

Paul Wood, University Hospital Birmingham NHS Trust, Queen Elizabeth Medical Centre, Birmingham, UK

Tom Woolley, Academic Department of Military Anaesthesia and Critical Care, Birmingham, UK

Patrick Wouters, Ghent University Hospitals, Department of Anesthesia and Perioperative Medicine, Ghent, Belgium

Arvi Yli-Hankala, Department of Anaesthesia, University of Tampere, Tampere, Finland

André van Zundert, Royal Brisbane & Women's Hospital & University of Queensland, Department of Anaesthesia & Perioperative Medicine, Herston, QLS, Australia

PART 7

Procedures, techniques, and therapies

Michel M. R. F. Struys

CHAPTER 48

The airway in anaesthetic practice

Christopher Frerk and Takashi Asai

Introduction

Airway management is a description of the synthesis of the knowledge, skills, and behaviours of a skilled professional working to keep a patient's breathing passages clear and, if necessary, assisting with his or her breathing. The main tasks of airway management during general anaesthesia are maintenance of oxygenation and elimination of carbon dioxide while protecting the lungs from aspiration. After induction of general anaesthesia, obstruction of the upper airway is almost inevitable without the intervention of an anaesthetist or other healthcare professional. Historically, the principal site of obstruction was believed to be the tongue pressing against the posterior pharyngeal wall but it is now accepted that the soft palate obstructing the nasal airway and the epiglottis obstructing the laryngeal inlet are equally common and important causes of upper airway obstruction in clinical practice.

Airway devices (facemasks, supraglottic airway devices, or tracheal tubes) are routinely used during anaesthesia to relieve upper airway obstruction and (particularly when positive pressure ventilation is used) to minimize leakage of gas at the interface of the patient and the anaesthesia apparatus. The choice of airway device should take into consideration the advantages, disadvantages, and likelihood of difficulty of each method, the type of operation, and the condition of the patient including an assessment of the risk of aspiration.

Anatomy and physiology

The front border of the oral cavity is the lips, the top border is the hard palate at the front and the soft palate at the back, the side borders are the cheeks, and the lower border is the 'floor of the mouth' which mainly consists of the tongue but also includes the space around the sides and undersurface of the tongue. At the back, the oral cavity connects with the pharynx at the fauces. The vallecula is the depression between the lateral glossoepiglottic folds which connect the lateral edges of the epiglottis to the base of the tongue.

The nasal cavity extends posteriorly from the nares or nostrils into the nasal vestibule (which bears short, thick hairs). The nasal cavity is lined with a moist mucosal membrane and is divided into two compartments (nostrils) by the nasal septum. The lateral wall of each nostril has three overhanging projections, the nasal conchae, running from the front to the rear. At the back of the nasal cavity, the space becomes the nasopharynx.

The pharynx is the space behind the oral cavity and it stretches above and below the level of the oral cavity. The top border is the base of the skull (sphenoid bone), the posterior border is the cervical spine, and inferiorly it becomes the oesophagus. The back of the nose connects with the pharynx at the top, the back of the oral cavity connects with the pharynx in the middle, and the larynx and oesophagus connect with the pharynx at the bottom. The pharynx is thus described in three parts: the nasopharynx is the portion above the soft palate, the oropharynx runs from there to the level of the hyoid bone, and the laryngopharynx runs from the level of the hyoid bone to the level of the lower border of the cricoid cartilage.

The larynx is situated at the upper end of the trachea, at the level of the third to sixth cervical vertebrae, extending from the tip of the epiglottis to the caudal border of the cricoid cartilage, where the trachea connects. In neonates, the larynx is positioned at the level of the second and third vertebrae, and descends as a baby grows.

The larynx consists of nine cartilages: epiglottis, thyroid, cricoid, and paired arytenoid, corniculate, and cuneiform cartilages. They are connected by fibroelastic membranes (thyrohyoid, cricothyroid, and cricotracheal membranes). The cricothyroid membrane is the most superficial, is relatively avascular, and has the widest anterior gap between the cartilages of the larynx and trachea, thus providing the best access for emergency percutaneous transtracheal access to the airway. The larynx is suspended from the hyoid bone by the thyrohyoid membrane. The caudal part of the epiglottis is attached to the posterior surface of the thyroid cartilage, and the anterior side is connected to the hyoid bone by the hyoepiglottic ligament. The cricoid cartilage is a complete ring which articulates with the thyroid and arytenoid cartilages. The larynx bulges posteriorly into the hypopharynx, leaving on each side a deep recess, the pyriform fossae.

The glottis (where the vocal cords are located) is situated at the mid level of the thyroid cartilage anteriorly, and at the upper edge of the cricoid cartilage posteriorly.

The trachea extends from the caudal edge of the cricoid cartilage to the carina. It consists of U-shaped cartilages joined by fibroelastic tissue and closed posteriorly by the longitudinal trachealis muscle.

The trachea divides into two main bronchi, left and right, at the carina. The left main bronchus is longer than the right and its axis makes a greater angle with the axis of the trachea. The right main bronchus subdivides into three lobar bronchi, whereas the left main bronchus divides into two.

Equipment

Facemasks

The oldest airway management manoeuvre, routinely used by clinicians for more than 100 years to maintain a patent airway, is to lift the mandible anteriorly, elevating the tongue and epiglottis. The application of a facemask allows administration of supplemental oxygen and anaesthetic vapours.

Facemasks are designed to form a seal around the mouth and the nose, and are connected to anaesthetic breathing systems, to allow spontaneous breathing or intermittent positive pressure ventilation. Historically, the body of a facemask was made of black rubber, but currently most are made of transparent plastics, with the advantage that it is possible to see lip colour, vomitus, and exhaled moisture. The rim of the mask is designed to achieve an airtight seal with the face, utilizing either an air-filled cushion (to which air can be added or removed to optimize the seal) or a flap.

Although facemask ventilation is a fundamental skill that all anaesthetists should master, it requires considerable skill to maintain a patent airway and a seal even in patients with normal airways. The optimal position for maintaining a clear airway is with neck flexed and the head extended on the neck (sniffing position). A pad or pillow under the head (not under the shoulders) aids optimum positioning. Jaw thrust is routinely required to prevent airway obstruction. Lifting the mandible anteriorly, so that the lower set of teeth is anterior to the upper set of teeth, lifts the tongue from the posterior pharyngeal wall and the epiglottis away from the glottis. This can be achieved by slightly opening the mouth and by applying forward force on the mandibular ramus. When there is difficulty in obtaining a patent airway, two-person/four-handed ventilation should be attempted. One person holds the mask with both hands, and lifts the rami of the mandible. The second person ventilates the patient's lungs by squeezing the reservoir bag. Jaw thrust with both hands, maximum head extension, and mouth opening ('triple airway manoeuvre') combine to provide optimal ventilation.

When these manoeuvres fail to maintain a patent airway, an oropharyngeal airway (Guedel airway) or a nasopharyngeal airway is used. An oropharyngeal airway increases the space at the back of the tongue, and helps lift the epiglottis from the posterior pharyngeal wall. A nasopharyngeal airway bypasses obstruction at the soft palate and the base of the tongue and is less likely to provoke airway reflexes such as coughing.

During positive pressure ventilation, anaesthetic gas may be insufflated to the stomach which increases the likelihood of regurgitation of gastric contents. This is especially likely when high airway pressures are necessary such as in obese patients, those with poor pulmonary compliance, or partial airway obstruction. Gastric distension leads to worsening diaphragmatic splinting (especially in small children), making continued positive pressure ventilation even more difficult.

The facemask is now rarely used for maintenance of anaesthesia as the anaesthetist is not able to easily perform other tasks such as record-keeping and administering fluids. In addition, the lungs are not protected from regurgitated stomach contents.

Supraglottic airways

Supraglottic airway devices are artificial airways inserted into the oropharynx with a 15 mm connector for attachment directly to a breathing system, providing hands-free airway maintenance. The first oropharyngeal airway devices were produced in the 1930s and were designed to provide a gastight seal, by forming a plug in the oropharynx. These devices needed constant manipulation to maintain a patent airway and the materials available at the time were too stiff to provide an effective sealing effect. Since the 1990s, several new pharyngeal plugs were developed with softer cuffs which provided relatively reliable sealing but they still had the problem of frequent upper airway obstruction.

As an advance on the simple pharyngeal plug, oesophageal obturators such as the Combitube and the laryngeal tube were developed with two cuffs: the distal cuff of the device sealing the oesophagus to prevent gas flow into the stomach, with the proximal cuff producing a seal within the oropharynx. Gases delivered between the two cuffs can thus only enter the trachea. Although these devices have been used for resuscitation and for prehospital care, they never achieved widespread popularity during anaesthesia practice.

The laryngeal mask airway was designed by Archie Brain in 1981 as a totally new concept and came to market in 1987. Brain designed the device based on the anatomy of the hypopharynx. When correctly positioned, the distal part of the mask conforms to the hypopharynx, and the inflatable cuff encircles and encloses the larynx, forming a gastight seal around it.

The laryngeal mask airway rapidly gained in popularity and soon overtook the facemask as the mainstay of airway maintenance during spontaneously breathing anaesthesia. Soon, because of its advantages (Box 48.1), it began to encroach on areas of anaesthesia where the tracheal tube had previously been the exclusive method of airway management.

Brain subsequently developed several variations on the Classic® (Teleflex, Inc., Wayne, PA, USA) laryngeal mask airway to address specific requirements. Concerns regarding infection led to the introduction of a disposable device (the Unique®; Teleflex, Inc., Wayne, PA, USA), difficulties using the classic device in head and neck surgery heralded development of the flexible version, and the specific requirement for use as a conduit for tracheal intubation led to the production of the Fastrach™ (intubating laryngeal mask airway) with a shorter wider rigid stem and different angle of approach to the laryngeal inlet. Subsequently, a video camera and screen were incorporated into the design of the Fastrach™ under the trade name CTrach™, allowing the previously blind intubation to be observed. In response to an increasing number of anaesthetists choosing to use positive pressure ventilation, the ProSeal™ and its disposable version the Supreme® (both Teleflex, Inc., Wayne, PA, USA) were added to the family.

The huge success of the laryngeal mask airway led to a variety of similar devices being brought to market. Since the patent expired on the laryngeal mask airway more than 20 versions have come to market from many manufacturers and although the evidence base for their efficacy does not match that available for the Classic® laryngeal mask airway, many healthcare providers are now using these devices throughout the world.

The next concept in supraglottic airway devices was the perilaryngeal airway, the most successful of which is the i-gel® (Intersurgical Ltd., Workingham, UK), launched in 2007. Although superficially similar in appearance to the laryngeal mask airway, the concept of the i-gel® is distinctly different: the i-gel® is designed based on the shape of the larynx and thus does not rely on inflation of a cuff to

Box 48.1 Advantages and disadvantages of supraglottic airways

Advantages

- Insertion of a supraglottic airway is generally easy to learn, and the success rate for placement by unskilled personnel is 94–100%.
- Compared with tracheal intubation and extubation, insertion of, and removal of, a supraglottic airway is associated with less haemodynamic and intraocular pressure changes.
- There is no risk of inadvertent endobronchial or oesophageal intubation.
- Compared with tracheal intubation, a supraglottic airway should be less likely to injure the teeth, the glottis, or the trachea.
- Compared with tracheal extubation, removal of a supraglottic airway during emergence from anaesthesia is associated with a lower incidence of airway complications and interruption of spontaneous breathing.
- Compared with a facemask, upper airway obstruction is infrequent during the use of a supraglottic airway (as the device bypasses the obstruction at the base of the tongue, soft palate, and the epiglottis), and thus holding the device and supporting the jaw are usually not necessary.
- Compared with a facemask, it is easier to obtain a gastight seal with a supraglottic airway.

Disadvantages

- First-generation supraglottic airways do not reliably prevent pulmonary aspiration of gastric contents.
- Anaesthetic gas may be insufflated to the stomach, and this may encourage regurgitation of gastric contents and may make positive pressure ventilation difficult.
- Supraglottic airways cannot prevent obstruction at the glottis or beyond.
- Supraglottic airways are less effective than cuffed tracheal tubes in preventing gas leakage when the airway pressure is high. Typical seal pressures have been recorded at 15–18 cm H_2O for the laryngeal mask airway classic, and 25–28 cm H_2O for the laryngeal mask airway ProSeal™ and the i-gel®.

seal the gap with the pharyngeal tissues (Fig. 48.1). The rim is made of a thermo-elastic polymer (ethylene butadiene styrene: SEBS), designed to conform to the anatomical shape of the larynx, changing its form dependent on individual laryngeal anatomy. Because of this, a gastight seal can be obtained without a cuff mechanism (Fig. 48.1), and thus the insertion time of the i-gel® is generally faster than that of any other supraglottic airways.

Supraglottic airways have several disadvantages (Box 48.1). Development in this field has concentrated on improving airway seal pressures to enable controlled ventilation at higher airway pressures, and on maintaining functional separation of the respiratory and gastrointestinal tracts with improved oesophageal venting via drain tubes overlying the top of the oesophagus to reduce the risk of gastric inflation, regurgitation, and aspiration.

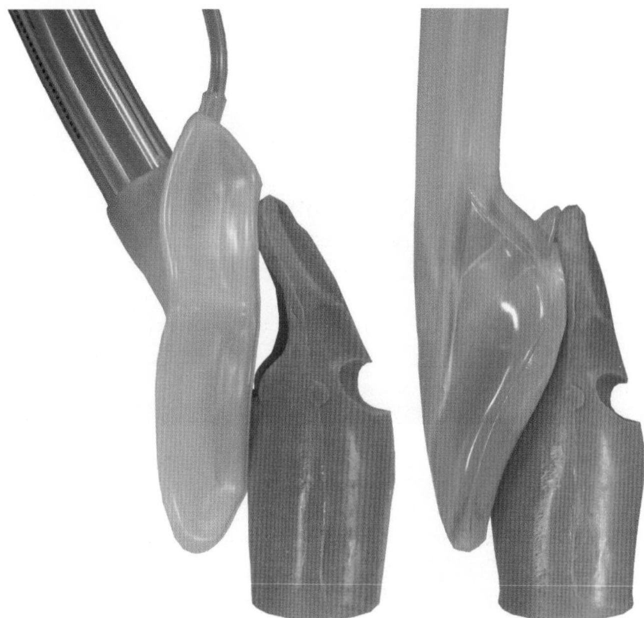

Figure 48.1 Anatomical position of the laryngeal mask airway (left), and the i-gel® (right). When correctly inserted, there is a gap between the laryngeal mask airway and the larynx, necessitating inflation of a cuff to obtain an airtight seal, whereas the i-gel® can provide an airtight seal without an inflatable cuff.

These second-generation supraglottic airway devices (such as the ProSeal™ and i-gel®) have an integral bite block, thus reducing the risk of airway obstruction during emergence from anaesthesia.

Practical use of the laryngeal mask airway

In anaesthesia training, little attention is given to laryngeal mask selection and insertion which is in large part testament to the design of the device in that untrained personnel can achieve good success rates with these devices. However, it is now recognized that we should afford the same attention to insertion technique of the laryngeal mask that we do to teaching tracheal intubation. While personal variations in technique (such as partly inflating the mask before insertion, folding the tip anteriorly, or rotating the mask laterally during insertion) may make insertion of the device easier, none have been proved to match (in terms of correct positioning of the mask) the standard method (Fig. 48.2, Box 48.2). For example, when the cuff is partially inflated, insertion of the device into the mouth is easier but is more likely to be associated with downfolding of the epiglottis. An incorrectly positioned device is more likely to be dislodged or to activate airway reflexes such as laryngospasm or severe coughing during emergence from anaesthesia.

In adults, the size of laryngeal mask airway should be determined by sex, as this provides a better sealing effect than selection based on body weight (with no differences in other factors, such as the ease of insertion). Larger sizes (size 4 or 5 in females and size 5 or 6 in males) usually provide a better gastight seal than smaller ones. Early versions of the manufacturer's instruction manual indicated that size selection should be based on weight, but the latest manual acknowledges the sex-based selection method. In children weighing less than 50 kg, size selection should be based on weight.

The manufacturer indicates a maximum volume of air for cuff inflation for each device which should not be regarded as the 'recommended inflation volume'. The cuff should be inflated with the

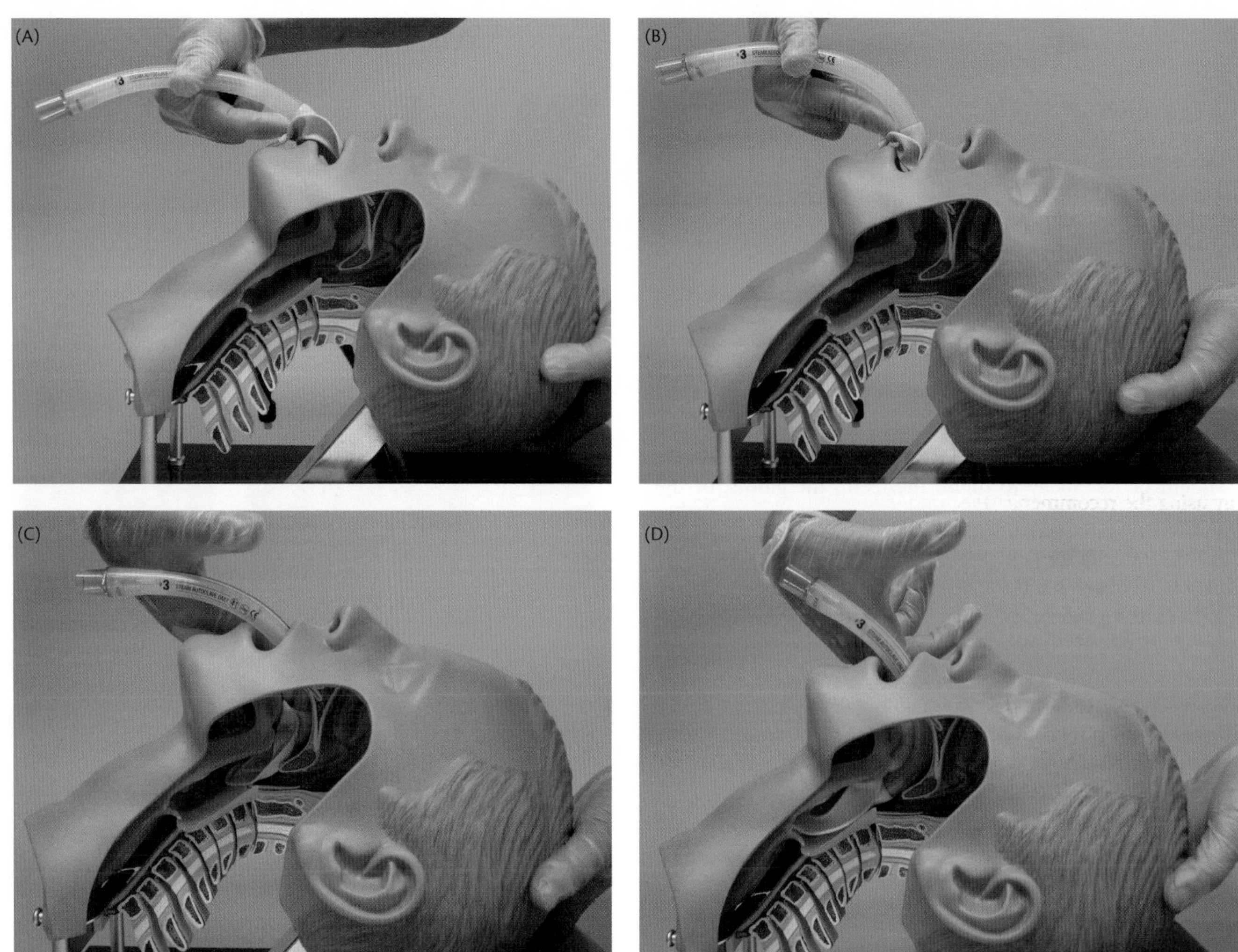

Figure 48.2 Insertion of the Classic® laryngeal mask airway.

Box 48.2 Standard insertion method of the laryngeal mask airway Classic®

1. The cuff must be fully deflated before placement. This imparts rigidity to the tip of the cuff. The deflated cuff should be free from wrinkles and its rim should face away from the mask aperture. This can be achieved by pressing the hollow side down onto a clean flat surface during deflation, with two fingers pressing down on a point just short of the tip.
2. A lubricant is applied only to the posterior surface of the mask just before placement.
3. While the non-dominant hand places the patient's head and neck to the sniffing position, the dominant hand holds the device, with the index finger placed at the junction of the tube and mask.
4. The tip of the mask is placed against the inner surface of the patient's upper incisor teeth. It is important that at this point the tube should be parallel to the floor rather than vertical. The mask is then pressed upwards against the hard palate and advanced into the oral cavity, maintaining upward pressure (Fig. 48.2A).
5. The device is advanced using the index finger located at the junction of the tube and the mask. It is essential that the tip of the cuff does not roll over while advancing the device (Fig. 48.2B, C).
6. The device is pushed as far as possible into the hypopharynx by the index finger. When the mask is fully advanced, resistance will be felt (Fig. 48.2D).
7. The cuff is inflated with *half the maximum recommended* volume of air. When correctly placed, the tube usually moves out of the mouth slightly, and the tissues overlying both the thyroid and cricoid cartilage bulge slightly when the cuff is inflated. The device should not be held or connected to the anaesthetic circuit during cuff inflation, as this may prevent optimum seating of the device, the tip of the mask is likely to be positioned too deeply if the tube is held during inflation.
8. After confirmation of adequate ventilation, a bite block is inserted, and the laryngeal mask and the bite-block are fixed.

minimum volume of air required to provide an effective seal. The best seal pressure is typically produced at approximately one-third to two-thirds the maximum recommended cuff volume. When the mask is inflated maximally, the more rigid cuff is less able to adapt to the variable contours of the pharynx. The cuff should initially be inflated with half the maximum recommended volume of air, and if there is a gas leak around the mask at an airway pressure of less than 15 cm H_2O, a further 5–10 ml of air should be added. If an acceptable seal has not been achieved with the maximum recommended volume, the use of a larger size laryngeal mask should be considered.

The failure rate of insertion of a supraglottic airway is likely to be higher in patients in whom difficult tracheal intubation is predicted, in particular, when neck movement or mouth opening is limited. For example, insertion of the Classic® laryngeal mask airway using the recommended technique becomes impossible when the angle between the oral and the pharyngeal axis is less than 90° at the back of the tongue. Several other reasons for difficulty in insertion have been reported (Box 48.3).

Supraglottic airways are well tolerated at light levels of anaesthesia and permit smooth emergence. However, in the UK national audit of serious complications of airway management, inadequate depth of anaesthesia was the most frequent associated factor with pulmonary aspiration which occurred during the use of a supraglottic airway (Cook et al. 2011). It is important to make sure that the depth of anaesthesia is sufficient to minimize the risk of breath holding, laryngospasm, or regurgitation in response to surgical stimuli or other physical stimuli such as changing the patient's position.

Tracheal intubation

The technique of tracheal intubation has been available to anaesthetists for more than 100 years. In the earliest days, a tracheal tube was passed into the trachea 'blindly' either by placing the fingers in the patient's mouth and guiding the tube by feel into the trachea (orotracheal intubation) or by manoeuvring the head and neck to direct the tube through the nose towards the trachea (blind nasotracheal intubation). Currently, the standard is that the tube should be placed into the trachea under vision.

Tracheal intubation has been considered for many years to be the gold standard of airway management. A correctly placed tube prevents obstruction in the upper airway, the glottis, and upper segments of the trachea. A cuffed tracheal tube (with the cuff inflated correctly) permits positive pressure ventilation in patients with poorly compliant lungs and is the most reliable method to minimize pulmonary aspiration during maintenance of anaesthesia.

A disadvantage of tracheal intubation is that to place the tube in the patient's trachea requires a laryngoscope and is thus an invasive procedure associated with increases in heart rate, blood pressure, and intraocular and intracranial pressures. Tracheal intubation using a Macintosh laryngoscope is difficult in about 1:65 cases, and fails in approximately 1:300 cases in obstetric patients and 1:2000 cases in general surgery. Repeated attempts at intubation are associated with injury to the airway and increased risk of mortality.

Route of tracheal intubation

Tracheal intubation can be achieved orally, nasally, or through a tracheostomy orifice. Oral intubation is less invasive than nasal intubation, and is usually chosen during routine anaesthesia. Nasal tubes are chosen for particular head and neck operations to facilitate surgical access. Tracheostomy is indicated when there is obstruction in the upper airway or in the larynx, or when a prolonged intubation is anticipated.

Box 48.3 Risk factors for difficult tracheal intubation and difficult ventilation

Tracheal intubation

- History of difficult intubation
- History of prolonged intubation, tracheostomy
- Sleep apnoea syndrome, snoring
- Obesity
- Obstetric anaesthesia
- Acromegaly
- Restricted cervical spine movement (e.g. rheumatoid arthritis, ankylosing spondylitis, fixed neck)
- Limited jaw movement
- Retrognathia
- Thyromental distance (<6.0 cm), sternomental distance (<12.5 cm)
- Limited mouth opening (interincisor distance <4–6 cm)
- Restricted view of the oropharynx (Mallampati score: 3 or 4)
- Deformity of the airway (e.g. thyroid tumour, glottic oedema, mediastinal mass).

Facemask ventilation

- History of neck radiation
- Beard
- Edentulous jaw
- Obesity
- Age older than 50 years
- Sleep apnoea syndrome, snoring
- Mallampati score 3 or 4.

Supraglottic airways

- Lack of experience
- Insufficient anaesthesia, muscle relaxation
- Limited mouth opening (interincisor distance <2 cm)
- Restricted cervical spine movement
- Mass in the oropharynx (e.g. large tonsils, oropharyngeal tumour)
- Laryngeal or tracheal obstruction (e.g. laryngospasm, laryngeal tumour, tracheal foreign body, compression to the airway)
- Cricoid pressure.

Direct laryngoscopy devices

Direct laryngoscopy is performed to obtain a straight line of view from the eye of the intubator to the glottis so that a tube can be passed into the trachea, under direct vision.

Alfred Kirstein was the first clinician to use a direct laryngoscopy device. In 1895, he used a modified oesophagoscope to observe the glottis. William Macewen performed the first tracheal intubation to maintain a patent airway during anaesthesia. Subsequently, in 1913, Chevalier Jackson and Henry Janeway independently developed direct laryngoscopes and described their usefulness for tracheal intubation. Both incorporated a distal light source, and a blade component to create room for passage of a tracheal tube. The first laryngoscopes were straight-bladed designs and two techniques developed for their use: a midline and a paraglossal approach both involving direct elevation of the epiglottis with the blade of the laryngoscope placed under the epiglottis. Tracheal intubation was subsequently popularized as a means of securing the airway during anaesthesia by Ivan Magill during his time working with the reconstructive surgeon Sir Harold Gilles. Magill refined the techniques of laryngoscopy, notably identifying the importance of appropriate head and neck position. Despite more than 100 laryngoscope blades being developed over the last 100 years, only two, the Macintosh (curved) and Miller (straight) blades, both of which were developed in the 1940s, have persisted in mainstream anaesthesia practice.

Macintosh and Miller laryngoscopes

The correct positioning of the tip of the blade differs between these two laryngoscopes. With the Macintosh laryngoscope, the tip of the blade is placed in the vallecula, and is designed to elevate the epiglottis indirectly by tensioning the hyoepiglottic ligament. With the Miller laryngoscope, the tip of the blade is advanced underneath the epiglottis which is lifted directly by the blade.

The method of tracheal intubation using a Macintosh laryngoscope is as follows. Place the patient's head and neck in the sniffing position with neck flexed, head extended, and mouth open. The laryngoscope is held in the left hand and introduced into the right-hand side of the mouth, displacing the tongue to the left. The blade is advanced along the tongue, observing the tip until the epiglottis comes into view, after which the tip of the blade is inserted into the vallecula. At this stage, applying a lifting force along the long axis of the handle will usually expose the glottis and permit tracheal intubation.

McCoy laryngoscope

The McCoy laryngoscope is the most widely used alternative direct laryngoscope. It is a modification of the Macintosh laryngoscope with a hinged tip extending approximately 25 mm from the end of the blade. The tip is controlled by a lever attached to the proximal end of the blade. It may be useful when it is difficult to elevate the epiglottis using a standard Macintosh blade. The McCoy is inserted into the vallecula (as for the Macintosh laryngoscope), and the thumb of the hand holding the laryngoscope is used to depress the lever to elevate the tip of the blade. This may elevate the epiglottis, by increasing the tension of the glossoepiglottic folds. It has been demonstrated to be a particularly useful laryngoscope for use during manual in-line stabilization of the cervical spine but in other cases it only improves the view in about 20% of difficult Macintosh laryngoscopies.

Rigid indirect laryngoscopes (videolaryngoscopes)

Increasing interest in the mechanisms of difficulty with direct laryngoscopy and tracheal intubation led to the development of rigid indirect laryngoscopes where the anaesthetist is able to view the larynx without the need to achieve a direct line of sight. The first commercially available indirect device was the Bullard laryngoscope, which used a fibreoptic bundle to carry the image of the larynx to a viewing lens. Since the turn of the century, several different types of indirect laryngoscopes have become available. These devices are often called videolaryngoscopes, as the majority of the currently available devices use video technology to transmit an image of the larynx to a video screen.

Videolaryngoscopes have several advantages over direct laryngoscopes (Box 48.4) and there are a number of different designs which vary in the way that they are used. The tip of the blade may be placed in the vallecula or underneath the epiglottis, some devices are designed to be used with the patient's head and neck position in the sniffing position, whereas others perform better with the head and neck in a neutral position.

Macintosh type

The first patent adding a video camera to a rigid laryngoscope was granted to Wood in 1998 (United States Patent US005800344A) and describes a curved Macintosh-like blade. The insertion method is basically the same as the conventional Macintosh laryngoscope, and thus it is possible to see the glottis either directly or on a video screen. One advantage is that it is not generally necessary to

Box 48.4 Advantages and disadvantages of rigid indirect laryngoscopes (videolaryngoscopes)

Advantages

- A videolaryngoscope usually provides a better view of the glottis.
- Two or more people can simultaneously see the same view. This is particularly useful for training, and also on the occasions when external laryngeal manipulation is necessary to aid the view or to help direct passage of the tracheal tube as the assistant applying pressure on the neck can see the glottic area on the video screen and optimize pressure to optimize view.
- Less cervical spine movement is required during tracheal intubation with a videolaryngoscope.
- Because the video image can be seen from any angle, it is unnecessary for the intubator to stand by the patient's head and instead can stand anywhere convenient as dictated by the suboptimal scenario.
- With some videolaryngoscopes, it is possible to record the images of tracheal intubation. This may be useful for teaching and training and in the future as a permanent record of the laryngoscopy and intubation.

Disadvantages

- Tracheal intubation becomes difficult if the video image is blurred by fogging, secretions, blood, or vomitus.
- For a videolaryngoscope without a tube guide, even when a clear view of the glottis is obtained, it may be difficult to manoeuvre the tip of a tracheal tube through the laryngeal inlet.
- Compared with a fibreoptic bronchoscope, it may be more difficult to insert the blade in patients with a limited mouth opening.

learn a new tube-insertion technique. Another advantage over the Macintosh laryngoscope is that the videolaryngoscope may provide a higher chance of obtaining a full view of the glottis, because the camera eye situated near the tip of the laryngoscope will be just a few centimetres from the glottis. Nevertheless, there is still insufficient evidence to support that the use of Macintosh-type videolaryngoscope would increase the chance of success of tracheal intubation in a patient in whom intubation using the conventional Macintosh blade has failed.

Anatomically shaped blade without a tube guide

Because it is unnecessary to obtain a line of sight to the glottis from outside the patient's mouth, videolaryngoscopes do not have to have the same shape as the Macintosh blade. Therefore, the blades are generally anatomically shaped to allow insertion without excessive movement of the head and neck and to deliver the camera to a position behind the tongue from where the larynx can be viewed. This means that it is usually not possible to direct a tube to the larynx without the use of a stylet with the same curve as the laryngoscope blade. The use of these devices therefore necessitates the acquisition of the new skill of manipulating the tube under video control. In addition, while the tip of the tube can be observed directly as it is placed into the mouth and is subsequently viewed indirectly via the video screen, there is usually a short period where the tip is not under vision and particular care needs to be taken to avoid trauma while advancing the tube.

Anatomically shaped blade with a tube guide

In an attempt to overcome these limitations, some new devices have been developed with a guide channel into which the tube is secured before starting laryngoscopy or through which the tube is passed under direct vision once the laryngoscope is in the patient's mouth. Assuming that a view of the larynx can be obtained, the channel directs the tube towards the larynx (Fig. 48.3). With these videoscopes the tube is steered towards the larynx by adjusting the position of the laryngoscope rather than by control of the hand advancing the tube, as is the case in direct laryngoscopy and when using other videoscopes. Even with a guide channel and a clear view of the larynx, the tip of the tracheal tube may impinge on arytenoids or the epiglottis, in which case a gum elastic bougie may be passed through the tracheal tube and advanced into the trachea (by manoeuvring the direction of the bougie tip as seen on the video screen); the tube can then be advanced over the bougie into the trachea.

Several studies have shown that some videolaryngoscopes enabled tracheal intubation with high success rates (Asai et al. 2009; Amathieu et al. 2011; Aziz et al. 2011) in patients in whom intubation with a Macintosh laryngoscope has been difficult.

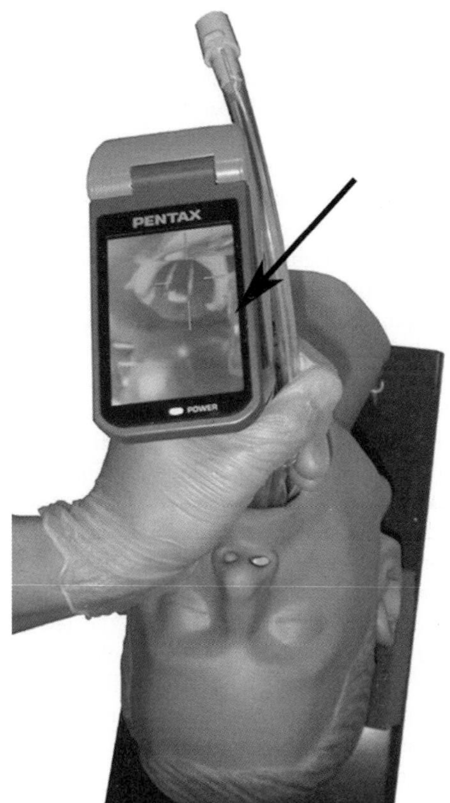

Figure 48.3 A videolaryngoscope with a tube guide (Pentax Airway Scope®). Both the glottis and the tip of the tube are seen on the video screen.

Fibreoptic laryngoscope

The first fibreoptic intubation was performed in 1967 using a choledocoscope. Purpose-built fibreoptic laryngoscopes were first produced in the 1970s using coherent bundles of glass fibres to transmit an image of the larynx to a viewing lens. These early fibrescopes required an external light source to provide illumination delivered via a second bundle of glass fibres. Improvements in technology allowed incorporation of greater numbers of smaller fibres giving better quality images, and improvements in battery technology have permitted fibrescopes to become readily portable. Since the 1990s, the use of cameras attached to the viewing lens with pictures displayed on video screens has facilitated teaching of the technique. The latest generation of 'fibreoptic' laryngoscope has utilized chip camera technology instead of glass bundles to transmit the images, giving much better quality pictures.

Fibreoptic laryngoscopy is currently considered the gold standard technique to facilitate tracheal intubation in patients with difficult airways. Nevertheless, there are difficulties associated with its use. As with all airway management techniques, it requires training and practice to become proficient in negotiating the fibrescope to and through the glottis. Importantly, even when the fibrescope has been inserted into the trachea, railroading a tracheal tube over the scope into the trachea may frequently be difficult, known as 'hold up'.

Several methods have been suggested for reducing difficulty in fibreoptic intubation.

A space needs to be created in the oropharynx in which to view the anatomy. The awake cooperative patient can protrude their tongue or take a deep breath on command, both of which increase the airspace in the oropharynx, permitting an improved view. In the anaesthetized patient, other techniques need to be used to create this space: jaw thrust provided by an assistant widens the oropharyngeal cavity and elevates the epiglottis, opening the laryngeal inlet and easing insertion of a fibrescope into the trachea; insertion of purpose-designed oral airways (e.g. Berman, Ovassapian, and Williams) may similarly be useful in bypassing the narrowed pharynx and also aid in guiding the fibrescope towards the glottis.

Premedication with an antisialagogue and removal of secretions and blood from the oropharynx by suction reduces the risk of an obscured view at fibreoptic laryngoscopy, by secretions ('white-out') or by blood ('red-out'). The laryngeal mask airway and other supraglottic airways can also be used as 'conduits' to fibreoptic intubation and enable delivery of oxygen and inhalation anaesthetics during attempts at fibreoptic intubation.

'Hold up' is usually caused by the left-facing bevel of the tracheal tube impacting on the right arytenoid as the tube is advanced over the fibrescope. Minimizing the gap between the fibrescope and tracheal tube reduces the incidence of this problem and there is rarely any value in choosing a tracheal tube larger than a 6.0 mm internal diameter (ID) for this reason.

It is the design of the tracheal tube tip, however, that has the most significant impact on ease of passage through the larynx. In the 1970s, a conical tipped tube was developed for fibreoptic intubation but the market could not support the development costs. The offset bevel of the tubes supplied with the intubating laryngeal mask (Fastrach™) has been shown to cause very little hold up and similar success has been demonstrated with Parker Flex-Tip® (Parker Medical, Inc., Highlands Ranch, CO, USA) (posterior bevel) tracheal tubes. The simplest aid to reducing hold up with standard tracheal tubes is to rotate the tube 90° anticlockwise, to orientate the bevel downwards. Many anaesthetists choose a spiral-wound reinforced tube for fibreoptic intubation, because they follow the curve of the fibrescope more readily.

Tracheal tubes

Tracheal tube design has remained essentially unchanged for many years although the materials used have improved. The first tracheal tubes were uncuffed and were hand-made from vulcanized rubber; today they are made from a variety of 'plastics', with polyvinylchloride (PVC), polyurethane, and siliconized PVC being the most common. The first cuffed tubes had low-volume, high-pressure spindle-shaped cuffs. When inflated, the cuff had a small area of contact with the tracheal wall and the pressure exerted by the cuff frequently exceeded the capillary perfusion pressure in the tracheal membrane, with the risk of ischaemic damage. With technological advancement, thinner, softer cuffs have been developed with higher volumes and lower pressures. These cuffs can provide a seal, without distending and deforming the trachea, and without exerting higher pressures than the mucosal perfusion pressure.

Selection of tracheal tube type

There are several different types of tracheal tubes.

Polar tubes (RAE tubes)

Polar tubes (RAE tubes, after the inventors, Ring, Adair, and Elwyn) are preformed so that the tube can be fixed to the chin (with an oral, south-facing tube) or to the forehead (with a nasal, north-facing tube), without kinking. Oral polar tubes are useful for minor oral surgery (e.g. tonsillectomy) or nasal surgery; nasal polar tubes may be indicated for improved surgical access or where fixation of a tube to the mandible may be undesirable. They have the disadvantage that the curve of the tube may not be at the right position to ensure correct tube tip placement.

Armoured or reinforced tubes

An armoured or a reinforced tube contains a spiral of metal wire so that it is unlikely to kink, making it suitable for surgery when pressure may inadvertently be applied to the tube, when the head and neck are in an unusual position, or when the tube needs to be moved or secured in an atypical position (e.g. facial surgery, thyroid surgery, or prone anaesthesia). A major disadvantage of armoured tubes is that they can become occluded if patients clench their teeth (such as during emergence from anaesthesia). The spiral winding then keeps the tube occluded even when biting is released. For this reason, armoured tubes should not be used without a bite block.

Microlaryngeal tubes

Microlaryngeal tubes are designed to facilitate endoscopic surgery to the larynx. They are longer than normal, have a small ID (typically 4.0–6.0 mm), and have larger cuffs to facilitate an effective seal in the adult trachea.

Double-lumen tubes and bronchial blockers

The double-lumen tube was invented by Eric Carlens, who designed the tube for bronchospirometry of each lung. The tube comprises two lumens; one is slightly longer than the other and is inserted into a bronchus. The distal aperture of the shorter lumen opens in the trachea above the carina. With a correctly placed double-lumen tube, either or both lungs can be ventilated as required.

A bronchial blocker consists of a long catheter with a balloon attached near the tip. After tracheal intubation, the blocker is advanced into a bronchus which is then occluded by inflating the balloon cuff. With a bronchial blocker in place it is only possible to ventilate the contralateral lung or both lungs. Historically, double-lumen tubes and bronchial blockers were placed blindly and their positions confirmed by clinical tests. Current best practice dictates that these devices should be placed under vision using a fibrescope.

Cuffed or uncuffed tubes

Cuffed tubes are generally used for adult anaesthesia. In addition to offering protection from pulmonary aspiration, they permit high inflation pressures to be used when needed and allow accurate monitoring of tidal volumes and end-tidal concentrations of gases. A cuffed tube also allows the anaesthetist to use low fresh gas flows and minimizes air pollution of the operating theatre.

In children, uncuffed tracheal tubes were still the mainstay into the first decade of the twenty-first century. In recent years, cuffed tubes are being increasingly used in children. This trend is primarily because of improvements in cuff material, shape and efficacy, and importantly, because several studies have confirmed that cuffed tracheal tubes do not increase the incidence of airway complications in children.

Appropriate tube size

The size of a tracheal tube is indicated as an internal diameter (ID) of the tube, in millimetres. The external diameter of a tube in relation to the ID differs between the types and the manufacturers of tubes. In the past, there was a considerable difference between the internal and external diameters, and thus the use of the largest possible tube was recommended. Currently, there is less difference between the internal and external diameters, and adequate ventilation can be obtained through a tube as small as 6.0 or 6.5 mm ID. The incidence of postoperative respiratory complications, such as hoarseness and sore throat, is lower with a small ID tube than a large ID tube. Therefore, in adults, it is advisable to use a tube with a small ID (7.0–8.0 mm in males, and 6.0–7.0 mm in females).

In children, selection of size of tracheal tube is usually based on the formula: [age (in years)/4] + 4 mm. For cuffed tubes, half a size smaller is usually an appropriate choice. It is important to ensure that the size chosen does not cause excessive pressure on mucosal surfaces.

Confirmation of correct tracheal intubation

Inadvertent oesophageal intubation is fatal if not recognized. Therefore, it is crucial to confirm that the tube has correctly been inserted into the trachea. Several methods have been reported to do this, but unrecognized oesophageal intubation still causes deaths related to anaesthesia.

Historically, clinical tests, such as chest expansion during inflation, auscultation of the chest and epigastrium, and anaesthesia reservoir bag movement were the only methods used to confirm tracheal tube placement. They should still be used routinely but can occasionally be difficult to interpret.

One of the first advanced tests used to distinguish between oesophageal and tracheal intubation was the use of an oesophageal detector device, where negative pressure is applied to the tracheal tube using either a 50 ml syringe or a self-inflating bulb. Gas can easily be aspirated from a tube placed in the trachea as the lumen is splinted open by cartilage rings. Inability to aspirate gas indicates that the tube is either occluded or misplaced into the oesophagus.

Capnography with waveform is the current gold standard for confirming tracheal intubation and ventilation and hence in detecting oesophageal intubation. When the tube is in the trachea, carbon dioxide will be exhaled during ventilation of the lungs and the capnograph will show an increase in carbon dioxide concentration. A carbon dioxide waveform will be seen even in cardiac arrest and is increasingly used as a guide to the effectiveness of resuscitation attempts. Absence of exhaled carbon dioxide indicates that the tube is not in the trachea or that the tracheal tube is obstructed.

Disposable carbon dioxide detectors use a pH-sensitive chemical indicator strip that responds quickly to exhaled carbon dioxide by a reversible colour change in semi-quantitative fashion. Nevertheless, they cannot be considered a reliable replacement for waveform capnography.

Fibreoptic endoscopy is a reliable method of confirming tracheal intubation but it is not often immediately accessible in cases of doubt over tube placement.

Even when clinical tests and capnography indicate oesophageal intubation, human factors such as fixation error and plan continuation bias may complicate decision-making and lead to persistent attempts to oxygenate with a misplaced tube. This is particularly likely when laryngoscopy and intubation have been difficult. If there are any concerns regarding the signs confirming effective ventilation, the tracheal tube should be removed.

Positioning of the tube

Having confirmed that the tube has passed into the trachea, it is important to ensure it is placed at the optimal depth, that is, with the tip well above the carina to avoid endobronchial intubation and with the proximal end of the cuff positioned more than 2 cm below the glottis to avoid the cuff compressing the recurrent laryngeal nerves. Optimal placement can usually be achieved by placing the printed guide mark on the tube (placed about 3 cm proximal to the cuff and about 8 cm proximal to the tip of the tube) at the level of the vocal cords. Because the size of the pharynx and the length of the trachea vary considerably between patients, the length of tube at the lips is not a reliable guide to correct placement and bilateral ventilation of the lungs should be confirmed by auscultation.

Even when a tracheal tube has been placed to the optimal position at the start of anaesthesia, the tip of the tube may be displaced towards or away from the carina (by up to 2 cm) during surgery. Flexion of the neck, pneumoperitoneum, and use of the Trendelenburg position typically lessen the distance between tube tip and carina, whereas extension of the neck displaces the tip away from the carina.

In children, several formulae have been suggested for optimal positioning of a tube but best practice is to use the same rules as in adults: the tube should be passed a sufficient distance beyond the cords to avoid accidental extubation using the depth marker on the tube as a guide, with auscultation used to confirm that the tube is not in too far. In critical care patients, a chest X-ray is a reliable method for confirming correct placement of the tube tip above the carina.

Inflation of the cuff

After tracheal intubation, the cuff should be inflated, with just enough air to prevent leakage of gas around the tube with airway pressures of 20–25 cm H_2O; this allows effective positive pressure ventilation, and minimizes the risk of pulmonary aspiration and of excessive cuff pressure on the tracheal mucosa. When nitrous oxide is used during anaesthesia, intracuff pressure will increase over time as nitrous oxide diffuses into the cuff. Assessing cuff pressure by palpation has proved to be unreliable and ideally a purpose-designed pressure gauge should be used to measure intracuff pressure at initial inflation and throughout anaesthesia.

Aids to tracheal intubation

Placing the tube under vision should be the goal of the anaesthetist but if it is not possible to see the cords at laryngoscopy (or if it is not possible to direct the tube through the cords despite being able to see them), a number of aids are available.

Stylets and bougies

Stylets are made of a malleable metal usually coated in a plastic. They are designed to be inserted inside the lumen of the tracheal tube which is then bent to an appropriate shape to direct the tip of the tube towards and through the laryngeal inlet. To reduce the risk of damage to the upper airway, the tip of the stylet should not protrude past the tube tip, and should be withdrawn before the tube is advanced fully into the trachea.

A modified version of this device is the lighted stylet, which has a light at its distal end. The tracheal tube is loaded as previously described, and when the tip of the tube is passed through the glottis, a bright patch of illumination is seen in the midline of the neck. If the tube has passed into the oesophagus, no such transillumination is seen. Lighted stylets can be used in conjunction with laryngoscopes and with the intubating laryngeal mask, but it is generally advocated for use as a sole device. Although some anaesthetists remain enthusiastic supporters of lighted stylets, the intubation is blind and injury to the delicate structures of the larynx may be more likely. Laryngeal pathology is a relative contraindication and bright ambient lighting and obesity increase the risk of failure. While the lighted stylet may retain a role in resource-poor locations, it seems to have little place in modern anaesthesia.

The gum elastic bougie (Eschmann tracheal tube intubator) was introduced into clinical practice in 1949 by Sir Robert Macintosh and is a simple and effective device to facilitate tracheal intubation, when the view of the glottis is obscured at laryngoscopy. The device is approximately 60 cm in length, and retains the approximate shape into which it is bent. The distal end of the bougie has an angulated tip.

Historically, a tube was preloaded over the bougie and the combination was advanced toward the glottis. In current practice, the bougie is inserted first and when correctly placed, the tube is loaded onto it and railroaded into the trachea. The angulated tip of the bougie is placed in the midline behind the epiglottis, and gently advanced along the posterior surface of the epiglottis into the trachea. As a bougie is generally used when the view at laryngoscopy is limited, it may be wrongly inserted into the oesophagus. Signs of correct (tracheal) placement include a 'clicking sensation', as the tip of the bougie runs over the tracheal cartilages, followed by 'hold up' (resistance to further gentle advancement when the tip of the bougie passes the carina and enters a smaller bronchus).

Many single-use bougies have been introduced in the first decade of the twenty-first century but their memory characteristics do not match the gum elastic bougie. With most it is possible to generate much higher forces than with the gum elastic device and as placing a bougie is a blind/semi-blind procedure, this increases the risk of airway trauma.

Bougies should be regarded as the first choice during difficult direct laryngoscopy, as they have been shown to be more effective than the stylets in this situation (Henderson et al. 2004). They have also been used successfully to facilitate intubation with guided videoscopes such as the Pentax Airway Scope® (Pentax Medical, Hoya Corporation, Tokyo, Japan), when the guide channel alone fails to direct the tube through the glottis. The memory of the bougie is not sufficient, however, to be used with videolaryngoscopes that do not have a tube guide, as the angle it needs to traverse is too great. The manufacturers of some videolaryngoscopes (e.g. the GlideScope®; Verathon Medical, Bothell, WA, USA) produce custom-made stylets preformed to the same shape as the blade of their laryngoscope.

Magill forceps

Sir Ivan Magill devised angulated forceps in 1920 to facilitate nasotracheal intubation. Magill forceps are still used today in the manner originally described. These are used principally in association with direct laryngoscopes and may not be suitable for use with videoscopes as the angulation does not match the shape of the blades.

Supraglottic airways

There are many reports of the successful use of several different supraglottic airways as aids to low-skill fibreoptic intubation after failed direct laryngoscopy, and the laryngeal mask airway is recognized in many national airway guidelines.

Retrograde intubation

Retrograde intubation describes a technique for managing difficult intubation where a needle is inserted through the cricothyroid membrane to allow passage of a wire cephalad into the patient's mouth. This proximal end of the wire is retrieved and used as a guide for passage of a tracheal tube. Commercial retrograde intubation kits are still available but the technique is rarely used today.

Cricothyroidotomy/tracheostomy

Percutaneous access to the airway is used electively for laryngeal surgery when it is desirable to have the entire glottis exposed for surgical access, or as an emergency procedure as the final common pathway in the 'cannot intubate, cannot ventilate' scenario. Access should usually be obtained through the cricothyroid membrane as this is the most superficial and relatively avascular part of the airway accessible from the front of the neck.

Narrow-bore cannula cricothyroidotomy (2 mm or less) requires a high-pressure gas source to enable adequate ventilation. For elective surgery, purpose-designed ventilators should be used which monitor and limit airway pressures to minimize the risk of barotrauma. Manually controlled high-pressure ventilation sources such as the Manujet™ (VBM Medizintechnik GmbH, Sulz, Germany) should only be used for emergency rescue where the benefits of quick set-up and ready availability outweigh the still-present risk of barotrauma.

Wide-bore cricothyroidotomy (typically 4 mm ID or greater) is generally only used to obtain emergency access to the airway which can be achieved using a purpose-designed device or with a surgical technique and a standard tracheal tube. Cuffed tubes should be used as they provide optimum ventilation and offer protection from aspiration.

Commercially available wide-bore cricothyroidotomy kits come in two forms: cannula over needle and Seldinger devices. There is currently little evidence to suggest that either is superior but both require regular retraining to maintain the practical skills necessary for prompt establishment of an airway. Surgical cricothyroidotomy involves using a scalpel to access the trachea through the cricothyroid membrane to allow placement of a standard 6.0 mm cuffed tracheal tube. A cricoid hook has been recommended to facilitate tube placement. The Fourth National Audit Project of the Royal College of Anaesthetists and the Difficult Airway Society (NAP4) showed that, in extremis, wide-bore cannula techniques failed in more than 40% of cases and that narrow-bore cannula techniques failed in more than 60% (Cook et al. 2011). In the same report, surgical techniques had a 100% success rate in accessing the airway, although this did not always prevent patient harm. Regardless of personal preferences and experience with cannula techniques, all anaesthetists should ensure they are also trained in the technique of surgical cricothyroidotomy.

Clinical practice

Preoperative evaluation of the airway

Difficult intubation/difficult ventilation

An airway assessment is essential to allow rational planning of an airway management strategy. Failure to secure a patent airway, although rare, can be fatal, and thus an assessment should be made of difficulty with facemask ventilation, placement of a supraglottic airway, tracheal intubation, and emergency access to the airway via the front of the neck (Box 48.3). Aspiration of blood or gastric contents into the airway remains the most common cause of death associated with airway management so assessment of aspiration risk is an essential part of routine preoperative assessment.

The usefulness of predictive testing for the rare occurrence of difficult laryngoscopy in otherwise normal patients has been repeatedly questioned because of the low positive predictive value of bedside tests. Nevertheless, it has been shown that, in a high proportion of cases in whom serious airway-related complications occurred, difficulty could have been anticipated at preoperative airway assessment (Cook et al. 2011), supporting the recommendation found in guidelines produced by many countries that an evaluation of the airway should always be performed. The fundamental purpose of all predictive tests (Box 48.5) is to identify techniques that have an increased likelihood of failure in the patient being tested so they are not relied upon as part of the overall airway management strategy. On their own, these lists do not provide a discriminatory test and each anaesthetist must decide which of the risk factors will determine that they should change from their default airway management technique. It must be accepted that all tests are inevitably associated with false-positive and false-negative results, and thus the anaesthetist should always plan for the possibility that their primary technique may fail.

A clinical judgement based on experience will inform the anaesthetist if patient cooperation is likely to be a problem; if this is the case, preoxygenation may be difficult and awake techniques such as awake fibreoptic intubation may not be easy.

In patients with predictors of difficulty with facemask ventilation or supraglottic airway devices (Box 48.3), the airway strategy should not rely on ability to oxygenate via these routes.

Regarding predictors of difficult tracheal intubation, most published research focuses on Macintosh laryngoscopy which relies on extension of the head on the neck and anterior displacement of the tongue to optimize the line of sight from the teeth to the vocal cords. The tests in Box 48.5 assess features that impede these processes, and it is important to recognize that they have not been evaluated for their usefulness in predicting difficult laryngoscopy and intubation with other laryngoscopes. Research into predictive tests for difficulty using videolaryngoscopes is limited and because the concepts and designs differ between devices, predictive tests for one may not transfer to others.

Surgical access to the airway is the final common pathway in airway management, and at the preoperative visit an assessment should be made as to the ease or difficulty of this strategy. Fixed

Box 48.5 Preoperative assessment of the airways

History of difficult airway management

A history of difficult airway management is one of the most reliable predictors of difficult airways. Therefore, confirm the presence or absence of such a history by checking the patient's previous anaesthetic records and by direct questioning. If the patient has a history of tracheostomy or prolonged tracheal intubation, the presence or absence of deformities should be checked by X-ray or by computed tomography.

Detection of known risk factors

Assess the presence or absence of congenital malformations (such as Robin's sequence or Treacher Collins syndrome) or acquired diseases (rheumatoid arthritis or ankylosing spondylitis) that are known to make airway management more difficult. Also assess whether or not the patient has pulmonary disease (e.g. asthma or chronic obstructive pulmonary disease), in whom ventilation (via a facemask, a supraglottic airway, or even via a tracheal tube) is more likely to be difficult.

History of airway obstruction

Assess the presence or absence of airway obstruction during daily life. This includes asthma, obstructive sleep apnoea syndrome, nasal obstruction, hoarseness, and difficulty in swallowing. Patients with respiratory infections including the common cold are known to have increased airway reactivity for up to 2 weeks after the disappearance of symptoms. There are several other causes of increased airway reflexes, so it is advisable to identify possible causes and the degree of severity. If necessary, a respiratory function test or arterial blood gas analysis should be carried out.

Obesity

Obesity is a risk factor of difficult tracheal intubation, difficult mask ventilation, and pulmonary aspiration, and is an independent risk factor for obstructive sleep apnoea syndrome so a history of snoring and daytime sleepiness should be sought. In addition, obese patients will more quickly become hypoxic during apnoea.

Restricted mouth opening

Laryngoscopy becomes difficult when the interincisor distance is less than 4–6 cm, and insertion of a supraglottic airway becomes difficult or impossible when this distance is less than 2 cm.

View of the oropharynx

The patient is asked to open the mouth as wide as possible and to protrude the tongue as far as possible. The view of the oropharynx has been categorized into four grades: Wilson's modification of the Mallampati score. In general, the greater the class, the more likely it is that tracheal intubation will be difficult.

Jaw thrust

Assess whether or not the lower teeth can protrude more anteriorly than the upper teeth. If this is not possible, both tracheal intubation and mask ventilation are more likely to be difficult.

Head and neck movement

Restricted head extension and limited neck mobility make both tracheal intubation and mask ventilation more difficult.

Thyromental distance, sternomental distance

A short thyromental distance (<6.0 cm) or sternomental distance (<12.5 cm) is associated with a higher incidence of difficult tracheal intubation.

Radiological or endoscopic investigation

For patients who are scheduled for head and neck surgery, any available X-rays, computed tomography, and magnetic resonance images should be reviewed (ideally with the operating surgeon), allowing the presence, location, and severity of airway pathology to be assessed to aid decision-making. If recent imaging studies are not available, preoperative endoscopy of the upper airway using a fibreoptic laryngoscope should be considered as a minimum level of assessment.

neck flexion, obesity, and neck pathology (such as a large thyroid gland or infection at the front of the neck) make planned or emergency access to the airway more difficult or impossible.

Risk of pulmonary aspiration

The danger of pulmonary aspiration was first acknowledged in the 1930s; since then much effort has been made to reduce its incidence. It is, however, still the commonest cause of death and brain damage during anaesthesia. In cases of serious aspiration reported to the NAP4 project, the risk was often underestimated, missed altogether, or was identified but not acted upon (Cook et al. 2011).

Patients who have not been fasted preoperatively or those with obstruction of the gastrointestinal tract are generally regarded as at increased risk but many other factors including patient, operation, anaesthesia, and airway device, should be taken into account when planning the airway management strategy (Box 48.6) (Asai 2004).

Box 48.6 Predisposing factors for pulmonary aspiration during anaesthesia

Patient factors

- Full stomach (e.g. emergency surgery)
- Inhibited gut function
- Diabetes mellitus
- Increased intracranial pressure
- Hiatus hernia
- Gastrointestinal obstruction
- Recurrent regurgitation
- Dyspeptic symptoms
- Achalasia, oesophageal diverticula
- History of upper gastrointestinal surgery
- Recent trauma
- Opioids
- Women in labour
- Morbid obesity.

Operation factors

- History of upper abdominal surgery
- Lithotomy, the head-down position
- Laparoscopic cholecystectomy.

Anaesthesia factors

- Insufficiently deep anaesthesia
- Intermittent positive pressure ventilation
- High pulmonary inflation pressures
- Prolonged anaesthesia.

Device factors

- Presence of a supraglottic airway
- Incorrectly inserted supraglottic airway.

As with other preoperative tests there are many uncertainties in estimating the risk of aspiration. The traditional cut-off value of residual gastric volume greater than 25 ml and pH less than 2.5 is not evidence based, but if this cut-off value is applied, as many as 50% of fasted patients can be regarded as at increased risk of aspiration. It is not clear how the known predisposing factors influence the risk of aspiration for individual patients.

Planning airway management

After preoperative airway assessment, it is important to develop a comprehensive airway strategy, particularly when airway management is predicted to be difficult. Failure of the primary airway technique can lead to hypoxia within a few minutes, necessitating plans B, C, and D being carried out rapidly, which is extremely challenging without appropriate planning and preparation.

All patients who are scheduled for elective surgery should be fasted routinely in accordance with local policy to minimize the risk of pulmonary aspiration. In patients who require emergency surgery or in those at increased risk of aspiration, attempts should be made to reduce the volume and acid contents of the stomach before the operation. Such strategies may include delaying the start of general anaesthesia, administration of an antacid, and emptying the stomach via nasogastric suction.

When difficulty in airway management is anticipated, an awake technique (e.g. awake fibreoptic intubation or awake tracheostomy/cricothyroidotomy) should be discussed with the team.

Even if no difficulty has been predicted at preoperative evaluation, it is important to recognize that any part of the airway plan may fail and an airway management strategy should always be formulated, with all necessary equipment and skills to carry it out being readily available.

If definitive airway management is planned for after induction of anaesthesia, it should be remembered that difficult ventilation is frequently associated with difficult tracheal intubation and pulmonary aspiration. Therefore, if one part of the airway management strategy fails, it is likely that rescue plans may also be more difficult than normal.

When tracheal intubation, ventilation, or both, are predicted to be difficult, a comprehensive airway management strategy is particularly important. It may be practical to avoid airway management altogether, by using local or regional anaesthesia. Nevertheless, even when this option is chosen, an airway management plan should be thought through, as the block may fail or start to wear off peroperatively if surgery is unexpectedly prolonged.

If general anaesthesia is necessary, a decision should be made as to the safest method of securing and maintaining the airway with the choice of primary airway plan guided by the preoperative airway assessment. Routine intravenous induction of anaesthesia and the use of a facemask or supraglottic airway is an appropriate primary plan in patients at low risk of aspiration, with reasonable pulmonary function, and no expected difficulty with device placement or maintenance of a clear airway.

Patients with poor pulmonary compliance may be safely managed, by maintaining spontaneous breathing via a supraglottic airway. If intermittent positive pressure ventilation is required, even a second-generation supraglottic airway may not be able to provide an airtight seal, with the attendant risks of hypoventilation and gastric insufflation. A particularly challenging group in this regard are patients with hyper-reactivity of the airway, such as those with asthma in whom tracheal intubation may provoke bronchospasm (particularly at light planes of anaesthesia). The risks and benefits of tracheal intubation should take into consideration the severity of asthma along with the expected duration of surgery, anticipated ease of intubation, and accessibility of the patient's airway during anaesthesia.

Choosing tracheal intubation as the primary plan for airway management necessitates further thought as to the safest technique for placing the tube. When there is a risk of pulmonary aspiration and tracheal intubation is predicted to be easy, a rapid sequence of induction of anaesthesia is indicated. When there is an increased risk of aspiration, and tracheal intubation is predicted to be difficult, the trachea should be intubated and the cuff inflated before induction of anaesthesia (awake intubation).

In a patient judged to be at low risk of aspiration with no expected difficulty with mask ventilation, tracheal intubation should be performed after intravenous induction of anaesthesia and non-depolarizing neuromuscular block. If, however, difficulty is anticipated with ventilation via a facemask or a supraglottic airway device, awake tracheal intubation is the safest option.

When preoperative assessment indicates that establishing an airway with facemask, supraglottic airway, and tracheal tube is likely to be very difficult, a surgical airway should be performed under local anaesthesia. This could be a formal tracheostomy or a cricothyroidotomy depending on the circumstances of the case and the skills available. It is important to remember that emergency cricothyroidotomy is the final common pathway rescue technique when standard airway management plans fail unexpectedly. Even when no difficulty has been anticipated, every operating list should start with a check that the anaesthetist and assistant are familiar with the location and use of the equipment available for emergency cricothyroidotomy and will be able to use it if required.

Awake intubation

General anaesthesia should not be induced when there is an increased risk of difficult intubation and difficult mask ventilation. In such a case, the airway should be secured with a tracheal tube before induction of anaesthesia.

Awake fibreoptic intubation has generally been regarded as the safest and most reliable method to achieve this. To facilitate this and to reduce psychological and physiological stress, sedative medication is often used in conjunction with local anaesthesia. Nevertheless, caution is required, as sedation and local anaesthesia may reduce pharyngeal integrity and may cause upper airway obstruction.

It is important to recognize that although the fibrescope is steered through the larynx into the trachea under vision, the intubation is a blind procedure as the tip of the tracheal tube is not seen as it is railroaded through the larynx. Repeated attempts at inserting a fibrescope into the trachea and advancing a tube over the scope increase the risk of injury to the larynx and surrounding tissues, leading to bleeding from, or oedema of, the tissues. Although rare, complete airway obstruction can occur during attempts at awake fibreoptic intubation. Therefore, even when awake intubation is planned, back-up plans, such as emergency tracheostomy, should be prepared.

Rapid sequence induction of anaesthesia

Rapid sequence induction of anaesthesia is indicated in patients who are at significantly increased risk of pulmonary aspiration where difficulty with laryngoscopy and tracheal intubation are not anticipated.

The essentials of the technique described in the 1950–60s involved preoxygenation, induction of anaesthesia with a predetermined dose of thiopental followed immediately by succinylcholine, and the application of cricoid pressure. Ventilation was avoided until the airway was protected by a cuffed tracheal tube after which cricoid pressure was released. Sellick's reasoning for cricoid pressure was that pressure on this complete ring of cartilage compresses and occludes the oesophagus between the cricoid and the cervical vertebral body (Sellick 1961).

The technique remained essentially unchanged for more than 30 years and the key premise of minimizing the period when the airway is not protected from pulmonary aspiration while permitting rapid wake up if intubation fails remains today; however, rapid sequence induction has been evolving since the mid 1980s.

Opiates are frequently administered before induction of anaesthesia to minimize the cardiovascular stimulation associated with laryngoscopy and tracheal intubation. Propofol is often substituted for thiopental as the induction agent, because of familiarity and because of its less frequent airway complications.

Since its introduction into clinical practice, high-dose rocuronium (1.0–1.2 mg kg^{-1}) has been increasingly used in place of succinylcholine as it has a comparable onset time and fewer side-effects. Pharmacologically, sugammadex at a dose of 16 mg kg^{-1} restores neuromuscular function more quickly than succinylcholine wears off, and if tracheal intubation failed and mask ventilation is difficult, allows the patient to resume spontaneous breathing. In clinical practice, however, there may be unacceptable delays in administering the correct dose of sugammadex.

Other developments in rapid sequence induction have included revision of the recommended force applied to the cricoid cartilage, as excessive force can distort or completely occlude the upper airway. It is currently recommended that 10 N should be applied before induction of anaesthesia, increasing to 30 N at loss of consciousness. Regular retraining of anaesthetic assistants has been shown to be necessary to avoid incorrectly applied and excessive force.

It is now recognized that cricoid pressure may worsen the view at laryngoscopy and make mask ventilation more difficult. If laryngoscopy is difficult, cricoid pressure should be temporarily reduced to see if the view improves. Similarly, if tracheal intubation fails and rescue mask ventilation is inadequate, oxygenation takes priority over potential aspiration risk, and cricoid pressure should be reduced or removed to determine if that is the cause of the difficulty. A laryngeal mask airway may maintain a patent airway in the presence of cricoid pressure but requires temporary release to ensure correct device placement.

Classic teaching was that preoxygenation should be carried out with a good facemask seal for 3 minutes to ensure optimum denitrogenation of the lungs. The first modification to this technique was to use three or four vital capacity breaths which if done correctly, paying particular attention to maximum exhalation with each breath, can be as effective as the timed method. The current gold standard is to monitor end-tidal oxygen concentrations (ETO_2) during preoxygenation, and to continue until the ETO_2 reaches at least 85%. This may take more or less than 3 min but is a reliable marker of completeness of denitrogenation.

In early descriptions of the technique, little attention was paid to airway management in the time between loss of consciousness and laryngoscopy; it is now recommended that the airway should be kept patent and the mask seal maintained during this period to allow mass transfer of oxygen from the breathing system to lungs. Mask ventilation is traditionally avoided to minimize gastric insufflation and the associated increased risk of regurgitation; however, effective cricoid pressure should prevent gas from passing into the stomach, and thus some clinicians gently inflate the lungs with low inflation pressures to help maintain oxygenation during the apnoeic period.

Anticipated or known difficult intubation is a relative contraindication for rapid sequence induction of anaesthesia in the patient at risk of regurgitation, and alternative anaesthetic techniques, such as awake intubation, should be considered. In the future, as more data is gathered about the effectiveness of various videolaryngoscopes, their role in rapid sequence induction may evolve.

Airway management during emergence from anaesthesia

At emergence from anaesthesia it is necessary to ensure adequate spontaneous breathing and safe removal of the airway device in use. Evidence continues to be published demonstrating that there are more airway problems associated with emergence from anaesthesia than occur at induction. Planning airway management during emergence from anaesthesia is important in all patients, but particularly in those in whom mask ventilation, tracheal intubation, or both, were difficult. Whereas guidelines for management of difficult intubation are well established, the first national guidelines for management of tracheal extubation at the end of anaesthesia were published in 2012 (Difficult Airway Society Extubation Guidelines Group 2012). Development of simple algorithms for prevention and treatment of airway problems along with training based on guidelines for anaesthetists and recovery nurses for management of postoperative respiratory complications is urgently required.

Extubation planning should include an evaluation of the risk of regurgitation and pulmonary aspiration, the incidence of which may be higher than during induction of anaesthesia (Warner et al. 1993) and is associated with mortality (Department of Health 1994). In patients identified to be at risk of aspiration, consideration should be given to emptying the stomach and administering antacid prophylaxis before tracheal extubation.

Tracheal extubation is associated with coughing, laryngospasm, and increases in arterial, intraocular, and intracranial pressure. Some anaesthetists will plan tracheal extubation under deep anaesthesia for patients undergoing intracranial or intraocular operation or for those in whom an increase in arterial pressure would be detrimental. This practice reduces the incidence and degree of straining (bucking) or coughing, and stimulating effects on arterial, intraocular, and intracranial pressures. However, the incidence of other complications, notably airway obstruction, is increased, both immediately after extubation and extending into the period in the recovery room. Continuing an infusion of remifentanil until after extubation has gained popularity in recent years as a method of trying to reduce coughing and straining but published evidence of its efficacy is lacking.

Supraglottic airway devices should be removed when the patient is awake and responds to verbal command, with a bite block left *in situ* until the device is removed. Unlike tracheal extubation, this task is often delegated to staff in recovery areas where monitoring and other equipment is more limited, and anaesthetists are not always immediately available, meaning detection of complications may be delayed and prompt treatment may be more difficult.

Complications associated with airway management

Complications associated with airway management range from minor self-limiting events with no long-term sequelae (such as needing to reposition an imperfectly placed laryngeal mask airway) through serious respiratory complications (such as airway obstruction, laryngospasm, and hypoxia), to those leading to continuing morbidity and mortality. They may occur during any phase of anaesthesia, but as mentioned previously, the incidence is higher during emergence from anaesthesia and in the recovery room than during induction of anaesthesia (Asai et al. 1998).

More than 20 years ago, a report of US closed claim analyses related to anaesthesia practice revealed that adverse outcomes involving the respiratory system comprised the single largest class of injury, and that the incidence of death or permanent brain damage associated with airway management was much higher than that associated with cardiovascular management (Caplan et al. 1990). More recent litigation analyses show that airway complications remain expensive and serious. The most thorough examination of serious airway complications arising from routine anaesthetic practice comes from the NAP4 project (Cook et al. 2011), carried out in the United Kingdom over a 1-year period from 2008 to 2009, which indicated that as many as 1:5000 anaesthetics result in a serious airway complication (death, brain damage, emergency surgical airway, or unexpected intensive care unit admission). The commonest factors associated with serious airway complications relate to difficulty with tracheal intubation, tracheal extubation, and removal of a supraglottic airway.

Trauma to the airway

The commonest airway injury is dental damage, which may be caused by a laryngoscope, bite block, or supraglottic airway. The state of dentition should be assessed preoperatively and any loose or damaged teeth, caps, crowns, or bridgework documented. Patients should be warned of the potential risk of damage. Cut or bruised lips are also common after laryngoscopy, and thus care should always be taken to avoid trapping the lip between laryngoscope blade and teeth.

Tracheal intubation may be associated with injury to the larynx, pharynx, or oesophagus and may be caused by a laryngoscope blade, airway adjuncts such as stylets or bougies, or by the tube itself. The design of bougies greatly influences the force that can be applied during placement, the traditional gum elastic bougie being associated with lower forces than new single-use devices.

Airway exchange catheters require particular skill to use safely. Depth of insertion should be strictly limited and extreme caution is needed if using these devices for oxygenation, as the risk of barotrauma exists if not used strictly according to the manufacturers' instructions.

Multiple attempts at tracheal intubation increases the risk of trauma including oedema of the glottis, and increases the likelihood of causing difficult or impossible mask ventilation.

Supraglottic airways may also cause mucosal injury with blood staining being apparent on removal in up to 30% of cases. Nerve injuries from pressure within the oropharynx have been recorded, leading to dysfunction of lingual and hypoglossal nerves. It is not possible to determine if one supraglottic device is more likely than another to cause this problem, but choosing the correct size and using the lowest possible inflation pressures for cuffed devices are sensible precautions to minimize the risk.

Laryngospasm

Laryngospasm is not a simple closure of the glottis, but involves a strong constriction of the false cords and periepiglottic tissues forming a ball valve, followed by a longer period of closure of the true vocal cords (Tagaito et al. 1998). It may occur at any phase of anaesthesia: induction, maintenance, or emergence, particularly when the cords are irritated by blood, secretions, or an artificial airway (Box 48.7). Inadequate depth of anaesthesia is a major contributory factor and minor degrees of laryngospasm are typically treated by increasing depth of anaesthesia and applying continuous positive airway pressure. For severe laryngospasm where oxygenation is at risk, a neuromuscular blocking agent should be given to relax the vocal cords to permit ventilation; the choice of drug and subsequent management will depend on the phase of anaesthesia and other patient factors.

Several drugs, including lidocaine, magnesium, diazepam, and doxapram, have been reported to be effective in resolving laryngospasm; it seems likely they exert that effect by either altering depth of anaesthesia or by decreasing tone in laryngeal musculature.

Box 48.7 Risk factors for laryngospasm and bronchospasm

Laryngospasm

- Younger age
- Respiratory infection
- Smoking, passive smoking
- Insufficient depth of anaesthesia
- Secretions or bleeding in the oral cavity
- Regurgitation
- Airway instrumentation (e.g. tracheal extubation)
- After oral surgery (e.g. tonsillectomy).

Bronchospasm

- ASA physical status 3–5
- Respiratory infection
- Smoking, passive smoking
- History of asthma attack
- Chronic bronchitis
- Chronic obstructive pulmonary disease
- Obesity
- Insufficient depth of anaesthesia
- Airway instrumentation (e.g. tracheal intubation).

Bronchospasm

Bronchospasm can occur in any anaesthetized patient, but is five times more likely to occur in patients with a history of asthma and in patients with a history of upper respiratory tract infections in the preceding 4–6 weeks. The principal underlying mechanism is stimulation of the airway at or below the level of the larynx at an insufficient depth of anaesthesia. The stimulus may be an airway device, aspirated secretions, or gastric contents. Several risk factors for bronchospasm are known (Box 48.7).

Supraglottic airways cause less airway stimulus than tracheal tubes and are the first choice in patients at risk of bronchospasm. If tracheal intubation is required, it should be performed at a deep level of anaesthesia with complete neuromuscular block, and particular care should be taken to avoid irritating the carina as this is a particularly potent stimulus for bronchospasm. If safe and practical, the tube should be removed before emergence from anaesthesia.

If practical, drugs associated with histamine release (e.g. thiopental, atracurium, and morphine) should be best avoided in patients at risk of bronchospasm. Non-steroidal anti-inflammatory drugs (NSAIDs) are associated with an increase in airway resistance, although many asthmatics regularly self-medicate with over-the-counter NSAIDs with no apparent problems.

All the volatile anaesthetic agents cause bronchodilation but isoflurane and desflurane are particularly irritant to the airway and may provoke coughing which is associated with bronchospasm. Sevoflurane may therefore be a better choice for the patient with irritable airways. Propofol and ketamine have bronchodilator properties and in theory make a good choice for at-risk patients.

Post-obstruction pulmonary oedema

Airway obstruction at the end of anaesthesia can lead to post-obstruction pulmonary oedema (negative pressure pulmonary oedema) which is usually self-limiting but can be associated with profound hypoxia, necessitating complex drug therapy and a period of ventilation on a critical care unit. The precipitating obstruction does not need to be prolonged and may occur as a result of the patient biting and occluding the airway device in use, or from laryngospasm during emergence from anaesthesia. Second-generation supraglottic airways have integral bite blocks built into the devices which reduce the risk of this complication. When using first-generation supraglottic airways or tracheal tubes, separate bite blocks should be used routinely to ensure airway patency during emergence. Early recognition and prompt treatment of airway obstruction at emergence reduces the risk of this complication.

Pulmonary aspiration

Aspiration of gastric contents or blood during anaesthesia was recognized as a major problem in the 1930s and remains the single largest cause of mortality associated with airway complications under general anaesthesia today. Several studies have highlighted risk factors (Caplan et al. 1990; Cook et al. 2011) and it is important to recognize that tracheal tube placement, even as part of rapid sequence induction, does not guarantee complete protection. There is a suggestion that a supraglottic airway such as the laryngeal mask airway, when placed correctly, may offer significant protection from aspiration of blood from above the airway, in comparison with a tracheal tube where blood and secretions above the level of the tube cuff may be aspirated at extubation. Second-generation supraglottic airways, such as the ProSeal™, Supreme®, and i-gel®, may offer some protection from above and also provide functional separation of the respiratory and digestive tracts, but they cannot be recommended when there is significant risk of aspiration.

Unrecognized oesophageal intubation

Unrecognized oesophageal intubation still occurs during anaesthesia. A misplaced tracheal tube should be easy to identify when capnography is in use, but in cardiac arrest or suspected anaphylaxis, the absence of carbon dioxide waveforms (indicating oesophageal intubation) may be misinterpreted as being as a result of low cardiac output. Even in cardiac arrest, carbon dioxide will be seen in exhaled breath and thus when no carbon dioxide waveform is detected, the tube should be removed and either replaced or, if this is not possible, an alternative means of ventilating the lungs attempted.

Failure to secure an airway

Difficult tracheal intubation is encountered in 1–2% of cases, using a Macintosh laryngoscope, and this figure may be higher in certain groups such as the obstetric population and in head and neck surgery. Difficulty in ventilation through a facemask may occur as frequently as difficulty in tracheal intubation during induction of anaesthesia. The reported incidence of difficult mask ventilation is 1–5 % (Asai et al. 1990; El-Orbanhy and Woehlck 2009; Kheterpal et al. 2009), and the incidence of impossible mask ventilation is approximately 0.2% (Kheterpal et al. 2009).

All anaesthetists should be aware of and follow published guidelines for difficult airway management such as those by the Difficult Airway Society in the United Kingdom (Frerk et al. 2015).

Failure of the primary airway plan (facemask, supraglottic airway, or tracheal intubation) does not by itself constitute an emergency situation. Maintaining oxygenation is the overriding goal of airway management rather than succeeding with any particular technique, and if the primary technique fails, it is important to move quickly through optimal attempts at alternative methods, which should include administration of a neuromuscular blocking agent to exclude laryngospasm as a cause of difficulty with ventilation (Cook et al. 2011; Difficult Airway Society Extubation Guidelines Group 2012). Having a comprehensive airway strategy in place before embarking on anaesthesia helps with this decision.

If attempts at maintaining oxygenation by all three methods have failed in the presence of neuromuscular block and immediate wakening of the patient is not possible, emergency rescue is needed. Manikin studies have shown that wide-bore cuffed cricothyroidotomy devices allow the best rescue ventilation, but in clinical practice in the emergency situation this technique fails in more than 40% of cases (Cook et al. 2011). Jet ventilation through a narrow-bore cannula has an even higher failure rate. These failures occur because of decision-making difficulties, equipment problems, poor technique, and patient factors. Simulator training has been shown to improve decision-making and adherence to published algorithms in these situations. Cardiopulmonary bypass could be used as a rescue technique, although this is unlikely to be readily available in an emergency situation.

Future perspective

Variations on videolaryngoscope design continue to emerge and are likely to continue to do so as technology improves. Devices with an interchangeable blade design are likely to become more common allowing a more versatile approach to difficult laryngoscopy. Improvements in chip camera and video screen technology will also influence the development of flexible 'fibreoptic' laryngoscopes, making them lighter, more durable, and more readily portable.

New-generation supraglottic airway devices continue to be developed with the aim of improving seal pressures and reducing the risk of pulmonary aspiration by improving separation of respiratory and gastrointestinal tracts. Despite this, there will certainly still be a need for tracheal intubation in the future. It is likely that cuffed tubes will become an increasingly common part of paediatric anaesthetic practice over the next decade. In adult practice, tracheal tubes have been produced with a suction port above a new design of tapered cuff; the intention is to provide improved seal characteristics and allow aspiration of material from within the larynx above the cuff to reduce the risk of aspiration. Changes in tube tip design to facilitate intubation using videolaryngoscopes are also on the horizon. Tracheal tubes with inbuilt chip cameras are being tested as an aid to difficult intubation; they are able to provide continuous visualization of the position of the tube in the trachea throughout anaesthesia in situations where tube placement is uncertain or changing.

Research into cricothyroidotomy equipment design, techniques, and training may help the profession be better prepared for the rare 'cannot intubate, cannot ventilate' scenario; meanwhile, computer-based decision support tools to aid preoperative airway assessment and airway management planning for the anticipated difficult airway are available and may become more widespread as the profession recognizes the potential hazards associated with airway management highlighted by NAP4 (Cook et al. 2011).

Conclusion

Airway management, when appropriately performed, is a safe procedure, but serious airway complications occur in a limited number of patients. Airway workshops prove popular at local and national educational meetings, major research projects have been carried out to improve our understanding of the nature and pattern of serious airway complications, and national guidelines and textbooks about difficult airway management have been published. In addition, new airway devices have been developed, and pulse oximetry and capnography have become routine. Despite these initiatives, airway complications remain commonly associated with poor standards of care. Our biggest future challenge is to better translate the available wealth of knowledge into changes in clinical practice.

Declaration of interest

None declared.

References

Amathieu R, Combes X, Abdi W, *et al.* An algorithm for difficult airway management, modified for modern optical devices (Airtraq laryngoscope, LMA CTrach™). *Anesthesiology* 2011; **114**: 25–33

Asai T. Who is at increased risk of pulmonary aspiration? *Br J Anaesth* 2004; **93**: 497–500

Asai T, Koga K, Vaughan RS. Respiratory complications associated with tracheal intubation and extubation. *Br J Anaesth* 1998; **80**: 767–75

Asai T, Liu EH, Matsumoto S, *et al.* Use of the Pentax-AWS in 293 patients with difficult airways. *Anesthesiology* 2009; **110**: 898–904

Aziz MF, Healy D, Kheterpal S, Fu RF, Dillman D, Brambrink AM. Routine clinical practice effectiveness of the Glidescope in difficult airway management. *Anesthesiology* 2011; **114**: 34–40

Caplan RA, Posner KL, Ward RJ, Cheney FW. Adverse respiratory events in anesthesia: a closed claim analysis. *Anesthesiology* 1990; **72**: 828–33

Cook TM, Woodall N, Frerk C. Major complications of airway management in the UK: results of the 4th National Audit Project of the Royal College of Anaesthetists and the Difficult Airway Society. Part 1 Anaesthesia. *Br J Anaesth* 2011; **106**: 617–31. [Full report can be downloaded from http://www.rcoa.ac.uk/nap4]

Department of Health. *Report on Confidential Enquiries Into Maternal Deaths in the UK, 1988–90.* London: HMSO, 1994

Difficult Airway Society Extubation Guidelines Group, Popat M, Mitchell V, *et al.* Difficult Airway Society Guidelines for the management of tracheal extubation. *Anaesthesia* 2012; **67**: 318–40

El-Orbanhy M, Woehlck HJ. Difficult mask ventilation. *Anesth Analg* 2009; **109**: 1870–80

Frerk C, Mitchell VS, McNarry AF, *et al.* Difficult Airway Society 2015 guidelines for management of unanticipated difficult intubation in adults. *Br J Anaesth* 2015; **115**: 827–48

Henderson JJ, Popat MT, Latto IP, Pearce AC. Difficult airway society guidelines for management of the unanticipated difficult intubation. *Anaesthesia* 2004; **59**: 675–94

Kheterpal S, Martin L, Shanks AM, Tremper KK. Prediction and outcomes of impossible mask ventilation. A review of 50,000 anesthetics. *Anesthesiology* 2009; **110**: 891–7

Sellick BA. Cricoid pressure to control regurgitation of stomach contents during induction of anaesthesia. *Lancet* 1961; **2**: 404–6

Tagaito Y, Isono S, Nishino T. Upper airway reflexes during a combination of propofol and fentanyl anesthesia. *Anesthesiology* 1998; **88**: 1459–66

Warner MA, Warner ME, Weber JG. Clinical significance of pulmonary aspiration during the perioperative period. *Anesthesiology* 1993; **78**: 56–62

CHAPTER 49

Vascular access during anaesthesia

Andrew R. Bodenham

Introduction

Vascular access, both arterial and venous, at peripheral and more central sites is relatively new in historical medical terms and has only really developed into mainstream practice in the last 60 years. Other routes of drug and fluid administration via the gut and inhalation preceded it by centuries (Dudrick 2006). It is a core skill for anaesthetists, yet is not always well taught or is left out of core training curricula, with the assumption that skills will just be picked up early along the way. Like many procedures, it can be surprisingly easy to learn the basics, but many hazards and difficulties await the less skilled or inexperienced operator.

Space precludes a detailed description of actual techniques for all routes of access; only general principles will be covered here.

General principles

Certain procedural steps are common to all devices and insertion sites: time should be taken to make an optimal choice of device and insertion site considering clinical needs, duration of therapy, and patient preferences. Adequate explanation/consent is needed from the patient. This may be an integral part of anaesthetic consent or requires separate consent similar to surgery for a stand-alone procedure. Verbal consent may be entirely appropriate for peripheral cannulation, but for more invasive stand-alone central procedures, written consent procedures should be used as in surgery. I explain and list general risks and benefits, and those particular to the site of access, for example, bleeding, infection, vein thrombosis, dislodgement, lung injury (pneumothorax), pain, and scars. Patients in an intensive care unit (ICU) may appear unconscious but may still be able to understand a basic explanation of procedures, and need adequate local anaesthesia (LA) and sedation.

Aseptic technique is essential for all insertion and aftercare procedures irrespective of site of access, because of the direct insertion into the circulation. This is an area of increasing scrutiny in hospital practice (Pronovast et al. 2006). Needlestick injury is also important as hollow needles and cannulae can carry a significant inoculum of blood.

In awake patients, all but the smallest-bore devices should be inserted under adequate LA, either topical or injected. For central access, wide infiltration anaesthesia is required, and often inadequate volumes are used (a minimum of 10 ml is needed in an adult). Intravenous sedation is very helpful for anxious patients. Some patients (e.g. children) will need general anaesthesia, or the procedure may be part of the anaesthetic sequence after induction. Sicker patients may benefit from insertion of central venous devices under LA, pre-induction (e.g. patient with severe heart failure or critical aortic stenosis).

The chosen access site vessel is approached by a number of techniques, including:

- under direct vision (e.g. superficial vessel, jugular venous pulse, or surgical cut-down)
- under indirect vision (e.g. infrared visualization devices)
- by palpation from arterial pulse, or a full vein from use of tourniquet
- using landmark orientation (e.g. adjacent to an artery, the clavicle, or heads of sternomastoid muscle)
- using ultrasound guidance (two-dimensional or acoustic Doppler signal)
- using X-ray guidance (after contrast enhancement of vessel by peripheral injection, e.g. subclavian).

Needle entry into the vessel is confirmed visually by backflow or aspiration of blood, then a catheter or guidewire can be passed over or through the needle respectively.

Guidewire and catheter insertion should be without resistance. Once the guidewire is in the vessel, a catheter with a preformed tip can be passed over the wire. Alternatively, a larger dilator and introducer sheath can be passed over the wire, and various catheters, wires, or devices can be inserted through the introducer sheath.

Verification of catheter position within the vessel is important and can be checked by aspiration/backflow of arterial or venous blood, successful flushing of the catheter, measurements of pressure via the cannula, or X-ray verification as appropriate. Ultrasound can be used to visualize catheters in the vessel near to the puncture site and at other more distant sites where vessels are visible with ultrasound (e.g. jugular veins). Verification of the position of a central catheter tip in the great vessels can be confirmed by plain X-ray, computed tomography (CT), ECG guidance (Lee et al. 2009), injection of contrast, transoesophageal echo (Koung-Shing et al. 2004), electromagnetic sensors, or direct vision/palpation during cardiac surgery.

Appropriate anchorage of devices is essential to avoid dislodgement, either by adhesive dressings or sutures, or internal anchoring cuffs. Purpose-designed adhesive devices such as StatLock® devices

(Bard Medical, Covington, GA, USA) are increasingly used to avoid sutures and increase the reliability of anchorage. Meticulous aftercare and observation is required to maintain catheter function and prevent problems. This includes regular flushing, safe removal before problems occur, and appropriate recognition and management of problems and complications (Association of Anaesthetists of Great Britain & Ireland 2016).

The vast majority of devices are currently inserted by percutaneous techniques but an alternative is the traditional surgical cut-down, which still has a place in emergency situations, in the very small child, and where percutaneous access has failed. Its use has declined dramatically due to the operative time and skills required, a larger scar, potential greater damage to the cannulated vessel (often tied off/thrombosed), and a higher incidence of local infection as a result of local tissue dissection (McBride et al. 1997). It remains a useful standby in operating theatres where, if necessary, a surgeon can temporarily divert from the original surgery to perform a cut-down at the operative site (e.g. neck or groin) or elsewhere.

Space precludes a detailed description of all different access sites and catheter management but there are many excellent sources elsewhere (Latto 2002; Pieters 2003; Hamilton and Bodenham 2009).

Peripheral intravenous cannulation

This is a core component of medical practice yet is often performed poorly by inexperienced staff. Significant skill is required in the more challenging cases (e.g. the infant or neonate with very small veins, the very elderly with fragile veins, and patients having chemotherapy), where all obvious veins have already been used and become thrombosed. It is by no means risk free (Box 49.1). It is revealing to be on the receiving end of such interventions or visit your local oncology unit to see the severe side-effects of extravasation injury, which may be bad enough to require skin grafting. There are less obvious sites other than upper and lower limbs which can be used, for example, scalp veins in infants, chest wall veins in adults with prominent collateral veins, and the external jugular vein.

Discomfort can be minimized by skilled operators using the smallest feasible gauge device, thoughtful preparation with topical LA creams, or injection of LA. Avoid insertion where possible over joint flexures. Check catheter patency and dilute drugs with a free-running saline infusion.

There is an increasing range of aids to peripheral vascular cannulation, typically based on enhancing the size or visibility of veins (and arteries), commonly used in small children. Traditionally these included transillumination with cold light sources (Goren et al. 2001), local warming (Lenhardt et al. 2002), and epidermal nitroglycerine (Vaksmann et al. 1987).

High-resolution ultrasound is very useful to aid peripheral venous puncture in adults and children (Samoya 2010). Newer devices utilize the differential absorption of infrared light (which penetrates deeper than visible light) by blood compared with surrounding tissues to generate an image of vessels using an infrared camera. This is either projected onto a screen or as a computer-generated image back onto the skin. Such devices are commercially available but costly and clinically, their true value is still under investigation (Perry et al. 2011).

Alternatives to venous access

It should always be questioned whether peripheral or central venous access is required, or essential, in the short or longer term. Other routes for drug administration exist (Box 49.2).

Fluid therapy can also be administered by subcutaneous infusion through a needle or cannula. Sites of injection are rotated around the body every 48 h, with typical injection sites in the axilla. It is frequently used for hydration in palliative care (Royal College of Nursing 2010).

Intraosseous injection

This route of access is now widely accepted in adult and paediatric resuscitation, where a needle with a trocar is inserted into the upper tibia to access the bony venous sinuses for administration of drugs and fluids. There are purpose-designed needles and powered drills available. Care must be taken to avoid extravasation injury with compartment syndromes, bony injury, and infection, and alternative venous access should be sought as soon as reasonably possible. The subject has been usefully reviewed, including its use during anaesthesia (Tobias and Kinder Ross 2010; Taylor and Clarke 2011).

Central venous catheters

Many patients undergoing anaesthesia will require central venous catheterization during surgery or in the early postoperative period

Box 49.1 Complications of peripheral cannulation

- Local or systemic infection
- Thrombosed, painful veins
- Leakage of fluids into tissue leading to:
  - ineffective drug administration (e.g. awareness with total intravenous anaesthesia)
  - drug extravasation with skin/tissue loss
- Compartment syndrome from pressurized infusions
- Inadvertent arterial cannulation
- Catheter fracture or damage.

Box 49.2 Other routes for drug administration

- Enteral and rectal
- Intramuscular, subcutaneous
- Sublingual
- Transdermal
- Nasal
- Inhalational
- Topical
- Intraventricular (cerebrospinal fluid), pleural, peritoneal, lymphatic, ocular.

Box 49.3 Indications for central venous access

- Monitoring of central venous pressure
- Drug administration
- Large-volume fluid resuscitation
- Pacing wires
- Insertion of pulmonary artery catheters
- Dialysis/haemofiltration
- Lack of peripheral venous access
- Cardiopulmonary bypass
- Parenteral nutrition.

(Box 49.3). More than an estimated 250 000 are inserted annually in UK hospitals.

Contraindications are relative, including limited sites for access, anatomical variants, acquired venous stenosis, previous difficulties/complications, severe coagulopathy, and local sepsis at the insertion site. Vascular surgical patients may have prosthetic material (typically radiolucent) at the proposed site of cannulation (e.g. carotid, femoral, or axillary patches or grafts). These are a strong contraindication to use of adjacent veins because of the risks of vessel damage, infection, or both.

Short-term central venous access

There is a very wide choice of devices. Most are inserted via a Seldinger guidewire technique, either directly over the guidewire or through an introducer sheath. Commoner devices in use for anaesthesia include a standard three- or four-multilumen central venous catheter (CVC), a 'long line' or peripherally inserted central catheter (PICC) inserted via arm veins (e.g. good for isolated vasopressor infusions), larger-bore valved introducer sheaths (e.g. pulmonary artery catheter introducer), and large-bore dialysis-type catheters for massive transfusion and postoperative dialysis/haemofiltration.

The risks of large-bore peripheral cannulae for large-volume pressurized fluid infusions (risk of extravasation/compartment syndrome) should be weighed against the risk of inserting a large-bore CVC (introducer sheath/dialysis catheter). If time, equipment, and expertise allows, the latter is generally better. Use large-bore dialysis-type catheters for predicted massive blood losses, or predicted need for dialysis/haemofiltration in the postoperative period (e.g. a patient with poor renal function needing complex cardiovascular surgery).

Some patients already have a long-term CVC *in situ* (e.g. Hickman, PICC, Port, or dialysis type). Consider their use during anaesthesia, rather than a new device insertion because of the frequent presence of narrowed central veins with increased risks/difficulty for further cannulation (see 'Short- *vs* long-term venous access').

A suitable range of catheter lengths should be stocked for each route of insertion. A minimal range of adult lengths would be 15 cm for the right internal jugular vein, 20 cm for the left internal jugular vein and right axillary/subclavian vein, and 24 cm for left axillary/subclavian and femoral veins. Use the narrowest gauge devices suitable for an individual indication to reduce trauma to the veins on insertion. Large-bore catheters and dilators devices do not traverse corners easily, so use right internal jugular or femoral veins in preference to the right subclavian vein or left-sided access sites. Compare the size of a vein with the diameter of the catheter using ultrasound. A catheter which occupies more than one-third of the diameter of the vein is likely to be associated with low venous flow and high risk of thrombosis over time.

Routes of access

Internal jugular vein

The right internal jugular vein is typically associated with the lowest risk of procedural complications and central catheter tip misplacement. There is wide variability in the relationship between the carotid artery and vein, and some patients will have a dominant venous circulation on one side of the neck. There may be higher risks in patients with carotid artery disease (patch, unstable plaque, scarring), where inadvertent arterial puncture may be dangerous, even with a green 21-gauge seeker needle. For postoperative ICU usage there is an increased risk of infection because of the close proximity of secretions from the oropharynx or tracheostomy stoma. Care needs to be taken to avoid carotid puncture or cannulation, which can be largely avoided with the routine use of ultrasound guidance. Low in the neck there is risk to other vessels, for example, the thyrocervical trunk and branches, the vertebral artery, and subclavian artery close behind the vein (visible with higher-resolution ultrasound, see Fig. 49.1). The vein is very superficial and easily transfixed. Catheters inserted from the left side have to traverse two corners on passage to the superior vena cava (SVC), making central placement more difficult.

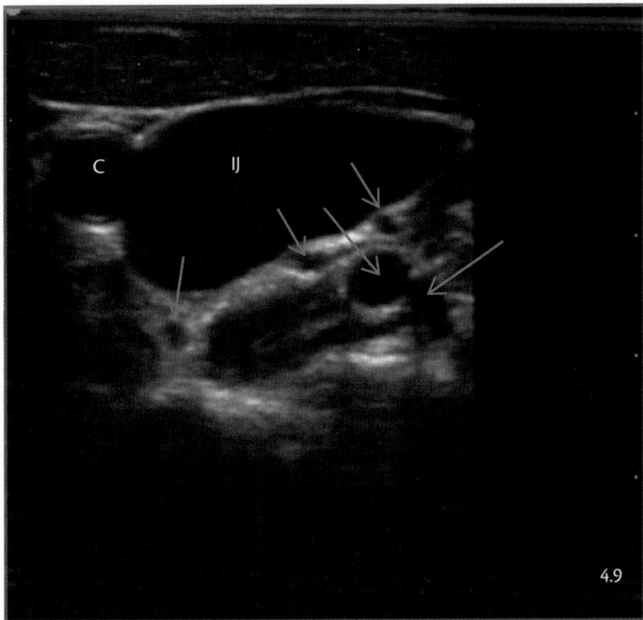

Figure 49.1 Cross-sectional ultrasound image of right internal jugular (IJ) and carotid (C), low in neck. Note the vessels immediately behind the vein, which are obviously at risk if the vein is transfixed at this level with the needle, thyrocervical trunk artery, and branches of thyrocervical trunk including the inferior thyroid artery (arrows). Such vessels should be avoided by adjusting the needle trajectory and avoiding transfixion by increasing venous pressure by head-down tilt, Valsalva manoeuvre, and application of intermittent positive pressure ventilation or positive end-expiratory pressure.

Landmark techniques

The internal jugular vein runs from the jugular foramen at the base of the skull (immediately behind the ear) to its termination behind the posterior border of the sternoclavicular joint, where it combines with the subclavian vein to become the brachiocephalic vein. Throughout its length it lies lateral, first to the internal and then common carotid arteries, within the carotid sheath, behind the sternomastoid muscle. Many landmark approaches to the internal jugular vein have been described (Latto 2000b), suggesting none is ideal. A typical approach is from the apex of the triangle formed by the two heads of the sternomastoid.

The procedure is as follows: slightly extend the neck and turn the head slightly to opposite side. Palpate the carotid artery at the level of the cricoid cartilage. Look for the internal jugular vein pulsation. If compressed, then released, the internal jugular can usually be seen to refill. To locate the vein, introduce the needle from the apex of the triangle at an angle of 30° and aim towards the ipsilateral nipple.

Often when attempting to puncture the vein it collapses under the pressure of the needle, which then transfixes it, and puncture is not recognized. The vessel may then be located by aspirating as the needle is slowly withdrawn. Blood will be aspirated as the needle tip passes back into the vein, which refills once the needle pressure has been released. It is a common mistake to assume the internal jugular vein is deep. Typically it is less than 2 cm from skin and can be easily located with a standard blue/green 'seeker' needle. Once the vessel has been identified, the seeker needle can be left in place as a guide to puncture with the introducer needle. The vein can be cannulated in the sitting/semi-recumbent patient in the case of heart failure or morbid obesity, where typically the venous pressure is very high.

Ultrasound guidance

There is very good evidence to support the routine use of ultrasound guidance for internal jugular puncture to reduce complications and increase success of procedures (Wu et al. 2013). You can see branches of the vein (e.g. facial vein), valves, and the carotid, subclavian, and thyroid arteries. The thyroid gland, cysts within it, and lymph nodes are relevant and visible. Choose a puncture site and needle direction such that overlap of the vein over the artery is minimized.

External jugular vein

This is useful in acute situations or coagulopathic patients when a standard large-bore short cannula can be inserted under direct vision. CVCs can be sited via the external jugular vein but the angles on passing through the deep fascia into the subclavian vein lead to potential problems with central passage of wires and catheters.

Subclavian vein

The subclavian vein is a continuation of the axillary vein. It runs from the apex of the axilla behind the posterior border of the clavicle and across the first rib to join the internal jugular vein, forming the brachiocephalic vein behind the sternoclavicular joint.

Landmark approaches are associated with a higher risk of complications compared with the internal jugular vein, particularly pneumothorax and incorrect tip placement (catheter ascending into the neck or contralateral side). However, it is more comfortable for the patient in the long term and is a potentially cleaner site in relation to infection risk. Avoid using the side of potential, or actual, dialysis arteriovenous fistulae because of the risk of bleeding from an arterialized vein or damage to the vein from thrombus formation. The subclavian vein may be preferred in the head-injured patient (less risk of effect on intracranial pressure).

Landmark techniques

The patient is positioned supine (some advocate placing a sandbag between the patient's shoulder blades). The junction of the medial third and outer two-thirds of the clavicle is marked and the needle introduced just beneath the clavicle at this point, and then redirected closely behind the clavicle towards the suprasternal notch, passing forward with continuous aspiration until blood is obtained. The vein may be transfixed, so aspiration is required as the needle is withdrawn. Many different approaches to infraclavicular axillary, subclavian, and supraclavicular subclavian veins are described, suggesting none are ideal (Ng 2000).

Ultrasound guidance

The clavicle impedes ultrasound imaging except in young children (Pirotte and Veyckemans 2007), but ultrasound can be used to guide puncture of the vein using a more lateral infraclavicular axillary approach (O'Leary et al. 2012) or supraclavicular site (Mallin et al. 2000). Recent studies have shown benefits of ultrasound similar to the internal jugular at the former site (Bodenham 2011a; Fragou et al. 2011). The close proximity of the pleura, axillary artery, and brachial plexus requires careful approaches to the vein. Ultrasound allows these structures to be visualized and avoided. In addition, branches of the axillary artery (thoracoacromial trunk, anterior to vein) and the cephalic vein can be visualized and avoided (Fig. 49.2). Further laterally, the operator will note a greater distance between vein and pleura, reducing the risk of pneumothorax. This advantage is balanced by a smaller diameter and deeper vessel compared with a more medial approach. It may be difficult to visualize and

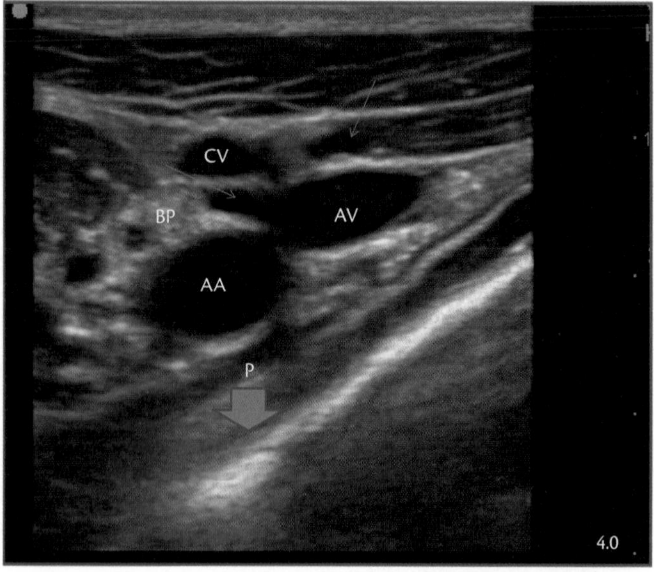

Figure 49.2 Cross-sectional ultrasound image of the right axillary vessels as seen from the right side. Note complexity of anatomy and close proximity of axillary vein (AV), axillary artery (AA), brachial plexus (BP), cephalic vein (CV) just proximal to where it enters the axillary vein, and branches (arrows) of the thoracoacromial arterial trunk (branch of the axillary artery) overlying the vein, the chest wall, and pleura (P).

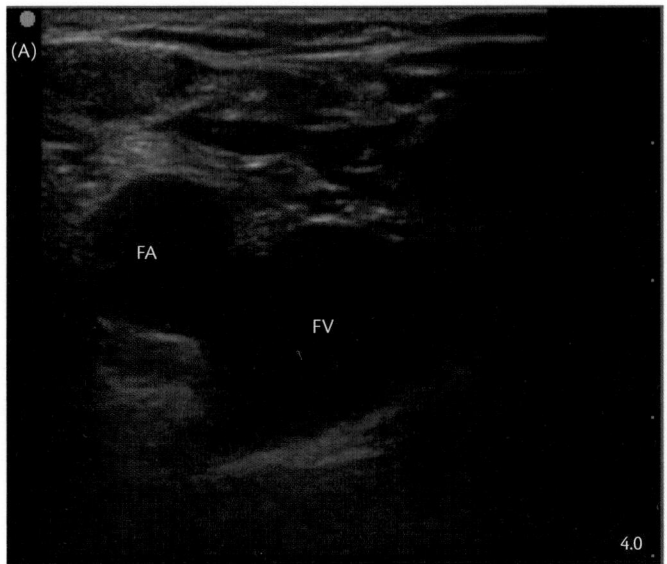

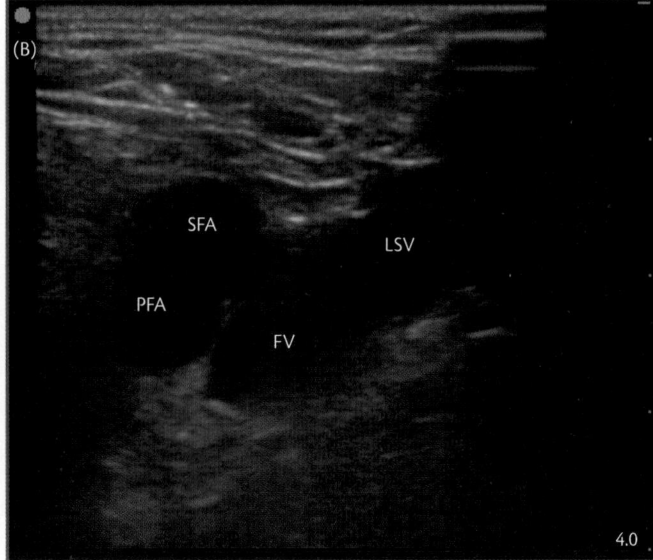

Figure 49.3 Cross-sectional image of left femoral vessels as seen from the patient's feet. (A) Vessels side by side at level of inguinal ligament, and (B) just below level of inguinal ligament. On image (B), note complexity of relations with superficial femoral artery (SFA) partially overlapping the femoral vein (FV), profunda (deep) femoral artery (PFA), and long saphenous vein entering the femoral vein (LSV). FA, femoral artery.

access the vein in obese or very muscular patients. The vein can also be visualized with an image intensifier after injection of peripheral contrast (Jaques et al. 1995).

Femoral vein

The anatomy is more complicated than the side-to-side orientation of vein and artery typically depicted in textbooks, which is only relatively true at the level of the inguinal ligament. The femoral vein is favoured in patients unable to tolerate head-down positioning and in children and emergency situations.

Landmark technique

Palpate the femoral artery and introduce the needle just medial to the femoral artery close to the inguinal ligament (actually not palpable, but a line from iliac crest to pubis tubercle). It is a common mistake to go too low where the superficial femoral artery overlies the vein and which may be the most easily palpable section.

Ultrasound guidance

Identify the femoral vein with the great saphenous vein entering it, and the common femoral artery dividing into deep and superficial branches (Fig. 49.3). Ensure that the vein is punctured near the inguinal ligament where the artery and common femoral vein lie side by side. The superficial femoral artery partially overlaps the vein just below this site (Hughes et al. 2000). Higher puncture sites risk incompressible damage to vessels, which can produce hidden bleeding into the peritoneal or retroperitoneal space (Taylor and Palagiri 2007).

Upper arm veins

High-frequency ultrasound can readily identify peripheral veins in the limbs. This is useful in intravenous drug users and the obese, and may facilitate central venous access with a PICC in the mid-upper arm to avoid flexure at the elbow.

PICCs can be inserted from antecubital veins which are visible or palpable. Veins in the upper arm away from the elbow flexure are an alternative and better for longer-term use (Sandhu and Sidhu 2004). The basilic, brachial, and cephalic veins are easily visualized with high-resolution ultrasound, together with accompanying artery and nerves (Fig. 49.4). There is wide anatomical variation. Access is best achieved with a small-bore needle, fine guidewire, dilator, and sheath (micropuncture kit). The catheter is measured for length from the proposed insertion site to third/fourth right intercostal space, or from X-ray screening (Parkinson et al. 1998). Regarding accompanying nerves, the median nerve adjacent to the brachial veins, and cutaneous nerves of forearm adjacent to the basilic vein should be identified where possible with ultrasound and avoided. The cephalic vein runs a more tortuous course where

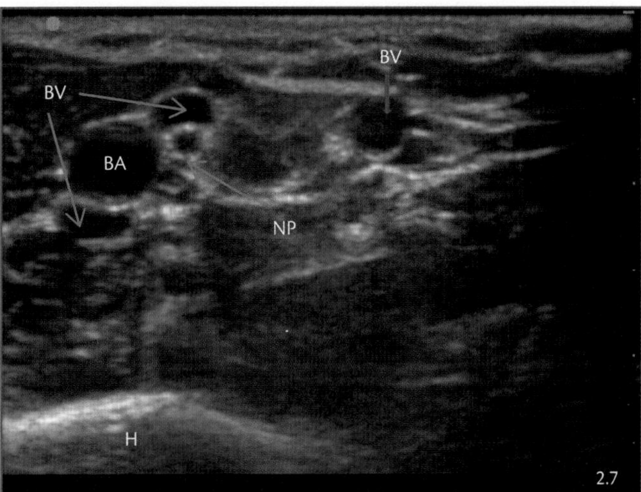

Figure 49.4 Cross-sectional image of vessels in right upper arm as seen from below. Basilic vein (BV), two brachial veins (arrows), humerus (H), nerve plexus (NP), and brachial artery (BA). There is significant variability in such relations between patients.

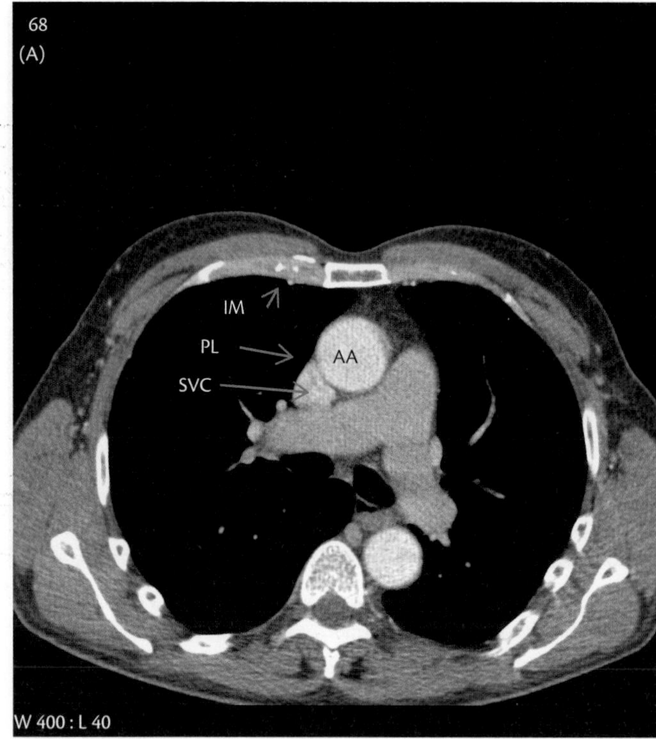

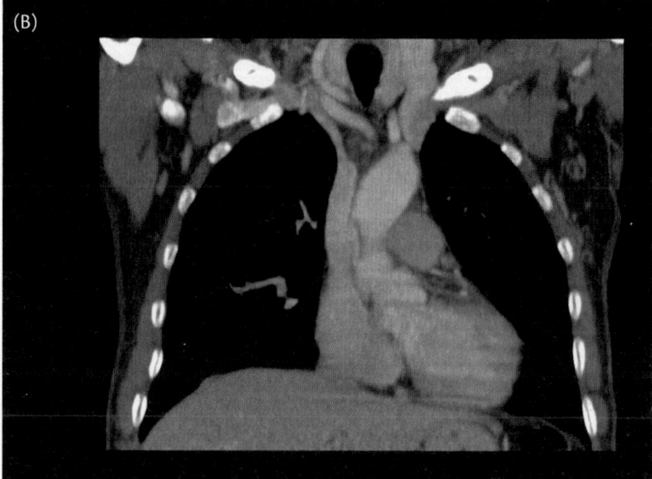

Figure 49.5 (A) Axial CT. (B) Coronal reconstruction to show superior vena cava (SVC). Note close relationship between SVC, right pleura (PL), and ascending aorta (AA), which overlie each other on anteroposterior X-ray imaging. IM, internal mammary vessels.

it penetrates the deep fascia to enter the axillary vein leading to potential difficulties in passing catheters.

Other routes of access are also used, for example, via the umbilical vein in neonates, direct access to the inferior vena cava (IVC) by radiologists, and mid-thigh femoral veins accessed with ultrasound.

Applied anatomy of the superior vena cava

The SVC drains venous blood from the upper half of the body and is the target site for CVC catheter tips from the upper-body insertion sites. The applied anatomy has been recently reviewed (Gibson and Bodenham 2013). It is formed by the confluence of the two brachiocephalic veins behind the first right costal cartilage. It is approximately 2 cm in diameter and 7cm long with no valves and descends to the upper part of the right atrium (Fig. 49.5). Its lateral right border is partially visible on anteroposterior chest X-ray but it is difficult to see where the right atrium begins.

The upper right border of the SVC bulges into the right pleural space such that a tear in this area risks major haemorrhage into the low-pressure pleural space. In the longer term, catheter tips (particularly from the left side) can perforate the vein wall and cause a hydrothorax when fluids are infused (Fig. 49.6). The lower half of the vessel is within the fibrous pericardium with relevance to the risk of pericardial tamponade (see 'Cardiac tamponade').

A major branch of the SVC is the azygous vein, which ascends on the right side in the posterior mediastinum, before arching forward to pierce the posterior wall of the mid section of SVC, at the level of the fourth thoracic vertebra. The tip of a catheter can lie at this junction or within the azygous vein.

Anatomical variations of central veins

Congenital

The commonest variant of the SVC is the so-called left SVC, which may occur with or without a normal right SVC, with an

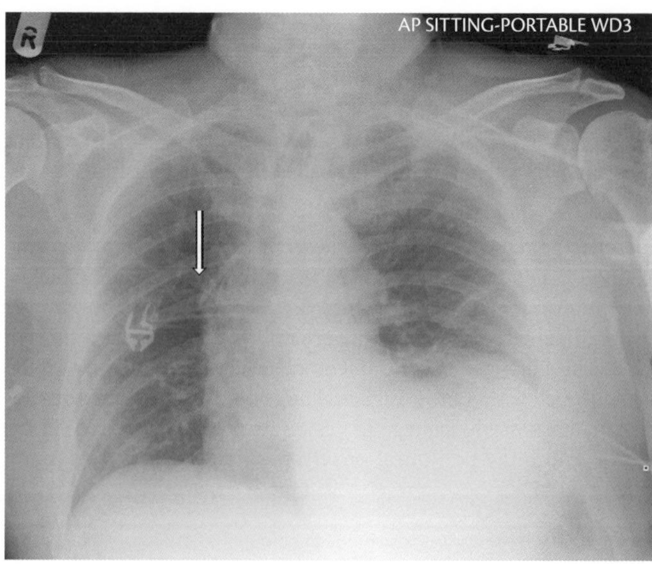

Figure 49.6 A stiff dual-lumen dialysis catheter has been inserted via the left subclavian vein and is abutting the wall of the superior vena cava (arrow). It is likely to cause discomfort, accelerated thrombosis, catheter failure, or erosion through the vein wall into the pleural space. To achieve adequate function including flows for dialysis it needs to be exchanged for a longer device whose tip lies in the long axis of the superior vena cava/right atrium.

incidence of approximately 0.5% in healthy individuals and 1–5% in those with additional cardiac defects. The left SVC is a persistence of the left cardinal vein present in the early fetal circulation, which normally atrophies with development. The right vein (if present) takes the normal course of the SVC. The left crosses the left side of the arch of the aorta, passes in front of the left pulmonary hilum, and passes posteriorly to enter the right atrium from behind, via a functionally enlarged coronary sinus. The two SVCs may communicate in the upper chest. A left-sided SVC can be used for access, but care should be taken as the vein may open into the left atrium with risks of systemic air or particulate embolism (Ghadiali et al. 2007).

Similarly, below the diaphragm, the IVC can show numerous variations. The IVC is normally formed from a bilateral circulation, which develops into a single large vessel through right-sided enlargement and left-sided regression. In the adult, the IVC may be represented below the level of the renal veins by two symmetrical vessels with an incidence of about 0.3%.

Rarely, patients present with dextrocardia, where the heart orientation is reversed so that it lies to the right of the midline. It is estimated to occur in 1 in 10 000 births. It can be associated with the reversal of abdominal/chest organs and blood vessels, so-called situs inversus, in which case the SVC and IVC also lie to the left of the midline (Evans et al. 2010).

Acquired

Any patient with a history of previous long-term central vein cannulation or a mass causing compression has the potential for an acquired SVC/IVC or great vessel abnormality. SVC compression from a tumour can cause oedema and venous engorgement in the upper body (SVC syndrome) (Cheng 2009). It is questionable whether a catheter should be passed through such a compressed vein as it may cause thrombosis and further SVC obstruction. Stenosis or thrombosis is common with long-term access (Galloway and Bodenham 2004), and is frequently asymptomatic as a result of collateral vein enlargement. This can present as a failure to pass a guidewire or catheter.

The presence of engorged venous collaterals on the chest wall, or engorged difficult-to-compress veins on ultrasound, or high venous pressure on cannulation are suggestive of such stenoses. Diagnosis of such problems can be confirmed by simple venography with an image intensifier, CT, or Doppler ultrasound studies (Fig. 49.7). With advanced age and disease, the SVC and other great veins may become increasingly tortuous. Mediastinal shift from effusions, lung collapse, or pneumonectomy will shift all structures including the SVC from the midline. This may cause confusion on X-rays if such changes are not understood.

Similar problems may also arise in the IVC. In the event of blockage or portal hypertension, the azygous system may massively enlarge and become the predominant route of venous drainage from the lower body.

Catheter tip position

Failure to achieve good catheter positions will increase the risk of the following: catheter-related thrombosis, arrhythmias, perforation of the vein wall (to cause hydrothorax, cardiac tamponade, extravasation), catheter failure and pain during injections, and later stenosis.

An adequate length of the distal catheter, lying in the long axis of the SVC with its tip above the pericardial reflection is ideal, approximately level with the carina on chest X-ray, often at the junction of the SVC/right atrium or upper right atrium. This is not always achievable, particularly with left-sided catheters, contrary to textbook guidance (Fletcher and Bodenham 2000; Vesely 2003; Stonelake and Bodenham 2006). The commonest problem is a catheter which is too short with its tip abutting vein wall at an acute angle (Fig. 49.6). A schematic representation of the areas where catheter tips can lie is shown (Fig. 49.8).

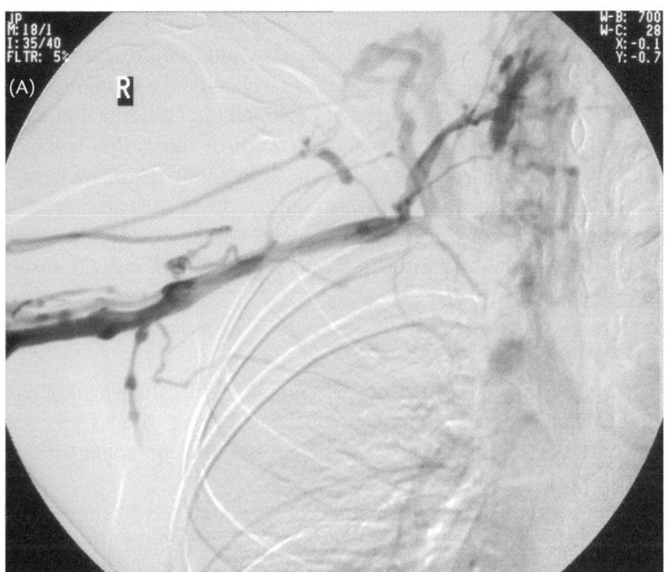

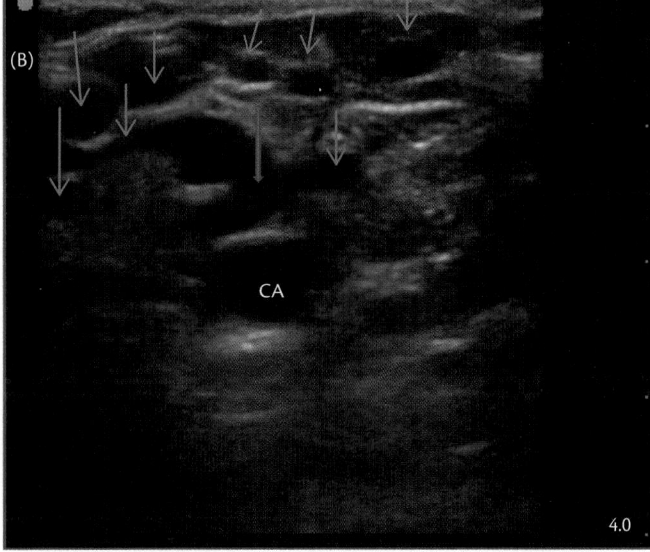

Figure 49.7 Blocked central veins following long-term venous access. (A) A venogram shows complete obstruction of the right subclavian vein with the venous return via collaterals to the internal jugular vein (also blocked low in neck) and thereafter to other collaterals into the chest. (B) Ultrasound examination of the right neck, where the original internal jugular vein (large arrow) has blocked and branches out into multiple engorged collaterals (small arrows). CA, carotid artery.

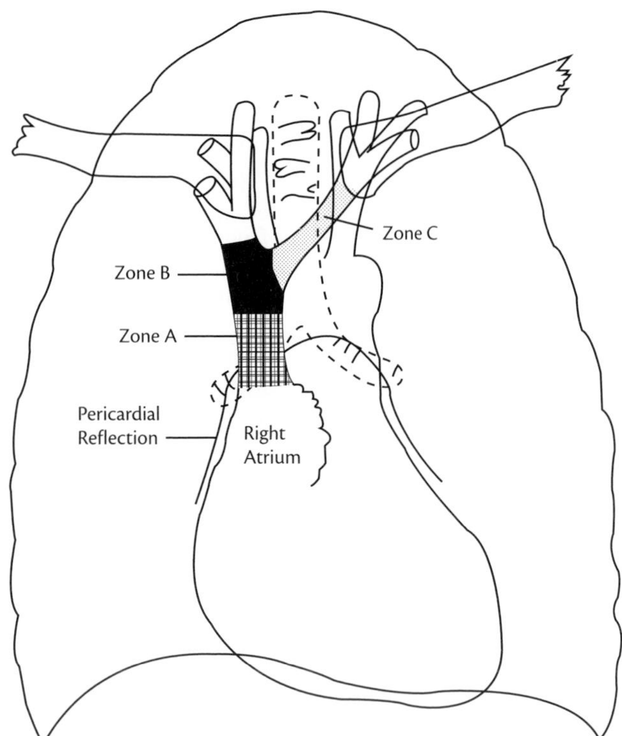

Figure 49.8 Stylized anatomical figure dividing the great veins and upper right atrium into three zones (A–C), representing different areas for placement of central venous catheter tips. A, Junction of right atrium and superior vena cava (SVC) suitable for all catheters, but below pericardial reflection. B, SVC above pericardial reflection, suitable for right internal jugular and sometimes right subclavian access. C, left innominate vein, suitable only for short-term fluids and central venous pressure monitoring from left-side access.

Reproduced with permission from Stonelake PA, Bodenham AR. The carina as a radiological landmark for central venous catheter tip position. *British Journal of Anaesthesia*, 2006, Volume 96, Issue 3, pp. 335–40, by permission of the Board of Management and Trustees of the British Journal of Anaesthesia.

Imaging

The majority of short-term CVCs are inserted without real-time imaging, with a subsequent chest X-ray to confirm central placement. The limitations of one-dimensional imaging must be understood (see 'Misplaced catheters'). Catheter tips move when a patient changes from lying to sitting/standing, or on deep breathing (Kowalski et al. 1997). On X-ray they will appear to be sited further centrally on supine/head-down imaging *vs* an erect posteroanterior film with deep inspiration. X-ray screening is ideal although infrequently used during anaesthesia but should be considered if difficulties occur.

Other aids including ECG guidance or electromagnetic sensors are increasingly used, but these do not distinguish between arterial, venous, and mediastinal placement, or a coiled tip, and compensation for right- and left-sided catheters is required (Kremser et al. 2011). Units need a suitable range of catheter lengths for each access site (see 'Short-term central venous access').

Misplaced catheters

Catheters may be misplaced within the venous system, following an abnormal path to the neck, the arm, or contralateral side. Such catheters need re-positioning if they are to stay *in situ* for anything more than a few hours. Alternatively, the patient may

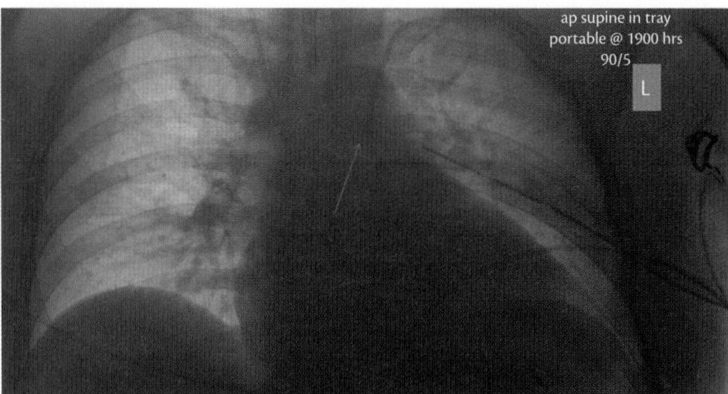

Figure 49.9 A chest X-ray showing two central venous catheters inserted by left and right internal jugular veins. The left-sided catheter fails to follow the path of the left innominate vein (arrow). This image cannot distinguish between a catheter in a vein (internal mammary or left superior vena cava), and artery (descending aorta), pleural space (actual site in this case), mediastinum, or other structure. It position was verified with computed tomography imaging and it was removed without complication.

have a normal variant of anatomy or acquired stenosis of the great veins leading to misplaced catheters in the great veins. Catheters are generally easily recognized in such positions and specialist advice is not required before using or removing such catheters.

Catheters may lie outside the vein in an obviously incorrect position. Of more concern is that catheters on a plain chest X-ray may appear to follow an approximate normal path, but are not correctly sited in the SVC. Analysis of cross-sectional anatomy shows that catheters in the SVC, right pleural space, right internal mammary vessels, azygous system, ascending aorta, or mediastinum cannot be reliably differentiated on a single plane X-ray (Fig. 49.9). Many clinicians rely too much on chest X-ray appearances, not appreciating that such images can only confirm that the catheter has passed centrally and is not kinked.

If a catheter is in an unusual position or malfunctions, time should be taken to ascertain its position, and it should not just be pulled out. Bedside tests include assessing the pressures in all lumens (via a fluid column or transducer) and aspiration of blood from the lumens for estimation of haemoglobin (systemic blood *vs* pleural collection), oxygen partial pressure, or saturation. None of these bedside tests are entirely reliable. If in doubt, definitive localization requires injection of X-ray contrast down the catheter with imaging (venogram) or cross-sectional CT imaging (Amerasekera et al. 2009; Bodenham 2011b). *If in doubt, don't pull it out* (Gibson and Bodenham 2013)!

Complications

Anaesthetists need knowledge of complications, their avoidance, and management. They may also be called upon to help sort out major CVC complications (e.g. major bleeding or upper airway obstruction).

Any anatomical structure adjacent or connected to the vascular tree may potentially be damaged during needle, catheter, and guidewire insertion, or later as a result of thrombosis, perforation, and infection (Box 49.4) (McGee and Gould 2003). Certain patterns are recognized as potentially life-threatening and a cause for high-value legal claims during or after anaesthesia (Domino et al.

Box 49.4 Complications of central venous catheterization

Early

- Arrhythmias
- Vascular injury
- Pneumothorax
- Haemothorax
- Cardiac tamponade
- Neural injury
- Embolization (including guidewire, catheter, or air).

Late

- Infection
- Thrombosis
- Embolization
- Erosion/perforation of vessels
- Cardiac tamponade
- Lymphatic damage
- Arteriovenous fistula.

2004; Hove et al. 2007; Cook 2010). These typically relate to local pressure effects from an arterial haematoma, massive bleeding into the chest/abdomen, and strokes from carotid cannulation.

Collateral damage from needle placement

This includes damage to adjacent arteries, lung, pleura, and nerves. Even if the original needle trajectory is correct, empty veins often have to be transfixed for cannulation. Structures behind the vein are then liable to injury (e.g. arteries in the neck: the carotid, subclavian, vertebral or thyrocervical trunk). Arteries may also overlie the vein, for example, the superficial femoral artery in the groin (Hughes et al. 2000) and thoracoacromial trunk in relation to the axillary vein (Smith et al. 2009; O'Leary et al. 2012). Needle damage is largely avoidable by the routine use of ultrasound (see main 'Ultrasound guidance' section).

Central insertion of devices

Guidewires generally pass with minimal resistance centrally, but may go astray from all access sites, including the right internal jugular vein. Without X-ray screening or other aids, there is no certainty that they have not passed across the midline, into venous branches, down an arm, or out of the vein. Excessive force must not be used as guidewires can easily exit veins, to pass into the pleura, mediastinum, or other structures.

Dilators and catheters passed over a guidewire will enlarge the tract to their outer diameter or larger if the vein tears. If a guidewire is kinked or acutely angulated, and further force is applied to the dilator/catheter, it will tear the vein wall and exit into adjacent structures. The guidewire should be repeatedly checked to ensure it moves freely through the dilator/catheter, to ensure no distortion or false passage. If any resistance is felt, the procedure must be stopped, or further imaging obtained to guide alternative approaches. Such judgement is very much an acquired skill. Mobile image intensifiers which are available in most theatre suites provide the optimal tool, but are rarely used by anaesthetists, outside pain management procedures.

Arterial damage

Insertion of needles, guidewires, dilators, and catheters may cause damage to arteries at the puncture site or more centrally. A local haematoma or false aneurysm may cause skin and tissue loss, nerve damage from compression (Chitwood et al. 1996), and upper airway compression (similar to bleeding after major neck surgery). Surgery will be required to decompress large haematomas urgently, irrespective of how the leak is eventually closed (surgery or radiology). Arterial dissection, thrombosis, embolus, and unintentional cannulation may cause distal ischaemic damage, with particular relevance to the carotid artery. If there is a needle puncture only, then removal and pressure for 5–10 min will usually suffice.

Case series suggest that accidental arterial catheter placement may be missed clinically, as staff seek to find alternative erroneous explanations for malfunctioning catheters, back-bleeding, infusion pump alarms, and signs of thrombosis including a stroke or transient ischaemic attack. Bleeding or a haematoma at the puncture site is not necessarily seen until removal of the catheter. A high index of suspicion is required.

Removal of large-bore catheters situated in the carotid artery needs careful consideration, to avoid emboli to the brain, and to seal the arterial defect. Systemic heparinization and removal of the device, with either a surgical procedure similar to a carotid endarterectomy (venting clot and suturing defect), or a radiological stenting procedure, are two preferred options (Guilbert et al. 2008). Removing such devices and pressing for 20 min to prevent carotid haemorrhage, will further risk brain ischaemia from haematoma, dislodged emboli, and a lack of blood flow. Similar considerations apply to larger arterial cannulae elsewhere. In the short term, it is generally safe to leave dilators, catheters, and guidewires in position, particularly in a heparinized patient, while the situation is evaluated. It is generally recommended not to remove catheters larger than 9 Fr from arteries without using a percutaneous occlusion device or surgical closure. If in doubt don't take it out! Seek advice from vascular surgery or interventional radiology.

Pleural collections

A pneumothorax typically results from needle damage during subclavian or jugular puncture but can occur from misplaced guidewires or catheters. Needle-based damage should be almost completely avoidable with routine skilled use of ultrasound. Ventilated patients are likely to need a chest drain after such needle damage. In the spontaneously breathing patient, the air leak may not be visible on chest X-ray until some hours later and patients can often be managed conservatively if asymptomatic and the degree of lung collapse is minimal.

Pleural catheter placement is important to recognize as infused fluids may cause an enlarging pleural effusion and if the catheter originates in the vein then there is the potential for massive bleeding into the low-pressure pleural space on catheter removal.

Haemothorax/peritoneum

Minor tears of great veins are probably more common during guidewire, dilator, or catheter insertion than is generally realized, because of thin vein walls. As a result of the low venous pressure, connective tissue, muscle, or other structures will usually tamponade local bleeding without further problems. Major bleeding occurs when a tear connects directly to the low-pressure pleural space (Jankovic et al. 2005). Chest veins at particular risk, immediately adjacent to the pleura, include the SVC (right border), azygous system, hemi-azygous system (on left), and internal mammaries. It is revealing to observe these vessels on CT (Fig. 49.5) scans, or at thoracotomy/thoracoscopy.

Damage to the arterial tree can cause similar problems, when a hole made by a needle alone is sufficient for massive bleeding. The subclavian arteries protrude into and can bleed directly into the apex of the pleural spaces. Alternatively, a more distant enlarging arterial haematoma may burst into the pleura. Similar mechanisms apply in the peritoneal space, with cases of fatal concealed haemorrhage from iliac vessels. Management relies on drainage, leaving dilators/catheters in place to reduce bleeding, and urgent repair by surgery or increasingly interventional radiology.

Lymphatic leaks result from either direct damage to the major thoracic lymphatics where they join the internal jugular vein or SCV, or thrombosis of the vein causing a back pressure effect. The leak can cause an external leak of lymph/chyle, a lymphocoele (localized collection), or a chylothorax. It can occur either side but is more commonly found on the left because of the much larger left thoracic duct (Mallick and Bodenham 2003).

Nerve damage

Major vessels at most cannulation sites are accompanied by nerves, which are at risk from needle or device damage, and stretching as a result of a haematoma. Reported damage includes that to the phrenic nerve, sympathetic chain (Horner's syndrome), femoral nerve, brachial plexus, and median nerve in the upper arm elbow region. At some sites (e.g. the axillary artery and vein) the brachial plexus can be visualized and specifically avoided with higher-resolution ultrasound. Deeper injection of LA may produce inadvertent reversible nerve block.

Cardiac tamponade

Reported series suggest that this occurs from two mechanisms: first, the pericardial space (reflection) extends up on to the arch of the aorta and the proximal part of its branches, so a needle puncture at this site may lead to bleeding into the pericardium. Surprisingly, this is a recognized problem, usually after attempted right subclavian approaches (Fangio et al. 2002). Second, erosion of catheters through the lower SVC or right atrium can occur, allowing infusion of fluid into the pericardium (Orme et al. 2007). Reported series suggest that it is pressurized fluid infusion, rather than low-pressure venous bleeding, that is the usual problem.

Box 49.5 Complications associated with central venous catheter removal

- Air embolism
- Catheter fracture and embolism
- Dislodgement or thrombus or fibrin sheath
- Haemorrhage
- Arterial complications—bleeding
- Infection—local and systemic
- Catheter trapped in vein/tissues.

Regrettably, cardiac tamponade is often a post-mortem finding. A high index of suspicion is required to prompt, and then confirm, this diagnosis by echocardiography in any collapsed patient with a CVC *in situ*. Management requires attempted aspiration of infused fluid through the catheter if still *in situ*, urgent pericardiocentesis, and stenting or surgical repair if required.

Removal of central venous catheters

CVCs should be removed as soon as they are either no longer required, or problems occur. Most devices can just be pulled out once anchorage devices are removed. The negative pressure in central veins can entrain air through an open/damaged catheter or through a well-formed tract, so devices should be removed in a head-down position, with applied pressure and occlusive dressing to the entry site. Air entrainment and embolization is at highest risk with large-bore devices, and well-established short tracts (e.g. jugular non-tunnelled dialysis catheter). This is a rare but recognized cause of collapse and death. The low venous pressure means bleeding is generally easily stopped with applied pressure and dressings. There are a number of other potential complications (Box 49.5).

Occasional long-term catheters cannot be removed because of the very tight constriction of a fibrin sleeve around the catheter or organized clot anchoring side holes in the catheter to the SVC or right atrium. Do not persist to the point of catheter breakage or vessel damage, seek specialist advice.

Removing a Hickman line/port

Anchored catheters need a cut-down procedure to free the cuff and avoid the catheter fracture on traction (Galloway and Bodenham 2003; Hudman and Bodenham 2013). Cuffed catheters may be pulled out if they have been in place less than 2–3 weeks, before adhesions form. Similarly, heavy infection breaks down adhesions, allowing the cuff to be pulled free.

Identify the cuff with palpation or ultrasound. Inject LA around the cuff site and tunnel tract then cut down (1 cm incision) on the venous side of the cuff. Use forceps to feel the catheter rolling beneath, as the incision is too small for a finger. Free up and remove the venous section first; typically a thin fibrin sheath will need to be incised. Then dissect around the cuff to free adhesions and remove it completely. Avoid sharp dissection until the venous section is removed to avoid catheter embolus. Similar principles apply to removing ports, which lie in a fibrous capsule with non-absorbable anchor sutures.

Short- *vs* long-term venous access

Cannulae in peripheral veins typically only last a few days but long-term devices can last months to years, and are in increasing use in hospitals and the community. The definition of long-term access is unclear, for example, predicted use greater than 6 weeks or the presence of internal anchoring devices.

Long-term devices can be used during anaesthesia and critical care with good attention to aseptic technique. Such devices are increasingly present so all anaesthetists should have a basic knowledge of their functions and use (Box 49.6). Such devices can be used for routine (e.g. anaesthesia induction) and emergency use (resuscitation). Some devices (e.g. Groshong catheters) have a valved tip or proximal hub, which will preclude CVP monitoring and may give pulsatile infusion of drugs (Rose and Bodenham 2010). The development of fibrin sleeves (Hemmelgarn et al. 2011), which commonly present after weeks/months around the internal section

Box 49.6 Common indications for long-term access

- Cancer chemotherapy
- Home parenteral nutrition
- Repeated blood transfusions
- Long-term intravenous fluid requirement
- Long-term antibiotics
- Haemodialysis
- Regular venesection.

of long-term catheters, can cause similar effects. Assess the risks and benefits of such use compared with new insertion of devices in a patient, who may already have very difficult access with blocked central veins.

Ports are accessed with non-coring Huber tip needles, although in practice any small-bore needle can be used. Some force is required to push the needle through the skin and then the thick silicone rubber membrane. The needle stops when it hits the back wall of the chamber.

Many devices are now inserted by anaesthetists during standalone procedures in the operating theatre. Points to consider when choosing devices include the following:

- The indication and duration of proposed treatment requiring venous access
- The proposed location for administration of therapy (e.g. hospital, outpatient clinic, or home)
- The risks of contamination
- The patient's clinical status (e.g. coagulation, platelets, sepsis) and whether the patient will self-administer drugs/fluids.

Devices

Shorter term

Mid-lines (10–20 cm soft catheters) are inserted via the antecubital fossa, with the tip in the upper third of the basilic/cephalic vein, short of the great veins, and are suitable for up to 3 weeks of infusion of non-irritant solutions.

Long term

PICCs are advanced centrally from the antecubital fossa/upper arm veins, and can last months to years, if managed correctly.

Cuffed, 'Hickman-type' catheters are tunnelled from the insertion site to chest/abdominal wall. A Dacron® cuff develops tissue ingrowth for anchorage and as an infection barrier (takes 3–4 weeks). Dialysis catheters (e.g. Tesio® type), are wide-bore, stiff catheters with dual lumens and an anchoring cuff.

Subcutaneous ports (titanium/plastic) are placed in a surgical cavity on the chest, abdominal wall, or upper arm. They are ideal for intermittent therapy (e.g. antibiotics for cystic fibrosis) and popular for use in children. The sealed system has an intact skin barrier between needle access episodes, which lowers the overall infection risk.

All the above-mentioned devices are available in single- and multiple-lumen versions. Some are CT compatible to allow high-pressure injection of X-ray contrast.

Site of access

Anecdotal evidence suggests that right-sided catheters have a lower risk of thrombosis, because of a shorter straighter route to the SVC, with easier catheter tip positioning. Choose a site after considering patient factors, previous venous access, and clinician experience.

Look for evidence of vein thrombosis, previous scars, or venous collaterals and use ultrasound to assess patency at access sites. Formal central vein imaging (venogram, CT, magnetic resonance imaging) is helpful in difficult cases. Arrange puncture sites and tunnel tract to avoid tight bends; if necessary, use multiple punctures to avoid bends and kinks of less than 90°.

Tips for insertion of long-term devices

Ask awake patients to inspire on insertion of guidewire/catheter to help central passage. Measure required catheter length from the positioned guidewire (using image intensifier), or measure predicted length externally over the chest wall.

Take care with rigid sheaths/dilators to avoid central vein damage. Do not insert too deeply (generally longer than required). Pinch the sheath (or use valved device) on removal of the obturator to avoid bleeding and air embolism. Sheaths readily kink—draw back until the catheter passes through it.

A long, thin, coated Terumo®-type (Somerset, NJ, USA) guidewire (70+ cm) can be passed via the sheath or through soft catheters to help central placement in difficult cases. Screen the guidewire, obturator sheath, and catheter insertion if any resistance is encountered.

Use venography through a needle, sheath, or catheter if you are uncertain as to the position of the device relative to the vein path (check contrast allergy first). For fixed-length catheters (e.g. Groshong/dialysis), choose the correct length for site of access, and adjust the length of tunnel to give a correct tip position. Move the anchor cuff along the tract to adjust the length of the venous section.

Ports can be inserted under LA with or without sedation, or general anaesthesia. Smaller low-profile versions can be sited in the arm. Minimize the incision and pocket size by placing anchor sutures in the pocket first, then slide the port in and tie off. Buried subcuticular sutures provide a good cosmetic result (Hudman and Bodenham 2013).

Aftercare

External anchoring sutures/devices should not be removed for at least 3 weeks to allow the Dacron® cuff to adhere. PICCs have no anchoring cuff and need a continued external anchor device. Adhesive external anchor devices (e.g. StatLock®) are thought to have a lower risk of infection than sutured devices.

If the patient is considered at high risk of thromboembolism, therapeutic dose anticoagulation may be indicated; low-dose regimens are not thought to work. Some units still lock dialysis catheters with heparin 1000 units ml^{-1}—always aspirate deadspace if in doubt. Thrombosed/blocked catheters may be unblocked, or prevented from blocking with low-dose urokinase (5000 units) injected into the catheter (Baskin et al. 2009; Hemmelgarn et al. 2011).

Arterial access

This is required for many elective and emergency operative procedures, for example, vascular, cardiothoracic, neurosurgical, and patients with severe cardiorespiratory disease. Relevant indications for anaesthesia and postoperative critical care include the following:

- Haemodynamic monitoring, when changes in blood pressure are likely to be sudden or profound
- Repeated arterial blood gas sampling
- Pulse contour analysis for cardiac output
- Aortic balloon pumps
- Cardiopulmonary bypass.

Common access sites include the radial, ulnar, brachial, dorsalis pedis, posterior tibial, and femoral arteries. Many patients have poor foot vessels so these are used less often than arm vessels. Occasionally, other sites such as the mid-arm brachial or infraclavicular axillary artery are used when other sites are blocked. Umbilical artery catheters are used in neonates.

The presence of dialysis arteriovenous fistulae or a future need for fistula requires consideration. In cardiac or vascular surgery, discussions with surgeons as to the optimal site are required, for example, during high aortic repairs and stents, the left subclavian or brachial artery may be occluded or accessed by vascular radiologists or surgeons.

Applied anatomy

Peripheral arterial cannulation is typically carried out via the radial artery of the non-dominant forearm, which is easily palpable at the wrist as a result of its superficial position. The presence of the ulnar artery means that the radial artery is generally not an end artery, and if damaged or thrombosed, tissue loss does not usually occur. Classically, the ulnar artery has been regarded as the dominant arterial supply to the forearm and hand but more recent studies have suggested that the radial artery is more likely to be the dominant vascular supply to the hand (Haerle and Häfner 2003). Alternatively, the brachial artery may be used, but as it is an end artery, the distal limb is at risk if occlusion occurs.

Many studies exist of applied arterial anatomy, including the use of ultrasound assessment, in the context of arterial cannulation, arteriovenous fistulae, and other surgical interventions. The detailed anatomy and relatively high frequency of normal variants may not be well recognized outside specialist surgery (Rodríguez-Niedenführ et al. 2003). Distal superficial radial and ulnar arteries may be clinically obvious, but cases of inadvertent cannulation during attempted venous access are described (Chin and Singh 2005). Variation in the proximal arterial supply to the upper arm and forearm are well recognized, and may not be obvious on palpation (e.g. high bifurcation of the brachial artery) (Çavdar et al. 2000) (Fig. 49.10).

Some patients with peripheral vascular disease have heavily diseased or blocked brachial, radial, or ulnar arteries, and rely on collateral supply. This should be identifiable clinically, and with ultrasound. It is intuitive that a site distal to such an obstruction should generally be avoided and a careful assessment of perfusion made. Allen's test—compression of the radial/ulnar artery while assessing hand blood flow—is useful conceptually, but has never been proved clinically to predict safe cannulation (Jarvis et al. 2000). Elderly patients tend to have more tortuous ectatic vessels which are more difficult to cannulate.

The femoral artery is a valuable access site widely used for diagnostic and interventional procedures. In the context of more prolonged catheterization, in anaesthesia or critical care it carries increased risks of infection and thrombosis. The superficial femoral artery is commonly more easily palpable than the common femoral artery but overlies the vein and is more likely to be diseased in the presence of atheroma. Higher damage to vessels can lead to hidden bleeding into the peritoneal or retroperitoneal spaces. Use ultrasound to cannulate the common femoral artery over the femoral head to allow compression against it. There is good evidence for the use of ultrasound for femoral artery cannulation (Seto et al. 2010).

Practical insertion tips

Consider the risk and benefits of multiple attempts at poor vessels in distal sites, *vs* a finite risk of cannulating an end artery

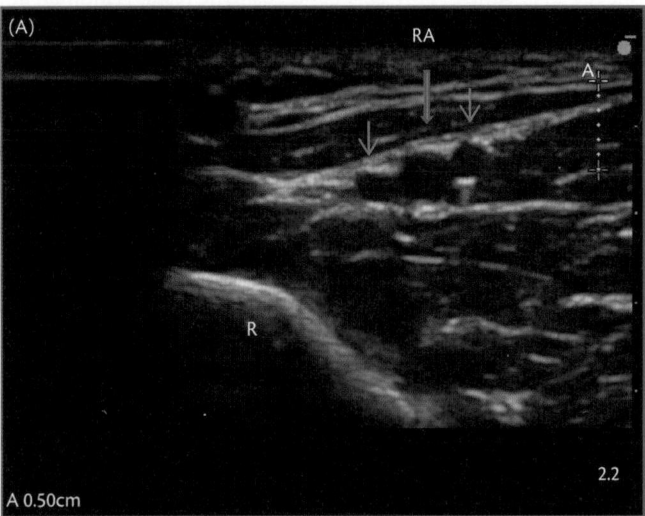

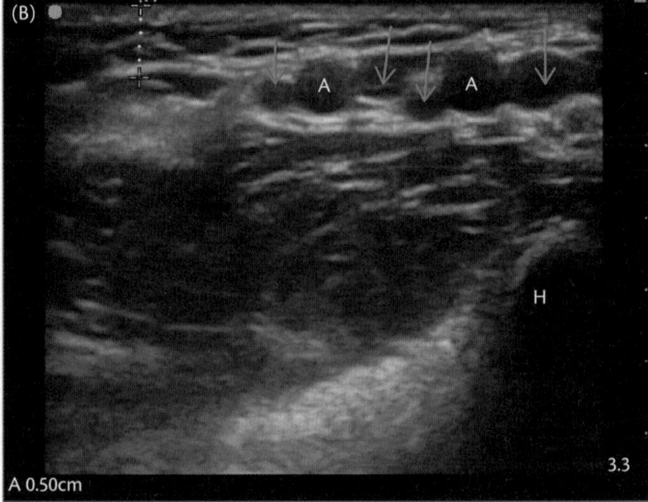

Figure 49.10 (A) Ultrasound image of radial artery just above wrist. Radial artery (RA) and paired compressible venae comitantes (small arrows) are seen either side of the artery. (B) Ultrasound image in the antecubital fossa, with venous tourniquet. There is a high bifurcation of the brachial artery in the upper arm but only one palpable pulse at the elbow. Two arteries (A) lie side by side with two sets of vena comitantes (arrows). This is a common anatomical variant.

more proximally. Do not persist with attempts at peripheral arterial cannulation in patients who are hypotensive and 'shut down'. The femoral and brachial arteries are useful during resuscitation of shocked patients; or use ultrasound guidance to visualize an impalpable artery.

Technically, procedures are typically easiest in awake patients, before anaesthesia, because of a stronger palpable pulse. Care should be taken with the length and size of catheters, particularly for deeper vessels such as the femoral and brachial arteries where short catheters can be dislodged with movement. Guidewire-based Seldinger devices are likely to have a higher success rate than catheter-over-needle devices in both routine and more difficult cases.

If using stitches, do not place stitches too deeply. It is possible to inadvertently damage peripheral arteries. Vessels may be calcified, making cannulation difficult and it may be impossible to close the vessels with pressure after removal of the cannula. Other vessels may have aneurysmal changes or dissection. If difficulties ensue, consider a vascular surgical cut-down to lessen the risk of iatrogenic injury. Larger sheaths left *in situ* in major arteries (femoral/brachial) need systemic heparinization to avoid thrombosis.

Removal

After catheter removal, press firmly on the site for at least 5 min. Occasionally persistent bleeding from the radial artery may require a fine suture (e.g. 5/0 nylon), to close the skin wound and stabilize the clot. Then apply further pressure. Radiological occlusion devices are required for removal of devices larger than 9 Fr, in the presence of severe coagulopathy, or in areas where pressure cannot be applied.

Complications

Complications can be divided into early and later but early complications may only be evident later (Box 49.7).

Vascular compromise may occur at any stage. Inadvertent injection of drugs into an arterial catheter is an important avoidable cause of morbidity. All cannulae and connecting tubes must be clearly labelled. Risks of infection increase with time and arterial catheters have been implicated in meticillin-resistant *Staphylococcus aureus* infection and other septicaemias. If concerns arise as to arterial patency and distal circulation, then urgent referral to vascular surgery or interventional radiology is required.

Box 49.7 Complications of arterial cannulation

Delayed

- Thrombus
- Embolism
- Nerve injury
- Infection
- Catheter dislodgement, fracture, embolism
- Arteriovenous fistula.

Early

- Bleeding
- Haematoma
- Arterial damage (dissection, thrombus, embolism).

Ultrasound guidance

Ultrasound imaging is not required routinely to cannulate arteries, although it has been used in difficult cases (Levin et al. 2003), and to reduce the number of attempts required at the wrist (Sandhu and Patel 2006; Schwemmer and Arzet 2006). Although not proved, it is likely that the frequency of vascular, tissue, or nerve damage and subsequent thrombotic or infectious complications is related in part to the number of needle passes. Ultrasound guidance for arterial access may be useful in patients with low blood pressure to identify flow and pulsatility, and to identify and avoid atheromatous vessels, stenosis, dissections, thrombosis, and congenital or acquired variations in anatomy. It helps in the presence of oedema, obesity, or multiple previous cannulations.

It is particularly useful at deeper sites such as the femoral artery to ensure access at the level to the common femoral as opposed to the lower superficial femoral artery. Look for and avoid vena comitantes and nerves. The low frequency of serious complications (e.g. tissue ischaemia and nerve damage) after radial cannulation make comparative studies difficult without very large numbers. Many anaesthetic departments will already have access to high-resolution ultrasound equipment suitable for assisting peripheral arterial access.

Ultrasound allows cannulation at a number of other deeper sites, for example, the impalpable radial and ulnar arteries in the mid forearm, so avoiding the flexures (Gratrix et al. 2009). There is increasing evidence for the benefit of ultrasound guidance in both the routine and more difficult case at peripheral and femoral sites (Shiver et al. 2006; Seto et al. 2010).

Principles of ultrasound guidance

There is a strong evidence base for the use of ultrasound in adult practice (Lamperti et al. 2012), in particular for the internal jugular vein with an improved first attempt success rate, reduced number of needle passes, and decreased frequency of complications compared with landmark techniques (Wu et al. 2013). Ultrasound also reduces the time to successful cannulation and potential costs, and infection risks (O'Grady et al. 2011). Trends are similar at other sites and paediatric practice.

Ultrasound allows:

- Direct visualization of the vessels (artery and vein) and their associated structures:
  - Identification of thrombosis, valves, dissection, atheroma, or anatomical abnormalities
  - Identification of an optimal target vessel and site along it
- First-pass cannulation in the midline of a vessel directly avoiding other vital structures
- Visualization of guidewire and cannulae entering vessel
- Reduction of puncture-related complications
- At-risk structures can be identified and specifically avoided (e.g. accompanying arteries, nerves, chest wall, and pleura).

Veins show respiratory fluctuation (if patent and no obstruction to right atrium) and are easily compressible. Arteries are round and non-compressible, and become easier to visualize with pressure. Arteries are seen to be relatively incompressible and pulsatile even in the shocked patient. Peripheral arteries have characteristic double vena comitantes. If in doubt, use colour Doppler to differentiate pulsatile arterial flow from more continuous venous signal. Limb veins will show flow with Doppler if the distal limb is squeezed or the patient is asked to contract their muscles.

Equipment preparation is important. The display should be positioned on the opposite side of the patient to the operator and the image should anatomically be in the orientation as seen from the position of the operator. An orientation marker in the image should be matched to a palpable marker on the probe. Correct orientation ensures that the image moves in a logical direction when the probe is moved and that the needle moves in the same direction in the patient as on the display. If in doubt, tap one end of the probe and watch for the accompanying display artifact.

Accurate needle-tip visualization is key. The spatial relationship between needle and probe may be in the 'short (out-of-plane)' or 'long (in-plane)' axis and the image cross-sectional or longitudinal. It is common to use a cross-sectional vessel view and short-axis insertion. This method provides good visualization of surrounding structures. It takes practice to maintain constant needle-tip visualization as the tip may inadvertently pass through the beam and the shaft is mistaken for the tip. Alternatively, the vein may be imaged longitudinally and the needle inserted in the long axis. This gives superior needle/wire views but does not provide concurrent images of surrounding structures. Hybrid approaches are increasingly used but the needle does need to be directed in the desired direction of guidewire travel. Some needles have their distal section machined to make them more echogenic (Chapman et al. 2006). Training and accreditation issues related to ultrasound have been discussed but not fully implemented in most centres (Bodenham 2006; Association of Anaesthetists of Great Britain & Ireland et al. 2011).

Conclusion

Vascular access is a core skill for anaesthetists in theatre and critical care practice. A thorough knowledge of applied anatomy, practical skills, and recognition and management of complications are essential for safe practice. The increasing use of ultrasound, ECG guidance, and X-ray screening, and improved design of devices allow much safer and more successful procedures. Many patients will now have long-term devices *in situ*, which can be used during anaesthesia and critical care. Such devices are increasingly inserted or removed by anaesthetists.

Declaration of interest

None declared.

References

Amerasekera SSH, Jones CM, Patel R, *et al.* Imaging of the complications of peripherally inserted central venous catheters. *Clin Radiol* 2009; **64**: 832–40

Association of Anaesthetists of Great Britain & Ireland. Safe vascular access guidelines 2016. *Anaesthesia* 2016; **71**: 573–85

Association of Anaesthetists of Great Britain & Ireland, The Royal College of Anaesthetists, The Intensive Care Society. *Ultrasound in Anaesthesia and Intensive Care: A Guide to Training*. London: AAGBI, 2011. Available from http://www.aagbi.org/sites/default/files/Ultrasound%20in%20Anaesthesia%20and%20Intensive%20Care%20-%20A%20Guide%20to%20Training.pdf

Baskin JL, Pui CH, Reiss U, *et al.* Management of occlusion and thrombosis associated with long-term indwelling central venous catheters. *Lancet* 2009; **374**: 159–69

Bodenham AR. Editorial II. Ultrasound imaging by anaesthetists: training and accreditation issues. *Br J Anaesth* 2006; **96**: 414–7

Bodenham AR. Ultrasound-guided subclavian vein catheterization: beyond just the jugular vein. *Crit Care Med* 2011a; **39**: 1819–20

Bodenham AR. Editorial. Reducing major procedural complications from central venous catheterisation. *Anaesthesia* 2011b; **66**: 6–9

Çavdar S, Zeybek A, Bayramiçli M. Rare variation of the axillary artery. *Clin Anat* 2000; **13**: 66–8

Chapman GA, Johnson D, Bodenham AR. Visualisation of needle position using ultrasonography. *Anaesthesia* 2006; **61**: 148–58

Cheng S. Superior vena cava syndrome: a contemporary review of a historic disease. *Cardiol Rev* 2009; **17**: 16–23

Chin KJ, Singh K. The superficial ulnar artery – a potential hazard in patients with difficult venous access. *Br J Anaesth* **94**: 692–3

Chitwood RW, Shepard AD, Shetty PC, *et al.* Surgical complications of transaxillary arteriography: a case-control study. *J Vasc Surg* 1996; **23**: 844–9

Cook T. Litigation related to central and peripheral venous access by anaesthetists: an analysis of claims against the NHS in England 1995–2009. *Anaesthesia* 2010; **65**: 56–7

Domino KB, Bowdle T, Posner A, *et al.* Injuries and liability related to central vascular catheters: a closed claims analysis. *Anesthesiology* 2004; **100**: 1411–4

Dudrick SI. History of vascular access. *J Parenter Enteral Nutr* 2006; **30**: S47–S56

Evans WN, Ruben J, Acherman RJ, *et al.* Dextrocardia: practical clinical points and comments on terminology. *Pediatr Cardiol* 2010; **31**: 1–6

Fangio P, Mourgeon E, Romelaer A, *et al.* Aortic injury and cardiac tamponade as a complication of subclavian venous catheterization. *Anesthesiology* **96**: 1520–2

Fletcher SJ, Bodenham AR. Safe placement of central venous catheters: where should the tip of the catheter lie? *Br J Anaesth* 2000; **85**: 188–91

Fragou M, Gravvanis A, Dimitriou V, *et al.* Real-time ultrasound-guided subclavian vein cannulation versus the landmark method in critical care patients: a prospective randomized study. *Crit Care Med* 2011; **39**: 1607–12

Galloway S, Bodenham A. Safe removal of long term cuffed Hickman type catheters. *Hosp Med* 2003; **64**: 20–3

Galloway S, Bodenham A. Long-term central venous access. *Br J Anaesth* 2004; **9**: 722–34

Ghadiali N, Teo LM, Sheah K. Bedside confirmation of a persistent left superior vena cava based on aberrantly positioned central venous catheter on chest radiograph. *Br J Anaesth* 2006; **96**: 53–6

Gibson F, Bodenham A. Misplaced central venous catheters: applied anatomy and practical management. *Br J Anaesth* 2013; **110**: 333–46

Goren A, Laufer J, Yativ N, *et al.* Transillumination of the palm for venipuncture in infants. *Pediatr Emerg Care* 2001; **17**: 130–1

Gratrix AP, Atkinson JD, Bodenham AR. Cannulation of the impalpable section of radial artery: preliminary clinical and ultrasound observations. *Eur J Anaesthesiol* 2009; **10**: 887–9

Guilbert MC, Elkouri S, Bracco D, *et al.* Arterial trauma during central venous catheter insertion: case series, review and proposed algorithm. *J Vasc Surg* 2008; **48**: 918–25

Haerle M, Häfner H. Vascular dominance in the forearm. *Plast Recons Surg* 2003; **111**: 1892–8

Hamilton H, Bodenham A (eds). *Central Venous Catheters*. Oxford: Wiley Blackwell, 2009

Hemmelgarn BR, Moist LM, Lok CE. Prevention of dialysis catheter malfunction with recombinant tissue plasminogen activator. *N Engl J Med* 2011; **364**: 303–12

Hove LD, Steinmetz J, Christoffersen JK. Analysis of deaths related to anesthesia in the period 1996-2004 from closed claims registered by the Danish Patient Insurance Association. *Anesthesiology* 2007; **106**: 675–80

Hudman L, Bodenham A. Practical aspects of long term venous access. *CEACCP* 2013; **13**: 6–11

Hughes P, Scott C, Bodenham A. Ultrasonography of the femoral vessels in the groin: implications for vascular access. *Anaesthesia* 2000; **55**: 1198–202

Jankovic Z, Boon A, Prasad R. Fatal haemothorax following large-bore percutaneous cannulation before liver transplantation. *Br J Anaesth* 2005; **95**: 472–6

Jaques PF, Campbell WE, Dumbleton S, *et al.* The first rib as a fluoroscopic marker for subclavian vein access. *J Vasc Interv Radiol* 1995; **6**: 619–22

Jarvis MA, Jarvis CL, Jones P. Reliability of Allen's test in selection of patients for radial artery harvest. *Ann Thorac Surg* 2000; **70**: 1362–5

Koung-Shing Chu KS, Hsu JH, Shan Wang SS, *et al.* Accurate central venous port-a catheter placement: intravenous electrocardiography and surface landmark techniques compared by using transesophageal echocardiography. *Anesth Analg* 2004; **98**: 910–4

Kowalski CM, Kaufman JA, Rivitz SM, Geller SC, Waltman AC. Migration of central venous catheters: implications for initial catheter tip positioning. *J Vasc Intervent Radiol* 1997; **8**: 443–7

Kremser J, Kleemann F, Reinhart K, *et al.* Optimized method for correct left-sided central venous catheter placement under electrocardiographic guidance. *Br J Anaesth* 2011; **107**: 567–72

Lamperti M, Bodenham AR, Pittiruti M, *et al.* International evidence-based recommendations on ultrasound-guided vascular access. *Intensive Care Med* 2012; **38**: 1105–17

Latto IP. The internal jugular vein. In: Latto IP, Ng WS, Jones PL, Jenkins BJ, eds. *Percutaneous Central Venous and Arterial Catheterisation*, 3rd Edn. London: WB Saunders, 2000; 136–95

Lee JH, Bahk JH, Ryu HG, *et al.* Comparison of the bedside central venous catheter placement techniques: landmark vs electrocardiogram guidance. *Br J Anaesth* 2009; **102**: 662–6

Lenhardt R, Seybold T, Kimberger O, *et al.* Local warming and insertion of peripheral venous cannulas: single blinded prospective randomised controlled trial and single blinded randomised crossover trial. *BMJ* 2002; **325**: 409–10

Levin PD, Sheinin O, Gozal Y. Use of ultrasound guidance in the insertion of radial artery catheters. *Crit Care Med* 2003; **31**: 481–4

Mallick A. Bodenham AR. Disorders of the lymph circulation: their relevance to anaesthesia and intensive care. *Br J Anaesth* 2003; **91**: 265–72

Mallin M, Louis H, Madsen T. A novel technique for ultrasound-guided supraclavicular subclavian cannulation. *Am J Emerg Med* 2000; **28**: 966–9

McBride KD, Fisher R, Warnock N, *et al.* A comparative analysis of radiological and surgical placement of central venous catheters. *Cardiovasc Intervent Radiol* 1997; **20**: 17–22

McGee DC, Gould MK. Preventing complications of central venous catheterization. *N Engl J Med* 2003; **348**: 1123–33

Ng WS. The subclavian vein. In: Latto IP, Ng WS, Jones PL, Jenkins BJ, eds. *Percutaneous Central Venous and Arterial Catheterisation*, 3rd Edn. London: WB Saunders, 2000; 91–134

O'Grady NP, Alexander M, Burns LA, *et al.* Summary of recommendations: guidelines for the prevention of intravascular catheter-related infections. *Clin Infect Dis* 2011; **52**: 1087–99

O'Leary R, Ahmed SY, McLure H, *et al.* Ultrasound-guided infraclavicular axillary vein cannulation: a useful alternative to the internal jugular vein. *Br J Anaesth* 2012; **109**: 762–8

Orme RML, McSwiney MM, Chamberlain-Webber RFO. Fatal cardiac tamponade as a result of a peripherally inserted central venous catheter: a case report and review of the literature. *Br J Anaesth* 2007; **99**: 384–8

Parkinson R, Gandhia M, Harpera J, Archibalda C. Establishing an ultrasound guided peripherally inserted central catheter (PICC) insertion service. *Clin Radiol* 1998; **53**: 33–6

Perry AM, Caviness AC, Hsu DC. Efficacy of a near-infrared light device in pediatric intravenous cannulation: a randomized controlled trial. *Pediatr Emerg Care* 2011; **27**: 5–10

Pieters P, Tisnado J, Mauro M. *Venous Catheters: A Practical Manual.* New York: Thieme Medical Publishers, 2003

Pirotte T, Veyckemans F. Ultrasound-guided subclavian vein cannulation in infants and children: a novel approach. *Br J Anaesth* 2007; **98**: 509–14

Pronovast P, Needham D, Berenholtz S, *et al.* An intervention to decrease catheter-related bloodstream infections in the ICU. *N Engl J Med* 2006; **355**: 2725–32

Rodríguez-Niedenführ M, Vázquez T, Parkin IG, *et al.* Arterial patterns of the upper limb: update of anatomical variations and embryological development. *Eur J Anat* 2003; 7(Suppl 1): 21–8

Rose A, Bodenham A. Vascular access services: an emerging role for anaesthetists. *R Coll Anaesth Bull* 2010; **61**: 15–8. Available from https://www.rcoa.ac.uk/system/files/CSQ-Bulletin61.pdf

Samoya SW. Real-time ultrasound-guided peripheral vascular access in pediatric patients. *Anesth Analg* 2010; **111**: 823–5

Sandhu NP, Sidhu DS. Mid-arm approach to basilic and cephalic vein cannulation using ultrasound guidance. *Br J Anaesth* 2004; **93**: 292–4

Sandhu NS, Patel B. Use of ultrasonography as a rescue technique for failed radial artery cannulation. *J Clin Anaesth* 2006; **18**:138–41

Schwemmer U, Arzet HA. Ultrasound-guided arterial cannulation in infants improves success rate. *Eur J Anesthesiol* 2006; **23**: 476–80

Seto AH, Abu-Fadel MS, Sparling JM, *et al.* Real-time ultrasound guidance facilitates femoral arterial access and reduces vascular complications: FAUST (Femoral Arterial Access With Ultrasound Trial). *JACC Cardiovasc Interv* 2010; **3**: 751–8

Shiver S, Blaivas M, Lyon M. A prospective comparison of ultrasound-guided and blindly placed radial arterial catheters. *Acad Emerg Med* 2006; **13**: 1275–79

Smith JA, Affolter JT, Patel JC, Broadhurst P. Arterial trauma during ultrasound-guided axillary vein puncture for endocardial lead placement. *Europace* 2009; **11**: 660–1

Stonelake PA, Bodenham AR. The carina as a radiological landmark for central venous catheter tip position. *Br J Anaesth* 2006; **96**: 335–40

Taylor CC, Clarke NMP. Amputation and intraosseous access in infants. *BMJ* 2011; **342**: d2778

Taylor RW, Palagiri AV. Central venous catheterization, a concise review. *Crit Care Med* 2007; **35**: 1390–6

Tobias JD, Kinder Ross A. Intraosseous infusions: a review for the anesthesiologist with a focus on pediatric use. *Anesthes Analg* 2010; **110**: 391–401

Vaksmann G, Rey C, Breviere GM, *et al.* Nitroglycerine ointment as an aid to venous cannulation in children. *J Pediatr* 1987; **111**: 89–91

Vesely TM. Central venous catheter tip position: a continuing controversy. *J Vasc Interv Radiol* 2003; **14**: 527–34

Wu SY, Ling Q, Cao LH, *et al.* Real-time two-dimensional ultrasound guidance for central venous cannulation. A meta-analysis. *Anesthesiology* 2013; **118**: 361–75

CHAPTER 50

Conscious sedation

Johannes (Hans) T. A. Knape

Introduction

The term sedation has its origin in the Latin verb '*sedo, sedare*' which literally means 'to calm down' and this is exactly how sedation is used in medicine. The interesting point is that the notion of '*sedare*' or 'to calm down' is usually associated with emotions of reassurance and smoothness, not only in general, but in medicine as well. Sedation, like anaesthesia, is a medical procedure with potential risks, but this is often poorly understood, not only by patients, but also by many health care professionals. This is especially true for moderate-to-deep sedation.

The use of intravenous sedation in medicine has increased exponentially in the last decades (Shah and Cohen 2010; Triantafillidis et al. 2013). Three factors are responsible for this.

First, the exponential increase in invasive diagnostic and therapeutic procedures being performed outside of the operating theatre (Seeff et al. 2004) being facilitated by sedation. Among these are many procedures in gastroenterology [e.g. colonoscopy, gastroscopy, endoscopic retrograde cholangiopancreatography (ERCP), and endoscopic ultrasound], and also in cardiology (interventional procedures such as pulmonary vein isolation and transoesophageal echocardiography), pulmonology (bronchoscopy, endobronchial ultrasound), intervention radiology and radiotherapy, gynaecology (labour pain, missed abortions, *in vitro* fertilization procedures), dentistry, and expanding indications. The most prominent example of this development is gastroenterology, a medical specialty which has evolved from a mainly contemplative medical specialty in the 1970s to a mainly invasive medical specialty today. Nowadays, gastroenterologists have great knowledge and skills in both invasive diagnostics and procedures of the oesophagus, and the whole intestinal tract including the pancreatobiliary tract.

Second, whole new groups of drugs have become available such as short-acting benzodiazepines, (ultra-)short-acting opioids, propofol, dexmedetomidine, and ketamine. These drugs enable the clinician to suppress the central nervous system and to sedate the patient quickly with a limited duration of action in an apparently straightforward way.

Third, the demand from the public for comfort and safety during painful and unpleasant medical procedures is rising sharply in most countries. Patients undergoing medical procedures for which they have given their consent also require that these procedures are performed effectively, safely, and efficiently, without unnecessary discomfort.

The increased demand for assistance for moderate (conscious)-to-deep sedation has not been met by anaesthetists in the majority of Western countries for a variety of reasons. The shortage of anaesthetists in many countries in the last decades has limited the efforts of anaesthesiology to take the lead in sedation procedures. Moreover, the absence of reasonable reimbursement for sedation in many countries has not stimulated anaesthetists to take an active role in the field of sedation. Another factor is that it has to be emphasized that training in moderate-to-deep sedation procedures has lagged behind in many anaesthesia training programmes until recently. When compared with providing general anaesthesia for a diagnostic colonoscopy, the moderate sedation of a patient for pulmonary vein isolation over the same time period is 'a whole new ball game' which has to be taught, including all the circulatory, pulmonary, and central nervous system complications associated with such procedures.

These circumstances were instrumental in prompting many non-anaesthesia specialties to develop sedation programmes for their respective patients (Dumonceau et al. 2010). For a long time, anaesthetists only highlighted the risks of the medical procedure of sedation, referring to many case reports on sedation procedures with a fatal outcome in the 1980s. These adverse events were mostly as a result of the use of combinations of sedative or analgesic drugs, or both, and the absence of adequate patient monitoring. Anaesthetists indicated that the administration of sedative drugs for sedation should be confined to medical practitioners who were trained to use these drugs for general anaesthesia and were familiar with handling complications associated with them. Correct as they were, however, anaesthetists often were not able to meet the quickly increasing demand for moderate-to-deep sedation.

Gastroenterology endoscopists in particular have taken the lead in many countries in setting up protocols and training not only medical specialists but also non-medical personnel to provide sedation to their patients. Currently, most clinical articles on sedation are published in non-anaesthesia journals (Rosow 2014). In the last few years, interest and involvement of anaesthetists have increased mainly as a result of the awareness that (1) moderate-to-deep sedation is an independent medical procedure and not just an adjunct of the diagnostic or therapeutic procedure in itself, and (2) that moderate-to-deep sedation is a medical procedure with potential risks for which a number of precautions and specific conditions are required to deliver a safe, efficient, and effective procedure.

The inclusion of moderate-to-deep sedation in the Helsinki Declaration of Patient Safety in Anaesthesiology from the European Board of Anaesthesiology and the European Society of Anaesthesiology has contributed strongly to this increased recognition of sedation in anaesthesiology (Mellin-Olsen et al. 2010).

Although the practice of sedation today is completely different from the sedation practice of 30 years ago, it is natural that anaesthetists, with their specific expertise in handling the side-effects of potent sedative and analgesic drugs, must take responsibility, together with other medical specialists, to lead in the design of sedation practices. Moderate-to-deep sedation today is provided by a variety of medical and non-medical practitioners. And in contrast to what was previously believed, a number of studies have made it clear that moderate-to-deep sedation implemented by non-anaesthesia sedation practitioners is associated with a similar incidence of respiratory and cardiovascular adverse events when compared with reports on sedation performed by anaesthetists, showing that it can be done safely (Clarke et al. 2002). These practices must be characterized by high quality, efficiency, effectiveness, safety, optimal conditions for the (endoscopic) practitioner, and comfort for the patient.

It is thus clear that anaesthesiology now holds a different position towards sedation when compared with 30 years ago. The challenges, however, to contribute to a high-quality and safe practice for moderate-to-deep sedation are the same and it is up to anaesthetists to take the lead in this field in close cooperation with gastroenterologists, cardiologists, gynaecologists, dentists, pulmonologists, radiologists, emergency physicians, nurse anaesthetists, endoscopic assistants, and other medical and non-medical personnel who are involved in the care for patients under sedation.

Definitions

Sedation (the artificial suppression of central nervous system functions) has to be considered to be an independent medical procedure with potential risks and complications. From experience in practice, it has become clear that not all parties involved speak the same language. Some medical specialists speak of 'sedation', but when asked to describe the desired condition, they mean, in fact, a state of deep general anaesthesia. In order to avoid misunderstandings, clear definitions are required.

It is important to realize that a number of factors determine the sedation technique which results in the best operative conditions, the best comfort for patients, the best controlled lowering of consciousness, and the safest procedure. Sedation for a procedure which is only unpleasant to undergo requires a sedation plan which differs from that for a therapeutic procedure which is not only unpleasant to undergo but also painful at times. The nature of the diagnostic or therapeutic procedure is foremost in the design of the sedation plan. Furthermore, the (co-)morbidity of the patient is crucial. This co-morbidity determines the cardiovascular, ventilator, and vital reserves of the patient. All these factors together govern the training level of the sedation practitioner, the level of monitoring conditions, and the competences of the healthcare personnel involved.

Anxiolysis is a medication or other intervention used to reduce the fear and stress level of the patient about to undergo an unpleasant medical procedure. When the level of consciousness is somewhat lowered, but remains intact during the performance of this technique, a state of light sedation is achieved.

Moderate sedation is the state of an artificial decrease of consciousness, where the patient may respond when stimulated by speech or by light tactile stimuli. The patient seems to be asleep.

In the condition of deep sedation, consciousness has been depressed such that the patient does not react when spoken to but does so when repeated or painful stimuli are applied.

In the conditions of moderate and deep sedation, the patient seems to be in a state of sleep. Both stages are characterized by a considerable likelihood to develop upper airway obstruction or depression of spontaneous ventilation. This is in contrast to anxiolysis and light sedation, where consciousness is maintained. The risk level in cases of moderate-to-deep sedation is higher than in cases of anxiolysis and light sedation. That is why procedures of moderate-to-deep sedation require better trained personnel and monitoring of a higher level than is demanded for anxiolysis and light sedation.

The definition of 'conscious sedation' is confusing for many and therefore a matter of debate. The word 'conscious' implies that consciousness is maintained: light sedation. In contrast, many physicians speak of conscious sedation where they mean, in fact, a condition where patients have lost consciousness and are asleep. This situation is in agreement with a state of moderate or even deep sedation. Moreover, many physicians use the term 'conscious sedation' to suggest that this a state of sedation with a certain continuity. In practice, the level of sedation of any individual patient is discontinuous as a result of the pharmacokinetic and pharmacodynamics properties of the drugs used, the intensity of painful stimuli, the sensitivity of the patient to the drugs used, the anxiety level of the patient, and his/her medical condition and reserves. Sedation which aimed to produce anxiolysis (with retainment of full consciousness) may produce a state of moderate sedation for a short period of time, and patients in a state of moderate sedation may develop short periods of unintended deep sedation. The term 'conscious sedation' trivialises the risk associated with the state of moderate-to-deep sedation, to which, in fact, the patient is exposed. By using the terms anxiolysis, light sedation, moderate sedation, and deep sedation the actual state of a patient undergoing sedation and its associated risks can be more precisely described and documented.

Morbidity, mortality, and safety

Most modern and international guidelines indicate that sedation, analgesia, or both in selected patients can be performed safely under certain conditions and prerequisites. The most frequent complication is hypoxaemia as a result of ventilatory depression, upper respiratory obstruction, or both (Sharma et al. 2007). Until the millennium, most data came from case reports and few well-founded prospective studies were available. Not only studies involving sedation provided by anaesthetists produced relatively safe reports. Clarke et al. (2002) reported a large study of 28 742 gastrointestinal endoscopy procedures with propofol sedation, mostly performed by non-anaesthesia sedation practitioners, which showed a similar low incidence of adverse events when compared with the results of studies performed by anaesthetists.

The risk of the whole medical procedure under sedation is determined by the risk of the diagnostic or therapeutic procedure, upon which the risk of the sedation procedure is superimposed. Both risks have to be identified, considered, and evaluated. As a number of studies have shown, the ASA classification of the patient is an important predictor for complications (Vargo et al. 2006; Sharma et al. 2007). More invasive procedures such as ERCP are associated with greater risks. The risk of developing cardiovascular complications is strongly associated with the condition of the patient and their co-morbidity, the executed procedure, and the medication used for sedation. Monitoring, pre-, per-, and post-sedation care, the competences of the sedation team, and the level of monitoring will have to be appropriate for the risks of the procedure and the condition of the patient.

Although American and some European anaesthetists maintain that patients requiring propofol for sedation should be sedated by anaesthetists because of the US Food and Drug Administration's statement that 'For general anesthesia or monitored anesthesia care (MAC) sedation, Propofol injectable emulsion should be administered only by persons trained in the administration of general anesthesia and not involved in the conduct of the surgical/diagnostic procedure' (Perel 2011), it is now clear that a considerable number of the sedation procedures of the 14 million colonoscopies performed annually in the United States are performed by gastroenterologists with propofol (Seeff et al. 2004). The same is happening in some European countries.

It is important to register sedation and sedation-associated procedures both by anaesthetists and by non-anaesthetists carefully and use these data to continuously improve the quality and safety of sedation procedures. Medical scientific societies must play a leadership role in this.

Preparing the patient

Irrespective of the type of sedation which will be required, it is important to be informed about the health condition of the patient, their co-morbidity, and their cardiopulmonary reserves. The ability of a patient to exercise can be expressed by a particular metabolic equivalent (MET) value. The MET value of a patient can be expressed as the utilization of oxygen per kg bodyweight per minute. One MET equals 3.5 ml oxygen per kg bodyweight per minute. The MET value of physical activities may vary from 0.9 MET when asleep to 18 MET during heavy exercise. Activities such as walking slowly are associated with MET values of about 2.0; cycling at 16 km h^{-1} is associated with a MET value of about 5.5, and for running a MET of 8 is required.

It must be emphasized that a patient with a certain co-morbidity such as type 2 diabetes without complications with a MET level of 3 has a higher risk when compared with a patient with the same co-morbidity but an exercise tolerance corresponding to a MET of 8.

The data from a health questionnaire will provide important first information about the condition of the patient.

Should the patient have fasted before sedation?

Data from the literature provide little evidence to require patients to have fasted before sedation which would reduce the risk of aspiration (Bahn and Holt 2005; Green et al. 2007). On the other hand, there are studies which show that contents of the oropharyngeal cavity may easily enter the trachea during sedation, not necessarily causing symptoms (Savilampi et al. 2014). Because the likelihood to develop reflux of gastric contents may be increased in some groups of patients (diabetes, those with renal failure) and because emptying of the stomach may be delayed in some patients and under some circumstances, it is recommended to stay on the safe side and to maintain the same regimen for pre-sedation fasting as is done for general anaesthesia. In patients who are considered to be at risk for aspiration of gastric contents or in emergency procedures, the sedation practitioner will have to weigh a potentially increased likelihood for aspiration against the risks associated with delay of the intended procedure. They have to include the choice of drugs, adaptation of the depth of the sedation and possible protection of the airway in their considerations.

Screening of patients for sedation

There are insufficient data from the literature to conclude that pre-sedation screening of the health status of patients would have a beneficial effect on the outcome of procedural sedation (American Society of Anesthesiologists 2002; Miller et al. 2005). On the other hand, there is sufficient evidence to relate some pre-existing patient characteristics to complications in the context of sedation. Information from the patient's medical history and selected data from a physical examination are extremely valuable for the sedation practitioner to assess the medical condition of the patient and their ability to cope with adverse effects on the ventilator and circulatory system associated with sedation.

The following information is valuable:

- Age, height, and body weight (BMI) and ASA classification
- Cardiovascular system: (unstable) chest pain, symptoms and signs of myocardial failure, its functional class
- Ventilatory system: chronic obstructive pulmonary disease (chronic bronchitis or emphysema), dependence on oxygen, ability to cough vigorously, swallowing disorders, functional abnormalities
- Gastrointestinal system: history of gastro-oesophageal reflux, hiatus hernia, ileus
- Airway problems, sleep apnoea
- Musculoskeletal disorders (rheumatoid arthritis, muscular dystrophy)
- Chromosomal aberrations (e.g. trisomy 21)
- Earlier complications associated with anaesthesia or sedation
- Drug history and allergies
- Limited physical exam:
    - Blood pressure and pulse rate
    - Heart and lungs
    - Airway (overweight, aberrations in the anatomy of the head and neck area).

If any suspicion arises from these data, additional laboratory investigations, consultations, or both, from an anaesthetist, pulmonologist, or cardiologist may be indicated. Studies have indicated that adequately trained non-anaesthetists are able to perform this screening procedure well, provided that the possibility exists of low threshold access to a dedicated anaesthetist for consultation.

When planning a diagnostic or therapeutic procedure, it is mandatory by law in most countries that the patient has to be informed about the intended goal of the procedure, given reasonable expectations of what the benefit(s) of the procedure will be, and the common complications associated with it. Moreover, the patient has to be informed about potential alternative approaches and their benefits and drawbacks.

As moderate-to-deep sedation is considered to be a medical procedure with potential risks, the same informed consent procedure has to be completed for sedation, including written permission of the patient for the sedation practitioner to proceed or to apply an alternative technique. These considerations and consent are documented in the medical record of the patient.

Qualifications of a sedation practitioner

Although sedation, being medical procedure with potential risks, is characterized by many similarities with general anaesthesia in terms of risk, it has to be recognized that an increasing percentage of moderate-to-deep sedation procedures are carried out by health professionals other than anaesthetists, in the United States, Europe, and elsewhere in the world (Clarke et al. 2002; Seeff et al. 2004; Rex et al. 2009). It also seems that the occurrence rate of adverse ventilator and cardiac events of sedation procedures carried out by non-anaesthetists is not essentially dissimilar from rates of adverse events of sedation procedures provided by anaesthetists.

It is mandatory that those practitioners who carry responsibility for performing moderate-to-deep sedation in patients have the knowledge and skills to screen the health conditions of patients, to inform patients about the proposed procedure, to practise moderate-to-deep sedation procedures in adult patients in good health or with minor co-morbidity (ASA I or II), and to monitor their recovery.

The following knowledge and skills are required to do this safely:

1. Knowledge of indications, contraindications, and necessary precautions of the anticipated sedation technique.
2. Selection of a sedation procedure which meets the requirement of the planned procedure and the needs of the patients, including their co-morbidities.
3. Thorough knowledge of the pharmacology, pharmacokinetics, and pharmacodynamics and sufficient experience of the application of the appropriate sedative and analgesic drugs, including their interactions.
4. Knowledge and skills to evaluate the health condition and physiological reserves of the patient, allowing the execution of a systematic and correct risk analysis.
5. Having the appropriate communication skills to inform the patient, the parents, or the legal representatives of the patient about the sedation procedure, its effects, its side-effects, the potential adverse effects, and, if possible, alternative techniques, including potential complications.
6. Knowledge of monitoring of vital parameters required for the intended sedation. Knowing how to evaluate and interpret the monitoring data, and the consequences for the conduct of the sedation procedure and the health status of the patient.
7. Ability to recognize the development of vital complications, and to treat them adequately and in a timely fashion to prevent permanent damage to the patient.
8. Being able to evaluate and interpret the depth of the sedation level on clinical grounds in relation to the medical condition of the patient and their reserves.
9. Organizing an adequate recovery phase by clinical and instrumental monitoring of the patient and being able to define adequate discharge criteria.
10. Being able to produce an adequate sedation report enabling reconstruction of the case and to register for quality control.
11. Knowledge of, and adequate performance of, airway management to guarantee an open airway and mask ventilation and advanced life support techniques, if needed.

It is imperative that sedation practitioners who apply a technique resulting in a state of moderate-to-deep sedation have no other concurrent tasks or responsibilities. In cases of light sedation, this person may execute other activities if they can be stopped or transferred to other healthcare workers instantly. This is only allowed when the sedation level is stable and when constant personal and instrumental monitoring is guaranteed.

Responsibilities of sedation practitioners

A recent study including various countries in Europe showed that moderate-to-deep sedation for gastrointestinal endoscopy procedures is performed by a diverse range of healthcare personnel: anaesthetists, endoscopy assistants, endoscopy nurses, sedation practitioners, nurse anaesthetists, and others (Vaessen and Knape 2014). The question of who carries responsibilities for performing the sedation procedure, whether the sedation practitioner is a qualified anaesthetist, a non-anaesthetist medical specialist or a doctor, or a non-medical practitioner (physician assistant, nurse anaesthetist, endoscopy assistant, and others), is a difficult subject, depending on diverse and variable legal regulations of the country involved. Although American certified nurse anaesthetists and European nurse anaesthetists have essentially different qualifications, competencies, and authorities and positions in healthcare, they seem ideal candidates to be trained as sedation practitioners because of their knowledge and experience in airway management and circulatory management, where the most cited complications of sedation seem to occur. Unfortunately, the range of the non-medical anaesthesia workforce in Europe, including their competences, is also quite diverse. Nurse anaesthetists work in some countries but are not active in others where, in contrast, circulation nurses, anaesthesia assistants, operating theatre assistants, anaesthesia technicians or anaesthesia physician assistants, all with varying qualifications and competencies, are employed.

The free movement of medical specialists and the mutual exchange and recognition of diplomas and qualifications of medical specialties which are included in the European Directive of Medical Specialties has been achieved by the activities of the European Union of Medical Specialists. In contrast, the diversity of legal regulations in Europe and the varying definitions of non-medical healthcare workers prevent harmonization of knowledge and competencies (Spritzer and Perrenoud 2006). The qualifications and authorities of non-medical professions in healthcare differ from country to country and obstruct the free movement of non-medical healthcare workers within Europe. Authorizations which apply to a certain non-medical profession in one country may not apply in other countries because of differences in training programmes.

In the future, harmonization of training programmes for non-medical healthcare professionals may stimulate the development of harmonization of qualifications of non-medical anaesthesia personnel and sedation practitioners.

Monitoring of patients undergoing moderate-to-deep sedation

The most frequent complications of sedation procedures fall within the domain of the ventilator and to a lesser extent of the circulatory domain. Fortunately their prevalence is limited but, depending on the diagnostic or therapeutic procedure and the co-morbidity of the patient, the rate of complications may be as high as 51% (Bhalla et al. 2006). Many of these complications are short-lasting and of limited nature but some may be the forerunner of a serious complication causing permanent damage. Continuous surveillance of the clinical condition of the patient, both by personal observation and by instrumental monitoring, is therefore required.

Important aspects of clinical observation of the patient include the level of consciousness, the reaction of the patient to physical stimuli associated with the diagnostic or therapeutic procedure, and the pattern of breathing. However, clinical observation alone is not enough in cases of moderate-to-deep sedation and additional instrumental monitoring is required to create safe conditions for the patient.

Monitoring of the ventilation: pulse oximetry

Upper airway obstruction and depression of ventilation are the most common adverse effects of pharmacological sedation techniques. As these adverse events, especially when undetected or when observed too late, may cause severe damage or life-threatening complications, it is important to apply the most appropriate monitoring techniques to enable early detection or early anticipation of imminent danger.

Hypoxaemia is the most frequent adverse event in moderate-to-deep sedation and, depending on the definition of hypoxaemia, may occur in 37% of patients (Bhalla et al. 2006). This is the reason why continuous pulse oximetry monitoring is recommended in patients undergoing moderate-to-deep sedation. The value of pulse oximetry, a simple and readily available non-invasive technique, is its ability to detect a decrease in oxygen saturation of the arterial blood early enough to take adequate measures to restore oxygen saturation and thus to prevent injury to the patient. It should be remembered, however, that pulse oximetry gives no information on the efficacy of the ventilator status of the patient whatsoever. Continuous clinical observation of the adequacy of the spontaneous ventilation of the patient is therefore mandatory. The use of a precordial stethoscope is a simple and effective means to acquire a semi-quantitative impression of the quality of the breathing pattern.

Monitoring the efficacy of spontaneous ventilation: capnography

Capnography is a monitoring method which results in a continuous representation of the CO_2 concentration of the exhaled gas mixture from the lungs in a non-invasive manner.

The interpretation of the graphic display allows an estimation of the effectivity of the ventilation. The important value of capnography in sedated patients is that it can effectively indicate an early ventilatory depression (e.g. because of opioids, sedatives, or both), which is a recognized risk of sedation techniques. Because a depression of the ventilation may frequently be followed by hypoxaemia during sedation, capnography is extremely useful as an early warning system. A recent study made it clear that capnography in some instances has no extra value, especially in those cases where bolus injection of propofol causes an abrupt cessation of breathing (van Loon et al. 2014). However, most regimens of sedation are based on continuous infusion techniques where an adverse event of cessation of breathing is forewarned by a gradual decrease in the effectiveness of the ventilation which can be excellently observed with capnography monitoring.

Until recently, technical problems of sampling exhaled gases in non-intubated sedation patients for capnography have prevented the widespread use of this valuable monitoring tool. The development of disposables allowing both the administration of oxygen on the one hand and sampling of exhaled gas on the other hand has improved the ease of the application of capnography (Sabatani and Mantovan 2013). Of course, the accuracy of the numerical CO_2 values is limited because of the inevitable blending of the exhaled gases with room air. But the interpretation of the CO_2 curve allows a fair estimate of the frequency of breathing and a rough estimate of the actual end-tidal CO_2. Continuous CO_2 monitoring is invaluable in sedation procedures where continuous visual and auditory observation of the patient is unreliable or even impossible, such as in magnetic resonance imaging investigations. It is expected that the role of capnography as a monitor of the ventilation in moderate-to-deep sedation will increase considerably in the near future.

Monitoring of the circulation

Following hypoxaemia as a relatively frequently occurring complication of moderate-to-deep sedation, periods of low blood pressure during moderate-to-deep sedation can be observed in up to 15% of cases (Heuss et al. 2003). Hypotension may occur as a consequence of latent hypovolaemia after fasting, of the use of diuretics and of antihypertensive drugs when the activation of the sympathetic system is reduced in association with the depression of the central nervous system by the sedative drugs. Frequent non-invasive blood pressure determination provides important additive information about the vital functions of the patient and is therefore recommended during moderate-to-deep sedation.

ECG monitoring

The evidence from the literature to support continuous ECG monitoring in all patients who undergo moderate-to-deep sedation, even in patients with relevant ischaemic cardiovascular disease, to improve outcome is very limited (Heuss et al. 2003; Godwin et al. 2005; Vargo et al. 2006; Sharma et al. 2007). Nevertheless, since ECG monitoring is familiar in all kinds of risky procedures and easy to apply, it is recommended in patients in all types of procedures and in particular it is recommended in patients who come for moderate-to-deep sedation, especially in patients with significant pulmonary or cardiac disease (or both), in older patients, and in patients for whom a longer-lasting procedure is anticipated.

Monitoring the depth of sedation

During moderate-to-deep sedation it is important to assess the effects of the sedative drugs used on the level of conscious. The level of suppression of the consciousness of the patient is correlated with the risk of developing adverse ventilator and cardiac effects. This can be assessed by continuous clinical observation of the patient.

Various methods have been introduced to objectively assess the level of suppression of the central nervous system with variable success. The very best known example is the Bispectral Index™ system, but the system has no additional or predictive values in monitoring patients undergoing moderate-to-deep sedation (American Society of Anesthesiologists 2002; Miner et al. 2005). The continuous clinical observation and assessment of the sedation level (using the Ramsey Sedation Scale or Modified Observer's Assessment of Alertness Scale) remains the basis for estimating the clinical depth of sedation.

Routine oxygen administration

It is a matter of debate of whether to routinely administer oxygen to patients undergoing moderate-to-deep sedation (Deitch et al. 2007). Opponents suggest that the administration of oxygen might mask the occurrence of hypoventilation and increased CO_2 content in the arterial blood. Although the scientific evidence is meagre, most sedation practitioners routinely administer oxygen. The philosophy is that a moderate-to-deep sedation technique inherently has a negative effect on the efficacy of the ventilation and thus increases the danger of developing hypoxaemia. Routine administration of oxygen under these circumstances may have a preventive effect on the development of hypoxaemia and reduce the associated risks. In cases where capnography is applied as a monitoring technique of ventilation in sedated patients, the administration of oxygen can only be beneficial.

Emergency interventions and resuscitation

Moderate-to-deep sedation procedures are characterized as high medical risk procedures and therefore serious morbidity and definitely mortality as a consequence of the sedation procedure in itself is not acceptable.

When for whatever reason an emergency situation develops, it is mandatory that rapid and optimal treatment of the patient can be offered. In all cases of sedation outside operating theatres, well-trained resuscitation personnel and equipment must be readily available. In cases of moderate-to-deep sedation procedures outside of a hospital, well-defined agreements must be in place to offer the patient being resuscitated rapid transport to a nearby hospital which can take charge of the resuscitation procedure.

Recovery of the patient after moderate-to-deep sedation

It would be a mistake to only consider the risks to the patient during the formal sedation procedure and not following the sedation. Although preferably most of the sedation drugs used are short-acting drugs, this does not mean that after waking up all risks to the patient have disappeared. An acceptable state of sedation is characterized by an equilibrium between the depth of sedation and the (painful) stimulus of the diagnostic or therapeutic procedure. When the (short-lasting) painful stimulus is over, the balance of the activation of the sympathetic system and the sedative effects can be disturbed such that the level of sedation unexpectedly increases, including the risks inherent to deep sedation levels: hypoventilation, airway obstruction, or both.

Clinical observation of the patient and registration of the ventilation, blood pressure, pulse rate, and oxygen saturation must be continued immediately post sedation in a well-equipped recovery facility with well-trained personnel after a moderate-to-deep sedation procedure. During this period, the same level of monitoring of the patient is required by personnel with the following competences:

Personnel should have the ability to observe and interpret the level of sedation and should be skilled enough to observe and monitor the vital parameters of the patient and to adequately interpret these data. Furthermore, recovery personnel must have knowledge of the clinical effects of the medication which was used for sedation and be skilled in basic resuscitation techniques, at least on the basic life support level to maintain an open airway, to adequately perform mask ventilation, and treat bradycardia and systole.

As during the sedation procedure, it is imperative to document the observations and register these in the patient files.

Discharge of the patient

As many patients who have been sedated are returning home afterwards, strict criteria have to be met for discharge of the patient. The decision to discharge a patient from the recovery room has to be considered to be a medical decision, including the associated responsibilities. The decision must be based on objective and fixed criteria which have to be documented in the patient's file.

Discharge of a patient after sedation has to meet the following requirements: the patient must be oriented in time and place, and have returned to the same level of consciousness as before the sedation procedure for at least a period of 1 h, unless the sedation has been terminated with antagonistic drugs. In that case, a stay in the recovery area of 2 h is required. The vital parameters of ventilation and circulation must have returned to normal and be stable.

The patient must be able to drink fluids, not suffer from nausea and vomiting, and benefit from adequate pain relief. Furthermore, it important for the patient to be accompanied by an adult person who can assist the patient if needed.

A document will be given to the patient with the following information: instructions for the post-sedation period; information about potential late effects of sedation and what to do if they occur; information on upcoming appointments with their physician; and the telephone number of the hospital, general physician, or both, in case a complication develops.

Techniques and drugs

The extensive discussion of all pharmacological properties of drugs which can be used for procedural sedation is not the purpose of this section; instead the reader is referred to Part 2 of this textbook. Here, the properties of those drugs which are favoured for use in procedural sedation are discussed.

Many of the drugs which are suitable to produce an adequate level of sedation are drugs which are commonly used for general anaesthesia. In this context, it is important to realize that a technique to produce a state of sedation is essentially different from a technique to produce general anaesthesia and that additional training for sedation is necessary. For general anaesthesia, the realization of loss of consciousness is usually achieved within a short period of time (seconds).

In contrast, for sedation, the suppression of the level of consciousness has to be achieved in a controlled way and may take some minutes. This statement has two important consequences. First, in order to gradually decrease the level of consciousness for sedation but also to be able to restore consciousness quickly (i.e. within minutes), only short-acting intravenous sedatives and intravenous opioids which are easily and rapidly titratable can be used. Second, it is impossible to give fixed-dose regimens for sedative drugs because of great interindividual variability in responses to sedative drugs. A sedation procedure has to be carried out with small doses of opioids and hypnotics where the resulting effects of the drugs on the level of consciousness, on the ventilation, and on cardiovascular events must be foremost in the decision for further dosing of the drugs, or for a restrictive policy.

Light sedation

To achieve light sedation or anxiolysis, where consciousness is retained, relatively simple sedation procedures can be used. Inhalation of a mixture of nitrous oxide and oxygen 50/50, which can be purchased in pre-mixed cylinders, may be helpful to cope with labour pain in obstetrics, or to reduce small fractures in children. The pain-relieving properties of nitrous oxide are of benefit. Nitrous oxide/oxygen works as an on/off sedative and its effects wear off quickly in practice.

Midazolam is a popular benzodiazepine in procedural sedation practice. The drug has a short distribution half-time contributing to short recovery times after small intravenous doses for sedation. Many adult patients are able to undergo simple but unpleasant gastrointestinal endoscopic procedures under sedation with small doses (1–2 mg intravenous increments) of midazolam. It is imperative to take sufficient time (minutes) to observe the effect of a single intravenous dose, because midazolam does not work 'on the needle': the resulting sedative/hypnotic effect takes some time to develop. When incorrectly deciding that too small a dose of midazolam has been given for the desired sedative effect, additional doses are given intravenously. Then a deep level of sedation may result, including apnoea and hypotension. In addition, the combination of midazolam and a short-acting opioid potentiates the dangerous adverse effects of the drug to an extreme extent. Fortunately, flumazenil, an antagonist of benzodiazepines, may be effective, but close observation and monitoring of the patient in combination with cautious dosing of the drugs is mandatory.

Most moderate-to-deep sedation procedures today are applied for moderately to highly complex, invasive gastrointestinal endoscopic procedures such as dilatation of the oesophagus, percutaneous endoscopic gastrostomy, ERCP, and endoscopic ultrasound. These procedures are not only unpleasant to undergo but also may be painful at times and a considerable number of patients present with significant co-morbidities. Highly skilled sedation practitioners are required to perform these moderate-to-deep sedation procedures safely.

Propofol is frequently used for moderate-to-deep sedation techniques. The continuous infusion of sedative (low) doses of propofol, combined with small doses of (ultra-)short-acting opioids such as remifentanil or alfentanil, is an excellent technique for this purpose. Remifentanil is ultra-short-acting as a result of its unique pharmacological properties. The preferred route of administration is as a continuous infusion (0.05–0.1 μg kg^{-1} min^{-1}); upon cessation of the infusion, both its analgesic and respiratory depressant effects will have worn off completely between 3 and 10 min. Alfentanil has been well-known as a short-acting opioid for some time and has been proved to be even more useful as an analgesic in sedation procedures. Intermittent doses of 100–200 μg alfentanil as an adjunct to a continuous low-dose propofol infusion permit the sedation practitioner to reliably anticipate painful moments of the diagnostic or therapeutic procedure, while producing fewer respiratory events and less nausea when compared with remifentanil.

The continuous dosing of propofol, if needed supplemented by small (15–25 mg), incremental doses of the drug, provides relatively stable sedation levels which can be terminated within minutes if required. Although they may have made small movements or have produced small sounds, patient satisfaction is high, usually because they have complete amnesia of the procedure.

The relatively new drug dexmedetomidine has been advocated for moderate-to-deep sedation. It is an α2 agonist with sedative, anxiolytic, and analgesic properties and promotes haemodynamic stability. This drug is also short-acting and until recently has been applied mainly in patients requiring intensive care treatment with good results. The experience with sedation for procedures outside of the operating theatre is limited. Its usefulness for procedural sedation is controversial (Parashchanka et al. 2014). Dexmedetomidine as mono-sedative is not considered to be the most practical drug. It may be used as a drug to enhance cooperation from the patient but does not provide amnesia which is so appreciated by patients. In order to achieve this, additional drugs such as benzodiazepines or opioids, or both, are required which in itself increases the recovery time and also the need to use antagonists to combat dangerous ventilatory and circulatory (hypotension) adverse effects.

Ketamine produces a dissociative-like state of anaesthesia but also analgesia. Moreover, it may also be a useful drug for sedation. Its particular values are its relative lack of haemodynamic and respiratory side-effects and that it can be administered in various ways: intravenously, intramuscularly, intranasally, intrathecally, and rectally. This makes it especially useful in patients with a mental handicap or in aggressive patients in whom sedation is mandatory. Unfortunately it has a limited applicability because of its well-known side-effects: emergency delirium, nightmares, and hallucinations. Supplemented by small doses of a benzodiazepine to prevent hallucinations, the drug is especially useful to produce analgo-sedation for painful wound dressing in burn patients, mainly because of its analgesic effects.

Sedation in children

For sedation of children (from a post-conceptual age of 44 weeks up to 15 years) who have to undergo unpleasant medical procedures, separate guidelines have been developed. For younger children, too little evidence is available to give recommendations. These young patients are mostly subjected to general anaesthesia if needed.

The need for sedation of children is huge and rising. Three problems come forward in this area of care. The number of unpleasant and uncomfortable invasive diagnostic and therapeutic procedures for children is quickly increasing, in particular in oncology.

Painless and stress-less medical care is more and more required by parents of children. The scientific evidence is that repeated painful procedures in children may have negative consequences for their emotional and cognitive development. Failure of costly and labour-intensive investigations as a consequence of inadequate sedation or of resistance of the patient is not acceptable.

And even more importantly, there is a safety problem in sedation for children. The incidence of mild, moderate, and potentially serious complications of sedation in children varies from 0.4% to 21.3% (Cravero and Blike 2004). These adverse events are usually the result of an unexpectedly deeper or longer sedation effect and insufficient precautions to identify these events. These events have lead to the development of guidelines for procedural sedation and analgesia in children and there is enough evidence which shows that the application of these guidelines has increased the safety of procedural sedation and analgesia in children (Coté et al. 2016). Further discussion is beyond the scope of this chapter.

Declaration of interest

None declared.

References

American Society of Anesthesiologists. Practice guidelines for sedation and analgesia by non-anesthesiologists: an updated report by the American Society of Anesthesiologists task force on sedation and analgesia by non-anesthesiologists. *Anesthesiology* 2002; **96**: 1004–17

Bahn EL, Holt KR. Procedural sedation and analgesia: a review and new concepts. *Emerg Med Clin North Am* 2005; **23**: 503–17

Bhalla A, Sood A, Sachdeva A, *et al.* Cardiorespiratory compromise under conscious sedation during upper gastrointestinal endoscopy. *J Coll Physicians Surg Pak* 2006; **16**: 585–9

Clarke AC, Chiragakis J, Hillman LC, Kaye GL. Sedation for endoscopy: the safe use of propofol by general practitioner sedationists. *Med J Aust* 2002; **176**: 158–61

Coté CJ, Wilson S, American Academy of Pediatrics; American Academy of Pediatric Dentistry. Guidelines for monitoring and management of pediatric patients before, during, and after sedation for diagnostic and therapeutic procedures: update 2016. *Pediatrics* 2016; **138**: e20161212.

Cravero JP, Blike GT. Review of pediatric sedation. *Anesth Analg* 2004; **99**: 1355–64

Deitch K, Chudnofsky CR, Dominici P. The utility of supplemental oxygen during emergency department procedural sedation and analgesia with midazolam and fentanyl: a randomized, controlled trial. *Ann Emerg Med* 2007; **49**: 1–8

Dumonceau JM, Riphaus A, Aparicio JR, *et al.* European Society of Gastrointestinal Endoscopy, European Society of gastroenterology and endoscopy nurses and associates, and the European Society of Anaesthesiology guideline: non-anesthesiologist administration of propofol for GI endoscopy. *Endoscopy* 2010; **42**: 960–74

Godwin SA, Caro DA, Wolf SJ. Clinical policy: procedural sedation and analgesia in the emergency department. American College of Emergency Physicians. *Ann Emerg Med* 2005; **45**: 177–96

Green M, Roback MG, Miner JR, Burton JH, Krauss B. Fasting and emergency department procedural sedation and analgesia: a consensus-based clinical practice advisory. *Ann Emerg Med* 2007; **49**: 454–61

Heuss LT, Schnieper P, Drewe J, *et al.* Safety of propofol for conscious sedation during endoscopic procedures in high-risk patients – a prospective, controlled study. *Am J Gastroenterol* 2003; **98**: 1751–7

Mellin-Olsen J, Staender S, Whitaker DK, Smith AF. The Helsinki declaration on patient safety in anaesthesiology. *Eur J Anaesthesiol* 2010; **27**: 592–7

Miller MA, Levy P, Patel MM. Procedural sedation and analgesia in the emergency department: what are the risks? *Emerg Med Clin North Am* 2005; **23**: 551–72

Miner JR, Biros MH, Seigel T. The utility of the bispectral index in procedural sedation with propofol in the emergency department. *Acad Emerg Med* 2005; **12**: 190–6

Parashchanka A, Schelfhout S, Coppens M. Role of novel drugs in sedation outside the operating room: dexmedetomidine, ketamine and remifentanil. *Curr Opin Anesthesiol* 2014; **27**: 442–7

Perel A. Non-anaesthesiologists should not be allowed to administer propofol for procedural sedation: a consensus statement of 21 European national societies of anaesthesia. *Eur J Anaesthesiol* 2011; **28**: 580–4

Rex DK, Deenadayalu VP, Eid E, *et al.* Endoscopist-directed administration of propofol: a world-wide safety experience. *Gastroenterology* 2009; **137**: 1229–37

Rosow C. Improving safety during sedation by nonanesthesiologists: do we lead or follow? *Anesth Analg* 2014; **119**: 7

Sabatani P, Mantovan R. Electrical cardioversion of atrial fibrillation: evaluation of sedation safety with midazolam by means of $EtCO_2$ and IPI algorithm analysis. *Int J Cardiol* 2013; **169**: 430–2

Savilampi J, Ahlstrand R, Magnuson A, Geijer H, Wattwil M. Aspiration induced by remifentanil. A double-blind, randomized, crossover study in healthy volunteers. *Anesthesiology* 2014; **121**: 52–8

Seeff LC, Richards TB, Shapiro JA, *et al.* How many endoscopies are performed for colorectal cancer screening? Results from CDC's survey of endoscopic capacity. *Gastroenterology* 2004; **127**: 1670–7

Shah B, Cohen LB. The changing faces of endoscopic sedation. *Expert Rev Gastroenterol Hepatol* 2010; **4**: 417–22

Sharma VK, Nguyen CC, Crowell MD, Lieberman DA, de Garmo P, Fleischer DE. A national study of cardiopulmonary unplanned events after GI endoscopy. *Gastrointest Endosc* 2007; **66**: 27–34

Spritzer A, Perrenaoud B. Reforms in nursing education across Western Europe: implementation process and current status. *J Prof Nurs* 2006; **22**, 162–71

Triantafillidis JK, Merikas E, Nikolakis N, Papalois AE. Sedation in gastrointestinal endoscopy: current issues. *World J Gastroenterology* 2013; **19**: 463–81

Vaessen HHB, Knape JTA. Considerable variability of procedural sedation and analgesia practices for gastrointestinal endoscopic procedures in Europe. *Clin Endosc* 2016; **49**: 47–55

van Loon K, van Rheineck Leyssius AT, van Zaane B, *et al.* Capnography during deep sedation with propofol by non-anaesthesiolgists: a randomized controlled trial. *Anesth Analg* 2014; **119**: 49–55

Vargo JJ, Holub JL, Faigel DO. Risk factors for cardiopulmonary events during propofol-mediated upper endoscopy and colonoscopy. *Aliment Pharmacol Ther* 2006; **24**: 955–63

CHAPTER 51

Blood conservation and transfusion in anaesthesia

Dafydd Thomas and Katy Beard

Introduction

The term blood conservation describes a clinical practice that attempts to minimize the use of allogeneic blood components and is not always fully understood. The reason for such clinical behaviour stems from a desire to prevent transfusion-transmitted disease and ensure a plentiful supply of blood components (Shander et al. 2010, 2012). The ability to store donated blood was a development of the second half of the twentieth century, but even with the use of current optimal storage mediums, shelf life remains between 35 and 42 days. It is apparent, therefore, that there is a continued need for blood donation if blood services are to keep pace with demand. The HIV epidemic (Busch et al. 2003) and changing population demographics have accentuated the need to ensure that blood component transfusion is used wisely and only when indicated. In addition, it has become apparent that blood transfusion is an independent risk factor for adverse outcomes (Tartter 1998; Rao et al. 2004; Isbister et al. 2011). These drivers have led to the development of clinicians who focus very closely on this area of clinical practice known as blood conservation (Maniatis et al. 2011). As a result of the confusion about the term blood conservation, a number of clinicians in this area have now developed the term patient blood management (PBM) which more accurately describes the treatment options available to manage a patient's anaemia, blood component transfusion becoming the line of last resort once all other options have failed to maintain an adequate concentration of haemoglobin, red cells, platelets, or coagulation factors in the patient. The patient-centric nature of this care allows treatment to be tailored specifically to the needs of the patient (Mercurali and Inghilleri 1996). Additional benefits have arisen as a result of this practice as it has proved possible to avoid blood transfusion in many patients, particularly surgical patients, who have demonstrated that haematological reserve can often obviate the need for blood component use (Goodnough and Shander 2012).

Background to challenges in the management of blood supply

Over the last 25 years, the indication for blood transfusion has come under considerable scrutiny for a number of reasons but mostly for the two reasons already mentioned related to infective risk resulting from transfusion and adequacy of blood supply for the ageing population. It has been appreciated for many years that blood transfusion has associated risks that range from mild febrile reactions to severe incompatibility reactions. In addition, the potential to transmit blood-borne infections such as malaria or syphilis was recognized early. The transmission of hepatitis was also documented but it was only later that the various viral diseases were more specifically identified. In fact, the two most devastating discoveries occurred in the 1980s when it was recognized that the retrovirus, human immunodeficiency virus (HIV), was causing an emerging illness known as acquired immunodeficiency syndrome (AIDS). The AIDS epidemic officially began on 5 June 1981, when the US Centers for Disease Control and Prevention in its Morbidity and Mortality Weekly Report newsletter reported unusual clusters of pneumocystis pneumonia caused by a form of *Pneumocystis carinii* (now recognized as a distinct species *Pneumocystis jirovecii*) in five homosexual men in Los Angeles, California. Shortly afterwards, in 1988, the previously recognized non-A, non-B hepatitis was reclassified as hepatitis C after Harvey Alter's successful research into the subject (Alter et al. 1989).

Discovery of the transmission of these two viruses created a reaction among governments, the public, and of course clinicians and scientists working in the field of blood transfusion. The fact that such widespread transmission was occurring as a result of the transfusion of blood components, which was always considered to be life-saving and of such benefit to patients, shook the blood establishment to the core and resulted in enormous research efforts to understand and categorize these viruses. It is a credit to the scientific endeavour displayed that we now have a much greater understanding of these viruses. In the case of both HIV and hepatitis C, we have developed treatment strategies to hold these viral illnesses in check if not completely eradicate them in some patients. Enormous resources have been invested into understanding the transmission and pathogenicity of these infections and immunological investigation of their impact in recipients. A necessary follow on once there were reliable tests to diagnose the presence of infective vectors in the donated blood was an application of this diagnostic knowledge to screen donated blood to ensure it was safe to transfuse into a patient. The commercial development of such tests meant that there was an added cost to the testing and provision of safe blood components, which saw the cost of blood components increase worldwide but more particularly in the developed countries where it was more affordable and the public demanded 'zero risk' from blood transfusion. This is of course idealistic and remains a goal to strive for, but little in life is completely risk free. The cost of testing has added considerably to the production of the final component. The introduction of nucleic acid testing within the United Kingdom has enabled the production of components that have a 1 in 45 million risk of transmitting hepatitis C, and HIV testing has decreased the risk of HIV transmission to 1 in 5 million. The risk of contracting hepatitis B remains the highest risk at 1 in 670 000 at the time of writing.

In addition to laboratory testing, there have been other pressures on the provision of a plentiful and safe supply of blood components: changing population demographics have started to alter the balance. As populations show increased longevity, in the main as a result of better healthcare and nutrition, life expectancy is increasing year on year. The birth rate has slowed in many countries and therefore there are fewer donors available to provide blood for an ageing population who are undergoing more extensive and complicated surgery, as surgical and anaesthetic techniques advance. Another pressure on blood collection has been the exclusion of precious donors as a result of stricter donor criteria; more affordable foreign travel to more exotic destinations has led to increased donor deferral (Advisory Committee on the Safety of Blood, Tissue and Organs 2011). All of these pressures have added to the challenge to recruit sufficient donors to maintain blood supplies.

There can be no argument with the principle that decreasing inappropriate use of blood components will decrease the demand on blood services and such initiatives need to be fully incorporated into blood service planning (American Society of Anesthesiologists 1996). We know that there are risks from blood transfusion no matter how finite and if there is not a physiological need to transfuse blood, other methods to improve anaemia, thrombocytopenia, and blood coagulation defects need to be tried first (Goodnough et al. 2011). This is particularly applicable to the elective surgical patient who can usually tolerate a degree of perioperative haemodilution (Habler and Messmer 1998). The effect of such rational blood component use means that demand decreases and will lead to wider availability of the blood components for those patients in whom there is no alternative treatment available (e.g. bone marrow transplant patients and massively haemorrhaging trauma victims).

Blood conservation and patient blood management

There are a number of aspects of blood management that relate particularly well to the perioperative nature of anaesthetic practice. The three main phases are preoperative, operative, and perioperative management of anaemia. Depending on the patient requiring treatment, different elements of patient-centred care may be used to avoid transfusion of allogeneic blood and to attempt to manage and correct anaemia using a variety of blood-sparing methods (Goodnough et al. 1997, 2011). Certain components require advanced planning such as preoperative optimization of anaemia while other intraoperative techniques such as red cell salvage can be quickly set up even in a surgical emergency. Figure 51.1 describes the three pillars and lists the various interventions that can be used.

Preoperative interventions before planned surgery

Historically, a preoperative visit the day or evening before surgery was usual practice. The more modern approach, to avoid unnecessary cancellation of surgery, is to organize preoperative assessment at least a month before planned surgery, allowing time for the correction of any reversible abnormal pathophysiology. The drive to ensure enhanced recovery from surgery and minimize last-minute cancellations means that issues such as poorly controlled hypertension, glycaemic control, and anaemia need correction in advance of surgery (NHS Improving Quality 2008; Pasricha et al. 2010; Kotze et al. 2012).

Paying particular attention to the correction of preoperative anaemia not only minimizes the risk of receiving a blood transfusion but may enhance outcome. It has been shown that in those patients undergoing non-cardiac surgery when anaemic, outcome is worse with increased morbidity and mortality (Musallam et al. 2011). The identification and adequate treatment of preoperative anaemia can result in decreased transfusion and possible cost savings as a result of a decrease in number of complications, length of stay, and mortality, when used as part of an organized patient blood management process (Goodnough et al. 2011; Na et al. 2011; Kotze et al. 2012; Weber et al. 2012).

Diseases associated with anaemia

There is a wide range of aetiological causes of anaemia but the commonest causes preoperatively are secondary to dietary iron deficiency anaemia, anaemia of chronic disease, blood loss as a result of either gastrointestinal malignancy or ulceration, and those patients with chronic kidney disease. In the majority of cases, correction of iron deficiency can be simply achieved and providing this occurs at least a month before planned surgery, exclusion of more sinister causes can be completed, allowing surgery to continue. In approximately 4–5% of patients there may be a malignant cause and then appropriate action can be taken to change the planned surgery to a more appropriate intervention. If anaemia is because of other causes then a more elaborate plan of haematinic treatment may be required. The discovery in 2000 of the 25-amino acid peptide hepcidin, which is secreted by the liver, has had a huge influence on understanding iron metabolism. It is now considered a master regulator of iron absorption from the intestines and inhibits iron transport by binding to the iron transport channel ferroportin. It plays a role in the anaemia of a number of chronic conditions such as inflammatory bowel disease, rheumatoid arthritis, renal failure, and chronic heart failure. Measurement of this peptide will alert the clinician that oral administration of oral iron may be futile (Goodnough 2011).

Treatment of anaemia

Pharmacological agents used to increase haemoglobin concentrations include erythropoietin (EPO), iron, folic acid, and vitamin B12 (Goodnough and Shander 2012).

Erythropoietin

The use of recombinant EPO to treat the anaemia of chronic kidney disease has led to remarkable improvements in both cardiac function and quality of life for these individuals, minimizing the need to resort to blood transfusion. A number of other uses became apparent for such erythropoietic-stimulating agents and some workers used recombinant EPO to try and improve the yield of donated blood during pre-deposit autologous programmes (Goodnough et al. 1989, 1997; Mercurali and Inghilleri 1996). The popularity of pre-deposit programmes has waned in recent years, particularly

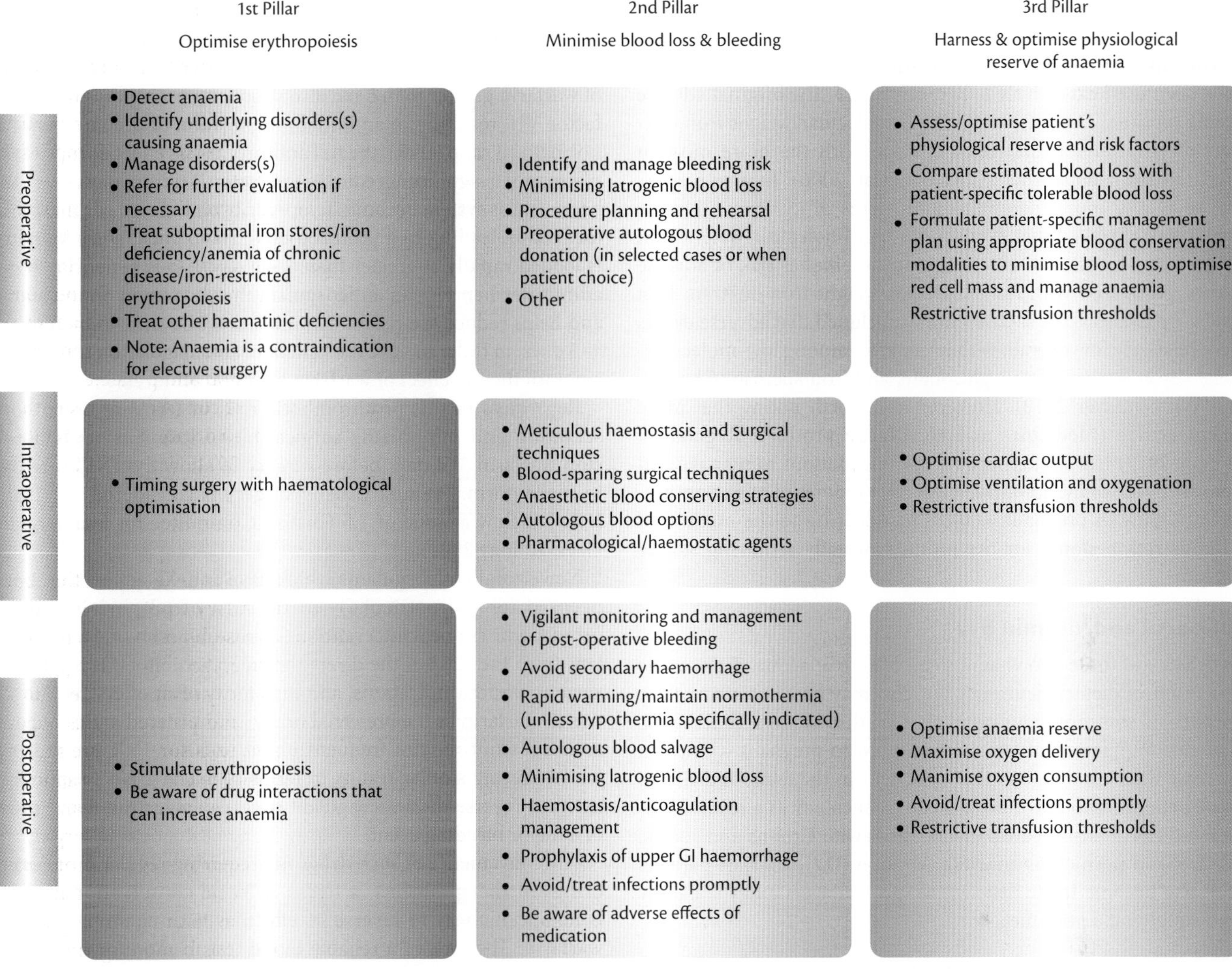

Figure 51.1 The three pillars of patient blood management listing the various interventions that can be used.
Reproduced with permission from Goodnough, L.T. and Shander, A. Patient blood management. *Anesthesiology*, Volume 116, Issue 6, pp. 1367–76, Copyright © 2012 the Journal of the American Society of Anesthesiologists, Inc.

in Europe. In addition, the cost of such programmes and marked reduced risk of infection from allogeneic blood, following improved testing of donated blood, together with advances in surgical techniques to minimize blood loss have made preoperative autologous donation poorly cost-effective (Billote et al. 2002). In addition, European legislation regarding blood establishments meant that many hospital blood banks who were supporting the programmes did not wish to be considered and inspected as such. Other reasons have also been responsible for a decline in the use of EPO in presurgical patients, particularly those with cancer, as the US Food and Drug Administration issued a warning regarding its use and studies have shown an increase in tumour growth and recurrence. There is also an increased risk of thromboembolic disease in patients receiving erythropoietic-stimulating agents. The decreased use of EPO has led to greater interest in the preoperative use of iron. Again, studies undertaken in patients with chronic kidney disease showed a significant improvement in haemoglobin concentrations even among EPO-naïve patients. In addition, other investigators have shown that the use of EPO to stimulate erythropoiesis can induce a state of functional iron deficiency in the treated patient (Na et al. 2011; Goodnough and Shander 2012).

Oral iron

The simplest and cheapest way of correcting iron deficiency is with the use of oral iron preparations. However, this form of treatment is often ineffective and although absorption from the gut can be a cause of limited effectiveness, patient compliance may also be poor, which may be as a result of forgetfulness or more frequently as a result of the gastrointestinal upset these preparations can cause. Anecdotally they are most effective in well-motivated patient groups, such as Jehovah's Witnesses.

Intravenous iron

As a result of the problems described with oral iron preparations, the use of i.v. iron has increased and has been further helped by the development of preparations that have dramatically lower adverse reaction rates than previously noted with parenteral iron dextran preparations.

The most commonly available agents include low-molecular-weight iron dextran, iron sucrose, iron carboxymaltose, ferric gluconate, and iron isomaltoside. All show good safety profiles and have been used extensively over recent years. The original adverse events reported from the use of high-molecular-weight iron dextran preparations are far less common with the more modern preparations listed earlier (Chertow et al. 2006). In a retrospective review of more than 30 million doses of i.v. iron, Chertow et al. (2006) showed that exposure to high-molecular-weight iron dextran was associated with a significantly higher risk of adverse events, compared with low-molecular-weight iron dextran. In a follow-up analysis, the same authors concluded that adverse events were relatively low overall, with lower rates among low-molecular-weight iron dextran, ferric gluconate, and iron sucrose (Chertow and Winkelmayer 2010). However it is worth noting that more recent advice (Medicines and Healthcare products Regulatory Agency 2013) has strengthened recommendations to manage and minimize risk of i.v. administration after reports of hypersensitivity, especially in pregnant women, by adhering to the method of administration stated for the product, usually requiring slower infusion.

Folic acid and vitamin B12

Deficiency of these two vitamins can lead to anaemia. This can be as a result of dietary deficiency but also may be associated with a number of common conditions that predispose to a macrocytic anaemia. Supplemental folic acid is given to pregnant women to decrease the neural defects that can occur in the fetus, and also to those patients who may have a dietary deficiency as a result of illness such as intensive care patients, those with Crohn's and coeliac disease, and pernicious anaemia (vitamin B12). Dialysis patients may also become folate deficient as can teenagers and the elderly who simply eat a poor diet.

Reversal of anticoagulation and antiplatelet drugs

Currently, many patients who present for both elective and emergency surgery may already be receiving drugs that are intended to prevent thromboembolic complications. The most common examples are those who may suffer from atrial fibrillation and are receiving warfarin to prevent embolic stroke. Other patients may be receiving antiplatelet therapy as secondary prevention for cardiac ischaemic events after myocardial infarction, percutaneous cardiac intervention, or both, resulting in stent implants. Consideration therefore needs to be given to stopping these agents in the preoperative phase if the risk:benefit assessment allows (Makris et al. 2012; Kozek-Langenecker et al. 2013; Lin et al. 2013).

Warfarin

Warfarin is a coumarin which interferes with the production of vitamin K-dependant clotting factors. Warfarin inhibits the vitamin K-dependent synthesis of biologically active forms of the calcium-dependent clotting factors II, VII, IX, and X, as well as the regulatory factors protein C, protein S, and protein Z.

When warfarin is newly started, it may promote clot formation temporarily. This is because the concentrations of protein C and protein S are also dependent on vitamin K activity. Warfarin causes a decline in protein C concentrations in the first 36 h. In addition, reduced concentrations of protein S lead to a reduction in activity of protein C (for which it is the co-factor) and therefore reduced degradation of factor Va and factor VIIIa. Although loading doses of warfarin greater than 5 mg also produce a precipitous decline in factor VII, resulting in an initial prolongation of the international normalized ratio (INR), the full antithrombotic effect does not take place until a significant reduction in factor II occurs days later. The haemostasis system becomes temporarily biased towards thrombus formation, leading to a prothrombotic state. Thus, when warfarin is loaded rapidly at greater than 5 mg day^{-1}, it is beneficial to co-administer heparin, an anticoagulant that acts upon antithrombin and helps reduce the risk of thrombosis, with warfarin therapy for 4–5 days, in order to have the benefit of anticoagulation from heparin until the full effect of warfarin has been achieved.

Regardless of this prothrombotic risk, in terms of blood conservation and minimizing surgical blood loss it is advisable to stop warfarin 3–4 days before surgery to allow the INR to return to more normal values. Usually surgery is considered safe if the INR is below a value of 1.5 (British Committee for Standards in Haematology 2004).

Newer oral anticoagulants which have anti-Xa action have been licensed for use particularly in the area of prophylaxis during orthopaedic surgical intervention. Dabigatran is an oral anticoagulant from the class of the direct thrombin inhibitors. It is used for various clinical indications, and in some cases it offers an alternative to warfarin as the preferred orally administered anticoagulant, as it does not require frequent blood tests for INR monitoring, while offering similar results in terms of efficacy. No specific way exists to reverse the anticoagulant effect of dabigatran in the event of a major bleeding event.

The convenience of such drugs not requiring regular monitoring brings further problems in terms of blood conservation as there is no specific way to reverse its effect, as with vitamin K use for warfarin. The lack of a reliable blood test to monitor dabigatran makes it difficult to determine if a given patient is experiencing a drug interaction. Testing of anticoagulant activity may be required in specific circumstances, such as surgery, overdose, and bleeding. The INR test should not be performed, as it is unreliable in patients on dabigatran. This can be done through thrombin time (TT), ecarin clotting time (ECT), and activated partial thromboplastin time (aPTT) tests. If ECT or TT is not available, the aPTT test provides an approximation of dabigatran's anticoagulant activity. An aPTT of longer than 80 s at trough was associated with an increased risk of bleeding when dabigatran was used in atrial fibrillation patients in a clinical study (Camm et al. 2012).

The Therapeutic Goods Administration in Australia published a Safety Advisory in November 2011 regarding the risk of bleeding in people using dabigatran. The analysis of these reports shows some of the bleeding adverse events occurred during the transition from warfarin to dabigatran; many of the adverse events occurred in patients on the reduced dosage regimen; and the most common site of serious bleeding for dabigatran was the gastrointestinal tract, whereas for warfarin it was intracranial. Risk factors for bleeding are age 75 years or older; moderate renal impairment (30–50 ml min^{-1})—severe renal impairment is a contraindication; concomitant use of aspirin (approximately twice the risk); clopidogrel (approximately twice the risk); and non-steroidal anti-inflammatory drugs including COX-2 inhibitors (50% more risk).

Antiplatelet drugs

Providing it is deemed safe to do so, stopping antiplatelet drugs approximately 7 days before surgery allows recovery of normal platelet function, allowing platelets to play a role in clot formation in response to surgically induced tissue damage. See Box 51.1 and Box 51.2.

Surgical techniques to minimize blood loss

Surgical technique is one of the most important determinants of blood loss. It is therefore imperative that there is adequate preoperative assessment and planning before an elective operation. During planning, considerations should include the use of an enlarged surgical team to help reduce the length of the operation and also the potential for blood loss during surgery, and the staging of complex procedures to reduce the potential for blood loss during surgery (Weltert et al. 2013). The increasing use of preoperative clinics allows such preparation to be undertaken some time in advance of the operation and it is advised that such a review occurs 4–6 weeks before the planned surgery, particularly if there are likely to be co-morbidities that would require correction or optimization before anaesthesia and surgery. Of course, in the context of this chapter, anaemia correction will need to be addressed but in addition poorly controlled angina, hypertension, or diabetes mellitus are also of concern to the operative team.

Meticulous haemostasis

When meticulous haemostasis is applied to surgical processes, less bleeding occurs.

The gentle and experienced surgeon will develop avascular planes and often use blunt dissection to expose the vascular bundles that then need a ligature or clip before cutting. Use of tourniquets and limb exsanguination is common among orthopaedic surgeons to help decrease operative loss but ischaemia of the tissues means that care must be taken to use such techniques for limited periods. Cross-clamping of major arteries (e.g. hepatic artery in liver surgery) or cross-clamping of the aorta controls bleeding but again can have deleterious effects on tissue perfusion if prolonged. Tissue hypoxia and oxidative stress during reperfusion are the drawbacks of prolonged use of cross-clamping. Elevating the operating field above the level of the heart can often have a minor effect on arterial pressures but more importantly significantly reduce venous congestion and subsequent bleeding.

Box 51.1 Operative and postoperative measures to minimize allogeneic transfusion

- Surgical techniques
- Pharmacological agents
- Anaesthetic techniques of blood conservation:
  - Acute normovolaemic haemodilution
  - Prevention of acidosis
  - Temperature
  - Judicious use of i.v. fluids
  - Positioning avoiding venous obstruction. When an operation site is above the level of the patient's heart, bleeding can often be reduced. Avoiding pressure on major veins also helps reduce blood loss.
- Intraoperative cell salvage
- Postoperative cell salvage
- Triggers to consider transfusion, liberal *vs* restrictive transfusion practice
- Point-of-care testing.

Box 51.2 Perioperative blood conservation strategy checklist

Does the patient require:

Preoperative

- Erythropoietin
- Iron, folate, vitamin B12 supplements
- Avoidance of drugs that can enhance bleeding:
  - NSAIDs
  - Antiplatelet drugs
- Heparin
- Warfarin
- Herbal preparations.

Intraoperative

- Autologous red cell provision:
  - Acute normovolaemic haemodilution
  - Preoperative autologous donation (rare red cell conditions)
  - Cell salvage—operative or postoperative
- Provision of coagulation components:
  - Component sequestration
  - Acute normovolaemic haemodilution
- Additional therapies
- Anaesthetic considerations:
  - Normothermia
  - Positioning
  - Drug therapy—aprotinin, tranexamic acid, desmopressin, factor VIIa
  - Deliberate hypotension
  - Avoid excessive crystalloid use
- Point-of-care testing
- Microsampling.

Postoperative period

- Washed or unwashed cell salvage
- EPO and i.v. iron
- Withholding transfusion according to clinical need.

Minimally invasive surgery

Laparoscopic surgical procedures using small surgical cuts, or simple dilatational access with virtually no cuts at all, can greatly reduce the trauma of access and reduce the amount of bleeding and are therefore of great importance to bloodless medicine.

Endoscopic and laparoscopic surgery

Endoscopy is used to examine, biopsy, or surgically treat a variety of conditions. Types of endoscopy include:

- arthroscopy (joints)
- bronchoscopy (bronchial tubes, lungs)
- colonoscopy/sigmoidoscopy (large intestine)
- colposcopy (vagina, cervix)
- gastroscopy (stomach, small intestine)
- laparoscopy (abdomen/thorax).

A rigid or flexible scope is used to visualize the inside of the body, either through insertion via a small incision or by passing the scope through a body opening (such as the mouth or anus).

In addition, more extensive surgical techniques can be undertaken in which a videoscope or fibreoptic endoscope is inserted via a tiny incision into the abdomen, joint, or anatomical space to be operated on. Laparoscopic surgery can be used to visualize and retrieve tissue samples by biopsy, but also to perform major surgery using instruments that are also passed into the abdomen through small incisions. The increased laparoscopic activity means that nephrectomy, colectomy, and cystectomy can be undertaken using these minimally invasive techniques.

Lithotripsy

Lithotripsy uses sound waves to break up a kidney stone or other stone into smaller pieces, allowing it to pass out of the urinary system without having created any incision at all.

Arterial embolization

There are various methods of blocking a bleeding blood vessel, preventing further blood loss. These include chemical agents that scar the inside of the blood vessel; mechanical agents that block a bleeding vessel, including metal coils and latex or silicone balloons; and particles or microspheres, including gelatine foam, an injected liquid that quickly turns into a thicker gel-like or spongy mass to prevent bleeding from a vessel. These techniques can be performed surgically or radiologically.

Cryosurgery

A surgical technique that uses extreme cold to destroy abnormal tissues in the body, and is sometimes used as a bloodless medicine technique by freezing tissue; bleeding is minimized.

Off-pump coronary artery bypass

This avoids the problems associated with cardiopulmonary bypass surgery including systemic inflammatory response, coagulopathies associated with platelet dysfunction, accelerated fibrinolysis, and consumption of clotting factors. This is not the place to describe surgical instruments in detail, but an outline of surgical principles may be of use. The improvement in surgical techniques and attention to haemostasis has led to a decrease in perioperative blood loss. The meticulous dissection and attention to haemostasis often prolongs the operative time but can be achieved with traditional surgical techniques. More technical approaches can be used and a number of aids can be used to achieve more rapid dissection while minimizing surgical loss. Such devices include laser dissection, harmonic scalpels, ultrasonic dissection, and LigaSure™ (Medronic, Minneapolis, MN, USA) forceps. It is probable that one of the most effective surgical interventions is early re-operation in patients who appear to be bleeding and in whom coagulation parameters appear to be within a normal range.

Haemostatic surgical instruments

Diathermy or electrocautery

Diathermy or electrocautery uses a device in which an electric current is used to heat a treatment instrument or probe. The heated probe cauterizes capillary vessels and small arteries, thus minimizing blood loss during surgery. This device does not transfer any electric current to the patient and is also known as thermal cautery.

Microwave scalpels

Microwaves are a form of electromagnetic energy that can be used to generate heat. The microwave scalpel uses an instrument that concentrates a localized high-power microwave field around the leading edge of a scalpel blade. As microwave energy is absorbed in tissue, this scalpel can provide coagulation during surgery on vascular organs such as the spleen or liver.

Lasers

Lasers when used in surgical instruments have a similar principle when in use to electrocautery devices, but use laser energy to cut, vaporize, and simultaneously coagulate a targeted area without disrupting adjacent tissue. Cutting is achieved precisely and haemostatically, making the systems suitable for endoscopic and open surgical procedures. Lasers promote clotting by localizing heat in bleeding vessels, resulting in coagulation.

Argon beam coagulator

A surgical instrument that uses a beam of ionized noble argon gas (argon 'plasma') to conduct a high-frequency electric current to bleeding tissues with limited tissue contact. Argon beam coagulation may be used for the haemostasis of diffuse surface bleeding from parenchymatous tissues (e.g. of the liver, spleen).

Cavitron ultrasonic surgical aspirator

The Cavitron ultrasonic surgical aspirator (CUSA®; Integra Lifesciences Corporation, Plainsboro, NJ, USA) is a powerful ultrasonic aspirator and dissector which can be used in a number of surgical situations but has been very successfully applied in the dissection of liver parenchyma, reducing perioperative blood loss and mortality (Storck et al. 1991).

Harmonic scalpels

The harmonic scalpel is an innovative way of cutting tissue using a rapidly vibrating blade to coagulate and create a cavitational effect in the tissue it is in contact with. It is activated by an ultrasonic method that results in less temperature increase, less smoke, and less lateral tissue damage compared to conventional electrocautery. It is for these reasons that it has become popular because of the decreased chance of unrecognized electrical arcing injuries, and it is accepted as a potentially safer instrument for tissue dissection. It has been available for approximately 20 years but is not widely used in open or laparoscopic procedures. It is more popular in Europe and has the potential for less traumatic dissection and decreased operative blood loss (Westervelt 2004).

Topical haemostatic agents

These should only be used when bleeding cannot be controlled by conventional methods such as sutures, ligatures, and diathermy. Once in contact with the bleeding area, they enhance clot formation.

They can be divided into two groups:

Haemostatic swabs

A chemical or biological compound, such as calcium alginate, oxidized cellulose, thrombin, or collagen promotes one or more steps of the clotting cascade therefore allowing a stable clot to build. These products are useful, inexpensive, and widely used.

Fibrin sealants

Fibrin sealants enhance the final stages of the clotting cascade, but their action is dependent on local concentration of clotting factors and they do not depend upon the body's normal clotting mechanism. Theoretically haemostasis can be achieved even in the presence of a coagulopathy. They comprise a source of fibrinogen, which is combined with thrombin plus, possibly, factor XIII or an antifibrinolytic agent (or both), such as bovine aprotinin or tranexamic acid, which stabilizes the clot. When the constituent parts are mixed, a cross-linked insoluble fibrin matrix is formed via the final common pathway. Commercially available fibrin sealants are manufactured from fibrinogen and thrombin derived from human plasma, and so there have been concerns over their use and possible transmission of infection. The use of pooled human plasma products introduces the risk of transmission of blood-borne pathogens. They have been reports of parvovirus B19 transmission but none of hepatitis or HIV transmission. The use of bovine products also raises concerns with regard to the transmission of bovine spongiform encephalitis. There are also risks associated with immunological sequelae, including anaphylaxis and coagulopathy.

The role of these sealants in facilitating haemostasis has become a part of the patient blood management programme and has the aim of aiding surgical haemostasis and reducing total blood loss for the patient undergoing the procedure. The contribution to total blood loss may be minimal, but the minimizing of surgical ooze or troublesome bleeding from surgical interventions may allow quicker closure and shorter surgical procedures.

These products may contain human or bovine thrombin and fibrinogen and so use of such products needs to be monitored by haemovigilance systems. Currently many such products are ordered by surgical teams and stored within a theatre pharmacy for immediate use when troublesome bleeding occurs. The traceability of such products may not be to the standard considered necessary by a haemovigilance scheme and is not usually under the control of the hospital blood bank. It is important to remember that the available fibrin sealants both in Europe and the United States tend to be of the new-generation virally inactivated or virus-removed fibrin sealants. However, before these products which have been available since 1998, there were a number of reports describing a variety of 'homemade' formulations. The use of plasma-derived products to facilitate haemostasis was first described in 1909. Concern over the transmission of hepatitis with the use of human thrombin led to its substitution with bovine thrombin. Commercial concentrates containing human fibrinogen plus fibrin stabilizing factor (factor XIII) together with bovine thrombin were available in Europe in the late 1970s. All of these products contained an antifibrinolytic agent. The viral risk was reduced through donor selection followed by heat treatment of the human fibrinogen component. In addition, human thrombin (virally inactivated) has now replaced bovine thrombin. Despite these advances in viral safety it is worth mentioning that a few cases have been reported with the use of fibrin glues which relate more to the mode of use of these products. Although it has to be stated that the use of generic 'fibrin glue' appears to be safe in the majority of cases, in one report of a fatality when a syringe was used to administer the glue to a deep hepatic wound, the fatal hypotension was thought to be related to a reaction to bovine thrombin. Another recently reported case highlighted significant morbidity after using a pressurized fibrin glue aerosol, again in liver surgery, resulting in air embolism and intravascular thrombus, identified with transoesophageal echocardiography, to be present in the right ventricle with some air even finding a passage through to the left ventricle leading to cardiovascular collapse.

In conclusion, the use of all types of fibrin glues appears to be increasing but the current practice seems to have little standardization of use with little attention being paid to the traceability of the product used. This is of course very important when human thrombin, albeit treated and virally inactivated, is being used. A better system needs to be used and a registry of patients who receive such products needs to be kept by the institution. In addition to the documentation, placement of a sticky label in the patient's notes precisely identifying the product needs to become a standard of care.

Pharmacological approaches

In cases of excessive blood loss in which no surgical or haemostatic abnormalities can be identified, a different approach is required, namely the use of pharmacological strategies. These can broadly be divided into preoperative prophylaxis for operations that confer a high risk of bleeding, and interventions for massive, refractory bleeding. The medications most widely used and evaluated include those that follow.

Serine protease inhibitors (e.g. aprotinin)

Aprotinin is a non-specific serine protease inhibitor (inhibits plasmin at low dose, kallikrein at high dose, activated protein C, and thrombin) derived from bovine lung. In addition to its antifibrinolytic properties, it may have effects on promoting platelet function by blocking the thrombin-activated protease-activated receptor 1 (PAR1), and appears to affect novel anti-inflammatory targets preventing transmigration of leucocytes. Efficacy is dose dependent. Due to its origin, there is a risk of allergy especially with repeated doses; therefore a test dose should always be performed. No cases of bovine spongiform encephalopathy transmission by aprotinin have been reported.

In cardiac surgery with a high risk of significant blood loss, aprotinin significantly reduced bleeding, mortality, and hospital stay. Beneficial effects were also reported in high-risk orthopaedic surgery. In liver transplantation, initial reports of benefit were overshadowed by concerns about toxicity. In a meta-analysis (Sedrakyan et al. 2004), transfusion requirements decreased by 39% in coronary artery bypass graft surgery. In orthopaedic surgery, a decrease of blood transfusions was likewise confirmed. However, in 2006, the use of aprotinin became controversial when the drug was associated with an increased risk of renal failure, myocardial infarction, stroke, and death in a couple of large observational studies (Mangano et al. 2007). Following the Blood Conservation Using Antifibrinolytics in a Randomized Trial (BART) study its use was suspended (Fergusson et al. 2008). This was a large, multicentre, randomized control trial that compared aprotinin, tranexamic acid, and aminocaproic acid. It concluded that the use of aprotinin was associated with a significant doubling of death from cardiac causes and only provided a modest reduction in the risk of bleeding when compared to the other antifibrinolytics.

Lysine analogue antifibrinolytics (e.g. ε-aminocaproic acid)

These antifibrinolytics work by inhibiting the binding of plasmin to fibrin by occupying the lysine-binding site of the proenzyme plasminogen (Mannucci and Levi 2007). Two meta-analyses have failed to demonstrate any statistically significant effect, at any dose, on the amount of allogeneic blood transfusion required in cardiac surgery. However, a study undertaken in major paediatric surgery patients found the effects of aminocaproic acid and tranexamic acid in reducing blood loss were comparable to that of aprotinin. There was found to be no increase in postoperative stroke in cardiac patients receiving aminocaproic acid during bypass surgery.

Tranexamic acid

This is a synthetically derived antifibrinolytic agent which acts like aminocaproic acid but is 10 times more potent.

Uncontrolled bleeding is an important cause of death in trauma victims. The 2011 Cochrane systematic review of antifibrinolytics concluded that tranexamic acid safely reduces mortality in bleeding trauma patients without the increase of adverse effects. The result of the CRASH-2 study also strongly endorses this (Shakur et al. 2010). Further trials are needed to determine the effects of tranexamic acid in patients with isolated brain injury.

The effect of tranexamic acid and its impact on platelet function remains controversial. A recent study supported its use to partially reverse the platelet aggregation dysfunction as a result of dual antiplatelet therapy, namely aspirin and clopidogrel. However, platelet aggregation was not aided by tranexamic acid in patients not on antiplatelet therapy.

Tranexamic acid is not licensed for the prophylaxis or treatment of bleeding after cardiac surgery in the United Kingdom. It is licensed for the prophylaxis and treatment of local fibrinolysis in patients at high risk of haemorrhage after prostatectomy, conization of the cervix, and surgical procedures or dental extractions in haemophiliac patients. It is also licensed in the management of general fibrinolysis associated with thrombolytic therapy and haemorrhage associated with disseminated intravascular coagulation with predominant activation of the fibrinolytic system.

Desmopressin

Desmopressin is a synthetic analogue of vasopressin (without the vasoconstrictive properties). Desmopressin increases factor VIII and von Willebrand factor and facilitates haemostasis by increasing platelet quality and adhesiveness. It is used routinely in mild haemophilia and von Willebrand disease, some platelet disorders, and occasionally in cardiac surgery to enhance platelet function. The therapeutic dose is 0.3 $\mu g\ kg^{-1}$ i.v. or s.c. before and shortly after surgery.

Overall, there have been 18 trials of desmopressin in a total of 1295 patients undergoing cardiac surgery. These show a small effect of perioperative blood loss with a median reduction of 115 ml. Further reviews have commented that although desmopressin helps to reduce perioperative blood loss, the effect is too small to influence more clinically relevant outcomes such as the need for transfusion and re-operation (Henry et al. 2001).

The most common adverse effects suffered with its use include facial flushing and transient hyponatraemia. There have been reports of an increased risk of arterial thrombotic events; however, some reviews concluded that the rate of thrombosis did not differ significantly.

Activated recombinant VIIa

This is a recombinant form of human factor VIIa. It is thought to act locally at the site of tissue injury and vascular-wall disruption by binding to exposed tissue factor, generating small amounts of thrombin that are sufficient to activate platelets. The activated platelet surface can then form a template on which recombinant factor VIIa directly or indirectly mediates further activation of coagulation, ultimately generating much more thrombin and leading to the conversion of fibrinogen to fibrin. Clot formation is stabilized by the inhibition of fibrinolysis as a result of recombinant factor VIIa-mediated activation of thrombin-activatable fibrinolysis inhibitor.

Despite some enthusiastic support for the use of the drug in massively bleeding patients, there are mixed reports of effectiveness in the peri-surgical setting (Ejlersen et al. 2001; Friederich et al. 2003; Boffard et al. 2005; Diprose et al. 2005; Ma et al. 2006; Essam 2007; Gill et al. 2009; Raobaikady et al. 2005; Levi et al. 2010).

Two reviews of recombinant factor VIIa for the prevention and treatment of bleeding patients without haemophilia, found no benefit from its use (Stanworth et al. 2007; Hsia et al. 2008). In a more recent review, the authors conducted an intervention review on the use of the drug, considering prophylactic and therapeutic studies. In the prophylactic group there was a trend towards lower transfusion and in the intervention group a trend to lower mortality. They concluded that there was in both groups a tendency for a greater incidence of thromboembolic events (O'Connell et al. 2006). The report concluded that the benefit in bleeding patients was weak and that unlicensed use should be restricted to clinical trials (Lin et al. 2011). In addition, other workers have found it difficult to evaluate its usefulness in trauma settings and intracranial bleeding (Diringer et al. 2008, 2010; Dutton et al. 2009).

Anaesthetic techniques of blood conservation

Pre-deposit autotransfusion

This method of providing autologous blood has become less popular because of some rather negative assessments in the late 1990s, and a Cochrane review and the European Directive on Blood resulted in a decline in its popularity and so it will not be considered further in this chapter (Goodnough et al. 1989; Brasher and Goodnough 1999; Henry et al. 2002).

Acute normovolaemic haemodilution

As has been described earlier, there is a need to ensure the haemoglobin concentration is as high as possible preoperatively. If this is achieved, acute normovolaemic haemodilution becomes possible as the removal of autologous blood in the immediate preoperative period (e.g. in the anaesthetic room immediately before surgery) will provide fresh blood which can be kept at room temperature, labelled with the patient's details, adjacent to the patient until reinfusion is undertaken towards the end of the procedure.

This technique relies on two basic principles. The first is the fact that the relative anaemia that develops as a result of this technique, means that the blood shed during surgical loss has a lower red blood cell content than would have been the case without haemodilution. The second is that the decrease in haemoglobin concentration is well tolerated as the patient is normovolaemic and well oxygenated under anaesthesia despite the lower haemoglobin concentration (Lieberman et al. 2000; Habler et al. 2004; Weiskopf et al. 2002, 2005).

Previous enthusiasts of the technique wanted to remove large volumes of blood but a mathematical model used to predict the volume of venesected blood necessary calculated that 4 units of blood were removed to conserve an equivalent 1 unit (Kick and Daniel 1997; Meier et al. 2003). To rely on this method alone for allogeneic blood avoidance is not possible in surgery that has a high blood loss. To save a 2-unit equivalent, 8 units of autologous blood would need to be removed, leaving very few red cells in the patient. A strategy of using a combination of colloid and an artificial oxygen carrier such as perfluorocarbon emulsion or haemoglobin solution as an oxygen-carrying bridge during surgery has not materialized because of the inability to manufacture a solution that has met with widespread acceptance because of safety issues. When such a product does become available, this method of blood conservation may gain more acceptance as the venesected autologous blood can be re-administered in the post-surgical phase. Obviously the process needs to offer less risk than current practice and with the caveats of the technique mentioned previously, both the safety of the technique and feasibility remain questionable.

Case reports have highlighted the risk of silent myocardial ischaemia in some at-risk surgical groups (Carvalho et al. 2003) and a meta-analysis done some years ago questioned the effectiveness of such procedures (Bryson et al. 1998; Segal et al. 2004). Having said that, in certain surgical procedures where blood loss is not extensive, the use of both normovolaemic and hypervolaemic haemodilution can be a very successful conservation strategy particularly when used in combination with hyperoxia (Habler and Messmer 1998; Boldt et al. 1999). Meier et al. (2004) showed the reversibility of silent myocardial ischaemia in the presence of hyperoxia without restoration of the haemoglobin concentration.

Prevention of acidosis

Associated with hypothermia and underperfusion during severe bleeding is a tendency towards acidosis secondary to decreased tissue oxygenation and carbon dioxide removal. A decreasing pH can have significant effects on the concentration of endogenous factor VII present and can inhibit clotting mechanisms. The administration of sodium bicarbonate is not particularly helpful and not used to reverse this acidosis. Treatment strategies to improve tissue oxygenation and improve microvascular flow are best used in these situations in an attempt to minimize a decrease of blood pH.

Judicious use of intravenous fluids

The use of crystalloid or colloid to restore intravascular volume is a useful treatment to maintain stroke volume and cardiac output. The delivery of oxygen to the tissues in healthy individuals, who are not anaemic, allows a surplus of oxygen delivery. This is one of the main reasons that patients can tolerate a lowering of haemoglobin concentrations to at least 50% of their normal values with no compromising of tissue oxygenation providing cardiac output is maintained in the presence of blood loss. There will come a point, however, in the face of ongoing haemorrhage that excessive haemodilution will occur, lowering haemoglobin concentrations to a critical level. The overuse of volume expanders also haemodilutes the essential clotting components and will compromise clot formation and clot strength.

Positioning avoiding venous obstruction

When an operation site is above the level of the patient's heart, bleeding can often be reduced. Avoiding pressure on major veins by careful positioning of the patient also helps reduce blood loss and preventing venous stagnation is also a simple measure that can be taken to reduce blood loss (Simpson 1992).

The use of a tourniquet and evacuation of venous blood before application is an efficient method of limiting blood loss in the surgical area (Mathru et al. 1996; Snyder 1997).

Normothermia

Maintaining a normal body temperature (normothermia) contributes to reducing blood loss (Schmied et al. 1996). Hypothermia reduces the function of both clotting factors and platelets, which will increase the tendency to bleed (Stainsby et al. 2006).

Neuroaxial analgesia techniques

Neuroaxial analgesia techniques, such as sympathetic nerve block, which may accompany epidural or intrathecal block can limit perioperative blood loss. A reduction of allogeneic blood transfusions by up to 50% has been described. Sympathetic nerve block causes peripheral vasodilation and regional flow redistribution (Sharrock et al. 1993; Sharrock and Salvati 1996).

Controlled hypotension by pharmacological methods

Blood pressure can be lowered in a controlled manner using pharmacological methods and this can contribute to decreased blood loss. Agents such as sodium nitroprusside or glyceryl trinitrate can be used for this or a combination of a vasodilator and an α- or β-receptor blocker. When such a technique is used, it is important to ensure relatively normal mean arterial pressures in the patient before surgical closure otherwise bleeding vessels can cause concealed haemorrhage. Elevation of the blood pressure towards the end of the procedure allows surgical ligation or diathermy to be undertaken before closure (Suttner et al. 2001).

Management of coagulation

Point-of-care testing

Excessive bleeding may be as a result of surgical causes, but in the absence of a surgical cause may be because of derangement of haemostasis. Haemostasis is a complex process that promotes clot formation and arrests bleeding providing there is sufficient stasis to allow this. When vessel damage is extensive, blood loss is often too brisk to allow clot formation and in this situation mechanical intervention will be required with either surgical or radiological methods. It refers to the process of keeping blood within a damaged blood vessel. Most of the time this includes the changing of blood from a fluid to a solid state. Intact blood vessels are central to moderating tendency of blood to clot. The endothelial cells of intact vessels prevent blood coagulation by secretion of heparin-like molecule and thrombomodulin and prevent platelet aggregation by the secretion of nitric oxide and prostacyclin. When endothelial injury occurs, the endothelial cells cease secretion of coagulation and aggregation inhibitors and instead secrete von Willebrand factor and tissue thromboplastin which initiate the maintenance of haemostasis after injury. Haemostasis has three major steps: (1) vasoconstriction, (2) temporary blockage of a break by a platelet plug, and (3) blood coagulation, or formation of a clot that seals the hole until tissues are repaired.

Methods of monitoring coagulation: laboratory tests

Laboratory tests are commonly carried out to assess coagulation and are usually performed on citrated plasma samples. The results are expressed as clotting time in seconds and compared with the mean plus or minus twice the standard deviation of results obtained from at least 20 normal individuals, usually laboratory staff. Platelet-poor plasma is used for testing. Commonly performed tests include prothrombin time (PT), which is a value used to calculate the INR and APTT, TT, and fibrinogen concentration.

Point-of-care tests of coagulation

Over recent years, tests that assess the haemostatic process in whole blood have gained popularity, reintroducing a previously developed test, the thromboelastogram, which measures the viscoelastic properties of whole blood as it clots

Haemostasis is a dynamic process and near-patient tests have the advantage of being quick with no delays incurred for transportation. They do not require special personnel or preparation providing the operator has been trained and deemed competent. They use whole blood, giving a better indication of all factors involved in the clotting process. Hence, therapeutic interventions can be made more rapidly. Studies have shown that the correct choice of near-patient test can reduce inappropriate blood transfusion, thromboembolism, major haemorrhage, and mortality.

However, these tests also have their limitations which include limited comparability with laboratory tests. Results may be unreliable in less experienced hands, may be inadequately documented, and equipment may lack adequate calibration and quality assurance.

Activated clotting time

The activated clotting time first came into clinical use in the mid 1970s to guide the administration and reversal of heparin during cardiopulmonary bypass procedures. Whole blood is incubated at 37°C with Celite® (diatomaceous earth). It is used to quantify the heparin. There is no laboratory equivalent. The normal range is 100–140 s. It is prolonged by inadequate mixing, thrombocytopenia, warfarin, and aprotinin. It cannot be used in cases of heparin resistance.

Platelet function analyser (PFA-100® System)

The PFA-100® System (Siemens Healthcare Diagnostics, Washington, DC, USA) measures primary haemostasis by assessing platelet adhesion, activation, and aggregation. It distinguishes the effects of aspirin from other abnormalities of platelet function.

Thromboelastography and thromboelastometry

Thromboelastography and thromboelastometry are near-patient tests to analyse the visco-elastic properties of whole blood or plasma and produce graphic displays, easily interpreted in operating theatres (Weber et al. 2012). These results can demonstrate primary fibrinolysis, secondary fibrinolysis, failure to reverse protamine, and whether blood products are required. The patient's progress can be monitored with successive tests. Two instruments are currently commercially available: the term thromboelastography refers to measurements made using the TEG® device (Haemonetics Corp., Braintree, MA, USA) and the ROTEM® (Tem International GmbH, Munich, Germany) which produces measurements termed thromboelastometry. See Figures 51.2 and 51.3. They are used in numerous cardiac and transplant surgery operating theatres and studies have shown that it is a significantly better predictor of postoperative haemorrhage and the need for re-operation than the conventional coagulation profile. It has also been reported they are of benefit in trauma patients in identifying coagulopathy and guiding transfusion therapy when compared with plasma-based routine coagulation tests. Both instruments can produce useful information within 5–10 min of initiation of the tests.

Intraoperative cell salvage

Cell salvage is the process by which blood from the surgical field is collected, filtered, and washed to produce autologous blood for transfusion back to the patient. The use of intraoperative cell salvage (ICS) reduces the demand on allogenic (donor) red cells and is a cost-effective measure (Ashworth and Klein 2010). It also reduces the risks associated with the immunological complications of allogenic blood transfusions. Analysis of a recent survey showed that 53% of UK hospitals now use ICS. Level one evidence of the efficiency of ICS is sparse but convincing, especially in vascular, cardiac, and orthopaedic surgery (Consensus Statement 1999; Carless et al. 2006). See Table 51.1.

Maximum benefit of cell salvage can be gained by capture of emergency cases which often require large-volume blood component support.

Indications for intraoperative cell salvage

ICS is indicated in surgery with:

- Anticipated blood loss of greater than 1000 ml or greater than 20% estimated blood volume

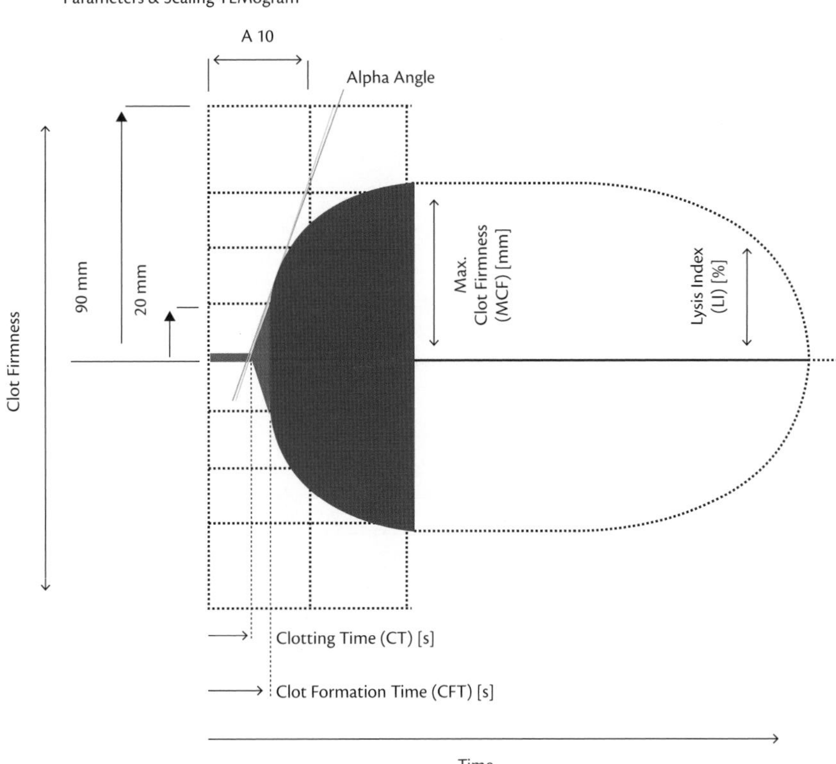

Figure 51.2 The outlines of the basic components of a ROTEM® graph.
Courtesy of TEM International.

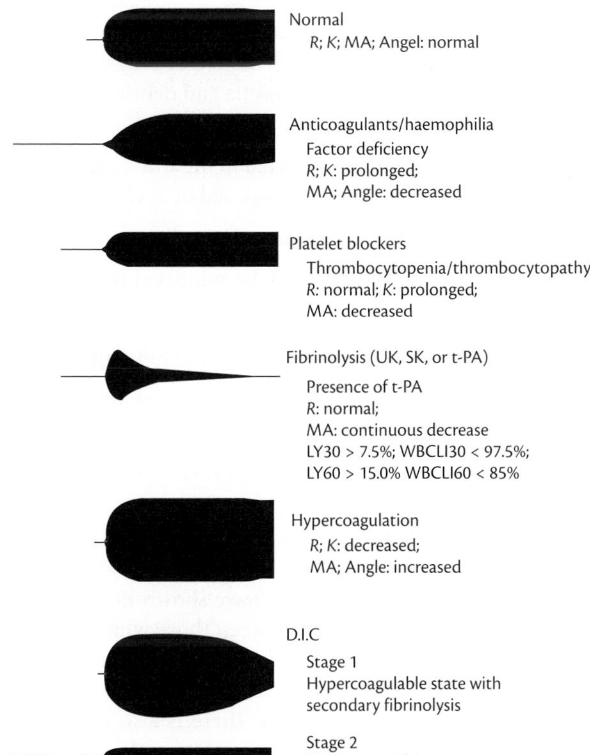

Figure 51.3 These outlines describe the various patters of graph obtained from a TEG® machine.
TEG® Hemostasis Analyzer tracing images used by permission of Haemonetics Corporation. TEG® is a registered trademark of Haemonetics Corporation.

Table 51.1 Advantages and disadvantages of cell salvage

Advantages	Disadvantages
Reduce the risk of transmission of infection	Initial equipment cost
No risk of ABO incompatibility	Cost of disposables
Option in the case of rare blood group and antibodies	Staff training and competencies
Acceptable for some Jehovah's Witnesses	Complex device
Reduce the demand for allogenic blood	Delay in processing red cells
Normal concentration of 2,3-DPG	Risk of bacterial contamination
Removal of activated clotting factors and inflammatory cytokines	Red cell lysis as a result of 'skimming'
Cells reinfused at room temperature	Electrolyte imbalance
	Air and fat embolism

Data from the Medicines and Health Regulatory Authority.

- Patients with a low haemoglobin or increased risk factors for bleeding
- Patients with multiple antibodies or rare blood types
- Patients with objections to receiving allogenic (donor) blood
- The American Association of Blood Banks suggest cell salvage is indicated in surgery where blood would ordinarily be cross-matched or where more than 10% of patients undergoing the procedure require transfusion.

See Table 51.2 for a summary of procedures and situations that may be suitable for ICS.

Table 51.2 Procedures and situations which may be suitable for ICS

Vascular surgery, trauma, and orthopaedics	Open aortic aneurysm repair—elective and emergency Splenic/liver trauma Spinal surgery Revision hip replacement Pelvic and femoral fractures (In primary hip and knee replacement it may be better to consider postoperative drainage system)
Urology	Radical cystectomy Radical prostatectomy Nephrectomy Pelvic clearance
General surgery	Hepatectomy Abdominal/thoracic trauma Emergency laparotomy
Cardiac	All major procedures (postoperative drainage may be of use if mediastinal drainage is of high volume)
Obstetric	*Emergency use*: major obstetric haemorrhage at caesarean section, laparotomy for post-partum haemorrhage, genital tract trauma, etc. *Elective use*: anticipated haemorrhage at caesarean section, e.g. placenta praevia/accrete, large fibroid uterus, etc.
Gynaecology	All major procedures, e.g. pelvic clearance
Head and neck	Major procedures
Jehovah's Witness or any patient refusing a blood transfusion	Consideration should also be given to postoperative drainage and reinfusion where indicated. All surgical procedures where blood loss is expected to have an impact

Data from the Medicines and Health Regulatory Authority.

Intraoperative cell salvage process

During surgery, blood loss can be removed from the operative site by a combination of suction and swabs. Depending on the type of surgery, blood loss to swabs has been estimated at between 30% and 50% (Haynes 2005) of the total surgical blood loss. By washing the swabs, the blood that is normally discarded can be collected and the overall efficiency of red cell recovery improved. To maximize quantity and minimize red cell damage, a large-bore suction tip (minimum 4 mm) should be used and surface skimming avoided. A low vacuum pressure should be also used to reduce haemolysis.

Separate suction needs to be used to discard substances that should not be aspirated into the ICS, such as antibiotics not licensed for i.v. use, iodine, chlorhexidine, hydrogen peroxide, alcohol, topical clotting agents, orthopaedic cement pleural effusions, amniotic fluid, and gastric and pancreatic secretions. These substances are harmful to the red cells and result in haemolysis and thus a decreased red cell yield. The pieces of topical clotting agents and bone cement are removed during filtration but are best avoided.

The cell salvage process involves the following six steps and is shown by Figure 51.4.

- Suction: blood is aspirated from the surgical site. It is transported via a dual-lumen tube and collected in a reservoir. It is immediately mixed with an anticoagulant at the end of the sucker where it joins the dual-lumen tube as acid citrate dextrose or heparinized saline is dripped down the smaller lumen and the mixture of blood and anticoagulant is aspirated up the other larger lumen.
- Filtration: this fluid is then filtered to remove debris and large clots. Filter sizes vary from 40–150 μm.
- Separation: the filtered fluid is drawn into a centrifuge. The force of the centrifuge holds the more dense red cells against the outer wall of the bowl. The less dense plasma and debris move into the centre of the bowel where it spills over into the waste bag.
- Washing: disposal products collected in the waste bag (e.g. platelets, fat, and clotting factors) are disposed of as clinical waste.
- Cell salvage: the red blood cells are collected in a separate bag.
- Reinfusion: collected red cells can be reinfused immediately or up to 4 h after processing.

Special circumstances and intraoperative cell salvage

The decision to use blood contaminated with bacteria, amniotic fluid, or malignant cells should be made by the clinicians caring for the patient.

Malignancy

The manufacturers of ICS devices do not recommend their use in surgery when the surgical site may contain malignant cells. However, recent reports and studies have shown no difference in recurrence risks or survival rates between those who received and did not receive salvaged blood. This led to approval of the use of ICS in urological malignancies by the UK National Institute for Health and Care Excellence (NICE). There is also evidence that blood filtration through leucodepletion filters also significantly reduces transmission of malignant cells.

Obstetrics

There are concerns over the use of ICS and the risk of causing an amniotic fluid embolus. In view that there are no proved cases

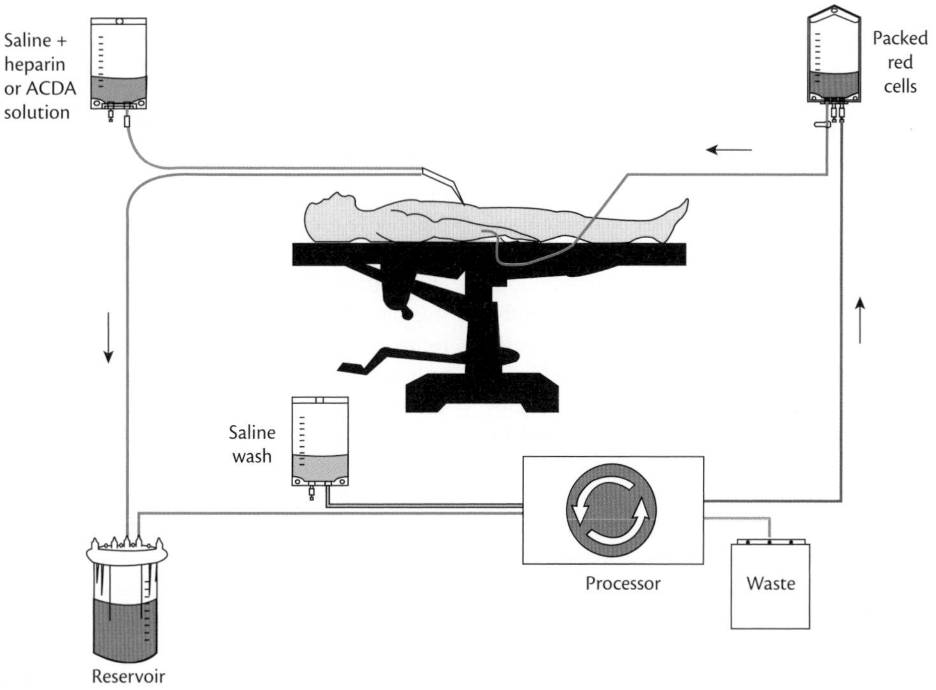

Figure 51.4 This diagram shows a schematic example of the intraoperative cell salvage set-up.
Drawn for the UK ICS Action Group by Medical Illustration Department – University of South Manchester NHS Foundation Trust. Reproduced with permission.

documented, NICE have approved the use in obstetrics. Again, the use of leucodepletion filters significantly reduces contamination. The rhesus status of the mother must also be checked during the use of ICS in obstetric cases. If the mother is rhesus negative (and fetus rhesus positive), they should undergo Kleihauer testing after use to determine the extent of maternal exposure and given a suitable dose of anti-D immunoglobulin.

Reports collected by the UK haemovigilance organization SHOT (Serious Hazards of Transfusion) have highlighted probable hypotensive episodes related to the use of near-patient leucocyte depletion filters in combination with warm salvaged red cells (Knowles and Cohen 2010).

Bowel contamination

In this instance, the manufacturers of ICS devices do not recommend the use of ICS unless there is catastrophic haemorrhage, although there is some evidence that there is no increase in postoperative infection or mortality. Cell salvage is not recommended by the manufacturers in the presence of sickle cell disease, sickle cell trait, and other red blood cell disorders.

Safety and management of intraoperative cell salvage

The successful use of ICS requires a team approach. Recommendations state that a lead clinician, ideally working in the theatre setting (i.e. consultant surgeon or anaesthetist), should provide information, support, and direction in promoting the service. A senior member of the theatre should be responsible for the organization and facilitation of the ICS service. All staff operating the cell saver should undergo rigorous training and supervision.

All cell salvage blood and procedures should be documented in patients' records. The UK Cell Salvage Action Group has developed a generic label for salvaged blood. Any adverse events should be reported to SHOT and the cell salvage service should be audited regularly to maintain the highest achievable standard.

In many operations where blood loss is expected to be more than 1 litre, the use of intraoperative cell salvage has now become an accepted and safe technique of minimizing operative blood loss. The use of a special dual-lumen suction which delivers anticoagulant to the end of the collection tubing allows admixture of the aspirated blood with either acid citrate dextrose or heparinized saline to prevent clot formation.

Aspiration from the wound, especially from pooled blood, using a specially designed sucker without air inlets in its tip prevents turbulent flow and enhances red cell recovery as a result of minimizing haemolysis of red cells. Limiting suction pressures also helps as does the less acute angle and wider bore of the suction catheter.

The collected blood is stored in a cardiotomy reservoir until there is sufficient blood to process. The use of 'standby' collection set-up means that the full processing kit is only opened if sufficient blood is collected, thus minimizing equipment costs. In standby mode, only a cardiotomy reservoir suction line and anticoagulant is used. In addition, if local information of expected blood loss and allogeneic blood transfusion usage is categorized by case complexity and surgeon then the deployment of cell salvage can be made using this local information, again enhancing the efficiency and cost-effectiveness of its use.

Once collected the blood is washed, concentrated, and filtered before reinfusion. In a situation of brisk bleeding, a unit of red cells can be processed in 10–15 min. One processing set can be used to collect and wash many litres of blood in a massive haemorrhage situation and becomes a very cost-effective and immediately available source of fresh red cells to aid the resuscitation process. It needs to be remembered that most platelets and clotting factors will be washed out of the resuspended red cells as the molecular weight of both means that they are separated by the centrifugal method used in these devices to separate plasma from the more dense red cells.

As shown in Figure 51.4, the salvage process can be set up to allow continuous collection and either continuous or discontinuous processing depending on the rate of bleeding and the type of machine used. The majority of such machines use a discontinuous method of processing while the C.A.T.S.® device (Fresenius Kabi, Bad Homburg, Germany) offers the opportunity to continuously process blood as a result of its different centrifugal system and lends itself to harvesting and processing of small volumes of red cells, ideal for use in paediatric surgery where only small volumes will be processed. See Figure 51.5.

Another advantage of the setting up of a continuous circuit is one of relative continuity with the patient's circulation, meaning that some Jehovah's Witness patients will accept collection and reinfusion of their own red cells which helps towards a successful outcome even in such extensive procedures as liver transplantation and cardiac surgery.

The quality of blood produced despite the presence of activated cytokines is very good and has a good 2,3-diphosphoglycerate (DPG) and a low potassium content as the red cell membranes remain active and therefore acidosis is minimized in massive haemorrhage as the red cells start carrying oxygen immediately after reinfusion.

Postoperative management

Postoperative cell salvage

Postoperative cell salvage is routinely used in some areas of surgical practice (e.g. cardiac and orthopaedic surgery), especially total knee arthroplasty (Bengtson et al. 1990; Newman et al. 1997; Weltert et al. 2013). This technique involves the collection of postoperative blood loss into a wound drain that is then either filtered and returned to the patient or washed before re-infusion. The volume of blood required for the technique to be justified is approximately 400 ml or more, but this loss should occur within 6 h of wound closure (Faris et al. 1991; Healy et al. 1994). If the patient is a suitable candidate for postoperative cell salvage it must be discussed with them in advance and documented. It is paramount that a strict sterile approach is followed and manufacturer's instructions followed. A 40-micron filter must be used during re-infusion. Intravenous fluids may be required in addition to salvaged blood. It is contraindicated if the patient declines the procedure. It cannot be used if the surgical field is contaminated with povidone-iodine, chlorhexidine, hydrogen peroxide, and antibiotics and cannot be used in patients with sickle cell disease, sickle cell trait, and other red

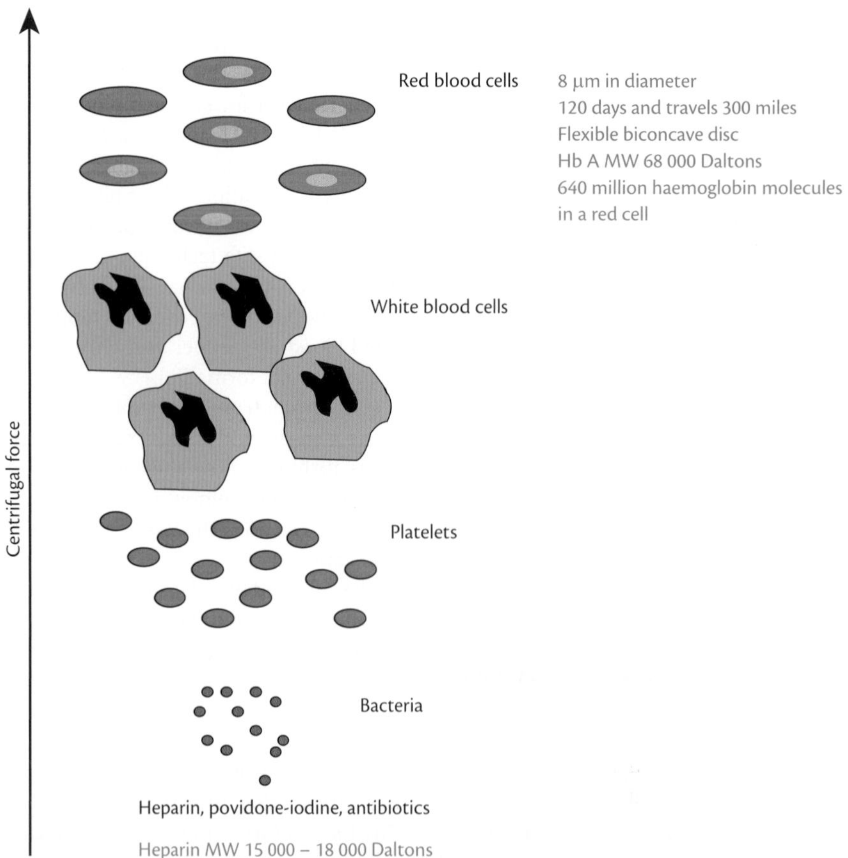

Figure 51.5 Diagrammatic representation of particle densities in whole salvaged blood to explain why the dense red cells are forced to the outside of the centrifuge bowl.

cell disorders. It should be avoided in cases of known or suspected infection or malignancy

An area where postoperative cell salvage is used extensively is in the field of orthopaedic surgery. Joint replacement surgery used to demand a very high level of allogeneic blood support but recent practice has led to a significant reduction in this area. A Cochrane review has shown that the various studies conducted over the years indicate a significant risk reduction for allogeneic transfusion with both washed and unwashed methods of red cell salvage (Carless et al. 2006). The combination of accepting a lower postoperative haemoglobin concentration combined with the use of cell salvage has dramatically reduced the need for allogeneic blood in the majority of these patients (Shenolikar et al. 1997; Thomas et al. 2001).

The blood conservation theme has continued to develop in these patients and the use of tranexamic acid has also reduced transfusion requirements. The drive to ensure enhanced recovery after surgery has led to the avoidance of wound drains, particularly in total knee replacement. This is said to minimize postoperative bleeding and the blood left in the joint does not seem to prevent early mobilization. Some surgeons are now advocating the use of no drainage and the insertion of tranexamic acid and local anaesthetic into the joint that minimizes blood loss and transfusion requirements and enhances early mobilization. However, a recent report showed that when properly blinded there was no difference in length of stay, blood loss, or pain scores between conventional treatment which included wound drainage (plus postoperative cell salvage) and enhanced recovery from surgery (Liu et al. 2016). Nevertheless, there was an increase in returns to theatre in the enhanced recovery from surgery group because of stiff knees and swelling and fracture blisters, related to the injection of local anaesthetic in large volumes.

Debate continues about the use of postoperative, unwashed cell salvage blood which is merely filtered and then returned to the patient (Vertrees et al. 1996). The re-infusate has a lower haematocrit and a large number of activated cytokines that may lead to non-haemolytic febrile reactions (Southern et al. 1995; Muñoz et al. 2005, 2006). Reports of decreased infection were not confirmed when reviewed by the Cochrane group but a study looking at natural killer cell function showed a significant increase in their numbers after re-infusion of wound drain blood (Mrózek et al. 1996; Tylman et al. 2001; Gharehbaghian et al. 2002, 2004; Dalén et al. 2003; Islam et al. 2011).

Minimize phlebotomy

There are a number of studies that have shown the impact of frequent venesection during the postoperative period (Vincent et al. 2002; Corwin et al. 2004). Several strategies can be implemented to decrease the effect of venesection. Obviously less frequent sampling and smaller samples will have an impact on patients who have a prolonged recovery from surgery. In addition, capillary haemoglobin assessment as with HemoCue® (HemoCue AB, Ängelholm, Sweden) or even a non-invasive haemoglobin monitor as with Masimo continuous pulse oximetry to trend haemoglobin concentrations in the postoperative period until it is felt that a formal laboratory test is required. Clearly in ITU patients other factors may increase the risk of anaemia, such as postoperative bleeding, development of acute kidney injury, and the suppressive effects on the bone marrow as a result of chronic illness, ongoing infection, and poor nutritional status.

Triggers to consider transfusion, liberal *vs* restrictive transfusion practice

Transfusion triggers have been used in many ITUs since the publication of the TRICC study (Hebert et al. 1999; Carless 2010). Two strategies can be described, one where a haemoglobin concentration is chosen which may trigger a transfusion, the other may be a desired target haemoglobin concentration (Carson et al. 1996, 2012).

One-unit transfusion may therefore be justified to achieve a target figure. Many clinicians, however, believe that a one-unit transfusion, 1 g litre^{-1} increase is rarely justified and probably not worth giving for physiological needs, but that does depend on whether oxygen delivery was critically necessary, that is, had a critical supply demand situation been reached? This is a very difficult decision and not easily made as there are no objective measures that can be easily used to help with this decision.

Oxygen postoperatively

The administration of added inspired oxygen ensures that the circulating haemoglobin is maximally saturated with oxygen and also helps minimize any ventilation/perfusion shunt that may be present postoperatively as a result of atelectasis or pneumonic changes in the postoperative patients who may have a distended abdomen with diaphragmatic splinting and deep breathing inhibited as a result of postoperative pain.

Iron and folic acid postoperatively

In patients who have a prolonged recovery from surgery, it may be difficult to recommence a normal diet and patients will become folate deficient very quickly and soon afterwards iron deficient, even if the acute blood loss operatively had not decreased their preoperative iron stores.

Deep vein thrombosis prophylaxis needs to be considered carefully although this should be started as soon as possible in the postoperative period. In those patients who have experienced extensive bleeding, prophylaxis is just as necessary as haemorrhage tends to promote a prothrombotic state in the patient.

Summary

The art of blood conservation requires fastidious attention to detail of the patient awaiting surgical intervention with measures to boost preoperative haemoglobin concentrations without resorting to allogeneic transfusion, combined with organized anaesthetic and surgical care to minimize operative blood loss and ensure that operative losses are recycled where appropriate. Avoidance of unnecessary allogeneic transfusion in the stable, non-symptomatic, postoperative patient plays at least an equal part to the preoperative and operative phases; it is important to treat the patient rather than a laboratory value which always needs to be considered when low, but only acted upon should the patient be symptomatic.

Declaration of interest

None declared.

References

Advisory Committee on the Safety of Blood, Tissue and Organs (SaBTO). *Donor Selection Criteria Review*. 2011. Available from http://webarchive.nationalarchives.gov.uk/+/www.dh.gov.uk/ab/SABTO/DH_129796 (accessed 2 June 2013)

Alter HJ, Purcell RH, Shih JW, *et al.* Detection of antibody to hepatitis C virus in prospectively followed transfusion recipients with acute and chronic non-A, non-B hepatitis. *N Engl J Med* 1989; **321**: 1494–500

American Society of Anesthesiologists. Practice guidelines for blood component therapy: a report by the American Society of Anesthesiologists task force on blood component therapy. *Anesthesiology* 1996; **84**: 732–47

Ashworth A, Klein A. Cell salvage as part of a blood conservation strategy in anaesthesia. *Br J Anaes* 2010; **105**: 401–16

Bengtson JP, Backman L, Stenqvist O, Heideman M, Bengtsson A. Complement activation and reinfusion of wound drainage blood. *Anesthesiology* 1990; **73**: 376–80

Billote DB, Glisson SN, Green D, Wixon RL. A prospective, randomised study of pre-operative autologous donation for hip replacement surgery. *J Bone Joint Surg Am* 2002; **84**: 1299–304

Boffard KD, Riou B, Warren B, *et al.* Recombinant factor VIIa as adjunctive therapy for bleeding control in severely injured trauma patients: two parallel randomized, placebo-controlled, double-blind clinical trials. *J Trauma* 2005; **59**: 8–15

Boldt J, Weber A, Mailer K, Papsdorf M, Schuster P. Acute normovolaemic haemodilution vs controlled hypotension for reducing the use of allogeneic blood in patients undergoing radical prostatectomy. *Br J Anaesth* 1999; **82**: 170–4

Brasher ME, Goodnough LT. The rise and fall of peroperative autologous blood donation. *Transfusion* 1999; **41**: 1495–62

British Committee for Standards in Haematology, Blood Transfusion Task Force, Duguid J, *et al.* Guidelines for the use of fresh-frozen plasma, cryoprecipitate and cryosupernatant. *Br J Haematol* 2004; **126**: 11–28

Bryson GL, Laupacis A, Wells GA. Does acute normovolaemic hemodilution reduce perioperative allogeneic transfusion? A meta-analysis, The International Study of Perioperative Transfusion. *Anesth Analg* 1998; **86**: 9–15

Busch MP, Kleinmann SH, Nemo GJ. Current and emerging infectious risks of blood transfusions. *JAMA* 2003; **289**: 959–62

Camm AJ, Lip GY, De Caterina R, *et al.* 2012 focused update of the ESC Guidelines for the management of atrial fibrillation: an update of the 2010 ESC Guidelines for the management of atrial fibrillation. Developed with the special contribution of the European Heart Rhythm Association. *Eur Heart J* 2012; **33**: 2719–47

Carless PA, Henry DA, Carson JL, Hebert PP, McClelland B, Ker K. Transfusion thresholds and other strategies for guiding allogeneic red blood cell transfusion. *Cochrane Database Syst Rev* 2010; **10**: CD002042

Carless PA, Henry DA, Moxey AJ, O'Connell DL, Brown T, Ferguson DA. Cell salvage for minimizing perioperative allogeneic blood transfusion. *Cochrane Database Syst Rev* 2006; **4**: CD001888

Carson JL, Carless PA, Hebert PC. Transfusion thresholds and other strategies for guiding allogeneic red blood cell transfusion. *Cochrane Database Syst Rev* 2012; **4**: CD002042

Carson JL, Duff A, Poses RM, *et al.* Effect of anaemia and cardiovascular disease on surgical mortality and morbidity. *Lancet* 1996; **348**: 1055–60

Carvalho B, Ridler BM, Thompson JF, Telford RJ. Myocardial ischaemia precipitated by acute normovolaemic haemodilution. *Transfus Med* 2003; **13**: 165–8

Chertow GM, Mason PD, Vaage-Nilsen O, Ahlmen J. Update on adverse drug events associated with parenteral iron. *J Dial Transplant* 2006; **2**: 378–82

Chertow GM, Winkelmayer WC. On the relative safety of intravenous iron formulations: new answers, new questions. *Am J Hematol* 2010; **85**: 643–4

Consensus statement. Autologous transfusion: 3 years on. What is new? What has happened? *Transfus Med* 1999; **9**: 285–6

Corwin HL, Gettinger A, Pearl RG, *et al.* The CRIT Study: Anemia and blood transfusion in the critically ill—current clinical practice in the United States. *Crit Care Med* 2004; **32**: 39

CRASH-2 Trial Collaborators, Shakur H, Roberts I, *et al.* Effects of tranexamic acid on death, vascular occlusive events, and blood transfusion in trauma patients with significant haemorrhage (CRASH-2): a randomised, placebo-controlled trial. *Lancet* 2010; **376**: 23–32

Dalén T, Bengtsson A, Brorsson B, Engström KG. Inflammatory mediators in autotransfusion drain blood after knee arthroplasty, with and without leucocyte reduction. *Vox Sang* 2003; **85**: 31–9

Diprose P, Herbertson MJ, O'Shaughnessy D, Gill RS. Activated recombinant factor VII after cardiopulmonary bypass reduces allogeneic transfusion in complex non-coronary cardiac surgery: randomized double-blind placebo-controlled pilot study. *Br J Anaesth* 2005; **95**: 596–602

Diringer MN, Skolnick BE, Mayer SA, *et al.* Risk of thromboembolic events in controlled trials of rFVIIa in spontaneous intracerebral hemorrhage. *Stroke* 2008; **39**: 850–6

Diringer MN, Skolnick BE, Mayer SA, *et al.* Thromboembolic events with recombinant activated factor VII in spontaneous intracerebral hemorrhage: results from the factor seven for acute hemorrhagic stroke (FAST) trial. *Stroke* 2010; **41**: 48–53

Dutton R, Hauser C, Boffard K, *et al.* Scientific and logistical challenges in designing the CONTROL trial: recombinant factor VIIa in severe trauma patients with refractory bleeding. *Clin Trials* 2009; **6**: 467–79

Ejlersen E, Melsen T, Ingerslev J, Andreasen RB, Vilstrup H. Recombinant activated Factor VIIa (rFVIIa) acutely normalizes prothrombin time in patients with cirrhosis during bleeding from oesophageal varices. *Scand J Gastroenterol* 2001; **10**: 1081–5

Essam MA. Prophylactic administration of recombinant activated factor VII in coronary revascularization surgery. *Int J Anesthesiol* 2007; **13**: 10

European Medicines Agency. *NovoSeven*. London (UK): The Agency; 2010. Available from http//www.ema.europa.eu/ema/index.jsp?curl=pages/medicines/human/medicines/000074/human_med_000936.jsp&murl=menus/medicines/medicines.jsp&mid=WC 0b01ac058001d125

Faris PM, Ritter MA, Keating EM, Valeri CR. Unwashed filtered shed blood collected after total hip and knee arthroplasties. A source of autologous red blood cells. *J Bone Joint Surg Am* 1991; **73**: 1169–78

Fergusson DA, PC Hébert PC, Mazer CD, *et al.* for the BART Investigators. A comparison of aprotinin and lysine analogues in high-risk cardiac surgery. *N Engl J Med* 2008; **358**: 2319–31

Friederich PW, Henny CP, Messelink EJ, *et al.* Effect of recombinant activated factor VII on perioperative blood loss in patients undergoing retropubic prostatectomy: a double-blind placebo-controlled randomised trial. *Lancet* 2003; **361**: 201–5

Gharehbaghian A, Haque KM, Truman C, *et al.* Effect of autologous salvaged blood on postoperative natural killer cell precursor frequency. *Lancet* 2004; **363**: 1025–30

Gharehbaghian A, Haque KM, Truman C, Newman J, Bradley BA. Quantitation of natural killer cell precursors in man. *J Immunol Methods* 2002; **260**: 69–77

Gill R, Herbertson M, Vuylsteke A, *et al.* Safety and efficacy of recombinant activated factor VII: a randomized placebo-controlled trial in the setting of bleeding after cardiac surgery. *Circulation* 2009; **120**: 21–7

Goodnough LT. Iron deficiency syndromes and iron restricted erythropoiesis. *Transfusion* 2011; **52**: 1584–92

Goodnough LT, Bravo JR, Hsueh Y, Keating LJ, Brittenham GM. Red blood cell mas in autologous and homologous blood units. Implications for risk/benefit assessment of autologous blood crossover and directed blood transfusion. *Transfusion* 1989; **29**: 821–2

Goodnough LT, Maniatis A, Earnshaw P, *et al.* Detection, evaluation, and management of preoperative anaemia in the elective orthopaedic patient: NATA guidelines. *Br J Anaesth* 2011; **106**: 13–22

Goodnough LT, Monk TG, Andriole GL. Erythropoietin therapy. *N Eng J Med* 1997; **336**: 933–8

Goodnough LT, Shander A. Patient blood management. *Anaesthesiology* 2012; **116**: 1367–76

Habler O, Schwenzer K, Zimmer K, *et al.* Effects of standardized acute normovolemic hemodilution on intraoperative allogeneic blood transfusion in patients undergoing major maxillofacial surgery. *Intl J Oral Maxillofac Surg* 2004; **33**: 467–75

Habler OP, Messmer KF. Hyperoxaemia in extreme haemodilution. *Br J Anaesth* 1998, **81**: 79–82

Haynes SL1, Bennett JR, Torella F, McCollum CN. Does swab washing increase the efficiency of red cell recovery by cell salvage in aortic surgery? *Vox Sang* 2005; **88**: 244–48

Healy W, Pfeifer BA, Kurtz SR, *et al.* Evaluation of autologous shed blood for autotransfusion after orthopaedic surgery. *Clin Orthop* 1994; **299**: 53–9

Hebert PC, Wells GA, Blajchman MA, *et al.* A multicenter, randomized, controlled clinical trial of transfusion requirements in critical care. Transfusion Requirements in Critical Care Investigators, Canadian Critical Care Trials Group. *N Engl J Med* 1999; **340**: 409–17

Henry DA, Carless PA, Moxey AJ, *et al.* Pre-operative autologous donation for minimising perioperative allogeneic blood transfusion. *Cochrane Database Syst Rev* 2002; **2**: CD003602

Henry DA, Mozey AJ, Carless PA, *et al.* Desmopressin for minimising perioperative allogeneic blood transfusions. *Cochrane Database Syst Rev* 2001: **1**: CD001884

Hsia CC, Chin-Yee IH, McAlister VC. Use of recombinant activated factor VII in patients without hemophilia: a meta-analysis of randomized control trials. *Ann Surg* 2008; **248**: 61–8

Isbister JP, Shander A, Spahn DR, Erhard J, Farmer SL, Hoffman A. Adverse blood transfusion outcomes; establishing causation. *Transfusion Med Rev* 2011; **25**: 89–101

Islam NWM, Mehandale S, Hall M, Blom A, Bannister G, Bradley B. Neopterin levels confirm immunostimulation by unwashed salvaged blood transfusion. *Transfus Altern Transfus Med* 2011; **12**: 28–9

Kick O, Daniel E. Mathematical considerations in the practice of acute normovolaemic hemodilution. *Transfusion* 1997; **37**: 141–3

Knowles S, Cohen H. The 2010 Annual SHOT report (on behalf of the serious hazards of transfusion steering group). 2011. Available from http://www.shotuk.org

Kotze A, Carter LA, Scally AJ. Effect of a patient blood management programme on preoperative anaemia, transfusion rate, and outcome after primary hip or knee arthroplasty: a quality improvement cycle. *Br J Anaesth* 2012; **108**: 943–52

Kozek-Langenecker SA, Afshari A, Albaladejo P, *et al.* Management of severe perioperative bleeding: guidelines from the European Society of Anaesthesiology. *Eur J Anaesthesiol* 2013; **30**: 270–382

Levi M, Levy JH, Andersen HF, *et al.* Safety of recombinant activated factor VII in randomized clinical trials. *N Engl J Med* 2010; **363**: 1791–800

Lieberman JA, Weiskopf RB, Kelley SD, *et al.* Critical oxygen delivery in conscious humans is less than 7.3 ml O2 x kg(-1) x min(-1). *Anesthesiology* 2000; **92**: 407–13

Lin DM, Murphy LS, Tran MH. Use of prothrombin complex concentrates and fibrinogen concentrates in the perioperative setting: a systematic review. *Transfus Med Rev* 2013; **27**: 91–104

Lin Y, Stanworth S, Birchall J, *et al.* Use of recombinant factor VIIa for the prevention and treatment of bleeding in patients without hemophilia: a systematic review and meta-analysis. *CMAJ* 2011; **183**: E9–19

Liu D, Dam M, Martinez Martos S, Beller E. Blood Management Strategies in Total Knee Arthroplasty. *Knee Surg Relat Res* 2016 Sep; **28**(3): 179–87

Ma B, Wang ZN, Zhang BR, *et al.* Effect of recombinant activated factor VIIa on early recovery of patients undergoing cardiac valve replacement under cardiopulmonary bypass: a randomized double-blind placebo-controlled trial. *Acad J Second Military Med Univ* 2006; **27**: 1110–13

Makris M, Van Veen JJ, Tait CR, Mumford AD Laffan M. on behalf of the British Committee for Standards in Haematology. Guideline on the management of bleeding in patients on antithrombotic agents. *Br J Haematol* 2012; **160**: 35–46

Mangano DT, Miao Y, Vuylsteke A, *et al.* Investigators of The Multicenter Study of Perioperative Ischemia Research Group; Ischemia Research and Education Foundation. Mortality associated with aprotinin during 5 years following coronary artery bypass graft surgery. *JAMA* 2007; **297**: 471–9

Maniatis A, Van der Linden P, Hardy J-F (eds). *Alternatives to Blood Transfusion in Transfusion Medicine*. Oxford: Wiley-Blackwell, 2011

Mannucci PM, Levi M. Drug therapy: prevention and treatment of major blood loss. *N Engl J Med* 2007; **356**: 2301–11

Mathru M, Dries DJ, Barnes L, Tonino P, Sukhani R, Rooney MW. Tourniquet-induced exsanguination in patients requiring lower limb surgery. An ischemia-reperfusion model of oxidant and antioxidant metabolism. *Anesthesiology* 1996; **84**: 14–22

Medicines and Healthcare products Regulatory Agency. Intravenous iron and serious hypersensitivity reactions: strengthened recommendations. *Drug Safety Update* 2013; **7**: A1

Meier J, Kemming G. I, Kisch-Wedel H, *et al.* Hyperoxic ventilation reduces 6-hour mortality at the critical hemoglobin concentration. *Anesthesiology* 2004; **100**: 70–6

Meier J, Kleen M, Habler O, *et al.* New mathematical model for the correct prediction of the exchangeable blood volume during acute normovolemic hemodilution. *Acta Anaesthesiol Scand* 2003; **47**: 37–45

Mercurali F, Inghilleri G. Proposal of an algorithm to help the choice of the best transfusion strategy. *Curr Med Res Opin* 1996; **13**: 465–78

Mrózek E, Anderson P, Caligiuri MA. Role of interleukin-15 in the development of human CD56+ natural killer cells from CD34+ hematopoietic progenitor cells. *Blood* 1996; **87**: 2632–40

Muñoz M, Cobos A, Campos A, Ariza D, Muñoz E, Gómez A. Impact of postoperative shed blood transfusion, with or without leucocyte reduction, on acute-phase response to surgery for total knee replacement. *Acta Anaesthesiol Scand* 2005; **49**: 1182–90

Muñoz M, Cobos A, Campos A, Ariza D, Muñoz E, Gómez A. Post-operative unwashed shed blood transfusion does not modify the cellular immune response to surgery for total knee replacement. *Acta Anaesthesiol Scand* 2006; **50**: 443–50

Musallam KM, Tamim HM, Richards T, *et al.* Preoperative anaemia and post-operative outcomes in non-cardiac surgery: a retrospective cohort study. *Lancet* 2011; **378**: 1396–407

Na HS, Shin SY, Hwang JY, Jeon YT, Kim CS, Do SH. Effects of intravenous iron combined with low-dose recombinant human erythropoietin on transfusion requirements in iron-deficient patients undergoing bilateral total Knee replacement arthroplasty. *Transfusion* 2011; **51**: 118–24

Newman JH, Bowers M, Murphy J. The clinical advantages of autologous transfusion. A randomized, controlled study after knee replacement. *J Bone Joint Surg Br* 1997; **79**: 630–2

NHS Improving Quality. Enhanced Recovery Programme. 2008. http://www.institute.nhs.uk/quality_and_service_improvement_tools/quality_and_service_improvement_tools/enhanced_recovery_programme.html

O'Connell KA, Wood JJ, Wise RP, *et al.* Thromboembolic adverse events after use of recombinant human coagulation factor VIIa. *JAMA* 2006; **295**: 293–8

Pasricha SR, Flecknoe-Brown SC, Allen KJ, *et al.* Diagnosis and management of iron deficiency anaemia: a clinical update. *Med J Aust* 2010; **193**: 525–32

Rao SV, Jollis JG, Harrington RA, *et al.* Relationship of blood transfusion and clinical outcomes in patients with acute coronary syndromes. *JAMA* 2004; **292**: 1555–62

Raobaikady R, Redman J, Ball JA, *et al.* Use of activated recombinant coagulation factor VII in patients undergoing reconstruction surgery for traumatic fracture of pelvis or pelvis and acetabulum: a double-blind, randomized, placebo-controlled trial. *Br J Anaesth* 2005; **94**: 586–91

Schmied H, Kurz A, Sessler DI Kozek S, Reiter A. Mild intraoperative hypothermia increases blood loss and allogeneic transfusion requirements during total hip arthroplasty. *Lancet* 1996; **347**: 289–92

Sedrakyan A1, Treasure T, Elefteriades JA. Effect of aprotinin on clinical outcomes in coronary artery bypass graft surgery: a systematic review and meta-analysis of randomized clinical trials. *J Thorac Cardiovasc Surg* 2004; **128**: 442–8

Segal JB, Blasco-Colmenares E, Norris EJ, *et al.* Preoperative acute normovolemic hemodilution: a meta-analysis. *Transfusion* 2004; **44**: 632–44

Shander A, Hofmann A, Ozawa S, Theysinger OM, Gombotz H, Spahn DR. Activity based costs of blood transfusions in surgical patients at four hospitals. *Transfusion* 2010; **50**: 753–65

Shander A, Van Aken H, Colomina MJ, *et al.* Patient blood management in Europe *Br J Anaesth* 2012; **109**: 55–68

Sharrock NE, Mineo R, Go G. The effect of cardiac output on intraoperative blood loss during total hip arthroplasty. *Reg Anaesth* 1993; **18**: 24–9

Sharrock NE, Salvati EA. Hypotensive epidural anesthesia for total hip arthroplasty: a review. *Acta Orthop Scand* 1996; **67**: 91–107

Shenolikar A, Wareham K, Newington D, Thomas D, Hughes J, Downes M. Cell salvage autotransfusion in total knee replacement surgery. *Transfus Med* 1997; **7**: 277–80

Simpson P. Perioperative blood loss and its reduction: the role of the anaesthetist. Review article. *Br J Anaesth* 1992; **69**: 498–507

Snyder SO Jr. The pneumatic tourniquet: a useful adjunct in lower extremity distal bypass. *Semin Vasc Surg* 1997; **10**: 31–3

Southern EP, Huo MH, Mehta JR, Keggi KJ. Unwashed wound drainage blood. What are we giving our patients? *Clin Orthop* 1995; **320**: 235–46

Stainsby D, MacLennan S, Thomas D, Isaac J, Hamilton PJ. Guidelines on the management of massive blood loss. *Br J Haematol* 2006; **135**: 634–41

Stanworth SJ, Birchall J, Doree CJ, *et al.* Recombinant factor VIIa for the prevention and treatment of bleeding in patients without haemophilia. *Cochrane Database Syst Rev* 2007; **2**: CD005011

Storck BH, Rutgers EJ, Gortzak E, Zoetmulder FA. The impact of the CUSA ultrasonic dissection device on major liver resections. *Neth J Surg* 1991; **43**: 99–101

Suttner SW, Piper SN, Lang K, Huttner I, Kumle B, Boldt J. Cerebral effects and blood sparing efficiency of sodium nitroprusside-induced hypotension alone and in combination with acute normovolemic haemodilution. *Br J Anasth* 2001; **87**: 699–705

Tartter PI. Blood transfusion and infectious complications following colorectal cancer surgery. *Br J Surg* 1998; **75**: 789–92

Thomas D, Wareham K, Cohen D, Hutchings H. Autologous blood transfusion in total knee replacement surgery. *Br J Anaesth* 2001; **86**: 669–73

Tylman M, Bengtson JP, Avall A, Hyllner M, Bengtsson A. Release of interleukin-10 by reinfusion of salvaged blood after knee arthroplasty. *Intensive Care Med* 2001; **27**: 1379–84

Vertrees RA, Conti VR, Lick SD, Zwischenberger JB, McDaniel LB, Shulman G. Adverse effects of postoperative infusion of shed mediastinal blood. *Ann Thorac Surg* 1996; **62**: 717–23

Vincent JL, Baron JF, Reinhart K, *et al.* Anemia and blood transfusion in critically ill patients. *JAMA* 2002; **288**: 1499–507

Weber CF, Gorlinger K, Meininger D, *et al.* Point-of-care testing: a prospective, randomised clinical trial of efficacy in coagulopathic cardiac surgery patients. *Anesthesiology* 2012; **117**: 531–42

Weiskopf RB, Feiner J, Hopf HW, *et al.* Oxygen reverses deficits of cognitive function and memory and increased heart rate induced by acute severe isovolemic anemia. *Anesthesiology* 2002; **96**: 871–7

Weiskopf RB, Toy P, Hopf HW, *et al.* Acute isovolemic anemia impairs central processing as determined by P300 latency. *Clin Neurophysiol* 2005; **116**: 1028–32

Weltert L, Nardella S, Rondinelli MB, Pierelli L, De Paulis R. Reduction of allogeneic red blood cell usage during cardiac surgery by an integrated intra- and postoperative blood salvage strategy: results of a randomised comparison. *Transfusion* 2013; **53**: 790–7

Westervelt J. Clipless cholecystectomy: broadening the role of the harmonic scalpel. *JSLS* 2004; **8**: 283–5

PART 8

Regional anaesthesia

Philip M. Hopkins

CHAPTER 52

General principles of regional anaesthesia

Andrew Berrill and Pawan Gupta

Brief history

Moreno y Maiz was the first researcher to study the medicinal effects of cocaine in frogs and postulated that cocaine could be used as a local anaesthetic. Later, Carl Koller demonstrated the local anaesthetic effects of cocaine on the eye and this led to widespread use of cocaine for eye surgery (Koller 1884). Halstead performed the first regional block, a mandibular block, using cocaine in 1885. However, the use of cocaine for local anaesthesia was not without problems. Mattison published a paper on cocaine dosage and cocaine addiction in 1887 after a Russian surgeon committed suicide from 'sorrow or remorse' because of his belief that a patient had died under his care from an overdose of cocaine. He collected and reported 126 cases of cocaine-induced toxicity, many of which were fatal (Mattison 1887). Research into local anaesthetics led to the development of safer anaesthetics, for example, procaine and lidocaine, which were introduced into anaesthetic practice in 1904 and 1943 respectively.

As safer local anaesthetics were introduced into clinical practice, the popularity of regional anaesthetic techniques increased. In the 1950s, as concerns were raised regarding severe neurological damage (Kennedy et al. 1950), there followed a sharp decline in the use of local anaesthetic techniques, especially spinal anaesthesia. Later, with the emergence of several large case series demonstrating the rarity of adverse neurological events, the use of local anaesthetic techniques increased again.

The use of peripheral local anaesthetic techniques has developed rapidly as more accurate methods of identifying nerves have emerged. The use of peripheral nerve stimulation was a major advance but the availability of portable high-definition ultrasound has led to an exponential increase in the use of regional techniques. Ultrasound-guided nerve block has led to a resurgence in the use of some older techniques (e.g. supraclavicular block and rectus sheath block) and the development of new approaches (e.g. pecs and serratus plane block) (Blanco et al. 2013). Evidence is emerging that the use of ultrasound may be associated with fewer complications (Barrington and Kluger 2013).

Factors affecting action of local anaesthetics

Local anaesthetics produce a reversible block of conduction along the nerve axons. Chemically, local anaesthetics are made up of a lipophilic aromatic ring and a hydrophilic amine that are linked together by an ester or amide bond. This forms the basis of classification of local anaesthetics into 'ester' and 'amide' local anaesthetics. Local anaesthetics can be applied topically over the skin, mucous membranes, subcutaneously, or injected directly around the nerves. If applied on the skin (EMLA® cream—eutectic mixture of local anaesthetics), dermal analgesia requires a contact time of about 30–60 min to allow the drug to penetrate 3–5 mm under the skin. On the other hand, if local anaesthetics are injected subcutaneously, the response is evident more quickly (i.e. 1–5 min) as the drug is being injected directly near the site of action.

The duration of the action of the drug depends upon the local blood flow, presence of vasoconstrictors, and local anaesthetic agent itself. High lipid solubility and low protein binding favour high tissue uptake. Local anaesthetic drugs are continuously metabolized and excreted. While ester local anaesthetics are metabolized by plasma esterase, amide local anaesthetics are metabolized in the liver and their metabolites excreted in the urine. Local anaesthetic bound to proteins acts as a reservoir replenishing the free amount as it is metabolized and excreted, thus determining the duration of action. C_m is the minimum concentration of the local anaesthetic that is needed to block action potential generation and nerve impulse generation. This mainly depends on lipid solubility. Lidocaine has a high lipid solubility, and therefore has a low C_m. The onset of action for local anaesthetics depends upon the pK_a which is defined as the pH at which the amount of ionized (charged) and unionized (uncharged) drugs are equal. Local anaesthetics have to enter the nerves to block conduction and can only enter the nerves in the unionized form. Therefore, the more unionized the drug, the faster would be the onset of action. This means that a high pK_a is associated with a fast onset of action.

In summary, the potency, onset of action, and duration of action of local anaesthetics depends upon the lipid solubility, dissociation constant (pK_a), and plasma protein binding (α1-acid glycoprotein) respectively. Table 52.1 shows the commonly used local anaesthetics and their pharmacokinetic characteristics.

Recommended doses of local anaesthetics

Local anaesthetic overdose can be potentially fatal. The ester and amide local anaesthetics cause toxicity by different mechanisms. The ester local anaesthetics are hydrolysed by plasma esterases, which lead to formation of para-aminobenzoic acid that can lead to anaphylactic reactions. On the other hand, amide-linked local anaesthetics are metabolized in the liver and the metabolites

Table 52.1 Characteristics of local anaesthetic agents

Local anaesthetic	Type	Lipid solubility (relative)	Potency	pK_a	Onset of action	Plasma protein binding %	Duration of action
Procaine	Ester	1	1	8.9	Slow	6	Short
Chloroprocaine	Ester	1	1	9.0	Fast	–	Short
Tetracaine	Ester	8	200	8.5	Slow	75	Long
Prilocaine	Amide	2	50	7.8	Fast	55	Medium
Lidocaine	Amide	2	200	7.8	Fast	64	Medium
Mepivacaine	Amide	2	50	7.6	Fast	78	Medium
Bupivacaine	Amide	8	1000	8.1	Medium	95	Long
Levobupivacaine	Amide	8	1000	8.1	Medium	95	Long
Ropivacaine	Amide	6	400	8.1	Medium	94	Long

are excreted in urine. Amide local anaesthetics cause toxicity by their direct action on different ion channels. Amide local anaesthetics are metabolized by the microsomal enzymes in the liver. Prilocaine is metabolized in the liver and kidney. One of its metabolites, ortho-toluidine, can accumulate after repeated or large doses. Ortho-toluidine can convert haemoglobin to methaemoglobin, limiting its ability to bind to oxygen, potentially leading to hypoxia.

Local vascularity and patient co-morbidities also impact the severity of toxicity. Local anaesthetics are bound to α1-acid glycoprotein in plasma, and conditions where the concentration of α1-acid glycoprotein is decreased are associated with higher concentrations of free drug and hence higher toxicity. High cardiac output states such as hyperthyroidism and pregnancy increase the rate of absorption from the local site of injection, and increase the likelihood of toxicity. Patients with problems of cardiac conduction, or mitochondrial defects, are also at a higher risk. The risk of toxicity is also increased in uraemia as the renal clearance is reduced and the rate of absorption is increased. The signs and symptoms of toxicity may be delayed because of prolonged absorption as a result of decreased muscle mass in elderly patients. A reduction in hepatic function (cirrhosis) or liver blood flow (congestive heart failure) reduces the rate of clearance and predisposes patients to local anaesthetic toxicity. While reducing the dose will increase the risk of inadequate analgesia/anaesthesia, a large dose increases the risk of toxicity. Table 52.2 shows the maximum recommended doses of local anaesthetics in different parts of the world.

Table 52.2 Maximum recommended doses of local anaesthetics

Local anaesthetic	Medicines and Healthcare products Regulatory Authority (UK)	Europe	USA	Our recommendations
Procaine	500 mg Maximum 1 g	500 mg	500 mg	500 mg
Chloroprocaine	50 mg (spinal)	–	800 mg	50–800 mg
Tetracaine (amethocaine)	Eye drops only	–	–	–
Prilocaine	400 mg	400 mg 600 mg (with adr)	400 mg 600 mg (with adr)	6 mg kg^{-1} 8 mg kg^{-1} with adr
Lidocaine	200 mg 500 mg (with adr)	200 mg 500 mg (with adr)	300 mg 500 mg (with adr)	200 mg 500 mg (with adr)
Mepivacaine	0.75 mg kg^{-1}	350 mg 350 mg (with adr)	400 mg 550 mg (with adr)	0.75 mg kg^{-1}
Bupivacaine	175 mg	150 mg	175 mg	150 mg
Levobupivacaine	150 mg	150 mg	150 mg	150 mg
Ropivacaine	3 mg kg^{-1}	225 mg	225 mg	3 mg kg^{-1} Max. 225 mg

adr, adrenaline (epinephrine).

Methods of identification of nerves

Anatomical landmarks

The most important factor that determines the success of a block is detailed knowledge of the surface and deeper anatomy of the target nerves. Many of the nerves in the human body form a part of a neurovascular bundle and their position can be estimated by relating it to the surrounding muscles and bones. Most blocks, such as supraclavicular block (contact with first rib), have previously been performed using the anatomical approach. Inter-individual variation in anatomy (Retzl et al. 2001) makes the success rate unpredictable and usually large amounts of local anaesthetics are injected to increase the chance of achieving the desired block. Peripheral nerve blocks performed with anatomical landmarks to localize nerves are therefore associated with a higher risk of failure and local anaesthetic toxicity.

Paraesthesia

Direct contact of any nerve with a needle may elicit paraesthesia. Needle-induced paraesthesia was a popular technique for nerve localization before the introduction of peripheral nerve stimulators. However, paraesthesia is unpredictable and is estimated to have a sensitivity for nerve localization of 38% (Perlas et al. 2006). Paraesthesia is also subjective and can be unpleasant. Clearly, the patient has to be conscious, cooperative, and able to reliably report any paraesthesia. Use of paraesthesia to localize nerves is not recommended.

Peripheral nerve stimulator

A peripheral nerve stimulator helps in localizing nerves by observation of twitches in the muscles supplied by the nerve elicited using an insulated needle. A minimum current (rheobase) is required to be applied for sufficient duration to elicit a response. The 'chronaxie' is defined as the stimulus duration that produces a response when the magnitude of the stimulus is twice the 'rheobase' (Fig. 52.1). The chronaxie for different nerve fibres (i.e. C and Aα) lies between 0.05 and 0.40 ms.

Modern nerve stimulators allow alteration of the current, pulse duration, and frequency of impulses. While lower frequencies may increase the time it takes to perform the block, higher frequencies are uncomfortable for the patient. Therefore, a frequency that allows the nerve action potential to return to baseline and is least uncomfortable to the patient should be used. The recommended initial settings of the peripheral nerve stimulator for peripheral nerve blocks are current 1–2 mA, pulse duration 0.1 ms, and frequency 1–2 Hz. Elicitation of muscle contraction between 0.4–0.5 mA is considered ideal for injection of local anaesthetic. If a response is obtained at a current amplitude of 0.3 mA or less, the needle is likely to be intraneural, thereby increasing the chances of nerve injury. However, if the contractions are obtained at greater than 0.5 mA, the needle may not be near the nerve, thereby increasing the chances of failure. However, a stimulus of 0.5 mA has a sensitivity of only 74.5% in producing a motor response when the needle is adjacent to the nerve (Perlas et al. 2006). Peripheral nerve stimulators are therefore better than paraesthesia for nerve localization, but do not offer complete protection against nerve injury or failed block.

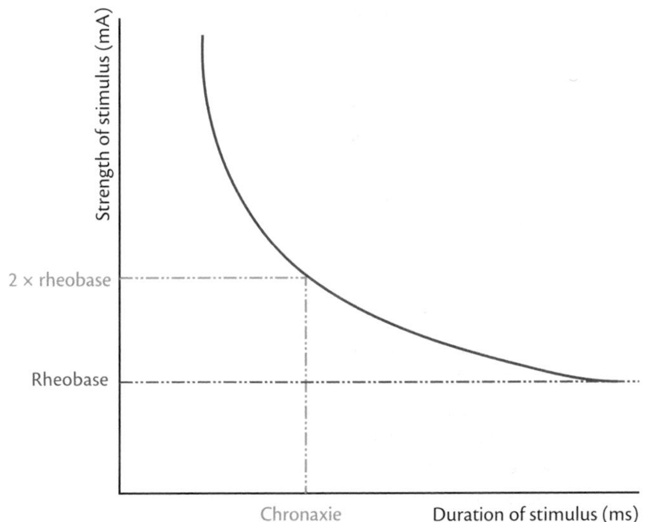

Figure 52.1 Strength–duration curve for peripheral nerve stimulation.

Ultrasound

Ultrasound allows real-time visualization of the block and is regarded as a gold standard in regional anaesthesia (Hopkins 2007). Ultrasound has been recommended for peripheral nerve blocks by national bodies such as the National Institute for Health and Care Excellence in the United Kingdom. An ultrasound probe consists of multiple piezoelectric crystals. These crystals vibrate at a high frequency when an alternating current is applied, which creates an ultrasound wave. This wave travels in the body at a constant speed (v). It is an acoustic (sound) wave which has a characteristic wavelength (λ) and frequency (f). The relationship between the three is shown in equation (52.1):

$$v = f \times \lambda \qquad (52.1)$$

The piezoelectric crystals in the ultrasound probe repeatedly switch between the emitter and receiver mode at about 7000 times per second. The ultrasound wave emitted by the probe is reflected back by the tissues and makes the piezoelectric crystals vibrate again. This vibration is converted to an electrical energy and generates an image on the machine. As this process happens at about 7000 times per second, the image on the ultrasound machine appears continuous and in real time.

Real-time visualization of the needle, nerves, blood vessels, muscles, bones, and other surrounding structures reduces the chances of complications and increases the chances of success. An understanding of ultrasound machines is essential for the safe use of this equipment. Three main factors that play an important role in optimization of the ultrasound machine image are the frequency of the ultrasound probe, gain, and angle of the probe to the skin. Ultrasound probes come in different shapes and frequencies. Curvilinear probes have lower frequencies. Lower-frequency ultrasound waves penetrate deeper and are therefore good for deeper structures. This, however, compromises the quality of the image (resolution). Straight probes have higher frequencies and are generally used for superficial structures. The frequency of ultrasound probes varies between 2 and 18 MHz and can be adjusted. The other important adjustable setting on the ultrasound machine is the 'gain' which allows brightening/lightening of the image at the level of interest. Nerves may appear hyperechoic (white) or hypoechoic (black) depending upon the surrounding structures and the angle of the probe to the skin. The best images of any nerve are obtained when the ultrasound probe is perpendicular to the nerve. As the course of nerves inside the body is not parallel to the skin, adjustments to the probe–skin angle are required to get the best image (anisotropy). The needle may be inserted along the long axis of the probe (in-plane) or perpendicular to the long axis of the probe (out-of-plane approach). The in-plane approach allows visualization of the full length of the needle, and is therefore safer as compared to the out-of-plane approach.

In summary, the first step in performing any nerve block is establishing familiarity with the relevant anatomy. If the anaesthetic practitioner is not aware of the detailed anatomy of the relevant nerve, a nerve block should not be attempted. The next step is localization of the nerve using ultrasound in combination with a peripheral nerve stimulator, ultrasound alone, or peripheral nerve stimulator alone. The final step is injection of local anaesthetic in the safe dose range which is determined by the site of nerve block and patient characteristics.

Types of needle

The incidence of nerve injury after peripheral nerve blocks is reported to be between 1:1000 and 1:10 000. Nerve damage could be attributed to chemical injury by the local anaesthetic or adjuncts, pressure effects from intraneuronal injection, or mechanical damage by the needle. The gauge and the angle of the bevel of the needle play a major role in mechanical nerve injury. The gauge of the needle is dictated by the depth of the nerve. Very small-gauge needles bend inside the body making it difficult to reach deeper structures. Twenty- to twenty-four-gauge needles are recommended for peripheral nerve blocks.

Long-bevel (Stimuplex® D, 15°) (B. Braun, Melsungen, Germany), medium-bevel (Stimuplex® A, 30°) (B. Braun), and short-bevel (Polymedic® US needle, 45°) (Polymedic, Singapore) needles are available for peripheral nerve blocks. A long bevel increases the chance of nerve puncture as compared to a short-bevel needle (Selander et al. 1979). On the contrary, the severity of nerve injury with a long-bevel needle is postulated to be less than a short-bevel needle (Rice and McMahon 1992). Therefore, medium-bevel (30°) needles are used by most anaesthetists.

Needle visualization under ultrasound is a limiting factor for deep nerves. The angle of insertion relative to the ultrasound probe is an important factor in needle visualization. As the angle of insertion becomes greater than 45°, all reflected ultrasound waves are directed away from the probe and needle visualization may not be possible. Ultrasound manufacturers use technology such as 'multi-beam technology' (e.g. SonoSite MB™, Fujifilm Sonosite, Bothell, WA, USA) to improve visualization at steeper angles.

When the angle of needle insertion is very steep or in an out-of-plane approach, tissue movement may be the only indicator of needle tip position. A rule of thumb for safe conduct of ultrasound-guided nerve blocks is that the needle should not be advanced unless the operator is aware of the position of the needle tip. Injection of a small amount of saline can be used as a guide to determine needle position to confirm needle tip position. Alteration to the needle outer surface has also been shown to improve needle visualization under ultrasound (e.g. Ultraplex® B. Braun, Melsungen, Germany).

Role of adjuncts

Peripheral nerve blocks can either be used as the sole anaesthetic or for postoperative analgesia. The main limitations of single-dose peripheral nerve blocks are the delay in onset time, safety of the dose required, duration of action, and the risk of local anaesthetic toxicity secondary to intravascular injection. Various adjuncts have been used which affect these characteristics of the local anaesthetics. Table 52.3 shows the adjuncts used and the impact on clinical practice.

Table 52.3 Local anaesthetic adjuncts for peripheral nerve blocks

Adjunct	Effect on			Amount used	Evidence
	Onset	Duration	Safe dose		
Adrenaline (epinephrine)	√	√	√	2.5–5.0 μg ml^{-1}	Yes
Clonidine	X	√	X	30–300 μg	Yes
Dexamethasone	X	√	X	4–8 mg	Yes
Sodium bicarbonate	X	√	X	0.1–1 mEq	Uncertain
Tramadol	X	√	X	50–200 mg	No
Buprenorphine	X	√	X	0.1–0.3 mg	No
Midazolam	X	√	X	50 μg kg^{-1}	No
Magnesium	X	√	X	50–100 mg	No
Dexmedetomidine	X	√	X	1 μg kg^{-1}	No

Out of these, only sodium bicarbonate, adrenaline (epinephrine), clonidine, and dexamethasone are discussed as only these agents have been shown to have a potentially useful effect.

Sodium bicarbonate

The pH of the pharmaceutical preparations of amide local anaesthetic solutions varies from 3.5 to 6.5 to ensure their stability and to increase shelf-life. The addition of adrenaline further reduces the pH of the local anaesthetic mixture. The pK_a of local anaesthetic agents lies between 7.6 and 8.1. Sodium bicarbonate solution has a pH of 8.4 and addition of sodium bicarbonate (0.05–1.0 ml) helps by increasing the pH of the local anaesthetic solution, thereby bringing the pH of the local anaesthetic mix towards the pK_a. An increase in pH of the solution by 1.0 leads to a 10-fold increase in the unionized form. This is postulated to lead to a faster onset, increased success rate, and a denser block. However the evidence to support the use of sodium bicarbonate is inconsistent (Capogna et al. 1989; Verborgh et al. 1991; Benzon et al. 1993; Ramos et al. 2001). The addition of too much sodium bicarbonate can lead to precipitation of local anaesthetic which reduces the potency and efficacy of the local anaesthetic. The reduction in the local anaesthetic onset time for peripheral nerve blocks is not clinically significant (Capogna et al. 1995). Routine use of sodium bicarbonate for peripheral nerve blocks is therefore not recommended.

Adrenaline (epinephrine)

Adrenaline acts by causing localized vasoconstriction, thereby decreasing the rate of uptake of local anaesthetic from the site of injection. Local anaesthetic is absorbed more slowly into the circulation and the peak plasma concentrations are reduced by

30–50% (Braid and Scott 1966; Raj et al. 1977). Adrenaline therefore increases the time to onset, duration of block (30–70%), and safe dose of local anaesthetics. Addition of adrenaline also helps in detection of inadvertent intravascular injection. Infiltration of adrenaline-containing local anaesthetics also helps by providing an avascular field and better identification of fascial planes.

Addition of adrenaline 1:400 000 (2.5 μg ml^{-1}) does not reduce the nerve blood flow (Partridge 1991) and leads to increases in the duration and safe dose of local anaesthetics (Bernards and Kopacz 1999). A lower concentration (i.e. 1:400 000) is recommended for peripheral nerve blocks to minimize its impact on neuronal blood flow. A higher concentration (1:200 000) is suggested where the principal purpose of the addition of adrenaline is to detect intravascular injection.

Clonidine

Addition of clonidine has been shown to increase the duration of surgical anaesthesia, postoperative analgesia (Singelyn et al. 1996), and improve haemodynamic stability (Gaumann et al. 1992a) with local anaesthetics. These effects are more evident with local anaesthetics that have a medium duration of action. The exact mechanism of action is not clear although it has been shown that clonidine has a local (Gaumann et al. 1992b) rather than a central effect (Singelyn et al. 1992).

Dexamethasone

Addition of dexamethasone phosphate (4–8 mg) has been shown to prolong the duration of analgesia after peripheral nerve blocks. The increase in duration is variable, from 2 h to more than 24 h. The exact mechanism of this effect is not known, although its direct action on C fibres (Williams et al. 2009) and a systemic effect (Desmet et al. 2013) after absorption have been postulated. A recent meta-analysis recommended the use of dexamethasone for brachial plexus block (Choi et al. 2014). More research, however, is required before its use and safety can be fully established in peripheral nerve block.

Aspects of management of nerve blocks

Consent

One of the key elements of success in regional anaesthesia is adequate preoperative preparation of the patient. The use of information such as patient leaflets, websites, DVDs, and so on can be a useful adjunct to a verbal explanation of the proposed techniques. Regional anaesthetic techniques may have particularly beneficial effects for patients with intercurrent illnesses (Gupta and Hopkins 2012).

A full explanation of the intended technique should be given along with the side-effects and complications. Cooperation of the surgical team is important and it is courteous to discuss the regional anaesthetic proposed. Clear documentation of the benefits and risks discussed should be made and filed within the patient record.

Use of sedation or general anaesthesia

Regional anaesthesia may be performed in the awake patient with or without sedation, or under general anaesthesia. Under heavy sedation or general anaesthesia, the patient may not be able to report pain, paraesthesia, or both, and therefore the risk of complications may be increased (Bromage and Benumof 1998; Benumof 2000). However, there is little evidence to support the assertion that regional anaesthetic techniques should be performed 'awake' other than isolated case reports. In a series of 4298 patients receiving lumbar epidural in combination with general anaesthesia, no neurological complications were recorded related to the block technique (Horlocker et al. 2003).

Many sedative techniques can be used to supplement regional block. The presence of a trained member of staff able to converse with the patient usually is sufficient to provide adequate support and reassurance for the patient. Where light sedation is deemed necessary, increments of midazolam (1–2 mg), propofol (10–20 mg), or fentanyl (25–50 mcg) are commonly used. The use of general anaesthesia may be necessary in some instances but there is the risk of profound hypotension if combined with central neuraxial block.

Complications of nerve blocks

Serious complications of nerve block are uncommon. A prospective study in France found the incidence of cardiac arrest and neurological injury to be very low but greater with spinal anaesthesia than after other regional techniques. Interestingly, two-thirds of patients with neurological deficits had either paraesthesia during needle placement or pain on injection (Auroy et al. 1997). An Australian prospective audit of neurological complications after peripheral nerve block found an incidence of block-related nerve injury of 0.4 per 1000 blocks, similar to the overall incidence in the French study of 0.02% (Barrington et al. 2009).

Systemic toxicity

Please refer to Chapter 17.

Neurological complications

Central neuraxial blocks

Incidence

The Royal College of Anaesthetists Third National Audit Project collected information on complications of neuraxial block over a period of a year. An estimate of the total numbers of procedures performed was extrapolated from a 2-week survey. The overall incidence of permanent injury was between 2 and 4.2 per 100 000 procedures (Cook et al. 2009). While the incidence of serious complications is low, the outcome may be devastating.

Direct injury

In most adults the spinal cord terminates at L1–2 and therefore spinal anaesthesia is performed at L3/4 or below. Identification of Tuffier's line (at the level of the iliac crests, usually corresponding to the L4/5 interspace) is traditionally used to help identify the appropriate interspace. Errors in identifying the correct level have been implicated in a series of patients with damage to the spinal cord from needles (Reynolds 2001). There is emerging evidence of the usefulness of ultrasound in identifying landmarks for neuraxial block (Perlas 2010).

During epidural placement, there is increased resistance to needle advancement through the ligamentum flavum and a subsequent loss of resistance when the epidural space is entered. In some cases, the ligamentous structures may be deficient in the midline, leading to a lack of resistance and potential damage to the spinal cord. Interestingly, spinal anaesthesia has been deliberately performed at the mid-thoracic level without sequelae (van Zundert et al. 2007).

Haematoma

Development of a haematoma in the vertebral canal is a serious occurrence as there is limited space and compression of the spinal cord and increased cerebrospinal fluid pressure leads to a high risk of neurological damage. Epidural haematomas can occur spontaneously. Structural abnormalities of the spinal canal (e.g. degenerative diseases) may increase the risk as can abnormal postural positioning (Beloeil et al. 2003). Around two-thirds of patients with a vertebral canal haematoma have a coagulation abnormality and most of these are associated with drug therapy (Vandermeulen et al. 1994). Guidelines to assist decision-making regarding regional anaesthesia and disorders of coagulation have been published by national associations (Horlocker et al. 2010; Harrop-Griffiths et al. 2013).

Infection

Epidural abscess and meningitis can occur both spontaneously and in association with neuraxial block. The risk factors for epidural abscess include immunosuppression (e.g. corticosteroid therapy), difficult neuraxial block and duration of catheterization (Grewal et al. 2006). Typically, epidural abscess presents with severe back pain and presence of a neurological deficit. However, the presentation may be more vague and may lead to a delay in diagnosis if a high index of suspicion is not maintained.

Injury from solutions injected

Local anaesthetic solutions used for neuraxial block should be preservative free. While local anaesthetic solutions do not cause neural damage in normal conditions, concerns were raised after reports of occurrence of cauda equina syndrome in patients receiving spinal anaesthesia via fine-bore intrathecal catheters (Rigler et al. 1991). Most of these cases involved the use of lidocaine 5% and it was postulated that a combination of maldistribution and a relatively high dose of local anaesthetic resulted in neurotoxicity.

Many agents have been used as adjuncts for neuraxial analgesia and while beneficial analgesic effects have been demonstrated, there is little safety data available.

Accidental contamination may occur with the solutions used to provide asepsis for skin preparation. These have been implicated as a cause of chronic adhesive arachnoiditis (Rice and McMahon 1992). It is important to allow the antiseptic skin preparation solution to dry fully on the skin before proceeding with neuraxial block.

Management

A rapid assessment should be performed on any patient receiving a neuraxial block who presents with back pain, increasing numbness, or loss of motor power. In patients with continuous infusions, the infusion should be stopped and signs of block regression looked for.

If there is any concern regarding an epidural haematoma or abscess, urgent imaging (normally magnetic resonance imaging) should be sought and urgent surgery performed where necessary.

Peripheral nerve blocks

Direct nerve injury

Peripheral nerves are covered by three layers of tissue: the epineurium, perineurium, and endoneurium. Injection within the perineurium potentially can cause significant injury (Hadzic et al. 2004). Injury to the nerve may be caused by direct trauma or by the effects of high pressure within the nerve. It has been suggested that short-bevel needles are less likely to cause nerve injury (Selander et al. 1977).

Nerve injuries can be classified into neurapraxia, axonotmesis, and neurotmesis (Seddon 1943). Neurapraxia refers to nerve dysfunction occurring from focal demyelination. The axons and connective tissues remain intact and recovery typically occurs in 6–8 weeks although some lesions may take several months to recover. Axonotmesis refers to disruption of axons but with intact connective tissue. As the nerve sheath is intact, axonal regeneration can take place though this may take several months as nerve fibres regenerate at 1–2 mm day^{-1}. Neurotmesis refers to complete interruption of the nerve. As nerve endings may be completely separated, effective recovery does not occur. Surgical exploration and nerve grafting may be required to enable recovery.

Numerous clinical indicators have been suggested as signs of intraneural placement of the needle and local anaesthetic. These include pain on needle placement or injection of local anaesthetic (or both), high injection pressure (Hadzic et al. 2004), low current threshold (<0.4 mA) (Chan et al. 2007), and evidence of expansion of nerve observed on ultrasound (Chan et al. 2007). Methods to avoid intraneural needle placement may reduce the risk of damage from direct needle trauma and compression from injection of local anaesthetic. Newer techniques such as sub-paraneural injection of the distal sciatic nerve in the popliteal fossa may potentially increase the risk of trauma because of the close proximity of nerve to needle (Abdallah and Chan 2013). The relationship of intraneural injection to the subsequent frequency of nerve damage is controversial, with several reports of inadvertent neural puncture occurring during regional anaesthesia without subsequent neurological damage (Bigeleisen 2006; Sala Blanch et al. 2009). Intraneural needle placement and injection should, however, be avoided until there is a greater body of evidence.

Injury from solutions injected

Little evidence exists that local anaesthetics have adverse effects on peripheral nerves in concentrations that are used clinically. It is prudent, however, to use the lowest concentration of drug that will produce the desired effect (Lambert et al. 1994).

Other factors

Many factors may lead to peripheral nerve injury such as direct surgical injury, haematoma formation, pressure from tourniquets, and poor positioning of the patient. Patients with pre-existing neurological injury (e.g. from diabetes mellitus or chemotherapy) may be at an increased risk for block-related nerve injury although there is little evidence to substantiate this. Consideration may be given to limiting the dose or concentration, or both, of local anaesthetic and avoiding the use of vasoconstrictors (Neal et al. 2008).

Management

Complete absence of nerve function beyond the expected duration of local anaesthetic should prompt immediate neurological consultation and evaluation. Magnetic resonance imaging may be useful in evaluating nerve lesions and, rarely, surgical exploration may be required.

Where nerve lesions are incomplete, prompt neurological evaluation should be sought and consideration given to early electrophysiological studies to establish baseline values and any pre-existing lesions (Neal et al. 2008). It is important that both anaesthetist and surgeon are fully involved with investigation and follow-up of suspected nerve injury. Factors not related to the specific anaesthetic technique should be explored. Most symptoms of nerve injury resolve in 4–6 weeks in 95% of patients and in 99% after 1 year (Borgeat et al. 2001).

Clinical pearls

Performing peripheral nerve blocks can be made safer by applying the following principles.

Fractionation of doses

Injection of small amounts of local anaesthetics (2–3 ml) probably may not lead to permanent nerve injury (Bigeleisen 2006). We therefore recommend injection of only a small amount of local anaesthetic solution at any one place and then re-directing the needle to another area around the nerve rather than injecting a large amount of local anaesthetic at one place. This also decreases the risk of local anaesthetic toxicity as a result of inadvertent intravascular injection of a large amount of local anaesthetic.

Local anaesthetic dose

The lowest possible dose should be used for any nerve block. This will vary with the anaesthetist's experience. Volumes as low as 4–5 ml have been shown to produce successful blocks with similar duration of analgesia and fewer side-effects (O'Donnell and Iohom 2009; Gautier et al. 2011).

Regular aspiration

Regular intermittent aspiration is essential to determine intravascular injection.

Addition of adrenaline

Adrenaline should be used only if indicated as it may decrease neural blood flow and contribute to neurapraxia. A concentration of 1:400 000 is recommended for use with peripheral nerve blocks if indicated.

Hydro-dissection

Injection of small amounts of saline or local anaesthetic helps to confirm the position of the needle and spread of local anaesthetic under ultrasound.

In-plane approach

Ultrasound is recommended for peripheral nerve blocks. Wherever possible, an in-plane approach should be used for peripheral nerve blocks as it allows full visualization of needle, thereby reducing the chances of damage to nerve and surrounding structures.

Declaration of interest

None declared.

References

Abdallah FW, Chan VW. The paraneural compartment: a new destination? *Reg Anesth Pain Med* 2013; **38**: 375–7

Auroy Y, Narchi P, Messiah A, Litt L, Rouvier B, Samii K. Serious complications related to regional anesthesia: results of a prospective survey in France. *Anesthesiology* 1997; **87**: 479–86

Barrington MJ, Kluger R. Ultrasound guidance reduces the risk of local anesthetic systemic toxicity following peripheral nerve blockade. *Reg Anesth Pain Med* 2013; **38**: 289–97

Barrington MJ, Watts SA, Gledhill SR, *et al.* Preliminary results of the Australasian Regional Anaesthesia Collaboration: a prospective audit of more than 7000 peripheral nerve and plexus blocks for neurologic and other complications. *Reg Anesth Pain Med* 2009; **34**: 534–41

Beloeil H, Albaladejo P, Hoen S, Eschwege P, Benhamou D. Bilateral lower limb hypoesthesia after radical prostatectomy in the hyperlordotic position under general anesthesia. *Can J Anaesth* 2003; **50**: 653–6

Benumof JL. Permanent loss of cervical spinal cord function associated with interscalene block performed under general anesthesia. *Anesthesiology* 2000; **93**: 1541–4

Benzon HT, Toleikis JR, Dixit P, Goodman I, Hill JA. Onset, intensity of blockade and somatosensory evoked potential changes of the lumbosacral dermatomes after epidural anesthesia with alkalinized lidocaine. *Anesth Analg* 1993; **76**: 328–32

Bernards CM, Kopacz DJ. Effect of epinephrine on lidocaine clearance in vivo: a microdialysis study in humans. *Anesthesiology* 1999; **91**: 962–8

Bigeleisen PE. Nerve puncture and apparent intraneural injection during ultrasound-guided axillary block does not invariably result in neurologic injury. *Anesthesiology* 2006; **105**: 779–83

Blanco R, Parras T, Mcdonnell JG, Prats-Galino A. Serratus plane block: a novel ultrasound-guided thoracic wall nerve block. *Anaesthesia* 2013; **68**: 1107–13

Borgeat A, Ekatodramis G, Kalberer F, Benz C. Acute and nonacute complications associated with interscalene block and shoulder surgery: a prospective study. *Anesthesiology* 2001; **95**: 875–80

Braid DP, Scott DB. Effect of adrenaline on the systemic absorption of local anaesthetic drugs. *Acta Anaesthesiol Scand Suppl* 1966; **23**: 334–46

Bromage PR, Benumof JL. Paraplegia following intracord injection during attempted epidural anesthesia under general anesthesia. *Reg Anesth Pain Med* 1998; **23**: 104–7

Capogna G, Celleno D, Laudano D, Giunta F. Alkalinization of local anesthetics. Which block, which local anesthetic? *Reg Anesth* 1995; **20**: 369–77

Capogna G, Celleno D, Tagariello V. The effect of pH adjustment of 2% mepivacaine on epidural anesthesia. *Reg Anesth* 1989; **14**: 121–3

Chan VW, Brull R, McCartney CJ, Xu D, Abbas S, Shannon P. An ultrasonographic and histological study of intraneural injection and electrical stimulation in pigs. *Anesth Analg* 2007; **104**: 1281–4

Choi S, Rodseth R, McCartney CJ. Effects of dexamethasone as a local anaesthetic adjuvant for brachial plexus block: a systematic review and meta-analysis of randomized trials. *Br J Anaesth* 2014; **112**: 427–39

Cook TM, Counsell D, Wildsmith JA. Major complications of central neuraxial block: report on the Third National Audit Project of the Royal College of Anaesthetists. *Br J Anaesth* 2009; **102**: 179–90

Desmet M, Braems H, Reynvoet M, *et al.* I.V. and perineural dexamethasone are equivalent in increasing the analgesic duration of a single-shot interscalene block with ropivacaine for shoulder surgery: a prospective, randomized, placebo-controlled study. *Br J Anaesth* 2013; **111**: 445–52

Gaumann D, Forster A, Griessen M, Habre W, Poinsot O, Della Santa D. Comparison between clonidine and epinephrine admixture to lidocaine in brachial plexus block. *Anesth Analg* 1992a; **75**: 69–74

Gaumann DM, Brunet PC, Jirounek P. Clonidine enhances the effects of lidocaine on C-fiber action potential. *Anesth Analg* 1992b; **74**: 719–25

Gautier P, Vandepitte C, Ramquet C, DeCoopman M, Xu D, Hadzic A. The minimum effective anesthetic volume of 0.75% ropivacaine in ultrasound-guided interscalene brachial plexus block. *Anesth Analg* 2011; **113**: 951–5

Grewal S, Hocking G, Wildsmith JA. Epidural abscesses. *Br J Anaesth* 2006; **96**: 292–302

Gupta PK, Hopkins PM. Regional anaesthesia for all? *Br J Anaesth* 2012; **109**: 7–9

Hadzic A, Dilberovic F, Shah S, *et al.* Combination of intraneural injection and high injection pressure leads to fascicular injury and neurologic deficits in dogs. *Reg Anesth Pain Med* 2004; **29**: 417–23

Harrop-Griffiths W, Cook TM, Gill H, *et al.* Regional anaesthesia and patients with abnormalities of coagulation: the Association of Anaesthetists of Great Britain & Ireland The Obstetric Anaesthetists' Association Regional Anaesthesia UK. *Anaesthesia* 2013; **68**: 966–72

Hopkins PM. Ultrasound guidance as a gold standard in regional anaesthesia. *Br J Anaesth* 2007; **98**: 299–301

Horlocker TT, Abel MD, Messick JM, Jr, Schroeder DR. Small risk of serious neurologic complications related to lumbar epidural catheter placement in anesthetized patients. *Anesth Analg* 2003; **96**: 1547–52

Horlocker TT, Wedel DJ, Rowlingson JC, *et al.* Regional anesthesia in the patient receiving antithrombotic or thrombolytic therapy: American

Society of Regional Anesthesia and Pain Medicine Evidence-Based Guidelines (Third Edition). *Reg Anesth Pain Med* 2010; **35**: 64–101

Kennedy F, Effron AS, Perry G. The grave spinal cord paralyses caused by spinal anesthesia. *Surg Gynecol Obstet* 1950; **91**: 385–98

Koller C. On the use of cocaine for producing anaesthesia on the eye. *Lancet* 1884; **124**: 990–2

Lambert LA, Lambert DH, Strichartz GR. Irreversible conduction block in isolated nerve by high concentrations of local anesthetics. *Anesthesiology* 1994; **80**: 1082–93

Mattison JB. Cocaine dosage and cocaine addiction. *Lancet* 1887; **129**: 1024–6

Neal JM, Bernards CM, Hadzic A, *et al.* ASRA Practice Advisory on Neurologic Complications in Regional Anesthesia and Pain Medicine. *Reg Anesth Pain Med* 2008; **33**: 404–15

O'Donnell BD, Iohom G. An estimation of the minimum effective anesthetic volume of 2% lidocaine in ultrasound-guided axillary brachial plexus block. *Anesthesiology* 2009; **111**: 25–9

Partridge BL. The effects of local anesthetics and epinephrine on rat sciatic nerve blood flow. *Anesthesiology* 1991; **75**: 243–50

Perlas A. Evidence for the use of ultrasound in neuraxial blocks. *Reg Anesth Pain Med* 2010; **35**: S43–6

Perlas A, Niazi A, McCartney C, Chan V, Xu D, Abbas S. The sensitivity of motor response to nerve stimulation and paresthesia for nerve localization as evaluated by ultrasound. *Reg Anesth Pain Med* 2006; **31**: 445–50

Raj PP, Rosenblatt R, Miller J, Katz RL, Carden E. Dynamics of local-anesthetic compounds in regional anesthesia. *Anesth Analg* 1977; **56**: 110–7

Ramos G, Pereira E, Simonetti MP. Does alkalinization of 0.75% ropivacaine promote a lumbar peridural block of higher quality? *Reg Anesth Pain Med* 2001; **26**: 357–62

Retzl G, Kapral S, Greher M, Mauritz W. Ultrasonographic findings of the axillary part of the brachial plexus. *Anesth Analg* 2001; **92**: 1271–5

Reynolds F. Damage to the conus medullaris following spinal anaesthesia. *Anaesthesia* 2001; **56**: 238–47

Rice AS, McMahon SB. Peripheral nerve injury caused by injection needles used in regional anaesthesia: influence of bevel configuration, studied in a rat model. *Br J Anaesth* 1992; **69**: 433–8

Rigler ML, Drasner K, Krejcie TC, *et al.* Cauda equina syndrome after continuous spinal anesthesia. *Anesth Analg* 1991; **72**: 275–81

Sala Blanch X, Lopez AM, Carazo J, *et al.* Intraneural injection during nerve stimulator-guided sciatic nerve block at the popliteal fossa. *Br J Anaesth* 2009; **102**: 855–61

Seddon H. Three types of nerve injury. *Brain* 1943; **66**: 237–88

Selander D, Brattsand R, Lundborg G, Nordborg C, Olsson Y. Local anesthetics: importance of mode of application, concentration and adrenaline for the appearance of nerve lesions. An experimental study of axonal degeneration and barrier damage after intrafascicular injection or topical application of bupivacaine (Marcain). *Acta Anaesthesiol Scand* 1979; **23**: 127–36

Selander D, Dhuner KG, Lundborg G. Peripheral nerve injury due to injection needles used for regional anesthesia. An experimental study of the acute effects of needle point trauma. *Acta Anaesthesiol Scand* 1977; **21**: 182–8

Singelyn FJ, Dangoisse M, Bartholomee S, Gouverneur JM. Adding clonidine to mepivacaine prolongs the duration of anesthesia and analgesia after axillary brachial plexus block. *Reg Anesth* 1992; **17**: 148–50

Singelyn FJ, Gouverneur JM, Robert A. A minimum dose of clonidine added to mepivacaine prolongs the duration of anesthesia and analgesia after axillary brachial plexus block. *Anesth Analg* 1996; **83**: 1046–50

Van Zundert AA, Stultiens G, Jakimowicz JJ, *et al.* Laparoscopic cholecystectomy under segmental thoracic spinal anaesthesia: a feasibility study. *Br J Anaesth* 2007; **98**: 682–6

Vandermeulen EP, Van Aken H, Vermylen J. Anticoagulants and spinal-epidural anesthesia. *Anesth Analg* 1994; **79**: 1165–77

Verborgh C, Claeys MA, Camu F. Onset of epidural blockade after plain or alkalinized 0.5% bupivacaine. *Anesth Analg* 1991; **73**: 401–4

Williams BA, Murinson BB, Grable BR, Orebaugh SL. Future considerations for pharmacologic adjuvants in single-injection peripheral nerve blocks for patients with diabetes mellitus. *Reg Anesth Pain Med* 2009; **34**: 445–57

CHAPTER 53

Regional anaesthesia of the trunk

Andrew Berrill, Will Jones, and David Pegg

Neuraxial anaesthesia

Neuraxial anaesthesia encompasses a range of techniques such as spinal, epidural, combined spinal–epidural (CSE), and caudal, all of which involve the injection of drugs into the spinal canal. These techniques can provide highly effective pain relief, improve patient satisfaction, and reduce postoperative morbidity. Approximately 700 000 such procedures are performed annually in the United Kingdom, with very few major complications (Cook et al. 2009).

Anatomy

In order to perform neuraxial anaesthesia, knowledge of the anatomy of the vertebral column, spinal cord, and spinal nerves is essential. The vertebral column consists of 33 vertebrae: 7 cervical, 12 thoracic, 5 lumbar, 5 sacral, and 4 coccygeal. The upper 24 vertebrae are articulating, with vertebral bodies separated by intervertebral discs, while the lower 9 vertebrae are fused, 5 as the sacrum, and 4 as the coccyx. The vertebral column contains three distinct curves; the cervical and lumbar regions are both convex anteriorly, whereas the thoracic region is convex posteriorly (Fig. 53.1).

A typical vertebra consists of an anterior segment, called the body, and a vertebral arch posteriorly. The arch consists of two pedicles and two laminae, which support seven processes: four articular, two transverse, and one spinous. This arch encloses the vertebral foramen. Articulation of the vertebrae forms a strong column, which supports the head and neck. The vertebral canal is formed by the vertebral foraminae, and offers protection to the delicate spinal cord. Between each pair of vertebrae are two intervertebral foramina, one on each side, which allow transmission of the paired spinal nerves and vessels (Fig. 53.2).

The vertebral column is held together by five ligaments (Table 53.1 and Fig. 53.3).

In adults, the spinal cord extends from the foramen magnum to the level of L1–2 where it tapers and terminates as the conus medullaris. It is 40–50 cm in length and 1–1.5 cm in diameter. Nerve roots emerge from each side to form 31 pairs of spinal nerves: 8 cervical, 12 thoracic, 5 lumbar, 5 sacral, and 1 coccygeal. These spinal nerves convey motor and sensory information to and from all parts of the body.

The spinal cord is surrounded by three membranes: the dura mater outermost, the arachnoid mater, and the pia mater innermost (Table 53.2).

Spinal anaesthesia

Background

The first operation carried out under spinal anaesthesia was performed in 1898 by August Bier (Bier 1899). Using a subarachnoid injection of cocaine, he successfully anaesthetized a series of six

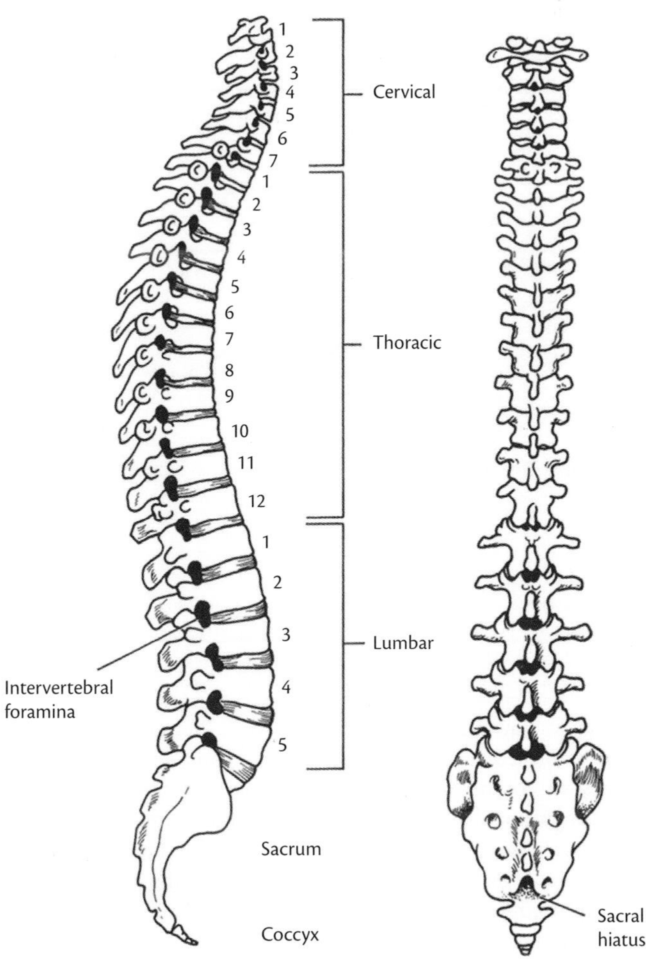

Figure 53.1 Lateral and posterior views of the vertebral column.
Reproduced with permission from Parkin, I., and Chambers, A. 'Anatomy and physiology of the vertebral canal', in McLeod, G. *et al.*, *Principles and Practice of Regional Anaesthesia, Fourth Edition*, 2012, Figure 12.1, Page 113, with permission from Oxford University Press.

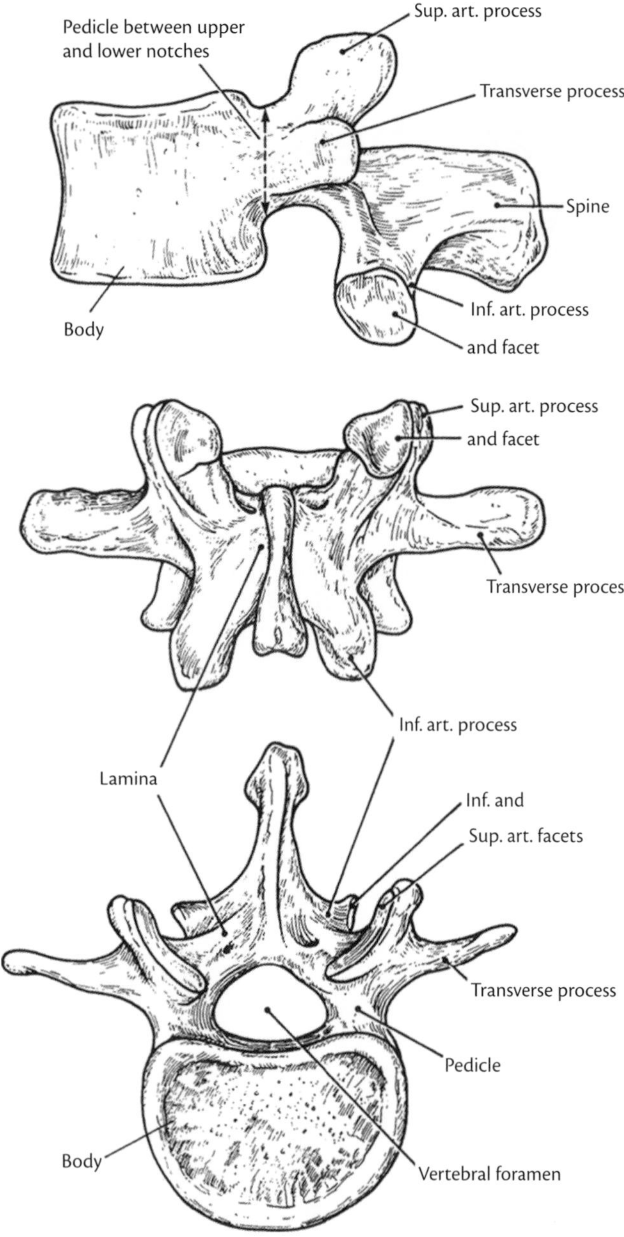

Figure 53.2 Anatomy of a typical vertebra.

Reproduced with permission from Parkin, I., and Chambers, A, 'Anatomy and physiology of the vertebral canal', in McLeod, G. *et al.*, *Principles and Practice of Regional Anaesthesia, Fourth Edition*, 2012, Figure 12.2, Page 114, with permission from Oxford University Press.

patients for lower limb surgery, after which Bier and his assistant both performed subarachnoid injections upon each other. During the first half of the twentieth century, spinal anaesthesia became an increasingly popular technique, but its use declined during the 1950s and 1960s following improvements in general anaesthetic techniques and reports of major complications in patients undergoing relatively minor procedures (Cope 1954). In recent decades, it has increased in popularity again, as it is a reliable and relatively simple form of anaesthesia to perform that is suitable for numerous clinical situations.

Anatomy

Spinal anaesthesia involves the injection of a small amount of local anaesthetic into cerebrospinal fluid (CSF) located within the

Table 53.1 Ligaments of the vertebral column

Ligament	Description
Supraspinous ligament	Situated most posteriorly. Connects the tips of the spinous processes from C7 to the sacrum
Interspinous ligament	Connects the lower edge of one spinous process to the upper edge of the next
Ligamentum flavum	Connects the lamina of the vertebrae, from C2 to the sacrum. Thinnest in the cervical region, becoming thicker further down the vertebral column
Posterior longitudinal ligament	Extends along the posterior surfaces of the vertebrae, from C2 to the sacrum
Anterior longitudinal ligament	Extends along the anterior surface of the spine for the whole length of the vertebral column

subarachnoid space. In the adult, the spinal cord most commonly ends at the level of the lower margin of the first lumbar vertebra but there is variability in this anatomical relationship, with the spinal cord extending to the second lumbar vertebra in 12–18% of the normal population, and to between the second and third lumbar vertebrae in 1–2%. In order to minimize the risk of needle trauma to the spinal cord, the most caudad possible of the intervertebral spaces between the third and fourth lumbar vertebrae (L3/4), the fourth and fifth lumbar vertebrae (L4/5), or the fifth lumbar vertebra and the sacrum (L5/S1) should be used (Reynolds 2000, 2001). If more cranial intervertebral spaces are used there is increasing risk of spinal cord damage. Some older textbooks suggest that L2/3 is a suitable level for spinal anaesthesia but evidence published in the early years of the new millennium demonstrated that this carried too high a risk of spinal cord damage. An imaginary line connecting the two iliac crests, called Tuffier's or the intercristal line, commonly crosses the spine at the L4 level, allowing estimation of a suitable interspace. However, it has been shown that it is difficult to accurately predict the level of the interspace using this technique (Broadbent et al. 2000).

Spread of local anaesthetic within the CSF results in rapid and dense block of the lower spinal nerve roots. This block is usually complete below the level of injection, with a reducing level of block spreading cranially. Sympathetic fibres are most sensitive, and will be blocked two to four segments higher than the moderately sensitive sensory fibres, which in turn, will be blocked two to four segments higher than the least sensitive motor fibres.

Indications

Spinal anaesthesia is commonly used for surgical procedures below the level of the umbilicus. High spinal block is now rarely used for procedures above this level because of the detrimental effects upon spontaneous ventilation and the difficulty in abolishing pain associated with peritoneal traction and diaphragmatic stimulation. A single-shot spinal injection will usually only last for 2–3 h so it is not suitable for prolonged procedures unless a catheter technique is used. It is of particular use in patients with co-morbidities that may make a general anaesthetic less desirable.

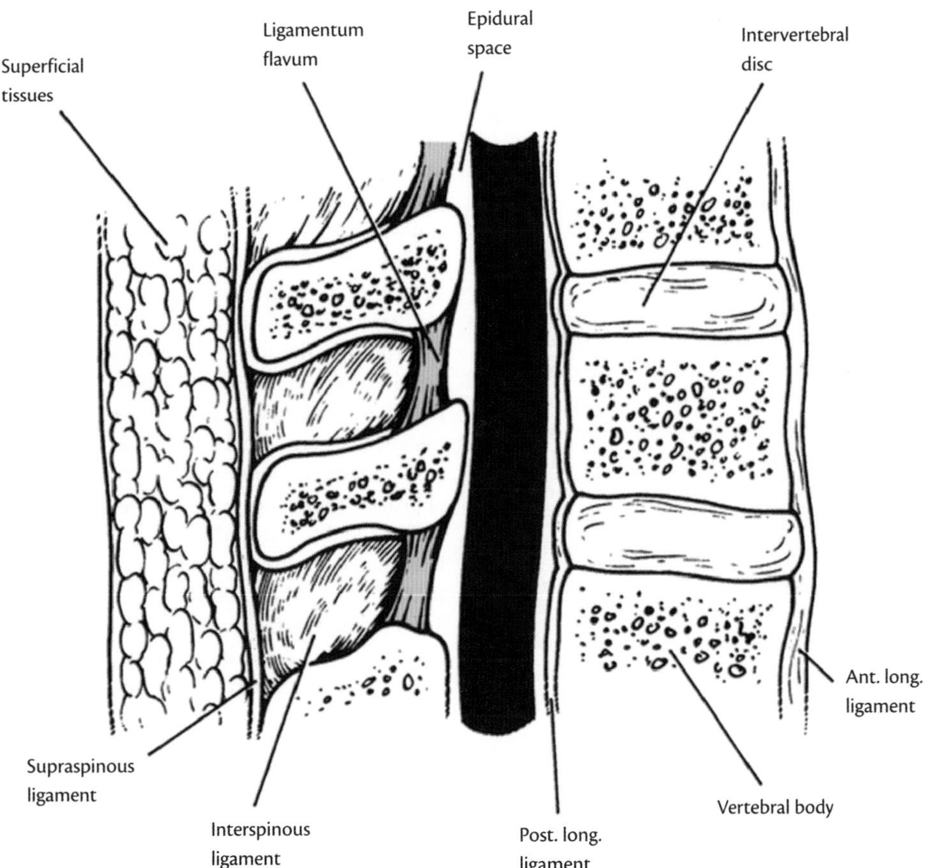

Figure 53.3 Ligaments of the vertebral column.
Reproduced with permission from Parkin, I., and Chambers, A. 'Anatomy and physiology of the vertebral canal', in McLeod, G. *et al., Principles and Practice of Regional Anaesthesia, Fourth Edition*, 2012, Figure 12.4, Page 116, with permission from Oxford University Press.

Table 53.2 Membranes and spaces surrounding the spinal cord

Membranes and spaces	Description
Pia mater	Innermost layer. Highly vascular. Closely adheres to the spinal cord and brain. Projects downwards from the conus medullaris, tethering the spinal cord to the coccyx
Subarachnoid space	Contains cerebrospinal fluid, spinal nerves, blood vessels, and the dentate ligaments, which attach the spinal cord to the dura mater laterally
Arachnoid mater	Middle layer. A delicate avascular membrane closely related to the dura mater. Terminates at S1
Subdural space	A potential space between the dura mater and the arachnoid mater
Dura mater	Outermost layer. A thick fibroelastic membrane. Forms a sac extending from the foramen magnum as an extension of the cranial dura to S1
Epidural space	Surrounds the dura mater, extending from the foramen magnum, for the entire length of the vertebral canal, terminating at the sacral hiatus Contains the paired spinal nerve roots, fat, blood vessels, lymphatics, and areolar tissue

Contraindications

These can be divided into absolute and relative contraindications (Table 53.3).

Equipment

Equipment should be prepared in a sterile field with full aseptic precautions—a hat, mask, gown, and sterile gloves should be worn. The patient's back should be cleaned using a sterilizing solution, with care taken to ensure that equipment does not become contaminated with the cleaning solution, and that the solution on the skin has dried fully before commencement of the procedure. An adhesive drape is then applied to the patient's back—a fenestrated drape is ideal as this leaves the target area uncovered and allows the anaesthetist to palpate anatomical landmarks while maintaining sterility.

Table 53.3 Contraindications to neuraxial block

Absolute contraindications	Relative contraindications
Patient refusal	Hypovolaemia
Local infection at insertion site	Aortic stenosis/mitral stenosis
Coagulopathies	Septicaemia
Systemic anticoagulation	Neurological disease
Raised intracranial pressure	Unknown duration of surgery

Technique

Pre-procedure preparation

After full preoperative assessment and the gaining of informed consent, the patient is transferred to a suitable environment in which monitoring, resuscitation equipment, and facilities for conversion to a general anaesthetic are available. Reliable intravenous access must be obtained before the procedure is commenced, and the patient should be fully monitored throughout.

Position

The patient is placed in either the sitting position, or in the lateral position. In the sitting position, the patient sits on a trolley with their legs supported by a stool. They are asked to place their chin on their chest, with their arms folded over a pillow placed beneath their armpits, flexing the lumbar region to open up the intervertebral spaces. An assistant should steady the patient at all times. Spinal anaesthesia is often easier in this position, especially in obese patients, as it is easier to locate the midline.

In the lateral position, the patient is laid on their side, with their back close to the edge of the trolley. It is important to ensure that the hips and shoulders both remain vertical. The patient's knees are brought up towards their chest, flexing the lumbar region, and opening up the intervertebral spaces. An assistant should steady the patient at all times. This position is more suitable in poorly cooperative patients or those who have received anxiolytic/sedative medications.

Approaches

The midline approach is used most commonly. Once a suitable interspace is selected, the midline is found by palpating the spinous processes. Local anaesthetic is infiltrated into the skin, subcutaneous tissues, and deeper ligaments, in the middle of the space. After this, an introducer needle is inserted into the centre of the space, in the midline, at right angles to the back or with a slightly cephalad angulation. This introducer needle provides stability for the smaller-gauge spinal needle, protects the spinal needle from coming into contact with potential contaminants from the patient's skin, and reduces transmission of skin tissue into deeper structures. In slim patients, care must be taken not to advance the introducer needle too far, as this can result in inadvertent dural puncture with the larger-gauge introducer needle, increasing the risk of post-dural puncture headache (PDPH). The smaller-gauge spinal needle should then be advanced; its passage is detailed in Box 53.1.

Box 53.1 Structures passed through by the spinal needle (midline approach)

1. Skin
2. Subcutaneous fat
3. Supraspinous ligament
4. Interspinous ligament
5. Ligamentum flavum
6. Epidural space
7. Dura mater
8. Arachnoid mater
9. Subarachnoid space.

With careful advancement of the needle, it is possible to detect the higher resistance of the ligamentum flavum, followed by a loss of resistance as the needle passes into the epidural space, and finally a click or pop as the needle pierces the tough dura mater and closely adherent arachnoid mater and enters the subarachnoid space. Removal of the stylet at this point will allow the visualization of the flow of CSF into the hub of the needle, confirming subarachnoid placement. If the needle encounters bone during insertion, the introducer position should be altered and the needle reinserted until dural puncture is successful.

Ultrasound assistance has been used to help identify the midline, predict the depth of the epidural space, and determine the optimum site for needle insertion. It has been shown to reduce the number of attempts to enter the epidural space. It may also help in instances where spinal anatomy is abnormal (Karmaker 2009).

In elderly patients with calcified ligaments, the paramedian approach may be of use. The needle is inserted 1 cm lateral and 2 cm caudal to the middle of the selected interspace. On insertion it is angled slightly towards the midline and slightly cephalad, so that its tip is in the midline at the point where it pierces the dura. This approach is technically more difficult as precise angles must be calculated in order to be successful, and may be more painful as the needle passes through the paraspinal muscles.

Injection

Once the spinal needle is in the correct position, it must be held firmly by the operator to ensure it does not migrate, while a syringe containing the desired local anaesthetic solution is attached. If the needle is correctly positioned, aspiration of CSF will result in a cloudy turbulence in the syringe, which confirms free flow of CSF along the needle. The local anaesthetic solution should then be injected slowly.

Needle types

Needles of different sizes and shapes have been developed for spinal anaesthesia. In order to reduce the risk of PDPH, it is important to use a needle that will leave the smallest perforation in the dura.

The main needle types available are cutting needles, such as the Quincke, and pencil-point needles, such as the Sprotte and Whitacre. Compared with pencil-point needles, cutting needles have a significantly higher chance of causing PDPH (Halpern and Preston 1994). Pencil-point needles are thought to separate the fibres of the dura, which then seal once the needle is removed, whereas cutting needles cut a hole in the dura, leaving a larger perforation.

Needle size is also an important factor to consider. Smaller-gauge needles are technically more difficult to use, with an increased risk of bending and decreased tactile feedback when compared with larger-gauge needles. However, smaller-gauge needles, of 26 G or smaller, have significantly less chance of causing PDPH than needles larger than 26 G (Halpern and Preston 1994).

Factors affecting the spread of local anaesthetic

An ideal spinal will spread far enough to provide sufficient anaesthesia for surgery without spreading so far so as to cause unwanted side-effects. Knowledge of the factors that may influence drug spread in the subarachnoid space is therefore essential. These factors can be divided into drug characteristics, patient characteristics, and technique (Table 53.4). The most important factors to consider are baricity, dose, and patient positioning—these are discussed in detail in the following subsections (Hocking and Wildsmith 2004).

Table 53.4 Factors affecting the spread of local anaesthetic in the subarachnoid space

Drug factors	Patient factors	Technique
Baricity	Patient positioning	Site of injection
Dose	Age	Speed of injection
Concentration	Weight	Barbotage
Volume	Height	Force of injection
	Gender	Direction of needle bevel
	Intra-abdominal pressure	
	Anatomical variations	

Baricity

Baricity of local anaesthetic refers to its density compared with CSF. The two anaesthetic solutions commonly available are plain solutions, which have approximately the same or slightly lower baricity as CSF, and hyperbaric solutions, which have an increased baricity as a result of a glucose additive. Hyperbaric solutions have been shown to produce a more predictable block, with greater spread in the direction of gravity. Conversely, plain solutions have been shown to be less predictable, with an increased risk of producing too high a block with unwanted side-effects, or too low a block which provides insufficient anaesthesia (Hocking and Wildsmith 2004).

Dose

The dose of drug injected has some effect. If no drug is injected, there will be no effect. If a very large dose is injected, such as inadvertent subarachnoid injection of an epidural bolus dose, a total spinal may result. However, there is not a linear relationship between these points. In the normal ranges of doses used, an increase in dose of 50% will only result in spread that is a dermatome or so higher. The resultant block will, however, have a longer duration (Hocking and Wildsmith 2004).

Patient position

Plain bupivacaine is actually slightly hypobaric with relation to CSF, and will therefore float upwards. If a patient is kept in the sitting position, after 2 min, this can lead to increase in block height of two to three segments. If the patient is kept in the sitting position for longer, the increase in block height may be even greater. However, as previously described, plain solutions produce a less predictable block, with greater inter-patient variability, and prolonged sitting can result in venous pooling in the lower limbs, worsening hypotension.

If kept in the sitting position with hyperbaric solutions, the block will be more limited to the lower segments. If the patient remains in the lateral position, the block will be more limited to the dependent side. Once the patient is supine, the block will then spread more cephalad, or to the other side respectively—this effect can be seen up to 30 min after injection. If a true saddle or unilateral block is to be achieved, the patient must remain in this position for a prolonged period of time (Hocking and Wildsmith 2004).

Testing the block

Before surgery can proceed it is necessary to ensure that the level of the block is adequate. Tests that are used can be split into those that assess afferent function, and those that assess efferent function.

Table 53.5 Anatomical landmarks of dermatomes

Dermatome	Anatomical landmark
T4	Nipple
T6	Xiphisternum
T10	Umbilicus

The most commonly used stimuli to test afferent function are cold, pinprick, and light touch. Usually, loss of sensation to cold will occur first, followed by pinprick, followed by light touch. This correlates with sequential blockade of C, Aδ, and Aβ nerve fibres respectively. Loss of sensation to pinprick correlates most closely with surgical anaesthesia and as a margin of safety should be demonstrated two to three dermatomes above the required level of block (Table 53.5).

Motor function is indicative of efferent function, and is commonly graded using the modified Bromage scale. Complete inability to straight-leg raise is a crude indicator that the block has reached the high lumbar segments. Higher levels of block will result in impairment of intercostal muscles, with impairment of pulmonary function. Such impairment is difficult to quantify clinically, but a patient who has the sensation of a heavy chest and difficulty breathing will likely have a mid to high thoracic block.

Other indicators of efferent function are the level of sympathetic block, which leads to cardiovascular changes such as hypotension and bradycardia. Such factors cannot, however, be used to accurately determine the extent of the block. Vasomotor changes such as skin colour and temperature may be detectable.

Side-effects

Cardiovascular

Subarachnoid blocks produce a sympathectomy, causing arterial and venous dilatation, with a resultant decrease in systemic vascular resistance of 15–18% (Rooke et al. 1997). If cardiac output is maintained, it follows that there will be a similar reduction in mean arterial pressure. The unblocked sympathetic fibres above the level of the block will produce a compensatory vasoconstriction, but in the presence of an extensive sympathetic block, the effect of this will be insufficient. If cardiac output decreases, as a consequence of a reduction in preload, as a result of hypovolaemia or patient positioning, the effect may be even more pronounced. A high block above the level of T4–5 may result in blockade of the cardioaccelerator fibres, with a resultant bradycardia.

Respiratory

A block below the level of the thoracic nerves will have little clinical effect upon respiratory function. Progressive block in a cephalad direction causes progressive paralysis of the intercostal muscles, which will alter respiratory mechanics more significantly. Expiration is mostly affected, and may be sensed by the patient as shortness of breath, heaviness on the chest, or the inability to cough effectively. Inspiration is largely unaffected as changes can be compensated for by an increase in diaphragmatic movement. Excessively high spread can cause paralysis of the phrenic nerve (C3–5) or hypoperfusion of the respiratory centres of the brainstem, leading to apnoea.

Gastrointestinal

Blockade of the thoracolumbar sympathetic nerves to the abdominal viscera by spinal anaesthesia results in unopposed parasympathetic stimulation, leading to an increase in secretions, relaxation of sphincters, and constriction of bowel. After spinal anaesthesia, approximately one in five patients will experience nausea and vomiting. Associated factors include blocks higher than T5, hypotension, and a history of motion sickness (Carpenter et al. 1992).

Epidural anaesthesia

Background

James Corning described the first documented central neuraxial block in 1885 (Corning 1885). Although he thought he was injecting cocaine into the subarachnoid space, analysis of his technique suggests that the drug was actually placed in the epidural space. Using a single-shot technique, Fidel Pagés developed the modern technique of lumbar epidural anaesthesia in the 1920s (Pagés 1921), and Dogliotti described the loss of resistance technique just over a decade later (Dogliotti 1933).

Indications

An epidural is commonly used to provide anaesthesia to the abdomen and lower limbs, often combined with a general anaesthetic. Compared with spinal anaesthetics, epidurals have a slower onset, require a larger volume of local anaesthetic to be administered, and give a less dense block. Their main advantage is that a catheter is usually left in the epidural space, allowing the duration of anaesthesia to be extended for longer procedures, and providing a means for pain relief to be continued in the postoperative period.

For suitable procedures, epidurals provide better postoperative analgesia than parenteral opioids (Block et al. 2003). In high-risk patients undergoing abdominal surgery, epidurals combined with general anaesthesia have not been shown to reduce the risk of most major postoperative morbidity, apart from respiratory failure (Rigg et al. 2002). However, the provision of excellent postoperative analgesia, and the reduction in the risk of postoperative respiratory morbidity mean that epidural analgesia clearly retains a place in the management of pain after major abdominal and thoracic surgery. Recently, interest has been shown in the role of regional anaesthetic techniques and prevention of cancer recurrence. More studies are underway in this area and the results may have implications for the type of analgesia used after major surgery (Colvin et al. 2012).

Contraindications

The contraindications for epidural anaesthesia are similar to those for spinal anaesthesia. As a result of the more gradual onset, epidurals are more suitable for patients with aortic or mitral stenosis, or both. They are also more suitable for surgery of uncertain duration, as their effects can be prolonged as required.

Equipment

Epidurals are commonly performed using a Tuohy needle. This specialized needle is hollow, allowing a catheter to be threaded, with a slight curve at the end, allowing the catheter to be directed. A stylet prevents clogging with tissues on insertion, which is then removed before the catheter is threaded. Tuohy needles are commonly 8 cm in length, and 18 or 16 G. Once a catheter is inserted into the epidural space, a 0.2-micron bacterial filter should be attached to reduce the risk of contamination.

Technique

Pre-procedure preparation and positioning are the same as for spinal anaesthesia. Vertebral level can be estimated using Tuffier's line as previously described, or counting down from the prominent spinous process of C7. To provide optimum analgesia, an interspace that corresponds with the middle of the surgical incision should be selected. Preparation of equipment and the back should be performed in the same aseptic manner as described for spinal anaesthesia. The epidural catheter and filter should be flushed with sterile saline before use.

For lumbar epidural block, the Tuohy needle is inserted in the midline, at right angles to the back in both planes. It is advanced until it is gripped firmly by the ligaments. At this point the stylet is removed and a syringe containing sterile normal saline is attached. The dorsum of one hand rests on the back, and grips the hub of the needle firmly. The needle and syringe is then advanced slowly while constant pressure is applied to the plunger of the syringe by the other hand. While the tip of the needle is within the dense ligaments, no saline will be injected. Advancement of the needle into the epidural space will result in a sudden loss of resistance, and the saline will inject easily. Care should be taken not to advance the needle too far, as this will result in inadvertent dural puncture.

Once the needle tip is in the epidural space, the catheter should be threaded through the needle. The needle should then be removed, while holding the catheter in place, leaving 3–6 cm of catheter in the epidural space. The catheter should be securely fixed to the patient's back to prevent migration or dislodgement.

Test dose

As large volumes of local anaesthetic are administered, a test dose is essential to rule out inadvertent intravascular or subarachnoid placement. An initial 3–4 ml of lidocaine 2% with 1:200 000 adrenaline (epinephrine) is one recommended regimen. If this test dose is injected intravascularly, a tachycardia will be observed. If this test dose is injected into the subarachnoid space, development of a rapid spinal block will be observed.

Injection of local anaesthetic

Once the test dose has been performed, and correct placement confirmed, local anaesthetic is injected via the catheter into the epidural space. This may require volumes up to 30 ml, and should therefore be done slowly, in divided doses, to minimize the risk of complications in case of catheter migration. After injection, the patient should be fully monitored, checking heart rate, blood pressure, oxygen saturations, and ECG.

Epidural opioids

After local anaesthetics the commonest drugs used in epidural anaesthesia are opioids. While they are in widespread clinical use, none are licensed for neuraxial administration in the United Kingdom. Most commonly, epidural opioids are used in combination with local anaesthetics. This results in an improved side-effect profile, use of lower doses of drugs, and increased effectiveness of block (Robinson et al. 2001).

Side-effects

Epidurals produce a sympathetic block in a similar manner to a spinal, with the result that the side-effects are similar. However, as the block achieved with an epidural is usually segmental and less complete, the magnitude of these side-effects will usually also be less.

Combined spinal–epidural anaesthesia

This technique combines a subarachnoid injection of local anaesthetic with placement of an epidural catheter. The aim of this is to achieve a rapid central neuraxial block, which can then be prolonged or modified.

The needle-through-needle technique involves location of the epidural space in the standard manner using a specialized Tuohy needle, through which a subarachnoid injection can also be performed using an extra-long spinal needle. Once the subarachnoid injection has been performed, the spinal needle is removed and the epidural catheter is threaded into the epidural space. An alternative method is to perform an epidural and a spinal in the standard manner but in separate interspaces.

Caudal anaesthesia

Caudal anaesthesia involves the injection of drugs into the epidural space in the sacrum. It is more commonly used in children, but can be used in adults to provide anaesthesia of the sacral and lower lumbar nerve roots.

Anatomy

The sacrum is a large triangular-shaped bone at the base of the spine, which is formed from the fusion of five sacral vertebrae. It articulates with L5 superiorly, the coccyx inferiorly, and the ilia laterally, via the sacroiliac joints. The sacral canal contains the filum terminale, fat, areolar tissue, blood vessels, sacral nerves, and the dural sac, which terminates at S2. The sacral hiatus is an opening at the bottom of the sacrum, which is covered by the sacro-coccygeal membrane, and is the entrance point for caudal anaesthesia.

Technique

The patient is placed in the lateral position. The posterior superior iliac spines and the sacral hiatus form an equilateral triangle, which can be used to identify the correct insertion point. After sterilization of the skin a needle or cannula is inserted in a cranial direction, at an angle of approximately 60° to the skin. A pop should be felt as it passes through the tough sacro-coccygeal membrane. At this point the needle is angled slightly more cranially, and advanced further. Aspiration should be carried out, looking for blood or CSF. In adults, 20–30 ml of bupivacaine or levobupivacaine 0.25–0.5% is then injected in divided doses—there should be little resistance encountered. While injecting, the other hand should feel for inadvertent subcutaneous injection.

Complications of neuraxial anaesthesia

Post-dural puncture headaches

PDPHs commonly present within a few days of dural puncture as a fronto-occipital headache with a strong postural element. They are worse on sitting up, standing, coughing, or straining, and relieved by lying down. The patient will often feel incapacitated with associated symptoms such as nausea, vomiting, photophobia, neck stiffness, and tinnitus. It should be noted that headache is a common complaint in the postoperative period and should not always be assumed to be a complication of a central neuraxial block. A full history and examination should be performed, considering all potential diagnoses.

The cause of PDPH is believed to be a leak of CSF through the dural puncture site, leading to intracranial hypotension. This is thought to cause a headache either as a result of traction on intracranial structures or a compensatory dilatation of intracranial blood vessels.

PDPH is less common with smaller-gauge needles, and atraumatic needles such as Sprotte and Whitacre designs, rather than cutting needles such as the Quincke. Use of atraumatic needles can result in a post-spinal dural puncture headache risk as low as 1:500. Patient factors associated with a reduced risk of developing PDPH include male sex and extremes of age. After inadvertent dural puncture with a 16 G Tuohy needle when siting an epidural, as many as 70% of patients may experience PDPH.

Most PDPH headaches will resolve spontaneously within 6 weeks. Conservative management involves explaining PDPH to the patient, bed rest with advice to avoid sitting up, and symptomatic relief with intravenous fluids, analgesia, and antiemetics. For patients in whom conservative management is not acceptable, an epidural blood patch may be offered. This involves injection of a sterile sample of 20–30 ml of the patient's blood into the epidural space. It is thought to relieve symptoms initially as a result of a pressure effect reducing intracranial hypotension, and prevents recurrence of symptoms by sealing the perforation in the dura, preventing further CSF leak. It is very effective, with immediate relief in more than 70% of patients (Turnbull and Shepherd 2003).

High or complete spinal block

The definition of a high spinal block is unclear, but some studies report incidences of about 1%. A block that has spread higher than the level required for surgery, with resultant unwanted side-effects is one definition. Total spinal block is much rarer, and its true incidence is unknown. Cephalad spread of local anaesthetic interferes with the function of thoracic nerves, cervical nerves, and the brainstem. This can be as a result of excessively high spread of a single-shot spinal injection, or more commonly, inadvertent injection of an epidural bolus dose into the subarachnoid space.

Drug factors associated with a high block include a higher dose of local anaesthetic, use of plain (i.e. not hyperbaric) local anaesthetics, and recent epidural drug administration, which is thought to reduce the volume of the spinal subarachnoid space. Patient factors include raised abdominal pressures, such as in obese or pregnant patients, or abnormal anatomy leading to a reduced volume of subarachnoid space. Procedural factors include high insertion site, and laying the patient supine rapidly after intrathecal injection, rather than staying sat upright for a period of time (Table 53.6).

Spinal haematoma formation

After spinal anaesthesia, the risk of vertebral canal haematoma is extremely low, with not a single case reported in more than 360 000 spinal anaesthetics (Cook et al. 2009). However, before spinal anaesthesia is performed, care must be taken to ensure the patient does not have any coagulation abnormalities to minimize the risk of this devastating consequence.

Vertebral canal abscess

Vertebral canal abscess is an extremely serious but rare complication of central neuraxial block, with an incidence of 1:47 000 procedures, causing permanent harm in 1:88 000 patients. Risk factors include compromised immunity, antithrombotic drug therapy, difficult or traumatic procedures, a source of infection, such as systemic sepsis, and a failure in aseptic technique.

Table 53.6 Symptoms of high or complete spinal block and their management

Symptom	Cause	Management
Hypotension	Sympathetic block	Vasopressors, e.g. phenylephrine, metaraminol Intravenous fluids Leg elevation
Bradycardia	Sympathetic block	Anticholinergics, e.g. atropine Sympathomimetics, e.g. ephedrine, adrenaline
Ventilatory dysfunction	Intercostal paralysis (T1–12) Accessory muscle paralysis Diaphragmatic paralysis (C3–5)	Oxygen Bag–mask ventilation Intubation
Loss of consciousness	Brainstem	Intubation

The classic presentation is described as back pain, systemic features of infection, and progressive neurological symptoms in the lower half of the body. Unfortunately, the clinical presentation often differs from this and therefore the presence of any of these symptoms should be treated with a high index of suspicion (Cook et al. 2009). Prompt diagnosis and treatment is required in order to minimize the risk of permanent neurological damage.

Bacterial meningitis

Bacterial meningitis is an extremely rare complication after central neuraxial block, with a reported incidence of less than 1:200 000 (Cook et al. 2009). Risk factors include reduced immunity, systemic sepsis, and prolonged central neuraxial catheterization. Prompt diagnosis can reduce morbidity and mortality, but can be difficult as the symptoms are similar to those of PDPH.

After spinal anaesthesia, the causative organisms are most commonly nasopharyngeal commensals, highlighting the need for a facemask to be worn when undertaking such procedures. After epidural anaesthesia, the most common causative organisms are skin commensals, suggesting spread along the epidural catheter tract. In patients with bacteraemia, contact of the needle with blood vessels during insertion may lead to contamination and transmission of infection into the CSF.

Wrong route administration

Wrong route administration refers to the infusion of a drug into an incorrect body compartment. This can be due either to inadvertent misconnection of an epidural infusion to an intravascular device, such as a cannula, or migration of an epidural catheter into the wrong compartment, such as a blood vessel or the subarachnoid space. Such problems can result in a total spinal, as previously discussed, or systemic effects of local anaesthetic toxicity. There have been attempts to minimize the likelihood of this happening by developing incompatible intravenous and epidural connectors, to prevent inadvertent misconnection. The more widespread use of less cardiotoxic local anaesthetics such as levobupivacaine and ropivacaine theoretically reduces the risk of wrong route administration causing permanent harm. Rapid recognition and treatment of systemic local anaesthetic toxicity with lipid emulsions may also reduce the risk of harm (Cook et al. 2009).

Permanent neurological injury

Although certainly rare, the exact incidence of permanent neurological injury after central neuraxial block, because of reasons other than haematoma and abscess formation, is unknown. Damage can occur as a result of direct trauma to a nerve root, by a needle or catheter, or secondary to drugs or chemicals. Other causes of nerve dysfunction, such as surgical positioning, labour, and pre-existing conditions such as diabetes, may also be implicated (Cook et al. 2009).

Paravertebral block

History

Sellheim of Lepzig performed the first recorded paravertebral block in 1905 for abdominal analgesia. Lawen refined this technique and it subsequently became popular for surgical analgesia. In 1919, Kappis used a similar technique to current practice to provide surgical anaesthesia for abdominal surgery. In the following years, thoracic paravertebral use decreased until a resurgence began after a publication by Eason and Wyatt (1979) who described a catheter technique. Numerous studies have now been published demonstrating its efficacy and safety as a regional anaesthetic technique in both adults and children (Karmakar 2001).

Anatomy

The thoracic paravertebral space is a potential wedge-shaped space. This three-sided wedge has posterior, medial, and anterolateral boundaries and it extends cranially and caudally in the thoracic region, allowing communication between each level. This is in contrast to the cervical and lumbar regions in which there is no direct communication between adjacent levels.

The medial border of the thoracic paravertebral space is formed by the structures that form the posterolateral border of the vertebral column. This comprises the vertebral body, intervertebral disc, and the intervertebral foramina. The anterolateral border is formed by the parietal pleura and internal intercostal membrane. The superior costotransverse ligament forms the posterior border of the thoracic paravertebral space. This ligament extends from the neck of a rib to the transverse process of the vertebra above (Ibrahim and Darwish 2005). The transverse processes and the head of the ribs also form the posterior border. The lateral edge of the superior costotransverse ligament is continuous with the internal intercostal membrane.

The thoracic paravertebral space communicates medially with the epidural space via the intervertebral foramen and laterally with the intercostal spaces. It is split into two compartments by the endothoracic fascia, an anterior extrapleural compartment, and a posterior subendothoracic compartment. The endothoracic fascia is continuous with the prevertebral fascia medially and the internal intercostal membrane laterally. It is currently unclear as to the relevance of this fascial plane in clinical practice although it has been proposed to be a reason why some paravertebral blocks have contralateral spread (Karmaker et al. 2000).

The paravertebral space contains fat, intercostal vessels, and nerves. At each level a spinal nerve emerges from the intervertebral foramen,

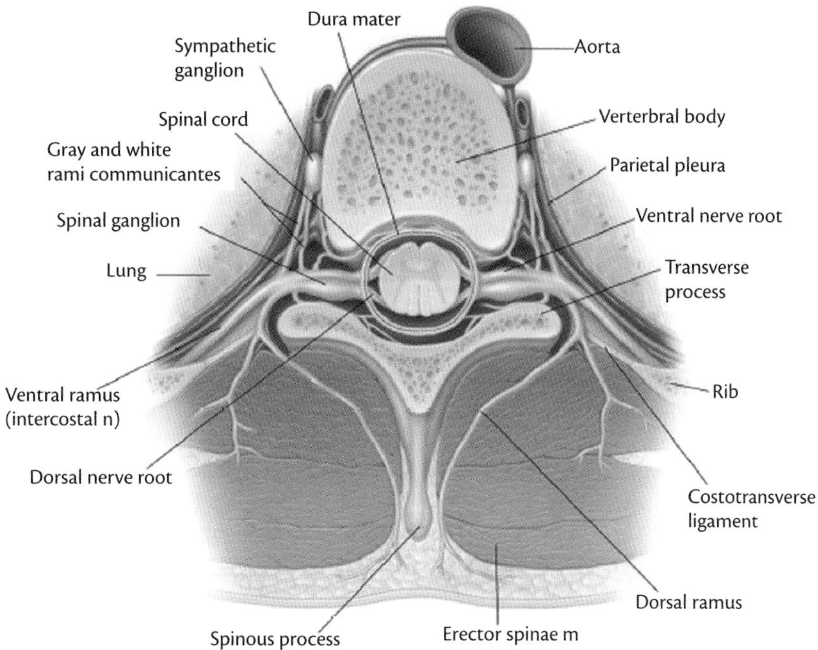

Figure 53.4 Paravertebral anatomy.
Reproduced from Hebl J, Lennon R (eds), *Mayo Clinic Atlas of Regional Anesthesia and Ultrasound-Guided Nerve Blockade*, Copyright © 2010 Mayo Foundation for Medical Education and Research/ Oxford University Press. By permission of Oxford University Press, USA, www.oup.com

posterior to the endothoracic fascia. At this point the nerve is not contained within a fascial sheath and it exists as small bundles, which increases its susceptibility to local anaesthetic block (Nunn and Slavin 1983). Shortly after the spinal nerve exits the intervertebral foramen, it branches into the dorsal ramus, ventral ramus, and rami communicantes. The ventral ramus then exits the paravertebral space as the intercostal nerve in the intercostal space. The sympathetic chain is also contained within the paravertebral space and this is located anterior to the endothoracic fascia. The rami communicantes connect the sympathetic chain with the spinal nerve (Fig. 53.4).

Indications

The main indication for the use of thoracic paravertebral block is for postoperative analgesia in unilateral surgical procedures in the thoracic and abdominal regions. More superficial procedures in these areas such as breast surgery can be performed using paravertebral block as the sole anaesthetic technique. It is also used in acute and chronic pain management (Tighe et al. 2010). Bilateral paravertebral blocks can also be used for midline surgical procedures but their role compared with epidural block has yet to be defined. They do provide a suitable alternative in those patients where an epidural is contraindicated, such as in anticoagulated patients (Richardson et al. 2011). Box 53.2 summarizes the various indications for the use of thoracic paravertebral block.

Contraindications

As with any regional anaesthetic technique there are absolute and relative contraindications to performing a paravertebral block. There are few absolute contraindications to paravertebral block and these are patient refusal, local anaesthetic allergy, local sepsis, empyema, and localized tumour occupying the paravertebral space. Relative contraindications include severe coagulopathy and

Box 53.2 Indications for the use of thoracic paravertebral block

Postoperative surgical analgesia

- Thoracic surgery
- Breast surgery
- Cholecystectomy
- Renal surgery
- Appendicectomy
- Inguinal hernia repair.

Surgical anaesthesia

- Plastic surgery
- Breast surgery
- Inguinal hernia repair.

Acute pain management

- Trauma—fractured ribs
- Trauma—liver capsule
- Infection—acute post-herpetic neuralgia.

Chronic pain

- Post-surgical neuropathic pain
- Chronic post-herpetic neuralgia
- Angina pectoris
- Cancer pain.

Other

- Hyperhydrosis—therapeutic control.

abnormal spinal anatomy (Richardson et al. 2011). Another relative contraindication is in patients with significant respiratory disease, where motor block of the intercostal muscles caused by a paravertebral block may cause further respiratory compromise.

Technique

Before performing a paravertebral block informed consent should be obtained from the patient. The patient must be monitored in an area where full resuscitation and skilled assistance are readily available. Intravenous access should be established and the procedure should be carried out in aseptic conditions.

The block can be performed with the patient awake, sedated, or in combination with general anaesthesia. If the patient is awake, the patient can be sitting with head and shoulders flexed forwards. In patients undergoing general anaesthesia or sedation, a lateral position with the side to be blocked uppermost is convenient. In the lateral position, the space between each transverse process can be increased by the use of a sandbag under the patient at the level to be blocked or adjusting the operating table to increase the curvature of the spine. There is no definitive evidence in terms of morbidity to advocate performing the block with either the patient awake or under general anaesthesia.

Irrespective of the technique used to perform a paravertebral block, it is necessary to first identify the correct anatomical level. The spinous process of each thoracic vertebrae is angled inferiorly to such a degree that its tip lies in the same horizontal spine as the transverse process of the vertebra located immediately below, such that the tip of the T2 spinous process lies adjacent to the transverse process of T1 and the paravertebral space anterior to this will contain the T1 nerve root. Therefore, correct identification of the level of the transverse process will determine which nerve roots will be subsequently blocked. This can be done via several different approaches:

1. Identify the spinous process of C7. It is the most superior process that is visible—*vertebra prominens*. From this point it is possible to count down each adjacent spinous process.
2. Identify the inferior tip of the scapula—this lies adjacent to the T7 spinous process. This method is less accurate than the identification of the vertebra prominens as described previously (Teogh et al. 2009).
3. Identify the 12th rib—this can be done either by a landmark technique or by ultrasound scanning. It is then possible to count each rib.

There are a variety of techniques that can be used to locate the paravertebral space. They either use a landmark technique or involve the use of ultrasound. Ultrasound can be used to either assist in identification of the landmarks or it can be used to provide a real-time ultrasound-guided paravertebral block. In the awake or sedated patient, it is necessary to infiltrate the skin with local anaesthetic before performing the block.

Landmark technique

The classical technique involves identification of the transverse process with a needle and then 'walking off' this to either a set predetermined distance, a loss of resistance technique, nerve stimulation, or a combination of these needle end-points.

At the appropriate level, the tip of the spinous process is palpated and the needle insertion point is marked at 25 mm lateral to this. Either an 18 G Tuohy needle or a 100 mm insulated nerve stimulator needle can be used. The needle is then inserted, perpendicular to the skin in all planes, and advanced to make contact with the transverse process. The transverse process should be encountered at a depth of 2–4 cm depending on patient habitus. It is important not to advance the needle too far initially as it is possible for the needle to be advanced beyond the transverse process and pleural puncture could occur. If the transverse process is not contacted within 3 cm then the needle should be reinserted and directed caudal and cranial to the same depth. If the transverse process is still not encountered then the depth of insertion can be increased by 1 cm and the process is repeated. This can be repeated until contact with the transverse process is made.

It is now possible to 'walk off' the transverse process and enter the paravertebral space. It is recommended to walk off caudally as there is a lower risk of pneumothorax with this approach (Hill and Greengrass 2000). The needle is then slowly advanced no further than 1 cm. A change in resistance or a subtle 'click' can sometimes be felt or heard as the needle passes through the superior costotransverse ligament (Greengrass et al. 1996). Compared with the loss of resistance encountered with epidural space location, the change in resistance is less evident because of the thinner costotransverse ligament. A complete loss of resistance may indicate pleural puncture. After a negative aspiration, local anaesthetic is injected which should occur with minimal resistance. The needle should only be advanced further than 1 cm if there is significant resistance to injection and then it should only be advanced in small increments until a change in resistance is felt (Tighe et al. 2010).

A nerve stimulator needle can also be used to detect an end-point for needle insertion (Naja et al. 2003). A current set at 1.5–2 mA with a frequency of 2 Hz and a pulse width of 0.1–0.3 ms will cause contraction of the intercostal muscles when the needle tip is in the correct position.

Ultrasound-assisted technique

This technique uses ultrasound to identify the location and depth of the transverse process and pleura. A 5–12 Hz linear probe is positioned in a parasagittal plane. A scan is performed and the transition between rib and transverse process is visualized. It is easier to identify this point if the scan is performed from lateral to medial, as the rib is easier to identify initially. The transverse process is always superficial to the rib and a characteristic 'double hump' can be seen. Now that the transverse process has been located the probe is turned obliquely away from the midline to obtain an optimum view of the pleura. It is now possible to measure the depths between the skin, transverse process, and pleura and to mark the midpoint of the transverse process. The probe is then removed and the paravertebral block is performed by the landmark technique described previously, using the depth and location measurements to assist needle placement.

Ultrasound-guided technique

This technique uses ultrasound to guide real-time needle placement and subsequent injection of local anaesthetic into the paravertebral space. There are a variety of different approaches; a brief description of some of the more common techniques are described in the following subsections.

Classic

The ultrasound probe is used in the same orientation as in the ultrasound-assisted technique. The transverse process and pleura are identified. It is then possible to view the costotransverse ligament. This can be seen as a less echogenic line connecting the hyperechoic transverse processes (Fig. 53.5). Both in-plane and out-of-plane needling techniques can be used. On injecting local anaesthetic within the paravertebral space, the pleura is pushed anteriorly. Scanning the levels above and below can also help in assessing the spread of local anaesthetic and therefore the need for subsequent injections.

Transverse

The ultrasound probe is placed in the transverse plane with the medial edge of the probe just over the spinous process. The intercostal space, transverse process, and the pleura are identified. It is possible then to view the internal intercostal membrane, which as previously described is continuous medially with the superior costotransverse ligament. An in-plane approach from lateral to medial can then be used to inject local anaesthetic into the paravertebral space. A disadvantage of this approach is an increased frequency of epidural spread of local anaesthetic (Luyet et al. 2009).

Intercostal

This approach is slightly different to the previous ultrasound techniques described, in that it does not image the paravertebral space. The ultrasound probe is positioned between the ribs at the appropriate level about 8 cm from the midline. The internal and innermost intercostal muscles are identified and the needle is placed in-plane from lateral to medial between these muscles (Ben-Ari et al. 2009). Local anaesthetic will enter into the paravertebral space because of the communication between the paravertebral space and this intercostal space.

Catheter technique

Continuous paravertebral block can be achieved by placing a catheter into the paravertebral space. Indications for its use include thoracotomy and multiple rib fractures (Karmakar et al. 2001).

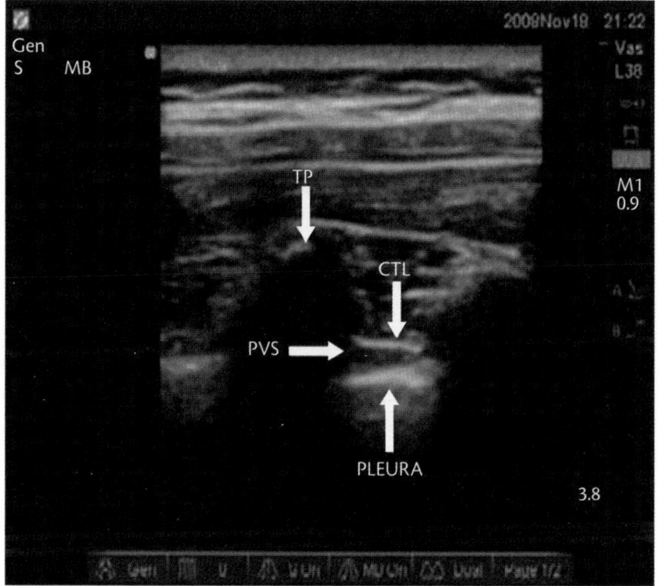

Figure 53.5 Ultrasound scan of the posterior chest wall to show the paravertebral space and related sonoanatomy. CTL, costotransverse ligament; PVS, paravertebral space; TP, transverse process.

Reproduced with permission from Tighe, SQM., *et al.* Paravertebral block. *Continuing Education in Anaesthesia, Critical Care, and Pain*, 2010, Volume 10, Issue 5, pp. 133–137, by permission of the British Journal of Anaesthesia.

Whichever technique is used to identify the paravertebral space it is necessary to expand the paravertebral space with either local anaesthetic or saline to aid catheter placement. Paravertebral catheter placement requires greater force to thread when compared with epidural catheter placement. It is recommended that less than 4 cm of catheter is inserted in adults to decrease the possibility of the catheter entering the intercostal space (Richardson and Lonnqvist 1998).

Paravertebral catheters can also be accurately placed under direct vision by the surgeon during thoracotomy and video-assisted thoracoscopic surgery.

Local anaesthetic volume and spread

Local anaesthetic injected into the paravertebral space will either remain at the level of injection or spread to the adjacent levels above and below. However, spread of local anaesthetic can also occur into the epidural space, intercostal space, and to the contralateral paravertebral space via prevertebral spread. Spread is less in females compared with males (Karmakar 2001).

The volume of local anaesthetic used will depend on how many dermatomes need to be blocked. Injections can either be made at a single or multiple levels. A single-level injection of 15 ml of local anaesthetic will produce a somatic block of at least three dermatomes and a mean distribution of sympathetic block over eight dermatomes (Cheema et al. 1995). Increasing the volume of injection to more than 25 ml at a single site is more likely to lead to a bilateral block (Gilbert et al. 1989). If a block is required over more than four dermatomes, then a single injection of 3–5 ml at each thoracic level (Greengrass et al. 1996) should be performed to ensure a sufficient block is achieved. Other options for larger areas include blocking alternate levels or blocking the upper and lower dermatomes required (Eason and Wyatt 1979).

Table 53.7 illustrates the commonly used drugs and their doses for single, multiple, and infusion regimens.

Complications

Thoracic paravertebral block has a very low risk of long-term morbidity and there have been no reported deaths as a direct result of paravertebral block.

The overall reported complication rate is low, between 2.6% and 5% of cases (Karmakar 2001). The frequency of specific complications has been reported as hypotension 4.6%, vascular puncture 3.8%, pleural puncture 1.1%, and pneumothorax 0.5% (Lonnqvist et al. 1995). A pneumothorax does not always occur after a pleural

Table 53.7 Commonly used local anaesthetic drugs and their doses for single, multiple, and infusion regimens

Patient group	Local anaesthetic	Single bolus	Multiple levels	Infusion ml kg^{-1} h^{-1}
Adult	Bupivacaine 0.25–0.5%	15 ml 0.3 ml kg^{-1}	3–5 ml	0.1
Adult	Ropivacaine 0.5–0.75%	15–20 ml	3–5 ml	
Paediatric	Bupivacaine 0.25%	0.5 ml kg^{-1}		0.2

puncture. If a pneumothorax does occur, it is usually small and can be managed conservatively (Coveney et al. 1998).

Epidural or paravertebral spread occurs in up to 10% of cases. This is caused by either epidural or prevertebral spread of local anaesthetic. High thoracic blocks causing ipsilateral Horner's syndrome is a recognized complication. Dural puncture resulting in spinal anaesthesia is very rare (Tighe et al. 2010).

The failure rate of thoracic paravertebral block is up to 10%, which is similar to other neuraxial regional anaesthetic techniques. The use of ultrasound to aid identification and placement of local anaesthetic within the paravertebral space may improve the success rate, but currently there is insufficient evidence to support this.

Summary

Thoracic paravertebral block has a high success rate coupled with a low rate of complications and morbidity.

It has proven benefits in a range of clinical scenarios. It is effective in providing analgesia for unilateral surgical cases including breast and thoracic surgery and in the acute management of rib fractures. It can be used as a sole anaesthetic technique for breast surgery. It may also reduce the incidence of tumour recurrence in breast cancer surgery (Exadaktylos et al. 2006). The prevalence of chronic pain after breast and thoracic surgery may also be reduced when paravertebral blocks are used at the time of surgery (Richardson et al. 1994; Kairaluoma et al. 2006).

Intercostal and intrapleural block

The intercostal nerves run in a small neurovascular bundle inferior to each rib. As a single block the duration of action is limited, therefore consideration should be given to continuous infusion depending on the duration of analgesia required. Intercostal blocks can be used for indications such as rib fractures, thoracotomy, and upper abdominal incisions (Hashimi et al. 1991; Barron et al. 1999). No fascial sheath surrounds the neurovascular bundle, therefore it is sufficient to deposit local anaesthetic close to the nerve. Multiple-level injections are often required.

Intrapleural block was introduced in the 1980s but its popularity has waned. Local anaesthetic is deposited between the parietal and visceral layers of the pleura. It has been shown to decrease analgesic requirements after a variety of unilateral surgical procedures including open cholecystectomy (Dravid and Paul 2007). Pneumothorax occurs in approximately 2% of patients.

Serratus anterior and 'pecs' block

Recently, there has been interest in novel ultrasound-guided techniques that provide analgesia to the chest wall for indications such as breast surgery or rib fractures as an alternative to paravertebral analgesia without an adverse side-effect profile. While promising, the so-called pecs I, pecs II, and serratus anterior plane blocks (Blanco et al. 2013) have limited evidence for their efficacy and further comparative randomized controlled studies are awaited.

Blocks of the anterior abdominal wall

A significant component of pain experienced after abdominal surgery is related to incision of the abdominal wall and adequate analgesia can be a challenge. Regional blocks of the anterior abdominal wall can significantly help with intraoperative and postoperative analgesia especially when used as part of a multimodal technique. It is important to note that blocks of the anterior abdominal wall do not provide analgesia to the abdominal viscera. However, abdominal wall blocks can be used even in major abdominal surgery when epidural analgesia is contraindicated. Haemodynamic effects are minimal as spread of local anaesthetic is confined to the abdominal wall. These blocks also provide a useful addition in ambulatory surgery, improving the quality of analgesia and reducing postoperative opioid requirements.

Traditionally these blocks relied on landmark techniques with detection of 'pops' to identify fascial planes and determine the correct location for local anaesthetic deposition. More recently, ultrasound techniques have been used to facilitate their performance. Relevant anatomical structures can be identified and complications from incorrect placement of local anaesthetic can be kept to a minimum.

Anatomical considerations

Within the abdominal wall there are three muscle layers, each with an associated fascial sheath. From superficial to deep these compromise the external oblique, internal oblique, and transversus abdominis muscles. Either side of the midline a fourth muscle layer is formed by the paired rectus abdominis muscles (Fig. 53.1). The anterior abdominal wall is bounded by the cartilages of the 7th to 10th ribs and xiphoid process of the sternum superiorly, the inguinal ligament and the pelvic bone inferiorly, and the mid axillary line laterally (Moore and Dalley 1999). The four muscles of the abdominal wall support the abdominal contents and the trunk. The main nerve supply to the anterior abdominal wall lies in a plane between the internal oblique and transversus abdominis. Below the muscles lie extraperitoneal fat and then the parietal peritoneum.

Each muscle layer is surrounded by a fascial plane. The external oblique muscle is the most superficial, arising from the middle and lower ribs; its fibres slope down and forward to the iliac crest, forming an aponeurosis below that level. The internal oblique attaches to the lateral two-thirds of the inguinal ligament and anterior iliac crest; its fibres slope forwards and upwards. The transversus abdominis muscle is the innermost layer with fibres running transverse towards the midline.

Medial to these is the principal vertical abdominal muscle, the rectus abdominis. This paired muscle is separated in the midline by the linea alba. The rectus abdominis muscle is wide and thin superiorly, and narrow and thick inferiorly. The majority of the rectus abdominis muscle is enclosed by the rectus sheath. The posterior layer of the rectus sheath is deficient over the lower quarter of the rectus abdominal muscle, marked by the arcuate line, which defines the point where the posterior aponeurosis layer of the internal oblique and the aponeurosis of the transversus abdominis become part of the anterior rectus sheath, leaving only the relatively thin transversalis fascia to cover the rectus abdominis muscle posteriorly. The arcuate line is found at one-third of the distance from the umbilicus to the pubic crest.

Between the internal oblique and transversus abdominis muscles lies a plane that corresponds with a similar plane in the intercostal spaces. This plane contains the anterior rami of the lower six thoracic nerves (T7–12) and first lumbar nerve (L1). These nerves supply the skin, muscles, and parietal peritoneum (McDonnell et al. 2007). At the costal margins, thoracic nerves T7–11 enter this neurovascular plane of the abdominal wall, travelling along it to pierce the posterior wall of the rectus sheath as anterior cutaneous branches supplying the overlying skin. The T7–9 nerves emerge to supply the skin superior to the umbilicus. The T10 nerve supplies the umbilicus while T11, the cutaneous branch of the subcostal T12, iliohypogastric nerve, and ilioinguinal nerve supply the skin inferior to the umbilicus.

The iliohypogastric nerve originates from the L1 nerve root and supplies the sensory innervation to the skin over the inguinal region. The nerve runs in the plane between the internal oblique and transversus abdominis muscle and later pierces the internal oblique to lie between this muscle and the external oblique before giving off cutaneous branches.

The ilioinguinal nerve also originates from the L1 nerve root and is found inferior to the iliohypogastric nerve perforating the transversus abdominis muscle at the level of the iliac crest running medially in a deeper plane than the iliohypogastric nerve. The ilioinguinal nerve innervates the inguinal hernia sac and medial aspect of thigh and anterior scrotum and labia (Van Schoor et al. 2005).

Rectus sheath block

The rectus sheath block was first described in 1899 and was initially used for the purpose of abdominal wall muscle relaxation during laparotomy before the advent of neuromuscular block. Now it is used for analgesia after umbilical or incisional hernia repairs and other midline surgical incisions. The aim of the block is to block the terminal branches of the 9th, 10th, and 11th intercostal nerves which run in-between the internal oblique and transversus abdominis muscles to penetrate the posterior wall of the rectus abdominis muscle and end in an anterior cutaneous branch supplying the skin of the umbilical area (Fig. 53.6).

The most widely described approach is a blind technique, passing the needle through the anterior rectus sheath and through the rectus abdominis muscle and injecting local anaesthetic onto the posterior wall of the rectus sheath.

With the patient lying supine, a point is identified 2–3 cm from the midline, slightly cephalad to the umbilicus at the apex of a bulge of the rectus abdominis muscle. A short-bevelled 5 cm needle inserted at right angles to the skin is passed through the skin until the resistance of the anterior sheath can be felt. A definitive 'pop' should be felt as it is passed through. The needle is advanced further until the firm resistance of the posterior wall is felt and injection of 15–20 ml of local anaesthetic is made. The procedure is repeated on the opposite side of the midline.

There is a poor correlation between the depth of the posterior sheath and the age, weight, or height of patients, meaning it can be difficult to predict the depth of the rectus sheath (Willschke et al. 2006). The use of ultrasound allows non-invasive, real-time imaging of the rectus sheath while the needle is placed under direct vision.

An in-plane approach can be taken to identify the posterior wall of the rectus sheath and direct visualization of local anaesthetic spread can be made. A higher success rate and lower doses of local anaesthetic have been described with ultrasound guidance. There are three tendinous intersections of the rectus abdominis muscle in the rectus sheath which can be identified on ultrasound. With real-time imaging, the free spread of local anaesthetic can confirm that these do not extend through the whole cross-section of the rectus abdominis muscle down to the posterior sheath, allowing for spread of anaesthetic with only one injection site on either side of the midline (Willschke et al. 2006).

Continuous rectus sheath blocks have been used as an alternative to epidural analgesia after major surgery with a midline abdominal incision, avoiding hypotension associated with central neuraxial block while providing equivalent analgesia (Godden et al. 2013).

With the posterior wall of the rectus sheath lying superficial to the peritoneal cavity, needle misplacement may lead to complications. Injection into the peritoneal cavity will lead to block failure and may risk bowel perforation or damage to blood vessels, usually the inferior epigastric vessels. In addition, block failure may result from anatomical variance as in up to 30% of the population the anterior cutaneous branches of the nerves are formed before the rectus sheath and so do not penetrate the posterior wall of the rectus sheath (Skinner and Lauder 2007).

Ilioinguinal and iliohypogastric nerve blocks

Inguinal herniorrhaphy pain can be severe and difficult to treat without opioid analgesia, but blocking the iliohypogastric and ilioinguinal nerves can provide good analgesia for many operations in the inguinal region. These blocks may be very effective, removing the need for opioids and in paediatric patients have been found to be as effective as caudal blocks, but with a higher failure rate (Van Schoor et al. 2005).

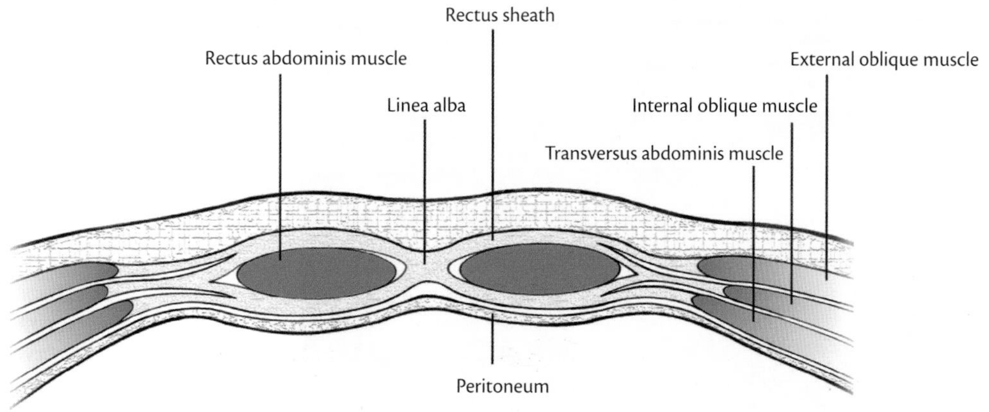

Figure 53.6 Anatomy of the rectus sheath.

The classical approach uses a landmark technique which blocks the nerves once they have separated into the different fascial layers. An injection is made at a point 2 cm medial and 2 cm superior to the anterior superior iliac spine. A short-bevelled needle is advanced perpendicular to the skin. After an initial pop sensation as the needle penetrates the external oblique aponeurosis, around 5 ml of local anaesthetic is injected. The needle is then inserted deeper until a second pop is felt penetrating the internal oblique, to lie between it and the transversus abdominis muscle. A further 5 ml of local anaesthetic is injected to block the ilioinguinal nerve. A fan-wise subcutaneous injection can be made to block any remaining sensory supply from the intercostals and subcostal nerve. This approach has a success rate of up to 70% with failure often as a result of the local anaesthetic being placed more than one anatomical layer away from the nerves (Weintraud et al. 2008).

Ultrasound guidance has been used with an increased success rate to block the nerves proximal to the anterior superior iliac spine when both nerves can be identified in the fascial layer between the internal oblique and transversus abdominis muscles, before the iliohypogastric nerve has penetrated the internal oblique to lie below the external oblique muscle. The ultrasound probe is placed obliquely on a line joining the anterior superior iliac spine and the umbilicus, immediately superior and posterior to the anterior superior iliac spine (Eichenberger et al. 2006) (Fig. 53.7). It may not be possible to identify each nerve exactly on ultrasound so the most important aspect is to ensure local anaesthetic is deposited in the correct fascial plane. When the correct plane between the internal oblique and transversus abdominis muscle is identified, 10 ml of local anaesthetic is injected.

It is worth noting, if used as the sole technique for inguinal herniorrhaphy, that the sac containing the peritoneum should be infiltrated with local anaesthetic by the surgeon as it is supplied by the abdominal visceral nerves. Placement of the needle and local anaesthetic too deep may result in block failure and an inadvertent femoral nerve block. Injection into the peritoneum and colonic puncture has been reported. Use of ultrasound guidance may reduce the incidence of these complications.

Transversus abdominis plane block

The aim of the transversus abdominis plane (TAP) block is to block the sensory nerves of the anterior abdominal wall before they pierce the musculature to innervate the abdomen. The block can be performed either by using a landmark technique or with the aid of ultrasound. The aim is to place a large volume of local anaesthetic in the fascial plane between internal oblique and transversus abdominis which contains the nerves from T7 to L1. Onset of sensory block appears to be relatively slow so ideally the block is placed at the start of surgery to give adequate time for onset of sensory analgesia (McDonnell et al. 2007).

The block was originally described using a landmark technique. The TAP is accessed from the lumbar 'triangle of Petit', bounded anteriorly by the external oblique, posteriorly by the latissimus dorsi, and inferiorly by the iliac crest (Fig. 53.8).

This landmark is normally easily palpable (McDonnell et al. 2007), although a cadaveric anatomical study noted a large variability in the position of the triangle of Petit (Jankovic et al. 2009) and its identification may be difficult in the obese patient. The triangle is identified just anterior to the latissimus dorsi muscle and a blunt tipped, short-bevelled needle is placed perpendicular to the skin immediately cephalad to the iliac crest. The needle is advanced through the external oblique and a first 'pop' sensation is felt when the needle enters the plane between external oblique and internal oblique. Further advancement of the needle results in a second 'pop' after passing through the internal oblique fascia into the TAP (Fig. 53.9). At this point, after careful aspiration, 20 ml of long-acting local anaesthetic is injected.

Ultrasound can also be used to identify the muscle layers and ensure accurate placement of local anaesthetic. The ultrasound probe is placed in-between the 12th rib and the iliac crest in the mid-axillary line. The TAP between internal oblique and transversus abdominis muscles can easily be observed on ultrasound (Fig. 53.10) and by using a 10 cm short-bevelled needle with an in-plane approach, the local anaesthetic spread distending the plane can be seen in real time.

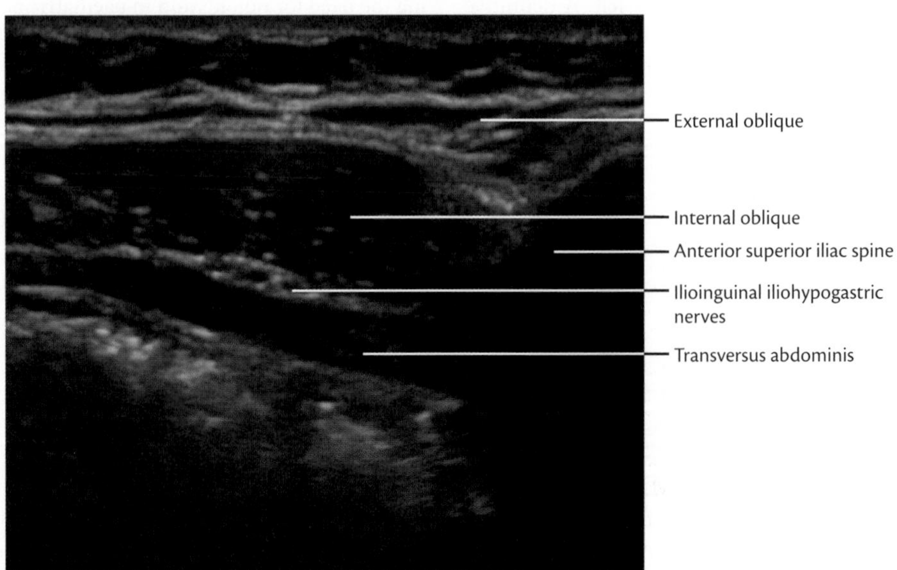

Figure 53.7 Ultrasound view of the Ilioinguinal iliohypogastric nerves.

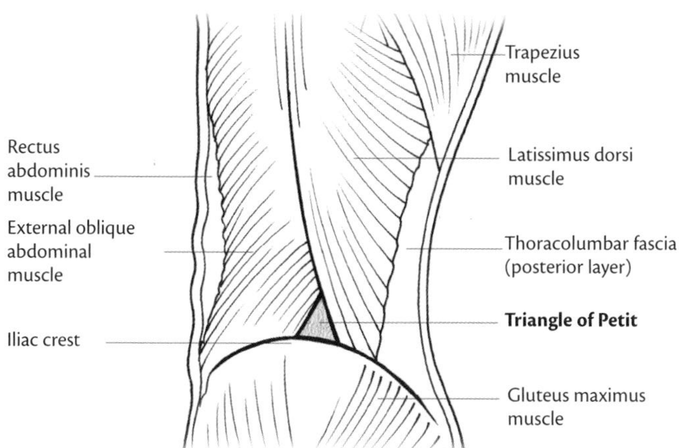

Figure 53.8 Triangle of Petit.

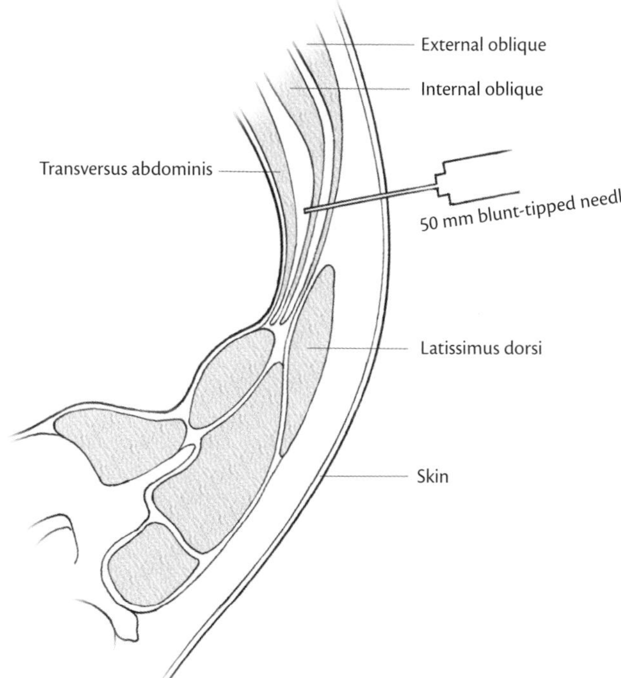

Figure 53.9 Injection into the transversus abdominis plane.

In order to facilitate higher dermatomal spread of analgesia, a second injection in the TAP in the subcostal area has been described (Barrington et al. 2009). The TAP block provides analgesia for the abdominal wall but not for the visceral contents and is ideally used as part of a multimodal approach to analgesia. Good postoperative analgesia and a decrease in morphine requirements for up to 48 h after operation has been demonstrated after a variety of surgical procedures including open colorectal surgery, retropubic prostatectomy, abdominal hysterectomy, and Caesarean section. It may be used as a simple alternative in patients for whom an epidural is not possible although there is little comparative data as to the relative effectiveness of the two techniques (Bonnet et al. 2009).

Complications include block failure, intravascular injection, or injection into the peritoneal cavity, with associated risks of damage

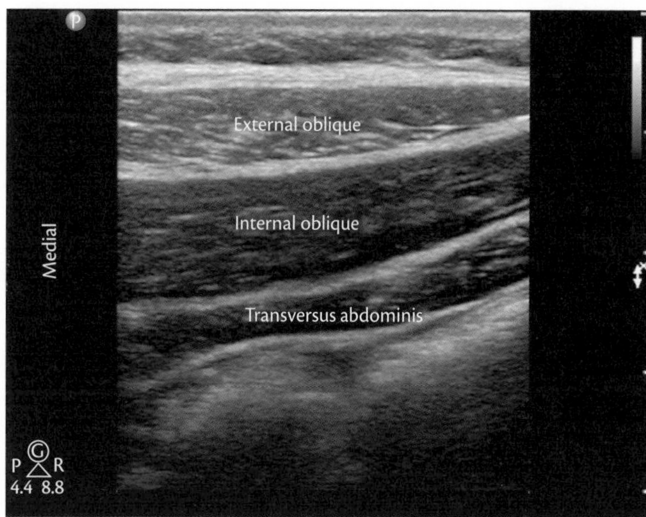

Figure 53.10 Ultrasound view of abdominal muscles in the mid-axillary line.
Reproduced with permission from McDonnell, J. and Harmon, D, 'Regional anaesthesia of the trunk', in McLeod, G. *et al.*, *Principles and Practice of Regional Anaesthesia*, 2012, Figure 16.14, Page 165, with permission from Oxford University Press.

to bowel and other abdominal viscera. There have been isolated case reports of complications both with the landmark (Farooq and Carey 2008) and ultrasound-guided techniques (Lancaster and Chadwick 2010). Large volumes of local anaesthetic are commonly injected with the potential for toxic blood levels (Griffiths et al. 2013) and there are case reports of convulsions associated with TAP block (Weiss et al. 2014). Absorption of local anaesthetic from the TAP may be significant. The use of an ultrasound-guided approach may reduce the risk of local anaesthetic systemic toxicity (Barrington and Kluger 2013). Attention should be paid to the total dose of local anaesthetic used and consideration given to the use of lower local anaesthetic concentrations in order to reduce the risk of toxic side-effects.

Numerous trials of TAP block have been published with variable results but with a trend towards superior early pain control (Abdallah et al. 2012). The exact role of the TAP block for procedure-specific indications remains to be defined. Different approaches to the TAP appear to result in contrasting patterns of local anaesthetic spread. Anterior subcostal and mid-axillary approaches result in predominantly anterior spread of local anaesthetic within the plane. Conversely the posterior landmark or ultrasound approaches result in predominantly posterior spread of local anaesthetic with extension into the paravertebral space (Carney et al. 2011). This may explain the apparently prolonged analgesic effects associated with the posterior approaches.

Local anaesthetic wound infiltration

Surgical wound infiltration catheters have been used after a variety of trunk procedures including mastectomy, laparotomy, and nephrectomy. Significant analgesic benefits have been demonstrated compared with placebo (Beaussier et al. 2007). Compared with epidural analgesia, continuous local anaesthetic wound infiltration can provide similar analgesia although epidural analgesia tends to reduce opioid requirements and is associated with lower pain scores. Further procedure-specific evidence is required regarding the efficacy of this technique (Ventham et al. 2013).

Penile block

Penile block is a useful technique for a variety of penile procedures (e.g. circumcision and meatotomy). It avoids the effects of other more central techniques such as caudal blocks and provides excellent analgesia usually in conjunction with general anaesthesia. The nerve supply to the penis arises from the second to fourth sacral nerve roots through the dorsal nerve of the penis. The dorsal nerves of the penis enter the subpubic space at the symphysis pubis. A needle is inserted in the midline into the sub-pubic space. Careful aspiration is required before injection as the area is highly vascular. Up to 5 ml of a non-adrenaline-containing local anaesthetic is injected either side of the midline. An alternative is to perform a subcutaneous ring block around the base of the penile shaft but there is a higher incidence of inadequate pain relief with this approach (Holder et al. 1997). Complications include haematoma formation.

Declaration of interest

None declared.

References

Abdallah FW, Chan VW, Brull, R. Transversus abdominis plane block: a systematic review. *Reg Anesth Pain Med* 2012; **37**: 193–209

Barrington MJ, Ivanusic JJ, Rozen WM, *et al.* Spread of injectate after ultrasound-guided subcostal transversus abdominis plane block: a cadaveric study. *Anaesthesia* 2009; **64**: 745–50

Barrington MJ, Kluger R. Ultrasound guidance reduces the risk of local anesthetic systemic toxicity following peripheral nerve blockade. *Reg Anesth Pain Med* 2013; **38**: 289–97

Barron DJ, Tolan MJ Lea RE. A randomized controlled trial of continuous extra-pleural analgesia post-thoracotomy: efficacy and choice of local anaesthetic. *Eur J Anesthesiol* 1999; **16**: 236–45

Beaussier, M, El'Ayoubi, H, Schiffer, E, *et al.* Continuous preperitoneal infusion of ropivacaine provides effective analgesia and accelerates recovery after colorectal surgery: a randomized, double-blind, placebo-controlled study. *Anesthesiology* 2007; **107**: 461–8

Ben-Ari A, Moreno M, Chelly JE, Biegelsen PE. Ultrasound guided paravertebral block using an intercostal approach. *Anesth Analg* 2009; **102**: 1691–4

Bier A. Versuche uber cocainisirung des ruckenmarkes [Experiments on the cocainization of the spinal cord]. *Deutsche Zeitschrift fur Chirurgie* 1899; **51**: 361–9

Blanco R, Parras T, McDonnell JG, Prats-Galino, A. Serratus plane block: a novel ultrasound-guided thoracic wall nerve block. *Anaesthesia* 2013; **68**: 1107–13

Block BM, Liu SS, Rowlingson AJ, *et al.* Efficacy of postoperative epidural analgesia: a meta-analysis. *JAMA* 2003; **290**: 2455–63

Bonnet F, Berger J, Aveline C. Transversus abdominis plane block: what is its role in postoperative analgesia? *Br J Anaesth* 2009; **103**: 468–70

Broadbent CR, Maxwell WB, Ferrie R, *et al.* Ability of anaesthetists to identify a marked lumbar interspace. *Anaesthesia* 2000; **55**: 1122–6

Carney J, Finnerty O, Rauf J, *et al.* Studies on the spread of local anaesthetic solution in transversus abdominis plane blocks. *Anaesthesia* 2011; **66**: 1023–30

Carpenter RL, Caplan RA, Brown DL, *et al.* Incidence and risk factors for side effects of spinal anesthesia. *Anesthesiology* 1992; **76**: 906–16

Cheema SPS, Isley D, Richardson J, Sabanathan S. A thermographic study of paravertebral analgesia. *Anaesthesia* 1995; **50**: 118–21

Colvin LA, Fallon MT, Buggy DJ. Cancer biology, analgesics, and anaesthetics: is there a link? *Br J Anaesth* 2012; **109**: 140–3

Cook TM, Counsell D, Wildsmith JA. Major complications of central neuraxial block: report on the Third National Audit Project of the Royal College of Anaesthetists. *Br J Anaesth* 2009; **102**: 179–90

Cope RW. The Woolley and Roe case. *Anaesthesia* 1954; **9**: 249–70

Corning, JL. Spinal anaesthesia and local medication of the cord. *N Y Med J* 1885; **42**: 483–5

Coveney E, Weltz CR, Greengrass R, *et al.* Use of paravertebral block anesthesia in the surgical management of breast cancer: experience in 156 cases. *Ann Surg* 1998; **227**: 496–501

Dogliotti AM. Research and clinical observations on spinal anesthesia: with special reference to the peridural technique. *Anesth Analg* 1933; **12**: 59–65

Dravid RM, Paul RE. Interpleural block—part 1. *Anesthesia* 2007; **62**: 1039–49

Eichenberger U, Greher M, Kirchmair L, *et al.* Ultrasound-guided blocks of the ilioinguinal and iliohypogastric nerve: accuracy of a selective new technique confirmed by anatomical dissection. *Br J Anaesth* 2006; **97**: 238–43

Eason MJ, Wyatt R. Paravertebral thoracic block—a reappraisal. *Anaesthesia* 1979; **34**: 638–42

Exadaktylos AK, Buggy DJ, Moriarty DC, *et al.* Can anesthetic technique for primary breast cancer surgery affect recurrence or metastasis? *Anesthesiology* 2006; **105**: 660–4

Farooq M, Carey M. A case of liver trauma with a blunt regional anesthesia needle while performing transversus abdominis plane block. *Reg Anesth Pain Med* 2008; **33**: 274–5

Gilbert J, Schuleman S, Sharp T. Inadvertent paravertebral block. *Anaesthesia* 1989; **33**: 561–4

Godden AR, Marshall MJ, Grice AS, *et al.* Ultrasonography guided rectus sheath catheters versus epidural analgesia for open colorectal cancer surgery in a single centre. *Ann R Coll Surg Engl* 2013; **95**: 591–4

Greengrass R, O'Brien F, Lyerly K, *et al.* Paravertebral block for breast cancer surgery. *Can J Anaesth* 1996; **43**: 858–61

Griffiths JD, Le NV, Grant S, *et al.* Symptomatic local anaesthetic toxicity and plasma ropivacaine concentrations after transversus abdominis plane block for Caesarean section. *Br J Anaesth* 2013; **110**: 996–1000

Halpern S, Preston R. Postdural puncture headache and spinal needle design. Metaanalyses. *Anesthesiology* 1994; **81**: 1376–83

Hashimi H, Stewart AL, Ah-Fat G. Continuous intercostal nerve block for postoperative analgesia after surgical treatment of the upper part of the abdomen. *Surg Gynecol Obstet* 1991; **173**: 116–8

Hill RP, Greengrass R. Pulmonary haemorrhage after percutaneous paravertebral block. *Br J Anaesth* 2000; **84**: 423–4

Hocking G, Wildsmith JA. Intrathecal drug spread. *Br J Anaesth* 2004; **93**: 568–78

Holder KJ, Peutrell JM, Weir PM. Regional anaesthesia for circumcision. Subcutaneous ring block of the penis and subpubic penile block compared. *Eur J Anaesth* 1997; **14**: 495–8

Ibrahim AF, Darwish HH. The costotransverse ligaments in human—a detailed anatomical study. *Clin Anat* 2005; **18**: 340–5

Jankovic ZB, du Feu FM, McConnell P. An anatomical study of the transversus abdominis plane block: location of the lumbar triangle of Petit and adjacent nerves. *Anesth Analg* 2009; **109**: 981–5

Kairaluoma PM, Bachmann MS, Rosenberg PH, Pere PJ. Preincisionalss paravertebral block reduces the prevalence of chronic pain after breast surgery. *Anesth Analg* 2006; **103**: 703–8

Karmakar MK. Thoracic paravertebral block. *Anaesthesiology* 2001; **95**: 638–42

Karmaker MK. Ultrasound for central neuraxial blocks. *Tech Reg Anesth Pain Manage* 2009; **13**: 161–70

Karmakar MK, Chui PT, Joynt GM, Ho AM. Thoracic paravertebral block for management of pain associated with multiple fractured ribs in patients with concomitant lumbar spinal trauma. *Reg Anaesth Pain Med* 2001; **26**: 169–73

Karmaker MK, Kwok WH, Kew J. Thoracic paravertebral block: radiological evidence of contralateral spread anterior to the vertebral bodies. *Br J Anaesth* 2000; **84**: 263–5

Lancaster P, Chadwick M. Liver trauma secondary to ultrasound-guided transversus abdominis plane block. *Br J Anaesth* 2010; **104**: 509–10

Lonnqvist PA, MacKenzie J, Soni AK, Conacher ID. Paravertebral blockade: failure rate and complications. *Anaesthesia* 1995; **50**: 813–5

Luyet C, Eichenberger U, Greif R, *et al.* Ultrasound-guided paravertebral puncture and placement of catheters in human cadavers: an imaging study. *Br J Anaesth* 2009; **102**: 534–9

McDonnell JG, O'Donnell B, Curley G, *et al.* The analgesic efficacy of transversus abdominis plane block after abdominal surgery: a prospective randomized controlled trial. *Anesth Analg* 2007; **104**: 193–7

McDonnell JG, O'Donnell B, Farrell T, *et al.* Transversus abdominis plane block: a cadaveric and radiological evaluation. *Reg Anaesth Pain Med* 2007; **32**: 399–404

Moore K, Dalley A. *Clinically Orientated Anatomy*, 4th Edn. Philadelphia, PA: Lippincott Williams and Watkins, 1999

Naja MZ, Ziade MF, Lonnqvist PA. Nerve stimulator guided paravertebral blockade vs general anaesthesia for breast surgery: a prospective randomised trial. *Eur J Anaesthesiol* 2003; **20**: 897–903

Nunn JF, Slavin G. Posterior intercostal nerve block for pain relief after cholecystectomy. Anatomical basis and efficacy. *Br J Anaesth* 1983; **55**: 521–4

Pagés, F. Anestesia metamérica. *Revista de Sanidad Militar* 1921; **11**: 351–4

Reynolds F. Logic in the safe practice of spinal anaesthesia. *Anaesthesia* 2000; **55**: 1045–6

Reynolds F. Damage to the conus medullaris following spinal anaesthesia. *Anaesthesia* 2001; **56**: 238–47

Richardson J, Lonnqvist PA. Thoracic paravertebral block: *Br J Anaesth* 1998; **81**: 230–8

Richardson J, Lonnqvist PA, Naja Z. Bilateral thoracic paravertebral block: potential and practice. *Br J Anaesth* 2011; **106**: 164–71

Richardson J, Sabanathan S, Mearns AJ, *et al.* Post-thoracotomy neuralgia. *Pain Clinic* 1994; **7**: 87–97

Rigg JR, Jamrozik K, Myles PS, *et al.* Epidural anaesthesia and analgesia and outcome of major surgery: a randomised trial. *Lancet* 2002; **359**: 1276–82

Robinson AP, Lyons GR, Wilson RC. Levobupivacaine for epidural analgesia in labor: the sparing effect of epidural fentanyl. *Anesth Analg* 2001; **92**: 410–4

Rooke G, Freund P, Jacobson A. Hemodynamic response and change in organ blood volume during spinal anaesthesia in elderly men with cardiac disease. *Anesth Analg* 1997; **85**: 99–105

Skinner AV, Lauder GR. Rectus sheath block: successful use in the chronic pain management of pediatric abdominal wall pain. *Pediatr Anesth* 2007; **17**: 1203–11

Teogh DA, Santosham KL, Lydell CC, *et al.* Surface anatomy as a guide to vertebral level for thoracic epidural placement: *Anesth Analg* 2009; **108**: 1705–7

Tighe SQM, Greene MD, Rajadurai N. Paravertebral block. *Cont Educ Anaesth Crit Care Pain* 2010; **10**: 133–7

Turnbull DK, Shepherd DB. Post-dural puncture headache: pathogenesis, prevention and treatment. *Br J Anaesth* 2003; **91**: 718–29

Van Schoor AN, Boon JM, Bosenberg AT, *et al.* Anatomical considerations of the pediatric ilioinguinal/iliohypogastric nerve block. *Pediatr Anesth* 2005; **15**: 371–7

Ventham NT, Hughes M, O'Neill S, *et al.* Systematic review and meta-analysis of continuous local anaesthetic wound infiltration versus epidural analgesia for postoperative pain following abdominal surgery. *Br J Surg* 2013; **100**: 1280–9

Weintraud M, Marhofer P, Bosenberg A, *et al.* Ilioinguinal/iliohypogastric blocks in children: where do we administer the local anaesthetic without direct visualisation? *Anesth Analg* 2008; **106**: 89–93

Weiss E, Jolly C, Dumoulin J, *et al.* Convulsions in 2 patients after bilateral ultrasound-guided transversus abdominis plane blocks for cesarean analgesia. *Reg Anesth Pain Med* 2014; **39**: 248–51

Willschke H, Bosenberg A, Marhofer P, *et al.* Ultrasonography-guided rectus sheath block in paediatric anaesthesia- a new approach to an old technique *Br J Anaesth* 2006; **97**: 244–9

CHAPTER 54

Regional anaesthesia of the upper limb

Colin J. L. McCartney and Alan J. R. Macfarlane

Upper limb blocks

Peripheral nerve blocks of the upper limb provide excellent anaesthesia and postoperative analgesia when performed by trained anaesthetists. The introduction of ultrasound guidance has generated significant excitement in the last 10 years by allowing the sonographic anatomy to be explored (Sites et al. 2010a, 2010b). Many studies performed have since demonstrated an improved efficacy using ultrasound compared with traditional techniques (Abrahams et al. 2009; Liu et al. 2010).

In order to understand the indications and techniques for each type of brachial plexus block it is important to appreciate the anatomy of the nerve supply to the upper limb. The upper limb is primarily supplied by the brachial plexus, which is formed by the ventral rami of C5–8 and T1, with a variable supply from C4 and T2 (Fig. 54.1). These roots (*interscalene block*) combine to form three trunks (superior, middle, and inferior) in the lower part of the neck (*supraclavicular block*), each of which then divides into anterior and posterior divisions as the nerves pass through the supraclavicular fossa, over the first rib, and under the clavicle. The three posterior divisions combine to form the posterior cord, the upper two anterior divisions form the lateral cord, and the lower anterior division forms the medial cord. The cords (*infraclavicular block*) lie, as their name describes, around the axillary artery before the plexus ends at the lower border of pectoralis minor by forming a number of terminal nerves. The four main terminal nerves are the radial, ulnar, musculocutaneous, and median nerves (*axillary block*). A variety of other nerves also branch from the plexus proximal to this point (Fig. 54.1), and where appropriate these are described in more detail in the following individual block sections, as are the anatomical relationships of the nerves and surrounding structures. The upper outer arm is supplied by the lateral cutaneous branch of the axillary nerve (C5, C6). The lateral cutaneous nerve of the forearm, a terminal branch of the musculocutaneous nerve (C5–7), supplies the lateral forearm. The medial cutaneous nerve of the forearm and the medial cutaneous nerve of the arm arise from the medial cord and supply the ulnar side of the forearm and arm respectively. The intercostobrachial nerve (T2), which does not arise from the brachial plexus, supplies the upper inner arm. This nerve is therefore not anaesthetized during a brachial plexus block and must be targeted separately for any skin incisions involving this area. Branches of the radial nerve (C5–T1) supply the extensor surfaces of the arm and forearm (the posterior cutaneous nerves of the arm and forearm), the thumb and radial three and a half digits, and the corresponding area on the dorsum of the hand (superficial branch). The median (C8, T1) and ulnar (C7, C8, and T1) nerves provide sensory innervation to the hand only. The median nerve supplies the flexor surface of the thumb and the lateral three and a half digits and nails, and the corresponding palmar area. The ulnar nerve supplies the remaining flexor and extensor surfaces of the medial one and a half digits and palm. See Figure 54.2.

Interscalene block

Indications

The interscalene block is generally performed at the level of the fifth or sixth cervical nerve roots (which subsequently form the superior trunk). The resulting anaesthesia and postoperative analgesia usually affects the C5–7 dermatomes (Fig. 54.1) and therefore this technique is most commonly utilized for shoulder or proximal upper limb and elbow procedures (Borgeat and Ekatodramis 2002). Many shoulder procedures are now commonly performed arthroscopically, with the ports being inserted posteriorly, laterally, and anteriorly. Despite this, shoulder surgery still produces significant postoperative pain (Ilfeld et al. 2003; Wilson et al. 2004). The interscalene block effectively reduces this pain (Wu et al. 2002), which in turn can decrease the length of in-patient stay and also allow certain procedures to be performed as a day case (Chelly et al. 2001). In addition, early mobilization after certain shoulder procedures is encouraged and therefore adequate dynamic pain control is important.

The lower trunk of the brachial plexus, and therefore the ulnar nerve, is often spared by interscalene block and so it is not an appropriate choice of block for medial forearm or hand surgery. More recently described alternatives to the interscalene block such as cervical paravertebral block, or combined suprascapular and axillary nerve blocks for shoulder surgery are not considered in this chapter (Verelst and van Zundert 2013).

An interscalene block may be undertaken as either a single injection or a continuous infusion technique. The use of a continuous catheter technique is useful in major arthroplasty procedures but these have also been shown to reduce pain more effectively compared with single-injection techniques even in ambulatory arthroscopic procedures (Fredrickson et al. 2010). Other authors, however, have reported satisfactory pain control with single-injection techniques and oral analgesia for these procedures. Catheters are more expensive, time-consuming, technically more challenging, and create management and follow-up issues so these factors must also

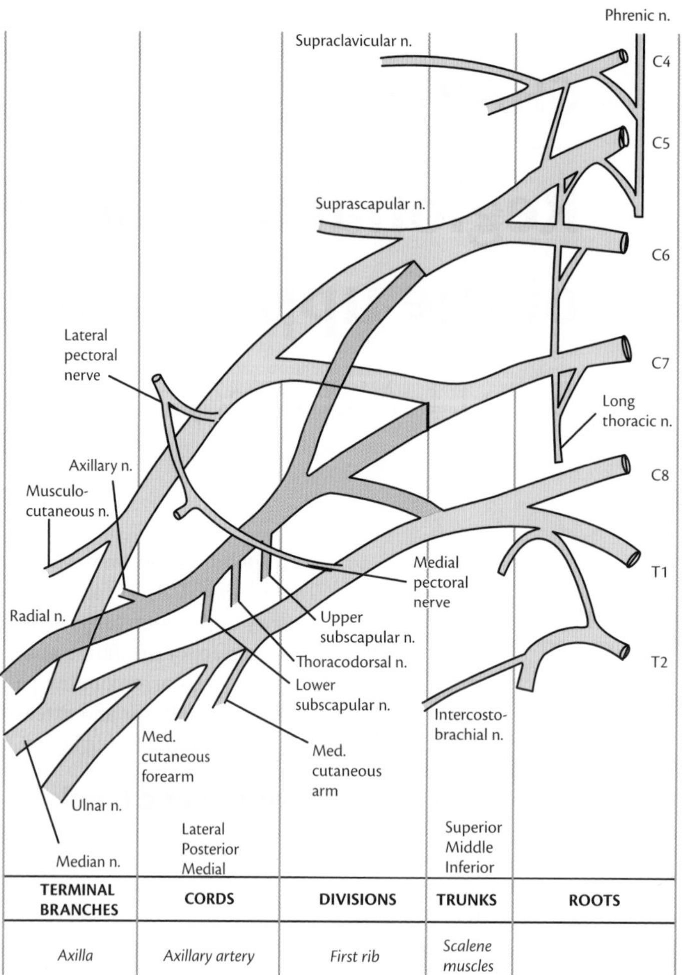

Figure 54.1 Formation and components of the brachial plexus.

Reproduced with permission from Coventry, D., 'Upper limb blocks', in McLeod, G. *et al.*, *Principles and Practice of Regional Anaesthesia, Fourth Edition*, 2012, Figure 54.1, Page 171, Oxford University Press 2012.

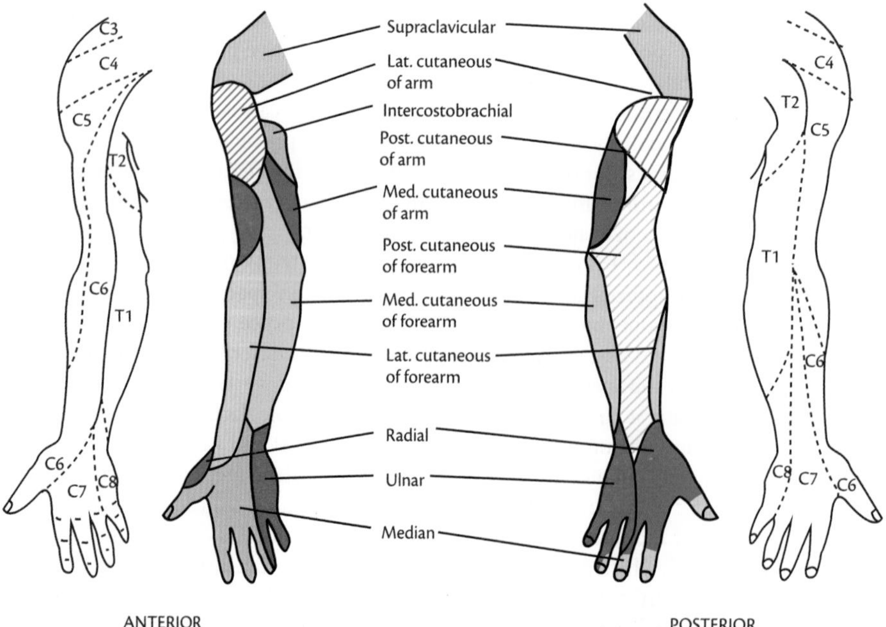

Figure 54.2 Cutaneous innervation and dermatomal maps of the upper limb. The segmental innervation of the deep structures is different from that of the skin: C5 supplies the shoulder, C7 the elbow, and T1 the hand.

Reproduced with permission from Coventry, D., 'Upper limb blocks', in McLeod, G. *et al.*, *Principles and Practice of Regional Anaesthesia, Fourth Edition*, 2012, Figure 54.2, Page 171, Oxford University Press 2012.

be accounted for before catheter insertion, especially if outpatient management is being considered.

An interscalene block can be used as the sole anaesthetic for shoulder surgery but it is often combined with general anaesthesia. As described later, the shoulder area receives innervation from a variety of sources. Achieving complete shoulder anaesthesia with a regional technique alone can therefore be more complex than for other upper limb procedures. Furthermore, the beach chair or lateral position is used in many shoulder procedures and so general anaesthesia may be chosen to ensure patient comfort, particularly for prolonged cases. Larger incisions such as those extending up into the C4 distribution (cape distribution) may require a larger volume technique or a superficial cervical plexus block (or individual block of the supraclavicular nerve branches of the cervical plexus) in combination with interscalene block.

Anatomy

The articular, ligamentous, capsular, and synovial membrane components of the shoulder are innervated by nerves arising predominantly from the brachial plexus (Romanes 1992). Specifically, the suprascapular nerve (C5, C6) arising from the superior trunk and the axillary nerve (C5, C6) arising from the posterior cord supply the majority, with variable contributions from the musculocutaneous (C5–7) and subscapular (C5, C6) nerves (Fig. 54.1). The cutaneous supply of the shoulder region arises from both the brachial plexus and branches of the superficial cervical plexus (Fig. 54.2). The transverse cervical nerve (C2, C3) innervates the skin of the front and side of the neck while the supraclavicular nerves (C3, C4) supply the 'cape distribution' of the clavicular area and the upper intercostal area anteriorly and the posterior cervical triangle. The skin over the deltoid muscle is innervated by the lateral cutaneous branch of the axillary nerve (C5, C6) while the medial upper arm is supplied by the intercostobrachial nerve (T2), and the medial cutaneous nerve of the arm which arises from the medial cord of the brachial plexus (C8, T1) (Fig. 54.1). If a regional *anaesthetic* technique is planned, the incision site for open procedures in particular must therefore be known. In addition, during arthroscopic procedures the posterior port may require additional local infiltration (or blockade of the supraclavicular nerves) if the procedure is to be performed solely using an interscalene block.

The fifth and sixth cervical nerves emerge from the intervertebral foramina above each of their corresponding cervical transverse processes. The anterior and middle scalene muscles arise from the anterior and posterior tubercles of the transverse processes and the nerves pass inferolaterally in the neck between these two muscles towards the first rib. The fifth and sixth roots unite to form the superior trunk of the brachial plexus but it is known that the anatomy can frequently vary from this classical description, and this can often be visualized when using ultrasound (Sites et al. 2010a).

Many of the potential complications of the interscalene block are as a result of the close proximity of a variety of important structures. The phrenic nerve arises from the third, fourth, and fifth cervical nerve roots and runs obliquely across the anterior scalene muscle. The vertebral artery enters the foramen transversarium at the sixth cervical vertebra and inferior to this lies exposed, anterior to the ventral rami of the seventh and eighth cervical nerves, medial to scalenus anterior. The dome of the pleura rises above the sternal end of the first rib, medial to scalenus anterior and covered by the suprapleural membrane, which itself arises from the seventh cervical transverse process. The thoracic duct also lies in the root of the neck on the left-hand side, while on both sides the recurrent laryngeal nerve is situated between the trachea and oesophagus. Finally, the cervical sympathetic chain runs anterior to the longus colli on the transverse processes, medial to the vertebral artery inferiorly.

Technique

Current guidelines (based on consensus evidence statements only) recommend undertaking all blocks in adults before the induction of general anaesthesia in order to reduce the risk of nerve injury and local anaesthetic toxicity (Neal et al. 2008a). Arguably this is particularly true for the interscalene block which appears to be at a higher risk of nerve injury than other nerve blocks (Brull et al. 2007). The anatomical structures to be blocked are superficial and a small dose of midazolam provides sufficient conditions to undertake the block in most patients. Either a landmark nerve stimulation or ultrasound technique may be used, or a combination of both. Nerve stimulation alone is still commonly used but ultrasound guidance has been shown to increase block success, reduce the number of needle passes, and decrease both postoperative pain and local anaesthetic volume requirements (Kapral et al. 2008; McNaught et al. 2011). Reducing the volume of local anaesthetic in ultrasound-guided interscalene block has been shown to reduce but not prevent the incidence of phrenic nerve palsy and respiratory complications, without compromising analgesia (Riazi et al. 2008; Renes et al. 2009).

Nerve stimulator

A variety of approaches exist. The classic approach described by Winnie involves directing the needle towards the cervical spine but is still commonly performed. The Pippa technique uses a posterior needle approach necessitating a longer, potentially more uncomfortable, distance to the target. The modified lateral technique aims to reduce the risk of complications by directing the needle away from the spine and is also best suited for catheter techniques as it follows more closely the path of the descending nerves and it is therefore described here. A 50 mm insulated block needle is chosen and an appropriate mixture of local anaesthetic prepared. The patient is positioned supine with the head turned slightly away from the side to be blocked, and on the edge of a pillow so as not to obstruct access to the neck. Standing at the head end of the patient, the groove between the scalene muscles should be palpated, posterior to the clavicular head of sternocleidomastoid muscle. Asking the patient to elevate the head helps identify the posterior border of the sternocleidomastoid while sniffing contracts the scalene muscles. Irrespective of body habitus the nerves are relatively superficial in the majority of patients. At 2 cm cranial to the level of the cricoid cartilage (Fig. 54.3) the skin above the interscalene groove is infiltrated with local anaesthetic. The nerve stimulator is set to 1.0 mA and the block needle advanced at a 30° angle from this position along the interscalene groove in a cephalad to caudad and slight lateral direction, aiming for the junction of the middle and lateral third of the ipsilateral clavicle. Deltoid or biceps muscle twitches indicate a successful end-point, and the current should be reduced to ensure a minimum stimulating current (MSC) of no less than 0.4 mA. Animal data has in general demonstrated a poor correlation between needle to nerve proximity and MSC (Macfarlane et al. 2011) and correspondingly one study has demonstrated equivalent

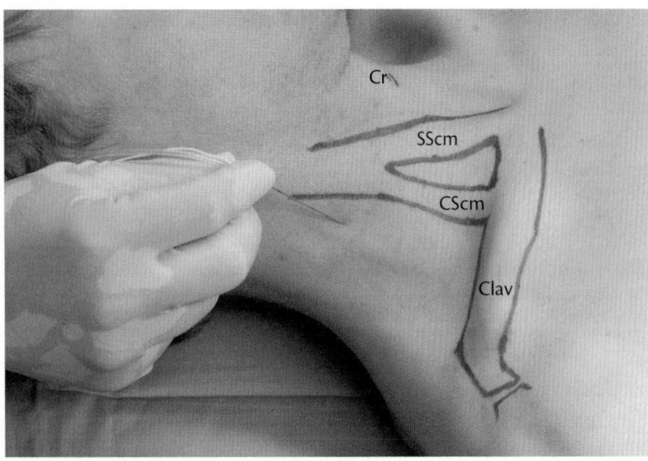

Figure 54.3 Surface landmarks and needle insertion for nerve stimulator-guided interscalene block. Clav, clavicle; Cr, cricoid cartilage; CScm, clavicular head of sternomastoid muscle; SScm, sternal head of sternomastoid muscle.

interscalene block duration and success irrespective of whether the current was above or below 0.5 mA when using ultrasound and nerve stimulation together (Sinha et al. 2007). Diaphragmatic stimulation indicates needle tip proximity to the phrenic nerve which lies anteriorly. The needle should therefore be directed posteriorly. Trapezius muscle stimulation indicates accessory nerve stimulation and suggests the needle is too posterior and should be redirected anteriorly.

Ultrasound

This is a basic level ultrasound-guided nerve block. Ultrasound allows direct visualization of the nerve roots between the anterior and middle scalene muscles and surrounding structures. A high-frequency linear probe should be chosen with depth settings around 2–3 cm. In the same supine or slightly head-up position as described previously, with the head turned slightly to the contralateral side, the neck is scanned in the transverse plane. The nerve roots at the level of the cricoid cartilage are generally visualized lying slightly obliquely as round, hypoechoic structures (Fig. 54.4). There are no large vascular landmarks at this level and

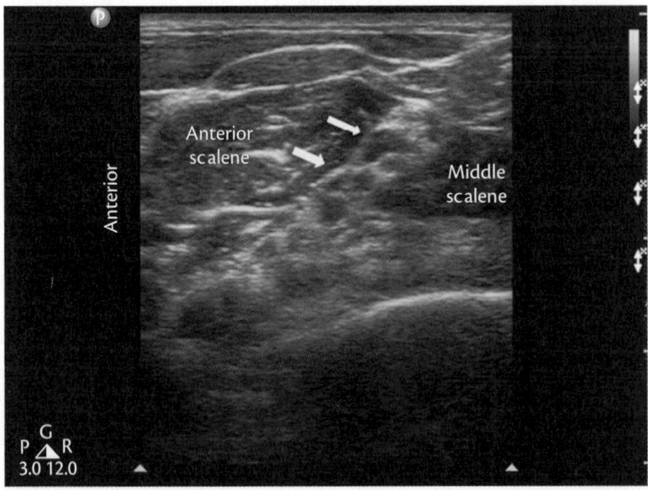

Figure 54.4 Ultrasound image of the interscalene brachial plexus.

tracing the nerves proximally from the supraclavicular region can facilitate nerve localization. Scanning from the midline may also be used to locate the nerves. Using this latter method, the trachea and overlying thyroid gland are identified, followed more laterally by the carotid and jugular vessels superficial to which lies the sternocleidomastoid muscle. The anterior scalene muscle subsequently lies lateral to the great vessels, underneath the tapering border of sternocleidomastoid. The vertebral artery may be visible medially below the level of C6. Doppler can be used to check for this and any other vessels. Once identified, the nerves may also be traced back to where they emerge from the intervertebral foraminae. The seventh cervical vertebra, which has no anterior tubercule, the prominent Chassaignac's (anterior) tubercle of C6, and the level of the vertebral artery can all aid in identification of the specific nerve roots. A nerve stimulator can also be used to confirm the identity of the nerves.

The needle may be introduced in plane or out of plane. An in-plane approach involves a lateral-to-medial direction with the needle passing through the middle scalene muscle towards the interscalene groove. As this direction is also towards the cervical spine and the vessels, care must be taken to ensure the needle tip is viewed at all times. It also technically risks damage to both the long thoracic and dorsal scapular nerves passing through this muscle. This method is still considered safer by some practitioners, however. As the block is superficial, the needle approach is relatively shallow and so good needle visualization should be possible. With the out-of-plane approach the needle tip is more difficult to visualize but it is inserted similarly to the nerve stimulator technique described earlier. This method, which follows the direction of nerve travel, may be particularly suited for catheter techniques. Unlike other blocks where circumferential spread is sought, this end-point for interscalene blocks has been called into question, particularly with the risk of nerve damage being higher in this block. A 'periplexus' injection (between the middle scalene muscle and plexus sheath) was just as effective as an intrasheath injection in one study, albeit slightly shorter in duration (Spence et al. 2011).

Authors' preferred technique

This is a combined ultrasound and nerve stimulation in-plane approach, maintaining good needle visualization at all times. A combined approach is used, the logic being that the nerve stimulator may provide additional information about intraneural needle placement (Neal and Wedel 2010). This is particularly important with the interscalene block as the risk of nerve damage may be greater with this block (see below). Using an in-plane needle approach the superior border of C6 nerve root or the upper trunk is the target, entering the fascial sheath. When the needle tip is next to the nerve the nerve stimulator is turned on, starting at 0 mA. The current is increased until an appropriate muscle twitch end-point is achieved, seeking only to ensure the MSC is greater than 0.4 mA. Animal studies, and some human data suggest a MSC of 0.2 mA is a relatively specific but non-sensitive indicator of intraneural needle placement (Macfarlane et al. 2011). Our practice in all US guided blocks is therefore to use nerve stimulation in conjunction with US, purely as an additional tool to try and prevent intraneural injection, and not for identification of nerves. In the absence of any evidence-based guidelines a MSC of 0.4 mA is chosen rather than 0.2 mA as an additional safety measure. The needle is only repositioned (usually withdrawn slightly) if the current is less than 0.4 mA. Local anaesthetic is then injected on the lateral side of the nerve roots aiming for spread cranially and caudally in the interscalene groove, but minimizing needle redirection to reduce iatrogenic nerve injury. Circumferential spread, as discussed above, is not sought. Levobupivacaine 0.375% 10 ml mixed with 1 mcg kg^{-1} clonidine (unless elderly when 0.5 mcg kg^{-1} is used) is injected for an analgesic block. Levobupivacaine 0.5% 15 ml is used for anaesthetic blocks and the supraclavicular nerves are blocked also if visible lying on the middle scalene muscle (Maybin et al. 2011). If spread to the anterior border of the anterior scalene muscle is observed the injection is halted, but even if this is not seen phrenic nerve palsy commonly still occurs albeit this rarely has a clinical effect in healthy patients.

Local anaesthetic choice and dosing

The choice of local anaesthetic is dependent on whether the block is for analgesia or anaesthesia and surgical factors such as operation, duration and magnitude. For shoulder surgery, a longer-acting agent such as ropivacaine or levobupivacaine is generally merited because of the significant postoperative discomfort and a single shot block may last up to 24 h if additives are used as described in 'Complications' (Cummings et al. 2011). Interestingly, addition of more rapid-onset local anaesthetic drugs has not been shown to hasten interscalene block onset and in fact reduced the block duration compared with longer-acting local anaesthetic alone (Gadsden et al. 2011). Levobupivacaine or ropivacaine 0.5–0.75% may be used for anaesthesia while lower concentrations are adequate for analgesia. Additives such as clonidine may be used but there is conflicting evidence as to whether this significantly prolongs block duration (Pöpping et al. 2009). Furthermore, larger doses of clonidine may contribute to hypotension in the deckchair position, particularly in elderly patients. Dexamethasone has, however, been reported to increase block duration by up to 12 h (Vieira et al. 2010; Cummings et al. 2011), possibly even if given intravenously rather than perineurally (Desmet et al. 2013).

The volume of local anaesthetic can influence the incidence of side-effects, although it is contentious as to whether this reduces efficacy. In one study, 5 ml reduced (but did not eliminate) the incidence of diaphragmatic palsy without affecting block success but other researchers found that reducing the volume to 5 ml increased the number of block failures (Riazi et al. 2008; Fredrickson et al. 2012). Reducing the volume to this level may also decrease proximal spread to branches of the superficial cervical plexus, which is important if the block is used as sole anaesthetic unless the surgeon infiltrates the port sites. A maximum of 15 ml should be sufficient with an accurate ultrasound-guided block. Volumes of 20–30 ml were previously recommended with nerve stimulation, although the minimum effective *analgesic* volume has been calculated to be 5.4 ml with nerve stimulation (albeit compared with 0.9 ml with ultrasound) (McNaught et al. 2011) with 10 ml also being shown to provide effective analgesia in other studies (Krone et al. 2001). If a catheter technique is used, a patient controlled bolus technique with either no or a very low continuous background rate (e.g. 5 ml bolus, 2 ml background rate) may be most appropriate, particularly in reducing unwanted motor block (Fredrickson et al. 2010). Levobupivacaine 0.125% or ropivacaine 0.2% are appropriate for continuous infusions.

Complications

Nerve damage is a potential complication of all nerve blocks but its incidence is reportedly higher for the interscalene block (Brull et al. 2007). This may be because of the relative lack of protective connective tissue surrounding the nerves at this level or as a result of the greater ratio of neural to connective tissue in proximal as opposed to distal nerves. Measures to reduce this risk, albeit not based on high-quality evidence, include not undertaking the block in an anaesthetized patient, ensuring no paraesthesia or pain on injection, careful needle tip visualization, avoidance of high injection pressures, and only injecting at a MSC above 0.2 mA (Gadsden et al. 2010). Local anaesthetic toxicity is another generic complication, the incidence of which should in theory be reduced by using ultrasound and lower doses of local anaesthetic as previously described. More specific complications include phrenic nerve palsy. Traditionally this was reported to occur in 100% of cases but using both ultrasound compared with nerve stimulation and reducing the volume of local anaesthetic independently reduce this figure (Riazi et al. 2008; Renes et al. 2009). However, in this latter study, even when using volumes of only 5 ml with ultrasound guidance, 45% of patients experienced diaphragmatic paralysis (although of a lesser severity than those who experienced paralysis at larger volumes of local anaesthetic). Bilateral interscalene blocks are therefore not recommended. Patients most sensitive to the reduction in lung function caused by phrenic nerve palsy include those with moderate to severe chronic obstructive pulmonary disease and obese patients. These conditions are not an absolute contraindication to an interscalene block but patients may require supplemental oxygen and overnight admission if desaturation occurs without supplemental oxygen. Contralateral lung pathologies such as a pneumothorax, pneumonectomy, or phrenic nerve palsy are also relative contraindications. Horner's syndrome results from proximal spread of local anaesthetic to the cervical sympathetic chain while recurrent laryngeal nerve palsy can cause hoarseness. Rare complications include spinal, epidural, or actual intervertebral injection. Avoidance of medial angulation or injecting close to where the roots emerge from the transverse processes should in theory reduce these complications. Vertebral artery or carotid injection can also occur with devastating effects. Finally, pneumothorax is also possible. In theory, ultrasound should reduce complications as many of the above-mentioned structures can be visualized. This has not been proved, however, and it must be remembered that ultrasound still relies upon good needle visualization and pattern recognition by the operator and therefore complications can still occur.

Supraclavicular block

Indications

The supraclavicular block targets the three trunks of the brachial plexus where they lie in close proximity to one another, before passing over the first rib. Kulenkampff introduced the block in 1911 and the predictable, rapid onset and dense anaesthesia resulted in it becoming referred to as the 'spinal of the arm'. However, because of the risk of pneumothorax (reported at rates of 6% in early studies) and the development of other approaches to the brachial plexus the popularity of the block declined (Brand and Papper 1961). Recently, with the advent of ultrasound and the ability to visualize the plexus and surrounding structures there has been a resurgence of interest in the supraclavicular block.

The only area of the upper limb not anaesthetized by a successful supraclavicular block is the inner aspect of the upper arm, which is supplied by the intercostobrachial nerve (a branch of the second intercostal nerve) (Figs 54.1, 54.2B). Nevertheless this does not generally affect tourniquet anaesthesia and the supraclavicular block alone provides excellent anaesthesia (and analgesia) for all surgical procedures on the upper outer arm, elbow, forearm and hand. Because the medial and lateral supraclavicular nerves (from the superficial cervical plexus) and the suprascapular nerve (see interscalene section) have already branched off proximally, the supraclavicular block has traditionally not been utilized for shoulder surgery. Recently, however, data from a large prospective registry revealed an ultrasound-guided supraclavicular approach was as effective for shoulder surgery anaesthesia as an interscalene block when used with fentanyl, propofol and midazolam sedation (Liu et al. 2010). The block appeared to function as a caudal approach to the interscalene block, but although hoarseness was less with the supraclavicular block there was no difference in respiratory complications. Hand procedures that require only a brief period of tourniquet time (< 30 min approximately) may be anaesthetized with more distal peripheral nerve blocks alone or intravenous regional anaesthesia to reduce the risk of complications discussed later. Catheter techniques are also possible, but the supraclavicular block is more commonly used as a single-injection technique. The infraclavicular region is a better location for securing a catheter and there is some evidence that an infraclavicular catheter provides superior analgesia when compared with the supraclavicular technique (Mariano et al. 2011).

One limitation with the ultrasound-guided supraclavicular block is that in a proportion of patients the ulnar nerve is not adequately blocked. This has been reported to be as high as 30% in some studies and 15% in other large series, despite targeting the 'corner pocket' described in the 'Ultrasound' subsection (Fredrickson et al. 2009; Brull and Chan 2011). While this can be easily rectified with supplementation in the forearm, elbow, or the axilla, this should be remembered when surgery involving the ulnar nerve distribution is planned.

Anatomy

The five main roots forming the brachial plexus (C5–8 and T1) pass inferolaterally in the neck between the anterior and middle scalene muscles, merging to form the superior, middle, and inferior trunks (Fig. 54.1) in the supraclavicular fossa. This fossa is bounded by the clavicle inferiorly, the trapezius muscle posterolaterally, and the sternocleidomastoid muscle medially. The scalene muscles insert onto the first rib, with the nerves between passing across the rib posterolateral to the supraclavicular artery, and then underneath approximately the mid-point of the clavicle where they split into the anterior and posterior divisions.

Most of the potential complications of the supraclavicular block, as discussed later, arise from the proximity of surrounding structures. Many of these are the same structures described previously for the interscalene block such as the phrenic nerve running obliquely across the anterior scalene muscle, the vertebral artery entering the foramen transversarium at the sixth cervical vertebra, medial to scalenus anterior, the dome of the pleura rising up above the sternal end of the first rib, again medial to scalenus anterior, and the thoracic duct lying in the root of the neck on the left-hand side. Again on both sides the recurrent laryngeal nerve lies between the trachea and oesophagus and the cervical sympathetic chain is located medial to the anterior scalene muscle.

Technique

As with all blocks, and as noted previously (Neal et al. 2008a), the supraclavicular block should be undertaken in awake or lightly sedated patients where possible. A small dose of sedative such as midazolam generally provides sufficient conditions. Only rarely should a small dose of fast-acting opioid also be required. Either nerve stimulator or ultrasound may be used, or a combination of both. The techniques are described in the following subsections. Ultrasound has been shown to improve the success rates of this block compared with using nerve stimulation alone (Williams et al. 2003).

Nerve stimulator

The most commonly used techniques are the plumb-bob approach, with or without minor modifications and the Winnie subclavian perivascular approach (Winnie and Collins 1964; Brown et al. 1993). The modified plumb-bob approach described in the following paragraph was designed to reduce the risk of pneumothorax, the prevalence of which has previously been reported to lie between 0.5% and 6% (Brand and Papper 1961). In theory this risk should be reduced using ultrasound but as yet there has been no large comparative trial, and indeed one case of pneumothorax has already been reported despite using ultrasound (Bhatia et al. 2010).

A 50 mm insulated block needle is chosen and an appropriate mixture of local anaesthetic prepared. The patient is positioned supine with the head turned slightly away from the side to be blocked, and the arm to be blocked adducted by the patient's side. The insertion of the clavicular head of sternomastoid on the clavicle is an important landmark as the dome of the pleura lies medially. The needle should therefore not pass medial to this point in the parasagittal plane. If possible, the groove between the scalene muscles should be palpated in the neck, and followed down to the supraclavicular fossa where, within a space 2.5 cm lateral to the insertion of the clavicular head of the sternomastoid, the brachial plexus may be palpable in thin individuals. The pulsation of the subclavian artery crossing above the first rib may also be palpable. In this case, the plexus is known to lie lateral and slightly posterior to the pulsation. A 50 mm needle connected to a nerve stimulator is then inserted about 1 cm behind the clavicle in an anteroposterior direction, with no medial but a slight caudal orientation (Fig. 54.5). It should be remembered that the depth of the plexus is sometimes

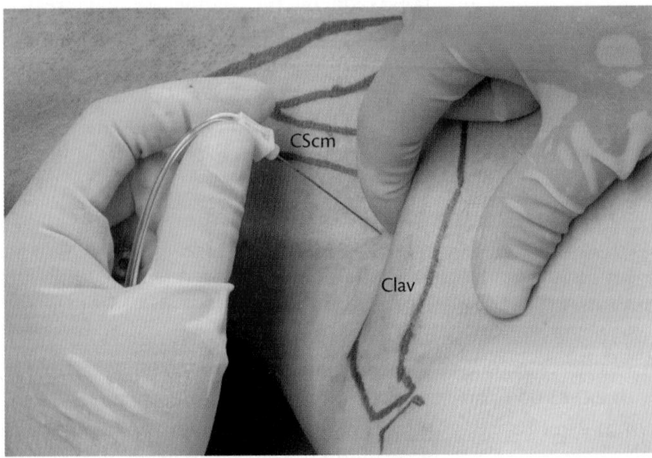

Figure 54.5 Surface landmarks and needle insertion for nerve stimulator-guided supraclavicular block. Clav, clavicle; CScm, clavicular head of sternomastoid muscle.

less than 2 cm and the lung lies medially. Shoulder twitches represent upper trunk stimulation. Ideally finger twitches should be obtained, as this represents stimulation of the lower trunk and may improve success rates (Franco et al. 2004). Injection can then be carried out after aspiration to exclude intravascular needle placement. Pectoralis muscle twitches suggest anterior needle placement, scapular twitches suggest posterior placement, while aspiration of blood may indicate the needle is too medial or too anterior. Magnetic resonance imaging studies suggest that initially the needle should be angulated slightly cephalad, particularly if no twitches are obtained (Klaastad et al. 2003).

Ultrasound

This is an intermediate level ultrasound-guided nerve block. A high-frequency linear probe should be chosen with depth settings around 2–4 cm. The patient should be positioned supine or slightly head-up with the head turned slightly to the contralateral side. The probe is then orientated in the supraclavicular fossa in the coronal oblique plane. The hypoechoic pulsatile subclavian artery should first be identified, lying on the hyperechoic first rib. The hyperechoic pleura, which 'slides' during respiration and lies underneath the first rib, should then be visualized at either edge of the first rib. The pleura are not visible underneath the rib with ultrasound. The brachial plexus trunks and divisions lie posterolaterally to the artery and are hypoechoic at this level. The probe should be tilted to ensure the plexus is visualized on top of the rib and not the pleura (Fig. 54.6). In this manner, the rib acts as a backstop, if the needle is in line with the ultrasound beam, and therefore is a safety feature in preventing a pneumothorax. Colour Doppler should be used to identify any vessels that may lie in the path or vicinity of the needle. Both the hypoechoic transverse cervical and suprascapular arteries may be seen in either longitudinal or transverse section among or above the plexus and may be confused with nerves unless Doppler is used. The plexus may be approached in plane in a medial-to-lateral, or lateral-to-medial direction. Large vessels, as previously described, may make a lateral to medial approach either technically more dangerous or indeed occasionally impossible. Both of these ultrasound techniques are a completely different approach to the classical nerve stimulator technique. With either approach, however, the aim is to initially target the 'corner pocket', ensuring local anaesthetic is deposited around the inferior trunk (Soares et al. 2007). The lateral-to-medial approach allows a more direct path to the corner pocket whereas the medial-to-lateral approach may be safer as the needle is moving parallel (as opposed to towards) the pleura. However, in this approach navigating around the subclavian artery makes reaching the 'corner pocket' technically more difficult. Neither technique has been shown to be superior (Subramanyam et al. 2011). With either approach, local anaesthetic is infiltrated in the skin and the needle carefully inserted towards the corner pocket. At all times, the needle tip must always be maintained in view or its position inferred by hydrolocation in order to minimize the risk of pneumothorax. A nerve stimulator may be used to confirm the identity of nerves, aiming to achieve hand twitches. After injecting at the corner pocket, the nerves are often seen to rise and 'float' towards the surface. The needle is then withdrawn and redirected towards the remaining trunks and divisions, ensuring all are surrounded by local anaesthetic. While some work has suggested that a double-injection technique rather than a single 'corner pocket' injection improves block onset, the extra time performing the block actually negated this benefit.

Authors' preferred technique

The authors' preferred technique is an ultrasound-guided approach, in plane and lateral to medial. After injecting in the corner pocket as previously described, each of the trunks and divisions in turn is targeted and circumferential spread sought as an end-point. Nerve stimulation is used to confirm absence of intraneural placement, as discussed previously, by keeping the output current at 0.4 mA and withdrawing the needle slightly if stimulation occurs at that current. A 50:50 mixture of lidocaine and adrenaline (epinephrine)

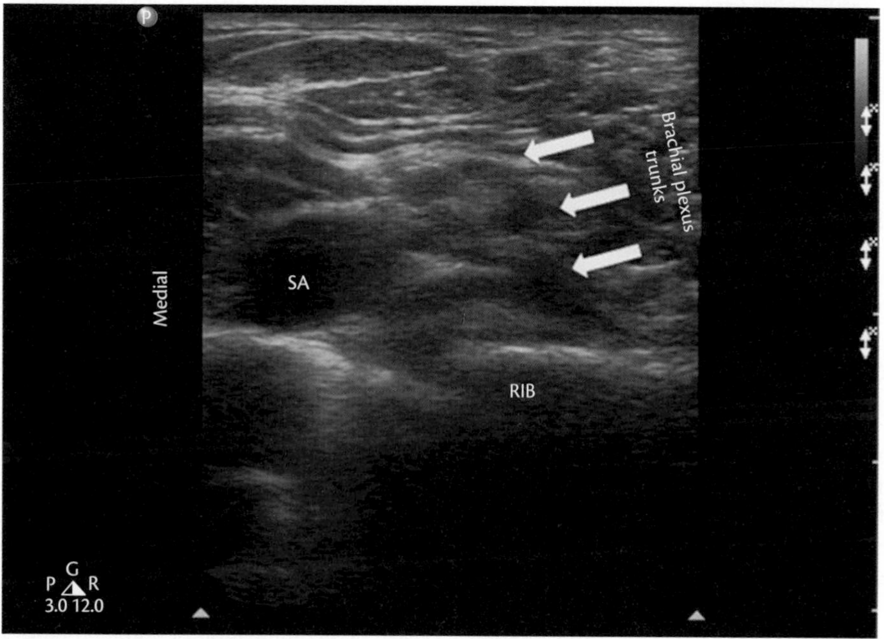

Figure 54.6 Ultrasound image of the supraclavicular brachial plexus.

1.5% and levobupivacaine 0.5% is used in a volume of around 25–30 ml for anaesthetic blocks, ensuring spread as already described. Levobupivacaine 0.25% is used for analgesic blocks.

Local anaesthetic choice and dosing

The choice of local anaesthetic is dependent on the duration and magnitude of surgery and whether analgesia or anaesthesia is the purpose of the block. For nerve stimulator blocks, 30–40 ml is required. When using ultrasound compared with a nerve stimulator, the volume of local anaesthetic required does not appear to be reduced, unlike other ultrasound-guided blocks. The ED_{50} with ultrasound was found to be 23 ml, with the more clinically relevant ED_{95} 42 ml (Duggan et al. 2009). Levobupivacaine 0.5% provides 3–4 h of anaesthesia. In longer cases, both tourniquet and general positioning discomfort can become limiting factors without additional analgesia and sedation. Adding dexamethasone to mepivacaine supraclavicular blocks has been shown to prolong block duration by approximately 100 min (Parrington et al. 2010).

Complications

Nerve damage is a rare but feared complication of all nerve blocks (Brull et al. 2007). More specifically, phrenic nerve palsy is reported to be as high as 67% (Knoblanche 1979) although it is generally asymptomatic in patients without underlying lung disease. Care must be taken, however, in those with severe pre-existing lung disease because a phrenic nerve palsy may further exacerbate respiratory function. A distal infraclavicular or axillary block is an alternative option in such patients. One comparative study demonstrated that when using the same volume (20 ml) of ropivacaine 0.75%, ultrasound reduced the risk of diaphragmatic palsy to 0% compared with 53% when using a nerve stimulator (Renes et al. 2009). This benefit of ultrasound has not been examined in other large studies as yet. The risk of pneumothorax was discussed previously and it must be remembered that this does not always present clinically at the time. For this reason, some practitioners prefer not to use supraclavicular blocks in day surgery although this is not the authors' practice. Ultrasound has been used routinely by some practitioners to exclude pneumothorax before discharge. Because of the risk of pneumothorax or phrenic nerve palsy, bilateral supraclavicular blocks should not be undertaken. Vascular puncture, involving either the subclavian artery or the other vessels in the vicinity of the plexus, is also a possible complication, leading to either local anaesthetic toxicity or haematoma. Ultrasound has been shown to reduce the incidence of vascular puncture during peripheral nerve blocks (Abrahams et al. 2009). Horner's syndrome and hoarseness are other possible side-effects. Suprascapular nerve palsy has also been reported after supraclavicular block.

Infraclavicular block

Indications

The infraclavicular block aims to place injectate at the level of the three brachial plexus cords lying around the second part of the axillary artery in the apex of the axilla. This block is suitable for all types of upper limb surgery except shoulder surgery and is also particularly suited to the placement of a continuous catheter as the catheter tip is deeply situated and not easily dislodged. In addition, a catheter is easily secured to the anterior chest wall at this location. Several different techniques and modifications have been developed since Bazy and Labat's original description of the block, but overall the infraclavicular block has a good success rate with a similar rate of complications to other brachial plexus blocks except for phrenic nerve palsy which is lower with the more distal infraclavicular approaches (see later) compared with supraclavicular block (Chin et al. 2013). Distal infraclavicular blocks therefore are a superior choice (as is the axillary block) in patients with respiratory disease. Recent studies comparing the infraclavicular and supraclavicular blocks have found the infraclavicular block to be superior (Fredrickson and Wolstencroft 2011). If the patient is unable to abduct their arm to allow access to the axilla then again the infraclavicular block may be indicated.

More recently, ultrasound-guided approaches have been described. While some studies have demonstrated shorter performance times these have not, unlike most other ultrasound-guided blocks, demonstrated any increased success with ultrasound (Sauter et al. 2008; Taboada et al. 2009; Gelfand et al. 2011). Insertion of a catheter using ultrasound guidance has been shown, however, to be more successful than with nerve stimulation (Mariano et al. 2009). Some ultrasound techniques also utilize a perivascular injection technique around the second part of the axillary artery, rather than targeting the cords themselves, necessitating fewer injection endpoints (Fredrickson et al. 2010). Success rates have been high and complication rates very low using this more simple method.

Anatomy

The boundaries of the infraclavicular fossa are the pectoralis minor and major muscles anteriorly, ribs and intercostal muscles medially, the clavicle and coracoid process superiorly, and the humerus laterally. The cords of the brachial plexus (Fig. 54.1) are formed as they cross the first rib, pass under the clavicle, and wrap around the second part of the axillary artery. Here, the lateral cord lies most superficial and is lateral to the artery. The posterior cord lies deeper to the lateral cord, posterior to the artery while the medial cord lies in a variable position from posterior to inferomedial to the artery. The pleura lies deep and medial to the plexus and therefore medial needle manipulation during infraclavicular block (especially with non-ultrasound techniques) is not advised. More laterally the subscapularis muscle lies deep to the plexus. The musculocutaneous nerve leaves the lateral cord in a variable manner, and sometimes quite proximal in the axilla (Pianezza et al. 2012). This may explain why failure to block this nerve can occur with the infraclavicular block, particularly when using techniques that aim more laterally (Minville et al. 2005).

Technique

A variety of techniques have been described including, from proximal to distal along the axillary artery, the vertical infraclavicular, the Raj, the coracoid, and the parasagittal approaches (Neal et al. 2008b). While complications, as discussed later, appear to reduce the more distal the plexus is approached, no technique has been shown to be superior in efficacy compared with another. As with all blocks, the infraclavicular block should preferably be undertaken in awake patients (Neal et al. 2008a). A small amount of sedative such as midazolam generally provides sufficient conditions but as the nerves in the infraclavicular approach are deeper and are approached by passage through the pectoralis muscles (particularly in the more distal techniques), a small amount of fast-acting opioid may also be required. Either nerve stimulator or ultrasound may be used, or a combination of both and these are described in the following subsections. Ultrasound, as noted previously, has not been found as yet to increase success rates of this block.

Nerve stimulator

The modified coracoid method, targeting the posterior cord to achieve high success rates, is described here (Wilson et al. 1998). This technique has the advantage of a consistent, palpable bony landmark (even in obese patients) and the arm does not need to be abducted. With the patient supine and the arm adducted, an 80 mm needle is inserted 2 cm medial and 2 cm inferior to the coracoid process, perpendicular to the skin until lateral cord stimulation is observed (Fig. 54.7). The needle should then be manipulated inferiorly and posteriorly until posterior cord stimulation is obtained. The cords are reached at a mean distance of 4.24 cm in men and 4.01 cm in women. A total of 30–40 ml of local anaesthetic is then injected with frequent negative aspiration. Several studies have determined that posterior cord or distal hand movement increases the success of the block (Bloc et al. 2007). This is logical because the posterior cord lies between the medial and lateral cords. Acceptance of proximal muscle twitches (biceps) or lateral cord stimulation can be associated with block failure in as many as 50% of patients (Borgeat et al. 2001). As noted previously, this is because the musculocutaneous nerve leaves the plexus before the coracoid process in a large proportion of patients. Dual (and triple) stimulation compared with single stimulation also appears to increase success (Rodriguez et al. 2004; Akyildiz et al. 2009) although it has been demonstrated that single stimulation of the posterior cord is actually more effective than dual stimulation of any other two non-posterior cord responses (Rodriguez et al. 2010).

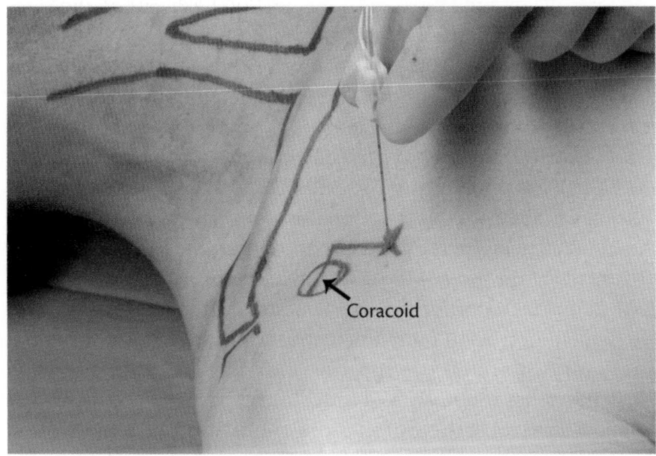

Figure 54.7 Surface landmarks and needle insertion for nerve stimulator-guided infraclavicular block (coracoid approach).

Ultrasound

This is an intermediate level ultrasound-guided block mainly because the target is relatively deep (4–6 cm) and the angle to reach the target can be steep in relation to the ultrasound probe making needle visualization difficult. In order to perform the block, a linear 10–13 MHz probe or a curvilinear probe can be used depending on availability and patient habitus. The patient is placed supine with the arm adducted, although abduction of the arm may improve visualization of the three cords. With the probe in a sagittal orientation, the second part of the axillary artery is visualized deep to pectoralis major and minor. During this pre-procedural scan the pleura should be visualized medially and the probe then moved laterally. The cords may be seen as hyperechoic structures posterior, medial, and lateral to the artery in varying positions (Fig. 54.8). Each cord can then be targeted, or more simply a needle insertion point can be chosen that allows approach to the posterior aspect of the artery (Fredrickson et al. 2010). In practice, this usually involves an insertion immediately inferior to the clavicle, usually at an angle greater than 45° (Kalagara et al. 2015). Successful placement is then associated with local anaesthetic spread immediately posterior to the artery that also causes the artery to be pushed anterior ('double-bubble' sign) (Tran et al. 2006). Spread that is too anterior without spread posterior to the artery or spread that is too deep and not well visualized will both either result in very slow block onset or block failure (Porter et al. 2005).

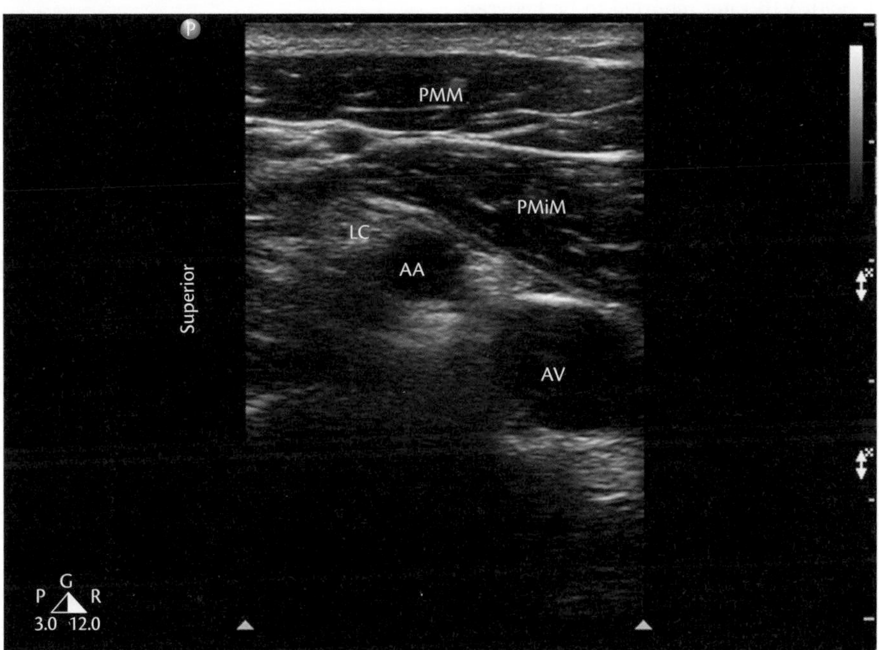

Figure 54.8 Ultrasound image of the infraclavicular brachial plexus. AA, axillary artery; AV, axillary vein; LC, lateral cord; PMiM, pectoralis minor muscle; PMM, pectoralis major muscle.

Authors' preferred technique

The perivascular ultrasound technique is the authors' preferred method because of the simplicity and lack of need to achieve stimulation end-points for block success. As before, nerve stimulation is used to confirm absence of intraneural placement by keeping the output current at 0.4 mA and withdrawing the needle slightly if stimulation occurs at that current. A total volume of approximately 30 ml of ropivacaine 0.5% is used. A catheter technique where the tip is placed immediately posterior to the axillary artery also provides very successful postoperative analgesia.

Local anaesthetic choice and dosing

The choice of local anaesthetic is dependent on the duration and magnitude of surgery and whether analgesia or anaesthesia is the purpose of the block. A systematic review concluded that at least 40 ml was required to improve the *anaesthetic* efficacy of the infraclavicular block (Chin et al. 2013). While the majority of the studies included in this review were nerve stimulator guided rather than ultrasound guided, it has been since shown that the minimum effective volume in 90% of patients was 35 ml when using a single-injection ultrasound-guided technique (Tran et al. 2011). The optimal dose when using a catheter has not been extensively studied but in one study the optimal regimen was found to be an 8 ml h^{-1} infusion with a 4 ml bolus compared with either a larger volume continuous infusion with no bolus or a bolus alone with no infusion (Ilfeld et al. 2004).

Complications

As previously noted, nerve damage is a potential complication of all nerve blocks. Most other complications of the infraclavicular block appear to be increased the more proximal/medial the approach. Phrenic nerve palsy, as previously discussed, is significantly less common with the infraclavicular block than the interscalene or supraclavicular blocks, with rates being reported as 25% with the (proximal) vertical infraclavicular block (VIB) but zero with the coracoid approach. Pneumothorax similarly is less common than the supraclavicular block, with VIB rates reported to be between 0.2% and 0.7% and 0.7% also for the coracoid approach (Desroches 2003). Vascular puncture is another possible complication, but this should be reduced by ultrasound (Abrahams et al. 2009). It is more difficult to compress a vessel in this location, however, than in the axilla. Other complications are rare but include Horner's syndrome, which again is more common in the proximal (vertical) approach.

Axillary block

Indications

The axillary block is a simple and safe brachial plexus block technique with a lower incidence of complications compared with more proximal approaches (Neal et al. 2008b). In particular, there is no risk of phrenic nerve palsy or pneumothorax making it a good choice in patients with significant respiratory disease. It provides suitable anaesthesia or analgesia, or both, for all types of forearm and hand surgery with one caveat being the musculocutaneous nerve must be blocked if surgery is performed on the lateral forearm or 'snuffbox' area of the wrist. The axillary block is less well suited to elbow or proximal arm surgery and in these cases a more proximal technique such as supraclavicular or infraclavicular block should be chosen. An axillary anaesthetic block has been shown to facilitate earlier discharge after hand surgery than a general anaesthetic technique but otherwise there is no evidence that long-term outcome is superior (McCartney et al. 2004). A continuous technique has been described for axillary block. However, the infraclavicular site is preferable for this purpose because of the closer proximity of nerves to each other (ensuring greater coverage of analgesia) and ease of securing the catheter to the anterior chest wall.

Anatomy

The axilla is a truncated pyramid in shape, with the apex directed upwards and medially towards the neck. The apex (bounded anteriorly by the clavicle, posteriorly by the scapula, and medially by the outer border of the first rib) is continuous with the superior aperture of the thorax and the root of the neck and it is through here that the cords of the brachial plexus travel, surrounding the axillary artery as described earlier. The other boundaries of the axilla are the pectoralis muscles anteriorly, the serratus anterior muscles and ribcage medially, while the posterior wall is formed by subscapularis above and teres major and latissimus dorsi below. The lateral boundary is formed by the humerus, coracobrachialis, and biceps. At the lateral border of the pectoralis minor muscle the cords divide into the four major terminal nerves of the plexus, namely the musculocutaneous, median, ulnar, and radial nerves. The median, ulnar, and radial nerves classically lie in characteristic positions within an incomplete sheath in close proximity to the axillary artery, but there can be significant variability in this traditional anatomy (Retzl et al. 2001). The musculocutaneous nerve generally arises from the lateral cord more proximally at the level of the coracoid and runs between biceps and coracobrachialis, outside the fascial sheath. At the level of the axilla, the median nerve and musculocutaneous nerves lie superior to the artery (musculocutaneous superior and more lateral) whereas the ulnar nerve lies inferiorly and radial more posteriorly. The medial cutaneous nerves of the arm and forearm have already branched off the medial cord and lie more superficially, sometimes also outside the fascial sheath. In addition to the brachial plexus and the axillary vessels, the contents of the axilla include lymph nodes, fat, and the intercostobrachial and long thoracic nerves. This lack of vital structures (other than the nerves and vessels) explains why this is the safest approach to the brachial plexus.

Technique

Before the use of ultrasound, two common methods of performing axillary brachial plexus block existed. The first was a transarterial technique using the axillary artery. This was commonly used, especially in North America, but while it had a reasonable success rate, high volumes of local anaesthetic were required (40–60 ml) and this approach will not be described further. The nerve stimulation technique then became increasingly popular, especially in the United Kingdom and Europe and this is described in the following subsections. Ultrasound, however, has now replaced nerve stimulation as the nerve localization method of choice in many centres. Ultrasound has been shown to reduce the time to perform the block and improve overall efficacy, and reduce overall incidence of minor adverse effects such as pain on injection and bruising as well as more serious adverse effects such as convulsions (Lo et al. 2008). Again, as with all blocks, it is recommended that this block is undertaken awake if possible (Neal et al. 2008a). A small dose of sedative such as midazolam is generally sufficient.

Nerve stimulation

The median, ulnar, radial, and musculocutaneous nerves all need to be anaesthetized for a successful block. However, studies have demonstrated that in order to block all four nerves it is only actually necessary to seek and deliver local anaesthetic around the radial, median, and musculocutaneous nerves (Koscielniak-Nielsen 2006). This is likely because the needle path often passes the ulnar nerve en route to the radial, and spread of local anaesthetic will usually reach the ulnar from the site of injection for the radial. Multiple injection techniques targeting the specific nerves with a nerve stimulator have clearly been shown to be superior to traditional single- and even double-injection techniques targeting only one or two nerves (Chin and Handoll 2011).

To undertake the block, the patient is positioned supine with the arm abducted to around 90° and the elbow flexed, resting on a pillow. The axillary artery is the major surface landmark for this block and should be palpated at the level of the pectoralis major muscle (Fig. 54.9). After local infiltration, a stimulating needle set at 2 Hz with a current of 1–1.5 mA is used to seek target nerves, remembering the anatomy as previously described whereby musculocutaneous (*elbow flexion*) and median nerves (*finger flexion, forearm pronation*) generally lie above the arterial pulsation while radial (*wrist, finger extension*) and ulnar (*thumb adduction* and *flexion of the ring and little fingers*) lie below. The radial nerve is usually located deeper to the ulnar nerve and so if the ulnar nerve is identified the needle should be advanced further and often upwards, behind the artery until a radial twitch is achieved. When the appropriate twitch is identified, the current should be reduced to reach no less than 0.4 mA and local anaesthetic injected. The intercostobrachial nerve lies superficially and can be blocked by subcutaneous infiltration from the superior margin of the biceps at the anterior axillary line to the border of the triceps muscle.

Ultrasound

A variety of ultrasound-guided techniques have been described, all of which are basic level blocks. Commonly the four individual nerves can be sought and anaesthetized. This may be undertaken at the level of the axilla or more distally at the level of the mid humerus. It is also possible, however, to use a simpler method such as that described by Bernucci et al. (2012) or Sites et al. (2006) who both used larger volumes at two sites around the axillary artery with a very high success rate.

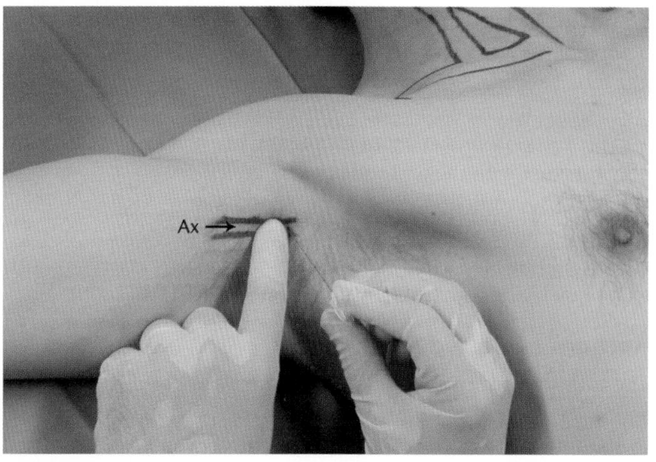

Figure 54.9 Landmarks and positioning for nerve stimulator-guided axillary nerve block. Ax, axillary artery.

For the axillary block, a high-frequency linear probe is chosen because of the superficial nature of the target structures (8–15 MHz). The arm is positioned as described for the nerve stimulator-guided block. The probe is placed transversely in the axilla where the nerves can be identified as hyperechoic structures surrounding the pulsatile, hypoechoic axillary artery. Enough pressure should be applied to occlude the axillary vein(s). In this short-axis view the median nerve usually lies in the 9–1 o'clock position, with the ulnar nerve between 1 and 4 o'clock and the radial nerve (often most difficult to identify) between 3 and 6 o'clock (Fig. 54.10). The musculocutaneous nerve appears flatter and lies between biceps and coracobrachialis and can be seen to move towards the artery when the probe is moved proximally. Either an in-plane or out-of-plane method can be used to approach the nerves. Using an in-plane approach, and after skin infiltration, a 22 G needle is introduced on the lateral/superior aspect of the probe (in which case the musculocutaneous and median nerves are closest to the needle tip). Approaching from medially/inferiorly is possible but can be ergonomically more challenging. Nerve stimulation may be used to confirm target identity but can be an unnecessary distraction as experience is gained. If the radial nerve is difficult to identify, local anaesthetic can be injected

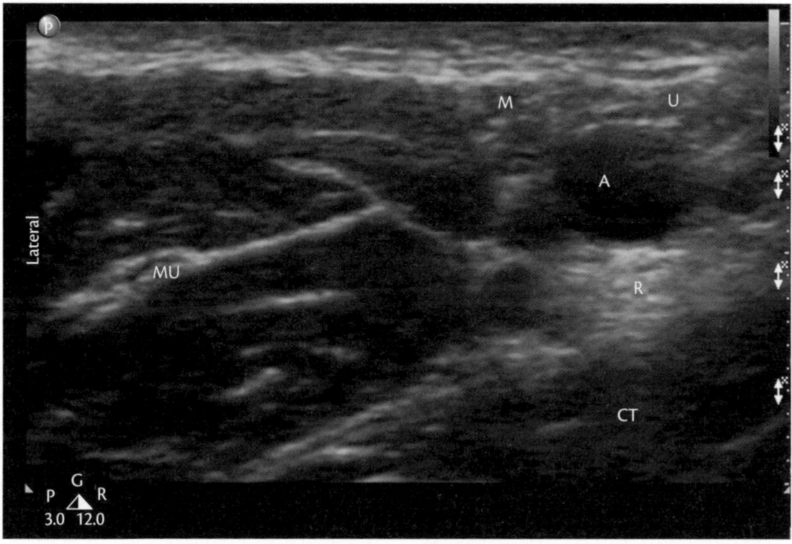

Figure 54.10 Ultrasound image of the axillary brachial plexus. A, axillary artery; CT, conjoint tendon; M, median nerve; MU, musculocutaneous nerve; R, radial nerve; U, ulnar nerve.

at around 6 o'clock, below the artery where it lies above the conjoint tendon of the latissimus dorsi and teres major muscles (Gray 2009). The radial nerve almost invariably is in this location and the contrast effect of the local anaesthetic often reveals the nerve. The nerve can also be traced from distally to proximally where it can be seen running together with the profunda brachii artery.

For those with less confidence about identifying individual nerves, the much simpler Sites technique involves injecting a larger volume (20 ml) both above and below the axillary artery and this technique has produced high success rates (Sites et al. 2006).

Authors' preferred technique

The authors' preferred technique is an ultrasound-guided, in-plane approach with the probe held in a transverse position just proximal to the mid-humeral level. A short-bevelled needle is introduced from the lateral side and usually the radial, ulnar, median, and musculocutaneous nerves are blocked sequentially. The authors currently only use nerve stimulation to confirm absence of intraneural placement by keeping the output current at 0.4 mA and withdrawing the needle slightly if stimulation occurs at that current. A volume of 15–30 ml of ropivacaine or levobupivacaine 0.5% is used.

Local anaesthetic choice and dosing

As with other brachial plexus techniques the choice of local anaesthetic depends on the duration and magnitude of surgery. A common choice is ropivacaine 0.5% in volumes of 15–30 ml depending on technique. Use of adrenaline in the solution (1:200 000) will provide a suitable marker of intravascular injection. Small volumes of local anaesthetic (3–5 ml) can be used at each nerve for successful block although volumes as low as 1 ml per nerve have been successful using ultrasound (O'Donnell et al. 2010). Such low-volume blocks, however, risk not providing cover to the cutaneous nerves of the forearm and arm. A medium duration local anaesthetic (e.g. lidocaine) may be used for the axillary block combined with forearm blocks using longer-acting local anaesthetic solution (bupivacaine or ropivacaine), especially when surgery only involves one or two terminal nerve distributions and sparing of long-lasting motor block in non-surgical areas is desired.

Complications

Transient neuropathy, as with all blocks, is a possibility. Permanent neuropathy, however, is much rarer (Brull et al. 2007). Pain, paraesthesia, or a high-pressure injection may indicate intraneural needle placement and should therefore alert the operator to stop injecting and reposition the needle. Other common complications of the axillary block include bruising, haematoma, and pain in the axilla although this has been reduced with ultrasound methods (Lo et al. 2008). Phrenic nerve block and pneumothorax are not features of the axillary block and as such make this technique very suitable for patients with severe respiratory disease. Vascular puncture is the commonest serious complication and therefore careful aspiration before and frequently during injection should be undertaken. In addition, the use of adrenaline, ensuring the axillary veins are compressed by adequate probe pressure, and stopping injection if no anaesthetic spread is visualized with ultrasound (possibly signifying intravascular injection) are further methods to reduce the possibility of intravascular injection. Compression of the artery in case of accidental puncture, unlike in the supraclavicular or infraclavicular regions, is easy in the axillary block. Convulsions, either through direct intravascular injection or local anaesthetic absorption (and so slower in onset) after axillary block, occur in approximately 1:1000 blocks, especially with non-ultrasound methods. Ultrasound itself, however, will not completely protect against this complication. As with all blocks, observation and standard monitoring of the patient should therefore be undertaken for signs of local anaesthetic toxicity.

Table 54.1 summarizes the advantages, disadvantages, and complications for the different approaches to the brachial plexus.

Forearm and wrist blocks

Indications

The median, radial, and ulnar nerve can all be anaesthetized at the elbow, forearm, or wrist. At this level these blocks are suitable primarily for hand surgery, either as supplementation for an incomplete brachial plexus block or for targeted analgesia in combination with a general anaesthetic. These blocks may also be used as the sole anaesthetic for short-duration hand procedures (longer operative times of more than 20–30 min are generally limited by tourniquet pain), therefore sparing the patient the risks of a general anaesthetic or proximal brachial plexus anaesthetic block (as described earlier). Applied anatomical knowledge is, as always, important. For example, forearm sensation arises from the medial and lateral cutaneous nerves of the forearm (Fig. 54.2) and therefore supplementing a failed block with median or ulnar block alone at the elbow will be of no value in providing complete anaesthesia for forearm surgery.

Whereas traditional landmark and nerve stimulator-based techniques rely upon vascular or tendon landmarks at the elbow or wrist to locate the nerves, ultrasound allows the nerve to be located and blocked anywhere in the forearm, away from vascular structures and potentially reducing the risk of vascular injury. Ultrasound also allows a reduced volume to be used compared with nerve stimulation techniques although this reduced the duration of the block (Ponrouch et al. 2010). Furthermore, high-resolution ultrasound can now also be used to reliably identify the smaller cutaneous nerves of the upper limb such as the medial and lateral cutaneous nerves of the forearm noted previously, although the reader is referred to specialist regional anaesthesia texts for descriptions of these latter nerve blocks.

Anatomy

The median nerve at the elbow is located medial to the brachial artery. In the cubital fossa it gives off branches to several of the forearm flexors before travelling distally between the superficial and deep flexor muscles, providing further motor supply (anterior interosseous nerve) en route. At the wrist, the nerve lies in the carpal tunnel, between and slightly underneath the tendons of flexor carpi radialis laterally and palmaris longus medially. Terminal digital branches supply the thumb, index, middle, and radial side of the ring fingers. The corresponding palmar area is supplied by the palmar cutaneous branch, which arises from the median nerve at or proximal to the wrist. The ulnar nerve enters the forearm via the condylar groove at the elbow. It travels on the medial side of the forearm, deep to the flexor carpi ulnaris before coming to lie medial to the ulnar artery in the distal half of the forearm. At the wrist it emerges lateral to the tendon of the flexor carpi ulnaris. The ulnar nerve supplies most of the intrinsic muscles of the hand with the dorsal and palmar branches, which branch off in the distal forearm, supplying sensation to the ulnar half of the ring finger and the little finger, and the corresponding dorsal and palmar areas of the hand. The radial nerve leaves the spiral groove of the humerus in the distal arm and passes between the

Table 54.1 Indications, advantages, and disadvantages for different brachial plexus nerve blocks

	Interscalene	Supraclavicular	Infraclavicular	Axillary
Indications	Shoulder Elbow	(Shoulder) Arm Elbow Forearm Hand	Arm Elbow Forearm Hand	(Elbow) Forearm Hand
Advantages	Shoulder analgesia Superficial Small volumes local anaesthetic possible	Nerves closest together at this point—rapid onset, high success, good coverage of upper limb Possible if unable to abduct arm	Good location for catheter insertion Lateral approach safer if respiratory disease Possible if unable to abduct arm No phrenic nerve palsy with lateral approaches	No risk in respiratory disease Safest Vessels easily compressible Small volumes local anaesthetic possible
Disadvantages	Phrenic nerve palsy (can still occur even in low-dose techniques) Highest risk of nerve injury	Phrenic nerve palsy in up to 50% Risk of pneumothorax More difficult to compress vessel if punctured	Risk of pneumothorax (reduces with more lateral approaches) More uncomfortable More difficult to compress vessel if punctured	Vascular puncture risk highest Not possible if arm cannot be abducted Need multiple injections for success
Other complications*	Spinal injection Epidural injection Vertebral artery injection Pneumothorax Horner's syndromes	Horner's syndrome		

* Nerve injury and local anaesthetic toxicity are possible complications of all blocks.

lateral intermuscular septum to lie between brachialis and brachioradialis. It branches into superficial (supplying the dorsum of the hand) and deep (motor and sensory) branches at around the level of the radio-humeral joint line. Distally, each of the branches can be traced in the forearm with ultrasound. The superficial branch runs lateral to the radial artery deep to brachioradialis and supplies the dorsal radial surface of the hand. The deep branch moves under supinator and winds round the radius supplying the hand extensor muscles and the wrist capsules. The terminal (sensory) branch of the musculocutaneous nerve, the lateral cutaneous nerve of the forearm, can be located with ultrasound at the elbow lateral to the biceps tendon and superficial to brachialis muscle. It is not discussed further here, however.

Cross-innervation of the hand can occur as a result of connections between the nerves at the level of either the brachial plexus or more distally. This combined with anatomical variations in the classical nerve supply to the hand means that relying on a single targeted nerve block may not provide complete anaesthesia. It has therefore been suggested that all nerves must be individually blocked for any hand procedure (Klezl et al. 2001). It should also be remembered that simple techniques such as local infiltration for carpal tunnel syndrome or a ring block for finger surgery using a finger tourniquet alone may be adequate, without exposing the patient to the (rare) risk of nerve injury or other complications of a brachial plexus nerve block.

Technique

Either a nerve stimulator or ultrasound may be used, or a combination of both. Using ultrasound allows a lower volume of local anaesthetic to be used (see earlier) and may also reduce the incidence of vascular puncture by allowing both direct visualization of the vessels and blockade of nerves distal from vascular landmarks.

Nerve stimulator

Median nerve

Position the arm in a supine, slightly abducted position with the elbow slightly flexed. Palpate the brachial artery and insert a 22 G needle 1 cm medially, at an angle of approximately 45°, 1–2 cm proximal to the elbow crease. After obtaining a motor response (finger flexion), 5–10 ml of local anaesthetic is injected.

Radial nerve

With the arm in the same position as for the median nerve procedure, palpate the biceps tendon in the antecubital fossa and feel for the groove laterally between biceps and brachioradialis. Insert a 22 G needle 2 cm above the elbow crease, aiming laterally towards the lateral epicondyle, and after obtaining an appropriate motor response (thumb and wrist extension) inject 5–10 ml of local anaesthetic.

Ulnar nerve

Position the arm across the body with the elbow flexed at 90°. Palpate the ulnar sulcus and insert a 22 G needle 2 cm proximal to the medial epicondyle, aiming cephalad in line with the sulcus. Inject 5–10 ml after the appropriate motor end-point is achieved (ring finger flexion, thumb adduction).

Ultrasound

These are all basic level ultrasound-guided nerve blocks. As the nerves are relatively superficial, a high-frequency linear probe should be used. Below the clavicle the nerves are all visible as hyperechoic, honeycomb structures (Fig. 54.11) and can be traced proximally and distally, unlike tendons which can have a similar appearance but become muscle in due course. The arm should be slightly abducted and supinated for both the median and ulnar blocks and slightly pronated for the radial block, as described in the following subsections.

Median nerve

The nerve can be visualized medial to the brachial artery in the antecubital fossa but is more easily blocked in the forearm between the superficial and deep flexor muscles where the nerve is not accompanied by the artery. Although the nerve can be visualized anywhere in the forearm, it must be remembered that the palmar cutaneous nerve branches from the median nerve approximately 5 cm proximal to the wrist crease so the nerve should be blocked proximal to this point. Either an in-plane or an out-of-plane approach can be taken, using a 22 G needle and 3–5 ml of local anaesthetic is usually sufficient to ensure a circumferential spread around the nerve. Ensure that when approaching the nerve in plane from laterally or medially, the needle does not traverse the radial or ulnar artery respectively.

Radial nerve

The simplest approach is to block this nerve above the elbow before its bifurcation. The probe is placed transversely, lateral to the biceps tendon where the nerve is generally visualized as an oblique hyperechoic structure medial to the brachioradialis muscle. As it is traced proximally it can be seen to course towards the humerus, before winding around the spiral groove. A 22 G needle inserted in plane, lateral to medial can be used to block the nerve several centimetres proximal to the elbow crease. Again, 3–5 ml is usually sufficient.

Ulnar nerve

The nerve can be visualized just proximal to the wrist, immediately medial to the ulnar artery. The nerve should be traced proximally to where it separates from the ulnar artery in the proximal third of the forearm and blocked at this point using an in-plane approach. Again, up to 5 ml local anaesthetic is sufficient. With the arm fully abducted, the ulnar nerve can also be blocked proximal to the cubital fossa in the distal arm, where the nerve will not be compressed by a local anaesthetic injection. At this level there are no vascular landmarks to guide identification of the nerve.

Authors' preferred technique

For each block, an ultrasound-guided, in-plane approach is preferred. The median nerve is blocked in the mid forearm, the radial nerve proximal to the elbow, and the ulnar nerve in the proximal third of the forearm as previously described. For each nerve the end-point is circumferential spread of local anaesthetic, using up to 5 ml of local anaesthetic.

(A)

(B)

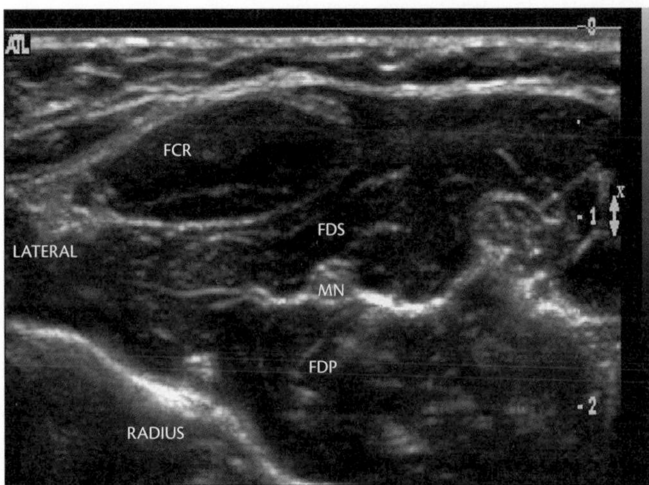

(C)

Figure 54.11 Images of the radial nerve at the elbow (A) and the median (B) and ulnar (C) nerves in the forearm. MN, median nerve; BR, brachioradialis; FCR, flexor carpi radialis; FDS, flexor digitorum superficialis; FDP, flexor digitorum profundus.

Local anaesthetic choice and dosing

The choice of local anaesthetic is dependent on whether the block is for analgesia or anaesthesia and surgical factors such as operation, duration, and magnitude. Levobupivacaine provides long-acting analgesia whereas lidocaine provides more rapid onset for short procedures with limited postoperative pain. Ultrasound allows a reduced volume of local anaesthetic to be used.

Complications

Nerve damage is a complication of all nerve blocks but there are few other complications of these peripheral nerve blocks. Care should be taken to avoid undertaking a mid-humeral block (not discussed here) if this is where a tourniquet is to be placed. There is some laboratory evidence that a 'double crush' phenomenon whereby compression from a tourniquet, may compound a block related nerve injury. The risk of vascular puncture can be reduced as already discussed with ultrasound by undertaking the block at areas away from surrounding vessels.

Declaration of interest

Professor McCartney currently acts as a consultant to Teleflex Medical who make regional anaesthesia needles and equipment.

References

Abrahams MS, Aziz MF, Fu RF, Horn JL. Ultrasound guidance compared with electrical neurostimulation for peripheral nerve block: a systematic review and meta-analysis of randomized controlled trials. *Br J Anaesth* 2009; **102**: 408–17

Akyildiz E, Gürkan Y, Cağlayan C, Solak M, Toker K. Single vs. double stimulation during a lateral sagittal infraclavicular block. *Acta Anaesthesiol Scand* 2009; **53**: 1262–7

Bernucci F, Gonzalez AP, Finlayson RJ, Tran de QH. A prospective, randomized comparison between perivascular and perineural ultrasound-guided axillary brachial plexus block. *Reg Anesth Pain Med* 2012; **37**: 473–7

Bhatia A, Lai J, Chan VW, Brull R. Case report: pneumothorax as a complication of the ultrasound-guided supraclavicular approach for brachial plexus block. *Anesth Analg* 2010; **111**: 817–9

Bloc S, Garnier T, Komly B, *et al.* Spread of injectate associated with radial or median nerve-type motor response during infraclavicular brachial-plexus block: an ultrasound evaluation. *Reg Anesth Pain Med* 2007; **32**: 130–5

Borgeat A, Ekatodramis G. Anaesthesia for shoulder surgery. *Best Pract Res Clin Anaesthesiol* 2002; **16**: 211–25

Borgeat A, Ekatrodamis G, Dumont C. An evaluation of the infraclavicular block via a modified approach of the Raj technique. *Anesth Analg* 2001; **93**: 436–41

Brand L, Papper EM. A comparison of supraclavicular and axillary techniques for brachial plexus blocks. *Anesthesiology* 1961; **22**: 226–9

Brown DL, Cahill DR, Bridenbaugh LD. Supraclavicular nerve block: anatomic analysis of a method to prevent pneumothorax. *Anesth Analg* 1993; **76**: 530–4

Brull R, Chan VW. The corner pocket revisited. *Reg Anesth Pain Med* 2011; **36**: 308

Brull R, McCartney CJ, Chan VW, El-Beheiry H. Neurological complications after regional anesthesia: contemporary estimates of risk. *Anesth Analg* 2007; **104**: 965–74

Chelly JE, Greger J, Al Samsam T, *et al.* Reduction of operating and recovery room times and overnight hospital stays with interscalene blocks as sole anesthetic technique for rotator cuff surgery. *Minerva Anestesiol* 2001; **67**: 613–9

Chin KJ, Alakkad H, Adikary SD, Singh M. (2013). Infraclavicular brachial plexus block for regional anaesthesia of the lower arm. *Cochrane Database Syst Rev* 2013; **8**: CD005487

Chin KJ, Handoll HH. Single, double or multiple-injection techniques for axillary brachial plexus block for hand, wrist or forearm surgery in adults. *Cochrane Database Syst Rev* 2011; **7**: CD003842

Cummings KC, 3rd, Napierkowski DE, Parra-Sanchez I, *et al.* Effect of dexamethasone on the duration of interscalene nerve blocks with ropivacaine or bupivacaine. *Br J Anaesth* 2011; **107**: 446–53

Desmet M, Braems H, Reynvoet M, *et al.* I.V. and perineural dexamethasone are equivalent in increasing the analgesic duration of a single-shot interscalene block with ropivacaine for shoulder surgery: a prospective, randomized, placebo-controlled study. *Br J Anaesth* 2013; **111**: 445–52

Desroches J. The infraclavicular brachial plexus block by the coracoid approach is clinically effective: an observational study of 150 patients. *Can J Anaesth* 2003; **50**: 253–7

Duggan E, El Beheiry H, Perlas A, *et al.* Minimum effective volume of local anesthetic for ultrasound-guided supraclavicular brachial plexus block. *Reg Anesth Pain Med* 2009; **34**: 215–8

Franco CD, Domashevich V, Voronov G, Rafizad AB, Jelev TJ. The supraclavicular block with a nerve stimulator: to decrease or not to decrease, that is the question. *Anesth Analg* 2004; **98**: 1167–71

Fredrickson MJ, Abeysekera A, White R. Randomized study of the effect of local anesthetic volume and concentration on the duration of peripheral nerve blockade. *Reg Anesth Pain Med* 2012; **37**: 495–501

Fredrickson MJ, Ball CM, Dalgleish AJ. Analgesic effectiveness of a continuous versus single-injection interscalene block for minor arthroscopic shoulder surgery. *Reg Anesth Pain Med* 2010; **35**: 28–33

Fredrickson MJ, Krishnan S, Chen CY. Postoperative analgesia for shoulder surgery: a critical appraisal and review of current techniques. *Anaesthesia* 2010; **65**: 608–24

Fredrickson MJ, Patel A, Young S, Chinchanwala S. Speed of onset of 'corner pocket supraclavicular' and infraclavicular ultrasound guided brachial plexus block: a randomised observer-blinded comparison. *Anaesthesia* 2009; **64**: 738–44

Fredrickson MJ, Wolstencroft P. Evidence-based medicine supports ultrasound-guided infraclavicular block over the corner pocket supraclavicular technique. *Reg Anesth Pain Med* 2011; **36**: 525–6

Fredrickson MJ, Wolstencroft P, Kejriwal R, Yoon A, Boland MR, Chinchanwala S. Single versus triple injection ultrasound-guided infraclavicular block: confirmation of the effectiveness of the single injection technique. *Anesth Analg* 2010; **111**: 1325–7

Gadsden J, Gratenstein K, Hadzic A. Intraneural injection and peripheral nerve injury. *Int Anesthesiol Clin* 2010; **48**: 107–15

Gadsden J, Hadzic A, Gandhi K, *et al.* The effect of mixing 1.5% mepivacaine and 0.5% bupivacaine on duration of analgesia and latency of block onset in ultrasound-guided interscalene block. *Anesth Analg* 2011; **112**: 471–6

Gelfand HJ, Ouanes JP, Lesley MR, *et al.* Analgesic efficacy of ultrasound-guided regional anesthesia: a meta-analysis. *J Clin Anesth* 2011; **23**: 90–6

Gray AT. The conjoint tendon of the latissimus dorsi and teres major: an important landmark for ultrasound-guided axillary block. *Reg Anesth Pain Med* 2009; **34**: 179–80

Ilfeld BM, Morey TE, Enneking FK. Infraclavicular perineural local anesthetic infusion: a comparison of three dosing regimens for postoperative analgesia. *Anesthesiology* 2004; **100**: 395–402

Ilfeld BM, Morey TE, Wright TW, Chidgey LK, Enneking FK. Continuous interscalene brachial plexus block for postoperative pain control at home: a randomized, double-blinded, placebo-controlled study. *Anesth Analg* 2003; **96**: 1089–95

Kalagara HK, Uppal V, McKinlay S, Macfarlane AJ, Anderson K. Effect of body mass index on angle of needle insertion during ultrasound-guided lateral sagittal infraclavicular brachial plexus block. *J Clin Anesth* 2015; **27**: 375–9

Kapral S, Greher M, Huber G, *et al.* Ultrasonography guidance improves the success rate of interscalene brachial plexus blockade. *Reg Anesth Pain Med* 2008; **33**: 253–8

Klaastad Ø, VadeBoncouer TR, Tillung T, Smedby O. An evaluation of the supraclavicular plumb-bob technique for brachial plexus block by magnetic resonance imaging. *Anesth Analg* 2003; **96**: 862–7

Klezl Z, Krejca M, Simcik J. Role of sensory innervation variations for wrist block anaesthesia. *Arch Med Res* 2001; **32**: 155–8

Knoblanche GE. The incidence and aetiology of phrenic nerve blockade associated with supraclavicular brachial plexus block. *Anaesth Intensive Care* 1979; **7**: 346–9

Koscielniak-Nielsen ZJ. Multiple injections in axillary block: where and how many? *Reg Anesth Pain Med* 2006; **31**: 192–5

Krone SC, Chan VW, Regan J, *et al.* Analgesic effects of low-dose ropivacaine for interscalene brachial plexus block for outpatient shoulder surgery-a dose-finding study. *Reg Anesth Pain Med* 2001; **26**: 439–43

Liu SS, Gordon MA, Shaw PM, Wilfred S, Shetty T, Yadeau JT. A prospective clinical registry of ultrasound-guided regional anesthesia for ambulatory shoulder surgery. *Anesth Analg* 2010; **111**: 617–23

Liu SS, Ngeow J, John RS. Evidence basis for ultrasound-guided block characteristics: onset, quality, and duration. *Reg Anesth Pain Med* 2010; **35**(Suppl): S26–35

Lo N, Brull R, Perlas A, *et al.* Evolution of ultrasound guided axillary brachial plexus blockade: retrospective analysis of 662 blocks. *Can J Anaesth* 2008; **55**: 408–13

Macfarlane AJ, Bhatia A, Brull R. Needle to nerve proximity: what do the animal studies tell us? *Reg Anesth Pain Med* 2011; **36**: 290–302

Mariano ER, Loland VJ, Bellars RH, *et al.* Ultrasound guidance versus electrical stimulation for infraclavicular brachial plexus perineural catheter insertion. *J Ultrasound Med* 2009; **28**: 1211–8

Mariano ER, Sandhu NS, Loland VJ, *et al.* A randomized comparison of infraclavicular and supraclavicular continuous peripheral nerve blocks for postoperative analgesia. *Reg Anesth Pain Med* 2011; **36**: 26–31

Maybin J, Townsley P, Bedforth N, Allan A. Ultrasound guided supraclavicular nerve blockade: first technical description and the relevance for shoulder surgery under regional anaesthesia. *Anaesthesia* 2011; **66**: 1053–5

McCartney CJ, Brull R, Chan VW, *et al.* Early but no long-term benefit of regional compared with general anesthesia for ambulatory hand surgery. *Anesthesiology* 2004; **101**: 461–7

McNaught A, Shastri U, Carmichael N, *et al.* Ultrasound reduces the minimum effective local anaesthetic volume compared with peripheral nerve stimulation for interscalene block. *Br J Anaesth* 2011; **106**: 124–30

Minville V, N'Guyen L, Chassery C, *et al.* A modified coracoid approach to infraclavicular brachial plexus blocks using a double-stimulation technique in 300 patients. *Anesth Analg* 2005; **100**: 263–5

Neal JM, Bernards CM, Hadzic A, *et al.* ASRA practice advisory on neurologic complications. *Reg Anesth Pain Med* 2008a; **33**: 404–15

Neal JM, Gerancher JC, Hebl JR, *et al.* Upper extremity regional anesthesia: essentials of our current understanding, 2008. *Reg Anesth Pain Med* 2008b; **34**: 134–70

Neal JM, Wedel DJ. Ultrasound guidance and peripheral nerve injury: is our vision as sharp as we think it is? *Reg Anesth Pain Med* 2010; **35**: 335–7

O'Donnell B, Riordan J, Ahmad I, Iohom G. Brief reports: a clinical evaluation of block characteristics using one milliliter 2% lidocaine in ultrasound-guided axillary brachial plexus block. *Anesth Analg* 2010; **111**: 808–10

Parrington SJ, O'Donnell D, Chan VW, *et al.* Dexamethasone added to mepivacaine prolongs the duration of analgesia after supraclavicular brachial plexus blockade. *Reg Anesth Pain Med* 2010; **35**: 422–6

Pianezza A, Salces y Nedeo A, Chaynes P, Bickler PE, Minville V. The emergence level of the musculocutaneous nerve from the brachial plexus: implications for infraclavicular nerve blocks. *Anesth Analg* 2012; **114**: 1131–3

Ponrouch M, Bouic N, Brinquier S, *et al.* Estimation and pharmacodynamic consequences of the minimum effective anesthetic volumes for median and ulnar nerve blocks: a randomized, double blind, controlled comparison between ultrasound and nerve stimulation guidance. *Anesth Analg* 2010; **111**: 1059–64

Pöpping DM, Elia N, Marret E, Wenk M, Tramèr MR. Clonidine as an adjuvant to local anesthetics for peripheral nerve and plexus blocks: a meta-analysis of randomized trials. *Anesthesiology* 2009; **111**: 406–15

Porter JM, McCartney CJ, Chan VW. Needle placement and injection posterior to the axillary artery may predict successful infraclavicular brachial plexus block: a report of three cases. *Can J Anaesth* 2005; **52**: 69–73

Renes SH, Rettig HC, Gielen MJ, Wilder-Smith OH, van Geffen GJ. Ultrasound-guided low-dose interscalene brachial plexus block reduces the incidence of hemidiaphragmatic paresis. *Reg Anesth Pain Med* 2009; **34**: 498–502

Renes SH, Spoormans HH, Gielen MJ, Rettig HC, van Geffen GJ. Hemidiaphragmatic paresis can be avoided in ultrasound-guided supraclavicular brachial plexus block. *Reg Anesth Pain Med* 2009; **34**: 595–9

Retzl G, Kapral S, Greher M, Mauritz W. Ultrasonographic findings of the axillary part of the brachial plexus. *Anesth Analg* 2001; **92**: 1271–5

Riazi S, Carmichael N, Awad I, Holtby RM, McCartney CJ. Effect of local anaesthetic volume (20 vs 5 ml) on the efficacy and respiratory consequences of ultrasound-guided interscalene brachial plexus block. *Br J Anaesth* 2008; **101**: 549–56

Rodríguez J, Bárcena M, Taboada-Muñiz M, Lagunilla J, Alvarez J. A comparison of single versus multiple injections on the extent of anesthesia with coracoid infraclavicular brachial plexus block. *Anesth Analg* 2004; **99**: 1225–30

Rodríguez J, Taboada M, Oliveira J, Ulloa B, Bárcena M, Alvarez J. Single stimulation of the posterior cord is superior to dual nerve stimulation in a coracoid block. *Acta Anaesthesiol Scand* 2010; **54**: 241–5

Romanes GJ. *Cunningham's Manual of Practical Anatomy. Volume One. Upper and Lower Limbs*. Oxford: Oxford University Press, 2010

Sauter AR, Dodgson MS, Stubhaug A, Halstensen AM, Klaastad Ø. Electrical nerve stimulation or ultrasound guidance for lateral sagittal infraclavicular blocks: a randomized, controlled, observer-blinded, comparative study. *Anesth Analg* 2008; **106**: 1910–5

Sinha SK, Abrams JH, Weller RS. Ultrasound-guided interscalene needle placement produces successful anesthesia regardless of motor stimulation above or below 0.5 mA. *Anesth Analg* 2007; **105**: 848–52

Sites BD, Beach ML, Spence BC, *et al.* Ultrasound guidance improves the success rate of a perivascular axillary plexus block. *Acta Anaesthesiol Scand* 2006; **50**: 678–84

Sites BD, Macfarlane AJ, Sites VR, *et al.* Clinical sonopathology for the regional anesthesiologist: part 1: vascular and neural. *Reg Anesth Pain Med* 2010a; **35**: 272–80

Sites BD, Macfarlane AJ, Sites VR, *et al.* Clinical sonopathology for the regional anesthesiologist: part 2: bone, viscera, subcutaneous tissue, and foreign bodies. *Reg Anesth Pain Med* 2010b; **35**: 281–9

Soares LG, Brull R. Lai J, Chan VW. Eight ball corner pocket: the optimal needle position for ultrasound-guided supraclavicular block. *Reg Anesth Pain Med* 2007; **32**: 94–5

Spence BC, Beach ML, Gallagher JD, Sites BD. Ultrasound-guided interscalene blocks: understanding where to inject the local anaesthetic. *Anaesthesia* 2011; **66**: 509–14

Subramanyam R, Vaishnav V, Chan VW, Brown-Shreves D, Brull R. Lateral versus medial needle approach for ultrasound-guided supraclavicular block: a randomized controlled trial. *Reg Anesth Pain Med* 2011; **36**: 387–92

Taboada M, Rodríguez J, Amor M, *et al.* Is ultrasound guidance superior to conventional nerve stimulation for coracoid infraclavicular brachial plexus block? *Reg Anesth Pain Med* 2009; **34**: 357–60

Tran de QH, Charghi R, Finlayson RJ. The "double bubble" sign for successful infraclavicular brachial plexus blockade. *Anesth Analg* 2006; **103**: 1048–9

Tran de QH, Dugani S, Dyachenko A, Correa JA, Finlayson RJ. Minimum effective volume of lidocaine for ultrasound-guided infraclavicular block. *Reg Anesth Pain Med* 2011; **36**: 190–4

Verelst P, van Zundert A. Respiratory impact of analgesic strategies for shoulder surgery. *Reg Anesth Pain M*ed 2013; **38**: 50–3

Vieira PA, Pulai I, Tsao GC, Manikantan P, Keller B, Connelly NR. Dexamethasone with bupivacaine increases duration of analgesia in ultrasound-guided interscalene brachial plexus blockade. *Eur J Anaesthesiol* 2010; **27**: 285–8

Williams SR, Chouinard P, Arcand G, *et al.* Ultrasound guidance speeds execution and improves the quality of supraclavicular block. *Anesth Analg* 2003; **97**: 1518–23

Wilson JL, Brown DL, Wong GY, Ehman RL, Cahill DR. Infraclavicular brachial plexus block: parasagittal anatomy important to the coracoid technique. *Anesth Analg* 1998; **87**: 870–3

Winnie AP, Collins VJ. The subclavian perivascular technique of brachial plexus anesthesia. *Anesthesiology* 1964; **25**: 353–63

Wilson AT, Nicholson E, Burton L, Wild C. Analgesia for day case shoulder surgery. *Br J Anaesth* 2004; **92**: 414–5

Wu CL, Rouse LM, Chen JM, Miller RJ. Comparison of postoperative pain in patients receiving interscalene block or general anesthesia for shoulder surgery. *Orthopedics* 2002; **25**: 45–8

CHAPTER 55

Regional anaesthesia of the lower limb

Pawan Gupta and Anurag Vats

Introduction

Carl Koller first described the use of cocaine for local anaesthesia of the eye in 1884 (Koller 1884). This generated interest in cocaine as a local anaesthetic and various investigators explored its use for other blocks. Ralph Stockman (1889) demonstrated the ability of cocaine to disrupt sensory and motor transmission of rabbit sciatic nerves. Cocaine was later used to block the sciatic nerve for anaesthesia and postoperative analgesia after amputation of the lower limb secondary to trauma or diabetic gangrene. George Hirschel (1911) described the axillary approach to brachial plexus block in 1911, but it took a further 62 years before Winnie et al. (1973) described the inguinal paravascular approach to the lumbar plexus for local anaesthesia of the lower limb. Compared with the axillary brachial plexus, the nerves of the lumbar plexus are deep. There are no clear bony or vascular landmarks to guide the needle and unlike in the upper limb, where the nerves lie in close association with each other and accompany major arteries, the branches from the lumbosacral plexus are widely separated. The popularity of lower limb nerve blocks is also constrained by availability of neuraxial techniques, which are easier to learn and provide complete and reliable anaesthesia for all operations on the lower limb.

Lower limb nerve blocks gained popularity with the introduction of better nerve localization techniques such as peripheral nerve stimulators and ultrasound. Compared with central neuraxial blocks, peripheral nerve blocks have many advantages. They do not affect the blood pressure, can be used in sick patients, provide longer-lasting analgesia, have less serious side-effects such as epidural haematoma or urinary retention, provide better patient satisfaction, and have acceptable success rates in experienced hands.

The nerve supply of the lower limb is from the lumbosacral plexus, which is formed from the anterior primary rami of the lumbar (L2–5) and the sacral (S1–3) nerve roots. The lumbosacral plexus provides sensory and motor innervation to the superficial tissues, muscles, and bones of the lower limb. Nerve blocks of the lower limb are often guided by the sensory distribution of the individual nerves rather than the dermatomal supply of individual nerve roots. The lumbosacral plexus is functionally divided into two parts (i.e. lumbar plexus and sacral plexus).

Lumbar plexus block (psoas compartment block)

The inguinal paravascular technique for lumbar plexus block was first described by Winnie et al. (1973). A year later they described the posterior approach to the lumbar plexus (Winnie et al. 1974). Chayen et al. (1976) modified this approach and noted that the lumbar plexus lies within the substance of the psoas major muscle and called this the 'psoas compartment block'. Both techniques aim to block the roots and divisions of the lumbar plexus.

Clinical application

A lumbar plexus block can be used as the sole anaesthetic for skin graft and muscle biopsy from the thigh, knee arthroscopy, patellar tendon repair, and anterior cruciate ligament reconstruction. In conjunction with a sciatic nerve block it can be used for any operation on the lower leg. The lumbar plexus block also provides good postoperative analgesia after hip arthroplasty, surgical fixation of fractured femur, knee arthroscopy, and knee arthroplasty.

Anatomy

The lumbar plexus is formed by the ventral (anterior) primary rami of the first four lumbar nerves (Fig. 55.1). The dorsal (posterior) rami of these nerves are sensory and carry the somatosensory input from the skin and muscles of the back. The lumbar plexus receives a contribution from the 12th thoracic nerve (subcostal nerve) in about half of the population. The L1, L2, L3, and L4 roots further divide into anterior and posterior branches. The anterior branch of the L1 root gives rise to the iliohypogastric and ilioinguinal nerves. The anterior branches of the L2, L3, and L4 roots join to form the obturator nerve. The posterior branches of the L1 and L2 roots join to form the genitofemoral nerve. The lateral cutaneous nerve of the thigh comes from the posterior branch of the L2 and L3 roots while the femoral nerve arises from the posterior roots of L2, L3, and L4.

The roots of the plexus lie in front of the transverse processes and lateral to the body of the lumbar vertebrae. The plexus lies within the body of the psoas major muscle before its branches emerge in the pelvis. The psoas major muscle has two parts: a superficial part and a deep part. The superficial part originates from the lateral surface of the body of the L1–5 vertebrae and the intervertebral discs. The deep part originates from the transverse processes of the L1–5 vertebrae.

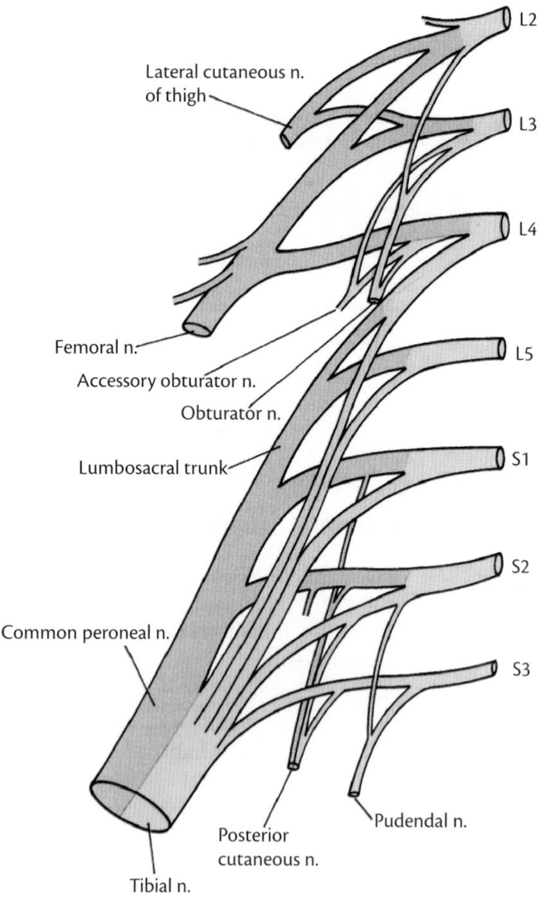

Figure 55.1 Lumbosaccral plexus: the anterior division of the nerve roots are shown in dark yellow colour.

Reproduced with permission from McCartney C., 'Lower limb blocks', in McLeod, G. *et al.*, *Principles and Practice of Regional Anaesthesia*, 2012, Figure 18.1, Page 188, with permission from Oxford University Press.

The muscle is inserted on the lessor trochanter of the femur along with the iliacus muscle. The roots and the anterior and posterior divisions of the lumbar plexus lie between the two parts of the psoas major muscle. The branches of the lumbar plexus emerge out of the muscle at the level of the L4–5 vertebrae and lie between the fascial compartment between the psoas major and the quadratus lumborum muscles.

The psoas muscle is enclosed in a facial sheath, which surrounds the branches of the lumbar plexus, that is, femoral nerve, obturator nerve, and lateral cutaneous nerve of thigh as they emerge from the muscle. The presence of this sheath around the femoral nerve is the proposed basis of the anterior para-vascular lumbar plexus or '3-in-1' block.

Landmarks

The lumbar plexus can be approached at L2–3, L3–4, or L4–5 levels. The landmarks that are used to guide the needle insertion point are the spinous processes of the lumbar vertebrae, the posterior superior iliac spine, and the inter-cristal line. A line is first drawn through the spinous processes of the lumbar vertebrae (inter-spinous line) followed by another line parallel to the inter-spinous line at the level of the posterior superior iliac spine. Finally, an intercristal line is drawn joining the highest points of the iliac crests. Figure 55.2 shows the point of insertion of the needle as advocated by different investigators.

We recommend Capedivilla's approach as it is based on sound evidence from robust computed tomography scan data. The point of insertion of the needle is the junction of the lateral one-third and the medial two-thirds on the line joining the L4 spinous process to the line drawn from the posterior superior iliac spine.

The patient is placed in the lateral position with the non-operative side down and the upper hip flexed at 30° and the knee flexed at 90°.

Conduct of the block

The lumbar plexus block has been performed using the nerve stimulator, ultrasound, and the fluoroscopic technique.

Peripheral nerve stimulator-guided technique

A 10–15 cm needle is required as the plexus is deep (5.7–10.1 cm under the skin). Insert the needle perpendicular to the skin slowly until the transverse process is contacted, then withdraw the needle by about 0.2 cm and advance very slowly in the cephalad direction. The needle should not be inserted any further than 1.5–2.0 cm beyond this point. Contraction of the paravertebral muscles will be observed when the needle is superficial, and will disappear when the transverse process is contacted. Once the needle is in close proximity to the femoral nerve, contraction of the quadriceps will be observed. The point of injection is when the quadriceps contractions are observed at a stimulating current between 0.4 and 0.5 mA. The psoas muscle is highly vascular and it is essential to inject the local anaesthetic in increments after repeated aspirations to reduce the risk of local anaesthetic toxicity.

If the transverse process is not contacted then the needle should be directed cephalad first and then caudad to locate it. If the transverse process cannot be identified in either direction, the insertion point should be moved slightly medial. The contraction of hamstring muscles indicates stimulation of the sacral plexus (i.e. the needle is too caudad). Flexion of the hip indicates direct stimulation of the psoas major muscle.

Ultrasound-guided technique

Ultrasound-guided lumbar plexus block is an advanced level block and requires detailed knowledge of the anatomy and considerable experience. As the plexus lies behind the vertebral bodies and within the body of the psoas muscle, visualization of the plexus is not easy. In lieu of the depth, a curvilinear probe is required. As the plexus is directly behind bony structures a lateral approach is useful.

Ultrasound offers the advantage of its ability to accurately identify the midline, the spinous processes, the level of the lumbar vertebrae, and the transverse processes. Identification of these landmarks is the first step when performing an ultrasound-guided lumbar plexus block. Once the landmarks are identified, these should be marked as in the landmark/peripheral nerve stimulator technique. Then place the ultrasound probe about 3 cm away from the inter-spinous line in the coronal plane and the space between the transverse processes is identified. In this view, the spinous process, the lamina, and the body of the vertebrae give the characteristic wave-like appearance, called the 'wave sign'. The lumbar plexus usually appears as a hyperechoic shadow within the substance of the psoas muscle (Fig. 55.3). This appearance, however, varies depending upon the patient's age and the echogenicity of surrounding

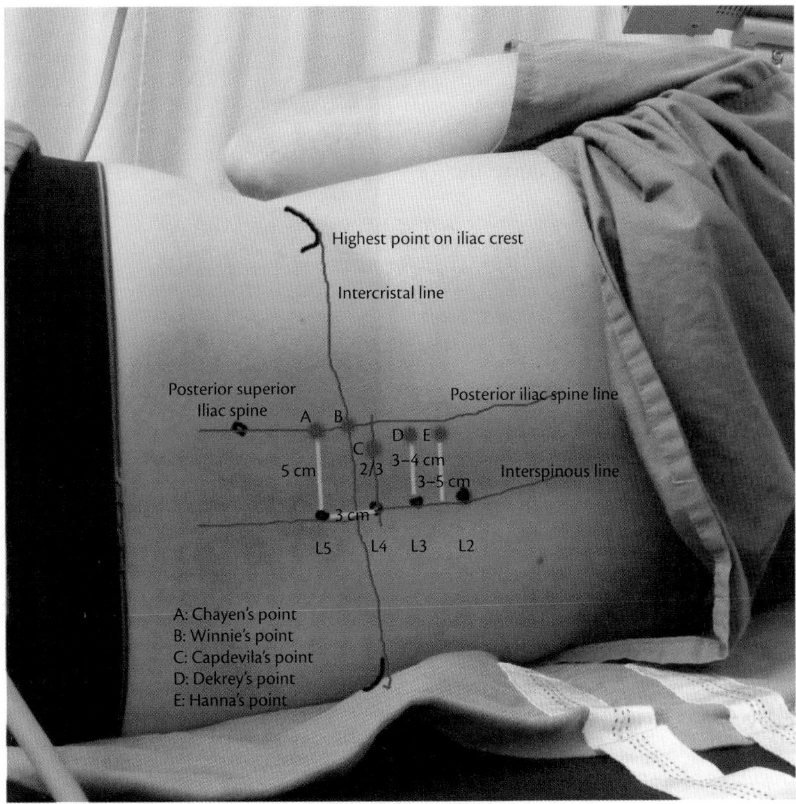

Figure 55.2 Different sites of needle insertion for the lumbar plexus block (*Capdevilla's point*: junction of medial 2/3 and lateral 1/3 on the perpendicular line from the L4 spinous process; *Chayen's point*: 3 cm caudad and 5 cm lateral to L4 spinous process; *Winnie's point*: point of intersection on the line drawn from the posterior superior iliac spine and intercristal line; *Dekrey's point*: 3–4 cm lateral to L3 spinous process; Hanna's point: 3–5 cm lateral to from the L2–3 interspace).

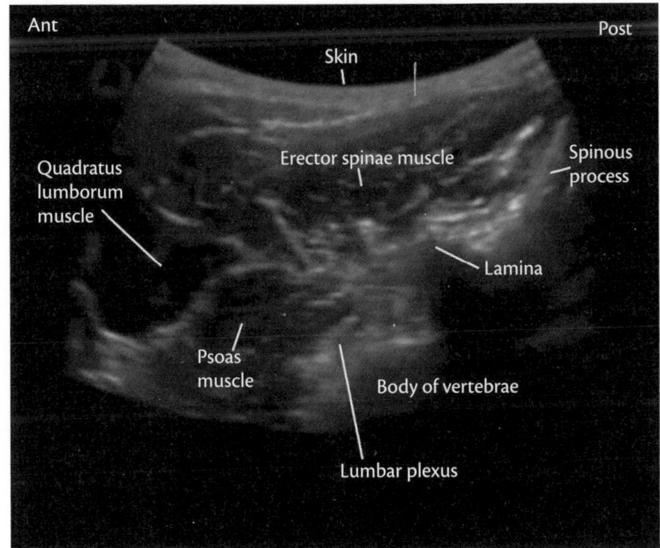

Figure 55.3 Ultrasound image of the lumbar plexus at the level of L4–L5 using a curvilinear probe. The lumbar plexus can be seen in the substance of psoas major muscle.

tissue. The lumbar plexus is located in a highly vascular area and pulsations of lumbar vessels can be seen close to the plexus. The authors recommend the 'in-plane' approach as it allows full visualization of the needle. Use of a peripheral nerve stimulator is also recommended to confirm needle position as the nerve structures are deep and may not be clearly visualized. Once the needle is in the right place, local anaesthetic should be injected in small increments after repeated aspirations.

Dose and choice of local anaesthetic

Twenty to forty millilitres of lidocaine, bupivacaine, or ropivacaine can be used as indicated.

Contraindications

Local sepsis, coagulation disorders (international normalized ratio >1.5), and patient refusal. The block should be performed carefully in patients with fixed cardiac output states and those with systemic sepsis.

Complications

The lumbar plexus area is very vascular and lies close to the spinal canal and visceral structures. The risk of complications is approximately 16 times higher than with other peripheral nerve blocks (Auroy et al. 2002).

The risks of lumbar plexus block include:

- Epidural diffusion of local anaesthetic leading to bilateral block
- Subarachnoid injection leading to total spinal block
- Retroperitoneal haematoma
- Renal subcapsular haematoma and damage to abdominal viscera
- Inadvertent intravascular injection

- Direct nerve damage and intraneural injection
- Psoas abscess
- Failure (failure rate is about 5% even in experienced hands).

The use of ultrasound to confirm bony landmarks, repeated aspiration before injection, and use of low volumes of local anaesthetics helps to reduce the risk of complications.

Femoral nerve block

Femoral nerve block is relatively simple to perform, requires basic skills and has low risks of complications. It benefits patients coming in for a range of lower limb operations.

Clinical application

Femoral nerve block provides anaesthesia for surgery of the anterior thigh, femur, and knee. It is indicated for postoperative analgesia for operations such as hip fractures, proximal femoral fractures, femoral shaft fracture, total knee arthroplasty, anterior cruciate ligament repair, and saphenous vein stripping, reducing the requirements of systemic analgesics or acting as a sole analgesic. Femoral nerve block provides excellent analgesia after total knee replacement and anterior cruciate ligament repair (Hadzic and New York School of Regional Anesthesia 2007; Association of Anaesthetists of Great Britain and Ireland 2012; Gupta et al. 2013). It is used as a sole anaesthetic for vastus medialis biopsy when testing patients for malignant hyperthermia susceptibility (Gupta et al. 2013). In conjunction with sciatic nerve block, it can provide analgesia for almost the entire lower limb.

Anatomy

The femoral nerve is the nerve of the anterior compartment of the thigh. It is the main branch of the lumbar plexus. The dorsal divisions of the anterior rami of the L2–4 spinal nerves combine to form the femoral nerve. It emerges from the lower lateral border of psoas muscle, passes between psoas and iliacus, and enters the thigh posterior to the inguinal ligament where it lies lateral to the femoral artery [a mnemonic, 'NAVY' (Nerve-Artery-Vein-'Y'-front) may prove useful in a busy clinical setting].

The femoral nerve runs deep to the fascia iliaca while the femoral blood vessels are superficial to it but deep to the fascia lata. It divides into anterior and posterior branches during its course through the thigh. Anterior branches supply sartorius and pectineus muscles and the skin of the anterior and medial part of the thigh. Posterior branches supply quadriceps muscle, the knee joint, and skin on the medial surface of the leg below the knee joint through the saphenous branch.

Sonoanatomy

The ultrasound probe is placed at the inguinal crease. The pulsating femoral artery, femoral vein (reducing pressure on the skin may bring it in view), and the ilio-psoas muscle with the overlying fascia iliaca should be identified. If more than one artery is visualized, the probe should be moved proximally, visualizing the femoral artery before its division (profunda femoris and superficial femoral artery). The femoral nerve is seen as a hyperechoic, oval-to-triangular structure lateral to the femoral artery (Fig. 55.4). It is located under the fascia iliaca and in the groove between the iliacus and the psoas muscles. Tilting the probe cranially or caudally may improve its definition and some rotation of the probe may be required to account for the pelvic tilt and slight medial-to-lateral course of the nerve, respectively. The femoral nerve is typically found at a depth of 2–4 cm.

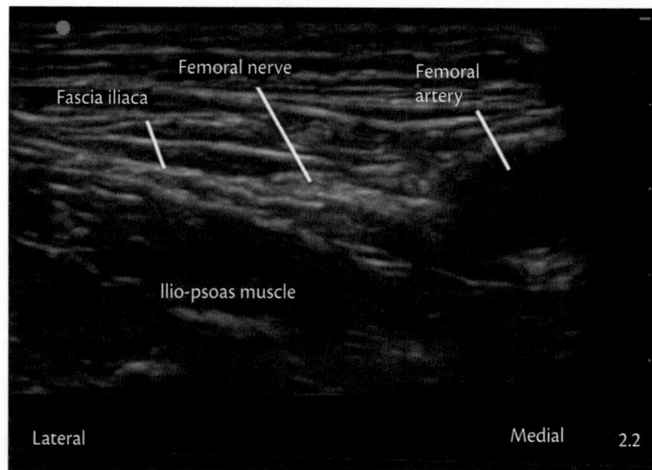

Figure 55.4 Ultrasound image of the femoral nerve, which is seen as a triangular hyperechoic structure lateral to the femoral artery and above ilio-psoas muscle.

The position of the lateral circumflex femoral artery is variable. It may lie deep to the femoral nerve, lateral to the femoral artery or may cross between the superficial and the deep branches of the femoral nerve or lie very close to the point of insertion of the needle at the inguinal crease. This variability may lead to inadvertent vascular puncture or intravascular injection of local anaesthetic (Orebaugh 2006). In some cases, inguinal lymph nodes may look similar to the femoral nerve. However, they are more superficial and can be differentiated by proximal and distal scanning. In some patients, the posterior division of the femoral nerve is far lateral to the femoral artery above the ilio-psoas muscle (Rigler et al. 1991).

Conduct of the block

The patient should be in the supine position with the leg abducted by 10–20°.

For the nerve stimulator-based technique, the mid point of the inguinal ligament is identified first. The femoral artery can be palpated at this level. A 22 G, 5 cm insulated nerve block needle is inserted 1 cm lateral to the femoral pulse, caudal to the inguinal ligament, after infiltrating a small volume of local anaesthetic in the skin. A nerve stimulator is connected to the needle. The starting current is set at 1.0 mA, and the needle advanced through the fascial planes aiming to find the femoral nerve. Correct placement of the needle tip is indicated by visible or palpable quadriceps muscle twitches at current levels of 0.4–0.5 mA. If there is no response or contact with the bone or local twitching (pectineus or iliopsoas), the needle should be withdrawn, and the landmarks should be reviewed. A vascular puncture indicates that the needle is inserted too medially. A sartorius twitch indicates stimulation of the branch to sartorius. The needle should be redirected laterally and advanced 1–3 mm deeper to block the main trunk of the femoral nerve.

If using ultrasound guidance, the out-of-plane or in-plane approach could be used. In the hands of an experienced operator, the in-plane orientation may allow better views of the needle tip than the out-of-plane approach. A 22 G, 5 cm needle should be inserted about 1 cm lateral to the edge of the ultrasound probe in short-axis view (at the level of the inguinal crease). The needle should be advanced until the tip is positioned under the fascia iliaca at the lateral edge of the femoral nerve. A small volume of local anaesthetic or other fluid such as saline 0.9% may help in accurate localization of the needle tip, particularly for the out-of-plane approach. Once the needle tip is in the correct plane, local anaesthetic should be deposited either anterior or posterolateral to the nerve. Circumferential spread of local anaesthetic is not essential but it may lead to faster onset of block (Morau et al. 2010; Hadzic and New York School of Regional Anesthesia 2012; Marhofer et al. 2014).

Block assessment

The sensory block to pinprick or cold should be tested over the medial and anterior thigh. Loss of sensation over the medial part of the leg indicates saphenous nerve block. Asking the patient to extend the knee (e.g. lifting foot off the bed with the knee supported) assesses quadriceps muscle strength (i.e. the motor block).

Dose and choice of local anaesthetic

Five to twenty millilitres of local anaesthetic is recommended for a successful block, especially with the use of ultrasound and multiple injection techniques (Casati et al. 2001, 2007; Marhofer 2010; Taha and Abd-Elmaksoud 2013). In a study using the continual reassessment method, Gupta et al. (2013) directly estimated the ED_{95} of 1% prilocaine as 17 ml. The choice of local anaesthetic depends on the indication of the block. For day case procedures where early ambulation is required, lidocaine or prilocaine is recommended. Bupivacaine (0.5%) or ropivacaine (0.75%) is recommended for prolonged postoperative analgesia. For total knee arthroplasty an infusion of dilute local anaesthetic such as ropivacaine (0.2%) at a rate of 5–10 ml h^{-1} provides excellent analgesia. This rate could be reduced to about 5 ml h^{-1} if patient-controlled boluses are added to the infusion regimen (Salinas et al. 2006; Brodner et al. 2007; Hadzic and New York School of Regional Anesthesia 2012).

Contraindications

Contraindications to femoral nerve block include patient refusal and true local anaesthetic allergy. Relative contraindications are inguinal lymphadenopathy, previous ilio-inguinal surgery and grafts, renal transplants, local infection, and pre-existing femoral neuropathy.

Complications

Femoral vessel puncture leading to local haematoma and intravascular injection leading to local anaesthetic toxicity are possible complications. Permanent nerve damage is rare. Patient falls as a result of attempted mobilization with ongoing motor block have been reported in the literature.

Fascia iliaca block

The fascia iliaca block was originally described in the paediatric population. It is a low-risk alternative which aims to block most of the nerves of the lumbar plexus. It mainly provides analgesia in the distribution of the femoral nerve and the lateral cutaneous nerve of the thigh. Success rates for the obturator nerve block are highly variable with fascia iliaca block.

Clinical application

Fascia iliaca block is indicated for analgesia after hip, anterior thigh, and knee surgery. It can be used in an emergency department providing analgesia to patients presenting with proximal femoral fractures. The Association of Anaesthetists of Great Britain and Ireland (2012) recommends considering fascia iliaca block for all patients presenting for proximal femoral fracture surgery. It reduces the requirements of systemic analgesics although the psoas compartment block is more reliable but has higher risks. It may be an alternative to the femoral nerve block in patients where the latter is contraindicated (e.g. vascular grafts or previous surgery leading to altered anatomy).

Anatomy

The fascia iliaca forms a partition between the inguinal ligament and the hip joint. The superolateral muscular compartment contains psoas major, iliacus, and the femoral nerve while the inferomedial compartment carries vascular structures. The fascia iliaca is attached to the inner lip of the iliac crest. It covers the iliacus muscle, which originates from the upper two-thirds of the iliac fossa and partly from the ventral sacroiliac ligament. Medially, it is attached to the pelvic brim blending with the periosteum.

Further down, it merges with the posterior margins of the inguinal ligament and the transversalis fascia and medially it passes behind the femoral vasculature continuing as the pectineal fascia attaching to the pecten pubis. It extends partly into the femoral sheath but otherwise does not extend into the thigh (Standring and Gray 2008; Sinnatamby and Last, 2011). The femoral nerve lies deep to this fascia at the level of the femoral crease.

Sonoanatomy

As detailed in the earlier femoral nerve section, the femoral blood vessels, the femoral nerve, the fascia iliaca, and the ilio-psoas muscle (large hypoechoic structure posterior to the femoral nerve) should be identified. Sliding the ultrasound probe laterally will bring the sartorius muscle into view, followed by the anterior superior iliac spine. During this scan the superficially placed fascia lata must be differentiated from the fascia iliaca (Fig. 55.5). This is crucial for correct placement of the local anaesthetic and success of the block.

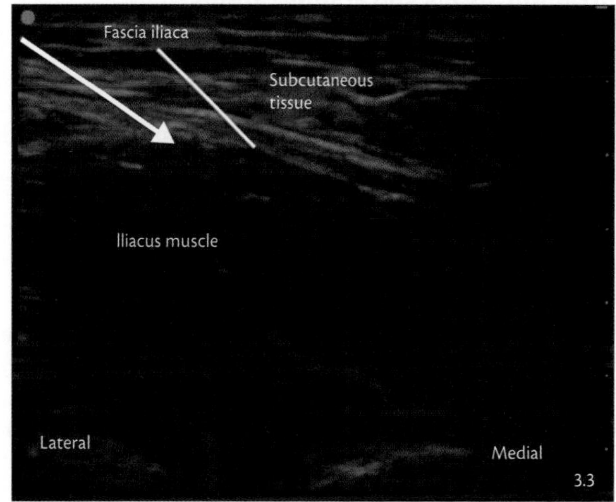

Figure 55.5 Ultrasound image to illustrate the key structures in fascia iliaca block. The fascia iliaca is seen covering iliacus muscle lateral to the femoral artery, which is not visible in this image. The arrow indicates the path of needle sited for conducting the block.

Conduct of the block

The patient should be in the supine position with the table as flat as possible to allow best access to the inguinal area. An ultrasound machine with a linear 6–13 MHz probe is used with the depth of view set at 2.5–3.0 cm. A 22 G, 5 cm short-bevel needle is chosen. A longer needle might be required in an obese patient. The block should be performed under standard aseptic conditions.

The femoral nerve, femoral artery, and the fascia iliaca covering iliopsoas muscles are identified in the short-axis view. The ultrasound transducer is moved laterally several centimetres to bring the sartorius muscle into view. Using the in-plane approach, the needle is inserted at the level of the femoral crease. The aim is to place the needle tip at approximately the lateral one-third of a line connecting the anterior superior iliac spine and pubic tubercle.

Use of ultrasound to assess and optimize spread of local anaesthetic by repositioning the needle may improve the success rate of lateral cutaneous nerve of thigh and obturator nerve block (Dolan et al. 2008).

Block assessment

A sensory block to cold in the distribution of the femoral nerve, the lateral cutaneous nerve of thigh (lateral part of the thigh), will indicate adequate spread of local anaesthetic. The obturator block will be indicated by a degree of motor weakness of the adductor muscles. The motor block could be weak if a very dilute local anaesthetic has been used.

Dose and choice of local anaesthetic

Fascia iliaca block is a fascial plane block requiring a high volume of local anaesthetic for success. Thirty to forty millilitres of the local anaesthetic is used for a successful block (Capdevila et al. 1998; Foss et al. 2007; Dolan et al. 2008). The choice of local anaesthetic agent is determined by the indication of the block. Agents such as lidocaine 1% with adrenaline, or mepivacaine 1% with adrenaline have been used for short-duration analgesia and quick onset of block (e.g. patient positioning or patient transfer) but long-acting local anaesthetic agents are used for postoperative analgesia (e.g. ropivacaine 0.2%).

Contraindications and complications

These are similar to other peripheral nerve blocks except there are no major blood vessels near the area of drug injection, minimizing the chances of intravascular injection. Failure to recognize a misplaced needle tip could lead to intramuscular injection of local anaesthetic and an ineffective block.

Lateral femoral cutaneous nerve block

Clinical application

This is used for providing anaesthesia and analgesia of the lateral part of the thigh (e.g. hip surgery and skin graft harvesting from the lateral thigh). It can be used in combination with femoral and sciatic blocks to supplement analgesia and for minimizing tourniquet pain. It has also been used for diagnosis and management of meralgia paraesthetica (Hurdle et al. 2007).

Anatomy

The lateral femoral cutaneous nerve (LFCN) is a branch of the lumbar plexus with contributions from L2–3. It emerges from the lateral border of the psoas muscle, and crosses the iliac crest laterally, anterior to iliacus muscle towards the anterior superior iliac supine. It enters the thigh either posterior to or through the inguinal ligament, 1–2 cm medial to the anterior superior iliac spine or through the origin of the sartorius muscle. As it courses inferolaterally on the anterior surface of sartorius, it forms anterior and posterior branches. The posterior branch pierces fascia lata providing cutaneous innervation to the lateral part of the thigh from the greater trochanter to mid thigh. The anterior branch becomes subcutaneous approximately 10 cm caudal to the anterior superior iliac spine. It supplies the anterolateral thigh as far as the knee joint. terminating by forming the patellar plexus, anastomosing with cutaneous branches of the anterior division of the femoral nerve and infrapatellar branches of the saphenous nerve. The anatomy of this nerve is variable, and it may exit the pelvis as four branches.

Sonoanatomy

The LFCN is easiest to identify between the tensor fascia lata and sartorius muscles (Ng et al. 2008; Zhu et al. 2012). Under aseptic conditions, a high-frequency linear probe set at a depth of 1.5–2.1 cm is placed just inferior and medial to the anterior superior iliac spine parallel to the inguinal ligament. Tensor fascia lata muscle is seen medial to the anterior superior iliac spine in the short-axis view. A space is seen between the medial end of tensor fascia lata muscle and the lateral end of sartorius. The fascia lata is seen 'dipping' between these structures forming a 'hammock.' The LFCN can be seen as a superficial hyperechoic structure in this hammock between the two layers of fascia lata (Fig. 55.6). It may be seen as a single nerve or multiple small branches. When scanning it proximally/distally, the nerve can be seen dividing or joining together as a single structure. Tilting or rotating the probe may make the image clearer, and the nerve may stand out from the fascia.

Conduct of the block

The patient is positioned supine with the leg extended in a neutral position. Any internal or external rotation of the leg should be avoided.

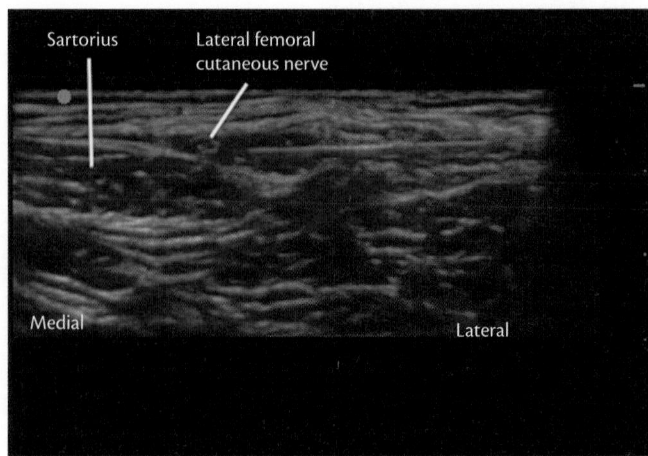

Figure 55.6 Sonoanatomy of the lateral femoral cutaneous nerve of thigh. The nerve can be seen as a small hyperechoic rim with a hypoechoic centre. In this image it has become more prominent after injection of local anaesthetic in the fascial plane lateral to sartorius muscle. Note image of nerve block needle *in situ* and tensor fascia lata muscle lateral to the sartorius muscle. The nerve is superficial and may require the use of the minimum depth setting on the ultrasound machine.

Ultrasound-guided technique

After identification of structures, as previously detailed, a 5 cm short-bevel needle is inserted in plane from lateral to medial. Injection of a small amount of local anaesthetic may help in accurate localization of the needle tip. Once the needle tip is in the correct fascial plane close to the nerve, the desired dose of chosen drug is injected after negative aspiration. The nerve may become clearer after injecting the drug.

Landmark technique

A short-bevel 5 cm needle is inserted 2 cm medial and caudal to the anterior superior iliac spine under aseptic conditions. The needle is advanced through the fascia lata as a 'give' is felt. Local anaesthetic is injected in a fan-wise fashion, from medial to lateral both above and below the fascia lata.

Block assessment

The block can be assessed using cold or pinprick on the lateral thigh between the anterior superior iliac spine and the knee joint. However, the range of blocked area is highly variable (Hopkins et al. 1991).

Dose and choice of local anaesthetic

Ten to fifteen millilitres of local anaesthetic is injected for the landmark technique. A high concentration of long-acting agent may increase the rate of success for landmark-based techniques. For ultrasound-guided techniques, successful block has been achieved with injectate volumes ranging from 1 ml to 10 ml (Hurdle et al. 2007; Hara et al. 2011).

Contraindications

Local infection or true allergy to local anaesthetics may contraindicate this block.

Complications

LFCN block has a low risk of complications. Direct nerve injury as a result of needle trauma or drug toxicity is theoretically possible but unlikely.

Obturator nerve block

Labat first described block of the obturator nerve in 1922. Since then Winnie, Wassef, and Pinnock have described various modifications. With the refinement of ultrasound guidance there is renewed interest in the use of this block. Recent studies have assessed the feasibility of ultrasound guidance and the correlation of anatomy to sonoanatomy and nerve blocks. Some authors describe it as a technically challenging block requiring advanced skills (Akkaya et al. 2009). The psoas plexus block is known to provide good obturator nerve anaesthesia.

Clinical application

There are very selected indications for this nerve block. It has been used to relieve spasms of the adductor muscle in patients with hemiplegia, paraplegia, and central neurological disorders such as cerebral palsy. It prevents adductor muscle contractions during transurethral bladder surgery. It can be blocked to supplement analgesia after major knee surgery.

Anatomy

The obturator nerve is a branch of the lumbar plexus with root value of L2–4 (Standring and Gray 2008; Hebl et al. 2010). It has a highly variable anatomy. It may have a contribution from the anterior primary rami of L5 or L1. The obturator nerve descends caudally within the substance of the psoas muscle (posteromedially) and divides into an anterior and a posterior branch within the pelvis. It enters the medial compartment of the thigh with the obturator vessels through the obturator foramen under the superior pubic ramus. In most cases, the division occurs within the foramen but in a minority of patients it may divide before the nerve leaves the foramen or after it leaves the pelvis. The anterior branch is in the fascial plane between the pectineus and the adductor brevis while the posterior branch is located between the adductor brevis and the adductor magnus. The anterior branch supplies cutaneous innervation to a variable area on the medial aspect of the thigh. It also supplies motor branches to the adductor muscles (pectineus, adductor brevis and longus, and gracilis). At the lower border of the adductor longus, it sends a branch to form the subsartorial plexus with the saphenous and the medial cutaneous branches of the femoral nerve. The posterior branch is the main motor supply to the deep adductor muscles but it may also provide a sensory branch to the medial part of the knee joint. The articular branches to the hip joint arise proximally before division of the obturator nerve.

The accessory obturator nerve is an anatomical variant. It passes above the superior pubic ramus and supplies the pectineus muscle and gives articular branches to the hip joint. It terminates by anastomosing with the anterior division of the obturator nerve.

Sonoanatomy

It is essential to recognize the muscles of the adductor compartment and fascial planes between them, as branches of the obturator nerve may not image well (Soong et al. 2007; Taha 2012). The patient is placed in the supine position with the thigh slightly abducted and externally rotated. Flexion of the knee joint may improve the image quality. A curved or linear ultrasound probe can be used with initial depth settings of 4–6 cm. Some authors have used musculoskeletal settings on the ultrasound machine to identify muscular planes and nerves. The anteromedial thigh is scanned in the short-axis view, identifying the femoral vessels at the level of the inguinal crease. The ultrasound probe is moved medially parallel to the inguinal crease to identify the adductor muscles. The fascial layers between the pectineus (inferolateral), adductor longus (superior) and the adductor brevis (inferomedial) may form a letter 'Y' configuration when scanned proximally. The anterior branch can be seen at the centre of the letter 'Y' or between pectineus and adductor brevis. Adductor brevis can be seen lying medially and deep to adductor longus at this level. The posterior branch is identified between the adductor brevis and the adductor magnus posteriorly (Fig. 55.7). Both divisions of this nerve appear as flattened hyperechoic structures. The obturator nerve may exhibit anisotropic behaviour. The ultrasound probe can be tilted cephalad/caudad to improve the image. Significant soft tissue compression may be required to improve the image quality but patient comfort must be considered.

Conduct of the block

Ultrasound-guided technique

Under aseptic conditions, a 10 cm short-bevel needle is inserted in plane from lateral to the medial side after infiltrating local anaesthetic in the skin. Attempts should be made to advance the needle in the inter-fascial plane between pectineus and adductor longus muscle avoiding tissue damage. The required dose of local

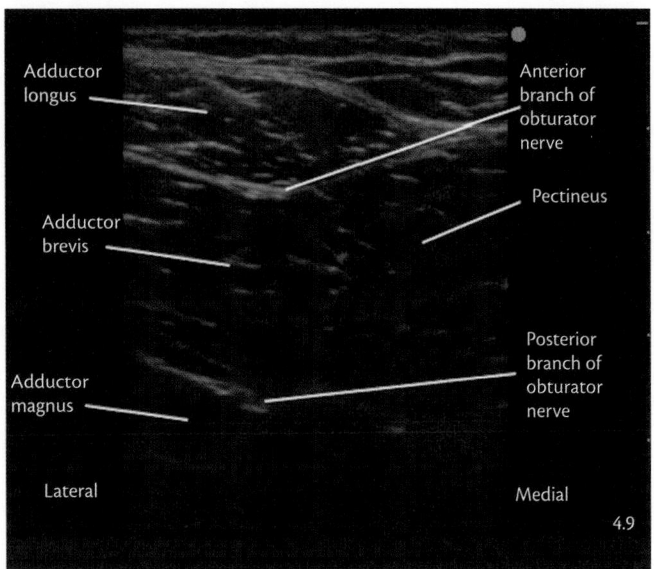

Figure 55.7 Sonoanatomy of the obturator nerve. The anterior branch of obturator nerve can be seen lying between fascial planes of the pectineus and adductor brevis muscles. The posterior branch of obturator nerve can be seen the fascial plane between the adductor brevis and adductor magnus muscles.

anaesthetic is injected near the anterior branch of the obturator nerve between pectineus and adductor longus. The needle is redirected to target the posterior branch between the adductor brevis and adductor magnus. It is important to recognize that local anaesthetic is injected in the fascial plane. If it is spreading intramuscularly, the needle tip should be repositioned. Care should be taken to avoid puncture of the femoral vessels lying superficially.

A proximal inter-fascial technique has been described by Taha (2012) where the author was able to block both divisions of the obturator nerve using a single inter-fascial injection. The pectineus muscle was identified, and ultrasound probe tilted 40–60° cranially. The inferior margin of the superior pubic ramus was visualized laterally. A well-defined fascial plane was seen posterior to the pectineus separating it from obturator externus. The local anaesthetic was injected at the most medial part of this plane. Sinha et al. (2009) made two inter-fascial injections with no attempt to identify the nerve division under ultrasound guidance. The first injection was at the middle and posterior one-third of the junction of the pectineus and adductor longus while the second injection was between the adductor brevis and adductor magnus.

Nerve stimulator-guided techniques

The main landmarks to be identified for this approach are the anterior superior iliac spine, pubic tubercle, inguinal ligaments, femoral artery, and the insertion of tendon of adductor longus. This tendon can be identified as a prominent structure on the medial side of the thigh when it is placed in extreme abduction. The patient is placed supine with the leg abducted by 30° degrees.

A modification of the classic Labat's approach (Labat 1922) (using a nerve stimulator) is described as insertion of an 8–10 cm insulated nerve block needle 2–3 cm medial and 2–3 cm caudad to the pubic tubercle perpendicular to the skin. The needle is withdrawn and redirected 45° laterally and caudad after it makes contact with the inferior border of the superior pubic ramus. The needle is advanced for 2–3 cm to elicit a motor response in the adductor compartment at 0.4–0.5 mA. The aim is to deposit a dose of local anaesthetic at the level of the obturator foramen where the obturator nerve emerges from the pelvis.

Wassef (1993) described an inter-adductor approach where a stimulating needle is inserted at the posterior border of the adductor longus tendon near its bony insertion. The needle is directed laterally at a point 1–2 cm medial to femoral pulse just under the inguinal ligament aiming to get appropriate motor response at 0.4–0.5 mA. The local anaesthetic is deposited proximally just as the obturator nerve leaves the pelvis.

For the paravascular inguinal approach, a line is drawn joining the medial border of adductor longus and the femoral pulse at the level of the inguinal crease. A 10 cm insulated needle is inserted at a 30° cepahalad angle to the skin at the midpoint of this line. At a depth of 1–2 cm, a motor response from the anterior branch of the obturator nerve can be elicited. The needle is then redirected slightly laterally to get a motor response from the posterior branch (hip adduction). An injection is made around the posterior branch followed by the anterior division as the needle is withdrawn. This is to prevent unrecognized trauma to the anterior branch. This approach may not provide pain relief for the hip joint as the nerve is blocked distally.

Block assessment

The obturator nerve supplies a highly variable area of the skin on the medial side of the thigh: assessing the sensory block may not be a reliable way to confirm obturator nerve block. Partial motor weakness of the adductor compartment is a good indicator of a successful block. The adductor group of muscles such as pectineus (femoral nerve) and adductor magnus (sciatic nerve) have some motor supply from other nerves. The patient should be asked to adduct their legs from an abducted position against resistance to assess the extent of motor block. Weakness in doing so may indicate a successful block.

Dose and choice of local anaesthetic

For single-injection techniques, where the nerve is blocked before it divides a volume of 10–15 ml of local anaesthetic has been used. If both branches of the obturator nerve are blocked separately with ultrasound guidance, 5–10 ml of local anaesthetic is used for each branch (Marhofer et al. 2010).

For supplemental analgesia after lower limb operations, long-acting agents such as bupivacaine 0.25–0.5% or ropivacaine 0.5–0.75% should be used. Lidocaine (1–2%) or prilocaine is adequate for transurethral bladder procedures. Neurolytic agents (phenol/ethanol) are used in combination with local anaesthetics and steroids for painful spasmodic conditions.

Contraindications

Relative contraindications are pre-existing neuropathies, inguinal lymph node enlargement, local infection, and coagulation disorders.

Complications

With Labat's approach, care should be taken to avoid damage to intra-pelvic organs such as the bladder, rectum, vagina, and spermatic cord. The obturator vessels are in close relation to the anterior division of the nerve and unintentional vascular damage or intravascular injections may occur.

Saphenous nerve block (also includes adductor/subsartorial canal block)

The saphenous nerve is the largest cutaneous branch of the femoral nerve. It arises from the posterior branch of the femoral nerve and is a terminal branch with pure sensory component. The nerve can be easily identified in the adductor canal in the lower thigh.

Clinical application

A saphenous nerve block is indicated in superficial procedures of the anteromedial and the posteromedial aspect of the leg (e.g. varicose veins surgery). Most often it is used in conjunction with sciatic or popliteal nerve block, providing analgesia for the medial aspect of the leg, medial malleolus, and ankle procedures (e.g. ankle fusion and fractures). The adductor canal block is emerging as an alternative to the femoral nerve block for postoperative analgesia after total knee arthroplasty. So far it has not shown any advantage in providing analgesia after anterior cruciate ligament repair but results are limited to a single study (Espelund et al. 2013). It provides analgesia similar to the femoral nerve block as part of a multimodal regimen. In healthy volunteers it preserves quadriceps motor strength significantly better than femoral nerve block but this does not translate into clinical benefit of early mobilization in patients undergoing total knee arthroplasty. Further work is required to understand the reasons behind this observation (Jenstrup et al. 2012; Jaeger et al. 2013; Kwofie et al. 2013; Kim et al. 2014; Mariano and Perlas 2014; Mudumbai et al. 2014).

Anatomy

The saphenous nerve descends thorough the thigh lateral to the femoral artery. It contributes to the subsartorial plexus at the mid-thigh level and continues distally entering the adductor canal anterior to the femoral artery. It crosses over the artery to lie medial to it. At the distal end of the canal, it leaves the artery, gives off an infrapatellar branch, which contributes to the peripatellar plexus and descends vertically behind the sartorius muscle. It emerges between the tendons of the sartorius and the gracilis muscles after piercing the fascia lata. As a subcutaneous structure, it descends along the medial border of the tibia along with the long saphenous vein, supplying the ankle and the skin on the medial side of the foot as far as the first metatarsophalangeal joint (Standring and Gray 2008).

The adductor canal also contains one motor nerve (nerve to vastus medialis) and many other sensory nerves supplying the cutaneous, capsular, and articular aspect of the knee joint and the lower leg (one or more branches of the infrapatellar nerve, the medial retinacular nerve, the superficial branches from the medial cutaneous femoral nerve and less consistently the articular branch of the obturator nerve) (Horner and Dellon 1994). Most of the motor branches of the femoral nerve do not traverse through the adductor canal as division occurs proximally within 5 cm of the inguinal ligament (Kwofie et al. 2013).

Sonoanatomy

The adductor canal occupies the distal two-thirds of the medial thigh. It extends from the apex of the femoral triangle to the distal insertion of the adductor magnus tendon (medial condyle of the femur). The anterolateral boundary of this triangular canal is formed by the vastus medialis muscle. Posteromedially it is bounded by the adductor longus proximally and the adductor magnus distally. The roof is made up of fascia underlying the sartorius muscle.

The sartorius muscle can be identified as an oval-shaped subcutaneous structure underneath the adipose tissue when the ultrasound probe is placed anteromedially at mid-thigh level. The vastus medialis can be identified anterolateral to the sartorius at this level. The femoral artery is seen as a pulsating structure in the adductor canal. The saphenous nerve appears as a small, round hyperechoic structure anterior to the artery. It may not always be possible to clearly identify the nerve (e.g. in obese patients). The sartorius muscle and the femoral artery can be tracked distally from the inguinal region if they are not well imaged. The use of colour Doppler imaging may help in delineating the artery.

In the distal thigh, other structures such as the vasto-adductor membrane and the perivascular sheath may have a hyperechoic echo texture. The saphenous nerve consistently lies sandwiched between the sartorius and the femoral artery during its course from the distal end of the adductor canal (2–3 cm proximal to the adductor hiatus) and the adductor hiatus (Fig. 55.8). At the level of the adductor hiatus, the femoral vessels can be seen diving posteriorly as they enter the popliteal fossa (Saranteas et al. 2011).

The saphenous nerve may also be visualized close to the long saphenous vein at the level of the tibial tuberosity at the medial border of the leg. A light contact should be made with the skin to avoid compressing the vein.

Conduct of the block

The patient is placed supine with the leg slightly abducted, externally rotated, and with minimal knee flexion. Using a high-frequency linear probe (6–13 MHz), the sartorius muscle, underlying femoral artery, and the vastus medialis muscle are identified at the mid-thigh level in the short-axis view. The saphenous nerve appears as a

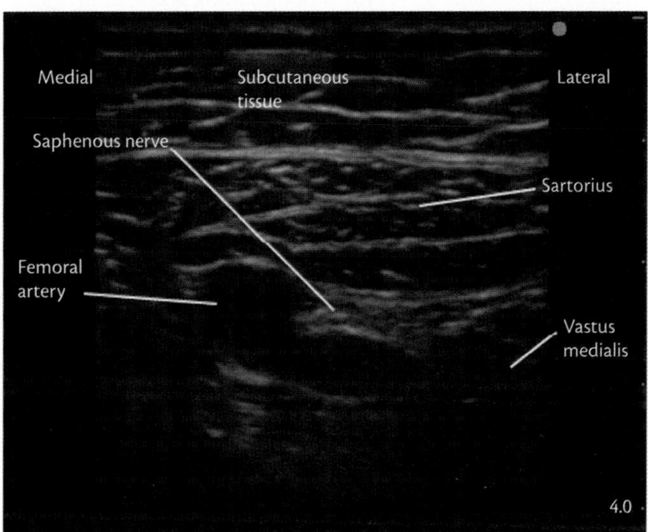

Figure 55.8 Ultrasound image of the right saphenous nerve in the adductor canal accompanying the femoral artery. The femoral vein can be seen just under the saphenous nerve. The vastus medialis forms the lateral boundary of the adductor canal, and fascia underlying the sartorius forms the roof.

small, round hyperechoic structure in the adductor canal lateral to the artery. A small volume of local anaesthetic is injected to numb the skin. Under aseptic conditions, a 5 cm, 22 G, short-bevel nerve block needle is advanced using the in-plane approach from lateral to medial direction. Once the needle tip is in proximity of the nerve, 3–5 ml of local anaesthetic is injected after negative aspiration. If the nerve is not well imaged, the needle tip should be placed medial to the artery and the local anaesthetic deposited there. Additional needle repositioning might be required if the spread of local anaesthetic does not occur in the desired area.

For the distal approach, the ultrasound transducer is moved caudally following the artery in the adductor canal until it is seen diving posteriorly through the adductor hiatus. The needle is inserted 2–3 cm proximal to it (using the approach previously described) and local anaesthetic is injected between the femoral artery and the sartorius muscle. The saphenous nerve lies just under the surface of the muscle and medial to the artery in this area.

Block assessment

A sensory block to cold over the medial aspect of the leg between the knee and the medial malleolus indicates a successful block. Some patients may exhibit some weakness in extending the knee joint if the flexed knee is supported off the bed.

Dose and choice of local anaesthetic

Five to ten millilitres of the local anaesthetic placed in the distal one-third of the canal provides excellent analgesia for the infrapatellar region, medial part of the leg, and ankle surgery (Krombach and Gray 2007; Manickam et al. 2009). A distal block may avoid motor weakness as a result of selective blockade of the saphenous nerve but may not provide complete analgesia for knee procedures.

Fifteen millilitres of local anaesthetic in the adductor canal at the mid-thigh level provides pain relief comparable to femoral nerve block, and better preserves the quadriceps motor power in patients undergoing total knee arthroplasty (Andersen et al. 2013; Kwofie et al. 2013; Kim et al. 2014). Local anaesthetics such as ropivacaine 0.75% or bupivacaine 0.5% provide long-lasting postoperative analgesia that can be further extended with a standard peripheral nerve infusion of 8 ml h^{-1} of ropivacaine 0.2%.

Higher volumes of local anaesthetic (20–30 ml) may lead to undesirable motor block (Chen et al. 2014). Anatomical studies have demonstrated that 30 ml of liquid dye injected into the adductor canal the distal one third of the femur could spread proximally up to the division of the femoral nerve and possibly up to the femoral triangle if injected under high pressure as there are no boundaries between the two (Davis et al. 2009).

So far there is no consensus on the ideal dose or site for adductor canal block (Bendtsen et al. 2014; Jaeger et al. 2014). The available literature combined with anatomical knowledge suggests that a higher volume block placed proximally provides excellent analgesia for knee surgery but may have an element of motor block while lower volumes at the distal end of the adductor canal are suitable for lower leg and ankle surgery. The choice of local anaesthetic agent is dictated by the indication of siting this block.

Contraindications

Patient refusal, true local anaesthetic allergy, local sepsis, and coagulation disorders.

Complications

Haematoma formation, intramuscular injection, nerve injury, and local infection.

Sciatic nerve block

L' Anesthésie Régionale is a fascinating book of regional anaesthesia published in 1920. Victor Pauchet (tutor and surgical colleague of Gaston Labat who was considered an expert in regional anaesthesia in France) describes infiltration of the great sciatic nerve as very difficult and uncertain. It was before the advent of nerve stimulators or ultrasound machines. Labat is credited with describing a reliable technique for sciatic nerve block but several different approaches have been reported subsequently.

Clinical application

Sciatic nerve block is indicated for surgical anaesthesia and analgesia of the knee, anterior (except anteromedial) and posterolateral leg, and ankle and foot (e.g. total knee arthroplasty, Achilles tendon repair, tibial plateau repair, ankle fracture and fusions). It is often combined with a femoral nerve block to provide complete analgesia of the lower limb from mid-thigh down. This is useful for the patient with significant cardiovascular disease to avoid the potential haemodynamic compromise associated with spinal anaesthesia.

Continuous sciatic nerve block, when added to a continuous femoral nerve block, provides better analgesia and reduces opioid requirements significantly when compared with continuous femoral block or continuous psoas compartment block for total knee arthroplasty. Use of dilute local anaesthetics for infusion avoids interference with early mobilization (Allen et al. 1998; Morin et al. 2005; Pham Dang et al. 2005; Cappelleri et al. 2011; Abdallah and Brull 2012; Luke and Chelly 2012; Sato et al. 2014).

Anatomy

The sciatic nerve is the nerve of the posterior compartment of the thigh (Standring and Gray 2008; Hadzic and New York School of Regional Anesthesia 2012). It is the largest peripheral nerve in the body arising from the lumbosacral plexus with root value of L4–S3. It is formed in the pelvis and enters the posterior leg through the greater sciatic foramen anterior to the piriformis muscle. The sciatic nerve descends between the ischial tuberosity and the greater trochanter deep to gluteus maximus but superficial to the lateral rotators of the hip (obturator internus, the gemelli muscles, and quadratus femoris). The posterior cutaneous nerve of thigh and the inferior gluteal artery lie lateral to the sciatic nerve at this level.

The sciatic nerve enters the posterior compartment of the thigh at the inferior border of the gluteus maximus posterior to the adductor magnus and anterior to the long head of biceps. It descends towards the popliteal fossa with the long head of biceps femoris laterally and the semimembranosus covered by the semitendinosus medially. Seen from the surface, the general direction of descent is from the midpoint between the greater trochanter and the ischial tuberosity to the apex of the popliteal fossa.

The sciatic nerve is in fact two nerves (tibial and common peroneal nerves) combined in one fascial sheath, and the nerves separate at a variable level. The division occurs most often near the level of the apex of the popliteal fossa. It may occur proximal (middle and lower third of the thigh) to but rarely distal to it. Both components

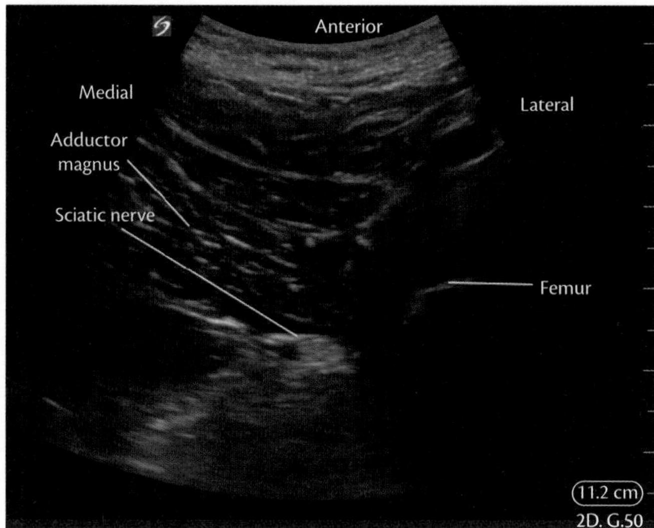

Figure 55.9 Short-axis ultrasound view of the sciatic nerve using the anterior approach. Note the depth settings on the ultrasound machine. The sciatic nerve is close to the lesser trochanter. In this case, external rotation of the thigh brought the sciatic nerve into view.

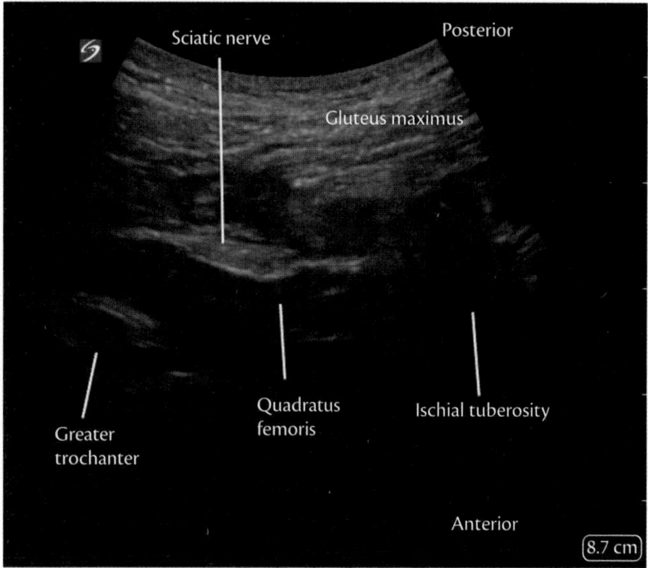

Figure 55.10 Ultrasound image of the sciatic nerve at the transgluteal level. The image was taken using a curved probe with high depth settings. The sciatic nerve is seen lying between the gluteus maximus and the quadratus femoris muscles.

may arise separately from the sacral plexus with the common peroneal nerve travelling through the piriformis and the tibial component entering the thigh below it.

Sonoanatomy

Anterior approach

The patient is placed supine with the leg slightly abducted and externally rotated. A curved ultrasound probe with a low-frequency range (2–8 MHz) is used. The initial depth settings are approximately 8–10 cm. The sciatic nerve is usually at a depth of 6–8 cm when accessed anteriorly. The probe is placed anteromedially in the proximal thigh (at the level of the lesser trochanter) to get short-axis views. Deep to sartorius muscle, the femoral vessels are identified. The femur is seen as a hyperechoic rim with an area of darkness underneath it. Just above the femur is the vastus medialis muscle while medial to the femur is the body of adductor magnus. The sciatic nerve is seen as a slightly flattened oval structure with hyperechoic texture deep to adductor magnus (Fig. 55.9). Posterior to the adductor magnus and the sciatic nerve are the hamstring muscles.

Transgluteal approach

The patient is placed in a modified Sims position. A low-frequency, curved ultrasound probe is placed over a line connecting the coccyx and the greater trochanter to attain a short-axis view (Marhofer 2010). The initial depth setting should be 8–10 cm in order to view both bony landmarks but can subsequently be reduced to improve image quality. Important landmarks are the greater trochanter and the ischial tuberosity, which are seen as areas of hyperechoic rims with areas of darkness underneath. The sciatic nerve is typically seen as a triangular hyperechoic structure between the two bony landmarks just deep to the gluteus maximus muscle (Fig. 55.10). A wide band of muscle posterior to the sciatic nerve, separated by a fascial layer, is the quadratus femoris.

Subgluteal approach

For the subgluteal approach, a higher-frequency linear probe can be used while imaging at the subgluteal fold as the sciatic nerve lies superficially (4–5 cm). Once the bony landmarks are identified, the sciatic nerve can be seen as a bright, hyperechoic, flattened oval structure sandwiched between the long head of biceps laterally, the semitendinosus medially, and the adductor magnus posteriorly (Fig. 55.11).

For any of these approaches, if the nerve is not well imaged, different manoeuvres can be tried to bring the nerve in to view, for example, tilting the probe cepahalad/caudad or scanning proximally/distally or asking the patient to plantarflex/dorsiflex the ankle.

Conduct of the block

Classic posterior and parasacral approaches are better suited for placement of peripheral nerve catheters than the anterior approach.

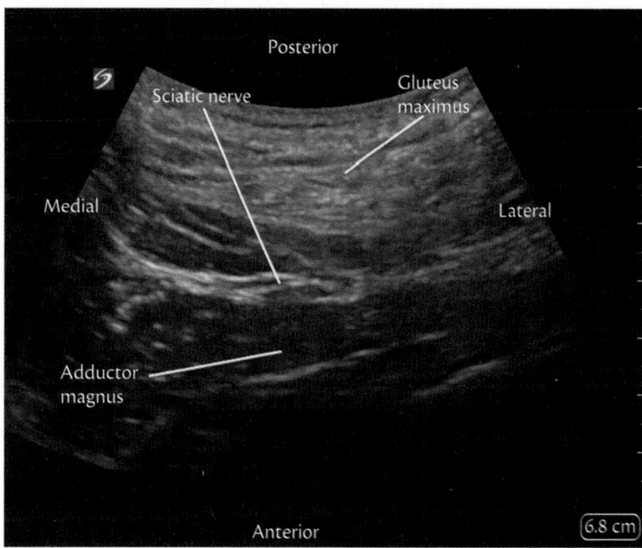

Figure 55.11 Sonoanatomy of the sciatic nerve at the subgluteal level showing the sciatic nerve as a flattened hyperechoic structure lying between the gluteus maximus and adductor magnus muscles.

Ultrasound-guided techniques

Anterior approach

All essential structures, as previously described, are identified using ultrasound. A 22 G, 15 cm short-bevel nerve block needle is introduced in-plane from the lateral to medial side with an ultrasound transducer on the anteromedial surface of the thigh. The out-of-plane approach can also be used. In both cases, extra care should be taken to identify the position of the tip of the needle as the nerve lies very deep. This can be facilitated by injecting a small amount (0.25–0.5 ml) of local anaesthetic solution or saline under real-time imaging. Once the needle tip is deemed to be in the correct position, 1–2 ml of local anaesthetic can be injected to assess the spread. This may further 'highlight' the boundaries of the sciatic nerve. If the distribution of the local anaesthetic is not appropriate, further re-positioning of the needle tip should be attempted. The chosen dose of local anaesthetic is injected after negative aspiration, assessing its spread in real time. Multiple injections for circumferential spread of the local anaesthetic are not essential but may hasten the onset of the block.

Transgluteal and subgluteal approach

All necessary structures, as previously described, are identified using ultrasound guidance. A 22 G, 10 cm short-bevel nerve block needle is introduced in-plane from the lateral to the medial side. The out-of-plane approach can also be used, in which case extra care should be taken to ascertain the position of the tip of the needle. Local anaesthetic is injected as described for the anterior approach.

Nerve stimulator-based techniques

Posterior approach

For the parasacral, modified Labat's, and subgluteal approaches, the patient is positioned laterally and rolled forward slightly with the block side non-dependent. The dependent leg should be fully extended. The operative leg is flexed at the hip and is rested on the partially flexed knee. The heel rests on the knee of the dependent leg such that the foot is clearly visible to assess the response to nerve stimulation (modified Sims position).

Parasacral approach (Mansour's description)

A line connecting the ischial tuberosity and the posterior superior iliac spine is drawn. An insulated nerve block needle is inserted 6 cm caudal to the posterior superior iliac spine on this line. It is inserted perpendicular to the skin and advanced slowly. Twitches of the hamstrings, calf, or toes are sought at a current intensity of 0.4–0.5 mA. The sciatic nerve is located at a depth of 6–8 cm. If bone is contacted by the needle tip then the needle is re-directed caudally and laterally to go past the wings of the sacrum or the iliac bone. However, care should be taken not to advance the needle by more than 2 cm after bone contact to avoid any damage to intra-pelvic organs. This block may achieve anaesthesia of the entire sacral plexus and motor block of the obturator nerve, but it is unreliable for this purpose. As a result, it may block the pudendal nerve leading to urinary retention (Mansour 1993; Mansour and Bennetts 1996; Morris et al. 1997; Helayel et al. 2006; Aissaoui et al. 2013). Ripart et al. (2005) reported a series of 400 successful cases of parasacral block.

Classic posterior approach

For Winnie's modification of Labat's approach see Labat (1922) and Winnie (1975). A line is drawn from the greater trochanter to the posterior superior iliac spine (ilio-trochanteric line). This line represents the upper border of the piriformis muscle and greater sciatic foramen. A second line is drawn from the greater trochanter to the sacral hiatus. A perpendicular is dropped from the midpoint of the ilio-trochanteric line to the second line. The intersection of these two lines marks the point of insertion of the needle. A 22 G, 10 cm long insulated needle is inserted perpendicular to the plane of the skin. The sciatic nerve lies at a depth of 5–8 cm. The needle should be advanced most carefully once it reaches a depth of 5 cm.

Initially, local twitches from the gluteal muscles may be observed. The aim is to attain twitches (visible or palpable) of the hamstrings, calf, foot, or toes at a current intensity of 0.4–0.5 mA. If bone is contacted or no twitches are obtained, the needle should be partially withdrawn and gradually directed caudally or cephalad until the twitches are obtained. If there is still failure to locate the sciatic nerve then anatomical landmarks should be reconsidered as adipose tissue over the gluteal region can easily mask landmarks or skin movement can change the point of entry.

A disadvantage of this approach is that the patient needs to be re-positioned and the needle travels through a thick layer of muscles that might be painful and uncomfortable for the patient. Incorrectly assessed landmarks can potentially lead to placement of the needle into the hip joint or inside the pelvis.

Sub-gluteal approach

The patient is positioned as for Labat's approach as previously described (di Benedetto et al. 2001). A line connecting the greater trochanter and the ischial tuberosity is drawn. A perpendicular is dropped caudally for 4 cm from the midpoint of this line to locate the point of entry of the needle. This usually corresponds to a furrow between the biceps and semitendinosus muscles. An insulated nerve stimulator needle is inserted perpendicular to the skin. The goal is to get an appropriate motor response (tibial or peroneal) distal to the knee joint. Failure to get a response may require redirection of the needle, medially or laterally, gradually until the desired response is achieved. Twitching of the hamstrings indicates direct muscular stimulation and this indicates that the needle is too medial. The sciatic nerve lies at a shallower depth in this region as compared with Labat's approach. This technique potentially causes less discomfort to the patient but the patient does need to be re-positioned.

Raj's approach

For the lithotomy position, see Raj et al. (1975). In this approach, a needle is inserted at the mid-point of a line connecting the greater trochanter and the ischial tuberosity while an assistant or a Mayo table supports the flexed thigh and the leg of the supine patient. It has the advantage that the patient does not need to be repositioned laterally, but an assistant is required to hold the leg and this can be challenging for the assistant.

Anterior approach

For Beck's description see Beck (1963). This position is advantageous when the patient cannot be placed in the lateral position. However, this block could be uncomfortable in an awake patient as the nerve is deeply situated and the needle travels through multiple muscles and fascial planes. There is a higher risk of complications as inaccurate landmark assessment can lead to neurovascular damage (femoral vessels and obturator nerve).

The patient is placed in the supine position. With the operative leg fully extended, a line is drawn between the anterior iliac superior spine and the pubic tubercle. At the junction of the medial and middle thirds of this line a perpendicular is drawn caudally, meeting another line drawn parallel to the inguinal ligament starting from the greater trochanter. The needle (22 G, 15 cm insulated needle) is inserted at this intersection perpendicular to the skin with slight lateral angulation. If the bone is contacted (minor trochanter), the needle is redirected medially in small increments and advanced further until a desired motor twitch (tibial or common peroneal) is achieved at 0.4–0.5 mA. The sciatic nerve is typically found at a depth of 10–12 cm. Slight internal rotation of the leg may help in finding the sciatic nerve if difficulty is faced, which also may reduce the risk of femoral vessel puncture (Vloka et al. 2001b; Moore et al. 2004). If all else fails then the needle should be reinserted 1–2 cm medial to the original point of insertion with lateral tilt.

Block assessment

The sciatic nerve supplies articular branches to the hip joint and the knee joint. It supplies motor branches to the muscles of the posterior compartment of the thigh, part of the adductor magnus, and all muscles below the knee joint. It provides sensory supply to the skin of the posterior thigh and almost all of the lower leg except the medial part of the lower leg, which is supplied by the saphenous nerve.

A block performed at the subgluteal, or lower level may not provide motor block of the hamstring group of muscles. Sensory block can be assessed using cold or pinprick in the sensory distribution as described earlier.

Dose and choice of local anaesthetic

Fifteen to 20 millilitres of the local anaesthetic is widely recommended in the literature for the nerve stimulator- and ultrasound-guided techniques (Taboada et al. 2006; Danelli et al. 2009). Use of ultrasound, particularly for the subgluteal approach, allows reduction in the dose, better sensory block, and faster performance time (Latzke et al. 2010; Salinas 2010). There are no studies that directly estimate the ED_{95} of local anaesthetics for sciatic nerve block. The choice of local anaesthetic depends on the purpose of the block. Short-acting local anaesthetics such as lidocaine 2% (onset within 10–20 min) provide analgesia lasting 5–8 h while longer-acting agent such as ropivacaine 0.5% and 0.75% have a slower onset (15–30 min) but analgesia may last up to 24 h. Bupivacaine 0.5% may provide analgesia for up to 48 h (Hadzic and New York School of Regional Anesthesia 2007).

Injection of 10 ml of local anaesthetic (bupivacaine 0.5% or ropivacaine 0.5%) under the common investing extraneural layer of the sciatic nerve at the subgluteal level may produce long-lasting (up to 24 h) motor and sensory block. A greater volume does not give any advantage while lower volumes reduce the duration of postoperative analgesia. However, this approach requires advanced expertise and may lead to intraneuronal injection, although Nader et al. (2013) reported no adverse sequelae in their study.

For analgesia after total knee arthroplasty, an initial bolus of 6–12 ml of ropivacaine 0.2% followed by infusion of 3–8 ml h^{-1} of ropivacaine 0.1–0.2% is one of the suggested regimens (Chelly et al. 2010).

Complications

Injury to pelvic organs can occur if the needle is inserted too deep while performing proximal approaches such as parasacral or transgluteal, especially using the nerve stimulator technique. An excessive volume of local anaesthetic can lead to spread proximally to the lumber sympathetic fibres.

Contraindications

There are very few contraindications to sciatic nerve block. They include local infection such as bedsores, pre-existing neuropathy, coagulation disorders, and a true allergy to local anaesthetics.

Popliteal nerve block

Block of the distal sciatic nerve in the popliteal fossa is a simple, safe, and reliable technique for analgesia and anaesthesia of the distal two-thirds of the leg, ankle, and foot. The success rate for popliteal block is quoted to be 92–97% (Perlas et al. 2009). It provides analgesia or anaesthesia of the entire distal extremity (except the medial part supplied by the saphenous nerve) and preserves hamstring motor power and knee joint function. The sciatic nerve in the popliteal fossa can be approached posteriorly (intertendinous approach) or laterally.

Clinical application

The popliteal nerve block is indicated for operations such as corrective foot surgery, ankle fracture repair, Achilles tendon repair, tibial plateau repair, tibial nailing (in conjunction with femoral nerve block), and short saphenous vein stripping. For calf tourniquets, the popliteal nerve block on its own may be sufficient. For ankle surgery, continuous popliteal blocks are more effective than ankle blocks for postoperative analgesia.

Anatomy

The popliteal fossa is bounded by the biceps femoris laterally and the semimembranosus and semitendinosus medially above the popliteal crease. Inferiorly, the medial and lateral heads of the gastrocnemius muscle form its boundaries. It contains the popliteal vessels and common peroneal nerve laterally, tibial nerve medially, connective tissue, and fat.

The sciatic nerve is lateral and superficial to the popliteal vessels and is contained in its own fascial layer. It divides 4–10 cm proximal to the popliteal crease.

The common peroneal nerve (L4–S2) descends along the medial border of the biceps femoris and continues laterally at its course along the head and neck of the fibula. It divides into the superficial and deep peroneal nerves.

The tibial nerve (L4–S3) is a larger branch descending centrally in the popliteal fossa. It crosses the popliteal vessels lateral to medial posteriorly. It terminates by dividing into medial and lateral plantar nerves. It supplies the muscles of the calf, ankle joint, and gives rise to the medial cutaneous sural nerve.

Ultrasound guidance helps in overcoming the challenge presented by variable anatomy of the sciatic nerve in the popliteal fossa. Images obtained by the ultrasound machine are similar regardless of the approach used. The operator must consider the orientation of the ultrasound image according to the patient's position. A high-frequency (6–13 MHz) linear probe is used with an initial depth setting of 3–4 cm. Imaging is started at the level of the popliteal crease with identification of the popliteal vessels in the short-axis view. Lateral to the artery is the biceps femoris while the semimembranosus covered by the semitendinosus is seen medially. Superficial and lateral to the artery is the tibial nerve with a hyperechoic echo texture and honeycomb appearance. Sliding the probe laterally will bring the common peroneal nerve in to view, which is more superficial than the tibial nerve and close to the medial border of the biceps femoris (Fig. 55.12). Both nerves should be traced proximally until they combine to form the sciatic nerve near the apex of the popliteal fossa. To help identify the nerves, the patient can be asked to flex the ankle. This may produce 'see-saw' movement of the nerves as they move within the soft tissues as the ankle is flexed. Tilting the probe proximally/distally or minor rotation at its axis may improve the image quality.

It can be technically challenging to scan the popliteal region in a trauma patient with a plaster cast or dressing on the leg. These may be removed after consulting the surgeons. Such patients are difficult to position as well. A Mayo table or tall wedge could be used to rest the leg supported by an assistant. The patient's thigh will be almost horizontal with acceptable space below the thigh for scanning. Resting the foot on the bed with the knee flexed may not provide ideal conditions for imaging or manoeuvring the needle especially in trauma patients or patients with shorter femoral length.

Conduct of the block

Both lateral and posterior approaches are suitable for siting a catheter for continuous nerve block.

Ultrasound-guided techniques

Posterior approach

The patient is placed in the prone position. Under aseptic conditions, the popliteal fossa is imaged as previously described, and relevant structures are identified. After infiltration of the skin with local anaesthetic, a 5–10 cm short-bevel nerve block needle is inserted in plane from the lateral to the medial side. The out-of-plane approach can also be used giving the advantage that the needle does not travel through muscular tissue. Placement of the needle tip under the common paraneural sheath at the level of the bifurcation of the sciatic nerve may be considered the optimal site. It allows faster onset of block with no increase in the incidence of neural injury (Perlas et al. 2013). It requires advanced ultrasound and needle manoeuvring skills. Once the needle tip reaches the desired site, the chosen dose of local anaesthetic is injected, initially in small doses to assess the spread of the drug. Needle repositioning may be required for correct placement and spread. Circumferential spread of local anaesthetic outside the paraneural sheath may hasten the onset of block but does not affect the success rates (Brull et al. 2011; Choquet et al. 2014).

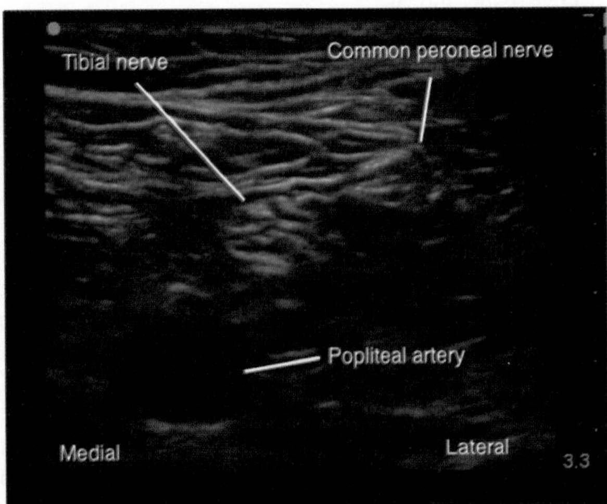

Figure 55.12 Ultrasound anatomy at the level of the popliteal fossa. The tibial nerve is slightly superficial and lateral to the popliteal artery. The common peroneal nerve is lateral and superficial to the tibial nerve.

Lateral approach

The patient is positioned supine and the leg is supported as previously described (see relevant section for 'Sonoanatomy'). Under aseptic conditions, the popliteal fossa is imaged as already described, and relevant structures are identified keeping patient orientation in mind. A 5–10 cm short-bevel nerve block needle is inserted in plane from the lateral border of the thigh 2–3 cm above the plane of the transducer. Once the needle tip is at the appropriate place (see previous paragraph under 'Posterior approach') a small volume of local anaesthetic is injected to confirm correct placement and assess the spread. Additional needle repositioning might be required for optimal spread of the local anaesthetic.

Nerve stimulator-guided techniques

For posterior and lateral approaches there is no significant difference between a single-injection and double-injection technique for onset time and success of block. Both common peroneal (i.e. dorsiflexion/eversion of the foot) and tibial response (i.e. plantar flexion/inversion) of the foot are acceptable when localizing the nerve, although the latter is preferable (Benzon et al. 1997; Hadzic and Vloka 1998; Taboada et al. 2005; March et al. 2006; Arcioni et al. 2007; Perlas et al. 2009).

Posterior approach

The patient is positioned prone on the bed with their foot and toes easily visible (Rorie et al. 1980; Vloka et al. 2001a). Three important landmarks to be identified are the popliteal crease, the tendon of biceps femoris (lateral), and the semimembranosus and semitendinosus (medial). The patient can be asked to flex the knee against resistance to make these tendons prominent. A needle insertion point is marked about 7 cm proximal to the popliteal crease, 0.5–1.0 cm lateral to the mid point between the two tendons. A 5 cm short-bevel insulated needle attached to a nerve stimulator is inserted at an angle of 45° anteriorly and superiorly. The needle is advanced, and motor response elicited between 0.4–0.5 mA. Once the needle tip is at a desirable site, the local anaesthetic is injected after ensuring negative aspiration.

Direct twitches in the biceps or the semimembranosus/semitendinosus indicate too lateral or too medial needle tip placement. Bone contact indicates that the needle is too deep. Calf twitches without toe/foot movement may indicate stimulation of motor branches to the calf muscle, which is not an acceptable response. Blood on aspiration may indicate that the needle tip is too deep or too medial.

Lateral approach

The lateral approach is advantageous for patients who cannot be turned prone (e.g. those with trauma or under general anaesthesia). Two different lateral approaches have been described in the literature. There are no studies directly comparing these two approaches. Arcioni et al. (2007) compared single- and double-injection lateral approach techniques where the needle was inserted 6 cm proximal to the popliteal crease.

Hadzic and Vloka (1998) suggest the needle insertion point as 7 cm proximal to the popliteal crease in the groove between the lateral border of vastus lateralis and the biceps femoris. Actively raising the foot off the bed may make these landmarks more prominent. A 10 cm short-bevel insulated needle connected to a nerve stimulator is placed in the groove parallel to the horizontal. After contact is made with the femur, the needle should be withdrawn and directed posteriorly at an angle of about 30° advancing it slowly until foot/toe twitches are obtained at a current intensity of 0.4–0.5 mA. At this point, the chosen dose of local anaesthetic is injected.

Zetlaoui and Bouaziz (1998) suggest the needle should be inserted at the intersection of the groove between biceps and vastus lateralis and a vertical line dropped from the superior pole of the patella. The needle is directed 30° posteriorly and the tibial nerve response is sought. The common peroneal nerve may get stimulated first as it is located laterally in which case the needle is withdrawn and directed more posteriorly. The authors recommended a two-injection technique for this approach.

When measured on the patient's leg there may not be much difference in point of needle insertion between the above two approaches.

Local muscle twitches may be seen when the needle is first inserted as a result of direct stimulation of biceps. These twitches will stop when the needle tip enters the popliteal fossa. If foot/toe twitches are not obtained within 2 cm of entering the fossa then the needle should not be advanced, as it may not be in the plane of the nerve and could cause vascular injury. Lateral rotation at the hip joint should be ruled out and functioning of the nerve stimulator should be checked. The needle should be withdrawn and redirected posteriorly by 5–10°. If all these measures fail, the anatomical landmarks should be reconsidered or an alternative technique, preferably ultrasound guided, should be used.

Block assessment

Adequate block of the sciatic nerve provides anaesthesia of the distal leg other than the anteromedial aspect. It also provides motor block of the leg muscles but the hamstrings are not affected. The skin on the posterior part of the knee is also anaesthetized.

Dose and choice of local anaesthetic

Thirty to forty millilitres of local anaesthetic has been used conventionally for nerve stimulator guided popliteal nerve block (Hebl et al. 2010; Miller 2010). With increased usage of ultrasound and paraneural injections, many authors have successfully used a volume of 30 ml (Perlas et al. 2008; Morau et al. 2010; Choquet et al. 2014). Sala-Blanch et al. (2012) has reported 100% success with 20 ml of mepivacaine 1.5% using ultrasound and a peripheral nerve stimulator with paraneural injection at the bifurcation of the sciatic nerve. Recently, Techasuk et al. (2014) suggested that 13.5 ml of a lidocaine–bupivacaine mixture provides adequate postoperative analgesia in 90% of patients using ultrasound-guided subparaneural popliteal sciatic nerve block (at the neural bifurcation). The choice of local anaesthetic depends on the purpose of the block. Lidocaine 2% with adrenaline provides analgesia for up to 8 h; ropivacaine 0.75% for up to 24 h; and bupivacaine 0.5% for up to 30 h (Hadzic and New York School of Regional Anesthesia 2007). For continuous infusions, an initial bolus of 10–20 ml of ropivacaine 0.2–0.5% followed by 5–10 ml h^{-1} of ropivacaine 0.1–0.2% is recommended (Chelly et al. 2010).

Contraindications

Patient refusal, infection at the injection site, and local anaesthetic allergy are contraindications. Relative contraindications include previous total knee arthroplasty, vascular bypass or grafts, and pre-existing neuropathy.

Complications

Patients may not be able to weight bear if undergoing ambulatory surgery. Haematoma formation, nerve injury, and local infection are possible complications with any peripheral nerve block.

Ankle block

Ankle block is a simple, safe, and effective way to block the terminal branches of the sciatic and saphenous nerves (Rudkin et al. 2005). It does not require any special equipment and has easily visible and palpable landmarks. The patient can walk with the help of crutches and be discharged home in the immediate postoperative period.

Clinical application

Ankle block can be used for anaesthesia and analgesia for all types of foot and toe surgery that does not require a tourniquet above the ankle (e.g. amputations, osteotomies, arthroplasty, and reconstruction). An ankle tourniquet may be tolerated for up to 30 min when sedation is used with the ankle block although patients more than 70 years of age may have a lower threshold of pain (Rudkin et al. 2004). For forefoot surgery, patients who had an ankle block required less analgesic as compared with popliteal block in the post-anaesthesia care unit (McLeod et al. 1995).

Anatomy

Five peripheral nerves need to be blocked for the ankle block (Fig. 55.13) (Standring and Gray 2008).

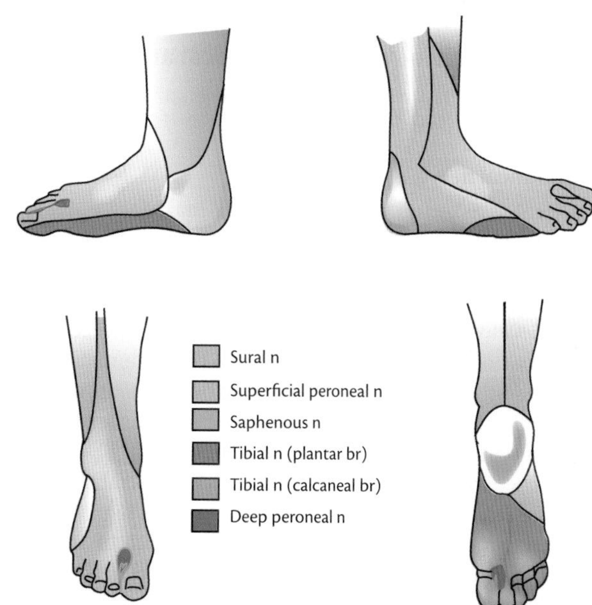

Figure 55.13 Cutaneous innervation of the foot and ankle.
Reproduced from Hebl J, Lennon R (eds), *Mayo Clinic Atlas of Regional Anesthesia and Ultrasound-Guided Nerve Blockade*, Copyright © 2010 Mayo Foundation for Medical Education and Research/Oxford University Press. By permission of Oxford University Press, USA, www.oup.com

The *deep peroneal nerve* runs its course between the tibialis anterior and the extensor digitorum longus muscles with the anterior tibial artery in the anterior compartment of the leg. It crosses the ankle between the tendons of extensor hallucis longus and extensor digitorum longus close to the anterior tibial artery. At this level, it divides into the medial and lateral branches. The medial branch crosses the dorsum of the foot lateral to the dorsalis pedis artery while the lateral branch supplies the muscles of the foot. The medial branch terminates by supplying a patch of skin in the first web space.

The *superficial peroneal nerve* supplies motor branches to the peroneus longus and brevis muscles in the anterolateral compartment of the leg. It becomes subcutaneous 5–10 cm above the lateral malleolus supplying the skin over the dorsum of the foot and terminates by communication with the saphenous nerve medially, deep peroneal nerve in the first web space, and the sural nerve laterally.

The *sural nerve* is formed by the combination of the medial sural nerve (from the tibial nerve) and the lateral sural nerve (from the common peroneal nerve). The sural nerve emerges on the lateral aspect of the Achilles tendon approximately 10 cm proximal to the lateral malleolus. It supplies the Achilles tendon, ankle joint, lateral malleolus, and skin over the lateral part of the foot extending to a small area of the sole, fourth interosseous space, and fifth toe.

The *posterior tibial nerve* emerges to lie superficial in the distal one-third of the leg on the medial side of the Achilles tendon. It initially runs between the tendons of tibialis posterior and flexor digitorum longus. It then passes behind the medial malleolus posterior to the posterior tibial artery. It divides into the medial and lateral plantar nerves and the medial calcaneal nerve. It supplies the ankle joint, the skin over most of the heel, the Achilles tendon and sensorimotor innervation of the sole.

The *saphenous nerve* (branch of the femoral nerve) travels subcutaneously on the medial aspect of the ankle and foot. It passes anterior to the medial malleolus supplying as far as the first metatarsophalangeal joint in some patients.

Conduct of the block and dose of local anaesthetic

See Hebl et al. (2010), Miller (2010), and Hadzic and New York School of Regional Anesthesia (2012).

Deep peroneal nerve

The patient is asked to dorsiflex the toes making the tendon of extensor hallucis longus more prominent. The dorsalis pedis artery can be felt pulsating just lateral to it. The deep peroneal nerve lies immediately lateral to these pulsations. Under aseptic conditions, a 1.5 cm, 25 G hypodermic needle is inserted under the skin until it contacts the bone. The needle is withdrawn by 2–3 mm and 2–4 ml of local anaesthetic is injected after ruling out intravascular placement. A fan-wise medial-lateral spread of local anaesthetic may improve success rates.

The deep peroneal nerve can be seen lying lateral to the dorsalis pedis artery in the short-axis view using a high-frequency (6–13 MHz, linear) ultrasound probe set at a depth of 1.5–2.2 cm (Fig. 55.14). The probe should be placed at the level of the extensor retinaculum. It can be blocked using an in-plane or out-of-plane approach. Often the nerve is distinguished better from neighbouring tissue after injection of local anaesthetic. The use of the colour Doppler setting on the ultrasound machine may help in locating the artery.

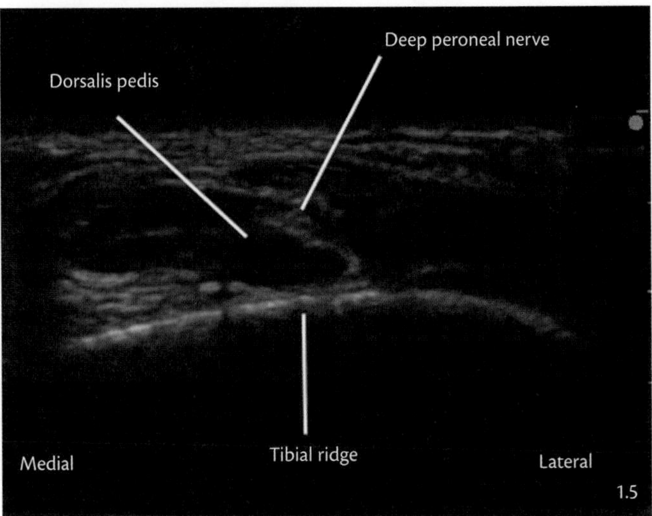

Figure 55.14 Ultrasound image of the deep peroneal nerve seen in the short-axis view lateral to the dorsalis pedis artery and superficial to the vein at the level of the extensor retinaculum.

Posterior tibial nerve

At the level of the medial malleolus, pulsations of the posterior tibial artery can be felt between the medial border of the Achilles tendon and the posterior margin of the medial malleolus. The posterior tibial nerve lies just posterior to the artery (Fig. 55.15). Under aseptic conditions, a 1.5 cm, 25 G hypodermic needle is inserted under the skin until it contacts the bone. The needle is withdrawn by 2–3 mm and 2–4 ml of local anaesthetic is injected after ruling out intravascular placement. A fan-wise anteroposterior spread of local anaesthetic may improve its success rates.

Similar to the deep peroneal nerve, an ultrasound machine can be used to locate the posterior tibial nerve behind the posterior tibial artery. The use of colour Doppler may help in locating the artery. The probe should be placed behind the medial malleolus. Anterior to the artery the tendons of tibialis anterior and flexor digitorum longus can be seen while flexor hallucis longus

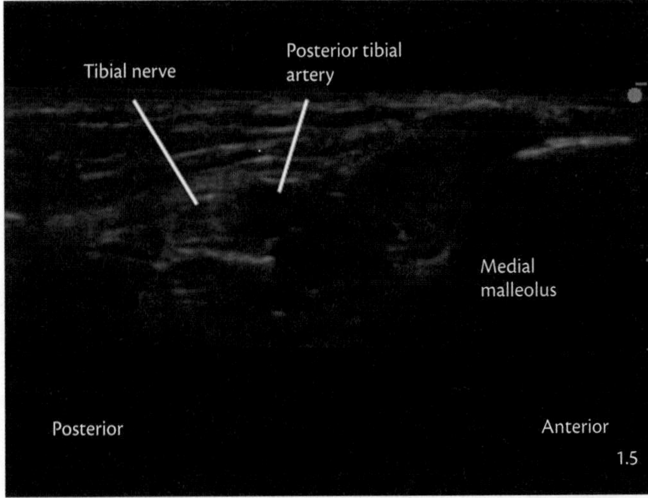

Figure 55.15 Ultrasound image of the posterior tibial nerve lying just behind the posterior tibial artery in the short-axis view at the level of the medial malleolus.

lies behind it: the tendons can have a similar appearance to the artery but they are non-pulsatile. Proximal/distal scanning may help in differentiating the nerve as it is intimately related to the artery.

Superficial peroneal nerve

This nerve lies on the anterolateral aspect of the leg. It may not be easily visible in the subcutaneous fascia with an ultrasound machine. It can be traced in the intermuscular septum between peroneus longus and extensor digitorum longus approximately 10–20 cm proximal to the lateral malleolus on the lateral side of the leg (Fig. 55.16). The prominent groove between these two muscles leads to the surface of the fibula.

The *superficial peroneal nerve, sural nerve*, and *saphenous nerves* are superficial branches of the femoral and sciatic nerves. They can be blocked by subcutaneous infiltration of local anaesthetic in a 'ring' fashion starting from the medial malleolus to the lateral border of the Achilles tendon. The first injection is made starting from the site of the deep peroneal nerve block to the medial malleolus. Approximately 4–5 ml of local anaesthetic is injected subcutaneously. This will cover branches of the saphenous nerve. The second injection is directed towards the lateral malleolus without fully withdrawing the needle from the skin, injecting 4–5 ml of local anaesthetic to raise a 'wheal' on the anterolateral part of the ankle to block the superficial peroneal nerve. The third injection is performed from the already anaesthetized part of the skin from just anterior to the lateral malleolus to the lateral border of the Achilles tendon. This will block branches of the sural nerve.

Block assessment

Sensory block to cold/pinprick is tested in the distribution of the nerves blocked. It may take up to 20 min for onset of the block depending on the drug used.

Choice of local anaesthetic

Agents such as bupivacaine 0.5% or ropivacaine 0.5% can provide analgesia lasting up to 24 h.

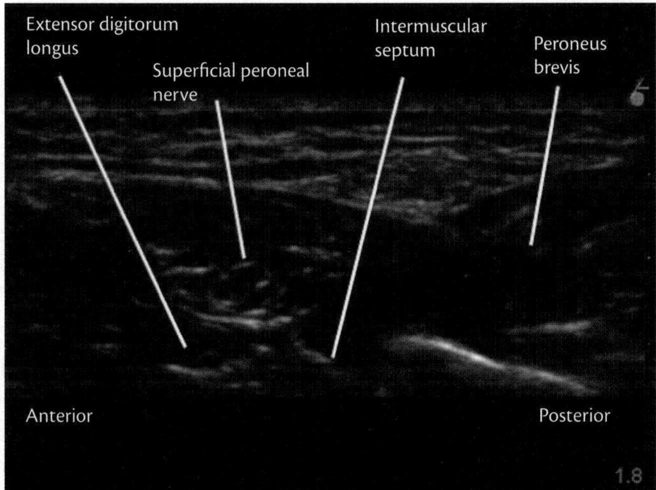

Figure 55.16 Ultrasound image of the superficial peroneal nerve which is seen between two layers of deep fascia soon after leaving the intermuscular septum between the extensor digitorum longus and peroneus brevis muscles to lie subcutaneously. This image was taken approximately 7 cm proximal to the lateral malleolus.

Contraindications

Patient refusal, a true local anaesthetic allergy, and local infection.

Complications

The ankle block is a safe block as most of the injections are subcutaneous. Residual paraesthesia as a result of inadvertent intraneural injections, haematoma formation, vascular injury, and infection are some other complications. The patient will lose proprioception from the ankle joint after this block.

Forefoot block

A popliteal nerve block in combination with a saphenous nerve block provides anaesthesia and analgesia for all operations on the foot. The ankle block alone can be used for forefoot operations. Forefoot blocks are mainly used for postoperative pain relief for operations performed under general anaesthesia.

Clinical application

Forefoot blocks can be used as the sole anaesthetic for metatarsophalangeal joint arthrodesis, modified McBride bunionectomy, interphalangeal arthrodesis, first metatarsophalangeal cheilectomy, paronychia, or amputation/ debridement of distal aspects of the toes. These blocks can also be used for postoperative analgesia and to supplement a partially effective or an incomplete popliteal or ankle block.

Anatomy

Dorsal (anterior) surface

The dorsum of the foot is supplied by the medial and intermediate branches of the superficial peroneal nerve, the deep peroneal nerve, and the sural nerve. The two branches of the superficial peroneal nerve further divide into digital branches as they enter the foot. The branches from the medial branch of the superficial peroneal nerve supply the medial side of the great toe and adjacent sides of the second and third toes. The digital branches of the intermediate nerve supply the adjacent sides of the third, fourth, and fifth toes. *All of these branches lie deep to the dorsal venous arch*. The deep peroneal nerve lies in the neurovascular bundle deep to the superficial fascia and becomes subcutaneous just above the first interphalangeal space when it emerges in the cleft between the first and second metatarsals. The deep peroneal nerve supplies the adjacent sides of the great toe and the second toe. The sural nerve runs subcutaneously under the skin on the lateral border of the foot and supplies the lateral aspect of the little toe.

Ventral (posterior) aspect

The posterior tibial nerve divides into the medial calcaneal nerve, medial plantar nerve, and the lateral plantar nerve just above the sole of the foot on the medial aspect of the ankle. The medial calcaneal nerve supplies the skin and superficial fascia of the sole in the region of the heel. The medial plantar nerve divides into two branches that supply the skin of the sole of the foot and the toes. The sole of the foot has five layers. The medial and lateral plantar nerves and vessels lie in the second layer under the plantar aponeurosis and the superficial layer of muscles. The lateral plantar nerve gives rise to a deep branch at the mid forefoot layer which lies in the deepest fifth layer.

Conduct of the block

Midfoot block

Palpate the dorsalis pedis artery and inject 2–3 ml of local anaesthetic on either side of the dorsalis pedis artery at any level to block the deep peroneal nerve in the forefoot. The medial and intermediate branches of the superficial peroneal nerve can be blocked by injecting 3–5 ml of local anaesthetic subcutaneously deep to the dorsal venous arch of the foot. This injection only leads to dermal analgesia on the anterior surface of the foot and is insufficient for any bony interventions in the blocked area.

Intermetatarsal block

Palpate the intermetatarsal area. Insert a 23/25 G needle slowly between the tarsal bones as far as possible until it can be felt on the other end. Withdraw the needle slightly and inject 3–5 ml of local anaesthetic (into the second layer of the sole of the foot). Then withdraw the needle under the skin and inject 3–5 ml of local anaesthetic. For a given toe, injections on either side of the metatarsal bone will be required to achieve complete analgesia.

Ring block

The local anaesthetic is injected subcutaneously under the skin in the web space, dorsal surface, and the plantar surface (i.e. on all sides of the relevant toe). Up to 5 ml of local anaesthetic may be required.

Dose and choice of local anaesthetic

Any local anaesthetic such as bupivacaine, ropivacaine, or lidocaine can be used. Local anaesthetic solutions containing adrenaline should be avoided.

Contraindications

Local infection and patient refusal

Complications

Local infection, haematoma, and failure.

Intra-articular injection of local anaesthetics

Local infiltration of local anaesthetic is gaining popularity with orthopaedic surgeons as an integral component of multimodal analgesia after hip, knee, and ankle surgery.

Anatomy

The articular surface of the joints is lined by hyaline cartilage, which expresses opioid, *N*-methyl-D-aspartate, and adrenergic receptors when inflamed.

Conduct of the block

These blocks are performed by the surgeons during the procedure.

Dose and choice of local anaesthetic

Large volumes (i.e. 150–200 ml) of local anaesthetic mixed with other drugs are used. The mixture usually contains dilute local anaesthetic such as ropivacaine (2 mg ml^{-1}), a non-steroidal anti-inflammatory such as ketorolac (30 mg), and adrenaline (0.1–0.5 mg). Opioids such as morphine are used by some surgeons. Some surgeons insert a catheter at the end of the operation. The catheter can be attached to an elastomeric balloon pump which delivers a constant rate of local anaesthetic mixture. The flow rate is adjustable. These devices are light and their function is not affected by gravity: therefore, they can be carried by the patient and do not impact mobility. The balloon pumps come in different capacities and can be used to provide a variable duration (up to 12 days) of analgesia after surgery. It is suggested that they do not pose an added infection risk as the catheters are sited and pump connected under sterile conditions.

Advantages

- Easy technique that does not require the skill of peripheral nerve blocks
- Early physiotherapy
- Early ambulation
- Better postoperative analgesia
- Shorter hospital stay
- Requires less time as compared with femoral nerve block
- No risk of nerve damage or urinary retention.

Complications

- Damage to articular cartilage
- Requires surgical expertise
- Chondrolysis
- Risk of local anaesthetic toxicity.

Limitations of intra-articular infusion of local anaesthetics

Haemarthrosis is often seen after joint surgery and this can limit the effectiveness of articular catheters as it lowers the concentration of local anaesthetics and increases the severity of the pain. If a drain is inserted into the joint space for the perioperative period, it may wash out the local anaesthetic solution being infused at the same time.

The articular surface of joints is avascular and meets its metabolic demands from the synovial fluid. Intra-articular administration of saline or local anaesthetic may dilute or alter the composition of synovial fluid and adversely affect the articular cartilage. Large volumes of local anaesthetic injected into the joint space may predispose to local anaesthetic toxicity, especially after major intra-articular trauma and when extensive raw surfaces within the joint have been created by the surgical procedure (increased absorption). The other concern is chondrotoxicity related to local anaesthetic agents. Bupivacaine, lidocaine, and ropivacaine have been shown to cause damage to articular cartilage and synovial membrane in animal and human models (Dogan et al. 2004; Karpie and Chu 2007; Piper and Kim 2008). The toxicity is agent dependent, dose dependent, and time dependent. The toxicity of the local anaesthetics is in the order bupivacaine > lidocaine > ropivacaine. Ropivacaine is therefore recommended for intra-articular infusions and periarticular analgesia. The infusion of local anaesthetics has been shown to significantly increase the risk of gleno-humeral chondrolysis after shoulder surgery (Matsen and Papadonikolakis 2013). Although no such association has been shown in lower limb surgery, caution is advised. A single injection into the joint has not been shown to cause any damage to the articular surface of the joint and these adverse effects are noticed only after continuous intra-articular infusions.

Periarticular local infiltration is also becoming popular among surgeons, but the published evidence does not suggest either a higher efficacy or increased safety of local infiltration analgesia over femoral nerve block or epidural analgesia (Kerr and Kohan 2008; Kehlet and Andersen 2011; McCartney and McLeod 2011; Raeder 2011).

Declaration of interest

None declared.

References

Association of Anaesthetists of Great Britain and Ireland, Griffiths R, Alper J, *et al.* Management of proximal femoral fractures 2011. *Anaesthesia* 2012; **67**: 85–98

Abdallah FW, Brull R. Sciatic nerve block for analgesia after total knee arthroplasty: the jury is still out. *Reg Anesth Pain Med* 2012; **37**: 122–3

Aissaoui Y, Serghini I, Qamous Y, Seddiki R, Zoubir M, Boughalem M. The parasacral sciatic nerve block does not induce anesthesia of the obturator nerve. *J Anesth* 2013; **27**: 66–71

Akkaya T, Ozturk E, Comert A, *et al.* Ultrasound-guided obturator nerve block: a sonoanatomic study of a new methodologic approach. *Anesth Analg* 2009; **108**: 1037–41

Allen HW, Liu SS, Ware PD, Nairn CS, Owens BD. Peripheral nerve blocks improve analgesia after total knee replacement surgery. *Anesth Analg* 1998; **87**: 93–7

Andersen HL, Gyrn J, Møller L, Christensen B, Zaric D. Continuous saphenous nerve block as supplement to single-dose local infiltration analgesia for postoperative pain management after total knee arthroplasty. *Reg Anesth Pain Med* 2013; **38**: 106–11

Arcioni R, Palmisani S, Della Rocca M, *et al.* Lateral popliteal sciatic nerve block: a single injection targeting the tibial branch of the sciatic nerve is as effective as a double-injection technique. *Acta Anaesthesiol Scand* 2007; **51**: 115–21

Auroy Y, Benhamou D, Bargues L, *et al.* Major complications of regional anesthesia in France: The SOS Regional Anesthesia Hotline Service. *Anesthesiology* 2002; **97**: 1274–80

Beck GP. Interior approach to sciatic nerve block. *Anesthesiology* 1963; **24**: 222–4

Bendtsen TF, Moriggl B, Chan V, Pedersen EM, Børglum J. Defining adductor canal block. *Reg Anesth Pain Med* 2014; **39**: 253–4

Benzon HT, Kim C, Benzon HP, *et al.* Correlation between evoked motor response of the sciatic nerve and sensory blockade. *Anesthesiology* 1997; **87**: 547–52

Brodner G, Buerkle H, Van Aken H, *et al.* Postoperative analgesia after knee surgery: a comparison of three different concentrations of ropivacaine for continuous femoral nerve blockade. *Anesth Analg* 2007; **105**: 256–62

Brull R, Macfarlane AJ, Parrington SJ, Koshkin A, Chan VW. Is circumferential injection advantageous for ultrasound-guided popliteal sciatic nerve block?: A proof-of-concept study. *Reg Anesth Pain Med* 2011; **36**: 266–70

Capdevila X, Biboulet P, Bouregba M, Barthelet Y, Rubenovitch J, D'Athis F. Comparison of the three-in-one and fascia iliaca compartment blocks in adults: clinical and radiographic analysis. *Anesth Analg* 1998; **86**: 1039–44

Cappelleri G, Ghisi D, Fanelli A, Albertin A, Somalvico F, Aldegheri G. Does continuous sciatic nerve block improve postoperative analgesia and early rehabilitation after total knee arthroplasty? A prospective, randomized, double-blinded study. *Reg Anesth Pain Med* 2011; **36**: 489–92

Casati A, Baciarello M, Di Cianni S, *et al.* Effects of ultrasound guidance on the minimum effective anaesthetic volume required to block the femoral nerve. *Br J Anaesth* 2007; **98**: 823–7

Casati A, Fanelli G, Beccaria P, Magistris L, Albertin A, Torri G. The effects of single or multiple injections on the volume of 0.5% ropivacaine required for femoral nerve blockade. *Anesth Analg* 2001; **93**: 183–6

Chayen D, Nathan H, Chayen M. The psoas compartment block. *Anesthesiology* 1976; **45**: 95–9

Chelly JE, Ghisi D, Fanelli A. Continuous peripheral nerve blocks in acute pain management. *Br J Anaesth* 2010; **105**(Suppl 1): i86–96

Chen J, Lesser JB, Hadzic A, Reiss W, Resta-Flarer F. Adductor canal block can result in motor block of the quadriceps muscle. *Reg Anesth Pain Med* 2014; **39**: 170–1

Choquet O, Noble GB, Abbal B, Morau D, Bringuier S, Capdevila X. Subparaneural versus circumferential extraneural injection at the bifurcation level in ultrasound-guided popliteal sciatic nerve blocks: a prospective, randomized, double-blind study. *Reg Anesth Pain Med* 2014; **39**: 306–11

Danelli G, Ghisi D, Fanelli A, *et al.* The effects of ultrasound guidance and neurostimulation on the minimum effective anesthetic volume of mepivacaine 1.5% required to block the sciatic nerve using the subgluteal approach. *Anesth Analg* 2009; **109**: 1674–8

Davis JJ, Bond TS Swenson JD. Adductor canal block: more than just the saphenous nerve? *Reg Anesth Pain Med* 2009; **34**: 618–9

Di Benedetto P, Bertini L, Casati A, Borghi B, Albertin A, Fanelli G. A new posterior approach to the sciatic nerve block: a prospective, randomized comparison with the classic posterior approach. *Anesth Analg* 2001; **93**: 1040–4

Dogan N, Erdem AF, Erman Z, Kizilkaya M. The effects of bupivacaine and neostigmine on articular cartilage and synovium in the rabbit knee joint. *J Int Med Res* 2004; **32**: 513–9

Dolan J, Williams A, Murney E, Smith M, Kenny GN. Ultrasound guided fascia iliaca block: a comparison with the loss of resistance technique. *Reg Anesth Pain Med* 2008; **33**: 526–31

Espelund M, Fomsgaard JS, Haraszuk J, Mathiesen O, Dahl JB. Analgesic efficacy of ultrasound-guided adductor canal blockade after arthroscopic anterior cruciate ligament reconstruction: a randomised controlled trial. *Eur J Anaesthesiol* 2013; **30**: 422–8.

Foss NB, Kristensen BB, Bundgaard M, *et al.* Fascia iliaca compartment blockade for acute pain control in hip fracture patients: a randomized, placebo-controlled trial. *Anesthesiology* 2007; **106**: 773–8

Gupta PK, Chevret S, Zohar S, Hopkins PM. What is the ED95 of prilocaine for femoral nerve block using ultrasound? *Br J Anaesth* 2013; **110**: 831–6

Hadzic A, New York School of Regional Anesthesia. *Textbook of Regional Anesthesia and Acute Pain Management*. New York: McGraw-Hill Medical, 2007

Hadzic A, New York School of Regional Anesthesia. *Hadzic's Peripheral Nerve Blocks and Anatomy for Ultrasound-Guided Regional Anesthesia.* New York: McGraw-Hill Professional, 2012

Hadzic A, Vloka JD. A comparison of the posterior versus lateral approaches to the block of the sciatic nerve in the popliteal fossa. *Anesthesiology* 1998; **88**: 1480–6

Hara K, Sakura S, Shido A. Ultrasound-guided lateral femoral cutaneous nerve block: comparison of two techniques. *Anaesth Intensive Care* 2011; **39**: 69–72

Hebl JR, Lennon RL, Hagen JV, Mayo Foundation for Medical Education and Research. *Mayo Clinic Atlas of Regional Anesthesia and Ultrasound-Guided Nerve Blockade.* New York: Oxford University Press, 2010

Helayel PE, Ceccon MS, Knaesel JA, Conceicao DB, De Oliveira Filho GR. Urinary incontinence after bilateral parasacral sciatic-nerve block: report of two cases. *Reg Anesth Pain Med* 2006; **31**: 368–71

Hirschel G. Anesthesia of the brachial plexus for operations of the upper extremity. *München Med Wochenschr* 1911; **58**: 2

Hopkins PM, Ellis FR, Halsall PJ. Evaluation of local anaesthetic blockade of the lateral femoral cutaneous nerve. *Anaesthesia* 1991; **46**: 95–6

Horner G, Dellon AL. Innervation of the human knee joint and implications for surgery. *Clin Orthop Relat Res* 1994; **301**: 221–6

Hurdle MF, Weingarten TN, Crisostomo RA, Psimos C, Smith J. Ultrasound-guided blockade of the lateral femoral cutaneous nerve: technical description and review of 10 cases. *Arch Phys Med Rehabil* 2007; **88**: 1362–4

Jaeger P, Lund J, Jenstrup MT, Brondum V, Dahl JB. Reply to Dr Bendtsen. *Reg Anesth Pain Med* 2014; **39**: 254–5

Jaeger P, Nielsen ZJ, Henningsen MH, Hilsted KL, Mathiesen O, Dahl JB. Adductor canal block versus femoral nerve block and quadriceps strength: a randomized, double-blind, placebo-controlled, crossover study in healthy volunteers. *Anesthesiology* 2013; **118**: 409–15

Jæger P, Zaric D, Fomsgaard JS, *et al.* Adductor canal block versus femoral nerve block for analgesia after total knee arthroplasty: a randomized, double-blind study. *Reg Anesth Pain Med* 2013; **38**: 526–32

Jenstrup MT, Jaeger P, Lund J, *et al.* Effects of adductor-canal-blockade on pain and ambulation after total knee arthroplasty: a randomized study. *Acta Anaesthesiol Scand* 2012; **56**: 357–64

Karpie JC, Chu CR. Lidocaine exhibits dose- and time-dependent cytotoxic effects on bovine articular chondrocytes in vitro. *Am J Sports Med* 2007; **35**: 1621–7

Kehlet H, Andersen LO. Local infiltration analgesia in joint replacement: the evidence and recommendations for clinical practice. *Acta Anaesthesiol Scand* 2011; **55**: 778–84

Kerr DR, Kohan L. Local infiltration analgesia: a technique for the control of acute postoperative pain following knee and hip surgery: a case study of 325 patients. *Acta Orthop* 2008; **79**: 174–83

Kim DH, Lin Y, Goytizolo EA, *et al.* Adductor canal block versus femoral nerve block for total knee arthroplasty: a prospective, randomized, controlled trial. *Anesthesiology* 2014; **120**: 540–50

Koller C. On the use of cocaine for producing anaesthesia on the eye. *Lancet* 1884; **124**: 990–2

Krombach J, Gray AT. Sonography for saphenous nerve block near the adductor canal. *Reg Anesth Pain Med* 2007; **32**: 369–70

Kwofie MK, Shastri UD, Gadsden JC, *et al.* The effects of ultrasound-guided adductor canal block versus femoral nerve block on quadriceps strength and fall risk: a blinded, randomized trial of volunteers. *Reg Anesth Pain Med* 2013; **38**: 321–5

Labat G. *Regional Anesthesia: Its Technic and Clinical Application.* Philadelphia, PA: W. B. Saunders Company, 1922

Latzke D, Marhofer P, Zeitlinger M, *et al.* Minimal local anaesthetic volumes for sciatic nerve block: evaluation of ED99 in volunteers. *Br J Anaesth* 2010; **104**: 239–44

Luke C, Chelly JE. Is a single sciatic really equivalent to a continuous sciatic block for total knee replacement? *Reg Anesth Pain Med* 2012; **37**: 234–5

Manickam B, Perlas A, Duggan E, Brull R, Chan VW, Ramlogan R. Feasibility and efficacy of ultrasound-guided block of the saphenous nerve in the adductor canal. *Reg Anesth Pain Med* 2009; **34**: 578–80

Mansour NY. Reevaluating the sciatic nerve block: another landmark for consideration. *Reg Anesth* 1993; **18**: 322–3

Mansour NY, Bennetts FE. An observational study of combined continuous lumbar plexus and single-shot sciatic nerve blocks for post-knee surgery analgesia. *Reg Anesth Pain Med* 1996; **21**: 287–91

March X, Pineda O, Garcia MM, Carames D, Villalonga A. The posterior approach to the sciatic nerve in the popliteal fossa: a comparison of single- versus double-injection technique. *Anesth Analg* 2006; **103**: 1571–3

Marhofer D, Karmakar MK, Marhofer P, Kettner SC, Weber M, Zeitlinger M. Does circumferential spread of local anaesthetic improve the success of peripheral nerve block? *Br J Anaesth* 2014; **113**: 177–85.

Marhofer P. *Ultrasound Guidance in Regional Anaesthesia: Principles and Practical Implementation.* Oxford: Oxford University Press, 2010

Marhofer P, Harrop-Griffiths W, Willschke H, Kirchmair L. Fifteen years of ultrasound guidance in regional anaesthesia: Part 2 – Recent developments in block techniques. *Br J Anaesth* 2010; **104**: 673–83

Mariano ER, Perlas A. Adductor canal block for total knee arthroplasty: the perfect recipe or just one ingredient? *Anesthesiology* 2014; **120**: 530–2

Matsen FA, 3rd, Papadonikolakis A. Published evidence demonstrating the causation of glenohumeral chondrolysis by postoperative infusion of local anesthetic via a pain pump. *J Bone Joint Surg Am* 2013; **95**: 1126–34

McCartney CJ, McLeod GA. Local infiltration analgesia for total knee arthroplasty. *Br J Anaesth* 2011; **107**: 487–9

McLeod D, Wong DW, Vaghadia H, Claridge R, Merrick P. Lateral popliteal sciatic nerve block compared with ankle block for analgesia following foot surgery. *Can J Anaesth* 1995; **42**: 765–9

Miller RD. *Miller's Anesthesia.* Philadelphia, PA: Churchill Livingstone/Elsevier, 2010

Moore CS, Sheppard D, Wildsmith JA. Thigh rotation and the anterior approach to the sciatic nerve: a magnetic resonance imaging study. *Reg Anesth Pain Med* 2004; **29**: 32–5

Morau D, Levy F, Bringuier S, *et al.* Ultrasound-guided evaluation of the local anesthetic spread parameters required for a rapid surgical popliteal sciatic nerve block. *Reg Anesth Pain Med* 2010; **35**: 559–64

Morin AM, Kratz CD, Eberhart, *et al.* Postoperative analgesia and functional recovery after total-knee replacement: comparison of a continuous posterior lumbar plexus (psoas compartment) block, a continuous femoral nerve block, and the combination of a continuous femoral and sciatic nerve block. *Reg Anesth Pain Med* 2005; **30**: 434–45

Morris GF, Lang SA, Dust WN, Van der Wal M. The parasacral sciatic nerve block. *Reg Anesth Pain Med* 1997; **22**: 223–8

Mudumbai SC, Kim TE, Howard SK, *et al.* Continuous adductor canal blocks are superior to continuous femoral nerve blocks in promoting early ambulation after TKA. *Clin Orthop Relat Res* 2014; **472**: 1377–83

Nader A, Kendall MC, De Oliveira GS, Jr, *et al.* A dose-ranging study of 0.5% bupivacaine or ropivacaine on the success and duration of the ultrasound-guided, nerve-stimulator-assisted sciatic nerve block: a double-blind, randomized clinical trial. *Reg Anesth Pain Med* 2013; **38**: 492–502

Ng I, Vaghadia H, Choi PT, Helmy N. Ultrasound imaging accurately identifies the lateral femoral cutaneous nerve. *Anesth Analg* 2008; **107**: 1070–4

Orebaugh SL. The femoral nerve and its relationship to the lateral circumflex femoral artery. *Anesth Analg* 2006; **102**: 1859–62

Perlas A, Brull R, Chan VW, McCartney CJ, Nuica A, Abbas S. Ultrasound guidance improves the success of sciatic nerve block at the popliteal fossa. *Reg Anesth Pain Med* 2008; **33**: 259–65

Perlas A, Chan VWS, Brull R. Several "correct" approaches to nerve stimulator-guided popliteal fossa block. *Reg Anesth Pain Med* 2009; **34**: 624–5

Perlas A, Wong P, Abdallah F, Hazrati L-N, Tse C, Chan V. Ultrasound-guided popliteal block through a common paraneural sheath versus conventional injection: a prospective, randomized, double-blind study. *Reg Anesth Pain Med* 2013; **38**: 218–25

Pham Dang C, Gautheron E, Guilley J, *et al.* The value of adding sciatic block to continuous femoral block for analgesia after total knee replacement. *Reg Anesth Pain Med* 2005; **30**: 128–33

Piper SL, Kim HT. Comparison of ropivacaine and bupivacaine toxicity in human articular chondrocytes. *J Bone Joint Surg Am* 2008; **90**: 986–91

Raeder JC. Local infiltration analgesia for pain after total knee replacement surgery: a winner or just a strong runner-up? *Anesth Analg* 2011; **113**: 684–6

Raj PP, Parks RI, Watson TD, Jenkins MT. A new single-position supine approach to sciatic-femoral nerve block. *Anesth Analg* 1975; **54**: 489–93

Rigler ML, Drasner K, Krejcie TC, *et al.* Cauda equina syndrome after continuous spinal anesthesia. *Anesth Analg* 1991; **72**: 275–81

Ripart J, Cuvillon P, Nouvellon E, Gaertner E, Eledjam JJ. Parasacral approach to block the sciatic nerve: a 400-case survey. *Reg Anesth Pain Med* 2005; **30**: 193–7

Rorie DK, Byer DE, Nelson DO, Sittipong R, Johnson KA. Assessment of block of the sciatic nerve in the popliteal fossa. *Anesth Analg* 1980; **59**: 371–6

Rudkin AK, Rudkin GE, Dracopoulos GC. Acceptability of ankle tourniquet use in midfoot and forefoot surgery: audit of 1000 cases. *Foot Ankle Int* 2004; **25**: 788–94

Rudkin G, Rudkin A, Dracopoulos G. Ankle block success rate: a prospective analysis of 1,000 patients. *Can J Anesth* 2005; **52**: 209–10

Sala-Blanch X, De Riva NS, Carrera A, López AM, Prats A, Hadzic A. Ultrasound-guided popliteal sciatic block with a single injection at the sciatic division results in faster block onset than the classical nerve stimulator technique. *Anesth Analg* 2012; **114**: 1121–7

Salinas FV. Ultrasound and review of evidence for lower extremity peripheral nerve blocks. *Reg Anesth Pain Med* 2010; **35**: S16–25

Salinas FV, Liu SS, Mulroy MF. The effect of single-injection femoral nerve block versus continuous femoral nerve block after total knee arthroplasty on hospital length of stay and long-term functional recovery within an established clinical pathway. *Anesth Analg* 2006; **102**: 1234–9

Saranteas T, Anagnostis G, Paraskeuopoulos T, *et al.* Anatomy and clinical implications of the ultrasound-guided subsartorial saphenous nerve block. *Reg Anesth Pain Med* 2011; **36**: 399–402

Sato K, Adachi T, Shirai N, Naoi N. Continuous versus single-injection sciatic nerve block added to continuous femoral nerve block for analgesia after total knee arthroplasty: a prospective, randomized, double-blind study. *Reg Anesth Pain Med* 2014; **39**: 225–9

Sinha SK, Abrams JH, Houle TT, Weller RS. Ultrasound-guided obturator nerve block: an interfascial injection approach without nerve stimulation. *Reg Anesth Pain Med* 2009; **34**: 261–4

Sinnatamby CS, Last RJ. *Last's Anatomy*. Edinburgh: Churchill Livingstone, 2011

Soong J, Schafhalter-Zoppoth I, Gray AT. Sonographic imaging of the obturator nerve for regional block. *Reg Anesth Pain Med* 2007; **32**: 146–51

Standring S, Gray H. *Gray's Anatomy: The Anatomical Basis of Clinical Practice*. Edinburgh: Churchill Livingstone, 2008

Stockman R. Report on the coca alkaloids. *Br Med J* 1889; **i**: 6

Taboada M, Atanassoff PG, Rodriguez J, *et al.* Plantar flexion seems more reliable than dorsiflexion with Labat's sciatic nerve block: a prospective, randomized comparison. *Anesth Analg* 2005; **100**: 250–4

Taboada M, Rodriguez J, Valino C, *et al.* What is the minimum effective volume of local anesthetic required for sciatic nerve blockade? A prospective, randomized comparison between a popliteal and a subgluteal approach. *Anesth Analg* 2006; **102**: 593–7

Taha AM. Ultrasound-guided obturator nerve block: a proximal interfascial technique. *Anesth Analg* 2012; **114**: 236–9

Taha AM, Abd-Elmaksoud AM. Lidocaine use in ultrasound-guided femoral nerve block: what is the minimum effective anaesthetic concentration (MEAC90)? *Br J Anaesth* 2013; **110**: 1040–4

Techasuk W, Bernucci F, Cupido T, *et al.* Minimum effective volume of combined lidocaine-bupivacaine for analgesic subparaneural popliteal sciatic nerve block. *Reg Anesth Pain Med* 2014; **39**: 108–11

Vloka JD, Hadzić A, April E, Thys DM. The division of the sciatic nerve in the popliteal fossa: anatomical implications for popliteal nerve blockade. *Anesth Analg* 2001a; **92**: 215–7

Vloka JD, Hadzic A, April E, Thys DM. Anterior approach to the sciatic nerve block: the effects of leg rotation. *Anesth Analg* 2001b; **92**: 460–2

Wassef MR. Interadductor approach to obturator nerve blockade for spastic conditions of adductor thigh muscles. *Reg Anesth Pain Med* 1993; **18**: 13–7

Winnie AP. Regional anesthesia. *Surg Clin North Am* 1975; **55**: 861–92

Winnie AP, Ramamurthy S, Durrani Z. The inguinal paravascular technic of lumbar plexus anesthesia: the "3-in-1 block". *Anesth Analg* 1973; **52**: 989–96

Winnie AP, Ramamurthy S, Durrani Z, Radonjic R. Plexus blocks for lower extremity surgery. *Anesthesiol Rev* 1974; **1**: 11–6

Zetlaoui PJ, Bouaziz H. Lateral approach to the sciatic nerve in the popliteal fossa. *Anesth Analg* 1998; **87**: 79–82

Zhu J, Zhao Y, Liu F, Huang Y, Shao J, Hu B. Ultrasound of the lateral femoral cutaneous nerve in asymptomatic adults. *BMC Musculoskelet Disord* 2012; **13**: 227

PART 9

The conduct of anaesthesia by surgical specialty

Philip M. Hopkins

CHAPTER 56

Anaesthesia for cardiac surgery

Uwe Schirmer and Andreas Koster

Introduction

The cardiac anaesthetist needs a thorough understanding of the principles of cardiopulmonary bypass (CPB) and techniques of extracorporeal circulation, the management of complex disorders of the coagulation system, and a comprehensive knowledge of pharmacological and mechanical management of the failing heart. With the widespread adoption of transoesophageal echocardiography (TOE) in the cardiac operating theatre, the cardiac anaesthetist has access to a sophisticated real-time monitoring tool that enables evaluation and treatment of cardiac function but also, with acquisition of the required competency, enables the diagnosis of cardiac and aortic pathology and evaluation of surgical results. This chapter provides an overview of the principles of cardiac anaesthesia and anaesthetic techniques for specific procedures.

General considerations

Preoperative evaluation and assessments

By the time of presentation for cardiac surgery, patients have invariably undergone a thorough evaluation of cardiovascular function and pathology. Of particular importance for the cardiac anaesthetist is to evaluate the preservation of left ventricular (LV) and right ventricular (RV) function and the extent of coronary artery and valvular disease. The results of (right and) left heart catheterization and echocardiography provide the necessary information. A L/RV ejection fraction (EF) (normal value 60–80%) of greater than 55% signals nearly complete preservation of myocardial function while an EF of 55–30% signals moderate impairment and an EF less than 30% severe impairment (see Box 56.1). However, in patients with mitral/tricuspid valve regurgitation, the EF is overestimated because large volumes are not ejected antegrade into the aorta or pulmonary artery but retrograde though the incompetent atrial valve.

Useful information can also be obtained from measurement of the LV end-diastolic pressure (LVEDP) (normal value 4–10 mm Hg), the LV end-diastolic diameter [normal value <55(–60) mm], and the pulmonary artery pressures. In addition to the absolute pressure, its relation to the systemic pressure may also be important. For example, an elevated LVEDP of 20–30 mm Hg associated with a mean systemic arterial pressure of 120 mm Hg indicates a less significant loss of cardiac contractility than a LVEDP of 30 mm Hg associated with a mean systemic arterial pressure of 60 mm Hg. The degree and location of coronary artery stenoses, the degree of regurgitation of incompetent valves, the pressure gradient measured across a stenotic valve, and the diameter and wall thickness of the ventricles all further help to evaluate the severity of cardiac disease.

Box 56.1 Preoperative evaluation of left/right ventricular function by ejection fraction (EF)

EF > 55%	Normal ventricular function
EF = 30–55%	Moderately reduced ventricular function
EF < 30%	Severely impaired ventricular function

In addition to a thorough cardiac evaluation, special consideration needs to be given to the cardiac surgery patient's coagulation status. This is because there are several factors that render patients undergoing cardiac surgery at increased risk of developing haemorrhagic complications. For example, as a result of changes in blood flow velocities, acquired von Willebrand syndrome is frequently (40–60%) associated with patients suffering from aortic valve stenosis. More general factors include preoperative anticoagulant and antiplatelet therapy, exposure of blood in the extracorporeal CPB circuit to a large non-endothelial surface area, and the tissue trauma of major surgery. The patient should be directly questioned about bleeding events after previous surgery, minor trauma, or dental treatment in order to identify those with a potential bleeding tendency who will need preoperative investigation: questionnaires have been designed for this purpose. The prothrombin time or international normalized ratio should be measured in patients who have been treated with warfarin preoperatively in order to identify those who may need replacement of vitamin K-dependent clotting factors in the perioperative period. New direct oral anticoagulants such as dabigatran and rivaroxaban are increasingly used in patients with atrial fibrillation. These drugs are mostly 'non-reversible' (dabigatran may be eliminated by haemodialysis or haemofiltration) and lead to severe bleeding complications when therapeutic plasma concentration are present during the time of surgery. Therefore, care has to be taken that such medication is stopped in a timely manner before elective surgery (usually 2 days preoperatively). If assays are available, plasma concentrations should be measured preoperatively to ensure that drug concentrations are decreased to sub-therapeutic concentrations. When antiplatelet drugs such as aspirin or clopidogrel have been given within 3–7 days of surgery, whole-blood aggregometers provide a quick and easy guide to evaluate the degree of inhibition of platelet function and the need for perioperative platelet transfusion.

Monitoring

Standard monitoring for a patient undergoing cardiac surgery includes five-lead ECG, pulse oximetry, capnography, core body (bladder and nasopharyngeal) temperature, continuous invasive measurement of arterial blood pressure, and continuous measurement of the central venous pressure. In patients with impaired ventricular function and patients undergoing complex surgery, extended haemodynamic monitoring, particularly of cardiac output (CO) is desirable (see Chapter 44). This can be accomplished by techniques combining an analysis of the arterial waveform (pulse contour analysis) and transthoracic thermodilution thereby providing continuous measurement of cardiac stroke volume (SV), CO and cardiac index (CI), global cardiac end-diastolic blood volume (GEDV), and thoracic blood/fluid volume, or with the use of a pulmonary artery catheter (PAC) which delivers information about CO/CI by pulmonary artery thermodilution (continuous online or manual), the pulmonary artery pressures including pulmonary capillary wedge pressure (PCWP), and allows determination of the mixed venous oxygen saturation (Sv_{O_2}) (continuous online or manually) and calculation of systemic and pulmonary vascular resistance (S/PVR).

In complex cases, before weaning from CPB, the surgeon may additionally insert a catheter via a right pulmonary vein into the left atrium (LA) for continuous measurement of the LA pressure thus providing valuable information about the LV preload.

CO can also be determined from measurement of LVEF and RVEF by TOE which also enables visualization of the response of the ventricles to changes in pre- and afterload, characterization of regional wall motion, and morphological abnormalities impairing cardiac function (see 'Intraoperative transoesophageal echocardiography').

Neuromonitoring may be accomplished by online EEG monitoring which additionally evaluates the depth of anaesthesia by calculation of the Bispectral Index™ (BIS™; Covidien, now Medtronic Minimally Invasive Therapies, Minneapolis, MN, USA) (see Chapter 44). Information about regional cerebral tissue oxygenation may be provided by near infrared spectroscopy (NIRS) (see Chapter 44).

For the authors' approach to monitoring, see Box 56.2.

Box 56.2 Authors' approach: monitoring

The relative merits of using arterial or preload pressures, CO, or measures of tissue perfusion and oxygenation such as the Sv_{O_2} to guide fluid volume therapy and use of inotropic or vasoactive agents is still much debated.

Pulse contour analysis (PCA) has emerged as a monitoring tool in non-cardiac and cardiac surgery. When an arterial line is already implicated, as in all cardiac surgery patients, it represents a much less invasive approach than using a PAC and is not associated with possible additional complications (see Chapter 44). Calculations of SV, CI, and GEDV are continuously recorded.

However, depending on the device, frequent calibrations may be necessary, particularly when major changes in fluid status or the clinical situation (chest closure etc.) occur. The GEDV as a marker of global cardiac preload cannot discriminate between RV and LV (over/under)load. No information about pulmonary artery pressures and the PVR is given, thus limiting the use particularly in RV failure, when selective reduction of PVR is a major objective (see 'Treatment of right ventricular failure'). No information about the Sv_{O_2}, which the authors deem to be a key decision parameter, is given.

Additionally, in cardiac surgery where an intra-aortic balloon-pump (IABP) is the mechanical support system of first choice (see 'Temporary mechanical support of the failing heart'), the signal of the arterial wave is changed by the IABP and PCA devices are not validated in this situation.

We also consider that monitoring of cardiac preload pressures is important, as acute massive volume overload, which will immediately be indicated by a dramatic increase in the filling pressures, may lead to distension of the RV or LV, which can become irreversible. The LV preload pressures (such as the PCWP or LA pressure) particularly help to calculate coronary artery perfusion pressure (diastolic arterial pressure–LVEDP) which is a key determinant of LV contractility.

Based on these considerations, the authors prefer the PAC intraoperatively. However we recommend the PCA as an additional monitoring for patients who might need a prolonged stay in the intensive care unit (ICU) where TOE is not continuously performed, the conditions are more stable than in the operating theatre, and calibrations of the devices are needed less frequently. Under these conditions, the continuous display of SV and CI facilitate immediate diagnosis of changes in the patient's condition and rapid adjustment of therapy.

Monitoring of regional (cerebral) tissue oxygenation by NIRS is increasingly used in more complex procedures; not only as a monitor of cerebral perfusion, but, as results correlate well to the Sv_{O_2}, as a non-invasive online monitoring of global tissue oxygenation.

Intraoperative transoesophageal echocardiography

The fundamental bases of modern echocardiography are anatomical B (M)-mode imaging and flow Doppler echocardiography including colour flow imaging. When ultrasound waves travel through tissue, they will be reflected when they reach an interface of different tissues with different impedances. The reflected waves are captured by the ultrasound transducer and after a complex process of computerization, visualized anatomically as grey scales in a nearly real-time online image (B-mode echocardiography).

The underlying principle of flow Doppler echocardiography is a change in the frequency (frequency shift) of received echoes reflected from flowing erythrocytes when compared with the interrogating transducer frequency. These echoes provide information about blood flow velocity, blood flow direction, and blood flow characteristics. Two Doppler techniques are currently used: (1) continuous wave (CW) Doppler (ultrasound is continually transmitted from one dedicated piezoelectric element and continually received by another; emitter ≠ receiver) allowing the measurement of fast blood streams (but, however, not discriminating the depth of sampled signals). CW Doppler is used clinically to quantify pressure decreases across a stenotic (particularly the aortic) valve or vessel using the Bernoulli equation. (2) Pulsed waved (PW) Doppler [after the transmission of a pulse, the piezoelectric element waits (time-gate) for the signal reflection from a selected depth before sending another signal; emitter = receiver] which gives information about blood flow velocities, blood flow direction, and blood flow pattern at a defined depth. Therefore, as the PW Doppler signal is time gated, a clean envelope across its beam path is achieved, enabling especially the measurement of lower blood flow velocities and directions at a defined localization, although higher flow velocities will be subjected to a Nyquist limit, thus causing aliasing artefacts. Therefore, PW Doppler is preferred clinically where lower blood velocities occur, such as in the mitral and tricuspid valves and the pulmonary veins.

This PW Doppler technique, after a complex computerization process, is also used in colour flow Doppler imaging which, by translating flow velocities and directions into defined colours (mapping), visualizes blood flow, for example, at an incompetent valve or tissue defect such as an atrial or ventricular septal defect (Fig. 56.1 and Fig. 56.2).

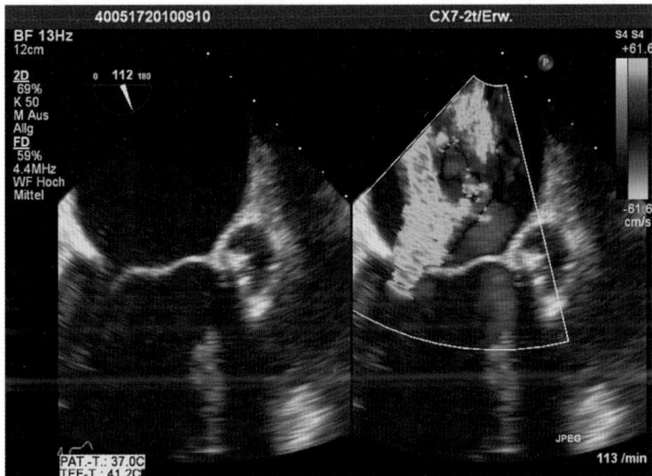

Figure 56.1 TOE image showing regurgitation of blood through the mitral valve in a modified two-chamber view using colour flow imaging.

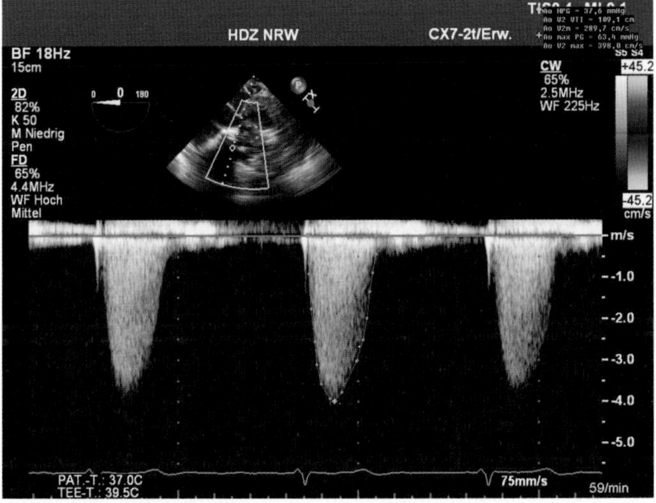

Figure 56.2 TOE image showing the CW Doppler envelope measured across a stenotic aortic valve in the deep gastric short-axis view. The gradient across the valve is calculated by the device when tracing the envelope.

In current multiplane TOE devices, the probe, apart from ante-/retroflexion and left-/right flexion, can be rotated from 0° to 180° thus allowing precise adjustment of the probe to achieve a desired slice even with complex anatomy.

With the introduction of TOE into the cardiac operating theatre, the anaesthetist has a powerful monitoring tool which, even with minimal training, gives a quick guide to RV and LV performance, response to changes in pre- and afterload. In skilled hands, TOE provides sophisticated insight into regional ventricular performance, function, and pathology of the heart structures and the thoracic aorta, thereby permitting immediate identification and quantification of cardiac dysfunction and immediate evaluation of the result of surgery.

As TOE may also involve complications, the American Society of Echocardiography and the American Society of Cardiovascular Anesthesiologists developed guidelines for performing a comprehensive intraoperative multiplane TOE. In these guidelines, indications and contraindications for intraoperative TOE are outlined and 20 cross-sectional views for complete evaluation of the heart and thoracic aorta are presented, thus serving as a standard for performance of intraoperative TOE (Fig. 56.3). Besides local courses addressing intraoperative TOE and comprehensive textbooks, online sites offer interactive courses to achieve an initial understanding of the complex technical basics and calculations and anatomical orientation for the different cross-sectional views

Cardiopulmonary bypass and extracorporeal circulation

Principles of cardiopulmonary bypass

CPB not only replaces the function of the heart with a pump and the function of the lungs with an oxygenator. It also provides the option to administer cardioplegic solution to arrest and protect the ischaemic heart, to decompress and protect the heart by venting volume from the aortic root, LA, or pulmonary artery into the CPB circuit, to perform selective regional perfusion thus providing oxygenation of tissue susceptible to ischaemia during systemic circulatory arrest. Moreover, it enables control of the patient's temperature and concentrates blood by haemofiltration when such filters are incorporated and serves like a cell saver when blood is aspirated from the operative field (cardiotomy suction) (Fig. 56.4 and Fig. 56.5).

In standard CPB systems for cardiovascular surgery, the patient's venous blood enters the circuit from cannulae placed in the right atrium or upper and lower venae cava. This drainage is achieved by gravity but can be augmented by vacuum assistance. The venous blood is collected in a collapsible soft- (closed CPB system; less blood–air interface) or hardshell cardiotomy (open CPB system; large blood–air interface) venous reservoir. Blood aspirated from the operative field and blood vented from the heart also returns into the cardiotomy reservoir after passing through a filter. From there, the blood is pumped through a heat exchanger, which allows regulation of blood temperature, into the membrane oxygenator. The oxygenated blood than passes through an arterial microfilter and bubble trap which prevents embolization with microfragments and air. The blood is returned to the patient through an arterial cannula, which is usually placed in the upper ascending aorta but may alternatively be placed in a femoral, subclavian, or carotid artery. Laminar flow of blood to the arterial circulation is achieved with a roller pump or centrifugal pump resulting in a non-pulsatile arterial blood pressure.

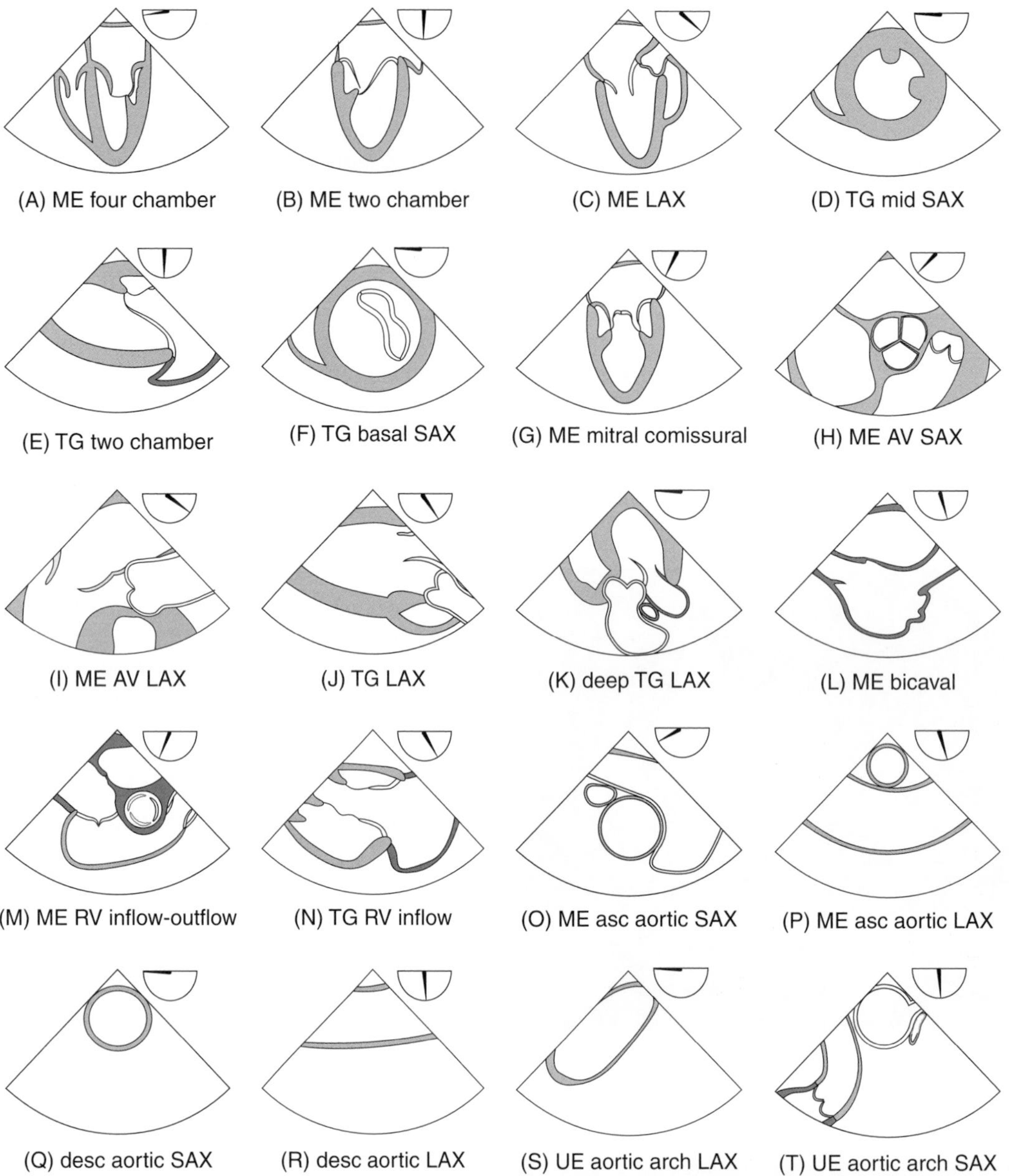

Figure 56.3 Scheme of the 20 cross-sectional views for performing a comprehensive intraoperative TOE.
Shanewise JS, Cheung AT, Aronson S, Stewart WJ, *et al.* ASE/SCA guidelines for performing a comprehensive intraoperative multiplane transesophageal echocardiography examination: recommendations of the American Society of Echocardiography Council for Intraoperative Echocardiography and the Society of Cardiovascular Anesthesiologists Task Force for Certification in Perioperative Transesophageal Echocardiography. *Anesthesia & Analgaesia*, Volume 89, Issue 4, pp. 870–84, Copyright © 1999 International Anesthesia Research Society.

Current CPB practice varies widely as custom-made circuits are modified by users according to specific preferences and demands. The tubing has a volume varying between approximately 800 to 2000 ml and is usually primed with crystalloid (and colloid) fluid. Depending on the priming volume, there is therefore moderate or severe haemodilution when the patient is connected to the system. Inexpensive and durable roller blood pumps or more elaborate biocompatible single-use centrifugal pumps may be used. Tubing lines and oxygenators may be coated with heparin or other materials to enhance biocompatibility of the non-endothelial surfaces and thereby reduce haemostatic/inflammatory activation. Circuits may or may not have a (hardshell and/or collapsible) cardiotomy reservoir, or may be nearly completely closed [such as the minimal (small priming volume of approximately 800 ml) extracorporeal circulation, MECC, system], thus permitting no or very limited entry of air and no cardiotomy suction into the circuit in order to increase biocompatibility and reduce blood trauma. However, where cardiotomy suction is not returned to the CPB circuit, a cell saver must be used, which can lead to a greater loss of coagulation factors and platelets. Moreover, as such systems are prone to air entry, despite sophisticated air removal devices, they are mostly used in 'closed-heart' procedures such as coronary artery bypass grafting (CABG). In extracorporeal life support systems (ECLSs), no reservoir is used and systems are completely closed. Moreover, biocompatible centrifugal pumps (providing improved drainage of the venous side by generating a suction) are incorporated thus allowing longer use (up to 2 months) while minimizing haemostatic activation and the need for anticoagulation (see 'Anticoagulation during

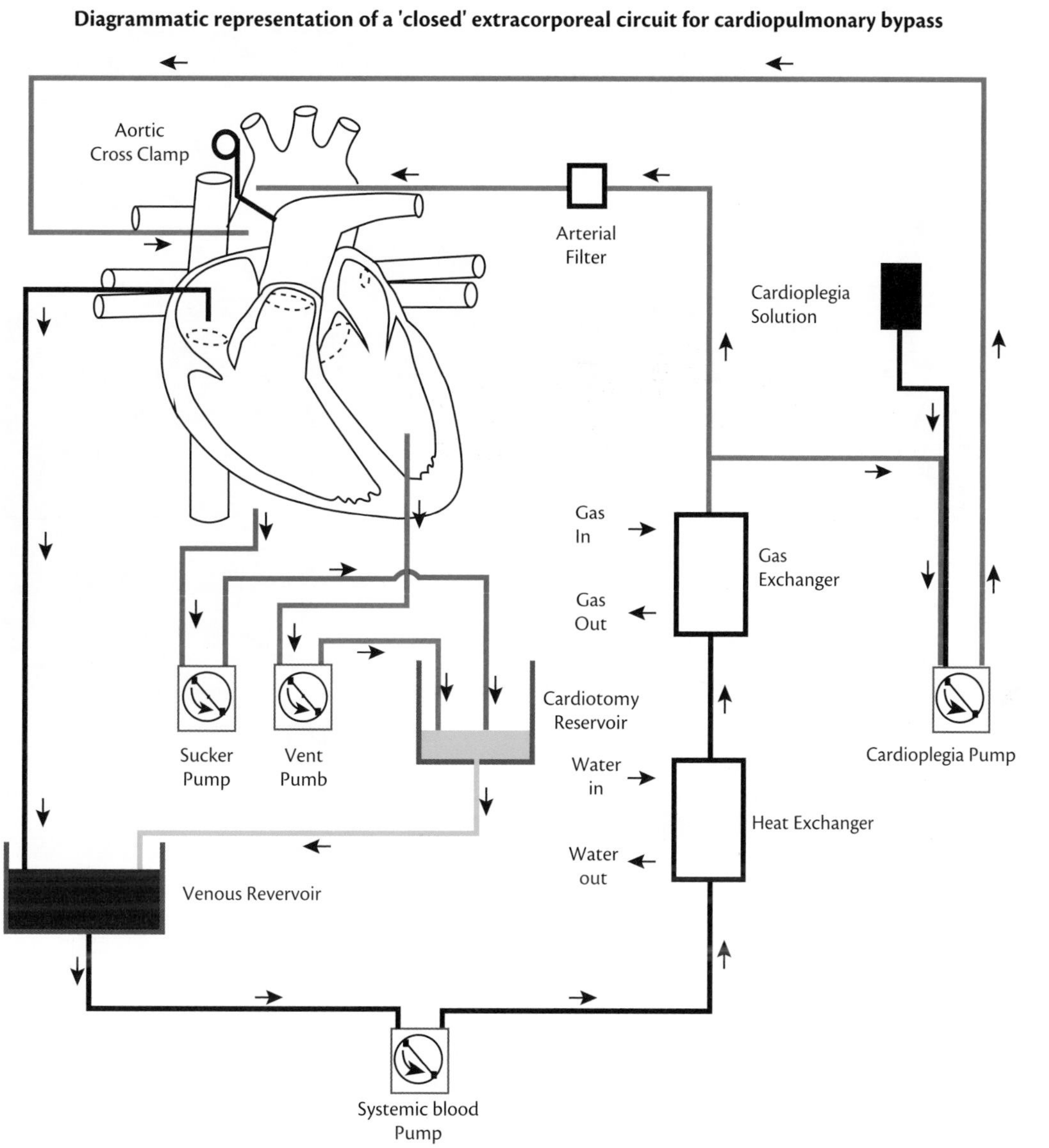

Diagrammatic representation of a 'closed' extracorporeal circuit for cardiopulmonary bypass

Figure 56.4 Scheme of a cardiopulmonary bypass system.

Reproduced with permission from Machin, D. and Allsager, C. Principles of cardiopulmonary bypass. *Continuing Education in Anaesthesia, Critical Care, and Pain*, 2006, Volume 6, Issue 5, pp. 176–181, by permission of the British Journal of Anaesthesia.

cardiopulmonary bypass'). An oxygenator can easily be added to the pump when necessary (bypassing the lungs in case of concomitant pulmonary failure). As such systems are small and portable, and femoral cannulation can be performed via percutaneous (Seldinger) techniques, these systems are not only inserted by a surgeon in the operating theatre but also by anaesthetists in the intensive care unit, catheter lab or even out of hospital. Such systems can also be used in case of pulmonary failure (mostly with venovenous cannulation) as extracorporeal membrane oxygenation systems. See Box 56.3.

Performance of and weaning from cardiopulmonary bypass

After placement of sutures for cannulation and systemic heparinization (see 'Anticoagulation during cardiopulmonary bypass'), venous and arterial cannulae are inserted, connected to the CPB circuit, and extracorporeal circulation started.

The target blood flow for the anaesthetized patient at a temperature of 35–37° and a haematocrit of approximately 25% is approximately 2.4 litres min^{-1} m^{-2} body surface area (BSA). Reduction of core body temperature reduces oxygen consumption by a factor of 0.5 for every 10°C decrease. The target arterial pressure is usually maintained at 50–60 mm Hg (compatible with autoregulation of blood flow in the vital organs) by adjustment of the CBP flow and the administration of vasoconstrictors or vasodilators. After achieving adequate blood flow at the start of CPB, the aorta is cross-clamped so that the heart is no longer perfused. Cardiac arrest and protection of the ischaemic heart is then achieved by continuous or intermittent infusion of cold/warm blood or crystalloid cardioplegia solution. The route of infusion can be either antegrade via the aortic root or coronary ostia or retrograde via the coronary sinus. The composition of these cardioplegic solutions varies greatly, although they all contain high concentrations

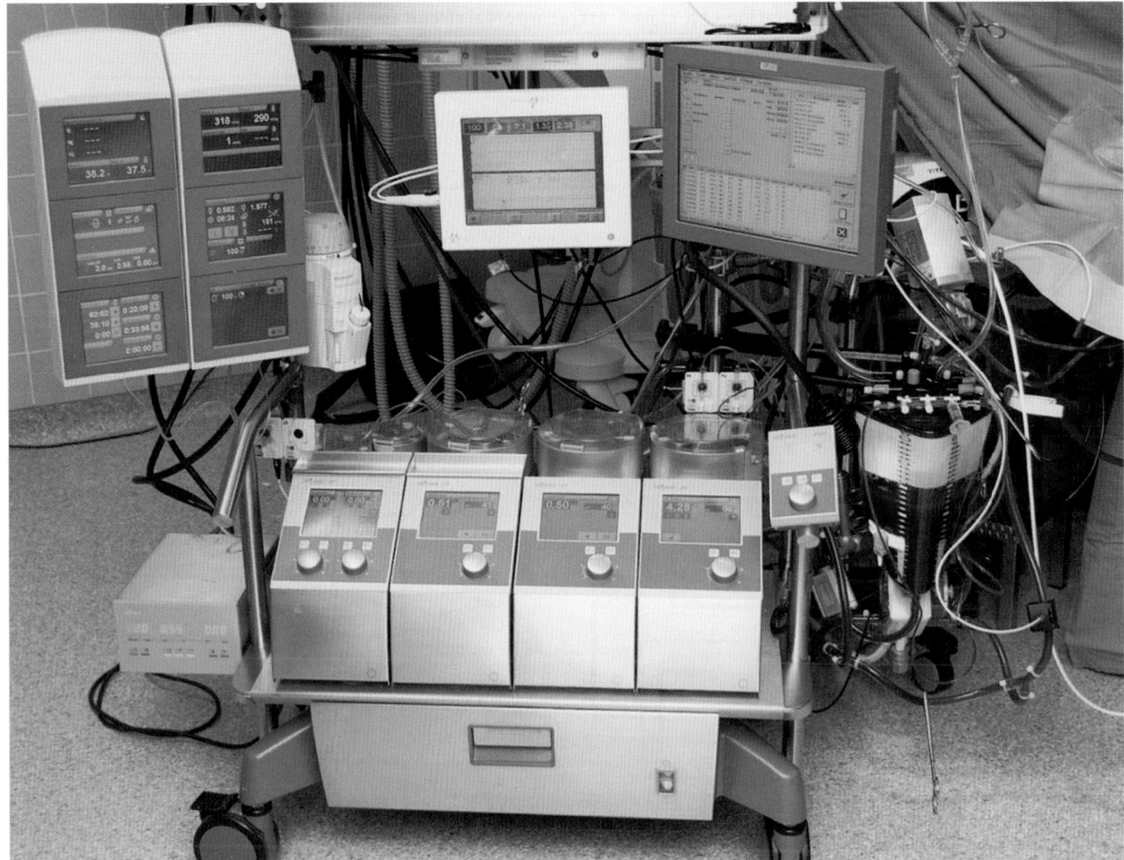

Figure 56.5 A contemporary heart–lung machine.

Box 56.3 Current cardiopulmonary bypass systems

Open system

Venous blood and blood from the operation field (cardiotomy suction) and vents are collected in a hard shell venous reservoir. Large air–blood interface; haemostatic activation because of cardiotomy suction.

Closed system

Venous blood drained in collapsible venous reservoir thus reducing air–blood contact. Cardiotomy suction and vented blood is directed into the hardshell reservoir.

MECC system

Mostly extremely small heparin-coated CPB circuit with centrifugal pump resulting in minimal haemodilution and blood trauma. Very limited options to remove air. Small venous reservoir (patient is the reservoir), venting in collapsible venous reservoir, no cardiotomy suction. Therefore, mostly used during closed-heart procedures, especially CABG.

ECLS system

Centrifugal pump and if needed an oxygenator. No reservoir, no cardiotomy suction. Heparinized circuit with small priming volume (400 ml) and lower degree of anticoagulation needed (ACT 160–180 s). ECLS systems can be used for temporary mechanical support (up to 2 months) of the left, right, or both ventricles. An oxygenator can be quickly added if pulmonary perfusion is bypassed or oxygenation is critically impaired. Mostly used via femorofemoral cannulation and because systems are very small and portable, often implanted outside the operating theatre via percutaneous (Seldinger) techniques

Extracorporeal membrane oxygenation system

Same principle as ECLS system, but always with oxygenator primarily for patients with pulmonary failure (venovenous cannulation).

of potassium to achieve cardiac arrest and additives to protect the heart. Further protection of the heart and other organ systems may be provided by systemic cooling which is mostly to between 34°C and 32°C. If larger periods of reduced blood flow are needed, temperature is further reduced to moderate or deep hypothermia or to profound hypothermia (18–16°C) (see Box 56.4) when total circulatory arrest is needed for longer periods. However, even during low/no-flow phases, regional blood flow may be maintained by selective perfusion, for example, of the brain to extend the safety window for organ systems which are most susceptible to ischaemia.

There are two approaches to pH/$P\text{CO}_2$ management during hypothermia (see Box 56.5): the pH stat method where the pH is

Box 56.4 Degrees of hypothermia

- Mild: 35–32°C
- Moderate: 31–26°C
- Deep: 25–20°C
- Profound: less than 20°C.

Box 56.5 pH/Pco_2 strategies during hypothermia

pH-stat

Correction of blood gas analysis to actual temperature. The pH is maintained during cooling and CO_2 added. Higher cerebral blood flow, pressure passive, and uncoupled from oxygen demand.

α-stat

Measurement of blood gas at 37°C. The pH becomes alkalotic during cooling. Lower cerebral blood flow, autoregulated, and coupled to cerebral oxygen demand.

maintained at a temperature-corrected value of 7.40 and requires addition of CO_2 when the patient is cooled; and the α-stat method where the pH is allowed to increase during cooling so that the blood becomes alkalotic. With the pH-stat method, cerebral blood flow is higher, pressure passive, and uncoupled from oxygen demand. With the α-stat method, cerebral blood flow is lower, autoregulated, and coupled to cerebral oxygen demand. The debate about which method is preferable is ongoing, although the pH-stat strategy may be better in adults while the α-stat strategy may be advantageous in paediatric cardiac surgery.

After rewarming and completion of the surgical procedure, the aortic cross-clamp is released and the period of reperfusion of the heart begins. Sometimes defibrillation is necessary if release of the aortic cross-clamp results in ventricular fibrillation. In this period of reperfusion, the heart is typically unloaded thus allowing recovery from ischaemia. The duration of this period of reperfusion varies greatly and depends on the aortic cross-clamp time, complexity of the procedure, and condition before the operation. The return of sinus rhythm indicates resumption of cardiac function, although temporary atrial and ventricular epicardial pacemaker wires are usually placed to enable control of the heart rate and rhythm if needed.

During the reperfusion phase, the anaesthetist facilitates weaning from CPB by the appropriate administration of fluid volume, blood products, and inotropic or vasoactive drugs. When a bladder temperature of 36.5°C is achieved, CPB venous return is gradually decreased and arterial pump flow reduced accordingly. With careful loading of the heart, the arterial pressure trace will change from the linear curve (caused by laminar CPB flow) to the pulsatile curve caused by systolic output of the loaded heart. Combined evaluation of the changes of the amplitude of the arterial pressure trace, cardiac filling pressures, and of the performance of the heart as assessed by TOE (contractility of the RV and anterior wall of the LV), will help guide the weaning process. After completion of weaning from CPB, the cannulae are removed, the action of heparin is reversed using protamine, and the remaining volume of the CPB circuit re-infused into the patient.

Treatment of vasoplegia during cardiopulmonary bypass

In selected patients, initialization of CPB (and near loss of active lung perfusion) leads to a massive loss of systemic vascular resistance (SVR) (arterial perfusion pressure <40 mm Hg despite CI of >2.5 litres min^{-1} m^{-2} BSA by CPB pump). Possible reasons include previous therapy with angiotensin-converting enzyme inhibitors, potent vasodilators, sepsis, and so on. First-line therapy in this situation is an infusion of noradrenaline (norepinephrine) (0.05–0.4 μg kg^{-1} min^{-1}). If this fails, an infusion of vasopressin (1–4 IU h^{-1}) may be considered. If this also fails, an infusion of methylthioninium chloride (2 mg kg^{-1} over 30 min) has been described with the intention of inhibiting the release of nitric oxide from the endothelium. In these patients, weaning from CPB and active perfusion of the lungs usually helps to reduce the requirement for vasoconstrictors but the weaning process may be complicated and requires a greater degree of inotropic support and larger volumes of intravenous fluid than usual.

Blood management

Transfusions of blood products during cardiac surgery not only have a dramatic financial impact for the hospital and society but also appear to be independently associated with a poor patient outcome. Therefore, blood management during surgery is a pivotal role for the cardiac anaesthetist.

Anticoagulation during cardiopulmonary bypass

As a result of clotting factor activation through contact of blood with the large non-endothelial surfaces of the CPB circuit, the re-infusion of highly activated tissue factor-enriched blood from the operation field and the release of tissue factor from the surgical trauma, a high degree of anticoagulation is necessary to prevent thrombosis within the CPB circuit. This is achieved by systemic heparinization with a bolus of, typically, 300–400 IU of unfractionated heparin. The adequacy of anticoagulation is monitored by measurement of the activated clotting time (ACT) as a point-of-care test in the operating theatre. For this test, blood is added to a cartridge containing an activator of the contact-activated clotting cascade (Celite® or kaolin). Clot formation is detected by inhibition of particle movement by the coagulation process. Prolongation of the ACT (baseline 120–140 s) to values of 400–480 s is regarded as safe for performing CPB. Monitoring of the ACT is performed at intervals of approximately 30 min and additional heparin given when the ACT decreases below the therapeutic range.

After discontinuation of CPB, protamine is given to reverse the effect of heparin. The dose of protamine is based on a 1:1 ratio relative to the dose of heparin required to achieve the target ACT value. The ACT, however, is a global coagulation test and is influenced by temperature, haematocrit, coagulation factor concentrations, platelet count, and so on. Therefore, the ACT may remain in the target range while heparin concentrations decrease during CPB. Protamine promotes coagulation only by reversing the effect of heparin and will even inhibit coagulation if given in excess. Methods for more precise calculation of the heparin concentration and therefore of the protamine requirement are available to maintain target heparin concentrations during CPB and prevent subsequent overdose of protamine after CPB.

Although high-dose heparinization prevents thrombosis of the CPB system, coagulation processes are not completely inhibited and consumption of coagulation factors and platelets occurs during CPB. This may lead to bleeding complications after CPB and further pharmacological targeting of haemostatic activation is used. Aprotinin, a kallikrein inhibitor, was demonstrated to be effective but, because of safety reasons, has been [temporarily (in Europe and Canada the suspension from the market has been lifted)] removed from the market in most countries. Alternative agents for this indication are tranexamic acid (TXA) and ε-aminocaproic acid but there seems to be little agreement as to the optimum dosing schedules for these drugs. Basically, a 'low-dose' TXA protocol, corresponding to a 10 mg kg^{-1} loading dose (an optional bolus of 1–2 mg kg^{-1} into the CPB prime), and 1 mg kg^{-1} h^{-1} infusion during surgery, and a 'high-dose' protocol with a 30 mg kg^{-1} bolus, 2 mg kg^{-1} into the CPB prime and constant infusion of 16 mg kg^{-1} h^{-1} during surgery are used. However, there is increasing evidence that in cardiac surgery TXA is associated with severe side-effects such as convulsive seizures.

Coagulation management after cardiopulmonary bypass

After prolonged CPB, transfusion of clotting factors and platelets will be required to prevent bleeding complications. The dilemma for the cardiac anaesthetist is that no current point-of-care test reliably quantifies these transfusion requirements. Modern viscoelastic coagulation tests using a modified thromboelastography technique such as the multichannel ROTEM™ (Tem International GmbH, Munich, Germany), visualize the clot formation processes activated by addition of different clotting activators to the individual channels (Fig. 56.6). The results are available after approximately 30 min (Fig. 56.7) and their interpretation can be used to predict if the administration of protamine, clotting factors, fibrinogen, platelets, or antifibrinolytic agents are likely to improve haemostasis. Nevertheless, the clinical value of these test systems still needs validation in large outcome trials. Additionally, there is no consensus on the relative benefits of administering clotting factors as fresh frozen plasma rather than as a concentrate of individual elements, such as prothrombin complex, fibrinogen, factor XIII, and so on.

In case of massive, uncontrollable bleeding, administration of recombinant activated coagulation factor VII is an ultimate option to promote coagulation and treat life-threatening bleeding. However, the use of this drug has been associated with thromboembolic complications, such that it can only be recommended when other measures have failed.

Optimal haemoglobin value

This is another area where opinion is divided for both during and after CPB. During CPB, a safe range of haemoglobin concentration is considered to be 6–8 g dl^{-1}, whereas after CPB, the target range is 7–10 g dl^{-1}.

The American Society of Thoracic Surgeons and the American Society of Cardiovascular Anesthesiologists have formulated guidelines and recommendations for blood management in cardiac surgery which provide valuable information in this complex area (Ferraris et al. 2007, 2011).

Despite the various controversies, attention to the following fundamental principles will best maintain adequate coagulation and reduce exposure to allogeneic blood products after CPB:

- To maintain core temperature after CPB, begin weaning from CPB only when a temperature of approximately 36.5–37°C is achieved.
- Use fluid warmers and warming blankets to avoid hypothermia if increased volume replacement and transfusions are expected.
- Use a cell saver when increased bleeding is expected.

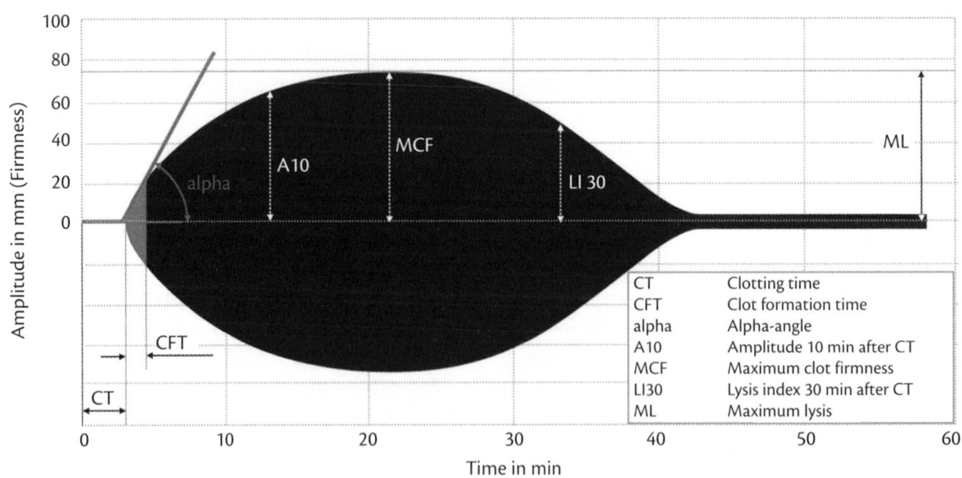

Figure 56.6 Diagram of the output and derived variables from a modified thromboelastography with the ROTEM™. A sample of whole blood is placed into a cuvette in which a cylindrical pin is placed. The gap of 1 mm between the pin and the cuvette is filled with the blood sample. The pin is rotated to the left and right. As long as the blood is liquid, movement of the pin is unrestricted. With the beginning of formation of a clot and ongoing firmness of the clot, the rotation is increasingly restricted. The degree of restriction is detected mechanically, calculated by a computer, and displayed as the thromboelastogram. The CT is the time from the beginning of the analysis to the initial formation of a weak clot (2 mm). This period depends on the presence of anticoagulants and status of the plasma coagulation system (fibrin formation). The CFT characterizes the time from the beginning of clot formation until achievement of a more stable clot with an amplitude of 20 mm. This period of clot polymerization depends on the plasma coagulation system as well as platelet function and fibrinogen levels. The maximum clot firmness (MCF) of the thromboelastogram indicates further clot polymerization and retraction and is influenced by platelet function, fibrinogen, and factor XIII. The maximal clot lysis (ML) indicates the lysis of the clot which is increased by fibrinolysis.

ROTEM™ modified thromboelastography. Homepage ROTEM Inc.

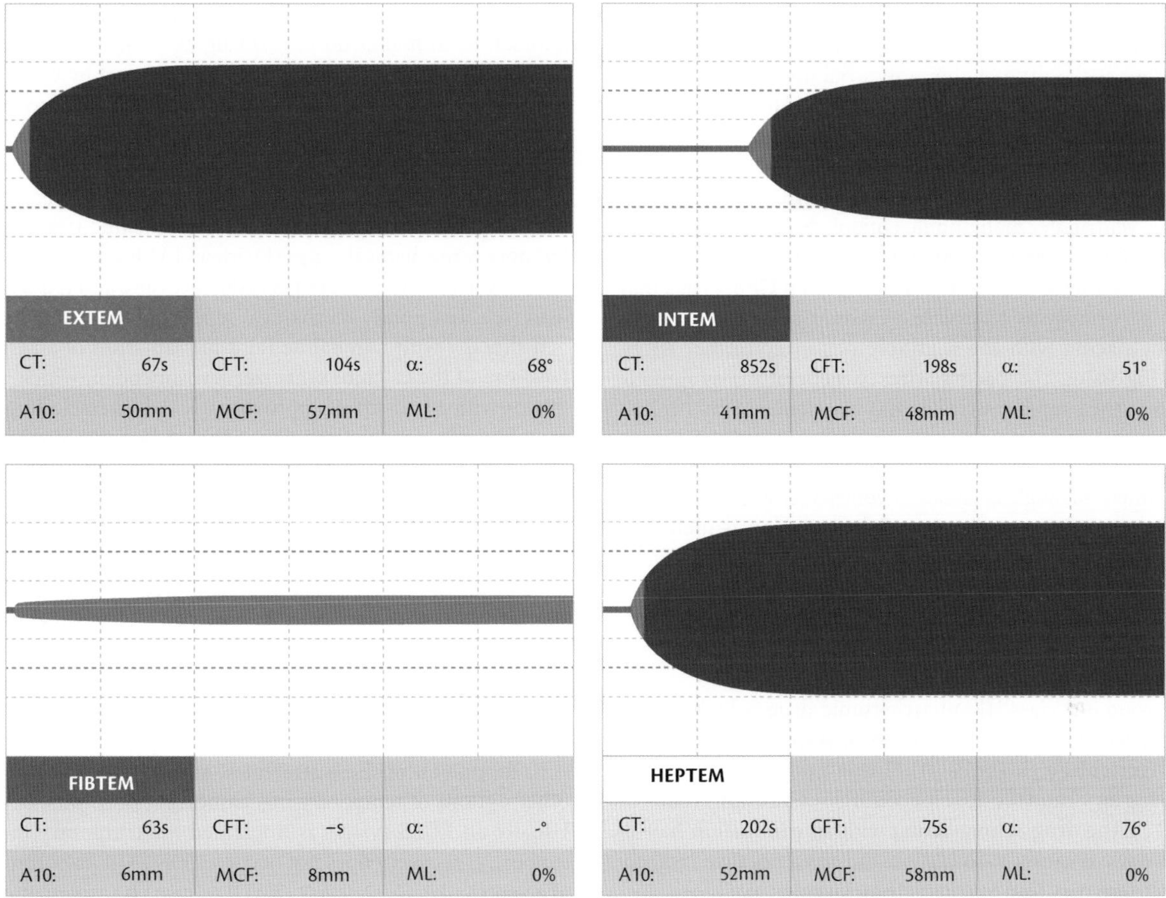

Figure 56.7 Diagram of four channels of the ROTEM™ for synoptical analysis of disturbances of clot formation. The INTEM channel is activated by adding an activator of the intrinsic (contact activation) system of coagulation. In the HEPTEM channel, the same reagent as in the INTEM channel is used, but heparinase is also added which inactivates heparin. A shorter CFT in the HEPTEM channel compared to the INTEM channel suggests heparin activity in the patient's blood. In the EXTEM channel, coagulation is activated by addition of an activator of the extrinsic system of coagulation. In the FIBTEM channel, the same reagent is used but platelets are also selectively inhibited thus showing the contributing effect of fibrinogen to the MCF. Both the EXTEM and the FIBTEM are not influenced by higher heparin concentrations as used during CPB. Therefore an analysis can be performed at the end of CPB during heparinization. Synoptically viewing the MCF in the EXTEM and FIBTEM channels therefore allows differentiation between bleeding due to impaired platelet function, impaired fibrinogen levels, or both. In the current example, the MCF in the FIBTEM is reduced to 8 mm (normal value 10–22 mm). Therefore, viewing the results of the four channels synoptically, it is likely that any patient bleeding will be caused by reduced fibrinogen levels and incomplete reversal of heparin.

ROTEM™ modified thromboelastography. Homepage ROTEM Inc.

For the authors' approach to coagulation management, see Box 56.6.

Box 56.6 Authors' approach: coagulation management

TXA (1 g bolus for the patient, 0.5 g added to the CPB prime, 200 mg h^{-1} during CPB) is given in patients with impairment of coagulation preoperatively, in procedures with an expected prolonged CPB duration, and procedures with increased bleeding risk. Before weaning from CPB, a ROTEM™ analysis is performed to evaluate the possible need for transfusion of clotting factors, platelets, and fibrinogen. However, these products are given after protamine and only when there is clinically evident microvascular bleeding.

We deem the FIBTEM channel of the ROTEM™ analysis to provide the most valuable information. Fibrinogen concentrate is given if the patient presents with diffuse bleeding and the maximum clot firmness of the FIBTEM is less than 8 mm. Usually, a bolus of 2 g is given (increase of the FIBTEM curve in a 70 kg patient 1 mm per 0.5 g fibrinogen concentrate). If necessary (clinically or after a second ROTEM™ analysis), a second bolus is given.

Before weaning from CPB, normothermia must be achieved and after weaning, care is taken to avoid hypothermia (warming blankets and fluid warming). A cell saver is used when large blood loss is expected. The residual volume of the CPB circuit is processed through the cell saver to avoid infusion of heparinized CPB blood when protamine has been given.

Antiarrhythmic therapy

Management of arrhythmias is complex and a large number of agents with complex pharmacology are available. Therefore, we recommend that the cardiac anaesthetist should select a smaller number of drugs with which they are most familiar.

Box 56.7 Authors' approach: antiarrhythmic therapy

Amiodarone is the drug of choice in atrial fibrillation and ventricular arrhythmias in heart failure patients. However, loading must be performed slowly because of haemodynamic side-effects. We administer the loading dose during CPB. In acute situations of supraventricular tachycardia but also ventricular tachycardia and other ventricular arrhythmia, sotalol given in intermittent boluses of 10 mg (maximum 80 mg) is the drug of choice.

When arrhythmia complicates weaning from CPB, drugs may be given generously as a possible atrioventricular block can be treated by pacing with the routinely placed epicardial wires. Overpacing using the pacing wires is generally a pragmatic approach to treat supraventricular and ventricular arrhythmias.

For treatment of single episodes of ventricular arrhythmia, after release of the aortic cross-clamp and defibrillation is ineffective, lidocaine, a short-acting (elimination half-life 15–20 min) class IB agent may be given as a bolus (1 mg kg^{-1}) (100 mg).

In case of supraventricular or ventricular arrhythmias, particularly in heart failure patients, drugs with a broad spectrum of supraventricular and ventricular effects are preferable.

Amiodarone is a class III antiarrhythmic drug, which is effective in supraventricular (the drug of choice in atrial fibrillation) and complex ventricular arrhythmias. The loading dose is approximately 300 mg (5 mg kg^{-1}) and the dose for continuous infusion is 600–900 mg $(24\ h)^{-1}$. The drug is long-acting with an elimination half-life of 10–100 days. It causes vasodilation and has a negative inotropic effect. Overdose may lead to complete atrioventricular block.

Sotalol is a class III antiarrhythmic drug which also provides class II (β-blocker) effects. It is effective in supraventricular (atrial fibrillation) and ventricular arrhythmia. The loading dose is approximately 40–80 mg (0.5–1.0 mg kg^{-1}), the elimination half-life approximately 7 h. Haemodynamic side-effects are moderate and even low bolus doses of 10–20 mg can provide rapid improvement of supraventricular tachycardia. Overdose may lead to atrioventricular block.

For the authors' approach to antiarrhythmic therapy, see Box 56.7.

Pharmacological treatment of post-cardiotomy left ventricular and right ventricular failure

Treatment of left ventricular failure

When weaning from CPB is not possible because of impaired LV function (low CO, high PCWP or LA pressure, impaired contractility, and volume overload of LV in the TOE), moderate inotropic support with a β-adrenergic agonist such as dobutamine (3–6 μg kg^{-1} min^{-1}) should be initiated. If this approach is unsuccessful, a phosphodiesterase-3 inhibitor such as milrinone (bolus of 50 μg kg^{-1} over 10 min and continuous infusion of 0.5–0.75 μg kg^{-1} min^{-1}) or enoximone (bolus of 1 mg kg^{-1} over 10 min followed by a continuous infusion of 5–10 μg kg^{-1} min^{-1}) can be added. However, as both drugs reduce SVR significantly, moderate vasoconstrictor therapy with noradrenaline (0.05.0.2 μg kg^{-1} min^{-1}) to maintain SVR and provide an adequate coronary artery perfusion pressure may be necessary. If this therapy fails, dobutamine may be replaced by adrenaline (epinephrine) (0.05–0.2 μg kg^{-1} min^{-1}). However, as adrenaline, in higher doses (>0.1 μg kg^{-1} min^{-1}), increases SVR, care must be taken to counterbalance this effect by vasodilation to reduce afterload, while still maintaining adequate coronary artery perfusion pressures. Vasodilation may be achieved with infusion of nitroglycerine or, if this fails, with sodium nitroprusside. Alternatively, before institution of aggressive inotropic therapy with possible detrimental effects on splanchnic tissue perfusion, temporary mechanical support with an IABP should be considered to increase coronary artery perfusion pressure and reduce LV afterload (see 'Temporary mechanical support of the failing heart').

If therapy with adrenaline (and implantation of an IABP) also fails, use of the calcium sensitizer levosimendan, which is an inodilator with a half-life of approximately 7 days (including its pharmacologically active metabolites), should be considered. Although not studied in large prospective trials for this indication, reports of large patient series demonstrated reversal of the post-cardiotomy low output syndrome when levosimendan therapy was initiated. In emergency situations, levosimendan is given with a bolus-infusion of 6–12 μg kg^{-1} (over 30–60 min) followed by a continuous infusion of 0.1–0.4 μg kg^{-1} min^{-1}. However, as levosimendan sometimes causes a severe decrease of SVR, a loading infusion over a period of 24 h is increasingly used. Nevertheless, therapy should be initiated cautiously and may need to be combined with vasoconstrictor therapy.

If, despite all of these strategies, a low CO syndrome persists, other options of temporary mechanical support must be initiated. Usually an ECLS system is implanted for temporary mechanical support. If recovery does not occur within 7–14 days, implantation of a ventricular assist device (VAD) or heart transplantation should be considered (see 'Temporary mechanical support of the failing heart').

Treatment of right ventricular failure

When RV failure is diagnosed as the underlying mechanism of cardiac failure (high CVP, low PCWP or LA pressure, RV impairment and dilation in TOE with septal flattening and shift to left, and tricuspid valve regurgitation) a stepwise approach of inotropic therapy is used as with LV failure. As a result of the reduced muscular mass, the ability of the RV to increase contractility is limited. The RV output can be increased by pacing the heart to a rate of 110–120 beats min^{-1} but this will reduce LV preload, increase LV work, and reduce coronary artery perfusion by shortening the duration of diastole. LV contractility normally makes an important contribution to RV performance, so maintenance of LV preload with vasopressors if necessary, is especially important in RV failure.

If increased afterload is contributing to RV failure, a reduction in PVR can be attempted using moderate hyperventilation, high inspired oxygen concentrations, moderate alkalosis, and low tidal volume ventilation (5–6 ml kg^{-1}). A moderate level of positive end-expiratory pressure (PEEP, 5–6 mm Hg) can be applied on the basis that mechanical compression of the pulmonary capillary bed by collapsed airways may compromise pulmonary capillary blood flow. When there is pre-existing pulmonary artery hypertension, more potent selective pulmonary artery vasodilation may be achieved with inhaled nitric oxide (20–40 ppm) or inhalation of aerosolized prostaglandins (iloprost 10–20 μg over 15–30 min, repeated after 1–24 h) or inhalation of milrinone (5 mg repeated after 1–2 h).

Box 56.8 Authors' approach: weaning from CPB

Basic conditions

In complicated weaning procedures, care must be taken to optimize conditions. The first step is to optimize the cardiac rhythm and optimize heart frequency. Thereafter, the afterload of the ventricles should be optimized. The afterload should be reduced as much as possible but adequate cardiac coronary perfusion pressures preserved. A SVR of approximately 800–1200 dyn s^{-1} cm^{-5} is the target. Preload pressures should be adequate (CVP 8–12 mm Hg, LA pressure/PCWP 8–12 mm Hg), but not exceeding a CVP of 12 (14) mm Hg in case of RV dysfunction and a LA pressure or PCWP of 12–15 (20 mm Hg dependent on values measured before surgery). If these conditions do not provide adequate CI (>2 litres min^{-1} m^{-2} BSA) and ventricular performance as assessed by TOE, inotropic support should be started. Volume therapy, positive inotropic support, and vasoactive therapy should be adjusted to achieve a CI greater than 2.2 litres min^{-1} m^{-2} BSA and a Sv_{O_2} of greater than 65–70%. If adrenaline is needed in doses exceeding 0.2 μg kg^{-1} min^{-1}, implantation of an IABP is performed. If even this strategy fails to establish adequate CO, temporary support with an ECLS system is used.

During use of an ECLS system, therapy with levosimendan may be initiated and a gradual attempt to wean from ECLS performed after 3–5 days.

Pharmacological preconditioning in high-risk patients

Patients at risk of developing post-cardiotomy cardiac failure are usually identified before surgery. In patients with preoperatively severely impaired ventricular function and patients with pulmonary artery hypertension we start therapy with an infusion of milrinone (0.5 mg kg^{-1} min^{-1}) after induction of anaesthesia to avoid a potentially rapid loss of SVR. (Preconditioning with levosimendan 24 h before surgery is an alternative approach.) Potential vasodilatory effects are counterbalanced by a continuous infusion of noradrenaline. Approximately 15 min before weaning from CPB, dobutamine (4–6 μg kg^{-1} min^{-1}) is added. If this approach fails, adrenaline is given with a maximum dose of approximately 0.2 μg kg^{-1} min^{-1}. In case of pre-existing pulmonary artery hypertension and RV failure, inhalation of aerosolized prostaglandins or milrinone is used. If pulmonary artery hypertension persists despite these efforts, sildenafil is administered intravenously. In severe cases, a bolus of 0.25 mg kg^{-1} is given as a rapid infusion over a period of 30 min. Thereafter, the dosing is adjusted according to the PVR.

Alternatively, an intravenous regimen with iloprost or sildenafil may be instituted. However, in this case, more pronounced effects on the SVR must be expected and may need to be counterbalanced by the systemic administration of vasoconstrictors such as noradrenaline or vasopressin.

If all these strategies remain ineffective to achieve an adequate CO, temporary mechanical support by insertion of an IABP is the next step. As the majority of RV coronary artery perfusion takes place during systole, IABP has a limited effect on RV coronary artery perfusion. However, maintenance of adequate LV coronary artery perfusion pressures via the IABP will improve LV function and consequently RV output. Nevertheless, because the IABP further reduces the afterload of the relatively unloaded LV, an increase in vasopressor therapy may be needed.

Even if these strategies achieve acceptable results when the chest is open, sternal closure and compression of the often swollen heart by the lungs sometimes has a tamponade-like effect and can impair RV function in particular. Therefore, chest closure has to be done very cautiously. If previously adequate cardiac performance becomes and remains unsatisfactory with sternal closure, re-opening the chest with a view to delayed sternal closure should be discussed with the surgeon. If even this strategy fails, temporary mechanical support with an ECLS system should be discussed (see 'Temporary mechanical support of the failing heart'). If recovery is not achieved after 7–14 days, implantation of a VAD system or heart transplantation is considered.

For the authors' approach to weaning from CPB, see Box 56.8.

Temporary mechanical support of the failing heart

If weaning from CPB fails despite the use of moderate or high doses of positive inotropic agents, temporary mechanical support of the failing heart has to be considered. The system of first choice, particularly in LV failure, is IABP counterpulsation. A balloon is placed (via the femoral artery or directly into the ascending aorta) into the descending part of the aorta, 2–3 cm distal to the origin of the left subclavian artery (Fig. 56.8). The balloon, triggered by the ECG or pulse curve, is inflated in diastole with helium thus providing an increase in diastolic artery pressure and thereby an increase in coronary artery perfusion pressure. During systole the balloon is deflated, thereby augmenting systolic arterial blood flow and decreasing LV afterload. While initially the balloon is inflated and deflated in a 1:1 ratio with the heartbeat, with ongoing recovery of the heart, weaning may be performed by successively changing the ratio to 1:2 and 1:3 and finally explantation of the device. In addition to its use in post-cardiotomy heart failure, the IABP is a helpful device when patients with acute myocardial infarction and (left) heart failure have to be bridged preoperatively until surgery can be performed. The value of an IABP in RV failure is still a matter of debate as the non-failing LV needs no reduction in afterload. Therefore, the only potential benefit of the IABP under this condition is an increase of diastolic artery pressure to preserve coronary artery perfusion pressure.

However, if the LV or RV fails completely, the IABP will not provide adequate flow for tissue oxygenation and improved mechanical support is necessary. This can be achieved by implantation of an ECLS system for selective bridging of the LV or RV or both ventricles (Fig. 56.9). An oxygenator can be easily added to the system if pulmonary blood flow is bypassed or oxygenation critically decreased. Implantation can be performed directly into the heart or pulmonary artery or peripherally into the femoral vessels (which allows closure of the chest and the option to wean the patient from mechanical ventilation). Gradual weaning may be accomplished by successively reducing pump flow and thus increasing work of the heart. When adequate cardiac function has been regained, the system can be explanted. However, if weaning is not possible, VAD implantation may be considered as definitive therapy or as a bridge to heart transplantation.

For the authors' approach to temporary mechanical support, see Box 56.9.

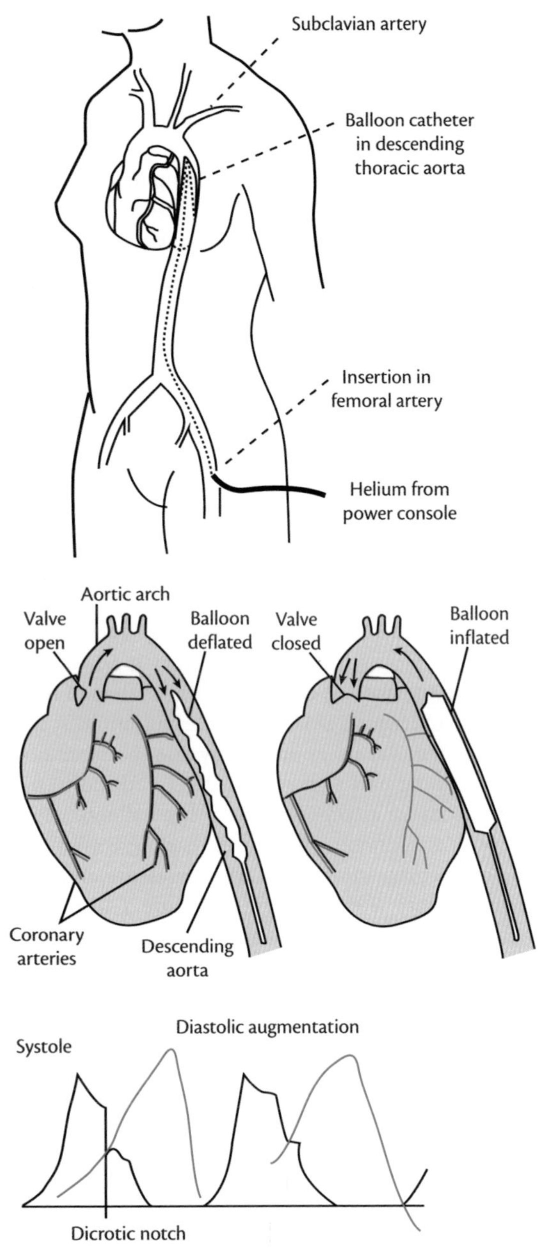

Figure 56.8 Diagram to show the placement of an IABP.
This figure was published in *Miller-Keane Encyclopedia & Dictionary of Medicine, Nursing & Allied Health, 7th edition*, O'Toole, M. T., Copyright © 2005 Elsevier.

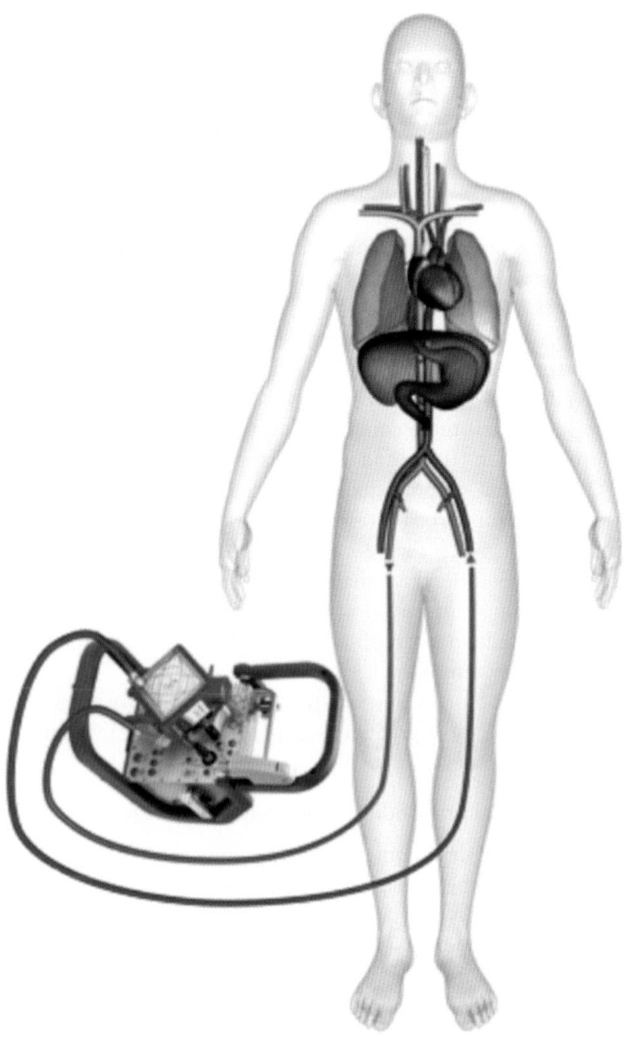

Figure 56.9 Picture of a contemporary ECLS system with a small console mounting on the centrifugal pump/oxygenator unit with venous inflow (from the patient) and arterial outflow lines (to the patient).
Maquet Cardiopulmonary Bypass Inc.

Box 56.9 Authors' approach: temporary mechanical support

If weaning with a moderate degree of positive inotropic therapy fails (adrenaline >0.2 μg kg^{-1} min^{-1}), the implantation of an IABP is usually the next step. If this also fails to generate adequate CO (<2 litres m^{-2} BSA) and acceptable Sv_{O_2} (<65%), before further increasing catecholamine therapy and the risk of decreased tissue perfusion, an ECLS system is used. Preferably this is performed using the femoral vessels to allow closure of the chest. However, in case of isolated right heart failure, arterial cannulation is preferentially performed with a graft sutured to the main pulmonary artery, tunnelled through the skin, and connected to the cannula out of the chest; this allows removal of the cannula without re-opening of the chest. Weaning is attempted after 3–5 days and usually preconditioned by administration of levosimendan. Further attempts are made as indicated until successful. If after 7–14 days of ECLS support no recovery of cardiac function is observed, implantation of a (more permanent) VAD and possible heart transplantation are considered.

Induction and maintenance of anaesthesia

Preparation of the anaesthesia induction room

Irrespective of whether an anaesthesia induction room is used or anaesthesia is induced in the operating theatre, syringes containing drugs for an emergency should be prepared. These should include a vasoconstrictor (e.g. noradrenaline 10 μg ml^{-1}) an inotrope (e.g. adrenaline 10 μg ml^{-1}), calcium chloride ($CaCl_2$) 2% 10 ml, and an antihypertensive agent (glyceryl trinitrate 0.1 mg ml^{-1}) (Box 56.10). A defibrillator should be available in the room or nearby, as should antiarrhythmic drugs,

Box 56.10 Emergency syringes for the anaesthesia induction room

- 10 ml noradrenaline 10 μg ml^{-1}
- 10 ml adrenaline 10 μg ml^{-1}
- 10 ml $CaCl_2$
- 10 ml glyceryl trinitrate 0.1 mg ml^{-1}.

which need not be drawn up unless they require dilution before administration.

Preparation of the patient

Usually the patient arrives in the anaesthesia induction room after having received premedication with a benzodiazepine on the evening before and morning of surgery. After placement of a five-lead ECG, pulse oximetry, and non-invasive measurement of blood pressure, a peripheral venous line is inserted. In patients with critically impaired cardiac function and in patients undergoing re-do or minimally invasive cardiac surgery, external defibrillator pads are also applied. A radial or femoral artery catheter for invasive monitoring of arterial blood pressure is inserted before induction of anaesthesia.

Induction of anaesthesia

Anaesthesia is induced with midazolam, an opioid such as fentanyl or sufentanil, and an intravenous induction agent (the authors prefer etomidate). A neuromuscular blocking agent is used to facilitate tracheal intubation. Changes in the blood pressure exceeding approximately 20% should be treated appropriately with a vasoconstrictor (noradrenaline 10 μg) or a vasodilator (glyceryl trinitrate 0.1 mg). If repeated boluses (two to three) of noradrenaline are not effective in treating hypotension, 10 ml $CaCl_2$ should be given. Only if the vasoconstrictor and $CaCl_2$ fail to restore the blood pressure should a bolus of adrenaline 10 μg be given. This is because adrenaline commonly causes a tachycardia which predisposes to ischaemia. If the heart rate exceeds 120 beats min^{-1} administration of, for example, 10–20 mg sotalol should be considered.

After induction of anaesthesia, a multilumen central venous catheter and, for higher-risk patients and procedures, a PAC introducer with or without the catheter, are placed in an internal jugular vein. In patients with critically impaired ventricular function, these lines may be inserted under local anaesthesia before anaesthetic induction. This enables continuous inotropic medication to be commenced before induction or emergency CPB to be instituted immediately if pharmacological therapy fails to stabilize the patient. Additionally, two large-bore peripheral venous catheters for volume replacement should be inserted. If the duration of surgery is anticipated to be long, there is a risk of excessive bleeding or with patients who have had previous cardiac surgery where there is a risk of injuring the aorta or RV during re-opening of the chest, a large-bore catheter for quick volume replacement may be inserted in an external jugular vein or, if this is not possible a second large-bore introducer (6–9 Gauge) or a 'Sheldon catheter' (particularly in patients who may later need renal replacement therapy), can be inserted in a femoral vein or the other internal jugular vein.

Maintenance of anaesthesia

Anaesthesia is maintained preferably with a continuous infusion of fentanyl, sufentanil, or remifentanil and either a propofol infusion or potent inhalation anaesthetics. Use of a potent inhalation anaesthetic such as sevoflurane or isoflurane may be continued during CPB if the facility for vaporization is available in the CPB circuit. The potent inhalation anaesthetics may be preferred as they may protect the heart and brain from ischaemia–reperfusion injury. The choice of neuromuscular blocking agent is especially important if 'fast-track' weaning from mechanical ventilation is planned. Shorter-acting neuromuscular blocking agents also have the advantage that they are less likely to accumulate, particularly when patients are hypothermic during CPB.

Anaesthesia for individual procedures

Anaesthesia for coronary artery bypass grafting (with cardiopulmonary bypass)

CABG with CPB (on-pump) surgery is the most common procedure in cardiac surgery. However, the preoperative condition of the patient can vary widely and this is a major determinant of the relative ease of management. Factors impacting the course of the patient include the following:

Acuity of the disease

The patient may be scheduled electively for treatment of chronic coronary artery disease or may arrive in the anaesthesia room with unstable angina, ST-segment changes on the ECG, or overt acute myocardial infarction.

Localization of the coronary artery stenoses

Patients with several distal coronary artery stenoses undergoing elective surgery rarely present acute signs of myocardial ischaemia during the induction of anaesthesia or preparation of the grafts before establishing CPB. However, patients with a critical (>80%) stenosis of the left main coronary artery are at high risk of developing acute ischaemia with low CO requiring urgent institution of CPB.

Regional stenosis *vs* diffuse coronary artery sclerosis

Additionally, in patients with regional stenosis of large vessels, an immediate improvement in distal tissue perfusion can be expected and weaning from CPB is likely to be uncomplicated. However, in patients with diffuse involvement of the smaller coronary arteries, the immediate benefit of surgery is limited and temporary impairment of cardiac function after cardioplegia might complicate weaning from CPB.

Preservation of cardiac function

A minority of patients develop an ischaemic cardiomyopathy with severe impairment of left ventricular function (LVEF <30%) and, particularly when accompanied by ischaemic mitral valve regurgitation, this may lead to increased pulmonary artery pressures. The consequence is an unexpected low CO state during weaning from CPB.

Management before CPB

Before induction of anaesthesia, all six leads of the ECG should be checked for signs of ischaemia and the time of the last episode of angina established with the patient. During induction, it is essential to avoid tachycardia as this increases myocardial oxygen demand while reducing supply by shortening diastole which is when the majority of coronary artery perfusion to the LV occurs. Similarly, care has to be taken to maintain the diastolic blood pressure in order to maintain coronary artery perfusion pressure. These aspects are of particular importance in patients with a critical stenosis of the left main coronary artery. In patients presenting with acute myocardial infarction and impaired cardiac function, the increase in afterload required to maintain the diastolic pressure might lead to development or aggravation of a low CO syndrome. Therefore, in these patients, preoperative percutaneous implantation of an IABP should be considered to reduce afterload and increase coronary artery perfusion pressures, as should inotropic support.

In complicated patients, when the chest is opened and before the grafts are harvested, the surgeon should prepare the sutures for the aortic and atrial cannulae so that CPB can be established rapidly if myocardial ischaemia or ventricular failure occurs.

Weaning from CPB

After completion of the coronary artery anastomoses and opening of the aortic cross-clamp the ECG is evaluated. Return of sinus rhythm without ventricular extrasystolic beats and normalization of ST segments indicate recovery of the heart from ischaemia and the effects of cardioplegia. In patients with previously impaired ventricular function or those presenting with acute myocardial infarction, a TOE probe should be inserted to assess regional wall motion and global contractility for evaluation of the need for inotropic support. In patients with acute myocardial infarction, ventricular dysfunction can extend to a penumbral region beyond the circumscribed area of the infarct. This area of 'myocardial stunning' is caused by an ischaemia–reperfusion injury which causes temporary (3–14 days) systolic and diastolic dysfunction. Dependent on the size of the infarction and the penumbral area, an IABP should be implanted pre-emptively and inotropic support started. If weaning is not possible under these conditions, further mechanical support may be necessary.

Bleeding in CABG patients

Patients with acute coronary syndromes and acute myocardial infarction often reach the operating theatre after having received dual antiplatelet therapy with aspirin and clopidogrel or other potent antiplatelet agents. In these patients, liberal transfusion of platelet concentrates is needed to prevent postoperative haemorrhage and pericardial tamponade which might further compromise ventricular performance.

For the authors' approach to anesthesia for CABG surgery, see Box 56.11.

Box 56.11 Authors' approach: anaesthesia for CABG surgery

In patients with a critical stenosis of the left main coronary artery and patients with acute myocardial infarction, repeated boluses of 10 mg sotalol (up to 40 mg) are given to avoid tachycardia and achieve a target heart rate of 80–90 beats min^{-1}. Diastolic pressure is maintained using carefully titrated boluses of noradrenaline.

In patients with acute myocardial infarction with impairment of cardiac performance, or patients with severely impaired LV function, an IABP is usually implanted preoperatively. Positive inotropic therapy with milrinone (0.5 $\mu g\ kg^{-1}\ h^{-1}$) is started after arrival in the operating theatre and dobutamine (3–5 $\mu g\ kg^{-1}\ min^{-1}$) added before weaning from CPB. If this approach fails, adrenaline (0.1–0.2 $\mu g\ kg^{-1}\ min^{-1}$) is added. If even this strategy fails, an ECLS system is implanted (see 'Temporary mechanical support of the failing heart'). On the ICU, early addition of levosimendan is used to aid the process of weaning from mechanical support. However, preoperative use of this new drug as a 'preconditioning' for special-risk patients is also under consideration.

Anaesthesia for off-pump coronary artery bypass graft surgery

Surgery for CABG can also be performed on the beating heart without the use of CPB. Several tools help the surgeon to expose the coronary arteries and stabilize the surgical field (Fig. 56.10):

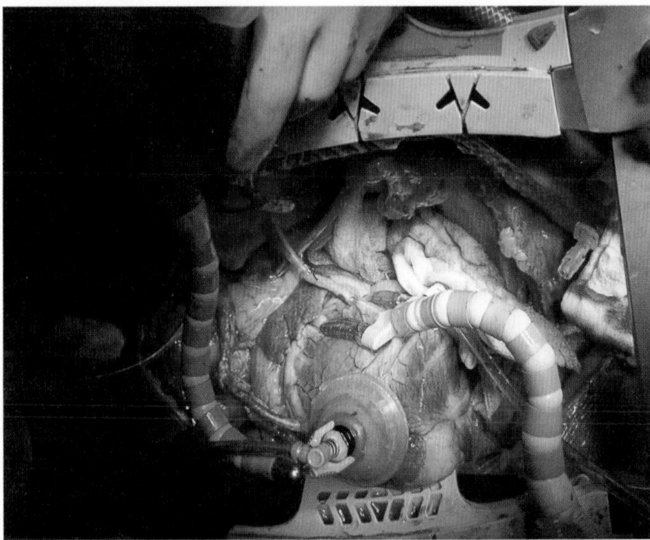

Figure 56.10 Photograph of a heart prepared for off-pump coronary artery bypass surgery. The heart is lifted and positioned using a pericardial sling and an apical suction device so that access even to the lateral branches and posterior branches of the coronary artery system is achieved. The surgical field around the coronary artery is 'fixed' using a stabilizer device so that the contractions of the heart will not hinder the surgeon.

Reproduced from Vettath MP, Ismail E and Kannan A. Re-engineering in OPCAB—A Vettath's perspective. *World Journal of Cardiovascular Diseases*, Volume 3, Issue 4a, pp. 33–44, Copyright © 2013 Murali P. Vettath et al.

- A pericardial sling is anchored at the posterior mediastinum by placement of a deep pericardial suture near the right lower pulmonary vein, under the LA. The sling thereby supports and elevates the LA and the LV without distortion of the atrioventricular axis. The deep pericardial traction lifts the atrioventricular groove and thereby optimizes access to the coronary vessels.
- Additionally, suction devices may be used to move and stabilize the heart so that surgery on the lateral branches of the left coronary artery and on the right coronary artery can be performed.
- A stabilizer is placed on the coronary artery where the anastomoses are performed to minimize movement by the beating heart during anastomosis.

- Small shunts are inserted into the vessel so that flow is provided despite clamping of the vessel in order to avoid ischaemia.

Intraoperative considerations

Induction of anaesthesia follows the same guidelines as during 'on-pump' CABG. However, cooling of the anaesthetized patient should be minimized by ensuring the use of intravenous warming devices and a warming blanket.

In some centres, a PAC is used to monitor CO and pulmonary artery pressures because the value of the TOE is limited when the heart is elevated. Temporary pacemaker wires are placed, so that the anaesthetist can control heart rhythm during the procedure which is an important tool to regulate CO.

During surgery, a cell saver should be used as bleeding might occur particularly when shunts are placed or are so small that blood floods the surgical field.

The need for circulatory support depends on how the 'positioning' of the heart is tolerated. In contrast to 'on-pump' CABG, off-pump CABG surgery usually begins with anastomosis of the left thoracic internal artery to the main branch of the left coronary artery. This anastomosis requires only moderate positioning of the heart and establishes adequate coronary blood flow to an important region. Also in contrast to on-pump CABG, the proximal anastomoses are usually performed first, so that after commencement of the distal anastomosis the blood flow is provided immediately.

Positive inotropic support may be necessary in patients who have impaired LV and RV function preoperatively (see 'Treatment of left ventricular failure'). In patients who undergo urgent surgery because of acute myocardial infarction, or patients with severely impaired LV function, placement of an IABP before performing the anastomoses should be considered.

If positioning of the heart for surgery cannot be achieved without compromising the circulation, conversion to CPB should be considered before proceeding because emergency conversion is associated with a poor patient outcome. Thereafter, CABG can be performed 'on pump' with a 'beating heart' without aortic cross-clamping and administration of cardioplegia.

For the authors' approach to off-pump coronary artery bypass surgery, see Box 56.12.

Box 56.12 Authors' approach: off-pump coronary artery bypass surgery

In an attempt to stabilize cardiac rhythm and avoid tachycardia, we administer a bolus of 40–80 mg sotalol before performing the anastomoses. Acute tachyarrhythmias are usually less well tolerated and more difficult to manage than bradyarrhythmias which can be easily overpaced.

In our experience, positioning for surgical access to the branches of the left lateral coronary artery is the main cause of severe haemodynamic instability. Maintenance of higher filling pressures is helpful to stabilize CO. Furthermore, particularly before moving the heart, small boluses of noradrenaline (5–10 μg) help to preserve systemic arterial pressure and maintain coronary artery perfusion pressure. We often use a highly diluted infusion (perfusion syringe with 0.5 mg/50 ml noradrenaline) for faster infusion rates. In our experience this quickly results in the desired effect along with the option to give small boluses (5–10 μg). Usually after a period of 1–2 min the heart adapts to its new position and no further noradrenaline is required. However, surgery on the vessel should only be started if positioning is tolerated without excessive pharmacological intervention.

More invasive monitoring for measurement of LV filling pressures and CO is only used in patients with acute myocardial infarction and patients with severely impaired LV function. A PAC is useful for monitoring LV filling pressures, while PCA devices quickly identify changes in cardiac SV and CO. Temporary monitoring of the LA pressure throughout the grafting procedure via a catheter inserted by the surgeon is an optimal addition to PCA monitoring in this special situation (see 'Section Monitoring' 'Box 56.2').

Anaesthesia for valvular heart disease

The more common valvular disorders in adult patients with non-congenital heart disease are tricuspid, mitral, or aortic regurgitation and mitral or aortic stenosis.

Mitral and aortic regurgitation lead to increased LV preload which, when chronic, may also lead to pulmonary artery hypertension and increased RV afterload. Tricuspid valve regurgitation leads to RV volume overload.

Chronic aortic stenosis leads to LV hypertrophy, while mitral stenosis usually results in increased RV afterload as a result of pulmonary artery hypertension. Therefore, the factors determining the complexity of anaesthetic management are the following:

Preservation of LV function

Particularly in patients with aortic and mitral regurgitation, chronic volume overload might cause progressive dilation of the ventricle and reduction of LVEF (note that in patients with mitral regurgitation, the LVEF is usually overestimated as a large proportion is ejected retrogradely through the incompetent mitral valve).

In patients with aortic stenosis, LV function is usually reasonably well maintained. However, chronic ischaemia of the subendocardial myocardium may cause progressive dilatation of the LV and further reduction of EF. In these patients, as the failing LV becomes unable to generate high systolic pressures, the pressure gradient across the aortic valve decreases

Preservation of RV function

In patients with tricuspid regurgitation, chronic volume overload leads to dilatation and impairment of the RV.

However, a chronic increase in RV afterload as a result of increased pulmonary artery pressure in aortic and mitral disease may also cause dilatation of the RV with impairment of RV function. Except in patients with atrial fibrillation or patients with endocarditis affecting the tricuspid valve, tricuspid regurgitation is often a consequence of RV dilatation as a result of the increased afterload caused by mitral or aortic regurgitation.

Induction of anaesthesia and the pre-CPB period

In patients with aortic or mitral stenosis, tachycardia has to be avoided as it shortens the diastolic period. In patients with mitral stenosis, this leads to a further reduction in LV preload. In patients with aortic stenosis, the shortening of diastole may critically reduce coronary artery perfusion of the hypertrophied LV, while the tachycardia causes an increase in myocardial oxygen demand. Acute LV decompensation may be the result. Additionally, any reduction of the diastolic pressure during induction may critically decrease coronary artery perfusion pressure and should be avoided.

Patients with severe aortic stenosis are highly susceptible to the development of ventricular extrasystoles because of LV hypertrophy. Care must be taken, for example, when advancing the guidewire during insertion of central venous catheters as ventricular exrasystoles predispose to ventricular fibrillation. Patients with aortic stenosis are also liable to acute LV decompensation which is resistant to pharmacological intervention. If this occurs, CPB must be established urgently.

Weaning from CPB

In patients with unimpaired or only moderately impaired ventricular function, weaning from CPB can usually be achieved without inotropic support. Patients with aortic stenosis and LV hypertrophy may benefit from an elevated diastolic blood pressure to ensure adequate coronary artery perfusion of the hypertrophied ventricle and infusion of a vasoconstrictor should be considered.

The intraoperative TOE will not only help to confirm the success of surgery but also provide important information about ventricular performance. In patients with chronic aortic or mitral regurgitation, positive inotropic pharmacological support may be necessary. If this fails, implantation of an IABP or further mechanical support may be required.

If RV failure is observed in patients after tricuspid, mitral, or aortic repair, RV afterload can be reduced by inhalation of nitric oxide or nebulization of prostaglandins in order to supplement inotropic support.

Surgical complications can also cause ventricular dysfunction. For example, in aortic valve replacement, particularly if the prosthesis is too large, the right coronary artery ostium may become obstructed leading to RV ischaemia and subsequent failure. Air embolism after aortic cross-clamp release can also cause ECG ST-segment elevation and impaired contractility but this is usually reversible within 5–10 min. If ischaemia and ventricular dysfunction from presumed air embolism do not resolve within this time then a problem with the prosthetic valve should be assumed: changing the prosthesis to a smaller size or CABG are the surgical options. After prolonged ischaemia, inotropic support or temporary mechanical support may be necessary to wean the patient from CPB.

In patients undergoing mitral valve surgery, the circumflex branch of the left coronary artery may be twisted or occluded causing LV dysfunction. Alterations in the ECG and impairment of regional wall motion visualized by TOE may suggest this rare complication, although definitive diagnosis may require coronary artery catheterization. Revision of the mitral valve reconstruction/prosthesis or CABG are the surgical options to treat this complication. Again, prolonged ischaemia may necessitate inotropic support or temporary mechanical support to wean the patient from CPB.

For the authors' approach to valvular heart disease, see Box 56.13.

Box 56.13 Authors' approach: valvular heart disease

In patients with severe aortic or mitral stenosis, care is taken that the patient is deeply anaesthetized to prevent tachycardia. Additionally, a bolus of 10–20 mg sotalol is given when inducing anaesthesia. When even a slight decrease in mean arterial (and diastolic) pressure is noted, (intermittent) small dosages of a vasoconstrictor (noradrenaline 5–10 μg) are given. In patients with impaired RV and LV function, particularly when pulmonary artery hypertension is diagnosed preoperatively, a continuous infusion of milrinone (0.25–0.5 $\mu g\ kg^{-1}\ h^{-1}$) is started after arrival in the operating theatre.

In patients with preoperative atrial fibrillation, 300 mg amiodarone is given during CPB in an attempt to synchronize heart rhythm or reduce the ventricular rate to enable external pacing and steady filling and emptying of the heart chambers.

Anaesthesia for minimally invasive valve surgery

Aortic valve surgery

Minimally invasive aortic valve surgery is performed through a partial sternotomy that enables visualization of, and surgical access to, the aorta and right atrium. The aortic cannula is inserted directly but the larger venous cannula is tunnelled under the skin so as not to restrict the surgical field. External defibrillator patches are applied as internal defibrillator paddles cannot be inserted through the small incision.

The main problem in minimally invasive aortic valve surgery is the prevention of systemic air embolus. Elimination of air from the heart needs to be meticulous and is therefore performed under TOE control. TOE is also helpful in evaluation of ventricular performance when weaning from CPB as the ventricles cannot be directly observed through the sternotomy.

Transcatheter aortic valve implantation

A relatively new method is transcatheter placement of a biological aortic valve prosthesis. This procedure is similar in principle to placement of a coronary artery stent. A large introducer is inserted in a femoral or axillary artery, through which is inserted the device containing the stented and compressed valve. Alternatively, a small left-sided thoracotomy is performed and the device inserted through the LV (transapical approach). Positioning of the valve is preceded by balloon valvuloplasty of the native aortic valve which is compressed into the aortic wall. This is performed under rapid pacing of the ventricle to avoid distension of the LV when the balloon occludes the LV outflow tract. The new valve is then positioned, again under rapid ventricular pacing and the prosthesis pressed into the tissue by expansion of a balloon catheter.

Patients selected for transcatheter aortic valve implantation (TAVI) are usually elderly or present severe co-morbidities, or both of these, that preclude them from conventional aortic valve replacement with CPB.

Possible complications of TAVI are:

- Acute decompensation as a result of massive acute aortic regurgitation after the balloon valvuloplasty
- Malpositioning of the prosthesis (possibly with coronary ostia occlusion causing myocardial ischaemia and acute decompensation) needing implantation of a second prosthesis (valve in valve) or emergency CPB and conventional aortic valve replacement
- Acute bleeding of the often fragile tissue of the LV when the large-calibre introducer is inserted or removed when the transapical approach is used
- Embolic stroke (particularly when transfemoral access is used).

TAVI is usually performed in the fully instrumented (arterial line, central venous catheter, large-bore introducer device) patient.

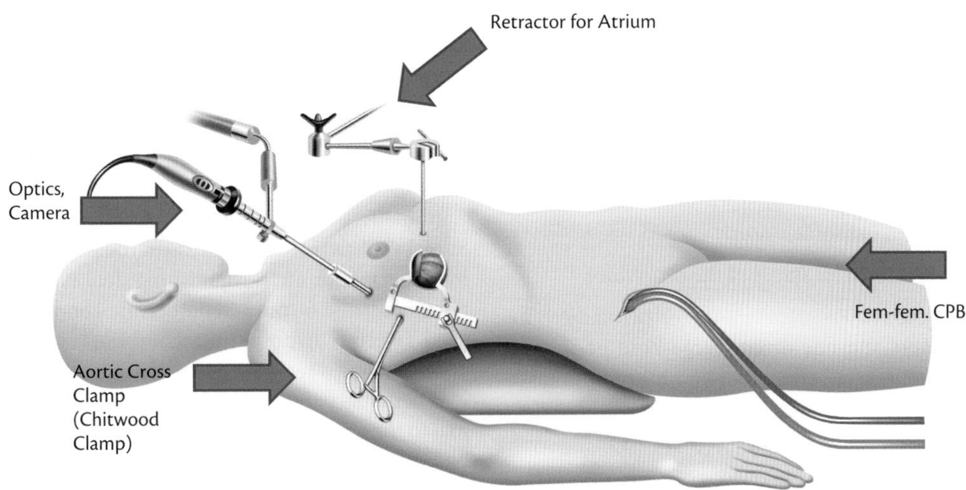

Figure 56.11 A montage summary of minimally invasive video-assisted mitral valve surgery. Cannulation for CPB is performed via the femoral vessels. A small thoracic incision is performed to gain access to the mitral valve. Also demonstrated are additional small incisions for placement of the aortic cross-clamp, the videoscope, and traction devices to improve exposure of the surgical field.

The transfemoral and transaxillary procedures may be performed under sedation (improved diagnostic of stroke etc.), or general anaesthesia with tracheal intubation or use of a laryngeal mask. The transapical approach requires general anaesthesia and tracheal intubation. One-lung ventilation is usually not required. When tracheal intubation is used, TOE is performed to help guide positioning and assess subsequent function of the prosthesis.

For all procedures, external defibrillator patches should be placed and a set of syringes with medication for emergency treatment of arrhythmias, systemic arterial hypo- and hypertension, and low CO should be available.

For transapical valve replacement, CPB and a cell saver should be ready for emergency use.

Mitral and tricuspid valve surgery

Minimally invasive mitral and tricuspid valve surgery is performed via a small, anterolateral sub-mammary thoracotomy (Fig. 56.11). Visualization of the surgical field is improved by inserting a small video camera inserted through the incision. Aortic cross-clamping is performed with a long clamp inserted through an additional small incision.

CPB is performed via the femoral vessels. In mitral valve surgery, a long two-stage cannula is passed through the inferior vena cava, the right atrium, and into the superior vena cava. This manoeuvre is guided by TOE. In tricuspid valve surgery, the superior vena cava is drained by a cannula through the right internal jugular vein inserted by the anaesthetist. As with minimally invasive aortic valve surgery, external defibrillator paddles are attached and elimination of air from the heart is confirmed by TOE. TOE also enables the ventricular performance and surgical result to be assessed.

For the authors' approach to minimally invasive valve surgery, see Box 56.14.

Box 56.14 Authors' approach: minimally invasive valve surgery

In some centres, minimally invasive mitral and tricuspid valve surgery is performed during one-lung ventilation. In our institution, the lung is disconnected after starting CPB. Thereafter, the small thoracotomy and surgery is performed with total collapse of the lungs. This helps to avoid the more traumatic and expensive placement of a double-lumen tracheobronchial tube or bronchial blocker system. Additionally, the surgeon places a small catheter into the wound for postoperative regional anaesthesia.

Anaesthesia for thoracic aortic surgery

Anaesthesia for surgery of the thoracic aorta is a specialized field within cardiovascular anaesthesia. The fact that the arteries providing perfusion and oxygenation of the brain originate from the aortic arch and arteries supplying the spinal cord originate from the descending thoracic aorta underlies the need for additional CPB techniques to prevent neurological damage. The basic strategies, which are often combined, are:

- Regional arterial perfusion
- Regional and particularly systemic hypothermia which reduces oxygen demand of ischaemic tissue
- Retrograde perfusion via the venous system to maintain hypothermia and eliminate air from the arterial vessels.

Besides possessing knowledge of these special perfusion techniques, the anaesthetist has to be aware that repair of thoracic aneurysms and acute dissections often require massive blood transfusion. Factors contributing to blood loss are:

- Deep or profound hypothermia and rewarming lead to a substantial prolongation of CPB which is associated with a severe coagulopathy
- The extent of the anastomoses of the aorta
- Friability or calcification (or both) of the aorta associated with aneurysm and dissection

- Erroneous administration of potent dual antiplatelet therapy because of misdiagnosis of dissection of the thoracic aorta as an acute myocardial infarction.

The volume of blood aspirated from the cardiotomy suction into the CPB system is a good predictor of the extent of bleeding after weaning from CPB. This information should be communicated by the perfusionist.

Principles for anaesthesia in thoracic aortic surgery are:

- Avoid high blood pressures at all stages of the procedure
- In addition to a central venous catheter, one or two large-bore central venous catheters and one or two large-bore peripheral venous lines should be inserted allowing rapid infusion of large volumes
- In the operating theatre, a cell saver should be available
- Patients should be placed on warming blankets and devices for warming infusions and blood products should be available to maintain the body temperature when massive transfusion is necessary.

Anaesthesia for elective surgery of the ascending aorta and aortic arch

Induction of anaesthesia, pre-CPB and CPB period

Arterial pressure is usually measured using both a right radial arterial catheter, for monitoring of brachiocephalic artery perfusion, and a femoral arterial catheter, for monitoring distal arterial perfusion. However, particularly in complex cases and revision surgery, the anaesthetist should discuss and plan the siting of lines for monitoring and CPB with the surgeon. Bladder and nasopharyngeal temperature should be measured. Neurological monitoring with EEG or NIRS is recommended.

Aortic valve disease often accompanies disease of the ascending aorta. If surgery is restricted to the aortic valve and ascending aorta, aortic cross-clamping can be performed proximal to the origin of the brachiocephalic artery using standard antegrade arterial perfusion and mild hypothermia. If, however, the aortic arch has to be examined or repaired, systemic deep or profound hypothermia may be necessary for periods of circulatory arrest, depending on whether regional cerebral perfusion is used or not.

Weaning from CPB

After rewarming to 36.5–37°C, weaning from CPB is begun. Preoperative ventricular function and the duration of aortic cross-clamping will determine the need for inotropic support. The TOE is very helpful in evaluating ventricular contractility.

After the administration of protamine, a massive transfusion of blood products may be necessary to maintain an adequate circulation and re-establish haemostasis.

Anaesthesia for surgery of the descending thoracic aorta

Induction of anaesthesia

Standard arterial blood pressure monitoring for surgery of the descending aorta consists of right radial and femoral artery catheters.

Surgery of the descending thoracic aorta is usually performed through a right-sided thoracotomy and requires one-lung ventilation. Intubation of the left main bronchus may be difficult as a result of distortion by the aortic aneurysm. Primary endoscopic placement of the tube preferably into the left main bronchus is recommended. Alternatively, a left-sided bronchial blocker may be used. As pulmonary bleeding might occur because of adhesion of the tissue of the left lung to the aneurysm the double-lumen tube may be left *in situ* and changed 24 h postoperatively.

Cardiopulmonary bypass

Cannulation for CPB usually involves a femoral artery and vein. Surgery is performed during circulatory arrest with profound hypothermia or after establishing dual parallel circulations under normothermic or mild hypothermic conditions. Some centres use mild systemic hypothermia combined with selective spinal cord cooling using a separate perfusion system.

When dual parallel circulations are used, organs and tissues proximal to the aortic cross-clamp are perfused via the beating heart with blood that is oxygenated by one-lung ventilation while the organs and tissues distal to the clamp are perfused and oxygenated via CPB. The point of communication between the two circulations is the right atrium. The perfusionist has to maintain a delicate balance between providing an adequate preload for the heart to perfuse the upper torso (but avoiding high arterial pressures) while providing adequate venous drainage for perfusion of the distal torso with the CPB.

Weaning from CPB

Weaning from CPB is commenced after rewarming to 36.5–37°C. Myocardial contractility is assessed using TOE. When surgery is performed with the heart beating, inotropic support is rarely necessary. However, after prolonged periods of deep circulatory arrest, inotropic support may be needed. After administration of protamine, a massive transfusion of blood products may be necessary to maintain an adequate circulation and re-establish haemostasis.

Anaesthesia for surgery of an acute type A dissection of the aorta

Dissections of the thoracic aorta are categorized using the DeBakey classification (I, II, IIIa, and IIIb) (Fig. 56.12) or the Stanford classification (type A = DeBakey I or II: type B = DeBakey IIIa or IIIb).

Stanford type A dissections include all dissections involving the ascending aorta, while type B dissections are restricted to the descending aorta. Type B dissections are usually not an indication for emergency surgery and are treated initially by pharmacological control of the arterial blood pressure and definitively with an endovascular stent. However, type A dissections are among the most dramatic indications for emergency surgery as mortality increases 1% per hour of delay in treatment.

Induction of anaesthesia and pre-CPB period

Patients may present which symptoms of cardiogenic shock if the ruptured aneurysm has caused pericardial effusion and cardiac tamponade or a coronary ostium is involved in the dissection causing symptoms of acute myocardial infarction. The arterial monitoring lines have to be inserted after consultation with the surgeon as they will usually need to cannulate the right subclavian artery, a carotid artery, or femoral artery because opening of the chest may release a tamponaded aneurysm resulting in massive bleeding. Central venous access is established as previously described for elective surgery of the thoracic aorta. Vasopressors or inotropes may be required to maintain a minimum blood pressure but hypertension could lead to increased haemorrhage or extension of the dissection and must be avoided.

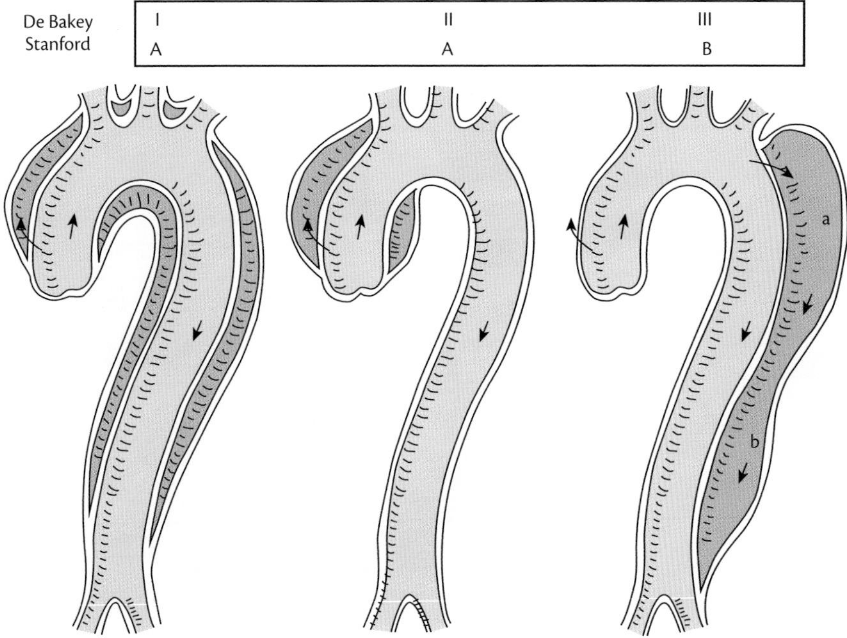

Figure 56.12 Scheme of the DeBakey and Stanford classifications for aortic dissections. In the Stanford classification, a type A dissection originates from the ascending aorta with exclusive dissection of this part of the aorta (DeBakey II) or additional involvement of the descending aorta (DeBakey I). Type B dissections according to the Stanford classification are limited to the descending part of the aorta (DeBakey IIIa and IIIb).

Reproduced from Aung Myat et al. (eds), *Challenging Concepts in Cardiovascular Medicine*, 2013, Figure 9.3, Page 99, with permission from Oxford University Press. DeBakey: Data from DeBakey MA, Henly WS, Cooley DA et al. Surgical management of dissecting aneurysms of the aorta. *Journal of Thoracic and Cardiovascular Surgery*, 1965, Volume 49, pp. 130–49. Stanford: Data from Daily PO, Trueblood HW, Stinson EB, Wuerflein RD, Shumway NE. Management of acute aortic dissections. *Annals of Thoracic Surgery*, 1970, Volume 10, Issue 3, pp. 237–47.

Anaesthesia during CPB and for weaning from CPB

After induction of anaesthesia, CPB is established, the patient cooled, and then the chest is opened and surgery performed. Depending on whether regional arterial cerebral perfusion is used, deep or profound hypothermia is established. Surgery can involve reconstruction or replacement of the aortic valve, reconstruction of the layers of the aortic wall and graft insertion above the coronary ostia, or placement of a valved conduit with re-implantation of the coronary ostia.

For weaning from CPB, inotropic support may be necessary especially if there was preoperative myocardial ischaemia. The ECG may suggest regional ischaemia or infarction, while TOE will provide important information about global and regional myocardial contractility and integrity of any aortic valve reconstruction. If there has been extensive myocardial ischaemia, mechanical support may be necessary. After administration of protamine, the anaesthetist should be prepared to manage extensive bleeding with red cell transfusion and coagulopathy with blood products.

For the authors' approach to surgery of the thoracic aorta, see Box 56.15.

Box 56.15 Authors' approach: surgery of the thoracic aorta

In all patients, bilateral cerebral NIRS is used, particularly when 'regional antegrade cerebral perfusion' is performed. During systemic cooling and rewarming from deep or profound hypothermia, a continuous infusion of sodium nitroprusside (60 mg/50 ml; 2–10 ml h^{-1}) is titrated to achieve vasodilation and faster cooling and re-warming. After CPB, sodium nitroprusside is useful to treat hypertension and its short elimination half-life means that its effects wear off soon after discontinuation should excessive bleeding occur.

We routinely give TXA (1 g intravenous bolus, 0.5 g into the CPB with a continuous infusion of 0.2 g h^{-1} during surgery) to inhibit haemostatic activation during CPB and attenuate postoperative bleeding.

Approximately 30 min before expected weaning from CPB a modified thromboelastogram using a TEG™ (Haemonetics Corp., Braintree, MA, USA) or ROTEM™ device is performed to guide the transfusion of platelets, coagulation factors, or fibrinogen concentrate.

Anaesthesia for implantation of total artificial heart or ventricular assist devices

The indications for VAD systems or a total artificial heart are:

- As a bridge to recovery after myocardial infraction or acute myocarditis
- As a bridge to heart transplantation
- As definitive treatment in patients with heart failure who are not eligible for heart transplantation because of advanced aged or severe co-morbidities.

Systems used are:

- A total artificial heart which is implanted in the mediastinum after resection of the native heart for biventricular support. The connection to the vascular bed is achieved by anastomosis to the atria, the pulmonary artery, and the aorta
- A single (L/R VAD) or biventricular (BVAD) extracorporeal pneumatic-chambered valved pump which is connected to the heart (LV and right atrium) and the pulmonary artery and aorta (Fig. 56.13).

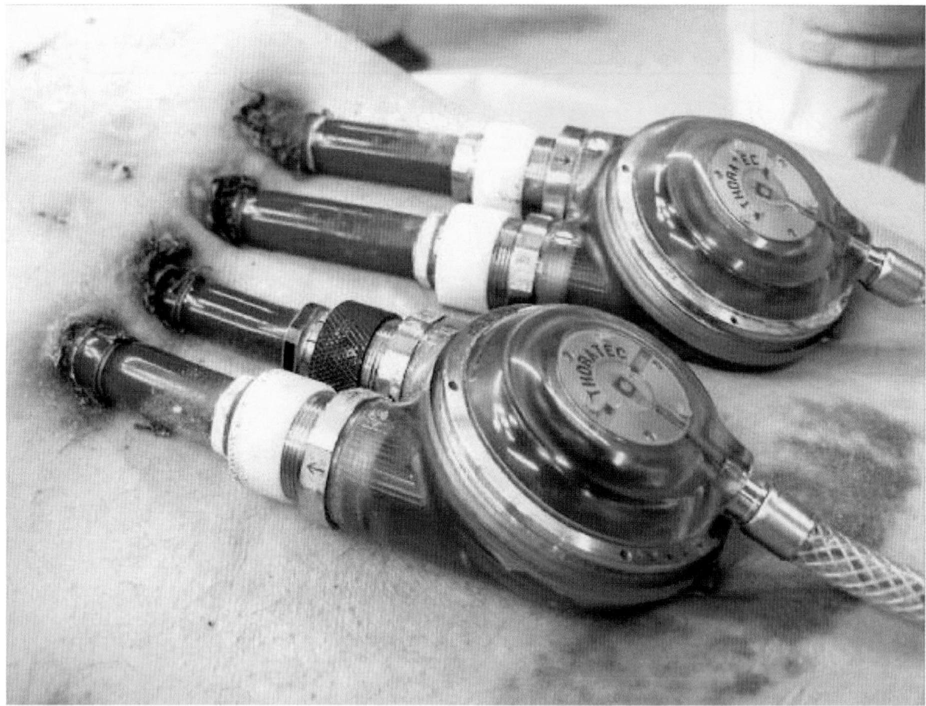

Figure 56.13 Photograph of an extracorporeal pneumatic BVAD with two pneumatic valved chambers which direct the blood from the left ventricle (left atrium) into the aorta and from the right atrium into the main pulmonary artery.

Both the total artificial heart and the pneumatic chambered and valved VAD generate a pulsatile blood flow:

- A usually left-sided (right-sided is possible) small, implantable non-valved impeller or centrifugal pump which is connected to the apex of the LV and the ascending aorta. These devices generate laminar blood flow, so no pulse is palpable (Fig. 56.14).

Because the modern LV laminar flow systems are small, light, non-valved, and therefore noiseless and electrically driven, mobility and comfort of life of the patient is dramatically increased. Therefore these systems are preferred if a longer duration of mechanical support is expected, especially when this is definitive treatment.

Induction of anaesthesia and pre-CPB period

Patients have terminal heart failure and need inotropic agents or an IABP (or both). Before induction of anaesthesia, the infusion rate of the inotropic agents may be increased to maintain blood pressure. In patients scheduled for implantation of a LVAD, insertion of a PAC is mandatory to measure pulmonary artery pressures and pulmonary vascular resistance after implantation of the device which will provide important information about RV afterload. In patients scheduled for implantation of a total artificial heart or BVAD, any PAC lines should be removed. A large-bore central venous line and peripheral large-bore venous catheter should be inserted to provide for massive transfusion.

Before implantation of the device, a TOE examination should be performed to exclude aortic valve regurgitation, a persistent foramen ovale, and presence of a ventricular thrombus which should be removed before implantation. In patients scheduled for LVAD implantation, RV function and competence of the tricuspid valve is also assessed.

Management of anaesthesia during CPB and weaning from CPB

The implantation of a total artificial heart or BVAD is performed with aortic cross-clamping while implantation of an LVAD is usually performed on the fibrillating heart. For LVAD implantation, aortic cross-clamping is only necessary if the aortic valve has to be replaced because of aortic regurgitation. If severe regurgitation of the tricuspid valve is necessary, this can also be accomplished on the fibrillating heart.

As inotropic agents are stopped during CPB and pulmonary blood flow reduced, higher infusion rates of vasoconstrictors or even methylthioninium chloride infusions might be necessary to maintain adequate arterial pressure in this period.

After implantation of a total artificial heart or BVAD, maintenance of CO and systemic perfusion pressure is achieved by replacement of volume and regulation of SVR. With perfusion of the pulmonary vascular bed, vasopressors can usually be incrementally reduced as adequate filling of the devices is reached.

After implantation of a LVAD, reduction of RV afterload and inotropic support of the RV is necessary to provide adequate filling of the LV (see 'Treatment of right ventricular failure'). The TOE is helpful to evaluate RV function, preload, and LV filling. A leftward shift of the ventricular septum is a sign of RV dysfunction and inadequate LV preload. The LV (VAD) preload may be optimized by adjusted the VAD output. In the case that moderate pharmacological treatment and optimized VAD blood flow does not achieve stable and adequate blood flow, temporary mechanical support of the RV via an ECLS system should be considered (see 'Temporary mechanical support of the failing heart').

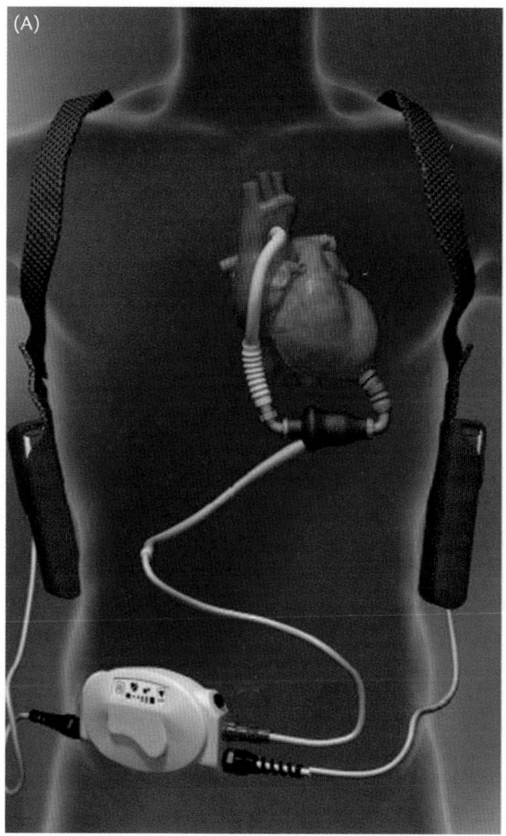

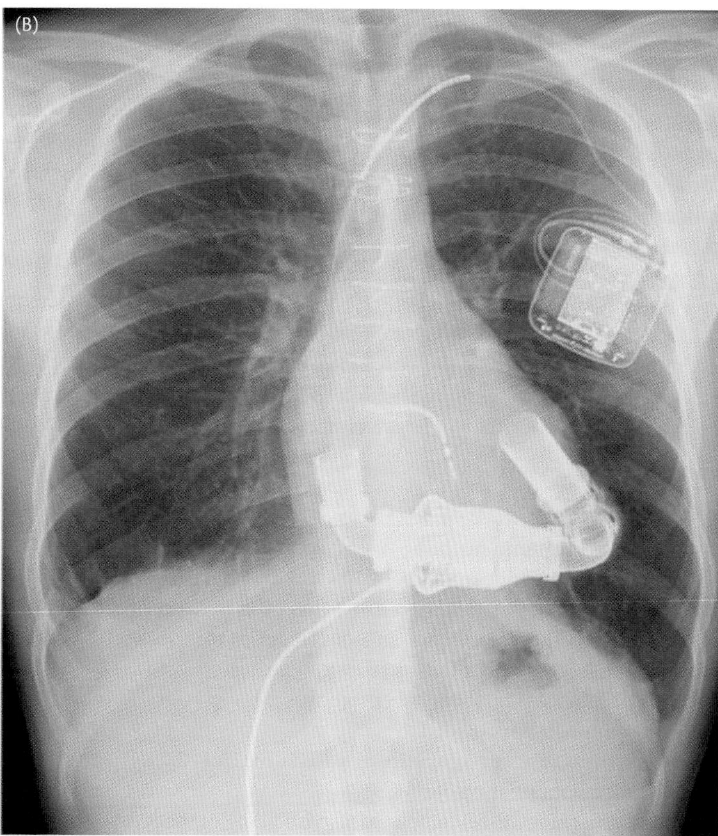

Figure 56.14 Cartoon and X-ray to show the positioning of a contemporary totally implantable axial flow LVAD with the inflow cannula in the apex of the left ventricle and outflow into the aorta. The driveline for receiving energy and control of the device is tunnelled through the abdominal wall to connect to the controller unit.
Reprinted with the permission of Thoratec Corporation.

Massive transfusion of red blood cells, platelet concentrates, and clotting factors may be necessary, especially when there has been previous cardiac surgery.

Some modern LVAD systems, such as the HVAD® (HeartWare® Inc, Miami Lakes, FL, USA), because of technical modifications of the ventriculotomy, can be implanted on an ECLS system even without the aid of CPB (however, the implantation strategy has to be modified). This helps to attenuate or prevent drawbacks associated with CPB. As these strategies do not allow elimination of air, they are only feasible when no procedures on the tricuspid valve, arterial septum, or aortic valve are necessary. Such a procedure is more challenging for the anaesthetist, because they must help to prevent air embolism using TOE, be aware of the fact that cardiotomy suction is not available, that they have to compensate for volume replacement in case of major blood loss and, in case of an 'off-pump' implantation, for haemodynamic stability throughout the implantation procedure.

For the authors' approach to VAD implantation, see Box 56.16.

General anaesthesia for patients with a VAD or total artificial heart

As there is an increasing number of patients with mechanical support, the general anaesthetist is increasingly confronted with the need to anaesthetize them for non-cardiac surgery. There are two main considerations when anaesthetizing this special patient group.

Management of coagulation and anticoagulation

In patients on mechanical support, there is always a delicate balance between the risk of bleeding and thrombosis. Thrombosis is promoted by the non-endothelial surface of the device and patients are anticoagulated with warfarin and usually with aspirin, other platelet inhibitors, or both. There is also emerging evidence that patients on mechanical support, especially with a laminar flow VAD, can develop von Willebrand syndrome because of loss of the high-molecular-weight von Willebrand factor, similar to patients with aortic stenosis. In order to prevent excessive bleeding, patients are usually bridged from warfarin with unfractionated heparin until surgery. Any prospect of stopping heparin or transfusing platelets or clotting factors should be initially discussed with the cardiac surgeon or VAD coordinator in order to balance the risks of bleeding and pump thrombosis with its dramatic consequences.

Monitoring in patients on laminar flow LVAD support

The laminar flow LVADs do not generate a pulsed arterial pressure. In patients who have some recovery of LV function, low-amplitude pulsatile flow is superimposed on the laminar flow and this may be sufficient to enable non-invasive blood pressure measurement and pulse oximetry. Otherwise non-invasive measurement of blood pressure and peripheral oxygen saturation is impossible, although CO is displayed on the control unit. For short, low-risk procedures, monitoring with an ECG and measurement of CO may be

Box 56.16 Authors' approach: VAD implantation

Induction of anaesthesia

In patients with a critical preoperative condition, the induction of anaesthesia is performed in the operating theatre with the surgical team scrubbed and ready to intervene should acute decompensation occur, so that extracorporeal support can be initiated immediately. Before induction of anaesthesia, adrenaline (0.05–0.1 μg kg^{-1} min^{-1}) is added or the infusion rate increased if it is already in use. For induction of anaesthesia, midazolam and ketamine (2 mg kg^{-1}) and a small bolus of etomidate (5 mg) are used.

For implantation of an LVAD with aid of an ECLS system, besides 'standard equipment' a 'Sheldon' dialysis catheter is inserted for rapid replacement of large volumes.

Haemodynamic management

LVAD implantation

As replacement of volume might be restricted as a result of RV failure, a haemoglobin concentration of 10–12 g dl^{-1} is desirable before weaning from CPB. This will ensure that even in cases of 'volume restriction' therapeutic amounts of platelet concentrates and coagulation factors can be transfused without causing a critical decrease of the haemoglobin concentration.

Inotropic support is provided by milrinone (0.5 μg kg^{-1} min^{-1}), dobutamine (3–5 μg kg^{-1} min^{-1}), adrenaline (0.1–0.2 μg kg^{-1} min^{-1}), or a combination of these.

Before weaning from CPB is completed, careful filling of the RV and ventilation of the lungs is performed to achieve lung perfusion while avoiding excessive RV preload. During this phase, iloprost (10–20 μg) or milrinone (5 mg) is nebulized over a period of 15–30 min to reduce PVR. Thereafter, CPB flow is slowly reduced and LVAD flow slowly increased. Preload of the RV is guided by TOE, direct visualization of RV performance, and response of the CVP to gradual fluid loading. Filling of the LV is monitored via the TOE or in complicated cases via measurement of the LA pressure (target approximately 8–12 mm Hg). If there is persistent elevation of pulmonary artery pressure and PVR, nebulization of iloprost or milrinone is continued. If chest closure leads to an impairment of haemodynamics, the chest may be left open. If stable adequate VAD flow cannot be provided by these strategies, temporary mechanical support of the RV via an ECLS system is initiated (see 'Temporary mechanical support of the failing heart').

Blood management

LVAD/BVAD/TAH implantation

In all patients TXA is given (1 g as bolus for the patient, 0.5 g into the CPB, continuous infusion of 0.2 g h^{-1} during surgery) to inhibit haemostatic activation during CPB and attenuate postoperative bleeding.

Approximately 30 min before expected weaning from CPB, a modified thromboelastography analysis using TEG™ or ROTEM™ is performed to guide transfusion of platelets and clotting. As a result of the increased blood flow, patients may quickly develop von Willebrand syndrome, so desmopressin (0.3 μg kg^{-1}) is given after CPB to promote coagulation.

If replacement of platelets and clotting factors does not prevent diffuse bleeding, the chest is left open to avoid acute tamponade with secondary closure after 1–3 days.

sufficient. With longer or higher-risk procedures, insertion of an arterial and central venous catheter is helpful. In the absence of a pulse, arterial cannulation is aided by ultrasound guidance.

TOE is helpful in detecting RV failure. Alternatively, a high level of suspicion should be maintained and, if CO decreases and CVP increases, positive inotropic therapy with milrinone (0.5 μg kg^{-1} min^{-1}) and dobutamine (3–6 μg kg^{-1} min^{-1}) should be started.

Anaesthesia for heart transplantation

RV failure is the main cause of early graft failure in heart transplantation. The RV of the donor heart, especially when it is young and comparably small, is not adapted to overcome the raised pulmonary artery pressure and PVR often present in the recipient. In addition, the contractility of the donor heart may be impaired by the ischaemia–reperfusion injury associated with organ preservation and the inflammatory response to CPB. Therefore, prevention and treatment of RV failure is a central aim in anaesthesia for heart transplantation. However, in some cases, severe reperfusion injury of the LV may lead to severe myocardial stunning, diastolic dysfunction, and LV failure. In cases of severe myocardial stunning, recovery of the heart may take 7–10 days if total recovery takes place at all. Kobashigawa et al. (2014) provide an excellent detailed overview of the pathophysiology and treatment strategies for early graft failure after cardiac transplantation.

Induction of anaesthesia and monitoring

Timing is a critical issue in heart transplantation as the period of ischaemia of the donor heart should be as short as possible to reduce ischaemia–reperfusion injury. Any delay in the preparation of the recipient should be minimized. Ideally, therefore, induction of anaesthesia and insertion of monitoring lines should be performed quickly, but this may be a problem as these patients have often experienced extended admissions to intensive care involving multiple arterial and central venous cannulations.

Usually the heart transplant recipient arrives in the anaesthesia induction room before the suitability of the organ is confirmed. Peripheral venous access and an arterial catheter are inserted. Placement of an arterial catheter can be difficult in patients with an axial flow LVAD as no arterial pulse can be palpated. Imaging of the radial artery by ultrasound and image-guided puncture is helpful in this situation. In those patients without a VAD, the pulse pressure curve provides a good estimate of the CO and informs the decision whether to start or increase inotropic therapy with dobutamine or adrenaline in order to maintain blood pressure and CO during the induction of anaesthesia and in the pre-CPB period.

After confirmation of suitability of the donor organ, anaesthesia is induced and a central multilumen venous catheter, an introducer with PAC, and large-bore central or peripheral venous access established. Patients who have been supported with a VAD or total artificial heart are especially likely to have severe bleeding and a second large-calibre central venous catheter for rapid infusion of large volumes is helpful.

Before initiation of CPB, the PAC should be briefly placed in the pulmonary artery to measure the actual pulmonary artery pressure, PVR, and transpulmonary gradient (TPG). Patients with an increased systolic pulmonary artery pressure of greater than 60 mm Hg, or a PVR greater than 200 dyn^{-1} s^{-1} cm^{-5}, or a TPG of greater than 15 mm Hg, or a combination of these, are considered to be at high risk of developing early postoperative RV failure

Box 56.17 Pulmonary vascular resistance and transpulmonary gradient

PVR = [80 × (mean pulmonary artery pressure − pulmonary capillary wedge pressure)/cardiac output ('s/cm^{-5}) (normal value approx. 100 dyn s^{-1} cm^{-5})].

Under the condition of hyper-oxygenation and deep anaesthesia the TPG is calculated by:

TPG = [mean pulmonary artery pressure − pulmonary capillary wedge pressure (mm Hg) (normal value approx. 6 mm Hg)].

(for calculation of PVR and TPG, see Box 56.17). Longer periods of bridging LVAD support are often associated with reductions in previously raised pulmonary artery pressure and PVR. The PAC should be withdrawn to lie in the superior vena cava before cannulation for CPB.

Weaning from CPB and post-CPB period

Reduction of RV afterload, while ideally maintaining LV afterload, and inotropic support of the RV is necessary to provide adequate filling of the LV. Basic inotropic support is achieved with milrinone (0.5 μg kg^{-1} min^{-1}) and dobutamine (3–6 μg kg^{-1} min^{-1}) and ventilation strategies to reduce PVR are instituted (see 'Treatment of right ventricular failure'). The RV is particularly sensitive to distension; care should be taken to avoid excessive preloading of the right heart. The central venous pressure should be kept below 10–12 mm Hg and RV function continuously evaluated by direct observation and TOE assessments.

If acceptable RV performance is not achieved with these measures, pharmacological support can be intensified [nebulization of iloprost, milrinone, or nitric oxide; infusion of adrenaline, noradrenaline (levosimendan; vasopressin, sildenafil)].

Closure of the chest and compression of the often swollen heart by the lungs or sometimes small intrapericardial cavity (e.g. after previous implantation of a TAH) may have a tamponade-like effect and compromise RV function. Therefore, chest closure has to be done very cautiously. If previously acceptable function is not maintained during chest closure, the chest should be re-opened and delayed closure discussed with the surgeon, being mindful that the patient will be immunosuppressed. If an adequate effect is still not achieved, temporary mechanical support via an ECLS system should be considered (see 'Temporary mechanical support of the failing heart'). This can be implanted as an isolated RV ECLS (only roller pump connected right atrium/femoral vein to pulmonary artery) or for biventricular support (right atrium/femoral vein to aorta/femoral artery) with use of an oxygenator.

Bleeding can be a problem, especially after the use of a VAD or total artificial heart. There are often extensive adhesions of the tissues and a coagulopathy. A modified thromboelastogram will provide useful information about the need for transfusion of platelets and clotting factors.

For the authors' approach to heart transplantation, see Box 56.18.

Box 56.18 Authors' approach: heart transplantation

Haemodynamic management in heart transplantation is similar to management in patients undergoing LVAD implantation. However, iloprost or milrinone is only nebulized pre-emptively if the pre-CPB measurements reveal a significant increase in pulmonary artery pressure and PVR.

In cases where moderate inotropic support will not provide stable and adequate haemodynamics (maximum dose of adrenaline 0.2 μg kg^{-1} min^{-1}), an IABP is implanted. If this does not result in adequate CO and tissue oxygenation (cerebral NIRS, mixed venous O_2 saturation, pH, serum lactate concentrations) an ECLS system is implanted as a bridge for recovery for both ventricles or only the 'right heart system' (see 'Temporary mechanical support of the failing heart'). Therapy with levosimendan may be instituted to prepare slow weaning from temporary mechanical support. The coagulation management also follows the strategy in VAD patients with the standard use of TXA and performance of a modified thromboelastogram shortly before weaning from CPB to guide transfusion therapy. Desmopressin (0.04 μg kg^{-1}) may be helpful in patients who previously had been on VAD support and developed von Willebrand syndrome.

Fast-track concepts in cardiac anaesthesia and cardiac surgery

With the development of less invasive cardiac surgery and the pressure on bed availability in the ICU, fast-track treatment concepts to minimize stay in, or even bypass, the ICU have been developed. The definition of 'fast-track' in cardiac surgery/anaesthesia varies although it certainly includes the scenario when tracheal extubation takes place in the anaesthetic recovery room within 2–4 h after surgery and the patient is subsequently managed in an intermediate care (high dependency) unit without the need for ICU. However, the concept of 'fast-track anaesthesia' may usefully be extended to include early tracheal extubation even of high-risk patients who are managed on the ICU.

Patient selection and premedication

Patients should be selected for 'fast-track' treatment preoperatively on the basis of an agreed risk evaluation by the anaesthetist and surgeon. Patients should not present severe co-morbidities and they should have good respiratory function. The surgical procedure should be low risk for perioperative complications such as development of low CO, postoperative bleeding, and so on.

Ideally, patients for fast-track management should be scheduled for surgery early in the morning to maximize the potential duration of stay in the anaesthesia recovery room. Surgery should be performed by a senior surgeon to provide the highest possible safety of the procedure. Premedication should reflect the need for early tracheal extubation. Longer-acting sedatives should not be given on the morning of surgery.

Induction of anaesthesia and perioperative care

A key principle of anaesthesia for fast-track procedures is that the drugs used should not impair the return of spontaneous ventilation and an adequate level of consciousness, to enable tracheal extubation as soon as the criteria for extubation have been met (see 'Anaesthesia recovery room'). Other important considerations are provision of analgesia for the conscious patient, antiemetic prophylaxis, and re-establishing normothermia at the completion of surgery with the use of a warming blanket and infusion warmers.

Box 56.19 Authors' approach: fast-track anaesthesia

Induction of anaesthesia is achieved using a bolus of an opioid (sufentanil 0.5–1.0 μg kg^{-1} or fentanyl 3–4 μg kg^{-1}), etomidate, and a short-acting neuromuscular blocking agent. Thereafter, hypnosis is maintained by a continuous infusion of propofol or volatile anaesthetic. Analgesia is achieved by a continuous infusion of remifentanil (0.2 μg kg^{-1} min^{-1}). For prevention of postoperative nausea and vomiting we use dexamethasone (4 mg) or ondansetron (4–8 mg). After closure of the chest, paracetamol (1 g) is given and continued 6-hourly. Sedation is maintained in the immediate postoperative period by infusions of propofol and remifentanil.

When the conditions for tracheal extubation are fulfilled, the infusion rates of propofol and remifentanil are reduced and a bolus of a longer-acting opioid such as piritramide (5.0–7.5 mg) is given.

Anaesthesia recovery room

After admission to the anaesthesia recovery room, sedation is maintained while a chest X-ray is obtained, blood gases optimized, and blood loss evaluated. The criteria for waking the patient with a view to tracheal extubation are:

- Haemodynamic stability
- Adequate pulmonary function with chest X-ray exclusion of pneumo-/haemothorax
- Exclusion of active bleeding
- Normothermia.

After tracheal extubation, the patient is instructed in the use of non-invasive ventilation as required. Analgesia is provided by regular paracetamol and patient-controlled administration of morphine. Assuming adequate cardiorespiratory function and establishing that there is good neurocognitive recovery, after 6–8 h a transthoracic echocardiogram is performed to rule out pericardial effusion. Thereafter, the patient may be transferred to the intermediate care unit.

For the authors' approach to fast-track anesthesia, see Box 56.19.

Declaration of interest

None declared.

Further reading

Cohn L, Edmunds LH. *Cardiac Surgery in the Adult*, 3rd Edn. New York: McGraw-Hill Medical Publishing, 2008

Gravlee GP, Davis RF, Stammers AH, Ungerleider RM. *Cardiopulmonary Bypass: Principles and Practice*, 3rd Edn. Philadelphia, PA: Lippincott & Wilkins, 2007

Guazzi M, Borlaug BA. Pulmonary hypertension due to left heart disease. *Circulation* 2012; **126**: 975–90

Hensley FA, Martin DE, Gravlee GP. *A Practical Approach to Cardiac Anesthesia*, 4th Edn. Philadelphia, PA: Williams & Wilkins, 2007

Kaplan JA, Reich DL, Savino JS. *Kaplan's Cardiac Anesthesia: The Echo Era* (Expert Consult Premium Edition), 6th Edn. Saunders, 2011

Perrino AC, Reeves ST. *A Practical Approach to Transesophageal Echocardiography*, 2nd Edn. Philadelphia, PA: Lippincott &Wilkins, 2007

Savage RM, Aronson S, Shernan ST. *Comprehensive Textbook of Perioperative Transesophageal Echocardiography*, 2nd Edn. Philadelphia, PA: Lippincott & Wilkins, 2010

Shanewise JS, Cheung AT, Aronson S, *et al.* ASE/SCA guidelines for performing a comprehensive multiplane intraoperative transesophageal echocardiography examination: recommendation of the American Society of Echocardiography Council for Intraoperative Echocardiography and the Society for Cardiovascular Anesthesiologists Task Force for Certification in Perioperative Transesophageal Echocardiography. *Anesth Analg* 1999; **57**: A153

References

Ferraris VA, Ferraris SP, Saha SP, *et al.* Perioperative blood transfusion and blood conservation in cardiac surgery: Society of Thoracic Surgeons and The Society of Cardiovascular Anesthesiologists clinical practice guideline. *Ann Thorac Surg* 2007; **83**(5 Suppl): S27–86

Ferraris VA, Brown JR, Despotis GJW, *et al.* 2011 update to the Society of Thoracic Surgeons and The Society of Cardiovascular Anesthesiologists blood conservation clinical practice guidelines. *Ann Thorac Surg* 2011; **91**: 944–82

Kobashigawa J, Zuckermann A, McDonald P, *et al.* ISHLT Consensus. Report from a consensus conference on primary graft dysfunction after cardiac transplantation. *J Heart Lung Transplant* 2014; **33**: 327–40

CHAPTER 57

Anaesthesia for thoracic surgery

Andrew Roscoe and Peter Slinger

Introduction

The conduct of thoracic anaesthesia requires a sound knowledge of tracheobronchial anatomy and a thorough understanding of thoracic physiology. This allows for the development of the fundamental skills essential to facilitate intrathoracic surgery: lung isolation and the management of one-lung ventilation (OLV) (Campos 2009a; Ishikawa and Lohser 2011). Thoracic surgery comprises both diagnostic and therapeutic procedures, involving the airways, lung parenchyma, pleura, pulmonary vasculature, and mediastinal structures.

Preoperative assessment

The aim of preoperative assessment is to gauge the patient's physiological reserve to tolerate the surgical intervention. The identification of factors associated with increased perioperative morbidity and mortality allows for patient risk stratification and more focused resource utilization in the perioperative period. With the development of newer surgical techniques and advances in anaesthetic and intensive care, patients previously labelled 'too high risk' for surgery are now presenting for surgical interventions (Linden et al. 2005). Scoring systems have been developed in an attempt to predict the risk of in-hospital mortality after lung resection (Harpole et al. 1999; Berrisford et al. 2005; Falcoz et al. 2007). Thoracoscore (Falcoz et al. 2007) is a logistic regression-derived model with nine variables (Box 57.1). It is currently recommended by the British Thoracic Society in the evaluation and consent of patients undergoing resection for lung cancer (Lim et al. 2010).

Respiratory function

Evaluation is aimed at predicting whether the patient will develop severe dyspnoea or ventilator dependency in the postoperative period. Initial assessment involves basic spirometry: a preoperative forced expiratory volume in 1 second (FEV_1) greater than 1.5 litres for lobectomy or greater than 2 litres for pneumonectomy are traditionally considered acceptable values to proceed to surgery (British Thoracic Society 2001). From this, the 'three-legged stool' approach (Fig. 57.1) was developed (Slinger and Johnston 2005), which consists of a measure of respiratory mechanics, lung parenchymal function, and cardiorespiratory interaction.

Lung mechanics are assessed using spirometry. The percentage predicted FEV_1 is used to calculate the predicted postoperative (ppo) FEV_1 percentage:

$$\text{ppoFEV}_1\% = \text{preoperative FEV}_1\% \times \left(1 - \%\text{functional lung tissue resected}/100\right) \quad (57.1)$$

Segmental division of the lungs can be used to calculate the amount of functional lung tissue due to be resected (Fig. 57.2) (British Thoracic Society 2001). However, the use of this equation often

Box 57.1 Variables included in the calculation of Thoracoscore

- Age
- Sex
- ASA class
- Performance status
- Dyspnoea score
- Priority of surgery (elective *vs* emergency)
- Procedure class (lobectomy *vs* pneumonectomy)
- Diagnosis group (benign *vs* malignant)
- Comorbidity score.

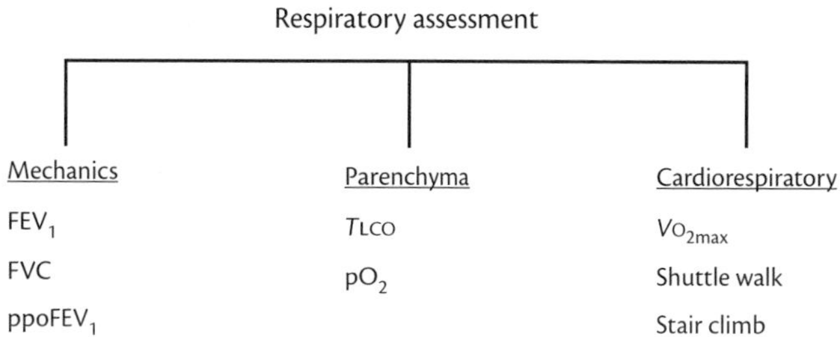

Figure 57.1 The traditional 'three-legged stool' approach to preoperative respiratory assessment. FEV_1, forced expiratory volume in 1 second; FVC, forced vital capacity; pO_2, partial pressure of oxygen; ppoFEV_1, predicted postoperative FEV_1; T_{LCO}, lung carbon monoxide transfer factor, $\dot{V}O_{2max}$: peak oxygen consumption.

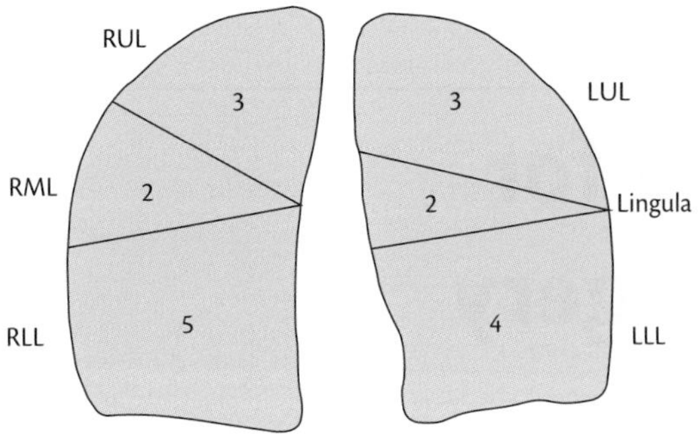

Figure 57.2 Segmental division of the lungs.

Reprinted from *The Annals of Thoracic Surgery*, Volume 63, Issue 5, Amar, D *et al.*, Effects of diltiazem versus digoxin on dysrhythmias and cardiac function after pneumonectomy, pp. 1374–81, Copyright © 1997 The Society of Thoracic Surgeons and the Southern Thoracic Surgical Association.

underestimates postoperative lung function (Bolinger et al. 1996), as the tumour may cause the affected segments to contribute less to overall function. In cases where further significant loss of lung function would render the patient unsuitable for surgery, additional evaluation of the functional contribution of the relevant segments includes scintigraphy (Win et al. 2006a), quantitative computed tomography (CT) scanning (Wu et al. 1994), and dynamic perfusion magnetic resonance imaging (Ohno et al. 2007).

A similar equation is used to calculate the predicted postoperative lung carbon monoxide transfer factor (*T*LCO) percentage, which is a measure of parenchymal function:

$$\text{ppo}T\text{LCO}\% = \text{preoperative } T\text{LCO}\% \times \left(1 - \%\text{functional lung tissue resected}/100\right) \quad (57.2)$$

Current recommendations (Lim et al. 2010) suggest the measurement of *T*LCO in all patients regardless of spirometric values to establish patient risk category (Fig. 57.3). Low-risk patients may proceed to surgery. Patients found to be at moderate or high risk of postoperative dyspnoea should be further differentiated using a marker of cardiorespiratory interaction.

Stair climbing is the simplest evaluation of cardiopulmonary function. In one study, the ability to walk up three flights of stairs was associated with reduced postoperative ventilation and hospital stay (Olsen et al. 1991). Other studies have used stair climbing to predict post-resection outcomes (Holden et al. 1992; Brunelli et al. 2002). However, routine application of this test should be viewed with caution, as the lack of standardization in stair height and outcome measures makes data difficult to interpret (Lim et al. 2010). Shuttle walk testing is a more cogent alternative. It involves increasing the pace of walking over a repeated 10 m distance. Studies suggest good reproducibility and correlation with formal cardiopulmonary exercise testing (Singh et al. 1994; Win et al. 2006b; Benzo and Sciurba 2010). A cut-off of 400 m has been proposed to differentiate moderate- and high-risk groups (Lim et al. 2010). Measurement of peak oxygen consumption ($\dot{V}O_{2max}$) may help further to delineate between moderate and high-risk groups (Benzo et al. 2007; Brunelli et al. 2009), although the recommended cut-off value of 15 ml kg^{-1} min^{-1} is arbitrary (Lim et al. 2010).

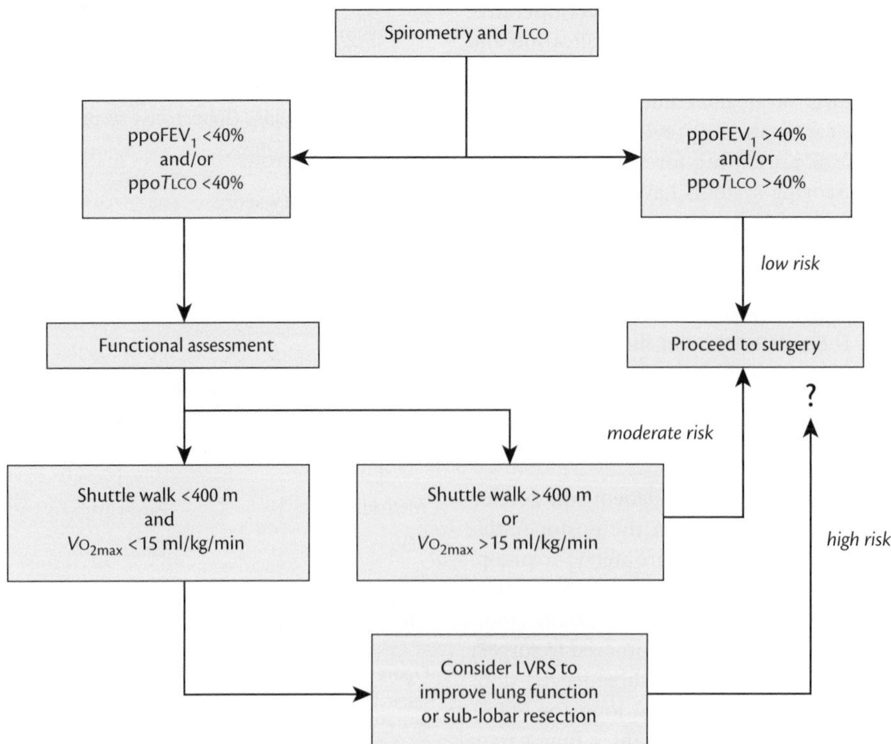

Figure 57.3 Risk assessment for postoperative dyspnoea after lung resection. FEV$_1$, forced expiratory volume in one second; LVRS, lung volume reduction surgery; ppo, predicted postoperative; *T*LCO, lung carbon monoxide transfer factor, VO_{2max}, peak oxygen consumption.

Reproduced from *Heart*, Albaladejo, P *et al.*, Non-cardiac surgery in patients with coronary stents: the RECO study, Volume 97, Issue 19, pp. 1566–72, Copyright © 2011 with permission from BMJ Publishing Group Ltd.

Patients at moderate risk may undergo lung resection after appropriate consent and acceptance of the risks of postoperative complications. Those in the high-risk group should be considered for sub-lobar resection (Ginsberg and Rubinstein 1994) or combined lung volume reduction surgery (Lim et al. 2010) to improve lung function.

Cardiovascular status

Cardiac morbidity is the second most common complication following thoracic surgery. Patients undergoing resection for lung cancer frequently have an extensive history of cigarette smoking, putting them at significant risk for coronary artery disease. The incidence of myocardial infarction or cardiac death after lung resection is approximately 1–5%. Myocardial ischaemia classically occurs on postoperative days 2 and 3. Cardiac risk assessment begins with history, examination, and evaluation of functional status. Patients with major clinical predictors of myocardial risk (Table 57.1) (Fleisher et al. 2007) should be referred for evaluation by a cardiologist for non-invasive testing and treatment of their underlying pathophysiology. Lung resection should be avoided within 30 days of a myocardial infarction (Lim et al. 2010). The revised cardiac risk index (Lee et al. 1999) is used to assess the non-high-risk group: risk factors include intrathoracic surgery, history of congestive heart failure, ischaemic heart disease, history of cerebrovascular disease, diabetes mellitus treated with insulin, and preoperative renal dysfunction (serum creatinine >177 μmol litre^{-1}). Those with two or fewer risk factors and good exercise capacity (ability to climb one flight of stairs or equivalent) may proceed to surgery without further investigations. Patients with three or more risk factors, or reduced functional capacity, require further investigation and cardiology review (Lim et al. 2010).

Table 57.1 Clinical predictors of increased perioperative cardiac risk

Level	Detail
Major	
Unstable coronary syndromes	Severe/unstable angina (CCSC 3 or 4)
	MI within 30 days
Decompensated heart failure	
Significant arrhythmias	High-grade atrioventricular block
	SVT with uncontrolled ventricular rate
	Symptomatic ventricular arrhythmias
Severe valvular disease	
Intermediate	
Coronary disease	Mild angina (CCSC 1 or 2)
	Previous MI
	Compensated heart failure
	Diabetes mellitus
	Renal insufficiency
Minor	
Advanced age	
Abnormal ECG	
Non-sinus rhythm	
Low functional capacity	
History of stroke	
Uncontrolled hypertension	

CCSC, Canadian Cardiovascular Society Class; MI, myocardial infarction; SVT, supraventricular tachycardia.

Reproduced with permission from Fleischer, L. et al. ACC/AHA 2006 Guideline Update on Perioperative Cardiovascular Evaluation for Noncardiac Surgery: Focused Update on Perioperative Beta-Blocker Therapy—A Report of the American College of Cardiology/American Heart Association Task Force on Practice Guidelines (Writing Committee to Update the 2002 Guidelines on Perioperative Cardiovascular Evaluation for Noncardiac Surgery). *Anesthesia Analgesia*, Volume 104, Issue 1, pp. 15–26, Copyright © 2007 International Anesthesia Research Society.

Therapeutic options in patients with coronary artery disease include optimization of medical therapy, percutaneous revascularization, and coronary artery bypass graft surgery. The current American College of Cardiology/American Heart Association (ACC/AHA) guidelines (Fleisher et al. 2007) suggest that β-blockers *may be considered* for patients in the intermediate- and high-risk groups undergoing intrathoracic surgery. Although the evidence for the routine use of β-blockade is still under debate (Bangalore et al. 2008), the withdrawal of β-blockers in the preoperative period is not recommended and may be detrimental to patient outcome (Shammash et al. 2001). The optimization of medical therapy should occur as early as possible in the preoperative pathway period. Both statins and aspirin should be continued throughout the perioperative period (Lim et al. 2010).

The dilemma with percutaneous coronary intervention lies with the type of intervention, the requirement for antiplatelet medication, and the duration of antiplatelet therapy. There are no studies specific to thoracic surgery, but in high-risk vascular surgery there is no benefit of prophylactic intervention (Godet et al. 2005) unless the patient has conventional indications for revascularization (Silber et al. 2005). A multidisciplinary approach involving cardiology, thoracic surgery, and anaesthesia is advocated to balance the risk of coronary stent thrombosis against the potential for intraoperative bleeding. Dual antiplatelet therapy (clopidogrel and aspirin) should continue for 3–4 weeks following a bare-metal stent and 6–12 months after placement of a drug-eluting stent (Silber et al. 2005). Surgery within 2 weeks of stent insertion is associated with an unacceptably high incidence of perioperative cardiac events and death (Kaluza et al. 2000). Interruption of antiplatelet therapy for more than 5 days before surgery is associated with a 10% incidence of major adverse cardiac and cerebrovascular events, typically occurring 3–5 days postoperatively (Albaladejo et al. 2011). Options include cessation of oral antiplatelet medication and bridging to surgery with intravenous antiplatelet therapy (Pickett et al. 2010). There is no evidence to support preoperative coronary artery bypass graft surgery unless the patient has conventional indications for such surgery (McFalls et al. 2007).

Arrhythmias are uncommon following minor wedge or segmental lung resection, but the incidence is 12–33% in patients undergoing lobectomy and larger resections (Roselli et al. 2005; Amar 2007). The most common dysrhythmia in the first postoperative week is atrial fibrillation (AF) (Ritchie et al. 1990). The use of a minimally invasive video-assisted thoracic surgery (VATS) approach does not appear to reduce the incidence of AF compared to open thoracotomy (Park et al. 2007). The proposed mechanisms for postoperative atrial arrhythmias include heightened sympathetic stimuli and oxygen requirements, usually maximal on the second postoperative day, and an increase in strain on the right ventricle (RV) associated with elevated right heart pressures (Amar et al. 1997; Slinger and Campos 2009). Predictors for the development of postoperative AF include male gender, advanced age, and a preoperative heart rate above 72 beats min^{-1} (Passman 2005). The ability to identify 'at-risk' patients allows for dysrhythmia prophylaxis, but it is still unclear if this improves patient outcome or reduces hospital length of stay (Amar 2007). Evidence suggests the use of diltiazem over amiodarone or β-blockers as the antiarrhythmic agent of choice in the treatment of AF after thoracotomy (Amar et al. 1997, 2000; Bayliff et al. 1999). Prophylactic magnesium sulfate may have a role in high-risk patients undergoing pneumonectomy (Saran et al. 2011) and the use of statins has been associated with a reduced incidence of post-thoracotomy AF (Amar et al. 2005). Thoracic epidural local anaesthetics may attenuate supraventricular tachycardias by their partial sympathetic blockade (Oka et al. 2001). Patients suffering from chronic obstructive pulmonary disease (COPD) are more resistant to treatment and polypharmacy is often necessary (Sekine et al. 2001).

Co-morbidities

Age

Age itself does not provide a contraindication to surgery. The perioperative mortality for elderly patients (>80 years) undergoing lobectomy is comparable to that of younger patients, but the complication rate is two to three times higher (Osaki et al. 1994; Fannuchi et al. 2011). However, the outcomes after pneumonectomy (especially right-sided) are significantly worse in the elderly (Spaggiari and Scanagatta 2007). It appears that functional exercise capacity is the major determinant of outcome in this population (Brunelli et al. 2004).

Chronic obstructive pulmonary disease

COPD is a disease state characterized by progressive airflow limitation, which is not fully reversible. The diagnosis is based on a history of dyspnoea and productive cough, and is confirmed by spirometry: an FEV_1/FVC less than 70% (where FVC is forced vital capacity) and a post-bronchodilator FEV_1 less than 80% predicted confirm the presence of airflow limitation. Severity of COPD is based upon FEV_1% predicted values—mild: FEV_1 greater than 80%; moderate: FEV_1 30–80%; and severe: $FEV_1 < 30\%$ (Pauwels et al. 2001).

Several issues must be addressed in patients with COPD. The anaesthetist must be aware of the effects of instituting positive pressure ventilation and potential life-threatening complications. Dynamic hyperinflation may lead to 'breath-stacking' and 'pulmonary tamponade' with eventual cardiac arrest, whilst rupture of a bulla can result in a tension pneumothorax (Myles et al. 1995; Gao et al. 2011; Marseu et al. 2011). RV dysfunction is common in COPD with a reduction in RV ejection fraction (Gao et al. 2011). The RV is intolerant of acute increases in afterload, which may be induced by positive pressure ventilation, and RV failure may ensue (MacNee 1994; Myles et al. 1995). In the postoperative period, identification of patients designated to be 'CO_2-retainers' and those with nocturnal hypoxaemia allows for vigilant monitoring, as postoperative oxygen therapy will be required in this population (Jokic and Fitzpatrick 1996).

Surgical resection in patients with severe COPD is feasible. The use of VATS, lung volume reduction surgery, and sub-lobar resections provide acceptable outcomes in this high-risk group, although there is an increased incidence of postoperative respiratory complications and prolonged length of stay (McKenna et al. 1996; Linden et al. 2005; Garzon et al. 2006; Lau et al. 2010; Raviv et al. 2011).

Renal dysfunction

Post-thoracotomy renal impairment occurs in up to 24% of patients (Golledge and Goldstraw 1994). The incidence of acute kidney injury is lower at 1–4% (Frumento et al. 2006), but the associated mortality can be as high as 19% (Golledge and Goldstraw 1994). Risk factors for the development of postoperative renal impairment include pneumonectomy, preoperative renal dysfunction, preoperative use of diuretics, intraoperative blood loss, and postoperative infection (Golledge and Goldstraw 1994). There is no evidence that the use of non-steroidal anti-inflammatory drugs precipitate renal dysfunction (Perttunen et al. 1991), but they should be used with caution in patients with kidney disease. Patients with pre-existing renal failure, requiring haemodialysis, can be managed successfully with good outcomes after lung resection (Obuchi et al. 2009). Careful fluid management is essential in the perioperative period, particularly in pneumonectomy patients (Slinger 2006a).

Obesity

For patients undergoing lobectomy, a body mass index (BMI) greater than 30 kg m^{-2} was not found to be associated with an increase in perioperative morbidity or mortality (Smith et al. 2007). However, a BMI greater than 25 kg m^{-2} has been shown to be a risk factor for postoperative respiratory complications after pneumonectomy (Petrella et al. 2001).

Tumour assessment

Lung cancer can be initially divided into non-small cell lung cancer (NSCLC), comprising 80% of lung cancers (Travis 1995), and small cell lung cancer (SCLC). Other less common tumours include carcinoid tumours, adenoid cystic carcinoma, and sarcomas. Tobacco smoking is responsible for approximately 90% of lung cancers (Felstein and Bach 2000), whilst pleural mesotheliomas are strongly linked to asbestos exposure (Peto et al. 1982).

Patients presenting with lung cancer should be assessed for the '4 M's' associated with malignancy. These are mass effects, metabolic derangements, metastases, and medications. Large tumours may compress both bronchial and important vascular structures, leading to cardiovascular compromise on induction of anaesthesia. Paraneoplastic syndromes are not uncommon with lung cancers and any systemic effect must be evaluated. Patients presenting for excision of a metastasis from a germ-cell tumour may have been exposed to bleomycin chemotherapy, putting them at risk of hyperoxic pulmonary toxicity (Mathes 1995).

Adenocarcinoma

The most common of NSCLC (Subramanian and Govindan 2007), these tumours tend be peripheral and slow growing, but metastasize early to the brain, liver, bone, and adrenal glands. They may spread to the chest wall, diaphragm, and pericardium and include the 'Pancoast tumour' which typically invades the ribs and vertebrae. Some secrete paraneoplastic metabolic substances, such as growth hormone and corticotrophin. Adenocarcinoma is associated with hypertrophic pulmonary osteoarthropathy ('clubbing').

A subtype of adenocarcinoma is bronchoalveolar carcinoma, which spreads along the alveolar membrane, and is seen more in female 'never-smokers' (Raz et al. 2006). Because of its lack of spread outside the lungs, transplantation is a treatment option (de Perrot et al. 2004).

Squamous cell carcinoma

Squamous cell carcinoma is the second most common NSCLC tumour and is strongly linked to cigarette smoking (Kenfield et al. 2008). It is more common in men than women. Tumours tend to be large and although they often metastasize to local hilar lymph nodes early in their course, they only disseminate outside the thorax much later than other tumours. Their large size causes local mass effects, with potential for bronchial and vascular obstruction. Central necrosis can lead to cavitation. The secretion of parathyroid-related peptide may render the patient hypercalcaemic (Takai et al. 1996).

Large cell carcinoma

Large cell carcinoma is the least common of the NSCLC (Subramanian and Govindan 2007) and comprises a group of undifferentiated neoplasms derived from lung epithelial cells. Tumours are typically large and found in the peripheries of the lung. Rapid growth, widespread metastases, and cavitation are features of this type of cancer.

Small cell lung cancer

SCLC is an undifferentiated neoplasm thought to originate from neuroendocrine cells in the bronchus. Early metastasis renders most patients inoperable at the time of presentation. It is divided in limited stage (LS) and extensive stage (ES). In LS-SCLC the mainstay of treatment is combination chemotherapy with concurrent radiotherapy. Small, solitary nodules may be suitable for surgical resection with adjuvant chemotherapy (Urschel et al. 1997). In ES-SCLC combination chemotherapy is the standard, with radiotherapy only added for palliation of symptoms.

SCLC is known for production of ectopic hormones: adrenocorticotropic hormone, leading to Cushing's syndrome, and antidiuretic hormone, resulting in hyponatraemia. Approximately half of patients with Eaton–Lambert myasthenic syndrome will eventually be diagnosed with SCLC (Titulaer et al. 2008). The syndrome is as a result of impaired release of acetylcholine from nerve terminals and presents with proximal muscle weakness. Unlike myasthenia gravis, repeated muscle contraction initially improves muscle strength. Patients are extremely sensitive to both depolarizing and non-depolarizing neuromuscular blocking agents and respond poorly to anticholinesterase reversal agents (Levin 1997).

Carcinoid tumours

Bronchial carcinoid represents the most indolent form of a group of neuroendocrine lung tumours, which includes SCLC. Carcinoid tumours typically occur in the gastrointestinal tract, but 10% are found in the lungs. Tumours develop within the airways and may present with bronchial obstruction or haemoptysis. Carcinoid syndrome occurs in approximately 2% of cases (Chong et al. 2006), usually associated with liver metastases. It is characterized by tachycardia, hypotension, and bronchoconstriction secondary to excess serotonin production. As a neuroendocrine tumour, secretion of adrenocorticotropic hormone and antidiuretic hormone and other biologically active peptides is possible.

Pleural tumours

Benign pleural tumours are much less common than diffuse malignant mesothelioma, but have the potential for successful resection. They are typically solitary fibrous tumours or nodular plaques, but rarer types also occur, such as mesothelial cysts and Schwannomas (Granville et al. 2005). The incidence of malignant pleural mesothelioma is increasing worldwide (Ceresoli et al. 2007). Patients often present with dyspnoea secondary to large pleural effusions. Early diagnosis and staging may provide patients with the option of 'trimodality' therapy: induction chemotherapy, surgical resection, and adjuvant radiotherapy (Buduhan et al. 2009). However, results of a recent trial suggest that the high perioperative morbidity associated with extrapleural pneumonectomy confers no benefit to patients and may cause harm (Treasure et al. 2011).

Airway assessment

In addition to the standard assessment of the airway, the thoracic anaesthetist must also ascertain the ease of endobronchial intubation. A history of difficult endobronchial intubation, previous intrathoracic or airway surgery, radiotherapy, and pulmonary infection should alert the anaesthetist. Review of imaging (chest X-ray and CT scan) is essential (Slinger and Campos 2009). The tracheal lumen of a left-sided double-lumen endobronchial tube (DLT) can become occluded in the presence of a 'sabre-sheath' trachea (Bayes et al. 1994) and the presence of an ascending thoracic aortic aneurysm may compress and distort the left main bronchus (Duke et al. 1987), making a left-sided DLT difficult and potentially hazardous to insert (Fitzmaurice and Brodsky 1999).

Patient optimization

Smoking

It would seem prudent to encourage patients to stop smoking before any major surgery. Ideally, cessation of smoking should be 6–8 weeks before surgery to allow for restoration of mucociliary function, reduction in sputum volume, and recovery of immune function (Pearce and Jones 1984). Although the majority of evidence suggests that cessation for greater than 4 weeks is associated with reduced postoperative morbidity and mortality (Nakagawa et al. 2001; Vaporciyan et al. 2002; Mason et al. 2009), some studies have shown that benefit can still be gained by stopping closer to the time of surgery (Barrera et al. 2005; Groth et al. 2009). Indeed, cessation of smoking for just 12 h will reduce blood carboxyhaemoglobin concentrations (Akrawi and Benumof 1997). However, current recommendations advocate counselling of patients to stop smoking as early as possible before lung resection (Mason et al. 2009).

Physiotherapy

Evidence suggests that patients with COPD undergoing lung resection benefit from intensive preoperative chest physiotherapy (Warner 2000), which aims to loosen and clear secretions. A multidisciplinary rehabilitation programme, comprising exercise, nutrition, education, and psychosocial support, shows improvements in patient functional capacity, but may not alter outcomes (Kesten 1997; Shannon 2010).

Medications

Although patients with COPD have, by definition, reduced reversal of airflow limitation by bronchodilators, the preoperative use of inhaled β_2-agonists and anticholinergics appears rational to optimize lung function (Behr 2001). The use of systemic corticosteroid therapy is advocated in acute exacerbations of COPD (Niewoehner et al. 1999), but the role of routine inhaled corticosteroids in stable COPD is less clear (Barnes 2005). Active chest infections should be treated aggressively with appropriate antimicrobial therapy and surgery should be postponed until infection control has been achieved (Behr 2001).

Medications for other comorbidities should be optimized appropriately. Good perioperative glucose control in diabetic patients will reduce the incidence of postoperative infections (Talbot et al. 2005).

Intraoperative management

Monitoring

Standard monitoring

For the safe conduct of induction and maintenance of anaesthesia the minimum required monitoring devices include pulse oximetry, ECG, non-invasive blood pressure monitor, airway gases (oxygen, carbon dioxide, and vapour), and airway pressure (Association of Anaesthetists of Great Britain and Ireland 2015). The use of invasive monitors (arterial, central venous, and pulmonary artery catheters) will depend on the extent of the surgery and the potential for complications. Specific to many thoracic procedures is the position of the patient in the lateral decubitus position, making intraoperative placement of invasive monitoring technically more difficult, so a low threshold for the insertion of invasive monitoring at the beginning is often preferred (Slinger and Campos 2009).

Current guidelines recommend the use of temperature monitoring and forced air warming devices in all cases expected to last more than 30 min, and the warming of intravenous fluids if more than 500 ml is being administered (NICE 2008). Intraoperative hypothermia (defined as core temperature <36°C) is associated with increased wound infection, adverse cardiac events, and prolonged length of hospital stay (Kurz et al. 1996; Frank et al. 1997; Lenhardt et al. 1997).

Fibreoptic bronchoscopy (FOB) should be performed to confirm the correct placement of DLTs and endobronchial blockers (EBBs) (de Bellis et al. 2011). After lateral positioning of the patient, confirmation of the correct position of the device should be repeated with FOB (Desiderio et al. 1997).

A nerve stimulator should be available whenever neuromuscular blocking agents are used. Current guidelines do not recommend the routine use of monitoring depth of anaesthesia with brain function monitors (ASA Task Force 2006).

Invasive monitoring

The use of invasive blood pressure monitoring via an arterial cannula is recommended for most intrathoracic procedures. Surgical manipulation may cause compression of the heart or great vessels and visualization of beat-to-beat pressure allows for more appropriate management. In addition, it provides for intermittent blood gas sampling, which may guide ventilatory settings. Insertion of the arterial cannula in the contralateral side to the surgery (lowermost side) may aid in safe lateral positioning of the patient by ensuring an adequate pulse waveform is still present, confirming that the axillary artery has not been compressed.

Intraoperative central venous pressure (CVP) monitoring is often difficult to interpret as a result of the effects of lateral patient position, lung collapse, and intermittent surgical manipulation. However, it is useful in postoperative fluid management (Slinger and Campos 2009). A CVP line also offers access for the infusion of potent vasoactive agents. It is generally inserted in either the internal jugular or subclavian vein on the same side as the ensuing surgery, as the complication of pneumothorax is readily resolved by the surgical thoracotomy.

Complications of pulmonary artery catheter (PAC) insertion are well documented (Pulmonary Artery Catheter Consensus Conference 1997) and the accuracy of thermodilution cardiac output measurements during OLV is debatable (Hasan et al. 1984). The insertion of a PAC is reserved for the very high-risk patient, when beat-to-beat pulmonary artery pressure monitoring is required or for the measurement of mixed venous oxygen saturation (Sv_{O_2}).

Minimally invasive cardiac output monitors

The use of a less invasive cardiac output monitor device appears an attractive alternative to the PAC. Devices based on pulse contour analysis make use of pulse pressure variation and stroke volume variation to detect fluid responsiveness and allow a 'goal-directed' approach to haemodynamic management (Brass et al. 2011). However, a consensus on the validation and accuracy of these devices has not yet been reached (Cecconi and Rhodes 2009).

The oesophageal Doppler monitor measures blood velocity in the descending thoracic aorta to calculate the stroke volume and cardiac output. Although its routine use is not associated with reduced mortality, reduction in perioperative morbidity and hospital length of stay have been consistently reported, leading to recommendations for its use in patients undergoing major or high-risk surgery (NICE 2011). Oesophagectomy provides a contraindication to its use.

Central venous and mixed venous O_2 saturation

The measurement of Sv_{O_2} as an indicator of the adequacy of body tissue oxygenation may improve patient outcomes (Pölönen et al. 2000; Holm et al. 2011), but requires the flotation of a PAC. Substitution of Sv_{O_2} with central venous oxygen saturation (Scv_{O_2}) monitoring requires only a CVP line, but may not provide as accurate an indicator of tissue oxygenation as Sv_{O_2} (Chawla et al. 2004). However, improved patient outcomes have been seen with goal-directed therapy using (Scv_{O_2}) (Donati et al. 2007).

Transoesophageal echocardiography

Although not recommended for routine thoracic surgery, the intraoperative management of specific thoracic procedures (pulmonary endarterectomy and lung transplantation) benefits from utilization of transoesophageal echocardiography (TOE). Visualization of RV function permits early detection of dysfunction and prompt intervention (Pedoto and Amar 2009). In haemodynamic instability, the left ventricle (LV) can be quickly assessed for contractility, volume status, and pericardial compression, with expeditious correction of any abnormality. Preload and filling status are more accurately evaluated by TOE than by PAC (Della Rocca et al. 2009). In lung transplantation, TOE should be used to assess the vascular anastomoses (Leibowitz et al. 1994; Michel-Cherqui et al. 1997). Stenosis of the pulmonary vein anastomosis is associated with graft failure (Huang et al. 2000).

Spirometry

Continuous measurement and display of intraoperative lung volumes, pressures, and flow alerts the anaesthetist to DLT malposition, bronchospasm, surgical air leak, acute changes in lung compliance, and the development of 'breath-stacking' and intrinsic positive end-expiratory pressure (PEEP) (Bardoczky et al. 1993a, 1993b; Iwasaka et al. 1996; Katsuno 1997).

Lung isolation techniques

Isolation and separation of the lungs is used to allow surgical access, prevent 'spillage' from one lung to the other, and to facilitate differential lung ventilation. Methods of lung isolation include DLTs, EBBs, and endobronchial tubes. Patients with a tracheostoma can present a challenge. A small DLT can be inserted through a well-formed stoma. A specific DLT has been designed for patients with a tracheostomy (Saito et al. 1998). Other options include positioning an EBB through a regular tracheostomy tube (Tobias 2001) and insertion of a double-lumen tracheostomy tube (Trachpart, Rüsch, Germany) (Fig. 57.4) (Alberti et al. 1992; Salluh et al. 2005). Options for lung isolation in a patient with a difficult airway include the use of an EBB through a single-lumen tracheal tube or changing a single-lumen tracheal tube for a DLT over a tube-exchange catheter.

Double-lumen endobronchial tubes

Since the introduction of the Carlens DLT in 1950 (Bjork and Carlens 1950), several modifications have produced a variety of DLTs (Bryce-Smith 1959; White 1960; Robertshaw 1962; Clapham and Vaughan 1985; Ghosh et al. 2008). The more modern polyvinyl chloride (PVC) tubes have a larger internal to external diameter ratio, are more compliant, and have been associated with easier, less traumatic insertion (Burton et al. 1983; Clapham and Vaughan 1985).

The first step for the anaesthetist is to select the size of DLT required for an individual patient. The red rubber 'Robertshaw' DLT offers extra-small, small, medium, and large sizes. The PVC tubes are 'French gauge' and are available in 26, 28, 32, 35, 37, 39, and 41 sizes (Table 57.2a and Table 57.2b) (Campos 2003). Selection of a DLT that is too large may lead to airway trauma, whilst an undersized tube is more prone to displacement and malposition during surgery (Wagner et al. 1985; Brodsky et al. 1989). Various methods have been proposed to calculate the ideal DLT size for an individual patient, based on height, tracheal diameter, and bronchial dimensions, using the chest X-ray, CT scan, and ultrasound (Hannallah et al. 1997; Eberle et al. 1999; Brodsky et al. 2001; Jeon et al. 2005; Sustic et al. 2008). However, the use of tracheal diameter for selection (Table 57.3) may result in overestimation of DLT size (Chow et al. 1998; Slinger 2001). A basic approximation for the selection of PVC DLT size based on patient height is shown in Table 57.4 (Slinger 2001).

Insertion of a DLT is generally performed using the 'blind' technique. Laryngoscopy is used to pass the tube through the vocal cords, the stylet is withdrawn and the tube is then advanced and rotated anticlockwise (left-sided DLT) or clockwise (right-sided

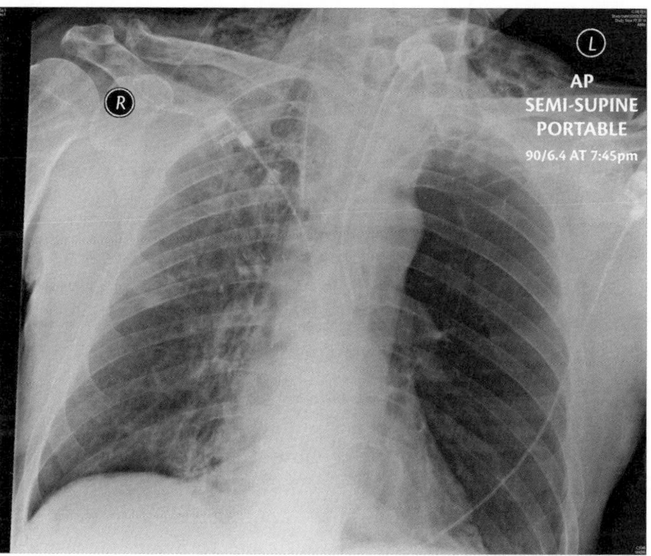

Figure 57.4 Chest X-ray showing a double-lumen tracheostomy tube used to facilitate differential lung ventilation, with the endobronchial lumen in the left main bronchus.

Table 57.2a Sizes and dimensions of double-lumen endobronchial tubes

DLT French gauge	OD (mm)	Tracheal ID (mm)	Bronchial ID (mm)
28	9.3	3.2	3.1
32	10.7	3.5	3.4
35	11.7	4.5	4.3
37	12.3	4.7	4.5
39	13.0	4.9	4.9
41	13.7	5.4	5.4

DLT, double-lumen endobronchial tube; ID, internal diameter; OD, outer diameter.

Data from Katsuno M, 1997, 'Usefulness of on-line spirometry in bronchospasm occurring during anaesthesia', *Masui* vol. 46, pp. 1599–601.

Table 57.2b Sizes and dimensions of Robertshaw double-lumen endobronchial tubes. The tracheal and bronchial lumens are D-shaped and the same dimension; the bronchial lumen cross-section becomes circular beyond the bronchial cuff (Phoenix Medical, UK)

Robertshaw size	OD (mm)	D-section ID (mm)	Bronchial tip ID (mm)
Extra-small	10.6	3.5 × 5.5	5.0
Small	12.5	4.0 × 6.5	5.5
Medium	14.8	5.4 × 7.2	7.2
Large	15.7	5.4 × 7.9	7.9

ID, internal diameter; OD, outer diameter.

Data from Phoenix Medical.

Table 57.3 Selection of double-lumen tube size based on tracheal diameter

Tracheal diameter (mm)	DLT size
> 18	41
16–18	39
15–16	37
< 15	35

DLT, double-lumen endobronchial tube.

Data from Brodsky JB et al., The relationship between tracheal width and left bronchial width: Implications for left-sided double-lumen tube selection, *J Cardiothorac Vasc Anesth*, 2001, vol. 15, pp. 216–7.

Table 57.4 Sizing of polyvinyl chloride double-lumen endobronchial tube

Male		Female	
Height	**DLT size**	**Height**	**DLT size**
>170 cm	41	>160 cm	37
160–170 cm	39	152–160 cm	35
<160 cm	37	<152 cm	32

DLT, double-lumen endobronchial tube.

Data from Slinger PD, Lung isolation in thoracic anesthesia, state of the art, *Can J Anaesth*, 2001, vol. 48, pp. R13–15.

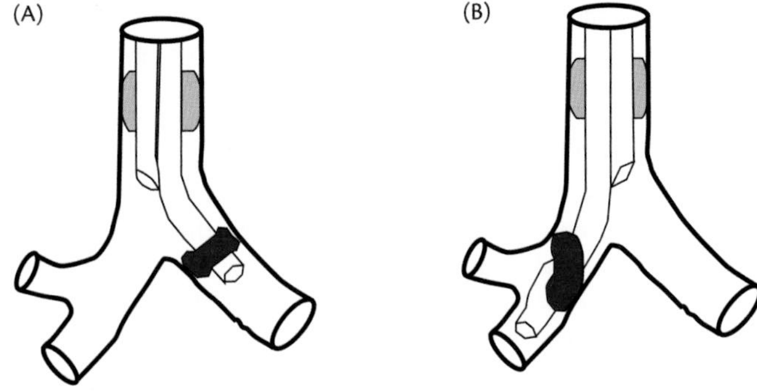

Figure 57.5 Endobronchial position of (A) left- and (B) right-sided double-lumen tubes.

DLT). Formulae exist to calculate the depth to which the tube should be inserted (Bahk and Oh 1999; Chow et al. 2002). The simplest is:

$$\text{Depth} = 12 + (\text{patient height in cm}/10) \quad (57.3)$$

In shorter-stature patients, there is less correlation between height and depth of insertion (Yasumoto et al. 2006). The anaesthetist should be aware that after confirming optimal tube depth with the DLT in the midline position, movement of the tube to the angle of the patient's mouth for fixation may cause the tube to withdraw from the left main bronchus by 10–15 mm (Sharma et al. 2009).

The alternative technique involves passing the FOB down the bronchial lumen, once the DLT has passed the vocal cords, to guide the tube into the correct bronchus (Boucek et al. 1998). Correct tube position should be confirmed by FOB, as auscultation by itself can be unreliable (Desiderio et al. 1997; Slinger and Campos 2009). The ideal position of a left-sided tube is shown in Fig. 57.5.

The majority of procedures can be undertaken with left-sided DLTs and are preferred by most anaesthetists as they are assumed to have a greater margin of error of placement (Slinger 2010). However, a right-sided DLT is indicated in certain circumstances (Box 57.2), so there is a strong argument for its use for all left-sided thoracotomies to maintain skills in its insertion and positioning (Campos and Gomez 2002; Ehrenfeld et al. 2010; Slinger 2010). Right-sided DLTs are designed with an orifice within the bronchial cuff to incorporate the higher take-off of the right upper lobe (Fig. 57.5). The use of FOB is recommended to ensure this orifice is accurately positioned (Slinger 2010). Knowledge of bronchial anatomy is key to the successful positioning of DLTs (Campos et al. 2006).

Endobronchial blockers

EBBs provide an alternative method for lung isolation. They are positioned into the main bronchus of the operative lung with the aid of FOB. The balloon is inflated under FOB visualization when the patient is in the lateral position. The balloon should be inflated when the lung to be isolated is deflated (end-expiration), as collapse of the lung through the narrow EBB lumen may take longer compared to a DLT (Narayanaswamy et al. 2009). In patients with severe COPD and gas-trapping, it may be beneficial to temporarily disconnect the ventilator to allow for maximal lung collapse before balloon inflation, before reconnection and recommencing ventilation.

Several types of EBB exist (Fig. 57.6): the Univent® torque control EBB (Fuji Systems Corporation, Tokyo, Japan) is a modified tracheal tube with an attached lumen for advancement of the EBB component. The Arndt wire-guided EBB (Cook Medical, Limerick, Ireland) is used with a conventional tracheal tube with a specific connector that allows lung ventilation during EBB placement. The wire is looped around a FOB, which guides the EBB into the appropriate bronchus. The Fuji Uniblocker™ (Fuji Systems Corporation, Tokyo, Japan) is designed with an angulation at the tip to allow the anaesthetist to twist the EBB to direct the tip into the correct bronchus. With the Cohen tip-deflecting blocker (Cook Medical, Limerick, Ireland) the anaesthetist turns the wheel control mechanism that deflects the tip towards the appropriate bronchus. Positioning of the tip into the left main bronchus may be facilitated by turning the patient's head to the right.

An advantage of EBBs includes the ability to achieve lung isolation in patients where it is only possible to intubate the trachea with a single-lumen tracheal tube (Campos 2010). Selective lobar blockade is also possible (Campos 2005).

Box 57.2 Indications for a right-sided double-lumen endobronchial tube

- Left-sided 'sleeve' resection
- Intraluminal tumour within left main bronchus
- External compression of left main bronchus: mediastinal tumour thoracic aortic aneurysm
- Left pneumonectomy
- Left single-lung transplantation
- Left-sided tracheobronchial disruption
- Stent within left main bronchus.

Data from Lim, E et al. 2010, 'Guidelines on the radical management of patients with lung cancer', *Thorax* vol. 65, pp. iii1–27.

Endobronchial tubes

Single-lumen endobronchial tubes (EBTs) are long, reinforced tubes with a modified, short cuff and non-bevelled tip (Fig. 57.7). They are designed to be placed within the main bronchus under FOB guidance. Although not commonly used, an indication for use may include ventilation of the contralateral lung early after a pneumonectomy, where it is desirable to avoid exposure of the bronchial stump to intermittent positive pressure ventilation (IPPV). Bilateral EBTs can be used for lesions close to the carina (Lobato et al. 1997).

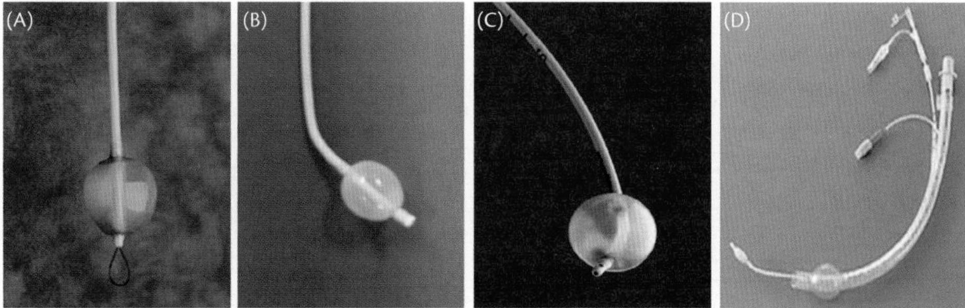

Figure 57.6 Several designs of endobronchial blocker: (A) Arndt wire-guided, (B) Fuji Uniblocker™, (C) Cohen tip-deflecting blocker, and (D) Univent® blocker.
Courtesy of Smiths Medical and Fuji Systems.

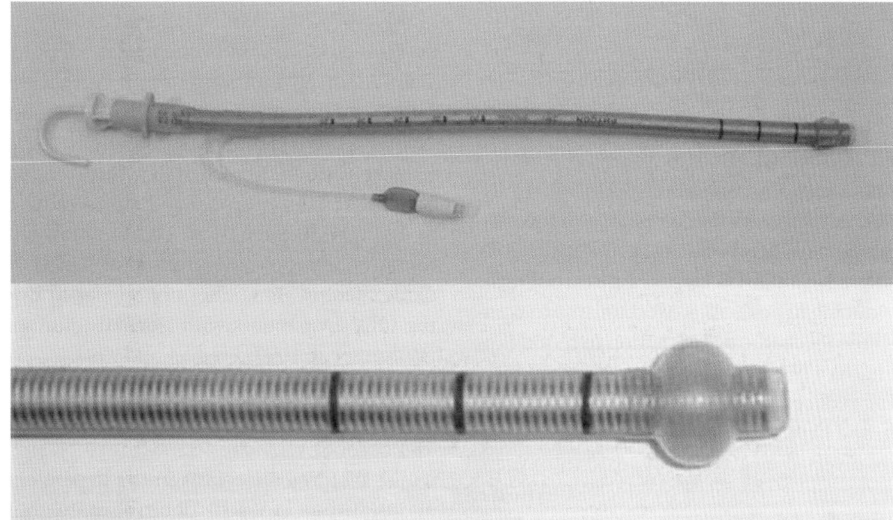

Figure 57.7 Single-lumen endobronchial tube.
Courtesy of Fuji Systems.

Complications of lung isolation

The most common complications of DLT placement are airway trauma and malposition. Airway trauma ranges from dental injury and pharyngeal abrasion to the more serious tracheobronchial rupture (Fitzmaurice and Brodsky 1999). Bronchial rupture has been reported with Carlens, PVC, and Robertshaw-type DLTs (Guernelli et al. 1979; Heiser et al. 1979; Yuceyar et al. 2003). DLT malposition will lead to failure of lung collapse, potential leakage of gases when performing OLV, and increased risk of hypoxaemia (Inoue et al. 2004). The tracheal or bronchial cuff may be damaged by the patient's teeth during passage through the mouth, resulting in failure to inflate the relevant cuff. Less common complications of DLTs include massive airway bleeding, development of a tension pneumothorax, subcutaneous emphysema, and kinking of the DLT tube (Sivalingham and Tio 1999; Weng et al. 2002; Ambrosio et al. 2011).

Malposition of an EBB, with herniation of the balloon back into the trachea, will result in inability to adequately ventilate, hypoxaemia, and eventually cardiorespiratory collapse (Sandberg 2005). Shearing of the balloon may occur when the EBB is withdrawn through the connector and recommendations advise removal of the EBB with the connector when the EBB is being extracted (Prabhu and Smith 2002). Poor communication with surgical colleagues during the procedure can lead to stapling of the EBB tip within the surgical field (Soto and Oleszak 2006).

A methodical approach for dealing with complications of lung isolation is required. The initial step is to increase the fraction of inspired oxygen $\left(FI_{O_2}\right)$ to 1.0, communicate the problem to the surgeon, and check the device position with FOB. With severe instability, a return to two-lung ventilation (TLV) is advised. Familiarity with tracheobronchial anatomy allows rapid recognition of a displaced device and prompt correction. Poor lung collapse despite appropriate device position may be improved by applying low-grade suction to the isolated lung (Campos 2008).

One-lung ventilation

Physiology

The majority of thoracic procedures requiring OLV will necessitate the patient being in the lateral decubitus position. In this position, gravity causes approximately 60% of the cardiac output to flow to the dependent lung. However, with the onset of positive pressure ventilation, the non-dependent lung preferentially receives more ventilation. This is secondary to reduced functional residual capacity and compliance of the dependent lung (Fig. 57.8), which is compressed

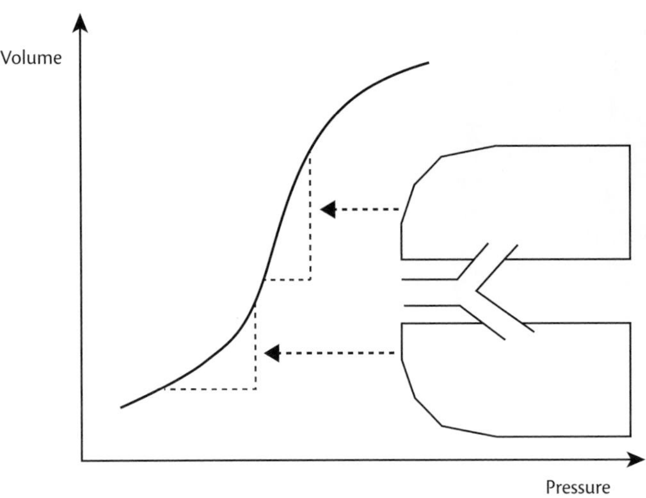

Figure 57.8 Differential lung compliance in the lateral decubitus position.

by the mediastinum and abdominal contents pushing against a paralysed diaphragm. This creates a ventilation/perfusion ($\dot{V}/\dot{Q}$) mismatch. Opening of the chest increases the compliance of the non-dependent lung, exacerbating the $\dot{V}/\dot{Q}$ mismatch (Levine et al. 2008).

At the onset of OLV there is initially a large shunt through the non-dependent lung, producing hypoxaemia. Mechanisms to compensate for this shunt include mechanical obstruction to blood flow to the non-dependent lung, as a result of lung collapse and surgical manipulation; pre-existing reduced blood flow to the diseased portion of the operated lung; and hypoxic pulmonary vasoconstriction (HPV), whereby blood is diverted away from hypoxic to oxygenated areas of lung tissue, which is triggered by alveolar hypoxia. This may reduce by half the blood flow to the non-dependent lung. These mechanisms result in overall cardiac output to the non-dependent lung to be approximately 20%. This shunt can usually be compensated for by an increase in $F\text{I}_{O_2}$ (Levine et al. 2008).

Several issues affect pulmonary blood flow: inhalation anaesthetic agents at concentrations above 1 minimal alveolar concentration (MAC) reduce HPV; vasodilators can inhibit HPV; vasoconstrictors may divert blood flow away from the dependent lung; increased $F\text{I}_{O_2}$ decreases vascular tone in the ventilated lung to increase blood flow; and increases in cardiac output augment blood flow to the non-dependent lung. A low cardiac output will result in low $S\text{v}_{O_2}$ and worsening of hypoxaemia (Karzai and Schwarzkopf 2009).

The adequacy of arterial oxygenation during OLV is multifactorial. Arterial oxygen content $\left(\text{Ca}_{O_2}\right)$ can be calculated form the following equation (Karzai and Schwarzkopf 2009):

$$Ca_{O_2} = Cc_{O_2} - (\dot{V}o_2 / \dot{Q}t) \times [(\dot{Q}s / \dot{Q}t) / 10(1 - \dot{Q}s / \dot{Q}t)] \qquad (57.4)$$

It can be seen that arterial oxygenation is dependent upon shunt ($\dot{Q}$s), HPV, $F\text{I}_{O_2}$, mixed venous oxygen content $\left(Cv_{O_2}\right)$, cardiac output ($\dot{Q}$t), oxygen consumption ($\dot{V}o_2$), pulmonary end-capillary oxygen content $\left(Cc_{O_2}\right)$, alveolar ventilation, and haemoglobin concentration.

Management of hypoxaemia

Hypoxaemia during OLV can often be predicted. Risk factors for desaturation include arterial oxygenation during TLV, high percentage of ventilation or perfusion to the operative lung on preoperative $\dot{V}/\dot{Q}$ scan, right-sided thoracotomy, and normal preoperative FEV_1 (Slinger and Campos 2009).

Development of hypoxaemia during OLV should prompt the anaesthetist to follow a systematic course of management (Karzai and Schwarzkopf 2009). Initially $F\text{I}_{O_2}$ is increased to 1.0 whilst correct placement of the DLT or EBB is confirmed. Oxygen may be insufflated into the non-dependent lung or continuous positive airway pressure (CPAP) can be applied. Although these manoeuvres will increase arterial oxygenation, they may expand the lung to a degree that makes surgical access unacceptable, particularly with VATS procedures (Hogue et al. 1994; Bailey et al. 1998). The next option is to perform a recruitment manoeuvre and apply PEEP to the ventilated lung. This may not reduce hypoxaemia and is determined by the patient's pre-existing lung pathology. COPD patients with significant intrinsic PEEP may deteriorate when further PEEP is added (Slinger and Hickey 1998; Brodsky 2001). Temporary surgical compression of the ipsilateral pulmonary artery will transiently reduce shunt and permit further limited surgery. The next option is re-ventilation of the collapsed lung, either intermittently or by high-frequency jet ventilation to allow surgery to continue (Abe et al. 2006; Russell 2009). Intravenous infusions of almitrine, which augments HPV, may help to reduce hypoxaemia (Dalibon et al. 2004), especially in combination with inhaled nitric oxide therapy (Silva-Costa-Gomes et al. 2005). However, inhaled nitric oxide therapy alone does not appear to improve oxygenation during OLV in patients with normal pulmonary vascular resistance (Wilson et al. 1997; Fradj et al. 1999).

Ventilation during OLV

The goals of OLV are to maximize collapse of the operated lung whilst avoiding atelectasis in the dependent lung. Providing a $F\text{I}_{O_2}$ of 1.0 during TLV will 'denitrogenate' the lungs, which will promote collapse of the non-dependent lung when OLV is commenced (Ko et al. 2003). At the start of OLV, a recruitment manoeuvre (CPAP 20 cm H_2O for 15 s) to the dependent lung to reduce atelectasis can be effective in reducing hypoxaemia during subsequent OLV (Tusman et al. 2004).

The use of inhalation anaesthetic agents at concentrations less than 1 MAC do not significantly impair HPV (Wang et al. 2000) and there does not appear to be any benefit of total intravenous anaesthesia (TIVA) over inhalation anaesthetic agents in terms of arterial oxygenation (Reid et al. 1996). The exception is nitrous oxide (N_2O). The use of N_2O with OLV is associated with increased postoperative atelectasis (Browne et al. 1970), increases in pulmonary artery pressure in patients with pulmonary hypertension (Schulte-Sasse et al. 1982) and inhibition of HPV (Bindslev et al. 1986). It is contraindicated in patients with large bullae. Generally N_2O is avoided in thoracic anaesthesia.

Traditional teaching advocates retaining tidal volumes of 10 ml kg^{-1} during OLV, as with TLV, and the avoidance of PEEP (Gal et al. 2006). The aim was to reduce atelectasis and maintain normocapnia. More recent evidence suggests that the higher airway pressure and the shearing forces generated by this strategy may be harmful (Slinger 2006b). Modern strategies for OLV have adopted the use of a smaller tidal volume (5–6 ml kg^{-1}) and the application of PEEP in individuals with little or no intrinsic PEEP. This has led to a reduction in post-lung resection acute lung injury (Licker et al. 2003; Fernandez-Perez et al. 2006; Jeon et al. 2009; Marret et al. 2010).

Pressure-controlled ventilation may offer a slight advantage over the more traditional volume-controlled ventilation. During OLV, peak airway pressures are lower with pressure-controlled ventilation compared with volume-controlled ventilation with the same tidal volume (Unzuetaet al. 2007; Pardos et al. 2009). Patients with COPD appear to benefit from pressure-controlled ventilation, shown by an increase in arterial oxygenation (Tugrul et al. 1997).

Anaesthesia for specific surgical procedures

Trachea

Bronchoscopy: diagnostic and therapeutic

Bronchoscopy can be a diagnostic or part of a therapeutic procedure. Flexible FOB can be performed in awake patients under topical local anaesthesia with or without sedation. Under general anaesthesia bronchoscopy may be undertaken during spontaneous or mechanical ventilation. The laryngeal mask airway allows the patient to breathe spontaneously and aids the surgeon in visualization of the vocal cords and sub-glottic structures. During ventilation, the flexible FOB may be passed through a conventional tracheal tube or a rigid bronchoscope. Anaesthesia options include TIVA or inhalation anaesthesia. Invasive monitoring is reserved for high-risk patients with severe cardiac disease.

Rigid bronchoscopic procedures create a different challenge for the anaesthetist. The 'shared airway' necessitates good communication with the surgeon. Ventilation options include spontaneous breathing; apnoeic oxygen insufflation with intermittent ventilation; IPPV via a side-port connector to the rigid bronchoscope; and jet ventilation. The patient breathing spontaneously requires excellent topical local anaesthesia and a deep plane of general anaesthesia, which may compromise haemodynamics in some patients. Short periods of apnoea allow only intermittent surgical intervention and this technique is best suited to shorter procedures. Attachment of a connector to the bronchoscope allows IPPV with delivery of inhalation anaesthetic agents, but significant air leaks can occur, especially when a smaller bronchoscope is used in a relatively large airway. Jet ventilation can be delivered via the handheld 'Sanders' injector (Sullivan and Neff 1979) or by a high-frequency jet ventilator (HFJV). This technique allows for adequate oxygenation, but hypercapnia occurs with prolonged procedures (Fernandez-Bustamante et al. 2006). TIVA is used in conjunction with jet ventilation to maintain anaesthesia. Neuromuscular blocking drugs are often required to facilitate tracheal intubation with the rigid bronchoscope, but successful techniques involving remifentanil with the avoidance of neuromuscular blocks have been described (Natalini et al. 1999). Remifentanil has also been shown to obtund the pressor response to tracheal intubation and provide haemodynamic stability during this stimulating procedure (Prakash et al. 2001). Antisialagogues are often administered to reduce secretions, but their clinical benefit is unclear (Cowl et al. 2000). There may be a role for the administration of dexamethasone, both as an antiemetic and to reduce post-bronchoscopy airway oedema (Abdelmalak 2011).

Interventional procedures include endobronchial ultrasound-guided transbronchial needle aspiration (Yasufuku 2010), tracheal dilatation, stent or T-tube insertion, and tumour debulking, with or without laser.

The neodymium-doped yttrium aluminium garnet (Nd-YAG) laser is used for tracheobronchial pathology. Standard laser safety precautions must be followed (Dumion et al. 1984). Both O_2 and N_2O are combustible. Recommendations advise delivery of an oxygen/air mixture with a FI_{O_2} of 0.3 (McRae 2001).

Complications of bronchoscopy and interventions include hypoxaemia, hypercapnia, haemorrhage, retention of stent pieces during extraction, barotrauma secondary to HFJV, pneumothorax, tracheal rupture, and laser fire (Abdelmalak 2011). Loss of tracheal integrity is more common during stent removal and dilatation. Risk factors include increased age, previous tracheal procedure, COPD, and current steroid therapy (Luna et al. 1993).

Tracheal resection

Major tracheal surgery is indicated for patients with significant tracheal obstruction secondary to tumour, post-intubation stenosis, congenital abnormalities, and vascular pathologies. The majority of resections involve reconstruction with a primary anastomosis.

Preoperative assessment should involve examination of the CT scan to define the exact location and extent of the lesion. Collaboration between anaesthetist and surgeon is essential to formulate a plan to provide adequate ventilation throughout the procedure. It is prudent to devise alternate 'back-up' strategies for each stage of the surgery. Knowledge of the proposed surgical approach is key. Invasive arterial monitoring is routine. The use of CVP lines is reserved for high-risk cases. The use of internal jugular CVP catheters may not be possible because of the close proximity to the surgical field. Subclavian and femoral veins provide alternative sites.

Induction of anaesthesia should only be performed with the surgeon present and prepared to intervene with a rigid bronchoscope if necessary (Pinsonneault et al. 1999). Inhalation induction with spontaneous ventilation is recommended (Slinger and Campos 2009). When an adequate depth of anaesthesia is achieved, topical local anaesthesia is applied to the upper airway before a tracheal tube, with FOB guidance, is passed through the stenotic region. Neuromuscular blocking agents are only given once the airway is secured. For the patient with a very narrow stenosis, an endotracheal catheter may be passed through the stenosis and HFJV used (Watanabe et al. 1988). The addition of helium to the inspired gas mixture may facilitate ventilation (Buczkowski et al. 2005). However, care must be taken to ensure the adequate exhalation of gases. 'Cross-field' intubation is often used during major tracheal surgeries. The surgeon is able to intubate the airway distal to the stenosis, which is then attached to a sterile anaesthesia circuit to provide ventilation (McRae 2001). A combination of several techniques may be utilized at different phases of the operation, frequently with periods of apnoea. Cardiopulmonary bypass is reserved for large carinal resections and inability to oxygenate the patient adequately by alternate means.

After resection, a suture is often placed from the patient's sternum to chin to limit tension on the tracheal anastomosis. Early tracheal extubation is desirable and, although challenging, can be achieved by using remifentanil (Saravanan et al. 2006) or by the use of a laryngeal mask airway.

Tracheo-oesophageal fistula

Malignancy is the main aetiology of tracheo-oesophageal fistula in the adult and fistulae can occur anywhere in the respiratory tract (Hindman and Bert 1987). Surgical management is typically palliative in nature, but resections can be successfully performed (Picone et al. 1989). The main anaesthetic consideration is to ventilate the airway beyond the level of the fistula. EBTs can be inserted into the distal trachea or even into the main stem bronchi (Chan 1984; Au et al. 1999).

Lung parenchyma

Lung resection

Resection of lung tissue runs the gamut from a small wedge biopsy to an extrapleural pneumonectomy. Although the less invasive VATS procedures produce less surgical stimulation and quicker patient recovery (Seder et al. 2009; Leshnower et al. 2010), they also present the anaesthetist with the challenge of older, more debilitated patients, deemed suitable for surgery (Linden et al. 2005). The anaesthetist should be prepared for conversion to open thoracotomy at any time or the extension of surgery from a lobectomy to bi-lobectomy or pneumonectomy.

Lung isolation and OLV is a standard requirement. Small resections in otherwise healthy patients do not require routine use of invasive monitoring. Surgical lobectomy warrants the insertion of invasive arterial monitoring. The use of CVP lines is not routine, but should be considered in high-risk patients, or where infusions of potent vasoactive agents are expected. The surgical approach will determine the mode of analgesia: VATS procedures can usually be managed with intercostal nerve blocks, inserted by the surgeon under thoracoscopic vision, combined with patient-controlled analgesia intravenous opiate (Taylor et al. 2004). Open thoracotomies require either epidural or paravertebral blocks to provide adequate postoperative analgesia (Savage et al. 2002; Conlon et al. 2008; Joshi 2008). Intrathecal morphine may be an effective alternative (De Cosmo et al. 2009).

Sleeve (bronchoplastic) resections are typically performed for tumours located at the origin of a lobar bronchus, precluding a simple lobectomy, but not infiltrating enough to warrant a pneumonectomy or in patients with borderline lung function not able to tolerate pneumonectomy. Lung isolation is achieved with a contralateral DLT or EBT. Patients undergoing angioplastic procedures, in addition to bronchoplasty, involving reconstruction of major pulmonary vessels, will require some degree of heparinization. The anaesthetist must be prepared for conversion to a pneumonectomy and insert monitoring accordingly.

Thoracotomy for pneumonectomy is usually undertaken through a posterolateral incision. Lung isolation may be achieved with a contralateral DLT or EBT, or via the insertion of an EBB into the ipsilateral side. Communication with the surgeon is paramount, as the device must be withdrawn from the bronchus immediately before stapling. Careful perioperative fluid management is essential because excessive fluid administration can lead to postoperative acute lung injury (Slinger 2006a). Insertion of a CVP catheter is standard. Risk factors for the development of post-pneumonectomy acute lung injury include excessive fluid administration, high intraoperative airway pressures, intraoperative tidal volume greater than 8 ml kg^{-1}, and preoperative alcohol abuse (Licker et al. 2003; Fernandez-Perez et al. 2006; Ramnath et al. 2007; Jeon et al. 2009). Postoperative acute lung injury is associated with a mortality of 25% (Alam et al. 2007). Early extubation is desirable to avoid barotrauma to the bronchial stump and risk of fistula formation (Pomerantz et al. 1988). RV function is another important consideration in the postoperative period. After pneumonectomy, pulmonary vascular resistance increases causing the RV to dilate, resulting in significant tricuspid regurgitation, and potential for RV failure (Foroulis et al. 2004; Venuta et al. 2007). A rare but potentially fatal complication of pneumonectomy is cardiac herniation or strangulation, where the heart prolapses through any surgically created defects in the pericardium, leading to immediate cardiovascular collapse. In situations where the pericardium has been breached, the patient should be nursed with a slight tilt to the non-operated side (Shimizu et al. 2003).

Extrapleural pneumonectomy is offered to patients with malignant mesothelioma, although the evidence is controversial (Treasure et al. 2011). It involves extensive surgery, with resection of lung, pleura, pericardium, and diaphragm. Anaesthetic management for extrapleural pneumonectomy is similar to a pneumonectomy with the additional risk of massive blood loss. Some patients will require a short period of postoperative ventilation because of the extensive surgery and large fluid shifts (Slinger and Campos 2009).

Patients with severe emphysema often develop bullae, caused by loss of normal alveolar architecture. Anaesthetic considerations for a bullectomy are similar to those for a patient with COPD: avoid high airway pressures and PEEP, allow for an adequate expiratory phase to reduce 'gas-trapping', and maintain a high vigilance for bulla rupture and the development of bronchopleural fistula and subsequent tension pneumothorax. The extension of bullectomy is lung volume reduction surgery. This can be performed via sternotomy, thoracotomy, or the VATS approach and is usually bilateral. The VATS approach offers a quicker recovery, which may in part be as a result of a reduced inflammatory response to the less invasive procedure (McKenna et al. 2004; Friscia 2007). Invasive monitoring is recommended and there is a low threshold for epidural insertion, even with VATS approach. The incidence of postoperative air leak is high (Moser 2008), so early extubation is advantageous.

Empyema and abscess

A lung abscess is an infection where an area of necrosis forms in the lung parenchyma, often secondary to aspiration of gastric contents or distal to an obstruction. An empyema is the accumulation of pus in the pleural cavity (pyothorax), typically complicating a pneumonia or post surgery. Treatment of an empyema involves drainage of the pus, either by thoracostomy or decortication. Patients should be on appropriate antimicrobial therapy, but may have signs of sepsis at the time of surgery. Decortication is associated with significant blood loss and invasive monitoring is advised.

Lung abscess is generally treated with antimicrobial agents, but surgery is indicated when there is failure to respond to intensive medical therapy or with the development of severe haemoptysis (Philpott et al. 1993; Hirshberg et al. 1999). The role of the thoracic anaesthetist is to achieve lung isolation without dissemination of infection to non-infected regions of the lung. This may involve induction of anaesthesia with the patient in the sitting of lateral position (Pfitzner et al. 2000). Insertion of a DLT allows for suctioning and drainage of the infected lung, whilst protecting the contralateral lung. An EBB can provide selective blockade of the infected lobe (Campos 2009b), protecting the remainder of the ipsilateral lung, but does not facilitate suctioning and drainage of infected secretions.

Pleura

Biopsy

Pleural biopsy can be generally be performed under local anaesthesia (Sakuraba et al. 2006). Patients that present for surgical biopsy may have had a failed attempt at biopsy under local anaesthesia or may have large pleural effusions requiring drainage. Thoracoscopic visualization will assist the surgeon in evaluating the extent of the underlying disease process. The patient frequently presents with dyspnoea, presumed to be related to the pleural collection. The anaesthetist must be alerted to the potential presence of an undiagnosed pericardial effusion, particularly where an underlying cancer is suspected (McKenna et al. 1985).

Pleurodesis/pleurectomy

Recurrent pleural effusions or pneumothoraces are typically treated by either partial pleurectomy (stripping of the parietal pleura) or pleurodesis (obliteration of the pleural cavity). Although frequently performed via the VATS approach, both procedures can be extremely painful to the patient in the postoperative period (Walker-Renard et al. 1994). In addition to standard opiates, analgesic options include epidural and intrathoracic spray of local anaesthesia (Kempen 1998; Lee and Colt 2007).

Bronchopleural fistula

A bronchopleural fistula (BPF) is an abnormal connection between the pleural space and the bronchial tree. It may result from infection, rupture of bullae, tumour erosion of bronchial wall, post radiotherapy, or, most commonly, post surgery. Risk factors for the development of post-pneumonectomy BPF are residual tumour in the stump, long bronchial stump, preoperative steroid use, and postoperative ventilation (Lois and Noppen 2005).

The initial step in the management of a patient with a BPF is the insertion of a functioning chest tube. The size of the BPF can be evaluated by the volume of air leak bubbling through the chest drainage system (Slinger and Campos 2009). Lung isolation is imperative. Although FOB awake intubation with a DLT provides the safest method of achieving lung isolation, this technique requires excellent topical anaesthesia and a cooperative patient (Patane et al. 1990; Salazar et al. 2010). The second option is inhalation induction and maintenance of spontaneous ventilation until the lung is isolated. This requires a relatively deep level of anaesthesia and may cause haemodynamic compromise in some patients. The third method is to use high-frequency oscillatory ventilation with permissive hypercapnia to avoid barotrauma and reduce air leak through the BPF (Tietjen et al. 1997; Poulin et al. 2009). Most anaesthetists opt for a modified rapid sequence induction and placement of a DLT, guided by FOB, with avoidance of IPPV until lung isolation is secured (Ross and McCormick 2011). The final approach includes regional anaesthesia, with the use of a thoracic epidural catheter (Williams and Kay 2000). After surgical repair of the BPF, early extubation is advisable to avoid any barotrauma.

Mediastinum

Mediastinoscopy

Cervical mediastinoscopy is the most common method for the evaluation and biopsy of lymph nodes in the staging of lung cancer. It involves a small transverse incision in the suprasternal region of the neck. The majority of cases are performed under general anaesthesia with a single-lumen tracheal tube. The patient's head is usually extended by the placement of a shoulder roll, to facilitate surgical access. It is necessary to monitor the pulse in the right upper limb as the surgeon may compress the innominate artery with the mediastinoscope. This can be achieved with the pulse oximeter and routine insertion of invasive arterial monitoring is not indicated. The surgeon should be alerted when there is loss of the pulse oximeter signal as the innominate artery also supplies the right common carotid artery and prolonged periods of occlusion put the patient at risk of cerebral ischaemia. A non-invasive blood pressure cuff should be placed on the patient's left arm to provide blood pressure measurements during periods of innominate artery compression.

Complications of mediastinoscopy include reflex arrhythmias, recurrent laryngeal nerve injury, pneumothorax, haemorrhage, tracheobronchial rupture, stroke, and air embolism (Ahmed-Nusrath and Swanevelder 2007; Benouaich et al. 2009).

Anterior mediastinoscopy involves a small, parasternal incision in the second intercostal space to facilitate surgical access to subaortic lymph nodes. It can also be used to biopsy anterior mediastinal masses. An additional complication includes bleeding from the internal mammary artery (Ahmad and Blum 2009).

Mediastinal tumours

The mediastinum lies between the left and right pleurae and extends from the sternum to the vertebral column. It is divided into superior and inferior portions, with the inferior part further subdivided into anterior, middle, and posterior parts. It contains the heart, major vessels, lymphatics, nerves, oesophagus, trachea, and thymus gland.

Masses in the mediastinum may be benign or malignant. Anterior mediastinal tumours include lymphomas, thymomas, germ cell tumours, and thyroid goitres (Slinger and Karsli 2007). Perioperative risks are increased when the patient is unable to lie supine, because of the development of orthopnoea, cough, or syncope. Initial anaesthetic evaluation requires assessment of the imaging (chest X-ray and CT scan) to ascertain the size, site, and involvement of important mediastinal structures. Biopsies of lesions to obtain tissue for diagnosis can frequently be performed under local anaesthesia. Resection of masses will require general anaesthesia.

Before induction, large-bore intravenous access must be established. In cases where superior vena cava flow is compromised by tumour, lower limb access is essential. Invasive arterial monitoring is also advocated. Inhalation induction, often in the semi-recumbent position, with maintenance of spontaneous ventilation, is the safest strategy (Gothard 2008; Blank and de Souza 2011), although not totally risk-free (Gardner and Royster 2011). Adequacy of ventilation with assisted manual ventilation should precede the administration of neuromuscular blocking drugs. Rigid bronchoscopy must be readily available. Cardiovascular collapse may be relieved by repositioning the patient, but immediate institution of cardiopulmonary bypass (CPB) may be necessary (Slinger and Karsli 2007). Some advocate the insertion of CPB cannulae under local anaesthesia before induction (Gardner and Royster 2011). In very high-risk cases, CPB can be established in the awake patient (Tempe et al. 2001).

Thymectomy for myasthenia gravis

Myasthenia gravis is an autoimmune disorder caused by circulating antibodies that block acetylcholine receptors at the postsynaptic neuromuscular junction. Patients are resistant to depolarizing neuromuscular blocking agents, but extremely sensitive to non-depolarizing neuromuscular blocking drugs. Thymectomy, even in the absence of thymoma, offers substantial improvements in the disease (Bachmann et al. 2008). Surgical approaches include full or partial sternotomy, thoracotomy, transcervical, and VATS.

Attention must be paid to the perioperative pyridostigmine dosing. Ideally, at the time of intubation, the patient should have some muscle weakness to facilitate tracheal intubation, whilst full muscle tone is desirable at the end of the procedure. This can be achieved by holding the morning dose of pyridostigmine until immediately before surgery. The anticholinesterase action should be working by the end of surgery. The use of neuromuscular blocking drugs is associated with prolonged postoperative ventilation (Chevally et al. 2001), and should be avoided. Intubation can be achieved with topical anaesthesia, propofol, and remifentanil. If necessary, small doses of neuromuscular blocking drugs can be given, with monitoring of the level of neuromuscular block. The choice of monitoring will depend on the invasiveness of the surgical approach. Patients may be on corticosteroid therapy or have had recent plasmapheresis. In the immediate postoperative period, anticholinesterase therapy should be continued. Minimally invasive approaches allow for immediate extubation and reduced hospital length of stay (de Perrot et al. 2003).

Vascular

Massive haemoptysis

Massive haemoptysis is defined by the volume of blood expectorated. Several definitions exist, ranging from 100 ml to 1000 ml in 24 h (Ibrahim 2008). However, quantification of blood loss is frequently inaccurate and may not be as important as the degree of haemodynamic instability and hypoxia (Jean-Baptiste 2000). The risk of death correlates with both the volume of blood lost and the rate of bleeding (Chun et al. 2010). Causes include tuberculosis, lung abscess, bronchial carcinoma, trauma, and iatrogenic.

Anaesthetic considerations include resuscitation, localization of the bleeding point to provide appropriate lung isolation, and definitive treatment. Initial assessment with clinical examination, chest X-ray, bronchoscopy, and CT scan is useful in localizing the site of bleeding. Lung isolation can be achieved by DLT, EBB, or EBT. After induction of anaesthesia, the surgeon may initially perform rigid bronchoscopy in an attempt to visualize the source of bleeding. This provides an opportunity to place an EBB with selective lobar or segmental blockade. Bronchial artery embolization is now considered the most effective procedure for massive haemoptysis (Chun et al. 2010).

Pulmonary endarterectomy

Pulmonary endarterectomy is the treatment of choice for patients suffering from chronic thromboembolic pulmonary hypertension (Hoeper et al. 2006). Patients presenting for surgery have severe pulmonary hypertension. Premedication is generally avoided because of the risk of precipitating hypercapnia and RV failure. Full invasive monitoring is required, including PAC and TOE. Trendelenburg position is avoided as the increase in preload may induce RV failure (Roscoe and Klein 2008). The combination of midazolam, fentanyl, and a neuromuscular blocking agent is the most common and safest drug combination for induction of anaesthesia (Manecke 2006). Ketamine is an alternative agent. Vasoactive support is often necessary during induction. The surgical procedure requires CPB and deep hypothermic circulatory arrest. Mannitol, methylprednisolone, and thiopental are administered in an attempt to provide cerebral protection. Weaning from CPB requires a balance between RV contractility and pulmonary vasoconstriction. Sufficient inotropy is needed to support RV function, but an excessive cardiac output is undesirable as it may cause reperfusion injury to the lungs. Inotrope and vasoconstrictor doses are titrated based upon cardiac output measurements. In the postoperative period, the patient usually remains sedated for the initial 24 h. Severe reperfusion pulmonary oedema can be managed successfully with extracorporeal membrane oxygenation (Thistlethwaite et al. 2006).

Lung transplantation

Lung transplantation is the treatment of choice for selected patients with end-stage respiratory failure or pulmonary hypertension (Christie et al. 2009). Recipient pathologies include COPD, α1-antitrypsin deficiency, idiopathic pulmonary fibrosis, cystic fibrosis, bronchiectasis, sarcoidosis, and primary pulmonary hypertension. Patients are listed when life expectancy after transplantation exceeds that without lung transplantation (Oren et al. 2006). Surgical lung transplantation procedures include single-lung transplantation (SLT), bilateral sequential-lung transplantation (BSLT), heart–lung transplant, and living-related lobar transplant, and depend on the patient's underlying pathology. Survival is better with BSLT compared with SLT. However, one donor could potentially offer organs to two SLT recipients in contrast to one BSLT recipient.

Full invasive monitoring is advocated, including PAC and TOE. In patients with copious secretions (cystic fibrosis), a single-lumen tracheal tube is initially inserted to facilitate bronchoscopic suctioning and lavage, before insertion of a DLT. Induction of anaesthesia can precipitate RV failure and cardiopulmonary collapse in patients with significant pulmonary hypertension. Emphysematous patients are prone to dynamic hyperinflation when IPPV is commenced and subsequent 'pulmonary tamponade.' Recipients with idiopathic pulmonary fibrosis often require high ventilatory pressures, leading to reduced venous return and cardiac output. The underlying pathophysiology should guide the anaesthetist to the most appropriate ventilatory and haemodynamic management (Roscoe 2011). Elective use of CPB is indicated in patients with severe pulmonary hypertension and undergoing heart–lung transplant. Routine use of CPB may be associated with worse outcomes (Dalibon et al. 2006; Ferrer et al. 2007). The anaesthetist should be prepared for the urgent institution of CPB if the patient develops severe instability, hypoxaemia, or hypercapnia. When BSLT is performed off-pump, the lung with the least perfusion (by $\dot{V}/\dot{Q}$ scan) is explanted first, with OLV of the contralateral lung. Once the initial donor lung is implanted, OLV is applied to the new lung during pneumonectomy of the remaining native lung. Once both donor organs are implanted TLV can be resumed. The transplanted lungs do not possess lymphatics, so any excess alveolar fluid results in pulmonary oedema. A restrictive fluid strategy is adopted. Ischaemia–reperfusion injury can lead to pulmonary oedema, hypoxaemia, pulmonary hypertension, and RV failure. Patients may require inhaled nitric oxide or extracorporeal membrane oxygenation therapy in the initial postoperative period until the lungs recover (Della Rocca et al. 2002; Hsu et al. 2008). Early extubation in the operating theatre is possible in selected patients, particularly with SLT (Hansen et al. 2003).

Bronchopulmonary lavage

Pulmonary alveolar proteinosis is a rare disorder characterized by the accumulation of abnormal lipoprotein in the alveoli. It may be primary (idiopathic) or secondary to haematological malignancies (Xue et al. 2010). Bronchopulmonary lavage provides symptomatic relief for patients suffering from idiopathic pulmonary alveolar proteinosis.

The most impaired lung is lavaged first. This can be determined by radiological imaging, although questioning the patient may provide this information.

The procedure necessitates precise lung isolation with a DLT. An arterial cannula is inserted for intermittent measurement of blood gases and electrolytes. A urinary catheter is inserted and a dose of diuretic is commonly given. TIVA is typically used to maintain anaesthesia and FI_{O_2} 1.0 is administered. The most impaired lung is then lavaged with 500–1000 ml aliquots of 0.9% saline at 37°C. Lavages are continued until the outflow fluid is clear (Bussieres 2011). The patient remains supine for the majority of the procedure apart from an episode of full lateral position for one lavage cycle. Chest percussion is used to facilitate efficacy of the lavage. After completion of the first side there is a period of TLV. A chest X-ray is performed to exclude hydrothorax, which may be suspected if the patient's lavage balance exceeds 10% (Bussieres 2011). The lavaged lung is allowed time to recovery before proceeding with lavage of the second lung. If arterial hypoxaemia is unacceptable, lavage of the second lung may be carried out at a later date. After the procedure, the patient remains sedated until arterial blood gases are acceptable for extubation. Observation for the initial 24 h in an intensive care unit is the standard (Bussieres 2011).

Postoperative care

Postoperative analgesia

Post-thoracotomy analgesia should be multimodal. Thoracic epidural analgesia (TEA) has traditionally been designated the 'gold standard' in thoracotomy analgesia (Joshi 2008). The use of TEA has consistently been shown to reduce postoperative pulmonary morbidity after thoracic surgery (Ballantyne et al. 1998; Popping et al. 2008). However, TEA can be associated with significant hypotension. The combination of low-dose local anaesthetic and opiate has a synergistic action, reducing the risk of hypotension and leading to a reduction in overall opiate consumption (Wiebalck et al. 1997; Joris et al. 2003). An alternative to TEA is paravertebral block (PVB, see Chapter 53). The thoracic paravertebral space is a wedge-shaped area, lateral to the vertebral bodies, anterior to the transverse processes of the vertebrae and posteromedial to the parietal pleura. Multiple studies have shown the efficacy of PVB for post-thoracotomy analgesia (Davies et al. 2006; Joshi 2008). Other local anaesthesia techniques include intercostal nerve blocks and intrapleural analgesia. Neither appears to be as effective as TEA or PVB.

Systemic opiates have been shown to provide inferior analgesia to TEA and PVB after thoracotomy, but mat be considered for patients with contraindications to the aforementioned techniques or in VATS procedures.

Non-steroidal anti-inflammatory drugs and paracetamol provide useful adjunctive analgesia. Ketamine provides excellent postoperative analgesia and the use of low-dose infusions is associated with significantly less opiate requirement, reduced nausea and vomiting, and with very few psychotomimetic side-effects (Bell et al. 2006).

Respiratory failure

Respiratory failure is the most common cause of morbidity and mortality after lung resection, occurring in up to 16% of cases (Lefebvre et al. 2009). Risk factors include advanced age, extent of lung resection, cardiac comorbidity, and inadequate postoperative analgesia (Slinger and Campos 2009). Chest physiotherapy and early ambulation help to reduce the risk. Non-invasive ventilation should be considered as first-line therapy and may be successful in 85% of patients. Failure to respond to non-invasive ventilation necessitates tracheal intubation and IPPV, with a significant increase in mortality (Freynet and Pierre-Emmanuel 2008; Lefebvre et al. 2009).

Declaration of interest

None declared.

References

Abdelmalak B. Anesthesia for interventional pulmonology. In: Urman DR, Gross W, Philip B, eds. *Anesthesia Outside of the Operating Room*. Oxford: Oxford University Press, 2011; 167–74

Abe K, Oka J, Takahashi H, Funatsu T, Fukuda H, Miyamoto Y. Effect of high-frequency jet ventilation on oxygenation during one-lung ventilation in patients undergoing thoracic aneurysm surgery. *J Anesth* 2006; **20**: 1–5

Ahmad US, Blum, MG. Invasive diagnostic procedures. In: Shields TW, LoCicero J, Reed CE, Feins RH, eds. *General Thoracic Surgery*. Philadelphia, PA: Lippincott, Williams & Wilkins, 2009; 301–10

Ahmed-Nusrath A, Swanevelder J. Anaesthesia for mediastinoscopy. *Cont Educ Anaesth Crit Care Pain* 2007; **7**: 6–9

Alam N, Park BJ, Wilton A, *et al.* Incidence and risk factors for lung injury after lung cancer resection. *Ann Thorac Surg* 2007; **84**: 1085–91

Albaladejo P, Marret E, Samama CM, *et al.* Non-cardiac surgery in patients with coronary stents: the RECO study. *Heart* 2011; **97**: 1566–72

Alberti A, Valenti S, Gallo F, Vincenti E. Differential lung ventilation with a double-lumen tracheostomy tube in unilateral refractory atelectasis. *Intensive Care Med* 1992; **18**: 479–84

Akrawi W, Benumof JL. A pathophysiological basis for informed preoperative smoking cessation counseling. *J Cardiothorac Vasc Anesth* 1997; **11**: 629–40

Amar D. Postthoracotomy atrial fibrillation. *Curr Opin Anaesthesiol* 2007; **20**: 43–7

Amar D, Roistacher N, Burt ME, *et al.* Effects of diltiazem versus digoxin on dysrhythmias and cardiac function after pneumonectomy. *Ann Thorac Surg* 1997; **63**: 1374–81

Amar D, Roistacher N, Rusch VW, *et al.* Effects of diltiazem prophylaxis on the incidence and clinical outcome of atrial arrhythmias after thoracic surgery. *J Thorac Cardiovasc Surg* 2000; **120**: 790–8

Amar D, Zhang H, Heerdt PM, Park B, Fleisher M, Thaler HT. Statin use is associated with a reduction in atrial fibrillation in noncardiac thoracic surgery independent of C-reactive protein. *Chest* 2005; **128**: 3421–7

Ambrosio C, Leykin Y, Pellis T, Brodsky JB. Endotracheal kinking of a double-lumen tube: a potential complication of inappropriate size tube selection. *Eur J Anaesthesiol* 2011; **28**: 607–8

ASA Task Force. Practice Advisory for Intraoperative Awareness and Brain Function Monitoring. Task Force Report. *Anesthesiology* 2006; **104**: 847–64

Association of Anaesthetists of Great Britain and Ireland. Recommendations for standards of during anaesthesia and recovery anaesthesia. *Anaesthesia* 2016; **71**: 85–93. Available from http://www.aagbi.org/sites/default/files/Standards_of_monitoring_2015_0.pdf

Au CL, White SA, Grant RP. A novel technique for tracheoesophageal fistula in adults. *Can J Anaesth* 1999; **46**: 688–91

Bachmann K, Burkhardt D, Schreiter I, *et al.* Long-term outcome and quality of life after open and thoracoscopic thymectomy for myasthenia gravis: analysis of 131 patients. *Surg Endosc* 2008; **22**: 2470–7

Bahk J, Oh YS. Prediction of double-lumen tracheal tube depth. *J Cardiothorac Vasc Anesth* 1999; **13**: 370–1

Bailey J, Mikhail M, Haddy S, Thangathurai D. Problems with CPAP during one-lung ventilation in thoracoscopic surgery. *J Cardiothorac Vasc Anesth* 1998; **12**: 239

Ballantyne JC, Carr DB, deFerranti S, *et al.* The comparative effects of postoperative analgesic therapies on pulmonary outcome: cumulative meta-analyses of randomized, controlled trials. *Anesth Analg* 1998; **86**: 598–612

Bangalore S, Wetterslev J, Pranesh S, Sawhney S, Gluud C, Messerli FH. Perioperative beta blockers in patients having non-cardiac surgery: a meta-analysis. *Lancet* 2008; **372**: 1962–76

Bardoczky GI, Engelman E, d'Hollander A. Continuous spirometry: an aid to monitoring ventilation during operation. *Br J Anaesth* 1993b; **71**: 747–51

Bardoczky GI, Levarlet M, Engelman E, deFrancquen P. Continuous spirometry for detection of double-lumen endobronchial tube displacement. *Br J Anaesth* 1993a; **70**: 499–502

Barnes PJ. Chronic obstructive pulmonary disease. *N Engl J Med* 2005; **343**: 269–80

Barrera R, Shi W, Amar D, *et al.* Smoking and timing of cessation: impact on pulmonary complications after thoracotomy. *Chest* 2005; **127**: 1977–83

Bayes J, Slater EM, Hedberg PS, Lawson D. Obstruction of a double-lumen endotracheal tube by a saber-sheath trachea. *Anesth Analg* 1994; **79**: 186–8

Bayliff CD, Massel DR, Inculet RI, *et al.* Propranolol for the prevention of postoperative arrhythmias in general thoracic surgery. *Ann Thorac Surg* 1999; **67**: 182–6

Behr J. Optimizing preoperative lung function. *Curr Opin Anaesthesiol* 2001; **14**: 65–9

Bell RF, Dahl JB, Moore RA, Kalso E. Perioperative ketamine for acute postoperative pain. *Cochrane Database Syst Rev* 2006; **1**: CD004603

Benouaich V, Marcheix B, Carfagna L, Brouchet L, Guitard J. Anatomical bases of left recurrent nerve lesions during mediastinoscopy. *Surg Radiol Anat* 2009; **31**: 295–9

Benzo R, Kelley GA, Recchi L, Hofman A, Sciurba F. Complications of lung resection and exercise capacity: a meta-analysis. *Respir Med* 2007; **101**: 1790–7

Benzo RP, Sciurba, FC. Oxygen consumption shuttle walking test and the evaluation of lung resection. *Respiration* 2010; **80**: 19–23

Berrisford R, Brunelli A, Rocco G, *et al.* The European Thoracic Surgery Database project: modeling the risk of in-hospital death following lung resection. *Eur J Cardiothorac Surg* 2005; **28**: 306–11

Bindslev L, Cannon D, Sykes MK. Reversal of nitrous oxide-induced depression of hypoxic pulmonary vasoconstriction by lignocaine hydrochloride during collapse and ventilation hypoxia of the left lower lobe. *Br J Anaesth* 1986; **58**: 451–6

Bjork VO, Carlens E. The prevention of spread during pulmonary resection by the use of a double-lumen catheter. *J Thorac Surg* 1950; **20**: 151–7

Blank RS, de Souza DG. Anesthetic management of patients with an anterior mediastinal mass: continuing professional development. *Can J Anaesth* 2011; **58**: 853–9

Bolinger CT, Jordan P, Solèr M, *et al.* Pulmonary function and exercise capacity after lung resection. *Eur Respir J* 1996; **9**: 415–21

Boucek CD, Landreneau R, Freeman JA, Strollo D, Bircher NG. A comparison of techniques for placement of double-lumen endobronchial tubes. *J Clin Anesth* 1998; **10**: 557–60

Brass P, Mills E, Latza J, *et al.* LiDCOrapid and PiCCOplus preload response parameter validation study. *Crit Care* 2011; **15**(Suppl 1): 61

British Thoracic Society. BTS Guidelines: guidelines on the selection of patients with lung cancer for surgery. *Thorax* 2001; **56**: 89–108

Brodsky JB. Approaches to hypoxemia during single-lung ventilation. *Curr Opin Anaesthesiol* 2001; **14**: 71–6

Brodsky JB, Adkins MO, Gaba D, *et al.* Bronchial cuff pressures of double-lumen tubes. *Anesth Analg* 1989; **69**: 608–10

Brodsky JB, Malott K, Angst M, *et al.* The relationship between tracheal width and left bronchial width: Implications for left-sided double-lumen tube selection. *J Cardiothorac Vasc Anesth* 2001; **15**: 216–7

Browne DR, Rochford J, O'Connell U, Jones JG. The incidence of postoperative atelectasis in the dependent lung following thoracotomy: the value of added nitrogen. *Br J Anaesth* 1970; **42**: 340–6

Brunelli A, Refai M, Monteverde M, *et al.* Stair climbing test predicts cardiopulmonary complications after lung resection. *Chest* 2002; **121**: 1106–10

Brunelli, A, Monteverde M, Refai M, *et al.* Stair climbing test as a predictor of cardiopulmonary complications after pulmonary lobectomy in the elderly. *Ann Thorac Surg* 2004; **77**: 266–70

Brunelli, A, Belardinelli R, Refai M, *et al.* Peak oxygen consumption during cardiopulmonary exercise test improves risk stratification in candidates to major lung resection. *Chest* 2009; **135**: 1260–7

Bryce-Smith R. A double-lumen endobronchial tube. *Br J Anaesth* 1959; **31**: 274–5

Buczkowski PW, Fombon FN, Russell WC, Thompson JP. Effects of helium on high frequency jet ventilation in model of airway stenosis. *Br J Anaesth* 2005; **95**: 701–5

Buduhan G, Menon S, Aye RW, *et al.* Trimodality therapy for malignant pleural mesothelioma. *Ann Thorac Surg* 2009; **88**: 870–5

Burton NA, Watson DC, Brodsky JB, *et al.* Advantages of a new polyvinyl chloride double-lumen tube in thoracic surgery. *Ann Thorac Surg* 1983; **36**: 78–84

Bussieres JS. Whole lung lavage. In: Slinger PD, ed. *Principles and Practice of Anesthesia for Thoracic Surgery*. New York: Springer, 2011; 497–510

Campos JH. An update on bronchial blockers during lung separation techniques in adults. *Anesth Analg* 2003; **97**: 1266–74

Campos JH. Progress in lung separation. *Thorac Surg Clin* 2005; **15**: 71–83

Campos JH. How to achieve successful lung separation. *SAJAA* 2008; **14**: 22–6

Campos JH. Update on tracheobronchial anatomy and flexible fiberoptic bronchoscopy in thoracic anesthesia. *Curr Opin Anaesthesiol* 2009a; **22**: 4–10

Campos JH. Update on selective lobar blockade during pulmonary resections. *Curr Opin Anaesthesiol* 2009b; **22**: 18–22

Campos JH. Lung isolation techniques for patients with difficult airway. *Curr Opin Anaesthesiol* 2010; **23**: 12–7

Campos JH, Gomez MN. Pro: right-sided double-lumen endotracheal tubes should be routinely used in thoracic surgery. *J Cardiothorac Vasc Anesth* 2002; **16**: 246–8

Campos JH, Hallam EA, Van Natta T, Kernstine KH. Devices for lung isolation used by anesthesiologists with limited thoracic experience: comparison of double-lumen endotracheal tube, Univent torque control blocker, and Arndt wire-guided endobronchial blocker. *Anesthesiology* 2006; **104**: 261–6

Cecconi M, Rhodes A. Validation of continuous cardiac output technologies: consensus still awaited. *Crit Care* 2009; **13**: 159

Ceresoli GL, Gridelli C, Santoro A. Multidisciplinary treatment of malignant pleural mesothelioma. *Oncologist* 2007; **12**: 850–63

Chan CS. Anaesthetic management during repair of tracheo-oesophageal fistula. *Anaesthesia* 1984; **39**: 158–60

Chawla LS, Zia H, Gutierrez G, *et al.* Lack of equivalence between central venous and mixed venous oxygen saturation. *Chest* 2004; **126**: 1891–6

Chevally C, Spiliopoulos A, de Perrot M, Tschopp JM, Licker M. Perioperative medical management and outcome following thymectomy for myasthenia gravis. *Can J Anaesth* 2001; **48**: 446–51

Chong S, Lee KS, Chung MJ, Han J, Kwon OJ, Kim TS. Neuroendocrine tumors of the lung: clinical, pathologic, and imaging findings. *Radiographics* 2006; **26**: 41–57

Chow MY, Goh MH, Ti LK. Predicting the depth of insertion of left-sided double-lumen endobronchial tubes. *J Cardiothorac Vasc Anesth* 2002; **16**: 456–8

Chow MY, Liam BL, Lew TW, Chelliah RY, Ong BC. Predicting the size of a double-lumen tube based on tracheal diameter. *Anesth Analg* 1998; **87**: 158–60

Christie JD, Edwards LB, Aurora P, *et al.* Registry of the International Society for Heart and Lung Transplantation: Twenty-sixth Official Adult Lung and Heart-Lung Transplantation Report-2009. *J Heart Lung Transplant* 2009; **28**: 1031–49

Chun JY, Morgan R, Belli AM. Radiological management of haemoptysis: a comprehensive review of diagnostic imaging and bronchial arterial embolization. *Cardiovasc Intervent Radiol* 2010; **33**: 240–50

Clapham MC, Vaughan RS. Bronchial intubation. A comparison between polyvinyl chloride and red rubber double lumen tubes. *Anaesthesia* 1985; **40**: 1111–4

Conlon NP, Shaw AD, Grichnik KP. Postthoracotomy paravertebral analgesia: will it replace epidural analgesia? *Anesthesiol Clin* 2008; **26**: 369–80

Cowl CT, Prakash UB, Kruger BR. The role of anticholinergics in bronchoscopy. A randomized clinical trial. *Chest* 2000; **118**: 188–9

Dalibon N, Moutafis M, Liu N, *et al.* Treatment of hypoxemia during one-lung ventilation using intravenous almitrine. *Anesth Analg* 2004; **98**: 590–4

Dalibon N, Geffroy A, Moutafis M, *et al.* Use of cardiopulmonary bypass for lung transplantation: a 10-year experience. *J Cardiothorac Vasc Anesth* 2006; **20**: 668–72

Davies RG, Myles PS, Graham JM. A comparison of the analgesic efficacy and side-effects of paravertebral vs epidural blockade for thoracotomy—a systematic review and meta-analysis of randomized trials. *Br J Anaesth* 2006; **96**: 418–26

de Bellis M, Accardo R, Di Maio M, *et al.* Is flexible bronchoscopy necessary to confirm the position of double-lumen tubes before thoracic surgery?. *Eur J Cardiothorac Surg* 2011; **40**: 912–16

De Cosmo G, Aceto P, Gualtieri E, Congedo E. Analgesia in thoracic surgery: review. *Minerva Anestesiol* 2009; **75**: 393–400

Della Rocca G, Brondani A, Costa MG. Intraoperative hemodynamic monitoring during organ transplantation: what is new? *Curr Opin Organ Transplant* 2009; **14**: 291–6

Della Rocca G, Pierconti F, Costa MG, *et al.* Severe reperfusion lung injury after double lung transplantation. *Crit Care* 2002: **6**: 240–4

de Perrot M, Bril V, McRae K, Keshavjee S. Impact of minimally invasive trans-cervical Thymectomy on outcome in patients with myasthenia gravis. *Eur J Cardiothorac Surg* 2003; **24**: 677–83

de Perrot M, Chernenko S, Waddell TK, *et al.* Role of lung transplantation in the treatment of bronchogenic carcinomas for patients with end-stage pulmonary disease. *J Clin Oncol* 2004; **22**: 4351–6

Desiderio DP, Burt M, Kolker AC, *et al.* The effects of endobronchial cuff inflation on double-lumen endobronchial tube movement after lateral decubitus positioning. *J Cardiothorac Vasc Anesth* 1997; **11**: 595–8

Donati A, Loggi S, Preiser JC, *et al.* Goal-directed intraoperative therapy reduces morbidity and length of hospital stay in high-risk surgical patients. *Chest* 2007; **132**: 1817–24

Duke RA, Barrett MR 2nd, Payne SD, *et al.* Compression of left main bronchus and left pulmonary artery by thoracic aortic aneurysm. *AJR Am J Roentgenol* 1987; **149**: 261–3

Dumion JF, Shapshay S, Bourcereau J, *et al.* Principles for safety in application of neodymium-YAG laser in bronchology. *Chest* 1984; **86**: 163–8

Eastwood J, Mahajan R. One-lung anaesthesia. *Cont Educ Anaesth Crit Care Pain* 2002; **2**: 83–7

Eberle B, Weiler N, Vogel N, *et al.* Computed tomography-based tracheobronchial image reconstruction allows selection of the individually appropriate double-lumen tube size. *J Cardiothorac Vasc Anesth* 1999; **13**: 532

Ehrenfeld JM, Mulvoy W, Sandberg WS. Performance comparison of right- and left-sided double-lumen tubes among infrequent users. *J Cardiothorac Vasc Anesth* 2010; **24**: 598–601

Falcoz PE, Conti M, Brouchet L, *et al.* The Thoracic Surgery scoring System (Thoracoscore): risk model for in-hospital death in 15,183 patients requiring thoracic surgery. *J Thorac Cardiovasc Surg* 2007; **133**: 325–32

Fannuchi O, Ambrogi MC, Dini P, *et al.* Surgical treatment of non-small cell lung cancer in octogenarians. *Interact Cardiovasc Thorac Surg* 2011; **12**: 749–53

Felstein MB, Bach PB. Epidemiology of lung cancer. *Chest Surg Clin N Am* 2000; **10**: 653–61

Fernandez-Bustamante A, Ibañez V, Alfaro JJ, *et al.* High-frequency jet ventilation in interventional bronchoscopy: factors with predictive value on high-frequency ventilation complications. *J Clin Anesth* 2006; **18**: 349–56

Fernandez-Perez ER, Keegan MT, Brown DR, Hubmayr RD, Gajic O. Intraoperative tidal volume as a risk factor for respiratory failure after pneumonectomy. *Anesthesiology* 2006; **105**: 14–8

Ferrer J, Rodriguez E, Roman A, *et al.* Factors related to postoperative mortality in lung transplantation for emphysema. *Transplant Proc* 2007; **39**: 3317–22

Fitzmaurice BG, Brodsky JB. Airway rupture from double-lumen tubes. *J Cardiothorac Vasc Anesth* 1999; **13**: 309–11

Fleisher LA, Beckman JA, Brown KA, *et al.* ACC/AHA 2006 Guideline Update on Perioperative Cardiovascular Evaluation for Noncardiac Surgery: Focused Update on Perioperative Beat-Blocker Therapy—A report of the American College of Cardiology/American Heart Association Task Force on Practice Guidelines. *Anesth Analg* 2007; **104**: 15–26

Foroulis CN, Kotoulas CS, Kakouros S, *et al.* Study on the late effect of pneumonectomy on right heart pressures using Doppler echocardiography. *Eur J Cardiothorac Surg* 2004; **26**: 508–14

Fradj K, Samain E, Delefosse D, Farah E, Marty J. Placebo-controlled study of inhaled nitric oxide to treat hypoxaemia during one-lung ventilation. *Br J Anaesth* 1999; **82**: 208–12

Frank SM, Zhu J, Kolff JW, *et al.* Perioperative maintenance of normothermia reduces the incidence of morbid cardiac events. A randomized controlled trial. *JAMA* 1997; **277**: 1127–34

Freynet A, Pierre-Emmanuel F. Does non-invasive ventilation associated with chest physiotherapy improve outcome after lung resection? *Interact Cardiovasc Thorac Surg* 2008; **7**: 1152–4

Friscia ME, Zhu J, Kolff JW, *et al.* Cytokine response is lower after lung volume reduction through bilateral thoracoscopy versus sternotomy. *Ann Thorac Surg* 2007; **83**: 252–6

Frumento, RJ, Logginidou HG, Wahlander S, Wagener G, Playford HR, Sladen RN. Dexmedetomidine infusion is associated with enhanced renal function after thoracic surgery. *J Clin Anesth* 2006; **18**: 422–6

Gal TJ. Con: low tidal volumes are indicated during one-lung ventilation. *Anesth Analg* 2006; **103**: 271–3

Gao Y, Du X, Qin W, Li K. Assessment of the right ventricular function in patients with chronic obstructive pulmonary disease using MRI. *Acta Radiol* 2011; **52**: 711–5

Gardner JC, Royster RL. Airway collapse with an anterior mediastinal mass despite spontaneous ventilation in an adult. *Anesth Analg* 2011; **113**: 239–42

Garzon JC, Ng CS, Sihoe AD, *et al.* Video-assisted thoracic surgery pulmonary resection for lung cancer in patients with poor lung function. *Ann Thorac Surg* 2006; **81**: 1996–2003

Ghosh S, Falter F, Goldsmith K, Arrowsmith JE. The Papworth BiVent tube: a new device for lung isolation. *Anaesthesia* 2008; **63**: 996–1000

Ginsberg RJ, Rubinstein L. The comparison of limited resection to lobectomy for T1N0 non-small cell lung cancer. *Chest* 1994; **106**: 318–9S

Godet G, Riou B, Bertrand M, *et al.* Does preoperative coronary angioplasty improve perioperative cardiac outcome? *Anesthesiology* 2005; **102**: 739–46

Golledge J, Goldstraw P. Renal impairment after thoracotomy: incidence, risk factors, and significance. *Ann Thorac Surg* 1994; **58**: 524–8

Gothard JW. Anesthetic considerations for patients with anterior mediastinal masses. *Anesthesiol Clin* 2008; **26**: 305–14

Granville L, Laga AC, Allen TC, *et al.* Review and update of uncommon primary pleural tumors: a practical approach to diagnosis. *Arch Pathol Lab Med* 2005; **129**: 1428–43

Groth SS, Whitson BA, Kuskowski MA, Holmstrom AM, Rubins JB, Kelly RF. Impact of preoperative smoking status on postoperative complication rates and pulmonary function test results 1-year following pulmonary resection for non-small cell lung cancer. *Lung Cancer* 1999; **64**: 352–7

Guernelli N, Bragaglia RB, Briccoli A, Mastrorilli M, Vecchi R. Tracheobronchial rupture due to cuffed Carlens tubes. *Ann Thorac Surg* 1979; **28**: 66–7

Hannallah M, Benumof JL, Silverman PM, Kelly LC, Lea D. Evaluation of an approach to choosing a left double-lumen tube based on chest computed tomographic scan measurement of left mainstem bronchial diameter. *J Cardiothorac Vasc Anesth* 1997; **11**: 168–7

Hansen LN, Ravn JB, Yndgaard S. Early extubation after single-lung transplantation: analysis of the first 106 cases. *J Cardiothorac Vasc Anesth* 2003; **17**: 36–9

Harpole DH, DeCamp MM Jr, Daley J, *et al.* Prognostic models of thirty-day mortality and morbidity after major pulmonary resection. *J Cardiovasc Thorac Surg* 1999; **117**: 969–79

Hasan FM, Malanga A, Corrao WM, Braman SS. Effect of catheter position on thermodilution cardiac output during continuous positive pressure ventilation. *Crit Care Med* 1984; **12**: 387–90

Heiser M, Steinberg JJ, MacVaugh H 3rd, Klineberg PL. Bronchial rupture, a complication of use of the Robertshawe double-lumen tube. *Anesthesiology* 1979; **51**: 88

Hindman BJ Bert AA. Malignant esophago-respiratory tract fistulas: anesthetic considerations for exclusion procedures using esophageal bypass. *J Cardiothorac Vasc Anesth* 1987; **1**: 438–44

Hirshberg B, Sklair-Levi M, Nir-Paz R, *et al.* Factors predicting mortality of patients with lung abscess. *Chest* 1999; **115**: 746–50

Hoeper MM, Madani MM, Nakanishi N, *et al.* Chronic thromboembolic pulmonary hypertension. *Circulation* 2006; **113**: 2011–20

Hogue CW Jr. Effectiveness of low levels of nonventilated lung continuous positive airway pressure in improving arterial oxygenation during one-lung ventilation. *Anesth Analg* 1994; **79**: 364–7

Holden DA, Rice TW, Stelmach K, Meeker DP. Exercise testing, 6-min walk, and stair climb in the evaluation of patients at high risk for pulmonary resection. *Chest* 1992; **102**: 1774–9

Holm J, Håkanson E, Vánky F, Svedjeholm R. Mixed venous oxygen saturation predicts short- and long-term outcome after coronary artery bypass grafting surgery: a retrospective cohort analysis. *Br J Anaesth* 2011; **107**: 344–50

Hsu HH, Ko WJ, Chen JS, *et al.* Extracorporeal membrane oxygenation in pulmonary crisis and primary graft dysfunction. *J Heart Lung Transplant* 2008; **27**: 233–7

Huang YC, Cheng YJ, Lin YH, Wang MJ, Tsai SK. Graft failure caused by pulmonary venous obstruction diagnosed by intraoperative transesophageal echocardiography during lung transplantation. *Anesth Analg* 2000; **91**: 558–60

Ibrahim WH. Massive haemoptysis: the definition should be revised. *Eur Respir J* 2008; **32**: 1131–2

Inoue S, Nishimine N, Kitaguchi K, Furuya H, Taniguchi S. Double-lumen tube location predicts malposition and hypoxemia during one-lung ventilation. *Br J Anaesth* 2004; **92**: 195–201

Ishikawa S, Lohser J. One-lung ventilation and arterial oxygenation. *Curr Opin Anaesthesiol* 2011; **24**: 24–31

Iwasaka H, Itoh K. Miyakawa H, *et al.* Continuous monitoring of ventilatory mechanics during one-lung ventilation. *J Clin Monit* 1996; **12**: 161–4

Jean-Baptiste E. Clinical assessment and management of massive hemoptysis. *Crit Care Med* 2000; **88**: 291–5

Jeon Y, Ryu HG, Bahk JH, Jung CW, Goo JM. A new technique to determine the size of double-lumen endobronchial tubes by the two perpendicularly measured bronchial diameters. *Anaesth Intensive Care* 2005; **33**: 59–63

Jeon K, Yoon JW, Suh GY, *et al.* Risk factors for post-pneumonectomy acute lung injury/acute respiratory distress syndrome in primary lung cancer patients. *Anaesth Intensive Care* 2009; **37**: 14–9

Jokic R, Fitzpatrick MF. Obstructive lung disease and sleep. *Med Clin North Am* 1996; **80**: 821–50

Joris, JL, Jacob EA, Sessler DI, *et al.* Spinal mechanisms contribute to analgesia produced by epidural sufentanil combined with bupivacaine for postoperative analgesia. *Anesth Analg* 2003; **97**: 1446–51

Joshi GP, Bonnet F, Shah R, *et al.* A systematic review of randomized trials evaluating regional techniques for postthoracotomy analgesia. *Anesth Analg* 2008; **107**: 1026–40

Kaluza GL, Joseph J, Lee JR, *et al.* Catastrophic outcomes of noncardiac surgery soon after coronary stenting. *J Am Coll Cardiol* 2000; **35**: 1288–94

Karzai W, Schwarzkopf K. Hypoxemia during one-lung ventilation. Prediction, prevention and treatment. *Anesthesiology* 2009; **110**: 1402–11

Katsuno M. Usefulness of on-line spirometry in bronchospasm occurring during anaesthesia. *Masui* 1997; **46**: 1599–601

Kempen PM. Complete analgesia during pleurodesis under thoracic epidural anesthesia. *Am Surg* 1998; **64**: 755–7

Kenfield SA, Wei EK, Stampfer MJ, Rosner BA, Colditz GA. Comparison of aspects of smoking among the four histological types of lung cancer. *Tob Control* 2008; **17**: 198–204

Kesten S. Pulmonary rehabilitation and surgery for end-stage lung disease. *Clin Chest Med* 1997; **18**: 173–81

Ko R, Kruger M, McRae K. Impact of inspired gas mixtures on oxygenation and surgical conditions during one lung ventilation. *Can J Anaesth* 2003; **50**: A13

Kurz A, Sessler D, Lenhardt R. Perioperative normothermia to reduce the incidence of surgical-wound infection and shorten hospitalization. Study of Wound Infection and Temperature Group. *N Engl J Med* 1996; **334**: 1209–15

Lau KK, Martin-Ucar AE, Nakas A, Waller DA. Lung cancer surgery in the breathless patient—the benefits of avoiding the gold standard. *Eur J Cardiothorac Surg* 2010; **38**: 6–13

Lee P, Colt HG. A spray catheter technique for pleural anesthesia: a novel method for pain control before talc poudrage. *Anesth Analg* 2007; **104**: 198–200

Lee TH, Marcantonio ER, Mangione CM, *et al.* Derivation and prospective validation of a simple index for prediction of cardiac risk of major Noncardiac surgery. *Circulation* 1999; **100**: 1043–9

Lefebvre A, Lorut C, Alifano M, *et al.* Noninvasive ventilation for acute respiratory failure after lung resection: an observational study. *Intensive Care Med* 2009; **35**: 663–70

Leibowitz DW, Smith CR, Michler RE, *et al.* Incidence of pulmonary vein complications after lung transplantation: a prospective transesophageal echocardiographic study. *J Am Coll Cardiol* 1994; **24**: 671–5

Lenhardt R, Marker E, Goll V, *et al.* Mild intraoperative hypothermia prolongs post anesthetic recovery. *Anesthesiology* 1997; **87**: 1318–23

Leshnower BG, Miller DL, Fernandez FG, *et al.* Video-assisted thoracoscopic surgery segmentectomy: a safe and effective procedure. *Ann Thorac Surg* 2010; **89**: 1571–6

Levin KH. Paraneoplastic neuromuscular syndromes. *Neurol Clinics* 1997; **15**: 597–614

Levine AI, Coetzee JF, Coetzee A. Arterial oxygenation and one-lung anesthesia. *Curr Opin Anaesthesiol* 2008; **21**: 28–36

Licker M, de Perrot M, Spiliopoulos A, *et al.* Risk factors for acute lung injury after thoracic surgery for lung cancer. *Anesth Analg* 2003; **97**: 1558–65

Lim E, Baldwin D, Beckles M, *et al.* Guidelines on the radical management of patients with lung cancer. *Thorax* 2010; **65**: iii1–27

Linden PA, Bueno R, Colson YL, *et al.* Lung resection in patients with preoperative FEV1 < 35% predicted. *Chest* 2005; **127**: 1984–90

Lobato EB, Risley WP 3rd, Stoltzfus DP. Intraoperative management of distal tracheal rupture with selective bronchial intubation. *J Clin Anesth* 1997; **9**: 155–8

Loi, M, Noppen M. Bronchopleural fistulas. *Chest* 2005; **128**: 3955–65

Luna CM, Legarreta G, Esteva H, Laffaire E, Jolly EC. Effect of tracheal dilatation and rupture on mechanical ventilation using a low-pressure cuff tube. *Chest* 1993; **104**: 639–40

MacNee W. Pathophysiology of cor pulmonale in chronic obstructive pulmonary disease. Part One. *Am J Resp Crit Care Med* 1994; **150**: 833–52

Manecke GR. Anesthesia for pulmonary endarterectomy. *Semin Thorac Cardiovasc Surg* 2006; **16**: 236–42

Marret E, Miled F, Bazelly B, *et al.* Risk and protective factors for major complications after pneumonectomy for lung cancer. *Interact Cardiovasc Thorac Surg* 2010; **10**: 936–9

Marseu K, Slinger P, de Perrot M, *et al.* Dynamic hyperinflation and cardiac arrest during one-lung ventilation: a case report. *Can J Anaesth* 2011; **58**: 396–400

Mason DP, Subramanian S, Nowicki ER, *et al.* Impact of smoking cessation before resection of lung cancer: a Society of Thoracic Surgeons General Thoracic Database study. *Ann Thorac Surg* 2009; **88**: 362–70

Mathes DD. Bleomycin and hyperoxia exposure in the operating room. *Anesth Analg* 1995; **81**: 624–9

McFalls EO, Ward HB, Moritz TE. Coronary-artery revascularization before elective major vascular surgery. *N Engl J Med* 2007; **351**: 2795–804

McKenna RJ Jr, Ali MK, Ewer MS, Frazier OH. Pleural and pericardial effusions in cancer patients. *Curr Prob Cancer* 1985; **9**: 1–44

McKenna RJ Jr, Benditt JO, DeCamp M, *et al.* Safety and efficacy of median sternotomy versus video-assisted thoracic surgery for lung volume reduction surgery. *J Thorac Cardiovasc Surg* 2004; **127**: 1350–60

McKenna RJ Jr, Fischel RJ, Brenner M, Gelb AF. Combined operations for lung volume reduction surgery and lung cancer. *Chest* 1996; **110**: 885–8

McRae K. Anesthesia for airway surgery. *Anesthesiol Clin North America* 2001; **19**: 497–541

Michel-Cherqui M, Brusset A, Liu N, *et al.* Intraoperative transesophageal echocardiographic assessment of vascular anastomoses in lung transplantation: A report on 18 cases. *Chest* 1997; **111**: 1229–35

Moser C, Opitz I, Zhai W, *et al.* Autologous fibrin sealant reduces the incidence of prolonged air leak and duration of chest tube drainage after lung volume reduction surgery: a prospective randomized blinded study. *J Thorac Cardiovasc Surg* 2008; **136**: 843–9

Myles PS, Madder H, Morgan EB. Intraoperative cardiac arrest after unrecognized dynamic hyperinflation. *Br J Anaesth* 1995; **74**: 340–2

Nakagawa M, Tanaka H, Tsukuma H, Kishi Y. Relationship between the duration of the preoperative smoke-free period and the incidence of postoperative pulmonary complications after pulmonary surgery. *Chest* 2001; **120**: 705–11

Narayanaswamy M, McRae K, Slinger P, *et al.* Choosing a lung isolation device for thoracic surgery: a randomized trial of three bronchial blockers versus double-lumen tubes. *Anesth Analg* 2009; **108**: 1097–10

Natalini G, Fassini P, Seramondi V, *et al.* Remifentanil vs fentanyl during interventional rigid bronchoscopy under general anaesthesia and spontaneous assisted ventilation. *Eur J Anaesthesiol* 1999; **16**: 605–9

NICE. *Perioperative Hypothermia (Inadvertent): The Management of Inadvertent Perioperative Hypothermia in Adults*. NICE Clinical Guideline 65. London: National Institute for Health and Clinical Excellence, 2008. Available from: www.nice.org.uk/CG065

NICE. *Cardio-Q Oesophageal Doppler Monitor*. NICE Medical Technology Guidance 3. London: National Institute for Health and Clinical Excellence, 2011. Available from: www.nice.org.uk/guidance/MTG3

Niewoehner DE, Erbland ML, Deupree RH, *et al.* Effect of systemic glucocorticoids on exacerbations of chronic obstructive pulmonary disease. *N Engl J Med* 1999; **340**: 1948–53

Obuchi T, Hamanaka W, Yoshida Y, *et al.* Clinical outcome after pulmonary resection for lung cancer patients on hemodialysis. *Ann Thorac Surg* 2009; **88**: 1745–8

Ohno Y, Koyama H, Nogami M, *et al.* Postoperative lung function in lung cancer patients: comparative analysis of predictive capability of MRI, CT, and SPECT. *AJR Am J Roentgenol* 207; **189**: 400–8

Oka T, Ozawa Y, Ohkubo Y. Thoracic epidural bupivacaine attenuates supraventricular tachyarrhythmias after pulmonary resection. *Anesth Analg* 2001; **93**: 253–9

Olsen GN, Bolton JW, Weiman DS, Hornung CA. Stair climbing as an exercise test to predict the postoperative complications of lung resection. *Chest* 1991; **99**: 587–90

Oren JB, Estenne M, Arcasoy S, *et al.* International guidelines for the selection of lung transplant candidates: 2006 update—a consensus report from the Pulmonary Scientific Council of the International Society for Heart and Lung Transplantation. *J Heart Lung Transplant* 2006; **25**: 745–55

Osaki T, Shirakusa T, Kodate M, Nakanishi R, Mitsudomi T, Ueda H. Surgical treatment of lung cancer in the octogenarian. *Ann Thorac Surg* 1994; **57**: 188–92

Pardos PC, Garutti I, Piñeiro P, Olmedilla L, de la Gala F. Effects of ventilatory mode during one-lung ventilation on intraoperative and postoperative arterial oxygenation in thoracic surgery. *J Cardiothorac Vasc Anesth* 2009; **23**: 770–4

Park B, Zhang H, Rusch VW, Amar D. Video-assisted thoracic surgery does not reduce the incidence of postoperative atrial fibrillation after pulmonary lobectomy. *J Thorac Cardiovasc Surg* 2007; **133**: 775–9

Passman RS, Gingold DS, Amar D, *et al.* Prediction rule for atrial fibrillation after major noncardiac thoracic surgery. *Ann Thorac Surg* 2005; **79**: 1698–703

Patane PS, Sell BA, Mahla ME. Awake fiberoptic endobronchial intubation. *J Cardiothorac Vasc Anesth* 1990; **4**: 229–31

Pauwels RA, Buist AS, Calverley PM, *et al.* Global strategy for the diagnosis, management, and prevention of chronic obstructive pulmonary disease. NHLBI/WHO Global Initiative for Chronic Obstructive Lung Disease (GOLD) Workshop summary. *Am J Respir Crit Care Med* 2001; **163**: 1256–76

Pearce AC, Jones RM. Smoking and anesthesia: preoperative abstinence and perioperative morbidity. *Anesthesiology* 1984; **61**: 576–84

Pedoto A, Amar D. Right heart function in thoracic surgery: role of echocardiography. *Curr Opin Anaesthesiol* 2009; **22**: 44–9

Perttunen K, Kalso E, Heinonen J, Salo J. IV diclofenac in post-thoracotomy pain. *Br J Anaesth* 1991; **68**: 474–80

Peto J, Seidman H, Selikoff IJ. Mesothelioma mortality in asbestos workers: implications for models of carcinogenesis and risk assessment. *Br J Cancer* 1982; **45**: 124–35

Petrella F, Radice D, Borri A, *et al.* The impact of preoperative body mass index on respiratory complications after pneumonectomy for non-small-cell lung cancer. Results from a series of 154 consecutive standard pneumonectomies. *Eur J Cardiothorac Surg* 2001; **39**: 738–44

Pfitzner J, Peacock MJ, Tsirgiotis E, Walkley IH. Lobectomy for cavitating lung abscess with haemoptysis: strategy for protecting the contralateral lung and also the non-involved lobe of the ipsilateral lung. *Br J Anaesth* 2000; **85**: 791–4

Philpott NJ, Woodhead MA, Wilson AG, Millard FJ. Lung abscess: a neglected cause of life threatening haemoptysis. *Thorax* 1993; **48**: 674–5

Pickett AM, Taylor DA, Ackman ML. Prolonged infusion of eptifibatide as bridge therapy between bare-metal stent insertion and cardiovascular surgery: case report and review of the literature. *Pharmacotherapy* 2010; **30**: 127e–33e

Picone A, Coleman JJ 3rd, Mansour KA. Surgical resection of high cervical esophageal carcinoma with malignant tracheoesophageal fistula: a case report. *J Thorac Cardiovasc Surg* 1989; **97**: 153–5

Pinsonneault C, Fortier J, Donati F. Tracheal resection and reconstruction. *Can J Anaesth* 1999; **46**: 439–55

Pölönen P, Ruokonen E, Hippeläinen M, Pöyhönen M, Takala J. A prospective, randomized study of goal-oriented hemodynamic therapy in cardiac surgical patients. *Anesth Analg* 2000; **90**: 1052–9

Pomerantz AH, Derasari MD, Sethi SS, Khan S. Early postpneumonectomy bronchial stump fistula. *Chest* 1988; **93**: 654–7

Popping DM, Elia N, Marret E, Remy C, Tramèr MR. Protective effects of epidural analgesia on pulmonary complications after abdominal and thoracic surgery: a meta-analysis. *Arch Surg* 2008; **143**: 990–9

Poulin V, Vaillancourt R, Somma J, Gagné N, Bussières JS. High frequency ventilation combined with spontaneous breathing during bronchopleural fistula repair: a case report. *Can J Anaesth* 2009; **56**: 52–6

Prabhu MR, Smith JH. Use of the Arndt wire-guided endobronchial blocker. *Anesthesiology* 2002; **97**: 1325

Prakash N, McLeod T, Gao Smith F. The effects of remifentanil on haemodynamic stability during rigid bronchoscopy. *Anaesthesia* 2001; **56**: 576–80

Pulmonary Artery Catheter Consensus Conference. Consensus statement. *Crit Care Med* 1997; **25**: 910–25

Ramnath N, Demmy TL, Antun A, *et al.* Pneumonectomy for bronchogenic carcinoma: analysis of factors predicting survival. *Ann Thorac Surg* 2007; **83**: 1831–6

Raviv S, Hawkins KA, DeCamp MM Jr, Kalhan R. Lung cancer in chronic obstructive pulmonary disease: enhancing surgical options and outcomes. *Am J Resp Crit Care Med* 2011; **183**: 1138–46

Raz DJ, He B, Rosell R, Jablons DM. Bronchoalveolar carcinoma: a review. *Clin Lung Cancer* 2006; **7**: 313–22

Reid CW, Slinger PD, Lenis S. A comparison of the effects of propofol-alfentanil versus isoflurane anesthesia on arterial oxygenation during one-lung ventilation. *J Cardiothorac Vasc Anesth* 1996; **10**: 860–3

Ritchie AJ, Bowe P, Gibbons JR. Prophylactic digitalization for thoracotomy: a reassessment. *Ann Thorac Surg* 1990; **50**: 86–8

Robertshaw FL. Low resistance double-lumen endobronchial tubes. *Br J Anaesth* 1962; **34**: 576–9

Roscoe A, Klein A. Pulmonary endarterectomy. *Curr Opin Anaesthesiol* 2008; **21**: 16–20

Roscoe A. Lung transplantation. In: Slinger PD, ed. *Principles and Practice of Anesthesia for Thoracic Surgery*. New York: Springer, 2011; 523–36

Roselli EE, Murthy SC, Rice TW, *et al.* Atrial fibrillation complicating lung cancer resection. *J Thorac Cardiovasc Surg* 2005; **130**: 438–44.

Ross N, McCormick B. Thoracic surgery. In: Allman KG, Wilson IH, eds. *Oxford Handbook of Anaesthesia*. Oxford: Oxford University Press, 2011; 365–402

Russell WJ. Intermittent positive airway pressure to manage hypoxia during one-lung anaesthesia. *Anaesth Intensive Care* 2009; **37**: 432–4

Saito T, Naruke T, Carney E, Yokokawa Y, Hiraga K, Carlsson C. New double intrabronchial tube (Naruke tube) for tracheostomised patients. *Anesthesiology* 1998; **89**: 1038–9

Sakuraba M, Masuda K, Hebisawa A, Sagara Y, Komatsu H. Thoracoscopic pleural biopsy for tuberculous pleurisy under local anesthesia. *Ann Thorac Cardiovasc Surg* 2006; **12**: 245–8

Salazar E, Gomez A, Ramasco F. Awake intubation with double-lumen tube in a patient with anticipated difficult airway. *Eur J Anaesthesiol* 2010; **27**: 273

Salluh JI, Martins GAR, Santino MS, *et al.* Independent lung ventilation and alveolar recruitment in tracheostomised patient with unilateral ARDS. *Internet J Emerg Intensive Care Med* 2005; **8**: 2

Sandberg WS. Endobronchial blocker dislodgement leading to pulseless electrical activity. *Anesth Analg* 2005; **100**: 1728–30

Saran T, Perkins GD, Jav MA, *et al.* Does the prophylactic administration of magnesium sulphate to patients undergoing thoracotomy prevent postoperative supraventricular arrhythmias? A randomised controlled trial. *Br J Anaesth* 2011; **106**: 785–91

Saravanan P, Marnane C, Morris EA. Extubation of the surgically resected airway—a role for remifentanil and propofol infusions. *Can J Anaesth* 2006; **53**: 507–11

Savage C, McQuitty C, Wang D, Zwischenberger JB. Postthoracotomy pain management. *Chest Surg Clin N Am* 2002; **12**: 251–63

Schulte-Sasse U, Hess W, Tarnow J. Pulmonary vascular responses to nitrous oxide in patients with normal and high pulmonary vascular resistance. *Anesthesiology* 1982; **57**: 9–13

Seder CW, Hanna K, Lucia V, *et al.* The safe transition from open to thoracoscopic lobectomy: a 5-year experience. *Ann Thorac Surg* 2009; **88**: 225–6

Sekine Y, Kesler KA, Behnia M, *et al.* COPD may increase the incidence of refractory supraventricular arrhythmias following pulmonary resection for non-small cell lung cancer. *Chest* 2001; **120**: 1783–90

Shammash JB, Trost JC, Gold JM, *et al.* Perioperative beta-blocker withdrawal and mortality in vascular surgical patients. *Am Heart J* 2001; **141**: 148–53

Shannon VR. Role of pulmonary rehabilitation in the management of patients with lung cancer. *Curr Opin Pulm Med* 2010; **16**: 334–9

Sharma K, Varshney M, Kumar R. Tracheal tube fixation: the effect on depth of insertion of midline fixation compared to the angle of the mouth. *Anaesthesia* 2009; **64**: 383

Shimizu J, Ishida Y, Hirano Y, *et al.* Cardiac herniation following intrapericardial pneumonectomy with partial pericardiectomy for advanced lung cancer. *Ann Thorac Cardiovasc Surg* 2003; **9**: 68–72

Silber S, Albertsson P, Avilés FF, *et al.* Guidelines for percutaneous coronary interventions. The Task Force for Percutaneous Coronary Interventions of the European Society of Cardiology. *Eur Heart J* 2005; **26**: 804–47

Silva-Costa-Gomes T, Gallart L, Vallès J, Trillo L, Minguella J, Puig MM. Low- vs high-dose almitrine combined with nitric oxide to prevent hypoxia during open-chest one-lung ventilation. *Br J Anaesth* 2005; **95**: 410–6

Singh SJ, Morgan MD, Hardman AE, Rowe C, Bardsley PA. Comparison of oxygen uptake during a conventional treadmill test and the shuttle walking test in chronic airflow limitation. *Eur Resp J* 1994; **7**: 2016–20

Sivalingham P, Tio R. Tension pneumothorax, pneumomediastinum, pneumoperitoneum, and subcutaneous emphysema in a 15-year-old Chinese girl after a double-lumen tube intubation and one-lung ventilation. *J Cardiothorac Vasc Anesth* 1999; **13**: 312–5

Slinger PD. Lung isolation in thoracic anesthesia, state of the art. *Can J Anaesth* 2001; **48**: R13–15

Slinger PD. Postpneumonectomy pulmonary edema: good news, bad news. *Anesthesiology* 2006a; **105**: 2–5

Slinger P. Pro: low tidal volume is indicated during one-lung ventilation. *Anesth Analg* 2006b; **103**: 268–70

Slinger P. The clinical significance of right-sided double-lumen tubes. *Can J Anaesth* 2010; **57**: 293–300

Slinger PD, Campos JH. Anesthesia for thoracic surgery. In: Miller RD, Eriksson LI, Fleisher LA, Wiener-Kronis JP, Young LJ, eds. *Miller's Anesthesia*. Philadelphia, PA: Churchill Livingstone, 2009; 1819–87

Slinger PD, Hickey DR. The interaction between applied PEEP and auto-PEEP during one-lung ventilation. *J Cardiothorac Vasc Anesth* 1998; **12**: 133–6

Slinger PD, Johnston M. Preoperative assessment: an anesthesiologist's perspective. *Thorac Surg Clin* 2005; **15**: 11–25

Slinger P, Karsli C. Management of the patient with a large anterior mediastinal mass: recurring myths. *Curr Opin Anaesthesiol* 2007; **20**: 1–3

Smith PW, Wang H, Gazoni LM, *et al.* Obesity does not increase complications after anatomic resection for non-small cell lung cancer. *Ann Thorac Surg* 2007; **84**: 1098–105

Soto RG, Oleszak SO. Resection of the Arndt bronchial blocker during stapler resection of the left lower lobe. *J Cardiothorac Vasc Anesth* 2006; **20**: 131–2

Spaggiari L, Scanagatta P. Surgery of non-small cell lung cancer in the elderly. *Curr Opin Oncol* 2007; **19**: 84–91

Subramanian J, Govindan R. Lung cancer in never smokers: a review. *J Clin Oncol* 2007; **25**: 561–70

Sullivan MT, Neff WB. A modified Sanders ventilating system for rigid-wall bronchoscopy. *Anesthesiology* 1979; **50**: 473–4

Sustic A, Miletić D, Protić A, Ivancić A, Cicvarić T. Can ultrasound be useful for predicting the size of a left double-lumen bronchial tube? Tracheal width as measured by ultrasonography versus computed tomography. *J Clin Anesth* 2008; **20**: 247–52

Takai E, Yano T, Iguchi H, *et al.* Tumor-induced hypercalcaemia and parathyroid hormone-related protein in lung carcinoma. *Cancer* 1996; **78**: 1384–7

Talbot TR. Diabetes mellitus and cardiothoracic surgical site infections. *Am J Infect Control* 2005; **33**: 353–9

Taylor R, Massey S, Stuart-Smith K. Postoperative analgesia in video-assisted thoracoscopy: the role of intercostal blockade. *J Cardiothorac Vasc Anesth* 2004; **18**: 317–21

Tempe DK, Arya R, Dubey S, *et al.* Mediastinal mass resection: femorofemoral cardiopulmonary bypass before induction of anesthesia in the management of airway obstruction. *J Cardiothorac Vasc Anesth* 2001; **15**: 233–6

Thistlethwaite PA, Madani MM, Kemp AD, *et al.* Venovenous extracorporeal life support after pulmonary endarterectomy: indications, techniques and outcomes. *Ann Thorac Surg* 2006; 2006; **82**: 2139–46

Tietjen CS, Simon BA, Helfaer MA. Permissive hypercapnia with high-frequency oscillatory ventilation and one-lung isolation for intraoperative management of lung resection in a patient with multiple bronchopleural fistulae. *J Clin Anesth* 1997; **9**: 69–73

Titulaer MJ, Wirtz PW, Kuks JB, *et al.* The Lambert-Eaton myasthenic syndrome 1988-2008: a clinical picture in 97 patients. *J Neuroimmunol* 2008; **201**: 153–8

Tobias JD. Variations on one-lung ventilation. *J Clin Anesth* 2001; **13**: 35–9

Travis WD, Travis LB, Devesa SS. Lung cancer. *Cancer* 1995; **75**: 191–202

Treasure T, Lang-Lazdunski L, Waller D, *et al.* 2011. Extra-pleural pneumonectomy versus no extra-pleural pneumonectomy for patients with malignant pleural mesothelioma: clinical outcomes of the Mesothelioma and Radical Surgery (MARS) randomised feasibility study. *Lancet Oncol* **12**: 763–72

Tugrul M, Camci E, Karadeniz H, *et al.* Comparison of volume controlled with pressure controlled ventilation during one-lung anaesthesia. *Br J Anaesth* 1997; **79**: 306–10

Tusman G, Böhm SH, Sipmann FS, Maisch S. Lung recruitment improves the efficiency of ventilation and gas exchange during one-lung ventilation anesthesia. *Anesth Analg* 2004; **98**: 160–9

Unzueta MC, Casas JI, Moral MV. Pressure-controlled versus volume-controlled ventilation during one-lung ventilation for thoracic surgery. *Anesth Analg* 2007; **104**: 1029–33

Urschel M, Antkowiak JG, Takita H. Is there a role for surgery in small cell lung cancer?. *J R Soc Med* 1997; **90**: 387–90

Vaporciyan AA, Merriman KW, Ece F, *et al.* Incidence of major pulmonary morbidity after pneumonectomy: association with timing of smoking cessation. *Ann Thorac Surg* 2002; **73**: 420–5

Venuta F, Sciomer S, Andreetti C, *et al.* Long-term Doppler echocardiographic evaluation of the right heart after major lung resections. *Eur J Cardiothorac Surg* 2007; **32**: 787–90

Wagner DL, Gammage GW, Wong ML. Tracheal rupture following the insertion of a double-lumen endotracheal tube. *Anesthesiology* 1985; **63**: 698–700

Walker-Renard PB, Vaughan LM, Sahn SA. Chemical pleurodesis for malignant pleural effusions. *Ann Intern Med* 1994; **120**: 56–64

Wang JY, Russell GN, Page RD, *et al.* A comparison of the effects of desflurane and isoflurane on arterial oxygenation during one-lung ventilation. *Anaesthesia* 2000; **55**: 167–73

Warner DO. Preventing postoperative pulmonary complications: the role of the anesthesiologist. *Anesthesiology* 2000; **92**: 1467–72

Watanabe Y, Murakami S, Iwa T, Murakami S. The clinical value of high-frequency jet ventilation in major airway reconstructive surgery. *Scand J Thorac Cardiovasc Surg* 1988; **22**: 227–33

Weng W, DeCrosta DJ, Zhang H. Tension pneumothorax during one-lung ventilation: a case report. *J Clin Anesth* 2002; **14**: 529–31

White GM. A new double-lumen tube. *Br J Anaesth* 1960; **32**: 232–4

Wiebalck A, Brodner G, Van Aken H. The effects of adding sufentanil to bupivacaine for postoperative patient-controlled epidural analgesia. *Anesth Analg* 1997; **85**: 124–9

Williams A, Kay J. Thoracic epidural anesthesia for thoracoscopy, rib resection, and thoracotomy in a patient with a bronchopleural fistula Postpneumonectomy. *Anesthesiology* 2000; **92**: 1482–4

Wilson WC, Kapelanski DP,Benumof JL, *et al.* Inhaled nitric oxide (40ppm) during one-lung ventilation, in the lateral decubitus position, does not decrease pulmonary vascular resistance or improve oxygenation in normal patients. *J Cardiothorac Vasc Anesth* 1997; **22**: 172–6

Win T, Jackson A, Groves AM, *et al.* Comparison of shuttle walk with measured peak oxygen consumption in patients with operable lung cancer. *Thorax* 2006b; **61**: 57–60

Win T, Tasker AD, Groves AM, *et al.* Ventilation-perfusion scintigraphy to predict postoperative pulmonary function in lung cancer patients undergoing pneumonectomy. *AJR Am J Roentgenol* 2006a; **187**: 1260–5

Wu MT, Chang JM, Chiang AA, *et al.* Use of quantitative CT to predict post-operative lung function in patients with lung cancer. *Radiology* 1994; **191**: 257–62

Xue Y, Han Y, Li T, *et al.* Pulmonary alveolar proteinosis as a terminal complication in a case of myelodysplastic syndrome with idic(20q-). *Acta Haematol* 2010; **123**: 55–8

Yasufuku K. Current applications of endobronchial ultrasound. *Expert Rev Respir Med* 2010; **4**: 491–8

Yasumoto M, Higa K, Nitahara K, Shono S, Hamada T. Optimal depth of insertion of left-sided double-lumen endobronchial tubes cannot be predicted from body height in below average-sized adult patients. *Eur J Anaesthesiol* 2006; **23**: 42–4

Yuceyar L, Kaynak K, Cantürk E, Aykaç B. Bronchial rupture with a left-sided polyvinylchloride double-lumen tube. *Acta Anaesthesiol Scand* 2003; **47**: 622–5

CHAPTER 58

Anaesthesia for vascular surgery

Jonathan P. Thompson

Introduction

The last two decades have seen changes in many aspects of vascular surgery, largely because of advances in radiological and cardiological practice. Examples include improvements in the treatment of myocardial infarction (MI) and coronary artery disease, and the development of endovascular aortic surgery and lower limb angioplasty; such progress is likely to continue (EVAR Trial Participants 2005a; Goodney et al. 2009).

The principles of preoperative preparation and perioperative care for vascular surgical patients are similar to any other major procedure. However, vascular surgical patients are at higher risk than other surgical patients from cardiovascular morbidity and death (Fleisher et al. 2007). There is a high prevalence of other coexisting medical disease, in particular ischaemic heart disease, hypertension, heart failure, diabetes mellitus, pulmonary disease, and renal disease (Fleisher et al. 2009; Poldermans et al. 2009). In addition to these risk factors for perioperative cardiac events, other important preoperative factors in patients undergoing major vascular surgery are advanced age and obesity (Back et al. 2004; Beck et al. 2009; Kheterpal et al. 2009). Only some of these are reversible but as the risks are high, it is vital that all aspects are assessed preoperatively and appropriate steps taken in order to optimize perioperative outcome. This requires meticulous attention to detail (especially to fluid management, maintenance of normothermia, and provision of effective analgesia), teamwork, and communication with surgical or radiological colleagues.

Preoperative risk assessment, investigations, and management

Previous recommendations on preoperative stress testing, referral for possible coronary revascularization, and management of medications (in particular β-blockade) have changed: it is now appreciated that non-invasive cardiac tests are relatively poor at predicting perioperative risk, and that the benefits of preoperative coronary revascularization are limited (McFalls et al. 2004; Fleisher et al. 2007, 2009). Testing in patients presenting for major vascular surgery should be reserved for those with:

- active symptoms of coronary artery disease
- known coronary artery disease and poor functional exercise capacity
- more than three clinical risk factors for cardiovascular disease (age > 70 years, a history of current or previous angina, MI, stroke, or heart failure) and poor or unknown functional capacity

It is important to remember that testing *should only be performed if it would change management* (i.e. the patient is a candidate for and would benefit from coronary revascularization) (Fleisher et al. 2007; Poldermans et al. 2009).

Functional exercise capacity relates to poor short- and long-term outcomes after major surgery but may be difficult to assess in vascular patients if exercise tolerance is limited by peripheral vascular insufficiency, respiratory disease, or other disease. Simple clinical assessment, graded walking tests (Struthers et al. 2008; Ross et al. 2010), or cardiopulmonary exercise (CPX) testing may be used; the latter allows quantification of a patient's oxygen uptake and utilization. Data have shown that CPX testing is reasonably reliable (Kothmann et al. 2009a), can be used to stratify patients according to perioperative risk, and correlates with outcome in patients undergoing vascular surgery (Carlisle and Swart 2007; Snowden et al. 2010), and it is recommended that CPX be used where facilities are available. Though it is intuitive that improved physical fitness is associated with improved perioperative outcome, most of the data showing that exercise training improves cardiopulmonary performance comes from studies of athletes: this may not be relevant to the vascular surgical population. However, a recent report describes improvements in variables measured by CPX testing in patients with abdominal aortic aneurysm (AAA) who underwent a supervised, tailored exercise regimen before surgery (Kothmann et al. 2009b), though this is not without risk in patients with cardiovascular disease. Further data on the role of CPX testing and the effects of interventions to improve physical fitness on postoperative outcome are required.

Preoperative risk assessment is best performed in a dedicated preoperative assessment clinic at least 2 weeks before surgery (Vascular Society of Great Britain and Ireland 2009; Wijeysundera et al. 2009). The clinic environment provides the best scenario for assessment and discussion of risks and allows the opportunity for general advice regarding nutrition, graded exercise, and modification of alcohol intake. The clinic should be led by a consultant anaesthetist experienced in anaesthesia for vascular surgery. There must be significant cooperation from both vascular surgeons and anaesthetists, with agreed pathways for investigations and referral. It is also helpful to identify consultant colleagues in other specialties (cardiology, respiratory, and renal medicine) to act as a point of contact for referrals. Referral to a cardiologist may be required to determine whether or not cardiac disease is optimally treated or whether coronary revascularization is indicated before AAA repair (Moll et al. 2011). Patients should be advised and helped to stop smoking, and prescribed antiplatelet drugs (if not contraindicated) and statins to reduce their long-term cardiovascular risks. β-blockade may be indicated in selected patients (Fleisher et al. 2007).

The likely outcomes of preoperative assessment are deferral for further investigations or other specialist opinion, a recommendation to proceed to surgery at a variable interval, to recommend a less invasive surgical procedure, or to advise against vascular surgery completely. It is also important to appreciate that some patients may not benefit from vascular interventions. The EVAR-2 study and other registries demonstrated no benefit from endovascular AAA repair in those with a limited life expectancy because of coexisting disease (Buth et al. 2002; EVAR Trial Participants 2005b) and therefore risk assessment must be realistic. Furthermore, the relative risks of surgery or some coexisting medical conditions (e.g. recent MI or coronary intervention) will change over time. Therefore, deferral for review (e.g. to reassess AAA size over several months and reconsider surgery if it increases significantly, or to allow an appropriate interval after coronary revascularization) can be the most appropriate course of action. An important part of preoperative assessment is advising against surgery where the risks outweigh the potential benefits. In practice, the highest-risk patients often decline surgery themselves when the estimated risks and benefits are explained.

Aortic surgery

Abdominal aortic aneurysm

An aortic aneurysm is defined as a permanent dilatation (of >3 cm) anywhere within the aorta (ascending, arch, thoracic, or abdominal sections). The prevalence of AAA in the population is estimated at 1.5–9.9% (Lederle et al. 1997; Vardulaki et al. 1999; Multicentre Aneurysm Screening Study Group 2002). The incidence is lower in women, though the risk of rupture is higher (UK Small Aneurysm Trial Participants 1998), and lower in patients of Asian or black ethnic origin (Metcalfe et al. 2011). Risk factors for the development of AAA include a positive family history, older age, and tobacco use, with the highest incidence in men aged more than 65 years. There is a weaker association with hypertension, though poorly controlled blood pressure may predispose to AAA rupture (UK Small Aneurysm Trial Participants 1998). Similarly, diabetes is associated with a decreased prevalence and expansion rate of AAA but an increased risk of rupture (Shantikumar et al. 2010; Metcalfe et al. 2011). Recent data have suggested that the prevalence of AAA may be decreasing, perhaps related to a reduction in cigarette smoking, better treatment of hypertension, and an increasing use of statin therapy.

Pathophysiology

Several factors are associated with aneurysm formation and development. There is a reduction in the number and quality of collagen and elastic fibres within the aneurysmal segment of the aorta, increased activity of elastase and protease enzymes, and other local inflammatory changes including plasminogen activation and thrombus formation. These combine to reduce the aortic wall strength and lead to progressive expansion over time (Sakalihasan et al. 2005). Inflammatory aneurysms comprise 3–10% of all AAAs and are characterized by a thickened aneurysm wall with marked peri-aneurysmal or retroperitoneal fibrosis and dense adhesions to adjacent organs. Many patients are asymptomatic but may present with a palpable pulsatile abdominal mass; symptoms of distal embolization; back, loin, or abdominal pain; or cardiovascular collapse if rupture has occurred.

Natural progression

The risk of rupture increases with aneurysm size, continued cigarette smoking, poorly controlled hypertension, a family history of AAA, and female sex (Fig. 58.1) (Brewster et al. 2003). The overall mortality from ruptured AAA is more than 80% (Holt et al. 2007). Many patients die before surgery can be performed and operative mortality is 37–45% (Bown et al. 2002; Lederle et al. 2002). Hence there have been initiatives to detect asymptomatic AAA in the population and intervene before rupture is likely. Large studies in the United Kingdom and the United States have shown that there is no long-term benefit in performing elective surgery unless the AAA diameter exceeds 5.5 cm (UK Small Aneurysm Trial Participants 1998; Lederle 2002). Currently, population screening has been introduced to detect and offer surgery to patients with asymptomatic AAA greater than 5.5 cm diameter and to allow smaller AAAs to be kept under surveillance. A meta-analysis of four large studies including 127 891 men and 9342 women found that screening is associated with a reduction in both AAA rupture and aneurysm-related mortality in men aged more than 65 years, but not in women (Cosford et al. 2007). The long-term benefits of screening and intervention for men aged 65–74 years have been confirmed (Thompson et al. 2012).

The current UK National Health Service AAA screening programme is targeted at men aged more than 65 years and accepts self-referrals from older patients. Males with an asymptomatic aneurysm of greater than 5.5 cm diameter or any symptomatic AAA should be referred rapidly for surgery. Data are limited but it has been recommended that the threshold for female patients should be slightly lower, and urgent referral for possible intervention considered at

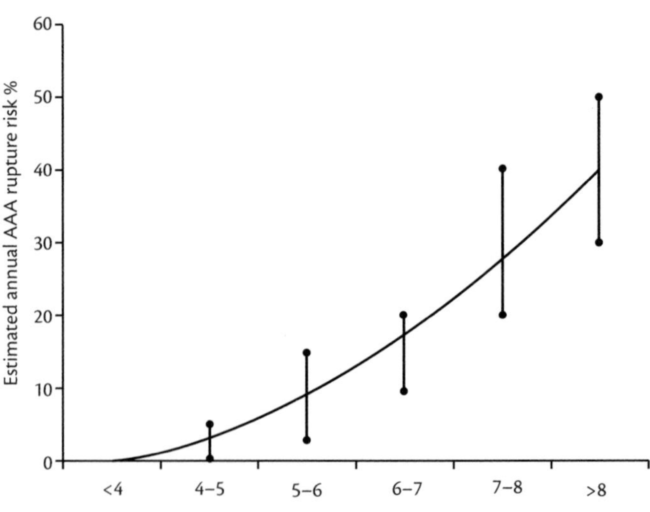

Figure 58.1 Annual risk of rupture according to abdominal aortic aneurysm (AAA) diameter. The error bars represent the mean range of mean values for the annual risk of rupture in published series, connected by a line indicating the polynomial trend of these values.

Adapted with permission from Al-Hashimi M, and Thompson J, Anaesthesia for elective open AAA repair. *Current Education in Anaesthesia & Critical Care*, 2013, Volume 13, Issue 6, pp. 208–212, by permission of the British Journal of Anaesthesia.

an aneurysm diameter of 5.2 cm (Moll et al. 2011). Perioperative mortality after elective AAA repair is approximately 5–8% though with the introduction of a quality improvement programme in the United Kingdom, mortality has reduced to 4.3% after open AAA repair (Vascular Society of Great Britain and Ireland 2010, 2012). Recent data have clearly shown that morbidity and mortality are reduced in larger units with higher caseloads (Holt et al. 2007) and it is recommended in the United Kingdom and the United States that services are concentrated in fewer centres with a higher caseload (Chaikof et al. 2009; Metcalfe et al. 2011).

Elective AAA repair is indicated for asymptomatic AAAs greater than 5.5 cm diameter in men and 5.2 cm diameter in women, providing that the patient is judged fit for intervention and that medical conditions have been optimized. In patients with aneurysm-related symptoms (back or abdominal pain, embolic events), the risk of rupture is thought to be higher so intervention on the next available operating list is advocated (Chaikof et al. 2009; Moll et al. 2011). The two main options for intervention are open surgery and endovascular aneurysm repair (EVAR), and the choice depends on the morphology of the aneurysm (i.e. its site, shape, angulation, involvement of renal arteries, and the size of the iliac arteries), the patient's age and life expectancy, and the presence and severity of coexisting medical conditions. It is important that the patient is fully informed of the risks of either technique and is involved in the decision-making process (Brewster et al. 2003; Moll et al. 2011). Though EVAR is increasingly becoming the preferred technique (Metcalfe et al. 2011), the aneurysm morphology is unsuitable in a significant proportion of patients and open surgery will be required.

Preoperative assessment

Morbidity and mortality of AAA repair are high (Table 58.1); most patients are elderly and surgery is prolonged with the potential for major haemorrhage and fluid shifts. Cardiovascular complications are the leading cause of early and late mortality after surgery but several other factors are associated with worse outcomes, including open surgery, increased age, respiratory and cerebrovascular disease, renal dysfunction, female sex, increased ASA grade, and diabetes (Brewster et al. 2003; Beck et al. 2004; Moll et al. 2011). Several attempts have been made to produce risk prediction models to inform decision-making before intervention. Of these, the Glasgow Aneurysm score, which includes cardiovascular disease (MI, angina), cerebrovascular disease, and renal disease, is perhaps the most well known but its predictive value is limited, particularly in the era of endovascular surgery (Patterson et al. 2011). The Medicare and Vascular Governance North West models both incorporate many of the established risk factors and have been shown to correlate well with outcome after open or endovascular AAA repair (Grant et al. 2012).

All patients presenting for AAA repair should undergo a formal assessment of cardiac risk before surgery and any coexisting medical conditions should be optimized before elective surgery (Moll et al. 2011; Vascular Society of Great Britain and Ireland 2012) (see Chapter 41). Hypertension and diabetes should be well controlled. All patients should be advised to stop smoking because by doing so the rate of aneurysm expansion and the incidence of cardiovascular, pulmonary, and wound-related complications are reduced (Metcalfe et al. 2011). Patients should be started on antiplatelet drugs (if not contraindicated) and statins to reduce their long-term cardiovascular risks. There is some evidence that statins and angiotensin-converting enzyme (ACE) inhibitors may also reduce the rate of aneurysm growth. Graded moderate exercise may also be helpful (Chaikof et al. 2009; Moll et al. 2011). Poorly controlled heart failure, renal dysfunction, chronic obstructive pulmonary disease (COPD), and anaemia are associated with increased perioperative complications and should be addressed (Brewster et al. 2003; Chaikof et al. 2009). Patients with significant renal dysfunction should be referred to a nephrologist before surgery. Patients with moderate or severe COPD may benefit from admission to hospital for preoperative optimization of respiratory function (Lawrence et al. 2006).

Table 58.1 Postoperative complications after open repair of infrarenal AAA

Respiratory complications (8–18%)	Pneumonia (5%) Respiratory failure Atelectasis Pulmonary thromboembolism
Cardiovascular complications (5–8%)	Myocardial ischaemia Myocardial infarction (1–8%) Dysrhythmias (3%) Congestive heart failure
Cerebrovascular complications (1–5%)	Stroke/transient ischaemic attack (1–2%) Postoperative cognitive dysfunction Carotid insufficiency Confusion/delirium
Renal complications (5–11%)	Acute kidney injury (5–11)% Chronic renal failure (<1%) Renal vascular injury Dialysis (0.5%) Ureteric injury (<1%)
Gastrointestinal complications (5–11%)	Bowel ischaemia (1–2%) Paralytic ileus (up to 11%) Abdominal compartment syndrome Incisional hernia (1–5%)
Neurological complications (<1%)	Spinal cord ischaemia Paraplegia
Surgical complications (5–25%)	Bleeding (primary and secondary) Wound infection (<5%) Wound dehiscence Leg ischaemia (1–4%) Graft thrombosis (<1%) Graft infection (<2%) Aortoenteric fistula (<1%) Incisional hernia Graft infection (<1%) Deep vein thrombosis (5–8%) Amputation (0.1%)

Data from Al-Hashimi M, and Thompson J, Anaesthesia for elective open AAA repair. *Current Education in Anaesthesia & Critical Care*, 2013, Volume 13, Issue 6, pp. 208–212, Oxford University Press.

Open surgery for abdominal aortic aneurysm

Open AAA repair involves sewing a prosthetic graft into the aortic lumen above and below the aneurysm. It can be performed through a transperitoneal (via a transverse or a longitudinal abdominal incision) or a retroperitoneal approach (usually via an incision in the left flank) (Chaikof et al. 2009). The transperitoneal approach provides the most rapid and easiest surgical access but is associated with a more prolonged postoperative ileus. The retroperitoneal approach is usually preferred in patients with a juxtarenal AAA, or a 'hostile' abdomen (previous abdominal surgery, presence of a stoma, inflammatory aneurysm, or horseshoe kidney). Laparoscopic-assisted AAA is reported but not widely practised. In most AAAs the origin is situated below the renal arteries (infrarenal AAA); in juxtarenal AAA the aneurysm begins close to the renal arteries but can often be isolated with a clamp at the neck of the aneurysm and below the renal arteries. However, there is a higher risk that embolization of atheromatous material may be dislodged into the renal arteries and cause renal damage. In a suprarenal or supracoeliac aneurysm, a clamp must be placed above the renal arteries (or coeliac axis) and re-implantation of one or several arteries into the graft may be required. The more proximal the aneurysm, the greater the complexity and duration of surgery and there is a corresponding increase in postoperative complications and mortality.

Once the aorta has been exposed, a cross-clamp is applied above the aneurysm to facilitate the insertion of a straight or bifurcated graft, depending on whether the iliac arteries are involved. If the aneurysm involves or is close to the renal arteries, the proximal clamp may be applied above the renal vessels; this significantly increases the overall morbidity. Cross-clamping of the aorta has a number of physiological effects. The extent of these depend on the level of the clamp in relation to the main branches of the aorta, and are more marked with more proximal (supracoeliac or suprarenal) clamp application. Changes are less marked if an extensive collateral circulation has developed, for example in the presence of aortoiliac occlusive disease. Clamp application leads to a sudden increase in afterload and left ventricular wall tension, with increases in arterial pressure and blood flow proximal to the clamp. Effects on preload are variable. Increased myocardial contractility and oxygen demand increase and are usually met by increased coronary blood flow but myocardial ischaemia, arrhythmias, and left ventricular failure may occur (Gelman 1995). During the period of cross-clamping, distal blood flow is via collateral vessels but is insufficient to meet oxygen demands so renal, mesenteric, pelvic, and lower limb ischaemia occur to a variable degree. Renal vascular resistance increases by up to 30% with decreased renal blood flow and perfusion pressures, related partly to turbulent flow within the aorta. These changes occur even with an infrarenal clamp, and may be worse in the presence of renal artery atherosclerosis. Inflammatory mediators (including reactive oxygen species, cytokines, and neutrophil proteases) and products of anaerobic metabolism accumulate. The extent of this may be reduced by minimizing the duration of cross-clamp application, but an ischaemia-reperfusion type injury with metabolic acidaemia occurs when the cross-clamp is released and these mediators are released into the systemic circulation. Peripheral vascular resistance decreases markedly (by up to 80%), related to myocardial depression and direct effects on the vasculature. Arterial pressure and coronary blood flow decrease, and myocardial ischaemia can occur. The cardiovascular effects of aortic unclamping are often greater in the presence of reduced circulating volume. They usually resolve within a few minutes but can be severe and cause cardiovascular collapse. Other complications of aortic clamping include distal embolization from dislodgement of atherosclerotic plaque within the aorta. Bleeding may occur at any time during the procedure and may be sudden; insidious back-bleeding from lumbar arteries after the aorta is opened is also common. Open AAA repair also has profound effects on respiratory function in the early postoperative period and transient acute kidney injury (AKI) is common. The overall incidence of postoperative complications is 27–40% (Table 58.1).

Anaesthesia for open aortic aneurysm repair

Anaesthesia for AAA repair is challenging because of the profound and widespread pathophysiological effects of the procedure in high-risk patients. The anaesthetist should aim to maintain cardiovascular stability and circulating volume, protect against organ dysfunction, and provide effective pain relief. Maintenance of normothermia, metabolic homeostasis, normal haematocrit blood coagulation, and gas exchange are all required. Some patients will benefit from a period of postoperative artificial ventilation. Probably the most commonly used technique is to provide balanced general anaesthesia with a volatile agent, opioid (fentanyl, remifentanil, morphine), and positive pressure ventilation. A thoracic epidural catheter is usually sited to provide postoperative analgesia. High-dose opioids may also be used. At least two large-bore i.v. cannulae, central venous access, a urinary catheter, and a nasogastric tube are needed. Minimal monitoring includes direct arterial pressure, central venous pressure, core body temperature, continuous ECG with ST-segment analysis, and urine output. Serial measurements of arterial blood gases and haematocrit are useful during surgery. Other monitors of cardiac output (including pulse contour analysis) may be used but there are few data on their use in AAA repair. Oesophageal Doppler readings are unreliable when the aorta is clamped and with the exception of transoesophageal echocardiography, most other cardiac output monitors may respond slowly to cardiovascular changes at aortic clamping and unclamping. All measures should be taken to maintain body temperature, using warmed i.v. fluids, forced air warming devices,,a heated mattress, and warmed humidified inspired gases, and all exposed areas should be covered. Active warming of the lower body distal to the cross-clamp is not encouraged while the clamp is still applied.

Specific measures should be taken to minimize the cardiovascular changes at aortic clamping. Available strategies include deepening of anaesthesia or administration of i.v. opioids, but vasodilator drugs such as glyceryl trinitrate (GTN) are often required, as an infusion from shortly before aortic clamping until before clamp release. Sodium nitroprusside is an alternative that is now used less frequently. Fluids should be administered to maintain circulating volume (or even produce mild hypervolaemia) during the period of clamping. The limitations of central venous pressure as a measure of intravascular volume status are recognized but it is common practice to titrate i.v. fluids to keep the central venous pressure at greater than 15 mm Hg before clamp release and by doing this, subsequent hypotension is reduced (Al-Hashimi and Thompson 2013). Other strategies should be used to prevent and manage cardiovascular changes at unclamping the aorta, including gradual or sequential cross-clamp release, and vasoconstrictor or positive inotropic drugs (e.g. ephedrine, phenylephrine, or metaraminol). Occasionally other drugs (noradrenaline, dobutamine, or adrenaline) may be required. Another important consideration is to avoid producing sympathetic blockade with epidural local anaesthetic until the cross-clamp has been released and it is established that the patient is stable. It is important to maintain mean arterial pressure within the range of autoregulation throughout surgery to ensure perfusion of vital organs and ameliorate organ dysfunction.

Bleeding can be brisk especially when the aortic sac is opened, when anastomoses are tested or when the cross-clamp is released. Continued back-bleeding from lumbar arteries into the aortic sac during graft placement may be insidious but considerable. Occasionally massive blood loss occurs. A rapid infuser device for administration of warmed blood and fluids should be available. A cell saver or other device should be used to re-transfuse washed autologous red blood cells, but homologous red blood cells are usually required. Other blood products such as fresh frozen plasma, platelets, and cryoprecipitate may be needed but are usually reserved until surgical haemostasis has been secured and the cross-clamp removed. Management of coagulopathy and requirements for transfusion should be determined by near-patient testing such as thromboelastography.

Organ protection during aortic surgery

The potential for marked cardiovascular changes during aortic surgery in patients with underlying cardiovascular disease renders several organs at risk of ischaemic damage, especially the kidneys and heart, and to a lesser extent the other abdominal viscera, gut, and the brain. Measures to minimize myocardial ischaemia include maintaining haemoglobin concentration greater than 100 g litre^{-1}, preventing tachycardia, hypotension, and attenuating the responses to aortic clamping and unclamping. ST-segment analysis allows early detection and treatment of ischaemia. Renal function during aortic surgery is harder to monitor and intraoperative urine output is a poor indicator of adequate or impaired renal function. Some degree of AKI is very common after aortic surgery. The causes of renal complications after AAA repair are reduced renal blood flow during aortic clamping, ischaemic–reperfusion injury, imbalance in intrarenal prostaglandins, and increased activity of the renin–angiotensin system (Sear 2005). Renal blood flow decreases by approximately 40% even after infrarenal clamping, with a reduction in renal vascular resistance of 75% (Gamulin et al. 1984). Myoglobin released from ischaemic muscles may also contribute to AKI. In many cases, AKI resolves spontaneously after a few days but renal replacement therapy may be required, and is associated with a worse outcome (Braams et al. 1999). Several drugs have been used to prevent AKI in patients undergoing aortic surgery. Mannitol and dopamine, or its analogue fenoldopam, may increase renal blood flow during cross-clamping; mannitol and acetylcysteine have theoretical scavenging effects on reactive oxygen species and other effects. Furosemide decreases renal tubular oxygen demand. However, none of these has been shown to be very effective and the most important interventions are to maintain extracellular fluid volume and renal perfusion pressure throughout the perioperative period (Sear 2005; Zacharias et al. 2008).

Patients are transferred to a critical care environment after surgery, but the trachea may be extubated at the end of surgery in low-risk patients undergoing uncomplicated surgery, providing they are stable, with normal cardiovascular and respiratory function, are normothermic, and have effective analgesia in place. Postoperative pain management is best provided with effective epidural analgesia via a catheter sited at the dermatome of the upper part of the incision (usually T6–T10). Patient-controlled analgesia with opioids can also be effective though a meta-analysis found epidural techniques provided better analgesia, a lower incidence of cardiorespiratory complications, and allowed earlier mobilization (Nishimori et al. 2006). Mortality, however, was not reduced. Heparin is administered during surgery, and so there is a potential risk of epidural haematoma, especially in the presence of coagulopathy. Five-year survival after successful AAA repair is approximately 75% (Lederle et al. 2012). Most deaths are unrelated to the aneurysm and are caused by cardiovascular disease or cancer.

Aortoiliac occlusive disease

Aortoiliac occlusive disease is a manifestation of generalized atherosclerosis and usually presents with symptoms of intermittent claudication, though disease can be present for many years before symptoms develop. Hence the incidence is hard to determine but population-based studies have found peripheral arterial disease in 4–5% of those aged more than 40 years, the incidence rising with increased age (Fowkes et al. 1991; Selvin and Erlinger 2004). Similar to patients with occlusive vascular disease of the lower limbs, there is a high incidence of diabetes, smoking, hypertension, hyperlipidaemia, coronary artery disease, and cerebrovascular disease, though patients are often younger than those with more peripheral disease. Because exercise capacity is limited by intermittent claudication, significant cardiorespiratory disease may be present without causing symptoms. The term critical limb ischaemia is defined as chronic ischaemic rest pain, ulcers, or gangrene attributable to objectively proved arterial occlusive disease, with symptoms present for more than 2 weeks. The natural history of occlusive arterial disease is that collateral vessels develop over time to supply the lower limbs. Hence critical limb ischaemia is less common in patients with aortoiliac disease compared with more distal disease. However, distal embolization from atherosclerotic plaques can occur. All patients should undergo lifestyle modification (cessation of smoking, weight loss) and cardiovascular risk factors treated with antihypertensive, lipid lowering, and antiplatelet drugs. Specific drugs such as cilostazol or naftidrofuryl may also be used (Norgren et al. 2007). Symptoms improve with graded exercise programmes, but intervention is considered earlier in patients with proximal (aortoiliac) disease compared with arterial occlusive disease in the femoral or distal arteries.

Aortobifemoral bypass

Aortoiliac disease may be treated using endovascular or open surgical techniques, depending on the anatomical site and length and severity of the lesions. The main surgical options are aortobifemoral bypass, or extra-anatomical graft placement including femorofemoral cross-over or axillobifemoral bypass. Aortic, iliac, and aortoiliac endarterectomy are occasionally used but have largely been replaced by endovascular techniques. Aortobifemoral bypass surgery is indicated for aortic occlusive disease or diffuse disease of the aorta and iliac arteries, with 5-year patency rates of 90%, and 5-year survival rates of 80–90%. Isolated or short iliac stenoses or occlusions are treated by percutaneous angioplasty with or without stenting, with patency rates of approximately 70% at 5 years (Norgren et al. 2007).

Aortobifemoral bypass and other open aortic procedures are usually performed through a midline transabdominal approach; iliac procedures may be performed through a lower retroperitoneal approach. The general considerations for preoperative assessment, anaesthesia, and postoperative management are similar to those for patients undergoing aortic aneurysm repair. Procedures involving the aorta are best performed under general anaesthesia with supplementary epidural anaesthesia, both to attenuate stress responses and provide postoperative analgesia. For procedures involving the iliac arteries performed through a retroperitoneal approach, regional anaesthesia alone (using a catheter-based technique) can be used. The cardiovascular and metabolic consequences of aortic cross-clamping are less than during AAA repair because a considerable collateral circulation has usually developed. In addition, the graft is often placed on the aorta rather than the aorta being opened and the graft placed within. Hence the aorta can be often side-clamped (rather than cross-clamped), maintaining distal flow while the graft is attached, and blood flow to the legs is restored sequentially.

Axillobifemoral bypass

Axillobifemoral bypass surgery is an alternative to aortic bypass procedures in patients considered unfit for open abdominal surgery. Long-term outcome is poor (1- and 5-year survival rates are 60% and 40% respectively) and graft patency rates in survivors are low (50–75% at 5 years) so it is only indicated in patients with critical limb ischaemia rather than claudication. It may also be performed in patients with an infected aortic graft. Patients are a particularly high-risk group, with perioperative mortality rates of 20% (Liedenbaum et al. 2009). During the procedure, a subcutaneous tunnel is created using a graft tunnelling device from the axillary artery area to the groin, and another tunnel formed between the two femoral arteries. Though the anastomoses between graft and axillary and femoral arteries can be performed under local anaesthesia, the tunnelling is painful and general anaesthesia is required, at least for this part of the procedure. Postoperative pain is modest, but patients may require postoperative monitoring in a high-dependency environment because of associated co-morbidities.

Thoracoabdominal aortic aneurysms

Thoracoabdominal aortic aneurysms (TAAAs) are classified according to their anatomical location (Fig. 58.2). The risk factors are similar to AAAs but differ in a number of respects. Although approximately 50% are associated with atherosclerosis, almost all patients are hypertensive. Other causes are trauma, previous repair of aortic coarctation, and congenital conditions such as Marfan's or Ehlers–Danlos syndrome. Most are asymptomatic until impending rupture, which is usually catastrophic. In patients presenting for elective surgery, renal impairment and old age are associated with worse outcome.

The principles of anaesthesia for open TAAA surgery are similar to those for infrarenal AAA repair, though the risks and morbidity are greater, and specific considerations apply for surgical access, ventilatory management, and spinal cord and organ protection. Some of these are circumvented by the use of endovascular or hybrid techniques (e.g. open infrarenal AAA repair with endovascular repair of a proximal thoracic aneurysm). Open thoracotomy and collapse of the left lung are required for surgical access, with one-lung ventilation using a double-lumen endobronchial tube or endobronchial blocker. Cardiovascular changes at aortic clamping and unclamping are more marked with proximal aortic clamping and vasoactive or positive inotropic drugs are always required. Intraoperative transoesophageal echocardiography may be useful to assess ventricular function and guide fluids and inotrope therapy. The surgeon may need to place separate grafts or implants to renal and other visceral arteries to maintain organ perfusion, though the overall clamp time is increased. Visceral ischaemia and metabolic acidaemia are common, even with the use of surgical bypass or re-implantation techniques. Mannitol is often used in an attempt to attenuate ischaemia–reperfusion injury. Blood loss can be rapid and enormous; specific wide-bore i.v. access with a rapid infusion device is needed. Near-patient testing should be used to monitor coagulation, haematocrit and acid–base status during surgery. Epidural catheters may be placed for postoperative analgesia, but local anaesthetics are often avoided as motor block may delay or confuse the diagnosis of spinal cord ischaemia. In contrast to infrarenal AAA surgery, all patients undergoing open TAAA require postoperative ventilation and possibly other organ support in the ICU.

Spinal cord protection

The blood supply to the spinal cord is derived from a single anterior and two posterior spinal arteries, with little overlap in the parts of the cord they supply. The anterior spinal artery arises from the vertebral arteries and runs down to supply the anterior two-thirds of the spinal cord. It receives multiple contributions from segmental arteries arising from the intercostal, lumbar, iliac, and other arteries. The most important of these segmental branches is the arteria radicularis magna (the artery of Adamkiewicz) which arises from between T5 and L3, but most commonly between T9 and T12. During aortic cross-clamping, spinal perfusion depends on the aortic pressure distal to the clamp and this may become critical when the clamp is placed more proximally, above the coeliac axis. Significant ischaemia of the spinal cord results in anterior spinal artery syndrome with motor weakness or paralysis and loss of distal pain and temperature sensation. Vibration, touch, and proprioception are maintained as their pathways are supplied by the posterior spinal arteries. The part of the spinal cord most at risk is the 'watershed' lower thoracic and high lumbar areas. Risk factors for spinal cord ischaemia are clamping on the proximal aorta, increased duration of clamping (especially > 60 min), intraoperative hypotension, ligation of spinal arteries, emergency surgery, old age, hyperglycaemia, diabetes, and severe atherosclerosis. The incidence of paraplegia after TAAA repair has been reported to be up to 25% in some series, but is 0–4% after elective type IV TAAA repair (Wahlgren and Wahlberg 2005) and has reduced with the introduction of endovascular procedures and specific preventative measures.

Spinal cord perfusion pressure (SCPP) is estimated as:

$$\text{Mean arterial pressure}\ (\text{in the distal aorta}) - \\ \text{cerebral spinal fluid}\ (\text{CSF})\ \text{or central venous pressure} \\ (\text{whichever is greater})$$

Spinal cord ischaemia is thought to cause cord oedema, which will increase CSF pressure, decrease SCPP, and exacerbate cord ischaemia. This is the rationale for CSF drainage during thoracic aortic surgery. Methods to monitor spinal cord function during surgery include somatosensory or motor-evoked potentials (see Chapter 44).

The other cause of spinal cord ischaemia during repair of a descending thoracic aortic (or supracoeliac) aneurysm is that the segmental arteries are often excluded from the circulation permanently by the graft. Several techniques are available to maintain

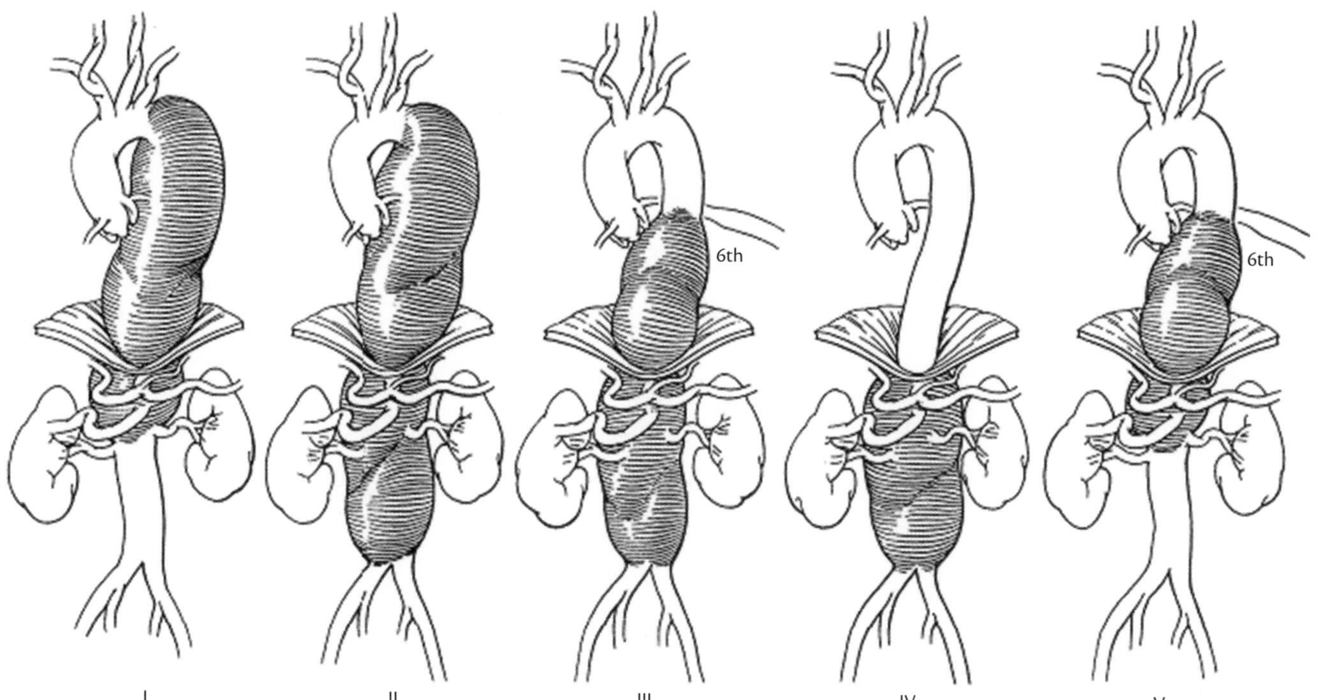

Figure 58.2 Thoracoabdominal aortic aneurysm classification. Type I, from below the left subclavian artery to above the coeliac axis, or opposite the superior mesenteric and above the renal arteries. Type II, from below the left subclavian and including the infrarenal abdominal aorta to the level of the aortic bifurcation. Type III, from the sixth intercostal space tapering to just above the infrarenal abdominal aorta to the iliac bifurcation. Type IV, from the 12th intercostal space, tapering to above the iliac bifurcation. Type V, from the sixth intercostal space, tapering to just above the renal arteries.

Reprinted from *Annals of Thoracic Surgery*, Volume 67, Issue 6, Safi HC, Miller CC., Spinal cord protection in descending thoracic and thoracoabdominal aortic repair. pp. 1937–9, Copyright © 1999 with permission from The Society of Thoracic Surgeons and the Southern Thoracic Surgical Association.

spinal cord perfusion during surgery. These include augmenting distal perfusion using bypass techniques such as atriofemoral bypass with sequential clamping or partial left heart bypass, with or without identification and preservation or selective re-implantation of segmental arteries (Jacobs et al. 2007). Cooling the spinal cord by infusion of cold fluid into the epidural space may be beneficial, though this is controversial, and many anaesthetists allow core temperature to decrease to 34–35°C. Barbiturates, steroids, and other drugs are not of proved benefit. In all cases, cross-clamp times, blood loss, and hypotension should be kept to a minimum. CSF drainage, using a standard epidural catheter and a purpose-made closed drainage system, is used to maintain the CSF pressure at approximately 10 mm Hg during surgery and for up to 72 h after surgery (Safi and Miller 1999). Mean arterial pressure should also be sustained at greater than 65 mm Hg to maintain SCPP throughout this period. Excessive CSF drainage may cause intracranial hypotension and haemorrhage in addition to other complications (Fedorow et al. 2010). However, when used in combination with other measures, CSF drainage has been shown to decrease the incidence of spinal cord ischaemia during thoracic aortic surgery (Coselli et al. 2002).

Endovascular aortic aneurysm repair

EVAR was first described in humans in 1991. It involves the placement of a self-expanding stent-graft within the lumen of the AAA to exclude the aneurysm sac from the circulation from within. The stent-graft is usually constructed from impervious graft material over an internal nickel–titanium skeleton; the device is compressed within a delivery device of approximately 7 mm diameter that is passed percutaneously through one or both femoral arteries and positioned within the aorta under fluoroscopic control. Once in position (usually with the proximal end just below the renal arteries and the distal end in the common iliac arteries) the device is deployed by retracting the delivery system and allowing the stent graft to emerge and expand to seal against the aortic wall just above the AAA. A balloon is expanded within the stent graft at proximal and distal ends to ensure full expansion. Multiple stent grafts are used to create bifurcated grafts into the iliac arteries (Fig. 58.3) More recent techniques include the use of fenestrated grafts that can be placed to allow perfusion of the renal and other visceral arteries. Deployment of the graft requires a short period of apnoea. Cardiovascular changes at deployment are modest.

In order that EVAR can be performed, the AAA must have certain characteristics including that the neck of the aneurysm (where the proximal part of the stent is deployed) should be of a minimum length (>10 mm), without excessive angulation and have a maximum diameter of 32 mm. To enable passage of the delivery system, the iliac vessels should be of greater than 7 mm diameter and not ectatic or tortuous (Moll et al. 2011). Developments in stent technology are permitting EVAR to be performed in an increasing number of cases, but approximately 20% will be unsuitable.

EVAR avoids the complications associated with a major abdominal incision and aortic cross-clamping. It has lower morbidity, hospital stay, and short-term mortality compared with conventional surgery (Cao et al. 2004; Schouten et al. 2007). Risk factors for patients undergoing EVAR are similar to those for open surgery and include significant cardiovascular disease, old age, COPD,

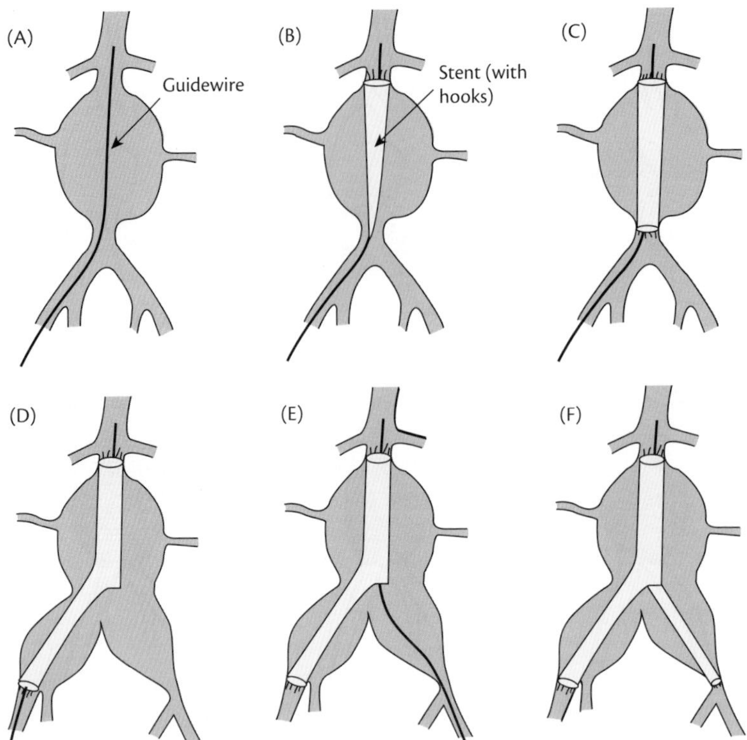

Figure 58.3 Deployment of an endovascular stent. A transfemoral guidewire is passed across the lumen of the abdominal aortic aneurysm (A) and both proximal (B) and distal (C) ends are deployed by balloon angioplasty. For bifurcated grafts, the first component enters through the original puncture site (D) before a second guidewire is introduced on the contralateral side (E) to facilitate deployment of the second component (F).

renal dysfunction, and increased ASA grade (Moll et al. 2011). As postoperative HDU or ICU care is not usually required after EVAR, late cancellations and overall hospital stay may be reduced. The main disadvantages of EVAR are that initial costs are higher and continued surveillance with computed tomography (CT) scanning is required to confirm the position of the graft. Leaks around or through the graft (endoleaks) may occur, requiring further or repeated radiological re-interventions (van Marrewijk 2002; Sampram et al. 2003). Furthermore, the long-term survival benefits of EVAR compared with open surgery are not clear, mainly because of late deaths from cardiac disease, cancer, or rupture of another aneurysm (Prinssen et al. 2004; Schermerhorn et al. 2008; UK EVAR Trial Investigators 2010; de Bruin et al. 2010; Lederle 2012). Postoperative renal function declines in the longer term to a greater extent after EVAR compared with open surgery (Mills et al. 2008). In addition, long-term outcome after EVAR in patients considered unfit for open repair is considerably worse than anticipated: 4-year survival in the EVAR-2 study was only 34% (EVAR Trial Participants 2005b). The lack of survival benefit from endovascular AAA repair in those with significant coexisting disease has been confirmed in other studies (Buth et al. 2002) and it remains uncertain whether EVAR improves life expectancy in patients unfit for open repair (Chaikof et al. 2009). Hence it should not be seen as a simple alternative in patients unfit for open surgery.

Anaesthesia for EVAR

EVAR is performed via groin incisions, usually below the inguinal ligament under local, regional, or general anaesthesia (Pichel and Serracino-Inglott 2008). Practice varies in respect of where endovascular surgery is performed—in the radiology suite or the operating theatre—and the choice is determined largely by local facilities and the preference of the operating practitioner. However, there are recommendations for the provision of adequate facilities including minimal standards for provision of anaesthesia (Medicines and Healthcare products Regulatory Agency 2010; Thompson and Danjoux 2014). Many centres are developing dedicated endovascular facilities where high-quality imaging is available within an environment equipped to operating theatre standards.

Outcome is more closely related to preoperative risk factors than to particular anaesthetic technique (Karthesalingam et al. 2012). The choice of anaesthesia should be determined by the presence and severity of co-morbidities, surgical factors (including type and anticipated duration of EVAR), local facilities, and expertise. Blood loss during EVAR is usually modest but may be significant. Large-gauge i.v. access should be secured and direct arterial pressure monitoring used. Imaging during the procedure may involve the use of high doses of radiocontrast with the potential to cause contrast-induced nephropathy, especially in patients with pre-existing renal dysfunction. The main measures to obviate this are to use the minimum dose of iso-osmolar contrast and to maintain hydration throughout the perioperative period (see 'Contrast-induced nephropathy'). Accurate deployment of the graft requires short periods of apnoea to avoid the effects of respiratory movements on the aorta.

EVAR can be performed entirely under local anaesthesia but leg ischaemia (caused by the insertion of the large delivery system into the iliac arteries) can be troublesome. Movements of gas within the bowel may also obscure the quality of imaging and this is more likely with local anaesthesia; an antispasmodic (hyoscine) may be needed. Neuraxial blocks are suitable for many patients in the absence of contraindications. General anaesthesia is also an option and avoids the difficulties some patients have in lying immobile and in breath-holding during the procedure. Postoperative pain requirements are modest and in the absence of severe coexisting diseases, most patients can return to the vascular ward after a few hours in the postoperative care unit.

Thoracic EVAR and hybrid procedures

Thoracic EVAR (TEVAR) is increasingly used for the management of isolated thoracic aortic aneurysms as it avoids many of the complications associated with open TAAA surgery (Scharrer-Pamler et al. 2003; Desai et al. 2012). Where the aneurysm involves the abdominal aorta and stenting would occlude major abdominal vessels (coeliac, renal or mesenteric), a 'hybrid' procedure is needed, involving anastomosis of these visceral arteries to distal vessels through an open surgical approach (Hughes and McCann 2009). Anaesthesia for TEVAR is similar to that for EVAR, with the exceptions that some surgeons may request a period of controlled hypotension during proximal stent placement. The other main consideration is that the brachial artery may be used for access; in this case it often leads to ischaemic pain in the arm and so general anaesthesia is preferable; alternatively an additional brachial plexus block can be used. Anaesthetic considerations for hybrid TEVAR are similar to those for open TAAA, except that one-lung ventilation is not required. Spinal cord ischaemia is less common than during open surgery, but spinal cord protection measures are often needed if the stent graft is long and likely to cause occlusion of multiple intercostal or segmental arteries. Long-term outcome after successful TEVAR is similar to open TAAA repair, with 5-year survival rates of 60%, though re-interventions may be required in 15% of patients after TEVAR (Desai et al. 2012).

Contrast-induced nephropathy

Contrast induced nephropathy (CIN) is defined as an increase in serum creatinine concentrations of greater than 44 μmol $litre^{-1}$ within 48–72 h after administration of i.v. radiocontrast, in the absence of other causes. CIN is a potential complication after endovascular surgery where large volumes of iodinated radio-contrast have been administered during the procedure. It may also occur after diagnostic contrast-enhanced CT scanning, angiography, or angioplasty. The aetiology is unknown but apoptosis of renal tubular cells and renal medullary hypoxia occur with the production of reactive oxygen species. Possible mechanisms include direct toxic effects of radio-contrast on tubular cells, ischaemia–reperfusion injury or reduced renal blood flow, or both. Although usually transient and self-limiting, permanent kidney damage has been reported. Risk factors include pre-existing chronic kidney disease, diabetes, hypertension, heart failure, dehydration, old age, the concurrent administration of other nephrotoxic drugs, and the use of hyper-osmolar contrast. Measures to prevent CIN are to maintain hydration before contrast administration with i.v. crystalloids [e.g. 0.9% saline or isotonic (1.26%) sodium bicarbonate at 1.5 ml kg^{-1} h^{-1} for 4–12 h pre-procedure and up to 48 h post-procedure (Hoste et al. 2010)], minimize the volume of contrast to less than 150 ml, use iso-osmolar (290 mOsm) contrast agents (e.g. iopamidol), and avoid vascular surgery or repeated administration of contrast within 48 h. Acetylcysteine (600 mg orally twice daily or 500 mg i.v. twice daily for 24 h pre-and post-procedure) may be used in high-risk groups. Theophyllines and statins may also be beneficial though the evidence is conflicting. Other drugs or interventions (dopamine, calcium channel blockers) are not effective and furosemide may be harmful (Kwok et al. 2013). In all cases, urine output should be monitored for at least 4 h after administration of contrast and oral hydration encouraged.

Carotid artery surgery

Stroke is the second most common cause of death in Europe, causing 1.1 million deaths each year, accounting for 10% of all deaths in men and 15% of all deaths in women. Worldwide, the annual incidence of stroke is approximately 15 million. Approximately 150 000 strokes occur in the United Kingdom each year with an annual incidence of 178 per 100 000 in men and 139 per 100 000 in women. In England and Wales, there are approximately 60 000 deaths each year from stroke. Though more common in the elderly, 25% of strokes occur in those aged less than 65 years. Stroke is a leading cause of disability and the majority of stroke survivors are dependent on others for everyday activities, with significant economic costs to society (Stroke Association 2013).

The majority (>70%) of strokes are ischaemic in aetiology, caused by atheroembolism arising from atheromatous plaques in the large arteries, particularly the common carotid bifurcation and internal and external carotid arteries. The other main causes are primary intracerebral or subarachnoid haemorrhage. In patients who have suffered a transient ischaemic attack (TIA) or minor stroke, the incidence and severity of major strokes or other events in the first few days relate to clinical features (Table 58.2); the risk of major stroke within 5 years depends on the degree of carotid stenosis (Table 58.3).

Carotid endarterectomy (CEA) is performed to prevent disabling or fatal embolic strokes in patients with significant carotid stenosis (>50%). It has well-defined indications based on the results of large-scale randomized prospective studies (North American Symptomatic Carotid Endarterectomy Trial

Table 58.2 $ABCD^2$ score

		Points
A	Age >60 years	1
B	Blood pressure >140/90	1
C	Clinical features	2
	Unilateral weakness	1
	Speech impairment without weakness	
D	Duration >60 min	2
	Duration 10–59 min	1
D	Diabetes mellitus	1

The $ABCD^2$ score can predict the incidence and severity of major strokes or other events in the first few days after TIA. A low score (<4) is associated with 2 and 7 day risks of major stroke of 1% and 1.2% respectively but also a higher 7 day risk of recurrent TIA. A high score (>5) is associated with 2 and 7 day risks of major stroke of 8.1% and 11.7% respectively.

Reprinted from *The Lancet*, Volume 369, Issue 9558, Johnston SC, Rothwell PM, Huynh-Huynh MN, Giles MF, Elkins JS, Sidney S, Validation and refinement of scores to predict very early stroke risk after transient ischemic attack, pp. 283–292, Copyright © 2007 Elsevier.

Table 58.3 Long-term risks of major stroke after transient ischaemic attack or minor stroke in patients with stable neurological symptoms

5-year risk of stroke after TIA or minor stroke without surgery		**% 5-year risk reduction for stroke or death conferred by CEA**		
>70% carotid stenosis	33%	>70% carotid stenosis	Absolute risk reduction	16%
			Relative risk reduction	48%
			Numbers needed to treat	6
50–69% stenosis	28%	50–69% stenosis	Absolute risk reduction	8%
			Relative risk reduction	28%
			Numbers needed to treat	13
<50% stenosis	25%	30–49%	Absolute risk reduction	2.6%
			Relative risk reduction	10%
			Numbers needed to treat	38
		<30% stenosis	Risks of CEA outweigh the benefits	

The risks in patients not undergoing surgery may improve with continuing advances in medical therapy (dual antiplatelet therapy, high-dose statin therapy, aggressive multi-agent antihypertensive therapy). Note that the benefits of CEA are greatest in patients with more severe carotid stenosis, and rely on low perioperative morbidity (30-day stroke or death rate <6%).

Adapted with permission from 'Carotid Artery Surgery and Stenting', in Thompson JP, Telford RJ, Howell SJ (eds) *Oxford Specialist Handbook of Vascular Anaesthesia*, 2014, Pages 377–378, with permission from Oxford University Press.

Collaborators 1991; Executive Committee for the Asymptomatic Carotid Endarterectomy Study 1995; European Carotid Surgery Trialists Collaborative Group 1998; MRC Asymptomatic Carotid Surgery Trial Trial Collaborative Group 2004). Patients have usually suffered a TIA or minor stroke but the carotid stenosis may be asymptomatic. CEA reduces the incidence of major disabling stroke after minor stroke or TIA, in patients with stable neurological symptoms. The approximate 5-year risks of stroke with medical therapy alone depend on the presence of symptoms, and in symptomatic patients the benefits are greatest in patients with the most severe carotid stenosis (Table 58.3). Paradoxically, the main risk of surgery is the production of a new neurological deficit (which may be fatal or cause permanent disability) and so the potential benefits of CEA are only realized if the overall perioperative risks of stroke or death are low (30-day stroke or death rate <6% in symptomatic patients and <3% in asymptomatic patients). In some patients who have had a TIA or minor stroke, CEA is not indicated, that is, the stroke was unrelated to carotid atherosclerosis, or the degree of carotid stenosis was less than 50% when assessed.

It is also important to recognize that the trials on which current practice and recommendations are made were performed 10–20 years ago. Stroke mortality has decreased over the last two decades and with the advent of thrombolysis for acute stroke, and further advances in medical therapy, the risks of stroke with medical therapy alone are likely to decrease. This is particularly relevant to asymptomatic patients in whom the risk:benefit ratio is lower (Table 58.4), and there have been calls for new trials in asymptomatic patients comparing CEA, carotid artery stenting, and medical therapy alone.

Timing of carotid surgery

Recent data have shown that the risks of major stroke are highest in the first few hours or days after TIA or minor stroke (Rothwell et al. 2006). The risks depend on the initial neurological event and increase in the order monocular amaurosis fugax < TIA < hemispheric stroke. The risks of major stroke after TIA at 7, 30, and 90 days are 8%, 12%, and 17% respectively (Lovett et al. 2003; Coull et al. 2004); the risks after minor stroke are 11.5%, 15.0%, and 18.5%, respectively. The highest absolute risk (up to 5%) is within the first 24 h. Within these groups, age greater than 60 years, duration of symptoms, and aetiology of stroke all contribute to increased risk of early stroke. Large artery atherosclerosis (mainly carotid disease) is associated with a 20% risk of stroke at 30 days after minor stroke (Fairhead et al. 2005). The EXPRESS study (Rothwell et al. 2007) showed that outcome after TIA and minor stroke was improved after investigations performed and medical therapy initiated urgently. Furthermore, the benefit of CEA is greatest in patients undergoing surgery within 2 weeks after TIA or minor stroke, with a number-needed-to treat of 5 to prevent 1 ipsilateral stroke in 5 years (Rothwell et al. 2006) (Table 58.5). Together these data have led to a change in philosophy and practice so that minor stroke or TIA is now treated without delay and if indicated CEA should be performed as soon as possible after the last event (Furie et al. 2011; Brott et al. 2011; Rothwell et al. 2011). The UK National Stroke Strategy states that 'carotid intervention for recently symptomatic severe carotid stenosis should be regarded as an emergency procedure in patients who are neurologically stable'. Interventions should be performed within 2 weeks of a TIA or minor stroke with the aim of reducing this to 2 days by 2017 (Department of Health 2007), though the benefits of performing surgery within 48 h are not clear. Adoption of this approach means that there is less time to optimize coexisting medical conditions before CEA, particularly hypertension or ischaemic heart disease. It is well established that cerebral pressure autoregulation is impaired early after TIA or minor stroke, but despite increased pressures for the anaesthetist, the available data suggest that outcome is not worse when carotid surgery is performed as an urgent procedure after the neurological event (Rerkasem and Rothwell 2009; Rantner et al. 2011; Lesech et al. 2012).

Preoperative assessment

In general, preoperative assessment should focus on identifying and optimizing reversible coexisting conditions before surgery. Many patients with carotid stenosis have coronary artery

Table 58.4 Long-term risks of major stroke in asymptomatic patients with carotid stenosis.Overall, the benefits are greater in men compared with women. However, the risks of stroke with medical therapy alone are likely to decrease in the future with improvements in treatment

5-year risk of stroke after TIA or minor stroke without surgery	5-year % risk reduction for stroke or death conferred by CEA		
5%, irrespective of the degree of stenosis	Carotid stenosis >60%	Absolute risk reduction	5%
		Relative risk reduction	46%
		Numbers needed to treat	19
	Carotid stenosis <60%	Risks of CEA outweigh the benefits	

Adapted with permission from 'Carotid Artery Surgery and Stenting', in Thompson JP, Telford RJ, Howell SJ (eds) *Oxford Specialist Handbook of Vascular Anaesthesia*, 2014, Pages 377–378, with permission from Oxford University Press.

disease, either occult or symptomatic. Most are elderly and there is a high prevalence of atrial fibrillation, hypertension, congestive heart failure, hyperlipidaemia, diabetes, and smoking-related respiratory disease. Patients presenting for CEA are therefore at increased risk for cardiovascular death and perioperative cardiovascular morbidity, principally MI. The major risks of CEA are stroke (3–4%), MI (0.5–1%), and death; cardiovascular complications account for 50% of the overall morbidity and mortality. As CEA is now considered an urgent procedure there is often limited time available for optimizing coexisting medical conditions, but surgery should be deferred if there is significant aortic stenosis, significant arrhythmias, uncompensated heart failure, or unstable angina. Wherever possible, other conditions (diabetes, hypertension, renal dysfunction) should be addressed and optimized (see Chapter 41).

Standard preoperative investigations include full blood count, biochemistry, ECG, and chest X-ray; others are determined by the presence of other coexisting conditions (see Chapters 41 and 42). In patients scheduled for CEA after recent TIA or minor stroke, these will already have been performed, and in addition, CT or magnetic resonance imaging (MRI) of the brain and Doppler ultrasound of the carotid arteries. After a recent neurological event, airway reflexes and swallowing may be impaired; these should be assessed formally (e.g. by nasendoscopy) if suspected on clinical evaluation. An algorithm for decision-making in patients after TIA or stroke presenting for CEA or other surgery is presented in Table 58.5. Most patients will be able to proceed to CEA with the exception of those requiring urgent cardiology interventions (e.g. coronary revascularization or urgent pacemaker insertion) (Thompson 2000a, 2000b, 2014). These patients should be referred to a cardiologist for consideration of interventions such as percutaneous coronary intervention (PCI), or in some cases combined CEA and coronary artery bypass grafting.

Diabetic control is important because hyperglycaemia occurs frequently after stroke and can worsen cerebral ischaemic damage; conversely, hypoglycaemia may mimic acute stroke and cause difficulties with diagnosis in the perioperative period. In all diabetic patients (except those controlled by dietary measures alone), an infusion of glucose with a variable rate insulin infusion should be started before CEA and continued after surgery until the patient resumes oral intake; a target blood glucose of 6–10 mmol litre^{-1} is recommended.

Almost all patients will be taking aspirin, clopidogrel, or both; and many will be receiving statin therapy. These medications should all be continued up to the day of surgery and restarted as soon as possible thereafter. In patients receiving warfarin (e.g. for atrial fibrillation), bridging therapy with heparin should be used. Some patients presenting with crescendo TIAs will also be receiving heparin; this should be continued up to a few hours before surgery. These decisions should be made in consultation with a stroke physician and a haematologist.

Table 58.5 Suggested algorithm for decision-making in patients after stroke or TIA

Scenario	Management
Recent non-disabling stroke or TIA not considered for CEA because mild or no carotid atherosclerosis or stroke not related to carotid disease	Evaluate and proceed to non-CEA surgery. Probably defer for 3 months to allow cerebral autoregulation to normalize, and correction of other medical risk factors, though there are few data to guide this
Recent disabling stroke, not considered for CEA but presenting for other surgery	Postpone non-carotid surgery for at least 3 months and re-evaluate extent of stroke and urgency of surgery. If reasonable recovery and life expectancy, evaluate. If benefits of surgery outweigh the risks, proceed with increased care and monitoring
Distant non-disabling stroke or TIA and not considered for CEA at the time	Reassess for CEA (? degree of carotid stenosis) and perform CEA first if indicated. If CEA not indicated, evaluate for non-carotid surgery
Recent stroke or TIA and candidate for CEA, no major cardiac risk factors but other disease process requiring urgent surgery, e.g. coexisting aortic aneurysm or critical limb ischaemia	Correct other medical problems and perform CEA first
Recent stroke or TIA and candidate for CEA with major cardiac risk factors (urgent treatment of cardiac risk factors, e.g. antiarrhythmic drugs, pacemaker, untreated heart failure	If cardiac revascularization indicated, consider PCI or combined CEA/CABG. Correct major cardiac risk factors first; proceed to CEA
Recent non-disabling stroke or TIA and has undergone successful CEA	Defer non-urgent surgery for at least 6 weeks

Reproduced from 'Management after recent stroke or TIA', in Thompson JP, Telford RJ, Howell SJ (eds), *Oxford Specialist Handbook of Vascular Anaesthesia*, 2014, Table 4.12, Page 194, with permission from Oxford University Press.

Control of blood pressure is often difficult in patients presenting for CEA because arterial baroreceptor function and cerebral autoregulation are impaired after TIA or stroke in addition to the effects of other factors that impair baroreflex sensitivity (Stoneham and Thompson 2009). Furthermore, haemodynamic instability is common during and after CEA, caused by the direct effects of surgery and anaesthesia. Hypertension occurs in 80% of patients in the first few days after TIA or minor stroke, though it usually decreases spontaneously. Conversely, hypotension could potentially worsen cerebral ischaemia, particularly in patients with uncorrected carotid stenosis. For these reasons routine, aggressive antihypertensive treatment is not currently recommended by stroke physicians early after ischaemic minor stroke or TIA. Trials are ongoing, but a target blood pressure of less than 180/110 is currently suggested. Untreated hypertension has historically been considered a risk factor for worse outcome after CEA (Table 58.6) but in symptomatic patients, it is now considered that the potential benefits of deferring urgent CEA to normalize blood pressure are outweighed by the increased risks of further stroke caused by the delay. Hence patients may present for CEA with blood pressures higher than those normally considered optimal before elective surgery. Wherever possible, however, it remains that blood pressure should be controlled before surgery and most vascular anaesthetists would aim for a systolic blood pressure less than 180 mm Hg before urgent CEA, and less than 160 mm Hg before elective CEA. There is no good evidence for the benefits of any particular antihypertensive drugs in this situation. ACE inhibitors and angiotensin II receptor blockers may cause refractory hypotension after induction of general anaesthesia and in this situation it is reasonable to omit them for 24 h before carotid surgery.

Anaesthesia for carotid endarterectomy

The principal aims of anaesthesia for carotid surgery are to maintain cerebral perfusion and oxygen delivery; to maintain cardiovascular stability before, during, and after surgery to minimize any stress to the myocardium; and to minimize the risk of postoperative complications such as hypertension, wound haematoma, or cerebral hyperperfusion syndrome. Postoperative recovery should be rapid to allow prompt detection of any new neurological deficits. General, local, or regional anaesthetic techniques can be used to achieve these goals.

Table 58.6 Perioperative risk factors for patients undergoing CEA

Clinical/radiological features	Ipsilateral hemispheric symptoms > ocular symptoms only > asymptomatic
	Ipsilateral ischaemic lesion on CT
	Urgent surgery in the presence of current neurological deficit
	Crescendo TIAs
Medical	Age > 75 years
	Angina
	Surgery immediately before CABG
	Hypertension (diastolic pressure >115 mm Hg or systolic pressure >180 mm Hg, or both)
	Chronic kidney failure
Surgical	Contralateral carotid occlusion
	Intraluminal thrombus
	Ulcerated or irregular plaque
	Stenosis near the carotid syphon

Adapted with permission from 'Principles of anaesthesia for Carotid Surgery', in Thompson JP, Telford RJ, Howell SJ (eds), *Oxford Specialist Handbook of Vascular Anaesthesia*, 2014, Box 9.1, Page 382, with permission from Oxford University Press.

General anaesthesia

General anaesthesia with controlled ventilation has a number of theoretical advantages. These include definitive airway control, the ability to maintain oxygenation and manipulate arterial $P\text{CO}_2$, cerebral protection, and reduced cerebral metabolic rate for oxygen ($CMRO_2$) by volatile or i.v. anaesthetic agents, and some monitoring modalities (such as transcranial Doppler) are easier. It also avoids problems of patient discomfort or movement during prolonged surgery, and positioning may be easier. However, the 'gold standard' for monitoring during CEA is the awake patient (see 'Monitoring') with surgery under local or regional anaesthesia.

General anaesthesia can be provided using balanced volatile or total i.v. anaesthesia. Cardiovascular instability is common, especially during induction of anaesthesia, manipulation of the carotid sheath during surgery, emergence from anaesthesia, and in the early postoperative period. Hypotension is common after induction of anaesthesia, caused by the cardiovascular effects of anaesthesia and artificial ventilation. This should be anticipated: drugs to treat hypotension should be prepared before induction of anaesthesia and be immediately available. An arterial catheter should be placed before induction of anaesthesia to monitor direct arterial pressure. Induction of anaesthesia must be smooth. The arm–brain circulation time is prolonged in the elderly and anaesthetic drugs must be titrated carefully to effect. It is preferable to secure the airway with tracheal intubation but a second-generation supraglottic airway device could be used. Coughing should be avoided as it can increase intracranial pressure; useful techniques include spraying the vocal cords or tracheal tube cuff with lidocaine 1%, and ensuring deep neuromuscular block before tracheal intubation. The pressor response to laryngoscopy and tracheal intubation should be attenuated using drugs such as alfentanil (15 μg kg^{-1}), remifentanil (slow bolus of 0.1–0.25 μg kg^{-1} or an infusion of 0.1–0.2 μg kg^{-1} min^{-1}, or both), or esmolol (1.0–1.5 mg kg^{-1}). Artificial ventilation is necessary to maintain normal Pa_{CO_2}, as hypo- or hypercapnia can cause unpredictable changes in cerebral blood flow. Anaesthesia can be maintained using volatile or i.v. anaesthetic agents. The former impair cerebral autoregulation at concentrations greater than 1 MAC so lower concentrations are used. Sevoflurane has theoretical beneficial effects on $CMRO_2$ but desflurane or isoflurane are also suitable. Nitrous oxide is often avoided because it increases cerebral metabolic rate and middle cerebral artery blood flow in the presence of both volatile agents and propofol. A low-dose remifentanil infusion (0.1–0.2 μg kg^{-1} min^{-1}), or incremental doses of fentanyl 50 μg may be used as adjuncts during surgery. CEA is not particularly painful and requirements for analgesia are modest. I.V. paracetamol and non-steroidal anti-inflammatory drugs (NSAIDs) (if not contraindicated) are usually adequate, in conjunction with either a superficial cervical plexus block or local anaesthetic infiltration of the wound.

Cardiovascular instability is common during carotid surgery. This relates to pre-existing baroreceptor dysfunction, the effects of antihypertensive medications, anaesthesia, and the surgery itself. Manipulation of the carotid sheath by the surgeon can cause hypertension or vagally mediated bradycardia. The latter may be sudden and severe, especially when using a propofol/remifentanil anaesthetic technique and atropine should be immediately available. Infiltration of the carotid sinus with local anaesthetic has not been shown to improve perioperative cardiovascular stability. It is often stated that blood pressure should be maintained during surgery to within 10–20% above preoperative values, though there is little evidence to support this. Cerebral blood flow is likely to be impaired in the presence of a carotid stenosis and particularly during cross-clamping of the carotid artery, but in the presence of good cerebral blood flow documented by transcranial Doppler or other monitoring, lower values may be preferable. Nevertheless, it is advisable to maintain a systolic pressure greater than 90 mm Hg at all times during general anaesthesia. Many anaesthetists augment blood pressure during closure of the carotid artery, so any minor bleeding (e.g. through suture holes) can be stopped by the surgeon before wound closure. A gentle 'Valsalva' manoeuvre may also make any venous oozing apparent before final closure of the wound. Minor oozing is often noticeable in patients receiving dual antiplatelet therapy and can usually be tamponaded with gentle pressure, but patience may be required.

Emergence from anaesthesia and tracheal extubation should be smooth and attempts made to prevent coughing, as this can be associated with increases in venous and arterial pressures, predisposing to postoperative haematoma. Titrated doses of i.v. β-blockers [e.g. atenolol 1–5 mg, labetalol (increments of 10 mg up to 100 mg), or metoprolol 2–15 mg] can be given before emergence from anaesthesia if hypertension is anticipated. Alternatively, esmolol 50–100 mg i.v. can be given shortly before extubation. Postoperative pain is modest, but a small proportion of patients may require increments of morphine 2–5 mg i.v. postoperatively.

Local/regional anaesthesia

Local or regional anaesthesia has a number of potential advantages for carotid surgery. It allows definitive (real-time and awake) monitoring of cerebral function, systemic and cerebral autoregulation is maintained, and it allows the selective use of surgical shunts, depending on the surgeons preferred technique. Furthermore, it avoids the adverse effects of general anaesthesia and mechanical ventilation on the cardiovascular system, and allows monitoring for symptoms of angina or hypoglycaemia. Disadvantages include potential patient discomfort (especially if the patient suffers from orthopnoea, if surgery is prolonged or technically difficult, e.g. in obese patients, or the carotid bifurcation is anatomically high). Discomfort from submandibular retractors is common and even with an apparently effective cervical plexus block, supplementary injections of local anaesthetic by the surgeon are usually required. Ipsilateral phrenic nerve palsy with diaphragmatic paralysis occurs commonly after deep cervical plexus block; this technique is best avoided in patients with severe COPD.

The pattern of blood pressure is different when CEA is performed under local/regional anaesthesia. Hypertension is much more common, especially during carotid cross-clamping, and hypotensive agents should be available. Intraoperative hypotension is less common and vasopressor requirements are lower (Stoneham and Thompson 2009).

Options for local or regional anaesthesia for CEA are superficial, intermediate, or deep cervical plexus block; local anaesthetic infiltration by the surgeon; or cervical epidural anaesthesia. Superficial cervical plexus block is performed by infiltration of local anaesthetic along the entire length of the posterior border of the sternomastoid muscle with 15–20 ml of local anaesthetic (e.g. levobupivacaine 0.25%). Intermediate cervical plexus block is performed by inserting a regional block needle perpendicular to the skin at the midpoint of the posterior border of sternomastoid until a loss of resistance is felt as the needle penetrates the investing layer of cervical fascia at a depth of 1–2 cm. Larger volumes (30 ml) of local anaesthetic solution are used to produce spread between the superficial and deep layers of cervical fascial layers, allowing spread to the cervical nerve roots. Deep cervical plexus block is performed as a single or separate injections at C2–4. Smaller volumes of local anaesthetic (5 ml) are used. Complications associated with deep cervical plexus block include epidural, subarachnoid, or vertebral artery injection, and phrenic nerve palsy.

The debate over whether local or regional anaesthesia improves outcome after CEA has been ongoing for a number of years and the GALA trial was performed in an attempt to address this (GALA Trial Collaborative Group 2008). Part of the rationale for this study was that local or regional anaesthesia can be used to determine aspects of surgical technique (specifically whether or not to use a shunt to maintain cerebral blood flow during carotid clamping), and that shunting is associated with morbidity by causing atheroembolism from a carotid plaque. The planned sample size in the GALA trial was 5000 patients, based on a predicted one-third reduction in risk of a primary outcome (30-day stroke MI or death) under local compared with general anaesthesia (from 7.5% to 5%). The trial recruited 3526 patients with symptomatic or asymptomatic carotid disease from 94 hospitals in 24 countries between 1999 and 2007, before recruitment stopped. The incidence of the primary outcomes in the trial population was lower than anticipated and no differences were found in the incidence of stroke, death, or MI between patients receiving local and general anaesthesia (GALA Trial Collaborative Group 2008). The study was a pragmatic trial with no standardization of technique, and some centres may not have engaged with the study because of a lack of equipoise about the superiority of local or regional anaesthesia. The GALA trial also found a non-significantly increased incidence of MI at 30 days in the local anaesthetic group, but conversely a non-significant trend towards fewer events (stroke, MI, or death) in the local anaesthetic group at 1 year. The trial concluded that 'The anaesthetist and surgeon, in consultation with the patient, should decide which anaesthetic technique to use on an individual basis'. Inclusion of the GALA results into a meta-analysis of the effects of anaesthetic technique on outcome after CEA confirms there is no effect of anaesthesia on stroke, death, or MI (Rerkasem and Rothwell 2008). This has been confirmed in recent large series and registry data (Menyhei et al. 2011; Schechter et al. 2012); medical and surgical factors are probably more important determinants of outcome.

Cervical epidural block at the level of C6–C7 or C7–T1 has been described for carotid surgery but almost always impairs respiratory function and may cause overt respiratory failure. There is also a theoretical risk of epidural haematoma as heparin is given during surgery and patients may be receiving dual antiplatelet therapy.

Monitoring

Although there is good collateral circulation to the brain via the circle of Willis, patients undergoing CEA often have generalized vascular disease and so some form of monitoring for cerebral ischaemia is required during surgery, especially during the period of carotid cross-clamping. Monitoring can be used to determine the need for insertion of an artificial shunt during the endarterectomy, or to monitor the adequacy of the shunt. Options include transcranial Doppler of middle cerebral artery blood flow velocity, EEG, and 'stump' pressure (pressure in the proximal carotid artery). Cerebral microdialysis has also been described. The 'gold standard' is considered to be the awake patient when surgery is performed under local/regional anaesthesia. All these monitoring techniques have advantages and disadvantages and are described in more detail in Chapters 44 and 59.

Postoperative care

Patients should be observed in a recovery or post-anaesthesia care unit (PACU) for at least 1–4 h after surgery as the majority of postoperative complications occur during this time. Close neurological and cardiovascular monitoring are required. Arterial pressure is often labile and direct pressure monitoring is indicated until blood pressure is stable. Postoperative hypertension is common. It predisposes to neck wound haematoma, haemorrhagic stroke, and myocardial ischaemia. In some cases it may herald the onset of cerebral hyperperfusion syndrome. After exclusion of simple remediable causes (pain, urinary retention), a systolic pressure greater than 170 mm Hg (or >30% of preoperative values) should be monitored closely and treated promptly if it persists for longer than 10–15 min (Box 58.1). In the presence of neurological symptoms, a lower threshold is used (aim for systolic pressure <140 mm Hg). Invasive arterial pressure monitoring should be continued for 2 h after administration of i.v. agents to observe for rebound effects. If drug infusions are needed to control arterial pressure, prolonged monitoring in a HDU environment is required.

Neck haematoma is a potentially dangerous complication after CEA. It is caused by arterial or venous bleeding after surgery and the onset may be insidious, leading to venous and lymphatic congestion, soft tissue oedema, and airway obstruction. Predisposing factors include early postoperative hypertension, coughing, vomiting, and dual antiplatelet therapy. The degree of external haematoma may not reflect the soft tissue oedema and possible airway obstruction. If airway compromise is suspected, surgical re-exploration of the wound should be arranged as soon as possible. This is best done under local anaesthesia as tracheal intubation is often very difficult. If surgery has been performed under local or regional anaesthesia, then the residual blocks may still sufficient; alternatively, further infiltration of local anaesthetic may be needed. After drainage of the haematoma, tissue oedema usually resolves but if tracheal intubation has been performed, the airway should be assessed carefully before extubation (Shakespeare et al. 2010). If there is any doubt, ventilation should be continued in the ICU until the residual oedema has subsided.

Box 58.1 Management of early postoperative hypertension in a PACU or HDU

1. Systolic pressure remains greater than 170 mm Hg despite simple measures. Patient unable to swallow tablets (early postoperative period)

First line: labetalol 10mg slow boluses every 2 min, up to 100 mg.

If blood pressure remains elevated after 20 min, move to second line agent.

If blood pressure decreases and does not rebound, continue regular blood pressure observations.

If blood pressure decreases initially but increases again, start infusion at 50–100 mg h^{-1}, titrating dose to blood pressure.

Second-line drugs: hydralazine or GTN.

Invasive arterial pressure monitoring should be continued for 2 h after parenteral agents to observe for rebound effects.

2. Systolic pressure remains greater than 170 mm Hg despite simple measures. Patient is able to swallow tablets

a. Patient not normally on antihypertensive therapy

First line: nifedipine retard (10 mg), repeated after 1 h if no change in blood pressure. DO NOT use crushed nifedipine capsules. If no reduction in blood pressure, move to second-line agent.

Second line: bisoprolol 5 mg.

Third line: ramipril 5 mg, repeated at 3 h if necessary.

b. Patient is normally on antihypertensive therapy

First line: administer patient's usual medication.

Second line: if patient is on ACE inhibitor or diuretic (or both), nifedipine LA 10 mg. If patient is on calcium channel blocker, ramipril 5 mg.

Other points

- If hypertension persists, contact hypertension specialists for clinical review. Observe closely for neurological signs or symptoms and treat immediately if these occur.
- Monitor and treat hypertension more aggressively in patients with risk factors for CHS. Aim to maintain systolic blood pressure in these patients below 140 mm Hg.

Adapted from University Hospitals of Leicester NHS Trust Guidelines for Blood Pressure Management after Carotid Endarterectomy. This is intended as a guide to treatment and other units may have their own policies. Adapted with permission from Stoneham MD, Thompson JP, Blood pressure management and carotid endarterectomy. *British Journal of Anaesthesia*, 2011, Volume 102, Issue 4, pp. 442–52, by permission of the Board of Management and Trustees of the British Journal of Anaesthesia.

Cerebral hyperperfusion syndrome

Cerebral blood flow increases after CEA, usually by 20–40% of preoperative values and for up to several hours. In some cases, the increase in cerebral blood flow is greater and may persist for several days. Cerebral hyperperfusion is defined as an increase in cerebral blood flow to greater than 100% of preoperative values. Cerebral hyperperfusion syndrome (CHS) is defined as severe ipsilateral migraine-like headache with transient focal neurological deficits or seizures, associated with cerebral hyperperfusion. These clinical features are similar to hypertensive encephalopathy, and are caused by ipsilateral vasogenic cerebral oedema in parts of the brain that were previously under-perfused. CHS typically develops within the first week after CEA. Predisposing factors include recent ipsilateral stroke, marked increases in cerebral perfusion during surgery, and severe postoperative hypertension. If suspected, CHS should be treated as an emergency and investigations (transcranial Doppler, CT, or MRI of the brain) performed. Blood pressure must be stabilized to systolic pressure less than 140 mm Hg or lower, dexamethasone 8 mg i.v. administered, and any seizures controlled promptly (Box 58.2). Admission to the HDU or ICU is usually required for invasive arterial pressure monitoring and management.

Box 58.2 Management of patient with suspected cerebral hyperperfusion syndrome. Systolic blood pressure greater than 160 mm Hg with headache/other neurological symptoms/deficit

Treatment should start *immediately* on the ward using non-invasive monitoring.

On-call surgical SpR/SHO must:

- Inform on-call consultant vascular surgeon of increase in blood pressure associated with seizure/headache or onset of neurological deficit.
- Contact on-call ICU team to arrange urgent transfer to HDU, or PACU for invasive arterial blood pressure monitoring.
- Administer 8 mg dexamethasone i.v.
- Check for and treat pain, urinary retention.
- Aim to reduce blood pressure gradually to <140 mm Hg systolic, and lower if symptoms persist.
- Seek expert advice early.

First line: labetalol 10 mg slow i.v. boluses every 2 min, up to 100 mg.

- If blood pressure remains elevated after 20 min, move to second-line agent.
- If blood pressure decreases and does not rebound, continue regular blood pressure observations.
- If blood pressure decreases initially but increases again, start labetalol infusion at 50–100 mg h^{-1}, titrating dose to blood pressure

Second-line drugs: hydralazine (2–10 mg slow i.v. injection) or GTN infusion (0–50 mg h^{-1}).

- If blood pressure remains elevated after 25 min, move to third-line agent.
- If blood pressure reduces and does not rebound, continue regular blood pressure observations.
- If blood pressure reduces but increases again, move to third-line agent.

Third line: GTN 50 mg in 50 ml 0.9% sodium chloride (i.e. 1 mg ml^{-1})

- Start infusion at 5 ml h^{-1} (5mg h^{-1}), increasing rate to 12ml h^{-1} (12 mg h^{-1}), titrated to blood pressure.

When blood pressure stable (in HDU/ICU), commence oral medication.

a. Patient *not* normally on antihypertensive therapy

- First line: nifedipine LA (10 mg), repeat after 1 h if no change in blood pressure.
- *Do not* use crushed nifedipine capsules. If no reduction in blood pressure, move to second-line agent.
- Second line: bisoprolol 5 mg.
- Third line: ramipril 5 mg, repeated at 3 h if necessary.

b. Patient *is* normally on antihypertensive therapy

- First line: administer patient's usual medication.
- Second line: if patient is on ACE inhibitor or diuretic (or both), nifedipine LA 10 mg. If patient is on calcium channel blocker, ramipril 5 mg.

After transfer, patient should remain in PACU or HDU while antihypertensive treatment ongoing. After cessation of treatment, the patient should remain in PACU, or HDU for a minimum of 6 further hours to minimize rebound hypertension.

Data from University Hospitals of Leicester NHS Trust Guidelines for Blood Pressure Management after Carotid Endarterectomy. This is intended as a guide to treatment and other units may have their own policies. Data from Stoneham MD, Thompson JP (2009). Blood pressure management and carotid endarterectomy. *British Journal of Anaesthesia*, 102, 442–52. Data from Thompson JP. Cerebral hyperperfusion syndrome in Thompson JP, Telford RJ, Howell SJ (eds) *Oxford Specialist Handbook of Vascular Anaesthesia*, OUP 2013.

Carotid artery stenting

Carotid angioplasty with stenting (CAS) is a less invasive alternative to CEA which is performed by radiologists, cardiologists, and vascular surgeons. It involves the endovascular placement of a stent across a carotid artery stenosis, usually accessed via a catheter passed via the femoral artery and into the carotid artery under fluoroscopic guidance. It is an alternative to CEA in patients with some surgical or anatomical considerations (e.g. previous radical neck dissection or irradiation, the presence of a tracheostomy, and restenosis after previous CEA) or in patients at particularly high medical risk for CEA. A meta-analysis including data from 16 randomized trials with long-term follow-up data showed that the risks of minor MI or cranial nerve injuries are lower with CAS, but the 30-day incidence of stroke is almost twice as high after CAS, with higher short-term mortality (Bonati et al. 2012). Hence the benefits of CAS compared with CEA are still not yet established, particularly in younger or asymptomatic patients. CAS is usually performed under local anaesthesia in the radiology or endovascular suite.

Carotid body tumours

A carotid body tumour (or chemodectoma) is a rare, glomus tumour arising from paraganglion cells in the carotid body. Paragangliomas are derived from chromaffin cells in ganglia and can occur at several sites including paravertebral ganglia, the adrenal gland (phaeochromocytoma), aortic body, tympanic membrane, vagus, jugular vein, ciliary ganglion, and the bladder. The incidence of carotid body tumours is 1–2 per 100 000 population and they account for 60–70% of head and neck paragangliomas, but only 0.5% of head and neck tumours overall. Patients are usually aged 40–60 years at presentation and usually asymptomatic, presenting with a slow-growing mass in the anterior triangle of the neck. In some cases, cranial nerve palsies (typically vagus or hypoglossal nerve) occur, leading to dysphonia, dysphagia, or other symptoms. In a small proportion (<3%) of cases, secretion of catecholamines leads to symptoms similar to phaeochromocytoma, including hypertension, flushing, and palpitations. Approximately 10% are bilateral; some may be familial and associated with other endocrine neoplasias. Most are benign but 3% metastasize. Carotid body tumours are located at the carotid bifurcation and cause characteristic splaying of the internal and external carotid arteries (the lyre sign).

Diagnosis is usually made by Doppler ultrasound, CT, or MRI scanning. Angiography is usually performed to determine the vascularity of the tumour and relationship to other vessels. Indirect laryngoscopy may be required to assess vocal cord function before surgery as the recurrent laryngeal nerve may be affected. If hormone secretion is suspected, urinary catecholamine concentrations should be determined.

The mainstay of treatment of a carotid body tumour is surgical resection, though radiotherapy may be used. Surgery involves resection of the tumour, but in some cases carotid bypass may be required. The surgical incision is usually more extensive than for CEA and occasionally the surgeon may need to access the skull base to gain access to the carotid canal. There is a significant risk of complications including cranial nerve damage, stroke (5%), or major haemorrhage. Anaesthetic considerations for carotid body tumour resection are similar to those for CEA, though most patients are younger with a lower incidence of cardiovascular and respiratory disease. General anaesthesia using a balanced technique is preferred; the airway is best secured using a tracheal tube and in some cases a nasotracheal tube may be requested to improve surgical access. Transcranial Doppler is useful to monitor for emboli and to assess shunt flow during cross-clamping. Some surgeons may use nerve stimulators to test the location and integrity of cranial nerves and so short-acting neuromuscular blocking agents are preferable. Continuous direct intra-arterial pressure monitoring and large-bore i.v. access are required.

Thoracic outlet syndrome

Thoracic outlet syndrome is caused by compression of the brachial plexus and subclavian artery between the uppermost rib and the scalenus anterior muscle or the clavicle within the thoracic outlet. The aetiology is usually a cervical rib, an abnormal first rib, or fibrous bands, but it may also follow a fracture of the clavicle. Symptoms mainly arise from compression of the nerve roots of C8 and T1, but subclavian artery stenosis with post-stenotic dilation and aneurysm formation, or subclavian vein thrombosis may occur. Surgery may be required for excision of fibrous bands or cervical rib, or subclavian artery reconstruction. Most patients are young and otherwise healthy. The main anaesthetic considerations are the potential for significant haemorrhage and pneumothorax as the pleura is often breached during procedures involving the first rib. These procedures are painful and multimodal analgesia, including local anaesthetic infiltration, NSAIDs, and opioids, should be used. Patient-controlled i.v. morphine is often needed.

Thoracoscopic sympathectomy

Surgery to the thoracic sympathetic chain is usually performed to treat palmar or axillary hyperhidrosis. Other less common indications are for complex regional pain syndromes affecting the upper limb, facial flushing or hyperhidrosis, and congenital long QT syndrome. The sympathetic chain runs below the posterior parietal pleura and is accessed using a thoracoscope. Surgical techniques include resection, electrocautery, or clipping. Patients are usually young and healthy. Visualization of the surgical field requires collapse or compression of the lung, with the intrathoracic insufflation of CO_2. Although thoracoscopic sympathectomy has been reported under local/regional anaesthesia, general anaesthesia with artificial ventilation is usually required, using one-lung ventilation via a double-lumen endobronchial tube or two-lung ventilation via a conventional tracheal tube. The latter avoids the difficulties of one-lung anaesthesia but continued insufflation of CO_2 is required and surgical access may be more difficult. Excessive intrathoracic pressures during thoracoscopy impair venous return and cardiac output and vasoactive drugs should be immediately available. One-lung ventilation causes a significant shunt in healthy patients and hypoxaemia is common. Measures to alleviate hypoxia are to increase FI_{O_2}, the application of continuous positive airway pressure and insufflation of oxygen to the non-ventilated lung, and maintenance of normal arterial pressure. In some cases, temporary re-inflation of the lung may be required. Large-bore i.v. access is needed to facilitate treatment of hypotension or haemorrhage, which is rare but may be catastrophic (Ojimba and Cameron 2004). Thoracoscopic sympathectomy is painful and instillation of local anaesthetic to the sympathetic chain and thoracoscope sites under direct vision are recommended, in addition to NSAIDs and morphine. Despite meticulous re-inflation of the lung at the end of surgery, almost all patients have a residual postoperative pneumothorax but these resolve over time and rarely require intervention. Routine chest X-ray is therefore often unhelpful and many clinicians rely on close observation for a significant pneumothorax using clinical signs.

Lower limb bypass surgery

Peripheral arterial disease causes symptoms progressing from cold extremities to paraesthesiae, intermittent claudication, rest pain, and gangrene. It affects 5–7% of the middle-aged and elderly population in the United Kingdom. Risk factors for peripheral arterial insufficiency are smoking, old age, diabetes, and hypertension. Many patients are elderly, frail, and relatively immobile. Approximately 90% of patients presenting for surgery have coronary artery disease (Hertzer et al. 1984) and many have COPD. However, because exercise tolerance is limited by intermittent claudication, many patients have no overt symptoms of respiratory or ischaemic heart disease. The poor overall condition of patients with critical limb ischaemia is shown by mortality rates of 15–25% at 12 months and 60% at 5 years after diagnosis. At 1 year, 30% will have undergone amputation, and only 45–50% will remain alive with both limbs (Hirsch et al. 2005; Norgren et al. 2007).

Symptoms may improve with cessation of smoking, moderation of alcohol intake, graded exercise programmes, and antiplatelet and statin therapy. If conservative measures fail, the primary treatment in many centres is radiological treatment such as percutaneous angioplasty (Goodney et al. 2009). However, studies have shown that though early morbidity is greater, long-term overall outcome after infra-inguinal bypass surgery using autologous vein grafting is better than angioplasty (Beard 2008).

The main indications for lower limb arterial reconstruction are ischaemic pain at rest, tissue loss (ulceration or gangrene), or failure of non-surgical treatment. Other indications include severe claudication with disease at certain sites (popliteal aneurysm or distal atherosclerosis). Peripheral arterial reconstructive surgery is often prolonged and patients with peripheral arterial disease are at high risk for perioperative morbidity and mortality. It is not always appreciated by anaesthetists that the overall perioperative risks of lower limb revascularization are similar to open aortic surgery (MI or cardiac death > 5%) (Fleisher et al. 2007).

Preoperative assessment is as for other major arterial surgery (see Chapter 41), with the important provisos that significant asymptomatic cardiac or respiratory disease may be present but the patient may be unable to undergo investigations which require exercise (e.g. CPX testing, exercise ECG). Surgery is usually performed on a semi-elective or urgent basis: major cardiac risk factors (unstable coronary syndromes, decompensated heart failure, significant arrhythmias, or valve disease) should be investigated and treated before surgery (Fleisher et al. 2007). The value of other invasive cardiological investigations is limited and should be reserved for those in whom the results would change management (Monahan et al. 2005). If surgery is urgent (e.g. to salvage a limb) or the patient is not a candidate for coronary interventions, further investigation is not appropriate. Pre-existing medical conditions should be optimized as far as possible before surgery. Patients are usually taking antiplatelet medications and statin therapy if there are no contraindications. If a patient is taking warfarin, the indications for this should be reviewed as in some cases (e.g. where the indication is atrial fibrillation with no other risk factors), warfarin may be omitted to lessen surgical bleeding and the consideration of regional anaesthesia.

Anaesthesia for lower limb revascularization

The main considerations are to maintain cardiovascular stability, normothermia, normal circulating volume, and provide good perioperative pain relief. These can be provided using regional anaesthesia, general anaesthesia, or a combination of techniques. Neuraxial anaesthetic techniques (subarachnoid or epidural) that provide sympathetic blockade have been shown to improve lower limb muscle blood flow, but they probably have no effect on surgical outcome (see 'Regional or general anaesthesia for lower limb revascularization surgery?').

Surgery is often prolonged (typically 2–6 h), and though blood losses are not usually large, they may be insidious. Minimum monitoring requirements include multilead ECG monitoring with ST-segment analysis, body temperature, and for procedures lasting more than 3 h, direct arterial pressure monitoring is recommended. The need for other monitors (cardiac output, central venous pressure) is determined by the presence and severity of coexisting diseases (Thompson and Smith 1999).

Balanced general anaesthesia can be provided using a volatile or total i.v. technique. Artificial ventilation is usually preferred via a tracheal tube or supraglottic airway. Fluids, vasopressors or positive inotropic drugs, or both, may be required to maintain cardiovascular stability. Heparin (5000 IU i.v.) is usually administered before the arterial supply is interrupted during surgery. When blood flow to the ischaemic limb is restored, vasoactive metabolites entering the systemic circulation can cause transient myocardial depression and hypotension requiring active treatment. It is essential that the patient remains normothermic during surgery, because hypothermia causes vasoconstriction (which may impair postoperative graft perfusion) and predisposes to myocardial ischaemia and dysrhythmias. Active warming devices (forced air warming, thermal mattress) should be used, exposed areas should be covered, i.v. fluids should be warmed, and pressure areas should be protected.

The surgical incision is often extensive and painful. If neuraxial anaesthesia is not used, i.v. morphine in combination with local anaesthetic infiltration is often required. Alternatively, femoral nerve or lumbar plexus blocks may be used. Patient-controlled analgesia is useful after surgery. Some patients may have been receiving chronic opioid medication and may be tolerant of opioids so may need higher doses. Postoperative care in stable uncomplicated patients may be provided on the ward, but a high-dependency environment may be required if the patient has significant comorbidities. Supplemental oxygen should be administered for at least the first postoperative night.

Regional or general anaesthesia for lower limb revascularization surgery?

A series of papers in the early to mid 1990s suggested that epidural analgesia resulted in a lower incidence of thrombotic complications and improved surgical outcomes after lower limb revascularization surgery (Breslow et al. 1993; Christopherson et al. 1993; Rosenfeld et al. 1993). These received much attention at the time, because they suggested that general anaesthesia impaired fibrinolysis and therefore contributed to a hypercoagulable state and perioperative thrombosis. However, the data in these three papers actually involved the same patient group, and the original study was designed to compare cardiac morbidity between regional and general anaesthesia. Several important surgical and other confounding factors were not included, and the incidence of primary graft failure was unusually high (13%). In a later, less cited paper, the authors re-analysed their data and found that poor run-off at operation was noted more frequently in the general anaesthesia group, and that after surgical re-exploration when needed, the secondary patency rates were similar between groups, suggesting that technical errors had been more frequent in the general anaesthesia group (Perler et al. 1995). Subsequent retrospective and randomized prospective trials have confirmed no difference in graft patency, mortality, or cardiac complications after lower limb vascular surgery performed under general or regional anaesthesia, suggesting that the potential benefits of regional anaesthesia are insignificant in the context of graft survival or cardiac outcomes (Bode et al. 1996; Pierce et al. 1997; Schunn et al. 1998). One of these also found a significantly higher mortality in a subgroup with inadequate regional anaesthesia (Bode et al. 1997).

It is important to note that lower limb revascularization procedures are associated with a lower stress response than major abdominal surgery and so the beneficial effects of regional anaesthesia on the stress response and perioperative thrombosis are probably limited. In terms of graft function after lower limb revascularization surgery, the most important considerations are disease severity and complexity, case selection, operator experience, and surgical technique rather than the effects of any single anaesthetic technique.

Nevertheless, regional anaesthesia (either alone, with sedative adjuncts, or light general anaesthesia) often works well as a technique for lower limb revascularization surgery. Because of the extended duration of surgery, continuous catheter techniques (epidural, combined spinal/epidural) are often preferred to single-shot regional methods. Contraindications to neuraxial anaesthesia are systemic anticoagulation and patient refusal; if the patient is unable to lie flat while awake for prolonged periods (e.g. in the presence of severe of cardiorespiratory disease or arthritis), general anaesthesia may be better. Current guidelines suggest that the administration of unfractionated heparin more than 4 h before or 1 h after neuraxial block is safe.

Vascular emergencies

Ruptured abdominal aortic aneurysm

The prognosis from rupture of an AAA is very poor. Free rupture into the peritoneal cavity results in cardiovascular collapse and almost certain death; if the aorta ruptures into the retroperitoneal space then haemorrhage may be limited by a tamponade effect and the outcome is better. However, despite improvements in many aspects of medical care over the last five decades, overall mortality is 80–90%. There has been no improvement in outcome for those patients who reach hospital and undergo surgery (Bown et al. 2002). In those who initially survive surgery, there is a high incidence of complications and both ICU and hospital stay are prolonged. In an attempt to stratify patients and improve emergency decision-making, scoring systems have been developed, similar to those used for elective surgery, but both the Hardman Index and the Glasgow Aneurysm Score are limited, especially for the highest-risk patients. The Vascular Study Group of New England developed a system based on age greater than 76 years (2 points), preoperative cardiac arrest (2 points), loss of consciousness, and the need for suprarenal cross-clamping (both 1 point). The predictive value of this score for in-hospital mortality was 8%, 25%, 37%, 60%, 80%, and 87% for scores of 0, 1, 2, 3, 4, and 5 or higher, respectively (Robinson et al. 2013) but further validation is needed in different populations. As rapid death is inevitable without treatment after ruptured AAA, intervention should be considered even in those patients who have been judged unfit for elective surgery or endovascular treatment, and many surgeons feel that the only firm contraindication to intervention is cardiac arrest. Many patients die without reaching hospital but the majority of those admitted to hospital survive for more than 2 h and it is now agreed that there is time to arrange imaging before intervention (Lloyd et al. 2004). Similarly, outcome is not worsened if patients are transferred to a specialist regional vascular unit (Adam et al. 2004).

Baseline investigations should be performed and blood cross-matched while resuscitation is ongoing. It is well established that the excessive administration of i.v. fluids is associated with clot disruption, dilution of clotting factors, hypothermia, further bleeding, and increased mortality after ruptured AAA (Hardman et al. 1996; Dick et al. 2013). Few prospective data are available but it is recommended that i.v. fluid resuscitation should be limited to maintain a systolic blood pressure of 50–100 mm Hg providing that the patient is conscious, until the patient is undergoing surgery and an aortic cross-clamp has been applied (Moll et al. 2011).

Open repair of ruptured AAA

Two anaesthetists are required to manage ruptured AAA. Catastrophic hypotension may occur at induction of anaesthesia because in addition to the cardiovascular effects of anaesthesia in the elderly hypovolaemic patient, relaxation of abdominal muscles reduces any tamponade effect. Therefore induction of anaesthesia should not occur until the patient is positioned on the operating table, fully prepared for surgery, and with blood immediately available for transfusion. Group-specific or group O blood may be required if cross-matched blood is not available. The hospital's major haemorrhage protocol should be activated, to allow release of packed red cells and other coagulation products without delay; the ratio of these may vary according to local policies. Direct arterial pressure monitoring is advisable before induction of anaesthesia but should not significantly delay surgery. Anaesthesia is induced using a rapid sequence technique with minimal doses of i.v. agents. General anaesthesia for surgery is then provided with a balanced technique aiming for cardiovascular stability with maintenance of circulating volume: high-dose opioids (fentanyl 5–20 $\mu g\ kg^{-1}$) with an oxygen/air/volatile agent are often used. Central venous access is required to administer inotropic and vasopressor drugs. Acid–base status and coagulation should be checked regularly during surgery; other monitors including cardiac output monitoring may be required.

It is common practice to withhold blood and coagulation products until early after the aortic cross-clamp has been applied. Massive transfusion requirements are common and should be guided by near-patient testing (e.g. thromboelastography) in conjunction with laboratory testing and advice from a haematologist. Hypocalcaemia may occur and require the administration of i.v. calcium salts. A rapid transfusion device and cell saver device should be used. It is difficult to maintain normothermia but all attempts should be made including the warming of all i.v. fluids. I.V. fluids are usually titrated to achieve a central venous pressure greater than 15 mm Hg before release of the aortic clamp. The main consideration is that aortic unclamping should be predicted and managed proactively in conjunction with the surgeon.

Some degree of renal and visceral ischaemia is almost inevitable after aortic rupture and intraoperative urine output is an unreliable guide to renal function. Circulating volume should be maintained, with a mean arterial pressure greater than 80 mm Hg after aortic clamping. Mannitol 0.5–1 $g\ kg^{-1}$ may be given before aortic clamping, though there are few good data to show an effect on outcome and postoperative renal replacement therapy is often required (Sear 1995). Ruptured AAA is commonly associated with the development of a retroperitoneal haematoma, which contributes to prolonged postoperative ileus, abdominal distension, intra-abdominal hypertension, and abdominal compartment syndrome. The surgeon may leave the abdomen open for 48–72 h. If not, intra-abdominal pressure monitoring should be used after surgery.

At the end of surgery the patient should be transferred to the ICU for further management. Artificial ventilation is continued until the patient is stable; this is usually at least 24 h. In contrast to elective surgery, there is no particular advantage in siting an epidural catheter at the time of ruptured AAA surgery and there are added risks as coagulopathy is often present.

Endovascular repair of ruptured AAA

Despite the logistical issues in provision of an emergency EVAR service (including the requirement for extensive experience with elective EVAR, and the rapid availability of dedicated equipment, facilities, and expertise), there is increasing enthusiasm for EVAR in the treatment of ruptured AAA. Several retrospective studies have shown good outcomes after EVAR compared with open surgery but are likely to have been affected by selection and performance bias and no firm conclusions can yet be made (Moll et al. 2011). However, randomized prospective trials of EVAR compared with open repair for ruptured AAA have shown no difference in 30-day mortality (Badger et al. 2014; IMPROVE Trial Investigators 2014).

The general considerations for anaesthesia for EVAR in ruptured AAA are similar to elective surgery and it can be performed under local, regional, or general anaesthesia. Advantages of local anaesthesia are that peritoneal tamponade is maintained, the adverse cardiovascular effects of general anaesthesia are avoided, and immediate postoperative recovery is quicker. Disadvantages include patients' difficulty in tolerating the procedure because of pain from an expanding retroperitoneal haematoma, iliac artery occlusion, or lower limb ischaemia. A femoro-femoral crossover graft may also be required to obviate distal ischaemia when an aorto-uni-iliac stent device is used (Moll et al. 2011). Despite adjunctive sedative or analgesic drugs, some patients require conversion to general anaesthesia (Leonard and Thompson 2008).

Acute limb ischaemia

Lower limb ischaemia

Acute limb ischaemia is a sudden reduction (<2 weeks' duration) in limb perfusion that threatens limb viability. The main causes are acute rupture and thrombosis *in situ* of a pre-existing atherosclerotic lesion, or embolization from a proximal arterial thrombus (spontaneously or after arterial surgery). Less commonly, acute limb ischaemia may occur after trauma, arterial aneurysm thrombosis (usually popliteal), after iatrogenic arterial damage or cardiac emboli in patients with atrial fibrillation, or after MI. In contrast to chronic ischaemia, acute ischaemia is often severe, because no collateral vessels have developed. Symptoms and signs may vary but it classically presents with pain, paraesthesia, paralysis, and absent pulses; the limb or affected part is cold and pale. The most important signs in the patient with a pulseless limb are sensory and motor loss; in these cases intervention is required immediately to prevent limb loss. When symptoms or signs are less severe, investigation and revascularization should be performed urgently. In some cases, particularly if presentation is delayed, the limb may not be salvageable. Indications of this include fixed skin mottling, and tense muscle compartments that are painful on passive movement. If there is uncertainty as to whether or not the ischaemic limb is potentially viable, surgical fasciotomies and inspection of the muscle for signs of necrosis may be required. It is important to assess the possibility of limb salvage and patient fitness to undergo possibly prolonged surgery, because attempts at revascularization may cause life-threatening reperfusion syndrome. In these circumstances the best option is primary amputation. In some patients with severe coexisting or terminal disease, palliative care may be appropriate. The 30-day mortality in patients with acute lower limb ischaemia is approximately 20% (Norgren et al. 2007). This is mainly related to coexisting cardiovascular or respiratory disease. Outcomes are worse in the elderly, those with active cardiac symptoms, and in the presence of proximal (e.g. aortoiliac) arterial occlusion (Hirsch et al. 2005).

Treatment options for acute lower limb ischaemia include embolectomy, thrombolysis, bypass procedures, radiological interventions, fasciotomies, or amputation. In many cases, diagnostic angiography is performed under local anaesthetic in the operating as a prelude to definitive treatment. Duplex imaging, CT, or MRI cross-sectional angiography are alternatives.

Embolectomy, using a catheter passed via the femoral or popliteal artery, is indicated as a primary procedure for most cases of acute limb ischaemia, to retrieve clot from the occluded artery. The exception to this is when thrombosis of a peripheral aneurysm has occurred. Embolectomy can be performed under local or regional anaesthesia. Radiological interventions include aspiration of thrombus with subsequent angioplasty, but these are usually performed as adjuncts to surgery. Radiological interventions alone can be performed in the radiology department under local anaesthesia with or without sedative adjuncts. Surgical revascularization is required if embolectomy is unsuccessful, arterial inflow is inadequate, or there is arterial trauma or thrombosis of a peripheral aneurysm. Common procedures include iliofemoral bypass or cross-over, or femoropopliteal or distal grafting. The latter usually involve a vein conduit from either the long saphenous or brachial/cephalic vein. Surgical bypass procedures can be performed under general or regional anaesthesia. General anaesthesia is preferred if a vein from the arm is being harvested and avoids the potential problems with regional anaesthesia and anticoagulation because heparin or thrombolytic drugs are often given before, during, or after the procedure.

Thrombolysis may be performed when acute lower limb ischaemia is thought to be caused by local thrombosis of a stenosed arterial segment, rather than distal embolism. However, it is usually only used as an adjunct to surgical and radiological attempts at revascularization. Fasciotomies are indicated to treat or prevent compartment syndrome or reperfusion injury caused by revascularization of an acutely ischaemic limb.

With the exception of ischaemia caused by trauma in younger patients, most patients with acute distal limb ischaemia have generalized cardiovascular disease and many are frail. Although emergency intervention may be required, the patient's medical condition must be assessed fully and appropriate investigations (including urea, electrolytes, full blood count, and ECG as a minimum) performed. Active ongoing resuscitation may be needed to treat acute conditions such as heart failure, atrial fibrillation, or electrolyte disturbances, but investigations to assess fitness should not be allowed to delay emergency surgery or radiological interventions. I.V. opioids are usually required and may already have been given.

It is essential that an anaesthetist is present during procedures performed under local anaesthesia to monitor the patient and to administer analgesic or sedative drugs (e.g. midazolam 0.5 mg increments or low-dose propofol infusion) as required. Oxygen should be given by face mask and continuous cardiovascular and respiratory monitoring is mandatory. Conversion to general anaesthesia may be required if the patient cannot tolerate the procedure or a more extensive procedure is needed. General anaesthesia may be required for surgical bypass procedures, fasciotomies, or prolonged procedures. A balanced technique is suitable, with measures to maintain circulating volume, cardiovascular stability, and normothermia. The precise technique depends on coexisting conditions and invasive monitoring may be required. Surgical bypass and fasciotomies are painful and local anaesthetic infiltration, nerve block, and i.v. opioids may be required during and after surgery. One of the main risks of surgical revascularization is the development of systemic reperfusion injury, caused by the release in to the systemic circulation of toxic metabolites (including lactic acid and potassium ions) on restoration of blood flow to the ischaemic tissues. Severe hyperkalaemia, arrhythmias, lactic acidosis, myocardial depression, and cardiac arrest may ensue, and the anaesthetist must be prepared to treat these complications. Release of myoglobin from damaged muscle causes myoglobinaemia with potential renal tubular damage and AKI. Systemic reperfusion syndrome can also cause systemic inflammatory response syndrome and occasionally multiorgan failure. It is important to maintain circulating volume and monitor urine output; forced alkaline diuresis may be used in an attempt to attenuate myoglobin-induced AKI but the evidence for its effectiveness is mixed. Where hyperkalaemia, renal injury, or other signs of reperfusion injury occur, the patient is best transferred to a HDU or ICU after surgery.

Upper limb ischaemia

Upper limb ischaemia is usually caused by cardiac emboli but may arise from an aneurysm of the subclavian artery in patients with thoracic outlet syndrome or cervical rib. Direct arterial injury from brachial artery catheterization, or accidental injection of drugs are rarer causes. Upper limb ischaemia is less common than lower limb ischaemia and occurs more frequently in women. Patients are usually younger, with a lower incidence of severe cardiovascular disease. The mortality and amputation rates are lower, but acute upper limb ischaemia is a surgical emergency because the upper limb cannot tolerate ischaemia as much as the lower limb. Treatment options are emergency brachial embolectomy or a bypass procedure using a vein graft from the saphenous vein. Compartment syndrome may occur in the forearm muscles and fasciotomies are occasionally needed. Embolectomy can be performed under local infiltration anaesthesia or a brachial plexus block, either as a single shot or infusion by a nerve sheath catheter. As for lower limb ischaemia, the anaesthetist should be present to monitor the patient and administer sedative or analgesic drugs as required. General anaesthesia may be needed for prolonged procedures, saphenous vein harvesting, or if the patient is unable to tolerate the procedure.

Lower limb amputation

The annual incidence of major amputation is decreasing in the United Kingdom but remains at approximately 5 per 100 000 population, which equates to more than 3000 amputations per year (Moxey et al. 2010). Lower limb amputation for vascular disease is performed in patients with acute or critical limb ischaemia, usually after failed attempts at limb salvage with reconstructive surgery or angioplasty, or in patients who are unfit to undergo lower limb revascularization. Other indications are infected gangrene with loss of limb function or the risk of systemic sepsis. In all cases, amputation is reserved for those cases where it is expected to save or prolong life, or improve the quality of life (Vascular Society of Great Britain and Ireland 2010).

The hospital mortality rate is approximately 21% after above-knee amputation and 11% after below-knee amputation (Campbell et al. 2001; Moxey et al. 2010; Vascular Society of Great Britain and Ireland 2010) and the long-term outcome is poor: 1-year survival is 75–80% after below-knee amputation and 60–65% after above-knee amputation. Corresponding 5-year survival rates are 45–60% and 30–45% respectively (Nehler et al. 2003; Sandnes et al. 2004; Ploeg et al. 2005).

Patients presenting for amputation have additional risk factors to other vascular surgical patients. They are usually frail, elderly, and have severe, widespread vascular disease but also have been immobile and in some cases bed-bound with the risk of debilitation and poor nutritional state. Approximately 40% have diabetes. Patients have frequently been receiving high doses of opioids and may be tolerant of these drugs. In acute limb ischaemia or the presence of potential sepsis, amputation is performed as an urgent procedure.

It is now accepted that the outcome after lower limb amputation is poor, and concerted efforts are made to improve outcome. Suggested measures including good pain control, involvement of a consultant anaesthetist in preoperative assessment, and treatment of modifiable conditions before surgery (Vascular Society of Great Britain and Ireland 2010, 2016a,b). Amputation should be performed in routine working hours wherever possible. Anaesthesia for lower limb amputation may be provided using general anaesthesia or neuraxial block. A balanced general anaesthetic technique is suitable. Particular attention should be paid to maintaining circulating volume and normothermia.

Postoperative pain control may be problematic because patients have frequently been receiving high doses of opioids and may be tolerant of these drugs. Sciatic or femoral nerve blocks (or both) are useful analgesic adjuncts and local anaesthetic infusions continued for several days via nerve sheath catheters. Patient-controlled analgesia is also often required after surgery. Regional anaesthesia with subarachnoid, epidural, or a combined technique is also useful. Some patients develop phantom limb pain or sensations after amputation. The incidence is difficult to determine as previous studies have not distinguished between pain arising directly from the stump (stump pain), non-painful phantom sensations, or neuropathic-type phantom perceived to be arising from the amputated limb (phantom pain). Phantom pain is probably more common in younger amputees after trauma. Once established, treatment of phantom pain may be difficult and amitriptyline, gabapentin, or pregabalin should be used early. Data suggesting a reduction in the incidence of phantom limb pain with regional anaesthesia or nerve sheath infusions of local anaesthetic after amputation have not been confirmed (Nikolajsen et al. 1997; Elizaga et al. 2004), though intrathecal ketamine may be beneficial (Wilson et al. 2008).

Declaration of interest

None declared.

References

Adam DJ, Mohan IV, Stuart WP, Bain M. Community and hospital outcome from ruptured abdominal aortic aneurysm within the catchment area of a regional vascular service. *J Vasc Surg* 2004; **39**: 788–910

Al-Hashimi M, Thompson J. Anaesthesia for elective open abdominal aortic aneurysm repair. *Contin Educ Anaesth Crit Care* 2013; **13**: 208–21

Back MR, Leo F, Cuthbertson D, *et al*. Long-term survival after vascular surgery: Specific influence of cardiac factors and implications for preoperative evaluation. *J Vasc Surg* 2004; **40**:7 52–60

Badger S, Bedenis R, Blair PH, *et al*. Endovascular treatment for ruptured abdominal aortic aneurysm. *Cochrane Database Syst Rev* 2014; **7**: CD005261

Beard JD. Which is the best revascularization for critical limb ischemia: endovascular or open surgery? *J Vasc Surg* 2008; **48**: 11S–16S

Beck AW, Goodney PP, Nolan BW, *et al*. Predicting 1-year mortality after elective abdominal aortic aneurysm repair. *J Vasc Surg* 2009; **49**: 838–43

Bode RH, Lewis KP, Zarich SW, *et al*. Cardiac outcome after peripheral vascular surgery. Comparison of general and regional anesthesia. *Anesthesiology* 1996; **84**: 3–13

Bonati LH, Lyrer P, Ederle J, Featherstone R, Brown MM. Percutaneous transluminal balloon angioplasty and stenting for carotid artery stenosis. *Cochrane Database Syst Rev* 2012; **9**: CD000515

Bown MJ, Sutton AJ, Bell PRF, Sayers RD. A meta-analysis of 50 years of ruptured abdominal aortic aneurysm repair. *Br J Surg* 2002; **89**: 714–30

Braams R, Vossen V, Lisman BA, *et al*. Outcome in patients requiring renal replacement therapy after surgery for ruptured and non-ruptured aneurysm of the abdominal aorta. *Eur J Vasc Endovasc Surg* 1999; **18**: 323–7

Breslow MJ, Parker S, Frank SM, *et al*. Determinants of catecholamine and cortisol responses to lower extremity revascularisation. *Anesthesiology* 1993; **79**: 1202–9

Brewster DC, Cronenwett JL, Hallett JW, Jr, *et al.* Guidelines for the treatment of abdominal aortic aneurysms. *J Vasc Surg* 2003; **37**: 1106–17

Brott TG, Halperin JL, Abbara S, *et al.* ASA/ACCF/AHA/AANN/AANS/ACR/ASNR/CNS/SAIP/SCAI/SIR/SNIS/SVM/SVS guideline on the management of patients with extracranial carotid and vertebral artery disease: executive summary: *Stroke* 2011; **42**: e464–e540

Buth J, van Marrewijk CJ, Harris PL, *et al.* Outcome of endovascular abdominal aortic aneurysm repair in patients with conditions considered unfit for an open procedure: a report on the EUROSTAR experience. *J Vasc Surg* 2002; **35**: 211–21

Campbell WB, Marriott S, Eve R, Mapson E, Sexton S, Thompson JF. Factors influencing the early outcome of major lower limb amputation for vascular disease. *Ann R Coll Surg Engl* 2001; **83**: 309–14

Cao P, Verzini F, Parlani G, *et al.* Clinical effect of abdominal aortic aneurysm endografting: 7-year concurrent comparison with open repair. *J Vasc Surg* 2004; **40**: 841–8

Carlisle J, Swart M. Mid-term survival after abdominal aortic aneurysm surgery predicted by cardiopulmonary exercise testing. *Br J Surg* 2007; **94**: 966–9

Chaikof EL, Brewster DC, Dalman RL, *et al.* The care of patients with an abdominal aortic aneurysm: The Society for Vascular Surgery practice guidelines. *J Vasc Surg* 2009; **50**(4 Suppl): S2–49

Christopherson R, Beattie C, Frank S, *et al.* Perioperative morbidity in patients randomised to epidural or general anesthesia for lower extremity vascular surgery. *Anesthesiology* 1993; **79**: 422–34

Coselli JS, LeMaire SA, Köksoy C, Schmittling ZC, Curling PE. Cerebrospinal fluid drainage reduces paraplegia after thoracoabdominal aortic aneurysm repair: results of a randomized clinical trial. *J Vasc Surg* 2002; **35**: 631–9

Cosford PA, Leng GC, Thomas J. Screening for abdominal aortic aneurysm. *Cochrane Database Syst Rev* 2007; **2**: CD002945

Coull AJ, Lovett JK, Rothwell PM, *et al.*, on behalf of the Oxford Vascular Study. Population based study of early risk of stroke after transient ischaemic attack or minor stroke: implications for public education and organisation of services. *BMJ*, 2004; **328**: 326–28

De Bruin JL, Baas AF, Buth J, *et al.* Long-term outcome of open or endovascular repair of abdominal aortic aneurysm. *N Engl J Med* 2010; **362**: 1881–9

Department of Health. National Stroke Strategy. 2007. Available from http://webarchive.nationalarchives.gov.uk/+/www.dh.gov.uk/en/Healthcare/Longtermconditions/Vascular/Stroke/DH_099065

Desai ND, Burtch K, Moser W, *et al.* Long-term comparison of thoracic endovascular aortic repair (TEVAR) to open surgery for the treatment of thoracic aortic aneurysms. *J Thorac Cardiovasc Surg* 2012; **144**: 604–11

Dick F, Erdoes G, Opfermann P, Eberle B, Schmidli J, von Allmen RS. Delayed volume resuscitation during initial management of ruptured abdominal aortic aneurysm. *J Vasc Surg* 2013; **57**: 943–50

Elizaga AM, Smith DG, Sharar SR, Edwards WT, Hansen ST Jr. Continuous regional analgesia by intraneural block: effect on postoperative opioids requirements and phantom limb pain following amputation. *J Rehabil Res Dev* 2004; **31**: 179–87

European Carotid Surgery Trialists Collaborative Group. Randomised trial of endarterectomy for recently symptomatic carotid stenosis: final results of the MRC European Carotid Surgery Trial (ECST). *Lancet* 1998; **351**: 1379–87

EVAR Trial Participants. Endovascular aneurysm repair versus open repair in patients with abdominal aortic aneurysm (EVAR trial 1): randomised controlled trial. *Lancet* 2005a; **365**: 2179–86

EVAR Trial Participants. Endovascular aneurysm repair and outcome in patients unfit for open repair of abdominal aortic aneurysm (EVAR trial 2): randomised controlled trial. *Lancet* 2005b; **365**: 2187–92

Executive Committee for the Asymptomatic Carotid Endarterectomy Study. Endarterectomy for asymptomatic carotid artery stenosis. *JAMA* 1995; **273**: 1421–8

Fairhead JF, Mehta Z, Rothwell PM. Population-based study of delays in carotid imaging and surgery and the risk of recurrent stroke. *Neurology* 2005; **65**: 371–75

Fedorow CA, Moon MC, Mutch WA, Grocott HP. Lumbar cerebrospinal fluid drainage for thoracoabdominal aortic surgery: rationale and practical considerations for management. *Anesth Analg* 2010; **111**: 46–58

Fleisher LA, Beckman JA, Brown KA, *et al.* ACC/AHA 2007 Guidelines on perioperative cardiovascular evaluation and care for noncardiac surgery: a report of the American College of Cardiology/American Heart Association Task Force on Practice Guidelines (Writing Committee to Revise the 2002 Guidelines on Perioperative Cardiovascular Evaluation for Noncardiac Surgery). *J Am Coll Cardiol* 2007; **50**: e159–241

Fleisher LA, Beckman JA, Brown, KA, *et al.* ACCF/AHA focused update on perioperative beta blockade incorporated into the ACC/AHA 2007 guidelines in perioperative cardiovascular evaluation and care for noncardiac surgery: a report of the American College of Cardiology Foundation/American Heart Association Task Force on Practice Guidelines. *Circulation* 2009; **120**: e169–276

Fowkes FG, Housley E, Cawood EH, *et al.* Edinburgh Artery Study: prevalence of asymptomatic and symptomatic peripheral arterial disease in the general population. *Int J Epidemiol* 1991; **20**: 384–92

Furie KL, Kasner SE, Adams RJ, *et al.* Guidelines for the prevention of stroke in patients with stroke or transient ischaemic attack. *Stroke* 2011; **42**: 227–76

GALA Trial Collaborative Group. General anaesthesia versus local anaesthesia for carotid surgery (GALA): a multicentre, randomised controlled trial. *Lancet* 2008; **372**: 2132–42

Gamulin Z, Forster A, Morel D, *et al.* Effects of infra-renal aortic cross-clamping on renal hemodynamics in humans. *Anesthesiology* 1984; **61**: 394–9

Gelman S. The pathophysiology of aortic cross-clamping and unclamping. *Anesthesiology* 1995; **82**: 1026–60

Goodney PP, Beck AW, Nagle J, Welch HG, Zwolak RM. National trends in lower extremity bypass surgery, endovascular interventions, and major amputations. *J Vasc Surg* 2009; **50**: 54–60

Grant SW, Grayson AD, Mitchell DC, *et al.* Evaluation of five risk prediction models for elective abdominal aortic aneurysm repair using the UK National Vascular Database. *Br J Surg* 2012; **99**: 673–9

Hardman DT, Fisher CM, Patel MI, *et al.* Ruptured abdominal aortic aneurysms: who should be offered surgery? *J Vasc Surg* 1996; **23**: 123–9

Hertzer NR, Young JR, Beven EG, *et al.* Coronary artery disease in peripheral vascular patients: a classification of 1000 coronary angiograms and results of management. *Ann Surg* 1984; **199**: 223–33

Hirsch AT, Haskal ZJ, Hertzer NR, *et al.* ACC/AHA 2005 practice guidelines for the management of patients with peripheral arterial disease (lower extremity, renal, mesenteric, and abdominal aortic): a collaborative report from the American Association for Vascular Surgery/Society for Vascular Surgery, Society for Cardiovascular Angiography and Interventions, Society for Vascular Medicine and Biology, Society of Interventional Radiology, and the ACC/AHA Task Force on Practice Guidelines (Writing Committee to Develop Guidelines for the Management of Patients With Peripheral Arterial Disease). *Circulation* 2005; **113**: 463–654

Holt PJ, Poloniecki JD, Loftus IM, Michaels JA, Thompson MM. Epidemiological study of the relationship between volume and outcome after abdominal aortic aneurysm surgery in the UK from 2000 to 2005. *Br J Surg* 2007; **94**: 441–8

Hoste EA, De Waele JJ, Gevaert SA, Uchino S, Kellum JA. Sodium bicarbonate for prevention of contrast-induced acute kidney injury: a systematic review and meta-analysis. *Nephrol Dial Transplant* 2010; **25**: 747–58

Hughes GC, McCann RL. Hybrid thoracoabdominal aortic aneurysm repair: concomitant visceral revascularization and endovascular aneurysm exclusion. *Semin Thorac Cardiovasc Surg* 2009; **21**: 355–62

IMPROVE Trial Investigators. Endovascular or open repair strategy for ruptured abdominal aortic aneurysm: 30 day outcomes from IMPROVE randomised trial. *BMJ* 2014; **348**: f7661

Jacobs MJ, Mommertz G, Koeppel TA, *et al.* Surgical repair of thoracoabdominal aneurysms. *J Cardiovasc Surg* 2007; **48**: 49–58

Karthesalingam A, Thrumurthy SG, Young EL, Hinchcliffe RJ, Holt PJE, Thompson MM. Locoregional anaesthesia for endovascular aneurysm repair. *Eur J Vasc Endovasc Surg* 2012; **56**: 510–9

Kheterpal S, O'Reilly M, Englesbe MJ, *et al.* Preoperative and intraoperative predictors of cardiac adverse events after general, vascular, and urological surgery. *Anesthesiology* 2009; **10**: 58–66

Kothmann E, Batterham AM, Owen SJ, *et al.* Effect of short-term exercise training on aerobic fitness in patients with abdominal aortic aneurysms: a pilot study. *Br J Anaesth* 2009a; **103**: 505–10

Kothmann E, Danjoux G, Owen SJ, *et al.* Reliablity of the anaerobic threshold in cardiopulmonary exercise testing of patients with abdominal aortic aneurysms. *Anaesthesia* 2009b; **64**: 9–13

Kwok CS, Pang CL, Yeong JK, Loke YK. Measures used to treat contrast-induced nephropathy: overview of reviews. *Br J Radiol* 2013; **86**: 20120272

Lawrence VA, Cornell JE, Smetana GW. Strategies to reduce postoperative pulmonary complications after non-cardiothoracic surgery: systematic review for the American College of Physicians. *Ann Intern Med* 2006; **144**: 596–608

Lederle FA, Freischlag JA, Kyriakides TC, *et al.* Long-term comparison of endovascular and open repair of abdominal aortic aneurysm. *N Engl J Med* 2012; **367**: 1988–97

Lederle FA, Johnson GR, Wilson SE, *et al.* Prevalence and associations of abdominal aortic aneurysm detected through screening. Aneurysm Detection and Management (ADAM) Veterans Affairs Cooperative Study Group. *Ann Intern Med* 1997; **126**: 441–9

Lederle FA, Wilson SE, Johnson GR, *et al.* Immediate repair compared with surveillance of small abdominal aortic aneurysms. *N Engl J Med* 2002; **346**: 1437–44

Leonard AD, Thompson JP. Anaesthesia for ruptured abdominal aortic aneurysm. *Cont Educ Anaesth Crit Care Pain* 2008; **8**: 11–5

Lesech G, Alsac J-M, Houbbala R, *et al.* Carotid endarterectomy in the acute phase of stroke in evolution is safe and effective in selected patients. *J Vasc Surg* 2012; **55**: 701–7

Liedenbaum MH, Verdam FJ, Spelt D, de Groot HG, van der Waal J, van der Laan L. The outcome of the axillofemoral bypass: a retrospective analysis of 45 patients. *World J Surg* 2009; **33**: 2490–6

Lloyd GM, Bown MJ, Norwood MGA. Feasibility of preoperative computer tomography in patients with ruptured abdominal aortic aneurysm: A time-to-death study in patients without operation. *J Vasc Surg* 2004; **39**: 788–91

Lovett J, Dennis M, Sandercock PAG, Bamford J, Warlow CP, Rothwell PM. The very early risk of stroke following a TIA. *Stroke* 2003; **34**: e138–40

McFalls EO, Ward HB, Moritz TE, *et al.* Coronary artery revascularisation before elective major vascular surgery. *N Engl J Med* 2004; **351**: 2795–804

Medicines and Healthcare products Regulatory Agency. Joint Working Group to Produce Guidance on Delivering an Endovascular Aneurysm Repair (EVAR) Service. Crown Copyright 2010. Available from http://www.mhra.gov.uk/NewsCentre/CON102998

Menyhei G, Björk M, Beiles B, *et al.* Outcome following carotid endarterectomy: lessons learned from a large international vascular registry. *Eur J Vasc Endovasc Surg* 2011; **41**: 735–40

Metcalfe D, Holt PJE, Thompson MM. The management of abdominal aortic aneurysms. *BMJ* 2011; **342**: d1384

Mills JL, Duong ST, Leon LR, *et al.* Comparison of the effects of open and endovascular aortic aneurysm repair on long-term renal function using chronic kidney disease staging based on glomerular filtration. *J Vasc Surg* 2008; **47**: 1141e9

Moll FT, Powell JT, Fraedrich G, *et al.* Management of abdominal aortic aneurysms. Clinical Practice Guidelines of the European Society for Vascular Surgery. *Eur J Vasc Endovasc Surg* 2011; **41**: S1–S58

Monahan TS, Shrikhande GV, Pomposelli FB, *et al.* Preoperative cardiac evaluation does not improve or predict perioperative or late survival in asymptomatic diabetic patients undergoing elective infrainguinal arterial reconstruction. *J Vasc Surg* 2005; **41**: 38–44

Moxey PW, Hofman D, Hinchliffe RJ, Jones K, Thompson MM, Holt PJE. Epidemiological study of lower limb amputation in England between 2003 and 2008. *Br J Surg* 2010; **97**: 1348–53

MRC Asymptomatic Carotid Surgery Trial (ACST) Collaborative Group. Prevention of disabling and fatal strokes by successful carotid endarterectomy in patients without recent neurological symptoms: randomised controlled trial. *Lancet* 2004; **363**: 1491–502

Multicentre Aneurysm Screening Study Group. The Multicentre Aneurysm Screening Study (MASS) into the effect of abdominal aortic aneurysm screening on mortality in men: a randomised controlled trial. *Lancet* 2002; **360**: 1531–9

Nehler MR, Coll JR, Hiatt WR, *et al.* Functional outcome in a contemporary series of major lower extremity amputations. *J Vasc Surg* 2003; **38**: 7–14

Nikolajsen L, Ilkjaer S, Kroner K, Christensen JH, Jensen TS. Randomised trial of epidural bupivacaine in prevention of stump and phantom pain in lower limb amputation. *Lancet* 1997; **350**: 1353–7

Nishimori M, Ballantyne JC, Low JH. Epidural pain relief versus systemic opioid-based pain relief for abdominal aortic surgery. *Cochrane Database Syst Rev* 2006; **3**: CD005059

Norgren L, Hiatt WR, Dormandy JA, *et al.* Inter-Society Consensus for the Management of Peripheral Arterial Disease (TASC II). *Eur J Vasc Endovasc Surg* 2007; **33**(Suppl 1): S1–75

North American Symptomatic Carotid Endarterectomy Trial Collaborators. Beneficial effect of carotid endarterectomy in symptomatic patients with high grade stenosis. *N Engl J Med* 1991; **325**: 445–53

Ojimba TA, Cameron AE. Drawbacks of endoscopic thoracic sympathectomy. *Br J Surg* 2004; **91**: 264–9

Patterson BO, Karthikesalingam A, Hinchliffe RJ, Loftus IM, Thompson MM, Holt PJ. The Glasgow Aneurysm Score does not predict mortality after open abdominal aortic aneurysm in the era of endovascular aneurysm repair. *J Vasc Surg* 2011; **54**: 353–7

Perler BA, Christopherson R, Rosenfeld BA, *et al.* The influence of anesthetic method on infrainguinal bypass graft patency: a closer look. *Am Surg* 1995; **61**: 785–9

Pichel AC, Serracino-Inglott F. Anaesthetic considerations for endovascular abdominal aortic aneurysm repair. *Curr Anaesth Crit Care* 2008; **19**: 150–62

Pierce ET, Pomposelli FB, Stanley GD, *et al.* Anesthesia type does not influence early graft patency or limb salvage rates of lower extremity arterial bypass. *J Vasc Surg* 1997; **25**: 226–32

Ploeg AJ, Lardenoye JW, Vrancken Peeters MP, Breslau PJ. Contemporary series of morbidity and mortality after lower limb amputation. *Eur J Vasc Endovasc Surg* 2005; **29**: 633–7

Poldermans D, Bax JJ, Boersma E, *et al.* Guidelines for pre-operative cardiac risk assessment and perioperative cardiac management in non-cardiac surgery of the European Society of Cardiology (ESC) and endorsed by the European Society of Anaesthesiology (ESA). *Eur Heart J* 2009; **30**: 2769–812

Prinssen M, Verhoeven EL, Buth J, *et al.* A randomised trial comparing conventional and endovascular repair of abdominal aortic aneurysms. *N Engl J Med* 2004; **351**: 1607–18

Rantner B, Kollerits B, Schmidauer C. Carotid endarterectomy within seven days after the neurological index event is safe and effective in stroke prevention. *Eur J Vasc Endovasc Surg* 2011; **42**: 732–9

Rerkasem K, Rothwell PM. Local versus general anaesthesia for carotid endarterectomy. *Cochrane Database Syst Rev* 2008; **4**: CD000126

Rerkasem K, Rothwell PM. Systematic review of the operative risks of carotid endarterectomy for recently symptomatic stenosis in relation to the timing of surgery. *Stroke* 2009; **40**: e564–e572

Robinson WP, Schanzer A, Li YF, *et al.* Derivation and validation of a practical risk score for prediction of mortality after open repair of ruptured abdominal aortic aneurysms in a U.S regional cohort and comparison to existing scoring systems. *J Vasc Surg* 2013; **57**: 354–61

Rosenfeld BA, Beattie C, Christopherson R, *et al.* The effects of different anesthetic regimens on fibrinolysis & the development of postoperative arterial thrombosis. *Anesthesiology* 1993; **79**: 435–43

Ross RM, Murthy JN, Wollak ID, Jackson AS. The six minute walk test accurately estimates mean peak oxygen uptake. *BMC Pulm Med* 2010; **10**: 31

Rothwell PM Algra A, Amarenco P. Medical intervention in acute and long-term secondary prevention after transient ischaemic attack and ischaemic stroke. *Lancet* 2011; **377**: 1681–92

Rothwell PM, Buchan A, Johnston SC. Recent advances in management of transient ischaemic attacks and minor ischaemic strokes. *Lancet Neurol* 2006; **5**: 323–31

Rothwell PM, Giles MF, Chandratheva A, *et al.* Effect of urgent treatment of transient ischaemic attack and minor stroke on early recurrent stroke (EXPRESS study): a prospective population-based sequential comparison. *Lancet* 2007; **370**: 1432–42

Safi HC, Miller CC. Spinal cord protection in descending thoracic and thoracoabdominal aortic repair. *Ann Thorac Surg* 1999; **67**: 1937–9

Sakalihasan N, Limet R, Defawe OD. Abdominal aortic aneurysm. *Lancet* 2005; **365**: 1577–89

Sampram E, Karafa MT, Mascha EJ, *et al.* Nature, frequency and predictors of secondary procedures after endovascular repair of abdominal aortic aneurysm. Nature, frequency and predictors of secondary procedures after endovascular repair of abdominal aortic aneurysm. *J Vasc Surg* 2003; **37**: 930–7

Sandnes DK, Sobel M, Flum DR. Survival after lower extremity amputation. *J Am Coll Surg* 2004; **199**: 394–402

Scharrer-Pamler R Kotsis T, Kapfler X, *et al.* Complications after endovascular treatment of thoracic aortic aneurysms. *J Endovasc Therapy* 2003; **10**: 711–8

Schechter MA, Shortell CK, Scarborough JE. Regional versus general anesthesia for carotid endarterectomy: The American College of Surgeons National Surgical Quality Improvement Program perspective. *Surgery* 2012; **152**: 309–14

Schermerhorn ML, O'Malley AJ, Jhaveri A, Cotterill P, Pomposelli F, Landon BE. Endovascular vs open repair of abdominal aortic aneurysms in the Medicare population. *N Engl J Med* 2008; **358**: 464–74

Schouten O, Dunkelgrun M, Feringa HH, *et al.* Myocardial damage in high-risk patients undergoing elective endovascular or open infrarenal abdominal aortic aneurysm repair. *Eur J Vasc Endovasc Surg* 2007; **33**: 544–9

Schunn CD, Hertzer NR, O'Hara PJ, Krajewski LP, Sullivan TM, Beven EG. Epidural versus general anesthesia; does anesthetic management influence early infrainguinal graft thrombosis? *Ann Vasc Surg* 1998; **12**: 65–9

Sear JW. Kidney dysfunction in the perioperative period. *Br J Anaesth* 2005; **95**: 20–32

Selvin E, Erlinger TP. Prevalence of and risk factors for peripheral arterial disease in the United States: results from the National Health and Nutrition Examination Survey, 1999–2000. *Circulation* 2004; **110**: 738–43

Shakespeare WA, Lanier WL, Perkins WJ, Pasternak JJ. Airway management in patients who develop neck hematomas after carotid endarterectomy. *Anesth Analg* 2010; **110**: 588–93

Shantikumar S, Ajjan R, Porter KE, Scott DJ. Diabetes and the abdominal aortic aneurysm. *Eur J Vasc Endovasc Surg* 2010; **39**: 200–7

Snowden CP, Prentis JM, Anderson HL. Submaximal cardiopulmonary exercise testing predicts complications and hospital length of stay in patients undergoing major elective surgery. *Ann Surg* 2010; **251**: 535–41

Stoneham MD, Thompson JP. Blood pressure management and carotid endarterectomy. *Br J Anaesth* 2009; **102**: 442–52

Stroke Association. Stroke statistics. 2013. Available from http://www.stroke.org.uk/sites/default/files/Stroke%20statistics.pdf

Struthers R, Erasmus P, Holmes K, *et al.* Assessing fitness for surgery: a comparison of questionnaire, incremental shuttle walk, and cardiopulmonary exercise testing in general surgical patients. *Br J Anaesth* 2008; **101**: 774–80

Thompson JP. Which non-cardiac medical conditions alter the operative risk? In: Naylor AR, Mackey, W, ed. *Carotid Artery Surgery: A Problem-Based Approach*. London: WB Saunders, 2000a; 149–55

Thompson JP. When is preoperative cardiac evaluation advisable? In: Naylor AR, Mackey W, ed. *Carotid Artery Surgery: A Problem-Based Approach*. London: WB Saunders, 2000b; 164–70

Thompson JP. Carotid and coronary disease management prior to open and endovascular aortic surgery. What are the current guidelines? *J Cardiovasc Surg* 2014; **55**(Supp 1–2): 1–14

Thompson JP, Danjoux GR. Guidance on the provision of vascular anaesthesia services. 2014. Available from http://www.rcoa.ac.uk/system/files/GPAS-2014-16-VASCULAR.pdf

Thompson JP, Smith G. Anaesthesia for vascular surgery of the lower limb. In: Bannister J, Wildsmith JA, eds. *Anaesthesia for Vascular Surgery*. London: Arnold, 1999; 267–93

Thompson SG, Ashton HA, Gao L, *et al.* Final follow-up of the Multicentre Aneurysm Screening Study (MASS) randomized trial of abdominal aortic aneurysm screening. *Br J Surg* 2012; **99**: 1649–56

UK EVAR Trial Investigators . Endovascular versus open repair of abdominal aortic aneurysm. *N Engl J Med* 2010; **362**: 1863–71

UK Small Aneurysm Trial Participants. Mortality results for randomised controlled trial of early elective surgery or ultrasonographic surveillance for small abdominal aortic aneurysms. *Lancet* 1998; **352**: 1649–55

van Marrewijk C BJ, Harris PL, *et al.* Significance of endoleaks after endovascular repair of abdominal aortic aneurysms: The EUROSTAR experience. *J Vasc Surg* 2002; **35**: 461–73

Vardulaki KA, Prevost TC, Walker NM, *et al.* Incidence among men of asymptomatic abdominal aortic aneurysms: estimates from 500 screen detected cases. *J Med Screen* 1999; **6**: 50–4

Vascular Society of Great Britain and Ireland. Quality Improvement Framework for Major Amputation Surgery. 2010. Available from http://www.vascularsociety.org.uk/doc-category/audit-qi/

Vascular Society of Great Britain and Ireland. Outcomes after Elective Repair of Infra-renal Abdominal Aortic Aneurysm. 2012. Available from http://www.vascularsociety.org.uk/vascular/wp-content/uploads/2012/11/VSGBI-Mortality-Report.pdf

Vascular Society of Great Britain and Ireland. A Best Practice Clinical Care Pathway for Major Amputation Surgery. 2016a. Available from https://www.vascularsociety.org.uk/_userfiles/pages/files/Resources/Vasc_Soc_Amputation_Paper_V2.pdf

Vascular Society of Great Britain and Ireland. Delivering a National Quality Improvement Programme for Patients with Abdominal Aortic Aneurysms. 2016b. Available from https://www.vascularsociety.org.uk/_userfiles/pages/files/Document%20Library/Final-AAAQIP-Public-Report-_VSGBI-August-2012_310812.pdf

Wahlgren C-M and Wahlberg E. Management of thoracoabdominal aneurysm type IV. *Eur J Vasc Endovasc Surg* 2005; **29**: 116–23

Wijeysundera DN, Austin PC, Beattie WS, *et al.* A population-based study of anesthesia consultation before major noncardiac surgery. *Arch Intern Med* 2009; **169**: 595–602

Wilson JA, Nimmo AF, Fleetwood-Walker SM, Colvin LA. A randomised double blind trial of the effect of pre-emptive epidural ketamine on persistent pain after lower limb amputation. *Pain* 2008; **135**: 108–18

Zacharias M, Conlon NP, Herbison GP, Sivalingam P, Walker RJ, Hovhannisyan K. Interventions for protecting renal function in the perioperative period. *Cochrane Database Syst Rev* 2008; **4**: CD003590

CHAPTER 59

Anaesthesia for neurosurgery and electroconvulsive therapy

Markus Klimek, Francisco A. Lobo, Luzius A. Steiner, and Cor J. Kalkman

Introduction

Neuroanaesthesia is the subspecialty of anaesthesiology that deals with patients undergoing surgical procedures in or close to the brain and the spinal cord. Neuroanaesthesia can be challenging, because sometimes apparently contradictory demands must be managed, for example, achieving optimal conditions for neurophysiological monitoring while maintaining sufficient anaesthetic depth, or maintaining oxygen delivery to neuronal tissue and simultaneously preventing high blood pressure that might induce local bleeding. Atypical patient positioning, management of increased intracranial pressure (ICP), and the need for early postoperative neurological evaluation are other typical challenges. This chapter addresses the general principles of neuroanaesthesia and special aspects of the most relevant procedures. A section on anaesthesia for electroconvulsive therapy (ECT) is also included.

Neuroanatomy, neurophysiology, and general principles of neuroanaesthesia including aspects of postoperative care

In neurosurgery, the surgeon and anaesthetist share the same target organ. Therefore, their mutual dependency is high and optimal collaboration is crucial. Such high-level teamwork requires a basic understanding of each other's field, including knowledge of the relevant neurophysiology, neuropathology, neurosurgical techniques, and neuroanaesthesia.

Weighing 1000–1500 g, the adult brain accounts for only 2–3% of total body weight, yet it receives 12–15% of the cardiac output and consumes 20% of all oxygen and 25% of all glucose. Thus, any disturbance of circulation or oxygenation, or both, will induce functional or even structural damage to the brain. 'Time is brain' is more than just a saying: the longer a disturbance lasts, the more severe the impact. Structural damage, such as destruction of neurones by trauma, resection, or ischaemia, cannot be repaired, and other neurones must take over the compromised functions. This often requires a long rehabilitation process. In contrast, functional damage (e.g. paraesthesia from ulnar nerve compression injury) can be reversible, but the recovery process may take a considerable time.

Adequate cerebral blood flow (CBF) and sufficient blood oxygen and blood glucose content are mandatory for normal brain function. CBF, however, cannot routinely be measured at the bedside or in the operating theatre. Cerebral perfusion pressure (CPP) is the driving force for CBF; it is defined as the difference between mean arterial pressure (MAP) and ICP:

$$CPP = MAP - ICP \tag{59.1}$$

Normal supine ICP is about 5–15 mm Hg. With normal blood pressure, CPP will be about 70–110 mm Hg. If ICP is increased as a result of, for example, a tumour or a haematoma, even a relatively minor decrease in MAP can result in cerebral ischaemia. Next to hypotension, hypoxaemia is another serious threat for the brain, as they both contribute to cerebral tissue hypoxia. Multiple studies have shown that preventing episodes of Sp_{O_2} less than 90% and systolic arterial blood pressure less than 90 mm Hg are the most important steps to take to achieve a good neurological outcome for a patient with brain injury (Chesnut et al. 1993; Citerio et al. 2000; Manley et al. 2001). In other terms, adequate cardiac output is required and sufficient oxygen delivery to the brain must be provided. This includes an appropriate haemoglobin concentration. However, the optimal transfusion threshold in patients with intracranial pathologies is still under debate.

Another important feature of the healthy brain is *cerebral autoregulation*. Cerebral autoregulation describes the ability of the brain to maintain a relatively constant level of CBF independent of current blood pressure. See Figure 59.1.

Contraction or dilation of cerebral blood vessels keeps CBF stable over a MAP range of 60–160 mm Hg. In patients with arterial hypertension, the range of autoregulation can shift upwards, which means that lower blood pressures are less well tolerated and may cause ischaemia. Therefore, blood pressure reduction in patients with cerebral pathologies and known hypertension should be performed very carefully, and in such patients the use of vasopressors or catecholamines, or both, to maintain arterial blood pressure during anaesthesia should be liberal. Furthermore,

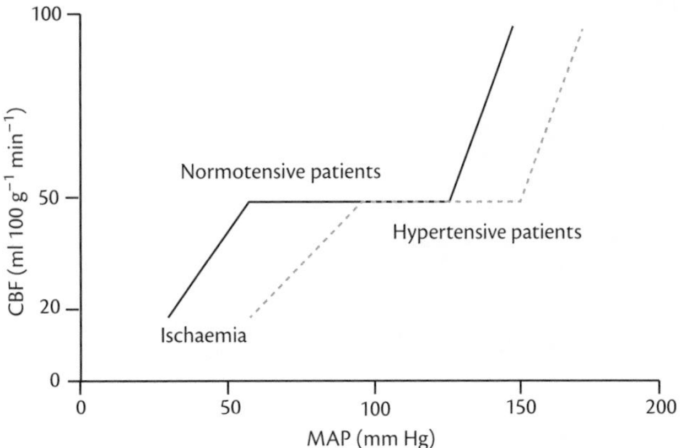

Figure 59.1 Cerebral autoregulation in normo- and hypertensive patients.

it is important to realize that in the presence of intracranial pathology (haematoma, tumour, etc.), cerebral autoregulation may be disturbed. In these cases, increasing arterial blood pressure will increase CBF via pressure-passive vasodilation, and ICP will increase via the increased cerebral blood volume. Regional CBF is also influenced by the metabolic activity of the respective parts of the brain. This flow–metabolism coupling enables functional magnetic resonance imaging (MRI) to image metabolically active brain regions.

Several factors other than MAP influence cerebrovascular tone: decreased pH, increased cerebral lactate, and, most importantly, hypercapnia will all induce cerebral vasodilation, which increases both CBF and cerebral blood volume. In contrast, hypocapnia induces vasoconstriction. Therefore, the neuroanaesthetist must be in control of arterial $P\text{CO}_2$ and pay close attention to any changes in end-tidal CO_2. Almost always the goal is to maintain strict normocapnia. Cross-checking end-tidal CO_2 with arterial blood gas analysis is standard practice. The regulative forces of the cerebral blood vessels should not be underestimated: pathological vasoconstriction from cerebral vasospasm can cause ischaemia and infarction of the brain distal to the constricted vessel.

At the skull base, the circle of Willis connects the two carotid arteries and the two vertebral arteries, providing communication between the blood supplies to the two brain hemispheres. At the cortical level, however, end-arteries provide the main blood supply, and, unlike other organs such as the gut, there is very limited collateral perfusion. This puts the cortex at a relatively high risk of ischaemia, especially at the peripheries of the main vascular territories.

The internal jugular veins provide the major venous drainage of the brain. Venous blood is the most important fluid component of the intracranial volume (three to four times more than arterial), and unobstructed venous drainage is important for haemostasis in the surgical field. A catheter directed upwards near the jugular bulb can be used to measure cerebral venous oxygen saturation Svj_{O_2}, which is one way of monitoring the adequacy of cerebral perfusion. Inadequate CBF will result in higher oxygen extraction and lower Svj_{O_2}. An Svj_{O_2} of 60–70% is considered normal, even in patients under general anaesthesia, illustrating the high oxygen extraction of the 'resting' brain. In the presence of epileptic activity, Svj_{O_2} can decrease dramatically. However, the clinical relevance of measuring Svj_{O_2} in daily neuroanaesthesia practice is limited because of its low sensitivity to detect focal ischaemia.

The cerebrospinal fluid (CSF) is the third relevant fluid component of the intracranial volume. An adult brain is surrounded by 120–150 ml of CSF, which acts as a type of protective 'bumper'. The daily production of CSF is around 500 ml. If this large amount of fluid cannot flow freely, hydrocephalus may develop within hours. CSF is produced in the ventricles, and reabsorbed into the venous blood by arachnoid granulations in the cerebral sinuses and along the spinal nerve roots. Epithelial cell layers with tight junctions create the blood–brain barrier, allowing free passage of O_2 and CO_2 but effectively shielding the brain from bacteria and larger molecules. This also provides a barrier to some therapeutic agents that must reach the brain to achieve their effects. In the presence of intracranial pathology (tumour, bleeding, trauma), this barrier can fail locally because of, for example, ensuing interstitial oedema.

Of the different fluid compartments in the brain, the volumes of venous blood and CSF have the highest variability. They can be displaced from the skull by an expanding intracranial mass. This mechanism can compensate for the increasing mass and maintain ICP in the normal range until they have been almost completely displaced from the cranium, when an abrupt increase in ICP occurs. Clinical signs may include a reduced level of consciousness, nausea and vomiting, and signs of focal brain herniation. This explains why intracranial mass lesions can often grow very large without any clinical signs or symptoms (see Fig. 59.2). On the other hand, it clearly highlights that symptomatic patients often require urgent therapeutic intervention, because compensatory mechanisms are exhausted. Infratentorial processes, in general, have an even higher need of urgent treatment compared with supratentorial processes, as the available space for compensation is smaller, and vital brainstem centres are close.

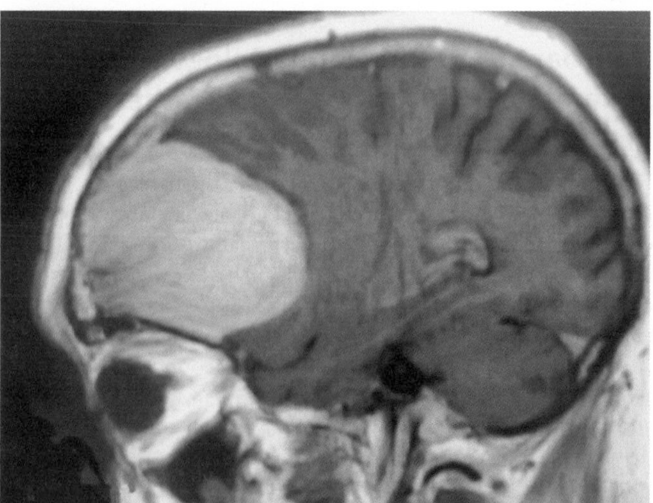

Figure 59.2 Frontal meningioma in a 57-year-old female patient without neurological deficits, who was treated for perimenopausal depression for 4 years before this scan was taken.

Courtesy: Erasmus MC, Rotterdam/NL.

Dealing with an increased ICP is one of the routine challenges of the neuroanaesthetist. Other than pharmacological measures, such as the infusion of mannitol (0.5 g kg^{-1}, approximately 200 ml of mannitol 15% in an adult patient) or hypertonic NaCl, deep anaesthesia, mild hyperventilation (intended Pa_{CO_2} not lower than 4.7 kPa), and physical measures such as 30° head-up tilt (anti-Trendelenburg) positioning are used to improve the drainage of CSF and venous blood. However, it is important to be aware that with head-up positioning, MAP must be maintained at a high enough level to secure adequate cerebral perfusion.

Perioperative management of the neurosurgical patient

The anaesthetist should be well informed about the patient's preoperative neurological condition, as it predicts postoperative performance, the need for planned intensive care unit (ICU) admission, and suitability for fast-track protocols. The eyes should be examined carefully, as the recognition and documentation of pre-existing anisocoria from previous eye surgery can prevent unnecessary postoperative emergency computed tomography scans. Many patients are understandably anxious before a neurosurgical procedure. Sedative agents must be used cautiously, however, because of their 'unmasking' effect. For example, a benzodiazepine may cause a patient in a 'compensated' neurological state to exhibit more serious neurological symptoms.

Positioning

Optimal access to the brain region of interest is essential for a safe and successful procedure. Therefore, neurosurgeons frequently use alternatives to the supine position. The long duration of neurosurgical procedures and the need for absolute immobility both increase the risk of pressure sores. Careful positioning with high-quality padding materials is mandatory. Flexion of the head is common and the anaesthetist needs to avoid accidental endobronchial intubation during positioning. Furthermore, excessive flexion or rotation restricts venous drainage of the brain. As a rule-of-thumb, at least three fingers should fit between the mandible and the clavicle of the patient. During the procedure, changes in table position are commonly requested: the patient must be well secured on the table to avoid accidents arising from such movements. As the patient's head will often be out of reach, all connections must be firmly secured and double-checked before the head is prepped and draped.

The brain itself has no nociceptors. Only craniotomy *per se* and manipulation of the dura and the cerebral blood vessels are painful. Critical phases of neurosurgery are frequently performed under the microscope, where inadvertent patient movement can be dangerous. Anaesthesia must therefore be deep enough to avoid any movements or coughing, especially while the patient's head is fixated in the Mayfield clamp. In patients who enter the operating theatre with a normal level of consciousness and undergo an uneventful procedure, a quick postoperative recovery is intended (fast-track neuroanaesthesia). Frequent neurological evaluation is the best diagnostic tool to detect postoperative complications. Therefore, the typical neuroanaesthesia regimen consists of short-acting agents for maintenance after an i.v. induction. If not contraindicated [because, e.g. facial nerve or motor-evoked potential (MEP) monitoring is to be performed], continuous use of neuromuscular blocking agents is common in neuroanaesthesia to prevent movement of the patient. However, the depth of anaesthesia should be sufficient to avoid awareness. The use of volatile anaesthetics for neurosurgical procedures is safe up to concentrations of 1.0 minimum alveolar concentration (MAC). However, total i.v. anaesthesia may be preferred when ICP is severely increased.

In craniotomy patients, postoperative pain can be severe, and sufficient postoperative pain therapy (including opioids with paracetamol) is encouraged. Because of concerns for increased risk of (intracranial) bleeding, non-selective non-steroidal anti-inflammatory drugs are not recommended for postoperative pain therapy in neurosurgical patients.

The most serious postoperative problems after craniotomy are reactive brain oedema causing increased ICP, and (re)bleeding in the surgical area. Therefore, most craniotomy patients have to be monitored in a high dependency unit (HDU), post-anaesthesia care unit (PACU), or ICU during the first postoperative night, and neurological function should be checked frequently. A possible exception is the patient who has undergone uncomplicated burr hole surgery: their postoperative complication risk is small and allows observation on a normal ward.

Postoperative hypertension is a risk factor for intracranial bleeding. Blood pressure must be monitored closely, preferably invasively, and systolic hypertension exceeding 140 mm Hg should be treated immediately by i.v. agents that are not cerebral vasodilators such as labetalol, nicardipine, or urapidil.

In all neurosurgical patients, special attention must be paid to the prophylactic use of antithrombotic agents during the early postoperative period. The risk of deep vein thrombosis is increased in brain tumour patients, but the impact of postoperative intracranial bleeding with re-trepanation on neurological recovery can be severe. Mechanical measures such as pneumatic stockings seem to be safe and effective, but should be combined with heparinoids when possible.

Because the brain reacts to the surgical trauma, the postoperative period is characterized by an increased risk of epileptic seizures. Patients who were treated with antiepileptic drugs before the procedure should continue these drugs in the perioperative period. Because some drugs are only available in an oral form, an alternative drug or application via the nasogastric tube must be used in patients who are not yet cooperative enough in the early postoperative period. There is, however, no evidence that routine prophylactic use of antiepileptic agents is beneficial and this is no longer practised in most centres. In the postoperative period, a non-convulsive status epilepticus is also possible. In case of doubt, EEG diagnosis of patients with a reduced level of consciousness should be performed early.

Anaesthesia for brain tumour surgery

The overall incidence of primary brain and central nervous system tumours is about 20 per 100 000 with most being non-malignant lesions [14 *vs* 7 per 100 000 in 2009 (Dolecek et al. 2012)]; the commonest in adults are gliomas (36%), meningiomas (32.1%), and pituitary adenomas (8.4%). The majority are located supratentorially (Fig. 59.3).

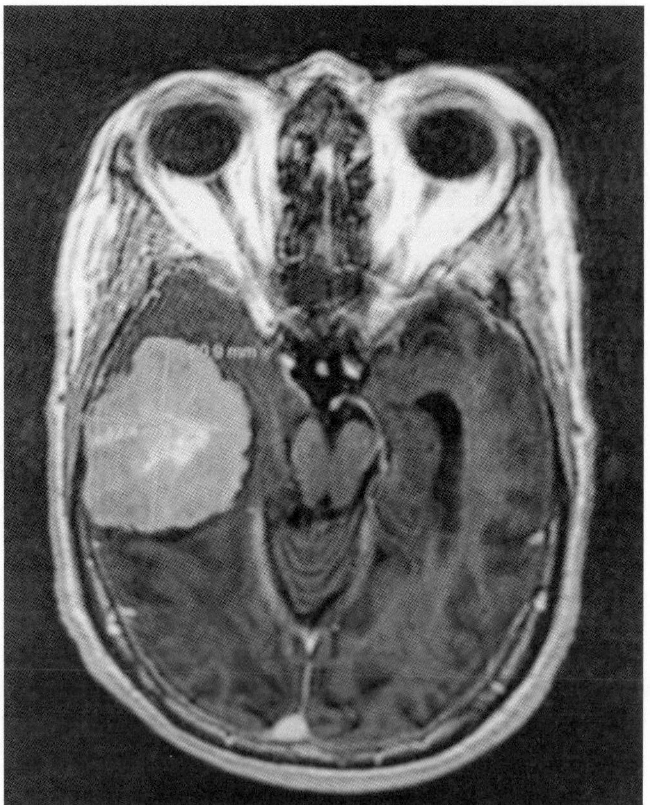

Figure 59.3 Large right convexity meningioma with uncal herniation.

The preoperative evaluation should include a complete neurological examination with particular emphasis on the level of consciousness, signs of raised ICP, existence of focal deficits, and the presence of seizures. Moreover, the knowledge of imaging data and the discussion with the neurosurgical team regarding positioning, surgical approach, risk of tumour bleeding, and vicinity of important cerebral structures such as vessels and cranial nerves are essential issues to address. In patients with poor cerebral compliance, premedication with sedative drugs may produce hypercapnia and must be used with caution.

Anaesthesia for brain tumour resection aims to optimize cerebral physiology already compromised by the intracranial mass. The goals are haemodynamic stability without swings in MAP and in CPP, and avoidance of drugs, techniques, and manoeuvres that increase ICP. The final end-point should be a fast and smooth emergence allowing an early neurological evaluation.

The search for an ideal neuroanaesthetic has remained inconclusive thus far. The cerebral vasodilating effect of volatile agents at higher concentrations (>1 MAC) is well known. In patients with relevant intracranial hypertension, many anaesthetists prefer to use an i.v. technique. Nitrous oxide is used increasingly less often for several reasons. Besides the known increases in cerebral metabolism, CBF, and ICP, and the increased risk of developing pneumocephalus, there is evidence for neurotoxic effects of nitrous oxide and increased postoperative nausea and vomiting (PONV), but initial fears for increased cardiac risk (Leslie et al. 2011) were not confirmed in a subsequent large randomized controlled trial (Myles et al. 2014). Propofol better maintains normal coupling between the cerebral metabolic rate of oxygen and CBF. However, in long procedures with high-dose propofol, one should consider the risk of the propofol infusion syndrome (Liolios et al. 2005).

As mentioned previously, the influence of Pa_{CO_2} on CBF necessitates maintenance of strict normocapnia. Failure to do so may either result in a bulging brain—when high Pa_{CO_2} causes cerebral hyperaemia—or increased risk of cerebral ischaemia when Pa_{CO_2} is low from inappropriate hyperventilation.

A slack brain will facilitate tumour resection, reduce the need for excessive retractor pressure, and reduce the incidence of ischaemic complications. If the general principles previously described are insufficient to decrease brain swelling, special measures may be needed. These include correcting head position to facilitate venous drainage, transient hyperventilation to manage extreme swelling and reduce the risk of brain herniation through the bone flap (realizing that excessive vasoconstriction in itself may produce cerebral ischaemia), and the use of osmotic diuretics such as mannitol. The use of hypertonic saline has gained renewed interest, providing effective brain relaxation without increased urine output.

Standard anaesthesia monitoring supplemented with invasive arterial blood pressure is standard practice. More advanced haemodynamic monitoring should be indicated by the patient's cardiac status. A second large-calibre peripheral or central venous line, or both, may be selected when location, size, or vascularization of the tumour represents a significant bleeding risk. The need for a central line and its preferred location should be discussed with the neurosurgeon. Subclavian, femoral, and cubital vein approaches are common in neuroanaesthesia, but internal jugular vein catheters are also possible without obstruction of the cerebral venous drainage (Mills and Tomlinson 2001).

Temperature should be measured during surgery to help maintain normothermia. The additional value of non-invasive cerebral oximetry monitoring or anaesthesia depth monitoring is limited by interference as a result of the proximity of the surgical field.

During haemostasis, neurosurgeons frequently request an increase of the blood pressure slightly above the normal awake blood pressure of the patient to be sure that no possible bleeding sources are missed. A small i.v. bolus of ephedrine or phenylephrine is sufficient in most cases.

Ideally, patients undergoing craniotomy for resection of a supratentorial lesion should be awake and extubated in the operating theatre at the end of the procedure, allowing early neurological evaluation. However, in some situations emergence may better be delayed until the patient is stable on the PACU or ICU. These include impaired preoperative consciousness, very large tumours, hypothermia, and the occurrence of surgical or anaesthetic complications (major bleeding, uncorrected electrolyte or metabolic disturbances, cerebral oedema, or seizures). The favourable pharmacokinetic properties of total i.v. anaesthesia with propofol and remifentanil allow predictable fast and smooth awakening. If the location of the craniotomy allows placement of a forehead sensor, an EEG monitor may be used to help titrate the i.v. anaesthetic. Remifentanil in combination with a low-dose volatile agent can also be used with similar results. One suggested technique to blunt deleterious haemodynamic responses during head bandaging and extubation at the end of the procedure is to keep a low-dose infusion of remifentanil [up to 0.05 $\mu g\ kg^{-1}\ min^{-1}$ (or if using target-controlled infusion: effect-site concentrations up to 2 $ng\ ml^{-1}$)] running during awakening and extubation. Alternatively, low-dose infusions of esmolol, labetalol, or lidocaine have been used for this purpose.

Finally, pain control is essential and there are several options. A preoperative scalp block with a local anaesthetic such as ropivacaine or levobupivacaine provides long-lasting analgesia when combined with i.v. paracetamol or cyclooxygenase-2 inhibitors. Nevertheless, many patients might need opioids for sufficient pain relief: despite the theoretical risk of respiratory depression, they can be given safely if titrated carefully on a HDU.

Surgery for infratentorial lesions

Neurosurgical procedures in the infratentorial compartment pose several challenges because of the involvement and manipulation of brainstem structures controlling regulation of respiration and the cardiovascular system. In children, the most common lesions are astrocytomas and neuroblastomas, while in adult patients, acoustic nerve tumours, metastatic masses, and meningiomas are the most common lesions, occurring in the cerebellar hemispheres, in the vermis, in the cerebello-pontine angle, in the clivus, or in the brainstem (Fig. 59.4).

There is no consensus among neurosurgeons regarding the best patient position for posterior fossa surgery, but sometimes the sitting position is requested and this constitutes a major challenge for anaesthetists. Other positions include the prone position, the 'park bench' position, and the lateral decubitus position (see Chapter 43). The sitting position deserves special attention: although it provides unrestricted mechanical ventilation of the lungs and access to the airway, it is associated with significant haemodynamic changes including decreased cardiac output and hypotension, pneumocephalus, venous jugular obstruction, peripheral nerve injury, and impaired cervical spinal cord blood flow, possibly leading to paraplegia. There is a high risk of venous air embolism from the entry of air into non-collapsible venous structures, such as bone and sinus. The occurrence of venous air embolism can be detected in several ways (see later paragraph) including capnography. The typical pattern is a rapid decrease of end-tidal CO_2, followed by a low-cardiac output state if large quantities of air have reached the lungs.

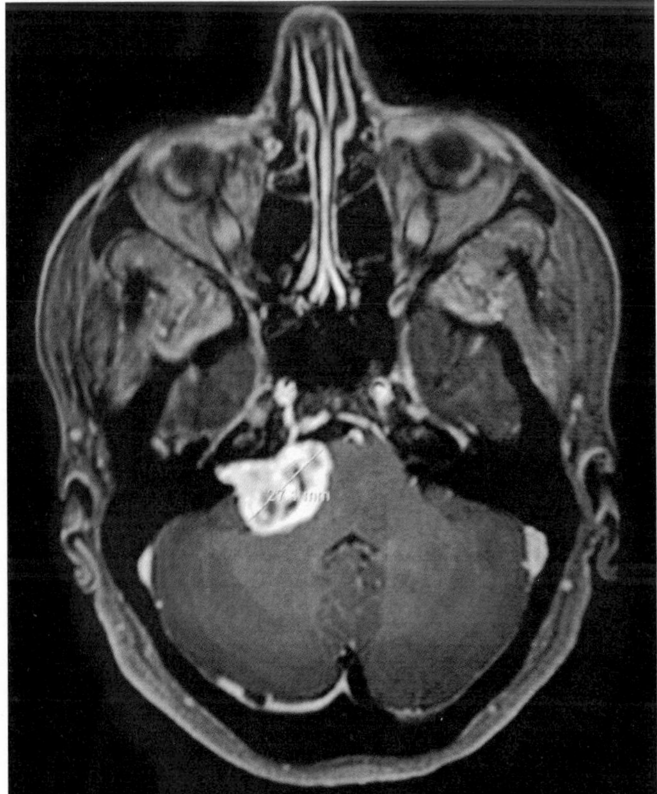

Figure 59.4 Right cerebellopontine angle schwannoma.

Because of the risk of a paradoxical right-to-left air embolism with serious cerebral complications in patients with a patent foramen ovale, preoperative echocardiography with a Valsalva manoeuvre is strongly recommended. Whether the surgery should be performed in the sitting position in patients with a patent foramen ovale (20% of the population) must be discussed with the neurosurgeon and the patient.

The anaesthetic technique for infratentorial approaches should be guided by the same principles as for the supratentorial approach. If the sitting position is to be used, monitoring should be compatible with early detection of common complications. Invasive cardiovascular monitoring is essential in patients with heart disease.

A precordial Doppler or transoesophageal echocardiogram can confirm the presence of air in the right atrium. The Doppler probe should be placed along the right parasternal border between the third and the sixth intercostal spaces. In the event of massive venous air embolism, withdrawal of air can be attempted from a properly positioned large-calibre, multiorifice central venous catheter, although it is unclear how often this has resulted in improved outcomes. This catheter should be positioned about 3 cm above the junction between the superior vena cava and the right atrium.

Venous air embolism is a neurosurgical emergency and the neurosurgeon should be informed immediately following detection so they can irrigate the surgical field and apply bone wax to the craniotomy edges to prevent any further air entry. Lowering the head to heart level will reduce the negative pressure gradient, while concomitant jugular vein compression may reduce the backflow of air to the heart. Aspiration of air from the central venous catheter can be attempted and administration of vasopressor drugs may help to overcome the increased pulmonary arterial resistance.

Immediate or delayed awakening and extubation at the end of the procedure again depend on the preoperative level of consciousness and on the occurrence of complications during surgery. Postoperative care should be directed towards the detection and treatment of complications resulting from perioperative manipulation of vital structures: airway patency may be decreased by facial oedema or effective ventilation may be impaired by surgical manipulation and oedema. The occurrence of a decreased level of consciousness, hypertension, bradycardia, and irregular breathing are signs of brainstem compression which requires reintubation and emergency re-craniotomy. Swallowing and other caudal brain nerve functions may be impaired. Because of these potentially life-threatening complications, all patients should be admitted to an ICU after infratentorial surgery.

Awake neurosurgery for brain tumour resection

Over the past decade, brain surgery that requires the patient to be awake has gained renewed interest among neurosurgeons, especially when tumours grow close to eloquent cortex (Fig. 59.5). It allows optimizing the extent of resection and minimizing the risk of permanent deficit. Awake craniotomy requires active anaesthetic management. Often, a brief period of general anaesthesia or

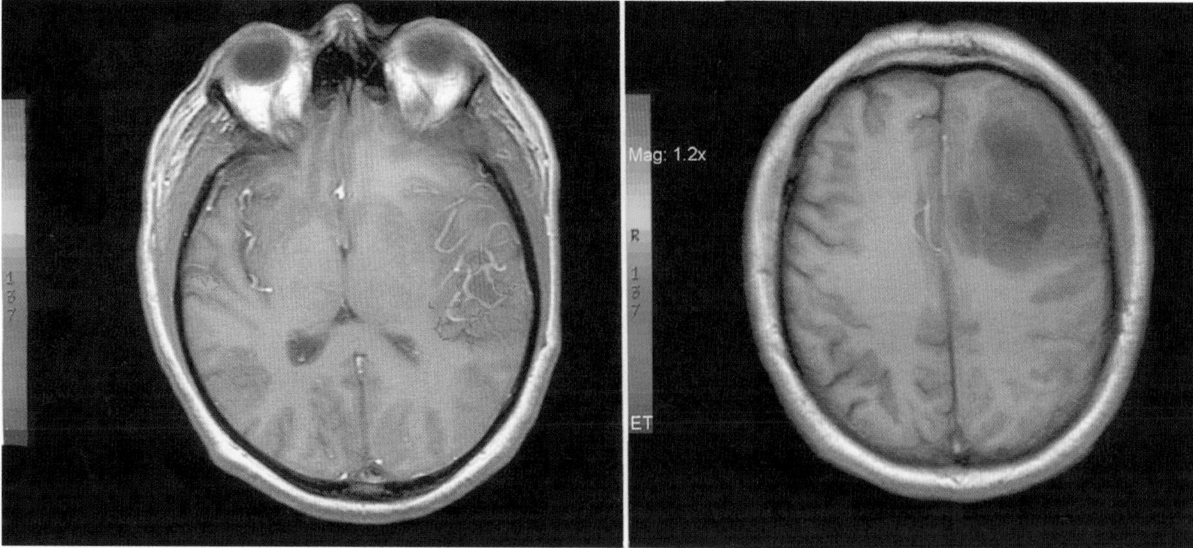

Figure 59.5 Functional MRI showing the close relation between a large brain tumour and a speech area.

sedation with an unprotected airway is used for craniotomy followed by the period of awake functional testing and lesion resection; a second period of general anaesthesia or sedation usually follows for craniotomy closure. Alternatively, the entire procedure is performed under conscious sedation.

The choice of the best combination of drugs and their optimum delivery is determined by the requirement to achieve an adequate level of anaesthesia and consciousness for each step of the procedure, allied to the challenge of suitable airway management throughout. Some authors who use the 'asleep–awake–asleep' technique use a laryngeal mask during the craniotomy phase under general anaesthesia with propofol and remifentanil, using target-controlled infusion, and Bispectral Index™ of the EEG (BIS™; Covidien, now Medtronic Minimally Invasive Therapies, Minneapolis, MN, USA) monitoring: this technique is associated with minimal incidence of complications and fast intraoperative awakening. Recently, dexmedetomidine has been suggested to provide good sedation and analgesia without ventilatory depression. Scalp block with local anaesthetic constitutes an essential component, providing important additional analgesia (Fig. 59.6).

Preoperative evaluation should assess the ability of the patient to cooperate (age and maturity, presence of psychiatric disorders or impaired consciousness from the primary disease), the airway (previous intubations, airway patency, ease of ability to perform mask ventilation, laryngeal mask airway insertion and intubation), presence and characteristics of seizures, and any clinical signs of increased ICP. Anticipation of specific difficulties and complications is a core task during awake craniotomies; for example, there is always the possibility of seizures occurring during the procedure. The surgeon can control most seizures by irrigating the cortical surface with iced saline; sometimes a small bolus (1–2 mg kg^{-1}) of thiopental might be necessary.

Positioning the patient is another essential issue when managing a patient undergoing awake resection of a brain tumour. Patients must be able to lie comfortably and be kept warm, with an adequate mattress and padding of the limbs, and with proper head and neck positioning avoiding excessive flexion or rotation. Communication between the patient and all relevant team members (anaesthetist, neurophysiologist, neuropsychologist, and neurosurgeon) must be assured in a sometimes frightening and noisy environment and enough space must be available in front of the patient (Fig. 59.7).

Monitoring is similar to that required for tumour surgery with general anaesthesia: invasive arterial blood pressure monitoring is recommended and allows arterial blood gas sampling. A central venous line is only indicated if a specific co-morbidity is present or if significant bleeding is anticipated. End-tidal CO_2 should also be monitored, both to detect hypoventilation and to help to control Pa_{CO_2} if controlled ventilation is used. Bladder catheterization is necessary, but the presence of the catheter may cause discomfort to the patient.

The increased extension of resection combined with a low incidence of complications and fast discharge home led some authors to suggest that awake craniotomy for brain tumour resection should be the rule, regardless of the lesion location and deficit risk (Brown et al. 2013).

Anaesthesia for patients with hydrocephalus

A hydrocephalus can be congenital, but also acquired as a result of intracranial haemorrhage or tumour in patients of all ages. A common feature is a mismatch between production and absorption of CSF or an obstruction of the circulation of the CSF, or both. Congenital hydrocephalus is frequently associated with other problems such as dysraphia, arachnoid cysts, or congenital tumours.

Patients with increased ICP as a result of hydrocephalus may have a decreased level of consciousness. Incontinence, nausea, and vomiting are common. Where there is severe intracranial hypertension, bradycardia and arterial hypertension will occur. This reflex hypertension (Cushing reflex) maintains cerebral perfusion and should not be treated with antihypertensive drugs, but indicates the need for urgent surgical intervention.

The surgical options for patients with CSF circulation disturbances depend on the cause of the hydrocephalus and the urgency of the problem. External drainage is a quick—but only temporary—option, while a ventriculoperitoneal shunt is the most common permanent solution. In the presence of abdominal infections or

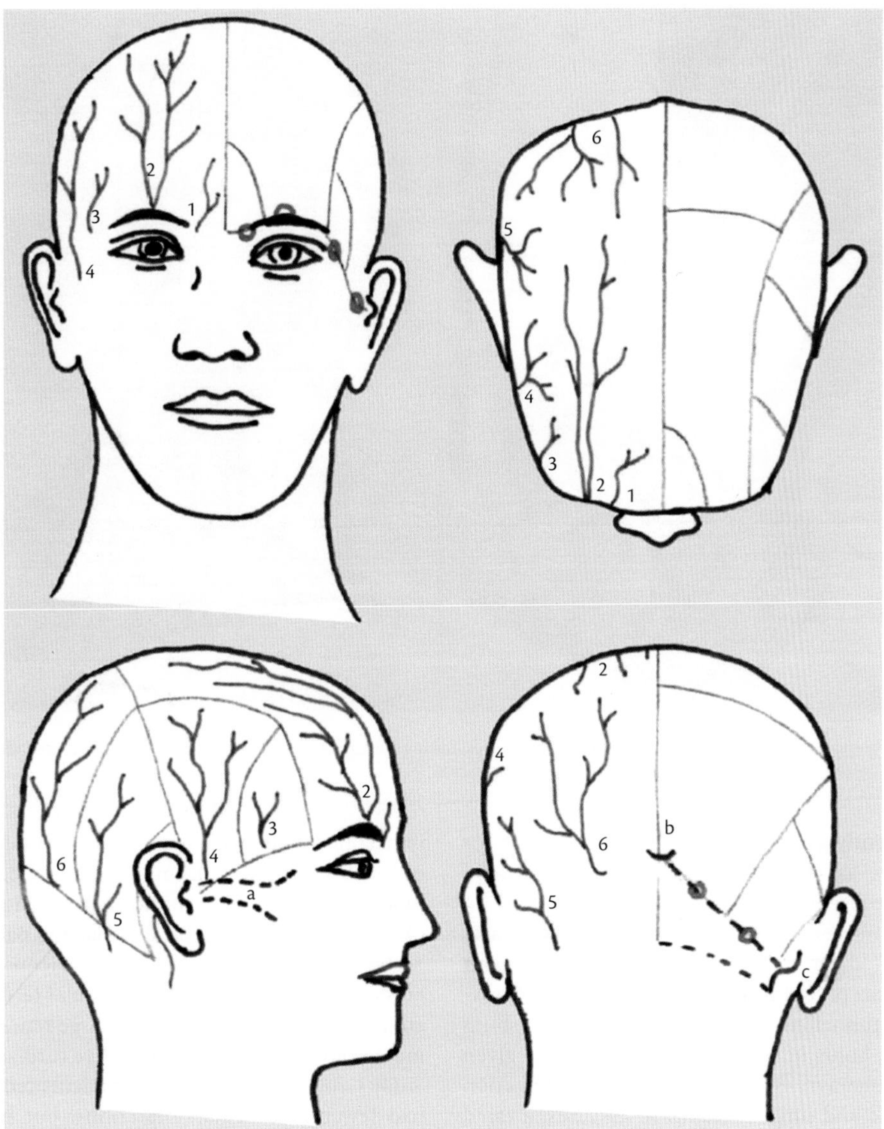

Figure 59.6 Nerves (N) to infiltrate for a unilateral scalp block and their respective sensory area: 1 = N. supratrochlearis (V1), 2 = N. supraorbitalis (V2), 3 = N. zygomaticotemporalis (V2), 4 = N. auriculotemporalis (V3), 5 = N. occipitalis minor (C2/C3), 6 = N. occipitalis major (C2). V = branch of trigeminal nerve, C = cervical spine nerve.

With kind permission from Springer Science+Business Media. *Der Anästhesist*, Kraniale Leitungsanästhesien. Volume 58, Issue 9, 2009, pp. 949–960, Kerscher, C. et al., Copyright © 2009 Springer Science and Business Media.

cerebral tumours with a tendency to induce metastases, a ventriculoatrial shunt is an alternative. In some cases, an endoscopic ventriculostomy can restore CSF circulation and no shunt is necessary. Unfortunately, all shunts are prone to infection and the need for revision, and very few patients will be cured with one single procedure. Especially in growing children, shunt dysfunction and dislocation are common, which may necessitate frequent urgent revision.

Shunt procedures require a patient with a sufficient depth of anaesthesia, especially during the tunnel manoeuvre of the shunt (subcutaneously from the neck to the middle of the abdomen), which is the most painful part of the procedure. In general, a first ventriculoperitoneal shunt can be placed within 45 min. In revision surgery, the procedure becomes much less predictable and can last from 15 min to hours. In relieving acute intracranial hypertension, severe brain-shifts are possible and these may cause bleeding as a result of sheared veins or herniation of the midbrain. Therefore, a careful reduction of the hydrocephalus is recommended. If the neurosurgeon plans a ventriculo-atrial shunt, the right jugular area should be kept free of other i.v. catheters to avoid contamination or knotting catheters. As soon as ICP normalizes, reflex hypertension will disappear, and vasoactive agents may be necessary to re-stabilize blood pressure.

If the level of consciousness is reduced, the risk of aspiration is increased. If the patient has been vomiting, fluid balance and electrolytes should be corrected. As most patients have to undergo several procedures, proper documentation of previous procedures enables optimal care during the following ones. Most patients with acute shunt dysfunction present in a much worse state and require more urgent therapy than those undergoing a first (elective, planned) shunt insertion.

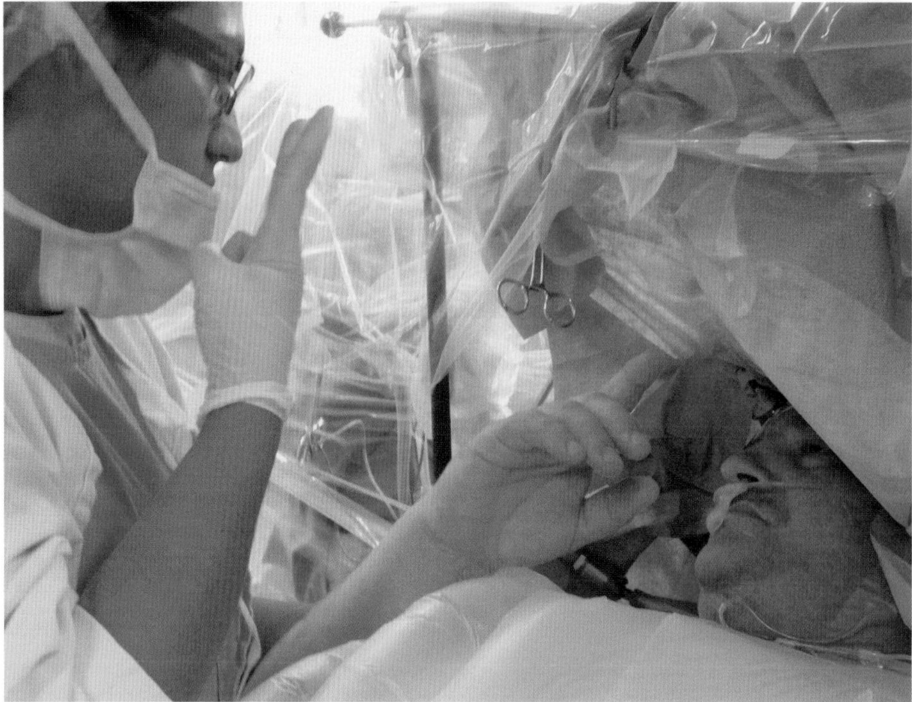

Figure 59.7 A patient undergoing resection of a tumour close to the speech area, talking with a neuropsychologist. Note the free space in front of the patient's head and how the transparent drapes contribute to a friendly environment.

Thiopental is frequently chosen as the induction agent for hydrocephalus surgery, as most patients will require a rapid sequence induction to prevent aspiration (Shapiro et al. 1973). In the presence of severe intracranial hypertension, total i.v. anaesthesia might be preferred for maintenance, but a volatile agent can also be used for these procedures. The response to acute noxious stimulation from tunnelling the ventriculoperitoneal shunt can be obtunded by a bolus of remifentanil (1 μg kg^{-1}) given 1–2 min before the manoeuvre. This requires a good interaction between the anaesthetic and surgical teams. In all cases, a rapid emergence is preferred to enable early assessment of neurological function. Postoperative pain intensity is relatively minor and can be reduced further by infiltration of the abdominal wound with local anaesthetic by the surgeon. In general, postoperative care can be provided on the ward, but in some cases ICU observation is necessary. HDU or ICU admission should be considered for very young patients and those who have a low level of consciousness or a high ICP.

Anaesthesia for neurovascular procedures

An intact cerebral circulation is critical to maintain normal neuronal function. As the brain has no energy stores, any disruption of CBF, for example during cardiac arrest, will result in dense global ischaemia, immediate loss of ATP generation, and rapid neuronal cell death.

Cerebral infarction

Cerebral infarction occurs after acute disruption of CBF as a result of the rupture of a vulnerable atherosclerotic plaque or from emboli originating upstream (left atrium, carotid arteries, paradoxical embolization via open foramen ovale). It presents clinically as acute ischaemic stroke, with neurological symptoms that represent loss of function in the ischaemic brain area. Less frequently, cerebral infarction results from prolonged cerebral ischaemia as a result of hypotension. This typical ischaemic pattern is often labelled a 'watershed' infarction, because ischaemia is most prominent in border zone areas of the main vascular territories. This stroke variant received new interest after a large randomized trial (POISE) of metoprolol to prevent perioperative cardiac complications (POISE Study Group 2008) found that patients receiving acute β-blockade had fewer myocardial infarctions, but higher mortality and a greater incidence of stroke. The latter might be related to perioperative hypotension.

Current treatment for acute stroke consists of revascularization by timely i.v. administration of recombinant tissue plasminogen activator. Apart from providing life support for comatose patients, this form of stroke treatment typically does not require active intervention by anaesthetists. However, the rapid development of interventional neuroradiology has renewed interest in endovascular removal of the embolic material using various retrieval devices. For these procedures, anaesthesia assistance is requested more frequently. The anaesthesia goals here are to maintain circulation and oxygenation and actively manage blood pressure as needed for the procedure, in particular the prevention of periprocedural hypotension. There is an ongoing debate about the use of general *vs* local anaesthesia for these procedures. At the time of writing, there are several ongoing studies on this topic (Simonsen et al. 2016).

Cerebral aneurysms

Genetic disposition combined with lifestyle (hypertension, smoking) may result in the development of a cerebral arterial aneurysm, a bulging protrusion of the weakened cerebral arterial wall. Aneurysms are preferentially located at bifurcations of the arteries originating from the circle of Willis (Brisman et al. 2006). Figure 59.8 shows angiographic images and a three-dimensional rendering of a large unruptured aneurysm of the anterior communicating artery.

Once the diameter of a cerebral aneurysm exceeds a critical threshold, it may rupture either spontaneously or in response to a stressful event that raises blood pressure. The resulting subarachnoid haemorrhage (SAH) typically causes immediate severe headache and can rapidly result in intense cerebral ischaemia as a result of raised ICP and loss of consciousness. SAH occurs more often in women (sex ratio: 2:1) and peaks between 40 and 60 years of age. The incidence of SAH is approximately 1:10 000, which translates to 74 000 new cases annually in all European countries combined. Outcome after SAH is poor. Of patients that reach the hospital alive, between 15% and 20% die within 6 months; another 20% survive with poor neurological outcome.

Symptoms of SAH vary from sudden headache only, to a life-threatening neurological emergency with coma and focal neurological deficit. The sudden loss of CPP can trigger massive release of adrenaline and noradrenaline which raises blood pressure. This autonomic storm can produce ECG abnormalities suggesting myocardial ischaemia and release of troponin as a result of subendocardial injury, even in patients with normal coronary arteries. The massive catecholamine release can also result in neurogenic pulmonary oedema.

The clinical severity of SAH is currently classified using the World Federation of Neurological Surgeons (WFNS) scale, a simple system to grade a patient with SAH that is less subject to interobserver variability than older scales (Table 59.1).

Treatment

Treatment of ruptured and unruptured aneurysms consists of excluding the aneurysm from the circulation by surgical ligation using small metal clips ('clipping': Fig. 59.9) or by percutaneous endovascular 'coiling'. With coiling, a fine metal wire mesh is inserted into the aneurysmal sac via the endovascular route. The resulting coiled wire mesh slows blood flow in the aneurysm and results in thrombus formation, effectively reducing the risk of (re) bleeding (Fig. 59.10). However, not all aneurysms are accessible to

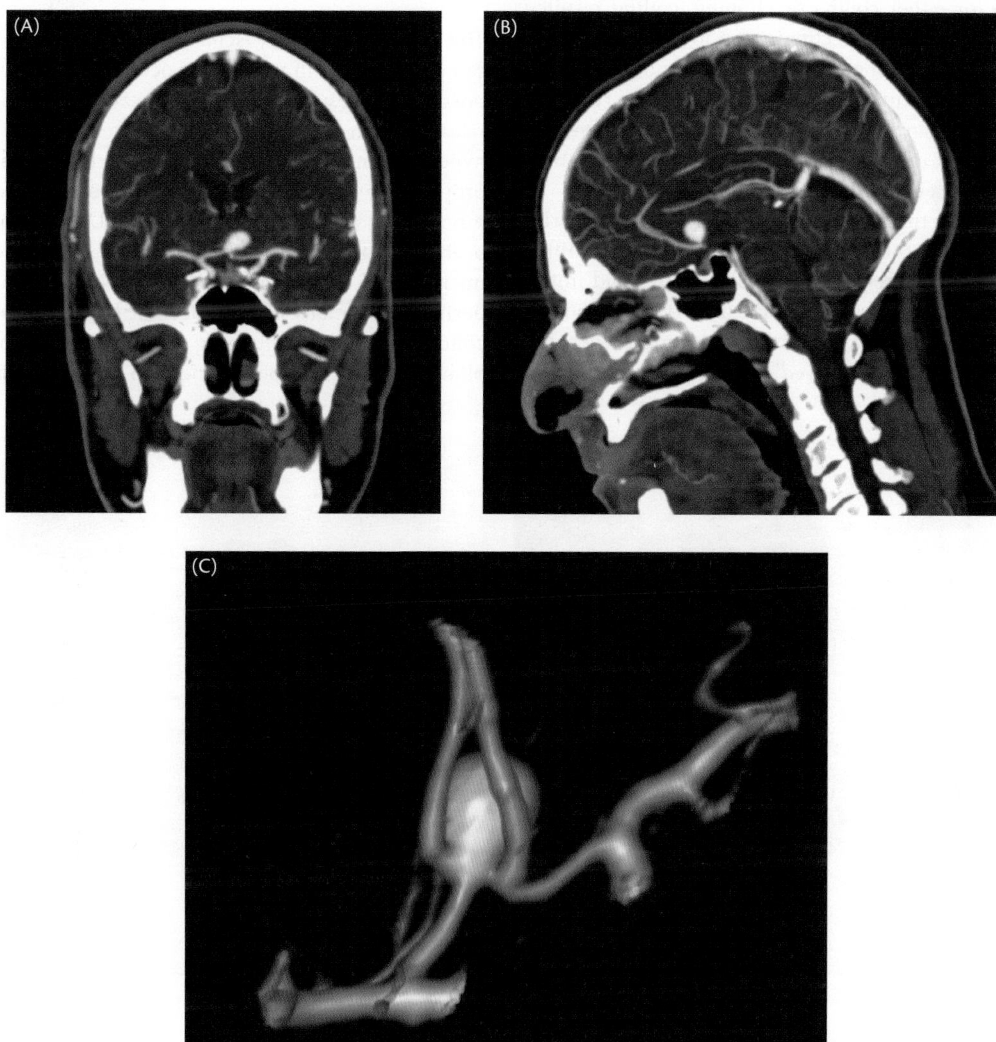

Figure 59.8 (A) and (B) Coronal and sagittal views of anterior communicating artery aneurysm. (C) Three-dimensional reconstruction of the same unruptured aneurysm.

Table 59.1 World Federation of Neurological Surgeons Grading System for Subarachnoid Haemorrhage (WFNS) scale

Glasgow Coma Score	Motor deficit	Grade
15	Absent	1
13–14	Absent	2
13–14	Present	3
7–12	Present or absent	4
3–6	Present or absent	5

Reproduced from *Journal of Neurology, Neurosurgery, and Psychiatry*, Teasdale, G.M., Drake, C.G., Hunt, W., *et al.*, A universal subarachnoid hemorrhage scale: report of a committee of the World Federation of Neurosurgical Societies. Volume 51, p. 1457, Copyright © 1988 with permission from BMJ Publishing Group Ltd.

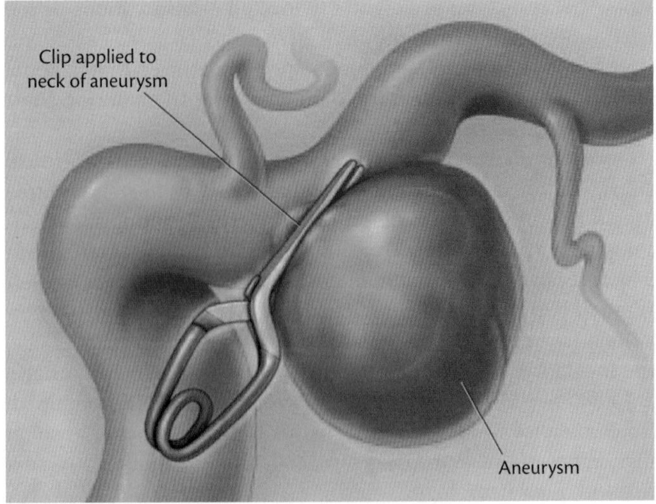

Figure 59.9 Cerebral aneurysm with permanent clip applied.
From *New England Journal of Medicine*, Ellegala, D.B. and Day, A.L., Ruptured cerebral aneurysms, 352, 2, pp. 121–4, Copyright © 2005 Massachusetts Medical Society. Reprinted with permission from Massachusetts Medical Society.

coiling. In order for the wire coil to stay in place, the neck of the aneurysm must be sufficiently narrow. Most 'wide-neck' aneurysms are therefore primary candidates for surgical clipping.

The results of coiling are as good as those of surgical clipping with less immediate postoperative neurological deficits. In a randomized trial of patients with ruptured intracranial aneurysms who were eligible for either coiling or clipping, coiling resulted in a better outcome than surgical clipping up to 7 years after the procedure. Endovascular coiling of aneurysms has now surpassed surgical clipping as the primary mode of treatment for ruptured and unruptured cerebral aneurysms. After coiling there is a low, but significantly higher risk of late rebleed or need for recoiling than after clipping (Molyneux et al. 2005).

If the patient survives the initial SAH, there is a substantial risk of rebleeding (15–20% in the first 2 weeks). Emphasis has shifted from a delayed operation after the acute episode, to rapid initiation of definitive treatment by securing the aneurysm as soon as possible. After surgery or coiling, there is a time window where the patient remains at high risk for *delayed cerebral ischaemia* (DCI). The cause of secondary ischaemia is incompletely understood, but can be explained in part by the occurrence of cerebral vasospasm, possibly as a result of nitric oxide scavenging by free haemoglobin released from erythrocytes. Deliberately producing hypertension, hypervolaemia, and haemodilution (triple 'H' therapy) has been proposed to prevent DCI, but it requires invasive haemodynamic monitoring and admission to an ICU. This therapy has never been subjected to rigorous testing in randomized trials. It is also unclear if all three components are necessary to improve cerebral perfusion. As many patients become hypovolaemic after SAH, it is conceivable that maintaining normovolaemia and (supra)normal blood pressure will be sufficient to maintain cerebral perfusion,

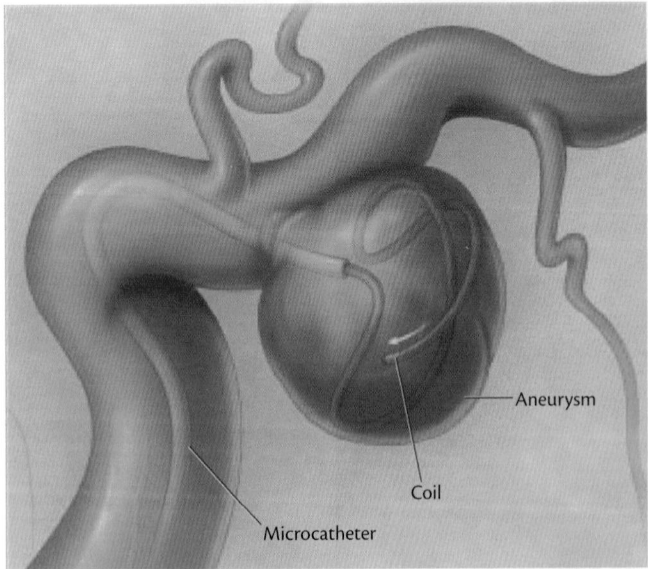

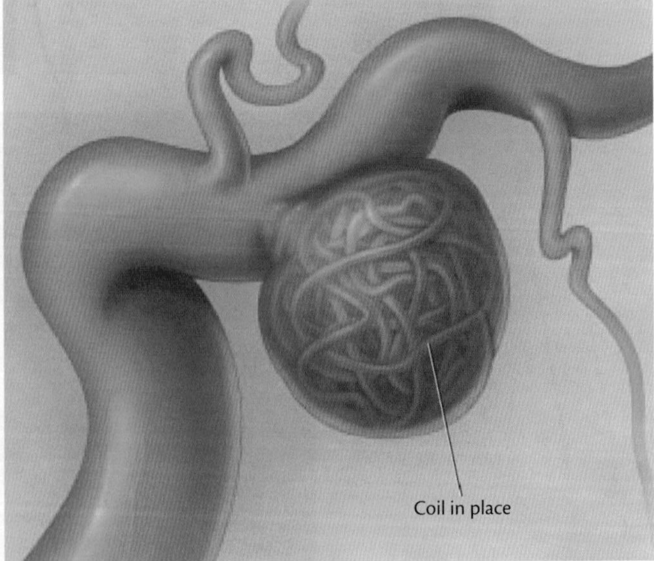

Figure 59.10 Insertion of a wire coil into a cerebral aneurysm and final completed coil.
From *New England Journal of Medicine*, Ellegala, D.B. and Day, A.L., Ruptured cerebral aneurysms, 352, 2, pp. 121–4, Copyright © 2005 Massachusetts Medical Society. Reprinted with permission from Massachusetts Medical Society.

without the attendant risks of pulmonary oedema from deliberate overfilling.

Anaesthesia for aneurysm surgery

Basic neuroanaesthesia goals

The basic anaesthesia goals for cerebral aneurysm surgery are creating an environment that facilitates optimal surgical access to the aneurysm, prevention of cerebral ischaemia, and dynamic maintenance of blood pressure at pre-agreed levels, according to the phase of the procedure. A pre-briefing with the entire surgical team allows clear communication about the surgical and anaesthesia goals and joint setting of targets for blood pressure.

Preoperative preparation of the patient

Review the patient's history and co-morbidity and identify the aneurysm's size, shape, and location from the imaging data. The preoperative ECG may be abnormal as a result of subendocardial injury resulting from the sympathetic discharge at the time of initial bleeding. Isolated ECG abnormalities are no reason to postpone surgery. Good-grade patients who are extremely anxious may benefit from premedication with a benzodiazepine. Monitoring of the arterial blood pressure waveform allows rapid intervention in case of imminent hypertension or hypotension; an arterial line before anaesthesia induction is therefore essential. Central venous pressure monitoring is of limited value. However, delivery of vasopressors via a central line will facilitate precise titration to the desired MAP values. Blood pressure targets should be guided by the patient's preoperative blood pressure values (if available) and the WFNS grade. Targeted blood pressure during temporary clipping will usually be higher than during maintenance.

Induction

During anaesthesia induction it is essential to maintain strict control over blood pressure in order to prevent a blood pressure spike that might result in rebleeding immediately before surgery. Make sure that the patient has received an adequate opioid dose before attempting intubation. A low dose of lidocaine i.v. (0.5 mg kg^{-1}) may help to mitigate the intense stimulation from laryngoscopy and tracheal intubation. In case of anticipated difficult intubation, it might be prudent to start a propofol infusion, with or without a remifentanil infusion to prevent arousal because of inadvertent return of consciousness when intubation takes longer than expected. Further high-risk stages are the application of the head pins and skin incision. Here, again, inadequate analgesia can increase blood pressure and possibly result in rebleeding. Some centres infiltrate the scalp with local anaesthetic to prevent this response.

Maintenance

Despite several comparative studies, including some randomized controlled trials, there is no evidence for a superior anaesthesia technique for cerebral aneurysm surgery. Most modern anaesthetic techniques allow the anaesthetist to achieve good surgical conditions and good blood pressure control when combined with a continuous vasopressor infusion via a syringe driver. Both sevoflurane and propofol are frequently used to produce unconsciousness. Continuous remifentanil infusions have become popular as remifentanil's predictable short duration of action allows stable intraoperative opioid concentrations during infusion and rapid recovery after discontinuation.

Temporary clipping

Once the aneurysm has been exposed, the surgeon can apply one or more clips directly on the neck of the aneurysm. This is the ideal situation. More often, it will be necessary to temporarily decrease blood flow to the aneurysm by occluding two or more afferent vessels with temporary clips (Fig. 59.11). Depending on the location of the aneurysm and the temporary clips, a smaller or larger brain region will become ischaemic (Ellegala and Day 2005). Increasing blood pressure during temporary clipping may restore some blood flow to the ischaemic area by increasing flow in collateral vessels. The surgeon will ask to record the time of temporary vessel occlusion. Several short episodes (2 min each) separated by a sufficient reperfusion interval may be better tolerated than one initial longer period of vessel occlusion.

Cerebral protection

Several strategies have been developed to increase cerebral tolerance to ischaemia and prevent ischaemic brain injury. Neuroprotective drugs either reduce cerebral metabolism or inhibit post-ischaemic

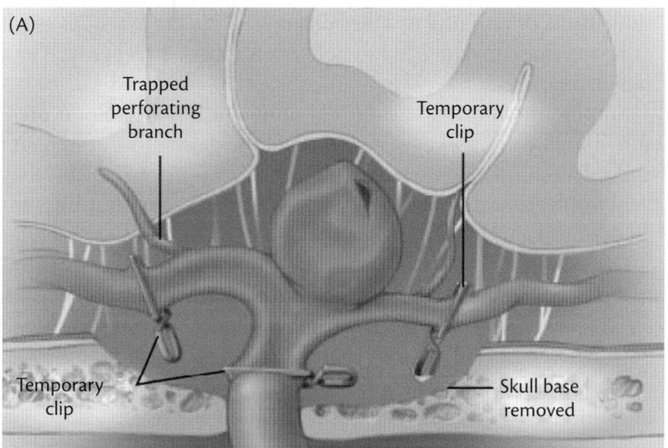

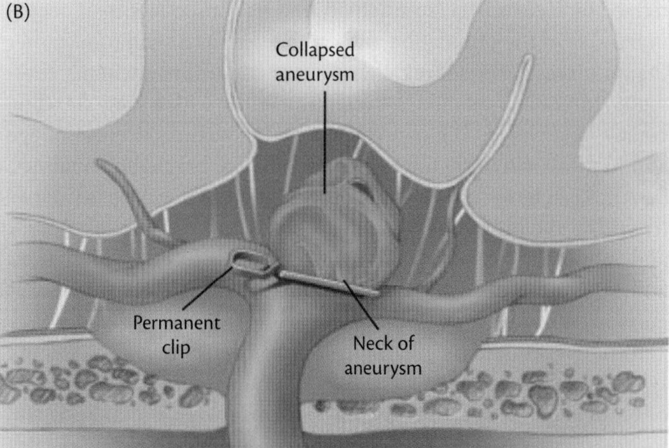

Figure 59.11 (A) Three temporary clips exclude a ruptured aneurysm from the arterial circulation; the brain areas behind the perforating branches are now ischaemic. (B) A permanent clip has been applied to the neck of the aneurysm.

From *New England Journal of Medicine*, Ellegala, D.B. and Day, A.L., Ruptured cerebral aneurysms, 352, 2, pp. 121–4, Copyright © 2005 Massachusetts Medical Society. Reprinted with permission from Massachusetts Medical Society.

injurious processes, but their effects in clinical studies have been disappointing. Reducing body temperature is an established neuroprotective strategy. Deep hypothermic circulatory arrest (core temperature 20°C) can extend ischaemic neuronal survival to 20 min. It has been applied in the treatment of complex basilar artery aneurysms. However, there is no benefit from routinely cooling all patients presenting for aneurysm surgery (Todd et al. 2005). Administering a bolus of thiopental, propofol, or etomidate to decrease cerebral metabolic rate immediately before temporary clipping or hyperoxygenation (FI_{O_2} 1.0) is also frequently performed, but there is no evidence that this results in better neurological outcomes (Hindman et al. 2010).

Disaster management

Immediate action is required when intraoperative haemorrhage from the aneurysm occurs. It may be necessary to decrease MAP transiently to 40–50 mm Hg and use temporary clips to regain control. This emergency situation requires optimal communication between the surgeon and anaesthetist.

Extubation

Assuming that the aneurysm is secured, extubation can proceed as after a regular craniotomy. To prevent an excessive blood pressure increase during emergence, one may decide to stop the volatile agent or propofol after the last suture and continue a remifentanil infusion until the head is bandaged and the patient is transferred to a bed. Obviously, only good-grade [WFNS 1–2–(3)] patients, who were awake and conversant before induction of anaesthesia should have their trachea extubated in the operating theatre. In all other cases it is safer to extubate after several hours in the ICU.

Postoperative care

Postoperative care will often be in the ICU or a HDU, depending on the preoperative grade of the patient. Blood pressure control should be continued after the operation and many patients will need antihypertensive medication to control post-craniotomy hypertension. However, if the aneurysm is secured by a clip, blood pressure ranges can be more liberal than before surgery.

Anaesthesia for epilepsy surgery

Epilepsy is a chronic and disabling neurological disorder, characterized by recurrent seizure activity and its consequences. It occurs in 0.5–1% of the population and can be seen as a symptom, rather than a disease, developing after several conditions (genetic, traumatic, tumours, metabolic), presenting either with a long-standing course or *de novo*. The incidence is higher at the extremes of age and in those with structural or developmental brain abnormalities. Seizures can be seen as a failure of regulation of the electrical activity within the brain, resulting in an imbalance between excitatory and inhibitory neuronal activity, which leads to burst discharges and generation of hyper-synchronous firing of a large number of cortical neurones.

Initial treatment is pharmacological, determined by seizure type and history, age, and side-effects, and combination therapy is often needed. Despite progress in pharmacological management, in 20–30% of cases medication alone cannot control seizure activity. Patients with a localized focus and drug-resistant seizures, or suffering from severe medication-related side-effects may benefit from ablation of the epileptogenic brain area in an attempt to improve seizure control, cognitive and psychosocial outcomes, and hence quality of life. Surgical treatment can be divided into curative (temporal lobectomy in temporal lobe epilepsy) or palliative surgery to decrease seizure severity or frequency, or both (corpus callosotomy in patients with disabling drop attacks, and vagal nerve stimulation).

In order to assess potential surgical candidates and determine the balance between risks and benefit for the individual patient, epileptogenesis must be determined by seizure characteristics (semiology), interictal and ictal EEG, and neuroimaging. Functional examination may include functional MRI, intra-carotid amobarbital procedure or Wada test, neuropsychological testing, and transcranial magnetic stimulation.

Anaesthesia planning for these procedures must consider potential recording of cerebral electric activity, activation of epileptic focus, and intraoperative cortical mapping with electrocorticography—spike activity monitoring via a small electrode placed over the cortex—in order to guide accurate definition of both seizure foci and eloquent cortices, and the resection margins.

Anaesthetic management

Patient history must include a detailed characterization of the disease including pattern, type, and frequency of seizures. Perioperative management of antiepileptic drug therapy is vital in maintaining seizure control. These are generally continued into the perioperative period and doses should be adjusted in order to keep adequate plasma concentrations (Perks et al. 2012). Side-effects, drug interactions, and maintenance dosing of antiepileptic drugs during periods of starvation are important considerations. Coexisting medical problems may be present and must be evaluated. An important contribution of the anaesthetist in the presurgical evaluation of the patient referred for surgical treatment of epilepsy is the anaesthetic management during performance of the Wada test. Temporary anaesthesia of one cerebral hemisphere with the patient awake, allowing the lateralization of language and memory, is required mostly when temporal lobectomy and amygdalohippocampectomy are planned. Although functional imaging has replaced this method for language mapping, it continues to be essential for memory study. For this purpose, a short-acting i.v. anaesthetic drug is administered into the internal carotid artery via an endovascular catheter. The possibility of occurrence of common side-effects of propofol or other drugs used for the Wada test such as myoclonic movements and confusion must be recognized and rapidly managed.

Routine monitoring is sufficient although invasive blood pressure measurement is suggested to avoid the discomfort of frequent cuff inflation. As mentioned previously, raw or processed EEG may help to titrate and guide anaesthetic dosing allowing fast intraoperative awakening if an 'asleep–awake–asleep' technique is used.

General anaesthesia management is similar to any other intracranial procedure, but anaesthetic agents that have minimal effects on electrocerebral activity and electrophysiological recordings should be used. The advantages of general anaesthesia include improved operating conditions, by controlling Pa_{CO_2} and MAP, and assurance of immobility and unconsciousness of the patient. Disadvantages include inability to assess speech and language. Benzodiazepines should be avoided and before electrocorticography, anaesthesia depth should be decreased. Burst suppression in the recordings suggests excessive depth of anaesthesia that needs to be addressed. During electrocorticography, neuromuscular blocking agents may be needed to avoid movement and several drugs may be used to elicit epileptiform activity. When seizure activity is provoked by a drug or by cortical stimulation, the cortical surface should be irrigated afterwards with iced saline to stop the epileptic activity.

In cases involving eloquent brain areas, electrocorticography is combined with intraoperative functional mapping requiring an awake and cooperative patient. This can be accomplished by combining local anaesthesia (field block or preferentially a scalp block) and sedation, or with an asleep–awake–asleep technique with a laryngeal mask for airway management, as described for resection of brain tumours located close to eloquent areas. Almost all considerations addressing the anaesthetic management of awake craniotomy for brain tumour resection may be applied for awake epilepsy surgery. Again, the selection of different options must be preceded by a detailed discussion between all members of the team and be adapted to their experience and skills. In every case, favourable conditions for the procedure and evaluation must be provided without compromising safety and comfort of the patient.

Administered drugs must provide anxiolysis, analgesia, and comfort without interfering with monitoring. Carefully titrated short-acting agents are preferred, minimizing interference of anaesthesia with functional evaluation. If an asleep–awake–asleep technique is chosen, the combination of remifentanil and propofol is usually used, but dexmedetomidine is a valuable alternative. It provides effective analgesia, sedation, and absence of interference with recordings at doses of 0.2 $\mu g\ kg^{-1}\ h^{-1}$ (Souter et al. 2007). Raw or processed EEG might be used throughout the procedure, helping to titrate the level of consciousness and reduce the time for emergence during the operation.

There are important interactions between antiepileptic drugs and drugs commonly used in anaesthesia, and these affect both drug efficacy and the risk of seizure activity intraoperatively. Induction and inhibition of the hepatic cytochrome P450 isoenzymes constitutes the most significant mechanism, especially with older-generation antiepileptic drugs. For example, chronic phenytoin therapy increases the clearance of rocuronium from 0.26 to 0.75 litres min^{-1} but has no effect on other pharmacokinetic parameters (Fernandez-Candil et al. 2008).

Many anaesthetic agents themselves affect the propensity to seizures, both in patients with epilepsy and in those with no prior history of seizures. Some agents have different effects depending on the dose: generally low doses are proconvulsant while higher doses have anticonvulsant activity. This is clearly the case with propofol: while it causes activation in small doses, it produces EEG burst-suppression at clinical doses. Propofol is currently used to treat refractory status epilepticus.

Benzodiazepines have well-known anticonvulsant activity. Thiopental is an anticonvulsant at clinical doses. Etomidate and methohexital activate the EEG and should be avoided, unless the desired effect is to activate seizure foci intraoperatively. As little as 25 mg of methohexital is enough to elicit epileptiform potentials in the epileptogenic area and this constitutes the drug of choice for this situation.

Volatile agents such as isoflurane, desflurane, and sevoflurane also have dose-dependent effects on seizure activity: epileptiform activity is suppressed by low doses and an isoelectric EEG is produced at 2 MAC; however, there are several reports of sevoflurane-induced seizures and epileptiform EEG.

None of the neuromuscular blocking agents appear to have proconvulsant effects, although they may interfere with intraoperative monitoring of myogenic motor-evoked potentials (MEPs).

Anaesthesia for patients undergoing pituitary gland surgery

Tumours of the pituitary gland are common in neurosurgery. They account for 10–15% of intracranial tumours and can be found in all ages with a peak around the third and fourth decades (Nemergut et al. 2005).

The symptoms from the tumour are either caused by endocrine activity or mass effect. Depending on the hormone produced, various endocrine syndromes are possible, for example, acromegaly in case of growth hormone or Cushing's syndrome in case of an adrenocorticotropic hormone-producing tumour. Mass-effects of the tumour may result in compression of the optic nerve and visual field disturbances, but bleeding inside the pituitary gland is also possible which can result in panhypopituitarism. In case of a hormone-producing tumour, involvement of an endocrinologist in a multidisciplinary team is common, as many of these patients have been treated conservatively before the decision for surgery has been made.

Another important aspect is the size and position of the tumour: the smaller the tumour and the more it is located in the (frequently enlarged) sella turcica, the more accessible it is for the transsphenoidal approach (often performed in cooperation with an ENT surgeon). Extremely big tumours with a relevant suprasellar part must be accessed by frontal or pterional craniotomy, which is a much more invasive procedure.

Patients with Cushing's syndrome frequently have hypertension and glucose intolerance that have to be controlled perioperatively. Patients with acromegaly show similar medical problems (hypertension, diabetes mellitus, coronary artery disease), but can also be challenging for the anaesthetist because of macroglossia obstructing the airway, a tough skin that is difficult to puncture, and body proportions that make positioning difficult. Furthermore, patients with acromegaly frequently have narcolepsy and sleep apnoea, which must be taken into account when organizing postoperative care.

All pituitary gland surgery is performed under general anaesthesia. In the transsphenoidal approach, the nasal mucosa is often infiltrated with local anaesthetics containing adrenaline to reduce bleeding. This infiltration is quite noxious and can induce vagal responses if anaesthesia is too light, while systemic absorption of adrenaline can induce arterial hypertension and tachycardia. Another stimulating part of the procedure is the drilling towards the sella. The transsphenoidal approach provides a small surgical field with a restricted view for the neurosurgeon. Accidental entry into the sinus cavernosus—which lies in close proximity to the sella turcica—can cause serious bleeding. Furthermore, at the end of the procedure it is important that any leakage of CSF is detected, as it might cause ascending meningitis. Therefore the neurosurgeon may request a Valsalva manoeuvre to increase the ICP. It is also common for an external lumbar spinal catheter to be placed at the end of the procedure to reduce CSF pressure during the early postoperative period.

Anaesthesia induction and maintenance are the same as for other types of brain tumour surgery. Because of the risk of bleeding and rapid changes in blood pressure, especially during the transsphenoidal approach, as well as the need for repeated blood sampling for glucose management, an arterial catheter is advisable. Procedures using the subfrontal or pteronial approach always require an advanced level of monitoring. As diabetes insipidus is common in all cases, a urinary catheter should be inserted.

Surgical manoeuvres during these procedures might induce kinking of the tracheal tube, and an armoured (Woodbridge) tube might be useful to prevent airway obstruction. In transsphenoidal surgery, a throat pack can be inserted after tracheal intubation to prevent blood entering the stomach and hence reduce the risk of PONV. In the rare cases of pronounced acromegaly with macroglossia, an awake fibreoptic intubation might be considered. Bleeding is rare, but if it occurs, it can be severe. Therefore, good peripheral venous access should be established. If a throat pack has been inserted, it must be removed before extubation of the trachea.

Postoperative pain after transsphenoidal surgery can be treated sufficiently with a combination of paracetamol and opioids.

After pituitary surgery, the need of hormonal replacement therapy must be kept in mind during the postoperative period. Patients with Cushing's syndrome might need higher doses of hydrocortisone perioperatively, but diabetes insipidus can also occur in the postoperative period, with the need for desmopressin treatment.

Immediately after transsphenoidal surgery the patient will not be able to breathe through the nose. While most patients can be discharged to normal wards after uneventful surgery and recovery, patients with obstructive sleep apnoea who normally use a continuous positive airway pressure mask at night may need postoperative care on a HDU. Many patients find removal of the nasal tampon to be painful, but in general this is performed by the surgeon without anaesthesia involvement.

To avoid CSF leakage, all activities that might increase ICP should be avoided in the first few postoperative days.

Finally, in patients who have undergone transsphenoidal surgery previously, the anaesthetist should avoid inserting nasotracheal or nasogastric tubes, as they might create a false passage and end up in the brain.

Anaesthesia for functional neurosurgery/stereotactic procedures

Functional neurosurgery is used for the treatment of a broad range of disorders characterized by changes of function of the central nervous system without major structural or anatomical changes. The initial indication for deep brain stimulation was Parkinson's disease, but its use has been extended to other neurological disorders such as dystonic syndromes and epilepsy, to some psychiatric illnesses such as depression, obsessive–compulsive disorders, and to chronic pain.

Changes in the physiology of the central nervous system, produced either by chronic electrical stimulation or by the generation of a lesion, are obtained after precise localization of structures such as the subthalamic nucleus, globus pallidus internus, and ventralis intermedius nucleus of the thalamus. These techniques require the use of a stereotactic frame but recent advances in imaging and neuronavigation systems allow the performance of frameless procedures. Besides the stereotactic and imaging approaches, neuroelectrophysiological techniques are used to localize the target structures.

Usually, these procedures entail fixing the patient's head within a rigid frame in the operating theatre or neuroradiology suite followed by an imaging study; the patient is then transferred to the operating theatre for the remainder of the procedure.

The use of general anaesthesia (reviewed by Poon and Irwin 2009; Venikatraghavan and Manninen 2011; Erickson and Cole 2012) or sedation is controversial because of suppression of neural recordings and, in Parkinson's disease, tremor. Local anaesthesia is the preferred anaesthetic technique in most centres but even then, monitoring by an anaesthetist is essential for a good outcome through provision of analgesia and sedation when necessary and management of complications (Harries et al. 2012).

Besides discussion with neurosurgical and neurological teams and the selection of appropriate patients, the anaesthetist should consider the implications of medical co-morbidities such as hypertension or obesity, and the impact of stopping the medications used to control the condition to be treated. Psychological preparation of the patient is important for a long day spent in the neuroradiology suite and operating theatre in an uncomfortable position. Airway evaluation should be performed even when general anaesthesia is not planned: dystonia in off-treatment Parkinson's disease can be problematic.

The choice of anaesthetic technique should be adapted to each patient and to the procedure: a patient with severe dystonia or psychotic symptoms probably needs general anaesthesia. Even when general anaesthesia is used, local anaesthesia or scalp block is used for head-frame placement; local anaesthetics such as ropivacaine provide long-lasting analgesia with low risk of toxicity (Costello et al. 2004). The anaesthetist must be aware of the effect of anaesthetic drugs on neural recordings and tremor: for example, drugs such as propofol, remifentanil, and β-blockers have been associated with temporary suppression of Parkinsonian tremor. Dexmedetomidine was shown to be a safe drug for use during neurophysiological recordings (Rozet 2008). The use of a low-dose infusion of propofol, especially if used with a target-controlled infusion system and tight titration of the target concentration, may improve patient comfort during periods when recordings and clinical evaluation are not being performed (Raz et al. 2010).

Blood pressure control is essential to minimize the risk of intracranial bleeding. The role of β-blocker drugs in Parkinson's disease and their effect on the intensity of the tremor is unclear, so these drugs are best avoided for blood pressure control; safe acceptable alternatives are i.v. calcium channel blockers such as nicardipine or clevidipine. Interestingly, there is evidence that deep brain stimulation modulates heart rate, blood pressure, heart rate variability, baroreceptor sensitivity, and blood pressure variability (Hyam et al. 2012).

After stimulation, electrodes are placed in the cerebral targets though a burr hole and the wires are tunnelled through the skin and connected to a stimulator inserted subcutaneously on the chest wall. This short last step, after removal of the stereotactic frame, may be performed under balanced or i.v. general anaesthesia using a laryngeal mask and controlled ventilation.

Proper positioning in the beach-chair position is essential, maximizing comfort and decreasing the risk of compression of anatomical structures. The neck should be positioned to avoid airway compromise, the legs flexed with support under the knees, and all pressure points should be padded. Again, a large free space around the patient improves their comfort and ensures contact with all the team members. Indeed, with an awake patient, environmental details are important: a comfortable room temperature should be maintained, while room noise and the number of people present should be minimized. Communication between the team and the patient must be possible at all moments.

Monitoring depends on the anaesthetic technique but ECG, oxygen saturation, and end-tidal CO_2 are mandatory. Because of the need for strict blood pressure control to avoid intracranial bleeding, invasive arterial blood pressure monitoring is advised, but the catheter may need to be sited in the brachial artery if wrist immobilization could interfere with intraoperative clinical evaluation. A bladder catheter may cause discomfort, especially in men in whom a sheath catheter is an option; if a catheter is not used, fluid administration should be restricted.

Intraoperative complications are uncommon, but may be serious. A review of 176 patients reported a 16% incidence of intraoperative adverse events including neurological (seizures, consciousness impairment, and neurological deficits), respiratory (airway obstruction and respiratory distress), and cardiovascular (hypertension) complications in addition to severe pain, nausea and vomiting, and blood loss (Venikatraghavan et al. 2006). Venous air embolism was also reported and should be remembered as a possible and life-threatening complication (Chang et al. 2011).

Respiratory complications are a concern. The fixed head with a stereotactic frame limits airway management. The key for opening and removing the frame must be readily available as release should be immediate if severe airway obstruction or respiratory depression occurs. Patients with Parkinson's disease may have restrictive pulmonary disease with the possibility of postoperative respiratory complications especially after general anaesthesia.

Neurological complications may appear during or after the procedure, demanding early diagnosis and treatment. Seizures are usually focal and self-limiting but tonic–clonic activity may be treated with small doses of propofol. A major neurological injury such as intracranial cerebral bleeding may cause a sudden impairment of consciousness; facilities to secure the airway for imaging and for craniotomy should be readily available. Postoperative cognitive disturbances may require multidisciplinary management.

Patients should resume their preoperative medication as soon as possible, particularly those with Parkinson's disease.

Stereotactic cerebral biopsy

Imaging techniques such as computed tomography or MRI allow accurate localization of lesions and their targeted biopsy using needle aspiration. This procedure requires the placement of a stereotactic head frame although frameless systems with fiducial markers over the scalp may be also used. Intra-hospital transport is required with a two- or three-stage process (neuroradiology suite and operating theatre; or operating theatre, neuroradiology suite, and operating theatre again).

Anaesthetic approaches include an awake patient with sedation and local anaesthesia or general anaesthesia (e.g. for an uncooperative patient or if the prone position is required). If position and patient condition allow, a possible technique is to perform a scalp block supplemented with a low-dose infusion of remifentanil and local anaesthetic injection at the pin sites.

If general anaesthesia is indicated, it should be induced and the trachea intubated before head-frame placement. Total i.v. anaesthesia with propofol and remifentanil is ideal to maintain anaesthesia during transport between different locations in the hospital.

Monitoring should be adapted to the anaesthetic technique. Nevertheless, even in the awake patient special attention should be paid to blood pressure, end-tidal CO_2, and, if sedation is used, processed EEG indices of consciousness.

Postoperative care should be provided at least initially on a HDU, as there is a risk of intracranial bleeding.

Stereotactic cerebral radiosurgery

The aim of cerebral radiosurgery is the ablation of small tumours or vascular lesions using focused appropriate radiation and it is performed in the radiotherapy department within a closed room with a linear accelerator. Children and non-cooperative patients need general anaesthesia for head-frame placement and immobilization during 1–3 h of treatment. Most radiotherapy departments have the appropriate anaesthesia equipment but sometimes it may be necessary to induce general anaesthesia in the operating theatre and then transfer the patient. The anaesthetist usually has to monitor the patient from outside the locked treatment room using a video camera system.

Anaesthesia for patients with traumatic brain injury

Patients of all ages are affected by traumatic brain injury: 'shaken' babies, infants after accidents, teenagers and young adults involved in sports and traffic accidents, and elderly people typically as a consequence of a fall. By far the largest group are young male adults. In patients with acute head injury, there must be a very high index of suspicion for trauma to other parts of the body: up to 40% of patients have further relevant trauma; in 10% the spine is affected (Fearnside and Simpson 2005). Hence, a stiff-neck collar should be fitted to all patients with a traumatic head injury at the scene of the accident. Other coexisting conditions are aspiration of gastric contents and occasionally neurogenic pulmonary oedema. Many patients who present with severe head injury are intoxicated with alcohol, cocaine, or other substances. Very often, patients suffering from acute traumatic brain injury were previously healthy. However, particularly in elderly patients, the use of warfarin or other drugs which interfere with coagulation (i.e. factor Xa inhibitors such as rivaroxaban or direct thrombin inhibitors such as dabigatran) should be ruled out.

Surgery aims at evacuation of haematomas or other space-occupying lesions such as large contusions and possibly at lowering ICP via craniectomy when massive brain swelling is present. In severe head injury, ICP monitoring or brain tissue oxygenation monitoring sensors, or both, will often be implanted by the neurosurgeon. The evidence that such monitoring improves patient outcome is controversial. Nevertheless, most management algorithms for severe head injury incorporate data from such devices. Typical complications of the procedures are rapidly developing brain oedema; lesions interfering with postoperative control of motor functions including airway control; and particularly with acute subdural haematomas and large contusions or intracerebral haemorrhage, considerable intraoperative blood loss and coagulation disorders. The surgical requirements of anaesthesia include stable haemodynamics with control of oxygenation, Pa_{CO_2}, blood glucose, and correction of coagulation abnormalities.

The initial Glasgow Coma Scale (GCS) score at the scene or after resuscitation may be used to judge the severity of the injury. However, the increasing use of tracheal intubation at the scene of the trauma and coexisting intoxication may obscure the severity of the injury. Moreover, many patients deteriorate in the hours after injury as a result of secondary brain injuries (i.e. brain injuries developing as a complication of the primary injury sustained at the time of trauma). Head injuries leading to an initial GCS score of 8 or less are considered to be severe. These patients typically have their trachea intubated as early as possible to protect the airway. Preoperative investigations include a cerebral computed tomography scan for which the patient usually requires tracheal intubation if this has not already occurred. At the same time, the cervical spine should be cleared and if possible the stiff-neck collar should be removed as it may cause venous congestion and, hence, an increase in ICP. Very early insertion of an arterial line, certainly before in-hospital induction of anaesthesia, facilitates blood pressure control and control of blood gases and blood glucose. The difference between Pa_{CO_2} and end-tidal CO_2 may vary considerably in head-injured patients (Seguin et al. 2001), hence the need for regular blood gases. Steroids have no role in the treatment of acute head injury (Alderson and Roberts 2005). If a relevant increase in ICP is suspected (e.g. unilateral or bilateral 'blown' pupil), boluses of mannitol (0.25–1 mg kg^{-1} i.v.) or hypertonic saline (e.g. 0.5 ml kg^{-1} of NaCl 20% i.v.) may be used. Hypertonic saline should be administered via a central line because of its potential to cause thrombosis and phlebitis.

A major concern during induction of anaesthesia is haemodynamic stability. Cerebrovascular pressure autoregulation should not be expected to be functional in contrast to CO_2 reactivity, which is only lost in very severe injury. Therefore, control of CPP or MAP is of utmost importance. There is no single best agent for anaesthetic induction, provided the changes in MAP or systolic pressure are anticipated and treated pre-emptively. If no ICP monitoring is available, systolic blood pressure should be maintained at greater than 90 mm Hg (Badjatia et al. 2008). Once ICP monitoring has been established, CPP should be monitored and the range between 50–70 mm Hg targeted (Brain Trauma Foundation et al. 2007a). In infants and children, lower thresholds (as low as 40 mm Hg in babies) are recommended (Kochanek et al. 2012). A rapid sequence induction is standard procedure. There is some debate regarding the ICP-raising effects of suxamethonium. With the introduction of sugammadex, rocuronium has become the first-choice neuromuscular blocking agent of many anaesthetists in this situation. For maintenance of anaesthesia, inhalation anaesthetics or propofol may be used. If inhalation anaesthetics are used, the cerebral vasodilator effects of higher doses (i.e. exceeding 1 MAC) should be anticipated and avoided, as they may cause an increase in ICP.

Blood glucose concentrations should be controlled. Although the evidence regarding which target value to use is unclear, 6–10 mmol $litre^{-1}$ is usually recommended (Oddo et al. 2008). Crystalloids (typically NaCl 0.9%) are used for volume replacement. Glucose-containing solutions and other hypo-osmolar solutions should not be used. Intraoperative blood loss—and if severe, coagulation—should be closely monitored and treated with a recommended target haemoglobin concentration of 7–9 g dl^{-1}. In patients with evidence of cerebral ischaemia, the target haemoglobin concentration should be greater than 9 g dl^{-1} (Retter et al. 2013). Prophylactic hypothermia is currently not recommended. The decision to extubate the patient's trachea immediately after the surgical procedure will depend on the GCS score at intubation and the extent of the surgical procedure. Frequently, in patients who are monitored with an ICP probe, extubation is only attempted when ICP has stabilized in the normal range and the increase in Pa_{CO_2} associated with weaning is tolerated. Subsequent postoperative management should be based on a current CPP/ICP algorithm (Protheroe and Gwinnutt 2011).

The primary task of the anaesthetist is to prevent secondary injury. The most important secondary insults are low CPP (<50 mm Hg), hypoxia, and raised ICP. For oxygenation, a peripheral saturation greater than 90% should be maintained whenever possible (Badjatia et al. 2008). The target value for Pa_{O_2} is controversial. At values less than 8 kPa, cerebral vasodilation and consequent increase in ICP must be anticipated. The role of (normobaric) hyperoxia is currently unclear. Many anaesthetists target values greater than 12 kPa, but this is an arbitrary threshold. A positive end-expiratory pressure (PEEP) trial may be used if PEEP is required for sufficient oxygenation. Often, if PEEP remains lower than ICP there are no repercussions on ICP. Pa_{CO_2} target values in the low normal range (3.5–4.5 kPa) are typically chosen (Brain Trauma Foundation et al. 2007b). ICP exceeding 20 mm Hg should be treated even if CPP is adequate. Head-up positioning, sedation, and analgesia together with neuromuscular blockade are initial measures. If further treatment is required, boluses of mannitol or hypertonic saline may be used up to an osmolarity of 320 mOsm $litre^{-1}$ or a Na^+ of 155 mmol $litre^{-1}$. Hypothermia and barbiturates are further options if these measures are insufficient. If the ICP increases unexpectedly, recurrent intracranial bleeding or increasing brain oedema and seizures should be ruled out. Seizures occurring within 7 days of brain injury are typically treated with phenytoin. However, this does not decrease the rate of seizures occurring late after trauma.

Anaesthesia for spinal surgery

Patients of all age groups may require spinal surgery; indications include congenital, degenerative, and traumatic pathologies. Commonly associated medical conditions include pre-existing neurological deficits related to the spinal pathology, disturbed respiratory mechanics as a result of cervical spinal lesions, and restrictive pulmonary disease as a result of kyphoscoliosis. However, cardiac co-morbidity is common given the large number of elderly patients undergoing spinal surgery. Particularly in patients with spina bifida and related conditions, there is a risk of latex allergy. Concurrent drugs with anaesthetic implications are pre-existing pain therapy (opioids, antidepressant therapy) and medication interfering with neuromuscular block such as baclofen. Furthermore, all drugs interfering with coagulation and platelet aggregation are important in these patients.

Surgery predominantly aims at decompression of neural structures as a result of blood, abscess, tumour, and disc herniation, stabilization of the vertebrae, or correction of malformations such as scoliosis. Complications include neurological deficits, severe bleeding particularly during cancer surgery, infection, CSF leakage, and postoperative deep venous thromboembolism. There are some specific issues regarding anaesthesia in spinal surgery. When the patient has an unstable cervical spine, particular attention must be paid to tracheal intubation in order to avoid spinal cord damage. Patient positioning is also crucial, again particularly in patients with an unstable spine. For some procedures on the ventral thoracic spine, single-lung ventilation via a double-lumen tube is required to expose the ventral parts of the vertebrae. Moreover, often an anaesthetic technique that does not interfere with spinal cord monitoring [somatosensory-evoked potentials (SSEPs) to monitor sensory function and MEPs to monitor motor pathways] must be carefully chosen (Raw et al. 2003). In some cases, the surgeon requests an intraoperative phase where the patient is deliberately awoken to assess neurological function. While it is possible to perform certain procedures such as lumbar intervertebral disc surgery under spinal anaesthesia, most surgeons are reluctant to operate under spinal anaesthesia because of the inability to assess neurological function immediately postoperatively.

The anaesthetist should be fully aware of the type of spinal pathology that is present. Mostly, any instability and any potential danger of neurological damage during tracheal intubation or positioning of the patient should be established. With instability of the cervical or upper thoracic spine, a detailed assessment of the airway is required to choose the least harmful method of intubation. In patients in whom a stiff-neck collar cannot be removed before intubation, the reduced mouth opening and rigidity of the neck need to be considered. Typically, in such patients and in those with potential instability, fibreoptic intubation is performed either after induction or in the awake patient. Preoperative assessment of neurological status is essential in all patients with compromised respiratory mechanics or airway protection. Pulmonary function testing may be required in patients with restrictive disease as a result of scoliosis or in patients with motor deficits that interfere with breathing or the clearing of secretions. In many centres, turning the patient into the prone position, which is required for the majority of procedures on the spine, is only performed in the presence of a senior surgeon and possibly with spinal cord monitoring before and after positioning the patient.

Tracheal intubation inevitably leads to movement of the spine, and the key issue with induction is how intubation will be performed, in the awake or sedated patient, and how movement of the cervical and upper thoracic spine can be minimized. There is no 'best' approach. The approach must be based on the individual patient and the preferences and skills of the anaesthetist (Crosby 2006). Any medication may be used irrespective of the airway management strategy. Like the brain, the spinal cord has pressure autoregulation of blood flow and marked CO_2 reactivity of the blood vessels (Hagberg et al. 1997). Hence, blood pressure changes and marked increases in Pa_{CO_2} during induction and maintenance should be avoided. Because of the risk of hyperkalaemia, succinylcholine should not be used in patients with an acute spinal cord injury from 3–4 days to at least 8 months post injury (Hagberg et al. 1997). Inhalation anaesthetics or propofol may be used for maintenance of anaesthesia unless SSEPs are monitored. In these patients, propofol should be used because inhalation anaesthetics change the latency and the amplitude of the monitored signal, making interpretation impossible. When MEPs are monitored, no neuromuscular block should be used. Ketamine can be added, as it has no negative influence on SSEPs or MEPs and even might increase the amplitude of the signals.

When intraoperative wake-up tests are planned, short-acting agents such as propofol and remifentanil should be used, possibly with depth-of-anaesthesia monitoring to help titrate anaesthesia. In order to allow immediate postoperative neurological assessment, most patients have their trachea extubated in the operating theatre. Possible exceptions are in cervical spine surgery with potential airway compromise and in patients suffering from tetraplegia with impaired respiratory mechanics.

Acute spinal cord injury demands pre- and postoperative treatment in specialized units (Stevens et al. 2003). The use of (high-dose) steroids early after spinal cord injury is controversial (Bracken 2012), and many units currently do not use them. Whenever there is hypotension early after acute spinal trauma, there should be a high index of suspicion for neurogenic shock, which is treated with volume and vasopressors. Later after injury, autonomic hyperreflexia presenting with hypertension, bradycardia, and sweating may occur with light anaesthesia during surgery below the level of the spinal injury. Tachycardia as a symptom of autonomic hyperreflexia is only seen in very high lesions where sympathetic activity is included in the autonomic efferent activity.

Spinal procedures can be very painful postoperatively, and postoperative pain therapy should be adapted to the individual patient while taking preoperative pain medication into account. Furthermore, the risk of deep venous thromboembolism must be considered, because many surgeons are reluctant to start patients on prophylactic low-molecular-weight heparin or alternative drugs because of the risk of postoperative haemorrhage. Graded compression stockings or, preferably, intermittent pneumatic leg compression devices should be used.

Most procedures are carried out under general anaesthesia. Any technique can be used provided it does not interfere with spinal cord monitoring. In contrast to brain injury, the concept of spinal perfusion pressure is not routinely used, and the impact on outcome is unclear. A reasonable approach would be to target the normal blood pressure range of the patient plus or minus 15% and normal Pa_{CO_2}. The lower limit of autoregulation will probably be encountered at MAP values of about 60 mm Hg. However, with trauma, autoregulation will be lost and spinal blood flow will vary with arterial pressure. It is also possible to improve spinal perfusion by CSF drainage. Vasodilators such as nitroglycerine and nitroprusside or hypercapnia may lower perfusion pressure as a result of an increase in spinal blood volume.

Postoperative care should be provided on dedicated wards; in patients with lesions or procedures of the cervical spine, respiratory depression might occur (phrenic nerve—C4), and care on a HDU might be necessary.

Anaesthesia for electroconvulsive therapy

ECT is indicated when pharmacological treatment of severe depression or schizophrenia is not effective (e.g. a catatonic patient refusing drug intake) or contraindicated (pregnancy, allergies). After intense debate regarding the ethics of ECT in the 1980s, it is now used more frequently. This is because of the proven efficacy of ECT with acceptable cognitive side-effects, but also because of the role of anaesthetists in increasing patient comfort and safety during and after ECT. ECT patients can be of any age, but the number of children is very low. Patients are scheduled for a series of several ECTs, often two per week for 6 weeks, but sometimes up to 12–16 weeks, with the option of a 'maintenance ECT' once a month after stabilization of psychological status.

A generalized motor seizure is induced by an electrical current that is applied to the patient's skull (mono- or bipolar stimulation). At the beginning of the treatment a 'dose finding' procedure is necessary to identify the individualized level of energy needed to induce an effective seizure in the patient. The seizure also induces an intense cardiovascular response consisting of tachycardia, hypertension, and (sometimes) arrhythmias (severe bradycardia). It results from massive central sympathetic stimulation together with increased adrenal catecholamine release. For effective treatment, a duration of the motor seizure response of more than 20 s seems to be necessary. If seizure duration is too short, a higher current may be applied within the same session.

Normally, both the seizure and the cardiovascular responses are self-limiting. However, extreme responses are possible. The anaesthetist should be ready to intervene when heart rate, blood pressure, or both, become unacceptably high (e.g. by administering a bolus dose of esmolol) (Saito 2005). In rare cases, the seizure lasts longer than 60 s, and pharmacological intervention is required (e.g. with small doses of midazolam or propofol).

To minimize muscle activity during the seizure and subsequent muscle pain, the procedure is performed using a tourniquet applied above the patient's knee or elbow (contralateral to i.v. access) before neuromuscular blocking agents are given: the isolated limb is used to observe the motor response. In general, the procedure lasts 5–10 min. Anaesthesia should be (1) long and deep enough to provide complete amnesia, (2) light enough to permit a sufficient seizure, and (3) short enough to enable a fast patient-turnover.

The interplay between the actions of the anaesthetist and the psychiatrist—both work with central-acting drugs on the same patient—requires optimal teamwork and collaboration, preferably within a small and experienced team.

Preoperative assessment of these patients can be a challenge, as their symptoms and complaints can reflect the psychiatric disease (e.g. subjective heart or 'total body' complaints, or both, in case of depression). Considering the impact of the treatment and the legal situation of these patients (are they really able to give informed consent?), a careful preoperative evaluation is recommended and symptoms of the patient should be verified whenever possible (Grundmann and Oest 2007).

All known induction agents have anticonvulsive properties. Methohexital and etomidate are the least anticonvulsive and both have been used with success for ECT. Propofol has been shown to shorten the seizure activity. Benzodiazepines should not be used.

As a result of its short duration of action, succinylcholine is still frequently used to achieve neuromuscular block, but mivacurium or a combination of rocuronium followed by sugammadex are alternatives.

A small bolus of alfentanil or remifentanil can help to reduce the dose of induction agent and does not interfere with the duration of the seizure. Because the entire ECT procedure takes only a few minutes, most patients (except pregnant and other non-fasted patients) do not require tracheal intubation. Brief mask hyperventilation before the current is applied may improve the quality of the seizure. Direct stimulation of the masseter muscle by the electrodes is common; therefore, some bite protection must be inserted to prevent damage to the tongue and lips.

Depending on the organization and logistics of the hospital, ECT is frequently performed in the recovery room, the PACU, or a special suite of the psychiatric department. In all cases, a defibrillator must be immediately available.

For a standard ECT, all patients are monitored with ECG, non-invasive blood pressure (every 2.5 min), and pulse oximetry. The tourniquet is applied but not inflated. Before induction of anaesthesia, a vagolytic drug (glycopyrronium bromide, atropine) should be given. A bolus of 10 mg metoclopramide might reduce PONV and the risk of regurgitation. Anaesthesia induction typically consists of 0.5 mg of alfentanil and 0.2 mg kg^{-1} of etomidate and as soon as the patient has lost consciousness and respiration ceases, mask (hyper)ventilation is started. The tourniquet is inflated, neuromuscular blocking agent (e.g. succinylcholine 1 mg kg^{-1}) is given, and after 50 s ventilation is stopped, bite-protection is inserted, and the current applied. During the seizure, ventilation is resumed and continued until the patient's spontaneous respiration is recovering. Tachycardia and hypertension are treated if necessary with a small bolus of esmolol (20 mg), which may be repeated.

Emergence delirium is quite common. During recovery, the patient must be monitored until the preoperative level of consciousness has returned.

Declaration of interest

None declared.

References

Alderson P, Roberts I. Corticosteroids for acute traumatic brain injury. *Cochrane Database Syst Rev* 2005; **1**: CD000196

Badjatia N, Carney N, Crocco TJ, *et al.* Guidelines for prehospital management of traumatic brain injury 2nd edition. *Prehosp Emerg Care* 2008; **12**(Suppl 1): S1–52

Bracken MB. Steroids for acute spinal cord injury. *Cochrane Database Syst Rev* 2012; **1**: CD001046

Brain Trauma Foundation, American Association of Neurological Surgeons, Congress of Neurological Surgeons, *et al.* Guidelines for the management of severe traumatic brain injury. IX. Cerebral perfusion thresholds. *J Neurotrauma* 2007a; **24**(Suppl 1): S59–64

Brain Trauma Foundation, American Association of Neurological Surgeons, Congress of Neurological Surgeons, *et al.* Guidelines for the management of severe traumatic brain injury. XIV. Hyperventilation. *J Neurotrauma* 2007b; **24**(Suppl 1): S87–90

Brisman JL, Song JK, Newell DW. Cerebral aneurysms. *N Engl J Med* 2006; **355**: 928–39

Brown T, Shah AH, Bregy A, *et al.* Awake craniotomy for brain tumor resection: the rule rather than the exception? *J Neurosurg Anesthesiol* 2013; 25, **3**: 240–7

Chang EF, Cheng JS, Richardson RM, Lee C, Starr PA, Larson PS. Incidence and management of venous air embolisms during awake deep brain stimulation surgery in a large clinical series. *Stereotact Funct Neurosurg* 2011; **89**: 76–82

Chesnut RM, Marshall LF, Klauber MR, *et al.* The role of secondary brain injury in determining outcome from severe head injury. *J Trauma* 1993; **34**: 216–22

Citerio G, Stocchetti N, Cormio M, Beretta L. Neuro-Link, a computer-assisted database for head injury in intensive care. *Acta Neurochir (Wien)* 2000; **142**: 769–76

Costello TG, Cormack JR, Hoy C, *et al.* Plasma ropivacaine levels following scalp block for awake craniotomy. *J Neurosurg Anesthesiol* 2004; **16**: 147–50

Crosby ET. Airway management in adults after cervical spine trauma. *Anesthesiology* 2006; **104**: 1293–318

Dolecek TA, Propp JM, Stroup NE, Kruchko C. CBTRUS statistical report: primary brain and central nervous system tumors diagnosed in the United States in 2005-2009. *Neuro-Oncology* 2012; **14**(Suppl 5): 1–49

Ellegala DB, Day AL. Ruptured cerebral aneurysms. *N Engl J Med* 2005; 352: 121–4

Erickson KM, Cole DJ. Anesthetic considerations for awake craniotomy for epilepsy and functional neurosurgery. *Anesthesiol Clin* 2012; **30**: 241–68

Fearnside MR, Simpson DA. Epidemiology. In: Reilly PL, Bullock MR, eds. *Head Injury*, 2nd Edn. London: Hodder Arnold, 2005

Fernandez-Candil J, Gambus PL, Troconiz IF, Valero R, Carrero E, Fabregas N. Feasibility of microdialysis to determine interstitial rocuronium concentration in the muscle tissue of anesthetized neurosurgical patients. *J Neurosurg Anesthesiol* 2008; **22**: 163–9

Grundmann U, Oest M. Anaesthesiological aspects of electroconvulsive therapy. *Anaesthesist* 2007; **56**: 202–11

Hagberg C, Welch WC, Bowman-Howard M. Anesthesia and surgery for spine and spinal cord procedures. In: Albin MS, ed. *Textbook of Neuroanesthesia with Neurosurgical and Neuroscience Perspectives*. New York: McGraw-Hill, 1997

Harries AM, Kausar J, Roberts SA, et al. Deep brain stimulation of the subthalamic nucleus for advanced Parkinson disease using general anesthesia: long-term results. *J Neurosurg* 2012; **116**: 107–13

Hindman BJ, Bayman EO, Pfisterer WK, Torner JC, Todd MM, IHAST Investigators. No association between intraoperative hypothermia or supplemental protective drug and neurologic outcomes in patients undergoing temporary clipping during cerebral aneurysm surgery: findings from the Intraoperative Hypothermia for Aneurysm Surgery Trial. *Anesthesiology* 2010; **112**: 86–101

Hyam JA, Kringelbach ML, Silburn PA, Aziz TZ, Green AL. The autonomic effects of deep brain stimulation—a therapeutic opportunity. *Nat Rev Neurol* 2012; **8**: 391–400

Kochanek PM, Carney N, Adelson PD, *et al.* Guidelines for the acute medical management of severe traumatic brain injury in infants, children, and adolescents--second edition. *Pediatr Crit Care Med* 2012; **13**(Suppl 1): S1–82

Leslie K, Myles PS, Chan MT, *et al.* Nitrous oxide and long-term morbidity in the ENIGMA trial. *Anesth Analg* 2011; **112**: 387–93

Liolios A, Guerit JM, Scholtes JL, Raftopoulos C, Hantson P. Propofol infusion syndrome associated with short-term large-dose infusion during surgical anesthesia in an adult. *Anesth Analg* 2005; **100**: 1804–6

Manley G, Knudson MM, Morabito D, Damron S, Erickson V, Pitts L. Hypotension, hypoxia, and head injury: frequency, duration, and consequences. *Arch Surg* 2001; **136**: 1118–23

Mills SJ, Tomlinson AA. The use of central venous cannulae in neuroanaesthesia. A survey of current practice in the UK. *Anaesthesia* 2001; **56**: 465–70

Molyneux AJ, Kerr RSC, Yu LM, Clarke M, Sneade M, Yarnold JA, Sandercock P, International Subarachnoid Aneurysm Trial (ISAT) Collaborative Group. International subarachnoid aneurysm trial (ISAT) of neurosurgical clipping versus endovascular coiling in 2143 patients with ruptured intracranial aneurysms: a randomised comparison of effects on survival, dependency, seizures, rebleeding, subgroups, and aneurysm occlusion. *Lancet* 2005; **366**: 809–17

Myles PS, Leslie K, Chan MT, *et al.* Avoidance of nitrous oxide for patients undergoing major surgery: a randomized controlled trial. *Anesthesiology* 2007; **107**: 221–31

Myles PS, Leslie K, Chan MT, *et al.* The safety of addition of nitrous oxide to general anaesthesia in at-risk patients having major non-cardiac surgery (ENIGMA-II): a randomised, single-blind trial. *Lancet* 2014; **384**: 1446–54

Nemergut EC, Dumont AS, Barry UT, Laws ER. Perioperative management of patients undergoing transsphenoidal pituitary surgery. *Anesth Analg* 2005; **101**: 1170–81

Oddo M, Schmidt JM, Mayer SA, Chiolero RL. Glucose control after severe brain injury. *Curr Opin Clin Nutr Metab Care* 2008; **11**: 134–9

Perks A, Cheema S, Mohanraj R. Anaesthesia and epilepsy. *Br J Anaesth* 2012; **108**: 562–71

POISE Study Group, Devereaux PJ, Yang H, Yusuf S, *et al.* Effects of extended-release metoprolol succinate in patients undergoing non-cardiac surgery (POISE trial): a randomised controlled trial. *Lancet* 2008; **371**: 1839–47

Poon CC, Irwin MG. Anaesthesia for deep brain stimulation and in patients with implanted neurostimulator devices. *Br J Anaesth* 2009; **103**: 152–65

Protheroe RT, Gwinnutt CL. Early hospital care of severe traumatic brain injury. *Anaesthesia* 2011; **66**: 1035–47

Raw DA, Beattie JK, Hunter JM. Anaesthesia for spinal surgery in adults. *Br J Anaesth* 2003; **91**: 886–904

Raz A, Eimerl D, Zaidel A, Bergman H, Israel Z. Propofol decreases neuronal population spiking activity in the subthalamic nucleus of Parkinsonian patients. *Anesth Analg* 2010; **111**: 1285–9

Retter A, Wyncoll D, Pearse R, *et al.* Guidelines on the management of anaemia and red cell transfusion in adult critically ill patients. *Br J Haematol* 2013; **160**: 445–64

Rozet I. Anesthesia for functional neurosurgery: the role of dexmedetomidine. *Curr Opin Anaesthesiol* 2008; **21**: 537–43

Saito S. Anesthesia management for electroconvulsive therapy: hemodynamic and respiratory management. *J Anesth* 2005; **19**: 142–9

Seguin P, Bleichner JP, Branger B, Guillou YM, Feuillu A, Malledant Y. The measurement of end-tidal carbon dioxide (PETCO2) is not a significant parameter to monitor in patients with severe traumatic brain injury. *Can J Anaesth* 2001; **48**: 396–400

Shapiro HM, Galindo A, Wyte SR, Harris AB. Rapid intraoperative reduction of intracranial pressure with thiopentone. *Br J Anaesth* 1973; **45**: 1057–62

Simonsen CZ, Sørensen LH, Juul N, *et al.* Anesthetic strategy during endovascular therapy: General anesthesia or conscious sedation? (GOLIATH - General or Local Anesthesia in Intra Arterial Therapy) A single-center randomized trial. *Int J Stroke* Advance access published on July 12, 2016, doi:10.1177/1747493016660103

Souter MJ, Rozet I, Ojemann JG, et al. Dexmedetomidine sedation during awake craniotomy for seizure reduction: effects on electrocorticography. *J Neurosurg Anesthesiol* 2007; **19**: 38–44

Stevens RD, Bhardwaj A, Kirsch JR, Mirski MA. Critical care and perioperative management in traumatic spinal cord injury. *J Neurosurg Anesthesiol* 2003; **15**: 215–29

Todd MM, Hindman BJ, Clarke WR, Torner JC. Intraoperative Hypothermia for Aneurysm Surgery Trial (IHAST) Investigators. Mild intraoperative hypothermia during surgery for intracranial aneurysm. *N Engl J Med* 2005; **352**: 135–45

Venikatraghavan L, Manninen P, Mak P, Lukitto K, Hodale M, Lozano A. Anesthesia for functional neurosurgery: review of complications. *J Neurosurg Anesthesiol* 2006; **18**: 64–7

Venikatraghavan L, Manninen P. Anesthesia for deep brain stimulation. *Curr Opin Anaesthesiol* 2011; **24**: 495–9

CHAPTER 60

Anaesthesia for ophthalmic surgery

Chris Dodds and Chandra M. Kumar

Introduction

Patients requiring anaesthesia for ophthalmology range across the extremes of age, from the premature neonate to the elderly. Anaesthesia is challenging in both. Detailed descriptions of anaesthesia for neonates, children, and the elderly are covered elsewhere in this book. This chapter is devoted to ophthalmic anaesthesia for adults. It is worth remembering that elderly patients have increased morbidity and receive multiple drugs that make even anaesthesia for minor surgery more risky than in fitter younger adults.

There has been a shift in the delivery of anaesthesia towards regional techniques although general anaesthesia remains the technique of choice for many intermediate and most complex ophthalmic operations. Ophthalmic surgical procedures range from simple cataract surgery to major procedures lasting several hours. Some patients require repeated surgical procedures at short intervals. It is essential to understand the physiology of the eye, the relevant anatomy, ophthalmic drugs they may receive, and their effects on drugs used during anaesthesia. Careful preoperative assessment and preparation of these patients are important factors towards a safe outcome. The choice and preferences for anaesthesia and techniques vary worldwide and several factors play an important part in choosing the type of anaesthesia.

Physiology

The perception of light requires normal functioning of both the eye and its central nervous system connections. Knowledge of the relevant ocular physiology behind this process is necessary for safe local and general anaesthesia. The protective homeostatic mechanisms of the eye are affected by anaesthesia in a similar way to the central nervous system and indeed the sclera and its contents are analogous to the skull and its contents. The compliance curve is similar but the underlying mechanisms are slightly different. This is as a result of the sclera being an elastic but completely full container unlike the rigid, but slightly empty cranium which has some room for expansion of its contents.

The intraocular pressure (IOP) and ocular blood flow are influenced by physiology and pharmacology that are relevant in every surgical and anaesthetic procedure. The mechanisms behind the effective transit of light through the relatively avascular structure of the eye on its way to the retina and the central nervous pathways, while complex and fascinating, have less relevance to anaesthesia.

Intraocular pressure

The IOP varies from 10 to 21 mm Hg. Diurnal variations in IOP of 4–6 mm Hg are considered normal, as are similar fluctuations with changes in body position or transient increases during coughing and straining. Pressure is distributed evenly throughout the eye, and the pressure is generally the same in the posterior vitreous as it is in the aqueous humour. Each eye may have a different pressure.

The IOP is determined by a careful balance of scleral rigidity, aqueous humour dynamics, volume of the other fluid contents (vitreous and choroidal blood) of the eye, and external forces acting on the eye such as extraocular muscle tone.

The aqueous humour is produced by an active secretory process in the non-pigmented epithelium of the ciliary body. Large molecules are excluded by the blood–aqueous barrier between the epithelium and iris capillaries. The Na/K ATPase pump is involved in the active transport of sodium into the aqueous and carbonic anhydrase catalyses water and CO_2 to acid and bicarbonate which passes passively into the aqueous. Acetazolamide is a carbonic anhydrase inhibitor used for the treatment of raised IOP by reducing bicarbonate and sodium transport into the aqueous.

In addition to this active secretory production there is a less important hydrostatic element dependent on ocular perfusion pressure. The ciliary body is highly vascular and is supplied by the ciliary arteries. Flow and corresponding vascular pressure is controlled by the autonomic nervous system and autoregulation exists similar to cerebral blood flow. Pressure within the pars plana and episcleral venules restricts the vascular outflow as does the IOP.

The aqueous humour flows from the ciliary body through the trabecular meshwork into the anterior chamber before exiting through the angle of Schlemm. Put simply, the sums of the hydrostatic inflow and the active aqueous production minus the active resorption and passive filtration must equal zero to achieve balance. Alteration of any individual process can lead to changes in IOP. This is invariably as a result of the increased hydrostatic pressure or the reduced removal of aqueous.

It is well known that the IOP can increase up to 40 mm Hg during coughing, bucking, during performing a Valsalva manoeuvre, and during retching and vomiting. Any pressure on the neck veins (e.g. a tight tie around the neck) can also interfere with drainage of the jugular veins resulting in increased IOP. A head-up position thus can facilitate jugular vein drainage and decrease IOP. It is also known that the IOP is higher in patients positioned prone or in Trendelenburg's position for a prolonged period. Although the exact reason is not known, it may presumably be as a result of a combination of increased episcleral venous pressure combined with an increase in end-tidal CO_2 and which is exacerbated by any fluid overload.

Increased tone of orbicularis oculi muscle and forceful squeezing of the eyelid can increase IOP up to 70–80 mm Hg. The application of an eye speculum can increase IOP by 4–5 mm Hg. Injection of local anaesthetic agents behind the globe during needle-based blocks is known to increase the IOP and the return of the IOP to baseline can take 5–10 min. Sustained compression with an external compression device, such as a Honan's balloon, for 5–10 min can decrease the IOP to below baseline values for as long as 20–25 min. Less than 25 mm Hg pressure should be applied when an oculocompression device is used as excessive external pressure can hamper perfusion of the eye.

Ocular blood flow and IOP

The blood supply to the optic nerve and retina depends on the intraocular perfusion pressure. Intraocular perfusion pressure is the difference between mean arterial pressure and IOP. Ocular perfusion pressure equals the mean arterial pressure minus the IOP (OPP = MAP − IOP).

An increase in arterial CO_2 tension increases the IOP. This is thought to be caused by hypercapnia-induced vasodilation and an increase in choroidal blood volume. Hyperventilation and a subsequent decrease in Pa_{CO_2} decreases IOP. Spontaneous respiration with an inhalation agent increases end-tidal CO_2 to greater than 7.5 kPa, resulting in a clinically significant increase in the IOP. It is important therefore to assist or control ventilation in patients with raised IOP undergoing intraocular surgery to prevent a further increase. During anaesthesia, increases in IOP also occur with hypoxia, hypertension, and venous congestion.

Blood pressure and IOP

Systolic hypertension is associated with an increase in IOP and an acute increase in arterial blood pressure is also accompanied by a corresponding increase in IOP (Murphy 1985).

Fluid intake and IOP

Prolonged fasting can result in a decrease in IOP and similarly an excessive amount of oral or intravenous fluid can increase IOP. Hyperosmotic agents such as mannitol decrease IOP by producing osmotic diuresis and probably by also decreasing vitreous volume. The effect usually starts 30 min after administration and returns to baseline after 2 h.

Effects of anaesthetic drugs on IOP

Most intravenous induction agents such as barbiturates, benzodiazepines, and propofol are known to decrease IOP. Ketamine may increase IOP; however, the effect may be less pronounced at lower doses (1–2 mg kg^{-1} intravenously) and in combination with agents which lower IOP (Nagdeve et al. 2006). Ketamine may keep IOP closer to pre-induction values and many centres use ketamine for IOP measurement under anaesthesia. All inhalation agents including sevoflurane and desflurane are also known to decrease IOP. Non-depolarizing neuromuscular blocking agents do not have any effect on IOP. Premedication with dexmedetomidine or gabapentin decreases IOP.

Suxamethonium (succinylcholine) and IOP

It is well known that suxamethonium increases IOP which peaks 90 s after administration and the increase can last for 3–6 min (Cunningham and Barry 1986). The exact cause of the increase in IOP is not clear. It was thought to be as a result of tonic contractions of extraocular muscle fibres but this theory is discounted because an increase in IOP has been observed when extraocular muscles are detached from the globe (Kelly et al. 1993). The combination of an increase in central venous pressure, choroidal blood flow, and the cycloplegic effect of succinylcholine is the postulated mechanism (Miller 2005). This increase in IOP after succinylcholine has been suggested to produce deleterious effects in perforating eye injury where extrusion of vitreous and eye contents can occur through the wound with an increase in IOP. However, there are no case reports in the literature to support this belief (Libonati et al. 1985).

The increase in IOP with suxamethonium and intubation can be attenuated by administration of thiopental or propofol before administering suxamethonium or pretreatment with short-acting opioids (remifentanil, alfentanil, sufentanil, or fentanyl). Administration of intravenous lidocaine 1.5 mg kg^{-1} at least 90 s before intubation is known to help. Clonidine, glyceryl trinitrate, and nifedipine have all been found to attenuate the increase in IOP.

IOP during airway management

The use of a laryngeal mask airway (LMA), by avoiding direct laryngoscopy and tracheal intubation, during the induction of GA offers the distinct advantage of having minimal effect upon IOP (Ismail et al. 2011). Equally, at the end of the anaesthetic a LMA is associated with far less airway irritation and there is rarely the precipitous increase in IOP which is associated with coughing or bucking at the time of extubation. Glaucoma patients may exhibit more pronounced increases in IOP with laryngoscopy and intubation and extubation, and use of a LMA theoretically may confer advantages.

The oculocardiac reflex

The oculocardiac reflex (OCR) was first described by Aschner (1908). The reflex is trigeminovagal and further details can be found in a textbook of physiology. The afferent limb is from orbital contents to ciliary ganglion to ophthalmic division of the trigeminal nerve to the sensory nucleus of the trigeminal near the fourth ventricle. The efferent limb is via the vagus nerve to the heart. The OCR is variously defined as a 10% or 20% decrease in heart rate, junctional rhythms, and asystole with or without hypotension (Kumar and Dowd 2006). It is observed during traction on the extraocular muscles, pressure on the globe mainly encountered during strabismus surgery, retinal detachment repair, or enucleation of the eyeball, and sometimes in the empty orbit (Kerr and Vance 1983). The OCR is one of a triad which also includes the oculorespiratory and oculovomiting reflexes (Blanc et al. 1988; van den Berg et al. 1989). An OCR leading to profound bradycardia is classically brought on by muscle traction. Traction on the extraocular muscles or pressure on the globe can also cause atrioventricular block, ventricular ectopy, or asystole. It is especially seen with traction on the medial rectus muscle, but can occur with stimulation of any of the orbital contents, including the periosteum. If this reflex is triggered, any of the triad of responses may occur including apnoea in spontaneously breathing patients.

The OCR is more common in children than adults and the incidence may be higher with medial rectus and inferior oblique manipulation than traction on the lateral rectus muscle. The OCR may occur in awake patients during the adjustment of sutures postoperatively in adjustable suture strabismus surgery. The greater the force applied on the muscle, the more likely is the OCR and the shorter the time taken to achieve a minimum heart rate. While the incidence of the OCR can be minimized by administering an ophthalmic regional block it can be precipitated by the process of instilling the block. The incidence can be reduced by instillation of topical lidocaine or proxymetacaine. An appropriate depth of anaesthesia results in a lower incidence of the OCR. Continuous (auditory) intraoperative monitoring of heart rate, ECG, and blood pressure should be performed during general anaesthesia. Agents with vagomimetic potential are more likely to be associated with the OCR, for instance, the opioids remifentanil, alfentanil, or sufentanil are associated with a high incidence of the OCR. Rocuronium and pancuronium are less likely to be associated with the OCR because of their vagolytic effects. Prophylactic administration of anticholinergics is known to significantly decrease the incidence of the OCR but not totally eliminate it. Intravenous glycopyrronium bromide may be as effective as atropine in preventing the OCR and is associated with less tachycardia and a lower incidence of arrhythmias (nodal rhythms and ventricular extrasystoles).

If an OCR is elicited during surgery, the surgeon is instructed to release any traction on the extraocular eye muscle immediately. Gentle traction can then be reapplied once the heart rate has returned to baseline. If the OCR recurs or is very severe, anticholinergics should be administered by the intravenous route.

Assessment and preparation

A standard preoperative assessment should be carried out for all patients irrespective of the anaesthesia they are likely to receive. Multiprofessional teamwork is the norm and the Joint Royal Colleges guidelines (Kumar et al. 2012) offer appropriate guidance in patients undergoing local anaesthesia. Appropriately trained nursing staff may carry out the bulk of pre-assessment and preoperative preparation under the guidance of a lead ophthalmic anaesthetist. A thorough history is required and together with the surgeon a decision concerning the likely choice of anaesthetic can be made. Investigations should be considered based on the relevant examination findings and guidelines (National Institute for Health and Care Excellence 2016). Age, co-morbidity (such as cardiorespiratory disease), and chronic drug treatments make routine investigations such as ECG, full blood count, and urea and electrolytes, potentially useful tests. However, if local anaesthesia is planned, investigations are usually reserved for very specific indications. Particular thought needs to be given to patients with hypertension, ischaemic heart disease, diabetes mellitus, and chronic obstructive pulmonary disease. It is important that the preoperative preparation includes checking that these patients are able to lie flat for up to an hour without becoming uncomfortable, claustrophobic, and, worse still, hypoxic or suffering ischaemic cardiac problems.

Chronic anticoagulation presents complications that are more relevant to the surgeon or those practising local anaesthesia (see 'Selection of patients and blocks').

It is imperative to make sure that the patient understands and consents to the choice of anaesthetic by taking part in an informed discussion. Patients (and surgeons) often request anaesthetic choices that appear contrary to the anaesthetic risk:benefit assessment.

Choice and preferences for anaesthesia

Risks and benefits of the technique used are assessed carefully and the type of anaesthesia is selected accordingly. Important factors such as urgency of procedure, duration of surgical procedures, age, ASA status of the patient, surgical conditions, preferences of the surgeon, and patient's choice influence the technique used. Regional and local anaesthesia are preferred in elderly patients with co-morbidities to reduce the stress response to surgery and postoperative complications such as nausea, vomiting, confusion, and urinary retention. Younger patients are frequently anxious and local anaesthesia can be used successfully but they are usually managed under general anaesthesia. The duration of the procedure and the patient's ability to lie still for a longer period is an important consideration. Children and adults with special needs or adults requiring potentially complex ophthalmic surgery usually require general anaesthesia. The indications for general anaesthesia are diminishing but still there are situations where there are benefits.

General anaesthesia

Indications for general anaesthesia

Most routine ophthalmic surgical procedures can be performed under regional and local anaesthesia. General anaesthesia is usually indicated in a patient who is unwilling or unable to tolerate local anaesthesia. The duration and complexity of the operation is an important determinant influencing the surgeon's and the patient's requests.

Contraindications to general anaesthesia

There are, of course, no absolute contraindications and it is not uncommon for patients with serious comorbidities, which cannot be improved, to undergo general anaesthesia without complications. Cardiovascular, respiratory, and neurological diseases increase in frequency with age and there is an increased incidence of adverse cardiac outcome, respiratory failure, and postoperative cognitive dysfunction. However, for the commonest procedures such as cataract surgery there is little evidence of a difference between regional and general anaesthesia in the incidence of these complications.

Induction of anaesthesia

A smooth induction is the goal of all anaesthetists and this is even more important in the ophthalmic setting. Avoidance of coughing, straining, and accidental increases in intrathoracic pressure and venous congestion is important so that optimal eye conditions are maintained. The choice of induction drug is of much less importance although propofol has a number of beneficial qualities in this setting, especially related to the ease of insertion of a LMA. In equipotent doses, propofol has a greater depressant effect on IOP than thiopental sodium and likewise on blood pressure (Mirakhur et al. 1987). Although suxamethonium, in isolation, causes an increase in IOP, this effect is more than balanced by the induction agent. Ketamine probably has little effect on the IOP.

Short-acting opioids such as fentanyl will act synergistically with the induction agent and obtund responses to airway manipulation.

Airway management

The airway may remain inaccessible throughout surgery and any need to adjust or reposition an airway device during surgery could cause disruption to surgery with potentially sight-threatening consequences. Thus, the safest option is to intubate the trachea and maintain ventilation and neuromuscular block throughout. Topical and intravenous lidocaine during laryngoscopy (and emergence) can help reduce airway stimulation. A south-facing RAE or other preformed tracheal tube which is securely stabilized with hypoallergenic tape (avoiding ties) is the best choice and along with mechanical ventilation provides ideal conditions for nearly all ophthalmic surgery. Guaranteed paralysis through the mandatory use of neuromuscular monitoring avoids the risks of patient and airway movement during surgery. However, intubation brings specific risks of increased IOP related to coughing and bucking during induction, the pressor response to laryngoscopy and intubation, laryngospasm during extubation or coughing, and postoperative nausea and vomiting related to the use of reversal agents. All of these complications assume much greater importance in open eye surgery.

The use of the LMA in tandem with propofol as the induction agent is popular, especially for short ophthalmic procedures; it reduces some of the above-mentioned risks but adds an increased risk of losing the airway during surgery if the mask is not well enough secured or positioned especially in patients who are covered under the surgical drape. The use of neuromuscular paralysis with the LMA may aid mechanical ventilation and tighter control of ocular physiology (Springer and Jahr 1995) but is seen by some as having a clinically significant increased risk of aspiration (Chmielewski and Snyder-Clickett 2004).

Therefore a risk:benefit assessment should be considered by the anaesthetist taking into account the relative importance of the following factors: body mass index, gastro-oesophageal reflux disease, hiatus hernia, ease of placement of tracheal tube or laryngeal mask, duration of operation, open eye status, fasting time, and, some might add, the opinion of the surgeon.

Maintenance of anaesthesia

Much of the choice of maintenance is related to personal preference and experience and the choice of airway. Inhalation anaesthesia is most commonly used because of its familiarity, controllability, and cost. Inhalation anaesthesia has a dose-dependent effect on reducing the IOP. Similarly virtually all sedative/hypnotic drugs reduce IOP. There is little difference between any individual inhalation agent and intravenous anaesthesia.

Nitrous oxide use may depend on local availability of medical air and personal preference. The benefits of nitrous oxide are well known but it brings two particular risks to ophthalmology that must be considered. These are the increase in postoperative retching and vomiting and the potentially catastrophic increase in IOP when intraocular gas mixtures are used for vitrectomy (see 'Vitreoretinal surgery').

Relative hypotension during anaesthesia combined with normoxia and normocarbia will provide a soft, well-perfused eye. A 15° head-up position may improve conditions. However, decreasing the blood pressure too far may prompt questions from the ophthalmologist noticing an absence of flow in the retinal arteries during some ocular surgery. It is a more common challenge in the elderly population to maintain normotension in the absence of significant surgical stimulation during ophthalmic surgery. Avoiding elevated IOP is necessary to avoid loss of ocular contents during open eye surgery.

The physiological challenge of most eye surgery can be considered to be low. There is little if any challenge to fluid balance and care should be taken not to be too liberal with intravenous fluids in case of overloading the myocardium or inducing urinary retention in the elderly population. Elderly patients are also vulnerable to hypothermia and with some ophthalmic operations taking more than an hour, close attention should be given to normothermia. Venous thromboembolism should likewise have prevention measures in place with mechanical compression devices. Diabetic eye complications mean that ophthalmic surgery is common in this population. Where general anaesthesia is required, local euglycaemia protocols must be followed. Analgesia requirements are based on intraoperative short-acting opioids. Paracetamol and non-steroidal anti-inflammatory drugs may be useful if there are no contraindications. Local anaesthesia with longer-duration local anaesthetic drugs is particularly useful provided that eye protection is maintained for the duration of action. It is unusual to require potent long-acting opioids and a cause for severe postoperative pain should always be sought, as this can be a sign of ophthalmic-related complications. Ophthalmic patients are particularly prone to suffer from nausea and vomiting despite the absence of long-acting opioid and prophylaxis with dexamethasone, ondansetron, or both, is useful.

Local anaesthesia for eye surgery

A well-drilled ophthalmic team can achieve a safe and efficient service with prompt patient turnaround and excellent operating conditions using injectable local anaesthesia. However, serious complications of ophthalmic injectable local anaesthesia including sub-Tenon's block can and do occur (Kumar and Dodds 2006; Kumar et al. 2011). A detailed knowledge of the anatomy of the eye and the relevant pharmacology is of paramount importance.

Nomenclature of blocks

The terminology used for ophthalmic blocks varies. Terminology based on the anatomical placement of the needle is widely accepted. The injection of local anaesthetic agent into the muscle cone behind the globe formed by the four recti muscles and the superior and inferior oblique muscles is known as intraconal (retrobulbar) block whereas in the extraconal (peribulbar) block the needle tip remains outside the muscle cone (Fanning 2003). Multiple communications exist between the two compartments and it is difficult in practice to differentiate whether the needle is intraconal or extraconal after placement (Ripart et al. 2001). Injected local anaesthetic agent diffuses easily across compartments and depending on its spread, anaesthesia and akinesia may occur. A faster onset of akinesia suggests that the block is intraconal. A combination of intraconal and extraconal block is described as the combined retro-peribulbar block (Hamilton 1996). In sub-Tenon's block, local anaesthetic agent is injected under the Tenon's capsule (Stevens 1992) and this block is also known as parabulbar block (Greenbaum 1992), pinpoint anaesthesia (Fukasaku and Marron 1994), or medial episcleral block (Ripart et al. 1998).

Relevant anatomy

Readers are advised to read a textbook of ophthalmic anatomy (Dutton 2011). Only brief and relevant anatomy is described in this chapter. The orbit is a four-sided irregular pyramid with its apex pointing posteromedially and its base anteriorly (Fig. 60.1). The annulus of Zinn is a fibrous ring arising from the superior orbital fissure. Eye movements are controlled by six extraocular muscles: inferior, lateral, medial, superior recti, and the superior oblique and inferior oblique muscles (Fig. 60.2). These muscles arise from the annulus of Zinn and insert on the globe anterior to the equator

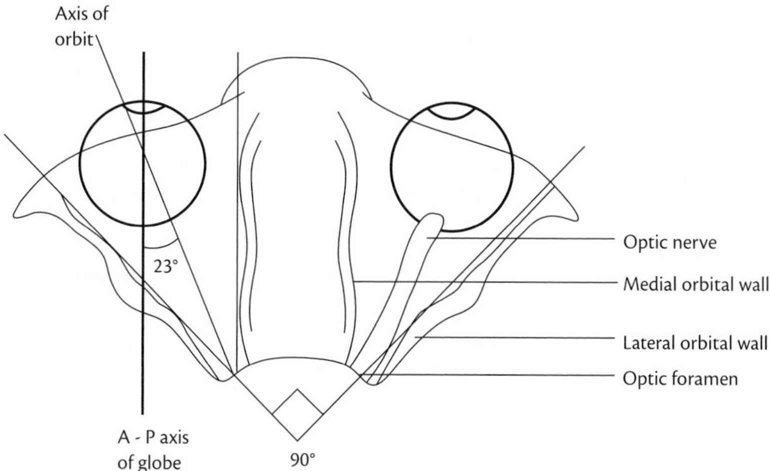

Figure 60.1 Diagram of the orbit as seen in a transverse section through the front of the skull to illustrate the shape of the orbit and the relative axes of the orbit and globe.

Reproduced from Gavin Parness et al., 'Regional Anaesthesia For Intraocular Surgery', *Continuing Education in Anaesthesia, Critical Care & Pain*, 2005, 5, 3, pp. 93–97, by permission of The British Journal of Anaesthesia.

to form an incomplete cone. The distance from annulus to inferior temporal orbital rim ranges from 42 to 54 mm. It is very important to bear in mind that the needle should not be inserted too far near the annulus where the vital nerves and vessels are tightly packed.

The optic nerve (cranial nerve II), oculomotor nerves (III, containing both superior and inferior branches), abducens nerve (VI), nasociliary nerve (a branch of the trigeminal nerve, V), ciliary ganglion, and vessels lie in the cone (Fig. 60.2). The ophthalmic division of the oculomotor nerve (III) divides into superior and inferior branches before emerging from the superior orbital fissure. The superior branch supplies superior rectus and the levator palpebrae superioris. The inferior branch divides into three to supply the medial rectus, the inferior rectus, and the inferior oblique muscles. The abducens nerve (VI) emerges from the superior orbital fissure beneath the inferior branch of the oculomotor nerve to supply the lateral rectus muscle. The trochlear nerve (IV) courses outside the cone but then branches and enters the cone to supply the superior oblique muscle. An incomplete block of this nerve leads to retained activity of the superior oblique muscle which may be frequently observed. Squeezing and closing of the eyelids are controlled by the zygomatic branch of the facial nerve (VII), which supplies the motor innervation to the orbicularis oculi muscle. This nerve emerges from the foramen spinosum at the base of the skull, anterior to the mastoid and behind the earlobe. It passes through the parotid gland before crossing the condyle of the mandible, and then passes superficial to the zygoma and malar bone before its terminal fibres ramify to supply the deep surface of the orbicularis oculi. The facial nerve also supplies secreto-motor parasympathetic fibres to the lacrimal glands, and glands of the nasal and palatine mucosa.

Tenon's capsule or bulbar fascia is a membrane that envelops the eyeball from the optic nerve to the sclerocorneal junction separating it from the orbital fat and forming a socket in which it moves. The capsule originates at the limbus and extends anteriorly to the optic nerve and as sleeves along the extraocular muscles. Tenon's capsule is arbitrarily divided by the equator of the globe into anterior and posterior portions. Anterior Tenon's capsule is adherent to episcleral tissue from the limbus posteriorly for about 5–10 mm and is fused with the intermuscular septum of the extraocular muscles and overlying bulbar conjunctiva. The conjunctiva fuses with Tenon's capsule in this area and the sub-Tenon space can easily be accessed through an incision 5–10 mm behind the limbus. The posterior sub-Tenon's capsule is thin and passes round to the optic

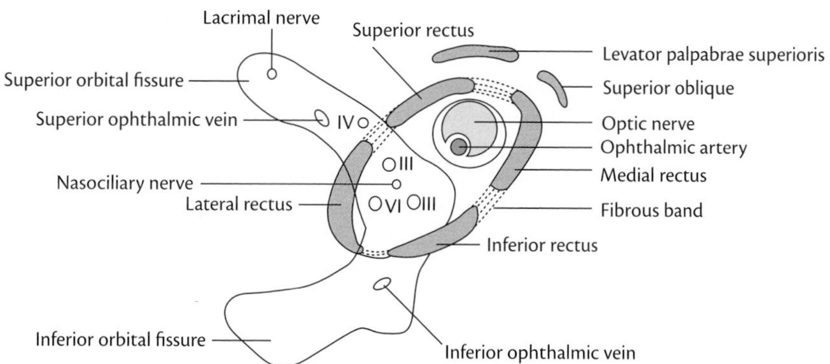

Figure 60.2 Diagram of a coronal section through the orbit to illustrate the left orbital fissure and the cone formed by the extraocular muscles.

Reproduced from Gavin Parness et al., 'Regional Anaesthesia For Intraocular Surgery', *Continuing Education in Anaesthesia, Critical Care & Pain*, 2005, 5, 3, pp. 93–97, by permission of The British Journal of Anaesthesia.

nerve, separating the globe from the contents of the retrobulbar space. Posteriorly, the sheath fuses with the openings around the optic nerve.

Sensation to the globe is supplied through the ophthalmic division of the trigeminal nerve (V). Just before entering the orbit, it divides into three branches: lacrimal, frontal, and nasociliary. The nasociliary nerve is sensory to the entire globe. It emerges through the superior orbital fissure between the superior and inferior branches of the oculomotor nerve and passes through the common tendinous ring. Two long ciliary nerves give branches to the ciliary ganglion and, with the short ciliary nerves, transmit sensation from the cornea, iris, and ciliary muscle. Some sensation from the lateral conjunctiva is transmitted through the lacrimal nerve and from the upper palpebral conjunctiva via the frontal nerve. Both nerves are outside the cone. Intraoperative pain may be experienced if these nerves are not adequately blocked.

The superomedial and superotemporal quadrants have abundant blood vessels but the inferotemporal and medial quadrants are relatively avascular and are the safer places to insert needles or cannulae.

To achieve adequate anaesthesia and akinesia, the above motor and sensory nerves must be blocked. However, it is very difficult to target these nerves individually and an adequate volume of local anaesthetic should be injected safely either into the intraconal or extraconal space and subsequent diffusion from one compartment to the other will ultimately block the nerves of interest.

Selection of patients and blocks

Numerous published studies confirm the preference of ophthalmologists, anaesthetists, and patients for local techniques but the decision is mostly made by the person performing the block. However, the decision should be based on factors which influence the choice of a particular technique. The preferred technique varies from topical anaesthesia, cannula-based block, to needle-based blocks. Published studies conflict on real differences between effectiveness of blocks suggesting peribulbar and retrobulbar anaesthesia produce equally good akinesia and equivalent pain control. There is insufficient evidence in the literature, however, to make a definitive statement concerning the relative effectiveness of sub-Tenon's block in producing akinesia when compared with peribulbar or retrobulbar block. The technique chosen should depend on a balance between the patient's wishes, the operative needs of the surgeon, the skills of the anaesthetist, and the type of surgery.

Preoperative assessment is generally limited to medical history, drug history, and physical examination. According to the UK Joint Colleges Working Party Report (Kumar et al. 2012), routine investigations are unnecessary and these are only performed to improve the general health of the patient. Patients are not fasted and this is especially helpful in managing patients with diabetes mellitus. They can therefore receive all of their normal medications and achieve better glycaemic control in the perioperative period. The blood sugar concentration must be checked. Patients receiving anticoagulants and antiplatelet agents are advised to continue their usual medications unless told otherwise. Warfarin therapy is not considered an absolute contraindication to local anaesthesia provided that preoperative international normalized ratio values are in the therapeutic target range. A sub-Tenon's block or topical anaesthesia is preferred. The axial length of the eye is usually measured before cataract surgery. Patients scheduled for glaucoma surgery are not usually scanned preoperatively and caution is required before considering a needle block. Patients whose axial length exceeds 26 mm are more prone to globe damage (Vohra and Good 2000). Antibiotics are not necessary in patients with valvular heart disease. Premedication is not usually necessary either but if needed may be given intravenously just before the local anaesthetic block is inserted.

Regional block techniques

Insertion of an intravenous cannula is good clinical practice and must be established if a sharp needle technique is planned (Kumar et al. 2012). Full cardiopulmonary resuscitation equipment and trained staff should be immediately available. Appropriate cardiorespiratory monitoring should be used. Ophthalmic regional anaesthesia should provide conditions appropriate for the surgeon's needs and planned surgery. The rapid advance of surgical techniques in recent years has necessitated rethinking of anaesthesia requirements. Ophthalmic akinetic blocks are either needle-based (intraconal, extraconal) or cannula-based (sub-Tenon's) blocks.

Needle-based blocks

The 'classical' retrobulbar block was described by Atkinson (1936). The patient is asked to look upward and inward and a 38 mm long needle is inserted at the junction of medial two-thirds and lateral one-third of the inferior orbital margin after raising a wheal of skin with local anaesthetic. The needle is directed towards the apex and 2–3 ml of local anaesthetic injected close to the optic nerve. Akinesia and analgesia results quickly but a facial nerve block is essential to block the orbicularis oculi muscle. Both classical retrobulbar and facial nerve blocks are associated with significant sight- and life-threatening complications (Kumar and Dowd 2006) and these techniques have been replaced by the modern retrobulbar block.

Modern retrobulbar block (inferotemporal approach)

Conjunctival anaesthesia is obtained with local anaesthetic drops (oxybuprocaine 0.4% or similar) (Kumar 2011). The conjunctiva is cleaned with aqueous 5% povidone iodine. Evidence-based literature suggests that the eye should be kept in the neutral (primary) gaze position at all times and a needle length shorter than 31 mm is inserted through the skin or conjunctiva in the inferotemporal quadrant as far lateral as possible below the lateral rectus. The needle is directed upwards and inwards with the needle always tangential to the globe (Fig. 60.3). A volume of 4–5 ml of local anaesthetic agent of choice such as lidocaine 2% is injected. A separate facial nerve block is not required.

Inferotemporal peribulbar block

Surface anaesthesia and asepsis is obtained as previously described. The globe is kept in a neutral gaze position and a needle less than 31 mm in length is inserted as far as possible in the extreme inferonasal quadrant through the conjunctiva or lower lid. A peribulbar block is essentially similar to a modern retrobulbar block but the needle is not directed upwards and inwards and the needle always remains tangential to the globe along the inferior orbital floor (Fig. 60.3). A volume of 5–6 ml of local anaesthetic agent is injected. However, more than 60% of patients require supplementary injection in the form of a medial peribulbar block.

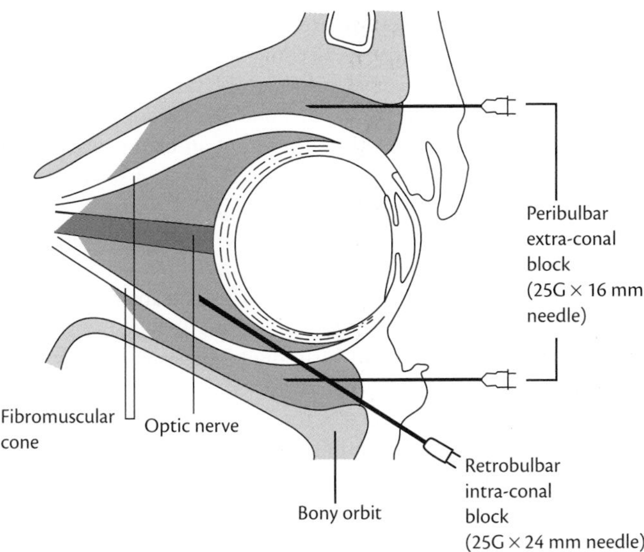

Figure 60.3 Diagram of a sagittal section through the orbit to demonstrate the position of needles for intra-conal and extra-conal regional anaesthetic blocks for ophthalmic surgery.
Reproduced from Gavin Parness et al., 'Regional Anaesthesia For Intraocular Surgery', *Continuing Education in Anaesthesia, Critical Care & Pain*, 2005, 5, 3, pp. 93–97, by permission of The British Journal of Anaesthesia.

Medial peribulbar block

A supplementary injection is often required either in the same quadrant or usually through an injection in the medial compartment termed a medial peribulbar block. A needle is inserted between the caruncle and the medial canthus to a depth of 1–1.5 cm and 3–5 ml of local anaesthetic is injected. A single medial peribulbar block with 6–8 ml of local anaesthetic has been advocated if akinesia is essential in patients with myopic eyes.

In practice, the differentiation between retrobulbar and peribulbar is more semantic than actual (Thind and Rubin 2001). If the onset of anaesthesia is rapid with a peribulbar anaesthetic, then the chances are that it has found a direct pathway or been injected directly into the cone (Kumar 2011).

The gauge of needle should be the finest that can be used comfortably but this is usually limited to a 25 or 27 G needle. Finer needles are difficult to manipulate but larger needles may cause more pain and damage. Sharp needles are used because blunt needles are painful to insert and cause vasovagal syncope. The operator should consistently use the same volume syringe with the same gauge needle, as it is then possible to feel and judge the resistance to injection. A correctly placed injection has minimal resistance.

Oculocompression

Gentle digital pressure and massage around the globe help to disperse the anaesthetic and reduce IOP. Alternatively, a pressure-reducing device such as Honan's balloon can be used. The maximum pressure should be limited to 25 mm Hg in order to avoid compromise to the globe blood supply.

Sub-Tenon's block

Sub-Tenon's block involves a minor surgical procedure, and although it avoids some of the complications of the two other techniques, it has its own problems. Surface anaesthesia and asepsis is obtained as previously described. The lower eyelid is retracted or a speculum can be used especially in patients who blink excessively. The patient is asked to look upwards and outwards. The conjunctiva and Tenon's capsule are gripped together with a non-toothed forceps 5–10 mm from the limbus in the inferonasal quadrant. A small incision is made through these layers with Westcott scissors until the white sclera is seen. A sub-Tenon cannula (19 G, curved, 2.54 cm long, metal, opening at the end) is gently inserted along the curvature of the globe and should pass easily without resistance. In the posterior capsule 3–5 ml of local anaesthetic of choice is injected slowly. The injected local anaesthetic agent diffuses around and into the intraconal space leading to anaesthesia and akinesia (Kumar and McNeela 2003). Inferotemporal, superotemporal, and medial quadrants may also be used to access the sub-Tenon's space (Kumar and Dodds 2006). A variety of cannulae, some are flexible and shorter in length, is available. This method reduces the risk of central nervous system spread, optic nerve damage, and global puncture but may be more likely to cause superficial haemorrhage. Akinesia may take longer to achieve and is volume dependent.

Local anaesthetic agents and adjuncts

The ideal local anaesthetic agent should be safe and painless to inject (McLure and Rubin 2005). It should quickly block motor and sensory nerves. The duration should be long enough to perform the operation but not so long as to cause persistent postoperative diplopia.

Lidocaine 2% remains the gold standard. It is safe and produces effective motor and sensory blocks. Bupivacaine has been largely superseded by its isomer levobupivacaine which is less likely to cause cardiovascular side-effects. It may be used in 0.5% concentration (McLure et al. 2005). Its onset of action is slower than that of lidocaine but it has a longer duration of action. The more concentrated solutions may cause prolonged diplopia or myopathy if accidentally injected directly into one of the extraocular muscles. Prilocaine 2–4% (Döpfmer et al. 1996) has a rapid onset of action, few side-effects, and duration of action comparable with that of bupivacaine but its use in ophthalmology is not recommended by its manufacturer. Ropivacaine 1% has also been shown to be effective (Seidenari et al. 2006). Mixtures of equal volumes of 2% lidocaine and either 0.5% or 0.75% levobupivacaine are commonly used for longer procedures (McLure and Rubin 2005). This combination has the dual effect of quick onset of action with prolonged postoperative analgesia.

Hyaluronidase is an enzyme which reversibly liquefies the interstitial barrier between cells by depolymerization of hyaluronic acid to a tetrasaccharide thus enhancing diffusion of molecules through tissue planes (McLure and Rubin 2005). The amount of hyaluronidase powder mixed with the local anaesthetic varies from 5 to 15 IU ml^{-1} but should not exceed 15 IU ml^{-1} (Joint Formulary Committee 2015). The use of hyaluronidase for ophthalmic blocks is controversial (Kumar and Dodds 2006) and its use for sub-Tenon's block is questioned for a short operation such as cataract surgery. Side-effects are rare but include allergic reactions, orbital cellulitis and formation of pseudotumours (Kumar et al. 2012).

A vasoconstrictor such as adrenaline (epinephrine) is commonly mixed with local anaesthetic solution to increase the intensity and duration of block and minimize bleeding from small vessels (McLure and Rubin 2005). Absorption of local anaesthetic is reduced which avoids any surge in plasma levels. Adrenaline may cause vasoconstriction of the ophthalmic artery compromising the retinal circulation. The use of adrenaline in blocks should be avoided in elderly patients suffering from cerebrovascular or cardiovascular diseases.

Commercial preparations of lidocaine and bupivacaine are acidic in solution and the basic local anaesthetic exists predominantly in the charged ionic form. The non-ionized form of the local anaesthetic agent that traverses the lipid membrane of the nerve produces the conduction block. At higher pH values, a greater proportion of local anaesthetic molecules exist in the non-ionized form which allows more rapid influx into the neuronal cells. Adjustment of the pH of levobupivacaine and lidocaine by the addition of sodium bicarbonate allows more of the local anaesthetic solution to exist in the uncharged form. Alkalinization has been shown to decrease the onset and prolong the duration after needle blocks but its role in clinical practice is probably unwarranted (McLure and Rubin 2005).

Complications of ophthalmic regional blocks

Complications of needle blocks from mild to serious, affecting the eye or acting systemically, are well documented (Kumar and Dowd 2006). Orbital complications include failure of the block, corneal abrasion, chemosis, subconjunctival haemorrhage, orbital haemorrhage, globe damage, optic nerve damage, and extraocular muscle dysfunction. Systemic complications such as local anaesthetic agent toxicity, brainstem anaesthesia, and cardiorespiratory arrest may occur as a result of intravenous injection, or spread or misplacement of drug in the orbit during or immediately after injection.

Sub-Tenon's block is considered a safe alternative to needle block; however, a number of complications both minor and major have been reported (Kumar et al. 2012). Minor and frequent complications such as pain during injection, reflux of local anaesthetic, chemosis, and subconjunctival haemorrhage occur with varying incidence. Visual analogue pain scores are typically low but even minor discomfort in the orbit may be interpreted as severe and unpleasant pain. Smaller cannulae may afford a marginal benefit. Anterograde reflux and loss of local anaesthetic upon injection occurs if the dissection is oversized relative to the gauge of the cannula. Inadequate access into the sub-Tenon's space can also promote chemosis. The incidence of chemosis varies with the volume of local anaesthetic, dissection technique, and choice of cannula. Shorter cannulae are associated with increased likelihood of conjunctival chemosis. Subconjunctival haemorrhage is common. According to one study, conjunctival haemorrhage occurred in 40% of patients treated with clopidogrel, 35% of patients treated with warfarin, 21% of patients treated with aspirin and 19% of patients receiving none of these drugs (Kumar et al. 2006). Occurrence can be reduced by careful dissection, application of topical adrenaline, or, controversially, the use of handheld cautery (Kumar and Williamson 2005; Gauba et al. 2007).

Orbital haemorrhage

Orbital haemorrhage is a sight-threatening complication of intraconal and extraconal anaesthesia and, rarely, sub-Tenon's block (Kumar and Dowd 2006; Kumar et al. 2012). It occurs with a frequency of between 0.1% and 3% after needle-based blocks. The haemorrhage may be venous or arterial in origin and may be concealed or revealed. The venous bleeding is slow and usually stops. Venous haemorrhage usually presents as markedly blood-stained chemosis and raised IOP. It may be possible to reduce the IOP by digital massage and cautious application of an oculocompression device to such an extent that surgery may proceed safely. Before the decision is made to proceed with surgery or postpone it for a few days, it is advisable to measure and record IOP. However, arterial bleeding is rapid with blood filling the periorbital tissues increasing tissue volume and pressure. This is transmitted to the globe, raising the IOP. Urgent measures must be taken to stop the haemorrhage and reduce IOP. Firm digital pressure usually stops the bleeding and, when it has been arrested, consideration must be given to reducing the IOP so that the blood supply to the retina is not compromised. Lateral canthotomy, acetazolamide or mannitol intravenously, or even paracentesis may need to be considered in consultation with the ophthalmologist.

Unduly anxious patients may strain while the procedure is taking place. The blood vessels behind the eye become engorged and are readily punctured. The anxious, straining patient may need some sedation and should be encouraged to breathe quietly through an open mouth and so prevent any Valsalva manoeuvre. The fewer injections that are made into the orbit, the less are the chances of damaging a blood vessel. Cutting and slicing movements at the needle tip should be avoided as should any attempt to move the eye when the needle is in the orbit. Fine needles are less traumatic than thicker ones. Deep intraorbital injections must be avoided. The inferotemporal quadrant has fewer blood vessels and is less hazardous. It is advisable to apply firm digital pressure to the orbit as soon as the needle is withdrawn after any intraorbital injection, as this reduces any tendency to ooze.

Central spread of local anaesthetic agent

Mechanism

The cerebral dura mater provides a tubular sheath for the optic nerve as it passes through the optic foramen. This sheath fuses to the epineurium of the optic nerve providing a potential conduit for local anaesthetic to pass subdurally to the brain. Central spread occurs if the needle tip has entered the optic nerve sheath and an injection is made. Cases of central spread after sub-Tenon's block have been reported (Ruschen et al. 2003). Even a small-volume injection may cross the optic chiasma to the opposite eye, or enter the central nervous system, or both, and may cause life-threatening sequelae, usually catastrophic cardiorespiratory collapse. The time of onset of symptoms is variable but usually appears in the first 15 min after injection (Kumar and Dowd 2006) but may be delayed (Pragt et al. 2006). Central spread may occur on rare occasions if an orbital artery is cannulated by the needle tip resulting in a retrograde spread up the artery until it meets a branch, where it can then flow in a cephalad direction. In addition to orbital haemorrhage, systemic collapse is almost instantaneous.

Signs and symptoms of central spread

The symptomatology of central spread is varied and depends upon which part of the central nervous system is affected by the local anaesthetic (Kumar and Dowd 2006). As a result of the anatomical proximity of the optic nerve to the midbrain, it is usual for this area to be involved. Signs and symptoms involving the cardiovascular and respiratory systems, temperature regulation, vomiting, temporary hemiplegia, aphasia, and generalized convulsions have been described. Palsy of the contralateral oculomotor and trochlear nerves with amaurosis (loss of vision) is pathognomonic of central nervous system spread and should be sought in any patient whose response to questions after block are not as crisp as they were beforehand.

Treatment of central spread

Cardiorespiratory arrest may occur and should be treated as any other arrest. Bradycardia requires treatment with an anticholinergic drug. Asystole has been reported rarely, but if it occurs, intravenous vasopressors and external pacing may be required. Respiratory depression or apnoea necessitates ventilatory support, intravenous fluid therapy, and administration of supplementary oxygen. Convulsions are treated with an intravenous induction agent such as propofol or benzodiazepines.

Prevention of central spread

Intraconal or extraconal injections should always be made with the patient looking in the neutral or the primary gaze position. The optic nerve is a C-shaped structure and there is slackness in the primary gaze position and it is out of the way of the advancing needle. If the needle encounters the optic nerve in this position, it is unlikely to damage or perforate its sheath, as slackness in the structure allows the nerve to be pushed aside (Kumar and Dowd 2006). The most dangerous position is when the patient looks upwards and inwards, as this presents the stretched nerve to a needle directed from the inferotemporal quadrant. The injection should not be made deep into the orbit, where the optic nerve is likely to be tethered.

Globe damage

Global puncture is a serious complication especially of ophthalmic needle-based blocks (Kumar and Dowd 2006). It has been reported after both intraconal and extraconal blocks and even after subconjunctival injection. Cases of globe damage after sub-Tenon's block have also been reported. Perforation of the globe means it has an entry and exit wound whereas penetration of globe has only the wound of entry. With appropriate care, it should be a very rare complication because the sclera is a tough structure and in most cases is not perforated easily. Puncture of the eyeball is most likely to occur in patients with high myopia, previous retinal banding, posterior staphyloma, or a deeply sunken eye with a narrow orbit. Not all globes are the same length and not all orbits are the same shape. In most patients who present for cataract surgery, an ultrasound measure is made of the axial length of the eyeball to calculate the power of the intraocular lens. Normal globes have an axial length of 20–24 mm. High myopes have much longer axial lengths and extreme caution with needle blocks should be exercised in these patients. The axial length in patients for glaucoma surgery is not usually measured and special care is required if a needle block is contemplated.

Globe damage is usually recognized at the time of surgery and presents as an exceptionally soft eye with a loss of red reflex. In cataract surgery, if the block is good, the surgeon should be encouraged to proceed with the lensectomy but to stitch up the eye with twice as many sutures as normal. Without lensectomy, it may not be possible to observe the damage to the posterior segment of the eye. It can be expected that the needle track through the vitreous will form a band of scar tissue. If this is not excised, it contracts and detaches the retina, sometimes causing sudden total blindness in the affected eye.

Optic nerve damage

This is a rare but late complication which usually results from obstruction of the central retinal artery or direct trauma after classical retrobulbar block with a long needle. This artery is the first and smallest branch of the ophthalmic artery arising from that vessel as it lies below the optic nerve. It runs for a short distance within the dural sheath of the optic nerve and about 35 mm from the orbital margin, pierces the nerve and runs forward in the centre of the nerve to the retina. Damage to the artery may cause bleeding into the confined space of the optic nerve sheath, compressing and obstructing blood flow. If the complication is recognized soon enough, surgical decompression of the optic nerve is performed.

Extraocular muscle malfunction

The inadvertent injection of a long-acting local anaesthetic into any extraocular muscle mass may result in muscle damage manifesting as prolonged weakness, fibrosis, or even necrosis of the muscle. The 'classical' retrobulbar description where the needle is inserted between the lateral one-third and medial two-thirds junction of the inferior orbital rim predisposes to this complication (Hamilton 2000). The safest site for inferotemporal injection is the extreme temporal area just below the lateral rectus and addition of hyaluronidase may facilitate local anaesthetic agent dispersal and minimize lasting damage. Persistent diplopia after local anaesthesia should be investigated with a suitable scan as urgent surgical intervention to the affected muscle may be required.

Ophthalmic drugs relevant to the anaesthetist

There are several drugs of importance which patients with ophthalmic conditions receive. Readers are advised to consult ophthalmic books for further details and a brief description of some of the important drugs are mentioned here for completeness. β-adrenergic blockade (e.g. with timolol) decreases IOP by reduction of aqueous humour production. Topical drugs can lead to clinically significant concentrations in the plasma via nasal drainage and the side-effects of timolol including hypotension, bradycardia, and bronchospasm are well reported. Similarly, phenylephrine applied to the eye intraoperatively, which dilates the pupil, may cause myocardial ischaemia and hypertension. Prostaglandin analogues (e.g. latanoprost) increase the uveoscleral outflow of aqueous, reducing IOP. α-adrenergic drugs (e.g. clonidine) cause the same effect. Carbonic anhydrase inhibitors (e.g. acetazolamide) reduce aqueous formation and are used orally or intravenously to treat or prevent increases in IOP. These are sulfonamides without bacteriostatic actions and should not be used in those with a relevant allergy. They can cause an acidosis (renal loss of bicarbonate) and a diuresis because of their effects on the renal tubules. The acidosis can be made worse in the perioperative period if the effect of opioids and anaesthesia reduce respiratory compensation. Hypertonic mannitol increases aqueous outflow. Initial blood pressure and systemic blood volume increases are followed by a diuresis. The use of intraoperative diuretics necessitates the use of urinary catheterization. Ecothiopate is of historical interest as a treatment for intraocular hypertension as it irreversibly binds to cholinesterase and can last for a week. The duration of action of succinylcholine is thus significantly prolonged.

Anaesthesia for specific ophthalmic procedures requiring general anaesthesia

Cataract surgery

Cataract surgical techniques have undergone recent changes and the procedure has become less invasive and rarely involves a big incision. Phacoemulsification surgery is increasingly performed with much smaller size phaco probes. The procedure can be performed under topical anaesthesia but many ophthalmologists and patients prefer a block technique. The use of sub-Tenon's block is common and needle-based block is avoided in many countries. General anaesthesia is now administered on rare occasions.

Eye trauma

The penetrating open eye injury attracts first place in the list, if only because of its importance in postgraduate examinations in anaesthesia. Eye injuries may be difficult to examine because of swelling and pain and may need to be explored under anaesthesia at the earliest opportunity. The potential for loss of intraocular contents exists even where penetration may not be obviously present preoperatively. Eye injury may also be coexistent with major head injury or polytrauma. This injury is commonest in young adult males although the advent of seatbelt use brought about a significant reduction in its incidence. As with any case of trauma there may be a short fasting time before the injury and subsequent delay in gastric emptying, especially after alcohol consumption pre injury or opioid use in the emergency department. The situation may therefore exist of anaesthesia for a patient with a full stomach.

In patients with penetrating eye injury alone or associated with other trauma, general anaesthesia is routine. Orbital regional anaesthesia has been used successfully in selected centres and patients (Scott et al. 2002). The classical dilemma of rapid intubation to prevent aspiration using suxamethonium and the subsequent risk of increased IOP causing loss of eye contents is a balance of anaesthesia risk *vs* surgical risk. The overwhelming importance is to choose the anaesthetic technique that prevents aspiration most effectively throughout the perioperative period and thought must also be given to reducing the IOP until the eye is made safe. In principle, therefore, suxamethonium as the neuromuscular blocking agent with the fastest onset of good or excellent intubating conditions, used in association with cricoid pressure is first choice. Large retrospective studies of penetrating eye injury have not shown vitreous loss to be clinically significant (Libonati et al. 1985).

The principal decision in making anaesthetic-related choices is the urgency of the surgery. Ophthalmologists are currently more likely to choose to wait for 6 h after the last meal or often, because of the time of day, to wait until morning before exploring the eye. This is dependent on the severity of the injury and the potential to produce a good ocular outcome. There is little incentive to risk aspiration and death if there is little likelihood of preserving vision as the benefit.

Where appropriate fasting delays have been followed, the anaesthetist is now in a position to make whatever anaesthetic choice is suitable for any other intraocular surgery with similar airway risk factors (see 'Airway managment').

Surgery may be bilateral and lengthy and subsequent return to theatre for repeated procedures is also common. Loss of vision in one or both eyes after accidental injury in the young population understandably heightens preoperative anxiety.

Vitreoretinal surgery

Vitreoretinal surgery covers a range of intra- and extraocular procedures that may involve lengthy periods of time in the dark. Anaesthetic considerations related to duration of procedure and individual choice of technique and airway were previously described in 'Airway managment'. The use of a local block is common and both needle- (Costen et al. 2005) and cannula-based blocks (Gill et al. 2012) are in use. General anaesthesia is used in younger, anxious patients and where surgery may be expected to last much longer than usual. Vitrectomy removes the vitreous from the eye for the purpose of clearing cloudy or bloody vitreous, and to perform intraocular procedures on the retina. The integrity and pressure of the vitreal cavity is set by the surgeon throughout the procedure while the structured jelly-like apparatus is removed. The cavity may then be filled with an air/gas mixture (commonly perfluoropropane or sulphur hexafluoride) or silicone. The surgeon may make a decision on which of these to use towards the end of surgery and as such it is sensible to avoid nitrous oxide use for vitrectomy surgery as a result of the fact that nitrous oxide in equilibrium in the eye cavity may diffuse out quickly, leaving a lower pressure in the eye than surgically intended, causing detachment or re-detachment of the retina. If nitrous oxide has been used it should be switched off well before the insertion of surgical gas into the vitreal cavity. Gases may persist for up to 3 months postoperatively and the non-ophthalmic anaesthetist needs to be aware of the relevance of ophthalmic gases (Yang et al. 2002). Wrist bands are placed on the patient after surgery to alert any subsequent anaesthetist to avoid nitrous oxide for all anaesthesia. Nitrous oxide would diffuse into the cavity faster than any nitrogen would diffuse out and the IOP could increase with serious consequences. Equally, flying will cause the bubble to expand. The gas is slowly removed by diffusion whereas silicone oil used for the same purpose will need to be surgically removed at a later stage.

Retinal surgery can also be performed from outside the sclera. Buckling, bands, cryotherapy, and laser therapies are used to repair breaks. The eye requires a lot of surgical manipulation during these procedures and the oculocardiac reflex can be profound and recurrent. Anticholinergic prophylaxis may be helpful. The vitreoretinal anaesthetist may find a very unpredictable list organization as different detachments (e.g. macular detachment) require urgent surgery and are therefore common additions at the end of the day.

Subsequent repeated operations are very common. General anaesthetic considerations will remain the same; however, local anaesthesia may become complicated by adhesions related to the original surgery.

Strabismus surgery

This is the most commonly performed paediatric ophthalmic procedure and is usually a day-case anaesthetic. Airway considerations of head and neck procedures apply but a laryngeal mask is the most commonly chosen airway, especially in older children. Long-acting opioids are not required and are only likely to increase an already high risk of postoperative nausea and vomiting. Surgery itself requires tension to be applied to the extraocular muscles. Steady deep anaesthesia with or without neuromuscular blockade (to guarantee immobility) will allow the surgeon to gauge how much muscle repositioning is required. Many surgeons prefer a non-paralysed patient if adjustable sutures are used. However, it is the tension applied by the surgeon to the muscle which can cause severe bradycardias especially in the vagally responsive child. Prophylaxis with glycopyrrolate is recommended. Temperature measurement is mandatory for children during general anaesthesia except for the shortest procedures but the historical association between strabismus surgery in children and malignant hyperthermia is probably spurious. Measures to control postoperative pain and reduction of nausea and vomiting should be instigated.

Glaucoma surgery

Where general anaesthesia is required, most of the considerations are the same as for cataract surgery. However, unlike most ocular surgery intraoperative miosis is required, but this is not a contraindication to intravenous atropine. Neuromuscular block and good anaesthetic control over IOP variables will produce the ideal conditions.

Dacrocystorhinostomy

Dacrocystorhinostomy (DCR) is a procedure performed for watering eyes, usually as a result of lacrimal duct stenosis. There is surgical exposure of the tear duct and a new opening is created into the nasal cavity. This is a relatively stimulating procedure and general anaesthesia is suitable although local anaesthesia (with or without sedation) has gained popularity (McNab and Simmie 2002). It can be performed with an open technique or through a nasal endoscope although anaesthetically the considerations are similar. All usual ophthalmic anaesthetic considerations apply. However, there is the additional risk of blood in the airway during and immediately after the procedure. Tracheal intubation and the safe use of a throat pack offer airway protection. Measures to prevent blood ooze at the site of surgery can aid the surgeon and these include hypotension, head-up position, and the use of vasoconstriction in the surgical field. Xylometazoline or cocaine provides vasoconstriction in the nose. Endoscopic laser DCR is another surgical operation and the anaesthetist should have additional training in the practicalities of laser airway surgery. The laser safety officer will provide the correct eye protection for the anaesthetist.

Other oculoplastic surgery

The range of surgery for this subspecialty relates to the lid, socket, or adnexae. Many procedures are short and lid surgery is generally performed under local anaesthesia. Longer procedures such as enucleation and tumour surgery are generally performed under general anaesthesia and appropriate measures are taken to control postoperative pain. Bilateral blepharoplasties for cosmetic reasons are increasingly frequent and in common with all oculoplastic surgery the requirements for a bloodless field are best met with controlled relative hypotension and surgical site vasoconstriction.

Paediatric procedures

In addition to strabismus surgery, children, including infants and neonates, may require other ophthalmic procedures. Readers are referred to Chapters 70 and 71 on anaesthesia for neonates and young children. Although the majority of children are ASA 1 or 2 and may be managed as day cases, there are a number of patients with associated comorbidities who require detailed examinations or ocular surgery. Congenital cataracts, glaucoma, vascular and lens disorders can occur in genetic diseases such as Down's syndrome, mucopolysaccharidoses, craniofacial, and connective tissue disorders. Anaesthetic considerations relevant to the condition balanced with the surgical requirements will guide anaesthesia choices. An infant with airway anomalies may require a complex anaesthetic skill set just to undergo ophthalmoscopy.

Sedation during ophthalmic blocks

Sedation is commonly used for topical anaesthesia (Greenhalgh and Kumar 2008). Selected patients, in whom explanation and reassurance have proved inadequate, may benefit from sedation. Short-acting benzodiazepines, opioids, and small doses of intravenous anaesthetic induction agents are favoured but the dosage must be minimal (Greenhalgh and Kumar 2008). The routine use of sedation is discouraged because of an increased incidence of adverse intraoperative events. It is essential that when sedation is administered, a means of providing supplementary oxygen is available. Equipment and skills to manage any life-threatening events must be immediately accessible.

Conclusion

The practice of anaesthesia has seen preferences for local or general anaesthesia for ophthalmology swing in both directions since Koller introduced a choice, using cocaine over 130 years ago. Currently the preference is firmly for local anaesthesia and a practising ophthalmic anaesthetist should have a range of different techniques to deal with the needs of different operations, operators, and, most importantly, patients. There is no place for *ad hoc* attendance in the eye unit and occasional practice. It is interesting and challenging work.

Declaration of interest

None declared.

References

Aschner B. Ueber einen bisher noch nicht beshriebenen Reflex vom Auge auf Kreislauf und Atmung. Verschwinden des Radialpulses bei Druck auf das Auge. *Wien Klin Wochenschr* 1908; **21**: 1529–30

Atkinson WS. Retrobulbar injection of anesthetic within the muscular cone. *Arch Ophthalmol* 1936; **16**: 494–503

Blanc VF, Jacob JL, Milot J, Cyrenne L. The oculorespiratory reflex revisited. *Can J Anaesth* 1988; **35**: 468–72

Chmielewski C, Snyder-Clickett S. The use of the laryngeal mask airway with mechanical positive pressure ventilation. *AANAJ* 2004; **72**: 347–51

Costen MT, Newsom RS, Wainwright AC, Luff AJ, Canning CR. Expanding role of local anaesthesia in vitreoretinal surgery. *Eye* 2005; **19**: 755–61

Cunningham AJ, Barry P. Intraocular pressure-physiology and implications for anaesthetic management. *Can Anaesth Soc* J 1986; **33**: 195–208

Döpfmer UR, Maloney DG, Gaynor PA, Ratcliffe RM, Döpfmer S. Prilocaine 3% is superior to a mixture of bupivacaine and lignocaine for peribulbar anaesthesia. *Br J Anaesth* 1996; **76**: 77–80

Dutton JJ. *Atlas of Clinical and Surgical Orbital Anatomy*, 2nd Edn. Philadelphia, PA: WB Saunders, 2011

Fanning GL. Orbital regional anesthesia: let's be precise. *J Cataract Refract Surg* 2003; **29**: 1846–7

Fukasaku H, Marron JA. Sub-Tenon's pinpoint anesthesia. *J Cataract Refract Surg* 1994; **20**: 468–71

Gauba V, Saleh GM, Watson K, Chung A. Sub-Tenon anaesthesia: reduction in subconjunctival haemorrhage with controlled bipolar conjunctival cautery. *Eye* 2007; **21**: 1387–90

Gill VS, Presland AH, Lord JA, Bunce C, Xing W, Charteris DG. Two-quadrant high-volume sub-Tenon's anaesthesia for vitrectomy: a randomised controlled trial. *Br J Ophthalmol* 2012; **96**: 189–92

Greenbaum S. Parabulbar anesthesia. *Am J Ophthalmol* 1992; **114**: 776

Greenhalgh DL, Kumar CM. Sedation during ophthalmic surgery. *Eur J Anaesthesiol* 2008; **25**: 701–7

Hamilton RC. Retrobulbar block revisited and revised. *J Cataract Refract Surg* 1996; **22**: 1147–50

Hamilton RC. A discourse on the complications of retrobulbar and peribulbar blockade. *Can J Ophthalmol* 2000; **35**: 363–72

Ismail SA, Bisher NA, Kandil HW, Mowafi HA, Atawia HA. Intraocular pressure and haemodynamic responses to insertion of the i-gel, laryngeal mask airway or endotracheal tube. *Eur J Anaesthesiol* 2011; **28**: 443–8

Joint Formulary Committee. *British National Formulary*, Volume 69. London: BMJ Group and Pharmaceutical Press, 2015

Kelly RE, Dinner M, Turner LS, Haik B, Abramson DH, Daines P. Succinylcholine increases intraocular pressure in the human eye with the extraocular muscles detached. *Anesthesiology* 1993; **79**: 948–52

Kerr WJ, Vance JP. Oculocardiac reflex from the empty orbit. *Anaesthesia* 1983; **38**: 883–5

Kumar CM. Needle-based blocks for the 21st century ophthalmology. *Acta Ophthalmol* 2011; **89**: 5–9

Kumar CM, Dodds C. Sub-Tenon's anesthesia. *Ophthalmol Clin North Am* 2006; **19**: 209–19

Kumar CM, Dodds C, Gayer S. *Oxford Handbook of Ophthalmic Anaesthesia.* Oxford: Oxford University Press, 2012

Kumar CM, Dowd TC. Complications of ophthalmic regional blocks: their treatment and prevention. *Ophthalmologica* 2006; **220**: 73–82

Kumar CM, Eid H, Dodds C. Sub-Tenon's anaesthesia—complications and their prevention. *Eye* 2011; **25**: 684–703

Kumar CM, Eke T, Dodds C, *et al.* Local anaesthesia for ophthalmic surgery – new guidelines from the Royal College of Anaesthetists and the Royal College of Ophthalmologists. *Eye* 2012; **26**: 897–8

Kumar CM, McNeela BJ. Ultrasonic localization of anaesthetic fluid using sub-Tenon's cannulae of three different lengths. *Eye* 2003; **17**: 1003–7

Kumar CM, Williamson S. Diathermy does not reduce subconjunctival haemorrhage during sub-Tenon's block. *Br J Anaesth* 2005; **95**: 562

Kumar N, Jivan S, Thomas P, McLure H. Sub-Tenon's anesthesia with aspirin, warfarin, and chlopidogrel. *J Cataract Refract Surg* 2006; **32**: 1022–5

Libonati MM, Leahy JJ, Ellison N. The use of succinylcholine in open eye surgery. *Anesthesiology* 1985; **62**: 637–40

McLure HA, Kumar CM, Ahmed S, Patel A. A comparison of lidocaine 2% with levobupivacaine 0.75% for sub-Tenon's block. *Eur J Anaesthesiol* 2005; **22**: 500–3

McLure HA, Rubin AP. Review of local anaesthetic agents. *Minerva Anestesiol* 2005; **71**: 59–74

McNab AA, Simmie RJ. Effectiveness of local anaesthesia for external dacryocystorhinostomy. *Clin Experiment Ophthalmol* 2002; **30**: 270–2

Miller RD. *Miller's Anesthesia.* Amsterdam: Elsevier Churchill Livingston, 2005

Mirakhur RK, Shepherd WF, Darrah WC. Propofol or thiopentone: effects on intraocular pressure associated with induction of anaesthesia and tracheal intubation (facilitated with suxamethonium). *Br J Anaesth* 1987; **59**: 431–6

Murphy DF. Anesthesia and intraocular pressure. *Anesth Analg* 1985; **64**: 520–30

Nagdeve NG, Yaddanapudi S, Pandav SS. The effect of different doses of ketamine on intraocular pressure in anesthetized children. *J Pediatr Ophthalmol Strabismus* 2006; **43**: 219–23

National Institute for Health and Care Excellence (NICE). *Routine Preoperative Tests for Elective Surgery.* NG45. London: NICE, 2016. Available from https://www.nice.org.uk/guidance/NG45

Pragt E, van Zundert AA, Kumar CM. Delayed convulsions and brief contralateral hemiparesis after retrobulbar block. *Reg Anesth Pain Med* 2006; **31**: 275–8

Ripart J, Lefrant JY, de La Coussaye JE, Prat-Pradal D, Vivien B, Eledjam JJ. Peribulbar versus retrobulbar anesthesia for ophthalmic surgery: an anatomical comparison of extraconal and intraconal injections. *Anesthesiology* 2001; **94**: 56–62

Ripart J, Prat-Pradal D, Charavel P, Eledjam JJ. Medial canthus single injection episcleral (sub-Tenon) anesthesia anatomic imaging. *Clin Anat* 1998; **11**: 390–5

Ruschen H, Bremmer FD, Carr C. Complications after sub-Tenon's eye block. *Anesth Analg* 2003; **96**: 273–7

Scott IU, McCabe CM, Flynn HW, *et al.* Local anesthesia with intravenous sedation for surgical repair of selected open globe injuries. *Am J Ophthalmol* 2002; **134**: 707–11

Seidenari P, Santin G, Milani P, David A. Peribulbar and retrobulbar combined anesthesia for vitreoretinal surgery using ropivacaine. *Eur J Ophthalmol* 2006; **16**: 295–9

Springer DK, Jahr JS. The laryngeal mask airway. Safety, efficacy, and current use. *Am J Anesthesiol* 1995; **22**: 65–9

Stevens J. A new local anaesthesia technique for cataract extraction by one quadrant sub-Tenon's infiltration. *Br J Ophthalmol* 1992; **76**: 620–4

Thind GS, Rubin AP. Local anaesthesia for eye surgery-no room for complacency. *Br J Anaesth* 2001; **86**: 473–6

van den Berg AA, Lambourne A, Clyburn PA. The oculo-emetic reflex. A rationalisation of postophthalmic anaesthesia vomiting. *Anaesthesia* 1989; **44**: 110–7

Vohra SB, Good PA. Altered globe dimensions of axial myopia as risk factors for penetrating ocular injury during peribulbar anesthesia. *Br J Anaesth* 2000; **85**: 242–3

Yang YF, Herbert L, Rüschen H, Cooling RJ. Nitrous oxide anaesthesia in the presence of intraocular gas can cause irreversible blindness. *BMJ* 2002; **325**: 532–3

CHAPTER 61

Anaesthesia for abdominal surgery

William J. Fawcett

Introduction

Major gastrointestinal (GI) surgery has always posed challenges for the anaesthetist. Patients are often elderly, with varying degrees of co-morbidities and malnutrition. Moreover, in the acute setting, there may be abdominal pain, distension, electrolyte imbalance, anaemia, and sepsis (see 'Emergency laparotomy'). After surgery, there will be varying degrees of pain and ileus and poor management of these is associated with significant morbidity and mortality. In addition, postoperative complications are not uncommon. These may be related to the surgery, such as anastomotic breakdown with associated leakage of GI contents. This will cause a marked inflammatory response and very often with superadded sepsis. Medical complications unrelated to the surgery are also relatively frequent. Major, open GI surgery puts significant demands on cardiorespiratory reserve, with large increases required in cardiac output and oxygen delivery. Patients with co-morbidities who are unable to meet these challenges may well enter a spiral of inadequate perfusion at cellular level, resulting in anaerobic metabolism, lactic acidosis, and eventually major organ dysfunction. Other medical postoperative complications that may be encountered include venous thromboembolism (VTE), pulmonary infections, and with those at risk, cardiac complications (such as myocardial infarction, arrhythmias, and cardiac failure). Cerebrovascular, renal, and hepatic complications may also be seen. Finally, as much of GI surgery is for malignancy, patients may well have recently completed treatment for this, in particular radiotherapy or chemotherapy. As a result, they may have a degree of immunosuppression, direct toxicity (e.g. cardiac), or both, from the treatment. Currently, there is major interest in how, to what extent, and for how long chemotherapy affects and impairs physiological reserve (West et al. 2015).

In the last 10 years, there have been some significant changes in the approach to major GI surgery. Preoperatively, timely surgery with preoperative optimization of concurrent medical conditions is seen as fundamental. Correction of major biochemical abnormalities and understanding the need for enteral nutrition (even in the preoperative period) may significantly benefit the patient. The use of Nutrition Risk Screening Scores and the administration of both nutritional support and oral nutritional supplements may reduce complications, stress response, and length of hospital stay (Weimann et al. 2006). Assessment of risk is fundamental to the planning of appropriate perioperative care for these patients. A major area is determining physiological reserve, which is the cornerstone of preoperative assessment. There are a number of simple, functional walk tests, such as the 6 min walk test, but many hospitals have introduced cardiopulmonary exercise testing (CPET), first popularized more than 15 years ago (Older et al. 1999). CPET is considered to be an objective and reproducible marker of reserve which is, in part, independent of patient effort and, as such, has some capacity to predict complications. Other methods, particularly the predictors of cardiac death such as ischaemic heart disease, ventricular failure, cerebrovascular disease, type 2 diabetes mellitus, and renal impairment (Auerbach and Goldman 2006) are fundamental for planning the type of anaesthesia, surgery, and, crucially, postoperative care. For example, high-risk patients may be better served by having more minor surgery, such as stenting of bowel tumours, or bypass procedures in preference to radical surgical resections.

Many patients might be expected to benefit from laparoscopic surgery, but this is not without risk and of itself causes marked cardiopulmonary changes (see 'Laparoscopic surgery'). Occasionally, it may be necessary to submit patients to prior interventions related to the intra-abdominal pathology (e.g. bile duct stenting, ureteric stenting) or even unrelated to the presenting pathology (such as percutaneous coronary interventions or carotid surgery). Postoperatively, the findings at preoperative assessment may guide whether or not a patient needs admitting to the intensive care unit (ICU), where they can receive, in particular, close monitoring and manipulation of cardiac physiology with i.v. fluids and sometimes inotropes or vasoactive drugs.

Key areas of change in gastrointestinal surgery

Laparoscopic surgery

The advent of laparoscopic surgery has been fundamental to improving the postoperative course of these patients. With appropriate expertise, it is associated with reduced length of stay, reduced complications, and reduced readmission rates, but it must also be remembered that prolonged procedures may be poorly tolerated. Carbon dioxide pneumoperitoneum has major physiological effects (Table 61.1). In addition, the patient is often then placed at extreme Trendelenburg (head-down) or reverse Trendelenburg (head-up) position. High intra-abdominal pressures (>20 mm Hg) exacerbate these changes and sometimes it may be safer to offer patients open surgery instead. The phrase 'minimal access surgery, maximum cardiopulmonary stress' is useful to remind both anaesthetists

Table 61.1 Physiological effects of laparoscopy

Cardiovascular	Respiratory	Other organs
Increased systemic vascular resistance	Reduced pulmonary compliance	Reduced intra- abdominal blood flow (gut/liver/ kidney)
Reduced venous return	Reduced functional residual capacity	Reduced cerebral venous drainage (may lead to cerebral oedema)
Reduction in cardiac output	Pulmonary atelectasis	Metabolic (lactic) acidosis if prolonged surgery
Blood pressure changes variable (very often reduces with reverse Trendelenburg)	Ventilation:perfusion mismatch	
	Carbon dioxide absorption with respiratory acidosis	

and surgeons that laparoscopic surgery is not without these risks. Currently, there are studies underway investigating whether performing laparoscopic surgery using deep neuromuscular block may improve surgical conditions at lower intra-abdominal pressures, thus reducing the cardiopulmonary sequelae.

Intravenous fluid therapy

Poor prescribing of fluids is disastrous to GI patients: too little fluid and there is a reduction in cardiac output, whereas fluid excess may cause oedema (particularly to the lungs but also to any anastomosis). Both extremes will ultimately impair tissue oxygenation. More than 40 years ago, intensivists first recognized the link between supranormal oxygen delivery ($\dot{D}o_2$) and consumption ($\dot{V}o_2$) and increased survival (Shoemaker et al. 1973). Later trials both from Shoemaker and others confirmed this hypothesis (Shoemaker et al. 1988; Hayes et al. 1993) in high-risk patients and indeed the concept of ensuring adequate or indeed supranormal $\dot{D}o_2$ to patients undergoing major surgery to reduce complications and death is now enshrined in modern anaesthetic practice. These measurements were derived using pulmonary artery flow catheters and using the well-known equation for indexed $\dot{D}o_2I$ (i.e. $\dot{D}o_2$ expressed per m^2):

$$\dot{D}o_2I = \frac{SV \times HR \times Sa_{O_2} \times [Hb] \times 1.34}{BSA} \qquad (61.1)$$

where SV = stroke volume, HR = heart rate, Sa_{O_2} = oxygen saturation (expressed as fraction), [Hb] = haemoglobin concentration, and BSA = body surface area.

Given that HR, Sa_{O_2} and [Hb] are often not markedly deranged, the major focus is directed at the optimization of SV according to the Frank–Starling curve. These measurements are commonly undertaken in theatres, no longer with a pulmonary artery flow catheter, but most commonly by either the oesophageal Doppler monitor or pulse contour analysis. Thus, perioperative fluid management is often guided by these flow measurements (i.e. $\dot{D}o_2I$) and not by pressure measurements [such as blood pressure or central venous pressure (CVP)]. Commonly used targets are a cardiac index of greater than 4.5 litres min^{-1} and a $\dot{D}o_2I$ of greater than 600 ml min^{-1} m^{-2} (Tote and Grounds 2006).

Although CVP measurements still have a place (using the assumption that CVP reflects left ventricular end-diastolic pressure and left ventricular end-diastolic volume) flow measurement technologies are being increasingly used, with the optimization of SV as the usual end-point. This is performed by measuring SV and then administering an i.v. bolus of 200–250 ml of colloid with the SV measured again 10–15 min later. If there has been more than a 10% increase in SV, further boluses are given until the SV no longer increases (i.e. SV optimization has occurred) (Fig. 61.1). Further boluses of fluid are potentially detrimental as SV can reduce with excess of fluid. This process is also referred to as goal-directed fluid therapy (GDFT).

The major issue is that there is a large inter-individual variation in fluid requirements (Levy et al. 2011) with fluid assessment and management by other means (e.g. on a ml kg^{-1} basis or using CVP) very much less accurate. Indeed, since the introduction of the oesophageal Doppler monitor, there has been a reduced need for CVP measurements with improved outcome and reduced hospital stay (NHS Technology Adoption Centre 2013). With patients undergoing major bowel surgery, the use of the oesophageal Doppler monitor not only reduced length of stay but was also associated with earlier recovery of gut function and less GI morbidity (Wakeling et al. 2005). Other studies and meta-analyses have confirmed these findings of reduced major and minor GI complications with the use of GDFT (Giglio et al. 2009). Furthermore, GDFT reduces aspects of the stress response such as reduced increases in interleukin 6 concentrations (Noblett et al. 2006). The importance attached to fluid management is now recognized widely within the UK National Health Service (NHS), and has been adopted by the UK National Institute for Health and Care Excellence (2011). Notwithstanding the above, many of the earlier studies were carried out before the improvements brought about by modern care pathways [such as enhanced recovery (ER), discussed later] which may attenuate some of these earlier benefits with major advantages of GDFT perhaps limited to the higher-risk patients (Rollins and Lobo 2016).

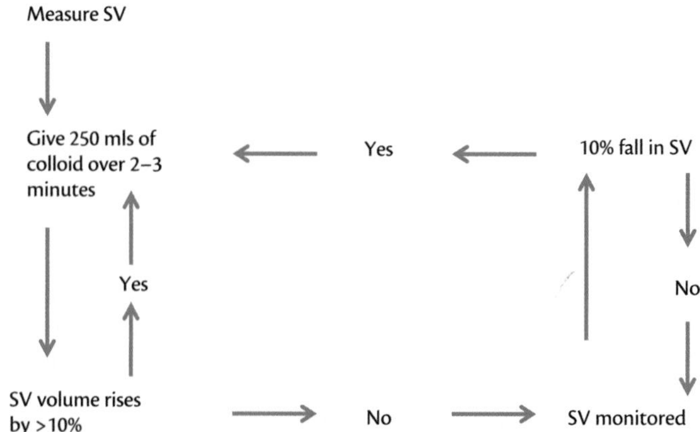

Figure 61.1 Algorithm for goal-directed fluid therapy.
Reproduced from HG Wakeling et al., Intraoperative oesophageal Doppler guided fluid management shortens postoperative hospital stay after major bowel surgery, *British Journal of Anaesthesia*, 2005, 95, 5, pp. 634–642, by permission of the Board of Management and Trustees of the British Journal of Anaesthesia.

For many years there has been a debate about the type of fluid to be used (crystalloid or colloid) and this continues. Another area of debate is whether to continue GDFT postoperatively, and if so, for how long. This will generally have to be carried out within an ICU setting. Other measurements have also been described to guide fluids once GDFT is no longer used: CVP, serum lactate, and central venous oxygen saturations (Scv_{O_2}). A serum lactate concentration greater than 1.5 mmol litre^{-1} may indicate a degree of hypoperfusion. Scv_{O_2} measurements were initially popularized in the treatment of septic patients (Rivers et al. 2001) but these findings have been used as an indicator of global oxygen extraction: low levels (e.g. <65%) imply that cardiac output is inadequate to meet oxygen demands and increased oxygen extraction is occurring. Moreover, Scv_{O_2} is an independent risk factor for complications (Pearse et al. 2005). A timely fluid challenge may increase $\dot{D}O_2$ and reverse these trends. They may also alert staff that the patient may need to return to ICU if there is no improvement to re-introduce GDFT.

Analgesia

The optimum analgesic modality after GI surgery is also a matter of debate. While the use of multimodal, opioid-sparing analgesia, with the regular use (if not contraindicated) of paracetamol and non-steroidal anti-inflammatory drugs (NSAIDs), is not controversial, this alone will not be adequate for these patients. GI surgery, in particular upper GI incisions, are very painful postoperatively and often require either regional block (e.g. epidural) or parenteral opioids. The latter cause nausea and vomiting and reduce GI motility and patients receiving large doses of opioids have a much slower return of GI function, (e.g. passage of flatus, stool, and tolerating fluids and diet). For many years, thoracic epidurals were seen as the gold standard after open GI surgery. The return of GI function was quicker, both as a result of reduced opioid requirements but also because of the sympathectomy and a relative increase in parasympathetic action on the gut. Other advantages claimed for epidurals were a reduced incidence of VTE, blood loss, and a reduction in some aspects of the stress response (pituitary, adrenocortical, and sympathetic responses). However, enthusiasm for epidurals has reduced somewhat. The failure rate of epidurals is often overlooked, with quoted ranges between 13% and 47%, with a large study describing an incidence of 32% for thoracic epidurals and 27% for lumbar epidural (Hermanides et al. 2012). Although in many cases re-siting or adding adjuvants (such as epidural diamorphine) may rectify the situation, a failed epidural not only leaves the patient in pain, but in addition it may deny them other alternatives (such as systemic opioids) as these drugs cannot be co-administered if the patient is receiving epidural opioids. In addition, although epidurals are widely perceived as safe, the 3rd National Audit Project highlighted the risks associated with central neural block, with postoperative epidurals having the highest incidence of permanent neurological harm, estimated at between 1:5700 and 1:12 200 (Royal College of Anaesthetists, 2009). Finally, patients with epidurals often receive a greater volume of fluids to combat hypotension, which predisposes to fluid overload and an increase in length of hospital stay (Levy et al. 2011). Ideally these patients should probably receive vasoactive drugs rather than fluids to combat the sympathetic-induced vasodilation, but these cannot be safely administered without intra-arterial monitoring and consequently require the patient to be nursed in an ICU or high dependency (HDU) environment. Other techniques have been used with success in open surgery such as rectus sheath catheters, transversus abdominis plane (TAP) block, and wound catheters infusing local anaesthetic into the wound edges as well as systemic adjuvants such as iv ketamine and lidocaine (Fawcett and Baldini 2015).

The marked increase in use of laparoscopic or small incision surgery has focused the debate on the best analgesic modality for these procedures too (Levy et al. 2010). Although epidurals provide better early pain relief, they are widely regarded as unnecessary as pain relief requirements are much more modest. This has also led to a number of techniques being used, with particular success with spinal anaesthesia (Levy 2011) but also others including TAP blocks.

Postoperative management

Anaesthetists and intensivists are key in the management of patients in the postoperative period. Early recognition of complications and access to outreach and ICU allow timely resuscitation, diagnosis, and treatment. The widespread adoption of early warning scores has been successful in alerting both medical and nursing staff to the deteriorating patient. In addition, early imaging with appropriate intervention (and in some cases reoperation) can be life-saving. The avoidance of major complications postoperatively is a cornerstone in the management of patients undergoing major GI surgery, as it is recognized that these not only have serious sequelae at the time but crucially impact patients for many years to come. In a huge study of more than 100 000 patients, the presence of major complications within 30 days of surgery was more important than preoperative and intraoperative risk factors in determining long-term survival. Overall, major complications reduced median survival by nearly 70%, from 18.4 years to 5.6 years (Khuri et al. 2005).

Others

There are a number of other key areas that are set to further transform the landscape of GI surgery over the next 5 years. Some of these are included within ER pathways (see 'Enhanced recovery'), and include pre-habilitation (optimizing physical, nutritional, and psychological status before surgery), intraoperative lung protective ventilation strategies, adequate antagonism of neuromuscular block (implicated in postoperative respiratory complications), possibly cerebral monitoring of anaesthetic agents (particularly in the elderly), and renewed emphasis on more fundamental aspects of care, such as glycaemic control, timely antibiotic prophylaxis (with repeat dosing during prolonged surgery), and prevention of hypothermia (Baldini et al. 2015).

Some of the above-mentioned changes have been driven by technology and innovation, other changes by audit, and addressing major complications. In particular, the UK National Confidential Enquiry into Patient Outcome and Death (NCEPOD) has produced many reports over the last 25 years, including two reports on 'Who Operates When', in 1997 and 2003, studying grade of surgeon and anaesthetists and the time of surgery (and indeed whether or not surgery is appropriate). The 2003 report (NCEPOD 2003) shows considerable improvements compared with the 1997 report. The specialization of services such as hepatopancreatobiliary has also generally led to marked improvements in patient care. The advent of care bundles or pathways has resulted in a consistent approach and quality improvement in patient management. Moreover, formal training and education at all grades, both within the operating theatres and outside (e.g. simulation) has also been seen as helping to drive up standards.

Liver surgery

Procedure

It has been recognized for centuries that the liver has a remarkable ability to regenerate. Without this, major liver resections would not be possible, although it is only relatively recently that safety has improved enough for resections to be carried out routinely. Liver resections are generally carried out for metastatic tumours. More rarely, patients undergo liver surgery for benign disease, primary liver tumours, or trauma. Colorectal metastases are the commonest cancer requiring liver surgery, but many other tumours may metastasize to the liver, including breast, melanoma, and carcinoid. Patients will most often have had definitive treatment of the primary tumour (including surgery, chemotherapy, and radiotherapy) and may present soon after for liver resection. However, in some cases liver metastases may occur months or years after seemingly successful eradication of the primary tumour. The majority of data is from patients with colorectal cancer, of whom about 50% will develop liver metastases.

Patient problems

Patients presenting for surgery are commonly in their fifties or sixties but given the diverse nature of the primary tumours, they can present in their twenties. Aside from incidental medication (such as for heart disease) a major factor is that these patients may have relatively recently undergone major surgery for the primary tumour (e.g. bowel) or more commonly, finished chemotherapy and may have decreased physiological reserve (such as cardiorespiratory and immunological). A minority of patients may also have undergone other procedures such as preoperative portal vein embolization or some ablative procedure (such as radiofrequency ablation or cryotherapy). The former will allow a degree of enlargement in the proposed liver remnant, thus minimizing the risk of postoperative liver dysfunction.

Nature and risk of surgery

The majority of hepatic resections are undertaken via open surgery although an increasing number are carried out laparoscopically, with excellent results (Nguyen et al. 2009). Most commonly the patient will have a large right subcostal incision, sometimes extending to the left subcostal area and even up to the xiphisternum ('Mercedes Benz' incision). Major, specific considerations for this procedure are perioperative haemorrhage and postoperative hepatic insufficiency.

The vast majority of liver resections are to attempt a cure. There is usually little merit in performing liver resection surgery if there is proved disease elsewhere, such as peritoneal involvement, and often a diagnostic laparoscopy is undertaken first to exclude this possibility. The advent of liver resection programmes (and advances in chemotherapy and radiology) has resulted in many centres reporting 5-year survival rates approaching 50% (Karanjia et al. 2009), whereas without treatment, the 5-year survival of the majority of people with secondary liver cancers is negligible.

Historically, liver surgery involved massive blood loss and was therefore associated with significant perioperative morbidity, and mortality of more than 20%. In the last 40 years, mortality has decreased to less than 5%. Improvements in surgery and anaesthesia have reduced blood loss substantially with many centres reporting blood transfusion rates of less than 5%. From a surgical perspective, the use of the Cavitron Ultrasonic Surgical Aspirator (CUSA™, Valleylab, Boulder, CO, USA), the harmonic scalpel, and the argon laser coagulator have been major advances. A key consideration for the anaesthetist is to reduce back-bleeding from the hepatic veins. The hepatic venous pressure is similar to the CVP, and achieving a low CVP is crucial during the resection. A number of studies have confirmed the importance of CVP reduction with a concomitant reduction in blood loss. This can be achieved by a number of techniques (see later).

Preoperative assessment

Patients will require a detailed assessment of physiological reserve not only with respect to the liver, but also for the cardiorespiratory and renal systems. The majority of these patients will need this overall assessment to undergo a major laparotomy and the detection and optimization of concurrent pathology is pivotal. In addition to the usual preoperative assessment (history and examination), further tests may be indicated such as echocardiography and CPET. These are useful for assessing risk and providing the correct level of care in the postoperative period.

In addition, the role of chemotherapy has to be considered. This is a complex area because of the rapidly changing regimens available for different types of tumour. In addition, whereas some patients receive postoperative (adjuvant) chemotherapy, others receive preoperative chemotherapy for resectable lesions in an attempt to increase survival (neoadjuvant chemotherapy) and others may have received chemotherapy in an attempt to make non-resectable lesions resectable (downsizing). Chemotherapeutic agents may cause significant toxicity to the heart, lungs, kidneys, liver, bone marrow, and nervous system (Allan et al. 2011).

Postoperative hepatic insufficiency is an ominous complication and carries a high mortality. Resections of up to 80% of the liver volume have been successfully undertaken, although a liver resection of this magnitude requires the liver remnant to have superlative function. Many patients will not tolerate liver resection of this magnitude, particularly if they have pre-existing liver impairment from alcohol or chemotherapy (see previous paragraph). It can sometimes be a difficult decision as to how much liver volume to safely remove and some centres use more specific indicators of liver function to provide further information.

For 50 years, gastroenterologists have used Child's score and its modifications, (the most common of which is the Child–Pugh score) which assess five markers: ascites, encephalopathy, serum albumin, serum bilirubin, and International normalized ratio (see Table 61.2), and although originally described for chronic liver disease outcome and not fully validated for liver resection, it is nevertheless generally accepted that patients with score A are suitable for major resection surgery.

In addition, there are various clearance (or retention) tests of which indocyanine green clearance is probably the best described. Indocyanine green is a dye that binds to albumin and α1-lipoproteins and its plasma clearance by active transfer into the liver parenchymal cells (assessed by serum blood sampling or more recently by pulsed spectrophotometry, using an optical sensor placed on the finger) is calculated. It is common to express this as a percentage of retention of indocyanine green—for example, more than 15% retention at 15 min is often used as a threshold of impairment (Imamura et al. 2005). Finally, portal venous pressure has been described as providing a further prognostic indicator

Table 61.2 Child–Pugh score

	Points		
	1	2	3
Ascites	None	Mild	Moderate or severe
Encephalopathy (grade)	None	1–2 (mild)	3–4 (significant)
Bilirubin (micromol/L)	<35	35–50	>50
Albumin (g/L)	>35	28–35	<28
International normalized ratio	<1.7	1.8–2.3	>2.3

Total scores a ranked as:
Score A, well-compensated disease (5–6 points)
Score B, significant functional compromise (7–9 points)
Score C, decompensated disease (10–15 points)
Reproduced with permission from Pugh RN, Murray-Lyon IM, Dawson JL, Pietroni MC, Williams R, Transection of the oesophagus for bleeding oesophageal varices. *British Journal of Surgery*, Volume 60, Issue 8, pp. 646–9, Copyright © 1973 British Journal of Surgery Society Ltd.

for patients with liver disease, although it is more common to use hepatic venous pressure (either a 'free pressure' or a 'wedged pressure' or the difference between the two—'gradient pressure') as this correlates well with portal venous pressure. High pressure gradients (>10 mm Hg) define portal hypertension and are closely associated with complications and mortality.

Provision of anaesthesia

Patients will require the standard set-up for major surgery with full monitoring, and large-bore peripheral venous, arterial, and central venous access. The advent of GDFT allows patients to leave the operating theatre with SV optimization. The provision of analgesia varies between centres: thoracic epidural anaesthesia has been successfully and most widely used providing that coagulation is normal, and is effective for analgesia, particularly in the early postoperative period. In recent years, a variety of other techniques have gained in popularity, such as intrathecal opioids, intrapleural block, paravertebral block, rectus sheath catheters, and wound catheters, many placed under direct vision by the surgeons. The use of epidurals has been reviewed (Tzimas et al. 2013). Areas of concern with epidurals include further postoperative coagulopathy, which peaks at days 1–2 but can last several days postoperatively and requires the use of fresh frozen plasma for the epidural catheter to be removed safely. In addition, the concern was raised about excess i.v. fluid requirements postoperatively, translating into poor return of GI function, increased length of stay, and even increased blood transfusion rates (Tzimas et al. 2013). Finally, epidural-induced hypotension has been implicated in a higher incidence of acute kidney injury after major hepatic resections (Kambakamba et al. 2015).

A combination of techniques may be used to lower CVP and hence hepatic venous pressure to reduce blood loss. A combination of an epidural (if used), fluid restriction, diuretics (e.g. furosemide), remifentanil, and glyceryl trinitrate may be used. The arterial blood pressure will often need to be supported by judicious use of a vasoconstrictor such as phenylephrine or noradrenaline. Blood loss can be restricted further by reducing the blood supply to the liver by clamping the portal vein and hepatic artery (Pringle's manoeuvre) or even by isolating the liver completely (total vascular exclusion) by clamping the hepatic vein as well. Both procedures may cause a reduction in cardiac output: the former by 20%, the latter by 60%, and may lead to marked circulatory instability. Another major drawback is that reducing the hepatic blood supply may predispose to ischaemia–reperfusion injury—particularly unwelcome in such a metabolically active organ at normothermia. The safe period and clamping times and protocols are unknown, as is the efficacy of ischaemic preconditioning (a short period of ischaemia before a longer period in an attempt to protect against tissue damage) in preserving postoperative liver dysfunction. Many surgeons have successfully limited the use of Pringle's manoeuvre, perhaps accepting a slightly higher blood loss without adverse sequelae. Unsurprisingly total vascular exclusion is associated with both marked intraoperative and postoperative complications, predisposing to a mortality of up to 10%. A CVP of less than 5 mm Hg is crucial and 2–3 mm Hg ideal. Some advocate the use of tranexamic acid or aprotinin to further reduce blood loss. It is particularly important for the anaesthetist to view the operating conditions of the cut liver and to communicate readily with the surgeon. Traction on structures such as the inferior vena cava or sudden blood loss are not tolerated well, and necessitate prompt intervention, sometimes with i.v. fluids. Finally, a close watch has to be kept for an air embolus, an ever-present risk when operating with low venous pressures which will cause marked reduction in end-tidal carbon dioxide concentration and cardiac output. For prolonged and difficult cases, with unavoidable periods of clamping, many extrapolate from experience with liver transplantation surgery and administer 5% glucose to prevent hypoglycaemia and *N*-acetylcysteine to reduce liver damage, although its role after liver resection surgery is unproven.

Where possible, drugs that do not rely on hepatic clearance are preferred and many favour the use of drugs that have organ-independent elimination such as remifentanil and atracurium or cisatracurium.

Once the liver resection is complete and haemostasis has been achieved, filling of the circulation may follow and the CVP allowed to increase. This may be guided by GDFT from oesophageal Doppler or other technologies (e.g. LiDCOrapid™, LiDCO Group PLC, London, UK). By the time surgery has been completed, the patient should be optimized in terms of fluid therapy, be normothermic, and have appropriate analgesia.

The vast majority of uncomplicated liver resections are sent to a level 1 or 2 environment after tracheal extubation. Postoperatively, a careful eye is kept on both haemodynamic variables (for early signs of haemorrhage) and the metabolic status. An increasing lactate and decreasing pH with haemodynamic stability suggest a degree of hepatic insufficiency and in the early stages optimizing the cardiac output is crucial.

In the later postoperative period, there is commonly a slight increase in coagulation times, sometimes associated with reduced platelet count, and a small degree of renal impairment. These are usually self-limiting. However, should lactic acidosis persist and in particular if it is associated with renal impairment then the patient may need to be moved to intensive care for closer haemodynamic manipulation and perhaps even renal and hepatic support. Major problems such as liver failure, renal failure, and biliary leak and coagulopathy will require continued monitoring and management in intensive care.

Analgesia is a key area here and the combination of local anaesthetic block (often an epidural) with judicious use of opioids is effective. Some units avoid paracetamol altogether or give a reduced dose (e.g. 2 g day^{-1}). Most avoid the use of NSAIDs in all but the smallest liver resections as significant renal impairment with liver impairment has a high mortality.

Patients undergoing liver resection surgery have usually had little bowel handling, and oral fluids and diet are usually rapidly resumed. Once any coagulopathy has resolved, low-molecular-weight heparin is commenced. Often by the third day most of the indwelling vascular lines may be removed as can epidural and urinary catheters.

Perhaps the greatest challenge for patients undergoing liver resection is the reconciliation of two divergent principles. On the one hand, the need to optimize $\dot{D}O_2$ with fluids, which has previously been described. On the other hand, the need for marked hepatic oligaemia during the resection, which has two advantages: it reduces the need for Pringle's manoeuvre and concomitant hepatic ischaemic damage and will also reduce blood loss and blood transfusion rates. Blood transfusion is seen as undesirable in these patients because of the risks of transmission of infectious agents, bilirubin load, and transfusion-related immunomodulation, which has been postulated to be linked to postoperative infections and even tumour recurrence.

A successful approach has been to submit the patient to a period of relative hypovolaemia peroperatively, the systemic arterial pressure supported by an infusion of a vasoconstrictor. Although this results in a reduction in cardiac output, and sometimes an increase in lactic acid and acidosis and a decrease in Scv_{O2}, this is tolerated well by the majority of patients for the duration of surgery and is rapidly corrected post liver resection. This aggressive approach to low CVP anaesthesia results in low median blood loss (250 ml), low transfusion rate (6%), with crucially a marked reduction in the use of vascular clamping (Lordan et al. 2009). The advent of ER programmes (see 'Enhanced Recovery') has led to further improvements. Protocolized pathways for liver resection surgery involving oral carbohydrate loading, perioperative GDFT, and early removal of epidural catheters have led to excellent results, reduced medical complications, and reduced length of stay (Jones et al. 2013).

Pancreatic surgery

Procedure

Pancreatic surgery presents several problems within the perioperative period. The pancreas is a relatively inaccessible structure and disturbances in both its endocrine and especially its exocrine function can cause significant morbidity and mortality. Generally pancreatic surgery is carried out on patients who have tumours within the pancreas (head, body, or tail) and for patients who have, or have had, pancreatitis.

Pancreatic tumours often present relatively late, usually with progressive jaundice (especially from the head of the pancreas), pain, or more rarely with neuroendocrine tumours (see Table 61.3). Unfortunately, for many patients the disease may have advanced too far for curative surgery, but patients may still undergo biliary bypass procedures to relieve obstructive jaundice.

Pancreatitis is a serious condition and is commonly secondary to gallstones or alcohol abuse, but other conditions may predispose to it such as trauma [including iatrogenic, e.g. post-endoscopic retrograde cholangiopancreatography (ERCP)], various viral infections, and hypothermia.

Table 61.3 Types of pancreatic neuroendocrine tumours

Tumour type	Clinical features	Pathology
Gastrinoma	Peptic ulceration, diarrhoea	Head of pancreas. Malignant
Insulinoma	Hypoglycaemia	Head, body, or tail of pancreas. Usually benign
Glucagonoma	Hyperglycaemia	Tail of pancreas. Malignant

VIPomas (vasoactive intestinal polypeptide) and somatostatinomas are rarer.

Pancreatic surgery will often involve pancreatic resection for tumours, for example, head of pancreas tumours which if operable will entail a pancreaticoduodenectomy, followed by a pancreaticojejunostomy, a hepaticojejunostomy, and a gastrojejunostomy (Whipple's procedure). A more major operation is undertaken for distal common bile duct carcinoma (cholangiocarcinoma), involving its excision, sometimes with a partial hepatectomy. For tail of pancreas disease (tumours and chronic inflammation), distal pancreatectomy often with splenectomy is undertaken. The other major group is patients with often severe pancreatitis, who may undergo repeated drainage procedures or necrosectomies, or at a later date excision of pancreatic pseudocyst or abscess.

Patient problems

Patients can present at any age for pancreatic surgery, particularly pancreatitis as both gallstones and alcohol abuse are not uncommon. Pancreatic tumours are often found in patients in their fifties or older, sometimes with painless and progressive jaundice which may be marked. Jaundice usually prompts patients to rapidly seek medical advice, but if the obstruction remains unrelieved, the patient may progress to coagulopathy, biliary tract sepsis, and liver dysfunction.

Although many of the patients with pancreatic tumours may present having been previously healthy, those with alcoholic pancreatitis may be well known to the hospital with multiple previous admissions related to chronic alcohol abuse. Of relevance to the anaesthetist are cardiovascular impairment (cardiomyopathy, hypertension, and arrhythmias), metabolic derangements (hypoglycaemia, hypokalaemia, and hypomagnesaemia), neurological impairment (peripheral and autonomic neuropathy), and haematological problems (prolonged clotting times and thrombocytopenia).

In addition, patients with pancreatitis may present acutely unwell with pancreatitis and its associated systemic inflammatory response. This can be relatively mild or progress, sometimes rapidly, to multiorgan failure and severe sepsis requiring cardiovascular, respiratory, and renal support and a prolonged stay in the ICU. Patients with longstanding pancreatitis may be markedly malnourished and cachectic with vitamin deficiency. Finally, endocrine pancreatic failure can result in diabetic patients, with secretory neuroendocrine tumours also causing glycaemic and other metabolic disturbances.

Patients with longstanding pancreatic disease may be receiving enzyme replacement drugs (amylase/lipase/protease) to combat the effects of pancreatic exocrine insufficiency. They may be receiving vitamin K (which rapidly corrects the coagulopathy as a result of obstructive jaundice). In addition, pain control may be a problem and some patients with acute pancreatitis may require patient-controlled analgesia. Patients with chronic pancreatitis may be on an array of analgesics, both opioids and sometimes other drugs (e.g. gabapentin). Patients may sometimes be receiving huge doses of opioids either orally or via other routes (e.g. transdermal). This may pose problems in the postoperative period. They may also be receiving antibiotics and drugs to combat associated organ impairment (e.g. heart failure).

Nature and risk of surgery

Commonly, major pancreatic resections for tumours or chronic pancreatitis are performed with a large upper abdominal incision, although there are some centres that perform laparoscopic pancreatic resections (particularly of the pancreatic tail). In well-prepared patients (e.g. with little co-morbidity and early relief of jaundice) and in high-volume centres, pancreatic resections carry a relatively low morbidity (18%) and mortality (1.6%) (Buchler et al. 2003). This situation changes significantly if the patient has pancreatitis and other organ insufficiency.

Patients may also undergo procedures other than pancreatic resection: they may require anaesthesia for detailed preoperative imaging such as endoscopic ultrasound, or drainage of the biliary tree and pancreas such as ERCP. These can be done under sedation or general anaesthesia. More recently, drainage and pancreatic necrosectomy (carried out laparoscopically) have been described. In addition, some tumours, in spite of extensive imaging, are inoperable or have spread distally (e.g. to the peritoneum) and the patients may undergo palliative biliary bypass surgery.

General complications of pancreatic surgery relate to those of a major laparotomy and include haemorrhage, wound infection, pulmonary thromboembolism, chest infections, and in susceptible individuals, myocardial infarction and worsening of renal function. Specific complications include worsening of pancreatitis, leakage of pancreatic contents (perhaps resulting in a fistula or anastomotic breakdown), prolonged starvation, and impaired glucose tolerance.

Preoperative assessment, investigations, and interventions

The majority of these patients are undergoing major surgery and therefore optimization of all physiological systems is mandatory. Of particular relevance to patients undergoing pancreatic surgery is nutrition and expert input preoperatively from a dietician is very useful. For patients with severe jaundice, biliary drainage is indicated. Routine investigations such as serum biochemistry, liver function tests, clotting, ECG, and chest X-ray may be supplemented by more detailed investigations if indicated such as echocardiography. In addition, there is growing evidence, as in liver surgery, for the use of CPET, which may be used to predict risk and plan the best location for patients postoperatively. Before major pancreatic resection, patents should, where possible, have jaundice relieved (e.g. stenting at ERCP) and coagulopathy treated.

Provision of anaesthesia

Patients undergoing pancreatic resections will generally have prolonged surgery and will require tracheal intubation and neuromuscular block. If there is gastric obstruction secondary to marked duodenal involvement then rapid sequence induction with cricoid pressure is mandatory. Good peripheral venous access is necessary and very commonly arterial and central venous access are used together with cardiac output monitoring and GDFT. There are likely to be major fluid shifts during the first 2–3 days and careful fluid balance (avoiding both fluid depletion and excess are essential). Perioperative monitoring of base excess, lactate, and Scv_{O_2} may also guide fluid therapy. Serum glucose concentrations need to be tightly controlled: this may require the use of insulin. There is no particular drug regimen for intraoperative management although many would choose atracurium or cisatracurium and remifentanil as they have organ-independent elimination. Some choose to provide intraoperative analgesia solely with the use of a thoracic epidural (mentioned previously). As the surgery may be prolonged, a low-flow maintenance of anaesthesia with desflurane will provide rapid and reliable awakening at the end of the case. Meticulous positioning to prevent nerve palsies and calf compression are also crucial, as is the avoidance of hypothermia.

Postoperative analgesia is key and, provided coagulation and platelets are normal, an epidural provides excellent analgesia. Other techniques previously described may also be used (rectus sheath or wound catheters). Large amounts of opioids via patient-controlled analgesia are to be avoided as they will prolong the return of gut function.

Providing early adequate nutrition has been a major advance in pancreatic surgery. The provision of nutrition intravenously (total parenteral nutrition) is generally less effective than foregut nutrition. This is more commonly achieved by gradual introduction of a diet, although some still favour the passage of a fine-bore nasojejunal tube (with wire) at induction with final placement under direct vision at operation. The wire is then removed.

Sometimes major blood loss is inevitable (particularly with patients with previous surgery or pancreatitis) and sometimes vascular reconstruction is required if the portal vein is encased in tumour and a sleeve of the vein has to be excised with the specimen.

Other specific treatment may be used. Octreotide, a somatostatin analogue, to reduce pancreatic secretion was formerly used once the resection is complete, but current evidence does not support its routine use. If used, it is important not to give this too early as it shrinks the gland markedly and can make any anastomosis on the pancreatic duct difficult or even impossible. The presence of jaundice, although usually relieved preoperatively, requires great attention to fluid balance to ensure that renal failure does not occur. Good hydration is more important than the use of other agents such as dopamine or mannitol (Clarke et al. 2006).

In spite of prolonged surgery—sometimes 6 h or much more—there is no reason why the patient's trachea cannot be extubated at the end of surgery, provided fluid management and analgesia are exemplary and hypothermia is avoided.

Postoperatively the patient is transferred commonly to a level 2 unit and should receive oxygen, fluid management guided as outlined earlier (CVP, GDFT, Scv_{O_2}, and lactate), analgesia, antibiotics, and thromboprophylaxis. Jejunal feeding is often instituted on the first day postoperatively. Any surgical drains inserted are to be handled with extreme care.

The situation is very different in patients with severe acute pancreatitis: these patients are usually level 3 patients requiring multiorgan support. They may require days or weeks of ventilation, inotropic support, renal support, and antibiotics.

Major pancreatic surgery rewards the meticulous anaesthetist. The author favours an ER pathway (see 'Enhanced Recovery') (Lassen et al. 2013), so that oral preload is used preoperatively where possible. Key components are early enteral feeding and a thoracic epidural (with or without remifentanil infusion intraoperatively), although other analgesic methods deserve consideration such as i.v. lidocaine, TAP blocks, and wound catheters. GDFT is ideal, with near zero fluid balance. Ideally GDFT should be used for several hours postoperatively to guide fluids (giving fluid boluses with colloid). Thereafter fluids can be guided by Scv_{O_2} and lactate levels. Early removal of surgical drains is now advocated.

Colorectal surgery

Procedure

Colorectal surgery has undergone huge changes in the last 10 years, which are perhaps best summarized by the ER programme (see 'Enhanced Recovery'). Large midline incisions, nasogastric tubes, routine epidural analgesia, bowel preparation, and nil by mouth for some days perioperatively (to name but a few) have been superseded by laparoscopic surgery and early resumption of oral diet and reduced length of hospital stay. Thirty per cent of patients present for their colorectal surgery as emergencies (Scott et al. 1995) (see 'Emergency laparotomy'), but this section will focus on elective surgery. The majority of patients presenting for major colorectal resections have malignant tumours, diverticular disease, or inflammatory bowel disease.

Laparoscopic colorectal resections have become increasingly popular although conversion rates to open surgery still remain at about 20–30% in some centres. Very low anterior resections are now performed, but there is a small group of patients in whom rectal tumours are too low and an abdominoperineal resection is required. Where possible, there is a primary anastomosis, but in those in whom this is felt to be too high a risk, a defunctioning colostomy is performed which is closed at a later date. In patients with inflammatory bowel disease, if medical treatment fails, small resections may be carried out for strictures (Crohn's disease) and with severe inflammation of the large bowel a panproctocolectomy may be undertaken, with either an ileostomy or with an ileo pouch–anal anastomosis. Finally, in the semi-emergency situation for colorectal cancers, there is an increase in the use of stenting for strictures.

Patient problems

Patients with colorectal cancer can present at any age but many present in their fifties or older. The advent of bowel cancer screening programmes offered in some areas to those aged more than 50 years and in other areas over the age of 60 years has reduced the mortality by more than 15%. Diverticular disease can also present in a similar age group. Inflammatory bowel disease can present in adolescence and young adults.

Patients with cancers may present symptom free from screening or from repeat colonoscopy, or with anaemia, but they are usually well. Patients with diverticular disease may have had a recent hospital admission and have received antibiotics. However, patients with severe inflammatory bowel disease presenting for surgery are often malnourished and may be taking a number of drugs—see Box 61.1. In addition, some patients may have received chemotherapy or radiotherapy before surgery.

Box 61.1 Drugs used to treat inflammatory bowel disease

- 5-aminosalicylates (5-ASA) such as sulfasalazine, mesalazine
- Steroids
- Azathioprine/6-mercaptopurine
- Methotrexate
- Ciclosporin
- Infliximab.

Nature and risk of surgery

The majority of colorectal surgery involves resection and anastomosis of large bowel. Aside from the expected complications of major surgery (wound infections and cardiorespiratory complications), the major specific risk is that of anastomotic leak. Such an event is a medical and surgical catastrophe, and requires prompt recognition and treatment. Various conditions will predispose to this, including poor blood supply and oxygen delivery to the bowel ends, poor healing from any cause (including chemoradiotherapy, steroids), sepsis, and very low rectal resections (<7 cm from the anal verge). An assessment has to be made as to whether or not it is safe to leave the anastomosis, or if a proximal, covering defunctioning ostomy is also required. Occasionally a smaller anastomotic leak may present as an abscess (e.g. pelvic).

The anaesthetist also has a perioperative role to play in anastomotic integrity. The principles of optimization of global oxygen delivery (see 'Intravenous fluid therapy') (Tote and Grounds 2006), is fundamental, with the maintenance of cardiac output, [Hb], and Sa_{O_2}. However, excess fluids will predispose the patient to anastomotic oedema and may ultimately threaten the integrity of the anastomosis. Finally, in addition to measuring and optimizing blood flow, maintenance of blood pressure is also important. This applies particularly in the postoperative period where hypotension from epidural anaesthesia adversely affects colonic blood flow which is corrected only by the use of vasopressors rather than i.v. fluids (Gould et al. 2002). Prolonged hypotension or an excess of i.v. fluids may therefore compromise gut blood flow and predispose to anastomotic leak.

Preoperatively, the patient needs to be assessed with a view to optimization of pre-existing conditions and assessment of their fitness to undergo colorectal surgery. There is an increasing trend for the use of laparoscopic surgery, but open surgery is still commonplace, particularly if there has been previous surgery. The physiological demands placed on patients undergoing open and laparoscopic surgery are hugely different. Open surgery will cause a marked physiological stress response (see Table 61.4), which will have a significant effect for some days postoperatively. There is the potential for large fluid shifts, but in addition, the systemic inflammatory response syndrome will cause an increase in $\dot{D}o_2$ and $\dot{V}o_2$. If these demands are unmet, there is a risk of anaerobic metabolism, organ impairment, and ultimately death. Therefore an assessment of the patient's ability to withstand these extra demands is fundamental and many now advocate the use of CPET for this purpose. In addition, open surgery is much more painful, involves more bowel handling, and is associated with a significant ileus. The patient needs to be assessed for the method of pain relief and

Table 61.4 'Stress response' to major surgery

	Examples
Endocrine	Pituitary and adrenal activation
Metabolic	Catabolism and nitrogen loss Hyperglycaemia Lipolysis Sodium and water retention Potassium loss
Inflammatory	Systemic inflammatory response syndrome response Cytokine production, e.g.: ◆ Interleukins (especially interleukin 6) ◆ Tumour necrosis factor ◆ Interferons ◆ Vascular endothelial growth factor

whether or not nutritional needs can be met by awaiting the return of bowel function or if parenteral nutrition is required.

In addition, aspects of the stress response can be magnified by adverse events: starvation, infection, hypovolaemia, and hypothermia

Assessment for laparoscopic surgery requires a different approach. The tissue damage and stress response is reduced, and is associated with less pain and earlier return of gut function, but there are marked cardiorespiratory physiological changes from laparoscopy (see Table 61.1). A careful decision has to made as to whether or not the patient can withstand these changes, and if so, for how long. For some patients with poor reserve, both the laparoscopy and subsequent positioning may cause significant problems and occasionally necessitate an open operation to be undertaken instead.

Patients with long-standing GI disorders, particularly those with inflammatory bowel disease, will need nutritional assessment and supplementation before surgery.

Provision of anaesthesia

All laparoscopic and the majority of open colorectal resections are performed under general anaesthetic. Under rare circumstances such as end-stage lung disease, or possibly with extreme airway difficulties, an open procedure may be performed under an epidural. Induction of anaesthesia has two major considerations. Firstly, is there a need for rapid sequence induction of anaesthesia with cricoid pressure? Occasionally colorectal patients present with an ileus, or with involvement of the upper GI tract, or after large doses of morphine. In these patients, consideration should be given to cricoid pressure, as there may be significant residual gastric volume. Secondly, careful pre-oxygenation and the use of a neuromuscular blocking agent that facilitates early paralysis (rocuronium is ideal) so as to avoid bag and mask ventilation—however expertly done, this always causes a degree of gastric distension. The patient then has their trachea intubated.

The surgeon requires a paralysed patient with minimum distension of the bowel, thus nitrous oxide is best avoided. In addition, anaesthetic access for all colorectal procedures is often limited by drapes, patient positioning, and perhaps a Mayo table. Therefore meticulous attention to securing the airway, cannulae (and ensuring they run freely), and monitoring (ECG and pulse oximetry) is required as access to the patient when surgery is underway is limited. There is no preferred technique for maintenance of anaesthesia but remifentanil and a volatile technique are popular, together with monitoring of neuromuscular block so that it does not wear off unexpectedly.

The execution of fluid balance and analgesia are seen as fundamental in colorectal anaesthesia. The use of arterial lines and central lines is standard both for intraoperative monitoring of pressures, but also perioperative monitoring of pH, base excess, lactate, and oxygen saturation (arterial and central venous). The low morbidity associated with central venous access, (particularly with the use of ultrasound) should encourage a low threshold for its use, especially in open colorectal surgery, where there may be a use for it up to several days postoperatively for pressure monitoring and in some cases, total parenteral nutrition. CVP lines are also very useful for rapid drug administration preoperatively. For laparoscopic colorectal surgery, the advent of GDFT, however, has lessened the need for CVP lines, but an arterial line is advisable for the monitoring of cardiovascular changes and arterial blood gas analysis. The usual perioperative goals of $\dot{D}O_2$ (>600 ml min^{-1} m^{-2}) cannot be readily obtained because of the cardiovascular effects of laparoscopy, and recently a target $\dot{D}O_2$ of greater than 400 ml min^{-1} m^{-2} during laparoscopic colorectal resection was shown to be a threshold predicting those who developed anastomotic leak and those who did not (Levy et al. 2012).

Perioperative analgesia can be a difficult decision. While the use of regular multimodal analgesia and minimal use of opioids is not controversial, supplementary analgesia is a matter of debate. It is made more difficult by the fact that 10% or more of planned laparoscopic procedures are converted to open. Thoracic epidurals have documented advantages and some disadvantages in open surgery (see 'Analgesia' and Table 61.5) but are still advocated in skilled hands for open surgery and where their good postoperative management can be assured. However, experience has also been directed elsewhere with rectus sheath blocks, TAP blocks, or local anaesthetic wound catheters, all of which have an opioid-sparing effect, but may nevertheless be used with, say, patient-controlled morphine (Table 61.6A). For laparoscopic resections, epidurals are

Table 61.5 Advantages and disadvantages of (thoracic) epidural anaesthesia in open colorectal surgery

Advantages	**Disadvantages**
Excellent pain control	Inadequate block with poor pain control
Quicker return of GI function	Hypotension and consequent fluid overload
Reduction in pulmonary thromboembolism	Poor mobilization
Reduction in pneumonia	Extra resources (e.g. nursing input)
Reduction in respiratory depression	Dural puncture headache
Reduction in blood loss and transfusion rates	Transient neurological injury
Debated effects on myocardial infarction, renal failure, and mortality	Permanent neurological injury

Table 61.6 Analgesia for colorectal surgery

Major analgesia (up to day 3)	Regular multimodal analgesia (days 0–5)	Rescue analgesia
(A) Open colorectal		
Thoracic epidural	Paracetamol oral or i.v.	Tramadol
TAP block	NSAIDs	Morphine
Rectus sheath catheter	Tramadol (if NSAIDs contraindicated)	
Wound catheter		
(B) Laparoscopic colorectal		
Wound infiltration with local anaesthetic	Paracetamol oral or i.v.	Tramadol
TAP block	NSAIDs	Morphine
Spinal	Tramadol (if NSAIDs contraindicated)	

now rarely used. Considerable success has been achieved with spinal anaesthesia with opioids but again TAP blocks have been used. The use of local anaesthetic into the wound edges, either by the surgeon, or with the use of a catheter postoperatively has also been successful (Table 61.6B). The use of other methods such as lidocaine, magnesium, ketamine, and pregabalin has been described some with considerable success (especially lidocaine) but are rarely used in the United Kingdom at present (Fawcett and Baldini 2015).

At the end of surgery, residual neuromuscular block is antagonized. In the past, there were suggestions that neostigmine, with its parasympathetic effect, may predispose to anastomotic dehiscence and postoperative nausea and vomiting. These have largely been discounted, but the advent of sugammadex, to antagonize rocuronium, provides a therapeutic alternative nevertheless. Good neuromuscular block is required for abdominal wall closure.

In the immediate postoperative period, attention is principally directed at analgesia and fluid balance. While there may be good theoretical indications for GDFT to continue into the postoperative period, from a practical standpoint this is usually not feasible and fluid management is guided by other means. The use of CVP monitoring may be used, but provided the patient is fluid optimized when leaving the operating theatre, postoperative fluids can be given relatively sparingly, with patients encouraged to drink at an early stage. An increasing lactate concentration and a decreasing Scv_{O_2} level are indicators that a fluid challenge (e.g. 250 ml of colloid) can be tried. In addition, oxygen therapy, antibiotics, VTE prophylaxis, and glycaemic control (if indicated) are fundamental.

Many of these patients are elderly and close observation is required to detect both medical and surgical complications. The advent of fever, ileus, pain, cardiac dysrhythmias, and rising inflammatory markers such as C-reactive protein and leucocytosis should lead to a careful search for the underlying cause. The use of early warning scores has aided this process, but remember that many conditions (e.g. myocardial ischaemia) may present silently or atypically. Any deteriorating patient will need careful cardiovascular and respiratory examination and assessment, including ECG, chest X-ray, arterial blood gas analysis, full biochemistry including cardiac troponins, and imaging of the bowel and perhaps of computed tomographic pulmonary angiography scan.

Miscellaneous procedures

Laparoscopic cholecystectomy

Laparoscopic cholecystectomy is the most common laparoscopic procedure worldwide, with more than 20 000 undertaken in England per year. It was the earliest major 'keyhole operation' performed nearly 30 years ago and has become the standard procedure for cholecystectomy. It is increasingly undertaken as a day-case procedure. Conversion rates are about 5% for elective procedures and nearly 10% for emergency procedures. Recently, single-incision laparoscopic surgery and natural orifice transluminal endoscopic surgery have been described, to reduce the number of abdominal port sites.

Although gallstones are associated with increasing age, patients may present very young, occasionally as young as their teens. Women are affected more commonly than men (particularly in younger age groups). Gallstones are associated with obesity and may occur in pregnancy. Patients may present in a number of ways, with pain (both moderate upper GI pain and biliary colic), jaundice, and much more seriously with acute pancreatitis and cholangitis. With the latter two conditions, patients may have some considerable physiological upset (necessitating treatment on ICU) and careful timing of surgery is important. Some advocate early intervention with success (i.e. within 48–72 h) before the onset of peritoneal adhesions. Others prefer to wait and perform the procedure some weeks later. The major complications of the procedure are bleeding and bile duct injury. The use of preoperative cholangiography may help to identify anatomy more clearly. Patients may have undergone procedures before laparoscopic cholecystectomy, to optimize biliary tree function, such as ERCP and sphincterotomy, to allow the passage of a gallstone into the duodenum.

Anaesthesia is generally straightforward and although it has been carried out using a laryngeal mask, this is not advised. There is a significant risk of bile aspiration and the stomach may be inflated inadvertently. Thus a tracheal tube and neuromuscular block are most commonly used, without the use of bag and mask ventilation. Nasogastric tubes were commonly used but are not required if distension of the stomach is avoided at induction. Antibiotic prophylaxis is administered (e.g. cefuroxime 1.5 g). Postoperatively diet is resumed early. Multimodal analgesia is used and a small amount of morphine may also be required too. The use of both TAP blocks (El-Dawlatly et al. 2009), and oral pregabalin preoperatively (150 mg) and intraperitoneal bupivacaine have all been shown to have an opioid-sparing effect. Analgesia is important as for a third of patients, poor analgesia is the most common reason for staying in hospital overnight.

Laparoscopic appendicectomy

Appendicitis is a very common surgical emergency. The first open appendicectomy was described more than 250 years ago and the first laparoscopic appendicectomy performed in 1980. This has revolutionized treatment as other causes of pain (e.g. endometriosis and ovarian cyst rupture) may also be visualized.

The highest incidence is in patients from 10 to 20 years of age with males more commonly affected than females. While most cases are as a result of obstruction of the lumen of the appendix with a faecolith or lymphoid tissue, appendicitis, particularly in older adults, may be a presenting complaint of caecal malignancy or carcinoid tumours. Although the classical signs of acute appendicitis are central abdominal pain localizing to the right iliac fossa, fever, and sickness are well known, the condition can present in a myriad of ways. Early diagnosis is essential, however, if perforation and peritonitis are to be avoided.

Laparoscopic appendicectomy should not be considered a minor procedure. Risks include major retroperitoneal vascular injury (causing haemorrhage or gas embolism) and bowel injury, which although uncommon, can be fatal. In those not expert at laparoscopic surgery, especially with children, an open procedure is advocated. In addition, in pregnancy and in those with obvious peritonitis, an open procedure or even a full laparotomy is indicated. Patients should receive timely surgery once the diagnosis is made to minimize the risk of perforation. In the early stages, i.v. fluids are all that is necessary, but once general peritonitis has occurred they should be treated as for emergency laparotomy (see 'Emergency laparotomy').

Patients should receive rapid sequence induction of anaesthesia with cricoid pressure and tracheal intubation, as the stomach may not be empty. Regular multimodal analgesia supplemented with opioids is required postoperatively. Perioperative antibiotics are required and i.v. fluids continued until the patient can drink. Complications include infection (wound or intra-abdominal collection), intestinal obstruction, and rarely fistula formation.

Splenectomy

This may be carried out with other operations (e.g. distal pancreatectomy) or as a result of trauma (including iatrogenic). It is also performed, both open and laparoscopically, for various haematological conditions, including idiopathic thrombocytopenic purpura, spherocytosis, and a number of malignancies such as myeloproliferative disorders and lymphoma. More rarely, the spleen is removed for infection. The spleen may be removed to arrest the disease process, or to relieve symptoms from splenomegaly.

Patients will need careful preoperative workup with respect to their haemoglobin and platelet counts. They may also be receiving chemotherapy. They may need haematological cover, particularly with platelets, for the procedure. Regional anaesthesia is often contraindicated because of quantitative or qualitative platelet abnormalities, or both. Major perioperative concerns are haemorrhage and infection. Patients should receive preoperative pneumococcal vaccination and perioperative antibiotic prophylaxis.

Transanal surgery

A number of procedures can be performed transanally. Haemorrhoids may be treated by excision or stapling but in recent years stapled transanal resection of the rectum for prolapse has gained popularity. In addition, transanal endoscopic microsurgery has been described for the management of early low rectal tumours. These patients may be in a variety of positions depending on tumour location (lithotomy, prone, or lateral). Muscular relaxation is required and a caudal epidural is ideal for postoperative analgesia. Routine prescription of laxatives is recommended with the avoidance of opioids where possible (including codeine).

Emergency laparotomy

While elective surgery permits a degree of investigation, optimization, and planning for patients undergoing major GI surgery, emergency laparotomy is seen as one of the most challenging areas for GI anaesthetists. It is a common operation and patients are often elderly with significant co-morbidities in addition to having an intra-abdominal emergency, which in advanced stages (e.g. dehydration and/or sepsis) can lead to multi-organ dysfunction. As in the approach to elective GI surgery, there has been a marked change in approach over the last 15 years. At that time, many of these patients were treated out of hours by inexperienced surgeons and anaesthetists, often with poor preoperative preparation and postoperative care, partly because of a lack of intensive care beds.

A number of reports in the United Kingdom (latterly from the Emergency Laparotomy Network) (Saunders et al. 2012), Europe, and the United States have highlighted two common themes. Firstly, overall the 30-day mortality rate was high (15%). Secondly, there was a marked variation in both mortality (3.6–42%) and in a number of other factors including both the grade of surgeon and anaesthetist involved and the time of day the surgery took place. Operations after midnight had a lower presence of consultants and a higher mortality. In addition, the use of GDFT was used in less than 15% of patients, again with marked variation (0–42%). Finally, there was huge variation in whether patients were sent to a surgical ward or ICU postoperatively. Although only about a quarter of hospitals' data were included in the Saunders et al. publication, the establishment of the National Emergency Laparotomy Audit in 2012 has provided more information from all hospitals. The first report published in 2015 provided data on more than 20 000 patients and has confirmed a number of themes, including the need for timeliness of care (both for assessment and administration of first dose i.v. antibiotic), assessment and appreciation of risk, input by consultant surgeon, anaesthetist, and radiologist, and access to theatres and postoperative intensive care. The mean overall death rate was 11%, but was 5% in those aged less than 50, rising to 18% in those more than 70 years of age.

There has also been a number of studies in this area, most recently the ongoing EPOCH study, which is a stepped-wedge cluster randomized trial (6 groups of 15 hospitals) over 85 weeks, looking at 90-day mortality.

The focus on these patients has led to changes in their management. Early patient assessment by a senior surgeon and recognition that the patient requires an emergency laparotomy is required. Coordination and communication between all those involved is crucial to allow prompt administration of antibiotics, timely diagnostic investigations, an operating theatre slot, and provision for the postoperative period (e.g. intensive care). In addition, the direct involvement of both a consultant surgeon and anaesthetist in the operating theatres is essential. Before surgery, the risk of death should be assessed with those patients in whom surgery is inappropriate or futile (because of their very poor condition) or in whom perhaps a lesser operation might be attempted before a definitive procedure when the patient is able to withstand a more major operation. Many hospitals also use a defined pathway for the perioperative care of these patients.

Procedure

Many patients presenting for emergency laparotomy have a segment of jeopardized bowel that may be at risk because of tumour, inflammation (e.g. diverticular disease), or from external pressure (e.g. adhesions). If left unresolved, bacterial translocation from a distended bowel or bowel perforation, or both, may lead to peritoneal soiling and sepsis. The clinical scenario may be further complicated by fluid loss from vomiting or diarrhoea and in prolonged cases, significant nutritional upset. These patients need a laparotomy (laparoscopy is usually not possible because of the dilated bowel) and depending on the findings may need a bowel resection. If there is a risk of anastomotic breakdown (e.g. as a result of sepsis or the poor condition of the patient), the surgeon may wish to defunction the bowel by means of a stoma.

Patient problems

These patients are often elderly. Many of the expected signs of an acute abdomen may be less pronounced in this age group, delaying the diagnosis further. For example, they may be apyrexial even with marked sepsis. In view of the age of the patients, significant co-morbidities are common, such as ischaemic heart disease, vascular disease, diabetes, and hypertension, and their physiological reserve may be minimal, putting them at grave risk with major surgery. Patients' medication may cause problems. On the one hand, the patient's usual medication may either have been omitted or not absorbed, leading to, say, poorly controlled blood pressure or atrial fibrillation. On the other hand, they may still be taking medication which has a marked effect on the proposed surgery such as antiplatelet drugs (especially clopidogrel) or warfarin or new oral anticoagulants (NOACs) such as rivaroxaban. There may be little time to reverse these effects and the patient may need blood products to ensure normal coagulation and platelet function.

Nature and risk of surgery

Emergency surgery has long been recognized as an independent risk factor adversely affecting outcome. Although the crude UK death rate was approximately 15%, it increases to 25% in those more than 80 years of age (Saunders et al. 2012). With 50 000 operations per year, this equates to 7500 deaths annually. No area of abdominal surgery requires such meticulous attention to detail. The surgeon requires good access with minimal distension of the bowel. The latter often precludes the use of nitrous oxide. In addition, visceral blood supply can be precarious and a good blood supply to the bowel is required particularly if anastomotic integrity is to be assured. This is best achieved with optimal fluid therapy (GDFT), perhaps supplemented by judicious use of vasoactive drugs. Poor cardiac output (and hence oxygen delivery) or excess fluids, especially crystalloids (which will predispose to anastomotic oedema), are to be avoided.

Preoperatively, early determination of major physiological upset including cardiovascular, respiratory, renal, and haematological systems is fundamental. This requires careful history-taking, examination, and investigations. Of particular note is biochemical analysis, including assessment of metabolic acidosis, serum lactate from arterial blood gas analysis, and C-reactive protein concentrations. In addition, many of these patients are prone to, or may have already developed, sepsis, even in the absence of a bowel perforation. The importance of early administration of appropriate antibiotics cannot be overemphasized. While simple in theory, their administration is often delayed as the patient moves from the emergency department to a ward. Appropriate imaging is very often required (e.g. computed tomography scan) and this must be expedited too, taking priority over elective radiology. Early resuscitation by i.v. fluids should be commenced and guided not just by capillary return, urine output, blood pressure, or heart rate, but by CVP (and even GDFT) and the impact on any deranged physiology assessed. There should be a dedicated emergency theatre with 'next slot' prioritization and senior surgical and anaesthetic involvement is mandatory. A urinary catheter and a nasogastric tube are invariably required.

Provision of anaesthesia

Anaesthetizing patients for an emergency laparotomy may be particularly hazardous, especially in elderly patients with unrecognized hypovolaemia, sepsis, or significant co-morbidities. These patients require their stomach contents to be aspirated through a nasogastric tube, followed by preoxygenation, and rapid sequence induction of anaesthesia with cricoid pressure. Classically, thiopental and suxamethonium were used (with a small dose of fentanyl or alfentanil), but many use propofol and rocuronium (providing sugammadex is readily available should a failed tracheal intubation occur). Catastrophic decreases in blood pressure may occur after induction of anaesthesia in sick and frail patients as vascular tone is reduced and vasoactive drugs (e.g. ephedrine, phenylephrine, or both) must be at hand. It may be wise to insert an arterial line before induction of anaesthesia to enable a swifter reaction to these changes. It must also be remembered that the arm–brain circulation may be very slow and rapid administration of an induction agent until loss of consciousness occurs will invariably lead to excessive drug administration and hypotension. Thereafter neuromuscular block is provided as required. Some prefer to use atracurium (or cisatracurium) if there is significant hepatorenal compromise because of the organ-independent biotransformation of these agents. Monitoring of neuromuscular block is essential. The patient is ventilated usually with air and oxygen and a short-acting volatile agent such as sevoflurane or desflurane.

Peroperatively, patients in all but the smallest cases should receive arterial and central venous access and have cardiac output monitoring and GDFT. Once fluid optimized, if cardiac output is low, inotropes such as adrenaline may be commenced; if mean arterial pressure is low in the face of normal or high cardiac output (such as in sepsis), then vasoconstrictors such as noradrenaline can be used. Current evidence for i.v. fluids suggests that starches may give poorer outcomes compared with crystalloid therapy (Perner et al. 2012), and if colloids are required, gelatins or albumin solution may be preferable. Analgesia may be difficult and epidurals are often contraindicated because of sepsis, hypotension, or coagulopathy. In spite of the disadvantages of opioids, patient-controlled morphine is commonly used. NSAIDs are often contraindicated, especially in the elderly or those with renal or cardiovascular dysfunction.

A key decision required regards the patient's immediate postoperative care. Ideally all patients should go to a level 3 or 2 environment (ICU/HDU) where they can continue to receive GDFT, with circulatory support if required. Some patients may also require renal support. Deranged biochemistry such as high serum lactate and acidosis can be regularly monitored here to ensure it is resolving. In addition, some patients will need a period of level 3 care for postoperative ventilation on ICU. This is generally required for patients with significant cardiovascular support (e.g. inotropes) or who have marked metabolic derangement such as a base deficit of greater than 10 mmol litre^{-1} or serum lactate concentration greater than 5 mmol litre^{-1}. In addition, pre-existing disease or the requirement of a high inspired oxygen, or marked abdominal distension, or hypothermia all suggest that the patient may not cope without ventilatory support.

Once over the acute episode, these patients are nursed on the surgical ward, but they need constant input to help their recovery, including physiotherapy and nutritional support (with early enteral feeding). Complications after emergency laparotomy are common and their early detection is paramount. Early warning scores should alert staff to access input from ICU or outreach teams with the patients started on appropriate therapy. Sudden deterioration is commonly as a result of abdominal sepsis (e.g. from anastomotic breakdown or from an intra-abdominal collection of pus), myocardial infarction (often silent), chest infection, or a pulmonary embolus.

The poor and varying results of emergency laparotomy have led some hospitals to aggressively target the management of these patients. The provision of a dedicated emergency theatre; surgeons, anaesthetists, and nurses available to rapidly see these patients; good monitoring in theatres (including GDFT); and adequate numbers of ICU beds should be able to transform results. The introduction of care bundles or pathways helps to ensure that staff recognize the severity of these cases and adhere to the principles of good practice. Regular audit of these patients should help to address any shortcomings. However, in spite of these points, one must always remember that whereas timely operating is fundamental, this does not equate to submitting the poorly resuscitated patient for surgery. Moreover, there will always be some patients in whom surgery is futile, and this requires senior clinical input with the patient and their family to ensure major surgery is not carried out inappropriately.

Enhanced recovery

ER has developed in the United Kingdom over the last decade to reduce the surgical stress response, minimize perioperative physiological dysfunction, and permit faster mobilization and hospital discharge after inpatient elective surgery. For GI surgery, a major area of focus has been a reduction in the duration of postoperative ileus via a multifactorial approach that includes minimally invasive surgery, opioid sparing analgesia, avoidance of salt and water overload, and early enteral nutrition (Scott et al. 2015). Overall, this initiative has improved the quality of patient care, with fewer complications, and permitted patients to return to their normal activities more quickly. It was initially carried out in four specialties: colorectal, orthopaedics, urology, and gynaecology. The biggest evidence base is in colorectal surgery. The concept is not new: Kehlet, a Danish surgeon, pioneered the concept of fast-track or accelerated recovery over 20 years ago. He showed that very short stays were possible for patients undergoing open colorectal surgery. The advent and adoption of many improvements in surgery (laparoscopic resections, avoidance of bowel preparation) and anaesthesia (GDFT, appropriate analgesia) and other areas (preoperative carbohydrate drinks) has led to marked reductions in length of stay, including 23 h stay colorectal resections (Levy et al. 2009). Although reduction in length of hospital stay (or more accurately time until medically fit for discharge from hospital) is seen as a major advantage for patients, healthcare workers, and hospital managers alike, the success of any ER programme revolves around good quality care and low complication rates, including readmission rates.

ER is essentially an evidence-based pathway, starting from referral from primary care. At every step of the way the patient is involved so that they are active, not passive in their care. There are many steps for ER in colorectal surgery (Fig. 61.2), and adherence to these steps is seen as fundamental in achieving optimal results. While some steps of the pathway have greater impact than others, the summation of the marginal gains for every step in this multistep pathway translates into a significant improvement in outcome. The Enhanced Recovery After Surgery Society has published a revised evidence base and recommendations in a number of areas, many of which are merely the formalization of established practice (Gustafsson et al. 2013).

Pre-admission information and optimization

Patients are given detailed information about their surgery. They should stop smoking, reduce alcohol consumption, and have comorbidities appropriately treated (e.g. hypertension and anaemia).

Preoperative fasting and oral carbohydrate loading

Prolonged fasting increases anxiety and may cause relative hypoglycaemia. The administration of oral preload helps to prevent this but also has other advantages including reducing insulin resistance and preserving nitrogen metabolism and muscle strength. A clear carbohydrate drink is given in two doses: the first dose (800 ml and containing 100 g of carbohydrate) approximately 12 h before surgery (or the night before) and the second dose (400 ml and containing 50 g of carbohydrate) 2–3 h before surgery (or the morning of surgery). The drink should contain maltodextrins which empty readily and predictably from the stomach, without increasing the risk of pulmonary aspiration while allowing the patient to arrive in theatres 'metabolically fed' (Scott and Fawcett 2014).

Anaesthetic considerations

The anaesthetist's role is pivotal in any ER programme. The two key areas are fluid balance and analgesia. Patients should receive balanced crystalloids (not 0.9% saline) or colloids to optimize cardiac output and SV. CVP is recognized as a poor indicator of fluid responsiveness although a central line can be useful for central venous saturation and thus to estimate oxygen extraction from Scv_{O2} in the early postoperative period to guide i.v. fluids. Patients should be encouraged to drink as early as possible and i.v. fluids discontinued. Analgesia is also a cornerstone of success: multimodal analgesia is used, with the addition of local or regional anaesthesia, to enable opioid sparing (with its problems of ileus and postoperative nausea and vomiting). Paracetamol and NSAIDs are widely used although there are currently some concerns about the use of NSAIDs and an increased rate of anastomotic dehiscence. The optimal method of regional block is debated. Thoracic epidural anaesthesia is advocated as the method of choice for open surgery, but is unproven and may even be detrimental for laparoscopic surgery, where other techniques particularly spinal or TAP blocks may be useful. Other anaesthetic issues include choice of anaesthetic technique and while no anaesthetic technique has proved superior, the use of agents that facilitate rapid awakening is clearly desirable. Minimizing postoperative nausea and vomiting is important and can be achieved with the regular use of multimodal antiemetics (particularly for those deemed to be at higher risk) together with attempts to reduce opioid consumption. Hypothermia (<36°C), which predisposes to wound infections, poor pain control, shivering, and concomitant hypoxia should also be avoided (Baldini and Fawcett 2015; Fawcett and Baldini 2015).

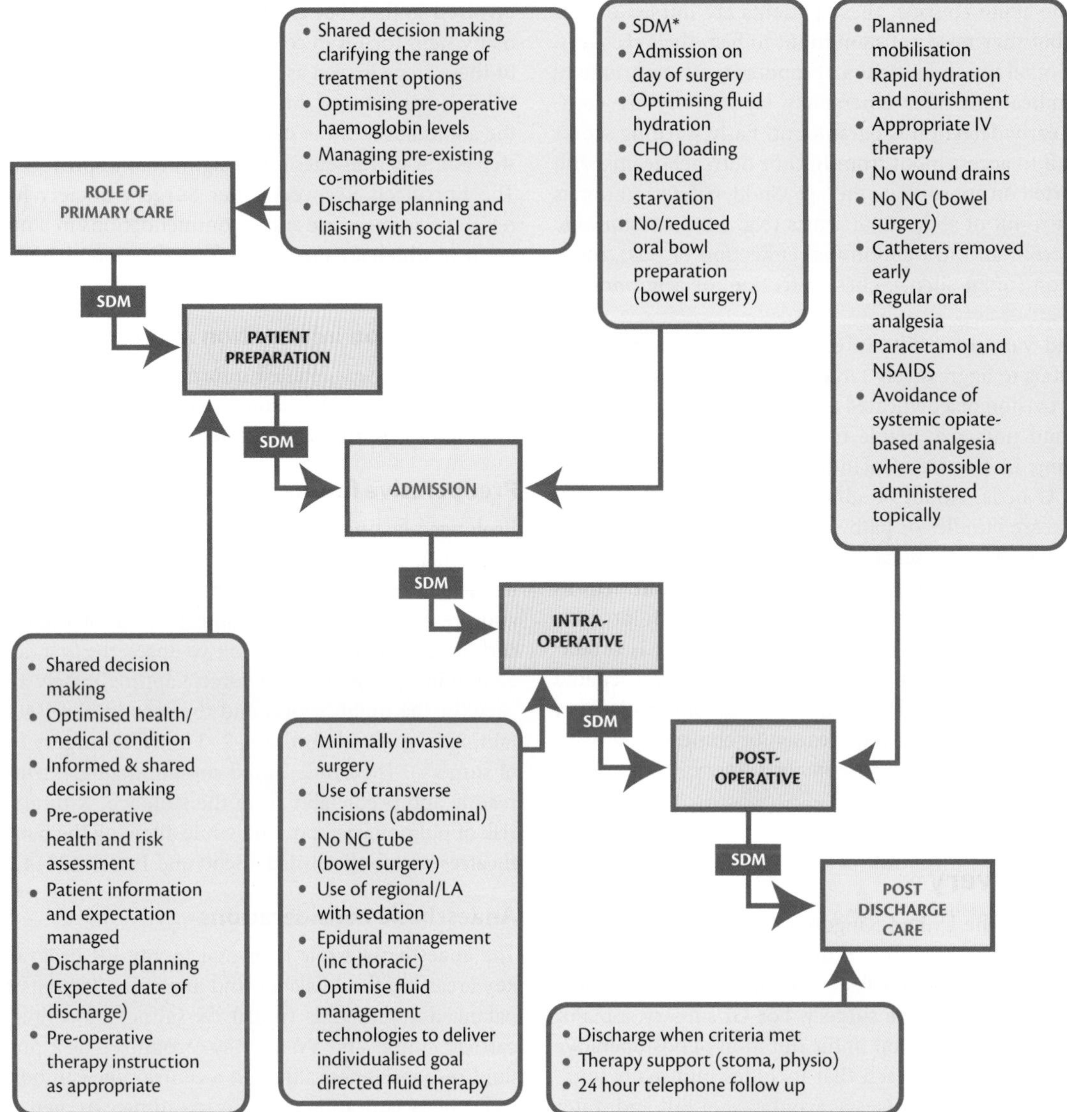

Figure 61.2 ER pathway for colorectal surgery. CHO, carbohydrate; LA, local anaesthetic; NG, nasogastric; SDM, shared decision-making.
Figure reproduced with thanks to NHSIQ.

Surgical considerations

Once viewed as mandatory, bowel preparation is now recognized as being often unnecessary, as well as being unpleasant, dehydrating, and predisposing to postoperative ileus. Laparoscopic surgery and small incision surgery are key factors in reducing length of stay. In addition, the use of various indwelling tubes has declined. Nasogastric tubes, also previously considered obligatory for patients undergoing colorectal surgery, are not only unnecessary, but also may increase pulmonary complications and slow GI motility. Abdominal drains are now also often regarded as unnecessary and prevent mobilization, while urinary catheters are generally removed after only 1 or 2 days.

Other considerations

Patients should receive appropriate antibiotics 30–60 min before surgery. Measures to prevent VTE perioperatively include the use of compression stockings, intermittent pneumatic calf compression during surgery, and low-molecular-weight heparin. Postoperatively, early enteral nutrition is strongly advocated, and there is some evidence to support giving nutritional supplements, such as arginine, glutamine, omega-3 fatty acids, and nucleotides. In addition, early mobilization and good glycaemic control are important. Finally, regular audit to examine compliance and results are key to the success of an ER programme. This whole area has recently been the subject of a detailed review (Feldheiser et al. 2015).

While many of the principles of ER have been practised in isolation, the concept of a structured pathway is seen as key to its success. It is desirable to include all the steps, although clearly some are more important than others, with oral carbohydrate loading and attention to fluid management described as the most important factors (Gustafsson et al. 2011). In addition, not all centres have the expertise to offer laparoscopic surgery, but ER patients still derive benefit from receiving ER programmes within open surgery compared with traditional care (Vlug et al. 2011). Finally, ER has been applied not only to colorectal surgery but has also been adopted in other areas of GI surgery. For example, in liver resections, an ER programme led to fewer medical complications and reduced length of stay (Jones et al. 2013).

As enthusiasm for ER grows, some of its principles have been applied to the emergency patient too. In addition, there is currently some interest in applying it to medical and other surgical patients. However, ER should not only be seen as reducing length of stay. The incidence of complications is reduced, and as mentioned previously, this has an effect not only on short-term morbidity and mortality, but also on long-term mortality (Khuri et al. 2005). In addition, there is now evidence that as patients recover more quickly they may be suitable for any adjuvant treatment (e.g. chemotherapy or radiotherapy) more quickly too, thus improving outcomes (Day et al. 2014). There is thus growing interest in the prospect that ER may play a part in improving survival (Fawcett et al. 2012).

Declaration of interest

None declared.

References

Allan N, Siller C, Breen A. Anaesthetic implications of chemotherapy. *Contin Educ Anaesth Crit Care Pain Med* 2011; **12**: 52–6

Auerbach A, Golman L. Assessing and reducing the cardiac risk of noncardiac surgery. *Circulation* 2006; **113**: 1361–76

Baldini G, Fawcett WJ. Anesthesia for colorectal surgery. *Anesthesiol Clin* 2015; **33**: 93–123

Buchler MW, Wagner M, Schmied BM, Uhl W, Friess H, Z'graggen K. Changes in morbidity after pancreatic resection toward the end of completion pancreatectomy. *Arch Surg* 2003; **138**: 1310–14

Clarke DL, Pillay Y, Anderson F, Thomson SR. The current standard of care in the periprocedural management of the patient with obstructive jaundice. *Ann R Coll Surg Engl* 2006; **88**: 610–6

Day AR, Middleton G, Smith RV, Jourdan IC, Rockall TA. Time to adjuvant chemotherapy following colorectal cancer resection is associated with an improved survival. *Colorectal Dis* 2014; **16**: 368–72

El-Dawlatly AA, Turkistani A, Kettner SC, *et al.* Ultrasound-guided transversus abdominis plane block: description of a new technique and comparison with conventional systemic analgesia during laparoscopic cholecystectomy. *Br J Anaesth* 2009; **102**: 763–7

Fawcett WJ, Baldini G. Optimal analgesia during major open and laparoscopic abdominal surgery. *Anesthesiol Clinics* 2015; **33**: 65–78

Fawcett WJ, Mythen MG, Scott MJ. Enhanced recovery: more than just reducing length of stay? *Br J Anaesth* 2012; **109**: 671–4

Feldheiser A, Aziz O, Baldini G, *et al.* Enhanced Recovery After Surgery (ERAS) for gastrointestinal surgery, part 2: consensus statement for anaesthesia practice. *Acta Anaesthesiol Scand* 2015; **59**: 1212–31

Giglio MT, Marucci M, Testini M, Brienza N. Goal-directed haemodynamic therapy and gastrointestinal complications in major surgery: a meta-analysis of randomized controlled trials. *Br J Anaesth* 2009; **103**: 637–46

Gould TH, Grace K, Thorne G, Thomas M. Effect of thoracic epidural anaesthesia on colonic blood flow. *Br J Anaesth* 2002; **89**: 446–51

Gustafsson UO, Hausel J, Thorell A, *et al.* Adherence to enhanced recovery after surgery protocol and outcomes after colorectal cancer surgery. *Arch Surg* 2011; **46**: 571–7

Gustafsson UO, Scott MJ, Schwenk W, *et al.* Guidelines for perioperative care in elective colonic surgery: Enhanced Recovery After Surgery (ERAS®) Society recommendations. *World J Surg* 2013; **37**: 259–84

Hayes MA, Yau EH, Timmins AC, Hinds CJ, Watson D. Response of critically ill patients to treatment aimed at achieving supranormal oxygen delivery and consumption. Relationship to outcome. *Chest* 1993; **103**: 886–95

Hermanides J, Hollmann MW, Stevens MF, Lirk P. Failed epidural: causes and management. *Br J Anaesth* 2012; **109**: 144–54

Imamura H, Sano K, Sugawara Y, Kokudo N, Makuuchi M. Assessment of hepatic reserve for indication of hepatic resection: decision tree incorporating indocyanine green test. *J Hepatobiliary Pancreat Surg* 2005; **12**: 16–22

Jones C, Kelliher L, Dickinson M, *et al.* Randomized clinical trial on enhanced recovery versus standard care following open liver resection. *Br J Surg* 2013; **100**: 1015–24

Kambakamba P, Slankamenac K, Tschuor C, *et al.* Epidural analgesia and perioperative kidney function after major liver resection. *Br J Surg* 2015; **102**: 805–12

Karanjia ND, Lordan JT, Fawcett WJ, Quiney N, Worthington TR. Survival and recurrence after neo-adjuvant chemotherapy and liver resection for colorectal metastases: a ten year study. *Eur J Surg Oncol* 2009; **35**: 838–43

Khuri SF, Henderson WG, DePalma RG, *et al.* Determinants of long-term survival after major surgery and the adverse effects of postoperative complications. *Ann Surg* 2005; **242**: 326–43

Lassen K, Coolsen MM, Slim K, *et al.* Guidelines for perioperative care for pancreaticoduodenectomy: Enhanced Recovery After Surgery (ERAS®) Society recommendations. *World J Surg* 2013; **37**: 240–58

Levy BF, Fawcett WJ, Scott MJ, Rockall TA. Intra-operative oxygen delivery in infusion volume optimized patients undergoing laparoscopic colorectal surgery within an enhanced recovery programme: effect of different analgesic modalities. *Colorectal Dis* 2012; **14**: 887–92

Levy BF, Scott MJ, Fawcett W, Fry C, Rockall TA. Randomized clinical trial of epidural, spinal or patient controlled analgesia for patients undergoing laparoscopic colorectal surgery. *Br J Surg* 2011; **98**: 1068–78

Levy BF, Scott MJ, Fawcett WJ, Rockall TA. 23-hour-stay laparoscopic colectomy. *Dis Colon Rectum* 2009; **52**: 1239–43

Levy BF, Tilney HS, Dowson HM, Rockall TA. A systematic review of postoperative analgesia following laparoscopic colorectal surgery. *Colorectal Dis* 2010; **12**: 5–15

Lordan JT, Worthington TR, Quiney N, Fawcett WJ, Karanjia ND. Operative mortality, blood loss and the use of Pringle manoeuvre in 526 consecutive liver resections. *Ann R Coll Surg Engl* 2009; **91**: 578–82

National Confidential Enquiry into Patient Outcome and Death. *Who Operates When? II.* London: NCEPOD, 2003. Available from http://www.ncepod.org.uk/2003wow.html

National Institute for Health and Care Excellence. *CardioQ-ODM Oesophageal Doppler Monitor.* NICE medical technology guidance [MTG3]. London: NICE, 2011. Available from https://www.nice.org.uk/guidance/mtg3

NHS Technology Adoption Centre. Intraoperative Fluid Management Technologies Adoption Pack. 2013. Available from http://webarchive.nationalarchives.gov.uk/20130701143131/http://ntac.nhs.uk/web/files/intra_operative_fluid_management/iofm_adoption_pack_update_jan_2013.pdf

Noblett SE, Snowden CP, Shenton BK, Horgan AF. Randomized clinical trial assessing the effect of Doppler-optimized fluid management on outcome after elective colorectal resection. *Br J Surg* 23006; **93**: 1069–76

Nguyen KT, Gamblin TC, Geller DA. World review of laparoscopic liver resection–2,804 patients. *Ann Surg* 2009; **250**: 831–41

Older P, Hall A, Hader R. Cardiopulmonary exercise testing as a screening test for perioperative management of major surgery in the elderly. *Chest* 1999; **116**:355–62

Pearse R, Dawson D, Fawcett J, Rhodes A, Grounds RM, Bennett ED. Changes in central venous saturation after major surgery, and association with outcome. *Crit Care* 2005; **9**: R694–9

Perner A, Haase N, Guttormsen AB, *et al.* Hydroxyethyl starch 130/0.42 versus Ringer's acetate in severe sepsis. *N Engl J Med* 2012; **367**: 124–34

Rivers E, Nguyen B, Havstad S, *et al.* Early goal-directed therapy in the treatment of severe sepsis and septic shock. *N Engl J Med* 2001; **345**: 1368–77

Rollins KE, Lobo DN. Intraoperative goal-directed fluid therapy in elective major abdominal surgery. *Ann Surg* 2016; **263**: 465–76

Royal College of Anaesthetists. *Major Complications of Central Neuraxial Blocks: The 3rd National Audit Project of the Royal College of Anaesthetists*. London: Royal College of Anaesthetists, 2009. Available from http://www.rcoa.ac.uk/nap3

Saunders DI, Murray D, Pichel AC, *et al.* Variations in mortality after emergency laparotomy: the first report of the UK Emergency Laparotomy Network. *Br J Anaesth* 2012; **109**: 368–75

Scott MJ, Fawcett WJ. Oral carbohydrate preload drink for major surgery—the first steps from famine to feast. *Anaesthesia* 2014; **69**: 308–13

Scott NA, Jeacock J, Kingston RD. Risk factors in patients presenting as an emergency with colorectal cancer. *Br J Surg* 1995; **82**: 321–3

Shoemaker WC, Montgomery ES, Kaplan E, Elwyn DH. Physiologic patterns in surviving and nonsurviving shock patients. *Arch Surg* 1973; **106**: 630–6

Shoemaker WC, Appel PL, Kram HB, Waxman K, Lee TS. Prospective trial of supranormal values of survivors as therapeutic goals in high risk surgical patients. *Chest* 1988; **94**: 1176–86

Tote SP, Grounds RM. Performing perioperative optimization of the high-risk surgical patient. *Br J Anaesth* 2006; **97**: 4–11

Tzimas P, Prout J, Papadopoulos G, Mallett SV. Epidural anaesthesia and analgesia for liver resection. *Anaesthesia* 2013; **68,** 628–35

Vlug MS, Wind J, Hollmann MW, *et al.* Laparoscopy in combination with fast track multimodal management is the best perioperative strategy in patients undergoing colonic surgery: a randomized clinical trial (LAFA-study). *Ann Surg* 2011; **254**: 868–75

Wakeling HG, McFall MR, Jenkins CS, *et al.* Intraoperative oesophageal Doppler guided fluid management shortens postoperative hospital stay after major bowel surgery. *Br J Anaesth* 2005; **95**: 634–42

Weimann A, Braga M, Harsanyi L, *et al.* ESPEN guidelines on enteral nutrition including organ transplantation. *Clinical Nutr* 2006; **25**: 224–44

West MA, Loughney L, Lythgoe D, *et al.* Effect of prehabilitation on objectively measured physical fitness after neoadjuvant treatment in preoperative rectal cancer patients: a blinded interventional pilot study. *Br J Anaesth* 2015; **114**: 244–51

CHAPTER 62

Anaesthesia for urological surgery and for robotic surgery in urology and gynaecology

Suzanne Odeberg-Wernerman and Margareta Mure

Introduction

Laparoscopic and robot-assisted laparoscopic surgical procedures have gained widespread use in both urology and gynaecology. Robotic instruments for surgical use have had, and continue to have, a huge developing potential. In the 1990s, the use of robots started with a voice-directed robotic arm holding the laparoscope. This device was developed into a robot including three robotic arms at the surgical table, controlled remotely from a console and spectacles providing three-dimensional vision.

Today, the robotic system is directed by the surgeon, with controls on a remote console, which also contains a viewer, creating a virtual three-dimensional stereoscopic image, with visual information being provided through an endoscope. A patient-side cart holds the robotic arms, one with the camera and the others with different instruments. The robotic instruments have a wrist-like mechanism that enables intra-abdominal articulation, thereby providing seven degrees of freedom, compared with the four degrees of freedom, plus the gripping function, of traditional laparoscopy.

Surgeons and patients increasingly favour robot-assisted operating techniques. Feasibility has been shown for a large number of robot-assisted operations. Compared with the two-dimensional view obtained in traditional laparoscopic procedures, the three-dimensional vision of the surgical field is a significant advantage, as are the more varied and precise movements of the instruments. Disadvantages are the high cost, first for purchasing the robot, then for disposable items, and the timely and costly training of surgeons and nurses.

The effect on long-term survival and cancer control after laparoscopic and robot-assisted laparoscopic procedures for cancer surgery is unclear, as follow-up through randomized controlled trials (RCT) is lacking. A recent meta-analysis has focused on positive surgical margin as an indicator of oncological control after open radical prostatectomy (ORP), laparoscopic radical prostatectomy (LRP), and robot-assisted laparoscopic radical prostatectomy (RALRP) (Tewari et al. 2012). They found that RALRP is equivalent to ORP and LRP in terms of margin rates.

Data on complications during and after laparoscopic and robot-assisted laparoscopic operations have been reported in single cohort studies and controlled clinical trials. Complication data are highly variable between series, and very few articles use a standardized method for complication reporting, such as the Clavien classification system (Dindo et al. 2004).

According to the above-mentioned meta-analysis (Tewari et al. 2012), complication rates for ileus, pulmonary embolism, myocardial infarction, and sepsis were not significantly different between the three surgical groups (ORP, LRP, and RALRP). Mortality rates were 0.1% (ORP) and 0.04% for LRP and for RALRP (Tewari et al. 2012).

Protocolized outcome measures of postoperative pain, blood loss, transfusion rates, discharge from hospital, etc. have not been compared. However, the general impression is that in conjunction with laparoscopic and robot-assisted laparoscopic procedures, postoperative pain is less, as are blood loss and need of transfusion. The patients are often discharged from hospital during the first or second postoperative day after robot-assisted prostatectomy. According to the meta-analysis of Tewari et al. (2012), RALRP has the shortest and ORP the longest length of stay in hospital, and ORP has the highest estimated blood loss and transfusion rate. Conversion to open surgery occurs in 0.7% (LRP) and 0.3% (RALRP).

Outcome data on sexual potency, urinary continence, and quality of life after robot-assisted laparoscopic prostatectomy and after robot-assisted gynaecological procedures, compared with other surgical approaches, are awaiting.

Overview of the pathophysiology of laparoscopic and robot-assisted laparoscopic surgery

Robot-assisted laparoscopic surgery produces a complex multifactorial pathophysiological response. In the clinical setting, it is difficult or impossible to define the precise origin of the various components of this response, but for didactic reasons the various factors are discussed separately here. See also Chapter 61.

Pneumoperitoneum with carbon dioxide

Carbon dioxide is commonly used to create a pneumoperitoneum. Carbon dioxide induces an increase in heart rate, blood pressure, and systemic vascular resistance, which is often seen immediately upon gas insufflation (Odeberg et al. 1994; Gannedahl et al. 1996). An elevated end-tidal CO_2 and Pa_{CO_2} is often seen, requiring increased minute ventilation. In susceptible patients or in lengthy procedures (or both), carbon dioxide retention and resulting acidosis can necessitate conversion to open surgery in rare cases.

Intra-abdominal pressure level

Most often, a pneumoperitoneum generating a pressure of 11–12 mm Hg or lower is required. Nevertheless, the circulatory effects of increased intra-abdominal pressure, such as increased blood pressure and systemic vascular resistance, and increased filling pressures of the right and left heart (Odeberg et al. 1994; Gannedahl et al. 1996; Andersson et al. 2003; Andersson et al. 2005b), are important. Inadvertent excessive abdominal pressure compromises venous return, which can lead to reduced cardiac output. Cardiac output is otherwise maintained in normovolaemic ASA I–II patients (Odeberg et al. 1994; Gannedahl et al. 1996; Andersson et al. 1999; Lestar et al. 2011).

Respiratory compliance is decreased (Odeberg and Sollevi 1995; Andersson et al. 2005a, 2005b), despite the use of positive end-expiratory pressure (PEEP) (Meininger et al. 2005). The decreased compliance often requires an increase in inspiratory pressure or frequency (or both), and change from volume-controlled to pressure-controlled ventilation, with or without adjustment of inspiratory:expiratory relationships.

Trendelenburg position

During gynaecological and urological laparoscopic and robot-assisted laparoscopic surgery, the Trendelenburg position is used to create a good view of the surgical field. This causes further increases of blood pressure and filling pressures of the heart (Odeberg et al. 1994; Gannedahl et al. 1996). Respiratory compliance is further decreased by the Trendelenburg position (Andersson et al. 2005b; Lestar et al. 2011). During robot-assisted urological surgery, the Trendelenburg positioning can be profound, as steep as 30–45°.

Robot-assisted laparoscopic surgery

Please see Figures 62.1 and 62.2.

Effects on haemodynamics and cardiac performance

The heart rate is initially unchanged (Meininger et al. 2002, 2004, 2005, 2006, 2008; Lestar et al. 2011), but after 2–4 h of surgery, an increased heart rate has been demonstrated (Meininger et al. 2002, 2004, 2005, 2006, 2008). During surgery, increased blood pressure is common (Meininger et al. 2002, 2004, 2005, 2006, 2008; D'Alonzo et al. 2009; Lestar et al. 2011), but hypotension can also occur (D'Alonzo et al. 2009). It is often difficult to identify the cause of hypotension and to judge whether it is caused by hypo- or hypervolaemia/overfilling, or myocardial dysfunction, or both.

With 20° head-down tilt, right-sided filling pressures are increased 1.5-fold during robot-assisted laparoscopic surgery (Meininger et al. 2006, 2008). Two-fold increases in left-sided filling pressures and three-fold increases in right-sided filling pressures have been demonstrated during robot-assisted laparoscopic surgery with 45° head-down tilt (Lestar et al. 2011). In this situation, pulmonary capillary wedge pressure (PCWP) was at a level seen during heart failure (Nieminen et al. 2005). However, echocardiography has revealed unchanged end-diastolic and end-systolic diameters (Lestar et al. 2011). Pulmonary hypertension (European Study Group on Heart Failure 1998) with right-sided filling pressures more than double compared with the usual situation during anaesthesia emphasizes the effects on right ventricular function.

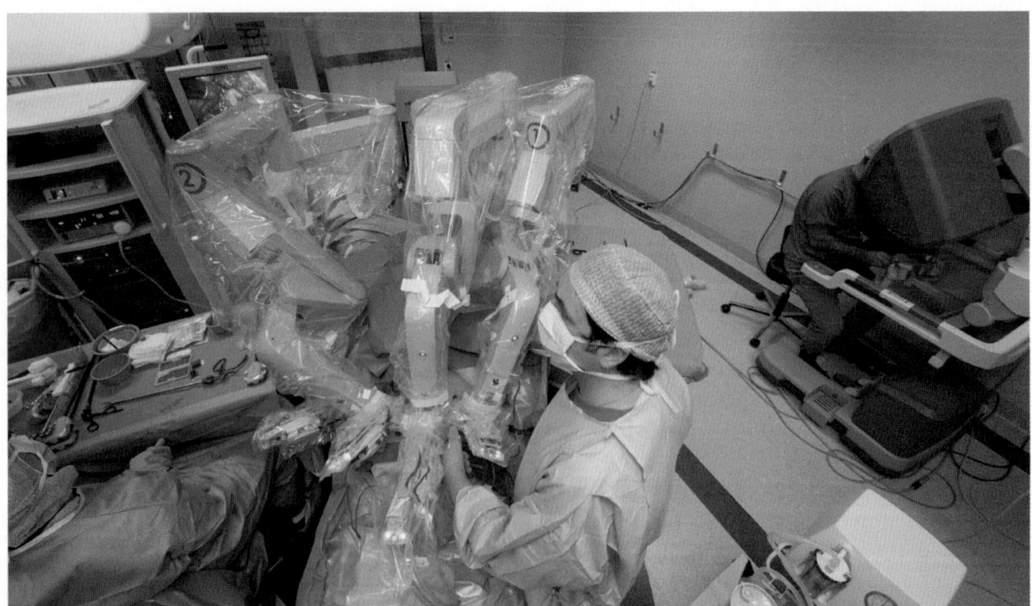

Figure 62.1 Robot-assisted laparoscopic radical prostatectomy procedure: sitting at the remote control to the right, the principal surgeon directs the instruments by tele-manipulation.

With thanks to Allan Larsen and the Department of Medicial Photography, Karolinska University Hospital. Reproduced with permission.

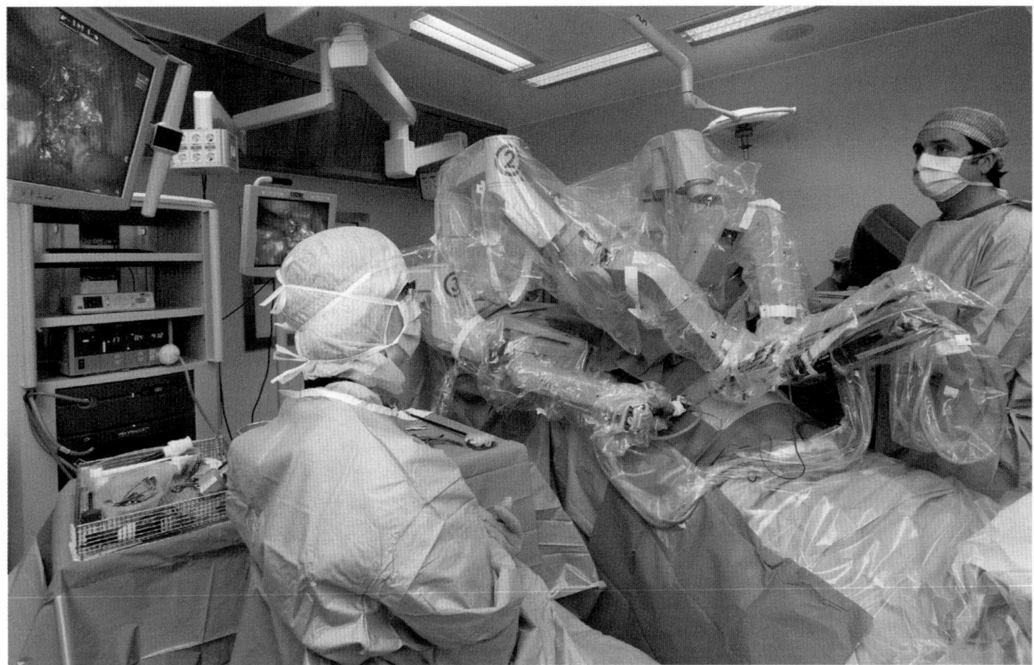

Figure 62.2 At the operating table, an assisting surgeon monitors and changes the instruments attached to the numbered robotic arms. The operation field is visualized on the screen.
With thanks to Allan Larsen and the Department of Medicial Photography, Karolinska University Hospital. Reproduced with permission.

Elevation of right-sided stroke work index by 65% and a less pronounced increase in left-sided stroke work index has been seen (Lestar et al. 2011).

During RALRP, unchanged intraventricular relaxation time and deceleration time has been shown, indicating unchanged diastolic function (Lestar et al. 2011). In contrast, during laparoscopic hysterectomy in the Trendelenburg position, diastolic dysfunction was indicated by increased deceleration time and intraventricular relaxation time in ASA I women with a mean age of 40 years (Russo et al. 2009). An altered relation between the early filling phase of the left atrium and the left atrial contraction time and increased early filling velocity has been shown in the Trendelenburg position (Lestar et al. 2011).

Despite these alterations, cardiac output has been shown to be maintained (Falabella et al. 2007; Choi et al. 2008; Meininger et al. 2008; Lestar et al. 2011). Cardiac output in this situation has been studied by different techniques, such as PiCCO (Meininger et al. 2008), transoesophageal Doppler measurements (Falabella et al. 2007), arterial pressure-based cardiac output (Choi et al. 2008), and bolus thermodilution technique (Lestar et al. 2011). Supporting the finding of unchanged cardiac output, mixed venous oxygen tension was also unaffected by RALRP (Lestar et al. 2011).

The pathophysiology during pneumoperitoneum and steep Trendelenburg positioning and the complex interaction between intra-abdominal and intrathoracic pressures and blood volume, cardiac filling pressures, intracardiac volumes, and ventilator pressures in the restricted space of the thoracic cavity are not yet fully understood or even characterized. It has been questioned whether the increased filling pressures during pneumoperitoneum and steep Trendelenburg position are of clinical relevance. Investigations in ASA I–II patients indicate that cardiac performance is maintained (Meininger et al. 2008; Lestar et al. 2011) despite significant increases in left ventricular filling pressures (Lestar et al. 2011). However, the increases in filling pressures may not correspond to transmural pressure increases but reflect the increase in intrathoracic pressure. It may also be that patients having sufficient cardiac reserve to permit an increase in myocardial contractility can compensate for increased pressure work during pneumoperitoneum and steep Trendelenburg positioning.

After release of the pneumoperitoneum and return to the supine position, a period with a hyperdynamic circulatory pattern with increased heart rate and cardiac index/cardiac output has been seen (Meininger et al. 2005, 2006, 2008; Lestar et al. 2011).

The circulatory pattern during laparoscopic robot-assisted urological surgery has not been systematically investigated in patients with cardiac disease. However, the substantial increases in pre-load and stroke work index may represent a risk for developing heart failure during the intervention.

Effects on respiratory physiology

Carbon dioxide pneumoperitoneum causes an increase in end-tidal CO_2 and Pa_{CO_2}, which can usually be prevented by increased ventilation, preferably first by increasing respiratory frequency, then by increasing tidal volume. Airway pressure is increased, which *per se* may require a slightly elevated inspiratory pressure. Respiratory compliance is reduced, being halved during robot-assisted prostatectomy (Lestar et al. 2011). Pneumoperitoneum-associated cranial displacement of the diaphragm, compression of basal lung zones, and atelectasis formation has been demonstrated (Andersson et al. 2005a). In spite of this, a reduced fraction of true shunt, unchanged venous admixture, and a reduction of ventilation–perfusion mismatch have been shown during robot-assisted laparoscopic prostatectomy (Lestar et al. 2011). These findings have been demonstrated previously during laparoscopic cholecystectomy (Odeberg et al.

1995; Andersson et al. 2005b). It has also been demonstrated that PEEP has a favourable effect on preserving arterial oxygenation during prolonged pneumoperitoneum for RALRP (Meininger et al. 2005; Park H-P et al. 2009).

Effects on splanchnic circulation

When splanchnic blood flow was estimated by hepatic blood flow measurements using the continuous infusion method, anaesthesia induction lowered splanchnic blood flow significantly. However, pneumoperitoneum with an intra-abdominal pressure level of 11–13 mm Hg and a duration of 1 h did not influence splanchnic blood flow. Splanchnic oxygen consumption, measured by the Fick principle, was not affected during this time (Odeberg et al. 1998). There are reports of increased oxidative stress during prolonged pneumoperitoneum (Luo et al. 2011), possibly as a result of compromised splanchnic microcirculatory flow (Arsalani-Zadeh et al. 2011).

Effects on kidney function

Urinary output and glomerular filtration rate have been shown to be decreased during pneumoperitoneum. After release of the pneumoperitoneum, urinary output is increased. These effects have been attributed to a pneumoperitoneum-induced increase of vasopressin release and to increased perirenal pressure (Ost et al. 2005).

Effects on central nervous system

Patients with cerebral aneurysms at risk of elevated intracranial pressure (ICP) or with glaucoma should be selected with caution. ICP is increased, as is intraocular pressure (Awad et al. 2009), during laparoscopic and robot-assisted laparoscopic procedures. There are case reports of blindness as a result of ischaemic optic neuropathy after robot-assisted procedures in the Trendelenburg position (Weber et al. 2007).

The clinical significance of the increased ICP is not clear. The majority of patients seem to tolerate this well, but caution is warranted, especially in patients with known aneurysms or risk factors for increased ICP. An experimental study in pigs has shown that the combination of pneumoperitoneum and Trendelenburg position with 20° head-down tilt increased ICP by more than 50%. The increase was immediate and linear when intra-abdominal pressure was 8 mm Hg or higher (Rosenthal et al. 1997). The cerebral perfusion pressure during robot-assisted laparoscopic surgery in the Trendelenburg position is influenced by the increase in mean arterial pressure (MAP) and central venous pressure (CVP), altering cerebral perfusion pressure (CPP), where CPP = MAP − CVP or CPP = MAP − ICP. The increased hydrostatic pressure during Trendelenburg position increases cerebral oedema which can also influence cerebral perfusion. Another factor of importance during robot-assisted laparoscopic surgery in the Trendelenburg position is the development of hypercarbia, which could influence cerebral autoregulation. However, several studies (Choi et al. 2008; Kalmar et al. 2012) indicate that cerebral autoregulation is intact during sevoflurane anaesthesia for robot-assisted laparoscopic surgery including a 30–40° Trendelenburg position for a time period of 2–3 h. Cerebral oxygenation, monitored by near-infrared spectroscopy, has been shown to be maintained in one study (Park EY et al. 2009) but reduced in another (Lee et al. 2006). In the latter study, two patients who were hypercapnic (Pa_{CO_2} > 6 kPa) had a regional cerebral oxygen saturation below 50%: postoperatively, one of them had a headache. This series included only healthy patients. The influence of pneumoperitoneum and Trendelenburg position on ICP, cerebral haemodynamics, and oxygenation in patients with compromised central nervous system function remains to be characterized.

Patients with high intraocular pressure are not suited for laparoscopic or robot-assisted procedures in the Trendelenburg position. For glaucoma patients, consulting an ophthalmologist should be considered preoperatively.

Overweight patients

In overweight patients during RALRP, arterial oxygenation was lower and alveolar–arterial difference in oxygen tension was increased under general anaesthesia in the Trendelenburg position compared with patients who were not overweight (Meininger et al. 2006). In overweight patients, pneumoperitoneum transiently reduced the impairment of arterial oxygenation and led to a decrease in alveolar–arterial difference in oxygen tension, whereas haemodynamic variables were not affected by body weight (Meininger et al. 2006).

Perioperative complications

Cardiovascular complications

Low blood pressure can occur as a result of cardiac failure caused by increased intravascular pressure or systemic vascular resistance (or both), hypovolaemia, decreased venous return, or pericardial restriction with a steep Trendelenburg position.

High blood pressure can result from the pneumoperitoneum and the Trendelenburg position *per se* but this may be difficult to distinguish from nociceptive responses. During RALRP, antihypertensive agents were used more often, whereas vasopressors were used less often compared with ORP (D'Alonzo et al. 2009), indicating increased intraoperative haemodynamic instability during RALRP. The approach to blood pressure management will be governed by patient co-morbidities and surgical requirements. The need for specific drugs to adjust blood pressure will depend on the anaesthetic agents used where, for example, ultrashort-acting opioids can be used for rapid adjustment of blood pressure.

Arrhythmias can be precipitated by high Pa_{CO_2} levels. They can also be a warning sign for cardiac failure or myocardial infarction. Left heart failure, myocardial infarction and pulmonary oedema can occur in patients with cardiac disease, supposedly when the combined effects of increased systemic vascular resistance, elevated filling pressures, and disturbed diastolic function cannot be compensated by increased cardiac contractility. During robot-assisted laparoscopic procedures in the steep Trendelenburg position (30–45°), the mean pulmonary artery pressure will reach values seen in pulmonary hypertension. There is a risk of right heart failure in this situation.

Circulatory complications may necessitate a return of the patient to the supine position. However, this may not be sufficient to restore the patient's cardiac function. It should be remembered that when the patient is connected to the robotic arms, postural changes first require disconnection from the instruments. Medical team training to manage acute emergency situations during robot-assisted surgery by using a simulator can be useful. The time to the start of chest compressions, removal of the robotic system, and first defibrillation were significantly improved at the second simulation (Huser et al. 2014).

Ocular complications

Posterior ischaemic optic neuropathy leading to loss of vision has been described after robotic prostatectomy (Weber et al. 2007). In a prospective study during robotic prostatectomy with a pneumoperitoneum of 15 mm Hg, the duration of the procedure and end-tidal CO_2 were significant predictors of intraocular pressure increase (Awad et al. 2009). During the intervention, the mean intraocular pressure was 13 mm Hg greater than pre-induction values. Patients reached intraocular pressure levels comparable to glaucoma patients who have temporarily stopped their medication and are placed in the Trendelenburg position.

Complications related to gas insufflation

Gas embolism is a rare complication, which can occur if carbon dioxide is accidentally insufflated into the circulation or if carbon dioxide diffuses into the circulation via open, bleeding venous plexa. In the case of a significant embolus, the monitor will display a decrease in blood pressure and absent end-tidal CO_2 curve.

Significant hypercarbia and acidosis can occur during lengthy exposure to pneumoperitoneum (several hours) (Hong et al. 2009). In severe cases, conversion to open surgery is necessary, but this is rare.

Subcutaneous emphysema is a common complication, which occurs more often after pelvic operations, as they involve a retroperitoneal approach. As the retroperitoneal space has communications with the thorax and subcutaneous tissue, subcutaneous emphysema can be significant and may even interfere with airway patency. This should be considered before tracheal extubation (Lam et al. 2009; Weingram et al. 2010).

Cystectomy is associated with hypothermia because of the duration of the operation and the insufflation of cold gas.

Complications related to position

Shoulder braces are used to prevent the patient from slipping during the Trendelenburg position. Swelling of the face and tongue is common, and there are cases where patients required mechanical ventilation postoperatively because of airway swelling (D'Alonzo et al. 2009). Conjunctival oedema and hyperaemia of the face are very common.

Reduced perfusion to the legs and compartment syndrome can occur after operations involving lengthy pneumoperitoneum and the Trendelenburg position. The pathophysiology is an ischaemic insult followed by reperfusion, which can result in a compartment syndrome necessitating fasciotomy. Myoglobinaemia should be treated by forced diuresis. If compartment syndrome is suspected, the pressure in the extremity should be monitored repeatedly and fasciotomy should be performed if needed.

During the operation, the patient's arms are placed at the sides of the body so as not to restrict the surgical access. Particular care must be taken in protecting pressure points. Extensions to the intravenous lines are needed to enable injections and infusions during the operation. IV lines must be well secured and handled carefully as they are difficult or impossible to replace during surgery.

Postoperative course

Monitoring of bleeding is essential in the early postoperative period. There may be venous bleeding, noticeable only after a couple of hours. The patients have no surgical drains, so bleeding is not visible and may be diagnosed too late unless the patient's clinical condition, blood pressure, and haemoglobin values are monitored in an appropriate setting during the first postoperative hours.

The need for postoperative transfusion seems to be low and postoperative haematocrit values have been reported to be higher than for open approaches (Tewari et al. 2012). However, outcome measures such as transfusion rate, postoperative haemoglobin, and haematocrit values are subject to significant bias in the absence of protocolized comparisons including transfusion targets and fluid treatment.

The need for postoperative analgesics is lower than after open surgery. Most patients do well with a dose of opioid at the end of surgery and intermittent doses after that.

After robot-assisted laparoscopic cystectomy, patient-controlled analgesia (PCA) can also be used. If needed, this can be combined with other analgesics. Experience is accumulating that spinal anaesthesia with morphine 0.1–0.4 mg decreases the need for other postoperative analgesics after robot-assisted laparoscopic cystectomy (authors' unpublished data, $n = 100$).

Despite the circulatory changes observed during surgery, patients are most often discharged early from hospital, the majority on the day after surgery, for example, after robot-assisted prostatectomy and hysterectomy. However, after robot-assisted cystectomy, patients stay approximately a week in hospital.

Preoperative evaluation

As the pathophysiological response to pneumoperitoneum and the Trendelenburg position includes predominantly haemodynamic disturbances, the focus during preoperative evaluation should be on circulatory status and reserve. As mentioned previously, the clinical significance of the complex cardiovascular response to robot-assisted laparoscopic surgery in the Trendelenburg position is still not clear. Nevertheless, patients with cardiac insufficiency, ischaemic heart disease, valvular disease, or a combination of these, should be selected with caution for robot-assisted laparoscopic surgery in the Trendelenburg position. In these compromised patients, a thorough preoperative evaluation should be carried out, defining the individual's myocardial performance and myocardial motility pattern by echocardiography and exercise testing. Patients with valvular disease require special preoperative attention, as valvular disease is often combined with heart failure, ischaemic heart disease, or both. In some cases, laparoscopic robotic operations are feasible with appropriate monitoring (see later).

In patients with severe stenosis of the aortic valve, robot-assisted laparoscopic surgery in the Trendelenburg position is contraindicated, and other treatment options should be offered to these patients.

Patients with a patent foramen ovale (PFO) are at risk of a paradoxical embolism should a gas embolism occur. It is worth noting that approximately 10% of the population have an unrecognized PFO.

Patients with restrictive pulmonary disease are not well suited to laparoscopic or robot-assisted laparoscopic surgery because of the marked decrease in respiratory compliance caused by the pneumoperitoneum and the further decrease as a result of the Trendelenburg position. Patients with severe restrictive pulmonary disease should be offered other therapy.

Patients with cerebral aneurysms and with a risk of elevated ICP or with glaucoma should be selected with caution. Both the surgeon and anaesthesiologist should evaluate ophthalmic concerns during preoperative assessment and if necessary refer the patient to an ophthalmologist. This is especially important should the patient have other co-morbidities such as hypertension, cardiac compromise, or diabetes mellitus. For glaucoma patients, it is important that the patient stays on his/her medication.

Choice of anaesthesia for robot-assisted surgery

General anaesthesia is required (Box 62.1). Induction can be performed with propofol or thiopental and maintenance with a volatile anaesthetic, sevoflurane or desflurane. An alternative is total intravenous anaesthesia, but because of difficulty inspecting the intravenous catheter during the operation, a combination of intravenous and inhalation anaesthesia is preferred. Neuromuscular block is used for tracheal intubation and maintained during the operation as required. Intraoperative analgesia with ultrashort-acting opioids is preferred. This can also aid rapid adjustment of blood pressure.

Monitoring

During laparoscopic and robot-assisted laparoscopic surgery, in addition to standard monitoring, an arterial line should be used for monitoring of blood pressure and for arterial blood gas sampling. In patients at risk of developing intraoperative heart failure or other cardiac complications, transoesophageal echocardiography or cardiac output monitoring by minimally invasive techniques, or both, should be performed. Body temperature should be monitored, as there is a risk of hypothermia during long operations.

Laparoscopic and robot-assisted radical prostatectomy

An increasing number of prostatectomies are performed using robot assistance with a system that generates a three-dimensional view of the operating field. This enables the surgeon to control the instruments using remote tele-manipulation, while the surgical assistant changes the instruments. With the patient in the horizontal position, a pneumoperitoneum is created by insufflation of carbon dioxide. The intra-abdominal pressure is monitored continuously and maintained at 11–12 mm Hg. During surgery, the patients are positioned in an extreme Trendelenburg position (up to 45° head-down tilt). After removal of the prostate gland, the urethra is reconnected to the urinary bladder over an indwelling urinary catheter. The advantage of the minimally invasive robot-assisted technique is that the majority of patients can leave the hospital the day after the operation.

Laparoscopic and robot-assisted radical cystectomy

Robot-assisted cystectomy has a growing role in the management of bladder cancer that has invaded the bladder muscle. Minimally invasive radical cystectomy techniques for the treatment of bladder cancer are being increasingly applied and offer potential benefits in terms of reduced blood loss and decreased transfusion rates, reduced analgesic requirements, and shorter hospital stay, whilst striving to provide similar oncological outcomes as open radical cystectomy (Cha et al. 2011; Challacombe et al. 2011).

Bleeding can be extensive during the procedure because of the proximity of the bladder to a large venous plexus.

Box 62.1 Summary of authors' approach to anaesthesia for laparoscopic and robotic major urological and gynaecological procedures

- Heating mattress or blanket
- General anaesthesia. Induction with propofol/thiopental and maintenance with a volatile anaesthetic (sevoflurane/desflurane) or with total intravenous anaesthesia
- Intraoperative analgesia with infusion of remifentanil or intermittent fentanyl
- Neuromuscular block for tracheal intubation and during the operation as needed
- Antibiotics according to local protocols
- Large-bore intravenous access is recommended
- Arterial catheter for monitoring of the arterial blood pressure and measurement of arterial blood gases
- Cardiac output monitoring in compromised patients
- PEEP 5–15 cm H_2O to minimize atelectasis
- Postoperative analgesia with morphine or ketobemidone
- Antithrombotic therapy.

Laparoscopic and robot-assisted nephrectomy

Laparoscopic living donor nephrectomy is an attractive surgical procedure (Ungbhakorn et al. 2012). Although the duration of the procedure and the warm ischaemic time were longer and the cost was higher than for open nephrectomy, there was less blood loss and lower pain scores. Robot-assisted partial nephrectomy is a minimally invasive option for patients undergoing nephron-sparing surgery. Kidney-sparing approaches have become the 'gold standard' for management of small renal tumours and have equivalent oncological outcomes to radical nephrectomy (Sukumar and Rogers 2011). Robot-assisted partial nephrectomy has emerged as a feasible alternative to other minimally invasive approaches. It has been used in patients with bilateral renal tumours. Anomalies in the kidney can also be corrected with these minimally invasive techniques.

Laparoscopic and robot-assisted gynaecological surgery

Advanced laparoscopic procedures are increasingly being used as an alternative to laparotomy in gynaecological surgery (Smith et al. 2009; Weinberg et al. 2011). In general and reproductive gynaecology, the robot is being used for procedures such as hysterectomies, myomectomies, adnexal surgery, and tubal anastomosis.

Lower overall hospitalization costs have been reported for robot-assisted surgery for endometrial cancer compared with open surgery as a result of the reduced length of stay and fewer complications (Bell et al. 2008). However, there is a lack of randomized controlled trials comparing robot-assisted gynaecological surgery to laparoscopic surgery or open surgery (or both) regarding primary outcome measures (survival) and complication rates, length of hospitalization, quality of life, costs, and so on. In a Cochrane review, it was concluded that there was no evidence from randomized controlled trials to support the use of robot-assisted gynaecological surgery for the treatment of gynaecological cancer (Lu et al. 2012). In another Cochrane review of surgery for benign gynaecological conditions (Liu et al. 2012), two randomized controlled trials comparing robot-assisted and laparoscopic surgery were identified (Sarlos et al. 2010; Paraiso et al. 2011) but these showed no benefits of robotic surgery.

The development of robotic technology has facilitated the application of minimally invasive techniques for the treatment and evaluation of patients with early, advanced, and recurrent cervical cancer (Magrina and Zanagnolo 2008). For early cervical cancer, radical parametrectomy and fertility-preserving trachelectomy have been performed using robotic technology and been shown to be feasible, safe, and easier to perform compared with laparoscopy for technically challenging operations performed to treat primary, early or advanced, and recurrent cervical cancer (Magrina et al. 2008).

Cystoscopy and ureteroscopy

Cystoscopy and ureteroscopy are performed to diagnose and treat lesions of the lower (urethra, prostate, bladder) and upper (ureter, kidney) urinary tract, respectively. Heated irrigation fluids are used to improve visualization and to remove blood, tissue, and stone fragments. Warm saline is used for cystoscopy.

Depending on the patient and the procedure, anaesthesia can range from topical to regional or general anaesthesia. Placement of a rigid cystoscope (particularly in males) and distension of the bladder and ureters can be painful. When regional anaesthesia is used, block to the level of the sixth thoracic dermatome (T6) is required for upper urinary tract instrumentation, whereas block to T10 is sufficient for lower urinary tract procedures. Spinal anaesthesia is commonly used for example with bupivacaine in doses of 5–15 mg with or without an opioid such as sufentanil 5 μg or fentanyl 10 mcg. Intravenous conscious sedation can be added.

Laser lithotripsy is used for kidney and ureteral stones that are not amenable to extracorporeal shock wave lithotripsy (ESWL). The laser beam is reflective so the user, other personnel, and the patient should wear protective eyeglasses. The smoke must also be evacuated. Stones in the kidney and ureter can be treated with a transurethral technique. If the stones are in the kidney, general anaesthesia is frequently used, with tracheal intubation and neuromuscular block to avoid patient movement. In patients with severe co-morbidity, spinal or epidural anaesthesia with or without an indwelling catheter can be used.

Extracorporeal shockwave lithotripsy

When kidney or ureteral stones are treated with ESWL, shockwaves are generated from a source external to the patient's body. The energy source rapidly generates pulses of energy into a fluid environment, which results in a shockwave. These waves move faster than the speed of sound. The stronger the initial shock, the faster the shockwave moves. Although the shockwaves in the lithotripters generate large pressures, they induce only slight compression and deformation of tissue. The uniqueness of the shockwave lithotripter is its ability to focus the shockwave. Relatively weak, non-intrusive waves are generated externally and transmitted through the body. The shockwaves build to sufficient strength only at the target, where they generate enough force to fragment a stone (Wein and Kavoussi 2011).

ESWL represents the initial treatment modality in approximately 90% of patients with urinary tract stones, and is done predominantly on an outpatient basis. Nearly 6% of patients experience an inadequate ESWL result, and may require endourological or operative stone removal. Pregnancy and the presence of coagulopathy are contraindications to ESWL. Patients with large calculi or with distal ureteral stricture or obstruction may not be candidates for ESWL monotherapy. Patients with calcium oxalate monohydrate, calcium phosphate, or cystine calculi, which are resistant to fracture with ESWL, may require alternative techniques. Percutaneous nephrolithectomy alone or with ESWL and open surgical intervention remain alternative treatment options for these patients (Gravenstein 2000).

Anaesthesia

The location of a stone influences the pain experienced; treatment of stones in the upper caliceal system is more painful than treatment of middle and lower caliceal stones. Furthermore, increased applied voltage, pressure, and energy density at the skin entry point and in the traversed tissues also heightens pain (Gravenstein 2000). Adequate pain control can generally be achieved with intravenous short-acting opioids such as remifentanil or alfentanil with additional sedation using midazolam or propofol.

Another approach to minimize anaesthesia requirements during ESWL has been the use of topical agents. A eutectic mixture of lidocaine and prilocaine has been shown to significantly reduce anaesthesia requirements during ESWL (Basar et al. 2003; Yilmaz et al. 2005). The topical anaesthetic agent should be applied at least 45 min before ESWL. The combination of topical agents and short-acting intravenous agents is likely to shorten recovery times.

Not all patients are well served by treatment with a low-energy ESWL technique, and therefore a variety of factors need to be considered in choosing the preferred approach for ESWL. Delivery of higher levels of shockwave energy will increase anaesthesia requirements (Wein and Kavoussi 2011). These procedures can be tolerated only under regional or general anaesthesia. Hyperbaric bupivacaine, administered as a continuous spinal infusion, has been shown to be effective for ESWL, with little hypotension (Gravenstein 2000). Epidural opioids alone (e.g. alfentanil, fentanyl, sufentanil) may be effective in providing comfort during ESWL.

Thin patients have more pain during ESWL because the converging shockwave is more concentrated at the point of skin penetration. Paediatric patients, who often require repeated treatments, and extremely anxious individuals may be best served by general anaesthesia.

Complications of ESWL

- Haematuria is very common and treated with hydration and diuretics.
- Renal contusion because of damage to renal vasculature.
- Cardiac arrhythmias such as bradycardia, premature atrial contractions, and premature ventricular contractions.
- Trauma to organs such as the liver and skeletal muscle, as evidenced by elevated concentrations of bilirubin, lactate dehydrogenase, serum aspartate transaminase, and creatine kinase within 24 h of treatment.

- Trauma to the intestine manifested as nausea, vomiting, or bradycardia.
- Pancreatitis.
- Pneumothorax.

Percutaneous nephrolithectomy

Stones and tumours in the kidney can also be treated with a percutaneous technique. If the procedure is performed in a radiology department, epidural anaesthesia with an indwelling catheter is often preferred. If the procedure is performed in the operating theatre, it can be performed either under epidural or general anaesthesia. Some surgeons will prefer general anaesthesia with neuromuscular block and tracheal intubation, as it is very important that the patient does not move during the procedure, especially if the tumour or stone is in the kidney as this can cause major bleeding or damage to the kidney. Some surgeons prefer that the patient is placed in the prone position during the procedure.

Laser is often used and the laser beam is reflective so the user, other personal and the patient should wear protective eyeglasses. The smoke must also be evacuated.

Transurethral resection of the prostate

Patients with symptomatic benign hypertrophy of the prostate gland with voiding difficulties or cancer are treated with transurethral resection of the prostate (TURP). During surgery, large venous sinuses are opened, which allows irrigation solution to be absorbed. If the gland is large (>60 g) and the resection time is prolonged, the patient is at risk of excessive absorption of hypotonic bladder irrigation fluid. When a monopolar cautery is used, non-electrolyte solutions have to be used (Michielsen et al. 2010a). Glycine, sorbitol, and mannitol are non-conductive but intravascular absorption can cause haemolysis and hyponatraemia.

Absorption of small amounts of fluid (1–2 litres) occurs in 5–10% of patients undergoing TURP and results in an easily overlooked mild TURP syndrome (Hahn 2006). When larger volumes of fluid are absorbed, overt TURP syndrome can develop. This is a potentially fatal condition (Cury et al. 2008). Technological advances using laser and bipolar cautery (Hawary et al. 2009; Michielsen et al. 2010b) together with advances in training of the surgeon have helped to minimize the risk of TURP syndrome. However, a high index of suspicion and intensive monitoring is vital.

Early symptoms of TURP syndrome

- Blurred vision
- Confusion
- Nausea, vomiting, or both
- Disorientation
- Dizziness
- Headache
- Hypertension
- Bradycardia
- Lethargy
- Hyponatraemia (serum sodium < 125 mmol litre^{-1})
- Abdominal distension.

Late symptoms

- Neuromuscular disturbances (i.e. twitching, seizures)
- Visual disturbances
- Hypotension
- Dyspnoea
- Cyanosis
- Myocardial ischaemia
- Renal tubular necrosis and decreased urinary output
- Cerebral oedema
- Coma
- Death.

Treatment of TURP syndrome

- Fluid restriction
- Loop diuretics such as furosemide
- Hypertonic saline in patients with hyponatraemia.

When using a laser or bipolar resection technique with saline irrigation, the risk of transurethral resection syndrome is much less. A bipolar resection technique is associated with a reduction in blood loss and improvement of voiding (Fagerstrom et al. 2009, 2011).

Even though there is a declining trend in the incidence of TURP syndrome, the risk still exists. To be able to monitor the patient's mental status during the operation and to detect the early symptoms of the TURP syndrome these patients are optimally anaesthetized using a regional technique: spinal anaesthesia, for example with bupivacaine in doses of 7–15 mg with or without an opioid such as sufentanil or fentanyl. General anaesthesia may be necessary in patients who have contraindications to regional anaesthesia, or who refuse regional anaesthesia.

Another common complication of TURP is perforation of the bladder. Most perforations are extraperitoneal. In a conscious patient the symptoms are obvious. Observation of the patient's vital signs is therefore very important. Also, the wall of the bladder can be perforated. In these cases, the patient will get pain in the upper part of the abdomen (for symptoms see 'Transurethral resection of bladder tumour').

In patients with an indwelling urinary catheter, there is an increased risk of bacteraemia that might lead to sepsis. In these cases, prophylactic antibiotics are used.

If the prostate gland is large, perioperative bleeding might be significant. The estimation of blood loss is difficult. The blood is mixed with a large volume of irrigation fluid and it is extremely difficult to quantify the bleeding.

Videos of the surgical procedure can be viewed at http://www.youtube.com/watch?v=Njm1BtrEf1w&feature=related and http://www.youtube.com/watch?v=Qn0Bo3GM4_w&feature=related.

Scrotal operations

Patients with torsion of the testis may require emergency reduction and orchidopexy to prevent ischaemia. Testicular cancer is treated with orchidectomy. These patients are often young and surgery is performed under general anaesthesia.

In patients with metastatic prostate cancer, bilateral orchidectomy is performed under spinal anaesthesia or under general anaesthesia, depending on the patient's general health.

Retroperitoneal lymph node dissection

In some types of testicular cancer, retroperitoneal lymph node dissection (RPLND) is performed in addition to orchidectomy. RPLND can be performed through an open abdominal approach or laparoscopically. RPLND may make the patient infertile by damaging sympathetic nerve fibres involved in ejaculation. A unilateral (ipsilateral to the tumour) nerve-sparing RPLND below the level of the inferior mesenteric artery can minimize the risk of this complication. The patients are often young and otherwise healthy, with anxiety about their prognosis often over-riding any concerns about the impending procedure: general anaesthesia is recommended. Regional anaesthesia for postoperative pain relief can be considered after open procedures.

Brachytherapy for prostate cancer

High-dose-rate (HDR) brachytherapy for cancer of the prostate gland is often performed under spinal anaesthesia giving good intra- and postoperative pain relief (Clarke et al. 2009). Brachytherapy requires a dedicated facility which is often separate from the operating theatre department. Patients with prostate cancer have a high incidence of cardiovascular and respiratory disease. They are often treated under spinal anaesthesia, for example with bupivacaine in doses of 10–15 mg with or without an opioid such as sufentanil or fentanyl, but general anaesthesia with or without tracheal intubation is an alternative.

Open radical prostatectomy

Open radical prostatectomy may be indicated in patients with prostate cancer or benign prostatic hyperplasia. Perioperative blood loss and postoperative pain need to be actively managed. General endotracheal anaesthesia combined with regional analgesia is associated with reduced blood pressure and significantly less blood loss compared with general anaesthesia alone (Tikuisis et al. 2009) and a reduced risk of clinical cancer progression (Biki et al. 2008; Wuethrich et al. 2010). The regional anaesthetic component may be provided using an epidural catheter technique or using spinal anaesthesia with a mixture of local anaesthetic and morphine, for example with bupivacaine in doses of 7–15 mg and morphine 0.2–0.4 mg.

Videos of the surgical procedure can be viewed at http://www.youtube.com/watch?v=FU6v_m9SFG4&feature=related and http://www.youtube.com/watch?v=QvHpHEYCA10&feature=related.

Incontinence

The increasing number of radical prostatectomies has resulted in increasing numbers of patients suffering from postoperative stress incontinence. This has a major impact on the quality of life of these patients. Some 2–5% of patients with incontinence after radical prostatectomy have persistent incontinence a year after surgery, despite conservative measures. For these patients, one of several surgical options is recommended (Bauer et al. 2009):

AdVance sling

The functional retro-urethral sling (AdVance sling) is a non-obstructive, functional therapeutic approach (Bauer et al. 2009). The sling lifts the supporting structures of the urethral sphincter to regain their anatomical position. Surgery is often performed under general anaesthesia but spinal anaesthesia is an alternative when there are relative contraindications to general anaesthesia.

Pro-ACT system

The proACT system is an adjustable physical device (Bauer et al. 2009). Two balloons are placed bilaterally at the bladder neck. Titanium ports are placed in the scrotum for volume adjustment. Surgery is often performed under general anaesthesia but spinal anaesthesia is again an option. Postoperative readjustment can be performed under local anaesthesia.

Artificial urinary sphincter

The artificial urinary sphincter (AS-800) is the gold standard for the surgical treatment of male incontinence (Bauer et al. 2009). Complications include a high rate of infection and a high occlusion pressure on the urethra with a risk of urethral atrophy. Surgery is often performed under general anaesthesia but spinal anaesthesia is an option.

Transurethral resection of bladder tumour

Patients with superficial tumours of the bladder are treated with transurethral resection. This treatment may cure the patient but in some patients the tumour will recur and may require regular transurethral resection of bladder tumour for the rest of the patient's life. Most patients are elderly and therefore have a high incidence of cardiovascular and respiratory disease.

Perforation of the bladder is a severe complication that is likely to be recognized earlier in a conscious patient (see Box 62.2 for a list of symptoms).

Spinal anaesthesia is therefore a good option using, for example, bupivacaine 5–15 mg with or without an opioid such as sufentanil 5 μg or fentanyl 10 μg. Patient anxiety can be managed using intravenous conscious sedation. If spinal anaesthesia is contraindicated or refused by the patient, general anaesthesia using a facemask or laryngeal mask may be used.

If the tumour is close to the lateral bladder wall, the obturator nerve can be stimulated during the resection, leading to involuntary

Box 62.2 Symptoms of bladder perforation

- Abdominal pain
- Shoulder pain
- Hiccups
- Bradycardia
- Hypotension
- Nausea
- Restlessness
- Dyspnoea.

leg movements with a risk of perforation of the bladder. The risk of activating the obturator jerk reflex may be reduced by using general anaesthesia with neuromuscular block. An alternative is to block the obturator nerve with local anaesthetic (Kuo 2008 and Chapter 55).

A video of obturator nerve block can be viewed at http://www.youtube.com/watch?NR=1&v=oynJgzUjTb0&feature=endscreen. A video of the surgical procedure can be viewed at http://www.youtube.com/watch?v=TuRoPGmR0io.

Open radical cystectomy

Radical cystectomy with pelvic lymph node dissection remains the standard treatment for patients with cancer invading the bladder muscle (Melnyk et al. 2011). Patients undergoing radical cystectomy are usually more than 60 years of age and often present late in the disease process. In addition, surgery is frequently prolonged involving cystoprostectomy (males), and cystectomy with hysterectomy and bilateral salpingo- oophorectomy (females), followed by bilateral pelvic lymph node dissection. The surgical procedure is completed with formation of an ileal conduit or orthotopic bladder reconstruction. Morbidity and mortality in these patients are associated with co-morbidities such as ischaemic heart disease, hypertension, and renal failure, and smoking history, gender, and age. The high postoperative mortality is linked to the functional status of the patient with an average 60-day mortality of 6% increasing to 11% in patients older than 65 years (Pillai et al. 2011).

Despite improvements in surgical techniques, preoperative preparation, and perioperative care, radical cystectomy is still associated with significant morbidity and mortality. The incidence of perioperative complications has been reported as 27% with a mortality of 0.8% (Novotny et al. 2007; Stimson et al. 2010). The most frequent complications are ileus, wound dehiscence, deep venous thrombosis, and pelvic lymphocoele. Major complications include bleeding, which can necessitate surgical re-exploration, myocardial infarction, stroke, respiratory failure, pulmonary embolus, bowel leak, urinary leak, sepsis, wound dehiscence, bowel obstruction, and death.

Enhanced recovery after surgery (ERAS) protocols, are multimodal perioperative care pathways designed to achieve early recovery after surgical procedures by maintaining preoperative organ function and reducing the profound stress response after surgery (Kehlet 1997; Melnyk et al. 2011) (see also Chapter 61). The key elements of ERAS protocols include preoperative counselling, optimization of nutrition, standardized analgesic and anaesthetic regimens, and early mobilization. For radical cystectomy, early postoperative provision of artificial nutrients (enteral and parenteral) has shown beneficial effects, with a return of bowel movements within a median of 2 days, and reinstitution of regular diet by a median of 4 days (Maffezzini et al. 2008). Multimodal perioperative management combining thoracic epidural analgesia, forced mobilization, and oral nutrition improved convalescence after major urological procedures, including radical cystectomy (Brodner et al. 2001).

Reconstructive surgery, without cystectomy, is performed in patients with bladder pain syndrome/interstitial cystitis. The decision to embark on this major reconstructive surgery should be preceded by a thorough preoperative evaluation (Rossberger et al. 2007).

Anaesthesia

The bladder is close to a large venous plexus and bleeding can be extensive during the operation. The combination of general and epidural anaesthesia is associated with reduced blood loss (Ladjevic et al. 2007) and with better postoperative analgesia without increased complications (Ozyuvaci et al. 2005). The afferent nerves sensation of stretch and fullness of the bladder are parasympathetic, whereas pain, touch, and temperature sensation are carried by sympathetic nerves. Sympathetic nerves to the bladder and urethra originate from the 11th thoracic to the second lumbar segments. Parasympathetic nerves arise from the second to fourth sacral segments and are the main motor supply to the bladder and far outnumber sympathetic fibres in the bladder. Effective epidural analgesia can therefore be provided by a catheter sited in the lower thoracic region.

The combination of general anaesthesia, epidural anaesthesia, potential for large blood loss, and a prolonged procedure in elderly patients with cardiovascular compromise necessitates advanced monitoring. An arterial catheter for continuous blood pressure measurement and a means of monitoring cardiac output using a dynamic non-invasive system are recommended. Vasoconstrictor therapy may be required to counteract excessive vasodilation. Perioperative fluid optimization has been associated with improvements in markers of postoperative outcome (Pillai et al. 2011).

For the authors' approach to anaesthesia for open radical cystectomy, see Box 62.3. A video of the surgical procedure may be viewed at http://www.youtube.com/watch?v=0nogrQQ10po&feature=related.

Nephrectomy

The kidneys have several functions, including excretion, regulation of electrolyte and water balance, maintenance of acid–base

Box 62.3 Authors' approach to anaesthesia for open radical cystectomy

- Heating mattress or blanket
- Thoracic epidural analgesia with indwelling catheter at T9–11 for intra-operative or postoperative pain relief, or both
- General anaesthesia. Induction with propofol/thiopental and maintenance with sevoflurane/desflurane or with total intravenous anaesthesia
- Neuromuscular block for tracheal intubation and during the operation as needed
- Arterial catheter to monitor the arterial blood pressure and arterial blood gases
- Large-bore intravenous access
- Noradrenaline if needed to counteract the vasodilator effect from the general and epidural anaesthesia
- Antibiotics according to local protocols
- Postoperative analgesia with an epidural infusion of ropivacaine 2 mg ml^{-1} in combination with sufentanil 0.5 μg ml^{-1} at an infusion rate of 4–10 ml h^{-1}
- Antithrombotic therapy.

homeostasis, and regulation of blood pressure. The kidneys produce hormones including calcitriol, erythropoietin, and renin. The kidneys are under the influence of antidiuretic hormone (ADH) and atrial natriuretic peptide. Impaired renal function can range from mild with no functional consequences to severe requiring dialysis.

The kidneys receive their blood supply through the renal arteries, which branch directly from the abdominal aorta. The kidneys receive approximately 20% of the cardiac output and so bleeding can be extensive during nephrectomy.

Cancer of the kidney is often treated with nephrectomy although partial resection is used where possible (Nabi et al. 2010). About 10–20% of renal tumours extend into the renal vein and the inferior vena cava (IVC) (Wagner et al. 2009). The tumour may partially or fully occlude the IVC. These patients are at risk of acute pulmonary embolization from tumour fragments during surgery. The full extent of the lesion must be defined preoperatively and further treatment planned. In rare cases a vena cava filter can be inserted.

Renal operations and pyeloplasties may be conducted in a near-full lateral position with some extension at the waist for a retroperitoneal approach or in the supine position with the affected side slightly elevated for a transabdominal approach.

Anaesthesia

The general principles of anaesthesia for open nephrectomy are largely similar to those for open radical cystectomy although on average, nephrectomy patients are younger and encompass a wide range of ASA physical status. Again it is useful to combine epidural with general anaesthesia to reduce blood loss and to optimize postoperative analgesia. Pain from the kidney and ureter is referred mainly to the somatic distribution of the 10th thoracic to the second lumbar segments. Effective neural block of these segments is necessary to provide adequate analgesia or anaesthesia. Sympathetic pre-ganglionic nerves originate from the eighth thoracic to the first lumbar spinal segments. From here, postganglionic fibres travel to the kidney via the autonomic plexus surrounding the renal artery. Parasympathetic fibres originate from the vagus nerve and travel with the sympathetic fibres to the autonomic plexus along the renal artery. It is interesting to note that the kidneys function well even without this innervation as evidenced by the successful function of transplanted kidneys (Wein and Kavoussi 2011).

For the authors' approach to anaesthesia for open nephrectomy, see Box 62.4.

Box 62.4 Authors' approach to anaesthesia for open nephrectomy

- Heating mattress or blanket
- Thoracic epidural analgesia with indwelling catheter at T7–11 for intra-operative and/or postoperative pain relief
- General anaesthesia. Induction with propofol/thiopental and maintenance with sevoflurane/desflurane or with total intravenous anaesthesia
- Neuromuscular block for tracheal intubation and during the operation as needed
- Arterial catheter to monitor the arterial blood pressure and arterial blood gases
- Large-bore intravenous access
- Noradrenaline if needed to counteract the vasodilator effect from the general and epidural anaesthesia
- Antibiotics according to local protocols
- Postoperative analgesia with an epidural infusion of ropivacaine 2 mg ml^{-1} in combination with sufentanil 0.5 μg ml^{-1} at an infusion rate of 4–10 ml h^{-1}
- Antithrombotic therapy.

Autonomic dysreflexia

Autonomic dysreflexia is also known as autonomic hyperreflexia and occurs most often in tetraplegic patients with a spinal cord injury above T6. These patients will often need urological surgery because of various voiding problems. Acute autonomic dysreflexia is a reaction of the autonomic nervous system to stimulation. It is associated with a sudden, uncontrolled sympathetic response, triggered by stimuli below a spinal cord injury (see Box 62.5 for clinical features). It is a potentially life-threatening condition which can be considered a medical emergency requiring immediate attention. For example, a blocked urethral catheter can induce life-threatening complications (Hagen et al. 2011). It can start to occur after the initial phase of spinal shock has passed, when the spinal reflexes return, and can occur throughout the patient's lifespan. It is believed that the afferent stimuli trigger and maintain an increase in blood pressure via a sympathetically mediated vasoconstriction in muscle, skin, and splanchnic vascular beds. The most common causes are irritation of the bladder, bowel, or skin.

Box 62.5 Clinical features of autonomic dysreflexia

- Severe paroxysmal hypertension
- Severe pounding headache
- Profuse sweating
- Flushing of the skin above the level of lesion
- Goose bumps
- Apprehension and fear
- Nasal stuffiness
- Bradyarrhythmias
- Hypotension
- Cognitive impairment
- Cerebral haemorrhage
- Death.

If the patient, when the bladder is full, experiences headache, profuse sweating, and flushing, the patient is at risk of developing severe autonomic dysreflexia during urological surgery. These procedures should then be performed under spinal anaesthesia with careful observation. Some tetraplegic patients may wish to undergo urological procedures without anaesthesia, but they will be at risk of developing autonomic dysreflexia during cystoscopy or vesical lithotripsy (Vaidyanathan et al. 2012a).

Box 62.6 Treatment of autonomic dysreflexia

- Removal of the triggering stimuli
- Catheterization of the bladder
- Relief of a blocked urinary catheter
- Hypertension is treated with rapidly acting vasodilators
- Bradycardia is treated with anticholinergic drugs
- Autonomic dysreflexia is abolished temporarily by spinal and epidural anaesthesia. General anaesthesia must be deep enough to prevent reactions from taking place. The concentration of sevoflurane required to block autonomic hyperreflexia is high (Yoo et al. 2008).

Treatment of autonomic dysreflexia (see Box 62.6) involves immediate identification and removal of the triggering stimuli (Vaidyanathan et al. 2012b) and administration of antihypertensives with short onset time such as nitrates, nifedipine, sodium nitroprusside, hydralazine, clonidine, or propranolol (Rabchevsky and Kitzman 2011). The rectum should be cleared of impacted stool. If the noxious precipitating trigger cannot be identified, drug treatment will be needed. Bradycardia is likely to be most profound in patients younger than 50 years (Huang et al. 2011).

Declaration of interest

None declared.

References

Andersson L, Wallin CJ, Sollevi A, Odeberg-Wernerman S. Pneumoperitoneum in healthy humans does not affect central blood volume or cardiac output. *Acta Anaesthesiol Scand* 1999; **43**: 809–14

Andersson L, Lindberg G, Bringman S, *et al.* Pneumoperitoneum versus abdominal wall lift: effects on central haemodynamics and intrathoracic pressure during laparoscopic cholecystectomy. *Acta Anaesthesiol Scand* 2003; **47**: 838–46

Andersson L, Bååth M, Thörne A, Odeberg-Wernerman S. Effect of carbon dioxide pneumoperitoneum on development of atelectasis during anesthesia, examined by spiral computed tomography. *Anesthesiology* 2005a; **102**: 293–9

Andersson L, Lagerstrand L, Thörne A, *et al.* Effect of CO2 pneumoperitoneum on ventilation-perfusion relationships during laparoscopic cholecystectomy. *Acta Anaesthesiol Scand* 2005b; **46**: 552–60

Arsalani-Zadeh R, Ullah S, Khan S, MacFie J. Oxidative stress in laparoscopic versus open abdominal surgery: a systematic review. *J Surg Res* 2011; **169**: e59–68

Awad H, Santilli S, Ohr M, *et al.* The effects of steep Trendelenburg positioning on intra-ocular pressure during robotic radical prostatectomy. *Anesth Analg* 2009; **109**: 473–8

Basar H, Yilmaz E, Ozcan S, *et al.* Four analgesic techniques for shockwave lithotripsy: eutectic mixture local anesthetic is a good alternative. *J Endourol* 2003; **1**: 3–6

Bauer RM, Bastian PJ, Gozzi C, Stief CG. Postprostatectomy incontinence: all about diagnosis and management. *Eur Urol* 2009; **55**: 322–33

Bell MC, Torgerson J, Seshadri-Kreaden U, Suttle AW, Hunt S. Comparison of outcomes and cost for endometrial cancer staging via traditional laparotomy, standard laparoscopy and robotic techniques. *Gyn Oncol* 2008; **11**: 407–11

Biki B, Mascha E, Moriarty DC, *et al.* Anesthetic technique for radical prostatectomy surgery affects cancer recurrence: a retrospective analysis. *Anesthesiology* 2008; **109**: 180–7

Brodner G, Van Aken H, Hertle L, *et al.* Multimodal peri-operative management—combining thoracic epidural analgesia, forced mobilization, and oral nutrition—reduces hormonal and metabolic stress and improves convalescence after major urologic surgery. *Anesth Analg* 2001; **92**: 1594–600

Cha E, Wiklund NP, Scherr DS. Recent advances in robot-assisted radical cystectomy. *Curr Opin Urol* 2011; **2**: 65–70

Challacombe BJ, Bochner BH, Dasgupta P, *et al.* The role of laparoscopic and robotic cystectomy in the management of muscle-invasive bladder cancer with special emphasis on control and complications. *Eur Urol* 2011; **60**: 767–5

Choi SH, Lee SJ, Rha KH, Shin SK, Oh YJ. The effect of pneumoperitoneum and Trendelenburg position on acute cerebral blood flow-carbon dioxide reactivity under sevoflurane anaesthesia. *Anaesthesia* 2008; **63**: 1314–8

Clarke HA, Tarshis J, Lam-McCulloch J, Kay J. Saddle block analgesia for high-dose-rate brachytherapy: a prospective study. *Brachytherapy* 2009; **8**: 335–8

Cury J, Coelho RF, Bruschini H, Srougi M. Is the ability to perform transurethral resection of the prostate influenced by the surgeon's previous experience? *Clinics (San Paulo)* 2008; **63**: 315–20

D'Alonzo RC, Gan TJ, Moul JW, *et al.* A retrospective comparison of anesthetic management of robot-assisted laparoscopic radical prostatectomy versus radical retropubic prostatectomy. *J Clin Anesth* 2009; **21**: 322–8

Dindo D, Demartines N, Clavien PA. Classification of surgical complications: a new proposal with evaluation in a cohort of 6336 patients and results of a survey. *Ann Surg* 2004; **240**: 205–13

European Study Group on Diastolic Heart Failure. Working group report. How to diagnose diastolic heart failure. *Eur Heart J* 1998; **19**: 990–1003

Fagerstrom T, Nyman CR, Hahn RG. Bipolar transurethral resection of the prostate causes less bleeding than monopolar technique: a single-centre randomized trial of 202 patients. *BJU Int* 2009; **105**: 1560–4

Fagerstrom T, Nyman CR, Hahn RG. Complications and clinical outcome 18 months after bipolar and monopolar transurethral resection of the prostate. *J Endourol* 2011; **25**: 1043–9

Falabella A, Moore-Jeffries E, Sullivan MJ, Nelson R, Lew M. Cardiac function during steep Trendelenburg position and CO_2 pneumoperitoneum for robotic-assisted prostatectomy: a transoesophageal Doppler probe study. *Int J Med Robotics and Comput Assist Surg* 2007; **3**: 312–5

Gannedahl P, Odeberg S, Brodin LA, Sollevi A. Effects of posture and pneumoperitoneum during anaesthesia on the indices of left ventricular filling. *Acta Anaesthesiol Scand* 1996; **40**: 160–6

Gravenstein D. Extracorporeal shock wave lithotripsy and percutaneous nephrolithotomy. *Anesthesiol Clin North Am* 2000; **18**: 953–71

Hagen EM, Faerestrand S, Hoff JM, Rekand T, Gronning M. Cardiovascular and urological dysfunction in spinal cord injury. *Acta Neurol Scand* 2011; Suppl, 71–8

Hahn RG. Fluid absorption in endoscopic surgery. *Br J Anaesth* 2006; **96**: 8–20

Hawary A, Mukhtar K, Sinclair A, Pearce I. Transurethral resection of the prostate syndrome: almost gone but not forgotten. *J Endourol* 2009; **23**: 2013–20

Hong JY, Lee SJ, Rha KH, *et al.* Effects of thoracic epidural analgesia combined with general anesthesia on intraoperative ventilation/oxygenation and postoperative pulmonary complications in robot-assisted laparoscopic radical prostatectomy. *J Endourol* 2009; **23**: 843–9

Huang YH, Bih LI, Liao JM, *et al.* Autonomic dysreflexia during urodynamic examinations in patients with suprasacral spinal cord injury. *Arch Phys Med Rehabil* 2011; **92**: 1450–4

Huser AS, Müller D, Brunkhorst V, *et al.* Simulated life-threatening emergency during robot-assisted surgery. *J Endourol* 2014; **28**: 717–21

Kalmar AF, Dewaele F, Foubert L, *et al.* Cerebral haemodynamic physiology during steep Trendelenburg position and CO2 pneumoperitoneum. *Br J Anaesth* 2012; **108**: 478–84

Kehlet H. Multimodal approach to control postoperative pathophysiology and rehabilitation. *Br J Anaesth* 1997; **78**: 606–17

Kuo JY. Prevention of obturator jerk during transurethral resection of bladder tumor. *Techn Urol* 2008; **19**: 27–31

Ladjevic N, Likic-Ladjevic I, Dzamic Z, Acimovic M, Dragicevic D, Durutovic O. Combined general and epidural anaesthesia versus general anaesthesia for radical cystectomy. *Acta Chir Lugosi* 2007; **54**: 89–91

Lam A, Kaufman Y, Khong SY, Liew A, Ford S, Condous G. Dealing with complications in laparoscopy. *Best Pract Res Clin Obstet Gynaecol* 2009; **23**: 631–46

Lee J-R, Lee PB, Do SH, *et al.* The effect of gynaecological laparoscopic surgery on cerebral oxygenation. *J Int Med Res* 2006; **34**: 531–6

Lestar M, Gunnarsson L, Lagerstrand L, Wiklund P, Odeberg-Wernerman S. Hemodynamic perturbations during robot-assisted radical prostatectomy in 45° Trendelenburg position. *Anesth Analg* 2011; **113**: 1069–75

Liu H, Lu D, Wang L, Shi G, Song H, Clarke J. Robotic surgery for benign gynaecological disease. *Cochrane Database Syst Rev* 2012; **2**: CD008978

Lu D, Liu Z, Shi G, Liu D, Zhou X. Robotic assisted surgery for gynaecological cancer. *Cochrane Database Syst Rev* 2012; **1**: CD008640

Luo C-F, Tsai YF, Chang CH, Wu CT, Yu HP. Increased oxidative stress and gut ischemia caused by prolonged pneumoperitoneum in patients undergoing robot-assisted laparoscopic radical prostatectomy. *Acta Anaesthesiol Taiwanica* 2011; **49**: 46–9

Maffezzini M, Campodonico F, Canepa G, Gerbi G, Parodi D. Current perioperative management of radical cystectomy with intestinal urinary reconstruction for muscle-invasive bladder cancer and reduction of incidence of postoperative ileus. *Surg Oncol* 2008; **17**: 41–8

Magrina JF, Zanagnolo VL. Robot surgery for cervical cancer. *Yonsei Med J* 2008; **49**: 879–85

Meininger D, Byhahn C, Bueck M, *et al.* Effects of prolonged pneumoperitoneum on hemodynamics and acid-base balance during totally endoscopic robot-assisted radical prostatectomies. *World J Surg* 2002; **26**: 1423–7

Meininger D, Byhahn C, Mierdl S, Westphal K, Zwissler B. Positive end-expiratory pressure improves arterial oxygenation during prolonged pneumoperitoneum. *Acta Anaesthesiol Scand.* 2005; **49**: 778–83

Meininger D, Byhahn C, Wolfram M, Mierdl S, Kessler P, Westphal K. Prolonged intraperitoneal versus extraperitoneal insufflations of carbon dioxide in patients undergoing totally endoscopic robot-assisted radical prostatectomy. *Surg Endosc* 2004; **18**: 829–33

Meininger D, Westphal K, Bremerich DH, *et al.* Effects of posture and prolonged pneumoperitoneum on hemodynamic parameters during laparoscopy. *World J Surg* 2008; **32**: 1400–5

Meininger D, Zwissler B, Byhahn C, Probst M, Westphal K, Bremerich DH. Impact of overweight and pneumoperitoneum on hemodynamics and oxygenation during prolonged laparoscopic surgery. *World J Surg* 2006; **30**: 520–6

Melnyk M, Casey RG, Black P, Koupparis AJ. Enhanced recovery after surgery (ERAS) protocols: time to change practice? *Can Urol Assoc J* 2011; **5**: 342–8

Michielsen DP, Coomans D, Braeckman JG, Umbrain V. Bipolar transurethral resection in saline: the solution to avoid hyponatraemia and transurethral resection syndrome. *Scand J Urol Nephrol* 2010; **4**: 228–35

Michielsen DP, Coomans D, Peeters I, Braeckman JG. Conventional monopolar resection or bipolar resection in saline for the management of large (> 60 g) benign prostatic hyperplasia: an evaluation of morbidity. *Min Invasive Ther Allied Technol* 2010; **19**: 207–13

Nabi G, Cleves A, Shelley M. Surgical management of localised renal cell carcinoma. *Cochrane Database Syst Rev* 2010; **3**: CD006579.

Nieminen M, Böhm M, Cowie MR, *et al.* Executive summary of the guidelines on the diagnosis and treatment of acute heart failure. The Task Force on Acute Heart Failure of the European Society of Cardiology. *Eur Heart J* 2005; **26**: 384–416

Novotny V, Hakenberg OW, Wiessner D, *et al.* Peri-operative complications of radical cystectomy in a contemporary series. *Eur Urol* 2007; **51**: 397–401

Odeberg S, Ljungqvist O, Svenberg T, *et al.* Haemodynamic effects of pneumoperitoneum and the influence of posture during anaesthesia for laparoscopic surgery. *Acta Anaesthesiol Scand* 1994; **38**: 276–83

Odeberg S, Sollevi A. Pneumoperitoneum for laparoscopic surgery does not increase venous admixture. *Eur J Anaesthesiol* 1995; **12**: 541–8

Odeberg S, Ljungqvist O, Sollevi A. Pneumoperitoneum for laparoscopic cholecystectomy is not associated with compromised splanchnic circulation. *Eur J Surg* 1998; **164**: 843–8

Ost MC, Tan BJ, Lee BR. Urological laparoscopy: basic physiological considerations and immunological consequences. *J Urol* 2005; **174**: 1183–8

Ozyuvaci E, Altan A, Karadeniz T, *et al.* General anesthesia versus epidural and general anesthesia in radical cystectomy. *Urol Int* 2005; **74**: 62–7

Paraiso MF, Jelovsek JE, Frick A, Chen CC, Barber MD. Laparoscopic compared with robotic sacrocolpopexy for vaginal prolapse: a randomized controlled trial. *Obstet Gynecol* 2011; **118**: 1005–13

Park EY, Koo BN, Min KT, Nam SH. The effect of pneumoperitoneum in the steep Trendelenburg position on cerebral oxygenation. *Acta Anaesthesiol Scand* 2009; **53**: 895–9

Park H-P, Hwang JW, Kim YB, *et al.* Effect of pre-emptive alveolar recruitment strategy before pneumoperitoneum on arterial oxygenation during laparoscopic hysterectomy. *Anaesth Intensive Care* 2009; **37**: 593–7

Pillai P, McEleavy I, Gaughan M, *et al.* A double-blind randomized controlled clinical trial to assess the effect of Doppler optimized intra-operative fluid management on outcome following radical cystectomy. *J Urol* 2011; **186**: 2201–6

Rabchevsky AG, Kitzman PH. Latest approaches for treatment of spasticity and autonomic dysrefexia in chronic spinal cord injury. *Neurotherapeutics* 2011; **8**: 274–82

Rosenthal RJ, Hiatt JR, Phillips EH, *et al.* Intracranial pressure. Effects of pneumoperitoneum in large-animal model. *Surg Endosc* 1997; **11**: 376–80

Rossberger J, Fall M, Jonsson O, Peeker R. Long-term results of reconstructive surgery in patients with pain syndrome/interstitial cystitis: subtyping is imperative. *Urology* 2007; **70**: 638–42

Russo A, Marana E, Viviani D, *et al.* Diastolic function: the influence of pneumoperitoneum and Trendelenburg positioning during laparoscopic hysterectomy. *Eur J Anaesthesiol* 2009; **26**: 923–7

Sarlos D, Kots LV, Stevenovic N. Robotic hysterectomy versus conventional laparoscopic hysterectomy: Costs and preliminary results of a randomized controlled trial. *Arch Gynecol Obstet* 2010; **282**(Suppl): 11–2

Smith AL, Pareja R, Ramirez PT. Robot radical hysterectomy. A literature review. *Minerva Ginecol* 2009; **61**: 339–46

Stimson CJ, Chang SS, Barocas DA, *et al.* Early and late peri-operative outcomes following radical cystectomy: 90-day readmissions, morbidity and mortality in a contemporary series. *J Urol* 2010; **184**: 1296–300

Sukumar S, Rogers CG. Robot partial nephrectomy: surgical technique. *BJU Int* 2011; **108**: 942–7

Tewari A, Sooriakumaran P, Bloch DA, Seshadri-Kreaden U, Hebert AE, Wiklund P. Positive surgical margin and perioperative complication rates of primary surgical treatments for prostate cancer: a systematic review and meta-analysis comparing retropubic, laparoscopic and robotic prostatectomy. *Eur Urol* 2012; **62**: 1–15

Ungbhakorn P, Kongchareonsombat W, Leenanupan C, *et al.* Comparative outcomes of open nephrectomy, hand-assisted laparoscopic nephrectomy, and full laparoscopic nephrectomy for living donors. *Transplant Proc* 2012; **44**: 22–5

Tikuisis R, Miliauskas P, Samalavicius NE, Zurauskas A, Sruogis A. Epidural and general anesthesia versus general anesthesia in radical prostatectomy. *Medicina* 2009; **45**: 772–7

Vaidyanathan S, Soni B, Oo T, Hughes P, Singh G, Pulya K. Autonomic dysreflexia in a tetraplegic patient due to a blocked urethral catheter: spinal cord injury patients with lesions above T-6 require prompt treatment of an obstructed urinary catheter to prevent life-threatening complications of autonomic dysreflexia. *Int J Emerg Med* 2012; **5**:6

Vaidyanathan S, Soni B, Selmi F, *et al.* Are urological procedures in tetraplegic patients safely performed without anesthesia? A report of three cases. *Patient Saf Surg* 2012; **6**: 3

Wagner B, Patard JJ, Méjean A, *et al.* Prognostic value of renal vein and inferior vena cava involvement in renal cell carcinoma. *Eur Urol* 2009; **55**: 452–60

Weber ED, Colyer MH, Lesser RL, Subramanian PS. Posterior ischemic optic neuropathy after minimally invasive prostatectomy. *J Neuroophtalmol* 2007; **27**: 285–7

Wein AJ, Kavoussi LR (eds). *Campbell-Walsh Urology*, 10th Edn. Philadelphia, PA: W.B. Saunders, 2011

Weinberg L, Rao S, Escobar PF. Robotic surgery in gynecology: an updated systematic review. *Obstet Gynecol Int* 2011; 2011: 852061

Weingram J, Sosa RE, Stein B, *et al.* Subcutaneous emphysema (SCE) during laparoscopic pelvic lymph node dissection (LPLND). *Anesth Analg* 2010; **76**: S460

Wuethrich PY, Hsu Schmitz SF, Kessler TM, *et al.* Potential influence of the anesthetic technique used during open radical prostatectomy on prostate cancer-related outcome: a retrospective study. *Anesthesiology* 2010; **113**: 570–6

Yilmaz E, Batislam E, Basar MM, Tuglu D, Ozcan S, Basar H. Effectiveness of eutectic mixture of local anesthetic cream and occlusive dressing with low dosage of fentanyl for pain control during shockwave lithotripsy. *J Endourol* 2005; **5**: 589–94

Yoo KY, Jeong CW, Kim SJ, *et al.* Sevoflurane concentrations required to block autonomic hyperreflexia during transurethral litholapaxy in patients with complete spinal cord injury. *Anesthesiology* 2008; **108**: 858–63

CHAPTER 63

Anaesthesia for orthopaedic and trauma surgery

Alex Sell, Paul Bhalla, and Sanjay Bajaj

Introduction

This chapter discusses surgery involving the skeletal system with the exception of the skull: it considers the patient population, specifically the chronic diseases that require orthopaedic services; general principles of anaesthesia for orthopaedic and trauma surgery; and then looks at specific surgical procedures and their anaesthetic considerations.

The patient population

The general population is ageing, so it comes as no surprise that the same is also true of the surgical population; along with this comes these patients' co-morbidities and polypharmacy. Although trauma conjures up images of high-speed impacts, one of the most common injuries is a fractured neck of femur resulting from simple slips, trips, and falls.

Rheumatoid arthritis

Rheumatoid arthritis affects between 1% and 3% of the population worldwide, with a peak prevalence between 30 and 50 years of age. Females are affected three times more frequently than males; other risk factors include a family history. There is a very strong association with the human leucocyte antigen (HLA)-DR4 subtype but the exact cause remains unidentified and is likely to be multifactorial. Rheumatoid arthritis is a chronic symmetrical polyarthritis with extra-articular organ involvement. The underlying pathology is inflammatory infiltration of the synovium, causing a proliferation of the synovium; this produces a pannus, which destroys the articular cartilage and subchondral bone. The typical manifestation is of insidious onset of pain, stiffness, and swelling in the small joints of the hands and feet; the pattern of joint involvement is typically one of a proximal progression with involvement of wrists, ankles, elbows, knees, shoulders, and cervical spine. Early features include swelling of joints, which leads to limitation of movement and wasting of muscles around the affected joints. Later features are of joint deformity, subluxation, and instability; this is the point at which patients present to orthopaedic surgeons. See Table 63.1.

When a patient with rheumatoid arthritis presents for orthopaedic surgery, aside from the specific considerations of the surgery, one has to take into account the other joints involved and how this will affect the positioning of the patient. The joint that deserves most attention is the atlantoaxial joint (Fig. 63.1). Problems with this joint can lead to instability in approximately 25% of rheumatoid patients and acute subluxation can result in compression of the cervical cord and the vertebral arteries with resultant neurological symptoms: in extreme cases, compression of the vertebral arteries can result in death.

Table 63.1 The extra-articular manifestations of rheumatoid arthritis

Systemic	Fever, fatigue, weight loss
Pulmonary	Pleural effusion, fibrosing alveolitis, rheumatoid nodules, small airways disease, costochondral disease, rheumatoid pneumoconiosis (Caplan's syndrome)
Cardiac	Pericarditis, pericardial effusion, amyloid disease, increased risk of ischaemic heart disease, diastolic heart failure
Renal	Amyloid disease, analgesic nephropathy
Neurological	Atlantoaxial subluxation, carpal tunnel syndrome, cord compression, polyneuropathy
Ocular	Secondary Sjögren's syndrome, scleritis
Haematological	Anaemia of chronic disease, iron deficiency secondary to NSAID-related gastrointestinal blood loss, haemolysis, thrombocytosis, drug-induced myelosuppression
Reticuloendothelial	Lymphadenopathy, Felty's syndrome (rheumatoid arthritis, splenomegaly, neutropenia)
Vascular	Vasculitis, leg ulcers, nail fold infarcts, gangrene of fingers and toes
Hepatic	Fibrosis secondary to drug therapy, amyloid disease, hypoalbuminaemia

Two other joints that can be affected that are of importance to anaesthetists are the temporomandibular and cricoarytenoid joints. Temporomandibular joint involvement can lead to a limitation in mouth opening, which can result in difficulty with direct laryngoscopy. Cricoarytenoid involvement is associated with dyspnoea, hoarseness, or other changes in the character of the voice, while stridor with airway obstruction may present during anaesthesia or postoperatively.

Rheumatoid patients will also be taking multiple medications: those that provide symptom control, those that modify and slow down disease progression, and also medications associated with extra-articular manifestations. It is important to be aware of the effects and side-effects of these medications.

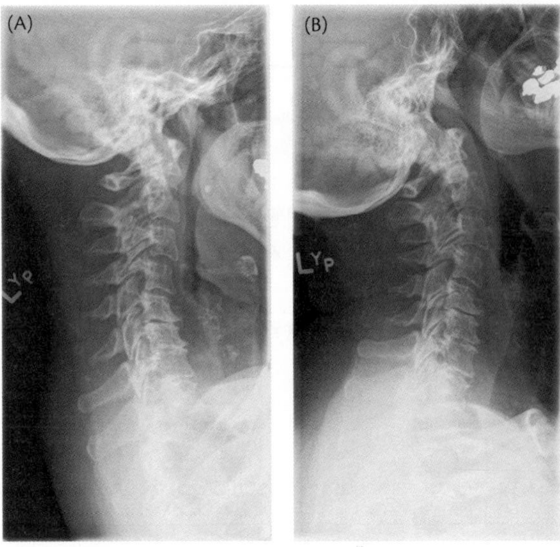

Figure 63.1 Flexion view (A) shows an 8.4 mm anterior translation of C1 in relationship to the odontoid peg on flexion as compared with the extension view (B).

Osteoarthritis

Osteoarthritis is a very common condition with approximately 50% of the population over the age of 60 having radiographic changes, although symptoms are present only in a proportion of these individuals. Females are twice as likely to be affected as males and there is a lower prevalence in the black, compared with the white, population. The underlying pathology is loss of articular cartilage, with the exposed subchondral bone becoming sclerotic, leading to increased vascularity and cyst formation. As the body attempts to repair the defect in the cartilage, cartilaginous growths at the joint margins become calcified to form osteophytes. The pathogenesis of primary osteoarthritis is thought to involve the production of metalloproteinases, which degrade collagen and proteoglycans. Secondary osteoarthritis occurs in abnormal joints, and is either congenital or traumatic.

Ankylosing spondylitis

Ankylosing spondylitis is one of the seronegative spondyloarthritides, which describes a group of arthritides that affect the spine and peripheral joints and are linked to HLA-B27. The synovitis is histologically similar to rheumatoid arthritis but is negative for production of rheumatoid factor and hence seronegative. The reason for the association with HLA-B27 is unknown but these conditions do tend to cluster in families. The other seronegative spondyloarthritides include psoriatic arthritis, reactive arthritis, and enteropathic arthritis. Ankylosing spondylitis typically affects young adults with increasing morning stiffness and pain in the lower back; although it affects males as commonly as females the condition is often more severe in males. In advanced cases, the patient will adopt a typical posture with loss of lumbar lordosis, exaggerated thoracic kyphosis, and a compensatory hyperextension of the neck. They will also develop fixed flexion of the hips and a compensatory flexion of the knees. Extra-articular features include iritis in about 25% of patients and, less commonly, apical lung fibrosis, aortic regurgitation, and cardiac conduction defects. The mainstay of treatment is physiotherapy to maintain posture and mobility as the disease-modifying drugs used in rheumatoid arthritis do not alter the progression of the spinal disease: more recently, anti-tumour necrosis factor (TNF) therapy has shown positive results in treating ankylosing spondylitis. The majority of patients will lead a normal life and be able to remain at work. At the severe end of the spectrum, the spine becomes completely fused; the fixed kyphosis of cervical and thoracic spine leads to impaired ventilation; and the spine becomes brittle and is at risk of fracture, which can cause cord compression. It is for one of these complications that patients with ankylosing spondylitis most commonly present for surgery. As indicated earlier, the patient's posture will lead to difficult intubating conditions, they will have restrictive lung disease, and, rarely, associated cardiac disease. They are also challenging to position on the operating table due to the fused spine; in extreme cases, a preoperative visit may involve assessment of patient positioning.

Medication

This section is not an exhaustive account of drug therapies that are commonly found when assessing orthopaedic patients, but it concentrates on the medications taken by the patient populations discussed in the previous section.

Non-steroidal anti-inflammatory drugs

Non-steroidal anti-inflammatory drugs (NSAIDs) are found almost ubiquitously in patients presenting for orthopaedic surgery unless they have suffered side-effects and are unable to take them due to co-morbid disease or allergy. The mechanism of action is that of non-selective reversible blockade of the cyclooxygenase (COX) enzyme and this prevents production of prostaglandins and thromboxanes from membrane phospholipids. Side-effects include gastric irritation, which can lead to erosions and substantial gastrointestinal blood loss. NSAIDs will cause bronchospasm in a significant minority of asthmatics; this is associated with chronic rhinitis or nasal polyps. Prostaglandins PGE_2 and PGI_2 produced in the kidney are required for vasodilation of the renal vasculature and maintaining the balance with renin, angiotensin, and noradrenaline (norepinephrine). In circumstances where the vasoconstrictor concentration is high and renal blood flow is low, inhibition of the renal prostaglandins may lead to acute kidney injury. Analgesic nephropathy is distinct from the acute kidney injury seen with NSAIDs. The underlying cause is poorly understood but chronic use of NSAIDs is associated with renal papillary necrosis leading to chronic interstitial nephritis and chronic renal failure. Chronic NSAID use can also lead to hepatotoxicity with an increase in serum transaminases; this can also be seen after a short course used in the acute setting. While aspirin is now rarely used for its analgesic properties, because it irreversibly binds to COX and is most commonly used for its anti-platelet action, the other non-selective NSAIDs were believed to be guilty by association; indeed, the majority of spinal surgeons at the authors' institution ask for NSAIDs not to be prescribed in the immediate postoperative period. Recently it has become evident that the pharmacology of NSAIDs is not as simple as this, probably highlighted by the development of COX-2 blocking drugs. COX exists in two forms, the constitutive form COX-1 and the inducible form COX-2. It was believed that COX-2 was mainly responsible for the production of inflammatory prostaglandins and COX-1 was directly involved in the production of prostaglandins necessary for renal blood flow and the gastric mucosal barrier. COX-2 is therefore an ideal target for pharmacological inhibition. Unfortunately, patients were shown to have an increased risk of myocardial infarction and stroke. This then led to non-selective NSAIDs being investigated and a meta-analysis (Trelle et al. 2011) showed the only NSAID that did not appear to cause an increase in relative risk for a cardiovascular event is naproxen. But what must be remembered is that postoperative pain carries with it its own morbidity and that alternative analgesics are not free of side-effects or risk.

Corticosteroids

As a result of the serious nature of side-effects observed with long-term corticosteroid therapy, it is less common to find patients on high-dose steroids for inflammatory disease control; this is also as a result of the development of newer biological therapies. Patients who are taking prednisolone need to be assessed for hypothalamic–pituitary axis suppression: those who are taking less than 10 mg a day are presumed to have a normal hypothalamic–pituitary axis and those who take 10 mg or more a day will require perioperative supplementation; the amount and duration is dependent on the nature of surgery, and up-to-date guidance is found in the British National Formulary. It is also worth remembering that the hypothalamic–pituitary axis is presumed to be suppressed for up to 3 months on cessation of steroid therapy.

Disease-modifying antirheumatoid drugs

Unlike analgesics, which provide symptomatic treatment, disease-modifying antirheumatoid drugs (DMARDs) target the underlying disease and reduce the disease load. First-line treatment is methotrexate, an antimetabolite, which first gained popularity in cancer chemotherapy. Methotrexate works by inhibiting dihydrofolate reductase, an enzyme required in the pathway for purine synthesis. Second-line DMARDs include hydroxychloroquine, leflunomide, ciclosporin, azathioprine, sulfasalazine, anakinra, and gold salts. While all of these have specific side-effects related to their mechanism of action, they are all capable of bone marrow suppression and therefore patients are at increased risk of infection.

Biological agents

Biological agents are now commonly prescribed to patients whose disease is resistant to DMARDs or in combination, there is also increasing use with other inflammatory diseases such as ankylosing spondylitis and inflammatory bowel disease. First-line biological agents target TNFα; as with DMARDs, they increase the risk of infection, particularly with opportunistic infections and re-activation of tuberculosis. Perioperatively, the obvious question is do DMARDs or biological agents increase the risk of surgical site infection? Unfortunately the evidence is inconclusive. Although a large retrospective observational study (den Broeder et al. 2007) from the Netherlands showed that the continuation of anti-TNF was not significantly associated with an increase in surgical site infection rates, it was an observational study and therefore not powered to answer the question. In practice, this is a question for the patient, the rheumatologist, and the surgeon looking after the patient; while the surgical site infection rate may or may not be increased, stopping therapy will put the patient at risk of a disease flare-up.

Surgical considerations

Positioning

Orthopaedic surgery involves many different positions to enable optimal access: lateral for hip surgery; 'beach chair' for shoulder surgery; and prone for posterior spinal surgery, and posterior access to the leg. Compared with the supine position, the other positions each carry extra potential risks that need to be balanced with the need for surgical access. While many orthopaedic procedures can be performed on conscious patients, for the purpose of this section we will assume the patient is unconscious and therefore the positioning of the patient is wholly the responsibility of the anaesthetist and theatre team. An analysis of litigation against the National Health Service in the United Kingdom over a 12-year period (Cook et al. 2007) showed that patient position was responsible for 31 (4%) claims, the majority of which were as a result of neurapraxia. This figure represents the number of claims, not the true incidence of patient injury related to positioning on the operating table. All positions create pressure areas and the risk of reduced tissue perfusion is dependent on the length of procedure and the underlying patient physiology and anatomy. Unfortunately we do not have much influence on the time taken to perform surgery but anatomically we need to concentrate on padding of these pressure points and physiologically maintaining adequate tissue perfusion.

Supine position

In all positions, care needs to be taken to prevent corneal dryness by assuring that the eye is closed; this will also reduce the risk of corneal abrasion. The supine position specifically puts the heel at risk from pressure; this can be reduced by the use of ankle gel pads that keep the heels off the operating table. The ulnar nerves are also vulnerable as they run through the ulnar groove. They can be damaged by direct pressure from the side of the operating table and arm supports, or from stretch related to excessive flexion at the elbow joint.

Lateral position

Care needs to be taken with excessive lateral positioning of the neck, which can lead to stretch on the brachial plexus; as with all positions, maintenance of a neutral neck position is paramount. The dependant axillary neurovascular bundle needs to be assessed and insertion of an appropriate axillary roll will reduce the compression. If the surgery does not involve frequent repositioning of the non-dependant leg then padding will need to be put between the legs. There is an exaggerated change in ventilation/perfusion mismatch with the dependant lung receiving more blood compared with the non-dependant lung but as a result of the position, the dependant lung is compressed by the mediastinum and abdominal contents, thus leading to reduced ventilation in comparison with the non-dependant lung.

Prone position

This position carries the greatest risk of injuries that are directly attributable to mal-positioning (Table 63.2). Again, the neck needs to be kept in a neutral position. For cervical spinal surgery the use of Mayfield pins inserted by the surgeon provides optimal access and has been shown to reduce pressure-related injuries when compared with a horseshoe head rest. If turning the patient prone for other procedures, there are many positioning aids for the face, head, and neck; the aim of all of them is to avoid direct pressure

Table 63.2 Complications of the prone position

Problem	Mechanism	Resulting issue
Cardiovascular	Abdominal compression causing inferior vena cava obstruction	Decreased cardiac index Increased bleeding at the surgical field
Respiratory	Increased functional residual capacity	Improved oxygenation
	Ventilation/perfusion changes	
	Tracheal tube movement	Endobronchial intubation
Central nervous system injury	Arterial occlusion from excessive neck rotation	Acute stroke
	Venous congestion from thoracic/abdominal pressure	Spinal cord ischaemia
Peripheral nervous system injury	Stretch or compression of nerves	Brachial plexus injury Ulnar nerve injury at the olecranon Peroneal nerve injury at the fibula head Lateral femoral cutaneous nerve injury at the iliac crest
Pressure injury	Excessive cutaneous pressure	Skin necrosis
	Peripheral vessel occlusion	Distal ischaemia
	Compression of viscera	Visceral ischaemia
	Excessive supraorbital pressure	Supraorbital nerve injury
Ophthalmic injury	Trauma to cornea	Corneal abrasion
	Direct increase in intraocular pressure	Retinal ischaemia
	Increased venous pressure causing decreased retinal nerve perfusion	Ischaemic optic neuropathy

to the eye, orbit, nose, and lips, while maintaining a neutral positioning of the neck. Apart from neck surgery, where the arms will be down by the sides, the arms will normally be brought up to either side of the head simultaneously. Careful attention needs to be paid to the axilla and pressure on the brachial plexus and the ulnar nerve that again will be at risk of compression and stretch. There are many types of surgical table available to improve surgical access and support the body. The most common is the Montreal mattress, which comes in different sizes. It is essential to get the correct size for the patient, in order that the abdomen is free to move with respiration—avoidance of abdominal pressure will reduce pressure on the inferior vena cava. Increased inferior vena cava pressure will lead to increased pressure in the venous epidural plexus—this can have a significant effect on blood loss during spinal surgery. Careful attention needs to be paid to the pressure areas created by whichever mattress, frame, or table that is used; the areas most at risk are breasts, genitalia, knees, and the dorsum of the feet. There have also been case reports of compartment syndrome of the anterior compartment of the thigh as a result of excessive pressure on the thigh secondary to mal-positioning for a long procedure. A single-centre observational study (Chang and Miller 2005) of 14 102 spinal operations showed an incidence of 0.028% of ischaemic optic neuropathy. The cause is unclear as ischaemic optic neuropathy is rarely associated with ischaemic injury of any other organ. The anaesthetist's role is to ensure there is no external pressure on the globe and maintain adequate tissue perfusion.

Beach-chair position

The beach-chair position is used for shoulder surgery and brachial plexus surgery; the most serious risk is cerebral ischaemia as a result of compromised perfusion pressure because of the elevation of the head and attenuation of cerebral autoregulation while under general anaesthesia. It has been demonstrated that the beach-chair position is associated with episodes of cerebral desaturation when compared with the lateral position (Murphy et al. 2010), which may also be used for shoulder arthroscopy. Despite this, strokes are a rare but devastating occurrence. While the obvious solution would be to perform this type of surgery in the lateral position, the authors' experience is that the majority of shoulder surgeons prefer the beach-chair position. Attention needs to be paid to the patient's blood pressure and also the alignment of the neck—not only does the neck need to be placed in the neutral position but also care must be taken to secure the head and neck, with regular checks under the drapes to make sure the alignment has not been changed by enthusiastic surgical manipulation of the arm and shoulder. When setting up the operating table in a beach-chair position, it is essential that blood pressure is maintained and that the patient's bottom is at the lowest point of the beach chair to avoid further movement of the patient during surgery.

Venous thromboembolism

When you consider that there were 25 000 deaths attributable to venous thromboembolism (VTE) in the United Kingdom in the period 2004–2005, VTE is an area of tremendous importance. Orthopaedic patients are at high risk as they often have the combination of major surgery followed by extended periods of immobility.

Surgical and trauma patients are considered to be at increased risk either from the nature or duration of the procedure:

- Combined surgical and anaesthetic time of greater than 90 min or greater than 60 min if the surgery involves the pelvis or lower limb
- Expected significant reduction in mobility
- Acute surgical admission with inflammatory or intra-abdominal condition.

They are also at increased risk if they have any pre-admission risk factors:

- Active cancer or treatment
- Over 60 years of age
- Admission to critical care
- BMI over 30 kg m^{-2}
- Hormone replacement therapy

- Oestrogen-containing contraceptive device
- Past medical history of VTE or a first-degree relative with a history of VTE
- Thrombophilia
- Significant medical co-morbidity
- Dehydration
- Varicose veins with phlebitis
- Pregnancy and up to 6 weeks postpartum.

The first line of treatment is to alter any risk factors, this includes advising patients to stop hormone replacement therapy or oestrogen-containing contraceptive devices 4 weeks before surgery. Regional anaesthesia should be considered but this needs to be balanced against patient and anaesthetist preference; if used, timing of pharmacological VTE prophylaxis needs to be planned.

Before prescribing pharmacological VTE prophylaxis, the individual patient needs to be assessed for bleeding risk:

- Active bleeding:
  - Untreated genetic bleeding disorder
  - Acquired bleeding disorder
- Acute stroke
- Thrombocytopenia
- Uncontrolled systolic hypertension
- Neuraxial block insertion or removal of catheter within the next 12 h or performed within the previous 4 h.

Specific guidelines exist for several orthopaedic procedures (National Institute for Health and Care Excellence 2010). For elective hip replacement, it is recommended to use mechanical VTE prophylaxis from admission, using antiembolism stockings and intermittent pneumatic compression devices. Provided there are no contraindications, pharmacological VTE prophylaxis should be started after surgery. Timing is dependent on the product manufacturer's recommendation; for low-molecular-weight heparin this is 6–12 h after surgery. Pharmacological VTE prophylaxis should then be continued for 28–35 days postoperatively, depending on local policy and the individual drug being used. Mechanical VTE prophylaxis should be continued until the patient no longer has significantly reduced mobility.

Elective knee replacements have the same recommendations as elective hip surgery, the only difference being that postoperative pharmacological VTE prophylaxis is used for 10–14 days. Recommendations for hip fracture surgery are similar to elective hip surgery, but the fact that immobility starts at the time of fracture requires the use of pharmacological prophylaxis from admission until 12 h before surgery. If surgery is to take place within 12 h of admission then pharmacological prophylaxis should be started 6–12 h after surgery. The regimen for other orthopaedic procedures will depend on an assessment of risk, and duration of therapy will depend on postoperative mobility.

VTE prophylaxis for spinal surgery depends on the nature of surgery and the individual risk. Mechanical VTE prophylaxis should be started on admission and pharmacological prophylaxis initiated when the spinal surgeon is satisfied that the risk of bleeding is low because of the potential devastating consequences of bleeding within the spinal canal.

Avoidance of hypothermia

National Institute for Health and Care Excellence (NICE) guidelines (2008) define inadvertent hypothermia as a core temperature below 36°C; the normal temperature range is between 36.5°C and 37.5°C and this is the optimum temperature range for homeostatic mechanisms. Hypothermia has been shown to increase the rate of surgical site infection, increase cardiac morbidity, and prolong clotting. Therefore NICE guidance recommends the use of fluid warmers if a volume greater than 500 ml of fluid is to be infused, and the use of forced air warmers for any procedure with a combined surgical and anaesthetic time of more than 30 min. They also recommend that the theatre temperature should be at 21°C while the patient is being exposed for surgery and any irrigation fluid should be warmed to a temperature between 38°C and 40°C. Consideration should also be given to preoperative warming of the patient. NICE recommends that elective surgery is not carried out in a patient with a temperature below 36°C, but notes that further research is required to identify the optimal pre-anaesthetic temperature.

Antibiotic prophylaxis

Antibiotic usage should be guided by microbiological advice; the exact antibiotic will depend on the local pathogens, patient factors and the surgical procedure.

Patient factors include drug allergies, bacterial colonization, and deep-seated infection. Surgical factors include the nature of surgery (diagnostic procedure, soft tissue surgery, or primary or revision arthroplasty surgery), use of a tourniquet, and blood loss greater than 1500 ml. All these factors need to be taken into account but for a patient undergoing a straightforward primary arthroplasty, the prophylactic antibiotic should be given less than 30 min before surgical incision with duration of therapy lasting no longer than 24 h.

Pneumatic tourniquet

Pneumatic tourniquets are used in distal limb surgery to provide a relatively bloodless field. The advantages of using a tourniquet are improved conditions for surgery and decreased blood loss at the time of surgery. The disadvantages relate to pressure exerted by the tourniquet and the reduction in blood supply to the limb. Interestingly, the inflation pressure of the tourniquet appears to be fixed in many surgeons' minds, with an inflation pressure of 300 mm Hg for the thigh and 250 mm Hg for the upper arm with a maximal duration of 2 h; there is rarely any thought given to the patient's preoperative or intraoperative blood pressure. Complications are rare but include injuries related to direct pressure effects of the tourniquet or ischaemia. These include nerve injuries, muscle injury, skin injury, and vascular injury. Nerve injury is believed to be secondary to direct pressure; the nerves most commonly affected are the sciatic nerve in the thigh and the radial nerve in the upper arm. Muscle injury results from ischaemia with a decrease in $P\text{O}_2$ and an increase $P\text{CO}_2$ within muscle cells. As ATP stores are used up, the muscles cells convert to anaerobic metabolism; this in turn increases lactate and CO_2 production leading to intracellular acidosis. If tourniquet duration exceeds 2 h, microvascular injury may occur, leading to increased vascular permeability. The muscles directly underneath the tourniquet exhibit fibre necrosis as a combination of ischaemia and compression if tourniquet times exceed 2 h; as mentioned previously, 2 h is an arbitrary figure and it is possible that patients may show these pathological changes with shorter tourniquet times.

Skin damage can occur in a poorly applied tourniquet, either by friction or by means of a chemical burn that occurs if a skin preparation that contains alcohol is applied in a manner that allows the solution to run under the tourniquet and then is held there under pressure. Vascular injury may occur as inadvertent damage is not revealed until after release of the tourniquet: frequently this is after skin closure and bandage application. Patients with peripheral vascular disease often have calcified arteries that will not be easily compressed and are at risk of plaque rupture, causing a further ischaemic assault that will not become apparent until the tourniquet is released. Patients with peripheral vascular disease will already have poor blood flow to the limbs and therefore ischaemic damage will occur at lower pressures of shorter duration and for both these reasons peripheral vascular disease is a relative contraindication to tourniquet use. A tourniquet provides an increasingly noxious stimulus over time and tourniquet pain may manifest in the awake patient having surgery under regional anaesthesia even though the block remains effective at the surgical site. In a patient under general anaesthesia, the noxious stimulus of the tourniquet will be reflected in increases in heart rate and blood pressure from sympathetic discharge. The application and release of tourniquets have a marked physiological effect as a result of the relative increase and then decrease of the circulating volume. The relative decrease in circulating volume that accompanies release of the tourniquet is compounded by the re-perfusion of an ischaemic limb and the release of ischaemic metabolites into the systemic circulation. This combination can lead to a profound decrease in blood pressure and an increase of up to 2.4 kPa in end-tidal carbon dioxide.

Blood conservation

This section discusses preoperative, intraoperative, and postoperative management and techniques that can be used to reduce the rate of allogenic blood transfusion. The evidence against use of allogenic blood transfusion is mounting; not only is it expensive and a limited resource, there are complications involved with transfusion, both immunological and infective.

Preoperative management

The World Health Organization defines anaemia as a haemoglobin concentration of less than 13 g dl^{-1} in men and less than 12 g dl^{-1} in women. Therefore the first measure that can be used to reduce transfusion rates is to make sure elective surgical patients are not already anaemic when they enter the anaesthetic room. An audit (Kotze et al. 2012) showed that length of stay and re-admission rates were both significantly reduced when blood transfusion rates were reduced by preoperative optimization of haemoglobin concentrations, when compared with a retrospective audit. This strategy at first seems straightforward but requires a pre-assessment service to take a full blood count and haematinic studies; this service needs to work in partnership with general practice to affect treatment. A significant proportion of patients do not have a straightforward iron deficiency anaemia and even those that do, may have an occult malignancy that will need further investigation. Pre-assessment will also identify those patients at increased risk of bleeding, either as a result of drug therapy or a genetic or acquired bleeding disorder. A management plan can be decided with regard to stopping medication if appropriate and discussion with a haematologist about pre-optimization of bleeding disorders. Autologous blood transfusion involves the patient's own blood being re-transfused back to them. In the preoperative period, autologous donation is possible—this involves the patient's own blood being collected preoperatively and then stored until it is required. This process will make the patient anaemic; they can be treated with iron therapy but some patients will not tolerate pre-donation. A large proportion of pre-donated blood is not required and is therefore wasted; the logistics and storage required for autologous blood means that it is more expensive than allogenic blood.

Intraoperative management

Management during the intraoperative period includes techniques to reduce red cell loss and also two techniques of autologous blood transfusion. Red cell loss can be reduced by avoidance of hypertension, low central venous pressure, and maintenance of haemostasis both surgically and pharmacologically. Autologous strategies include acute normovolaemic haemodilution and the use of cell salvage. Acute normovolaemic haemodilution involves collection of the patient's blood in the anaesthetic room immediately before surgery: volumes of 15–20 ml kg^{-1} are standard for this technique with volume being replaced by crystalloid or colloid fluids. As a result of this acute fluid shift and reduction in circulating volume, some patients will be excluded by co-morbid cardiac disease. The blood will be transfused at the end of surgery. Several meta-analyses (Bryson et al. 1998; Segal et al. 2004) did not find a reduction in rates of allogenic transfusion although they did find a reduction in volume of allogenic blood transfused. Cell salvage involves collection of blood that is lost from the surgical field via a suction catheter, the blood is then collected and mixed with an anticoagulant before being filtered, washed, and spun down before red cells are re-transfused back to the patient. The obvious advantage is the more blood that is lost from the surgical field, the more blood that is salvaged and re-transfused. As the system is a virtual loop, some patients who normally refuse blood transfusion will allow cell salvage. Cell salvage cannot be used for all operations, the exceptions within the realm of orthopaedic surgery include exploration or revision of an infected prosthesis and malignancy. Although now accepted for some tumours, there have been no studies looking at bone and soft tissue malignancy. Caution also needs to be exercised with revision arthroplasty as cement should be avoided and this necessitates the use of a second suction system during cement removal. The American Association of Blood Banks recommends the use of cell salvage for any case in which a patient would normally be cross-matched preoperatively or where more than 10% of patients undergoing this procedure would require transfusion.

Pharmacological strategies include controlled hypotension and the use of antifibrinolytics. Hypotension has been shown to reduce blood loss but the quality and size of studies mean that there are no substantial data on the safety of induced hypotension, while the benefits of reduced blood loss and clearer surgical field need to be balanced against a patient's co-morbidities. Two meta-analyses of hip (Sukeik et al. 2011) and knee (Alshryda et al. 2011) surgery have shown that there is a significant reduction in blood loss and the need for allogenic blood transfusion with the use of tranexamic acid. No increase of VTE has been found with tranexamic acid; high-dose regimens used in cardiac surgery have been linked with an increased risk of non-ischaemic epilepsy.

Postoperative management

Acceptance of restrictive transfusion thresholds will also help reduce the use of allogenic transfusion; a widely accepted trigger is a haemoglobin concentration below 7 g dl^{-1} (Herbert et al. 1999; The Association of Anaesthetists of Great Britain and Ireland 2008) but the trigger for patients with known ischaemic heart disease is not straightforward and many doctors now quote a concentration of 10 g dl^{-1}. This figure is derived from a retrospective sub-group analysis with a trend towards improved survival but which is not statistically significant (Herbert et al. 1999). One study looking specifically at elderly patients undergoing lower limb arthroplasty and the risk of silent myocardial ischaemia found no difference between a transfusion threshold of 8 g dl^{-1} compared with 10g dl^{-1} (Grover et al. 2006). Autologous transfusion is possible in the post-operative period with the re-transfusion of wound drainage, most commonly used after total knee replacement. In one randomized trial (Thomas et al. 2001), transfusion of wound drainage showed a significant reduction of allogenic transfusion and furthermore in those patients that did not require an allogenic transfusion, there was a significant reduction in postoperative infections.

Bone cement implant syndrome

The majority of hip replacements are cemented, which involves the use of polymethylmethacrylate to affix the femoral stem and acetabular cup into place, as opposed to uncemented prosthesis, which involves a force fit. The implication for the anaesthetist is that of bone cement implantation syndrome (BCIS). BCIS may be a slight misnomer, however, as although it has been shown to be significantly more common when the prosthesis is cemented, the same collection of physiological changes may be seen with an uncemented implant, indeed these same changes may be seen as early as reaming of the femur. BCIS is associated with an up to 20-fold increase in intramedullary pressure (IMP), from a normal IMP of 30–50 mm Hg to 800 mm Hg. The IMP is further increased up to 1400 mm Hg during the insertion of a cemented femoral prosthesis. The physiological changes present as hypoxia and hypotension, and these changes have been graded (Donaldson et al. 2009) (Table 63.3).

The changes are a result of increased pulmonary vascular resistance that leads to a ventilation/perfusion mismatch that is exacerbated by the lateral position. The acute increase in pulmonary vascular resistance leads to an increase in pulmonary artery pressure, which will reduce right ventricular output. Grade 3 BCIS results from severe right ventricular failure to the extent that the right ventricle becomes severely dilated and the interventricular septum is shifted to the left, thereby compressing the left ventricle which is already struggling to maintain cardiac output as left ventricular filling is greatly reduced as a result of right ventricular failure. Whist these features are clearly demonstrated on transoesophageal echocardiography, the exact pathophysiology is not clearly understood but it is likely to be immunological as well as a result of any mechanical obstruction secondary to emboli. Treatment is supportive once the BCIS has occurred, therefore avoidance and prevention is the key. Surgical measures include the use of non-cemented prostheses, thorough lavage of the femoral shaft to remove debris, use of a suction catheter placed into the distal tip of the shaft during cementing (this creates a vacuum in the medullary cavity), and use of a cement gun that leads to a more uniform IMP. Although low-viscosity cement is associated with a lower incidence of BCIS compared with high-viscosity cement, its physical properties will lead to a higher failure rate of a load-bearing joint such as a hip prosthesis.

Table 63.3 Bone cement implant syndrome classification

Grade	Description
Grade 1	Sp_{O_2} <94% or a decrease in systolic arterial pressure >20%
Grade 2	Sp_{O_2} <88% or a decrease in systolic arterial pressure >40% or in the awake patient loss of consciousness
Grade 3	Cardiorespiratory arrest

Reproduced with permission from Donaldson, A. J. et al., Bone cement implantation syndrome, *British Journal of Anaesthesia*, 2009, Volume 102, Issue 1, pp 12–22, by permission of the Board of Management and Trustees of the British Journal of Anaesthesia.

Surgical procedures

This section looks at specific procedures and gives a brief overview, as the areas already discussed earlier in the chapter underpin all of these operations from an anaesthetic perspective.

Hip surgery

Primary total hip arthroplasty is one of the most common operations performed; it increases function and reduces pain. As a result of the profound positive effect this operation can have on a patient's life, there are few contraindications; they focus on factors likely to lead to failure, such as infection or absolute dysfunction of the abductor mechanism of the hip. Positioning of the patient can be either supine with a sandbag under the pelvis or more commonly the lateral position. Anaesthetic technique will consist of either general anaesthesia, neuraxial anaesthesia, or a combination of the two. Recently, two contrasting studies have been published ; one, a large retrospective data analysis of 382 236 primary hip or knee arthroplasties, showed superior perioperative outcomes with significant reductions in length of stay and morbidity and mortality for neuraxial anaesthesia, either alone or in combination with general anaesthesia, compared with general anaesthesia alone (Memtsoudis et al. 2013). Conversely, a small randomized trial of 120 patients undergoing primary knee arthroplasty, comparing general anaesthesia with local anaesthetic infiltration against spinal anaesthesia, sedation, and local anaesthetic infiltration showed a significant reduction in length of stay and overall morphine consumption in the general anaesthesia group (Harsten et al. 2013). The study was not designed to look at morbidity and mortality. Local anaesthetic infiltration is gaining popularity in hip and knee arthroplasty and what is clear, as with all techniques, is that its results are operator dependant.

Indications for revision include aseptic loosening, deep infection, instability resulting in recurrent dislocation, and periprosthetic fracture. Revision hip arthroplasty is surgically more challenging with higher expected blood loss, even when revision of only component is required. The set-up for revision hip surgery is similar to primary arthroplasty, with precautions for major blood loss. One of the reasons for hip resurfacing is that the femoral neck is preserved and therefore if and when it requires revising to a total hip replacement, there is no femoral stem to be removed, but because of the uncertainty surrounding metal-on-metal joint replacements and joint resurfacing, this operation is unlikely to be a common operation in the near future, until further research has been carried out.

Hip arthroscopy as a diagnostic and therapeutic tool is widely practised; patients are normally young with little co-morbidity. Positioning is supine or lateral with a pulley system to distract the hip to enable camera insertion. General anaesthetic with local anaesthetic infiltration by the surgeon is often the preferred choice.

The estimated risk of primary hip prosthetic dislocation is 3%. The main reason for urgent relocation is pain, but if the head has dislocated posteriorly then the sciatic nerve is at risk of compression. Emergency departments will often attempt re-location but if they are unsuccessful with analgesia and sedation then a general anaesthetic is often required with normal precautions against gastric aspiration; occasionally neuromuscular block is required and, if still unsuccessful, then an open reduction will be required.

Knee surgery

The anaesthetic requirements for knee surgery are very similar to hip surgery, the obvious differences are supine positioning and use of a thigh tourniquet. Intraoperative blood loss is minimal unless surgical preference is to deflate the tourniquet to allow surgical haemostasis before closure. The majority of surgeons deflate the tourniquet after closure and bandage application and blood loss, seen in drainage bottles, occurs in the postoperative period. Provided there is no contraindication, the blood can be re-infused after processing, a technique that reduces allogenic blood transfusions in total knee replacements (Thomas et al. 2001). The other main difference is that total knee replacements are more painful then total hip replacements. Techniques include neuraxial anaesthesia alone or in combination with general anaesthesia, or general anaesthesia in combination with peripheral nerve block or local anaesthetic infiltration. Most important is the use of multimodal analgesia in combination with an enhanced recovery programme that is discussed later in this chapter. Revision surgery is essentially similar to primary arthroplasty but surgery is more challenging and will therefore take longer, so careful attention should be paid to the tourniquet time; the expected blood loss will be greater and may only reveal itself in the post-anaesthetic recovery room when the drain clamp is released. Frank bleeding at this time can quickly lead to hypovolaemia in a patient population with little cardiovascular reserve.

Foot and ankle surgery

This ranges from complex ankle replacements and reconstruction to simple forefoot surgery. Both types of surgery lend themselves to peripheral nerve blocks; indeed, it is common for foot and ankle surgery to be performed under regional anaesthesia alone, the limiting factor is often the use of a tourniquet and where it is placed.

Shoulder and elbow surgery

Like foot and ankle surgery, upper limb surgery lends itself to regional anaesthesia; this is covered in great detail in a separate chapter (see Chapter 54). The type of surgery encountered will depend on the institution; this will also dictate the patient population which can range from an athlete having a diagnostic shoulder arthroscopy to a patient with severe rheumatoid arthritis having a revision shoulder replacement. Patient positioning will be beachchair for open shoulder surgery and is often used for shoulder arthroscopy; the alternative for shoulder arthroscopy is lateral positioning. Elbow surgery will often require access to the posterior elbow, the most reliable position is the lateral position with the cubital fossa resting on a padded bar.

Spinal surgery

There is crossover between neurosurgery and orthopaedic surgery—in the authors' institution, the spinal surgery department consists of both orthopaedic surgeons and neurosurgeons. This section concentrates on spinal deformity surgery as other forms of spinal surgery are covered in a separate chapter on neurosurgery (see Chapter 59) and traumatic spinal injury is covered later in this chapter. Thoracic decompression, fixation, and fusion is usually performed by a posterior approach but a combined approach with anterior instrumentation may be required if adequate surgical correction cannot be performed by a posterior approach alone. Anterior approach is a slight misnomer as the patient is positioned in the lateral position and refers to surgical exposure of the anterior vertebral column. The pleura is incised with careful retraction of the lung in order to expose the spine, therefore poor respiratory function contraindicates an anterior approach. Thoracolumbar surgery is performed for unstable fractures, cord compression secondary to tumours or a degenerative process, and coronal or sagittal deformity correction. Scoliosis is a sign present in a diverse range of underlying conditions; planning of surgery and anaesthesia needs to reflect this. These conditions can be divided into idiopathic, neuromuscular, congenital, and degenerative (Table 63.4).

The indications for surgery are severe deformity, curve progression, cosmesis, back pain or radicular pain in degenerative cases, and the inability to sit unaided with progressive neuromuscular orders. The severity of the curve is measured by drawing perpendicular lines from the maximally tilted upper and lower vertebrae, the angle at which these lines intersect is known as the Cobb angle (Fig. 63.2).

Anaesthetic management depends on the underlying cause for the scoliosis and also the surgical plan. Surgical treatment can range from plaster jacket casting, which often has to be performed under general anaesthesia in very young or syndromic children,

Table 63.4 Scoliosis classification

Classification	Description
Idiopathic	Infantile 0–3 years Juvenile 4 years–puberty Adolescent puberty–skeletal maturity Adult
Neuromuscular	Cerebral palsy Spinal muscular atrophy Myopathies
Congenital	Syndromes involving vertebral anomalies, will often also have rib anomalies and may have associated cardiac, renal defects with a high incidence of cord abnormality especially spinal dyraphism
Degenerative	Trauma Infection Radiation

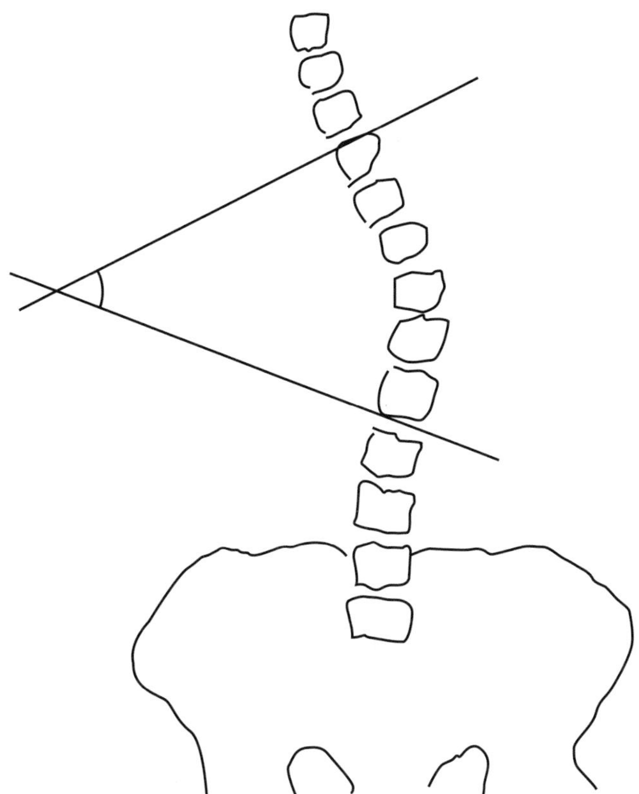

Figure 63.2 Measurement of the Cobb angle.

to anterior and posterior correction. If surgery is to involve both posterior and anterior approaches this may be done in one theatre session or it can be staged, normally with a week between the two operations. A combined approach carries with it an increased risk of complications compared with a single approach, an anterior approach has an increased risk of complications compared with a posterior approach (Memtsoudis et al. 2011). In the authors' institution, when spinal deformity surgery is carried out, continuous neurophysiological monitoring in the form of somatosensory-evoked potentials and transcranial motor-evoked potentials (MEPs) are recorded. Depression of intrinsic spinal cord activity is greatest with halogenated anaesthetic agents and nitrous oxide. While it is possible to obtain MEP recordings with low-dose halogenated agents, it appears that end-tidal concentration is not the only factor. For this reason, in the authors' institution, if MEP recordings are being monitored then maintenance of anaesthesia is with a total intravenous anaesthetic of propofol and remifentanil. There are a few cautions to be observed with transcranial MEP recording: they are related to the passage of an electrical stimulus from a cranial electrode, therefore this is best avoided in epileptics and any patient with an implanted electrical device. With the widespread use of continuous intraoperative neurophysiological monitoring, the wake-up test is rarely performed; as the wake-up test is not continuous it only gives a snapshot of the patient's motor pathways, but as mentioned previously, there are contraindications to transcranial MEPs. If the wake-up test is to be performed, then after turning off the anaesthetic agent the patient will have to be gently restrained to avoid injury and accidental extubation by excessive movement. At the authors' institution, all patients who have undergone major spinal correction are admitted to a high dependency setting postoperatively. This enables close neurovascular observation and careful titration of analgesic medication; organ support is rarely needed. One of the more unusual complications of scoliosis correction is superior mesenteric artery syndrome, also known as cast syndrome. The superior mesenteric artery normally leaves the abdominal aorta at an angle between 38° and 52°; the third part of the duodenum passes underneath the superior mesenteric artery, therefore if this angle is decreased, which may occur in correction of severe scoliosis, there is a risk of partial or complete duodenal obstruction. Symptoms are of upper abdominal pain, nausea, and vomiting, all of which could be ascribed to the surgery and opioid medication, so a high index of suspicion is required. Diagnosis is made with contrast radiography demonstrating extrinsic obstruction of the third part of the duodenum; the patient should be referred to a general surgeon. Treatment is initially conservative as for any small bowel obstruction although total parental nutrition will need to be initiated as this patient population will be in a catabolic state. Occasionally a laparotomy is required for surgical intervention.

Paediatric orthopaedic surgery

Paediatric anaesthesia is covered in more detail in Part 10 of this textbook, but it is worth briefly looking at the type of surgery and the underlying conditions that present for orthopaedic surgery in the paediatric population. Paediatric orthopaedic surgery concentrates on scoliosis (discussed previously in 'Spinal surgery') or conditions which affect the child's ability to walk. Cerebral palsy is an umbrella term for a vast array of neurological disorders, therefore a definition is difficult but the underlying problem is a non-progressive abnormality of the immature brain. This may occur during pregnancy, the peripartum period, during the first 2 years of life, or as a result of a congenital disorder. Patients will present with a varying degree of neurological impairment, both at an intellectual level and with regard to motor function. Treatment is aimed at improving posture and mobility; this requires a multidisciplinary approach as any surgical treatment offered will need to be in conjunction with physiotherapists, occupational therapists, and paediatricians. Treatments offered range from botulinum toxin injections for muscle spasticity to surgical correction of hip subluxation and scoliosis surgery. Arthrogryposis multiplex congenita is a term that implies the child is born with multiple curved joints, therefore like cerebral palsy it is a descriptive term as the underlying causes are many. The child presents with multiple rigid joint contractures, frequently involving all four limbs; tracheo-oesophageal fistulae are often also present. Initial treatment is with stretching and splinting of the affected joints but corrective surgery is often required. Unsurprisingly, difficult airways and difficulty in obtaining intravenous access are encountered in this patient population. There are also reports of intraoperative pyrexia (Hopkins et al. 1991) but there has been no positive diagnosis of malignant hyperthermia; in the same series of case reports, pyrexia was reported despite all malignant hyperthermia triggers being avoided.

Tumour surgery

As a result of the relatively low incidence of bone and connective tissue malignancy (3.2:100 000 in the United Kingdom population compared with an incidence of 125.9:100 000 for breast cancer), this type of surgery is only performed in specialist centres that have both the surgical experience and extensive multidisciplinary set-up, requiring expert histopathologists and radiologists for accurate diagnosis and staging of the disease. Surgery ranges from computed tomography (CT)-guided biopsies, which will require general anaesthesia for children or lesions that are hard and lesions that are difficult to access, to sacrectomy and hemipelvectomy.

Orthopaedic tumour surgery

A list of the most commonly performed procedures is given in Box 63.1.

As can be seen from the list in Box 63.1, which is by no means exhaustive, tumour surgery is extremely varied and preoperative planning is paramount. These patients may have had radiotherapy and chemotherapy. Almost all chemotherapeutic agents will cause myelosuppression, cisplatin can cause nephrotoxicity; and doxorubicin can cause a cardiomyopathy with reduced left ventricular ejection fraction. Positioning of the patient will depend on location of the lesion and may require a change of position during the operation. Major tumour resection will often require involvement of vascular, plastic, spinal, and general surgeons. Sacrectomy carries with it a high morbidity rate. Surgical factors that improve a favourable oncological outcome are clear margins and en bloc resection as opposed to piecemeal resection of the tumour (Schwab et al. 2009). Because of the uncommon nature of these tumours, it has not been possible to carry out trials of surgical treatment of total sacral tumour resection. One recent case series of 25 patients that included 8 staged and 17 non-staged procedures showed a trend of improved clinical outcome and reduced intensive care stay for those patients that underwent a staged procedure (Brown et al. 2011).

Box 63.1 Orthopaedic tumour procedures

- Biopsy, both open and CT guided
- Curettage of benign and locally aggressive bone tumours
- Excision of soft tissue masses
- Synovectomy
- Distal femur resection with reconstruction
- Proximal femur resection with reconstruction
- Proximal tibia resection with reconstruction
- Proximal humerus resection with reconstruction
- Long-stem arthroplasty
- Fixation of pathological fracture and prophylactic fixation
- Amputation:
  - Above and below knee
  - Above elbow
  - Hip disarticulation
  - Shoulder disarticulation
  - Hindquarter
  - Forequarter
- Scapulectomy
- Radical sarcoma resection requiring soft tissue reconstruction
- Radical pelvic resection with limb preservation
- Vertebrectomy
- Hemipelvectomy
- Sacrectomy.

Analgesia in orthopaedic surgery

Adequacy of postoperative pain control determines the postoperative mobility and overall patient satisfaction. Good pain relief is one of the most important factors in determining a patient's safe discharge.

Opioids

Opioids are the mainstay in postoperative pain control in orthopaedic surgery. The μ-agonist opioids such as morphine, fentanyl, and oxycodone are the cornerstone of moderate to severe acute pain management.

Opioid analgesics are available in several formulations and can be administered by a variety of routes, the most common of which are oral, subcutaneous, and intravenous. Oral opioids are available in short-acting and long-acting (modified, controlled, or extended-release) preparations. Parenteral formulations of opioids are available for subcutaneous, intramuscular, or intravenous administration. Intravenous patient-controlled analgesia allows patients to manage their pain by self-administering opioid doses and is one of the most commonly used methods to treat acute postoperative pain.

Preservative-free preparations are available for epidural and intrathecal delivery, which can be administered as single injections or in solutions for epidural analgesia. The intramuscular route for opioid administration is not recommended as injections are painful and have highly variable absorption, with a 30–60 min lag to peak effect.

The most common adverse effects of opioids are nausea, vomiting, pruritus, constipation, and sedation. Antiemetics, antihistamines, and stool softener plus a laxative should be prescribed to tackle the adverse effects. The combination of an opioid with very low-dose naloxone in oral form is now being used in practice. One such oral preparation of naloxone with oxycodone reduces constipation by blocking the effect of the opioid on receptors in the gut. With the exception of constipation, opioid adverse effects are dose related. The most dangerous adverse effect of opioids is respiratory depression.

The intrathecal opioids bind to G-protein-linked pre- and postsynaptic opioid receptors of the dorsal horn to activate potassium channel opening (μ and δ) and calcium channel closure (κ), with an overall reduction in intracellular calcium. This reduces the release of excitatory transmitters (glutamate and substance P) from presynaptic C fibres with consequent reduction in nociceptive transmission. Other possible target sites for intrathecal opioids have been proposed: fentanyl and pethidine have demonstrable local anaesthetic effects on sensory C primary afferent nerve fibres, which may facilitate analgesic effects. Intrathecal morphine increases adenosine concentration in cerebrospinal fluid (CSF), which opens potassium channels with consequent hyperpolarization of nerve fibres and reduction in neuronal activity. Intrathecal opioids also reduce the release of γ-amino butyric acid (GABA) and glycine by a calcium-independent process from dorsal horn neurones. Opioids may disinhibit inhibitory pathways, thereby reducing nociceptive transmission.

Fentanyl is the most frequently used intrathecal lipophilic opioid and, when administered in single doses of 10–30 μg, it has a rapid onset (10–20 min) and short duration of action (4–6 h) with minimal cephalad spread, and hence is suitable for day case arthroscopic procedures.

The combination of fentanyl (20–30 μg) or sufentanil (5–7.5 μg) with bupivacaine or lidocaine leads to a faster onset of block and better intraoperative and immediate postoperative analgesia without increasing the degree of motor block or the time until discharge (Bujedo 2012). Fischer and Simanski (2005) state that intrathecal morphine (preservative free) can provide excellent analgesia after arthroplasty surgery. A European collaborative (PROSPECT) has recommended intrathecal morphine 0.1–0.2 mg after total hip arthroplasty without the need for supplementation by patient-controlled analgesia or monitoring on a high dependency unit.

Intrathecal morphine has been reported to be a superior analgesic to diamorphine for arthroplasty surgery at the comparative doses investigated. Morphine is 1000 times more hydrophilic than fentanyl and it crosses the blood–brain barrier slowly, binds to the epidural fat to a lesser extent, and more strongly to specific receptors in the grey matter, and has a slow plasma reuptake, maintaining higher concentrations in the CSF and for longer. After intrathecal morphine administration, CSF concentrations are maintained with a long cord exposure time of around 12 h; hence there is a potential for delayed respiratory depression as a result of rostral spread.

Intrathecal morphine is an effective pain control technique after multilevel spinal surgery. Some authors have found that a dose of 20 μg kg^{-1} of morphine (0.14 mg for a 70 kg adult) reduced the need for supplemental analgesia for the first 12 h after lumbar fusion surgery. However, Boezaart et al. (1999) recommended 20–40 μg kg^{-1} (0.15–0.3 mg for a 70 kg patient) for lumbar intrathecal surgery. The extended-release epidural morphine (EREM) intended for single-dose administration by epidural route at the lumbar level, with mean duration of analgesia of 48 h after a single injection, has been studied extensively in recent years. The peak concentration in CSF is delayed until 3 h after epidural injection of the liposomal EREM. In a review of five controlled clinical trials in knee replacement surgery, abdominal surgery and caesarean sections ($n = 913$), comparing intravenous patient-controlled analgesia combined with epidural placebo, with a group receiving epidural administration of 5 mg of morphine sulphate and with another given EREM at various different doses (5–30 mg), it was demonstrated by Mhuircheartaigh et al. (2009), that the EREM group was the most effective at controlling postoperative pain after a single administration before surgery and also as preventive analgesia.

Diamorphine is a lipophilic prodrug with an octanol:water coefficient of 280 that makes it more likely to partition across the dura more readily than morphine but more slowly than fentanyl. Its low pK_a (7.6) at physiological pH produces a 34% unionized fraction (fentanyl 9%) available for diffusion onto the dorsal horn opioid receptors.

A variety of doses of intrathecal diamorphine have been tested. A study by Hammell et al. (2009) included 194 patients who received intrathecal diamorphine during lumbar fusion surgery with a mean dose of 1.6 mg (range 1–4 mg or 20–50 mcg kg^{-1}). Only 9% of patients had a pain score of 2/10 or greater within the first 24 h. No patients required rescue analgesia with intravenous opiates. Apart from pruritus (9%), other side-effects were rare.

Multimodal pain relief

It has been suggested that excessive use of postoperative opioids leads to decreased patient satisfaction and carries the potential of the development of acute tolerance.

Multimodal analgesic techniques involving the use of smaller doses of opioids in combination with non-opioid analgesic drugs (e.g. local anaesthetics, ketamine, paracetamol, NSAIDs, and anticonvulsants) are becoming increasingly popular approaches to postoperative pain relief.

The non-opioid options in orthopaedic pain relief are as follows:

Local anaesthetics

When administered before surgery, local anaesthetics can decrease anaesthetic and analgesic requirements during surgery, and reduce the need for opioid-containing analgesics postoperatively. More effective pain relief in the early postoperative period, as a result of the residual sensory block produced by local anaesthetics, facilitates recovery by enabling earlier mobilization and discharge. The use of local anaesthetic-based techniques for preventing pain can decrease the incidence of postoperative nausea and vomiting and is suitable for superficial procedure.

Commonly used local anaesthetic techniques in orthopaedic procedures are:

1. Nerve blocks: commonly performed blocks are femoral/obturator/lateral cutaneous nerve of thigh/sciatic/fascia iliaca block for lower limb and brachial plexus/ axillary/ulnar/radial/median for upper limb surgeries.It has been suggested that performing neural blockade with local anaesthetics before surgical incision prevents the nociceptive input hence altering excitability of the central nervous system by pre-emptively blocking the *N*-methyl-D-aspartate (NMDA)-induced 'wind up' phenomena, and subsequent release of inflammatory mediators.
2. Local infiltration: this is common after arthroscopic procedures of knees and shoulders. In addition to the local anaesthetics, a wide variety of other adjuvants (e.g. morphine, ketorolac, steroids, and clonidine) have also been injected into the intra-articular space to decrease post-arthroscopic pain.
3. Continuous local anaesthetic infusion systems, where the catheter is placed at the sub-fascial level or near a peripheral nerve, have shown better patient satisfaction and decreased opioid use (e.g. continuous popliteal-sciatic or brachial plexus blocks).The availability of longer-acting local anaesthetic suspensions and 'delayed-release' formulations containing liposomes or polymer microspheres may minimize the need for a continuous infusion catheter delivery system in the near future. Liposomal bupivacaine appears to be a promising therapeutic option for prolonged reduction of postsurgical pain in soft tissue and orthopaedic surgeries. Currently it is only licensed for wound infiltration, but various ongoing trials in peripheral nerve blocks and wound infiltration of sustained-release bupivacaine have shown pain relief for up to 3–4 days with good acceptability by patients.

NSAIDs

Oral NSAIDs are used for treating surgical pain because of their well-known anti-inflammatory and analgesic properties. When parenteral preparations of NSAIDs (e.g. ketorolac, diclofenac, and ibuprofen) became available, these drugs were more widely used in the management of acute perioperative pain. NSAIDs block the synthesis of prostaglandins by inhibiting cyclooxygenase (COX)-2, thereby reducing production of mediators of the acute inflammatory response, and COX-1. It has been shown that the central response to painful stimuli is modulated by NSAID-induced inhibition of prostaglandin synthesis in the spinal cord.

The benefits of NSAIDs are improved recovery profile, including less vomiting, no urinary retention, and faster mobilization with earlier discharge home. They also include better global patient satisfaction and less constipation than opioid-containing oral analgesics.

Despite the obvious benefits of using NSAIDs in the perioperative period, controversy still exists regarding their use because of the potential for gastrointestinal mucosal and renal tubular damage, platelet dysfunction, and potential delayed bone healing.

Selective COX-2 inhibitors have the advantage of fewer gastrointestinal complications. Both preoperative and postoperative administration of COX-2 inhibitors resulted in significant opioid-sparing effects, reduced adverse effects, and improved the quality of recovery and patient satisfaction with their postoperative pain management

The studies suggested that parecoxib (40–80 mg intravenously) was as effective and longer-acting than ketorolac (30 mg intravenously) in reducing pain after surgery. Unfortunately, there is a growing controversy regarding the potential adverse cardiovascular risks of the COX-2 inhibitors as discussed earlier in the chapter. In addition, many orthopaedic surgeons are also concerned about the negative influence of these compounds on bone growth as COX-2 activity appears to play an important role in bone healing.

Paracetamol

Paracetamol is perhaps the safest and most cost-effective non-opioid analgesic when it is administered in analgesic doses. Although both parenteral and rectal paracetamol produce analgesic effects in the postoperative period, concurrent use with a NSAID is superior to paracetamol alone.

NMDA antagonists

The use of small doses of ketamine (0.1–0.2 mg kg^{-1} intravenously) appears to be associated with an opioid-sparing effects and a less frequent incidence of adverse events. It is frequently used in multimodal analgesic regimens for spinal and major joint surgeries.

Dextromethorphan, another NMDA receptor antagonist that inhibits wind-up and NMDA-mediated nociceptive responses in dorsal horn neurones, has been proposed to enhance opioid, local anaesthetic, and NSAID-induced analgesia.

α_2-agonists

The α_2-adrenergic agonists, clonidine and dexmedetomidine, produce significant anaesthetic and analgesic-sparing effects. Clonidine also has been shown to improve and prolong central neuraxial and peripheral nerve blocks. However, their use is associated with potentially increased postoperative sedation and bradycardia.

Anticonvulsants

Gabapentin and pregabalin (structural analogues of GABA) are anticonvulsants and have proved useful in the treatment of chronic neuropathic pain and may also be useful adjuvants in the management of acute postoperative pain. Many studies have demonstrated an opioid dose-sparing effect of both gabapentin and pregabalin in the perioperative period. These anticonvulsants act by stabilizing nerve membranes, reducing excitability, and reducing spontaneous neuronal firing. They may have a role in the prevention of persistent postsurgical pain syndromes.

Miscellaneous

A bolus dose of magnesium (50 mg kg^{-1} intravenously) at induction of anaesthesia also led to improved pain control and better patient satisfaction with less opioid requirement after major orthopaedic surgery (Levaux et al. 2003). Benzodiazepines are analgesic only for pain associated with muscle spasm, especially in major spinal surgery.

Tramadol is a dual-mechanism analgesic. It binds to μ-receptors and it also weakly inhibits noradrenaline and serotonin reuptake, which is believed to augment pain signal transmission inhibition.

Tapentadol is a newer medication, is considered an opioid agonist, and binds to the μ-receptor. Unlike other opioid medications, except tramadol, its μ-receptor activity is supplemented by its inhibition of noradrenaline reuptake, believed to enhance the inhibition of pain signal transmission.

Methadone is a μ-agonist opioid. However, it is also a NMDA antagonist and produces excellent pain relief. As methadone has a very long half-life, caution must be used in its administration, dosage adjustments must be made slowly, and it should be used by experts only.

Enhanced recovery

The concept of 'enhanced recovery' was described and promoted by Henrik Kehlet in patients after colonic surgery, with its principles centred on a multimodal rehabilitation programme to reduce postoperative pain and accelerate rehabilitation. The enhanced recovery model has successfully been used in major joint replacement and spinal surgeries. Since its implementation across various NHS hospitals in the United Kingdom, there have been various reports of positive results such as reduced length of stay, better patient satisfaction, and reduced co-morbidities after primary joint surgery.

Generic principles of enhanced recovery

Preoperatively

The steps involve thorough preoperative assessment and intervention to optimize health and medical conditions before surgery. In addition, adequate patient education and making discharge arrangements are very important in preoperative preparation. All this preparation facilitates the admission on the day of surgery and avoids prolonged fasting. The pre-emptive use of analgesics such as paracetamol and gabapentinoids (pregabalin or gabapentin) as premedication has been used in many hospitals in the enhanced recovery programme protocols for orthopaedic surgery (Dauri et al. 2009).

Intraoperatively

The steps include minimally invasive surgical techniques with shortened surgical times and optimized anaesthesia, preferably regional anaesthetic techniques with or without sedation. Maintenance of normovolaemia, normothermia, and prevention of hypoxia ensures a better outcome. For enhanced recovery for major joint surgery, intraoperative local infiltration analgesia is recommended;

this involves the surgeon injecting a high volume, about 100–150 ml, of very dilute local anaesthetic into all the tissues that are traumatized during surgery. When done meticulously, this can provide high-quality pain relief without the need for strong opioids.

Postoperatively

The aim is to achieve early mobilization with early physiotherapy and multimodal analgesia. Early mobilization reduces the incidence of deep vein thrombosis, a major cause of death.

Multimodal analgesia attempts to limit the use of morphine, which causes sedation and nausea, and epidurals or nerve blocks that cause muscle weakness, thereby aiding same-day mobilization. Intraoperative local anaesthetic infiltration and postoperative oral analgesics are the main components of pain relief after the effect of regional block starts wearing off. The anaesthetist should prescribe regular oral analgesics such as paracetamol and anti-inflammatory drugs, if not contraindicated. Pregabalin or gabapentin may also be used in the perioperative period.

Removal of catheters, drains and drips as soon as possible can promote the sense of well-being after surgery. The reduced length of hospital stay might also reduce the incidence of hospital-acquired infections such as MRSA and *Clostridium difficile*.

Patients are discharged home with clear instructions on how to progress with rehabilitation independently and appropriate use of prescribed analgesic medication.

In-hospital anaesthetic management of orthopaedic trauma

Major trauma consists of multiple, serious injuries that could result in death or serious disability. These might include serious head injuries, severe gunshot wounds, or road traffic accidents. Orthopaedic trauma is injury specific to the musculoskeletal system.

Injuries account for 17 000 deaths per year in the United Kingdom. The most common cause of major trauma in the United Kingdom is road traffic accidents, accounting for more than 21 000 cases and approximately 1713 deaths in 2013 (Department for Transport 2014).

Trauma management begins at the scene of the injury, and can be seen as a continuum of care to the point of rehabilitation. The initial priorities of in-hospital trauma management are control of haemorrhage; resuscitation to address shock, coagulopathy, and hypothermia; pain relief; and infection control. Management of orthopaedic trauma then progresses to fracture stabilization, mobilization, and return of function.

Initial assessment

In-hospital trauma generally begins in the emergency department. In the severely injured patient, a dedicated trauma team will take a handover from pre-hospital care providers. A standard protocol will be followed for initial assessment and stabilization of the patient, along the lines of those taught in the Advanced Trauma Life Support algorithm. The priority is to determine the patient's physiological status using the 'ABCDE' approach—airway, breathing, circulation, disability, and exposure. Severe trauma, particularly pelvic and long-bone fractures, may cause hypovolaemic shock resulting in tissue hypoperfusion and hypoxaemia. Injuries are triaged by location and severity and more life-threatening issues are addressed. Early reduction of fractures may be necessary to control haemorrhage and shock and therefore can be a part of the initial resuscitation. Alternatively, assessment of orthopaedic injuries may have to wait until other life-threatening issues are dealt with.

The initial role of the anaesthetist within a trauma team is rapid airway assessment and control, with stabilization of the cervical spine. They may also be called on to help with securing intravenous access, placement of chest drains, and providing pain relief and sedation or anaesthesia for other procedures or investigations that form part of the initial survey, such as CT scanning.

If emergency surgery is indicated, the anaesthetist must facilitate this as safely as possible by identifying and addressing key areas of risk. There has been a shift in trauma surgery toward early fracture stabilization and fixation (Bone et al. 1989; Pape et al. 2002). The exact timing of surgery depends upon the overall risk:benefit ratio, and good communication between the surgeon, trauma team, and anaesthetist is vital to balance the decision-making process. Concepts relevant to this decision-making process are discussed in the following subsections.

Timing of trauma surgery

The ultimate aim of orthopaedic intervention in fracture management is the restoration of function with avoidance of complications. Generally, early fracture fixation has numerous advantages:

- Decreased pain
- Decreased fat embolism
- Improvement in respiratory function
- Decreased sepsis
- Earlier mobility
- Easier wound care.

Timing of orthopaedic intervention therefore depends upon the precise anatomical site of fracture(s), the mechanism of injury, and the presence and severity of other non-orthopaedic injuries or co-morbidities. The purpose of a trauma team is to identify and triage life- and limb-threatening injuries and address them in order to minimize mortality and morbidity. Table 63.5 outlines examples of musculoskeletal trauma with respect to urgency.

Acute traumatic coagulopathy

The classic view of coagulopathy in trauma victims is as a triad of dilution of clotting factors from haemorrhage and fluid administration, acidaemia, and hypothermia (Lier et al. 2008). More recently, the concept of acute traumatic coagulopathy has emerged after evidence that shock and tissue hypoperfusion is the most significant initial cause of coagulopathy, via activation of the protein C pathway and hyperfibrinolysis (Brohi et al. 2007; Mercer et al. 2013). This is then exacerbated in the resuscitation phase by hypothermia, haemodilution, and acidosis. A large randomized controlled trial of more than 20 000 patients across 40 countries, the CRASH-2 trial, showed a significant reduction in all-cause mortality and death as a result of bleeding when the antifibrinolytic agent tranexamic acid was administered within 8 h of injury (CRASH-2 Trial Collaborators et al. 2010). Metabolic acidosis as a marker of tissue hypoperfusion can be assessed by measurement of blood pH, lactate, or base deficit; normalization of these values within 24 h of injury is a predictor of survival. In particular, base deficit is a reasonable indicator of resuscitation and is used as a guide to volume

Table 63.5 Urgency of musculoskeletal injuries

Musculoskeletal emergencies	Life-threatening	Pelvic ring fractures
		Long bone fractures (bilateral femoral shaft or multiple long bone)
	Limb-threatening	Traumatic amputation
		Vascular injury
		Compartment syndrome
Urgent musculoskeletal problems	Surgery within 6–8 h	Open fracture
		Traumatic arthrotomy
		Dislocations
		Displaced neck of femur in young adults
	Surgery within 24 h	Unstable pelvis or femoral fracture
		Proximal femoral fracture in the elderly
		Femoral neck fractures
		Intertrochanteric fractures

status and tissue oxygenation (Davis et al. 1988; Pape et al. 2001). Acute traumatic coagulopathy has been shown to predict death, prolonged intensive care stay, multiorgan failure, and acute lung injury (MacLeod et al. 2003; Maegele et al. 2007).

Traditional 'massive transfusion protocols' do not address acute traumatic coagulopathy, as they tend to focus on initial infusion of packed red blood cells, followed by laboratory-guided infusion of clotting factors and platelets. These protocols have largely been replaced by 'major haemorrhage protocols', which have been shown to improve delivery of blood components, reduce waste, and improve outcomes such as length of stay of survivors (Khan et al. 2013). An example of a trauma haemorrhage management algorithm is shown in Figure 63.3.

Damage-control resuscitation

Permissive hypotension

An adequate circulating volume is required in order to allow perfusion of vital organs. However, administration of too much fluid contributes to dilutional coagulopathy and hypothermia. Furthermore, an increase in blood pressure beyond the minimum required for perfusion will result in increased haemorrhagic loss. Thus the current approach of permissive hypotension limits fluid therapy and allows a lower systolic pressure until bleeding is controlled (Jansen et al. 2009). The National Institute for Health and Care Excellence has endorsed permissive hypotension, at least in the civilian pre-hospital setting, and advises against fluid administration in patients without head injury if a radial pulse is palpable (Dretzke et al. 2004).

Haemostatic resuscitation

The replacement of circulating volume while limiting coagulopathy and further loss of blood is termed haemostatic resuscitation, a concept that has largely emerged from military trauma experience over the last decade (Kirkman et al. 2007; Mercer et al. 2013). Strategies include earlier administration of fresh frozen plasma and platelets; use of recombinant factor VIIa, cryoprecipitate, and tranexamic acid; and calcium replacement. Blood and blood products are used as the primary resuscitation fluid after severe injury rather than crystalloid or colloid solutions in an attempt to limit acute traumatic coagulopathy and prevent the development of dilutional coagulopathy. Suggested ratios of 1:1:1 of red blood cells:fresh frozen plasma:platelets are becoming more widely used in civilian trauma centres. However, the recent multicentre PROPPR (Pragmatic, Randomized Optimal Platelet and Plasma Ratios) trial looked at this 1:1:1 strategy and found that while it enabled haemostasis to be achieved more effectively, it conferred no mortality benefit at 1 day or at 1 month (Holcomb et al. 2015).

Diagnosing coagulopathy and monitoring the response to resuscitation remains challenging. Commonly available laboratory tests such as full blood count, prothrombin time, activated partial thromboplastin time, and fibrinogen concentration are often unhelpful in a traumatic haemorrhage situation because of the delay in sending samples and obtaining results. Furthermore, there is a lack of consensus on the definition of traumatic coagulopathy and on values that should be used to trigger treatment (Curry et al. 2011). More recently, near-patient testing using thromboelastography or thromboelastometry has been used to provide a rapid real-time picture of clot formation and lysis and guide management.

Damage-control surgery

The concept of damage-control surgery involves minimizing the physiological 'hit' to the patient caused by invasive surgery. In the two-hit model of organ dysfunction, the first hit consists of the systemic inflammatory response syndrome that may occur in severely injured patients. A subsequent secondary inflammatory event, such as an orthopaedic fracture fixation, can result in a secondary insult leading to multiple organ failure (Pape et al. 2003). Adequate resuscitation of a patient is vital in order to minimize the impact of the second hit. Damage-control surgery therefore involves limited resuscitative surgery in order to control haemorrhage and reduce contamination. An example would be an initial washout and external fixation of compound femoral fracture in a patient with multiple injuries. This would be prioritized in order to limit further insult to the patient. Delaying surgery to obtain laboratory or radiological studies, await cross-matched blood products, or place invasive monitors is contraindicated. Instead, these activities should occur in parallel without delaying the transfer of the patient to theatre. This limited surgery would be followed by a period of intensive care for correction of coagulation, hypothermia, and acidosis. Only once the patient is stable with normal physiology would the definitive intramedullary nailing be undertaken (Scalea et al. 2000).

Damage-control surgery has been shown to be beneficial, but it is not applicable to all cases of trauma. For example, not all fractures can be externally fixed. It also requires a second surgical procedure with all its associated risks and costs. It is likely that careful clinical judgement and patient selection is required for damage-control surgery to be of significant benefit (Rixen et al. 2005).

Other preoperative considerations

In addition to the traumatic injury itself, the manner of the initial presentation of patients can make planning of anaesthesia more difficult. They may be confused, intoxicated, or unconscious, making it

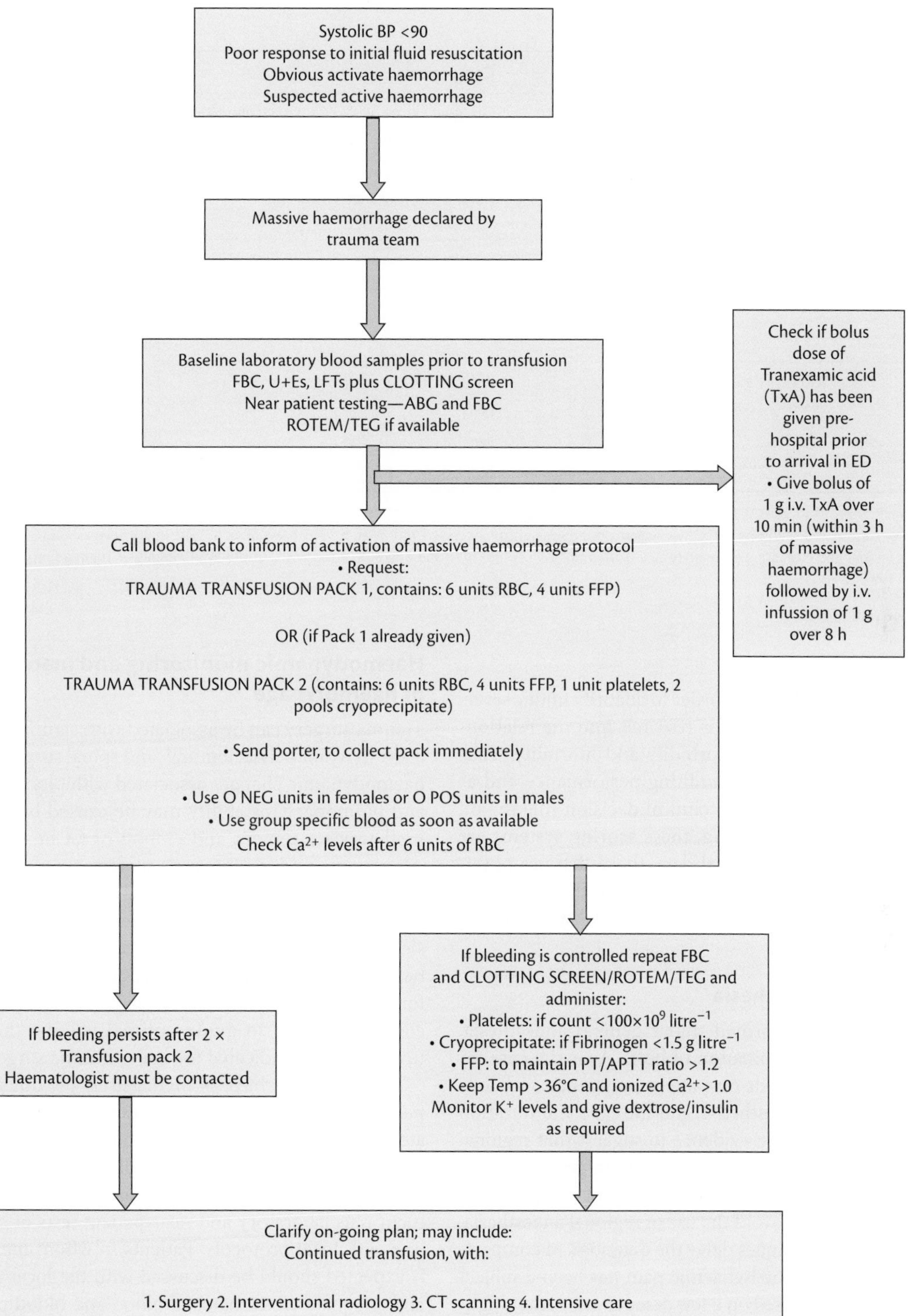

Figure 63.3 Trauma haemorrhage algorithm.

Reproduced with permission from Sengupta, S. and Shirley, P. Trauma anaesthesia and critical care: the post trauma network era. *Continuing Education in Anaesthesia, Critical Care, and Pain*, 2014, Volume 14, Issue 1, pp. 32–37, by permission of the British Journal of Anaesthesia.

difficult or impossible to obtain an adequate medical history including allergies, medications, and co-morbidities. Intoxication with alcohol or illicit substances can cause agitation, confusion, or unconsciousness, and changes in cardiovascular and respiratory physiology.

There is also the risk associated with a full stomach and uncleared spine, both of which must be assumed in the absence of an adequate history. These risks may combine with those present in other higher-risk groups: extremes of age, the obese patient, and the pregnant patient.

Table 63.6 Examples of trauma scoring systems in use

Type of scoring system	Example	Components	Limitations
Physiological	Revised Trauma Score (RTS) (Champion et al. 1989)	Glasgow Coma Score (GCS); systolic blood pressure; respiratory rate	GCS difficult to measure in sedated, ventilated, or intoxicated patients
Anatomical	Abbreviated Injury Scale (AIS) (Association for the Advancement of Automated Medicine 2016)	Grades injuries from 0 (no injury) to 6 (fatal injury) by anatomical site	Consensus-derived coding, requires dedicated manual and does not reflect increasing severity of multiple injuries
	Injury Severity Score (ISS) (Baker et al. 1974)	Sum of the squares of the highest AIS scores in three defined body regions	Cannot account for multiple injuries in the same body region Limited to three most severe injuries Non-linear scoring
Combined scores	TRISS (TRauma score and Injury Severity Score) (Boyd et al. 1987)	RTS ISS Age Blunt or penetrating injury	Limited accuracy in predicting survival Combines limitations of its individual components

Data from: Champion HR, Sacco WJ, Copes WS, Gann DS, Gennarelli TA, Flanagan ME (May 1989). "A revision of the Trauma Score". *The Journal of Trauma* 29(5): 623–9; Association for the Advancement of Automated Medicine. http://www.aaam.org/about-ais.html. Accessed 14th March 2016; Baker SP, et al, "The Injury Severity Score: a method for describing patients with multiple injuries and evaluating emergency care", *J Trauma* 14: 187–196; 1974; and Boyd CR, Tolson MA, Copes WS: "Evaluating Trauma Care: The TRISS Method", *J Trauma* 27: 370–378; 1987.

Trauma scoring systems

A number of scoring systems exist in order to quantify injury severity. These have arisen from a need for research into the relationship between injury severity and morbidity and mortality. Thus their use is primarily intended for auditing performance and as quality indicators and not to inform clinical decision-making on an individual basis. Broadly speaking, these scoring systems are divided into those that use anatomical data, those that use physiological data, and those that use a combination of the two. All of them attempt to categorize injury severity by mortality risk (Yates 1990). See Table 63.6.

General *vs* regional anaesthesia

Trauma surgery may be performed under general anaesthesia, regional anaesthesia, or a combination of both. As is the case for all surgery, the decision depends on patient preference and consent, the preference of the anaesthetist, and the type and duration of surgery. There is currently no evidence to suggest that regional anaesthesia provides a better overall outcome than general anaesthesia (Bonnet 2005). In trauma surgery, the risk of compartment syndrome may be a reason to avoid the use of regional anaesthesia, although whether these techniques delay the diagnosis of compartment syndrome by masking the ischaemic pain has been a subject of some controversy, and is based on a few case reports rather high-quality evidence (Walker et al. 2012).

In general, most isolated extremity trauma surgery can be performed under regional anaesthesia if the benefits are judged to outweigh the risks. However, in major polytrauma involving multiple limbs plus other soft tissue or visceral injury, the benefit of superior postoperative pain relief and avoidance of opioids offered by regional anaesthesia diminishes greatly, particularly as these patients face a period of sedation and invasive ventilation in an intensive care unit. The issue of a coagulopathy in the presence of peripheral nerve catheters or epidural catheters must also be taken into account.

Haemodynamic monitoring and management of haemorrhage

Trauma surgery can be associated with significant blood loss, especially in major pelvic, femoral, and spinal surgery. In addition to the haemodynamic changes associated with blood loss, cardiovascular and pulmonary instability may be caused by reactions to methyl methacrylate cement and emboli of fat or bone during surgery. All patients undergoing such surgery should have two large-bore peripheral intravenous lines, and if massive haemorrhage is suspected, then large-bore central venous access should also be considered. Arterial line placement is usually indicated for accurate beat-to-beat blood pressure measurement and sampling of blood for blood gas analysis and coagulation tests. It also allows for pulse contour analysis to guide optimal volume therapy. Monitoring urine output is indicated for major trauma surgery.

Major haemorrhage is managed as previously described, with permissive hypotension and volume replacement with appropriate fluid including blood and blood products. Equipment for rapid transfusion of fluid should be available to use if required.

Administration of blood products is guided by clinical judgement plus laboratory and near-patient tests of coagulation, and in line with local protocols. Patients in whom massive haemorrhage is expected should be discussed with the local transfusion service and adequate cross-matched blood and blood products should be available. Use of autologous blood using a cell saver is also possible in trauma surgery.

Acute compartment syndrome

Compartment syndrome is a condition in which increased pressure within a closed compartment compromises the circulation and function of tissues within that space. A direct injury causes an initial increase in compartmental pressure, which reduces perfusion and causes local ischaemia. Ischaemic damage to tissue membranes causes fluid leak and further increases in pressure, eventually compromising venous outflow and causing further fluid transudation and tissue swelling. Once capillary pressure is exceeded, local perfusion is no longer possible and infarction of tissue is inevitable. Irreversible tissue damage can occur within 4 h of injury. Ischaemia and necrosis of muscle tissue may result in rhabdomyolysis and renal failure secondary to muscle breakdown. Trauma involving limb injury, with or without a fracture, is a common cause of acute compartment syndrome. Fractures of the tibial shaft and of the distal forearm are particularly at risk (McQueen et al. 2000). Soft tissue injuries, injuries to vasculature, and excessively tight dressings or plaster casts may also cause compartment syndrome.

Diagnosis

Early diagnosis is paramount to the successful treatment of compartment syndrome. Pain that is disproportionate to the injury is the cardinal sign. This may present as an increased analgesic requirement, particularly in patients who are unable to communicate pain magnitude effectively. Paraesthesia, weakness, and pulselessness may present as late signs, but sensitivity is poor. Diagnosis of compartment syndrome relies on well-trained staff maintaining a high index of suspicion. Measurement of compartment pressure can aid diagnosis and be used for monitoring high-risk patients, but thresholds for diagnosis and treatment vary. The choice of analgesic technique is an area of controversy in patients who are at risk of compartment syndrome. It has been advocated that regional anaesthesia may mask the pain of compartment syndrome and delay diagnosis. However, there is no good evidence of this occurring with epidural analgesia or peripheral nerve block if patients are monitored adequately (Farrow et al. 2011).

Treatment

Any suspicion of compartment syndrome should prompt removal of any external dressings or plaster casts and rapid assessment by a surgeon. Compartment syndrome requires urgent surgical decompression in order to restore tissue perfusion and prevent tissue necrosis and subsequent loss of function. This is achieved by open fasciotomy and debridement of any necrosed tissue, followed by splinting to prevent contractures. Any delay from diagnosis to fasciotomy increases the risk of loss of function.

Fat embolism syndrome

Fat embolism occurs relatively frequently in patients with orthopaedic trauma, and a proportion of these develop adverse clinical symptoms and signs, termed fat embolism syndrome. After trauma, fat particles enter the circulation and damage capillary beds resulting in an intense inflammatory response. Capillary beds develop increased permeability and inflammatory mediators damage surrounding tissues (Kwiatt and Seamon 2013). Depending on the criteria used for diagnosis, fat embolism syndrome can develop in 9–29% of patients with a long bone fracture (Mellor and Soni 2001).

Diagnosis

The features are non-specific, with the classical presentation of a triad of hypoxia, neurological disturbance, and a petechial rash. Respiratory failure is the most commonly seen manifestation. Pulmonary hypertension and decreased cardiac function may also be present. Thrombocytopenia and unexplained anaemia are common, and fat globules may appear in blood and urinary analysis. A chest X-ray classically shows multiple bilateral patchy areas of consolidation typically in the middle and upper zones, while a chest CT scan will show diffuse areas of vascular congestion and pulmonary oedema.

Treatment

Numerous pharmacological treatment strategies have been tried. The administration of glucose, ethanol, heparin, and corticosteroids in numerous trials has not shown any clear clinical benefit (Kwiatt and Seamon 2013).

Treatment therefore centres on close monitoring and organ support. Lung involvement may manifest as acute respiratory distress syndrome and require mechanical ventilation; shock requires fluid resuscitation and cardiovascular support with inotropes or vasopressors; neurological injury as a result of cerebral oedema may require monitoring of intracranial pressure.

Surgery may also influence the incidence and severity of fat embolism syndrome (Mellor and Soni 2001). Early fracture fixation may reduce the incidence, as the movement of fracture ends during conservative management causes showering of fat emboli. Specific surgical techniques aimed at decreasing intramedullary pressure during operative fixation have not been shown to reduce the incidence of fat embolism syndrome.

Management of specific fractures

Fractures of the hip

Hip fractures are seen most commonly in the elderly population, with 30% being seen in those more than 85 years old. This group is associated with prolonged hospital stays and high morbidity and mortality (Kearns et al. 2012). Mortality at 30 days is over 10%, rising to over 25% at 1 year (Foss and Kehlet 2005). With a projected incidence of 100 000 cases in England alone by 2033 at an annual cost of £3.6–5.6 billion (White and Griffiths 2011), there is also a growing public health issue relating to hip fractures.

Anaesthetic management of these patients must take into account the high chance of co-morbidity and frailty in this group. On the one hand, optimizing them for safe anaesthesia may mean delaying surgery while unstable medical conditions are treated. On the other hand, early fixation of hip fractures has been shown to be beneficial. A review of the evidence concluded that patients who underwent surgery earlier had lower rates of non-union, avascular necrosis of the femoral head, urinary tract infections, decubitus ulcers, pneumonia, VTE, and death, and better long-term functional status than those who underwent surgery later (Whinney 2005). The same review found that delaying surgery also resulted in increased pain, leading to delayed discharge, delayed rehabilitation, and postoperative delirium. When UK national guidelines on the management of proximal femoral fracture were examined, all were found to emphasize the advantages of expedited surgery, with all but one setting a standard of surgical repair on the day of or day after injury, and within daylight hours. The exception was the 2009 Scottish Intercollegiate Guidelines Network guideline, which reduced this to within 24 h (Kearns et al. 2012).

Fractures of the pelvis

Relatively high force is required to fracture the bones of the pelvic ring, and so the incidence of pelvic fractures is low compared with all other orthopaedic fractures. They are usually associated with high-speed road traffic accidents. As the bony pelvis is closely related to the arterial supply, this type of injury can result in rapid massive haemorrhage and carries a relatively high mortality rate among orthopaedic injuries. Major pelvic trauma with haemodynamic instability has a mortality rate of 42% (Mucha and Welch 1988), although rapid blood loss may be slowed by tamponade within the retroperitoneal pelvis. External devices such as pneumatic antishock trousers can play a role in limiting blood loss and certain types of fracture may be amenable to external fixation. However, with ongoing life-threatening haemorrhage, the options are limited to therapeutic embolization within an angiography suite or immediate transfer to theatre for open surgery.

Whether surgery is performed for a life-threatening emergency or as a delayed urgent procedure, surgery involving the pelvis and acetabulum are major interventions associated with significant blood loss, and careful anaesthetic preparation is vital. Between 30% and 49% of unstable pelvic fractures require over 10 units of blood during operative fixation (Cryer et al. 1988). Large-bore intravenous access, rapid infusion devices, and adequate blood and blood products are all essential. Positioning of the patient depends on the fracture location and may be supine, lateral, or prone. There may also be a requirement for neurological monitoring of the sciatic nerve, which may present a significant challenge for the anaesthetist. High-dose volatile agents or benzodiazepines interfere with somatosensory-evoked potentials, and neuromuscular blocking agents cannot be used if MEPs are monitored. Propofol may not be tolerated in haemodynamically unstable patients, and nitrous oxide is contraindicated in trauma patients because of its potential to expand gas-filled spaces. Opioids and α_2-agonists may be used for analgesia and sedation, but the risk of awareness during general anaesthesia in these patients is increased.

Fractures of the spine

Traumatic spinal injuries can present multiple challenges to the anaesthetist, which vary depending on their site and severity. Loss of neurological function should be looked for and documented. Loss of neurological function and involvement of the autonomic nervous system is determined by the level of the trauma. Spinal cord transections at and above C5 require constant artificial ventilation. Injury from T1 to L2 may result in sympathectomy, and above T6 the parasympathetic system may be unopposed, causing the neurogenic shock picture of hypotension, bradycardia, and hypothermia.

Initial management of spinal injury

Management of spinal cord injury begins with control of the airway and breathing to ensure adequate oxygenation followed by optimization of circulation by controlling haemorrhage, fluid resuscitation, and use of vasopressors if required. Concurrent injuries are evaluated and managed in accordance with standard ATLS protocols (ATLS Subcommittee et al. 2013). A high index of suspicion for unstable spine injury should be maintained in any high-energy trauma even in the absence of neurological signs or symptoms. Such patients should be treated with complete spine immobilization until the possibility of spine injury has been formally excluded. Neurological deficit such as numbness, paraesthesia, weakness, or bowel or bladder dysfunction is suggestive of a spinal cord injury and requires urgent radiological investigation. Magnetic resonance imaging in a haemodynamically unstable patient is not advised.

An unstable fracture of the spine with acute neurological impairment requires urgent surgical intervention in order to reduce the fracture, decompress the spinal canal, and then stabilize unstable segments by fusion and instrumentation (Stahel et al. 2012). There is no clear evidence from clinical trials to support early surgical decompression in improving neurological outcomes when compared with those performed after 72 h. However, earlier surgery does appear to result in shorter hospital stays, shorter intensive care unit stays, less days on mechanical ventilation, and lower pulmonary complications (Carreon and Dimar 2011).

Other strategies that have been used in the past in neurological injury include therapeutic hypothermia and corticosteroid administration. Hypothermia has shown neuroprotective benefit in animal models (Maybhate et al. 2012), but its use in humans remains experimental and must be balanced with the potential deleterious effect on coagulation and cardiovascular function. Corticosteroid therapy was popular a few decades ago but its use has become obsolete after the 'CRASH' trial (Corticosteroid randomization after significant head injury), which showed an increased mortality in acutely head-injured patients who were given methylprednisolone (Roberts et al. 2004).

Anaesthetic management of the patient with spine injury

Anaesthetic management of patients with acute spinal cord injuries must involve an understanding of the pathophysiology of the injury. Neurogenic shock may be confused with late hypovolaemic shock. A decrease in vascular resistance requires administration of a vasopressor, and atropine may be required to treat increased vagal tone.

Other precautions may need to be taken depending on the duration of time since the injury. For example, autonomic hyperreflexia may present from a few days to several years after an injury, usually transections at T5 or above. A profound autonomic response can result from minor stimulation below the level of injury, such as during bladder catheterization or skin incision. Marked vasoconstriction below the level of the lesion causes hypertension and reflex bradycardia. Dysrhythmias and myocardial infarct may result. Prevention or early recognition of the phenomenon is important and requires knowledge of the level of injury, careful history-taking in those with long-standing injuries, and appropriate monitoring of the patient during anaesthesia. Vasodilating agents and β-blockers should be immediately available during the procedure.

Patients presenting for surgery after the acute phase of injury are at risk of succinylcholine-induced hyperkalaemia as a result of upregulation of acetylcholine receptors, and this agent is generally avoided for 24 h after spinal cord injury (Martyn and Richtsfeld 2006).

In addition to the pathophysiological changes of neurological injury, spine surgery itself can present major challenges to the anaesthetist. An anterior approach to the thoracic spine may require lung isolation, and for lumbar surgery necessitates a laparotomy, both of which can contribute to blood loss and fluid shifts.

Declaration of interest

None declared.

References

Alshryda S, Sarda P, Sukeik M, *et al.* Tranexamic acid in total knee replacement a systematic review and meta-analysis. *J Bone Joint Surg Br* 2011; **93**: 1577–85

ATLS Subcommittee, American College of Surgeons' Committee on Trauma, International ATLS Working Group. Advanced trauma life support (ATLS®): the ninth edition. *J Trauma Acute Care Surg* 2013; **74**: 1363–6

Boezaart AP, Eksteen JA, Spuy GV, Rossouw P, Knipe M. Double blind evaluation of optimal dosage for analgesia after major lumbar spinal surgery. *Spine* 1999; **24**: 1131–7

Bone LB, Johnson KD, Weigelt J, Scheinberg R. Early versus delayed stabilization of femoral fractures. A prospective randomized study. *J Bone Joint Surg Am* 1989; **71**: 336–40

Bonnet F. Influence of anaesthetic and analgesic techniques on outcome after surgery. *Br J Anaesth* 2005; **95**: 52–8

Brohi K, Cohen MJ, Davenport RA. Acute coagulopathy of trauma: mechanism, identification and effect. *Curr Opin Crit Care* 2007; **13**: 680–5

Brown MJ, Kor DJ, Curry TB, *et al.* Sacral tumour resection. *Spine* 2011; **36**: 1570–8

Bryson GL, Laupacis A, Wells GA. Does acute normovolemic hemodilution reduce perioperative allogenic transfusion? A meta-analysis. The International Study of Perioperative Transfusion. *Anesth Analg* 1998; **86**: 9–15

Bujedo BM. A clinical approach to neuraxial morphine for the treatment of postoperative pain. *Pain Res Treat* 2012; **2012**: 612145

Carreon LY, Dimar JR. Early versus late stabilization of spine injuries: a systematic review. *Spine* 2011; **36**: E727–3

Chang SH, Miller NR. The incidence of vision loss due to perioperative ischemic optic neuropathy associated with spine surgery: The John Hopkins experience. *Spine* 2005; **30**: 1299–302

Cook TM, Bland L, Mihal R, Scott S. Litigation related to anaesthesia: an analysis of claims against the NHS in England 1995–2007. *Anaesthesia* 2009; **64**: 706–18

CRASH-2 trial collaborators, Shakur H, Roberts I, *et al.* Effects of tranexamic acid on death, vascular occlusive events, and blood transfusion in trauma patients with significant haemorrhage (CRASH-2): a randomised, placebo-controlled trial. *Lancet* 2010; **376**: 23–32

Cryer HM, Miller FB, Evers BM, Rouben LR, Seligson DL. Pelvic fracture classification: correlation with hemorrhage. *J Trauma Injury Infect Crit Care* 1988; **28**: 973

Curry N, Stanworth S, Hopewell S, Dorée C, Brohi K, Hyde C. Trauma-induced coagulopathy--a review of the systematic reviews: is there sufficient evidence to guide clinical transfusion practice? *Transfus Med Rev* 2011; **25**: 217–231.e2

Dauri M, Faria S, Gatti A, Celidonio L, Carpenedo R, Sabato AF. Gabapentin and pregabalin for the acute post-operative pain management. A systematic-narrative review of the recent clinical evidences. *Curr Drug Targets* 2009; **10**: 716–33

Davis JW, Shackford SR, Mackersie RC, Hoyt DB. Base deficit as a guide to volume resuscitation. *J Trauma* 1988; **28**: 1464–7

den Broeder AA, Creemers MCW, Fransen J, *et al.* Risk factors for surgical site infections and other complications in elective surgery in patients with rheumatoid arthritis with special attention for anti-tumour necrosis factor: a large retrospective study. *J Rheumatol* 2007; **34**: 689–95

Department for Transport. Reported road casualties Great Britain: annual report 2013. 2014. Available from https://www.gov.uk/government/statistics/reported-road-casualties-great-britain-annual-report-2013

Donaldson J, Thomson HE, Harper NJ, Kenny NW. Bone cement implantation syndrome. *Br J Anaesth* 2009; **102**: 12–22

Dretzke J, Sandercock J, Bayliss S, Burls A. Clinical effectiveness and cost-effectiveness of prehospital intravenous fluids in trauma patients. *Health Technol Assess* 2004; **8**: iii–1–103

Farrow C, Bodenham A, Troxler M. Acute limb compartment syndromes. *Cont Educ Anaesth Crit Care Pain* 2011; **11**: 24–8

Fischer HBJ, Simanski CJP. A procedure specific systematic review and consensus recommendations for analgesia after total hip replacement. *Anaesthesia* 2005; **60**: 1189–202

Foss NB, Kehlet H. Mortality analysis in hip fracture patients: implications for design of future outcome trials. *Br J Anaesth* 2005; **94**: 24–9

Grover M, Talwalkar S, Casbard A, *et al.* Silent myocardial ischaemia and haemoglobin concentration: a randomized controlled trial of transfusion strategy in lower limb arthroplasty. *Vox Sanguinis* 2006; **90**: 105–12

Hammell C, Barrett P, Shackleford I. Intrathecal diamorphine for analgesia following lumbar spinal surgery. *J Bone Joint Surg Br* 2009; **9**(Suppl III): 477

Harsten A, Kehlet H, Toksvig-Larsen S. Recovery after total intravenous anaesthesia or spinal anaesthesia for total knee arthroplasty: a randomized trial. *Br J Anaesth* 2013; **111**: 391–9

Herbert PC, Wells G, Blajchman MA, *et al.* A multicenter randomized controlled clinical trial of transfusion requirements in critical care. Transfusion Requirements in Critical Care Investigators, Canadian Critical Care Trials Group. *N Engl J Med* 1999; **340**: 490–17

Holcomb JB, Tilley BC, Baraniuk S, *et al.* Transfusion of plasma, platelets, and red blood cells in a 1:1:1 vs a 1:1:2 ratio and mortality in patients with severe trauma: the PROPPR Randomized Clinical Trial. *JAMA* 2015; **313**: 471–82

Hopkins PM, Ellis FR, Halsall PJ. Hypermetabolism in arthrogryposis multiplex congenital. *Anaesthsia* 1991; **46**: 374–5

Jansen JO, Thomas R, Loudon MA, Brooks A. Damage control resuscitation for patients with major trauma. *BMJ* 2009; **338**: b1778

Kearns RJ, Moss L, Kinsella J. A comparison of clinical practice guidelines for proximal femoral fracture. *Anaesthesia* 2012; **68**: 159–66

Khan S, Allard S, Weaver A, Barber C, Davenport R, Brohi K. A major haemorrhage protocol improves the delivery of blood component therapy and reduces waste in trauma massive transfusion. *Injury* 2013; **44**: 587–92

Kirkman E, Watts S, Hodgetts T, Mahoney P, Rawlinson S, Midwinter M. A proactive approach to the coagulopathy of trauma: the rationale and guidelines for treatment. *J R Army Med Corps* 2007; **153**: 302–6

Kotze A, Carter LA, Scally AJ. Effect of a patient blood management programme on preoperative anaemia, transfusion rate, and outcome after primary hip or knee arthroplasty: a quality improvement cycle. *Br J Anaesth* 2012; **108**: 943–52

Kwiatt ME, Seamon MJ. Fat embolism syndrome. *Int J Crit Illn Inj Sci* 2013; **3**: 64–8

Levaux C, Bonhomme V, Dewandre PY, *et al.* Effect of intra-operative magnesium sulphate on pain relief and patient comfort after major lumbar orthopaedic surgery. *Anaesthesia* 2003; **58**: 131–5

Lier H, Krep H, Schroeder S, Stuber F. Preconditions of hemostasis in trauma: a review. The influence of acidosis, hypocalcemia, anemia, and hypothermia on functional hemostasis in trauma. *J Trauma* 2008; **65**: 951–60

MacLeod JBA, Lynn M, McKenney MG, Cohn SM, Murtha M. Early coagulopathy predicts mortality in trauma. *J Trauma* 2003; **55**: 39–44

Maegele M, Lefering R, Yucel N, *et al.* Early coagulopathy in multiple injury: an analysis from the German Trauma Registry on 8724 patients. *Injury* 2007; **38**: 298–304

Martyn JAJ, Richtsfeld M. Succinylcholine-induced hyperkalemia in acquired pathologic states: etiologic factors and molecular mechanisms. *Anesthesiology* 2006; **104**: 158

Maybhate A, Hu C, Bazley FA, *et al.* Potential long-term benefits of acute hypothermia after spinal cord injury: assessments with somatosensory-evoked potentials. *Crit Care Med* 2012; **40**: 573–9

McQueen MM, Gaston P, Court-Brown CM. Acute compartment syndrome. Who is at risk? *J Bone Joint Surg Br* 2000; **82**: 200–3

Mellor A, Soni N. Fat embolism. *Anaesthesia* 2001; **56**: 145–54

Memtsoudis SG, Sun X, Chiu Y, *et al.* Perioperative comparative effectiveness of anesthetic technique in orthopedic patients. *Anesthesiology* 2013; **118**: 1046–58

Memtsoudis SG, Vougioukas VI, Ma Y, *et al.* Perioperative morbidity and mortality after anterior, posterior and anterior/posterior spine fusion surgery. *Spine* 2011; **36**: 1867–77

Mercer SJ, Tarmey NT, Woolley T, Wood P, Mahoney PF. Haemorrhage and coagulopathy in the Defence Medical Services. *Anaesthesia* 2013; **68**(Suppl 1): 49–60

Mhuircheartaigh RJN, Moore RA, McQuay HJ. Analysis of individual patient data from clinical trials: epidural morphine for postoperative pain. *Br J Anaesth* 2009; **103**: 874–81

Mucha P Jr, Welch TJ. Hemorrhage in major pelvic fractures. *Surg Clin North Am* 1988; **68**: 757–73

Murphy GS, Szokol JW, Marymont JH, *et al.* Cerebral oxygen desaturation events assessed by near-infrared spectroscopy during shoulder arthroscopy in the beach chair and lateral decubitus positions. *Anesth Analg* 2010; **111**: 496–505

National Institute for Health and Care Excellence. *Reducing the Risk of Venous Thromboembolism in Patients Admitted to Hospital.* Clinical Guideline 92. London: NICE, 2010 [updated 2015]. Available from https: //www.nice.org.uk/guidance/cg92

National Institute for Health and Care Excellence. *Perioperative Hypothermia (Inadvertent): The Management of Inadvertent Perioperative Hypothermia in Adults.* Clinical Guideline 29. London: NICE, 2008. Available from www.nice.org.uk

Pape HC, Giannoudis P, Krettek C. The timing of fracture treatment in polytrauma patients: relevance of damage control orthopedic surgery. *Am J Surg* 2002; **183**: 622–9

Pape HC, Grimme K, Van Griensven M, *et al.* Impact of intramedullary instrumentation versus damage control for femoral fractures on immunoinflammatory parameters: prospective randomized analysis by the EPOFF Study Group. *J Trauma* 2003; **55**: 7–13

Pape HC, Van Griensven M, Rice J, *et al.* Major secondary surgery in blunt trauma patients and perioperative cytokine liberation: determination of the clinical relevance of biochemical markers. *J Trauma* 2001; **50**: 989–1000

Rixen D, Grass G, Sauerland S, *et al.* Evaluation of criteria for temporary external fixation in risk-adapted damage control orthopedic surgery of femur shaft fractures in multiple trauma patients: "evidence-based medicine" versus "reality" in the trauma registry of the German Trauma Society. *J Trauma* 2005; **59**: 1375–94

Roberts I, Yates D, Sandercock P, *et al.* Effect of intravenous corticosteroids on death within 14 days in 10008 adults with clinically significant head injury (MRC CRASH trial): randomised placebo-controlled trial. *Lancet* 2004; **364**: 1321–8

Scalea TM, Boswell SA, Scott JD, Mitchell KA, Kramer ME, Pollak AN. External fixation as a bridge to intramedullary nailing for patients with multiple injuries and with femur fractures: damage control orthopedics. *J Trauma* 2000; **48**: 613–21

Schwab JH, Healey JH, Rose P, *et al.* The surgical management of sacral chordomas. *Spine* 2009; **34**: 2700–4

Segal JB, Blasco-Colmenares E, Norris EJ, Gullar E. Preoperative acute normovolemic hemodilution: a meta-analysis. *Transfusion* 2004; **44**: 632–44

Stahel PF, VanderHeiden T, Finn MA. Management strategies for acute spinal cord injury: current options and future perspectives. *Curr Opin Crit Care* 2012; **18**: 651–60

Sukeik M, Alshryda S, Haddad FS, Mason JM. Systematic review and meta-analysis of the use of tranexamic acid in total hip replacement. *J Bone Joint Surg Br* 2011; **93**: 39–46

The Association of Anaesthetists of Great Britain and Ireland. *Blood Transfusion and the Anaesthetist: Red Cell Transfusion.* London: AAGBI, 2008. Available from https: //www.aagbi.org/publications

Thomas D, Wareham K, Cohen D, Hutchings H. Autologous blood transfusion in total knee replacement surgery. *Br J Anaesth* 2001; **85**: 669–73

Trelle S, Reichenbach S, Wandel S, *et al.* Cardiovascular safety of non-steroidal anti-inflammatory drugs: network meta-analysis. *BMJ* 2011; **342**: c7086

Walker BJ, Noonan KJ, Bosenberg AT. Evolving compartment syndrome not masked by a continuous peripheral nerve block: evidence-based case management. *Reg Anesth Pain Med* 2012; **37**: 393–7

Whinney CM. Do hip fractures need to be repaired within 24 hours of injury? *Cleve Clin J Med* 2005; **72**: 250–2

White SM, Griffiths R. Projected incidence of proximal femoral fracture in England: a report from the NHS Hip Fracture Anaesthesia Network (HIPFAN). *Injury* 2011; **42**: 1230–3

Yates DW. ABC of major trauma. Scoring systems for trauma. *BMJ* 1990; **301**: 1090

CHAPTER 64

Anaesthesia for plastic surgery and burns

Sandip K. Pal

Introduction

Plastic surgery is a branch of medicine concerned with correction and restoration of form and function of tissues. The term *plastic* denotes 'sculpting' and is derived from the Greek word *plastikē* meaning 'art of modelling' of malleable tissue ('Plastic', 1996).

Plastic surgery originated in India as early as 600 BC (Rana and Arora 2002). An Indian surgeon, Sushruta, performed rhinoplasty in that era. Amputation of the nose was performed as a punishment for committing adultery and hence the need for nasal reconstruction.

Anaesthesia was non-existent and surgeons used wine to dull the pain of surgical incisions. With the introduction of anaesthetics, surgery became painless and with advances in anaesthesia it became possible to perform longer and more complex surgical procedures safely, and major advances in surgery took place.

In World War I, (Sir) Harold Gilles, while caring for soldiers suffering from horrific facial injuries, developed techniques of plastic surgery which are still practised. During World War II, (Sir) Archibald McIndoe pioneered a treatment strategy for Royal Air Force aircrew with severe burns.

Plastic surgery is a broad field, and may be subdivided into:

- Reconstructive surgery:
  - Trauma (e.g. laceration, scar, hand surgery)
  - Congenital abnormalities (e.g. cleft lip and palate, craniofacial abnormalities, and congenital hand deformities such as brachial plexus injury)
  - Cancer/tumour (e.g. skin cancer—basal cell carcinoma/squamous cell carcinoma, tumour removal, breast reconstruction after mastectomy)
- Cosmetic (aesthetic) surgery
- Burns.

Anaesthesia for free flap surgery

Free flap surgery is a complex method of large wound closure used when it is not possible to close the wound directly (primary closure). The term 'free' denotes vascular detachment of an isolated region of the body (skin, fat, muscle, bone, bowel, or any combination) followed by transfer of that tissue to another region where tissue loss has occurred; the circulation is restored by reattachment of the divided vessels using microvascular anastomoses. The tissue loss may be caused by trauma, infection, burn, extensive surgery for head and neck cancer, or after mastectomy.

The first reported experimental free flap surgery was carried out by Krizek in 1965 (Krizek et al. 1965). The first free microvascular flap surgery in a patient was carried out by Antia and Buch (1971) when they used a lower abdominal flap to reconstruct a post-traumatic facial defect. However, the flap developed partial necrosis. The following year, McLean and Buncke (1972) successfully carried out microvascular free tissue transfer using an omental flap to fill a large scalp defect. Since then, free tissue transfer has become commonplace in many centres around the world. The advantages of a free tissue transfer include stable wound coverage, improved aesthetic and functional outcomes, and minimal donor site morbidity. With improved safety and advanced surgical and anaesthetic techniques, the success rate has improved substantially and is currently higher than 95% among experienced surgeons and anaesthetists working together in established centres. However, postoperative flap perfusion failure still occurs even in the most experienced hands, requiring immediate surgical exploration and restoration of perfusion in the flap. Early detection of compromised flap perfusion is imperative, allowing timely re-exploration and salvaging of failing flaps. Various objective monitoring devices apart from close clinical observation have been developed and used clinically. Postoperative free flap salvage rates exceeding 50% have been reported (Wei et al. 2001; Top et al. 2006).

Types of free flap

Examples of free flaps are free fibular flap for mandibular reconstruction; transverse rectus abdominis myocutaneous (TRAM), muscle-sparing TRAM, microsurgical inferior epigastric vessel enhanced pedicled TRAM flap which can be either 'supercharged' (venous) or 'turbocharged' (arterial and venous); deep inferior epigastric perforator (DIEP), superficial inferior epigastric artery, thoracodorsal artery perforator, superior and inferior gluteal perforator flaps for breast reconstruction; anterior lateral thigh and gracilis flaps for lower limb trauma; and toe transfer for trauma or congenital deformities of the hand.

The use of perforator flaps minimizes donor site morbidity (Blondeel et al. 1997). Supercharge and turbocharge can increase the length of operating time which the anaesthetist should be aware of.

In trauma patients, the timing of free-flap reconstruction is of prime importance (Nahabadian et al. 2004). Free tissue transfer should be carried out within 6 days to allow time for adequate debridement and declaration of the zone of injury, but before colonization of the wound takes place with resultant risk of complications. In patients with multiple trauma, it is vital that any life-threatening injury is addressed first and the patient's haemodynamic status stabilized before contemplating reconstructive surgery.

Steps of flap surgery

The stages of free flap transfer are as follows:

1. If cancer is involved, it is removed (perhaps by a different team of surgeons).
2. Flap elevation: the flap is dissected and freed from the surrounding tissue.
3. Before the vascular pedicle is clamped and divided, the area the flap will be attached to is prepared by identifying a recipient artery and vein to which the free flap's vascular pedicle can be attached.
4. The blood supply including at least one vein and one artery is dissected. This segment is called the vascular pedicle. The vascular pedicle is clamped and divided. Primary ischaemia develops as blood flow ceases and intracellular metabolism becomes anaerobic (this is dependent on surgical time taken to anastomose the vessels and lasts 60–90 min in experienced hands).
5. The vein and artery from the flap (vascular pedicle) are anastomosed to the vein and artery identified in the wound using a microscope. Clamps are released allowing reperfusion of the flap.
6. The free flap is sutured to the defect area.
7. The donor site area is sutured closed.

Characteristics of free vascularized tissue include the following:

- Denervated hence no sympathetic innervation to respond to autonomic regulation.
- Responds to local and humeral factors including circulating catecholamines, pharmacological agents, and cold.
- No lymphatic drainage (at least initially) and therefore susceptible to interstitial oedema.
- Usually only a single (and damaged) feeder artery and vein.
- Subject to ischaemia during transfer which causes alteration in the microcirculation (discussed in detail in the next section, 'Physiology of free flap surgery') leading to a decrease in blood flow to the flap itself. This may take a few days to recover.

Physiology of free flap surgery

A sound understanding of the physiology of the circulation and of denervated tissue, and pharmacology is essential when providing anaesthesia for free flap surgery. The following will provide that understanding:

Microcirculation

The microcirculation in the free flap provides oxygen delivery and is vital to its viability. Regulation of blood flow through a series of successive branching of arterioles and venules from central vessels is achieved in three distinct regions: resistance vessels, capillaries, and venules.

Resistance vessels are the arterioles, ranging in diameter from 20 to 50 μm and containing large amounts of smooth muscle in their walls that control regional blood flow. The arteriolar muscular wall can constrict the vessels completely or dilate them several-fold. The vascular tone in the resistance vessels responds to adrenergic stimulation.

Capillaries consist of a single layer of endothelial cells, and are responsible for exchange of nutrients, hormones, electrolytes, and other substances between the blood and the interstitial fluid. Precapillary sphincters containing a band of smooth muscle are located at the arterial end of capillaries and they control blood flow into the capillaries. Blood flow in the capillaries is controlled mainly by local factors such as hypoxia, hypercapnia, and increases in potassium, osmolality, and magnesium, which may cause relaxation; although adrenergic stimulation may have an effect. Other vasoactive hormones (e.g. renin, vasopressin, prostaglandins, and kinins) also play a role in controlling microvascular circulation.

The venules located beyond the capillaries collect blood from the capillaries and act as capacitance vessels. Venous tone is important for maintenance of the return of blood to the heart (e.g. in severe haemorrhage) when adrenergic stimulation causes venoconstriction (Guyton and Hall 2006).

Primary ischaemia

When the flap is raised, clamped, and divided, blood ceases to flow into the flap which then becomes anoxic. In the absence of oxygen, anaerobic metabolism sets in which leads to an accumulation of lactate, depletion of ATP, reduction in intracellular pH, and a rise in calcium concentration, and pro-inflammatory mediators. The extent of damage caused by anoxia is directly proportional to the duration of ischaemia. Tissues with a high metabolic rate such as muscle are more susceptible to ischaemia, hence a TRAM flap (myocutaneous flap) is more sensitive to ischaemia than a DIEP flap (cutaneous flap). At the end of primary ischaemia the following changes take place in the flap ready to be reperfused (Anaesthesia UK 2006):

- Endothelial swelling, vasoconstriction, and interstitial oedema leading to narrow capillaries
- Leucocyte migration and sequestration
- Endothelial cells become less capable of releasing vasodilators and degrading vasoconstrictors
- Cell membrane dysfunction leading to accumulation of toxic products
- Release of inflammatory mediators.

Reperfusion and ischaemia-reperfusion injury

When the vascular clamps are released, blood flow is re-established and in the majority of cases it reverses the changes produced by primary ischaemia and the flap recovers fully. However, if the conditions are not favourable, it may result in an ischaemia–reperfusion injury (I/R injury).

Reperfusion after a prolonged ischaemic insult initiates a multifaceted cascade of pathological events that can paradoxically cause severe tissue injury, resulting in tissue necrosis and systemic effects. This fascinating phenomenon is termed I/R injury, where tissue injury is exacerbated by the restoration of a blood supply rather than the ischaemia itself. Several theories have been proposed over recent years to explain the mechanisms of I/R injury (especially in myocardium). Although there are likely to be multiple components involved, it is generally accepted that oxidative stress plays a central role in mediating the destructive effects. This is further reinforced by the observation that ischaemic tissues must be exposed to molecular oxygen upon reperfusion for I/R injury to occur (Hearse 1977). During a prolonged phase of ischaemia, ATP is broken down under anaerobic metabolism, leading to an accumulation of hypoxanthine within cells (Balakumar et al. 2008). Ischaemic conditions also promote the conversion of xanthine dehydrogenase to xanthine oxidase (Granger and Korthuis 1995). Consequent reperfusion with oxygenated blood enables xanthine oxidase to metabolize hypoxanthine; crucially this reaction converts molecular oxygen to free radicals, thereby generating reactive oxygen species (ROS). This pathway appears to be the principal source of ROS in reperfused tissue (McCord 1985). ROS are cytotoxic molecules that can directly lead to cell death by interacting with cellular proteins, DNA, and membrane lipids.

Another focus of investigation more recently has implicated the extent of opening of the mitochondrial permeability transition pore (MPTP) as a major determinant of I/R injury. The MPTP is a non-specific pore located in the inner mitochondrial membrane that is closed under physiological conditions (Halestrap et al. 2004). However, under conditions of cellular stress (especially mitochondrial Ca^{2+} overload) it can open, which interferes with the permeability barrier of the inner membrane that usually affords protection to the mitochondria. This transition can have devastating impacts—it causes an imbalance in the osmotic pressure gradient that results in mitochondrial swelling, which in turn leads to the release of proteins associated with apoptosis. Also, the mitochondria become permeable to H^+ ions (mitochondrial proton leak), causing the ATPase enzyme involved in oxidative phosphorylation to reverse direction and hydrolyse ATP instead. The decline in ATP means that ionic pumps and other metabolic reactions are eventually inhibited. The cell cannot maintain homeostasis and subsequently faces irreversible damage and death. It has been shown that MPTP opening occurs upon reperfusion, but not during the ischaemic period (Javadov et al. 2003). The conditions that exist during reperfusion are favourable for opening the MPTP to produce the deleterious effects mentioned previously. Generation of ROS during reperfusion enables Ca^{2+} to accumulate in mitochondria, which is the main stimulus for MPTP opening (Halestrap et al. 2004).

I/R injury can produce systemic effects leading to pulmonary oedema and myocardial depression.

Prevention of I/R injury

- Limit ischaemia time to a minimum.
- Ultimately it is the preservation of ATP and subsequent reduction in ROS production that is thought to offer protection against I/R injury.
- Dexamethasone has been reported to reduce IR injury in flaps in an animal study (Dolan et al. 1995). Currently all patients (except patients with diabetes mellitus) receive dexamethasone on induction of anaesthesia in the author's centre. Many clinicians use it as an antiemetic without realizing its potential beneficial effect in reducing I/R injury.
- Is there a place for preconditioning? Ischaemic preconditioning has been shown to reduce mitochondrial proton leak and ROS production in post-ischaemic heart in rats (Quarrie et al. 2011); however, earlier studies claim that temperature (cold) preconditioning has better outcomes than ischaemic preconditioning (Khaliulin et al. 2007).
- Preconditioning with remifentanil has been shown to attenuate liver I/R injury in animals via inducible nitric oxide synthase expression (Yang et al. 2011). Its use during maintenance of anaesthesia for free flap may be beneficial.
- Exogenous adenosine is controversial. Some workers have demonstrated that in addition to its vasodilator effects, exogenous adenosine inhibits neutrophil-mediated cellular injury and free radical production after prolonged ischaemia (Ely and Berne 1992; Bouma et al. 1997). However, this has been challenged by Ulusal et al. (2006).
- Nicorandil, a nitrovasodilator and adenosine triphosphate-sensitive potassium channel opener has been shown in animals to be a potential prophylactic treatment against skeletal muscle I/R injury in reconstructive surgery (Cahoon 2013).
- Activated protein C may be beneficial (Park et al. 2009).
- Further clinical studies are needed to translate the above-mentioned findings in animal studies to clinical situations.

Secondary ischaemia

Secondary ischaemia occurs after the flap is reperfused and may be as a result of intravascular thrombosis, pressure effects of interstitial oedema, or both, and kinking of the anastomosed vessels. Associated findings are raised concentrations of fibrinogen and platelets. Close observation of the flap and quick surgical intervention may salvage a failing flap. Thrombolytic therapy has been shown to have a role in free flap salvage (Yii et al. 2001).

Factors determining perfusion of free flap

The outcome of free flap surgery depends on the physiological status of the patient. Adverse outcomes occur as a result of poor surgical technique; prolonged surgery; poor conduct of anaesthesia; and postoperative management which leads to hypovolaemia, hypotension, hypothermia, haematoma formation, inadequate analgesia, bleeding, and sepsis; leading to flap failure and deterioration in the patient's condition.

To understand the factors which determine good perfusion of free flaps one needs to understand the factors that influence blood flow through the vessel. Laminar flow through a rigid tube is described by the Poiseuille–Hagen equation (Davis and Kenny 2013):

$$\text{Blood Flow} = \frac{\Delta P \pi r^4}{8\eta l} \qquad (64.1)$$

where ΔP = pressure difference between two ends of a tube (perfusion pressure), r = radius of the tube, η = viscosity, and l = length of the tube.

Although the equation applies to a rigid tube and not entirely to the circulation, it can be assumed, however, that alterations in the diameter, perfusion pressure, and viscosity will influence blood flow to the flap.

Perfusion pressure

The systemic arterial pressure will determine the pressure gradient across the flap. Maintaining a good perfusion pressure with a wide pulse pressure will ensure good perfusion of the flap. Use of an appropriate depth of anaesthesia and optimum fluid therapy are usually sufficient. However, if they are not, the situation may be tricky because many surgeons request that inotropes are not given, as they believe that systemically administered catecholamines adversely affect flap blood flow, even though there is little evidence to support this view. In fact, inotropes may actually improve blood flow to the flap by increasing mean arterial pressure. Some centres use dopexamine or dobutamine because these agents will increase cardiac output (CO) with systemic vasodilation.

Radius of the vessel

This is the most important determinant of blood flow to the flap. According to equation (64.1), flow is related to the fourth power of the radius, hence a small decrease in vessel diameter will result in a large drop in blood flow. Also the blood vessel diameter follows Laplace's law which states that intraluminal pressure can influence blood vessel diameter. Transmural pressure may be decreased by either an extravascular pressure rise (e.g. interstitial oedema, haematoma, application of tight dressing, or awkward positioning creating direct pressure on the vessels) or a fall in intravascular pressure (e.g. hypovolaemia) (Adams 2003). Vasodilation should be aimed at in order to improve perfusion of the flap. Vasodilation is dependent on (a) temperature, (b) fluid, (c) type of anaesthesia, and (d) sympathetic innervation. The patient should be kept warm (cold can cause vasoconstriction) in the theatre, recovery, and high dependency unit (HDU)/ward. This can be achieved by increasing the ambient temperature in the theatre or HDU and by using a warm air blanket and a fluid warmer. Hypothermia not only causes vasoconstriction but also raises haematocrit and viscosity, rouleaux formation of red blood cells, and platelet aggregation leading to a reduction in perfusion of the flap. Underestimation of fluid loss is common as insensible loss can be quite large and this can lead to vasoconstriction. The type of anaesthesia can influence the perfusion of a flap. Isoflurane can cause vasodilation with minimal myocardial depression. Propofol inhibits platelet aggregation and increases synthesis of nitric oxide by leucocytes, thereby reducing the risk of thrombosis. Vasospasm of the flap pedicle vessels during surgery is common because of surgical handling and intimal damage of the vessels. This can be treated with topical application of vasodilators [e.g. papaverine, lidocaine, or verapamil (a calcium channel blocker)]. Regional anaesthesia has been used to provide sympathetic blockade to facilitate further vasodilation. However, this can be counterproductive as the denervated transplanted vessels are unable to dilate in response to sympathetic blockade and the normal vessels will dilate, resulting in a 'steal' effect diverting blood flow away from the flap. Furthermore, sympathetic blockade can also cause hypotension which may require vasoconstrictor in addition to fluid therapy. Concerns have been raised in patients who are hypovolaemic as animal models have demonstrated that in the presence of only 10% hypovolaemia, epidural anaesthesia may reduce the blood flow in the flap by 40% (Adams and Charlton 2003). The disadvantages may outbalance the advantages of sympathetic blockade viz. reduction in blood loss, lower incidence of deep vein thrombosis (DVT), and good analgesia which reduces the concentration of circulating catecholamines (causing vasoconstriction) released in response to pain.

Viscosity

The relationship between blood viscosity and haematocrit is non-linear in that viscosity rises steeply when haematocrit exceeds 40%. Isovolaemic haemodilution to 30% increases blood flow. Further reduction of blood viscosity does not improve blood flow markedly and any advantage may be offset by a reduction in oxygen-carrying capacity. In patients with poor cardiac reserve, a low haematocrit could be detrimental as it increases myocardial work.

Length of the pedicle

Blood flow is inversely proportional to the length of the vessel. Blood flow through a long pedicle may have reduced flow.

Practical conduct of anaesthesia

Pre-anaesthetic assessment

All patients presenting for free flap surgery must be thoroughly assessed and investigated in the pre-assessment clinic before anaesthesia. The author's centre has a joint clinic with surgeons and patients are pre-assessed by both teams on the same day. Surgeons can identify the perforator vessels with a hand-held Doppler probe and plan the flap surgery. Risk factors are identified, for example, smoking, obesity, use of alcohol, hypertension, diabetes mellitus, and previous chemotherapy or radiotherapy. Patients with head and neck cancer are generally elderly with poor nutritional status, heavy smokers and drinkers, and may have significant cardiac and respiratory co-morbidities. Some patients may need a percutaneous endoscopic gastrostomy tube inserted and feeding commenced to improve their nutritional status before major head and neck surgery. Airway anatomy may be distorted as a result of the presence of a mass in the neck or as a result of previous chemotherapy or radiotherapy, and a difficult tracheal intubation must be anticipated. A full explanation of awake fibreoptic intubation should be given to the patient if this is planned. Routine investigations should include a full blood count, urea and electrolytes, clotting screen, and group and save. Chest X-ray, ECG, respiratory function tests, arterial blood gases, echocardiogram, and cardiopulmonary exercise testing should be considered in patients with cardiac and respiratory risk factors. Blood should be cross-matched if extensive dissection and reconstruction is planned where excessive blood loss may be anticipated. A careful explanation to the patient about the anaesthetic is required, including prolonged surgery and anaesthesia, pain relief, invasive monitoring, urinary catheter, possible blood transfusion, and postoperative care. A benzodiazepine premedication is often prescribed (e.g. temazepam 10–20 mg or lorazepam 1–2 mg orally 1 h before surgery) in anxious patients.

Monitoring

Routine monitoring should include ECG, non-invasive blood pressure, pulse oximetry, and core and peripheral temperature. In the author's centre it is routine practice to monitor (continuous, non-invasive) CO, stroke volume (SV), and corrected flow time using an oesophageal Doppler probe. This may not be practical in patients undergoing free flap surgery for head and neck cancer. In such cases, a femoral central line and an arterial line are placed. The majority of DIEP cases are performed with non-invasive monitoring;

however, it must be emphasized that oesophageal Doppler is not a substitute for invasive monitoring. For example, an arterial line can provide information about the acid–base status of the patient; a central venous pressure (CVP) line can be useful to administer drugs that will reach the right heart quickly. It has been debated that CVP readings may not truly reflect the fluid status (Marik 2008). Care should be taken to prevent complications, for example, compartment syndrome; alopecia; fluid overload—generalized oedema, pleural effusion; pulmonary oedema; bleeding diathesis; haematoma; and sepsis.

Prophylaxis against DVT is essential using subcutaneous enoxaparin (Clexane®) perioperatively, antiembolism stockings, and intermittent calf compression devices.

Induction of anaesthesia

Usually intravenous induction of anaesthesia is used and total intravenous anaesthesia (TIVA) is a popular technique. Midazolam 1–2 mg intravenously at the start ensures a smooth induction. The airway may be maintained either by a ProSeal™ (Teleflex, Inc., Wayne, PA, USA) laryngeal mask airway (LMA) or cuffed tracheal tube. Advantages of the ProSeal™ LMA are that it is quick and easy to insert, avoids coughing and bucking on the tube on extubation which raises venous pressure leading to poor perfusion of flap: an oesophageal Doppler probe can be inserted via the side port. However, a cuffed tracheal tube isolates the airway completely and has less chance of misplacement and partial obstruction of the airway during crucial parts of the surgery.

Maintenance of anaesthesia

Free flap surgery is a lengthy procedure and so careful positioning to prevent pressure injuries such as nerve paralysis, alopecia, compartment syndrome, and eye damage are vitally important. Anaesthesia can be maintained, for example, by either of the following: (a) a volatile agent (isoflurane preferred) and remifentanil infusion, or (b) TIVA with a target-controlled infusion (TCI) of propofol and target-controlled remifentanil.

- TCI propofol—induction target is around 4.0 ng ml^{-1} and maintenance between 2.6–4.0 ng ml^{-1}.
- Remifentanil—concentration of 40–80 μg ml^{-1} at 0.1–0.5 μg kg^{-1} min^{-1} (equates to a TCI target of 2.0–4.0 ng ml^{-1}) for maintenance.

Remifentanil has the advantages of enabling mechanical ventilation of the lungs without the need for neuromuscular blockade and it is rapidly metabolized. If remifentanil is used, then morphine 10–20 mg (for adults) should be given at least 40 min before the end of surgery to avoid patients waking up in pain as remifentanil clears from plasma very rapidly when the infusion is stopped. Prolonged use of remifentanil is also associated with hyperalgesia. Pain can cause release of catecholamines, which cause vasoconstriction and may compromise flap perfusion. Exadaktylos et al. (2006) reported that the breast cancer recurrence rate was higher in patients who received a volatile agent and morphine analgesia than those who received propofol and paravertebral block for their anaesthesia. However, this study was retrospective with low power. There is also experimental evidence to suggest that morphine can suppress tumour growth (Sasamura et al. 2002; Koodie et al. 2010). Further prospective clinical trials in patients are warranted before abandoning morphine use in free flap surgery for cancer. Whatever the outcome, it would seem sensible to use remifentanil in reducing the morphine requirement during surgery while local anaesthesia block/infiltration at the donor site will reduce pain and intake of morphine postoperatively (see 'Reperfusion and reperfusion–ischaemia injury' for other actions of remifentanil and other anaesthetic agents).

Papaverine or lidocaine is used topically by the surgeon to vasodilate the anastomotic vessels.

Some plastic surgeons prefer heparin 5000 IU to be given intravenously on releasing clamps.

Perioperative fluid therapy

Fluid should be started at induction through a fluid warmer. The type and amount of fluid can influence the outcome of free flap surgery.

Type of fluid

- Crystalloids: electrolytes (Na^+, K^+, Cl^-) in water (e.g. normal saline, Hartmann's solution). Normal saline contains 150 mmol $litre^{-1}$ of Na^+ and equal amount of Cl^-. Hartmann's is a balanced solution containing Na^+ 131 mmol $litre^{-1}$, K^+ 5 mmol $litre^{-1}$, Cl^- 112 mmol $litre^{-1}$, and Ca^{2+} 4 mmol $litre^{-1}$.
- Colloids: a homogenous mixture of one or more solutes dissolved in a solvent. These contain large molecules which do not cross semipermeable membranes easily and hence stay intravascular for a longer period of time. Examples include gelatins—Gelofusine® and Volplex®, and hetastarches—Voluven® and Volulyte®. Gelatins are derived from animal protein whereas hetastarch is a plant product. The solvent in Voluven® is saline and in Volulyte® is balanced solution. Hetastarches have been withdrawn from the market because of their adverse effect on renal function. Currently gelatins are commonly used as colloid.
- Plasma: Na^+ 140 mmol $litre^{-1}$, K^+ 5.0 mmol $litre^{-1}$, Cl^- 102 mmol $litre^{-1}$ and Ca^{2+} 2.4 mmol $litre^{-1}$.
- 5% glucose: contains glucose in water and no electrolytes.

Normal saline contains too much Na and Cl: too much chloride leads to hyperchloraemic acidosis.

When compared with crystalloids, colloid solutions cause rapid intravascular expansion and therefore less volume can be administered so there is a low risk of oedema. However, there is an increased risk of allergic reaction, they are more expensive, and some patients raise religious objections to gelatine administration.

The following is a guide to intraoperative fluid management:

- Crystalloids:
  - 10–20 ml kg^{-1} to replace preoperative deficit
  - 4–8 ml kg^{-1} h^{-1} to replace insensible losses
- Colloids: goal-directed therapy.

Goal-directed fluid therapy

The relationship of pressure and flow in the circulation is given by:

$$\text{Flow (CO)} = \frac{\text{BP}}{\text{SVR}} \tag{64.2}$$

Or

$$\text{BP} = \text{HR} \times \text{SV} \times \text{SVR} \tag{64.3}$$

where SVR = systemic vascular resistance, BP = blood pressure, SV = stroke volume, and HR = heart rate.

Thus when SVR is kept low, SV or HR (or both) needs to increase to improve perfusion pressure.

Currently goal-directed fluid therapy is practised in the author's centre. Invasive monitoring is now not routinely used in DIEP flap surgery because of the advantages of oesophageal Doppler: Several studies show that CVP (and pulmonary artery wedge pressure) does not correlate well with volume or flow status (Sakka et al. 1999; Kumar et al. 2004; Kuntscher et al. 2006). In addition, CVP does not give any information about SV. Marik et al. (2008) recommended that CVP should not even be used in ICUs, emergency departments, and operating rooms because of its lack of accuracy. In a retrospective study, Sasai et al. have suggested CVP unreliably reflects left ventricular preload for fluid management during initial phase of septic shock (Sasai et al. 2014).

Optimizing SV in surgical populations has resulted in a substantial decrease in hospital length of stay and the frequency of postoperative complications (Sinclair et al. 1997; Gan et al. 2002; McKendry et al. 2004).

The trend of using corrected flow time as a goal has been shifted to SV because concerns have been raised that corrected flow time does not reflect preload (Singer 2006; Bundgard et al. 2007).

Fluid algorithm when using stroke volume as a goal

When SV is used as the end-point, fluid is administered rapidly and if the SV increases by more than 10% then more fluid is needed. The concept of Starling's law of SV and left ventricular end-diastolic volume is used at this point. Fluid is stopped when SV does not increase by more than 10% (Fig. 64.1). This algorithm allows the anaesthetist to administer fluids precisely and the patient does not receive too much or too little fluid.

Postoperative care

Patients are nursed in the HDU by nurses specially trained in plastic surgery. They maintain a HDU observation chart that includes a flap monitoring chart. The goals of perioperative care are listed in Box 64.1.

Fluids

- Crystalloid as maintenance fluid at 1.0–1.5 ml kg^{-1} h^{-1}.
- Colloid (gelatins in the author's centre): boluses of 250 ml to challenge mean arterial blood pressure above 60 mm Hg or urine output greater than 0.5 ml kg^{-1} h^{-1}.
- Reassess response.

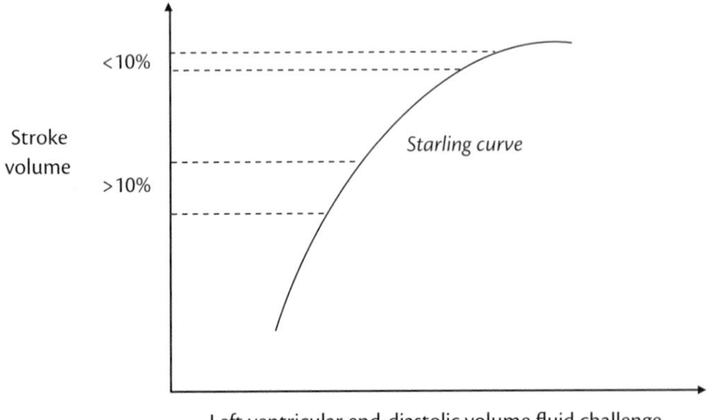

Fig. 64.1 Optimizing dynamic (flow-related) goals.

Box 64.1 Goals of perioperative care for free flap surgery

- Maintain normal blood pressure
- Low systemic vascular resistance and high cardiac output
- Isovolaemic haemodilution with haematocrit 30–35%
- Haemoglobin not more than 100 g $litre^{-1}$
- Normothermia with a difference between core and peripheral temperature of less than 2°C
- Urine output greater than 0.5 ml kg^{-1} h^{-1}
- Goal-directed fluid therapy: maintain stroke volume index at greater than 35 ml m^{-2}
- Sa_{O_2} greater than 96%
- Effective analgesia with oral or subcutaneous morphine—patient-controlled analgesic morphine not needed
- Monitor flap perfusion to detect early signs of failure.

Analgesia

Regular simple analgesic plus subcutaneous morphine or oxycodone is sufficient. A recent audit in the author's centre showed this regimen is very satisfactory.

Patient-controlled morphine analgesia is not essential [it may increase the incidence of postoperative nausea and vomiting (PONV)].

Flap monitoring

Apart from monitoring vital signs of the patient to gather information about oxygenation, fluid balance, CO, urine output, acid–base balance, and signs of sepsis, the following specific observations are made with regard to flap monitoring:

- Flap observation—hourly for the first 24 postoperative hours, then every 2 h for the next 1–2 days, and thereafter every 4–8 h until discharge.
  - Colour score: white (0), blue/white (2), paler (4), normal (6), darker (8), mauve/blue (10), or purple/black (12)
  - Temperature (touch chart): cold, cooler, warm, or hot
  - Texture: spongy, soft, firm, or hard
  - Capillary refill (press firmly for 10 s and release): no blanch, longer than 3 s, slow, 3 s, less than 3 s, or no refill
  - Light source—: natural, ward lights, lamps, torch, or other.
  - Leeches applied: no, yes; result = good, no difference, or poor
  - Heparin: soak, injected; result = good, no difference, or poor
  - Divet bleeding: fast, medium, or slow
- Objective measurements—several techniques and monitoring devices have been used for assessing tissue perfusion postoperatively in an attempt to find one that is non-invasive, accurate, continuous, easy to use, reproducible and inexpensive:
  - Temperature of the flap using a temperature probe into the flap tissue
  - Tissue pH monitor
  - Transcutaneous Po_2 using polarographic microcatheter (Serafin et al. 1982)

- Laser Doppler flowmetry (Jones and Mayou 1982)
- Doppler ultrasound (Lorenzetti et al. 1999)
- Microdialysis (Setala et al. 2006)
- Near infrared spectroscopy (Repez et al. 2008)
- Plethysmography (Stack et al. 2003)
- Orthogonal polarization spectral imaging: (Langer et al. 2001)
- Positron emission tomography scanning (Schrey et al. 2006)
- Pulse transit time index (Visscher et al. 2010).

All of these techniques share advantages and disadvantages, and have limitations that preclude their routine application for monitoring perfusion in skin flaps. Therefore, to date, there is no widely accepted and readily available intraoperative or postoperative technique to reliably assess the viability of free flaps.

There should be a high degree of suspicion and clinical observation is still the mainstay of monitoring flaps. The author, in collaboration with City University, London, United Kingdom, has successfully developed and completed a clinical trial using a new non-invasive opto-electronic measuring device. The results are encouraging (Zaman et al. 2011, 2013).

Anaesthesia for cleft lip/palate surgery

Cleft lip, cleft palate, or both, have a huge impact on the life of a patient and their family. Management of these congenital abnormalities requires a multidisciplinary team (comprising surgeons, anaesthetists, orthodontists, paediatricians, speech therapists, special nurses, and psychologists), to look after them. Surgery aims to correct anatomical defects and restore normal function. It is a worldwide problem and in the United Kingdom the incidence of cleft lip is 1:600 live births and cleft palate is 1:2000 live births. Twenty-five per cent of cleft lip cases are bilateral and 85% of these are associated with cleft palate. Cleft lip/palate is more common in males and cleft lips are usually left sided. The aetiology is unknown, but is likely to include environmental and genetic factors that combine to cause defects in palatal growth during the first trimester.

As with any other congenital abnormality, the presence of other associated congenital abnormalities including cardiac and renal should be looked for. Many syndromes have been associated with cleft lip/palate (Box 64.2) with considerable anaesthetic implications including potential airway problems (Hatch 1996).

Box 64.2 Common syndromes associated with cleft lip/palate

Pierre Robin

Micrognathia, glossoptosis, atrial septal defect, ventricular septal defect, and patent ductus arteriosus.

Treacher Collins

Maxillary, zygomatic, and mandibular hypoplasia, retrognathia, narrow nasopharynx, basilar kyphosis, and hearing difficulties.

Goldenhar

Hemifacial microsomia, micrognathia, vertebral hypoplasia, and cardiac anomalies.

Fortunately these are rare. The most well known are (a) Pierre Robin (cor pulmonale as a result of chronic upper airway obstruction, difficult laryngoscopy and intubation, feeding difficulties), (b) Treacher Collins (obstructive sleep apnoea, difficult mask ventilation and intubation), and (c) Goldenhar (difficult mask fit, laryngoscopy, C1–2 subluxation). Other anomalies such as Klippel–Feil syndrome include abnormalities of the cervical spine.

Other syndromes associated with cleft lip/palate are velocardiofacial, hemifacial microsomia, Stickler, Downs, and fetal alcohol syndromes.

Changes have taken place in the organization of cleft services in the United Kingdom following the recommendations of the Clinical Standards Advisory Group (1998) that the number of hospitals providing cleft lip/palate surgery be reduced to 8–15 units managing 40–50 cases of primary cleft lip and cleft palate per annum. This has resulted in care being centralized with the potential advantages of improved outcomes.

Cleft surgery is divided into primary or secondary. Primary surgical repair is to repair the primary cleft lip/cleft palate defect. Secondary surgical repair may be required well into adulthood consisting of, for example, to improve lip aesthetics, close residual palatal defects, bone graft, and align alveolar and dental defects.

Primary cleft repair

Children with cleft lip/palate usually present for correction in infancy. Primary repair of cleft lip is done at 3 months when body weight of 4.5 kg and haemoglobin concentration of 100 g litre^{-1} have been achieved, because waiting until that age gives time to detect most congenital abnormalities, and allows anatomical and physiological maturation. However, in some centres neonatal repair of cleft lip is undertaken using the argument that early repair may improve mother–infant bonding and maintain the infant's normal cognitive development (Murray et al. 2008).

Primary cleft palate repair is usually carried out at 9–12 months as further delay may cause speech impairment. However, it may be delayed until 18 months by the investigation of other problems or ongoing airway difficulties (e.g. in patients with Pierre Robin syndrome).

Preoperative assessment

All children with cleft lip/palate are seen in the pre-assessment clinic. A detailed history is taken and a thorough clinical examination is carried out to rule out any associated abnormalities. Assessment of the degree of difficulty of intubation preoperatively may not be possible because the method of assessment requires the infant's cooperation which is not easy to achieve. It is important to record preoperative oxygen saturation and consider echocardiography (Black and Nadarajan 2010). The weight of the baby is recorded. Preoperative investigations include only haemoglobin in a healthy baby and a 'group and save' for palate repair. Some patients may require stabilization in terms of nasogastric feeding, airway management such as continuous positive airway pressure, or even temporary tracheostomy to cover the perioperative period (Bull et al. 1990). Upper respiratory tract infection is common in cleft palate as a result of nasal regurgitation during feeds. If there is active infection then the surgery is postponed.

Preparation for anaesthesia includes cessation of breastfeeding for 4 h and formula feeds for 6 h with unlimited clear oral fluids being given up to 2 h before induction.

Premedication

No premedication is given in the author's centre; however, in some centres atropine 0.02 mg kg^{-1} is administered in order to dry oral secretions (Blogg 1994).

Induction

ECG and pulse oximetry is begun before induction. Inhalation induction with sevoflurane in 100% oxygen ensures that spontaneous ventilation is maintained as manual ventilation with a facemask may be difficult if the mask cannot fit closely. Peripheral venous access is achieved when anaesthesia is sufficiently deep. A non-depolarizing neuromuscular blocking agent is administered intravenously only after effective bag and mask ventilation is confirmed. Neuromuscular blocking agents are contraindicated before intubation if there is any doubt about the ability to inflate the lungs. Tracheal intubation is straightforward in the majority of cases and in one series of 800 cases, Gunawardane (1996) found that despite difficulty in laryngoscopy, failure to intubate occurred in only 1% of patients. Various methods have been used in managing the child with a difficult airway, including firm pressure over the larynx to aid laryngoscopy and a bougie to assist in intubation, a paraglossal approach using a straight laryngoscope blade, packing gaps in the palate with gauze, laryngeal mask, retrograde wire technique, digital-assisted intubation, video laryngoscopy, and fibreoptic techniques.

- Intubation is performed using a non-kinking, preformed RAE tube which is fixed in the midline to allow insertion of a surgical retractor without obstructing the airway. A throat pack is used. Controlled ventilation is used to achieve normocapnia. Use of an overhead heater in the induction room helps prevent heat loss.
- Dexamethasone 0.1 mg kg^{-1} is given at induction.

Maintenance

Anaesthesia is maintained with oxygen, air, and sevoflurane. Standard monitoring in theatre includes ECG, Sa_{O2}, non-invasive blood pressure, end-tidal CO_2, agent monitoring, temperature, and ventilator alarm. The airway is shared between the anaesthetic and surgical access hence extra care should be taken to avoid inadvertent extubation or endobronchial intubation especially during positioning which requires neck extension (Jordi Ritz et al. 2008). Local anaesthetic is infiltrated by the surgeon.

Analgesia is maintained with a remifentanil infusion 20 mcg kg^{-1} added to 50 ml normal saline and run at 4 ml kg^{-1} h^{-1} (0.2 mcg kg^{-1} min^{-1}). Paracetamol intravenously is given at a dose of 10 mg kg^{-1}. In cleft lip, infraorbital nerve block is performed. In cleft palate, local anaesthetic infiltration is done instead by the surgeon. Additionally rectal diclofenac 1–1.5 mg kg^{-1} is administered. Morphine 100 mcg kg^{-1} is administered.

- Tranexamic acid 10 mg kg^{-1} is sometime administered to reduce bleeding.
- Fluids—boluses of 10 ml kg^{-1}. Hartmann's solution is given. Blood is administered if loss of more than 10% of blood volume.
- Theatre temperature is maintained at 22–24°C to minimize heat loss.

Recovery and postoperative care

Neuromuscular blockade is antagonized and the trachea extubated in theatre.

Postoperative care is focused initially on ensuring the child is well oxygenated and maintaining a clear airway. Patients with potential for airway problems will benefit from a nasopharyngeal airway during the recovery period.

Postoperative analgesia—oral morphine, paracetamol and ibuprofen/diclofenac is usually sufficient. In some centres, nurse-controlled 'patient-controlled analgesic' morphine has been used successfully.

Postoperative complications include airway obstruction, laryngospasm, retained throat pack, swelling of tongue as a result of gag pressure, obstructive sleep apnoea, and bleeding; leading to hypoxaemia and hypovolaemia. The child should be monitored postoperatively with Sa_{O_2}, respiratory rate, pulse rate, blood pressure, and apnoea monitors.

Feeding can be commenced at 2 h postop.

Other techniques of anaesthesia for cleft surgery

A range of techniques have been used around the world with various modifications depending on the availability of drugs, equipment, skilled personnel, and facilities for postoperative care. Some are summarized briefly as follows:

- Cleft lip can be repaired under infraorbital nerve block alone.
- Ketamine and atropine, suxamethonium for intubation, and spontaneous ventilation with halothane and oxygen-enriched air.
- Halothane for induction and maintenance and intubation as previously mentioned.
- Morphine for analgesia. Precordial stethoscope for continuous monitoring of heart rate and breathing (can act as disconnection monitor as well). Pulse oximetry may not be available everywhere.

Future developments

There is experimental evidence to suggest that *in utero* surgery for cleft lip and palate repair provides superior wound healing without scarring (Lorenz and Longaker 2003).

Anaesthesia for burns

A burn is a type of injury to the surface layers of the body resulting from heat, electricity, chemicals, light, radiation, or friction causing coagulative destruction. The commonest cause of burns in adults is flame burn and in children is scald. Patients at the extremes of age, with pre-existing morbidities such as epilepsy and alcoholism, and psychiatric illness are more vulnerable to burn injury. Many children admitted with burns suffer non-accidental injuries. The annual incidence of patients with severe burn injury in Europe has been reported to be between 0.2 and 2.9:10 000 inhabitants (Brusselaers et al. 2010). In the United Kingdom, about 10 000 patients are seriously injured requiring hospital admission each year and out of these, 10% need formal fluid resuscitation and surgery. Most burns occur at home and are preventable. The incidence has reduced in the past three decades as a result of improved socioeconomic status and preventive measures being taken to reduce injury at work. In recent years, there has been a decrease in mortality which has been attributed to modern techniques of prompt resuscitation and wound care (Roberts et al. 2012).

All anaesthetists should be competent in assessing burn injuries and safely managing their transfer to a specialist burns unit. Anaesthetic personnel have a major role to play in the management of burn injuries which requires a thorough understanding of pathophysiological changes and treatment strategies. The anaesthetic team in the specialized units must have specialized skills in resuscitation, airway management, intensive care, care of extremes of ages, and should have access to expert help in managing non-burn co-morbidity. Burn patients are best managed by a multidisciplinary team which includes burn surgeons (plastic or general surgeons with special interest in burns), anaesthetists, operating department practitioners, nursing staff (theatre, ICU), microbiologists, pharmacists, pain team, nutritionists, psychologists, physiotherapists, occupational therapists and play specialists. For such a diverse team to deliver in an effective manner, it is vital to have great communication skills in dealing with patients and their relatives. Regular commitment to burn care by each member of the multidisciplinary team is required. A dedicated theatre for burn cases is essential in a specialized burn centre.

Classification of burns

Skin is made up of the outer epidermis and inner dermis. The deeper layer of dermis is termed adnexa and contains the hair follicle and sweat and sebaceous glands. The adnexa provides keratinocytes needed for epithelialization of the burn wound.

Burn injury to the skin can be classified according to depth of burn as partial or full thickness. Partial-thickness injury can be subdivided into superficial and deep.

First-degree burn

See Figure 64.2. Erythema, for example, sunburn:

- Involves epidermis only
- Erythematous, pain, no blisters, but desquamation can occur later
- Not life-threatening, do not require intravenous fluid.

Second-degree (superficial partial-thickness) burn

See Figure 64.3. Involves the epidermis and part of the dermis sparing a significant proportion of adnexa:

- Red or mottled, swelling, blisters
- Weeping wet appearance
- Blanch on pressure
- Painfully hypersensitive even to air current.

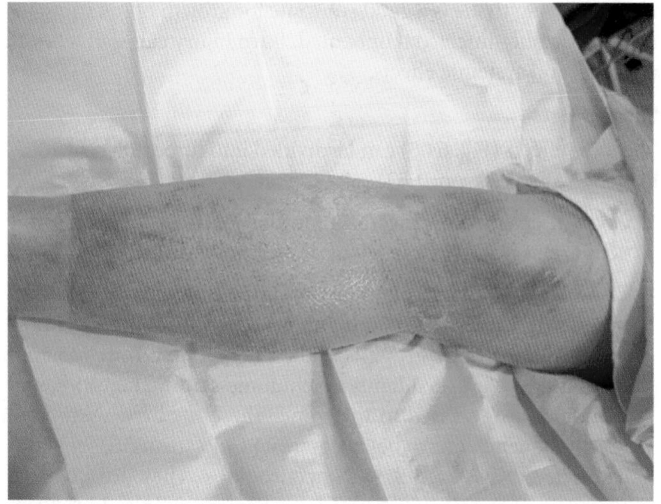

Figure 64.2 First-degree burn.

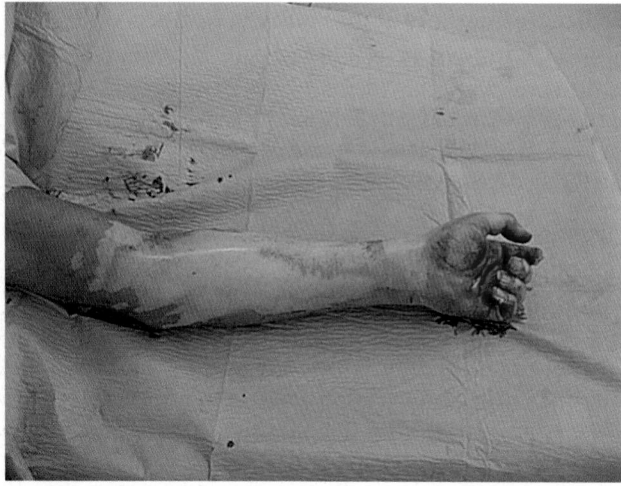

Figure 64.3 Second-degree burn.

Second-degree (deep partial-thickness) burn

Burns destroy a larger proportion of the dermis and associated adnexa:

- White or red with fixed staining
- Do not blanch on pressure
- Diminished sensation.

Third-degree (full-thickness) burn

See Figure 64.4. Burns destroy all of the epidermis, dermis, and all adnexal structures:

- Dark and leathery
- Charring, fixed staining, and haemorrhage areas
- Surface painless and generally dry.

First-degree burn usually heals without any problem. Superficial partial-thickness burn heals spontaneously with little or no scarring. Deep partial-thickness burn heals with hypertrophic scarring and often needs skin grafting. Full-thickness burn requires surgical intervention and skin grafting.

According to size of burn

- Major: more than 15% total body surface area (TBSA) in adults, and more than 10% in children
- Minor: less than 15% TSBA in adults and less than 10% in children.

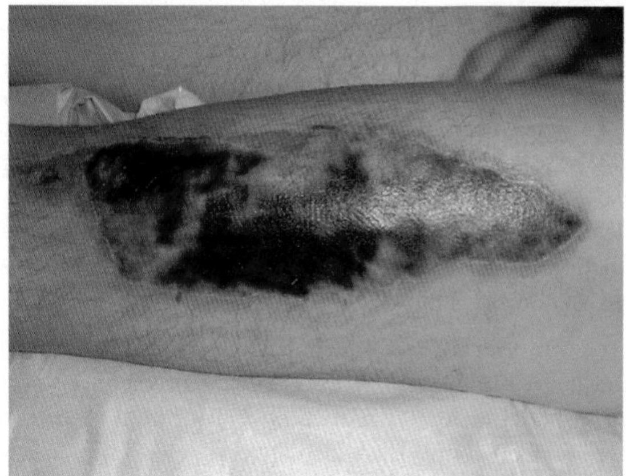

Figure 64.4 Third-degree burn.

Prediction/markers of mortality in burns

Being able to accurately predict probability of death is important for the burn care team. There is no single parameter which can accurately predict mortality in burn patients. Objective estimates and a few markers discussed next give indications for clinicians to plan the management of these patients.

Objective estimates

- Baux Score (Baux 1961): it is well known that the elderly are vulnerable and especially likely to die of burns. Burn mortality in the elderly may be calculated by the Baux formula—age plus percentage body surface area (BSA) burned equals mortality. When the TBSA of burn in an elderly patient is more than 70%, or if the Baux score is greater than 130, mortality is nearly 100%. The formula is less accurate at extremes of age, and a significant number of patients survive despite Baux scores reaching more than 100 (Wassermann and Schlotterer 1985; Bang and Ghoneim 1996; Cadier and Shakespeare 1995).
- Revised Baux Score (Osler et al. 2010): Osler et al. revised the Baux score to include inhalation injury. They developed a single-term logistic regression model using data on 39 888 burned patients and showed that age and percentage burn contribute almost equally to mortality, while the presence of inhalation injury added the equivalent of 17 years (or 17% burn). The Revised Baux Score performed well.
- Probability with three identifiable risk factors (Ryan et al. 1998): three risk factors for death were identified by Ryan et al.: age greater than 60 years, more than 40% of TBSA burned, and presence of inhalation injury. The mortality formula predicts 0.3%, 3%, 33%, or approximately 90% mortality, depending on whether zero, one, two, or three risk factors are present, respectively.
- The mortality rate after smoke inhalation varies depending on the presence or absence of cutaneous burns. Mortality rate in the absence of cutaneous burn is less than 10%; however, it rises considerably to 25–65% in the presence of cutaneous burns (Herndon et al. 1986, 1987; Haponic and Summer 1987).

Markers

- Cytokine concentrations: serum cytokine concentrations are important markers of sepsis in burns patients. Gauglitz et al. (2008) found that interleukin (IL)-10 on admission, or IL-6 and IL-7 5–7 days later, may predict outcome. Mortality is increased as serum IL-6 and IL-10 concentrations increase and serum IL-7 concentrations decrease. However, the validity of the results of this study has been questioned by Myrianthefs and Baltopoulos (2008) who argued that there are a variety of factors that are capable of affecting circulating cytokines even in a subgroup of critically ill patients and recommended serum cytokine-based prediction models need to be compared with prediction models based on clinical parameters.
- Microalbuminuria (Yew and Pal 2006): microalbuminuria or albumin–creatinine ratio (ACR) is a useful predictor of mortality in burns patients. ACR of more than 20 mg $mmol^{-1}$ is associated with poorer outcome. There also appears to be a biphasic variation of mean ACR in patients who die, with either an early peak in the first week of injury, or a later peak a month later. The two peaks of ACR observed in Yew and Pal's study (2006) in the mortality group correlate with the two cascades of multiorgan failure as described by Goodwin (1990). The early cascade, occurring within the first week, is characterized by failure of reversal of burn shock. The late cascade is typified by an infectious process, and is usually associated with pneumonia. In a study of 50 patients in a heterogeneous ICU population, MacKinnon et al. (2000) calculated probability of death and suggested that ACR can give a rapid indication of outcome within 6 h of ICU admission. Other researchers have shown that microalbuminuria can predict mortality within 15 min of admission in ICU (Gosling et al. 2003). Microalbuminuria has also been shown to increase glomerular permeability in post-septic patients (De Gaudio et al. 2000).
- Antithrombin III (Del Principe 2003): the plasma antithrombin III concentration falls significantly in severe burns patients. Antithrombin III concentration at the onset of burn injury correlates significantly with mortality.
- C-reactive protein and lipoprotein(a). There is a major increase in plasma C-reactive protein concentrations, whereas lipoprotein(a) declines abruptly and transiently in burns and severe sepsis (Mooser et al. 2000). These markers are not specific for burns.
- Other markers: biphasic activated partial thromboplastin time waveform (also termed A2 flag) has been shown to be a predictor of mortality in burn patients (Mathew and Pal 2002). Lactate clearance (Nguyen et al. 2004, 2010) and soluble L-selectin (Seidelin et al. 2002) are shown to predict mortality in severe sepsis in general ICU; however, an association with burn mortality has not been studied.

Spies et al. (2003) showed prospectively that outcome in severely burned children cannot be reliably predicted on the basis of patient characteristics and injury characteristics alone. They also suggested that all severely burned children should be given a course of treatment before consideration of withdrawal of treatment (Spies et al. 2003).

Pathophysiology of burns

Burn injury leads to tissue necrosis; the resultant tissue is termed 'eschar'. If untreated, the eschar slowly separates allowing viable tissue underneath to grow and cover the exposed wound. Because the underlying tissue is a good substrate for growth of microorganisms, it becomes infected if untreated. Burn injury can lead to local, regional, and systemic effects.

Local effects

The local effects (Fig. 64.5) can be divided into three different zones histologically (Jackson 1953):

1. Zone of coagulation (necrosis): in the centre of the wound the cells are necrosed as a result of destruction by burn.
2. Zone of stasis (ischaemia): surrounds the central zone of coagulation where microvascular injury is occurring. There is priming and attraction of neutrophils to the site of injury. Inflammatory mediators such as oxidants, arachidonic acid metabolites, and cytokines are released in this zone. These mediators although locally beneficial have been implicated in causing tissue damage when they reach high concentrations. They are involved in causing arteriolar and venular dilatation followed by platelet aggregation resulting in vascular stasis (Rose and Herndon

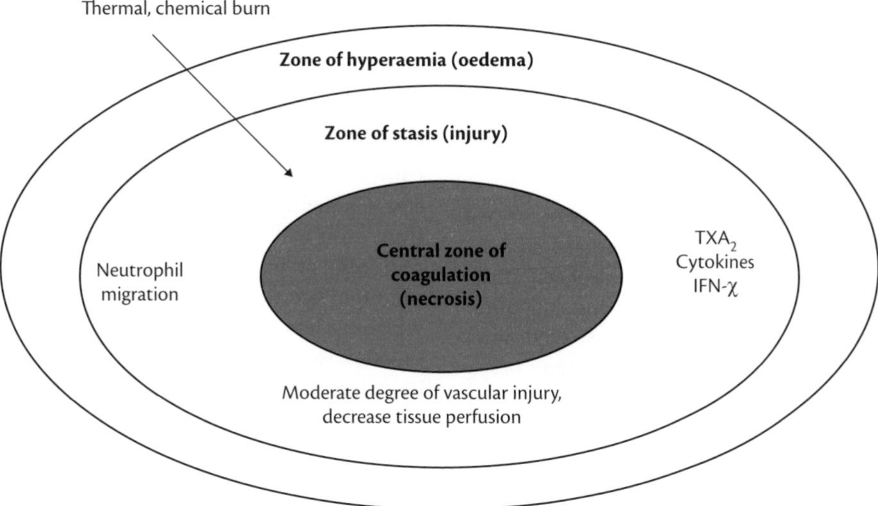

Figure 64.5 Pathophysiology of burns—local effects. IFN, interferon; IL; interleukin; TNF, tumour necrosis factor; TXA2, thromboxane A2.

1997). Inflammatory mediators that are implicated are histamine, prostaglandins, leukotrienes B4–D4, thromboxanes A2 and B2, kinins, serotonin, catecholamines, free O_2 radicals, tumour necrosis factor α, IL-1, IL-2, IL-4, IL-6, IL-8, IL-12, and interferon-γ (Young et al. 1992). These inflammatory mediators can cause increased permeability of the microvasculature leading to tissue oedema, and can also cause microvascular stasis and thrombosis (see earlier). The resultant effect is deepening of the area of tissue burned. This zone is of tremendous interest to scientists and clinicians as modulation of this zone can prevent further progress of tissue injury.

3. Zone of hyperaemia (inflammation): the outer area of hyperaemia with increased permeability of vasculature leading to tissue oedema.

Regional effects

Regional effects include compromised limb circulation as a result of gross oedema in a limb resulting in venous obstruction. In circumferential burn, the eschar formed is incapable of distending which, in the chest, can lead to ventilatory problems (hypoventilation leading to hypoxaemia), while in the limbs compartment syndrome can result: the treatment in each case is immediate escharotomy (Fig. 64.6). The circulation of the intrinsic muscles of the hand may be compromised because of oedema.

Systemic effects

Fluid loss

Fluid from damaged capillaries leaks out either as external loss or accumulates internally into the tissues in the region of the burn as oedema. In fact it may extend and involve the entire body. The increased permeability of the capillaries is mediated by cytokines and other inflammatory mediators acting on the microcirculation. Effective fluid replacement will prevent hypovolaemia and minimize the risk of other systemic complications.

Altered cellular membranes and cellular oedema

There is a change in the membrane potential (from −90 mV to −70 mV) in cells in non-burned area similar to the effect seen in haemorrhage; however, it is different in that resuscitation of burn injury only partially restores the membrane potential unlike in haemorrhage where rapid restoration is seen. It results in increased intracellular Na^+ and water. Cell death occurs at −60 mV. There is generalized oedema in burns affecting more than 25% TBSA. The water content of burned tissue is increased by 70–80% within 30 min. Decreased oncotic pressure of plasma occurs as a result of denatured proteins. Water content of all tissues gradually increases over 12–24 h.

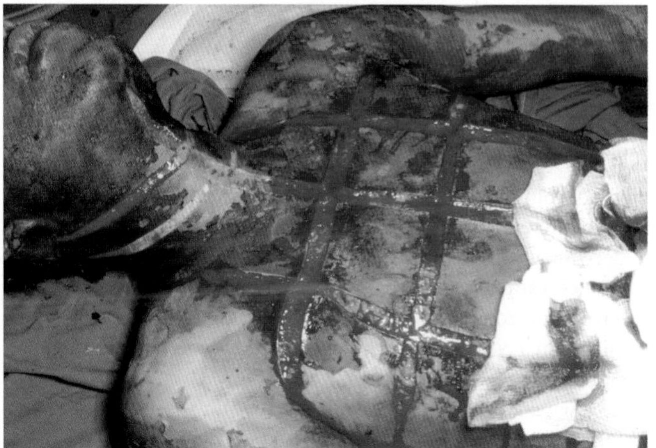

Figure 64.6 Escharotomy.

Haemodynamic consequences of acute burns

Burn shock hypodynamic phase (first 48 h) The CO is reduced immediately before any reduction in plasma volume is detected suggesting a neuronal response to increased circulating vasoconstrictor mediators. The SVR decreases, leading to reductions in blood pressure, perfusion, urine output, and oxygen delivery. There is some response to fluid challenge.

Burn shock hyperdynamic phase (after 48 h and lasts up to 9 months) In this phase, the SVR is reduced markedly and there is a pathological inability to respond to hypovolaemia and vasoconstriction. The CO rises markedly and the urine output falls further. There is a poor response to fluid challenge and patients can get easily overloaded with oedema formation. There is a marked increase in energy expenditure. The immune status is reduced.

Multiple organ failure

In the course of burn injury, multiple organ failure may occur (e.g. progressive failure of renal or hepatic and myocardial function). The cause of multiple organ failure is varied and has been attributed to fluid loss, 'toxaemia' from infection, or systemic inflammatory response to sepsis (systemic inflammatory response syndrome). Multiple organ failure may develop without any obvious signs of systemic infection.

Systemic complications

There are well-documented systemic complications which can occur in association with burns such as:

- Curling's (gastric or duodenal) ulcer that may result in acute upper gastrointestinal bleeding
- Immunosuppression which increases the risk of sepsis
- Later in the course of burn injury, weight is lost as a result of a catabolic response to trauma
- Other non-specific complications include urinary tract infection from catheterization, DVT, and pulmonary embolism.

Electrical burn

Electrical burn is identifiable by a small entry and exit wound. Even though there is only a small burn superficially there is massive underlying muscle damage as current flows through the path of least resistance leading to potential myocardial damage. Hence serial ECG and troponin concentrations should be performed to rule out myocardial damage. Delayed arrhythmias are common. Compartment syndrome is a possibility requiring fasciotomy. Urine shows myoglobinuria which can lead to renal failure. The aim should be to achieve a high urine output of 1.5–2.0 ml kg^{-1} h^{-1} using mannitol.

Chemical burn

Acids, alkali, and organic substance such as petrol can cause chemical burn. Immediate management includes irrigation with water to neutralize the acid or alkali for several hours. When systemically absorbed, these substances can cause metabolic acidosis and alkalosis (as the case may be). Hydrofluoric acid can lead to hypocalcaemia.

Burns in children

Children have thin skin hence the burn is deeper and more extensive. Compared with adults, children have different body proportions so it can be difficult to assess burn size accurately. Fluid requirement is greater and glucose solution may be included. Maintenance fluid (Hartmann's) should be added for children weighing less than 30 kg which should be titrated against oral intake/nasogastric feed. In massive burn, intravenous access may be extremely difficult if not impossible; however, intraosseous access is a good alternative. Non-accidental injury is a common cause of burns in children.

Management of burns

Pre-hospital management: first aid

Stop the burning process—removal of clothing and irrigation of the burnt area with tepid water (at least 15°C for 20–30 min). Chemical powder should be brushed away.

Initial care in the emergency department

- History is obtained from relatives/ambulance staff regarding the mechanism and time of burn and associated injuries.
- Taking universal precautions when examining the patient and carrying out any invasive procedure until the drug abuse status is known is good practice.

Primary survey: ABCDEF

Airway and control of cervical spine

- Initial compromise of the airway is almost always as a result of a low Glasgow Coma Scale score and not the burn
- Coma as a result of trauma, drugs, alcohol, carbon monoxide, and smoke inhalation
- Early maintenance of airway is important (Fig. 64.7)
- If there is history of trauma, the C-spine is immobilized
- Once the airway is clear, high-flow oxygen is administered

(A)

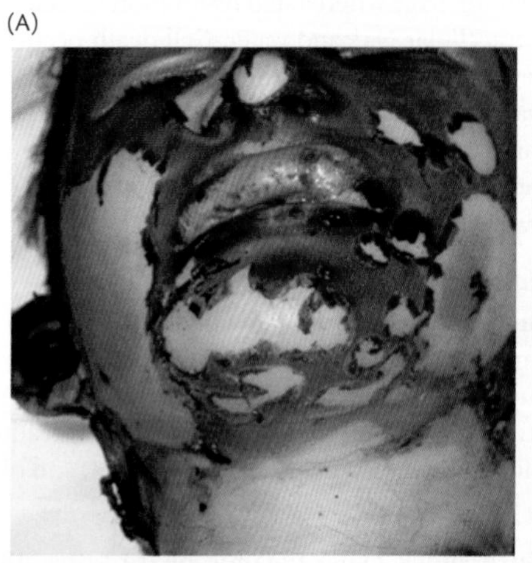

(B)

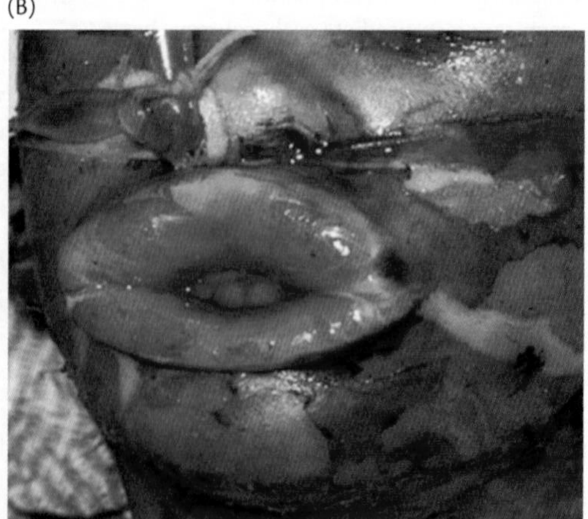

Figure 64.7 Airway burn on admission (A) and a few hours later (B).

Breathing and control of ventilation

Breathing may be compromised as a result of a depressed conscious level. Exclude trauma, smoke inhalation, and a constricting circumferential burn to chest wall:

- A pulse oximeter can give a spuriously high reading if the carbon monoxide concentration is high
- Tracheal position is checked—exclude tension pneumothorax
- Tracheal intubation at early stage is technically easy
- Suxamethonium can safely be used in the first 24 h
- Escharotomy is performed in circumferential burn.

Circulation and control of breathing

Rapid assessment of circulation in burned and unburned limbs: blood pressure, pulse, and capillary refill.

- Pressure is applied to bleeding points
- Hypovolaemic shock is never because of burn alone—look for underlying trauma
- Intravenous access and baseline carboxyhaemoglobin
- Two large-bore intravenous cannulae placed preferably through unburned skin. Options: saphenous cut-down, femoral line, and intraosseous in children less than 6 years old
- Escharotomy in circumferential burn causing compartment syndrome.

Disability

- AVPU score: alert, vocalizing, responding to pain, unconscious
- Pupils checked.

Exposure and estimation

- Expose patient completely and remove all jewellery
- Keep patient warm
- Log roll, inspect back for injuries and burns
- Estimate burn size and depth. The 'rule of nines' (Fig. 64.8) is a simple way of estimating size of burn. In an adult who has been burned, the percent of the body involved can be calculated as follows:
  - Head = 9%
  - Chest (front) = 9%
  - Abdomen (front) = 9%
  - Upper/mid/low back and buttocks = 18%
  - Each arm = 9% (front = 4.5%, back = 4.5%)
  - Groin = 1%
  - Each leg = 18% total (front = 9%, back = 9%).[1]
- As an example, if both legs (18% × 2 = 36%), the groin (1%), and the front chest (9%) and abdomen (9%) were burned, this would involve 55% of the body
- BSA of an infant's head is twice that of an adult
- Palm (excluding fingers) represents 1%
- Laser Doppler is a useful tool to estimate depth of burn.

[1] (Reprinted from *The Lancet*, 257, 6653, Wallace AB, 'The exposure treatment of burns', pp. 501–504, Copyright 1951, with permission from Elsevier.)

Fluids

- Burns of more than 15% in adults and 10% in children will require fluid resuscitation
- Rate of fluid administration:
  - 3–4 ml kg^{-1} (% $burn)^{-1}$ in 24 h
  - ½ in first 8 h, rest in the next 16 h
- Calculation based on the time from injury
- Lactated Ringer's solution is fluid of choice
- Glucose-containing solution in children
- Aim for urine output:
  - Adults 0.5 ml kg^{-1} h^{-1}
  - Children 1 ml kg^{-1} h^{-1}
- Frequent clinical assessment
- Any formula provides only an estimate of fluid need.

Secondary survey

- History—AMPLE (Allergy, Medications, Past medical history, Last meal, Event—what happened?):
  - Mechanism of injury
  - Head to toe examination
  - Tetanus prophylaxis
  - Burn dressing with cling film
- Lab investigations as in trauma patient—full blood count, urea and electrolytes, blood gas analysis, and, if indicated, toxicology analysis. ECG, chest X-ray, and other investigations (CT scan) may be required as guided by clinical situation
- Transfer arrangements—follow established guidelines.

British Burns Association referral criteria for burned patients

(See http://www.britishburnassociation.org/referral-guidance.)

- More than 10% TBSA in adults and 5% in children
- Burns of special areas: face, hands, feet, genitalia, perineum, major burns
- Full-thickness burns more than 5% TBSA
- Burns with associated inhalation injury
- Electrical and chemical burns
- Circumferential burns of limbs and chest
- Burns of patients at the extremes of age
- Burns in patients with pre-existing disease which may affect management, recovery or mortality
- Any burn associated with trauma.

Inhalation injury

Inhalation injury occurs when the victim is trapped in enclosed spaces. Excessive consumption of alcohol may lead to a fire being accidentally started and impairs judgement which can delay escaping and reporting a fire. Oxygen is consumed by a fire so the FI_{O_2} may be as low as 12%. The degree of airway injury sustained is related to the length of exposure to smoke, amount of smoke inhaled, type of smoke inhaled, and depth of respiration (can be

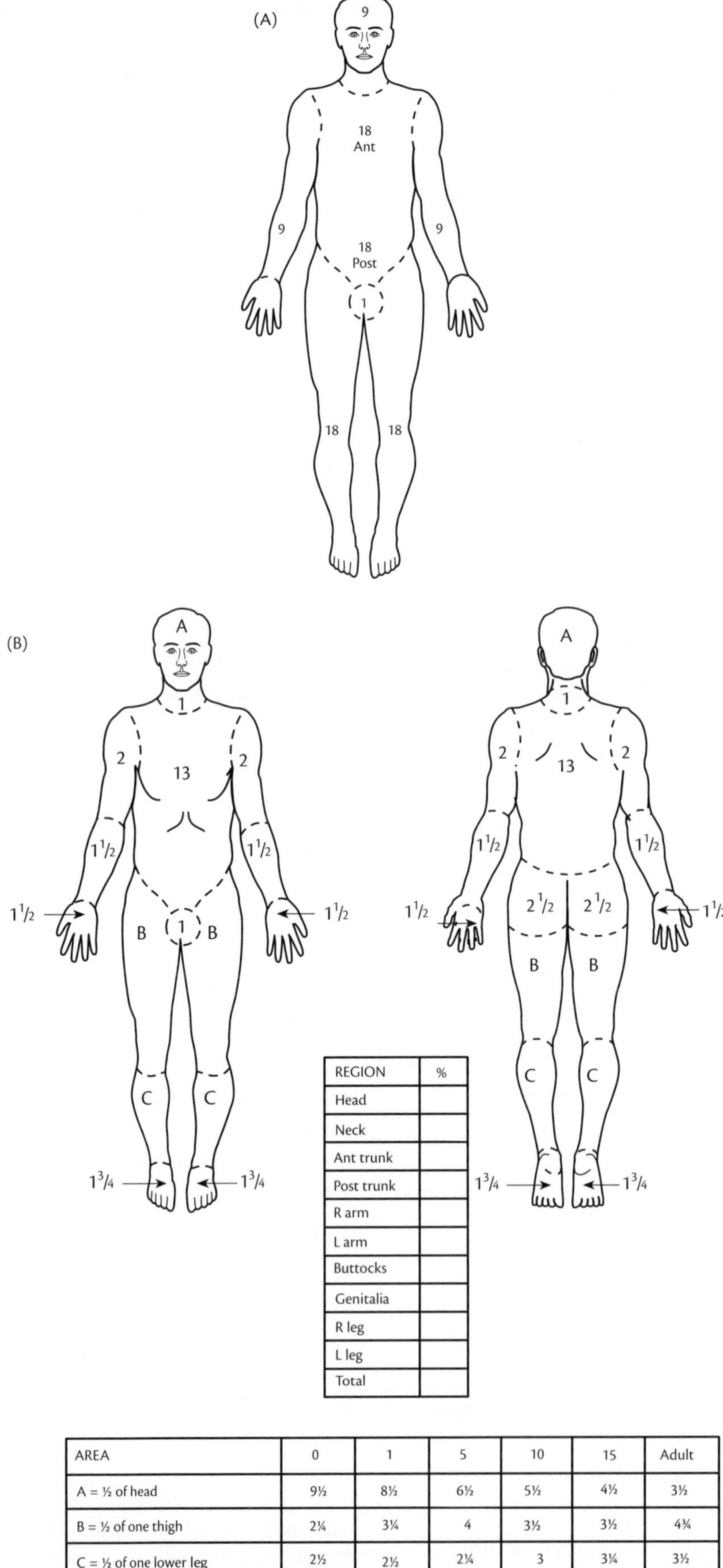

REGION	%
Head	
Neck	
Ant trunk	
Post trunk	
R arm	
L arm	
Buttocks	
Genitalia	
R leg	
L leg	
Total	

AREA	0	1	5	10	15	Adult
A = ½ of head	9½	8½	6½	5½	4½	3½
B = ½ of one thigh	2¾	3¼	4	3½	3½	4¾
C = ½ of one lower leg	2½	2½	2¾	3	3¼	3½

Figure 64.8 Calculating total body surface area (TBSA) burnt. (A) Rule of nines. (B) Lund and Browder chart.

(A) Reproduced from McLatchie, G., Borley, N., and Chikwe, J., *Oxford Handbook of Clinical Surgery, Fourth Edition*, 2013, Figure 16.4, Page 605, with permission from Oxford University Press.

(B) Reproduced from McLatchie, G., Borley, N., and Chikwe, J., *Oxford Handbook of Clinical Surgery, Fourth Edition*, 2013, Figure 16.5, Page 605, with permission from Oxford University Press.

influenced by alcohol and CO_2). It should be suspected in patients with burns of the head and neck if there are two or more of the following factors present: history of fire in enclosed space, carbonaceous sputum, perioral burn, altered level of consciousness, symptoms/signs of respiratory distress, hoarseness/loss of voice/stridor, carboxyhaemoglobin greater than 15%, and impaired gas exchange. The risk of impending airway obstruction increases in the following order:

- Burns around nose/mouth
- Soot in nostrils or singed nasal hair
- Burns of tongue
- Intra-oral swelling
- Hoarse voice
- Oedema on laryngoscopy
- Stridor.

Various parts of the airway may be injured which may be as a result of heat (thermal burn) or inhalation of toxic gases (chemical burn). The inhalation of hot gases causes a thermal burn to the upper airway. This is manifest by hoarseness, cough, stridor, and respiratory obstruction. Inhalation of the products of combustion (toxic gases) causes a chemical burn to the bronchial tree and lung parenchyma. This is manifest by hypoxia, acute respiratory distress syndrome, and respiratory failure; it may be of delayed onset. The location of injury in the airway depends on particle size, solubility of the substance, and duration of exposure. Particles larger than 10 μm are deposited in the upper airway and those smaller than 3 μm into the alveoli. Highly soluble chemicals (e.g. hydrochloric acid, sulphur

Box 64.3 Guidelines for management of airway burns

Suspect if:

- Burns in closed space.
- Stridor, hoarseness, or cough.
- Burns to face, lips, tongue, mouth, pharynx, or nasal mucosa and soot in sputum, nose, mouth.
- Dyspnoea, decreased level of consciousness or confusion.
- Clinical hypoxaemia (Sa_{O_2} < 94%), increased carbon monoxide concentrations (>2%).

The consultant anaesthetist must be informed of admission of *all* inhalation injuries.

Upper airway burns

- Must intubate the trachea early to avoid respiratory compromise when swelling increases.
- Early assessment may not be impressive. Later intubation may be very difficult.
- If in doubt, intubate.

Lower airway burns

Control airway

- Intubate with large low-pressure/high-volume cuffed tube using sterile technique.
- Nasal intubation in children.

Confirm diagnosis

- All patients with suspected inhalation injury should have bronchoscopy with or without lavage/culture on admission and 24 h after admission.
- Repeat bronchoscopy if persistent lobar collapse or for culture.
- Chest X-ray (initial may be normal) on admission and first thing each morning.
- Carbon monoxide concentration (on admission and repeated hourly until normal).

Specific treatment

- 100% oxygen until carbon monoxide concentrations are less than 2%.
- Pressure-controlled ventilation, permissive hypercapnia, positive end-expiratory pressure (<7.5 cm H_2O).
- Nebulized heparin 5000 IU diluted with 3 ml normal saline 4-hourly for 5–7 days. Monitor coagulation daily and discontinue if activated partial thromboplastin time is greater than 1.5.
- Nebulized 20% acetylcysteine solution 3 ml every 4 h (may be irritant to airway and should be discontinued if bronchospasm unresponsive to bronchodilation develops). Alternate medications so patient receives 2-hourly treatments.
- Nebulized salbutamol 2.5–5 mg 4-hourly if wheezing present.
- Aggressive pulmonary toilet—at least every 4 h—30 min after acetylcysteine nebulization.
- Chest physiotherapy at least four times a day. More frequently if persistent plugging or poor gas exchange. Daily sputum bacterial surveillance.
- Increased fluid requirements by as much as 50%. Restricting fluids is detrimental to the pulmonary insult and does not reduce oedema.
- All patients with severe lower airway burns and those that remain hypotensive or with poor urine output should have continuous invasive/non-invasive cardiac output monitoring and O_2 delivery optimized with inotropic support.
- Suspect cyanide poisoning if persistent acidosis (treatment with 0.3 ml kg^{-1} of 10% sodium nitrate and 1.6 ml kg^{-1} of 25% sodium thiosulfate as a single dose).
- Prophylactic antibiotics should not be given. Antibiotics according to culture reports for clinical infection.
- Early enteral feeding—nasogastric/nasojejunal tube on admission and feed immediately.
- Reduce risk of infection from remote sites (frequent line changes, evaluate cutaneous burn sites).
- Early surgical debridement.
- Early mobilization/ambulation.

Pulmonary function tests before discharge and at return clinic visits.

This table is adapted from that published in *Anaesthesia Review*, Kaufman et al. (eds), Akinniranya AK and Pal SK, 'Inhalational injury: current concepts and management', Table 6.3, Copyright Elsevier 1999.

dioxide, ammonia, and aldehydes) cause damage to upper airway and bronchioles. Less soluble chemicals (e.g. nitrogen dioxide, nitrous oxide, ozone, and phosgene) affect mainly distal airways and the onset of symptoms is delayed (hours to days). Airway injury includes direct mucosal injury; increased bronchial blood flow and capillary permeability; mediator-induced actions such as oedema, capillary leak, and bronchoconstriction; and loss of surfactant with resultant impaired alveolar function. Consequences of these airway injuries are bronchoconstriction, reduced lung compliance with increased work of breathing, and secondary infection leading to acute lung injury. Systemic absorption of toxic gases, in particular, carbon monoxide (but also hydrogen cyanide from burning plastics) causes poisoning. Carbon monoxide has more affinity (240 times) than oxygen to haemoglobin, and displaces oxygen from haemoglobin to form carboxyhaemoglobin, thereby reducing the oxygen-carrying capacity of the blood. It also has deleterious intracellular effects. Patients who survive the original incident may arrive confused or unconscious. The presence of inhalation injury in cutaneous burn increases mortality.

Management of inhalation injury

The guideline shown in Box 64.3 (Akinniranye and Pal 1999) was first introduced by the author in 1996 in the burns unit at St Andrew's Centre for Plastic Surgery and Burns (Broomfield Hospital, Chelmsford, United Kingdom). Since then, the protocol has worked well in these patients. Internal audit has shown good compliance with the protocol and good outcome of inhalation injury. As evident from the guideline, inhalation injury is a dynamic process and early intervention can prevent a disastrous situation developing. Fibreoptic bronchoscopy is the gold standard in diagnosing inhalation injury (Fig. 64.9).

The decision to intubate a patient's trachea in the referring hospital may be difficult as delay can make it a 'can't intubate, can't ventilate' scenario. The reasons to intubate are to protect the airway, maintain patency of upper airway, ventilatory support, and to facilitate safe transfer to a regional burns centre. There are, however, some clear indications when to intubate, that is, reduced level of consciousness; impending signs of airway obstruction (see list in 'Inhalation injury'); and symptoms and signs of respiratory distress—tachypnoea, nasal flaring, intercostal recession, hypoxia, and hypercarbia. If there is any doubt, it is better to intubate for safe transfer to a regional burns centre where the patient can be extubated if needed. If the decision is made to proceed to intubate then it is advisable to place an appropriate size of tracheal tube for long-term ventilation; not to cut the tracheal tube as progressive oedema can cause it to protrude with loss of airway; check and, if necessary, adjust tube ties as oedema forms.

Patients with cutaneous burns and coexisting inhalation injury require more resuscitative fluid especially in the first 24–48 h by as much as 40–75%. The treatment of carbon monoxide poisoning is to give 100% oxygen until the carboxyhaemoglobin concentration is less than 7%. Hyperbaric oxygen therapy is controversial as a result of the difficulties of managing a major burn patient who is intubated and ventilated in a hyperbaric chamber. Additionally, there are risks of barotrauma in an already friable respiratory tract. Use of nebulized heparin and acetylcysteine (mucolytic agent) has been shown to improve lung function in paediatric burns patients by decreasing cast formation, small airway obstruction, and barotrauma (Desai et al. 1998). Sepsis or inflammation can cause thrombin to trigger a change in endothelial cell shape to produce microvascular gaps leading to increased endothelial permeability. Heparin improves oxygenation by preventing microvascular permeability caused by thrombin-mediated microvascular injury.

The ventilation strategy should aim to prevent barotrauma and includes permissive hypercapnia, low tidal volume, positive end-expiratory pressure, limiting peak pressure, and 35–45° head-up tilt.

Tertiary burn care

Patients with burn injuries are assessed in the admission room in the tertiary centre. Depending on the severity of the burn (Fig. 64.10), patients are admitted either to a burns ICU (if a major burn needing fluid resuscitation, invasive monitoring, cardiovascular and respiratory support) or rehabilitation unit (if a minor burn). If the patient has sustained a major burn, venous access and invasive monitoring is established if not already in place from the referring centre. After a thorough handover, the burn size is estimated using the 'rule of nine' (see 'Exposure and estimation' and Fig. 64.8). Fluid resuscitation is carried out as outlined in a later subsection.

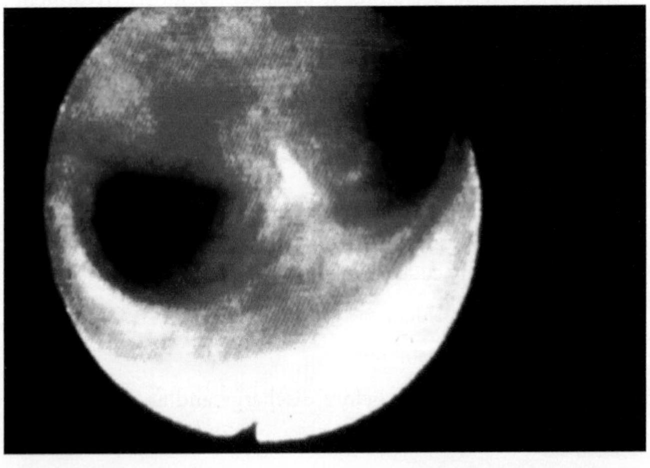

Figure 64.9 Bronchoscopic view of major airway burn showing redness, oedema, and ulceration of bronchial mucosa.

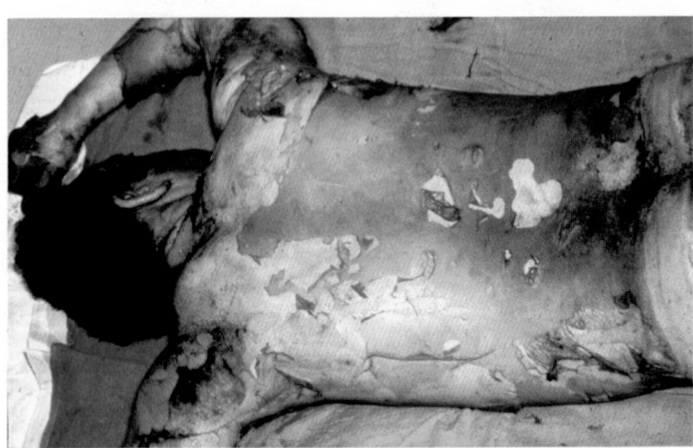

Figure 64.10 Major burn.

The burn wound is cleaned and dressed and the patient is stabilized before proceeding to early surgical excision of burn wound and skin grafting. It may take 6–12 h to stabilize the patient. Often inotropic and ventilator support is needed.

Estimation of burn depth

Currently, burn depth is determined clinically by visual and tactile assessment by an experienced burn specialist. However, clinical estimation of burn depth can be inaccurate. Various objective methods have been developed to define the depth of burn injury, including wound biopsy, vital dyes (Zawacki and Walker 1970—animal study), fluorescent fluorometry (Gatti et al. 1983), ultrasonography (Wachtel et al. 1986), thermography (Cole et al. 1990), light reflectance (Afromowitz et al. 1988), laser Doppler imaging (O'Reilly et al. 1989) (Fig. 64.11), and magnetic resonance imaging (MRI) (Koruda et al. 1986—animal study). These methods have used different technologies to determine the depth of burn wound, for example, by detecting dead cells or denatured protein (ultrasound, vital dyes), the changes in blood flow (fluorescin, laser Doppler, thermography), the colour of the wound (light reflectance), and the presence of oedema (nuclear MRI). Thermography is highly dependent on room and patient temperature. Light reflectance uses a portable, non-invasive electronic device which instantly measures spectral characteristics of light reflected from the skin. However, it is inaccurate in partial-thickness burns. Reliability is inconsistent with all these methods except histological sections of wound biopsy which is invasive and requires an experienced histopathologist.

Resuscitation of adult burn patients

All pre-admission fluid is added up and documented as pre-admission fluid. The 24 h predicted resuscitation fluid is calculated. Hourly cumulative fluid input (including preadmission fluid, oral intake, and drug infusions) is documented. Vital signs and urine output are monitored, aiming to achieve a urine output of 0.5–1.0 ml kg^{-1} h^{-1}. Hartmann's solution is started at the rate of 4 ml kg^{-1} (% of burn)$^{-1}$. Half of the calculated resuscitation fluid is given in the first 8 h from the time of burn and half is given in the next 16 h. The patient is assessed hourly and fluids adjusted accordingly. If the urine output is less than

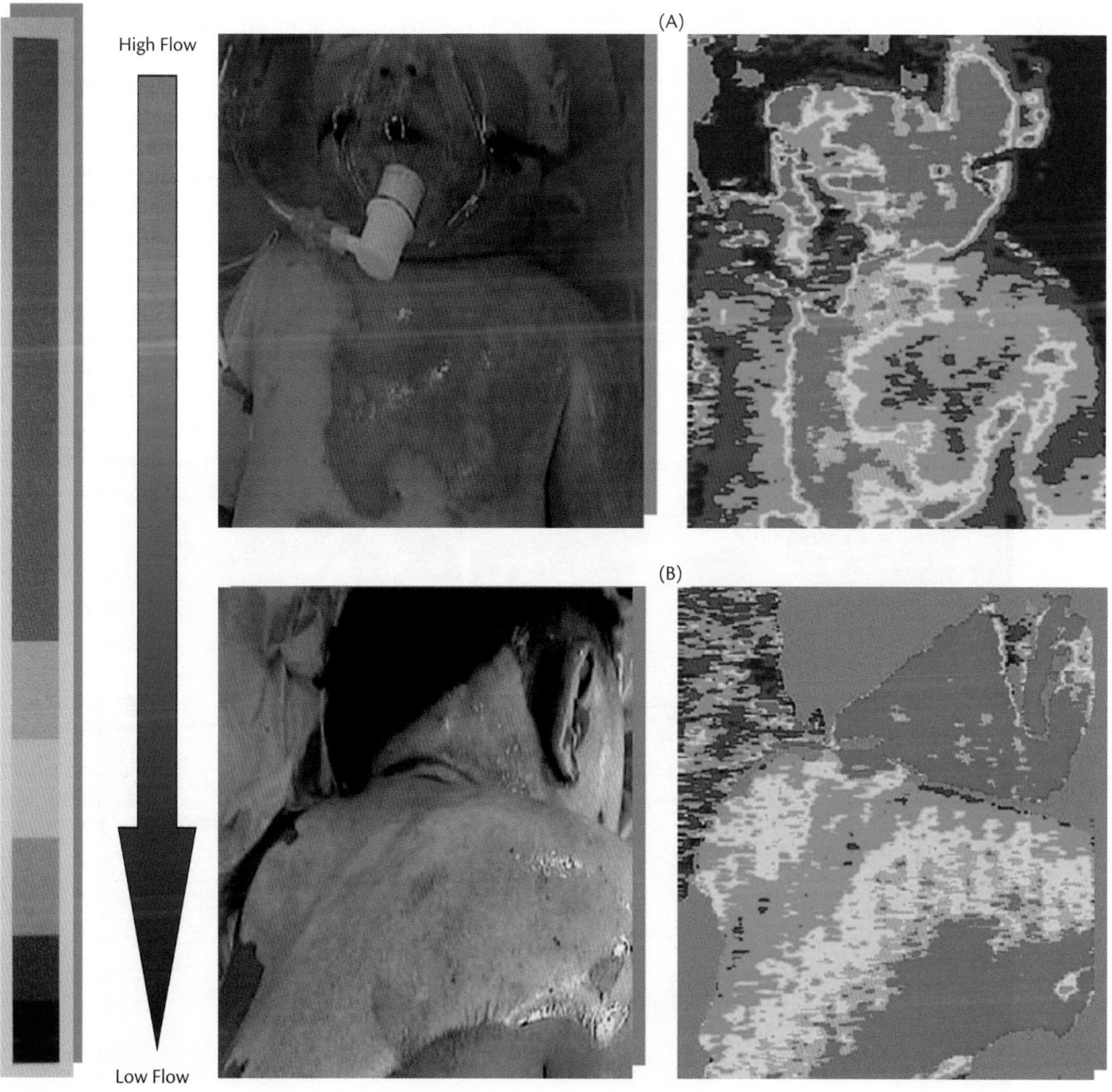

Figure 64.11 Laser Doppler to measure depth of burn objectively. (A) Front and (B) Back.

0.5 ml kg^{-1} h^{-1}, a fluid bolus of 250 ml is administered and the patient is reassessed at 1 h. However, if the patient becomes clinically unwell then a fluid bolus of 250 ml of gelatin (Volplex®) is given over 10 min and the patient reassessed. The bladder should be catheterized and invasive lines (arterial and CVP) established if not already done so.

Additional monitoring with pulse-induced contour cardiac output, lithium indicator dilution cardiac output, or oesophageal Doppler is commenced. Goal-directed fluid therapy (SV as indicator) with 250 ml of Volplex® over 10 min is commenced. If an internal jugular or subclavian venous line (not femoral) is in place, the Sv_{O_2} is checked. The patient may require inotropic, ventilatory, and renal (haemofiltration) support. The SVR is expected to be low in major burns as the resistance vessels are burned and one should not aim to achieve a 'normal' peripheral vascular resistance with an α-adrenergic drug (noradrenaline) as this would compromise perfusion to the vital organs. If the urine output is greater than 1 ml kg^{-1} h^{-1}, the rate of i.v. fluid administration should be reduced by 25–50%. If the urine output is between 0.5 and 1.0 ml kg^{-1} h^{-1}, the rate of i.v. fluid administration is maintained but reassessed hourly. If the calculated 24 h target for cumulative fluid input is achieved, before 24 h from the time of the burn, then the patient should be reassessed (check catheter/palpable bladder)—heart rate, urine output, capillary refill, and mean arterial pressure. The initial burn assessment on which the resuscitation fluid was calculated should be revisited and other (missed) injuries considered. There is no point chasing false targets such as isolated base deficit. If there is inhalation injury with severe metabolic acidosis or high lactate and the patient is unresponsive to fluid administration then consider carbon monoxide and cyanide poisoning (Box 64.3). It is important to note that too much fluid is as harmful as too little. There is ongoing trauma in major burns from the hypermetabolic state, burn wound toxicity, repeated surgical procedures, repeated dressing changes and showers, and massive fluid shift. In addition, there is psychological trauma including social deprivation, disfiguring scars, and prolonged reconstructive surgery. There is often a traumatic history and difficult family background (e.g. suicide attempts, house fires, and multiple casualties from the same incident). Psychological support and stress counselling must be available for patients, relatives, and all members of staff involved in caring for burn patients.

Anaesthesia for burn surgery

Working in the burn theatre environment can be quite daunting and requires a highly motivated team to work long hours in a heated environment involving a variety of case mix and patient dynamics which are complex (Fig. 64.12). The technical aspect is quite challenging and demanding. The course of burn treatment involves multiple surgical episodes requiring repeated exposure to anaesthesia. Preoperative assessment requires careful attention to anaemia, airway difficulty, catabolic state, coagulopathy, cardiac dysfunction, hyponatraemia, thermoregulation, immunosuppression, nutrition, intravenous access, monitoring, multiple general anaesthetics, multiple organ failure, and sepsis. Compatible monitoring systems should be in place in theatres, for transport, and intensive care rooms. Infection is a major problem in a burn unit hence extra care is needed to minimize infection, for example, single-use items; reserving equipment for the burn unit without sharing with general theatres; storing only the required equipment in theatre; changing gloves when drugs and equipment are to be taken into the theatre from the anaesthetic room; and using plastic gown, face mask, gloves, and glasses for eye protection. Vigorous cleaning of theatres between cases means inevitable delay between cases. Staffing the recovery room postoperatively can be a problem even in a burn unit setting with a dedicated theatre for burns.

Practical conduct of anaesthesia

Local and regional anaesthesia is often not feasible.

General anaesthesia with either (a) conventional propofol induction, LMA/cuffed oral tracheal tube, maintenance with oxygen, air,

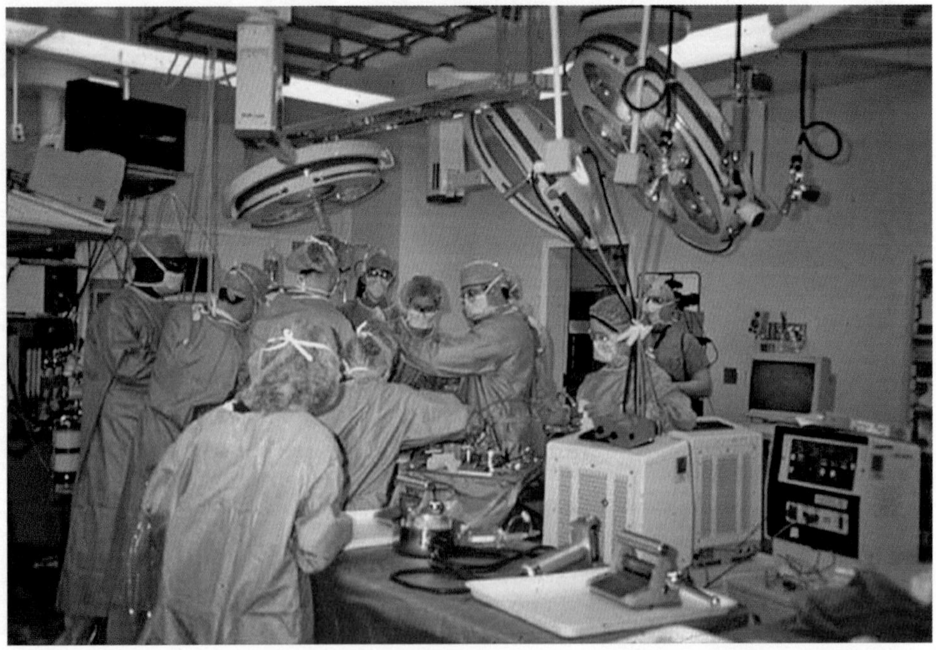

Figure 64.12 Multidisciplinary team working in an operating theatre to carry out a burn surgical procedure in a patient with major burn.

and inhalation agent (isoflurane or sevoflurane), non-depolarizing neuromuscular blocking agent when needed (avoid suxamethonium as it causes release of K^+ in the circulation leading to arrhythmias and even cardiac arrest); morphine for analgesia; (b) TIVA induction and maintenance; airway as for (a); or (c) propofol induction and maintenance with oxygen, air, and inhalation agent and remifentanil infusion; airway as for (a); morphine before end of anaesthesia.

Considerations in anaesthesia for burns

Venous access

Venous access can be technically difficult. However, the use of ultrasound has made line placement easier in burn patients. Patients with major burns undergoing surgical debridement of a burn wound invariably have all the lines *in situ* (being placed on admission).

Airway problems

The airway can be compromised if there is inhalation injury with swelling of the face, soot in the nostril, and difficulty in visualizing the larynx because of oedema (Box 64.3). A difficult airway trolley should be available in theatre before starting anaesthesia. Surgical intervention (tracheostomy) may be required. Another situation where the anaesthetist will face a challenging airway is when the patient has developed a neck contracture later in the course of burn rehabilitation, requiring surgical correction.

Temperature loss

Temperature regulation is altered in burn patients with the result that the patient may experience hyper- or hypothermia. A high metabolic rate may contribute to changes in temperature. In the operating theatre, a combination of lengthy procedures, exposure of large areas of the body, and administration of large volumes of fluids can cause hypothermia. Hence it is imperative to monitor both the peripheral and core temperature. The aim should be to keep the body temperature above 35°C and the difference between the core and periphery less than 4°C (a difference of greater than 4°C signifies that the patient is peripherally shut down). The ambient temperature of the room should be above 27°C. Use of overhead radiant heaters is very effective. In addition, fluid should be warmed using a fluid warmer and in major surgery a level 1 infusion system is useful for rapid transfusion of warm fluid and blood.

Infants aged less than 6 months lack the mechanism to shiver and prolonged hypothermia can lead to hypoxia and acidosis through adaptive brown fat metabolism (Langley and Sim 2002). Infants and children quickly lose heat because they have a higher relative evaporative heat loss than adults.

The 'Thermogard' Intravascular Temperature Management System (IVTM™, Zoll Medical Corporation, Chelmsford, United Kingdom) has recently been introduced for clinical use. Thermoregulation is achieved by circulation of saline around a ballooned catheter inserted into a central vein, with automatic adjustment of saline temperature controlled by remote monitoring of the patient's temperature. It has been successfully used in regulating labile body temperature associated with severe burns (Mavrogordato et al. 2009).

Monitoring difficulties

In the operating theatre, continuous monitoring of the patient's vital signs is essential to the safe conduct of anaesthesia. Essential monitoring devices include ECG, pulse oximeter, non-invasive blood pressure, and capnography. Burn patients pose particular challenges in achieving this essential standard of monitoring because of difficulties in placement of monitoring equipment (e.g. standard sites for ECG, pulse oximeter probe, and blood pressure cuff are often unavailable or do not stick on damaged skin). Pulse oximetry may be unreliable in the presence of carboxyhaemoglobin in inhalation injury or in shocked vasoconstricted patients. Siting of the pulse oximeter probe may be a problem in a patient with major burns because of lack of access to the usual sites. Access to neck veins, groin, and the infraclavicular region may be difficult because of burn wounds. These difficulties can be overcome in the following manner:

1. Attaching ECG leads to staples placed in burned areas.
2. Using specially designed metallic ECG electrodes which can be screwed onto the burned area.
3. A blood pressure cuff can be placed in the burned area or in extensive procedures, invasive measurement is justified with the added advantage of arterial blood gas and other analyses.
4. Attaching a pulse oximeter probe to central sites such as ears, nose, lips, or tongue. A modification of Guedel's airway whereby the Nellcor™ (Medtronic, Minneapolis, MN, USA) probe is inserted into the airway and the airway is inserted over the tongue in the usual manner. However, it may not give reliable results and in fact it can give a falsely high reading.
5. Use of a reflectance oesophageal photoplethysmographic probe utilizing miniature surface mount infrared and red emitters and a photodetector placed inside a modified nasogastric tube (Pal et al. 2005). The device is placed non-invasively in the patient's oesophagus and it gives a continuous recording of Sa_{O_2}. This has been shown to give accurate levels of oxygen saturation.

Blood loss

Blood loss can be massive and may reach twice the circulating volume. However, advances in surgical technique using subcutaneous adrenaline 1:1 000 000 infiltration under pressure (tumescence) before excising the wound or taking a skin graft has reduced blood loss considerably (Robertson et al. 2001). While estimating blood loss, consider donor site loss and the excision area. Blood loss is estimated according to area in cm^2. It depends on the time since injury, surgical plan, presence of infection, and whether a primary or repeat harvest is being done. The calculation is based on:

- Less than 24 h-old burn = 0.45 ml cm^{-2}
- 1–3-day-old burn = 0.65 ml cm^{-2}
- 2–16-day-old burn = 1.25 ml cm^{-2}.

Blood loss can be sudden as multiple surgical teams work at different sites. Therefore it is wise to confirm the availability of cross-matched blood and blood products before commencing anaesthesia. If there is sudden massive blood loss, surgery may need to be stopped temporarily while hypovolaemia is corrected. Assessing blood loss by weighing swabs is inaccurate and measuring haemoglobin and haematocrit using a blood gas analyser gives a fairer estimate. Additionally, it gives an indication of how well the vital organs are perfused with oxygenated blood. One needs to determine what haemoglobin target should be achieved. It is considered that up to 30% of the circulating volume can be replaced by crystalloid or colloid solutions alone (Carson et al. 1998) and a haemoglobin concentration of greater than 80 g $litre^{-1}$ should be sufficient without impairing wound healing (Wahr 1998; Hopf et al. 2000).

Drug pharmacokinetics

Burns patients exhibit altered pharmacokinetics as a result of changes in volume of distribution (V_d), and excretion of drugs. V_d is altered as a result of changes in the protein binding and extracellular fluid volume resulting from intravascular fluid loss, fluid administration, and increased capillary permeability. Losses may occur through burn wounds. In the acute hypometabolic phase, plasma protein concentrations change—albumin concentrations fall and α1-acid glycoprotein concentrations rise. Also in this phase the circulating blood volume and CO decrease and tissue perfusion is reduced as a result of increased fluid loss and increased vascular permeability. This in turn reduces renal and hepatic blood flow affecting drug clearance. In the hypermetabolic phase, there is restoration of vascular permeability; however, renal and hepatic function may still be impaired, therefore restoration of drug clearance may not be seen in this phase.

Burn injury affects the efficacy of neuromuscular blocking agents. Proliferation of extrajunctional acetylcholine receptors occurs in response to burn injury. This leads to resistance to non-depolarizing neuromuscular blocking agents and hypersensitivity to depolarizing neuromuscular blocking agents (Marathe et al. 1989). These changes are proportional to TBSA burn and may occur within a week of the injury and persist for up to a year. Hyperkalaemia occurs with a depolarizing neuromuscular blocking agent as a result of proliferation of the acetylcholine receptors and may lead to life-threatening arrhythmias (Allan et al. 1961). The maximum risk of hyperkalaemia in burn patients occurs between 9 and 60 days after the burn. The use of succinylcholine in the first 24 h after a severe burn injury is regarded as safe.

Because of the hyperdynamic circulation and hypermetabolic state, the dose requirement of all anaesthetic agents is increased and their duration of action is decreased. The MAC value for volatile anaesthetic agents is increased. Tolerance develops to a wide range of drugs including analgesics, sedatives, and inotropic agents.

Fluid requirement

Patients undergoing surgical debridement of burn wounds will require, in addition to maintenance fluid with crystalloid fluid, replacement with crystalloid, colloid, blood, and blood products for losses during surgery. Traditionally, albumin was used in the author's centre after the leaky capillary stage; however, controversy surrounded its use in a published report of a meta-analysis of albumin in critical care patients (Cochrane Injuries Group Albumin Reviewers 1998) leading to the introduction of other colloids. However, albumin is used when the serum albumin concentration falls below 15 g $litre^{-1}$. Hydroxyethyl starch (Volulyte®) has the advantages of efficient volume expansion, a prolonged duration of effect, being less expensive than human albumin, and with no possibility of transmitting infection. However, concerns have been raised that the use of starch may cause acute kidney injury in sepsis (Schortgen et al. 2001). Moreover it can cause itching (Sirtl et al. 1999) which is problematic in burn patients. Currently it has been withdrawn from the market. The colloid of choice now is gelatins (Volplex® or Gelofusine®). Blood is transfused to maintain the haemoglobin concentration at higher than 80 g $litre^{-1}$.

Infection control

Burn patients are at a greater risk of infection as the natural barrier of the skin is lost and the immune system is depressed. Topical antimicrobials are useful. These are silver-containing—flamazine, silver nitrate, and acticoat; hypochlorite (0.025%); and betadine. Washing wounds reduces the bacteria count, for example, taking a bath or shower results in a reduction from 10^6 to 10^2 organisms g^{-1} of tissue. Microbiological surveillance with regular wound swabs, tissue microbiology, and close liaison with a microbiologist is essential. Prophylactic systemic antibiotics are not prescribed unless patients are undergoing surgical procedures. In theatres, the patient routinely receives benzylpenicillin 1.2 g and gentamicin 3–5 mg kg^{-1} intravenously. Further systemic antibiotics are guided by culture and sensitivity reports.

Patients may develop infections caused by bacteria that are resistant to antibiotics and these are often difficult to treat, leading to sepsis which can be fatal. Colistin has been reported to be effective in treating multiresistant Gram-negative organisms in burn patients (Ganapathy et al. 2010).

Nutrition

Burn patients develop a high basal metabolic rate in the hyperdynamic phase. This leads to increased oxygen consumption. The Harris–Benedict equation (Harris and Benedict 1919) is used to calculate resting energy expenditure (REE), along with the usual multiplication factors to provide adequate calorie intake:

$$\text{Women: REE} = 655 + (9.6 \times \text{weight in kg}) + (1.7 \times \text{height in cm}) - (4.7 \times \text{age in years}) \quad (64.4)$$

$$\text{Men: REE} = 66 + (13.7 \times \text{weight in kg}) + (5.0 \times \text{height in cm})\ (6.8 \times \text{age in years}) \quad (64.5)$$

$$\text{Calorie requirements day}^{-1} = 1.25 \times \text{REE} \quad \text{(for each 1°C above 37 add 10\% extra allowance)} \quad (64.6)$$

A dietitian is a useful member of the burn team and carries out daily assessment of calorie requirement and intake is accordingly adjusted.

Gut motility is commonly affected and nasojejunal feeding is instituted early. Nasojejunal feeding is preferred to nasogastric feeding because repeated interruptions to the latter for surgical procedures can restrict the required calorie intake which may delay wound healing and recovery. With a nasojejunal feeding tube in place, the intubated patients can be fed through the surgical procedures without the fear of aspiration. Anaesthetic technique can be modified to reduce gut motility impairment. Functioning bowel is essential to reduce burns sepsis. Total parenteral nutrition is instituted if the gut becomes non-functioning. Abdominal girth is measured at intervals to detect any intra-abdominal pressure increase which can lead to bowel necrosis. Selective decontamination of the gastrointestinal tract may be considered in selected cases.

Glycaemic control is vitally important as hyperglycaemia is associated with increased mortality in burn patients (Gore et al. 2001).

Pain control in burns

Burn pain is one of the most severe forms of acute pain, necessitating the use of opioids. Opioid requirements are increased as a result of changes in V_d, protein binding, metabolism, and excretion. Altered pharmacokinetics, difficulty in assessing pain, and fear of addiction in the past has led to undermedication. There may be little or no pain for the first few hours because of release of endogenous opioids providing stress-induced analgesia. Pain is influenced by the following factors: depth of burn, stage of healing, nature of care procedures, and patient characteristics (age, ethnic origins, etc.). Often the pain experienced by the patient is complex as a result of the factors that led to the injury and they may have minimal pain and an increased level of anxiety. Pain receptors in skin around the exposed wound are stimulated and sensitized. Nerve damage can lead to neuropathic pain. It is important to differentiate various types of pain (Pal et al. 1997):

- Resting pain: constant and dull in nature, when the patient is resting between procedures
- Procedural pain: shorter in duration but much greater in intensity during procedures such as wound cleaning, debridement, and physiotherapy
- Breakthrough pain: generally associated with resting pain and is of shorter duration.

Psychological factors (depression/anxiety) become a part of the experience of pain if pain medication is not initiated before unpleasant procedures.

Endogenous pain modulation

Neural systems are involved in pain modulation. The endogenous opioid peptides met-enkephalin, leu-enkephalin, β-endorphin, and dynorphin are implicated. Receptor sites are μ, δ, and κ. There is an inverse association between β-endorphin immunoactivity and pain levels. The circadian rhythm is lost. The potency of opioid analgesics is increased acutely after burn injuries and augments stress-induced analgesia.

Patients with a major burn require sedation (propofol or midazolam) and infusion of opioids (morphine or remifentanil) to control pain in burn ICUs. If tracheal extubation is planned, sedation and analgesia are changed to propofol and remifentanil which are cleared rapidly from the plasma. In renal failure, morphine is replaced with alfentanil, and midazolam boluses are administered instead of using an infusion to prevent accumulation of these drugs. Gabapentin and clonidine can be added to the usual sedation. In patients with a minor burn, simple analgesics (paracetamol, ibuprofen) and opioid (morphine sulfate oral solution) are administered on admission. Pain scores and clinical signs are monitored regularly. If the pain score deteriorates, slow-release morphine is added to simple analgesics and morphine sulfate oral solution is given for breakthrough pain. In elderly patients, oxycodone is preferred. Pain is assessed, evaluated, and reviewed regularly. Intranasal fentanyl is useful in procedural pain (Borland et al. 2005). Intranasal diamorphine can be used effectively as analgesia for procedural pain and also to control breakthrough pain rapidly. If itching develops and is not helped by a moisturizer then gabapentin is administered. Antihistamine is usually effective (cyproheptadine and cetirizine initially and chlorphenamine later) in severe cases.

Adjuvant therapies include clonidine, local anaesthetics, ketamine, amitriptyline, methadone, and anticonvulsants which are effective in the treatment of sympathetically maintained pain (Pal et al. 1997). Psychological therapies include cognitive interventions, preparatory information, behavioural interventions, and hypnosis. These adjunctive methods enhance strategies to cope with pain and aid relaxation which benefit many patients (Pal et al. 1997).

Anaesthesia for hand surgery

Hand surgery involves treatment of acute injuries and chronic diseases such as rheumatoid arthritis of the hand and wrist; correction of congenital malformations of the upper extremities; and peripheral nerve disorders such as brachial plexus injuries at birth and carpal tunnel syndrome. There is an overlap of surgical skills of orthopaedic and plastic surgeons to perform some of the surgical procedures of the upper extremity. Acute injuries of the hand may involve replanting an amputated extremity or a finger requiring microsurgery. In some hand centres, hand transplant has been carried out successfully.

Various options are available to the anaesthetist for upper extremity surgery and each technique has particular benefits and risks. However, the goal should be to provide a safe technique and a comfortable experience for the patient during surgery. The anaesthetic technique is dependent on various factors such as the extent, site, and expected length of surgery; anxiety levels of the patient and the need for sedation; physical status of the patient; and among others, the patient's and anaesthetist's personal preferences.

The following techniques are used.

Local anaesthesia

Local anaesthetic is injected directly into the site where the procedure will be performed. It is commonly used for simple, small procedures which can be performed quickly. Advantages are quick onset, simplicity, and avoidance of complications of general anaesthesia. The surgeon usually administers the local anaesthetic. Disadvantages of this technique include discomfort and pain associated with injection of local anaesthetic and use of a tourniquet; inability to anaesthetize a large area or an inflamed area; and distortion of tissues from the local anaesthetic injection. In anxious patients and if the duration of surgery is anticipated to be prolonged, intravenous sedation is beneficial.

Regional anaesthesia (nerve) blocks

Regional anaesthesia involves injection of local anaesthetic to block the sensory (and motor) functions of specific nerves in the extremities. Regional anaesthesia techniques include digital blocks, wrist blocks, intravenous regional anaesthesia blocks, and brachial plexus blocks. These are described in detail in other chapters and readers are advised to refer to Part 8 of this textbook. Surgery can be performed under regional anaesthesia alone or a combination of regional anaesthesia with intravenous sedation or general anaesthesia.

General anaesthesia

Usual pre-anaesthetic assessment is done to assess fitness of the patient for general anaesthesia. Anaesthetic technique may include intravenous induction, LMA, or tracheal tube if indicated and maintenance with a volatile agent or TIVA. Regular simple analgesic postoperatively is sufficient. Opioids may be supplemented if required. Local anaesthesia and regional anaesthesia usually last 4–12 h and provide useful pain relief postoperatively.

Anaesthesia for aesthetic (cosmetic) surgery

Aesthetic or cosmetic surgery is performed to improve the appearance of the body. Physical appearance plays an important role in our lives and how we are perceived by others. This is influenced by current standards and fashion in society. Often these factors lead to dissatisfaction with body image and result in patients considering sometimes quite extensive and invasive aesthetic surgery to enhance their self-esteem and attractiveness. Please refer to Pal and Kumar (2010) for further reading.

Selection of patients

Patients presenting for aesthetic surgery are generally healthy (ASA 1 or 2) in comparison to other surgical patients. It is important to understand the psychological issues of the patient. Patients' expectations are often unrealistic in terms of what can be achieved surgically. Consequently changes and 'improvement' in their physical appearance may not satisfy their needs and this may lead to deterioration in their psychological status. Therefore patients' psychological status and their expectations have to be evaluated preoperatively before undertaking any surgical aesthetic procedure. The presence of an active psychotic disorder is commonly thought to contraindicate cosmetic surgery (Sarwer 1997; Sarwer et al. 1998).

Choice of anaesthesia

As a result of the range of aesthetic surgical procedures that are performed, various options are available to the anaesthetist to provide the patient with a safe and comfortable experience. Aesthetic surgery on the face poses many challenges to the anaesthetist including careful attention to securing the airway device requiring close cooperation between anaesthetic and surgical teams. The options that are available to the anaesthetist are:

- Infiltration of local anaesthetic agent with or without sedation
- Regional anaesthesia with or without intravenous sedation
- General anaesthesia alone or supplemented by the above-listed options.

Patients should be assessed preoperatively to exclude any pre-existing medical conditions and to optimize these if necessary before contemplating surgery. Patients booked to have their surgery under local anaesthesia should be prepared as for general anaesthesia.

Local anaesthesia and regional anaesthesia

The essential requirements for aesthetic surgery under local or regional anaesthesia are that patients should be safe, comfortable, and stable. It is desirable for them to be immobile (hence not suitable for too lengthy procedures) and not too talkative. Local or regional anaesthesia techniques, or both, have the advantages of (a) reducing the overall stress of surgery and anaesthesia, (b) providing better postoperative pain control, (c) reducing PONV, (d) reducing dysphoria because of opiates, and (e) possibly improving wound healing. However, there are disadvantages of local or regional anaesthesia—allergy, neurotoxicity, and systemic toxicity. Please refer to Chapter 17 for the detailed pharmacology of local anaesthetics.

Conscious sedation

Conscious sedation describes a state that allows patients to tolerate and sometimes forget unpleasant procedures by relieving anxiety, discomfort, or pain while maintaining cardiovascular and respiratory functions and the ability to respond to verbal commands and tactile stimulation. Too much sedation can rapidly change the depth of consciousness and expose the patient to the risks associated with an unsecured airway and lack of protective reflexes. Patients must be carefully selected for conscious sedation as in a cardiorespiratory compromised patient, a 'normal' dose of sedation may prove too much and the situation described earlier in this paragraph can arise. This is also the reason why conscious sedation should be used by trained anaesthetists in an environment where the patient's vital signs can be monitored and there is access to resuscitation equipment.

General anaesthesia

Preoperative anaesthetic consideration

General anaesthesia is popular for aesthetic surgery in the United Kingdom while local anaesthesia and conscious sedation is popular in the United States. The proposed aesthetic surgery can dictate the type of anaesthesia. For example, rhinoplasty and breast augmentation are almost always done under general anaesthesia although local anaesthesia has been used successfully. Adult patients and many teenagers will accept local anaesthesia with or without conscious sedation for a pinnaplasty. It may not be possible to perform some aesthetic procedure under local or regional anaesthesia because of the duration of the procedure. Lengthy operations make it difficult to maintain uncomfortable positions for a prolonged period and can deter even the most motivated of patients. Sedation must be judiciously used and oversedation must be avoided as it can lead to disinhibition, agitation, dysphoria, and unconsciousness (Fiset et al. 1992). In terms of cardiovascular stability and recovery from anaesthesia, there are distinct advantages of using target-controlled infusion of propofol or remifentanil to sedate these patients (Pal and Kumar 2010).

Types of aesthetic surgery

The following are some of the common aesthetic surgical procedures carried out in the United Kingdom:

- Head and neck:
  - Facelift
  - Blepharoplasty
  - Rhinoplasty
  - Otoplasty (pinnaplasty)
  - Laser resurfacing of face
- Breast: breast augmentation, breast reduction, mastopexy
- Abdomen: abdominoplasty, liposuction.

Rhinoplasty

Cosmetic rhinoplasty is the surgical manipulation of the nose to improve its appearance. It may involve nasal hump reduction, or augmentation or improvement of nasal tip definition. Rhinoplasty is performed as an open or closed technique depending on the patient's requirement and the surgeon's preference. The anaesthetic technique is the same for both surgical techniques. Rhinoplasty is routinely performed under general anaesthesia. Ideal conditions for surgery include patient immobility, a clear surgical field with minimal bleeding, and smooth recovery. General anaesthesia with an oral tracheal tube with a throat pack, or flexible LMA with either spontaneous or controlled ventilation, can be used. Local anaesthetic infiltration is also used with general anaesthesia.

It is important to know the anatomy and sensory nerve supply of the nose before embarking on local anaesthesia. The skin of the nose is supplied by the supratrochlear branch of the frontal nerve of the ophthalmic, the anterior ethmoidal branch of the nasociliary (ophthalmic), and infraorbital branch of the maxillary branch of the trigeminal nerve. The fifth cranial nerve provides the sensory supply to the anterior one-third of the septum and the lateral walls are innervated by the anterior ethmoidal branch of the nasociliary nerve. The long sphenopalatine nerves from the sphenopalatine ganglion innervate the posterior two-thirds of the septum and lateral walls.

The nasal cavities are either sprayed or packed with gauze soaked in 4–5% cocaine. Cocaine paste is also applied to the area of the sphenopalatine ganglion behind the middle turbinate. The mucosa becomes avascular as a result of the vasoconstrictor properties of cocaine. Cocaine is a powerful vasoconstrictor so adrenaline is not necessary. Alternatively, Moffett's solution, a mixture of 2 ml of cocaine hydrochloride 8%, 2 ml of sodium bicarbonate 1%, and 1 ml of 1:200 000 adrenaline solution, is used.

Blockade of the sphenopalatine ganglion gives a clear surgical field. If the septum is to be operated on, 2 ml of lidocaine 1% with adrenaline should be injected into the columella and base of the septum as this area is covered by squamous epithelium which does not absorb the topically applied agents. However, use of the combination may precipitate cardiac arrhythmias and should be avoided.

Various techniques for general anaesthesia are available to the anaesthetist ranging from intravenous induction with propofol followed by inhalation agents to very rapidly acting propofol and remifentanil TIVA. The author's preference is to use TIVA which allows flexibility in quickly modulating the systemic blood pressure by altering the target, that is, rate of remifentanil infusion. This, combined with regional local anaesthetic block as previously described, provides a clear surgical field. Additionally, maintaining a head-up tilt during surgery and recovery (equally important) reduces venous congestion and bleeding. A recent trend is to use a flexible LMA for rhinoplasty which the author is not in favour of. The rationale for using LMA is probably to reduce the incidence of postoperative sore throat (which can be a significant factor in a professional singer) which can be distressing. However, it must be remembered that the LMA does not protect the airway in an anaesthetized patient and a cuffed tracheal tube [Ring–Adair–Elwyn (RAE) tube] should be used. The RAE tube is south-facing and can be taped on the chin to keep it out of the surgeon's field. Part of the procedure may involve using nasal osteotomies to straighten the nasal bones and this can lead to blood pooling in the nasopharyngeal area. The presence of a throat pack will soak up the blood and protect the airway. It also reduces the amount of blood which can trickle into the stomach via the oesophagus. Ingested blood is an irritant and a known factor for PONV. Even though the throat pack is soaked with saline it is still very abrasive to the pharyngeal mucosa and the patient may complain of a sore throat postoperatively. Careful attention must be paid to removing the throat pack at the end of surgery as it can cause airway obstruction leading to hypoxia, respiratory arrest, and death. Leaving a throat pack in after surgery is a 'never event' and each department should develop their own policy on how to remind the clinician to remove the throat pack at the end of surgery. These may include one or more of placing a printed sticker on the forehead indicating throat pack *in situ*, tying the throat pack tail to the tracheal tube, noting the status of throat pack on the theatre notice board, including the throat pack in the mandatory World Health Organization checklist in theatre, keeping accurate records, and performing a complete handover when transferring care.

At the end of surgery a surgical splint is applied. The splint should be allowed to stiffen and contour before waking the patient up. Recovery should be smooth. Excessive coughing increases venous pressure which can increase bleeding. However, the patient must be fully awake before extubation as the application of a face mask to maintain the airway may be difficult, especially if the nostrils are packed, and too much pressure by the facemask can spoil the surgeon's work. If the nostrils are packed, the patient may wake up in recovery in a panic unable to breathe through the nose, hence it is wise to warn the patient preoperatively and ask them to practise mouth breathing. Patients are usually pain free postoperatively; however, mouth dryness as a result of mouth breathing may be distressing.

Facelift

A surgical facelift involves removing excess facial folds and tightening underlying facial muscles to create a more youthful appearance. Incisions are usually made above the hairline to hide any scarring after the facelift. Facial skin is separated from the underlying tissue first and excess fat excised. The underlying muscles are tightened and redundant skin is excised. The skin is then stitched and the area is bandaged. A facelift is often combined with other aesthetic procedures such as blepharoplasty or forehead (brow) lift, and submandibular liposuction.

Patients presenting for facelift surgery usually tend to be between 45 and 65 years and they are generally fit and well. It can be performed under local anaesthetic with or without sedation but a general anaesthetic is preferred by many patients. When a general anaesthetic is used, the main challenge for the anaesthetist is to make sure the tracheal tube does not interfere with the surgical field and that it does not get displaced. Options for general anaesthesia include TIVA or propofol induction followed by an inhalation agent. Local anaesthetic infiltration helps although one should remember that it can block the branches of the facial nerve if not performed carefully and it may create confusion (until the local anaesthetic wears off) with regard to the integrity of the nerve in the postoperative period. The continued use of a neuromuscular blocking agent is avoided if intraoperative testing of the facial nerve is intended. Usual measures to prevent heat loss and DVT should be taken.

Blepharoplasty

Blepharoplasty involves resection of skin, orbicularis muscle, and fat in the periorbital region to rejuvenate the aged appearance of the eyes. As an isolated procedure it can be done under local anaesthetic with or without sedation. Too much sedation is avoided as patient cooperation may be needed in opening and closing the eye during the procedure to ensure a perfect result. When using local anaesthetic infiltration, care must be taken to avoid causing haematomas and injections into muscle. Many patients opt for a general anaesthetic. TIVA or propofol induction followed by inhalation agents can be used. The airway is maintained either with a LMA or tracheal tube if indicated. The usual anaesthetic precautions for head and neck surgery apply.

Pinnaplasty

Patients with prominent ears presenting for correction are usually children and a number of them develop psychological issues secondary to bullying and harassment in school. Surgery involves flattening the antihelical fold and may require reshaping. An elliptical skin incision is made behind the ear followed by dissection, cartilage resection, and suturing. When children present for pinnaplasty, the generic considerations of paediatric anaesthesia apply (see Part 10 of this book). Gas induction or intravenous induction with propofol followed by anaesthetic maintenance with an inhalation agent is usually used. The airway can be maintained with a LMA but a tracheal tube may be preferred if there is a risk of the LMA becoming dislodged during surgical positioning or repositioning of the patient, or both, during the procedure or during application of bandages. Local anaesthetic and adrenaline infiltration is commonly performed to create a clear surgical field, provide pain relief, and reduce PONV. Adult patients presenting for pinnaplasty will accept local anaesthetic with or without sedation. Local anaesthetic is infiltrated in each ear with 10 ml of 1% lidocaine in 1:200 000 adrenaline. The general anaesthesia technique is similar to that for facelift or blepharoplasty described previously.

As the dermatomes supplying the back of the ears correspond to the vomiting centre in the brain, the incidence of PONV is much higher in this cohort of patients and prophylactic antiemetic(s) should be considered. This must be explained to the patient (and the parents in case of children) in the preoperative consultation. Postoperative pain usually requires paracetamol only. Some surgeons prefer non-steroidal anti-inflammatory agents not to be used because even a small haematoma is likely to require surgical evacuation. Excessive pain could mean haematoma formation and the dressing should be released and the surgical site examined. The dressing stays on for a week or two depending on the surgeon's preference, and this can cause scalp discomfort and itching.

Laser resurfacing of the face

Laser resurfacing of the face is performed to reduce fine lines, wrinkles, and skin discolouration. It is claimed to avoid scarring and recovery is quicker and hence sometimes preferred to a surgical facelift. A carbon dioxide laser is useful for resurfacing of the face. After laser application, the skin healing is quicker and the connective tissue becomes stronger leading to tightening of the facial skin.

It is important to take a general medical history including information about wound healing, bleeding disorders, and any history of infectious diseases particularly hepatitis and HIV infection. The HIV proviral DNA has been detected in the laser plume generated by carbon dioxide laser irradiation of HIV-infected tissue culture (Baggish et al. 1991).

Laser treatment usually causes a transient stinging sensation, however cumulative pulses of laser may be uncomfortable and increasingly intolerable. In many instances, especially if the area of treatment is small, use of topical anaesthetics such as EMLA™ or Ametop® cream alone is sufficient. For maximal effectiveness, the local anaesthetic cream is applied under an occlusive dressing for 60 min followed by removal 10–30 min before treatment.

If general anaesthesia is planned then a minimally explosive mixture of inspired gases such as less than 30% oxygen-enriched air should be used. Dedicated laser protective airway devices should be used and protected from the laser beam by means of saline-soaked dressing gauze. The cuff of the tracheal tube should be filled with saline instead of air. Intravenous induction is followed by controlled ventilation via a tracheal tube and anaesthesia is maintained with an inhalation agent or preferably TIVA.

Postoperative pain or discomfort experienced by patients undergoing laser resurfacing is similar to that of a severe burn. Intraoperative and postoperative analgesics are required to keep the patient comfortable.

Abdominoplasty

Abdominoplasty is a surgical procedure to remove excess fat and skin from the abdomen and to tighten the abdominal wall to improve the shape of abdomen. It can also remove or reduce the appearance of stretch marks and unwanted scars on the abdomen. Patients presenting for abdominoplasty may have various reasons to have the surgery, for example, to remove folds of skin left behind after losing a lot of weight or to tighten stretched skin after pregnancy. The former group of patients may have had bariatric surgery such as gastric banding to reduce weight and may still be overweight and carry a higher incidence of morbidity. The latter group of patients may or may not be obese. It is important to tell the patient that abdominoplasty is not a treatment for weight control or a substitute for regular physical activity and a healthy balanced diet and that it will not stop the patient from gaining weight in future.

The majority of cases are done under general anaesthesia; however, in patients where only a small area of excess fat and skin is removed (miniabdominoplasty), which does not require repositioning of the umbilicus, local anaesthesia with or without sedation can be considered. When general anaesthesia is planned, the author prefers TIVA induction with propofol and remifentanil and maintenance with either a LMA or tracheal tube if indicated. Intraoperative opioids are given. The usual precautions to prevent DVT and heat loss are taken. In the postoperative period, patients require simple analgesics and oral opiates: patient-controlled analgesia may be required over the first 12 h after surgery, especially when divarication of the rectus abdominis muscles is repaired. It is important that patients keep their knees bent when lying in bed to prevent putting strain on the abdominal stitches. Complications may include infection, haematoma, and seroma which may require surgical exploration.

Breast reduction

Breast reduction surgery involves reshaping and reducing the size of enlarged breasts. Patients presenting for breast reduction surgery, apart from being self-conscious about the way they look, often complain of discomfort as a result of back, neck, and shoulder pain; and sweating, rashes, and skin infections under the breasts. Although females present for this type of surgery, males also present for breast reduction surgery for gynaecomastia (enlarged breasts). Gynaecomastia may result from a hormonal imbalance, a typical example being an athlete using steroids to improve muscle mass and athletic performance. This has anaesthetic implications.

Patients presenting for breast reduction are advised to reduce weight if they are overweight as breast size alters with body weight.

Breast reduction surgery is usually carried out under general anaesthesia. The operation typically takes approximately 2 h but some surgeons may take up to 4 h. Bleeding is minimized by infiltration of a local anaesthetic and adrenaline mixture by the surgeon or careful surgical technique, or both. The author's preferred choice is TIVA and either a LMA or tracheal tube as indicated. Intraoperative opioids and postoperative simple analgesic and oral opioids are usually sufficient. There are various techniques to perform this operation but essentially excess breast tissue is removed through the lower parts of the breasts and the nipples are moved to suit the new shape. Patients may be unable to breastfeed after the operation. Complications may include infection, haematoma, fat necrosis, and rarely loss of part or even the entire nipple as a result of alterations in the blood supply to the breast.

Breast augmentation

Breast enlargement (or breast augmentation) surgery usually involves putting an artificial implant either under the breast tissue, or under the pectoral muscles deep to the breast. Patients presenting for breast augmentation include women who feel that their breasts are too small after losing weight or after a pregnancy, or to correct unequal breast sizes. Breast augmentation using an implant is also considered if the patient is having surgery as treatment for breast cancer or other conditions that may have affected the size and shape of the breasts. It is also considered in patients with Poland's syndrome—a congenital anomaly with a unique pattern of one-sided malformation at birth with underdevelopment or absence of chest wall including pectoralis major and breast tissue and ipsilateral cutaneous syndactyly.

Various types of breast implants are available; however, popular ones have an outer layer of firm silicone, and are usually filled with silicone gel. Manufacturers of breast implants claim that they last for at least 10 years, but they may last for longer than this without problems. Patients may still be able to breastfeed after breast augment surgery with breast implants. Breast implants can interfere with mammography so the radiographer should be informed accordingly if breast screening is planned.

The operation is usually carried out under general anaesthesia although in some countries local anaesthesia with sedation is quite acceptable to the patients. The duration of the procedure is usually 1–2 h. It tends to be a more painful procedure than a breast reduction even though the latter involves more extensive skin incisions. This is because of the extent of tissue dissection required and the stretching of the skin caused by the presence of an implant, especially if a large implant is placed. Intraoperative and postoperative opioids and regular simple analgesics are required. The usual precautions to prevent DVT and extra precautions to prevent infection because of the implant are taken. The author's experience is that a TIVA anaesthetic produces a smooth recovery and a low incidence of PONV. The airway is maintained with a LMA or tracheal tube if indicated. Often the operation may be carried out as a day-case procedure. Complications include infection, haematoma, DVT, capsular contracture, ruptured implant, and leaking implant.

Liposuction

Liposuction is an operation involving application of a negative pressure to suck excess unwanted body fat to change the shape of the body. Liposuction is not a treatment for reducing weight or obesity and patients need to understand that it will not remove stretch marks. Areas that can be treated are the abdomen, hips, buttocks, neck, arms, thighs, knees, and ankles. The body will not replace the fat cells that have been sucked out, however gaining weight after surgery can cause the remaining fat cells to enlarge.

Liposuction is usually carried out under general anaesthesia but small areas can be done under local anaesthesia with or without sedation. The procedure takes between 1 and 3 h depending on how extensive the area is to be treated.

Tumescent liposuction technique

This technique involves subcutaneous infiltration of very large volumes of isotonic solution (normal saline or Hartmann's solution) containing a dilute mixture of local anaesthetic and adrenaline into the fatty area being treated. The technique was first described by Klein (1990) in which he used a dilute solution of adrenaline and lidocaine 1% (35 mg kg^{-1}). The aim was to avoid the risks of general anaesthesia, reduce blood loss, and provide postoperative pain relief for up to 18 h. The technique is mainly used in the United States and Germany. The dose recommended by Klein is five times the recommended toxic dose of lidocaine (7 mg kg^{-1} with adrenaline). The arguments in favour of using such a toxic dose of local anaesthetic are that local anaesthetic is absorbed fairly slowly from subcutaneous tissue as a result of poor vascularity and much of the drug is initially absorbed into fat, while the vasoconstriction produced by adrenaline further slows the absorption. Additionally, a proportion (35%) of the lidocaine administered for liposuction is removed in the aspirate. However, this would still leave a potentially lethal amount of lidocaine. There have been published reports of plasma lidocaine concentrations with this technique and associated claims of safety with as much as 55 mg kg^{-1} (Ostad et al. 1996). The plasma concentration of lidocaine, however, continues to rise for up to 23 h after the procedure. Also the sampling times in the studies were wide and variable. Therefore the evidence is not strong enough and further research is needed.

The injectate helps to remove the fat cells easily, reducing bleeding and bruising. Through a small skin incision a long metal cannula is inserted into the subcutaneous area. The cannula is then connected to a vacuum pump or a syringe. The cannula is pushed and pulled carefully through the fat layer to break it up and then the fat and fluid is sucked out. If the fat is very dense, ultrasound can be used to break up the fat before it is removed. The anaesthetist must keep an eye on the fluid balance as hypovolaemia can ensue rapidly. Simple analgesics are sufficient for postoperative pain relief. In the postoperative period, the patient may experience some bruising, swelling, numbness, and thrombophlebitis. Complications include local anaesthetic toxicity, infection, fluid imbalance leading to pulmonary oedema, damage to internal organs, fat embolism, and death. There are still questions about the safety of tumescent anaesthesia. In 1999, five deaths were reported after tumescent anaesthesia in New York between 1993 and 1998 (Rao and Hoffman 1999). The authors linked two deaths to lidocaine toxicity, one to fluid overload, and one to thromboembolic complications. Several deaths associated with tumescent anaesthesia have been reported in the literature (Barillo et al. 1998). However, safety of tumescent anaesthesia has improved over the years with better application of knowledge of drug absorption, safety profile, and management of the technique. In tumescent anaesthesia, lidocaine injected in subcutaneous tissue is absorbed very slowly resulting in lower and delayed peak blood levels compared to other routes (Conroy and O'Rourke 2013). Conroy and O'Rourke also suggested absorption of local anaesthetic administered in this way is similar to depot injection as slow systemic absorption allows rapid plasma clearance to maintain safe local anaesthetic blood levels. Drugs which affect hepatic drug clearance will adversely influence the local anaesthetic blood levels. Wang et al. (2015) have measured the local anaesthetic blood levels in tumescent anaesthesia. After injecting lidocaine 40.7 mg kg^{-1} with a total dose of 2528 mg injected they reported lidocaine peak level of 0.63 μg ml^{-1} after 12–20 h. The study also showed no significant correlation between dose per kg body weight or total dose of lidocaine infiltrated and its peak levels or time (Wang et al. 2015). A recent survey from the American Society of Plastic Surgeons revealed that a small number of plastic surgeons (7% of responders) in the United States are using bupivacaine in their tumescent solution and have reported no toxicity and better postoperative pain control (Paik et al. 2015).

Declaration of interest

The author, in collaboration with City University, London, United Kingdom, has successfully developed and completed a clinical trial using a new non-invasive opto-electronic measuring device. The author has no financial benefit that may be accrued from this device.

References

Adams J, Charlton P. Anaesthesia for microvascular free tissue transfer. *Br J Anaesth CEPD Rev* 2003; **3**: 33–7

Afromowitz MA, Callis JB, Heimbach DM, DeSoto LA, Norton MK. Multispectral imaging of burn wounds: a new clinical instrument for evaluating burn depth. *IEEE Trans Biomed Eng* 1988; **35**: 842–50

Akinniranye OA, Pal SK. Inhalation injury: current concepts and management. *Anaesth Rev* 1999; **15**: 81–102

Allan CM, Cullen WG, Gillies DMM. Ventricular fibrillation in a burned boy. *Curr Med Assoc* 1961; **85**: 432–4

Anaesthesia UK. Anaesthesia for Reconstructive Free Flap Surgery. 2006. Available from http://www.frca.co.uk/article.aspx?articleid=100376

Antia NH, Buch VI. Transfer of an abdominal dermo-fat graft by direct anastomosis of blood vessels. *Br J Plast Surg* 1971; **24**: 15–9

Baggish MS, Poiesz BJ, Joret D, Williamson P, Refai A. Presence of human immunodeficiency virus DNA in laser smoke. *Laser Surg Med* 1991; **11**: 197–203

Balakumar P, Rohilla A, Singh M. Pre-conditioning and post-conditioning to limit ischaemia-reperfusion-induced myocardial injury: what could be the next footstep? *Pharmacol Res* 2008; **57**: 403–12

Bang RL, Ghoneim IE. Epidemiology and mortality of 162 major burns in Kuwait. *Burns* 1996; **22**: 433–8

Barillo DJ, Cancio LC, Kim SH, Shirani KZ, Goodwin CW. Fatal and near fatal complications of liposuction. *South Med J* 1998; **91**: 487–92

Baux S. *Contribution a l'etude du traitement local des brulures thermiques etendues*, Paris: These, 1961

Black A, Nadarajan S. Anaesthesia for paediatric maxillofacial surgery. In: Shaw I, Kumar C, Dodds C, eds. *Oixfiord Textbook of Anaesthesia for Oral and Maxillofacial Surgery*. Oxford: Oxford University Press, 2010; 253–68

Blogg CE. Anaesthesia for plastic surgery. In: Nimmo W, Rowbotham DJ, Smith G, eds. *Anaesthesia*. Oxford: Blackwell Scientific Publication, 1994; 1037–41

Blondeel N, Vanderstraeten GG, Monstrey SJ, *et al.* The donor site morbidity of free DIEP flaps and free TRAM flaps for breast reconstruction. *Br J Plast Surg* 1997; **50**: 322–30

Borland ML, Bergesio R, Pascoe EM, Turner S, Woodger S. Intranasal fentanyl is an equivalent analgesic to oral morphine in paediatric burns patients for dressing changes: a randomised double blind crossover study. *Burns* 2005; **31**: 831–7

Bouma MG, van den Wildenberg FA, Buurman WA. The anti-inflammatory potential of adenosine in ischemia-reperfusion injury: established and putative beneficial actions of a retaliatory metabolite. *Shock* 1997; **8**: 313–20

Brusselaers N, Monstrey S, Vogelaers D, Hoste E, Blot S. Severe burn injury in Europe: a systematic review of the incidence, etiology, morbidity, and mortality. *Crit Care* 2010; **14**: R188

Bull MJ, Givan DC, Sadove AM, Bixler D, Hearn D. Improved outcome in Pierre Robin sequence: effect of multidisciplinary evaluation and management. *Pediatrics* 1990; **86**: 294–301

Bundgaard-Nielsen M, Ruhnau B, Secher NH, Kehlet H. Flow-related techniques for preoperative goal-directed fluid optimization. *Br J Anaesth* 2007; **98**: 38–44

British Burn Association. *National Burn Care Referral Guidance*. London: British Burn Association, 2012. Available from http:www.britishburnassociation.org/referral-guidance

Cadier MA, Shakespeare PG. Burns in octogenarians. *Burns* 1995; **21**: 200–4

Cahoon NJ, Naparus A, Ashrafpour H, *et al.* Pharmacologic prophylactic treatment for perioperative protection of skeletal muscle from ischaemia-reperfusion injury in reconstruction surgery. *Plast Reconstr Surg* 2013; **131**: 473–85

Carson JL, Duff A, Berlin JA, *et al.* Perioperative blood transfusion and postoperative mortality. *JAMA* 1998; **279**: 199–205

Clinical Standards Advisory Group. *Cleft Lip and Palate*. London: The Stationery Office, 1998

Cochrane Injuries Group Albumin Reviewers. Human albumin administration in critically ill patients: systematic review of randomised controlled trials. *BMJ* 1998; **317**: 235–40

Cole RP, Jones SG, Shakespeare P. Thermographic assessment of hand burns. *Burns* 1990; **16**: 60–3

Conroy PH, O'Rourke J. Tumescent anaesthesia. *Surgeon* 2013; **11**: 210–21

Davis PD, Kenny GNC. Fluid flow. In: *Basic Physics and Measurement in Anaesthesia*, 5th Edn. London: Butterworth-Heinemann, 2003; 13

De Gaudio AR, Adembri C, Grechi S, Novelli GP. Microalbuminuria as an early index of impairment of glomerular permeability in postoperative septic patients. *Int Care Med* 2000; **26**: 1364–8

Del Principe D. [Antithrombin III in burned children] [Article in Italian]. *Minerva Anestesiol* 2003; **69**: 376–80

Desai MH, Mlcak R, Richardson J, Nichols R, Herndon DN. Reduction in mortality in paediatric patients with inhalation injury with nebulised heparin/acetylcysteine therapy. *J Burn Care Rehabil* 1998; **19**: 210–12

Dolan RW, Kerr D, Arena S. Reducing ischemia-reperfusion injury in rat island groin flaps by dexamethasone and BW755C. *Laryngoscope* 1995 **105**: 1322–5

Ely SW, Berne RM. Protective effects of adenosine in myocardial ischemia. *Circulation* 1992; **85**: 893–904

Exadaktylos AK, Buggy DJ, Moriarty DC, Mascha E, Sessler DI. Can anesthetic technique for primary breast cancer surgery affect recurrence or metastasis? *Anesthesiology* 2006; **105**: 660–4

Fiset I, Milgrom P, Beirne OR, Roy-Byrne P. Disinhibition of behaviour with midazolam: report of a case. *J Oral Maxillofac Surg* 1992; **50**: 645–9

Gan TJ, Soppitt A, Maroof M, *et al.* Goal-directed intra-operative fluid administration reduces length of hospital stay after major surgery. *Anesthesiology* 2002; **97**: 820–6

Ganapathy H, Pal SK, Teare L, Dziewulski P. Use of colistin in treating multi-resistant Gram-negative organisms in a specialised burns unit. *Burns* 2010; **36**: 522–7

Gatti J, LaRossa D, Silverman D, Hartford CE. Evaluation of the burn wound with perfusion fluorometry. *J Trauma* 1983; **23**: 202–6

Gauglitz GG, Finnerty CC, Herndon DN, Mlcak RP, Jeschke MG. Are serum cytokines early predictors for the outcome of burn patients with inhalation injuries who do not survive? *Crit Care* 2008; **12**: R81

Goodwin CW. Multiple organ failure: clinical overview of the syndrome. *J Trauma* 1990; **30**: S163–5

Gore DC, Chinkes D, Heggers J, Herndon DN, Wolf SE, Desai M. Association of hyperglycemia with increased mortality after severe burn injury. *J Trauma* 2001; **51**: 540–4

Gosling P, Brudney S, McGrath L, Riseboro S, Manji M. Mortality prediction at admission to intensive care: a comparison of microalbuminuria with acute physiology scores after 24 hours. *Crit Care Med* 2003; **31**: 98–103

Granger DN, Korthuis RJ. Physiologic mechanisms of post-ischaemic tissue injury. *Annu Rev Physiol* 1995; **57**: 311–32

Gunawardane RH. Difficult laryngoscopy in cleft lip and palate surgery. *Br J Anaesth* 1996; **76**: 757–9

Guyton AC, Hall JE. *Textbook of Medical Physiology*, 11th Edn. Philadelphia, PA: Elsevier Inc, 2006

Halestrap AP, Clarke SJ, Javadov SA. Mitochondrial permeability transition pore opening during myocardial reperfusion: a target for cardioprotection. *Cardiovasc Res* 2004; **61**: 372–85

Haponic ER, Summer W. Respiratory complication in burn patient: pathogenesis and spectrum of inhalation injury. *J Crit Care* 1987; **2**: 49

Harris JA, Benedict FG. *A Biometric Study of Basal Metabolism in Man*. Washington, DC: Carnegie Institute of Washington, Publication No 279, 1919

Hatch D. Editorial II: Airway management in cleft lip and palate surgery. *Br J Anaesth* 1996; **76**: 755–6

Hearse DJ. Reperfusion of ischaemic myocardium. *J Mol Cell Cardiol* 1977; **9**: 605–15

Herndon DN, Thompson PB, Brown M, Traber DL. Diagnosis, pathophysiology and treatment of inhalation injury. In: Boswick JA, ed. *The Art and Science of Burn Care*. Rockville, MD: Aspen, 1987; 153

Herndon DN, Thompson PB, Linares HA, Traber DL. Postgraduate course: respiratory injury. Part 1: Incidence, mortality, pathogenesis and treatment of pulmonary injury. *J Burn Care Rehabil* 1986; **7**: 84

Hopf H W, Viele M, Watson JJ, *et al.* Subcutaneous perfusion and oxygen during acute severe isovolemic hemodilution in healthy volunteers. *Arch Surg* 2000; **135**: 1443–9

Jackson DM. The diagnosis of the depth of burning. *Br J Surg* 1953; **40**: 588

Javadov SA, Clarke S, Das M, Griffiths EJ, Lim KH, Halestrap AP. Ischaemic preconditioning inhibits opening of mitochondrial permeability transition pores in the reperfused rat heart. *J Physiol* 2003; **549**: 513–24

Jones BM, Mayou BJ. The laser Doppler flowmeter for microvascular monitoring: a preliminary report. *Br J Plast Surg* 1982; **35**: 147–9

Jordi Ritz EM, Von Ungern-Sternberg BS, Keller K, Frei FJ, Erb TO. The impact of head position on the cuff and tube tip position of preformed oral tracheal tubes in young children. *Anaesthesia* 2008; **63**: 604–9

Khaliulin I, Clarke SJ, Lin H, Parker J, Suleiman MS, Halestrap AP. Temperature preconditioning of isolated rat hearts—a potent cardioprotective mechanism involving a reduction in oxidative stress and inhibition of the mitochondrial permeability transition pore. *J Physiol* 2007; **581**: 1147–1161

Klein JA. Tumescent technique for regional anaethesia permits lidocaine doses of 35 mg/kg for liposuction. *J Dermatol Surg Oncol* 1990 **16**: 248

Koodie L, Ramakrishnan S, Roy S. Morphine suppresses tumor angiogenesis through a HIF-1alpha/p38MAPK pathway. *Am J Pathol* 2010; **177**: 984–97

Koruda MJ, Zimbler A, Settle RG. Assessing burn wound depth using in-vitro nuclear magnetic resonance (NMR). *J Surg Res* 1986; **40**: 475–81

Kumar A, Anel R, Bunnell E, *et al.* Pulmonary artery occlusion pressure and central venous pressure fail to predict ventricular filling volume, cardiac performance, or the response to volume infusion in normal subjects. *Crit Care Med* 2004; **32**: 691–9

Kuntscher MV, Germann G, Hartmann B. Correlations between cardiac output, stroke volume, central venous pressure, intra-abdominal pressure and total circulating blood volume in resuscitation of major burns. *Resuscitation* 2006; **70**: 37–43

Langer S, Biberthaler P, Harris AG, Steinau HU, Messmer K. In vivo monitoring of microvessels in skin flaps: introduction of a novel technique. *Microsurgery* 2001; **21**: 317–24

Langley K, Sim K. Anaesthesia for patients with burns injuries. *Curr Anaesth Crit Care* 2002; **13**: 70–5

Lorenz HP, Longaker MT. In utero surgery for cleft lip/palate: minimizing the "Ripple Effect" of scarring. *J Craniofac Surg* 2003; **14**: 504–11

Lorenzetti F, Salmi A, Ahovuo J, Tukiainen E, Asko-Seljavaara S. Postoperative changes in blood flow in free muscle flaps: a prospective study. *Microsurgery* 1999; 19: 196–9

MacKinnon KL, Molnar Z, Lowe D, Watson ID, Shearer E. Use of microalbuminuria as a predictor of outcome in critically ill patients. *Br J Anaesth* 2000; **84**: 239–41

Marathe PH, Dwersteg JF, Pavlin EG, Haschke RH, Heimbach DM, Slattery JT. Effect of thermal injury on the pharmacokinetics and pharmacodynamics of atracurium in humans. *Anesthesiology* 1989; **70**: 752–5

Marik P, Baram M, Vahid B. Does central venous pressure predict fluid responsiveness? A systematic review of the literature and the tale of seven mares. *Chest* 2008; **134**: 172–8

Mathew M, Pal SK. Is A2 flag a predictor of mortality in burns patients. *Br J Anaesth* 2002; **89**: 198–9

Mavrogordato AE, Wagstaff MJD, Fletcher AJP, Wilson DI, Jayamaha JEL. A novel method to treat hyperthermia in a burns case: use of a catheter-based heat exchange system. *Burns* 2009; **35**: 141–5

McCord JM. Oxygen-derived free radicals in post-ischaemic tissue injury. *N Engl J Med* 1985; **312**: 159–63

McKendry M, McGloin H, Saberi D, Caudwell L, Brady AR, Singer M. Randomized controlled trial assessing the impact of a nurse delivered, flow-monitored protocol for optimization of circulatory status after cardiac surgery. *BMJ* 2004; **329**: 258

Mooser V, Berger MM, Tappy L, *et al.* Major reduction in plasma Lp(a) levels during sepsis and burns. *Arterioscler Thromb Vasc Biol* 2000; **20**: 1137–42

Murray L, Hentges F, Hill J, *et al.* The effects of cleft lip and palate, and the timing of lip repair on mother-infant interactions and infant development. *J Child Psychol Psychiatry* 2008; **49**: 115–23

Myrianthefs PM, Baltopoulos GJ. Circulating cytokines and outcome prediction of burned children with concomitant inhalation injury. *Crit Care* 2008; **12**: 155

Nahabedian MY, Momen B, Manson PN. Factors associated with anastomotic failure after microvascular reconstruction of the breast. *Plast Reconstr Surg* 2004; **114**: 74–82

Nguyen HB, Loomba M, Yang JJ, *et al.* Early lactate clearance is associated with biomarkers of inflammation, coagulation, apoptosis, organ dysfunction and mortality in severe sepsis and septic shock. *J Inflammation* 2010; **7**: 6

Nguyen HB, Rivers EP, Knoblich BP, *et al.* Early lactate clearance is associated with improved outcome in severe sepsis and septic shock. *Crit Care Med* 2004; **32**: 1637–42

O'Reilly TJ, Spence RJ, Taylor RM, Scheulen JJ. Laser Doppler flowmetry evaluation of burn depth. *J Burn Care Rehabil* 1989; **10**: 1–6

Osler T, Glance LG, Hosmer DW. Simplified estimates of the probability of death after burn injuries: extending and updating the baux score. *J Trauma* 2010; **68**: 690–7

Ostad A, Kageyama N, Moy RL. Tumescent anesthesia with a lidocaine dose of 55 mg/kg is safe for liposuction. *Dermatol Surg* 1996; **22**: 921–7

Paik AM, Daniali LN, Lee ES, *et al.* Local anaesthetic use in tumescent liposuction: an American Society of Plastic Surgeons survey. *Ann Plast Surg* 2015; **74**: 145–51

Pal SK, Kumar C. Anaesthesia for aesthetic surgery. In: Shaw I, Kumar C, Dodds C, eds. *Oxford Textbook of Anaesthesia for Oral and Maxillofacial Surgery*. Oxford: Oxford University Press, 2010; 131–41

Pal SK, Cortiella J, Herndon D. Adjunctive methods of pain control in burns patients. *Burns* 1997; **23**: 404–12

Pal SK, Kyriacou PA, Kumaran S, et al. Evaluation of oesophageal reflectance pulse oximeter in major burns patients. *Burns* 2005; **31**: 337–41

Park SW, Chen SW, Kim M, D'Agati VD, Lee HT. Human activated protein C attenuates both hepatic and renal injury caused by hepatic ischemia and reperfusion injury in mice. *Kidney Int* 2009; **76**: 739–50

Plastic. In: *Oxford English Dictionary* (Hanks P, ed). Oxford: Oxford University Press, Oxford, 1996

Quarrie R, Cramer BM, Lee DS, *et al.* Ischemic preconditioning decreases mitochondrial proton leak and reactive oxygen species production in the postischemic heart. *J Surg Res* 2011; **165**: 5–14

Rana RE, Arora BS. History of plastic surgery in India. *J Postgrad Med* 2002; **48**: 76–8

Rao RB, Ely SF, Hoffman RS. Deaths related to liposuction. *N Engl J Med* 1999; **340**: 1471–5

Repez A, Oroszy D, Arnez ZM. Continuous postoperative monitoring of cutaneous free flaps using near infrared spectroscopy. *J Plast Reconstr Aesthetic Surg* 2008; **61**: 71–7

Roberts G, Lloyd M, Parker M, *et al.* The Baux score is dead. Long live the Baux score: a 27-year retrospective cohort study of mortality at a regional burns service *J Trauma* 2012; **72**: 251–6

Robertson R D, Bond P, Wallace B, Shewmake K, Cone J. The tumescent technique to significantly reduce blood loss during burn surgery. *Burns* 2001; **27**: 835–8

Rose JK, Herndon DN. Advances in the treatment of burns patients. *Burns* 1997; **23**(Suppl 1): S19–S26

Ryan CM, Schonfeld DA, Thorpe WP, Sheridan RL, Cassem EH, Tompkins RG. Objective estimates of probability of death from burn injuries. *N Engl J Med* 1998; **338**: 362–6

Sakka SG, Reinhart K, Meier-Hellmann A. Comparison of pulmonary artery and arterial thermodilution cardiac output in critically ill patients. *Intensive Care Med* 1999; **25**: 843–6

Sarwer DB. The obsessive cosmetic surgery patient: a consideration of body image dissatisfaction and body dysmorphic disorder. *Plast Surg Nurs* 1997; **17**: 193–209

Sarwer DB, Wadden TA, Pertschuk MJ, Whitaker LA. Body image dissatisfaction and body dysmorphic disorder in 100 cosmetic surgery patients. *Plast Reconstr Surg* 1998; **101**: 1644–9

Sasai T, Tokioka H, Fukushima T, *et al.* Reliability of central venous pressure to assess left ventricular preload for fluid resuscitation in patients with septic shock. *J Intensive Care* 2014; **2**: 58

Sasamura T, Nakamura S, Iida Y, *et al.* Morphine analgesia suppresses tumor growth and metastasis in a mouse model of cancer pain produced by orthotopic tumor inoculation. *Eur J Pharmacol* 2002; **441**:185–91

Schortgen F, Lacherade J C, Bruneel F, *et al.* Effects of hydroxyethylstarch and gelatin on renal function in severe sepsis: a multicentre randomised study. *Lancet* 2001; **357**: 911–6

Schrey AR, Aitasalo KM, Kinnunen IA, *et al.* Functional evaluation of microvascular free flaps with positron emission tomography. *J Plast Reconstr Aesthet Surg* 2006; **59**: 158–65

Seidelin J B, Nielsen O H, Strøm J. Soluble L-selectin levels predict survival in sepsis. *Intensive Care Med* 2002; **28**: 1613–18

Setala L, Papp A, Romppanen EL, Mustonen P, Berg L, Harma M. Microdialysis detects postoperative perfusion failure in microvascular flaps. *J Reconstr Microsurg* 2006; **22**: 87–96

Sinclair S, James S, Singer M. Intraoperative intravascular volume optimization and length of hospital stay after repair of proximal femoral fracture: randomized controlled trial. *BMJ* 1997; **315**: 909–12

Singer M. The FTc is not an accurate marker of left ventricular preload. *Intensive Care Med* 2006; **32**: 1089

Sirtl C, Laubenthal H, Zumtobel V, Kraft D, Jurecka W. Tissue deposits of hydroxyethyl starch (HES): dose-dependent and time-related. *Br J Anaesth* 1999; **82**: 510–5

Spies M, Herndon DN, Rosenblatt JI, Sanford AP, Wolf SE. Prediction of mortality from catastrophic burns in children. *Lancet* 2003; **361**: 989–94

Stack BC, Jr, Futran ND, Zang B, Scharf JE. Initial experience with personal digital assistant-based reflectance photoplethysmograph for free tissue transfer monitoring. *Ann Plast Surg* 2003; **51**: 136–40

Ulusal BG, Ulusal AE, Hung LM, Wei FC. The effect of A2A adenosine receptor agonist on composite tissue allotransplant survival: an in vivo preliminary study. *J Surg Res* 2006; **131**: 261–6

Visscher K, Boyd K, Ross DC, Amann J, Temple C. Refining perforator selection for DIEP breast reconstruction using transit time flow volume measurements. *J Reconstr Microsurg* 2010; **26**: 285–90

Wachtel TL, Leopold GR, Frank HA, Frank DH. B-mode ultrasonic echo determination of depth of thermal injury. *Burns Incl Therm Inj* 1986; **12**: 432–7

Wahr JA. Myocardial ischaemia in anaemic patients. *Br J Anaesth* 1998; **81**(Suppl1): 10–15

Wang G, Cao WG, Li SL, *et al.* Safe extensive tumescent liposuction with segmental infiltration of lower concentration lidocaine under monitored anaesthesia care. *Ann Plast Surg* 2015; **74**: 6–11

Wassermann D, Schlotterer M. Survival rates of patients hospitalized in French burns units during 1985. *Burns* 1989; **15**: 261–4

Yang LQ, Tao KM, Liu YT, *et al.* Remifentanil preconditioning reduces hepatic ischemia-reperfusion injury in rats via inducible nitric oxide synthase expression. *Anesthesiology* 2011; **114**: 1036–47

Yew WS, Pal SK. Correlation of microalbuminuria and outcome in patients with extensive burns. *Br J Anaesth* 2006; **97**: 499–502

Yii NW, Evans G, Miller M, *et al.* Thrombolytic therapy: what is its role in free flap salvage? *Ann Plast Surg* 2001; **46**: 601–4

Young YK, LaLonde C, Demling R. The role of mediators in the response to thermal injury. *World J Surg* 1992; **16**: 30–6

Zaman T, Pal SK, Kyriacou PA. Development of a reflectance photoplethysmographic sensor used for the assessment of free flap perfusion. *Conf Proc IEEE Eng Med Biol Soc*, 2011; **2011**; 4006–9

Zaman T, Pal SK, Kyriacou PA. Pilot investigation of DIEP free flap perfusion utilising a multi-wavelength non-invasive optical sensor. *Br J Anaesth* 2013; **110**: 884–5

Zawacki BE, Walker HL. An evaluation of patent blue V, bromphenol blue and tetracycline for the diagnosis of burn depth. *Plast Reconstr Surg* 1970; **54**: 459–65

CHAPTER 65

Anaesthesia for ENT, dental, and maxillofacial surgery

Michael G. Irwin, Chi Wai Cheung, and Gordon Tin Chun Wong

Introduction

The principles of anaesthesia management for otolaryngological and maxillofacial surgery share some similarities and unique challenges. Patients present at all ages and surgery can range from simple, short interventions to major, prolonged, and complicated cases with potential for massive blood loss. Some procedures can be performed under local anaesthesia with sedation whereas, at the other extreme, general anaesthesia with invasive monitoring is required. Microsurgery will necessitate a bloodless field, nerve monitoring is often required, and there is a susceptibility to postoperative nausea and vomiting (PONV). Patients with cancer often have poor nutritional status because of catabolism and eating difficulties and, as many head and neck cancers are associated with smoking and excessive alcohol consumption, significant co-morbidity is not unusual. Airway management particularly can be challenging because of abnormal anatomy, pathology in this area, and the inherent difficulties of a shared airway. Postoperative management of the airway is particularly challenging as alteration to the anatomy and tissue swelling may have occurred during the course of surgery or thereafter. Last but not least, patients may present acutely with airway complications that require emergent management.

Preoperative assessment

The patient population ranges from neonates to geriatrics and the general principles of assessment will be the standard issues applicable to these age groups and their respective co-morbidities. There are, however, certain problems that will be more common in patients presenting for this type of surgery. Airway assessment, including planning for both intra- and postoperative management, cannot be overemphasized both because airway anomalies are a common reason for surgery and procedures may involve sharing the airway or impact upon its structure.

Obstructive sleep apnoea

Patients with obstructive sleep apnoea (OSA) may present for anatomical correction surgery, or the pathology may be coexistent owing to upper airway abnormalities. Depending on the duration and severity, OSA is not only associated with a difficult airway but also respiratory and cardiovascular co-morbidities. Preoperative screening can be performed with a clinical questionnaire, such as the STOP-BANG (Chung et al. 2008) (Fig. 65.1), or the Berlin Questionnaire, and should be considered routine in any patient with such anomalies. Although patients with suspected OSA undergoing elective surgery should be referred for specialist assessment and optimization, in ENT surgery the diagnosis is likely to have been made already and the patient will be using a continuous positive airway pressure device during sleep. The device should be brought to hospital for use when sleeping and postoperatively. Preoperative sedation should be avoided and short-acting anaesthetic drugs used where possible. Patients who are able to understand the procedure, and to communicate and cooperate throughout are suitable candidates for local anaesthesia with or without sedation. Patients with OSA are particularly prone to the ventilatory depressant effect and

		Yes	No
1.	Snoring Do you snore loudly (louder than talking or loud enough to be heard through closed doors)?		
2.	Tired Do you often feel tired, fatigued, or sleepy during daytime?		
3.	Observed Has anyone observed you stop breathing during your sleep?		
4.	Blood pressure Do you have or are you being treated for high blood pressure?		
5.	BMI BMI more than 35 kg/m^2?		
6.	Age Age over 50 years old?		
7:	Neck circumference Neck circumference greater than 40 cm?		
8.	Gender Gender male?		
High risk of OSA: answering yes to three or more items			
Low risk of OSA: answering yes to less than three items			

Figure 65.1 STOP-BANG scoring model.

Reproduced with permission from Chung *et al.* STOP Questionnaire: a tool to screen patients for obstructive sleep apnoea. *Anesthesiology*, Volume 108, Issue 5, pp. 812–821, Copyright © 2008 American Society of Anesthesiologists.

the decrease in muscle tone seen with many sedative and analgesic drugs. Consequently, vigilant postoperative monitoring is mandatory and high dependency care is often appropriate.

Identification of the challenging airway

The approach needs to be age and presentation appropriate and history is of paramount importance. Difficulties in mask ventilation, intubation, or both, might be anticipated. Previous anaesthetic records documenting airway findings are valuable if available although this only represents a snapshot of the patient's airway status as changes since the last intervention are possible, particularly in the growing child or with changes in body habitus. Those with identifiable or diagnosed syndromes associated with a known difficult airway should be approached with caution. While traditional bedside predictors and tests for a difficult airway (see chapter 48 of this book) should be sought, they have notoriously poor sensitivity, specificity (Shiga et al. 2005), and low positive predictive value. In addition, the pathological basis of the operative lesions should be meticulously explored. Patients presenting with tonsillar or other intra-oral mass should be questioned regarding obstructive or invasive symptoms such as dysphagia or stridor. Patients may also have breathing difficulties in certain positions (e.g. supine). Computed tomography (CT), magnetic resonance imaging, or even positron emission tomography is often available as part of surgical planning. Some patients will have also undergone direct laryngoscopy. These investigations should be reviewed for any anatomical distortion of the lower airway that may preclude placement of a supraglottic airway, for example, laryngeal mask airway (LMA) or tracheal intubation.

Co-existing conditions

Patients with laryngeal tumours are often smokers and may have a history of chronic excessive alcohol consumption. Supraglottic and glottic tumours are more common than subglottic carcinoma. Chronic obstructive airway disease is common. Stopping smoking can reduce the carboxyhaemoglobin concentration within 12 h but mucociliary clearance and airway hyperactivity may take more than 3 weeks to improve (Egan and Wong 1992). Chest physiotherapy can help encourage expectoration and inhalation of bronchodilators or steroids (or both) should be continued. Ventilation of the lungs using a bag and mask and tracheal intubation can be difficult in patients with laryngeal tumours or pathology. Symptoms of hoarseness of voice, stridor, and shortness of breath can indicate large upper airway tumours. Physical examination may reveal tracheal deviation, possible upper airway anatomy distortion, and positional effects on breathing. Patients have sometimes had radiotherapy which can reduce soft tissue movement and cause scarring with attendant reduction in elasticity of soft tissues and increased difficulty with laryngoscopy. Local application of vasoconstrictors and cocaine is common in ENT surgery but they should be used with great caution or avoided altogether in patients with a history of coronary artery disease, myocardial infarction, congestive heart failure, cardiac arrhythmia, poorly controlled hypertension, and in those taking monoamine oxidase inhibitors (Harper and Jones 2006).

Anaesthetic requirements

Provision of a bloodless field for endoscopic surgery

Patients can be positioned slightly (20–30°) head-up in the 'deck chair' position. This will decrease venous congestion and arterial pressure at the surgical site while avoiding venous pooling in the lower limbs. The head position should not be higher than this to minimize the risk of air entrainment in transected veins. Bone wax should be used on exposed areas of bone for this reason also. Drapes and ties should be carefully placed so as not to interfere with venous return from the head and neck and positive end-expiratory pressure and hypercapnia are avoided during ventilation. Attention to the patient's head positioning is important to avoid venous obstruction and congestion. In addition, extreme hyperextension or torsion can cause injury to the brachial plexus and the cervical spine. In patients with carotid atherosclerosis, carotid blood flow may be compromised or plaque emboli dislodged and it is worth auscultating for carotid bruits before surgery.

Blood conservation techniques

Blood loss may be quite extensive during neck dissection, tumour resection, and reconstructive procedures requiring flaps (Krupp et al. 2003). Orthognathic surgery involves mandibular and maxillary transection and is also associated with significant haemorrhage (Krohner 2003). Careful preoperative, intraoperative, and postoperative planning and a team approach are required to reduce transfusion when extensive surgery is proposed.

A full blood count will determine haemoglobin concentration and platelet count. Coagulation status can also be measured if there is clinical evidence of a potential problem but is not necessary as a routine. Bleeding time is affected by platelet function, certain vascular disorders, and von Willebrand disease. Liver disease, uraemia, and antiplatelet medication, in particular the use of aspirin, are likely to increase bleeding. Many patients take herbal supplements for perceived health benefits and some of these (e.g. garlic and *Ginkgo biloba*) can increase bleeding. The American Society of Anesthesiologists recommends that all herbal supplements be stopped 2–3 weeks before surgery (American Society of Anesthesiologists Task Force on Perioperative Blood Transfusion and Adjuvant Therapies 2006). If anaemia is discovered, red blood cell morphology, vitamin B12 concentration, and ferritin can help establish the aetiology. Treatment can then be appropriately tailored. Iron therapy is necessary to support erythropoiesis and increase red blood cell production (by increasing and maintaining transferrin saturation). Vitamin B12 or folic acid may be helpful in megaloblastic anaemia. Occasionally, recombinant erythropoietin therapy is recommended in the management of preoperative anaemia especially where there is expected high blood loss or in patients who are Jehovah's witnesses. Recombinant erythropoietin is a biosynthetic form of the natural human hormone responsible for stimulation of red cell production. Response to erythropoietin is dose dependent and shows interindividual variability. Intravenous iron significantly increases the haematopoietic response to erythropoietin therapy (Rohling et al. 2000). If coagulopathy is identified, especially if associated with anticoagulant or antiplatelet use, measures should be taken to correct the coagulopathy without putting the patient at risk of thrombotic events. This is a fine balance and close collaboration with medical colleagues is essential. Aspirin is the most widely used antiplatelet agent. The drug works on the cyclooxygenase enzyme system to irreversibly inhibit platelet aggregation. It takes 5–7 days to produce new platelets after cessation of therapy. In primary coronary prevention, it is probable that the anti-inflammatory properties of aspirin are extremely important also (Hennekens 2007). While increased surgical bleeding is generally evident, it is usually not clinically significant and transfusion requirements have been found to be similar (Burger et al. 2005). In the more recent and larger POISE II trial, however, major bleeding was significantly higher in aspirin-treated patients than in the placebo group, at 4.6% *vs* 3.8% (95% confidence interval 1.01–1.49, $P = 0.04$) and appeared to be a predictor of cardiac morbidity. While one study found that there is an approximate two- to three-fold increase in subsequent death or myocardial infarction if aspirin is stopped before surgery (Gerstein et al. 2012), POISE II found the primary outcome of death or non-fatal myocardial infarction at 30 days was no different between the two groups, at 7% in the aspirin group and 7.1% in the placebo group (Devereaux et al. 2014). The cardioprotective benefits of aspirin may have been offset by the increased risk of bleeding such that in surgery with a high risk of bleeding, aspirin cessation should be considered. However, in patients with coronary stents *in situ*, it is still strongly advised to continue aspirin especially in the period when in-stent thrombosis is prevalent and can cause mortality of 5–30% depending on how recently the stent has been inserted. It is also important to point out that aspirin protection cannot be substituted by anticoagulant medications, for example, low-molecular-weight heparin (often used for deep venous thrombosis prophylaxis), as they do not inhibit platelet function or decrease inflammation.

From a surgical perspective, preoperative interventional radiology may be helpful in surgery involving vascular malignancies in the head and neck region. Preoperative embolization has been shown to significantly decrease blood loss in vascular tumours and to control epistaxis. In certain high-risk situations, performing complex surgery in stages has been shown to be an effective way of decreasing blood loss. Various novel agents can be used by the surgical team, for example, in sinus surgery, purified plant polysaccharide (HemoStase®) and gelatin-thrombin matrix (FloSeal®) (Baumann and Caversaccio 2003). Ankaferd BloodStopper® was shown to be effective in decreasing intraoperative blood loss and reducing operative time when compared with traditional haemostasis methods in curette adenoidectomy (Iynen et al. 2011). Quick and effective haemostasis not only reduces blood loss but improves visibility of the surgical site, facilitates tissue handling, and reduces operation time. Electrosurgical dissection was shown to reduce blood loss in head and neck surgery (Weber et al. 1989). The use of the Harmonic® Scalpel (Ethicon, Cincinnati, OH, USA) is safe and confers some advantages over conventional methods of head and neck dissection (Salami et al. 2008). Ultrasonic scalpels and tissue fibrin sealants have been shown to reduce blood loss and so reduce allogenic blood transfusion (Baumann and Caversaccio 2003; Chung et al. 2012). Ultrasonic scalpels use ultrasound to make incisions with minimal tissue damage. Other haemostatic instruments include bipolar scissors, argon beam coagulators, and lasers. Bipolar scissors are scissors with two normal blades that have been modified to allow the use of bipolar electrocautery without excessive collateral tissue damage. The argon bean coagulator uses a beam of ionized argon gas to conduct a high-frequency electric current to bleeding tissues with limited tissue contact. It causes minimal tissue damage, coagulates large vessels, reduces the risk of postoperative haemorrhage, and reduces operation time (Ward et al. 1989). Laser energy can cut, vaporize, and simultaneously coagulate a targeted area without disrupting adjacent tissue.

A reliable model for predicting perioperative blood transfusion requirements in patients undergoing major head and neck surgery requiring free-flap reconstruction has been described (Shah et al. 2010). It was found that some preoperative variables were significantly associated with perioperative transfusion: sex, body mass index, T stage, preoperative haemoglobin concentration, and type of free-flap reconstruction used (i.e. osseous *vs* non-osseous).

Controlled hypotension

The efficacy of controlled hypotension to reduce allogenic blood transfusion and improve the operative field is difficult to confirm from current evidence (Choi and Samman 2008). However, the potential complications of this technique need to be considered and a large number of studies investigating the physiological changes following controlled hypotension noted it as a potential cause of damage to vital organs as a result of hypoperfusion, especially the brain, heart, kidneys, and liver. Induction of hypotension should only be carried out for that part of the surgery where there is a high risk of bleeding and normal blood pressure resumed as soon as possible thereafter, both to minimize adverse effects and to ensure no bleeding vessels have been missed before the end of surgery.

The targeted blood pressure should be individualized, balancing the age and cardiovascular status of each patient. It is generally believed that the safety margin for blood pressure in patients of ASA I is a mean arterial pressure of at least 55 mm Hg or a systolic blood pressure of at least 80 mm Hg or a reduction of 30% of baseline mean arterial pressure in patients with hypertension (Degoute et al. 2001). Patients with ischaemic heart disease, diabetes, cerebrovascular disease, impaired renal function, and hypertension are generally not suitable for controlled hypertension, although a modest reduction in blood pressure is likely to be safe.

Systemic vascular resistance can be reduced by:

- blockade of α-adrenoreceptors (e.g. labetalol, phentolamine)
- relaxation of vascular smooth muscle [e.g. direct acting vasodilators such as sodium nitroprusside (SNP) or calcium channel blockers].

It is apparent that many of these drugs have undesirable side-effects such as reflex tachycardia with calcium channel blockers and SNP. SNP is very potent but titratable. It releases cyanide ions but toxicity can usually be avoided if the dose is less than 0.5 mg kg^{-1} h^{-1} with normal renal function. It also induces tachyphylaxis. Anaesthesia drugs themselves can induce hypotension in high doses generally as a result of negative inotropic effects and vasodilation, but deliberately overdosing patients with anaesthesia may have other untoward effects that preclude such techniques. Dexmedetomidine is a highly selective α_2-agonist that reduces anaesthetic requirements by around 20–50%. It produces a modest reduction in blood pressure and heart rate that can be useful in this situation.

Meticulous monitoring is crucial for the safety of patients during controlled hypotension to reduce morbidity and mortality. Apart from regular monitoring, urine output and direct arterial blood pressure are important particularly when using very potent drugs such as SNP. Patients receiving SNP should also have hourly blood gas measurement for cyanide toxicity (acidosis) and arterial carbon dioxide tension can be accurately assessed. The ECG can be monitored for ST-segment changes and temperature monitoring is indicated as vasodilators facilitate more heat loss. Fluid balance and blood loss must also be carefully monitored because the normal physiological response to blood loss is impaired by many of these drugs. Blood loss must be replaced with an equal amount of colloid or three times the amount of crystalloid. Generally, colloid with a background crystalloid infusion may be better as excessive crystalloid can contribute to oedema around the surgical site.

Choice of airway management

For all procedures involving the head and neck region, the choice of airway depends on patient, surgical, and anaesthetic factors. Consideration of the type of surgery and surgical plan allows formulation of an airway management plan to maximize surgical access and at the same time minimize the risk of airway dislodgement or displacement during surgery.

Nasal endotracheal intubation

Cuffed nasal endotracheal intubation is preferable for procedures in the oral cavity as it facilitates good surgical access and is easy to secure (Hall and Shutt 2003). Soft, preformed north-facing tubes/nasal Ring–Adair–Elwyn (RAE) tracheal tubes can be secured to the forehead without obscuring the oral cavity or facial bony contours and are less likely to kink. Before intubation, the patient should be asked about nostril patency and consideration given to the use of a topical vasoconstrictor such as xylometazoline. The tube should be placed carefully in the most patent nostril after being warmed in water at body temperature and well lubricated. Gentle rotation may assist insertion but it should never be forced in order to avoid epistaxis or damage to the delicate nasal bones and turbinates. A Macintosh laryngoscope and Magill forceps can be used but it is preferable, and possibly less traumatic, to use a fibreoptic bronchoscope. Awake fibreoptic intubation with topical anaesthesia is the safest approach if difficult ventilation and intubation is suspected. On securing the tracheal tube, make sure there is no pressure on the external nares as this can lead to avascular necrosis. While wire-reinforced tracheal tubes are more resistant to kinking, they have the disadvantage of having a greater external diameter for a given internal diameter. They are also less compliant compared with standard polyvinylchloride tracheal tubes and may exert greater pressure on the external nares. Nasotracheal intubation is contraindicated in patients with fronto-basilar or nasal fractures, where the tube can be inadvertently passed intracranially and can increase the risk of meningitis.

Oral endotracheal intubation

Oral tracheal tubes are suitable for surgery not involving the oral cavity and where dental occlusion is not required (e.g. functional endoscopic sinus surgery, cleft lip/palate repair, and rhinoplasty/septoplasty). South-facing preformed tracheal tube and oral RAE tubes may be more suitable compared with standard tracheal tubes as they can direct the connectors and circuit away from the surgical field. Caution should be taken when the surgeons place a mouth guard during tonsil or cleft surgery as this can compress the tracheal tube. As blood and tissue debris can still pass along the outer surface of the tracheal tube to the level of the vocal cords and subglottis, it is common to insert a moistened, protective throat pack. The insertion of a pack should be clearly documented and acknowledged by anaesthetic, nursing, and surgical personnel as part of a checklist so that it is removed before extubation.

Supraglottic airway devices

These versatile devices are now available in a variety of modifications of the original Laryngeal Mask Airway™. Particularly useful are those with a channel for gastric drainage and the wire-reinforced, flexible airway tube. Flexible reinforced supraglottic airway devices (SADs) are a suitable alternative to tracheal intubation for simple dental extractions and nasal, zygomatic, superficial facial, and cleft lip/palate surgery. Patients can either breathe spontaneously through the SAD or their lungs can be ventilated. This is especially useful with total intravenous anaesthesia (TIVA) using propofol and remifentanil (Atef and Fawaz 2008) and it provides an acceptable barrier against soiling of the lower airway during nasal surgery such as functional endoscopic sinus surgery (FESS) (Ahmed and Vohra 2002). The SAD helps facilitate a smooth recovery without coughing and straining on emergence and does not traumatize the lower airway. Dental extractions can be performed around a reinforced SAD as it can be moved from side to side. The SAD does, however, take up more surgical space which may obscure the intraoral field. Obstruction and dislodgement can also occur, especially when the mandible is moved and they are not suitable where alignment and occlusion need to be assessed.

Microlaryngoscopy tube

The microlaryngoscopy tracheal tube is a small-diameter tracheal tube with an extended length as most 'regular' tracheal tubes (size 5.0 and smaller) are not long enough to span the distance between the oral commissure and subglottic airway in an adult. Lesions located on the anterior two-thirds of the larynx (membranous vocal folds) can be exposed with a microlaryngoscopy tube, although there is often reduced access and the operative field is relatively mobile, moving with respiration. This has the advantage, however, of allowing the use of standard anaesthetic equipment in normal operating mode. As they are composed of polyvinylchloride, they are not laser resistant and should not be used without modification if a laser procedure is planned.

Laser-resistant tubes

There are commercially available tubes that are rendered resistant to the effect of laser beam impaction by means of coating the cuff or the tube (or both) with a laser-reflective compound and thus reducing the chance of being ignited by the energy of the laser. None of the designs are ideal as in some the cuff is still susceptible. Examples are described in Box 65.1.

Box 65.1 Examples of commercially available laser-resistant tubes

Sheridan Laser-Trach™ (Teleflex Medical Europe Ltd, Athlone, Ireland)	Red rubber shaft embossed with copper wrapped Unprotected red rubber cuff and tip
Mallinckrodt Laser-Flex™ (Medtronic Parkway, Minneapolis, MN, USA)	Stainless steel shaft with an unprotected plastic cuff and tip
Rüsch Lasertubus™ (Teleflex Medical Europe Ltd, Athlone, Ireland)	Soft white rubber with Murphy eye Reinforced with corrugated copper foil Absorbent sponge Laser-resistant foam surrounds the lower portion Double-cuff design

Care should be taken to avoid the use of other materials that could act as fuel for a fire such as sponges, flammable drapes and gauze, or alcohol-based cleaning fluids. Should an airway fire occur with the tracheal tube, disconnect the circuit, irrigate and suction the airway with cold water, extubate the patient, use a mask with 100% O_2 (once the fire is extinguished), and start TIVA to maintain anaesthesia. The damage can then be evaluated with direct laryngoscopy/bronchoscopy, debris removed, and the patient reintubated if necessary. Severe damage may require tracheostomy. A chest X-ray and blood gas analysis should be performed with further management in intensive care recognizing the possibility of pulmonary injury and airway oedema.

Submental endotracheal intubation

This is an uncommon technique but it can be used as an alternative to tracheostomy (Caron et al. 2000) as the latter is associated with significant morbidity (complications include haemorrhage, recurrent laryngeal nerve damage, subcutaneous emphysema, tracheal stenosis, and a cosmetically undesirable scar). It may be useful when surgery requires both assessment of dental occlusion and access to the upper part of the face, or when nasal or oral intubation is not possible, for example, complex craniofacial trauma or oncological cranial base surgery (Biglioli et al. 2003). It also permits considerable downward retraction of the maxilla after a Le Fort I osteotomy, is associated with good clival exposure, and does not interfere with maxillomandibular fixation at the end of surgery (Jundt et al. 2012).

The trachea is initially intubated orally and a path is created surgically from the floor of the mouth to a skin incision adjacent to the lower border of the mandible. This allows the proximal end of the tube to pass over the tongue and out through the submental skin (Fig. 65.2). The tracheal tube is then sutured into place and the surgery can proceed. At the end of surgery, the process is reversed to re-establish oral intubation and allow a normal extubation. Complications include bleeding, trauma to the sublingual glands or lingual nerve, fistula formation, scarring, and infection.

Intermittent apnoeic technique, tubeless spontaneous respiration, and jet ventilation

Lesions of the posterior third of the larynx (vocal processes and posterior commissure/arytenoids) will be obscured by a tracheal tube. A tubeless technique is useful, therefore, to facilitate certain airway procedures such as laser resection of laryngeal papillomatosis (Judelman 1974; Talmage 1981). Intermittent apnoea, jet ventilation, or tubeless spontaneous respiration can provide an unobstructed view of the vocal cords (Xiao and Zhang 2010). In addition, if a laser is to be used, there will be no combustible material in the airway, thus decreasing the risk of fire.

Apnoeic oxygenation involves ventilating the patient with a tracheal tube and then intermittently removing it for a few minutes at a time to provide an unobstructed surgical view. The time period for the surgeon to operate is limited to only a few minutes

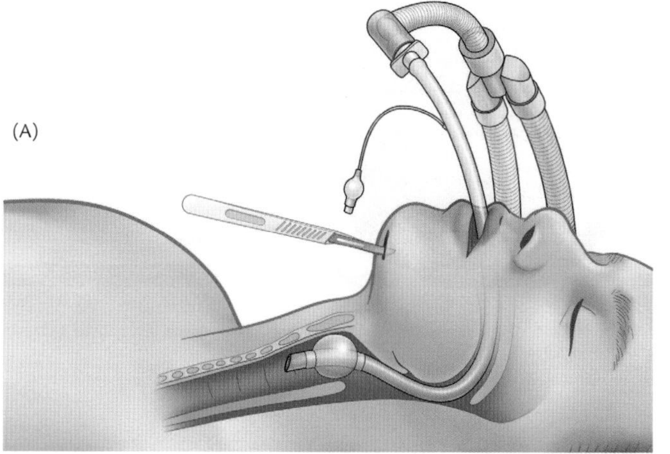

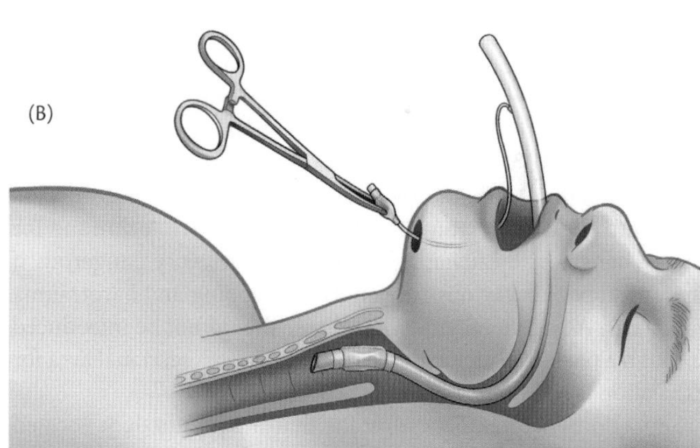

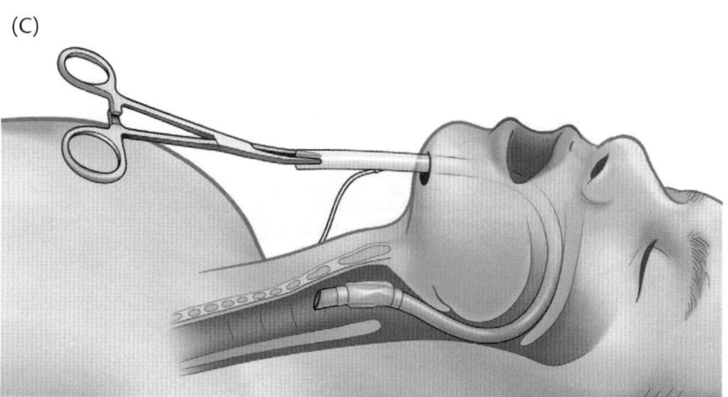

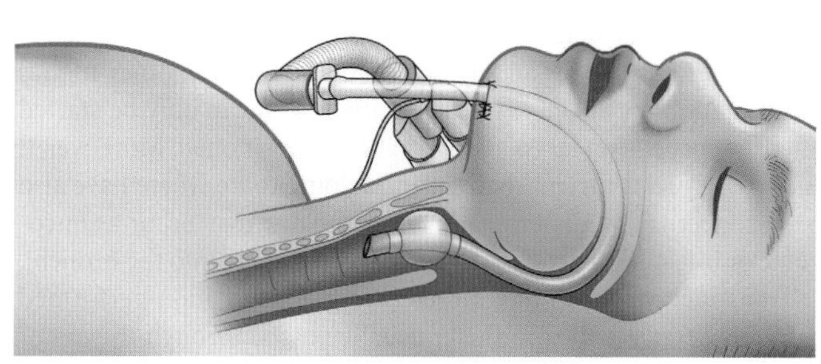

Figure 65.2 The patient's airway is first secured by intubating the trachea via the oral route. A small paramedian incision is then made in the floor of the mouth near the lower border of the mandible. (A) A passage through the floor is created by blunt dissection using curved forceps. After removing the universal connector from the endotracheal tube, the pilot balloon (B) followed by the free end of the endotracheal tube (C) is passed through the opening. The universal connector is then replaced and the endotracheal tube reattached to the breathing circuit. The tube is fixed to the patient using sutures (D).

for each sequence because the patient's functional residual capacity limits the oxygen reserve. Oxygen saturation needs to be carefully observed and ventilation reinstituted immediately the saturation starts to decrease as detection and calculation take approximately 30–40 s before they are displayed. The disadvantages of this technique are that repetitive intubation and extubation may cause damage to the vocal cords and also prolong the procedure. It can also introduce laser debris and tumour tissue to the lower airway tract and is less suitable for patients with underlying pulmonary disease with reduced functional residual capacity.

Spontaneous respiration anaesthesia relies on maintenance of a patient's own respiration while keeping an adequate depth of intravenous anaesthesia. It is a challenging balance. Propofol is a suitable hypnotic but does not provide analgesia. Supplemental easily titratable opioids such as remifentanil, sufentanil, or alfentanil can help but, obviously, increase the likelihood of respiratory depression and can cause muscle rigidity. Dexmedetomidine can be infused along with propofol as it reduces hypnotic drug requirement, is analgesic, and has an antisialagogue effect which helps facilitate the application of local anaesthetic and decrease airway secretions. As capnography is not practical, inspection and palpation of chest movement is important. This special technique provides adequate ventilation for the patient and an open view for the surgeon. It is also the only method for functional assessment of the vocal cords.

Jet ventilation relies on air entrainment around a jet catheter to provide ventilation without endotracheal intubation. It is generally classified according to the position of the jet nozzles in relation to the airway: infraglottic (Fig. 65.3), supraglottic (Fig. 65.4), or transtracheal (Fig. 65.5) (Biro 2010).

The thin jet catheter is located below the vocal cords in the trachea. This is occasionally used in laryngeal surgery and in rigid bronchoscopy. It allows continuous ventilation throughout the procedure, without the need to occasionally stop and change to other ventilation methods. Moreover, the insufflation of gas occurs deep into the airway, thus it is the most effective technique for gas exchange. Its disadvantage is that it can be very dangerous if there is upper airway obstruction as air trapping and barotrauma can occur. As a general guide, a catheter should not be introduced through a narrowed airway if the remaining cross sectional area for exhalation is less than 50% of normal.

Supraglottic jet ventilation means that the jet nozzle is located proximal to the vocal cord level. Modified suspension laryngoscopes with multiple channels are used in conjunction with this technique. It offers excellent visibility and accessibility of the larynx as it remains completely free of tubing. Most importantly, the risk of barotrauma is reduced as the jet nozzle is located proximal to any possible obstruction. This feature makes it the best choice for jet ventilation in lower airway obstruction. However, other modes of ventilation may have to be used initially as it can only be started after the suspension laryngoscope has been positioned. Moreover, it is obviously less efficient than the infraglottic route. There have also been concerns that dissemination of pathology may occur as oncogenic or infectious particles can be dragged distally into the bronchi.

Transtracheal jet ventilation refers to gas insufflation performed through a transtracheal catheter usually passed through the cricothyroid membrane. It is familiar to anaesthetists as a very important rescue oxygenation technique in extremely urgent situations where intubation and ventilation have failed. Although it is relatively avascular and straightforward to perform a cricothyroid

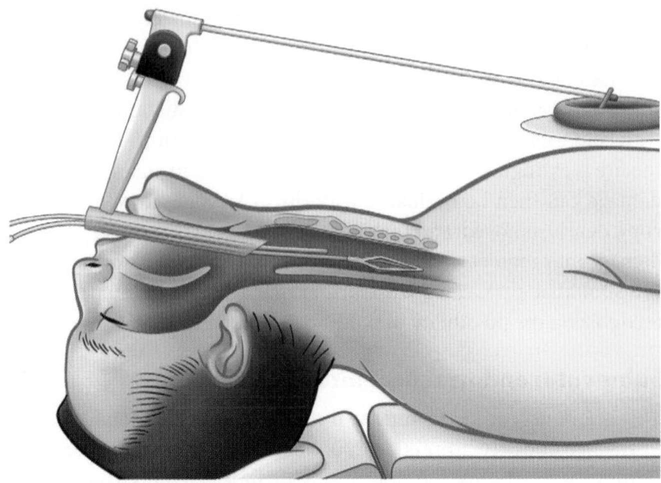

Figure 65.3 Infraglottic jet ventilation

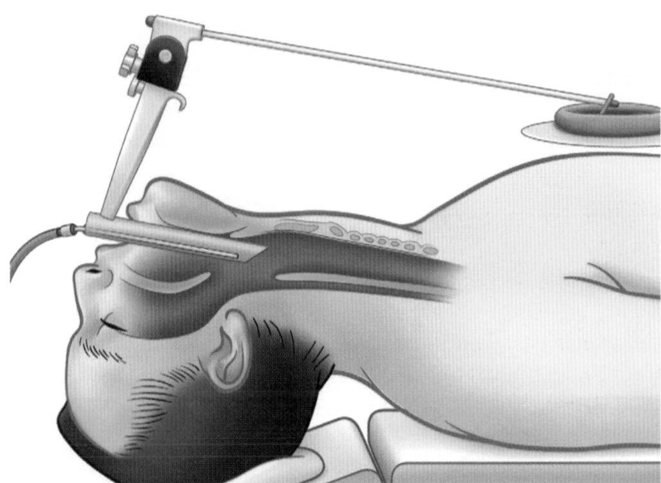

Figure 65.4 Supraglottic jet ventilation.

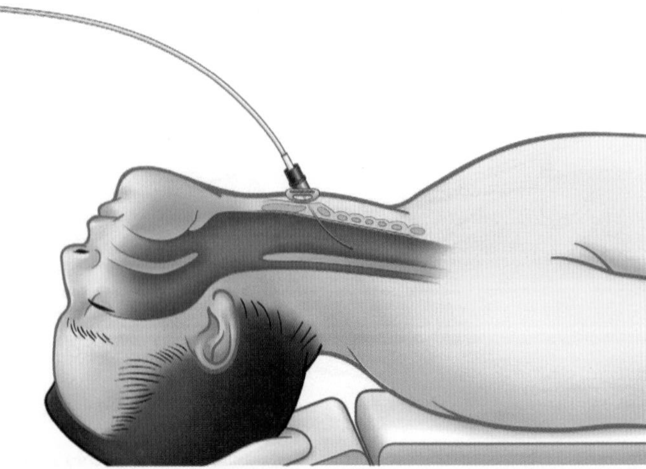

Figure 65.5 Transtracheal jet ventilation.

puncture, it can be difficult in obesity, restricted neck extension, and anatomical abnormality. Serious complications can occur such as misplacement, displacement, subcutaneous emphysema, and posterior tracheal wall puncture. If there is upper airway obstruction to gas outflow, barotrauma may result.

Tracheostomy

An initial tracheostomy can be performed in the awake or sedated patient with local anaesthesia for seriously compromised airways. It is also used following major ENT and maxillofacial surgery where significant postoperative airway swelling is anticipated. Although this can be managed with a normal tracheal tube, it requires postoperative intensive care and expertise in airway management. It has to be recognized that such capability is not available in all centres in the world and temporary tracheostomy will be safer in such circumstances. In this situation, tracheostomy can be performed at the beginning of surgery after initial endotracheal intubation.

Anaesthesia management for specific ENT procedures

Special considerations for ENT surgery include provision of a bloodless surgical field, attention to the patient's head position, airway management, facial nerve monitoring, the effect of nitrous oxide on the middle ear, a smooth and calm recovery, and prevention of PONV.

Middle ear surgery

For adults, simple middle ear surgery can be performed under local or general anaesthesia, although complicated or long procedures should be performed under general anaesthesia. Patients who are able to understand the procedure, and to communicate and cooperate throughout, are suitable candidates for local anaesthesia with or without sedation (Yung 1996). Patients may suffer from extensive hearing loss which will hinder their ability to cooperate with local anaesthesia. Leaving the hearing aid *in situ* in the non-surgical ear before induction and replacement before emergence may help to minimize anxiety and facilitate communication. A bloodless operative field is essential because even a few drops of blood can obscure the surgical field and a head-up tilt of 15–20°, avoidance of venous obstruction, normocapnia, and controlled hypotension may be considered.

The advantages of performing middle ear surgery under local anaesthesia include less bleeding, reduced pain in the immediate postoperative period, early mobilization, cost-effectiveness, and the ability to test hearing restoration during surgery (Caner et al. 2005). When required to be done under general anaesthesia, a total intravenous technique (TIVA) has the advantage of enhancing early recovery of consciousness and reducing nausea and vomiting. The use of nitrous oxide in anaesthetic practice has declined in recent years as a result of concerns over both physical and metabolic effects (Sanders et al. 2008; Irwin et al. 2009). The use of nitrous oxide in middle ear surgery is particularly controversial as it is more soluble than nitrogen in blood and enters the middle ear cavity more rapidly than nitrogen leaves, causing an increase in middle ear pressure if the Eustachian tube is obstructed (Miller 2005; Morgan et al. 2006). During tympanoplasty, the middle ear is open to the atmosphere, thus there is no build-up of pressure but once a tympanic membrane graft is placed, the continued use of nitrous oxide might cause displacement. At the end of surgery, when it is discontinued, nitrous oxide is rapidly absorbed which may then result in negative pressure which may cause graft dislodgement, serous otitis media, disarticulation of the stapes, or impaired hearing (Miller 2005; Morgan et al. 2006). Thus, the use of nitrous oxide is not recommended in tympanoplasty. Nitrous oxide also increases PONV which may further increase the incidence above that already associated with this type surgery.

Functional endoscopic sinus surgery

FESS is now the main technique for the surgical treatment of sinusitis and nasal polyposis, including bacterial, fungal, and recurrent acute and chronic sinus problems. The rationale behind FESS is that localized pathology in the ostiomeatal complex blocks the ostia and leads to inflammation in the dependent sinuses. Using fibreoptic endoscopes, it is possible to access the postnasal space from the anterior nares and to remove the ostiomeatal blockage. This restores normal sinus ventilation and mucociliary function with no need for external incisions and has a high success rate. It is sometimes performed with CT-navigational assistance to improve anatomical identification and avoid damage to neighbouring structures such as the brain and eyes. The surgical approach can also be used for resection of inverted papilloma, skull base tumour excision, treatment of vascular malformations associated with hereditary haemorrhagic telangiectasia, and transsphenoidal pituitary tumour resection. Patients may be taking steroids, although these are usually topical or short-term oral. There is a high incidence of atopy and asthma in conjunction with perennial and allergic rhinitis and nasal polyposis. Non-steroidal anti-inflammatory drug (NSAID) sensitivity can also coexist.

Minor FESS procedures can be performed under local anaesthesia in selected patients but comfort and surgical conditions are much better under general anaesthesia and, consequently, fewer complications ensue (Baker and Baker 2010). The SAD, especially the flexible one, has been used for FESS with good results. Patients managed with a flexible SAD are no more likely to have blood in the airway at completion of surgery compared with patients managed with a tracheal tube (Kaplan et al. 2004). At the end of surgery, the nasal airway is usually blocked by surgical packing making mouth breathing obligate. Awake extubation is safer but there is also the possibility of laryngospasm, coughing, and bucking with subsequent oxygen desaturation, and increased risk of bleeding. The SAD may make this process smoother. If choosing tracheal intubation then an oral RAE tracheal tube can be used with a throat pack in the oropharynx.

Blood loss during FESS is usually around 100–300 ml. Moderate hypotension with intraoperative β-blockade, α_2-agonists, or magnesium is associated with better operating conditions than when vasodilating agents are used even with similar levels of blood pressure. Interestingly, control of carbon dioxide does not show any effect on the surgical field but normocapnia is prudent. TIVA with propofol and remifentanil has been reported to have the advantage of decreased bleeding compared with conventional inhalation agents (Tirelli et al. 2004). It also reduces PONV with smooth emergence and less agitation than inhalation agents such as sevoflurane (Gupta et al. 2004; Dahmani et al. 2010). High-frequency jet ventilation has been used to reduce bleeding during FESS, possibly as a consequence of increased venous return caused by lower intrathoracic pressures but this technique has other risks. Monitoring of intraoperative visual-evoked potentials has been advocated as injury to the eye and blindness may occur by direct injury or by increased orbital pressure as a result of a retrobulbar haemorrhage. However, current visual-evoked potential technology is cumbersome, can cause corneal injury itself, and has relatively poor sensitivity so it is not commonly used. FESS is not associated with significant postoperative pain and analgesia is generally provided with multimodal techniques, minimizing the use of opioids. Paracetamol is safe and can be given orally preoperatively or as an intravenous pro-drug. Some patients may have NSAID sensitivity and there is concern over the bleeding risk. Sensitivity also occurs with cyclooxygenase 2 inhibitors but they have no effect on platelet function.

Adenotonsillectomy

Tonsillectomy is one of the oldest surgical procedures in the world and, although the efficacy has been questioned in management of recurrent infection (Friedman et al. 2009), it is still very commonly performed, particularly in children where it appears to have benefits in OSA. For children, the adenoids are removed at the same time, a procedure called adenoidectomy (this is uncommon in adults in whom the adenoids are usually vestigial). The American Academy of Otolaryngology–Head and Neck Surgery Foundation has published clinical practice guidelines on indications and management (Baugh et al. 2011). In addition to sleep apnoea, children may have other co-morbid conditions that might improve after tonsillectomy, including failure to thrive, poor school performance, enuresis, and behavioural problems. Those with severe OSA may have right heart symptoms such as cor pulmonale and are generally more susceptible to the inhibitory effect of sedative and anaesthetic drugs on pharyngeal muscle tone. Despite having their enlarged lymphoid tissues removed, these children are still prone to develop airway obstruction in the first postoperative night and, therefore, careful monitoring is essential.

Tonsillectomy has traditionally been performed by dissecting the tonsil from its surrounding fascia, a so-called total, or extracapsular tonsillectomy. Recently, there is increasing interest in sub-total tonsillectomy or 'tonsillotomy' in an effort to reduce complications such as pain and bleeding (Walton et al. 2012). Removal is typically achieved using a scalpel and blunt dissection or with electrocautery, although the Harmonic® Scalpel or lasers have also been used. Bleeding is stopped with electrocautery, ligation of sutures, and the topical use of thrombin.

There is a considerable range of opinion as to the optimal anaesthetic technique. The decision of whether or not to administer sedative premedication to the child should be made on a case-by-case basis as it can cause preoperative airway compromise, delay emergence, and the return of protective reflexes. On the other hand, it may help with the management of the otherwise inconsolable or uncooperative child who poses a danger to him- or herself. Both inhalation and intravenous induction are acceptable but one must be aware of potential difficulty in bag and mask ventilation with OSA. Jaw thrust with or without continuous positive airway pressure is usually effective in overcoming the obstruction and improving ventilation (Bruppacher et al. 2003). A reinforced SAD has been shown to be a valid alternative to the tracheal tube and has the advantage of reducing airway complications (Williams and Bailey 1993). If a neuromuscular blocking agent is to be used, a non-depolarizing one with a short duration of action should be selected. Suxamethonium should be reserved for emergency use only because of its well-known adverse effects. A spontaneous breathing technique using either a tracheal tube or SAD is also acceptable. Extreme care and good cooperation must be exercised at the time of placing the mouth gag in the oral cavity for surgical exposure as it is stimulating and can kink or displace the airway device. Some have advocated temporarily disconnecting the circuit from the SAD until the gag is securely placed (Jöhr 2006).

Emergence from anaesthesia is another period of challenge. Awake extubation is preferable as it ensures the return of protective airway reflexes. However, if the timing is not right, a partially conscious child is at risk of laryngospasm from oral bleed and secretions. Placing the child in the recovery position with head down and minimizing stimulation while the child recovers from the anaesthetic may reduce this occurrence (Tsui et al. 2004). Significant debate exists regarding the optimal postoperative analgesia regimen. Morphine, while providing good pain relief, increases the likelihood of PONV and respiratory depression. NSAIDs and paracetamol provide a good baseline and can be used in combination as there is evidence of additive effects. A small dose of fentanyl can help. The use of NSAIDs remains controversial with respect to the clinical significance of platelet inhibition. A systematic review that included 13 trials with 955 children, however, did not find an increase in bleeding that required a return to the operating theatre but did demonstrate significantly less nausea and vomiting with the use of NSAIDs (Cardwell et al. 2005). Local anaesthetic also seems to provide a modest reduction in post-tonsillectomy pain (Grainger and Saravanappa 2008). Topical local anaesthetic on swabs appears to provide a similar level of analgesia to that of infiltration without the potential adverse effects and should be the method of choice for providing additional postoperative analgesia. The incidence of postoperative nausea is high in this surgical group and prophylaxis has been recommended in the form of ondansetron 0.05 mg kg^{-1} with dexamethasone 0.15 mg kg^{-1} (Carr et al. 2009).

As the risk of severe re-bleeding some hours after surgery in routine cases is very low, discharge on the day of surgery is usually justified provided institutional protocols are in place and strict instructions are given to the parents. Those with a history of sleep apnoea or below 3 years of age should be observed in hospital overnight.

Anaesthesia for bleeding tonsils is very challenging as the patient is at risk of hypovolaemic shock, pulmonary aspiration, and may present as a difficult intubation because of an obscured view of the airway. Administering a second anaesthetic to the child within a short period may result in prolonged sedation in the recovery phase, although this is less likely with drugs such as sevoflurane and propofol. One must, therefore, take into account any sedative analgesics administered in the original operation. Although the patient usually requires fairly urgent surgery, adequate fluid resuscitation should be performed before induction. This should be guided by clinical parameters and haemoglobin concentration as estimating blood loss is notoriously difficult. 'Type and screen' ('group and save') should be available in case of significant bleeding requiring transfusion. The surgeons should be ready before induction and a large-bore suction catheter available. Either inhalation induction in the head-down lateral position or rapid sequence induction can be used, each with its pros and cons (Table 65.1).

Before tracheal extubation, some practitioners would place a wide-bore orogastric tube under direct vision to empty the stomach. The child is then placed in the lateral head-down position and the trachea extubated when the child is awake.

Table 65.1 Advantages and disadvantages of inhalation induction and rapid sequence induction in emergency anaesthesia for bleeding tonsils

Inhalation induction	Rapid sequence induction
Advantages	**Advantages**
Maintains spontaneous ventilation	Good intubating conditions: ◆ Supine position ◆ Neuromuscular block
Drains blood and secretions away from the airway	
Avoids succinylcholine	Cricoid pressure can be applied
Disadvantages	Less stressful for the child if an intravenous catheter is *in situ*
May be difficult in an anxious child	
Inadvertent deep anaesthesia (recent general anaesthesia)	**Disadvantages**
Difficult to intubate in the lateral position	Difficult to pre-oxygenate
	Risk of hypoxia if intubation is difficult

Peritonsillar abscess

Peritonsillar abscess can arise near the superior pole of the palatine tonsil, or from infection in the tonsillar fossa as a result of adjacent acute tonsillitis. Many cases can be managed with antibiotics and conservative management or needle aspiration under local anaesthesia. Management can be complicated, however, in paediatric patients who are too young to tolerate bedside drainage under local anaesthesia and with large abscesses potentially compromising breathing. Diagnosis is historically by physical examination but intra-oral ultrasound and CT are commonly used nowadays. Delayed diagnosis and treatment may lead to local extension of the infection and further compromise the airway. Cephalad spread can lead to facial oedema and difficulty with mask ventilation; spread into the masticator space can limit mouth opening; and caudal spread can result in glottic swelling and upper airway obstruction (Ono et al. 2004). Incision and drainage with possible tonsillectomy may be required under general anaesthesia and management is similar to the bleeding tonsil as the abscess can easily rupture with airway manipulation and discharge pus into the lower airway. Particular attention needs to be paid to more gentle manipulation and the possibility of partial or even complete airway obstruction during induction.

Paediatric airway procedures

Microlaryngeal procedures can be performed using the suspension laryngoscope and various combinations of inhalation and intravenous anaesthetics. Clear communication between the surgeon and anaesthetist is of supreme importance as the surgical requirements determine the anaesthetic options. Children presenting for these types of procedures usually have some degree of airway obstruction and it is very important to maintain spontaneous ventilation and avoid neuromuscular blocking agents unless it is clear that positive ventilation is possible. Spontaneous ventilation is also essential for functional assessment of the vocal cords or for malacia. A delicate balance has to be achieved between providing sufficient depth of anaesthesia to prevent movement and not excessively deep to impair normal respiratory mechanics. Strict adherence to fasting guidelines must be enforced to reduce the risk of aspiration.

Both inhalation insufflation and total intravenous anaesthesia or a combination of both of these have been described with spontaneous breathing. In the authors' institution, the child receives either inhalation induction with sevoflurane to secure intravenous access or is induced directly with a propofol medium-chain triglyceride preparation if intravenous access is available. Infusion may be started at relatively high doses in the range of 200–300 μg kg^{-1} min^{-1} and supplemented with a low-dose remifentanil infusion and or dexmedetomidine infusion and then titrated down. The vasoconstrictor xylometazoline is applied to both nostrils. A flexible bronchoscopy can then be performed through one nostril to evaluate the movement of the cords. A soft catheter can be passed through the other nostril for oxygenation.

At the completion of the nasal endoscopy, the depth of anaesthesia is then tested against the haemodynamic response to direct laryngoscopy performed by the anaesthetist. Local anaesthesia is then applied to the glottic areas and, if necessary, through the vocal cords into the trachea. It is important to calculate the total dose of local anaesthesia that can be used for the entire procedure and divide it up between the anaesthetist and surgeon to prevent inadvertent overdose. Intermittent ventilation and interruption to the procedure may be required should the patient develop apnoea.

Adult airway procedures

Direct laryngoscopy using a suspension laryngoscope is performed for both the diagnosis and treatment of vocal cord pathology. Apart from simple fibreoptic procedures that can be performed under local anaesthesia, the patients will require general anaesthesia with paralysis to provide an immobile operative field. Placement of the surgical equipment may cause intense sympathetic stimulation and it is necessary to obtund this response to avert myocardial ischaemia in this susceptible patient population. After achieving adequate anaesthesia, the effects of surgical stimulation can be ameliorated by the adjunct use of dexmedetomidine and/or short-acting opioids or β-receptor antagonists. Dexmedetomidine also has the advantage of reducing airway secretions in a situation where anticholinergic medication is undesirable. Options for managing the airway include intermittent apnoea without endotracheal intubation, intubation with a microlaryngoscopy tube, and positive pressure ventilation either with an inhalation anaesthetic or with oxygen/air in combination with TIVA.

Dealing with pathology further down the respiratory track requires the use of a rigid bronchoscope. Instrumentation through the vocal cords usually precludes the use of tracheal tubes. The principles are the same as that for laryngoscopy and topical anaesthesia applied to the glottic area is advisable to reduce the stimulation from instrumentation through the vocal cords. Jet ventilation can be performed down the bronchoscope or a circuit can be attached to a ventilating side arm.

Laser procedures

Lasers can cause biological tissue destruction through both thermal and mechanical effects leading to coagulation, carbonization, and vaporization of target tissues. The beam can be manipulated to remove unwanted tissue such as tumours or haemangioma with precision. However, its use can be hazardous to both the patient and theatre staff if safety guidelines are not strictly followed. In addition to damage caused by a misdirected or reflected beam, tissue vaporization by lasers creates plumes of fine particulates that can deposit in alveoli causing interstitial pneumonia, bronchiolitis, and may even be carcinogenic. Laser energy can strike anything in the operating room causing damage to patients, staff, or equipment. Consequently when laser is being used, a warning should be placed on the entrance to the room with protective shutters. Those inside the room should have appropriate protective eyewear when the laser is being delivered (see Table 65.2). The patient's eyes must also be protected and be closed and covered with moist gauze.

Laser energy can also provide the spark for an operating room fire but of particular concern is the risk of airway fire. This depends on the relative flammability of various tracheal tubes and the gas composition therein. Laser being the ignition source, fuels such as surgical preparation solutions or the tracheal tube and oxidizers such as oxygen or nitrous oxide can quite easily complete the 'fire triangle'. Precautions should be taken to minimize the combination of these factors. A tubeless technique can be used when feasible. If not, laser-resistant tubes should be considered as they can either deflect or absorb some of the laser energy. Essentially a minimal $F_{I_{O_2}}$ to maintain adequate oxygen saturation should be used and nitrous oxide avoided. A cuffed tube is strongly preferred but, if uncuffed tubes are used, moist gauze packs should be placed to reduce leakage of oxygen-enriched gas into the oropharynx. The cuff should be inflated with 0.9% saline, preferably dyed to indicate cuff damage. The duration and intensity of laser delivery should be kept to a minimum.

Should an airway fire occur, ventilation must be stopped immediately, the oxygen source disconnected, and the surgical field flooded with water or saline. The burned tracheal tube should be removed and the extent of injury may then be assessed by bronchoscopy after re-establishing a means of ventilation. The patient should be monitored and reintubated and ventilated if necessary while steroids may be considered to reduce airway oedema. In severe cases, tracheostomy will be required and all patients will need monitoring in intensive care for 24 h as swelling may not develop immediately.

Inhaled foreign bodies

Once the diagnosis and the nature of the inhaled foreign body have been confirmed, a definitive management plan should be made in consultation with the surgeon. General anaesthesia is almost always required for a small child. Laryngoscopy and bronchoscopy is required to retrieve objects in the trachea, typically with the aid of a ventilating rigid bronchoscope. The maintenance of spontaneous respiration is encouraged in those with partial obstruction as positive pressure ventilation may push the object further down the bronchial tree. Inhalation anaesthesia may be delivered via the bronchoscope and supplemented with intravenous agents such as propofol, remifentanil, or dexmedetomidine. The last listed agent is attractive for this procedure given its minimal depressant effect on respiration. Complications can result from inadequate anaesthesia leading to coughing and bronchospasm or excessive anaesthesia causing respiratory depression, hypercapnia, and hypoxia. Occasionally the retrieved object may be sufficiently large to necessitate the removal of the bronchoscope along with the object. If a foreign body in the pharynx is dislodged from the retrieving forceps, it has the potential to cause total obstruction should it fall into the trachea. If the object cannot then be retrieved in a timely manner, pushing it more distally to allow ventilation is warranted followed by a second attempt at removal. Dexamethasone should be considered to reduce airway oedema if multiple insertion and removal of the bronchoscope was required.

Table 65.2 Laser type and colour of protective eyewear

Laser type	Wavelength	Colour of protective eyewear
Carbon dioxide (CO_2)	10.6 μm	Clear
Potassium titanyl phosphate (KTP)	532 nm	Orange
Neodymium: yttrium aluminium garnet (Nd:YAG)	1062 nm	Clear
Argon	514 nm	Orange

Sleep naso-endoscopy

This technique, which is also referred to as drug-induced sleep endoscopy, is a powerful tool for studying the dynamic airway in the supine position during a sleep-like state in patients with possible OSA. The knowledge gained from sleep endoscopy helps delineate the anatomical basis for obstruction and, therefore, the most suitable surgical procedure (Kezirian et al. 2011). Sleep endoscopy may also provide information that erases the need for surgery altogether. The procedure was first proposed in 1991 by Pringle and Croft who later developed a grading scale that utilized sleep endoscopy to categorize snoring and obstruction (Pringle and Croft 1993). Grading was based on whether the obstruction was palatal, multilevel, or tongue-based. Another grading system that uses sleep endoscopy to assess airway obstruction uses three separate evaluations of the pharynx. The first two ascertain individual areas of obstruction in the palate and hypopharynx while the third assesses the percentage of obstruction in each area: less than 50%, 50–75%, and more than 75%, representing mild, moderate, and severe obstruction, respectively.

The patient should be in the supine position without a shoulder roll, mimicking the position of natural sleep as much as possible. Topical local anaesthesia with a vasoconstrictor should be used on the nasal mucosa and oxygen can be given via a nasal cannula in the contralateral nares. Midazolam was the first drug to be used for sedation but it is apparent that propofol and dexmedetomidine may be better alternatives: propofol because of its more suitable pharmacokinetic properties and excellent titratability, particularly using target-controlled infusion; dexmedetomidine because it does not induce respiratory depression, produces non-rapid eye movement phase II sleep which better mimics the natural state and it has an antisialagogue effect. Once a rhythmic pattern of respiration is established, a flexible fibreoptic laryngoscope is passed through the nose into the nasopharynx. For visualization and documentation, a digital video camera is used with the endoscope.

In children, a suggested technique is that anaesthesia is induced either by inhalation or intravenously as usual, and then maintained with an infusion of dexmedetomidine at 1–2 $\mu g\ kg^{-1}\ h^{-1}$ without a loading dose, and with a concurrent ketamine bolus of 1 $mg\ kg^{-1}$ (Lin and Koltai 2012). This technique causes less muscle relaxation and a more sustained respiratory effort than a propofol infusion and the dexmedetomidine antagonizes the increased secretions produced by ketamine.

Transoral robotic surgery

Transoral robotic surgery (TORS) has been increasingly used for the management of early benign and malignant tumours in the head and neck, having received US Food and Drug Administration approval for these indications. It is also used to treat lingual tonsillar hypertrophy in patients with OSA. The daVinci® Surgical Robot (Intuitive Surgical, Sunnyvale, CA, USA) consists of a surgeon's console and a surgical cart. It is minimally invasive and considered to have many advantages over conventional techniques. These include easier manipulation of tissues within a limited space with multiple degrees of motion and a three-dimensional vision to enhance depth perception. It has been reported that transoral robotic surgery can reduce blood loss, wound infection, and postoperative pain with faster recovery and return to preoperative speech and swallowing. This results in better overall quality of life (O'Malley et al. 2006; Weinstein et al. 2007).

There are additional challenges to the anaesthetist as access to the airway may be even more restricted by the surgical cart. Generally, both console and cart are situated at the same side of the patient but the former is away from the patient and the latter is in the vicinity of the patient's head. The nurse and other equipment are located at the opposite side so that the surgeon can communicate with the nurse and assistant. During the operation, the anaesthetic machine is required to be located at the feet end of the patient and, therefore, appropriate plans need to be made regarding the configuration of the machine and the operating table during the induction of anaesthesia. A wire-reinforced tracheal tube is generally used or one that is laser resistant if laser use is to be considered. The patient's eyes should be protected with safety goggles. The mouth gag and retractor are placed by the surgeon. Neuromuscular block is not mandatory, although ventilation should be controlled, but may be required to reduce contraction of the pharyngeal muscles during electrocautery.

As with most head and neck surgery, an anaesthetic technique that facilitates rapid recovery of consciousness and less PONV is best (e.g. propofol/remifentanil). At the end of surgery, haemostasis should be checked with the Valsalva manoeuvre and restoration of normal blood pressure. The robotic arms, mouth gag or retractor (or both), and the dental guard are then removed. Laryngopharyngeal oedema compromising the airway can occur which can result in serious morbidity and mortality. An appropriate extubation plan should be considered if airway oedema is anticipated (see later). It has been suggested that patients should be kept intubated after transoral robotic surgery when there has been dissection adjacent to the vallecula or epiglottis, in prolonged cases, and after supraglottic partial laryngectomy. Tracheostomy is usually performed in patients with resection involving the tongue base and a portion of the epiglottis. Otherwise the early complication rate of transoral robotic surgery is comparable to that of conventional non-robotic transoral surgery.

Nasopharyngeal carcinoma

As a result of geographic, ethnic, and environmental factors, nasopharyngeal carcinoma is endemic in Southern China and Southeast Asia (10–50 per 10 000 population affected) but relatively rare in Europe and North America (Chan and Wei 2012). Nasopharyngeal carcinoma occurs in the epithelial lining of the nasopharynx at the centre of the head and often measures more than 10 cm from the surface of all directions (Wei 2003). Important structures including the skull base and internal carotid artery are also located near the nasopharynx. It is a radiosensitive tumour and, therefore, radiotherapy is the first-line treatment with good results. If the disease is persistent or recurrent, a second phase of external radiotherapy may be considered but will damage the surrounding tissues and produce functional disturbance such as dysphagia and xerostomia. Moreover, generally, the response is not as good such that surgical intervention is required (Wei et al. 2011). Minimally invasive endoscopic nasopharyngectomy has been reported for central roof or floor lesions with minimal lateral extension. There are various open approaches for nasopharyngectomy including superior, transcervical, lateral, anterior, and anterolateral (maxillary swing). The choice depends on the size, location, and the extent of the tumour and each has its own advantages, disadvantages, and limitations. The anterolateral approach is now generally advocated and adopted. It involves hemi-maxillectomy and, as a result, the nasopharynx and paranasopharyngeal region can be widely exposed for much easier and extensive resection. The maxilla is then reinserted as a free bone graft after tumour resection.

Patients undergoing nasopharyngectomy may have poor general health and nutritional status as a result of the disease itself or poor oral intake. Previous radiotherapy can have implications perioperatively. Xerostomia often results in poor dental hygiene and a dental referral is usual before surgery. Trismus-limited neck movement and general loss of soft tissue elasticity can make intubation difficult. Elective tracheostomy is generally done before nasopharyngectomy. There are major blood vessels around the maxilla and the nasopharynx so sudden massive blood loss should be anticipated. After surgery, patients can breathe spontaneously through the tracheostomy tube. Pain can be moderate to severe for in the first 2 days so patient-controlled opioid analgesia is useful along with paracetamol and NSAID which can be given either intravenously or in syrup form via a nasogastric enteral feeding tube.

Surgery for malignancies requiring flap reconstruction

Anaesthetic technique can affect the success rate of flap reconstruction. Different factors including intravenous fluid therapy, blood pressure, ventilation settings, choice of anaesthetic agent, and vasoactive drugs can affect the flap survival rate (Xiao and Zhang 2010). The blood supply to the flap is reduced with arterial vasoconstriction after anastomosis and an increase in venous pressure as a result of oedema so these should be avoided. Dopamine infusion was found to have no effect on blood flow to flaps (Cordeiro et al. 1997) while dobutamine increased both cardiac output and flap blood flow (Scholz et al. 2009). Phenylephrine infusion was shown to reduce flap blood flow in doses greater than 1 $\mu g\ kg^{-1}\ min^{-1}$ (Cordeiro et al. 1997). Hypovolaemia will reduce cardiac output and impair perfusion and microcirculatory flow. Goal-directed fluid therapy optimizes cardiac output and intraoperative oesophageal Doppler monitoring has shown some promise in improving flap perfusion (Figus et al. 2011). Colloids may be preferable to crystalloids to reduce oedema. Mild haemodilution will decrease blood viscosity which is helpful (Qiao et al. 1996) and a haematocrit between 30% and 35% is generally recommended. Dextran is a water-soluble polymer derived from sucrose and is commonly used in flap surgery. It can remain in the intravascular space from 2 to 12 h depending on the molecular weight and decreases platelet aggregation and activities of clotting factors V, VII, and IX which can help to improve the microcirculation and reduce thromboembolism. Disadvantages include an allergic potential (less in low-molecular-weight dextran) and its interference with cross-matching because of rouleaux formation. Other goals such as normocapnia and normothermia should also be adopted during flap surgery. Vasodilators such as SNP will reduce mean arterial pressure with a concomitant decrease in blood flow to the flap (Banic et al. 1999).

Anaesthesia for dental procedures

While the majority of dental procedures are satisfactorily performed under local anaesthesia, there are clear indications where general anaesthesia is required. These include patients with special needs in whom cooperation is not possible, such as small children, those with mental disabilities, or those with severe dental phobia. General anaesthesia may also be required when the proposed dental work is extensive or if acute inflammation is present that may render the local anaesthetic ineffective. Though very rare, allergy to local anaesthetic agents is also an indication for general anaesthesia.

Premedication may be required for those with challenging behaviour. Midazolam can be given orally (0.5–0.75 mg kg^{-1}), either alone or mixed with juice to disguise the taste, or intranasally (0.2–0.3 mg kg^{-1}). More recently, dexmedetomidine given via the nasal route has been shown to be equally effective compared with intranasal midazolam in decreasing anxiety upon separation from parents, though midazolam is superior in providing satisfactory conditions during inhalation induction (Akin et al. 2012).

Inhalation induction with sevoflurane is a commonly used method for very young children but intravenous induction may be offered to older children. The application of topical local anaesthetic cream such as EMLA® (Eutectic Mixture of Local Anaesthetic containing lidocaine and prilocaine) or Ametop® (containing tetracaine) 30–40 min beforehand should reduce the discomfort of intravenous cannula insertion.

The choice of airway for simple procedures such as exodontia depends on the expected duration of the procedure and clear communication with the dental surgeon is paramount. Nasal masks may be used for uncomplicated extraction of deciduous teeth. Measures such as packing the buccal sulci with gauze may reduce the amount of mouth breathing and aspiration of debris. Alternatively, a SAD is useful for longer procedures, although it occupies more room within the oral cavity and can be dislodged. Conservation work requires a longer operative time, drilling with irrigation, and, therefore, may warrant endotracheal intubation with the placement of a throat pack for ventilation and protection against aspiration respectively.

Although traditional teaching stipulates the use of prophylactic antibiotics for patients with cardiac valve lesions undergoing dental procedures, more recent recommendations are more conservative, balancing the risk of antibiotic-associated problems (allergic reactions, breeding of resistant strains) against the exceedingly small number of infective endocarditis cases. The guidelines from the 2007 American Heart Association have been adopted by professional dental bodies such as the American Academy of Pediatric Dentistry and can be accessed online (Wilson 2007, available at http://circ.ahajournals.org/content/116/15/1736.long).

Anaesthesia for maxillofacial surgery

Maxillofacial surgery involves a broad scope of procedures ranging from tooth extraction to major orthognathic and facial reconstruction surgery. Some of this may be cosmetic or functional in nature but there is also a significant amount of maxillofacial trauma and cancer surgery. Local anaesthesia, monitored anaesthetic care, general anaesthesia, or a combination of these can be used depending on the pathology, surgical requirements, and the patient's preference. Owing to the nature of the patients and the type of surgery, a difficult airway is quite common both pre- and postoperatively. Fixation devices that restrict mouth opening may be required at the end of surgery to stabilize facial and mandibular fractures. This, coupled with a propensity for postoperative airway oedema, mandates a detailed and safe plan for postoperative airway management and an appropriate location for patient monitoring.

Orthognathic procedures

This type of surgery is intended to correct conditions of the jaw and face related to structure, growth, temporomandibular joint disorders, and dental malocclusion. Osteotomies are performed usually of the maxilla and mandible and the bones re-aligned, then held in place with either screws or plates. Patients may present with problems such as difficulties with chewing or speaking, chronic maxillomandibular pain, cosmetic issues, or OSA. Common procedures are presented in Table 65.3. In a report of a single-centre experience over 20 years, airway obstruction requiring emergency tracheostomy has been reported only once but the authors reported several incidences where fixation devices had to be removed to relieve obstruction (Teltzrow et al. 2005).

Endotracheal intubation is the most common way to secure the airway in maxillofacial surgery. The skill of fibreoptic intubation is essential in this field. It can be performed safely and comfortably after regional anaesthesia to the airway. Concomitant sedation may be used carefully with dexmedetomidine as it has an antisialagogue effect and doesn't depress respiration. Low-dose propofol infusion or a benzodiazepine can also be used carefully but opioids only with the utmost caution. If difficult ventilation is not expected, fibreoptic intubation can be done under anaesthesia as it is less traumatic for nasal use and provides an opportunity to maintain the experience and skills required. Like all potential difficult airway situations, a clear plan is required and a backup plan should this fail. A difficult airway equipment trolley should be ready for emergency use. For simple third molar surgery, either oral or nasal intubation is

Table 65.3 Common orthognathic procedures

Procedure	Comments
Bilateral sagittal split osteotomy	Osteotomy through the mandibular ramus; access via intraoral incision
Vertical ramus osteotomy	Divides the mandibular ramus from the sigmoid notch down to the angular region; access via intraoral or external incision
Le Fort osteotomies	Osteotomies performed across the lines of facial fractures as described by Le Fort; an incision made in the vestibular sulcus from the first molar toward of one side all the way to its contralateral counterpart
Le Fort I (horizontal)	Nasal septum to the lateral pyriform rims
Le Fort II (pyramidal)	Pyramidal naso-orbito-maxillary direction

possible and an oral reinforced tube or RAE tube useful. The SAD is also feasible for such surgery, although it somewhat restricts access. However, for mandibular and maxillary surgery nasotracheal intubation is preferred whether intraoral fixation is required or not. The nasal mucosa should be prepared with topical vasoconstrictors or cocaine as described in the ENT section.

The nasotracheal tube should be warmed to body temperature in order to make it softer during intubation. Portex® Ivory (Smiths Medical, Hythe, Kent, UK) PVC preformed tube may be less traumatic for nasal intubation and the overall curve is preserved when warmed but its length and contour make postoperative ventilation and tracheal toileting more difficult. The nasotracheal tube should be longer and usually 1–2 mm smaller in diameter than that used orally. The tube should be fully deflated and inserted through the nostril at right angles to the face. Once the tube reaches the oropharynx, it can be advanced into the larynx under direct vision with conventional laryngoscopy. Sometimes, Magill forceps are useful in assisting advancement of the tube. With better equipment and drugs, blind nasal intubation is not commonly used now. The most common complication is epistaxis which is mainly as a result of direct trauma to Kisselbach's plexus of Little's area but can also occur from damage to other structures and the delicate mucosa from the nose to the pharynx. Using a smaller-diameter, warmed tube and vasoconstrictor will help. It is absolutely essential not to force the tube and a gentle rolling or tube rotation may assist. If epistaxis occurs, nasotracheal intubation should be completed as soon as possible and the tube left in place in order to produce a tamponade effect and to protect the airway. Most nose bleeding can be controlled adequately like this but it may resume when the tube is removed at the end of surgery so great care should also be taken at this time. Other rare complications include traumatic avulsion of structures in the nasopharynx, aryepiglottic folds, valleculae, pyriform sinuses and vocal cords, bacteraemia, sinusitis, and necrosis of the nasal ala. The overall complication rate is reported to be 20% but most of these are mild bleeding. Absolute contraindications include base of skull fracture and bleeding diathesis. A moistened throat pack is normally put around the tube in the oropharynx as during ENT surgery.

During maxillofacial surgery, movement of the head and neck may cause the tube to move up and down in the trachea risking extubation, or endobronchial intubation. Kinking or twisting of the tracheal tube is possible. Compression of the tube can also obstruct ventilation both during inspiration and expiration. Wire-reinforced tubes are commonly used for this reason, although they can cause more trauma during insertion. Accidental extubation and cutting of the tube have also been reported. Care must also be taken to protect the eyes as inadvertent pressure by the surgeons' hands or instruments can easily occur. Steroids are commonly administered perioperatively to reduce oedema. Although evidence seems to support this indication, the dose and timing remains contentious (Dan et al. 2010; Chegini and Dhariwal 2012). Dexamethasone has the added benefit of reducing PONV.

Blood loss is more prevalent with maxillary than mandibular surgery. If heavy blood loss is anticipated, preoperative autologous blood donation and isovolaemic haemodilution may be arranged. As in major ENT surgery, moderate controlled hypotension is also commonly utilised to improve surgical conditions and reduce blood loss especially during bimaxillary osteotomy (Choi and Samman 2008). Tranexamic acid (TXA) is a synthetic derivative of the amino acid lysine that is used to treat or prevent excessive blood loss during surgery. It is an antifibrinolytic that competitively inhibits the activation of plasminogen to plasmin, by binding to specific sites of both plasminogen and plasmin, a molecule responsible for the degradation of fibrin. The effect of tranexamic acid on reducing blood transfusion during surgery was recently supported in a meta-analysis (Ker et al. 2012). Of the 129 trials recruited, 7 involved cranial and orthognathic surgery. Preoperative intravenous bolus administration of tranexamic acid at 20 mg kg^{-1} reduced blood loss compared with placebo during bimaxillary osteotomy (Choi et al. 2009). Tranexamic acid has now been included in the WHO list of essential medicines (World Health Organization 2011) as it is inexpensive and treatment would be considered highly cost-effective in high-, middle-, and low-income countries (Guerriero et al. 2011). Topical application of tranexamic acid is also effective (Ker et al. 2013) and it can even be given orally. Dexmedetomidine produces a modest reduction in blood pressure and heart rate that can be useful in this situation.

Generally, maxillofacial surgery is not associated with significant pain postoperatively and, in fact, there is often paraesthesia after osteotomies. Some surgical sites such as dental sites can be blocked with local anaesthetic. Respiratory depression and vomiting could be particularly dangerous after maxillofacial surgery so minimizing opioid use and utilizing multimodal analgesia is important. NSAIDs can be used if bleeding is not a problem otherwise cyclooxygenase-2 selective NSAIDs can substitute. Paracetamol and intraoperative low-dose ketamine are helpful and patient-controlled opioid analgesia is usually not required. As with all head and neck surgery, great care must be taken with tracheal extubation and subsequent airway monitoring. Some surgery requires maxillomandibular fixation which is usually applied by wiring together the fixed upper and lower arch bars. Propofol-based TIVA reduces PONV and facilitates rapid recovery of consciousness. Wire cutters should be kept on the patient's bed and the attendant staff instructed in their use should an airway emergency arise.

Facial trauma

Facial trauma can range from simple lacerations to pan-facial injury with airway comprise that makes intubation difficult. These injuries are usually blunt or crushing in nature caused by motor vehicle accidents or assault. Massive bleeding can cause acute airway obstruction while progressive swelling can insidiously lead to total airway obstruction. Management of these patients should follow the ABC of trauma protocol with a priority to secure the airway early as obstruction is the leading cause of death in maxillofacial trauma. Concomitant head injury with alteration in the level of consciousness is another indication for early airway and ventilatory control.

Damage to other surrounding structures such as the hypopharynx and larynx must be suspected. As cervical spine injury is possible, the head and neck must be maintained in the neutral position during intubation, usually with manual in-line stabilization avoiding extension and flexion of the neck. There should be a low threshold for fibreoptic intubation and this should be considered awake if possible with the use of topical local anaesthetics and nerve block of the airway. Great caution should be used with concomitant sedation, although patients intoxicated or with obtunded consciousness may be uncooperative. Nasotracheal intubation is (relatively) contraindicated in patients with potential base of skull fracture or unstable mid-face injuries in whom oral fibreoptic intubation is preferable using a split airway device such as the Ovassapian intubator. Surgical airway such as tracheostomy should be an early option if the facial trauma is so severe that orotracheal intubation seems to be impossible or if the airway is severely comprised. Other injuries should also be attended to and general resuscitative measures implemented at the same time. Other airway management devices may be necessary and used according to the skill and experience of the practitioner. A SAD or the Combitube® (Tyco-Healthcare-Kendall-Sheridan, Mansfield, MA, USA), can be inserted blindly but there are also a plethora of other direct insertion devices now available such as the videolaryngoscopes.

The timing of definitive repair of facial injuries depends largely on other significant injuries. Soft tissue injury should be cleaned and sutured as soon as feasible. Mandibular fractures should be fixed within 24–48 h as they are very painful and interfere with swallowing. Other fractures may need CT scanning to properly assess, and should be fixed within 7–10 days before the fractures begin to set and become more difficult to reduce.

The choice of airway management depends largely on the surgical requirements and the effect of the injury upon the patient's airway anatomy. The usual airway assessment should be performed, paying special attention to the pattern of swelling, mouth opening, nasal patency, or any dental damage. Mouth opening is often limited by trismus in early fractures and should disappear following induction but one has to be aware of the possibility of mechanical interference of the temporomandibular joint by a bone fragment or an unusual fracture. An assessment has to be made as to the ease of face mask ventilation and, if in any doubt, awake fibreoptic intubation is safest. Mid-facial fracture reduction usually requires temporary intraoperative dental occlusion and usually precludes the use of an oral tracheal tube. In contrast, oral RAE tubes are suitable for zygomatic and orbital fractures. Pan-facial fractures may require access to both the nose and dental occlusion, in which case submental intubation or tracheostomy may have to be considered.

Postoperative management of the airway

Rescuing patients from postsurgical airway obstruction is fraught with difficulties as patients may have depleted oxygen reserves from respiratory compromise and airway distortion secondary to the surgical procedure. Therefore, it is prudent to formulate a stepwise and logical postoperative airway management plan in consultation with the surgeons to avoid such occurrence and to rapidly re-secure the airway should extubation fail. The plan should identify patients at high risk for complications following extubation, a means of physical airway assessment, monitoring after extubation, and the provision of airway devices to facilitate oxygenation and possible re-intubation. Before enacting such plans, the patient should fulfil general criteria for extubation which include haemodynamic stability, adequate respiratory strength, airway patency, normothermia, and a conscious level enabling clearance of secretions and airway protection.

A useful way to conceptualize and identify patients at anatomical risk of failing extubation is to use the three-column model proposed by Greenland (2010), where the posterior focuses on the cervical spine, the middle column is the airway passage, and the anterior is the mandible, tongue, and submandibular tissues (Fig. 65.6). Delaying extubation should be considered when a problem with the middle column is anticipated. Anomalies in the anterior and posterior columns can independently distort the middle column, thus constituting a 'difficult airway'. Patients undergoing prolonged anaesthesia requiring moderate to high doses of opioids are at risk of depressed genioglossus and pharyngeal muscle tone that, in turn, narrows the middle column. Diminished airway protective reflexes from residual drug effects place them at risk of aspiration. Those patients requiring massive fluid resuscitation and subjected to airway soft tissue trauma during surgery are at risk of mucosal swelling that further exacerbates airway narrowing.

Physical assessment of the airway may include direct inspection by the surgeon, anaesthetist, or both, and the use of the cuff leak test. The former can be achieved using direct laryngoscopy or fibreoptic bronchoscopy. An *in situ* tracheal tube can give a false impression of the ease with which the larynx may be visualized should reintubation be required. The airway should be inspected for swelling, anatomical distortions, vocal cord function, and appearance. The cuff leak is suggested by some as an indicator of airway patency and can be performed qualitatively by listening for an audible leak when a positive pressure of 20 mm Hg is delivered through the tracheal tube or during spontaneous respiration. Alternatively, it may be quantified by calculating the tidal volume difference between inspiration with the cuff inflated and expiration when deflated. A test is said to be positive when the leak volume is less than 110 ml. A positive test, which indicates a failure, has a positive predictive value of 80% for failed extubation when the test is conducted 24 h before the extubation after extended critical care intubation (Francon et al. 2008).

Strategies should be available for re-securing the airway when trial of extubation is contemplated. A supraglottic device such as a SAD may be placed before extubation. This will facilitate inspection of the vocal cords and as a conduit for re-intubation. The use of an airway exchange catheter provides a means of rapid reintubation, oxygenation, and monitoring of end-tidal carbon dioxide. The airway exchange catheter is a long. semi-rigid hollow device that enjoys a high success rate as a conduit for railroading a tracheal tube and has a low complication rate (Mort 2007). The 11- and 14-French gauge devices are well tolerated and should be placed to the same distance as the tip of the tracheal tube to avoid stimulation of the carina. After careful removal of the tracheal tube, the airway exchange catheter should be firmly secured to the face or forehead and clearly labelled to avoid inadvertent removal or other misadventures. The duration of placement is variable and depends on the risk of developing delayed airway complications. Although periglottic oedema contributing to airway compromise usually develops within the first 45 min after extubation, laryngeal oedema as late as 8 h post extubation has been reported (Mort 2007).

After extubation, patients deemed at risk of developing airway compromise should be monitored in a high dependency area with staff experienced in recognizing warning signs (Greenland et al. 2011). Emphasis should be placed on early symptoms and signs such as sore throat, hoarse or weak voice, poor cough, and dysphagia or drooling rather than the late signs of stridor or orthopnoea which herald imminent respiratory arrest. The Difficult Airway Society (UK) has developed guidelines for the safe management of tracheal extubation in adult perioperative practice, many of which are applicable to head and neck surgery (Difficult Airway Society Extubation Guidelines Group 2012). See Fig. 65.7.

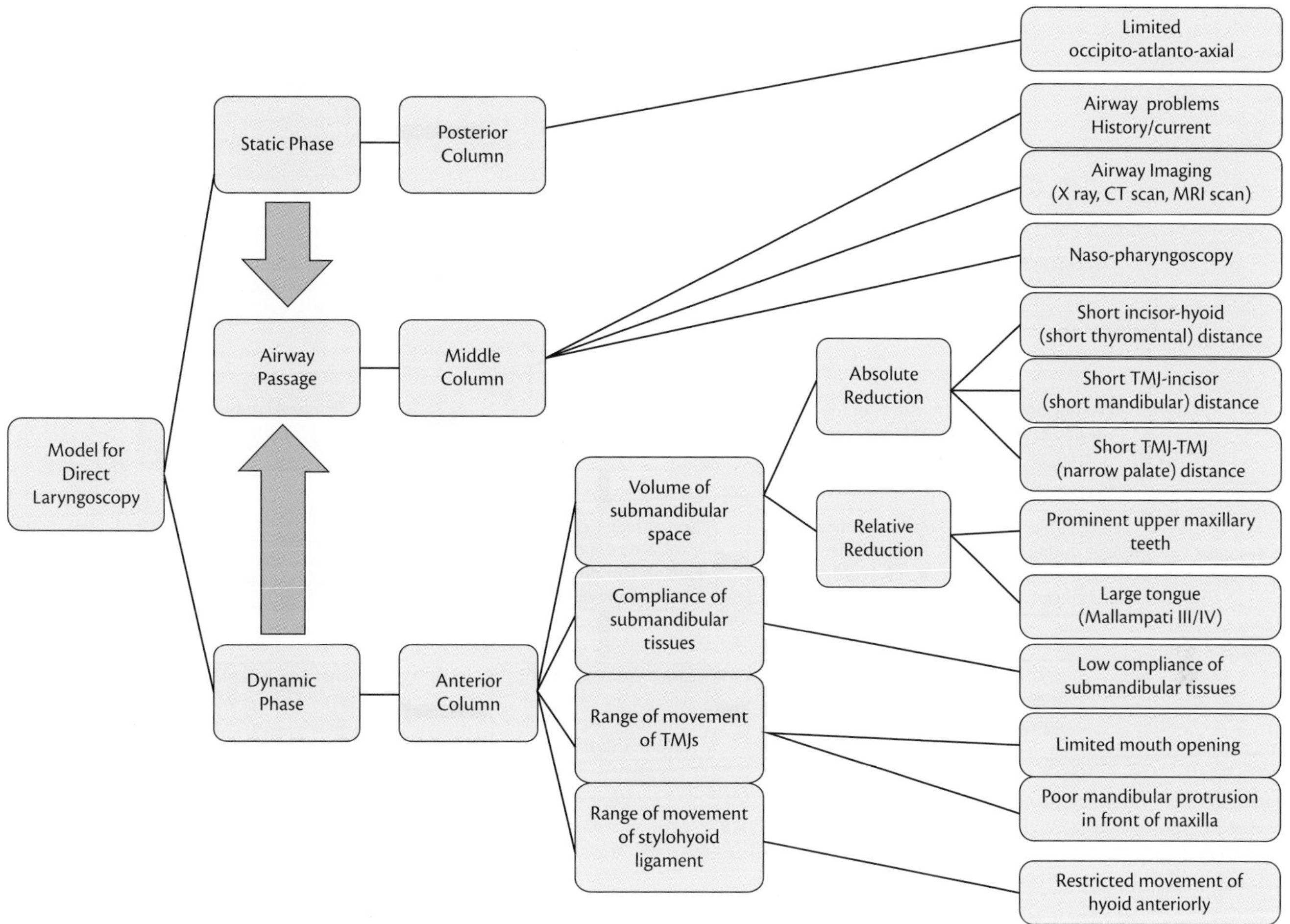

Figure 65.6 Integrated assessment of all three columns using the proposed 'model for direct laryngoscopy'. Incisor, lower front mandibular incisors; TMJ, temporomandibular joint.

Reproduced with permission of the Australian Society of Anaesthesiologists: Greenland, K. B., Airway assessment based on a three column model of direct laryngoscopy. *Anaesthesia Intensive Care*, Volume 38, Issue 1, pp. 14–9, Copyright © 2010 Australian Society of Anaesthetists.

Regional anaesthesia techniques

Regional anaesthesia has a role in head and neck surgery both as a sole technique for more minor procedures and as a method of adjunct intra- and postoperative analgesia. Some of the procedures are described in the following subsections. Choice of local anaesthetic solution depends on desired duration of block and drug availability.

Cocaine

Cocaine is an alkaloid extracted from the leaves of the South American shrub *Erythroxylum coca*. Its discovery as a local anaesthetic dates back to 1884 when Carl Koller, an ophthalmologist, demonstrated topical local anaesthesia of the eye (Goerig et al. 2012). It is commonly used topically in ENT surgery because of its potent local anaesthetic and vasoconstrictive effects that can reduce blood loss and improve the surgical field. Although there are safer alternatives available, cocaine is still the preference of many otorhinolaryngologists. Cocaine is an ester local anaesthetic that is rapidly absorbed by the nasal mucosa but there is individual variation in its local absorption. Its half-life is 45–90 min and it is metabolized in the plasma and the liver with its metabolites (benzoylecgonine, ecgonine methyl ester, and active norcocaine) excreted in the urine. Its vasoconstrictive effect is related to inhibiting the presynaptic reuptake of noradrenaline (norepinephrine) and dopamine and this also accounts for the central CNS effects of euphoria and hyperactivity (Latorre and Klimek 1999; Lange and Hillis 2001; Kloner and Rezkalla 2003). Cardiovascular effects include myocardial ischaemia and necrosis, uncontrolled hypertension, arrhythmias, aortic dissection, myocarditis, endocarditis, and cardiomyopathies (Latorre and Klimek 1999; Lange and Hillis 2001; Pozner et al. 2005; Torres et al. 2007). These cardiovascular complications are also the potential serious adverse effects of cocaine.

It is prepared as a 4–10% (40–100 mg ml^{-1}) clear solution. The recommended safe dose is 1.5 mg kg^{-1} (Harper and Jones 2006). Local absorption varies among different individuals depending on the degree of vasoconstriction (Latorre and Klimek 1999). Irrigation of the nasal mucosa enhances the absorption with an increase in cardiovascular adverse effects, although these are rare. It was found that mild adverse reactions, severe reactions, and mortality were 0.3%, 0.04%, and 0.005% respectively in a registry (Fleming et al. 1990). Adrenaline (epinephrine) may be used with cocaine to reduce local absorption and further improve haemostasis. However, there is a risk of potentiation of cocaine's sympathomimetic effect. It has been recommended that with careful selection and avoiding cocaine in patients with cardiovascular risks, a dose of 200 mg cocaine with

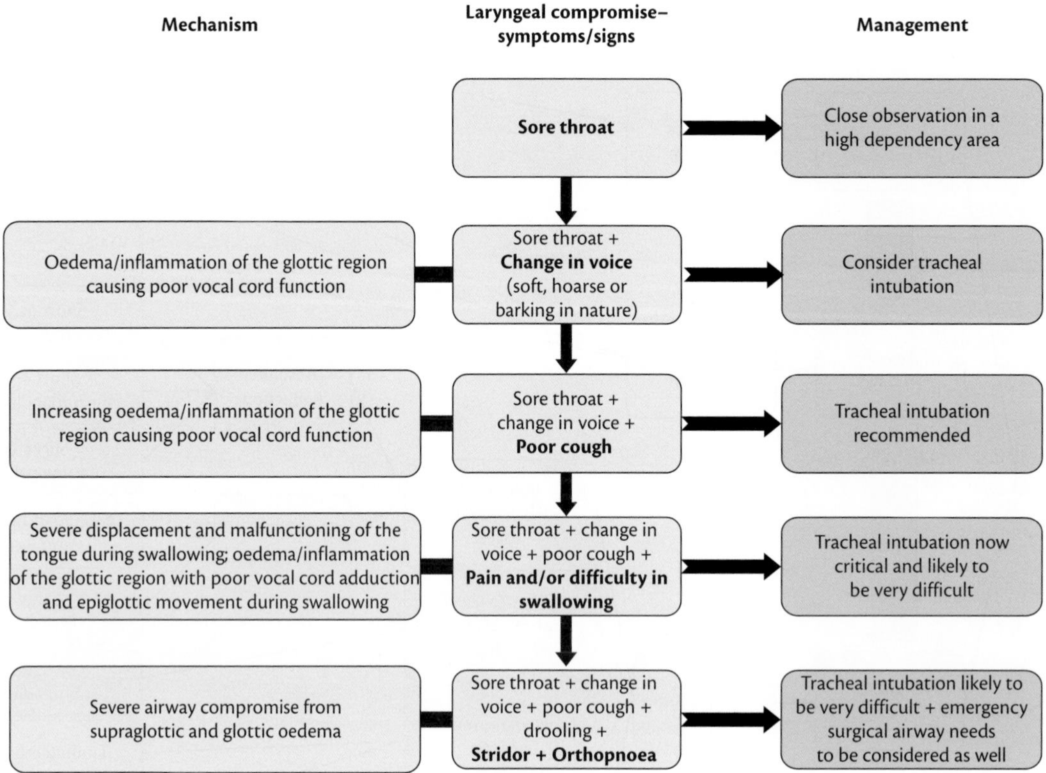

Figure 65.7 Signs and symptoms of laryngeal compromise with suggested clinical management.
Reproduced with permission of the Australian Society of Anaesthetists: Greenland, K. B., et al. Delayed airway compromise following extubation of adult patients who required surgical drainage of Ludwig's angina: comment on three coronial cases, *Anaesthesia Intensive Care*, Volume 39, Issue 3, pp. 506–8, Copyright © 2011 Australian Society of Anaesthetists.

10 ml lidocaine 2% and 1:100 000 adrenaline was found to avoid cardiovascular toxicity (Kara et al. 2001). Equally efficacious alternatives include lidocaine with 1:100 000 adrenaline or proprietary mixtures such as lidocaine 5% with phenylephrine 0.5% (Lennox et al. 1996). It has been recommended that non-cocaine preparations should be used in outpatient settings (Harper and Jones 2006).

Nasociliary nerve block

Anatomy

The ophthalmic nerve runs from the trigeminal ganglion to the eye via the cavernous sinus and the superior orbital fissure. The nasociliary nerve gives off the anterior ethmoid, the infratrochlear, and the long ciliary nerve. Block of this nerve gives anaesthesia of the anterolateral portions of the nose.

Technique

Injection is performed 1.5 cm above the medial canthus at the medial orbital wall with the needle advanced 2–3 cm posteriorly; 2 ml of local anaesthetic is injected.

Supraorbital and supratrochlear nerve block

Anatomy

The frontal nerve enters the orbit at the superior orbital fissure and divides into the supraorbital and supratrochlear nerves. This block can be used for forehead anaesthesia.

Technique

Palpation is performed to find the supraorbital notch and the needle is advanced until paraesthesia is felt in the distribution of the nerve: injection of 3 ml of local anaesthetic is made at this point. Then another 2 ml is injected at the point where the bridge of the nose meets the supraorbital ridge (i.e. the superior medial corner of the orbit).

Maxillary nerve block

Anatomy

The maxillary nerve starts from the trigeminal ganglion, travels through the cavernous sinus, and leaves the skull at the foramen rotundum to enter the pterygopalatine fossa where it gives off several branches to the mid face.

Technique

A needle is inserted just below the zygomatic arch midway between the coronoid and condyle of the mandible. It is inserted perpendicular to the skin until the pterygoid plate is felt. The needle is then withdrawn and guided anteriorly towards the eye to enter the pterygopalatine fossa. An injection of 5 ml of local anaesthetic is made when paraesthesia of the upper jaw is elicited. It should be noted that haemorrhage of the maxillary artery can cause haematoma in the hard and soft palate.

Infraorbital nerve block

Anatomy

This is the largest terminal branch of the maxillary nerve. It enters though the inferior orbital fissure and travels in the infraorbital foramen to innervate the incisors and canines and anterior gingival mucosa along with the skin and soft tissues of the cheek. It should be noted that blocking the infraorbital nerve does not provide anaesthesia to all the upper dentition. Maxillary nerve block should be used for this purpose.

Technique

The infraorbital foramen is located in a line between the pupil and the corner of the mouth just below the infraorbital rim. An injection of 3 ml of local anaesthetic is made at the site of exit of the nerve. The foramen can be approached from the skin or sublabially.

Sphenopalatine ganglion block

Anatomy

The sphenopalatine ganglion sits in the pterygopalatine fossa. Its main innervation is from the maxillary nerve, the greater superficial petrosal nerve, and sympathetic from the deep petrosal nerve. It supplies the periostium of the orbit and lacrimal gland, and gives off the posterior superior nasal nerve and the nasal palatine nerves that supply the gums, hard palate, soft palate, uvula, and part of the tonsils.

Technique

The greater palatine foramen is located at the posterior portion of the hard palate just medial to the gum line opposite the third molar. A needle is advanced 5 cm through the foramen and 3 ml of local anaesthetic is injected.

Mandibular nerve block

Anatomy

The mandibular nerve exits the foramen ovale and divides into an anterior motor branch and a posterior branch. The anterior motor branch supplies the medial pterygoid, tensor tympani, and tensor palatine muscles. The posterior branch supplies sensation for the lower third of the face and the pre-auricular area.

Technique

The patient is asked to open their mouth and the needle is advanced just below the zygomatic arch at the midpoint of the notch of the mandible until the pterygoid plate is felt. The needle is then withdrawn slightly and redirected posteriorly in the direction of the ear; 4–5 ml of local anaesthetic is injected here and upon withdrawal of the needle.

Inferior alveolar and lingual nerve blocks

Anatomy

The inferior alveolar nerve is the largest branch of the mandibular nerve and enters the mandibular canal giving off several branches in the canal to give sensation to the teeth before exiting the mental foramen to supply sensation to the chin. The lingual nerve travels anteriorly just medial to the mandible on the floor of the mouth where it is joined by the corda tympani nerve before travelling to the tongue. It also gives off branches to the submandibular and sublingual glands.

Technique

The inner surface of the mandible is infiltrated with 5 ml of local anaesthetic after advancing the needle about 4–5 cm deep, 2 cm superior, and just medial to the third mandibular molar tooth.

Auriculotemporal nerve block

Anatomy

The auriculotemporal nerve is the posterior branch of the mandibular branch of the trigeminal nerve. It passes between the external auditory canal and the temporomandibular joint and passes through the parotid gland to ascend with the superficial temporal artery over the zygomatic arch. It provides sensory intervention to the external auditory meatus, tympanic membrane, portions of the pinna, and the temporomandibular joint, and the skin of the temporal region and lateral part of the scalp.

Technique

Palpation of the temporal artery as it crosses the zygomatic arch near the root of the zygoma gives the approximate location of the nerve. Infiltration with 3 ml of local anaesthetic is given in this area.

Mental nerve block

Anatomy

The mental nerve is one of two terminal branches of the inferior alveolar nerve. It emerges from the mental canal to innervate the lower lip and gingival surface from the corner of the mouth to the midline. It is located just below or slightly posterior to the second premolar midway between the inferior and superior borders of the mandible.

Technique

The foramen is approached intraorally or through the skin with a 25 G needle and 2–3 ml of local anaesthetic is injected. It should be noted that entrance into the foramen with the needle poses risk of permanent nerve damage.

Nasal surgery blocks

Anatomy

The nose is supplied by the anterior and posterior ethmoidal nerves, multiple branches of the olfactory nerves, terminal branches from the sphenopalatine ganglion, and branches of the supratrochlear, nasociliary, and infraorbital nerves.

Technique

The nose is first sprayed with topical lidocaine 4%. Infiltration of the infraorbital, supratrochlear, and supraorbital nerves is next done with 5–10 ml of local anaesthetic, with 1 in 100 000 adrenaline. Pledgets of 4% cocaine are next used to further provide topical anaesthesia. Additional anaesthesia can be performed with injection of the sphenopalatine ganglion by an endoscopic technique just posterior to the medial attachment of the middle turbinate or via the greater palatine foramen.

Ear surgery blocks

Anatomy

The ear is innervated by branches of the greater auricular nerve and the auriculotemporal nerve. The external auditory canal is innervated by branches of the seventh, ninth, and tenth cranial nerves.

Technique

If surgery is to be done on the auricle, injection completely around the ear, with additional injection of the greater auricular nerve (see later) and the auriculotemporal nerve (as previously described above) is adequate. If surgery of the external auditory canal and middle ear is contemplated, an additional four-quadrant injection of 0.25–0.5 ml of local anaesthetic is necessary.

Cervical plexus blocks

Anatomy

The cervical plexus is formed by the ventral primary rami of the first four cervical nerves. Each ramus gives a superior and inferior branch that forms the nerve bundle of the cervical plexus. The deep nerves give off more superficial cutaneous branches that are the lesser occipital nerve, the greater auricular nerve, the suprascapular nerves, and smaller cutaneous branches. The deep cervical plexus gives motor supply to the deep musculature of the neck. The superficial branches merge from behind the midpoint of the sternocleidomastoid muscle, or Erb's point, to supply the overlying skin of the neck from the base of the skull to the clavicle.

Technique

Deep block

The patient is positioned with head turned away. A line drawn between the mastoid tip and the insertion of the sternomastoid muscle on the clavicle approximates the transverse processes of the cervical spine. Approximately 5 cm below the mastoid tip is the level of C3. A needle is inserted until the level of the transverse process of the spine is reached, then 5–10 ml of local anaesthetic is injected. This is done both above and below this mark by about 1 cm to achieve blocks of C2–C4. Care is taken to withdraw on the needle before injection to assure that CSF or blood is not aspirated. The deep block will produce some paralysis of the musculature of the neck. Bilateral deep nerve blocks can result in bilateral phrenic nerve paralysis with possible respiratory difficulty.

Superficial block

Erb's point is found midway between the origin and insertion of the sternomastoid muscle. An injection of 10 ml of local anaesthetic is made at the posterior border of the sternomastoid muscle and then 3–4 cm up and down the border.

Greater and lesser occipital nerve blocks

Anatomy

The greater occipital nerve arises from the dorsal primary ramus of the second and third cervical nerve. It gives sensation to the medial portion of the posterior scalp. The lesser occipital nerve arises from the ventral primary rami of the second and third cervical roots and supplies the cranial surface of the pinna and adjacent scalp.

Technique

The greater occipital nerve runs with the occipital artery and can be blocked by injecting 5–10 ml of local anaesthetic at the level of the superior nuchal line midway between the midline of the neck and the posterior border of the mastoid process. The lesser occipital nerve can be blocked by injecting 2.5 cm inferior and medial to this area. The occipital artery can often be palpated and used as a landmark for injection of both areas.

Greater auricular nerve block

Anatomy

The greater auricular nerve arises from the ventral rami of C2 and C3. It passes Erb's point to supply the skin in the region of the ear, angle of the jaw, and over the parotid gland.

Technique

See 'Superficial blocks' in 'Cervical plexus blocks'.

Glossopharyngeal nerve block

Anatomy

The glossopharyngeal nerve exits the jugular foramen and passes between the internal jugular vein and internal carotid artery staying lateral to the vagus and spinal accessory nerves to pass anteriorly in the neck. It gives off the tympanic nerve to the middle ear, the carotid nerve to the baroreceptors of the carotid body, the pharyngeal nerve which gives sensation to the pharynx, and the tonsillar nerve and sensory branches to the posterior one-third of the tongue.

Technique

This block can be used to treat glossopharyngeal neuralgia. The nerve is blocked just after leaving the jugular foramen. At 1 cm anterior and 1 cm inferior to the mastoid tip, a needle is inserted 2–3 cm until the styloid process is contacted. At this point, the needle is directed posteriorly and advanced another 1–2 cm. Aspiration is advised before injection of 3–5 ml of local anaesthetic. Block of the spinal accessory and hypoglossal nerves is usually achieved at the same time.

Laryngeal blocks

Anatomy

The nerve supply to the larynx is largely via the superior laryngeal nerve with a small contribution from the recurrent laryngeal nerves. The superior laryngeal nerve is a branch of the vagus nerve. It passes lateral to the pharynx and behind the internal carotid artery to divide into internal and external branches at the level of the hyoid bone. The internal branch gives sensation to the mucous membranes of the supraglottis and glottis, and the external branch supplies motor innervation to the cricothyroid muscle.

Technique

The larynx is best blocked either with a transcricothyroid injection or superior laryngeal nerve block or a combination of both. The cricothyroid membrane is palpated and 2 ml of 2% lidocaine is injected with a 22 G needle. The patient should be asked to take a deep breath before injection as they will cough after the injection, spreading the local anaesthetic towards the larynx. The hyoid bone and thyroid cartilage are palpated, and midway between these two structures 2 ml of 2% lidocaine is injected bilaterally. It is possible to feel a 'popping' sensation if the thyrohyoid ligament is pierced.

Declaration of interest

None declared.

References

Ahmed MZ, Vohra A. The reinforced laryngeal mask airway (RLMA) protects the airway in patients undergoing nasal surgery – an observational study of 200 patients. *Can J Anaesth* 2002; **49**: 863–6

Akin A, Bayram A, Esmaoglu A, *et al.* Dexmedetomidine vs midazolam for premedication of pediatric patients undergoing anesthesia. *Pediatric Anesthesia* 2012; **22**: 871–6

American Society of Anesthesiologists Task Force on Perioperative Blood Transfusion and Adjuvant Therapies. Practice guidelines for perioperative blood transfusion and adjuvant therapies: an updated report by the American Society of Anesthesiologists Task Force on Perioperative Blood Transfusion and Adjuvant Therapies. *Anesthesiology* 2006; **105**: 198–208

Atef A, Fawaz A. Comparison of laryngeal mask with endotracheal tube for anesthesia in endoscopic sinus surgery. *Am J Rhinol* 2008; **22**: 653–7

Baker AR, Baker AB. Anaesthesia for endoscopic sinus surgery. *Acta Anaesthesiol Scand* 2010; **54**: 795–803

Banic A, Krejci V, Erni D, Wheatley AM, Sigurdsson GH. Effects of sodium nitroprusside and phenylephrine on blood flow in free musculocutaneous flaps during general anesthesia. *Anesthesiology* 1999; **90**: 147–55

Baugh RF, Archer SM, Mitchell RB, *et al.* Clinical practice guideline: tonsillectomy in children. *Otolaryngol Head Neck Surg* 2011; **144**: S1–30

Baumann A, Caversaccio M. Hemostasis in endoscopic sinus surgery using a specific gelatin-thrombin based agent (FloSeal). *Rhinology* 2003; **41**: 244–9

Biglioli F, Mortini P, Goisis M, Bardazzi A, Boari N. Submental orotracheal intubation: an alternative to tracheotomy in transfacial cranial base surgery. *Skull Base* 2003; **13**: 189–95

Biro P. Jet ventilation for surgical interventions in the upper airway. *Anesthesiol Clin* 2010; **28**: 397–409

Bruppacher H, Reber A, Keller JP, Geiduschek J, Erb TO, Frei FJ. The effects of common airway maneuvers on airway pressure and flow in children undergoing adenoidectomies. *Anesth Analg* 2003; **97**: 29–34

Burger W, Chemnitius JM, Kneissl GD, Rucker G. Low-dose aspirin for secondary cardiovascular prevention—cardiovascular risks after its perioperative withdrawal versus bleeding risks with its continuation—review and meta-analysis. *J Intern Med* 2005; **257**: 399–414

Caner G, Olgun L, Gultekin G, Aydar L. Local anesthesia for middle ear surgery. *Otolaryngol Head Neck Surg* 2005; **133**: 295–7

Cardwell M, Siviter G, Smith A. Non-steroidal anti-inflammatory drugs and perioperative bleeding in paediatric tonsillectomy. *Cochrane Database Syst Rev* 2005; **2**: CD003591

Caron G, Paquin R, Lessard MR, Trepanier CA, Landry PE. Submental endotracheal intubation: an alternative to tracheotomy in patients with midfacial and panfacial fractures. *J Trauma* 2000; **48**: 235–40

Carr AS, Courtman S, Holtby H, *et al. APA Guidelines on the Prevention of Post-operative Vomiting in Children.* Association of Paediatric Anaesthetists of Great Britain and Ireland, 2009. Available from http://www.apagbi.org.uk/sites/default/files/APA_Guidelines_on_the_Prevention_of_Postoperative_Vomiting_in_Children.pdf

Chan JY, Wei WI. Critical appraisal of maxillary swing approach for nasopharyngeal carcinoma. *Expert Opin Ther Targets* 2012; **16**(Suppl 1): S111–7

Chegini S, Dhariwal DK. Review of evidence for the use of steroids in orthognathic surgery. *Br J Oral Maxillofac Surg* 2012; **50**: 97–101

Choi WS, Irwin MG, Samman N. The effect of tranexamic acid on blood loss during orthognathic surgery: a randomized controlled trial. *J Oral Maxillofac Surg* 2009; **67**: 125–33

Choi WS, Samman N. Risks and benefits of deliberate hypotension in anaesthesia: a systematic review. *Int J Oral Maxillofac Surg* 2008; **37**: 687–703

Chung CU, Yu JW, Bastidas N, Bartlett SP, Taylor JA. Utility of the ultrasonic scalpel in mandibular distraction osteogenesis. *J Craniofac Surg* 2012; **23**: 1279–82

Chung F, Yegneswaran B, Liao P, *et al.* STOP questionnaire: a tool to screen patients for obstructive sleep apnea. *Anesthesiology* 2008; **108**: 812–21

Cordeiro PG, Santamaria E, Hu QY, Heerdt P. Effects of vasoactive medications on the blood flow of island musculocutaneous flaps in swine. *Ann Plast Surg* 1997; **39**: 524–31

Dahmani S, Stany I, Brasher C, *et al.* Pharmacological prevention of sevoflurane- and desflurane-related emergence agitation in children: a meta-analysis of published studies. *Br J Anaesth* 2010; **104**: 216–23

Dan AEB, Thygesen TH, Pinholt EM. Corticosteroid administration in oral and orthognathic surgery: a systematic review of the literature and meta-analysis. *J Oral Maxillofac Surg* 2010; **68**: 2207–20

Degoute CS, Ray MJ, Manchon M, Dubreuil C, Banssillon V. Remifentanil and controlled hypotension; comparison with nitroprusside or esmolol during tympanoplasty. *Can J Anaesth* 2001; **48**: 20–7

Devereaux PJ, Mrkobrada M, Sessler DI, *et al.* Aspirin in patients undergoing noncardiac surgery. *N Engl J Med* 2014; **370**: 1494–503

Difficult Airway Society Extubation Guidelines Group, Popat M, Mitchell V, *et al.* Difficult Airway Society Guidelines for the management of tracheal extubation. *Anaesthesia* 2012; **67**:318–40

Egan TD, Wong KC. Perioperative smoking cessation and anesthesia: a review. *J Clin Anesth* 1992; **4**: 63–72

Figus A, Wade RG, Oakey S, Ramakrishnan VV. Intraoperative esophageal Doppler hemodynamic monitoring in free perforator flap surgery. *Ann Plast Surg* 2013; **70**: 301–7

Fleming JA, Byck R, Barash PG. Pharmacology and therapeutic applications of cocaine. *Anesthesiology* 1990; **73**: 518–31

Francon D, Jaber S, Pean D, Bally B, Marciniak B. [Difficult extubation: extubation criteria and management of risk situations: question 6. Societe Francaise d'Anesthesie et de Reanimation]. *Ann Fr Anesth Reanim* 2008; **27**: 46–53

Friedman M, Wilson M, Lin HC, Chang HW. Updated systematic review of tonsillectomy and adenoidectomy for treatment of pediatric obstructive sleep apnea/hypopnea syndrome. *Otolaryngol Head Neck Surg* 2009; **140**: 800–8

Gerstein NS, Schulman PM, Gerstein WH, Petersen TR, Tawil I. Should more patients continue aspirin therapy perioperatively?: clinical impact of aspirin withdrawal syndrome. *Ann Surg* 2012; **255**: 811–9

Goerig M, Bacon D, Van Zundert A. Carl Koller, cocaine, and local anesthesia: some less known and forgotten facts. *Reg Anesth Pain Med* 2012; **37**: 318–24

Grainger J, Saravanappa N. Local anaesthetic for post-tonsillectomy pain: a systematic review and meta-analysis. *Clin Otolaryngol* 2008; **33**: 411–9

Greenland KB. Airway assessment based on a three column model of direct laryngoscopy. *Anaesth Intensive Care* 2010; **38**: 14–9

Greenland KB, Acott C, Segal R, Riley RH, Merry AF. Delayed airway compromise following extubation of adult patients who required surgical drainage of Ludwig's angina: comment on three coronial cases. *Anaesth Intensive Care* 2011; **39**: 506–8

Guerriero C, Cairns J, Perel P, Shakur H, Roberts I. Cost-effectiveness analysis of administering tranexamic acid to bleeding trauma patients using evidence from the CRASH-2 trial. *PLoS One* 2011; **6**: e18987

Gupta A, Stierer T, Zuckerman R, Sakima N, Parker SD, Fleisher LA. Comparison of recovery profile after ambulatory anesthesia with propofol, isoflurane, sevoflurane and desflurane: a systematic review. *Anesth Analg* 2004; **98**: 632–41

Hall CE, Shutt LE. Nasotracheal intubation for head and neck surgery. *Anaesthesia* 2003; **58**: 249–56

Harper SJ, Jones NS. Cocaine: what role does it have in current ENT practice? A review of the current literature. *J Laryngol Otol* 2006; **120**: 808–11

Hennekens CH. Aspirin in the treatment and prevention of cardiovascular disease: current perspectives and future directions. *Curr Atheroscler Rep* 2007; **9**: 409–16

Irwin MG, Trinh T, Yao CL. Occupational exposure to anaesthetic gases: a role for TIVA. *Expert Opin Drug Saf* 2009; **8**: 473–83

Iynen I, Bozkus F, San I, Alatas N. The hemostatic efficacy of Ankaferd Blood Stopper in adenoidectomy. *Int J Pediatr Otorhinolaryngol* 2011; **75**: 1292–5

Jöhr M. Anaesthesia for tonsillectomy. *Curr Opin Anesthesiol* 2006; **19**: 260–1

Judelman H. Anaesthesia for laryngoscopy and microsurgery of the larynx. *S Afr Med J* 1974; **48**: 462–4

Jundt JS, Cattano D, Hagberg CA, Wilson JW. Submental intubation: a literature review. *Int J Oral Maxillofac Surg* 2012; **41**: 46–54

Kaplan A, Crosby GJ, Bhattacharyya N. Airway protection and the laryngeal mask airway in sinus and nasal surgery. *Laryngoscope* 2004; **114**: 652–5

Kara CO, Kaftan A, Atalay H, Pinar HS, Ogmen G. Cardiovascular safety of cocaine anaesthesia in the presence of adrenaline during septal surgery. *J Otolaryngol* 2001; **30**: 145–8

Ker K, Edwards P, Perel P, Shakur H, Roberts I. Effect of tranexamic acid on surgical bleeding: systematic review and cumulative meta-analysis. *BMJ* 2012; **344**: e3054

Ker K, Beecher D, Roberts I. Topical application of tranexamic acid for the reduction of bleeding. *Cochrane Database Syst Rev* 2013; **23**: CD010562

Kezirian EJ, Hohenhorst W, De Vries N. Drug-induced sleep endoscopy: the VOTE classification. *Eur Arch Otorhinolaryngol* 2011; **268**: 1233–6

Kloner RA, Rezkalla SH. Cocaine and the heart. *N Engl J Med* 2003; **348**: 487–8

Krohner RG. Anesthetic considerations and techniques for oral and maxillofacial surgery. *Int Anesthesiol Clin* 2003; **41**: 67–89

Krupp NL, Weinstein G, Chalian A, Berlin JA, Wolf P, Weber RS. Validation of a transfusion prediction model in head and neck cancer surgery. *Arch Otolaryngol Head Neck Surg* 2003; **129**: 1297–302

Lange RA, Hillis LD. Cardiovascular complications of cocaine use. *N Engl J Med* 2001; **345**: 351–8

Latorre F, Klimek L. Does cocaine still have a role in nasal surgery? *Drug Saf* 1999; **20**: 9–13

Lennox P, Hern J, Birchall M, Lund V. Local anaesthesia in flexible nasendoscopy. A comparison between cocaine and co-phenylcaine. *J Laryngol Otol* 1996; **110**: 540–2

Lin AC, Koltai PJ. Sleep endoscopy in the evaluation of pediatric obstructive sleep apnea. *Int J Pediatr* 2012; **2012**; 576719

Miller RD. *Miller's Anesthesia*. Hershey, PA: Elsevier Churchill, 2005

Morgan EG, Mikhail MS, Murray MJ. *Clinical Anesthesiology* New York: Lange Medical Books/McGraw-Hill, 2006

Mort TC. Continuous airway access for the difficult extubation: the efficacy of the airway exchange catheter. *Anesth Analg* 2007; **105**: 1357–62

O'Malley BW, Jr, Weinstein GS, Snyder W, Hockstein NG. Transoral robotic surgery (TORS) for base of tongue neoplasms. *Laryngoscope* 2006; **116**: 1465–72

Ono K, Hirayama C, Ishii K, Okamoto Y, Hidaka H. Emergency airway management of patients with peritonsillar abscess. *J Anesth* 2004; **18**: 55–8

Pozner CN, Levine M, Zane R. The cardiovascular effects of cocaine. *J Emerg Med* 2005; **29**: 173–8

Pringle MB, Croft CB. A grading system for patients with obstructive sleep apnoea--based on sleep nasendoscopy. *Clin Otolaryngol Allied Sci* 1993; **18**: 480–4

Qiao Q, Zhou G, Chen GY, Ling YC, Zhang F, Buncke HJ. Application of hemodilution in microsurgical free flap transplantation. *Microsurgery* 1996; **17**: 487–90

Rohling RG, Zimmermann AP, Breymann C. Intravenous versus oral iron supplementation for preoperative stimulation of hemoglobin synthesis using recombinant human erythropoietin. *J Hematother Stem Cell Res* 2000; **9**: 497–500

Salami A, Dellepiane M, Crippa B, Barettini L, Mora R. Visual-vestibular interaction test in the diagnosis of vertigo in children. *Int J Pediatr Otorhinolaryngol* 2008; **72**: 1–7

Sanders RD, Weimann J, Maze M. Biologic effects of nitrous oxide: a mechanistic and toxicologic review. *Anesthesiology* 2008; **109**: 707–22

Scholz A, Pugh S, Fardy M, Shafik M, Hall JE. The effect of dobutamine on blood flow of free tissue transfer flaps during head and neck reconstructive surgery. *Anaesthesia* 2009; **64**: 1089–93

Shah MD, Goldstein DP, McCluskey SA, *et al.* Blood transfusion prediction in patients undergoing major head and neck surgery with free-flap reconstruction. *Arch Otolaryngol Head Neck Surg* 2010; **136**: 1199–204

Shiga T, Wajima Z, Inoue T, Sakamoto A. Predicting difficult intubation in apparently normal patients: a meta-analysis of bedside screening test performance. *Anesthesiology* 2005; **103**: 429–37

Talmage EA. Endotracheal tube is not necessary for laryngeal microsurgery. *Anesthesiology* 1981; **55**: 332

Teltzrow T, Kramer F-J, Schulze A, Baethge C, Brachvogel P. Perioperative complications following sagittal split osteotomy of the mandible. *J Craniomaxillofac Surg* 2005; **33**: 307–13

Tirelli G, Bigarini S, Russolo M, Lucangelo U, Gullo A. Total intravenous anaesthesia in endoscopic sinus-nasal surgery. *Acta Otorhinolaryngol Ital* 2004; **24**: 137–44

Torres M, Rocha S, Rebelo A, *et al.* Cardiovascular toxicity of cocaine of iatrogenic origin. Case report. *Rev Port Cardiol* 2007; **26**: 1395–404

Tsui BCH, Wagner A, Cave D, Elliott C, El-Hakim H, Malherbe S. The incidence of laryngospasm with a "no touch" extubation technique after tonsillectomy and adenoidectomy. *Anesth Analg* 2004; **98**: 327–9

Walton J, Ebner Y, Stewart MG, April MM. Systematic review of randomized controlled trials comparing intracapsular tonsillectomy with total tonsillectomy in a pediatric population. *Arch Otolaryngol Head Neck Surg* 2012; **138**: 243–9

Ward PH, Castro DJ, Ward S. A significant new contribution to radical head and neck surgery. The argon beam coagulator as an effective means of limiting blood loss. *Arch Otolaryngol Head Neck Surg* 1989; **115**: 921–3

Weber RS, Byers RM, Robbins KT, *et al.* Electrosurgical dissection to reduce blood loss in head and neck surgery. *Head Neck* 1989; **11**: 318–24

Wei WI. Cancer of the nasopharynx: functional surgical salvage. *World J Surg* 2003; **27**: 844–8

Wei WI, Chan JY, Ng RW, Ho WK. Surgical salvage of persistent or recurrent nasopharyngeal carcinoma with maxillary swing approach—critical appraisal after 2 decades. *Head Neck* 2011; **33**: 969–75

Weinstein GS, O'Malley BW, Jr, Snyder W, Sherman E, Quon H. Transoral robotic surgery: radical tonsillectomy. *Arch Otolaryngol Head Neck Surg* 2007; **133**: 1220–6

Williams PJ, Bailey PM. Comparison of the reinforced laryngeal mask airway and tracheal intubation for adenotonsillectomy. *Br J Anaesth* 1993; **70**: 30–3

Wilson W, Taubert KA, Gewitz M, *et al.* Prevention of infective endocarditis: guidelines from the American Heart Association: a guideline from the American Heart Association Rheumatic Fever, Endocarditis, and Kawasaki Disease Committee, Council on Cardiovascular Disease in the Young, and the Council on Clinical Cardiology, Council on Cardiovascular Surgery and Anesthesia, and the Quality of Care and Outcomes Research Interdisciplinary Working Group. *Circulation* 2007; **116**: 1736–54

World Health Organization. *Summary of the Report of the 18th Meeting of the WHO Expert Committee on the Selection and Use of Essential Medicines*. Available from http://www.who.int/selection_medicines/committees/TRS_web_summary.pdf?ua=1

Xiao P, Zhang XS. Adult laryngotracheal surgery. *Anesthesiol Clin* 2010; **28**: 529–40

Yung MW. Local anaesthesia in middle ear surgery: survey of patients and surgeons. *Clin Otolaryngol Allied Sci* 1996; **21**: 404–8

CHAPTER 66

Obstetric anaesthesia and analgesia

Peter Biro and Marc Van de Velde

Physiological changes associated with pregnancy

Major changes in normal female physiology occur during pregnancy, labour, delivery, and in the immediate postpartum period. These changes have to be considered during anaesthetic practice. Hence, anaesthetists should recognize and understand these physiological adaptations. These changes are induced by hormonal mechanisms and the enlarging uterus and are present from the first weeks of pregnancy, peaking around 34 weeks of gestation.

Respiratory system

Oxygen demand and consumption are increased during pregnancy. Oxygen delivery to tissue is increased because cardiac output is higher and the maternal oxyhaemoglobin dissociation curve is shifted to the right. Minute ventilation is also significantly increased. As a result, a mild respiratory alkalosis is present during pregnancy, partly compensated by decreased bicarbonate concentrations. Functional residual capacity is lower by approximately 20%. Airway management becomes more demanding when gestation progresses because of higher body weight, short neck, enlarged breasts, nasopharyngeal oedema, capillary engorgement, and the increased susceptibility of the mucosa of the respiratory tract and the pharynx to be traumatized.

The pregnant patient is more prone to hypoxaemia because of decreased functional residual capacity and increased oxygen consumption. Careful denitrogenation before induction of general anaesthesia is therefore recommended. Mild respiratory alkalosis and reduced arterial $P\text{CO}_2$ levels should be maintained during artificial ventilation as both hyper- and hypocarbia can compromise uteroplacental perfusion.

Cardiovascular system

The total blood volume increases by 35% with a red blood cell volume increase of 20% and a plasma volume increase of approximately 45%. Hence, a state of pregnancy-induced relative anaemia develops. Cardiac output, stroke volume, and heart rate are increased. Myocardial contractility is unchanged and systemic vascular resistance is decreased. Despite increased blood volume and increased cardiac output, the enlarged uterus causes compression of the inferior vena cava and the aorta resulting in the so-called supine hypotensive syndrome. Positioning of the patient with left lateral displacement of the uterus is required to avoid the supine hypotensive syndrome.

A state of hypercoagulability develops. Pregnant patients are more prone to thromboembolic complications, and therefore adequate prophylactic measures should be taken including prophylactic administration of low-molecular-weight heparin.

Gastrointestinal changes

The enlarging uterus causes increased gastric pressure. Combined with a decreased lower oesophageal sphincter tone and delayed gastric emptying, the chance of gastric regurgitation is increased: the acidity of the gastric contents is also increased. Acid aspiration prophylaxis is therefore recommended to reduce gastric content and raise gastric pH.

Central nervous system

Central nervous system depression occurs secondary to increased progesterone concentrations. There is increased peripheral nerve sensitivity. The epidural space capacity is reduced as a result of engorgement of the epidural venous plexus. Pregnant patients are more prone to the effects of inhalation anaesthetics, neuromuscular blocking agents, and local anaesthetics.

Renal physiological changes

Renal anatomy and physiology are significantly affected by pregnancy with changes to kidney size as well as glomerular and tubular function. Healthy women accommodate to the changes of pregnancy by the up-regulation of vasodilatory and the down-regulation of vasoconstricting hormones. In the kidneys, these hormonal alterations result in dilatation of the collecting system with a small increase in renal size as well as vasodilation with increased renal plasma flow and glomerular filtration rate. The decreased renal tubular threshold for bicarbonate reabsorption results in a net decrease in serum bicarbonate by 4–5 mmol litre^{-1}, despite progesterone-governed stimulation of the respiratory centre.

Labour analgesia

Although many women will deliver without needing pain relief, many prefer some form of analgesia during the birth process. Worldwide, pethidine (meperidine) and nitrous oxide analgesia are used most frequently, but particularly in the developed world, more and more women opt for neuraxial blocks to alleviate labour pain. When providing neuraxial analgesia, the anaesthetist has to make several choices: how will analgesia be initiated, how will analgesia be maintained, which local anaesthetic will be used for neuraxial analgesia, and with which adjuvant drugs?

Initiation of neuraxial analgesia

Initiation of neuraxial labour analgesia is possible using either conventional epidural analgesia or combined spinal–epidural (CSE) analgesia (Escarment and Clement 1989; Camann et al. 1993; Collis et al. 1994; Rawal et al. 2000; Paech 2003; Rawal 2005; Van Houwe et al. 2006; Fun et al. 2008; Petre et al. 2008). Obstetric anaesthetists are divided when questioned on the place of CSE to produce labour analgesia (Russell 1999; Collis 2002; Russell 2002; Kuczkowski 2007; Preston 2007). Simmons et al. (2007) published a Cochrane review concluding that CSE offers little benefit as compared with conventional epidural analgesia. However, the authors did acknowledge that CSE produced faster analgesia, resulted in less need for rescue analgesia, and was associated with less urinary retention. This Cochrane review can be criticized. Firstly, a number of well-performed studies were excluded from analysis for obscure reasons. Secondly, a number of outcomes were not considered in the analysis such as unilateral analgesia, epidural catheter reliability, anaesthetist intervention rate, local anaesthetic consumption, and the occurrence of fetal heart abnormalities.

Consistently, effective labour analgesia is accomplished within 4–6 min after intrathecal injection (Camann et al. 1993; Stacey et al. 1993; Abouleish et al. 1994; Collis et al. 1994, 1995; Joos et al. 1995; Gautier et al. 1997; Palmer et al. 1998; Van de Velde et al. 1999, 2004; Nickells et al. 2000; Comparative Obstetric Mobile Epidural Trial Study Group 2001; Hughes et al. 2001; Vercauteren et al. 2001b; Vernis et al. 2004). After conventional epidural analgesia, pain reduction is usually achieved after 15–25 min. Moreover, with epidural analgesia a wide inter-patient variability exists depending on parity, stage of labour, and other obstetric and non-obstetric factors. Especially during late labour, analgesia after an epidural injection is often delayed and only successful if large doses are administered.

Some trials demonstrated lower visual analogue (pain) scale (VAS) scores with CSE as compared with epidural analgesia (Collis et al. 1995; Stocks et al. 2001; Kayacan et al. 2006), but others noticed no difference (Price et al. 1998; Hepner et al. 2000; Nickells et al. 2000).

Most anaesthetists would agree that CSE provides better quality analgesia throughout the course of labour (Landau 2002). Vernis et al. (2004) reported unilateral analgesia with CSE. Interestingly, Hess et al. (2001) found that patients treated with conventional epidural analgesia were three times as likely to experience recurrent breakthrough pain as compared with CSE-treated women. In contrast, however, Goodman et al. (2009) noted no difference.

The presence of a dural puncture may facilitate the passage of epidurally administered drugs during maintenance of analgesia to the cerebrospinal fluid (Leighton et al. 1996; Swenson et al. 1996). Cappiello et al. (2008) performed a randomized, double-blind study in which the dura was perforated with a 25 G Whitacre needle without administration of spinal drugs. The control group had no dural puncture. Patients treated with a dural puncture had better sacral spread, shorter time to onset of analgesia, and better quality pain relief. Thomas et al. (2005) performed a similar study using a 27 G Whitacre needle and could not find a difference between patients treated with or without a dural puncture. Several studies have demonstrated that CSE results in less local anaesthetic consumption (Collis et al. 1995; Comparative Obstetric Mobile Epidural Trial Study Group 2001; Van de Velde et al. 2004; Vernis et al. 2004).

After initial spinal analgesia, bilateral analgesia and sensory changes occur, making testing of the epidural catheter difficult. However various investigators noted that the reliability of epidural catheters after CSE was significantly increased as compared with stand-alone epidural catheters (Norris 2000; Norris et al. 2001; Van de Velde et al. 2001a; Wilson et al. 2002; Thomas et al. 2005; Cappiello et al. 2008; Miro et al. 2008; Lee et al. 2009) (Table 66.1). There was less need for epidural catheter replacement and a reduced incidence of unilateral analgesia requiring catheter manipulation.

When using a CSE technique, a perfect midline approach is required to identify the subarachnoid space and consequently the epidural catheter is more reliably positioned in the epidural space (Van de Velde et al. 2001a). Thomas et al. (2005) interestingly noted that when no cerebrospinal fluid was obtained after attempted CSE, more epidural catheters required replacement as compared with those catheters placed when cerebrospinal fluid was noted.

Overall, CSE analgesia seems to confer some advantages in terms of quality of pain relief as compared with a conventional epidural technique. However, this may come at the expense of an increased incidence of side-effects. Pruritus is the most common side effect of intrathecal opioids, occurring in almost all patients, if directly questioned (Collis et al. 1995; Van de Velde et al. 2004; Vernis et al. 2004; Miro et al. 2008). It usually develops shortly after onset of analgesia. It is mild and hardly ever requires antipruritic therapy. Nausea and vomiting are very rare complications during CSE and conventional epidural analgesia. Miro et al. (2008) reported more nausea and vomiting in patients treated with epidural analgesia.

Both CSE and conventional epidural analgesia have been associated with mild hypotension, which is easily treated by avoiding the supine position and by intravenous fluids or, if necessary, vasopressors such as ephedrine or phenylephrine (Norris et al. 1994; Shennan et al. 1995; Moschini et al. 2006).

There have been several reports of respiratory depression after intrathecal administration of lipid-soluble opioids (Palmer 1991; Hays and Palmer 1994; Baker and Sarna 1995; Greenhalgh 1996; Ferouz et al. 1997; Lu et al. 1997; Katsiris et al. 1998; Hughes et al. 2001; Pan et al. 2004). Fortunately symptoms typically occurred within the first 30 min and were easily treated and reversed by naloxone. In one patient, chest compressions and resuscitation was

Table 66.1 Reliability of epidural catheters: percentage of failed epidural catheters not producing adequate analgesia and that were resited

	Combined–spinal epidural	Epidural
Norris (2000)	0.2%	1.3%
COMET Study Group (2001)	4.0%	6.8%
Van de Velde (2001a)	1.49%	3.18%
Thomas et al. (2005)	9.3%	8.0%*
Cappiello et al. (2008)	3%	13%
Lee et al. (2009)	1%	6%
Miro et al. (2008)	3.4%	6.2%

* Thomas et al. reported more catheter replacement when the spinal component failed (22.2%).

Data from various sources, see references.

required (Pan et al. 2004). Ferrouz et al. (1997) performed a retrospective medical records analysis and reported one respiratory arrest in more than 5000 CSE cases performed with 10 μg of spinal sufentanil. As this complication is rare, most authors advocate vigilance and advise the use of lower doses of intrathecal opioids then those initially suggested on empirical grounds (Albright and Forster 1999). Other complications related to excessive rostral spread of opioids and local anaesthetics include aphonia, aphagia, dysphagia, altered levels of consciousness, high sensory block, and transient swallowing difficulties (Hamilton and Cohen 1995; Currier et al. 1997; Fragneto and Fisher 2000; Scavone 2002; Kuczkowski and Goldsworthy 2003; Coleman et al. 2009). Sudden hypoglycaemia has also been described (Crites and Ramanathan 2000; Kuczkowski 2003a).

Some authorities claim that the risk of central nervous system infection is increased secondary to the breach of the dura with CSE (Bromage 1999). However, two publications both agree that there is currently no scientific evidence indicating that CSE analgesia is associated with more infections than epidural analgesia (Camann et al. 2000; Birnbach and Ojea 2002). Indeed, several case reports of meningitis or epidural abscess have been described after CSE and epidural anaesthesia in obstetric patients (Berga and Trierweiler 1989; Harding et al. 1994; Aldebert and Sleth 1996; Cascio and Heath 1996; Bouhemad et al. 1998; Pickering et al. 1999; Vernis et al. 2004; Davies et al. 2009). Despite these occasional case reports, central nervous system infections remain extremely rare irrespective of the neuraxial technique used. Five publications evaluate the risk of infections after neuraxial anaesthesia in obstetric patients (Crawford 1985; Scott and Hibbard 1990; Palot et al. 1994; Paech et al. 1998; Albright and Forster 1999). In more than 900 000 patients, only two cases of epidural abscess and three cases of meningitis were reported.

Several cases of damage to the conus medullaris in pregnant women have been reported when using CSE (Reynolds 2001). Especially with CSE, it is imperative to perform the block as low as possible as the conus medullaris might extend below the L2 vertebral body, which is the case in 5% of parturients (Carvalho 2008). To avoid conus damage, careful recognition of the correct interspace is required. By means of radiography and ultrasound, it has been clearly demonstrated that most anaesthetists who used anatomical landmarks, erred by one to four interspaces from the intended interspace (Whitty et al. 2007; Carvalho 2008). Ultrasound may be useful, especially in obese patients, to identify or confirm the correct interspace (Carvalho 2008).

As CSE includes a dural puncture, there is a theoretical risk of post-dural puncture headache. This is a disabling complication in an otherwise healthy mother, keen on taking care of her newborn child. However the introduction of small-gauge atraumatic spinal needles (26–29 G) has dramatically decreased the problem. From the available literature it seems that post-dural puncture headache occurs in no more than 1% of patients. Furthermore the incidence is not increased as compared with conventional epidural analgesia (Norris et al. 1994; Collis et al. 1995; Mandell et al. 1996; Nageotte et al. 1997; Norris 2000; Norris et al. 2001; Birnbach and Ojea 2002; Landau 2002; Wilson et al. 2002; Vernis et al. 2004; Miro et al. 2008; Van de Velde et al. 2008). Rarely the spinal needle itself is responsible for post-dural puncture headache. Usually a dural tap with either the Tuohy needle or the epidural catheter causes the headache. After an accidental dural tap, threading the epidural catheter intrathecally seems to reduce the incidence and severity of post-dural puncture headache (Cohen et al. 1989; Norris and Leighton 1990; Rutter et al. 2001; Van de Velde et al. 2008).

Low-dose epidurals are successfully used to allow labouring women to maintain mobility whilst being fairly pain free (Nageotte et al. 1997; Comparative Obstetric Mobile Epidural Trial Study Group 2001). With CSE it is easier to provide effective analgesia with no or very small doses of local anaesthetics. As already described, CSE decreased total local anaesthetic consumption (Collis et al. 1995; Comparative Obstetric Mobile Epidural Trial Study Group 2001; Van de Velde et al. 2004) and decreased the occurrence of motor block compared with standard epidural techniques (Collis et al. 1995; Nageotte et al. 1997; Comparative Obstetric Mobile Epidural Trial Study Group 2001; Van de Velde et al. 2004). Especially, when labour is prolonged, CSE results in more women with normal motor power as was demonstrated by Wilson et al. (2009).

Some authors have questioned the safety of walking during labour when using neuraxial analgesia. However, others have demonstrated that motor function and balance remained intact with CSE, whilst low-dose epidurals induced clinically detectable dorsal column deficits (Davis et al. 1993; Buggy 1999; Pickering et al. 1999). Ambulation has become common practice and can be advised, provided adequate precautions, written protocols, and testing of motor function after initiation of analgesia are performed. It is also advisable to ask the partner to stand and go with the mother when she is moving in order to give support when necessary. Motor function testing is straightforward and includes the ability to perform a deep knee bend unassisted and to perform a straight leg lift for 30 s with the eyes closed. Caution is required when using epidural test doses after insertion of an epidural catheter, as test doses can significantly impair motor strength (Cohen et al. 2000). Controversy also exists regarding the effects of spinally administered adrenaline (epinephrine) (28,106) on motor block. Whilst minute doses do not impair motor function, larger doses have a significant impact (Palmer 1991; Gurbet et al. 2005).

Epidural analgesia has been implicated in prolonged labour, an increased instrumental delivery rate, and a higher Caesarean section rate. There is expert consensus that epidural analgesia does not produce more operative deliveries. However, epidural analgesia prolongs the duration of the first stage of labour and may increase the need for exogenous oxytocin.

Abnormal fetal heart rate recordings and fetal bradycardia are worrisome side-effects that may follow any type of effective labour analgesia. Some authors reported that this complication could be more common after intrathecal opioids than after conventional epidural analgesia (Honet et al. 1992; Cohen et al. 1993; Clarke et al. 1994; Kuczkowski 2004). Clarke et al. (1994) were the first to describe in detail the association between intrathecal opioids, uterine hyperactivity, and fetal bradycardia in the absence of maternal hypotension. Since then, several non-randomized trials have evaluated the incidence of fetal heart rate changes after either intrathecal opioids or conventional epidural analgesia (Nielsen et al. 1996; Palmer et al. 1999; Van de Velde et al. 2001a, 2001b). Nielsen et al. (1996) and Eberle et al. (1998) did not observe an increased incidence of fetal heart rate abnormalities, whilst all other non-randomized reports noted at least a doubling of the incidence of worrisome fetal heart rate changes.

Mardirossof et al. (2002) performed a meta-analysis of several prospective trials comparing intrathecal opioid analgesia with non-intrathecal opioid analgesia with respect to fetal bradycardia. These authors concluded that intrathecal opioids were associated with significantly more fetal heart rate abnormalities. Vercauteren et al. (1997) suggested that the incidence of fetal bradycardia depended on the dose of the intrathecal opioid. Van de Velde et al. (2004) concluded that high doses of intrathecal opioids increased the incidence of fetal heart rate abnormalities despite a reduced incidence of hypotension. Similar results were published by Nicolet et al. (2008). These authors also indicated that older age and higher VAS scores before analgesia were risk factors associated with fetal heart rate abnormalities after CSE. Gaiser et al. (2005) suggested that the risk of abnormalities in the fetal heart rate is increased when the baby's head is not engaged or when decelerations are already present before initiation of analgesia. The presumed mechanism of opioid-induced fetal heart rate abnormalities is uterine hyperactivity caused by rapid analgesia and, as a result, a rapid decrease in circulating maternal catecholamines. Abrao et al. (2009) measured uterine tone using an intrauterine pressure catheter after either CSE or conventional epidural analgesia and noticed slight increases in uterine tone.

However, in this context it is important to note that neonatal and obstetric outcome is not affected by the use of intrathecal opioids. Abrao et al. found no changes in fetal oxygen saturation after CSE analgesia (Abrao et al. 2009). In none of the reports was emergency Caesarean section required as a result of opioid-induced fetal heart rate abnormalities (Nielsen et al. 1996; Eberle et al. 1998; Kahn and Hubert 1998; Palmer et al. 1999; Van de Velde et al. 2001a; Vercauteren et al. 2001b; Van de Velde et al. 2004; Gaiser et al. 2005). Neither was neonatal outcome, as assessed by Apgar scores, umbilical artery pH, or admission to the neonatal intensive care, affected by the chosen technique. Albright and Forster (1997) performed an institutional retrospective survey involving 2500 patient records and observed no increase in emergency Caesarean delivery associated with the use of intrathecal opioids. In contrast, Gambling et al. (1998) reported an increased Caesarean section rate as a result of fetal heart rate abnormalities. However, they also found that neonatal outcome was good and similar to the epidural group.

As epidural catheters can inadvertently be misplaced in either the cerebrospinal fluid or in an epidural vein, test doses to verify the correct position of the catheter are commonly used. Unfortunately, test doses are neither sensitive nor specific (Colonna-Romano et al. 1992; Norris et al. 1999). Furthermore, test doses containing adrenaline can induce motor impairment sufficient to impair ambulation during labour (Cohen et al. 2000). Some authors also suggest that an adrenaline-containing test dose has potential adverse effects on uteroplacental perfusion (Marcus et al. 1998). As a result, it has been proposed to abandon the routine use of a test dose after placement of an epidural catheter for labour analgesia, as adequate analgesia confirms the correct position of the catheter (Birnbach and Chestnut 1999).

With CSE, analgesia occurs rapidly and testing the functionality of the epidural catheter is not possible until the initial spinal dose wears off. Many authors consider the fact that the reliability of the epidural catheter is uncertain during this period as a major disadvantage. Their concern is related to the possibility that the catheter may be dysfunctional when an emergency Caesarean section is required. Especially in high-risk pregnancies this is considered a major drawback. However, it is important to note that even with a well-tested epidural catheter, one can never be absolutely sure that several hours later the catheter remains correctly positioned. Even with conventional epidural catheters, fractioned dosing or a *de novo* test dose is required before the catheter is used for the injection of high doses of local anaesthetics.

Some anaesthetists are reluctant to initiate epidural analgesia immediately after the spinal dose, preferring to wait for the spinal dose to have worn off before testing the epidural catheter for subsequent use throughout labour. As a result, most patients will experience breakthrough pain. However, several authors initiate an epidural infusion immediately after the initial spinal dose. With low-volume, low-dose techniques, the risk of total spinal anaesthesia or toxic side-effects is minimal. These doses cannot produce systemic toxicity or total spinal anaesthesia even when direct intravascular or intrathecal injection occurs. However, if a continuous epidural infusion or patient-controlled epidural analgesia (PCEA) does not produce adequate analgesia, one must consider an intravascular position of the catheter.

Currently, a local anaesthetic (bupivacaine, ropivacaine, or levobupivacaine)/opioid (fentanyl/sufentanil) mixture is used to initiate spinal analgesia. Van de Velde et al. (2007) were the first to construct the full dose–response relationship of spinal ropivacaine, levobupivacaine, and bupivacaine combined with opioids for labour analgesia. These investigators noted that bupivacaine was significantly more potent then both of the other local anaesthetics and that ropivacaine and levobupivacaine were of similar potency (Van de Velde et al. 2007). They also noted that in active labour much more local anaesthetic was required to produce effective analgesia in all parturients than previously described on empirical grounds.

Several authors have suggested prolonging the initial intrathecal analgesia by the addition of various adjuvant drugs such as clonidine, adrenaline, or neostigmine. Although these drugs were successful in prolonging analgesia, they also produced significantly more side-effects.

Maintenance of analgesia

Maintenance of analgesia can be achieved using intermittent top-up doses, continuous epidural infusions, or PCEA with or without a background infusion. In California, only 25% of obstetric anaesthesia units used PCEA in 2005 (Carvalho et al. 2006). In the United Kingdom only 5% of units used PCEA in 1999 (Burnstein et al. 1999). However, in Belgium in 2005, the majority of hospitals used PCEA (Van Houwe et al. 2006).

Intermittent top-up dosing, by an anaesthetist or trained midwife, was the original method for maintaining epidural analgesia with a bolus of local anaesthetic administered either on patient request or after a fixed interval. Intermittent top-up dosing has several disadvantages: administration of large bolus doses of local anaesthetic can lead to systemic toxicity; maternal hypotension and fetal heart rate abnormalities; and periods of inadequate pain control.

Compared with intermittent top-up dosing, continuous epidural infusions have variously been shown to be associated with better analgesia (D'Athis et al. 1988; Lamont et al. 1989), no difference in analgesic quality (D'Athis et al. 1988; Smedstad and Morison 1988; Purdie et al. 1992), or inferior analgesia (Boutros et al. 1999; Salim et al. 2005). Most studies also showed that local anaesthetic consumption is reduced with intermittent top-up doses (D'Athis et al. 1988; Smedstad and Morison 1988; Purdie et al. 1992; Boutros et al.

1999). Despite less anaesthetic consumption, obstetric outcome is usually similar between the two methods (Purdie et al. 1992; Tan et al. 1994; Boutros et al. 1999; Usha Kiran et al. 2003; Salim et al. 2005; Fettes et al. 2006), although Smedstad and Morison (1988) found an increased incidence of spontaneous deliveries with intermittent top-up doses. In summary, continuous epidural infusions and intermittent top-up doses are quite similar in terms of quality of analgesia and incidence of side-effects with a tendency towards better performance for the intermittent top-up dosing technique.

Numerous studies have evaluated PCEA since its introduction into obstetric analgesia by Gambling et al. (1988). PCEA produced similar levels of pain relief in most studies in terms of VAS for pain (Lysak et al. 1990; Ferrante et al. 1991; Viscomi and Eisenach 1991; Purdie et al. 1992; Gambling et al. 1993; Curry et al. 1994; Tan et al. 1994; Boutros et al. 1999; Collis et al. 1999; Sia and Chong 1999; Smedvig et al. 2001; Ledin Eriksson et al. 2003). PCEA is associated with fewer medical staff interventions (van der Vyver et al. 2002). Some studies also showed that patient satisfaction was increased with PCEA (Sia and Chong 1999). PCEA is also associated with 20–55% less local anaesthetic consumption (van der Vyver et al. 2002). As a result, significantly less motor block is observed with PCEA (van der Vyver et al. 2002). It remains unclear whether this results in a better obstetric outcome.

The use of background infusions combined with PCEA is controversial. Some authors found that a background infusion confers no benefit while others suggest better pain scores with a background infusion (Missant et al. 2005; Vallejo et al. 2007; Lim et al. 2008). However the difference may be that a background infusion seems particularly useful when analgesia is initiated with CSE, where the background infusion ensures epidural priming when the patient requests the first epidural bolus. More rapid and effective analgesia follows priming of the epidural space (Missant et al. 2005; Lim et al. 2008; Okutomi et al. 2009).

Several studies compared PCEA with intermittent top-up dosing techniques for maintaining epidural analgesia during labour (Gambling et al. 1988; Gambling et al. 1990; Purdie et al. 1992; Tan et al. 1994; Paech, Pavy et al. 1995; Boutros et al. 1999; Halonen et al. 2004). The quality of pain relief was similar between the two methods, except in the studies of Paech et al. (1995), where intermittent top-up doses resulted in higher maximal pain scores, and Halonen et al. (2004) who found that PCEA produced better analgesia. Gambling et al. (1990) reported increased satisfaction scores with PCEA as compared with intermittent top-up doses, but other authors could not confirm these results. Most studies show no difference in local anaesthetic consumption, while some report an increased consumption and others a decreased consumption with PCEA (Paech et al. 1995; Boutros et al. 1999; Halonen et al. 2004). Two studies demonstrate a negative effect on obstetric outcome with PCEA (Paech et al. 1995; Halonen et al. 2004). Paech et al. (1995) observed a prolonged second stage of labour, while Halonen et al. (2004) observed more Caesarean sections as well as a longer second stage.

In more recent years, several authors have evaluated the use of PCEA combined with automated intermittent boluses. Both Wong et al. (2006) and Sia et al. (2007) compared automated boluses with continuous background infusion, both combined with PCEA. In both studies, automated boluses performed better resulting in less local anaesthetic consumption, less clinician intervention, and better quality of pain relief. Several studies are emerging looking at computer-integrated PCEA. Computer-integrated PCEA is a conventional PCEA system but with an automated feedback loop: the rate of a continuous background infusion is adapted according to the administered PCEA boluses during the previous hour (Lim et al. 2006). Computer-integrated PCEA resulted in less breakthrough pain and higher parturient satisfaction.

In conclusion, the literature suggests that PCEA and intermittent top-up doses seem to be superior compared with continuous epidural infusions for maintenance of labour analgesia with less local anaesthetic consumption, less motor block and increased patient satisfaction as compared with continuous epidural infusions. PCEA may be slightly more expensive then intermittent top-up doses, but results in much reduced medical staff workload. Depending on local legislation, intermittent top-up doses may not be an option. PCEA with a background infusion, especially when CSE is used, may be a good option. However the background infusion rate should be low (no more than 25% of total hourly consumption).

Choice of local anaesthetic

Bupivacaine is probably the most commonly used drug worldwide for obstetric neuraxial regional anaesthesia and analgesia. Reports of bupivacaine cardiotoxicity after unintentional intravascular injection, mainly in obstetric patients, prompted the development of ropivacaine and levobupivacaine (Albright 1979). These drugs appear to be safer than bupivacaine while also producing a greater differential between sensory and motor blockade, an especially advantageous feature during labour analgesia.

All local anaesthetics can produce systemic toxicity by direct and indirect mechanisms that derive from their mode of local anaesthetic actions, that is, inhibition of voltage-gated ion channels and by interference with mitochondrial respiration by impeding oxidative phosphorylation, thus depleting the cell's energy reserve. Ropivacaine and levobupivacaine both have lower systemic toxicity than bupivacaine (Mather and Chang 2001). Ropivacaine seems to be the least toxic, levobupivacaine has intermediate toxicity and bupivacaine is most toxic. Reduced systemic toxicity has also been demonstrated in pregnant animals (Santos et al. 1995).

It is essential that clinicians use the customary precautions to minimize the risk of systemic toxicity such as standard monitoring, aspiration of the catheter before injection of the drugs, use of a test dose (but see previous discussion), dividing the injected dose, and use of the lowest local anaesthetic concentration feasible.

One of the factors implicated in the association between epidural analgesia and increased rates of operative delivery is motor block from epidural local anaesthetic. Motor block can be minimized by reducing the concentration of local anaesthetic, by decreasing the total dose used, or by choosing a drug with a high differential sensory-motor block ratio.

Several trials have evaluated conventional labour analgesia using rather high concentrations of different local anaesthetics (≥0.2%) (Writer et al. 1998; Asik et al. 2002). Using high doses, bupivacaine resulted in more motor block and worse labour outcome.

However, modern labour analgesia uses lower concentrations of local anaesthetics. The advantages in terms of motor block and labour outcome of lower epidural local anaesthetic concentrations were well demonstrated by the COMET trial (Comparative Obstetric Mobile Epidural Trial Study Group 2001). Halpern and Walsh (2003) performed a meta-analysis of 23 randomized trials that compared ropivacaine and bupivacaine during labour analgesia. Onset, duration, and quality of analgesia were comparable between the two local anaesthetics. No differences in mode of delivery or other outcome variables were identified, except for a higher incidence of motor block with bupivacaine. The data for motor block were not combined statistically because of the large amount of heterogeneity among studies resulting from the large differences in drug doses and concentrations used.

However, several studies using low concentrations of local anaesthetic (≤0.125%) did demonstrate differences in motor block with ropivacaine producing less motor block then bupivacaine (Gautier et al. 1999; Campbell et al. 2000; Fischer et al. 2000; Meister et al. 2000; Chua et al. 2001; Owen et al. 2002; Gogarten et al. 2004; Lee et al. 2004; Atienzar et al. 2008). Gautier et al. (1999) clearly demonstrated that, especially if the cumulative epidural dose of local anaesthetic increased, the risk of motor block was higher with bupivacaine. This difference persisted if lower concentrations of epidural bupivacaine were used to provide analgesia. Table 66.2 gives an overview of motor block reported in several studies that compared low concentrations of ropivacaine and bupivacaine during labour analgesia. Combined, it becomes clear that motor block occurs much less frequently with ropivacaine. Atienzar et al. (2008) demonstrated that both ropivacaine and levobupivacaine produced less motor block.

This has been confirmed using the 'minimum local analgesic concentration' (MLAC) methodology. Lacassie et al. (2002) determined the motor block MLAC concentration of ropivacaine and bupivacaine using a model of up-and-down sequential allocation. These authors noted that ropivacaine was significantly less potent for motor block than bupivacaine, at 66% that of bupivacaine.

Similar observations can be made for intrathecal ropivacaine and bupivacaine. Excellent analgesia is achieved with both agents using similar spinal doses but with less motor impairment in patients treated with ropivacaine. Table 66.3 gives an overview of the number of patients developing detectable motor block in various studies that compare intrathecal ropivacaine and bupivacaine (Levin et al. 1998; Hughes et al. 2001; Lim et al. 2004; Camorcia et al. 2005).

Table 66.2 Number of patients with motor block in bupivacaine- or ropivacaine-treated patients using similar and low (≤0.125%) concentrations of local anaesthetic

	Bupivacaine	Ropivacaine	Number of patients
Campbell et al. (2000)	5	0*	40
Meister et al. (2000)	18	8*	50
Gautier et al. (1999)	15	3*	90
Lee et al. (2004)	21	10	346
Owen et al. (2002)	12	8	50
Gogarten et al. (2004)	11	4	109
Chua et al. (2001)	5	3	32
Fischer et al. (2000)	19	10	189
Atienzar et al. (2008)	18	13	65
Total	124	59	971

* $P < 0.05$ *vs* bupivacaine.

Data from various sources, see references.

Table 66.3 Number of patients with motor block in bupivacaine- or ropivacaine-treated patients using similar doses of local anaesthetic administered intrathecally

	Bupivacaine	Ropivacaine	Number of patients
Levin et al. (1998)	0	0	48
Hughes et al. (2001)	8	1*	40
Lim et al. (2004)	5	2*	40
Camorcia et al. (2005)	8	1	64
Total	21	4	192

* $P < 0.05$ *vs* bupivacaine.

Data from various sources, see references.

For levobupivacaine, less information is available. Lacassie and Columb (2003) determined the motor block MLAC concentration of levobupivacaine and bupivacaine using a model of up-and-down sequential allocation. These authors noted that levobupivacaine was significantly less potent for motor block then bupivacaine, at 87% the potency of bupivacaine. Vercauteren et al. (2001a) observed no clinical differences between spinal levobupivacaine and racemic bupivacaine except for less motor block with levobupivacaine.

MLAC studies have repeatedly demonstrated that ropivacaine and levobupivacaine are less potent during labour analgesia at the ED_{50} point of the dose–response curve then bupivacaine (Capogna et al. 1999; Polley et al. 1999; Polley et al. 2003). Although MLAC studies have undoubtedly added to our understanding of local anaesthetics and their relative potency, there are several caveats when applying these results to the clinical situation of labour analgesia. First, MLAC studies only focus on one point of the dose–response curve and provide no information on the slopes of the dose–response curves. Second, MLAC studies only focus on the concentration used and not on the total dose. However, total dose determines the intensity of sensory and motor block (Duggan et al. 1988). Third, it is difficult to analyse these reports for confounding factors such as stage of labour, parity, type of labour, and so on, factors that each impact labour pain intensity. Fourth, MLAC studies determine relative potency for initiation of analgesia during labour, but do not provide information on relative potency during maintenance of analgesia (which might be influenced by factors such as local anaesthetic lipid solubility or effects of local anaesthetics on epidural vessels). However, despite these criticisms, most clinicians would agree that new local anaesthetics are indeed less potent then bupivacaine. This has been confirmed by the first full dose–response comparison of levobupivacaine, ropivacaine, and bupivacaine, used for spinal labour analgesia (Van de Velde et al. 2007). Other authors did propose a potency hierarchy: bupivacaine > levobupivacaine > ropivacaine (Camorcia et al. 2005).

Usually clinicians are not interested in the ED_{50}, but want all patients to be without pain. This means we will use higher doses than needed for some patients, to achieve good analgesia for all. Various solutions to minimize overdosing have been successfully investigated such as PCEA.

Adjuvant drugs

Various adjuvant drugs have been tested for use in neuraxial labour analgesia: opioids, clonidine, neostigmine, adrenaline, magnesium, and adenosine.

Opioids

Opioids used for labour pain relief act through agonistic mechanisms in the dorsal horn. Activation of μ, δ, and κ receptors induces presynaptic inhibition of neurotransmitter release and produces postsynaptic neuronal membrane hyperpolarization.

Pure epidural opioid analgesia is feasible in the early stages of labour. Capogna et al. (2003) determined the ED_{50} of epidural fentanyl and sufentanil using the MLAC methodology. To produce analgesia in 50% of patients, a dose of 124 μg of fentanyl and 21 μg of sufentanil was necessary, establishing a potency ratio of 5.9 between sufentanil and fentanyl.

However, usually opioids are combined with local anaesthetics. It has been repeatedly shown that opioids have a synergistic effect with various local anaesthetic agents. Opioids reduce the ED_{50} of local anaesthetics (Polley et al. 1998). In clinical practice, the addition of opioids reduces the onset of analgesia, prolongs the duration of epidural analgesia, reduces local anaesthetic consumption, and decreases the incidence of patients with insufficient analgesia (Vertommen et al. 1991). The incidence of troublesome motor block is reduced and the rate of spontaneous vaginal delivery is increased (Vertommen et al. 1991). Unfortunately, more patients experience pruritus (Vertommen et al. 1991).

Plain intrathecal opioids are successful in producing labour analgesia. Palmer et al. (1998) established that 25 μg of fentanyl was the optimal intrathecal dose. Increasing the dose above 25 μg did not improve the duration or quality of analgesia, but increased the incidence of side-effects. For sufentanil, an ED_{95} of 8.9 μg was established (Herman et al. 1997). However, certainly in Europe, most anaesthetists prefer the intrathecal combination of local anaesthetic and opioid. Adding opioids to the chosen local anaesthetic reduces the ED_{50} of the latter and prolongs dose-dependently the duration of initial spinal analgesia (Stocks et al. 2001).

Clonidine

Clonidine is an α_2-receptor agonist that acts on receptors located in the dorsal horn to produce labour analgesia. Presynaptic stimulation of α_2-receptors inhibits neurotransmitter release and postsynaptic stimulation, preventing neuronal transmission through hyperpolarization. Animal safety studies established that clonidine was not neurotoxic and did not affect spinal cord blood flow (Gordh et al. 1986; Eisenach and Grice 1988).

A limited number of clinical trials have studied various doses (30–150 μg) of epidural clonidine during labour. Based on the MLAC methodology, a minimum of 60 μg of clonidine is required to reduce the ED_{50} of ropivacaine for labour analgesia (Aveline et al. 2002). Doses above 100 μg induce maternal hypotension, bradycardia, and sedation and in some trials also new-onset fetal heart rate changes (Chassard et al. 1996). Based on work by Landau et al. (2002) it can be concluded that the optimal epidural dose of clonidine is probably 75 μg. Prolonged analgesia, reduced local anaesthetic consumption, and fewer epidural top-ups for breakthrough pain without an increase in side-effects were noted (Landau et al. 2002).

Chiari et al. (1999) studied the use of pure spinal clonidine labour analgesia and found that doses producing adequate analgesia also induced unacceptable side-effects such as hypotension. Adding lower doses of clonidine (15–45 μg) to spinal analgesics does improve the duration and quality of initial spinal analgesia (Mercier et al. 1998; Paech et al. 2002; Missant et al. 2004). However, especially when clonidine is combined with local anaesthetic agents, significant and prolonged hypotension is likely to occur (Paech et al. 2002; Missant et al. 2004).

Adrenaline

Adrenaline also acts on α_2-receptors. However vascular effects, especially with epidural administration might also be involved.

Epidurally administered adrenaline significantly reduces the MLAC concentration of bupivacaine in labouring patients and improves the quality of analgesia (Polley et al. 2002). Spinal administration of adrenaline combined with local anaesthetics and opioids has been evaluated in a wide range of doses from 2.25 to 100 μg. Duration of intrathecal analgesia was consistently prolonged (Gautier et al. 1997).

Unfortunately, adrenaline also induces an increased incidence of maternal motor deficit (Cohen et al. 2000; Goodman et al. 2002). Epidural adrenaline might also prolong labour duration by β-agonist effects, especially when higher doses are infused into the epidural space (Dounas et al. 1996; Cohen et al. 2000; Okutomi et al. 2000; Okutomi et al. 2000; Goodman et al. 2002). Furthermore adding adrenaline to pre-prepared solutions complicates storage and significantly increases the price of handling and preparation. Thus, the authors have abandoned the addition of adrenaline from the local anaesthetic solution used for spinal and epidural administration.

Neostigmine

Acetylcholine is an important neurotransmitter in the dorsal horn of the spinal cord for the descending inhibitory pathways. Neostigmine, a cholinesterase inhibitor, increases the concentration of acetylcholine in the synapses and thus produces analgesia by stimulating acetylcholine mediated mechanisms. Naguib and Yaksh (1994) demonstrated that the analgesic effects of neostigmine and clonidine are synergistic. After reassuring safety studies, in which no neurotoxic effects and no detrimental effects on spinal cord perfusion were identified, neostigmine has been evaluated for labour pain relief (Hood et al. 1995; Yaksh et al. 1995).

Several trials evaluated the effects of epidural neostigmine (Habib and Gan 2006; Roelants 2006). Neostigmine seems to be promising as an adjuvant drug for labour analgesia. Both Roelants (2006) and Van de Velde et al. (2009) successfully added epidural neostigmine to the analgesic mixture, improving the quality and duration of effective analgesia.

Nelson et al. (1999) investigated the analgesic potential and side effect profile of 5, 10, and 20 μg of intrathecal neostigmine alone. From this first phase, these investigators chose 10 μg as the optimal dose to be added to intrathecal sufentanil and determined the ED_{50} of spinal sufentanil with and without neostigmine. Neostigmine successfully reduced the ED_{50} of spinal sufentanil. In a further step, they compared twice the ED_{50} of spinal sufentanil with neostigmine to twice the ED_{50} of plain spinal sufentanil. A synergistic effect on duration of analgesia of neostigmine was observed. D'Angelo et al. (2001), however, reported no increase in analgesic duration with neostigmine as part of a multidrug combination (local anaesthetic, opioid, clonidine, and neostigmine). Furthermore several authors reported a very high incidence of severe nausea and vomiting (Owen et al. 2000).

Other drugs (magnesium and adenosine)

Both adenosine and magnesium have been added to intrathecal opioids to relieve labour pain (Owen et al. 2000; Buvanendran et al.

2002; Rane et al. 2003). No significant advantages of adding adenosine to the analgesic mixture were observed. Magnesium prolonged intrathecal fentanyl analgesia.

In conclusion, local anaesthetic agents combined with opioids remain the cornerstone of effective spinal and epidural labour analgesia. Epidural clonidine is a valuable adjuvant drug, especially in cases when it becomes difficult to control labour pain. An epidural dose of 75 μg of clonidine seems safe and effective. Spinal clonidine is effective but has been shown to induce hypotension and should therefore be reserved for specific situations. Routine use cannot be recommended. Adrenaline is a valuable drug but potential problems such as motor block, detrimental effects on the progress of labour, and storage problems limit its usefulness. With neostigmine, only limited clinical experience is available. Spinal neostigmine may cause unacceptable nausea and vomiting. Adenosine and magnesium have recently been studied during labour analgesia, but preliminary data are disappointing.

Anaesthesia for Caesarean section

Caesarean section represents by its nature an intervention with all concomitant perioperative and anaesthetic implications of surgery in the abdominal cavity. As it is usually performed on young, healthy women, there might be an impression that it is not a particularly difficult anaesthetic challenge. But this procedure is much more than a surgical opening of the abdominal cavity. Higher degrees of stress, tissue trauma, and impaired homeostasis are encountered than, for example, surgery on the body surface or extremities. In addition, significant intra- and postoperative pain might complicate the perioperative course and well-being of mother and newborn. However, the physiological and potentially pathophysiological changes of late pregnancy can increase the challenges of anaesthesia. Furthermore, in contrast to all other surgical procedures, it also concerns at least two individuals.

The choices of today's anaesthesia allow for a differentiated approach in which the treatment of the mother can guarantee the integrity of her vital functions as well as those of the fetus. Additionally, it is also important to provide optimal surgical conditions to the obstetrician to facilitate a rapid and careful delivery of the newborn.

Preoperative investigations and preparation

The time available for preoperative investigations before a Caesarean section varies from zero for the very urgent case to several months if it is known in advance that a surgical delivery will be carried out. In accordance with these different prerequisites, pre-anaesthetic evaluation may vary widely in its extent and focus.

Pre-anaesthetic evaluation before extremely urgent cases is very brief. It is essentially limited to questions regarding the feasibility of general anaesthesia and tracheal intubation. Of prominent importance is the assessment of the airway and the probability of problems when performing a rapid sequence induction. Of course, there are many other relevant questions, in particular if there is any type of pregnancy-associated or independent maternal morbidity. In most cases, there is an urgent fetal problem that needs immediate delivery, while the mother usually is a healthy young woman (Spitzer 1992). Fortunately, severe co-morbidities are usually known in advance obviating the need for a time-consuming interview of the otherwise highly stressed parturient, the midwife, or obstetrician. Urgency nevertheless is no sufficient reason to expose the mother to any unnecessary risk by a too hasty and superficial pre-anaesthetic evaluation that might result in wrong decisions concerning the choice of technique.

In a grade II or III Caesarean section, there is usually enough time to perform regional anaesthesia, either by extending an existing epidural or a single-shot spinal. Therefore, all relevant facts concerning the application of a regional technique should be considered. A possible difference to the elective situation might be that one should not delay anaesthesia by waiting for laboratory results, unless there is a reason from the history (e.g. in case of known or suspected coagulopathy). Last but not least, in elective surgery, there is plenty of time to make all necessary investigations, but if these have been made longer than 2 weeks before surgery, a fresh reassessment of relevant findings is appropriate and justified in the light of possible (patho)physiological changes during late pregnancy.

The goal of any assessment is to quantify functional limitations of individual organ systems, with the ultimate scope to optimize the parturient's and her fetus's conditions by the time of surgery. Common problems in this context are connected to the coagulation system, which targets primarily the question of the feasibility of regional anaesthesia and the risk of haemorrhage and the necessary volume and blood replacement. Sometimes these questions arise at very short notice if there is severe pre-eclampsia or HELLP (haemolysis, elevated liver enzymes, and low platelet count) syndrome. Other problems requiring clarification are pre-existing cardiovascular pathologies (e.g. valvular heart disease, pulmonary hypertension) that require extensive investigation and if necessary, must be reassessed immediately before the operation.

Electrocardiogram or chest X-ray is not necessary in healthy subjects. In principle, further investigation should be adopted only if the history leads to a reasonable likelihood of pathological findings. However, laboratory results alone are of limited value unless they are seen in the context of the clinical situation. For example, borderline coagulation parameters have to be carefully interpreted in particular if they are used in deciding for or against using neuraxial anaesthesia: one should be aware of the inherent risks of the alternative. For example, a low platelet count that might otherwise be a contraindication for a spinal anaesthetic may be the better choice if the patient shows signs of airway-related risks. In any case, the decision has to be made on an individual basis, by carefully weighing the risk:benefit ratios of the alternative procedures. Further information on neuraxial techniques in the presence of possible coagulopathy and after drugs that inhibit coagulation can be found in Chapter 52.

The pre-anaesthetic visit has to include provision of detailed information to the patient and a description of the planned anaesthetic techniques, including their risks and complications. The appropriate informed consent must be documented according to local guidelines. The woman in labour should not be coerced into agreeing to any specific technique; her decision based on comprehensive and complete information must be respected, even if not the preferred or recommended technique of the anaesthetist (Wyatt et al. 2001).

A complete pre-anaesthetic preparation includes voiding the bladder, giving a gastric acid buffer (e.g. 30 ml of sodium citrate orally) and the correct orientation of the operation table in a left-tilt position to avoid caval compression syndrome (Kjaer et al. 2006).

A sensitive psychological approach, possibly with involvement of the partner, is also essential. The presence of the partner in the operating theatre during delivery might be dependent on the type of anaesthesia, or local traditions and considerations. We recommend their presence only when regional anaesthesia is used, and only after adequate anaesthesia has been established and all preparations have been concluded. Whenever a critical situation arises (e.g. marked bleeding), the partner should be politely asked to leave the operation theatre.

Anaesthetic techniques

Types of anaesthesia

Caesarean delivery can be performed under general anaesthesia, neuraxial regional anaesthesia, or local infiltration anaesthesia. Infiltrative local anaesthesia is mentioned only for completeness, but because of its technical complexity, lower safety and higher risk, its use is restricted to very rare circumstances. This technique will not be described further.

General *vs* regional anaesthesia

The decision between general and regional anaesthesia is guided by parturient characteristics, the urgency of the Caesarean section, and the existing technical and infrastructure capabilities of the unit and the needs of the operator. The final decision on the choice of the appropriate anaesthesia procedure is ultimately left to the anaesthetist in charge in agreement with the parturient (or in special cases with their families or guardians) (Ranganathan and Raghuraman 2003; Carvalho et al. 2005).

The current state of knowledge is that, given the relative benefit and risk profiles, regional anaesthesia is the preferred technique unless there are medical contraindications or evident anatomical or pathophysiological circumstances which would indicate a preference for general anaesthesia (Bloom et al. 2005; Lyons and Akerman 2005; Reynolds and Seed 2005; Stamer et al. 2005). This conclusion is based on the belief that in pregnant women after the 12th week of gestation, regional anaesthesia is the better alternative. The reasons for the preference for regional anaesthesia for Caesarean section are:

- Fewer concerns about transplacental passage of anaesthetics to the fetus: in general anaesthesia, the drugs given to the parturient pass to a varying extent to the fetus and may complicate their postpartum adaptation. As a result of fewer drugs required for regional anaesthesia and because of the primarily non-systemic route of administration (with a considerably delayed systemic appearance after epidural or spinal application), virtually no clinically relevant transplacental transfer of anaesthetics occurs (Littleford 2004; Reynolds and Seed 2005).
- No or fewer problems with airway management: in regional anaesthesia, consciousness, protective reflexes of the airway, and spontaneous breathing are maintained, and therefore there is no need to interfere with the airway. This issue is even more relevant in late pregnancy, when tracheal intubation is frequently more difficult, and failure to secure the airway may have more severe consequences for both mother and the newborn (Kuczkowski 2003b; Biro 2011).
- Lower risk of aspiration: during tracheal intubation and extubation, there is an increased risk for aspiration of possibly acidic stomach contents, for which reason any pregnant woman beyond the 16th week of gestation is *a priori* considered to be not fasted (Malan and Johnson 1988).
- Easier maintenance of homeostasis and organ function: the stress level caused by surgery and anaesthesia may be lower in regional anaesthesia. This also applies to the immediate postoperative period; for example, by having better respiratory function, improved bowel movements and a better analgesia (Shyken et al. 1990; Ramin et al. 1991).
- Birth experience and emotional bonding: the conscious witnessing of the birth while having a regional anaesthetic has emotional value and supports the bond between the mother and her newborn. As the woman's partner is usually permitted to be present with a regional anaesthetic technique, this approach also permits a greater involvement of the partner in the birth (Cakmak and Kuguoglu 2007).

Indications and contraindications of various methods of anaesthesia

Indications and contraindications of suitable anaesthetic procedures for Caesarean section can be considered systematically. Because of the generally accepted superiority of regional anaesthesia in obstetric interventions, an escalating scheme of indications can be applied that should precede all other considerations in the choice of the individually chosen technique:

1. In the absence of any limitation of, or contraindication to, regional anaesthesia, this technique is *a priori* preferable.
2. Within the regional anaesthesia category, spinal or CSE anaesthesia is preferable to epidural or any other variant of locoregional technique.
3. An epidural as the primary technique is indicated when there is already a functioning epidural catheter *in situ* (e.g. for a previously attempted vaginal delivery and subsequent switch to operative delivery or in the case of the intended use of a vacuum or forceps).
4. If general anaesthesia is the primary choice for whatever reason, a rapid sequence induction technique has to be adopted, unless a difficult airway is anticipated.
5. If a difficult airway is expected, an awake fibreoptic intubation should be considered as the primary choice of securing the airway.
6. With unexpected difficult or failed intubation, the most important issue is to maintain oxygenation of the mother by the most suitable alternative method. Repeated attempts at tracheal intubation with a technique which has failed should not be made. However, in the case of unpredicted difficult intubation, recently introduced alternative equipment based on video-assisted display of the relevant structures and the intubation pathway (video-laryngoscopes or video stylets) should be considered in the hands of well-trained users.

Regional anaesthesia

The preferred technique in the context of a Caesarean section is spinal anaesthesia (either single shot or as part of a CSE technique), in which the local anaesthetic is injected via a fine needle through all layers of the meninges surrounding the spinal cord into the cerebrospinal fluid. In some publications, this technique is also termed 'subdural', which, however, is not as commonly used but means the same as 'spinal' anaesthesia.

Epidural anaesthesia can be performed either as a 'single shot' through the epidural needle or using an epidural catheter, which permits the continuous or repeated administration of anaesthetic agents for almost any duration. Although a single-shot epidural may be suitable for a Caesarean section, a catheter provides more options to prolong or to modify ongoing anaesthesia, analgesia, or both. This represents a significant advantage, so that in everyday clinical practice only the catheter-based version is used. In the context of catheter-based epidural anaesthesia, there again are two possible variants, namely, the primary form, when the epidural is used explicitly and exclusively for a surgical delivery, and the secondary form, if a previously inserted and functioning epidural catheter is *in situ* (e.g. for epidural analgesia for a planned vaginal delivery) and which must be converted to an epidural suitable for the abdominal surgery of Caesarean section (Yentis 2006).

Single-shot spinal anaesthesia

This method involves the puncture of the subarachnoid space with a very thin, specially shaped spinal needle (e.g. a pencil-point needle, 25 or 27 G), which penetrates the dura by creating a small hole that might seal easily after withdrawal. Spinal anaesthesia is considered by many to be the first choice for elective Caesarean section. Also in unplanned or emergent cases, spinal anaesthesia might be the preferred option especially if the operator is experienced and the puncture can be performed without delay.

Absolute contraindications to spinal anaesthesia are coagulopathy and hypovolaemic shock (Bloom et al. 2005).

Spinal anaesthesia can be performed with the patient sitting or in the left lateral position. This choice depends on the patient and physician preference and anatomical patient factors. A midline approach is considered standard. The best possible access to the subdural space is either at the L3/4 or L4/5 level. The L4/5 level can be identified as at the same level as a line connecting the two iliac crests ('Tuffier's line'). Insertion at levels higher than L3/4 are not recommended because the conus medullaris of the spinal cord might be injured with the spinal needle.

There is clear evidence that non-cutting, pencil-point spinal needles and needles not exceeding 25 G are associated with a lower incidence of post-dural puncture headache in the obstetric population which is prone to this complication (Hafer et al. 1997). In very obese women, an extra-long needle might be necessary, which has the disadvantage of being floppier and requires an experienced user (Roofthooft 2009).

The most commonly used local anaesthetic for spinal anaesthesia is hyperbaric bupivacaine 0.5% (5 mg ml^{-1}), which is usually given in a dose of 10–12 mg. It has become popular to add a small amount of a μ-opioid agonist (e.g. 25 μg of fentanyl or 2–5 μg of sufentanil) in order to achieve a more profound and prolonged analgesic effect. Some anaesthetists prefer hyperbaric mepivacaine 2% (20 mg ml^{-1}) with an added opioid, in particular for shorter procedures (Meininger et al. 2003). Ropivacaine is another option that enables earlier postoperative mobilization compared with bupivacaine. As the spinal block takes effect rapidly, the parturient should be moved into the supine position as soon as possible, but always with a slight left lateral tilt to avoid vena cava compression syndrome. The ongoing spread of the anaesthetic effect should be regularly checked (described later) and if necessary the patient's position changed in order to achieve an upper limit close to the fourth thoracic segment. The extent of spread of the block can be influenced by careful tilting of the operating table in the Trendelenburg direction to give a higher spread and in the reverse Trendelenburg direction to avoid excessive cephalad spread. The insertion of a triangular pillow under the upper thorax, neck, and head may help to prevent unwanted spread above the desired limit (Yun et al. 1998). The ability to influence the spread (by tilting the operation table) is only possible if a hyperbaric agent has been used. With an isobaric agent, the local anaesthetic dosage (in mg) and its volume are determinants of the expected spread, which cannot be influenced after injection.

The immediate side-effects of spinal anaesthesia are haemodynamic instability, nausea, dyspnoea, restlessness, and panic attacks. These are mostly caused by the upper thoracic spread of the block to cause sympatholytic symptoms. With an appropriate intravenous infusion regimen to maintain normovolaemia and the repetitive administration or continuous infusion of suitable vasoconstricting agents (e.g. phenylephrine, ephedrine, and noradrenaline), the haemodynamic side-effects of systemic vasodilation can be avoided (Kee et al. 2005). The vasopressor of choice, based on extensive work by Ngan Kee and Khaw (2006), is phenylephrine.

An especially important application of spinal anaesthesia is its use as a rescue technique in the case of failed epidural anaesthesia. As long as there is no contraindication to spinal anaesthesia and there is still enough time to establish the block, it seems a reasonable approach instead of directly resorting to general anaesthesia.

Combined spinal epidural anaesthesia

Several authors advocate the use of low-dose spinal anaesthesia for Caesarean section using a CSE technique. The initial spinal dose of local anaesthetic can be reduced (e.g. hyperbaric bupivacaine <8 mg). The advantages of this technique include increased haemodynamic stability with less hypotension, less risk of fetal acidosis, less maternal nausea and vomiting and less need for vasopressors (Roofthooft et al. 2011). However, concerns may arise that with such a low spinal dose, intraoperative discomfort and pain may arise (Arzola and Wieczorek 2011). Indeed low spinal doses result in a shorter duration of anaesthesia and the epidural catheter is required to manage and prevent breakthrough pain. The epidural catheter also enables the use of epidural volume extension (EVE), where saline can be injected into the epidural space to enhance the spread of spinally administered local anaesthetic (Lew et al. 2004; Tyagi et al. 2009; Loubert et al. 2011; Salman et al. 2013).

Epidural anaesthesia

Epidural anaesthesia is no longer the first-choice technique for Caesarean section, but may be used if an already sited labour analgesia catheter needs to be topped up for operative delivery. In contrast to this 'usual' way of secondarily adopting epidural anaesthesia for Caesarean delivery, some anaesthetists favour it as the primary choice in cases of haemodynamic instability (e.g. in severe pre-eclampsia), or if anaesthesia has to be extended slowly as is the case in parturients with cardiovascular morbidity such as pulmonary hypertension or valvular disease (Dyer et al. 2004). Another good reason for primary epidural anaesthesia (eventually with an additional spinal component) might be an anticipated extended surgical procedure, as is possible if extended adhesions are expected or myomas need to be resected. In these cases, an additional benefit of the epidural technique is the ability to prolong the use of the epidural catheter for subsequent postoperative pain treatment.

Usually, with a flawless technique, surgery can begin approximately 20 min after the first epidural dose. If the epidural anaesthetic is given through a catheter that has been previously used for labour analgesia, and there is still residual analgesic effect, the added doses should be administered stepwise under careful control of their effect, which needs additional time. However, experience shows in these cases that a full epidural anaesthetic dose is usually necessary to achieve adequate surgical conditions. In such 'upgrading' of residual analgesia to full anaesthesia, care needs to be exercised to avoid cephalad spread of the block beyond the desired limit of T4.

The immediate side-effects of epidural anaesthesia resemble those of spinal anaesthesia, but usually appear later and are less pronounced. The management of hypotension is similar and is based on adequate intravenous fluid administration and administration of vasoactive drugs (Ngan Kee and Khaw 2006). A specific difference is in post-dural puncture headache; if this occurs after epidural anaesthesia, it usually has been caused by accidental dural perforation with the Tuohy needle and is likely to lead to a more severe and persisting headache than is the case after spinal anaesthesia.

If an accidental dural puncture with the Tuohy needle is recognized, the catheter can be inserted into the subdural space to convert the epidural into a spinal anaesthetic (Ng et al. 2004). This accidental and unintended approach at least offers the possibility to exploit the mishap to the benefit of the parturient. The sealing of the dura by the catheter at least delays the onset of the otherwise very likely post-dural puncture headache. If the epidural was intended to alleviate labour pain, this aim can be achieved by providing catheter-based subdural analgesia with appropriate medication and dosage through the spinal catheter (Robbins et al. 1995). However, it is of utmost importance to clearly label the catheter as 'spinal' in order to prevent the severe consequences of administering epidural doses into the subdural space. The spinal catheter can also be used to provide excellent anaesthesia for an operative intervention.

Rescue techniques in case of insufficient regional anaesthetic effect

For any variant of neuraxial anaesthesia there are three possible outcomes in terms of efficacy: (1) anaesthesia with a complete spread over the required dermatomes and with a sufficient anaesthetic depth (which is the ideal situation); (2) partially successful anaesthesia, which covers most but not all the required dermatomes, and is associated with some pain perception (which might have a broad range from mild discomfort to severe pain); and (3) only a very limited or even no anaesthetic effect (which represents a full failure of neuraxial blockade).

A full anaesthetic block can be confirmed by complete lack of pain sensations in the affected dermatomes. A full motor blockade need not be present for sufficient analgesia; however, its presence indicates also a sensory blockade. Insufficient or even no analgesic effect can be occasionally seen in distinct dermatomes or there may be unilateral block. This may happen as a result of impeded spread of the anaesthetic in the epidural space. Usually, the loss of normal temperature sensation (as tested with a cold spray or a piece of ice) indicates the onset and presence of anaesthesia/analgesia in the respective dermatome.

Even with a good block [as delineated in point (1)], the parturient might sense movements and pressure in the abdomen during the procedure and, in the worst case, some vague discomfort transmitted by the unblocked vagal nerves. These are transient symptoms and, after preoperative counselling and reassurance, most parturients can cope with them. Some patients who expect total paralysis may object to still being able to move their legs. One should assure them, that this is normal and does not indicate less sensory blockade than necessary. However, the latter has to be checked carefully and insufficient anaesthesia should be excluded. If the spinal or epidural anaesthetic evidently fails [as delineated in point (3)], there are two options: either to reattempt a regional technique, or revert to general anaesthesia. This choice should be made with consideration of the available resources and the estimated chances for success. A decision to reattempt regional anaesthesia, which should be a simple spinal anaesthetic at a different level than before or by a paramedian approach, is appropriate if the anatomy permits such a choice, if there is still sufficient time for another attempt and the parturient is able to tolerate it. Converting to general anaesthesia is appropriate if the parturient is exhausted by long labour and previous interventions, the Caesarean section is urgent, or the anatomy of the spinal column presents unusual difficulties. However, the decision should be balanced by the perceived risks of general anaesthesia, especially any suspicion of potential airway difficulties.

The decision how to continue is more difficult in the case of a partially effective regional anaesthesia [as delineated in point (2)]. In this case, a wide range of spread or intensity deficits is possible and it is of primary importance for the anaesthetist to recognize clearly the qualitative and quantitative characteristics of the block. The larger the deficits, the more difficult it is to manage the situation with additional systemic analgesics and one might revert to another solution as previously described for failed regional anaesthesia. A second attempt at regional anaesthesia should be made, recognizing that the spinal cord and spinal nerves might be partially blocked by local anaesthetic and therefore less responsive to mechanical irritation. This implies that the second attempt should be performed by the most experienced available anaesthetist, who should use careful advancement of the needle and immediate retraction if paraesthesia is elicited. These considerations are less relevant if the initial regional technique was an epidural. There might be a fair chance to improve the anaesthetic effect if the catheter was placed too deep into the epidural space (>4 cm) (Ithnin et al. 2006). A slight retraction to the minimum necessary depth of 3.5 cm bears a fair chance of improvement, in particular if it is followed by injection of a more concentrated local anaesthetic that may also contain adjuvant drugs such as fentanyl 50 μg or clonidine 75 μg (Karaman et al. 2006b).

The systemic administration of analgesics, sedatives, or both, has to be limited to amounts that do not interfere with maternal well-being and the adaptation of the newborn. Therefore only limited doses of drugs known to cross the placenta are permitted (Littleford 2004; Reynolds and Seed 2005). An example of appropriate adjuvant analgesic treatment is a single bolus of 0.1 mg of remifentanil (Draisci et al. 2008). If this is still not sufficient to proceed with surgery, a different approach should be adopted instead of a repeated dose of opioid. A subanaesthetic but analgesic dose of ketamine up to 1 mg kg^{-1} (as a cumulative total amount of repetitive 10 μg boluses) might represent an acceptable compromise between maternal and fetal tolerance and requirements (Sen et al. 2005). Ketamine does not alter respiration and also leaves the airway reflexes intact. However, it might cause a temporary loss of consciousness, and the mother might not later remember the birth. Even worse, sometime it can induce bad dreams and so the anaesthetist should avoid unnecessary visual or auditory stimulation of the parturient while she is under the influence of the drug. Soon after delivery, an empathetic debriefing with both parents is recommended if more than a strictly analgesic dose of ketamine has been administered, or if the parents request this (Hobson et al. 2006). Indeed, if anaesthesia at any time has shown deficiencies or was associated with discomfort or complications, a detailed debriefing with both parents should be conducted, including a discussion of an alternative approach for subsequent pregnancies.

General anaesthesia

Technical details

As described previously, general anaesthesia is not the technique of choice for Caesarean section, but in certain cases remains the only available alternative. As a result of the relative rarity of this approach, it is not surprising that less experienced anaesthetists may feel uncomfortable with the technique. They also might be intimidated by the fact that in late pregnancy, fasting does not guarantee an empty stomach, and the physiological changes in the parturient that increase the anaesthesia-related airway risks. The elevated intra-abdominal pressure, the reduced tone of the lower oesophageal sphincter, the delayed gastric emptying, the lower pH, and the higher volume of gastric secretions contribute to a substantially higher risk for pulmonary aspiration of gastric contents. In addition, from the onset of apnoea the time for arterial desaturation to occur in late pregnancy is less than half of that in non-pregnant women (McClelland et al. 2009).

In light of these considerations, tracheal intubation remains the only acceptable means of securing the airway, a technique that has to be carried out by the most experienced available person and in the fastest possible way. Thus, it has to be performed strictly according to the locally adopted 'rapid sequence induction' protocol. This means the fastest possible anaesthesia induction and tracheal intubation using intravenous administration of a potent and rapidly acting hypnotic (e.g. thiopental 5 mg kg^{-1}) and a rapidly acting neuromuscular blocking drug (suxamethonium 1 mg kg^{-1}), assuming no specific contraindications such as porphyria for thiopental (Consolo et al. 2005) and malignant hyperthermia susceptibility for suxamethonium. In these rare cases, alternative induction agents (etomidate, propofol), or neuromuscular blocking drugs (e.g. rocuronium) should be chosen at an appropriate dose.

Measures to reduce the risk of aspiration of gastric contents and its impact should it occur begin with the oral administration of 30 ml of sodium citrate solution to reduce the volume and buffering of acidic gastric juice (Imarengiaye and Ekwere 2005) before induction. The anaesthetic equipment should have been checked and optimally prepared intubation equipment (e.g. a styleted tracheal tube and availability of 'difficult intubation' aids) available along with a readily to hand functioning suction device. The lungs should be denitrogenated by pre-oxygenation and the patient positioned in a slight Trendelenburg position with left lateral tilt to in order to avoid vena cava compression syndrome. The rationale for the use of 'cricoid pressure' has been questioned and is increasingly abandoned in some centres (Paech 2010).

The administration of an opioid for induction must be handled very cautiously. Before cutting the umbilical cord it can be assumed that the child's adaptation will be delayed if opioids were given, which implies that suitable arrangements for optimal neonatal care have to be present (Giriyappa et al. 2006; Heard and Langley 2006; Kee et al. 2006). Most authors thus refrain from giving opioids before delivery. However, more and more well respected authorities in obstetric anaesthesia are suggesting that remifentanil administered at induction is a good and safe option. Recently Heesen et al. (2013) performed a meta-analysis of published trials and concluded that remifentanil before induction produced haemodynamic stability and only minimal and short-lived effects on the neonate which are easily treated. In addition to haemodynamic stability the advantages of remifentanil at induction include reduced risk of awareness and major complications such as intracranial haemorrhage.

For maintenance of anaesthesia, an easily adjustable (with low blood–gas partition coefficient) potent inhalation anaesthetic may be used (e.g. sevoflurane or desflurane) (Karaman et al. 2006a). However, in the rare case of malignant hyperthermia susceptibility, a safe alternative is to use propofol by infusion at initially 8–12 mg kg^{-1} h^{-1} or by target-controlled infusion with a calculated effect site concentration of 3.5–4.5 μg ml^{-1}. Mechanical ventilation of the lungs is adjusted according to the end-tidal CO_2 and with the aim of maintaining normocarbia. After cord clamping, fentanyl or analogues can be administered in the usual dose according to the individual clinical needs. The oxygen concentration can be reduced to 40–50% in air or nitrous oxide. As a 'normal' Caesarean delivery only takes about 20–30 min, the continuation of the initial neuromuscular block should be handled cautiously and most probably it is best to avoid further neuromuscular block after tracheal intubation.

During emergence from anaesthesia, residual neuromuscular block must be excluded with certainty and, if a non-depolarizing neuromuscular blocking drug has been used, a suitable reversal agent administered according to response to nerve stimulation. Tracheal extubation takes place only upon unequivocal establishment of confirmed normal neuromuscular function, return of airway reflexes, and responsiveness of the parturient. Adequate postoperative analgesia is commenced immediately.

Management of the airway

For the reasons delineated previously, the increased risk of aspiration requires special attention. In the previous section, the procedures for general anaesthesia are described in the context of normal circumstances, that is, with not a particularly difficult airway. However, in late pregnancy, a difficult airway is more frequently encountered than in non-pregnant women because of physiological and pathophysiological changes that affect the visibility of the larynx during direct laryngoscopy (Kuczkowski et al. 2003; Saravanakumar and Cooper 2005). These include an increase in mass of the breasts and shift of the rib cage towards a position of inspiration, and oedematous swelling of the neck and of laryngeal/pharyngeal mucous membranes, which are more vulnerable to external force and therefore bleed easily. There is also a less favourable working environment because of limited space, lack of time, and situation-related stress factors. Respiratory difficulty, insufficient oxygenation, or failure to secure the airway and related complications are the major cause of anaesthesia-associated mortality in obstetric patients (Mhyre 2010).

By definition, a difficult airway is present when an experienced anaesthetist with specialist expertise cannot persistently maintain the oxygen saturation above 90% with the usual means of airway management; either with face mask ventilation (having a difficult mask ventilation), or with tracheal intubation in a maximum of 3 attempts, or until a desaturation (Sp_{O_2} < 90%) occurs (having a difficult or failed intubation) (Heidegger et al. 2005). This situation is sometimes predictable, but often it occurs unexpectedly. When airway difficulties are predicted, flexible fibreoptic tracheal intubation in the awake patient is considered to be the safest technique. There is only one specific limitation in late pregnancy: the nasal route should be avoided because of the increased vulnerability of the physiologically oedematous mucosa.

It is an absolutely mandatory precondition of each anaesthesia service covering obstetrics to have made provisions for the possibility of unexpected airway difficulties (Malan and Johnson 1988; DeMask 1993; Thind and Nagaraja 2001; Trevisan 2002). There need to be standardized and locally adapted algorithms while all personnel must know of the location of equipment prepared specifically for this purpose, and how to use it. At an operational level, each anaesthetist who practises in this area should be able to provide a professional service under prevailing conditions, such as in a remote location devoid of additional support and outside regular working hours. The anaesthetist in charge should be able to protect the parturient from two potentially fatal hazards, namely, hypoxaemia and gastric aspiration. This begins with the routine search and detection of possible predictors of a difficult airway, which would be the indication for low-risk alternative techniques such as elective, awake fibreoptic intubation (Malan and Johnson 1988; Wong et al. 2003).

The standard technique of rapid sequence induction as described earlier already contains certain safety-enhancing elements that might limit the risks and avoid complications of airway difficulties. However, in pregnant women some further precautions are necessary. When difficulty is encountered during attempted tracheal intubation, the anaesthetist must recognize the most probable reason for the difficulty in order to appropriately choose the next step. Throughout, emphasis must be given to the primacy of oxygenation over ventilation and the primacy of ventilation over tracheal intubation, that is, first avoid hypoxaemia, second avoid aspiration. Furthermore, it should be considered whether a return to baseline (spontaneous breathing with preserved protective reflexes) might be the best course of action. This choice is more difficult in the presence of fetal distress, which represents an urgent indication for the fastest possible implementation of the Caesarean section. However, this cannot be established categorically, but requires a joint assessment with the obstetrician to decide whether to proceed further with the intervention (escalation strategy) or to step back to wakefulness (de-escalation strategy). In the case of a pro-escalation decision, it has to be emphasized that such a strategy does not permit repeated intubation attempts; implementation of an alternative technique is more appropriate. Certainly it may be more prudent to relinquish attempts at tracheal intubation, while a cautious face or laryngeal mask ventilation is maintained (Bailey and Kitching 2005; Cook et al. 2005). Other supraglottic airway instruments such as the i-gel® (Intersurgical Ltd., Workingham, UK), Combitube® (Tyco-Healthcare-Kendall-Sheridan, Mansfield, MA, USA), EasyTube™ (Teleflex Rusch, Research Triangle Park, NC, USA), laryngeal tube, and so on, may be considered as well. The point is not the choice of any specific instrument or technique, but a rational restriction on the selection of a small number of reliable alternatives, which are part of a local standard difficult airway procedure (Biro 2011).

Combined anaesthetic techniques

This heterogeneous category refers to the simultaneous and combined use of different anaesthesia techniques at the same time in the same patient. Each of these techniques may be individually sufficient for surgery alone, but in combination they have synergistic effects while less pronounced or fewer side-effects. The combination of regional anaesthesia with general anaesthesia for Caesarean delivery is not standard care, but can be considered if regional anaesthesia alone is likely to be inadequate in terms of intensity, duration, or both. This can occur when an operation under spinal anaesthesia unexpectedly lasts longer because of unforeseen surgical circumstances such as extensive adhesiolysis or problems with haemostasis. The addition of general anaesthesia to an otherwise functioning regional anaesthesia represents a gradual switch of techniques, which should be considered when an ensuing adverse situation is developing for the mother. Examples might include if severe fetal distress or death occurs, or if there is a severe uterine atony, abnormal bleeding, or both. In such situations, unconsciousness might represent a benefit for the mother, even though the regional technique alone may sufficiently cover the surgical pain.

CSE anaesthesia may be indicated when on the one hand a rapid onset and a profound block are needed in a patient undergoing surgery with an uncertain duration (Tyagi et al. 2009). Another indication for CSE is existing haemodynamic instability or in moderate to severe maternal cardiovascular disease (pre-existing heart disease, pulmonary hypertension). If haemodynamic changes need to be absolutely minimized, a stepwise increase of anaesthetic effect might be possible by performing a CSE based on a low concentration of local anaesthetic and adjuvants for the spinal component (e.g. ropivacaine 0.2% with fentanyl 25 µg), and a slow build-up of the epidural component by repeated administration of small volumes of ropivacaine 0.35% or 0.5% (Macfarlane et al. 2009). Specially manufactured spinal/epidural sets are available for CSE, in which the epidural needle has a separate lumen for the spinal needle thus allowing the two punctures to be performed via one system at the same vertebral column level.

Special situations

Highly urgent caesarean section

With sudden and sustained deterioration of fetal well-being, operative delivery is needed as soon as is possible. If an epidural catheter is *in situ*, the fastest possible onset of surgical anaesthesia can be achieved by a bolus of 8–12 ml of 2% carbonized lidocaine immediately after the alarm has been sounded. Alternatives include ropivacaine 0.75% which in a meta-analysis was found to be superior to lidocaine (Hillyard et al. 2011). Chloroprocaine has recently become available in many European countries and is a good alternative to top-up an epidural for Caesarean section as it has an extremely fast onset. However, because of its short duration of action, it will need supplementation with another local anaesthetic. This might even happen before the transport of the parturient to the operating theatre. Further doses of 6–10 ml during transport with or without additional opioid can produce sufficient anaesthesia to permit skin incision. If this approach does not yield the desired anaesthetic effect for the surgery, one should not hesitate to switch to general anaesthesia in order to avoid unnecessary delay. In this context, one should also consider the side-effects of common obstetric medications such as magnesium and antibiotics that might prolong the action of neuromuscular blocking drugs, and of tocolytics that might interfere with heart rate, heart rhythm, and blood pressure.

Unexpectedly longer duration of operation

In parturients with additional diseases, or in women who have had multiple abdominal surgical procedures (e.g. repeated Caesarean deliveries), the duration of the operation may be significantly extended (Raffin et al. 2006). This is also the case if additional surgical measures are undertaken such as myomectomy or appendectomy. If general anaesthesia has been adopted or an epidural catheter is in place, this will not be a major problem, whereas a single-shot spinal anaesthetic may wear off before the operation is completed. This is especially the case when a local anaesthetic without any additive is used (Sanli et al. 2005). The management of this situation depends on whether there is just a slightly premature anaesthetic regression towards the end of surgery, or the end of the operation remains distant. In the first case, one can get by with the measures that are described in detail in the earlier section on 'Rescue techniques in case of insufficient regional anaesthetic effect'. Otherwise, conversion to general anaesthesia will be required.

Atonic haemorrhage

Atonic bleeding occurs when the uterus does not contract as a result either of normal physiological (humoral) processes or after pharmacological stimulation with uterotonics. If uterine contraction does not happen, sustained bleeding results from the surface where the placenta was adhered. This most often occurs when a placenta praevia, accreta, or vasa praevia was present during the pregnancy (Kuczkowski 2006; Oyelese and Smulian 2006). Usually, atonic bleeds are not self-limiting and therefore they can lead to life-threatening haemorrhage and circulatory failure and, if not treated rapidly, may result in morbidity or death of the mother. The anaesthetist should begin aggressive volume replacement therapy with replacement of clotting factors (fibrinogen, fresh frozen plasma, cryoprecipitate) and platelets (Weiniger et al. 2005). In case of uncertainty about which clotting factor might be mostly deficient, consider fibrinogen to be the first compound that needs substitution in the range of 2–4 g. If the preceding Caesarean section was performed under regional anaesthesia, conversion to general anaesthesia is strongly advisable, regardless of the quality or function of the still effective regional anaesthesia technique. When volatile anaesthetic agents are used, their uterine relaxing effect must be taken into account, and over-dosage avoided. Early siting of a sufficient number of large peripheral intravenous cannulae, and an arterial line are essential: delay is likely to increase the technical challenge. The emphasis is on maintenance of circulating volume, oxygen delivery, and haemostasis (using point-of-care monitors of coagulation when available) with continuous and meticulous efforts to keep the relevant variables within an acceptable range.

Pre-eclampsia, eclampsia, and HELLP syndrome

The anaesthetic concerns in pre-eclampsia, eclampsia, and HELLP syndrome focus on the proper indications for the most suitable anaesthetic technique, as well as the preservation, stabilization, or restoration of vital functions and of homeostasis. With high priority, careful attention has to be given to clotting function, where single laboratory values are of less significance than the general direction and speed of their change. Thus, for example an acute decrease in platelet count from 200 000 to 100 000 over a few hours is much more concerning than a relatively constant value around 80 000. In marked hypertension with concomitant sequestration of intravascular fluid into the interstitial space (which inevitably is associated with pronounced hypovolaemia), a suddenly expanding sympathectomy after spinal anaesthesia may produce severe haemodynamic insufficiency (Santos and Birnbach 2005; Tihtonen et al. 2006). Therefore, if sufficient time is available, invasive blood pressure measurement should be instigated and the insertion of an epidural catheter should be preferred to spinal anaesthesia. With this, a stepwise build-up of anaesthesia with a sufficient spread can be achieved by repetitive administration of epidural local anaesthetics (Visalyaputra et al. 2005). The more organ systems that are affected by the underlying disease and the more pronounced the associated symptoms, the indications of the basic anaesthesia technique should move from spinal to epidural or even towards general anaesthesia (Kamilya et al. 2005; Richa et al. 2005). Full attention has to be devoted to the oxygen supply of mother and fetus and the maintenance of uterine blood flow. While hypovolaemia is in any case deleterious, aggressive intravenous fluid replacement may produce pulmonary oedema because of capillary leak. In this situation good monitoring (possibly with measurement of cardiac filling pressures, non-invasive cardiac output devices) is essential in order to guide carefully tailored therapy. As with atonic haemorrhage, in HELLP syndrome one has to deal with an increasingly impaired coagulation, which involves several levels of the clotting cascade and requires careful monitoring (e.g. by using bedside function tests such as thromboelastography) (Beilin et al. 2006) and an appropriate replacement of factors which are recognized as deficient. Thus, the individual components such as fibrinogen, platelets, plasma coagulation factors, and calcium are targeted to achieve sufficient plasma concentrations. Additionally, one has to take into account the actual as well as the expected further blood loss (Wulf 1990). Finally, normothermia, a normal pH, and water–electrolyte balance must be constantly maintained.

Amniotic fluid embolism

Amniotic fluid embolism accounts for the highest maternal mortality during, closely before, and after childbirth (Tramoni et al. 2004; Moore and Baldisseri 2005; Schoening 2006). Its immediate cause lies in the passage of amniotic fluid and meconium into the maternal circulation, by penetration through the placental attachment to the endometrial surface. The immediate consequences are pulmonary embolism with amniotic fluid components, concomitant pulmonary microvascular obstruction, pulmonary hypertension, right heart overload, and heart failure. Another important feature is disseminated intravascular coagulation caused by activation of the clotting cascade and formation of microthrombi in peripheral arterioles. These vessels become obstructed resulting in subsequent ischaemia and organ failure, ultimately with cardiovascular shock. Of utmost importance is the differential diagnosis of local anaesthetic toxicity, for example, by accidental intravascular injection during epidural anaesthesia.

Amniotic fluid embolism requires aggressive initial therapy to safeguard and restore vital organ function, circulation, coagulation, and respiration. These include tracheal intubation, ventilation of the lungs with oxygen, adequate intravascular volume administration, and administration of vasoactive and inotropic drugs. At the same time one has to ensure haemostasis and control of coagulation with fibrinogen, tranexamic acid, clotting factor concentrates, and possibly antithrombin-III. Therapy also encompasses normalization of acid–base and water–electrolyte balance and adequate renal function (dopamine 2–3 μg kg^{-1} min^{-1}, furosemide) (Beilin et al. 1996). All these measures should be performed with the aid of invasive arterial blood pressure monitoring, which implies that an arterial line should be sited as early as possible. After having achieved stable haemodynamic conditions, vasodilators should be carefully introduced to off-load the (right) heart. Invasive haemodynamic monitoring is necessary because of the severity of the disease, the necessity to obtain fast and frequent blood gas samples, and other laboratory results. As a result of the sudden onset of symptoms, the necessary monitoring can only be installed parallel to the treatment, but naturally the resuscitation measures have priority. Significant bleeding complications have to be expected, therefore, sufficient venous access lines must be established as early as possible.

Postoperative care

Adequate and complete perioperative care covers the immediate postoperative period, which extends from the emergence from anaesthesia usually for 24 h. This period encompasses several important issues, such as pain control and attempts to start lactation, which in turn might be affected by possible side-effects and complications of anaesthesia. Analgesia should be adapted to the prevailing after-effects of the anaesthetic, which usually is characterized by an earlier and more intense analgesic therapy after general anaesthesia than after a regional technique (Pan et al. 2006). When preserving the epidural catheter for further use, one has an elegant opportunity to provide effective and safe postoperative analgesia, which is superior to any form of systemic pharmacological pain treatment. The latter remains the best choice in the absence of an epidural catheter and is best adopted using a multimodal approach, where several pharmacologically different but mutually synergistic analgesic agents are combined. When using a lumbar epidural catheter to provide postoperative analgesia, one should decrease the local anaesthetic concentration to the lowest possible level and it should be combined with analgesic adjuvant drugs in order to limit motor blockade, which during convalescence may hinder early mobilization. This treatment principle encompasses combination of opioids with non-opioids and adjuvant drugs that do not interfere with the post-partum adaptation of the breast-fed newborn (Siddik et al. 2001; Jakobi et al. 2002). It should be remembered that traditional non-steroidal anti-inflammatory drugs (NSAIDs) are associated with persistent patent ductus arteriosus of the infant and should be withheld from the breast-feeding mother. Paracetamol and novaminsulfone can substitute for NSAIDs. As for opioids, both morphine and weaker μ-receptor agonists can be used.

Postoperative fasting longer than 2 h is not necessary (Guedj et al. 1991), but it is advisable to delay oral intake until regional anaesthesia has regressed below the 10th thoracic segment (level at the umbilicus). Abstinence is also recommended if there is an increased probability of further surgical intervention, for example, because of bleeding. Regional anaesthesia can lead to back pain at the puncture site, temporary nerve irritation, and post-dural puncture headache. The latter is caused by loss of cerebrospinal fluid through the hole in the dura. This occurs more frequently when the puncture was difficult and the subdural space was repeatedly punctured. Post-dural puncture headache is even more likely after an accidental puncture of the dura with a Tuohy needle. Depending on the severity of the symptoms, one should first attempt to treat the headaches by pharmacological means, strict bed rest, and generous fluid intake. If no sustained improvement can be achieved this way, the use of an epidural 'blood patch' should be considered (Gunaydin and Karaca 2006; Raffin et al. 2006).

Outcome

Mortality

Anaesthesia in obstetric surgery can be regarded as overwhelmingly safe. During the last decade, the careful observance of contraindications and knowledge of risk factors associated with the various anaesthesia techniques, the routine use of pulse oximetry and capnography, and improvements in equipment have contributed to a significant increase in anaesthesia safety. Kuklina et al. (2009) reported a cross-sectional study of obstetric complications that were retrieved from the 1998–2005 Nationwide Inpatient Sample of the Healthcare Cost and Utilization Project (Mhyre 2010). They found that the frequency of hospitalizations as a result of severe obstetric complications markedly increased from 0.64% in 1998–99 to 0.81% in 2004–05, which was caused by an even more accentuated increase in Caesarean sections at the expense of vaginal births. Even so, there was a decrease of 40% in the rate of severe anaesthesia related complications. The ASA Closed Claims Database also confirms the tendency for increased safety of obstetric anaesthesia for the period from 1990 to 2003 as compared with the period before 1990 (Davies et al. 2009; Kuczkowski et al. 2010). Respiratory complications decreased after 1990 from 24% to 4%. A similar trend was observed for claims connected to inadequate oxygenation or aspiration of gastric contents.

A detailed analysis of anaesthesia-related maternal mortality during childbirth in the United States indicates a significant decrease of mortality in the period 1979 to 1990 (Hawkins et al. 1997). The number of deaths among parturients related to Caesarean section under regional anaesthesia decreased by a factor of 4.5 while for general anaesthesia it increased by a factor of 1.6. The Confidential Enquiries into Maternal Mortality in the United Kingdom convincingly show that the maternal mortality rate has decreased constantly. Between 1994 and 1996, a single death was directly associated with regional anaesthesia, in which there were multiple drug overdoses administered during a CSE. Some other cases of maternal deaths were related to insufficient perioperative surveillance (Lewis et al. 1998).

Morbidity

Complications associated with obstetric regional anaesthesia are usually multifactorial, involving complicated pregnancies, difficult childbirth, maternal co-morbidities and their treatment, inadequate care, urgency of surgery, and poor local structures. Injuries have also been directly associated with anaesthesia, mostly caused by inadequate perioperative surveillance, poor positioning, or both. Problems clearly caused by anaesthesia *per se* are rare. The detailed interpretation of 670 closed liability cases of nerve injuries linked to anaesthesia showed the following frequencies and locations (Cheney et al. 1999): ulnar nerve 28%, brachial plexus 20%, lumbosacral nerve roots 16%, and spinal cord 13%. In a comparison of anaesthesia-related complications between obstetric and non-obstetric cases from the years 1985–1995, difficult intubation had a comparable incidence, but pulmonary aspiration of gastric contents was significantly more frequent in obstetrics. The use of epidural anaesthesia was associated with a slightly increased frequency of seizures, neurological disorders and in a few cases with death of mother, newborn, or both. The majority of claims dealt with cramps, awareness under anaesthesia, as well as headaches and back pain, which in turn represented the most frequent complication in obstetric regional anaesthesia. There was a single case of hypoxic brain damage associated with both non-obstetric and obstetric anaesthesia.

In an Australian analysis (Sinclair et al. 1999) of 203 events from obstetric anaesthesia, 33% of cases were related to documented problems with the regional technique itself in (in particular as the result of accidental dural puncture during epidural anaesthesia). Problems with the equipment accounted for 13% of cases, errors in drug administration were present in 10%, other problems associated with drugs in 16%, difficult or impossible intubation 9%, and technical problems with the tracheal tube in 9%. Difficult but ultimately successful intubations were found with equal incidence in both obstetric anaesthesia and in non-obstetric anaesthesia, but the rare situation of impossible intubation was more common in pregnant women. In the United Kingdom, difficult intubations occurred more frequently in the night, over the weekend, and in emergency situations (Barnardo and Jenkins 2000), which clearly indicates that the level of training and the experience of the involved anaesthetists plays an important role.

Complications after regional anaesthesia

A comparison between spinal anaesthesia and CSE shows that there are no significant differences in the incidence of nerve damage (Holloway et al. 2000). After more than 17 000 consecutive neuraxial regional anaesthetics (Dahlgren and Tornerbrandt 1995) there were 17 neurological complications, 13 of which were irreversible. Three cases involved spinal anaesthesia and 10 followed epidural anaesthesia. According to current data neurological complications in obstetrics are extremely rare after neuraxial regional anaesthesia, which in turn supports the generally accepted dogma that in pregnancy regional anaesthesia has the better benefit/risk ratio compared with general anaesthesia (Loo et al. 2000).

Declaration of interest

None declared.

References

Abouleish A, Abouleish E, Camann W. Combined spinal-epidural analgesia in advanced labour. *Can J Anaesth* 1994; **41**: 575–8

Abrao KC, Francisco RP, Miyadahira S, Cicarelli DD, Zugaib M. Elevation of uterine basal tone and fetal heart rate abnormalities after labor analgesia: a randomized controlled trial. *Obstet Gynecol* 2009; **113**: 41–7

Albright GA. Cardiac arrest following regional anesthesia with etidocaine or bupivacaine. *Anesthesiology* 1979; **51**: 285–7

Albright GA, Forster RM. Does combined spinal-epidural analgesia with subarachnoid sufentanil increase the incidence of emergency cesarean delivery? *Reg Anesth* 1997; **22**: 400–5

Albright GA, Forster RM. The safety and efficacy of combined spinal and epidural analgesia/anesthesia (6,002 blocks) in a community hospital. *Reg Anesth Pain Med* 1999; 24: 117–25

Aldebert S, Sleth JC. [Bacterial meningitis after combined spinal and epidural anesthesia in obstetrics]. *Ann Fr Anesth Reanim* 1996; **15**: 687–8

Arzola C, Wieczorek PM. Efficacy of low-dose bupivacaine in spinal anaesthesia for Caesarean delivery: systematic review and meta-analysis. *Br J Anaesth* 2011; **107**: 308–18

Asik I, Goktug A, Gulay I, Alkis N, Uysalel A. Comparison of bupivacaine 0.2% and ropivacaine 0.2% combined with fentanyl for epidural analgesia during labour. *Eur J Anaesthesiol* 2002; **19**: 263–70

Atienzar MC, Palanca JM, Torres F, Borras R, Gil S, Esteve I. A randomized comparison of levobupivacaine, bupivacaine and ropivacaine with fentanyl, for labor analgesia. *Int J Obstet Anesth* 2008; **17**: 106–11

Aveline C, El Metaoua S, Masmoudi A, Boelle PY, Bonnet F. The effect of clonidine on the minimum local analgesic concentration of epidural ropivacaine during labor. *Anesth Analg* 2002; **95**: 735–40

Bailey SG, Kitching AJ. The Laryngeal mask airway in failed obstetric tracheal intubation. *Int J Obstet Anesth* 2005; **14**: 270–1

Baker MN, Sarna MC. Respiratory arrest after second dose of intrathecal sufentanil. *Anesthesiology* 1995; **83**: 231–2

Barnardo P, Jenkins J. Failed tracheal intubation in obstetrics: a 6-year review in a UK region. *Anaesthesia* 2000; **55**: 690–4

Beilin Y, Arnold I, Hossain S. Evaluation of the platelet function analyzer (PFA-100) vs. the thromboelastogram (TEG) in the parturient. *Int J Obstet Anesth* 2006; **15**: 7–12

Beilin Y, Bodian CA, Haddad EM, Leibowitz AB. Practice patterns of anesthesiologists regarding situations in obstetric anesthesia where clinical management is controversial. *Anesth Analg* 1996; **83**: 735–41

Berga S, Trierweiler MW. Bacterial meningitis following epidural anesthesia for vaginal delivery: a case report. *Obstet Gynecol* 1989; **74**: 437–9

Birnbach DJ, Chestnut DH. The epidural test dose in obstetric patients: has it outlived its usefulness? *Anesth Analg* 1999; **88**: 971–2

Birnbach DJ, Ojea LS. Combined spinal-epidural (CSE) for labor and delivery. *Int Anesthesiol Clin* 2002; **40**: 27–48

Biro P. Difficult intubation in pregnancy. *Curr Opin Anesthesiol* 2011; **24**: 249–54

Bloom SL, Spong CY, Weiner SJ, *et al.* Complications of anesthesia for cesarean delivery. *Obstet Gynecol* 2005; **106**: 281–7

Bouhemad B, Dounas M, Mercier FJ, Benhamou D. Bacterial meningitis following combined spinal-epidural analgesia for labour. *Anaesthesia* 1998; **53**: 292–5

Boutros A, Blary S, Bronchard R, Bonnet F. Comparison of intermittent epidural bolus, continuous epidural infusion and patient controlled-epidural analgesia during labor. *Int J Obstet Anesth* 1999; **8**: 236–41

Bromage PR. Problems with combined spinal and epidural anesthesia. *Reg Anesth Pain Med* 1999; **24**: 191

Buggy D. Ambulation during regional analgesia for labour should be discouraged. *Int J Obstet Anesth* 1999; **8**: 179–83

Burnstein R, Buckland R, Pickett JA. A survey of epidural analgesia for labour in the United Kingdom. *Anaesthesia* 1999; **54**: 634–40

Buvanendran A, McCarthy RJ, Kroin JS, Leong W, Perry P, Tuman KJ. Intrathecal magnesium prolongs fentanyl analgesia: a prospective, randomized, controlled trial. *Anesth Analg* 2002; **95**: 661–6

Cakmak H, Kuguoglu S. Comparison of the breastfeeding patterns of mothers who delivered their babies per vagina and via cesarean section: an observational study using the LATCH breastfeeding charting system. *Int J Nurs Stud* 2007; **44**: 1128–37

Camann W, Norris M, Rawal N, Crowhurst J, Vercauteren M, Holmstrom B. Alleged problems with combined spinal and epidural anesthesia. *Reg Anesth Pain Med* 2000; 25: 104–6

Caman WR, Minzter BH, Denney RA, Datta S. Intrathecal sufentanil for labor analgesia. Effects of added epinephrine. *Anesthesiology* 1993; **78**: 870–874

Camorcia M, Capogna G, Columb MO. Minimum local analgesic doses of ropivacaine, levobupivacaine, and bupivacaine for intrathecal labor analgesia. *Anesthesiology* 1995; **102**: 646–50

Campbell DC, Zwack RM, Crone LA, Yip RW. Ambulatory labor epidural analgesia: bupivacaine versus ropivacaine. *Anesth Analg* 2000; **90**: 1384–9

Capogna G, Camorcia M, Columb MO. Minimum analgesic doses of fentanyl and sufentanil for epidural analgesia in the first stage of labor. *Anesth Analg* 2003; **96**: 1178–82

Capogna G, Celleno D, Fusco P, Lyons G, Columb M. Relative potencies of bupivacaine and ropivacaine for analgesia in labour. *Br J Anaesth* 1999; **82**: 371–3

Cappiello E, O'Rourke N, Segal S, Tsen LC. A randomized trial of dural puncture epidural technique compared with the standard epidural technique for labor analgesia. *Anesth Analg* 2008; **107**: 1646–51

Carvalho B, Cohen SE, Lipman SS, Fuller A, Mathusamy AD, Macario A. Patient preferences for anesthesia outcomes associated with cesarean delivery. *Anesth Analg* 2005; **101**: 1182–7

Carvalho B, Wang P, Cohen SE. A survey of labor patient-controlled epidural anesthesia practice in California hospitals. *Int J Obstet Anesth* 2006; **15**: 217–22

Carvalho JC. Ultrasound-facilitated epidurals and spinals in obstetrics. *Anesthesiol Clin* 2008; **26**: 145–58, vii–viii

Cascio M, Heath G. Meningitis following a combined spinal-epidural technique in a labouring term parturient. *Can J Anaesth* 1996; **43**: 399–402

Chassard D, Mathon L, Dailler F, Golfier F, Tournadre JP, Bouletreau P. Extradural clonidine combined with sufentanil and 0.0625% bupivacaine for analgesia in labour. *Br J Anaesth* 1996; 77: 458–62

Cheney FW, Domino KB, Caplan RA, Posner KL. Nerve injury associated with anesthesia. A closed claims analysis. *Anesthesiology* 1999; **90**: 1062–9

Chiari A, Lorber C, Eisenach JC, *et al* Analgesic and hemodynamic effects of intrathecal clonidine as the sole analgesic agent during first stage of labor: a dose-response study. *Anesthesiology* 1999; **91**: 388–96

Chua NP, Sia AT, Ocampo CE. Parturient-controlled epidural analgesia during labour: bupivacaine vs. ropivacaine. *Anaesthesia* 2001; **56**: 1169–73

Clarke VT, Smiley RM, Finster M. Uterine hyperactivity after intrathecal injection of fentanyl for analgesia during labor: a cause of fetal bradycardia? *Anesthesiology* 1994; **81**: 1083

Cohen S, Daitch JS, Goldiner PL. An alternative method for management of accidental dural puncture for labor and delivery. *Anesthesiology* 1989; **70**: 164–5

Cohen SE, Cherry CM, Holbrook RH, Jr, el-Sayed YY, Gibson RN, Jaffe RA. Intrathecal sufentanil for labor analgesia – sensory changes, side effects, and fetal heart rate changes. *Anesth Analg* 1993; **77**: 1155–60

Cohen SE, Yeh JY, Riley ET, Vogel TM. Walking with labor epidural analgesia: the impact of bupivacaine concentration and a lidocaine-epinephrine test dose. *Anesthesiology* 2000; **92**: 387–92

Coleman L, Carvalho B, Lipman S, Schmiesing C, Riley E. Accidental intrathecal sufentanil overdose during combined spinal-epidural analgesia for labor. *Int J Obstet Anesth* 2009; **18**: 78–80

Collis R. Combined spinal epidural (CSE) analgesia is the preferred technique for labour pain relief. *Acta Anaesthesiol Belg* 2002; **53**: 283–7

Collis RE, Baxandall ML, Srikantharajah ID, Edge G, Kadim MY, Morgan BM. Combined spinal epidural (CSE) analgesia: technique, management, and outcome of 300 mothers. *Int J Obstet Anesth* 1994; **3**: 75–81

Collis RE, Davies DW, Aveling W. Randomised comparison of combined spinal-epidural and standard epidural analgesia in labour. *Lancet* 1995; **345**: 1413–6

Collis RE, Plaat FS, Morgan BM. Comparison of midwife top-ups, continuous infusion and patient-controlled epidural analgesia for maintaining mobility after a low-dose combined spinal-epidural. *Br J Anaesth* 1999; **82**: 233–6

Colonna-Romano P, Lingaraju N, Godfrey SD, Braitman LE. Epidural test dose and intravascular injection in obstetrics: sensitivity, specificity, and lowest effective dose. *Anesth Analg* 1992; **75**: 372–6

Comparative Obstetric Mobile Epidural Trial Study Group, UK. Effect of low-dose mobile versus traditional epidural techniques on mode of delivery: a randomised controlled trial. *Lancet* 2001; **358**: 19–23

Consolo D, Ouardirhi Y, Wessels C, Girard C. Obstetrical anaesthesia and porphyrias. *Ann Fr Anesth Reanim* 2005; **24**: 428–31

Cook TM, Brooks TS, Van der Westhuizen J, Clarke M. The Proseal LMA is a useful rescue device during failed rapid sequence intubation: two additional cases. *Can J Anaesth* 2005; **52**: 630–3

Crawford JS. Some maternal complications of epidural analgesia for labor. *Anaesthesia* 1985; **40**: 1219–25

Crites J, Ramanathan J. Acute hypoglycemia following combined spinal-epidural anesthesia (CSE) in a parturient with diabetes mellitus. *Anesthesiology* 2000; **93**: 591–2

Currier DS, Levin KR, Campbell C. Dysphagia with intrathecal fentanyl. *Anesthesiology* 1997; **87**: 1570–1

Curry PD, Pacsoo C, Heap DG. Patient-controlled epidural analgesia in obstetric anaesthetic practice. *Pain* 1994; **57**: 125–7

D'Angelo R, Dean LS, Meister GC, Nelson KE. Neostigmine combined with bupivacaine, clonidine, and sufentanil for spinal labor analgesia. *Anesth Analg* 2001; **93**: 1560–4

D'Athis F, Macheboeuf M, Thomas H, *et al.* Epidural analgesia with a bupivacaine-fentanyl mixture in obstetrics: comparison of repeated injections and continuous infusion. *Can J Anaesth* 1988; **35**: 116–22

Dahlgren N, Tornerbrandt K. Neurological complications after anaesthesia. A follow-up of 18000 spinal and epidural anaesthetics performed over three years. *Acta Anaesthesiol Scand* 1995; **39**: 872–80

Davies JM, Posner KL, Lee LA, Cheney FW, Domino KB. Liability associated with obstetric anesthesia: a closed claims analysis. *Anesthesiology* 2009; **110**: 131–9

Davis L, Hargreaves C, Robinson PN. Postpartum meningitis. *Anaesthesia* 1993; **48**: 788–9

DeMask DR. A system of airway risk management in obstetric anesthesia. *Nurse Anesth* 1993; **4**: 62–72

Dounas M, O'Kelly BO, Jamali S, Mercier FJ, Benhamou D. Maternal and fetal effects of adrenaline with bupivacaine (0.25%) for epidural analgesia during labour. *Eur J Anaesthesiol* 1996; **13**: 594–8

Draisci G, Valente A, Suppa E, *et al.* Remifentanil for cesarean section under general anesthesia: effects on maternal stress hormone secretion and neonatal well-being: a randomized trial. *Int J Obstet Anesth* 2008; **17**: 130–6

Duggan J, Bowler GM, McClure JH, Wildsmith JA. Extradural block with bupivacaine: influence of dose, volume, concentration and patient characteristics. *Br J Anaesth* 1988; **61**: 324–31

Dyer RA, Rout CC, Kruger AM, van der Vyver M, Lamacraft G, James MF. Prevention and treatment of cardiovascular instability during spinal anaesthesia for caesarean section. *S Afr Med J* 2004; **94**: 367–72

Eberle RL, Norris MC, Eberle AM, Naulty JS, Arkoosh VA. The effect of maternal position on fetal heart rate during epidural or intrathecal labor analgesia. *Am J Obstet Gynecol* 1998; **179**: 150–5

Eisenach JC, Grice SC. Epidural clonidine does not decrease blood pressure or spinal cord blood flow in awake sheep. *Anesthesiology* 1988; **68**: 335–40

Escarment J, Clement HJ. [Use of epidural and intrathecal opiates in obstetrics]. *Ann Fr Anesth Reanim* 1989; **8**: 636–49

Ferouz F, Norris MC, Leighton BL. Risk of respiratory arrest after intrathecal sufentanil. *Anesth Analg* 1997; **85**: 1088–90

Ferrante FM, Lu L, Jamison SB, Datta S. Patient-controlled epidural analgesia: demand dosing. *Anesth Analg* 1991; **73**: 547–52

Fettes PD, Moore CS, Whiteside JB, McLeod GA, Wildsmith JA. Intermittent vs continuous administration of epidural ropivacaine with fentanyl for analgesia during labour. *Br J Anaesth* 2006; **97**: 359–64

Fischer C, Blanie P, Jaouen E, Vayssiere C, Kaloul I, Coltat JC. Ropivacaine, 0.1%, plus sufentanil, 0.5 microg/ml, versus bupivacaine, 0.1%, plus sufentanil, 0.5 microg/ml, using patient-controlled epidural analgesia for labor: a double-blind comparison. *Anesthesiology* 2000; **92**: 1588–93

Fragneto RY, Fisher A. Mental status change and aphasia after labor analgesia with intrathecal sufentanil/bupivacaine. *Anesth Analg* 2000; **90**: 1175–6

Fun W, Lew E, Sia AT. Advances in neuraxial blocks for labor analgesia: new techniques, new systems. *Minerva Anestesiol* 2008; **74**: 77–85

Gaiser RR, McHugh M, Cheek TG, Gutsche BB. Predicting prolonged fetal heart rate deceleration following intrathecal fentanyl/bupivacaine. *Int J Obstet Anesth* 2005; **14**: 208–11

Gambling DR, Huber CJ, Berkowitz J, *et al.* Patient-controlled epidural analgesia in labour: varying bolus dose and lockout interval. *Can J Anaesth* 1993; **40**: 211–7

Gambling DR, McMorland GH, Yu P, Laszlo C. Comparison of patient-controlled epidural analgesia and conventional intermittent top-up injections during labor. *Anesth Analg* 1990; **70**: 256–61

Gambling DR, Sharma SK, Ramin SM, *et al.* A randomized study of combined spinal-epidural analgesia versus intravenous meperidine during labor: impact on cesarean delivery rate. *Anesthesiology* 1998; **89**: 1336–44

Gambling DR, Yu P, Cole C, McMorland GH, Palmer L. A comparative study of patient controlled epidural analgesia (PCEA) and continuous infusion epidural analgesia (CIEA) during labour. *Can J Anaesth* 1988; **35**: 249–54

Gautier P, De Kock M, Van Steenberge A, Miclot D, Fanard L, Hody JL. A double-blind comparison of 0.125% ropivacaine with sufentanil and 0.125% bupivacaine with sufentanil for epidural labor analgesia. *Anesthesiology* 1999; **90**: 772–8

Gautier PE, Debry F, Fanard L, Van Steenberge A, Hody JL. Ambulatory combined spinal-epidural analgesia for labor. Influence of epinephrine on bupivacaine-sufentanil combination. *Reg Anesth* 1997; **22**: 143–9

Giriyappa R, Jefferson P, Ball DR. Remifentanil for tracheal intubation. *Anaesthesia* 2006; **61**: 194–5

Gogarten W, Van de Velde M, Soetens F, *et al.* A multicentre trial comparing different concentrations of ropivacaine plus sufentanil with bupivacaine plus sufentanil for patient-controlled epidural analgesia in labour. *Eur J Anaesthesiol* 2004; **21**: 38–45

Goodman SR, Kim-Lo SH, Ciliberto CF, Ridley DM, Smiley RM. Epinephrine is not a useful addition to intrathecal fentanyl or fentanyl-bupivacaine for labor analgesia. *Reg Anesth Pain Med* 2002; **27**: 374–9

Goodman SR, Smiley RM, Negron MA, Freedman PA, Landau R. A randomized trial of breakthrough pain during combined spinal-epidural versus epidural labor analgesia in parous women. *Anesth Analg* 2009; **108**: 246–51

Gordh T, Jr, Post C, Olsson Y. Evaluation of the toxicity of subarachnoid clonidine, guanfacine, and a substance P-antagonist on rat spinal cord and nerve roots: light and electron microscopic observations after chronic intrathecal administration. *Anesth Analg* 1986; **65**: 1303–11

Greenhalgh CA. Respiratory arrest in a parturient following intrathecal injection of sufentanil and bupivacaine. *Anaesthesia* 1996; **51**: 173–5

Guedj P, Eldor J, Stark M. Immediate postoperative oral hydration after caesarean section. *Asia Oceania J Obstet Gynaecol* 1991; **17**: 125–9

Gunaydin B, Karaca G. Prevention strategy for post dural puncture headache. *Acta Anaesthesiol Belg* 2006; 57: 163–5

Gurbet A, Turker G, Kose DO, Uckunkaya N. Intrathecal epinephrine in combined spinal-epidural analgesia for labor: dose-response relationship for epinephrine added to a local anesthetic-opioid combination. *Int J Obstet Anesth* 2005; 14: 121–5

Habib AS, Gan TJ. Use of neostigmine in the management of acute postoperative pain and labour pain: a review. *CNS Drugs* 2006; **20**: 821–39

Hafer J, Rupp D, Wollbrück M, Engel J, Hempelmann G. The effect of needle type and immobilization on postspinal headache. *Anaesthesist* 1997; **46**: 860–6

Halonen P, Sarvela J, Saisto T, Soikkeli A, Halmesmaki E, Korttila K. Patient-controlled epidural technique improves analgesia for labor but increases cesarean delivery rate compared with the intermittent bolus technique. *Acta Anaesthesiol Scand* 2004; **48**: 732–7

Halpern SH, Walsh V. Epidural ropivacaine versus bupivacaine for labor: a meta-analysis. *Anesth Analg* 2003; **96**: 1473–9

Hamilton CL, Cohen SE. High sensory block after intrathecal sufentanil for labor analgesia. *Anesthesiology* 2005; **83**: 1118–21

Harding SA, Collis RE, Morgan BM. Meningitis after combined spinal-extradural anaesthesia in obstetrics. *Br J Anaesth* 1994; **73**: 545–7

Hawkins J, Koonin L, Plamer S, Gibbs C. Anesthesia-related deaths during obstetric delivery in the United States, 1979-1990. *Anesthesiology* 1997; **86**: 277–84

Hays RL, Palmer CM. Respiratory depression after intrathecal sufentanil during labor. *Anesthesiology* 1994; **81**: 511–2

Heard A, Langley K. Remifentanil for tracheal intubation. *Anaesthesia* 2006; **61**: 194

Heesen M, Klohr S, Hofmann T, *et al.* Maternal and foetal effects of remifentanil for general anaesthesia in parturients undergoing caesarean section: a systematic review and meta-analysis. *Acta Anaesthesiol Scand* 2013; **57**: 29–36

Heidegger T, Gerig HJ, Henderson JJ. Strategies and algorithms for management of the difficult airway. *Best Pract Res Clin Anaesthesiol* 2005; **19**: 661–74

Hepner DL, Gaiser RR, Cheek TG, Gutsche BB. Comparison of combined spinal-epidural and low dose epidural for labour analgesia. *Can J Anaesth* 2000; **47**: 232–6

Herman NL, Calicott R, Van Decar TK, Conlin G, Tilton J. Determination of the dose-response relationship for intrathecal sufentanil in laboring patients. *Anesth Analg* 1997; **84**: 1256–61

Hess PE, Pratt SD, Lucas TP, *et al.* Predictors of breakthrough pain during labor epidural analgesia. *Anesth Analg* 2001; **93**: 414–8

Hillyard SG, Bate TE, Corcoran TB, Paech MJ O'Sullivan G. Extending epidural analgesia for emergency Caesarean section: a meta-analysis. *Br J Anaesth* 2011; **107**: 668–78

Hobson JA, Slade P, Wrench IJ, Power L. Preoperative anxiety and postoperative satisfaction in women undergoing elective caesarean section. *Int J Obstet Anesth* 2006; **15**: 18–23

Holloway J, Seed P, O'Sullivan G, Reynolds F. Paraesthesiae and nerve damage following combined spinal epidural and spinal anesthesia: a pilot survey. *Int J Obstet Anesth* 2000; **9**: 151–5

Honet JE, Arkoosh VA, Norris MC, Huffnagle HJ, Silverman NS, Leighton BL. Comparison among intrathecal fentanyl, meperidine, and sufentanil for labor analgesia. *Anesth Analg* 1992; **75**: 734–9

Hood DD, Eisenach JC, Tong C, Tommasi E, Yaksh TL. Cardiorespiratory and spinal cord blood flow effects of intrathecal neostigmine methylsulfate, clonidine, and their combination in sheep. *Anesthesiology* 1995; **82**: 428–35

Hughes D, Hill D, Fee JP. Intrathecal ropivacaine or bupivacaine with fentanyl for labour. *Br J Anaesth* 2001; **87**: 733–7

Imarengiaye CO, Ekwere IT. Acid aspiration prophylaxis and caesarean delivery: time for another close look. *J Obstet Gynaecol* 2005; **25**: 357–8

Ithnin F, Lim Y, Sia AT, Ocampo CE. Combined spinal epidural causes higher level of block than equivalent single-shot spinal anesthesia in elective cesarean patients. *Anesth Analg* 2006; **102**: 577–80

Jakobi P, Solt I, Tamir A, Zimmer EZ. Over-the-counter oral analgesia for postcesarean pain. *Am J Obstet Gynecol* 2002; **187**: 1066–9

Joos S, Servais R, van Steenberge A. Sequential spinal epidural analgesia for pain relief in labour: an audit of 620 parturients. *Int J Obstet Anesth* 1995; **4**: 155–7

Kahn L, Hubert E. Combined spinal epidural (CSE) analgesia, fetal bradycardia, and uterine hypertonus. *Reg Anesth Pain Med* 1998; **23**: 111–2

Kamilya G, Bharracharyya SK, Mukherji J. Changing trends in the management of eclampsia from a teaching hospital. *J Indian Med Assoc* 2005; **103**: 132, 134–5

Karaman S, Akercan F, Aldemir O, Terek MC, Yalaz M, Firat V. The maternal and neonatal effects of the volatile anaesthetic agents desflurane and sevoflurane in caesarean section: a prospective, randomized clinical study. *J Int Med Res* 2006; 2006a; **34**: 183–92

Karaman S, Kocabas S, Uyar M, Hayzaran S, Firat V. The effects of sufentanil or morphine added to hyperbaric bupivacaine in spinal anaesthesia for caesarean section. *Eur J Anaesthesiol* 2006b; **23**: 285–91

Katsiris S, Williams s, Leighton BL, Halpern S. Respiratory arrest following intrathecal injection of sufentanil and bupivacaine in a parturient. *Can J Anaesth* 1998; **45**: 880–3

Kayacan N, Ertugrul F, Cete N, *et al.* Comparison of epidural and combined spinal-epidural analgesia in the management of labour without pain. *J Int Med Res* 2006; **34**: 596–602

Kee WD, Khaw KS, Ma KC, Wong AS, Lee BB, Ng FF. Maternal and neonatal effects of remifentanil at induction of general anesthesia for cesarean delivery: a randomized, double-blind, controlled trial. *Anesthesiology* 2006; **104**: 14–20

Kee WD, Khaw KS, Ng FF. Prevention of hypotension during spinal anesthesia for cesarean delivery: an effective technique using combination phenylephrine infusion and crystalloid cohydration. *Anesthesiology* 2005; **103**: 744–50

Kjaer K, Comerford M, Kondilis L, *et al.* Oral sodium citrate increases nausea amongst elective Cesarean delivery patients. *Can J Anaesth* 2006; **53**: 776–80

Kuczkowski KM. Acute hypoglycaemia in a healthy parturient following induction of a combined spinal-epidural analgesia for labour. *Anaesthesia* 2003a; **58**: 488–9

Kuczkowski KM. Post-dural puncture headache, intracranial air and obstetric anesthesia. *Anaesthesist* 2003b; **52**: 798–800

Kuczkowski KM. Severe persistent fetal bradycardia following subarachnoid administration of fentanyl and bupivacaine for induction of a combined spinal-epidural analgesia for labor pain. *J Clin Anesth* 2004; **16**: 78–79

Kuczkowski KM. Anesthesia for the repeat cesarean section in the parturient with abnormal placentation: what does an obstetrician need to know? *Arch Gynecol Obstet* 2006; **273**: 319–21

Kuczkowski KM. Labor pain and its management with the combined spinal-epidural analgesia: what does an obstetrician need to know? *Arch Gynecol Obstet* 2007; **275**: 183–5

Kuczkowski KM, Goldsworthy M. Transient aphonia and aphagia in a parturient after induction of combined spinal-epidural labor analgesia with subarachnoid fentanyl and bupivacaine. *Acta Anaesthesiol Belg* 2003; **54**: 165–6

Kuczkowski KM, Reisner LS, Benumof JL. Airway problems and new solutions for the obstetric patient. *J Clin Anesth* 2003; **15**: 552–63

Kuklina EV, Meikle SF, Jamieson DJ, *et al.* Severe obstetric morbidity in the United States: 1998–2005. *Obstet Gynecol* 2009; **113**: 293–9

Lacassie HJ, Columb MO The relative motor blocking potencies of bupivacaine and levobupivacaine in labor. *Anesth Analg* 2003; **97**: 1509–13

Lacassie HJ, Columb MO, Lacassie HP, Lantadilla RA. The relative motor blocking potencies of epidural bupivacaine and ropivacaine in labor. *Anesth Analg* 2002; **95**: 204–8

Lamont RF, Pinney D, Rodgers P, Bryant TN. Continuous versus intermittent epidural analgesia. A randomised trial to observe obstetric outcome. *Anaesthesia* 1989; **44**: 893–6

Landau R. Combined spinal-epidural analgesia for labor: breakthrough or unjustified invasion? *Semin Perinatol* 2002; **26**: 109–21

Landau R, Schiffer E, Morales M, Savoldelli G, Kern C. The dose-sparing effect of clonidine added to ropivacaine for labor epidural analgesia. *Anesth Analg* 2002; **95**: 728–34

Ledin Eriksson S, Gentele C, Olofsson CH. PCEA compared to continuous epidural infusion in an ultra-low-dose regimen for labor pain relief: a randomized study. *Acta Anaesthesiol Scand* 2003; **47**: 1085–90

Lee BB, Ngan Kee WD, Ng FF, Lau TK, Wong EL. Epidural infusions of ropivacaine and bupivacaine for labor analgesia: a randomized, double-blind study of obstetric outcome. *Anesth Analg* 2004; **98**: 1145–52

Lee S, Lew E, Lim Y, Sia AT. Failure of augmentation of labor epidural analgesia for intrapartum cesarean delivery: a retrospective review. *Anesth Analg* 2009; **108**: 252–4

Leighton BL, Arkoosh VA, Huffnagle S, Huffnagle HJ, Kinsella SM, Norris MC. The dermatomal spread of epidural bupivacaine with and without prior intrathecal sufentanil. *Anesth Analg* 1996; **83**: 526–9

Levin A, Datta S, Camann WR. Intrathecal ropivacaine for labor analgesia: a comparison with bupivacaine. *Anesth Analg* 1998; **87**: 624–7

Lew E, Yeo SW, Thomas E. Combined spinal-epidural anesthesia using epidural volume extension leads to faster motor recovery after elective cesarean delivery: a prospective, randomized, double-blind study. *Anesth Analg* 2004; **98**: 810–4

Lewis G, Drife J, Botting B. *Why Mothers Die. Report on Confidential Enquiries into Maternal Deaths in the United Kingdom 1994–1996.* London: Department of Health and MSO, 1998

Lim Y, Ocampo CE, Sia AT. A comparison of duration of analgesia of intrathecal 2.5 mg of bupivacaine, ropivacaine, and levobupivacaine in combined spinal epidural analgesia for patients in labor. *Anesth Analg* 2004; **98**: 235–9

Lim Y, Ocampo CE, Supandji M, Teoh WH, Sia AT. A randomized controlled trial of three patient-controlled epidural analgesia regimens for labor. *Anesth Analg* 2008; **107**: 1968–72

Lim Y, Sia AT, Ocampo CE. Comparison of computer integrated patient controlled epidural analgesia vs. conventional patient controlled epidural analgesia for pain relief in labour. *Anaesthesia* 2006; **61**: 339–44

Littleford J. Effects on the fetus and newborn of maternal analgesia and anesthesia: a review. *Can J Anaesth* 2004; **51**: 586–609

Loo C, Dahlgren G, Irestedt L. Neurological complications in obstetric regional anaesthesia. *Int J Obstet Anesth* 2000; **9**: 99–124

Loubert C, O'Brien PJ, Fernando R, *et al.* Epidural volume extension in combined spinal epidural anaesthesia for elective caesarean section: a randomised controlled trial. *Anaesthesia* 2011; **66**: 341–7

Lu JK, Manullang TR, Staples MH, Kem SE, Balley PL. Maternal respiratory arrests, severe hypotension, and fetal distress after administration of intrathecal, sufentanil, and bupivacaine after intravenous fentanyl. *Anesthesiology* 1997; **87**: 170–2

Lyons G, Akerman N. Problems with general anaesthesia for caesarean section. *Minerva Anestesiol* 2005; **71**: 27–38

Lysak SZ, Eisenach JC, Dobson CE, 2nd. Patient-controlled epidural analgesia during labor: a comparison of three solutions with a continuous infusion control. *Anesthesiology* 1990; **72**: 44–9

Macfarlane AJ, Pryn A, Litchfield KN, *et al.* Randomised controlled trial of combined spinal epidural vs. spinal anaesthesia for elective caesarean section: vasopressor requirements and cardiovascular changes. *Eur J Anaesthesiol* 2009; **26**: 47–51

Malan TP, Jr, Johnson MD. The difficult airway in obstetric anesthesia: techniques for airway management and the role of regional anesthesia. *J Clin Anesth* 1988; **1**: 104–11

Mandell GL, Jamnback L, Ramanathan S. Hemodynamic effects of subarachnoid fentanyl in laboring parturients. *Reg Anesth* 1996; **21**: 103–11

Marcus MA, Vertommen JD, Van Aken H, Gogarten W, Buerkle H. The effects of adding isoproterenol to 0.125% bupivacaine on the quality and duration of epidural analgesia in laboring parturients. *Anesth Analg* 1998; **86**: 749–52

Mardirosoff C, Dumont L, Boulvain M, Tramer MR. Fetal bradycardia due to intrathecal opioids for labour analgesia: a systematic review. *BJOG* 2002; **109**: 274–81

Mather LE, Chang DH. Cardiotoxicity with modern local anaesthetics: is there a safer choice? *Drugs* 2001; **61**: 333–42

McClelland SH, Bogod DG, Hardman JG. Pre-oxygenation and apnoea in pregnancy: changes during labour and with obstetric morbidity in a computational simulation. *Anaesthesia* 2009; **64**: 371–7

Meininger D, Byhahn C, Kessler P, *et al.* Intrathecal fentanyl, sufentanil, or placebo combined with hyperbaric mepivacaine 2% for parturients undergoing elective cesarean delivery. *Anesth Analg* 2003; **97**: 926–7

Meister GC, D'Angelo R, Owen M, Nelson KE, Gaver R. A comparison of epidural analgesia with 0.125% ropivacaine with fentanyl versus 0.125% bupivacaine with fentanyl during labor. *Anesth Analg* 2000; **90**: 632–7

Mercier FJ, Dounas M, HBouaziz H, *et al.* The effect of adding a minidose of clonidine to intrathecal sufentanil for labor analgesia. *Anesthesiology* 1998; **89**: 594–601

Mhyre JM. What's new in obstetric anesthesia in 2009? An update on maternal patient safety. *Anesth Analg* 2010; **111**: 1480–7

Miro M, Guasch E, Gilsanz F. Comparison of epidural analgesia with combined spinal-epidural analgesia for labor: a retrospective study of 6497 cases. *Int J Obstet Anesth* 2008; **17**: 15–9

Missant C, Teunkens A, Vandermeersch E, Van de Velde M. Intrathecal clonidine prolongs labour analgesia but worsens fetal outcome: a pilot study. *Can J Anaesth* 2004; **51**: 696–701

Missant C, Teunkenst A, Vandermeersch E, Van de Velde M. Patient-controlled epidural analgesia following combined spinal-epidural analgesia in labour: the effects of adding a continuous epidural infusion. *Anaesth Intensive Care* 2005; **33**: 452–6

Moore J, Baldisseri MR. Amniotic fluid embolism. *Crit Care Med* 2005; **33**(10 Suppl): S279–85

Moschini V, Marra G, Dabrowska D. Complications of epidural and combined spinal-epidural analgesia in labour. *Minerva Anestesiol* 2006; **72**: 47–58

Nageotte MP, Larson D, Rumney PJ, Sidhu M, Hollenbach K. Epidural analgesia compared with combined spinal-epidural analgesia during labor in nulliparous women. *N Engl J Med* **337**: 1715–9

Naguib M, Yaksh TL. Antinociceptive effects of spinal cholinesterase inhibition and isobolographic analysis of the interaction with mu and alpha 2 receptor systems. *Anesthesiology* 1994; **80**: 1338–48

Nelson KE, D'Angelo R, Foss ML, Meister GC, Hood DD, Eisenach JC. Intrathecal neostigmine and sufentanil for early labor analgesia. *Anesthesiology* 1999; **91**: 1293–8

Ng A, Shah J, Smith G. Is continuous spinal analgesia via an epidural catheter appropriate after accidental subarachnoid administration of 15 mL of bupivacaine 0.1% containing fentanyl 2 micrograms/mL? *Int J Obstet Anesth* 2004; **13**: 107–9

Ngan Kee WD, Khaw KS. Vasopressors in obstetrics: what should we be using? *Curr Opin Anaesthesiol* 2006; **19**: 238–43

Nickells JS, Vaughan DJ, Lillywhite NK, Loughnan B, Hasan M, Robinson PN. Speed of onset of regional analgesia in labour: a comparison of the epidural and spinal routes. *Anaesthesia* 2000; **55**: 17–20

Nicolet J, Miller A, Kaufman I, Guertin MC, Deschamps A. Maternal factors implicated in fetal bradycardia after combined spinal epidural for labour pain. *Eur J Anaesthesiol* 2008; **25**: 721–5

Nielsen PE, Erickson JR, Abouleish EI, Perriatt S, Sheppard C. Fetal heart rate changes after intrathecal sufentanil or epidural bupivacaine for labor analgesia: incidence and clinical significance. *Anesth Analg* 1996; **83**: 742–6

Norris MC. Are combined spinal-epidural catheters reliable? *Int J Obstet Anesth* 2000; **9**: 3–6

Norris MC, Ferrenbach D, Dalman H, *et al.* Does epinephrine improve the diagnostic accuracy of aspiration during labor epidural analgesia? *Anesth Analg* 1999; **88**: 1073–6

Norris MC, Fogel ST, Conway-Long C. Combined spinal-epidural versus epidural labor analgesia. *Anesthesiology* 2001; **95**: 913–20

Norris MC, Grieco WM, Borkowski M, *et al.* Complications of labor analgesia: epidural versus combined spinal epidural techniques. *Anesth Analg* 1994; **79**: 529–37

Norris MC, Leighton BL. Continuous spinal anesthesia after unintentional dural puncture in parturients. *Reg Anesth* 1990; **15**: 285–7

Okutomi T, Amano K, Morishima HO. Effect of standard diluted epinephrine infusion on epidural anesthesia in labor. *Reg Anesth Pain Med* 2000; **25**: 529–34

Okutomi T, Mochizuki J, Amano K, Hoka S. Effect of epidural epinephrine infusion with bupivacaine on labor pain and mother-fetus outcome in humans. *Reg Anesth Pain Med* 2000; **25**: 228–34

Okutomi T, Saito M, Mochizuki J, Amano K, Hoka S. A double-blind randomized controlled trial of patient-controlled epidural analgesia with or without a background infusion following initial spinal analgesia for labor pain. *Int J Obstet Anesth* 2009; **18**: 28–32

Owen MD, Ozsarac O, Sahin S, *et al.* Low-dose clonidine and neostigmine prolong the duration of intrathecal bupivacaine-fentanyl for labor analgesia. *Anesthesiology* 2000; **92**: 361–6

Owen MD, Thomas JA, Smith T, Harris LC, D'Angelo R. Ropivacaine 0.075% and bupivacaine 0.075% with fentanyl 2 microg/mL are equivalent for labor epidural analgesia. *Anesth Analg* 2002; **94**: 179–83

Oyelese Y, Smulian JC. Placenta previa, placenta accreta, and vasa previa. *Obstet Gynecol* 2006; **107**: 927–41

Paech M. Newer techniques of labor analgesia. *Anesthesiol Clin North America* 2003; **21**: 1–17

Paech M.J. Pregnant women having caesarean delivery under general anaesthesia should have a rapid sequence induction with cricoid pressure and be intubated. Can this 'holy cow' be sent packing? *Anaesth Intensive Care* 2010; **38**: 989–91

Paech MJ, Banks SL, Gurrin LC, Yeo ST, Pavy TJ. A randomized, double-blinded trial of subarachnoid bupivacaine and fentanyl, with or without clonidine, for combined spinal/epidural analgesia during labor. *Anesth Analg* 2002; **95**: 1396–401

Paech MJ, Godkin R, Webster S. Complications of obstetric epidural analgesia and anaesthesia: a prospective analysis of 10,995 cases. *Int J Obstet Anesth* 1998; **7**: 5–11

Paech MJ, Pavy TJ, Sims C, Westmore MD, Storey JM, White C. Clinical experience with patient-controlled and staff-administered intermittent bolus epidural analgesia in labour. *Anaesth Intensive Care* 1995; **23**: 459–63

Palmer CM. Early respiratory depression following intrathecal fentanyl-morphine combination. *Anesthesiology* 1991; **74**: 1153–5

Palmer CM, Cork RC, Hays R, Van Maren G, Alves D. The dose-response relation of intrathecal fentanyl for labor analgesia. *Anesthesiology* 1998; **88**: 355–61

Palmer CM, Maciulla JE, Cork RC, Nogami WM, Gossler K, Alves D. The incidence of fetal heart rate changes after intrathecal fentanyl labor analgesia. *Anesth Analg* 1999; **88**: 577–81

Palot M, Visseaux H, Botmans C, Pire JC. [Epidemiology of complications of obstetrical epidural analgesia]. *Cah Anesthesiol* 1994; **42**: 229–33

Pan PH, Coghill R, Houle TT, *et al.* Multifactorial preoperative predictors for postcesarean section pain and analgesic requirement. *Anesthesiology* 2006; **104**: 417–25

Pan PH, Moore CH, Ross VH. Severe maternal bradycardia and asystole after combined spinal-epidural labor analgesia in a morbidly obese parturient. *J Clin Anesth* 2004; **16**: 461–4

Petre E, Dylst D, Vandermeersch E, Van de Velde M. Obstetric anesthesia in Belgium: the First nationwide survey of current practice. *Int J Obstet Anesth* 2008; **14**: S17–S21

Pickering AE, Parry MG, Ousta B, Fernando R. Effect of combined spinal-epidural ambulatory labor analgesia on balance. *Anesthesiology* 1999; **91**: 436–41

Polley LS, Columb MO, Naughton NN, Wagner DS, van de Ven CJ. Relative analgesic potencies of ropivacaine and bupivacaine for epidural analgesia in labor: implications for therapeutic indexes. *Anesthesiology* 1999; **90**: 944–50

Polley LS, Columb MO, Naughton NN, Wagner DS, van de Ven CJ. Effect of epidural epinephrine on the minimum local analgesic concentration of epidural bupivacaine in labor. *Anesthesiology* 2002; **96**: 1123–8

Polley LS, Columb MO, Naughton NN, Wagner DS, van de Ven CJ Goralski KH. Relative analgesic potencies of levobupivacaine and ropivacaine for epidural analgesia in labor. *Anesthesiology* 2003; **99**: 1354–8

Polley LS, Columb MO, Wagner DS, Naughton NN. Dose-dependent reduction of the minimum local analgesic concentration of bupivacaine by sufentanil for epidural analgesia in labor. *Anesthesiology* 1998; **89**: 626–32

Preston R. The role of combined spinal epidural analgesia for labour: is there still a question? *Can J Anaesth* 2007; **54**: 9–14

Price C, Lafreniere L, Brosnan C, Findley I. Regional analgesia in early active labour: combined spinal epidural vs. epidural. *Anaesthesia* 1998; **53**: 951–5

Purdie J, Reid J, Thorburn J, Asbury AJ. Continuous extradural analgesia: comparison of midwife top-ups, continuous infusions and patient controlled administration. *Br J Anaesth* 1992; **68**: 580–4

Raffin L, Batiste C, Noel D, Serbouh A. Epidural blood patch, never too late. *Ann Fr Anesth Reanim* 2006; **25**: 201–5

Ramin SM, Porter JC, Gilstrap LC, 3rd Rosenfeld CR. Stress hormones and acid-base status of human fetuses at delivery. *J Clin Endocrinol Metab* 1991; **73**: 182–6

Rane K, Sollevi A, Segerdahl M. A randomised double-blind evaluation of adenosine as adjunct to sufentanil in spinal labour analgesia. *Acta Anaesthesiol Scand* 2003; **47**: 601–3

Ranganathan M, Raghuraman G. Ethical considerations in obtaining consent under anaesthesia. *Anaesthesia* 2003; **58**: 1250–1

Rawal N. Combined spinal-epidural anaesthesia. *Curr Opin Anaesthesiol* 2005; **18**: 518–21

Rawal N, Holmstrom B, Crowhurst JA, Van Zundert A. The combined spinal-epidural technique. *Anesthesiol Clin North America* 2000; **18**: 267–95

Reynolds F. Damage to the conus medullaris following spinal anaesthesia. *Anaesthesia* 2001; **56**: 238–47

Reynolds F, Seed PT. Anaesthesia for Caesarean section and neonatal acid-base status: a meta-analysis. *Anaesthesia* 2005; **60**: 636–53

Richa F, Yazigi A, Nasser E, Dagher C, Antakly MC. General anesthesia with remifentanil for Cesarean section in a patient with HELLP syndrome. *Acta Anaesthesiol Scand* 2005; **49**: 418–20

Robbins PM, Fernando R, Lim GH. Accidental intrathecal insertion of an extradural catheter during combined spinal-extradural anaesthesia for caesarean section. *Br J Anaesth* 1995; **75**: 355–7

Roelants F. The use of neuraxial adjuvant drugs (neostigmine, clonidine) in obstetrics. *Curr Opin Anaesthesiol* 2006; **19**: 233–7

Roofthooft E. Anesthesia for the morbidly obese parturient. *Curr Opin Anaesthesiol* 2009; **22**: 341–6

Roofthooft E, Walters M, Van de Velde M. Low dose spinal anesthesia for Cesarean section to prevent spinal hypotension. *Reg Anesth Pain Med* 2011; **36**: E2–E5

Russell R. The dura is too vulnerable to be breached routinely in labour. *Int J Obstet Anesth* 1999; **8**: 56–61

Russell R. Combined spinal epidural analgesia is the preferred technique for labour analgesia. *Acta Anaesthesiol Belg* 2002; **53**: 331–4

Rutter SV, Shields, F, Broadbent CR, Popat M, Russell R. Management of accidental dural puncture in labour with intrathecal catheters: an analysis of 10 years' experience. *Int J Obstet Anesth* 2001; **10**: 177–181

Salim R, Nachum Z, Moscovici R, Lavee M, Shalev E. Continuous compared with intermittent epidural infusion on progress of labor and patient satisfaction. Obstet Gynecol 2005; **106**: 301–6

Salman C, Kayacan N, Ertugrul F, Bigat Z, Karsli B. Combined spinal-epidural anesthesia with epidural volume extension causes a higher level of block than single-shot spinal anesthesia. *Braz J Anesthesiol* 2013; **63**: 267–72

Sanli S, Yegin A, Kayacan N, Yilmaz M, Coskunfirat N, Karsli B. Effects of hyperbaric spinal ropivacaine for caesarean section: with or without fentanyl. *Eur J Anaesthesiol* 2005; **22**: 457–61

Santos AC, Arthur GR, Wlody D, De Armas P, Morishima HO, Finster M. Comparative systemic toxicity of ropivacaine and bupivacaine in nonpregnant and pregnant ewes. *Anesthesiology* 1995; **82**: 734–40

Santos AC, Birnbach DJ. Spinal anesthesia for cesarean delivery in severely preeclamptic women: don't throw out the baby with the bathwater! *Anesth Analg* 2005; **101**: 859–61

Saravanakumar K, Cooper GM. Failed intubation in obstetrics: has the incidence changed recently? *Br J Anaesth* 2005; **94**: 690

Scavone BM. Altered level of consciousness after combined spinal-epidural labor analgesia with intrathecal fentanyl and bupivacaine. *Anesthesiology* 2002; **96**: 1021–2

Schoening AM. Amniotic fluid embolism: historical perspectives & new possibilities. *MCN Am J Matern Child Nurs* 2006; **31**: 78–83

Scott DB, Hibbard BM. Serious non-fatal complications associated with extradural block in obstetric practice. *Br J Anaesth* 1990; **64**: 537–41

Sen S, Ozmert G, Aydin ON, Baran N, Caliskan E. The persisting analgesic effect of low-dose intravenous ketamine after spinal anaesthesia for caesarean section. *Eur J Anaesthesiol* 2005; **22**: 518–23

Shennan A, Cooke V, Lloyd-Jones F, Morgan B, de Swiet M. Blood pressure changes during labour and whilst ambulating with combined spinal epidural analgesia. *Br J Obstet Gynaecol* 1995; **102**: 192–7

Shyken JM, Smeltzer JS, Baxi LV, Blakemore KJ, Ambrose SE, Petrie RH. A comparison of the effect of epidural, general, and no anesthesia on funic acid-base values by stage of labor and type of delivery. *Am J Obstet Gynecol* 1990; **163**: 802–7

Sia AT, Chong JL. Epidural 0.2% ropivacaine for labour analgesia: parturient-controlled or continuous infusion? *Anaesth Intensive Care* 1999; **27**: 154–8

Sia AT, Lim Y, Ocampo C. A comparison of a basal infusion with automated mandatory boluses in parturient-controlled epidural analgesia during labor. *Anesth Analg* 2007; **104**: 673–8

Siddik SM, Aouad MT, Jalbout MI, Rizk LB, Kamar GH, Baraka AS. Diclofenac and/or propacetamol for postoperative pain management after cesarean delivery in patients receiving patient controlled analgesia morphine. *Reg Anesth Pain Med* 2001; **26**: 310–5

Simmons SW, Cyna AM, Dennis AT, Hughes D. Combined spinal-epidural versus epidural analgesia in labour. *Cochrane Database Syst Rev* 2007; **3**: CD003401

Sinclair M, Simmons S, Cyna A. Incidents in obstetric anaesthesia and analgesia: an analysis of 5000 AIMS reports. *Anaesth Intensive Care* 1999; **27**: 275–81

Smedstad KG, Morison DH. A comparative study of continuous and intermittent epidural analgesia for labour and delivery. *Can J Anaesth* 1988; **35**: 234–41

Smedvig JP, Soreide E, Gjessing L. Ropivacaine 1 mg/ml, plus fentanyl 2 microg/ml for epidural analgesia during labour. Is mode of administration important? *Acta Anaesthesiol Scand* 2001; **45**: 595–9

Spitzer LE. Preoperative evaluation of the patient for regional anesthesia. *CRNA* 1992; **3**: 147–53

Stacey RG, Watt S, Kadim MY, Morgan BM. Single space combined spinal-extradural technique for analgesia in labour. *Br J Anaesth* 1993; **71**: 499–502

Stamer UM, Wiese R, Stuber F, Wulf H, Meuser T. Change in anaesthetic practice for Caesarean section in Germany. *Acta Anaesthesiol Scand* 2005; **49**: 170–6

Stocks GM, Hallworth SP, Fernando R, England AJ, Columb MO, Lyons G. Minimum local analgesic dose of intrathecal bupivacaine in labor and the effect of intrathecal fentanyl. *Anesthesiology* 2001; **94**: 593–8

Swenson JD, Wisniewski M, McJames S, Ashburn MA Pace NL. The effect of prior dural puncture on cisternal cerebrospinal fluid morphine concentrations in sheep after administration of lumbar epidural morphine. *Anesth Analg* 1996; **83**: 523–5

Tan S, Reid J, Thorburn J. Extradural analgesia in labour: complications of three techniques of administration. *Br J Anaesth* 1994; **73**: 619–23

Thind GS, Nagaraja SV. Airway management/failed intubation drill. *Anaesthesia* 2001; **56**: 385

Thomas JA, Pan PH, Harris LC, Owen MD, D'Angelo R. Dural puncture with a 27-gauge Whitacre needle as part of a combined spinal-epidural technique does not improve labor epidural catheter function. *Anesthesiology* 2005; **103**: 1046–51

Tihtonen K, Koobi T, Yli-Hankala A, Huhtala H, Uotila J. Maternal haemodynamics in pre-eclampsia compared with normal pregnancy during caesarean delivery. *BJOG* 2006; **113**: 657–63

Tramoni G, Valentin S, Robert MO, *et al.* Amniotic fluid embolism during caesarean section. *Int J Obstet Anesth* 2004; **13**: 271–4

Trevisan P. Fibre-optic awake intubation for caesarean section in a parturient with predicted difficult airway. *Minerva Anestesiol* 2002; **68**: 775–81

Tyagi A, Girotra G, Kumar A, Kumar S, Sethi AK, Mohta M. Single-shot spinal anaesthesia, combined spinal-epidural and epidural volume extension for elective caesarean section: a randomized comparison. *Int J Obstet Anesth* 2009; **18**: 231–6

Usha Kiran TS, Thakur MB, Bethel JA, Bhal PS, Collis RE. Comparison of continuous infusion versus midwife administered top-ups of epidural bupivacaine for labour analgesia: effect on second stage of labour and mode of delivery. *Int J Obstet Anesth* 2003; **12**: 9–11

Vallejo MC, Ramesh V, Phelps AL, Sah N. Epidural labor analgesia: continuous infusion versus patient-controlled epidural analgesia with background infusion versus without a background infusion. *J Pain* 2007; **8**: 970–5

Van de Velde M, Berends N, Kumar A, *et al.* Effects of epidural clonidine and neostigmine following intrathecal labour analgesia: a randomised, double-blind, placebo-controlled trial. *Int J Obstet Anesth* 2009; **18**: 207–14

Van de Velde M, Dreelinck R, Dubois J, *et al.* Determination of the full dose-response relation of intrathecal bupivacaine, levobupivacaine, and ropivacaine, combined with sufentanil, for labor analgesia. *Anesthesiology* 2007; **106**: 149–56

Van de Velde M, Mignolet K, Vandermeersch E, Van Assche A. Prospective, randomized comparison of epidural and combined spinal epidural analgesia during labor. *Acta Anaesthesiol Belg* 1999; **50**: 129–36

Van de Velde M, Schepers R, Berends N, Vandermeersch E, De Buck F. Ten years of experience with accidental dural puncture and post-dural puncture headache in a tertiary obstetric anaesthesia department. *Int J Obstet Anesth* 2008; **17**: 329–35

Van de Velde M, Teunkens A, Hanssens M, van Assche FA, Vandermeersch E. Post dural puncture headache following combined spinal epidural or epidural anaesthesia in obstetric patients. *Anaesth Intensive Care* 2001a; **29**: 595–9

Van de Velde M, Teunkens A, Hanssens M, Vandermeersch E, Verhaeghe J. Intrathecal sufentanil and fetal heart rate abnormalities: a double-blind, double placebo-controlled trial comparing two forms of combined spinal epidural analgesia with epidural analgesia in labor. *Anesth Analg* 2004; **98**: 1153–9

Van de Velde M, Vercauteren M, Vandermeersch E. Fetal heart rate abnormalities after regional analgesia for labor pain: the effect of intrathecal opioids. *Reg Anesth Pain Med* 2001b; **26**: 257–62

van der Vyver M, Halpern A, Joseph G. Patient-controlled epidural analgesia versus continuous infusion for labour analgesia: a meta-analysis. *Br J Anaesth* 2002; **89**: 459–65

Van Houwe P, Heytens L, Vercruysse P. A survey of obstetric an aesthesia practice in Flanders. *Acta Anaesthesiol Belg* 2006; **57**: 29–37

Vercauteren M, Bettens K, Van Springel G, Schols G, Van Zundert J. Intrathecal labor analgesia: can we use the same mixture as is used epidurally? *Int J Obstet Anesth* 1997; **6**: 242–6

Vercauteren MP, Hans G, De Decker K, Adriaensen HA. Levobupivacaine combined with sufentanil and epinephrine for intrathecal labor analgesia: a comparison with racemic bupivacaine. *Anesth Analg* 2001a; **93**: 996–1000

Vercauteren MP, Jacobs S, Jacquemyn Y, Adriaensen HA. Intrathecal labor analgesia with bupivacaine and sufentanil: the effect of adding 2.25 microg epinephrine. *Reg Anesth Pain Med* 2001b; **26**: 473–7

Vernis L, Duale C, Storme B, Mission JP, Rol B, Schoeffler P. Perispinal analgesia for labour followed by patient-controlled infusion with bupivacaine and sufentanil: combined spinal-epidural vs. epidural analgesia alone. *Eur J Anaesthesiol* 2004; **21**: 186–92

Vertommen JD, Vandermeulen E, Van Aken H, *et al.* The effects of the addition of sufentanil to 0.125% bupivacaine on the quality of analgesia during labor and on the incidence of instrumental deliveries. *Anesthesiology* 1991; **74**: 809–14

Visalyaputra S, Rodanant O, Somboonviboon W, Tantivitayatan K, Thienthong S, Saengchote W. Spinal versus epidural anesthesia for cesarean delivery in severe preeclampsia: a prospective randomized, multicenter study. *Anesth Analg* 2005; **101**: 862–8

Viscomi C, Eisenach JC. Patient-controlled epidural analgesia during labor. *Obstet Gynecol* 1991; **77**: 348–51

Weiniger CF, Elram T, Ginosar Y, Mankuta D, Weissman C, Ezra Y. Anaesthetic management of placenta accreta: use of a pre-operative high and low suspicion classification. *Anaesthesia* 2005; **60**: 1079–84

Whitty R, Goldszmidt E, Parkes RK, Carvalho JC. Determination of the ED95 for intrathecal plain bupivacaine combined with fentanyl in active labor. *Int J Obstet Anesth* 2007; **16**: 341–5

Wilson MJ, Cooper G, MacArthur C, Shennan A, U. K. Comparative Obstetric Mobile Epidural Trial Study Group. Randomized controlled trial comparing traditional with two mobile epidural techniques: anesthetic and analgesic efficacy. *Anesthesiology* 2002; **97**: 1567–75

Wilson MJ, MacArthur C, Cooper GM, Shennan A, COMET Study Group UK. Ambulation in labour and delivery mode: a randomised controlled trial of high-dose vs mobile epidural analgesia. *Anaesthesia* 2009; **64**: 266–72

Wong CA, Ratliff JT, Sullivan JT, Scavone BM, Toledo P, McCarthy RJ. A randomized comparison of programmed intermittent epidural bolus with continuous epidural infusion for labor analgesia. *Anesth Analg* 2006; **102**: 904–9

Wong SY, Wong KM, Chao AS, Liang CC, Hsu JC. Awake fiberoptic intubation for cesarean section in a parturient with odontoid fracture and atlantoaxial subluxation. *Chang Gung Med J* 2003; **26**: 352–6

Writer WDR, Stienstra R, Eddleston JM, *et al.* Neonatal outcome and mode of delivery after epidural analgesia for labour with ropivacaine and bupivacaine: a prospective meta-analysis. *Br J Anaesth* 1998; **81**: 713–7

Wulf H. Anesthesia and intensive therapy of pregnant women with the HELLP syndrome. *Anaesthesist* 1990; **39**: 117–21

Wyatt SS, Jones DA, Peach MJ, Gurrin L. Anxiety in patients having caesarean section under regional anaesthesia: a questionnaire and pilot study. *Int J Obstet Anesth* 2001; **10**: 278–83

Yaksh TL, Grafe MR, Malkmus S, Rathbun ML, Eisenach JC. Studies on the safety of chronically administered intrathecal neostigmine methylsulfate in rats and dogs. *Anesthesiology* 1995; **82**: 412–27

Yentis SM. Height of confusion: assessing regional blocks before caesarean section. *Int J Obstet Anesth* 2006; **15**: 2–6

Yun EM, Marx GF, Santos AC. The effects of maternal position during induction of combined spinal-epidural anesthesia for cesarean delivery. *Anesth Analg* 1998; **87**: 614–8

CHAPTER 67

Anaesthesia for transplant surgery

Michael A. E. Ramsay

Introduction

The provision of anaesthesia for organ transplantation requires a team of specialist anaesthetists who are available 24 h a day. The cold and warm ischaemia times may have very deleterious effects on the graft. The team must have a basic understanding of the immune system and the strategies of immunosuppression therapy. The preoperative assessment of the patient requires an understanding of the cause and effects of the compromised organ that is to be replaced. The procedure in many instances will result in a reperfusion syndrome when the graft is revascularized and also an ischaemia–reperfusion (I–R) injury. The understanding of these entities is essential as is the preparation and protocols to treat or ameliorate the effects of these syndromes if they occur.

The preparation for many organ transplants includes invasive monitoring of haemodynamics, cardiac function, pulmonary function, and acid–base balance. Access for massive transfusion therapy and coagulation assessment is essential for many transplant procedures. The maintenance of body temperature and fluid balance may be challenging. The protection and monitoring of the function of major organs such as the brain, heart, lungs, and kidneys is essential but the homeostasis of endocrine function and electrolytes is also important.

The provision of excellent anaesthesia is a key component of a successful transplant programme. A small team of highly trained professionals with extensive training and experience in transplant anaesthesia provide the best results.

Innate and adaptive immunity, organ transplantation, and immunosuppression

The immune system provides the body with protection from foreign pathogens such as infections. It responds rapidly to repel microorganisms that have penetrated our protective epithelial and endothelial borders. The initial response is termed the innate response and is the first line of defence against pathogens with the production of macrophages and dendritic cells that are activated to engulf and kill the invader. Inflammatory cytokines are produced such as interleukin 12 and the pathogens are contained. The dendritic cells orchestrate this innate response and also an adaptive response (Kreisel and Goldstein 2012). The adaptive response takes time to develop but is very specific for the antigens presented and has a durable memory to provide resistance to re-infection. The dendritic cells take antigen particles to the lymph nodes where T cells are produced that will target and kill the antigen-presenting cells (Banchereau and Steinman 1998). The innate immune response may be activated by the I–R injury that occurs when a transplanted organ undergoes reperfusion after an ischaemic period. The dendritic cells orchestrate the responses of both the innate and adaptive immune responses to induce immunity or tolerance (Steinman and Banchereau 2007; Ueno et al. 2007, 2010). Overactivity may cause harm in the form of autoimmune disease, organ rejection, and graft-*vs*-host disease while underactivity may allow tolerance or exacerbation of infection and cancer.

Immunosuppressant therapy is designed to prevent rejection of the allograft but also minimizes the adverse effects on the recipient such as increased propensity for infection, malignancy, and other adverse reactions. Over time, some organ recipients may develop tolerance and be successfully weaned off immunosuppressant therapy. The majority of major organ recipients will require immunosuppressant drugs for the rest of their lives (Olson and Wiesner 2012). Therefore, from the anaesthetist's perspective, it is important that immunosuppression therapy be administered before reperfusion of the graft and maintained if the patient returns for further surgery.

The regimens for major organ transplants are dependent on centre and type of organ. The drugs are divided into two main categories: pharmacological- and biological-based therapies. The pharmacological therapies are small-molecule drugs and consist of corticosteroids, calcineurin inhibitors, antimetabolites, and mTOR inhibitors. The corticosteroids inhibit transcription of important inflammatory cytokines and induce apoptosis of T lymphocytes, reduce the number of dendritic cells, and impair adhesion molecules thereby impeding T-cell migration to target zones. High doses of steroids are often given at the time of organ implantation to induce immunosuppression and they are then tapered down over time (3–6 months) to reduce side-effects (Zarrinpar and Busuttil 2012).

Calcineurin inhibitors interfere with signalling and impede the activation of T cells. Ciclosporin was the first isolated and resulted in a major advance in the success of organ transplantation. Later, tacrolimus was developed, which is absorbed from the intestine with better predictability. These agents are associated with nephrotoxicity, neurotoxicity, hypertension, and hyperlipidaemia. Antimetabolites are often administered, including azathioprine and mycophenolate mofetil, which block lymphocyte proliferation. mTOR inhibitors prevent the proliferation of T lymphocytes: sirolimus is an example, and does have significant side-effects including poor wound healing, cytopenia, arthralgia, and mouth ulcers.

Biological therapies are also available and these are divided into a group that depletes antibodies and a non-depleting group. The former group includes polyclonal antithymocytes, monoclonal anti-CD3 antibodies (e.g. muromonab), and an anti-CD52 antibody, alemtuzumab. The non-depleting antibodies include the anti-CD25 antibody basiliximab, which has few side-effects.

Ischaemia–reperfusion injury

All major organs when transplanted will undergo an I–R injury. This is caused by a period of ischaemia, when the blood supply has been clamped off; a period of cold ischaemia followed by a period of warm ischaemia when the organ is being re-implanted; and finally reperfusion, when the clamps are removed and blood flows again through the organs. During the ischaemic period the endothelium is damaged, leucocytes become adherent to the damaged endothelial cells, and inflammatory cytokines are activated, as is complement and reactive oxygen species. On reperfusion, macrophages cross the endothelium and cause apoptosis of the organ cells; the complement activation results in an explosive release of inflammatory cytokines, platelet adhesion, and potential no-reflow in the small arterioles. Oxidative stress results in an increase in reactive oxygen species that include superoxide, hydrogen peroxide, and hydroxyl ions. These molecules cause apoptosis, cellular necrosis, and damage to DNA. The outcome if severe may result in primary non-function of the graft. The damage also occurs in distant organs (Ramsay 2008; Weyker et al. 2012; Zhai et al. 2013).

To ameliorate the I–R injury two approaches can be made. The first is an attempt to provide remote ischaemic preconditioning (Brevoord et al. 2012). In this manner, a series of short non-lethal periods of ischaemia are applied to a more readily accessible remote organ such as a tourniquet on a limb. This has been demonstrated in some studies to ameliorate the end-organ damage in the target organ (Candilio et al. 2013). The second approach is to attempt to ameliorate the inflammation that occurs at reperfusion (Gorsuch et al. 2012). This is predominantly an innate immune-dominated response that is mediated by the sentinel pattern recognition receptor system. This proinflammatory immune response triggers an adaptive immune response that culminates in allograft rejection. Studies are underway to attempt to block the cell adhesion cascade in an effort to mitigate the I–R injury. Inhaled nitric oxide decreases platelet adhesion and leucocyte adherence to injured endothelium (Bahde and Spiegel 2010). The volatile anaesthetic sevoflurane has been shown in one randomized prospective clinical trial (Beck-Schimmer et al. 2008) to have a protective effect if administered before reperfusion in patients undergoing liver surgery with inflow occlusion (Van Allen et al. 2012).

Major organ transplantation

Liver transplantation

The indications for liver transplantation include viral hepatitis, alcoholic liver disease (Laennec's cirrhosis), non-alcoholic fatty liver disease, autoimmune hepatitis, primary biliary cirrhosis, primary sclerosing cholangitis, drug-induced liver damage (paracetamol, methotrexate), genetic causes (Wilson's disease, α1-antitrypsin deficiency, haemochromatosis), contained hepatocellular cancer, and cryptogenic causes.

Pathophysiology of liver disease

An understanding of the pathophysiology of end-stage liver disease and cirrhosis is required in order to manage the patient undergoing transplantation. Some genetic aetiologies may affect more than just one organ system such as the patient with amyloidosis who may have significant cardiac amyloid infiltration as well. The synthetic liver function of some patients such as those with early hepatocellular cancer may be well preserved while in others severe dysfunction may be present. The patient who has developed severe cirrhosis will have a liver wherein the response to damage has been fibrosis and nodular regeneration. This is frequently associated with portal hypertension causing widespread varices with bleeding, a profound coagulopathy as a result of impaired synthetic function, severe ascites and pleural effusions, cirrhotic cardiomyopathy, hepatorenal syndrome (HRS), and encephalopathy.

To assess the severity of the liver disease and determine risk for survival, two classification systems have been developed: the Child–Turcotte–Pugh (CTP) system (see Table 67.1) and the Model for End-stage Liver Disease (MELD) (see Table 67.2). Both are designed to assess the risk for mortality of patients on the waiting list for liver transplantation, so that organs can be allocated to those in greater need.

The 3-month mortality for a patient with a CTP score of 5–6 points is 4%; 7–9 points is 14%; and 10–15 points is 51%.

The MELD score is a more precise calculation that is based on serum creatinine, bilirubin, and international normalized ratio (INR) (Table 67.2). Both scores assess the patient's risk for survival.

Table 67.1 The Child–Turcotte–Pugh score

	1 Pt	2 Pts	3 Pts
Encephalopathy	0	1–2	3–4
Ascites	Slight	Moderate	Severe
Bilirubin (μmol/L)	<34	34–50	>50
Albumin g/L	>35	28–35	< 28
INR	<1.7	1.8–2.3	>2.3
OR PT (sec)	1–4	5–6	>6

Reproduced with permission from Pugh RN, Murray-Lyon IM, Dawson JL, Pietroni MC, Williams R, Transection of the oesophagus for bleeding oesophageal varices. *British Journal of Surgery*, Volume 60, Issue 8, pp. 646–9, Copyright © 1973 British Journal of Surgery Society Ltd.

Table 67.2 Three-month mortality according to MELD score. The MELD score: $10 \times [0.957 \times \log_e(\text{creatinine}) + \log_e(\text{bilirubin}) + 1.12 \times \log_e(\text{INR})] + 6.43$

Meld score	9 or less	10–19	20–29	30–39	>40
In Hospital	4%	27%	76%	83%	100%
Out Patient	2%	6%	50%		

Reproduced with permission from Malinchoc M, Kamath PS, Gordon FD, Peine CJ, Rank J, ter Borg PC, A model to predict poor survival in patients undergoing transjugular intrahepatic portosystemic shunts. *Hepatology*, Volume 31, Issue 4, pp. 864–71, Copyright © 2000 The American Association for the Study of Liver Diseases.

Preoperative assessment

The patient presenting for liver transplantation is frequently severely debilitated with multiple organ system malfunctions. The time to assess the patient may be limited by the arrival of an organ for which the ischaemia time is limited. The major concerns should be focused on a patient with severe muscle wasting, severe ascites and pleural effusions, renal dysfunction, cardiomyopathy, coagulopathy, encephalopathy, respiratory compromise, electrolyte derangements, altered physiology and pharmacology, and potentially an increased aspiration risk. The patient may have deteriorated significantly from the last full assessment and this may be the reason that the patient is now receiving a transplant. It is paramount that the anaesthesia team are involved in the selection process for liver transplant candidates but also kept in close communication on the results of ongoing assessments that occur while the patient is on the waiting list. Careful assessment for specific pathological changes that may have taken place since the previous evaluation include a cardiac assessment for progression of cardiomyopathy, portopulmonary hypertension (POPH), and hepatopulmonary syndrome (HPS). The use of cardiac echocardiography may be extremely helpful in this regard. Renal function needs to be rapidly assessed to determine if intraoperative continuous venovenous haemodialysis will be useful.

Cardiovascular system

The usual haemodynamic picture of the cirrhotic patient is that of high cardiac output and low systemic vascular resistance (Kowalski and Abelmann 1953). This reduced afterload can make a preliminary assessment of ventricular function to be excellent, but it is important to take into consideration that nearly 100% of cirrhotic patients will exhibit a cardiomyopathy even if it is just a down-regulation of the β-receptor (Lee 1989). This may be further compromised by the chronic use of β-blocking agents used to control portal hypertension. Close examination by transoesophageal echocardiography (TOE) may demonstrate both systolic and diastolic dysfunction. The diagnostic features include an E/A ratio less than 1, a prolonged deceleration time greater than 200 ms, a prolonged isovolumetric relaxation time greater than 80 ms, an enlarged atrium, and overall decreased pattern of contractility (Zardi et al. 2010) (Fig. 67.1).

Coronary artery disease is also prevalent in this population and careful screening should be undertaken during the initial assessment (Carey et al. 1995). Non-invasive stress testing may be considered in liver transplantation candidates with no active cardiac conditions on the basis of the presence of multiple coronary artery disease risk factors regardless of functional status. Relevant risk factors among transplantation candidates include diabetes mellitus, prior cardiovascular disease, left ventricular hypertrophy, age greater than 60 years, smoking, hypertension, and dyslipidaemia. The specific number of risk factors that should be used to prompt testing remains to be determined, but three or more appear to be reasonable. A stress test assessment should be made; the type of test is dependent on what the physical condition of the patient will allow (Lentine et al. 2012). The dobutamine stress echocardiogram

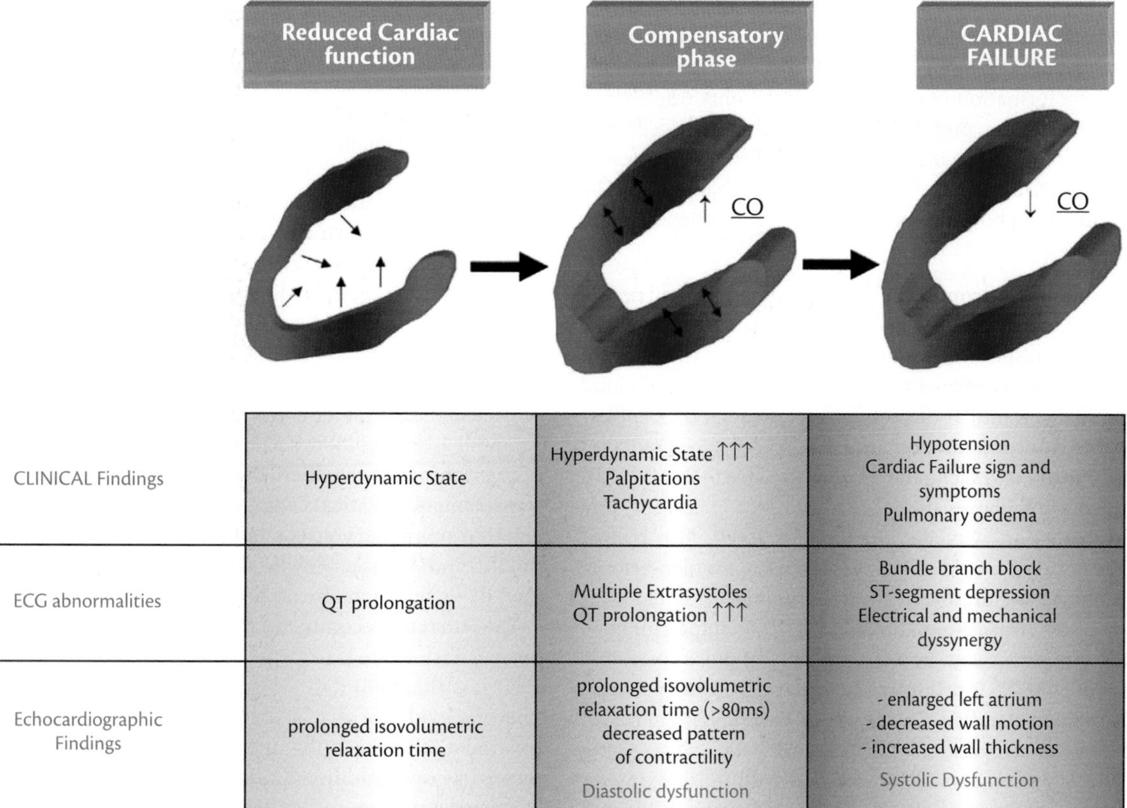

CLINICAL Findings	Hyperdynamic State	Hyperdynamic State ↑↑↑ Palpitations Tachycardia	Hypotension Cardiac Failure sign and symptoms Pulmonary oedema
ECG abnormalities	QT prolongation	Multiple Extrasystoles QT prolongation ↑↑↑	Bundle branch block ST-segment depression Electrical and mechanical dyssynergy
Echocardiographic Findings	prolonged isovolumetric relaxation time	prolonged isovolumetric relaxation time (>80ms) decreased pattern of contractility Diastolic dysfunction	- enlarged left atrium - decreased wall motion - increased wall thickness Systolic Dysfunction

Figure 67.1 The progression of cirrhotic cardiomyopathy.

test has been demonstrated to have a strong positive predictive value and detection capability (Plotkin et al. 2000). If ischaemia is demonstrated then coronary arteriograms should be obtained. If arterial obstructive lesions can be dilated and a bare-metal stent placed then liver transplantation may be an acceptable risk. If coronary artery bypass surgery is necessary then the decision has to be made how best to manage this (Morris et al. 1995). However, once treated the patient may undergo liver transplantation with similar outcomes as those patients without coronary artery disease (Wray et al. 2013).

Pulmonary system

The severe cirrhotic patient may have restricted ventilation because of pleural effusions but also severe abdominal ascites making it impossible for the patient to lie down without respiratory distress. When patients such as this are met in the operating theatre, anaesthesia should be induced with the patient breathing comfortably with the back raised up. The patient should only be laid flat when the airway and ventilation are controlled. A sepsis syndrome is seen in some patients with end-stage liver disease and this presents with an adult respiratory distress syndrome with bilateral pulmonary infiltrates. Resolution of this syndrome has been reported with liver transplantation suggesting that it is the result of endotoxins and not infection (Doyle et al. 1993).

Hepatopulmonary syndrome and portopulmonary hypertension

These are pathological conditions that result from changes in the pulmonary arteriolar wall. When the pulmonary vascular endothelium is dysfunctional, as may occur in liver disease or with portal hypertension because of exposure to inflammatory cytokines, increased stress forces caused by high cardiac output, and increased exposure to oxidants, several effects may occur. These include vasodilation, the formation of aneurysms and shunts resulting in HPS, or vasoconstriction, proliferation of smooth muscle cells, and microthrombosis causing an increase in pulmonary vascular resistance (PVR) and POPH. These two pathological changes may be seen in the same lung but one entity usually predominates (Pham et al. 2010).

Hepatopulmonary syndrome The HPS is defined as the triad of liver disease and increased alveolar–arterial oxygen gradient in the presence of intrapulmonary vascular dilations. The diameter of pulmonary capillaries is normally between 8 and 15 μm. Red blood cells, which possess a similar diameter, travel through the capillaries in single file. This configuration minimizes the distance required for oxygen diffusion and facilitates oxygen transfer to red cells. In HPS, pulmonary capillaries dilate to a diameter of 50–500 μm, impeding oxygenation (Umeda and Kamath 2009). The HPS is defined as the triad of liver disease and increased alveolar–arterial oxygen gradient in the presence of intrapulmonary vascular dilatations (Fig. 67.2). Thus, the hallmark of HPS is impairment in oxygenation, and can easily be screened for by pulse oximetry. A unique feature of HPS is orthodeoxia, which is a decrease in oxygen saturation upon standing. This is caused by preferential perfusion of the lung bases in a standing patient. All patients presenting for liver transplantation should be screened with pulse oximetry while breathing room air in both the sitting and supine positions. Platypnoea, shortness of breath worsened by sitting, results from the same mechanism. Again, most patients with dyspnoea prefer to sit up but not the patient with HPS. The diagnostic test is the delayed passage (4–6 heart beats) of echogenic material (agitated saline) passing from right heart to left heart with echocardiography. HPS has a prevalence of 15–20% in patients undergoing evaluation for liver transplantation (Fallon and Abrams 2000). Other clinical features of HPS when severe are finger clubbing and cyanosis. It is a progressive syndrome but is reversed by liver transplantation. Intraoperative management focuses on the provision of adequate oxygenation. Given that HPS is typically responsive to supplemental oxygen, this goal is usually attainable. The prevention of embolic material, especially air bubbles, from entering the venous circulation is imperative as these may traverse through the shunts to the systemic circulation. The more severe the hypoxia, the higher the risk for undergoing liver transplantation and the longer the period of post-transplant intensive care needed (Gupta et al. 2010; Zhang and Fallon 2012).

Portopulmonary hypertension If the pulmonary vascular remodelling results in vascular smooth muscle proliferation, vasoconstriction, intimal proliferation, and fibrosis, then an obstructive pathology exists that causes an increased resistance to blood flow and pulmonary hypertension. When this is associated with portal hypertension it is termed POPH. The diagnostic criteria for POPH include a mean pulmonary artery pressure (MPAP) of greater than 25 mm Hg at rest, and a PVR greater than 240 dyn s^{-1} cm^{-5} (Ramsay 2010). The transpulmonary gradient of greater than 12 mm Hg (MPAP – pulmonary arteriolar occlusion pressure) reflects the obstruction to flow and distinguishes the contribution of volume and resistance to the increase in MPAP (Safdar et al. 2012) (Fig. 67.3).

POPH may be classified as mild (MPAP 25–35 mm Hg), moderate (MPAP >35 and <45 mm Hg), and severe (MPAP >45 mm Hg) (Krowka et al. 2006). Mild POPH is not associated with increased mortality at liver transplantation, although the immediate recovery period may be challenging if there is a significant increase in cardiac output after reperfusion of the new graft. Moderate and severe POPH are associated with significant mortality at transplantation. However, the key factor is not MPAP, but rather right ventricular (RV) function (Ramsay 2010).

Transthoracic echocardiography is an effective, non-invasive method of screening for POPH. Positive screening necessitates right-heart catheterization for definite diagnosis. The right ventricular systolic pressure (RVSP) is estimated based upon the velocity of tricuspid regurgitation (TR) using the Bernoulli equation, RVSP (in mm Hg) = $4 \times (\text{TR m s}^{-1})^2$ + right atrial pressure. Any dilatation of the right heart chambers must be noted as a risk factor for liver transplantation. Patients with fluid overload may also present with elevated pulmonary artery pressure, particularly in the presence of HRS and oliguria. However, these patients also have normal (or low) PVR, and therefore do not fulfil POPH criteria.

The current recommendation of the European Respiratory Society Task Force is to target a MPAP of less than 35 mm Hg and PVR less than 400 dyn s^{-1} cm^{-5} (Rodriguez-Roisin et al. 2004). There is evidence that a portion of POPH patients respond to treatment, and that subsequent liver transplantation can be performed without additional risk if these treatment goals are reached. However, the course of POPH after successful transplant is, unlike HPS, not one of progressive improvement. Thus, POPH monitoring and treatment is indicated after successful transplantation. The key to how well the patient will tolerate liver transplantation may

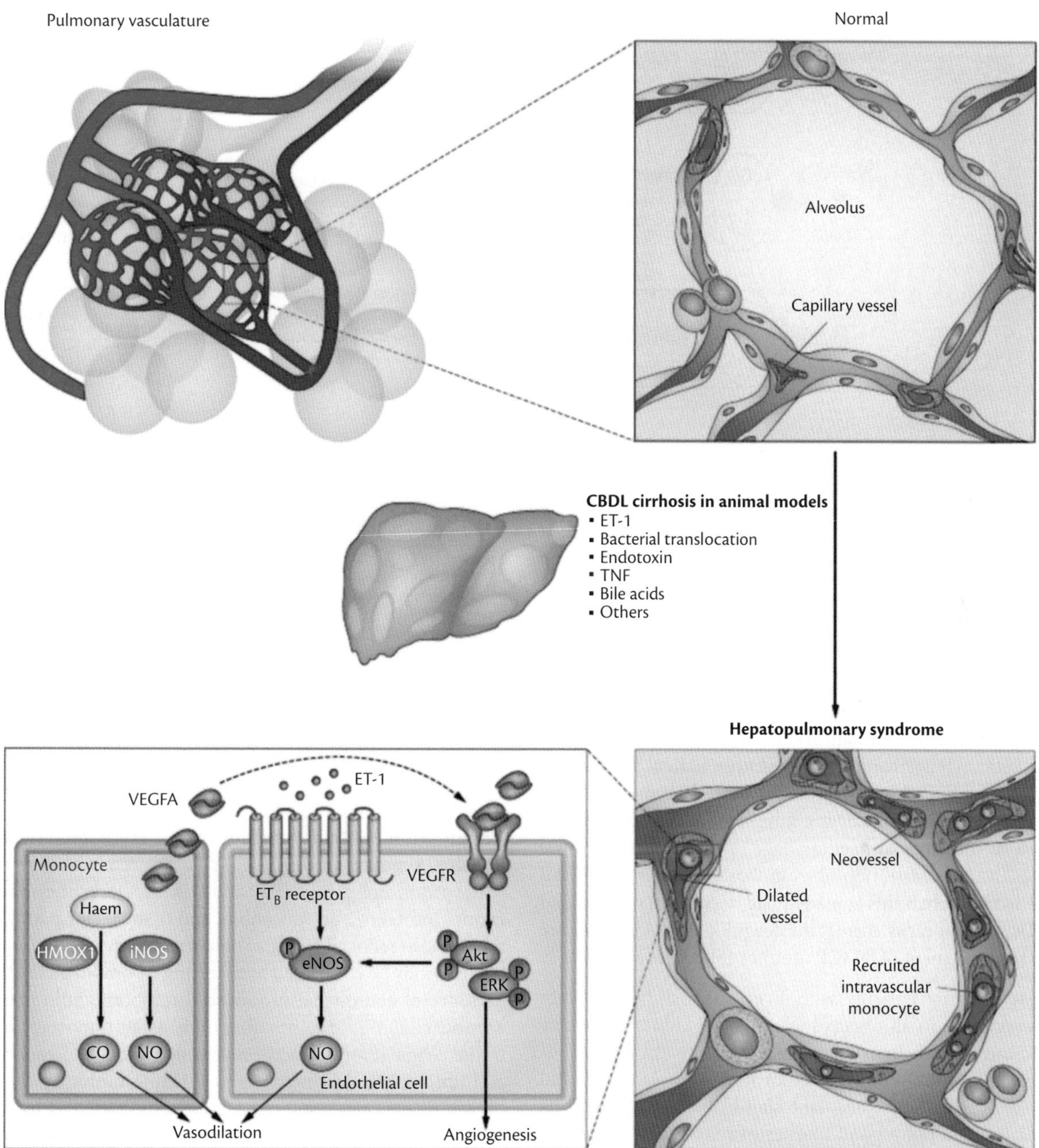

Figure 67.2 The key pathological features of HPS are pulmonary microvascular alterations including vasodilation, intravascular monocyte accumulation, and angiogenesis.

rest with RV function more than any other factor. If the RV has accommodated the increase in PVR and has hypertrophied, is contracting well, and is no longer dilated, this may facilitate a successful outcome (Ramsay 2010).

Central nervous system Mild encephalopathy has been found in up to 84% of patients with chronic liver failure (Moore et al. 1989). Hepatic encephalopathy is characterized by alterations in mental status with fluctuating neurological signs (asterixis, hyperreflexia, or an inverted plantar reflex) and characteristic electroencephalographic changes (symmetric high-voltage, slow-wave activity). Some patients especially with fulminant hepatic failure may have elevated intracranial pressure (ICP) from cerebral oedema. The cause of hepatic encephalopathy has been associated with increased γ-aminobutyric acid (GABA) neurotransmitter in the brain (Bakti et al. 1987). This excess GABA neurotransmitter effect may be potentiated by benzodiazepine drugs, so these should be avoided as they may precipitate hepatic coma (Basile et al. 1991). Flumazenil, the reversal agent for benzodiazepine drugs, may also temporarily reverse hepatic coma (Barbaro et al. 1998; Dursun et al. 2003). The failure of the liver to convert ammonia to urea results in the accumulation of ammonia

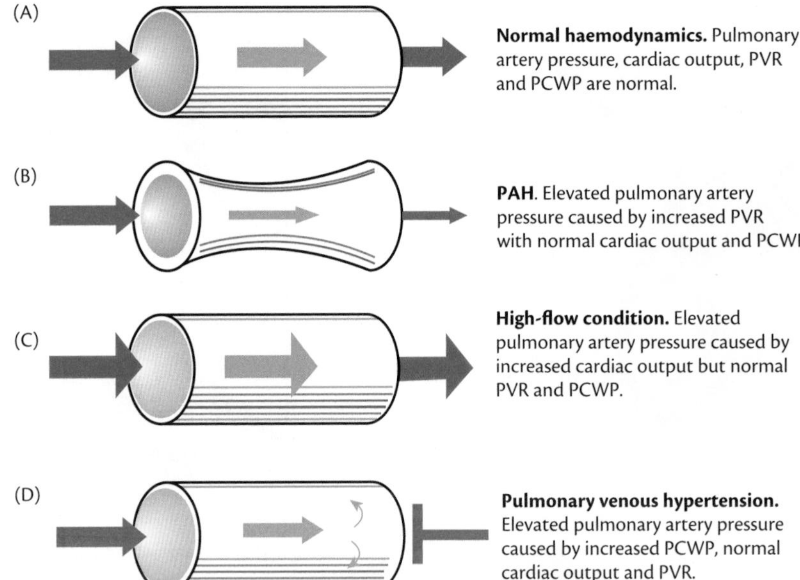

Figure 67.3 Portopulmonary hypertension: an update.
Reproduced with permission from Safdar, Z., Bartolome, S. and Sussman, N., Portopulmonary hypertension: an update, *Liver Transplantation*, 18, pp. 881–891, Copyright © 2012 American Association for the Study of Liver Diseases.

that exacerbates the encephalopathy. If the encephalopathy worsens as the patient becomes obtunded, early intervention to protect the airway and maintain ventilation and oxygenation is warranted. The anaesthetic management of the comatose patient with raised ICP is greatly facilitated by the presence of an ICP monitor. The severe coagulopathy associated with fulminant hepatic failure presents a risk of intracranial haemorrhage on placing an epidural transducer. The administration of fresh frozen plasma may be all that is needed but when this is inadequate, recombinant activated factor VII will temporarily correct the coagulopathy of liver failure and allow the placement of an ICP monitor (Shami et al. 2003).

Renal system Many patients with liver cirrhosis will sustain endothelial damage in all organs including the kidney. This may progress to cause parenchymal damage and eventually acute tubular necrosis. This will not be reversed by liver transplantation and a combined liver–kidney transplant should be considered. The serum creatinine is not a good marker of renal function in this patient population as there is frequently severe muscle wasting and reduced production of creatinine. Renal dysfunction may also present as HRS, in which there is no parenchymal damage, but there is profound hypoperfusion of the kidney caused by vasoconstriction in the setting of systemic and splanchnic arterial vasodilation in patients with advanced cirrhosis (Nadim et al. 2012). HRS is classified as type 1 when there is rapid deterioration in kidney function and type 2 with a more moderate deterioration in renal function. HRS diagnosis is based on the absence of primary renal disease, proteinuria, hypovolaemia, and renal hypoperfusion. It is characterized by normal urinary sediment, low urinary sodium (<10 mmol litre^{-1}), uraemia, and oliguria. HRS is reversible with liver transplantation. The recommendation from the Acute Dialysis Quality Initiative Group is that patients with HRS type 1 be resuscitated with albumin in combination with a vasoconstrictor, preferentially terlipressin (Nadim et al. 2012). If terlipressin is not available then alternative vasoconstrictors such as noradrenaline, vasopressin, or a combination of octreotide and midodrine should be considered. If the patient is unresponsive to therapy, early institution of intraoperative continuous venovenous haemodialysis should be considered. It can easily be accomplished in the operating room and greatly facilitates fluid and electrolyte management.

Coagulation system Liver cirrhosis is characterized by the impaired synthesis of coagulation factors, resulting in prolongation of the prothrombin time (PT) and INR. However, the anticoagulant factors (protein C, antithrombin, and tissue factor pathway inhibitor) are also reduced and may balance out any effect of a prolonged PT. This may be confirmed by assessing thrombin generation in the presence of endothelial-produced thrombomodulin (Tripodi and Mannucci 2007). The liver functions as an important modulator of the coagulation balance, preventing hyper- or hypocoagulation and fibrinolysis. An alteration in this fine-tuning by the presence of liver disease can result in coagulopathy caused by hypocoagulation, excessive fibrinolysis, or a hypercoaguable state, resulting in thrombosis or disseminated intravascular coagulation (Hambleton et al. 2002). The state of coagulation should be monitored both by laboratory testing and by intraoperative viscoelastic tests. These include the thromboelastography and rotational thromboelastometry or Sonoclot® (Sienco Inc., Morrison, CO, USA) analysis. These instruments allow the state of coagulation in whole blood to be monitored and can provide an early indication of the presence and severity of fibrinolysis (Furnary et al. 2003). In this manner, the accurate administration of antifibrinolytic agents can be made.

Fulminant hepatic failure

Fulminant liver failure results from severe hepatocellular injury and necrosis. Hepatic encephalopathy develops early, together with deep jaundice. Laboratory findings include hyperbilirubinaemia, marked elevation of the serum aminotransferase concentration, hypoglycaemia, hyperammonaemia, and hypoalbuminaemia. Severe coagulopathy develops because there is impaired liver synthesis of coagulation factors; a prolongation of the PT is a sensitive index of hepatocyte dysfunction. Depressed liver gluconeogenesis results in increased anaerobic metabolism and generation of lactic acid, creating a severe metabolic lactic acidosis. Some patients in fulminant liver failure will recover, therefore guidelines for the selection of patients for orthotopic liver transplantation were developed so that transplantation can occur before grade IV coma sets in (de Knegt and Schalm 1991; Saibara et al. 1991). Criteria include any three of the following variables: younger than 10 years or older than 40 years of age, non-A, non-B hepatitis, halothane hepatitis, idiosyncratic drug reaction, jaundice for at least 7 days before the onset of encephalopathy, PT greater than 50 s, and serum bilirubin concentration greater than 300 mmol litre^{-1}. Arterial ketone body ratio is a predictor of prognosis in fulminant liver failure (Ellis and Wendon 1996). As the patient becomes obtunded, airway control and ventilation are indicated because there is a risk of pulmonary aspiration, hypercarbia, and hypoxia. Elevation of the patient's head to 25° and maintenance of cerebral perfusion pressure by supporting systemic arterial blood pressure and reducing central venous pressure are essential. Cerebral perfusion pressure should be maintained above 50 mm Hg (Husberg et al. 1991).

Anaesthesia management Adequate venous access must be obtained so that massive rapid transfusions may be administered if necessary. Large-bore peripheral and central venous catheters may be placed in the upper part of the body because fluid given through lower body venous catheters may be lost in the surgical field or obstructed in passage to the heart. A radial arterial catheter is inserted for continuous blood pressure monitoring and access for arterial blood gas measurement. A single large-bore catheter or two catheters are placed percutaneously in the right internal jugular vein, if venovenous bypass is contemplated. One, a 12-French catheter, is used for rapid volume replacement and as the return limb of a venovenous bypass circuit. The other, an internal jugular catheter, is used as a pulmonary artery catheter introducer. A pulmonary artery catheter, although not used in all centres, may prove valuable in diagnosing pulmonary hypertension and managing haemodynamic instability. All fluids should pass through warming devices to assist in temperature maintenance. A rapid infusion system may be necessary for those times when massive blood loss occurs.

A modified rapid-sequence induction technique is used in the majority of patients. Preoxygenation is followed by the administration of propofol (1.5 mg kg^{-1}). Tracheal intubation is assisted by neuromuscular block, for example, by vecuronium (0.2 mg kg^{-1}), and cricoid pressure is applied until the airway is secured. Anaesthesia is maintained with isoflurane in an air–oxygen mixture, supplemented with fentanyl and vecuronium. Isoflurane provides an optimal relationship between liver oxygen supply and demand; however, in this extensive procedure, this may be only a theoretical consideration. The use of neuromuscular blocking agents that are metabolized by the liver, such as vecuronium or rocuronium, should be accompanied by monitoring of neuromuscular block with a nerve stimulator.

The anaesthetic management of the operation can be considered with respect to three phases: preanhepatic, anhepatic, and neohepatic. The preanhepatic phase includes dissection and isolation of infra- and suprahepatic vena cava, exposure of the porta hepatis and hilar structures of the liver, and preparation for venovenous bypass when used. The anhepatic phase begins with isolation of the liver and extends until the time of reperfusion of the donor liver. The neohepatic phase begins at reperfusion and lasts until the end of the procedure. During the preanhepatic phase, significant blood loss may occur, particularly in patients with portal hypertension. Massive volumes of ascitic fluid may be drained, and volume shifts need to be anticipated and corrected. The most common cause of a low cardiac output at the start of liver transplantation is hypovolaemia. Good volume replacement is required for adequate tissue perfusion, and more especially for adequate renal perfusion. A non-lactate balanced electrolyte solution can be used as maintenance fluid. This solution will not exacerbate lactic acidosis in patients with little or no liver function.

Venovenous bypass is used in some centres while others use a 'piggy-back' technique where the inferior vena cava is partially occluded and the hepatic vein caval patch is parachuted down on to the cava. Careful attention to volume management is essential, as the new liver when reperfused will be injured by congestion if the central venous pressure is allowed to be high. Immunosuppression needs to be administered before reperfusion and this usually consists of 1 g of hydrocortisone. Reperfusion of the graft liver via the portal vein marks the beginning of the neohepatic phase.

Reperfusion is complicated by the reperfusion syndrome and I–R injury. The reperfusion syndrome is the result of cold blood, with acids, and other toxic molecules from the new liver graft being flushed directly into the heart. This causes hypotension, arrhythmias and rarely a transient cardiac arrest (Ramsay 2008; Paugam-Burtz et al. 2009).

I–R injury may result in an impaired reperfusion of the new graft. Prostaglandin E1 (PGE1) has been reported to improve the survival of livers that appeared marginal at reperfusion (Greig et al. 1989). The effect of PGE1 on vascular endothelium may enhance perfusion of the graft both generally and in areas of 'no reflow'.

The third stage or neohepatic stage consists of the hepatic artery reconstruction and bile duct anastomosis. This is the time to obtain good haemostasis before closing.

Signs of a good functioning graft include good hepatic arterial flow, early bile formation, increasing body temperature, improvement in coagulation status, correction of acidosis, a decrease in potassium, and an increase in carbon dioxide production.

Postoperative care

The patient's lungs are ventilated until full recovery from anaesthesia and their trachea is then extubated. This may be performed safely in many patients at the end of the procedure on the operating room table or on arrival in the intensive care unit (Mandell et al. 2002). Sepsis and retransplantation are major risk factors for the development of adult respiratory distress syndrome (Takaoka et al. 1989).

Kidney transplantation

The patient with end-stage renal disease may be treated with haemodialysis, peritoneal dialysis, or undergo renal transplantation. The patient who undergoes renal transplantation has a better survival than those patients who remain on dialysis (Wolfe et al. 1999). There are considerable co-morbidities associated with chronic kidney disease and some can be anticipated from the aetiology of the disease such as diabetes mellitus, hypertension, chronic glomerulonephritis, lupus nephritis, and renal toxic medications. The major cause of death for the renal failure patient either before transplant

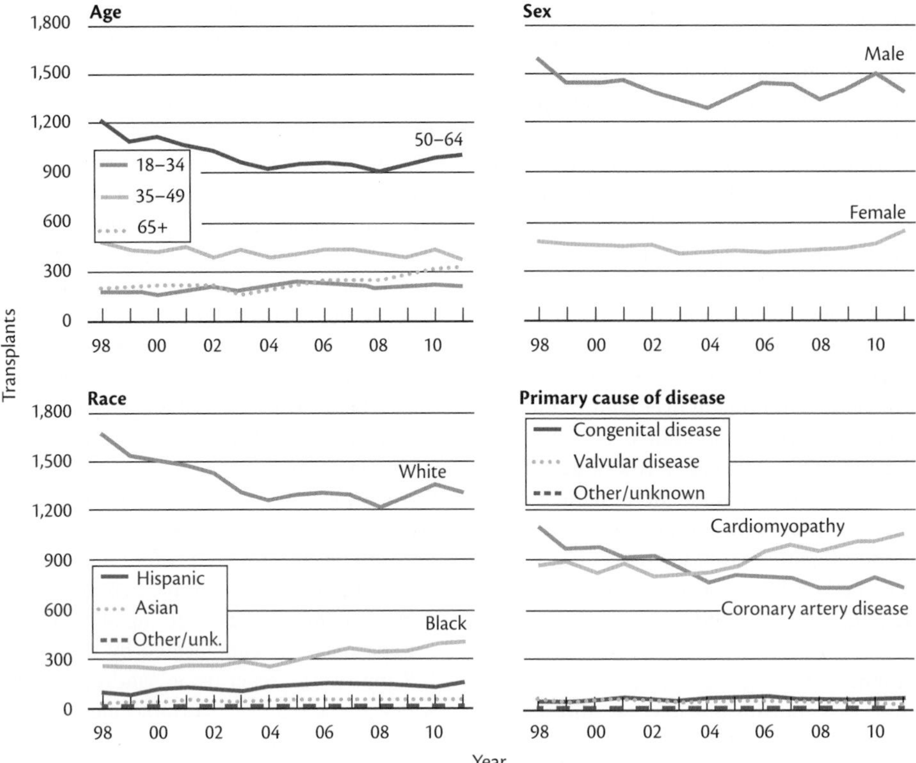

Figure 67.4 Adult heart transplants.
Data from 2011 Annual Report of the U.S. Organ Procurement and Transplantation Network and the Scientific Registry of Transplant Recipients; http://optn.transplant.hrsa.gov

or afterwards is related to cardiovascular disease. Accelerated arteriosclerosis and cardiomyopathy may both be found in this patient population.

Preoperative assessment

Careful assessment of this high-risk group of patients is essential. The combination of diabetes mellitus and cardiovascular disease allows symptoms to be minimized as the diabetic autonomic neuropathy may eliminate angina. Diabetes is seen in up to 30% of patients and by its deleterious effect on the vascular endothelium can increase the risk for myocardial infarction and stroke (Gaston et al. 2003). The incidence of coronary artery disease in patients with chronic kidney disease is 25% (McClellan and Chertow 2005) and this is the most important factor affecting perioperative morbidity and mortality (Kasiske et al. 2006). The risk of cardiovascular disease is 10–30 times higher in the chronic kidney disease patient than in the normal population. It is further complicated by the high incidence of hypertension that is difficult to control, often requiring multiple therapies. The hypertension may be the result or cause of the kidney disease, or both, and may be sustained in a progressive cycle. Congestive heart failure is also prevalent in patients with end-stage kidney disease and will increase the risk of transplantation, but after a successful transplant left ventricular function has been shown to improve (Wali et al. 2005). Basic laboratory analysis will be required to assess electrolytes, especially serum potassium, glucose, and haemoglobin, as many of these patients will be chronically anaemic. Volume status is important and will depend on timing of last dialysis. If the patient is volume overloaded then preoperative dialysis will be warranted.

The anaesthetic technique is dictated by local preference, and both general anaesthesia and regional techniques have been used successfully. One important facet of the anaesthetic technique is good postoperative pain management. This is not only for good patient care but in many of these recipients significant pain will cause extreme hypertension and tachycardia unless well β-blocked because of their non-compliant vasculature. The addition of a transverse abdominis plane block has had reported mixed results, from being very effective to completely ineffective (Mukhtar and Khattak 2010; Freir et al. 2012). This may represent the quality of technique used when administering the block. The diabetic recipients will benefit from close glucose control with an insulin infusion.

Intravenous access may be challenging for those patients who have undergone years of haemodialysis. Ultrasound technology may be helpful for both peripheral and central venous access. The type of fluid administered is a matter of debate. Some centres use normal saline, as it contains no potassium, but this does cause an increase in total body sodium and a hyperchloraemic acidosis that will cause an increase in serum potassium. Other centres use a balanced crystalloid solution. The better course is to monitor the electrolytes during the procedure and adjust fluids accordingly (Schmid and Jungwirth 2012).

Basic monitoring is required but centres differ in the use of invasive monitors (Niemann and Eilers 2010; Othman et al. 2010). Their use is probably best guided by the clinical condition of the patient. To improve renal perfusion 'renal dose' dopamine is often infused ($3\ \mu g\ kg^{-1}\ min^{-1}$) but there is little evidence to demonstrate efficacy and significant data that it may be harmful (Marik 2002). The best therapy is to maintain a good perfusion pressure and cardiac output.

Anaesthetic drugs that do not rely primarily on excretion by the kidney are recommended but as long as repeated doses are not administered this may not be relevant (Lepage et al. 1987).

Postoperative care will vary from routine recovery room care to intensive care depending on the initial status of the patient and the state of the new kidney graft.

Heart transplantation

This has been the best option for selected patients with end-stage heart failure for many years, but ventricular assist devices (VADs) are approaching similar 1-year survival rates. The projected duration of current VADs is at least 5 years and many VADs are inserted as destination devices with no plans for transplantation. The most common causes in the United States for heart transplants are dilated and ischaemic cardiomyopathy with a consistent average of 2000 adult heart transplants performed annually (Fig. 67.4). The number of recipients who have had VADs placed in the months or years before transplant is increasing and this adds extra challenges in recipient management (Fig. 67.5). The placement of an arterial catheter for monitoring blood pressure perioperatively may need a Doppler probe or ultrasound to identify the artery in patients with non-pulsatile VADs. Surgically, the removal of an established VAD may result in significant bleeding.

Overall 5-year graft survival is 74.9% and is similar between all status codes and disease groups.

The timing of the recipient procedure is often set as an emergency basis as the ischaemia time is kept to a minimum. The timing of the procedure will depend on location of the donor and whether the recipient has had previous heart surgery or VAD placement.

Anaesthesia management

The time from the patient being scheduled for surgery and the induction of anaesthesia may be very short. A rapid but precise preoperative assessment is made followed by placement of an arterial monitoring catheter. Once the organ recovery team have given the go ahead, the anaesthesia is induced using a minimally cardiodepressant technique and with inotropes standing at the ready.

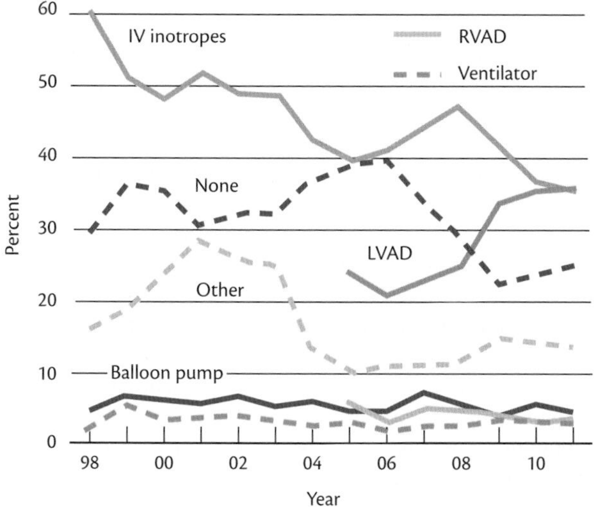

Figure 67.5 Adult heart recipients on circulatory support prior to transplant.
Data from 2011 Annual Report of the U.S. Organ Procurement and Transplantation Network and the Scientific Registry of Transplant Recipients; http://optn.transplant.hrsa.gov

A large-bore central venous catheter is placed plus a multilumen catheter for infusion of vasoactive drugs. A pulmonary artery catheter may be placed or just passed into the vena cava for placement after implantation of the graft. A TOE probe is placed and native cardiac function assessed. If a left ventricular assist device (LVAD) is in place there may be minimal flow through the aortic valve. Immunosuppression therapy is administered and the patient heparinized and placed on cardiopulmonary bypass. The diseased heart is excised, and haemostasis obtained. The donor heart is removed from ice and implanted into the recipient. Right heart failure is the main contributor to early graft failure so pulmonary vasodilators and inotropes are prepared including the immediate availability of inhaled nitric oxide (Shanewise 2004; Koster et al. 2011).

After rewarming, the function of the graft is examined for ventricular contractility and for any retained air in the chambers. Inotropic support is started initially with dobutamine 5 μg kg^{-1} min^{-1} and if there is any concern about ventricular function adrenaline infusion is added at 0.05 μg kg^{-1} min^{-1}. If there is any concern for RV dysfunction, milrinone 0.5 μg kg^{-1} min^{-1} is also started. After a period of rest for the new graft, the patient is gradually weaned from cardiopulmonary bypass. If there is evidence of RV strain then inhaled nitric oxide at 20–40 ppm is started or inhalation of aerosolized prostaglandins may be used, iloprost 20–30 μg over 15 min (Khan et al. 2009). If the right heart is still seen to be dysfunctional by TOE then the heart should be put back on cardiopulmonary bypass and rested for 30 min and then retried. Finally if the right heart continues to function poorly then extracorporeal membrane oxygenation should be considered or finally the placement of a right ventricular assist device (RVAD) (Marasco et al. 2005).

Lung transplantation

Indications of lung transplantation include pulmonary fibrosis (33%), chronic obstructive pulmonary disease (29%), cystic fibrosis (16%), α1-antitrypsin deficiency, and primary pulmonary hypertension.

The anaesthetic management requires an excellent skill set in endobronchial intubation and lung isolation, including the ability to manage optimal gas exchange during one-lung ventilation, the ability to support right and left ventricular dysfunction, and expertise with TOE (Myles et al. 2007). Early post lung graft implantation therapy may be needed with inhaled nitric oxide, RVAD, and extracorporeal membrane oxygenation (ECMO).

Donor lungs are matched by ABO compatibility and anatomical size. Donor organ allocation is assigned on the basis of estimated pretransplant mortality and postoperative survival (Merion et al. 2004). Bilateral lung transplantation appears to offer better outcomes than single-lung transplantation (Chang et al. 2007; Nwakanma et al. 2007) (Figs 67.6 and 67.7).

Anaesthetic management

Preoperative assessment must include the current respiratory status of the patient and this will frequently demonstrate a patient with end-stage pulmonary disease, sitting up to breathe, and with continual supplemental oxygen. A review of the haemodynamic data is also paramount to understand the degree of pulmonary hypertension that exists before isolation of one lung. Most centres will plan to stay off cardiopulmonary bypass for the transplant procedure but pulmonary hypertension may lead to RV dysfunction

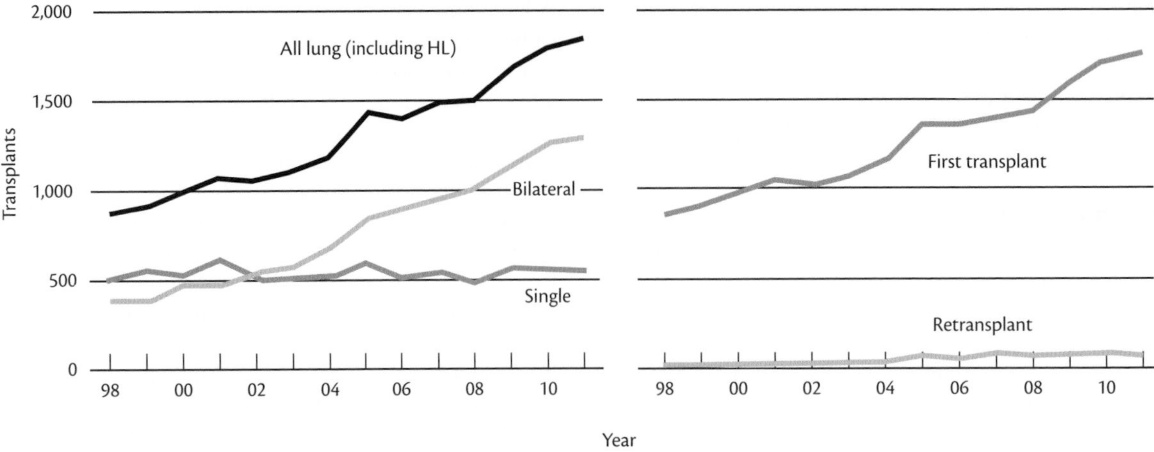

Figure 67.6 Total adult lung transplants.
Data from 2011 Annual Report of the U.S. Organ Procurement and Transplantation Network and the Scientific Registry of Transplant Recipients; http://optn.transplant.hrsa.gov

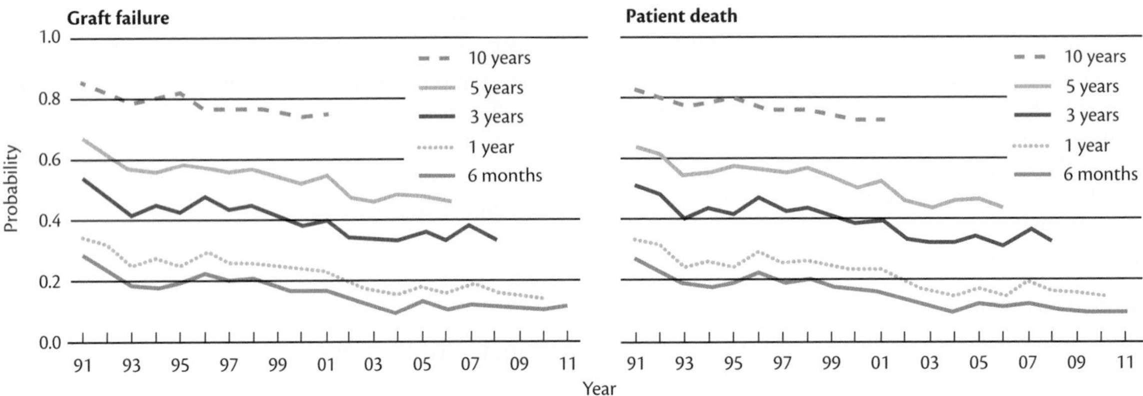

Figure 67.7 Graft failure and patient death among adult lung transplant recipients.
Data from 2011 Annual Report of the U.S. Organ Procurement and Transplantation Network and the Scientific Registry of Transplant Recipients; http://optn.transplant.hrsa.gov

intraoperatively so these patients are often electively placed on cardiopulmonary bypass from the start.

Induction of anaesthesia and the onset of mechanical ventilation may lead to profound hypotension; therefore an intra-arterial monitoring catheter should be placed before induction. A central venous volume catheter and a monitoring catheter follow the placement of a double-lumen endobronchial tube with a fibreoptic bronchoscope to confirm position. A multilumen catheter allows access for pharmacological infusions. If a pulmonary artery catheter is placed it should be withdrawn back into the RV before clamping of the pulmonary artery. A TOE probe allows assessment of ventricular function; especially RV function when one pulmonary artery is clamped and ventilation may be impaired. The imaging may also be used to review the arterial and venous anastomoses to ensure that there is no obstruction or rotation of the vessels. Mechanical ventilation will be adjusted according to the disease process and the arterial blood gas analysis. Patients with chronic obstructive pulmonary disease may be vulnerable to air trapping so longer expiratory times may be necessary with occasional disconnection of the circuit to allow adequate lung deflation, with occasional assistance by the surgeon compressing the lung. One-lung ventilation may cause significant shunting of blood before clamping of the pulmonary artery. If this is severe, the surgeon may be able to place a temporary snare around the vessel and prevent the shunting. If the pulmonary artery pressure increases and compromises the right ventricle, pulmonary vasodilators may be helpful such as inhaled nitric oxide or inhaled epoprostenol (Khan et al. 2009). If this intervention does not help the RV then cardiopulmonary bypass should be instituted. Some centres will use cardiopulmonary bypass consistently while others are concerned that there will be increased bleeding. However, outcomes are the same between groups that use cardiopulmonary bypass routinely and those that use it selectively.

Once the pulmonary arterial and venous anastomoses are complete, the bronchial anastomosis is completed and it is aspirated under direct vision through a fibreoptic bronchoscope to remove any blood or mucus and also the anastomoses are inspected. The lung is then reperfused and ventilation resumed. The allograft is very susceptible to pulmonary oedema and protective lung ventilation strategies should be implemented. This includes low tidal volumes with increased frequency, high levels of PEEP at 10 cm H_2O, and the use of the lowest inspired oxygen concentration that will allow adequate oxygenation. Avoidance of fluid overload is essential.

Good postoperative analgesia is necessary to enable early tracheal extubation in selected patients. Thoracic epidural or paravertebral blocks may be very effective (Davies et al. 2006). Opioid reduction to avoid respiratory depression by using non-steroidal anti-inflammatory drugs and α_2 agonists such as dexmedetomidine can be very useful.

Severe postoperative graft dysfunction from reperfusion injury is the most common cause of death in the immediate postoperative period. Strategies to counteract this include inhaled nitric oxide (Pasero et al. 2010), PGE1, and intravenous nitroglycerine. It has also been treated successfully by the temporary implementation of ECMO (Oto et al. 2004; Mason et al. 2006; Lucangelo et al. 2012).

Pancreas transplantation and islet cell transplantation

Type 1 diabetes is an autoimmune disease in which pancreatic islet insulin-producing cells, β cells, are selectively destroyed by autoantibodies. The scourge of diabetes may be devastating with loss of renal function, accelerated atherosclerosis, diabetic retinopathy, and autonomic and peripheral neuropathy, therefore pancreatic transplantation or transplantation of islet cells offers great promise. The most successful therapy is auto-islet cell transplantation where, after a total pancreatectomy, the islet cells are salvaged and infused via the portal vein into the liver where they survive and produce insulin. Immunosuppression therapy is not required. In the United States, 1500–2000 pancreas transplants are performed each year. Frequently a combined kidney–pancreas transplant is performed, as there is renal failure as the result of the diabetes. Pancreatic graft survival with insulin independence is around 80% at 1 year. Survival rates have increased as a result of improved surgical techniques, improved organ preservation, and improved immunosuppression (Fisher et al. 2010).

The preoperative assessment includes determining the effects of diabetes on major organ systems, including cardiovascular, renal, and the nervous system. Ischaemic heart disease may be harder to assess in the diabetic patient as diabetic neuropathy may prevent the sensation of chest pain because of the autonomic dysfunction. Therefore, non-invasive cardiac stress evaluation is required for most recipients (Rabbat et al. 2003). More invasive testing may be indicated depending on the stress test results. Most deaths related to this procedure are the result of cardiovascular disease. The patients may also be at an increased aspiration risk because of diabetic-induced gastroparesis, therefore the routine precautions should be instituted.

In patients with concomitant renal dysfunction, medications that rely on renal excretion may be avoided. Monitoring should include intra-arterial catheter and central venous catheter placements. Blood glucose homeostasis should be instituted with an initial insulin infusion but as the islet cells begin to function this may need to be reduced or stopped. Close monitoring of blood glucose is essential.

Islet cell transplantation with autotransplantation after a total pancreatectomy has had some excellent results with the report of insulin independence for more than 16 years (Robertson 2004). However, allotransplants do not do as well with a reported efficacy of only 12% of recipients being insulin independent at 1 year.

Anaesthetically, the procedure consists of managing a total pancreatectomy for which direct arterial blood pressure monitoring is helpful, and the presence of a central venous multilumen catheter. The resected pancreas is transferred to a laboratory where the islet cells are recovered by enzymatic isolation and then purified and returned to the operating room. This may take several hours. The prepared islet cells are then transfused via the portal vein and 'seed' into the liver.

Small intestine transplantation

Intestinal transplantation may replace long-term parenteral nutrition in patients with 'short gut syndrome'. The patient and graft survival at 1 year is 81% and 73.4%, respectively (Pascher et al. 2008). A combined liver and intestinal transplant is sometimes performed especially in the paediatric population. The preoperative assessment includes assessing a patient who is often afflicted with chronic pain, and very limited vascular access because of long-term parenteral nutrition. Venous mapping may need to be performed to find access to the central venous circulation. Intraoperative monitoring will require central venous access and intra-arterial catheter placement. There is a significant aspiration risk at induction, therefore precautionary measures should be taken. Regional anaesthesia may be useful in managing postoperative pain and allowing early tracheal extubation but a coagulopathy is frequently present that will rule out a neuraxial technique. Significant blood and fluid losses may take place, requiring careful attention to fluid resuscitation and coagulation management. The reperfusion syndrome with this transplant procedure may be significant, causing severe haemodynamic instability (Planinsic 2004). Maintaining normothermia may be challenging so all appropriate measures should be taken. Postoperative pain management requires extensive skill and experience, as this too will be complex (Lomax et al. 2011).

Extremity transplantation

Hand, forearm, and arm transplants are termed vascularized composite allografts. They consist of multiple transplanted tissues unlike solid organ transplants. The first successful hand transplant was reported from Lyon in 1998. Now nearly 100 upper extremity allografts have been transplanted (Lanzetta et al. 2007). The anaesthetic management of these recipients has been described by the Pittsburgh group as the Pittsburgh Upper Extremity Transplant Anesthesiology Protocol (PUETAP) (Lang et al. 2012). This protocol focused on fluid management, intraoperative monitoring, and regional anaesthesia. The protocol includes good regional analgesia by placing ultrasound-guided supraclavicular catheters, central venous and arterial catheters, coagulation monitoring with thromboelastography and the availability of a rapid infuser device. Adequate pain control in the postoperative period is challenging and essential.

Face transplantation

There are a few centres around the world that have successfully performed face transplants. The first face transplant was described in 2005 (Devauchelle et al. 2006) and since then fewer than 25 have been reported. The reasons to perform this procedure include severe burn and blast injuries, animal bites, and disfiguring diseases such as neurofibromatosis (Edrich et al. 2012). Two major impacts on the anaesthesia team have been reported. The first is a very prolonged procedure—median 19 h. The second is major blood loss that occurs after the transplanted face has been reperfused. Much of the blood loss is hard to detect, as it is mainly occult to the anaesthesia team as it drains into the surgical drapes and is not collected by sucker canisters. The median blood transfusions were 20 units of packed red cells. Most of the recipients required a tracheostomy for protection of the airway but also to facilitate surgical access to the whole face. An armoured tracheal tube was inserted into the tracheostomy site so that it could be easily manipulated without kinking. Arterial and venous access was via the femoral artery and vein to avoid the risk of thrombosis in the neck area from the usual sites. Successful outcomes have led to measurable improvements in depression, body image, quality of life, and social integration (Coffman et al. 2010).

Tracheal transplantation

Resection of a severe tracheal stenosis or a trachea with a tumour and replacing it with a tracheal transplant is a surgical and anaesthesia challenge (Delaere 2012). The trachea lacks a well-defined blood supply so the implantation of an allograft with a microvascular reconstruction is not possible. Therefore a significant advance in tissue engineering has taken place wherein a donor allograft trachea 10 cm in length is wrapped in the recipients forearm fascia and after 2 months it becomes revascularized. The donor respiratory epithelium is then removed and replaced by a full-thickness buccal mucosa graft from the recipient (Fig. 67.8). Three months after implantation the graft is revascularized by the recipient and can be placed in the tracheal defect. This tracheal chimera will only need short-term or no immunosuppression (Sykes 2010). The use of ECMO has alleviated some of the anaesthetic difficulties of

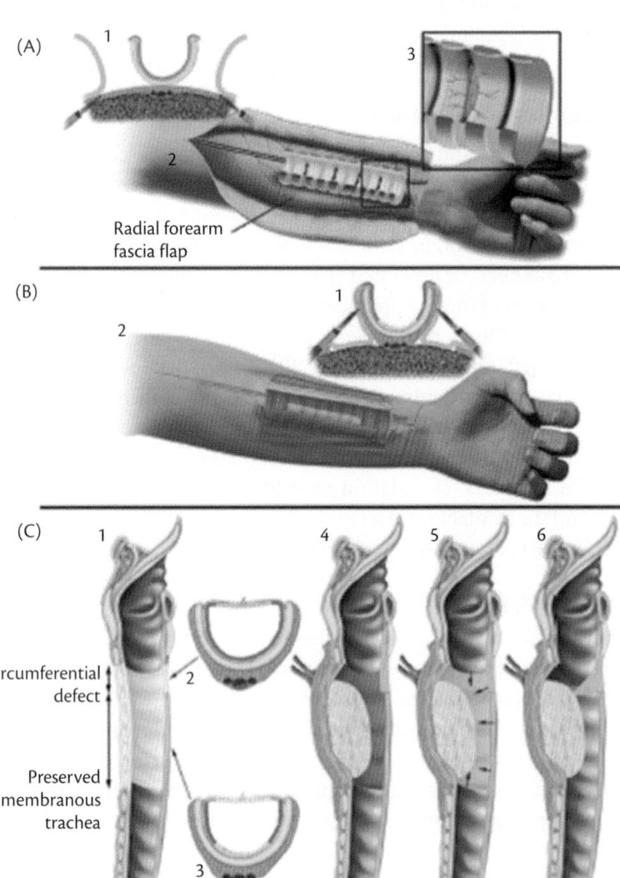

Figure 67.8 Tracheal allotransplant being revascularized in the recipient forearm.
Reproduced with permission from Delaere, P. R. Tracheal transplantation. *Current Opinion in Pulmonary Medicine*, Volume 18, Issue 4, pp. 313–320, Copyright © 2012 Wolters Kluwer Health.

maintaining oxygenation during the procedure and early after the operation (Roman et al. 2013).

The anaesthetic management of the transplanted patient undergoing non-transplant surgery

As the number of transplanted patients increases, it is likely that many anaesthetists will be required to manage patients that have undergone an organ transplant and now present for additional surgery. This will require consideration of the function of the transplanted organ, the side-effects of immunosuppressant drugs and managing the risks of infection, and the potential for enhanced rejection.

Nearly all the patients will be on immunosuppressant therapy. Those taking corticosteroids will need to be covered by stress doses of steroids until they are able to resume oral intake. Protective drug therapy for gastrointestinal bleeding should be considered. Steroidal side-effects may be seen and need to be managed, such as fragility of the skin and increased infection risk. The calcineurin inhibitors require to be kept at a therapeutic drug concentration so care needs to be taken in the administration of the preoperative dose and consultation with the immunosuppressant therapist regarding perioperative management of the drugs (Kostopanagiotou et al. 1999).

The preoperative assessment should specifically include an evaluation of the graft function, and the side-effects of graft dysfunction and immunosuppression therapy on major organs, especially the kidney. Great care should be exercised not to introduce infection into the immunosuppressed patient when inserting catheters or tracheal tubes. Patients who have received a heart transplant may still have an autonomic denervation and may not respond to vagolytic drugs. Lung transplant recipients may have an impaired cough reflex below the bronchial anastomosis. Small intestine graft recipients and kidney recipients may have very limited venous access and often require ultrasound to find an open vein.

The anaesthetic care of the living donor

The use of living donors for many transplant recipients is increasing as it may be the only source of organ supply when religious or cultural reasons prevent cadaveric donation, or because of organ shortage: in these circumstances they offer a lifeline to a recipient. The ethical issues raised by living donors are significant as the risks of morbidity and mortality are not zero (Calne 2012). The first successful kidney transplant was from a living donor who was an identical twin of the recipient (Murray et al. 1955). During the early years of transplantation, immunosuppression strategies had not been elucidated. Today, because the risks are relatively low, living kidney donation is increasing and now accounts for about 40% of all kidney transplants in the United States. Most kidney donations are performed laparoscopically so that there are faster recovery times and less pain than with open procedures (Jankovic 2008). Anaesthesia should be routine with good intravenous access and maintenance of perfusion pressure. The value of 'renal dose' dopamine has not been substantiated and may be harmful (Marik 2002). Living donor liver transplants are the most frequent donors in Asian countries but form only a small percentage in the United States. The left or right lobe of the liver may be resected for transplantation. In the United States, the right lobe is usually used as it is the larger of the two lobes. There are good data to suggest that keeping the central venous pressure low will reduce the hepatic venous volume and thereby reduce bleeding during the resection (Lautt and Greenway 1976; Jones et al. 1998). Intra-arterial monitoring of blood pressure and central venous access with a volume catheter are helpful in patient management as well as good postoperative analgesia to allow tracheal extubation at the end of the procedure (Merritt 2004; Feltracco and Ori 2010). Early postoperative coagulation dysfunction may be noted (Borromeo et al. 2000). The logistics of having the donor surgery and recipient surgery overlapping in order to minimize the ischaemia time will engage a significant number of the transplant team.

Living donor lung transplantation is performed in some centres wherein a lobe of the lung may be resected from a donor or two lobes from two donors and implanted into a recipient. Many recipients are children as cadaveric donors are scarce. Excellent postoperative analgesia for the donor is essential so that tracheal extubation may take place at the end of the procedure. The donor anaesthetic management is similar to a routine lobar lung resection.

The future

The future of major organ transplantation will rest in many different approaches, including:

1. The maintenance of good function of existing organs by better prevention of disease and better therapeutic options
2. The improved development of immunosuppression therapy to prevent loss of transplanted organs
3. The development of immunotolerance so that immunosuppressive drugs are no longer required, resulting in great savings of cost and morbidity
4. The development of xenotransplantation particularly in the field of pancreatic islet cell transplantation
5. The development of more advanced devices to support failing organs, including LVADs, RVADs, and ECMO, in addition to even newer devices such as the total artificial heart, which is now under clinical trial (Kobashigawa 2012)
6. Regenerative medicine: stem cells and tissue engineering will be used to develop new organs that do not require immunosuppression therapy (Taylor 2009).

Declaration of interest

None declared.

References

Bahde R, Spiegel HU. Hepatic ischaemia-reperfusion injury from bench to bedside. *Br J Surg* 2010; **97**: 1461–75

Bakti G, Fisch HU, Karlaganis G, Minder C, Bircher J. Mechanism of the excessive sedative response of cirrhotics to benzodiazepines: model experiments with triazolam. *Hepatology* 1987; **7**: 629–38

Banchereau J, Steinman RM. Dendritic cells and the control of immunity. *Nature* 1998; **392**: 245–52

Barbaro G, Di Lorenzo G, Soldini M, *et al.* Flumazenil for hepatic encephalopathy grade III and IVa in patients with cirrhosis: an Italian multicenter double-blind, placebo-controlled, cross-over study. *Hepatology* 1998; **28**: 374–8

Basile AS, Hughes RD, Harrison PM, *et al.* Elevated brain concentrations of 1,4-benzodiazepines in fulminant hepatic failure. *N Engl J Med* 1991; **325**: 473–8

Beck-Schimmer B, Breitenstein S, Urech S, *et al.* A randomized controlled trial on pharmacological preconditioning in liver surgery using a volatile anesthetic. *Ann Surg* 2008; **248**: 909–18

Borromeo CJ, Stix MS, Lally A, Pomfret EA. Epidural catheter and increased prothrombin time after right lobe hepatectomy for living donor transplantation. *Anesth Analg* 2000; **91**: 1139–41

Brevoord D, Kranke P, Kuijpers M, Weber N, Hollmann M, Preckel B. Remote ischemic conditioning to protect against ischemia-reperfusion injury: a systematic review and meta-analysis. *PLoS One* 2012; **7**: e42179

Calne RY. "It can't be done". *Nat Med* 2012; **18**: 1493–95

Candilio L, Malik A, Hausenloy DJ. Protection of organs other than the heart by remote ischemic conditioning. *J Cardiovasc Med (Hagerstown)* 2013; 14: 193–205

Carey WD, Dumot JA, Pimentel RR, *et al.* The prevalence of coronary artery disease in liver transplant candidates over age 50. *Transplantation* 1995; **59**: 859–64

Chang AC, Chan KM, Lonigro RJ, *et al.* Surgical patient outcomes after the increased use of bilateral lung transplantation. *J Thorac Cardiovasc Surg* 2007; **133**: 532–40

Coffman KL, Gordon C, Siemionow M. Psychological outcomes with face transplantation: overview and case report. *Curr Opin Organ Transplant* 2010; **15**: 236–40

Davies RG, Myles PS, Graham JM. A comparison of the analgesic efficacy and side-effects of paravertebral vs epidural blockade for thoracotomy--a systematic review and meta-analysis of randomized trials. *Br J Anaesth* 2006; **96**: 418–26

de Knegt RJ, Schalm SW. Fulminant hepatic failure: to transplant or not to transplant. *Neth J Med* 1991; **38**: 131–41

Delaere PR. Tracheal transplantation. *Curr Opin Pulm Med* 2012; **18**: 313–20

Devauchelle B, Badet L, Lengele B, *et al.* First human face allograft: early report. *Lancet* 2006; **368**: 203–9

Doyle HR, Marino IR, Miro A, *et al.* Adult respiratory distress syndrome secondary to end-stage liver disease-successful outcome following liver transplantation. *Transplantation* 1993; **55**: 292–6

Dursun M, Caliskan M, Canoruc F, *et al.* The efficacy of flumazenil in subclinical to mild hepatic encephalopathic ambulatory patients. A prospective, randomised, double-blind, placebo-controlled study. *Swiss Med Wkly* 2003; **133**: 118–23

Edrich T, Cywinski JB, Colomina MJ, *et al.* Perioperative management of face transplantation: a survey. *Anesth Analg* 2012; **115**: 668–70

Ellis A, Wendon J. Circulatory, respiratory, cerebral, and renal derangements in acute liver failure: pathophysiology and management. *Semin Liver Dis* 1996; **16**: 379–88

Fallon MB, Abrams GA. Hepatopulmonary syndrome. *Curr Gastroenterol Rep* 2000; **2**: 40–5

Feltracco P, Ori C. Anesthetic management of living transplantation. *Minerva Anestesiol* 2010; **76**: 525–33

Fisher JS, Mirbolooki MR, Lakey JRT, Robertson RP, Marsh CL. Pancreas and islet transplantation. In: *Comprehensive Clinical Nephrology*, 4th Edn. London: Mosby, 2010; 1232–44

Freir NM, Murphy C, Mugawar M, Linnane A, Cunningham AJ. Transversus abdominis plane block for analgesia in renal transplantation: a randomized controlled trial. *Anesth Analg* 2012; **115**: 953–7

Furnary AP, Gao G, Grunkemeier GL, *et al.* Continuous insulin infusion reduces mortality in patients with diabetes undergoing coronary artery bypass grafting. *J Thorac Cardiovasc Surg* 2003; **125**: 1007–21

Gaston RS, Danovitch GM, Adams PL, *et al.* The report of a national conference on the wait list for kidney transplantation. *Am J Transplant* 2003; **3**: 775–85

Gorsuch WB, Chrysanthou E, Schwaeble WJ, Stahl GL. The complement system in ischemia-reperfusion injuries. *Immunobiology* 2012; **217**: 1026–33

Greig PD, Woolf GM, Abecassis M, *et al.* Prostaglandin E1 for primary nonfunction following liver transplantation. *Transplant Proc* 1989; **21**: 3360–1

Gupta S, Castel H, Rao RV, *et al.* Improved survival after liver transplantation in patients with hepatopulmonary syndrome. *Am J Transplant* 2010; **10**: 354–63

Hambleton J, Leung LL, Levi M. Coagulation: consultative hemostasis. *Hematology Am Soc Hematol Educ Program* 2002; **2002**: 335–52

Husberg BS, Goldstein RM, Klintmalm GB, *et al.* A totally failing liver may be more harmful than no liver at all: three cases of total hepatic devascularization in preparation for emergency liver transplantation. *Transplant Proc* 1991; **23**: 1533–5

Jankovic Z. Anaesthesia for living—donor renal transplant. *Curr Anaesth Crit Care* 2008; **19**: 175–80

Jones RM, Moulton CE, Hardy KJ. Central venous pressure and its effect on blood loss during liver resection. *Br J Surg* 1998; **85**: 1058–60

Kasiske BL, Maclean JR, Snyder JJ. Acute myocardial infarction and kidney transplantation. *J Am Soc Nephrol* 2006; **17**: 900–7

Khan TA, Schnickel G, Ross D, *et al.* A prospective, randomized, crossover pilot study of inhaled nitric oxide versus inhaled prostacyclin in heart transplant and lung transplant recipients. *J Thorac Cardiovasc Surg* 2009; **138**: 1417–24

Kobashigawa JA. The future of heart transplantation. *Am J Transplant*, **12**: 2875–91

Koster A, Diehl C, Dongas A, Meyer-Jark T, Lüth IU. Anesthesia for cardiac transplantation: a practical overview of current management strategies. *Applied Cardiopulm Pathophysiol* 2011; **15**: 213–9

Kostopanagiotou G, Smyrniotis V, Arkadopoulos N, Theodoraki K, Papadimitriou L, Papadimitriou J. Anesthetic and perioperative management of adult transplant recipients in nontransplant surgery. *Anesth Analg* 1999; **89**: 613–22

Kowalski HJ, Abelmann WH. The cardiac output at rest in Laennec's cirrhosis. *J Clin Invest* 1953; **32**: 1025–33

Kreisel D, Goldstein DR. Innate immunity and organ transplantation: focus on lung transplantation. *Transpl Int* 2012; **26**: 2–10

Krowka MJ, Swanson KL, Frantz RP, McGoon MD, Wiesner RH. Portopulmonary hypertension: results from a 10-year screening algorithm. *Hepatology* 2006; **44**: 1502–10

Lang RS, Gorantla VS, Esper S, *et al.* Anesthetic management in upper extremity transplantation: the Pittsburgh experience. *Anesth Analg* 2012; **115**: 678–88

Lanzetta M, Petruzzo P, Dubernard JM, *et al.* Second report (1998-2006) of the International Registry of Hand and Composite Tissue Transplantation. *Transpl Immunol* 2007; **18**: 1–6

Lautt WW, Greenway CV. Hepatic venous compliance and role of liver as a blood reservoir. *Am J Physiol* 1976; **231**: 292–5

Lee SS. Cardiac abnormalities in liver cirrhosis. *West J Med* 1989; **151**: 530–5

Lentine KL, Costa SP, Weir MR, *et al.* Cardiac disease evaluation and management among kidney and liver transplantation candidates: a scientific statement from the American Heart Association and the American College of Cardiology Foundation. *J Am Coll Cardiol* 2012; **60**: 434–80

Lepage JY, Malinge M, Cozian A, Pinaud M, Blanloeil Y, Souron R. Vecuronium and atracurium in patients with end-stage renal failure. A comparative study. *Br J Anaesth* 1987; **59**: 1004–10

Lomax S, Klucniks A, Griffiths J. Anaesthesia for intestinal transplantation. *Contin Educ Anaesth Crit Care Pain* 2011; **11**: 1–4.

Lucangelo U, Del Sorbo L, Boffini M, Ranieri VM. Protective ventilation for lung transplantation. *Curr Opin Anaesthesiol* 2012; **25**: 170–4

Mandell MS, Lezotte D, Kam I, Zamudio S. Reduced use of intensive care after liver transplantation: influence of early extubation. *Liver Transpl* 2002; **8**: 676–81

Marasco SF, Esmore DS, Negri J, *et al.* Early institution of mechanical support improves outcomes in primary cardiac allograft failure. *J Heart Lung Transplant* 2005; **24**: 2037–42

Marik PE. Low-dose dopamine: a systematic review. *Intensive Care Med* 2002; **28**: 877–83

Mason DP, Boffa DJ, Murthy SC, *et al.* Extended use of extracorporeal membrane oxygenation after lung transplantation. *J Thorac Cardiovasc Surg* 2006; **132**: 954–60

McClellan WM, Chertow GM. Beyond Framingham: cardiovascular risk profiling in ESRD. *J Am Soc Nephrol* 2005; **16**: 1539–41

Merion RM, Hulbert-Shearon TE, Bustami RT, *et al.* Proposed lung allocation system based on medical urgency and transplant benefit. *Am J Transplant* 2004; **4**: 414 (abstract 936)

Merritt WT. Living donor surgery: overview of surgical and anesthesia issues. *Anesthesiol Clin North America* 2004; **22**: 633–50

Moore JW, Dunk AA, Crawford JR, *et al.* Neuropsychological deficits and morphological MRI brain scan abnormalities in apparently healthy nonencephalopathic patients with cirrhosis. A controlled study. *J Hepatol* 1989; **9**: 319–25

Morris JJ, Hellman CL, Gawey BJ, *et al.* Case 3-1995. Three patients requiring both coronary artery bypass surgery and orthotopic liver transplantation. *J Cardiothorac Vasc Anesth* 1995; **9**: 322–32

Mukhtar K, Khattak I. Transversus abdominis plane block for renal transplant recipients. *Br J Anaesth* 2010; **104**: 663–4

Murray JE, Merrill JP, Harrison JH. Renal homotransplantation in identical twins. *Surg Forum* 1955; **6**: 432–6

Myles PS, Snell GI, Westall GP. Lung transplantation. *Curr Opin Anaesthesiol* 2007; **20**: 21–6

Nadim MK, Kellum JA, Davenport A, *et al.* Hepatorenal syndrome: the 8th international consensus conference of the Acute Dialysis Quality Initiative (ADQI) Group. *Crit Care* 2012; **16**: R23

Niemann CU, Eilers H. Abdominal organ transplantation. *Minerva Anestesiol* 2010; **76**: 266–75

Nwakanma LU, Simpkins CE, Williams JA, *et al.* Impact of bilateral versus single lung transplantation on survival in recipients 60 years of age and older: analysis of United Network for Organ Sharing database. *J Thorac Cardiovasc Surg* 2007; **133**: 541–7

Olson JC, Wiesner RH. Immunomodulating therapy in liver transplantation: principles and practice. *Immunotherapy* 2012; **4**: 793–805

Othman MM, Ismael AZ, Hammouda GE. The impact of timing of maximal crystalloid hydration on early graft function during kidney transplantation. *Anesth Analg* 2010; **110**: 1440–6

Oto T, Rosenfeldt F, Rowland M, *et al.* Extracorporeal membrane oxygenation after lung transplantation: evolving technique improves outcomes. *Ann Thorac Surg* 2004; **78**: 1230–5

Pascher A, Kohler S, Neuhaus P, Pratschke J. Present status and future perspectives of intestinal transplantation. *Transpl Int* 2008; **21**: 401–14

Pasero D, Martin EL, Davi A, Mascia L, Rinaldi M, Ranieri VM. The effects of inhaled nitric oxide after lung transplantation. *Minerva Anestesiol* 2010; **76**: 353–61

Paugam-Burtz C, Kavafyan J, Merckx P, *et al.* Postreperfusion syndrome during liver transplantation for cirrhosis: outcome and predictors. *Liver Transpl* 2009; **15**: 522–9

Pham DM, Subramanian R, Parekh S. Coexisting hepatopulmonary syndrome and portopulmonary hypertension: implications for liver transplantation. *J Clin Gastroenterol* 2010; **44**: e136–40

Planinsic RM. Anesthetic management for small bowel transplantation. *Anesthesiol Clin North America* 2004; **22**: 675–85

Plotkin JS, Johnson LB, Rustgi V, Kuo PC. Coronary artery disease and liver transplantation: the state of the art. *Liver Transpl* 2000; 6(4 Suppl 1): S53–6

Rabbat CG, Treleaven DJ, Russell JD, Ludwin D, Cook DJ. Prognostic value of myocardial perfusion studies in patients with end-stage renal disease assessed for kidney or kidney-pancreas transplantation: a meta-analysis. *J Am Soc Nephrol* 2003; **14**: 431–9

Ramsay M. The reperfusion syndrome: have we made any progress? *Liver Transpl* 2008; **14**: 412–4

Ramsay M. Portopulmonary hypertension and right heart failure in patients with cirrhosis. *Curr Opin Anaesthesiol* 2010; **23**: 145–50

Robertson RP. Islet transplantation as a treatment for diabetes—a work in progress. *N Engl J Med* 2004; **350**: 694–705

Rodriguez-Roisin R, Krowka MJ, Herve P, Fallon MB. Pulmonary-hepatic vascular disorders (PHD). *Eur Respir J* 2004; **24**: 861–80

Roman PE, Battafarano RJ, Grigore AM. Anesthesia for tracheal reconstruction and transplantation. *Curr Opin Anaesthesiol* 2013; **26**: 1–5

Safdar Z, Bartolome S, Sussman N. Portopulmonary hypertension: an update. *Liver Transpl* 2012; **18**: 881–91

Saibara T, Onishi S, Sone J, *et al.* Arterial ketone body ratio as a possible indicator for liver transplantation in fulminant hepatic failure. *Transplantation* 1991; **51**: 782–6

Schmid S, Jungwirth B. Anaesthesia for renal transplant surgery: an update. *Eur J Anaesthesiol* 2012; **29**: 552–8

Shami VM, Caldwell SH, Hespenheide EE, Arseneau KO, Bickston SJ, Macik BG. Recombinant activated factor VII for coagulopathy in fulminant hepatic failure compared with conventional therapy. *Liver Transpl* 2003; **9**: 138–43

Shanewise J. Cardiac transplantation. *Anesthesiol Clin North America* 2004; **22**: 753–65

Steinman RM, Banchereau J. Taking dendritic cells into medicine. *Nature* 2007; **449**: 419–26

Sykes M. Immune evasion by chimeric trachea. *N Engl J Med* 2010; **362**: 172–4

Takaoka F, Brown MR, Paulsen AW, Ramsay MA, Klintmalm GB. Adult respiratory distress syndrome following orthotopic liver transplantation. *Clin Transpl* 1989; **3**: 294–9

Taylor DA. From stem cells and cadaveric matrix to engineered organs. *Curr Opin Biotechnol* 2009; **20**: 598–605

Tripodi A, Mannucci PM. Abnormalities of hemostasis in chronic liver disease: reappraisal of their clinical significance and need for clinical and laboratory research. *J Hepatol* 2007; **46**: 727–33

Ueno H, Klechevsky E, Morita R, *et al.* Dendritic cell subsets in health and disease. *Immunol Rev* 2007; **219**: 118–42

Ueno H, Schmitt N, Palucka AK, Banchereau J. Dendritic cells and humoral immunity in humans. *Immunol Cell Biol* 2010; **88**: 376–80

Umeda N, Kamath PS. Hepatopulmonary syndrome and portopulmonary hypertension. *Hepatol Res* 2009; **39**: 1020–2

Van Allen NR, Krafft PR, Leitzke AS, *et al.* The role of volatile anesthetics in cardioprotection: a systematic review. *Med Gas Res* 2012; **2**: 22

Wali RK, Wang GS, Gottlieb SS, *et al.* Effect of kidney transplantation on left ventricular systolic dysfunction and congestive heart failure in patients with end-stage renal disease. *J Am Coll Cardiol* 2005; **45**: 1051–60

Weyker PD, Webb CA, Kiamanesh D, Flynn BC. Lung ischemia reperfusion injury: a bench-to-bedside review. *Semin Cardiothorac Vasc Anesth* 2013; **17**: 28–43

Wolfe RA, Ashby VB, Milford EL, *et al.* Comparison of mortality in all patients on dialysis, patients on dialysis awaiting transplantation, and recipients of a first cadaveric transplant. *N Engl J Med* 1999; **341**: 1725–30

Wray C, Scovotti JC, Tobis J, *et al.* Liver transplantation outcome in patients with angiographically proven coronary artery disease: a multi-institutional study. *Am J Transplant* 2013; **13**: 184–91

Zardi EM, Abbate A, Zardi DM, *et al.* Cirrhotic cardiomyopathy. *J Am Coll Cardiol* 2010; **56**: 539–49

Zarrinpar A, Busuttil RW. Immunomodulating options for liver transplant patients. *Expert Rev Clin Immunol* 2012; **8**: 565–78

Zhai Y, Petrowsky H, Hong JC, Busuttil RW, Kupiec-Weglinski JW. Ischaemia-reperfusion injury in liver transplantation-from bench to bedside. *Nat Rev Gastroenterol Hepatol* 2013; **10**: 79–89

Zhang J, Fallon MB. Hepatopulmonary syndrome: update on pathogenesis and clinical features. *Nat Rev Gastroenterol Hepatol* 2012; **9**: 539–49

CHAPTER 68

Anaesthesia for day-stay surgery

Jan Jakobsson

Introduction

During the last two to three decades, there has been an increasing interest in and adoption of day surgery. Thus, almost 60–80% of surgery today is performed on an ambulatory basis in many countries across the world. There are several reasons for the increase in day surgery cases: the healthcare cost constraints; decreasing number of hospital beds; expanding developments in minimally invasive surgery; and introduction of new drugs and perioperative anaesthetic techniques, promoting rapid recovery and early ambulation allowing safe discharge of the patient to return home and sleep in their own beds. These have had a major impact in promoting day surgery. The benefits of early ambulation and shortening the time spent in hospital, thus reducing the risk of thromboembolism and hospital-acquired infections, have also contributed to the expanding interest in day surgery.

The positive experience from day surgery, from the adoption of a multidisciplinary commitment in order to facilitate efficient and rapid patient turnover, has led to an increasing interest and adoption of programmes aimed at shortening the hospital stay, through various accelerated recovery programmes. The anaesthetist and the perioperative anaesthetic care form vital and fundamental parts of the success of such programmes. Effective preparation and planning, including structured intraoperative care and multimodal pain and postoperative nausea and vomiting (PONV) management, are cornerstones of this work. The present chapter provides a guide to the basic and general aspects of the anaesthetic perioperative care of the day-stay surgical patient.

Patient selection, preoperative assessment, and evaluation

Preoperative management

Previous boundaries and limitations to day surgery have been stretched in recent years to include sicker patients undergoing not only minor or intermediate-risk surgery but also major surgery, and the boundaries for day surgery are likely to expand further in the future (see Fig. 68.1). Thus, we first need to ask ourselves whether the patient can be safely operated on a day-stay basis or if outcome and quality of care is significantly improved through inpatient care. A detailed preoperative assessment, in order to identify medical conditions that potentially increase the risk for an adverse outcome, or that have a significant impact on quality of care associated with surgery and anaesthesia, is important. Preoperative assessment must therefore take into consideration not only the surgical trauma but also the pathophysiological stress associated with the planned procedure (see Fig. 68.2). In addition, preoperative assessment should also identify anaesthetic and analgesic techniques that would be suitable, taking into consideration the patient's preference, and the availability of support services after discharge, while at home.

Preoperative assessment

Preoperative assessment is often based on age, procedure, or both. In many institutions, preoperative assessment follows a standardized pathway. A regular review and possible revision of such

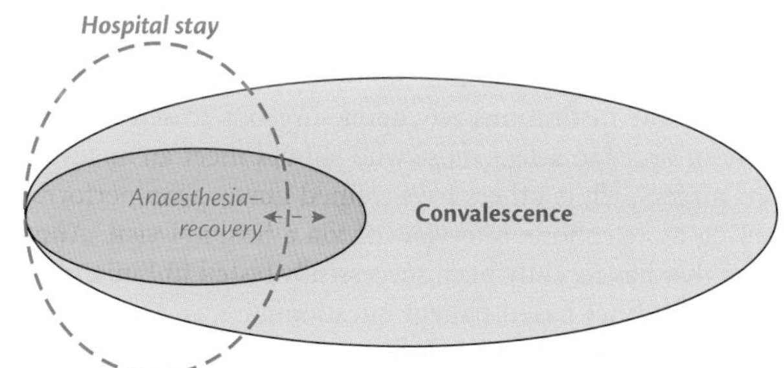

Figure 68.1 Day surgery.

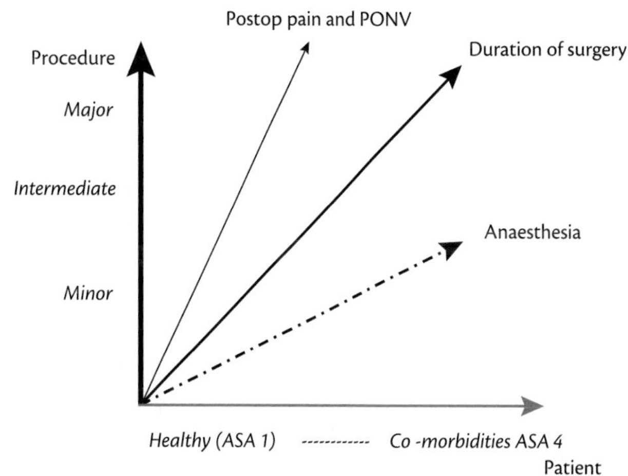

Figure 68.2 Day-stay assessment guide.

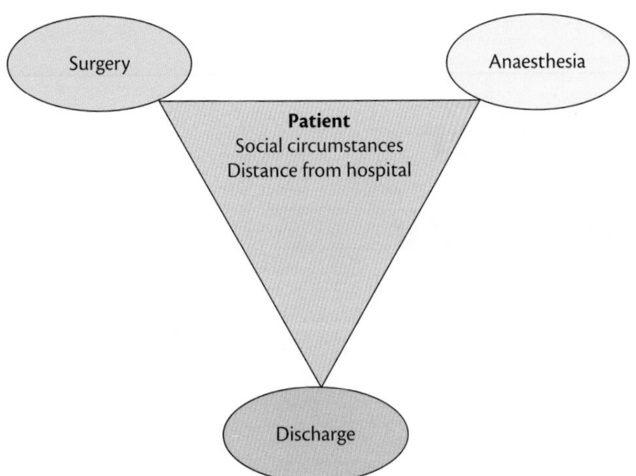

Figure 68.3 Selection criteria for day-stay surgery must consider four variables.

routine practices needs to be done in view of the continuous expansion of day surgery. ASA class I–II patients scheduled for minor or intermediate-risk surgery may not exhibit a substantial anaesthetic risk when operated as day cases and routine preoperative assessment in the preoperative anaesthetic clinic may not be necessary, thus avoiding an extra hospital visit.

The use of patient questionnaires for assessment of general health which incorporate questions on physical activity and capacity, smoking and substance abuse, prior anaesthetic or surgical outcome, allergies, and unfavourable experiences from medications provides some effective screening questions that may be appropriate for most patients. These can be completed during the preoperative surgical consultation or submitted electronically using the Internet. Many institutions rely upon surgeons to screen patients initially in order to select those who should meet an anaesthetist before surgery, while others have trained nurses who perform the screening by telephone interview or via a hospital visit. Another method that has recently been successfully tested in Finland is the use of an Internet-based patient questionnaire as a tool to avoid an additional hospital visit before a day surgical procedure. Each method has its advantages and disadvantages and none can be considered to be universally applicable. The choice is often dependent on such factors as local institutional practices, patient and procedure characteristics, preferences of the attending anaesthetist, and the costs involved.

Selection criteria for accepting patients for day surgery need to take several features into account. Essentially, four variables need to be considered: the patient, the type of surgery, the planned anaesthesia technique, and plans for the extended recovery and rehabilitation in the home environment (see Fig. 68.3). In addition, the duration of surgery is sometimes considered to be an independent but important factor. Thus, anticipated surgical times exceeding 120 min should preclude day surgery.

The patient

Previously, extremes of age, weight, and ASA classification were the primary determinants of whether or not to perform day surgery. Over time, each of these has proved to be more or less irrelevant. Age limits have never independently been shown to affect outcome in prospective, randomized studies. Body mass index (BMI) has also not been shown to be an independent risk factor for outcome and, although ASA classification continues to be used as a criterion for day surgery, it is likely that factors other than the ASA physical status are much more important for outcomes after day surgery. For instance, a healthy 90-year-old patient with no concomitant disease and undergoing minor surgery cannot be denied day surgery because of age limitations. Cataract surgery is nowadays almost exclusively performed as a day-stay procedure and, in many institutions, as office-based practice in the elderly patient. Similarly, a patient with a BMI of 55 with no attendant co-morbidities undergoing minor surgery should not be denied day surgery on the basis of weight. In contrast, a 30-year-old type 1 diabetic with hypertension and mild heart failure undergoing laparoscopic cholecystectomy may not be an ideal candidate for day surgery.

The type of surgery

Surgical procedures have been classified into three categories, based on the risks involved: minor-, intermediate- and major-risk surgery. Major-risk surgery should certainly not be performed as day surgery, although enthusiastic surgeons have performed endovascular aortic aneurysm repair on an ambulatory basis, which most would consider to be undesirable. Intermediate-risk surgical procedures can be performed in a day-stay setting provided the supporting services (nursing, home-doctor, physiotherapists, etc.) are well developed, the patient is motivated to go home and has the support services needed while at home, and is not living far away from the hospital so that potential complications can be managed quickly without putting the patient at major risk. Minor-risk surgery is ideally suited for day surgery provided the postoperative pain is likely to be manageable using simple analgesic techniques.

The anaesthetic technique

Procedures that can be performed under sedation or local anaesthesia are almost invariably suitable for day surgery, independent of patient- or surgical-risk factors. For instance, inguinal hernia repair may be performed under local anaesthesia with sedation even in patients with compromising co-morbidities. Although procedures that may be accomplished under spinal anaesthesia may also be acceptable in day surgery, a somewhat delayed home discharge might be anticipated. Newer spinal anaesthetics (chloroprocaine and articaine) with a shorter duration of action that will soon be available may change this scenario in the future. Regional blocks, specifically of the upper extremity, in otherwise sick patients may be suitable for day surgery. However, general anaesthesia in sick patients undergoing moderately invasive surgery should preferably not be performed as day surgery as the risk for admission or readmission may be high.

The after-discharge planning

The socioeconomic situation and travel times from home to the hospital are aspects that need to be taken into consideration when planning day-stay surgery. There are several examples of successful implementation of extensive surgical procedures in dedicated centres. This is certainly possible for experienced teams working in a specifically designed and organized unit but it cannot be universally recommended. There are no randomized trials that have compared alternative standardized clinical pathways for patients undergoing intermediate risk surgery and no such trials are likely in the future. However, experience from accelerated rehabilitation programmes that encourage early home discharge has been positive. Therefore, a proper benefit *vs* risk assessment should be made in each case and the merits of inpatient management weighed against home discharge the same day. Nonetheless, day surgery should not put the patient at any risk. Day-stay anaesthesia and surgery should provide an adequate, safe, and cost-effective alternative to traditional in-hospital care.

In summary, each patient has to be considered individually and the balance and interactions between surgical procedure, the patient's functional capacity, planned anaesthesia, and the management of pain, PONV, and all other aspects of the more extended recovery/rehabilitation process should influence whether surgery should be performed on a day-care basis. It is important to know that there are no strict criteria as to which patients are suitable for day surgery but patients unsuitable for day surgery can often be identified. Local practices, the level of experience of personnel, patient motivation, and bed availability all interact in deciding the best management for each patient. Whatever the decision made, in each establishment, implementation of day surgery should never put patients at any but minimal added risk.

Preoperative investigations

Whether day surgical patients should be exposed to investigations based on predefined criteria or not has been much debated. Essentially, investigations should be performed in day surgical patients if they are needed or would change patient management and should follow the same basic principles as for in-patients. Chung et al. (2009) published a study to elucidate the value of routine preoperative laboratory testing and found that routine testing did not have any significant or clinically meaningful impact on outcome. The question of routine ECG in elderly patients has also been addressed in several studies. The consensus of opinion seems to suggest that routine ECG does not lead to improved outcome in day surgical (or indeed any) patients and that testing, both laboratory and cardiac, should be performed only if it may change patient management. Thus, a patient with ischaemic heart disease should have an ECG performed before day surgery while a diabetic patient should have a blood glucose checked before induction of anaesthesia.

Preoperative information

Verbal information given by the surgeon and anaesthetist is mandatory. Informed consent about the surgical procedure, acceptance of short stay schedule, and the type of anaesthesia is strongly recommended, although not obligatory, in most countries. Furthermore, information about the time schedule, preoperative preparations, and aspects of postoperative care, wound care and hygiene, mobilization, and limitations in activities of daily living should be provided to all patients. Information should preferably be both verbal and written: nurses may easily provide many aspects of this. Other cost-effective strategies for optimal information may include brochures, video-tapes, Internet-based resources, and other interactive media. Information should not be limited to surgical intervention but also include aspects of anaesthesia and postoperative care and convalescence, pain management at home, and ways to improve mobilization and early return to work. Information about take-home analgesics should preferably be provided, or patients should be encouraged to buy these medicines preoperatively in order that that they are available on returning home from the hospital. Finally, information about preoperative medications, personal hygiene, and when to stop eating, smoking, and drinking are important and help in allaying anxiety, improving patient outcome, and promoting good clinical practice. Elective day-stay patients with no risk factors for delayed gastric emptying should be encouraged to take clear fluids up to 2 h before anaesthesia, thus reducing preoperative fluid restriction and perioperative fluid replacement.

Patients on regular medications should be provided with explicit and detailed information about what to do on the morning of surgery with regard to regular medication. In general, regular medications to control cardiovascular disease should be continued, with the possible exception of angiotensin-converting enzyme inhibitors for hypertension. Other non-essential drugs that could be omitted on the morning of day surgery include digoxin for atrial fibrillation, thyroxine for hypothyroidism, and oral antidiabetics. Although local hospital practices should guide therapy, interrupting these medications for a short period of time does not appear to cause harm. Most institutions currently allow continuation of low-dose aspirin, while oral anticoagulation therapy may be interrupted, depending on its indication, and on an individual basis, taking into account the type of surgery, the risk of bleeding, and the risk of thromboembolic complications.

Type 2 diabetic patients should be accepted for day surgery if the diabetes is stable and well controlled. Co-morbidities in these patients must be optimally controlled before surgery. The management of patients with diabetes mellitus should follow general guidelines (see Chapter 79).

Premedication

Anxiolytic premedication is not commonly needed in day-stay anaesthesia. Patients should be well informed and waiting time minimized. The preoperative holding area should be comfortable and relaxing and patients should have the opportunity if they wish to read, watch TV, listen to music, and even have access to the Internet. Children should have the option of watching films while waiting for their operation. These multimedia possibilities help to divert attention and thereby reduce anxiety in the holding area. A patient beeper or mobile contact may allow those who wish to relax outside the hospital atmosphere to do so with the possibility of coming to the day-care centre only shortly before surgery. However, clear instructions on when to eat and drink have to be given if the patient is not in the day centre. In certain anxious patients and specifically when waiting times may be long, administration of an anxiolytic preoperative medication may be appropriate. *Benzodiazepines* have been the drugs of choice in this situation and intravenous midazolam 1–2 mg in an adult is usually adequate. *Clonidine* has also been used, specifically in children, and has the benefit of having both anxiolytic and postoperative analgesic effects. Doses of about 4 $\mu g\ kg^{-1}$ orally may be administered but the time to onset can be up to 1 h. *Topical anaesthesia* with a local anaesthetic cream should be applied in children and even adult patients who have a fear of needles.

It has become increasingly popular to administer peripheral analgesics such as non-steroidal anti-inflammatory drugs (NSAIDs) and paracetamol orally preoperatively as premedication in order to have analgesic effects perioperatively and thus reduce postoperative pain. This has become a standard of care in day-stay surgery for preventive analgesia. Administration of a cyclooxygenase (COX)-2 inhibitor such as etoricoxib has been shown to be effective and does not cause increased bleeding. However, if the surgeon is concerned about the potential impact of bleeding on surgical outcome, such as during plastic surgery, parecoxib, which has a short time to onset of action, may be an option and can be given intravenously at the end of surgery. The potential concerns about cardiovascular complications associated with the prolonged use of NSAIDs and selective COX-2 inhibitors ('coxibs') are well known. However, the risks associated with their short postoperative use seem low. Naproxen has been shown to be associated with the lowest risk, and can be recommended as the drug of first choice in patients at risk of cardiovascular complications.

Preoperative fasting

Patients undergoing day surgery should follow the same guidelines for preoperative fasting as in-patients. Prolonged fasting and withholding of fluids should be avoided. Whether administration of preoperative nutritional drinks has any major impact on outcome in day surgery has not yet been established. In consideration of the risk of fluid deprivation from prolonged fasting, maintaining fluid homeostasis by oral intake of clear fluids up to 2 h before anaesthesia should be encouraged in all patients who are not at risk. Similarly, early fluid intake during recovery should also be encouraged.

Anaesthetic practice

Preparation for induction of anaesthesia

Establishment of intravenous access in the preoperative preparation area may facilitate logistics and patient turnover. Inhalation of nitrous oxide in oxygen by mask for 1–2 min makes intravenous access more comfortable in children and may also be an option in adults with needle phobias.

After intravenous access, a small dose of midazolam (1–2 mg) or propofol (10–30 mg) may be an option in order to reduce anxiety. The latter may be repeated during preparation of the patient in the operating theatre, which is usually appreciated by the patient.

Anaesthesia

There are many anaesthetic techniques that can be safely and effectively used for day-stay surgery (Kumar et al. 2014). However, the main principle should be to use drugs with a short duration of action in order that recovery is rapid. Postoperative analgesics should be administered pre- or intraoperatively in order to have a good effect at the time of awakening. This helps to shorten postoperative recovery. *Multimodal pain management* (see Fig. 68.4) has become a standard of care in day surgery. This necessitates the administration of several analgesics with different mechanisms of action in order to reduce postoperative pain. Whenever feasible, the surgical field should be infiltrated with local anaesthetic before or at the end of surgery. Administration of local anaesthetic before surgery reduces the noxious afferent impulses and has benefits both intra- and postoperatively. The use of a peripheral nerve block may be an option and offers similar benefits, providing good intraoperative analgesia and reducing postoperative pain. However, patients should be explicitly instructed to proactively take oral pain medication during the recovery period and up to 24–48 h after the operation in order to avoid breakthrough pain, which commonly occurs when the residual effects of local anaesthetic wear off.

General or regional anaesthesia and intravenous or inhalation anaesthesia all have benefits and side-effects. It would be impossible to describe all of the advantages and disadvantages of each technique in this short chapter. However, the salient features of these techniques in relation to day surgery are outlined in the following sections (see Fig. 68.5).

General anaesthesia

This is still the commonest technique for day-stay surgery. The advantage of rapid induction and easy maintenance of anaesthesia means that the operating lists can easily be managed without inconvenience for patient or surgeons. The disadvantage of general anaesthesia is that early recovery from anaesthesia can sometimes be delayed as a result of residual effects of general anaesthetics and intermediate recovery sometimes delayed because of pain, dizziness, and PONV, leading to loss of efficiency in a busy unit.

Propofol

Propofol is the drug of choice for day-stay anaesthetic induction. Inhalation anaesthetic induction is an option in children and adults with needle phobia. Thiopental (thiopentone) may also be used for induction of anaesthesia.

Maintenance of anaesthesia may be achieved effectively and safely with both inhaled anaesthetics and intravenous drugs. The choice is based on the experience of the anaesthetist and the anaesthesia

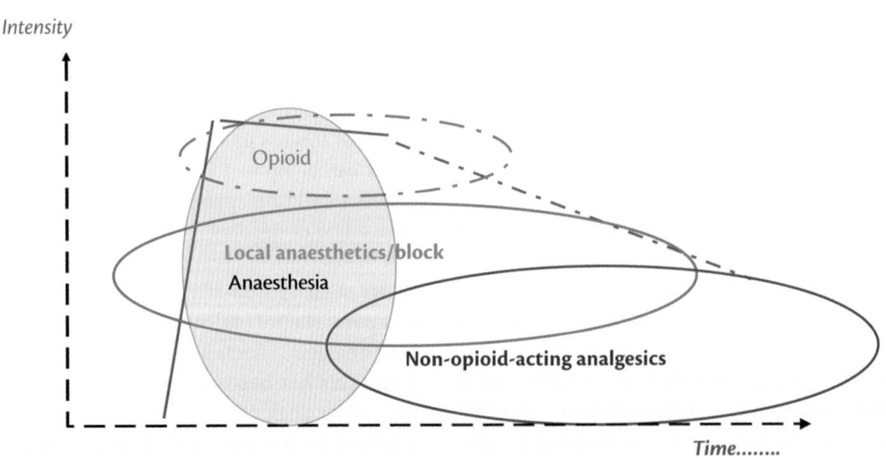

Figure 68.4 Multimodal approach for use in day surgery.

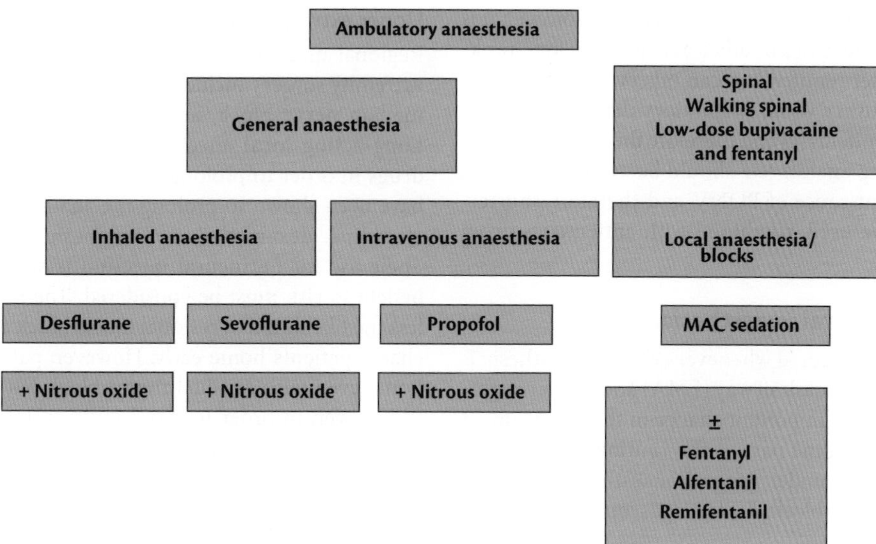

Figure 68.5 Anaesthesia for day surgery.

team. It is often more important as to how the drugs are used than what drugs are chosen for maintenance of general anaesthesia. Thus, knowing the pharmacokinetics of the drugs used and maintaining a close cooperation with the surgeon ensures that a vaporizer or infusions can be turned off well ahead of the end of surgery thus ensuring quick and smooth recovery. Similarly, analgesics and antiemetics can be given well before the end of surgery so they are acting when the patient is awakening from anaesthesia.

Propofol-based total intravenous anaesthesia

This is a safe and effective technique. Target-controlled propofol infusion has improved drug delivery and, using different pharmacokinetic models programmed into infusion pumps, ensures correct and adequate propofol delivery in conjunction with total intravenous anaesthesia (TIVA) for day surgery. The target concentration of propofol must be individualized but target values between 3 and 8 $\mu g\ ml^{-1}$ may be safely used, depending on which agents are used in conjunction with propofol. There are also pumps with algorithms for effect site concentration dosing which further enhance fine tuning of administration.

As an alternative to propofol for maintenance of anaesthesia, the inhaled anaesthetics desflurane and sevoflurane have gained huge popularity for use in day surgery.

Sevoflurane

Sevoflurane has several advantages and has therefore become a very popular anaesthetic. Its low propensity for airway irritation makes it a popular option for induction of anaesthesia in children and even adults who are afraid of needles. Sevoflurane has the additional advantage that it has only mild effects on the heart rate and blood pressure, and adequate spontaneous respiration is usually maintained when sevoflurane is used as the sole agent.

Desflurane

Desflurane is another potent halogenated inhaled anaesthetic with the advantage of a low blood:gas solubility and therefore, both induction and recovery are faster compared with sevoflurane and isoflurane. However, desflurane is known to cause airway irritation and when used as a sole agent, the risk of airway irritability and coughing is a potentially significant problem. Small doses of short-acting opioids have been shown to effectively reduce airway irritation. The increase in heart rate and blood pressure that may be seen in conjunction with rapid increases in the inhaled concentration of desflurane can also be suppressed by the use of opioids. The rapid emergence from desflurane anaesthesia may have clinical advantages in obese and in elderly patients undergoing day surgery, ensuring rapid elimination and emergence.

Nitrous oxide

Nitrous oxide may be used as a component of inhalation anaesthesia. The favourable pharmacokinetic and -dynamic properties of nitrous oxide, including low blood:gas solubility, combined with the minimal effects on cardiovascular and respiratory functions have promoted its use in day surgery. It facilitates the ability to maintain spontaneous breathing and shortens emergence. The effect of nitrous oxide on the occurrence of PONV is important and nitrous oxide should be avoided in patients at a high risk for PONV and in procedures lasting for more than 1 h.

Opioids during general anaesthesia

Opioids during general anaesthesia are commonly used in order to reduce the concentration of inhalation or intravenous anaesthetics and thereby reduce side-effects and facilitate emergence from these anaesthetics. In addition, they prevent the stress response by reducing perioperative pain. A low dose of any of the fast-acting opioid analgesics may be used and the lowest effective dose should be sought. In the spontaneously breathing patient, monitoring of the respiratory rate and end-tidal CO_2 and in all patients, the heart rate and blood pressure help in dose titration during the intraoperative period.

Remifentanil infusion

Remifentanil infusion has gained increasing popularity, specifically during TIVA. The combination of remifentanil with propofol and sometimes with sevoflurane or desflurane is efficacious and enhances early recovery. Thus, remifentanil infusion titrated to effect site concentration between 3 and 8 $ng\ ml^{-1}$, reduces the dose of propofol or inhaled anaesthetic considerably. However, it is important to give adequate doses of other analgesics before awakening as hyperalgesia after remifentanil can otherwise become difficult to treat in the recovery ward. Respiratory depression is also common when using remifentanil and therefore the option for controlled ventilation during anaesthesia should be available. Finally, opioids are an important cause of PONV and therefore shorter-acting opioids should be used, combined with antiemetics given prophylactically.

The airway during general anaesthesia

The airway must be safely secured whenever general anaesthesia is administered. The laryngeal mask airway (LMA) and similar supraglottic devices have led to an important change in the management of the airway and have become part of the routine management of day surgical procedures under general anaesthesia, reducing the need for neuromuscular blockade, laryngoscopy, and tracheal intubation.

Laryngeal mask airway

The LMA is still used during laparoscopic surgery by some practitioners for selected patients and has also become an acceptable alternative for shorter procedures with the patient in the lateral or even prone position. Some LMA devices have reduced the risk of unanticipated gastro-oesophageal reflux, allowing gastric contents to drain away from the glottis thereby avoiding aspiration of gastric contents. The use of the supraglottic airway allows spontaneous respiration or pressure-assisted ventilation during anaesthesia. There are several supraglottic devices that have gained widespread use for day-stay anaesthesia and local practices and personal choice should dictate the type of device used as differences between them are minor.

Perioperative monitoring

Monitoring of patients undergoing day surgery should follow the same international standards as for those undergoing in-patient surgery. The underlying disease should determine the level of monitoring in an individual patient rather than the surgical setting. In general, pulse oximetry, non-invasive blood pressure monitoring, ECG, and anaesthetic gas monitoring are basic requirements during day surgical procedures performed under general anaesthesia. In addition, the use of a depth of anaesthesia monitor has been shown to reduce anaesthetic consumption and increase fast tracking (see later) when used in day surgery. The use of these monitors may also have an impact on quality of recovery, promoting a rapid emergence, lowering the occurrence of PONV and the risk for cognitive impairment after day surgery.

Regional anaesthesia

With the increasing availability of ultrasound devices to better visualize peripheral nerves, both upper and lower extremity surgery may be performed using regional blocks. The use of regional anaesthesia has major advantages for the patient as the side-effects of general anaesthesia are avoided and postoperative pain relief can be prolonged, specifically when catheters are left *in situ*. Low-dose spinal anaesthesia may be used during lower abdominal surgery and hernia repair. The major disadvantages of regional anaesthesia are that ultrasound devices are expensive and require considerable training before a high success rate can be achieved. Block failures occur even in expert hands.

Upper extremity surgery

Regional anaesthesia techniques that are commonly used for upper extremity surgery include brachial plexus block, ulnar nerve block, median nerve block, and digital nerve block (see Chapter 54). Long-acting local anaesthesia may be combined with adjuvant drugs in order to prolong analgesia postoperatively. Several drugs have been shown to prolong the analgesic effects: buprenorphine, clonidine, dexamethasone, magnesium, and dexmedetomidine. Their use for perineural injection is still, however, off-label and benefit *vs* risk must be considered. The more distal the block, the less the likelihood of residual motor block and the easier it is to discharge patients home early. However, patients may be discharged home even with residual motor block but clear instructions need to be given in order to avoid injuries. In addition, oral analgesic supplementation needs to be provided as severe pain can be experienced when the residual sensory block wears off.

Lower extremity surgery

Although almost all procedures on the lower extremity are amenable to spinal anaesthesia, many anaesthetists prefer peripheral nerve blocks of the lower extremity because these have the major advantage of being side specific and, when effective, allow specific regions of the lower extremity to be blocked rather than the entire extremity, which can be considered by many patients to be distressing. Common blocks of the lower extremity used in day surgery include femoral, sciatic, and popliteal nerve blocks (see Chapter 55).

The use of ultrasound increases block success rate and lowers the volume of local anaesthetic injected and has become increasingly popular during regional anaesthesia and analgesia.

Selective spinal anaesthesia

Selective spinal anaesthesia can be achieved by the administration of a low dose of bupivacaine and fentanyl/sufentanil mixture injected slowly in a lateral position and allowing the patient to remain in this position for 10–15 min so that the block remains preferentially one-sided. It has been shown to provide rapid onset, effective anaesthesia and analgesia, and is associated with a relatively quick recovery and only minor side-effects. Doses of 4–8 mg of bupivacaine mixed with 5–15 μg of fentanyl or an equivalent dose of sufentanil have been successfully administered for arthroscopic procedures of the knee and for open inguinal hernia repair.

Local anaesthesia

Local anaesthetics can be used alone for perioperative anaesthesia and analgesia and many procedures in day surgery are performed using local anaesthetic infiltration only. Not only is this cost-effective, but it allows rapid recovery and home discharge, which is appreciated by both patients and healthcare givers. Specifically, procedures commonly performed using local anaesthetic alone include plastic and aesthetic surgery, hand and arthroscopic surgery, eye surgery, and minor general surgery. When feasible, peripheral or central blocks using local anaesthetic alone or in combination with adjuvants to facilitate the block and analgesic duration should be considered in the day-stay setting.

Infiltration of local anaesthetic into the wound before incision is strongly recommended but when this is not possible, local anaesthetic infiltration should be done at the end of the procedure in order to prolong postoperative analgesia. Administration of long-acting local anaesthetics in the wound and the surgical field can reduce postoperative pain and the need for early postoperative opioid analgesics. The combination of local anaesthesia, paracetamol, and NSAIDs or COX-2 inhibitors administered preoperatively should constitute the basis of postoperative pain management. The potential risks associated with NSAIDs/COX-2 inhibitors are well known but the risk associated with their short-term use after ambulatory surgery is probably low.

The use of wound catheters and intermittent injection of local anaesthetic for postoperative pain management is becoming increasingly popular. Catheters placed subfascially may reduce pain and the use of rescue analgesics. However, their efficacy has been questioned and, except in special situations, their routine use is not recommended. Large-volume, local infiltration of local anaesthetic into different tissue planes during surgery has been found to be efficacious, specifically during orthopaedic surgery, but attention to the technique used is required for a high success rate.

Postoperative recovery

In day surgery, three phases of recovery have been described: early, intermediate, and late recovery. These phases are characterized by specific end-points and are commonly assessed using well-defined protocols. Fulfilling recovery criteria is an important part of the decision to change the level of care such as during fast-tracking or home-discharge. No easy and objective methods are currently available to assess street fitness or fitness to drive and return to work, which remain poorly explored and very subjective.

Early recovery

Several end-points are used to assess early recovery including time to opening eyes, obeying commands, and full orientation. Mostly, these end-points are achieved in the operating theatre and within minutes after the end of the anaesthetic. Therefore, using modern anaesthetic agents, almost all patients are able to retain a free airway, are oriented, and have protective reflexes when they leave the operating theatre. Early recovery, however, continues into the post-anaesthesia care unit (PACU) and ends when stable vital signs are achieved and patients have only mild pain and minimal nausea or vomiting. They can then be transferred into the step-down unit where intermediate recovery can be followed up. In the last decade, the concept of 'fast-tracking' has been introduced, which means that patients can bypass the early phase of recovery if they fulfil all the above-mentioned criteria and move into a step-down unit. This can be achieved through the use of very short-acting drugs and is believed to reduce costs by moving patients rapidly from the operating theatre to the step-down unit. It is, however, important that early recovery is not initiated in the operating theatre in order to fast-track patients as operating theatre occupancy is much more expensive than early recovery in the PACU.

Intermediate recovery

This is characterized by continued stable vital signs, mild pain, and return of functional status to preoperative levels. Thus, the patient should be mobilized without any evidence of deterioration in vital signs and be able to walk independently, with no or minimal assistance (non-lower limb surgery), eat and drink without vomiting, and pass urine without the need for catheterization. This last criterion is especially important after spinal anaesthesia, in elderly men, and in patients living far away from a hospital but is otherwise not necessary for discharge home. When there is concern about the possibility of urinary retention, an ultrasound scan of the bladder is useful. Intermediate recovery ends when the patients have achieved a score on the Post-Anaesthesia Discharge Scoring System (PADSS), which is considered satisfactory for home readiness. Shorter, user-friendly versions of this scoring system are described but have not been documented to provide similar results.

Late recovery

This is the time from discharge from the PACU to the time when the patient returns to work or full normal function. This process can take anything from 1 day up to 6 weeks, or even longer depending on the type of surgery and possible complications. Patients should be given goal-oriented skills that need to be achieved in order to accelerate this process otherwise there is a risk that late recovery can be prolonged. Patients should be advised not to drink alcohol or drive during the first 24 h after the anaesthetic and longer if motor or cognitive skills have not returned to normal. Unfortunately, this area is poorly researched and information is mostly obtained from questionnaires on subjective well-being and not objective measures of recovery. Driving skills have been tested in several studies under very controlled circumstances and mostly in simulator situations. Therefore, these tests, although objective, cannot be applied to individual patients. Follow-up should be done over a few weeks, if not months, and recent studies have focussed on this important area, albeit using questionnaire techniques.

There are several multi-dimensional scales for assessment of recovery. The Quality of Recovery Scale and Postoperative Quality of Recovery Scale (PQRS) (Bowyer et al. 2014) assess recovery in multiple domains, including physiological, nociceptive, emotive, activities of daily living, cognition, and patient satisfaction. They address recovery over time and compare individual patient data with baseline, thus describing resumption of capacities, and are acceptable methods for detailing individual patient recovery. They include follow-up until 7 days after surgery and can also be used for a more remote follow-up.

Postoperative pain management

Adequate management of postoperative pain is one of many important aspects of good day surgical practice. Procedure-specific and structured plans should be adopted. Pain management should start preoperatively as pain is inevitable after surgery, if inadequately managed. Several approaches have been used in the management of pain including preventive, proactive, and multimodal approaches. *Preventive analgesia* implies the use of analgesics pre- or peroperatively in order to reduce the likelihood of development of postoperative pain (see Fig. 68.6). *Proactive management* means that pain should be anticipated, treatment initiated, and analgesics taken regularly in the presence or absence of postoperative pain as pain is more difficult to treat than prevent. *A multimodal approach* means that several drugs with different mechanisms of action need to be used to prevent or treat pain as one drug in larger doses would inevitably lead to side-effects and poor pain control. Patients should be informed about how to manage post-discharge pain at home and also be given clear and explicit written instructions including how and when to take prescribed basic pain medication and the use of rescue analgesics in case of insufficient analgesia from this base medication.

The concept of multimodal or balanced analgesia has become a standard of care. Combining local anaesthetics and non-opiate

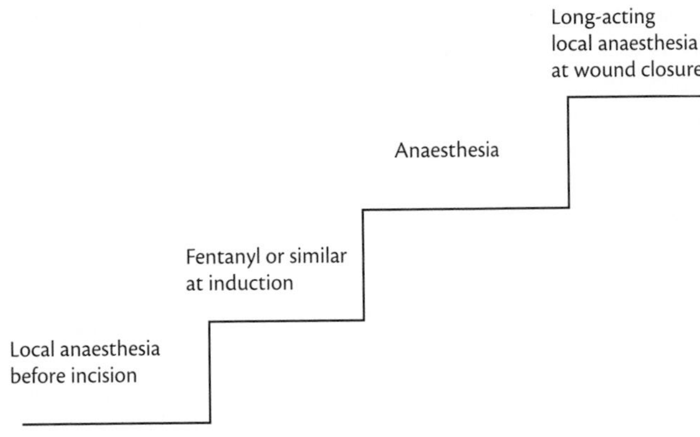

Figure 68.6 Preventive pain management.

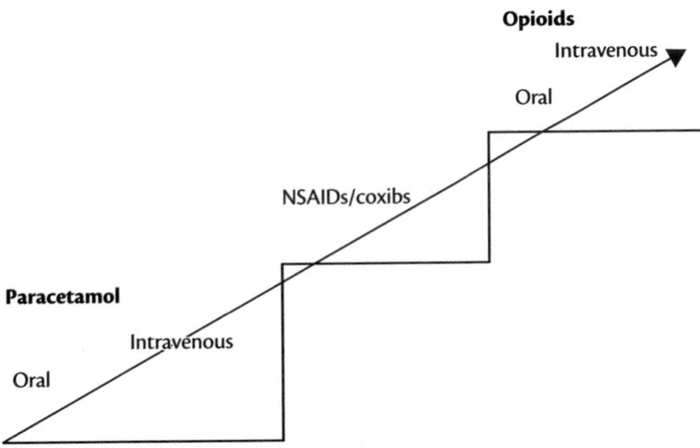

Figure 68.7 Preventive pain management in day surgery.

analgesics including paracetamol and NSAIDs provides superior analgesia than one drug alone. The lowest effective dose of all drugs should be used for the management of pain after day surgery (see Fig. 68.7).

Local anaesthesia

Local anaesthetics have been used routinely in the wound as a single injection, which is effective but has a short duration. Many patients may not experience postoperative pain until they arrive home when the effect of the local anaesthetic has worn off. This could be a problem unless proactive pain management with other analgesics is started early. Newer techniques whereby local anaesthetic is injected into different tissue planes during surgery may further improve pain management postoperatively in the future.

Regional analgesia

Regional analgesia with or without a catheter has been used successfully for many decades. Recently, the use of ultrasound techniques has made regional anaesthesia popular. However, it requires experience and training to achieve a high success rate and is sometimes time-consuming, which could be a problem in a busy ambulatory surgical practice. Technical difficulties in nerve identification, specifically in the obese, could also be a problem.

Catheter techniques

Catheter techniques for continuous administration of local anaesthetics in the wound have been used successfully and safely in conjunction with more extensive surgery performed on a day-stay basis. This technique requires proper education and training of the entire day-stay team, and adequate information given to patients on how to manage the use of analgesic pumps at home after discharge. They appear to have some analgesic effects in certain types of surgery and are a good option when more invasive methods cannot be used. However, the results show a weak analgesic effect and, when possible, other methods should be used in the first instance.

Oral analgesics

Paracetamol

Paracetamol is commonly administered preoperatively and many hospitals in Sweden use a loading dose of 20–30 mg kg^{-1} orally. When oral intake is not an option, intravenous paracetamol at the end of the procedure ensures adequate plasma concentration at awakening and some hours postoperatively. Because of the relatively few side-effects in otherwise healthy patients, and the of ease of administration, a standard prescription of 1 g of paracetamol four times daily is recommended as basic pain medication in adult patients. In children, the total dose of paracetamol should not exceed 80–100 mg kg^{-1} day^{-1}.

NSAIDs and COX-2 inhibitors

NSAIDs and COX-2 inhibitors have also been shown to be efficacious and reduce the need for opiate analgesics thus minimizing opiate-induced side-effects, and improving and accelerating recovery. As the analgesic properties are similar to NSAIDs, the benefit of COX-2 inhibitors which have a lower risk for gastrointestinal side-effects and with minimal effects on platelet function must be weighed against their somewhat higher cost. However, caution must be taken when using NSAIDs in patients with ischaemic heart disease, hypertension, or renal impairment, and the benefit *vs* risk of these drugs must be weighed in each patient. The potential risk for negative effects on the healing process, specifically in orthopaedic surgery, has been a matter of debate and the data are still insufficient to make any general recommendation. The short-term use of NSAIDs or COX-2 inhibitors in post-surgical patients without other risk factors for impaired healing such as diabetes, concomitant steroid medication, or excessive smoking is unlikely to have long-term effects. A standard dose of ibuprofen 400 mg three times daily has been shown to be an effective basal pain medication after day-stay surgery. Other NSAIDs may be chosen, depending on availability and local practices. If surgeons are concerned about the risk of bleeding when using NSAIDs, celecoxib 200 mg twice daily is an option and this also reduces the risk of gastric irritation in patients prone to it. Combining paracetamol and a NSAID/COX-2 inhibitor during the early postoperative course has been shown to be effective. The potential risk for cardiovascular side-effects associated with the prolonged use of COX-2 inhibitors and NSAIDs are clearly recognized. Naproxen is the NSAID associated with the lowest risk, and should thus be the first-line choice.

Level I pain management

Paracetamol alone or in combination with a NSAID/COX-2 inhibitor is considered to be level I pain management in a 'pain ladder' approach recommended by the World Health Organization.

Level II pain management

Weak opioids such as codeine or tramadol should be considered after procedures with expected moderate postoperative pain. Codeine is considered a pro-drug as it is metabolized *in vivo* to the active compounds morphine and codeine-6-glucoronide. It can be useful as an oral supplement after moderately painful procedures, specifically as a medication for use at home. Tramadol possesses weak agonist actions at the μ-opioid receptor, releases serotonin, and inhibits the reuptake of noradrenaline (norepinephrine). Like codeine, tramadol is used to treat moderate to severe pain. However, there is a high incidence of nausea and vomiting and therefore some are reluctant to prescribe it for pain management at home.

Level III pain management

This includes the classical slow-release or regular opioid tablet. The use of oral oxycodone has also become widely accepted either as slow-release oral oxycodone or as intravenous oxycodone for severe postoperative pain. The potential risk for addiction when using oxycodone at home must be considered. Clinical experience suggests that oxycodone can be used safely when indicated.

Box 68.1 summarizes how to handle pain after discharge.

The place for other medications such as clonidine, gabapentin, and pregabalin is not well established for routine use in day surgery. The use of clonidine has been shown to have opiate-sparing effects but the overall effects on enhancing rapid and safe discharge is not equally well documented. Gabapentin and pregabalin have also been studied in patients undergoing ambulatory surgery with some benefit. Several studies have been published using gabapentin for ambulatory surgery with mixed results. The benefits appear to be small and side-effects such as tiredness and giddiness are common. Therefore, the precise role of these drugs in routine clinical practice during ambulatory surgery also remains unclear.

In summary, a structured strategy for the management of pain is of utmost importance. The multimodal or balanced analgesia approach has become the gold standard. Procedure-specific programmes should be implemented. Supportive information on pain management is available from the Prospect Group and Bandolier website (http://www.postoppain.org/).

Box 68.1 Handling pain after discharge

- Level I:
  - Paracetamol 1 g four times daily
  - NSAID/COX-2 inhibitors:
    - Naproxen 500 mg twice daily
    - Etoricoxib 120 mg once daily
- Level II:
  - Codeine or tramadol
- Level III:
  - Classic opioid: oxycodone slow-release
- Rescue analgesic:
  - Oxycodone.

Postoperative nausea and vomiting

PONV is also a common minor but annoying complication of surgery and anaesthesia and requires considerable resources in time and money: when possible, it should be prevented. Persistent PONV may have a major impact during day surgery, as it is a common reason for delayed discharge and unplanned hospital admission. Post-discharge nausea and vomiting also has a major impact on patient satisfaction. In addition, inability or unwillingness to drink or eat properly may also require readmission. Several risk-scoring systems have been developed for the identification of patients at risk of PONV and these should be used in each individual patient. Factors identified to be associated with a high incidence of PONV include female gender, history of PONV or motion sickness, non-smoking status, and the need for postoperative opiates (Apfel risk score).

Prophylactic measures

Prophylactic measures should be taken in order to minimize the occurrence and severity of PONV. Nausea and vomiting is one of the most important factors determining a negative patient experience after anaesthesia. It is important that each department develops policies and protocols for the prevention of PONV as standard therapy in all patients may not be successful. However, some common measures to reduce the incidence of PONV should be taken and include avoiding/minimizing the use of opiates; avoiding hypotension; use of oral fluids up to 2 h before induction of anaesthesia; and liberal perioperative fluid therapy. In addition, avoiding nitrous oxide, use of propofol for induction and maintenance of anaesthesia, and avoiding the use of neostigmine for reversal of neuromuscular blocking agents have all been shown to have some impact on the risk of PONV. In patients at very high risk of PONV, regional anaesthetic techniques that avoid general anaesthesia may be advantageous. In addition to these measures, drugs may be used, alone or in combination, to prevent PONV. Non-pharmacological measures such as acupressure at the P6 point at the wrist have been successfully used in preventing PONV. The drugs used for prevention are the same as for treatment of PONV and therefore discussed in the following paragraphs. All drugs lead to a similar reduction in PONV and therefore, no one drug can be considered to be better than another for preventing PONV. Local traditions, costs, and personal choice may sometimes dictate the use of these drugs in the individual patient. A structured risk-based stepwise approach is recommended which has been shown effective in reducing the risk for PONV. There is, however, still no strategy that guarantees avoiding PONV. The drugs used in the pharmacological management of emesis should be based on their pharmacokinetic and pharmacodynamic profile, such as time to onset, duration of action, and side-effects. Ondansetron, with a rather short duration of action, may be best administered at the end of surgery or used for treatment of PONV. The onset of action of corticosteroids can be up to 2 h and therefore, these should be used for prophylaxis (not treatment) of PONV and given early so that their effect can be evident even in the early postoperative period.

Treatment of established PONV

Emetic agents act through different neurotransmitters at different receptors in the central nervous system and therefore drugs with different mechanisms need to be used in combination in order to block several receptors for best effect. When one drug has been administered, a different drug with a different mechanism of action should be chosen. Repeating the same drug for prophylaxis and treatment of PONV may be ineffective. Drug combinations produce additive effects.

Dexamethasone and *betamethasone* have been shown to exhibit antiemetic effects. The use of a single preoperative intravenous dose of dexamethasone or betamethasone 4–8 mg has become well established in the prevention of PONV. Not only does it prevent PONV, it has also been shown to reduce pain and the need for rescue analgesics thus having a dual function. A single preoperative 0.1 mg kg^{-1} intravenous dose of dexamethasone has been shown to exhibit a dual action in preventing PONV and reducing postoperative pain. It has also been shown that a single dose of dexamethasone may improve and prolong the effects of peripheral blocks.

Droperidol (0.5–1 mg intravenous) is also efficacious and should be administered early in order to monitor the ECG because of a minor but significant risk for prolongation of the QT interval, which could lead to malignant arrhythmias.

The *serotonin antagonists* differ somewhat in their duration of action. Thus, ondansetron, with a rather short duration of action, should be administered at the end of surgery in order to have prolonged postoperative effects. On the other hand, granisetron has a longer duration of action and may thus be a good alternative in order to cover an extended postoperative period.

Non-pharmacological management of PONV should not be forgotten. The P6 acupressure point has been shown to be equi-efficacious as pharmacological management without the side-effects of these drugs.

In summary, liberal risk-adjusted PONV prophylaxis should be administered. The use of double antiemetic prophylaxis using steroids and droperidol is useful in the high-risk patient while the serotonin antagonists may be reserved for treatment thus providing a cost-effective approach to the pharmacological management of PONV. Post-discharge nausea and vomiting should not be forgotten and adequate information and provision of an oral rescue antiemetic may be appropriate in high-risk patients (see Box 68.2).

Conclusion

Effective day-stay anaesthesia practice means careful preparation, planning, and logistics combined with a good understanding of the pharmacology of drugs to be used. Day-stay anaesthesia can be performed with most of the fast- and short-acting anaesthetics available, both intravenous and inhaled. Success is more a matter of how the drugs are used and combined than which drugs are chosen. Early recovery and rapid home discharge must be planned before the start of surgery and detailed information and education of patients provided before the operation helps achieve these goals. Effective planning for the management of postoperative pain and minimizing nausea and vomiting is of outmost importance. Multimodal pain and PONV management has become a standard of care in day-stay anaesthesia. Day-case surgery is a multidisciplinary commitment; personnel working in day-stay surgical establishments should be dedicated, and documentation, follow-up, case discussions, regular reviews, and audits should be undertaken in order to help identify problems and improve quality. In any well-functioning ambulatory surgical unit, postoperative complications should be low, patient satisfaction high, and unanticipated hospital admissions exceptional.

Box 68.2 Antiemetic strategy

- Female
- History of PONV: motion sickness
- Non-smoking
- Need for postoperative opioid
- Steroid:
  - Droperidol
  - Metoclopramide
- 5-HT3 blocker: scopolamine
- TIVA: consider the need for a rescue antiemetic.

Key messages

- Day-stay surgery/anaesthesia demands proper patient selection.
- Day-stay anaesthesia should be based on standardized and structured procedure-specific anaesthesia planning.
- Planning for the handling of postoperative pain and protocols for minimizing PONV are of utmost importance.
- Multimodal analgesia should be used intra- and postoperatively.
- Postoperative quality of care should be ensured while achieving rapid recovery.
- A patient who can walk, drink, and make an unassisted visit to the rest room with adequate control of pain and PONV is generally considered ready for discharge.
- Ready for discharge is not the same as street-fit. The latter requires patients to have recovered fully, both physically and psychologically, and even to have returned to normal working life.

Declaration of interest

Professor Jakobsson has taken part in advisory boards for Pfizer, MSD, Grunenthal, Abbott, Baxter, Onysis, Medipharm, and Nycomed and has also lectured on pain and pain management. He also has a consultant agreement with Linde Healthcare.

Further reading

Apfel CC, Korttila K, Abdalla M, *et al.* A factorial trial of six interventions for the prevention of postoperative nausea and vomiting. *N Engl J Med* 2004; **350**: 2441–51

Coxib and Traditional NSAID Trialists' (CNT) Collaboration, Bhala N, Emberson J, *et al.* Vascular and upper gastrointestinal effects of non-steroidal anti-inflammatory drugs: meta-analyses of individual participant data from randomised trials. *Lancet* 2013; **382**: 769–79

Dahl JB, Kehlet H. Preventive analgesia. *Curr Opin Anaesthesiol* 2011; **24**: 331–8

Dahl JB, Mathiesen O, Kehlet H. An expert opinion on postoperative pain management, with special reference to new developments. *Expert Opin Pharmacother* 2010; **11**: 2459–70

De Oliveira GS Jr, Almeida MD, Benzon HT, McCarthy RJ. Perioperative single dose systemic dexamethasone for postoperative pain: a meta-analysis of randomized controlled trials. *Anesthesiology* 2011; **115**: 575–88

Diakos EA, Gallos ID, El-Shunnar S, Clarke M, Kazi R, Mehanna H. Dexamethasone reduces pain, vomiting and overall complications following tonsillectomy in adults: a systematic review and meta-analysis of randomised controlled trials. *Clin Otolaryngol* 2011; **36**: 531–42

Elvir-Lazo OL, White PF. The role of multimodal analgesia in pain management after ambulatory surgery. *Curr Opin Anaesthesiol* 2010; **23**: 697–703

Eriksson H, Tenhunen A, Korttila K. Balanced analgesia improves recovery and outcome after outpatient tubal ligation. *Acta Anaesthesiol Scand* 1996; **40**: 151–5

Fortier J, Chung F, Su J. Unanticipated admission after ambulatory surgery – a prospective study. *Can J Anaesth* 1998; **45**: 612–9

Gan TJ, Diemunsch P, Habib AS, *et al.* Consensus guidelines for the management of postoperative nausea and vomiting. *Anesth Analg* 2014; **118**: 85–113

Gupta A, Stierer T, Zuckerman R, Sakima N, Parker SD, Fleisher LA. Comparison of recovery profile after ambulatory anesthesia with propofol, isoflurane, sevoflurane and desflurane: a systematic review. *Anesth Analg* 2004; **98**: 632–41

Jacob AK, Walsh MT, Dilger JA. Role of regional anesthesia in the ambulatory environment. *Anesthesiol Clin* 2010; **28**: 251–66

Jakobsson J. *Anaesthesia for Day Case Surgery*. Oxford: Oxford University Press, 2009

Jakobsson J. Preoperative single-dose intravenous dexamethasone during ambulatory surgery: update around the benefit versus risk. *Curr Opin Anaesthesiol* 2010; **23**: 682–6

Jildenstål PK, Hallén JL, Rawal N, Berggren L, Jakobsson JG. AAI-guided anaesthesia is associated with lower incidence of 24-h MMSE < 25 and may impact the IL-6 response. *Int J Surg* 2014; **12**: 290–5

Jildenstål PK, Hallén JL, Rawal N, Gupta A, Berggren L. Effect of auditory evoked potential-guided anaesthesia on consumption of anaesthetics and early postoperative cognitive dysfunction: a randomised controlled trial. *Eur J Anaesthesiol* 2011; **28**: 213–9

Keay L, Lindsley K, Tielsch J, Katz J, Schein O. Routine preoperative medical testing for cataract surgery. *Cochrane Database Syst Rev* 2009; **2**: CD007293

Le TP, Gan TJ. Update on the management of postoperative nausea and vomiting and postdischarge nausea and vomiting in ambulatory surgery. *Anesthesiol Clin* 2010; **28**: 225–49

Leslie K, Myles PS, Chan MT, *et al.* Risk factors for severe postoperative nausea and vomiting in a randomized trial of nitrous oxide-based vs nitrous oxide-free anaesthesia. *Br J Anaesth* 2008; **101**: 498–505

Michaloliakou C, Chung F, Sharma S. Preoperative multimodal analgesia facilitates recovery after ambulatory laparoscopic cholecystectomy. *Anesth Analg* 1996; **82**: 44–51

Ong CK, Seymour RA, Lirk P, Merry AF. Combining paracetamol (acetaminophen) with nonsteroidal antiinflammatory drugs: a qualitative systematic review of analgesic efficacy for acute postoperative pain. *Anesth Analg* 2010; **110**: 1170–9

White PF, Ma H, Tang J, Wender RH, Sloninsky A, Kariger R. Does the use of electroencephalographic bispectral index or auditory evoked potential index monitoring facilitate recovery after desflurane anesthesia in the ambulatory setting? *Anesthesiology* 2004; **100**: 811–7

White PF, Tang J, Wender RH, *et al.* The effects of oral ibuprofen and celecoxib in preventing pain, improving recovery outcomes and patient satisfaction after ambulatory surgery. *Anesth Analg* 2011; **112**: 323–9

Wong J, Tong D, De Silva Y, Abrishami A, Chung F. Development of the functional recovery index for ambulatory surgery and anesthesia. *Anesthesiology* 2009; **110**: 596–602

References

Bowyer A, Jakobsson J, Ljungqvist O, Royse C. A review of the scope and measurement of postoperative quality of recovery. *Anaesthesia* 2014; **69**: 1266–78

Chung F, Yuan H, Yin L, Vairavanathan S, Wong DT. Elimination of preoperative testing in ambulatory surgery. *Anesth Analg* 2009; **108**: 467–75

Kumar G, Stendall C, Mistry R, Gurusamy K, Walker D. A comparison of total intravenous anaesthesia using propofol with sevoflurane or desflurane in ambulatory surgery: systematic review and meta-analysis. *Anaesthesia* 2014; **69**: 1138–50

PART 10

Paediatric anaesthesia

Jonathan G. Hardman and Neil S. Morton

CHAPTER 69

Anatomy, physiology, and pharmacology in paediatric anaesthesia

Niall Wilton, Brian J. Anderson, and Bruno Marciniak

Introduction

We develop from a small mass of undifferentiated cells to a highly complex organism that is the adult human. Various systems develop and mature at different rates and these differences affect anaesthesia care. The neonate undergoes a rapid period of growth and development continuing into the first few years of life. These anatomical, physiological, and behavioural changes affect the child's response to disease, drugs, and the environment. Growth is an increase in size while development is an increase in complexity and function. Prenatal growth is the most important phase of development, comprising organogenesis in the first 8 weeks (embryonic growth), followed by the functional development of organ systems to full-term gestation (fetal growth).

Growth and maturation

While rapid growth occurs particularly in the second trimester, a major increase in weight from subcutaneous tissue and muscle mass occurs in the third trimester. Prematurity is defined relative to gestation age with a preterm infant defined as one born before 37 completed weeks of gestation. A term or full-term infant is one born between 37 and 42 completed weeks of gestation. A post-term infant is one born after 42 completed weeks of gestation.

Preterm infants are further classified according to their actual birth weight. A low-birth-weight infant is one weighing less than 2500 g regardless of the duration of the pregnancy. A very low-birth-weight infant weighs less than 1500 g, and an extremely low-birth-weight infant weighs less than 1000 g. A summary of the more significant neurological and physical signs of maturity at birth is presented in Table 69.1.

After birth, physical growth continues at a rapid pace during the first 6 months of extrauterine life but slows by about 2 years of age. Physical growth accelerates a second time during the pubertal period (Fig. 69.1). A simple way to remember how rapidly the infant grows is that birth weight doubles by 6 months of age and triples by 1 year. Length doubles by 4 years of age. The different organs increase in size at different rates (Fig. 69.2).

Assessment of growth is measured by changes in weight, length, and head circumference. Percentile charts (e.g. Ogden et al. 2002; de Onis et al. 2007) are valuable for monitoring the child's growth and development. Weight is a more sensitive index of well-being, illness, or poor nutrition than length or head circumference and is the most commonly used measurement of growth. Change in weight reflects changes in muscle mass, adipose tissue, skeleton, and body water and thus is a non-specific measure of growth. Measurement

Table 69.1 Neurological and external physical criteria used to assess gestational age

Physical examination	Preterm (<37 weeks)	Term (≥37 weeks)
Ear	Shapeless, pliable, slow recoil	Firm, well formed
Skin	Oedematous, thin skin	Thick skin, wrinkled
Sole of foot	Anterior transverse crease only	Whole foot creased
Breast tissue	Less than 1 mm diameter	More than 5 mm diameter
Genitalia		
Male	Scrotum poorly developed, faint rugae	Scrotum rugated
	Testes undescended	Testes descended
Female	Large clitoris, gaping labia majora	Labia majora developed and cover clitoris
Limbs	Hypotonic	Tonic (flexed)
Grasp reflex	Weak grasp	Can be lifted by reflex grasp
Moro reflex	Complete but exhaustible (>32 weeks)	Complete
Sucking reflex	Weak	Strong, synchronous with swallowing

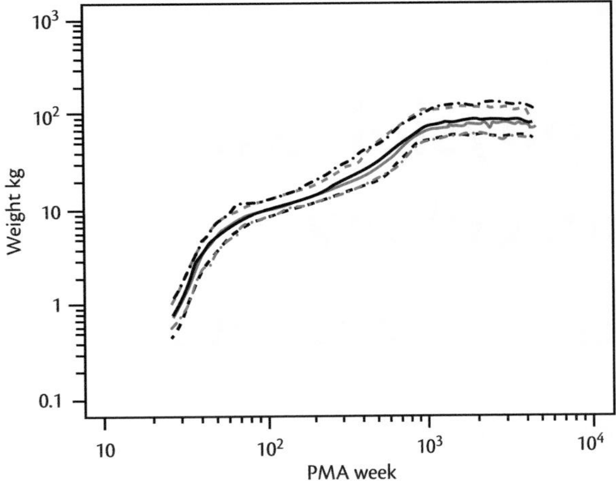

Figure 69.1 Observed weights across the human age range with 90% prediction intervals for females (dashed line) and males (solid line). These demonstrate growth spurts in infancy and puberty. PMA, postmenstrual age.

Reproduced with permission from Sumpter A and Holford NHG, Predicting weight using postmenstrual age – neonates to adults. *Pediatric Anesthesia*, Volume 21, pp. 309–15, Copyright © 2011 John Wiley and Sons Ltd.

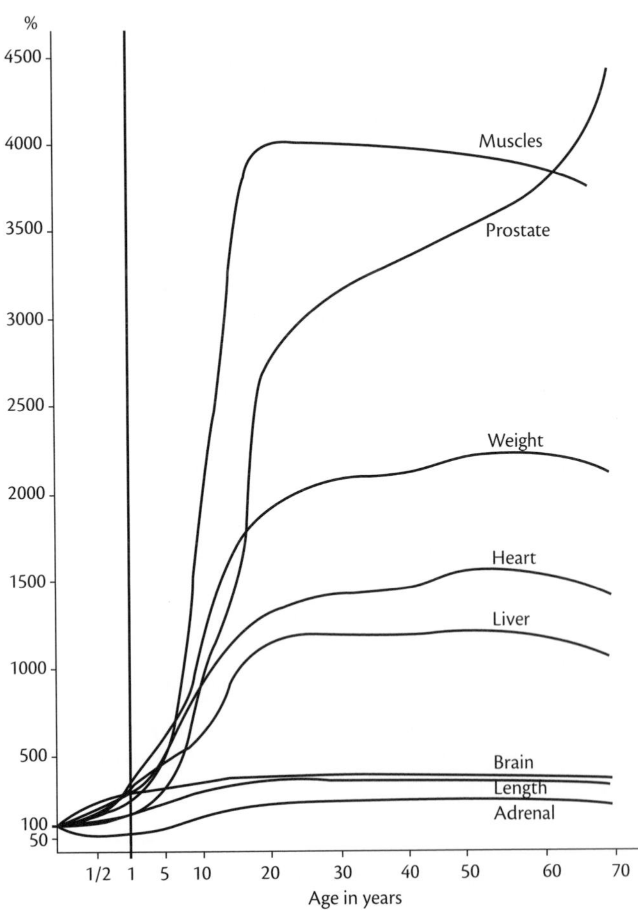

Figure 69.2 The increase in weight of different organs expressed as a percentage of their weight in the newborn.

Reproduced with permission from Friis-Hansen B, Body composition during growth. In vivo measurements and biochemical data correlated to differential anatomical growth, *Pediatrics*, 47, Suppl 2, pp. 264–274, Copyright © 1971 by the AAP.

of length provides the best indicator of skeletal growth because it is not affected by changes in adipose tissue or water content.

Term infants may lose 5–10% of their body weight during the first 24–72 h of life from loss of body water. Birth weight is usually regained in 7–10 days. A daily increase of 30 g is satisfactory for the first 3 months. Thereafter, weight gain slows so that at 10–12 months of age it is 70 g each week. Plots (see the World Health Organization charts at http://www.who.int/childgrowth/standards/en/) should be made using corrected gestational age [also known as postmenstrual age (PMA)]. Post-conception age is taken from conception and is approximately 10 days to 2 weeks shorter, while postnatal age (PNA) is the chronological age from birth. Growth and development continue during gestation and PNA is unsatisfactory for size monitoring during the first 2 years of the infant's life.

Head size reflects growth of the brain and correlates with intracranial volume and brain weight. Changing head circumference reflects head growth and is a part of the total body growth process; it may or may not indicate underlying involvement of the brain. An abnormally large or small head may indicate abnormal brain development, which can be an alert to possible underlying neurological problems. A large head may indicate a normal variation, familial features, or a pathological condition (e.g. hydrocephalus or increased intracranial pressure), whereas a small head may indicate a normal variant, a familial feature, or a pathological condition such as craniosynostosis or abnormal brain development. During the first year of life, head circumference normally increases by 10 cm, and it increases by 2.5 cm in the second year. By 9 months of age, head circumference reaches 50% of adult size, and by 2 years it is 75%.

Body composition changes with age. Total body water decreases at the expense of the extracellular compartment, with adult proportions attained at 1 year of age. Total body water and extracellular fluid (ECF) (Friis-Hansen 1961) are increased in neonates and reduction tends to follow PNA while the percentage of body weight contributed by fat is 3% in a 1.5 kg premature neonate and 12% in a term neonate. This proportion further doubles by 4–5 months of age (Fig. 69.3). These body component changes affect volumes of

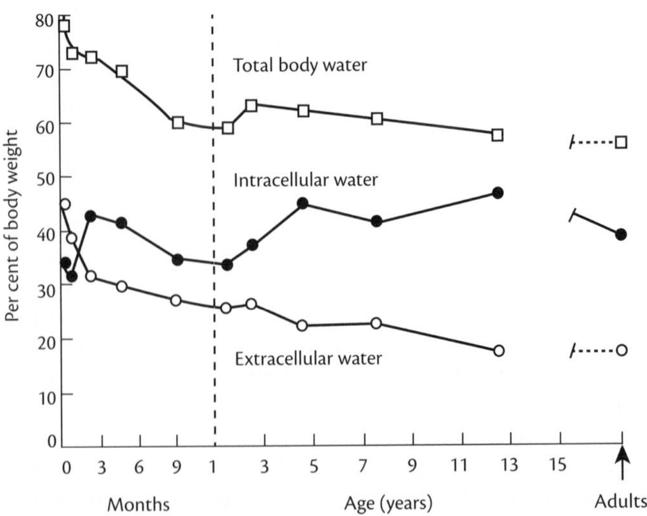

Figure 69.3 Changes in total body water (TBW), intracellular water (ICW), extracellular water (ECW), and the fat content of the body from early fetal life to old age.

Reproduced with permission from Holzman R (ed), *A Practical Approach to Pediatric Anesthesia*, Copyright Wolters Kluwer Health 2015.

distribution of drugs. Polar drugs such as aminoglycosides distribute rapidly into the ECF, but enter cells more slowly. The initial dose of such drugs is consequently higher in the neonate compared with a child or adult.

Fentanyl has an increased volume of distribution in neonates. The volume of distribution at steady-state is 5.9 (SD 1.5) litres kg^{-1} in a neonate compared with 1.6 (SD 0.3) litres kg^{-1} in an adult (Johnson et al. 1984). This may contribute to the reduced degree of respiratory depression seen after doses as high as 10 mcg kg^{-1} in infants. However, a higher dose results in a prolonged effect in neonates as a result of reduced clearance. Reduction of propofol concentrations after induction is attributable to redistribution rather than rapid clearance. Neonates have low body fat and muscle content and so less propofol is apportioned to these 'deep' compartments. Delayed awakening occurs because central nervous system (CNS) concentration remains higher than that observed in older children as a consequence of this reduced redistribution. This observation can also be demonstrated with thiopental (Fig. 69.4).

Pharmacology and size

Drug clearance in children 1–2 years of age, expressed as litres h^{-1} kg^{-1}, is commonly greater than that observed in older children and adolescents. This is consistent with metabolic processes that are faster in small children (e.g. oxygen consumption). This is a size effect and is not as a result of bigger livers or increased hepatic blood flow in that subpopulation. This 'artifact of size' disappears when alternate scaling is used such as body surface area (BSA) (Mosteller 1988):

$$\mathrm{BSA}\,(\mathrm{m}^2) = \sqrt{\frac{\text{height (cm)} \times \text{weight (kg)}}{3600}} \qquad (69.1)$$

BSA can also be described using an allometric equation with an exponent of ⅔. Allometry is a term used to describe this non-linear relationship between size and function such as metabolic rate. This non-linear relationship is expressed as:

$$y = a \times \text{body mass}^{PWR} \qquad (69.2)$$

where y is the variable of interest (e.g. basal metabolic rate), a is a scaling parameter, and PWR is the allometric exponent. The value of PWR has been the subject of much debate. Basal metabolic rate is the commonest variable investigated and camps advocating for a PWR value of ⅔ (i.e. BSA) are at odds with those advocating a value of ¾. It has been demonstrated that cardiac output (Vinet et al. 2003; Chantler et al. 2005) and oxygen consumption (West et al. 1997) (other physiological functions related to basal metabolic rate) are better scaled with an allometric exponent closer to ¾ than with BSA.

Support for a value of ¾ comes from investigations that show the log of basal metabolic rate plotted against the log of body weight produces a straight line with a slope of ¾ in all species studied, including humans (Fig. 69.5).

The ¾-power law for metabolic rates was derived from a general model that describes how essential materials are transported through space-filled fractal networks of branching tubes (West and Brown 2005). A great many physiological, structural, and time-related variables scale predictably within and between species with weight (W) exponents (PWR) of ¾, 1, and ¼ respectively. These exponents have applicability to pharmacokinetic parameters such as clearance (CL exponent of ¾ because this is a metabolic process related to metabolic rate), volume (V exponent of 1), and half-time ($T_{1/2}$ exponent of ¼) (Anderson and Holford 2008). The factor for size ($Fsize$) for total drug clearance may be expressed as:

$$Fsize = \left(W/_{70} \right)^{3/4} \qquad (69.3)$$

Remifentanil and atracurium are degraded by non-specific esterases in tissues and erythrocytes. Clearance, expressed per kilogram, is increased in younger children, likely attributable to size

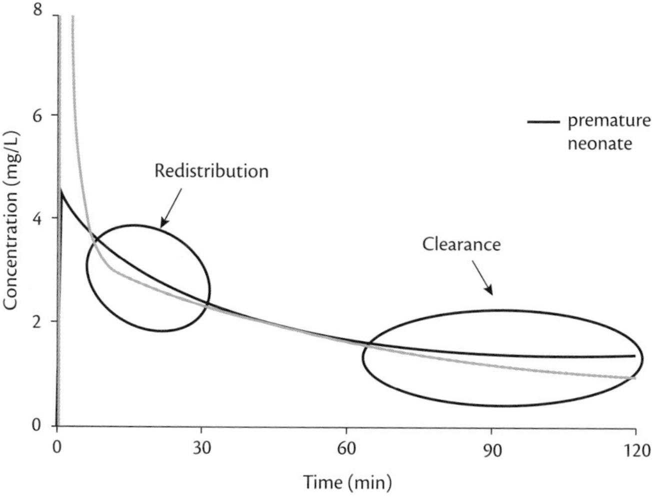

Figure 69.4 Time–concentration profiles for a premature neonate (30 weeks' PMA) and an adult given 3 mg kg^{-1} of thiopental. Neonates have low body fat and muscle content and so less thiopental is apportioned to these 'deep' compartments, resulting in the higher concentrations in the first 30 min. Later concentrations are higher in neonates because clearance is lower than in adults (shown as grey line).
Data from Larsson P *Acta Anaesth Scand* 2011; 55: 444–51. Adult parameters are from Stanski D. *Anesthesiology* 1990; 72: 421–22.

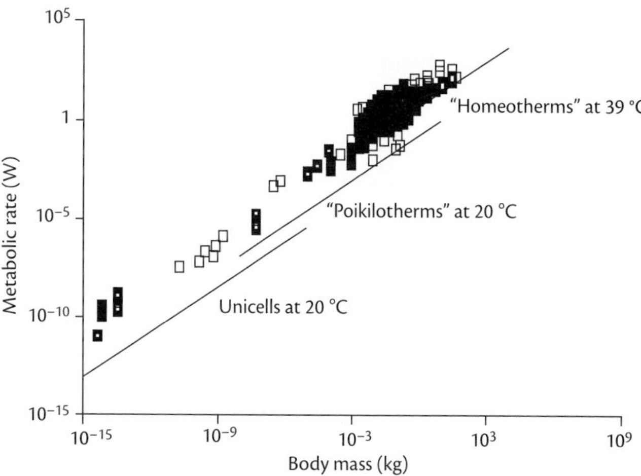

Figure 69.5 A comparison of the temperature-standardized relation for whole-organism metabolic rate as a function of body mass. The 'allometric ¾ power model' fits for unicells, poikilotherms, and homeotherms, uncorrected for temperature, are also shown.
From Gillooly, J. F. *et al.*, Effects of Size and Temperature on Metabolic Rate, *Science*, 2001, Volume 293, No. 5538, pp. 2248–2251, Reprinted with permission from AAAS.

because clearance is similar when scaled to a 70 kg person using allometry (Rigby-Jones et al. 2007). Non-specific blood esterases that metabolize remifentanil are mature at birth (Welzing et al. 2011). Suxamethonium clearance is also increased in neonates suggesting butyrylcholinesterase activity is mature at birth and can be described using allometry.

Maturation of drug clearance

Unlike remifentanil clearance, allometry alone is insufficient to predict clearance in neonates and infants from adult estimates for most drugs. The addition of a model describing maturation is required (Holford et al. 2013). The sigmoid hyperbolic or Hill model (Hill 1910) has been found useful for describing this maturation process (MF):

$$MF = \frac{PMA^{Hill}}{TM_{50}^{Hill} + PMA^{Hill}} \quad (69.4)$$

The TM_{50} describes the maturation half-time, while the Hill coefficient relates to the slope of this maturation profile. Maturation of clearance begins before birth, suggesting that PMA would be a better predictor of drug elimination than PNA. Figure 69.6 shows the maturation profile for dexmedetomidine expressed as both the standard per kilogram model and using allometry with a maturation factor. Clearance is immature in infancy. Clearance is greatest at 2 years of age, decreasing subsequently with age. This 'artifact of size' disappears with use of the allometric model.

Neurobehavioral

The nervous system is anatomically complete at birth, but functionally it remains immature with the continuation of myelination and synaptogenesis. Myelination is usually complete by 7 years of age. An infant's normal mental development depends on the maturation of the CNS.

Development of the nervous system

The brain weighs about 335 g at birth and grows rapidly in the first year of life, doubling its size by 6 months (Fig. 69.2) and reaching its adult size by 12 years. Brain development starts with the formation of the neural tube (neurulation) and forebrain (prosencephalon) from the third week of gestation. Intensive growth and proliferation of the brain cells then follow, during which time the cells migrate to genetically programmed areas, gradually forming the layers and structures of the brain. This involves processes of neurogenesis, migration, synaptogenesis, apoptosis, and myelination that follow a definite timeline in each region of the brain resulting in different rates of neurocognitive development (Table 69.2). Neurulation refers to the events that result in formation of the brain and spinal cord and this occurs during days 20–23. Cells at the tip of the neural folds are not incorporated into the neural tube but form the neural crest, which together with some neural tube cells form the peripheral nervous system. By 7 weeks, these cells move to either side of the spinal cord forming the dorsal root ganglia. Neural crest cells link the periphery and CNS via dorsal roots. Axons from the developing motor roots join with sensory afferents distal to the dorsal root ganglia to form spinal nerves. Spina bifida and neural tube defects occur during this period. Prosencephalic development then results in paired optic and olfactory structures, the cerebral hemispheres (telencephalon), plus the thalamus and hypothalamus (diencephalon). Finally, other midline structures such as the corpus callosum, septum pellucidum, optic chiasm, and hypothalamus are formed, and completed by about 20 weeks of gestation. Congenital hydrocephalus probably originates during this period. Brain growth then shifts to developing connections between the various cell groupings.

During the remainder of the fetal period, proliferation of the brain neurones occurs together with migration of these cells to specific sites in the CNS. Increasing organization results in the intricate circuitry that defines the human brain and is followed by myelination. During organization (which continues through childhood), neuronal differentiation results in the establishment of the six layers of the cortex with the subplate neurones being particularly important. They form an extensive dendritic network, receive synaptic inputs, and extend axonal projections linking the cortical and subcortical sites (synaptogenesis). Several pathways are involved in development and remodelling of the dendritic spines which involve a number of neurotransmitters [γ-aminobutyric acid (GABA), excitatory amino acids], neuropeptides, and trophic factors. Cell death and selective elimination of neuronal processes and synapses are an integral part of brain development. Importantly, up to 90% of the subplate neurones and 50% of the neurones in the cortical region undergo programmed cell death (or apoptosis) in the final trimester. This appears to be triggered by neuronal competition for limited amounts of trophic factors and allows elimination of incorrect

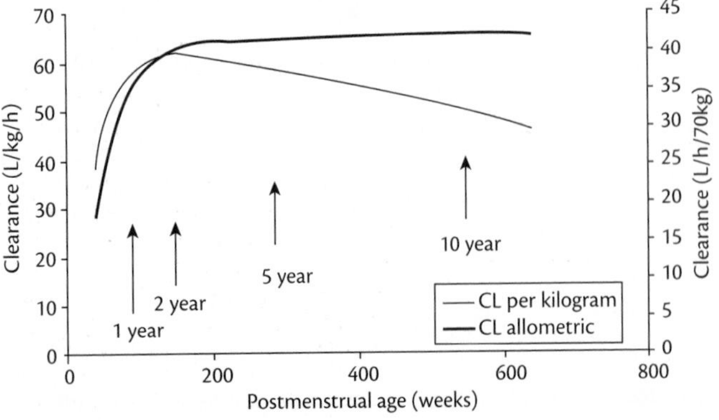

Figure 69.6 The clearance maturation profile of dexmedetomidine expressed using the per kilogram model and the allometric ¾-power model. This maturation pattern is typical of many drugs cleared by the liver or kidneys.
Data from Potts et al. *Pediatr Anesth* 2009; 19: 1119–29, with permission.

Table 69.2 Major events in human brain development and peak times of occurrence

Major developmental event	Peak time of occurrence
Primary neurulation	3–4 weeks of gestation
Prosencephalic development	2–3 months of gestation
Neuronal proliferation	3–4 months of gestation
Neuronal migration	3–5 months of gestation
Organization	5 months of gestation to years postnatally
Myelination	Birth to years postnatally

or aberrant connections. Further organizational refinement occurs by selective pruning of neuronal processes and synapses, which is mediated and controlled by activation of a *N*-methyl-D-aspartate mediated type of glutamate receptor. Importantly, these processes may be altered by anaesthetic agents (see 'The immature brain and anaesthesia'). The most common disorders occurring throughout this developmental process are shown in Table 69.3 Myelination begins in the second trimester, peaks immediately after birth but continues into adult life. Myelination begins in the peripheral nervous system before birth and then in the CNS where, in contrast to the peripheral nervous system, the sensory system precedes the motor system.

Table 69.3 Central nervous system anomalies and development

Development event	Peak time	Examples of anomalies
Primary and secondary neurulation	3–4 weeks	Anencephaly
		Encephalocoele
		Myeloschisis
		Myelomeningocele
		Dysraphic states
Prosencephalic development	5–6 weeks	Holoprosencephaly
		Agenesis of the corpus callosum
		Septo-optic dysplasia
Neuronal proliferation		
Cerebral	2–4 months	Microcephaly and macrocephaly
		Tuberous sclerosis
Cerebellar	2–10 months postnatal	Dandy-Walker malformation
		Cerebellar hypoplasias
Neuronal migration		
Cerebral	3–5 months	Schizencephaly
		Lissencephaly-pachygyria
		Heterotopias
Cerebellar	4–10 months postnatal	Joubert syndrome
Neuronal differential		
Axon outgrowth	3 months–birth	Agenesis of the corpus callosum
Dendritic growth and synapse formation	6 months–1 year postnatal	Mental retardation
Synaptic rearrangement	Birth–years postnatal	Autism
		Angelman syndrome
		Down syndrome
		Rett syndrome
Myelination	Birth–years postnatal	Cerebral white matter hypoplasia
		18q syndrome
		Cerebral white matter disease of prematurity
		Nutritional and metabolic disturbances

Further brain development

The period between the seventh month *in utero* and the age of 2 years sees the greatest activity in growth and synaptic organization (Davies 2011). The rapid synaptogenesis that occurs during this period gives rise to the whole range of human functioning, including motor abilities, sensory capacities, cognitive skills, emotional responses, and some pain processing. Myelination allows faster transmission of neural impulses, a process that increases gradually until mid adolescence. Increased processing speed improves as pruning of the synaptic circuits plus myelination allows them to function more efficiently. As myelination proceeds, new functions develop, for example, walking becomes possible when nerve pathways and the spinal cord become myelinated. The brain is genetically programmed to over-produce synapses during the early growth period with synaptic production also being influenced by use. Neurones that are frequently stimulated grow denser dendritic branches, whereas those that are not are gradually pruned away. Synaptogenesis and myelination occur at different rates as different brain regions with particular functions develop. Motor reflexes and sensory abilities including hearing and vision are fairly well developed at birth and undergo rapid maturation during the first 6 months of life. Synaptogenesis in the visual and auditory cortices peaks at about 3 months and then a pruning process begins. Other areas mature over much longer periods for example, synapses in the neocortex (which controls high cognitive functions), continue to be over-produced, pruned, and myelinated throughout childhood and do not attain their final organization until late adolescence (Huttenlocher and Dabholkar 1997).

It is during these periods of development that the brain may be affected by environmental factors, but the impact of these is complicated as the brain also shows a great deal more plasticity during this during this time than in later years. Because of this plasticity, risk and opportunity factors during the early years have more influence on how the brain ultimately functions (Nowakowski and Hayes 1999). As an opportunity example, children with early damage to the left cerebral cortex (the side of language ability), can go on to normal language development because the brain compensates by relying on the right hemispheres (Bates et al. 2001). A number of biological and environmental factors may compromise brain development. These include genetic disorders, exposure to toxic substances, poor nutrition, prematurity, stress, deprivation, and trauma. Anaesthesia and surgery may need to be added to this list (see next section).

The immature brain and anaesthesia

Cell death can occur by two main routes—apoptotic or necrotic. Apoptosis is used synonymously with 'programmed cell death'; this is an intrinsic mechanism of cell suicide. Apoptosis is important in the developing nervous system but is also prominent in brain injury or disease. It is an active process which leads to the progressive dismantling of cell components such as proteins and DNA. Packaging of the cell components into apoptotic bodies then occurs, which are removed by phagocytic cells without any evidence of inflammation. This process is distinct from necrosis where there is disruption of cellular contents with associated inflammation (Pirianou et al. 2011).

Anaesthetic drugs disrupt synaptogenesis and cause or accelerate apoptosis and programmed cell death of many neurones that would have otherwise have survived and contributed to brain function (Creeley and Olney 2010). Most classes of anaesthetic drugs, *N*-methyl-D-aspartate antagonists (ketamine), GABA agonists (benzodiazepines, thiopental, and propofol), plus inhalational agents, cause apoptotic neurodegeneration and long-term locomotor and cognitive defects in rats. These detrimental effects appear to be age dependent with maximal effects being seen at the peak of synaptogenesis (Jevtovic-Todorovic 2011). Similar effects are demonstrated in subhuman primates (rhesus and macaque monkeys). Ketamine exposure produces long-lasting cognitive defects in rhesus monkeys (Paule et al. 2011). Drug combinations appear to be detrimental as clinically relevant doses of isoflurane and nitrous oxide when administered together, but not alone, result in increased cell death of both apoptotic and necrotic nature (Zou et al. 2011). Initial work with propofol in rats has suggested that at later stages of development (equivalent to infancy), an effect on synaptogenesis still occurs (Briner et al. 2011). The relevance of these animal models to human neonates and infants is contentious as our development is more prolonged and neurocognitive development performance more complicated. It may be that the dramatic effects observed in the 7-day-old rodent model widely used represent effects likely to be seen in a 20–22-week-old human fetus rather than later preterm or term neonates as was originally thought. Furthermore, in rodents 'environmental enrichment' (representing nurturing, stimulation, and learning in humans) has been shown to reverse the adverse effects on performance demonstrated after anaesthesia (Shih et al. 2012).

Clinical studies in humans are mixed. Studies where children have been anaesthetized for major surgery show an association between anaesthesia for surgery and poor neurodevelopmental outcome but this can be explained by confounding factors such as prematurity and congenital malformation. Clinical studies in infants undergoing single exposure for inguinal hernia repair have not yet confirmed the animal data (Hansen et al. 2011) but there is the suggestion that multiple anaesthetic exposures may result in limited neurocognitive deficits (Flick et al. 2011). Review of the published human studies to date suggests little or no association with single brief exposures confirmed in a recent randomized controlled clinical trial (the GAS study) (Davidson et al. 2016). Some association, however, between repeated exposure and poor performance on a variety of non-specific tests of cognition and behaviour is apparent. The hazard ratio in almost all of these studies is lower than 2, implying that bias or confounding factors could easily account for the association (Gleich et al. 2013).

Development and behaviour

The stages of developmental behaviour are outlined in Table 69.4. These stages may overlap and are influenced by many social factors such as family environment, socioeconomics, and culture (Dixon and Stein 2006). Children's concepts and understanding of disease follow this development and young children are likely to have misconceptions about anaesthetic and surgical procedures (Bibace and Walsh 1980). This may increase the likelihood of anxiety and stress in the perioperative period although children are also more amenable to distraction and storytelling at this age.

Temperament appears to be hardwired and comprises four broad groups in infancy: 'easy' (40%)—regular routines, cheerful, and adaptable; 'difficult' (10%)—irregular routines, slow to accept change, and tendency to respond negatively; 'slow to warm up' (15%)—inactive, negative or neutral mood, and slow to adjust; and 'mixture' (35%) (Dixon and Stein 2006).

Table 69.4 Perspectives of human behaviour

Development stage skill areas				
Age	**Piaget**	**Language**	**Motor**	**Possible psychopathology**
Birth–18 months	Sensorimotor	Body actions; crying; naming; pointing; shared social communication	Reflex; sitting; reaching; grasping; walking; mouthing	Autism; colic; disorders of attachment; feeding and sleeping problems
18 months–3 years	Symbolic, preoperational	Sentences: unique utterances; sharing of events	Climbing; running; jumping; use of tools; using toilets; early self-care	Separation issues; negativism; fearfulness; shyness; withdrawal; aggressiveness
3–6 years	Intuition, preoperational	Connective words; can be readily understood; tells and follows stories; questions	Increased coordination: tricycle; jumping; writing	Enuresis; encopresis; anxiety, aggressive acting, and phobias
6–12 years	Concrete operational	Subordinate sentences: reading and writing; language; reasoning	Increased skills: sports; cooperative games	School phobias: obsessive reactions; conversion reactions; depressive equivalents; anxiety; ADHD
12–17 years	Formal operational	Reason abstract: using language; abstract mental manipulation	Refinement of skills	Delinquency: promiscuity; schizophrenia; anorexia; suicide

Responses to separation have been identified as secure, avoidant, resistant, or disorganized. 'Securely attached' infants tend to deal well with separation; 'avoidant' infants do not resist separation but will avoid the parent afterwards; 'resistantly attached infants' cling to the parent and become distressed and angry at separation. 'Disorganized attachment' describes the apathetic, flat child on separation and reunification, which suggests poor attachment and may have long-term implications (Dixon and Stein 2006). Consequentially, children aged 1–5 years are at greatest risk of separation anxiety and distress in the perioperative period (Kain et al. 1996). Emergence delirium occurs in up to 20% of children after anaesthesia. Younger age (particularly preschoolers), anaesthesia with short-acting inhalational agents, and previous surgery are risk factors (Voepel-Lewis et al. 2003). Negative behaviour and temporary psychosocial regression is not uncommon after surgery, occurring in up to 50% of children and may persist for as long as 6 months. Younger age, temperament, and parental anxiety are risk factors (Kain et al. 1996).

The spinal cord

During the early stages of development the spinal cord extends the entire length of the embryo, but with increasing age the vertebral column and dura lengthen more rapidly than the neural tube. At birth, the cord (conus medullaris) ends at L3 and the dura mater ends at the level of S3–4. It is only at the end of the first year of life that adult levels are attained; namely L2 for the conus medullaris and S2 for the dural and subarachnoid space (Sadler 2012) (Fig. 69.7). Delayed myelination of the spinal cord is a feature of infancy. Although myelination begins during the fourth month of fetal life it continues throughout infancy (Tanaka et al. 1995).

Development of nociceptive pathways and pain expression

Neurophysiological, behavioural, and molecular nociceptive processes undergo significant changes during early development that affect the response to noxious stimuli, injury, and analgesia. Although peripheral nociceptive responses mature early, there is a tendency to increased excitatory and reduced inhibitory modulation in the spinal cord during early development. Nociceptors, which develop from the neural crest cells, have their cell body in the dorsal root ganglion and synapse centrally in the spinal cord. Nociceptors (both myelinated A-δ fibre axons and unmyelinated C fibre axons) as well as A-β low pressure mechanoreceptors both synapse in the superficial laminae of dorsal horn during the early neonatal period providing a mechanism for central sensitization (Walke 2008). The balance between excitatory and inhibitory neurotransmission at the dorsal horn is tipped towards enhanced excitability during early infant development probably related to the absence of specific afferent and descending inputs to the inhibitory neurones (Fig. 69.8) (Fitzgerald 2005). There is clinical evidence of lower thresholds for withdrawal reflexes, larger receptive field size, and lack of specificity of withdrawal responses in the neonate (Walker 2008). As a result of the plasticity of the developing nervous system, there are concerns that early, untreated, or poorly

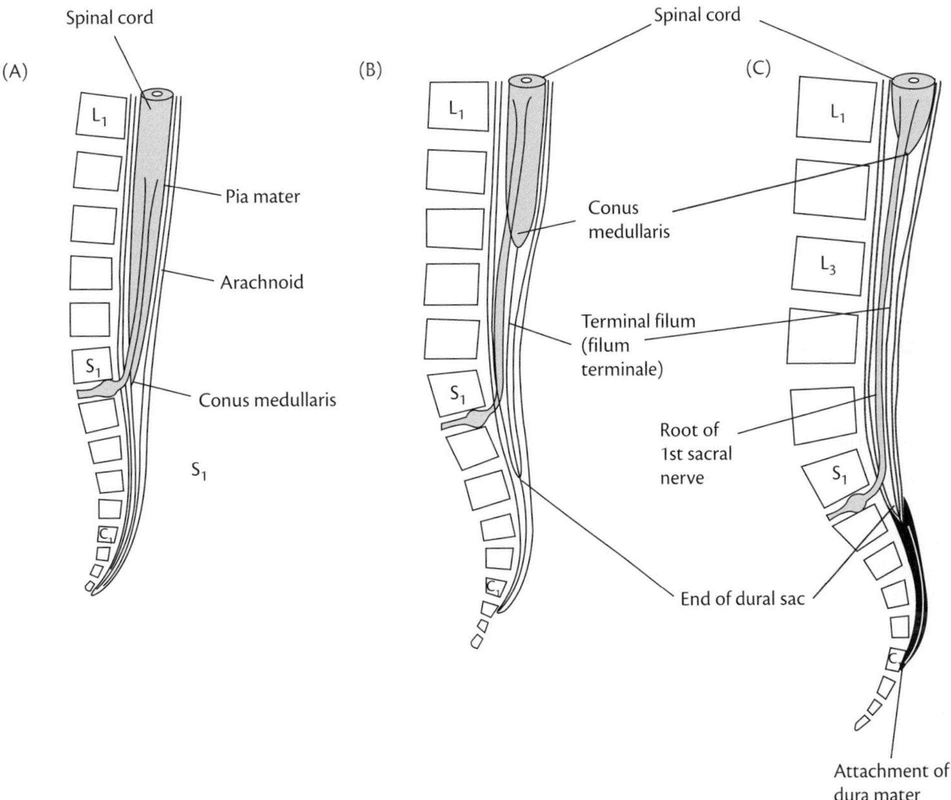

Figure 69.7 Diagram showing the position of the caudal end of the spinal cord (conus medullaris) and dural sac relative to the spinal column at various stages of development. (A) 24 weeks, (B) newborn, and (C) adult.

This figure was published in *The Developing Human: Clinically-Oriented Embryology*, Moore K et al., Copyright © Elsevier 2015.

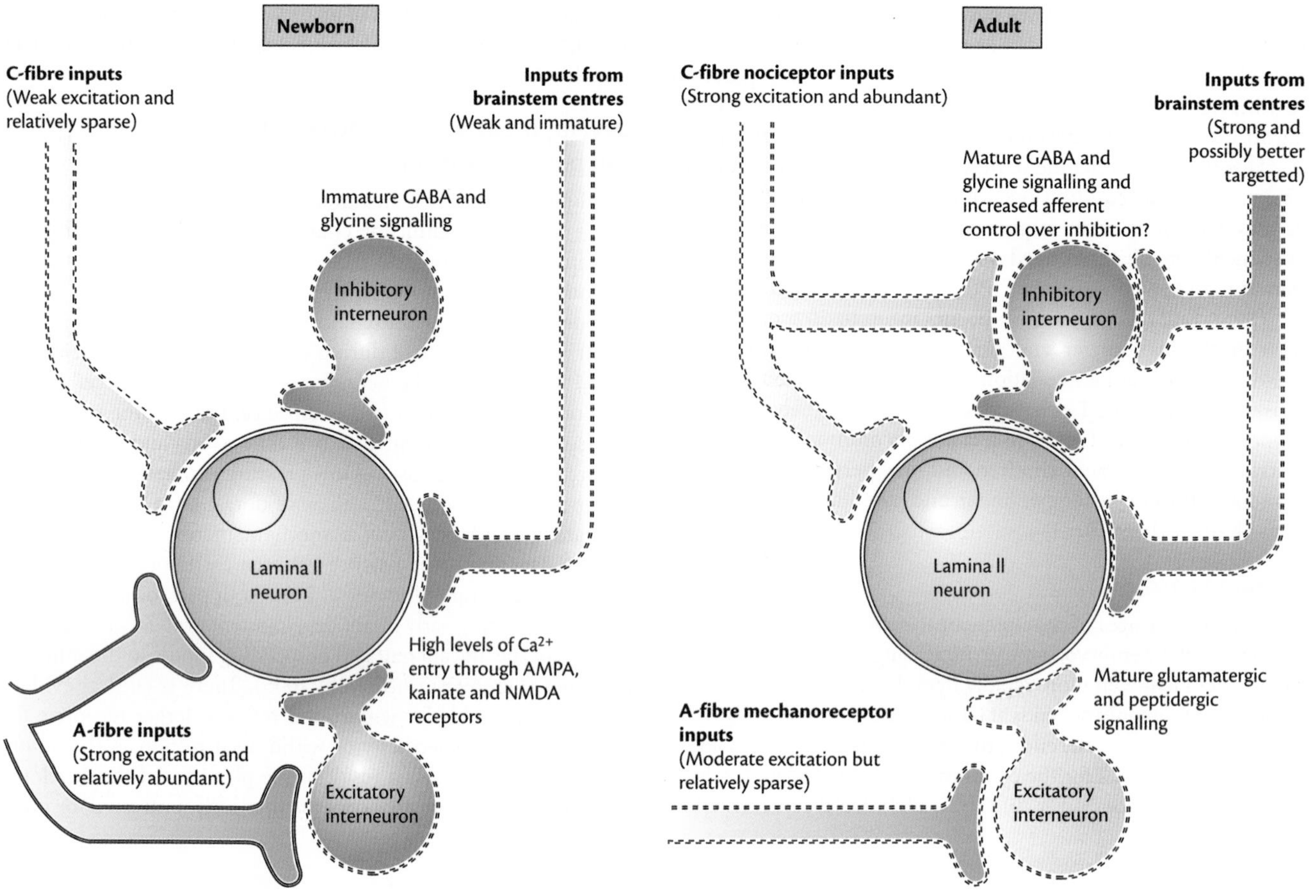

Fig 69.8 Schematic diagram of synaptic changes in the superficial laminae of the dorsal horn during the neonatal period, comparing the changing balance of excitation and inhibition in the neonate and adult.

Reprinted by permission from Macmillan Publishers Ltd: *Nature Reviews Neuroscience*, Fitzgerald, M. The development of nociceptive circuits. Volume 6, Issue 7, pp. 507–520, Copyright © 2005 Nature Publishing Group.

treated pain and injury may be associated with long-term changes in sensory function and future responses to painful stimuli and injury. Limited clinical evidence supports this perspective (Taddio et al. 1997a; Peters et al. 2005b).

Central nervous system pharmacology implications

Pharmacodynamics in neonates and infants are altered. The minimal alveolar concentration (MAC) is commonly used to express anaesthetic vapour potency. The MAC for almost all these vapours is lower in neonates than in infancy (Lerman 1992; Warner et al. 1987; Molin and Bendhack 2004). MAC of isoflurane in preterm neonates less than 32 weeks' gestation was 1.28 (SD 0.17%), and MAC in neonates 32–37 weeks' gestation was 1.41 (SD 0.18%) (Fig. 69.9) (LeDez and Lerman 1987). Similarly, the MAC of halothane in neonates [0.87 (SEM 0.03%)] was lower than that in infants [1.20 (SEM 0.06%)], while the decrease in blood pressure and the incidence of hypotension in neonates were similar to those in infants at approximately 1 MAC of halothane (Lerman et al. 1983). MAC peaks at 1–6 months age before decreasing to adult values in adolescence (Lerman 1992). The reason for these age differences is uncertain. Changes in regional blood flow may influence the amount of drug going to the brain. $GABA_A$ receptor numbers or developmental shifts in the regulation of chloride transporters in the brain may change with age, altering response (e.g. midazolam). Data from rodents over an age range from immediate newborn to PNA 40 days have shown developmental pharmacodynamic changes

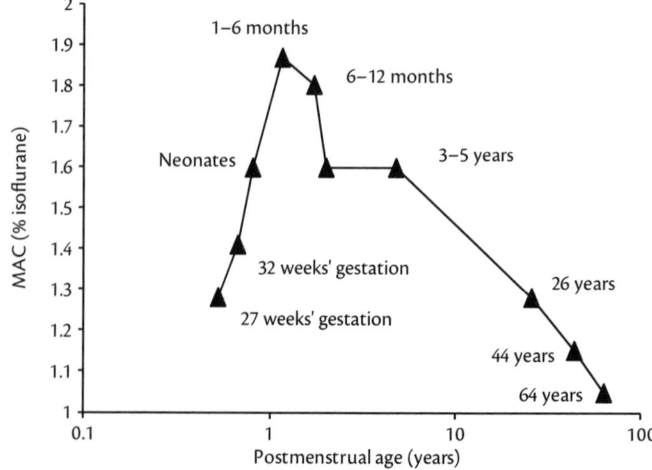

Figure 69.9 Changes in the minimum alveolar concentration (MAC) of isoflurane with age.

Data from Stevens W et al. *Anesthesiology* 1975; 42: 197–200 and LeDez K et al. *Anesthesiology* 1987; 67: 301–7 and Cameron C et al. *Anesth Analg* 1984; 65: 418–20.

for sedation that mimic those seen in human childhood (Koch et al. 2008).

Infants have a propensity to develop bradycardia during induction with halothane. Decreased solubility (i.e. smaller volume of distribution) and size factors (i.e. faster physiological processes) increase speed of onset. The increased MAC (i.e. a pharmacodynamic difference) and a rate-dependent cardiac output set the scene for a relative overdose. A lack of awareness of what constitutes bradycardia in neonates and infants completes the recipe (Keenan et al. 1994).

Blood–brain barrier

The blood–brain barrier (BBB) is a network of tight junctions that restricts paracellular diffusion of compounds between blood and brain. Confusion over the importance of this barrier in the neonate exists, partly because of early studies on respiratory depression caused by morphine and pethidine (Way et al. 1965). Early investigations found that the respiratory depression after morphine was greater than that after pethidine. This difference was attributed to greater brain concentrations of morphine because of the poorly developed BBB in the neonate (Way et al. 1965). It was postulated that BBB permeability to water-soluble drugs such as morphine changed with maturation (Way et al. 1965). However, the neonatal respiratory depression observed after morphine could have been explained by pharmacokinetic age-related changes. For example, the volume of distribution of morphine in term neonates of 1–4 days (1.3 litres kg^{-1}) is reduced compared with that in infants 8–60 days of age (1.8 litres kg^{-1}) and in adults (2.8 litres kg^{-1}) (Pokela et al. 1993). Consequently, we might expect greater initial concentrations of morphine in neonates than in adults, resulting in more pronounced respiratory depression in the former. Respiratory depression, measured by carbon dioxide response curves or by arterial oxygen tension, are similar from 2 to 570 days of age at the same morphine blood concentration (Lynn et al. 1993). The BBB theory in this particular circumstance lacks strong evidence. It is more likely that the increased neonatal respiratory depression after morphine is as a result of pharmacokinetic age-related changes.

The BBB may have effects, however, in other ways. Small molecules are thought to access fetal and neonatal brains more readily than in adults (Engelhardt 2003). BBB function improves gradually, possibly reaching maturity by full-term age (Engelhardt 2003). Kernicterus, for example, is more common in preterm neonates than in full-term neonates. In contrast to drugs bound to plasma proteins, unbound lipophilic drugs passively diffuse across the BBB, equilibrating very quickly. This may contribute to bupivacaine's propensity for seizures in neonates. Decreased protein binding, as in the neonate, results in a greater proportion of unbound drug that is available for passive diffusion.

In addition to passive diffusion, there are specific transport systems that mediate active transport. Pathological CNS conditions can cause BBB breakdown and alter these transport systems. Fentanyl is actively transported across the BBB by a saturable ATP-dependent process, while ATP-binding cassette proteins such as P-glycoprotein actively pump out opioids such as fentanyl and morphine (Henthorn et al. 1999). P-glycoprotein modulation significantly influences opioid brain distribution and onset time, magnitude, and duration of analgesic response (Hamabe et al. 2007). Modulation may occur during disease processes, fever, or in the presence of other drugs (e.g. verapamil or magnesium) (Henthorn et al. 1999). Genetic polymorphisms that affect P-glycoprotein-related genes may explain differences in CNS-active drug sensitivity (Choudhuri and Klaassen 2006).

Central blockade

The distance from the skin to the subarachnoid space is very small in neonates (approximately 10 mm) and increases progressively with age [(age in years × 2) + 10 mm]. The ligamentum flavum is much thinner and less dense in infants and children than in adults; this makes dural puncture more likely because the characteristic resistance as the epidural needle enters the ligaments is softer.

Preterm and full-term infants have a much greater cerebrospinal fluid volume relative to weight (10–14 ml kg^{-1}) than a child (4 ml kg^{-1} in children <15 kg) or adult (2 mg kg^{-1}); this may account in part for the increased dose (mg kg^{-1}) of local anaesthetic required in infants to produce a successful subarachnoid block. Duration of blockade is shorter in neonates and this may be as a result of a higher cerebrospinal fluid turnover rate than adults.

The nature of the epidural space in infants is different from adults with increased vascularity and a smaller absorptive surface for local anaesthetics. Anatomical studies have shown that the epidural fat is spongy and gelatinous in appearance with distinct spaces between individual fat globules (Bosenberg et al. 1988). With increasing age, fat becomes more tightly packed and fibrous. The absorption half time of epidural levobupivacaine decreased from 0.36 h at 1 month of PNA to 0.14 at 6 months of PNA (Fig. 69.10). This, combined with reduced clearance (the cytochrome P450, CYP3A4), caused time to maximum plasma concentration (T_{max}) to decrease from 2.2 h at 1 month of PNA to 0.75 h by 6 months of PNA (Chalkiadis and Anderson 2006).

The spinal cord ends at the intervertebral level of L3–4 at birth and 'recedes' to the adult level of L1 by the age of 1 year—attributable to a differential growth between the bony spinal column and the cord (Fig. 69.7). Lumbar puncture for subarachnoid block in neonates and infants should be performed at the L4–L5 or L5–S1 interspace to avoid spinal cord injury. The vertebral laminae are poorly calcified at this age, so a midline approach is preferable to a paramedian one where the needle is 'walked off' the soft laminae. The sacrum

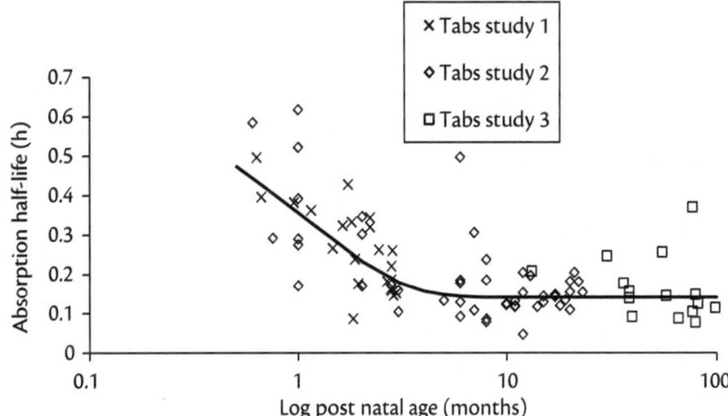

Figure 69.10 Individual predicted levobupivacaine absorption half-time (Tabs), standardized to a 70 kg person, are plotted against postnatal age (PNA). The solid line represents the non-linear relation between Tabs and PNA. The absorption half-time is mature at 6 months' PNA.

Reproduced with permission from Chalkiadis, G. and Anderson, B. Age and size are the major covariates for prediction of levobupivacaine clearance in children. *Pediatric Anesthesia*, Volume 16, pp. 275–282, Copyright © 2006 John Wiley and Sons Ltd.

is narrower and flatter in neonates than in adults, allowing a more direct approach to the caudal canal in neonates than in adults. Dural puncture is possible if the needle is advanced deeply in neonates. The presence of a deep sacral dimple may be associated with spina bifida occulta, greatly increasing the probability of dural puncture.

Peripheral nervous system

Neonates demonstrate an increased sensitivity to the effects of neuromuscular blocking drugs (NMBDs) (Fisher et al. 1982). The reason for this sensitivity is unknown but the finding is consistent with the observation that there is a three-fold reduction in the release of acetylcholine from the infant rat phrenic nerve compared with the adult nerve (Meakin et al. 1992; Wareham et al. 1994). Reduced clearance and increased sensitivity prolong the duration of neuromuscular effect.

The duration of regional block with amide local anaesthetic agents in infants is reduced compared with older children. Onset time and duration of blockade are reduced because the myelin sheath does not have to be penetrated and less anaesthetic is retained within it.

Developmental issues

Normal neonates show various primitive reflexes, which include the Moro response and grasp reflex. Milestones of development are useful indicators of mental development and possible deviations from normal. Children with developmental issues are delayed in many aspects of both cognitive and motor development. Smiling, vocalization, sitting, walking, speech, and sphincter control are delayed. When there is a delay with visual fixing and following or response to sound, blindness and deafness may erroneously be diagnosed. Drooling, common in young infants, is frequently prolonged for years in neurologically delayed children. Initially, an infant with learning disabilities appears to be inactive and may be seen as a 'good child'. The child later demonstrates constant and sometimes uncontrollable over-activity. Infants born prematurely will be delayed and should be assessed in terms of their PMA. Infants with cerebral palsy or sensory deficits (auditory and visual) may have normal mental development, but the disability may interfere with assessment of mental status.

Analgesic medications and delivery systems commonly used in adults may not be possible or practicable in children or in those with developmental delay. Preschool children are unable to use patient-controlled analgesia devices; continuous infusion pumps or nurse-controlled analgesic devices are used instead (McDowall, 1993). Buccal and sublingual administration in children requires prolonged exposure to the mucosal surface. Younger children find it difficult to comply with instructions to hold drug in their mouth for the requisite retention time (particularly if taste is unfavourable) and this results in more swallowed drug or drug spat out than in adults (Karl et al. 1993). Bioavailability of an oral transmucosal fentanyl formulation was lower than adults, suggesting that many children swallowed a large fraction of the dose (Wheeler et al. 2002). If the drug has a high first-pass effect then the lower relative bioavailability results in lower plasma concentrations (Johnson et al. 2005a; Michel et al. 2011).

Cardiovascular system

Embryology, normal development, and fetal circulation

The heart originates as a flat sheet of mesodermal cells that form a linear heart tube, which starts beating at 14 days. The next phase, looping, starts on day 21 and over the next 7 days differential growth leads to differentiation of the left and right ventricles plus a common atrium. During the next weeks the atria septate so that by day 50 the septum primum has fused with the endocardial cushions and the septum secundum partly overlaps the septum primum. The orifice between the two septums (foramen ovale) remains patent until birth allowing oxygenated blood from the maternal circulation (placenta via inferior vena cava to right atrium) to flow through the heart. Functional closure of the foramen ovale occurs at birth. Over a similar time period (days 34–56) outflow tract separation occurs as the truncus arteriosus, which starts as a single tube connected to both ventricles, rotates and divides to form the aortic and pulmonary outflow tracts which arise from the left and right ventricles respectively. Ventricular separation (days 38–46) occurs simultaneously as upward growth of a thick ridge of cells towards the endocardial cushion form the ventricular septum. This is incomplete until later in development when the membranous septum forms, joining the endocardial cushions to the muscular septum (Fig. 69.11).

The fetus has a very different circulation from that seen postnatally, as the placenta rather than the lungs is the source of oxygenated blood and both ventricles, rather than just the left ventricle, contribute to systemic blood flow: a parallel circuit arrangement. This requires two additional channels that usually close at birth: the ductus venosus and the ductus arteriosus in addition to the foramen ovale already mentioned. In the fetus, oxygenated blood from the placenta flows via the umbilical vein, into the inferior vena cava and then via the ductus venosus, bypassing the liver, to the right atrium, where the Eustachian valve directs it through the foramen ovale to the left atrium. This is then ejected into the aorta by the left ventricle to supply the developing fetus (predominantly head and upper body). Deoxygenated blood returns to the right atrium, where flow from the upper body streams preferentially into the right ventricle, but as a result of the high pulmonary vascular resistance (as the lungs are not yet expanded), it then flows through the second channel, the ductus arteriosus, and into the descending aorta, mixing with blood from the head and upper body (Fig. 69.12) (Rudolph 2001).

Transitional circulation, persistent fetal circulation, and persistent pulmonary hypertension of the newborn

Several changes are initiated subsequent to lung expansion and spontaneous respiration plus the sudden decrease in placental flow at birth. This results in the fetal parallel circulation transitioning to the adult series circulation with separate systemic and pulmonary circulations (Fig. 69.12). Lung expansion and oxygenation decreases the pulmonary vascular resistance, allowing blood flow to the lungs and increased filling of the left atrium. In response to the increasing oxygen tension, the ductus arteriosus vasoconstricts with closure occurring in the first 24 h after birth. Simultaneous decrease in placental flow results in an increase in systemic vascular resistance (from ligation of the umbilical arteries) and decreased filling pressures in the portal vein and right atrium (from ligation of the umbilical vein). The change in atrial pressures closes the foramen ovale and the decrease in portal vein flow leads to closure of the ductus venosus. These changes comprise the transitional circulation. These changes may not be completed if adequate oxygenation is not achieved early after birth.

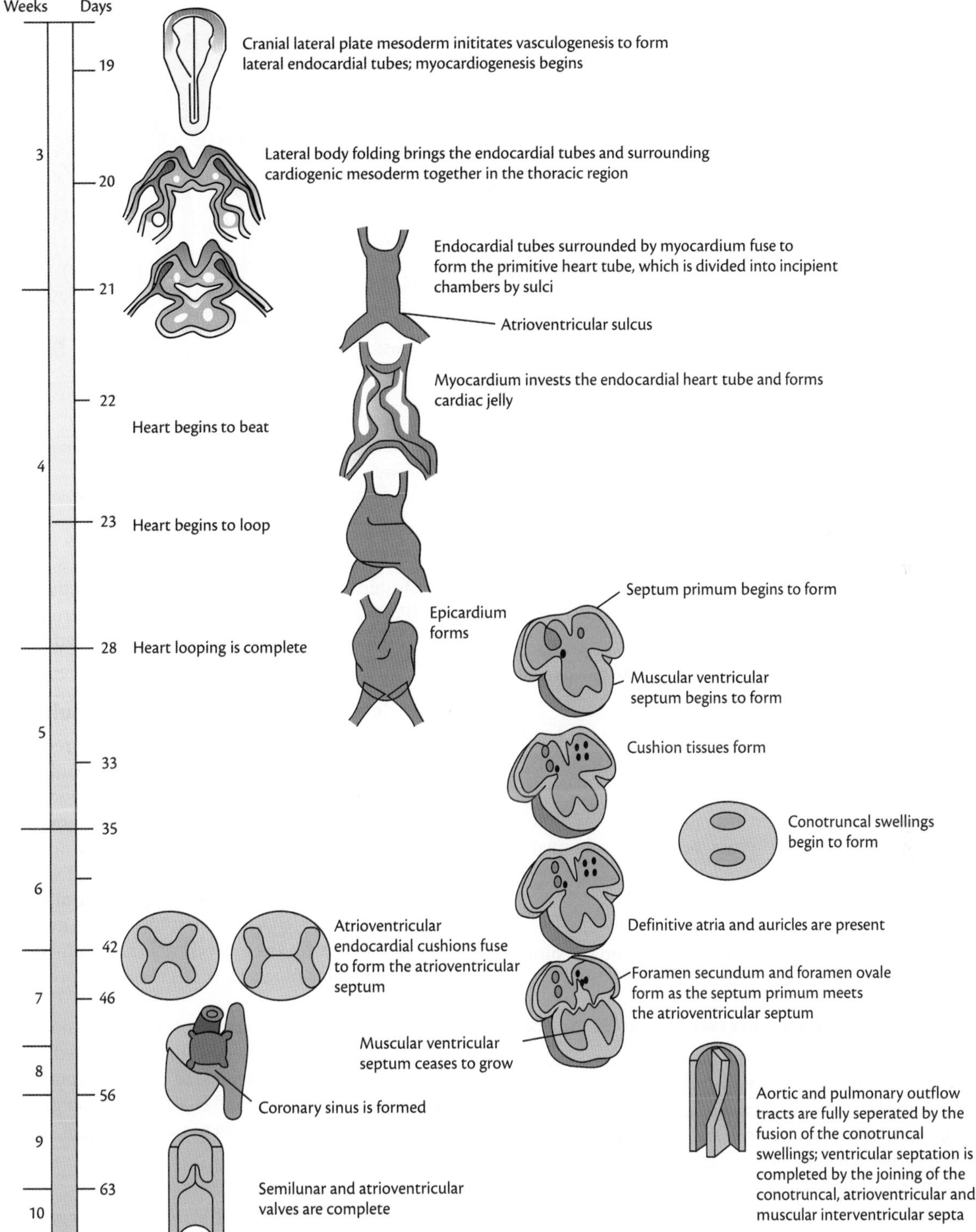

Figure 69.11 Timeline of the formation of the heart.

Reproduced from Andropoulos, D. B. et al., *Anaesthesia for Congenital Heart Disease, Third Edition*, Copyright © John Wiley and Sons Ltd 2015. This image was originally published in *Larsen's Human Embryology*, Schoenwolf, G. et al., Copyright © Elsevier 2014.

The neonate is very susceptible to conditions that trigger an increase in pulmonary vascular resistance. Right ventricular diastolic dysfunction may promote a right-to-left shunt through the foramen ovale and if pulmonary vascular resistance exceeds systemic vascular resistance, a right-to-left shunt develops via the ductus arteriosus as well. This is called persistent fetal circulation or persistent pulmonary hypertension of the newborn (Konduri and Kim 2009). Causes of persistent fetal circulation are shown in Box 69.1. The ductus arteriosus may be kept open in neonates with cyanotic heart defects by

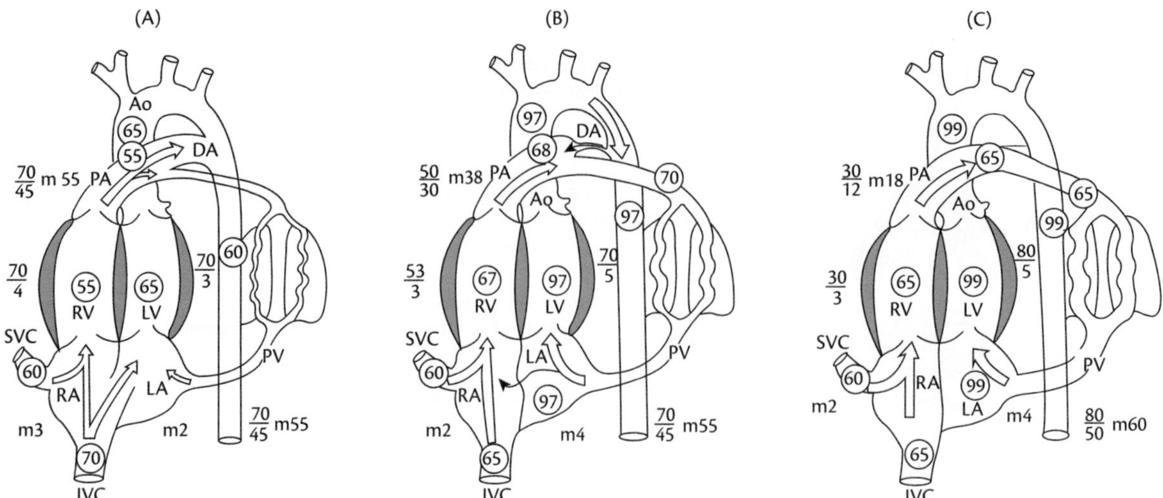

Figure 69.12 Transition from fetal to mature circulation showing (A) fetal circulation, (B) transitional circulation, and (C) mature circulation. Circled numbers represent % oxygen saturation; uncircled numbers are pressure (mm Hg). DA, ductus arteriosus; PV, pulmonary vein.

Box 69.1 Conditions leading to persistent fetal circulation

- Prematurity
- Physiological and metabolic disturbances: hypoxaemia, hypercarbia, acidosis, hypothermia, sepsis, high altitude
- Congenital heart disease especially cyanotic congenital heart disease: tetralogy of Fallot, pulmonary atresia, tricuspid atresia, transposition of the great arteries
- Respiratory disorders: meconium aspiration, bronchopulmonary dysplasia, diaphragmatic hernia, persistent pulmonary hypertension of the newborn.

using prostaglandin infusions to augment pulmonary blood flow and oxygenation.

Neonatal circulation and cardiovascular performance

Further postnatal changes occur as the pulmonary vascular bed remodels so that pulmonary artery pressures decrease to those of adults by about 4 weeks with resistance continuing to decrease over the first 3 months. Congenital defects, if not diagnosed prenatally, may become apparent during this period, particularly those that result in a left-to-right shunt (ventricular septal defect, atrioventricular septal defect, patent ductus arteriosus, atrial septal defect). Non-steroidal anti-inflammatory drugs (NSAIDs) may be used during this time to close a patent ductus arteriosus.

The neonatal myocardium differs from the adult myocardium histologically, in that it contains fewer muscle cells (poorly organized rather than in parallel) and more connective tissue; plus functionally it is more dependent on free cytosolic ionized calcium for contractility (Nayler and Fassold 1977; Baum and Palmisano 1997). These differences result in limited improvement of cardiac output (stroke volume) with increasing preload, greater sensitivity to increased afterload, and decreased ionized calcium concentrations compared with adult myocardium. Immature autonomic regulation is also a feature of the neonate with parasympathetic tone predominating (Papp 1988). This results in a limited inotropic response to catecholamine administration and a more marked vagal response to stimulation such as intubation.

Further development from infancy to adulthood

Further development reflects the changing requirements of the systemic and pulmonary circuits. As the individual grows, both ventricles increase in size to provide the increased cardiac output required. The left ventricle increases mass mainly by hyperplasia of the myocytes, as it is required to work against a higher systemic vascular resistance to sustain normal blood pressures. The right ventricle, which has a similar myocardial wall thickness to the left ventricle at birth, does not demonstrate the changes seen with the left ventricle as its function adapts to provide pulmonary blood flow at pressure approximately one-third of systemic values.

Neonatal heart rate (110–160 beats min^{-1}) is much higher than adults (60–100 beats min^{-1}) reflecting the limited compliance of the neonatal heart and the increased cardiac output relative to per kilogram body weight (Southall et al. 1980). Changes in heart rate with age are shown in Table 69.5. Cardiac output decreases from

Table 69.5 Heart rate and systolic blood pressure by age

Age (years)	Heart rate (bpm)	Systolic BP (mm Hg)
		50th centile
<1	110–160	80–90
1–2	100–150	85–90
2–5	95–140	90–95
5–12	80–120	100–105
>12	60–100	110–120

300 ml min^{-1} kg^{-1} in neonates to 100 ml min^{-1} kg^{-1} in adolescence, decreasing further to 70–80 ml min^{-1} kg^{-1} by adulthood (Samuels 2011). The relatively large cardiac output (expressed as ml min^{-1} kg^{-1}) in neonates reflects their greater metabolic rate and oxygen consumption compared with adults. Basal metabolic rate has been shown to increase as size decreases in all species (West and Brown 2005).

Mean systolic blood pressure in neonates and infants increases from 65 mm Hg in the first 12 h of life to 75 mm Hg at 4 days and 95 mm Hg at 6 weeks. Pooled data showing normal mean and systolic blood pressures for premature infants and neonates 2 weeks after birth are shown in Figure 69.13 (Dionne et al. 2012) There is little change in mean systolic pressure between 6 weeks and 1 year of age; between 1 year and 6 years, there is only a slight change, followed by a gradual increase (Horan 1987). Representative blood pressures with age are shown in Table 69.5. More detailed changes of blood pressure with age can be found in the *Report of the Second Task Force on Blood Pressure Control in Children – 1987* (Horan 1987).

ECG changes from infancy to adolescence are as follows. The P wave changes little with age but the PR interval increases from 0.10 s in infancy, to 0.14 s by adolescence. The duration of the QRS complex increases with age, but prolongation greater than 0.10 s is abnormal at any age. At birth, the QRS axis is right sided, reflecting predominant right ventricular intrauterine development. It moves leftward during the first month as left ventricular muscle

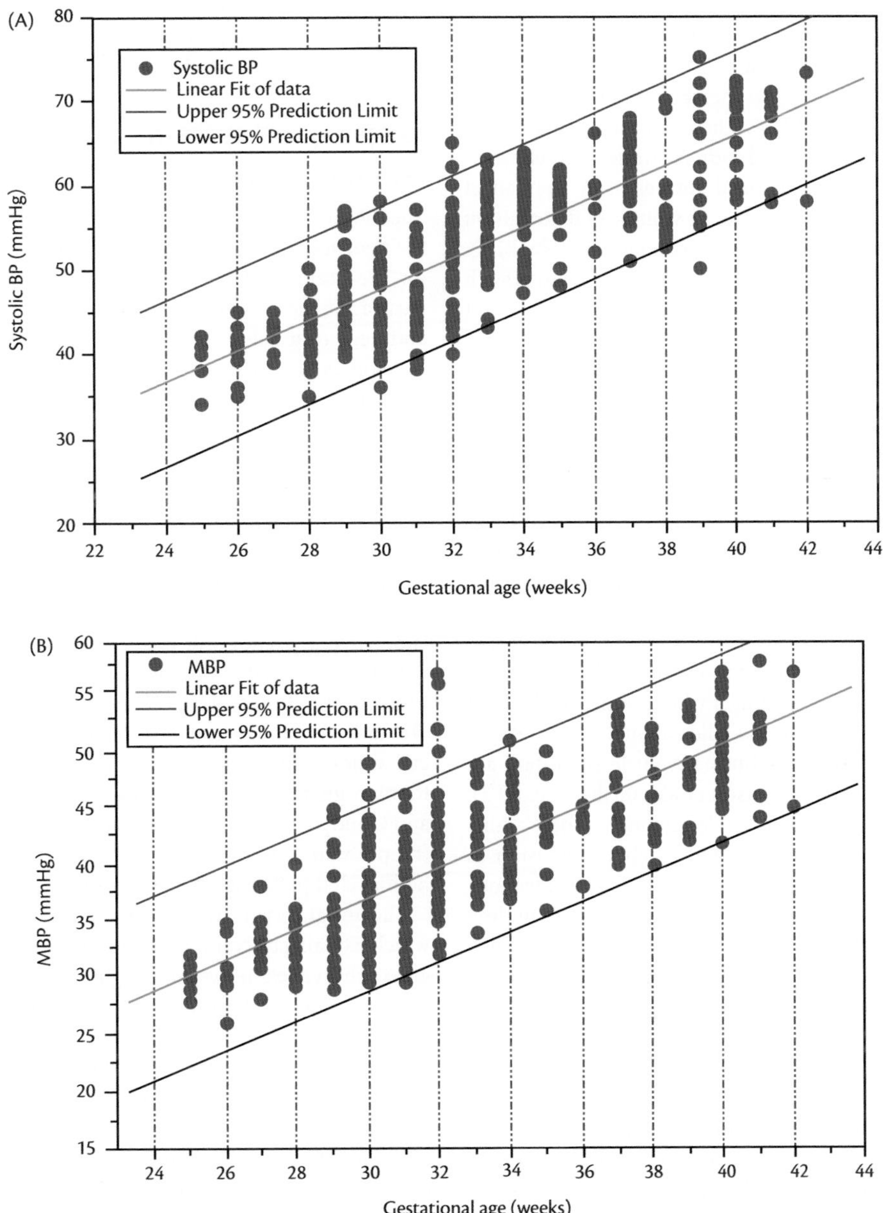

Figure 69.13 Changes in systolic and mean blood pressures (MBP) by gestational age measured on the first day of life.

Adapted from Pejovic, B., *et al.* Blood pressure in non-critically ill preterm and full-term neonates. *Pediatric Nephrology*, Volume 22, Issue 2, pp. 249–57, Copyright © 2006 International Pediatric Nephrology Association. With kind permission from Springer Science and Business Media.

hypertrophies. Thereafter, the QRS follows a gradual change away from its right-sided axis. T waves are upright in all chest leads at birth but within hours, they become isoelectric or inverted over the left chest. By the seventh day, the T waves are inverted in V4R, V1, and across to V4; from then on, the T waves remain inverted over the right chest until adolescence, when they become upright over the right side of the chest again. Failure of T waves to become inverted in V4R and V1 to V4 by 7 days may be the earliest ECG evidence of right ventricular hypertrophy (Southall et al. 1976; Dickinson 2005).

Pharmacological aspects

Transition from the intrauterine to the extrauterine environment is associated with major changes in blood flow. There may also be an environmental trigger for the expression of some metabolic enzyme activities resulting in a slight increase in maturation rate above that predicted by PMA at birth (Allegaert et al. 2007b; Anderson and Holford 2011). The opening or closing of a patent ductus may have profound effects on drug delivery to metabolizing organs in preterm infants (Gal and Gilman 1993). The open ductus may cause reduced perfusion of to the liver and kidney, influencing elimination dependent on blood flow. Reduced gut perfusion may affect absorption. Fluid overload may increase the volume of distribution of drugs confined to the ECF (e.g. aminoglycosides and NMBDs). Cardiac depression by volatile agents, although less obvious with modern agents than halothane, is greater in the neonate than adult (Friesen et al. 2000).

The initial phase of distribution reflects the magnitude of regional blood flow. Consequently, the brain, heart, and liver, which receive the largest fraction of cardiac output, are first exposed. Drugs are then redistributed to other relatively well-perfused tissues, such as skeletal muscle. There is a much slower tertiary distribution to relatively under-perfused tissues of the body that is noted with long-term drug infusions. In addition to perinatal circulatory changes (e.g. ductus venosus and ductus arteriosus), there are maturational differences in relative organ mass and regional blood flow while a symptomatic patent ductus arteriosus may also result in differences in distribution. Blood flow as a fraction of the cardiac output to the kidney and brain increases with age, whereas that to the liver decreases through the neonatal period (Bjorkman 2005). Cerebral and hepatic mass as proportions of body weight in the infant are much greater than in the adult (Johnson et al. 2005b) (Fig. 69.2). While onset times are generally faster for neonates than adults (a size effect), reduced cardiac output and cerebral perfusion in neonates means that the expected onset time after an intravenous induction is slower in neonates, although reduced protein binding may counter this observation for some drugs. Offset time is also delayed because redistribution to well-perfused and deep under-perfused tissues is more limited.

Cardiac calcium stores in the endoplasmic reticulum are reduced in the neonatal heart because of immaturity. Exogenous calcium has a greater impact on contractility in this age group than in older children or adults. Catecholamine release and response to vasoactive drugs vary with age. These pharmacodynamic differences are based in part upon developmental changes in myocardial structure, cardiac innervation, and adrenergic receptor function. For example, the immature myocardium has fewer contractile elements and therefore a decreased ability to increase contractility; it also responds poorly to standard techniques of manipulating preload (Steinberg and Notterman 1994). Dopaminergic receptors are present in the pulmonary vasculature and are believed to be responsible for pulmonary vasoconstriction in preterm neonates. However, systemic vasoconstriction is greater than that observed in the pulmonary circulation and this differential response contributes to the use of dopamine in neonates with known pulmonary hypertension after cardiac surgery. Neonates have underdeveloped sympathetic innervation and reduced stores of noradrenaline. Signs of cardiovascular α-receptor stimulation may occur at lower doses than β-receptor stimulation because β-receptor maturation lags behind α-receptor maturation during the development of the adrenergic system (Seri et al. 1984). The preterm neonate has immature metabolic and elimination pathways leading to increased dopamine concentrations after prolonged infusions (Seri et al. 1984, 1985, 1990; Cuevas et al. 1991). These maturational changes in pharmacokinetics and pharmacodynamics may contribute to dopamine's continued popularity in the neonatal nursery while its popularity wanes in the adult population.

Respiratory system

Face and upper airway

The development of the skull can be divided into two major parts, the neurocranium, which is the part that forms the protective case for the brain, and the viscerocranium, which forms the skeletal part of the face (Pohunek 2004). Most of the structures of the face and neck originate from the pharyngeal (branchial) arches. These develop as paired structures lateral to the developing foregut and laryngotracheal groove. Each pharyngeal arch consists of a variety of cell types that includes the neural crest cells, which contribute to the skeletal components, mesodermal cells which contribute to the muscular components, as well as a nerve and arterial components. Each arch is separated by a pouch medially (endoderm) and a groove laterally (ectoderm).

The first three pharyngeal arches give rise to the maxilla, mandible, and hyoid bone with their accompanying nerves and muscles, whereas arches four to six give rise to the laryngeal cartilages with their associated muscles and are supplied by branches of the vagus nerve. The tonsils arise from the second pharyngeal pouch. Disruption of the neural crest cell development results in craniofacial abnormalities. Interruption of mandibular development leads to micrognathia and retrodisplacement of the tongue (Mankarious and Goudy 2011). This may manifest as Treacher Collins syndrome (mandibulofacial dysostosis) or Pierre Robin sequence (micrognathia, cleft palate, and glossoptosis).

The tongue is derived from the first four pharyngeal arches, which explains its complicated innovation via the trigeminal nerve, glossopharyngeal nerve, and vagus nerves. The anterior two-thirds of the tongue are derived mostly from the first arch and the posterior one-third from the third and fourth arches. At birth, the entire tongue lies within the mouth and the posterior third descends into the oropharynx over the first 4 years of life. The palate is formed from lateral palatine processes which project medially on each side of the tongue and fuse with the nasal septum. Cleft lips and palates result from failure of this process.

Active, synchronized muscle tone during the respiratory cycle is required for patency of the upper airway; the pharynx is the most compliant area and therefore prone to collapse. During inhalation induction, loss of tone in the upper airway muscles occurs at lower

MAC values than depression of the intercostal and diaphragm muscles and is further exaggerated in the young (Ochiai et al. 1992).

Infants are obligatory nasal breathers (except when crying). Occlusion of one nare by a nasogastric tube increases resistance by up to 50% and may precipitate ventilatory failure (Stocks 1980). Lymphatic tissue known as Waldeyer's ring, mainly comprising the adenoids in the nasopharynx and the faucial tonsils, undergo periods of hyperplasia/hypertrophy as a defensive mechanism against infection. Both increase progressively in size during the first decade. Maximal adenoid hypertrophy compromising the nasopharyngeal airway occurs in the early childhood years and tonsillar enlargement from this age until the first decade is the most common cause of obstructive sleep apnoea in children (Vogler et al. 2000; Arens et al. 2002).

The epiglottis, larynx, and cricoid region

The fourth to sixth pharyngeal pouches give rise to the larynx, trachea, bronchi, and lungs by initially forming a laryngotracheal groove that evaginates to form the pouch-like respiratory diverticulum. Abnormalities in partitioning of the oesophagus and trachea by the tracheoesophageal septum result in oesophageal atresia and tracheoesophageal fistulae. The epiglottis develops from the hypopharyngeal eminence (third and fourth pharyngeal arches) which also forms the posterior third of the tongue. The epiglottis is intimately related to the base of the tongue superiorly, suspended from the hyoid bone and attaches inferiorly to the larynx, explaining the high position of the larynx in the newborn. Differences between the infant and adult larynx are shown in Figure 69.14. At birth, the relative position of the larynx is at C3–4, higher than in older children and adults (C4–5), which facilitates simultaneous breathing and early liquid feeding. During infancy, the epiglottis is attached to the arytenoid cartilages by relatively prominent aryepiglottic folds, an arrangement which protects the larynx from aspiration of fluids. Active, synchronized muscle tone during the respiratory cycle is required for patency of the upper airway and larynx. Lack of maturation of this system leads to the most common upper airway problems in early infancy: laryngomalacia and vocal cord paresis.

Subsequent laryngeal growth and descent occurs as the posterior third of the tongue develops, predominantly during the first 3 years of life, allowing for the formation of sounds of adult speech. The epiglottis changes shape from its infantile omega shape with

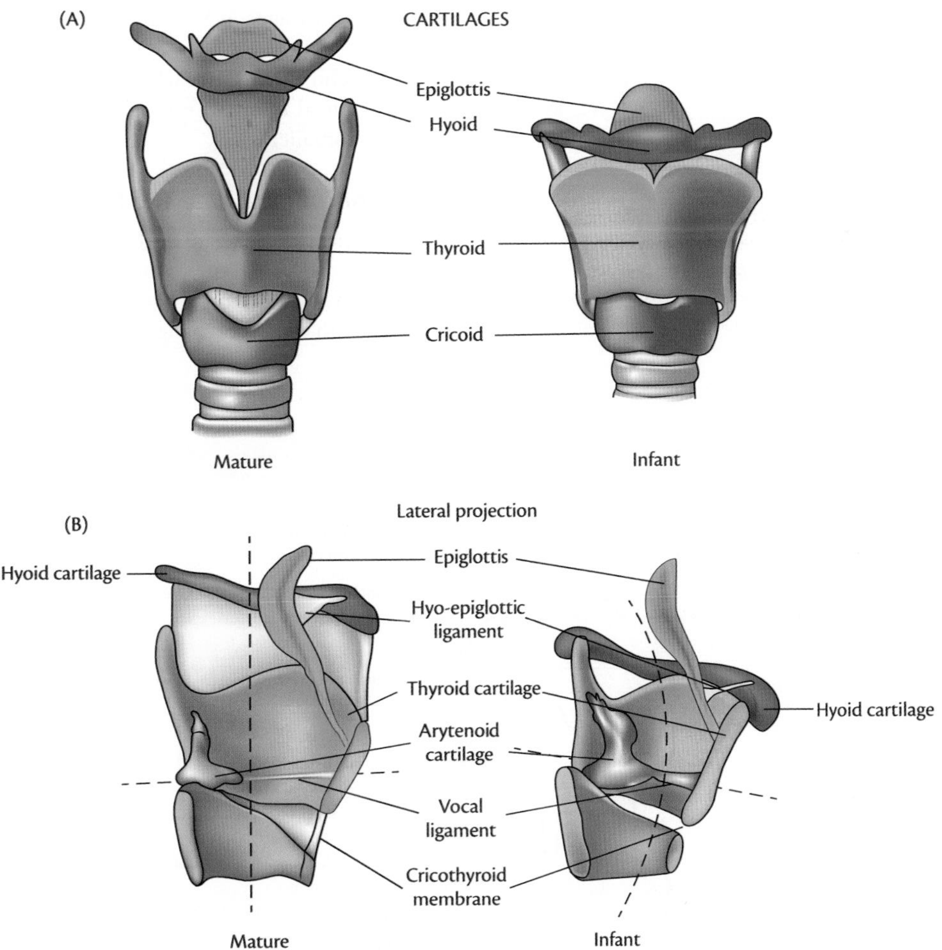

Figure 69.14 Comparison between the infant and adult larynx showing caudad attachment of the hyo-epiglottic ligament, compact nature of the hyo-thyrocricoid complex with poorly developed cricothyroid ligament, relatively large size of arytenoid cartilages, and caudad position of the anterior attachment of the vocal cords. (A) Anteroposterior projection. (B) Lateral projection.

This figure was published in *Atlas of the Difficult Airway*, Martin L Noughton and Allan CD Brown (eds), Copyright Elsevier 1991.

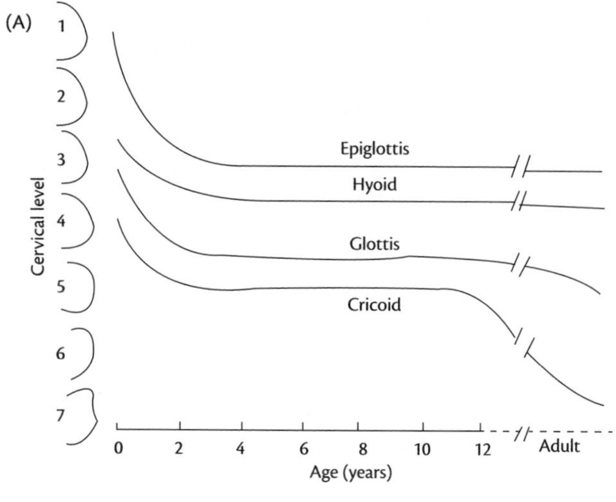

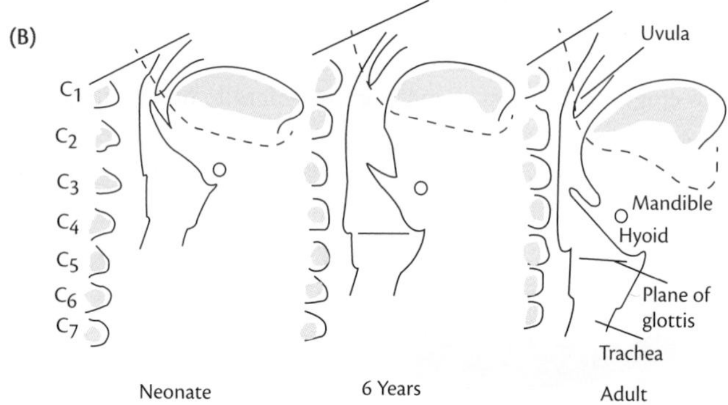

Figure 69.15 (A) Changes in the level of laryngeal structures at different ages relative to the cervical spine. (B) The relative positions of the upper airways with growth.
Reproduced with permission from Westhorpe RN. The position of the larynx in children and its relationship to the ease of intubation. *Anaesthesia Intensive Care*, Volume 15, pp. 384–8, Copyright © 1987 Australian Society of Anaesthetists. Reproduced with permission from the Australian Society of Anaesthetists.

well-defined attachments to the arytenoid cartilages (via the ary-epiglottic folds) to its adult U-shape during this time. The hyoid–laryngeal complex descends during postnatal life relative to the jaw, face, and cranial base from C4 to C5. From the end of the second year of life, its position relative to the vertebral column remains relatively stable (Westhorpe 1987) (Fig. 69.15).

Development of the cricoid ring is important in determining tracheal tube selection and complications that arise from prolonged intubation (subglottic stenosis). The classical teaching is that the cricoid is the narrowest part of the upper airway in infants and children. This is based on data from moulages and anatomical sections and may not be applicable to the living (Eckenhoff 1951). More recent data from detailed magnetic resonance imaging and bronchoscopy studies suggests this is not so and that the glottis is the narrowest part of the upper airway throughout life (Litman et al. 2003; Dalal et al. 2009). With the smaller cross-sectional area of the paediatric airway, comparatively minor degrees of inflammation, oedema, and secretions may result in significant airway obstruction.

Uncuffed tracheal tubes are commonly calculated according to a formula:

$$\text{Tracheal tube size (internal diameter, mm)} = 4 + (\text{PNA}/4) \quad (69.5)$$

after 1 year of age. A 3.5 mm tracheal tube is commonly used in infants less than 3.5 kg, a 3.0 mm tracheal tube for neonates 1–3.5 kg, and a 2.5 mm tracheal tube in those less than 1 kg. If a cuffed tracheal tube (>3 mm internal diameter) is used, the size is 0.5 mm smaller.

Tracheobronchial tree and lungs

Growth and development of the airways proceed through four well-defined periods; the pseudo-glandular, canalicular, saccular, and the alveolar periods (Fig. 69.16) (Kotecha 2000). Elements involved with the gas exchange are not formed until the canalicular

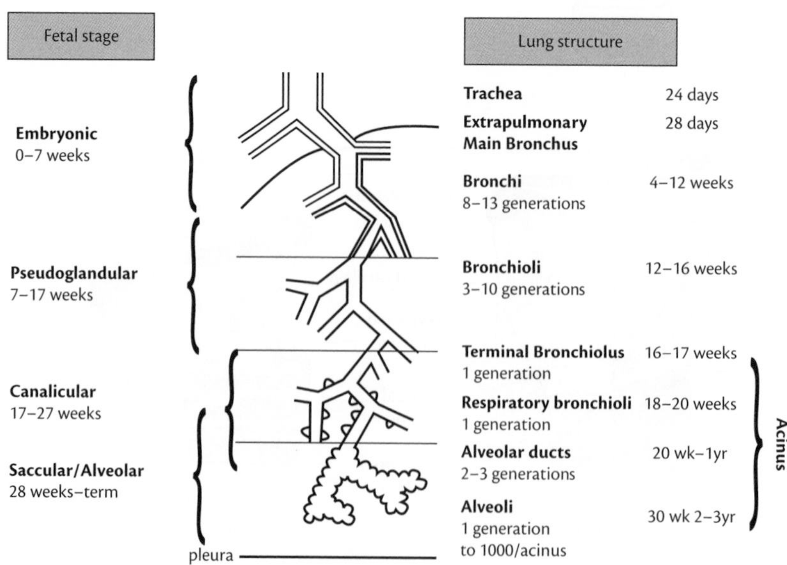

Figure 69.16 Development of the bronchial tree.
Reproduced with permission from Kotecha, S. Lung growth for beginners. *Paediatric Respiratory Reviews*, Volume 1, Issue 4, pp. 308–13, Copyright © 2000 Elsevier. Adapted from that used by Dr Alison Hislop, personal communication.

period. During this period the acina structures comprising the respiratory bronchioles, alveolar ducts, and primitive aveoli are formed. The peripheral airways enlarge and the gas-exchanging surface area increases as the airway walls thin during the saccular phase. Type 1 alveolar cells associated with blood and lymph capillaries and type 2 alveolar cells that produce surfactant develop during this period. During the alveolar phase, definitive formation of the alveoli occurs. At birth, less than one-tenth of the terminal air sacs are developed and 95% of the alveoli develop postnatally, a process of growth that continues through infancy, when there are approximately 300–600 million alveoli in the lung, approximately 1000 per acinus (Thurlbeck 1982). Impaired alveolar growth occurs in infants who develop chronic lung disease of prematurity, hyaline membrane disease, or who require positive pressure ventilation in the neonatal period (Hislop et al. 1987).

Perinatal adaption, control of breathing, and postoperative apnoea

At birth, during the first few breaths, the neonate has to develop a large negative intrapleural pressure to overcome the high surface tension within the collapsed, fluid-filled alveoli. With lung expansion, the arterial oxygen Pa_{O_2} increases rapidly causing a decrease in pulmonary resistance and facilitating the cardiovascular changes. Neonates are unlikely to self-resuscitate in response to hypoxia and hypercarbia. The neonatal response to hypoxia is a transient increase in ventilation followed by sustained respiratory depression unlike the sustained increase seen in older children and adults (Rigatto et al. 1975a, 1975b). The slope of the CO_2 response curve is less in preterm and term neonates than older infants and adults. Under hypoxic conditions, this response curve is right shifted and further decreased, unlike adults, who show an increase in slope with a left shift (Rigatto et al. 1975b).

Premature and term neonates breathe irregularly. Periodic breathing (apnoea <10 s without cyanosis or bradycardia) occurs in most premature neonates and many term neonates, and decreases significantly after 44 weeks post-conception age, but may still persist throughout the first year of life. It is of little significance. Central apnoea, however (apnoea >15 s alone or <15 s associated with hypoxia or bradycardia), occurs in many premature infants but is rare in term neonates. Postoperative apnoea in premature and ex-premature infants can be a significant problem with the risk decreasing exponentially to less than 1% by 56 weeks post-conception age. Degree of prematurity and anaemia are additional risk factors (Cote et al. 1995).

Lung volumes, mechanics, and work of breathing

The chest wall is very compliant in the young infant (three to six times higher than the lung compliance), whereas the inward recoil of the lungs is only slightly less than adult values. As a result, the functional residual capacity (FRC) of young infants is only 10–15% of total lung capacity and is well below closing capacity leading to ventilation/perfusion mismatch and atelectasis with oxygen desaturation (Motoyama 2011). Under anaesthesia, greater decreases in FRC are seen in infants compared with older children and adults, which can be restored by positive end-expiratory pressure (von Ungern-Sternberg et al. 2006). Despite the compliant chest wall and the tendency for static FRC to decrease, the dynamic FRC in awake infants is maintained near the values of older children and adults by a number of active mechanisms including laryngeal braking, maintenance of respiratory muscle tone during expiration, early activation of inspiratory muscles during expiration, and a short expiratory time (high respiratory rate). Transition from this dynamic maintenance of FRC to the more static methods in adults occurs as the chest wall stiffens during the first year of life (Motoyama 2011). Changes in the more common lung function values with age are shown in Table 69.6.

Tidal volumes of approximately 7 ml kg^{-1}, similar to adults, are achieved soon after birth in preterm and term infants. In the neonatal period, resting respiratory rates of 30–40 breaths min^{-1} are seen (Al-Hathlol et al. 2000). Dead-space ventilation is proportionally similar to that in adults but oxygen consumption is two to three

Table 69.6 Normal values for lung function of children and young adults

	Age								
							Male	Male	Female
	1 week	1 year	3 years	5 years	8 years	12 years	15 years	21 years	21 years
Weight (kg)	3.3	10	15	18	26	39	57	73	57
VC (ml)	100	475	910	1100	1855	2830	4300	4620	3380
FRC (ml)	75	263	532	660	1174	1855	2800	3030	2350
FRC/weight (ml kg^{-1})	25	26	37	36	46	48	49	42	41
V_D (ml)	7.5	21	37	49	75	105	141	150	126
V_T (ml)	17	78	112	130	180	260	360	500	420
V_D/V_T	0.44	0.27	0.33	0.38	0.42	0.40	0.39	0.30	0.30
f (frequency)	30	24	22	20	18	16	14	12	12
V_E (litres min^{-1})	0.55	1.8	2.5	2.6	3.2	4.2	5	6	5
C_l (ml cm H_2O^{-1})	5	16	32	44	71	91	130	163	130
R (cm H_2O $litre^{-1}$ s^{-1})	29	13	10	8	6	5	3	2	2

times higher explaining the higher respiratory rates seen in infants. In preterm infants particularly, the work of breathing is significantly increased to about three times that in adults. Infants do not tolerate increased resistance to breathing as the respiratory muscles are prone to fatigue. This is because of the relatively low percentage of type I (slow-twitch, high-oxidative) muscle fibres compared with type II (fast-twitch, low-oxidative) during infancy compared with adults (Keens et al. 1978).

The increase in alveolar ventilation in neonates and infants results in a faster uptake of inhalation anaesthetics resulting in more rapid induction of anaesthesia. This may be partially offset by the increase in MAC values associated with this age group (Lerman et al. 1994). The increased metabolic demands and reduced FRC contribute to an increased speed of desaturation with decreasing age during anaesthetic induction (Xue et al. 1996).

Pharmacology implications

Inhalation anaesthetic delivery is determined largely by alveolar ventilation and FRC. Neonates have increased alveolar ventilation and a smaller FRC compared with adults because of increased chest wall compliance. Consequently, pulmonary absorption is generally more rapid in neonates (Salanitre and Rackow 1969). The higher cardiac output and greater fraction of the cardiac output distributed to vessel-rich tissues (i.e. a clearance factor) and the lower tissue/blood solubility (i.e. a volume factor) further contribute to the more rapid wash-in of inhalation anaesthetics in early life (Malviya and Lerman 1990; Lerman 1992).

Disease characteristics further contribute to the variability in inhalation absorption. Induction of anaesthesia may be slowed by right-to-left shunting of blood in neonates suffering cyanotic congenital cardiac disease or intrapulmonary conditions. This slowing is greatest with the least soluble anaesthetics (e.g. nitrous oxide and sevoflurane). Left-to-right shunts usually have minimal impact on uptake because cardiac output is increased so that systemic tissue perfusion is maintained at normal levels. The flow of mixed venous blood returning to the right heart ready for anaesthetic uptake is normal. If cardiac output is not increased, and peripheral perfusion is reduced, then there will be less anaesthetic uptake in the lung. Although alveolar anaesthetic partial pressure may be observed to increase rapidly, there is a slower increase in tissue partial pressure and anaesthetic effect is delayed.

The factors that determine anaesthetic absorption through the lung (alveolar ventilation, FRC, cardiac output, solubility) also contribute to elimination kinetics. We might anticipate more rapid wash-out in neonates for any given duration of anaesthesia because of the greater alveolar ventilation to FRC ratio, greater fraction of cardiac output perfusing vessel-rich tissues, reduced solubility in blood and tissues, and a reduced distribution to fat and muscle content. Furthermore, younger age (as in the neonate) will speed the elimination of more soluble anaesthetics such as halothane to a greater extent than the less soluble anaesthetics, desflurane and sevoflurane primarily. Halothane, and to a far lesser extent isoflurane (1.5%) and sevoflurane (5%), undergo hepatic metabolism. Halothane is reported to undergo as much as 20–25% metabolism but at typical anesthetizing concentrations, hepatic halothane removal is extremely small (Sawyer et al. 1971).

Bronchodilators are ineffective in neonates because of the paucity of bronchial smooth muscle that can cause bronchospasm.

The renal system

Anatomy

Nephrogenesis starts in the embryo at approximately week 5 of gestation and nephrons become functional by week 8. Nephrogenesis is complete at gestational week 36 when there are about 1 000 000 nephrons in each kidney, after which no new nephrons are produced (Potter 1965). Renal tubular growth, rather than an increase in the number of glomeruli, accounts for the large increase in renal mass after 36 weeks' gestation (Potter 1965; Robillard et al. 1975).

At birth, renal blood flow is only 5–6% of cardiac output and reaches adult values (15–25%) by 1 year of age when adjusted for BSA (Hook and Bailie 1979). This increase in blood flow is as a result of both an increase in cardiac output and a decrease in renal vascular resistance.

Physiology

The kidneys are responsible for water and electrolyte status. They are active before birth and urine production begins at 10–12 weeks of gestation. Urine contributes to amniotic fluid volume. Maturation of the glomerular filtration rate (GFR) correlates closely with PMA (Fig. 69.17A) (Rhodin et al. 2009). GFR at 36 weeks is only 20% the mature rate (Rhodin et al. 2009) and renal blood flow is similarly reduced. Parturition results in a slight (approximately 10%) increase in maturation, attributed to an increase in cardiac output and a decrease in renal vascular resistance (Fig. 69.17B) (Anderson and Holford 2011). GFR is approximately 30% of the mature value at birth in a term neonate and increases rapidly around 40 weeks' PMA (Leake et al. 1976; Fawer et al. 1979; Aperia et al. 1981). Adult renal function is reached within 2 years of age; 90% of which is achieved in the first year (Rhodin et al. 2009). Tubular function begins to develop after 34 weeks of gestation and increases during the first 2 years of life (Arant 1978, 1987). The processes that determine GFR, tubular secretion, and tubular reabsorption all undergo independent maturation and the mature kidney emerges within the first few years of life (Hook and Hewitt 1977; Haycock 1998).

Difficulties arise in determining renal function in children although a number of formulae have been published that allow estimation of GFR from clinical characteristics (Paap and Nahata 1995). These formulae use simple markers such as height, creatinine concentration in plasma, and BSA. Estimation of GFR is acceptable in adults, but prediction is poor in children with a GFR value less than 40 ml min^{-1} (Cole et al. 2004). Serum creatinine, especially in the first days of life, reflects the maternal serum creatinine and therefore cannot be used to predict neonatal renal function until at least 2 days after birth (Guignard and Drukker 1999). Creatinine production in neonates is reduced when compared with adults because of immature muscle development, resulting in low serum creatinine concentrations in the presence of immature renal function. Tubular reabsorption of creatinine may also occur in the immature kidney (Guignard and Drukker 1999). The increase of creatinine production in childhood is assumed to be a consequence of increasing muscle bulk

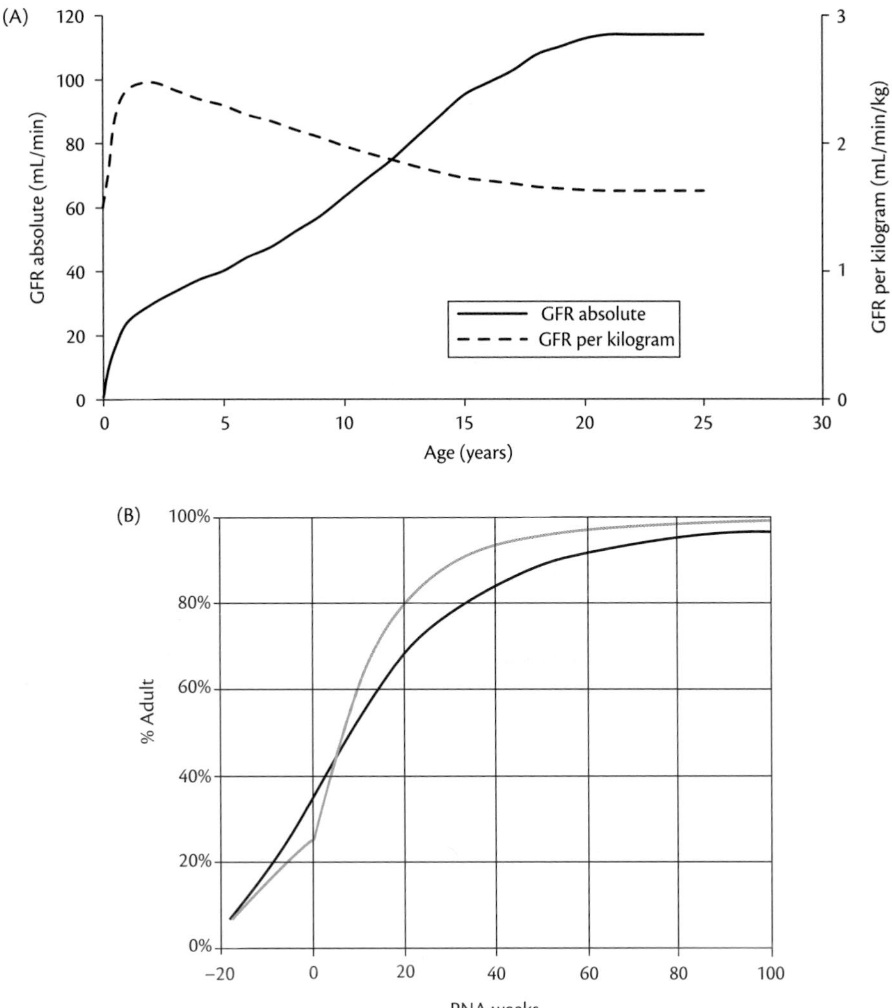

Figure 69.17 (A) GFR maturation in relation to postnatal age, expressed as absolute and as per kilogram. (B) GFR maturation over the first few years of life in relation to postnatal age, expressed as a percentage of adult values using the allometric ¾-power size model, demonstrating maturity by 2 years. This figure uses the same data as that shown in part (A). GFR is 35% mature at birth in a term neonate, but parturition (grey line) does have a small effect on maturation rate.

(A) Reproduced with permission from Rhodin M. Human renal function maturation: a quantitative description using weight and postmenstrual age. *Pediatric Nephrology*, Volume 24, pp. 67–76, Copyright © 2008 International Pediatric Nephrology Association. With kind permission from Springer Science and Business Media. (B) Reproduced with permission from Anderson, B. Developmental pharmacology; filling one knowledge gap in pediatric anesthesiology. *Pediatric Anesthesia*, Volume 21, pp. 222–237, Copyright © 2011 John Wiley and Sons Ltd.

as opposed to the decrease in muscle bulk that occurs with older age in adults. Attempts to use the Cockcroft and Gault models (Cockcroft and Gault 1976) to predict creatinine production rate fail. Estimation methods such as those of Schwartz incorporate a size factor (body length or height, Ht) and a scaling factor (k) that is age dependent (e.g. $k = 0.33$, premature neonates; $k = 0.45$, term infants 0–1 years; $k = 0.45$, 1–12 years; $k = 0.7$ 13–21 years adolescent males) (Schwartz et al. 1976, 1984; Brion et al. 1986) to account for reduced creatinine production:

$$\text{Creatinine clearance} = \left[\mathrm{k} \times \left(\mathrm{Ht/Cr}\right)\right] \ \mathrm{ml\ min^{-1} 1.73\ m^{-2}} \quad (69.6)$$

Creatinine clearance estimation over-predicts GFR in children, possibly because of tubular secretion. Other formulae may be useful in children out of infancy (Leger et al. 2002; Cole et al. 2004).

The kidney is responsible for the regulation of total body sodium balance and for maintenance of a normal extracellular and circulating volume. There are a number of hormones that play a role in this autoregulation, for example, vasodilators (prostaglandins E and I_2, dopamine, and nitric oxide) and vasoconstrictors (angiotensin II, thromboxane, adrenergic, antidiuretic hormone). Renal biochemical processes (e.g. Na^+/K^+-ATPase transporters) are immature at birth and this immaturity contributes to an inability to concentrate urine and a loss of bicarbonate. Physiological acidaemia (pH 7.37) and the lower serum bicarbonate concentration (22 mEq litre^{-1}) observed in neonates is partially attributable to renal bicarbonate wasting as a result of a diminished tubular threshold and partially because of the deposition of calcium in bone, a process that produces 0.5–1 mEq (litre of acid)$^{-1}$ day^{-1} (Edelmann et al. 1967). Infants are also obligate salt losers and

Table 69.7 Normal values for blood chemistry

	Neonate		>2 years
	Preterm	Term	
Chloride	100–117	90–115	98–106
Potassium	4.6–6.7‡	4.3–7.6‡	3.5–5.6
Sodium	133–146	136–148	135–145
Glucose (mmol litre^{-1})	2.2–3.5*	2.2–4.5*	3.6–5.4
Total protein (g dl^{-1})	3.9–4.7	4.6–7.7	5.5–7.8
Pa_{CO_2} (mm Hg)	30–35	33–35	35–40

* Although 2.2 mmol litre^{-1} may be the lower limit of 'normal', most practitioners would treat a serum glucose <2.6 mmol litre^{-1}.
‡ K^+ >6 should be regarded with caution.

Table 69.8 Daily maintenance requirements for fluid, electrolytes, and carbohydrates

Weight	H_2O (ml kg^{-1})	Na^+ (mEq kg^{-1})	K^+ (mEq kg^{-1})	Carbohydrate (g kg^{-1})
1000 g	200	3	2–2.5	10
1000–1499 g	180	2.5	2–2.5	9
1500–2499 g	160	2	1.5–2	8
2500 g	150	1.5–2	2	5
4–10 kg	100–120	2–2.5	2–2.5	5–6
10–20 kg	80–100	1.6–2	1.6–2	4–5
20–40 kg	60–80	1.2–1.6	1.2–1.6	3–4
Adult 70 kg	40–50	0.8–1.4	0.8–1.4	1.5–2.5

can only concentrate urine to 700–800 mOsm litre^{-1} (half that of adults), but can dilute urine down to 50 mOsm litre^{-1} (Robillard et al. 1977). Immaturity of distal tubular function and relative hypoaldosteronism explain slight hyperkalaemia (4–6 mEq litre^{-1}) in preterm infants. See Table 69.7.

The relative inability of neonates to conserve or excrete water when compared with older children makes perioperative fluid management more complex. Neonates can maintain acid–base homeostasis but are limited in their ability to respond to an acid load. The 'threshold' or the plasma concentration at which HCO_3^- is no longer completely reabsorbed by the kidney is reduced. Table 69.8 shows daily fluid and electrolyte requirements based on weight. Fluid requirements parallel the changes in metabolic rate that relate to weight in a non-linear manner (allometric theory) rather than directly. This is reflected in the commonly used maintenance fluid requirements known as the 4–2–1 rule (Table 69.9) (Holliday and Segar 1957).

Pharmacology implications

Renal elimination of drugs and their metabolites is determined by three processes: glomerular filtration, tubular secretion, and tubular reabsorption. Aminoglycosides are almost exclusively cleared by GFR and maintenance dose is predicted by PMA because it

Table 69.9 Hourly weight-based maintenance fluid requirements for children

Weight	Hourly rate
<10 kg	4 ml kg^{-1}
10–20 kg	40 ml + 2 ml kg^{-1} for every kg >10 kg
>20 kg	60 ml + 1 ml kg^{-1} for every kg >20 kg

predicts the time course of renal maturation (Langhendries et al. 1998). Similarly the clearance of the NMBD, d-tubocurarine, can be directly correlated with GFR (Fisher et al. 1982). GFR and active tubular secretion processes contribute to digoxin clearance, which is higher than might be expected from GFR alone (Halkin et al. 1978; Ng et al. 1981).

Intrauterine growth retardation can be associated with reduced renal function at birth, influencing aminoglycoside elimination (Allegaert et al. 2007a). Some drugs such as the NSAIDs may compromise renal clearance in early life: ibuprofen reduces GFR by 20% in preterm neonates, independent of gestational age (Allegaert et al. 2004, 2005). The kidney is also capable of metabolizing drugs; CYP2E1, which metabolizes ether anaesthetics, is active in the kidney. The very presence of CYP2E1 in the kidney has been held responsible for the degradation of ether anaesthetics and the release of nephrotoxic fluoride (Kharasch et al. 1995).

Immaturity of the clearance pathways can be used to our advantage when managing apnoea after anaesthesia in the preterm neonate. N_7-methylation of theophylline to produce caffeine is well-developed in the neonate whereas oxidative demethylation (CYP1A2) responsible for caffeine metabolism is deficient. Theophylline is effective for the management of postoperative apnoea in the preterm neonate, in part because it is a prodrug of caffeine, which is effective in controlling apnoea in this age group and can only be cleared slowly by the immature kidney (McNamara et al. 2004).

The hepatic system

Anatomy

The liver and biliary systems are derived from the endoderm of the dorsal foregut during the late third to the early fourth week of gestation. The liver weighs between 120 and 160 g in the term neonate, but remains structurally and physiologically immature. Peripheral branches of the intrahepatic biliary system require an additional 4–8 weeks before portal bile ducts can be identified histologically. Fetal vitelline veins give rise to the portal and hepatic veins. The liver is composed of eight structurally independent segments, each containing a feeding hepatic artery, portal vein, draining hepatic vein, and bile duct. Segment 1 is the caudate lobe. Segments 2 and 3 form the left lateral segment; and with segment 4, the left lobe of the liver is defined. Segments 5, 6, 7, and 8 constitute the right lobe of the liver.

The liver receives blood from two sources: the portal vein, which drains the spleen and intestine, and the hepatic artery, which provides systemic oxygenated blood directly to biliary epithelium and to the hepatic sinusoids. The portal vein accounts for approximately

70% of the blood flow to the liver. In the sinusoids, the hepatic arterial and portal venous blood mix, and intercalate among the hepatocytes, fenestrated sinusoidal cells and a host of resident immune cells (e.g. Kupffer cells). Sinusoids drain into terminal hepatic venules, which eventually coalesce to form the left and right hepatic veins, which in turn merge into the inferior vena cava just below the level of the right atrium. The liver is a large reservoir of blood and contains approximately 13% of the circulating blood volume.

The fetal and neonatal liver account for a greater percentage of body weight than the adult counterpart (3.6% of body weight *vs* 2.4% in adults) (Haddad et al. 2001). Hepatic organ blood flow in the neonate is 0.58 litres min^{-1} kg^{-1} tissue, and is reduced to 0.4 litres min^{-1} kg^{-1} tissue by 12 months' PNA. Adult rates of 0.25 litres min^{-1} kg^{-1} tissue are reached in teenage years (Bjorkman 2005). The neonatal liver contains approximately 20% fewer hepatocytes than adult livers, and the cells are nearly half the size of adult hepatocytes.

Physiology

Most critical biological functions such as glycolysis, bile acid synthesis, and removal of metabolic wastes for the fetus are managed by the maternal liver through the feto-placental circulation until birth. Gluconeogenesis and protein synthesis are active at 12 weeks' gestation. Although glycogen may be found in liver cells by 14 weeks' gestation, large amounts do not appear until the late third trimester. Consequently, those neonates born prematurely or who are small for gestational age have meagre glycogen stores and may develop hypoglycaemia. The liver function is still immature at birth, even in neonates born at term, and many of the hepatic enzyme systems responsible for drug and xenobiotic clearance develop within the first few years of postnatal life. This is exemplified by immature uridine diphosphoglucuronosyl transferase (UGT)-1A1 responsible for the conjugation of bilirubin that contributes to physiological jaundice of the newborn. This jaundice peaks on the fifth to seventh postnatal day. After this period, the concentration gradually decreases as UGT1A1 maturation occurs (Miyagi and Collier 2011), reaching adult values of less than 2 mg dl^{-1} by 1–2 months in both term and preterm infants. Sick preterm infants are especially at risk for kernicterus and are more aggressively treated to lower bilirubin concentrations than full-term infants.

For many drugs, the reduced metabolism in neonates relates to reduced total quantities of CYP enzymes in the hepatic microsomes. CYP activity measured in hepatic microsomes obtained from term neonates approached half of the activity found in adults (Fig. 69.18) (Aranda et al. 1974).

The liver plays a major role in metabolism, carbohydrate production, and regulation, and lipid and protein delivery to the tissues. α-Fetoprotein, the principal protein in the fetus, appears at 6 weeks' gestation and albumin synthesis starts at the end of the first trimester. Haematopoiesis starts in the liver at 6 weeks' gestation, moving exclusively to bone marrow after 6 weeks' PNA. Proteins involved in coagulation are reduced in the neonate. Albumin and α1-acid glycoprotein (AAG) concentrations are also reduced in neonates, albeit with a broad range of scatter (e.g. AAG 0.32–0.92 g $litre^{-1}$), but are similar to those in adults by 6 months (Luz et al. 1996, 1998). Binding capacity approaches adult values by 1 year of age. In addition, free fatty acids and unconjugated bilirubin compete with acidic drugs for albumin binding (e.g. ibuprofen and ceftriaxone). Neonates also have a tendency to manifest a metabolic acidosis that alters ionization and binding properties of plasma proteins. Bile acid secretion in neonates is reduced, and malabsorption of fat occurs.

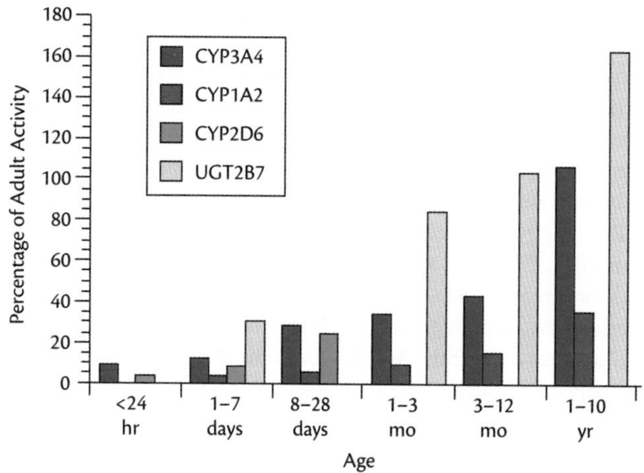

Figure 69.18 The activity of cytochrome P450 changes with age. Maturation of these enzyme systems is compared to glucuronide conjugation (UGT2B7).
From *New England Journal of Medicine*, Kearns G, Developmental Pharmacology—Drug Disposition, Action, and Therapy in Infants and Children, 349, 12, pp. 1157–67, Copyright © Massachusetts Medical Society. Reprinted with permission from Massachusetts Medical Society.

The liver plays an important role in coagulation. Although the haemostatic system is functionally adequate at birth, the system is immature. At birth, the vitamin K-dependent factors (II, VII, IX, and X), the contact factors (XII, XI, high-molecular-weight kininogen, and prekallikrein) and the four inhibitors (antithrombin III, heparin cofactor II, protein C, and protein S) are approximately half that of adult values (Andrew et al. 2000). The pattern of maturation in the postnatal period differs for different proteins, but most approach adult values within the first year of life (Andrew et al. 2000). The neonate's ability to generate thrombin is reduced, and remains 26% less than adult throughout childhood (Schmidt et al. 1989; Andrew et al. 1994). The lower vitamin K-dependent factors at birth (Andrew et al. 1987) increases the risk of haemorrhagic diseases of the newborn, while a lower production of thrombin in infancy may reduce the risk of thromboembolic complications.

Pharmacology aspects

The liver is one of the most important organs involved in drug metabolism. Hepatic clearance pathways can be broadly divided into two types: phase I reactions transform the drug via oxidation, reduction, or hydrolysis; while phase II reactions transform the drug via conjugation reactions, such as glucuronide conjugation, sulphation, conjugation, and acetylation, into more polar forms that can be eliminated through the kidney. Hepatic drug metabolism activity appears as early as 9–22 weeks' gestation when fetal liver enzyme activity may vary from 2% to 36% of adult activity (Pelkonen and Karki 1973).

Microsomal enzyme activity can be classified into three groups: (1) mature at birth but decreasing with age (e.g. CYP3A7 responsible for methadone clearance in neonates (Ward et al. 2014); (2) mature at birth and sustained through to adulthood [e.g. plasma esterases that clear remifentanil (Welzing et al. 2011)]; (3) immature at birth (Hines 2013). The latter accounts for the majority of clearance pathways.

CYPs are haem-containing proteins that provide many of the phase I drug metabolism for lipophilic compounds. The different pathways develop at different rates and are dependent on growth hormone and other mediators. Different enzymes develop within different hepatic zones and the maturity of some components may take months. Some appear to be switched on by birth, while in others birth is necessary but not sufficient for the onset of expression. CYP2E1 activity surges after birth, CYP2D6 becomes detectable soon after, CYP3A4 and CYP2C family appear during the first week, whereas CYP1A2 is the last to appear (Kearns et al. 2003). Neonates are dependent on the immature CYP3A4 for levobupivacaine clearance and CYP1A2 for ropivacaine clearance, dictating reduced epidural infusion rates in this age group (Berde 1992; Anderson and Hansen 2004).

The other major route of drug metabolism, designated phase II reactions, involves synthetic or conjugation reactions that increase the hydrophilicity of molecules to facilitate renal elimination. The phase II enzymes include UGT, sulfotransferase, *N*-acetyltransferase, glutathione *S*-transferase, and methyl transferase. One of the most familiar synthetic reactions in young infants is UGT; this enzyme system includes numerous isoforms and is also responsible for glucuronidation of endogenous compounds, such as bilirubin (UGT1A1). Chloramphenicol is also cleared by this route and failure to account for its immaturity caused infants to suffer fatal circulatory collapse, a condition known as the grey baby syndrome (Burns and Hodgman 1959; Sutherland 1959).

Morphine, paracetamol, dexmedetomidine and lorazepam also undergo glucuronidation. The maturation of UGT enzymes varies among isoforms, but, in general, adult activity is reached by 6–18 months of age (Miyagi and Collier 2011). Some of the confusion relating to maturation rates is attributable to the use of the per kilogram size model. The use of allometry with a maturation model has assisted understanding. The time courses of maturation of drug metabolism [morphine (Anand et al. 2008), paracetamol (Anderson and Holford 2009), and dexmedetomidine (Potts et al. 2008)] and GFR (Rhodin et al. 2009) are strikingly similar (Fig. 69.19) with 50% of size-adjusted adult values being reached between 8 and 12 weeks (maturation half-time, TM_{50}) after full term delivery. All three drugs are cleared predominantly by UGT that converts the parent compound into a water-soluble metabolite that is excreted by the kidneys, and maturation rates are similar to that described for GFR. Glucuronidation is the major metabolic pathway of propofol metabolism and this pathway is immature in neonates, although multiple CYP isoenzymes, including CYP2B6, CYP2C9 or CYP2A6 also contribute to its metabolism and cause a faster maturation profile than expected from glucuronide conjugation alone (Allegaert et al. 2007b). A phase I reaction (CYP3A4) is the major enzyme system for oxidation of levobupivacaine and clearance through this pathway is faster than those associated with UGT maturation.

Some enzyme systems are inducible before birth through maternal exposure to drugs, cigarette smoke, or other inducing agents. Other pathways may be induced through drug exposure after birth [e.g. phenobarbital induces CYP1A2, CYP2C9, CYP2C19, CYP3A4, and UGT (Perucca 2006, Strolin Benedetti et al. 2005, Corcos and Lagadic-Gossmann 2001)] and may be slowed by hypoxia, organ damage, or illness. Morphine clearance is reduced in very sick neonates who are candidates for extracorporeal membrane oxygenation, but clearance increases dramatically a few days after extracorporeal membrane oxygenation is started (Peters et al. 2005a).

Single nucleotide changes or polymorphisms in the DNA sequence in CYP enzymes may cause decreased or increased metabolic activity for a specific drug substrate. Polymorphism in the CYP2D6 isoenzyme results in some individuals exhibiting normal or reduced metabolic activity (poor metabolizers) while others are

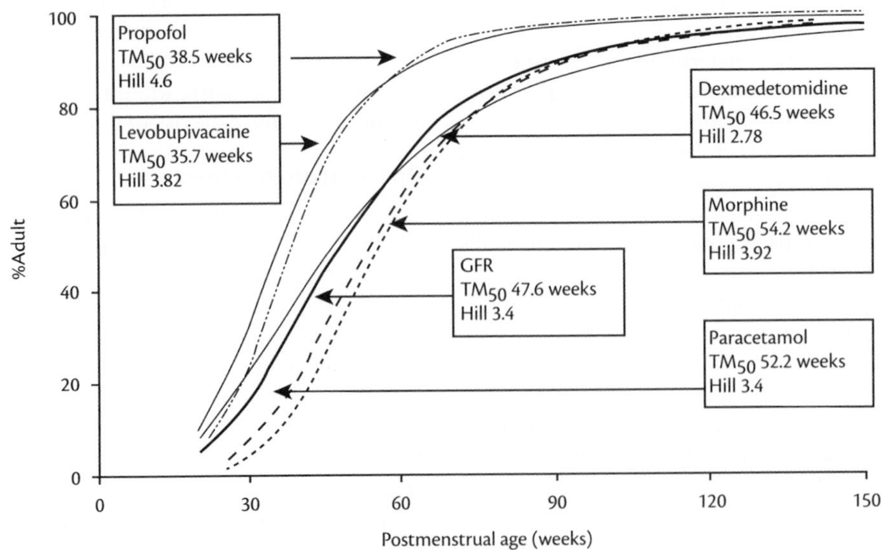

Figure 69.19 Clearance maturation, expressed as a percentage of mature clearance, of drugs where glucuronide conjugation (paracetamol, morphine, dexmedetomidine) plays a major role. These profiles are closely aligned with glomerular filtration rate (GFR). In contrast, cytochrome P450 isoenzymes also contribute to propofol and levobupivacaine metabolism and cause a faster maturation profile.

ultrafast metabolizers. The frequency of poor metabolizers varied among ethnic groups, occurring in approximately 7% of Caucasians and 0% to 1% of Chinese and Japanese (Bertilsson 1995).

Codeine is primarily a prodrug that undergoes metabolic activation by CYP2D6 *O*-demethylation to morphine. Poor metabolizers get little analgesia from codeine. We might anticipate that neonates achieve limited analgesia from codeine because CYP2D6 activity is minimal at birth. Its subsequent maturation after birth, however, is rapid. The active metabolite of tramadol (M1, *O*-desmethyl tramadol), which is produced by *O*-demethylation in the liver (CYP2D6), has been used to plot this rapid maturation (Fig. 69.20) using an activity score to differentiate metabolizer phenotypes (Allegaert et al. 2008).

AAG is an acute-phase reactant that increases after surgical stress. This causes an increase in total plasma concentrations for low to intermediate extraction drugs such as bupivacaine (Erichsen et al. 1996). The unbound concentration, however, will not change because clearance of the unbound drug is affected only by the intrinsic metabolizing capacity of the liver. Any increase in unbound concentrations observed during long-term epidurals is attributable to reduced clearance rather than AAG concentration (Anderson et al. 1997). Total bupivacaine concentrations increase in the first 24 h after surgery in neonates given analgesia by continuous epidural infusion, attributable to an increase of AAG. This increase, combined with reports of seizures in infants given epidural bupivacaine infusion, has led to recommendations to stop epidural infusion at 24 h. However, it is the unbound bupivacaine that is responsible for effect and this unbound concentration may not change, implying that the infusion could be run for longer (Bosenberg et al. 2005; Calder et al. 2012). Clearance is the key parameter and this is reduced in neonates. Unfortunately, clearance is associated with large between-subject variability and this means that unbound bupivacaine concentrations may continue to increase in some individuals with very low clearance. The induction dose of thiopental is lower in neonates than children. It is possible that this is related to decreased binding of thiopental to plasma albumin; 13% of the drug is unbound in newborns compared with 7% in adults (Russo and Bressolle 1998).

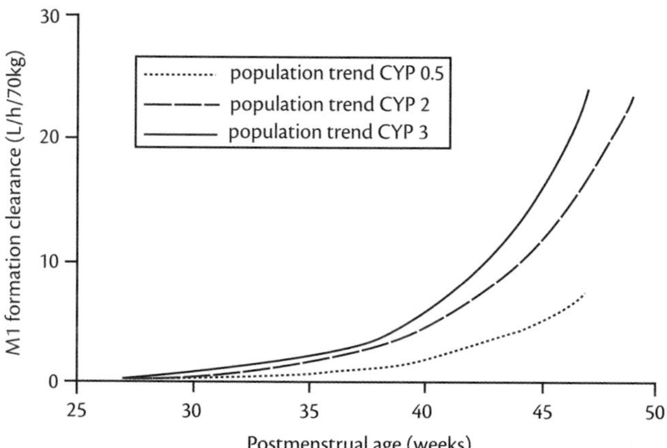

Figure 69.20 Tramadol M1 metabolite formation clearance (CYP2D6) increases with postmenstrual age. Rate of increase varies with genotype expression.
Reproduced with permission from Allegaert et al. Covariates of tramadol disposition in the first months of life. *British Journal of Anaesthesia*, 2008, Volume 100, Issue 4, pp. 525–532, by permission of the Board of Management and Trustees of the British Journal of Anaesthesia.

Coagulation system components mature at different rates and altered blood coagulation factor ratios may contribute to different responses to therapy in infants. The reduced vitamin K-dependent enzyme metabolism in the immature liver may increase resistance to warfarin therapy (Takahashi et al. 2000). The response to heparin may be less because antithrombin III concentrations in the first 3 months are reduced (Andrew et al. 1988, 1990), although this effect may be counteracted by an increased inhibition of thrombin from higher concentrations of α2-macroglobulin, resulting in negligible clinical differences between infants and older children.

Haematopoietic system

The blood volume of a full-term neonate depends on the time of cord clamping, which modifies the volume of placental transfusion. The blood volume is 93 ml kg^{-1} when cord clamping is delayed after delivery, compared with 82 ml kg^{-1} with immediate cord clamping (Usher et al. 1963; Usher and Lind 1965). Within the first 4 h after delivery, however, fluid is lost from the blood and the plasma volume contracts by as much as 25%. The larger the placental transfusion, the larger this loss of fluid in the first few hours after birth, with resultant haemoconcentration. The blood volume in preterm infants is greater (90–105 ml kg^{-1}) than it is in full-term infants because of increased plasma volume.

The normal haemoglobin range in the neonate is between 14 and 20 g dl^{-1}. The site of sampling must be considered when interpreting these values for the diagnosis of neonatal anaemia or hyperviscosity syndrome. Capillary sampling (e.g. heel stick) generally overestimates the true haemoglobin concentration because of stasis in peripheral vessels that results in a loss of plasma and produces haemoconcentration. The net effect may be an increase in haemoglobin by as much as 6 g dl^{-1} As a result, venepuncture is preferred over capillary sampling. In 1% of infants, fetal–maternal transfusion before the umbilical cord is cut may explain much of the 'lower normal' haemoglobin values reported.

Erythropoietic activity from the bone marrow decreases immediately after birth in both full-term and preterm infants. The cord blood reticulocyte count of 5% persists for a few days and declines below 1% by 1 week. This is followed by a slight increase to 1–2% by the 12th week, where it remains throughout childhood. Preterm infants have greater reticulocyte counts (up to 10%) at birth. Abnormal reticulocyte values reflect haemorrhage or haemolysis.

In term infants, the haemoglobin concentration decreases during the 9th to 12th week to reach a nadir of 10–11 g dl^{-1} (haematocrit 30% to 33%) and then increases. This decrease in haemoglobin concentration is as a result of a decrease in erythropoiesis and to some extent as a result of a shortened lifespan of the red blood cells. In preterm infants, the decrease in the haemoglobin concentration is greater and is directly related to the degree of prematurity; also, the nadir is reached earlier (4–8 weeks) (O'Brien and Pearson 1971). In infants weighing 800–1000 g, the decrement may reach a very low concentration, 8 g dl^{-1}. This 'anaemia' (physiological anaemia of the newborn) is a normal physiological adjustment to extrauterine life. Despite the reduction in haemoglobin, the oxygen delivery to the tissues may not be compromised because of a shift of the oxygen–haemoglobin dissociation curve (to the right), secondary to an increase of 2,3-diphosphoglycerate. In addition, fetal haemoglobin is replaced by adult-type haemoglobin, which also results in a shift in the same direction. In neonates, especially preterm infants, reduced haemoglobin concentrations may be associated with apnoea and tachycardia (Ross et al. 1989). Infants with anaemia of prematurity have been found to have an inadequate production of erythropoietin and recombinant human erythropoietin in these infants stimulates erythropoiesis and decreases the need for transfusions (Shannon et al. 1995).

After the third month, the haemoglobin concentration stabilizes at 11.5–12.0 g dl^{-1}, until about 2 years of age. The haemoglobin values of full-term and preterm infants are comparable after the first year. Thereafter, there is a gradual increase in the haemoglobin concentration to mean values at puberty of 14.0 g dl^{-1} for females and 15.5 g dl^{-1} for males.

Immunological system

The white blood cell count may normally reach 21 000 mm^{-3} in the first 24 h of life and 12 000 mm^{-3} at the end of the first week, with the number of neutrophils equalling the number of lymphocytes. It then decreases gradually, reaching adult values at puberty. At birth, neutrophil granulocytes predominate but rapidly decrease in number so that during the first week of life and through 4 years of age the lymphocyte is the predominant cell. After the fourth year, the values approximate an adult's. Neonates have an increased susceptibility to bacterial infection, which is related in part to immaturity of leucocyte function. Sepsis may be associated with a minimal leucocyte response or even with leucopenia. Spurious increases in the white blood cell content may be because of drugs (e.g. adrenaline). The incidence of neonatal sepsis correlates inversely with gestational age and may be as great as 58% in very low-birth-weight infants (Stoll et al. 2010).

Neuromuscular system

Physiology

A number of changes occur in the first few years of life. The neuromuscular junction is immature and structurally different in neonates. Fetal neonatal postjunctional acetylcholine receptors differ from adult receptors (Mishina et al. 1986; Jaramillo and Schuetze 1988). Adult receptors possess five subunits—two α, one β, one δ, and one ε subunits. Preterm neonates (<31 weeks' PMA) have a γ-subunit instead of an ε-subunit in their neuromuscular receptor (Hesselmans et al. 1993). Fetal receptors have a greater opening time than adult receptors, allowing more sodium to enter the cell with a consequently larger depolarizing potential. The resulting increased sensitivity to acetylcholine is at odds with the observed increased sensitivity to NMBDs, but may compensate for reduced acetylcholine stores in the terminal nerve endings (Jaramillo et al. 1988).

Skeletal muscle properties change in infancy. Muscle fibres can be grouped into two broad types: type I fibres are rich in oxidative enzymes and type II fibres that are rich in glycolytic enzymes. Preterm infants tolerate respiratory loads poorly. The diaphragm in the preterm neonate contains only10% of the slowly contracting type I fibres. This proportion increases to 25% at term and to 55% by 2 years of age (Keens et al. 1978). A similar maturation pattern has been observed for the intercostal muscles (Keens et al. 1978). Type I fibres tend to be more sensitive to NMBDs than type II fibres and consequently the diaphragmatic function in neonates may be better preserved and recover earlier than peripheral muscles (Donati et al. 1986; Laycock et al. 1988a, 1988b; Meretoja 1990).

The proportion of muscle in relation to body weight is reduced, but there is a dramatic increase in muscle bulk from 5 to 10 years (Fig. 69.2). The ECF that NMBDs distribute to is increased (Fig. 69.3). In addition, the metabolic clearance pathways for NMBDs are often immature and the relationship between parasympathetic and sympathetic tone is unbalanced in early life.

Pharmacology

The dose of NMBDs at different ages depends on a complex interweaving of pharmacodynamic and pharmacokinetic factors. The volume of distribution mirrors ECF changes and can be predicted using either an allometric ¾-power model or the surface area model, both of which approximate ECF changes with weight (Anderson and Meakin 2002). This occurs because ECF is a major contributor to the volume of distribution at steady-state (V_{ss}). These volume changes are true for both depolarizing (suxamethonium) (Cook and Fisher 1975; Meakin et al. 1989) and non-depolarizing NMBDs (Cook 1981).

The age-related dose required to achieve a predetermined level of neuromuscular block varies. The ED_{95} of vecuronium, for example, is 47 (SD 11) mcg kg^{-1} in neonates and infants, 81 (SD 12) mcg kg^{-1} in children between 3 and 10 years of age and 55 (SD 12) mcg kg^{-1} in patients aged 13 years or older (Meretoja et al. 1988). Similar profiles have been reported for other NMBDs (Basta et al. 1982; Laycock et al. 1988a; Meakin et al. 1988; Goudsouzian et al. 1993; Woelfel et al. 1993). The increased dose in children may be attributable to increased muscle bulk. Dose is greater than anticipated in neonates who have immaturity of the neuromuscular junction because the extracellular volume is increased but the duration of neuromuscular block is greater in neonates because of immature clearance pathways. The plasma concentration required in neonates to achieve the same level of neuromuscular block as in children or adults is 20–50% less (Fisher et al. 1982, 1985; Kalli and Meretoja 1988; Fisher et al. 1990; Wierda et al. 1997).

The onset time for NMBDs in neonates is faster than it is in older children than adults. Onset time (time to maximal effect) after vecuronium 70 mcg kg^{-1} is most rapid for infants [1.5 (SD 0.6] min compared with that for children [2.4 (SD 1.4) min] and adults [2.9 (SD 0.2) min] (Fisher and Miller 1983). Similar observations are reported for other intermediate- and long-acting NMBDs (Meretoja 1990). The more rapid onset of these drugs in neonates has been attributed to a greater cardiac output seen with the per kilogram model (Meretoja 1990).

Suxamethonium remains the NMBD with the most rapid onset. The onset time of a paralysing dose (1.0 mg kg^{-1}) of suxamethonium 1 mg kg^{-1} is 35–55 s in children and adolescents. The onset time after 3 mg kg^{-1} in neonates is faster (30–40 s) (Meakin et al. 1990). Onset time is dependent on both age and dose; the younger the child and the greater the dose, the shorter the onset time. Suxamethonium may also be given as an intramuscular injection for intubation in children (Gronert and Brandom 1994). There are few data available from neonates, but infant studies suggest that a dose of up to 5 mg kg^{-1} may be required to achieve satisfactory intubating conditions (Sutherland et al. 1983). Onset to maximum blockade is slow [4 (SD 0.6) min] and mean full recovery of T1 occurred in 15.6 (SD 0.9) min after injection (Sutherland et al. 1983).

Total plasma clearance of non-depolarizing NMBDs cleared by renal (alcuronium and d-tubocurarine) or hepatic pathways (pancuronium, rocuronium, and vecuronium), or both, are all reduced in neonates (Matteo et al. 1984; Fisher et al. 1985; Tassonyi et al. 1995; Wierda et al. 1997; Meretoja and Erkola 1997). In contrast, the clearances of atracurium and cisatracurium are neither renal nor hepatic dependent bur rather depend on Hofmann elimination, ester hydrolysis, and other unspecified pathways (Fisher et al. 1986). Clearance of these drugs is increased in neonates when expressed as per kilogram (Brandom et al. 1986; Reich et al. 2004; Imbeault et al. 2006). When clearance is standardized using allometric ¾-power scaling, the clearances for atracurium and cisatracurium are similar throughout all age groups. The clearance of suxamethonium, expressed per kilogram, also decreases as age increases (Cook et al. 1976; Goudsouzian and Liu 1984). Suxamethonium is hydrolysed by butyrylcholinesterase. These observations are consistent with that observed for the clearance of remifentanil (Rigby-Jones et al. 2007), which is also cleared by plasma esterases. These clearance pathways are mature at birth.

Regarding reversal of neuromuscular block, the distribution volumes of neostigmine are similar in infants (2–10 months), children (1–6 years), and adults (V_{ss} 0.5 litres kg^{-1}) whereas the elimination half-life is less in the paediatric patients (Fisher et al. 1983). Clearance decreases as age increases (Fisher et al. 1983). The train-of four (TOF) ratio recovers to 0.7 in less than 10 min when a 90% neuromuscular block from pancuronium is antagonized with neostigmine 30–40 μg kg^{-1} in infants, children, or adults (Meakin et al. 1983; Meistelman et al. 1988; Debaene et al. 1989; Meretoja et al. 1996). Neonates have the most rapid times to full recovery after neostigmine antagonism (Meakin et al. 1983; Bevan et al. 1994). For example, reversal of an atracurium-induced 90% neuromuscular block in infants and children by neostigmine 50 μg kg^{-1} was fastest in the youngest age group (Kirkegaard-Nielsen et al. 1995). The time to a TOF-ratio of 0.7 was 4 min in neonates and infants, 6 min in 2- to 10-year-old children, and 8 min in adolescents.

Sugammadex, a relatively new drug that reverses the neuromuscular blocking effects of rocuronium and, to a lesser extent, vecuronium, at a dose of 2 mg kg^{-1} reverses a rocuronium-induced moderate neuromuscular block in infants, children and adolescents (Plaud et al. 2009). The average time to recover a TOF-ratio of 0.9 at the time of appearance of the second twitch response was 1.2, 1.1, and 1.2 min in children, adolescents, and adults, respectively.

The gastrointestinal tract

Anatomy

In the fetus, the digestive tract consists of the developing foregut and hindgut. These rapidly elongate so that a loop of gut is forced into the yolk sac. At 5–7 weeks, this loop twists around the axis of the superior mesenteric artery and returns to the abdominal cavity. Maturation occurs gradually from the proximal to the distal end. Blood vessels and nerves (Auerbach and Meissner plexuses) are developed by 13 weeks of gestation, and peristalsis begins. The pancreas arises from two outgrowths of the foregut; a diverticulum of the foregut gives rise to the liver.

Physiology

Enzyme concentrations of enterokinase and lipase increase with gestational age but are reduced at birth compared with older children. Full-term neonates and preterm infants handle protein loads reasonably well, although preterm infants may have difficulty with large loads. Fat digestion is limited, particularly in preterm infants, who absorb only 65% of adult levels. Neonatal duodenal motility undergoes marked maturational changes between 29 and 32 weeks of gestation. This is one factor limiting tolerance of enteral feeding before 29 to 30 weeks of gestation (Morriss et al. 1986).

Swallowing is a complex process that is under central and peripheral control. The reflex is initiated in the medulla, through cranial nerves to the muscles that control the passage of food through the pharyngo-oesophageal sphincter. In the process, the tongue, soft palate, pharynx, and larynx all are smoothly coordinated. Any pathological condition of these structures can interfere with normal swallowing. Neuromuscular incoordination, however, is more likely to be responsible for any dysfunction. This is particularly evident when the CNS has sustained damage either before or during delivery.

Meconium is the material contained in the intestinal tract before birth. It consists of desquamated epithelial cells from the intestinal tract and bile, pancreatic and intestinal secretions, and water (70%). Meconium is usually passed in the first few hours after birth; virtually all term neonates pass their first stool by 48 h. However, passage of the first stool is usually delayed in low-birth-weight neonates, probably because of immaturity of the motility and lack of gut hormones as a result of delayed enteral feeding. Meconium ileus occurs in cystic fibrosis or Hirschsprung disease. Lower oesophageal pressures are reduced at birth but increase steadily reaching adult values 3–6 weeks postnatally. Daily vomiting or 'spitting up' may be seen in half of all infants between 0 and 3 months of age and up to two-thirds of 4- to 6-month-old infants. Most of these infants suffer no ill-effect ('happy spitter') and grow well. This condition usually begins in the first weeks of life and resolves spontaneously by 9–24 months of age as solid food is introduced and the child assumes the upright position. Between 1:300 and 1:1000 infants have reflux that is significant enough to warrant treatment to avoid complications.

The gastrointestinal transit time in the infant is less than that of an adult and increases with increasing age. The normal physiological range of stool frequency varies greatly (from 10 times a day to 1–2 times a week and more often in breast-fed infants. The frequency of bowel movements gradually declines over the first years of life, reaching adult habits at about 4 years of age.

Necrotizing enterocolitis is an acquired gastrointestinal disease associated with significant morbidity and mortality in prematurely born neonates. Necrotizing enterocolitis affects about 10% of preterm neonates weighing less than 1500 g or 1–5% of all neonatal intensive care unit admissions. Combined with enteral feeds and bacterial colonization, inflammatory mediators are released, leading to a propagated inflammatory response with both pro- and anti-inflammatory influences (Lahmiti and Aboussad 2011).

Pharmacology aspects

Anaesthetic drugs are mainly administered intravenously or through inhalation, but premedication and postoperative pain relief are commonly administered enterally. Absorption after oral administration is slower in neonates than in children as a result of delayed gastric emptying. Adult rates may not be reached until 6–8 months (Grand et al. 1976; Liang et al. 1998). Congenital malformations (e.g. duodenal atresia), co-administration of drugs (e.g. opioids), or disease characteristics (e.g. necrotizing enterocolitis) may further contribute to absorption variability. Slow gastric emptying and reduced clearance may dictate reduced doses and frequency of administration (Fig. 69.21). For example, a mean steady-state

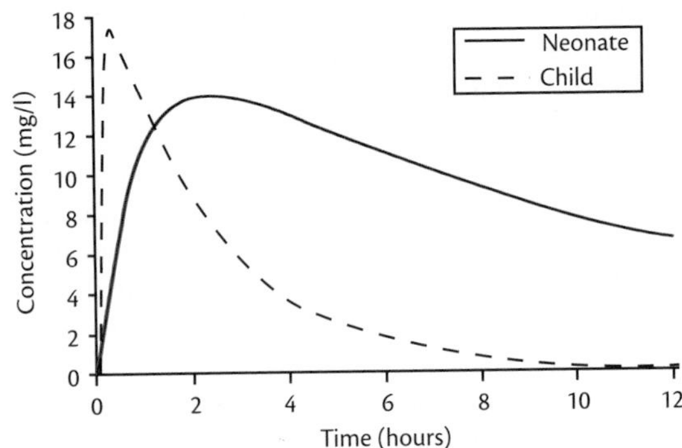

Figure 69.21 Simulated mean predicted time–concentration profiles for a term neonate and a 5-year-old child given paracetamol elixir. The time to peak concentration is delayed in neonates because of slow gastric emptying and reduced clearance.

Data from Anderson, BJ et al. *Anesthesiology* 2002; 96: 1336–45.

target paracetamol concentration above 10 mg litre^{-1} at trough can be achieved by an oral dose of 25 mg kg^{-1} day^{-1} in premature neonates at 30 weeks, 45 mg kg^{-1} day^{-1} at 34 weeks, and 60 mg kg^{-1} day^{-1} at 40 weeks of PMA (Anderson et al. 2002). Because gastric emptying is slow in premature neonates, dosing may only be required twice a day (Anderson et al. 2002). Rectal administration (e.g. thiopental and methohexital) is speedier for neonates undergoing cardiac catheter study or radiological sedation. However, the between-individual absorption and relative bioavailability variability may be more extensive compared with oral administration, making rectal administration less suitable for repeated administration (van Hoogdalem et al. 1991).

There is an age-dependent expression of intestinal motilin receptors and the modulation of antral contractions in neonates. Prokinetic agents may not be useful in very preterm neonates, useful only in part, in older preterm infants, but very useful in full-term infants.

Intragastric pH is elevated (>4) in neonates (Rodbro et al. 1967; Agunod et al. 1969) increasing the bioavailability of acid-labile compounds (penicillin G) and decreasing the bioavailability of weak acids (phenobarbital) when given orally (Huang and High 1953). The infant gut is more permeable to large molecules (e.g. proteins and high-molecular-weight drugs) than that of older children. Many of the effects of the immature gastrointestinal system are either not characterized or the effect of immaturity uncertain. Immature conjugation and transport of bile salts into the intestinal lumen may effect lipophilic drug blood concentrations (Poley et al. 1964; Suchy et al. 1981), while splanchnic blood flow changes in the first few weeks of life may alter concentration gradients across the intestinal mucosa and consequent absorption. The role of altered intestinal microflora in neonates and its effect on drugs [e.g. digoxin inactivation (Linday et al. 1987)] is uncertain.

The skin and thermoregulation

Neonates and particularly preterm neonates are susceptible to hypothermia. Heat loss in children occurs by four possible routes: convection (34%), conduction (3%), radiation (39%), and evaporation (24%). Evaporative heat loss and insensible fluid loss are increased in the preterm neonate because the epidermis is 'thinner' and has less keratin and subcutaneous fat (Hammarlund et al. 1986). Loss through conduction and convection are also increased because of the large surface area to mass ratio. Thermoregulation is poorly developed. Adults and children can generate heat by shivering. Premature neonates are compromised because brown fat stores, used for non-shivering thermogenesis are low; they are accumulated around the kidneys, adrenal glands, scapulae, and in the mediastinum during the last trimester of pregnancy. This brown adipose tissue comprised 2–6% of the term neonate's weight. In addition, regulation of skin blood flow is less efficient in the preterm neonate (Jahnukainen et al. 1993). Anaesthesia further disrupts the normal thermoregulation (Fig. 69.22).

Pharmacology implications

General anaesthetics depress the thermoregulatory response in children, widening the 'set' point and decreasing the gain of the vasoconstrictor response (Bissonnette and Sessler 1990; Bissonnette and Sessler 1992; Nebbia et al. 1996). Heat is also lost from the core to peripheral tissues. Hypothermia can contribute to a metabolic acidosis, impaired peripheral perfusion, increased risk of infection, and coagulation abnormalities. The reduced basal metabolic rate associated with hypothermia reduces the clearance of almost all drugs. The use of forced air warmers has greatly improved temperature regulation during anaesthesia. The use of thermoneutral incubators for transport and warming of the operating room up to 26°C before exposing the neonate also helps. A warming pad on the

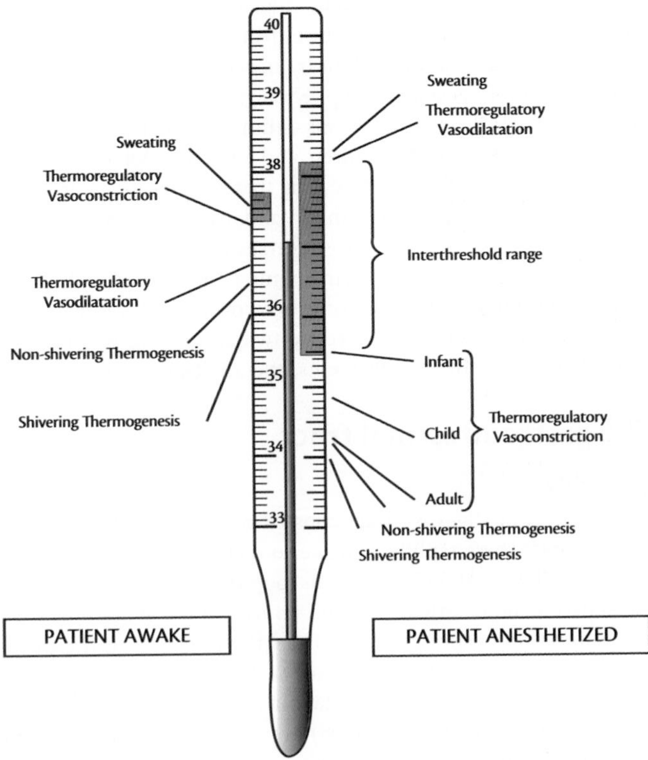

Figure 69.22 Schematic illustration of thermoregulatory thresholds and gains in awake and anaesthetized states, demonstrating a broadening of the response thresholds for compensatory mechanisms under anaesthesia but earlier vasoconstriction in infants during hypothermia.

Reproduced with permission from *Pediatric Anesthesia*, editor Bisonnette B, 2011. Chapter 14 temperature Regulation: Physiology and Pharmacology, fig 14.2, p229 PMPH-USA, Shelton., Connecticut. Adapted from Bissonnette B, Thermoregulation and Paediatric Anaesthesia, *Current Opinion in Anaesthesiology*, 6, pp. 537–542, Copyright © Wolters Kluwer Health Ltd.

operating table reduces conductive heat loss; use of overhead heat lamps reduces radiant heat loss; and keeping the skin dry reduces evaporative heat loss. Warming and humidifying inspired gases should be considered when high fresh gas flows are used.

The larger relative skin surface area, increased cutaneous perfusion, and thinner stratum corneum in neonates increase systemic exposure of topical drugs (e.g. corticosteroids, local anaesthetic creams, and antiseptics). Neonates have a tendency to form methaemoglobin because they have reduced methaemoglobin reductase activity and fetal haemoglobin is more readily oxidized compared with adult haemoglobin. This, combined with increased percutaneous absorption resulted in a reluctance to use repeat lidocaine-prilocaine cream in this age group (Taddio et al. 1997b). Similarly, cutaneous application of iodine antiseptics can result in transient hypothyroidism.

Declaration of interest

None declared.

References

Agunod M, Yamaguchi N, Lopez R, Luhby AL, Glass GB. Correlative study of hydrochloric acid, pepsin, and intrinsic factor secretion in newborns and infants. *Am J Dig Dis* 1969; **14**: 400–14

Al-Hathlol K, Idiong N, Hussain A, *et al.* A study of breathing pattern and ventilation in newborn infants and adult subjects. *Acta Paediatrica* 2000; **89**: 1420–5

Allegaert K, Anderson BJ, Van Den Anker JN, Vanhaesebrouck S, De Zegher F. Renal drug clearance in preterm neonates: relation to prenatal growth. *Ther Drug Monit* 2007a; **29**: 284–91

Allegaert K, Cossey V, Debeer A, *et al.* The impact of ibuprofen on renal clearance in preterm infants is independent of the gestational age. *Pediatr Nephrol* 2005; **20**: 740–3

Allegaert K, Cossey V, Langhendries JP, *et al.* Effects of co-administration of ibuprofen-lysine on the pharmacokinetics of amikacin in preterm infants during the first days of life. *Biol Neonate* 2004; **86**: 207–11

Allegaert K, Peeters MY, Verbesselt R, *et al.* Inter-individual variability in propofol pharmacokinetics in preterm and term neonates. *Br J Anaesth* 2007b; **99**: 864–70

Allegaert K, Van Den Anker JN, De Hoon JN, *et al.* Covariates of tramadol disposition in the first months of life. *Br J Anaesth* 2008; **100**: 525–32

Anand KJ, Anderson BJ, Holford NH, *et al.* Morphine pharmacokinetics and pharmacodynamics in preterm and term neonates: secondary results from the NEOPAIN trial. *Br J Anaesth* 2008; **101**: 680–9

Anderson BJ, Hansen TG. Getting the best from pediatric pharmacokinetic data. *Paediatr Anaesth* 2004; **14**: 713–5

Anderson BJ, Holford NH. Mechanism-based concepts of size and maturity in pharmacokinetics. *Annu Rev Pharmacol Toxicol* 2008; **48**: 303–32

Anderson BJ, Holford NH. Mechanistic basis of using body size and maturation to predict clearance in humans. *Drug Metab Pharmacokinet* 2009; **24**: 25–36

Anderson BJ, Holford NH. Tips and traps analyzing pediatric PK data. *Paediatric Anaesthesia* 2011; **21**: 222–37

Anderson BJ, McKee AD, Holford NH. Size, myths and the clinical pharmacokinetics of analgesia in paediatric patients. *Clin Pharmacokinet* 1997; **33**: 313–27

Anderson BJ, Meakin GH. Scaling for size: some implications for paediatric anaesthesia dosing. *Paediatr Anaesth* 2002; **12**: 205–19

Anderson BJ, Van Lingen RA, Hansen TG, Lin YC, Holford NH. Acetaminophen developmental pharmacokinetics in premature neonates and infants: a pooled population analysis. *Anesthesiology* 2002; **96**: 1336–45

Andrew M, Mitchell L, Vegh P, Ofosu F. Thrombin regulation in children differs from adults in the absence and presence of heparin. *Thromb Haemost* 1994; **72**: 836–42

Andrew M, Monagle P, Brooker L. Developmental hemostasis: relevance to thrombotic complications in pediatric patients. In: *Thromboembolic Complications During Infancy and Childhood.* Hamilton. London: B.C. Decker. Inc, 2000; 5–46

Andrew M, Paes B, Johnston M. Development of the hemostatic system in the neonate and young infant. *Am J Pediatr Hematol Oncol* 1990; **12**: 95–104

Andrew M, Paes B, Milner R, *et al.* Development of the human coagulation system in the healthy premature infant. *Blood* 1988; **72**: 1651–7

Andrew M, Paes B, Milner R, *et al.* Development of the human coagulation system in the full-term infant. *Blood* 1987; **70**: 165–72

Aperia A, Broberger O, Elinder G, Herin P, Zetterstrom R. Postnatal development of renal function in pre-term and full-term infants. *Acta Paediatr Scand* 1981; **70**: 183–7

Aranda JV, Macleod SM, Renton KW, Eade NR. Hepatic microsomal drug oxidation and electron transport in newborn infants. *J Pediatrics* 1974; **85**: 534–42

Arant BS, Jr. Developmental patterns of renal functional maturation compared in the human neonate. *J Pediatr* 1978; **92**: 705–12

Arant BS, Jr. Postnatal development of renal function during the first year of life. *Pediatric Nephrology* 1987; **1**: 308–13

Arens R, Mcdonough JM, Corbin AM, *et al.* Linear dimensions of the upper airway structure during development: assessment by magnetic resonance imaging. *Am J Respir Crit Care Med* 2002; **165**: 117–22

Basta SJ, Ali HH, Savarese JJ, *et al.* Clinical pharmacology of atracurium besylate (BW 33A): a new non-depolarizing muscle relaxant. *Anesth Analg* 1982; **61**: 723–9

Bates E, Reilly J, Wulfeck B, *et al.* Differential effects of unilateral lesions on language production in children and adults. *Brain Lang* 2001; **79**: 223–65

Baum VC, Palmisano BW. The immature heart and anesthesia. *Anesthesiology* 1997; **87**: 1529–48

Berde C. Convulsions associated with pediatric regional anesthesia. *Anesth Analg* 1992; **75**: 164–6

Bertilsson L. Geographical/interracial differences in polymorphic drug oxidation. Current state of knowledge of cytochromes P450 (CYP) 2D6 and 2C19. *Clin Pharmacokinet* 1995; **29**: 192–209

Bevan JC, Purday JP, Reimer EJ, Bevan DR. Reversal of doxacurium and pancuronium neuromuscular blockade with neostigmine in children. *Can J Anaesth* 1994; **41**: 1074–80

Bibace R, Walsh ME. Development of children's concepts of illness. *Pediatrics* 1980; **66**: 912–7

Bissonnette B, Sessler DI. The thermoregulatory threshold in infants and children anesthetized with isoflurane and caudal bupivacaine. *Anesthesiology* 1990; **73**: 1114–8

Bissonnette B, Sessler DI. Thermoregulatory thresholds for vasoconstriction in pediatric patients anesthetized with halothane or halothane and caudal bupivacaine. *Anesthesiology* 1992; **76**: 387–92

Bjorkman S. Prediction of drug disposition in infants and children by means of physiologically based pharmacokinetic (PBPK) modelling: theophylline and midazolam as model drugs. *Br J Clin Pharmacol* 2005; **59**: 691–704

Bosenberg AT, Bland BA, Schulte Steinberg O, Downing JW. Thoracic epidural anesthesia via caudal route in infants. *Anesthesiology* 1988; **69**: 265–9

Bosenberg AT, Thomas J, Cronje L, *et al.* Pharmacokinetics and efficacy of ropivacaine for continuous epidural infusion in neonates and infants. *Paediatr Anaesth* 2005; **15**: 739–49

Brandom BW, Stiller RL, Cook DR, Woelfel SK, Chakravorti S, Lai A. Pharmacokinetics of atracurium in anaesthetized infants and children. *Br J Anaesth* 1986; **58**: 1210–3

Briner A, Nikonenko I, De Roo M, Dayer A, Muller D, Vutskits L. Developmental Stage-dependent persistent impact of propofol anesthesia on dendritic spines in the rat medial prefrontal cortex. *Anesthesiology* 2011; **115**: 282–93

Brion LP, Fleischman AR, McCarton C, Schwartz GJ. A simple estimate of glomerular filtration rate in low birth weight infants during the first year of life: noninvasive assessment of body composition and growth. *J Pediatr* 1986; **109**: 698–707

Burns LE, Hodgman JE. Fatal circulatory collapse in premature infants receiving chloramphenicol. *N Engl J Med* 1959; **261**: 1318

Calder A, Bell GT, Andersson M, Thomson AH, Watson DG, Morton NS. Pharmacokinetic profiles of epidural bupivacaine and ropivacaine following single-shot and continuous epidural use in young infants. *Paediatr Anaesth* 2012; **22**: 430–7

Chalkiadis GA, Anderson BJ. Age and size are the major covariates for prediction of levobupivacaine clearance in children. *Paediatr Anaesth* 2006; **16**: 275–82

Chantler PD, Clements RE, Sharp L, George KP, Tan LB, Goldspink DF. The influence of body size on measurements of overall cardiac function. *Am J Physiol Heart Circ Physiol* 2005; **289**: H2059–65

Choudhuri S, Klaassen CD. Structure, function, expression, genomic organization, and single nucleotide polymorphisms of human ABCB1 (MDR1), ABCC (MRP), and ABCG2 (BCRP) efflux transporters. *Int J Toxicol* 2006; **25**: 231–59

Cockcroft DW, Gault MH. Prediction of creatinine clearance from serum creatinine. *Nephron* 1976; **16**: 31–41

Cole M, Price L, Parry A, *et al.* Estimation of glomerular filtration rate in paediatric cancer patients using 51CR-EDTA population pharmacokinetics. *Br J Cancer* 2004; **90**: 60–4

Cook DR. Muscle relaxants in infants and children. *Anesth Analg* 1981; **60**: 335–43

Cook DR, Fisher CG. Neuromuscular blocking effects of succinylcholine in infants and children. *Anesthesiology* 1975; **42**: 662–5

Cook DR, Wingard LB, Taylor FH. Pharmacokinetics of succinylcholine in infants, children, and adults. *Clin Pharmacol Ther* 1976; **20**: 493–8

Corcos L, Lagadic-Gossmann D. Gene induction by Phenobarbital: an update on an old question that receives key novel answers. *Pharmacol Toxicol* 2001; **89**: 113–22

Cote CJ, Zaslavsky A, Downes JJ, *et al.* Postoperative apnea in former preterm infants after inguinal herniorrhaphy. A combined analysis. *Anesthesiology* 1995; **82**: 809–22

Creeley CE, Olney JW. The young: neuroapoptosis induced by anesthetics and what to do about it. *Anesth Analg* 2010; **110**: 442–8

Cuevas L, Yeh TF, John EG, Cuevas D, Plides RS. The effect of low-dose dopamine infusion on cardiopulmonary and renal status in premature newborns with respiratory distress syndrome. *Am J Dis Child* 1991; **145**: 799–803

Dalal PG, Murray D, Messner AH, Feng A, Mcallister J, Molter D. Pediatric laryngeal dimensions: an age-based analysis. *Anesth Analg* 2009; **108**: 1475–9

Davidson, AJ, Disma N, de Graaff JC, *et al.* Neurodevelopmental outcome at 2 years of age after general anaesthesia and awake-regional anaesthesia in infancy (GAS): an international multicentre, randomised controlled trial. *Lancet* 2016; **387**: 239–50

Davies D. Brain development. In: *Child Development: A Practitioners Guide*, 3rd Edn. New York: The Guildford Press, 2011; 39–59

De Onis M, Onyango AW, Borghi E, Siyam A, Nishida C, Siekmann J. Development of a WHO growth reference for school-aged children and adolescents. *Bull World Health Organ* 2007; **85**: 660–7

Debaene B, Meistelman C, D'hollander A. Recovery from vecuronium neuromuscular blockade following neostigmine administration in infants, children, and adults during halothane anesthesia. *Anesthesiology* 1989; **71**: 840–4

Dickinson DF. The normal ECG in childhood and adolescence. *Heart* 2005; **91**: 1626–30

Dionne JM, Abitbol CL, Flynn JT. Hypertension in infancy: diagnosis, management and outcome. *Pediatr Nephrol* 2012; **27**: 17–32

Dixon SD, Stein MT. Understanding children: theories, concepts and insights. In: Dixon SD, Stein MT, eds. *Encounters with Children. Pediatric Behavior and Development*, 4th Edn. Philadelphia, PA: Mosby Elsevier, 2006; 12–43

Donati F, Antzaka C, Bevan DR. Potency of pancuronium at the diaphragm and the adductor pollicis muscle in humans. *Anesthesiology* 1986; **65**: 1–5

Eckenhoff JE. Some anatomic considerations of the infant larynx influencing endotracheal anesthesia. *Anesthesiology* 1951; **12**: 401–10

Edelmann CM, Soriano JR, Boichis H, Gruskin AB, Acosta MI. Renal bicarbonate reabsorption and hydrogen ion excretion in normal infants. *J Clin Invest* 1967; **46**: 1309–17

Engelhardt B. Development of the blood-brain barrier. *Cell Tissue Res* 2003; **314**: 119–29

Erichsen CJ, Sjovall J, Kehlet H, Hedlund C, Arvidsson T. Pharmacokinetics and analgesic effect of ropivacaine during continuous epidural infusion for postoperative pain relief. *Anesthesiology* 1996; **84**: 834–42

Fawer CL, Torrado A, Guignard JP. Maturation of renal function in full-term and premature neonates. *Helvetica Paediatrica Acta* 1979; **34**: 11–21

Fisher DM, Canfell PC, Fahey MR, *et al.* Elimination of atracurium in humans: contribution of Hofmann elimination and ester hydrolysis versus organ-based elimination. *Anesthesiology* 1986; **65**: 6–12

Fisher DM, Canfell PC, Spellman MJ, Miller RD. Pharmacokinetics and pharmacodynamics of atracurium in infants and children. *Anesthesiology* 1990; **73**: 33–7

Fisher DM, Castagnoli K, Miller RD. Vecuronium kinetics and dynamics in anesthetized infants and children. *Clin Pharmacol Ther* 1985; **37**: 402–6

Fisher DM, Cronnelly R, Miller RD, Sharma M. The neuromuscular pharmacology of neostigmine in infants and children. *Anesthesiology* 1983; **59**: 220–5

Fisher DM, Miller RD. Neuromuscular effects of vecuronium (ORG NC45) in infants and children during N2O, halothane anesthesia. *Anesthesiology* 1983; **58**: 519–23

Fisher DM, O'keeffe C, Stanski DR, Cronnelly R, Miller RD, Gregory GA. Pharmacokinetics and pharmacodynamics of d-tubocurarine in infants, children, and adults. *Anesthesiology* 1982; **57**: 203–8

Fitzgerald M. The development of nociceptive circuits. *Nat Rev* 2005; **6**: 507–20

Flick RP, Katusic SK, Colligan RC, *et al.* Cognitive and behavioral outcomes after early exposure to anesthesia and surgery. *Pediatrics* 2011; **128**: e1053–61

Friesen RH, Wurl JL, Charlton GA. Haemodynamic depression by halothane is age-related in paediatric patients. *Paediatr Anaesth* 2000; **10**: 267–72

Friis-Hansen B. Body water compartments in children: changes during growth and related changes in body composition. *Pediatrics* 1961; **28**: 169–81

Gal P, Gilman JT. Drug disposition in neonates with patent ductus arteriosus. *Ann Pharmacother* 1993; **27**: 1383–8

Gleich S, Nemergut M, Flick R. Anesthetic-related neurotoxicity in young children: an update. *Curr Opin Anaesthesiol* 2013; **26**: 340–7

Goudsouzian NG, Denman W, Schwartz A, Shorten G, Foster V, Samara B. Pharmacodynamic and hemodynamic effects of mivacurium in infants anesthetized with halothane and nitrous oxide. *Anesthesiology* 1993; **79**: 919–25

Goudsouzian NG, Liu LM. The neuromuscular response of infants to a continuous infusion of succinylcholine. *Anesthesiology* 1984; **60**: 97–101

Grand RJ, Watkins JB, Torti FM. Development of the human intestinal tract: a review. *Gastroenterology* 1976; **70**: 790–810

Gronert BJ, Brandom BW. Neuromuscular blocking drugs in infants and children. *Pediatr Clin North Am* 1994; **41**: 73–91

Guignard JP, Drukker A. Why do newborn infants have a high plasma creatinine? *Pediatrics* 1999; **103**: e49

Haddad S, Restieri C, Krishnan K. Characterization of age-related changes in body weight and organ weights from birth to adolescence in humans. *J Toxicol Environ Health A* 2001; **64**: 453–64

Halkin H, Radomsky M, Millman P, Almog S, Blieden L, Boichis H. Steady state serum concentrations and renal clearance of digoxin in neonates, infants and children. *Eur J Clin Pharmacol* 1978; **13**: 113–7

Hamabe W, Maeda T, Kiguchi N, Yamamoto C, Tokuyama S, Kishioka S. Negative relationship between morphine analgesia and P-glycoprotein expression levels in the brain. *J Pharmacol Sci* 2007; **105**: 353–60

Hammarlund K, Stromberg B, Sedin G. Heat loss from the skin of preterm and fullterm newborn infants during the first weeks after birth. *Biol Neonate* 1986; **50**: 1–10

Hansen TG, Pedersen JK, Henneberg SW, *et al.* Academic performance in adolescence after inguinal hernia repair in infancy: a nationwide cohort study. *Anesthesiology* 2011; **114**: 1076–85

Haycock GB. Development of glomerular filtration and tubular sodium reabsorption in the human fetus and newborn. *Br J Urol* 1998; **81**(Suppl 2): 33–8

Henthorn TK, Liu Y, Mahapatro M, Ng KY. Active transport of fentanyl by the blood-brain barrier. *J Pharmacol Exp Ther* 1999; **289**: 1084–9

Hesselmans LF, Jennekens FG, Van Den Oord CJ, Veldman H, Vincent A. Development of innervation of skeletal muscle fibers in man: relation to acetylcholine receptors. *Anat Rec* 1993; **236**: 553–62

Hill AV. The possible effects of the aggregation of the molecules of haemoglobin on its dissociation curves. *J Physiol* 1910; **14**: iv–vii

Hines RN. Developmental expression of drug metabolizing enzymes: impact on disposition in neonates and young children. *Int J Pharmaceutics* 2013; **452**: 3–7

Hislop AA, Wigglesworth JS, Desai R, Aber V. The effects of preterm delivery and mechanical ventilation on human lung growth. *Early Hum Dev* 1987; **15**: 147–64

Holford N, Heo YA, Anderson B. A pharmacokinetic standard for babies and adults. *J Pharm Sci* 2013; **102**: 2941–52

Holliday MA, Segar WE. The maintenance need for water in parenteral fluid therapy. *Pediatrics* 1957; **19**: 823–32

Hook JB, Bailie MD. Perinatal renal pharmacology. *Ann Rev Pharmacol Toxicol* 1979; **19**: 491–509

Hook JB, Hewitt WR. Development of mechanisms for drug excretion. *Am J Med* 1977; **62**: 497–506

Horan MJ. Report of the Second Task Force on Blood Pressure Control in Children – 1987. Task Force on Blood Pressure Control in Children. National Heart, Lung, and Blood Institute, Bethesda, Maryland. *Pediatrics* 1987; **79**: 1–25

Huang NN, High RH. Comparison of serum levels following the administration of oral and parenteral preparations of penicillin to infants and children of various age groups. *J Pediatr* 1953; **42**: 657–8

Huttenlocher PR, Dabholkar AS. Regional differences in synaptogenesis in human cerebral cortex. *J Comp Neurol* 1997; **387**: 167–78

Imbeault K, Withington DE, Varin F. Pharmacokinetics and pharmacodynamics of a 0.1 mg/kg dose of cisatracurium besylate in children during N2O/O2/propofol anesthesia. *Anesth Analg* 2006; **102**: 738–43

Jahnukainen T, Van Ravenswaaij-Arts C, Jalonen J, Valimaki I. Dynamics of vasomotor thermoregulation of the skin in term and preterm neonates. *Early Hum Dev* 1993; **33**: 133–43

Jaramillo F, Schuetze SM. Kinetic differences between embryonic- and adult-type acetylcholine receptors in rat myotubes. *J Physiol* 1988; **396**: 267–96

Jaramillo F, Vicini S, Schuetze SM. Embryonic acetylcholine receptors guarantee spontaneous contractions in rat developing muscle. *Nature* 1988; **335**: 66–8

Jevtovic-Todorovic V. Anesthesia and the developing brain: are we getting closer to understanding the truth? *Curr Opin Anaesthesiol* 2011; **24**: 395–9

Johnson KL, Erickson JP, Holley FO, Scott JC. Fentanyl pharmacokinetics in the paediatric population. *Anesthesiology* 1984; **61**: A441

Johnson RE, Fudala PJ, Payne R. Buprenorphine: considerations for pain management. *J Pain Symptom Manage* 2005a; **29**: 297–326

Johnson TN, Tucker GT, Tanner MS, Rostami-Hodjegan A. Changes in liver volume from birth to adulthood: a meta-analysis. *Liver Transpl* 2005b; **11**: 1481–93

Kain ZN, Mayes LC, O'Connor TZ, Cicchetti DV. Preoperative anxiety in children. Predictors and outcomes. *Arch Pediatr Adolesc Med* 1996; **150**: 1238–45

Kalli I, Meretoja OA. Infusion of atracurium in neonates, infants and children. A study of dose requirements. *Br J Anaesth* 1988; **60**: 651–4

Karl HW, Rosenberger JL, Larach MG, Ruffle JM. Transmucosal administration of midazolam for premedication of pediatric patients. Comparison of the nasal and sublingual routes. *Anesthesiology* 1993; **78**: 885–91

Kearns GL, Abdel-Rahman SM, Alander SW, Blowey DL, Leeder JS, Kauffman RE. Developmental pharmacology--drug disposition, action, and therapy in infants and children. *N Engl J Med* 2003; **349**: 1157–67

Keenan RL, Shapiro JH, Kane FR, Simpson PM. Bradycardia during anesthesia in infants. An epidemiologic study. *Anesthesiology* 1994; **80**: 976–82

Keens TG, Bryan AC, Levison H, Ianuzzo CD. Developmental pattern of muscle fiber types in human ventilatory muscles. *J Appl Physiol* 1978; **44**: 909–13

Kharasch ED, Hankins DC, Thummel KE. Human kidney methoxyflurane and sevoflurane metabolism. Intrarenal fluoride production as a possible mechanism of methoxyflurane nephrotoxicity. *Anesthesiology* 1995; **82**: 689–99

Kirkegaard-Nielsen H, Meretoja OA, Wirtavuori K. Reversal of atracurium-induced neuromuscular block in paediatric patients. *Acta Anaesthesiol Scand* 1995; **39**: 906–11

Koch SC, Fitzgerald M, Hathway GJ. Midazolam potentiates nociceptive behavior, sensitizes cutaneous reflexes, and is devoid of sedative action in neonatal rats. *Anesthesiology* 2008; **108**: 122–9

Konduri GG, Kim UO. Advances in the diagnosis and management of persistent pulmonary hypertension of the newborn. *Pediatr Clin North Am* 2009; **56**: 579–600

Kotecha S. Lung growth for beginners. *Paediatr Respir Rev* 2000; **1**: 308–13

Lahmiti S, Aboussad A. Neonatal necrotizing enterocolitis. *ScientificWorldJournal* 2011; **11**: 655–6

Langhendries JP, Battisti O, Bertrand JM, *et al.* Adaptation in neonatology of the once-daily concept of aminoglycoside administration: evaluation of a dosing chart for amikacin in an intensive care unit. *Biol Neonate* 1998; **74**: 351–62

Laycock JR, Baxter MK, Bevan JC, Sangwan S, Donati F, Bevan DR. The potency of pancuronium at the adductor pollicis and diaphragm in infants and children. *Anesthesiology* 1988a; **68**: 908–11

Laycock JR, Donati F, Smith CE, Bevan DR. Potency of atracurium and vecuronium at the diaphragm and the adductor pollicis muscle. *Br J Anaesth* 1988b; **61**: 286–91

Leake RD, Trygstad CW, Oh W. Inulin clearance in the newborn infant: relationship to gestational and postnatal age. *Pediatr Res* 1976; **10**: 759–62

Ledez KM, Lerman J. The minimum alveolar concentration (MAC) of isoflurane in preterm neonates. *Anesthesiology* 1987; **67**: 301–7

Leger F, Bouissou F, Coulais Y, Tafani M, Chatelut E. Estimation of glomerular filtration rate in children. *Pediatr Nephrol* 2002; **17**: 903–7

Lerman J. Pharmacology of inhalational anaesthetics in infants and children. *Paediatr Anaesth* 1992; **2**: 191–203

Lerman J, Robinson S, Willis MM, Gregory GA. Anesthetic requirements for halothane in young children 0–1 month and 1–6 months of age. *Anesthesiology* 1983; **59**: 421–4

Lerman J, Sikich N, Kleinman S, Yentis S. The pharmacology of sevoflurane in infants and children. *Anesthesiology* 1994; **80**: 814–24

Liang J, Co E, Zhang M, Pineda J, Chen JD. Development of gastric slow waves in preterm infants measured by electrogastrography. *Am J Physiol* 1998; **274**: G503–8

Linday L, Dobkin JF, Wang TC, *et al.* Digoxin inactivation by the gut flora in infancy and childhood. *Pediatrics* 1987; **79**: 544–8

Litman RS, Weissend EE, Shibata D, Westesson PL. Developmental changes of laryngeal dimensions in unparalyzed, sedated children. *Anesthesiology* 2003; **98**: 41–5

Luz G, Innerhofer P, Bachmann B, Frischhut B, Menardi G, Benzer A. Bupivacaine plasma concentrations during continuous epidural anesthesia in infants and children. *Anesth Analg* 1996; **82**: 231–4

Luz G, Wieser C, Innerhofer P, Frischhut B, Ulmer H, Benzer A. Free and total bupivacaine plasma concentrations after continuous epidural anaesthesia in infants and children. *Paediatr Anaesth* 1998; **8**: 473–8

Lynn AM, Nespeca MK, Opheim KE, Slattery JT. Respiratory effects of intravenous morphine infusions in neonates, infants, and children after cardiac surgery. *Anesth Analg* 1993; **77**: 695–701

Malviya S, Lerman J. The blood/gas solubilities of sevoflurane, isoflurane, halothane, and serum constituent concentrations in neonates and adults. *Anesthesiology* 1990; **72**: 793–6

Mankarious LA, Goudy SL. Craniofacial and upper airway development. *Paediatr Respir Rev* 2011; **11**: 193–8

Matteo RS, Lieberman IG, Salanitre E, Mcdaniel DD, Diaz J. Distribution, elimination, and action of d-tubocurarine in neonates, infants, children, and adults. *Anesth Analg* 1984; **63**: 799–804

Mcdowall RH. Anesthesia considerations for pediatric cancer. *Semin Surg Oncol* 1993; **9**: 478–88

Mcnamara DG, Nixon GM, Anderson BJ. Methylxanthines for the treatment of apnea associated with bronchiolitis and anesthesia. *Paediatr Anaesth* 2004; **14**: 541–50

Meakin G, Mckiernan EP, Morris P, Baker RD. Dose-response curves for suxamethonium in neonates, infants and children. *Br J Anaesth* 1989; **62**: 655–8

Meakin G, Morton RH, Wareham AC. Age-dependent variation in response to tubocurarine in the isolated rat diaphragm. *Br J Anaesth* 1992; **68**: 161–3

Meakin G, Shaw EA, Baker RD, Morris P. Comparison of atracurium-induced neuromuscular blockade in neonates, infants and children. *Br J Anaesth* 1988; **60**: 171–5

Meakin G, Sweet PT, Bevan JC, Bevan DR. Neostigmine and edrophonium as antagonists of pancuronium in infants and children. *Anesthesiology* 1983; **59**: 316–21

Meakin G, Walker RW, Dearlove OR. Myotonic and neuromuscular blocking effects of increased doses of suxamethonium in infants and children. *Br J Anaesth* 1990; **65**: 816–8

Meistelman C, Debaene B, D'hollander A, Donati F, Saint-Maurice C. Importance of the level of paralysis recovery for a rapid antagonism of vecuronium with neostigmine in children during halothane anesthesia. *Anesthesiology* 1988; **69**: 97–9

Meretoja OA. Neuromuscular blocking agents in paediatric patients: influence of age on the response. *Anaesth Intens Care* 1990; **18**: 440–8

Meretoja OA, Erkola O. Pipecuronium revisited: dose-response and maintenance requirement in infants, children, and adults. *J Clin Anesth* 1997; **9**: 125–9

Meretoja OA, Taivainen T, Wirtavuori K. Cisatracurium during halothane and balanced anaesthesia in children. *Paediatr Anaesth* 1996; **6**: 373–8

Meretoja OA, Wirtavuori K, Neuvonen PJ. Age-dependence of the dose-response curve of vecuronium in pediatric patients during balanced anesthesia. *Anesth Analg* 1988; **67**: 21–6

Michel E, Anderson BJ, Zernikow B. Buprenorphine TTS for children—a review of the drug's clinical pharmacology. *Pediatr Anesth* 2011; **21**: 280–90

Mishina M, Takai T, Imoto K, *et al.* Molecular distinction between fetal and adult forms of muscle acetylcholine receptor. *Nature* 1986; **321**: 406–11

Miyagi SJ, Collier AC. The development of UDP-glucuronosyltransferases 1A1 and 1A6 in the pediatric liver. *Drug Metab Dispos* 2011; **39**: 912–9

Molin JC, Bendhack LM. Clonidine induces rat aorta relaxation by nitric oxide-dependent and -independent mechanisms. *Vascul Pharmacol* 2004; **42**: 1–6

Morriss FH, Jr, Moore M, Weisbrodt NW, West MS. Ontogenic development of gastrointestinal motility: IV. Duodenal contractions in preterm infants. *Pediatrics* 1986; **78**: 1106–13

Mosteller RD. More on simplified calculation of body-surface area. *N Engl J Med* 1988; **318**: 1130

Motoyama EK. Respiratory physiology. In: Bissonnette B, ed. *Pediatric Anaesthesia: Basic Principles, State of the Art, Future.* Shelton, CT: Peoples Medical Publishing House, 2011; 106–39

Nayler WG, Fassold E. Calcium accumulating and ATPase activity of cardiac sarcoplasmic reticulum before and after birth. *Cardiovasc Res* 1977; **11**: 231–7

Nebbia SP, Bissonnette B, Sessler DI. Enflurane decreases the threshold for vasoconstriction more than isoflurane or halothane. *Anesth Analg* 1996; **83**: 595–9

Ng PK, Cote J, Schiff D, Collins-Nakai RL. Renal clearance of digoxin in premature neonates. *Res Commun Chem Pathol Pharmacol* 1981; **34**: 207–16

Nowakowski RS, Hayes NL. CNS development: an overview. *Dev Psychopathol* 1999; **11**: 395–417

O'Brien RT, Pearson HA. Physiologic anemia of the newborn infant. *J Pediatr* 1971; **79**: 132–8

Ochiai R, Guthrie RD, Motoyama EK. Differential sensitivity to halothane anesthesia of the genioglossus, intercostals, and diaphragm in kittens. *Anesth Analg* 1992; **74**: 338–44

Ogden CL, Kuczmarski RJ, Flegal KM, *et al.* Centers for Disease Control and Prevention 2000 growth charts for the United States: improvements to the 1977 National Center for Health Statistics version. *Pediatrics* 2002; **109**: 45–60

Paap CM, Nahata MC. Prospective evaluation of ten methods for estimating creatinine clearance in children with varying degrees of renal dysfunction. *J Clin Pharm Ther* 1995; **20**: 67–73

Papp JG. Autonomic responses and neurohumoral control in the human early antenatal heart. *Basic Res Cardiol* 1988; **83**: 2–9

Paule MG, Li M, Allen RR, *et al.* Ketamine anesthesia during the first week of life can cause long-lasting cognitive deficits in rhesus monkeys. *Neurotoxicol Teratol* 2011; **33**: 220–30

Pelkonen O, Karki NT. Drug metabolism in human fetal tissues. *Life Sci* 1973; **13**: 1163–80

Perucca E. Clinically relevant drug interactions with antiepileptic drugs. *Br J Clin Pharmacol* 2006; **61**: 246–55

Peters JW, Anderson BJ, Simons SH, Uges DR, Tibboel D. Morphine pharmacokinetics during venoarterial extracorporeal membrane oxygenation in neonates. *Intensive Care Med* 2005a; **31**: 257–63

Peters JW, Schouw R, Anand KJ, Van Dijk M, Duivenvoorden HJ, Tibboel D. Does neonatal surgery lead to increased pain sensitivity in later childhood? *Pain* 2005b; **114**: 444–54

Pirianou G, Mehmet H, Taylor DT. Apoptotic cell death. In: Polin RA, Fox WW, Abman SH, eds. *Fetal and Neonatal Physiology.* Philadelphia, PA: Elsevier Saunders, 2011; 93–101

Plaud B, Meretoja O, Hofmockel R, *et al.* Reversal of rocuronium-induced neuromuscular blockade with sugammadex in pediatric and adult surgical patients. *Anesthesiology* 2009; **110**: 284–94

Pohunek P. Development, structure and function of the upper airways. *Paediatr Respir Rev* 2004; **5**: 2–8

Pokela ML, Olkkola KT, Seppala T, Koivisto M. Age-related morphine kinetics in infants. *Dev Pharmacol Ther* 1993; **20**: 26–34

Poley JR, Dower JC, Owen CA, Jr, Stickler GB. Bile acids in infants and children. *J Lab Clin Med* 1964; **63**: 838–46

Potter EL. Development of the human glomerulus. *Arch Pathol* 1965; **80**: 241–55

Potts AL, Warman GR, Anderson BJ. Dexmedetomidine disposition in children: a population analysis. *Paediatr Anaesth* 2008; **18**: 722–30

Reich DL, Hollinger I, Harrington DJ, Seiden HS, Chakravorti S, Cook DR. Comparison of cisatracurium and vecuronium by infusion in neonates and small infants after congenital heart surgery. *Anesthesiology* 2004; **101**: 1122–7

Rhodin MM, Anderson BJ, Peters AM, *et al.* Human renal function maturation: a quantitative description using weight and postmenstrual age. *Pediatr Nephrol* 2009; **24**: 67–76

Rigatto H, Brady JP, De La Torre Verduzco R. Chemoreceptor reflexes in preterm infants: I. The effect of gestational and postnatal age on the ventilatory response to inhalation of 100% and 15% oxygen. *Pediatrics* 1075a; **55**: 604–13

Rigatto H, De La Torre Verduzco R, Gates DB. Effects of O2 on the ventilatory response to CO2 in preterm infants. *J Appl Physiol* 1975b; **39**: 896–9

Rigby-Jones AE, Priston MJ, Sneyd JR, *et al.* Remifentanil-midazolam sedation for paediatric patients receiving mechanical ventilation after cardiac surgery. *Br J Anaesth* 2007; **99**: 252–61

Robillard JE, Kulvinskas C, Sessions C, Burmeister L, Smith FG, JR. Maturational changes in the fetal glomerular filtration rate. *Am J Obstet Gynecol* 1975; **122**: 601–6

Robillard JE, Sessions C, Kennedey RL, Hamel-Robillard L, Smith FG, JR. Interrelationship between glomerular filtration rate and renal transport of sodium and chloride during fetal life. *Am J Obstet Gynecol* 1977; **128**: 727–34

Rodbro P, Krasilnikoff PA, Christiansen PM. Parietal cell secretory function in early childhood. *Scand J Gastroenterol* 1967; **2**: 209–13

Ross MP, Christensen RD, Rothstein G, *et al.* A randomized trial to develop criteria for administering erythrocyte transfusions to anemic preterm infants 1 to 3 months of age. *J Perinatol* 1989; **9**: 246–53

Rudolph AM. *Congenital Disease of the Heart: Clinical-Physiological Considerations.* Chicago, IL: Futura Publishing Company, 2001

Russo H, Bressolle F. Pharmacodynamics and pharmacokinetics of thiopental. *Clin Pharmacokinet* 1998; **35**: 95–134

Sadler T. *Langman's Medical Embryology*. Baltimore, MD: Lippincott, Williams and Wilkins, 2012

Salanitre E, Rackow H. The pulmonary exchange of nitrous oxide and halothane in infants and children. *Anesthesiology* 1969; **30**: 388–94

Samuels M (ed); Advanced Life Support Group. *Advanced Paediatric Life Support* Chichester: Wiley-Blackwell, 2011

Sawyer DC, Eger EI, 2nd, Bahlman SH, Cullen BF, Impelman D. Concentration dependence of hepatic halothane metabolism. *Anesthesiology* 1971; **34**: 230–5

Schmidt B, Ofosu FA, Mitchell L, Brooker LA, Andrew M. Anticoagulant effects of heparin in neonatal plasma. *Pediatr Res* 1989; **25**: 405–8

Schwartz GJ, Feld LG, Langford DJ. A simple estimate of glomerular filtration rate in full-term infants during the first year of life. *J Pediatr* 1984; **104**: 849–54

Schwartz GJ, Haycock GB, Edelmann CM, Jr, Spitzer A. A simple estimate of glomerular filtration rate in children derived from body length and plasma creatinine. *Pediatrics* 1976; **58**: 259–63

Seri I. Dopamine and natriuresis. Mechanism of action and developmental aspects. *Am J Hypertens* 1990; **3**: 82S–86S

Seri I, Tulassay T, Kiszel J, Machay T, Csomor S. Cardiovascular response to dopamine in hypotensive preterm neonates with severe hyaline membrane disease. *Eur J Pediatr* 1984; **142**: 3–9

Seri I, Tulassay T, Kiszel J, *et al.* Effect of low-dose dopamine infusion on prolactin and thyrotropin secretion in preterm infants with hyaline membrane disease. *Biol Neonate* 1985; **47**: 317–22

Shannon KM, Keith JF, 3rd, Mentzer WC, *et al.* Recombinant human erythropoietin stimulates erythropoiesis and reduces erythrocyte transfusions in very low birth weight preterm infants. *Pediatrics* 1995; **95**: 1–8

Shih J, May LD, Gonzalez HE, *et al.* Delayed environmental enrichment reverses sevoflurane-induced memory impairment in rats. *Anesthesiology* 2012; **116**: 586–602

Southall DP, Richards J, Mitchell P, *et al.* Study of cardiac rhythm in healthy newborn infants. *Br Heart J* 1980; **43**: 14–20

Southall DP, Vulliamy DG, Davies MJ, Anderson RH, Shinebourne EA, Johnson AM. A new look at the neonatal electrocardiogram. *Br Med J* 1976; **2**: 615–8

Steinberg C, Notterman DA. Pharmacokinetics of cardiovascular drugs in children. Inotropes and vasopressors. *Clin Pharmacokinet* 1994; **27**: 345–67

Stocks J. Effect of nasogastric tubes on nasal resistance during infancy. *Arch Dis Child* 1980; **55**: 17–21

Stoll BJ, Hansen NI, Bell EF, *et al.* Neonatal outcomes of extremely preterm infants from the NICHD Neonatal Research Network. *Pediatrics* 2010; **126**: 443–56

Strolin Benedetti M, Ruty B, Baltes E. Induction of endogenous pathways by antiepileptics and clinical implications. *Fundam Clin Pharmacol* 2005; **19**: 511–29

Suchy FJ, Balistreri WF, Heubi JE, Searcy JE, Levin RS. Physiologic cholestasis: elevation of the primary serum bile acid concentrations in normal infants. *Gastroenterology* 1981; **80**: 1037–41

Sutherland GA, Bevan JC, Bevan DR. Neuromuscular blockade in infants following intramuscular succinylcholine in two or five per cent concentration. *Can Anaesth Soc J* 1983; **30**: 342–6

Sutherland JM. Fatal cardiovascular collapse of infants receiving large amounts of chloramphenicol. *Am J Dis Child* 1959; **97**: 761–767

Taddio A, Katz J, Ilersich AL, Koren G. Effect of neonatal circumcision on pain response during subsequent routine vaccination. *Lancet* 1997a; **349**: 599–603

Taddio A, Stevens B, Craig K, *et al.* Efficacy and safety of lidocaine-prilocaine cream for pain during circumcision. *N Engl J Med* 1997b; **336**: 1197–201

Takahashi H, Ishikawa S, Nomoto S, *et al.* Developmental changes in pharmacokinetics and pharmacodynamics of warfarin enantiomers in Japanese children. *Clin Pharmacol Ther* 2000; **68**: 541–55

Tanaka S, Mito T, Takashima S. Progress of myelination in the human fetal spinal nerve roots, spinal cord and brainstem with myelin basic protein immunohistochemistry. *Early Hum Dev* 1995; **41**: 49–59

Tassonyi E, Pittet JF, Schopfer CN, *et al.* Pharmacokinetics of pipecuronium in infants, children and adults. *Eur J Drug Metab Pharmacokinet* 1995; **20**: 203–8

Thurlbeck WM. Postnatal human lung growth. *Thorax* 1982; **37**: 564–71

Usher R, Lind J. Blood volume of the newborn premature infant. *Acta Paediatr Scand* 1965; **54**: 419–31

Usher R, Shephard M, Lind J. The blood volume of the newborn infant and placental transfusion. *Acta Paediatr* 1963; **52**: 497–512

Van Hoogdalem E, De Boer AG, Breimer DD. Pharmacokinetics of rectal drug administration, Part I. General considerations and clinical applications of centrally acting drugs. *Clin Pharmacokinet* 1991; **21**: 11–26

Vinet A, Mandigout S, Nottin S, *et al.* Influence of body composition, hemoglobin concentration, and cardiac size and function of gender differences in maximal oxygen uptake in prepubertal children. *Chest* 2003; **124**: 1494–9

Voepel-Lewis T, Malviya S, Tait AR. A prospective cohort study of emergence agitation in the pediatric postanesthesia care unit. *Anesth Analg* 2003; **96**: 1625–30

Vogler RC, Ii FJ, Pilgram TK. Age-specific size of the normal adenoid pad on magnetic resonance imaging. *Clin Otolaryngol Allied Sci* 2000; **25**: 392–5

Von Ungern-Sternberg BS, Hammer J, Schibler A, Frei FJ, Erb TO. Decrease of functional residual capacity and ventilation homogeneity after neuromuscular blockade in anesthetized young infants and preschool children. *Anesthesiology* 2006; **105**: 670–5

Walker, SM. Developmental neurobiology of nociception. In: Macintyre PE WS, Rowbotham DJ, eds. *Acute Pain.* 2nd Edn. London: Hodder Arnold, 2008; 32–52

Ward RM, Drover DR, Hammer GB, *et al.* The pharmacokinetics of methadone and its metabolites in neonates, infants, and children. *Pediatr Anesth* 2014; **24**: 591–601

Wareham AC, Morton RH, Meakin GH. Low quantal content of the endplate potential reduces safety factor for neuromuscular transmission in the diaphragm of the newborn rat. *Br J Anaesth* 1994; **72**: 205–9

Warner MA, Kunkel SE, Offord KO, Atchison SR, Dawson B. The effects of age, epinephrine, and operative site on duration of caudal analgesia in pediatric patients. *Anesth Analg* 1987; **66**: 995–8

Way WL, Costley EC, Way EL. Respiratory sensitivity of the newborn infant to meperidine and morphine. *Clin Pharmacol Ther* 1965; **6**: 454–461

Welzing L, Ebenfeld S, Dlugay V, Wiesen MH, Roth B, Mueller C. Remifentanil degradation in umbilical cord blood of preterm infants. *Anesthesiology* 2011; **114**: 570–7

West GB, Brown JH. The origin of allometric scaling laws in biology from genomes to ecosystems: towards a quantitative unifying theory of biological structure and organization. *J Exp Biol* 2005; **208**: 1575–92

West GB, Brown JH, Enquist BJ. A general model for the origin of allometric scaling laws in biology. *Science* 1997; **276**: 122–6

Westhorpe RN. The position of the larynx in children and its relationship to the ease of intubation. *Anaesth Intens Care* 1987; **15**: 384–8

Wheeler M, Birmingham PK, Dsida RM, Wang Z, Cote CJ, Avram MJ. Uptake pharmacokinetics of the Fentanyl Oralet in children scheduled for central venous access removal: implications for the timing of initiating painful procedures. *Pediatr Anesth* 2002; **12**: 594–9

Wierda JM, Meretoja OA, Taivainen T, Proost JH. Pharmacokinetics and pharmacokinetic-dynamic modelling of rocuronium in infants and children. *Br J Anaesth* 1997; **78**: 690–5

Woelfel SK, Brandom BW, McGowan FX, Jr, Cook DR. Clinical pharmacology of mivacurium in pediatric patients less than off years old during nitrous oxide-halothane anesthesia. *Anesth Analg* 1993; **77**: 713–20

Xue FS, Luo LK, Tong SY, Liao X, Deng XM, An G. Study of the safe threshold of apneic period in children during anesthesia induction. *J Clin Anesth* 1996; **8**: 568–74

Zou X, Liu F, Zhang X, *et al.* Inhalation anesthetic-induced neuronal damage in the developing rhesus monkey. *Neurotoxicol Teratol* 2011; **33**: 592–7

CHAPTER 70

Neonatal anaesthesia

Andrew Davidson, Adrian Bosenberg, and Stephen Stayer

Introduction

Neonatal anaesthesia is one of the most challenging areas of anaesthesia. Neonates have a significantly different physiology and pharmacology from adults and older children; their small size can make procedures such as intravenous or arterial access more difficult, and they have a reduced physiological reserve. One of the greatest challenges is the lack of knowledge. We have very little data on the basic pharmacology of even our most commonly used anaesthesia drugs in neonates (Anderson 2012b). Similarly, there are few data on anaesthesia techniques and outcomes. We also have a relatively poor understanding of neonatal physiology; for example, what blood pressure is acceptable in a neonate? Given the challenges, it is not surprising that several studies have shown that neonates have a relatively high risk of anaesthesia-related morbidity and mortality (van der Griend et al. 2011).

This chapter outlines relevant aspects of neonatal physiology and pharmacology and describes some of the anaesthetic challenges for several of the more common neonatal surgical procedures.

General principles

Safe neonatal anaesthesia requires a good understanding of normal neonatal anatomy, physiology, and pharmacology. The anaesthetist should also have a good understanding of the pathology needing surgery. Neonatal surgical conditions are frequently associated with syndromes or other pathologies that will have an impact on perioperative care. Safe care of a neonate also requires excellent teamwork and good communication with a neonatologist, nursing staff, surgeons, and specialist referral teams. The preoperative assessment should be thorough. There should be a plan for the perioperative respiratory, fluid and glucose management, and for postoperative pain control. There should be discussion about when the surgery should take place: in an emergency, is there time for more thorough preoperative assessment (e.g. echocardiography to assess heart disease), or for less urgent cases, can the surgery wait until the child is more mature? There should also be discussion about where the surgery should be performed: regional or tertiary centre, in the neonatal intensive care unit (NICU), or in the operating theatres? Lastly, the anaesthetist should discuss the plan with the parents, understanding that parents are likely to be highly anxious when their newborn child requires surgery.

Safe neonatal anaesthesia also requires a sufficient level of experience and assistance. In some situations, only dedicated paediatric anaesthetists, or general anaesthetists with a dedicated interest in paediatric anaesthesia, should attempt to anaesthetize neonates. There should be a low threshold for having two senior anaesthesia staff present, particularly if the neonate has significant co-morbidity or if the anaesthetists do not anaesthetize neonates regularly.

Being well prepared is important for neonatal anaesthesia. The child has limited reserve and access to the child is very difficult once surgery has commenced. Events happen quickly and need a rapid response. If the surgery is major, then make sure red cells and clotting factors are readily available. In some cases, it is useful to draw them up, have them connected, and ready to go. Similarly, if the child is septic then consider getting inotropic infusions established and connected beforehand. If the child already has a tracheal tube then it should be checked for patency and tip position, and be well secured. Make sure you can get to the tube under the drape to correct any disconnection or kink. Ventilator requirements may change substantially during major neonatal surgery so have a plan for how to provide greater levels of support. Once surgery starts, it will be very difficult to establish further intravenous access, thus ensure access is reliable. Intravenous lines can also easily disconnect. Check all connections before the drapes are placed and have a high index of suspicion for intravenous line disconnection if the child appears to be failing to respond to intravenous medication or fluid bolus.

Neonatal anatomy and physiology

Growth

The most obvious aspect of neonatal anatomy is size. A normal term neonate is usually a little more than 3 kg in weight and 50 cm long. The head is relatively large with a long trunk and short arms and legs. A term baby loses 5–10% of their body weight in the first few days as a result of loss of extracellular body water. A neonate gains weight at approximately 30 g day^{-1}, regaining their birth weight by about 10 days of age.

The neonatal airway

At birth, the mandible is relatively small and, in the absence of teeth, the tongue is relatively large, increasing the risk of airway obstruction during anaesthesia. Jaw thrust is a particularly useful technique to relieve obstruction. The larynx is more cephalad (C4), and on laryngoscopy appears more anterior, and the axis is directed more posterosuperior to inferoanterior. The large U-shaped epiglottis may obscure the view of the larynx. Placing the laryngoscope blade in the vallecula lifts the epiglottis out of the line of sight and aids laryngoscopy. To do this, a straight blade may be more suitable than a curved blade.

During quiet awake respiration, most neonates prefer to breathe through their nose; nasal breathing is essential for breastfeeding. The nasal passages are narrow and thus nasogastric tubes or even moderate amounts of secretion may cause significant obstruction and exacerbate any existing respiratory distress. The neonatal trachea is also narrow with the narrowest point at the cricoid ring. Minor mucosal trauma and subsequent oedema can produce a significant reduction in the cross-sectional area and restrict airflow. In addition, because the diameter is small, airflow is more likely to become turbulent, further impeding ventilation. Care must be taken to minimize tracheal mucosal injury during tracheal intubation. Cuffed tracheal tubes may allow the use of smaller tubes, eliminate the need for a leak and reduce mucosal injury; however, to avoid injury, the cuff pressure must not be excessive and the pressure must be carefully monitored.

Respiratory drive

At birth, onset of respiration is triggered by cold, touch, acidosis, and the relative hyperoxia compared with the intrauterine environment. Unlike adults, neonates may respond to hypoxaemia with suppression of respiration. The response to hypercapnia is also moderately reduced in the neonate.

Periodic breathing, defined as a brief pause in breathing usually less than 15 s without desaturation or bradycardia, occurs commonly in newborns. Apnoea is defined as a more prolonged pause and may be associated with desaturation and bradycardia. Apnoea may be obstructive (airway obstruction with continued respiratory effort) or central (loss of respiratory drive with no effort). Obstructive apnoea may progress to central apnoea. Neonates may also become apnoeic after stimulation of the carina or areas supplied by the superior laryngeal nerve. Central apnoea may be a sign of underlying disease and may occur with sedative medication or after anaesthesia. Central apnoea may be treated with caffeine or theophylline.

Postoperative apnoea is a major issue in neonatal anaesthesia. It is more common in children born prematurely and the risk is inversely related to postmenstrual age. Anaemia and a history of lung disease or previous apnoea are also risk factors (Cote et al. 1995). The true incidence of postoperative apnoea is difficult to determine as definitions of apnoea vary between studies and some methods of detection are more sensitive than others. Awake regional anaesthesia reduces the risk compared with general anaesthesia; however, if any sedatives are given to supplement the block, the risk of apnoea is increased (Davidson et al. 2009). This may be as a result of the sedative or because of the fact that neonates who need sedation are more likely to have apnoea for some other reasons. Most apnoea studies were performed before modern shorter-acting anaesthetic agents were introduced, thus the incidence after use of sevoflurane and remifentanil is largely unknown.

The risk of postoperative apnoea is very pertinent to the timing of surgery and where it is performed. Data are too few to form firm guidelines on monitoring and discharge time. Guidelines are also difficult to prepare as many babies have a very small background risk of apnoea and the clinical significance of a brief self-correcting apnoea is unclear. In general, the risk appears to be small in term babies and in preterm babies the risk probably becomes no greater than normal background risk at about 56 weeks post-menstrual age. Thus most institutions would monitor an ex-premature baby that had surgery before they were 46–50 weeks post-menstrual age in hospital for at least a 12 h apnoea period, though some monitor for longer.

Caffeine (5–10 mg kg^{-1}) can be used to prevent postoperative apnoea in preterm infants; however, these trials only included small numbers of infants and caffeine is not considered routine (Henderson-Smart and Steer 2010).

Respiratory mechanics

The spontaneous tidal volume of a neonate is 6–8 ml kg^{-1} and the dead space is about a third of this. On a ml kg^{-1} basis, tidal volume and dead space are relatively the same as adults while the oxygen consumption is relatively higher in neonates (6–8 ml kg^{-1} min^{-1} in neonates compared with 4–6 ml kg^{-1} min^{-1} in adults). Consequently, the minute ventilation and respiratory rate is also higher. A healthy term neonate has a respiratory rate of between 20 and 60 breaths min^{-1}. The functional residual capacity (FRC) of neonates and adults is also similar on a ml kg^{-1} basis but the higher oxygen consumption results in a more rapid fall in Pa_{O_2} with apnoea.

The neonate is highly dependent on the diaphragm for breathing, making abdominal excursion more obvious even during quiet breathing. The ribs are more horizontally orientated and the diaphragm less domed. This results in a relatively lower total lung capacity. The chest wall is compliant and thus the outward recoil of the thorax is considerably less than in adults. In contrast, the lung elasticity is only slightly less. Accessory muscles are needed to maintain FRC and prevent the chest wall collapsing during inspiration. FRC is also maintained by the use of laryngeal adductors breaking the expiratory airflow (grunting). Anaesthesia relaxes these muscles resulting in a significant fall in FRC. Closing volume is higher in neonates and therefore hypoxia occurs more readily if the FRC decreases.

Surfactant, produced after 36 weeks' gestation, promotes alveolar stability by reducing surface tension. Lack of surfactant in premature neonates favours atelectasis that, if untreated, can lead to respiratory distress syndrome.

Neonatal ventilation requires meticulous attention to detail. Continuous positive end-expiratory pressure or continuous positive airway pressure is required to maintain FRC during anaesthesia. Gentle recruitment manoeuvres may be required to open atelectatic alveoli. Neonatal lungs are at particular risk of barotrauma or volutrauma that could lead to interstitial lung damage or pneumothorax. Excessive inflation pressures and tidal volumes should therefore be avoided—in high-risk babies this can occur with only a few breaths. High FI_{O_2} can also lead to lung damage so the inspired oxygen fraction should be kept as low as possible. Over-ventilation can also lead to hypocapnia that may impede cerebral and coronary perfusion. In contrast, hypercapnia, particularly chronic hypercapnia, is well tolerated by neonates, Neonates should ideally only be ventilated with machines that are designed to accommodate neonatal ventilation. Moving an unstable neonate from the NICU to the operating theatre may significantly impact ventilation. Thus for neonates with critical or very unstable ventilatory requirements it is wise to consider surgery in the NICU using the NICU ventilator.

Transition to extrauterine life

During delivery, compression of the chest expels fluid from the lungs through the mouth. Lung fluid continues to be reabsorbed into lymphatics after birth. Retained fetal lung fluid may complicate the transition from fetal to adult circulatory physiology and thereby contribute to the development of persistent pulmonary hypertension.

In utero, the organ of gas exchange is the placenta, which has low-resistance/high-capacitance flow, whereas the pulmonary vasculature has high resistance. This circulation favours flow of oxygenated blood returning from the placenta (via the umbilical vein and ductus venosus) across the right atrium through the foramen ovale to the left atrium and into the systemic circulation. The ductus arteriosus connects the pulmonary artery and the aorta allowing the majority of blood ejected by the right ventricle to bypass the lungs and empty into the aortic arch to supply the systemic circulation. The well-oxygenated blood returning from the placenta is ejected into the arch vessels preferentially supplying the developing brain with a higher oxygen content, while desaturated blood returning from the infant's circulation is ejected by the right ventricle and mixes with the better oxygenated blood at the level of the ductus arteriosus to supply the rest of the body.

At birth, the first breath and subsequent crying fills the lungs with air; oxygen tension across the alveolar capillary bed increases and surfactant maintains alveolar patency producing a decrease in pulmonary vascular resistance. At the same time, clamping the umbilical cord removes the placenta from the systemic circulation and the systemic vascular resistance increases. These changes in resistance cause left atrial pressure to exceed right atrial pressure, resulting in functional closure of the foramen ovale. The increase in oxygen tension also reduces flow through constriction of the ductus arteriosus by approximately 24% soon after birth, but is not sufficient to eliminate ductal flow for 48 h after birth. Complete cessation of ductal blood flow, as this structure fibroses to become the ligamentum arteriosum, occurs over the first 2–3 weeks of life.

Even though pulmonary vascular resistance decreases significantly in the first hours of life, it does not achieve adult levels for months, and the pulmonary vasculature in the neonate is prone to vasoconstriction in response to hypoxia, hypercarbia, acidosis, cold, pain, and other stressors. If pulmonary vascular resistance is increased, right-to-left shunting can occur resulting in further hypoxia that in turn can result in further pulmonary vasoconstriction. This vicious cycle partly explains why neonates are characteristically slow to recover from an acute episode of hypoxia.

Persistent pulmonary hypertension of the newborn, also known as persistent fetal circulation, may develop in association with septicaemia or meconium aspiration, but can be idiopathic in nature (Steinhorn 2009). It is characterized by supra-systemic right ventricular pressures, right-to-left flow of deoxygenated blood through the ductus arteriosus or foramen ovale (or both), and severe hypoxaemia. Treatment requires optimizing oxygenation and ventilation while providing pulmonary vasodilation with nitric oxide. Extracorporeal membrane oxygenation (ECMO) may be needed for refractory cases.

Cardiovascular physiology

In utero, both ventricles are of similar size. After birth, there is a greater workload on the left ventricle that responds by rapidly increasing in size. The myocytes increase in size and number. Cardiac output is relatively greater in neonates in response to the greater metabolic demands that increase oxygen consumption. The resting cardiac output is 350 ml kg^{-1} min^{-1} with only limited capacity for further increase. Resting heart rate is between 95 and 145 beats min^{-1}. Normal mean blood pressure is between 40 and 60 mm Hg in a full-term neonate. In premature babies, the mean blood pressure is roughly equivalent to the postmenstrual age in weeks, that is, a 30-week premature neonate has a mean blood pressure of 30. The total blood volume is relatively high in neonates at 80–90 ml kg^{-1} while adult values are closer to 70 ml kg^{-1}. The left ventricle also has a greater basal level of contractility. This may be as a result of loss of increased cardiac sympathetic activity. During infancy there is a gradual decrease in adrenergic and an increase in cholinergic tone.

Neonates have a reduced capacity to accommodate changes in either preload or afterload. This is in part as a result of loss of the immature intracellular and extracellular structure of the heart. The myocardium is relatively less compliant than adult myocardium, reducing its capacity to increase stroke volume in response to an increasing preload. Thus, neonates are vulnerable to fluid overload. Acute overload can lead to acute distension of the liver. This can make abdominal surgery more difficult. A distended liver is more easily injured by retractors that can cause substantial haemorrhage. Traditionally heart rate was considered the predominant determinant of cardiac output in neonates, however in spite of the myocardial immaturity and poorer diastolic function there is indeed still some capacity to increase stroke volume in spite of their relatively decreased diastolic function (Gullberg et al. 1999).

Renal function and fluid management

As a general principle, neonates have immature organ function and thus tend to have a more limited range of function. For example, neonates are less able to concentrate urine or excrete a water load. Similarly, neonates have a lesser capacity for renal clearance of drugs. This limitation in renal function is due both to the relatively lesser renal blood flow and glomerular filtration rate, and the immature nephron structure and tubular function.

Neonates have a total body water content of 70–75% with a relatively higher proportion of extracellular fluid compared with intracellular fluid. The newborn initially has a lower replacement requirement and for the first 3 days requires only 40–60 ml kg^{-1} day^{-1}. This requirement gradually increases up to 150 ml kg^{-1} day^{-1}.

Healthy term neonates have sufficient liver glycogen to allow up to 12 h of fasting without risk of hypoglycaemia. However, preterm, small for gestation, or sick neonates have limited glycogen reserve and require 5–6 mg kg^{-1} min^{-1} of glucose (equivalent to approximately 4 ml kg^{-1} h^{-1} of 10% dextrose) to prevent hypoglycaemia. Neonates having major surgery or those that come to the operating room already on a glucose infusion should have glucose continued intraoperatively and have blood glucose concentrations monitored. Hypoglycaemia can be difficult to detect clinically and can cause substantial neurological injury. In contrast to adults, there is some evidence that hyperglycaemia is relatively neuroprotective in neonates (Loepke and Spaeth 2004). Hyperglycaemia can, however, cause an osmotic diuresis.

Haematology

Haemoglobin concentration may range between 14 and 20 g dl^{-1} with a higher percentage of fetal haemoglobin. The haemoglobin concentration may vary depending on circumstances; for example, placental insufficiency is associated with high haemoglobin concentrations while premature babies may be anaemic if born before iron stores are laid down. The haemoglobin concentration decreases to a nadir by about 2–3 months and then increases.

Neurological development

The brain is relatively large at birth weighing about 300 g and receives a similar proportion of cardiac output compared with adults. Neonates thus have a relatively low brain blood flow despite the relatively greater mass. Neonates also have a narrower range of blood pressures where autoregulation is effective. Thus, blood pressure control is vital in neonates.

At birth, there is an overabundance of neurones and glia and with maturation, excess cells undergo programmed cell death (apoptosis). While the number of neurones decreases, their dendritic arborization increases and synaptic connections become more complex. Myelination also increases during development.

Neonates have no explicit memory, but they do form some rudimentary implicit memory. In particular, there is evidence for persisting altered behaviour after painful procedures. There is considerable discussion with regard to the nature of consciousness in neonates; though this debate is driven mostly by the problems in defining consciousness, there is some evidence that neonates do have rudimentary forms of cognition.

Pharmacology

There are few data on which to base dosing recommendations for neonates—even less for premature neonates. For many drugs, the optimal plasma concentration to achieve a desired effect and the dose required to achieve that level is unknown. Both the pharmacokinetics and pharmacodynamics are different in neonates compared with adults and older children. These differences are a consequence of different body fluid composition, plasma protein composition, relative organ size and perfusion, and the maturity of organ function and enzyme systems. In general, the relatively larger blood volume and total body water results in larger central compartments, particularly for water-soluble drugs. Thus, initial doses may be relatively larger. Drugs are frequently given on a mg kg^{-1} basis but the difference in the relative size of organs in neonates will result in a difference in doses when computed by mg kg^{-1}. Other methods have been proposed which may give a more consistent basis for dosing (Anderson 2012a).

The proportion of cardiac output supplying skeletal muscle is only half that of adults, and therefore relatively more blood goes to other organ systems influencing the onset of action and the redistribution of drugs. Although the relative size of organs such as kidney, brain, and liver is great, the blood flow to these organs is not simply related to size. The liver and kidneys are larger in neonates but have lower relative blood flows. The maturity of organ systems influences how the organs handle the drugs independent to blood flow. Thus, clearance is often lower because of immature renal tubular or hepatic enzyme function. Dosing intervals need be greater to cater for this difference.

In terms of pharmacodynamics, neonates differ in the number of drug receptors or in the subtypes of receptors. Consequently, they may be more resistant or sensitive to a particular drug effect. Lastly, neonates have less reserve to compensate for unwanted drug effects, resulting in an apparent greater sensitivity to some effects.

Inhaled anaesthetic agents

Inhalation induction is faster in the neonate. This is the result of several factors: the ratio of alveolar minute ventilation to FRC is greater and an increased proportion of the cardiac output is delivered to the vessel-rich group and hence there is less uptake into muscle and fat. The increase in alveolar concentration may be slower if there is a substantial right-to-left shunt, particularly for agents with low blood solubility.

The minimum alveolar concentration (MAC) of isoflurane, desflurane and halothane is greatest in children at about 1 year of age; the MAC in neonates is slightly less, but still greater than seen in older children or adults. The MAC for sevoflurane, however, is highest in both neonates and infants. Although neonates have a relatively high MAC they are more sensitive to cardiovascular depression at these values. The MAC awake for neonates is unknown.

Intravenous anaesthetics and analgesic agents

The dose of propofol for induction is poorly described in neonates but is approximately 3 mg kg^{-1}. The lower muscle and fat content results in a slower redistribution of propofol and hepatic clearance is reduced. The result is a slower offset of action and delayed awakening.

Fentanyl and morphine have decreased clearance as a result of reduced hepatic clearance. Fentanyl may cause increased chest wall rigidity, increased vagal tone, and decreased baroreceptor reflex. In contrast, remifentanil clearance, by tissue and plasma esterases, is similar or even increased in neonates. Respiratory depression to opiates is increased probably as a result of increased penetration of the blood–brain barrier and central nervous system sensitivity.

Dexmedetomidine is highly protein bound and has been used as an adjuvant or as a sole agent in neonates. The half-life is dependent on both hepatic metabolism and renal excretion. It may have neuroprotective properties but may cause significant bradycardia particularly if given rapidly.

Ketorolac and intravenous paracetamol have been used effectively for surgical and procedural pain. There is some concern regarding prostaglandin inhibition in newborns.

Neuromuscular blocking agents

Both depolarizing and non-depolarizing agents are water-soluble. The increased volume of distribution, decreased clearance, as well as decreased muscle mass and smaller myoneural junctions all affect the dose response. The potency and duration is therefore unpredictable and longer-acting agents (rocuronium, pancuronium) should be carefully titrated.

Anaesthetic neurotoxicity to the developing brain

Over the past decade, considerable concern over the potential neurotoxic effects of general anaesthetics on the developing brain has been expressed. These concerns arose from two parallel perspectives: laboratory data and human cohort data. Ikonomidou et al. (1999) demonstrated that blockade of *N*-methyl-D-aspartate (NMDA) receptors resulted in widespread apoptosis in the brain of 7-day-old rats. Since then, many studies have found accelerated neuronal apoptosis in newborn animal models after exposure to commonly used general anaesthetics such as ketamine, propofol, nitrous oxide, sevoflurane, isoflurane, and benzodiazepines (Loepke and Soriano 2008). Some researchers have also demonstrated long-term cognitive and learning defects in the exposed animals. Most of the experiments have been in rodents; however, data are also emerging in the non-human primate model. Increased apoptosis is seen in monkeys exposed to 24 h of ketamine at late gestation or at 5 days of age but not at 35 days of age and not with only 3 h of ketamine (Slikker et al. 2007).

In another study, apoptosis was seen after 5 h of ketamine in 6-day-old monkeys and apoptosis was also seen in 6-day-old monkeys exposed to 5 h of isoflurane (Brambrink et al. 2010). The monkeys exposed to 24 h of ketamine at 5 days of age were found to have persistent learning deficits (Paule et al. 2011). The mechanism for anaesthesia-induced apoptosis is still not entirely clear.

We are born with an excess of neurones and apoptosis is a normal process to cull unnecessary neurones. Inactivity results in fewer trophic factors that accelerate apoptosis. It is possible that anaesthesia induces inactivity via γ-aminobutyric acid (GABA) receptors and thus enhances this process. However, against this argument, GABA receptors are excitatory at this phase of development and giving a GABA agonist with an anaesthetic does not reduce the effect. Another possibility is that NMDA blockade leads to upregulation and subsequent excitatory neurotoxicity. However, against this argument is that racemic and S-ketamine have similar degrees of toxicity. Interestingly, apoptosis is not seen with xenon or dexmedetomidine.

Apoptosis is not the only effect that is seen. Exposure to propofol and inhalation anaesthetics can lead to changes in dendritic spine morphology, changes in the neuronal cytoskeleton. and abnormal re-entry into cell cycle. While apoptosis is only seen when animals are exposed at very specific developmental periods, these effects and other effects may be seen in animals at later stages of development.

Translating animal data to humans is very difficult. The age of exposure is difficult to interpret. A 7-day-old rat may correspond to a late-trimester fetus or a neonate but such comparisons are far from straightforward. It is also difficult to interpret duration of exposure. Development in a rodent is rapid. Compared with humans, several hours in a rat represent a substantially greater fraction of time when the brain is undergoing development. Given our longer period of development, a human may have more time for plasticity or recovery. However, human development is far more complex so an injury at a critical period may have a more profound effect on later development. Translating neurobehavioural effects is also difficult. Only crude measures are available in the rodent. Doses are also different. While the dose of inhalation anaesthetic required to produce unconsciousness is fairly constant across species, the dose of intravenous anaesthetics varies enormously. Lastly, the experimental conditions may not be the same as in humans as small animals are difficult to anaesthetize with increased risk of respiratory acidosis and death.

The other area of investigation is human cohort studies. For some time neonatologists have known that neonates who have surgery have an increased risk of poorer neurobehavioural outcome—especially premature babies and babies having major surgery. Once the animal data linking anaesthesia and apoptosis emerged, many more studies have been done examining the neurobehavioural outcome in children who have had surgery. Using an existing birth cohort, two studies found evidence that children exposed to more than one anaesthetic before the age of 2 or 3 years had a greater risk of learning disability. A study examining the RAINE birth cohort in Western Australia also found an association between exposure to anaesthesia before the age of 3 years and poor performance in language at 10 years of age (Ing et al. 2012). A retrospective cohort study from New York, United States (Di Maggio et al. 2009) found that children who had hernia repair before the age of 3 years also had an increased risk of a diagnosis of a developmental or behavioural disorder and a population-based study from Iowa, United States (Block et al. 2012) found evidence for an association between minor surgery and poor performance at school; however, in contrast, a large population-based study in Denmark (Hansen et al. 2011) found no evidence that children who had hernia repair had any increased risk of poor performance at school. Lastly, a twin study found no evidence for any difference in school performance between twin pairs where one twin had surgery in infancy and the other did not (Bartels et al. 2009).

There are many limitations to the human cohort data. The biggest limitation is the presence of strong confounding factors. Infants and children who have anaesthesia usually have significant pathology such a sepsis or are also more likely to have other conditions associated with poor outcome such as prematurity or chromosomal abnormalities. The inflammatory and neurohumoral effect of surgery itself may also increase the risk of poor outcome. Thus, it is unclear if any association is as a result of loss of anaesthesia exposure, pathology, or surgery. It is also unknown which neuropsychological domain would be affected. Crude composite tests such as school performance may miss subtle changes in specific domains. It is also unclear which age group is most at risk or the duration of exposure most likely to cause a significant injury. Thus, the human cohort studies cannot confirm or rule out any significant injury as a result of anaesthesia.

Given the difficulty in translating animal and human studies, regulatory authorities have avoided any formal recommendations and instead have emphasized the danger in delaying essential surgery. Similarly, it should be remembered that neonates and infants are at high risk of respiratory and circulatory complications. Anaesthesia-related morbidity is highest in this age group. Thus, it would be very unwise to adopt new anaesthetic techniques that increase risk from respiratory or circulatory complications. Finally, even if it is demonstrated that anaesthesia does not cause any significant neurotoxic injury, there is still strong evidence that surgery in infancy is associated with poor outcome. This reinforces the need to further investigate and improve all aspects of perioperative management in this vulnerable age group.

Two recently published multi-centre large prospective studies have added evidence that a short exposure to general anaesthetics do not produce measureable declines in neurocognition. A sibling-matched cohort study compared the neurocognitive and behavioural outcomes of children with a single exposure to surgery/anaesthesia before 36 months of age with their siblings who were not exposed (Sun et al. 2016). There were no significant differences in IQ scores in later childhood. The GAS trial randomized infants to receive general anaesthesia or awake-regional anaesthesia. The primary outcome for this study is the Wechsler Preschool and Primary Scale of Intelligence that is administered at age 5 years. This study presented the results of the secondary outcome, the composite cognitive score of the Bayley Scales of Infant and Toddler Development, which was assessed at 2 years; finding the groups to be equivalent (Davidson et al. 2106).

Do neonates need an anaesthetic?

Up until relatively recently, neonates were often given just nitrous oxide and neuromuscular blocking agents for anaesthesia. There was a perception that neonates did not feel pain or were not robust enough to tolerate a general anaesthetic. However, in the 1980s, several studies demonstrated that the type of anaesthetic given could influence outcome. Anand et al. (1987) compared nitrous oxide to nitrous oxide and fentanyl in neonates having a ductal ligation. The fentanyl group had better outcome (fewer cerebral haemorrhages, shorter ventilation postoperatively, and less cardiovascular instability). Anand et al. (1988) also compared nitrous oxide to nitrous oxide and halothane and found neonates in the halothane group required less respiratory support and had less cardiovascular instability. In another study, high-dose sufentanil produced less mortality than low-dose morphine and halothane in neonates having cardiac surgery (Anand and Hickey 1992).

There is strong evidence that neonates do indeed feel pain; painful stimuli increase cortical activation, and several clinical studies have demonstrated that neonates given analgesia for painful non-surgical procedures have better outcomes. From these studies, it is clear that neonates need adequate analgesia for surgery and other painful procedures. However, if there is adequate analgesia, do neonates still need a general anaesthetic? This question is very pertinent if general anaesthetics are neurotoxic or if neonates are at risk of significant cardiovascular depression.

The classic components of anaesthesia are lack of movement, loss of consciousness, amnesia, and analgesia. Neonates have no explicit memory so the need for amnesia is moot. They do form some rudimentary implicit memory, but the significance of this is unclear. They need to be immobile and, as mentioned previously, they need analgesia, but do they need to be unconscious? Does it matter if some sensory information is perceived provided the neonate has no pain? The problem is more acute as it is very difficult to monitor or measure consciousness in a neonate and little is known of what dose of general anaesthetic produces unconsciousness. This need for unconsciousness is perhaps best considered given the fundamental humane aim to reduce distress, and with the knowledge that distressed neonates have poorer outcomes in the NICU. The aim of anaesthesia should thus be to ensure the neonate is comfortable and not distressed. Neonates have a poorer outcome with cardiovascular instability, or inflammatory or neurohumoral stress. The aim of anaesthesia in neonates is thus also to reduce this stress. Giving a hypnotic agent such as an inhalation anaesthetic or regional anaesthesia may be the best way to ensure this. However, the question remains of how much is needed.

General principles of neonatal anaesthesia

Temperature management

Temperature management in neonates is critical. Heat loss and gain is more rapid because of the large surface area-to-weight ratio. In the normal newborn, the surface area-to-volume ratio is approximately 1.0, whereas the adult ratio is closer to 0.4. Lack of insulating fat allows more heat loss from the core to the surface particularly in preterm neonates. All efforts to maintain body temperature should be instituted and temperature should be routinely monitored. Core temperature monitoring (nasopharyngeal, oesophageal, or rectal) should be used for major thoracic or abdominal surgery. Hypothermia, even exposure to a cold environment, increases the metabolic rate and oxygen consumption of infants (by mobilizing glycogen from brown fat) and this may cause hypoxaemia, acidosis, apnoea, or respiratory distress (Hazan et al. 1991). Warming the operating theatre remains the most effective method of maintaining normothermia by reducing the two most important factors in heat loss—radiation and convection. Radiant heat loss is a consequence of the transfer of heat from the patient to surrounding objects. In a neutral thermal environment, radiant heat loss accounts for about 39% of total heat loss, whereas at 22°C, radiant losses increase to nearly 80% of the total (Hardy 1934). Convective heat loss occurs from the transfer of heat to the surrounding air and depends on the velocity of air movement and the difference between the temperature of the patient and surrounding air. This accounts for approximately 34% of heat loss in a neutral thermal environment. Other mechanisms of heat loss, evaporation, and conduction can be reduced by use of forced air warming, heating and humidifying gases, warming intravenous fluids, and warming surgical solutions. A neonate exposed to cold vasoconstricts to conserve heat and increases metabolic rate by oxidizing brown fat (non-shivering thermogenesis). Both these mechanisms to generate heat are impaired by general anaesthetics. Preterm neonates have low brown fat stores.

Airway equipment

Airway equipment appropriate for neonates must be available whenever neonatal anaesthesia is provided. This includes facemasks, oral airways, laryngeal mask airways (size 1), suction catheters, stylets, tracheal tubes, and laryngoscope blades. Difficult intubation equipment for neonatal patients is limited. Many video laryngoscopes that have neonatal blades are effective for term infants, but are often too large for preterm or low-birth-weight babies. The smallest flexible fibreoptic scopes do not have suction channels, and do not fit through tracheal tubes smaller than 3.0 mm. Double-lumen tubes or bronchial blockers appropriate for lung isolation in neonates are not universally available and lung isolation is generally achieved by endobronchial intubation.

Monitoring

Routine monitoring equipment for the neonate should comply with basic standards and should include ECG, pulse oximetry, non-invasive blood pressure, capnography, temperature, and, where possible, anaesthetic agent monitoring. Simultaneous monitoring of pre- and post-ductal saturations is useful in certain situations. Specific non-invasive blood pressure cuff sizes for neonates and preterm infants should be used; an appropriately sized cuff covers roughly two-thirds the length of the upper arm. Most monitors use different (less compliant) tubing for neonatal cuffs to produce more accurate blood pressure measurements from the reduced pulse pressure in neonates. If the cuff is improperly matched with the tubing, the built-in algorithm displays inaccurate information. It is common practice to place the cuff on the calf; however, the correlation between arm and calf blood pressures is poor and the arm should be utilized whenever possible (Crapanzano et al. 1996). Mean calf pressure is significantly lower than mean arm pressure (Short 2000).

Pulse oximetry should be used to monitor oxygenation continuously during anaesthesia as well as transport. Recent evidence has suggested that there is a lower incidence of retinopathy of prematurity when oximeter alarms for premature infants are set lower. It is considered better practice to keep the Sa_{O_2} during anaesthesia at the same levels as used in the intensive care nursery, usually between 87% and 94% (Carlo et al. 2010). To achieve this, neonates should not be routinely transported with 100% oxygen, but rather with an oxygen blender to reduce oxygen exposure during transport.

Monitoring of ventilation

Accurate monitoring of ventilation presents unique challenges in neonates. Capnography and end-tidal CO_2 is the most common non-invasive method of estimating Pa_{CO_2} and hence adequacy of ventilation. In neonates, end-tidal CO_2 will be falsely low when there is a leak around the tracheal tube. In addition, the end-tidal CO_2 is lower in neonates because it is usually measured at the Y-piece of the ventilator circuit where the flow of fresh gas can wash out the small volume of CO_2 sampled (Badgwell et al. 1987). Exhaled tidal volumes can also be used as an indication of alveolar ventilation. Exhaled tidal volume is typically measured by a spirometer located at the end of the expiratory limb. Unless the ventilator has the ability to measure the compliance of the breathing circuit, this measurement will commonly overestimate tidal volume because it reflects the patient's exhaled tidal volume *as well as* the compression volume in the breathing circuit. However, if there is a leak around the tracheal tube, the spirometer will underestimate the exhaled gas volume. Transcutaneous CO_2 is also frequently monitored in NICUs as an estimate of Pa_{CO_2}; however, these are difficult to use in an operative setting. Without reliable estimates of Pa_{CO_2} or tidal volume, the anaesthetist may have to rely on chest expansion and inspiratory pressure measurements. When monitoring, ventilation is critical, blood gases should be measured frequently in order to ensure adequate ventilation and to recognize changes in acid–base status. Newer monitoring systems allow for measurement of flow and pressure at the tracheal tube, assisting the anaesthetist in determining optimal ventilation in patients with poorly compliant lungs. Newer anaesthesia machines that compensate for breathing circuit compliance provide accurate measures of delivered tidal volume (Bachiller et al. 2008).

Fluids

Glucose-containing maintenance fluids or parenteral nutrition should be continued at the same rate for neonates and preterm infants transferred from the NICU. Discontinuation or suddenly reducing a hyperglycaemic infusion may precipitate hypoglycaemia in view of their limited glycogen stores. When sequential blood glucose concentrations can be measured during surgery, the glucose infusion should be adjusted to maintain normoglycaemia. A second infusion containing a balance salt solution (lactated Ringer's, Plasma-Lyte®) should be used to replace volume losses from surgical trauma. This may be large for major abdominal or thoracic procedures, and significantly less for peripheral procedures. Fluid administration system should be controlled (buretrol or infusion device) to prevent unintended volume overload. Replacing losses with 0.2 or 0.3 normal saline is dangerous because it leads to hyponatraemia, water overload, and potentially death (Moritz and Ayus 2010). Alternatively, colloid (albumin or blood) may be used to treat hypovolaemia. Accurately monitoring volume status is difficult. Central venous pressure can be used, as can mean arterial pressure, urine output and just looking at the adequacy of perfusion clinically. In smaller preterm infants, monitoring urine output can be challenging because relatively large volumes of urine (>5 ml) are required before the urine is seen in standard tubing.

Peripheral venous access

Venous access is necessary for all neonatal surgical procedures because of the frequent need for medication to assist intubation, to administer glucose, treat bradycardia, or for resuscitation. The most recent evaluation of the Pediatric Perioperative Cardiac Arrest Registry (POCA) found a higher incidence of arrest related to cardiovascular causes, emphasizing the need for adequate peripheral venous or central venous access when caring for paediatric patients (Ramamoorthy et al. 2010). Peripheral veins may be seen through the skin of preterm or even term neonates who are lightly pigmented. When peripheral veins cannot be seen, anatomical landmarks may assist cannulation of anatomically constant veins, for example, saphenous (just lateral to the medial malleolus) or distal cephalic vein (medial aspect of the wrist, typically just lateral to a line from the thumb). Ultrasound guidance can be used when peripheral veins cannot be easily seen (Bodenham et al. 2016).

Percutaneous central venous access is more challenging in newborns. The umbilical vein is the most accessible central vein, and a catheter can be passed 'blindly' through the ductus venosus into the inferior vena cava. The position of the catheter tip should be confirmed radiographically. If the ductus venosus is not patent, the catheter passes into branches of the hepatic veins, and is visible in the liver. When this occurs, the catheter should be repositioned and only used for emergencies as central venous pressure monitoring will be inaccurate, and portal vein thrombosis or hepatic injury can occur when hyperosmolar or vasoactive drugs (sodium bicarbonate, dopamine) are infused. Surgically placed central catheters or PICC lines (percutaneous intravenous central catheters) are most commonly used for long-term venous access, and rarely for monitoring.

Invasive arterial monitoring is commonly used in the NICU and for large abdominal or thoracic surgical procedures. In the first week of life, the umbilical artery is the most accessible artery. If the umbilical artery is not available, or ligated during abdominal surgery, the radial artery is generally used, typically cannulated with a 24 g cannula with or without assistance of a 0.015 inch (0.381 mm) guidewire. The ulnar, dorsalis pedis or posterior tibial arteries can also be used when indicated.

Considerations for the premature and extreme premature infant

Preterm infants are commonly divided into three groups: borderline premature (36–37 weeks' gestation), moderately premature (31–35 weeks' gestation), and severely premature ('micropremies', 24–30 weeks' gestation). Sixteen per cent of infants are born borderline premature and generally only have mild symptoms of prematurity such as difficulty with temperature maintenance and poor feeding. Six to seven per cent of infants are moderately premature and are at increased risk to develop intracranial haemorrhage, sepsis, and respiratory distress syndrome. Even though only 1% of all infants are micropremies, they account for more than 70% of neonatal mortality and represent a large portion of neurologically damaged infants later in life. The causes of death include birth asphyxia, acidosis, necrotizing enterocolitis, intracranial haemorrhage, and respiratory failure (congestive heart failure, patent ductus arteriosus, respiratory distress syndrome, infections, especially group B *Streptococcus* and listeria).

Several complications of prematurity require surgical intervention and include ligation of patent ductus arteriosus, repair of retinopathy of prematurity, abdominal exploration and bowel resection for necrotizing enterocolitis, ventriculo-peritoneal shunt or reservoir placement for intraventricular haemorrhage with hydrocephalus, and inguinal hernia repair. Those infants who require significant respiratory or cardiovascular support often have their surgical procedures performed in the NICU. Infection rates do not differ from surgery performed in the operating theatre. Performing surgery in the NICU reduces risks associated with transport and altering ventilation; however, it reduces the anaesthetist's ability to access the patient or use inhalation anaesthesia.

The premature infant is typically fragile, requiring precise titration of anaesthetics, fluids, and cardiovascular and ventilatory support. It is critical for the anaesthesia team to thoroughly review the patient's current management and discuss the patient's status with the neonatologists before assuming care of the patient. The operating theatre must be warmed, infusions prepared (preferably with the use of an infusion pump), and precise doses of resuscitation medications prepared before transport. Even though the MAC requirements for the premature infant are reduced, insufficient anaesthesia will cause hypertension, tachycardia, and release of stress hormones. Premature infants typically show a more profound reduction in blood pressure from inhaled anaesthetics and therefore a narcotic-based technique is often utilized. Premature infants have poor respiratory control and are at significant risk of postoperative apnoea; therefore, most of these infants remain intubated after major surgical procedures, and if extubated should be monitored in an intensive care environment where apnoea can be readily detected and the infant rescued. The incidence of respiratory distress syndrome is directly related to maturity at birth, and many of these infants require mechanical ventilatory support. The anaesthesia team should try to match the ventilator settings used in the NICU because higher pressures and volumes can further injure the premature lung. Commonly these infants are ventilated with some degree of respiratory acidaemia to avoid excess pressures from mechanical ventilation, and this strategy should be continued during surgery. It is often difficult to manage ventilation precisely when intrathoracic and intra-abdominal contents are compressed from surgery. In this situation, manual ventilation with careful observation of the surgical field is commonly used. In addition, the oxygen concentration should be titrated to maintain the Sp_{O_2} between 87% and 94%, and a blender used to maintain these saturations for transport. Blood loss is often difficult to determine, but transfusion is commonly necessary for major abdominal and thoracic procedures because 10 ml of blood loss is equivalent to 10% of the circulating blood volume for a 1000 g infant. Red cells and potentially plasma and platelets should be available and irradiated before use for large operations. Typically, glucose-containing solutions from the NICU are continued intraoperatively to avoid hypoglycaemia as the glycogen stores of the premature infant are often depleted. The evaporative losses should be replaced with a balanced salt solution such as lactated Ringer's, Plasma-Lyte® or normal saline. Temperature maintenance is critical and the most effective method is to cover the infant for transport and use chemical warming pads; in the operating theatre, the most effective method to avoid heat loss is to warm the theatre. Warming fluids, use of convection warmers, and warming respiratory gases are also helpful in preventing heat loss.

Fetal anaesthesia

Fetal interventions require a large specialized team of fetal surgeons, maternal fetal medicine specialists, sonographers, paediatric cardiologists, anaesthetists, and operating room nurses. Fetal surgical interventions can be categorized into three types of procedures: open fetal surgery, minimally invasive 'fetoscopic' procedures, and *ex utero* intrapartum treatment (EXIT) procedures. Open fetal procedures are performed under general anaesthesia with the same maternal and fetal considerations for non-obstetric surgery performed during pregnancy. High concentrations of volatile anaesthetics are used to provide profound uterine relaxation. Therefore, the mother requires invasive pressure monitoring and treatment with vasopressors to maintain adequate blood pressure. The fetus is partially delivered and monitored by pulse oximetry and intermittent echocardiography. Additional anaesthetics or resuscitative medications are generally delivered to the fetus via the intramuscular route. When necessary, venous access can be obtained in the fetus by use of a peripheral vein or the umbilical vein in order to deliver additional medications, fluids, and blood. A multicentre study of meningomyelocele repair demonstrated a reduction in the need for venticuloperitoneal shunt and improved motor function; however, the fetal intervention group had a higher incidence of preterm birth and uterine dehiscence (Adzick et al. 2011). Other open procedures performed include resection of congenital cystic adenomatoid malformations of the lung and large sacrococcygeal teratomas. Attempts at fetal repair of congenital diaphragmatic hernia have not shown an improvement in outcome over that of conventional therapy.

Minimally invasive procedures can be performed through endoscopy and the introduction of fibreoptic scopes and instruments. Common procedures include photocoagulation of abnormal vascular connections in twin–twin transfusion syndrome, insertion of vesico-amniotic shunts for obstructive uropathy, and intraperitoneal transfusion for haemolytic anaemia. Most of these procedures can be performed with the use of local anaesthesia for port placements, with sedation of the mother. Remifentanil readily crosses the placenta and has been shown to reduce fetal movement during procedures (Van de Velde et al. 2005).

Similar to open fetal surgery, the EXIT procedure requires the mother to be deeply anaesthetized in order to provide extreme uterine relaxation. Invasive arterial monitoring of maternal blood pressure and treatment with vasoactive agents is commonly required. A hysterotomy is performed and the term or near-term infant is partially delivered while placental gas exchange is maintained. During this time, a difficult airway can be secured, or a thoracotomy performed to control a cystic malformation of the lung before positive pressure ventilation. Immediately after the umbilical cord is clamped and the fetus delivered, the volatile agent is reduced or discontinued and oxytocin administered to restore uterine tone.

Newborn resuscitation

Anaesthetists may be involved in resuscitation of the newborn at birth and some principles are common to resuscitation that may be required after birth. The algorithm presented here is based on the 2015 guidelines from the Resuscitation Council (UK), which are the same as the European guidelines (http://www.resus.org.uk).

For uncompromised term infants, cord clamping should be delayed for at least 1 min after delivery. However, if an infant requires resuscitation, this should not be delayed. Term babies should be dried and placed in a dry towel or blanket; significantly, preterm infants should be covered with food-grade plastic wrap and placed under a radiant warmer without drying of the skin and the delivery room temperature should be at least 26°C. In the first 30 s after delivery, the infant's tone, respiratory effort, and heart rate should be assessed. If the baby is not breathing effectively, first open the airway by placing the infant on their back, head in neutral position, and possibly a jaw thrust or chin lift if the infant has significant hypotonia. If the airway is not improved, give five inflation breaths.

High oxygen concentrations and high pulmonary inflating pressures should be avoided during neonatal resuscitation. If the baby's respiratory effort is inadequate, usually indicated by a heart rate less than 100 beats min^{-1}, perform assisted ventilation using air and positive pressure ventilation using pressures of 30 cm H_2O and inspiratory pause of 2–3 s. These breaths are commonly delivered with a T-piece resuscitator. For preterm infants, the inspiratory pressure should initially be 25 cm H_2O. Pulse oximetry should be used to guide supplemental oxygen therapy. An acceptable preductal Sp_{O_2} at 2 min after delivery is 60%, at 2 min is 70%, at 3 min is 80%, at 4 min is 85% at 5 min, and at 10 min is 90%

Adequate ventilation typically improves the heart rate, and if the heart rate does not improve, reassess the airway, and consider tracheal intubation. If the baby is breathing spontaneously, it is acceptable to initiate nasal CPAP. If the heart rate does not increase, or decreases below 60 beats min^{-1}, chest compressions should begin. This is most effectively administered with the infant's chest held in the hands of the resuscitator with thumbs on the lower third of the sternum and fingers along the spine posteriorly. The sternum should be compressed by about one-third of the antero-posterior diameter of the chest with a 3:1 compression to inflation ratio. If the heart rate remains below 60, obtain venous access (either peripheral intravenous or umbilical vein cannulation) and administer adrenaline (epinephrine) 10 μg kg^{-1} (0.1 ml kg^{-1} of 1:10 000 solution) and possibly $NaHCO_3$ and 10% glucose. If the initial dose is ineffective, the dose can be increased to 30 μg kg^{-1}. The dose of $NaHCO_3$ is 1–2 mmol of bicarbonate kg^{-1}, and it is preferable to use 4.2% $NaHCO_3$ (2–4 ml); the dose of glucose is 250 mg kg^{-1} (2.5 ml kg^{-1} of 10% glucose). If these manoeuvres do not improve the circulation, consider volume expansion with 10 ml kg^{-1} of normal saline, which may need to be repeated.

Specific neonatal surgical conditions and anaesthetic considerations

Congenital diaphragmatic hernia

Congenital diaphragmatic hernia has an incidence of 1:2000–3000 live births. The majority are left-sided (80%); a small percentage may be bilateral. Ten per cent present later in life. More than half are associated with other anomalies, some life-threatening. Prematurity, chromosomal abnormalities, significant cardiac defects, and central nervous system and spinal anomalies are associated with poor prognoses. Approximately half are diagnosed prenatally. The most significant issue in these children is pulmonary hypoplasia and pulmonary hypertension. Prognosis is most closely linked to the degree of lung hypoplasia and may be calculated with Bohn's Ventilation Index (Bohn et al. 1987) or the simple formula Pa_{O_2} [max] – P_{CO_2} [max], in the initial 24 h of life (Schultz et al. 2007).

Preoperatively, the neonate may require high-frequency oscillatory ventilation, inhaled nitric oxide, or ECMO. Sildenafil, prostacyclins, and non-specific endothelin inhibitors may also be used to control pulmonary hypertension. Surgical repair of the hernia is not urgent and should be performed when the child's respiratory status is stable. Indeed, respiratory function may acutely deteriorate after surgery (Sakai et al. 1987). Surgery is usually performed via the abdominal approach. Large defects have been closed using prosthetic patches, tissue-engineered grafts, and primary abdominal flaps. Minimally invasive surgery using a thoracoscopic approach may offer some advantages. Most infants will be intubated before surgery; however, if bag and mask ventilation is needed for induction it should be brief and inspiratory pressures minimized to avoid gastric insufflation. However, it should also be remembered that hypoxia may worsen pulmonary hypertension.

No particular anaesthetic regimen has been proved to be superior; most are opiate-based that provide haemodynamic stability. Epidural analgesia can be used provided the neonate is not anticoagulated or on ECMO. High-frequency oscillatory ventilation may be continued intraoperatively—requiring a total intravenous anaesthesia technique. A sudden decrease in oxygen saturation and haemodynamic instability may indicate pulmonary hypertension or a pneumothorax in the contralateral lung. Nitric oxide should be available. The vast majority remain intubated for ongoing ventilatory support after surgery.

Oesophageal atresia and tracheo-oesophageal fistula

Oesophageal atresia and tracheo-oesophageal fistula is the result of failure of the mesenchyme of the upper foregut to separate between the fourth and sixth weeks of gestation. Interruption of the elongation and partitioning of the foregut causes incomplete development of the oesophagus and persistent fistulae or clefts between the oesophageal and tracheal tubes. Up to 90 variations have been described but the rare tracheo-oesophageal clefts are the most challenging to treat. The most common anomaly (Fig. 70.1) is a blind-ending upper pouch with a distal tracheo-oesophageal fistula. The distal fistula is classically situated 1 cm above the carina but often lies at the carina.

Oesophageal atresia may be suspected antenatally if there is maternal polyhydramnios or a small gastric bubble on ultrasound. Clinical features strongly suggestive of oesophageal atresia include excessive frothy saliva and respiratory distress at birth; coughing and cyanosis during first and subsequent feeds; or the inability to pass a nasogastric tube. A chest radiograph confirms the diagnosis. Late presentation may be complicated by aspiration pneumonia or gastric distension (or both); distressed babies in particular 'air swallow' through the fistula. Type II or 'H' fistulae usually present late, often when the baby is investigated for recurrent chest infections or even bronchiectasis. Other anomalies are common particularly the VACTERL association (Box 70.1).

Cardiac and renal abnormalities are the most important and should be identified before surgery by echocardiography and abdominal ultrasound. A right-sided aortic arch requires a different surgical approach. Aspiration pneumonia and gastric reflux can be reduced by nursing the baby prone or in a head-up position,

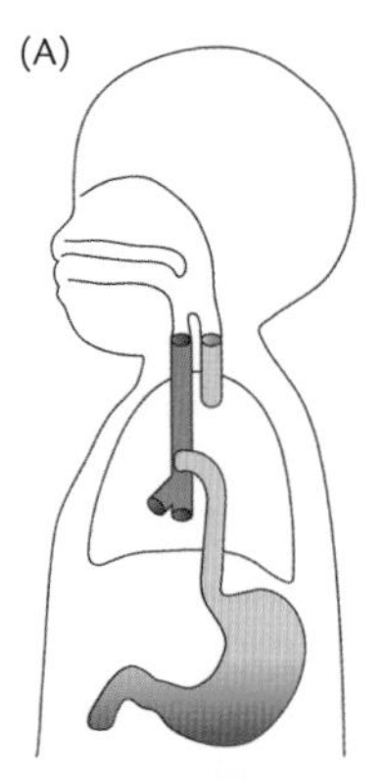

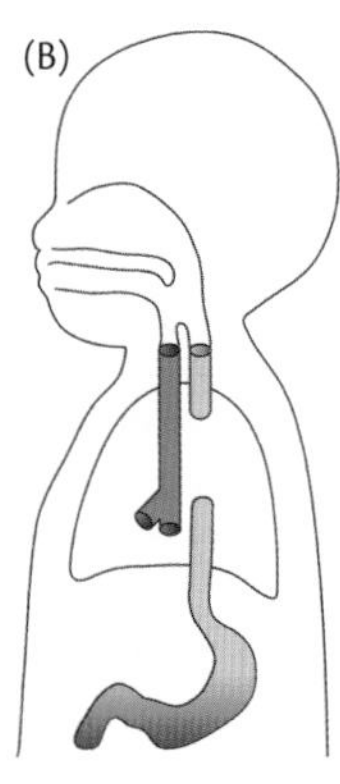

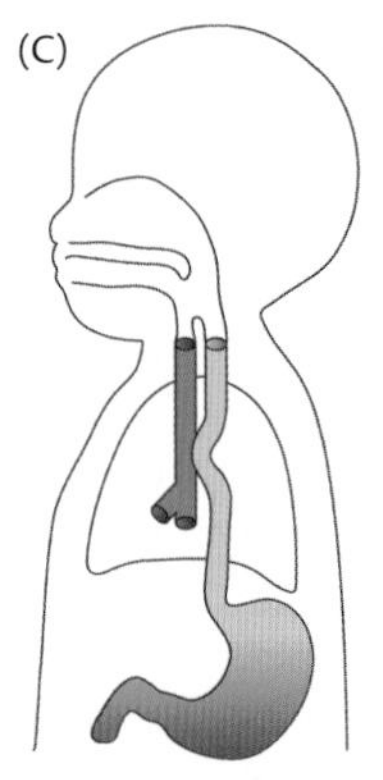

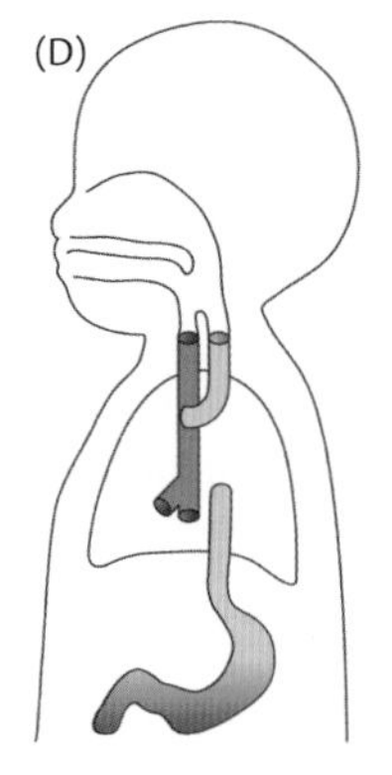

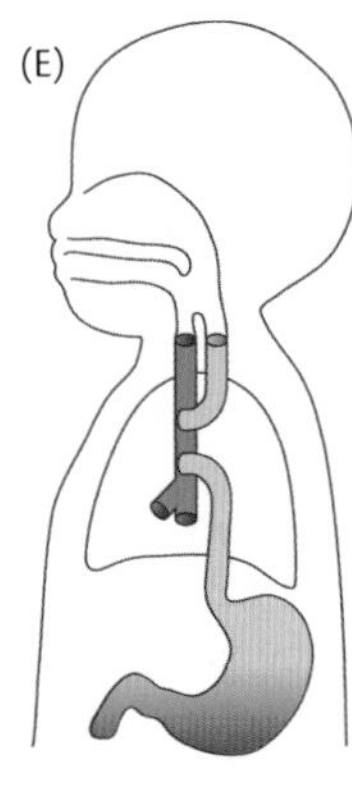

Figure 70.1 Classification and relative frequency of oesophageal atresia.

Box 70.1 The VACTERL association

- **V**ertebral (absent, fused vertebra, hemivertebra, absent, extra ribs)
- **A**nal or **A**limentary tract (Anorectal malformation, sacral anomalies, duodenal atresia, Meckel's diverticulum, malrotation, pyloric stenosis)
- **C**ardiac: congenital heart defects (incidence 20–25%) include ASD, VSD, PDA or tetralogy of Fallot
- **T**racheo-o**E**sophageal fistula
- **R**enal (renal agenesis, lobulation, hydronephrosis, hypospadias). Impact: renal function affects prognosis, renal agenesis may be associated with ipsilateral pulmonary agenesis or hypoplasia
- **L**imb (radial dysplasia, thenar defects, abnormal defective limbs). Impact: difficult vascular access and invasive monitoring

ASD, atrial septal defect; PDA, patent ductus arteriosus; VSD, ventricular septal defect.

and by draining the upper pouch using suction (continuously using low-grade suction through a double-lumen Replogle tube, or intermittently through a large nasogastric tube).

Positive pressure ventilation may result in gas passing preferentially through the fistula causing gastric distension and diaphragmatic splinting. The risk is greater with large fistulae and non-compliant lungs. High-frequency oscillatory ventilation may reduce the risk of gastric distension. Inability to ventilate effectively as a result of loss of gastric distension may require urgent gastrostomy.

Primary anastomosis is the goal whenever possible. The surgery is performed through a right thoracotomy using an extrapleural approach. Thoracoscopic closure has not been universally adopted. Positive pressure ventilation should ideally be avoided until the fistula is ligated. This may involve an inhalation induction without use of paralysis. Preoperative bronchoscopy has significant advantages. Ideally, it should be undertaken with the neonate breathing spontaneously so that the airway dynamics can be assessed. A Fogarty catheter—or a simple feeding tube—can be used to occlude the fistula when necessary. To avoid positive pressure ventilation it is again ideal to intubate the child without paralysis and then maintain spontaneous ventilation until the fistula is ligated, though this is not always possible and frequently assisted ventilation is required. It is preferable to place the tip of the tracheal tube distal to the fistula. This may not be feasible for distal fistulae. If there is a large fistula, the tracheal tube may be inadvertently placed into the fistula. A large fistula may also result in an inability to ventilate the lungs and gastric distension as a result of preferential ventilation of the stomach. If this occurs, withdrawing slightly or rotating the tracheal tube may help (Knottenbelt et al. 2012). In some cases, urgent gastric decompression is needed and if ventilation is still compromised, the intra-abdominal oesophagus can be urgently clamped through an abdominal incision.

Other causes of intraoperative desaturation include pulmonary compression, mediastinal retraction causing tracheal deviation or compression, or loss of cardiac output. Hand ventilation with a T-piece can be used while the chest is open to coordinate ventilation with the surgery. The anaesthetist can assist the surgeon identify the proximal pouch by moving the Replogle tube in the upper pouch. Once the anastomosis is almost complete, a smaller trans-anastomotic tube may be passed through the nose into the stomach under direct vision. This acts as a stent and facilitates subsequent feeding. Primary anastomosis of the oesophagus may be impossible if there is a long gap between the proximal and distal oesophagus. If so, the surgeon will ligate the fistula and fashion a feeding gastrostomy, delaying definitive repair.

Some surgeons prefer to ventilate all babies postoperatively, while others ventilate only those with anastomosis under tension or those with other significant anomalies. Epidural or extrapleural catheters can provide effective postoperative analgesia and increase the chance of successful extubation at the completion of surgery.

Gastroschisis and omphalocele

Gastroschisis and omphalocele are embryological defects that have antenatal herniation or evisceration of abdominal contents through the abdominal wall. Their differences are described in Table 70.1. Gastroschisis is a lateral defect, 2–5 cm long, usually to the right of, and separated by a skin bridge from, a normally situated umbilicus. There is no sac and the herniated bowel becomes thickened, matted, oedematous, and covered with a film that envelops the bowel. The risk of infection is proportional to the length of exposure to infected amniotic fluid or contaminated environment. The size of the defect influences the degree of evaporative fluid loss and cooling. Gastroschisis is seldom associated with other congenital anomalies except those in the gastrointestinal tract.

Table 70.1 Differences between exomphalos and gastroschisis

	Exomphalos	Gastroschisis
Incidence	1–5:10 000	1:30 000 may be on increase
		Associated maternal cocaine abuse
Site of defect	Herniation through umbilicus	Lateral defect to right of umbilicus
	Defect 2–10 cm	Defect 2–5 cm
	Sac (amnion, peritoneum)	No sac
		Risk of sepsis
Fetus	Premature 30%	Premature 60%
	Intrauterine growth retarded 35%	Intrauterine growth retarded 60%
Associated anomalies	Common	Rare
	Cardiac; cleft lip palate	
	Beckwith–Wiedemann syndrome	
	Trisomy 13, 18	
Problems with bowel	Usually normal structure, function	Becomes thickened, damaged
	Malrotation	Delayed return of function (2–5 weeks)
		Risk of atresia, ischaemia stenosis, adhesions, perforation
Outcome	Good dependent on size	Depends on state of bowel, time of closure, sepsis-associated anomalies

Omphalocele (exomphalos), a central defect that herniates through the base of the umbilical cord, is covered by a sac comprising amnion and peritoneum and usually with the cord at the apex. It may be 2–12 cm in size. Omphalocele is associated with other serious congenital abnormalities or chromosomal defects in up to 70% of cases. Beckwith–Wiedemann syndrome is characterized by macroglossia, organomegaly, and hypoglycaemia.

Gastroschisis and ruptured omphalocele require urgent closure, whereas closure of an exomphalos can be delayed to investigate associated cardiac or chromosomal defects. The goals of preoperative management include protection of the herniated viscera; antibiotics; minimize heat and fluid loss; prevent and decompress gastric or bowel distension with a nasogastric tube; and correct fluid, metabolic, and electrolyte disturbances. The protein and fluid loss from the exposed bowel in gastroschisis may be substantial. Cardiac abnormalities should be ruled out before surgery—particularly with exomphalos.

With large defects, the eviscerated bowel can be placed in a Bentec bag to allow gradual reduction before attempting primary closure. If primary closure is impossible, then a silastic pouch (silo) is fashioned to cover and protect the bowel. This pouch can be gradually reduced over subsequent days until a delayed closure is possible. The timing of the closure is balanced between the size of the defect and the infant's cardiorespiratory reserve.

Measurement of central venous, ventilatory (<30 cm H_2O), intragastric (<20 cm H_2O), or intravesical pressure has been used to gauge the risk of abdominal compartment syndrome and predict successful primary closure. Absent dorsalis pedis pulse, sluggish capillary refill, and a decrease in urine output suggest a dangerously elevated intra-abdominal pressure, which can lead to gastrointestinal or renal ischaemia.

Nitrous oxide should be avoided because of its propensity to cause bowel distension that can prevent abdominal closure. Continuing fluid resuscitation and maintenance of body temperature is essential. Opioid analgesia with a low concentration of volatile anaesthetic and full muscle paralysis is often required. Continuous epidural infusions, which provide analgesia and a degree of motor blockade without respiratory depression, can reduce the need for postoperative ventilation. Most babies require postoperative ventilatory support; some requiring continuous muscle paralysis for 24–48 h. Fluid requirements may also be increased in the face of a prolonged ileus. These babies are dependent on total parenteral nutrition until normal bowel function returns. Subsequent surgery may be required for undetected intestinal atresias, malrotation, or adhesive obstruction.

Necrotizing enterocolitis

Necrotizing enterocolitis is an incompletely understood intestinal complication with a high morbidity and mortality almost exclusively seen in premature infants.

The aetiology is probably multifactorial but is probably as a result of ischaemia of the bowel making it susceptible to bacterial and hyperosmolar damage. Bowel gas or gas-forming bacteria may enter the submucosa and the portal circulation giving rise to the classic, but transient, radiological signs of 'pneumatosis intestinalis' or gas in the portal system. Management is primarily conservative (stop feeds, fluid resuscitation, nasogastric drainage, and antibiotic therapy) unless complications that warrant surgical intervention occur (e.g. peritonitis, bowel perforation, progressive acidosis, and uncontrolled sepsis). Surgical intervention may be required in 25–50% of cases.

Vigorous fluid therapy may be indicated (crystalloids, blood, platelets, and fresh frozen plasma). The baby may be coagulopathic and septic. Inotropes are often needed. An intraperitoneal drain placed under local anaesthesia may form part of the resuscitation in very unstable low-birth-weight babies (<1.5 kg). Most neonates with necrotizing enterocolitis are already intubated and ventilated before surgery. If not, then measures to prevent aspiration should be instituted. Renal function and diaphragmatic action may be compromised by raised intra-abdominal pressure. Opioid-based anaesthesia is often used and inhalation agents should be used with caution. Nitrous oxide should be avoided. The intraoperative course can be stormy. Good intravenous access is necessary for the potential blood loss and frequent need for inotropic support.

Pyloric stenosis

Infantile pyloric stenosis (idiopathic circular muscle hypertrophy of the pylorus) is the commonest gastrointestinal abnormality in infancy. The aetiology is unknown; it has a polygenic mode of inheritance and the incidence is higher in the children of affected parents. Worldwide, the incidence is 3:1000 live births but with large regional variations and it is more common in white populations than black African or Asian populations. Males predominate by about 4:1. There are usually no associated congenital anomalies.

Infants generally present at 3–5 weeks with a typical history of progressive non-bile-stained vomiting (which becomes projectile and occasionally blood-stained) and failure to thrive. Infants are usually ravenously hungry. Visible peristalsis may be seen, particularly after feeding. Varying degrees of dehydration may be present. An olive-sized mass may be felt below the liver in the right upper quadrant. Mild jaundice is common and usually disappears 4–5 days after surgery. Hyponatraemic, hypokalaemic, and hypochloraemic metabolic alkalosis with a compensatory respiratory acidosis in varying degrees of severity is seen. Pyloromyotomy is the definitive treatment, but surgery is not urgent and should only be undertaken after adequate resuscitation. Correction of the alkalosis may take 24–48 h. Target values for resuscitation are serum Na greater than 135 mmol $litre^{-1}$, Cl greater than 100 mmol $litre^{-1}$, HCO_3 less than 28–30 mmol $litre^{-1}$, and K greater than 3 mmol $litre^{-1}$. Failure to correct hypokalaemia can lead to intraoperative cardiac arrhythmias and postoperative muscle weakness. Failure to correct metabolic alkalaemia leads to postoperative hypoventilation, particularly after intraoperative hyperventilation or opioid administration.

It is common practice before induction to insert a nasogastric tube (8 or 10 FG) to decompress the stomach. Some anaesthetists advocate rolling the baby from side to side while aspirating. Both intravenous and inhalation inductions are considered safe after this manoeuvre. Short-acting neuromuscular blocking agents may improve the surgical conditions and allow the inspired concentration of the inhalation agent to be reduced. Similar conditions can be achieved with regional anaesthesia; spinal, caudal, rectus sheath block, and local infiltration have all been described. The abdominal incision may be midline, right subcostal or umbilical. Laparoscopic approach is used with increasing frequency.

The surgeon may request a volume of air to be injected down the nasogastric tube to test the integrity of the gastric mucosa. An undetected gastric perforation may cause significant morbidity. Oral feeds may be started as early as 4–6 h after surgery in some cases. Paracetamol, 20–30 mg kg^{-1}, combined with regional anaesthesia, usually provides adequate analgesia.

Intestinal obstruction

Neonatal intestinal obstruction occurs in about 1:2000 births and may be the result of intrinsic developmental defects arising from disordered embryogenesis such as anorectal malformation or malrotation, abnormalities of peristalsis such as Hirschsprung's disease, or a secondary insult *in utero* after normal intestinal development such as an atresia, stenosis, or web.

Clinical presentation is determined by the cause and time of presentation. Most are diagnosed early, either *in utero* or soon after birth, and the babies are generally well and easily resuscitated. Abdominal distension may compromise breathing by splinting the diaphragm. These neonates are also at risk of aspiration, which may further compromise respiratory function. Broadly speaking, more proximal obstructions have greater electrolyte disturbance (duodenal atresia) while more distal lesions are more distended. Bowel perforation may cause septicaemia, coagulopathy, or further distension.

Initial resuscitation should include bowel decompression and correction of fluid and electrolyte disturbance. Coagulopathy, a feature of unstable septic neonates, should be corrected. Surgery can be delayed to optimize the neonate's condition provided there is no compromised bowel, perforation, or peritonitis. Other anomalies, particularly in association with duodenal atresia and anorectal malformations, are common and must be identified and optimized before surgery. The nasogastric tube should be aspirated before induction to reduce the risk of pulmonary aspiration. Rapid sequence induction and cricoid pressure may further reduce the risk. Invasive monitoring is indicated in sick or unstable babies and a central line may be required for intravenous feeding postoperatively. Maintenance of anaesthesia is determined by the condition of the baby. Relaxant opioid and volatile anaesthesia is commonly used. Nitrous oxide causes further abdominal distension and should be avoided. Epidural analgesia has been described (Table 70.2).

Inguinal herniotomy

The incidence of inguinal hernia(e) increases with the degree of prematurity. The risk of incarceration and strangulation is also higher in the more premature baby. The timing of surgery should take into account the risks of incarceration *vs* the risk of perioperative complications. The risk of postoperative apnoea decreases with increasing post-menstrual age. Awake spinal or caudal anaesthesia is reported to have fewer episodes of apnoea, hypoxaemia, and bradycardia than when the repair is performed under general anaesthesia or performed under spinal anaesthesia when additional sedatives are required. However, infants receiving spinal rather than general anaesthesia had an increased risk of anaesthetic failure (Jones et al. 2015). Most paediatric anaesthetists use a combination of general and some form of local anaesthesia (caudal, ilioinguinal block, or local infiltration). Infants with risk factors for apnoea should be monitored at least overnight, or until a 12 h apnoea-free period is achieved, before discharge. An incarcerated or strangulated inguinal hernia should be managed as for intestinal obstruction.

Table 70.2 Causes of intestinal obstruction and their associations

Diagnosis	Incidence	Clinical features	Associated anomalies	Specific problems
Pyloric stenosis	1:200–500 Geographic variability	Male: female 4:1 Usually present at 2–6 weeks Projectile vomiting Failure to thrive	Uncommon	Correct metabolic alkalosis Fluid resuscitation Aspiration risk
Duodenal atresia	1:6000–20 000	Early copious vomiting may be bile stained Hypochloraemia Metabolic alkalosis 'Double-bubble' on radiograph	Maternal diabetes in 50–70% Congenital HD in 20% Urogenital anomalies Gastrointestinal tract anomalies (anorectal; malrotation oesophageal atresia) Genetic disorders (trisomy 21, cystic fibrosis, trisomy 11)	Prematurity 50% (1 in 5 <2 kg) Aspiration risk Hypoglycaemia Correct electrolyte disturbance
Intestinal atresia	1:1500–3000	Bile-stained vomiting Meconium absent Abdominal distension Bowel perforation	Ileal atresia 25% Jejunal atresia 15% Colonic atresia 5% Multiple 10% Familial incidence	Prematurity Aspiration risk Respiratory compromise Correct electrolyte disturbance
Malrotation	1:600	50% present as neonates History of normal feed and stool; then colic and bilious vomiting X-ray findings: normal or dilated stomach, duodenum, small bowel; small bowel right of midline	Exomphalos Duodenal atresia Diaphragmatic hernia Midgut volvulus	Abdominal distension Suspicion of volvulus (blood per rectum) Urgent surgery
Anorectal malformation		Low or high depending on relation to levator ani 60% High lesions associated with other anomalies	VACTERL association Genitourinary fistula common (high lesion in males)	Cardiac assessment Pass nasogastric tube to exclude oesophageal atresia Abdominal distension Anoplasty for low lesion Colostomy or primary repair for high lesion Caudal block may be difficult; sacral anomaly
Meconium ileus	1:20 000	No meconium at 48 h Signs of obstruction or complications Visible peristalsis Radiograph: multiple dilated bowel loops of varying diameter, bowel 'ground glass' appearance, microcolon	Uncommon 10–15% of cases cystic fibrosis Complications: atresia, meconium-peritonitis, perforation, gangrene, volvulus	Gastrografin swallow Fluid resuscitation Surgery for complications Correct metabolic disturbances Treat sepsis Aspiration risk Humidify gases Avoid anticholinergics that thicken secretions
Hirschsprung's disease	1:5000–10 000	Functional obstruction: parasympathetic ganglion cells absent in rectal mucosa and variable distance proximally Abdominal distension, vomiting, constipation Radiograph: multiple fluid levels, no gas in rectum	Uncommon Congenital heart disease in 5% Trisomy 21 in 5% Recto-sigmoid disease more common in males Familial occurrence, long segment disease in females Recto-sigmoid 70% Left colon 20% Whole colon 5% Small intestine 1–2%	Enterocolitis carries significant mortality in neonatal period Antibiotics Fluid resuscitation Rectal washout Procedures include definitive resection, colostomy or rectal biopsy

Congenital lobar emphysema

Congenital lobar emphysema is characterized by over-inflation and air trapping in a lobe of the lung—usually the left upper lobe. This may cause compression atelectasis of the adjacent lobe(s), and mediastinal displacement with reduced venous return. The aetiology is unknown. Fifty per cent of affected babies have associated airway abnormalities such as deficiency or stenosis of the bronchial cartilage, vascular compression, or intra-bronchial obstruction. Congenital heart defects are present in 10–35%. Babies with congenital lobar emphysema present with varying degrees of respiratory distress and cyanosis with or without hypotension, the severity of which determines the urgency of surgery.

Inhalation induction with spontaneous ventilation is recommended to prevent further expansion of the affected lobe caused by positive-pressure ventilation. Selective bronchial intubation may be necessary if positive-pressure ventilation is needed. Inotropic support may be required. Nitrous oxide should be avoided. Once the chest is opened, the affected lobe herniates through the incision and ventilation becomes easier. Before closure of the chest, the lungs should be re-expanded to reduce atelectasis. Early extubation should be the goal in order to reduce the risks associated with positive-pressure ventilation such as rupture of the bronchial stump, air leaks, or broncho-pleural fistula. Regional anaesthesia (epidural infusion or paravertebral block) provides good analgesia that may facilitate successful extubation.

Patent ductus arteriosus

In the neonatal period, a patent ductus arteriosus is largely a problem of prematurity. It causes a varying degree of left-to-right shunt across the ductus resulting in excessive pulmonary circulation, left-sided strain, or high output cardiac failure. In severe cases, reversal of blood flow during diastole can contribute to hypoperfusion of the gut and necrotizing enterocolitis. Pharmacological closure is often achieved using indometacin, diuretics, and fluid restriction. Indometacin inhibits prostaglandin synthetase, reducing the prostaglandin E_1 and E_2 activity that maintains duct patency. Surgical closure is indicated if medical treatment fails, in longstanding cases, or if the duct is large.

Cardiac failure with fluid retention may be present. Usually a baby with a significant patent ductus arteriosus is treated with fluid restriction or diuretics, or both, which may render them relatively hypovolaemic. Diuretics can also cause significant potassium deficits. The anaesthetic technique and drugs used for induction and maintenance of anaesthesia are determined by the degree of cardiac failure. Intraoperative problems include lung compression and hypotension. Lung compression may produce periods of desaturation but may need to be tolerated to allow surgery to be completed. Hypotension may be as a result of hypovolaemia or surgical impairment of venous return. Volume expansion with a fluid bolus (colloid, 10–15 ml kg^{-1}) or inotropic support may be required to restore blood pressure.

For postoperative analgesia, a paravertebral or intercostal block can be placed with ultrasound guidance or under direct vision by the surgeon. Continuous epidural infusion is also occasionally used. Before closing the chest, the lung should be carefully re-expanded to reduce atelectasis.

Laparoscopy and thoracoscopy

Laparoscopic and thoracoscopic techniques are increasingly used for neonatal surgery. Insufflation of the abdomen or thorax commonly leads to hypoxia and hypotension. These complications can be reduced by limiting the inflation pressure. Hypothermia is related to the flow rate and duration of surgery and can be reduced by warming the gases used for insufflation. Abdominal insufflation shifts the diaphragm cephalad, compresses the lungs, and may cause endobronchial intubation. Higher ventilator pressures may be required to maintain tidal volumes. End-tidal CO_2 monitoring is less reliable during thoracic insufflation. Acute reductions in end-tidal CO_2 may be as a result of obstruction of the tracheal tube, surgical compression of the airway, increased leak around the tracheal tube, or cardiac shunt from increased pulmonary artery pressure related to hypercarbia and acidosis in patients with a transitional circulation. Hypotension may require a bolus of fluid or inotropic support.

Regional anaesthesia in neonates

Regional anaesthesia, although technically challenging in newborns, has wide-ranging benefits (Bosenberg 2012). Most blocks are placed under general anaesthesia to ensure an immobile patient. However, in certain situations spinals, epidurals, caudal catheters, and peripheral nerve blocks can be placed in awake newborns.

Opinions remain divided over the safely and effectiveness of regional anaesthesia in newborns (Chalkiadis 2003; Bosenberg et al. 2011). Some consider the risks too high for routine use by individuals who do not have the necessary expertise. Based on recent UK audits, there is little risk associated with epidural analgesia in children (Llewellyn and Moriarty 2007); however, the risks associated with epidural analgesia or peripheral nerve blocks in neonates are less clear. Newborns are considered to be at greater risk of local anaesthetic toxicity as a result of loss of reduced clearance (Chalkiadis et al. 2005); however, the actual plasma concentration that is toxic is unknown in neonates.

Portable high-frequency ultrasound has improved our ability to place epidurals and peripheral nerve blocks safely. Neonates are ideal subjects for ultrasound-guided blocks given that most peripheral nerves are superficial and the nerves and surrounding structures can be readily defined. Even the spinal cord can be visualized as ossification of the vertebrae in newborns is limited.

Spinal blockade

Bainbridge described the first spinal anaesthetic performed on an infant in 1899 and early in the twentieth century, Lord H. Tyrell Gray suggested that spinal anaesthesia 'would occupy an important place in the surgery of children in the future'. Although the popularity of spinal anaesthesia waned as the safety of general anaesthesia improved, it remains a popular technique in some centres—particularly for infants at risk of apnoea. Spinal anaesthesia can also be combined with caudal blockade. Spinal anaesthesia, with or without caudal blockade, has been described in a wide variety of surgeries including inguinal hernia repair, ligation of patent ductus arteriosus, pyloromyotomy, gastrostomy, gastroschisis, omphalocele, exploratory laparotomy, colostomy, anoplasty, rectal biopsy, circumcision, meningomyelocele repair, or orthopaedic surgery (Frawley and Ingelmo 2010). Spinal blockade has also been described as an adjunct to cardiac anaesthesia in infants (Humphreys et al. 2005).

With spinal alone, the duration of action is much shorter than in adults despite the relatively higher doses (typically 0.2 ml kg^{-1} of bupivacaine 0.5% with a minimum of 0.5 ml). The duration of blockade allows approximately 1 h of surgery (Frawley et al. 2004), although longer surgery may be possible if further local anaesthetic is delivered via a caudal catheter. Some also place a one-off caudal block at the end of surgery to provide postoperative analgesia.

Spinal anaesthesia rarely produces significant changes in heart rate or blood pressure; however, elevating the legs immediately post spinal may lead to a high block with apnoea and a loss of cardiac output. Reduced cortical arousal caused by peripheral de-afferentation results in most babies drifting off to sleep during spinal anaesthesia. If the baby is unsettled, oral glucose may help settle the child. Brief volatile anaesthesia or sedation may also settle the child, although it may increase the risk of postoperative apnoea (Davidson et al. 2009). The incidence of serious complications is low, but includes infection and intracranial bleed. Failure rates range from 5% to 20%.

Caudal block

Caudal anaesthesia is frequently used to provide analgesia for surgery below the umbilicus. It can be performed as a sole anaesthetic in an awake neonates but more frequently is used to supplement general anaesthesia. Caudal catheters may be used to top-up the block. Complications apart from failed block are rare but include inadvertent subarachnoid injection leading to apnoea and loss of cardiac output, nerve injury, and infection. Adjuvants such as clonidine prolong the block in older children but some data exist in neonates that show it may cause apnoea.

Lumbar and thoracic epidural block

Lumbar epidural blocks have been described for lower abdominal, pelvic, and lower limb surgery, and thoracic epidural blockade has been used for upper abdominal or thoracic surgery. Experience in neonates is relatively limited. Epidural are usually performed under general anaesthesia but can also be performed under sedation or spinal blockade. The T12–L1 and L1–2 interspaces are the largest and most easily palpable. The skin–epidural distance ranges from 5 to 12 mm depending on the gestational age and weight. Ultrasound can be used to measure this distance.

Sacral inter-vertebral block is also possible as the sacral vertebrae have not fused in newborns and is particularly useful in those where the sacral hiatus cannot be identified (e.g. obese newborns or high anorectal malformations with associated sacral abnormalities). This approach has less risk of spinal cord damage or dural puncture.

Caudal catheters can be passed up to lumbar and thoracic levels to provide effective analgesia for abdominal and thoracic surgery. This technique may be easier and safer than direct lumbar and thoracic blocks; however, confirming the correct position of the catheter tip is essential as misplacement is common (Valairucha et al. 2002).

Peripheral nerve blocks

Most well-known peripheral nerve blocks can be performed on newborns. Blocks can be placed using anatomical landmarks, nerve stimulation, or ultrasound guidance.

Axillary blocks can be used to provide vasodilation to facilitate PICC line placement or for limb salvage after misadventures with arterial catheterization. Femoral nerve blocks can be used for PICC line placement in the lower limbs, muscle biopsy, skin graft, and clubfoot repair in infants. Infraorbital nerve block has been described for neonatal cleft lip repair. Ilioinguinal nerve block can provide analgesia comparable to caudal blockade after inguinal herniotomy or orchidopexy. The ilioinguinal and iliohypogastric nerves lie between the transversus abdominis and internal oblique muscles 3–5 mm medial to the anterior superior iliac spine. Transabdominal plane block has been explored as an alternative for intraoperative and early postoperative analgesia for selected upper or mid-abdominal procedures involving the abdominal wall. However, the muscle layers are thin and compliant and the risk of penetrating the peritoneal cavity is high with both transabdominal plane and ilioinguinal blocks.

Intercostal blocks can be placed under direct vision at surgery or using ultrasound guidance to provide analgesia after thoracotomy or chest tube placement. Paravertebral block under direct vision immediately before chest closure is a viable alternative for management of post-thoracotomy pain. Extrapleural catheters can also be effective for postoperative analgesia.

Declaration of interest

None declared.

References

Adzick NS, Thom EA, Spong CY, *et al.* A randomized trial of prenatal versus postnatal repair of myelomeningocele. *N Engl J Med* 2011; **364**: 993–1004

Anand KJ, Hickey PR. Halothane-morphine compared with high-dose sufentanil for anesthesia and postoperative analgesia in neonatal cardiac surgery. *N Engl J Med* 1992; **326**: 1–9

Anand KJ, Sippell WG, Aynsley-Green, A. Randomised trial of fentanyl anaesthesia in preterm babies undergoing surgery: effects on the stress response. *Lancet* 1987; **1**: 62–6

Anand KJ, Sippell WG, Schofield NM, Aynsley-Green A. Does halothane anaesthesia decrease the metabolic and endocrine stress responses of newborn infants undergoing operation? *Br Med J (Clin Res Ed)* 1988; **296**: 668–72

Anderson BJ. My child is unique; the pharmacokinetics are universal. *Paediatr Anaesth* 2012a; **22**: 530–8

Anderson BJ. Pharmacology in the very young: anaesthetic implications. *Eur J Anaesthesiol* 2012b; **29**: 261–70

Bachiller PR, McDonough JM, Feldman JM. Do new anesthesia ventilators deliver small tidal volumes accurately during volume-controlled ventilation? *Anesth Analg* 2008; **106**: 1392–400

Badgwell JM, McLeod ME, Lerman J, Creighton RE. End-tidal PCO2 measurements sampled at the distal and proximal ends of the endotracheal tube in infants and children. *Anesth Analg* 1987; **66**: 959–64

Bartels M, Althoff RR, Boomsma DI. Anesthesia and cognitive performance in children: no evidence for a causal relationship. *Twin Res Hum Genet* 2009; **12**: 246–53

Block RI, Thomas JJ, Bayman EO, Choi JY, Kimble KK, Todd MM. Are anesthesia and surgery during infancy associated with altered academic performance during childhood? *Anesthesiology* 2012; **117**: 494–503

Bodenham CA, Babu S, Bennett J, *et al.* Association of Anaesthetists of Great Britain and Ireland: Safe vascular access 2016. *Anaesthesia* 2016; **5**: 573–85

Bohn D, Tamura M, Perrin D, Barker G, Rabinovitch M. Ventilatory predictors of pulmonary hypoplasia in congenital diaphragmatic hernia, confirmed by morphologic assessment. *J Pediatr* 1987; **111**: 423–31

Bosenberg A. Benefits of regional anesthesia in children. *Paediatr Anaesth* 2012; **22**: 10–8

Bosenberg AT, Johr M, Wolf AR. Pro con debate: the use of regional vs systemic analgesia for neonatal surgery. *Paediatr Anaesth* 2011; **21**: 1247–58

Brambrink AM, Evers AS, Avidan MS, *et al.* Isoflurane-induced neuroapoptosis in the neonatal rhesus macaque brain. *Anesthesiology* 2010; **112**: 834–41

Carlo WA, Finer NN, Walsh MC, *et al.* Target ranges of oxygen saturation in extremely preterm infants. *N Engl J Med* 2010; **362**: 1959–69

Chalkiadis G. The rise and fall of continuous epidural infusions in children. *Paediatr Anaesth* 2003; **13**: 91–3

Chalkiadis GA, Anderson BJ, Tay M, Bjorksten A, Kelly JJ. Pharmacokinetics of levobupivacaine after caudal epidural administration in infants less than 3 months of age. *Br J Anaesth* 2005; **95**: 524–9

Cote CJ, Zaslavsky A, Downes JJ, *et al.* Postoperative apnea in former preterm infants after inguinal herniorrhaphy. A combined analysis. *Anesthesiology* 1995; **82**: 809–22

Crapanzano MS, Strong WB, Newman IR, Hixon RL, Casal D, Linder CW. Calf blood pressure: clinical implications and correlations with arm blood pressure in infants and young children. *Pediatrics* 1996; **97**: 220–4

Davidson AJ, Disma N, de Graff JC, *et al.* Neurodevelopmental outcome at 2 years of age after general anaesthesia and awake regional anaesthesia in infancy (GAS): an international multicentre, randomised controlled trial. *Lancet* 2016; **387**: 239–50

Davidson A, Frawley GP, Sheppard S, Hunt R, Hardy P. Risk factors for apnea after infant inguinal hernia repair. *Paediatr Anaesth* 2009; **19**: 402–3

Di Maggio C, Sun L, Kakavuoli A, Byrne M, Li G. A retrospective cohort study of the association of anesthesia and hernia repair surgery with behavioral and developmental disorders in young children. *J Neurosurg Anesthesiol* 2009; **21**: 286–91

Frawley G, Ingelmo P. Spinal anaesthesia in the neonate. *Best Pract Res Clin Anaesthesiol* 2010; **24**: 337–51

Frawley GP, Farrell T, Smith S. Levobupivacaine spinal anesthesia in neonates: a dose range finding study. *Paediatr Anaesth* 2004; **14**: 838–44

Gullberg N, Winberg P, Sellden H. Changes in stroke volume cause change in cardiac output in neonates and infants when mean airway pressure is altered. *Acta Anaesthesiol Scand* 1999; **43**: 999–1004

Hansen TG, Pedersen JK, Henneberg SW, *et al.* Academic performance in adolescence after inguinal hernia repair in infancy: a nationwide cohort study. *Anesthesiology* 2011; **114**: 1076–85

Hardy JD. The radiation of heat from the human body: III. The human skin as a black-body radiator. *J Clin Invest* 1934; **13**: 615–20

Hazan J, Maag U, Chessex P. Association between hypothermia and mortality rate of premature infants – revisited. *Am J Obstet Gynecol* 1991; **164**: 111–2

Henderson-Smart DJ, Steer PA. Caffeine versus theophylline for apnea in preterm infants. *Cochrane Database Syst Rev* 2010; **1**: CD000273

Humphreys N, Bays SM, Parry AJ, Pawade A, Heyderman RS, Wolf AR. Spinal anesthesia with an indwelling catheter reduces the stress response in pediatric open heart surgery. *Anesthesiology* 2005; **103**: 1113–20

Ikonomidou C, Bosch F, Miksa M, *et al.* Blockade of NMDA receptors and apoptotic neurodegeneration in the developing brain. *Science* 1999; **283**: 70–4

Ing C, Dimaggio C, Whitehouse A, *et al.* Long-term differences in language and cognitive function after childhood exposure to anesthesia. *Pediatrics* 2012; **130**: e476–85

Jones LJ, Craven PD, Lakkundi A, *et al.* Regional (spinal, epidural, caudal) versus general anaesthesia in preterm infants undergoing inguinal herniorrhaphy in early infancy. *Cochrane Database Syst Rev* 2015; **6**: CD003669

Knottenbelt G, Costi D, Stephens P, Beringer R, Davidson A. An audit of anesthetic management and complications of tracheo-esophageal fistula and esophageal atresia repair. *Paediatr Anaesth* 2012; **22**: 268–74

Llewellyn N, Moriarty A. The national pediatric epidural audit. *Paediatr Anaesth* 2007; **17**: 520–33

Loepke AW, Soriano SG. An assessment of the effects of general anesthetics on developing brain structure and neurocognitive function. *Anesth Analg* 2008; **106**: 1681–707

Loepke AW, Spaeth JP. Glucose and heart surgery: neonates are not just small adults. *Anesthesiology* 2004; **100**: 1339–41

Moritz ML, Ayus JC. New aspects in the pathogenesis, prevention, and treatment of hyponatremic encephalopathy in children. *Pediatr Nephrol* 2010; **25**: 1225–38

Paule MG, Li M, Allen RR, *et al.* Ketamine anesthesia during the first week of life can cause long-lasting cognitive deficits in rhesus monkeys. *Neurotoxicol Teratol* 2011; **33**: 220–30

Ramamoorthy C, Haberkern CM, Bhananker SM, *et al.* Anesthesia-related cardiac arrest in children with heart disease: data from the Pediatric Perioperative Cardiac Arrest (POCA) registry. *Anesth Analg* 2010; **110**: 1376–82

Sakai H, Tamura M, Hosokawa Y, Bryan AC, Barker GA, Bohn DJ. Effect of surgical repair on respiratory mechanics in congenital diaphragmatic hernia. *J Pediatr* 1987; **111**: 432–8

Schultz CM, Digeronimo RJ, Yoder BA. Congenital diaphragmatic hernia: a simplified postnatal predictor of outcome. *J Pediatr Surg* 2007; **42**: 510–6

Short JA. Noninvasive blood pressure measurement in the upper and lower limbs of anaesthetized children. *Paediatr Anaesth* 2000; **10**: 591–3

Slikker W, Jr, Zou X, Hotchkiss CE, *et al.* Ketamine-induced neuronal cell death in the perinatal rhesus monkey. *Toxicol Sci* 2007; **98**: 145–58

Steinhorn RH. Neonatal pulmonary hypertension. *Crit Care Med* 2009; **11**: S79–84

Sun LS, Li G, Miller TL, *et al.* Association between a single general anesthetic exposure before 36 months and neurocognitive outcomes in later childhood. *JAMA* 2016; **315**; 2312–20

Valairucha S, Seefelder C, Houck CS. Thoracic epidural catheters placed by the caudal route in infants: the importance of radiographic confirmation. *Paediatr Anaesth* 2002; **12**: 424–8

Van de Velde M, Van Schoubroeck D, Lewi LE, *et al.* Remifentanil for fetal immobilization and maternal sedation during fetoscopic surgery: a randomized, double-blind comparison with diazepam. *Anesth Analg* 2005; **101**: 251–8

van der Griend BF, Lister NA, *et al.* Postoperative mortality in children after 101,885 anesthetics at a tertiary pediatric hospital. *Anesth Analg* 2011; **112**: 1440–7

CHAPTER 71

Anaesthesia for the infant and older child

Erin A. Gottlieb, Anthony Moores, Tom Pettigrew, and Alyson Walker

Introduction

Anaesthesia for infants and older children is, in many respects, similar to the practice of anaesthesia in adults. However, there are important differences in physiology, pathology, and pharmacology between children and adults, and there are the additional overlays of childhood personality and parental involvement. This chapter considers anaesthesia for children beyond the neonatal stage. It deals with the important aspects of the pre-, intra-, and postoperative periods, and particularly details those aspects of paediatric anaesthesia where practice differs from that in adult patients.

Preparation and assessment

The majority of infants and older children presenting for surgery are fit and healthy. Much of the effort in preparation and assessment will therefore be directed at offering relevant preoperative information and attempting to allay patient and parental anxiety. The incidence of preoperative anxiety and subsequent behavioural change is high, and there are a number of pharmacological and non-pharmacological strategies to address this problem. Paediatric anaesthetists continue to face common preoperative dilemmas, including those related to undiagnosed murmurs or coexistent upper respiratory tract infection. Most paediatric surgery is conducted on a day-case basis. Individual hospitals need to agree on selection criteria based on appropriate patient and surgical factors.

Information for children and families

The increase in ambulatory surgery has reduced the time available to the anaesthetist for interaction with children and families. The delivery of information to children and their parents will often begin at the pre-admission clinic. As with any patient for surgery, they should receive written information relating to the proposed procedure and clear guidelines on what they can eat and drink before surgery.

Medical professionals have known for a long time that anaesthesia and surgery can have a significant psychological impact on children (Kain et al. 1996; Wollin et al. 2003; Fortier et al. 2010). The development of behavioural rating scales has demonstrated postoperative maladaptive changes including postoperative anxiety, sleep disturbance, eating disorders, separation anxiety, aggression towards authority, and withdrawal. About two-thirds of children may exhibit such behaviours initially, but fortunately the changes are usually not long-lasting. Younger children have consistently been shown to be more susceptible to these problems. These behavioural changes are often associated with preoperative anxiety leading to a lack of cooperation and traumatic induction. Predicting preoperative anxiety is notoriously difficult, but factors such as parental anxiety, shy temperament, and previous hospital experience are indicators.

Written preoperative information may go some way to allaying prehospital anxiety, particularly parental, but may have little impact on the induction period and postoperative behavioural changes discussed. However, children and parents desire to receive such written information (Fortier et al. 2009). The Royal College of Anaesthetists has three patient information leaflets specifically designed for young children, older children, and teenagers. There are further guides for parents and all are freely available from the college website (www.rcoa.ac.uk/childrensinfo). Although complex cognitive behavioural preparation programmes have been shown to be effective in targeting anxiety and behavioural change in older children, they are unlikely to be deliverable in a resource-limited service.

Assessment

The majority of children presenting for surgery are fit and healthy. Anaesthetic assessment is often concentrated on providing age-appropriate information and reassurance, while making a plan for induction and postoperative analgesia. Specific to paediatric anaesthesia, a birth and neonatal history may provide useful information regarding previous long-term ventilation or complications of prematurity. The incidence of difficult direct laryngoscopy or difficult mask ventilation in otherwise fit and healthy children is low, and airway assessment is primarily concerned with the detection of loose deciduous teeth. Previous anaesthetic charts provide useful information on cooperation with induction and any technical difficulties, particularly difficult vascular cannulation. It is routine for pre-assessment services to record an immunization history, although recent immunization is not an absolute contraindication to anaesthesia. Surgery may be delayed after immunization to avoid confusion between the febrile symptoms of inoculation and surgical complications. Occasionally, children will have extremely complex congenital or acquired disease with multidisciplinary and multisystem involvement. The assessment of this group of children is beyond the scope of this section, but covered comprehensively in widely available review articles (von Ungern-Sternberg and Habre 2007a, 2007b).

Fasting

Starvation guidance for infants and children in many ways mirrors adult practice with recommendations of 2 h for clear fluids and 6 h for solid food (Smith et al. 2011). Breast milk is cleared rapidly from the stomach and most guidelines suggest a 4 h fasting time is sufficient. Most formula preparations take longer to empty and are therefore grouped with non-human milk and solid food. Gastric emptying of formula feeds may be faster in children less than 6 months of age and guidelines from Scandinavia support 4 h fasting times for this group. Children should be encouraged to drink clear fluids up to 2 h before surgery to decrease thirst and avoid preoperative dehydration. The volume of preoperative fluid does not appear to influence residual gastric volumes.

Preoperative assessment clinics

Consideration should be given to the development of pre-assessment clinics to facilitate same-day surgery, in particular to ameliorate the stress of admission and avoid unnecessary same-day cancellation. Nurse-led pre-assessment through structured questionnaires is now the norm in the United Kingdom and has been shown to be safe and effective (Varughese et al. 2006). It is still imperative that the child meets the surgeon and the anaesthetist on the day of surgery to confirm the need for the procedure and make anaesthetic plans for induction, recovery, and analgesia.

The child with an upper respiratory tract infection

A child is likely to have six to eight viral respiratory illnesses per year (Tait and Malviya 2005). Airways can remain hyper-responsive for up to 6 weeks after an illness. This creates a dilemma for the assessing anaesthetist who must weigh up the risks and benefits of continuing with anaesthesia and surgery. Postponing elective surgery in a child with a upper respiratory tract infection (URTI) is inconvenient to the family and wastes healthcare resources. Conversely, there is little doubt that URTI leads to an increase in perioperative respiratory adverse events (although generally these events, such as laryngospasm, bronchospasm, and atelectasis, are easily manageable with no permanent sequelae).

There remains little agreement on which patients can safely proceed to surgery. It would seem sensible that children with productive coughs, heavy purulent nasal secretions, fever (>38.5°C), or other signs of systemic illness (e.g. malaise, lethargy, or lack of appetite) should have their surgery postponed (for a minimum of 4 weeks). In the context of milder illness, factors such as age (<1 year), co-morbidities, urgency of surgery, and the planned procedure will guide decision-making. Young children, in whom the baseline incidence of respiratory events is higher, and those children with coexisting respiratory disease (e.g. asthma) make the most sensible choices for postponement of surgery in the context of a URTI. Traditionally, it has been demonstrated that procedures involving endotracheal intubation are associated with a higher incidence of adverse respiratory events in the context of coexisting URTI. Although there are widespread recommendations for the avoidance of endotracheal intubation, this would still seem to represent the safest, secure airway in this group of patients.

The child with a heart murmur

Heart murmurs are extremely common in the infant population. Nearly all of these are innocent murmurs occurring in structurally normal hearts. A number of authors have suggested decision-making algorithms to identify children at low risk of significant cardiac disease. Most of these algorithms begin with auscultatory features suggesting a benign murmur. It should be cautioned, however, that the nature of a murmur cannot always be determined by auscultatory features alone. Clinicians should adopt a high index of suspicion in children with syndromes that are associated with cardiac disease. In many paediatric centres, a cardiology opinion is always sought when the patient is less than a year old as clinical features are likely to be subtle in this population. Children aged more than 1 year with a systolic murmur, who are thriving, with no symptoms or signs suggestive of cardiovascular disease (cyanosis, tachypnoea, frequent respiratory tract infections. palpitations, syncope, reduced exercise tolerance) can proceed to surgery (Bhatia and Barber 2011). It should always be remembered that transthoracic echocardiography is non-invasive and can provide a quick, definitive answer.

The child with asthma

Asthma is one of the most common chronic illnesses affecting up to 10% of children (Doherty et al. 2005). Its great prevalence (which is currently rising) will ensure that many anaesthetists will encounter patients with the characteristic symptoms of cough and wheeze related to reversible airways obstruction. All patients with a history of reactive airways disease are at risk of bronchospasm in the perioperative period. The incidence of laryngospasm or bronchospasm during the perioperative period in asthmatics is low but the consequences are potentially serious.

Although there is scanty evidence to determine the optimal anaesthetic management of the asthmatic child, there are a number of important issues to address during assessment (Doherty et al. 2005). Firstly, asthma is extremely difficult to diagnose, and it is always important to consider alternative diagnoses. Clinicians should maintain vigilance for the unremitting wheeze or stridor indicating a fixed airway obstruction, patients with potentially chronic suppurative lung conditions, or children with tracheomalacia or bronchomalacia. The assessment of disease severity should include questions relating to poor control such as frequent hospital admissions or use of oral steroids. The severity of the child's asthma can be stratified by the level of treatment required to control symptoms as found in the 2008 British Thoracic Society guidelines (British Thoracic Society and Scottish Intercollegiate Guidelines Network 2008). Caution should obviously be taken in anaesthetizing children on step 4 or 5 of the British Thoracic Society guidelines. These children may have the wrong diagnosis, may not be complying with treatment, or may rarely have life-threatening exacerbations.

Anaesthetists should bear in mind that those with atopy may be at greater risk of allergic reactions. Additional i.v. corticosteroids may be required in those taking systemic corticosteroid therapy and occasionally those taking high-dose inhaled steroids. Despite these many considerations most children with asthma undergo uneventful anaesthesia.

Premedication and non-pharmacological interventions for anxiety

Ideal premedication

Despite adequate information and preparation, a minority of particularly anxious children, including many with special needs, will require sedative premedication to enable cooperation, avoid restraint, and prevent some of the behavioural complications that were described earlier. Ideally, a premedicant drug would provide reliable anxiolysis and sedation, possibly with amnesia, although this is debated. It would have a predictable but short duration of action and simple mode of delivery (or pleasant taste). Unfortunately, there is no single drug that meets all these criteria, but agents commonly used in the United Kingdom are discussed in the following sections.

Benzodiazepines

Oral midazolam remains the mainstay of anxiolytic premedication in children despite occasional unpredictable effects. It has a rapid onset of action (approximately 30 min) in a dose of 0.5 mg kg^{-1}. It produces sedation, anxiolysis, and amnesia with little effect on postoperative recovery. Rectal preparations are available but rarely used. Temazepam and lorazepam tend to be avoided in children because of prolonged drowsiness.

α-Agonists

Clonidine is emerging as a potentially useful agent. In addition to sedation, it has widespread useful properties including analgesia, reduction in emergence delirium, reduction in volatile requirements, and improved perioperative haemodynamic stability. The dose for oral clonidine is 4 μg kg^{-1}, and the neutral taste has been demonstrated to be superior to midazolam. It requires longer to work (approximately 40–60 min) but appears to have better levels of sedation, recovery profiles, and parental satisfaction when compared with midazolam (Almenrader et al. 2007). Clonidine appears particularly suited to the technique of steal-induction where the anaesthetist attempts a smooth transition between physiological and anaesthetic sleep by quiet, gentle inhalation induction. Dexmedetomidine may have a future role, but availability remains restricted.

Ketamine

The *N*-methyl-D-aspartate (NMDA) antagonist ketamine remains a useful paediatric premedicant despite its well-known psychotomimetic side-effects. An oral dose of 3–5 mg kg^{-1} will generally provide profound sedation in 30–40 min. It has an extremely bitter taste and may not be tolerated. For extremely anxious and uncooperative children, the i.m. route may have to be used. In about 15 min, doses in the range 4–10 mg kg^{-1} will provide deep sedation and analgesia bordering on anaesthesia. The latter technique obviously requires careful planning and discussion with parents.

Other agents

Alimemazine (trimeprazine) is still used as a sedative in critical care settings and occasionally for procedural sedation at a dose of 2 mg kg^{-1}. Although historically used for premedication, a relatively prolonged duration of action and cardiorespiratory depression make this antihistamine drug unsuitable for modern day-case anaesthesia. Similarly, the virtually prehistoric chloral hydrate or triclofos sodium (the more palatable metabolite of chloral hydrate) needs to be given in large volumes (50–100 mg kg^{-1}), effectively limiting their role to nasogastric delivered sedation in critical care.

Non-pharmacological interventions

Parental presence at induction undoubtedly alleviates parental anxiety, but the effect on the child is more variable. It has been almost universally adopted in the United Kingdom despite disagreement on the benefits to the child (Chundamala et al. 2009). To most clinicians, it seems to afford the best balance of addressing the rights of the parent and child, ameliorating parental anxiety, and possibly reducing anxiety and improving cooperation in the child. Interestingly, a study showed that clowns provided lower child anxiety scores in the anaesthetic room than midazolam premedication (Vagnoli et al. 2010). Low ambient lighting, single operators, and relaxing classical music in the anaesthetic room appear to also lower anxiety scores. Video games and other distraction techniques are also effective. With the increasing availability and familiarity with portable electronic devices these may prove to be an important tool in the armoury of the paediatric anaesthetist.

Topical anaesthesia for venepuncture

LMX-4® is a topical liposomal formulation of 4% lidocaine. It is rapidly absorbed and produces anaesthesia within 20–30 min that lasts for 1 h after removal. It appears to be as efficacious as EMLA® (Eutectic Mixture of Local Anaesthetics) and has a better adverse effect profile, including fewer cutaneous responses (Koh et al. 2004). LMX-4® has become the standard topical anaesthetic in many paediatric hospitals in the United Kingdom.

EMLA® is a 1:1 mixture of 2.5% lidocaine and 2.5% prilocaine as an oil-in-water emulsion. Anaesthesia is achieved in approximately 45–60 min and last for about 2 h after removal. There is a theoretical risk of methaemoglobinaemia, and care should be taken in neonates, especially those less than 37 weeks of gestation.

Ametop™ gel contains the local anaesthetic tetracaine (4%). It is effective in about 30–45 min lasting 4–6 h. It often causes a local reaction (erythema) and effective alternatives have reduced its use.

Topical anaesthesia appears to have no bearing on the success of i.v. cannulation in children, and therefore it should be considered mandatory if time permits (Arendts et al. 2008). Sucrose may be more effective than topical anaesthetics in ameliorating cannulation responses in newborns, although doubts continue as to whether this constitutes analgesia (Wilkinson et al. 2012).

Selection for day-case surgery

Children make ideal day surgery candidates. In addition to being generally fit and healthy, many of the common surgical procedures are of short duration with modest analgesic requirements. For these reasons, surgery is increasingly being carried out on a day-case basis. Children are no different from adults in that a number of patient, surgical, and social factors will need to be considered (Patil and Brennan 2007). Individual units will need to produce their own selection criteria to outline the patient and surgical factors that can lead to safe anaesthesia and surgery with their individual resource pool.

Neonatal surgery

The lower limit for consideration for day surgery will depend on a number of factors including the experience of the personnel. Many units will now consider day-case surgery for otherwise healthy babies at term. Preterm infants are not normally considered suitable until between 50 and 60 weeks post-conceptual age because of the risk of postoperative apnoea. This period may be longer for those with complex lung disease, anaemia, or neurological impairment.

Day-case surgery for tonsillectomy

In many countries around the world, tonsillectomy (or adenotonsillectomy as is often carried out in children) has now become a day surgery procedure. Many UK audits have demonstrated the introduction of safe and effective care pathways for day case tonsillectomy with strict inclusion criteria and standardized analgesic and antiemetic regimens (Robb and Ewah 2011). Despite this, tonsillectomy has remained an inpatient procedure in many centres. There remains concern among clinicians about complications such as primary haemorrhage and the applicability of studies to differing populations. Further barriers to implementation include large numbers of children that fail to meet social support criteria and a lack of enthusiasm for discharge among parents. It should also be noted that many tonsillectomies performed in the paediatric population are in patients with obstructive sleep apnoea. Many of these patients have clinical diagnoses of obstructive sleep apnoea without polysomnography. Admission for this subset of patients would always seem prudent.

Checklists and safety

Since the World Health Organization (WHO) launched the Safe Surgery Checklist as part of the 'Safe Surgery Saves Lives' campaign, many countries have made efforts to incorporate checklists into numerous aspects of the patient perioperative care journey. There is evidence that such checklists can reduce perioperative morbidity and mortality across a diverse range of surgical populations (Haynes et al. 2009). The National Patient Safety Agency in England and Wales has adapted the WHO checklist, but retained the 'sign in, time out, sign out' format. Many hospitals have tailored the checklist to their specific requirements, but all contain similar checks to confirm the identity of the patient, nature and site of surgery, staff and equipment availability, and delivery of appropriate antimicrobial and thromboembolic prophylaxis. Other similar initiatives include the 'Stop Before you Block' campaign led by the Safe Anaesthesia Liaison Group in the United Kingdom and designed with the intention to avoid wrong site regional anaesthesia. In Scotland, the Scottish Patient Safety Programme works on similar principles and has similar perioperative interventions, but has a wider remit to improve consistency of care throughout the hospital and beyond.

Intraoperative care

Induction

Induction of anaesthesia in paediatric patients can be achieved via inhalation of volatile anaesthetics, or by i.v. or i.m. administration of sedative hypnotic drugs. Each induction technique has unique advantages and disadvantages. When selecting a technique for induction, the anaesthetist should consider patient preference, health, anxiety level, ability to cooperate, and nil by mouth status. The anaesthetist must also consider the planned procedure and their level of comfort with these techniques (Zielinska et al. 2011).

Inhalation

An inhalation induction can be accomplished safely and easily in the cooperative paediatric patient. This induction technique is especially attractive in the outpatient setting, where most patients are healthy and fasted. Oral premedication or parental presence might be desirable for the anxious child.

For the cooperative patient, a smooth technique is to have the patient breathe nitrous oxide for 1 min and then introduce sevoflurane which is gradually increased. Alternatively, overpressure can speed induction by setting the vaporizer to deliver 8% concentration of sevoflurane in oxygen. Finally, the circuit can be flushed with 8% sevoflurane and the patient coached to fully exhale, then inhale a maximum tidal volume of sevoflurane and hold their breath, the single-breath technique. When delivering high concentrations of sevoflurane, the second gas effect from nitrous oxide does not affect the rate of induction (Banchs et al. 2013). Sevoflurane and halothane (no longer available in the United States) are the potent agents selected for inhalation induction because of their lack of noxious odour, acceptability and low incidence of airway irritation, breath holding, and laryngospasm (Lee et al. 2013). After the patient is anaesthetized, an i.v. catheter can be placed and the airway manipulated.

It is important to recognize that patients undergoing this method of induction pass through stage 2, the excitement phase, with an unsecured airway and without i.v. access. Patients in stage 2 are vulnerable to breath-holding, airway obstruction, laryngospasm, and regurgitation and aspiration of stomach contents. The anaesthetist should monitor the airway carefully during this time and be ready to suction any vomitus and treat laryngospasm.

Intravenous

I.V. induction of anaesthesia is achieved by the administration of a sedative hypnotic agent such as propofol, thiopental, etomidate, or ketamine through an i.v. catheter. Each of these drugs has unique advantages and disadvantages. Dosages of these common induction agents are found in Table 71.1.

Cases in which an i.v. technique might be preferable to an inhalation induction include patients at increased risk for aspiration of gastric contents, those with increased airway reactivity who might be predisposed to laryngospasm or bronchospasm, patients at risk for malignant hyperthermia, and some patients with cardiac disease such as left ventricular outflow tract obstruction, cardiomyopathy, or pulmonary hypertension (Sümpelmann and Osthaus 2007; White 2011).

Advantages of propofol include a quick onset of action, quick redistribution and cessation of effect, clear wakeup, and antiemetic properties. It can also be used to treat laryngospasm through a rapid increase in anaesthetic depth. Disadvantages of propofol include pain on injection, a decrease in myocardial contractility, and decreases in preload and afterload. This drug should be used with caution in patients with decreased myocardial function and in hypovolaemic patients.

Thiopental has similar properties to propofol in terms of quick onset of action and redistribution phase. Thiopental can also be associated with airway reactivity and bronchospasm.

Table 71.1 Common induction drugs in paediatric anaesthesia

Drug	Dosage (mg kg^{-1})
Propofol	I.V.: 1.0–2.5
Etomidate	I.V.: 0.2–0.3
Thiopental	I.V.: 3–5
Ketamine	I.V.: 1–2
	I.M.: 4–6
Midazolam	I.V.: 0.1–0.3

Cardiovascular effects include a decrease in myocardial contractility and decreases in preload and afterload.

Etomidate is distinctive in that it does not affect myocardial contractility. It can be a good choice in the setting of decreased myocardial function or hypovolaemia. Unfortunately, even one dose of etomidate is associated with adrenal suppression in adults and children. Etomidate is associated with pain on injection and myoclonus (Scherzer et al. 2012).

Ketamine, an NMDA receptor antagonist, has sympathomimetic properties. It is a wise choice for the induction of hypovolaemic patients or for patients with cardiac tamponade, asthma, or decreased myocardial function. It should be used with caution in patients with severe cardiac failure, as direct myocardial depressant effects are unmasked in catecholamine-depleted patients (Scherzer et al. 2012).

Intramuscular

I.M. administration of ketamine can also be used for induction of anaesthesia. This technique is useful for patients who are uncooperative or combative and will not accept i.v. cannulation or an inhalation technique. This induction technique is also considered safe for paediatric patients with cardiac disease including cardiomyopathy, left ventricular outflow tract obstruction, and cyanotic congenital heart disease (Sungur Ulke et al. 2008; Jamora and Iravani 2010).

Airway management for infants and older children

Depending on the planned surgical procedure, choices for airway management in infants and older children include endotracheal intubation, supraglottic airway device, face mask, and natural airway with or without supplemental oxygen via nasal cannula or simple face mask.

Endotracheal intubation provides the most protected and controlled airway. The patient can be orally or nasally intubated, and ventilation can be spontaneous or assisted. Uncuffed tracheal tubes were once preferred over cuffed tubes because of concerns about tracheal mucosal damage from excess cuff pressure. However, recent evidence does not support this, and the incidence of post-extubation airway morbidity is not increased when cuffed tubes are used (Weiss et al. 2009). Cuffed tubes confer the advantage of providing a good fit with fewer laryngoscopies, and more accurate monitoring of lung mechanics, less pollution of the operating theatre with inhalation agents, and decreased risk of microaspiration (Litman and Maxwell 2013). Cuffed tubes are preferred when it is critical to effectively control ventilation (e.g. in patients with pulmonary hypertension) or in situations where changes in pulmonary compliance are anticipated (e.g. laparoscopy and insufflation, transoesophageal echocardiography probe placement, burns, and cardiopulmonary bypass). Cuffed tracheal tubes should be used in cases in which the patient is at increased risk for aspiration of gastric contents. Cuffed tracheal tube size estimations can be made based on age, weight, or height (Xue et al. 2008). A common age-based sizing formula for cuffed tracheal tubes in children more than 1 year of age is (Duracher et al. 2008): tube internal diameter (mm) = (age/4) + 3.5.

Supraglottic airway devices, which include the laryngeal mask airway, are commonly used for airway management during general anaesthesia and as a rescue tool when a difficult airway is encountered. Although the technical skills for proper insertion are much more easily mastered than endotracheal intubation, practise is required to master these skills (Ghai and Wig 2009). The cuff of the supraglottic airway device can also be hyperinflated. Hyperinflation and associated higher cuff pressures (>60 cm H_2O) are associated with sore throat and dysphagia postoperatively. In addition, hyperinflation is associated with an increased leak of anaesthetic gases around the cuff. The use of cuff manometry should reduce leakage around the cuff and reduce pharyngeal morbidity (Licina et al. 2008; Ghai and Wig 2009; Schloss et al. 2012). Although less invasive than endotracheal intubation, airway stability, surgical field avoidance, the ability to deliver positive pressure ventilation, and the risk of aspiration should be considered before choosing a supraglottic airway device (White et al. 2009).

Mask ventilation is often used for cases of short duration. The airway is unprotected, and both aspiration and laryngospasm are possible. Mask ventilation is an important skill to master, as discussed later. The teaching of proper technique and strategies to produce and maintain a patent mask airway can be life-saving.

A natural, unsupported airway can be used for patients undergoing a total i.v. anaesthetic. A nasal cannula or simple face mask can be applied, and oxygen or air can be administered to the patient. Newer cannula and face mask designs contain a port through which end-tidal carbon dioxide is monitored. The airway must be continuously monitored for patency throughout the case. This can be a useful technique for non-painful procedures such as magnetic resonance imaging or proton therapy in which patient immobility is critical (Schulte-Uentrop and Goepfert 2010; McFadyen et al. 2011).

Difficult airway in children

Children with a difficult airway can be classified into one of three groups: those who appear normal and have an unexpected difficult airway; those with a normal airway who have trauma, burn, radiation, or swelling producing a difficult airway; and those with anatomical abnormalities producing a difficult paediatric airway. Difficulty can be encountered with mask ventilation, direct laryngoscopy, or passing the tracheal tube below the glottic opening. With any of these scenarios, the goal is to maintain oxygenation and ventilation, to have airway adjuncts available with which there are local training and expertise, and to refer patients with known difficult airways to appropriately experienced and staffed hospitals, if time permits (Engelhardt and Weiss 2012; Sims and von Ungern-Sternberg 2012).

There are a few differences between children and adults. First of all, the incidence of unanticipated difficult mask ventilation is probably lower in children. The cause of difficult mask ventilation in adults is commonly associated with the presence of a beard, and neck radiation changes (Kheterpal et al. 2006, 2009). An additional difference when managing the difficult airway of a child *vs* an adult is that children are typically unable to cooperate with an awake or lightly sedated fibreoptic intubation of the trachea that is topicalized with local anaesthetic. Most children must be heavily sedated or anaesthetized to allow airway instrumentation.

A difficult airway should be anticipated in patients with congenital syndromes affecting craniofacial anatomy such as Treacher Collins, Goldenhar, and Pierre Robin sequence; those with acquired facial pathology such as infection and burns; and those with other congenital airway abnormalities such as vascular or lymphatic malformations. It is critical to identify such patients and consider the anatomical site of airway difficulty in order to formulate an optimal plan (de Beer et al. 2011). These patients should be treated electively in experienced centres, and a difficult airway plan should be devised preoperatively. Anaesthesia can be induced intravenously or via inhalation, and ability to mask ventilate should be determined. Controversy exists over the use of neuromuscular block *vs* spontaneous respiration if mask ventilation is possible (Engelhardt and Weiss 2012; Sunder et al. 2012). Airway adjuncts that are available in paediatric patients include supraglottic airway devices, video laryngoscopes, optical stylets, and flexible and rigid fibrescopes. It is critical that staff be trained and have experience with the available equipment (Engelhardt and Weiss 2012; Sunder et al. 2012; Krishnan and Thiessen 2013).

In the paediatric patient that cannot be ventilated and cannot be intubated, few options exist. It should be recognized that needle cricothyrotomy in infants and children is extremely difficult with a low success rate. A surgical tracheostomy performed by a skilled practitioner is a better option. For this reason, such a surgeon should be available and present when a difficult airway is anticipated (Sunder et al. 2012).

The key to managing the anticipated or unanticipated difficult airway is to have a planned and practised approach with an armamentarium of airway adjuncts and well trained staff who are familiar with these tools (Best 2012). Simulation of difficult airway scenarios can be useful in teaching difficult airway skills to trainees. It is important to start with more simple techniques and advance to more complicated ones. A major advantage of simulation is that the primary teaching occurs without risk of injury to the patient. Clinical learning on patients is reserved for trainees who have developed skill with specialized airway equipment in simulation (Schaefer 2004).

Finally and importantly, mask ventilation needs to be recognized and taught as the primary life-saving skill and manoeuvre when a difficulty airway is encountered (Engelhardt and Weiss 2012). Some authors suggest that the routine use of the laryngeal mask airway and other supraglottic airways for elective anaesthetics has led to a decrease in the use of mask ventilation and a reduction in mask ventilation skills (Sims and von Ungern-Sternberg 2012).

Maintenance of anaesthesia

In paediatric patients, anaesthesia can be maintained with inhaled or i.v. medications, or a combination. Inhaled anaesthetics that are available include sevoflurane, isoflurane, and desflurane. Halothane is not readily available and is primarily of historical interest. Nitrous oxide can be added to increase the depth of anaesthesia and reduce the concentration of the potent inhalation agent required. There is some evidence that nitrous oxide may reduce the development of chronic post-procedural pain in adults; however, data is lacking in paediatric patients (Chan et al. 2011).

Short-acting i.v. anaesthetics can be administered as infusions and include propofol, ketamine, dexmedetomidine, etomidate, and remifentanil. Each of these anaesthetics has a unique profile in terms of pain control, amnesia, immobility, and effect on respiration, and typically, a hypnotic agent is combined with an analgesic. For example, it is often necessary to administer a combination of infusions to achieve complete anaesthesia (e.g. propofol/remifentanil or propofol/ketamine).

An i.v. infusion can be added to an inhaled anaesthetic with an opioid as part of a balanced technique. Neuromuscular block for paediatric surgery is not commonly required because of the reduced muscle mass (strength) of children and their ability to tolerate the haemodynamic effects of higher concentrations of inhaled anaesthetics that produce some degree of neuromuscular block. Neuromuscular blockers are used to facilitate laryngoscopy and intubation, to produce a dense block for certain surgeries (e.g. gastroschisis repair), and to reduce the anaesthetic requirement in sick patients (Meakin 2007).

Analgesia

Analgesics used in paediatric anaesthesia include opioids, non-steroidal anti-inflammatory drugs (NSAIDs), and central α_2-agonists such as dexmedetomidine. Regional techniques such as caudal, lumbar, and thoracic epidural analgesia, spinal anaesthesia, and peripheral nerve blocks are also widely used. The location and type of procedure, inpatient or outpatient status of the patient, and patient co-morbidities should be considered (Association of Paediatric Anaesthetists of Great Britain and Ireland 2012).

Opioid analgesics can be administered as a bolus or as an infusion. They include morphine, fentanyl, sufentanil, alfentanil, remifentanil, hydromorphone, and pethidine. All produce some degree of sedation and respiratory depression. Some narcotics and other analgesics can be administered neuraxially and produce analgesia from binding to opioid receptors in the spinal cord or parts of the brain, or both.

NSAIDs do not produce the same sedation and respiratory depression that are associated with opioid administration. Paracetamol is available for oral, rectal, and i.v. administration, and it is widely used in paediatric anaesthesia. Ketorolac is administered intramuscularly or intravenously. Concerns about increasing bleeding tendencies or the risk of renal injury may steer some practitioners away from this drug.

Fluids

Intraoperative fluid administration should consider the pre-existing fluid deficit, third-space loss, and blood loss. Glucose-free balanced salt solutions such as normal saline and lactated Ringer's solution are usually used intraoperatively.

Glucose-containing solutions sometimes produce hyperglycaemia and are not needed for healthy day surgery patients. Glucose should be considered when providing care for infants, patients receiving total parenteral nutrition, or patients with a history of hypoglycaemia. Another alternative is to monitor serum glucose during surgery and adjust fluid administration accordingly.

In general, the patient's fluid deficit should be calculated by multiplying the calculated maintenance rate by the number of hours that the patient has been without fluids (maximum of 8 h). Fifty per cent of the deficit is replaced over the first hour of the anaesthetic and 25% each in the second and third hours (Furman 1975). (See Table 71.2.)

Third-space losses should be replaced as well. These losses are quite variable depending on the invasiveness of the operation and the presence of fever or increased metabolic demand (Leelanukrom and Cunliffe 2000; Bailey et al. 2010).

In addition, blood loss should be replaced by crystalloid or colloid. Replacement by crystalloid is 3 ml for every 1 ml of blood loss. Replacement with colloid is 1:1 for every millilitre of blood loss. If the haematocrit decreases below a certain transfusion trigger or if blood loss exceeds the maximum allowable blood loss, transfusion of packed red blood cells may be required.

Table 71.2 Formula for maintenance fluid calculations (the 4–2–1 rule)

Body weight (kg)	Fluid requirement
0–10	4 ml $kg^{-1} h^{-1}$
10–20	40 ml h^{-1} + 2 ml $kg^{-1} h^{-1}$ above 10 kg
>20	60 ml h^{-1} + 1 ml $kg^{-1} h^{-1}$ above 20 kg

Data from Furman EB, Roman DG, Lemmer LA, et al. (1975) Specific therapy in water, electrolyte and blood-volume replacement during pediatric surgery. *Anesthesiology*, 42: 187–193.

If the patient has a known coagulopathy or thrombocytopenia, fresh frozen plasma, platelets, or cryoprecipitate is administered as indicated by the coagulation profile. In infants and small children, the citrate preservative in blood products can quickly produce transient hypocalcaemia. Replacement with calcium chloride or calcium gluconate may be necessary.

Postoperative care

The post-anaesthesia care unit (PACU) provides monitoring, analgesia, treatment of complications, and assessment of readiness for discharge to a ward or critical care environment. It should be warm, child friendly, contain paediatric equipment, and be staffed by nurses with paediatric training. It should be close to theatres but separate from the adult PACU, admission area, and preoperative patients (Royal College of Surgeons 2013; Royal College of Anaesthetists 2016).

Children are transferred from theatre with oxygen therapy in place, accompanied and closely monitored by the anaesthetist. Nursing is on a one-to-one basis. Patient care is formally handed over to a PACU nurse once the anaesthetist is satisfied with the patient's stability [The Association of Anaesthetists of Great Britain and Ireland (AAGBI) 2002]. The anaesthetist should communicate pertinent information about past medical history, airway, surgery, and the postoperative plan. Written instructions should include an analgesic regimen, antiemesis, i.v./oral fluid instructions, and duration of oxygen therapy.

I.V. access should be bandaged to prevent dislodgement, and flushed intraoperatively to prevent administration of residual drugs from within the i.v. chamber. This is of particular importance in infants and neonates (e.g. small volumes of residual neuromuscular blocking agent may cause paralysis). Warming measures should be used if a patient's temperature is below 36°C (e.g. overhead heaters, forced air warmers). Capnography is required if a tracheal tube or supraglottic airway is *in situ* (Royal College of Anaesthetists 2016). As capnography aids early detection of airway obstruction, it must be available in recovery and used in high-risk cases (Quinn and Woodall 2011). Tracheal tube removal is the responsibility of the anaesthetist (AAGBI 2002). Once the child starts to waken, the parents should be allowed into the PACU if stable (Royal College of Surgeons 2007).

Postoperative pain management

Assessment of pain in children requires a holistic approach (e.g. the extent of surgery, analgesia administered, and parental attitudes). Several scoring systems are available to aid objective pain assessment; some rely on the child being able to self-report (e.g. Wong–Baker Faces scale, visual analogue scale) (Wong and Baker 1988) while others require observation of behaviour parameters (e.g. FLACC: Faces, Legs, Activity, Cry, Consolability) (Merkel et al. 1997). The FLACC scale has been adapted for children with cognitive impairment (Malviya et al. 2006). Parental input is invaluable as they know their child's normal 'baseline' behaviour. Pain must be reassessed after analgesic administration to ascertain its efficacy.

A local analgesia protocol should be in place to ease consistent and safe pain management (Royal College of Surgeons 2007). Basic strategies (e.g. parental comfort, breathing techniques, distraction, and ensuring the child is not cold) should be used alongside pharmacological treatment if the child is in pain. Ensure loading doses of paracetamol and NSAIDs (e.g. ibuprofen or diclofenac) have been administered as these have an opioid-sparing effect. If opioid use is required, avoid i.m. administration. Concomitant administration of an antiemetic should be considered if using morphine.

After major surgery, patient-controlled analgesia (appropriate for age 5 and above), nurse-controlled analgesia, or morphine infusions may be used (Table 71.3). Background i.v. fluid should run alongside patient-controlled morphine analgesia if no continuous infusion is being used as this prevents cannula occlusion. A one-way valve must be included in the administration set to prevent morphine entering the i.v. fluid bag and resulting in inadvertent administration of a large opioid bolus. Children on morphine or epidural infusions should be cared for by staff trained in these techniques, and the Acute Pain Service should review these patients on their daily ward round.

Analgesia at home

Clear instructions must be given for the analgesic plan once home. Parents are advised to administer regular analgesia rather than waiting for the child to express discomfort. The analgesic protocol will depend upon the extent of the surgery and may consist of paracetamol, with or without NSAIDS (e.g. ibuprofen), with or without dihydrocodeine or oral morphine. When regional techniques are used, parents should be warned when the analgesic effects are expected to 'wear off' so that transition to oral analgesia can be commenced in advance. Topical preparations may be useful after some procedures (e.g. lidocaine gel after circumcision, diclofenac eye-drops after strabismus surgery).

Postoperative complications

Complications in the PACU are commoner in younger patients and those with higher ASA scores (Murat et al. 2004). Risk factors for postoperative respiratory complications include recent URTIs (within 2 weeks), asthma, passive smoking, nocturnal dry cough, and history of hay fever/eczema (von Ungern-Sternberg et al. 2010). Resuscitation drugs and equipment, high-flow oxygen, suction, and a defibrillator (with paediatric pads) should be immediately available. This may include emergency boxes and protocols for treatment of cardiovascular collapse, anaphylaxis, and malignant hyperthermia (AAGBI 2002). The PACU should have an emergency call system in place (AAGBI 2002).

Laryngospasm

Children have more reactive airways and develop laryngospasm readily, more commonly after extubation than induction (Asai et al. 1998). Blood or secretions increase the risk of laryngospasm, and so pharyngeal suctioning is performed before extubation, particularly after ENT/dental procedures. Laryngospasm must be recognized and managed quickly and effectively to avoid rapid desaturation and bradycardia. Patients may first breath hold, cough, and display

Table 71.3 Suggested postoperative analgesia regimen

STEP 1—simple analgesia: paracetamol with or without diclofenac or ibuprofen			
Paracetamol	20 mg kg^{-1}	P.O.	Loading dose
	15 mg kg^{-1}	P.O.	4–6-hourly maintenance dose
Paracetamol	7.5 mg kg^{-1}	I.V.	6-hourly if < 10kg
	15 mg kg^{-1} (max. 1 g)	I.V.	6-hourly if > 10kg
Diclofenac	1 mg kg^{-1}	PO	8-hourly
	0.5–1 mg kg^{-1}	P.R.	8–12-hourly
Ibuprofen	5 mg kg^{-1}		6–8-hourly (3–6 months old)
	10 mg kg^{-1} (max. 400 mg)	P.O.	6–8-hourly (>6 months old)
STEP 2—opioid bolus			
Dihydrocodeine	0.5 mg kg^{-1}	P.O.	
Fentanyl	1–2 μg kg^{-1}	I.V.	
Morphine (p.o.)	0.1–0.2 mg kg^{-1}	P.O.	4–6 hourly
Morphine (i.v.)	50 μg kg^{-1}	I.V.	Repeated up to 4 times
STEP 3—morphine PCA/NCA/infusion			
Morphine	I.V./S.C. infusion	10–40 μg kg^{-1}/h	
	PCA		20 μg kg^{-1} bolus with 5 min lockout
			With or without background infusion 4 μg kg^{-1} h^{-1}
		NCA	20 μg kg^{-1} bolus with 30 min lockout
			With or without background infusion 20 μg kg^{-1}/h
STEP 4—adjuncts			
Clonidine, ketamine, gabapentin and regional techniques should be considered if appropriate			

NCA, nurse-controlled analgesia; PCA, patient-controlled analgesia.

Data from Lonnqvist, P.-A. and Morton, N.S. (2005). Postoperative analgesia in infants and children. *British Journal of Anaesthesia*, 95(1), 59–68.

increased work of breathing (increased abdominal and chest wall movements and recession) (Sims and Farrell 2011). Inspiratory stridor may become silent in complete obstruction.

Laryngospasm may be managed as follows (Hampson-Evans et al. 2008; Ungern-Sternberg and Sims 2011; Orliaguet et al. 2012):

- Jaw thrust and continuous positive airway pressure with 100% oxygen
- Deepen anaesthesia (1–3 mg kg^{-1} propofol)
- Neuromuscular block [0.5–2 mg kg^{-1} suxamethonium (succinylcholine) i.v. or 4 mg kg^{-1} i.m.]
- Re-intubation is rarely required.

Co-administration of atropine i.v./i.m. (0.02 mg kg^{-1}) is useful to treat or prevent bradycardia (Hampson-Evans et al. 2008). If suxamethonium is absolutely contraindicated, 1 mg kg^{-1} of rocuronium may be used and can be reversed with sugammadex, if necessary.

Pharyngeal suctioning and aspiration of the stomach via an orogastric tube if distended can be performed while the neuromuscular block is still effective. If there has been a delay in the management, negative pressure pulmonary oedema may be seen after laryngospasm. This is usually seen within a minute of relieving the obstruction, but delayed presentation up to 6 h later has been reported (Orliaguet et al. 2012). Treatment is oxygen supplementation, positive end-expiratory pressure, and furosemide.

Postoperative stridor

Postoperative stridor usually presents within an hour of extubation and is caused by subglottic oedema particularly if a large tracheal tube has been used, in those with a history of croup or recent URTI, and in children who have subglottic stenosis (e.g. Down's syndrome).

Management

- Humidified oxygen
- I.V. dexamethasone (0.5–0.6 mg kg^{-1}, maximum 8 mg): this should be administered slowly because of the side-effect of perineal pain and burning on rapid injection
- Nebulized adrenaline (epinephrine): 0.5 ml kg^{-1} of 1:1000 (i.e. 0.1% adrenaline).

If severe, re-intubation with a smaller tracheal tube may be necessary. Overnight admission should be considered if nebulized adrenaline was required.

Postoperative apnoea

Premature infants less than 46 weeks post-conceptual age should undergo continuous postoperative apnoea monitoring for at least 12 h. In patients between 46 and 60 weeks post-conceptual age with risk factors for postoperative apnoea (i.e. apnoea at home, chronic lung disease, neurological disease, or anaemia), overnight apnoea monitoring is recommended (Walther-Larsen and Rasmussen 2006).

Postoperative nausea and vomiting

Murat et al. (2004) reported the incidence of postoperative vomiting to be 6%. Risk factors include age more than 3 years, patient or family history of previous postoperative nausea and vomiting (PONV), motion sickness, duration of surgery longer than 30 min, strabismus surgery, adenotonsillectomy, volatile anaesthesia, and use of longer active opioids (Eberhart et al. 2004; Association of Paediatric Anaesthetists of Great Britain and Ireland 2009). PONV may be a manifestation of pain, so ensure adequate analgesia.

First-line treatment of PONV is ondansetron 0.15 mg kg^{-1} (p.o./i.v.) (maximum 4 mg) (Association of Paediatric Anaesthetists of Great Britain and Ireland 2015). If this has already been administered, a second dose is unlikely to be beneficial. Children at high risk should also be given dexamethasone 0.15 mg kg^{-1} (i.v.) (maximum 8 mg). The combination of ondansetron and dexamethasone increases the effectiveness of PONV prevention. Efficacy of metoclopramide, cyclizine, and prochlorperazine are unproved for the treating PONV in children (Association of Paediatric Anaesthetists of Great Britain and Ireland 2009).

Agitation and emergence delirium

Children can be agitated postoperatively for many reasons (e.g. pain, full bladder, disorientation, parental separation, hypoxia, or delirium) (Sims and Farrell 2011). A difficult induction often predicts a difficult emergence.

Emergence delirium, commonest in preschool children, is distressing for the patient, parents and staff as the child may cry inconsolably, kick, scream, thrash about, and hallucinate. Midazolam has not been shown to be preventative (Dahmani et al. 2010). There is decreased incidence after propofol total i.v. anaesthetic use. Although it is usually a self-limiting condition after 20–30 min, medication may be useful (Sims and Farrell 2011): propofol 0.2–2.0 mg kg^{-1} or clonidine 0.5–1.0 μg kg^{-1} or fentanyl 0.5–1.0 μg kg^{-1}.

In children with learning disabilities (LDs) and those who have received ketamine in the previous hour, waking up in a dimly lit 'quiet room' aids a smooth emergence.

Discharge criteria

Local criteria should be in place to facilitate safe decision-making for discharge from the PACU (AAGBI 2002). Such criteria should include the following:

- Regained consciousness
- Maintaining own airway
- Cardiorespiratory stability
- Normothermia
- Adequately controlled pain and PONV
- Absence of surgical complications (e.g. bleeding)
- I.V. fluids prescribed if required.

Nursing staff should give a formal 'hand-over' to ward staff. If postoperative complications occur, discharge may be delayed and may result in an unplanned admission overnight. The commonest causes for this are PONV or uncontrolled pain.

Discharge home

In addition to an analgesia plan, parents should be advised about wound care and when their child can resume activities (e.g. swimming after ear surgery). Nightmares, eating problems, behavioural change, and enuresis may be observed up to 1 year postoperatively, and are commoner in children with higher levels of preoperative anxiety (Zain et al. 1996). Clear written instructions should be issued specific to that patient and their procedure including a contact in case of problems and a follow-up plan.

Special requirements in other conditions

Congenital heart disease

Congenital heart disease (CHD) is the commonest congenital anomaly. It accounts for nearly one-third of all congenital anomalies and has an incidence of 1:125 live births in the developed world. Patients with CHD may have an associated congenital malformation syndrome. These may be as a result of chromosomal abnormalities (trisomy 21, Down syndrome; trisomy 18, Edwards syndrome), exposure to teratogens *in utero* (fetal alcohol syndrome, congenital rubella), or it may feature as part of a syndrome complex (CHARGE syndrome, VATER association, or DiGeorge sequence). Consequently, approximately 30% of these patients will have extracardiac abnormalities requiring surgery in their first year of life (e.g. anorectal abnormalities, trachea-oesophageal fistulae, and cleft lips and palates).

Advances in the multidisciplinary approach to these children have meant that 85% will survive into adulthood. It is therefore possible for a child with CHD to present for elective or emergency anaesthesia in the same way that any other 'normal' child may do so. These children may have had multiple medical and surgical admissions, and good communication with the child and family is important. Hospital admission may be associated with a high level of anxiety, and practical procedures such as venous access, blood sampling, and anaesthetic induction require a sensitive approach.

CHD is a spectrum of simple to extremely complex anatomical lesions with their corresponding physiological consequences (Lake and Booker 2005). Septal wall defects, disruption or obstruction of the great arteries, absent or defective valves, and abnormally small or absent chambers can create complex haemodynamic circulations and place a great strain on myocardial function. The result of this may be increased or decreased pulmonary blood flow, or increased myocardial work to overcome an obstruction to flow. Common consequences of these anomalies are cyanosis, cardiac failure, pulmonary hypertension, and an increased likelihood of perioperative arrhythmias. The approach to these patients must therefore be individualized. This will depend on the situation in which the patient presents, the nature of surgery required, and local expertise of the medical and surgical staff. It is essential that the anaesthetic and surgical team have a good understanding of the effects anaesthesia and surgery will have on the child's circulation and myocardial function (White 2011, 2012).

Children with heart disease have an increased risk of perioperative morbidity and mortality (Pediatric Perioperative Cardiac

Arrest (POCA) registry 2010; Thiagarajan and Laussen 2011; Gottlieb and Andropoulos 2013). Patients identified to be at highest risk are children less than 2 years of age, infants with a functional single-ventricle lesion, and patients with dilated cardiomyopathy or left ventricular outflow tract obstruction. Patients presenting for emergency operations are also at increased risk.

It is normal practice in the developed world for children with CHD to undergo non-cardiac surgery in a specialist paediatric centre familiar with the management of these patients and able to provide perioperative paediatric intensive care support (Walker et al. 2009). Where a child with CHD presents to a hospital not equipped with the specialist skills and facilities to manage these patients, advice and support should be sought early from the specialist centre. Where possible, the child should be transferred to the specialist centre for further care.

Cystic fibrosis

Cystic fibrosis (CF) is an autosomal recessive disorder affecting 1:2500 live births in the United Kingdom. It is the commonest fatal inherited disease in white populations. The mutations occur in a single gene on the long arm of chromosome 7 responsible for encoding a chloride channel found in epithelial cells of exocrine glands in the body called cystic fibrosis transmembrane regulator (CFTR). It is a multisystem disease affecting the lungs, pancreas, biliary tract, bowel, and sweat glands.

Approximately two-thirds of children with CF will be diagnosed before the age of 1 year. Improved survival is attributed to aggressive management of these patients by their CF multidisciplinary team: chest physiotherapy, exercise to optimize sputum clearance, nutrition for normal growth, and aggressive antibiotic treatment of infections.

Children with CF can present for surgery relating to their condition or for operations common to the general population. Neonates with CF may present with intestinal obstruction in their first few days of life secondary to meconium ileus or an intestinal atresia. In childhood, they may require central venous catheter insertions, Portacaths, bronchoscopies and ENT procedures.

Active involvement of the CF team in the preoperative preparation of these patients is essential for both elective and emergency surgery. Where time allows, their chest should be optimized with chest physiotherapy, postural drainage, inhaled bronchodilators, mucolytics (dornase alfa), or inhaled hypertonic saline. This should continue right up until the patient goes to theatre. Intraoperative chest physiotherapy is occasionally undertaken in intubated patients allowing endobronchial toilet and bronchoalveolar lavage if necessary. On return to the ward, physiotherapy will continue again once the patient is awake and comfortable enough to allow this.

It is important to use short-acting drugs intraoperatively to ensure rapid return of function postoperatively (Rocca 2002; Fitzgerald and Ryan 2011). Propofol and sevoflurane are both well tolerated for induction, maintenance, or both (Pandit et al. 2014). Nitrous oxide should be avoided in children with poor lung function and evidence of bronchiectasis because of the risk of pneumothorax. Anaesthetic gases and oxygen administered postoperatively must be humidified to avoid drying of secretions. Sedative drugs should be avoided and where possible local anaesthetic infiltration, regional blocks, or epidurals used to achieve adequate analgesia to allow cooperation with physiotherapy after surgery. Where use of regional analgesia is contraindicated, regular simple analgesics and careful use of opioids to ensure an adequate analgesia/sedation balance is recommended.

Cerebral palsy

Cerebral palsy is a term that encapsulates a diverse group of neurological disorders affecting motor, sensory, and intellectual function resulting from a non-progressive injury to the developing brain during the antenatal, perinatal, or postnatal period. It is the leading cause of childhood motor disability with a prevalence of 1–2.5:1000 live births in babies of normal birth weight (Cans et al. 2008). Aetiology is multifactorial and causation in individual cases often difficult to establish. Risk factors antenatally include cerebral mal-development, prenatal stroke, congenital abnormalities, prenatal infection (TORCH), genetic predisposition, and trauma. In preterm infants, it is more likely to be a result of periventricular haemorrhage and ischaemia.

Classification describes the predominant motor defect present: spasticity (70%), ataxia (10%), dyskinesia (10%), or mixed (10%). Approximately two-thirds of patients are intellectually impaired; however, communication disorders and sensory deficits may mask normal intellect. Epilepsy is common in this patient group (approximately 30%). Pseudobulbar palsy, hyperactive salivary glands, and gastro-oesophageal reflux disease can lead to recurrent chest infections, poor nutritional status, low weight for age, dehydration, anaemia, and electrolyte disturbance. Often nutrition is supplemented overnight via nasogastric tube or gastrostomy feeding.

Patients often receive medications to control muscle tone: oral or intrathecal baclofen, diazepam, i.m. botulinum toxin type-A injection, vigabatrin, or tizanidine. These are combined with physiotherapy and splints to improve the range of movement and reduce pain from contractures. They may also be on antiepileptic, antispasmodic, anti-reflux, antidepressant, anticholinergic, prophylactic antibiotic, and laxative medications.

Patients with cerebral palsy can present for general surgical procedures or for interventions resulting from their cerebral palsy (e.g. imaging, dental restorative/extractions, surgery for gastro-oesophageal reflux, gastrostomies, spinal corrective surgery for scoliosis, orthopaedic bone and soft tissue release, tendon transfers, osteotomies, and botulinum toxin injections). It is important to establish the patient's level of communication and cognition preoperatively and have a full appreciation of the role the carer has in communication, alleviating anxiety, and assessment of pain and distress in their child during the hospital stay. Good communication and involvement of a multidisciplinary team from the outset is an essential part of their care. Patients may have had multiple previous surgical procedures, so previous anaesthetic charts should be reviewed,and screening questions should enquire about a history of latex allergy. Coexisting medical conditions must be optimized preoperatively and normal medications continued where possible.

Anaesthetic induction may be challenging with difficult i.v. access, gastro-oesophageal reflux disease, excessive drooling, communication difficulties, anxiety, and poor patient cooperation (Wongprasartsu and Stevens 2002; Prosser and Sharma 2010). The presence of the primary carer at induction and in recovery may help alleviate some of this stress. Sedative premedication may be useful but best avoided in hypotonic patients with poor upper airway tone. Often a second pair of hands may be of help during a gas induction.

Hypothermia is a significant problem in this patient group (Wass et al. 2012). They are predisposed to this as a result of hypothalamic dysfunction, a lack of insulating tissues, and malnourishment. Patients should be actively warmed perioperatively. Limb contractures and scoliosis make careful positioning with protective padding important to avoid nerve, soft tissue, or bone injury. Intraoperatively volatile minimum alveolar concentration values have been found to be approximately 20% lower and more so if taking anticonvulsants. Resistance to vecuronium has also been reported.

Postoperative emergence problems can include irritability, delayed emergence as a result of volatile sensitivity, hypothermia, postoperative nausea and vomiting, especially with opioid use. Pain assessment can be difficult often relying on behavioural indicators (groaning, face grimacing, moaning, and altered sleep patterns) or the primary carer's assessment. 'On-demand' analgesia techniques should therefore be avoided in favour of 'continuous' multimodal analgesia. Epidural infusion techniques combining local anaesthetic agents with clonidine have been shown to be beneficial for controlling pain and muscle spasm especially after major orthopaedic surgery (Nolan et al. 2000). Postoperative muscle spasms are triggered by hypothermia, pain, and anxiety causing acute pain and distress. Regular oral or rectal diazepam is often given prophylactically and in cases where spasms are resistant to this, a low-dose midazolam infusion usually in a high dependency environment may be necessary.

Postoperative care must also concentrate on ensuring adequate hydration, providing regular chest physiotherapy, and care with positioning to avoid pressure sores. Often after orthopaedic surgery there is extensive plaster casting which can restrict respiration, cause acute gastric dilatation, or mask lower limb compartment syndrome.

Neuromuscular disease

Neuromuscular disorders in children are a relatively rare heterogeneous group of conditions that raise specific concerns for the conduct of anaesthesia. These children may present for surgery related to determining a definitive diagnosis (muscle biopsy and magnetic resonance imaging) or managing a particular consequence of their condition (gastrostomy and corrective orthopaedic procedures). Occasionally, the diagnosis may not be known or even suspected for a child presenting for incidental surgery and in this situation there is always the potential risk of complications occurring that relate to these disorders. The specific diagnosis of the presenting condition is important in both the risk assessment and anaesthetic management and so wherever possible it should be ascertained before any surgery is undertaken. This may be ascertained from genetic studies, family history, examination, investigations, and a discussion of the possible diagnosis with the patient's paediatric neurologist. Because of the rarity of some of these conditions, it is always useful to review case reports, review articles, or refer to information websites such as OrphanAnesthesia (http://www.orphananesthesia.eu/en/) (Becke et al. 2011).

Perioperative care for a child with a neuromuscular disorder can be complex and requires the input from multiple disciplines to minimize the morbidity and mortality associated with anaesthetic and surgical interventions in this group. A paediatric intensive care bed should be considered for even the most minor of procedures. Neuromuscular diseases are multiorgan diseases. In particular, the cardiorespiratory function of these patients requires thorough investigation before embarking on any surgery. Cardiac abnormalities that must be sought include cardiomyopathy, conduction defects, and arrhythmias. Respiratory complications are common in these patients and relate to weak diaphragmatic and intercostal muscles, inadequate cough, poor pharyngeal tone, spinal deformities resulting in restriction of chest wall movement, obstructive sleep apnoea, and recurrent respiratory tract infections (Blatter and Finder 2013). It is common for the degree of severity of function not to correlate with progression of their underlying disorder. It can also be difficult to assess the physiological reserve of patients who are unable to challenge themselves physically because of their muscle weakness.

Suxamethonium should be avoided in patients with neuromuscular disorders because of the high risk of rhabdomyolysis. The use of halogenated inhalation anaesthetic agents in any patient with a known or suspected muscle disease needs to be carefully considered because on rare occasions they too can cause rhabdomyolysis giving rise to acute hyperkalaemic cardiac arrest, notably in Duchenne and Becker muscular dystrophy (Segura et al. 2013). This anaesthesia-related rhabdomyolysis is distinct from malignant hyperthermia but the use of volatile anaesthetics agents in patients with muscular dystrophies remains controversial (see Chapter 80). Central core myopathies, minicore or multicore myopathy with *RYR1* mutation, and King Denborough syndrome may be associated with malignant hyperthermia susceptibility (Davis and Brandom 2009; Brislin and Theroux 2013).

With the development of faster onset non-depolarizing neuromuscular blocking agents such as rocuronium and an available antagonist agent to this drug (sugammadex) we have potentially safer alternatives to suxamethonium for (modified) rapid sequence inductions. Where non-depolarizing neuromuscular blocking drugs are used, careful titration with neuromuscular block monitoring is essential. Neostigmine should be used with caution for neuromuscular reversal in patients with myotonic dystrophy because of a potential risk of incomplete reversal or curarization.

Myopathic patients with underlying mitochondrial dysfunction present a unique type of challenge (Niezgoda and Morgan 2013). The stress of surgery and anaesthesia poses significant perioperative risks. Respiratory depression, cardiac depression, conduction defects, and problems with coordinating swallowing resulting in aspiration can all occur as a result of the depressant effects of anaesthetic agents on the mitochondria. Avoidance of prolonged fasting, PONV, hypoglycaemia, hypovolaemia, lactate-containing solutions, and hypothermia help to minimize the metabolic burden for these children. Mitochondrial disease probably represents hundreds of different defects with different sensitivities to anaesthetic agents. It is generally considered though that propofol is perhaps not a good choice of agent as it is well known to inhibit mitochondrial function. Bupivacaine should also be used with caution in patients with defects in fatty acid metabolism because of increased sensitivity to its cardiotoxic effects (Weinberg et al. 2000).

Children with learning disabilities

Children with LDs have an intelligence quotient (IQ) of less than 70 as a result of cognitive impairment which has occurred before the age of 18 and is associated with declining social functioning (Courtman and Mumby 2008). Severity can vary from mild to profound. Communication can be difficult as many children with a severe LD do not develop speech and a significant number have problems with their sight and hearing. The input of the parents/caregiver is invaluable as they understand the child's behaviour and communication styles. It is important not to dismiss a child's behaviour (e.g. screaming, pulling) as being simply attributable to the LD: one must ensure that it is not because of pain or anxiety, for example.

Keys to successful management include preparation and a team approach with involvement of the parents/caregiver. The surgical team should inform the anaesthetic team before the day of surgery that a child with a LD is on the operating list. This allows thorough preparation and appropriate allocation of theatre and anaesthetic time. Anaesthetists should read the patient's notes before the preoperative consultation to avoid repetition of history-taking (Department of Health 2003). Parents/carers may have a folder containing information on the child's behaviour, likes and dislikes, comfort items, medical problems, and medications. Children with LDs often have complex health needs, including medical conditions (Box 71.1).

The anaesthetist should assess how cooperative the child will be/has been on previous occasions and consider the parent/caregiver's opinion. Children with LDs are less likely to cooperate on induction and are more likely to require premedication. This can be administered in a favourite drink to improve compliance and to disguise any bitter taste. Flexibility of approach (e.g. plans A, B, and C) should be agreed in advance so that staff and parents know what to expect. Suggested premedication regimens are shown in Table 71.4.

If the child has a 'comfort object' (e.g. blanket or favourite toy), bring this into the induction room. The anaesthetic room/operating theatre should be as calming an environment as possible: low lighting, minimal outside noise, a familiar voice, and as few people as possible in the room. If the child is very uncooperative despite premedication, re-premedication or postponement of surgery may be necessary. Restraint should be avoided if at all possible. If unavoidable, ensure adequate members of trained staff are available to control the situation as quickly and effectively as possible (Royal College of Nursing 2010). Parents should be forewarned about what to expect. It is good practice to record how the child acted during induction and postoperatively to inform future anaesthetists. Postoperatively, bring the parents/caregiver into the PACU as soon as possible. Careful assessment of behaviour is required to identify and manage postoperative pain.

Box 71.1 Medical problems associated with learning disabilities

- Difficult airway (e.g. Down's syndrome)
- Increased risk of chest infections
- Congenital cardiac disease
- Epilepsy (note: some anticonvulsants can reduce MAC values, increasing recovery time from anaesthesia and the risk of airway compromise) (Prosser and Sharma 2010)
- Increased sensitivity to opioids (Down's syndrome) (Mafrica and Fodale 2006)
- Gastro-oesophageal reflux (Bohmen et al. 1999)
- Increased salivation
- Impaired postural control, requiring mobility or transfer equipment and care when positioning (e.g. cerebral palsy)
- Difficulty maintaining normothermia
- Visual or hearing impairment
- Psychiatric disorders
- Increased risk of latex allergy if repeated catheterization
- Poor dental hygiene
- Some neuroleptics (e.g. risperidone) can increase the risk of post-induction hypotension
- Difficult vascular access.

Data from various sources, see references.

Autistic spectrum disorders ('autism')

Autism is a group of disorders characterized by impaired social development and communication, delayed and deviant language development, and repetitive or unusual behaviours with an onset before the age of 3 years (Rainey and Van der Walt 1998; Carlyle and Lim 2011). It affects 0.6% of children, 40–62% of whom will also have a LD (Rice 2007). As autistic children are often upset by changes in their routines, a hospital admission can be upsetting and stressful.

An 'early warning system' should be in place so that the patient's management can be planned and coordinated in advance (Rainey and Van der Walt 1998). Inviting the parents/carer to attend a preoperative assessment in advance is useful for forming an anaesthetic plan, and signing consent forms. Such planning minimizes the waiting time on the day of surgery. The anaesthetic team should find out the child's likes, dislikes, and phobias in order to create as stress-free an environment as possible. A premedication is often

Table 71.4 Suggested premedication regimens

Drug	Administration route	Dose	Onset time (min)
Midazolam	P.O.	0.25–1 mg kg^{-1} (max. 20 mg)	20–30
Ketamine	P.O.	3–5 mg kg^{-1}	30–60
	I.M.	2–5 mg kg^{-1}	3
Midazolam and ketamine	P.O.	0.5 mg kg^{-1} 3 mg kg^{-1}	
Clonidine	P.O.	4 μg kg^{-1}	45–60
Dexmedetomidine	P.O.	2–4 μg kg^{-1}	30–60
	Buccal	1 μg kg^{-1}	30–60

required, and regular regimens may not suffice. A suitable preoperative sedative is oral ketamine (6–7 mg kg^{-1}) (Rainey and Van der Walk 1998). Alternatively, 3–5 mg kg^{-1} of oral ketamine and 0.3–0.5 mg kg^{-1} of midazolam can be administered simultaneously. Clonidine can also be useful for these patients. Oral midazolam alone (0.5 mg kg^{-1}) may be unpredictable and insufficient and is not recommended for these cases (Roy 1996; Rainey and Van Der Walt 1998). The parent's assistance may be required in convincing the child to take the premedication. I.M. premedication should only be used as a last resort; 4–5 mg kg^{-1} of ketamine will produce a sedative effect.

On hospital arrival, a 'quiet room' should be available and the time from admission to surgery should be as streamlined a possible. Having the same nurse care for them throughout the operative journey may be beneficial. If possible, the child should be allowed to wear their regular clothes rather than changing in to a hospital gown. Anaesthetists may have a lower threshold for intraoperative antiemetic administration in these cases. Postoperatively, the aim is to return to the child's routine as soon as possible, and so hospital discharge is advised as soon as safely possible.

The anxious child

Perioperative anxiety is common in children and can lead to poor compliance or refusal to cooperate. Lowering anxiety levels decreases the rates of emergence delirium, postoperative pain, and maladaptive postoperative behavioural changes (Kain et al. 2007). Recognition of the anxious child can be difficult, particularly because the way a child behaves when they are anxious varies with age (e.g. toddlers may cry while older children may remain silent). There are some recognized risk factors:

- Children aged 1–5 years
- Parental anxiety (Fortier et al. 2010)
- Shy/dependent/withdrawn child
- Lack of eye contact
- Poor social adaptive qualities
- Multiple previous admissions
- Previous negative hospital/vaccination/dentist experience
- Communication difficulties.

Behaviour in the anaesthetic room can be difficult to predict and so a flexible approach is required. Anxiety can present in different ways: either apparently cooperative children become uncooperative in the anaesthetic room, or children may be uncooperative from the outset. Listen to the parent if they say that they think the child will be uncooperative.

The behaviour of the healthcare workers and parents can influence the anxiety levels and therefore cooperation of the child. Martin et al. (2011) describe 'coping promoting' and 'distress promoting' behaviours (Box 71.2). Some elements of hypnosis can be used by anaesthetists in the induction room (e.g. story- telling, speaking in a slow calming voice).

During the preoperative visit, body language and tone of voice are equally as important as the content of what is said. The anaesthetist should adopt age-appropriate communication techniques. Simple strategies include getting down to the child's level, being reassuring and confident, listening and responding sympathetically

Box 71.2 Coping-promoting and distress-promoting behaviours

'Coping-promoting' behaviours

- Distracting talk, not related to the procedure
- Joke telling
- Describing the medical equipment as something fun (e.g. spaceman's mask)
- Offering the child choices which does not allow them to refuse the procedure (e.g. the choice of smell coming through the mask).

'Distress-promoting' behaviours

- Reassurance, apologies, and empathy (as these make the child concentrate on any anxiety they may be feeling)
- Offering a choice that they cannot control (e.g. would you like to come to theatre?)
- Providing too much medical/technical information
- Describing the medical equipment when it is not visible.

Data from Martin, S.R., MacLarn Chorney J., Tan E.T., Fortier M.A., Blount R.L., Wald S.H., Shapiro N.L., Strom S.L., Patel S. and Kain Z.N. (2011) Changing healthcare providers' behaviour during pediatric inductions with an empirically based intervention. *Anesthesiology*, 115, 18–27.

to the child's concerns, and avoiding words which may worry them (e.g. 'needle', 'jab', or 'jag'). Find out what the child's concerns are and listen actively. Different age groups have different worries. Children aged 6 months to 3 years may have separation anxiety and distraction techniques (e.g. stickers, bubbles, toys, puzzles, magic, and video media) are useful. Children aged 3–6 years may accept some explanation about what to expect, alongside play and distraction techniques. Children aged 7–12 years enjoy rewards and maintaining a feeling of control (e.g. they may enjoy the challenge of blowing up the 'balloon' on the anaesthetic circuit). Adolescents may fear loss of control, lack of privacy, pain or awareness, and may like to be involved in decisions. Involving older children in forming your anaesthetic plan empowers them and helps them maintain a sense of control over the situation.

For the child with extreme anxiety, preoperative psychological preparation may be beneficial. A preoperative visit to meet the anaesthetist, tour the hospital, and visit the anaesthetic room provides an opportunity to address the child's concerns and remove the 'fear of the unknown'. This is useful 5 or more days preoperatively in children above the age of 6 while visits the day before theatre are the least beneficial (McCann and Zain 2001). Information can be reinforced using DVDs, leaflets, and Internet websites. Training in relaxation or coping skills, play therapy, or a desensitization programme with graded exposure to the theatre environment may also have a place in equipping the anxious child with skills to deal with their anxiety.

Separation anxiety is a particular problem in the pre-school group, but can affect older children who have regressed behaviourally because of the acute stress of the situation. For this reason, parental presence is permitted in many hospitals during induction. While research has not proved parental presence to decrease anxiety levels in children during induction, it improves parental satisfaction. Parental presence can increase or decrease anxiety levels depending upon the parents' behaviour and anxiety levels (Kain et al. 2000). Parental anxiety transfers to the child, so it is important to address parental concerns preoperatively and treat their anxiety as necessary (e.g. educational videos and preoperative counselling). After auricular acupuncture, anxiety levels decreased in anxious mothers and consequently improved cooperation of the child on induction (Wang et al. 2004).

Restraining patients should only ever be used as a last resort and always discussed with the parents beforehand to minimize distress. Consent must always be obtained from the parents/guardian and recorded (Royal College of Nursing 2010).

Declaration of interest

None declared.

References

Almenrader N, Passariello M, Coccetti B, Haiberger R, Pietropaoli P. Premedication in children: a comparison of oral midazolam and oral clonidine. *Paediatr Anaesth* 2007; **17**: 1143–9

Arendts G, Stevens M, Fry M. Topical anaesthesia and intravenous cannulation success in paediatric patients: a randomized double-blind trial. *Br J Anaesth* 2008; **100**: 521–4

Asai T, Koga K, Vaughan, RS. Respiratory complications associated with tracheal intubation and extubation. *Br J Anaesth* 1998; **80**: 767–5

Association of Paediatric Anaesthetists of Great Britain and Ireland. Good practice in postoperative and procedural pain management, 2nd edition. *Pediatr Anesth* 2012; **22**(Supp 1): 1–79

Association of Paediatric Anaesthetists of Great Britain and Ireland. *Guidelines on the Prevention of Post-operative Vomiting in Children*. London: Association of Paediatric Anaesthetists of Great Britain and Ireland, 2015. Available from http://www.apagbi.org.uk/sites/default/files/APA_Guidelines_on_the_Prevention_of_Postoperative_Vomiting_in_Children.pdf

Bailey AG, McNaull PP, Jooste E, Tuchman JB. Perioperative crystalloid and colloid fluid management in children: where are we and how did we get here? *Anesth Analg* 2010; **110**: 375–90

Banchs R, Lerman J, Wald SH. The use of nitrous oxide as an adjuvant for inhalation inductions with sevoflurane: a pro-con debate. *Paediatr Anaesth* 2013; **23**: 557–64

Becke K, Ayme S, Straub J, *et al.* The OrphanAnaesthesia project. *Eur J Anaesthesiol* 2011; **28**: 678–9

Best C. Paediatric airway anaesthesia. *Curr Opin Anesthesiol* 2012; **25**: 38–41

Bhatia N, Barber N. Dilemmas in the preoperative assessment of children. *Contin Educ Anaesth Crit Care Pain* 2011; **11**: 214–8

Blatter JA, Finder JD. Perioperative respiratory management of paediatric patients with neuromuscular disease. *Paediatr Anaesth* 2013; **23**: 770–6

Bohmen CJ, Niezen-de Boer MC, Klinkenberg-Knol EC, *et al.* The prevalence of gastroesophageal reflux in institutionalized intellectually disabled individuals. *Am J Gastroenterol* 1999; **94**: 804–10

Brislin RP, Theroux MC. Core myopathies and malignant hyperthermia susceptibility: a review. *Paediatr Anaesth* 2013; **23**: 834–41

British Thoracic Society and Scottish Intercollegiate Guidelines Network. *British Guideline on the Management of Asthma. A National Clinical Guideline*. London: British Thoracic Society, 2008 (revised January 2012)

Cans C, De-La-Cruz J, Mermet M-A. Epidemiology of cerebral palsy. *Paediatric Child Health* 2008; **18**: 393–8

Carlyle A, Lim SI. Chronic diseases of childhood. In: Sims C, Johnson C, eds. *Your Guide to Paediatric Anaesthesia*. Sydney: McGraw-Hill, 2011; 179–94

Chan MT, Wan AC, Gin T, *et al.* Chronic postsurgical pain after nitrous oxide anesthesia. *Pain* 2011; **152**: 2514–20

Chundamala J, Wright JG, Kemp SM. An evidence-based review of parental presence during anesthesia induction and parent/child anxiety. *Can J Anaesth* 2009; **56**: 57–70

Courtman S, Mumby D. Children with learning disabilities. *Paediatr Anaesth* 2008; **18**: 198–207

Dahmani S, Stany I, Brasher C, *et al.* Pharmacological prevention of sevoflurane- and desflurane-related emergence agitation in children: a meta-analysis of published studies. *Br J Anaesth* 2010; **104**: 216–23

Davis P, Brandom W. The association of malignant hyperthermia and unusual disease: when you're hot you're hot or maybe not. *Anesth Analg* 2009; **109**: 1001–3

De Beer D, Bingham R. The child with facial abnormalities. *Curr Opin Anesthesiol* 2011; **24**: 282–288

Department of Health. *Getting the Right Start: National Service Framework for Children, Standards for Hospital Services*. London: Department of Health, 2003

Doherty GM, Chisakuta A, Crean P, Shields MD. Anesthesia and the child with asthma. *Paediatr Anaesth* 2005; **15**: 446–54

Duracher C, Schmautz E, Martinon C, *et al.* Evaluation of cuffed tracheal tube size predicted using the Khine formula in children. *Paediatr Anaesth* 2008; **18**: 113–18

Eberhart LH, Gelgner G, Kranke P, *et al.* The development and validation of a risk score to predict the probability of post-operative vomiting in pediatric patients. *Anesth Analg* 2004; **99**: 1630–7

Engelhardt T, Weiss M. A child with a difficult airway: what do I do next? *Curr Opin Anesthesiol* 2012; **25**: 326–32

Fitzgerald M, Ryan D. Cystic fibrosis and anaesthesia. *Contin Educ Anaesth Crit Care Pain* 2011; **11**: 204–9

Fortier MA, Chorney JM, Rony RY, Perret-Karimi D, Rinehart JB, Camilon FS. Children's desire for perioperative information. *Anesth Analg* 2009; **109**: 1085–90

Fortier MA, Del Rosario AM, Rosenbaum A, Kain ZN. Beyond pain: predictors of postoperative maladaptive behavior change in children. *Pediatr Anesth* 2010; **20**: 445–53

Fortier MA, Del Rosario AM, Martin SR, Kain ZN. Perioperative anxiety in children. *Paediatr Anaesth* 2010; **20**: 318–22

Furman EB, Roman DG, Lemmer LA, *et al.* Specific therapy in water, electrolyte and blood-volume replacement during pediatric surgery. *Anesthesiology* 1975; **42**: 187–93

Ghai B, Wig J. Comparison of different techniques of laryngeal mask placement in children. *Curr Opin Anesthesiol* 2009; **22**: 400–4

Gottlieb E.A. and Andropoulos D.B. Anesthesia for the patient with congenital heart disease presenting for noncardiac surgery. *Curr Opin Anesthesiol* 2013; **26**: 318–26

Hampson-Evans D, Morgan P, Farrar M. Pediatric laryngospasm. *Paediatr Anaesth* 2008; **18**: 303–7

Haynes AB, Weiser TG, Berry WR, *et al.* A surgical safety checklist to reduce morbidity and mortality in a global population. *N Engl J Med* 2009; **360**: 491–9

Jamora C, Iravani M. Unique clinical situations in pediatric patients where ketamine may be the anesthetic agent of choice. *Am J Ther* 2010; **17**: 511–5

Kain ZN, Mayes LC, Wang SM, *et al.* Parental presence and a sedative premedicant for children undergoing surgery: a hierarchical study. *Anesthesiology* 2000; **92**: 939–46

Kain ZN, Mayes LC, O'Connor TZ, Cicchetti DV. Preoperative anxiety in children. Predictors and outcomes. *Arch Pediatr Adolesc Med* 1996; **150**: 1238–45P

Kain, ZN, Caldwell-Andrews AA, Mayes LC, *et al.* Family-centred preparation for surgery improves perioperative outcomes in children: a randomized controlled trial. *Anesthesiology* 2007; **106**: 65–74

Kheterpal S, Han R, Tremper KK, *et al.* Incidence and predictors of difficult and impossible mask ventilation. *Anesthesiology* 2006; **105**: 885–91

Kheterpal S, Martin L, Shank AM, Tremper KK. Prediction and outcomes of impossible mask ventilation: a review of 50,000 anesthetics. *Anesthesiology* 2009; **110**: 891–7

Koh JL, Harrison D, Myers R, Dembinski R, Turner H, McGraw T. A randomized, double-blind comparison study of EMLA and ELA-Max for topical anesthesia in children undergoing intravenous insertion. *Pediatr Anesth* 2004; **14**: 977–82

Krishnan PL, Thiessen BH. Use of the Bonfils intubating fiberscope in a baby with a severely compromised airway. *Paediatr Anaesth* 2013; **23**: 670–2

Lake CL, Booker PD. *Pediatric Cardiac Anesthesia*, 4th Rev Edn. Philadelphia, PA: Lippincott Williams & Wilkins, 2005

Lee SY, Cheng SL, Ng SB, Lim SL. Single-breath vital capacity high concentration sevoflurane induction in children: with or without nitrous oxide. *Br J Anaesth* 2013; **110**: 81–6

Leelanukrom R, Cunliffe M. Intraoperative fluid and glucose management in children. *Paediatr Anaesth* 2000; **10**: 353–9

Licina A, Chambers NA, Hullett B, *et al.* Lower cuff pressures improve the seal of pediatric laryngeal mask airways. *Paediatr Anaesth* 2008; **18**: 952–6

Litman RS, Maxwell LG. Cuffed versus uncuffed endotracheal tubes in pediatric anesthesia: the debate should finally end. *Anesthesiology* 2013; **118**: 500–1

Lonnqvist P-A, Morton NS. Postoperative analgesia in infants and children. *Br J Anaesth* 2005; **95**: 59–68

Mafrica F, Fodale V. Opioids and Down syndrome. *J Opioid Manage* 2006; **2**: 93–8

Malviya S, Voepel-Lewis T, Burke C, Merkel S, Tait AR. The revised FLACC observational pain tool: improved reliability and validity for pain assessment in children with cognitive impairment. *Paediatr Anaesth* 2006; **16**: 258–65

Martin SR, MacLarn Chorney J, Tan ET, *et al.* Changing healthcare providers' behaviour during pediatric inductions with an empirically based intervention. *Anesthesiology* 2011; **115**: 18–27

McCann ME, Kain ZN The management of preoperative anxiety in children: an update. *Anesth Analg* 2001; **93**: 98–105

McFadyen JG, Pelly N, Orr RJ. Sedation and anaesthesia for the pediatric patient undergoing radiation therapy. *Curr Opin Anesthesiol* 2011; **24**: 433–8

Meakin GH. Role of muscle relaxants in pediatric anesthesia. *Curr Opin Anesthesiol* 2007; **20**: 227–31

Merkel SI, Voepel-Lewis T, Shayevitz JR, Malviya S. The FLACC: a behavioural scale for scoring postoperative pain in young children. *Pediatr Nurs* 1997; **23**: 293–7

Murat I, Constant I, Maud'huy H. Perioperative anaesthetic morbidity in children: a database of 24165 anaesthetics over a 30-month period. *Paediatr Anaesth* 2004; **14**: 158–66

Niezgoda J, Morgan PG. Anaesthetic considerations in patients with mitochondrial defects. *Paediatr Anaesth* 2013; **23**: 785–93

Nolan J, Chalkiadis G, Low J, Olesch CA, Brown TCK. Anaesthesia and pain management in cerebral palsy. *Anaesthesia* 2000; **55**: 32–41

Orliaguet GA, Gall O, Savoldelli GL, Couloigner V. Case scenario: perianesthetic management of laryngospasm in children. *Anesthesiology* 2012; **116**: 458–71

Pandit C, Valentin R, De Lima J, *et al.* Effect of general anaesthesia on pulmonary function and clinical status on children with cystic fibrosis. *Paediatr Anaesth* 2014; **24**: 164–9

Patil V, Brennan LJ. Day surgery for children. *Anaesth Intensive Care Med* 2007; **8**: 176–9

Prosser DP, Sharma N. Cerebral palsy and anaesthesia. *Contin Educ Anaesth Crit Care Pain* 2010; **10**: 72–6

Quinn A, Woodall N. The end of anaesthesia and recovery. In: Royal College of Anaesthetists. *Report and Findings of the 4th National Audit Project of The Royal College of Anaesthetists*. London: Royal College of Anaesthetists, 2011; 62–70

Rainey L, Van Der Walt JH. The anaesthetic management of autistic children. *Anaesth Intensive Care* 1998; **26**: 682–6

Rice C. Prevalence of autism spectrum disorders: Autism and Developmental Disabilities Monitoring Network, United States. *Surveill Summ MMWR* 2007; **56**: 1–27

Robb PJ, Ewah BN. Post-operative nausea and vomiting following paediatric day-case tonsillectomy: audit of the Epsom protocol. *J Laryngol Otol* 2011; **125**: 1049–52

Rocca GD. Anaesthesia in patients with cystic fibrosis. *Curr Opin Anaesthesiol* 2002; **15**: 95–101

Roy WL. Anaesthetising children in remote location: necessary expeditions or anaesthetic misadventures? *Can J Anaesth* 1996; **43**: 764–8

Royal College of Anaesthetists. Post-operative care. In: *Guidance for the Provision of Anaesthetic Services*. Royal College of Anaesthetists, 2016; Chapter 4. Available from http://www.rcoa.ac.uk/gpas2016

Royal College of Nursing. *Restrictive Physical Intervention and Therapeutic Holding for Children and Young People: Guidance for Nursing Staff*. London: Royal College of Nursing, 2010

Royal College of Surgeons of England. *Standards for Children's Surgery: Children's Surgical Forum*. London: Royal College of Surgeons of England, 2013. Available from http://www.rcseng.ac.uk/publications/docs/standards-in-childrens-surgery

Schaefer JJ. Simulators and difficult airway management skills. *Paediatr Anaesth* 2004; **14**: 28–37

Scherzer D, Leder M, Tobias JD. Pro-con debate: etomidate or ketamine for rapid sequence intubation in pediatric patients. *J Pediatr Pharmacol Ther* 2012; **17**: 142–9

Schloss B, Rice J, Tobias JD. The laryngeal mask in infants and children: What is the cuff pressure? *Int J Pediatr Otorhinolaryngol* 2012; **76**: 284–6

Schulte-Uentrop L, Goepfert MS. Anaesthesia or sedation for MRI in children. *Curr Opin Anaesthesiol* 2010; **23**: 513–7

Segura LG, Lorenz JD, Sprung J, *et al.* Anaesthesia and Duchenne or Becker muscular dystrophy: review of 117 anesthetic exposures. *Paediatr Anaesth* 2013; **23**: 855–64

Sims C, von Ungern-Sternberg BS. The normal and the challenging pediatric airway. *Paediatr Anaesth* 2012; **22**: 521–6

Sims, C. Behavioural management of children. In: Sims C, Johnson C, eds. *Your Guide to Paediatric Anaesthesia*. Sydney: McGraw-Hill, 2011; 40–54

Sims C, Farrell T. An overview of paediatric anaesthesia. In: Sims C, Johnson C, eds. *Your Guide to Paediatric Anaesthesia*. Sydney: McGraw-Hill, 2011; 1–19

Smith I, Kranke P, Murat I, *et al.* Perioperative fasting in adults and children: guidelines from the European Society of Anaesthesiology. *Eur J Anaesthesiol* 2011; **28**: 556–69

Sümpelmann R, Osthaus WA. The pediatric cardiac patient presenting for non-cardiac surgery. *Curr Opin Anesthesiol* 2007; **20**: 216–20

Sunder RA, Haile DT, Farrell PT, Sharma A. Pediatric airway management: current practices and future directions. *Paediatr Anaesth* 2012; **22**: 1008–15

Sungur Ulke Z, Kartal U, Orhan Sungur M, *et al.* Comparison of sevoflurane and ketamine for anesthetic induction in children with congenital heart disease. *Paediatr Anaesth* 2008; **18**: 715–21

Tait AR, Malviya S. Anesthesia for the child with an upper respiratory tract infection: still a dilemma? *Anesth Analg* 2005; **100**: 59–65

The Association of Anaesthetists of Great Britain and Ireland. *Immediate Post-anaesthetic Recovery*. London: AAGBI, 2002

Thiagarajan RR, Laussen PC. Mortality as an outcome measure following cardiac surgery for congenital heart disease in the current era. *Paediatr Anaesth* 2011; **21**: 604–8

Vagnoli L, Caprilli S, Messeri A. Parental presence, clowns or sedative premedication to treat preoperative anxiety in children: what could be the most promising option? *Pediatr Anesth* 2010; **20**: 937–43

Varughese AM, Byczkowski TL, Wittkugel EP, Kotagal U, Dean Kurth C. Impact of a nurse practitioner-assisted preoperative assessment program on quality. *Pediatr Anesth* 2006; **16**: 723–33

Von Ungern-Sternberg BS, Habre W. Pediatric anesthesia: potential risks and their assessment: part I. *Paediatr Anaesth* 2007a; **17**: 206–15

Von Ungern-Sternberg BS, Habre W. Pediatric anesthesia: potential risks and their assessment: part II. *Paediatr Anesth* 2007b; **17**: 311–20

Von Ungern-Sternberg BS, Sims C. Airway management. In: Sim C, Johnson C, eds. *Your Guide to Paediatric Anaesthesia*. Sydney: McGraw Hill, 2011; 55–82

Von Ungern-Sternberg S, Boda K, Chambers NA, *et al.* Risk assessment for respiratory complications in paediatric anaesthesia: a prospective cohort study. *Lancet* 2010; **376**: 773–83

Walker A, Stokes M, Moriarty A. Anesthesia for major general surgery in neonates with complex cardiac defects. *Paediatr Anaesth* 2009; **19**: 119–25

Walther-Larsen S, Rasmussen LS. The former preterm infant and risk of post-operative apnoea: recommendations for management. *Acta Anaesthesiol Scand* 2006; **50**: 888–93

Wang SM, Maranets I, Weinberg ME, Caldwell-Andrews AA, Kain ZN. Parental auricular acupuncture as an adjunct for parental presence during induction of anesthesia. *Anesthesiology* 2004; **100**: 1399–404

Wass C, Warner ME, Worrell GA, *et al.* Effect of general anesthesia in patients with cerebral palsy at the turn of the New Millennium: a population based study evaluating perioperative outcome and brief overview of the anesthetic implications in this coexisting disease. *J Child Neurol* 2012; **27**: 859–66

Weinberg GL, Palmer JW, VadeBoncouer TR, *et al.* Bupivacaine inhibits acylcarnitine exchange in cardiac mitochondria. *Anesthesiology* 2000; **92**: 523–8

Weiss M, Dullenkopf A, Fischer JE, *et al.* Prospective randomized controlled multi-centre trial of cuffed or uncuffed endotracheal tubes in small children. *Br J Anaesth* 2009; **103**: 867–73

White MC. Approach to managing children with heart disease for noncardiac surgery. *Paediatr Anaesth* 2011; **21**: 522–9

White MC. Anaesthetic implications of congenital heart disease for children undergoing non-cardiac surgery. *Anaesth Intensive Care Med* 2012; **13**: 432–7

White MC, Cook TM, Stoddart PA. A critique of elective pediatric supraglottic airway devices. *Paediatr Anaesth* 2009; **19**(Suppl. 1): 55–65

Wilkinson DJ, Savulescu J, Slater R. Sugaring the pill: ethics and uncertainties in the use of sucrose for newborn infants. *Arch Pediatr Adolesc Med* 2012; **166**: 629–33

Wollin SR, Plummer JL, Owen H, Hawkins RM, Materazzo F. Predictors of preoperative anxiety in children. *Anaesth Intensive Care* 2003; **31**: 69–74

Wong DL, Baker CM. Pain in children: comparison of assessment scales. *Pediatric Nurse* 1988; **14**: 9–17

Wongprasartsu P, Stevens J. Cerebral palsy and anaesthesia. *Paediatr Anaesth* 2002; **12**: 296–303

Xue FS, Xu YC, Liao X, Zhang YM. Does an age-based formula predict the appropriate tracheal tube sizes in children? *Paediatr Anaesth* 2008; **18**: 901–2

Zielinska M, Holtby H, Wolf A. Pro-con debate: intravenous vs inhalation induction of anesthesia in children. *Paediatr Anaesth* 2011; **21**: 159–68

CHAPTER 72

Procedural sedation in children

Michael Sury

Introduction

This chapter describes the principles of paediatric procedural sedation and the effective drug techniques that could be used in four common scenarios. It should be appreciated that with potent fast-acting drugs, such as propofol, conscious level can change quickly so that sedation easily becomes anaesthesia, albeit at a 'light' level. Such techniques will cause airway obstruction and apnoea, but if they are managed well, as they should be in conventional anaesthesia, the target level of unconsciousness could be considered unimportant if the patient is safe and recovery is rapid. For this reason, both sedation and short-acting anaesthesia techniques are included here.

Drugs that do not cause unconsciousness are usually not potent and do not require 'anaesthesia skills'. It is, therefore, the level of training that defines the type of sedation technique that can be used safely. Unsafe acts, with catastrophic consequences (Cote et al. 2000), occur with all types of sedation and these stories have driven the development of guidelines.

Demand

In large paediatric hospitals, approximately 30% of all procedures carried out under anaesthesia take place outside the operating theatres. The expansion of services such as magnetic resonance imaging (MRI), interventional radiology, oncology, and gastrointestinal endoscopy have increased demand for anaesthesia and, when anaesthesia services have become limited, sedation techniques have been used by non-anaesthetists. In emergency departments, procedural sedation and analgesia techniques using ketamine have become established, and in dentistry, dentists are using a wide range of sedation methods. 'Paediatric' is different to 'adult' sedation because children are often uncooperative and will not accept procedures while they are conscious. Many adults, in contrast, prefer to be conscious rather than undergo anaesthesia. Nevertheless, conscious sedation is possible and important in children but is more difficult to achieve without causing unconsciousness by accident. It is crucial to appreciate that the type of procedure dictates the sedation method and therefore influences the training of the practitioners to make sedation effective and safe.

Training and personnel

All healthcare practitioners using sedation should be trained to use the drugs effectively and safely. To begin, however, the staff performing a procedure itself will need to be skilled so that time is not wasted and that any pain or discomfort from the procedure is minimized; the success of sedation may depend on how long and how painful the procedure is. Behavioural management of distressed and frightened children will be important. The 'specifics' of the training depends on the characteristics of the drugs and the depression of conscious level caused. Nitrous oxide (up to 50%) alone almost never causes unconsciousness, and therefore advanced airway training may not be necessary. Other techniques that cause unconsciousness, even if the risk is small, will require practitioners to have the training to manage airway obstruction (National Institute for Health and Care Excellence 2010).

Anaesthetists rarely use sedation because anaesthesia techniques are often preferred; consequently, training opportunities are limited. Non-anaesthetists, such as dentists or emergency medicine doctors, who frequently use sedation techniques, need to establish training schemes to enable safe sedation. All recent recommendations have emphasized the importance of training, and each specialty will need to develop their own schemes. Individual hospitals or clinics could take the lead and develop their own courses that may be adapted for other providers (Krauss and Green 2008). Clinical governance processes should make clinical directors and managers aware of the importance of training. Healthcare insurance and purchasing organizations have changed the quality control of sedation (in the United States, for example) so that standards of care must be met before costs are reimbursed. In the United Kingdom, annual appraisal and revalidation of doctors and dentists are required to show evidence of good practice and of keeping up to date: this should enable appraisers to persuade practitioners to stop performing tasks for which their training is inadequate or whenever practice is outside recommendations. The practitioner responsible for delivery of sedation will need to monitor and manage the patient and not be distracted by being involved in the procedure itself. If the sedation technique risks causing anaesthesia, there should be a trained assistant present. Guidance should be provided by specialist groups.

Perception of risk

The risk of death from anaesthesia may be between 1:10 000 and 1:200 000 and will depend mainly upon the medical status of the patient (van der Griend et al. 2011). Sedation managed by adequately trained professionals, whether anaesthetists or non-anaesthetists, should be, in principle, equally safe. The main factors therefore that influence the safety of sedation are the training of staff and the medical status of the patient. There are no large studies that have randomized children to sedation or anaesthesia, and it would not be reasonable to compare sedation with anaesthesia unless staff have been adequately trained to manage complications. Observational studies of large cohorts have shown that children can be sedated, even with propofol, with a low rate of complications by non-anaesthetists (van Beek and Leroy 2012).

The public may perceive that sedation is safer than anaesthesia. For example, falling asleep after taking an oral sedative seems less involved and inherently safer than anaesthesia by inhalation or injection, but there is no evidence for this and parents and children should understand the pros and cons of both methods.

Definitions

Standard definitions published by the American Society of Anesthesiologists are widely accepted and are summarized in Table 72.1 (American Society of Anesthesiologists Task Force on Sedation and Analgesia by Non-Anesthesiologists 1996). Minimal sedation involves only anxiolysis. Moderate sedation is a sleep state from which the patient can be roused easily and deep sedation is a sleep state from which the patient can be roused but only with repeated or painful stimuli. These definitions do not cover all situations and other descriptive terms or definitions are being used (Table 72.2).

'Conscious sedation' is favoured in the United Kingdom (Royal College of Anaesthetists and Royal College of Radiologists 1992), especially by dentists and is equivalent to moderate sedation but with the proviso that patients can be roused easily by verbal command; this is necessary in dentistry because the patient has to cooperate and open their mouth. Patient assent is crucial for conscious sedation. If assent is not given, as is common in children, drugs rarely gain it. A further characteristic of a conscious sedation technique is that the margin of safety should be wide enough to make the loss of consciousness unlikely. 'Margin of safety' means that the doses causing deep sedation or anaesthesia are much larger or easily distinguished from conscious sedation doses.

Table 72.1 Summary of characteristics of ASA levels of sedation

Sedation level	Characteristics	
	Conscious state	**Respiratory depression**
Minimal sedation	Awake and calm Normal response to commands Impaired cognitive function and coordination	None
Moderate sedation	Sleepy Responds purposefully to commands or gentle stimulation (NB reflex withdrawal is not a purposeful response)	Intervention rarely necessary
Deep sedation	Sleep and cannot be easily roused Responds purposefully to repeated or painful stimuli	Intervention often necessary Cardiovascular function is usually maintained
Anaesthesia	Asleep and unrousable	Usual, requiring routine airway intervention Cardiovascular depression common

Data from American Society of Anesthesiologists Task Force on Sedation and Analgesia by Non-Anesthesiologists 1996.

Table 72.2 Characteristics of alternative sedation terms

Sedation term (common scenario)	Characteristics	
	Conscious state	**Respiratory intervention**
Conscious sedation (dental procedures)	Sleepy Opens mouth to command	Rarely necessary with basic techniques To be expected with advanced techniques
Safe sleep (painless imaging)	Asleep Rousability not tested	Rarely necessary
Ketamine (painful procedures)	Eyes open Unresponsive Immobile	1% brief apnoea or laryngospasm, or both
Minimal anaesthesia (see 'Painless imaging' and 'Gastrointestinal endoscopy' in chapter text)	Sleep with short-acting drug/s Not easily roused or unrousable for brief periods Rapid recovery	Routine airway intervention Other respiratory and cardiovascular intervention unlikely

In painless imaging, a child will need to remain still enough and this is not likely unless they are asleep. Testing whether they can be roused is counter-productive and therefore the true sedation level cannot be assessed. In such a situation, successful sedation could be termed 'safe sleep' and defined as a sleep state in which the patient is unconscious (or appears to be) and that appreciable airway and breathing effects are unlikely.

Ketamine produces a range of dose-related effects. Its analgesia is intense and at low doses, the patient may not look asleep but will be unreactive (sometimes called a dissociative state). It may be reasonable to assume that the patient is deeply sedated but the characteristics are different to other techniques. Nevertheless, laryngospasm occurs in approximately 0.5% of patients and practitioners need airway skills.

Minimal anaesthesia could be used to describe a technique that induces anaesthesia but thereafter the dose is reduced so that the patient remains 'lightly' asleep. The dose is insufficient to carry out a surgical procedure. The true conscious level is undetermined because the procedure does not stimulate; when it ends, recovery is rapid (Sury and Smith 2008).

Guidelines and recommendations

Several UK reports have made important recommendations. The Chief Dental and Medical Officers have issued guidance on sedation in primary dental care (Department of Health 2000); more recent dental recommendations are available. The Academy of Medical Royal Colleges report of 2001 is about sedation of adults and specifies the need for training (Academy of Medical Royal Colleges 2001); its principles apply to children. The Royal College of Nursing has advised nurses on restraining children (Royal College of Nursing 2010). The Scottish Intercollegiate Guidelines Network (SIGN) produced *Safe Sedation of Children Undergoing Diagnostic and Therapeutic Procedures* in 2004 (SIGN 2004); it was limited to techniques intended for moderate sedation. In 2010, the National Institute for Health and Care Excellence (NICE) published *Sedation for Diagnostic and Therapeutic Procedures in Children and Young People* (NICE 2010). This large report contains 34 recommendations, based on consensus and evidence, and covers how patients should be managed and which drug techniques are effective; the main recommendations are discussed later in this chapter. The Royal College of Emergency Medicine (2009) has, online, a 'Guideline for ketamine sedation in emergency departments' with specific guidance on doses and fasting.

General principles

The following principles are based on the 'patient journey' recommendations of NICE Clinical Guideline 112 (National Institute for Clinical Excellence 2010; Sury et al. 2010).

Pain

Overcoming the pain of a procedure will reduce the dose of sedative required. Local anaesthesia should be used whenever appropriate; for example, in dentistry, once the local anaesthesia has become effective, sedation requirements are markedly reduced. Opioid analgesia should not be used for painless procedures because it is unnecessary and can cause respiratory depression and vomiting.

Immobility

Immobility is necessary for imaging, and sleep is usually needed for young and uncooperative children. The length of time of the scan will influence the choice of technique. Computed tomography (CT) scans are short whereas some nuclear medicine scans take hours. Long or unpredictable scanning requires immobility that can be extended which generally means that an i.v. or inhalation method is preferred.

Disease-related behaviour

The behaviour of the patient who requires the procedure influences the technique. Children needing endoscopy, for example, teenagers who are unwell with active inflammatory bowel disease, may prefer a minimal anaesthetic technique rather than sedation. MRI may be needed for investigation of autism and sedation is unlikely to succeed for this and other behavioural problems.

Need for cooperation

In sleep, the mouth tends to close. For dentistry, cooperation with mouth opening can only be achieved with a conscious patient. A closing mouth may indicate that sedation is becoming deep and that airway obstruction might occur. A mouth gag removes this useful sign.

Drug choice and dose limits

Bearing in mind the aforementioned factors, sedation protocols will be needed to guide practitioners to achieve the best outcome with minimum risk. The appropriate use of analgesia and sedation are the most common considerations. The training limits the type of drug. Staff without anaesthesia training can only use non-potent drugs (drugs with a wide margin of safety). High doses of non-potent drugs are unsafe too often. I.V. drugs can be titrated to effect but not beyond dose limits and therefore a sedation failure has to be accepted rather than risk accidental anaesthesia. Oral drugs have to be given according to a best estimate and, here also, sedation failure should be accepted. Only effective drugs (those with a low failure rate) should be chosen. The choice of the drug and its dose will depend on both the procedure and the child. Techniques recommended in the NICE guideline are grouped into four common scenarios: painless imaging, painful emergency department procedures, gastrointestinal endoscopy, and dentistry. Doses are not included in the NICE guidance but, in the following sections, doses are suggested.

Patient assessment

Probably the most important factor in safety is the avoidance of sedation in unfit children. Airway and breathing problems are notorious in the presence of some medical problems. It is the lack of anaesthetic expertise that contraindicates sedation more than the drug techniques themselves. Non-anaesthetists should not be managing children in whom airway and breathing problems are likely. A list of the common contraindications to sedation for children presenting for nurse-led MRI sedation has been useful in the author's hospital but may not be applicable in other situations (Table 72.3) (Sury et al. 1999). An exhaustive list is not practicable but another list is provided by the SIGN (2004) guideline. NICE Clinical Guideline 112 provides recommendations on the important features of clinical assessment that are similar to a standard assessment for anaesthesia.

Fasting

Fasting before anaesthesia or sedation is established practice and aspiration is a rare event. Pulmonary aspiration of gastric contents is possible in unconscious patients whose airway is unprotected by a tracheal tube. It is reasonable to think that fasting reduces gastric contents and protects against aspiration. Virtually all sedation techniques risk unconsciousness and therefore patients may be safer if they are fasted. The standard anaesthesia fasting protocol (6 h for solids or non-breast milk, 4 h for breast milk, 2 h for clear fluids) should be applied to sedated patients in most situations (Royal College of Nursing 2005).

It is possible that fasting may reduce the success of sedation and there is evidence that children having painless procedures need a lower dose of chloral if they are not fasted (Keidan et al. 2004). In this situation, 4 h of fasting after food may be acceptable instead of 6 h (Marti-Bonmati et al. 1995). In dentistry, confidence in maintaining consciousness during sedation may justify a liberal approach to fasting but the avoidance of a recent large meal is sensible; in this scenario, conscious sedation with nitrous oxide alone or midazolam alone are considered safe in unfasted patients.

In the emergency department, patients are often unfasted and the risk of delaying a procedure may need to be balanced against the small risk of inhalation of gastric contents during unintended unconsciousness. Guidance on which technique to use, based on a consensus of US emergency physicians, has been published (Green et al. 2007). The guidance is summarized in two matrices, one each for low and high health risk patients. Each matrix shows the maximum sedation depth recommended according to a particular

Table 72.3 Common contraindications to sedation

Airway problems	Actual or potential airway obstruction, e.g. snoring or stridor, blocked nose, small mandible, large tongue
Apnoeic spells	Related to: ◆ Brain damage ◆ Drug treatment
Respiratory disease	Sp_{O_2} less than 94% in air Respiratory failure (high respiratory rate, oxygen treatment) Inability to cough or cry
High intracranial pressure	Drowsiness Headache Vomiting
Epilepsy	Convulsions requiring rectal diazepam within the last 24 h Rectal diazepam used more frequently than once in 2 weeks Seizure related to sedation Resuscitation within the last month. Major neurological or neuromuscular disease associated with, e.g. apnoeic spells or hypotonia Intracranial hypertension Convulsions with cyanosis more frequent than once per day Convulsion less than 4 h before sedation Failure to regain full consciousness and mobility after a recent convulsion
Risk of pulmonary aspiration of gastric contents	Abdominal distension Appreciable volumes draining from NG tube Vomiting
Severe metabolic, liver or renal disease	Requiring i.v. fluids or glucose Jaundice or abdominal distension Requiring peritoneal or haemodialysis

NG, nasogastric.

combination of fasting status and the urgency of the procedure. The matrices and guidance are detailed and should be consulted for various combinations of fasting status and degree of urgency. Briefly however, in an emergency, any level of sedation is reasonable, whatever the fasting status. For non-urgent procedures, only minimal sedation is reasonable. If the procedure is urgent, a 'dissociative' or 'moderate' sedation technique is acceptable in unfasted children.

Intravenous access

I.V. access is vital if i.v. drugs or fluids are essential to the procedure or the sedation technique; i.v. contrast media and i.v. sedation are clear indications. Access may be needed to manage complications such as laryngospasm or bradycardia. If access is not essential and complications are considered unlikely, it may be omitted if it causes unnecessary problems. I.V. access can be difficult or distressing and it can waste valuable time and risk sedation failure. Access is not necessary for nitrous oxide alone (for dental treatment) or for oral chloral hydrate (for painless imaging).

Consent

The principles of informed consent, as for anaesthesia, should be applied to sedation (Department of Health 2001). Carers (and children, if old enough) need to understand what the procedure involves and what they have to gain from it before the choices and hazards of the sedation techniques can be explained. It is convention that the referring clinician begins the consenting process and then other professionals can follow. If the procedure (its purpose and its value) is understood by all, then some regard it as reasonable for the sedation or anaesthesia team to take written consent for the procedure itself if they agree and this is explicit in governance processes. Many, however, regard specific separate consents for procedure and sedation or anaesthesia as best practice and in some countries, this is mandatory.

Psychological preparation

Anxiety can be reduced by behavioural management techniques and a full review is available in the NICE guideline. Painless procedures can be achieved in cooperative children if they are calmed by skilled and experienced play specialists (and others). This approach can be time-consuming but may save time and resources in the long term if the procedure has to be repeated: extensive dental treatment and regular MRI scans to check for cancer recurrence are two good examples. Psychological and behavioural techniques also help children to cope with their fears and smooth the induction of sedation; in some circumstances, the dose of sedation may be reduced.

Common scenarios

Four different scenarios are described here, and they cover approximately 90% of all current procedural sedation. Other scenarios such as cardiac angiography or eye examinations are not discussed because these are relatively uncommon and carried out in specialist hospitals; specialist anaesthesia services should be provided for them. If sedation is considered, the elements of techniques used to provide sleep, immobility, analgesia, reflex control, and conscious sedation, which are described in the following sections, can be applied appropriately. Only drug techniques recommended by the NICE guidance are described. These were based on evidence from publications investigating efficacy (randomized controlled trials with at least 20 patients in each group) or safety (randomized controlled trials or observations on cohorts of at least 200 patients).

Painless imaging

Patients need to be immobile for MRI, CT, and nuclear medicine scans. MRI is especially difficult for frightened children because of the noisy confined space. Some children will lie still, however, and they should be identified by a selection process. Young infants (less than 3 months old) may sleep peacefully after a feed if they are warm and comfortable. A strategy is presented in Figure 72.1.

Almost all children who cannot lie still enough with behavioural methods need to be asleep either with deep sedation or anaesthesia; conscious sedation is rarely effective because most of the patients have problems that prevent them cooperating. Many are ill, in pain, or have behavioural difficulties. In this scenario *safe sleep* and *minimal anaesthesia*, as defined previously, are practicable. If an anaesthesia service is available, short-acting potent drugs such as sevoflurane or propofol are preferred over less reliable sedation drugs.

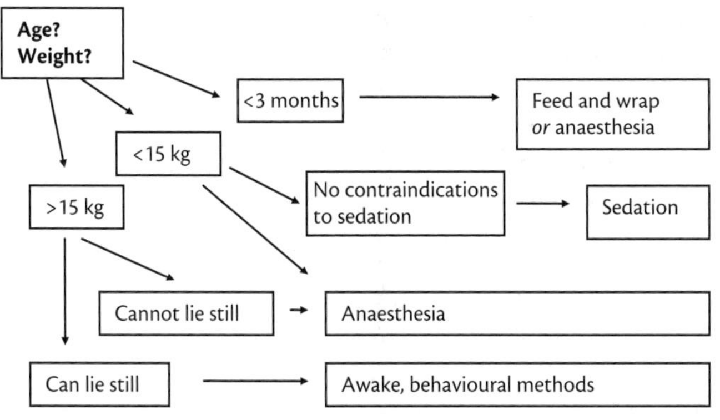

Figure 72.1 Sedation strategy for MRI.

There are major problems with equipment in MRI. Setting up a sedation or anaesthesia service requires thorough planning and special consideration of the options (The Association of Anaesthetists of Great Britain and Ireland 2002). Ferromagnetic items are unsafe unless they are sufficiently remote and fixed securely. Steel oxygen cylinders are especially dangerous and should not be in the vicinity. Syringe drivers are a common hazard. Electrical apparatus may not function or can cause image artifacts. All wires going into the scanning room must be filtered. Electrical cables touching the skin can burn. MRI pulse oximeters have fragile fibreoptic cables.

Minimal anaesthesia

Sevoflurane inhalation anaesthesia is the standard technique and is the most reliable. I.V. access can be sited after induction. To maintain anaesthesia, inspired concentrations of 3% are effective and a laryngeal mask airway (LMA) is commonly used. Lower doses of sevoflurane can be used once the child is asleep which may make the use of any airway device or intervention unnecessary (De Sanctis Briggs 2005). If an LMA is not used, both capnography monitoring and oxygen administration are essential. Capnography can be best achieved by purpose-built oral or nasal sampling tubes that are combined with the delivery of oxygen.

Occasionally, the movement of breathing causes 'head nodding' that cannot be restrained by mechanical measures, and this is an indication for controlled breathing, neuromuscular block, and tracheal intubation. These measures are necessary whenever LMA or spontaneous breathing is contraindicated (e.g. high intracranial pressure, or full stomach).

Some children, perhaps as many as 30%, are distressed when they awaken in recovery after sevoflurane anaesthesia and this may be a delirium reaction. The problem is usually brief and seems to need only time and comforting by parents or carers. Propofol maintenance seems to cause less crying in recovery and it can be used either exclusively or after a sevoflurane induction (Bryan et al. 2009).

A propofol infusion technique is almost 100% successful and has a rapid, pleasant recovery profile. An induction dose of 2–3 mg kg^{-1} can be followed by 10 mg kg^{-1} min^{-1} (Frankville et al. 1993). There is variation and dose adjustments are sometimes necessary. The airway remains patent in most children, some need head positioning, and less than 5% need further airway intervention. Occasionally there are extra-pyramidal movements or hiccoughs that cause too much movement. The addition of ketamine, an opioid, or midazolam reduces this problem (Machata et al. 2008).

Safe sleep

'Safe sleep' is a sleep state in which airway and breathing effects are unlikely. Two techniques are considered.

Oral chloral hydrate (100 mg kg^{-1}, maximum dose 1 g) sedates more than 90% of children weighing less than 15 kg for approximately 1 h (Greenberg et al. 1993; Ronchera-Oms et al. 1994). Supplementation with i.v. midazolam is necessary in 5–10% of children. The induction time is usually within 20 min but can take up to 1 h. Doses larger than 1 g are associated with vomiting.

I.V. midazolam alone is a common technique. Published data on the necessary doses are lacking, but the 2016 British National Formulary for Children recommends that increments of 25–50 μg kg^{-1} of midazolam can be injected over 2–3 min and titrated to effect up to maximum doses of 6 mg, 10 mg, and 7.5 mg for children aged 1 month–6 years, 6–12 years, and 12–18 years respectively.

Other drug techniques have been described, including barbiturates, major tranquilizers, paraldehyde, and melatonin but, whereas they may be effective in some children, the evidence of reliability is lacking (Sury et al. 2005).

I.V. dexmedetomidine, given in high doses, is also effective at achieving moderate sedation for imaging (Koroglu et al. 2006). It is not available in the United Kingdom. Its mechanism of action (α2-adrenergic agonism) may produce a natural sleep state from which the patient can be roused and in which vital breathing reflexes may be preserved. It is associated with marked cardiovascular changes (Mason et al. 2008).

Painful procedures

The range of painful procedures is wide but many children present to emergency departments with minor trauma such as skin lacerations and forearm fractures (Pena and Krauss 1999; Krauss and Green 2006). Sedation for the treatment of burns is a specialist subject and is not discussed here in detail. The oncology department is another setting where painful procedures such as intrathecal chemotherapy and bone marrow sampling are commonplace. The need for sedation or anaesthesia will depend on the coping ability of the child. Some will tolerate treatment with local anaesthesia alone and others will need anaesthesia. Techniques aimed at delivering minimal, moderate, and deep sedation are described here but it should be appreciated that conscious level can change with almost any technique.

Minimal sedation

If the child can cooperate with insertion of local anaesthesia but needs help with reducing anxiety, behavioural management alone may be sufficient. Potent systemic analgesia such as fentanyl or diamorphine is valuable (Atkinson et al. 2009). Nitrous oxide, alone, up to an inspired concentration of 50% in oxygen can be 'self-administered' by the patient. This technique is largely analgesic but does have a sedative component. It is remarkably safe because consciousness is almost always preserved (Gall et al. 2001). Unconsciousness is possible if the patient is taking other sedatives or if there is another cause of altered consciousness. Midazolam, taken orally (0.5 mg kg^{-1}), is an effective anxiolytic within 30 min. The buccal route is faster alternative. Nasal midazolam (0.25 mg kg^{-1}) is as fast as the i.v. route (Connors et al. 1994); atomized midazolam is much less painful than drops.

Moderate to deep sedation

Two techniques are effective. The sedation level achieved is largely dependent on the dose and the stimulation of the procedure.

Ketamine causes an unresponsive state that is unique. The child is immobile, calm, and their eyes may be open—they appear 'dissociated'. Whether this state is moderate or deep is uncertain. The analgesia of ketamine is intense yet, unlike opioids, airway and breathing reflexes are usually maintained which makes it ideal for short painful procedures. Doses recommended are 2 mg kg^{-1} i.v. (additional doses of 1 mg kg^{-1} if necessary) or 5–10 mg kg^{-1} i.m. (The Royal College of Emergency Medicine 2009). I.M. ketamine is painful but may be appropriate if i.v. access causes more distress. Vomiting is a common problem. Dysphoric reactions occur in a minority and do not appear to be prevented by midazolam (Wathen et al. 2000). Airway secretions cause laryngospasm in approximately 0.5% of cases (Green et al. 1998). In high doses, ketamine is an anaesthetic. Even standard doses may anaesthetize some children. Ketamine has been used extensively for the management of children having treatment for burns (Emerson et al. 2008).

An alternative technique involves the combination of i.v. midazolam and fentanyl. The doses vary and both drugs should be titrated carefully. Initial doses are 25–50 μg kg^{-1} for midazolam and 0.25–0.5 μg kg^{-1} for fentanyl (Krauss and Green 2000) Fentanyl causes respiratory depression especially when the pain of the procedure is over. The reversal agents, flumazenil and naloxone, should be available and ready for prompt use. Ketamine is the more reliable technique. Even though ketamine causes sedation deeper than the 'moderate' level it has fewer respiratory effects, and requires less judgement and less intervention than a combination of midazolam and fentanyl (Kennedy et al. 1998).

Deep sedation or anaesthesia

Propofol combined with an opioid is an effective short-acting anaesthetic technique for short procedures. Fentanyl, alfentanil, or remifentanil are suitable. Lumbar puncture and bone marrow aspirate procedures, common in oncology departments, can be achieved under short-acting anaesthesia using propofol (2–3 mg kg^{-1}) and remifentanil (1 μg kg^{-1}) (Glaisyer and Sury 2005). Remifentanil almost always causes apnoea so that a short period of assisted ventilation via a face mask is usual; airway devices are rarely necessary. Indwelling central venous catheters (CVCs) are common in oncology patients and allow a painless i.v. method. Neither postoperative analgesia (other than local anaesthesia) nor antiemetics are necessary after this technique for oncology procedures. Recovery is faster than after inhalation of sevoflurane and children are able to eat and drink a few minutes afterwards.

Gastrointestinal endoscopy

Upper endoscopy should take no more than 10 min. Colonoscopy is more variable and lasts 20–40 min. The discomfort of colonoscopy is appreciable only when the colon is stretched, often during biopsy of the terminal ileum. Many adults tolerate upper and lower endoscopy without any sedation but sedation or anaesthesia is necessary in children and both methods are used widely in the United Kingdom.

Moderate sedation

I.V. midazolam can be titrated for upper gastrointestinal endoscopy; a starting dose is 25–50 μg kg^{-1}. Patients should be in the lateral position. A mouth guard precedes oesophagoscopy. Insertion of the gastroscope often causes struggling and retching, so that mild restraint is often necessary and someone should suction secretions or regurgitant fluid from the pharynx. Retching and bradycardia can occur with duodenoscopy. Capnography is the best indicator of respiratory difficulty. Sedation is easier for colonoscopy. Midazolam combined with fentanyl (initial dose 0.25–0.5 μg kg^{-1}), or an equivalent opioid can be used (Mamula et al. 2007). Reversal of sedation with flumazenil and naloxone may be necessary.

Minimal anaesthesia

I.V. propofol alone or with low doses of opioids has become widespread for both upper and lower endoscopy (Barbi et al. 2006; van Beek and Leroy 2012). The anaesthetist should take control of the airway. Few cases need an intervention other than a jaw thrust and pharyngeal suction, but oxygen desaturation can occur either from obstruction caused by the endoscope or from the respiratory depression of propofol. These problems are detected by capnography before pulse oximetry. Capnography via purpose-made nasal and oral speculums incorporating oxygen delivery is reliable. The dose of propofol required for oesophagoscopy is approximately 2–3 mg kg^{-1} and further bolus doses of 0.5–1 mg kg^{-1} are frequently necessary. Target-controlled infusion of propofol is practical but the minimum blood concentration required for successful oesophagoscopy is uncertain; preliminary data showed that the median effective target blood concentration was 3.7 μg ml^{-1} (Hammer et al. 2009). An infusion of remifentanil (0.025 μg kg^{-1} min^{-1}) reduces the required dose of propofol (Drover et al. 2004). The discomfort of colonoscopy can be minimized by an opioid. An infusion of remifentanil 0.05 μg kg^{-1} min^{-1} is effective and respiratory depression is unusual at this dose rate. Recovery is rapid and neither analgesia nor antiemetic is necessary. Other standard methods of anaesthesia with short-acting inhalation agents may also have a fast recovery profile.

Dentistry

Dental treatment causes considerable anxiety because it can be exquisitely painful. Extractions can take 10–15 min. Conservation treatment can take an hour. Effective local anaesthesia reduces the need for sedation but its injection is also distressing. Dentists have been pioneers of sedation and they understand the needs of their patients and the limitations of the sedation techniques. Their skill in behaviour management is invaluable. Having time to reassure and reward children is important and this is possible if the dental treatment is not urgent. When sedation methods are necessary, it is agreed widely that uncontrolled deep sedation is not helpful because the airway may become obstructed during treatment—the desired target level is either conscious sedation or anaesthesia. The airway is safe in conscious sedation but does require the child's cooperation. During anaesthesia the dentist and the anaesthetist need to cooperate to maintain airway patency.

In the United Kingdom, dental conscious sedation was divided into standard and alternative techniques—and recently these have become basic and advanced.

Standard conscious sedation

Two techniques are recommended. Nitrous oxide alone (termed relative analgesia) is administered via a nasal mask. The mask incorporates scavenging. When it is effective, inspired concentration of 30% is sufficient; higher concentrations may be needed but they cause dysphoria. Severely anxious children may not tolerate this method (Lahoud and Averley 2002), but for those who do, neither fasting nor i.v. access is necessary. In anxious adolescents, midazolam can be titrated intravenously starting with 25–50 μg kg^{-1}.

Both techniques are successful in selected children. If they are not sufficient, advanced sedation or anaesthesia are indicated.

Advanced conscious sedation

Combinations of potent drugs, given i.v. or via inhalation, can be used to deliver conscious sedation. The risk of unintended deep sedation or anaesthesia depends on the drugs and their doses, but only adequately trained staff, in a fully equipped facility, should use advanced sedation methods. Inhaled nitrous oxide can be combined with low concentrations of sevoflurane and this has the advantage of rapid onset and offset (Averley et al. 2004); the combination of inhaled with i.v. midazolam also has potential (Averley et al. 2004). Combinations of midazolam, fentanyl, and ketamine with sub-anaesthetic doses of propofol are being used by some specialists but these techniques probably have a narrow margin of safety. Recovery after drug combinations may be prolonged and, if so, a brief propofol anaesthetic may have the advantage.

Common or important problems

Difficult procedures

Prolonged procedures or those when the time taken is uncertain should be managed with techniques that can be extended to allow completion of the procedure without necessarily causing prolonged recovery. Pain that is not brief or not nullified with local anaesthetic is an indication for anaesthesia. Cardiac angiography is associated with life-threatening events (Bennett et al. 2005) and should be managed using anaesthesia and controlled ventilation; the same applies whenever haemorrhage is possible. Multiple procedures are ideally completed under the same sedation or anaesthetic technique to minimize fasting. When this is not possible, children should undergo only short-acting sedation techniques.

Difficult behaviour

Uncooperative children, in any setting, need to be given special consideration. Their age and mental capacity dictate their rights of consent (Department of Health 2001). In England, children older than 16 years can consent for treatment but not refuse it. Those older than 18 years have full rights of adulthood. Children under 16 years are able to consent without their carer's permission if they are competent. Healthcare workers are obliged always to act in the best interests of the patient and this may mean acting against the child's wishes in an emergency. There is, however, nearly always time for a more cautious course of action. Anxiety can be managed by skilled staff and permission is usually given for anxiolytics if necessary.

Intravenous access

Local anaesthesia creams and ethyl alcohol sprays reduce the pain of venepuncture. Nitrous oxide inhalation may also be tried. Many children, however, need long-term venous access and the distress of venepuncture can be avoided by inserting appropriate CVCs. CVCs can be inserted by an open 'cut-down' technique or by venous cannulation using a 'guidewire-through-needle' technique. The aid of ultrasound has transformed CVC placement because it detects the position and the patency of suitable large veins (NICE 2002). Needle techniques minimize damage to the vessel and may allow the vein to be used again years later. CVCs should be inserted by specialists in an interventional radiology suite. Anaesthesia with controlled ventilation is preferred to prevent movement and air embolism.

Infection of CVCs should be minimized by adherence to clean handling protocols. Children with bowel failure are dependent on their i.v. feeding venous catheter and anxiety about infection prevents their use unless there is no alternative. Some venous catheters contain concentrated heparin solutions and must be aspirated before use. After use, all lines should be cleared of residual anaesthetic; 20 ml normal saline is standard.

Unintended deep sedation

The pharmacokinetic and dynamic characteristics of almost all sedation drugs vary sufficiently to make unintended deep sedation possible. Nitrous oxide is the exception and anxiolysis with i.v. midazolam is similarly safe but the risk is dose dependant. Two principles are important in avoiding deep sedation: careful titration and not exceeding agreed dose limits. Higher doses will be necessary for some patients and a protocol should be agreed locally or by professional groups to limit the maximum dose. The British National Formulary for Children provides advice. Flumazenil (10 $\mu g\ kg^{-1}$) and naloxone (100 $\mu g\ kg^{-1}$) may be necessary for the reversal of deep sedation and respiratory depression effects of midazolam and opioids. An international panel of experts has agreed definitions of complications that could be used to audit sedation practice (Mason et al. 2012).

Delayed unconsciousness and respiratory depression can occur after the pain of the procedure has elapsed. This is a particular problem of potent opioids whose action outlasts the pain of the procedure (Strunin 2007). The pain of a dental extraction, for example, is brief. Staff in the recovery area must be ready to detect and respond to respiratory depression. Suitable criteria for discharge must be adhered to.

Excitement

A small minority of children are distressed by sedation and increasing the dose can worsen the situation. Midazolam can cause excitement that may be reversed by flumazenil. Ketamine can cause distressing hallucinations. Sedation may need to be abandoned in these circumstances.

Monitoring

Monitoring standards of sedated children who are at risk of unconsciousness should be similar to those used for anaesthesia. If a child is insufficiently sedated to tolerate the monitor, it should be applied. A finger pulse oximeter is usually tolerated in sleepy children. Capnography is the most useful monitor to prevent oxygen desaturation and should be used in all unconscious children; it is practical in children under 'safe sleep' with chloral hydrate, ketamine sedation, and all minimal anaesthesia techniques. ECG and blood pressure monitoring should be available and used appropriately in children at risk of a cardiovascular problem. Processed electroencephalography devices are not used widely but may be useful in prolonged procedures.

Procedural errors

The injection of vincristine into the cerebral spinal fluid instead of intravenously is almost always fatal. This error has occurred because the two drugs, methotrexate and vincristine, meant for i.v. and intrathecal administration respectively, became swopped accidentally. Systems were not in place to prevent it (Toft 2001).

Now, recommendations prevent the proximity of the two drugs in both time and place. Currently, manufacturers have been directed to introduce spinal needles (and syringes) with connectors that are incompatible with i.v. syringes. Patient harm involving misconnections to epidural and gastrostomy catheters have occurred. Mistakes are possible in any situation, but patients can be protected by effective safety strategies. Institutional complacency is a common factor in disastrous errors.

A recent strategy of the surgical safety checklist may help to prevent many mistakes. All procedures, even the most minor, should only take place after team briefing, pre-anaesthesia checks (patient identity, consent, allergy, body weight, and fasting) and a 'surgical pause' (World Health Organization 2009).

Declaration of interest

None declared.

References

Academy of Medical Royal Colleges. *Safe Sedation Practice for Healthcare Procedures in Adults: Standards and Guidance*. London: Academy of Medical Royal Colleges, 2013

American Society of Anesthesiologists Task Force on Sedation and Analgesia by Non-Anesthesiologists. Practice guidelines for sedation and analgesia by non-anesthesiologists. *Anesthesiology* 1996; **84**: 459–71

Atkinson P, Chesters A, Heinz P. Pain management and sedation for children in the emergency department. *BMJ* 2009; **339**: b4234

Averley PA, Girdler NM, Bond S, Steen N, Steele J. A randomised controlled trial of paediatric conscious sedation for dental treatment using intravenous midazolam combined with inhaled nitrous oxide or nitrous oxide/sevoflurane. *Anaesthesia* 2004; **59**: 844–52

Barbi E, Petaros P, Badina L, *et al.* Deep sedation with propofol for upper gastrointestinal endoscopy in children, administered by specially trained pediatricians: a prospective case series with emphasis on side effects. *Endoscopy* 2006; **38**: 368–75

Bennett D, Marcus R, Stokes M. Incidents and complications during pediatric cardiac catheterization. *Paediatr Anaesth* 2005; **15**: 1083–8

Bryan YF, Hoke LK, Taghon TA, *et al.* A randomized trial comparing sevoflurane and propofol in children undergoing MRI scans. *Paediatr Anaesth* 2009; **19**: 672–81

Connors K, Terndrup TE, Connors K, Terndrup TE. Nasal versus oral midazolam for sedation of anxious children undergoing laceration repair. *Ann Emerg Med* 1994; **24**: 1074–9

Cote CJ, Notterman DA, Karl HW, Weinberg JA, McCloskey C. Adverse sedation events in pediatrics: a critical incident analysis of contributing factors. *Pediatrics* 2000; **105**: 805–14

De Sanctis Briggs V. Magnetic resonance imaging under sedation in newborns and infants: a study of 640 cases using sevoflurane. *Paediatr Anaesth* 2005; **15**: 9–15

Department of Health. *Consent—What You Have a Right to Expect: A Guide for Children and Young People*. London: Department of Health, 2001

Department of Health. *A Conscious Decision: A Review of the Use of General Anaesthesia and Conscious Sedation in Primary Dental Care*. Report by a Group chaired by the Chief Medical Officer and Chief Dental Officer. London: Department of Health, 2000. Available from http://www.dh.gov.uk/en/Publicationsandstatistics/Publications/PublicationsPolicyAndGuidance/DH_4074702

Drover DR, Litalien C, Wellis V, Shafer SL, Hammer GB. Determination of the pharmacodynamic interaction of propofol and remifentanil during esophagogastroduodenoscopy in children. *Anesthesiology* 2004; **100**: 1382–6

Emerson BM, Martin R. Burns. In: Bingham R, Lloyd-Thomas A, Sury M, eds. *Hatch & Sumner's Textbook of Paediatric Anaesthesia*, 3rd Edn. London: Hodder Arnold, 2008; 647–57

Frankville DD, Spear RM, Dyck JB. The dose of propofol required to prevent children from moving during magnetic resonance imaging. *Anesthesiology* 1993; **79**: 953–8

Gall O, Annequin D, Benoit G, Glabeke E, Vrancea F, Murat, I. Adverse events of premixed nitrous oxide and oxygen for procedural sedation in children. *Lancet* 2001; **358**: 1514–5

Glaisyer HR, Sury MR. Recovery after anesthesia for short pediatric oncology procedures: propofol and remifentanil compared with propofol, nitrous oxide, and sevoflurane. *Anesth Analg* 2005; **100**: 959–63

Green SM, Rothrock SG, Lynch EL, *et al.* Intramuscular ketamine for paediatric sedation in the emergency department: safety profile in 1,022 cases. *Ann Emerg Med* 1998; **31**: 688–97

Green SM, Roback MG, Miner JR, Burton JH, Krauss, B. Fasting and emergency department procedural sedation and analgesia: a consensus-based clinical practice advisory. *Ann Emerg Med* 2007; **49**: 454–61

Greenberg SB, Faerber EN, Aspinall CL, Adams RC. High-dose chloral hydrate sedation for children undergoing MR imaging: safety and efficacy in relation to age. *AJR Am J Roentgenol* 1993; **161**: 639–41

Hammer GB, Sam WJ, Chen MI, Golianu B, Drover DR. Determination of the pharmacodynamic interaction of propofol and dexmedetomidine during esophagogastroduodenoscopy in children. *Paediatric Anaesthes* 2009; **19**: 138–44

Keidan I, Gozal D, Minuskin T, Weinberg M, Barkaly H, Augarten, A. The effect of fasting practice on sedation with chloral hydrate. *Pediatr Emerg Care* 2004; **20**: 805–7

Kennedy RM, Porter FL, Miller JP, Jaffe DM. Comparison of fentanyl/midazolam with ketamine/midazolam for pediatric orthopedic emergencies. *Pediatrics* 1998; **102**: 956–63

Koroglu A, Teksan H, Sagir O, Yucel A, Toprak HI, Ersoy OM. A comparison of the sedative, hemodynamic, and respiratory effects of dexmedetomidine and propofol in children undergoing magnetic resonance imaging. *Anesth Analg* 2006; **103**: 63–7

Krauss B, Green SM. Sedation and analgesia for procedures in children. *N Engl J Med* 2000; **342**: 938–45

Krauss B, Green SM. Procedural sedation and analgesia in children. *Lancet* 2006; **367**: 766–80

Krauss B, Green SM. Training and credentialing in procedural sedation and analgesia in children: lessons from the United States model. *Paediatr Anaesth* 2008; **18**: 30–5

Lahoud GY, Averley PA. Comparison of sevoflurane and nitrous oxide mixture with nitrous oxide alone for inhalation conscious sedation in children having dental treatment: a randomised controlled trial. *Anaesthesia* 2002; **57**:446–50

Machata AM, Willschke H, Kabon B, Kettner SC, Marhofer P. Propofol-based sedation regimen for infants and children undergoing ambulatory magnetic resonance imaging. *Br J Anaesth* 2008; **101**: 239–43

Mamula P, Markowitz JE, Neiswender K, *et al.* Safety of intravenous midazolam and fentanyl for pediatric GI endoscopy: prospective study of 1578 endoscopies. *Gastrointest Endosc* 2007; **65**: 203–10

Marti-Bonmati L, Ronchera-Oms CL, Casillas C, Poyatos C, Torrijo C, Jimenez NV. Randomised double-blind clinical trial of intermediate-versus high-dose chloral hydrate for neuroimaging of children. *Neuroradiology* 1995; **37**: 687–91

Mason KP, Green SM, Piacevoli Q. Adverse event reporting tool to standardize the reporting and tracking of adverse events during procedural sedation: a consensus document from the World SIVA International Sedation Task Force. *Br J Anaesth* 2012; **108**: 13–20

Mason KP, Zurakowski D, Zgleszewski SE, *et al.* High dose dexmedetomidine as the sole sedative for pediatric MRI. *Paediatr Anaesth* 2008; **18**: 403–11

National Institute for Health and Care Excellence. *Guidance on the Use of Ultrasound Locating Devices for Placing Central Venous Catheters*. Technology Appraisal No. 49. London: NICE, 2002. Available from https://www.nice.org.uk/guidance/ta49

National Institute for Health and Care Excellence. *Sedation for Diagnostic and Therapeutic Procedures in Children and Young People*. Clinical

Guideline 112. London: NICE, 2010. Available from https://www.nice.org.uk/Guidance/cg112

Pena BM, Krauss B. Adverse events of procedural sedation and analgesia in a pediatric emergency department. *Ann Emerg Med* 1999; **34**: 483–91

Ronchera-Oms CL, Casillas C, Marti-Bonmati L, *et al.* Oral chloral hydrate provides effective and safe sedation in paediatric magnetic resonance imaging. *J Clin Pharm Ther* 1994; **19**: 239–43

Royal College of Anaesthetists and Royal College of Radiologists. *Sedation and Anaesthesia in Radiology. Report of a Joint Working Party.* London: Royal College of Anaesthetists, 1992

Royal College of Nursing. *Restrictive Physical Intervention and Therapeutic Holding for Children and Young People: Guidance for Nursing Staff.* London: Royal College of Nursing, 2010. Available from https://www2.rcn.org.uk/__data/assets/pdf_file/0016/312613/003573.pdf

Royal College of Nursing. *Perioperative Fasting in Adults and Children Clinical Practice Guidelines. An RCN Guideline for the Multidisciplinary Team.* London: Royal College of Nursing, 2005. Available from https://www2.rcn.org.uk/__data/assets/pdf_file/0009/78678/002800.pdf

Scottish Intercollegiate Guidelines Network. *Safe Sedation of Children Undergoing Diagnostic and Therapeutic Procedures. A National Clinical Guideline.* Edinburgh: Scottish Intercollegiate Guidelines Network, 2009

Strunin L. Intravenous conscious sedation for dental treatment: am I my brother's keeper? *Anaesthesia* 2007; **62**: 645–7

Sury M, Bullock I, Rabar S, Demott K. Sedation for diagnostic and therapeutic procedures in children and young people: summary of NICE guidance. *BMJ* 2010; **341**: c6819

Sury MR, Harker H, Begent J, Chong WK. The management of infants and children for painless imaging. *Clin Radiol* 2005; **60**: 731–41

Sury MR, Hatch DJ, Deeley T, Dicks-Mireaux C, Chong WK. Development of a nurse-led sedation service for paediatric magnetic resonance imaging. *Lancet* 1999; **353**: 1667–71

Sury MR, Smith JH. Deep sedation and minimal anesthesia. *Paediatr Anaesth* 2008; **18**: 18–24

The Association of Anaesthetists of Great Britain and Ireland. *Provision of Anaesthetic Services in Magnetic Resonance Units.* London: AAGBI, 2002. Available from https://www.aagbi.org/sites/default/files/mri02.pdf

The Royal College of Emergency Medicine. *Guideline for Ketamine Sedation in Emergency Departments.* 2009. Available from http://secure.rcem.ac.uk/code/document.asp?ID=4880

Toft B. *External Inquiry into the adverse incident that occurred at Queen's Medical Centre, Nottingham, 4th January 2001.* London: Department of Health, 2001

van Beek EJ, Leroy PL. Safe and effective procedural sedation for gastrointestinal endoscopy in children. *J Pediatr Gastroenterol Nutr* 2012; **54**: 171–85

van der Griend BF, Lister NA, McKenzie IM, *et al.* Postoperative mortality in children after 101,885 anesthetics at a tertiary pediatric hospital. *Anesth Analg* 2011; **112**: 1440–7

Wathen JE, Roback MG, Mackenzie T, Bothner JP. Does midazolam alter the clinical effects of intravenous ketamine sedation in children? A double-blind, randomized, controlled, emergency department trial. *Ann Emerg Med* 2000; **36**: 579–88

World Health Organization. *Surgical Safety Checklist.* 2009. Available from http://www.who.int/patientsafety/safesurgery/checklist/en/

CHAPTER 73

Acute paediatric pain management

Tom G. Hansen

Introduction

Safe and effective treatment of acute pain in children within hospital settings has gained huge attention in the past two to three decades. It is widely accepted that the nervous system is sufficiently developed to process nociception before birth, and therefore, children must be assumed to experience pain from birth onward. Long-term effects of pain in young infants can occur, resulting in behavioural changes and a lowered pain threshold for months after a painful event.

Advances in developmental neurobiology and pharmacology are continuing to improve the available methods of both assessing and managing paediatric pain. Around the world, formalized paediatric pain services have now been established in most paediatric centres (Lonnqvist and Morton 2005).

The safe and effective management of pain in children includes the prevention, recognition, and assessment of pain, early and individualized treatment, and evaluation of the efficacy of treatment. This chapter discusses selected topics in paediatric acute pain management, with more specific emphasis placed on acute postoperative pain management.

Age-appropriate pain assessment

A main prerequisite for satisfactory pain management is proper and age-appropriate pain assessment. However, children's pain may be difficult to recognize and measure reliably. Pain assessment tools are used to quantify and guide the treatment of pain. Self-reported pain assessment tools are the standard, and many validated developmentally appropriate tools are available in which the child rates the pain intensity on a numeric scale, a colour scale, or a face picture scale (Rose and Logan 2004) (Fig. 73.1). Preverbal children or cognitively impaired children are unable to provide a self-report, so physiological and behavioural measures must be used as indicators of pain. The perception and communication of an individual's pain depend on their intellectual and social development. Expression of pain relies on the child's ability to understand, quantitate, and communicate it (Solodiuk and Curley 2003). Self-reporting which is the gold standard for pain assessment is possible only in older children or those with cognitive and communicative skills. For the youngest children, the measurements are usually based on behaviours typically known to be associated with pain (e.g. grimacing, body movements, posture, and vocalization). Albeit not specific to pain, physiological measurements (e.g. blood pressure, heart rate, and sweating) are also used in some pain rating scales. Moreover, in acute (and chronic) pain situations, the physiological responses quickly return to baseline as the body more or less adapts to the stimuli, further reducing the specificity of these measures. Examples of assessment tools used for neonatal pain assessment are PIPP (Premature Infant Pain Profile), CRIES, NFCS, and COMFORT scale. For older children and adolescents, most pain rating scales rely on self-reports similar to the situation in adults. Frequently used scales include the Faces Pain Scale, the Pieces of Hurt Tool, the Oucher, and the visual analogue scale. The younger the child, the less likely it is that they can distinguish between the levels of pain using face pain scales. The Pieces of Hurt Tool is used in 4- to 6-year-olds and involves the child selecting one to four poker chips that represent pieces of hurt such that one chip is 'a little bit of hurt' and four chips represent 'the most hurt.' The Oucher scale is aimed at 3- to 12-year-olds and requires a set of colour photographs that show children with different expressions of pain that the individual patient correlates to their own pain. The Faces Pain Scale use drawings of facial expressions to assess for pain intensity and is also focused for 3- to 12-year-old children. The visual analogue scale is age-appropriate for children older than 6 years and requires that they express their degree of pain on a 10 cm line in which the range is from no pain (0 cm) to worst pain possible (10 cm). The verbal numeric scale is reliable and valid for acute pain in from 8 years and only requires that the patient rate their pain on a 0–10 scale verbally.

Developmental neurobiology

Neonates including very premature infants clearly perceive pain, as demonstrated by their integrated behavioural and physiological responses to nociceptive stimuli (Fitzgeralds and Howard 2001). In fact, pain in neonates may be accentuated as a result of the fact that descending inhibitory pathways to the dorsal horn of the spinal cord are not fully developed at birth and they have wider receptive fields and lower excitatory thresholds than those of older children (Pattinson and Fitzgerald 2004). Repeated painful stimuli (e.g. heel lancing or i.v. placement) further lower the excitatory thresholds of dorsal horn neurones (Taddio et al. 1997; Lidow 2002). The neural transmission in peripheral nerves is slower in neonates as a result of incomplete myelination. The major nociceptive neurones in neonates and in adults are either unmyelinated C-fibres or thinly

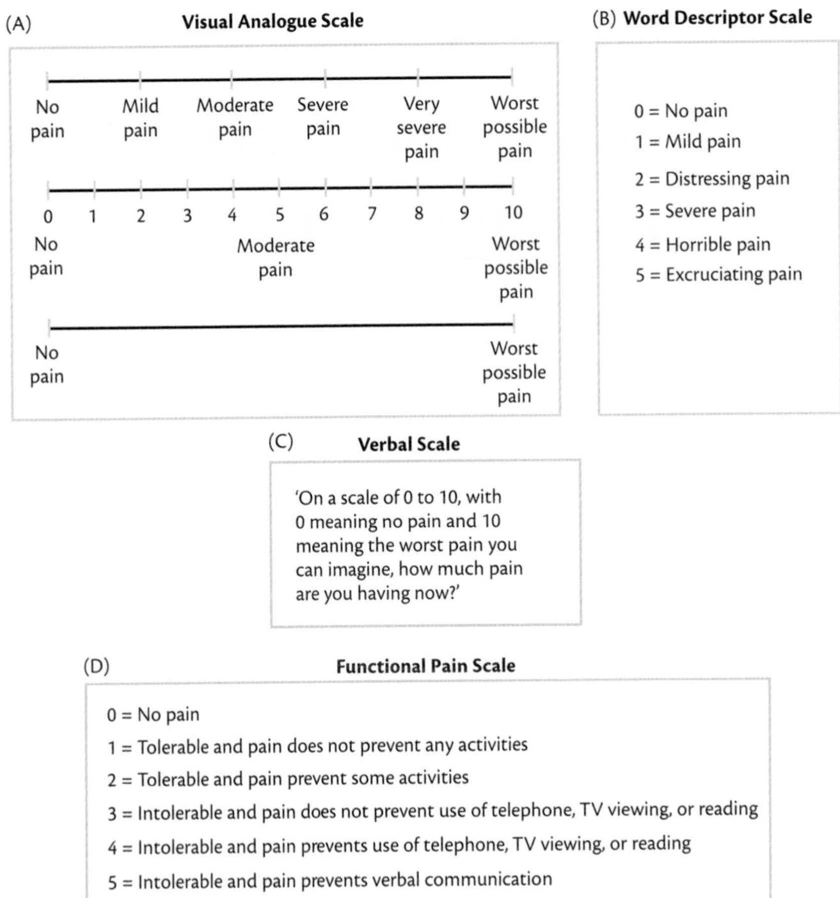

Figure 73.1 Examples of pain scales used in children. (A) Visual analogue scale. (B) Word descriptor scale. (C) Verbal scale. (D) Functional Pain Scale.
(D) Reprinted from *Journal of the American Medical Directors Association*, Volume 2, Issue 3, Gloth, F. M. *et al. The Functional Pain Scale*: reliability, validity and responsiveness in the elderly population, pp. 110–114, Copyright © 2001, with permission from Elsevier and AMDA: The Society for Post-acute and Long-term Care Medicine.

myelinated Aδ-fibres. Repeated stimulation of these nociceptive fibres causes decreased excitatory thresholds resulting in peripheral sensitization (hyperalgesia).

Allodynia, another consequence of peripheral sensitization in which non-nociceptive fibres transmit noxious stimuli, results in the sensation of pain from non-noxious stimuli. In addition, repeated nociceptive input to the dorsal horn of the spinal cord causes the amplification of pain intensity and duration, which is termed 'wind-up' or 'central sensitization' (Fitzgeralds and Howard 2001).

Developmental pharmacology

There is a growing body of experience with the use of analgesic drugs in children (Kearns et al. 2003). Most analgesics are lipophilic drugs and thus require transformation into water-soluble substances for the body to be able to excrete the substances in the urine or bile. Pharmacokinetic variations in children are significant and have implications for the dosage and intervals of analgesics. For example, body composition affects the volume of distribution of drugs. The higher body water content in neonates and infants results in a larger volume of distribution of water-soluble drugs and the potential for a longer elimination half-life (and duration of action). Smaller fat and muscle stores in neonates result in higher plasma concentrations of drugs because there is less drug uptake by these pharmacodynamically inactive sites. With a higher percentage of cardiac output going to organ systems known as the vessel-rich group (e.g. the brain) in neonates, the brain concentration of drugs may be higher in neonates than in older children and adults. It is the general belief that an immature blood–brain barrier in neonates may further facilitate (hydrophilic) drug transportation into this pharmacologically active site. Protein binding of drugs is reduced in neonates compared with older children and adults because of lower plasma concentrations and reduced binding affinity of albumin and α1-acid glycoprotein. Drugs that are highly protein bound, such as opioids, non-steroidal anti-inflammatory drugs (NSAIDs), and local anaesthetics, will be present in a higher unbound concentration in plasma, leading to increased effects, toxicity, or both (Hansen et al. 2001). Hepatic metabolism of drugs involves either phase I reactions (oxidation, reduction, hydroxylation, and hydrolysis) or phase II reactions (conjugation). The cytochrome P450 (CYP) system is the most important phase I enzyme family and is responsible for the metabolism of many analgesics. At birth, the hepatic enzymes responsible for drug metabolism are immature; resulting in a reduced clearance of drugs (Yaster 2001). The concentrations of these hepatic enzymes quickly increase to adult levels in the first few months of life. Drug clearance in the 1- to 6-year-old age group is often higher than adult levels because of the larger hepatic mass relative to body weight and increased activity of enzymes, thus higher doses and shorter intervals of analgesics may be required. The renal excretion of drugs depends on renal blood flow, glomerular filtration rate, and tubular secretory function, all of which are decreased in neonates, especially in the young neonate and in premature infants. Renal function reaches adult levels by 1 year of age. With decreased renal function, parent compounds or active drug metabolites can accumulate to toxic concentrations (e.g. the morphine-6-glucuronide metabolite) (Bouwmeester et al. 2004).

Pain management strategies

Acute pain in children in hospital settings encountered by the anaesthetist is usually postoperative in nature, related to medical conditions, cancer, or the result of trauma. Acute pain management should always include both non-pharmacological and pharmacological strategies.

Non-pharmacological pain management

Non-pharmacological strategies are used to supplement analgesic drugs and are particularly suitable in relation to procedural pain. Non-pharmacological techniques such as cognitive behavioural therapies (distraction, guided imagery, and relaxation) and physical therapy are essential modalities of acute pain management (Lonnqvist and Morton 2005) (readers are referred to the many texts and articles on this topic). A child-friendly environment with a strong and parental involvement is essential. More specific strategies include massage, heat therapy, and transcutaneous electrical nerve stimulation. Psychological techniques are also used, including distraction, hypnosis, breathing techniques, play therapy, and imagery. Oral sucrose provides safe and effective analgesia in neonates and infants less than 3 months of age in relation to procedural pain for single minor painful procedures (e.g. heel lance and venepuncture) (Johnston et al. 2011). A dose–response relationship has been suggested; however, effective and optimal dosing remains to be established particularly in the tiniest premature infants. Interestingly, infants less than 31 weeks of gestational age who receive more than 10 doses of sucrose are at risk for poorer neurodevelopmental scores (Johnston et al. 2007).

Pharmacological pain management

Paracetamol

Paracetamol is the most widely used analgesic in children. It possesses both antipyretic and analgesic properties. Paracetamol's mechanism of action is still not fully understood, but involves inhibition of central prostaglandin synthesis in the hypothalamus and a central activation of descending serotonergic pathways. A cannabinoid-mediated mode has also been suggested. Paracetamol is different from the NSAIDs in that it does not inhibit peripheral cyclooxygenase (COX) (Arana et al. 2001). It lacks the troublesome side-effects of NSAIDs, and as such it has no antiplatelet or anti-inflammatory effects. Paracetamol can be given orally or rectally, although the initial rectal dose needs to be higher to achieve appropriate blood concentrations (Anderson et al. 2002).

Paracetamol is usually the first-line analgesic administered for mild to moderate pain. However, it is also useful in other clinical settings, for example, weaning from more advanced pain treatment regimens such as continuous regional techniques. For practitioners adhering to the concept of multimodal analgesia in which pain should be treated at all levels within the nociceptive system, paracetamol constitutes the basic drug. Paracetamol is metabolized extensively in the liver by three main pathways: sulphation, glucuronidation, and oxidation. In therapeutic doses, most of it undergoes glucuronidation or sulphation, producing non-toxic metabolites that are excreted in the urine. The rate constant for paracetamol glucuronide formation in neonates is considerably smaller than in older children and adults whereas the rate constant for sulphate formation is larger. Thus, the pronounced immaturity of the phenolic glucuronidation process in the neonate is offset by a well-developed capacity for the conjugation of a phenolic group with sulphate. This makes conjugation with sulphate quantitatively the most important pathway for paracetamol metabolism in young children. A maturational increase in urinary glucuronide metabolite elimination has been described partly explained by postnatal age, postmenstrual age, and repeated administration. Interestingly, unconjugated hyperbilirubinaemia concentrations of 150 μmol litre^{-1} or higher are associated with a 40% reduction in paracetamol clearance. Approximately 5% is excreted unchanged in the urine, and the remainder is metabolized by the hepatic mixed function oxidase system. The product of oxidation is a highly reactive arylating metabolite, *N*-acetyl-p-benzoquinone imine (NAPQI), which normally is rendered non-toxic by preferential conjugation with the intracellular tripeptide glutathione and excreted as mercapturic acid and cysteine conjugates in the urine. As sulphation and glucuronidation pathways become saturated, an increasing proportion and quantity of the drug is metabolized by the CYP system, resulting in an increased production of NAPQI when the hepatic synthesis of glutathione is overwhelmed and manifestations of toxicity appear, producing centrilobular necrosis. The isoenzyme CYP2E1 is primarily involved in paracetamol hepatotoxicity. In particular, bioactivation of paracetamol via CYP2E1 produces high concentrations of NAPQI. Children, particularly young children, appear to have a lower incidence of liver failure as a result of paracetamol overdose than adults, but neonates are known to be capable of forming the reactive intermediate metabolites that cause hepatocellular damage. The high therapeutic ratio in neonates may be related to reduced rates of metabolism by the CYP system in the neonatal liver and the neonate's increased ability to synthesize glutathione relative to adults (Arana et al. 2001).

The therapeutic index of paracetamol in older children is relatively narrow and doses of 5–10 times normal can be dangerous. The analgesic therapeutic plasma paracetamol concentration is generally considered to be 10 mg litre^{-1} (= 66 μmol litre^{-1}), whereas the antipyretic paracetamol concentrations may be slightly lower, 5–10 mg litre^{-1}. However, the evidence for this belief is poor, and there are studies showing a dose–response relationship for analgesia in children. For analgesia and antipyresis the recommended oral dosing regimen is 15–20 mg kg^{-1}, 4–6-hourly, with a maximum dose of 90–100 mg kg^{-1} in 24 h in children aged 3 months or older. Neonates and premature infants have reduced clearance of paracetamol; indeed, clearance is inversely associated with gestational age, and doses should be reduced in infants less than 1 months of age (Table 73.1) (Anderson et al. 2002).

The rectal route for administration of paracetamol is convenient when the oral route cannot be used (e.g. postoperatively, postoperative nausea and vomiting). However, bioavailability with this route is relatively poor and slow (particularly in older children) with C_{max} occurring 2–3 h after administration (Hansen 1999).

Table 73.1 Recommended dosing of oral and rectal paracetamol in infants and children aiming at a plasma concentration of approximately 10 mg $litre^{-1}$

Age (postconceptual weeks)	Route	Loading dose ($mg\ kg^{-1}$)	Maintenance dose ($mg\ kg^{-1}$)	Interval (hourly)	Maximum dose per 24 h ($mg\ kg^{-1}$)	Duration of treatment (h)
28–32 PCA	Oral	20	10–15	8–12	30	48
	Rectal	20	15	12		
32–52 PCA	Oral	20	10–15	6–8	60	48
	Rectal	30	20	8		
>3 months	Oral	20	15	4	90	48
	Rectal	40	20	6		

PCA, post-conceptual age (in weeks).

Data from Anderson B. J. et al. (2002). Acetaminophen developmental pharmacokinetics in premature neonates and infants: a pooled population analysis. *Anesthesiology*, 96, 1336–45.

Therefore, the rectal loading dose of paracetamol should be larger, but the daily maximum rectal doses are similar compared with oral recommendations.

The use of i.v. paracetamol (Perfalgan®) circumvents the bioavailability problems and has a more rapid and predictable onset of action with peak paracetamol concentrations in the cerebrospinal fluid occurring at about 45–60 min (Allegaert et al. 2011). Perfalgan® is a mannitol solubilized formula, ready-for-use preparation. Perfalgan® should be infused over 15 min to reduce the risk of local adverse events. Perfalgan® has been studied in most age groups of children including neonates and premature infants; however, it should be used with great caution in premature infants less than 32 weeks of gestation because of a lack of clinical studies in this age group (Table 73.2) (van den Anker and Tibboel 2011). Although paracetamol is generally considered a very safe drug with few side-effects, hepatotoxicity has been reported in children after chronic ingestion of doses less than 150 mg kg^{-1} day^{-1} for 2–8 days and routine doses (75–90 mg kg^{-1} day^{-1}), thus the recommended daily maximum doses should be adhered to and only used for 48–72 h (Arana et al. 2001).

Non-steroidal anti-inflammatory drugs

NSAIDs are used for the management of mild to moderate pain in children, particularly if there is significant associated inflammation (Maunuksela and Olkhola 2003). Their advantage is that they do not cause respiratory depression or sedation. In single doses they have analgesic efficacy comparable to that of paracetamol (Berde and Sethna 2002). They are used either alone or in combinations with paracetamol, local anaesthetics, opioids, or a mix of these. As a rule of thumb, the NSAID reduces morphine requirements by 25–30%. Their mechanism of action is through the inhibition of COX, the enzyme responsible for metabolizing arachidonic acid. When arachidonic acid is released from traumatized cell membranes, it is metabolized by COX to form prostaglandins and thromboxanes, which in turn sensitize peripheral nerve endings and vasodilate vessels, causing pain, erythema, and inflammation. There are two COX isoenzymes in humans. The constitutive form of COX (COX-1) is found in high concentrations in platelets, vascular endothelial cells, stomach, and in the kidneys, where prostaglandins and thromboxanes are essential for gastric mucosal protection, regulation of renal blood flow, and aggregation of platelets. COX-2 is called an 'inducible COX' and is present only in traumatized cells or inflamed tissue and is almost undetectable in most normal tissues. Most NSAIDs are non-selective COX inhibitors, but during the search for NSAIDs with fewer side-effects, selective COX-2 inhibitors were developed. Selective COX-2 inhibitors have been used extensively in adults, and some COX-2 inhibitors (e.g. rofecoxib and celecoxib) have also been studied in children (Turner and Ford 2004). Unfortunately, since their release, COX-2 inhibitors have been shown to increase cardiovascular morbidity in adults and their use subsequently ceased. At this point, the future of COX-2 inhibitors in children remains uncertain. This is unfortunate because short-term therapy for acute postoperative pain in children may not be associated with an increased risk for cardiovascular complications, however due to the above-mentioned reasons, future paediatric studies comprising COX-2 inhibitors are unlikely to be conducted.

Table 73.2 Recommended doses of i.v. paracetamol in children

Age group	Dose	Maximum daily dose	Dose interval
PCA 32–44 weeks	10 mg/kg	40 mg/kg/d	6 hourly
PCA >44 weeks	15 mg/kg	60 mg/kg/d	6 hourly

I.V. paracetamol is as yet not recommended in children born before 32 weeks post-conceptual age (PCA) because of a lack of PK/PD studies. Duration of treatment should be restricted to 48 h in the youngest infants.

Although there are many NSAIDs available for use in adults, few are licensed for use in children and there are only some marketed in liquid form or in age-appropriate doses suppository for children. Acetylsalicylic acid (aspirin) is the oldest NSAID. Because of its association with Reye's syndrome, it is used rarely in children. Ibuprofen, diclofenac, ketoprofen, and ketorolac are the most commonly used NSAIDs in paediatrics. Ibuprofen is available in oral suspension, infant drops, tablets, and i.v. formulations. Diclofenac is available as tablets, suppository, and parenteral formulations. Ibuprofen dosing is 5–10 mg kg^{-1} every 6–8 h in children, with the low dose generally recommended for children less than 6 months. Diclofenac suppositories are available in many countries; rectal and oral dosing is 1 mg kg^{-1} every 8 h (maximum 3 mg kg^{-1} day^{-1}). Indeed, rectal absorption of diclofenac is faster than paracetamol. Ketorolac is the only parenteral NSAID used in children at a dose

Table 73.3 Dosing of NSAIDs used in children

NSAID	Dose ($mg\ kg^{-1}$)	Intervals (h)	Maximum daily dosing [$mg\ kg^{-1}\ (24\ h)^{-1}$]	Licensed from age
Ibuprofen	5–10	6–8	30	3 months
Diclofenac	1	8	3	6 months
Ketorolac	0.5	6	2	n/l
Piroxicam	0.5	24	0.5	n/l
Naproxen	7.5	12	15	n/l
Ketoprofen	1	6	4	n/l

n/l, not licensed.

of 0.5–1.0 mg kg^{-1} (maximum 10–15 mg kg^{-1}), but it is not yet licensed for use in children. Concerns regarding acute kidney injury in healthy young adults receiving i.v. ketorolac have resulted in its use being rather limited in children. Ketoprofen is not yet recommended in many countries because of insufficient data on safety and efficacy (Table 73.3) (Maunuksela and Olkhola 2003).

Widespread usage of NSAIDs is limited by contraindications and side-effects, albeit these are generally believed to occur less frequently in children than in adults and serious toxicity associated with NSAIDs appears to be very rare in children. Although several studies have indicated that the short-term use of NSAIDs is safe in asthmatic children, severe asthma and coexistent nasal polyps remains a particular concern. NSAIDs should generally be avoided in infants less than 6 months of age; children with known allergy to aspirin and NSAIDs; dehydration or hypovolaemia; renal, hepatic, or coagulation impairments; peptic ulcers; or in clinical settings where significant bleeding can be anticipated. They are generally used with caution in tonsillectomy because of the risk of bleeding (Dsida and Coté 2004). A concern in orthopaedic surgery is that NSAIDs may interfere with osteoclast activity and thus prevent bone healing (Gerstenfeld et al. 2003). In addition, the NSAIDs should not be administered together with anticoagulants, steroids, and nephrotoxic drugs. The most commonly reported side-effects of NSAIDs are gastrointestinal and bleeding followed by skin reactions, central nervous system, pulmonary, hepatic, and renal effects. Much severer (but far less common) side-effects such as bone marrow depression and Stevens–Johnson syndrome have also been reported. Limiting NSAID exposure to the lowest effective dose and shortest duration may reduce the risk of adverse events.

Opioids

Opioids are used for moderate to severe nociceptive pain, although they are sometimes used for neuropathic pain. Opioid receptors are classified as μ (mu), κ (kappa), δ (delta), and σ (sigma). The μ-receptor is further sub-divided into subclasses: μ_1, which mediates supraspinal analgesia and dependence, and μ_2, which mediates respiratory depression, intestinal dysmotility, sedation, and bradycardia. Most commonly used opioids work through μ_1-mediated analgesia. Examples of the μ_1-agonists include morphine, pethidine (meperidine), methadone, fentanyl, alfentanil, sufentanil, remifentanil, codeine, and oxycodone. Side-effects common to opioid agonists include respiratory depression, sedation, nausea, vomiting, pruritus, urinary retention, and constipation. Less common effects are dysphoria, hallucinations, seizures, cough, and myoclonic movements (Stein and Rosow 2004). There is significant *individual* variability in the side-effect profiles of the different opioid analgesics. In the presence of unacceptable side-effects, switching to a different opioid may result in lessened side-effects (Quigley 2004).

Morphine

Morphine is the standard opioid with which all other opioids are compared (Esmail et al. 1999; Berde and Sethna 2002; Lonnqvist and Morton 2005; Morton and Errera 2010). It has been extensively studied in virtually all age groups of children. Neonates, particularly if born prematurely, have extreme inter-individual variability in morphine clearance and terminal elimination half-life that is inversely related to post-menstrual age. Thus, clearance is lower with lower post-menstrual age and elimination half-life is prolonged. Morphine clearance in full term neonates aged less than 1 month is about one-third of that in older children and about one-half of that in adults (Kart et al. 1997; Bouwmeester et al. 2004). It is generally believed by clinicians that small infants are more prone to respiratory depression induced by opioids than older children and adults. However, hard scientific evidence for this contention has been quite difficult to establish. Nevertheless, it is clear that inter-individual variation in pharmacokinetics and pharmacodynamics is huge in the youngest infants and morphine (and other opioids) should be administered with great caution, particularly in postoperative infants with an unprotected airway (Table 73.4).

Morphine can be given via multiple routes (i.v., oral, s.c., i.m., intrathecal, epidural, and intra-articular). It is metabolized in the liver to morphine-3-glucuronide (inactive) and morphine-6-glucuronide (active), both of which are excreted by the kidneys. Less morphine is protein bound in neonates, allowing a greater proportion of unbound morphine to penetrate the brain, thus increasing the risk for respiratory depression. The elimination half-life and clearance reach adult values within 2 months of age. The optimal plasma concentration of morphine needed to achieve analgesia in children is variable based on the existing data.

Methadone

Methadone is a synthetic opioid with a long elimination half-life and duration of action (12–36 h). It has a relatively high bioavailability (80–85%), thus it appears to be an attractive oral analgesic. The primary metabolite of methadone is morphine (Yaster 2001). Methadone acts as both a μ-receptor agonist and an *N*-methyl-D-aspartate (NMDA) receptor antagonist, resulting in incomplete cross-tolerance between methadone and morphine, which must be taken in to consideration when switching from morphine to methadone (Table 73.4) (Ripamonti et al. 1998).

Fentanyl

Fentanyl is a synthetic opioid structurally related to meperidine and approximately 100 times more potent than morphine. It is highly lipophilic, thus it easily passes through the blood–brain barrier. A single bolus dose of fentanyl has a relatively short duration of action because of redistribution into body tissues. However, once these sites are saturated, the elimination half-life is actually quite long. Indeed, the context-sensitive half-life of fentanyl progressively increases with the duration of infusion. Fentanyl is highly protein bound to α1-acid glycoprotein in the plasma. Neonates have reduced concentrations of α1-acid glycoprotein, resulting in higher concentrations of free unbound fentanyl. Metabolisms occur

Table 73.4 Recommended opioid doses in different age groups of children

Opioid	Route/age group	Dosing	Intervals
Morphine	Oral:		
	Preterm neonates	n/r	
	Term neonates	n/r	
	Infants and children	0.2–0.3 mg kg^{-1}	As needed (2–4 h)
	I.V. bolus:		
	Preterm neonates	5–10 μg kg^{-1}	As needed (2–4 h)
	Term neonates	25–50 μg kg^{-1}	
	Infants and children	50–100 μg kg^{-1}	
	I.V. infusion:		
	Preterm neonates	2–5 μg kg^{-1} h^{-1}	
	Term neonates	5–10 μg kg^{-1} h^{-1}	
	Infants and children	10–40 μg kg^{-1} h^{-1}	
Fentanyl	Intranasal:		
	Infants and children	1–2 μg kg^{-1}	1–2 h
	Transdermal patches:		
	Infants and children	12.5, 25, 50, 75, 100 μg h^{-1}	
	I.V. bolus:		
	Neonates	0.25–0.5 μg kg^{-1}	
	Infants and children	0.5–1.0 μg kg^{-1}	
	I.V. infusion:		
	Neonates:	n/r*	
	Infants and children	0.5–2.5 μg kg^{-1} h^{-1}	
Tramadol	Oral/rectal:		
	Infants and children	1–2 mg kg^{-1}	4–6 h
	I.V. bolus:		
	Infants and children	1 mg kg^{-1}	4–6 h
	I.V. infusion:		
	Infants and children	0.1–0.4 mg kg^{-1} h^{-1}	
Codeine	Oral:		
	Infants and children	0.5–1.0 mg kg^{-1}	4–6 h
Methadone	Oral or i.v.:		
	Infants and children	0.1–0.2 mg kg^{-1}	12–36 h
Oxycodone	Oral:		
	Infants and children	0.1–0.2 mg kg^{-1}	4–6 h

* Please note that careful administration of opioids under adequate monitoring in neonates and premature infants is necessary postoperatively, particularly if the airway is unprotected. n/r, not recommended.

through glucuronidation in the liver to inactive metabolites that are excreted by the kidney. The clearance of fentanyl is significantly decreased and the elimination half-life prolonged in neonates and young infants. Similarly to morphine, neonates and young infants are more prone to adverse effects of fentanyl, especially sedation and respiratory depression (Koren and Maurice 1989). As a result of its high lipophilicity, fentanyl can be given by multiple routes: i.v., epidural, nasal, transmucosal, and transdermal. Given nasally (2 μg kg^{-1}), fentanyl provides good analgesia in children who are undergoing myringotomy tube insertion. Fentanyl is also available for transmucosal administration with an onset time of 20 min and duration of 2 h (Yaster 2001). Transmucosal fentanyl provides good analgesia, but the incidence of nausea and vomiting is troublesome. Transdermal fentanyl administration is also possible (patches available in 12.5, 25, 50, 75, and 100 μg h^{-1}). It has a long onset time but also a long duration even after the patch is removed (Collins et al. 1999).

Other potent synthetic opioid such as alfentanil, sufentanil, and remifentanil are usually reserved for perioperative use in the anaesthetic practice as a result of their potency and adverse effects associated with their use, particularly in higher doses, limit their use outside operating theatres (Table 73.4).

Pethidine (meperidine)

Pethidine is a synthetic opioid and a phenylpiperidine derivative. It has 10% of the potency of morphine and is metabolized in the liver by hydrolysis and *N*-demethylation. It has an elimination half-life of approximately 3 h. Pethidine is used infrequently in children as an analgesic; however, it is still used for postoperative shivering. Its metabolite, norpethidine, may cause seizures particularly in relation to long-term use; hence, it is generally not recommended in children (Koren and Maurice 1989; Berde et al. 1991).

Codeine

Codeine is a μ-agonist and a derivative of morphine. Codeine is at least 10 times less potent than morphine. Its bioavailability is 60% after oral administration, with an onset time of 20 min and an elimination half-life of 2.5–3 h. Approximately 10% of codeine is hepatically demethylated to morphine by *O*-demethylation in the liver (CYP2D6); a prerequisite for analgesia to occur. An important characteristic of this metabolic process is the effect of genetic polymorphism (Williams et al. 2001). Four to ten per cent of the population lack the CYP2D6 isoenzyme responsible for this conversion and therefore receive little if any analgesic effect from codeine. Overall a large number of different genetic variants of CYP2D6 (>50) are known to exist, resulting in a wide range of possible effects from codeine, from no analgesia to increased analgesia and enhanced side-effects (extensive metabolizers) (Caraco et al. 1996). Very few studies on efficacy and safety of codeine in infants and children have been published. Much of the known pharmacokinetics of codeine is derived from adult studies. Because of the unpredictability of the analgesic effect and the significant incidence of nausea and vomiting associated with it, codeine is being used less as a first-line oral analgesic.

Oxycodone

Oxycodone (13-hydroxy-7,8-dihydrocodeinone) is a semisynthetic thebaine derivative, with effects similar to morphine. Oxycodone is metabolized in the liver by means of *N*- and *O*-demethylation, 6-ketoreduction, and conjugation with glucuronic acid. Oxymorphone, the end-product of *O*-demethylation of oxycodone, has marked opioid activity, whereas the *N*-demethylation end-product, noroxycodone, has only weak affinity for opioid receptors. Oxymorphone may accumulate in renal failure. Bioavailability is 50–60% after oral administration, with an onset time of 20–30 min and duration of action of 4–5 h. Although there are some paediatric studies, oxycodone is not licensed for children and studies on efficacy and tolerability should be performed before it is used clinically (Kokki et al. 2004).

Tramadol

Tramadol is an atypical opioid that structurally resembles morphine and codeine. It is available as a racemic mixture of two enantiomers that provide synergistic analgesia. Its interesting mechanism of action involves both central inhibition of noradrenaline (norepinephrine) and serotonin reuptake and a weak μ-receptor agonism by an active metabolite. Hepatic biotransformation via CYP2D6 results in the formation of *O*-demethyl-tramadol, which has a μ-receptor affinity 200 times greater than the parent compound. Tramadol's huge variation in pharmacokinetics may at least partly be ascribed to CYP2D6 polymorphism. It is available in oral, sublingual, slow-release, rectal, and parenteral formulations. Tramadol is 10–15 times less potent than morphine. It may have fewer side-effects than other opioids, albeit nausea and vomiting occur with the same incidence as with other opioids (Finkel et al. 2002). Seizures are a known but rare complication of tramadol. It is a safe and effective analgesic for mild to moderate pain in children. The recommended dose of tramadol is 1–2 mg kg^{-1} (maximum 100 mg) every 6 h, with a maximum daily dose of 8 mg kg^{-1} day^{-1} or 400 mg day^{-1} (Table 73.4).

Naloxone

Naloxone is an antagonist at all opioid receptors. It is used in emergency treatment of respiratory depression at a dose of up to 10 μg kg^{-1} i.v. It is also used in smaller doses for pruritus (0.5–2 μg kg^{-1} i.v.). Naloxone is metabolized in the liver and has an elimination half-life of 60 min. Because this is a shorter half-life than most μ-receptor agonists continued monitoring of the patient is required to ensure that side-effects do not recur (Lonnqvist and Morton 2005).

Other analgesics

Nitrous oxide

Nitrous oxide (N_2O) can be used for procedural sedation and analgesia in children. It is a weak anaesthetic with analgesic properties that if (self-)administered by inhalation via a face or nasal mask will be rapidly absorbed as a result of a very low blood/gas partition coefficient. Fifty per cent nitrous oxide in oxygen is available in premixed cylinders; however, N_2O can also be administered in inspired concentrations of up to 70–75% in oxygen. N_2O is widely used for minor procedures such as venepunctures, change of dressings, and physiotherapy after major surgery. It is not suitable for very painful procedures such as reduction of fractures. Analgesia is usually achieved after three to four breaths and recovery is rapid once N_2O is discontinued. Side-effects include nausea and vomiting, agitation, and dizziness. N_2O may cause central nervous system depression and deep sedation in concentrations higher than 50%; as such, it also potentiates the central nervous system depressant effects of other drugs. Prolonged and repeated usage of N_2O may affect folate metabolism resulting in megaloblastic anaemia and peripheral neuropathy (Lonnqvist and Morton 2005). Furthermore, the potential impact of N_2O on the developing brain is a particular concern at present.

Ketamine

Ketamine, a phencyclidine derivative and a dissociative anaesthetic, is a potent analgesic in sub-anaesthetic doses that is often used for short painful procedures in children in the emergency room and intensive care unit settings. It can be administered via multiple routes, for example, orally, rectally, intramuscularly, and intravenously; and has been used epidurally as well (Roelofse 2010). The analgesic effects of ketamine are mediated by NMDA receptor antagonism and possibly also by μ-receptor agonism. Ketamine is very lipid-soluble drug with an oral bioavailability of 20–25% (Malinovsky et al. 1996). It is *N*-demethylated in the liver by the CYP system into various metabolites, for example, norketamine, which has an analgesic effect of up to one-third that of ketamine itself. Small i.v. doses of ketamine (0.25–0.5 mg kg^{-1}) can produce intense analgesia for 10–15 min, despite an elimination half-life of 2–3 h. Anaesthetic doses (1–2 mg kg^{-1} i.v.) may be needed for more painful procedures such as fracture reduction. Adult and paediatric studies are increasing on the intraoperative and postoperative use of ketamine as an adjunct to opioid analgesia, for example, low-dose infusion (0.2 mg kg^{-1} h^{-1}) (Himmelseher and Durieux

2005). Ketamine is a racemic mixture. Its S-isomer (S-ketamine) is believed to possess approximately twice the analgesic potency of the racemate. S-ketamine may have fewer side-effects than racemic ketamine; however, there are only few paediatric studies on S-ketamine. The use of ketamine to supplement caudal analgesia with a local anaesthetic has been shown to prolong postoperative analgesia, but safety issues regarding epidural administration of ketamine have not been properly addressed. Furthermore, although its role as an analgesic or preventive analgesic is well established in adults, it is less clear in children. As with N_2O, concern about ketamine's potential neurotoxic effects on the developing brain remains an important issue.

α2-Adrenergic agonists

Clonidine

Clonidine is an α2-adrenergic agonist that is used increasingly as an anxiolytic and analgesic in paediatrics. Clonidine is also used to control opioid and benzodiazepine withdrawal symptoms in intensive care unit settings. Given orally preoperatively (4–5 μg kg^{-1}) or i.v. (2 μg kg^{-1}), clonidine decreases both intraoperative anaesthetic requirements and postoperative opioid consumption. It is also used as an adjunct to local anaesthetics to prolong or increase the quality of analgesia in regional blocks (1–2 μg kg^{-1}) (Nishina et al. 1999). Compared with opioids, clonidine has a much better side-effect profile (less postoperative nausea and vomiting and respiratory depression and no pruritus). Clonidine is almost completely bioavailable when given orally as a result of its high lipid solubility and it easily passes the blood–brain barrier. Epidural clonidine may cause sedation and hypotension (Constant et al. 1998; Hansen and Henneberg 2004; Hansen et al. 2004).

Dexmedetomidine

Dexmedetomidine is a relatively new α2-receptor agonist, which has an affinity for the receptor that is eight times that of clonidine. Although dexmedetomidine is primarily used as a sedative in intensive care unit settings, it appears to have analgesic effects by reducing opioid requirements. Additionally, its use seems to be associated with minimal respiratory depression (Lonnqvist and Morton 2005). To date, dexmedetomidine is only licensed in a few countries worldwide, and although paediatric studies are mounting up, its safety and efficacy profile is still to be clarified.

Local anaesthetics

Local anaesthetics are drugs that reversibly block electric impulse conduction along nerve fibres mainly by interfering with sodium channels, thus preventing pain transmission. There are two classes of local anaesthetics: amides and esters. The amides are metabolized in the liver, whereas the esters are metabolized via plasma esterases. Local anaesthetics may be administered intrathecally or epidurally, in close proximity to peripheral nerves, subcutaneously, or applied topically in creams or ophthalmic drops. They differ in onset of action, potency, duration, and potential for toxic reactions (Mazoit 2012). The maximum dosages and duration of action of the local anaesthetics are listed in Table 73.5 (Lonnqvist and Morton 2005). Bupivacaine is the most commonly used local anaesthetic for both central and peripheral local anaesthesia, although the newer local anaesthetics ropivacaine and levobupivacaine are increasingly being used (Casati and Putzy 2005). Several studies have shown that ropivacaine has less potential for cardiovascular toxicity compared with bupivacaine. Because of reduced clearance and lower protein binding of bupivacaine, levo-bupivacaine, and ropivacaine, dosages of these drugs must be reduced in neonates and young infants to avoid toxicity (Hansen et al. 2000, 2001; Hansen 2004; Lonnqvist and Morton 2005).

Table 73.5 Suggested maximum dosages of the commonest used amide local anaesthetics: bupivacaine, levobupivacaine, and ropivacaine

	Maximum bolus dose	Maximum continuous infusion rate
Neonates	2 mg kg^{-1}	0.2 mg kg^{-1} h^{-1}
Children	2.5 mg kg^{-1}	0.4 mg kg^{-1} h^{-1}

In children older than 6 months, clonidine (1–1.5 μg ml^{-1}) or fentanyl (2 μg ml^{-1}) can be added to the solution for sedation or to improve the quality of analgesia, or both.

Topical applied local anaesthetics, for example, eutectic mixture of local anaesthetics (EMLA®) cream or 4% tetracaine (Ametop™), may provide children with analgesia for many painful procedures, for example, venepuncture, i.v. placement, lumbar punctures, and laceration suturing.

Postoperative pain management strategies

Successful acute pain management targets all of the elements in the complex nociceptive system. Analgesia balanced with a combination of opioid therapy, regional techniques, and NSAIDs (multimodal analgesia) is being used successfully in paediatric patients. Such a balanced approach results in a reduction in systemic opioid administration and occasionally also opioid-related side-effects (Yaster 2010). There is a huge inter-individual variation in the amount of pain experienced by different children with similar conditions and undergoing similar surgeries (Hansen et al. 1996, 2004). Children also have fluctuating analgesic needs. During rest, the child's analgesic requirements are less than when the child is physical active in attempting to change positions, breathe deeply, or undergo dressing changes, diagnostic tests, therapeutic procedures, physiotherapy, or nursing care. Thus, a prerequisite for effective paediatric pain management requires a proactive plan for managing background and breakthrough pain.

Specialized pain management techniques

Postoperative pain management in the recovery room

In the recovery room, children can appear distressed for a variety of reasons, for example, anxiety, hunger, thirst, emergency delirium, and pain. Most experienced recovery nurses can distinguish inadequate analgesia from other causes of distress. Moderate to severe pain in the recovery room is best treated with intermittent i.v. bolus doses of opioids with subsequent adjustment of any chosen analgesia regimen (e.g. increasing opioid infusion rate, checking the quality of the epidural block) if needed before the child is returned to the ward (Berde and Sethna 2002).

Intermittent bolus doses of opioids

The i.v. route of administration is the route of choice for opioids for the management of acute severe pain. It ensures a rapid and efficient titration of analgesia. I.M. or s.c. injections should never be used because of the painful nature of the injections, but absorption following these routes is also erratic and unpredictable. Intermittent i.v. morphine bolus doses are suitable for all children suffering from moderate to severe acute short-term pain and as rescue for children who experience breakthrough pain and those who are weaned off from any mode of continuous analgesia (Table 73.4) (Berde and Sethna 2002; Lonnqvist and Morton 2005).

Patient-controlled analgesia

Patient-controlled analgesia (PCA) is used for moderate to severe pain in children more than 5–6 years of age. The PCA concept requires a cooperative, awake child who understands that administration of analgesics requires that he or she pushes a button to activate the pump (Berde et al. 1991). PCA is mainly used in the postoperative context, but has also been used in children who have more chronic opioid needs (e.g. children with malignant conditions) (Anghelescu et al. 2011).

PCA is safe, effective, and highly satisfactory to patients, families, and nursing staff. The technique is considered safe because if a child has a high demand for an opioid, he or she will eventually become sedated and stop pushing the demand button. If another individual pushes the button, however, there is potential for severe sedation and respiratory depression. Therefore, only the patient is allowed to press the button. However, PCA by proxy (nurse- and parent-controlled analgesia) has been shown to be safe and effective in younger children and infants or in cognitively impaired older children (Monitto et al. 2000; Anghelescu et al. 2011). PCA is effective because it allows patients (or proxies) to titrate the amount of analgesic drugs they require to the degree of pain of the individual patient. Plasma concentrations of opioid are thus maintained in a narrower range with lower peak concentrations and higher trough concentrations than with intermittent injections. This may help reducing the incidence and severity of side-effects, particularly respiratory depression and sedation. PCA is well suited to deal with inter- and intra-variation in analgesia experienced by patients with similar and different conditions. The PCA infusion pumps are programmed to deliver a preset (on-demand) dose of opioid when the patient pushes a button in a specified period of time (lockout interval) irrespective of how many times the patient pushes the on-demand button. The pump also is programmed only to deliver a preset maximum amount of opioid in the course of a 1 h limit. The pump records both the patient's history of attempts and actual opioid injections. The infusion pumps can also be programmed to deliver a continuous background infusion of opioid regardless of whether the patient uses the demand button (Berde and Sethna 2002; Lonnqvist and Morton 2005). However, there is an ongoing debate regarding the use of PCA background infusions. The argument against using background infusions is that it removes the inherent safety of the patient titrating the analgesic drug to the desired analgesic effect, thereby increasing the risk for side-effects, of which respiratory depression is the most feared. Several studies have shown that background infusions merely increase the risk for side-effects without improving analgesia. The argument for background PCA infusions is that they allow the patient to sleep uninterruptedly without wake-up events as a result of severe pain arising from having not activated the button. Background PCA infusions may be necessary in older children and adolescents after spinal surgery. Even with a background opioid infusion, some children may experience severe pain if they have been asleep for a prolonged period of time without having activated the on-demand button. Additionally, standing orders for respiratory depression and *too* deep sedation (naloxone 10 μg kg^{-1} i.v., as needed), nausea and vomiting (e.g. ondansetron 100 μg kg^{-1} i.v., every 8 h), and pruritus (naloxone 0.5–1 μg kg^{-1} i.v., as needed) should be prescribed for all children on PCA. For children with muscle spasms, an adjunct such as diazepam, 0.1 mg kg^{-1}, orally or rectally, every 6 h, may be helpful. Morphine is the first-line opioid used in PCA in children. Alternatively, fentanyl can be used if there are too severe side-effects to morphine. For PCA dosing see Tables 73.6 and 73.7.

Continuous intravenous opioid infusion

Continuous intravenous opioid infusion (CIV) is used in patients who are unable to use PCA because of age, physical disability, or cognitive impairment. Compared with intermittent opioid administration, CIV ensures a stable plasma opioid concentration without major fluctuations with a reduced reliance on nursing staff (Esmail et al. 1999). A constant infusion will not cover breakthrough incident pain, so rescue doses of opioid may be needed. Morphine is the most common opioid used for CIV, with doses adjusted for age and clinical status Table 73.4. Morphine infusions are associated with an increased risk of respiratory depression in preterm and full-term neonates, so further reductions are required in this age group (Table 73.4). Fentanyl and tramadol can also be administered as a CIV. Pethidine should never be used in this context because of the risk of accumulation of its metabolite—norpethidine—which is known to cause convulsions.

Continuous epidural analgesia

Continuous epidural analgesia (CEA) provides pain relief for surgical procedures below the fourth thoracic dermatome. Patients on CEA obtain excellent dermatomal analgesia. Epidural catheters may be placed via the caudal, lumbar, or thoracic route (Berde and

Table 73.6 Intravenous patient-controlled analgesic dosing guidelines for the most commonly used opioids

Opioid	On demand dose (μg kg^{-1})	Lockout interval (min)	Background infusion (μg kg^{-1} h^{-1})
Morphine	10–25	5–10	0–4.0
Fentanyl	0.5–1.0	5–10	0–1.0

Other opioids have been used for i.v. patient-controlled analgesic in children (e.g. tramadol and oxycodone) but cannot be recommended at present.

Table 73.7 Intravenous nurse-controlled analgesia dosing guidelines for morphine in children

Opioid	On demand dose (μg kg^{-1})	Lockout interval (min)	Background infusion (μg kg^{-1} h^{-1})
Morphine	10–20	20–30	0–20

Caution should be taken when using background infusion in young infants.

Sethna 2002; Lonnqvist and Morton 2005). In infants, thoracic dermatomal analgesia may be often obtained by threading a catheter from a caudal route of insertion to the thoracic region (Tsui et al. 2004). This indirect method of placement is often confounded by incorrect dermatomal placement of the catheter. A stylet-guided catheter may be helpful in these situations although the risk of vascular or dural puncture is increased. An X-ray intensifier using non-ionic radio contrast agent can help ensuring catheter position. The stimulating catheter technique as described by Tsui et al. (2004) may also be used to ensure the reliability of this technique.

The use of CEA requires a hospital organization with the ability to immediately act and solve problems. Daily rounds should be performed by a team of nurses and physicians who have expertise in CEA to ensure proper analgesia and to proactively address expected adverse effects such as nausea, vomiting, pruritus, motor block, epidural site inflammation, and less frequent and more severe sequelae such as respiratory and central nervous system depression. Additionally, regular monitoring comprising respiratory rate, blood pressure, heart rate, mental status, and pain scores is essential.

The postoperative epidural analgesic solution may contain a single local anaesthetic agent or a combination of different classes of analgesics (Table 73.5).

The most common problems with CEA are ineffectiveness caused by incorrect dermatomal location, catheter problems (obstruction, kinking, leaking, or breaking), infusion pump failure, inappropriate infusion rate or solution, or accidental displacement of the catheter from its original location (Giaufré et al. 1996; Llewellyn and Moriarty 2007). In the event of motor block, the concentration of the local anaesthetic can be decreased. If significant opioid-related side-effects occur, the epidural opioid should be discontinued. A rare but serous complication is the development of local anaesthetic toxicity from systemic absorption. This is very unlikely if the concentrations and infusion rates recommended are adhered to, although extra caution is needed in patients with a reduced capacity for local anaesthetic metabolism and excretion (e.g. neonates). CEA can be combined with PCA to patient-controlled epidural analgesia (PCEA), which may be of particular benefit for predictable episodes of incident pain such as getting out of bed, physical therapy, or dressing changes (Birmingham et al. 2003).

Transition to oral analgesics

The transition from specialized techniques such as CIV, PCA, CEA, and PCEA may be challenging. In neonates and young infants, weaning is usually considered after 36–48 h as opposed to older children, where this is usually not attempted before 48–72 h. Certain surgeries require significantly longer pain treatment (e.g. spinal fusion or pelvic osteotomies). Oral analgesic therapy can begin when the child's pain subsides and oral medications are tolerated. Epidural infusions and CIV are discontinued before oral analgesics are started. Patients on PCA may start oral analgesics and be allowed to use demand-only PCA (no background infusion) for a brief period to make certain that the dose of oral analgesic is sufficient (Berde and Sethna 2002; Lonnqvist and Morton 2005). A co-analgesic such as paracetamol or NSAIDs may be helpful in facilitating the transitional phase. During the transition, a rescue i.v. dosage of morphine 50 μg kg^{-1} as needed may be necessary. The instructions delivered to the parents at discharge about use of analgesics at home after an inpatient hospital stay or from the post-anaesthesia care unit after outpatient surgery are important. The parents should be very clear on the specific analgesics, doses, and frequency, and the importance of proper pain management for their child. Pain management after paediatric day surgery is still an area in need of improvement (Wolf 1999).

Regional techniques

Many regional techniques are being used increasingly in paediatric anaesthesia both as an adjunct to anaesthesia and as a modality of postoperative analgesia (McCann et al. 2001). It is generally believed that performing regional blocks in anaesthetized children is actually much safer rather than in a struggling child (Krane et al. 1998).

Caudal analgesia

Caudal block is one of the most commonly performed regional techniques in children (Constant et al. 1998; Hansen et al. 2001, 2004; Passariello et al. 2004). It provides excellent analgesia for lower extremity or superficial lower abdominal surgeries using volumes of 0.75–1 ml kg^{-1} of local anaesthetic solution (bupivacaine/levobupivacaine 0.125–0.25%, ropivacaine 0.2%). To reach T10 dermatomal levels, volumes of 1.25 ml kg^{-1} are required, but caution is needed to ensure that the dosage of bupivacaine or ropivacaine does not exceed 2.5 mg kg^{-1}. Bupivacaine 0.25% provides excellent analgesia, but in ambulatory children, the potential motor block can be avoided by using bupivacaine 0.125%. The use of clonidine (1–2 μg kg^{-1}) as an adjunct significantly prolongs the duration of caudal analgesia by about 40% (Constant et al. 1998; Hansen et al. 2004; Passariello et al. 2004). Additional adjuncts such as preservative-free S-ketamine, neostigmine, tramadol, and midazolam are being studied for their efficacy in augmenting and prolonging analgesia with single-dose caudal administration, but cannot be recommended at this point.

Peripheral nerve blocks

Peripheral nerve blocks are being used with increasing frequency in children. The potential advantages of using peripheral nerve blocks as adjuncts to general anaesthesia and to postoperative analgesia are improved and more prolonged analgesia and fewer opioid-induced side-effects, especially nausea and vomiting (Polaner and Drescher 2011). The volume of local anaesthetic solution needed to cause a suitable block in children is relatively higher (per kg) than in adults; hence caution is needed to use the lowest concentration of local anaesthetic necessary. Peripheral blocks may be performed as a single injection technique or as a continuous infusion through a percutaneous catheter.

The use of ultrasound-guided peripheral nerve block ensures proper visualization of anatomical structures, facilitates the procedure, and shows how the local anaesthetic solution spread when injected within the desired tissue. Furthermore, the use of ultrasound for peripheral nerve block lowers the volume of local anaesthetics applied, shortens the onset time, results in higher success rates, and may reduce the incidence of complications. The use of ultrasound, however, requires significant training and skills before it can be implemented successfully and universally in paediatrics (Marhofer et al. 2005).

It is very likely that in the near future we may experience significant advancements in paediatric regional analgesia. In addition to the increasing use of ultrasound, use of long-acting local anaesthetic microsomal spheres seems particularly promising (Curley et al. 1996).

Conclusion

Paediatric pain management has made great strides in the past few decades, in the understanding of developmental neurobiology, developmental pharmacology, the use of analgesics in children, the use of regional techniques in children, and of the psychological needs of children in pain. A wide range of various analgesic drugs is available to ensure proper paediatric pain management. More pharmacological research is required, especially in the youngest and most vulnerable infants. Children now benefit from many of the techniques for effective pain management in adults and there are reasons to be optimistic that ongoing research together with political and public pressure will promote even further advancements in pain management for children.

Declaration of interest

None declared.

References

Allegaert K, Palmer GM, Anderson BJ. The pharmacokinetics of intravenous paracetamol in neonates: size matters most. *Arch Dis Child* 2011; **96**: 575–80

Anderson BJ, van Lingen RA, Hansen TG, Lin YC, Holford NH. Acetaminophen developmental pharmacokinetics in premature neonates and infants: a pooled population analysis. *Anesthesiology* 2002; **96**: 1336–45

Anghelescu DL, Kaddoum RN, Oakes LL, Windsor KB, Faughnan LG, Burgoyne LL. An update: the safety of patient-controlled analgesia by proxy for pain management in pediatric oncology: 2004 to 2010. *Anesth Analg* 2011; **113**: 1525–6

Arana A, Morton NS, Hansen TG. Treatment with paracetamol in infants. *Acta Anaesthesiol Scand* 2001; **45**: 20–9

Berde CB, Lehn BM, Yee JD, Sethna NF, Russo D. Patient-controlled analgesia in children and adolescents: a randomized, prospective comparison with intramuscular administration of morphine for postoperative analgesia. *J Pediatr* 1991; **118**: 460–6

Berde CB, Sethna NF. Analgesics for the treatment of pain in children. *N Engl J Med* 2002; **347**: 1094–103

Birmingham PK, Wheeler M, Suresh S, *et al.* Patient-controlled epidural analgesia in children: can they do it? *Anesth Analg* 2003; **96**: 686–91

Bouwmeester NJ, Anderson BJ, Tibboel D, Holford NH. Developmental pharmacokinetics of morphine and its metabolites in neonates, infants and young children. *Br J Anaesth* 2004; **92**: 208–17

Caraco Y, Sheller J, Wood AJ. Pharmacogenetic determination of the effects of codeine and prediction of drug interactions. *J Pharmacol Exp Ther* 1996; **278**: 1165–74

Casati A, Putzy M. Bupivacaine, levobupivacaine and ropivacaine: are they clinically different? *Best Pract Res Clin Anaesthesiol* 2005; **19**: 247–68

Collins JJ, Dunkel IJ, Gupta SK, *et al.* Transdermal fentanyl in children with cancer pain: feasibility, tolerability, and pharmacokinetic correlates. *J Pediatr* 1999; **134**: 319–23

Constant I, Gall O, Gouyet L, Chauvin M, Murat I. Addition of clonidine or fentanyl to local anaesthetics prolongs the duration of surgical analgesia after single shot caudal block in children. *Br J Anaesth* 1998; **80**: 294–8

Curley J, Castillo J, Hotz J, *et al.* Prolonged regional nerve blockade. Injectable biodegradable bupivacaine/polyester microspheres. *Anesthesiology* 1996; **84**: 1401–10

Dsida R, Coté CJ. Nonsteroidal antiinflammatory drugs and hemorrhage following tonsillectomy: do we have the data? *Anesthesiology* 2004; **100**: 749–51

Esmail Z, Montgomery C, Courtrn C, Hamilton D, Kestle J. Efficacy and complications of morphine infusions in postoperative paediatric patients. *Paediatr Anaesth* 1999; **9**: 321–7

Finkel JC, Rose JB, Schmitz ML, *et al.* An evaluation of the efficacy and tolerability of oral tramadol hydrochloride tablets for the treatment of postsurgical pain in children. *Anesth Analg* 2002; **94**: 1469–73

Fitzgeralds M, Howard R. The neurobiologic basis of pediatric pain. In: Schechter NL, Berde CB, Yaster M, eds. *Pain in Infants, Children, and Adolescents*, 2nd Edn. Baltimore, MD: Lippincott Williams & Wilkins, 2001; 19–42

Gerstenfeld LC, Thiede M, Seibert K, *et al.* Differential inhibition of fracture healing by non-selective and cyclooxygenase-2 selective non-steroidal anti-inflammatory drugs. *J Orthop Res* 2003; **21**: 670–5

Giaufré E, Dalens B, Gombert A. Epidemiology and morbidity of regional anesthesia in children: a one-year prospective survey of the French-Language Society of Pediatric Anesthesiologists. *Anesth Analg* 1996; **83**: 904–12

Hansen TG. Plasma paracetamol concentrations and pharmacokinetics following rectal administration in neonates and young infants. *Acta Anaesthesiol Scand* 1999; 43: 855–9

Hansen TG. Ropivacaine: a pharmacological review. *Expert Rev Neurother* 2004; **4**: 781–91

Hansen TG, Henneberg SW. Caudal clonidine in neonates and small infants and respiratory depression. *Paediatr Anaesth* 2004; **14**: 529–30

Hansen TG, Henneberg SW, Hole P. Age-related postoperative morphine requirements in children following major surgery – an assessment using patient-controlled analgesia (PCA). *Eur J Pediatr Surg* 1996; **6**: 29–31

Hansen TG, Henneberg SW, Walther-Larsen S, Lund J, Hansen M. Caudal bupivacaine supplemented with caudal or intravenous clonidine in children undergoing hypospadias repair: a double-blind study. *Br J Anaesth* 2004; **92**: 223–7

Hansen TG, Ilett KF, Lim SI, Reid C, Hackett LP, Bergesio R. Pharmacokinetics and clinical efficacy of long-term epidural ropivacaine infusion in children. *Br J Anaesth* 2000; **85**: 347–53

Hansen TG, Ilett KF, Reid C, Lim SI, Hackett LP, Bergesio R. Caudal ropivacaine in infants: population pharmacokinetics and plasma concentrations. *Anesthesiology* 2001; **94**: 579–84

Himmelseher S, Durieuex ME. Ketamine for perioperative pain management. *Anesthesiology* 2005; **102**: 211–20

Johnston CC, Fernandes AM, Campbell-Yeo M. Pain in neonates is different. *Pain* 2011; **152**: S65–73

Johnston CC, Filion F, Snider L, *et al.* How much sucrose is too much sucrose? *Pediatrics* 2007; **119**: 226

Kart TT, Christrup LL, Rasmussen M. Recommended use of morphine in neonates, infants and children based on a literature review: Part 1—Pharmacokinetics. *Paediatr Anaesth* 1997; **7**: 5–11

Kearns GL, Abdel-Rahman SM, Alander SW, *et al.* Developmental pharmacology--drug disposition, action, and therapy in infants and children. *N Engl J Med* 2003; **349**: 1157–67

Kokki H, Rasanen I, Reinikainen M, Suhonen P, Vanamo K, Ojanperä I. Pharmacokinetics of oxycodone after intravenous, buccal, intramuscular and gastric administration in children. *Clin Pharmacokinet* 2004; **43**: 613–22

Koren G, Maurice L. Pediatric uses of opioids. *Pediatr Clin North Am* 1989; **36**: 1141–56

Krane EJ, Dalens BJ, Murat I, Murrell D. The safety of epidurals placed during general anesthesia. *Reg Anesth Pain Med* 1998; **23**: 433–8

Lidow MS. Long-term effects of neonatal pain on nociceptive systems. *Pain* 2002; **99**: 377–83

Llewellyn N, Moriarty A. The national pediatric epidural audit. *Paediatr Anaesth* 2007; **17**: 520–33

Lonnqvist PA, Morton NS. Postoperative analgesia in infants and children. *Br J Anaesth* 2005; **95**: 59–68

Malinovsky JM, Servin F, Cozian A, Lepage JY, Pinaud M. Ketamine and norketamine plasma concentrations after i.v., nasal and rectal administration in children. *Br J Anaesth* 1996; **77**: 203–7

Marhofer P, Greher M, Kapral S. Ultrasound guidance in regional anaesthesia. *Br J Anaesth* 2005; **94**: 7–17

Mazoit JX. Local anesthetics and their adjuncts. *Pediatr Anesth* 2012; **22**: 31–8

Maunuksela EL, Olkhola KT. Nonsteroidal anti-inflammatory drugs in pediatric pain management. In: Schechter NL, Berde CB, Yaster M, eds. *Pain in Infants, Children, and Adolescents*, 2nd Edn. Baltimore, MD: Lippincott Williams & Wilkins, 2003; 170–80

McCann ME, Sethna NF, Mazoit JX, *et al.* The pharmacokinetics of epidural ropivacaine in infants and young children. *Anesth Analg* 2001; **93**: 893–7

Monitto CL, Greenberg RS, Kost-Byerly S, *et al.* The safety and efficacy of parent-/nurse-controlled analgesia in patients less than six years of age. *Anesth Analg* 2000; **91**: 573–9

Morton NS, Errera A. APA national audit of pediatric opioid infusions. *Pediatr Anesth* 2010; **20**: 119–25

Nishina K, Mikawa K, Shiga M, Obara H. Clonidine in paediatric anaesthesia. *Paediatr Anaesth* 1999; **9**: 187–202

Passariello M, Almenrader N, Canneti A, Rubeo L, Haiberger R, Pietropaoli P. Caudal analgesia in children: S(+)-ketamine vs S(+)-ketamine plus clonidine. *Paediatr Anaesth* 2004; **14**: 851–5

Pattinson D, Fitzgerald M. The neurobiology of infant pain: development of excitatory and inhibitory neurotransmission in the spinal dorsal horn. *Reg Anesth Pain Med* 2004; **29**: 36–44

Polaner DM, Drescher J. Pediatric regional anesthesia: what is the current safety record? *Pediatr Anesth* 2011; **21**: 737–42

Quigley C. Opioid switching to improve pain relief and drug tolerability. *Cochrane Database Syst Rev* 2004; **1**: CD004847

Ripamonti C, Groff L, Brunelli C, *et al.* Switching from morphine to oral methadone in treating cancer pain: what is the equianalgesic dose ratio? *J Clin Oncol* 1998; **16**: 3216–21

Roelofse JA. The evolution of ketamine applications in children. *Pediatr Anesth* 2010; **20**: 240–5

Rose JB, Logan DE. Pediatric pain assessment. In: Litman RS, ed. *Pediatric Anesthesia: the Requisites in Anaesthesiology*. Philadelphia, PA: Mosby Inc, 2004; 191–5

Solodiuk J, Curley MA. Pain assessment in nonverbal children with severe cognitive impairments: the Individualized Numeric Rating Scale (INRS). *J Pediatr Nurs* 2003; **18**: 295–9

Stein C, Rosow CE. Analgesia: receptor ligands and opiate narcotics. In: Evers AS, Maze M, eds. *Anesthetic Pharmacology: Physiologic Principles and Clinical Practice*. Philadelphia, PA: Churchill Livingstone, 2004; 451–71

Taddio A, Katz J, Ilersich AL, Koren G. Effect of neonatal circumcision on pain response during subsequent routine vaccination. *Lancet* 1997; **349**: 599–603

Tsui BC, Wagner A, Cave D, Kearney R. Thoracic and lumbar epidural analgesia via the caudal approach using electrical stimulation guidance in pediatric patients: a review of 289 patients. *Anesthesiology* 2004; **100**: 683–9

Turner S, Ford V. Role of the selective cyclo-oxygenase-2 (COX-2) inhibitors in children. *Arch Dis Child Educ Pract Ed* 2004; **89**: ep46–ep49

van den Anker JN, Tibboel D. Pain relief in neonates: when to use intravenous paracetamol. *Arch Dis Child* 2011; **96**: 573–4

Williams DG, Hatch DJ, Howard RF. Codeine phosphate in paediatric medicine. *Br J Anaesth* 2001; **86**: 413–21

Wolf AR. Tears at bedtime: a pitfall of extending paediatric day-case surgery without extending analgesia. *Br J Anaesth* 1999; **82**: 319–20

Yaster M. Clinical pharmacology. In: Schechter NL, Berde CB, Yaster M, eds. *Pain in Infants, Children, and Adolescents*, 2nd Edn. Baltimore, MD: Lippincott Williams & Wilkins, 2001; 71–84

Yaster M. Multimodal analgesia in children. *Eur J Anaesthesiol* 2010; **27**: 851–7

CHAPTER 74

Resuscitation, stabilization, and transfer of sick and injured children

Ian A. Jenkins and David A. Rowney

Introduction

Critically ill children come under the care of anaesthetists, whether working in children's hospitals or in the district hospital. In the non-specialist setting, anaesthetists will be called to attend these children and help stabilize them in the emergency department (ED), paediatric ward, paediatric high dependency unit, or general intensive care unit (GICU). Transfers to a tertiary paediatric specialist centre will more usually involve a specialist paediatric intensive care transport or 'retrieval' team but, for certain time-critical conditions, the local anaesthetic/intensive care team may be required to transfer the child (Welsh Assembly 2005; Department of Health 2006; Scottish Executive 2006; Royal College of Anaesthetists 2009; Paediatric Intensive Care Society 2015). These conditions include intracranial emergencies needing surgical intervention, such as evacuation of haemorrhage or drainage of cerebrospinal fluid for cerebral oedema or acute hydrocephalus; intra-abdominal emergencies, such as volvulus and intussusception; and thoracic burns that need urgent escharotomies.

Advanced life support measures are usually commenced by the staff of the ED or general paediatric wards. Having reached the end of the advanced life support repertoire, the ED or ward staff will be hoping for more expert help from their anaesthetic and critical care colleagues.

In the absence of a clear history of trauma, the differential diagnosis of a collapsed infant or child may lie between disparate conditions such as sepsis, dehydration, intussusception, cardiomyopathy, coarctation of the aorta, metabolic disease, or non-accidental injury. This chapter seeks to help non-specialist anaesthetists navigate through what may appear to be an alarming array of differential diagnoses by focusing on key elements.

How much paediatric critical care is out there?

According to data from the UK Paediatric Intensive Care Audit Network (PICANet), there were approximately 49 000 paediatric intensive care unit (PICU) admissions to 28 National Health Service Hospital Trusts in the United Kingdom in the 3 years between 2007 and 2009, of which 16 800 (34%) had been transported to these PICUs (PICANet 2010). Nearly a quarter of all these transfers were carried out by non-PICU teams. Additionally, there is no sign that the number of children admitted to GICUs in the United Kingdom is decreasing (PICANet 2010). This should come as no surprise; children continue to be admitted to the ED and to general hospital paediatric inpatient services, and they continue to be subject to acute trauma or critical illness and need the services of their local clinicians to resuscitate and stabilize them. Data from South West England for 2001–2010 showed there were 2307 admissions to district general hospital (DGH) ICUs across this single region, that is, more than 200 children per year for a total population of 4.5 million (Southwest Audit of Critically Ill Children 2012). However, of these, only 39% were transferred to a PICU (Figure 74.1), with the rest returning mainly to local paediatric areas. The reasons for this will include that the ICU admission can be predicted to be short (e.g. after a febrile convulsion, or with mild, rapidly resolving croup, asthma, or bronchiolitis) or where the child is well known to the local DGH and may have a terminal condition and moving the child would, at that point, be neither in the child's best interest nor that of the family.

Risk-adjusted outcomes, validated for use in the GICU setting, of children who remained in these GICUs were shown to be comparable to national PICU outcomes (Fraser et al. 2004). This would indicate that, in a region where such outcomes have been consistently and carefully audited within an active network for 10 years, not all children admitted to GICUs need to be transferred to the regional PICU; see Figure 74.1 (Southwest Audit of Critically Ill Children 2012).

When the incidence of all critical illness in children in the same region was examined, only a tenth of children meeting high dependency unit (HDU) or ICU admission criteria ever get to an ICU (Southwest Audit of Critically Ill Children 2009, 2012). It is important to appreciate, therefore, that ICU admissions represent only the tip of a critical illness iceberg.

The type of diagnosis seen in the GICUs compared with that seen in the PICUs is compared in Figures 74.2 and 74.3 (PICANet 2009, 2010). Respiratory, neurology, and trauma make up the largest groups in children admitted, albeit temporarily, to general hospital ICUs.

PICU case-mix is affected by their tertiary specialist role and resulting elective admissions and, in particular, by the high volume

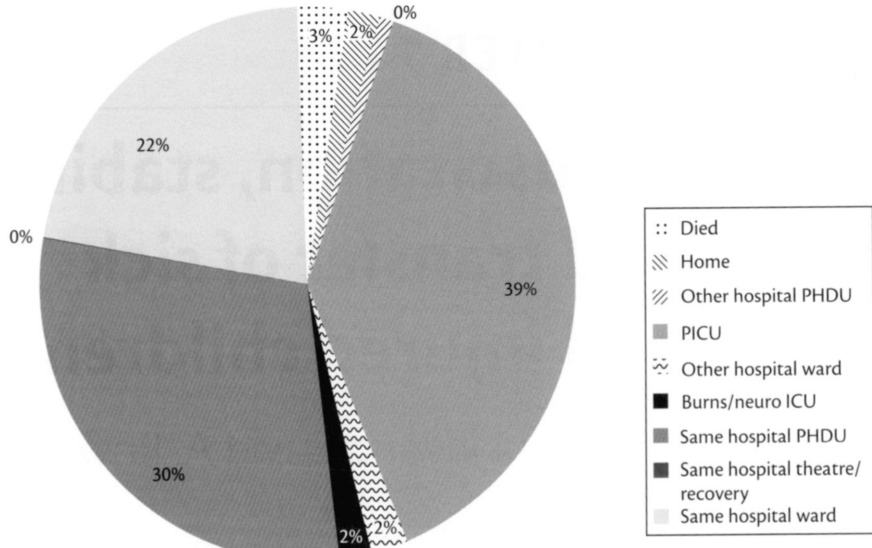

Figure 74.1 Discharge destination of paediatric admissions to GICUs (n = 583)—South West England, 2008–2010.
Data from SWACIC. Southwest Audit of Critically Ill Children; a ten year report. (2012): http://www.picanet.org.uk

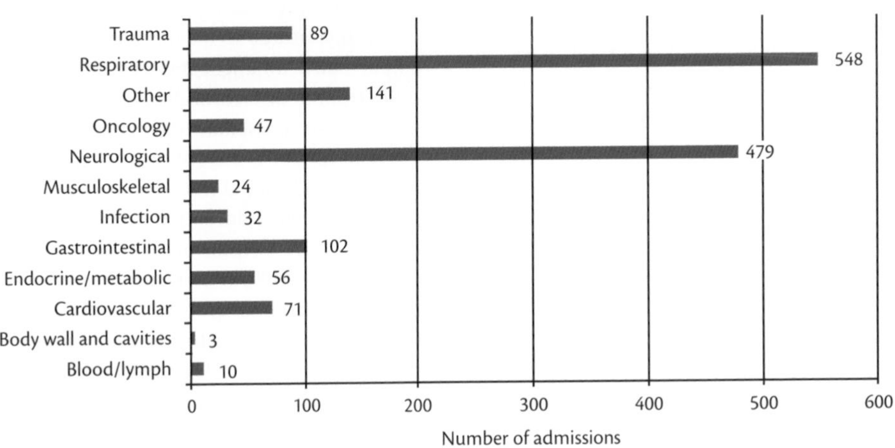

Figure 74.2 Diagnostic groups in GICUs nationally 2008–2010 (ICNARC figures).
Data from PICANet. National Report of the Paediatric Intensive Care Network. 2010: http://www.picanet.org.uk/

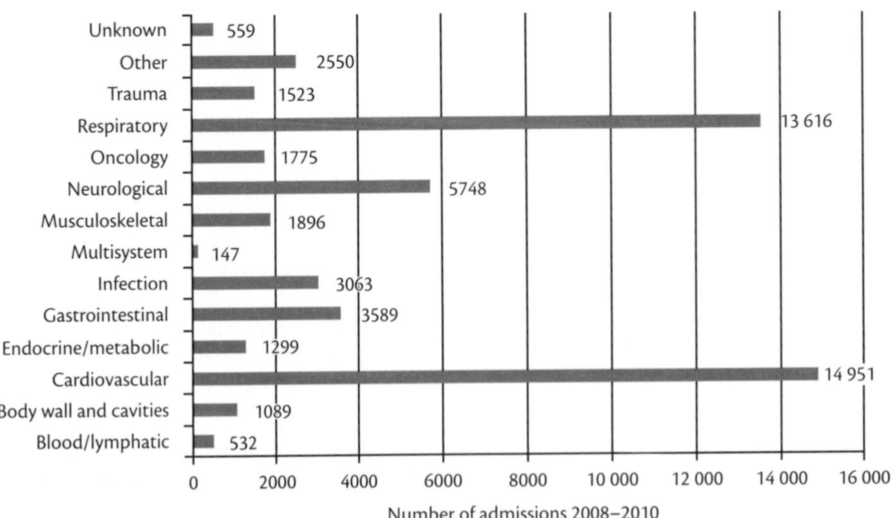

Figure 74.3 Diagnostic groups in PICUs 2008–2010.
Data from PICANet. National Report of the Paediatric Intensive Care Network. 2009: http://www.picanet.org.uk/

of cardiovascular surgery passing through the UK PICU population as a whole. When this is discounted, the patterns seen in PICUs and GICUs are fairly similar, reflecting rather more urgent and emergency presentations.

Essentially, PICUs see far more infants and this is driven to some extent by the large number of cardiovascular operations performed across the country in this age group, whereas the age distribution in GICUs is far more evenly distributed where trauma, acute neurology, head injury, and respiratory emergencies are more prevalent (Figures 74.4 and 74.5).

Regarding potential de-skilling in district hospitals, studies have been performed in the United Kingdom to assess the impact of the establishment of paediatric retrieval teams on the skill retention amongst DGH teams. In contrast to the hypothesis that de-skilling may have occurred, a study covering the period 1994–2001, thus before and after the wide establishment of paediatric intensive care retrieval teams in the United Kingdom in 1997–1998, found that core interventions by general hospital teams such as intubations and inserting of arterial and central venous catheters had increased with time (Ramnarayan et al. 2003; Lampariello et al. 2010). A later, similar study in 2010 showed that these core interventions were achieved on a higher number of patients overall, indicating that appropriate care was still being given by DGH staff (Lampariello et al. 2010).

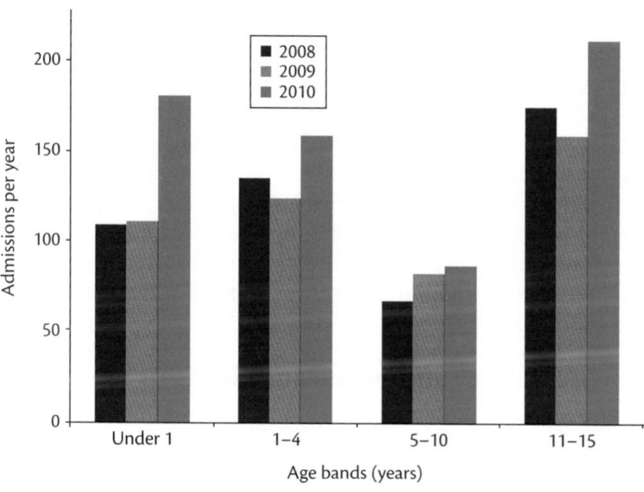

Figure 74.4 Admissions to reporting GICUs by age.
Data from SWACIC. Southwest Audit of Critically Ill Children; a ten year report. (2012): http://www.picanet.org.uk

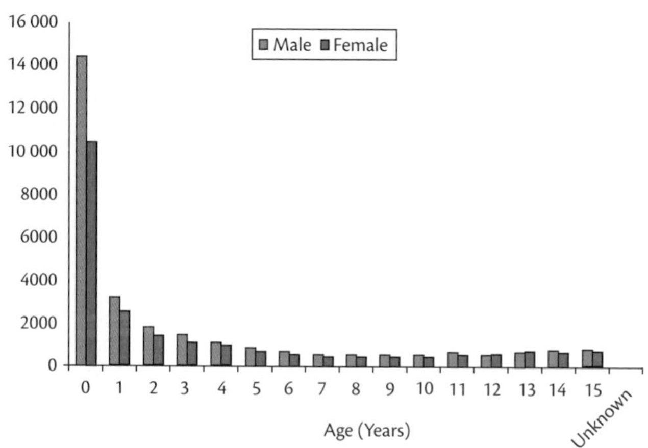

Figure 74.5 Admissions to PICUs 2008–2010.
Data from PICANet. National Report of the Paediatric Intensive Care Network. 2011: http://www.picanet.org.uk/

What needs to be addressed for the future is the acquisition and maintenance of relevant knowledge and skills for staff dealing with critically ill children in the DGH setting. Both doctors and nurses should be given the opportunity to acquire and maintain paediatric knowledge and skills relevant to their practice and can access relevant updates in tertiary centres (Royal College of Anaesthetists 2009). Some of this already occurs but it is yet to become widespread and will require specific funding.

Respiratory emergencies: general considerations

Factors in respiratory inadequacy in children

Infants have small airways and therefore, according to the Hagen–Poiseuille equation ($Q = \Delta P\pi r^4/8\eta l$), a reduction in airway diameter has a dramatic effect on flow and work of breathing. Infants have horizontal and cartilaginous ribs. These factors cause both a difficulty in increasing tidal volumes via rib movement and a mechanical disadvantage from thoracic cage flexibility. In croup and bronchiolitis, these factors result in the mechanical inefficiency of subcostal and substernal in-drawing and exacerbation of work of breathing. In view of the lack of ability to increase tidal volumes, infants must rely on tachypnoea.

Clinical indicators of respiratory inadequacy

Apart from those signs seen in adults, children exhibit additional signs, particularly infants. These derive from the anatomical factors previously described: subcostal and sternal recession; lack of inspiratory reserve; and smaller cricoid rings that cause stridor when oedematous as a result of croup or after tracheal intubation. These factors may cause an increase in Pa_{CO_2} associated with conditions that might otherwise be expected to cause primarily 'type 1' respiratory failure. This is as a result of the interplay of decreased lung and thoracic compliance with these anatomical mechanical factors having earlier effects on the mechanical efficiency of the child's respiratory system. As in adults, respiratory failure is demonstrated by increases in respiratory rate, heart rate, use of accessory muscles, deteriorating conscious level, and ultimately cyanosis. Peculiar to infants and young children with croup is the appearance of expiratory stridor where initially only inspiratory stridor existed. This is a sign that the airway compromise caused by croup is advancing and signals the need for intubation if other measures such as steroids and adrenaline (epinephrine) have already been tried (see 'Croup, epiglottitis, and tracheitis').

Intubation: principles—when, how, and where

Intubation should be undertaken by those who have had training in this procedure and who understand how things can go wrong and what to do about it. This means that failed intubation drills should be just as much a part of airway management skills as simply the ability to intubate. This will also entail knowledge and skills regarding effective mask ventilation, use of Guedel and laryngeal mask airways, appropriate knowledge of anaesthetic pharmacology, and how certain agents may affect the patient cardiovascularly and biochemically. All locations where children might be intubated and ventilated such as EDs, HDUs, and intensive care units (ICUs) should be fully equipped to deal with this scenario with a full range of child-specific equipment. A list of suitable drugs and equipment for these areas is indicated in the *Standards for the Care of Critically Ill Children* (Paediatric Intensive Care Society 2015).

Besides clear ventilatory compromise, other indications for intubation include the following:

1. Decreased conscious level. Conventionally this becomes definitely indicated with a Glasgow Coma Score of 8 or less.
2. Smoke inhalation—even when no respiratory effects are present at that time because respiratory compromise from airway swelling, pneumonitis, or carbon monoxide poisoning can ensue quickly.
3. Severe sepsis necessitating large amounts of intravenous fluids (e.g. >60 ml kg^{-1}). In these situations, pre-emptive control with intubation and ventilation is necessary to offset the development of respiratory compromise as a result of increased lung water. It also permits insertion of central venous and arterial catheters, monitoring central venous and arterial pressures, and the administration of inotropes, which would be indicated in these circumstances. This line of action with aggressive fluid resuscitation, control of ventilation, and administration of inotropes is often underdone (Inwald et al. 2009).

Drugs for intubation in the critically ill child

'Which drugs should be used?' is one of the most frequently asked questions paediatric intensive care retrieval services receive when other hospitals are referring and dealing with a seriously ill child. As in any other emergency situation, the effects of anaesthetic induction agents on the circulation of a shocked patient still apply. Agents that affect the systemic vascular resistance the least and are less likely to exacerbate any residual occult hypovolaemia are the ones to be chosen. Even when children are ostensibly normovolaemic, intrinsic cardiovascular compromise still exists in sepsis, metabolic conditions, arrhythmias, and cardiomyopathies. Arguably, the ubiquity and familiarity of propofol may lead to problems caused by its depressant effects on the systemic vascular resistance. Those experienced with critically ill children, particularly those with cardiovascular compromise, find that agents such as ketamine, with *small* doses of fentanyl or midazolam, or both, and neuromuscular block with pancuronium are found to cause less instability and have much to commend them. Additionally, ketamine may be safely used in head injury according to more recent studies (Sehdev et al. 2006). In cases of suspected tachyarrhythmia, pancuronium with its specific effect on heart rate is best avoided and agents such as vecuronium or rocuronium used. Atracurium often releases histamine and is therefore not so useful in situations with cardiovascular compromise.

Respiratory support in children

Continuous positive airways pressure can decrease the work of breathing by decreasing the pressure gradient across the narrowed airways. It is frequently used in infants with less severe forms of croup, bronchiolitis, and pneumonias, often obviating the need for intubation and ventilation, and enables the child to remain safely in the district hospital. In smaller infants (<6 kg), this is usually delivered via short nasal prongs connected to a humidified gas supply from a purpose-built 'driver' and small nasal masks are now being marketed. It is increasingly used in purpose-built, staffed, and equipped paediatric HDUs. Older children may manage with small (adult) nasal masks. Some conventional ventilators are now having software fitted that will allow them to deliver the necessary free-flowing gases without alarming continually for the large leaks that inevitably result.

For larger children, the various purpose-built non-invasive ventilators used in adults can be used and can deliver either continuous positive airways pressure or patient-triggered bi-level positive airway pressure via nasal masks or facemasks covering nose and mouth. Even 'total' facemasks, covering the whole face, can be used successfully, particularly in children whose face shapes do not match conventional masks.

In children up to the age of 5 years or so requiring ventilation on the ICU, nasal intubation is better tolerated than oral, with decreased requirements for sedation. Additionally, nasal tubes are more stable, easier to fix, and permit easier mouth care.

Pressure-cycled ventilation is very common in paediatric practice because leaks round uncuffed tracheal tubes are rendered less significant but, on the other hand, changes in lung or thoracic compliance will alter alveolar ventilation. Volume-cycled ventilation is less vulnerable to compliance changes but is affected by the leaks around non-cuffed tubes. Monitoring of expired tidal volumes is therefore vital. As in adult practice, there is an increasing trend to use non-invasive monitoring with peripheral oxygen saturations and end-tidal CO_2.

Tracheal tubes: cuffed *vs* uncuffed in PICUs

The increasing use of cuffed tubes in PICUs lends itself to greater use of volume-cycled ventilation modes, as in adult practice, but caution needs to be taken with cuff pressures and it is suggested that these should remain below 25 cm H_2O (Weber et al. 2009). However, this may not prevent a leak in conditions requiring high-pressure ventilation, and there are no reliable data yet on prolonged use of such cuffed tubes and their effects on tracheal integrity nor is there consensus on the methodology of cuff pressure monitoring in children. In children with prolonged length of stay on the PICU, tracheostomies are less readily used as a result of anatomical difficulties (short necks, short trachea lengths) and their use is associated with longer-term problems such as local tracheomalacia or stenosis (even with more modern surgical techniques).

Respiratory emergencies: specific conditions

In paediatric practice, viral disease accounts for much of the respiratory pathology seen on the PICU. Nasopharyngeal aspirates are commonly taken for immunofluorescence and polymerase chain reaction to detect viruses against a set screen of those commonly occurring locally. However, where the pathology is in the lower respiratory tract, it is more logical to send either endotracheal aspirates or bronchoalveolar lavage specimens. These need to be sent to the local virology laboratory promptly to ensure the maximum yield of detection.

Croup, epiglottitis, and tracheitis

The differing clinical features of these conditions are outlined in Table 74.1 (Denny et al. 1983; Mayo-Smith et al. 1995; Hopkins et al. 2006; Jenkins and Saunders 2009).

For croup, glucocorticoids are best administered parenterally and can avoid or shorten intubation. Intubation in upper airway conditions such as these is best achieved by inhalation anaesthesia with a range of 'smaller-for-age' tubes available and, if possible, an ENT surgeon present. The tubes are left in place until there is a clear leak in croup or, in epiglottitis, until laryngoscopy reveals resolution of the oedema above the glottis.

The incidence of bacterial tracheitis appears to be on the increase. Although presenting also with stridor, the key features differ from the other two conditions with cough, pyrexia, and sometimes overt sepsis predominating but with no dysphagia or drooling (see Table 74.1). Pseudomembranous tracheitis has been reported, requiring repeated bronchoscopic lavage (Salamone et al. 2004).

Bronchiolitis

Acute bronchiolitis is an infection of the lower respiratory tract usually involving infants but can be seen in children of up to 3 years of age. It is characterized by cough and tachypnoea with other signs of increased respiratory work such as nasal flaring and subcostal recession. Usually there are signs of small airway compromise with widespread crepitations and coarse wheeze indicating increased airways resistance. Many can be managed conservatively with attention to treating the pyrexia, ensuring adequate hydration, and the use of continuous positive airway pressure delivered by nasal prongs or nasal mask.

No benefit from steroids has been demonstrated and no sustained effects from bronchodilators have been shown although some temporary improvements in clinical variables have been observed (Hartling et al. 2004).

Where indicated in terms of actual or impending respiratory fatigue judged on clinical grounds (see 'General principles of resuscitation and stabilization') intubation and ventilation is indicated. Pulmonary compliance can be very poor so 'permissive' degrees of hypercarbia (6.5–8 kPa), respiratory acidosis (≥7.25), and desaturation (92–95%) should be accepted until the viral condition improves, allowing ventilation to be weaned.

Table 74.1 Principal clinical features of croup, epiglottitis, and bacterial tracheitis

	Croup	Epiglottitis	Bacterial tracheitis
Age range (peak)	6 m–3 yr (1.5 yr)	3 m–5 yr (2.5 yr)	8 m–14 yr (3.75 yr)
Cough	+ + + (barking, non-productive)	Minimal	+ + + (productive)
Stridor timing	Early	Late	Early
Stridor onset	Gradual	Sudden + + +	Sudden
Toxic	No, mild pyrexia	Yes	Yes
Dysphagia	Minimal	Pronounced	Minimal
Drooling	No	Yes	No

Status asthmaticus

Children with severe asthma present with respiratory distress cough and wheeze. The factors that indicate that ICU admission is indicated are pleomorphic but might include history of previous ICU admissions or rapid deterioration, or both; severe distress despite nebulized bronchodilators including inability to phonate, limited air entry, and inspiratory and expiratory wheezing; altered conscious level; and, if blood gases are being taken, a rising CO_2 with signs of fatigue (National Institutes of Health 2007).

Once a decision is made to intubate and ventilate the child, care needs to be taken, as there may be occult hypovolaemia secondary to a period of decreased fluid intake. Drugs that release histamine, such as morphine and atracurium, are best avoided. Ketamine is useful in preserving blood pressure and in its bronchodilator action. A cuffed tube might be useful, given the anticipated high inflation pressures. Ventilation should adopt the following strategy: accept hypercarbia, accepting an arterial pH of greater than 7.2, slow rates to allow for prolonged expiratory time and to avoid air-trapping, short inspiratory times to keep an adequate respiratory rate, and low positive end-expiratory pressure. Avoidance of positive end-expiratory pressure is a mistake as this only encourages small airway closure and exacerbates air trapping but if flow–time curves are available, then the optimal positive end-expiratory pressure and expiratory times can be estimated. Antibiotics are only required where there is evidence of bacterial infection, that is, any of raised inflammatory markers such as raised neutrophil count and C-reactive protein; positive cultures of tracheal aspirates; radiological evidence; or combinations of these. Macroscopically purulent sputum may be misleading as this may contain large amounts of eosinophils.

Sedation on ventilation could include ketamine and fentanyl and possibly a neuromuscular blocking agent if it is better to obtund the patient's respiratory activity and coughing in the early stages. It should be remembered that the presence of the tracheal tube may be an ongoing stimulus for bronchospasm and so the tube should be removed at the earliest opportunity, even if there is still some wheeze.

The agents that have most effect are glucocorticoids, but they may not exert any effect for up to 8 h. In the meantime, β-agonists should be given either by nebulization or intravenously. Methylxanthines, theophylline or aminophylline, are used in children, often to supplement β-agonists, as is ipratropium, but the evidence for their efficacy has not been established. The same also applies to magnesium but this is becoming used more often after some studies have suggested its use in the ED setting (Cheuk et al. 2005).

Cardiovascular emergencies: general considerations

Fluid requirements

Children have a proportionately ml kg^{-1} larger extracellular fluid compartment, particularly infants. This leads to higher maintenance fluid requirements but also, in cases of sepsis, increased circulatory effects of capillary leak. Such children will also have increased requirements for fluid supplementation on a ml kg^{-1} basis than may be anticipated from adult practice. However, children are also more prone to developing inappropriate antidiuretic hormone secretion in respiratory conditions such as bronchiolitis. If given 'normal for age' intravenous fluid maintenance they can develop hyponatraemia which can be quite severe. Therefore, in these instances, maintenance fluids are cut back to 80% of normal for that age. If fluid boluses are needed for ongoing deficits then isotonic fluids should be used. With greater surface area for their body weight, smaller children have higher insensible losses on a volume/weight basis and this is exaggerated in pyrexia. In infants, it is reasonable to allow an extra 10% of maintenance fluids for every degree centigrade of pyrexia above 37°C.

Cardiac physiology

Infants have hearts that differ structurally from older children and adults with less concentration of contractile elements and a relative preponderance of collagen and elastin. The cardiac compliance is diminished and the Starling curve of stroke force *vs* fibre length is flatter with an earlier downward inflection point at shorter fibre lengths (i.e. lower filling pressures). Thus, cardiac output is less responsive to volume loading and more dependent on heart rate. Myocyte β-receptor populations are normal after term and the heart is responsive to catecholamines and phosphodiesterase inhibitors; however, the infant heart remains particularly sensitive to and dependent on ionized calcium concentrations in the extracellular fluid and hypocalcaemia is not well tolerated.

Cardiovascular emergencies: specific conditions

Balanced circulations

Children may present with congenital cardiac anomalies that give rise to 'balanced circulations'. The paradox here is that these children may well deteriorate with added inspired oxygen. Conditions such as persistent ductus arteriosus, ventricular septal defect, and truncus arteriosus may worsen because increased inspired O_2 or decreasing Pa_{CO_2}, if ventilated, leads to pulmonary vasodilation and increased shunt flow into the lungs and a decrease in systemic perfusion.

Children with congenital cyanotic heart disease may have had modified Blalock–Taussig shunts (a GoreTex® tube) inserted between the subclavian artery and the pulmonary arteries to augment pulmonary blood flow. Again, because added inspired oxygen or decreased CO_2 dilates the pulmonary arteries and increases pulmonary blood flow, this may cause an excessive 'steal' directly from the systemic circulation, and these children may then show decreased systemic perfusion *even though they remain cyanosed.*

Obstructive lesions

Children with obstructive lesions may deteriorate with systemic vasodilation (or hypovolaemia), for example, in aortic stenosis, myocardial ischaemia results from decreased coronary perfusion and in Fallot's tetralogy, with obstruction at the right ventricular outflow, profound hypoxaemia will result from increased right-to-left shunting across the ventricular septal defect.

Such situations that lead to decreased systemic perfusion or hypoxaemia, or both, in neonates and young infants will compromise splanchnic O_2 delivery, which may lead to necrotizing enterocolitis.

In a baby who has been discharged from the maternity unit perfectly well but re-presents to the hospital in a collapsed state in the first few days of life, there should be a high index of suspicion for coarctation of the aorta or congenital aortic stenosis. In these children, the patency of the ductus arteriosus protects them immediately after birth by perfusing the aorta distal to the obstruction. However, as the duct closes over the next few days, ductal tissue in the wall of the coarcted area will also constrict thus accentuating the effect of any coarctation. Administering prostaglandins in this situation may not reopen the duct but may give partial relief to the obstruction and improve distal perfusion to a degree. In aortic stenosis, amelioration does depend on re-opening the duct.

Gastrointestinal emergencies

Volvulus is a condition caused by malrotation of the gut and is heralded by bilious vomiting or bilious nasogastric aspirates. It is usually seen in the neonate but can occur later. It is a surgical emergency and it may be faster and therefore more appropriate if the referring team transfers the child to a paediatric surgical centre, rather than waiting for a retrieval team which may double the transfer time and could result in an necrotic intestine with disastrous results.

Intussusception can present rather vaguely with lethargy and intermittent pain rather than the classical vomiting and red currant jelly stools, which is seen in only a third of cases. It can develop into a time-critical emergency where the viability of the intestine and of the child itself are at stake. A number of these children develop a marked systemic inflammatory response with circulatory failure. Again, it is often best that the referring team transfers these patients into the tertiary centre rather than incurring delays caused by retrieval. Local protocols must allow for this.

Diarrhoeal conditions may go on to develop haemolytic uraemic syndrome, particularly associated with *Escherichia coli* O157:H7 but also with *Salmonella* and *Campylobacter*. It is a condition caused by diffuse small vessel occlusion by thrombotic microangiopathy with a triad of haemolysis, thrombocytopenia, and renal failure. Its complications are diffuse: cerebral compromise (fits, coma), cardiac failure, pancreatitis, and ischaemic colitis, where frank necrosis and perforation can occur. The treatment is to support the failing kidney with peritoneal dialysis or haemofiltration and, where possible, avoid platelet transfusion and systemic antibiotics that may fuel the condition. The progress of the disease can be tracked with serial lactate dehydrogenase concentrations. Where central nervous system involvement occurs, then it more resembles thrombotic thrombocytopenic purpura and is often treated with plasmapheresis with replacement of circulating proteins with fresh frozen plasma.

Neurological emergencies and traumatic brain injury

Cerebral blood flow accounts for a third of the cardiac output at birth and, up to 4 years of age, is still double in flow per kilogram compared that of adults. Thus, in cardiovascular compromise, it should be expected that brain function and conscious levels consequently deteriorate. In sick children, this may be demonstrated in the early inconsolable irritability that later develops into the somnolence of the seriously ill child. It is helpful to characterize decreased consciousness reproducibly in terms of a modified Glasgow Coma Scale (see Table 74.2).

Table 74.2 Children's Glasgow Coma Score

	1	2	3	4	5	6
Eyes	No eye opening	Opens eyes to pain	Opens eyes to speech	Opens eyes spontaneously		
Verbal	No verbal response	Inconsolable, agitated	Inconsistently consolable, moaning	Cries but consolable, inappropriate interactions	Smiles, follows objects and sounds, interacts	
Motor	No motor response	Extension to pain (decerebrate)	Flexion to pain (decorticate)	Withdraws from pain	Withdraws from touch	Infant moves spontaneously or purposefully

The lowest score possible is 3; any score less than 8 is associated with poor outcomes and is the accepted level for mandatory tracheal intubation & ventilation.

Reproduced with permission from Morray, J. *et al.* Coma scale for use in brain-injured children. *Critical Care Medicine*, Volume 12, Issue 12, pp. 1018, Copyright © Wolters Kluwer Health 1984.

Amongst the diagnoses that produce primary neurological dysfunction, consideration should be given to trauma (which may be as a result of non-accidental injury), meningoencephalitis (viral or bacterial—including tuberculous), tumours, spontaneous haemorrhage, hydrocephalus, and metabolic causes (diabetic ketoacidosis, hyperammonaemia or lipid handling disorders—see 'Metabolic disorders').

Some of these conditions may lead to coma or seizures and status epilepticus. Regarding infection, meningitis would have to be excluded if the history is suggestive. These days there is no longer the imperative to perform early lumbar puncture, recognizing the potential hazard in removing lumbar cerebrospinal fluids when there is brain swelling. It is important to take blood cultures and throat swabs and to start antibacterials and aciclovir to treat potential herpes infection. A retrospective lumbar puncture can be performed some days later, after brain swelling has diminished, and then the polymerase chain reaction technique can be used to detect the presence of microorganisms.

The most common cause of seizures in the preschool child (3 months to 5 years old) are so-called febrile convulsions. These appear to be worse where the increase in temperature is fastest, hence a lack of prodromal history is often seen and they can be resistant to conventional antiepileptic protocols. These children can often present with alarming unilateral and prolonged fits and the fits are sometimes only controlled with anaesthetic drugs requiring intubation. When the fits are unilateral, precautionary computed tomography (CT) scanning is inevitable to exclude a more sinister cause. Generally, after a few hours of ventilation and control of temperature where indicated, these children wake up entirely normally. Further investigation is usually not undertaken unless fits recur.

The acute management of status epilepticus should follow internationally accepted guidelines (European Resuscitation Council 2015; Advanced Life Support Group 2016). This starts with ensuring a patent airway, administering oxygen, and checking the blood glucose. If no immediate intravenous access is present, then rectal diazepam or buccal midazolam is given, both at 0.5 mg kg^{-1}; if intravenous access is present, then lorazepam 0.1 mg kg^{-1} is given. This can be repeated, but if there is no response then intravenous phenytoin 20 mg kg^{-1}, or if already receiving phenytoin, phenobarbital 20 mg kg^{-1}, is given. If these agents do not stop the seizures, then thiopental 4–8 mg kg^{-1} should be given as part of an intubation procedure.

Some centres continue to use paraldehyde rectally, 0.4 ml kg^{-1} suspended in a 50:50 mixture with olive oil or normal saline (avoiding arachis oil which would be harmful to children with peanut allergy).

In traumatic brain injury, the two pivotal decisions are the need for CT imaging and decision to intubate. Both decisions are based on the nature of the injury mechanism (velocity or height fallen), degree of impairment of conscious level and the appearance of abnormal posture. For intubation, a Glasgow coma score (GCS) of 8 or less is commonly taken to be the trigger level, though if other features are present such as airway and breathing compromise, abnormal posture and fitting, then intubation and controlled ventilation should commence at higher GCS levels. Criteria for imaging are similar but with lower thresholds such that any impairment of conscious level with abnormal neurological features, especially with a skull fracture, should warrant a CT scan.

When the head CT scan is performed, it is logical to extend this down the neck to the thoracic inlet to check for obvious injury. However, this may not detect ligamentous ruptures that may exist without any bony misalignment but, nevertheless, if the head were to be moved, may lead to cervical spinal cord damage. Magnetic resonance imaging is a better modality to identify such abnormalities, while the best of all is a clinical evaluation of the conscious patient. However, this may not be possible for some time and, in some cases, not at all. The neck must therefore be protected with a hard collar and in-line logrolling of the patient undertaken until such 'clearance' of the cervical spine is possible.

Most centres insert intracranial pressure monitoring after traumatic brain injury and aim for a minimal cerebral perfusion pressure of at least 40 mm Hg (cerebral perfusion pressure = mean arterial blood pressure minus the greater of intracranial pressure and central venous pressure). However, in these situations, cerebral blood flow autoregulation is abnormal and there is recognition that pushing cerebral perfusion pressure higher risks over-perfusion of the brain and thereby raising intracranial pressure. There is no evidence of benefit of hypothermic treatment of paediatric traumatic brain injury (Hutchison et al. 2008). Jugular venous saturation measurement, although it has been studied in research to a limited extent, has not proved to be consistently useful in practice and may also interfere with jugular venous drainage.

External ventricular drains are often inserted to decrease a raised intracranial pressure by controlled release of cerebrospinal fluid and are also used for draining obstructed hydrocephalus which can occur in haemorrhagic brain injury. These external ventricular drains are used over the full age range down to the smallest preterm neonates. When moving patients with external ventricular drains one has to control the level of the drain carefully where these are usually set at 5–10 cm above a zero-point taken as being the mid-point between the lateral edge of the orbit and the tragus of the ear. Dropping the drain level may cause precipitant and excessive drainage. If it is raised then there may be some inadvertent but limited reflux back into the patient leading to an increase in intracranial pressure and increasing danger of infection. Generally, it is safer to *briefly* clamp these drains for transfer to between beds and trolleys for transport to scanners and operating rooms but, once this is completed, to replicate its setting in ICU and maintain controlled drainage. Above all, it is important to remember to unclamp the drain and then ensure that free drainage has returned. If not, the drain may have blocked and will need attention. These drains should not be laid flat as the porous ventilation holes in the collection chamber that allow air escape on fluid ingress will get wet and the drain will no longer function correctly.

Burns

Scalds are the commonest form of burn in childhood, most occurring in the pre-school child, when hot liquids are pulled over. Non-accidental injury should be suspected when the history is implausible or the distribution of injury is inconsistent with a child's likely behaviour. Older children, particularly boys, experiment with fire.

Practically, there are five modes of burn injury: cutaneous, airway, electrical, chemical, and infective.

Cutaneous burns are judged on depth and surface area. The area of a burn depends on the variations in the surface areas of differing part of the body at different ages. The 'rule of nines' does not apply and a 'Lund and Browder Chart' is commonly used to estimate the area of the burn (Lund and Browder 1944). Alternatively, at all ages, the area of one side of the patient's palm and closed fingers equates to 1% of body surface area (BSA).

If the estimated surface of the burn equals 10% or more of BSA in a child, fluid resuscitation should be undertaken. There are many fluid regimens in the literature that seek to address this. The 'Parkland Formula' is one that has been widely adopted (Baxter and Shires 1968); Hartmann's solution is given to treat burn losses *in addition to* normal maintenance fluids for the age and weight of child. The burn deficit for the first 24 h is calculated as 4 ml kg^{-1} (% $BSA)^{-1}$ burned. Half of this calculated amount is given over 8 h, the rest over the subsequent 16 h.

Airway burns should be suspected if there is evidence of soot particles or burn around the mouth, if the patient is coughing up soot particles, or the patient was evacuated from a room containing smoke. Further deterioration can arise from peri-oral or airway oedema, so it is prudent to secure the airway early with endotracheal intubation. Soot particles in the lower airway often cause chemical pneumonitis and bronchial lavage may be indicated.

Electrical burns have three significant extra features: disturbance of electrical activity of the heart—either fibrillation or asystole, either of which can be delayed for up to 24 h (George et al. 2005); concentrated internal burns conducted through blood vessels causing distal ischaemia and infarction; and mechanical injuries from being thrown from the source of the current.

Chemical burns may be topical to skin or eyes, particularly from acids or alkalis. Acid burns can cause severe damage but remain at a more superficial level, but alkalis will penetrate deeper if not washed off. Chemical burn injuries are often caused by ingestion. This needs early irrigation and intervention by gastrointestinal surgeons before burned tissue adheres and blocks the affected organ, usually the oesophagus, which is very difficult to treat.

Infective burns include toxic epidermal necrolysis, necrotizing fasciitis, and staphylococcal scalded skin syndrome.

Referral of patients to an expert burns centre should take place if any of the following features exist: age under 5 years; any burn greater than 5% of BSA; sites such as face, hands, perineum, and flexures, such as axillae and neck; and types of burn including full thickness, circumferential, airway, electrical, chemical, or infective.

Metabolic disorders

Inborn errors of metabolism usually declare themselves in early childhood but occasionally this does not happen until young adulthood. Whereas many such conditions result in slowly developing conditions manifest by delayed growth and development and 'failure to thrive', there are a few that can present as medical emergencies, sometimes catastrophically. These children can be developing quite normally and then a trigger, such as intercurrent infection, precipitates an acute collapse with features that many include any of lactic acidosis, hypoglycaemia, and hyperammonaemia. The presentation can be a drowsy, 'shut-down', hypoglycaemic, and poorly perfused infant and thus the presentation can be easily confused with other conditions. Where doubt exists, it is important to measure blood glucose (one reason why this is emphasized in life support courses) and lactate, and a sample for ammonia must go to the lab *on ice*. A glucose infusion must be started containing 10% glucose and run at a minimum of 90 ml kg^{-1} h^{-1} (to give approximately 6 mg kg^{-1} min^{-1} of glucose) and all feeds stopped (which may be a substrate for the toxic by-products the child is now failing to clear). Giving adequate carbohydrate will switch off protein and lipid metabolism, which may be the root cause of the crisis. When the dust has settled, there will be time to set in motion more detailed metabolic investigations and to start ammonia-scavenging medications and co-enzymes. Very high ammonia concentrations (>500 μmol $litre^{-1}$) will require haemofiltration to clear this neurotoxic substance as an emergency.

Diabetic ketoacidosis in children behaves differently from that seen in adults and must be managed differently and within tight guidelines. The principal difference is danger of the development of cerebral oedema. It is thought that this disastrous complication is as a result of the rapidity with which pathology manifestations are corrected, most probably associated with rapid changes in serum osmolality, whether as a result of fluids used in rehydration, reduction of the high glucose with or without correction of the acidosis, particularly associated with the use of bicarbonate—or any combination of these. Hence, the internationally accepted guidelines give quite didactic instructions on the administration of fluids, the very gradual correction of the glucose and the acidosis, and the avoidance of bicarbonate. Shock, as a result of dehydration, should of course be treated with fluids, but even this should be done carefully and any such fluids should be deducted from the calculation of fluid replacement necessary over the next 48 h (body weight × % dehydration × 10). If cerebral oedema is suspected from a deteriorating GCS, then mannitol 10% (1 ml kg^{-1}) or hypertonic saline 3% (5 ml kg^{-1}) should be given, and all intravenous fluids slowed. If this does not procure a lasting improvement, the child should be intubated, ventilated, and nursed in a head-up position. Hyperventilation must be avoided because of worse outcomes (Marcin et al. 2002) though some recognition that a low normal Pa_{CO_2} may be physiologically appropriate (Tasker et al. 2005). A CT scan should be performed to exclude cerebral venous thrombosis, a recognized complication from the profound dehydration.

Sepsis

In severe sepsis, where volumes administered equal or exceed 60 ml kg^{-1}, it is advisable to consider intubation. Not only does this counteract the effects of the pulmonary oedema that often develops to a degree in these situations, but it also presents an opportunity to insert central venous and arterial catheters for more accurate monitoring and to treat more effectively with inotropes. It is a common mistake to underestimate the amount of fluid a child needs to maintain cardiac output in sepsis and not to intervene aggressively with inotropes (Inwald et al. 2009).

Similar considerations apply as in adults in dealing with 'warm' or 'cold' shock by responding to a lack of intravascular volume by administering fluids to ensure the heart is well filled and then using either selective inotropes or adding in agents with vasoconstrictive effects or even vasodilatory effects (such as with phosphodiesterase inhibitors), depending on the perceived tonicity of the vascular bed (Carcillo and Fields 2002).

Limb compromise can be seen in the purpuric septicaemias, as a result of either meningococci or pneumococci, and this can be because of either embolic deficits or more global deficits consequent to 'compartment syndromes'. However, compartment involvement can be quite diffuse, involving multiple compartments, even in the same limb. Fasciotomies have been tried in the past but have had disappointing results, perhaps because the vessel compromise has not been as a result of any relievable local pressure and, in turn, the operative wounds also go on to be a source of secondary infection themselves.

Non-accidental injury, child protection, and ethics

Child abuse comprises four main aspects: physical, sexual, emotional abuse, and neglect; the latter being the most common. Anaesthetists may encounter any of these in the course of their duties and have an obligation to have at least some basic training both in recognition and in knowing what subsequent course of action to take. Non-accidental injury may present as overt trauma but may 'masquerade' with fits, as 'failure to thrive', or as a 'collapse' in the ED. An ever-present index of suspicion is unfortunately necessary.

Anaesthetists may have to consider the ethics of a procedure in which they are to take part and to consider whether this is, indeed, in the best interests of the child. Sometimes this takes place in the context of a child who is frequently admitted to the ICU and may have already been subjected to considerable 'heroic' therapy or may have already undergone many invasive and painful procedures. The ethics and legalities of such situations, including the balance to be achieved between the assent—or dissent—of the child, their mental 'capacity', the legal context of 'consent' (which is not the same as capacity) (Wellesley and Jenkins 2009), the desires of the family, and, indeed, other specialists can be very complex and is beyond the scope of this chapter. The reader is referred to a comprehensive review of such matters (Anderson 2009) and to Chapter 75 in this textbook.

General principles of resuscitation and stabilization

Thorough preparation and stabilization of the child before transport will significantly reduce the likelihood of adverse events occurring during transportation, whichever team performs this. Rapid resuscitation, with initiation of all necessary supportive therapies and monitoring, should lead to a stabilization phase with the goal of reversing deterioration and, ideally, improving the child's clinical condition before embarking on transportation. Proactive management should be instituted to avoid problems in transit. A systematic 'ABC' approach, including assessment, optimization, preparation for transportation, and frequent reassessment of the airway, breathing, circulation, neurological status, temperature, and blood glucose is recommended. The child is transferred onto transport equipment that can provide continuous therapy and monitoring throughout the journey.

Airway and breathing

Respiratory compromise can be the cause or the result of multi-system dysfunction in children. It is fundamental that the airway and breathing be assessed in the context of the full clinical picture. A classic example is the child with meningococcal disease and septic shock, where respiratory failure is rarely an early presenting feature. It is widely accepted that early intubation and ventilation (after 40–60 ml kg^{-1} of resuscitation fluid and the commencement of a peripheral or intraosseous inotrope infusion) is advantageous in many respects: reducing the risk of hypoxaemia secondary to fluid overload and pulmonary oedema, and facilitating central venous and arterial catheter insertion. It also reduces the work of breathing, which can account for 40% of cardiac output and oxygen consumption, and maximize oxygen delivery to other vital organs, enhance cardiac output via reduction in left ventricular work, and facilitate temperature control measures that may reduce global oxygen consumption further. However, excessive ventilation, impairing venous return to the heart and hence cardiac output, and further reducing cerebral blood flow through hypocapnia, must be avoided. In other situations, the decision to intubate for transport may not be straightforward. There will inevitably be a lower threshold for intubation and ventilation for transportation than in routine intensive care practice recognizing the importance of securing airway and ventilation before departure on the grounds of safety. Pre-departure clinical data should include Sp_{O_2} capnography, airway pressures, ECG, arterial blood gas analysis, and chest radiograph to confirm the correct position of a tracheal tube. Reliable tracheal tube fixation is essential and sedative and neuromuscular blocking drugs should generally be given to intubated children during transportation to minimize the risk of accidental extubation, facilitate controlled ventilation with the transport ventilator, and decrease awareness and anxiety. It is recommended practice to insert an orogastric or nasogastric tube to decompress the stomach of intubated children. Pneumothoraces require draining before departure. Positive pressure ventilation or flying at altitude can rapidly expand pneumothoraces causing significant respiratory and cardiovascular compromise. A one-way flutter (Heimlich) valve in place of a bottle and underwater seal system for chest drains is the preferred option during transportation.

Circulation

Hypovolaemic or shocked children do not tolerate the g-forces associated with transport. It is important that hypovolaemia is reversed with adequate fluids before transportation and, if required, an inotrope infusion started. Preparing an inotrope infusion in an ambulance is difficult so there should be a low threshold for doing this before departure. Children with ongoing haemorrhagic shock should not be transported until the bleeding has been controlled. It is advisable to have a minimum of two securely fixed intravenous cannulae. The requirement for central venous and arterial cannulae depends on the clinical condition but they are not required for transport *per se*. Non-invasive blood pressure monitoring technology in modern transport monitors provides reliable readings despite effects of movement and vibration. However, regular use will be a significant drain on the battery life of the monitor if an alternative power source is not available in the vehicle. Arterial lines should be easily accessible for inspection as bleeding can be profound if they become disconnected. Maintenance fluid requirements remain unchanged during transportation and are best administered by syringe driver. A urinary catheter is usually inserted and hourly urine output monitored.

Infants presenting with congenital heart disease may require a prostaglandin infusion to maintain patency of the ductus arteriosus for duct-dependent systemic circulations (e.g. coarctation of the aorta, critical aortic stenosis, or interrupted aortic arch) or duct-dependent pulmonary circulations (e.g. pulmonary or tricuspid atresia).

Referral to a transport team

Referrals should be made as soon as it is evident that the child is critically ill and needs transportation to a tertiary service for surgery or intensive care. Children often compensate and appear 'well' in the early stages of critical illness, then rapidly deteriorate when their compensatory mechanisms start to fail. A 'physiological' approach to criteria for PICU referral is given in Box 74.1. The referring hospital team is responsible for the resuscitation, stabilization, and transport of children with time-critical pathologies where mobilizing a remote specialized paediatric intensive care retrieval team would introduce unacceptable delays in getting the child to definitive emergency surgery. This should be undertaken by the most senior staff available, following widely accepted advanced life support principles (European Resuscitation Council 2015; Advanced Life Support Group 2016) and other available guidelines (Brierley et al. 2009; National Institute for Health and Care Excellence 2010). Preparation should take place in an appropriate location equipped for instigating intensive care (usually ICU, HDU, operating theatre, or recovery area). The receiving PICU or the transport service can guide management and decision-making throughout this process by telephone or video conferencing link.

Most critically ill children that present to general hospitals in the United Kingdom are 'retrieved' by a specifically trained and equipped team from the regional PICU or a centralized retrieval service. However, one has to consider the inevitable situations where cases are so time-critical that they require primary *transfer* by the referring team. This includes not only intracranial emergencies, but also intra-abdominal catastrophes (e.g. volvulus or intussusception) and burns where there is a 4 h window to perform potentially life- or limb-saving escharotomies (Paediatric Intensive Care Society 2015).

In traumatic brain injury, where the child has no emergent surgically remediable lesion, the child should be *retrieved* by the PICU.

Where there is a time-critical surgical lesion, then the fastest way of getting the child to the neurosurgeon is the right one. This depends on geography, mode of transport (road or air, fixed-wing or rotary), and available suitable landing sites (which often depend on daylight and weather). For the larger, more widespread regions, the distances are such that if the neurosurgical centre's transport team comes out and back, then this may take at least twice the time it would take for a primary transfer, as has been shown in one study in the United Kingdom (Tasker et al. 2006). Each hospital should consider how this eventuality can best be addressed and have a 'game plan' prepared before the event actually occurs (Department of Health 2006; Jenkins et al. 2010; Paediatric Intensive Care Society 2015).

Box 74.1 Physiological criteria for PICU referral

- Deteriorating airway:
  - Chest wall recession
  - 'See-saw' breathing
  - Stridor
- Respiratory distress:
  - Rate greater than 60 beats min^{-1}
  - Chest wall recession
  - Sa_{O_2} less than 94% or Pa_{O_2} less than 8 kPa (with O_2)
  - P_{CO_2} greater than 6 or less than 3.5 kPa
- Shock:
  - Heart rate greater than 180 or less than 80 beats min^{-1}
  - Absent peripheral pulses
  - Cold peripheries
  - Capillary refill greater than 2 s
  - Systolic blood pressure less than 70 + (age in years × 2) mm Hg
- Deteriorating level of consciousness
- Recurrent or resistant seizures
- Burns greater than 10%
- Multiple trauma
- Severe metabolic acidosis.

Background to paediatric transport

In the developed world, centralization of paediatric intensive care services in large PICUs rather than in multiple GICUs results in improved survival for critically ill children (Pollack et al. 1991; Pearson et al. 1997; Shann and Pearson 1999).

This centralization has resulted in increasing numbers of critically ill children who present to a general hospital (the 'referring' hospital) that require subsequent inter-hospital transport to the tertiary services in the 'receiving' hospital (American Academy of Pediatrics 2000). The initial resuscitation and stabilization is undertaken by the local team at the referring hospital, often with real-time support by telephone or video link from the PICU. The transport episode can be undertaken by the referring hospital team or a specialist retrieval service, which is either independent of, or integral to, the receiving PICU. Several groups have reported higher-quality care delivered during transport with fewer critical incidents when the transport episode was undertaken by specialist transport teams compared with *ad hoc* teams assembled by the referring hospital (Macnab 1991; Kanter et al. 1992; Barry and Ralston 1994; Edge et al. 1994; Britto et al. 1995; Hatherill et al. 2003; Vos et al. 2004).

In response to these findings, the UK Paediatric Intensive Care Society published a standard-setting report in 1996 recommending that critically ill children admitted to a local hospital should receive the best available assessment, resuscitation, and stabilization by senior local clinicians, followed by transportation to a regional PICU by a specialized transport team (Paediatric Intensive Care Society 1996). Subsequent to further developments and experience, these have been revised in 2010 and 2015 with input from bodies representing stakeholder staff groups in general hospitals (Paediatric Intensive Care Society 2015).

The model of using a specialized transport team functioning as an 'intensive care bed on the move' is now accepted as the ideal throughout the developed world. Specialized teams have training and experience in both paediatric intensive care and transportation, using dedicated transportation equipment, and should function without leaving either the PICU base or referring hospital short-staffed (Paediatric Intensive Care Society 2015), and published quality indicators support the ongoing use and development of specialized retrieval services (Lutman et al. 2008; Ramnarayan 2009).

With the majority of inter-hospital transport episodes in critically ill children now being undertaken by specialized paediatric intensive care teams, it was feared that referring hospital staff, particularly general anaesthetists, would become deskilled and lose confidence in managing critically ill or injured children. However, when looked at longitudinally over time, there is evidence that referring hospital teams have not become deskilled and continue to perform the majority of initial stabilization procedures, including intubation and ventilation, insertion of central venous lines, and initiation of inotrope therapy, before the arrival of a specialist retrieval team and that these skill levels have not decreased since the inception of dedicated transport teams; in fact they may well be increasing (Ramnarayan et al. 2003; Lampariello et al. 2010).

Inter-hospital transport delivered by specialized teams involves a time period for the team to mobilize and travel to the patient. In view of this, there are a number of time-critical pathologies that may necessitate rapid transport by a referring hospital team. The classic example is the expanding intracranial haematoma requiring urgent neurosurgical intervention. Referring hospitals, therefore, need to maintain a high-quality transport capability. Referring hospital teams are often assembled around an anaesthetist as the central figure (The Association of Anaesthetists of Great Britain and Ireland 2006, 2009).

Planning for inter-hospital transport by the referring hospital

Inter-hospital transport, regardless how infrequent an occurrence, should not be organized on an *ad hoc* basis. In the event that a referring hospital is required to undertake inter-hospital transport of a critically ill or injured child, it must have contingency plans in place to ensure the provision of high-quality care equivalent to an 'intensive care bed on the move' (Warren et al. 2004). This is a significant challenge for hospitals that undertake this activity infrequently. A senior doctor and nurse should have clinical responsibility for procuring the necessary transport equipment and medical supplies, development of basic transport protocols, and auditing transport activity. However, there must be 'board-level' hospital management responsibility for the provision of such facilities and measures (Paediatric Intensive Care Society 2015). Careful planning will ensure that the hospital is not left short of staff when a transport team is mobilized. This necessitates the availability of two transport personnel, usually one doctor and one nurse, in addition the ongoing requirements of the hospital. The logistics around staff availability are often dictated by the size and resources of the hospital. From a nursing perspective, this requires staffing of an extra 'transport bed' in the ICU or ED. Medical staffing is often achieved by a system of 'second on-call' or cross-cover within a hospital. The issue of supervision of trainee doctors during transport is important. An ambulance or indeed an aircraft in the air is the extreme of geographical isolation for a trainee doctor. Adequate training and experience and a robust means of communication with the supervising consultant are essential.

Advance planning requires prior liaison with the local ambulance service to determine the type of equipment and modes of transportation available. An increasingly popular option is to purchase a custom-built transport trolley, which must be compatible with the loading and fixation systems in the local ambulances. These can be used for inter-hospital transportation of critically ill patients of all ages. Other solutions are based around packaging the child and equipment onto an adult-sized vacuum mattress, which can then be fixed onto any stretcher on a road, helicopter, or fixed-wing ambulance.

Liaison with the pharmacy department is helpful in selecting which drugs to carry and how best to store them.

Referring hospital transport personnel and training

A transport team assembled by a referring hospital will usually comprise an experienced doctor and nurse. Ideally the doctors should be senior members of staff or senior trainees, with several years of experience in anaesthesia and intensive care medicine, or other equivalent discipline (Royal College of Anaesthetists 2009; The Association of Anaesthetists of Great Britain and Ireland 2006, 2009).

Nurses have independent professional responsibility towards the child and, ideally, should have intensive care training.

Critically ill children should be transported by individuals capable of providing the appropriate level of intensive care and to manage possible complications and adverse events that can occur in transit. There currently are no agreed international standards for, or certification of, transport personnel. Doctors performing transport should be able to determine diagnostic and therapeutic priorities in critically ill children and be skilled in airway management including endotracheal intubation, venous and arterial cannulation, and chest drain insertion, and should be able to manage the transport of critically ill children with a variety of conditions including respiratory failure, shock, and traumatic brain injury. It is prudent that all transport personnel should have advanced life support knowledge and skills (such as those gained on EPLS or APLS courses) and have undergone a specialist transport-training course that includes elements of team training and non-technical skills, now often taught using simulation. Ongoing training and continuous professional development can be achieved through refresher courses, audit, debriefing, and the reporting and discussion of critical incidents and adverse events that have occurred during transportation.

Transport equipment

The team should carry all the necessary equipment and drugs for ongoing resuscitation and stabilization during transportation. Equipment and drugs can be packed in wheeled transport kit bags with multiple, labelled, and well-padded compartments to allow rapid access to the contents. All equipment and drugs should be inventoried on laminated checklists. Transport equipment should be checked and serviced regularly. A battery usage and recharging log can be useful to ensure the battery-operated equipment does not fail in transit. The transport bags are restocked after each transport episode using the checklist and sealed ready for immediate use. Guidelines on the requirements for transport equipment have been published (Warren et al. 2004), stating that equipment should:

- Facilitate paediatric resuscitation and stabilization in the transport setting
- Be durable and portable
- Be readily secured to the trolley, vacuum mattress, or vehicle for transportation
- Include a self-contained power supply or battery back-up
- Connect to ambulance power and oxygen supplies
- Be electronically compatible with flight electrical systems and avionics.

It is fundamental that personnel who undertake transport, even (or indeed especially) where this is infrequent, should maintain familiarity and competence with all items of equipment, from being able to locate an item of equipment in the bags quickly to safe operation of the ventilator, patient monitor, and infusion pumps. Several strategies can be used: yearly update and competency checks, using the transport set-up for internal hospital patient transfers, or using transport equipment in daily practice (e.g. the monitor or infusion pumps).

Transport trolley/stretcher

Several generic transport trolleys are available on the worldwide market. They are often transport certified (crash-tested) by the manufacturer with various configurations of user-mounted equipment. It is important to ensure that the trolley is fitted with a fixation system that is compatible with the local transport (ambulance) vehicles. Typically, they incorporate a metal pole or shelf system to secure the ventilator, pumps, and monitor in accessible positions and an adjustable patient restraint system. The power cables for electrical equipment can be connected together to allow mains-charging via one lead. An inverter, converting ambulance 12/24V DC to 240V AC, is usually available as a factory-fitted option. The trolley oxygen supply should be easily switchable from trolley-mounted cylinders to the ambulance oxygen supply.

Transport drugs

Drug bags (or boxes) should be well padded to protect glass ampoules, and should contain the full range of commonly used resuscitation, anaesthesia, sedation, and vasopressor drugs. Box 74.2 lists the minimum recommended range; other drugs may need to be added depending on the patient diagnosis (e.g. mannitol or hypertonic saline for a child with a head injury).

Box 74.2 Minimum recommended transport drugs

Resuscitation

- Adenosine
- Amiodarone
- Atropine
- Calcium gluconate
- Dobutamine
- Dopamine
- Adrenaline (epinephrine)
- Noradrenaline (norepinephrine)
- Sodium bicarbonate 8.4%

Anaesthesia, sedation, and analgesia

- Ketamine
- Midazolam
- Morphine
- Propofol
- Rocuronium
- Suxamethonium
- Thiopental

Miscellaneous

- Cefotaxime
- Furosemide
- Hydrocortisone
- Ipratropium nebulizer
- Magnesium sulfate
- Mannitol
- Phenytoin
- Salbutamol (intravenous)
- Salbutamol nebulizer

Transport ventilators

A selection of portable mechanical ventilators is required to deliver the range of tidal volumes required for infants and children of all ages. They should have disconnection and high-pressure alarms, variable FI_{O_2}, respiratory rate, duty cycle, tidal volume, and end-expiratory pressure. There are a number of commercially available transport ventilators of varying degrees of sophistication. Ideally, a simple, gas-driven ventilator will be easy to use and not be reliant on a power supply that may fail. More sophisticated, portable, battery-powered ventilators can replicate most of the commonly used ICU modes of ventilation. They have become more popular after the recent improvements in battery technology and the increasing availability of ambulance or trolley-mounted inverters making power failure in transit a rare occurrence.

Oxygen supply

The amount of oxygen that the team should take with them will depend on the amount available in the ambulance or aircraft. The rate of oxygen consumption can be estimated from the predicted minute volume of the patient and the amount of gas required to drive the ventilator (as specified by the manufacturer). Hand-ventilating usually consumes considerably more oxygen than a mechanical ventilator. The required amount can be calculated using a nomogram for cylinder size and duration of transport episode (Lutman and Petros 2006). The commonly used, steel construction, oxygen cylinders (sizes D, E, and F) have a capacity of 340, 680, and 1360 litres, respectively. Lightweight aluminium cylinders (e.g. ZD with integral regulator) can be pressurized to much higher levels than standard steel cylinders, thereby increasing the amount of oxygen which can be carried by the transport team. ZD and D cylinders, both approximately 2 litres in volume, have a compressed gas capacity of 605 and 340 litres of oxygen, respectively.

Suction apparatus

Battery-powered suction apparatus is usually available in the ambulance or aircraft or can be carried by the transport team. Venturi suction systems rapidly consume oxygen supplies and should be avoided. Foot- or hand-pump mechanical suction systems are useful as an emergency back-up.

Infusion pumps

Intravenous infusion pumps should be robust, compact, lightweight, have a simple user interface, visible and audible alarms, and a long, predictable battery life.

Patient monitor

The patient monitor should be robust, portable, battery powered (with the option of being powered by 12/24V DC or 240V AC in transit), and have a clear illuminated display with a wide viewing angle. There are an increasing number of transport monitors available, some combined with a portable transport defibrillator/pacer. Modern portable monitors can be used from neonates to adults and offer ECG, pulse oximetry, non-invasive blood pressure, temperature, capnography, respiratory rate, and multiple simultaneous invasive pressure measurements. Most monitors now incorporate sophisticated software/hardware solutions to minimize effects of movement and cold extremities on pulse oximetry and blood pressure measurement. Non-invasive blood pressure monitoring on transport monitors is now sufficiently accurate and reliable that invasive blood pressure recording is no longer indicated for transport of the critically ill child. Most monitors now also have data storage with download or printing capabilities to facilitate accurate data recording in transit. It is important that patient alarms are visible, red being ideal, and audible because of high ambient noise in transport vehicles. It is worth noting that the major power usage of a monitor is by the non-invasive blood pressure, end-tidal CO_2 and sophisticated high-resolution colour screens. Modern battery technology and the availability of AC power sources in transit circumvent the risk of power failure on long journeys.

Additional equipment

Additional equipment includes a document folder containing the recording chart, audit form, information for parents, infusion and resuscitation drug charts, a mobile telephone, warm protective high-visibility clothing for staff, and a sharps disposal box.

Modes of transportation

The mode of transportation can be by road or air—either helicopter or fixed-wing. The choice depends on pre-existing local arrangements, familiarity and competency of staff in the various modes of transport, the severity of illness of the child, urgency of the transportation, availability of vehicles, distances involved, proximity of the hospitals to airfields, time of day, weather conditions, and the amount and type of equipment to be carried. All modes of transport should have easy access for patient loading, adequate lighting and heating, space for the transport team at the head and side of the patient, an adequate supply of oxygen, integrated power source (either 12/24V DC or 240V AC), suitable storage space, and acceptable levels of noise and vibration. There should be restraints for the staff, patient, trolley, and equipment. An effective communications system both internal and external to the vehicle is essential.

Road transportation

Road ambulance transport is rapidly organized and 'door to door' and is therefore usually more time-efficient for distances less than 75 miles (120 km). The ambulance can stop at the roadside to facilitate clinical procedures and divert to the nearest hospital if a serious complication arises en route.

Air transportation

Air ambulance transportation takes longer to organize and, if the landing sites are not integral to the respective hospitals, will require secondary road transportation. The slower and more complicated loading and unloading of patients on exposed airfields and helipads can increase the risk of critical incidents and expose the patient to adverse weather conditions with the risk of hypothermia. Helicopter transport is a realistic option for distances further than 75 miles (120 km) and fixed-wing transport for distances of greater than 150 miles (240 km). Transport personnel will usually travel as 'medical passengers' concentrating on patient management. However, an understanding of how to load the patient, set-up and mount equipment in the aircraft, and the emergency in-flight aircraft procedures is very important. This can be covered by pre-flight briefings at the time or by 'medical passenger' orientation courses run by providers. Helicopters and small fixed-wing air ambulances are not pressurized whereas larger fixed-wing air ambulances and commercial aircraft have pressurized cabins. It should be borne in mind, however, what is meant by 'pressurized'.

Altitude physiology

Pressurized aircraft usually fly with a 'cabin altitude' of up to 8000 feet (2500 m). Atmospheric pressure decreases with altitude from approximately 760 mm Hg (101 kPa) at sea level to 565 mm Hg (75 kPa) at 8000 feet (2500 m). This will have an effect on enclosed gas spaces, mechanical ventilation, and patient oxygenation.

Enclosed air spaces can expand by up to 35% at standard cabin pressure. Clinical sequelae of this can include ear, sinus, and dental pain; expansion of pneumothoraces and tracheal tube cuffs; and gaseous abdominal distension requiring decompression with a nasogastric or orogastric tube.

The ambient oxygen fraction remains at 21% at 8000 feet (2500 m). As atmospheric pressure decreases, the Po_2 in dry air decreases from 21 kPa at sea level to 16 kPa at standard cabin pressure. The reduction in the partial pressure of oxygen becomes clinically significant for children with high oxygen requirements at sea level and when $F\text{I}_{O_2}$ cannot be readily increased during transportation (e.g. those breathing spontaneously on high-flow face-mask oxygen or ventilated with 100% oxygen). To compensate, children on high-flow face-mask oxygen can be electively intubated and ventilated before transportation and for children requiring 100% oxygen at sea-level, the effective cabin altitude of pressurized aircraft *can* be reduced to near sea-level and military helicopters can fly as low as 500 feet (150 m), weather permitting (Barry and Leslie 2003).

Transport considerations

Isolation and the unfamiliar environment

The transport team is isolated from assistance and working in a relatively unfamiliar environment. Use of a mobile phone en route to communicate with the receiving hospital, including other tertiary specialists besides intensive care, is mandatory.

Movement and vibration

In transit, passengers are subjected to various types of movement including acceleration, deceleration, head-up and head-down tilt, and vibration. Generally, in level flight, helicopters travel nose-down and fixed wing aircraft nose-up. With the patient positioned with their head towards the front of the vehicle, acceleration will cause venous pooling in the legs and reduced cardiac output. Normal baroreceptor compensation is obtunded in patients with septicaemia, hypovolaemia, central nervous system injury, and under the effects of sedative drugs. Acceleration can be minimized by the ambulance driver or pilot and is usually clinically insignificant. Deceleration can be more unpredictable (e.g. emergency braking). It usually involves greater forces and may be clinically significant. It will cause an increase in venous return and intracranial pressure, which may be exacerbated by a head-down orientation (e.g. sharp braking while travelling downhill). The effects of these forces can be minimized by sympathetic driving and using a police escort to clear road junctions. Other important strategies include appropriate patient positioning (e.g. head-up tilt on landing), adequate fluid resuscitation, and the use of appropriate inotropes in shocked patients and optimizing other treatment strategies (e.g. for raised intracranial pressure). In wider aircraft, it is possible to place the patient across the line of travel thus minimizing these positional and inertial forces.

Motion sickness can affect the patient and transport team members and is made worse by excessive head movement and reading in transit. Antiemetics (e.g. antihistamines, ondansetron) are usually effective treatments.

Movement and vibration can also cause displacement of tracheal tubes, chest drains, and intravascular cannulae.

Communication

Effective communication between the referring/transport team, ambulance service, and receiving team is important at all stages of transportation. Most retrieval services have a dedicated telephone 'hotline'. Referrals should be made direct from the referring to receiving team at a senior medical level. The PICU or transport consultant can remain in regular contact by mobile phone with the referring team and the transporting team during transit to give additional advice and to receive clinical updates. The transport team should then also be able to access advice in transit from colleagues in other tertiary specialities such as neurosurgery and cardiology.

Patient packaging

The ambulance environment can be challenging and confined. There is limited space, in the back of an ambulance, to perform procedures such as intubation or venous cannulation. The child's head, tracheal tube, and ventilator tubing should be securely fixed, while ensuring easy, rapid access for airway management. Pressure areas require additional padding. An extension line attached to a peripheral intravenous cannula is useful for administering drugs or fluid without the need to unfasten seatbelts or expose the child. The transport environment can be hostile. Infants, with a large surface area-to-weight ratio, large head, thin skin, and neuromuscular block preventing shivering are at risk of hypothermia on airport runways in winter. The use of a vacuum mattress, insulation blankets, chemical warming packs (which can be placed directly against the skin of an infant without causing thermal injury), a hat, and warm ambient temperature within the vehicle is sufficient to maintain body temperature in infants with a body weight of more than 5 kg. Babies weighing less than 5 kg are usually transported by intensive care teams using a portable 'Baby Pod' or incubator to maintain body temperature.

All equipment, syringe pumps, and the monitor must be secured and readily visible to the team while seated. Equipment can be mounted on a commercially available transport trolley, which can be used for inter-hospital transportation of critically ill patients of all ages. These must be compatible with the loading and fixation systems in the local ambulances. Alternatively, the child and equipment can be secured within an adult-sized vacuum mattress that can then be fixed onto any stretcher on a road, helicopter, or fixed-wing ambulance.

Emergency drugs, fluids, and airway and ventilation equipment (including a self-inflating resuscitation bag–valve–mask system) must be immediately available. Completing a pre-departure checklist will avoid accidental omissions in the stabilization process or inadvertently leaving equipment behind (see Table 74.3).

Table 74.3 Pre-departure checklist

Patient	**Item**
Airway	Airway patent Chest X-ray—correct tracheal tube position Tracheal tube secured and suctioned
Breathing	On transport ventilator—settings checked Arterial blood gases OK End-tidal CO_2 and Sa_{O_2} traces OK Nasogastric and orogastric tube *in situ* and draining
Circulation	Heart rate/perfusion/blood pressure OK Vascular access patent/secure/accessible Urinary catheter *in situ* ECG and non-invasive blood pressure OK Invasive pressure zeroed/traces OK
Neurology	GCS documented Pupil reaction documented
Temperature	Warming measures *in situ* Core/peripheral temperature monitor
Fluids/infusions	Blood sugar documented Maintenance fluid running Sedation/neuromuscular block running Other required drugs running
Logistics	**Item**
Communication	Receiving PICU informed of estimated time of arrival/ clinical condition Ambulance informed of clinical condition/any requirements Relatives briefed/information leaflet/map/contact number Documentation- notes, X-rays/CT scan, lab results, Team—comfort stop and refreshments
Patient packaging	Name bracelets × 2, check details correct Padding: Gamgee®/harness/vacuum mat/gel pads Vacmat secured to ambulance trolley Monitor/pumps/ventilator secured to ambulance trolley Invasive lines transducers padded and accessible Scan patient: head to toe/monitor/ventilator/pumps
Equipment	Monitor/ventilator/pump alarms set and activated Bags closed and secured Oxygen sufficient/accessible/T-piece connected to cylinder Suction apparatus checked/accessible Emergency bag: bag–valve–mask/suction/drugs/fluids/torch Mobile phone accessible

Avoiding adverse events in transit

The child should only be transported when their clinical condition has been optimized, the benefits of transfer outweigh the risks, and the parents have consented to the transportation (Warren et al. 2004). Transferring a critically ill child between trolleys, around the hospital, and into and out of vehicles with the associated switching between oxygen and power supplies are risk factors for critical incidents. Despite optimum stabilization and preparation, children may deteriorate in transit and the transport team must recognize this early and respond effectively. Published series (Kanter et al. 1989) highlight the critical incidents that can occur during transportation of children, which can be classified as physiological deterioration or equipment problems. Staff performing patient transport should have regular audit and risk management meetings to discuss any adverse events or critical incidents that have occurred.

During transportation, the transport team should adopt a routine of regular assessment and recording using a systematic 'ABC' approach. The position, patency, and fixation of the tracheal tube are confirmed. Capnography is essential to monitor airway security in the intubated child, particularly during periods of maximal risk such as loading and unloading from vehicles when clinical observation is difficult. Small-diameter tracheal tubes (<5.0 mm internal diameter) are prone to blockage by secretions. This can be avoided by humidifying inspired gas using a heat and moisture exchanging bacterial filter and by regular tracheal suction. Adequacy of ventilation is assessed by the 'triple-check': observing chest movement, the airway pressure gauge on the ventilator, and the capnograph trace (Barry and Leslie 2003). The ventilator settings, connections, and oxygen source should be inspected and recorded regularly. The well-known mnemonic, 'DOPES' is a useful method of troubleshooting airway and breathing problems: consider *D*isplacement or *O*bstruction of the tube, *P*neumothorax, *E*quipment problems, and gaseous *S*tomach distension (European Resuscitation Council 2015).

Assessment of circulation includes evaluation of heart rate, peripheral and central pulses, capillary refill, blood pressure, and central venous pressure if monitored. Intravenous access sites should be inspected regularly for signs of blockage or extravasation. Neurological status is assessed by evaluating pupil size and reactivity and fontanelle pressure, where appropriate. Seizure activity, which is masked by neuromuscular block, should be suspected by the sudden occurrence of tachycardia, hypertension, or pupil dilatation. Body temperature and blood glucose in infants can decrease during transportation and should be monitored regularly.

It is advisable to carry back-up equipment in the event of a ventilator, monitor, or infusion pump failure. Inexpensive, compact, battery-operated end-tidal CO_2 and Sp_{O_2} monitors are commercially available. Several 'golden rules' of transport have become standard teaching (see Box 74.3).

Documentation

Documentation, like communication, is central to high-quality inter-hospital transportation. Each referring hospital should

Box 74.3 Golden rules of transportation

- Boring transfers make good transfers
- No form of transportation is ideal for every patient
- Any hospital is a better hospital than an airplane or ambulance
- If it is possible for a sick child to become sicker, he/she probably will
- Big problems are simply small problems you have not anticipated
- Nothing lasts forever: oxygen cylinders, batteries
- Plan ahead.

develop documentation best suited to their needs. It should include a comprehensive medical and nursing record from the time of initial presentation of the sick child until the child arrives in the receiving PICU. Thorough documentation facilitates debriefing, audit, and risk management. Movement and vibration can inhibit and reduce the quality of hand-written records. Information stored in the monitor memory should be printed if possible and attached to the observation chart. A recent development, inspired by the aviation industry, is the use of Standard Operating Procedures to guide the whole process of patient resuscitation, stabilization, and transportation and 'Emergency Action Cards' outlining the team management of rare or complex activities (e.g. equipment or oxygen failure, or rapid sequence induction in the back of an ambulance). The required documentation is described in Box 74.4.

Debriefing, audit, and risk management

Routine debriefing of the team after each transport episode will support the team members and identify any shortfall in the quality of the service. The responsible senior doctor and nurse should audit and review all transport episodes examining the justification for referring hospital team transportation, clinical standards, communication, documentation, critical incidents, and outcome. It is beneficial if the receiving paediatric intensive care retrieval teams are involved in this important process.

Family-orientated care

This is an extremely distressing time for parents and family that is exacerbated by the news that their child requires transportation to a different hospital. Most PICUs have booklets for parents and some have websites containing much of this useful information to inform the parents about the need for transfer and what to expect when they arrive in the PICU. It is becoming more common to get informed consent from parents for the transfer. Parents often want to accompany their child during transportation. Considerations include the available space within the vehicle, the distance to be travelled, the availability of alternative transport, and the severity of illness of the child. It is usual for a parent to accompany a conscious child. If the parents are not travelling with their child, alternative transportation should be arranged.

Box 74.4 Documentation of paediatric transportation

- Patient characteristics/location data—patient and referring/receiving doctor and hospital
- Rational for transportation
- Advice given by PICU
- Treatment during resuscitation, stabilization, and transportation
- Clinical observations
- Operational data—mode of transport, personnel, and timings
- Pre-departure checklists
- Drug infusion and resuscitation charts
- Standard Operating Procedures
- Emergency Action Cards
- Adverse events in transit
- Transport consent form
- Parent information

Special circumstances

Occasionally it is not possible to fully stabilize a child before transportation because of an evolving surgical pathology such as intracranial haemorrhage or the need for advanced intervention, for example, balloon atrial septoplasty for transposition of the great arteries or support such as extracorporeal life support. Difficult decision-making should be undertaken by senior staff in discussion with the receiving PICU. Avoiding unnecessary delay is more important than speed when dealing with time-critical pathologies. Cardiac arrest or death occurring in transit is fortunately rare. A decision must be made, in discussion with the PICU team, about the duration of attempted resuscitation and whether to proceed towards the PICU or return to the referring hospital. It may appropriate to divert to another appropriate hospital en route.

Safety

Transport team and patient safety is of prime importance. Accident rate data are widely available (Kahn et al. 2001; Lutman et al. 2008). Safety issues should be addressed in team training, Standard Operating Procedures, and risk management activities. The use of tail-lift or ramp and winch systems is important when loading heavy transport trolleys into ambulances. Most inter-hospital transport episodes do not warrant use of lights and sirens, and speed limits should generally be adhered to (Hunt et al. 1995; Brown et al. 2000; Kahn et al. 2001).

A police escort is advisable for negotiating traffic congestion at a steady speed. The patient and all equipment should be firmly secured to the trolley and ambulance. The wearing of seat belts should be mandatory at all times while the ambulance is moving. Airfield and aircraft hazards include propellers, rotor blades, fuel, noise, and severe weather conditions. It is usually mandatory to wear high-visibility clothing when working on airfields or helicopter landing pads. Approaching an aircraft can be dangerous. The transport team should always seek permission from a crewmember, ideally the pilot, before approaching the aircraft. Fixed-wing aircraft should not be approached when the engines are running. Helicopters should only be approached from the front and sides to avoid the tail rotor that is often difficult to see.

Medical indemnity and personal insurance

Professional indemnity for the team is usually provided by the employing hospital or health authority. Personal professional medical defence indemnity cover is also recommended. Arrangements for providing life insurance for transport personnel vary widely. Sources of insurance cover include personal life and disability, hospital insurance, and ambulance service insurance policies. Individuals need to confirm the terms and conditions of their personal life policies, especially for air transportation. Some national and international organizations and societies provide insurance cover for their members while undertaking transport duties (e.g. Paediatric Intensive Care Society, The Association of Anaesthetists of Great Britain and Ireland, and the Intensive Care Society).

Declaration of interest

None declared.

Further reading

American Academy of Pediatrics. *Guidelines for Air and Ground Transport of Neonatal and Pediatric Patients*, 4th Edn. Washington, DC: American Academy of Pediatrics, 2015

Hammer GB, Holzki J, Morton NS (eds). The pediatric airway. *Paediatr Anaesth* 2009; **19**(Suppl 1): 1–197

Murphy PJ, Marriage SC, Davis PJ. *Case Studies in Pediatric Critical Care*. Cambridge: Cambridge University Press, 2009

Nichol DG (ed). *Rogers' Textbook of Pediatric Intensive Care*, 4th edn. Philadelphia, PA: Lippincott, Williams & Wilkins, 2008

References

Advanced Life Support Group. *Advanced Paediatric Life Support: The Practical Approach (APLS)*, 6th Edn. Oxford: Wiley-Blackwell, 2016

American Academy of Pediatrics. Committee on Pediatric Emergency Medicine. American College of Critical Care Medicine. Society of Critical Care Medicine. Consensus report for regionalization of services for critically ill or injured children. *Pediatrics* 2000; **105**: 152–5

Anderson BJ. Special themed issue on Ethics. *Pediatric Anesthesia* 2009; **19**: 931–1033

Barry P, Leslie A. *Paediatric and Neonatal Critical Care Transport*. London: BMJ Books, 2003

Barry PW, Ralston C. Adverse events occurring during interhospital transfer of the critically ill. *Arch Dis Child* 1994; **71**: 8–11

Baxter CR, Shires T. Physiological response to crystalloid resuscitation of severe burns. *Ann N Y Acad Sci* 1968; **150**: 874–94

Brierley J, Carcillo JA, Choong K, *et al*. Clinical practice parameters for hemodynamic support of pediatric and neonatal septic shock: 2007 update from the American College of Critical Care Medicine. *Crit Care Med* 2009; **37**: 666–88

Britto J, Nadel S, Maconochie I, *et al*. Morbidity and severity of illness during interhospital transfer: impact of a specialised paediatric retrieval team. *BMJ* 1995; **311**: 836–9

Brown LH, Whitney CL, Hunt RC, *et al*. Do warning lights and sirens reduce ambulance response times? *Prehosp Emerg Care* 2000; **4**: 70–4

Carcillo JA, Fields AI. Clinical practice parameters for hemodynamic support of pediatric and neonatal patients in septic shock. *Crit Care Med* 2002; **30**: 1365–78

Cheuk DK, Chau TC, Lee SL. A meta-analysis on intravenous magnesium sulphate for treating acute asthma. *Arch Dis Child* 2005; **90**: 74–7

Denny FW, Murphy TF, Clyde WA, Jr, *et al*. Croup: an 11-year study in a pediatric practice. *Pediatrics* 1983; **71**: 871–6

Department of Health. *The Acutely or Critically Sick or Injured Child in the District General Hospital: A Team Response*. London: Department of Health, 2006

Edge WE, Kanter RK, Weigle CG, *et al*. Reduction of morbidity in interhospital transport by specialized pediatric staff. *Crit Care Med* 1994; **22**: 1186–91

European Resuscitation Council. *Paediatric Life Support*. London: European Resuscitation Council, 2015. Available from https://cprguidelines.eu/

Fraser J, Maskrey C, Taylor H. Evaluation of the Paediatric Index of Mortality in children managed on adult intensive care units. *Arch Dis Child* 2004; **89**: 974–6

George EN, Schur K, Muller M, *et al*. Management of high voltage electrical injury in children. *Burns* 2005; **31**: 439–44

Hartling L, Wiebe N, Russell K, *et al*. Epinephrine for bronchiolitis. *Cochrane Database Syst Rev* 2004; **1**: CD003123

Hatherill M, Waggie Z, Reynolds L, *et al*. Transport of critically ill children in a resource-limited setting. *Intensive Care Med* 2003; **29**: 1547–54

Hopkins A, Lahiri T, Salerno R, *et al*. Changing epidemiology of life-threatening upper airway infections: the reemergence of bacterial tracheitis. *Pediatrics* 2006; **118**: 1418–21

Hunt RC, Brown LH, Cabinum ES, *et al*. Is ambulance transport time with lights and siren faster than that without? *Ann Emerg Med* 1995; **25**: 507–11

Hutchison JS, Ward RE, Lacroix J, *et al*. Hypothermia therapy after traumatic brain injury in children. *N Engl J Med* 2008; **358**: 2447–56

Inwald DP, Tasker RC, Peters MJ, *et al*. Emergency management of children with severe sepsis in the United Kingdom: the results of the Paediatric Intensive Care Society sepsis audit. *Arch Dis Child* 2009; **94**: 348–53

Jenkins I, Waldman C, Taylor B. Critical care for children—"back to the future." *J Intensive Care Soc* 2010; **11**: 160–2

Jenkins IA, Saunders M. Infections of the airway. *Paediatr Anaesth* 2009; **19**(Suppl 1): 118–30

Kahn CA, Pirrallo RG, Kuhn EM. Characteristics of fatal ambulance crashes in the United States: an 11-year retrospective analysis. *Prehosp Emerg Care* 2001; **5**: 261–9

Kanter RK, Boeing NM, Hannan WP, *et al*. Excess morbidity associated with interhospital transport. *Pediatrics* 1992; **90**: 893–8

Kanter RK, Tompkins JM. Adverse events during interhospital transport: physiologic deterioration associated with pretransport severity of illness. *Pediatrics* 1989; **84**: 43–8

Lampariello S, Clement M, Aralihond AP, *et al*. Stabilisation of critically ill children at the district general hospital prior to intensive care retrieval: a snapshot of current practice. *Arch Dis Child* 2010; **95** 681–5

Lund CC, Browder NC. The estimation of areas of burns. *Surg Gynecol Obstet* 1944; **79**: 352–8

Lutman D, Montgomery M, Ramnarayan P, *et al*. Ambulance and aeromedical accident rates during emergency retrieval in Great Britain. *Emerg Med J* 2008; **25**: 301–2

Lutman D, Petros AJ. How many oxygen cylinders do you need to take on transport? A nomogram for cylinder size and duration. *Emerg Med J* 2006; **23**: 703–4

Macnab AJ. Optimal escort for interhospital transport of pediatric emergencies. *J Trauma* 1991; **31**: 205–9

Marcin JP, Glaser N, Barnett P, *et al*. Factors associated with adverse outcomes in children with diabetic ketoacidosis-related cerebral edema. *J Pediatr* 2002; **141**: 793–7

Mayo-Smith MF, Spinale JW, Donskey CJ, *et al*. Acute epiglottitis: an 18-year experience in Rhode Island. *JAMA* 1995; **108**: 1640–7

National Institute for Health and Care Excellence. *Meningitis (Bacterial) and Meningococcal Septicaemia in under 16s: Recognition, Diagnosis and Management*. Clinical Guideline 102. London: National Institute for Health and Care Excellence, 2010 (updated 2015)

National Institutes of Health. *Expert Panel Report: Diagnosis and Management of Asthma*, EPR-3 edn. Bethesda, MD: National Institutes of Health, 2007. Available from http://www.nhlbi.nih.gov/guidelines/asthma/11_sec15_exacerb.pdf

Paediatric Intensive Care Audit Network (PICANet). *National Report of the Paediatric Intensive Care Network*. 2009. Available from http://www.picanet.org.uk/

Paediatric Intensive Care Audit Network (PICANet). *National Report of the Paediatric Intensive Care Network*. 2010. Available from http://www.picanet.org.uk/

Paediatric Intensive Care Society. *Standards for Paediatric Intensive Care including Standards of Practice for the Transportation of the critically ill child*. Bishop's Stortford: Saldatore Ltd, 1996

Paediatric Intensive Care Society. *Standards for the Care of Critically Ill Children*, 5th edn. London: Paediatric Intensive Care Society, 2015

Pearson G, Shann F, Barry P, *et al*. Should paediatric intensive care be centralised? Trent versus Victoria. *Lancet* 1997; **349**: 1213–17

Pollack MM, Alexander SR, Clarke N, *et al*. Improved outcomes from tertiary center pediatric intensive care: a statewide comparison of tertiary and nontertiary care facilities. *Crit Care Med* 1991; **19**: 150–9

Ramnarayan P, Britto J, Tanna A, *et al*. Does the use of a specialised paediatric retrieval service result in the loss of vital stabilisation skills among referring hospital staff? *Arch Dis Child* 2003; **88**: 851–4

Ramnarayan P. Measuring the performance of an inter-hospital transport service. *Arch Dis Child* 2009; **94**: 414–6

Royal College of Anaesthetists. *Guidelines for the Provision of Anaesthetic Services (Paediatric Anaesthesia & Critical Care Sections)*. London: Royal College of Anaesthetists, 2009. Available from http://www.rcoa.ac.uk/system/files/GPAS-2009-FULL_0.pdf

Salamone FN, Bobbitt DB, Myer CM, *et al.* Bacterial tracheitis reexamined: is there a less severe manifestation? *Otolaryngol Head Neck Surg* 2004; **131**: 871–6

Scottish Executive. *Emergency Care Framework for Children and Young People in Scotland.* Edinburgh: Scottish Executive, 2006. Available from https://www.scottishpatientsafetyprogramme.scot.nhs.uk/Media/Docs/MCQIC/Paediatric%20Care/Emergency%20Care%20Framework%20for%20Children%20and%20Young%20People.pdf

Sehdev RS, Symmons DA, Kindl K. Ketamine for rapid sequence induction in patients with head injury in the emergency department. *Emerg Med Australas* 2006; **18**: 37–44

Shann F, Pearson G. Paediatric intensive care—specialisation reduces mortality. *Anaesthesia* 1999; **54**: 809–10

Southwest Audit of Critically Ill Children. 2009. Available from http://www.picanet.org.uk/research_projects.html

Southwest Audit of Critically Ill Children. *A Ten Year Report*. 2012. Available from http://www.picanet.org.uk

Tasker RC, Lutman D, Peters MJ. Hyperventilation in severe diabetic ketoacidosis. *Pediatr Crit Care Med* 2005; **6**: 405–11

Tasker RC, Morris KP, Forsyth RJ, *et al.* Severe head injury in children: emergency access to neurosurgery in the United Kingdom. *Emerg Med J* 2006; **23**: 519–22

The Association of Anaesthetists of Great Britain and Ireland. *Interhospital Transfer*. 2009. Available from https://www.aagbi.org/sites/default/files/interhospital09.pdf

The Association of Anaesthetists of Great Britain and Ireland. *Recommendations for the Safe Transfer of Patients with Brain Injury.* 2006. Available from https://www.aagbi.org/sites/default/files/braininjury.pdf

Vos GD, Nissen AC, Nieman FH, *et al.* Comparison of interhospital pediatric intensive care transport accompanied by a referring specialist or a specialist retrieval team. *Intensive Care Med* 2004; **30**: 302–8

Warren J, Fromm RE, Jr, Orr RA, *et al.* Guidelines for the inter- and intrahospital transport of critically ill patients. *Crit Care Med* 2004; **32**: 256–62

Weber T, Salvi N, Orliaguet G, *et al.* Cuffed vs non-cuffed endotracheal tubes for pediatric anesthesia. *Paediatr Anaesth* 2009; **19**(Suppl 1): 46–54

Wellesley H, Jenkins IA. Consent in Children. *Anaesth Intensive Care Med* 2009; **19**: 196–9

Welsh Assembly. *Children's National Service Framework for Wales. Acute and Chronic Illness or Injury*. Cardiff: Welsh Assembly, 2005

CHAPTER 75

Ethics, consent, and safeguarding in paediatric anaesthesia

Alistair Cranston, Jillian McFadzean, and Robert Wheeler

Child protection and safeguarding in anaesthesia

Background

The terms 'child protection' and more recently 'child safeguarding' are often used interchangeably. Safeguarding is a wide concept embracing measures to promote children's welfare generally and the implementation of measures to improve safety and prevent abuse. Child protection refers to that part of the safeguarding process where intervention is necessary if it is believed that a child is at risk of significant harm.

Anaesthetists may encounter children in a variety of settings who are at risk of harm or who have been harmed. This may include resuscitation, care of an injured child in the intensive care or theatre setting, and, occasionally, in the conduct of a forensic examination under anaesthesia. Often there will be a professional colleague involved in the care of the child who has a wider knowledge of the subject, but not always. An anaesthetist may be the first to discover signs that may lead to a suspicion of physical or other abuse and so a background knowledge of the subject and knowing how to raise and pursue concerns is essential.

In England and Wales, the overall responsibility for child protection lies with the Department for Education which issues both statutory and advisory guidance to local authorities to aid in the production of procedural guidelines to be followed by practitioners in that local authority area. Similar systems exist in Scotland (via the Scottish Executive) and Northern Ireland. In England and Wales, the legislative framework for the child protection system is the Children Act 1989, amended and revised in the Children Act 2004. (Readers should note that there are differences in the legal framework in different regions of the United Kingdom and further afield.)

Legislation has been in place for well over a century to deal with child cruelty but in recent times, high-profile child abuse deaths, such as that of Victoria Climbié in 2000, and the subsequent inquiry by Lord Laming (Department of Health 2003) have highlighted the incidence of such abuse and the importance of awareness and action on the part of healthcare professionals and other agencies in its detection and prevention. The importance of involvement of, and training for, health professionals has been reinforced in a major review of child protection in England and Wales commissioned by the Department for Education (2011b).

In England, in 2010, there were approximately 11 million children of whom some 350 000 were categorized as 'in need', requiring the provision of one or more additional services and 65 000 were 'looked after', that is, subject to some form of local authority care. Some 39 000 of these were subject to a child protection plan (Department for Education 2011a). Of the 5000 child deaths in England each year, some 150 to 200 will have preventable factors.

Child maltreatment is usually categorized as physical, sexual, or emotional abuse or neglect. Although physical and sexual abuse is often highlighted, in fact neglect and emotional abuse may be far more widespread than is generally appreciated (National Society for the Prevention of Cruelty to Children (NSPCC) 2011).

Enactment of legislation to protect children from maltreatment places obligations on all healthcare institutions and professionals who work with children to act in the best interests of children at all times. The responsibilities of health professionals, institutions, and local authority bodies are set out in the document 'Working Together to Safeguard Children: A guide to inter-agency working to safeguard and promote the welfare of children' (Department for Education 2015). This is the main reference document for all professionals involved in safeguarding children. It defines Local Safeguarding Boards, sets out roles and responsibilities of practitioners in different agencies, guides inter-agency working to safeguarding children, and summarizes evidence-based approaches to child protection procedures. The importance of understanding risk factors and recognition of the risks for and indicators of abuse is stressed. Effective communication with children, families, other health professionals, and agencies is emphasized as well as involvement in planning to meet the needs of children at risk or who are vulnerable. In 2012, the General Medical Council issued a document setting out the responsibilities of all doctors in respect of the protection of children and young people (General Medical Council 2012).

Child protection training

Training for professionals working with children is of key importance and levels of training and expected competencies are set out in an intercollegiate document, last revised in 2014 (Royal College of Paediatrics and Child Health 2014). Currently, most anaesthetists will be expected to maintain 'level 2' competencies as set out in the document. Within a department, at least one individual, but more in larger departments of paediatric anaesthesia, will need training to 'level 3, core' standard (Royal College of Anaesthetists and Association of Paediatric Anaesthetists of Great Britain and Ireland 2010). The range of competencies described apply to many health professionals, from those who will rarely encounter children to those who are child protection experts. Much of the training at level 2 can be delivered in e-learning packages, although this should be supplemented by local teaching, ideally with relevance to anaesthesia. It is recognized that anaesthetists do not, in general, have the same degree of contact with children as do paediatricians, some surgeons, and others; hence, level 2 competencies are appropriate. The role of the 'anaesthetic safeguarding lead' trained to level 3 will be to act as a source of knowledge and to assist in training for colleagues and liaison with other child protection team members. Training for these individuals will require the delivery of some specific materials targeted to the role. Some specific practical guidance for anaesthetists was developed by the Royal College of Paediatrics and Child Health together with the Association of Paediatric Anaesthetists of Great Britain and Ireland (2007). A recent revision of this guidance, including a section on anaesthesia for forensic examinations, has been published by the Royal College of Anaesthetists (2014).

Child safeguarding and the anaesthetist

Anaesthetists may be in contact with children who are at risk of, or who have suffered, abuse in a number of settings. Commonly this will be during resuscitation from or investigation of serious injury or in the intensive care setting. Rarely, anaesthesia may be requested for forensic examination procedures. In such situations, others with expertise in child protection matters will be involved. Occasionally, however, an anaesthetist may be the first to suspect abuse, for instance, during a scan for head trauma or when unexplained injuries are noted during anaesthesia for an unrelated procedure. An awareness of the possibility of abuse is of paramount importance but confident interpretation of physical findings or other signs may be very difficult. Inconsistencies in the medical history, unexplained injuries, or those inconsistent with the purported mechanism of injury must be considered as suspicious. The National Institute for Health and Care Excellence (2009) has produced guidance on when to suspect abuse and a useful summary of those injuries often associated with abuse was published in 2010 (Maguire 2010). Much useful information about injuries associated with abuse is available via the website of the Welsh Child Protection Systematic Review Group (http://bit.ly/1GZdL8J).

Given the nature of the contact that anaesthetists generally will have with children and their carers, other aspects of child maltreatment such as emotional abuse or neglect will rarely be suspected. However, unusual behaviour by children or inappropriate attitudes or interactions by parents or other carers may indicate the possibility of difficulties and should not be ignored. It may be necessary to broach concerns with others involved in the care of the child such as a general practitioner or social worker.

The discovery of unexplained or suspicious findings does not necessarily mean that a child has been abused and most anaesthetists in this position will not be confident to make a definitive interpretation. In this situation, it is important to know how to seek assistance and essential not to ignore potentially important signs. Any concerns should be acted upon without fear of embarrassment or censure should they subsequently prove unfounded.

In most hospital settings, there will be a child protection team or designated paediatrician with responsibility for safeguarding matters, or both, and it is advisable to seek their views if there are suspicions of abuse injuries. It is also sensible to consult colleagues in the theatre setting, particularly those with level 3 training so that the findings may be confirmed and discussed. An inspection of the child's injuries by a more experienced colleague is acceptable and helpful but this cannot constitute a formal examination for child protection purposes. It is important to understand that such an examination, making photographs, or otherwise investigating the injury can only occur after specific consent for this has been obtained, either from a parent, the child if competent, or if necessary, the appropriate legal body. At this stage, a clear and unambiguous documentation of the findings including a note of other individuals consulted must be made. This should describe the findings and indicate that further investigation is necessary but should not pre-judge the cause of any injuries. A common theme in reports and enquiries into cases of child maltreatment is the lack of clear, legible, and attributable written records. It is of great importance to pay particular attention to good note keeping.

If concerns persist about the nature of the findings then an interview with the child's parents or guardian is conducted. This would generally be led by a paediatrician or designated member of the safeguarding team but may include the anaesthetist in some circumstances. The interview is formal but non-confrontational and seeks an explanation for the findings and to convey, if necessary, the need for further examination and investigation of the child to determine how the injuries might have been sustained.

If this interview fails to resolve concerns as to how the injuries were sustained or if there are no satisfactory explanations then further action will be necessary. In the first instance, this would involve a referral to the local authority child-protection team (or rarely to police) who is then responsible for deciding what action to take. Although in the hospital setting this would usually be made by the safeguarding team, anyone with concerns may make such a referral. If there are worries that the child is in immediate danger from further harm then it may be sensible to keep the child in hospital (effectively a 'place of safety') while arrangements are made for their continuing care. It must be remembered that healthcare professionals have no authority to enforce this and cannot physically prevent a parent removing their child. If this does happen and the child is considered to be in immediate danger, then the police have emergency powers to intervene and should be informed.

Implicit in the nature of a referral to the local authority team is the sharing of important and often sensitive information with others. The nature of the information and concerns about confidentiality may be troubling under some circumstances and may lead to some difficulty in understanding what to reveal and to whom. What is clear, however, is that sharing information with other relevant bodies and individuals is a duty and one that is supported by the legal authorities in situations where the best interests of a child are concerned. The common law duty of confidentiality in the special relationship between doctor and patient is not absolute and disclosure of information can be justified in such circumstances. The principle of information sharing set out in 'Working Together to Safeguard Children' (Department for Education 2015) is that information sharing is necessary to keep children safe. Generally, personal information should be disclosed to third parties only with the consent of the subject of that information but consent may be dispensed with if seeking it may place the child at increased risk of harm. Such an approach is also in keeping with the guidance for doctors regarding confidentiality (General Medical Council 2009). It is stressed that good practice is to involve families and children, where appropriate, in decisions about their care and to seek consent to share information, but that the overriding concern is to act in the best interests of a child and this may mean proceeding without consent. Where doubt exists, it may be helpful to seek advice from a senior colleague in the child protection team. All information shared should be accurate, up to date, and necessary for the purpose for which it is shared and only revealed to people who need to have it. The reasons for a decision about whether or not to share information should be recorded. Doctors should not fear criticism, or worse, if they are acting in what they believe genuinely to be a child's best interests. Not to pass on information that could help in the prevention of harm is a failure of duty to that child.

Child protection procedures

After a referral to the local authority child-protection team, a brief assessment is made to determine whether the child is in need, or at risk, the nature of any services that may be required, and the necessity to undertake a detailed assessment. This will usually involve the use of the 'Common Assessment Framework', a key component in the 'Every Child Matters' programme (Department for Education and Skills 2004). This is a standard form, common to all services, based on discussions with the child, family, and other practitioners. It helps to record and share information and is used to determine what might be needed to help in responding to the needs of a child and his or her family.

If it is determined that a child needs further support then he or she will be designated as a 'child in need' under section 17 of the Children Act 1989. This places upon the local authority a duty to safeguard and promote the welfare of that child. In general, this section of the Act applies when a child is not considered to be at risk of actual harm and additional services are usually delivered in the setting of the family.

If a child is judged to have suffered or to be at risk of 'significant harm' this may lead to proceedings under section 47 of the Act. Such proceedings will determine whether to place the child on a Child Protection Plan and how the needs of the child can be met. In addition, the involvement of the child's parents and other family members in their care and the necessity for legal action against any individuals will be considered. 'Significant harm' is the term used to define a threshold that justifies compulsory intervention in family life in a child's best interests. There are no absolute criteria upon which to decide whether significant harm is present but often this results from a compilation of events, acute and longstanding, that interrupt or damage a child's physical and psychological well-being.

Additional to these processes are a range of powers available to local authorities and others (NSPCC, police) to take emergency action immediately to remove a child from a harmful environment. An emergency protection order under section 44 of the Children Act 1989 requires a court order but a police officer may use a police protection order under section 46 of the Act without recourse to a court in the first instance.

Summary

Child maltreatment is not uncommon. Anaesthetists should be aware of the key features that may indicate child abuse and be trained, to a level appropriate to their practice, in the principles of safeguarding and child protection. This will include maintaining competencies commensurate with their involvement in the care of children and a working knowledge of local and national service provision, guidance, and legal requirements in relation to the welfare of children.

Ethics and paediatric anaesthesia

From the Hippocratic Oath, 2500 years ago, to the present day, doctors have applied ethical principles to clinical practice relevant to the culture or society they live in. Society has weaved into, and moulded, these principles, and governments have added to (and sometimes interfered with) the debate. As we stretch the scientific boundaries in medicine, ethical dilemmas are prevalent, complex, and high profile with individual cases attracting media speculation and attention. The ethical issues around the beginning and end of life, together with access to medical care, have dominated moral debates in the last 50 years. The developments in technology have often advanced at a faster rate than our understanding of the consequences of that technology and the ethics that surround it. It is unquestionable that rapid scientific advances have conveyed huge benefits to the health of many people, allowing them to live longer, healthier lives. However, it has come at a cost, and sometimes a compromise on the quality of a life, and we need to increasingly question as doctors whether in some cases we *should* be embarking on a particular treatment pathway. In medicine, we aim to restore health, sustain life, and prevent disease. With children, their family, and the doctor there is a special triangular relationship created to try to achieve these goals. The rationale for treatments, present and future, is that decisions should be in the interests of the child. Absolute agreement in decision-making between a doctor and parent or child may not be achievable or practical especially if it concerns value but there is an obligation to seek as much common ground as possible, and sometimes acknowledge those differences in a sincere, honest, and transparent way. In this section of the chapter, we will provide a brief overview of the ethical framework which underpins our decision making and practice. Following this, we will consider some specific scenarios that cause ethical dilemmas for paediatric anaesthetists.

Teaching in medical ethics is introduced early in the modern medical curriculum, emphasizing how fundamentally important it is to apply moral thinking and basic ethical principles to decision making at the very start of training to be a doctor. The four underlying ethical principles which patients have a right to expect in their relationship with a doctor are maleficence (do not harm), beneficence (do good), justice, and respect for autonomy (Beauchamp and Childress 2001; Hope et al. 2008). The final principle, the respect for autonomy, is probably the commonest ethical principle that has a practical application for a paediatric anaesthetist on a daily basis because it underpins consent. Autonomy describes the rights of the individual parent or patient to process, rationalize, and express their views during decision-making for treatment plans, without coercion. The process of consent attracts considerable interest in paediatric practice, because there are many patients who do not have the capacity to take part in decision-making. Because society views most family relationships to have inherent value, the parents have the right to give consent and make decisions for their children. The doctor and the parents are advocates for the child, and have a duty to act in their best interests. Increasingly, and correctly in our view, there is a growing recognition that these rights are accrued gradually by children, rather than the all-or-nothing situation with adults. Children and young people often understand more than we think they do, and 4- and 5-year-olds can express meaningful views on their care if age-appropriate techniques are used (Curtis et al. 2004).

Children can often be in a more fearful state if they are excluded from decision-making. These rights have a legislative framework within United Nations Convention on the Rights of the Child and the Council of Europe, both of which strongly emphasize that children should be listened to (Lansdown and Karkara 2006) and their views considered when decisions are made about them in all areas of their lives. The concerns children have need to be taken seriously and their right to self-determination under the age of 18 years needs to be evaluated based on their maturity rather than the arbitrary age definitions within the law. The interests of an individual child must be considered in their own right, but also as part of a family and community. There is a growing recognition that children can effectively contribute to health policy giving reasoned, articulate, and informed recommendations when consulted (Department of Health 2002; Lansdown and Karkara 2006). They need to be given the opportunity to take responsibility for their lives and health, and adults need to appreciate the benefits that come from direct engagement with children and young people on these important issues, and how it enhances society, and advances our understanding and development.

As doctors who work with children, we also have a duty to consider the overall welfare of the child, and intervene swiftly if there is a suspicion of abuse. This issue will be dealt with later in this chapter under safeguarding.

Consent

For any procedure to go ahead, consent must be obtained, and the first hurdle to cross in paediatric practice is establishing who has parental responsibility if the child is not competent to give consent (Hope 2008). The decision is taken by a competent adult, usually the parent or guardian of the child, who has a duty to act reasonably, and make that decision in the best interests of the child. For most minor patients there will be a gradual maturity and ability to understand and interpret complex issues as we have discussed before. Even if a child does not have the maturity to make a fully competent decision they should be involved as much as possible in the decision-making process even if they do not have the final say, or sign the form. Children can become fearful and un-cooperative if they are excluded from the decision-making process. It is part of a doctor's role in caring for children to help them make good decisions and support their fledgling attempts to contribute to them, however small that contribution is. The legal implications around consent will be considered in detail later in the chapter.

Refusal of consent

The way in which we deal with refusal by a patient under the age of 18 years is interesting, and is probably a good example of where the law takes precedence over the ethical principles involved. It would seem logical that if a minor was assessed to be competent to make decisions they should be able to refuse them, even if we do not agree with them. This is how we treat competent adults where, although decision making may be seen as ill informed or illogical, the ultimate right to self-determination is paramount. However, in the case of young people, even if decision making is thought to be competent, the law heavily favours treatment to avoid serious harm. Within our society, it would seem that the assent of the medical profession or the parents, or both of these, outweighs the dissent of the minor patient. Alternatively, it could be considered as a situation of competing rights: of the minor, doctor, parents, and sometimes even society. It is an anomaly ethically that is understandable, but an anomaly no less. It may be a remnant of paternalism in our practice where we are not able to rationalize or bear the thought that a child may choose not to do something that we think is in their best interests, particularly a decision which may have devastating or fatal consequences. We have taken the view with other potentially vulnerable groups in the past, such as mentally ill patients or pregnant women, where the law has strongly ruled to treat when doctors have brought refusal of consent cases to the court. In the present day, it would be hard to argue that pregnant women are not competent to refuse treatment, and even harder to argue it on ethical grounds, so perhaps in the future there will be a change in the way cases of refusal of treatment by a competent minor are handled by the courts. It is also at odds with the age of criminal responsibility that is less than 18 years, where a minor in this case may be found responsible for a crime, but have no accompanying rights. As in all cases of dispute, it is important to explore the reasons for that dispute and seek advice. Societies across the world almost universally recognize the age of adulthood as 18 years. In general, there is an underestimation of how much a young person approaching adulthood can be involved with decision-making. It would be of huge benefit to empower this group of often poorly represented young people if the legislation improved (Aynsley-Green et al. 2000).

Refusal of parental consent

This fortunately does not happen often, but an example of this area of contention where an anaesthetist may be involved has been the refusal of blood transfusions by Jehovah's Witness parents. While there needs to be a respect for the autonomy of parents, and tolerance of religious beliefs, the overwhelming consideration is to act in the best interests of the child. It could be argued that if a blood transfusion is necessary to save the life of the child, there is a moral obligation to give that transfusion. The doctor may have to justify not giving the blood transfusion if the child died or came to serious harm. All efforts should be made to explore the issue beforehand with the parents if time allows, or to discuss the decision-making afterwards, but ultimately this type of case can end in the courtroom. In the United Kingdom, most cases of this type have ruled to give the blood transfusion, but not in other jurisdictions.

Confidentiality

The relationship between a doctor and a patient is unique, and the fact that the information divulged during each consultation is confidential is at the heart of the doctor–patient relationship. Even though the patient is a child the same rules apply, and if the child is considered competent, as described previously, then the doctor has a duty to maintain the confidentiality of the competent minor even if a parent demands to know the content of a consultation. There are notable exceptions to this, for example, if a crime is being committed, where the doctor has a duty to pass on the information.

Unavailability of parents

If a child has not reached competence to consent, authorization is needed by the parent or legal guardian before a procedure being carried out. In exceptional circumstances, the local authority may be the legal guardian. Consent in this situation may be obtained over a telephone, with a witness recording the call. It is quite common with the high number of day-case procedures in paediatric practice for the child to be accompanied by someone other than the parent and it is important to establish who the adults are accompanying the child at the beginning of an anaesthetic consultation. If the child requires an emergency procedure in the absence of a parent, the anaesthetist has a duty to provide emergency treatment that is in the child's interests until the parents are located.

Under-age mother

It is not unknown for the mother of a baby to be under the age of 16 years. In those circumstances, there is a need, similar to the previous discussion of patients under the age of 16 years, to establish whether the mother is competent to give consent. There is a general acceptance that close family members, particularly the maternal grandparents, would be present during discussions about treatment plans, but this can be fraught with problems and conflict between family members, and potentially a young father of the baby. It is advised to seek legal advice to establish who has parental responsibility in these circumstances.

Ethical dilemmas for the paediatric anaesthetist

The child refuses

Over the years, there have been changes in the behaviour and expectation of the public. A generation ago, it may have been uncommon to have a child refuse to have a procedure performed in hospital if it was requested by a doctor or a parent, but in modern practice, this situation is increasing. It is distressing for all involved. There may have been an expectation that a child would automatically respond to an adult giving a command such as 'lie down' without any questions or dissent. In the few cases where this did not suffice, physical restraint may have been used to achieve the end-point of a successful induction of anaesthesia. It is difficult to justify any role for the anaesthetist using physical restraint if you consider the previous narrative of the growing recognition and acceptance of the rights of the child, and it could be viewed as assault. The anaesthetist may even be asked by a parent to use restraint, but the duty of care is to the child. There is no duty of care to the parents, only an obligation to listen and consider their wishes. Investigating and exploring why the child is refusing to have the procedure serve the interests of the child. These reasons will be wide, and range from deep-rooted fear to triviality. It must always be balanced against how urgent the procedure really is but few will fall into the emergency category. It is important, together with the surgeon, to discuss with the child the consequences of not having the surgery, which will vary, depending on the age and understanding of the child. In all situations such as this, there will be multifactorial reasons for the refusal and the dynamics between the child and parents/guardians will be central to finding a solution. Communicating with the child and the parents with insight and compassion is central, with forward planning strategies to try to prevent this happening again in the future.

Non-therapeutic interventions

This can be a difficult area for paediatric anaesthetists. Children will be scheduled, from time to time, for a procedure that may have limited therapeutic value to them, or appear unnecessary. Examples could include male circumcision, or cosmetic procedures such as correction of prominent ears. There may be very good social, cultural, or religious reasons for these procedures to convey benefit but they need to be balanced against the potential harm to the child from having the procedure carried out. It can be difficult ethically to justify such procedures. The rights of the child are paramount, and the concept behind the parents providing consent by proxy is that they protect those rights, by acting in their child's best interests. The argument that the child is not likely to be harmed by the procedure so making it acceptable is limited. However, this is usually not a type of practice the anaesthetist can tackle alone, or single out a family as an example, but rather raises the issue in a multidisciplinary forum presenting all sides of the conundrum, trying to change practice through consensus within the constitution. Society values parental views and often favours preserving family relationships, giving parents a unique role in evaluating what is best for their child.

Children in research

There would be little controversy in saying that research in children is very important, and helps us understand the difference between them and adults, progresses our understanding of how to focus treatment for disease with drugs or other interventions, and prevents poor health in the future. As children are more vulnerable, and the potential for causing pain and distress higher, the research question must be expected to lead to a significant benefit in their health. There has been a paucity of good quality clinical research in children in the recent decade compared with adults because of these difficulties, in addition to issues of consent. It may be easier to obtain consent if the research is likely to convey a benefit to the child in question, but it is obviously important for the researcher to make sure that clear information is presented to the parents, and in some cases the child, to convey the risks and benefits before obtaining consent. Despite all the obstacles, it is important to take all possible opportunities to carry out objective high-quality clinical research in children that ultimately may benefit future generations.

Prematurity and surgery

The consequences of extreme prematurity (22–27 weeks of gestation) have been extensively investigated, and neurological impairment is strongly associated with gestational age, with greater impairment being associated with decreasing gestational age. The pivotal age where a higher proportion of babies can survive without significant disability appears to be between 24 and 25 weeks (Moore et al. 2012). These small babies can present for procedures and the anaesthesia and operation may carry substantial risks. It is extremely important that the anaesthetist is involved with the planning of the case and the discussion of those risks with the parents together with the surgeon, neonatologist, and other members of the multidisciplinary team rather than be presented with the patient on the emergency board.

Anaesthetists are responsible for their own judgement and practice and their central role of being the patient's advocate during surgery makes their contribution invaluable. If they feel a procedure carries too large a burden or risk they must voice their concerns.

Children with 'do not attempt resuscitation' or treatment-limitation orders

The number of children with complex or chronic conditions who have a treatment limitation order or a do not attempt resuscitation order being scheduled for procedures under anaesthesia is increasing in number. The child may have multiple medical problems and be considered at high risk of harm from the anaesthesia or the procedure itself. It is important to balance these risks against the perceived benefits to the child of proceeding with the operation. It may be a quality of life issue, or the likely benefits may be equivocal; but how a life is valued is in itself a value judgement, and the doctor's view may not be the same as that of a parent. In a situation such as this, the parents are very likely to have a strong view that should be seriously considered. If there is a reasonable possibility that the child may suffer a life-threatening event under anaesthesia, this must be explained and discussed with the parents beforehand. However, having a treatment limitation order and a procedure are ethically compatible with continuing, as long as the benefit expected from the procedure is thought to outweigh the burden of that treatment. It is perfectly defendable ethically to provide anaesthesia to place a feeding tube if that was the only means to provide nutrition. The parents' understanding of the treatment limitation order may be completely different from the doctor's expectation and this must be fully explored and documented before the procedure. An order such as this does not override clinical discretion and judgement, and they may not be followed if the child suffers a cardiac or respiratory arrest from a reversible cause, such as a blocked tracheal tube.

Parental presence

There has been a metamorphosis in practice over the years in the United Kingdom in the attitude to a parental presence at the induction of anaesthesia and it is now common to have the parents present with the child at this time, and then in the recovery area when the child wakes up after the procedure. It is beneficial to most children to have their parents present at these moments. There is more controversy around whether parents have a right to be present during an emergency, such as a cardiac arrest. It is difficult to argue that their presence has an ethical basis as they convey no tangible benefit to the child by being there, but parents may argue that it is their right as a parent to be present at such a crucial life-or-death moment. There is no correct or incorrect solution to this high-tension scenario but if it is thought to be beneficial for the parents to witness such a scene, it is important that a member of staff can be devoted to them to try to communicate what is happening at such a distressing time. While it is preferable not to get into conflict with parents at this time, if the team leader felt that the parents' presence was hampering the ability of the team to give the best possible treatment to the child, she or he should be able to take the final decision.

End of life care

Paediatric anaesthetists in many departments play an important role in contributing to end of life, or palliative, care providing expertise in the pharmacological control of symptoms. This is an active approach to care from the decision being made for palliation until the end of a child's life. It is an attempt to enhance the quality of that life, empowering the child, and the family's ability to fulfil whatever plans they may have. We increasingly understand the importance of creating memories for the child and for the family of that child. It is crucial that a short life is valuable, and has meaning, even if it is tragically short (Hain 2015). We should not underestimate the importance of this process or the role an anaesthetist may have in helping achieve this.

Ethical dilemmas often occur in clinical practice, and they should be debated within teams, hospitals, and societies. How we deal with them defines us as individual doctors and people, and helps us to make better decisions and promote lifelong learning about our teams and ourselves.

Clinical Ethics Committees, which have been created in many large hospitals, have a growing role in helping clinical staff with difficult ethical questions. They promote transparent, honest, and inclusive decision-making. They can offer mediation where communication has become difficult between the doctor and the parents. They help examine why communication has broken down, offer practical and reasonable support, help define goals, reconcile entrenched views, and sometimes offer an alternative or second opinion. In times of conflict, support from an ethical team may make a favourable or tolerable outcome more likely for all concerned. Finally, listening to children and young people, and truly valuing what they say, is a fundamental human right. It enhances our understanding of each other, and provides an essential contribution to achieving good outcomes in our clinical practice.

Consent for children's anaesthesia

What is consent and why is it needed?

'Choice' has achieved high priority in our society. It appears that politicians believe that citizens' choices in education, transport structure, and healthcare provision must be constantly and publically acknowledged.

The necessity for 'choice' reflects the fundamental role of autonomy in our society; that is, the right of every citizen to influence their own destiny. In healthcare terms, this has two important consequences. First, that a patient must agree, in advance, to being physically touched before any intervention can ensue. Second, that a patient must agree, in advance, before any of the confidential information that they impart when dealing with their doctor can be further disclosed.

These two agreements can occur only after a formal conversation, disclosing information about the matter itself, its benefits, risks, and alternatives, has occurred. The patient (or person with parental responsibility) must have the mental capacity to engage in the conversation, and be able to make the appropriate decision. The final agreement, in both cases, is known as consent.

In the great majority of cases, it is consent for anaesthesia that is uppermost in the anaesthetist's mind, and rightly so. However, at this early stage, it should be noted that the rules of consent encompassing, as they do, capacity, correct disclosure, and appropriate recording, are equally applicable to both clinical interventions and to confidentiality. Consent is the legal key that makes both physical intervention and sharing of information lawful.

From this point in the text, the discussion will be of consent to clinical intervention ... but forget its application in confidentiality at your peril.

The standard of clinical management that patients receive is judged against several yardsticks:

The most straightforward of these is that clinicians should not touch patients without their consent. The need for consent for the otherwise unwanted touch is self-evident. Unwelcome attention from another person, who tries to touch you against your wishes, is repellent. There are times when such touches are unavoidable—packed like a sardine on the London Underground or jostling fellow shoppers (and their trolleys) in the Christmas Eve supermarket, there is little choice but to resign yourself to being touched.

However, in less frenetic circumstances, there is an absolute understanding that we are entitled to choose who touches us, and when. The patient who is lying on her hospital bed, when suddenly confronted with a surgeon who puts his hand on her abdomen, without first asking if he may do so, would justifiably complain that her treatment fell below the reasonable standard she was entitled to expect. Such behaviour is simple rudeness, irrespective of the legal context. However, the legal context is suddenly placed into stark relief when a patient complains that an intimate procedure (such as the insertion of a suppository while she was asleep) was performed without consent; and further still when such an examination was irrelevant to her clinical presentation.

These latter actions move the lack of consent into the arena of professional disciplinary regulation, civil litigation, and potentially criminal prosecution. The medical defence organizations' case reports are a testament to this frequent and devastating error of judgement.

A second standard that clinicians must attain is that they should supply the patient with enough information to make an informed decision as to whether they wish to undergo the proposed intervention. This is entirely separate from the need to ensure that patients are not subjected to an unwanted touch.

Doctors often fail to appreciate how little patients understand about the consequences of intervention. How many patients appreciate that epidural anaesthesia could result in urinary and faecal incontinence, or failure to move their legs? Or that misdirection of a subclavian needle may lead to a thoracotomy, to arrest the haemorrhage thus caused?

While training ensures that anaesthetists are acutely aware of these hazards, the patients are not. The process of consent, with disclosure of risks and side-effects, is designed to allow patients an insight into the risks that they and the anaesthetist jointly face.

It is very unusual for cases where patients claim that they were not provided with valid disclosure (and thus that their consent was invalid) to reach court. However, when this happens, English courts do not rely on expert witnesses to set the standard for what the appropriate disclosure should have been. This is in contradistinction to the great majority of clinical negligence cases, where a medical expert will be asked to set the standard of care (Bolam v Friern Barnet Hospital Management Committee 1957), against which the defendant doctor will be judged.

This gives an insight into the importance that the judiciary sets on disclosure for consent. They put themselves in the shoes of the 'reasonable' patient, and enquire what such a person would want to know, before giving consent in the particular set of clinical circumstances. This position was articulated in 1998, and remains the standard for disclosure of risk (Pearce v United Bristol Healthcare NHS Trust 1999) (a decision now confirmed by the Supreme Court in Montgomery v Lanarkshire Health Board (Scotland)[2015] UKSC 11). See 'What should be disclosed?'.

Treating children

From the legal perspective (in England, Wales, and Northern Ireland), a child is someone who has not yet reached 18 years of age. Legal synonyms include 'minor' and 'infant'. The latter is instructive, as it is derived from the Latin: *infans*, unable to speak. This reflects the legal rules that prevent children from speaking for themselves in court, although this impediment has been at least partly addressed over the last two decades. Nevertheless, it begs a fundamental question, as to whether children can provide their own consent, or whether they depend upon their parents to provide it for them.

People under 18 years can be considered in three broad groups:

Children under the age of 16 who lack capacity

This is the simplest group. Although presumed to lack capacity, some will be able to demonstrate their competence to provide independent consent for treatment (see later).

For those who cannot, a person with parental responsibility has the right to provide consent where necessary. The child's mother (the woman who gave birth to the baby, rather than the person who provided the egg from which he or she was conceived, if different) has parental responsibility automatically. The child's father gains parental responsibility automatically if married at the time of the birth registration, or if the parents marry subsequent to the birth. Since 2003, unmarried fathers also gain parental responsibility automatically when they register the birth. Alternatively, parental responsibility can be acquired by the unmarried father, either with the agreement of the child's mother, or by application to a court.

Parental responsibility is passed to adoptive parents on legal adoption. It may be shared with guardians appointed by parents or with local authorities, and is linked to various legal orders (Bainham and Gilmore 2013).

The person with parental responsibility who provides consent for a child's treatment must act in the child's best interests in so doing. These are usually self-evident, and the agreement between parents and clinician is reached after full disclosure of the relevant information.

This agreement is not invariable. In a case concerning a child with biliary atresia [Re T (Wardship: Medical Treatment) 1997], the clinicians wished to perform a liver transplant, and considered the prospects of success to be good. The parents refused their consent, on the grounds that the surgery was not in the child's best interests. The Court of Appeal held that the assessment of the child's best interests went wider than the narrower medical best interests, and that T's connection with his family held great weight in this regard. Accordingly, the court refused to enforce the hospital's request that the mother would bring T in for surgery. The judgement could be criticized, in failing to differentiate between the interests of the child and those of his mother. However, the case provides an example of the balancing act performed by courts.

Children under 16 who can demonstrate their capacity

Depending on their maturity and the intervention that is proposed, children from a young age may be able to provide independent consent. A 4-year-old may be able to consent to a blood pressure measurement; a 6-year-old to a venepuncture; and a 10-year-old to an anaesthetic for the treatment of an early stage appendicitis. No one is suggesting that the parents should be excluded from this process: such an exclusion would be quite wrong. It is for the family as a whole to decide what part the child's potential capacity should play in the consenting process. However, the involvement of children in this process will strengthen the therapeutic relationship, and is to be encouraged.

A child's previous experience is of great importance. It is submitted that after the very recent diagnosis of leukaemia, a 15-year-old, who has been healthy up to this point, may be so horrified by the dissolution of his comfortable and well-organized life as to be incoherent, entirely incapable of consenting for the anaesthetic necessary to insert a tunnelled central venous catheter. Contrast this child with a 10-year-old on the same ward, suffering relapsed leukaemia. He has already undergone three line insertions and two removals. He knows (effectively) everything there is to know about the anaesthetic for central venous catheter placement. Now facing his fourth insertion, he will very likely be competent to provide independent consent.

Therefore, it is important objectively to determine whether a child of 15 years or younger has capacity to provide independent consent for the proposed intervention.

For this assessment, the Gillick test is used, derived from a landmark case where it was established that a child with capacity to provide consent should be allowed to do so, independently of her parents. The test requires that the child has sufficient understanding and intelligence to enable them to understand fully what is involved in a proposed intervention (Gillick v West Norfolk & Wisbech AHA 1986). Thus, if a child can understand:

- that a choice exists
- the nature and purpose of the procedure
- the risks and side-effects
- the alternatives to the procedure

... and is able to:

- retain the information long enough
- weigh the information
- arrive at a decision
- be free from undue pressure

then she would be deemed competent for the proposed intervention. It will be seen that competence rests on intelligence, maturity and experience—and not on age.

During the Gillick case, an additional set of guidelines were suggested by Lord Fraser, specifically for doctors who assist with reproductive decision-making by children under 16. It should be noted that these do not replace the Gillick test, nor are they synonymous with it (Wheeler 2006).

Gillick provides a high threshold for consent, consistent with public policy. It would be highly undesirable to allow incompetent children to provide consent for interventions that they could not fully understand. The fact that a child has to 'prove' their competence places a barrier to children that is never experienced by adults, whose capacity is presumed. One can only speculate how many adults would 'pass' the test in the Gillick case.

The Gillick-competent child does not enjoy an equal right to refuse treatment. Only those cases in which the refusal of life-saving treatments in these children is at issue have reached the court. However, given this opportunity, courts have resolutely denied the (otherwise) competent minor the right to choose death. A 15-year-old girl [Re M (Medical Treatment: Consent) 1999] refusing her consent for a life-saving heart transplant had her refusal overridden by the courts. M's reason was that she 'would rather die than have the transplant and have someone else's heart ... I would feel different with someone else's heart ... that's a good enough reason not to have a heart transplant, even if it saved my life.'

The court authorized the operation, as being in her best interests.

In another case [Re L (Medical Treatment: Gillick Competency) 1998], a 14-year-old girl with serious scalding required a blood transfusion. She was a Jehovah's Witness, and refused the treatment. The court found that even if she had been Gillick competent, her grave condition would have led the court to authorize the transfusion. As it was, the girl was unaware of the manner of death from anaemia, and was basing her views of on those of her congregation, rather than on her own experiences. For these reasons, she was judged incompetent to make this decision for herself.

It is crucial to remember that the vast majority of Gillick-competent children who refuse treatment are refusing relatively trivial procedures. You would be entitled to rely upon their parents' consent if necessary, but it is a matter for clinical judgement whether the procedure could be deferred, to allow the child further time to consider, and be reconciled with what is likely to be an inevitable outcome. The problem of refusal in Gillick-competent children is dealt with in the same way as for the 16- and 17-year-age group, in the following section.

People of 16 and 17 years of age

People of 16 and 17 years of age are presumed to have the capacity to provide consent for anaesthesia. This was made possible by a law enacted in 1969 (Family Law Reform Act 1969), which recognized that the decisions that teenagers were taking, irrespective of the law, contrasted sharply with the age of majority at the time (21 years). The new law reduced the age of majority to 18 years, and introduced the presumption of capacity for 16- and 17-year-olds.

What the new law did not do was extend this right to consent for research, or interventions that do not potentially provide a direct health benefit to the individual concerned. However, if competent along 'Gillick' lines, a young person may be able to provide consent for these activities.

Young people of 16 and 17 years are thus able to provide consent for treatment in the absence of their parents. However, the parental right to provide consent for treatment lasts until the end of childhood. This has the effect of providing a 'safety net'; allowing a 16/17-year-old the opportunity of consent for herself; or deferring to her parents, if she sees fit. Once the child reaches adulthood on her 18th birthday, her parents' right disappears. For the rest of her life, she alone can provide consent: directly, in person, or in some circumstances, by a proxy method. If parents and a child of this age disagree, it is wise to exercise caution.

If a 16/17-year-old wishes to exercise his right to consent, and his parents oppose the decision, then you would be entitled to rely on this consent. However, it would be important to understand the basis for their disagreement. For instance, if you suspected that the young person was not competent, you should challenge the presumption. This can simply be done by establishing whether he understands the relevant information; can retain the information, believe it, weigh it up, and communicate his decision. If he can, then he has capacity. However, it is still wise to tease out where the problem lies, as this is a most unusual situation, and it would be in the young person's best interests to resolve the issue before anaesthesia, if that is feasible.

The problem, reversed, is of a young person who refuses treatment, but who is accompanied by a parent who provides consent. Valid parental consent will make the procedure 'legal', but as with the situation of consent withdrawal, you will have to make a clinical judgement as to whether proceeding with the treatment against the young person's wishes is both practicable, and in their best interests. In summary, it is recommended that an elective procedure should be abandoned until the dispute is resolved.

A withdrawal of consent

A child with capacity (or a person providing consent on behalf of a child) may withdraw consent at any stage (Department of Health 2009). In practical terms, the withdrawal needs to be made without ambiguity. What happens next is largely dependent on whether the patient is about to undergo general anaesthesia, or a procedure under local blockade; in paediatric practice, the former situation is the most likely (Nair et al. 2012).

Withdrawal of consent is seen in starkest relief when it occurs in the anaesthetic room, before a general anaesthetic is administered.

For elective surgery, if a competent child indicates that they have changed their mind, the clinical situation must be reviewed. He or she should be moved out of the anaesthetic room, and taken to a quiet location in the theatre complex. Here, their capacity can be assessed. It should be noted that a child who was competent to consent for surgery may have been rendered incompetent by premedication. However, if they still have capacity, and despite being aware of the consequences of not receiving the intervention still refuse to proceed, the withdrawal must be honoured, and the procedure cancelled. Alternatives to the original procedure could be offered; perhaps a lesser procedure or conservative management may be agreed upon. In children *whose parents* withdraw consent in the anaesthetic room, the procedure should be cancelled and completely re-discussed, unless a simple misunderstanding is identified which can be rapidly rectified.

If an emergency procedure is required within the next few minutes to save a child's life or limb, or prevent irremediable harm, the best interests of the child will overcome the child's (or their parents') lack of consent, and the procedure should be performed on the basis of necessity, without consent. In the situation where there is no choice but to provide an anaesthetic and start surgery, then reluctantly, it may be necessary to restrain the child or the parents, and proceed. This is an experience that few paediatric anaesthetists will have to endure. It should be noted that in reality, the amount of resistance that a child of any age puts up is usually inversely proportional to their malaise and discomfort. In the gravely ill, refusal is rare.

There are those who are gravely ill, but need urgent rather than emergency treatment. If a 16/17-year-old in this category refuses treatment for the preservation of their life, such as the transfusion of blood [Re P (Medical Treatment: Best Interests) 2004], or feeding [Re W (A Minor) (Medical Treatment: Court's Jurisdiction) 1992] (in anorexia), courts invariably choose to override the child's autonomy, and provide an order which allows lawful provision of the treatment against the child's wishes. This either upholds the parental wishes for treatment, or overrides parental refusal. These cases are rare, but the timescale within which the decision needs to be made usually allows sufficient time for the court to be contacted, providing the anaesthetist with the necessary authority to proceed.

What should be disclosed, and by whom?

Judges now feel able to put themselves in the position of claimant patients, asking themselves whether, in the circumstances of the case, they would regard the disclosure as adequate. The courts do not feel the need to ask an expert doctor's view on this matter. They consider themselves, as reasoning citizens, amply equipped to set the standard. Thus, the stage is set for the 'reasonable patient'. This patient is a fictional creation of the court, imbued with all of the characteristics of the claimant patient, but whose sense of reasonableness is provided by the court:

> If there is a significant risk which would affect the judgement of a reasonable patient, then in the normal course it is the responsibility of a doctor to inform the patient of that significant risk, if the information is needed so that the patient can determine … what course he or she should adopt. (Pearce v United Bristol Healthcare NHS Trust 1999)

This leaves open to question what a 'significant risk' entails. However, if you apply your personal criteria to the phrase, you are likely to consider that some of the unintended harms that flow from anaesthesia could be construed as 'significant'. The great difficulty is that there exists a gap between what you, as an experienced clinician, and what an average patient might foresee as the result of an anaesthetic complication.

As previously noted, how many citizens, whom you might encounter walking down your local high street, will be aware of the risks of epidural techniques, or central venous access?

To address this imbalance created by the doctor's professional knowledge, the General Medical Council makes it clear that the duty to disclose is onerous:

> You must tell patients if an investigation or treatment might result in a serious adverse outcome, even if the likelihood is very small. (General Medical Council 2008)

The risk may be tiny, but of great importance when deciding whether or not to have anaesthesia and surgery, which may be elective.

Statistics are a valuable form of description when articulating risk to patients. In one case, the court confirmed the importance of comparative statistics when describing alternative procedures that a patient might want to consider in deciding which intervention to which they should consent. Faced with a choice between a catheter cerebral angiography and an MR angiogram, the patient was not informed of the comparative risks of stroke (Birch v University College London Hospital NHSFT 2008). The court held that the patient, as a result, could not provide properly informed consent.

However, although risk needs to be articulated, is there a numeric risk threshold; how common does a risk have to be before we disclose it to the patient (Wheeler 2012)?

The concept of a numeric threshold for disclosing risk is outdated from the legal point of view. There is no reference whatsoever to a threshold either from the General Medical Council (2008) or the Department of Health (2009) other than to give information about all significant adverse outcomes. It is submitted that doctors should follow the lead of the courts, because the formula from the General Medical Council that identifies what needs to be disclosed has been provided for our use. It is better because it provides an assurance that patients will not be 'ambushed' by a serious complication which the doctor could foresee, but of which the patient remained oblivious until it was too late for her to avoid it.

As it is very clear that every significant risk should be disclosed, there is no doubt that the person best placed to disclose is a person who is familiar with the procedure, as he or she has performed it many times. Some anaesthetists prefer to delegate this duty to trainees. It is recommended that the consent for anaesthesia, and the disclosure that makes it valid, should be taken by the person who is about to perform, or at least who is capable of performing, the anaesthetic.

Declaration of interest

None declared.

References

Association of Paediatric Anaesthetists of Great Britain and Ireland. *Safeguarding Training*. London: APAGBI. Available from http://www.apagbi.org.uk/professionals/education-and-training/safeguarding-training

Aynsley-Green A, Barker M, Burr S, *et al.* Who is speaking for children and adolescents and for their health at policy level? *BMJ* 2000; **321**: 229–32

Bainham A, Gilmore S. *Children: The Modern Law*, 4th edn. Bristol: Jordan Publishing, 2013

Beauchamp TL, Childress JF. *Principles of Biomedical Ethics*, 5th Edn. New York: Oxford University Press, 2001

Birch *v* University College London Hospital NHSFT [2008] EWHC 2237

Bolam *v* Friern Barnet Hospital Management Committee [1957] WLR 582

Children Act 1989. HM Government. Available from http://bit.ly/1QoOeXt

Children Act 2004. HM Government. Available from http://bit.ly/1BHbKqo

Curtis K, Liabo K, Roberts H, Barker M. Consulted but not heard: a qualitative study of young people's views on their local health service. *Health Expect* 2004; **7**: 149–56

Department for Education. *Characteristics of Children in Need in England 2010–11*. 2011a. Available from http://bit.ly/1Gk69PD

Department for Education. *The Munro Review of Child Protection*. 2011b. Available from http://bit.ly/1SVucI5

Department for Education. *Working Together to Safeguard Children: A Guide to Inter-Agency Working to Safeguard and Promote the Welfare of Children*. 2015. Available from http://www.gov.uk/government/publications/working-together-to-safeguard-children--2

Department for Education and Skills. *Every Child Matters: Change for Children*. 2004. Available from http://bit.ly/1FT8oGj

Department of Health. *Listening, Hearing and Responding*. London: Department of Health, 2002

Department of Health. *Reference Guide to Consent for Examination or Treatment*, 2nd Edn. London: Department of Health, 2009

Department of Health. *The Victoria Climbié Inquiry*. 2003. Available from http://bit.ly/1ANlVjo

Family Law Reform Act 1969 s8. HM Government. Available from http://www.legislation.gov.uk/ukpga/1969/46/contents

General Medical Council. *Consent: Patients and Doctors Making Decisions Together*. 2008. Available from http://www.gmc-uk.org/guidance/ethical_guidance/consent_guidance_contents.asp

General Medical Council. *Confidentiality—Guidance for Doctors*. London: General Medical Council, 2009. Available from http://bit.ly/1cxf5Dd

General Medical Council. *Protecting Children and Young People: The Responsibilities of All Doctors*. London: General Medical Council, 2012. Available from http://bit.ly/1qnMces

Gillick v West Norfolk & Wisbech AHA [1986] AC 112

Hain R. Teddy Houlston's short life tells us so much about what it is to be human. *The Guardian*, 26 April 2015. Available from http://bit.ly/1GZeBCG

Hope T, Savulescu J, Hendrick J. *Medical Ethics and Law: The Core Curriculum*, 2nd Edn. Edinburgh: Churchill Livingstone, 2008

Lansdown G, Karkara R. Children's right to express views and have them taken seriously. *Lancet* 2006; **367**: 690–2

Maguire S. Which injuries may indicate child abuse? *Arch Dis Child Educ Pract Ed* 2010; **95**: 170–7

Moore T, Hennessy EM, Myles J, *et al.* Neurological and developmental outcome in extremely preterm children born in England in 1995 and 2006: the EPICure studies. *BMJ* 2012; **68**: 274–5

Nair R, Holroyd DJ. *Handbook of Surgical Consent*. Oxford: Oxford University Press, 2012

National Institute for Health and Care Excellence. *Child Maltreatment: When to Suspect Maltreatment in Under 18s*. Clinical Guideline 89. London: NICE, 2009. Available from http://bit.ly/1og8FHB

National Society for the Prevention of Cruelty to Children. Available from http://bit.ly/1KDfn7g

Pearce v United Bristol Healthcare NHS Trust [1999] 48 BMLR 118

Re L (Medical Treatment: Gillick Competency) [1998] 2 FLR 810

Re M (Medical Treatment: Consent) [1999] 2 FLR 1097

Re P (Medical Treatment: Best Interests) [2004] 2 All ER 1117

Re T (Wardship: Medical Treatment) [1997] FLR 502

Re W (A Minor) (Medical Treatment: Court's Jurisdiction) [1992] 3 WLR 758

Royal College of Anaesthetists, Association of Paediatric Anaesthetists of Great Britain and Ireland. *Lead Anaesthetist for Child Protection/Safeguarding*. 2010. Available from http://bit.ly/1JpC4gx

Royal College of Anaesthetists. *Child Protection and the Anaesthetist. Safeguarding Children in the Operating Theatre*. 2014. Available from http://bit.ly/1M4g3mF

Royal College of Paediatrics and Child Health. *Child Protection Reader*. 2007. Available from http://bit.ly/1FsVXgS

Royal College of Paediatrics and Child Health. *Safeguarding Children and Young People: Roles and Competencies for Health Care Staff*, 3rd Edn. London: Royal College of Paediatrics and Child Health, 2014. Available from http://bit.ly/1qnLtKx

Wheeler RA. Gillick or Fraser? A plea for consistency over competence in children. *BMJ* 2006; **332**: 807

Wheeler RA. The numeric threshold for the disclosure of risk. *Ann R Coll Surg Engl* 2012; **94**: 81–2

PART 11

The conduct of anaesthesia outside the operating theatre

Peter F. Mahoney and Michel M. R. F. Struys

CHAPTER 76

Pre-hospital care for the anaesthetist

Nicholas Crombie, G. Boukes Eindhoven, and Bert Dercksen

Pre-hospital care

History of pre-hospital care

Care of casualties at the scene of injury has been recognized for thousands of years. In the New Testament, the story of the Good Samaritan tells of a passer-by finding a beaten and injured stranger on the road:

> A man was going down from Jerusalem to Jericho, when he was attacked by robbers. They stripped him of his clothes, beat him and went away, leaving him half dead. ... A Samaritan, as he travelled, came where the man was; and when he saw him, he took pity on him. He went to him and bandaged his wounds, pouring on oil and wine. Then he put the man on his own donkey, brought him to an inn and took care of him.[1] (Luke 10: 30–34, New International Version)

This example illustrates care of a casualty at the scene with subsequent use of transport to convey the casualty to a place where further resources, assistance, and shelter are available. This early tale has had a profound effect on pre-hospital care, with the phrase 'Good Samaritan' still in widespread use today.

During the intervening years, many advances in care of the casualty have been documented, often during times of war. In 1792, Dominique-Jean Larrey was appointed Surgeon Major of the French army and during the sacking of the city of Spire noted that:

> The wounded were left on the field, until after the engagement, and were then collected at a convenient spot, to which the ambulances speeded as soon as possible; but the number of wagons interposed between them and the Army, and many other difficulties so retarded their progress that they never arrived in less than 24 or 36 hours, so that most of the wounded died for want of assistance. (Larrey 1814, pp. 27–28)

Over the following years, he developed a horse-drawn ambulance service which was staffed with dedicated officers. There was great detail provided regarding equipment, uniform, and staffing, as well as regarding the ambulances themselves:

> The frame ... resembled an elongated cube, curved on the top: it had two small windows on each side, a folding door opened before and behind. The floor of the body was moveable; and on it were placed a hair mattress, and a bolster of the same, covered with leather. This floor moved easily on the sides of the body by means of four small rollers; on the sides were four iron handles through which the sashes of the soldiers were passed, while putting the wounded on the sliding floor. These sashes served instead of litters for carrying the wounded; they were dressed on these floors when the weather did not permit them to be dressed on the ground. (Larrey 1814, p. 81)

The next real advance in care came with the introduction of the modern vehicle. Motorized ambulances had taken the place of the horse-drawn carriage around 1900, but little else had changed. Captain G.H.R. Gosman, Medical Corps, United States Army, was undoubtedly the first to point out in 1910 the great possibilities of aeroplanes to transport patients. The Department of War denied his plea for funding his plans. In 1912, a French surgeon, Emile Raymond, suggested using biplanes to spot casualties on the field during World War I. The use of a hot air balloon for casualty evacuation was investigated the following year by Gautier. During the Korean War in the 1950s, helicopters were used to evacuate injured soldiers from the battlefield to military field hospitals, and in spite of few significant advances in medicine since the conclusion of World War II, the death rate of injured personnel fell from 4.5% to 2.5% (Edwards et al. 2010). Efforts were made to further improve this statistic during the Vietnam War with the inclusion of a trained medic on board the helicopter providing fluids, haemorrhage control, and basic airway management.

At the same time, civilian ambulances were beginning to move from a transportation to a treat and transport model with the introduction of defibrillators and pharmaceuticals (Briggs et al. 1976). In 1991, the 'chain of survival' was introduced by Cummins et al. (1991). The concept of the life support chain implies early recognition and call for help (early access), early Basic Life Support by laymen, early defibrillation, and early initiation of advanced care and treatment. In this concept, the importance of an early (pre-hospital) start of life-saving measurements was emphasized.

Current pre-hospital care

Modern pre-hospital care in Europe is now being delivered by a variety of state, private, charitable, and voluntary providers. The organization of pre-hospital care is diverse and depends on national or regional requirements and regulations. In the United Kingdom, the vast majority of cases are dealt with by the National Health Service ambulance trusts through emergency and urgent care pathways. Through a combination of rapid-response vehicles and ambulances, delivery of a level of pre-hospital care is provided

[1] Scripture taken from the Holy Bible, NEW INTERNATIONAL VERSION®, NIV® Copyright © 1973, 1978, 1984, 2011 by Biblica, Inc.® Used by permission.

to the entire population. In most European countries, a two-tier model is in use. Basic pre-hospital medical care is provided by emergency medical technicians (EMTs) or paramedics. If advanced care such as sedation, anaesthesia, surgery, or special paediatric care is required, emergency medical services physicians may be assigned. In the Netherlands and some other European countries, specialized registered nurses may be involved in providing some levels of this advanced care.

Across Europe and many other areas of the world, helicopter emergency medical services (HEMS) offer varying levels of pre-hospital emergency medical coverage. These services may be paramedic- or doctor-led models of care. The cost-effectiveness of helicopter-based delivery of pre-hospital care has been frequently questioned (Taylor et al. 2010). Much evidence, however, is based upon historical and North American models which differ from European operations in terms of crewing and funding. Current operations with advanced paramedics and pre-hospital specialist doctors who possess significant experience in trauma and pre-hospital medicine can deliver targeted evidence-based care followed by rapid transport to the most appropriate hospital (Biewener et al. 2004). By way of example, an air ambulance crew dispatched to a patient with chest pain in a rural area may diagnose a myocardial infarction and transfer that patient directly to a hospital offering percutaneous coronary intervention overflying several hospitals where this service is not available. This service may therefore decrease the time from symptoms to definitive intervention by several hours.

Until recently, pre-hospital emergency medicine has been limited to enthusiastic doctors drawn from all specialities but predominantly from anaesthesia, surgery, emergency medicine, and general practice. In Europe, formal training, education, or assessment differs, resulting in a wide variation in knowledge and skills with subsequent uncertainty by paramedic staff about what level of support may be available (Hyde et al. 2012). One of the biggest variations between existing practitioners is the provision of advanced sedation and anaesthesia—this is currently restricted to anaesthetists and some experienced emergency medicine physicians with training in the pre-hospital environment. In some countries, pre-hospital training has become a recognized sub-speciality and a formal curriculum and assessment programme has been developed which is now establishing a standard of advanced practitioner operating within a firm national framework.

Principles

The role of pre-hospital care has evolved with time. Until recent decades, the initial focus of care was to remove the casualty from the scene of injury with rapid transfer to medical care ('scoop and run') with minimal interventions at scene or en route to hospital. As the understanding of trauma pathophysiology grew, more emphasis was placed upon the delivery of immediate medical care before and during transfer. At the same time, pre-hospital services developed and more equipment became available, resulting in scene times lengthening as efforts were made to treat casualties at the site of the incident (Birk and Henriksen 2002). Over time it became clear that the pendulum might have swung too far in the direction of treatment at scene ('stay and play') when often casualties were developing coagulopathy, hypothermia, and being denied definitive care by prolonged times in the pre-hospital phase. This point was brought into the public arena during the enquiry into the death of Diana, Princess of Wales on 31 August 1997. During the investigation it emerged that more than 1.5 hours elapsed between the emergency services arriving at the incident and the Princess' arrival at the Pitié-Salpétrière Hospital (Metropolitan Police 2006). This comprised treatment for 57 min on scene and 40 min in the ambulance, despite the distance between the accident site within the Alma tunnel and the hospital being just 4 miles. She subsequently died from a partial rupture of her left pulmonary vein ('Coroner's Inquests into the death of Diana, Princess of Wales and Mr Dodi Al Fayed' 2008).

The decision to effect a rapid removal and transfer to hospital has the advantage of reducing time for deterioration in basic physiology to occur (Gonzalez et al. 2009). This includes the development of hypothermia, acidosis, coagulopathy (termed the 'lethal triad'), and associated continuing blood loss. This approach is often appropriate in the urban setting where transfer times to hospital are short and risks associated with pre-hospital interventions are offset by the ability to perform them in the setting of a fully equipped emergency department (Smith et al. 1985). In this environment, the pre-hospital focus can be limited to immediate threats to life such as control of catastrophic haemorrhage, the management of airway compromise with support of respiration, and prompt departure from scene while ongoing circulatory support is provided en route to definitive care. This is known as the CABC approach to resuscitation (where the first C stands for catastrophic haemorrhage). However, as times spent effecting transfer from scene increase, so too do the effects of uncontrolled secondary injury (Seamon et al. 2007).

Complex triage and incidents which occur at long travel times away from hospital present difficulties as the effects of secondary injury become more pronounced. By way of an example, uncontrolled hypoventilation in a patient with head injury may result in progressive hypercarbia and subsequent potential rise in intracranial pressure. It should be noted that uncontrolled hyperventilation in these patients also has its disadvantages: hypocarbia may result in cerebral vasoconstriction. In cases such as these, the ability to perform a smooth rapid sequence induction (RSI) and maintain anaesthesia might be considered time well spent on scene if that patient was then subject to controlled mean arterial blood pressure, normocarbia, and reduced chances of coughing and straining during transfer. This type of targeted intervention can greatly improve the physiological condition of patients on arrival to definitive care (Davis et al. 2006).

The range and nature of interventions therefore depend upon the level of skill of the practitioner, the equipment, monitoring, drugs, and assistance available at the scene. A RSI of anaesthesia performed by a HEMS consultant, assisted by a specialized paramedic or nurse, with full monitoring including side-stream capnography might well be associated with improved patient outcomes when compared with a non-anaesthetist assisted by an unskilled assistant using only basic monitoring equipment. In interventions that are not carried out in a smooth and controlled manner, further secondary injury can occur as a result of those interventions (Davis et al. 2003).

The current model accepted in pre-hospital practice is to perform only those interventions that are within the practitioner's regular skill set and that are necessary to provide the physiological stability required to transfer the patient to definitive care with the minimum of deterioration en route.

Mechanism of injury

Pre-hospital practice differs from almost every other branch of medicine in that decisions to perform major invasive procedures may have to be made over the space of a few minutes without any investigations, imaging, or consultation with colleagues. Interventions such as thoracostomy, cricothyrotomy, and amputation of a limb are all procedures that may be carried out by pre-hospital physicians based only on recognition of clinical signs and symptoms and the mechanism of injury. Evacuation of a cardiac tamponade through a clamshell thoracostomy is a resuscitation procedure appropriate in a small subgroup of patients which should be completed within less than 10 min of a witnessed cardiac arrest based on history and the briefest of examinations (Davies 2011). It is essential that the mechanism is understood and applied to all trauma patients to ensure that injuries are found and appropriately treated. Often there is an enormous amount of information to be gathered, including personal and team safety, approaching the scene of a road traffic collision by assessing the resting position of vehicles, looking for points of bodywork damage (principle of 'reading the wreck'), identifying activated safety devices (airbags), ascertaining likely transmitted and rotational forces sustained by the occupants, and estimating distances travelled after impact. This scene survey may only take 30 s but may allow an experienced practitioner to accurately predict likely injuries and actively treat them before they exert a pathophysiological effect. This understanding is also very important at the point of handover from pre-hospital to hospital teams where the receiving physicians may not fully appreciate the course of events leading up to the patient's arrival in the emergency department (Bond et al. 1997).

Understanding the mechanical forces of trauma is of utmost importance. It is however, beyond the scope of this chapter to provide an extensive discussion on the details of mechanism, but blunt forces sustained in trauma can be broadly classified into acceleration, deceleration, rotational, and direct force. Acceleration and deceleration often cause internal injuries as solid organs are sheared from their supporting structures, as well as injuries to the cervical, thoracic, and lumbar spine. Rotational forces commonly cause cervical spine injuries and, depending on their force, may cause shear injuries within tissue. The brain is particularly susceptible to these forces. Direct force may cause injury at the point of impact such as contusions or fractures, or may be transmitted to areas away from the point of impact through the skeletal system (Smith et al. 2010). An example of this is a fall from height in which the patient lands on their feet—as well as fractured calcanea one might expect the femoral heads to impact within the acetabula causing pelvic disruption, possibly involving the sacroiliac joints, as well as compression fractures of the lumbar and thoracic vertebrae. The wave of deceleration force may also result in traumatic tears to the liver and spleen, and possibly a ruptured diaphragm. It is with this expectation that the patient should be approached, rather than concentrating on the visible injuries to the feet and ankles.

ABCD principle

Baker et al. (1980) formulated a classification of immediate, early, and late trauma-related deaths. In this trimodal distribution, the immediate deaths occur at the scene within minutes after getting injured, the early deaths occur within hours as a result of hypoxia and haemorrhage, and the late deaths occur in hospital days to weeks after the incident as a result of trauma-related complications. See Figure 76.1. A more recent study (Gunst et al. 2010) suggests a change from trimodal to bimodal caused by a large reduction of the late deaths group.

Modern pre-hospital trauma systems focus mainly on the first and second peaks in the tri- or bimodal distribution but accepting the fact that the first group (immediate deaths) are frequently beyond help by the time emergency services arrive.

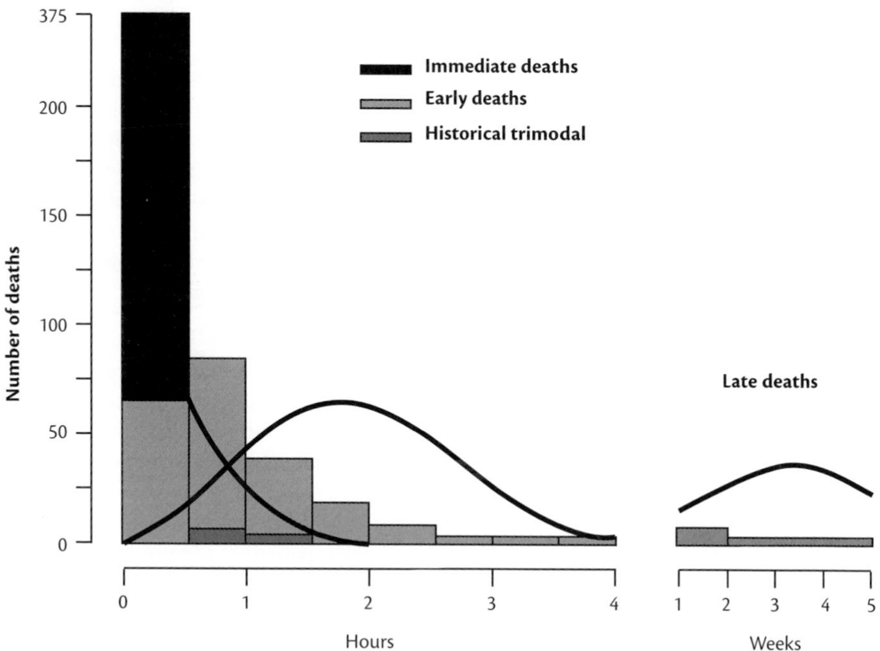

Figure 76.1 The trimodal model of mortality following traumatic injury.

Reprinted from *The American Journal of Surgery*, Volume 140, Issue 1, Baker, C.C. *et al.* Epidemiology of trauma deaths, pp. 144–150. Copyright © 1980, with permission from Elsevier.

It is accepted that in order to reduce the number of early trauma deaths, aggressive correction of vital functions is necessary. The traditional history–examination–investigation–diagnosis model is rarely appropriate in this patient group. Instead, a rapid identification of immediately life-threatening injuries and associated treatment must be provided within a timespan often of only a few minutes.

In the early 1980s, the Advanced Trauma Life Support (ATLS) course was developed in the United States.

The ATLS is based on three concepts:

1. Treat the greatest threat to life first.
2. The lack of a definitive diagnosis should never impede the application of an indicated treatment.
3. A detailed history is not essential to begin the evaluation of a patient with acute injuries.

A similar standard approach to treatment is delivered by the European Trauma Course. These and other systematic management plans for emergency care have led to the widespread uptake of the CABCD approach to evaluate and treat the injured patient.

Based on the likely physiological course of a trauma casualty, the following areas should be addressed in turn as part of a seamless and simultaneous assessment and treatment.

C: Catastrophic haemorrhage

A: Airway continuity

B: Breathing abnormalities

C: Circulatory problems as a result of hypovolaemia or cardiac failure.

D: Disability.

Special considerations of pre-hospital practice

Equipment

One of the significant challenges of pre-hospital practice is the dependence upon the equipment carried on the vehicle used to access the scene. The range of equipment is often limited to two or three manufacturers and may be purpose-designed for the environment or adapted from existing designs. There are many specific requirements for pre-hospital equipment and choosing the best design depends greatly on the predicted usage. Unlike planned transfers between hospitals which involve specific equipment carried for the task, pre-hospital equipment must reflect a balance of weight and complexity against ease of use and reliability in the pre-hospital environment. Moreover, electrical equipment carried in helicopters and aeroplanes needs to be certified for aviation usage.

Monitoring

Monitoring equipment will normally be splash-resistant and battery-operated. Displays will need to be viewable in bright direct sunlight and low ambient light; battery changes should be able to be performed without loss of function and so dual batteries may be an advantage; and buttons and keypads should be usable while wearing gloves. Reliability should be tested after impact, in a wide range of ambient temperatures and conditions such as dust and moisture, and also in the presence of electromagnetic interference.

Typical monitor functions might include 3-lead and 12-lead electrocardiographs with the ability to print captured recordings, pulse oximetry, non-invasive blood pressure (NIBP), and waveform capnography. In addition, defibrillation and cardiac pacing may be integrated into the device. Dependent upon usage, invasive blood pressure channels and temperature monitoring may also be included in the specification. The device should be portable with a weight that permits carriage on foot over considerable distances. The limited monitoring and diagnostic equipment readily available results in much reliance on the use of clinical signs and symptoms linked to an understanding of mechanisms of injury and likely diagnoses to guide treatment.

Ventilators

Ventilators should be robust, simple to operate, and use the minimum amount of compressed gas to preserve cylinder endurance. Pre-hospital ventilators fall into one of three categories:

- Simple resuscitation ventilators that produce a fixed regular tidal volume delivering either 50% or 100% oxygen
- Intermediate ventilators which allow more manipulation of parameters including PEEP, inspiratory:expiratory ratio, and inspired oxygen fraction which are suitable for on-scene anaesthesia
- Advanced ventilators allowing significant control of multiple parameters which are appropriate for transfer of intensive care patients and children.

Drivers and pumps

Syringe drivers and volumetric pumps are increasingly found in immediate medical care practice. Bulk, weight, and complexity have historically weighed against their use in favour of bolus techniques of fluid and drug administration. In recent years, however, small, reliable, effective battery-operated devices have become available. In a growing number of countries they have now become part of the standard configuration of advanced pre-hospital teams.

Environment

A significant step in the transition from hospital or practice-based practice into the pre-hospital environment is recognizing and preparing for the change in ambient working conditions that may be encountered. The majority of clinical staff work in conditions of steady temperature, light, humidity, and cleanliness with easy access to refreshment and rest areas. This is in sharp contrast to pre-hospital medicine in which none of these factors can be provided with any degree of reliability.

Temperature

Across Europe, pre-hospital practitioners operate in temperatures ranging from −40°C in northern Scandinavia to +40°C in southern Spain and Greece. This can only be achieved with the use of substantial levels of personal protective equipment (PPE) which is discussed later in this chapter.

Of equal importance is the effect that this ambient temperature has on the patient in the pre-hospital environment. Cold temperatures are often combined with precipitation, winds, wet ground, and cold or frozen surfaces which result in massive heat loss through the processes of convection, conduction, and radiation (Kornfält and Johansson 2010). This heat loss can result in rapid and significant hypothermia which can exacerbate underlying coagulopathy. The focus of pre-hospital care is to prevent further heat loss rather than to attempt rewarming. The equipment used to perform rewarming effectively is often bulky and dependent on significant amounts of electrical power which may not be readily available. Instead, removal of wet clothing, wrapping in thermally insulating material, the delivery of warmed fluids if appropriate, along with short exposure times is often the most effective way of limiting hypothermic insult.

High temperatures are less of a problem with regard to patient management, but may pose a significant threat to the pre-hospital practitioner in terms of dehydration and heat exhaustion. Physical work with little shade for prolonged periods of time can rapidly cause loss of physical and mental performance.

Light

In a similar way to extremes of temperature, light can interfere with pre-hospital practice. Sun in the presence of lying snow can create very high levels of ambient light which may interfere with the use of visual displays on monitors and cause eye strain.

Darkness can pose many hazards in terms of personal safety, team functioning, patient assessment, and treatment. High-visibility clothing is essential for all staff working in low light, but this can make identification of individuals difficult, especially in a complex or crowded scene. Patient assessment can become more difficult, with subtle signs such as uneven chest wall movement or misting of an oxygen mask becoming impossible to detect. The use of torches can help, but their efficacy is often limited to a small task-focused area such as cannulation (Lockey et al. 2005). Fire and rescue services often provide scene floodlighting from purpose-designed vehicles.

Humidity

A relative humidity of 30–70% is often described as the zone of comfort. In a pre-hospital environment, air humidity can be very high. In a humid environment, growth of microorganisms and fungi is promoted. This can lead to allergic reactions, headache, irritation of the airways, and shortness of breath for the healthcare provider. High humidity in combination with high temperature can lead to heat stroke and collapse because of the inability to sweat.

Cleanliness

A considerable problem for pre-hospital practice is that of infection prevention and control. Unlike the clean working environment of practice-based colleagues, many foreign materials such as ditch or canal water, mud, oil, bodily fluids, and other scene-related contaminants are usually present to some degree in most pre-hospital trauma and equipment may be heavily contaminated during routine use. The introduction of single-use consumables, cleaning schedules for vehicles and equipment, and evidence-based wound care are all helping to reduce sources of pre-hospital infection (McDonell 2008). Although prevention of contamination is preferable, the prophylactic, pre-hospital use of antibiotics (e.g. in patients with open fractures) is sometimes advised where administration does not prolong scene times (Gosselin et al. 2009).

Personal protective equipment

The primary role of PPE is to protect the user from environmental or related harm. The nature of PPE may vary widely depending on the type and location of work within pre-hospital care but should allow the user to carry out the functions required of them without hindrance. Pre-hospital practitioners should be highly visible at all times, protected from sharp or mechanical injury as best as possible, insulated from the effects of water, extremes of temperature, electrical current, and able to avoid contamination of their skin and mucous membranes by bodily fluids and noxious chemicals or gas. This suggests that a minimum of fire-retardant, high-visibility clothing with water resistance incorporated into the fabric, eye and ear protection, helmet, examination gloves, and steel-capped insulating boots are required for safe practice. Further items are added dependent upon specific need. As the working environment becomes more hostile, more PPE is usually required. The drawback is that the user will be progressively more remote from their patient: thermal or reinforced gloves lack tactile sensitivity, bulky clothing may hinder movement, and hearing protection may mask subtle changes in respiratory noise.

It follows that good quality and appropriate PPE is of paramount importance for the safe and efficient care of trauma patients at the scene of injury while protecting the pre-hospital team from potential harm (Krzanicki and Porter 2009).

Isolation from support

Knowledge

The pre-hospital practitioner may often work in complete isolation. Specialist advice, reference literature, and additional treatment options may be totally inaccessible at the scene of injury or during transportation. As practice has evolved in line with governance, the variation of independent practice based on individual experience and skills has waned, with standardized operating procedures offering a more reproducible, reliable, and evidence-based service. Other than small and portable aide memoirs and checklists, there are limited sources of diagnostic or treatment information available. Furthermore, in most cases time is limited and decisions have to be taken in a short time span. It is for these reasons that much emphasis remains on understanding of patterns and mechanisms of injury, the prediction of likely injury, and reliable management techniques to allow stable transfer to definitive care.

Equipment

The availability of blood in the military pre-hospital teams has had a dramatic effect on survival after polytrauma, but this has yet to become widely available within routine civilian practice (Barkana et al. 1999). Prolonged incidents (e.g. complex extrication) and incidents involving multiple casualties may rapidly deplete resources available at the scene of the incident and resupply may not be easy or even possible. Rationing of resources such as fluid therapy, oxygen delivery, and personnel is therefore a necessary and important aspect of pre-hospital practice. It is for this reason that in major incident planning, triage of casualties ensures that the maximum number of patients are treated effectively with the resources available at any given time.

Major incidents

A major incident is any emergency that requires the implementation of special arrangements by one or more of the emergency services and will generally include the involvement, either directly or indirectly, of large numbers of people. For specific health purposes, a major incident may be defined as 'Any occurrence which presents a serious threat to the health of the community, disruption to the service, or causes (or is likely to cause) such members or types of casualties as to require special arrangements to be implemented by hospitals, ambulance services or health authorities'.

Common examples may be single events such as a railway collision or an aeroplane crash, multiple isolated events such as widespread rioting, or a steady drain on resources such as an outbreak of influenza or severe winter weather. Major incidents may affect one or more public services—rioting may severely affect the fire and police services but if few injuries occur it may leave the health services operating under relatively normal conditions. Most major incidents, however, involve all emergency services and it is vital that any pre-hospital practitioner understands what role they will play in the organization of such an event.

Within many European countries, established major incident plans exist which allow the fundamental principles of major incident management to occur: command and control. With respect to an isolated major incident, the site will be treated as a crime scene with the police having control of the outer cordon to minimize disturbance of the area. Meanwhile, the fire service will retain responsibility for the incident itself and the safety of all personnel within the inner cordon. Any practitioners wishing to access a major incident will therefore require identification and correct PPE to pass the cordons.

In the United Kingdom, within the incident, health command rests with a 'Silver' ambulance incident officer and 'Silver' medical officer. These are non-clinical roles and provide an overview of the process of casualty triage, extrication, treatment, and transport to receiving hospitals. Further personnel will be allocated pre-defined roles to manage the various stages of treatment. At the site of patient contact, a 'Bronze' officer will oversee the initial triage and extrication of casualties to a casualty clearing station where immediate medical treatment is provided while awaiting transfer to hospital. It is often the casualty clearing station that most doctors are deployed to, while those within the 'bronze' area will be mostly paramedics or rescue teams. If the incident is likely to have adverse effects on the regional health service structure, a 'Gold' command may be set up remote from the incident to coordinate resources across the area. In other European countries, stepped organizations similar to this 'gold/silver/bronze' system are used although the nomenclature is different.

Established triage systems are in use and initially rely on the most basic of observations to identify those that need immediate or delayed treatment. Once initial triage has occurred and those with life-threatening injuries have been identified, a secondary triage system applies further classification to prioritize casualties according to physiological disturbance (Aylwin et al. 2006). Little provision is made for anything other than immediate stabilizing treatment on scene. The limitations of personnel and equipment mean that resources are directed towards those with the greatest chance of survival and away from those unlikely to survive. The allocation of limited resources is based on a strategy to maximize the number of survivors. This shift in focus from routine pre-hospital work can be a difficult adjustment to make and post-event stress can be a common feature among even the most experienced practitioners (Alexander and Klein 2001; Fullerton et al. 2004).

Specific interventions

Haemorrhage management

Management of haemorrhage is widely recognized as one of the principal goals of trauma control. There are many ways of describing haemorrhage, classifying shock, and estimating blood loss in trauma patients. These guides provide a useful snapshot of the condition of the patient, but do little to reflect the dynamic nature of immediate trauma. In the pre-hospital arena, the guiding principle is to prevent secondary injury and this applies firmly to the management of haemorrhage (Hodgetts et al. 2006; Beekley et al. 2008).

Table 76.1 Progressive blood loss and associated signs (estimated fluid and blood losses for a 70 kg man based on patient's initial presentation)

	Class I	Class II	Class III	Class IV
Blood loss (ml)	Up to 750	750–1500	1500–2000	>2000
Blood loss (% blood volume)	Up to 15%	15–30%	30–40%	>40%
Heart rate (beats min^{-1})	<100	>100	>120	>140
Blood pressure (mm Hg)	Normal	Normal	Decreased	Decreased
Pulse pressure (mm Hg)	Normal or increased	Decreased	Decreased	Decreased
Respiratory rate (breaths min^{-1})	14–20	20–30	30–40	>35
Urine output (ml h^{-1})	>30	20–30	5–15	Negligible
Central nervous system/mental status	Slightly anxious	Mildly anxious	Anxious, confused	Confused, lethargic

Haemorrhage can occur internally as well as externally, and may vary from a catastrophic major arterial haemorrhage to a slow ongoing bleed into a hidden area such as the retroperitoneal space. Regardless of the origin of the haemorrhage there is a loss of circulating volume and therefore oxygen-carrying capacity within the blood. Taken in isolation this may result in an initial mild tachycardia but at the scene of an incident with the attendant stresses, this variation in heart rate could also be explained by high levels of fear, anxiety, and pain. Therefore the pre-hospital practitioner should look towards mechanism of injury, likely sources of bleeding, and available treatment strategies rather relying purely on non-specific clinical signs.

As bleeding continues, however, the symptoms and signs become increasingly clear and should direct the practitioner towards the presence of developing hypovolaemia or shock (Table 76.1).

'Blood on the floor and four more'

When presented with a patient exhibiting symptoms and signs that could be attributed to hypovolaemic shock, great care must be taken to ensure that all available methods of arresting ongoing haemorrhage are used. In order to achieve this in a timely and efficient manner, the prompt review of sites where bleeding may occur is an important task. The casualty should be inspected closely for external haemorrhage ('blood on the floor … '). To be performed to an adequate standard the casualty must be stripped and fully examined where possible as clothing such as motorcycle leathers or padded jackets can conceal significant volumes of blood.

The other areas that may accommodate blood (' … and four more') are the chest, the abdomen, the pelvis, and the long bones of the limbs (Battlefield Advanced Trauma Life Support 2001).

A systematic review of the chest looking for signs of injury, bruising, deformity, or poor expansion should be carried out as soon as possible. The ribs should be examined for any displaced fractures or flail segments, and the chest wall, neck, and back tested for the crepitus of surgical emphysema. Auscultation, percussion, and ultrasound should be performed where possible. Auscultation and percussion are often hindered by ambient noise (Hunt et al. 1991).

A similar examination should be carried out around the abdomen, noting the forces that may have acted upon the patient. Assessment of signs such as guarding may be hindered by the conscious level of the patient, but a thorough examination will make it quicker to detect the presence of increasing distension.

The pelvis is a common source of major blood loss in trauma, which occurs when the pelvic ring is disrupted with associated damage to the intraosseous and intrapelvic vessels. Any high-mechanism force to the lower half of the body may result in pelvic injury, and it is commonly seen in road traffic collisions (Dalal et al. 1989). Motorcyclists may suffer serious disruptions when riding into the side of a car that pulls out of a junction; a motorcycle fuel tank dented where it meets the seat may suggest a substantial injury. Upon impact, the motorcycle rapidly decelerates although the rider continues to move forwards in the sitting position. This effectively results in the tank driving backwards into the pelvis opening it as would a wedge (de Peretti 1994). Another group of patients susceptible to pelvic injuries are heavy goods vehicle (HGV) drivers who collide with an immovable object, or another stationary HGV. Due to the configuration of most vehicles, the driver sits at the very front of the vehicle with little material to absorb the considerable impact. As a result of this, the dashboard is often pushed backwards and into contact with the knees of any occupants with considerable force upon impact. This compressive force is then applied to the femurs which transmit it up into the acetabula and then on into the pelvic ring which may then sustain various fractures.

Lastly, fractures of the long limb bones may result in substantial blood loss and care should be taken to evaluate each limb looking for signs of swelling or deformity (Lieurance et al. 1992). Upon fracture, bleeding may occur into the surrounding tissues in the case of a closed fracture, or externally in the case of an open fracture.

Prompt and effective management of haemorrhage is a vital core component of pre-hospital emergency medicine as ongoing loss of blood will result in immediate cardiovascular compromise in terms of both oxygen delivery and loss of clotting factors, resulting in a worsening coagulation profile. As blood loss continues, the delayed effects on end-organ function as a result of hypoperfusion with increasingly deranged acid–base balance and rising lactate becomes significant. The immediate and delayed effects of haemorrhage account for a significant proportion of the morbidity and mortality after trauma (Blow et al. 1999).

'The first clot is often the best clot'

Control of haemorrhage is very dependent upon the source of bleeding, the skill of the operator, and equipment available, but the fundamental principles remain the same—reduce blood flow to the bleeding point and encourage a stable clot to form at that same point. Simple wounds such as lacerations of vascular tissue or peripheral arteries such as the radial may be easily managed by elevation and direct pressure with a dressing. More significant blood loss from larger wounds or less accessible bleeding points may benefit from a pressure dressing and haemostatic agent (see next paragraph). Larger wounds still, or those involving large arteries, may not be amenable to management at the bleeding point and use of a tourniquet or surgical technique might be necessary (Rossaint et al. 2010). Once the haemorrhage is controlled, the coagulation that occurs will often be fragile—clotting factors can be rapidly diluted and consumed in polytrauma. If hypothermia occurs, this can further reduce the effectiveness of clot formation. It is therefore of paramount importance that dressings are not removed or tourniquets released for inspection of the wound until the patient reaches a place where formal surgical haemostasis is available.

Haemostatic agents are now readily available and can broadly be divided into those with active ingredients derived from aluminiosilicate minerals (zeolites) and from crustacean shells (chitosans). These materials can be presented in granule form for direct application to a wound, or bound to a dressing to facilitate the application of direct pressure. They act to promote the production of a stable clot and have been extensively tested in active military service (Granville-Chapman et al. 2011).

The use of tourniquets has been debated for many years, but recent military experience has proved their worth beyond doubt. In cases of substantial bleeding from a limb, application of a modern tourniquet device, often incorporating a windlass for accurate application of pressure, can significantly reduce bleeding and allow dressing of a wound with haemostatic agents. As with haemostatics, once applied tourniquets should not be released until the patient is within a facility offering definitive care as any formed clot may be dislodged causing further bleeding (Rossaint et al. 2010).

Hypotensive resuscitation

Until recently, the guidance of the American College of Surgeons through the Advanced Trauma Life Support (ATLS) programme was that signs of bleeding and hypotension should be treated by up to 2 litres of warmed crystalloid solution. This strategy has been shown to increase uncontrolled haemorrhage through a combination of increased mean arterial pressure and dilution of clotting factors (Cotton et al. 2006). The focus of circulatory management has instead shifted to permissive hypotension, also termed hypotensive resuscitation. This strategy requires the use of small boluses of fluid to achieve a targeted end-point of a systolic pressure of 80–90 mm Hg (often defined as the presence of a radial pulse) in blunt or penetrating trauma, or 100 mm Hg in trauma with head injury.

This strategy has been widely adopted because of the evidence of reduced blood loss and transfusion requirements, and survival in animal studies although there are limited high-quality human trials (Morrison et al. 2011). There is increasing interest in prehospital administration of blood products, with several randomised controlled trials underway to establish whether early intervention with packed red blood cells and plasma confers patient benefit (RePHILL, PAMPer, COMBAT).

Access

Vascular access can be a significant problem for pre-hospital practitioners—a triad of hypovolaemia, hypothermia, and high sympathetic drive is present to some degree in many patients encountered. These combine to cause considerable difficulty in securing a venous cannula, especially in stressful adverse circumstances such as the confined physical space and darkness of a night-time road traffic collision entrapment.

Alternative devices are available to specialist practitioners including large-bore central vein cannulae and the increasingly popular intraosseous needle devices. These products can secure intraosseous access within a matter of seconds either through the firing of a hollow needle into a bone such as the sternum, or by using a powered drill to drive a needle into a long bone such as the tibia or the humerus. The time to circulation for drugs administered in this way is very similar to direct venous access, and the advantage of being able to site these needles by a landmark technique provides a reliable method to fall back on should standard cannulation techniques fail. The technique is in fact so easy to learn and use that in some parts of Europe it has become first choice in gaining access to the circulation in, for example, resuscitation scenarios.

Advanced analgesia

Provision of analgesia is a requirement for any patient in pain. The humanitarian aspect to this is obvious, but the physiological response to pain is also well documented. Uncontrolled pain causes an increase in sympathetic tone which can alter several physiological systems: oxygen consumption may be increased; increases in heart rate and blood pressure can worsen existing myocardial ischaemia; hyperventilation may exacerbate chest injury; and together they may cause reduced cerebral perfusion as a result of hypocapnic-induced vasoconstriction and reduction in oxygen delivery to brain tissue. Pain also increases anxiety and may reduce patient compliance during complicated procedures such as extrication from a vehicle or building.

The first and one of the most powerful methods of providing analgesia is reassurance. The effect of the appearance of the emergency services at an incident should not be underestimated and early contact with a patient in a calm and professional manner can often reduce the anxiety associated with pain. Continued calm and confident explanations of what is happening around the patient can significantly reduce pain scores before any analgesia is administered. In the case of paediatric patients, engaging with any available parents or carers is important. The injured child will often look to them for emotional prompts and if they are seen to be calm and in control of their anxiety the child will usually respond in a similar manner.

Another key concept in providing excellent pre-hospital analgesia is immobilization of injured tissues. The manipulation of fractures and damaged tissues can be extremely painful during movement of patients, and the application of splints may greatly facilitate patient handling. Various splints may be used dependent upon the site and nature of injury—simple box splints and straps are of use in sprains and soft tissue injuries but often lack the rigidity required to fully immobilize fractures. Vacuum splints are relatively simple devices which allow air to be sucked out of a plastic bag containing polystyrene beads. As the air is withdrawn, the bag forms a firm moulded splint around the injured part. Larger vacuum splints are often used as whole-body immobilization for infants and small children. Advanced splint devices can apply traction to a fractured femur, or compression to a fractured pelvis, significantly reducing pain with the added benefit of reducing internal haemorrhage.

Often, when considering the application of splints or for short periods of movement such as the extrication of a patient from a confined space, a short period of analgesia is all that is required. One effective method of providing this is through the provision of 50% nitrous oxide in oxygen (Entonox®). This gas is dealt with extensively in Chapter 14 but for the purposes of pre-hospital analgesia it provides a safe and reliable method of inducing short periods of analgesia. There are two issues relevant to its use in trauma patients, however, which need to be addressed before it is offered to a patient. Firstly, a careful history and examination and assessment of the mechanism of injury should be undertaken to ensure no contraindications exist. Secondly, Entonox® should be stored above its pseudo-critical temperature of −6°C to avoid the nitrous oxide returning to the liquid phase. If this occurs, administration will initially deliver a high fraction of oxygen with little clinical effect, followed by a high fraction of nitrous oxide with the risk of delivering a hypoxic mixture. Often in pre-hospital practice these cylinders are stored in vehicles which, during winter, may often become colder than −6°C when unused. Short journeys to the scene of an incident may allow little time for adequate rewarming and so care must be taken in cold environments that cylinders are stored in warmed buildings until needed.

Morphine or other opioids such as fentanyl or sufentanil are indicated for moderate to severe pain and according to country and region may be given by paramedic staff. Used in conjunction with non-pharmacological methods as previously described, they are a safe and effective form of analgesia and are presented either in intravenous, oral, transmucosal (nasal), or transdermal forms. Difficulties may arise, however, when injuries are severe or when the patient falls outside of the criteria set out by regional or national regulations for administration.

Pre-hospital doctors, suitably qualified nurses, and advanced paramedics operating under a patient group directive are able to administer ketamine to provide further analgesia, procedural sedation, or anaesthesia. Ketamine is a dissociative anaesthetic with pharmacological properties that make it highly suitable for the pre-hospital environment. In intravenous or intraosseous doses of 0.5 mg kg^{-1} it provides excellent analgesia without causing respiratory depression or loss of airway reflexes. Further doses up to 1 mg kg^{-1} offer a smooth continuum into sedation while preserving respiratory and cardiovascular stability. It is often suggested that in order to avoid emergence phenomena of hallucinations and delirium the patient should be recovered in a quiet, calm, and dark environment with the minimum of physical stimuli. This is, however, difficult to achieve in the pre-hospital environment and management of these phenomenon is instead often managed using small doses of midazolam (0.03 mg kg^{-1}) before emergence. The physiology, pharmacology, and effects of ketamine are fully described in Chapter 15.

In addition to non-pharmacological and intravenous methods of analgesia, some pre-hospital practitioners advocate the use of regional anaesthesia for specific indications such as femoral nerve blocks for femoral fractures. The success of these blocks in pre-hospital practice is variable and without peripheral nerve stimulators or handheld ultrasound devices should generally be avoided. Simple blocks that can be achieved through landmark techniques such as digit, wrist, or ankle blocks, however, can be an effective method of managing localized pain before transportation. After arrival at the hospital, peripheral nerve blocks may hinder physical examination while sensory and motor neurones are blocked. With the range of interventions available, spending time on scene performing regional anaesthesia is rarely justifiable.

There is considerable interest in alternative methods of delivering analgesia, especially in paediatrics. Nasal administration of fentanyl and diamorphine is well established, and fentanyl 'lollipops' are now in use.

Advanced airway interventions including rapid sequence induction of anaesthesia

Induction of anaesthesia in hospital, but in particular out of the controlled clinical environment of the anaesthetic room, is

Box 76.1 Training requirements for pre-hospital anaesthesia

The individual will require skills in both anaesthesia and working in the pre-hospital environment. Competence should be defined by these skills rather than by the primary specialty of the individual.

A 2-year acute care common stem (ACCS) training programme provides individuals with 6 months of training in emergency medicine and acute medicine, and 1 year in anaesthesia and critical care medicine.

The ACCS programme, or equivalent training, should be regarded as the absolute minimum required by an individual practising pre-hospital anaesthesia. However, specific training for working in the pre-hospital environment is also essential.

Having achieved competence in pre-hospital RSI, the practitioner and assistants will need to maintain their skills by undertaking the procedure regularly. The precise number of drug-assisted tracheal intubations required to maintain competence has not been defined, but an average of at least once a month would seem reasonable. Unless an individual is working in a very busy pre-hospital programme, it is likely that RSI competence will be achieved only with regular in-hospital RSI experience or simulator experience.

All pre-hospital organizations should provide a clinical governance structure that ensures that each practitioner is competent. The individual undertaking pre-hospital RSI should keep a log of all procedures and be included in a clinical governance structure that incorporates regular review of cases managed by that individual in addition to an adverse incident reporting system.

considered to be a high-risk procedure because of the relative lack of support, equipment, and familiarity of the environment. It therefore follows that induction of anaesthesia outside hospital in uncontrolled public areas, subject to environmental factors such as noise, temperature, and ambient light, with relatively unskilled assistance, limited equipment, and basic monitoring is extremely hazardous. RSI should only be attempted by appropriately trained and equipped practitioners.

There has been much debate around the subject of the benefits, risks, and practice of pre-hospital anaesthesia and these debates continue to cast much doubt on when and if it should occur. What is clear is that anaesthesia induced out of hospital by a team which lacks appropriate experience and governance often results in significant morbidity and delays transfer to definitive care. The Association of Anaesthetists of Great Britain and Ireland (AAGBI) has produced clear guidance on the requirements for pre-hospital anaesthesia, and these are outlined in Box 76.1.

Teamwork

The provision of pre-hospital anaesthesia is a team exercise led by a suitably qualified doctor. At least one other member of the team must act as a trained assistant in a similar fashion to the operating department practitioner. This is often an advanced paramedic who may have undertaken training in assisting in RSI. As paramedics are trained in tracheal intubation it may be that the doctor administers drugs and assistance while the paramedic manages the airway, or vice versa. Either way, in the pressure of the pre-hospital environment it is essential that both team members are working to a standard operating procedure which clearly sets out the indications, preparation, equipment, and technique for RSI, with clear failed intubation pathways to follow.

Pharmaceutical agents

There is wide variation between providers in which pharmaceutical agents are used, which in part reflects how a lack of standardized pre-hospital training has allowed significant differences in practice to develop. Induction agents are commonly ketamine and thiopental with etomidate still available but declining in popularity because of the growing evidence of adrenal cortex inhibition after a single dose. Propofol is used in European countries but concerns exist over the profound hypotension that may occur in shock. Neuromuscular block is commonly achieved with either suxamethonium (succinylcholine) or rocuronium. Maintenance of anaesthesia is commonly provided by boluses of analgesia (morphine or fentanyl), sedative (midazolam), and long-acting neuromuscular blocking agent (e.g. pancuronium, rocuronium) as required. Some providers that operate considerable time distances from hospital may opt to achieve maintenance with infusions; this has advantages of steady levels of sedation (e.g. propofol) and paralysis (e.g. rocuronium) but with the added complexity of infusion lines and battery-powered devices.

Equipment

The airway equipment available for pre-hospital use is limited by what can reasonably be carried by the practitioner as patients may only be accessible by foot. By the nature of indications for pre-hospital anaesthesia, there is rarely an opportunity to take a history or assess a patient's airway beyond immediate visualization of the face, jaw, and neck. Taking into account the lack of opportunity for formal assessment, the possibility of facial injuries and bleeding, the assumption that any trauma patient has a full stomach, and the position of the patient, often on the floor, it is important that failed airway algorithms are clear, practised, and adhered to. These differ from hospital-based practice in that equipment may be limited, and allowing a patient to spontaneously breathe and regain consciousness would rarely be appropriate.

Indications

Reflecting on an intervention that carries significant chance of harm or death to the patient if unsuccessful, the indications for performing it need to be clear and well defined. In broad terms there are three main groups of indications:

1. For immediate safety (e.g. risk of compromise to the airway in facial trauma, inadequate spontaneous ventilation, risk of vomiting, regurgitation and aspiration)
2. To reduce the severity of secondary injury (e.g. control of ventilation and prevention of hypercarbia in turn limiting intracranial pressure rise in acute head injury)
3. For humanitarian reasons (e.g. significant injury).

Box 76.2 reflects commonly accepted indications.

Safe working practices in the pre-hospital environment

Safe induction of anaesthesia relies on good communication and understanding between team members. Within the anaesthetic room, the anaesthetic practitioner and assistant will usually operate within a controlled and familiar environment along a predictable

Box 76.2 Indications for pre-hospital RSI

- Airway obstruction (actual or impending)
- Anticipated airway problem during transport
- Risk of aspiration
- Oxygenation with or without ventilatory failure
- Unconsciousness
- Severe haemorrhagic shock
- Major cutaneous burns (>40%)
- Humanitarian reasons: analgesia, planned surgical intervention
- Anticipated clinical course
- Transport/management considerations:
  - Aeromedical evacuation
  - Agitated/combative patient (GCS score ≤15)
  - Anticipated clinical problems (e.g. the need to amputate a limb).

sequence of events and actions. These working conditions require a minimum of briefing, preparation, and planning as team members will be working well within their abilities and scope of practice. The uncontrolled and unpredictable pre-hospital environment can severely test levels of concentration, situational awareness, and focus at the point of induction and intubation. A thorough understanding of human factors and crew resource management is essential to compensate for multiple distractions and uncontrolled variables while maintaining a safe and reproducible technique. It is now accepted that the use of challenge–response checklists which are read out and positively responded to, are a crucial part of preparation (Fig. 76.2).

Beginning intubation

Once the team have confirmed that basic and failed intubation equipment, drugs, monitors, and briefings are all in place, the process of intubation may occur. It may seem that these procedures, checklists, and briefings may delay the process and ultimately delivery to definitive care. In part this may be true, but the complexity, noise, presence of distracting bystanders, and environmental considerations of pre-hospital anaesthesia make a practised, reproducible, and methodical approach essential.

Boxes 76.3–76.15, Tables 76.2 and 76.3, and Figure 76.3 summarize the process of intubation in the pre-hospital environment.

Use of stethoscopes and other methods for assessing tube placement are unreliable with the noise normally associated with an ongoing incident, and should not be relied on. It is for this reason among others that immediate detection of exhaled carbon dioxide is mandatory. These may take the form of colorimetric end-tidal carbon dioxide detection devices that change colour in the presence of carbon dioxide, or measured levels or waveform capnography. Colorimetric devices are useful for the immediate confirmation of tracheal placement of a tracheal tube, but provide no reliable assessment of ventilation beyond the first breath. There are several devices available that provide a simple digital measurement of carbon dioxide, or more complex devices that display side-stream or mainstream capnography. Use of such devices is mandatory in pre-hospital anaesthesia.

Apply tight-fitting oxygen mask or bag–valve mask whilst this checklist is performed.

CONFIRMATION
Are we agreed why we are anaesthetizing this patient?
Does any one have any questions?

PREPARATION
Is this the best place to perform this? ON TROLLEY? 360° ACCESS?
NO DIRECT SUNLIGHT/WIND?
Oxygen supply confirmed
Oxygen mask on tight and reservoir bag moving with ventilation
Capnograph trace with ventilation during pre-oxygenation
BP monitor on cycle and baseline BP seen
Pulse oximeter
ECG
Suction working

Cricoid pressure ready:	CONFIRM TECHNIQUE	

In-line immobilization person briefed/collar open (if indicated)
Team member watching monitors

IVI/IO DRUGS
Cannula connected to fluid and runs easily

Spare cannula *in situ* and flushed	(consider this)	
Induction agent:	drug/dose	SHOW ME
Paralysing agent:	drug/dose	SHOW ME
Long-acting paralysis (if indicated):	drug/dose	SHOW ME
Resuscitation drugs:	(alpha and beta agonists)	SHOW ME

AIRWAY/VENTILATION

Primary laryngoscope:	accessible and working
Primary ETT:	size/cuff checked
Alternate laryngoscope:	accessible and working
Alternate ETT:	size/cuff checked
Bougie	
Syringe	
Tube tie or holder	
Stethoscope	
Ventilator settings:	confirmed and attached to O_2

AIRWAY RESCUE

LMA and syringe available:	accessible and working	SHOW ME
Surgical airway kit available:	accessible and working	SHOW ME
OPA and NPA available		
Verbally confirm failed airway plans		

READY TO PROCEED?
Does any one have any questions?
EVERYONE AROUND THE AREA IS NOW TO BE SILENT EXCEPT FOR EMERGENCIES

Figure 76.2 Challenge–response checklist: prehospital emergency anaesthesia.

Once induction and intubation has occurred, maintenance of anaesthesia must be provided. Some pre-hospital providers carry automated infusion devices such as syringe drivers. The speed and limitations of primary pre-hospital interventions mean that most providers continue to rely on bolus sedation techniques. A common strategy is to provide morphine (0.1 mg kg^{-1}) and midazolam (0.1 mg kg^{-1}) in divided doses titrated to simple variables such as heart rate and blood pressure. This has the advantages of requiring minimum equipment to be carried, the absence of multiple infusion lines, and time saved in setting up the devices and infusions. However, in Europe and areas with longer transfer times, infusions of sedatives including propofol are in routine use.

A full review of the condition of the patient in a systematic manner is essential immediately after intubation. Injuries that may have

Box 76.3 Access

- Confirm scene safety.
- 360° access with patient on ambulance trolley is desirable.
- Move patient if necessary.
- Anaesthesia in a confined space is hazardous (e.g. patient still trapped in vehicle). Consider airway adjunct (i.e. laryngeal mask airway) to relieve airway obstruction/respiratory distress until access is optimized.
- Do not anaesthetize a patient in a confined space unless there is no alternative

Box 76.4 Patient optimization: pre-oxygenation (1)

- All efforts must be made to pre-oxygenate the patient to prolong the time before life-threatening desaturation occurs after induction of anaesthesia if problems occur. Adjuncts, sedation, and assisted ventilation may all be required. Do not abandon patient optimization unless there is no feasible alternative.
- High-flow O_2 via tight fitting facemask with reservoir bag while preparing for RSI.
- Manual manoeuvres may be required to hold the airway open.
- Insert airway adjuncts (oro- or nasopharyngeal, or both) as required to achieve best possible airway opening.
- Suction as necessary.
- Support ventilation if required with bag and mask.
- In some patients the supine position for pre-oxygenation may not be the best choice. Consider using the position where the patient is most comfortable and can maintain their airway themselves (e.g. severe maxillofacial injuries).
- In most patients, a head-up position will improve the efficacy of pre-oxygenation.

Box 76.5 Intravenous access

- Secure large-bore i.v. access (two lines are preferable).
- If i.v. access is not possible, site i.o. access.
- Confirm correct placement with saline flush (especially if cannula not sited by you). Attach free-running crystalloid infusion.
- If patient too agitated for adequate pre-oxygenation, administer sedation:
  - *Either* midazolam 1 mg i.v. (repeat to effect)
  - *Or* ketamine 20 mg i.v. (repeat to effect).

Box 76.6 Monitoring

- Minimum monitoring standards apply as per AAGBI recommendations.
- Attach ECG, Sp_{O_2}, and NIBP (2–3 min cycles).
- Capnography is mandatory (see Box 76.8).

Box 76.7 Preparation

The equipment that is prepared should be organized in a standardized layout on a 'kit dump'. This includes drugs, airway devices and adjuncts, bougie, suction, adequate oxygen, a breathing and ventilation system, and monitoring equipment. An example of a kit dump list is shown in Table 76.2.

Box 76.8 Ventilator

- Ensure ventilator turns on
- Set to 100% oxygen (no air mix)
- Tidal volume: 6–8 ml kg^{-1}
- Respiratory rate: 12 breaths min^{-1}
- Check capnograph function.

Box 76.9 Personnel

Ideally, four people are required although given operational constraints this may not be achievable at all times.

Intubation will be performed by an appropriately skilled operator.

Other crucial tasks to be completed by the team will include:

- Cricoid pressure/laryngeal manipulation
- Administration of drugs
- Manual in-line stabilization (MILS) as indicated by clinical condition and history
- Monitoring the patient.

When MILS is performed, remove the front of the cervical collar.

Box 76.10 Patient optimization: pre-oxygenation (2)

- All efforts must be made to pre-oxygenate the patient to prolong the time before life-threatening desaturation occurs after induction of anaesthesia if problems occur. Adjuncts, sedation, and assisted ventilation may all be required. Do not abandon patient optimization unless there is no feasible alternative.
- Continue pre-oxygenation via bag with reservoir and mask for at least 1 min in addition to the time spent with a Hudson mask *in situ*. If the condition of the patient allows continue preoxygenation of the patient using oxygen at 15 litres min^{-1} via a tight-fitting non-rebreather mask for at least 3 min. If Sp_{O_2} is less than 95% after 60 s or there is poor respiratory effort/apnoea, assist with bag–valve–mask (BVM) ventilation.
- Ensure that mask is tight fitting and airway unobstructed (use manual manoeuvres, adjuncts, and suction as necessary). Attach capnograph to BVM to ensure adequate ventilation during this phase and to establish baseline CO_2 trace.
- During this time, complete the challenge–response checklist, see Figure 76.2.

Box 76.11 Intubation

- Ensure all of team are ready.
- Identify correct anatomical position and apply cricoid pressure.
- Administer induction agent STAT.
- Flush line with running i.v. infusion.
- Administer neuromuscular blocking agent STAT.
- Wait for 30 s before commencing attempt at intubation. Fasciculations may occur if suxamethonium is used, but not if rocuronium is used.
- Intubate the trachea.
- This attempt must last no longer than 30 s (timed by team member).
- Inflate cuff until air leak disappears.
- If the trachea cannot be intubated on the first attempt (usually as a result of a poor view of the cords), undertake the '30 s drills' as described in Box 76.12.
- Inability to intubate the trachea within three attempts despite performing the 30 s drills mandates using the failed intubation drill, see Figure 76.3.

Box 76.12 30 s drills

- These are to be undertaken if the trachea cannot initially be intubated.
- They must be completed within 30 s. A properly pre-oxygenated patient should not desaturate within this time.
- Reposition yourself.
- Reposition the patient.
- Suction as necessary.
- Reduce downward cricoid pressure in favour of BURP—backwards, upwards, and right pressure to counter the opposing forces exerted by the laryngoscope.
- Try an alternative laryngoscope blade.

Box 76.13 Confirm tube position

- Watch for chest movement
- Auscultate in both axillae and over the epigastrium
- Attach catheter mount, filter, and capnograph
- Confirm presence of end tidal CO_2
- Remove cricoid pressure only on the instruction of the intubator
- Secure tube
- Repeat NIBP while securing tube.

Box 76.14 Attach ventilator

Ventilate with bag and mask for as little time as possible.

Box 76.15 Transport

- Secure all lines, tubes, and tubing.
- Administer:
  - Morphine 0.1 mg kg^{-1} in divided doses
  - Midazolam 0.1 mg kg^{-1} in divided doses
  - Rocuronium 0.6 mg kg^{-1} (if suxamethonium used at induction—not required if rocuronium used at induction)
  - Metaraminol 0.5 mg i.v. repeated to effect
- Thiopental (small doses titrated to effect) may be useful if the (head-injured) patient remains very hypertensive.
- Adjust ventilation to maintain end-tidal CO_2 at 4.5–5.0 kPa.
- If there is evidence of imminent coning, ventilate to end-tidal CO_2 of 4.0–4.5 kPa.
- Avoid further hyperventilation completely.
- Alert the receiving hospital.

been undiagnosed before anaesthesia may become apparent. These may take the form of occult pneumothorax which is converted to a tension pneumothorax under positive pressure ventilation, undiagnosed haemorrhage which presents as a substantial hypotension with the vasodilation and reduction in endogenous catecholamines after induction, or injuries that may not have been observed in a previously agitated or combative patient. Full documentation of the procedure must be made and Box 76.16 shows an example of the minimum data required from a UK air ambulance service.

Transfer to definitive care after anaesthesia and intubation must be controlled and prompt. As with in-hospital patient care, close

Table 76.2 Intubating kit

Equipment	Notes
Bag and mask attached to oxygen	
Laryngoscopes	For adult patients, begin with a size 4 Mackintosh blade. Have an alternative laryngoscope available Check size, patency, cuff, and presence of 22 mm attachment. Lubricate cuff
Tracheal tube	
Gum elastic bougie	Use bougie for every pre-hospital RSI
20 ml syringe	To inflate cuff
Suction device	Positioned to the right of patient's head
Catheter mount and filter	Assembled
Tube tie	

Table 76.3 Pharmaceutical agents for rapid sequence induction

Indication	Drug	Intravenous/intraosseous dosage	Notes
Pre-treatment	Fentanyl	1–3 μg kg^{-1}	Pre-treatment is designed to reduce swings in blood pressure and intracranial pressure, to allow pre-oxygenation to occur and to allow preparation for anaesthesia to occur safely
	Midazolam	10–30 μg kg^{-1}	
	Ketamine	200–400 μg kg^{-1}	
Induction of anaesthesia	Ketamine	1–2 mg kg^{-1}	Provides cardiovascular stability. May cause increased salivation
	Thiopental	1–4 mg kg^{-1}	May cause precipitous drop in blood pressure so careful dose titration is required. Commonly used for isolated head injury and status epilepticus
	Etomidate	150–300 μg kg^{-1}	Cardiovascularly stable but associated with adrenocortical suppression
	Propofol	1–2 mg kg^{-1}	Not used in UK pre-hospital practice because of significant reductions in mean arterial blood pressure after administration
Neuromuscular block	Rocuronium	0.6–1.2 mg kg^{-1}	Medium-acting non-depolarizing neuromuscular blocking agent which is gaining popularity as a first-line treatment
	Suxamethonium (succinylcholine)	1–2 mg kg^{-1}	Short-acting depolarizing neuromuscular blocking agent
Maintenance	Morphine	100 μg kg^{-1}	Usually given in titrated doses with midazolam
	Midazolam	100 μg kg^{-1}	Usually given in titrated doses with morphine
	Propofol infusion	1.5–4.5 mg kg^{-1} h^{-1}	Not common in UK practice
	Pancuronium	20 μg kg^{-1}	Long-acting non depolarizing relaxant
	Rocuronium	150 μg kg^{-1} or 300 μg kg^{-1} h^{-1} as infusion	See 'Neuromuscular block'

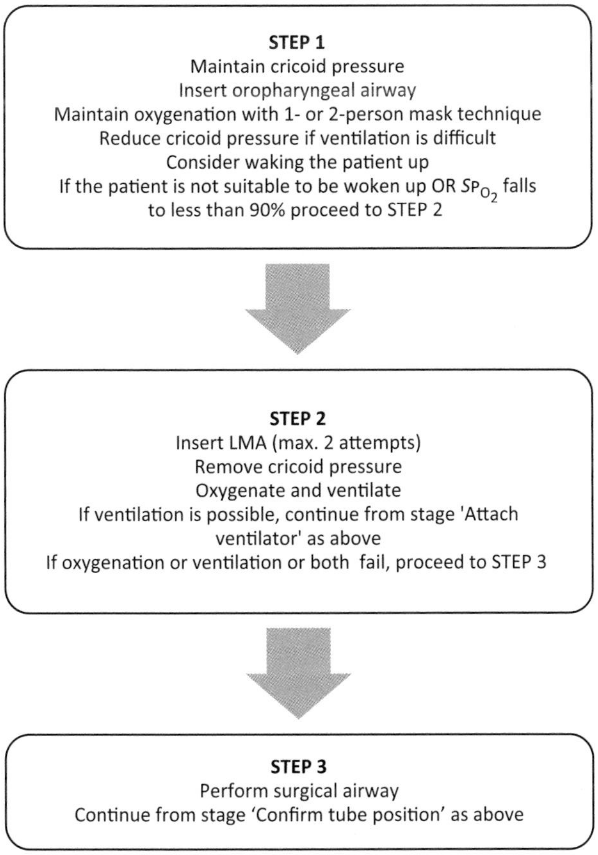

STEP 1
Maintain cricoid pressure
Insert oropharyngeal airway
Maintain oxygenation with 1- or 2-person mask technique
Reduce cricoid pressure if ventilation is difficult
Consider waking the patient up
If the patient is not suitable to be woken up OR Sp_{O_2} falls to less than 90% proceed to STEP 2

STEP 2
Insert LMA (max. 2 attempts)
Remove cricoid pressure
Oxygenate and ventilate
If ventilation is possible, continue from stage 'Attach ventilator' as above
If oxygenation or ventilation or both fail, proceed to STEP 3

STEP 3
Perform surgical airway
Continue from stage 'Confirm tube position' as above

Figure 76.3 Failed intubation drill.

attention must be given to patient safety. Positioning is often managed through the use of a vacuum mattress, spinal board, or scoop stretcher with straps, neck collar, and head blocks. However, great care must be taken to ensure that there are no articles left between the patient and the stretcher; these may take the form of medical devices such as infusion-giving set caps, environmental debris such as gravel or glass, or other items such as mobile telephones. These may all cause significant pressure necrosis which is a particular issue in the presence of relative hypotension.

Monitoring of physiological variables must be continuous, visible, and with the benefit of audible and visual alarms. The visual alarm is especially important when the background noise of sirens or ambient helicopter cabin noise is considered. It is also worth considering that reliability of NIBP and pulse oximetry is very variable in these environments and often the presence of end-tidal carbon dioxide must act as a surrogate marker for the adequacy of circulation.

When preparing for departure it is worth considering a pre-departure checklist to ensure that all equipment used on scene is retrieved, and all equipment and drugs that might be required en route is carried. The possibility of vehicle breakdown or adverse weather necessitating aircraft diversion should always be considered when assessing supplies of oxygen and pharmaceutical agents available.

Thoracostomy

Lungs are particularly sensitive organs to trauma. Pneumothorax can be considered in blunt, penetrating, blast, and diving-related injuries. Any injury where a rib fracture is suspected should alert the pre-hospital practitioner to the possibility of underlying lung

Box 76.16 Data to be recorded after rapid sequence induction

- Indication
- Estimate of weight
- Pre-RSI observations: heart rate, NIBP, Sp_{O_2}, respiratory
- Pre-RSI neurology: GCS score and gross neurology
- Pre-oxygenation duration
- MILS used or not
- Cricoid used or not
- Blade size and type
- View obtained
- Bougie used or not
- Size of tracheal tube and length at teeth
- Position confirmed with:
  - capnography
  - auscultation
- Post-RSI observations: heart rate, NIBP, Sp_{O_2}, respiratory rate
- Adverse events *or* none
- All drugs and times each bolus given.

injury. In the pre-hospital environment, diagnostic techniques are often limited to observation, auscultation, percussion, and manual palpation when circumstances permit and measurement of pulse oximetry. More recently, handheld ultrasound devices have been developed which will clearly demonstrate the presence of a small pneumothorax but these are not currently widely available.

Therefore, the practitioner is often faced with a likely diagnosis based upon observed mechanism, basic examination techniques, and limited monitoring devices. In circumstances where a patient with a possible pneumothorax is awake and alert, this can be supplemented by the symptoms being experienced. These may include shortness of breath, pleuritic pain, and dyspnoea. However, in a polytrauma patient with a reduced level of consciousness, these symptoms may not be readily communicated. If intubation and ventilation of such a patient is being considered, the presence of a small pneumothorax becomes an important diagnosis to make or exclude.

If a pneumothorax is suspected, there is a balance of risks to consider when deciding how to proceed. The risks of leaving the pneumothorax untreated or partially treated are those associated with tension pneumothorax and inadequate ventilation (especially in head injury). These risks present an immediate and delayed morbidity and potential mortality. The risks associated with decompressing a suspected pneumothorax are operator dependent but include immediate bleeding, damage to structures and causing a pneumothorax if one did not exist, and delayed risks of infection as this is often performed in unclean conditions.

If, based on mechanism and injury pattern, a pneumothorax might be present in an otherwise stable patient ready for transfer to a nearby hospital, it might be perfectly reasonable to observe the patient and ensure that the suspected diagnosis is clearly handed over on arrival. However, if the likely course of events is that the patient will require pre-hospital intubation, then being faced with an uncontrolled tension pneumothorax during transfer would swing the balance in favour of decompressing the chest before or immediately after intubation.

There are two common methods for formal decompression of a simple pneumothorax: finger thoracostomy and tube thoracostomy. In addition, an immediate but temporary procedure in patients suffering from a tension pneumothorax is a needle decompression. After acute decompression a tube thoracostomy needs to be performed.

Needle decompression is an emergency procedure during which a large-bore cannula (commonly a 14 or 12 G venous cannula) is inserted through the second intercostal space in the mid-clavicular line. This technique is one that is intended to allow the release of extrapleural gas under pressure via the cannula. It is associated with several complications, the most significant of which are the failure of the cannula to reach the pleural cavity and subsequent dislodgment or kinking of the cannula. It is, however, currently the only technique available to the majority of paramedics.

Finger thoracostomy is a technique that allows manual examination of the pleural cavity along with decompression of a pneumothorax. The technique is commonly described as forming a 2.5–5 cm incision along the upper border of the sixth rib in the mid-axillary line to the depth of the sub-cutaneous fat. This is followed by blunt dissection with a forceps until the pleural cavity is reached. A finger is then inserted into the track to open it up, allow the escape of gas and assess for inflation of the lung. Once this is achieved, a dressing which allows one-way gas flow is applied to create a seal permitting escape of further gas. Should ventilation become difficult or signs suggest a recurrence of the pneumothorax, a finger can simply be reinserted into the existing hole to re-form the pathway. Extreme caution should be exercised when performing this procedure as there is a significant risk of rib fractures around the site of thoracostomy. Insertion of a gloved finger may result in fragments of rib piercing the glove and skin of the operator with an associated chance of blood-borne infection.

Tube thoracostomy is an extension of the finger thoracostomy technique in which a chest drain is inserted into the hole to allow formal drainage. The time spent performing the insertion and securing the tube, along with the chance of damaging underlying structures during insertion, mean that in most cases finger thoracostomy is often the preferred technique. Occasions that might warrant a tube thoracostomy include an obviously damaged chest wall when finger thoracostomy would be impossible, or in the case of significant haemothorax to minimize the spread of external haemorrhage and risk to attendants.

Handover

On arrival in hospital, it is of great importance that what has happened to the patient during and immediately after the incident is relayed clearly to the waiting emergency department team. It is often poorly appreciated that the course of the patient through the hospital is frequently determined well before that patient arrives. Structured handovers are used to maximize the information passed in a concise manner. One such structure is ATMIST:

A: Age and gender of patient

T: Time of incident and key timings thereafter

M: Mechanism of injury/illness

I: Injuries observed and suspected from mechanism

S: Signs and symptoms

T: Treatment given.

In addition, other key information that has been learnt during the pre-hospital phase such as co-morbidities, allergies, and social circumstances should be clearly passed on to the receiving team as the patient may no longer be in a position to give these details.

Ongoing developments

Areas of current interest in trauma and medical pre-hospital care relate to evolving technologies in terms of materials and electronics.

Temperature regulation is recognized as being a major contributor to secondary injury. The benefits of therapeutic hypothermia after non-traumatic cardiac arrest are well documented, as are the harmful effects of hypothermia in trauma with regard to physiological effects such as tissue perfusion and coagulation. It is beyond the ability of most pre-hospital services to actively cool or warm patients because of the significant amounts of power required to perform this. Much research and development is being directed towards reduction of heat loss, however, with pocket-sized fluid warmers, materials which limit conduction, convection and radiation heat loss, and more accurate means of measuring core temperature. While this development continues, the basic techniques of protecting the patient from the environment, minimizing scene times, and good technique in packaging patients in dry and insulative materials for transfer must not be forgotten.

Another area of interest is diagnostic equipment that is durable and portable. Handheld ultrasound is becoming readily available and may be used to guide the pre-hospital clinician as to likely injuries, and assist in securing vascular access in hypovolaemic patients. Uses are likely to include identification of pneumothorax and pericardial tamponade which require on-scene treatment, but may also distract practitioners into abdominal examinations that will not ultimately affect the pre-hospital management.

In a similar way, point-of-care testing such as blood-gas analysers, haemoglobin assays, and suchlike are becoming available in small portable devices. These may be of interest to isolated practitioners to assist in referral decisions, but are unlikely to find a place in acute pre-hospital medicine.

Declaration of interest

None declared.

References

Alexander DS, Klein S. Ambulance personnel and critical incidents. *Br J Psychiatry* 2001; **178**: 76–81

Aylwin CJ, König TC, Brennan NW, *et al.* Reduction in critical mortality in urban mass casualty incidents: analysis of triage, surge, and resource use after the London bombings on July 7, 2005. *Lancet* 2006; **368**: 2219–25

Baker CC, Oppenheimer L, Stephens B, Lewis FR, Trunkey DD. Epidemiology of trauma deaths. *Am J Surg* 1980; **140**: 144–50

Barkana Y, Stein M, Maor R, Lynn M, Eldad A. Prehospital blood transfusion in prolonged evacuation. *J Trauma* 1999; **46**: 176–80

Battlefield Advanced Trauma Life Support (BATLS). *J R Army Med Corps* 2001; **147**: 187–91

Beekley AC, Sebesta JA, Blackbourne LH, *et al.* Prehospital tourniquet use in Operation Iraqi Freedom: effect on hemorrhage control and outcomes. *J Trauma* 2008; **64**: s28–s37

Biewener A, Aschenbrenner U, Rammelt S, Grass R, Zwipp H. Impact of helicopter transport and hospital level on mortality of polytrauma patients. *J Trauma* 2004; **56**: 94–8

Birk HO, Henriksen LO. Pre-hospital interventions: on-scene times and ambulance technicians' experience. *Prehosp Disaster Med* 2002; **17**: 167–9

Blow O, Magliore L, Claridge JA, Butler K, Young JS. The golden hour and the silver day: detection and correction of occult hypoperfusion within 24 hours improves outcome from major trauma. *J Trauma* 1999: **47**: 964–9

Bond RJ, Kortbeek JB, Preshaw RM. Field trauma triage: combining mechanism of injury with the prehospital index for improved trauma triage tool. *J Trauma* 1997; **43**: 283–7

Briggs RS, Brown PM, Crabb ME, *et al.* The Brighton resuscitation ambulances: a continuing experiment in prehospital care by ambulance staff. *Br Med J* 1976; **2**: 1161–5

Coroner's Inquests into the Deaths of Diana, Princess of Wales and Mr Dodi Al Fayed. 2008. Available from http://webarchive.nationalarchives.gov.uk/20090607230252/http:/www.scottbaker-inquests.gov.uk/

Control of Major Bleeding after Trauma (COMBAT) Trial; NCT01838863

Cotton BA, Guy JS, Morris JA Jr, Abumrad NN. The cellular, metabolic and systemic consequences of aggressive fluid resuscitation strategies. *Shock* 2006; **26**: 115–21

Cummins RO, Ornato JP, Thies WH, Pepe PE. Improving survival from sudden cardiac arrest: the "chain of survival" concept. A statement for health professionals from the Advanced Cardiac Life Support Subcommittee and the Emergency Cardiac Care Committee American Heart Association. *Circulation* 1991; **83**: 1832–47

Dalal SA, Burgess AR, Siegel JH, *et al.* Pelvic fracture in multiple trauma: classification by mechanism is key to pattern of organ injury, resuscitative requirements, and outcome. *J Trauma* 1989; **29**: 981–1000

Davies G. Thirteen survivors of prehospital thoracotomy for penetrating trauma: a prehospital physician-performed resuscitation procedure that can yield good results. *J Trauma* 2011; **70**: 75–8

Davis DP, Hoyt DB, Ochs M, *et al.* The effect of paramedic rapid sequence intubation on outcome in patients with severe traumatic brain injury. *J Trauma* 2003; **54**: 444–53

Davis DP, Idris AH, Sise MJ, *et al.* Early ventilation and outcome in patients with moderate to severe traumatic brain injury. *Crit Care Med* 2006; **34**: 1202–8

de Peretti F, Cambas PM, Hovorka I, Veneau B, Argenson C. Motorcycle tanks and their role in severe pelvic injuries. *Injury* 1994; **25**: 223–5

Edwards PM. *Historical Dictionary of the Korean War*. Lanham, MD: Scarecrow Press, 2010

Fullerton CS, Ursano RJ, Wang L. Acute stress disorder, posttraumatic stress disorder, and depression in disaster or rescue workers. *Am J Psychiatry* 2004; **161**: 1370–6

Gonzalez RP, Cummings GR, Phelan HA, Mulekar MS, Rodning CB. Does increased emergency medical services prehospital time affect mortality in rural motor vehicle crashes? *Am J Surg* 2009; **197**: 30–4

Gosselin RA, Roberts I, Gillespie WJ. Antibiotics for preventing infection in open limb fractures. *Cochrane Database Syst Rev* 2004; **1**: CD003764

Granville-Chapman J, Jacobs N, Midwinter MJ. Pre-hospital haemostatic dressings: a systematic review. *Injury* 2011; **41**: 447–59

Gunst M, Ghaemmaghami V, Gruszecki A, *et al.* Changing epidemiology of trauma deaths leads to a bimodal distribution. *Proc (Bayl Univ Med Cent)* 2010; **23**: 349–54

Hodgetts TJ, Mahoney PF, Russell MQ, Byers M. ABC to <C>ABC: redefining the military paradigm. *Emerg Med J* 2006; **23**: 745–6

Hunt RC, Bryan DM, Brinkley VS, Whitley TW, Benson NH. Inability to assess breath sounds during air medical transport by helicopter. *JAMA* 1991; **265**: 1982–4

Hyde P, Mackenzie R, Ng G, Reid C, Pearson G. Availability and utilisation of physician-based pre-hospital critical care support to the NHS ambulance service in England, Wales and Northern Ireland. *Emerg Med J* 2012; **29**: 177–81

Kornfält J, Johansson A. Occurence of hypotherima in a pre-hospital setting, southern Sweden. *Int Emerg Nurs* 2010; **18**: 76–9

Krzanicki DA, Porter KM Personal protective equipment provision in pre-hospital care: a national survey. *Emerg Med J* 2009; **26**: 892–5

Larrey DJ. *Memoirs of Military Surgery and Campaigns of the French Armies* (trans. Richard Wilmott Hall), Vol I. Baltimore, MD: Joseph Cushing/ University Press of Sergeant Hall, 1814

Lieurance R, Benjamin JB, Rappaport WD. Blood loss and transfusion in patients with isolated femur fractures. *J Orthop Trauma* 1992; 6: 175–9

Lockey DJ, Mackenzie R, Redhead J, *et al.* London Bombings July 2005: the immediate pre-hospital medical response. *Resuscitation* 2005; **66**: 9–12

McDonell A. Issues of infection control in pre-hospital settings. *J Emerg Primary Health Care* 2008; **6**: 1

Metropolitan Police. *The Operation Paget Inquiry Report into the Allegation of Conspiracy to Murder*. London: Metropolitan Police, 2006

Morrison CA, Carrick MM, Norman MA, *et al.* Hypotensive resuscitation strategy reduces transfusion requirements and severe postoperative coagulopathy in trauma patients with hemorrhagic shock: preliminary results of a randomized controlled trial. *Trauma* 2011; **70**: 652–63

PreHospital Air Medical Plasma Trial (PAMPer): NCT01818427

Resuscitation with PreHospital Blood Products (RePHILL) EudraCT: 2015-001401-13

Rossaint R, Bouillon B, Cerny V, *et al.* Management of bleeding following major trauma: an updated European guideline. *Crit Care* 2010; **14**: R52

Seamon MJ, Fisher CA, Gaughan J, *et al.* Prehospital procedures before emergency department thoracotomy: "scoop and run" saves lives. *J Trauma* 2007; **63**: 113–20

Smith J, Greaves I, Porter K. *Oxford Desk Reference: Major Trauma*. Oxford: Oxford University Press, 2010

Smith JP, Bodai BI, Hill AS, Frey CF. Prehospital stabilization of critically injured patients: a failed concept. *J Trauma* 1985; **25**: 65–70

Taylor CB, Stevenson M, Jan S, Middleton PM, Fitzharris M, Myburgh JA. A systematic review of the costs and benefits of helicopter emergency medical services. *Injury* 2010; **41**: 10–20

CHAPTER 77

Anaesthesia for medical imaging and bronchoscopic procedures

Sebastian Brandt and Hartmut Gehring

Anaesthesia for neuroradiology imaging and interventional procedures

In recent years, there has been significant progress in the field of interventional neuroradiology. Indications, treatment options, and the number of cases have all increased significantly and anaesthetists are involved in a large number of interventions. For neuroradiological procedures, anaesthesia can represent a significant challenge for the anaesthetist that should not be underestimated. The procedures are often of long duration on elderly patients with a variety of comorbidities. The neuroradiological intervention units are often located far away from the operating theatre so that in emergencies it can be difficult to get help. In addition, the patient is often inaccessible under sterile dressings. The anaesthetist with their anaesthesia workstation cannot remain close to the patient, but must instead adopt a position at the foot or on the side of the patient and must take care to ensure that the ventilation circuit and i.v. tubing (and the monitoring cables) are not within reach of the rotating radiology unit (C-arms).

Neuroradiological interventions can be carried out either in an elective or an emergency setting and can be roughly categorized as purely diagnostic (angiography), embolization, or recanalization interventions.

Table 77.1 provides an overview of the various types of endovascular neuroradiological intervention.

Table 77.1 Examples of endovascular interventions in neuroradiology

Intervention: coiling, embolization	Intervention: recanalization
Use (1): Tumour embolization: (meningioma, glomus tumour, angiofibroma, haemangioma)	Use (1): Treatment of acute ischaemic stroke: stenting, angioplasty, mechanical thrombectomy, local intra-arterial lysis
Use (2): Endovascular treatment of acute bleeding: intractable epistaxis (e.g. hereditary haemorrhagic telangiectasia), carotid blowout (tumour, infection), carotid cavernous sinus fistula (traumatic or spontaneous), dural arteriovenous fistula, arteriovenous malformation	Use (2): Treatment of intracerebral vasospasms (e.g. after subarachnoid bleeding): angioplasty, local intravascular spasmolysis
Risk: Rupture of cerebral aneurysm (acute subarachnoid bleeding) Danger of acute intracranial bleeding (cerebral aneurysm)	Risk: Danger of acute ischaemic stroke: stenting or angioplasty of stenosis (supra-aortic or intracranial vessels)

Radiation protection

As neuroradiological interventions are often time-consuming procedures, the cumulative dose of radiation received during surgery can be considerable. One should also remember that the neuroradiological unit is designed to protect the operator as much as possible (such as through the use of built-in protective panels, etc.). The design of the apparatus takes no consideration of an anaesthetist who might also be present in the room. It is therefore of prime importance for the anaesthetist to take their own personal radiation protection measures. This includes wearing adequate protective clothing (with thyroid protection), radiation protection glasses, and a personal dosimeter (worn under clothing), using appropriate movable shields, and (perhaps most importantly) maintaining as large a distance as possible from the radiation source (think of the inverse square law).

Acute stroke

Recanalization can be achieved by a number of interventions: angioplasty, thrombectomy, stenting, intra-arterial lysis, and spasmolysis (e.g. vasospasm after subarachnoid haemorrhage). When (and if) the patient with an acute stroke should be intubated before a recanalization procedure often depends on the anaesthesia department's protocols. The scientific literature on this subject is inconclusive, and more recent studies seem to indicate that avoiding intubation has a positive effect on patient outcome (Jumaa et al., 2010; Nichols et al., 2010).

There is a balance of risks. The patient with a decreased conscious level is at risk of aspiration during the intervention and the movement of the microcatheter within the brain can lead to nausea, vomiting, and acute cardiovascular reactions.

The intracranial navigation in an anaesthetized, immobile (and even briefly apnoeic) patient is easier, making the interventions shorter and safer, but this clearly has a cost in terms of anaesthesia resources. There is also the risk of haemodynamic instability after induction of anaesthesia.

Immediately after the intervention weaning can be complicated to perform, so the option of postoperative ventilation must be available.

In order to decide which anaesthetic approach to use, a risk:benefit assessment must be undertaken for the individual patient in cooperation with the other relevant specialities (e.g. neuroradiology, neurology, and intensive care).

Embolization of intracranial aneurysms and vascular malformations

With such procedures, one needs to distinguish between elective and emergency interventions. Emergency interventions are generally for acute subarachnoid haemorrhage. In all cases, deep general anaesthesia with tracheal intubation and invasive blood pressure measurement is required as navigation of microcatheters within small intracranial vessels is performed, and there is a great risk of an acute subarachnoid haemorrhage if the aneurysm is perforated. Navigation is often technically demanding; no movement of the patient can be tolerated. Sometimes phases of apnoea are required. The interventions often last several hours. If acute perforation occurs, blood pressure must be lowered immediately to the lowest acceptable value (consult immediately with the attending neuroradiologist), and consider emergency transport to the computed tomography scanner or the neurosurgical operating theatre.

Pure angiography and extracranial interventions

If general anaesthesia is not needed for these patients, sedation and analgesia may be appropriate. Nevertheless, a careful assessment of the individual patient and their risk profile is needed.

Preoperative assessment

- Pre-existing conditions, medical history, medication, and intubation anatomy
- Coagulation history
- Neurological status
- Laboratory values
- Glycaemic status (patients after a stroke must have normoglycaemic sugar concentrations strictly maintained).

Anaesthetic management

- Standard monitoring for all patients (ECG, Sp_{O_2}, non-invasive blood pressure, respiratory gases including end-tidal CO_2). In high-risk patients (e.g. those having intracranial interventions, those who have had acute stroke), place intra-arterial pressure monitoring—ideally before induction of anaesthesia—to help avoid rapid changes in blood pressure.
- If a difficult intubation is anticipated, consider inducing anaesthesia in a suitable location—such as the emergency department or the operating theatre—rather than the intervention suite.
- In patients at risk of aspiration, perform a rapid sequence induction of anaesthesia.
- Establish at least two venous cannulae if there is no central access. One access point is for vasopressors and antihypertensives.
- Use total i.v. anaesthesia (TIVA) where possible—volatile anaesthetics increase cerebral blood flow.
- Place a urinary catheter for longer interventions.
- Patient warming: use equipment compatible with the radiology suite. Consider a heated mattress—blankets alone are insufficient. Temperature can be measured via the urinary catheter.

Top priorities

- Work rapidly but safely ('after injury, time is brain'!)
- Normotension (allow neuroradiologists to specify target values), normocapnia, and normoglycaemia
- Coagulation management should be planned on an interdisciplinary basis and responsibilities should be agreed.

Anaesthesia for magnetic resonance imaging

Magnetic resonance imaging (MRI) is a diagnostic imaging procedure where strong magnetic fields are used to produce images with good spatial resolution and high soft tissue contrast. As such, MRI is particularly well suited for imaging the brain and spinal cord, abdominal parenchymal organs, lungs, and muscles and tendons. The examination of the heart by MRI is also growing in importance. A major advantage of MRI is that no ionizing radiation is used.

Special hazards in MRI

In addition to the general problems of an anaesthesia workstation away from the operating theatre, there are a number of hazards that are specific for MRI. In MRI, although there is no ionizing radiation, a very strong magnetic field is omnipresent. A distinction needs to be made here between the effects of static and alternating magnetic fields. The static magnetic field of a clinical MRI scanner has a strength of between 0.5 and 3 tesla (T). For research purposes, devices are also available where much stronger magnetic fields (currently up to 11.7 T) are used. Very strong magnetic fields can exert direct effects on the human body; this includes stimulation of peripheral nerves. Devices that are currently used clinically, however, operate below the threshold for peripheral nerve stimulation. For systems using 3 T or higher, it is possible that a metallic taste will be noticed or that dizziness and nausea will be caused by inner ear irritation. The main danger in using MRI, however, is when ferromagnetic, paramagnetic, or electrically conductive objects in the vicinity of the MRI scanner interact in harmful ways with the human body. This can happen, for example, if a 'missile effect' occurs. In such a case, a rogue ferromagnetic or paramagnetic object in the MRI room can act as a projectile and injure patients or staff. If the object is large, such as a bed, a person can also become trapped between the object and the scanner.

A strong high-frequency field is generated (radio frequency, or RF field) inside the scanner room. This is usually well shielded from the outside world by using a Faraday cage. Electrically conductive objects (e.g. objects made of metal or carbon fibres) interact with the high-frequency field and can, under certain circumstances, become hot. If the human body has contact with these objects, severe burns may result. Ultimately, any piece of electrical and electronic equipment inside the scanner room that has not been extensively tested and declared fit for MRI may malfunction or stop working. Also, the quality of the magnetic resonance images obtained can be affected by 'image noise' and artifacts if metallic or electrical devices not fit for MRI have been used in the MRI scanner room.

During the examination, the MRI scanner produces a very loud noise that can achieve levels of greater than 100 dB. Patients (even those under anaesthesia) and attending staff (radiologist, anaesthetist, nurses, etc.) need to be protected with adequate ear defences.

Anaesthesia in MRI

Anaesthetists will be involved in caring for patients undergoing MRI when a sedation or general anaesthesia is required for the examination. MRI examinations may require patients to lie absolutely still in the narrow MRI tube for up to 2 h. As such, anaesthetic management is required for the following patient groups:

- Children up to school age
- Patients with severe claustrophobia
- Patients with involuntary movement disorders
- Patients with severe pain
- Patients with learning disabilities
- Disoriented patients
- Critically ill patients with continuous monitoring, mechanical ventilation, or both.

The attending anaesthetist must be competent to identify and manage critical situations that may arise at any time. They must be able to carry out a change in procedure, for example, from a sedation to general anaesthesia with a protected airway. This requires them to have completed specialist training with close supervision by a consultant.

Preparation

The patient (and staff!) must be checked thoroughly before entering the scanner room for the presence of any metallic or paramagnetic objects and implants. Intensive care patients are frequently particularly problematic, as a variety of monitor cables, infusion tubes, dressings, and so on, need to be assessed for MRI compatibility. In these patients in particular there is also the risk that some information (e.g. about implants) may not be documented and can often not be queried.

If the patient wears implants or has medical devices implanted in their body, the attending radiologist is responsible for determining whether a scan can be carried out, as they also have access to extensive Internet databases that they can refer to (such as http://www.MRIsafety.com or http://www.magresource.com).

There are both American and European standards concerning the classification of a medical device into magnetic resonance safety categories (Table 77.2). The responsibility of the anaesthetist is to ensure that all medical materials on the patient, and all anaesthesia equipment to be used in the MRI room, are suitable. It is important to stress that a medical device which has been approved for a certain field strength (e.g. 3 T) is not necessarily suitable for a weaker magnetic field (e.g. 1.5 T). The approval for specific areas of application can be referred to in the product information, and any restrictions should always be followed. For instance, the use of a certain device may be restricted to 'out of the 5000 gauss-field line'. Magnetic field lines are typically painted or taped onto the floor of the scanner room. Details have to be checked beforehand with the local magnetic resonance safety officer.

The anaesthesia workstation in the MRI room

The induction of and recovery from anaesthesia should ideally take place in a dedicated area close to the scanner room. Here the patient should be switched to an MRI-compatible monitoring system. Another advantage is that special, non-MRI-compatible equipment (fibreoptics, defibrillator, difficult airway equipment) for emergency situations can be used and stored here. All specialists involved should be aware of which items are MRI compatible and which are not. An appropriate form of labelling is required.

Minimum requirements and desirable options for anaesthesia work in the MRI room can be found in Table 77.3. The safety standards should be as strictly adhered to as they are in the operating theatre. This means that any compromise leading to an unauthorized

Table 77.2 Definitions of magnetic resonance (MR) safety

MR safety category	Definition
MR safe MR	Item poses no known hazard in all MR environments
MR conditional MR	Item poses no known hazards in a specified MR environment with specified conditions of use
MR unsafe MR	Item poses hazards in all MR environments

Data from ASTM F2503-E and DIN 6877-1.

Table 77.3 Minimum technical requirements and desirable options for anaesthesia care in a MR-environment

Minimal equipment	Options
MR-compatible anaesthesia machine	Operable and monitorable wirelessly from the outside Vapour Ventilation modes for assisted ventilation
MR-compatible patient monitoring (ECG, Sp_{O_2}, blood pressure, end-tidal CO_2)	Operable and monitorable wirelessly from the outside Invasive pressure and temperature measurement
MR-compatible syringe pump(s)	Operable and monitorable wirelessly from the outside Multiple pumps (e.g. for additional vasopressors)
Gas supply from wall connection or MR-compatible gas cylinders (oxygen)	Additional compressed air, vacuum Anaesthesia gas extraction
	Video surveillance communications system

use of non-MRI-suitable equipment must be rejected. For the purposes of operating non-MRI-compatible syringe pumps from outside the scanner room, excessively long syringe pump lines are sometimes improvised by combining multiple lines. This practice is not safe; volumes of drugs delivered cannot be accurately calculated because of the high tube compliance. Just as unacceptable is the use of highly extended ventilation tubes as this results in the creation of unacceptably large dead-space volumes.

Anaesthesia management

Anaesthesia for MRI covers the entire range of anaesthesia services provided by monitored anaesthesia care with or without sedation: with or without a preserved spontaneous breathing right up to deep general anaesthesia with mechanical ventilation. Knowing the precise requirements for the planned examination, the anaesthetist decides on the appropriate anaesthetic procedure based on the individual patient's risk profile. As an example, the radiologist might desire brief periods of apnoea during imaging to avoid any artifacts as a result of breathing movements (e.g. a cardiac MRI). This would require deep general anaesthesia with a neuromuscular block. The anaesthetist must then decide whether they remain in the scanner room or whether monitoring the anaesthesia from outside the room is sufficient. In addition to the patient's condition, spatial issues also play a role. Modern MRI-compatible patient monitors and syringe pumps allow for wireless monitoring and operation from outside the scanner room. In this scenario, video monitoring of the patient in MRI is also desirable.

If the MRI scan is performed under sedation with preserved spontaneous breathing, a continuous monitoring of end-tidal CO_2 is recommended so that apnoea can be recognized in good time. For general anaesthesia, a TIVA with propofol (sometimes in combination with an opioid such as remifentanil) is carried out in the MRI room. However, if the option of volatile anaesthesia is available, a balanced anaesthesia can be provided—as long as this is not contraindicated for the patient.

The heat balance of infants and young children can be disrupted by MRI. Although children in the MRI room can become hypothermic as a result of cold exposure and the effects of the anaesthetic, some 3 T MRI cases have been reported where hyperthermia has been induced by the magnetic field. Unfortunately, accurate temperature monitoring cannot be performed with many of the standard MRI patient monitors. Active warming using patient warming devices, as has long been established for surgical operations, is not currently possible with MRI.

Management of critical situations

In critical situations, the risk is particularly high that metallic objects are unwittingly or unknowingly brought into the scanner room. Clear visual alerts and metal detectors at the door to the MRI room can help to prevent this. If there is an incident or a critical situation in the MRI, the following decisions must be made as quickly as possible:

1. Can the situation be managed with the help of the available equipment (MRI compatible) in the MRI room? If not, an immediate evacuation must be carried out.
2. Is there a life-threatening situation involving a person being trapped by a large magnetic object (e.g. a hospital bed). If so, press the 'magnetic quench' button immediately.

Serious incidents generally require an immediate evacuation. Implementing this quickly and safely is not a trivial matter and requires regular training of the staff involved (anaesthetist, anaesthesia nurses, technicians, and radiologists).

The 'magnetic quench' should only be activated if an individual's life is at risk because of the strong magnetic field and where the situation cannot be controlled by other measures. During quenching, the liquid helium used to cool the magnetic coils is abruptly evaporated. Restoration of the operation readiness of the MRI costs €10 000 and takes a number of working days to complete.

The future

It is likely that both the number of anaesthetically supervised MRI scans and the field strength of the scanners themselves will increase over the coming years. In addition, the thresholds for magnetic fields in the workplace will be reduced so far that the presence of an anaesthetist in the scanner room shall no longer be possible. A European Union directive on this already exists (2004/40/EC). These facts and the currently developing area of 'Interventional MRI' will present a range of new technical and clinical challenges for anaesthesia in the future.

Anaesthesia for bronchoscopy

Diagnostic and therapeutic bronchoscopy can be implemented using a flexible fibreoptic bronchoscope, a rigid bronchoscope, or a combination of the two. By using a flexible fibreoptic bronchoscope, deeper regions within the bronchial-tracheal system can be reached, but because of the small size of the working channel, the spectrum of therapeutic and diagnostic procedures that can be carried out is restricted. Through a rigid bronchoscope, however, a multitude of instruments can be introduced and applied. Another advantage for a rigid tube is that it can also be used for ventilation. Although in most cases flexible bronchoscopy can be carried out without any anaesthesiological care and using just local anaesthesia with mild sedation, rigid bronchoscopy requires a deep general anaesthesia. Anaesthesia is always indicated for a bronchoscopy wherever the patient cannot tolerate the procedure (children, excessive restlessness, anxiety disorders), or where the patient is in too poorly a condition to undergo a local anaesthesia and sedation.

Table 77.4 provides an overview of the common indications for a bronchoscopy.

Table 77.4 Common indications for bronchoscopy

Procedure	Indications
Diagnostic	Bronchial and transbronchial biopsies (preferentially ultrasound guided, e.g. EBUS)
	Cytology (brush, lavage)
	Source of haemoptysis, unexplained cough
Therapeutic	Extraction of foreign bodies
	Reduction of obstructive tumours (e.g. laser, cryotherapy)
	Dilatation
	Palliative procedures (e.g. stenting, bronchial valves)
	Control haemorrhage
	Occlusion of fistulae

The patient for rigid bronchoscopy

A high proportion of patients for whom diagnostic or therapeutic interventions involving bronchoscopy are planned are also severely disabled as a result of underlying disease and pulmonary comorbidities. Patients with suspected lung cancer are often afflicted with an additional pulmonary impairment because of long-standing nicotine abuse (chronic obstructive pulmonary disease, hypertension, coronary heart disease). Lambert–Eaton syndrome, a neuromuscular paraneoplastic syndrome, occurs in approximately 60% of patients with small-cell bronchial carcinoma. In such patients, a prolonged duration of action of neuromuscular blocking agents can be expected.

The rigid bronchoscope

The rigid bronchoscope consists of a metal tube with an attached eyepiece and a connector for a cold light source. In addition, there are also connections for a ventilation tube. Ventilation can be carried out manually, or mechanically with the help of an anaesthesia ventilator, or using a jet ventilator. Often during a procedure a flexible bronchoscope is inserted through the rigid endoscope so that distal regions of the bronchial tree can be reached. For diagnostic purposes, an ultrasound probe can also be fitted to the tip of the flexible fibreoptic [endobronchial ultrasound (EBUS)].

Anaesthesia procedure for rigid bronchoscopy

1. Monitoring (ECG, Sp_{O_2}, blood pressure, end-tidal CO_2)
2. Anaesthesia induction after pre-oxygenation (e.g. with propofol or remifentanil)
3. Checking of mask ventilation
4. Neuromuscular block (short acting, e.g. with mivacurium or suxamethonium)
5. Positioning of the patient
6. Introduction of the bronchoscope
7. Connection of the ventilation tube (100% FI_{O_2}, high flow > 10 litres min^{-1})
8. Test ventilation and estimation of ventilation efficiency (end-tidal CO_2, tidal volume, chest excursions, noise)
9. Release for bronchoscopy
10. After completion of the intervention, removal of the rigid bronchoscope, termination of anaesthetic dosing, and introduction of a laryngeal mask airway or a conventional tracheal tube
11. After awakening of the patient, removal of the laryngeal mask and extubation.

An estimation of the efficiency of ventilation through the rigid bronchoscope requires experience. The ventilators depict the tidal volumes and end-tidal CO_2 unreliably. As such, the most important method used for monitoring during a bronchoscopy is pulse oximetry. If there is excessive leakage, application of cricoid pressure, or switching to a larger tube diameter can be of assistance. Sometimes the leak might be from the bronchoscope itself (open working channel, eyepiece not attached properly, constant suction by the pulmonologist). When ventilation problems occur it is often easier to ventilate manually rather than by mechanical ventilation.

During the intervention, it may be necessary to maintain a brief phase of apnoea, but one must of course remember that a typical pulmonary patient has only limited reserves. If a jet ventilator is available, the procedure can be simplified. Before the intervention, one should in any case set clear individual limits with the bronchoscopist for the patient's lowest tolerable Sp_{O_2} levels and clearly communicate when any falling saturation levels occur.

Anaesthesia procedure

The anaesthesia should be maintained using i.v., short-acting anaesthetics (e.g. propofol and remifentanil) as inhaled anaesthetics are not suitable because of the leakages that tend to occur. Even when choosing a neuromuscular blocking agent, briefly effective and well-controllable substances should be preferred, such as mivacurium and cisatracurium. Before ending anaesthesia one must always check for any persisting neuromuscular blocking action using a nerve stimulator. Patients with a 'difficult airway' always represent a particularly problematic challenge where the procedure has to be planned very carefully. A fibreoptic awake intubation may be considered, but is only of limited use wherever a rigid bronchoscopy is planned. Alternative respiratory aids (e.g. intubating laryngeal mask airways, laryngeal tubes, etc.) and emergency tracheotomy or cricothyrotomy sets must always be within reach. For patients at risk of aspiration, the anaesthesia is introduced by rapid sequence induction, which is followed by an intubation using a rigid bronchoscope. The rigid bronchoscope, however, provides no protection from aspiration. Depending on the planned intervention and the patient's condition, it can make sense to monitor blood pressure using an invasive arterial catheter. This also provides the benefit that blood gas measurements can also be performed.

The anaesthesia workstation in bronchoscopy

When equipping the anaesthesia workstation in the bronchoscopy laboratory, it must be considered that even rarely used emergency equipment must be readily at hand. The complications listed in Table 77.5 should all be manageable with the materials and equipment available.

Laser procedures

Laser procedures are often performed in order to eliminate narrowing and obstruction of the respiratory tract, such as that caused by tumours. Sometimes stents are applied afterwards to

Table 77.5 Overview of complications during bronchoscopy

Complication	Therapy/prophylaxis
Acute endobronchial bleeding	Local haemostasis (adrenaline, coagulation) Bronchial blocker, double-lumen tube
Bronchospasm	Glucocorticoid administration (i.v.)
Laryngeal, tracheal, dental trauma	Depending on complication
Pneumothorax	Pleural drainage
Hypoxaemia/hypercarbia	Improving ventilation
Awareness	Adequate depth of anaesthesia

keep the airways open in the long term. These patients are often severely impaired by their cancer, and curative treatment is not possible. In order to prevent life-threatening burns in the airways, it is vital that ventilation be carried out with a low FI_{O_2} of 21% oxygen. This means that the bronchoscopist can only activate the laser when a FI_{O_2} is displayed for the exhaled air by the respiratory gas measurement device. Nitrous oxide (acts as an incendiary) and volatile anaesthetics (can break down into toxic derivatives) are contraindicated. Often oxygen desaturation occurs which can only be treated by interrupting the laser therapy and ventilating with 100% oxygen. After recovery of saturation the FI_{O_2} can then be reduced again and the laser therapy can be resumed. Here, good communication and clear agreements on limits are the keys to success. The vapours resulting from laser therapy are often highly irritating to the airways. In patients at risk of, or with evidence of, bronchospasm, an i.v. glucocorticoid injection is indicated. It should also not be forgotten that the eyes of anyone involved in the therapy need to be protected with suitable laser safety goggles.

Anaesthesia procedure in special situations

Removal of a foreign body in a child

Aspiration of a foreign body is the most common cause of acute respiratory distress in children. A typical patient will be less than 3 years old and will have aspirated a small foreign body (e.g. a peanut). The foreign body can dislodge at any time and cause a complete obstruction, so that an immediate removal is required even if the child shows no outward signs of distress. As children usually have no i.v. access and should also not be additionally distressed, an inhalation induction with sevoflurane is recommended. After this, placement of i.v. access, administration of neuromuscular blockers, followed by ventilation via a rigid bronchoscope are recommended. Now the foreign body can be removed via the rigid bronchoscope. In order to bridge the time until the patient breathes spontaneously and is fully awake the airway can be secured with a tracheal tube or a laryngeal mask. In order to prevent post-intervention swelling of the airways, glucocorticoids can be applied prophylactically. Another option is to maintain spontaneous breathing during the entire procedure.

Mediastinal mass syndrome

When investigating mediastinal masses, a transbronchial biopsy should sometimes be performed. When these lesions reach a certain size, a so-called mediastinal mass syndrome can result. Upon initiation of general anaesthesia, and even with analgesic sedation, an acute perioperative cardiovascular failure might occur that can remain uncontrollable and even lead to the death of the patient. These patients generally have a difficult airway and anaesthesia or sedation should therefore be avoided. The attending anaesthetist must decide the level of risk associated with a general anaesthesia on the basis of clinical and radiological findings. Tables 77.6 and 77.7 provide a classification and breakdown of the risks of anaesthesia. If a procedure involving general anaesthesia is unavoidable, all patients with the classification 'unsafe' or 'uncertain' should have a cardiac surgical team on standby so that support can be provided using cardiopulmonary bypass. This usually means providing a femoral cannulation under local anaesthesia to patients who are fully awake.

Table 77.6 Mediastinal mass syndrome (MMS) anaesthesiological risk classification

Classification	
Safe	Asymptomatic patients (computed tomography finding), negative dynamic evaluation*
Unsafe	Symptomatic patients (MMS clinical syndrome and positive dynamic evaluation*)
Uncertain	Patients with moderate clinical symptoms Asymptomatic patients with obstruction of the tracheobronchial tree (<50% of normal diameter) Asymptomatic patients with positive dynamic evaluation* Adults without possibility of dynamic evaluation

* Dynamic evaluation: awake fibreoptic tracheobronchoscopy, pneumotachography, echocardiography with change of patient position.

Reproduced with permission from Erdos, G. and Tzanova, I. Perioperative anaesthetic management of mediastinal mass in adults. *European Journal of Anaesthesia*. Volume 26, Issue 8, pp. 627–632, Copyright © 2009 European Society of Anaesthesiology.

Table 77.7 Mediastinal mass syndrome (MMS): grading of clinical symptoms

Grading	
Asymptomatic	Can lie supine without symptoms
Mild	Can lie supine with some cough, pressure sensation
Moderate	Can lie supine for short periods only
Severe	Cannot tolerate supine position

Reproduced with permission from Erdos, G. and Tzanova, I. Perioperative anaesthetic management of mediastinal mass in adults. *European Journal of Anaesthesia*. Volume 26, Issue 8, pp. 627–632, Copyright © 2009 European Society of Anaesthesiology.

Acute endobronchial bleeding

There is always a risk of triggering an acute endobronchial haemorrhage when a bronchoscopy is performed. The risk of this is particularly great in patients with endobronchial tumours, in those with bleeding disorders, and of course while invasive procedures are being carried out (e.g. biopsy, tumour debulking, and stenting). A severe endobronchial bleeding is always a potentially life-threatening situation. The anaesthetist must always bear in mind the risk of bleeding and the coagulation status of the patient before the procedure is carried out. Precautions must be taken on the basis of a patient's individual risk profile (e.g. availability of homologous blood, provision of wide-lumen venous access, and invasive blood pressure measurement). Acute endobronchial bleeding leads to an immediate massive impairment for the bronchoscopist so that the possibilities for intervention are then greatly restricted. At the same time, usually before the effects of acute blood loss are felt, there are also massive problems associated with oxygenation. The aim should now be to control the bleeding as quickly as possible so that oxygenation becomes possible again. If an immediate local haemostasis is not possible, single-lung ventilation (e.g. using a double-lumen tube, or a bronchus blocker) might stabilize the situation. This can gain time for diagnostic (e.g. localization of bleeding) and therapeutic (e.g. correction of the coagulation status, angiography, and thoracic surgery) procedures to be carried out.

Acute bronchospasm

Patients who have to undergo a diagnostic or therapeutic bronchoscopy also have an increased risk of bronchospasm during surgery. On the one hand, the manipulation of the airways themselves can stimulate the cholinergic system, which can induce acute bronchospasm; on the other hand, a significant proportion of typical pulmonological patients also suffer obstructive airway diseases such as asthma, chronic obstructive pulmonary disease, or chronic bronchitis.

Prophylactically, all patients should have taken their anti-obstructive medication (inhalers) before any anaesthesia is induced. An intraoperative prophylaxis for high-risk patients can also be given by administering i.v. glucocorticoids. A patient with significant bronchospasm must not be extubated. Immediately after diagnosis, the patient is ventilated with 100% oxygen (usually manual ventilation is required) and the depth of anaesthesia is deepened. Propofol and ketamine can be used because of their bronchodilatory effect. A glucocorticoid can also be administered i.v. With severe bronchospasm, adequate ventilation via the rigid bronchoscope is no longer possible, so that switching to a tracheal tube or insertion of a supraglottic airway may become necessary. After that, volatile anaesthetics (if available) can also be of use because of their bronchodilatory effects. After resolution of the bronchospasm, it must be decided if the patient can be safely extubated or needs further mechanical ventilatory support in an intensive care unit. However, even if immediate extubation was possible, post-interventional patient monitoring, for example, at the post-anaesthesia care unit, is indicated.

Declaration of interest

None declared.

Further reading

Erdos G, Tzanova I. Perioperative anaesthetic management of mediastinal mass in adults. *Eur J Anaesthesiol* 2009; 26: 627–32

Farling PA, Flynn PA, Darwent G, *et al.* Safety in magnetic resonance units: an update. *Anaesthesia* 2010; 65: 766–70

Hushek SG, Russell L, Moser RF, *et al.* Safety protocols for interventional MRI. *Acad Radiol* 2005; 12: 1143–8

Metzner J, Posner KL, Domino KB. The risk and safety of anesthesia at remote locations: the US closed claims analysis. *Curr Opin Anaesthesiol* 2009; 22: 502–8

Morris CG, McBrien ME, Farling PA. Anticipation and planning for anaesthesia provision within MR units in the UK. *Br J Radiol* 2004; 77: 216–8

Odegard KC, DiNardo JA, Tsai-Goodman B, Powell AJ, Geva T, Laussen PC. Anaesthesia considerations for cardiac MRI in infants and small children. *Paediatr Anaesth* 2004; 14: 471–6

Schulte-Uentrop L, Goepfert MS. Anaesthesia or sedation for MRI in children. *Curr Opin Anaesthesiol* 2010; 23: 513–7

Van De Velde M, Kuypers M, Teunkens A, Devroe S. Risk and safety of anesthesia outside the operating room. *Minerva Anestesiol* 2009; 75: 345–8

References

Jumaa MA, Zhang F, Ruiz-Ares G, *et al.* Comparison of safety and clinical and radiographic outcomes in endovascular acute stroke therapy for proximal middle cerebral artery occlusion with intubation and general anesthesia versus the nonintubated state. *Stroke* 2010; **41**: 1180–4

Nichols C, Carrozzella J, Yeatts S, Tomsick T, Broderick J, Khatri P. Is periprocedural sedation during acute stroke therapy associated with poorer functional outcomes? *J Neurointerv Surg* 2010; **2**: 67–70

CHAPTER 78

Military anaesthesia

Peter F. Mahoney, Emrys Kirkman, Sarah Watts, Karen Smyth, Giles Nordmann, Nicholas T. Tarmey, Simon J. Mercer, Tom Woolley, Dominic Aldington, Simon Turner, Charlotte Small, and Paul Wood

Introduction

War and conflict have long been associated with improvements in medical care. The recent conflicts in Afghanistan and Iraq have been no exception. The high tempo of operations has presented the UK's Defence Medical Services (DMS) with the need to care for injured service personnel and local nationals with highly complex patterns of injury. Patients have presented to the DMS with injuries not commonly encountered in civilian practice—typically the result of blast and ballistic mechanisms. The deployed anaesthetist is involved in all stages of the patient pathway from point of wounding to the emergency department (ED), through the resuscitative period encompassed by the damage control construct, to the critical care delivered on the ground and in the air, and finally back in the United Kingdom at the interface with the civilian National Health Service (NHS).

The high quality of care delivered in association with rigorous clinical audit and research, including laboratory physical science, has produced developments that not only impact military outcomes, but which are being introduced in wider civilian practice.

This chapter covers all these areas from first principles to the management of pain and advances in the understanding of coagulopathy.

Mechanisms of wounding

Explosions are the primary mechanism of wounding in recent military conflicts and represent an increasing mode of battlefield injuries (Kelly et al. 2008; Champion et al. 2009). A comprehensive review (Eastridge et al. 2011) of 558 combat casualties injured between 2001 and 2009 who died of wounds (i.e. those who survived the pre-hospital phase but succumbed to their injuries after reaching a medical treatment facility) found that 72% were injured in explosions, 25% by gunshot, and the remaining 3% by a mixture of helicopter and motor vehicle crashes. The casualties were further sub-divided into those with non-survivable injuries and those whose injuries were 'potentially survivable'. While traumatic brain injury predominated (83%) in those with non-survivable injuries, haemorrhage was the primary cause of death in 80% of those who were deemed to be potential survivors (Eastridge et al. 2011). Other studies have focused on describing and mapping the anatomical location of injuries (Kelly et al. 2008; Sohn et al. 2008; Champion et al. 2009); however, this is outside the scope of this chapter which will focus on generic aspects of the injuries, the pathophysiological responses, and implications for clinical treatment.

Explosions cause a complex pattern of injury, some aspects of which are normally only seen after explosions while others such as penetrating injuries and blunt injuries are also seen in gunshot wounds and blunt collisions respectively. Descriptions of penetrating injuries from fragments energized by explosions are also relevant for penetrating injuries from gunshots. The relative contribution of the different forms of blast injuries depend on a number of factors which include the nature of the explosive device, distance of the casualty from the device, the environment in which the explosion occurred (open space or enclosed), and any protective equipment worn (e.g. ballistic armour) by the casualty. The various categories of blast injury are based upon the component of the explosion which caused them as shown in Table 78.1 (Stuhmiller 2008; Champion et al. 2009).

Primary blast injury

Blast lung is one of the most notable forms of primary blast injury. There has been considerable debate regarding the precise mechanism of coupling the shock wave into the body to cause the injuries. Current thinking suggests that the shock wave causes a brief acceleration of the thoracic wall, leading to a mechanical stress in the underlying lung tissue. Because of the foam-like characteristics of lung tissue, it is thought that the stress wave propagates into the tissue developing into a high-stress wave as it does so, ultimately leading to damage at the liquid–gas interfaces of the alveoli and small airways and concurrently damaging small blood vessels (e.g. pulmonary capillaries). Although the nature of this coupling is of paramount importance to those developing protection systems (Cooper 1996), it is the pathophysiological consequences of widespread haemorrhage into the small airways and lung parenchyma that are of medical importance.

Blast lung is therefore characterized by the influx of blood and extravasation of oedema fluid into lung tissue (Brown et al. 1993), giving rise to haemorrhagic foci which can be substantial depending

Table 78.1 Classification of blast injuries

Category	Definition	Typical injuries
Primary	Injuries caused by the blast shock wave (unique to high-order explosives) Stress and shear waves occur in tissues Waves reinforced and reflected at tissue density interfaces Gas-filled organs (lungs, ears, etc.) at particular risk	Tympanic membrane rupture Blast lung Eye injuries Concussion
Secondary	Ballistic wounds produced by primary fragments (originating from the explosive device) and secondary fragments (originating from the environment) Threat of fragment injury extends further than the blast wave	Penetrating injuries Blunt injuries from large fragments Eye injuries Lacerations Concussion
Tertiary	Whole-body acceleration caused by the blast wind	Blunt injuries Concussion Compartment syndrome Older texts categorize traumatic amputations as tertiary although they are more likely to be a combination of primary and tertiary
Quaternary	All explosion-mediated injuries not associated with pressure or wind effects High temperature Toxic gases	Burns Toxic gas and other inhalation injuries Injuries from environmental contamination
Quinary (or collateral)	Clinical consequences of 'post detonation environmental contaminants' including bacterial (deliberate and commensal), radiation ('dirty bombs'), and tissue reaction to fuel and materials Systemic response to massive trauma	

Adapted with permission from Champion, H. R. *et al.* Injuries From Explosions: Physics, Biophysics, Pathology, and Required Research Focus. *Journal of Trauma and Acute Care Surgery*. Volume 66, Issue 5, pp. 1468–1477. Copyright © 2009 Wolters Kluwer Health and American Association for the Surgery of Trauma; and from Stuhmiller JH. Blast injury: translating research into operational medicine. Office of The Surgeon General, Borden Institute, US Army Medical Department Center & School, 2008.

on the level of blast loading. The intrapulmonary haemorrhage and oedema contribute to the initial respiratory compromise in blast lung (Gorbunov et al. 2006a). The problem is exacerbated because free haemoglobin and extravasated blood have been shown to induce free radical reactions which cause oxidative damage and initiates/augments a pro-inflammatory response (Gorbunov et al. 2006a). Free haemoglobin also causes an accumulation of inflammatory mediators and chemotactic attractants (Gorbunov et al. 2005), thereby amplifying the problem.

Within 3 h, leucocytes can be demonstrated within the haemorrhagic areas and concentrations increase for 24 h or more after exposure (Gorbunov et al. 2006a). This accumulation of leucocytes is associated with increasing levels of myeloperoxidase activity, which in turn is indicative of oxidative events and developing inflammation in the affected areas (Gorbunov et al. 2006a). Histological and electron microscopic examination reveal prominent perivascular oedema and extensive alveolar haemorrhages without widespread visible damage to endothelial cells during the first 12 h after exposure (Gorbunov et al. 2006a). Thereafter, 12–24 h after exposure, type 1 epithelial cells show evidence of developing damage followed later (24–56 h after exposure) by secondary damage to endothelial cells which become detached from their basement membrane into the capillary lumen (Gorbunov et al. 2006a).

This picture of pulmonary inflammation can develop further into acute lung injury and acute respiratory distress syndrome (ARDS). The likelihood of developing ARDS is dependent in part on the severity of the initial blast lung, which has been defined on the basis of functional (pulmonary gas transfer) and radiographical findings (Table 78.2). Civilian data based on casualties of terrorist bombings in Israel suggest that all of those with severe and approximately one-third of those with moderate blast lung injury develop ARDS, while none of those with mild blast lung develop ARDS (Pizov et al. 1999).

Physiological response to primary blast injury

A number of experimental studies and clinical reports indicated that primary blast injury to the thorax produces bradycardia, prolonged hypotension, and apnoea followed by rapid shallow breathing (Barrow and Rhoads 1944; Cernak et al. 1996; Guy et al. 1998; Ohnishi et al. 2001). The respiratory disturbance has been shown to be as a result of a reflex with an afferent vagal pathway, the bradycardia is as a result of vagal efferent activation, and the hypotension is due in part to profound systemic vasodilation which may be mediated by nitric oxide release from the pulmonary circulation (Zunic et al. 2000; Ohnishi et al. 2001; Gorbunov et al. 2006b).

Initial management of blast injury

The guidelines provided by the American College of Surgeons allow a uniform and systematic approach to the management of major trauma. The ABCDE resuscitation principle is the first priority because these basic measures apply to all severe trauma patients. Secondary and even tertiary surveillance is then used to aid identification of immediately life-threatening injuries and facilitate appropriate intervention. The six immediately life-threatening injuries comprise airway obstruction, tension pneumothorax, open pneumothorax, massive haemothorax, flail chest, and cardiac tamponade.

Table 78.2 Blast lung injury severity score

	Blast lung severity		
	Mild	**Moderate**	**Severe**
Pa_{O_2} / FI_{O_2} (kPa)	>26.6	8.0–26.6	<8.0
Chest radiograph	Localized lung infiltrates	Bilateral or unilateral lung infiltrates	Massive bilateral lung infiltrates
Bronchial pleural fistula	No	Yes/No	Yes

Republished with permission of American College of Chest Physicians, from *Chest*, Pizov, R. et al. Blast Lung Injury From an Explosion on a Civilian Bus, Volume 115, Issue 1, pp. 165–172, 1999; permission conveyed through Copyright Clearance Center, Inc.

When indicated, three initial radiographical examinations should be performed in the resuscitation room, which are radiographs of the chest, lateral C-spine, and pelvis. Further computed tomography (CT) imaging must be deferred until the patient has been adequately resuscitated. While a CT of the thorax is not mandatory in the management of blast lung injury this should not detract from the important information that may be yielded, for example, a CT of the thorax is the definitive diagnostic test for injury to the aorta.

The mainstay of management of parenchymal injury to the lung is mechanical ventilation. This intervention may in itself exacerbate the initial injury by direct mechanical damage, induction of surfactant failure, and stimulation of pulmonary and systemic inflammatory cytokines (Pinhu et al. 2003). Research pertaining to the reduction of this iatrogenic injury in the setting of ARDS is applicable to the management of blast lung injury because of the similar pathological end-points. It is now widely recognized that a conservative ventilation strategy (The Acute Respiratory Distress Syndrome Network 2000), whereby plateau airway pressures are limited to 30 cm H_2O and tidal volumes to 6 ml kg^{-1}, is associated with improved clinical outcomes. However, this strategy mandates a degree of hypoxaemia and hypercapnia. The application of positive end-expiratory pressure (PEEP) is a key component of a protective ventilatory strategy because it theoretically reduces atelectotrauma. Higher PEEP levels may lead to recruitment of collapsed alveoli with concomitant improvement in shunt fraction and arterial oxygenation. However, if the recruitment potential is low, there is a risk of further injury by over-distension of open alveoli. The optimum level of PEEP is controversial, but there is evidence that high levels are beneficial in severe lung injury (Grasso et al. 2002; Meade et al. 2008; Mercat et al. 2008). The choice of mode of ventilation depends on local factors, such as the technology available and the experience of the physician. There is very little evidence to favour one mode over another in adult patients. In a small number of cases, high-frequency oscillatory ventilation (HFOV) can be utilized in patients that are refractory to conventional ventilation (Wunsch et al. 2005). High-frequency, low-volume ventilation may reduce atelectotrauma and volutrauma to the alveoli. However, a recent trial was terminated early because patients receiving HFOV with a mean airway pressure of 31 ± 2.6 cm H_2O and frequency of 5.5 ± 1 Hz for new onset moderate-severe ARDS had excess mortality when compared to those receiving a conservative ventilation strategy (Ferguson et al. 2013).

The intensity of mechanical ventilation can be greatly reduced by using an extracorporeal membrane oxygenation system. However, complications associated with removing blood from the patient and circulating it through an artificial membrane may preclude its widespread use. The system has been proved to be of benefit in the paediatric population, but remains of uncertain importance in adults (Zapol et al. 1979; Anderson et al. 1994; Morris et al. 1994; Plotkin et al. 1994; Peek et al. 2009). Although a recent large clinical trial has reported that the strategy improved survival of patients with severe ARDS, the lack of standardized management of the control group makes definite conclusions difficult (Peek et al. 2009). The Novalung® system (Inspiration Healthcare Ltd, UK) uses the arterial pressure to drive blood across a membrane to remove carbon dioxide only. Although it offers fewer treatment options, it has the benefits of being compact, less invasive, and a lower anticoagulation requirement.

Despite the challenges presented by the pathology of lung injury, dramatic improvements in outcome have been borne out of preventing secondary injury by mechanical ventilation.

Secondary and tertiary blast injuries: haemorrhage, tissue injury, and resuscitation of casualties with concomitant primary blast injury

Blast-injured casualties often sustain haemorrhage as a consequence of their injuries (Cooper et al. 1983). The casualties may therefore suffer profound haemorrhagic shock and so require resuscitation to sustain life while they are evacuated to hospital.

A multidisciplinary task force has recommended low-volume fluid resuscitation in the initial phase of resuscitation in patients without brain injury (Spahn et al. 2007; Rossaint et al. 2010). The strategy aims to reduce the risk of re-bleeding by:

- minimizing the hydrostatic pressure on clot forming over the wound
- minimizing dilutional coagulopathy
- reducing the volume of cool fluid that is infused.

However, a Cochrane systematic review of randomized clinical trials failed to show any difference in outcome when compared with a traditional resuscitative strategy (Kwan et al. 2003), and concluded that 'We found no evidence from randomised controlled trials for or against early or larger volume of intravenous fluid administration in uncontrolled haemorrhage. There is continuing uncertainty about the best fluid administration strategy in bleeding trauma patients. Further randomised controlled trials are needed to establish the most effective fluid resuscitation strategy' (Kwan et al. 2014). However, amongst those practicing pre-hospital resuscitation it is generally held that there is a body of evidence to support a restricted pre-hospital resuscitation strategy in penetrating injury when evacuation timelines are short (Bickell et al. 1994).

The clinical picture during resuscitation is complicated by the pathophysiological changes associated with blast lung and hypoxaemia, together with a range of cardiovascular (Harban et al. 2001; Sawdon et al. 2002) and microcirculatory (Zunic et al. 2005) disturbances which may further compromise nutritative tissue blood flow. The combination of the low tissue blood-flow state inherent in hypotensive resuscitation can therefore be compounded by poor arterial oxygenation and can lead to an overwhelmingly inadequate tissue oxygen delivery. Although the reduced risk of re-bleeding outweighs the deleterious effects of poor tissue oxygen delivery when evacuation times are short, the physiological penalties of low-flow states can become overwhelming during extended resuscitation timelines, particularly when this is compounded by hypoxaemia as a result of blast lung (Garner et al. 2010).

An experimental study conducted at the Defence Science and Technology Laboratory (Dstl) at Porton Down investigated an alternative strategy for extended evacuation timelines, developed jointly by Dstl and RCDM. This new strategy involves initial resuscitation to a hypotensive end-point to allow time for clot stabilization, followed after the first hour by a revised (normotensive) target. This alternative strategy (termed 'novel hybrid', NH) was found to increase survival time and reverse a severe metabolic acidosis that developed during the hypotensive phase, without causing re-bleeding (Kirkman et al. 2011) (Fig. 78.1).

The new resuscitation strategy also attenuated other sequelae such as the early acute trauma coagulopathy and inflammatory response associated with prolonged hypotensive resuscitation (Hypot) (Fig. 78.2). The peak prothrombin times (PTs) attained are shown in Figure 78.2. NH resuscitation was associated with significantly lower PT compared with Hypot ($P = 0.001$). In contrast, blast injury (*vs* sham blast) had no significant effect ($P = 0.56$) on the peak levels of PT. Peak concentrations of interleukin 6 (IL6) were also significantly higher in the Hypot groups compared with NH (Fig. 78.2) ($P = 0.001$), but overall there was no significant effects of blast ($P = 0.34$) on the inflammatory marker. However, survival time was significantly shorter in the blast-injured animals given Hypot ($P = 0.017$). Due to the expected time course of IL6 release the levels seen in the short-lived Blast/Hypot group may be reduced. When the effects of blast was examined only in those given NH resuscitation (where survival times were similar between NH and Hypot, $P = 0.45$), IL6 concentrations were found to be significantly higher in animals given blast injury ($P = 0.009$). In contrast, when a similar analysis was taken, examining PT levels only in those given NH, there was no significant difference in maximum PT between blast and sham blast groups ($P = 0.24$).

More recent considerations focus on the nature of the resuscitation fluids, with increased emphasis on proactive use of blood products to treat and, if possible, avoid the development of acute trauma coagulopathy. Adjuvant therapies, such as coagulation factors and antifibrinolytics have an important role in the management of haemorrhage. Recommendations for the management of haemorrhage in the civilian setting are provided in a set of European guidelines (Spahn et al. 2007; Rossaint et al. 2010). Although the military regimen appears more liberal, it can be appreciated that both regimens have similar physiological targets.

Blast-induced brain injury

In recent years, there has been a myriad of anecdotal reports suggesting that mild blast exposure causes mild traumatic brain injury, leading to symptoms which include difficulties with concentration,

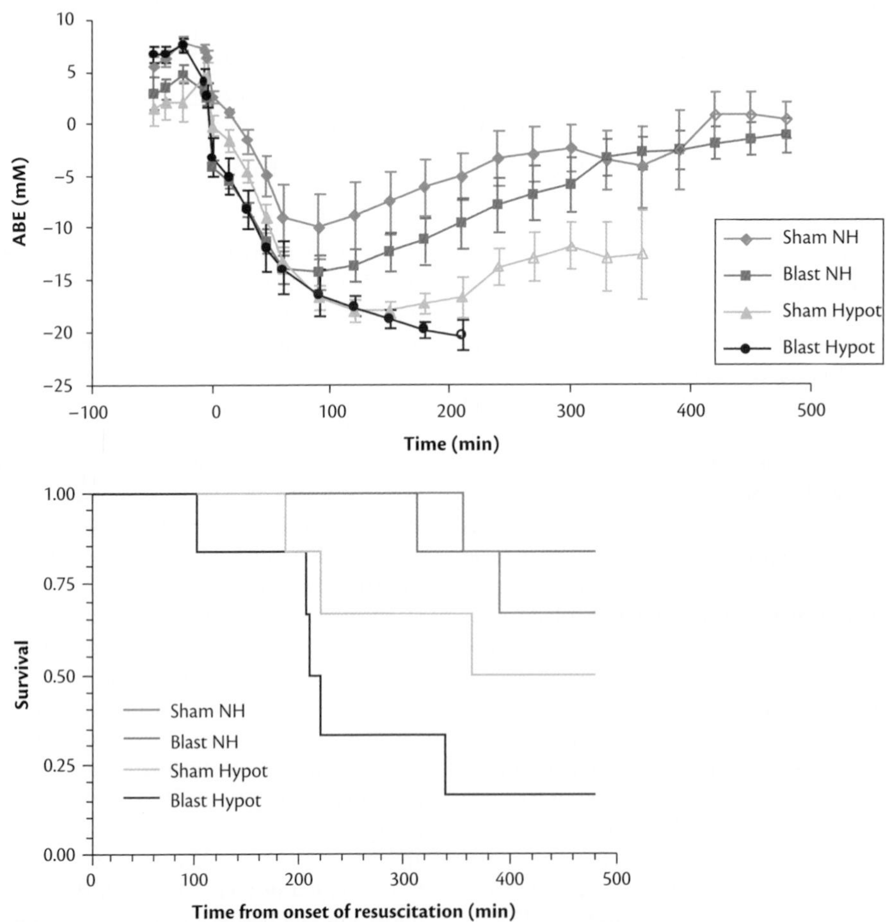

Figure 78.1 Kaplan–Meier survival plot and arterial base excess (ABE) for four groups of animals subjected to either sham blast (S) or blast (B), haemorrhagic shock, and resuscitation following either the novel hybrid (NH) or hypotensive (Hypot) arterial blood pressure profile. For ABE, time indicates time from onset of resuscitation. First three values represent Baseline 1, Baseline 3, and Blast (or Sham Blast). Mean values (with SEM).

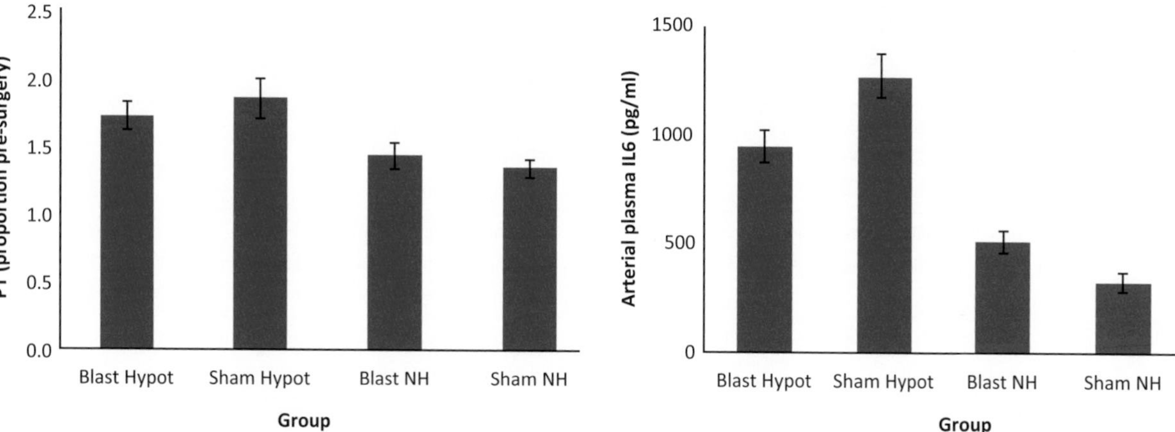

Figure 78.2 Peak prothrombin time (PT) and arterial interleukin 6 (IL6) in the four groups of animals described in Figure 78.1. Mean values (with SEM).
Reproduced from C Doran et al., Targeted resuscitation improves coagulation and outcome, *The Journal of Trauma and Acute Care Surgery*, 72, 4, pp. 835–843, Copyright 2012, American Association for the Surgery of Trauma.

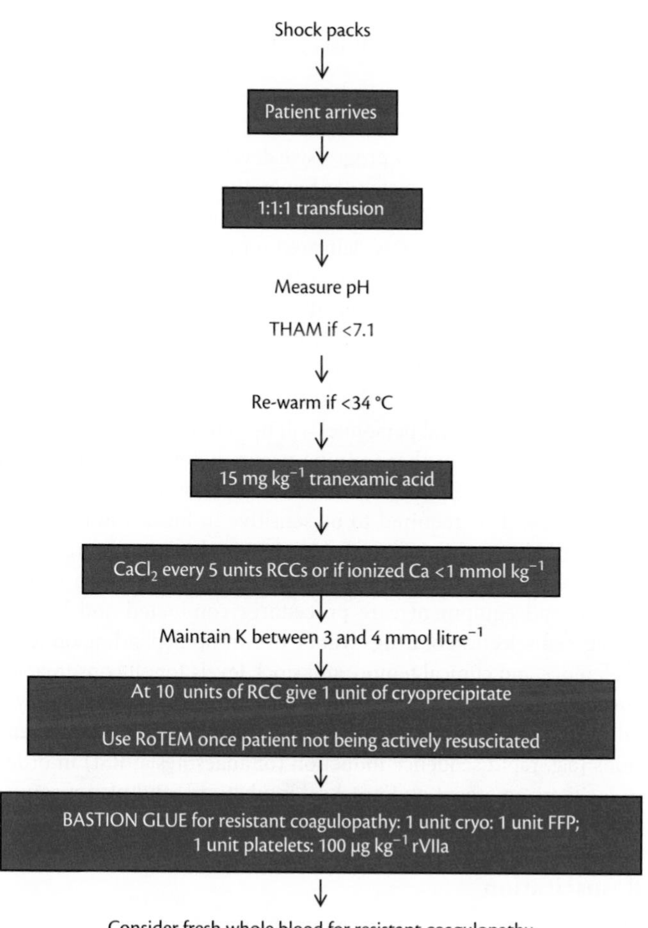

Figure 78.3 UK Military Guideline for the treatment of traumatic haemorrhage. 1:1:1, packed red cells (RCC): fresh frozen plasma (FFP): platelets in a 1:1:1 ratio; THAM, tromethamine; RoTEM, rotational thromboelastometry; BASTION GLUE, components listed in final box of the flow diagram.
Data from Surgeon General's Operational Policy Letter SGOPL Number: 08/09, due revision: 06/14, dated: 10 June 09, reference: DMSD: /29/15/01 Management of massive haemorrhage on operations.

irritability, sleep, and memory problems (Okie 2005). A number of these symptoms may overlap with post-traumatic stress disorder (Rosenfeld and Ford 2010). Experimental studies have shown that blast exposure leads to expression of biomarkers of brain injury and apoptosis (Cernak et al. 2010) and electrophysiological changes consistent with damage to long axonal tracts (Park et al. 2011). Conversely, recent controlled studies have found no evidence of neuronal injury in humans exposed to low levels of blast (Blennow et al. 2011). A comprehensive retrospective study has been published by Fear et al. (2009) highlighting the difficulties associated with specifically linking the neuropsychological disturbances with blast exposure. The mechanism underpinning any blast-induced mild traumatic brain injury is also a matter of debate. It is uncertain whether the shock wave itself couples directly into brain tissue (via the skull) or whether more conventional acceleration of the head is responsible, or whether brief changes in intravascular pressure caused by the impact of the blast wave on the body may play a part. Recent studies have raised the interesting possibility that a spill-over of inflammatory mediators from other organs (e.g. the lungs) may contribute to brain injury (Cernak 2010). All of these issues are profoundly important not only for clinical treatments but also for the development of protection systems and strategies.

At higher levels of blast exposure there is accumulating evidence that exposure to blast leads to alterations in the brain (possibly the microvasculature) which increase the likelihood and severity of cerebral oedema caused by other concomitant injuries (e.g. penetrating brain injury) (Armonda et al. 2006). Currently there is no specific treatment for this condition (Armonda et al. 2006; Risdall and Menon 2011). The mechanisms underpinning mild traumatic brain injury and cerebral oedema with more severe blast loading may be different and it is clear that the debate and investigational studies will continue in the short to mid term.

Summary: mechanisms of wounding

Blast (explosions) is currently the predominant mechanism of battlefield injury, while haemorrhage is the principal cause of battlefield deaths. Although serious primary blast injury (e.g. blast lung caused by the shock wave) is seen in the minority of casualties, it does complicate the response to and treatment of secondary (e.g. haemorrhage as a result of penetrating injuries from energized fragments) and tertiary (translational) blast injuries. The effectiveness

Table 78.3 Physical restraints to delivery of care in flight

Constraint	Effect	Result
Enemy threat	Personal danger from ballistics requires personnel to wear helmet, body armour, ballistic glasses, fire-retardant clothing Carry personal weapons	Additional weight Restricted movement Physical fatigue
Noise	Auscultation and percussion impossible Difficulty communicating by voice Threat to hearing	Impaired diagnostic skills Communication by radio and hand signals Hearing protection worn
Vibration	Monitoring unreliable (Sp_{O_2} and NIBP especially) Increased equipment failure rate Equipment will move if not secured Fine motor skills impaired	Impaired diagnostic skills, decreased situation awareness Daily equipment checks vital Difficult to locate equipment Cannulation and intubation more difficult
Temperature	Cold at night especially at altitude (−15°C) resulting in hypothermia and coagulopathy Hot during day especially in summer (40°C)	Warming blankets (e.g. Blizzard, Blizzard Protection Systems Ltd, Gwynedd,UK) and fluid warmers (e.g. enFlow™, Becton, Dickinson and Company Franklin Lakes, NJ, USA) Hyperthermia, heat injury
Light	Light at night kept to a minimum for aircraft protection White light avoided as it interferes with night-vision equipment	Difficult to locate equipment in preparation phase of mission Patient signs (e.g. cyanosis) and monitor colours difficult to ascertain
Aircraft	Rotors, jets, and counter-measures represent significant danger for embarking/disembarking personnel	Team, crew must be familiar with dangers areas of each aircraft type

of hypotensive resuscitation is significantly limited by concomitant hypoxaemia. A new strategy, termed 'novel hybrid', which replaces hypotensive resuscitation with a revised normotensive target after the first hour, increases survival time. In-hospital management of blast lung is currently supportive using conservative ventilation strategies. New directions for resuscitation currently focus on pro-active treatment of acute trauma coagulopathy using blood products, which can now be projected into the pre-hospital arena.

Military pre-hospital critical care

The majority of military patients are suffering from traumatic injuries and, as such, the focus of military pre-hospital critical care is geared towards providing damage control resuscitation forward of the field hospital. In current operations, the enemy threat results in a non-permissible environment mandating that minimal treatment occurs on the ground before evacuation, resuscitation therefore is commenced on the transport on the way to hospital from the battlefield.

Preparation and training

The military deliver critical care forward of the hospital in a variety of locations around the world. Many of these are in austere environments with potential physical and health risks from enemy threat and local endemic disease. It is therefore imperative that all personnel involved in this role are properly selected, trained, and prepared. As such, individuals will undertake a variety of personal military and medical training in line with current pre-deployment instructions, which will include physical fitness, weapons handling, health screening, and appropriate vaccinations. Pre-deployment training will include Battlefield Advanced Trauma Life Support (BATLS), Advanced Paediatric Life Support (APLS), Major Incident Medical Management and Support (MIMMS), and other bespoke courses specific to roles before progressing into integrated simulation training as part of the wider deploying medical force. These individual elements of training allow progressive development of team performance while working to standard operating procedures to ensure a consistent high level of care. Currently the majority of military pre-hospital critical care is delivered on aeromedical evacuation helicopters; however, teams are expected to deliver care on the ground or using maritime assets if required. Training is tailored to the requirements to provide medical support to that specific operation. While the bulk of the workload is likely to be trauma, there will be a significant proportion that will be medical or paediatric and deploying medical personnel will need to be prepared for this.

Once deployed, further training occurs before integrating into their team under supervision to ensure maximum clinical output. Personnel will be required to be sensitive to local traditions and religious beliefs, while often working in a multinational force.

Before the beginning of each shift, the incoming team is fully briefed and equipment care procedures conducted and logged. An agreed selection of drugs will be drawn up depending on team preference and clinical tempo, and stock levels for all consumables checked. Teams will conduct low-level simulation training to crystallize clinical roles and responsibilities, practise complex interventions [e.g. rapid sequence induction (of anaesthesia; RSI) in order to facilitate emergent endotracheal intubation], and plan resource management in the event of multiple casualties.

Resuscitation

The resuscitation goal is to maintain the radial pulse/systolic blood pressure of 90 mm Hg for the first hour after wounding and then aim for normotension. This is particularly pertinent for blast injuries (Kirkman et al. 2011). Exceptions to this rule include head injuries and pregnancy. This aim remains unchanged whether the patient and team are on the ground or if they are in the air. The provision of care in flight provides clinicians with considerable physical constraints (Table 78.3).

In line with the principles of BATLS, haemorrhage control is the key priority for severely injured patients; however, practically, this occurs concurrently with other treatments. Indeed, it may be impossible in some circumstances to achieve adequate haemostasis without adequate analgesia or anaesthesia. In the present area of operations, amputations are common and require the application of tourniquets with further control gained through the use of haemostatic agents such as Celox™ (Medtrade Products Ltd, Crewe, UK) to the remaining stumps. There is a high incidence of pelvic ring fractures, requiring the use of pelvic slings prophylactically, and perineal injuries, requiring improvisation of dressings such as Celox™ and abdominal dressings with anaesthesia being commonly required in order to achieve adequate haemostasis.

Access

Access to the vascular space is achieved as rapidly as possible by whatever methods are most appropriate. Large-bore intravenous cannulae would be ideal; however, particularly on aircraft in hypovolaemic patients, these are difficult, take a great deal of time, and are associated with high failure rates. Intraosseous access is the route of choice as it is quicker, more reliable, and more secure, with comparable flow rates. Intraosseous access is most commonly achieved in the humeral heads with EZIO™ (Teleflex, Wayne, PA, USA) or the sternum with FAST™ (Pyng Medical Richmond, British Columbia Canada). Tibial or pelvic crest access can be used when limbs are present, but is inappropriate in significant abdominal or thoracic injuries as venous bleeding relating to the inferior vena cava will prevent resuscitative fluids reaching the heart. Intraosseous fluids need the use of a 50 ml syringe and three-way tap having been warmed (Enflow™) (Becton, Dickinson and Company Franklin Lakes, NJ, USA) as flow rates through intraosseous needles via gravity only are slow. Central venous cannulation via the subclavian vein has been used, in spite of the difficulty, when all limbs are unusable and haemorrhage is non-compressible or hypovolaemic cardiac arrest is *in situ* (or both). Once access has been established in very severely injured patients often the next task is anaesthesia allowing for further interventions.

Rapid sequence intubation

In-flight RSI is a complex intervention in a demanding environment requiring high levels of team work, with potential devastating complications. Team training and simulation is imperative with the need to establish exact roles, actions, tracheal tube sizes, bougie use, and failed intubation procedures, including cricothyroidotomy; all practised before deployment. Despite the austere conditions (moving aircraft, patient on floor, poor lighting, and excessive noise), successful intubation is achieved in 98.8% of patients (Kehoe et al. 2011).

- *Preparation*. All intubation equipment and pre-drawn drugs are checked at the beginning of the shift.
- *Indications*. A diminished Glasgow Coma Score as a result of hypovolaemia and humanitarian (severely injured with multiple amputations) are the commonest followed by airway compromise and ventilatory failure.
- *Position*. The patient is on a stretcher on the floor with the physician kneeling over them.
- *Pre-oxygenation* is achieved with a Hudson mask and oxygen reservoir or by bag–valve mask while monitoring is established (ECG (Defib pads), Sp_{O_2} × 2, non-invasive blood pressure, end-tidal CO_2). Intraosseous access is usually achieved concurrently.
- *Induction* is with ketamine 1–2 mg kg^{-1} and suxamethonium (succinylcholine) 1.5–2 mg kg^{-1}.
- *Laryngoscopy* is performed in the best position to gain a view (prone/kneeling/sitting); tube position is confirmed visually and with end-tidal CO_2 with or without an Easy Cap® detector (Medline Industries, Inc, IL, USA). The tube is secured with tube ties or a Thomas™ tracheal tube holder (Laerdal Medical, Stavanger, Norway).
- *Ventilation* is with a portable ventilator (Oxylog® 1000, Draeger Medical Lubeck, Germany) and enables the physician to perform other tasks.
- *Cervical collars* are used to protect the tracheal tube position and stabilize the cervical spine which is at risk in certain explosive injury patterns.
- *Maintenance*. Intermittent ketamine or midazolam/morphine boluses are used depending on blood pressure in addition to vecuronium.

Establishing anaesthesia allows further access to be gained for blood products and advanced procedures to be performed.

Blood products

Blood products are carried in temperature-regulated containers ensuring temperature stability for 24 h. All patients receive products from universal donors, O-negative packed red cells, and AB-positive fresh frozen plasma (FFP) and are administered in a ratio of 1:1. The administration of these products is indicated by:

- injury pattern
- anticipation of a massive transfusion
- absence of radial pulse
- heart rate higher than 120 beats min^{-1}.

Tranexamic acid is administered early in anticipation of massive transfusion for prevention of fibrinolysis (CRASH-2 Collaborators 2011) and 10 ml of CaCl 10% is administered after the third unit of FFP to prevent hypocalcaemia. The initiation of transfusion is communicated to the receiving hospital via radio for resupply of blood products to the pre-hospital team, and to alert the ED of the requirement for ongoing transfusion.

Advanced resuscitative techniques

Thoracic injuries may result in pneumothorax, haemothorax, and significant vascular injury. Clinical signs are difficult to elicit in this environment. Bilateral thoracotomies should be performed immediately after intubation to diagnose pneumothorax, large haemothorax, and release/prevent tension pneumothorax.

Resuscitative thoracotomy in traumatic cardiac arrest secondary to penetrating injury has been performed; however, the high energy levels of ballistic injuries mean cardiac tamponade is unlikely to be the cause of arrest. Significant large vessel injury is more likely and as such, a pre-hospital thoracotomy is unlikely to be successful. Pulseless electrical activity cardiac arrest secondary to hypovolaemia in the presence of a normal cardiac ECG is a low cardiac output/blood pressure state that does not necessitate cardiopulmonary resuscitation (CPR). Blood products are needed rapidly. Ventilation of these casualties in a low-output state needs low respiratory rates and low tidal volumes to achieve the correct balance between oxygenation and minimizing hindrance to venous return.

Post-mission considerations

Handover

Limited information is passed from the aircraft to the receiving hospital to enable the hospital to prepare appropriate resources. On arrival at the receiving hospital, a succinct, accurate handover is needed in the ATMIST format:

A: Age of patient

T: Time of injury

M: Mechanism of injury

I: Injuries sustained

S: Symptoms and signs

T: Therapeutic interventions.

The handover should provide enough detail to allow the receiving trauma team a high standard of continuity of care while being brief enough not to delay further assessment and treatment. A more detailed history is usually given to the team scribe to be referred back to as necessary.

Resupply

Once the handover is complete then it is necessary to replenish the items used. The priorities are blood products and drugs. Usually there are adequate reserves of other consumables for back-to-back missions to take place. The other responsibilities include clinical documentation, mission debrief, and completion of audit data.

Debrief

The debrief process is vital to ensure that strengths and weaknesses are identified and can be acted on. It should encompass all aspects from equipment performance and problems through to psychological impact for team members. The cumulative impact of multiple casualties and missions should not be underestimated. Incident reports must be completed for potential or actual patient safety events, and these are all reviewed at weekly clinical governance meetings, which will highlight emerging themes, examples of excellent practice, all reported critical incidents, and a review of activity statistics. Further information is sought from weekly telephone conference clinical updates with the patients' home nations. Regular audit should be conducted to ensure that standards are being met, that weaknesses can be identified, and measures put in place to ensure that the risk is minimized. Clinical governance processes need to be in place and strong to ensure high standards of care are maintained.

Resuscitation (including traumatic cardiac arrest) and human factors in the initial management of the military casualty

Resuscitation in the military setting presents a unique challenge, with a number of striking differences from civilian practice. Firstly, the case-mix is different, with a high incidence of blast and penetrating trauma as the cause of arrest (Hodgetts et al. 2007). Additionally, care must be delivered in a range of environments on land, at sea, or in the air—all of which may be hostile or hazardous. Finally, the military setting may involve significant constraints on resources, with an impact on the level or extent of treatment that is available.

Successful resuscitation from military trauma depends on care that is appropriate to the military casualty and delivered by effective teams from the point of wounding all the way to rehabilitation (an end-to-end approach). Recent research and training by the UK DMS has focused on these key areas, by adapting civilian protocols to the military setting (Ministry of Defence 2013) and by emphasizing the importance of human factors for effective resuscitation (Mercer et al. 2010).

Military traumatic cardiorespiratory arrest

Traumatic cardiorespiratory arrest (TCRA) is defined as the loss of central pulses and respiratory effort after trauma, and is associated with a very poor overall prognosis both in civilian and in military practice (Rosemurgy et al. 1993; Fulton et al. 1995; Battistella et al. 1999; Hopson et al. 2003). Although most evidence for the management of military TCRA is extrapolated from civilian studies, a recent observational study of 52 military TCRA patients treated in a UK field hospital in Afghanistan highlighted some key differences in the military trauma population (Tarmey et al. 2011).

Overall rates of survival from military TCRA were 8%, broadly in keeping with published civilian data, where rates of survival are usually considerably less than 10% (Rosemurgy et al. 1993; Fulton et al. 1995; Battistella et al. 1999; Hopson et al. 2003). The pattern of injury, however, is very different in military trauma: 65% of military TCRA victims suffered a combination of blast and penetrating injuries from improvised explosive device explosions, while the remainder were injured by gunshot wounds or grenade fragments. Consequently, more than 80% of military TCRA victims arrested as a result of hypovolaemia from exsanguination. In contrast with civilian experience, where TCRA as a result of hypovolaemia is almost universally associated with death (Lockey et al. 2006; Soar et al. 2010), 75% of survivors of military TCRA had arrested as a result of exsanguination.

A number of civilian studies have attempted to define criteria for withdrawing or withholding resuscitation from TCRA in order to reduce the burden of futile care (Margolin et al. 1996; Battistella et al. 1999; Cera et al. 2003). Based on these studies, the American College of Surgeons and the National Association of EMS Physicians issued guidelines in 2003 recommending that resuscitation should be withheld in the field for TCRA with ECG evidence of electrical asystole, or when the expected transfer time to hospital is more than15 min (Hopson et al. 2003). However, these guidelines have been limited in their acceptance after reports of a number of survivors who would have met the proposed criteria for withdrawal of care (Pickens et al. 2005; Lockey et al. 2006). This is reflected in current European Resuscitation Council guidelines that recognize the lack of reliable predictors of survival after TCRA (Soar et al. 2010).

Similarly, in military TCRA, electrical asystole and arrest beginning in the field were associated with unsuccessful resuscitation, but occasional survivors defied these predictions: one patient survived to discharge despite suffering arrest as a result of massive haemorrhage requiring 24 min of CPR en route to hospital. A recent development in the initial assessment of TCRA victims in the ED is the use of ultrasound to assess cardiac activity before commencing resuscitation (Schuster et al. 2009). In keeping with emerging civilian evidence, the presence of cardiac movement on ultrasound during arrest is strongly associated with successful resuscitation. In the future, this may prove useful for identifying potential survivors on arrival in the ED.

Because of the pattern of injury, resuscitation from military TCRA is particularly focused on the treatment of exsanguinating haemorrhage with immediate transfer for damage-control surgery. In the field, catastrophic external haemorrhage may be controlled with limb tourniquets, which were carried by all soldiers deployed in Afghanistan. Resuscitation with un-cross-matched blood products is then commenced during helicopter transfer to hospital, while advance communication with the field hospital trauma team allows immediate thoracotomy on arrival in the ED. Other potentially reversible causes of arrest are treated concurrently during the transfer, by securing the airway, assessing for tension pneumothorax, and decompressing the chest if necessary.

Resuscitative thoracotomy is an important part of the management of TCRA after penetrating trauma, and may take place in the operating theatre, the ED, or potentially during helicopter transfer to hospital. From the group of military patients studied, all four survivors of TCRA received resuscitative thoracotomy, with interventions including compression of the descending thoracic aorta, release of pericardial tamponade, non-anatomic lung resection and open-chest CPR.

The conventional therapies of external chest compressions, positive-pressure ventilation, and intravenous adrenaline (epinephrine) are of questionable value in TCRA. Logically, compressing an empty heart will be ineffective and positive-pressure ventilation may further reduce venous return by increasing intrathoracic pressure (Pepe et al. 2005; Ho et al. 2009). Vasopressors may also be deleterious in the treatment of hypovolaemic shock (Sperry et al. 2008). In practice, while CPR and adrenaline are often used in the treatment of military TCRA, these should never take precedence over treating the cause of arrest, and care should be taken not to do more harm than good.

Resuscitation from military TCRA is costly in terms of medical resources, particularly in the use of blood products. More than 900 donor units of packed red blood cells (PRBCs) and FFP were used in treating 52 military TCRA patients over a 6-month period, placing significant strain on the transfusion service, but resulting in the survival of four patients with good neurological outcome. In the absence of any absolute predictors of successful or unsuccessful resuscitation, decision-making on the management of military TCRA remains dependent on a rapid appraisal of the clinical and tactical situation by medical teams at the time of presentation. A summary of the approach to resuscitation from military TCRA is shown in Figure 78.4.

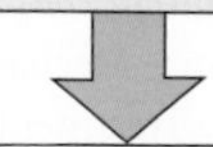
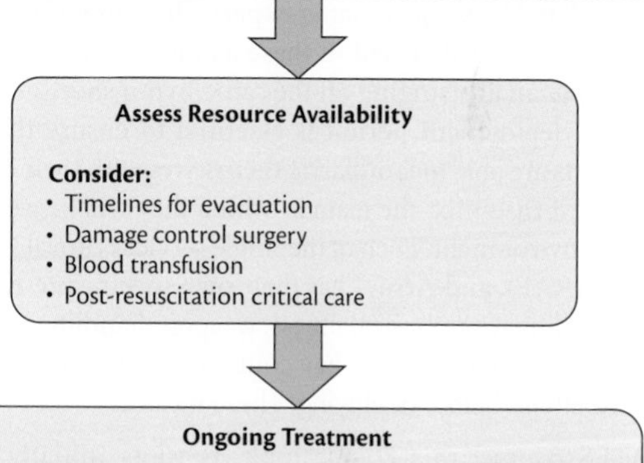

Figure 78.4 A summary of the approach to resuscitation from military traumatic cardiorespiratory arrest.

Military paradigms and human factors

Care of the military casualty starts at the point of wounding and is taught specifically on the UK BATLS Course (Hodgetts et al. 2008). This describes four levels of care as follows:

1. Care Under Fire: initial treatment and evacuation of the casualty, while still under enemy attack, in a non-permissive environment
2. Tactical Field Care: delivered at the point of wounding in a permissive or semi-permissive environment
3. Field Resuscitation Care: delivered in a smaller field medical facility, before transfer to a field hospital
4. Advanced Resuscitation: team-based and consultant-directed resuscitation in a field hospital.

The UK military paradigm of <C>ABC, where <C> stands for catastrophic haemorrhage, differs from the civilian ABC as it recognizes the importance of catastrophic external haemorrhage as a common cause of early and avoidable battlefield mortality (Hodgetts et al. 2006). The aim is to deal rapidly with life-threatening external bleeding using either field-dressings, the combat-application-tourniquet, or topical haemostatic agents. When control of catastrophic haemorrhage has been achieved, ABC is dealt with according to the conventional trauma paradigm.

DMS anaesthetists spend the majority of their clinical practice in the NHS. When deployed, they are primarily involved in advanced resuscitation whether as part of the helicopter-based pre-hospital Medical Emergency Response Team (MERT) or in the field hospital.

It is well documented that the trauma managed in deployed field hospitals in Iraq and Afghanistan is far more severe than in the NHS (Soar et al. 2010). The success of the multidisciplinary trauma team is heavily reliant on excellent human factors or non-technical skills, as described by Rall and Gaba (2005). For anaesthetists, these have been described by Fletcher et al. (2003) as anaesthetists' non-technical skills and the importance of these human factors has recently been described specifically for the defence anaesthetist (Mercer et al. 2010). In the trauma setting, this means that there must be an identified team leader who is supported by others performing with good followership.

There must also be clear communication at every stage. This is particularly important during the handover from the MERT team to clinicians in the ED, where a standardized 'AT-MIST' handover is used every time (Age, Time of Injury, Mechanism of Injury, Injuries sustained, Signs and Symptoms, Treatment Given). Situational awareness is also very important, as anticipation and planning are vital in severely injured patients who have the potential to deteriorate very quickly. As anaesthetists deploy more frequently, the opportunity to develop mental models then increases and this is advantageous.

Specific Standard Operating Procedures (SOPs) for use in the deployed environment have been laid down in the Clinical Guidelines for Operations (Ministry of Defence 2013) and are constantly updated by subject matter experts. It is important that DMS anaesthetists are well versed in these as they ensure that all members of the team are 'singing off the same hymn sheet'.

The pre-deployment period is essential to ensure that defence anaesthetists are able to familiarize themselves with their equipment, the deployed case-mix, the team in which they will be working, and also their environment. Each of the single services [Royal Navy, Royal Air Force (RAF), and Army] has their own specific pre-deployment training dealing with physical fitness, weapons handling, and theatre-specific briefs. There are also key courses that defence anaesthetists also must attend before deploying. These include:

1. BATLS course: this course took its roots initially from the Advanced Trauma Life Support course and is constantly adapted with evidence-based practice and subject matter expert input.
2. Triservice Anaesthetic Simulation Course: this course focuses on a piece of anaesthetic equipment, the Triservice Anaesthetic Apparatus (Houghton 1981) that is not used routinely in the NHS, but may be required on operation.
3. Military Operational Surgical Training course: this is a bespoke course with the whole deploying surgical trauma team training together through cadaveric and high-fidelity simulation scenarios designed to reflect current practice in the field hospital. There is significant input from subject matter experts who have recently returned from the conflict to ensure that lessons learnt are incorporated.
4. Hospital Exercise (HOSPEX) (Arora and Sevdalis 2008): this is a macrosimulation that takes place in a converted aircraft hangar. It is 'mocked up' as realistically as possible to represent the deployed field hospital and allows systems to be tested in real time.

Summary: resuscitation and human factors in the initial management of the military casualty

Resuscitation from military trauma involves treating very severely injured patients in an often dangerous and unfamiliar environment. Despite these challenges, excellent clinical outcomes can still be achieved by using a tailored approach to resuscitation and strong non-technical skills in well-rehearsed teams.

Coagulation and the complex trauma casualty

Trauma results in a complex disturbance of coagulation that is no longer thought to be simply as a result of acidosis, consumption, and dilution (Hesset al. 2008). Recent work has identified that about 30% of civilian trauma patients arrive at hospital with a coagulopathy soon after injury, and that these patients have an increased mortality (Brohi et al. 2003; MacLeod et al. 2003; Maegele et al. 2007). Some studies conclude that this early coagulopathy is a primary event, possibly related to the degree of shock that occurs before any significant fluid therapy (Brohi et al. 2007).

Understanding of early coagulopathy after trauma is limited. Current opinion is that this is tri-modal, with an immediate, short lived, hypercoagulable state, followed by a hypocoagulable period, and ending in a later hypercoagulable state (Allen and Kashuk 2011). Timings are unclear as some authors regard early as the first 24–48 h, while others talk about the first few hours (Brohi et al. 2007; Hayakawa et al. 2011). Likewise, the transition between the various phases is not well characterized. The early hypocoagulable state appears to be driven by poor tissue perfusion leading to alterations in normal endothelial haemostatic mechanisms. Coordinated surgical and anaesthetic treatment should therefore be directed toward restoration of tissue perfusion (Midwinter and Woolley 2011).

Over the last few years, there has been a move towards an increased ratio of packed red blood cells:FFP with earlier use of platelets either in an empiric or targeted fashion. Traditional resuscitation would utilize a certain number of PRBCs before contemplating the use of FFP, and platelets were often not considered until the platelet count fell below 50×10^9 cells litre^{-1} (Theusinger et al. 2009). Replacing lost whole blood with component products in a bleeding patient is an obvious concept; however, evidence determining exactly how this should be achieved is still evolving.

Transfusion guidelines from Europe and the United States have suggested that a ratio approaching 1:1 (PRBC:FFP) should be used, with platelets given either to a target count of greater than 100×10^9 cells litre^{-1}, or in an empiric 1:1:1 (PRBC:FFP:platelets) ratio (Ministry of Defence 2009). There is still some controversy over the exact ratio with some centres feeling that a ratio nearer 2:1 or 3:1 may be better than 1:1, however there are no prospective randomized trials to fully elucidate the answer (Kashuk et al. 2008). The military trauma population differs from the civilian trauma population in that casualties are predominantly male (93%), young (mean 27 years), and involved in blast or penetrating trauma, or both. Extrapolation of civilian data is therefore debatable; however, UK military survival figures support this approach over traditional Advanced Trauma Life Support-style resuscitation. The UK military has adopted a massive transfusion policy with 'shock packs' of prepositioned thawed plasma immediately available, enabling 1:1 resuscitation to begin immediately and avoiding delays caused by the thawing of plasma.

Other therapies used to treat the coagulopathy of trauma include recombinant activated factor VII (rFVIIa) and tranexamic acid (TXA). rFVIIa was developed and licensed initially as a haemostatic agent to treat bleeding patients with haemophilia and factor inhibitors. In pharmacological doses, it works by inducing thrombin generation in locally activated platelets, and by contributing to the formation of a stabilized fibrin clot at the site of vessel injury. Early case reports, followed by a series of observational studies, showed rFVIIa to be effective in reducing blood loss and transfusion requirements for military and civilian trauma patients (Boffard et al. 2005; Wade et al. 2010). Evidence of survival benefit in these studies was inconsistent, especially when hypothermia, acidosis, and platelet and clotting factor deficiencies were not adequately corrected.

In 2010, a multinational phase III trial of rFVIIa in trauma was terminated early, when an interim analysis showed little effect on mortality, despite a significant reduction in transfusion requirements (Hauser et al. 2010). Recent advances in trauma care had reduced underlying mortality, rendering the study underpowered. The safety of rFVIIa has also been questioned, following a 2010 meta-analysis showing increased thromboembolic events, particularly in older patients given rFVIIa (Levi et al. 2010). Despite these concerns, rFVIIa does still have a role in military trauma, especially when resource or practical constraints prevent resuscitation with a 1:1:1 ratio of PRBC:FFP:platelets from the time of wounding.

Tranexamic acid (TXA) is a serine protease inhibitor that binds plasminogen to inhibit fibrinolysis. Although most evidence for TXA is from its use during cardiac surgery, recent research has focused on its potential role in treating hyperfibrinolysis associated with major trauma. In a large randomized controlled trial published in 2010, more than 20 000 trauma patients with, or at risk of, significant bleeding were randomized to receive TXA or placebo within 8 h of injury (Shakur et al. 2010). TXA significantly reduced mortality and death as a result of bleeding, without increasing vascular occlusive events. Surprisingly, this was achieved without a significant reduction in blood transfusion, suggesting a previously unrecognized mechanism of action. TXA is now being used increasingly for military trauma patients, both empirically and in response to laboratory evidence of hyperfibrinolysis.

Although desirable, massive transfusion policies have not been universally adopted in civilian practice, and their implementation is variable and often poorly rehearsed (Malone et al. 2006). Any patient with complex trauma and haemorrhagic shock requires immediate and aggressive resuscitation in order to restore tissue oxygen delivery. This will usually require surgery and the continuum of resuscitation will include management of massive haemorrhage and critical care (Midwinter and Woolley 2011). Management of coagulopathy is an integral part of this process.

Military massive transfusion policies are used early on in the resuscitation during the 'life-saving' period of treatment. However, a 'one-size-fits-all' approach is not ideal for managing complex trauma coagulopathy. Not every patient is the same and differences in demographics, mechanism of injury, and treatment received mean that the resuscitation should become bespoke as soon as is practical. Management of coagulopathy in military circles has been improved by the use of rotational thromboelastometry (ROTEM®, Tem Innovations, Munich, Germany).

Determining coagulopathy using traditional laboratory tests generally takes 40–60 min. Detecting coagulopathy using viscoelastic methodology, where the viscosity of the developing clot is measured, is potentially a more useful tool in trauma because of its relevance as a whole-blood assay, and the speed of results. ROTEM® is a recent, more robust, improvement on existing viscoelastic methodologies that has been evaluated by the UK military since January 2009 (Doran et al. 2010). Its use has been adopted clinically and it is proving to be a useful tool, although it has yet to be fully evaluated and its use has not yet been included in military massive transfusion protocols. ROTEM® can be used to assess the coagulation within 15 min, proving useful in three ways: determining the presence of coagulopathy, monitoring the effect of administered products, and targeting component therapy.

After coagulopathy has been corrected and resuscitation is complete, the casualty will enter a hypercoagulable state as a result of the body's inflammatory response to injury (Allen and Kashuk 2011). Compounded with the administration of procoagulant therapies, it is clear that successful resuscitation may lead to a more significant, and earlier than expected, hypercoagulable state. Great care and thought must be given to the ongoing thromboprophylaxis after injury in these casualties.

Summary: coagulation and the complex trauma casualty

Coagulopathy after major trauma is complex and poorly understood but treatment is crucial to improve mortality. Current challenges include detecting coagulopathy promptly, determining the appropriate form of treatment, and optimizing the timing of thromboprophylaxis.

Military pain management

When examining military pain management requirements there are several issues to consider. One of these clinical issues, and preeminent here, is a recognition of the importance of pain and of treating it robustly. The traditional view is often that combatants rarely feel pain when injured. It is true that survivors of catastrophic injury may deny pain at the point of injury. Indeed, the author has met individuals who describe applying tourniquets to their own thighs while maintaining an awareness of the tactical environment in which they are placed. However, these are the exception. A survey of UK battle casualties has shown that two-thirds of them with a memory of the event described their pain as severe at the point of wounding (Aldington et al. 2011).

As with any medical condition, the first step in treating pain is to identify it and a simple scale that helps treatment decision-making is invaluable. The UK DMS use a scale of 0–3 where 0 is no pain and 3 is the top score, severe pain. The aim is to intervene with pain scores of 2 and 3 and the higher the score, the stronger the analgesic used. This scale is used throughout the chain of evacuation from the point of wounding to the point of rehabilitation (Looker and Aldington 2009).

The initial provision of analgesia is provided by the casualty themselves as all UK servicemen and servicewomen are issued with 10 mg of intramuscular morphine in an automatic injector. Of course, this has no greater analgesic efficacy than 400 mg of ibuprofen or 1g of paracetamol (Moore and McQuay 2003). However, it does have the advantage of being relatively well understood by all, repeatable, and reversible. Further analgesia in the pre-hospital environment will depend upon the skills of the providers. More morphine may be used, but it may also be augmented with intravenous paracetamol, ketamine, and oral transmucosal fentanyl citrate.

Arrival at the field hospital will typically provide access to greater expertise. Together with the agents already mentioned, use can be made of patient-controlled analgesic (PCA) devices, continuous peripheral nerve block (CPNB) infusions, and epidural infusions. The patient-controlled analgesic devices are best managed with a standard solution that does not change. The UK's current approach is to use plain morphine in a mechanical device that will deliver 1 mg every 5 min (Connor et al. 2009).

The advent of portable ultrasound machines has made the use of CPNB catheters viable; traditional peripheral nerve stimulators rely on an intact distal limb to provide evidence of location and this is not always possible. Again, standardized solutions and infusion rates should be used, and great care should be taken to confirm catheters are secured in place and well labelled. Concerns about masking compartment syndrome are not directly relevant as prophylactic fasciotomies should be performed to ensure this does not develop during repatriation. Surgical management and analgesic management are different (Hayakawa et al. 2009; Clasper and Aldington 2010).

During the initial phases of a military operation, the conditions of cleanliness may not be sufficient to allow the use of epidural infusions. However, once these are met, epidurals can be of great value, particularly in the presence of bilateral lower limb, perineal, and abdominal injuries.

Early use of antineuropathic agents is encouraged; 50 mg amitriptyline and a rapid upward titration of pregabalin are used as soon as casualties are able to take them.

Once stabilized, a casualty will be repatriated. As with any patient transfer the secret to success is appropriate preparation of the patient and to ensure that they have sufficient supplies of their analgesics to last the anticipated duration of the transfer, and a little longer to cover any unexpected delays (Flutter et al. 2009).

The arrival back in the United Kingdom, or in an appropriate staging post, provides an opportunity for a review of everything that has gone before. This must include a review of the effectiveness of any catheters that have been sited together with their inspection to ensure no visible signs of infection or catheter migration. A review of all analgesic techniques must be undertaken at this point (Edwards et al. 2009; Devonport et al. 2010).

This is also when patient education must begin in earnest. Patients must be encouraged to understand what analgesic options they have, what the risks and benefits are, and to take responsibility for them. Very few service personnel are happy taking analgesics unless is it is explained that appropriate analgesia will support rehabilitation and thus expedite their recovery.

After the acute phase of care, rehabilitation becomes the focus of medical management. It is essential to understand that the only role of a Pain Service is to augment the rehabilitation of the casualty and this includes consideration of the occupational issues that are so important for military patients. The fundamental tenets are of continued patient education and empowerment. Very often the aim is for down-titration of the medication that was introduced early on and it is not unknown for casualties to wish for a 'little more brain', while understanding that this may result in a 'little more pain' (Jagdish et al. 2009).

After the clinical issues, audit and research are important issues that must be addressed. These are never easy at the best of times but every effort should be made to ensure they are undertaken and the results promulgated and used to influence clinical practice.

The next issue to consider is that of education. The education of the patients has been mentioned but we need to consider the education of the healthcare providers themselves, and it was against this background that the Army's entry officer's course now includes more than a day of training in pain. The staff deploying to the field hospital also get several hours of training in pain management techniques immediately before their deployment, and analgesic techniques are a part of the Military Operating Surgical Team course (Mercer et al. 2010).

The final issue to consider, and possibly the most important, is that of organization. None of the techniques previously described are unknown in civilian circles. However, what is relatively novel is the way they have been put together in an attempt to provide a seamless provision of pain management techniques from point of wounding to point of leaving the service. Thus each process must dovetail with what has gone before and what will follow afterwards. Things cannot change with every change of personnel and so they must be unified and regulated.

These clinical, audit, research, educational, and structural issues are all overseen by the Pain Special Interest Group that in turn comes under the auspices of the Defence Consultant Adviser in Anaesthesia.

Deployed critical care

Critical care is needed whenever conflicts generate casualties that exceed the current definitions of level 2 nursing care. How this capability appears will depend on the maturity of the military operation.

Definitions exist for the different medical capabilities that are deployed and critical care is typically found at Role 2 or 3 facilities. These may be land or sea based. The differences between Roles 2 and 3 are due fundamentally to the surgical capabilities found therein. As a medical facility becomes more sophisticated, then so does its requirement to care for the critically ill patient with multiple organ failures.

Critical care resources

One of the biggest differences from civilian critical care services is the requirement to rapidly move potentially many thousands of miles and set up a critical care service in a foreign land. It is essential that critical care can cope with critically injured personnel as soon as possible and the initial footprint is very different to that seen in mature operations such as in the recent conflict in Afghanistan.

Deployed critical care units are resourced via the medical module. This contains all the equipment required to enable critical care to take place in addition to the staff who typically are derived from a formed unit or field hospital. Since the closure of the Military Hospitals (Royal Hospital Haslar was the last to close in 2007), these staff currently practice in a mixed military and civilian arena. Such staff will come from a variety of medical and nursing backgrounds in order to ensure an adequate skill mix. Training is of major importance and thus within the land arena, field hospital units have been created which allow for the training and administration of personnel. Currently this includes real-time simulation-based training based at Strensall Barracks, York at the Hospital Exercise (or HOSPEX) run by the Army Medical Services Training Centre.

Critical care capabilities

These will be dependent on the type of medical facility. Thus there will be a range of deployed critical care units from the forward unit perhaps attached to the Light Surgical Group of the Medical Regiment where a ventilated patient is held after damage control surgery before onward transfer to a more sophisticated medical facility. Even the recent (2014) 'state-of-the-art' Role 3 facility at Camp Bastion in Southern Helmand Province did not have access to all surgical specialties. Patients attending the Role 3 facility may need to be moved elsewhere for neurosurgical care, for example.

Critical care throughput

Patients are admitted to critical care after admission to the hospital via the ED or after theatre, or both. However, the critical care services also need to be able to look after patients suffering from organ failures as a result of non-traumatic injuries and illnesses. During a typical tour the critical care physician caring may encounter many of the conditions that are typical for the civilian intensivist in addition to infective illnesses not commonly seen in the developed world.

Due to the inherent acute nature of the field hospital, however, the majority of admissions will be unplanned and timely communication with the theatres, ED, and the hospital management are essential. Due to the relative lack of theatre capacity compared with a civilian hospital, the critical care facility needs to be actively involved in the dynamic triage and damage control sequencing procedures that take place. In this way, patients may require active ongoing resuscitation and may also present to critical care when the capacity for the ED to take patients has been exhausted.

With a finite number of beds that can care for level 3 patients, there is a far greater reliance on the ability to transfer patients out of critical care. This role is undertaken by the Critical Care Air Support Team (CCAST) of the RAF. This team comprises an anaesthetic consultant, two critical care nurses, a medic, and an equipment technician who serve to transfer patients for tertiary referral, step-down, and definitive repatriation to the home nation.

Limitations of deployed critical care services

These will very much depend on the size of the medical facility that the critical care services are held within. Numbers of beds and staff to care for the patients will always be a limiting factor. As previously mentioned, not all surgical sub-specialities will be available and typically the training and experience of staff with regard to dealing with paediatric patients is limited. The length of time that a deployed unit can care for a critically ill patient will vary depending on the size of the field hospital and resupply is vital to maintain ongoing capability.

It is not possible to deploy with the ability to care for all eventualities and thus critical care services are initially established with the trauma victim as the main effort. However, as operations mature and become more sophisticated, so do the critical care services. It is commonplace now for a critically injured service person to return to the United Kingdom after resuscitation, surgery, and stabilization in critical care within 36 h of the initial injury. In this way certain complications that arise later than this timeframe may be dealt with in the critical care of the Role 4. Examples of this include renal failure requiring support and ARDS. There have been few occasions to date requiring continuous venovenous haemofiltration in the deployed field hospital. Patients at risk of ARDS from blast lung, for example, are repatriated within the initial 48 h window of opportunity whenever possible.

Critical Care Air Support Team

The RAF CCAST provide a worldwide aeromedical transfer service to critically ill and injured service personnel and entitled civilians. The teams provide cover 365 days a year and can be tasked, mobilized, and airborne within 6 h from their base at RAF Brize Norton.

CCAST can be classified as either strategic, the UK-based repatriation service, or tactical, whereby patients are transferred within a military theatre of operation. The service provides a vital link in the chain between the field hospitals and UK critical care units and the teams are trained to provide the same standard of care as that expected in UK civilian practice.

Each team consists of a consultant anaesthetist, anaesthetic specialist trainee, two intensive care nurses, a medical technician, and a medical assistant. Teams can be augmented with extra staff for simultaneous transfers of three or more patients. All team members receive generic military training and in-depth training on CCAST equipment, aeromedical physiology, and the management of in-flight aircraft emergencies. While not on call for CCAST, they will maintain medical currency and skills while working at a number of intensive care units around the United Kingdom. During flights, the team are relatively isolated from specialist interventions and advice, though communication links do exist via the flight crew and diversions can be arranged to suitable facilities en route in the event of an emergency.

The equipment used must be portable, robust, and function reliably on battery power in the aircraft without causing interference with the aircraft systems, such as avionics (Box 78.1). Monitoring, including invasive lines, is entirely compatible with that used in the field hospital units. Drugs and fluids, including blood products if required, are carried and the teams aim to take sufficient supplies to maintain self-sufficiency for 72 h in the event of an unexpected delay en route.

Patient oxygen requirements are calculated using the formula:

$$\text{Delivered oxygen flow (litres min}^{-1}) \times \text{duration of transfer (min)} = \text{oxygen required (litres)}$$

BOC medical size ZX cylinders are used, which each contain 3040 litres of oxygen. Thus, anticipating a requirement of 15 litres min^{-1} of oxygen flow, each cylinder lasts approximately 3 h. As a contingency measure, this figure is usually doubled to allow for unexpected delays.

Box 78.1 CCAST equipment (list not exhaustive)

- Portable ventilator
- Vacuum mattress
- Monitor with inbuilt defibrillator
- Infusion pumps
- Syringe drivers
- Suction—mechanical and manual
- Point-of-care blood testing
- Pacemaker
- Nerve stimulator
- Oxygen analyser
- Oxygen
- Batteries
- Airway equipment
- Invasive monitoring lines
- Urinary catheters
- Nasogastric tubes
- Warming blankets
- Disposables
- Personal protective equipment
- Waste disposal bags and bins
- Hand hygiene facilities.

Box 78.2 Challenges of the aeromedical environment

- Pressure changes (acceleration/deceleration)
- Gravitational forces
- Vibration
- Noise
- Limited lighting during take-off and landing in hostile airspace
- Temperature
- Restriction of movement
- Isolation
- Motion sickness
- Patient anxiety.

The flexibility of the team and equipment allows transfers to be undertaken on a variety of aircraft, most commonly the C17 Globemaster, Tristar, and C130 Hercules, and helicopters over shorter distances.

Caring for patients in the aeromedical environment presents a number of challenges (Box 78.2). It is important to be aware of the potential for the physical environmental challenges of flight to impact patient physiology. The most important considerations are those related to pressure changes. With a cruising altitude of 30 000–45 000 feet, cabin altitude is usually 6000–8000 feet above sea level, resulting in an ambient pressure of approximately 75.3 kPa (565 mm Hg) (Martin 2006). This exposes patients to gaseous expansion within body cavities by a factor of 1.35 and a reduction in capillary oxygen saturation to 93–94% in normal subjects. Thus, supplementary oxygen is often required, pneumothoraces must be drained, nasogastric tubes placed on free drainage, and, if necessary, cabin altitude can be reduced to ground level (e.g. for cases of intraocular and intracranial air) at the expense of flight duration and aircraft fuel efficiency.

Aircraft vibration necessitates meticulous securing of lines and tubes. Most critical care patients are transferred on a vacuum mattress to minimize movement. This is then secured to the stretcher by a five-point harness and the stretcher is secured to the aircraft via fixed stanchion posts.

The physiological effects of changes in gravitational forces exerted during take-off and landing can be exaggerated in haemodynamically unstable and hypovolaemic patients, thus haemodynamic stability should be optimized before and during flight. Patient temperature is monitored and managed either by warming or cooling devices or by altering the ambient cabin temperature.

With limited lighting in hostile airspace, and considerable noise levels especially in certain aircraft, communication between medical and nursing staff, patients, and aircrew can be difficult and monitor alarms are often rendered inaudible. Staff must remain vigilant and patients and monitors are watched at all times.

Non-intubated patients may be anxious, uncomfortable, and suffer motion sickness (Demmons and Cook 1997). This can be managed pre-emptively with patient reassurance, optimum positioning and movement in flight, and use of antiemetics. All patients undergo regular rolling, pressure area monitoring, and care.

Pain management, particularly in awake patients, requires careful consideration. Both aircraft movement and prolonged patient immobility can aggravate pain that was well controlled before transfer. A multimodal technique is used, utilizing regional anaesthesia where appropriate (Flutter et al. 2010).

Current practice is to avoid feeding intubated patients during the transfer because of concerns regarding micro-aspiration in flight (Turner et al. 2008). Careful fluid management is needed because of the dehydrating effects of the reduced ambient humidity.

Poor communication has been associated with detrimental patient outcomes after transfer (Beckmann et al. 2004), thus detailed records are kept during each transfer, allowing thorough handover of patients at the receiving units, with copies kept for clinical governance purposes. The unique environment provides opportunities for research and development, and the RAF maintains a growing audit and research compendium.

Specialist roles include support of the air transportable isolator, a Department of Health asset maintained by the RAF and used for international transfer of patients with highly contagious and virulent diseases such as viral haemorrhagic fevers. Strategic paediatric critical care transfers are provided by a specialist civilian team with RAF support, while CCAST members moving paediatric patients in the tactical environment have received additional paediatric training. Box 78.2 summarizes the special challenges of an aeromedical environment.

Conduct of the complex military anaesthetic

Definition

Complex military anaesthesia (CMA) may be defined as anaesthesia required during the damage control phase of the patient's clinical care (Box 78.3). It is associated with surgery directed at control of physiology rather than definitive restoration of function, requiring active management of the lethal triad of coagulopathy, acidosis, and hypothermia (Dawes and Thomas 2009; Midwinter and Woolley 2011).

CMA will be associated with the most severely injured (injury severity scores >16). As defined by recent conflicts, these patients will usually have been injured by improvised explosive devices with signature injuries characterized by limb amputation(s) and severe hypovolaemia. Some 10% of these patients will require a massive transfusion.

Massive transfusion has been variously defined but operational military criteria include the transfusion of more than 4 units of

Box 78.3 Clinical features of the damage control philosophy

- Anaesthesia and surgery are contemporary—surgery is part of resuscitation
- The surgeon's efforts are directed at haemorrhage control, wound debridement, and prevention/limitation of contamination
- Management of the lethal triad includes the use of massive transfusion and haemostatic resuscitation with specialized blood products as necessary
- Surgical episodes are often time limited by the patient's physiological status—periods of 'catch up' may be necessary in critical care.

blood within 1 h (alternatively replacement of 50% of the blood volume within 3 h or continuing haemorrhage at a rate exceeding 150 ml min^{-1}).

Specialized surgical procedures required for restoration of function can be demanding of anaesthetic expertise but these take place during the prolonged phase of the patient's care, and will not be discussed here.

Resources

CMA is intensive and demanding of logistics and personnel both within and outside the operating theatre. Success is improved by pre-planning and training via a concerted effort of crew resource management (Mercer et al. 2010).

Practical conduct

Anaesthesia will be contemporary with resuscitative surgery. Teamwork is critical and a constant dialogue is required between all members—in particular, technical and nursing staff must be empowered to highlight problems that medical staff may have overlooked.

When dealing with the most severely injured, one patient may require the attention of two anaesthetists and two operating department practitioners.

A practical sequence of anaesthesia is outlined as follows:

- Pre-oxygenation and induction—oxygen should be administered via a high-flow non-re-breathing system until such time as an anaesthetic face mask can be substituted. Intravenous induction of anaesthesia should occur through a secure intravenous/intraosseous cannula, Suitable induction agents are ketamine (1.5 mg kg^{-1}) or sodium thiopentone at a tenth to a half of normal dose. Ketamine has the advantage of maintaining blood pressure because of its sympathomimetic action; a disadvantage is the consequent tachycardia. With subsequent controlled ventilation, ketamine's action on *N*-methyl-D-aspartate receptors affords neuroprotection by reducing cerebral oxygen consumption.
  - Muscle relaxation for tracheal intubation should be ensured with 1.5 mg kg^{-1} of suxamethonium; 1.5 mg kg^{-1} of rocuronium is an alternative.
- Airway—this may have already been secured pre-hospital either via a tracheal tube or surgical airway. In-hospital RSI must include the facility to rapidly achieve a surgical airway should tracheal intubation fail.
  - Single-lumen tracheal tubes are used—when required, control of intrathoracic haemorrhage is undertaken via a clamshell thoracotomy and if required, lung deflation can be achieved by temporary disconnecting the ventilator.
  - Tracheal tubes should not be cut—this is particularly relevant in the presence of facial burns with progressive oedema. Facial burns or maxillofacial trauma may involve a gas induction with a patient in the sitting position. Tape fixation of tracheal/cricothyroidotomy tubes must not be too tight as this can raise intracranial pressure by obstructing jugular venous return. Consideration should always be given to securing a cricothyroidotomy tube with sutures.
- Cervical spine control—this is less of an issue in military patients but in blunt trauma associated with reduced consciousness levels, the usual precautions apply and more difficult laryngoscopy anticipated during in-line immobilization.
- Intravenous access—in the severely hypovolaemic patient it is usual to establish subclavian central venous access with a 7.5 FG catheter. On occasions both subclavian veins will be cannulated. Subsequent fluid administration is via a rapid fluid infuser. A recent refinement is to use a multiple access catheter which permits rapid infusion and drug infusion/pressure monitoring via one device.
- Arterial cannulation—the choice of vessel may be constrained by the injury pattern and arterial access should not be attempted until correction of hypovolaemia has improved the chance of successful first-time insertion.
- Ventilation—adequacy of ventilation must be confirmed by visual inspection and capnography. Barotrauma should be minimized by avoiding excessive inflation pressures. An evolving blast lung injury may require permissive hypercapnia—the respiratory rate should be increased in preference to tidal volume which should be capped at 8 ml kg^{-1} with peak inspiratory pressures not exceeding 30 cm H_2O. PEEP values should be matched to the inspired oxygen concentrations as shown in Table 78.4 (The Acute Respiratory Distress Syndrome Network 2000).

Established blast lung injury may require that the patient is ventilated in the operating theatre with that individuals critical care ventilator, whose settings have been optimized to best permit the requirements outlined.

- Massive transfusion—current doctrine is to administer PRBCs and FFP in a 1:1 ratio, supported by platelets, cryoprecipitate, and antifibrinolytics (Ministry of Defence 2009) (Box 78.4).
- Haemostatic resuscitation—this is a necessary by-product of trauma-induced coagulopathy, including dilutional effects from fluid resuscitation and MT. Therapy must be directed by laboratory tests of coagulation and where possible near-patient testing. Currently the UK DMS use thromboelastometry (ROTEM™) to supplement laboratory assays and guide component therapy.
- Treatment of fibrinolysis which is increasingly recognized as a sentinel feature of the acute coagulopathy of trauma (ATC) requires early intervention with intravenous tranexamic acid. In the presence of ongoing MT, the recommended loading dose of 1 g may need repeating.
- A continued failure of haemostasis may prompt consideration of recombinant factor VIIa (rFVIIa). This is only effective at pH levels above 7.2. If successful, a dose of 100 μg kg^{-1} will likely achieve clinical efficacy within 15–20 min. If ineffective, a second dose can be administered but subsequent repetitions are unlikely to help.

Table 78.4 PEEP values matches to inspired O_2 concentrations

FI_{O_2}	0.3	0.4	0.5	0.8	0.9	1.0
PEEP	5 to 8	8 to 10	10 to 14	14 to 16	16	16 to 18

Box 78.4 Essential components of the military massive transfusion protocol

- Initial reception pack containing 4 units each of RBCs (group O Rh Neg or group specific) and FFP (group AB)
- Transfuse PRBCs: FFP in 1:1 ratio
- Second pack to contain 4 units each of RBCs and FFP plus platelets
- After second pack and thereafter anticipate need for further platelets and cryoprecipitate
- Frequent measurement and control of calcium and potassium
- Monitor transfusion with laboratory and near-patient testing: PT, APTT, fibrinogen, arterial blood gases, and ROTEM®
- Consider early use (within 3 h of injury) of tranexamic acid to correct anticipated or established fibrinolysis
- Red cell function deteriorates significantly after 14 days of storage—hence the administration policy should be 'last in, first out'.

- It is also necessary to frequently measure potassium and calcium levels, with correction as necessary. Immediately treat hyperkalaemia greater than 6.0 mmol litre^{-1} with 10 ml calcium gluconate 10% (2.32 mmol calcium) or 10 ml calcium chloride 10% (6.8 mmol calcium) followed by 25 ml glucose 50% + 10 units soluble insulin over 15 min. Ionized calcium should be aggressively maintained above 1.0 mmol litre^{-1} using bolus injections of calcium preparations as mentioned previously. Note these are not equivalent doses. Calcium chloride should be given via a central vein.
- Crystalloid/non-blood product infusion—in the presence of a massive transfusion, the use of crystalloid is limited as a vehicle for drug delivery only. This prevents further dilution of clotting factors or the subsequent development of oedema in acute lung injury.
- Patient warming—the ambient theatre temperature should be increased as high as 29°C (84°F). Patients should be managed on a warming mattress and covered where possible by warmed air blankets. Rapid fluid infusion devices should ensure all intravenous fluids are administered at 37°C.
- Anaesthetic/analgesia agents—it is essential to ensure good tissue perfusion as hypoperfusion is implicated as a direct cause of the coagulopathy of trauma. Perfusion results from combining vasodilation with aggressive fluid resuscitation, using high-dose, potent opiate analgesia with judicious use of low-concentration volatile agents. Skeletal muscle paralysis should be maintained with train-of-four monitored doses of non-depolarizing relaxants, particularly where access to a body cavity is anticipated.

Complications

The maintenance phase is a continuation of resuscitation and during this period the anaesthetist should be in frequent dialogue with the surgical team. The physiological consequences of injuries may still be developing or not have initially been recognized. Any deterioration in the patient's physiology requires reconsideration of the possible cause.

Table 78.5 lists potential complications, while Box 78.5 describes key features of blast lung injury.

End-points

Successful management may be bluntly defined as returning a patient to critical care in as good a physiological condition as possible within as short a period as possible. The UK military criteria for haemostatic resuscitation are more prescriptive than corresponding civilian guidelines—desirable parameters are listed in Table 78.6.

Table 78.5 Differential diagnoses of complications during maintenance phase of anaesthesia

	Possible mechanism	Management/comment
Hypoxia	Tracheal tube malposition	Check position/patency
	Tension pneumothorax	May only be revealed after positive pressure ventilation—in extremis, thoracostomy then intercostal drain
	Evolving injury—blast lung	Permissive ventilation strategies—if complicated by pulmonary oedema consider use of rFVIIa
	Obstruction to pulmonary outflow tract as confirmed by capnography	Air embolism or pulmonary embolism (see row below)
Hypotension	Continuing haemorrhage	Check coagulation status—coagulation of trauma (COT) may mandate return to critical care once surgical bleeding is controlled. Failure of haemostasis may be corrected with rFVIIa
	Myocardial contusion/fluid overload	Normalize CVP—check Ca^{2+} and further inotropic support as required.
	Cardiac tamponade	Hypotension with raised CVP—confirmation by surgical inspection
	Cardiac micro air embolism	A possible squeal of blast injury—ventilate with 100% O_2
	SIRS—sepsis	Sepsis may become a feature during the damage control phase—particularly with heavily contaminated wounds associated with blast injury
	Pulmonary embolism	This can occur during damage control associated with massive transfusion—inferior vena cava filter may be considered

Box 78.5 Clinical features of blast lung injury

- Depending upon exposure, characteristic signs and symptoms may be immediate or delayed for 24–48 h
- Pathology is result of disruption of air–tissue interface with symptoms ranging from mild hypoxia through to severe ARDS
- In severe cases, haemorrhagic pulmonary oedema may be an early feature
- Between 6 and 48 h the haemorrhagic state is superseded by an inflammatory response
- Complications such as pneumothorax and air embolism are potentially worsened by intermittent positive pressure ventilation—ventilator management requires pressure limitation with or without permissive hypercapnia.

Postoperative management

Other than in exceptional cases, the recipient of such anaesthesia will postoperatively be directed to the critical care unit. This allows the opportunity where necessary to catch up on physiological normalization with ongoing haemostatic resuscitation. This may be one of several such pauses in the initial series of damage control surgeries.

Table 78.6 Physiological targets after damage control resuscitation with massive transfusion

Parameter	Target value	Comment
Haemoglobin	10 g dl^{-1}	A balance between O_2-carrying capacity and rheology is achieved with a haematocrit of 0.3
Platelets	>100 × 10^9 cells litre^{-1}	Component of massive transfusion
Fibrinogen	1.5–2.0 g litre^{-1}	Coagulation of trauma associated with fibrinolysis
PT ratio	<1.2	Values >1.2 are a marker of need for massive transfusion
APTT ratio	<1.2	As for PT
Core temperature	>35°C	All components of haemostasis are temperature dependant
pH	>7.3	Acidosis—negative effect on O_2 delivery and haemostasis
Base deficit	0 to −2 mmol litre^{-1}	Reflects correction of metabolic acidosis
Lactate	<2 mmol litre^{-1}	Raised lactate is a marker of tissue hypoperfusion
Potassium	<5.5 mmol litre^{-1}	Hyperkalaemia is a feature of massive transfusion worsened by metabolic acidosis
Calcium	≥1.9 mmol litre^{-1}	Ionized calcium reduced by citrate toxicity

Box 78.6 Essential requirements for reception of casualties at Role 4

- Secure signals detailing numbers of expected casualties and nature of injuries
- Trauma coordinators to ensure key clinical personnel are aware of incoming casualties, operating theatre space and critical care beds—organized as necessary
- Sufficient and appropriately trained staff available to receive patients at ward and critical care locations
- Dedicated laboratory support, particularly with respect to blood and blood products.

The initial phase of critical care will mandate continued ventilation of the patient with analgesic and sedative infusions. When coagulation has been normalized, consideration may be given to siting an epidural or equivalent regional analgesia before extubation or further surgery.

Anaesthesia at Role 4

Philosophy and infrastructure

The aims of anaesthesia at Role 4 may be described as a horizontal integration with the care given in operational theatres. While easily stated, this is not without its challenges.

Clinical expertise and adequate infrastructure are required to maintain and improve clinical care. In addition, consideration must be given to support the workload of these (resource-intensive) patients without interrupting the hospital's usual activity. This is particularly important during periods of increased operational activity.

The logistical requirements require a system of command and communication which cascades from the care given at Roles 1–3 down to the receiving clinical and planning teams at Role 4. The details of such a model as it may apply to an institution staffed jointly by military and civilian clinicians are detailed in Box 78.6.

At Role 4, the contribution of anaesthesia is improved if there is anaesthetic representation wherever there is a multidisciplinary review of the clinical care of patients. This may involve a regular formal ward round or as part of scheduling the daily operating theatre list. In either case, it enables manpower and clinical planning particularly in respect of anticipated difficult surgical episodes.

Patient admissions and theatre allocation

Injured military personnel are transported by 'routine' aeromedical evacuation, or in the case of the critically ill, by specially trained and tasked CCASTs. Repatriation can be expected within 24–48 h of wounding and because of these timelines, seriously injured personnel will often still be in the 'damage control phase' of their surgical journey (Midwinter and Woolley 2011).

On admission to the Role 4 facility, CCAST patients enter the critical care unit where an immediate assessment of their injuries and physiological status is undertaken before continued stabilization or immediate surgery. Frequently this surgery will be the 'second look' after resuscitative surgery at Role 3, and will be limited by the physiology of the patient. It is often the first of repeated visits

Box 78.7 Anaesthetic considerations for the critically injured military patient

- Anaesthesia continues as part of damage control philosophy: rigorous attention to managing the lethal triad of coagulation, hypothermia, and lactic acidosis
- Use of blood/FFP with platelet, cryoprecipitate, and antifibrinolytic therapy as necessary. Haemostatic resuscitation guided by standard laboratory tests plus near-patient assessment with thromboelastometry (Rugeri et al. 2007)
- Crystalloid restriction—to allow better haemostatic resuscitation and decrease oedema
- Awareness of evolving blast injury—with appropriate ventilator strategies (Mackenzie and Tunnicliffe 2011)
- Recognize that within 48 h, patients will develop and maintain a florid systemic inflammatory response syndrome (SIRS)
- If necessary, change resuscitative central lines established at Role 3 and ensure nasogastric feeding tube *in situ*.

Box 78.8 Anaesthetic considerations for patients on the military surgical ward

- Patients may require preoperative intravenous fluids after prolonged starvation when surgery has been anticipated during aeromedical evacuation
- The nature of the wounds may not be clear from the signals sent from Role 3—patients may need cross-matching before surgery
- The effectiveness of in-transit analgesia should be assessed as CPNB/epidural catheters may need revision or *de novo* insertion perioperatively
- As with the critically injured, ensure normothermia
- A sub-group of patients admitted from critical care may still need high dependency care and will continue to sustain a marked SIRS
- 'Flashbacks' during awakening requires sensitive management by recovery staff
- Postoperative analgesic 'failure' requires prompt rescue.

to the operating theatre until their clinical condition improves enough to consider definitive surgery for restoration of function.

Less severely injured aeromedical admissions should be admitted directly to an appropriate surgical ward, where an early review of their wounds is similarly undertaken. Where necessary, within 2–8 h they will also be in an operating theatre having their wounds inspected, with definitive management at this time or as the first procedure in a consequent series.

The anaesthetic considerations for these two groups are somewhat distinct—the essential elements are detailed in Box 78.7 and Box 78.8 and includes comments (Box 78.8) relevant to patients recently discharged from critical care.

Anaesthesia and restorative surgery

The complex nature of ballistic wounds means that as the patient's condition stabilizes, multiple surgical interventions are the norm. Particular challenges for anaesthesia include pain control, establishing and maintaining intravascular access, and avoiding undue perioperative starvation. Preoperative omission of solids should be limited to 6 h, with clear fluids permitted up to 2 h before surgery. Many of the operations are prolonged with the recognized attendant anaesthetic considerations. Frequent extensive

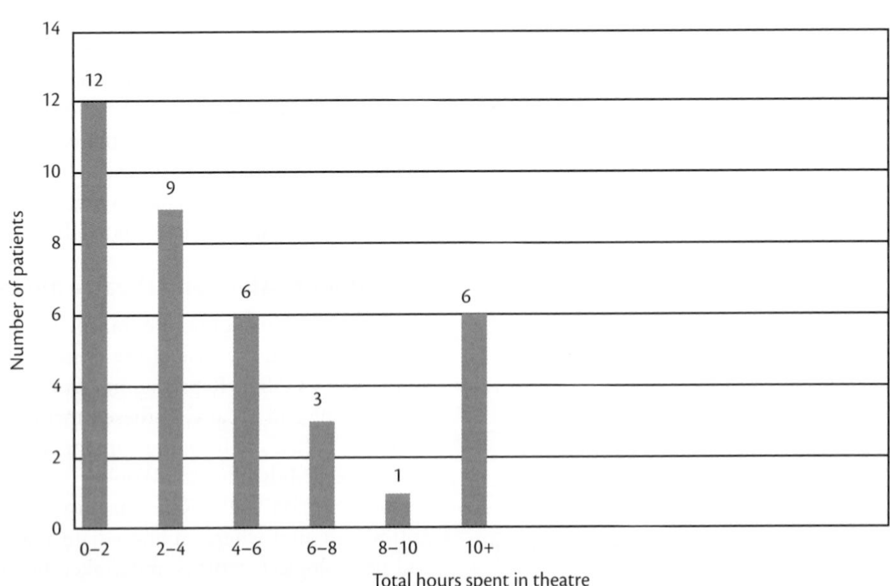

Figure 78.5 Operating time required for military patients at Role 4 (United Kingdom) during February 2010.

Reproduced with permission from Wood PR, Haldane AG, Plimmer SE. Anaesthesia at Role 4. *Journal of the Royal Army Medical Corps*, Volume 156, Issue 4, Suppl. 1, pp. 308–310, Copyright © BMJ Publishing Ltd 2010.

Box 78.9 Analgesic features of military polytrauma

- Multimodal oral analgesia regimen necessary, often characterized by maximum permitted doses of anticonvulsants and frequent/high dosage opiate requirements
- While theoretically attractive, use of multiple CPNB catheters in one patient is often limited by practical constraints and overall local anaesthetic dose
- Epidural analgesia may be restricted in the presence of spinal injury
- Neurological assessment of epidural complications more problematical when the injury pattern involves high lower limb amputation and associated perineal injury
- As a consequence, the threshold for suspecting epidural complications must be low.

surgical episodes have implications for operating theatre logistics. Figure 78.5 details the surgical activity for all the military patients operated upon at the UK Role 4 facility during February 2010. The six casualties whose theatre time exceeded 10 h are of particular note. One patient required 45 h of surgery—his operative interventions continued in the following month.

Postoperative care

Critically injured patients are returned directly to the critical care unit. Non-critical patients are admitted to the recovery unit and returned to the ward when vital signs and analgesia are optimized. See Box 78.9.

Perioperative analgesia

Any system which manages severely injured military personnel requires a robust acute pain team (Devonport et al. 2010). A multimodal analgesic regimen is necessary, including prescription for neuropathic injury. It is essential that familiarity and expertise with continuous peripheral nerve block (CPNB) and epidural analgesia use is developed, while at all times recognizing some of the limitations and particular difficulties in this group of patients. See Box 78.9.

Research and development

Anaesthesia directly contributes to the care of injured military personnel at Role 4 but new lessons are continually being absorbed. Future progress will continue to depend upon close support and cooperation between civilian clinicians and the DMS.

Acknowledgement

With regards to the section on 'Mechanisms of wounding' authored by Emrys Kirkman, Sarah Watts, and Karen Smyth: © Crown copyright (2015), Dstl/MOD. This material is licensed under the terms of the Open Government Licence except where otherwise stated. To view this licence, visit http://www.nationalarchives.gov.uk/doc/open-government-licence/version/3 or write to the Information Policy Team, The National Archives, Kew, London TW9 4DU, or email psi@nationalarchives.gsi.gov.uk.

Declaration of interest

At the time of writing, Dr Aldington was a Serving Officer in the Royal Army Medical Corps. Dr Aldington has received honoraria from Grünenthal, Pfizer, and Napp for delivering educational presentations and from Grünenthal for consultancy work.

References

Aldington DJ, McQuay HJ, Moore RA. End-to-end military pain management. *Philos Trans R Soc Lond B Biol Sci* 2011; **366**: 268–75

Allen SR, Kashuk JL. Unanswered questions in the use of blood component therapy in trauma. *Scand J Trauma Resusc Emerg Med* 2011; **19**: 5

Anderson HL, III, Shapiro MB, Delius RE, Steimle CN, Chapman RA, Bartlett RH. Extracorporeal life support for respiratory failure after multiple trauma. *J Trauma* 1994; **37**: 266–72

Armonda RA, Bell RS, Vo AH, *et al.* Wartime traumatic cerebral vasospasm: recent review of combat casualties. *Neurosurgery* 2006; **59**: 1215–25

Arora S, Sevdalis N. HOSPEX and concepts of simulation. *J R Army Med Corps* 2008; **154**: 202–5

Barrow DW, Rhoads HY. Blast concussion injury. *JAMA* 1944; **125**: 900–2

Battistella FD, Nugent W, Owings JT, Anderson JT. Field triage of the pulseless trauma patient. *Arch Surg* 1999; **134**: 742–5

Beckmann U, Gillies DM, Berenholtz SM, Wu AW, Pronovost P. Incidents relating to the intra-hospital transfer of critically ill patients. An analysis of the reports submitted to the Australian Incident Monitoring Study in Intensive Care. *Intensive Care Med* 2004; **30**: 1579–85

Bickell WH, Wall MJ, Pepe PE, *et al.* Immediate versus delayed fluid resuscitation for hypotensive patients with penetrating torso injuries. *N Engl J Med* 1994; **331**: 1105–9

Blennow K, Jonsson M, Andreasen N, *et al.* No neurochemical evidence of brain injury after blast overpressure by repeated explosions or firing heavy weapons. *Acta Neurol Scand* 2011; **123**: 245–51

Boffard KD, Riou B, Warren B, *et al.* Recombinant factor VIIa as adjunctive therapy for bleeding control in severely injured trauma patients: two parallel randomized, placebo-controlled, double-blind clinical trials. *J Trauma* 2005; **59**: 8–15

Brohi K, Cohen MJ, Ganter MT, Matthay MA, Mackersie RC, Pittet JF. Acute traumatic coagulopathy: initiated by hypoperfusion: modulated through the protein c pathway? *Ann Surg* 2007; **245**: 812–8

Brohi K, Singh J, Heron M, Coats T. Acute traumatic coagulopathy. *J Trauma* 2003; **54**: 1127–30

Brown RF, Cooper GJ, Maynard RL. The ultrastructure of rat lung following acute primary blast injury. *Int J Exp Pathol* 1993; **74**: 151–62

Cera SM, Mostafa G, Sing RF, Sarafin JL, Matthews BD, Heniford BT. Physiologic predictors of survival in post-traumatic arrest. *Am Surg* 2003; **69**: 140–4

Cernak I. The importance of systemic response in the pathobiology of blast-induced neurotrauma. *Front Neurol* 2010; **1**: 151

Cernak I, Noble-Haeusslein LJ. Traumatic brain injury: an overview of pathobiology with emphasis on military populations. *J Cereb Blood Flow Metab* 2010; **30**: 255–66

Cernak I, Savic J, Malicevic Z, *et al.* Involvement of the central nervous system in the general response to pulmonary blast injury. *J Trauma* 1996; **40**: S100–S104

Champion HR, Holcomb JB, Young LA. Injuries from explosions: physics, biophysics, pathology, and required research focus. *J Trauma* 2009; **66**: 1468–77

Clasper JC, Aldington DJ. Regional anaesthesia, ballistic limb trauma and acute compartment syndrome. *J R Army Med Corps* 2010; **156**: 77–8

Connor DJ, Ralph JK, Aldington DJ. Field hospital analgesia. *J R Army Med Corps* 2009; **155**: 49–56

Cooper GJ. Protection of the lung from blast overpressure by thoracic stress wave decouplers. *J Trauma* 1996; **40**: S105–S110

Cooper GJ, Maynard RL, Cross NL, Hill JF. Casualties from terrorist bombings. *J Trauma* 1983; **23**: 955–67

CRASH-2 Collaborators. The importance of early treatment with tranexamic acid in bleeding trauma patients: an exploratory analysis of the CRASH-2 randomised controlled trial. *Lancet* 2011; **311**: 1096–101

Dawes R. Thomas GO. Battlefield resuscitation. *Curr Opin Crit Care* 2009; **15**: 527–35

Demmons LL, Cook EW. Anxiety in adult fixed-wing air transport patients. *Air Med J* 1997; **16**: 77–80

Devonport L, Edwards D, Edwards C, Aldington DJ, Mahoney PF, Wood PR. Evolution of the role 4 U.K. military pain service. *J R Army Med Corps* 2010; **156**(4 Suppl 1): 398–401

Doran CM, Woolley T, Midwinter MJ. Feasibility of using rotational thromboelastometry to assess coagulation status of combat casualties in a deployed setting. *J Trauma* 2010; **69**(Suppl 1): S40–8

Eastridge BJ, Hardin M, Cantrell J, *et al.* Died of wounds on the battlefield: causation and implications for improving combat casualty care. *J Trauma* 2011; **71**: S4–S8

Edwards D, Bowden M, Aldington DJ. Pain management at role 4. *J R Army Med Corps* 2009; **155**: 58–61

Fear NT, Jones E, Groom M, *et al.* Symptoms of post-concussional syndrome are non-specifically related to mild traumatic brain injury in UK Armed Forces personnel on return from deployment in Iraq: an analysis of self-reported data. *Psychol Med* 2009; **39**: 1379–87

Ferguson N, Cook D, Guyatt G, et al. High-frequency oscillation in early acute respiratory distress syndrome. *N Engl J Med* 2013; **368**: 795–805

Fletcher G, Flin R, McGeorge P, Glavin R, Maran N, Patey R. Anaesthetists' Non-Technical Skills (ANTS): evaluation of a behavioural marker system. *Br J Anaesth* 2003; **90**: 580–8

Flutter C, Ruth M, Aldington D. Pain management during Royal Air Force strategic aeromedical evacuations. *J R Army Med Corps* 2009; **155**: 61–63

Fulton RL, Voigt WJ, Hilakos AS. Confusion surrounding the treatment of traumatic cardiac arrest. *J Am Coll Surg* 1995; **181**: 209–14

Garner J, Watts S, Parry C, Bird J, Cooper G, Kirkman E. Prolonged permissive hypotensive resuscitation is associated with poor outcome in primary blast injury with controlled hemorrhage. *Ann Surg* 2010; **251**: 1131–9

Gorbunov NV, Asher LV, Ayyagari V, Atkins JL. Inflammatory leukocytes and iron turnover in experimental hemorrhagic lung trauma. *Exp Mol Pathol* 2006a; **80**: 11–25

Gorbunov NV, Das DK, Goswami SK, Gurusamy N, Atkins JL. Nitric oxide (NO), redox signaling, and pulmonary inflammation in a model of polytrauma. Proceedings of the XIII Congress of the Society for Free Radical Research International. Davos, Switzerland: 2006b; 2–4

Gorbunov NV, McFaul SJ, Januszkiewicz A, Atkins JL. Pro-inflammatory alterations and status of blood plasma iron in a model of blast-induced lung trauma. *Int J Immunopathol Pharmacol* 2005; **18**: 547–56

Grasso S, Terragni PP, Mascia L. Dynamic airway pressure/time curve in experimental ARDS. *Intensive Care Med* 2002; **28**: A727

Guy RJ, Kirkman E, Watkins PE, Cooper GJ. Physiologic responses to primary blast. *J Trauma* 1998; **45**: 983–7

Harban FMJ, Kirkman E, Kenward CE, Watkins PE. Primary thoracic blast injury causes acute reduction in cardiac function in the anaesthetised pig. *J Physiol Lond* 2001; **533**: 81P

Hauser CJ, Boffard K, Dutton R, *et al.* Results of the control trial: efficacy and safety of recombinant activated factor vii in the management of refractory traumatic hemorrhage. *J Trauma* 2010; **69**: 489–500

Hayakawa H, Aldington D, Moore R. Acute traumatic compartment syndrome: a systematic review of results of fasciotomy. *Trauma* 2009; **11**: 5–15

Hayakawa M, Sawamura A, Gando S, *et al.* Disseminated intravascular coagulation at an early phase of trauma is associated with consumption coagulopathy and excessive fibrinolysis both by plasmin and neutrophil elastase. *Surgery* 2011; **149**: 221–30

Hess JR, Brohi K, Dutton RP, *et al.* The coagulopathy of trauma: a review of mechanisms. *J Trauma* 2008; **65**: 748–54

Ho AM, Graham CA, Ng CS, *et al.* Timing of tracheal intubation in traumatic cardiac tamponade: a word of caution. *Resuscitation* 2009; **80**: 272–4

Hodgetts T, Mahoney P, Clasper J (eds). *Battlefield Advanced Trauma Life Support*, 5th Edn. London: UK Defence Medical Services, 2008

Hodgetts TJ, Davies S, Russell R, McLeod J. Benchmarking the UK military deployed trauma system. *J R Army Med Corps* 2007; **153**: 237–8

Hodgetts TJ, Mahoney PF, Russell MQ, Byers M. ABC to <C>ABC: redefining the military trauma paradigm. *Emerg Med J* 2006; **23**: 745–6

Hopson LR, Hirsh E, Delgado J, *et al.* Guidelines for withholding or termination of resuscitation in prehospital traumatic cardiopulmonary arrest. *J Am Coll Surg* 2003; **196**: 475–81

Houghton IT. The Triservice anaesthetic apparatus. *Anaesthesia* 1981; **36**: 1094–108

Jagdish S, Davies M, Aldington D. Military chronic pain management. *J R Army Med Corps* 2009; **155**: 67

Kashuk JL, Moore EE, Johnson JL, *et al.* Postinjury life threatening coagulopathy: Is 1: 1 fresh frozen plasma: packed red blood cells the answer? *J Trauma* 2008; **65**: 261–70

Kehoe A, Jones A, Marcus S, Nordmann G, Pope C, Reavley P, Smith C. Current controversies in military pre-hospital critical care. *JR Army Med Corps* 2011; **157**: 305–9

Kelly JF, Ritenour AE, McLaughlin DF, *et al.* Injury severity and causes of death from Operation Iraqi Freedom and Operation Enduring Freedom: 2003-2004 versus 2006. *J Trauma* 2008; **64**: S21–S27

Kirkman E, Watts S, Cooper GJ. Blast injury research models. *Philos Trans R Soc Lond B Biol Sci* 2011; **366**: 144–59

Kwan I, Bunn F, Chinnock P, Roberts I. Timing and volume of fluid administration for patients with bleeding. *Cochrane Database Syst Rev* 2014; **5**: CD002245

Kwan I, Bunn F, Roberts I. Timing and volume of fluid administration for patients with bleeding. *Cochrane Database Syst Rev* 2003; **3**: CD002245

Levi M, Levy JH, Andersen HF, Truloff D. Safety of recombinant activated factor vii in randomized clinical trials. *N Engl J Med* 2010; 363: 1791–800

Lockey D, Crewdson K, Davies G. Traumatic cardiac arrest: who are the survivors? *Ann Emerg Med* 2006; **48**: 240–4

Looker J, Aldington D. Pain scores-as easy as counting to three. *J R Army Med Corps* 2009; **155**: 42–43

Mackenzie IMJ, Tunnicliffe B. Blast injuries to the lung: epidemiology and management *Phil Trans R Soc B* 2011; **366**: 295–9

MacLeod JB, Lynn M, McKenney MG, Cohn SM, Murtha M. Early coagulopathy predicts mortality in trauma. *J Trauma* 2003; **55**: 39–44

Maegele M, Lefering R, Yucel N, *et al.* Early coagulopathy in multiple injury: an analysis from the German trauma registry on 8724 patients. *Injury* 2007; **38**: 298–304

Malone DL, Hess JR, Fingerhut A. Massive transfusion practices around the globe and a suggestion for a common massive transfusion protocol. *J Trauma* 2006; **60**: S91–6

Margolin DA, Johann DJ, Jr, Fallon WF, Jr, Malangoni MA. Response after out-of-hospital cardiac arrest in the trauma patient should determine aeromedical transport to a trauma center. *J Trauma* 1996; **41**: 721–5

Martin T. *Aeromedical Transportation: A Clinical Guide*. Aldershot: Ashgate Publisher Limited; 2006

Meade MO, Cook DJ, Guyatt GH, *et al.* Ventilation strategy using low tidal volumes, recruitment maneuvers, and high positive end-expiratory pressure for acute lung injury and acute respiratory distress syndrome: a randomized controlled trial. *JAMA* 2008; **299**: 637–45

Mercat A, Richard JC, Vielle B, *et al.* Positive end-expiratory pressure setting in adults with acute lung injury and acute respiratory distress syndrome: a randomized controlled trial. *JAMA* 2008; **299**: 646–55

Mercer SJ, Whittle C, Siggers B, Frazer RS. Simulation, human factors and defence anaesthesia. *J R Army Med Corps* 2010; **156**(4 Suppl 1): 365–9

Mercer SJ, Whittle CL, Mahoney PF. Lessons from the battlefield: human factors in defence anaesthesia. *Br J Anaesth* 2010; **105**: 9–20

Midwinter MJ, Woolley T. Resuscitation and coagulation in the severely injured trauma patient. *Phil Trans R Soc B* 2011; **366**: 192–203

Ministry of Defence. *Clinical Guidelines for Operations*. Joint Service Publication 999. London: Ministry of Defence, 2013

Ministry of Defence. *Management of Massive Haemorrhage on Operations*. Surgeon General's Operation Policy Letter. London: Ministry of Defence, 2009

Moore A, McQuay HJ. Acute pain. *Bandolier* 2003; **4**: 1–22

Morris AH, Wallace CJ, Menlove RL, *et al.* Randomized clinical trial of pressure-controlled inverse ratio ventilation and extracorporeal CO2 removal for adult respiratory distress syndrome. *Am J Respir Crit Care Med* 1994; **149**: 295–305

Ohnishi M, Kirkman E, Guy RJ, Watkins PE. Reflex nature of the cardiorespiratory response to primary thoracic blast injury in the anaesthetised rat. *Exp Physiol* 2001; **86**: 357–64

Okie S. Traumatic brain injury in the war zone. *N Engl J Med* 2005; **352**: 2043–7

Park E, Gottlieb JJ, Cheung B, Shek PN, Baker AJ. A model of low-level primary blast brain trauma results in cytoskeletal proteolysis and chronic functional impairment in the absence of lung barotrauma. *J Neurotrauma* 2011; **28**: 343–57

Peek GJ, Mugford M, Tiruvoipati R, *et al.* Efficacy and economic assessment of conventional ventilatory support versus extracorporeal membrane oxygenation for severe adult respiratory failure (CESAR): a multicentre randomised controlled trial. *Lancet* 2009; **374**: 1351–63

Pepe PE, Roppolo LP, Fowler RL. The detrimental effects of ventilation during low-blood-flow states. *Curr Opin Crit Care* 2005; **11**: 212–8

Pickens JJ, Copass MK, Bulger EM. Trauma patients receiving CPR: predictors of survival. *J Trauma* 2005; **58**: 951–8

Pinhu L, Whitehead T, Evans T, Griffiths M. Ventilator-associated lung injury. *Lancet* 2003; **361**: 332–40

Pizov R, Oppenheim-Eden A, Matot I, *et al.* Blast lung injury from an explosion on a civilian bus. *Chest* 1999; **115**: 165–72

Plotkin JS, Shah JB, Lofland GK, DeWolf AM. Extracorporeal membrane oxygenation in the successful treatment of traumatic adult respiratory distress syndrome: case report and review. *J Trauma* 1994; **37**: 127–30

Rall M, Gaba D. Human performance and patient safety. In: Miller R, ed. *Miller's Anesthesia.* Philadelphia, PA: Elsevier Churchill Livingstone, 2005; 3021–72

Risdall JE, Menon DK. Traumatic brain injury. *Philos Trans R Soc Lond B Biol Sci* 2011; **366**: 241–50

Rosemurgy AS, Norris PA, Olson SM, Hurst JM, Albrink MH. Prehospital traumatic cardiac arrest: the cost of futility. *J Trauma* 1993; **35**: 468–73

Rosenfeld JV, Ford NL. Bomb blast, mild traumatic brain injury and psychiatric morbidity: a review. *Injury* 2010; **41**: 437–43

Rossaint R, Bouillon B, Cerny V, *et al.* Management of bleeding following major trauma: an updated European guideline. *Crit Care* 2010; **14**: R52

Rugeri L, Levrat A, David JS, Delecroix E, Floccard B, Gros A, Allaouchiche B, Negrier C. Diagnosis of early coagulation abnormalities in trauma patients by rotation thrombelastography. *J Thromb Haemost* 2007; **5**: 289–95

Sawdon M, Ohnishi M, Watkins PE, Kirkman E. The effects of primary thoracic blast injury and morphine on the response to haemorrhage in the anaesthetised rat. *Exp Physiol* 2002; **87**: 683–9

Schuster KM, Lofthouse R, Moore C, Lui F, Kaplan LJ, Davis KA. Pulseless electrical activity, focused abdominal sonography for trauma, and cardiac contractile activity as predictors of survival after trauma. *J Trauma* 2009; **67**: 1154–7

Shakur H, Roberts I, Bautista R, *et al.* Effects of tranexamic acid on death, vascular occlusive events, and blood transfusion in trauma patients with significant haemorrhage (CRASH-2): a randomised, placebo-controlled trial. *Lancet* 2010; **376**: 23–32

Soar J, Perkins GD, Abbas G, *et al.* European Resuscitation Council Guidelines for Resuscitation 2010 Section 8. Cardiac arrest in special circumstances: Electrolyte abnormalities, poisoning, drowning, accidental hypothermia, hyperthermia, asthma, anaphylaxis, cardiac surgery, trauma, pregnancy, electrocution. *Resuscitation* 2010; **81**: 1400–33

Sohn VY, Arthurs ZM, Herbert GS, Beekley AC, Sebesta JA. Demographics, treatment, and early outcomes in penetrating vascular combat trauma. *Arch Surg* 2008; **143**: 783–7

Spahn DR, Cerny V, Coats TJ, *et al.* Management of bleeding following major trauma: a European guideline. *Crit Care* 2007; **11**: R17

Sperry JL, Minei JP, Frankel HL, *et al.* Early use of vasopressors after injury: caution before constriction. *J Trauma* 2008; **64**: 9–14

Stuhmiller JH. *Blast Injury: Translating Research into Operational Medicine.* Washington, DC: Office of The Surgeon General, Borden Institute, US Army Medical Department Center & School, 2008

Tarmey NT, Park CL, Bartels OJ, Konig TM, Mahoney PF, Mellor A. Outcomes following military traumatic cardiorespiratory arrest: a prospective, observational study. *Resuscitation* 2011; **84**: 1194–7

The Acute Respiratory Distress Syndrome Network. Ventilation with lower tidal volumes as compared with traditional tidal volumes for acute lung injury and the acute respiratory distress syndrome. *N Engl J Med* 2000; **342**: 1301–8

Theusinger OM, Spahn DR, Ganter MT. Transfusion in trauma: why and how should we change our current practice? *Curr Opin Anaesthesiol* 2009; **22**: 305–12

Turner S, Ruth MJ, Bruce DL. "In flight catering": feeding critical care patients during aeromedical evacuation. *J R Army Med Corps* 2008; **154**: 282–3

Wade CE, Eastridge BJ, Jones JA, *et al.* Use of recombinant factor viia in us military casualties for a five-year period. *J Trauma* 2010; **69**: 353–9

Wunsch H, Mapstone J, Takala J. High-frequency ventilation versus conventional ventilation for the treatment of acute lung injury and acute respiratory distress syndrome: a systematic review and Cochrane analysis. *Anesth Analg* 2005; **100**: 1765–72

Zapol WM, Snider MT, Hill JD, *et al.* Extracorporeal membrane oxygenation in severe acute respiratory failure. A randomized prospective study. *JAMA* 1979; **242**: 2193–6

Zunic G, Pavlovic R, Malicevic Z, Savic V, Cernak I. Pulmonary blast injury increases nitric oxide production, disturbs arginine metabolism, and alters the plasma free amino acid pool in rabbits during the early post-traumatic period. *Nitric Oxide* 2000; **4**: 123–8

Zunic G, Romic P, Vueljic M, Jovanikic O. Very early increase in nitric oxide formation and oxidative cell damage associated with the reduction of tissue oxygenation is a trait of blast casualties. *Vojnosanit Pregl* 2005; **62**: 273–80

PART 12

Anaesthesia and concurrent disease

Philip M. Hopkins

CHAPTER 79

Endocrine disease and anaesthesia

Peter A. Farling and Michael F. M. James

Introduction

Anaesthesia for patients with endocrine disorders involves the management of both extremely common and extremely rare conditions. There is a high incidence of diabetes, hypothyroidism, and hyperthyroidism in the population but pituitary apoplexy, phaeochromocytoma, and insulinoma may never be encountered during the career of the general anaesthetist. Whenever possible, elective surgery should await normalization of abnormal endocrine function. For example, patients with uncontrolled hyperthyroidism are at risk of developing a thyroid crisis so elective surgery should be delayed until they are euthyroid. Endocrine emergencies may mimic other causes of cardiovascular collapse and successful management requires a multidisciplinary approach involving anaesthetists, endocrinologists, surgeons, accident and emergency and intensive care specialists. This chapter covers issues relating to patients with diabetes mellitus and discusses the anatomy and anaesthetic management for surgery on each of the endocrine glands. Applied physiology of neuroendocrine regulation has been discussed in Chapter 8 of this textbook, so only essential details will be repeated in this chapter.

Pituitary

Anatomy and physiology

The pituitary gland weighs less than 1 g and sits at the base of the brain within the pituitary fossa, which is formed by the sella turcica and the diaphragma sella, a fold of dura. The pituitary stalk passes through the diaphragma sella and connects the pituitary gland to the hypothalamus. Important anatomical relations of the pituitary gland include the optic chiasma and third ventricle above, cranial nerves III, IV, V, and VI, the carotid arteries, and the cavernous sinus laterally, and the sphenoid air sinuses inferiorly (Standring 2008).

The pituitary gland comprises two distinct lobes, the adenohypophysis or anterior lobe and the neurohypophysis or posterior lobe. Embryologically the anterior lobe of the pituitary gland is derived from Rathke's pouch in the roof of the mouth. It synthesizes, stores, and secretes a number of hormones in response to releasing factors from the supraoptic nuclei of the hypothalamus. These releasing factors are delivered to the pituitary gland via portal veins. The anterior pituitary secretes growth hormone, thyroid-stimulating hormone (TSH), adrenocorticotrophic hormone (ACTH), prolactin, and the gonadotrophins. The posterior lobe is an extension of neural tissue and produces oxytocin and antidiuretic hormone (ADH) (Ganong 2005).

Anaesthetic considerations

Surgery is required for excision of pituitary adenomas that are causing a mass effect, visual disturbance, or hormonal over-production, and rarely as an emergency for pituitary apoplexy. Pituitary tumours comprise about 10% of intracranial neoplasms.

Preoperative assessment

Preoperative assessment will detect any symptoms and signs of excess hormone production. Patients with a prolactinoma will appear normal but tumours that secrete an excess of ACTH or growth hormone will have typical features affecting all systems and difficult airway management should be anticipated (Smith and Hirsch 2000).

Cushing's disease

Cushing's disease is caused by an excess of glucocorticoid after hypersecretion of ACTH from a pituitary adenoma. Cushing's syndrome is a term used for any chronic glucocorticoid excess, regardless of cause. The typical appearance is of a moon face with central obesity, limb wasting, and a dorsocervical fat pad. The skin is friable and there may be striae, hyperpigmentation, and hirsutism. The features that present difficulties to the anaesthetist include hypertension, congestive cardiac failure, sleep apnoea, muscle weakness, oesophageal reflux, glucose intolerance, and hypokalaemia. Postoperative infection and poor wound healing may occur.

Acromegaly

Acromegaly is caused by an excess of growth hormone from a pituitary adenoma. Gigantism will occur if this develops before puberty. Patients may be unaware of the typical features as they develop slowly—one memorable patient was a 'spot' diagnosis, at an airport, by a professor of endocrinology! Typical features include thickening of the skin, hirsutism, increasing hand and foot size, deepening of the voice, macrognathia, and malocclusion. The features that present difficulties to the anaesthetist include hypertension, ischaemic heart disease, arrhythmias, cardiomyopathy, sleep apnoea, and glucose intolerance. Patients with acromegaly may also present with nerve entrapment syndromes such as carpal tunnel syndrome.

Surgical considerations

The usual approach is via the sphenoidal sinus but bifrontal craniotomy may be required occasionally for large supratentorial tumours. Transsphenoidal hypophysectomy usually involves approaching the pituitary fossa through the sphenoidal sinus via the nasal passages. Some surgeons may choose the sublabial, or rarely these days, the infraorbital approach. Preoperative discussion with the surgeon is required to ensure an appropriate choice, and position, of the tracheal tube. RAE south-facing or flexible armoured tubes allow adequate surgical access. The nose is infiltrated or packed with ribbon gauze soaked in a suitable local anaesthetic and vasoconstrictor. A throat pack is placed in the oropharynx to collect blood and debris. The patient remains supine with the head slightly flexed as most surgeons rely on image intensification to locate the pituitary fossa. The operating microscope will also be used so anaesthetic access to the patient during the procedure will be limited. Towards the end of the procedure, the surgeon may request that intracranial pressure (ICP) is allowed to increase so that any remaining pituitary tumour will be pushed down into the field of view. This can be achieved by reducing ventilation and allowing the Pa_{CO_2} to increase. The resulting intracranial vasodilation will increase ICP. Another technique that produces the same effect requires the placement of a lumbar spinal drain after induction of anaesthesia. Injecting saline or, less commonly, air via the intrathecal catheter will increase ICP and promote descent of the remaining tumour (Nath et al. 1995). A Valsalva manoeuvre may be requested to assess the presence of a cerebrospinal fluid (CSF) leak. If a CSF leak has occurred some form of packing with harvested adipose tissue will be required and insertion of a spinal drain may be required. As with all neurosurgery, rapid recovery allows the surgeon to assess the patient's level of consciousness and detect any postoperative complications.

Anaesthetic technique

The possibility of difficult airway management should be anticipated and appropriate preparations completed. The usual technique involves intravenous induction, neuromuscular block, positive pressure ventilation, and maintenance of anaesthesia with volatile agents and short-acting narcotics. Remifentanil reduces the response to the surgical stimulus during the approach via the nose but will require administration of longer-acting analgesics before emergence. Bilateral intraoral, infraorbital nerve block has been described for perioperative analgesia, but is not commonly used (McAdam et al. 2005). Administration of prophylactic antibiotics and hydrocortisone supplements will be required. Intra-arterial blood pressure monitoring is used as significant haemorrhage is possible and these patients often have concurrent hypertension or cardiac disease. Rapid recovery allows the patient to sit up and be aware of the nasal packing. Postoperative care involves neurological and visual field assessment. Airway obstruction and bleeding are potential immediate complications. The possibility of diabetes insipidus should be considered and special attention given to fluid balance. Postoperative airway management requires special consideration as these patients may have redundant upper airway soft tissue predisposing to sleep apnoea and will have an obstructed nasal passage. Other later complications include infection, CSF leak, and carotid–cavernous fistula. Endocrine and electrolyte disturbances may occur and shared follow-up with endocrinologists is essential.

Craniopharyngioma

Craniopharyngioma is a tumour that arises from the remnants of Rathke's pouch and may present with similar features to pituitary tumours. There are two types, adamantinous and papillary. The adamantinous type occurs in childhood, is often cystic, and contains cholesterol crystals. These crystals may irritate the cortex and cause seizures postoperatively. The papillary type is found in adults and arises in the third ventricle. Craniopharyngiomas may present with raised ICP, visual disturbance, or impaired pituitary function, including diabetes insipidus, hypothyroidism, and failure to thrive. Resection of a craniopharyngioma is uncommon and neuroendoscopic techniques may be used to reduce cystic lesions (Komotar et al. 2009).

Thyroid

Anatomy and physiology

The thyroid gland weighs 10–20 g and is found at the level of C5 to T1 vertebrae. It is butterfly-shaped with two lobes joined anteriorly by the isthmus (Standring 2008). A pyramidal lobe is found in 50% of the population. The relationship to the recurrent laryngeal nerve and the external laryngeal nerve is important during thyroidectomy. A layer of epithelial cells filled with colloid forms thyroid follicles. Thyroxine (T_4) and triiodothyronine (T_3) are synthesized by iodination, coupling, and condensation of tyrosine molecules. TSH from the anterior pituitary gland increases the synthesis of T_3, T_4, and thyroglobulin. Calcitonin is produced by clear or C-cells and is involved in calcium metabolism (Ganong 2005).

Hypothyroidism

The causes of hypothyroidism, or myxoedema, include iodine deficiency, autoimmune thyroiditis, treatment of hyperthyroidism, and under-activity of the pituitary gland. Drugs such as lithium, amiodarone, and interferon may also induce hypothyroidism. In the developed world, congenital hypothyroidism is usually detected during the neonatal screening process.

The signs and symptoms of hypothyroidism include fatigue, sluggishness, weight gain, cold sensitivity, dry skin, brittle nails and hair, puffy face, and hoarse voice.

Hypothyroidism results in depression of myocardial function, decreased spontaneous ventilation, abnormal baroreceptor function, reduced plasma volume, anaemia, hypoglycaemia, hyponatraemia, and impaired hepatic drug metabolism. Psychiatric presentations include cognitive dysfunction, depression, and psychosis. Hypothyroid patients should be rendered euthyroid before elective surgery and close communication with the metabolic physicians is advised.

The decision whether or not to postpone surgery in a patient with hypothyroidism will depend on a number of factors, not least the urgency of the procedure. Pre-assessment clinics should detect clinical or poorly controlled hypothyroidism and thyroxine treatment should be optimized before elective surgery.

It is logical to avoid premedication in hypothyroid patients and to use regional anaesthesia wherever possible. Careful perioperative cardiovascular monitoring and judicious use of anaesthetic drugs because of the hypo-metabolic state is essential.

Preventative measures should be adopted to protect against hypothermia (Murkin 1982). Myxoedema coma will be discussed later in this chapter in the section on endocrine emergencies.

Hyperthyroidism

Hyperthyroidism or thyrotoxicosis affects approximately 2% of women and 0.2% of men in the general population. The commonest cause of primary hyperthyroidism is Graves' disease, an autoimmune condition. Other causes include toxic nodular goitre, thyroiditis, and drug-induced hyperthyroidism. Secondary hyperthyroidism is as a result of excessive circulating TSH. The classical features of thyrotoxicosis include heat intolerance, hyperactivity, weight loss, tremor, and eye signs including exophthalmos, and ophthalmoplegia. Of importance to the anaesthetist are the cardiovascular effects of hyperthyroidism including atrial fibrillation, congestive cardiac failure, and ischaemic heart disease. In an attempt to prevent the dreaded complication of thyroid storm, patients should be rendered euthyroid before surgery. This is achieved by the use of anti-thyroid drugs such as carbimazole, propylthiouracil, and β-blockers. Pre-assessment clinics should detect clinical or poorly controlled hyperthyroidism and anti-thyroid treatment should be optimized before elective surgery (Stehling 1974).

Thyroidectomy

This procedure is commonly performed for colloid goitre, thyroid malignancy, hyperthyroidism unresponsive to medical treatment, and occasionally Hashimoto's disease. The goitre will present particular problems if it is large, retrosternal, or intrathoracic. If thyroidectomy is required during pregnancy, it should be performed during the second trimester to avoid teratogenicity.

Preoperative assessment

Thyroid function should be assessed clinically and biochemically. Where possible, elective surgery should be delayed until the patient is euthyroid in order to prevent the risk of hyperthyroid crisis. Associated endocrine disorders should be considered: patients with multiple endocrine neoplasia type 2 with medullary thyroid cancer may have an associated phaeochromocytoma. The social history is important as singers, teachers, and other 'voice professionals' should be warned of the risk of postoperative hoarseness. Problems with airway management will be the main concern of the anaesthetist and patients with retrosternal goitre may exhibit signs of vena caval obstruction. Pemberton's sign is the development of facial cyanosis, distension of neck veins, stridor, and elevation of the jugular venous pressure as the patient raises their arms above their head (Pemberton 1946).

Routine investigations include thyroid function tests, full blood count, urea and electrolytes including serum calcium, chest X-ray, and indirect laryngoscopy. Patients may also have had fine-needle aspiration under local anaesthesia as a diagnostic test in the outpatient clinic. The usefulness of respiratory function tests is debatable. Respiratory flow–volume loops may show evidence of upper airway obstruction in those patients presenting with thyroid enlargement but this is usually evident during preoperative clinical assessment. An ENT colleague routinely performs the indirect laryngoscopy in order to document any preoperative vocal cord dysfunction. This investigation is useful to the anaesthetist. If indirect laryngoscopy was unsuccessful, and a fibreoptic nasendoscope had to be used to view the vocal cords, the anaesthetist will be alerted to the probability of a difficult intubation. However, the patient may simply have had difficulty with gagging and the ability of an ENT surgeon to visualize the larynx does not equate with the ability of anaesthetist to intubate the trachea.

A chest X-ray, and lateral thoracic inlet views, may show evidence of tracheal compression and deviation. Computed tomography (CT) and magnetic resonance imaging (MRI), although not routine, can provide excellent views of retrosternal goitres. Detailed non-invasive imaging is considered to be valid when it provides information that influences the preoperative decision-making process regarding airway management (Gillespie and Farling 2004).

Anaesthetic technique

While it is possible to perform thyroidectomy under bilateral deep or superficial cervical plexus blocks (Kulkarni et al. 1996), the usual technique involves balanced anaesthesia with intravenous induction, neuromuscular block, positive pressure ventilation, and maintenance of anaesthesia with volatile agents and short-acting narcotics. Routine monitoring, including ECG, pulse oximetry, and non-invasive blood pressure, is attached to the patient and intravenous access secured. The increasing utilization of remifentanil by infusion has reduced the need for nitrous oxide. Intravenous paracetamol 1 g and morphine 5–10 mg, combined with infiltration of local anaesthetic into the incision by the surgeon, provide postoperative analgesia. Morphine should be given at least 30 min before the end of the procedure in order to have a sufficient effect during emergence (Farling 2000).

Airway management

Although in the majority of cases the trachea is intubated directly using conventional laryngoscopy, the anaesthetic team must be experienced and prepared to cope with difficult situations. Difficult intubation is not more frequent than in the general population and is predicted by the same criteria. The complicating factor is the absence of the option of cricothyroid puncture should the airway become compromised. North-facing oral tracheal tubes are used as they keep the respiratory filter away from the surgical field. Small, reinforced tracheal tubes should be considered when there is significant tracheal compression. The laryngeal mask airway has been used although there is a risk that it will be displaced during surgery and obstruction may occur as a result of laryngospasm after surgical manipulation (Hobbiger et al. 1996).

If a difficult intubation is anticipated, the anaesthetist must have a clear intubation strategy. Awake fibreoptic intubation is the method of choice whenever there is concern that the airway will be lost after intravenous induction of anaesthesia. Before the widespread availability of fibreoptic equipment, inhalation induction was used. If respiratory obstruction occurred, the induction was abandoned and the patient should, theoretically, wake up without serious consequences. If inhalation induction was successful then anaesthesia was deepened so that gentle laryngoscopy could be performed before the administration of a neuromuscular blocking drug. If the larynx was visualized then the neuromuscular blocking drug could be given and tracheal intubation performed. However, the possibility to withdraw existed at any point in this strategy. This traditional technique has regained acceptability as a result of the introduction of sevoflurane.

Airway equipment must be available to deal with difficult mask ventilation and difficult intubation. This will include various sizes of tracheal tubes, gum elastic bougies, a video-laryngoscope, and laryngeal mask airways. There should be ready access to an intubating fibrescope (Farling 2000). Should airway access prove impossible, consideration should be given to femoro-femoral bypass to maintain oxygenation while airway access is obtained surgically.

Surgical considerations

The patient is positioned with a sandbag below the shoulder blades and the head resting on a padded 'horseshoe'. As the surgeon will need to stand on both sides of the patient during the procedure, the patient's arms are tucked into their sides and a long connector for the intravenous infusion allows access from the foot of the bed. A 25° head-up tilt will assist venous drainage, although this should be performed with careful attention to the blood pressure, particularly in patients who have been receiving β-blockers. Slight head extension will allow the surgeon excellent access to the thyroid gland. The use of head towels prevents the anaesthetist from inspecting the patient's face during the procedure. It is therefore important to check and secure the position of the tracheal tube. The patient's eyes are protected and particular care should be taken when the patient has exophthalmos. The surgeon infiltrates local anaesthetic along the line of the incision, skin flaps are raised, and the strap muscles separated in the midline. The upper pole is mobilized and the superior thyroid vessels ligated. Mobilization of the lobe is completed and the parathyroid glands and recurrent laryngeal nerve are routinely identified and protected during dissection of the thyroid from the trachea. Haemostasis is secured and the strap muscles and platysmal layers apposed. The skin is closed with staples or subcutaneous sutures.

Monitoring of the recurrent laryngeal nerve

Some surgeons find it useful to monitor recurrent laryngeal nerve function during complex re-operative procedures or operations on large goitres. Intraoperative nerve monitoring requires placement of detecting electrodes close to the vocal cords. Special tracheal tubes with surface electrodes may be used or electrodes may be placed directly into the muscles of the larynx (National Institute for Health and Care Excellence 2008). When the recurrent laryngeal nerve is identified, it is stimulated with a small current until an evoked electromyographic trace is obtained. The anaesthetist must choose an appropriate neuromuscular blocking agent for endotracheal intubation, and a suitable anaesthetic technique to facilitate this process. Communication between the anaesthetist and clinical physiologist before induction of anaesthesia is essential. Observation of the vocal cords with a fibrescope through a laryngeal mask has been used successfully. The surgeon is alerted if an instrument comes close to the recurrent laryngeal nerve.

Postoperative care

Residual neuromuscular block is reversed and the patient is allowed to recover from anaesthesia. If there has been any concern during dissection of the recurrent laryngeal nerve, the vocal cords are visualized and the surgeon reassured. If there is no immediate respiratory obstruction after extubation, the patient is transferred to the recovery ward. Experienced recovery staff should be aware of the potential postoperative complications that include haematoma, damage to the recurrent laryngeal nerve, and rarely tracheomalacia (Lacoste et al. 1993). Early re-intubation is recommended as tracheal intubation becomes more difficult as a haematoma expands, laryngeal oedema develops, and the airway becomes compressed. In the event of bilateral recurrent laryngeal nerve damage, vocal cord paralysis will lead to stridor at tracheal extubation. Re-intubation will be required and tracheostomy should be considered. Unilateral vocal cord paralysis leads to glottic incompetence, hoarseness, and aspiration. Tracheomalacia or softening of the tracheal rings is rare and follows prolonged compression of the trachea by a large goitre. Collapse of the trachea after extubation may lead to life-threatening airway obstruction that will require urgent re-intubation.

Unintentional parathyroidectomy will result in temporary or permanent hypocalcaemia. Symptoms and signs of hypocalcaemia include numbness and paraesthesia in the hands and feet, which may progress to carpopedal spasm and tetany. Treatment is by calcium supplements. After total thyroidectomy, thyroxine 50–100 μg is prescribed daily. Postoperative vocal cord function is examined by indirect laryngoscopy before hospital discharge.

Parathyroid

Anatomy and physiology

There are usually four parathyroid glands on the posterior surface of the thyroid gland. They are in pairs, two superior and two inferior, and weigh 25–40 mg each. The superior glands develop from the fourth pharyngeal pouch. The inferior pair develops from the third pharyngeal pouch and usually descends below the superior pair. As the thymus also develops from the third pharyngeal pouch, the inferior glands may be found within the mediastinum (Standring 2008).

Calcium control

Calcium is the most abundant mineral in the body and is vital for muscle contraction, nerve conduction, and coagulation. The concentration of calcium in the blood is detected by a receptor on the parathyroid chief cells. Low concentrations of calcium cause parathyroid hormone (PTH) to be secreted from the chief cells and high calcium concentrations inhibit PTH secretion. Vitamin D and magnesium also inhibit the release of PTH.

Parathyroid hormone

PTH is a peptide containing 84 amino acids that is metabolized rapidly in the Kupffer cells of the liver. It increases the availability of free extracellular calcium and decreases serum phosphate. Its actions are on bone, kidney, and the intestine. PTH stimulates the release of calcium from bone into extracellular fluid and stimulates calcium reabsorption in the renal tubules. It also activates the conversion of vitamin D into calcitriol in the kidney and thus indirectly stimulates absorption of calcium from the gut (Ganong 2005).

Hypoparathyroidism

Hypoparathyroidism may be congenital but is usually iatrogenic after inadvertent removal of parathyroid glands during thyroidectomy. Symptoms of hypocalcaemia include numbness and paraesthesia in the hands and feet. This may progress to carpopedal spasm and tetany. Chvostek's sign is facial twitching in response to tapping the facial nerve and Trousseau's sign is carpal spasm after inflation of a sphygmomanometer cuff. ECG changes include a prolonged ST segment and prolonged QT interval. Treatment is with oral or intravenous calcium supplements and vitamin D.

Primary hyperparathyroidism

Primary hyperparathyroidism is usually caused by a parathyroid adenoma and is diagnosed by elevated serum calcium and PTH concentrations. It may also be caused by parathyroid hyperplasia and rarely a parathyroid carcinoma. Symptoms and signs of hypercalcaemia include osteopenia, hypertension, lethargy, and nephrolithiasis. Asymptomatic hyperparathyroidism is often detected during routine electrolyte testing and treatment is recommended as hyperparathyroidism has been shown to be a risk factor for cardiovascular disease and glucose intolerance. Medical treatments include calcimimetics such as cinacalcet and bisphosphonates such as pamidronate. Surgical management involves parathyroidectomy and is the only curative treatment. Hypercalcaemic crisis is dealt with later in this chapter in the section on endocrine emergencies.

Secondary hyperparathyroidism

Secondary hyperparathyroidism is caused by stimulation of the parathyroid glands by hypocalcaemia leading to increased PTH concentrations. This may be a result of malabsorption or dietary deficiencies of calcium or vitamin D. Chronic renal failure results in reduced calcium reabsorption in the renal tubules, reduced concentrations of calcitriol, and hyperphosphataemia. The resulting stimulation of the PTH production causes hypertrophy of the parathyroid glands. The autonomous PTH secretion has been referred to as tertiary hyperthyroidism and may result in nephrocalcinosis of the transplanted kidney. Parathyroidectomy is therefore recommended.

Multiple endocrine neoplasia

Multiple endocrine neoplasia (MEN) is a rare autosomal dominant condition where tumours coincide in two or more endocrine glands. Gene abnormalities are responsible for the recognized types MEN 1, MEN 2A, and MEN 2B. These disorders may be sporadic or familial. Parathyroid tumours are associated with pancreatic and anterior pituitary tumours in MEN 1. Hyperparathyroidism occurs in 20–30% of patients with MEN 2A associated with medullary thyroid carcinoma and phaeochromocytoma. Parathyroidectomy is recommended and MEN should be considered in young patients with primary hyperparathyroidism.

Parathyroidectomy

Preoperative assessment

Careful assessment is required, as these patients may be elderly with concurrent cardiac disease. Routine investigations will include full blood count, urea and electrolytes, PTH concentration, thyroid function tests, chest X-ray, ECG, and possibly echocardiography. Total calcium concentration is dependent upon albumin, therefore total serum calcium should be corrected for hypoalbuminaemia. Indirect laryngoscopy is often performed to exclude preoperative vocal cord paralysis. Patients with renal disease may require dialysis before surgery.

Surgical considerations

Preoperative location of parathyroid adenomas is usually performed by technetium isotope scanning. This is taken up by both thyroid and parathyroid tissue and subtraction techniques reveal the abnormal parathyroid glands. If a single adenoma is detected, a limited, minimally invasive procedure may be offered. Other methods of localization include ultrasound, MRI, CT, and single photon-emission computed tomography.

The patient is positioned as for thyroidectomy, supine with a head-up tilt and the neck slightly extended. A head ring or horseshoe rest and a sandbag between the scapulae allow excellent surgical access. Usually a transverse midline cervical incision is performed with the length dependent upon the extent of the expected dissection. Video-assisted endoscopic techniques are offered in some centres via small lateral incisions (Miccoli et al. 2005).

Most experienced endocrine surgeons rely upon careful dissection and direct visualization for intraoperative location of parathyroid glands. This has also been achieved by preoperative intravenous methylthioninium chloride or by γ-probe after radioactive technetium. Intraoperative PTH assay is used in some centres. Samples taken before and after removal of abnormal parathyroid tissue may confirm adequate excision (Chen et al. 2005). Some centres will monitor recurrent laryngeal nerve function intraoperatively as for thyroid surgery.

When there is no definite abnormal parathyroid gland identified, a prolonged neck dissection and exploration may be required. The parathyroid may be found within the thyroid or it may be necessary to extract the thyrothymic ligament via the cervical incision. On rare occasions a median sternotomy has been used to locate and excise a parathyroid adenoma within the mediastinum.

Anaesthetic technique

Local anaesthetic infiltration and cervical plexus blocks may be considered, but the usual technique involves intravenous induction, neuromuscular block, positive pressure ventilation, and maintenance of anaesthesia with volatile agents and short-acting narcotics. Theoretically, hypercalcaemia may increase the requirement for non-depolarizing neuromuscular blocking agents so intraoperative monitoring of neuromuscular block is advised. Temperature monitoring and prevention of heat loss is important. Adequate venous access is essential and intra-arterial monitoring should be considered for patients with concurrent cardiac disease. Central venous access is usually unnecessary but, if required, a subclavian line is preferred. As the surgeons operate from both sides of the patient it may be beneficial to have both arms by the sides of the patient. A suitable extension set, or using the long saphenous vein for intravenous access, should be considered. A north facing tracheal tube will ensure that the breathing filter is outside the surgical field. As with any neck dissection, bradycardia should be anticipated.

Excessive coughing is avoided during extubation and the anaesthetist should be vigilant for signs of recurrent laryngeal nerve damage. Routine postoperative care is instigated and experienced recovery ward staff will be aware of the risks of haematoma formation after cervical surgery. Early re-intubation is advocated in the event of postoperative airway obstruction. Patients undergoing minimally invasive procedures may be considered for discharge on the day of surgery. Hypocalcaemia in the postoperative period may require temporary or permanent supplements.

Adrenal

Anatomy and physiology

The adrenal glands are found on the anterosuperior surface of each kidney and normally weigh 10–20 g each. There are two distinct parts, the cortex and medulla (Standring 2008). There are three zones within the cortex: the zona glomerulosa produces mineralocorticoids, the zona fascicularis produces glucocorticoids, and the zona reticularis produces androgens. The medulla contains chromaffin cells that produce catecholamines in response to sympathetic stimulation via pre-ganglionic nerve fibres. Details of hormone synthesis within the adrenal gland may be found in Chapter 8.

Pathology

The pathological conditions of the adrenal gland, of interest to anaesthetists, include adrenal insufficiency, Conn's disease, Cushing's syndrome, phaeochromocytoma, and incidental tumours of the adrenal.

Adrenal insufficiency

Adrenal insufficiency, or Addison's disease, is usually caused by autoimmune adrenalitis but other causes include tuberculosis, septicaemia, HIV, haemorrhage, and tumours. Primary insufficiency involves a decrease in both glucocorticoid and mineralocorticoid activity. Secondary adrenal insufficiency is as a result of a lack ACTH because of suppression by exogenous steroids, hypopituitarism, pituitary tumours, or after hypophysectomy. Clinical features include weakness, fatigue, postural hypotension, nausea, vomiting, diarrhoea, weight loss, and hyperpigmentation. Routine blood tests will show hyponatraemia, hyperkalaemia, and eosinophilia. Low cortisol concentration confirms the diagnosis. In primary adrenal insufficiency, ACTH concentration will be high while in secondary adrenal insufficiency, ACTH concentration will be low. Treatment involves glucocorticoid replacement with hydrocortisone 15–25 mg day^{-1} in divided doses. Fludrocortisone 0.05–0.2 mg day^{-1} is given for substitution in mineralocorticoid deficiency. Patients with known adrenal insufficiency should carry steroid cards or medic-alert bracelets to avoid developing an Addisonian crisis.

Anaesthetic implications

Perioperative supplements for patients on long-term steroid therapy will depend upon the degree of surgical stress. Patients who have been taking the equivalent of 10 mg of prednisolone in the previous 3 months who are undergoing minor surgery should receive hydrocortisone 25 mg at induction. For moderate surgery this should be followed by hydrocortisone 100 mg in divided doses for 24 h. Patients undergoing major surgery should receive hydrocortisone 25–50 mg at induction followed by 100 mg for 3 days.

Conn's syndrome

Conn's syndrome or hyperaldosteronism is caused by bilateral adrenal hyperplasia or by an adenoma of the zona glomerulosa. The usual presentation is of hypertension and hypokalaemia in a young patient. Diagnosis is confirmed by measuring the ratio between aldosterone and renin activity in the plasma. Localization of the lesions will involve CT, MRI, and possibly sampling from the adrenal veins during angiography. Treatment is by an aldosterone antagonist such as spironolactone and adrenalectomy.

Cushing's syndrome

Cushing's syndrome is caused by an excess of glucocorticoids from an adenoma or carcinoma of the zona fascicularis, ectopic ACTH production or exogenous steroid therapy. (Cushing's disease is caused by a basophilic adenoma of the pituitary.) The typical appearance is of a moon face with central obesity, limb wasting, and a dorsocervical fat pad. The skin is friable and there may be striae, hyperpigmentation, and hirsutism. A high cortisol concentration and a dexamethasone suppression test confirm diagnosis, which is then followed by radiological localization. The features that present difficulties to the anaesthetist include hypertension, congestive cardiac failure, sleep apnoea, muscle weakness, oesophageal reflux, glucose intolerance, hypokalaemia, and postoperative infection. Medical management includes metyrapone which blocks the synthesis of cortisol by inhibiting 11β-hydroxylase. Unilateral or bilateral adrenalectomy may be required.

Incidental adrenal tumour

There is an increase in the number of patients who are found to have a tumour of the adrenal during investigations for other conditions. The term VOMIT refers to 'victims of modern imaging techniques' and applies to many surgical specialities. The protocol for the investigation of patients with adrenal 'incidentalomas' involves a careful history and examination, including blood pressure, and assessment of signs of virilization or feminization. Urea and electrolytes, cortisol, aldosterone, renin activity and sex hormones will be measured, and dexamethasone suppression tests will be done. Samples will be required for urinary cortisol and urinary catecholamines.

Phaeochromocytoma

Phaeochromocytoma is a rare tumour of the adrenal medulla that secretes an excessive amount of catecholamines. The estimated incidence in the population is 1:1.5–2.0 million people year^{-1}. Similar tumours, arising from chromaffin cells in the sympathetic chain, are termed paragangliomas. Traditional teaching is that 10% of phaeochromocytomas are extra-adrenal. They may be familial or occur as part of MEN 2 syndromes, along with medullary thyroid carcinoma and parathyroid tumours. They may also be associated with von Hippel–Lindau disease or neurofibromatosis type 1. The symptoms are a result of episodic release of catecholamines and include sweating, pallor, palpitations, and headache. Hypertension is usually episodic. Other presenting features include anxiety, tremor, weight loss, nausea and vomiting, chest pain, abdominal pain, cardiac failure, and cerebrovascular disease. Diagnosis was based on the presence of catecholamine metabolites, for example, vanillylmandelic acid (VMA) in the urine. More sensitive investigations include raised plasma catecholamines and fractionated metanephrines in urine or plasma. Localization is then established by MRI, CT, or radioactive I-MIBG (meta-iodobenzylguanidine).

Preoperative preparation

Preoperative α-blockade is recommended before surgery for phaeochromocytoma and this is usually managed by an endocrinologist. The aim is to prevent surges in blood pressure and normalize blood volume by counteracting the vasoconstricting effects of the excessive catecholamines. Traditionally, phenoxybenzamine has been used but other α-blockers such as doxazosin, have become popular. Some patients will require the addition of a β-blocker, such as atenolol or propranolol, to control tachycardia. It is important to establish α-blockade before prescribing a β-blocker as severe hypertension will occur. This is because β-blockers will prevent vasodilation that offsets the α-mediated vasoconstriction. Patients do not like being on α-blockers for prolonged periods as they experience postural hypotension, stuffy noses, and feel generally lethargic without the stimulating effects of the catecholamines. One patient's main complaint was the adverse effect of the α-blockade on his sex life!

All patients who are scheduled for adrenalectomy should be carefully assessed for the effects of hypertension and diabetes. Cushingoid patients may present difficulties with airway management. The anaesthetist should note the position and size of the tumour, as this will give an estimate of the likelihood of an open or laparoscopic procedure. Postoperative analgesia strategies such as epidural or patient-controlled analgesia should be mentioned. The potential for postoperative care in a high dependency or intensive care unit should be discussed with the patient. The anaesthetist should be aware of the extent and type of catecholamine over-production as this will give an indication of the requirement for inotropes after removal of the tumour. Most phaeochromocytomas secrete a mixture of adrenaline (epinephrine) and noradrenaline (norepinephrine), some secrete only one of these and, rarely, the only abnormally raised catecholamine is dopamine.

Surgical considerations

Laparoscopic adrenalectomy will be offered whenever possible but large tumours or those invading surrounding structures, particularly major blood vessels, will require an open procedure. The patient is placed in a lateral position and the table broken to extend the patient's flank. Attention to detail is required by the anaesthetist to prevent pressure sores and to allow for ease of access to intravenous and arterial lines.

Anaesthetic technique

Large-bore intravenous access is established and drugs for controlling blood pressure and arrhythmias should be prepared. The use of magnesium by intravenous infusion is recommended for patients with a phaeochromocytoma. An epidural is recommended for bilateral open procedures. A balanced technique with intravenous induction, neuromuscular block, positive pressure ventilation, and maintenance with inhalation agents and short-acting narcotics is standard. Anticholinergic and histamine-releasing drugs, such as succinylcholine (suxamethonium), should be avoided if possible. Intra-arterial measurement of blood pressure may be established before induction, particularly for patients with a phaeochromocytoma. A smooth induction and tracheal intubation is necessary to minimize any pressor response. The need to measure central venous pressure, or infuse vasoactive agents via a central line, should be assessed. If there is any catecholamine-induced cardiomyopathy, a pulmonary artery catheter, or transoesophageal echocardiography should be considered. Care is taken during positioning as hypotension can occur when the operating table is 'broken', particularly in those patients who have received β-blockers.

Intraoperative problems

Hypertension is likely to occur when the phaeochromocytoma is manipulated and this is just as likely during laparoscopic surgery. Retroperitoneal insufflation has also been implicated in producing hypertension. Severe hypertensive episodes may cause myocardial infarction, pulmonary oedema, cardiac failure, or cerebrovascular ischaemia so the anaesthetist must deal with these promptly. Sodium nitroprusside is a potent arteriolar and venodilator that has a rapid onset and offset. An intravenous infusion can be titrated against increases in blood pressure but it must be protected from light by silver foil as its metabolites include thiocyanate. Other agents that may be used include phentolamine, nicardipine, esmolol, and magnesium (James 2010).

Once the adrenal veins have been ligated the excessive catecholamine efflux will diminish. This can lead to hypotension that may require inotropic support. It is logical to assume that if the tumour secreted large amounts of noradrenaline preoperatively then this will need to be replaced in the immediate postoperative phase. Withholding the dose of phenoxybenzamine on the morning of surgery is advised to reduce the need for inotropes postoperatively. Vasopressin may be valuable in patients resistant to noradrenaline. Blood loss will be poorly tolerated in those patients who have received α-blockers and the need for transfusion should be anticipated.

Postoperative care should focus on the restoration of normal fluid balance after the removal of the catecholamine stimulus. This will require the continuation of invasive monitoring in intensive care or high dependency units. Blood glucose should be monitored as hypoglycaemia can occur with the reduced catecholamine effect on insulin.

Diabetes mellitus

Diabetes mellitus is a metabolic disorder of energy metabolism as a consequence of inadequate insulin production or function (Nolan et al. 2011). The number of adults with diabetes may have doubled within the past three decades from 153 million in 1980 to 347 million in 2008. Although 70% of the observed increase is attributed to population growth and ageing, the number also reflects the global shift towards a Western lifestyle of unhealthy diet and physical inactivity, with obesity as the outcome (Anonymous 2011). The disease now affects up to one in four adults in the United States.

The American Diabetes Association currently recognizes four types of diabetes mellitus: (a) type 1 as a result of β-cell destruction and absolute insulin deficiency; (b) type 2 characterized by insulin resistance or secretory defects, or both; (c) specific causes of diabetes mellitus including genetic defects of β-cell function, diseases of the exocrine pancreas, endocrinopathies, drug- or chemical-induced diabetes mellitus, infections and genetic defects associated with diabetes; (d) and finally gestational diabetes (Garber et al. 2004).

Diabetes is defined on the results of a fasting glucose greater than 7.0 mmol litre^{-1}; a random non-fasting glucose greater than 11.1 mmol litre^{-1}; or a blood glucose greater than 11.1 mmol litre^{-1} in a sample taken 2 h after a 75 g glucose tolerance test. The normal value for fasting glucose is less than 5.6 mmol litre^{-1} and impaired glucose tolerance is defined as a fasting glucose between 5.6 and 7.0 mmol litre^{-1}, or a 2 h post-prandial value greater than 7.8 and less than 11.1 mmol litre^{-1}.

Pathophysiology

Under normal circumstances, the blood concentration of glucose is kept remarkably constant with the liver acting as both a reservoir for excess glucose and a source of glucose when the demand is increased. In exercise, glucose can be supplied through the Cori cycle in which lactate from muscle is converted back to glucose in the liver. In starvation, glucose demand is diminished by fat adaptation of the peripheral tissues using free fatty acids and ketone bodies for energy, so that glucose availability can be limited to those organs, particularly the brain, that have an absolute requirement for glucose. Glucose can be rapidly mobilized from glycogen reserves and additional glucose can be synthesized through gluconeogenesis from deaminated amino acids. Although it was thought that the liver was the prime organ involved in gluconeogenesis, it is now recognized that the kidney plays a major role in the synthesis of new sugar and glucose uptake (Gerich 2010). Fat is the major energy storage mechanism, and excess glucose, beyond the need to maintain the glycogen reserves, is converted to fat. In humans, fat cannot be converted back to glucose to any useful degree. The energy stores from fat must be consumed through direct oxidation of fatty acids and via acetyl Co-A into the citric acid cycle.

Insulin is the major hormone regulating energy metabolism, controlling not only glucose utilization, but also fat metabolism and amino acid turnover. The hormone is released from the β-cells of the pancreas in response to an increase in blood glucose concentration as well as by various gastrointestinal hormones including glucagon-like peptide (GLP-1) and glucose-dependent insulinotropic peptide (GIP). Feedback links also exist creating cross-talk between the β-cells and insulin-sensitive tissues and these and other pathophysiological issues have recently been extensively reviewed (Kahn et al. 2014). In response to an increase in blood sugar, insulin promotes the removal of glucose from the blood by stimulating glucose uptake into skeletal muscle and liver with the formation of glycogen and by stimulating the uptake of glucose into adipose tissue. Insulin is not necessary for glucose uptake and utilization by most tissues in the body. It is, however, absolutely required for fat deposition and it is the main inhibitor of gluconeogenesis and glycogenolysis.

Glucagon is generated by the α cells of the pancreas, and its secretion is decreased by an increase in the blood glucose concentration. In general, its effects are opposite to those of insulin, stimulating glycogenolysis, gluconeogenesis, lipolysis, and ketogenesis.

Energy balance is tightly regulated through a complex neurohumoral network in which central signals (from the brainstem and higher cortical centres, e.g. cognitive, visual, and other reward cues) and peripheral signals of energy stores (from adipose tissue, e.g. leptin) are integrated. Stimuli including hunger and satiety messages feed into the hypothalamus and other key central nervous system areas to control appetite, physical activity, and body weight. This network is also regulated by the circadian clock and sleep disorders may play a key role in the development of obesity and type 2 diabetes (Nolan et al. 2011). In the stress response, insulin release is inhibited and other stress hormones (catecholamines, glucagon, growth hormone, and thyroid hormone) stimulate increased concentrations of plasma glucose.

Type 1 diabetes

In type 1 diabetes, absolute insulin deficiency leads to disorders of glucose, fat, and protein metabolism. The characteristic hyperglycaemia is not primarily a failure of glucose utilization as many tissues can use glucose in the absence of insulin. Rather, the primary lesion is a failure of regulation of gluconeogenesis leading to excessive glucose production from the liver and other organs together with breakdown of protein to liberate amino acids for this process. The mechanism is similar to that seen in starvation and has been described as 'starvation in the midst of plenty'. The hyperglycaemia leads to an osmotic diuresis that results in severe fluid and electrolyte depletion with loss of water, sodium, potassium, and magnesium.

Absolute insulin deficiency also results in a failure of regulation of fat metabolism. The primary lipolytic regulator, hormone-sensitive lipase, is activated by the absence of insulin and leads to the breakdown of fat with the liberation of fatty acids. Most tissues in the body become fat-adapted, but in the liver, the excess fatty acids are converted to ketones. The ketones can be used by many organs in the body for energy, but are produced in excess of the ability of the tissues to metabolize them, so that the consequence is ketoacidosis (see Fig. 79.1).

Thus, type 1 diabetics generally present with a combination of hyperglycaemia and ketoacidosis with dehydration and electrolyte deficiencies. The age of onset is generally in children and young adults and the patients present with an acute illness and a lean body habitus.

Type 2 diabetes

Type 2 diabetes is associated with either a relative insulin deficiency or insulin resistance. Again, there is a failure of regulation of gluconeogenesis leading to hyperglycaemia, but fat metabolism is usually adequately regulated and ketoacidosis is a less common feature of this version of the disease. Consequently, symptoms of type 2 diabetes may be more subtle and patients can present with severe hyperglycaemia, together with dehydration and electrolyte deficiencies (Fig. 79.2). Handling of glucose by the kidney is altered in type 2 diabetes mellitus. Renal gluconeogenesis and renal glucose uptake are increased in both the post-absorptive and postprandial states, and renal glucose reabsorption is increased (Gerich 2010).

The age of onset is generally middle-aged to elderly, although increasing juvenile obesity is leading to an increase in the incidence of type 2 diabetes in younger people. Certain patient groups are more susceptible to early onset of the disease (especially native Americans, African Americans, and Hispanics). It accounts for about 90% of all diabetics (and has a prevalence of about 6.6% in the United States, equating to about 15–20 million of the population). The incidence of type 2 diabetes has increased two-fold over the last decade; and currently affects between 8% and 10% of all Americans. This is related to alterations of diet and an increasing prevalence of obesity.

Hyperglycaemia

Glucose is normally filtered at the glomerulus and reabsorbed in the proximal convoluted tubule. However, when the renal threshold for glucose is exceeded (at approximately 10 mmol litre^{-1}), reabsorption is incomplete and glucose appears in the urine.

Urinary glucose stimulates an osmotic diuresis which leads to increased water excretion and an increase in the plasma osmolality. In turn, the latter leads to stimulation of the thirst centre in the floor of the fourth ventricle. This combination of an osmotic diuresis (with fluid deficits of 5–6 litres, and Na^+, K^+, and Mg^{2+} deficiency) and thirst lead to the development of polyuria and polydipsia that are typical of this condition.

Chronically elevated blood glucose concentrations decrease microcirculatory dilatation, and cause endothelial dysfunction. In particular, the coronary circulation is affected with reductions in coronary vasodilatory reserve and collateral blood flow, decreasing the development of collateral blood vessels. At a cellular level, hyperglycaemia leads to decreased signal activation (as occurs with ischaemic and anaesthetic preconditioning) and K^+-ATP channel activation. There is also increased production of reactive oxygen species, protein glycosylation, and decreased production of nitric oxide. Consequently, diabetic patients have an increased incidence of cardiovascular co-morbidities. Cardiac pathologies are the main cause of death in diabetic patients. These changes affect both the microvascular and the macrovascular components of the circulation.

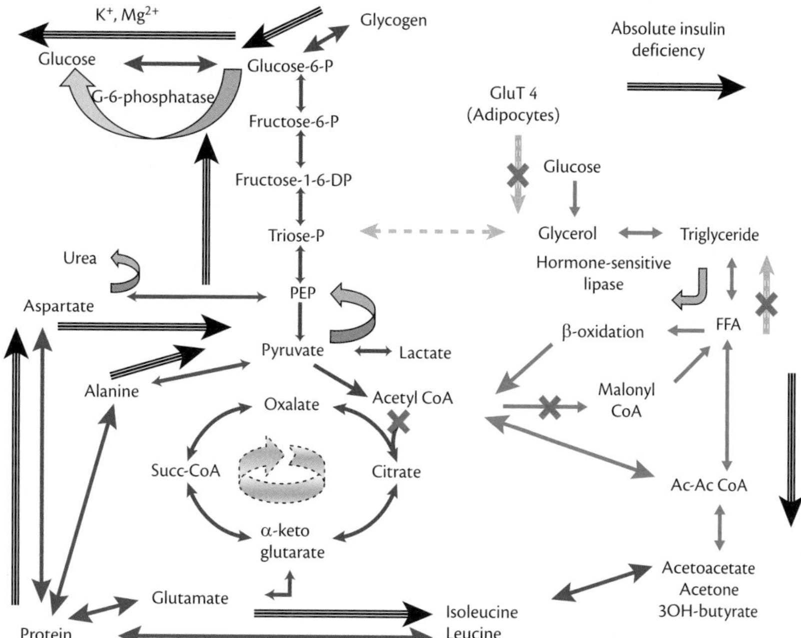

Figure 79.1 The effects of absolute insulin deficiency (usually type 1 diabetes) on intermediary metabolism.

→ Major carbohydrate pathways and citric acid cycle.

→ Interlinking energy pathways for protein.

→ Interlinking energy for fat metabolism.

Ac-Ac CoA, aceto-acetyl co-enzyme A; FFA, free fatty acids; ✖, inhibited pathways.

Note that fat metabolism is markedly impaired resulting in keto-acidosis. Relative impairment of the citric acid cycle in the liver leads to ketones becoming a major source of energy.

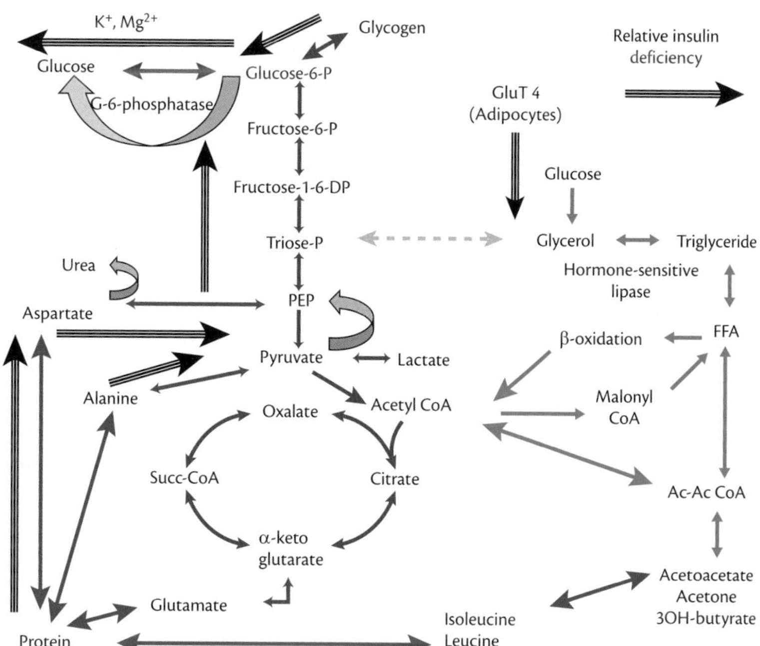

Figure 79.2 The effects of relative insulin deficiency (only type 2 diabetes) on intermediary metabolism.

→ Major carbohydrate pathways and citric acid cycle.

→ Interlinking energy pathways for protein.

→ Interlinking energy for fat metabolism.

Note that fat metabolism is usually preserved as minimal amounts of insulin are required for this pathway. Ketosis is thus uncommon but severe hyperosmolar, non-ketotic states may occur.

The microvascular pathology affects many organs and leads to the complications of renal damage, neuropathy, and retinopathy characteristic of this disease. In addition, the accumulation of sorbitol in the cells causes osmotic injury and increased formation of glycosylated proteins alters the cross-linkages between molecules leading to structural and functional damage. Hyperglycaemia also enhances the formation of free radicals and activation of tissue injury responses. The content of oxidized fatty acids is increased and the anti-inflammatory and antioxidant activities of high-density lipoproteins are impaired in type 2 diabetes. At a macrovascular level, diabetic patients are more likely to develop atherosclerosis. While there is clear evidence that improved glucose control decreases the incidence of microvascular complications, this is not is clearly demonstrated for macrovascular pathology.

Management of the diabetic patient

Patients with type 1 diabetes will require insulin at all times. Initially many type 2 diabetic patients manage their blood sugar control by diet alone but some will progress to need oral agents and insulin as the disease progresses. Normoglycaemia decreases the incidence of complications in all types of diabetes. In addition, it enhances cellular immune function and red cell production, reduces the tendency to cholestasis, and minimizes the adverse effects on the microcirculation and on nerve axons.

Insulins

There are a number of different types of insulin based on their physiological profiles and sources (bovine, porcine, and human). When switching from an animal source to human insulin, a reduction of 10–20% of the overall daily dose is usually required to avoid episodes of hypoglycaemia. There is evidence that early use of low-dose insulin in type 2 diabetes mellitus may improve glycaemic control and decrease insulin resistance.

Soluble insulins

These preparations are usually administered subcutaneously or intramuscularly and when given by these routes have an onset of action of 30–60 min, a peak effect at 2–4 h, with a duration of effect of up to 8 h. Intravenously, soluble insulins have a very short half-life of around 5 min and a duration of action of less than 30 min. Intermittent intravenous bolus injections of soluble insulin do not provide good control and pose the risk of alternating hypo- and hyperglycaemia. After an initial bolus dose, maintenance doses should be given by infusion or by subcutaneous or intramuscular injection.

Initially, soluble insulins were derived from animal sources but modern human insulin preparations are produced using recombinant technology (insulin aspart, glulisine, and lispro). These products have a faster onset of action and a shorter duration than earlier soluble insulins that more closely match normal mealtime peaks of plasma insulin and result in a more normal pattern of periprandial glycaemic control. Given that insulin is a major growth factor, there is concern of an increased risk of cancer in patients on long-acting insulins. However, the risk:benefit ratio of better glycaemic control is likely to remain favourable. The modern formulations of insulin have been reviewed (Nicholson and Hall 2011).

Soluble insulins are generally used in combination with intermediate- or long-acting insulin with the purpose of optimizing blood sugar control. They are particularly useful for immediate blood sugar control in the perioperative period.

Intermediate- and long-acting insulins

When given by subcutaneous injection, these preparations have a dynamic profile with an onset of 1–2 h, maximal effect at 4–12 h, and duration of 16–35 h. They may be given twice daily in conjunction with short-acting (soluble) insulin; or once daily, especially in elderly patients. Soluble insulin can often be mixed with other preparations in the same syringe (except with detemir and glargine insulin) with each formulation essentially retaining their own properties.

- Isophane: this is a mixture of insulin and protamine, and is of particular value in the initiation of twice-daily insulin regimens. It can be reliably mixed with soluble insulin; and is also prepared as 'ready-mixed' preparations (e.g. biphasic isophane insulin; biphasic insulin aspart or biphasic insulin lispro).
- Insulin zinc suspension (PZI): this is a mixture of 30% amorphous and 70% crystalline insulin, giving the insulin a more prolonged duration of action (24–46 h). PZI is usually given once a day, but the formulation cannot be given by the intravenous route.
- Glargine and detemir: these are both human insulin analogues with prolonged durations of action. Glargine is given once a day; detemir once or twice a day.

Biphasic insulins

- Biphasic insulin aspart—30% aspart and 70% aspart protamine
- Biphasic insulin lispro—25% lispro; 75% lispro protamine
- Biphasic isophane insulin—30% soluble; 70% isophane.

Oral glycaemic-control agents

There has been a rapid expansion in the range of oral agents available for the management of hyperglycaemia and increasing understanding of the pathophysiological processes involved in the disease has led to new lines of drug development. The older oral agents are still the first line of treatment for most patients, but an array of new agents is being developed that may enhance glycaemic control.

Sulfonylureas

These drugs act on the pancreas to increase β-cell sensitivity and augment insulin secretion by binding to ATP-dependent K^+ channels. They may also have some long-term effects by increasing the numbers of insulin receptors on cell membranes.

There is a range of different types of sulfonylureas available including the older tolbutamide and chlorpropamide, and the more recent agents glibenclamide, glyburide, glipizide, and glimepiride.

In general, these drugs should be withheld on the day of surgery if a disruption of normal times of food intake is anticipated. Chlorpropamide should normally be stopped for 48 h because of its longer half-life. These drugs can safely be combined with insulin therapy.

The major side-effect of sulfonylureas is hypoglycaemia with minor episodes occurring in up to 20% of patients. The elderly are especially prone to these episodes, and use of longer-acting drugs, such as chlorpropamide and glibenclamide, are best avoided in these patients. The primary failure rate with sulfonylurea drugs is about 15%.

Chlorpropamide is now less commonly used as a result of its side-effect profile and its very prolonged duration of action that increases the risk of hypoglycaemia. Other side-effects of chlorpropamide include facial flushing after drinking alcohol, enhanced ADH secretion, and very rarely hyponatraemia (which has also been reported after glimepiride and glipizide).

Other side-effects seen with the sulphonylureas include rare episodes of cholestatic jaundice; hypersensitivity reactions within first 6–8 weeks of starting therapy; rare blood dyscrasias; and photosensitivity reactions (especially with chlorpropamide and glipizide).

Biguanides

Metformin is the only agent in this group currently in use. Although these are the oldest of the oral hypoglycaemic agents, they have recently seen an increased popularity as they mainly affect gluconeogenesis, which is now recognized as the primary source of hyperglycaemia. Metformin may also inhibit intestinal glucose absorption and improve weight reduction. Compared with the sulphonylureas, metformin is also associated with a reduction in mortality. The risk of hypoglycaemia is lower with this drug. The major adverse effect is the risk of type 2 lactic acidosis as a consequence of the inhibition of gluconeogenesis and impaired lactate metabolism. The drug should therefore not be used where there is a significant risk of lactate production including tissue hypoxia and severe sepsis. The risk of lactic acidosis is also greater in the elderly and in patients with renal or hepatic failure and those undergoing major surgery. However, continuing metformin in patients undergoing cardiac surgery has not been associated with harm and may have been related to improved outcome (Duncan et al. 2007).

α-glucuronidase inhibitors

These drugs, of which acarbose is the archetypical agent, decrease intestinal absorption of saccharides and are usually used as an adjunct to metformin or the sulphonylureas. The major side-effect of these drugs relate to incomplete glucose absorption leading to flatulence and diarrhoea. There is no need to withdraw these drugs before surgery. Other agents in this group are miglitol and voglibose.

Thiazolidinediones

The thiazolidinediones activate one or more of the peroxisome proliferator-activated receptors which regulate gene expression in response to ligand binding. They increase insulin sensitivity, increase insulin secretion, and act on the liver to inhibit gluconeogenesis and may also reduce concentrations of glycosylated haemoglobin and free fatty acids. There is a high primary failure rate of around 25% and these agents are generally limited to second-stage diabetic treatment and are usually given in combination with metformin or the sulphonylureas.

The two prominent drugs in this category, rosiglitazone and pioglitazone, have both been linked with adverse clinical effects, with rosiglitazone being associated with an increased incidence of cardiac failure, while pioglitazone has been reported to increase the risk of bladder cancer. Consequently, rosiglitazone should not be used in patients with a history of heart failure and probably should be avoided in patients with acute ischaemic cardiac disease. As a group, these drugs increase oedema retention and may be associated with weight gain.

Thiazolidinediones may induce hypoglycaemia with starvation and should therefore be stopped on the morning of surgery.

Meglitinides

Meglitinides stimulate pancreatic β cells to produce insulin by binding to ATP-dependent K^+ channels. They include repaglinide, nateglinide, and mitiglinide. These drugs are rapidly metabolized and short-acting. Taken shortly before meals, they mimic the normal effects of insulin after eating. These drugs may be particularly helpful in combination with metformin or other drugs. They may also be a good choice for people with potential kidney problems.

Side-effects include diarrhoea and headache. As with the sulfonylureas, repaglinide poses a slightly increased risk for cardiac events, and should be stopped on the morning of surgery.

Incretins

The incretins are endogenous gut hormones which stimulate the secretion of insulin in response to oral glucose loads to concentrations that are greater than that seen when a similar intravenous glucose load is given. The main incretins are GIP (glucose-dependent insulinotrophic polypepetide) and GLP-1 (glucagon-like peptide-1). The utility of GIP is limited by the fact that its insulinotropic effect is lost in diabetic patients, but the action of GLP persists. Within a few minutes of food intake, GLP-1 concentrations in the blood increase three- to five-fold, suggesting a fast endocrine or neural mechanism is involved in addition to simple detection of food in the gastrointestinal tract.

The first GLP-1 agents to become available are exenatide and liraglutide. They have an onset of action of 6–12 h after intravenous injection. They increase insulin secretion, suppress glucagon secretion, and slow gastric emptying, reducing appetite and decreasing glucagon concentration. Liraglutide provides greater improvements in glycaemic control, induces weight loss, improves obesity-related risk factors, and reduces pre-diabetes. It is also associated with reductions in glycated haemoglobin (HbA_{1c}) and blood pressure (Nicholson and Hall 2011).

The most common adverse events are gastrointestinal symptoms, including nausea and, rarely, vomiting or diarrhoea. Patients receiving both exenatide and a sulfonylurea have an increased risk of mild to moderate hypoglycaemic events. However, the risk was not increased in patients receiving concurrent exenatide and metformin. These agents require parenteral administration. Possible risks include medullary thyroid carcinoma and pancreatitis, but these remain to be established. Given that these agents decrease gastric emptying and may compound the reduced gastric emptying associated with long-standing diabetes, it is recommended that they are stopped 24 h before anaesthesia, but there is no evidence for or against this recommendation.

GLP-1 is broken down by the enzyme peptidase dipeptidyl peptidase IV (DPP-IV), to which exenatide and liraglutide are resistant. A second approach to use the 'incretin effect' to enhance glucose control is to inhibit DPP-IV with sitagliptin, saxagliptin, or vildagliptin as sole agents and also combined with metformin. Unlike exenatide, these agents do not affect gastric emptying and are well tolerated. A combination tablet with sitagliptin and metformin is now available. Unlike exenatide, these drugs can be taken orally and have few adverse effects apart from diarrhoea. Potential adverse effects of inhibition of DPP-IV activity include increased blood pressure, neurogenic inflammation, and immunological reactions. None of these have yet been described clinically. There is low potential for hypoglycaemia and gastric emptying is not affected. However, the current recommendation is to stop this agent preoperatively.

Amylin

Pancreatic β cells produce another gastrointestinal hormone called amylin. The secretion of this substance is increased by ingestion of food, and it decreases blood glucose concentrations in an insulin-independent manner. A synthetic analogue, pramlintide, acts in an additive fashion with insulin and can enhance glucose control in patients on insulin. In addition to improving post-prandial glucose concentration, pramlintide decreases the HbA_{1c} concentration, and post-prandial triglyceride profiles. The main adverse effect is that of nausea. As with the other agents cessation of administration in the day of surgery is recommended.

Consequences of hyperglycaemia in the surgical patient

Diabetic patients have an increased incidence of cardiovascular co-morbidities including arterial hypertension, coronary artery disease, peripheral vascular disease, and systolic and diastolic left ventricular dysfunction, possibly leading to congestive cardiac failure. Cardiac pathologies are the main cause of death in diabetic patients and they are at particular risk in the perioperative period. They are also at risk of silent myocardial ischaemia. The overall risk of postoperative mortality and morbidity for non-cardiac surgery in these patients has been reported as 24% at a median follow-up time of 10 months (Juul et al. 2004).

Preoperative preparation

Patients with diabetes presenting for elective surgery require careful screening for secondary organ dysfunction, paying particular attention to cardiovascular disease, renal disease, neurovascular and neurological disorders, and peripheral neuropathies. Whether or not intensive cardiac screening for these patients is justified, given the risk of silent myocardial ischaemia, remains currently unresolved and is an issue that should probably be decided on a case-by-case basis in consultation with the medical and surgical teams. Although the measurement of HbA_{1c} is not a particularly valuable predictor of long-term outcome in diabetics, it does provide useful information on the quality of glycaemic control over the recent past. For all but minor surgery, diabetic patients should probably undergo routine ECG examination, standard biochemical measurements, and urinalysis together with a careful clinical assessment. Appropriate cardiac protection strategies should be adopted depending on the risk stratification of the patient.

The risk of gastric regurgitation needs to be considered, but the risks have probably been overstated in the past. Unless there is clear evidence of autonomic dysfunction, the usual risk factors for regurgitation can be applied to diabetic patients. The anaesthetist should consider the balancing risks of a rapid sequence intubation in a patient with possible underlying myocardial ischaemia against the much less common risk of aspiration and make an informed decision. Consideration may be given to the use of H_2-antagonists with or without prokinetic agents to improve gastric emptying and decrease the risk should regurgitation occur. The risks associated with glycosylated collagen and the possibility that this may make intubation more difficult needs to be assessed.

Operative management

There is a wide range of recommended approaches to the diabetic patient, which indicates that no single policy has been established as being superior. The objective at all times should be to maintain blood sugar within a reasonable range while at the same time submitting the patient to the least possible risk from the combination of preoperative starvation and the persistent presence of hypoglycaemic agents. It is a good basic principle to minimize the period of preoperative starvation and clear glucose-containing drinks may be given up to 2 h preoperatively. Ideally, diabetic patients should be placed early on an operating list with the objective of reinstating their normal daily routines as quickly as possible.

A number of approaches have been suggested depending on the type of diabetes and the nature of the surgical procedure. The following is a suggested approach, but there are numerous differing opinions and individual anaesthetists should adopt an approach with which they are comfortable. The older laissez-faire attitudes in which no effective control of blood glucose was conducted with the emphasis placed on the avoidance of hypoglycaemia is no longer acceptable.

Surgery initiates a stress response related to the severity of the surgical insult that includes increased circulating catecholamines and an increase in blood sugar as a consequence of the release of the array of stress hormones. This metabolic response may be more pronounced in diabetic patients undergoing surgery compared with non-diabetic patients (Schricker et al. 2005). There is little evidence that tight intraoperative glycaemic control affects the outcome in diabetic patients. Peak glucose concentration has been shown to be a risk factor for mortality and morbidity in cardiac surgical patients (Gandhi et al. 2005), patients undergoing carotid endarterectomy (McGirt et al. 2006), and in patients undergoing infra-inguinal arterial bypass surgery (Malmstedt et al. 2006). However, the small number of prospective studies so far conducted have failed to demonstrate that intraoperative tight glucose control improves outcome. Nevertheless, there is probably sufficient evidence that good control of hyperglycaemia perioperatively is associated with better postoperative outcomes and that patients without hyperglycaemia have fewer complications, including wound infections.

Elective surgery for the type 1 diabetic

Minor surgery

For this category of patient, the simplest approach for patients with good glycaemic control is to continue with their normal diabetic medication up until the evening before surgery, including a bedtime snack. Patient should be scheduled early on the operating list and allowed free intake of clear liquids, usually containing glucose, up until 2 h preoperatively. On arrival in the operating room, blood sugar should be measured and appropriate procedures introduced on the basis of that result. If the patient is hypoglycaemic, a glucose infusion should be started. If the blood sugar is high, an appropriate bolus dose of soluble insulin should be administered, repeated at 30 min if necessary. Should sugar concentrations be in the acceptable range (4.6–8.0 mmol $litre^{-1}$), hourly measurement of the blood sugar is all that is required. Regional anaesthesia is appropriate for these patients as it allows early return to normal diabetic control.

Major surgery

For major surgery, and in patients in whom preoperative glycaemic control is poor, it could be justified to admit the patient electively and stabilize blood sugar on soluble insulin preoperatively, although it is generally acceptable for patients with good glycaemic control to continue with their standard insulin regimen until the night before surgery.

- When the patient comes to theatre, blood sugar should be measured and a treatment plan instituted considering the duration and severity of the surgery and the level of blood sugar control. If the initial blood sugar is in an acceptable range, it is reasonable to give a glucose-free infusion, no insulin, and hourly monitoring the blood sugar. Should the blood sugar (BS) increase, an infusion of insulin should be commenced at a rate adjusted to the concentration of glycaemia as follows: 50 U of insulin in 500 ml saline

- Initial infusion rate 1–2 U h^{-1} from a syringe pump
- BS <4.5: stop infusion, give glucose
- BS 4.6–5.5: decrease insulin by 50%
- BS 5.6–7: maintain infusion rate
- BS 7.1–8.5: increase insulin by 0.5 U h^{-1}
- BS 8.6–11: increase insulin by 1.5 U h^{-1}
- BS greater than 11.1: increase insulin by 2 U h^{-1}.

Postoperatively, clear instructions must be given to the ward regarding the reinstatement of appropriate diabetic control.

Elective surgery for the type 2 diabetic

For all types of surgery, oral medications should probably be omitted on the morning of the operation. Patients undergoing minor surgery should be managed in a similar fashion to that for type 1 diabetic patients. The older policy of converting all patients undergoing major surgery on to insulin for 24 h before surgery is no longer considered necessary. Provided that preoperative glycaemic control is good, it is reasonable to continue standard diabetic medication up until the night before surgery and then to manage the patient according to the blood sugar measurement as for type 1 diabetics.

Postoperative care

Tight diabetic control in the postoperative and critical care areas has become fairly controversial in the last few years. A study in intensive care patients found that intensive insulin therapy in which the blood glucose was maintained within a narrow range of 4.4–6.1 mmol $litre^{-1}$ compared with conventional therapy in which the blood sugar was allowed to increase to around 10 mmol $litre^{-1}$ showed a significant reduction in mortality for the tight glucose control group (Van den Berghe et al. 2001). Subsequent studies have failed to support this approach and the NICE-SUGAR study found that tight glucose control was associated with an increased risk of hypoglycaemia and a higher mortality compared with a group in which the blood glucose concentration was maintained between 8.0 and 10.0 mmol $litre^{-1}$ (Finfer et al. 2009).

Overall, current evidence suggests that reasonable control of blood glucose over the perioperative period is appropriate but that attempts to maintain blood sugar within a very narrow, normal range may be associated with more harm than good.

Diabetic emergencies

Patients with either form of diabetes may present to the anaesthetist requiring urgent surgery together with acute management of severely arranged biochemistry.

Diabetic ketoacidosis

This is generally seen in type 1 diabetes and patients may present in a state of hyperglycaemia, ketosis, and metabolic acidosis, together with intracellular and extracellular dehydration and electrolyte depletion. Although this may be the first presentation of diabetes, the anaesthetist is more commonly involved with patients in whom there is an acute stressor event precipitating a stress response and failure of diabetic control. These stressors include apparently minor skin and peri-anal infections, to which diabetic patients are prone, and intra-abdominal pathology such as appendicitis. Other precipitants include myocardial infarction, trauma, pregnancy, acute pancreatitis, surgery, catecholamine excess, and drugs with hyperglycaemic effects such as glucocorticoids and thiazides.

Patients may have a variety of symptoms including polydipsia and polyuria and may progress to neurologically depressed states including coma. On examination, the patients are usually dehydrated, may have a typical smell of acetone on the breath and may have acidosis-induced hyperventilation (Kussmaul breathing).

Investigation should include urinalysis, which should demonstrate glycosuria and positive ketone bodies, and blood gas analysis to determination of the severity of the acid–base disturbance. Most modern analysers include electrolyte, glucose, and lactate measurements that will aid in the management of the patient. In patients requiring urgent surgery, placement of an arterial line will significantly aid management, not only in terms of fluid resuscitation, but also will facilitate regular blood gas measurements that assist in determining appropriate therapeutic strategies. The placement of a urine catheter is also of assistance. These patients will usually have hypernatraemia and hyperkalaemia. However, these measurements may be misleading as these patients are frequently sodium, potassium, and magnesium depleted.

The initial aim of therapy is to restore adequate tissue perfusion and to obtain reversal of ketoacidosis, with gradual control of blood sugar. Traditional teaching holds that 0.9% saline should be used for initial resuscitation as it contains no potassium, but this may not be a valid argument. The hyperchloraemia that can accompany large volume saline resuscitation may in fact worsen both the acidosis and hyperkalaemia. Compared with 0.9% saline, a balanced salt solution, Plasma-Lyte A® gave faster initial resolution of metabolic acidosis and less hyperchloraemia, together with a transiently improved blood pressure profile and urine output (Chua et al. 2012). Ringer's lactate solution may also be a more appropriate resuscitation solution than saline and will not cause an increase in potassium concentration. The argument that lactate may be metabolized to glucose, making control of blood sugar more difficult, is also fallacious. Excessively aggressive fluid resuscitation should be avoided in these patients as there is a risk of developing cerebral oedema and 1–2 litres of crystalloid solution should be administered and the response of the patient carefully assessed before further fluids are given. A more gradual further volume resuscitation over the next few hours is probably more appropriate than continued rapid administration of crystalloid solutions.

Blood glucose control should be commenced with an infusion of short-acting insulin at 0.1 U kg^{-1} h^{-1} and adjusted according to the rate of change in plasma glucose concentrations aiming for a decrease of 2.5–4 mmol $litre^{-1}$ h^{-1}. There appears to be no advantage in an initial bolus of insulin provided an infusion can be started without excessive delay. Hourly blood gas, blood sugar, and electrolyte estimations should be performed and replacement of potassium and magnesium concentrations commenced once the potassium concentration decreases into the normal range and urine output is established.

The timing of surgery in these patients is always problematic, as the presence of sepsis will impede the establishment of good diabetic control. As a general rule, where sepsis is the precipitating cause, surgery should commence once acceptable control of the acid–based abnormalities is established (pH > 7.25). The use of bicarbonate is controversial, and is now not generally recommended unless there is life-threatening acidosis (pH < 6.9) together with haemodynamic instability, but the evidence for its use is weak.

Postoperatively, careful fluid balance management should be continued together with an insulin infusion adjusted against blood sugar concentration until such time as the patient is able to take an oral diet again.

Hyperglycaemic hyperosmolar states

Hyperglycaemic hyperosmolar state, previously known as hyperosmolar non-ketotic coma (HONK), is much less common than diabetic ketoacidosis, but carries a higher mortality and, like diabetic ketoacidosis, may present in the perioperative period or require treatment in a critical care unit. The onset is frequently insidious and severe hyperglycaemia with coma may be the first presenting feature (Nugent 2005). The patients are often elderly type 2 diabetics with some degree of diminished renal function.

The predominant features relate to hyperglycaemia, osmotic diuresis, and resultant electrolyte depletion, often exacerbated by inability to drink adequate free water to replace urinary losses. Again, an acute stressor is frequently the precipitating event.

Neurological deficits are common, with alterations in conscious level ranging from mild drowsiness to coma, closely related to serum osmolality. Hyperglycaemia is typically severe, usually at greater than 35 mmol $litre^{-1}$ and occasionally up to 100 mmol $litre^{-1}$. Serum osmolality is elevated above 320 mOsm kg^{-1} and occasionally as high as 400 mOsm kg^{-1}, reflecting hyperglycaemia and a water deficit of up to 25% (8–12 litres in a 70 kg adult). Serum sodium may be low, normal, or high, although total body sodium is invariably low. Plasma potassium may be elevated, but total body potassium, magnesium, and phosphate are invariably depleted and plasma concentrations will decrease during resuscitation.

As these patients are not usually acidotic, the use of 0.9% saline as the initial resuscitation fluid is acceptable, particularly given the fact that all of the intravenous solutions have a substantially lower osmotic pressure than that of the plasma of these seriously ill patients. Although the water deficit is considerable, rapid fluid replacement should be limited to 1–2 litres initially in the average adult and the patient then reassessed. It is important that the osmotic pressure is not allowed to decrease too rapidly as this may be associated with central pontine myelinolysis. A rate of decline in effective serum osmolality no greater than 3 mOsm h^{-1} has been suggested as a target. Potassium replacement should be started early and magnesium supplementation may also be necessary. Insulin should not be given until the potassium is at least normal or slightly elevated as it will cause significant hypokalaemia. Typically, an intravenous insulin infusion at 0.1 units kg^{-1} h^{-1} will lower plasma glucose at an acceptable rate of 2.5–4 $mmol^{-1}$ h^{-1}.

Surgery should only be contemplated once the patient is stable and an acceptable plasma osmolality has been established—usually lower than 320 mOsm $litre^{-1}$. The hyperosmolar state may also increase the risk of hypercoagulation and thrombotic prophylaxis with low-molecular-weight heparin should be considered. The overall mortality is in the order of 15%, which has to do with the age and health of the patients and the underlying condition.

Carcinoid tumours

Carcinoid tumours represent about 2% of all malignant tumours of the gastrointestinal tract, with an overall incidence of tumours found at autopsy of 2–10:100 000 population, although the incidence at post-mortem maybe as high as 8%, indicating that most tumours remain undiagnosed. These APUD tumours are derived from enterochromaffin cells and may be found in any tissue derived from endoderm, including the lungs, although the gastrointestinal tract is the most common site for their development. Carcinoid tumours contain and secrete a large number of amine and peptide hormones including serotonin, corticotrophin, histamine, dopamine, substance P, neurotensin, prostaglandins, and kallikrein (which stimulates the production of bradykinin and tachykinins). Despite this array of biologically active substances contained within these tumours, only a minority (15–18%) of patients with carcinoid tumours progress to develop carcinoid syndrome.

Classification

Traditionally, carcinoid tumours were classified according to their embryonic site of origin, arising from the foregut, midgut, and hindgut. Although it is now more customary to classify the tumours according to their functional status, the anatomical classification is still of some value, as the tumours arising from each of these anatomically distinct areas may behave quite differently (Table 79.1).

Table 79.1 Abbreviated table of sites, secretions, behaviour, and associations of carcinoid tumours

Site	Secretion	Behaviour	Comment
Respiratory			
Typical carcinoid	Serotonin, corticotrophin	Indolent	
Atypical carcinoid	Serotonin, histamine	Malignant, metastasizing	
Gastric			
Type 1	Nil, hypergastrinaemia from hypochlorhydria	Well differentiated, non-invasive	CAG-A, multiple, fundus, body
Type 2		Well differentiated, non-invasive	ZE syndrome, MEN 1
Type 3		Invasive	Sporadic, solitary
Small bowel	Serotonin, substance P	Indolent	Carcinoid syndrome
Appendix	Serotonin, substance P	Indolent	
Colon	Serotonin, substance P	Invasive	Right sided
Rectum	Nil	Well differentiated	

CAG-A, chronic atrophic gastritis type A; ZE, Zollinger–Ellison.
From *New England Journal of Medicine*, Kulke, M. H. and Mayer, R. J., Carcinoid Tumors. Volume 340, Issue 11, pp. 858–868,

Tumours arising from embryological foregut may occur in the lung and the stomach, with occasional occurrences in the thymus, pancreas, and proximal duodenum. Tumours arising from the lung are particularly likely to contain histamine and may give rise to a very vivid red and patchy flushing. They may also secrete adrenocorticotrophic hormone, resulting in Cushing's syndrome (Fink et al. 2001). Bronchial carcinoids are generally very slow-growing and have a very low level of metastatic activity. They may be detected on routine chest X-ray in an otherwise asymptomatic patient. However, these tumours may also present with bronchial obstruction, obstructive pneumonitis, pleuritic pain, atelectasis, and dyspnoea (41%). Gastric carcinoid may take various forms. Benign tumours arise from mucosal cells and occur as multiple tumours in the fundus or body of the stomach and may be associated with atrophic gastritis and pernicious anaemia. Tumours associated with MEN 1 are more likely to be malignant and to metastasize.

The midgut is the commonest site of carcinoid tumours, particularly the appendix. These tumours generally present with symptoms related to anatomical distortion such as abdominal pain and intestinal obstruction, rather than hormone-related symptomatology. Midgut tumours are generally small (5–10 mm in diameter) and are particularly likely to produce large quantities of serotonin; however, metastases arising from these sites may be large. They are multiple in up to one-third of patients.

Hindgut tumours of the distal colon and rectum generally secrete hormones (pancreatic polypeptide, peptide YY, human chorionic gonadotropin, and chromogranin A) that do not cause any specific clinical symptoms and most commonly present with problems related to the mass, including abdominal pain, intestinal obstruction, and bleeding. Other sites for the development of carcinoid tumours include the kidney, ovary, testes, and prostate. As it is almost exclusively the midgut carcinoids that produce the classical features of carcinoid disease, it has been suggested that the term 'carcinoid tumour' should be assigned only to midgut carcinoid while carcinoid tumours arising from elsewhere are termed neuroendocrine tumours related to their anatomical site.

Signs and symptoms

The majority of gastrointestinal carcinoid tumours do not present with the classical hormone-related constellation of symptoms. Symptoms are often vague, generalized, and diffuse abdominal symptoms of discomfort, borborygmus, and diarrhoea that may be misdiagnosed as irritable bowel syndrome. As a result, patients may present for surgery without the diagnosis having been made, with the consequent risk of the development of carcinoid crisis during the surgical procedure. Some of the gastrointestinal symptoms experienced by patients with carcinoid tumours may be as a result of local secretion of some of the hormonally active substances produced by the tumour.

Carcinoid syndrome

The carcinoid syndrome occurs when the various hormones produced by the tumour are released into the systemic circulation. Carcinoid syndrome usually only becomes manifest once metastatic disease is present, as the liver normally metabolizes the active peptides and amines before they reach the systemic circulation. However, in rare cases, notably, but not exclusively, those where the tumours occur in regions not drained by the portal system (such as the lungs or ovaries), carcinoid syndrome may occur without hepatic metastases. Rectal carcinoid, despite having direct access to the systemic circulation, rarely causes carcinoid syndrome, as these tumours do not produce the classical array of active amines and peptides. Ovarian carcinoid represents a special case as these carcinoids generally arise from ovarian dermoid cysts or teratomas rather than from ovarian tissue and may present with the full carcinoid syndrome picture.

Flushing and diarrhoea are the commonest symptoms of the carcinoid syndrome. The flush reaction may range from the typical varying, patchy red, plethoric appearance thought to be related to the production of tachykinins, to more serious generalized facial flushing with swelling and lachrymation associated with excess histamine release. This is the most severe type of flush reaction and is sometimes part of the carcinoid crisis. However, upper airway oedema and difficulties with intubation have not been reported as a feature. The diarrhoea is characterized by watery stools, colicky abdominal pain, and urgency of defecation, and may be associated with significant fluid and electrolyte abnormalities. These symptoms may respond to ondansetron. Bronchoconstriction and hypotension may be severe and resistant to conventional therapy, particularly in the perioperative period.

Carcinoid heart disease occurs in the majority of patients with the carcinoid syndrome, with abnormal echocardiographic findings in up to 70% of patients. The characteristic lesions are plaque formation and thickening of the pulmonary and tricuspid valves leading to valvular insufficiency and occasionally stenosis. Left-sided valvular lesions are uncommon as the lung metabolizes the high concentrations of serotonin and the tachykinins to which the right heart is subject. They may be associated with patent foramen ovale or pulmonary carcinoid (Pellikka et al. 1993). Valve surgery is the only definitive treatment. Although cardiac surgery carries a high perioperative mortality, marked symptomatic improvement occurs in survivors. Surgical intervention should therefore be considered when cardiac symptoms become severe.

Diagnosis

The diagnosis of carcinoid syndrome is based initially on the symptomatology and supported by biochemical tests. Urinary 5-hydroxyindoleacetic acid (5-HIAA) is the standard initial confirmatory test although false-positives may occur in patients taking chlorpromazine or who have recently ingested bananas, avocado, pineapple, walnuts, chocolate, or coffee. Plasma chromagranin is almost invariably elevated in metastatic carcinoid and is both prognostic and a useful marker of the success of treatment. Ultrasound and CT have been used for the detection of the metastases, with contrast-enhanced CT being superior to MRI scanning. Tumour localization with somatostatin scintigraphy is extremely useful in identifying multiple tumours, and positron emission tomography offers high detection rates.

Treatment

The introduction of somatostatin (Marsh et al. 1987) and its longer-lasting analogue, octreotide, has revolutionized the medical treatment and perioperative care of patients with carcinoid syndrome and may delay tumour progression.

Surgery is the definitive treatment for carcinoid tumours and surgical excision of a localized bowel tumour has a high cure rate and 5-year survival of 60–70%. The presence of local and hepatic metastases substantially worsens the prognosis, but hepatic resection has been associated with 5-year survival rates ranging from 45% to 80%. These tumours are generally resistant to radio- and chemotherapy, but the use of hepatic arterial procedures including ligation and chemoembolization combined with systemic chemotherapy has reduced tumour size in 78% of patients (Ruszniewski et al. 2004). Nevertheless, most patients with carcinoid disease will come to some form of surgical management. Where hepatic resection is contemplated for carcinoid syndrome in the presence of significant right-sided cardiac valvular lesions, valve replacement surgery should precede hepatic surgery otherwise the congested liver may bleed profusely.

Perioperative care

Preoperative evaluation of a patient with carcinoid syndrome should always include echocardiography as the incidence of right-sided cardiac lesions is so high. Where diarrhoea is a prominent feature, careful fluid and electrolyte assessment and correction may be required and the need for intraoperative measurements of electrolytes and glucose should be anticipated.

The major intraoperative concern is the occurrence of carcinoid crisis with severe hyper/hypotension and bronchospasm. The introduction of somatostatin and its analogues has relegated previous forms of perioperative management (antagonists of serotonin and histamine) to the status of secondary level therapy. The half-life of somatostatin is 3 min, whereas that of its analogues octreotide, lanreotide, and octastatin (all of which are octapeptides) is of the order of 100–120 min, making these agents easier to use in the treatment of patients with carcinoid syndrome. Sedative premedication with a benzodiazepine and possibly a histamine antagonist may be helpful. Preoperative preparation with octreotide 100 μg subcutaneously before surgery is generally recommended followed by octreotide 50–100 μg given intravenously at induction. An intravenous infusion at a rate of 50–100 μg h^{-1} can be used intraoperatively, with further bolus doses given intraoperatively as required for the control of symptoms. Doses in excess of 500 μg h^{-1} have been given without untoward effect (Mancuso et al. 2011). As intraoperative blood loss may be considerable, the presence of hypovolaemia must always be considered should hypotension prove unresponsive to octreotide. Hypotension refractory to octreotide may respond to the kallikrein inhibitor, aprotinin, and histamine antagonists (usually as a combination of H_1 and H_2 receptor blockers) may be helpful, particularly in predominantly histamine-secreting tumours such as a gastric or bronchial carcinoid. Invasive monitoring should be used in most cases, and may include central venous pressure monitoring, direct arterial pressure measurement, and possibly the use of pulmonary artery catheters. Whether or not it is advisable to place a pulmonary artery catheter in a patient with tricuspid and pulmonary valvular disease is unclear. Theoretically, transoesophageal echocardiography should provide more useful information than pulmonary artery catheterization, as pulmonary artery dynamics may be significantly disrupted particularly during a carcinoid crisis. There is, however, no firm scientific evidence on which to base recommendations. The use of newer techniques, such as oesophageal Doppler or systolic pressure variation might be helpful but have not been described in this condition as yet.

There is no scientific basis for recommending any one anaesthetic technique in preference to any other. Histamine-releasing agents should, theoretically, be avoided, but most of the currently available anaesthetic agents have been used in conjunction with carcinoid syndrome. Shorter-acting agents may be preferred as increased concentrations of serotonin may be associated with delayed emergence from anaesthesia, and agents that release catecholamines should be avoided. Regional anaesthesia is controversial, as the high-quality postoperative pain relief available from regional techniques is likely to be advantageous, but intraoperative management of hypotension associated with neuraxial block may be problematic. Most texts recommend the avoidance of catecholamines, as all of the catecholamines have been reported to trigger carcinoid crises. However, there are also reports of good responses to adrenaline and phenylephrine in patients with otherwise unresponsive hypotension (Hamid and Harris 1992). Judicious use of small doses of direct-acting catecholamines, titrated against patient responsiveness, may be justified for both refractory bronchospasm and for cardiovascular support. Both phenylephrine and ephedrine have been extensively used during carcinoid resections (Kinney et al. 2001). Bronchospasm should be managed in the first instance with deepening levels of volatile anaesthesia, and non-catecholamine bronchodilators such as ipratropium bromide. Antihistamines may be useful, but inhaled β-agonists should not be withheld if bronchospasm fails to respond to other measures. There are no reports of catecholamine-induced carcinoid crisis in association with octreotide treatment.

Surgical aspects

Pulmonary carcinoids

The principles of surgery are complete removal of the primary tumour, with a draining lymphadenectomy. There are numerous surgical strategies, and these depend on the stage of the lesion. Wedge or segmental resections are usually undertaken. Endoscopic approaches are unlikely to achieve full tumour removal, and should probably only be used palliatively. Imprint cytology or frozen section histology will help plan the extent of resection and lymphadenectomy. A multidisciplinary team approach offers potentially excellent results (Fischer et al. 2001).

Gastric carcinoids

The majority of gastric carcinoids are type 1, and associated with chronic atrophic gastritis. Most tumours are encountered in later life, and have multiple lesions situated in the fundus or body of the stomach. Type 2 gastric carcinoids are also attributed to the hypergastrinaemia found in the Zollinger–Ellison syndrome. These are usually found in patients with MEN 1, and it is important that the other components of the syndrome (pituitary, pancreatic islet, parathyroid) be sought. Type 3 carcinoids are sporadic and malignant.

The surgical strategy chosen depends on the type, size, and number of the lesions. Because of the indolence of the first two types, small lesions (1 cm) are usually removed endoscopically and the biopsy site regularly monitored. Larger lesions may require segmental resection, or gastrectomy. Multiple lesions may require a total gastrectomy. The inherent malignancy of the type 3 lesions mandates an approach similar to that for gastric carcinoma.

Carcinoids of small bowel

Carcinoid tumours of the small bowel are usually located in the distal ileum, and are frequently multiple. Presenting in later life, they usually cause anaemia and abdominal pain, and the diagnosis is made with difficulty; as a result, many present with nodal and liver metastases.

The management is by surgical resection of both the affected bowel and mesentery, often in the presence of hepatic metastases. The lesions may be accompanied by extensive mesenteric fibrosis that may make surgery technically very difficult and occasion significant bleeding. This is also true of ovarian carcinoids where thickening of pelvic structures may lead to severe haemorrhage.

Liver transplantation has been used successfully in cases with extensive hepatic metastases.

Colonic and rectal carcinoids

Most tumours are found in the right side of the colon, usually the caecum. The symptoms are the same as those for colonic cancer and the carcinoid syndrome is found in less than 5% of them.

The surgical management strategies are the same as those for carcinoma of the colon; small rectal carcinoid are excised locally, with expectation of cure (Mani et al. 1994), but the larger ones are managed using the surgical principles that govern rectal carcinoma.

Postoperative care

Postoperatively, patients should be managed in a high-care environment as ongoing haemodynamic disturbances, metabolic disruptions, and release of mediators from residual tumour may pose significant problems. Good quality analgesia should improve the management of these patients, although there are no specific studies to support this proposition. As it is impossible to predict likelihood of continued mediator release, octreotide infusions should be continued postoperatively. Although it is generally recommended that histamine-releasing drugs should be avoided, there is no evidence that morphine, which releases histamine only at a cutaneous level, is contraindicated. Other short-acting, potent opioids such as fentanyl and sufentanil have been used successfully, and there would seem no reason to avoid non-steroidal anti-inflammatory agents as part of a planned postoperative analgesic regimen. Epidural analgesia is widely recommended. Antiemetic treatment is best provided with a serotonin antagonist such as ondansetron.

Kinney et al. (2001) concluded that most people with metastatic carcinoid tumours can undergo intra-abdominal surgery safely. In their series, no intraoperative complications occurred in patients who received octreotide intraoperatively. Overall, perioperative complications and death were strongly associated with the presence of carcinoid heart disease and high elevated urinary 5-HIAA output.

Endocrine emergencies (non-diabetic)

Emergency situations involving the endocrine system are rare and may mimic other causes of life-threatening cardiovascular collapse (Farling and Silversides 2010). However, if recognized and managed appropriately, the patient may survive without significant sequelae. Endocrine emergencies include pituitary apoplexy, thyroid storm, myxoedema coma, hyperparathyroid crisis, hypocalcaemia, adrenal insufficiency, phaeochromocytoma, hypoglycaemia, diabetic ketoacidosis, hyperglycaemic hyperosmolar state, and carcinoid. Successful management of endocrine emergencies requires a multidisciplinary approach that will include anaesthetists, endocrinologists, surgeons, accident and emergency specialists, and intensive care specialists (Mullan 2010).

Pituitary apoplexy

Pituitary apoplexy is a rare clinical syndrome caused by sudden haemorrhage or infarction of the pituitary gland, generally within a pituitary tumour. The sudden increase in size of the contents of the sella turcica causes compression of surrounding structures, including the portal veins, giving rise to the classical signs and symptoms. There is significant morbidity and mortality and diagnosis may be delayed if the patient and clinicians are unaware of the underlying adenoma.

Simmonds' syndrome is the term for panhypopituitarism after trauma, vascular lesions, or tumour. Sheehan's syndrome is a complication of pregnancy caused by hypotension and ischaemia of the anterior pituitary after major obstetrical haemorrhage.

The classical presentation of pituitary apoplexy is of a sudden severe headache, reduced level of consciousness, vomiting, visual impairment, caused by displacement of the optic chiasma and ocular motor nerves, and reduced function of the pituitary gland. Damage to the anterior pituitary leads to multiple acute hormonal deficiencies. Tests of hypothalamic and pituitary dysfunction will include TSH, T_4, and insulin tolerance test for adrenocorticotropic hormone deficiency, leading to secondary adrenal failure, and may be life-threatening if untreated. Ophthalmic examination, imaging, and measurement of pituitary hormones confirm the diagnosis and CT or MRI will show a pituitary tumour with haemorrhagic or necrotic components.

Initial management of patients with pituitary apoplexy includes administration of intravenous fluids and corticosteroids. Hydrocortisone treatment must be initiated immediately, at a dose of 50 mg $(6\ h)^{-1}$. Urgent transsphenoidal surgical decompression is an option particularly for patients with reduced levels of consciousness and visual field defects. All patients presenting with pituitary apoplexy will require long-term follow-up to treat any residual tumour or pituitary dysfunction.

Thyrotoxic crisis

Thyrotoxic crisis, also known as thyroid storm, is a rare, life-threatening condition that occurs in uncontrolled hyperthyroid patients as a result of triggers such as surgery, infection, or trauma. It occurs predominantly in elderly patients and is three to five times more common in women than in men. The overall mortality is 10–20%.

The diagnosis of a thyrotoxic crisis is made entirely on clinical grounds. There is no difference in thyroid hormone concentration between patients with uncomplicated thyrotoxicosis and those undergoing a thyroid storm.

Medical management aims to counteract the peripheral effects of thyroid hormones, inhibit thyroid hormone synthesis, and treat systemic complications.

β-blockade and anti-thyroid drugs are used as the first line of treatment. Dantrolene has been used successfully to treat a thyroid crisis and magnesium sulfate could be beneficial as it reduces the incidence and severity of dysrhythmias as a result of catecholamines. Supportive management of thyroid crisis includes hydration, cooling, and inotropes and is often best managed in intensive care. Early thyroidectomy should be considered if medical treatment fails to result in clinical improvement.

Myxoedema coma

Myxoedema coma is a rare, life-threatening complication of hypothyroidism that may be precipitated by infection, environmental exposure, trauma, or certain drugs, particularly diuretics and sedatives. Patients exhibit disorientation, lethargy, and psychosis that may proceed to coma. The diagnosis should be considered when hypothermia, respiratory depression, and unconsciousness are present in a patient with known, or clinical evidence of, hypothyroidism.

Investigations should include thyroid function tests, electrolytes, blood gas analysis, chest X-ray and ECG. TSH is elevated in primary hypothyroidism but may be normal or low if the hypothyroidism is secondary. T_4 will be low and T_3 resin uptake is increased. Hyponatraemia is common because of elevated ADH. Blood glucose concentrations range from normal to low because of decreased gluconeogenesis and reduced insulin clearance. Hypoventilation will cause hypoxia and hypercapnia. A chest X-ray may show signs of a chest infection or pericardial effusion. ECG will confirm bradycardia, low voltage, prolonged PR interval, T-wave abnormalities, and possibly electrical alterans, if an effusion is present.

In addition, abdominal radiology will show an associated ileus and CT will rule out other causes of coma, including intracerebral haemorrhage.

Treatment will include careful T_3 replacement, passive re-warming, cautious plasma volume expansion, and correction of hypoglycaemia. Ventilatory support in intensive care may be required. Aggressive replacement with T_3 should be avoided as myocardial ischaemia may be precipitated and aggressive re-warming will cause vasodilation and hypotension. Severe hyponatraemia will require hypertonic saline therapy and blood glucose will need to be monitored frequently. Adrenal insufficiency has a high association with thyroid failure so patients with myxoedema coma should be treated with hydrocortisone. Sedatives and narcotics should be avoided. Early recognition and improved management has reduced mortality.

Parathyroid crisis

Parathyroid crisis is an uncommon endocrine emergency resulting in severe hypercalcaemia, usually greater than 3.5 mmol litre^{-1}, and dehydration. It is an extreme manifestation of primary hyperparathyroidism and may be known as acute hyperparathyroidism, parathyroid storm, and parathyrotoxicosis. Neurological disturbances include lethargy, confusion, coma, and seizures. Symptoms include nausea, anorexia, vomiting, abdominal pain, and muscular weakness. Polyuria and polydipsia result from a nephrogenic diabetes insipidus leading to dehydration and a decrease in glomerular filtration rate. Acute kidney injury may develop. ECG changes include shortened QT interval and ST elevation, tachyarrhythmias, conduction defects, bradyarrhythmias, and asystole. There is an association between parathyroid crisis and acute pancreatitis.

There are many causes of severe hypercalcaemia so the key investigation is serum PTH concentration, which, if not suppressed in the presence of hypercalcaemia, is diagnostic of PTH-dependent hypercalcaemia. Treatment involves volume replacement, with large volumes of 0.9% saline, increasing elimination of calcium, and surgical excision of the parathyroid glands. Furosemide promotes loss of calcium in the urine but should only be given once adequate volume replacement has been completed. Other diuretics that cause calcium absorption should be discontinued. Bisphosphonates such as pamidronate and zoledronic acid are effective calcium-lowering agents. Calcitonin is used in the emergency situation and cinacalcet has been used with good effect. Haemodialysis with a calcium-free dialysate may be used to lower the calcium concentration. With effective medical therapy, parathyroidectomy should be delayed until dehydration has been treated and hypercalcaemia at least partially controlled.

The mortality from this condition has decreased dramatically and death from parathyroid crisis is now rare.

Adrenal insufficiency

Adrenal insufficiency is also known as Addisonian crisis. It is a rare disorder and the most common cause is autoimmune adrenalitis. Other causes include tuberculosis, septicaemia, advanced AIDS, haemorrhage, and tumours. Primary insufficiency involves a decrease in both glucocorticoid and mineralocorticoid activity. Secondary adrenal insufficiency is as a result of a lack of ACTH because of suppression by exogenous steroids, hypopituitarism, pituitary tumours, or after hypophysectomy. Most crises occur in undiagnosed Addison's disease and failure to increase the dose after infection or stress in patients on steroid replacement therapy. The clinical features of an Addisonian crisis include hypotension, hypoglycaemia, hyponatraemia, and hyperkalaemia, as a result of reduced aldosterone, in a patient with abdominal, leg, or back pain. Random cortisol concentrations will be low. In primary adrenal insufficiency, ACTH concentrations will be high. In secondary adrenal insufficiency, ACTH concentrations will be low.

The initial treatment involves fluid replacement with 2–3 litres of 0.9% saline and glucocorticoid replacement. Hydrocortisone 100 mg intravenously 6-hourly should commence immediately without waiting for tetracosactide testing. Careful and repeated education of patients and their partners is the best strategy to avoid adrenal crises. Patients with known adrenal insufficiency should carry steroid cards or medic-alert bracelets and they should be taught how to use an emergency intramuscular injection of hydrocortisone.

Phaeochromocytoma

A hypertensive crisis in a patient with a phaeochromocytoma may present with a severe pounding headache, sweating, pallor, palpitations, and numbness or tingling. The onset may be sudden and can be precipitated by straining, exercise, pressure on the abdomen, and drugs such as anaesthetic agents.

It is important to consider the possibility of an undiagnosed phaeochromocytoma in any patient when extreme hypertension occurs during induction of anaesthesia. The differentiation of causes of hypertensive crises is difficult and other endocrine causes include excesses of glucocorticoids, aldosterone, and renin. Non-endocrine causes include subarachnoid haemorrhage, acute glomerulonephritis, and eclampsia. These will require detailed clinical, biochemical, and radiological assessment. Severe hypertension has the potential to cause cerebrovascular, cardiovascular, renal, and eye damage. Urgent treatment is required to reduce the blood pressure in a progressive but controlled manner. The choice will depend upon the experience of the individual clinician. Infusions of sodium nitroprusside, glyceryl trinitrate, or magnesium with intra-arterial monitoring of blood pressure, to avoid rebound hypotension, are recommended. After control of the hypertensive crisis, the patient will require referral for surgical excision of the phaeochromocytoma.

Carcinoid crisis

Carcinoid is an APUD tumour derived from argentaffin cells. A carcinoid crisis is the result of a massive outpouring of vasoactive peptides such as serotonin, bradykinin, histamine, and prostaglandins. A crisis is distinguished from a severe episode of the carcinoid syndrome by the simultaneous sudden onset of different symptoms. Crises may be precipitated by endogenous or exogenous catecholamines so anxiety and various forms of stress have been implicated. Triggers of a crisis include mechanical stimulation of the tumour, hypotension, hypertension, hypercapnia, hypothermia, and administration of histamine-releasing drugs.

Serotonin and its metabolites (5-HIAA) are raised while tryptophan is reduced. Management includes the use of octreotide and ketanserin. Hypertension is controlled by labetalol and esmolol. Volume replacement and octreotide should be the first line of treatment of hypotension. The use of inotropes containing catecholamines to manage episodes of hypotension might be counterproductive as they may stimulate further serotonin secretion, but they should not be withheld in refractory hypotension once octreotide has been administered in appropriate doses.

In summary, endocrine emergencies are rare but increased awareness and understanding of pathophysiology combined with improved diagnosis and management has decreased the mortality associated with these conditions.

Declaration of interest

None declared.

References

Anonymous. The diabetes pandemic. *Lancet* 2011; **378**: 99

Chen H, Pruhs Z, Starling JR, Mack E. Intraoperative parathyroid hormone testing improves cure rates in patients undergoing minimally invasive parathyroidectomy. *Surgery* 2005; **138**: 583–7

Chua HR, Venkatesh B, Stachowski E, *et al.* Plasma-Lyte 148 vs 0.9% saline for fluid resuscitation in diabetic ketoacidosis. *J Crit Care* 2012; **27**: 138–45

Duncan AI, Koch CG, Xu M, *et al.* Recent metformin ingestion does not increase in-hospital morbidity or mortality after cardiac surgery. *Anesth Analg* 2007; **104**: 42–50

Farling PA. Thyroid disease. *Br J Anaesth* 2000; **85**: 15–28

Farling PA, Silversides JA. Endocrine emergencies. In: James MFM, ed. *Anaesthesia for Patients with Endocrine Disease.* Oxford: Oxford University Press, 2010; 169–203

Finfer S, Chittock DR, Su SY, *et al.* Intensive versus conventional glucose control in critically ill patients. *N Engl J Med* 2009; **360**: 1283–97

Fink G, Krelbaum T, Yellin A, *et al.* Pulmonary carcinoid: presentation, diagnosis, and outcome in 142 cases in Israel and review of 640 cases from the literature. *Chest* 2001; **119**: 1647–51

Fischer S, Kruger M, Mcrae K, Merchant N, Tsao MS, Keshavjee S. Giant-bronchial carcinoid tumors: a multidisciplinary approach. *Ann Thorac Surg* 2001; **71**: 386–93

Gandhi GY, Nuttall GA, Abel MD, *et al.* Intraoperative hyperglycemia and perioperative outcomes in cardiac surgery patients. *Mayo Clin Proc* 2005; **80**: 862–6

Ganong WF. *Review of Medical Physiology.* New York: McGraw-Hill, 2005

Garber AJ, Moghissi ES, Bransome ED, Jr, *et al.* American College of Endocrinology position statement on inpatient diabetes and metabolic control. *Endocr Pract* 2004; **10**: 77–82

Gerich JE. Role of the kidney in normal glucose homeostasis and in the hyperglycaemia of diabetes mellitus: therapeutic implications. *Diabet Med* 2010; **27**: 136–42

Gillespie S, Farling PA. III. Preoperative assessment of the airway: should anaesthetists be making use of modern imaging techniques? *Br J Anaesth* 2004; **93**: 758–60

Hamid SK, Harris DN. Hypotension following valve replacement surgery in carcinoid heart disease. *Anaesthesia* 1992; **47**: 490–2

Hobbiger HE, Allen JG, Greatorex RG, Denny NM. The laryngeal mask airway for thyroid and parathyroid surgery. *Anaesthesia* 1996; **151**: 972–4

James MFM. Adrenal medulla: the anaesthetic management of phaeochromocytoma. In: James MFM, ed. *Anaesthesia for Patients with Endocrine Disease.* Oxford: Oxford University Press, 2010; 149–69

Juul AB, Wetterslev J, Kofoed-Enevoldsen A. Long-term postoperative mortality in diabetic patients undergoing major non-cardiac surgery. *Eur J Anaesthesiol* 2004; **21**: 523–9

Kahn SE, Cooper ME, Del Prato S. Pathophysiology and treatment of type 2 diabetes: perspectives on the past, present, and future. *Lancet* 2014; **383**: 1068–83

Kinney MA, Warner ME, Nagorney DM, *et al.* Perianaesthetic risks and outcomes of abdominal surgery for metastatic carcinoid tumours. *Br J Anaesth* 2001; **87**: 447–52

Komotar RJ, Roguski M, Bruce JN. Surgical management of craniopharyngiomas. *J Neurooncol* 2009; **92**: 283–96

Kulkarni RS, Braverman LE, Patwardhan NA. Bilateral cervical plexus block for thyroidectomy and parathyroidectomy in healthy and high risk patients. *J Endocrinol Invest* 1996; **19**: 714–8

Lacoste L, Gineste D, Karayan J, *et al.* Airway complications in thyroid surgery. *Ann Otol Rhinol Laryngol* 1993; **102**: 441–6

Malmstedt J, Wahlberg E, Jorneskog G, Swedenborg J. Influence of perioperative blood glucose levels on outcome after infrainguinal bypass surgery in patients with diabetes. *Br J Surg* 2006; **93**: 1360–7

Mancuso K, Kaye AD, Boudreaux JP, *et al.* Carcinoid syndrome and perioperative anesthetic considerations. *J Clin Anesth* 2011; **23**: 329–41

Mani S, Modlin IM, Ballantyne G, Ahlman H, West B. Carcinoids of the rectum. *J Am Coll Surg* 1994; **179**: 231–48

Marsh HM, Martin JK, Jr, Kvols LK, *et al.* Carcinoid crisis during anesthesia: successful treatment with a somatostatin analogue. *Anesthesiology* 1987; **66**: 89–91

Mcadam D, Muro K, Suresh S. The use of infraorbital nerve block for postoperative pain control after transsphenoidal hypophysectomy. *Reg Anesth Pain Med* 2005; **30**: 572–3

McGirt MJ, Woodworth GF, Brooke BS, *et al.* Hyperglycemia independently increases the risk of perioperative stroke, myocardial infarction, and death after carotid endarterectomy. *Neurosurgery* 2006; **58**: 1066–73

Miccoli P, Barellini L, Monchik JM, Rago R, Berti PF. Randomized clinical trial comparing regional and general anaesthesia in minimally invasive video-assisted parathyroidectomy. *Br J Surg* 2005; **92**: 814–18

Mullan B. Thyroid function in critical care. In: Hall GM, Hunter JM, Cooper MS, eds. *Core Topics in Endocrinology in Anaesthesia and Critical Care.* Cambridge: Cambridge University Press, 2010; 168–74

Murkin JM. Anesthesia and hypothyroidism: a review of thyroxine physiology, pharmacology, and anesthetic implications. *Anesth Analg* 1982; **61**: 371–83

Nath G, Korula G, Chandy MJ. Effect of intrathecal saline injection and Valsalva maneuver on cerebral perfusion pressure during transsphenoidal surgery for pituitary macroadenoma. *J Neurosurg Anesthesiol* 1995; **7**: 1–6

National Institute for Health and Care Excellence. *Intraoperative Nerve Monitoring During Thyroid Surgery.* Interventional procedure guidance 255. 2008. Available from http://www.nice.org.uk/guidance/IPG255

Nicholson G, Hall GM. Diabetes mellitus: new drugs for a new epidemic. *Br J Anaesth* 2011; **107**: 65–73

Nolan CJ, Damm P, Prentki M. Type 2 diabetes across generations: from pathophysiology to prevention and management. *Lancet* 2011; **378**: 169–81

Nugent BW. Hyperosmolar hyperglycemic state. *Emerg Med Clin North Am* 2005; **23**: 629–48

Pellikka PA, Tajik AJ, Khandheria BK, *et al.* Carcinoid heart disease. Clinical and echocardiographic spectrum in 74 patients. *Circulation* 1993; **87**: 1188–96

Pemberton H. Sign of submerged goitre. *Lancet* 1946; **248**: 509

Ruszniewski P, Ish-Shalom S, Wymenga M, *et al.* Rapid and sustained relief from the symptoms of carcinoid syndrome: results from an open 6-month study of the 28-day prolonged-release formulation of lanreotide. *Neuroendocrinology* 2004; **80**: 244–51

Schricker T, Gougeon R, Eberhart L, *et al.* Type 2 diabetes mellitus and the catabolic response to surgery. *Anesthesiology* 2005; **102**: 320–6

Smith M, Hirsch NP. Pituitary disease and anaesthesia. *Br J Anaesth* 2000; **85**: 3–14

Standring S. *Gray's Anatomy*. Edinburgh: Elsevier Churchill Livingstone, 2008

Stehling LC. Anesthetic management of the patient with hyperthyroidism. *Anesthesiology* 1974; **41**: 585–95

Van Den Berghe G, Wouters P, Weekers F, *et al.* Intensive insulin therapy in the critically ill patients. *N Engl J Med* 2001; **345**: 1359–67

CHAPTER 80

Musculoskeletal disorders and anaesthesia

Philip M. Hopkins

Introduction

Musculoskeletal disorders constitute the most common reason for patients to consult their general practitioner. The majority of these consultations, however, relate to self-limiting mechanical problems. The focus of this chapter is the less common, but chronic, disorders where the musculoskeletal system is either primarily affected or forms an important component of a multisystem disorder not covered elsewhere in this textbook. The chapter is divided into three parts dealing separately with the polyarthropathies, the connective tissue disorders, and the myopathies. In each part the generic implications for anaesthesia of patients with each set of conditions are discussed followed by an account of individual disorders. The individual disorders covered are not exhaustive but are limited to those conditions that have implications for anaesthesia in addition to the generic considerations for the group of conditions as a whole.

Polyarthropathies

Joint symptoms and mobility

While each of the polyarthropathies has a distinct pattern of the joints most commonly and primarily affected, all joints can be affected to a greater or lesser degree. Many of these conditions have a fluctuating pattern of disease progression in which flare-ups can be generalized or limited to only a few joints. A useful initial question in the history is to ask the patient which joints are presently most affected before asking the patient to demonstrate to you the full range of movement for all joints that may be passively moved during anaesthesia and surgery. This will obviously depend on the nature of the surgery and the patient positioning required during the procedure but will almost invariably include the joints of the upper limb and those of the neck (see 'Airway assessment'). Any limitation of pain-free movement should be documented.

Airway assessment

The ease of airway management can be compromised by involvement of the cervical spine and temporomandibular joints. The joints may have restricted movement because of joint fusion or destruction (or both) and, in the awake patient, pain and muscle spasm in acutely inflamed joints. There may also be joint instability which is of particular concern if it affects the cervical spine with the atlantoaxial joint the most commonly vulnerable. Although the incidence of atlantoaxial subluxation is decreasing with modern biological therapies for inflammatory polyarthropathies, the potential for catastrophic compression of the spinal cord or vertebral arteries is such that every effort should be made to determine the presence and extent of cervical spine instability. With the patient presenting for elective procedures, it may be appropriate to defer surgery until after operative fixation of a newly diagnosed significant atlantoaxial subluxation. It is therefore appropriate to seek definitive radiological diagnosis of atlantoaxial subluxation in elective surgical patients with a history of cervical spine involvement in longstanding polyarthropathy where manipulation of the neck may be required for airway intervention. The radiological features of atlantoaxial subluxation or inferior cervical pathology (Table 80.1) require both lateral views (neutral and flexion) and anteroposterior films (including an open mouth odontoid view). See Figure 80.1 (Fombon and Thompson 2006).

Temporomandibular joint involvement is assessed by determining the incisor gap on full mouth opening. To complete the assessment, the patient should be directly questioned for features of cricoarytenoid involvement. The anaesthetist may be alerted to this by a patient with a hoarse voice or one who whispers, but in any case the patient should be asked if they have noticed any change in the character of their voice or if they have any difficulties with swallowing or perhaps a feeling of fullness in their throat which can result from inflammation of the cricoarytenoid joints.

Assessment of body system function

An extrinsic restrictive respiratory defect can result from involvement of the thoracic spine or articulations of the ribs, or both, but

Table 80.1 Identification of cervical spine pathology by X-ray of the neck

Radiological view	Pathological radiological features	
Lateral (flexion)	>3 mm separation of odontoid from arch of atlas	Loss of odontoid
Lateral (neutral)	>4.5 mm vertical migration of odontoid	
AP (open mouth odontoid)	>2 mm lateral atlantoaxial misalignment	
AP	>2 mm lateral misalignment of adjacent subaxial vertebrae	

AP, anteroposterior.

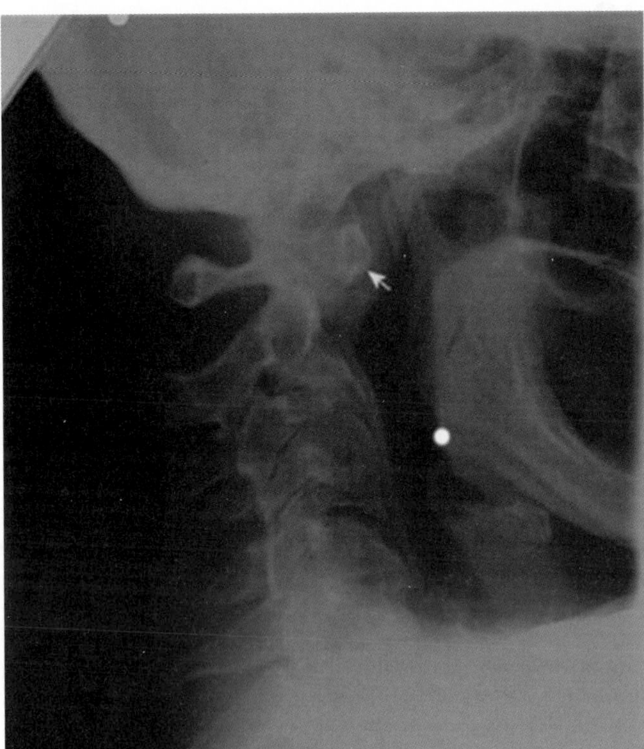

Figure 80.1 Lateral neck X-ray in flexion in a patient with rheumatoid arthritis. Note the position of dens axis (arrow). There is a 13 mm dislocation between atlas and odontoid peg. C3 shows degenerative changes. This patient had been receiving long-term steroid treatment.

Reproduced from Fombon, F. and Thompson, J. P. Anaesthesia for the adult patient with rheumatoid arthritis. *Continuing Education in Anaesthesia, Critical Care, and Pain*, Volume 6, Issue 6, pp. 235–239, Copyright © 2006, by permission of the *British Journal of Anaesthesia*.

some of the polyarthropathies, notably rheumatoid arthritis, are systemic diseases that can be associated with, for example, interstitial pulmonary fibrosis. Cardiovascular compromise can result from myocardial or pericardial involvement. It is, however, difficult to make an assessment of cardiorespiratory reserve because exercise capacity is often limited by the joint disease. Clinical examination should include assessment of chest expansion and auscultation for the presence of adventitious breath sounds along with auscultation of the heart, being alert to the possibility of quiet heart sounds or a pericardial rub. Even in the absence of a relevant clinical history and the presence of a normal clinical examination, an ECG is recommended in any polyarthropathy patient of 40 years of age or more. The need for a chest X-ray is determined by abnormal features, clinical assessment, ECG, or a combination of these.

Medication history

Medications for polyarthropathies include analgesics, anti-inflammatories, steroids, disease-modifying antirheumatic drugs, and the newer biological treatments. For analgesia, the majority of patients are managed with any combination of paracetamol, weak opioid, and non-steroidal anti-inflammatory drugs (NSAIDs) (selective or non-selective cyclooxygenase 2 inhibitors). A minority of patients are managed with more potent preparations such as sustained relief morphine sulfate, complicating postoperative pain management. Corticosteroids are now reserved for the management of acute flare-ups although there are still some patients on chronic low-dose prednisolone. While such patients are unlikely to have significant adrenocortical suppression, the normal physiological increase in corticosteroid production in response to major surgery or trauma rarely results in plasma steroid concentrations greater than therapeutic levels. It is important to substitute equivalent doses of parenteral steroid during periods of perioperative starvation but it is invariably unnecessary to exceed the equivalent of the patient's usual maintenance dose. Table 80.2 provides equivalent doses for commonly used glucocorticoids.

Table 80.2 Relative potency and plasma half-life of commonly used glucocorticoid medications

Glucocorticoid	Equivalent dose (mg)	Half-life (h)
Hydrocortisone	25	8–12
Prednisolone	5	18–36
Methylprednisolone	4	18–36
Prednisone	5	18–36
Dexamethasone	0.75	36–54

The disease-modifying agents all act on the immune system (Table 80.3). They render the patient susceptible to infection and there is uncertainty whether they should be discontinued ahead of elective surgery. They all have the potential to suppress bone marrow function and many also have additional selective toxic effects (Table 80.3). Patients prescribed these medications therefore undergo regular clinic and blood test screening.

Table 80.3 Disease-modifying therapies for rheumatoid arthritis

Drug	Mechanism of action	Specific potential toxicities
Methotrexate	Antimetabolite, folate poison	Interstitial lung disease Liver toxicity
Hydroxychloroquine	Blocks toll-like receptor on dendritic cells	Ocular toxicity
Ciclosporin	Calcineurin inhibitor, prevents IL-2 action	Hypertension Nephrotoxicity
Leflunomide	Anti-proliferative, inhibits pyrimidine synthesis	Liver toxicity. Extensive hepato-enteric re-circulation
Anakinra	IL-1 receptor antagonist, reduces IL-1 signalling	Pneumonia
Sulfasalazine	Immunomodulation	Stevens–Johnson syndrome
Azathioprine	Anti-proliferative, inhibits purine synthesis	Toxicity in slow acetylators Pancreatitis
Gold salts	Unknown immunomodulation	Glomerulonephritis

IL, interleukin.

Reproduced with permission from Samanta, R. *et al.* Rheumatoid arthritis and anaesthesia. *Anaesthesia*, Volume 66, Issue 12, pp. 1146–1159, Copyright © 2011, The Association of Anaesthetists of Great Britain and Ireland.

The newer biological therapies have been shown to be efficacious especially in rheumatoid arthritis. They are either monoclonal antibodies or other proteins that act against tumour necrosis factor (TNF)-α or other cytokine mediators (Table 80.4).

Their immunosuppressive effects again may place the surgical patient at increased risk of infection and they are usually withheld in the month preceding elective surgery. Patients receiving biological therapies are closely monitored for organ toxicity and there is some evidence that they are associated with congestive heart failure and development of lymphoma (Samanta et al. 2011).

Investigations

In addition to the X-rays and ECG already mentioned, pulmonary function tests may be indicated. For anything but the most minor surgical procedures a full blood count is advisable. In addition to the myelosuppressive effect of disease-modifying drugs, patients with polyarthropathy are at risk of anaemia associated with chronic disease. Renal and liver function will need to be assessed in patients taking medications that affect these organs and additionally blood glucose should be tested in patients with continued or frequent steroid use.

Planning for anaesthesia

Wherever feasible according to the planned surgery, regional or local anaesthesia is invariably a good option for patients with polyarthropathy. Avoidance of general anaesthesia removes the considerable problem of airway management, provides reassurance that the patient can be positioned comfortably, and is associated with lower overall risk in patients with significant systemic disease (Gupta and Hopkins 2012). It is worth remembering that the skill of the surgeon is an important variable in determining whether some procedures are tolerable for the patient under regional anaesthesia.

Table 80.4 Biological agents for the treatment of rheumatoid arthritis

Anti-TNFa directed (first-line)	
Infliximab	Chimaeric monoclonal anti-TNFa antibody
Adalimumab	Human monoclonal anti-TNFa antibody
Etanercept	TNFa receptor-IgG fusion protein (inactivates membrane-bound and free receptors)
Certolizumab	PEGylated Fab fragment of humanized monoclonal anti-TNFa antibody
Golimumab	Human monoclonal anti-TNFa antibody
Other agents (second-line)	
Abatacept	Anti-CTLA4 monoclonal antibody
Tocilizumab	Anti-IL-6 receptor
Rituximab anti-CD20 monoclonal antibody	

Ig, immunoglobulin; IL, interleukin; TNF, tumour necrosis factor.

Reproduced with permission from Samanta, R. *et al.* Rheumatoid arthritis and anaesthesia. *Anaesthesia*, Volume 66, Issue 12, pp. 1146–1159, Copyright © 2011, The Association of Anaesthetists of Great Britain and Ireland.

The management plan should therefore be discussed with the surgeon who will be performing the operation. It is also appropriate to discuss with the surgeon and the patient's rheumatologist about the need to stop disease-modifying agents or biological therapies ahead of elective surgery.

Where general anaesthesia cannot be avoided, a plan for airway management should be devised and discussed with the patient. It is vital that this plan includes a strategy for tracheal extubation as well as induction of anaesthesia and tracheal intubation.

Conduct of anaesthesia

The main additional implication for patients with polyarthropathy is prevention of damage to diseased joints. No joint should be moved beyond the range of pain-free movement that the patient could demonstrate preoperatively. This is of course especially important for the neck where subluxation or fracture can result in cervical spinal cord damage. This may well mean that tracheal intubation should be achieved through a fibreoptic technique in the conscious patient. Once the patient is anaesthetized, a safe position of the neck must be maintained. This can be achieved with any combination of a head ring, sand bags to prevent lateral movement, and use of adhesive tape to stabilize the head in position. It should be remembered, however, that many of these patients have fragile skin which can be damaged by less than careful removal of adhesive tape. If a patient uses a cervical support collar, this should not necessarily be relied upon to maintain stability of the neck but assuming that it does not impede the surgery, it can be worn by the patient to remind theatre staff that there is a risk to the cervical spine.

Careful patient positioning is also paramount because of the generalized frailty of many of these patients. There can be thin skin with a loss of muscle mass and subcutaneous tissues, which is often compounded by chronic steroid use. There is therefore an increased risk of pressure sores and nerve compression injuries during general or regional anaesthesia. Additional padding of the vulnerable pressure points is indicated.

Venous access can be difficult because of fragility and mobility of the peripheral veins. This can be further complicated by the inability to manipulate joints of the upper limb, especially the wrist, where these are involved in the disease. Internal jugular vein cannulation can also be difficult because of inability to position the patient's head and neck optimally.

Individual polyarthropathies

Although osteoarthritis is the most prevalent polyarthropathy affecting, to a greater or lesser degree, 50% of the population aged more than 60 years of age, there are no implications for anaesthesia other than the generic implications for polyarthropathy patients described previously. I will therefore consider rheumatoid arthritis and the spondyloarthropathies.

Rheumatoid arthritis

Rheumatoid arthritis affects 1–2% of the global population. It is a chronic, symmetrical inflammatory polyarthropathy that most commonly begins in the fourth decade of life. The aetiology of rheumatoid arthritis is unclear but there is a genetic component with an association in 70% of most populations with human leucocyte antigen (HLA)-DR4. The mechanism of the disease involves inflammation and proliferation of the synovium of joints. The proliferating synovium extends over adjacent cartilage and the inflammatory mediators destroy the latter producing the arthritis. The inflammatory process also results in a release of inflammatory mediators into the circulation leading to a systemic inflammatory response. Although there are widespread immune changes, TNF-α has been highlighted as a key mediator, hence the development of drugs and biological agents acting against TNF-α.

Joint involvement in rheumatoid arthritis

The joints of the hands, feet, and wrists are most commonly affected with a typical symmetrical distribution. In the hands, classically the metacarpophalangeal joints and proximal interphalangeal joints are affected and this pattern is reproduced in the feet. As the disease progresses, the larger joints of the upper and lower limbs are affected, with the hip joints typically the last of these to produce symptoms. The cervical spine, temporomandibular joints, and cricoarytenoid joints can all be affected. The thoracic and lumber spine is usually spared.

Periarticular soft tissue involvement

Inflammatory bursitis can cause swelling but also leads to weakening of adjacent ligaments causing joint laxity. This is the mechanism of atlantoaxial subluxation where weakening of the transverse ligament of the atlas allows separation of the odontoid process from the anterior arch of the atlas and posterior movement of the odontoid on cervical spine flexion with the potential for cervical cord compression. Tenosynovitis can lead to flexion deformities and erosion and even rupture of tendons. Joint mobility can also be diminished by periarticular muscle wasting. Rheumatoid nodules are inflammatory masses that can occur anywhere including within internal organs.

Systemic manifestations

Cardiovascular system

Some degree of pericarditis is present in up to 30% of patients with rheumatoid arthritis but it is uncommon for there to be functional compromise secondary to either a large pericardial effusion or constrictive pericarditis. The myocardium is a site for rheumatoid nodules but more significant from a functional point of view is ischaemic heart disease resulting from coronary artery thrombo-atherosclerosis or from the small vessel vasculitis associated with rheumatoid arthritis. Congestive cardiac failure is more prevalent in age- and sex-matched rheumatoid arthritis patients than those not affected.

Respiratory system

Some degree of lung involvement is relatively common in rheumatoid arthritis. The commonest manifestation is pleural effusion which is much more prevalent in men than women. Fortunately, interstitial fibrosis is rare but rheumatoid arthritis seems to predispose to chronic obstructive pulmonary disease in smokers. Isolated rheumatoid nodules can be mistaken for carcinoma while the more diffuse nodular fibrosis of Caplan's syndrome is much less common than previously as a result of the decline in exposure to industrial atmospheric particulate matter.

Nervous system

Symptomatic cervical myelopathy is uncommon and is not a sensitive indicator of cervical spine and specifically atlantoaxial instability. Peripheral nerve compression syndromes such as carpal tunnel syndrome are more common in patients with rheumatoid arthritis and rarely there is a peripheral polyneuropathy. Fifteen per cent of rheumatoid arthritis patients have Sjögren's syndrome which combines rheumatoid arthritis with dry eyes and dry mouth. Scleritis may also occur.

Haematopoietic system

A normochromic, normocytic anaemia should be anticipated but this may be combined with iron deficiency secondary to occult gastrointestinal bleeding in patients taking non-steroidal anti-inflammatories or steroids themselves. Neutropenia with splenomegaly in patients with rheumatoid arthritis is known as Felty's syndrome and these patients are prone to recurrent infections. Skin pigmentation may be associated with Felty's syndrome. Active rheumatoid disease is associated with thrombophilia although thrombocytopenia may be consequent to immunosuppressive medication or rarely as part of a pancytopenia in Felty's syndrome.

Renal system

The presence of proteinuria may indicate secondary amyloidosis of the kidneys. This can be associated with nephrotic syndrome and may progress to chronic renal failure.

The spondyloarthropathies

These are a group of conditions characterized by inflammatory back pain, asymmetrical synovitis especially of the lower limbs, anterior uveitis, and absence of rheumatoid factor. There is a genetic predisposition with an association with HLA-B27. The spondyloarthropathy of principal concern to the anaesthetist is ankylosing spondylitis but there is considerable overlap with the other conditions listed in Box 80.1.

Ankylosing spondylitis

Ankylosing spondylitis occurs in approximately 1% of the population but there is a very wide clinical spectrum of disease with only a minority severely affected. It is a progressive disease of the joints principally affecting the intervertebral articulations of the spine with the sacroiliac joints the most commonly involved. Ankylosing spondylitis is characterized by calcification of the soft tissues leading to restricted movements of the spine. Other joints that can be affected include the temporomandibular joint, the cricoarytenoid joints, and articulation of the ribs, involvement of which can reduce compliance of the chest wall and therefore restrict breathing. With increasing severity, ankylosing spondylitis is more likely to be

Box 80.1 The spondyloarthropathies

- Ankylosing spondylitis
- Psoriatic arthritis
- Reiter's disease
- Acute anterior uveitis
- Seronegative juvenile chronic arthropathies
- Undifferentiated spondyloarthropathy
- Enteropathic synovitis.

associated with systemic involvement including the eye, the cardiovascular system, the lungs, and the nervous system.

Patients with ankylosis of the cervical spine are at increased risk of sustaining a cervical fracture, which can occur after even mild trauma. The combination of a rigid neck and limited mouth opening places patients severely affected by ankylosing spondylitis at high risk of being difficult patients in whom to perform tracheal intubation.

The ankylosed spine is at real risk of damage in the anaesthetized patient (Woodward and Kam 2009) and manipulation of the spine beyond the limits of pain-free awake movements should be avoided. For this reason, the gold standard for tracheal intubation in the patient with significant cervical spine ankylosis is awake fibreoptic intubation. Neuraxial regional anaesthesia may also be difficult because of the inability of the patient to flex the spine and also because of ligamentous calcification. A paramedian approach to the epidural space may be necessary.

Osteogenesis imperfecta

This is a series of conditions resulting from different gene defects affecting collagen formation. The major clinical features are fragile and brittle bones but the tendons, skin, and eyes (blue sclera) can also be affected. The most common type is osteogenesis imperfecta tarda which is a relatively mild and dominantly inherited condition with relatively mild bony deformities, blue sclera, hypermobility of the joints, and occasionally heart valve disorders. The other types of osteogenesis imperfecta are more severe with some forms being incompatible with life.

The main implication for anaesthesia is avoidance of iatrogenic fracture. There have been reports of malignant hyperthermia (MH) associated with osteogenesis imperfecta but in the great majority of cases this is a false association brought about by the observation of a perioperative pyrexia thought to be associated with inflammatory responses to tissue damage resulting from the connective tissue defect (Bojanic et al. 2011). However, the author is aware of at least one case of the coexistence of MH and osteogenesis imperfecta.

Connective tissue diseases

The connective tissue diseases encompass systemic lupus erythematosus, systemic sclerosis, and polymyositis/dermatomyositis. There is considerable overlap between the conditions which have in common vasculitis, arthralgia, immunological activation, and multisystem involvement. The features of all three conditions can occur together in mixed connective tissue disease. The anaesthetic implications of the connective tissue diseases (Ben-Menachem 2010) are related to the systemic involvement which will be described for each condition in turn.

Systemic lupus erythematosus

This is the most common connective tissue disease occurring in approximately 0.1% of the population. It is up to 10 times more common in women than men with a usual age of onset of 20–40 years. It is more prevalent in Africans and Polynesians than other races.

The most common features are small joint arthralgia and rashes with organ system involvement as follows:

- Cardiovascular system: subclinical pericarditis and pericardial effusion are common as is a myocarditis that is rarely of functional significance. Endocarditis typically involving the mitral valve is very rare although aortic valve lesions can occur more commonly.
- Respiratory system: the majority of patients with systemic lupus erythematosus experience pleurisy and pleural exudates at some stage in the course of their disease. Interstitial lung disease can also occur as an inflammatory pneumonitis although this only rarely progresses to pulmonary fibrosis.
- The nervous system: some form of nervous system involvement is seen in the majority of patients. This may manifest as psychiatric symptoms, most commonly depression, but epilepsy, cerebellar ataxia, stroke, and aseptic meningitis have all been reported.
- The renal system: proteinuria is common and may progress to glomerulonephritis as a result of immune complex deposition. The renal disease may progress to nephrotic syndrome or chronic renal failure either of which can be accompanied by hypertension.

Systemic sclerosis

Systemic sclerosis is rarer than systemic lupus erythematosus and is characterized by involvement of the skin and Raynaud's disease (Muangchan et al. 2013). Again it has a female preponderance and usually appears before 50 years of age. Sclerosis of the skin commonly affects the fingers and the skin around the mouth, making mouth opening difficult. The changes in the hands can be accompanied by oedema and soft tissue swelling, making venous access in the dorsum of the hands difficult or even impossible. Areas of calcinosis can be acutely tender.

- Gastrointestinal system: reduced distal oesophageal peristalsis and lower oesophageal sphincter tone is almost invariable and should be assumed even in the absence of symptoms. Manoeuvres to protect the airway from aspiration of regurgitated gastric contents should be used but it should be noted that myopathy or myositis are relatively common and these predispose to succinylcholine (suxamethonium)-induced rhabdomyolysis.
- Cardiovascular system: myocardial fibrosis can occur predisposing to arrhythmias and conduction defects. Pericardial involvement with pericardial effusion is also recognized.
- Respiratory system: pulmonary fibrosis tends to be confined to the lower lobes but a restrictive deficit can be sometimes found with pulmonary function testing.
- The renal system: chronic renal failure can result from renal vessel endarteritis. The associated hypertension can be difficult to manage.

CREST syndrome is a variant of systemic sclerosis where calcinosis is a prominent feature but is accompanied by Raynaud's disease, oesophageal involvement, sclerodactyly, and telangiectasia.

Polymyositis/dermatomyositis

Polymyositis is characterized by muscle weakness and muscle wasting of the proximal muscles of the shoulder and pelvic girdles caused by vasculitic necrosis of muscle fibres with inflammation and regeneration. It can occur at any age but like the other connective tissue disorders is more common in females than males.

The onset may be acute with rhabdomyolysis. Succinylcholine should be avoided during active disease as it may induce or exacerbate rhabdomyolysis. The activity of the disease can be assessed using serum creatine kinase concentration.

Dermatomyositis refers to polymyositis accompanied by a rash.

Treatment of connection tissue disorders

The mainstay of treatment for acute phases of systemic lupus erythematosus and polymyositis/dermatomyositis are corticosteroids. Where remission of the disease is relatively slow, maintenance therapy with other immunosuppressant drugs may be indicated. There are no effective treatments in terms of slowing the progress of systemic sclerosis.

Muscle diseases

Skeletal muscle typically constitutes 40% of body mass and therefore any generalized skeletal muscle disorder can have systemic effects. Many muscle diseases, however, affect some muscle groups more than others, while there may also be myocardial muscle involvement. The implications for anaesthesia in generic terms are as follows:

1. Involvement of bulbar muscles. Bulbar muscle integrity is important for airway maintenance and airway protection. Patients with bulbar muscle involvement are at risk of recurrent episodes of pneumonia and will have reduced protection from regurgitated stomach contents, upper airway secretions, blood, and debris from upper airway surgery. Bulbar muscle weakness should be anticipated to be compounded by the effects of anaesthesia and airway protection should be maintained until the patient is fully awake.
2. Respiratory muscle involvement. Fortunately the diaphragm seems to be spared from the majority of muscle diseases but the accessory muscles are more commonly involved. In these patients, neuromuscular blocking drugs should be used most judiciously and complete reversal of their effects ensured. This is a scenario where the use of sugammadex after neuromuscular block with rocuronium or vecuronium is highly recommended when neuromuscular block is required. Respiratory function may also be compromised by kyphoscoliosis which is common in patients with muscle diseases. Kyphoscoliosis tends to be particularly severe in patients confined to a wheelchair. Problems should be anticipated after general anaesthesia with a patient having a preoperative forced vital capacity of less than 1.5 litres. Such patients may also be compromised by brachial plexus regional anaesthesia using the interscalene or supraclavicular approaches, where there is a high incidence of phrenic nerve paralysis by the local anaesthetic.
3. Risk of rhabdomyolysis. Instability of skeletal muscle membranes is associated with an increased risk of rhabdomyolysis from any known cause. A list of factors that can trigger rhabdomyolysis is given in Box 80.2. Suxamethonium should be avoided in any patient with primary or secondary myopathy.
4. Cardiac involvement. Depending on the myopathy, cardiac involvement may be manifest as a cardiomyopathy, conduction defects, or arrhythmias.
5. Risk of MH. Over the last 50 years the medical literature includes suggestions for virtually every neuromuscular condition to be associated with an increased risk of MH. Most of these associations are spurious and reflect the lack of specificity of the individual features of MH. MH is strictly defined as a progressive life-threatening hyperthermic and hypermetabolic reaction to general anaesthetic agents. Using this strict definition enables association with MH to be confined to a subset of myopathies that share genetic defects with MH susceptibility.
6. Myotonia. This results from failure of muscle relaxation after normal muscle activation. Depending on the cause of the myotonia, symptoms may be activated either by inactivity or excessive muscle activity. A common precipitating factor is cold which is a risk in the perioperative period unless preventative measures are implemented. Surgical handling of muscle tissue or surgical diathermy may also precipitate myotonia. The defect in the myotonias is distal to the neuromuscular junction and myotonia can therefore occur in a patient having surgery under regional anaesthesia or under general anaesthesia with neuromuscular block. Suxamethonium may produce sustained and generalized myotonia in an undiagnosed patient. Intravenous lidocaine and phenytoin have been proposed as treatments because of their inhibition of skeletal muscle membrane sodium channels. Volatile anaesthetics tend to reduce myotonia rather than increase it and there are theoretical reasons to anticipate that dantrolene may be beneficial.

Box 80.2 Causes of rhabdomyolysis

- Muscle ischaemia
- Crush injury
- Intense muscle activity
- Metabolic derangement
- Extremes of temperature
- Infection
- Drug toxicity or idiosyncrasy
- Poisoning (classically with hemlock)
- Envenomation
- Myopathies: structural, metabolic, and inflammatory.

Preoperative considerations for patients with muscular diseases

The most important task for the anaesthetist is to establish an accurate diagnosis for the muscle disease. Definitive diagnosis is nowadays invariably achieved through genetic testing and this has revealed considerable overlap in clinical and histopathological findings between disorders that were once considered to be clinically and histologically distinct. This is particularly the case in babies and infants presenting as floppy infants or with delayed motor milestones who often have only non-specific features on histopathology. It is entirely appropriate therefore for the anaesthetist to insist on molecular genetic investigation where this has not been undertaken before elective surgery.

Once the correct diagnosis is established, then the possibility of bulbar muscle, respiratory muscle, and cardiac involvement can be established. Physical examination can determine the extent of bulbar muscle involvement through assessment of the gag reflex, and respiratory excursion through clinical and formal respiratory function tests. Assessment of cardiorespiratory reserve is rarely possible because of the limitations on exercise imposed by the skeletal muscle defect. Echocardiography is therefore indicated in patients with muscle diseases associated with cardiomyopathy.

Throughout the perioperative period it is important to maintain hydration, electrolyte balance, body temperature, and metabolic substrate provision. This applies to all muscle diseases and reflects the inter-relationship between membrane potential, calcium release and sequestration, and the balance between mitochondrial oxidative phosphorylation and regulation of reactive oxygen species. Throughout the preoperative period, the patient with muscle disease (other than those identified in later sections of this chapter) should therefore receive intravenous hydration and glucose provision while external body warming using warm air convection blankets should be instituted on the preoperative ward and continued during transfer to the operating theatre department.

The muscular dystrophies

The muscular dystrophies are characterized by instability of the skeletal muscle plasma membrane (sarcolemma) resulting from defects in one of the structural proteins forming the proteoglycan scaffold of the muscle fibres (Fig. 80.2). Membrane instability produces a loss of integrity of the sarcolemma, muscle cell necrosis, loss of muscle tissue, and infiltration with fibroblasts and fatty tissue to produce fibrotic, fatty tissue. The clinical features of the various dystrophies depend on the gene involved and, in some cases, the specific defect in the gene. The most severe dystrophies can be lethal at birth or in infancy but all are progressive. The rate of progression is another highly variable feature between the different dystrophies.

Duchenne muscular dystrophy

Duchenne muscular dystrophy (DMD) is one of the commonest sex-linked genetic disorders affecting approximately 1:3500 live male births. The gene affected, and the protein it encodes, are both known as dystrophin, with the gene located on the short arm of the X chromosome (Xp21). DMD results from a complete lack of expression of the dystrophin protein that normally links the cytoplasmic actin scaffold to β-dystroglycan of the transmembrane proteoglycan complex. Dystrophin is normally expressed in skeletal, cardiac, and smooth muscle.

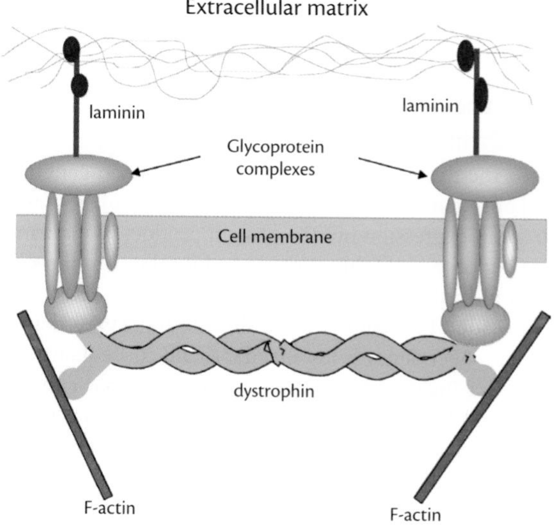

Figure 80.2 The proteoglycan scaffold of striated muscles.

Skeletal muscle involvement is responsible for the presenting features of rapidly progressive muscle weakness. Symptoms typically become apparent in the third year of life, with proximal limb muscle, neck, and abdominal muscle weakness the most obvious feature along with pseudohypertrophy of the calf muscles. Muscle weakness progresses, becoming more generalized until use of a wheelchair is required from the early teenage years. Confinement to a wheelchair is associated with kyphoscoliosis, fixed joint contractures, obesity, impaired circulation to the lower limbs with dependent oedema, and psychological problems. From the second decade, these boys are prone to frequent chest infections as a result of impaired ventilatory effort. Death, as a result of pneumonia, respiratory failure, or cardiac disease, is usual in the third or fourth decades.

Classical symptoms of heart failure are deceivingly uncommon because of the enforced sedentary existence but echocardiography highlights the prevalence of myocardial dysfunction (Goldberg et al. 1982). Symptoms that do occur tend to be vague and include fatigue, inability to concentrate, irritability, sleep disturbance, nausea, loss of appetite and weight loss. Dyspnoea may be the presenting feature of myocardial deterioration but may also represent progression of respiratory muscle weakness or its resulting pulmonary complications. The principal pathological process in DMD cardiomyopathy is fibrosis commencing posteriorly with apically directed circumferential spread. As the myocardial disease progresses, a dilated cardiomyopathy can evolve with mitral regurgitation. Regular echocardiography is recommended from the age of 6 years, initially every 2 years but then annually. If severe, kyphoscoliosis can present technical challenges in obtaining high-quality echocardiographic images such that the ejection fraction can only be estimated visually rather than calculated. The echocardiographic incidence of reduced ejection fraction therefore may underestimate the true incidence. Magnetic resonance imaging is becoming a valuable tool with late gadolinium enhancement a sensitive indicator of myocardial fibrosis (Romfh and McNally 2010). Patients with DMD often have a relatively low blood pressure with reduced vascular tone resulting from smooth muscle involvement compounding the effects of the cardiomyopathy.

There have been significant improvements in life expectancy of patients with DMD over the past 25 years. Treatment with corticosteroids invariably is commenced soon after diagnosis. Non-invasive nocturnal ventilatory support (BiPAP or CPAP) and treatment of myocardial dysfunction (angiotensin-converting enzyme inhibitors or angiotensin II receptor antagonists plus β-blockade if tolerated) have each been demonstrated to independently reduce symptoms and prolong life. When the left ventricular ejection fraction decreases below 35% despite maximal medical therapy, an implantable cardioverter-defibrillator device may be considered: cardiac transplant has been used successfully in DMD.

There is a large historical experience of anaesthesia for diagnostic muscle biopsy in boys with DMD, before the introduction of genetic diagnosis in the 1990s. Orthopaedic procedures for releasing fixed joint contractures to improve the duration of mobility are now the most prevalent indication for anaesthesia in patients with DMD.

Anaesthetic problems are related to myocardial involvement, respiratory function, and the effects of drugs on the diseased skeletal muscles (Sethna et al. 1988). A thorough preoperative evaluation is essential, specifically assessment of cardiorespiratory function. Discussion with the child's neurologist and cardiologist can be invaluable. An echocardiograph should be requested unless one has been done within the previous 12 months (25% of 6-year-olds with DMD have evidence of myocardial dysfunction) or if there is onset or deterioration of symptoms since the last echocardiograph.

There is controversy over the choice of general anaesthetic technique for patients with a sex-linked dystrophy, specifically the use of potent inhalation anaesthetics. Concern about these agents stems principally from reports of profound rhabdomyolysis occurring during anaesthesia or in the postoperative period, including several cases of hyperkalaemic cardiac arrest and death. There are also isolated reports of tachycardia, hypercarbia, and raised temperature. These latter features are seen in MH where they are progressive and life-threatening, which does not appear to be the case in the reports in dystrophic patients. However, the pathophysiological process in the dystrophic patients may involve leak of Ca^{2+} from the sarcoplasmic reticulum, as occurs in MH, but through an indirect mechanism (nitrosylation of the Ca^{2+} release channel secondary to a chronic increase in cytoplasmic Ca^{2+} concentration) rather than primary genetic defects as seen in MH.

Marked sarcoplasmic reticulum Ca^{2+} release by potent inhalation anaesthetics is unlikely to be implicated in the cases of profound rhabdomyolysis, however, because such a mechanism would be associated with a substantial hypermetabolic reaction (as in MH), which is not a feature of the cases reported (e.g. Poole et al. 2010). This does not exclude the potent inhalation anaesthetics being implicated in rhabdomyolysis but it is worth considering other mechanisms. Rhabdomyolysis, with loss of large intracellular proteins such as myoglobin and creatine kinase, involves significant loss of integrity of the sarcolemma. In healthy muscle this occurs through natural cell turnover or from the mechanical stresses on the sarcolemma imposed by contractile activity, which causes microscopic tears in the sarcolemma (McNeil and Khakee 1992; McNeil and Steinhardt 2003). These tears are normally repaired within 1 min (Bansal et al. 2003) by energy-dependent mechanisms (Warren et al. 2002). With defects in metabolic capacity, such as in a variety of metabolic myopathies, rhabdomyolysis can occur with increased demand for muscle repair with exercise, or when energy substrates are lacking as in fasting (Warren et al. 2002).

Episodes of spontaneous acute rhabdomyolysis have been reported in dystrophic patients (Doriguzzi et al. 1993) and the increased susceptibility to mechanically induced damage (Petrof et al. 1993) inevitably predisposes DMD patients to any of the reported triggers of rhabdomyolysis (Warren et al. 2002). Of these, the most likely to have a potential role in the perioperative period include excessive muscle activity (agitated or physically struggling child, drug-induced rigidity), impaired metabolic repair (hypoxia, ischaemia, acidosis, reduced oxidative phosphorylation capacity), or direct membrane toxicity (drugs, reactive oxygen species). It may be relevant that muscle from a mouse model of DMD has a markedly impaired mitochondrial metabolic capacity (Kuznetsov et al. 1998). In a similar way to patients with metabolic myopathies, fasted dystrophic patients may thus be at increased risk of developing rhabdomyolysis and may therefore benefit from an intravenous dextrose infusion during perioperative fasting.

Choice of anaesthetic technique in patients with DMD

For older children and adults, peripheral regional anaesthesia is preferred for appropriate surgical procedures. Neuraxial regional anaesthesia may be poorly tolerated by patients with cardiomyopathy because of reduced preload and afterload caused by peripheral vasodilation. When general anaesthesia is necessary, there is no 'ideal' anaesthetic. Propofol and ketamine have been associated with rhabdomyolysis (Warren et al. 2002) and, along with etomidate, can be associated with an increase in muscle tone. Propofol infusion syndrome, which can cause profound rhabdomyolysis, is postulated to result from disruption of mitochondrial fatty acid oxidation (Vasile et al. 2003). As there is reduced mitochondrial oxidative capacity in muscular dystrophies (Kuznetsov et al. 1998), propofol infusions pose at least a theoretical risk. NSAIDs can cause rhabdomyolysis in healthy patients (Delrio et al. 1996) and were used preoperatively in two cases of perioperative rhabdomyolysis in Becker dystrophy (Hopkins 2010).

The unwelcome possibility of rhabdomyolysis, a life-threatening but rare complication in DMD, should not override other considerations when planning general anaesthesia for patients with DMD, as attempting to eliminate this risk may expose the patient to more likely complications, such as those related to airway management or the underlying cardiorespiratory dysfunction (Hopkins 2010). If, in the anaesthetist's judgement, the overall risks of potent inhalation agents or other drugs that might contribute to acute rhabdomyolysis indicate their use, the risk of rhabdomyolysis should be accepted and the patient monitored appropriately (for evidence of hyperkalaemia). If a patient develops signs of increased CO_2 production during inhalation anaesthesia, it would be prudent, after excluding inadequate anaesthesia or analgesia (or both), to switch to an alternative maintenance anaesthetic technique, such as remifentanil with midazolam.

Neuromuscular blocking agents are often unnecessary in patients with DMD because of the inherent lack of muscle tone. Suxamethonium is absolutely contraindicated because of the risk of acute rhabdomyolysis and hyperkalaemic cardiac arrest. If non-depolarizing neuromuscular blocking agents are used, it is essential to ensure their complete reversal at the end of the procedure: this is a good indication to use rocuronium or vecuronium as the neuromuscular blocking drug so that sugammadex can be used as the reversal agent.

Becker muscular dystrophy

Becker muscular dystrophy (BMD), like DMD, is caused by defects in the dystrophin gene and is a sex-linked genetic disorder. Becker mutations are not as severe as those in DMD and there is dystrophin expression but the protein product is abnormal. The clinical phenotype is highly variable and is related to the nature of the dystrophin defect. The myopathy is typically detected in the second decade of life and is more slowly progressive than DMD. Wheelchair dependency is not inevitable and consequently there is a much lower incidence of kyphoscoliosis and fixed contractures. Depending on the genetic defect there can be a marked difference in the relative effects on cardiac *vs* skeletal muscle. In some patients the cardiomyopathy is the presenting feature.

The principles of anaesthetic management for a patient with BMD are similar to those for patients with DMD. There are cases of hyperkalaemic cardiac arrest in BMD patients who have received potent inhalation anaesthetics but no suxamethonium. Indeed, it may be that the risk of rhabdomyolysis is higher in BMD than DMD depending on the prevailing activity of necrosis and repair. The serum creatine kinase concentration will provide an indication of these processes and therefore the risk of rhabdomyolysis, whatever the cause (see earlier).

Female carriers of dystrophin gene defects

These women have one normal allele for the dystrophin gene which produces sufficient functioning protein for there to be no overt myopathy. There may, however, be some increased muscle cell turnover with a concomitant increase in basal creatine kinase concentration and consequently increased risk of rhabdomyolysis secondary to, for example, suxamethonium. Dystrophinopathy carrier status may also be associated with an increased incidence of heart failure in the elderly.

Other muscular dystrophies

These are usually less severe than the X-linked dystrophies and the distribution of muscle weakness and wasting is apparent from the name of the disease, although other muscle groups may become involved with disease progression. I will outline those dystrophies with particular anaesthetic implications.

- Oculopharyngeal dystrophy: this condition is characterized by dysphagia and progressive ptosis beginning in later life (fourth to the seventh decade). It is inherited in an autosomal dominant manner and is caused by a mutation in the gene encoding poly(A)-binding protein-2 (*PABPN1*) on chromosome 14q11. Bulbar muscle involvement increases the risk of pulmonary aspiration.
- Facioscapulohumeral dystrophy: this is the third most prevalent hereditary muscle disease, after DMD and myotonic dystrophy. It results from a chromosomal rearrangement within the subtelomeric region of chromosome 4q. Clinical onset and severity are variable. It is usually diagnosed in late childhood or adolescence. As the name implies, there is facial weakness but with sparing of bulbar and extraocular muscles. The scapulae, foot dorsiflexors, and hip girdle are also affected, but the respiratory muscles are not.
- Humeroperoneal (Emery–Dreifuss) dystrophy: this exists in an X-linked (mutations in the gene encoding emerin) and an autosomal dominant (mutations in the lamin A/C gene) form. Early contractures involve the posterior cervical muscles. A predictable feature is atrioventricular block that predisposes to recurrent episodes of syncope and embolic disease.

Congenital myopathies

The congenital myopathies are a heterogeneous group of rare primary muscle diseases characterized by weakness. The severity of the different conditions covers a spectrum from death in early infancy to non-progressive weakness that is not recognized as abnormal by the patient, their parents, or their primary care physicians and which therefore goes undiagnosed. Within some of the individual myopathies there can be a range of severity of symptoms and their rate of progression. The congenital myopathies are characterized by distinct morphological features and sub-classified, where relevant, by the predominant clinical features.

Central core disease

Central core disease (CCD) derives its name from the histological features of central demarcated areas (cores) extending the length of type 1 muscle fibres that do not take up stains for oxidative enzymes (Fig. 80.3). Common early clinical features are floppy infant syndrome and delayed motor milestones. Sometimes the condition presents later in childhood with weakness and generalized muscle hypotonia. Secondary skeletal abnormalities such as club foot, scoliosis, or hip dysplasia may be the presenting clinical feature. There is no bulbar muscle or diaphragmatic weakness. Beyond childhood, CCD is typically non-progressive and indeed functional improvement occurs to the extent that many affected adults consider themselves to be asymptomatic. Some, however, have a severe disability with wheelchair dependence.

CCD is usually inherited in an autosomal dominant pattern and at least 90% of cases are associated with defects in the *RYR1* (ryanodine receptor type 1) gene that is also implicated in the majority of patients with MH. Some patients with CCD give a history of MH under anaesthesia and have abnormal *in vitro* contracture tests for MH susceptibility (see Chapter 22) but other CCD patients have no adverse anaesthetic history and normal responses to the *in vitro* contracture tests (Halsall et al. 1996). This is explained by the functional characterization of CCD-associated *RYR1* mutations

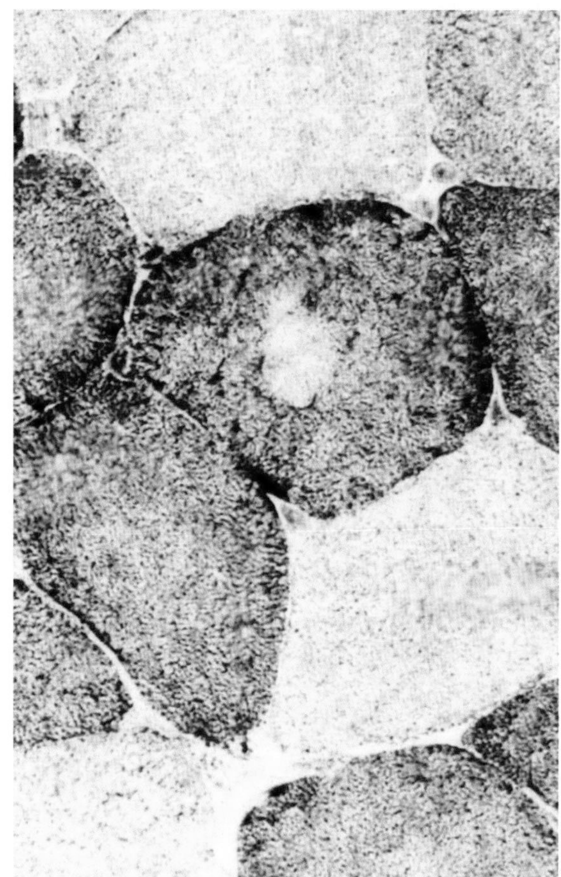

Figure 80.3 Histology of central core disease: muscle fibres containing unstructured cores and no mitochondria (NADH reductase staining).
Reproduced with permission from Klingler, W, Rueffert H, Lehmann-Horn F, Girard T, Hopkins PM. Core myopathies and the risk of malignant hyperthermia. *Anesthesia and Analgesia*, Volume 109, Issue 4, pp. 1167–73, Copyright © 2009 International Anesthesia Research Society.

into either loss of function mutations (not associated with MH susceptibility) or gain-of-function mutations (associated with MH susceptibility) (Dirksen and Avila 2004). CCD patients with *RYR1* mutations that have not been functionally characterized should be assumed to be at risk of developing MH under anaesthesia unless their mutation has been associated with a negative *in vitro* contracture test.

Multiminicore disease

Multiminicore disease (MmD) is characterized histologically by multiple cores lacking oxidative enzyme activity that are less clearly defined than the single cores found in CCD. MmD is recessively inherited with a pattern of weakness that differs from CCD. Severe axial involvement is a common feature, with respiratory, bulbar, and extraocular muscles also commonly affected. There are four clinical subtypes of MmD and these have different genetic aetiologies (Klingler et al. 2009). The moderate form of MmD with hand involvement is usually associated with *RYR1* variants but the most prevalent, or classical, form is associated with mutations in the selenoprotein N gene (*SEPN1*). There are no convincing reports of MH associated with MmD but caution should be exercised where *RYR1* variants are implicated until they have been functionally characterized or if the patient has had a normal *in vitro* contracture test (Table 80.5).

Nemaline rod myopathy

Nemaline rod myopathy derives its name from clusters of dense rod-shaped cytoplasmic inclusions. In 10% of cases there are also intranuclear inclusions. There is marked genetic and clinical heterogeneity with six clinical forms and five associated genes (Table 80.6) The majority of cases result from *de novo* mutations in the nebulin (*NEB*) gene but recessive and dominant forms occur. Most commonly, nemaline rod myopathy presents with feeding difficulties and hypotonia in infancy with proximal muscle weakness. Weakness may also affect the distal limb, neck flexor, and trunk (including intercostal) muscles. Dysmorphic features are common and include narrow, high-arched palate and micrognathia or marked prognathism. Other skeletal malformations include kyphoscoliosis, hand contractures, pes cavus, and talipes equinovarus. Nemaline rod myopathy is not associated with MH.

Table 80.5 Core myopathies and genes associated with the diseases and estimated risk of malignant hyperthermia (MH) (given there is no particular MH history in family)

Disease	Gene	MH risk
Central core disease	*RYR1*	High*
Multiminicore disease	*SEPN1*	Low
	ACTA1	Low
	RYR1	High*
Nemaline rod myopathy	*NEB, TPM3, TNNT1, TPM2, ACTA1*	Low

* Dependent on the underlying mutation; to be on the safe side, risk to be considered high until more information becomes available. Abbreviations for myopathies and genes encoding the channels: *RYR1* = Ryanodine receptor Type 1, *SEPN1* = selenoprotein N, *ACTA1* = alpha-actin, *NEB* = Nebulin, *TPM3* = Tropomyosin 3, *TNNT1* = troponin T1, *TPM2* = beta-tropomyosin. The table summarizes molecular genetic knowledge, i.e. involved genes, of the different core myopathies. Emphasis should be on the underlying molecular pathology rather than phenotypic presentation. In patients where the genes associated with MH (*RYR1* and the alpha-1 subunit of the dihydropyridine receptor, *CACNA1S*) are involved, a non-triggering anaesthesia technique is to be chosen.

Type 1 fibre hypotrophy with central nuclei

Also known as centronuclear or myotubular myopathy. It covers a wide range of clinical presentations from a fatal congenital form to a slowly progressive late-onset form. The predominant clinical feature is weakness.

The skeletal muscle membrane ion channelopathies

Chapter 7 described the physiology of muscle contraction with the generation of the muscle action potential dependent on activation followed by inactivation of voltage-gated Na^+ channels, activation of voltage-gated K^+ channels, and restoration of the resting membrane potential by activation of Cl^- channels. The action potential is sensed as it spreads into the T-tubules by $Ca_V1.1$ which couples with the sarcoplasmic reticulum Ca^{2+} release channel, RyR1. Skeletal muscle membrane ion channelopathies have been described in association with defects in the sodium, chloride, and calcium channels.

The two main features of the ion channelopathies are muscle weakness and myotonia. Myotonia describes delayed relaxation of muscles after contraction but mechanistically results from repetitive firing of action potentials. Patients with myotonia commonly describe their symptoms to improve with repeated activity or warmth and to be exacerbated by cold. Myotonia can be induced

Table 80.6 Tabular list of myotonias, genes encoding associated channels and estimated risk of malignant hyperthermia (MH) (in the absence of a family history of MH)

Disease	Gene	MH risk
Chloride channelopathies Myotonia congenita, Becker, or Thomsen	*CLCN1*	Low
Sodium channelopathies HyperPP, paramyotonia congenita, PAM, HypoPP-2	*SCN4A*	Low
Calcium channelopathies HypoPP-1	*CACNA1S*	Unclear
Myotonic dystrophy, type 1 (DM1, Steinert's disease)	Expanded trinucleotide repeat, CTG, 3′ untranslated region of *DMPK* gene	Low
Myotonic dystrophy, type 2	Tetranucleotide repeat, CCTG, of 1st intron, *ZNF9* gene	Low

The table summarizes the known molecular genetics of the different myotonias and estimation of associated risk of MH. Estimation of risk of MH emphasizes the underlying molecular pathology rather than phenotypic presentation. PAM, potassium-aggravated myotonias; HyperPP, hyperkalaemic periodic paralysis; HypoPP, hypokalaemic periodic paralysis; *CLCN1*, skeletal muscle chloride channel; *SCN4A*, sodium channel, α-subunit; *CACNA1S*, α_1-subunit of L-type, voltage-dependent calcium channel; MH, malignant hyperthermia.

by mechanical stimulation of the muscles, including during surgery which may be a life-threatening complication if it affects the laryngeal or respiratory muscles. As the causative molecular defect lies distal to the neuromuscular junction, myotonia cannot be treated using neuromuscular blocking drugs or by local anaesthetic nerve conduction block. Prevention is best achieved by maintaining normothermia and careful handling of the patient. If sustained myotonia does occur, treatment is aimed at reducing action potential firing with Na^+ channel blocking drugs such as lidocaine (1 mg kg^{-1} intravenously) or phenytoin. If these are not sufficiently effective, it may be worth trying dantrolene which theoretically will reduce the muscle rigidity.

Although muscle rigidity occurs in patients susceptible to MH when they are given suxamethonium and in the later stages of a MH reaction, most patients with myotonic disorders are not at increased risk of developing MH. The possible exception is patients with hypokalaemic periodic paralysis where the cause is a mutation in the *CACNA1S* gene (Lambert et al. 1994). This gene is also implicated in approximately 1% of MH cases. Until there is a complete understanding of the pathophysiological mechanisms of hypokalaemic periodic paralysis and MH it would be prudent to treat patients with hypokalaemic periodic paralysis having *CACNA1S* gene mutations as at risk of developing MH unless they have been shown not to be at risk by muscle biopsy and *in vitro* contracture tests (see Chapter 22).

Myotonic dystrophy (dystrophia atrophica)

Although I have included this condition, which is the second most common inherited muscle disease with the ion channelopathies, the primary genetic defect does not involve a gene encoding an ion channel. Indeed, genetic characterization has identified two subtypes with the most common (type 1 or Steinert's disease) resulting from an expanded trinucleotide repeat in the 3' untranslated region of the myotonic dystrophy protein kinase gene located on chromosome 19. The less common type 2 myotonic dystrophy is caused by a tetranucleotide repeat in the zinc finger protein 9 gene. The multisystem disease, which involves the eyes (cataracts), hair (frontal baldness), bones (skull thickening), endocrine and metabolic function (hypogonadism, insulin resistance), immune system, cognitive function (reduced intelligence and somnolence), and skeletal, cardiac, and smooth muscle, results from interference of expression of multiple genes by the bulk of the mRNA from the expanded genes within the nucleus. The skeletal muscle involvement is a consequence of altered splicing of the Cl^- channel gene resulting in expression of its embryonic form. Muscle weakness, predominantly of the facial, oropharyngeal, and distal limb muscles, is invariably the major symptom; myotonia becomes less apparent as the dystrophy progresses but is relatively mild even in the early stages of the disease. Heart muscle involvement leads to dysrhythmias or conduction defects (or both) in about 60% of cases and is progressive.

As with any myopathy, the key to reducing the risk of anaesthesia for patients with myotonic dystrophy is to make the diagnosis preoperatively. Previously undiagnosed patients can present for surgery because disease expression varies considerably, even between members of the same family. If a patient does present with any features of myotonic dystrophy, the anaesthetist should elicit a detailed family history and seek a neurological opinion if indicated.

Local and regional anaesthetic techniques overcome many of the potential problems of general anaesthesia in patients with myotonic dystrophy but not myotonia. If general anaesthesia is necessary, short-acting drugs should be used where possible. Aspiration pneumonia is a risk because of oesophageal dilation caused by smooth muscle involvement, bulbar muscle weakness, and, in the postoperative setting, by prolonged somnolence after the use of thiopental (Aldridge 1985; Pollard and Young 1989). Prompt postoperative awakening has been reported after induction with propofol (Pollard and Young 1989) and after a 4 h propofol infusion (White and Smyth 1989). Neuromuscular blocking drugs may not be required but if they are, reduced doses can be sufficient. Muscle depolarization can provoke myotonia and therefore suxamethonium and, at least theoretically, neostigmine should be avoided. The use of steroidal neuromuscular blocking drugs enabling reversal with sugammadex is a logical choice in patients with myotonic dystrophy. Respiratory muscle weakness may lead to retention of sputum and persistent atelectasis in the postoperative period, increasing the risk of chest infection. Hypercapnia may contribute to postoperative somnolence.

Chloride channelopathies

Myotonia congenita

This rare condition is usually inherited in an autosomal dominant manner (Thomsen's disease) and is characterized by diffuse muscle hypertrophy and generalized myotonia. The myotonia, which may present as muscle cramps or stiffness, is provoked by cold or inactivity. Marked muscle hypertrophy may cause ischaemic damage within a limited fascial compartment and intermittent claudication. In the rarer autosomal recessive variety (Becker) muscle weakness may be apparent but is usually confined to the limbs. The disorder does not affect the heart or other tissues.

Sodium channelopathies

These conditions are caused by mutations in *SCN4A*, the gene encoding the skeletal muscle membrane sodium channel, $Na_v1.4$.

Paramyotonia congenita

In this autosomal dominant condition, generalized myotonia develops in response to cold, vigorous exercise (in contrast to myotonia congenita, where muscle stiffness usually improves with exercise), and in some cases to hyperkalaemia. Indeed there is considerable overlap between paramyotonia congenita and hyperkalaemic periodic paralysis (see later). The myotonia may be followed by a prolonged flaccid paresis. As with myotonia congenita, there is no involvement of other body systems.

Hyperkalaemic periodic paralysis

The predominant symptom is episodic weakness associated with an increase in the serum potassium concentration (although not necessarily above the upper limit of normal). In some cases there are also myotonic symptoms which may occur at any time, or be limited to the period preceding or during an episode of weakness. In addition to the same precipitating factors as paramyotonia congenita, an attack of hyperkalaemic periodic paralysis can be induced by fasting, sleep, and anaesthesia. Anaesthetic considerations include the administration of intravenous glucose (with no potassium!) during fasting, general measures for myotonic disorders (careful handling of muscles, and avoidance of suxamethonium, neostigmine and cold), and monitoring of the serum potassium concentration. An attack can be treated with intravenous glucose and insulin.

Potassium-aggravated myotonias

There are three clinical entities characterized by myotonia, or worsening myotonia after ingestion of potassium, or after exercise but not exacerbated by cold. The name of each condition—myotonia fluctuans, myotonia permanens, and acetazolamide-responsive myotonia—describe their distinguishing features. Muscle rigidity and rhabdomyolysis can occur during surgery. The features of myotonia fluctuans can be so subtle that the patient considers their symptoms to be normal.

Calcium channelopathies

Hypokalaemic periodic paralysis

This condition is characterized by intermittent episodes of muscle weakness that are associated with a low serum potassium concentration. The attacks vary between and within individuals in their severity, frequency and duration. The mechanism whereby mutations in *CACNA1S*, the gene encoding the skeletal muscle calcium channel/voltage sensor, $Ca_V1.1$, lead to hypokalaemia is not understood. A minority of cases are associated with mutations in *SCN4A* rather than *CACNA1S*. A severe attack may leave the patient unable to move their limbs but their respiratory function is maintained. Bulbar and extraocular muscles are also minimally affected. Some attacks appear to have no obvious trigger but exercise, excessive carbohydrate intake, stress, trauma, and cold are recognized precipitating factors. In the perioperative setting it is impossible to avoid the trauma of surgery but attempts to limit psychological stress and the neuroendocrine stress response should be made. Active warming to maintain normothermia should be begun preoperatively, maintained during transfer to the operating theatre department, and continued until the patient returns to the postoperative ward. An infusion of potassium chloride should be titrated against frequent monitoring of the serum potassium concentration. Hypokalaemic periodic paralysis is an exception among muscle diseases in that an intravenous glucose infusion during fasting may be detrimental.

There is an acquired form of hypokalaemic periodic paralysis. It is a recognized but rare complication of thyrotoxicosis and renal or gastrointestinal conditions associated with potassium wasting.

Metabolic muscle diseases

The glycogenoses

Alternatively called glycogen storage diseases, these inherited disorders of defective glycogen or glucose metabolism (or both) collectively affect 1:20 000–1:40 000 live births. The liver and skeletal muscles are the principal tissues involved. Muscle symptoms predominate in McArdle's disease (type V), Tarui's disease (type VII), and Pompe's disease (type II).

McArdle's disease

McArdle's disease is caused by a deficiency of muscle glycogen phosphorylase with the consequent inability to utilize stored muscle glycogen. The metabolic substrate demands of the muscle are therefore dependant on the availability and uptake of glucose and fatty acids. Patients with McArdle's disease are prone to rhabdomyolysis when there is an imbalance between energy requirements and the supply of substrate. Conditions associated with increased metabolic demands, such as exercise, or reduced supply of substrate, such as fasting or ischaemia, are associated with muscle cramps or pain and myoglobinaemia can be severe enough to precipitate occlusive acute kidney injury. Before surgery, an intravenous infusion of glucose should be commenced and maintained throughout the perioperative period until oral intake is tolerated. During surgery on the limbs, tourniquets should not be used. Should rhabdomyolysis and myoglobinuria occur, renal injury may be prevented by establishing an alkaline diuresis.

Tarui's disease

Muscle phosphofructokinase deficiency produces a condition with similar clinical features to McArdle's disease. In this case, however, glucose is not utilized as the enzyme defect lies distal to the entry of glucose in the glycolytic pathway. An intravenous fatty acid solution should be infused during periods of starvation.

Pompe's disease

Pompe's disease is caused by a deficiency in acid maltase. There is an infantile variety where all tissues are affected leading to accumulation of glycogen, with death from cardiac failure usually before the age of 2 years. In the adult variety, the condition only affects the skeletal muscles to cause weakness, ultimately involving the respiratory muscles.

Disorders of muscle lipid metabolism

Sustained muscle activity exhausts glycogen stores and becomes dependent on the oxidation of fatty acids by the mitochondria. The uptake of long-chain fatty acids by the mitochondria utilizes carnitine as a carrier. Muscle cells cannot synthesize carnitine (it is produced in the liver) and are dependent on active uptake from the plasma.

Carnitine deficiency

Systemic primary carnitine deficiency is as a result of defective renal tubular reuptake. The condition is characterized by either a cardiomyopathy or by hypoglycaemia. Muscle weakness may accompany either of the main clinical presentations. An infusion of glucose should be maintained during perioperative fasting in order to prevent a potentially fatal acidosis.

Myopathic carnitine deficiency is caused by defective muscle uptake. It usually presents in childhood with proximal muscle weakness. A fatal cardiomyopathy may also occur.

Carnitine palmitoyl transferase II deficiency

Carnitine palmitoyl transferase II (CPT-II) is an enzyme found on the inner mitochondrial membrane that is involved in the transfer of long-chain fatty acids into mitochondria where they can be metabolized by β-oxidation. Various mutations in the *CPT2* gene lead to distinct phenotypes so that CPT-II deficiency ranges from a lethal neonatal form, through infantile onset to late onset. Muscle symptoms include weakness, painful cramps, and susceptibility to rhabdomyolysis, the latter two features associated with exercise. Anaesthetic management includes intravenous glucose administration throughout the fasting period in order to provide a usable substrate and avoidance of succinylcholine.

Myoadenylate deaminase deficiency

Myoadenylate deaminase, alternatively known as adenosine monophosphate deaminase (gene name *AMPD1*), is a key enzyme in the purine nucleotide cycle which enables fumarate to be generated from aspartate, thus enhancing the capacity for oxidative phosphorylation in muscle through the ability of fumarate to act as a terminal acceptor of electrons as an alternative to oxygen. Myoadenylate deaminase deficiency (MADD) is purported to be the most prevalent human genetic disease but many of the approximately 2% of homozygotes are asymptomatic (Genetta et al. 2001; Castro-Gago et al. 2011). When symptoms occur they include muscle cramps and pain with exercise and these can be associated with rhabdomyolysis. It would be prudent to avoid the use of suxamethonium in patients with MADD. There is no good evidence that patients with MADD are at increased risk of developing MH under anaesthesia despite the report of Fishbein et al. (1985).

Mitochondrial myopathies

Mitochondrial disorders may be caused by defects in genes encoded either by mitochondrial or nuclear DNA. Defects in mitochondrial DNA are inherited down the maternal line. The principal organs affected are the liver, brain, and cardiac and skeletal muscles. Anaesthetic management of these rare conditions will require consideration of the child's psychological and emotional status, potential sensitivity to sedative drugs, cardiac conduction defects, substrate provision, tendency to develop lactic acidosis and muscle weakness, including bulbar and respiratory muscle weakness. Potent inhalation agents have been used without adverse effects as have induction doses of propofol (Footitt et al. 2008). As disruption of mitochondrial metabolism has been implicated in the aetiology of propofol infusion syndrome (Vasile et al. 2003), infusions of propofol should be avoided.

Declaration of interest

None declared.

References

Aldridge LM. Anaesthetic problems in myotonic dystrophy. *Br J Anaesth* 1985; **57**: 1119–30

Bansal D, Miyake K, Vogel SS, *et al.* Defective membrane repair in dysferlin-deficient muscular dystrophy. *Nature* 2003; **423**: 168–72

Ben-Menachem E. Systemic lupus erythematosus: a review for anesthesiologists. *Anesth Analg* 2010; **111**: 665–76

Bojanic K, Kivela JE, Gurrieri C, Deutsch E, Flick R, Sprung J, Weingarten TN. Perioperative course and intraoperative temperatures in patients with osteogenesis imperfecta. *Eur J Anaesthesiol* 2011; **28**: 370–5

Castro-Gago M, Gomez-Lado C, Perez-Gay L, *et al.* Primary adenosine monophosphate (AMP) deaminase deficiency in a hypotonic infant. *J Child Neurol* 2011; **26**: 734–7

Delrio FG, Park Y, Herzlich B, Grob D. Case report: diclofenac-induced rhabdomyolysis. *Am J Med Sci* 1996; **312**: 95–7

Dirksen RT, Avila G. Distinct effects on Ca^{2+} handling caused by malignant hyperthermia and central core disease mutations in RyR1. *Biophys J* 2004; **87**: 3193–204

Doriguzzi C, Palmucci L, Mongini T, Chiado-Piat L, Restagno G, Ferrone M. Exercise intolerance and recurrent myoglobinuria as the only expression of Xp21 Becker type muscular dystrophy. *J Neurol* 1993; **240**: 269–71

Fishbein WN, Muldoon SM, Deuster PA, Armbrustmacher VW. Myoadenylate deaminase deficiency and malignant hyperthermia susceptibility: is there a relationship? *Biochem Med* 1985; **34**: 344–54

Fombon FN, Thompson JP. Anaesthesia for the adult patient with rheumatoid arthritis. *Contin Educ Anaesth Crit Care Pain* 2006; **6**: 235–9

Footitt EJ, Sinha MD, Raiman JAJ, Dhawan A, Moganasundra S, Champion MP. Mitochondrial diseases: a case series and review. *Br J Anaesth* 2008; **100**: 436–41

Genetta T, Morisaki H, Morisaki T, Holmes EW. A novel bipartite intronic splicing enhancer promotes the inclusion of a mini-exon in the AMP deaminase 1 gene. *J Biol Chem* 2001; **276**: 25589–97

Goldberg S, Stern L, Feldman L. Serial two-dimensional echocardiography in Duchenne muscular dystrophy. *Neurology* 1982; **10**: 1101–5

Gupta PK, Hopkins PM. Regional anaesthesia for all? *Br J Anaesth* 2012; **109**: 7–9

Halsall PJ, Bridges LR, Ellis FR, Hopkins PM. Central core disease and malignant hyperthermia are not always associated. *J Neurol Neurosurg Psychiatry* 1996; **61**: 119–21

Hopkins PM. Anaesthesia and the sex-linked dystrophies: between a rock and a hard place. *Br J Anaesth* 2010; **104**: 397–400

Klingler, W, Rueffert H, Lehmann-Horn F, Girard T, Hopkins PM. Core myopathies and the risk of malignant hyperthermia. *Anesth Analg* 2009; **109**: 1167–73

Kuznetsov AV, Winkler K, Wiedemann FR, von Bossanyi P, Dietzmann K, Kunz WS. Impaired mitochondrial oxidative phosphorylation in skeletal muscle of the dystrophin-deficient mdx mouse. *Mol Cell Biochem* 1998; **183**: 87–96

Lambert C, Blanloeil Y, Krivosic Horber R, Berard L, Reyford H, Pinaud M. Malignant hyperthermia in a patient with hypokalemic periodic paralysis. *Anesth Analg* 1994; **79**: 10124

McNeil PL, Khakee R. Disruptions of muscle fiber plasma membranes. Role in exercise-induced damage. *Am J Pathol* 1992; **140**: 1097–109

McNeil PL, Steinhardt RA. Plasma membrane disruption: repair, prevention, adaptation. *Annu Rev Cell Dev Biol* 2003; **19**: 697–731

Muangchan C, Canadian Scleroderma Research Group, Baron M, Pope J. The 15% rule in scleroderma: the frequency of severe organ complications in systemic sclerosis. A systematic review. *J Rheumatol* 2013; **40**; 1545–56

Parness J, Banschapp O, Girard T. The myotonias and susceptibility to malignant hyperthermia. *Anesth Analg* 2009; **109**: 1054–64

Petrof BJ, Shrager JB, Stedman HH, Kelly AM, Sweeney HL. Dystrophin protects the sarcolemma from stresses developed during muscle contraction. *Proc Natl Acad Sci U S A* 1993; **90**: 3710–4

Pollard BJ, Young TM. Anaesthesia in myotonia dystrophica. *Anaesthesia* 1989; **44**: 699

Poole TC, Lim TYJ, Buck J, Kong AS. Perioperative cardiac arrest in a patient with previously undiagnosed Becker's muscular dystrophy after isoflurane anaesthesia for elective surgery. *Br J Anaesth* 2010; **104**: 487–9

Romfh A, McNally EM. Cardiac assessment in Duchenne and Becker muscular dystrophies. *Curr Heart Fail Rep* 2010; **7**: 212–18

Samanta R, Shoukrey K, Griffiths R. Rheumatoid arthritis and anaesthesia. *Anaesthesia* 2011, **66**: 1146–59

Sethna SF, Rockoff MA, Worthen HM, Rosnow JM. Anesthesia-related complications in children with Duchenne muscular dystrophy. *Anesthesiology* 1988; **68**: 462–5

Vasile B, Rasulo F, Candiani A, Latronico N. The pathophysiology of propofol infusion syndrome: a simple name for a complex syndrome. *Intensive Care Med* 2003; **29**: 1417–25

Warren JD, Blumbergs PC, Thompson PD. Rhabdomyolysis: a review. *Muscle Nerve* 2002; **25**: 332–47

White DA, Smyth DG. Continuous infusion of propofol in dystrophia myotonica. *Can J Anaesthesiol* 1989; **36**; 200–3

Woodward LJ, Kam PCA. Ankylosing spondylitis: recent developments and anaesthetic implications. *Anaesthesia* 2009; **64**: 540–8

CHAPTER 81

Central nervous system pathologies and anaesthesia

Steven J. Gill and Michael H. Nathanson

Introduction

While any patient presenting for anaesthesia (general, sedation, neuraxial, or regional) requires a thorough evaluation and assessment, those with neurological disease present the greatest challenge in that the very action of the anaesthetic technique must directly alter neurological function in order to produce the desired effect. Thus, patients with neurological disease provide three challenges: assessment of the disease itself—including its course or stage, its prognosis, and current or recent treatment; pharmacodynamic or pharmacokinetic interactions that may require a modification of the proposed anaesthetic technique or influence the intra- or postoperative care; and the possibility that the patient or their carers in some way attach blame to the anaesthetist for any contemporaneous deterioration in neurological status. The latter, while sounding defensive, is more than that, as such impressions may influence future care.

The importance of a good history and physical examination are described elsewhere. Neurological diseases are often chronic and the history may stretch back many years, if not the whole of life. Some neurological diseases have a remitting/relapsing course or have years of relative stability interspersed with more acute deteriorations. Thus, the present state of the patient and how that relates to current treatment is important. Detailed examination may be felt to be the role of the neurologist, but an assessment of current disability (and, if necessary, of consciousness using the Glasgow Coma Scale) is easy to perform, to record, and to relay to other carers. Furthermore, motor weaknesses and abnormal sensation will inform positioning of the patient, as will fixed skeletal deformities.

There is no evidence that the process of anaesthesia in itself, providing it is conducted carefully, influences the course of the majority of neurological diseases. Of course, some agents can cause short-term adverse events, an example being succinylcholine (suxamethonium) causing rhabdomyolysis in patients with a myopathy. There is much debate about the role of anaesthetics in causing postoperative cognitive dysfunction and whether chronic deterioration is accelerated after anaesthesia and surgery. There is also concern that anaesthesia may affect the growing brain (particularly in neonates), but this topic is not discussed further here.

In general, the role of the anaesthetist is to adapt their technique in the light of the pre-existing disease, reassure the patient that their condition will not be affected, and to provide safe and secure postoperative care.

Cerebral palsy

Like many other neurological conditions, anaesthetizing children and adults with cerebral palsy requires a sympathetic understanding of the underlying condition, and the degree and type of disability it causes in the individual patient, rather than a specific anaesthetic technique. There are, however, some commonly used drug therapies that the anaesthetist should be aware of and knowledge of the common types of surgery and associated risks is useful.

Cerebral palsy is a term to describe a range of disabilities—mental and physical—that occur perinatally or in early life. It was thought that most were due to hypoxia at the time of birth, but in many the damage occurs before birth. The risk is higher with multiple births, prematurity, prenatal infections, and peripartum maternal haemorrhage. Acquired causes include infections (meningitis, encephalitis), seizures, head injury, intracerebral haemorrhages, and hyperbilirubinaemia. While the degree of physical disability can vary hugely, by far the most common symptom is muscle spasticity, particularly in the lower limbs. If the patient can walk, this leads to a spastic gait and walking on 'tip toes'. Many patients have associated impaired mental function and communication difficulties. Epilepsy is common.

While many patients with cerebral palsy are children, many survive into adulthood. Common operations include release of contractures, scoliosis surgery, insertion of baclofen pumps, diagnostic procedures including endoscopy, antireflux surgery, and dental surgery. Release of contractures, for example by the use of tenotomies, tendon lengthening, or osteotomies, improves patient comfort and eases nursing difficulties.

Spasticity can be eased by antispasmodics—in particular baclofen, a γ-aminobutyric acid $(GABA)_B$ agonist. Baclofen is given orally or intrathecally via an implanted catheter and pump. Patients may present for a test dose, for catheter and pump insertion, or for a pump refill. Baclofen should not be stopped abruptly as there may be 'rebound' seizures, disorientation, and dyskinesia (Siegfried et al. 2001). Oral baclofen has been associated with delayed recovery after anaesthesia and with intraoperative bradycardia and hypotension (Sill et al. 1986; Gomar and Carrero 1994).

More severely disabled patients may have a number of co-morbidities, including gastro-oesophageal reflux, drooling, repeated lung infections (in part due to chronic aspiration) and subsequent bronchiectasis, pressure sores, and poor nutrition. A significant scoliosis may cause restrictive lung disease and cardiac impairment. It is important to assess the extent of the disability and assess the patient's general condition. Co-morbidities may determine the need for high dependency or intensive care unit admission postoperatively. Spasticity and contractures can cause difficulties with positioning, and increase the likelihood of pressure damage, for example, to nerves and skin. Postoperative muscle spasms may be a sign of pain. Careful attention to postoperative care, particularly pain control, is essential in view of the intellectual disability and communication difficulties in many patients with cerebral palsy (Nolan et al. 2000). The minimum alveolar concentration (MAC) of halothane is approximately 20–30% lower in children with cerebral palsy than in controls (Frei et al. 1997). Although an upper motor neurone lesion, cerebral palsy is not associated with increased release of potassium compared with controls after administration of succinylcholine (Dierdorf et al. 1985).

Dementia

Dementia is a chronic, irreversible, global decline in cognitive function, without clouding of consciousness. Diagnosis, while frequently suggested by carers or relatives, requires specialist assessment. Some therapeutic options, such as anticholinesterases, are available, and it is important to ensure that neither depression nor acute delirium is mistaken for dementia. Of note, a pre-existing diagnosis of dementia is a risk factor for the development of acute delirium after surgery (Smith et al. 2009). The relationship of pre-existing dementia to postoperative cognitive dysfunction is less clear, as studies of postoperative cognitive dysfunction usually exclude such patients.

The main anaesthetic implications are consent in patients who are not competent, the management of concurrent medication, and the care of patients who are often frail or have other co-morbidities.

The overall epidemiology is well known to physicians and laypeople. Dementia is predominantly a disease of the elderly; the idiopathic type is known as Alzheimer's disease. However, variants in young (<65 years) patients are seen, and other common causes include multi-infarct dementia in arteriopaths, and the advanced stages of Parkinson's disease. The presence of cognitive decline (as assessed preoperatively by the mini mental test score) is associated with an increase in mortality after surgery (Maxwell et al. 2008). A more complete test of cognitive function is the Mini-Mental State Examination (Folstein et al. 1975).

Some patients with dementia are agitated and a small dose of a benzodiazepine may help (Verbough 2004). The concurrent use of anticholinesterases (such as donepezil and rivastigmine) does not appear to increase early mortality or the risk of respiratory complications in hip fracture patients (Seitz et al. 2011). However, long-term anticholinesterase therapy may reduce heart rate variability (Masuda and Kawamura 2003), and bradycardia should be managed with an anticholinergic that does not cross the blood–brain barrier (e.g. glycopyrronium bromide). Anticholinesterases may induce a degree of resistance to non-depolarizing neuromuscular blockers (Sanchez Morillo et al. 2003).

There may be other changes that affect the anaesthetic. For example, the baseline Bispectral Index™ (BIS™, Covidien, now Medtronic Minimally Invasive Therapies, Minneapolis, MN, USA) value is lower in patients with Alzheimer's disease. In a group of patients aged more than 75 years, the mean (95% confidence interval) baseline BIS™ (Ver. 4.0) value was 89.1 (86–92) and 94.7 (93–96) in patients with Alzheimer's disease or multi-infarct dementia [mean (SD) MMSE 16.5(8.1)] and controls, respectively (Renna et al. 2003). However, there are no hard data on which to base further titration of anaesthetic agents. The increased sensitivity of the elderly to anaesthetic agents (intravenous and inhalation) is well known. Algorithms can assist in predicting the likely MAC value of inhalation agents (Nickalls and Mapleson 2003).

In other respects, care of these usually frail, elderly patients is similar to that of other elderly patients.

Epilepsy

Epilepsy is a disorder of the brain characterized by the enduring propensity to generate seizures (Fisher et al. 2005). Seizures are a symptom of an underlying abnormality within the brain and are a relatively common phenomenon; up to 5% of the population will suffer a single non-febrile seizure during their lifetime. Most, however, do not go on to develop epilepsy, which has a population incidence of up to 2%. Between a quarter and a third of patients with epilepsy have an identifiable underlying cause (The National Society for Epilepsy). This is typically a structural lesion within the brain, such as a tumour or previous injury which may have been traumatic, ischaemic, or hypoxic. Drugs and toxins may also cause seizures, either in excess or upon abrupt withdrawal. There are also a number of genetic, infective, and metabolic conditions that predispose to seizures. Where seizure activity is recurrent and no cause is identified, the term idiopathic or primary epilepsy is applied.

A seizure is caused by abnormal, excessive, and oscillating discharge from a group of neurones, analogous to feedback through a microphone-amplifier circuit (Voss et al. 2008). The clinical manifestation of this neuronal activity, sometimes termed a convulsion, can vary greatly and depends on the anatomical location of this group of neurones; hence seizures can be motor, sensory, or autonomic in nature (Table 81.1). If the seizure focus is surrounded by hyperpolarized and

Table 81.1 Different types of seizure

Seizure type	Subtypes
Partial Motor, sensory, autonomic or psychiatric symptoms according to which part of the brain is involved	Simple—without impairment of consciousness Complex—with impairment of consciousness Partial onset developing into generalized
Generalized A large portion or all of the brain is affected, consciousness is reduced	**Inhibitory** Absence—abrupt onset of impaired consciousness and interruption of activity, blank stare, unresponsive, rapid recovery Atonic—loss of skeletal muscle tone also called 'drop attacks' **Excitatory** Myoclonic—brief involuntary contraction of muscle group Clonic—rhythmic muscular contractions Tonic—involuntary stiffness Tonic-clonic
Pseudo or non-epileptic	Varied but often stereotyped and convincing

inexcitable neurones, the seizure activity remains localized or focal. If the seizure activity spreads into neighbouring regions and then gathers sufficient energy to spread through non-synaptic pathways the seizure becomes generalized (Stoetling and Dierdorf 2008).

Pharmacological treatment of epilepsy controls seizures completely or almost completely in the majority of cases. However, even the newer anticonvulsant medications have a number of side-effects. Some are mild such as skin rashes or gastrointestinal upset, but more serious complications such as aplastic anaemia or drug-induced systemic lupus erythematosus are well recognized (Herman and Pendley 1998). Treatment of women of childbearing age is challenging, as many drugs have a risk of teratogenicity; however, seizures in pregnancy increase the risk of morbidity and mortality to mother and fetus (Tomson and Hiilesma 2007). Drug interactions are also a common problem and may alter the efficacy of many drugs, including other antiepileptic drugs.

Implications for anaesthesia

A patient with epilepsy may present a number of challenges for the anaesthetist. The patient may have an associated disorder or underlying cause for their epilepsy. These conditions are dealt with elsewhere and this section is primarily targeted at the patient with idiopathic epilepsy. The anaesthetic considerations can be divided into two parts. Firstly, it is important to consider how a patient's epilepsy and its treatment may affect the delivery of anaesthesia; this is particularly significant when considering the pharmacology of anaesthesia. It is unsurprising that antiepileptic drugs and anaesthetic drugs influence a number of shared neurotransmitters and receptors. It is also unsurprising that much of their actions and interactions are not fully understood. Secondly, one must consider how the proposed anaesthetic may affect the patient's epilepsy, in particular keeping the patient safe and avoiding perioperative seizures.

Pre-anaesthetic assessment

When discussing epilepsy during the pre-anaesthetic interview, the anaesthetist must establish the nature and frequency of the patient's seizures. This should include any triggering factors such as sleep deprivation or stress (which might be avoided with appropriately timed sedative pre-medication). A detailed medication history including the timing of antiepileptic drugs should be taken and the patient should be advised to continue this medication as normal before anaesthesia. Many antiepileptic drugs are not available in an intravenous preparation, and some cannot be crushed to administer via a nasogastric tube, or require the nasogastric feed to be discontinued. If the patient's usual drugs cannot be continued orally, a plan should be established in discussion with a neurologist or pharmacist, and it may be appropriate to stabilize the patient on a treatment which can be given parenterally before anaesthesia.

Assuming that any perioperative seizure is dealt with quickly and safely, the most significant implication for the patient may be on their ability to drive. In the United Kingdom, a period of 1 year free from seizures is required in order to hold a driving licence (Driver and Vehicle Licensing Agency 2011). It may therefore be pertinent to enquire about the patient's driving status and discuss the implications of perioperative seizures with them.

The impact of epilepsy and antiepileptic drugs on anaesthesia

The major impact of epilepsy on the delivery of anaesthesia is that of the drugs used to prevent or control seizures. Antiepileptic drugs have a number of relevant actions and side-effects that must be considered by the anaesthetist (Table 81.2). Two common effects of antiepileptic drugs are sedation and hepatic enzyme induction, in particular the cytochrome P450 pathway. The drugs with sedative effects will reduce the required dose of anaesthetic agent, a familiar effect that is often utilized by pre-medicating patients with benzodiazepines. Antiepileptic drugs that induce liver enzymes (such as carbamazepine, phenytoin, and topiramate) lead to increased metabolism and hence reduced efficacy or duration of action of drugs such as the aminosteroid non-depolarizing neuromuscular blocking agents and some opioids, local anaesthetics, and non-steroidal anti-inflammatory drugs (Sweeney and Bromilow 2006). These effects are difficult to quantify accurately and careful clinical monitoring, possibly in conjunction with enhanced monitoring such as a peripheral nerve stimulator or a depth of anaesthesia monitor may be appropriate, especially in patients taking multiple antiepileptic drugs (Voss et al. 2008). Sodium valproate inhibits hepatic enzymes and so can prolong the effects of other drugs, including antiepileptic drugs.

Many antiepileptic drugs are highly protein bound, a feature they share with a number of anaesthetic drugs. When given in combination the resultant increase in the unbound fraction of either or both drugs can quickly produce toxicity. This is particularly a problem with phenytoin which is typically more than 90% protein bound. Its therapeutic range is just below the concentrations associated with zero-order kinetics, so any change to its protein binding not only affect the concentration of free drug but may dramatically alter its rate of elimination, leading rapidly to toxicity (Craig 2005).

Finally, some antiepileptic drugs have unique effects, such as the reduction in platelet number or function caused by sodium valproate or the antiarrhythmic effects of phenytoin, which may or may not be relevant to the delivery of anaesthesia (Table 81.2).

The impact of anaesthesia on epilepsy

There are three possible relevant effects of an anaesthetic drug on the epileptic patient (Voss et al. 2008). Firstly, epileptiform activity may be seen on the electroencephalogram (EEG) and is as a result of small areas (<1 cm^2) of neuronal hypersynchrony. This is best detected on cortical rather than scalp EEG and rarely produces any clinically detectable activity. They are commonly caused by anaesthetic drugs, but rarely evolve in to a clinically detectable phenomenon; only a weak correlation between epileptiform spikes and clinically detectable seizures has been described (Garcia-Morales et al. 2002; Bromfield et al. 2006). Secondly, the EEG may demonstrate widespread epileptiform oscillations. This is termed a seizure, though it may not be clinically apparent in the case of non-convulsive seizures. Typically seizures are evident without EEG monitoring, most commonly leading to tonic–clonic movements of the limbs and a reduction in consciousness. This is the third possible effect of anaesthesia on the patient with epilepsy and is often referred to as a convulsion. Almost all anaesthetic drugs have been associated with EEG changes or seizure activity to a greater or lesser extent (Gratrix and Enright 2005). This is often based upon animal studies or single case reports. Animal studies are difficult to translate to human practice with any degree of accuracy and should generally be considered as hypothesis-forming only. Similarly any anaesthetic is likely to involve numerous drugs given in rapid succession making it very difficult to establish the causative drug in a case report of possible anaesthetic-related seizure. Furthermore, many of the same anaesthetic drugs have been associated with

Table 81.2 Relevant effects and side-effects of antiepileptic drugs

Drug	Effects relevant to anaesthesia
Carbamazepine	Reduces duration of activity of aminosteroid neuromuscular blocking drugs Induces hepatic metabolism of itself and other drugs
Phenytoin	Potent inducer of hepatic enzymes and multiple interactions More than 90% protein bound May decrease MAC of volatile agents Increases CNS toxicity of local anaesthetics Increases required dose of all neuromuscular blocking drugs except atracurium Vaughan Williams class 1 antiarrhythmic effects Metabolic effects include hyperglycaemia, hypocalcaemia and suppressed ADH secretion
Sodium valproate	Induces hepatic enzymes 90% protein bound High doses may displaces barbiturates and benzodiazepines from binding sites May reduce platelet function or number, though in isolation of limited clinical significance Contraindicated in acute liver disease
Lamotrigine	Fewer interactions and less enzyme induction than other antiepileptic drugs Duration of action reduced if taken with enzyme inducing drugs (e.g. other antiepileptic drugs) Associated with leucopenia Possible reduced analgesia requirements
Levetiracetam	May cause drowsiness Low protein binding and no hepatic metabolism make interactions very uncommon Possible use in status epilepticus

Data from Smith S, Scarth E and Sasada M (2011) *Drugs in Anaesthesia and Intensive Care.* Oxford University Press; and Bonicalzi V, Canavero S, Cerutti F, Piazza M, Clemente M, Chio A (1997). Lamotrigine reduces total postoperative analgesia requirement: A randomised double-blind, placebo controlled pilot study. *Surgery*, 122(3), 567–570.

Table 81.3 Relative pro- and anticonvulsant effects of various anaesthetic drugs

Anaesthetic agent	Proconvulsant effect	Anticonvulsant effect
Nitrous oxide	+	–
Halothane	+	++
Isoflurane	++	+++
Sevoflurane	++	
Desflurane	–	
Thiopental	++	++++
Etomidate	+++	+++
Benzodiazepines		+++
Ketamine	++	+
Propofol	++	++
Opioids	+++	

Reproduced from Gratrix, A. P., and Enright, S. M. Epilepsy and anaesthesia in intensive care. *Continuing Education in Anaesthesia, Critical Care and Pain.* Volume 5, Issue 4, pp. 118–121, Copyright © 2005, by permission of the British Journal of Anaesthesia.

control of seizure activity. Table 81.3 quantifies the relative convulsant or anticonvulsant activity of some common anaesthetic drugs (Gratrix and Enright 2005). These drugs are thought to have multiple binding sites with both excitatory and inhibitory actions, and this probably accounts for the varied effects on seizure threshold. The overall clinical effect depends on the balance of the drug's pro- and anticonvulsant properties and the use of other drugs and the patient's physiological status.

The clinician is left with a dilemma—how to balance the incomplete theory of neuropharmacology and physiology, with at times conflicting animal studies and case reports to deliver a safe anaesthetic. What follows is a pragmatic and practical guide to safe anaesthesia of a patient with epilepsy.

Benzodiazepine premedication delivered orally on the ward may be useful in those patients with poor seizure control or stress-related seizures. An intravenous dose of midazolam is a commonly used co-induction technique and may produce some seizure prophylaxis during anaesthesia. However, in the event of an overdose, the benzodiazepine antagonist flumazenil has been associated with seizures (British National Formulary 2014). Etomidate has been shown to induce epileptiform changes in the EEG (Ebrahim et al. 1986) and is effective in identifying the seizure focus during epilepsy surgery (Pastor et al. 2010). It seems prudent to avoid this drug when anaesthetizing patients with epilepsy.

Ketamine is used for its haemodynamic stability or preservation of airway reflexes and spontaneous ventilation. Its effect on epilepsy is not clear. Ketamine has been shown to produce epileptiform EEG changes and commonly produces abnormal movements at induction (Ferrer-Allando et al. 1973), but it is probably more anticonvulsant than proconvulsant (Celsia et al. 1975) and has been used in resistant status epilepticus (Borris et al. 2000). Thiopental is a thiobarbiturate with anticonvulsant properties typical of barbiturates and for many years has been considered the anaesthetic agent of choice in status epilepticus (Brown and Horton 1967). The recovery characteristics, lack of airway reflex attenuation, and greater risk of anaphylaxis compared with propofol deter some from using this drug; however, it is undoubtedly anticonvulsant and the lasting impact of all these problems, with the exception of anaphylaxis, is minimal. There is no consensus on the use of propofol in patients with epilepsy. Excitatory phenomena associated with its use, including seizures, are described at both anaesthetic and sub-anaesthetic doses (Sneyd 1992). However, it has also been shown to be effective in resistant status epilepticus (Parviainen et al. 2006) and also shortens seizure duration in electroconvulsive therapy when compared with thiopental (Fear et al. 2005). The current prescribing data in the United Kingdom recommends avoiding it in patients with epilepsy, as do other experts in the field (Sneyd 1999). While our understanding of the full mechanisms of action of propofol is limited it is unlikely that consensus will be established. Pragmatically, when faced with the choice of an induction agent with proven anticonvulsant activity and one where there remains doubt it would seem prudent to choose the anticonvulsant agent when anaesthetizing a patient with epilepsy, unless there is a contraindication such as allergy or a strong indication for propofol.

The major metabolite of atracurium and cisatracurium, laudanosine, crosses the blood–brain barrier easily and at high concentrations is neurotoxic. However, there is no evidence to suggest this is a clinically relevant issue and animal studies have suggested its use is safe (Tateishi et al. 1989). All other neuromuscular blocking agents are considered safe in epilepsy.

All of the volatile anaesthetic agents have been associated with epileptiform EEG changes to varying extents and, at times, abnormal movements (Ito et al. 1988). The clinical significance of these and the incidence of progression to clinically evident seizure activity are probably very small. Conversely, there are case reports of volatile anaesthesia being used to treat refractory status epilepticus with some success though its application is limited by side-effects and logistical problems (Shorvon and Ferlisi 2011). Sevoflurane has been widely studied and a review concluded that no lasting neurological or EEG sequelae of these changes had been demonstrated. The authors recommended that these EEG changes could be reduced by avoiding hypocapnia, limiting the end-tidal concentration to less than 1.5 MAC, and by the use of benzodiazepine pre-medication, opioids, and nitrous oxide (all of which may in themselves offer some anticonvulsant effects). The authors also recommended cerebral function monitoring in high-risk cases to titrate sevoflurane dose and detect major epileptiform changes (Constant et al. 2005).

Opioid drugs have both pro- and anticonvulsant properties, which probably relates to their ability to bind to both opioid and non-opioid receptors, which exert opposing effects on seizure threshold (Cheng and Templehoff 1999). Studies suggest that doses far in excess of those used in the opioid-naive surgical patient are needed to induce seizures and it may be that receptor down-regulation protects chronic opioid users. However, intrathecal morphine has been associated with seizures (Kronenberg et al. 1998) and small intravenous doses of alfentanil, and possibly fentanyl, have been shown to induce EEG changes (Manninen et al. 1999). Given the popularity of these drugs it is unlikely that these effects are of clinical relevance. Tramadol is known to reduce the seizure threshold, especially if used in combination with selective serotonin reuptake inhibitors or tricyclic antidepressants, and should be avoided in patients with epilepsy. Most other commonly used analgesics are safe in epilepsy.

Avoidance of general anaesthesia may seem a sensible approach for the patient with epilepsy. Local anaesthetics are another group of drugs with varied effects on the likelihood of seizures. Low doses of local anaesthetic reduce cerebral blood flow, metabolic activity, and electrical activity, producing an anticonvulsant effect. This is utilized in neonatal medicine where lidocaine is used for resistant seizures (Shany et al. 2007). At higher doses, local anaesthetics are neurotoxic and commonly cause convulsions. Some have suggested that patients with seizure disorders are more likely to develop local anaesthetic-related seizures and that regional techniques should be modified by selecting a low-potency local anaesthetic and minimizing the dose (Faccenda and Finucane 2001). There is, however, little evidence for this, and a retrospective review of 411 procedures undertaken with regional or central neuraxial anaesthesia in patients with epilepsy found that the timing of the most recent preoperative seizure was the best predictor of postoperative seizures (Kopp et al. 2009). The anaesthetist must therefore balance the likelihood and the risk of an intraoperative seizure based on the patient's seizure frequency, any precipitating factors such as stress or anxiety, and the nature of the surgery.

Perioperative seizures

Abnormal perioperative movements have a wide differential diagnosis and it may be difficult to accurately diagnose what is a true seizure, and even harder to attribute a specific drug as a cause. A careful clinical assessment of the whole episode including any impairment in consciousness and the recovery from any possible seizure is essential and should be carefully documented. True perioperative seizures should be managed in the same manner as any other seizure. If local anaesthetic toxicity is suspected then Intralipid®, which was initially recommended only for the treatment of cardiac arrest as a result of local anaesthetic toxicity, may be effective in managing seizures and arrhythmias (Foxall et al. 2007) and guidelines have changed to encourage its use earlier (The Association of Anaesthetists of Great Britain and Ireland 2010).

With careful pre-assessment, an understanding of the pharmacology of anaesthetic and antiepileptic drugs and their interactions, along with consideration of the patient and the surgical intervention, safe and effective anaesthesia can be delivered to patients with epilepsy or a propensity for seizures with a high degree of safety.

Multiple sclerosis

Multiple sclerosis (MS) is a chronic inflammatory disease of the central nervous system (CNS), characterized by axonal demyelination. Its clinical course is varied and, although there are common clinical syndromes associated with MS, theoretically any nerve within the CNS can be affected, producing an almost infinite number of signs and symptoms. The prevalence varies geographically, with the highest rates in Northern and Western Europe, Australasia, and central North America and a very low incidence in those of African or Asian origin (Kurtzke 1991). There is significant evidence of genetic predisposition with monozygotic twin concordance rate six times higher than that of dizygotic twins (Sadovnick et al. 1993), and a high prevalence of human leucocyte antigen (HLA)-DR and -DQ genotypes in sufferers (Weinshenker et al. 1998). There are also suggestions of environmental and infectious triggers including human herpes virus 6 and *Chlamydia pneumoniae* (Challoner et al. 1995; Sriram et al. 1999).

The diagnosis is based on clinical features initially, typically after detection of two separate episodes of possible symptoms which are distant both in time and their focus within the CNS. Common early symptoms include optic neuritis, paraesthesia, ataxia, bladder dysfunction, or neuropathic pain including trigeminal neuralgia. Magnetic resonance imaging typically reveals 'plaques' of demyelination (Goodkin et al. 1994). Examination of the cerebrospinal fluid may also be useful, with elevated concentrations of immunoglobulin (Ig)-G, oligoclonal bands, and lymphocytic pleocytosis common. Visual and somatosensory-evoked potentials may demonstrate sub-clinical evidence of impaired neuronal conduction secondary to demyelination (Noseworthy et al. 2000).

The subsequent clinical course varies greatly but typically follows one of four patterns (Hauser and Goodwin 2008):

- *Relapsing and remitting*: discrete episodes of symptoms, with complete or near complete recovery in between.

- *Secondary progressive*: after a period of relapsing/remitting MS, symptoms become permanent and more severe over time.
- *Primary progressive*: similar to secondary progressive MS, but without the preceding period of relapsing and remitting symptoms.
- *Progressive and relapsing*: episodes of acute exacerbations of symptoms with partial recovery but an overall chronic deterioration.

There is no cure for MS and although treatment is not always needed, the aims of treatment are to reduce the duration and frequency of exacerbations with disease-modifying therapies such as corticosteroids, plasma exchange, and interferon beta. Symptomatic treatment is essential (Cree 2007).

Anaesthetic implications

Patients may present for a wide range of surgical interventions both related and unrelated to their MS. As the disease may develop relatively early in adult life it is also one of the more common neurological diseases encountered during pregnancy. For some time it has been thought that both emotional and physiological stress may produce a relapse of MS, although the strength of this relationship is probably weak and may relate to number of stressors rather than their severity (Brown et al. 2006). This makes it very difficult to establish the cause of a postoperative exacerbation, and particularly difficult to prove any association with a particular anaesthetic drug or technique.

Preoperative assessment

During preoperative assessment, attention must be given to the patient's current neurological symptoms, in particular those affecting the airway, respiratory system, and cardiovascular system. Various respiratory effects may be seen ranging from diaphragmatic weakness or paralysis secondary to cervical cord lesions, altered response to arterial tension of carbon dioxide, or impaired bulbar function affecting coughing and swallowing. While total lung volume and vital capacity may remain within normal ranges, maximal inspiratory and expiratory efforts may be reduced by up to 50%, reducing the functional residual capacity and good pre-oxygenation will be important (Smeltzer et al. 1992). A simple bedside assessment of cough strength, ability to clear secretions, and exhale deeply may be as useful as formal pulmonary function testing and arterial blood gas analysis (Tantucci et al. 1994).

Demyelination within the high thoracic cord may lead to autonomic neuropathy causing intraoperative haemodynamic instability; there are reports of severe hypotension resistant to fluid and vasopressor, in particular related to central neuraxial anaesthesia (Kattula et al. 1999). Patients with a history of syncope, impotence, bladder or bowel dysfunction, or orthostatic hypotension should alert the clinician to the possibility of autonomic dysfunction (Darotta and Schubert 2002).

Finally, it is essential to consider recent and current drug history. Significant steroid use may necessitate perioperative supplementation or have caused side-effects such as myopathy. Baclofen may also cause weakness and increased sensitivity to non-depolarizing neuromuscular blocking agents. Anticonvulsants used either for seizures or neuropathic pain may lead to resistance to these drugs. Immunosuppressant drugs may have significant side-effects such as pulmonary fibrosis or myocarditis, and the obvious increased risk of perioperative infection.

Choice of anaesthetic technique

For many years, there have been concerns that central neuraxial and regional anaesthesia may increase the risk of relapse in patients with MS. There are three potential mechanisms for this. The first is that of mechanical trauma at the time of injection (either by the needle or increased pressure) may provide a 'focus' for demyelination to occur. Second, demyelinated nerves (which may not be clinically evident) may be more susceptible to neurotoxicity from local anaesthetic drugs, a concern particularly during spinal anaesthesia. Finally, these same nerves may be more at risk of ischaemia secondary to compression by injectate within the nerve sheath, or from additives to the local anaesthetic. There are no large prospective studies comparing anaesthetic techniques in patients with MS. The published retrospective data are from small cohorts, but do not support these concerns about regional or central neuraxial techniques. The largest study to date included 139 patients with CNS disease, 25% of whom had MS, undergoing epidural, combined spinal–epidural, 'single-shot', or continuous spinal anaesthesia. They found no documented new or worsening neurological symptoms, with a mean duration of follow-up of approximately 6 weeks (Hebel et al. 2006).

The anaesthetist must balance the risks and benefits of each possible technique on an individual patient basis and after discussion help the patient make an informed decision. Where a central neuraxial technique is needed, there may be a theoretical advantage to choosing an epidural if possible as lower concentrations of local anaesthetic can be used, and direct contact with the spinal cord is avoided.

There are few specific concerns about general anaesthesia in patients with MS. Attention should be given to positioning in patients with contractures or altered posture, and the general principles of maintaining oxygen delivery to potentially 'at-risk' neuronal tissue should be observed. In patients with significant upper motor neurone weakness, the risk of significant hyperkalaemia with suxamethonium should be considered carefully (Cooperman 1970).

Irrespective of the technique chosen, careful attention to perioperative temperature control is essential. Conduction in demyelinated nerves slows as temperature increases and may lead to new or worsened postoperative symptoms (Guthrie and Nelson 1995). Postoperatively, the patient should be carefully assessed for new symptoms or signs and if there is concern discussion with a neurologist is advisable.

Multiple sclerosis and pregnancy

MS is one of the more common neurological diseases in women of childbearing age. Seventy per cent of cases present between the ages of 20 and 40 years, and 1 in 10 cases in this age group present in pregnancy (Drake et al. 2006). A study assessing relapses of MS in pregnancy followed a total of 227 pregnancies. The authors found a reduced incidence of relapse during pregnancy, especially the third trimester. In the first 3 months postpartum the relapse rate was higher than the pre-pregnancy risk, after which it reduced back to baseline. Epidural analgesia was used in 42 cases and was not identified as a risk factor for relapse (Confavreux et al. 1988). Data on spinal anaesthesia for delivery is more limited but does not support the theoretical concerns of relapse as a result of increased local anaesthetic neurotoxicity in demyelinated nerves. Careful antenatal assessment and planning is essential to consider each patient individually and agree and plan which she finds agreeable.

Myasthenia gravis

Myasthenia gravis (MG) is an auto-immune disease in which antibodies are generated against the postsynaptic nicotinic acetylcholine receptors of the neuromuscular junction. This results in weakness and the cardinal clinical feature of fatigability in voluntary muscle. The exact pathophysiology is not fully understood; however, the thymus gland is abnormal in many patients with MG with the majority showing hyperplasia and a thymoma is present in 10–15% (Hughes et al. 2004). The severity of clinical manifestations is variable; though many patients will go on to develop severe weakness. Table 81.4 shows a widely used classification of myasthenic symptoms (Osserman and Genkins 1971).

The diagnosis is based on history and examination suggesting fatigability of muscle, supported by detection of auto-antibodies to the acetylcholine receptor (typically IgG) which are present in 80–90% of cases (Lindstrom et al. 1976). Electromyography usually demonstrates a reduction in compound muscle action potentials with repeated stimulation despite normal conduction velocities (Baraka 1992). The Tensilon (edrophonium) test may also be performed, where a dose of edrophonium (a synthetic acetylcholinesterase inhibitor) is administered and a there is transient improvement in power and reduction in fatigability (Osserman and Kaplan 1952). This is measured in an easily quantifiable muscle group, for example, by assessing grip strength (forearm and hand muscles) or forced vital capacity (FVC) respiratory muscles.

Treatment of mild disease is with acetylcholinesterase inhibitors, such as pyridostigmine, to reduce the clearance of acetylcholine from the neuromuscular junction, a therapy with clear relevance to the anaesthetist. The usefulness of these drugs is usually limited by muscarinic side-effects. In more severe disease, immunosuppressive therapy is used, typically with steroids with or without azathioprine or cyclophosphamide. A myasthenic crisis is an acute exacerbation of MG causing respiratory weakness necessitating ventilatory support, and is often accompanied by severe bulbar muscles weakness. This life-threatening complication is often treated with plasma exchange or intravenous immunoglobulin therapy which may provide rapid but short-term improvement. When a thymoma is present, thymectomy is recommended to avoid local invasion, and may improve myasthenic symptoms. Similarly in patients with thymic hyperplasia, thymectomy may improve symptoms or lead to remission (Kumar and Kaminski 2011).

Table 81.4 The Osserman and Genkins classification system of severity of myasthenia gravis

Type	Clinical appearance
1	Ocular signs and symptoms only
2A	Generalized mild muscle weakness responding well to treatment
2B	Generalized moderate muscle weakness responding less well to treatment
3	Acute fulminating presentation and/or respiratory dysfunction
4	Myasthenic crisis requiring invasive ventilation

Anaesthetic implications

The focus of anaesthetic management is to preserve and support respiratory function as much as possible in the perioperative period. This requires preoperative assessment and possibly optimization, intraoperative considerations of the use of neuromuscular blocking agents and analgesics, and postoperative monitoring and support.

Preoperative assessment

Preparation for elective surgery should involve a multidisciplinary team of neurologist, surgeon, anaesthetist, and critical care team. Careful assessment of respiratory function is essential and regular measurement of FVC may be most useful. In patients with severe disease or limited response to treatment, preoperative plasma exchange may be considered. Factors associated with the need for postoperative respiratory support include a FVC less than 40 ml kg^{-1}, a pyridostigmine dose greater than 750 mg day^{-1}, other chronic respiratory disease, grade 3 or 4 MG, and disease duration of longer than 6 years (Thavasothy and Hirsch 2002; Hines and Marshall 2008). Medications need reviewing carefully and plans may be needed for corticosteroid supplementation and alternative routes of administration if surgery involves the gastrointestinal tract. It is usual to omit acetylcholinesterase inhibitors on the morning of surgery.

Anaesthetic management

Whenever possible, it is best to avoid general anaesthesia. It is important, however, to consider that certain regional anaesthetic techniques, such as interscalene blockade, may reduce respiratory function, which can be critical in patients with borderline respiratory function preoperatively. When general anaesthesia is unavoidable then neuromuscular blocking agents should not be used if possible, and often tracheal intubation can be achieved under deep anaesthesia and opioids alone. When this is not possible, especially when rapid sequence induction is necessary, a thorough understanding of the pathology of MG and the pharmacology of neuromuscular blocking agents is essential.

Succinylcholine binds to the same postsynaptic acetylcholine receptors as are affected by MG. The reduction in functional receptors results in resistance to the effects of suxamethonium and, theoretically requires, an increase in dose to achieve sufficient neuromuscular block for intubation. A dose–response study suggested that MG increases the ED_{50} and ED_{95} of suxamethonium by a factor of 2–2.6; however, the commonly used dose of 1–1.5 mg kg^{-1} is three to five times the normal ED_{95}, and hence no dose increase may be needed (Eisenkraft et al. 1988). This was supported by a subsequent study which demonstrated a dose of 1 mg kg^{-1} to be fully effective in patients with MG (Wainwright and Brodrick 1987).

Conversely, patients with MG are markedly more sensitive to the effects of non-depolarizing neuromuscular blocking agents (Thavasothy and Hirsch 2002), an effect which may be significant even in those with minimal disease (including patients in remission and those with clinical undetectable MG) (Enoki et al. 1989; Kim and Mangold 1989; Lumb and Calder 1989). The ED_{50} and ED_{95} of atracurium and vecuronium are reduced by approximately 50% (Baraka 1992). When rapid sequence induction is not required, small doses can be titrated while monitoring neuromuscular function with a peripheral nerve stimulator, and further doses titrated intraoperatively. Such small doses will probably reverse spontaneously and an anticholinesterase will not be required. Caution is required if neostigmine is needed, especially if the patient has taken their usual acetylcholinesterase inhibitors that day, as a cholinergic crisis (excessive acetylcholine producing flaccid weakness and respiratory failure along with other cholinergic symptoms such as sweating, salivation, meiosis, and bradycardia) may develop. Sugammadex has been used in a patient with MG, and may be useful in preventing residual weakness causing respiratory compromise, or in permitting use of rocuronium as a rapid sequence induction agent (Unterbuchner et al. 2010).

When respiratory function is significantly impaired by MG or surgery (e.g. thoracotomy), effective analgesia is essential. A multimodal approach to reduce opioid use is essential, and epidural analgesia should be considered when appropriate. Postoperatively, it should be possible to extubate the trachea of most patients with reasonable preoperative respiratory function. Most patients should be observed in a critical care unit, for respiratory monitoring and optimization of myasthenia treatment.

Lambert–Eaton myasthenic syndrome

The Lambert–Eaton myasthenic syndrome (LEMS) is a relatively common disorder of the neuromuscular junction, often associated with neoplasia, most typically small cell lung cancer. Autoantibodies are formed which interact with voltage-gated calcium channels in the pre-synaptic cleft, resulting in reduced release of acetylcholine and hence weakness which typically improves with repetition as more acetylcholine is released. Patients with the Lambert–Eaton myasthenic syndrome are sensitive to both depolarizing and non-depolarizing neuromuscular blocking agents, and doses should be reduced, though there is limited data to guide this (Baraka 1992).

Table 81.5 Clinical features of Parkinson's disease of relevance to anaesthetist

Central nervous system
◆ Tremor (pill rolling)
◆ Rigidity (cogwheel or lead-pipe)
◆ Bradykinesia
◆ Postural imbalance
◆ Expressionless face
◆ Slow gait
Cardiovascular system
◆ Orthostatic hypotension
Respiratory system
◆ Restrictive and/or obstructive lung defect
◆ Obstructive sleep apnoea
◆ Aspiration
Others
◆ Excess salivation
◆ Dysphagia
◆ Nausea
◆ Depression
◆ Dementia
◆ Flexion deformity of neck

Parkinson's disease and parkinsonism

Parkinson's disease is an idiopathic form of parkinsonism and accounts for the majority of cases. Other causes of parkinsonism include atherosclerotic multi-infarct disease, drugs [such as phenothiazines, butyrophenones (e.g. droperidol), and metoclopramide], repeated head trauma (as was said to affect the boxer Mohammed Ali), some types of poisoning, and other neurodegenerative diseases including progressive supranuclear palsy, multiple system atrophy, Shy–Drager syndrome, and Lewy body disease (early dementia and hallucinations). The prevalence of Parkinson's disease increases with age, with 1.6–3% of those older than 65 years affected (Moghal et al. 1994; de Rijk et al. 1997). There may be a familial factor or subtype.

The classic features are tremor, rigidity, and bradykinesia often associated with postural imbalance. Other features of relevance to an anaesthetist are described in Table 81.5; some are the result of autonomic dysfunction. There is, however, no specific test for Parkinson's disease.

Parkinson's disease arises as a result of depletion of dopaminergic neurones in the substantia nigra of the basal ganglia. There are two main therapies—to pharmacologically increase the amount of dopamine in the basal ganglia, or neurostimulation to mimic the actions of dopamine. The commonly used drugs are listed in Table 81.6.

Dopamine does not cross the blood–brain barrier. Instead, a prodrug, levodopa (L-dopa), is used, which is enterally absorbed and crosses the blood–brain barrier. In the brain, is it converted to dopamine, while peripheral conversion is blocked by co-administration of a peripheral dopa decarboxylase inhibitor (such as carbidopa or benserazide) to reduce systemic side-effects. Levodopa requirements increase over time and 'on/off' effects may be seen. When 'on' the levodopa is working and voluntary

Table 81.6 Common drug therapies for Parkinson's disease

Drug	Anaesthetic considerations
Levodopa (L-dopa)	Dyskinesia; neuroleptic malignant syndrome; do not stop abruptly
Oral dopamine agonists (e.g. ropinirole, pergolide, bromocriptine)	
Apomorphine	Nausea and vomiting, severe hypotension
Type B monoamine oxidase inhibitors (e.g. selegiline)	Possible interaction with pethidine (Zornberg et al. 1991) and sympathomimetics
Anticholinergics (e.g. orphenadrine)	Central anticholinergic syndrome
Catechol-O-methyl transferase inhibitors	Interaction with other drugs using COMT pathway (e.g. adrenaline)
Others: amantadine	

Data from Zornberg GL, Bodkin JA, Cohen BM (1991). Severe adverse interaction between pethidine and selegiline. *The Lancet*, 337, 246.

movement may be good; however, as the concentration of dopamine decreases towards the end of a dosing interval. the patient can rapidly go into an 'off' period marked by a rebound increase in rigidity and bradykinesia (fixed dyskinesias). Long-term use of levodopa can be associated with extrapyramidal dyskinesias and choreiform movements. Alternatively, dopamine agonists, type B monoamine oxidase inhibitors, or catechol-*O*-methyl transferase inhibitors can be used. The purpose of these drugs is to delay the onset of use of levodopa and its associated adverse effects, or to be used with levodopa to smooth out the 'on/off' fluctuations. Apomorphine, which must be given subcutaneously or sublingually, is a short-acting dopamine agonist that, while very emetogenic, can dramatically smooth out 'on/off' effects, or be given while patients are 'nil by mouth'. Domperidone is given concurrently to reduce nausea.

A sudden cessation of treatment can precipitate a dramatic worsening of the symptoms of the disease. If levodopa is stopped or withdrawn abruptly, the neuroleptic malignant syndrome (rigidity, hyperthermia, autonomic dysfunction, and muscle breakdown) can be precipitated.

Some patients with very debilitating or refractory disease have brain electrodes inserted to enable deep brain stimulation. More experimental treatments include cell transplantation. Long-term care of patients with Parkinson's disease requires specialist neurologist and nursing inputs, and these professionals will usually be involved in planning elective surgery.

Perioperative care and anaesthetic considerations

The basis of perioperative care is to continue the patient's usual treatment for as long as possible, and to restart it as soon as possible afterwards. If necessary, a nasogastric tube can be used to administer levodopa, which must be taken enterally. If levodopa cannot be restarted, or the 'off' effects are very severe, apomorphine can be given. However, this drug should only be used under expert supervision because of the complexities of dosing and managing the problematic side-effects.

Centrally acting anticholinergic drugs should be avoided, along with those known to be associated with parkinsonism (e.g. some antiemetics). If an antisialagogue is required for drooling, glycopyrrolate should be used. Patients with severe lung disease or chronic aspiration may have worsened respiratory function postoperatively. Regional anaesthesia may offer a way to avoid general anaesthesia and allow earlier resumption of oral therapy. However, tremor and rigidity may hamper attempts to place neuraxial blocks or to use regional techniques.

There is little evidence on which to base the choice of general anaesthetic drugs or techniques (Zornberg et al. 1991). For example, while inhalation anaesthetics have complex interactions with dopaminergic pathways, there is no known contraindication to their use in patients with Parkinson's disease. Parkinsonism has been seen after use of thiopental, but the clinical significance of the few available reports is unclear (Nicholson et al. 2002). The lack of evidence is particularly pertinent to the use of propofol, as it is, otherwise, a useful agent for patients undergoing asleep–awake–asleep surgery for insertion of deep brain electrodes to manage their Parkinson's disease. Propofol induced dyskinesias in two Parkinson's patients temporarily off treatment (Kraus et al. 1996) and in a patient undergoing deep brain electrode placement (Deogaonkar et al. 2006), and it reduces neuronal activity in the subthalamic nucleus, interfering with accurate placement of the electrodes (Raz et al. 2010), although it has been used successfully for this procedure.

Morphine and other opioids may interact with dopamine pathways. In two patients morphine caused a reduction of dyskinetic movements at low doses and akinesia at higher doses (Berg et al. 1999). An acute dystonic reaction was observed after alfentanil 20 $\mu g\ kg^{-1}$ in a patient with untreated Parkinson's disease (Mets 1991). A possible association between Parkinson's disease and suxamethonium-related hyperkalaemia has been reported, but others have failed to find a link (Gravlee 1980; Muzzi et al. 1989).

Stroke and cerebrovascular disease

Stroke is defined by the World Health Organization as a clinical syndrome of rapid onset of focal (or global, as in subarachnoid haemorrhage) cerebral deficit, lasting more than 24 h (unless interrupted by surgery or death), with no apparent cause other than a vascular one. With the ageing population, the incidence of stroke is rising. More than 150 000 people in the United Kingdom have a stroke each year (Stroke Association 2016), and many hundreds of thousands of patients are alive in the United Kingdom having suffered a stroke in the past.

Pathophysiology

About 85% of strokes are ischaemic (most commonly thrombotic, and less commonly embolic) and the rest are haemorrhagic. The immediate importance of this distinction is that thrombotic stroke may be suitable for acute thrombolysis, whereas haemorrhagic strokes are not. The important risk factors are hypertension, diabetes, smoking, high cholesterol, and atrial fibrillation (embolic stroke). Patients with atrial fibrillation are likely to receive warfarin; other patients surviving a thrombotic stroke will have medical conditions treated and lifestyle factors modified. Secondary prevention with low-dose aspirin is common, while the benefits of other antiplatelet agents are less clear. High cholesterol will be treated with diet and statins and blood pressure will be controlled.

Previous stroke or transient ischaemic attack is a significant risk factor for a perioperative stroke. In general, patients with symptomatic carotid stenosis should undergo carotid endarterectomy before major surgery (Selim 2007). The use of such surgery in patients with asymptomatic carotid bruits is much less clear, and referral for specialist advice is warranted (Selim 2007).

Recent stroke

The immediate management of stroke (ischaemic, haemorrhagic including subarachnoid haemorrhage, and embolic) is not the remit of this chapter. Some stroke patients require urgent anaesthesia for thrombectomy or other interventional neuroradiology procedures, or for decompressive craniectomy for malignant middle cerebral artery syndrome. Again, these conditions, as well anaesthesia for carotid artery disease, are covered elsewhere. In nearly all other situations surgery in patients with a recent stroke can be deferred. If urgent anaesthesia is required, they are best served by treating them like any other patient with a recent brain injury—with careful attention to blood pressure control, hydration, oxygenation, and blood sugar concentration.

Perioperative management of patients with a previous stroke

There is very little data on how long-standing stroke patients should be managed. Many will present with the same conditions requiring surgery seen in other elderly patients needing urological, ophthalmic, or orthopaedic procedures. Previous stroke is often but one of their co-morbidities, and their care should be tailored to these conditions; a good common-sense approach with maintenance of normal (for that patient) blood pressure, good hydration, and monitoring after surgery for adequate recovery of respiratory function is required.

Patients with significant upper motor neurone loss are at risk of an exaggerated hyperkalaemic response to succinylcholine (as mentioned elsewhere). While one approach would be to balance the risks and benefits of using this agent, rocuronium is a satisfactory alternative in many circumstances.

Managing antiplatelet and anticoagulant therapies

Many patients will be taking aspirin and may also be taking clopidogrel (or other antiplatelet agents). Alternatively, warfarin is commonly given to patients with atrial fibrillation. Statins will also be commonly prescribed and, of course, should be continued in the perioperative period. A number of guidelines about the management of these agents in patients undergoing surgery have been produced (Gogarten et al. 2010; Horlocker et al. 2010; Harrop-Griffiths et al. 2013). Chronic use of aspirin rarely leads to difficulty, but use of clopidogrel and, of course, warfarin can lead to bleeding problems. Similarly, these agents will preclude the use of central neuraxial blockade.

Rare neurological conditions

Intermittently an anaesthetist will be asked to care for a patient with a condition they have never encountered, or possibly never heard of, before. A good grasp of the basic science underlying both the intended anaesthetic and the condition involved can help immensely. Rather than provide a commentary on an endless list of rare neurological conditions, what follows is a summary of some related conditions and their implications for anaesthesia. While this may not cover every condition that an anaesthetist may encounter, it is hoped that the basic principles and science can be transferred to manage such patients.

The core principles of careful preoperative assessment to establish the deficit and problems caused by the condition, with a careful assessment of airway, breathing, and circulation are essential and must be coupled with an understanding of the pathophysiology of the disease and relevant pharmacology in order to provide a safe anaesthetic. An awareness of associated conditions and diseases is also important and where relevant these are outlined in the following sections.

Muscle diseases, including myotonic dystrophy, are covered in Chapter 80.

Movement disorders

The basal ganglia are found at the base of the forebrain and interlink with the upper cortex, brainstem, and cerebellum. This allows them to act as a coordinating centre that moderates and fine-tunes movement initiated in the motor cortex. Consequently dysfunction of the basal ganglia can result in abnormal movement or difficulties controlling movement. This dysfunction may result from degenerative or inherited disease, drug toxicity, or injury from hypoxia or trauma. The anaesthetic management of these conditions is broadly similar as the underlying abnormalities are also similar. Table 81.7 summarizes some of the basal ganglia disorders that are seen in clinical practice. Parkinson's disease is the most common of these disorders and is dealt with in more detail elsewhere in this chapter.

Consideration of the individual's health, reserve, and frailty is an important part of the anaesthetic assessment and perioperative plan. Careful attention should be paid to medications and potential interactions with anaesthetic drugs. Drugs acting on dopaminergic pathways may exacerbate movement disorders and should be avoided where possible and the patient's regular drug therapy should be continued wherever possible.

Patients with Sydenham's chorea need to be assessed carefully for evidence of cardiovascular compromise as a result of rheumatic fever. In particular, mitral valve stenosis may cause significant perioperative cardiovascular instability. In Huntington's chorea, basal ganglia GABA concentrations are decreased and somatostatin concentrations are increased (Benumof 1998). Despite this there are no

Table 81.7 Summary of the commoner basal ganglia related movement disorders

Parkinson's disease	Idiopathic onset aged 4–70 years Characterized by bradykinesia, pill-rolling tremor, shuffling gait, and expressionless face Caused by dopamine deficiency in caudate and putamen Autonomic dysfunction and dementia may occur Treated with dopamine or drugs to boost CNS dopamine
Huntington's chorea	Autosomal dominant trinucleotide repeat disorder Onset typically 35–40 years Chorea, ataxia, and dysarthria initially Dementia increases as disease progress No treatment
Sydenham's chorea	Also known as 'St. Vitus's dance' Typically seen in children as an auto-immune complication of group A β-haemolytic streptococcal infection Seen in 20–30% of cases of rheumatic fever Chorea, dysarthria, and loss of fine motor control Associated with endocarditis and ECG abnormalities
Spasmodic torticollis (and other craniocervical spasms)	Intermittent irregular spasms of the muscles of head and/or neck, typically sternocleidomastoid Onset is early to mid adulthood Possibly due to hypersensitivity to dopamine in striatum Surgical interruption of spinal accessory nerve and C1–3 motor roots is effective
Torsion dystonia	Also known as Oppenheim's disease Genetic disease with varied inheritance and onset Gradual onset involuntary writhing movements and torsion spasms Spasms may cause spinal deformity needing correction or making airway management difficult

convincing reports of complications of anaesthetic drugs acting on GABA-ergic pathways (Gaubatz and Wehner 1992). Plasma cholinesterase activity may be decreased and may result in prolonged duration of muscle weakness after succinylcholine, although this is not a consistent finding and should not be considered a contraindication to its use (Costarino and Gross 1985). Anticholinergic agents which cross the blood–brain barrier, such as atropine, may exacerbate chorea.

Diseases causing motor neurone degeneration

A wide variety of degenerative, acquired, and inherited diseases can lead to weakness and muscle wasting without sensory deficit. The most common form is motor neurone disease (also known as amyotrophic lateral sclerosis).

Motor neurone disease

This is a pre-junctional condition that causes upper and lower motor neurone degeneration. Its most common form is sporadic, but inherited forms sometimes associated with dementia have been described. It causes a rapidly progressive weakness of skeletal, respiratory, and bulbar muscles (McDermott and Shaw 2008). There is no curative treatment and death from neuromuscular respiratory failure is typical, although this may be delayed with the use of non-invasive ventilation and tracheostomy. The glutamate release inhibitor riluzole can extend survival by a few months. Its important side-effects include interstitial lung disease, bone marrow suppression, and hepatitis (Lacomblez et al. 1996). The numbers of extra-junctional acetylcholine receptors increase in denervated muscle, leading to the risk of significant hyperkalaemia with suxamethonium, which should be avoided. The effective dose of non-depolarizing neuromuscular blocking agents is reduced and their effect should be closely monitored (Marsh and Pittard 2011). Patients with significant respiratory muscle weakness pose a clinical and ethical challenge for the anaesthetist.

As with most patients suffering from respiratory disease, regional or central neuraxial anaesthesia may be considered superior; however, care must be taken with techniques which can cause respiratory muscle weakness such as interscalene block, or respiratory depression such as intrathecal opioids.

Postoperative respiratory failure is common in these patients. This may not be easily reversed as the remaining respiratory muscle mass will atrophy rapidly limiting their ability to wean back to unsupported spontaneous breathing. Detailed preoperative assessment and discussion with the patient is essential, and, if appropriate, limitations of care or plans for a tracheostomy at the time of surgery may need to be made. Ideally postoperative respiratory support is provided with non-invasive ventilation only and weaned rapidly.

Other conditions that involve motor neurone degeneration are summarized in Table 81.8. The anaesthetic considerations are largely similar to those described previously for patients with motor neurone disease.

Table 81.8 Summary of conditions involving degeneration of motor neurones

Spinal muscular atrophy Type 1 to 4	Inherited condition ranging from rapidly progressive weakness usually fatal in the first year of life (type 1), to chronic indolent weakness developing in adulthood (type 4)
Friedrich's ataxia	Inherited progressive ataxia with degeneration of motor neurones within spinal cord. Typical signs include upper and lower motor neurone and cerebellar deficits
Guillain–Barré syndrome	Acquired typically post-infectious autoimmune demyelination of lower motor neurones Autonomic dysfunction is common. Respiratory support may be required
Acute disseminated encephalomyelitis (ADEM)	Immune mediated demyelination of brain and spinal cord closely related to multiple sclerosis. Typically following infection or occasionally vaccination or sporadic. Recovery is seen in 50–70% but a more aggressive necrotizing form also exists

Spinal cord injury

The anaesthetic management of patients sustaining an acute spinal cord injury is dealt with elsewhere within this text; however, patients with an established spinal cord injury and neurological deficit will present for a variety of surgical procedures. During preoperative assessment it is essential to consider the level and nature of the cord lesion and its subsequent neurological deficit, and any previous surgical interventions.

Neck movement may be limited as a result of muscular contractions or surgical fixation leading to potential difficulty achieving satisfactory laryngoscopy for intubation. Any deficit originating from a thoracic vertebral level will reduce intercostal muscle function, though after a period of adaption this is often well tolerated. For quadriplegic patients dependent on diaphragmatic breathing, respiratory function is optimal in the supine or mild Trendelenburg position (Baydur et al. 2001). Assessment of respiratory function and planning for postoperative care or support may be informed by spirometry and arterial blood gases. Tracheal intubation and mechanical ventilation of the lungs is likely to be necessary for most patients with high thoracic or cervical cord injury and the choice of anaesthetic agents and analgesic strategy should be aimed at minimizing respiratory depression postoperatively. It may be necessary to plan for a period of postoperative ventilation and slow weaning of support depending on the baseline function of the patient and the expected impact of surgery on the respiratory system.

High thoracic and cervical cord lesions will produce significant reduction in sympathetic tone below the lesion resulting in vasodilation, relative hypotension, and a reduction in the tachycardic response to hypotension. The impact of this will need to be considered carefully by the anaesthetist as it will be exacerbated by most anaesthetic agents, and may mask the typical signs of hypovolaemia. The inability to vasoconstrict below the level of the cord lesion also has implications for thermoregulation. Careful attention should be paid to monitoring and maintaining a normal temperature, especially during long procedures.

Chronic kidney disease is common as a result of urinary retention, infection, and calculus formation. Baseline renal function should be checked and when abnormal the patient should be assessed for common complications of chronic kidney disease. Extra-junctional proliferation of nicotinic acetylcholine receptors is common in denervated muscle after spinal cord injury and can cause life-threatening hyperkalaemia even with normal renal function (Martin and Richtsfeld 2006). Suxamethonium is best avoided in patients with an established spinal cord injury.

It may seem logical to question the necessity of any form of anaesthesia when a patient has been rendered insensate below the level of their spinal cord lesion; however, spinal and autonomic reflexes often persist and can lead to significant problems. Autonomic hyperreflexia is a generalized autonomic over-activity in response to stimulus below the level of the cord lesion. This typically may include bowel or bladder distension or other intra-abdominal pathology such as appendicitis or labour, or soft tissue or bone injury including surgery. The physiological effects may be mild or can be life-threatening. Severe hypertension may lead to pulmonary oedema, cardiac failure, and intracranial haemorrhage. The risk of autonomic hyperreflexia increases with higher cord lesions. It is said to be very rare below T10, but occurs in 65–85% of patients with a lesion above T7 (Lindan et al. 1980). The best management is to avoid triggers by good bowel management, catheter care, and anaesthesia for surgical interventions, even minor procedures.

The choice of anaesthetic technique will depend on many patient factors and the proposed surgery. Central neuraxial techniques are not always contraindicated; however, there may be difficulties positioning the patient or identifying the relevant anatomy. The procedure itself may cause an autonomic hyperreflexia and the extent of the block may be impossible to assess. This means that the first sign of an inadequate block or missed segment may be significant autonomic hyperreflexia in response to surgical stimulus.

Diseases of the autonomic nervous system

Autonomic neuropathy is most commonly encountered as a secondary effect of another pathology. Rarely it may be seen as a congenital disease or an isolated idiopathic acquired disease. Table 81.9 summarizes the different aetiologies within these categories.

These conditions cause varying severity of autonomic dysfunction but as a rule the inherited forms and acquired pandysautonomia are the most severe forms. These lead to a patient with a low systemic vascular resistance and a cardiac output which is largely pre-load dependent. Inotropic and chronotropic responses to increased demand are poor and responses to adrenoceptor stimulation by drugs acting either by intrinsic or extrinsic (direct or indirect) mechanisms are variable. Respiratory impairment is common as responses to hypoxia and hypercapnia may also be impaired; some of these conditions are associated with scoliosis and subsequent restrictive lung disease.

When severe, these disorders present a significant challenge to the anaesthetist. Preoperative aims are to ensure respiratory function is optimized with physiotherapy and antibiotics where required. Circulating volume should be restored and maintained at normal levels during preoperative fasting. Ensuring euvolaemia at the time of induction may reduce the risk of severe hypotension in response to anaesthetic agents. Delayed gastric emptying may not be clinically evident and rapid sequence induction should be considered for all patients with autonomic neuropathy. Atropine is usually effective at reversing bradycardia and hypotension should be managed with fluid challenges and a directly acting alpha-agonist. Invasive monitoring and central venous access is recommended (Lindan et al. 1980). Postoperative care should be undertaken in a high-dependency environment where respiratory and cardiovascular monitoring and support can be offered. Non-opioid analgesia is preferable, when possible.

Table 81.9 Causes of autonomic neuropathy

Classification	Diseases
Congenital	Familial amyloid polyneuropathy
	Hereditary sensory autonomic neuropathy I–V
	Fabry disease
	Acute intermittent and variegate porphyria
Primary acquired	Pandysautonomia
	Idiopathic distal small fibre neuropathy
	Holmes–Adie syndrome
	Ross syndrome
	Chronic amyloid anhidrosis
	Amyloid neuropathy
	Postural orthostatic tachycardia syndrome (POTS)
Secondary acquired	Diabetes
	Uraemia
	Liver disease
	Vitamin/nutrient deficiency
	Infections (Lyme disease, HIV, Chagas disease, botulism; diphtheria, leprosy)
	Autoimmune diseases (coeliac disease, Sjögren's syndrome, rheumatoid arthritis, systemic lupus erythematosus, Guillain–Barre syndrome, Lambert–Eaton myasthenic syndrome, paraneoplastic neuropathy, inflammatory bowel disease)

In less severe cases, autonomic neuropathy may be suggested by exercise intolerance, postural hypotension, or resting tachycardia in a patient with an associated disease—typically diabetes mellitus. Further detection may be undertaken by assessing heart rate responses to deep breathing, a Valsalva manoeuvre or standing, or analysis of R-R variability on an ECG. The anaesthetist should be wary of the risks of aspiration at the time of induction and disordered cardiorespiratory autoregulation during, and after, an anaesthetic (Oakeley and Emond 2011).

Neurofibromatosis

Neurofibromatosis type 1 and 2 are autosomal dominant conditions, although a high number of cases are as a result of a spontaneous mutation. The characteristic lesions are tumours arising from nerve tissue. Neurofibromatosis type 1 is the more common form with predominantly cutaneous lesions. The main complication of these lesions is compression of the involved nerve leading to pain or neuropathy. Renal artery stenosis occurs in 1–2% of cases. Neurofibromatosis type 2 is a rarer, but more serious, form with tumours originating from the central nervous system including acoustic neuromas (more correctly called vestibular Schwannomas; typically bilateral) and meningiomas. Epilepsy is common. The most important anaesthetic consideration in a patient with neurofibromatosis is to understand and recognize the associated conditions. These include pulmonary fibrosis, phaeochromocytoma (occasionally as part of multiple endocrine neoplasia type 3), and skeletal deformity including scoliosis. There are no specific reports of complications arising from anaesthetic agents in patients with neurofibromatosis (Hirsch et al. 2001).

Declaration of interest

None declared.

References

Stroke Association. *About Stroke*. 2016. Available from http://www.stroke.org.uk/about-stroke

Baraka A. Anaesthesia and myasthenia gravis. *Can J Anaesthesiol* 1992; **39**: 476–86

Baydur A, Adkins RH, Milic-Emili J. Lung mechanics in individuals with spinal cord injury: effects of level of injury and posture. *J Appl Physiol* 2001; **90**: 405–11

Benumof JL. *Anaesthesia and Uncommon Diseases*, 4th Edn. Philadelphia, PA: WB Saunders Company, 1998

Berg D, Becker G, Reiners K. Reduction of dyskinesia and induction of akinesia induced by morphine in two Parkinsonism patients with severe sciatica. *J Neural Transm (Vienna)* 1999; **106**: 725–8

Bonicalzi V, Canavero S, Cerutti F, Piazza M, Clemente M, Chio A. Lamotrigine reduces total postoperative analgesia requirement: a randomised double-blind, placebo controlled pilot study. *Surgery* 1997; **122**: 567–70

Borris DJ, Bertram EH, Kapur J. Ketamine controls prolonged status epilepticus. *Epilepsy Res* 2000; **42**: 117–22

Bromfield EB, Cavazos JE, Sirven JI. *An Introduction to Epilepsy*. West Hartford, CT: American Epilepsy Society, 2006

Brown AS, Horton JM. Status epilepticus treated by intravenous infusions of thiopentone sodium. *Br Med J* 1967; **1**: 27–8

Brown RF, Tennant CC, Sharrock M, *et al*. Relationship between stress and relapse in multiple sclerosis: Part 1. Multiple sclerosis, 2006; **12**: 453–64

Celesia CG, Chen R-C, Bamforth BK. Effects of ketamine in epilepsy. *Neurology* 1975; **25**: 169

Challoner PB, Smith KT, Parker JD, *et al*. Plaque associated expression of human herpes virus in multiple sclerosis. *Proc Natl Acad Sci U S A* 1995; **92**: 7440–4

Cheng MA, Templehoff R. Epilepsy and anaesthesia. *Curr Opin Anaesthesiol* 1999; **12**: 523–8

Confavreux C, Hutchinson M, Hours M, Cortinovis-Tourniaire P, Moreau T. For the Pregnancy in Multiple Sclerosis Group. Rate of pregnancy-related relapse in multiple sclerosis. *N Engl J Med* 1988; **339**: 285–91

Constanst I, Seeman R, Murat I. Sevoflurance and epileptiform EEG changes. *Paediatr Anaesth* 2005; **15**: 266–74

Cooperman LH. Succinylcholine induced hyperkalemia in neuromuscular disease. *JAMA* 1970; **213**: 1867–71

Costarino A, Gross J. Patients with Huntington's disease may respond normally to succinylcholine. *Anesthesiology* 1985; **63**: 570

Craig S. Phenytoin Poisoning. *Neurocrit Care* 2005; **3**: 161–70

Cree BAC. Multiple sclerosis. In: Brust JCM, ed. *Current Diagnosis and Treatment in Neurology.* New York: Lange Medical Books/McGraw-Hill Medical, 2007

Darotta IR, Schubert A. Multiple sclerosis and anaesthetic implications. *Curr Opin Anaesthesiol* 2002; **15**: 365–70

de Rijk MC, Tzourio C, Breteler MM, *et al*. Prevalence of parkinsonism and Parkinson's disease in Europe: the EUROPARKINSON Collaborative Study. *J Neuro Neurosurg Psych* 1997; **62**: 10–15

Deogaonkar A, Deogaonkar M, Lee JK, Ebrahim Z, Schubert A. Propofol-induced dyskinesias controlled with dexmedetomidine during deep brain simulation surgery. *Anesthesiology* 2006; **104**: 1337–9

Dierdorf SF, McNiece WL, Rao CC, *et al*. Effect of succinylcholine on plasma potassium in children with cerebral palsy. *Anesthesiology* 1985; **62**: 88–90

Drake E, Drake M, Bird J, Russell R. Obstetric regional blocks for women with multiple sclerosis: a survey of UK experience. *Int J Obstetr Anesth* 2006; **15**: 115–23

Driver and Vehicle Licensing Agency (DVLA). *At a Glance Guide to the Current Medical Standards of Fitness to Drive*. August 2011. Available from http://www.dft.gov.uk/dvla/medical/ataglance.aspx

Ebrahim ZY, DeBoer GE, Luders H, Hahn J, Lesser P. Effect of etomidate on electroencephalogram of patients with epilepsy. *Anesth Analg* 1986; **65**: 1004–6

Eisenkraft JB, Brook WJ, Mann SM, Papatestas AE, Hubbard M. Resistance to succinylcholine in myasthenia gravis: a dose-response study. *Anesthesiology* 1988; **69**: 760–3

Enoki T, Yoshiyuki N, Hirokawa Y, Nomura R, Hatano Y and Mori K. Marked sensitivity to pancuronium in a patient without clinical manifestations of myasthenia gravis. *Anesth Analg* 1989; **69**: 840–2

Faccenda KA, Finucane BT. Complications of regional anaesthesia. Incidence and prevention. *Drug Saf* 2001; **24**: 413–2

Fear CF, Littlejohns CS, Rouse E, McQuail P. Propofol anaesthesia in electroconvulsive therapy. Reduced seizure duration may not be relevant. *Br J Psychiatry* 2005; **165**: 506–9

Ferrer-Allado T, Brechner VL, Dymond A, Cozen H, Crandall P. Ketamine induced electroconvulsive pehnomena in human limbic and thalamic regions. *Anesthesiology* 1973; **38**: 333–44

Fisher RS, van Emde Boas W, Blume W, *et al*. Epileptic Seizures and Epilepsy: Definitions Proposed by the International League Against Epilepsy and the International Bureau for Eiplepsy. *Epilepsia* 2005; **46**: 470–2

Folstein MF, Folstein SE, McHugh PR. Mini-Mental State: a practical method for grading the cognitive state of patients for the clinician. *J Psychiatr Res* 1975; **12**: 189–98

Foxall G, McCahon R, Lamb J, Hardman JG, Bedforth NM. Levobupivicaine-induced seizures and cardiovascular collapse treated with Intralipid. *Anaesthesia* 2007; **62**: 516–8

Frei FJ, Haemmerle MH, Brunner R, Kern C. Minimum alveolar concentration for halothane in children with cerebral palsy and severe mental retardation. *Anesthesia* 1997; **52**: 1056–60

Garcia-Morales I, Garcia MT, Galari-Davila L, *et al*. Periodic lateralized epileptiform discharges: etiology, clinical aspects, seizures and evolution in 130 patients. *J Clin Neurophysiol* 2002; **19**: 172–7

Gaubatz CL, Wehner RJ. Anesthetic considerations for the patient with Huntington's disease. *AANA* 1992; **60**: 40–44

Gogarten W, Vandermeulen E, Van Aken H, *et al*. Regional anaesthesia and antithrombotic agents: recommendations of the European Society of Anaesthesiology. *Eur J Anaesthesiol* 2010; **27**: 999–1015

Gomar C, Carrero EJ. Delayed arousal after general anesthesia associated with baclofen. *Anesthesiology* 1994; **81**: 1306–7

Goodkin DE, Rudick RA, Ross JS, *et al*. The use of brain magnetic resonance imaging in multiple sclerosis. *Arch Neurol* 1994; **51**: 505–16

Gratrix AP, Enright SM. Epilepsy in anaesthesia and intensive care. *Contin Educ Anaesth Crit Care Pain* 2005; **5**: 118–21

Gravlee GP. Succinylcholine-induced hyperkalemia in a patient with Parkinson's disease. *Anesth Analg* 1980; **59**: 444–6

Guthrie TC, Nelson DA. Influence of temperature changes on multiple sclerosis: critical review of mechanisms and research potential. *J Neurosci* 1995; **129**: 1–8

Harrop-Griffiths W, Cook T, Gill H, *et al*. Regional anaesthesia and patients with abnormalities of coagulation. *Anaesthesia* 2013; **68**: 966–72

Hauser SL, Goodwin DS. Multiple sclerosis and other demyelinating diseases. In: Fauci AS, Braunwald E, Kasper DL, Hauser SL, eds. *Harrison's Principles of Internal Medicine*, vol. II, 17th ed. New York: McGraw-Hill Medical, 2008; 2611–21

Hebel JR, Horlocker TT, Schroeder DR. Neuraxial anaesthesia and analgesia in patients with pre-existing central nervous system disorders. *Anesth Analg* 2006; **103**: 223–8

Hepner DL, Castells MC. Anaphylaxis during the perioperative period. *Anesth Analg* 2003; **97**: 1381–95

Herman ST, Pedley TA. New options for the treatment of epilepsy. *JAMA* 1998; **280**: 693–4

Hines R, Marshall K (eds). *Stoelting's Anesthesia and Co-existing Disease*, 5th Edn. Philadelphia, PA: Saunders Publishers, 2008

Hirsch NP, Murphy A, Radcliffe J. Neurofibromatosis: clinical presentation and anaesthetic implications. *Br J Anaesth* 2001; **86**: 555–64

Horlocker TT, Wedel DJ, Rowlingson JC, *et al*. Regional anesthesia in the patient receiving antithrombotic or thrombolytic therapy. *Reg Anesth Pain Med* 2010; **35**: 64–101

Hughes BW, Moro De Casillas ML, Kaminski HJ. Pathophysiology of myasthenia gravis. *Semin Neurol* 2004; **24**: 21–30

Ito BM, Sato S, Kufta CV, Tran D. Effect of isoflurane and enflurane on the electrocorticogram of epileptic patients. *Neurology* 1988; 38: 924–8

Joint Formulary Committee. *British National Formulary*, 65th Edn. London: BMJ Group and Pharmaceutical Press, March 2014

Kattula A, Kranner P, Arndt G. Regional anesthesia in the presence of neurological disease. In: Finucane BT, ed. *Complications of Regional Anesthesia*. New York: Churchill Livingstone, 1999; 294–6

Kim JM, Mangold J. Sensitivity to both vecuronium and neostigmine in a seronegative myasthenic patient. *Br J Anaesth* 1989; **63**: 497–500

Kopp SL, Wynd KP, Horlocker TT, Hebl JR, Wilson JL. Regional blockade in patients with a history of seizure disorder. *Anesth Analg* 2009; **109**: 272–8

Kraus JK, Akeyson EW, Giam P, Jankovic J. Propofol-induced dyskienesias in Parkinson's disease. *Anesth Analg* 1996; **83**: 420–2

Kronenberg MF, Laimer I, Rifici C, *et al*. Epileptic seizure associated with intracerebroventricular and intrathecal morphine bolus. *Pain* 1998; **75**: 383–7

Kumar V, Kaminski HJ. Treatment of myasthenia gravis. *Curr Neurol Neurosci Rep* 2011: **11**: 89–96

Kurtzke JF. Multiple sclerosis: changing times. *Neuroepidemiology* 1991; **10**: 1–8

Lacomblez L, Bensimon G, Leigh PN, Guillet P, Meininger V. Dose-ranging study of riluzole in amyotrophic lateral sclerosis. Amyotrophic Lateral Sclerosis/Riluzole Study Group II. *Lancet* 1996; **347**: 1425–31

Lindan R, Joiner F, Freechafer A, Hazel C. Incidence and clinical features of autonomic dysreflexia in patients with spinal cord injury. *Paraplegia* 1980; **18**: 285–92

Lindstrom JM, Seybold MD, Lennon VA, Whittingham S, Duane DD. Antibody to acetylcholine receptor in myasthenia gravis: prevalence, clinical correlates, and diagnostic value. *Neurology* 1976; **26**: 1054–9

Lumb AB, Calder I. "Cured" myasthenia gravis and neuromuscular blockade. *Anaesthesia* 1989; **44**: 828–30

Manninen PH, Burke SJ Wennberg R, Lozano AM, El Beheiry H. Intraoperative localization of an epileptogenic focus with alfentanil and fentanyl. *Anesth Analg* 1999; **88**: 1101–6

Marsh S, Pittard A. Neuromuscular disorders and anaesthesia. Part 2: specific neuromuscular conditions. *Contin Educ Anaesth Crit Care Pain* 2011; **11**: 119–23

Martin JA, Richtsfeld M. Succinylcholine-induced hyperkalemia in acquired pathologic states: etiologic factors and molecular mechanisms. *Anesthesiology* 2006; **104**: 158–69

Masuda Y, Kawamura A. Acetylcholinesterase inhibitor (donepezil hydrochloride) reduces heart rate variability. *J Cardiovasc Pharmacol* 2003; **41**(Suppl. 1): S67–71

Mathias CJ. Autonomic diseases: clinical features and laboratory evaluation. *J Neurol Neurosurg Psychiatry* 2003; **74**: iii31–41

Maxwell MJ, Moran CG, Moppett IK. Development and validation of a preoperative scoring system to predict 30-day mortality in patients undergoing hip fracture surgery. *Br J Anaesth* 2008; **101**: 511–7

McDermott CJ, Shaw PJ. Diagnosis and management of motor neurone disease. *BMJ* 2008; **336**: 658

Mets B. Acute dystonia after alfentanil in untreated Parkinson's disease. *Anesth Analg* 1991; **72**: 557–8

Moghal S, Rajput AH, D'Arcy C, Rajput R. Prevalence of movement disorders in elderly community residents. *Neuroepidemiology* 1994; **13**: 175–8

Muzzi DA, Black S, Cucchiara RF. The lack of effect of succinylcholine on serum potassium in patients with Parkinson's disease. *Anesthesiology* 1989; **71**: 322

Nicholson G, Periera AC, Hall GM. Parkinson's disease and anaesthesia. *Br J Anaesth* 2002; **89**: 904–16

Nickalls RWD, Mapleson WW. Age-related iso-MAC charts for isoflurane, sevoflurane and desflurane in man. *Br J Anaesth* 2003; **91**: 170–4

Nolan J, Chalkiadis GA, Low J, Olesch CA, Brown TCK. Anaesthesia and pain management in cerebral palsy. *Anaesthesia* 2000; **55**: 32–41

Noseworthy JH, Lucchinetti C, Rodriguez M, Weinshenker BG. Multiple sclerosis. *N Engl J Med* 2000; **343**: 938–52

Oakely I, Emond L. Diabetic cardiac autonomic neuropathy and anaesthetic management: review of the literature. *AANA J* 2011; **79**: 473–9

Osserman KE, Genkins G. Studies in myasthenia gravis: Review of a twenty-year experience in over 1200 patients. *Mt Sinai J Med* 1971; **38**: 497–537

Osserman KE, Kaplan L. Rapid diagnostic tests for myasthenia gravis: Increased muscle strength, without fasciculations, after intravenous administration of edrophonium (Tensilon®) chloride. *JAMA* 1952; **150**: 265–8

Parviainen I, Uusaro A, Kalviainenr, Mervaala E, Ruokenen E. Propofol in the treatment of resistant status epilepticus. *Intensive Care Med* 2006; **32**: 1075–9

Pastor J, Wix R, Meilan ML, *et al*. Etomidate localizes the epileptic area in patients with temporal lobe epilepsy. *Epilepsia* 2010; **51**: 602–9

Raz A, Eimerl D, Zaidel A, Bergman H, Israel Z. Propofol decreases neuronal population spiking activity in the subthalamic nucleus of Parkinsonism patients. *Anesth Analg* 2010; **111**: 1285–9

Renna M, Handy J, Shah A. Low baseline Bispectral index on the electroencephalogram in patients with dementia. *Anesth Analg* 2003; **96**: 1380–5

Sadovnick AD, Armstrong H, Rice GP, *et al*. A population-based study of multiple sclerosis in twins: update. *Ann Neurol* 1993; **33**: 281–5

Sanchez Morillo J, Demartini Ferrari A, Roca de Togores Lopez A. Interaction of donepezil and muscular blockers in Alzheimer's disease. *Rev Esp Anestesiol Reanim* 2003; **50**: 97–100

Seitz DP, Gill SS, Gruneir A, Austin PC, Anderson G, Reimer CL, Rochon PA. Effects of cholinesterase inhibitors on postoperative outcomes of older adults with dementia undergoing hip fracture surgery. *Am J Geriatr Psychiatry* 2011; **19**: 803–13

Selim M. Perioperative stroke. *N Engl J Med* 2007; **356**: 706–13

Shany E, Benzaqen O, Watemberg N. Comparison of continuous drip of midazolam or lidocaine in the treatment of intractable neonatal seizures. *J Child Neurol* 2007; **22**: 255–9

Shorvon S, Ferlisi M. The treatment of super-refractory status epilepticus: a critical review of available therapies and a clinical treatment protocol. *Brain* 2011; **134**: 2802–18

Siegfried RN, Jacobson L, Chabal C. Development of an acute withdrawal syndrome following the cessation of intrathecal baclofen in a patient with spasticity. *Anesthesiology* 1992; **77**: 1048–50

Sill JC, Schumacher K, Southorn PA, Reuter J, Yaksh TL. Bradycardia and hypotension associated with baclofen used during general anesthesia. *Anesthesiology* 1986; **64**: 255–8

Smeltzer SC, Skurnick JH, Troiano R. Respiratory function in multiple sclerosis. Utility of clinical assessment of respiratory muscle function. *Chest* 1992; **101**: 479–84

Smith PJ, Attix DK, Weldon C, Greene NH, Monk TG. Executive function and depression as independent risk factors for postoperative delirium. *Anesthesiology* 2009; **110**: 781–7

Smith S, Scarth E, Sasada M. *Drugs in Anaesthesia and Intensive Care*. Oxford: Oxford University Press, 2011

Sneyd JR. Excitatory events associated with propofol anaesthesia: a review. *J R Soc Med* 1992; **85**: 288–91

Sneyd JR. Propofol and epilepsy. *Br J Anaesth* 1999; **82**: 168–9

Sriram S, Stratton CW, Yao S, *et al*. Chlamydia pneumoniae infection of the central nervous system in multiple sclerosis. *Ann Neurol* 1999; **46**: 6–14

Sweeney BP, Bromilow J. Liver enzyme induction and inhibition: implications for anaesthesia. *Anaesthesia* 2006; **61**: 159–77

Tantucci C, Massucci M, Piperno R. Control of breathing and respiratory muscle strength in patients with multiple sclerosis. *Chest* 1994; **105**: 1163–70

Tateishi A, Zornow M, Scheller M, Canfell P. Electroencephalographic effects of laudanosine in an animal model of epilepsy. *Br J Anaesth* 1989; **62**: 548–52

Thavasothy V, Hirsch N. Myasthenia gravis. *BJA CEPD Rev* 2002; **2**: 88–90

The Association of Anaesthetists of Great Britain and Ireland. *AAGBI Safety Guideline Management of Severe Local Anaesthetic Toxicity*. 2010. Available from http://www.aagbi.org/sites/default/files/la_toxicity_2010_0.pdf

The National Society for Epilepsy. *Facts about Epilepsy*. Available from https://www.epilepsysociety.org.uk/facts-and-statistics#.WBzxp_mLSM8

Tomson T, Hiilesma V. Epilepsy and pregnancy. *BMJ* 2007; **335**: 769–73

Unterbuchner C, Fink H, Blobner M. The use of sugammadex in a patient with myasthenia gravis. *Anaesthesia* 2010; **65**: 302–5

Verbough C. Anaesthesia in patients with dementia. *Curr Opin Anaesthesiol* 2004; **17**: 277–83

Voss LJ, Sleigh JW, Barnard JPM, Kirsch HE. The howling cortex: seizures and general anaesthetic drugs. *Anesth Analg* 2008; **107**: 1689–703

Wainwright AP, Brodrick PM. Suxamethonium and myasthenia gravis. *Anaesthesia* 1987; **42**: 950–57

Weinshenker BG, Santrach P, Bissonet AS, *et al.* Major histocompatibility complex class II alleles and the course and outcome of MS: a population based study. *Neurology* 1998; **51**: 742–7

Zornberg GL, Bodkin JA, Cohen BM. Severe adverse interaction between pethidine and selegiline. *Lancet* 1991; **337**: 246

CHAPTER 82

Pulmonary disease and anaesthesia

Gary H. Mills

Why is pulmonary disease important?

Pulmonary disease predisposes patients to intra- and postoperative complications and in some cases may be so severe that the proposed surgery is impossible. Knowledge of the type and severity of the pulmonary disease enables clinicians to determine risk, inform patients, and plan therapy (Featherstone 1932) that may be needed before, during, or after surgery and could also affect the timing of an operation.

Postoperative pulmonary complications are arguably the most common complications in the perioperative period, ranging in incidence from 2% to 19% for non-cardiac elective surgery (Rosen et al. 1992; Pedersen, 1994; Escarce et al. 1995; Lawrence et al. 2002; Mazo et al. 2014). Many are related to underlying pulmonary disease. In the ARISCAT study, postoperative complications leading to respiratory failure occurred in 2.6% of patients in all surgical groups. Postoperative pulmonary complications are at least as common as cardiac complications after non-cardiac surgery (Pedersen 1994; Pedersen et al. 1990, 1992; Lawrence et al. 1996) and in some situations the rate is higher (Khuri et al. 1995). They may create serious morbidity or death. The most common postoperative pulmonary complications are atelectasis, pneumonia (Khuri et al. 1995), respiratory failure, and exacerbation of an underlying chronic lung disease (Smetana et al. 2006). This is important not just in the short term, but also because pulmonary complications are a predictor of longer-term survival. Postoperative pneumonia is, for example, a strong indicator of longer-term outlook after oesophagectomy (Kinugasa et al. 2004). Therefore, it is vital to understand and prepare for the effects of pre-existing respiratory disease or for clinical issues that will expose the respiratory system to more risk.

Preoperative risk prediction

Intuitively, diseases of the respiratory system are likely to have a major impact in the perioperative period. However, there are other factors that also impact respiratory outcomes, and it is important to understand these as they will greatly affect who with respiratory disease is most at risk.

Arozullah et al. (2000) looked at 81 719 male patients undergoing major non-cardiac surgery and examined how many developed respiratory failure, which was defined as more than 48 h of postoperative mechanical ventilation or unplanned tracheal intubation and ventilation. This work divided the risk into operative- and patient-specific factors and led to the development of a risk algorithm (Arozullah et al. 2000, 2001). The operation-specific factors relate largely to the proximity of the incision to the diaphragm, respiratory system, or its control. Abdominal aortic aneurysm surgery, thoracic surgery, upper abdominal surgery, peripheral vascular surgery, neurosurgery, and head and neck surgery topped the list, with emergency surgery adding to the likelihood compared to elective surgery. Patient factors added to this, including plasma albumin concentration, renal function, age and dependency, and chronic obstructive pulmonary disease (COPD). There was 23% mortality where tracheal extubation had not been achieved within 2 days postoperatively, while reintubation of the trachea was associated with 31% mortality: 3.6% of patients developed postoperative pneumonia and 3.4% respiratory failure.

Later, Arozullah et al. (2001) examined the ability to predict the 30-day risk of postoperative pneumonia. This involved gathering data from 160 805 patients for the initial derivation sample and another 155 266 patients for the validation sample. A major disadvantage of this very large study was that 700 patients with respiratory failure requiring mechanical ventilation were excluded because pneumonia had not been formally diagnosed at this point, even though pneumonia would be expected to be affecting at least some of these patients. Despite this, some of the factors identified were similar, including site of surgery, emergency *vs* elective surgery, and age. Importantly, the study included a measure of dependency, which proved influential and also found a history of cerebrovascular accident, renal impairment, and COPD to be significant. The impact of COPD has often been controversial, especially when classified according to spirometry only. Clinical features appeared more important than spirometry.

Smetana et al. (2006) looked at postoperative complications and found a slightly higher incidence of respiratory complications (2.6%) compared to cardiac problems (2.0%). Advanced age, higher ASA class, congestive heart failure, functional dependency, albumin concentration below 35 g litre^{-1}, and abnormal preoperative chest X-ray, all produced an odds ratio greater than 2. Smetana et al. examined chronic lung disease and found COPD confirmed in 13 of 15 studies containing multivariate analysis as a risk factor for postoperative pulmonary complications with an odds ratio of 1.79 [95% confidence interval (CI) 1.44–2.22]. In these patients the cough test also indicated an increased risk. This is when a patient takes in a deep breath, then coughs and continues to cough. It suggests a 3.8 times higher risk of postoperative pulmonary complications. Abnormal findings on chest examination such as crackles or wheezes were a strong predictor of postoperative pulmonary complications with an odds ratio of 5.8 (95% CI 1.04–32.11).

More recently, respiratory outcomes have been examined in a prospective multicentre study of 2500 patients, finding seven key factors that predicted the risk of postoperative respiratory complications, including respiratory failure, with an 88% area under the receiver operating characteristic curve (Canet et al. 2010). These independent risk factors were age, preoperative Sp_{O_2}, respiratory infection in the last month, preoperative anaemia (haemoglobin concentration <100 g litre^{-1}), upper abdominal or thoracic surgery, duration of procedure over 2 or 3 h, and whether the surgery was an emergency procedure. These were weighted as part of the ARISCAT score. A score of 26 indicated a moderate risk and a score higher than 45 indicated a high risk of postoperative pulmonary complications.

Functional dependence

In the United States, the National Surgical Quality Improvement Program data generated two studies that looked at postoperative pulmonary complications and functional dependence (Arozullah et al. 2000, 2001). These examined the difference between no dependence, partial dependence (requiring help with some activity of daily living), and total dependence (unable to perform any activities of daily living). Partial dependence increased the odds ratio by 1.65 (95% CI 1.34–2.01) and total dependence by 2.51 (95% CI 1.99–3.15).

Principles of ventilation and anaesthesia in patients with lung disease

It is vital to be aware of the diagnosis, severity, and current state of control of lung disease as they will affect the decision to proceed to surgery and the perioperative provision that is needed. Consideration must be given to the current status of the disease and the therapies the patient may be using, which could include steroids and immunosuppressive drugs. Some patients with lung disease or diaphragmatic paralysis may not tolerate lying flat and will be unsuitable for a regional anaesthetic technique if the supine position is required for the surgery. Often, it is not necessary for the patient to be fully supine from the surgical perspective and regional anaesthesia will be an option. Lung disease may impact the difficulty of the airway or the speed and risks associated with securing the airway. There may be a risk of pneumothoraces in patients with bullous disease and there is a potential lack of recruitability and increased lung stiffness in patients with fibrotic or inflammatory lung diseases. Obstructive lung disease may involve limited expiratory flow and the risk of air trapping. Consideration needs to be given to what is the most protective form of ventilation for the patient (PROVE Network Investigators 2014). Lung disease may create pulmonary hypertension. Therefore, it is important to determine the appropriate fluid balance to maintain cardiac output, but not exacerbate right ventricular failure. Prevention or reduction of bronchospasm with preoperative bronchodilators may reduce the stress on the respiratory and cardiovascular systems. These can be nebulized in theatre, providing a suitable system is available, and may allow timely tracheal extubation. Reversal of residual neuromuscular block is important. Tracheal extubation with the patient sitting upright when feasible, followed by direct application of continuous positive airway pressure (CPAP) (Squadrone et al. 2005, 2010) or non-invasive ventilatory support may avoid extra atelectasis. In patients with severe lung disease, it is important to discuss the risks of respiratory failure and the potential need for postoperative ventilation on the intensive care unit (ICU), which could involve weaning with the aid of a tracheostomy.

This chapter considers the respiratory tract and intrinsic lung disease, disorders of the chest wall, including the pleura, diaphragm, and respiratory muscles, and the impact of problems below the diaphragm. It also looks at those conditions that affect the drive to breath and obstructive sleep apnoea (OSA).

Diseases of the respiratory system

Upper respiratory tract infection

Patients presenting with a cold (rather than influenza) may have surgery postponed. However, patients may require urgent surgery, so an assessment of the balance of risks should be made and in some cases the symptoms are mild and a pragmatic judgement as to whether to proceed is needed (Fendrick et al. 2003). Studies so far have looked at the risk to the patient with a cold, but have not considered the effect of spread to staff or to other patients.

Viral upper respiratory tract infections (URTIs) may lead to airway hyper-reactivity and narrowing of upper airway passages, especially in the nose and throat as a result of inflammation, congestion, and nasal discharge. There is an increased risk of perioperative adverse events including coughing, breath-holding, laryngospasm, bronchospasm, atelectasis, post-extubation breathing difficulties, and pneumonia. The effects of viral URTIs are mediated by chemical transmitters such as bradykinin, prostaglandins, interleukins, and histamine. Vagal reflexes are produced by inhibition of muscarinic receptors, so increasing acetylcholine release and increasing the risk of bronchospasm. Viral URTIs may inhibit endopeptidases, which would normally reduce tachykinin activity. This increases tachykinin-induced smooth muscle contraction (Empey et al. 1976).

Despite these effects, studies have shown that in some circumstances it may be reasonable to proceed with elective surgery, providing the diagnosis is clear (Tait and Knight 1987; Tait and Malviya 2005). Positive signs to proceed would include a patient who looks well, who is apyrexial with clear nasal secretions, normal peripheral oxygen saturation on air, and with no abnormal physical signs in the chest. However, if the patient looks unwell, is pyrexial, has purulent nasal discharge, nasal congestion (Tait et al. 2001), a productive cough, or signs in the chest, then postponement is indicated, unless the surgery is urgent. The type of anaesthesia and surgery will also influence cancellation. If the surgery is major, especially if it impacts the airway, chest, or abdomen and if a tracheal tube is required, this would indicate an increased risk. A history of asthma and, in children, paternal smoking (Skolnick et al. 1998) and prematurity (Tait et al. 2001) increase risk. Common complications include laryngospasm and bronchospasm (Tait and Knight 1987), increased breath-holding, oxygen desaturation below 90%, and a greater incidence of overall respiratory adverse events (Tait et al. 2001). The need for an inhalation induction or the use of thiopental are also risk factors. Tracheal intubation may increase the risk of intra- or postoperative adverse events, especially in patients under 5 years of age. Anaesthesia via a laryngeal mask up to 2 weeks after the URTI appears to have settled, may also increase perioperative problems (von Ungern-Sternberg et al. 2007). Patients who are very young, especially if less than 1 year old, are at increased risk.

The common cold is implicated in acute sinusitis, otitis media, and lower respiratory tract infection. Common colds may also exacerbate COPD and asthma and impact immune-suppressed patients.

Patients who have recovered from an URTI may have reactive airways producing respiratory complications during and after anaesthesia. Therefore a further period of 4–6 weeks should be avoided unless surgery is required urgently (McGill et al. 1979; Tait and Malviya 2005).

Trachea and bronchi

The average tracheal coronal and sagittal diameters for men aged 20–79 are 25 mm and 23 mm, with the lower limit for normal being 13 mm and 10 mm respectively (Breatnach et al. 1984). The trachea is D-shaped with incomplete cartilaginous rings lying anteriorly and laterally with a flat membranous part posteriorly. The trachea extends from the cricoid complete ring of cartilage immediately below the larynx down an average of 11 cm to the carina at the level of the space between the fourth and fifth thoracic vertebrae, where it bifurcates into the two main bronchi. The left main bronchus is angled at 45° to the line of the trachea and the right main bronchus is angled at 25–30°. The left main bronchus bifurcates after 5 cm, but the right has an early branch into the 'clover leaf' of the right upper lobe. The right main bronchus is about 2.5 cm long. Occasionally, the entrance to the right upper lobe can even lie in the trachea. These dimensions can be impinged upon by extrinsic compression or by diseases affecting the airway wall of lumen.

Anterior to the trachea lies the thyroid, which is a common cause of extrinsic compression, especially if it is enlarged posterior to the sternum, causing upper airway obstruction beneath the vocal cords (Fig. 82.1). Other benign causes include a thymoma, mediastinal lymphadenopathy, such as that caused by tuberculosis

(A)

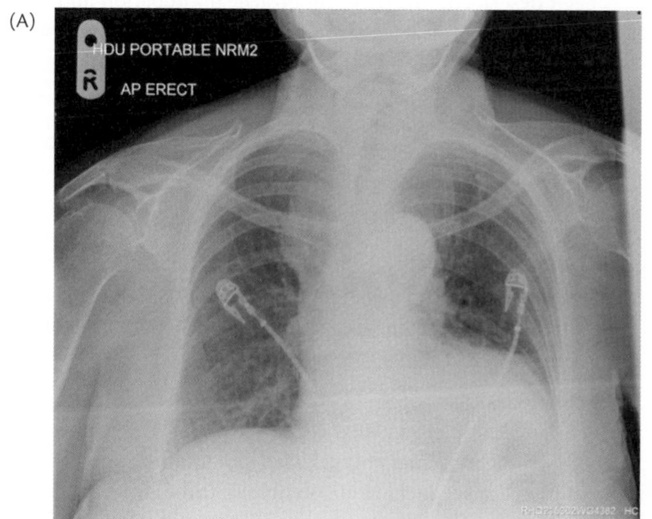

(B)

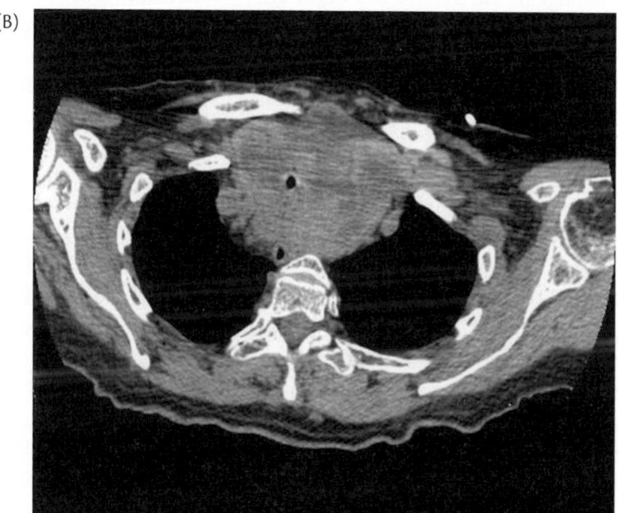

(C)

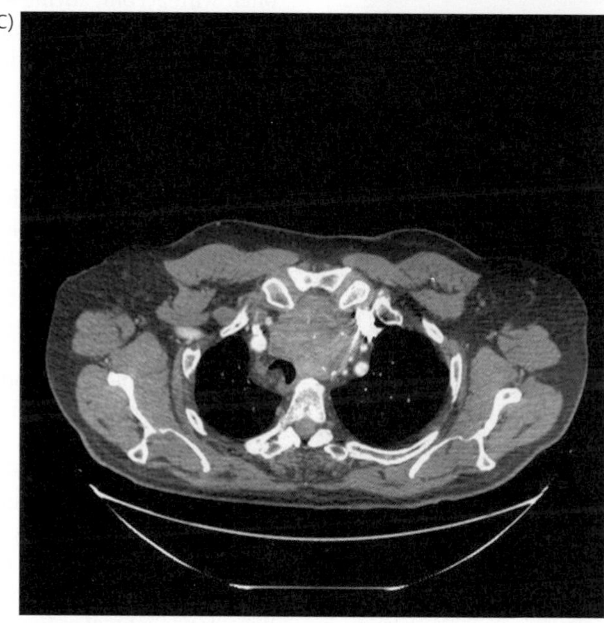

Figure 82.1 Upper airway obstruction due to retrosternal thyroid compressing the trachea and presenting with breathlessness and ventilatory failure. (A) Plain Chest Xray shows upper midline radioopacity (B and C) CT scans show a retrosternal mass encircling and compressing the trachea.

or lymphoma, and vascular anomalies such as enlargement of the innominate artery. Malignant causes include thyroid cancer, lymphoma, and lung cancer with related lymphadenopathy.

Compression can itself lead to tracheomalacia, which can also be associated with rheumatoid disease. Intrinsic narrowing may occur as a result of laryngeal trauma or burns, bilateral vocal cord paralysis, foreign bodies, sarcoidosis, or amyloidosis. Impairment of vocal fold mobility can occur with rheumatoid arthritis, intubation-related damage, infections such as epiglottitis and diphtheria, respiratory papilloma or polyps, congenital laryngeal stenosis, or atresia. Cancer of the thyroid, oesophagus, lung cancer, or primary tracheal cancers can erode into the airway. Below the larynx, intubation can damage or render the trachea ischaemic. The trachea may also be damaged by inflammatory or connective tissue diseases, such as granulomatosis with polyangiitis (formerly known as Wegener's granulomatosis), amyloidosis, relapsing polychondritis, tracheomalacia, or bronchomalacia. Other abnormal tissue may be present in the airway such as haemangiomata or tracheal cysts.

Damage to the trachea can occur after tracheostomy, with clinically significant, usually subglottic tracheal stenosis occurring in approximately 1% of cases of percutaneous dilatational tracheostomies, with death in 0.6% (Walz et al. 1998). Occasionally, this may not be discovered until intubation is attempted for a subsequent operation.

Tracheo-oesophageal fistulae can present at birth or occur as a result of malignancy or injury, sometimes secondary to trauma (Fig. 82.2), oesophageal or tracheal surgery, or tracheostomy. To provide a safe airway, the lesion will have to be passed by a tracheal tube or tracheostomy tube. A tracheo-oesophageal fistula sometimes presents as excessive belching or air filling of the nasogastric tube, with or without surgical emphysema. It may be possible to stent the lesion, or perform an awake fibreoptic intubation to get past the lesion under visual guidance. Sometimes it is possible to pass a tracheal tube into a main bronchus and then pull it back into the trachea to a point still distal to the lesion.

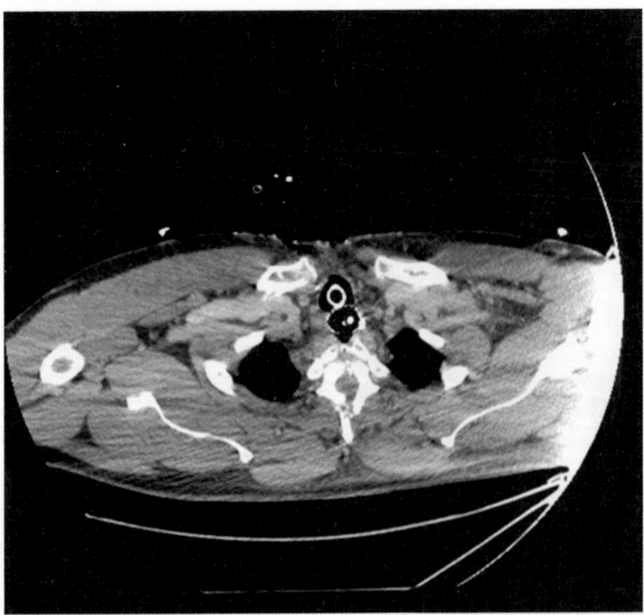

Figure 82.2 Trauma to the trachea, oesophagus, and spine after gunshot injury.

Epidermolysis bullosa

Epidermolysis bullosa is a defect in the dermoepidermal junction. It affects the skin and upper airway, leading to blistering and bullae formation on handling. Even heavy pressure to achieve a well-fitting face mask may be too much for the skin to remain intact. Similar problems can occur in the mouth and pharynx and this can result in poor mouth opening or tracheal stenosis. Patients may also develop oesophageal stenosis and reflux as part of the disease and so reflux precautions may be needed. From the anaesthetic perspective, the greatest hazards are from mucous membrane and skin damage. This is especially an issue in the airway. Despite this, patients with epidermolysis bullosa can be anaesthetized relatively safely, but patients do require extremely careful handling, which may involve the omission of ECG monitoring and non-invasive blood pressure monitoring—used in only 16.6% of one paediatric series (Iohom and Lyons 2001). In this series, 73% underwent inhalation anaesthesia and 65% had tracheal intubation. Despite these problems, successful prolonged anaesthesia for a 12 h operation has been described, involving endotracheal intubation and careful airway handling (Yonker-Sell and Connolly 1995). Management of the airway by face mask or by laryngeal mask has been described. Ketamine monoanaesthesia has been reported (Idvall, 1987). Regional anaesthesia has been used for vaginal and Caesarean section delivery (Baloch et al. 2008) and other regional techniques, especially involving ultrasound guidance (Englbrecht et al. 2010), have been described for limb surgery.

Diseases of the bronchi

Obstructive lesions can develop in the bronchi and the trachea and many of the causes are the same. These can be benign or neoplastic.

Bronchopleural fistulae

Bronchopleural fistulae are formed by a connection between the bronchi and the pleura. Most commonly they are caused by the breakdown of bronchial stumps after pneumonectomy or lobectomy. Other causes include abscess break through or erosion as a result of cancer. This results in contamination of the pleural space, often with accompanying sepsis and a pneumothorax on the side of the leak, which will require urgent drainage and isolation of the relevant lung, usually with the aid of a double-lumen tube (see Chapter 57).

Carcinoid

Carcinoid tumours most commonly develop in the small intestine (40%) or the area around the appendix, but they can occur in many other areas including the lung in 25%, where they may occlude a bronchus (Powell et al. 2010). However, they account for only 2% of primary lung tumours (Fig. 82.3). They are usually perihilar and present with pneumonia, cough, haemoptysis, and occasionally chest pain.

Lung carcinoid may produce cushingoid or acromegalic effects. They may also be present as carcinoid miliary lung with many deposits. Those primarily occurring within the gastrointestinal tract may manifest themselves by obstruction, perforation, bleeding, and weight loss, or even malnutrition, anaemia, and electrolyte imbalance. However, once they spread into the liver, or if they have developed in a site outside the gastrointestinal tract, they begin to show the effects of hormonal secretion. It is this behaviour that makes them particularly important to anaesthesia. The main compounds produced include 5-hydroxyindoleacetic

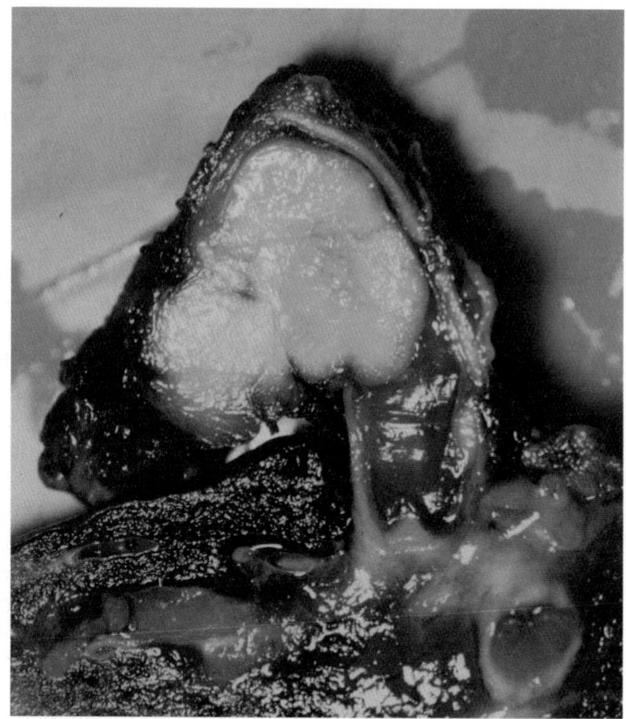

Figure 82.3 Carcinoid occluding main bronchus.
Reproduced from Powell B, Al Mukhtar A, Mills GH. Carcinoid: the disease and its implications for anaesthesia. *Continuing Education in Critical Care, Anaesthesia, and Pain*, Volume 11, Issue 1, pp. 9–13, Copyright © 2011, by permission of the British Journal of Anaesthesia.

acid (5-HIAA), which produces the classic signs of flushing and diarrhoea, and these may be exacerbated by consumption of serotonin-containing foods such as chocolate or bananas (Veall et al. 1994). Stimulation of a carcinoid tumour may lead to asthma, hypotension, or hypertension. Right-sided cardiac lesions may occur with pulmonary and tricuspid stenosis and right ventricular hypertrophy, and consequent high right-sided pressures and a pulsatile liver. High serotonin formation may lead to tryptophan and niacin deficiency. Handling of the tumour during surgery causes release of the hormones and most commonly causes flushing, a decrease in blood pressure, and bronchoconstriction (Mason and Steane 1976). It is therefore a priority to reduce the effect of these hormones by commencing octreotide in advance of surgery and continuing the infusion through the whole perioperative period. Octreotide has an action very similar to somatostatin, inhibiting growth hormone, insulin, glucagon, luteinizing hormone, splanchnic blood flow, as well as serotonin, vasoactive intestinal peptide, secretin, motilin and pancreatic polypeptide. It also can cause QT prolongation on the ECG, bradycardia, nausea, and vomiting.

Epidural techniques reduce the stimulus to the carcinoid tumour, provide good pain relief, and reduce the incidence of pneumonia. General anaesthesia may be required separately or in addition, depending on the nature of the operation. Drugs with the potential to release histamine (e.g. atracurium and morphine) are normally avoided. Invasive monitoring is usually utilized and in terms of vasoactive drugs, vasopressin is commonly used. Noradrenaline can activate kallikrein that leads to activation of bradykinin and so is not normally used. Small doses of phenylephrine have been used cautiously in some patients. To counter hypertension related to the carcinoid, labetalol or α-blockade has been used.

Some procedures are debulking in nature and the carcinoid remains *in situ*, limiting potential treatments in the postoperative period, so complicating provision of analgesia and necessitating the continued use of octreotide. Postoperative monitoring for 48 h on a high dependency unit (HDU) or ICU is usually necessary.

Lung cancers

Lung cancers are grouped into small cell and non-small cell lung cancers and are important to anaesthetists because of potential involvement in their treatment, and also because of the effects these diseases have on body systems outside the lung, which may be encountered during the perioperative period or as part of a critical care referral.

Non-small cell lung cancers include squamous, adenocarcinoma, and bronchoalveolar. Small cell lung cancers are very aggressive and fatal in a few weeks if not treated. They spread early to the liver, bones, brain, and adrenal glands and produce the syndrome of inappropriate antidiuretic hormone (SIADH). The lung may also be attacked by other tumours such as lymphoma, carcinoid, and metastases from distant sources.

The primary lung cancers can themselves produce widespread effects, which may be local as a result of obstruction or invasion including cough; pneumonia; pleural effusions; haemorrhage; damage to the phrenic nerves (hemidiaphragm paralysis) or left recurrent laryngeal destruction (vocal cord paralysis); or sympathetic chain involvement producing miosis, ptosis, enophthalmos, and anhidrosis on the ipsilateral half of the face (Horner's syndrome). Superior vena cava obstruction may occur, which may have been treated with dexamethasone, radiotherapy, or intraluminal stents with or without anticoagulation. Hormonal effects include SIADH or ectopic ACTH production. SIADH increases vascular volume and so may lower urea. Hyponatraemia is usually the alerting feature with urinary sodium greater than 40 mmol litre^{-1} (sometimes confused by loop diuretics which elevate this figure) and urine osmolarity greater than 100 mOsm kg^{-1} (usually lower in water overload). Normally treated with fluid restriction, demeclocycline, or tolvaptan. Hyperparathyroidism can occur either from ectopic production of parathyroid hormone, producing high calcium and low phosphate concentrations, or bone metastases which will elevate both. It is treated with rehydration with saline and sometimes furosemide to help eliminate calcium. Bisphosphonates may be indicated to reduce bone resorption. Bone metastases may present at surgery as pathological fractures or as a cause of cord compression. Cerebral metastases may present as raised intracranial pressure, confusion, or seizures (which may present in the perioperative period).

Thoracic surgery and preoperative prediction of outcome

One of the first areas where attempts were made to predict the impact of surgery on lung function, especially in patients with lung disease, was lung resection surgery. This was important because these patients commonly have more than one lung disease, including those related to smoking. Assessments of the respiratory system are vital when assessing suitability for lung resection, because postoperative ventilator dependency is a real risk and achieving a reasonable quality of life after surgery is crucial. Traditionally, patients who could not climb two flights of stairs needed very careful consideration and might not be suitable for pneumonectomy. Unfortunately, the lack of a standard staircase and standard speed up the staircase made this imprecise and not easily compared. Although decisions should not be wholly made on the basis of lung function and exercise testing, these can be helpful, because they have a degree of objectivity. The downside is that they are at least to some degree volitional and affected by technique.

Predicted postoperative forced expiratory volume in 1 s (ppo-FEV_1) is useful in choosing further tests or even demonstrating patients are unsuitable for lung resection. A ppo-FEV_1 of less than 40% or less than 30% of predicted is associated with mortalities of 16–50% (Markos et al. 1989; Wahi et al. 1989; Holden et al. 1992; Pierce et al. 1994; Bolliger et al. 1995) and 60% (Nakahara et al. 1985, 1988) respectively. However, a recent study showed a ppo-FEV_1 of less than 40% to be associated with a mortality of 4.8%. This could be because of the lung volume-reducing effect of a lobectomy, which may diminish over-inflation. Therefore, a value of 30% has been assessed as more appropriate. Low preoperative transfer factor (ppo-TLco) of less than 30% predicted is suggested as a high-risk threshold. The equations used to calculate predicted postoperative values for FEV_1, TLco, and maximal oxygen consumption ($\dot{V}O_{2max}$) rely on the ratio of postoperative functioning segments divided by the functioning preoperative lung segments times the preoperative values. An algorithm for assessing cardiopulmonary reserve has been produced. In patients with a ppo-$\dot{V}O_2$ peak of less than 40% or less than 10 ml kg^{-1} min^{-1}, surgical therapy is contraindicated, unless either PPO-FEV_1 or TLco are greater than 40%. Exercise tests are recommended in anyone with a FEV_1 or TLco less than 80% of normal predicted values. An alternative is the shuttle test, as recommended by the British Thoracic Society. This consists of repeatedly walking between two cones placed 10 m apart. The time allowed progressively diminishes and failure to complete 25 shuttles may indicate high risk.

The Thorascore was derived from a study of 15 183 patients with a mortality of 2.2% and is a model of in-hospital mortality (Falcoz et al. 2007). Respiratory symptoms featured strongly in the score, which included age; ASA score; performance status; dyspnoea score; elective, emergency, or urgent classification of surgery; procedure; diagnosis of benign or malignant; and co-morbidity score. Age, procedure group, and dyspnoea score were also identified as important by Harpole et al. (1999) and Berrisford et al. (2005).

Bronchiectasis

This is an abnormal widening of the airways, which makes sputum hard to clear. This results in frequent respiratory infections, which in turn lead to further lung damage. Patients often show signs of clubbing and lung crackles and may cough up blood. Bronchiectasis may follow pneumonia or tuberculosis or problems associated with abnormal sputum clearance such as primary ciliary dyskinesia, which also affects the ciliary motility in the fallopian tubes, sinuses, middle ear, and sperm flagella (or Kartagener's syndrome, when associated with situs inversus, chronic sinusitis, and bronchiectasis), or the more common chloride ion transport disease known as cystic fibrosis. Bronchiectasis may also be associated with inflammatory bowel disease, especially Crohn's disease. Prompt appropriate antibiotic use is needed to combat infections, although development of resistant organisms is common. Staphylococcal, *Klebsiella*, or *Bordetella pertussis* infections are commonly associated with bronchiectasis. HIV and related infections may also cause bronchiectasis. Prophylactic antibiotics may be used. Chemical damage as a result of aspiration of gastric contents may cause bronchiectasis, as may inhalation of toxic gases. Traction bronchiectasis is often seen with inflammatory lung diseases (Fig. 82.4).

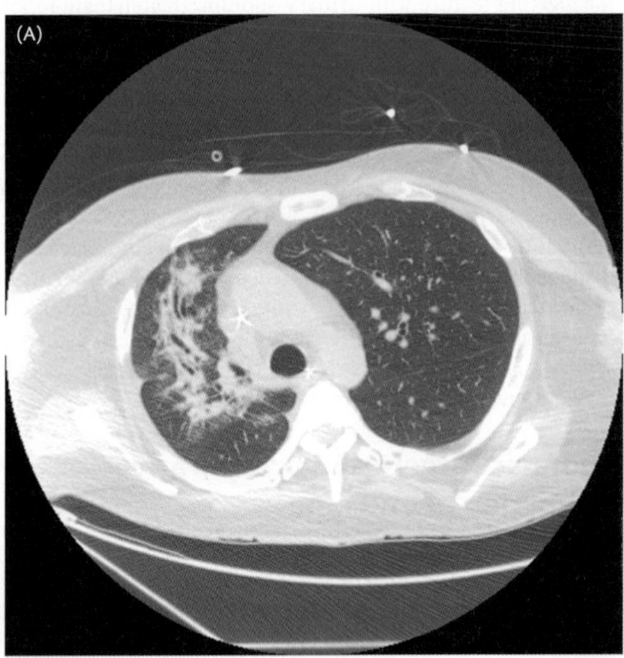

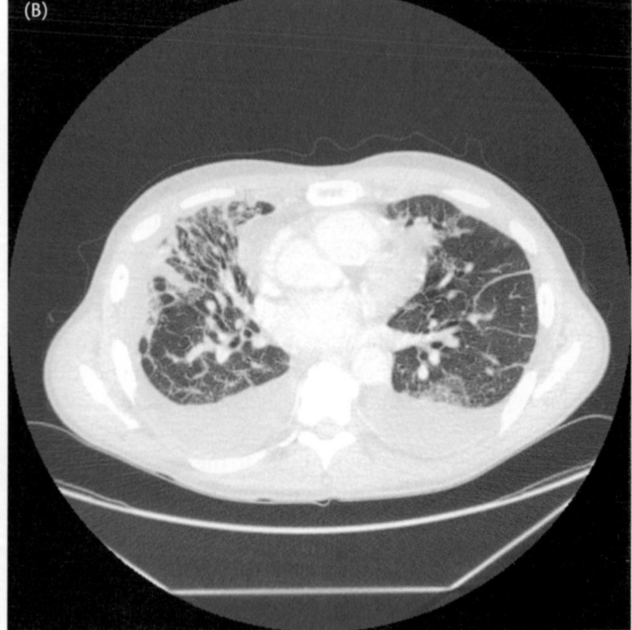

Figure 82.4 Computed tomography scans that show (A) bronchiectasis, with traction on surrounding tissues and cuffing of bronchi and (B) worsening bronchiectasis with fibrosis in left lung and empyema.

Cystic fibrosis

Cystic fibrosis is a multisystem disease caused by an autosomal recessive genetic abnormality, affecting 1:2500 births, that causes bronchiectasis and other major problems. Cystic fibrosis is caused by a mutation on the long arm of chromosome 7 resulting in major issues for anaesthesia and complications that may need surgical intervention. Traditionally it is diagnosed by applying pilocarpine to stimulate sweating and then using iontophoresis to drive the medication into the skin. One electrode is placed on the pilocarpine and the other on normal skin. An electric current is passed through the electrodes and sweating is produced. The sweat has an abnormally high NaCl content in patients with cystic fibrosis. Screening tests that detect raised blood concentrations of immunoreactive trypsinogen are now used and genetic testing is possible. Cystic fibrosis used to cause death in infancy or childhood, but median survival is now in the 30s or 40s. It affects the production of the cystic fibrosis transmembrane regulator protein, which controls a chloride channel. If chloride cannot be transported, this disturbs the sodium and chloride balance in mucous making it too thick to be moved by cilia. This means bacteria are not eliminated and a biofilm is generated leading to infection and inflammation and blockage of small airways. This produces bronchiectasis and chronic colonization with *Pseudomonas aeruginosa, Staphylococcus aureus, Haemophilus influenza, Stenotrophomonas maltophilia, Burkholderia cepacia, Mycobacterium avium*, and *Aspergillus fumigatus*. Recurrent infections eventually destroy lung tissue leading to right heart failure and respiratory failure. Lung function tests usually show an obstructive picture, but patients may develop pneumothoraces. Eventually lung damage leads to increased pulmonary vascular resistance and then pulmonary hypertension and right heart failure. Prolonged antibiotic use and the use of steroids to damp down inflammation increases the risk of fungal growth and also promote an inflammatory response to the fungi, producing allergic bronchopulmonary aspergillosis, which is an immune response to *Aspergillus*.

Cystic fibrosis also leads to nasal polyps, paranasal sinusitis, pancreatic fibrosis, osteoporosis from impaired vitamin D and calcium absorption, infertility, focal biliary cirrhosis, and meconium ileus in neonates. Patients also have clubbing. Liver diseases may include fatty infiltration, cirrhosis and portal hypertension, cholelithiasis and cholecystitis, and hepatocellular carcinoma. The damage to the pancreas is as a result of the absence of the cystic fibrosis transmembrane regulator, which impairs chloride–bicarbonate exchange. Pancreatic secretions become more viscous and lower in pH, resulting in pancreatic autodigestion and fibrosis. This causes malabsorption, pancreatitis, and eventually destruction of pancreatic B cells. This leads to diabetes requiring insulin in approximately 30% of patients by the age of 30. Intestinal obstruction may be caused by intussusception, constipation, or distal intestinal obstruction syndrome. Lung, pancreas, and liver transplants are needed for end-stage disease and so patients may present for this type of surgery. However, they may also present for other surgery partially or not at all related to cystic fibrosis. All these issues will complicate the likelihood of a patient presenting for surgery, and how best to conduct anaesthesia, the physical handling of the patient, and management in the perioperative period.

Cystic fibrosis cannot be cured, but it can be ameliorated, such that patients now survive well into adulthood. All these issues mean that patients with cystic fibrosis now have a much greater chance of surviving to present with surgical conditions later in life. It is essential that sufferers receive good nutrition, avoid dehydration, have suitable antibiotic therapy and physiotherapy, and keep as active as possible—all of which may be disrupted by surgery. Drug therapy incorporates prophylactic antibiotics including nebulized tobramycin, and additional antibiotics during chest infections, which may be administered by many routes including Hickmann lines. Mucolytics and other treatments to clear sputum or open airways include saline or a recombinant human deoxyribonuclease (dornase), which decreases sputum viscosity. Steroids may be used to reduce inflammation. Later in the disease course patients may present on oxygen or non-invasive ventilation (NIV) as they develop type 1 and type 2 respiratory failure. Some patients may be suitable for lung transplantation.

Patients with cystic fibrosis who present for surgery are at elevated risk, particularly from respiratory complications. A clear understanding of their current respiratory status, together with sputum production and exercise tolerance is vital. Up-to-date lung function is important in addition to information on their respiratory therapy, including any requirement for supplemental oxygen or NIV. Chest X-rays will give an indication of heart size and degree of lung inflation. Peribronchial thickening and cyst formation, consistent with bronchiectasis may be visible. Chest computed tomography (CT) will quantify these findings (Fig. 82.5). Lung function tests usually show signs of obstruction (worsening FEV_1 and reduced FEV_1/forced vital capacity ratio, with an increase in residual volume compared with total lung capacity). Initially this will lead to a decrease in oxygenation and then eventually raised Pa_{CO_2}, so where this is suspected, baseline blood gases are important to provide an understanding of risk and how to manage oxygen and ventilator therapy. Patients with cystic fibrosis may also be predisposed to bronchospasm. Nasal polyps and sinuses may be a reservoir for

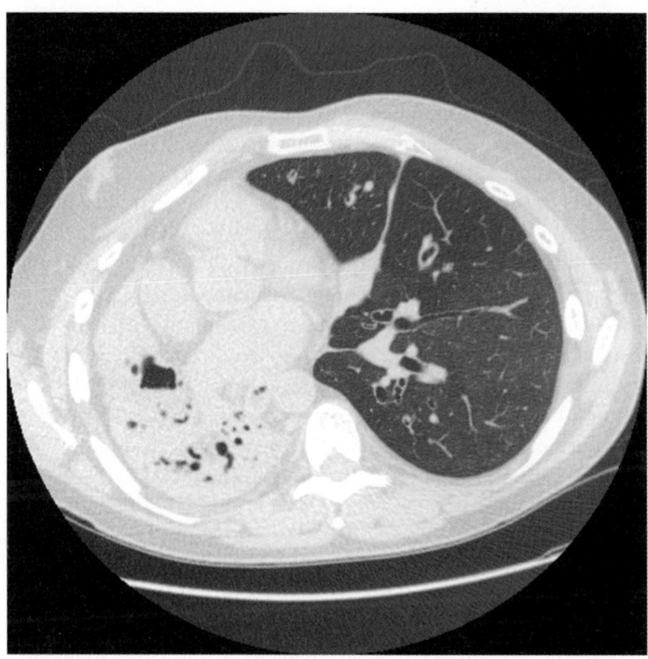

Figure 82.5 Computed tomography scan of a patient with cystic fibrosis, showing complete occlusion of the left lung by secretions, with resulting collapse and midline shift.

infection, which may be aspirated during anaesthesia or intubation. The nasal route may be difficult for passage of tracheal, nasogastric, and nasojejunal tubes, which can become very important in patients unfortunate enough to have a difficult airway.

Obstetric anaesthesia and pregnancy bring physiological changes that may further load the right ventricle. This is particularly a problem in patients with a FEV_1 of less than 50% predicted.

Anaesthesia should be designed to minimize the impact on the respiratory system with local or regional options considered first. However, where a general anaesthetic is needed, efforts should be made to use short-acting agents. Volatile anaesthetic agents normally have bronchodilatory properties so should be helpful. Gases should be warmed and humidified and every effort made to avoid further damage to the respiratory system. Endobronchial suction may well be needed and protective ventilation, although unproved, is probably beneficial. The aim should be to allow patients to breath as normally as they can as soon as possible after surgery. NIV or CPAP should be started very early in the postoperative period (Huffmyer et al. 2009), together with physiotherapy.

Alveoli and small airways

Asthma

Asthma is characterized by an increased airway reactivity related to airway inflammation, which leads to bronchoconstriction, with oedema and increased mucous production, resulting in variable small airways obstruction, which may be responsive to treatment. It causes the death of around 250 000 people a year worldwide. Anaesthesia often involves instrumenting the airway or giving drugs, which could trigger bronchospasm or inflammation. Airborne allergens and viral infections are very important in the development of immunoglobulin E-mediated allergic asthma, together with genetic components and other factors such as obesity.

Non-allergic asthma occurs in adults and is associated with aspirin-induced asthma related to the inhibition of cyclooxygenase enzymes and eosinophilic rhinosinusitis, nasal polyps, and non-steroidal anti-inflammatory drug-induced bronchospasm.

The degree of preoperative control is very important when planning anaesthesia. A history of a recent cold or a patient demonstrating reduced peak flows or feeling their asthma is not under control should be regarded as a major risk factor for surgery. Current and recent drug therapy is important, especially steroid use, which may need restarting or supplementing. Bronchospasm can be life-threatening in the perioperative period, particularly on induction (Cook et al. 2011), where it may be part of an exacerbation of asthma, an anaphylactic response, or may be mediated through mechanical or drug factors. In its most extreme form, the anaesthetist will be faced with intubating a patient, who moments earlier appeared relatively well, but now is extremely difficult to ventilate, who demonstrates an inadequate end-tidal CO_2 trace, perhaps with unilateral or bilateral wheeze and markedly reduced breath sounds. At this point the anaesthetist needs to consider whether this is asthma, some other cause of bronchospasm such as an anaphylactic reaction, blockage of the airway with mucous or a foreign body, a blockage of the tracheal tube, or an oesophageal intubation. Sometimes the cause of wheeze may be severe pulmonary oedema or the difficulty in ventilation may be unilateral or bilateral pneumothoraces (Dewachter et al. 2011). The treatment of anaphylaxis and airway emergencies is dealt with elsewhere (Chapters 22 and 48).

Chronic obstructive pulmonary disease and anaesthesia

Chronic obstructive pulmonary disease (COPD) is most commonly caused by cigarette smoking, affects 3 million people in the United Kingdom, and may be present in 5–10% of general surgical patients. It is the fifth most common cause of death and causes 30 000 deaths per year in the United Kingdom, 90% of which involve people above the age of 65 years. It is a chronic inflammatory condition of the airways and lung parenchyma, which can also lead to pulmonary hypertension and right heart failure. Patients produce large amounts of sputum as a result of increased numbers of mucus secreting cells. There is poorly reversible narrowing of small airways resulting in airways obstruction and destruction of lung parenchyma reducing the elastic recoil of the lung. This causes air trapping and hyperinflation. The loss of lung tissue reduces the surface area for gas exchange and the number of capillaries through the lung and ventilation/perfusion ($\dot{V}/\dot{Q}$) mismatching occurs. The National Institute for Health and Care Excellence (NICE) and the Global Initiative for Chronic Obstructive Lung Disease (GOLD) have produced guidelines on COPD management (NICE 2010; GOLD 2013). Patients with COPD are at increased risk after surgery and anaesthesia and frequently exhibit the other complications of smoking. Five-year survival from COPD may be an important factor when we consider the risk:benefit balance of surgery. Severe disease, requiring oxygen or nebulized therapy, results in a 30% survival in men and 24% in women (Soriano et al. 2000). See Table 82.1.

COPD may also be caused by α1-antitrypsin deficiency and has been associated with the FAM13A genetic variant (Cho et al. 2010), which leads to more emphysema and thicker airway walls on CT. Higher concentrations of CD46 can reduce inflammation in smokers; however, proline–glycine–proline (PGP) causes persistent neutrophil release leading to chronic inflammation in COPD. LTA4H is a proinflammatory enzyme that produces leukotriene B4, but in acute inflammation LTA4H degrades PGP, so reducing inflammation (Snelgrove et al. 2010). Unfortunately, LTA4H is reduced by smoking, so promoting chronic inflammation. There is also evidence for elevated C-reactive protein and tumour necrosis factor even in stable COPD patients (Gan et al. 2004).

The combination of small airway inflammation and repeated damage to the lung tissue leads to loss of alveolar tissue and airways obstruction. This leads to air-trapping and over-distension, with an increase in functional residual capacity. The loss of tissue then also leads to a loss of support for small airways so increasing their tendency to narrow on expiration (Fig. 82.6). There has frequently been debate as to whether the respiratory muscles are weak. Much of this is accounted for by the hyperinflation of the chest (Hamnegard et al. 1995), which puts the diaphragm in a poor position to generate inspiratory force. However, some patients do generate an inflammatory response and become generally weak and also develop disuse weakness in their leg muscles. This may be combined with weight loss. COPD is an independent risk factor for mortality in critically ill patients presenting with ventilator-associated pneumonia (Makris et al. 2011) and is linked to a higher rate of reintubation of the trachea (Ramachandran et al. 2011), morbidity, and mortality after major surgery (Greenblatt et al. 2011). COPD produces an increased risk for major surgery of the chest or abdomen. Treatment of COPD requires smoking cessation,

Table 82.1 Severity classification for COPD

Post-bronchodilator FEV_1/FVC	FEV_1% predicted	Severity of airflow obstruction			
		NICE Clinical Guideline 12 (2004)	**ATS/ERS (2004)**	**GOLD (2008)**	**NICE update Clinical Guideline 101 (2010)**
			Post-bronchodilator	Post-bronchodilator	Post-bronchodilator
<0.7	≥80%		Mild	Stage 1—mild	Stage 1—mild*
<0.7	50–79%	Mild	Moderate	Stage 2—moderate	Stage 2—moderate
<0.7	30–49%	Moderate	Severe	Stage 3—severe	Stage 3—severe
<0.7	<30%	Severe	Very severe	Stage 4—very severe†	Stage 4—very severe†

* Symptoms should be present to diagnose COPD in people with mild airflow obstruction.

† Or FEV_1 < 50% with respiratory failure.

National Institute for Health and Clinical Excellence (2010). *CG 101 Chronic obstructive pulmonary disease: Management of chronic obstructive pulmonary disease in adults in primary and secondary care (partial update)*. Manchester: NICE. Available from www.nice.org.uk/CG101. Reproduced with permission. Information accurate at time of press. For up-to-date information, please visit www.nice.org.uk. ATS/ERS Score: Reproduced with permission of the European Respiratory Society ©: *European Respiratory Journal* Jun 2004, 23 (6) 932–946; DOI: 10.1183/09031936.04.00014304. GOLD 2008 Score: Reproduced with permission from Global Initiative for Chronic Obstructive Lung Disease (GOLD) Global Strategy for the Diagnosis, Management, and Prevention of COPD 2016, ©.

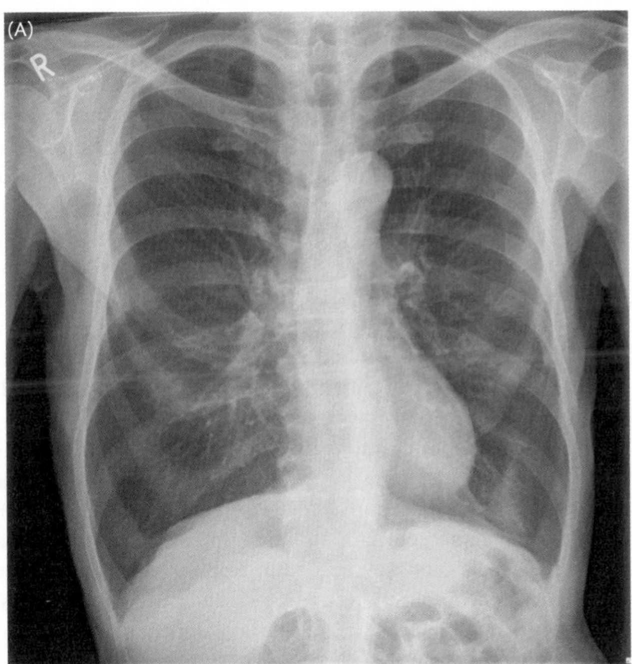

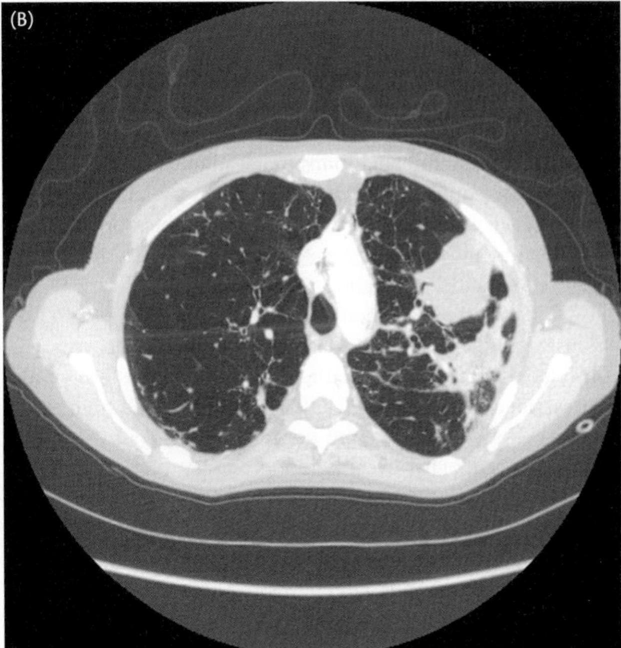

Figure 82.6 (A) Emphysema and kyphoscoliosis with hyperinflation on chest X-ray. (B) Chest computed tomography scan shows severe emphysema with bullae and lung masses.

exercise where possible, bronchodilator therapy, oxygen to reduce pulmonary vasoconstriction, NIV (Lightowler et al. 2003), lung volume reduction surgery to reduce the effects of high lung volume on chest wall and diaphragm mechanics, and sometimes lung transplantation.

Patients are likely to be on theophylline drugs, which have a narrow therapeutic window and also have metabolism changed by other drugs, plus inhaled therapy. Patients may be on long-term, 15 h day^{-1} oxygen if their Pa_{O_2} is less than 7.3kPa. Patients who suffer frequent exacerbations are at increased risk. The ECG may show right heart strain or ischaemic heart disease. A Pa_{O_2} of less than 7.9 kPa and Pa_{CO_2} greater than 5.9 kPa suggest a worse prognosis, especially if accompanied by malnutrition (albumin <35 mg $litre^{-1}$).

Many patients are likely to be smokers. It is helpful if they can stop smoking 8 weeks or more before surgery. Regional or local anaesthesia is preferable to general anaesthesia where possible. Epidural anaesthesia reduces the incidence of postoperative pneumonia by 50%. However, some patients are unable to lie sufficiently flat while awake to facilitate surgery. A combined technique is likely to help in patients where general anaesthesia is required (van Lier et al. 2011). There are concerns about the risk of blocking the phrenic nerves with cervical epidural, interscalene, or supraclavicular blocks.

During surgery under general anaesthesia, patients are likely to show signs of cardiovascular disease, exacerbated by smoking, and may develop right ventricular failure secondary to the COPD and increased pulmonary vascular resistance during

COPD. As with asthma, airways obstruction will slow expiration and may lead to a failure to reach a plateau on the capnography trace and an expiratory flow pattern that does not return to zero flow before another breath is delivered. This results in air trapping and further hyperinflation, which may raise intrathoracic pressure further and prevent venous return to the heart. Longer expiratory times are needed and are achieved by lengthening the I:E ratio and slowing the respiratory rate. There may be an element of reversibility, so bronchodilator therapy may be helpful. Sometimes positive end-expiratory pressure (PEEP), at levels up to intrinsic PEEP, may help keep airways open and allow expiration. However, it is difficult to set a PEEP that is ideal for all the different regions of the lung.

Experience with COPD in intensive care has shown the usefulness of NIV in the management of exacerbations of COPD (Lightowler et al. 2003). NIV is being investigated as a means of weaning, allowing early tracheal extubation onto NIV in patients receiving invasive ventilation after an acute exacerbation of COPD. Similarly, NIV may have a role in COPD patients in the immediate postoperative period. This is especially the case in patients with elevated Pa_{CO_2}.

Oxygen-induced hypercapnia in chronic obstructive pulmonary disease

Patients with a number of conditions that lead to chronically raised Pa_{CO_2}, most commonly COPD, develop ventilatory failure characterized by hypercapnia and an elevated plasma bicarbonate as a result of renal metabolic compensation for what would otherwise be a respiratory acidosis. Traditionally, following the work in the 1940s by Davies and Mackinnon (1949), the explanation was a loss of response to high Pa_{CO_2}; patients become acclimatized to this and rely on hypoxic drive to maintain the drive to breathe. Donald (1947) described a patient with COPD, who developed high Pa_{CO_2} (16 kPa) when given oxygen and became unconscious. This was explained as a result of hypoventilation secondary to loss of hypoxic drive and so oxygen was discontinued and the patient woke up. However, the explanation is more complicated than this (Abdo and Heunks 2012). The effect of high-flow oxygen, at 15 litres min^{-1}, on Pa_{CO_2} was studied by Aubier et al. (1980b, 1980a). This produced very high Pa_{O_2} levels, with dramatic increases from 4.9 to 29 kPa, with an accompanying increase in Pa_{CO_2} from 8.4 to 11.4 kPa. There was an initial decrease in minute ventilation, which then started to recover, but Pa_{CO_2} continued to increase. In addition, the drive to breathe as indicated by $P_{0.1}$ fell from a very high average of 8.3 cm H_2O to a still high 4.9, when oxygen was given, but minute ventilation and change in Pa_{CO_2} did not correlate well (Aubier et al. 1980a). Therefore the change in hypoxic drive is not the whole explanation of the worsening hypercapnia seen in these patients (Hanson et al. 1996). The situation is explained by the impact of $\dot{V}/\dot{Q}$ mismatch and the Haldane effect (Hanson et al. 1996).

$\dot{V}/\dot{Q}$ mismatch can be countered by hypoxic pulmonary vasoconstriction. Alveoli with poor ventilation would normally shut down their pulmonary arterial supply, allowing blood to flow preferentially to well-ventilated alveoli. High-flow oxygen will increase oxygen tension in these poorly ventilated alveoli and reduce hypoxic pulmonary vasoconstriction, so producing increased physiological dead space (Aubier et al. 1980b; Milic-Emili and Aubier 1980; Robinson et al. 2000).

The Haldane effect also contributes as haemoglobin combines with CO_2 to form carbamino compounds, especially in its deoxygenated form. Therefore if we administer high flow and high concentrations of oxygen the haemoglobin will bind more oxygen and be less able to combine with CO_2, which will be made available to increase the Pa_{CO_2}. If the Pa_{CO_2} then reaches high enough levels, the patient will become narcotized.

These effects have great implications for general anaesthesia and recovery of COPD patients after waking from anaesthesia. Controlled oxygen therapy is needed to target oxygen saturations between 88% and 92%, to achieve a compromise, whereby these patients are not so hypoxaemic that they deprive the body of oxygen and the Pa_{O_2} is not so high that hypercarbia is produced by the effects described previously. To minimize the work of breathing and to reduce increasing $\dot{V}/\dot{Q}$ mismatch and increasing dead space, CPAP and NIV may be required. During anaesthesia, volatile anaesthetic agents impact hypoxic pulmonary vasoconstriction and so worsen $\dot{V}/\dot{Q}$ mismatch, while opioid drugs decrease the drive to breathe.

Smoking

Smoking is at least partly responsible for many of the diseases that require surgery, including thoracic surgery, coronary artery bypass grafting, gastrectomy, bladder cancer, and femoral neck fracture in addition to affecting plastic surgery flaps, vascular surgery, colorectal anastomoses, and wound healing. Intraoperatively irritable airway effects, including bronchospasm, laryngospasm, hypoxaemia, and retained secretions, are more common. Smoking also increases gut diseases such as Crohn's, peptic ulcer disease, and gastro-oesophageal reflux (Moppett and Curran 2001).

Originally, Morton described a six-fold increase in postoperative respiratory morbidity in patients smoking more than 10 cigarettes per day. Smoking 40 pack-years increased the odds of postoperative respiratory complications by a factor of 5.7 (McAlister et al. 2003). Smoking 21–50 pack-years showed a significant increase in pulmonary complications (Warner et al. 1984). Unfortunately, when patients succeeded in stopping smoking before coronary artery bypass surgery they needed to stop for more than 8 weeks for pulmonary complications to drop significantly. There may even have been a small increase in those who stopped for 2–4 weeks. In non-cardiac surgery, an increase in risk was found in those who stopped for a similar period (Bluman et al. 1998). This may be as a result of a combination of factors including a transient increase in tracheo-bronchial secretions, which become more viscous, the respiratory epithelium is altered, and ciliary activity poor. Therefore smokers are more reliant on coughing to clear secretions. In thoracic surgery, stopping smoking for a short period did not appear to help (Barrera et al. 2005). However, short-term preoperative smoking abstinence may benefit the patient by reducing carbon monoxide concentrations within a day. Airway irritability may improve within 2–10 days of smoking cessation. A regional anaesthetic technique improves postoperative lung function where feasible. Past-smokers who underwent a general anaesthetic *vs* regional anaesthesia were four times as likely to suffer postoperative pulmonary complications.

Smokers have a faster yearly decline in FEV_1 than non-smokers. The rate of decline decreases from 60 ml year^{-1} to 20 ml year^{-1} within 1 year of stopping smoking and 6 months' cessation may bring the postoperative pulmonary complications rate down to the level of those who have never smoked (Fletcher and Peto 1977). Unfortunately, a lower percentage of lung volume is available to smokers compared with non-smokers (Woodhouse et al. 2005) and cigarette smoke contains the highest concentrations of nitric oxide to which humans are commonly exposed, which produces a major oxidative and nitrosative effect in asymptomatic current chronic smokers and GOLD stage 0 COPD (Rytila et al. 2006). Recent smoking increases ST depression in humans during general anaesthesia (Woehlck et al. 1999). Carbon monoxide combines with haemoglobin and so reduces oxygen carriage, which because of the similar light absorbance characteristics of carboxyhaemoglobin and oxyhaemoglobin may confuse pulse oximeters, producing an overestimate of oxygen saturation. Smoking also increases platelet aggregation and fibrinogen concentration (Levine 1973), while nicotine may lower tissue oxygenation and slow wound healing (Jensen et al. 1991). Smoking damages collagen production by affecting the conversion of proline to hydroxyproline (Jorgensen et al. 1998) in addition to reducing bone and tendon healing (Galatz et al. 2006).

Other effects of oxygen on the lung

Obesity and sleep apnoea

Obesity is a cause of restrictive lung physiology, which may combine with the atelectasis associated with anaesthesia and postoperative complications such as pain, to worsen atelectasis. Its prevalence is increasing, affecting approximately one-third of adults in developed countries. Importantly, obesity causes severe practical problems once complications become serious and invasive ventilation and invasive monitoring is needed. Obesity increases the risk of pulmonary aspiration during anaesthesia. It also causes airway collapse, increasing atelectasis and $\dot{V}/\dot{Q}$ mismatch. This results in a more rapid desaturation after induction of anaesthesia, because of a rapid and major reduction in end-expiratory lung volume.

A high FI_{O_2} increases absorption atelectasis, especially above FI_{O_2} levels of 0.7–0.8 (Edmark et al. 2003). When this is combined with $\dot{V}/\dot{Q}$ mismatch we see even more rapid absorption (Hedenstierna and Rothen 2012) and further atelectasis (Magnusson and Spahn 2003). This occurs in all patients, but is more prominent, because of increased airway compression, closure, and partial closure, in the obese. PEEP with recruitment manoeuvres helps reduce atelectasis and $\dot{V}/\dot{Q}$ mismatch (Rothen et al. 1995; Reinius et al. 2009) and on intensive care may reduce the incidence of ventilator-associated pneumonia (Manzano et al. 2008). During general anaesthesia in the operating theatre, protective ventilation using tidal volumes of 6–8 ml kg^{-1} ideal body weight appears to reduce respiratory complications in the perioperative period (Futier et al. 2013). However, when the role of PEEP in patients beginning with normal or near-normal lungs was investigated during surgery (low tidal volumes were combined with either no or very low PEEP *vs* 12 cm H_2O PEEP plus recruitment manoeuvres), no benefit was seen in the PEEP group in terms of survival (Imberger et al. 2010) or reduced perioperative respiratory complications (PROVE Network Investigators 2014). In fact, there was an increase in intraoperative hypotension. Therefore, whether intraoperative PEEP has a positive effect on patient perioperative outcomes is in doubt (Serpa Neto et al. 2015). It may be that lower levels such as 6 cm H_2O are more appropriate, similar to those used by Futier et al. (2013). This is an area of continued study, especially in the obese patient.

Obesity is also often accompanied by other co-morbidities that may affect the respiratory system, such as OSA. Gupta showed a 20% *vs* 6% rate of unplanned intensive care transfers in obese compared with non-obese patients, a rate of serious complications of 24 *vs* 9%, and a length of stay of 6.8 days *vs* 5.1 days (Gupta et al. 2001).

OSA is a common sleep disorder characterized by intermittent obstruction of the upper airway, together with periods of apnoea lasting longer than 10 s. It is exacerbated by anaesthetic and analgesic drugs (Chung et al. 2008c). One screening method to detect undiagnosed OSA is the STOP-BANG questionnaire (Chung et al. 2012). Unfortunately, even when a history is present it remains undetected by surgeons in 58% of cases and by anaesthetists in 15% of cases (Singh et al. 2013) and unless screened for, it remains undiagnosed in the majority of cases of previously undiagnosed OSA. This is a particular problem, because we know that in non-cardiac surgery there is an increased risk of postoperative hypoxia, complications, ICU transfers, and length of stay (Kaw et al. 2012). There is also an increased risk of pulmonary complications (Memtsoudis et al. 2011), delirium (Bateman and Eikermann 2012; Flink et al. 2012), and pulmonary aspiration (Valipour et al. 2002). OSA is also associated with myocardial infarction and cerebrovascular accident. Pulmonary aspiration may contribute to the increased risk of acute respiratory distress syndrome (ARDS) in these patients, combined with evidence of an upregulation of the proinflammatory transcription factor nuclear factor kappa-light-chain-enhancer of B cells and related proinflammatory genes (enhanced by repetitive hypoxaemia) (Greenberg et al. 2006). Patients with OSA undergoing orthopaedic arthroplasty procedures have an elevated risk of pulmonary embolism over other similar patients (Memtsoudis et al. 2009). Spontaneous platelet aggregation and activation were elevated in patients with OSA and reduced to normal with effective treatment with CPAP (Bokinsky et al. 1995). There was also an increased risk of unplanned tracheal intubation and mechanical ventilation in the perioperative period (Memtsoudis et al. 2011).

OSA occurs in adults and children and also occurs with craniofacial and palatal abnormalities (such as in trisomy 21 and Pierre–Robin syndrome). In children, it is commonly associated with tonsillar hypertrophy but now, as in adults, obesity-related obstruction is increasing and is becoming a major issue for anaesthetists. The patient with disordered breathing during sleep is likely to have even more disturbed breathing when sedated, because the normal arousal process that opens the airway and stimulates breathing is obtunded. The upper airway abnormalities that predispose to breathing obstruction during sleep may also make tracheal intubation difficult (Chung et al. 2008a), although this has been disputed in one study, which found a Mallampati score of 3 or 4 or male gender predictive of difficult tracheal intubation in morbidly obese patients (average BMI 49 kg m^{-2}) in the ramped position (Neligan et al. 2009).

The main group with sleep apnoea are overweight middle-aged men in whom increasing fatty tissue within the oropharynx tips the balance against the oropharyngeal dilator and abductor muscles, which normally maintain airway patency, in favour of airway closure. This produces periods of apnoea, until increased oxygen and carbon dioxide chemoreceptor activity and general arousal produces an increased inspiratory effort and oropharyngeal tone that opens the airway (Chung et al. 2008b). The STOP-BANG questionnaire is a screening tool. More formal diagnostic sleep studies are available including polysomnography and may well already have been carried out on patients with known sleep apnoea. These tests range from simple overnight pulse oximetry to simultaneous pulse oximetry, ECG, electroencephalography (to look at the phases of sleep and arousal), snoring volume, oro-nasal air flow, and video recordings of body position. These more complex recordings also allow the temporal relationship of any abnormalities to be examined. This allows the calculation of the apnoea/hypopnoea index, which examines the number of periods of hypopnoea or apnoea lasting more than 10 s. Defining apnoea is relatively straightforward, but hypopnoea requires the setting of definitions such as greater than 30% airflow reduction and greater than 4% desaturation or greater than 50% reduction in the change in nasal pressure during inspiration with 3% desaturation.

These patients are at risk from cerebrovascular accidents and cardiovascular problems, including myocardial infarction, brady- and tachyarrhythmias, biventricular failure, and pulmonary hypertension. Obesity and OSA are also associated with myocardial infarction as a result of the pro-inflammatory condition with endothelial dysfunction, increased platelet aggregation, low antioxidant levels, and raised inflammatory cytokines (Hung et al. 1990). These features are also seen in metabolic syndrome, which occurs in central obesity and includes raised triglycerides, reduced high-density lipoprotein, raised blood pressure, and raised fasting glucose (diabetes) and may be associated with lowered testosterone and catecholamine concentrations. It is also associated with fatty liver disease and steatohepatitis. All these features add to the risks during stressful surgery and mean that these patients may become too sedated when exposed to opiates or benzodiazepines and this may exacerbate sleep apnoea and atelectasis. Therefore, postoperative CPAP is important and in severe cases tracheal extubation directly onto CPAP may be needed. Patients should always bring their CPAP machines with them to hospital, because although CPAP may be available on the HDU, this may not be the case on the surgical ward, where they will be at ongoing increased risk of obstruction and ventilatory failure. In patients where hypoventilation is severe, NIV may be needed and in some patients there may be difficulty in tracheal extubation or recovery from anaesthesia and mechanical ventilation, especially after longer-acting opioid drugs. Therefore, short-acting agents such as desflurane and a multimodal or regional approach to analgesia may be beneficial.

Central sleep apnoea

This may occur with disordered peripheral chemosensitivity. It is seen in obesity, OSA, cardiac failure, after bilateral carotid body surgery, and in disordered central ventilatory control, which can occur after strokes or head injury. Other causes include neuromuscular disorders such as poliomyelitis, motor neurone disease, or muscular dystrophy and rarely in acromegaly. In these situations, NIV will be needed postoperatively. Bariatric surgery is increasing in frequency and most patients suffer from OSA and may continue to need CPAP for some months after surgery. Morbidity after Caesarean section surgery is frequently associated with sleep-disordered breathing, because a large proportion of patients are obese.

Obesity hypoventilation syndrome occurs in about 11% of OSA patients and is characterized by a raised Pa_{CO_2}, a BMI higher than 30 kg m^{-2}, and daytime somnolence. Preoperative blood gases will help identify a high Pa_{CO_2} and an elevated bicarbonate, suggesting a condition that has been present for some time (Loadsman and Hillman 2001). These patients are at high risk of respiratory failure in the postoperative period (Kaw et al. 2011a, 2011b) and should receive NIV, with enough expiratory positive airway pressure to combat upper airway obstruction (10–13 cm H_2O and enough inspiratory positive airway pressure to maintain adequate ventilation). Pulmonary hypertension occurs secondary to chronic hypoxaemia, resulting in right heart failure. Therefore, preoperative assessment with echocardiography may be helpful. Anaesthesia involves avoiding respiratory depression and residual effects of anaesthetic drugs as far as possible.

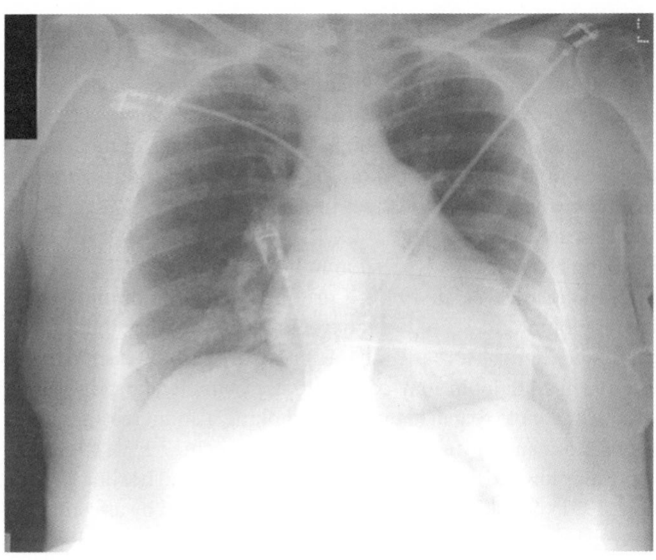

Figure 82.7 Pulmonary arterial hypertension. Chest X-ray can be normal, but can demonstrate cardiomegaly with prominent pulmonary arteries together with peripheral pruning of vessels.

Pulmonary hypertension

Progressive breathlessness that is not easily explained by left heart dysfunction or intrinsic lung disease may suggest pulmonary hypertension or chronic thromboembolic pulmonary hypertension (CTEPH) if persisting after pulmonary embolism (Fig. 82.7).

Pulmonary hypertension is defined as a mean pulmonary artery pressure of 25 mm Hg or higher at rest or 30 mm Hg on exercise (British Cardiac Society et al. 2001). At the World Symposium on Pulmonary Arterial Hypertension in 2003, the clinical classification of pulmonary hypertension was revised to identify five major groups (Elliot and Kiely 2006) and then updated in 2013 (Simonneau et al. 2013). These five groups now include the following aetiologies:

1. Pulmonary arterial hypertension (PAH):
   - 1.1 Idiopathic PAH
   - 1.2 Heritable PAH:
     - 1.2.1 BMPR2
     - 1.2.2 *ALK-1* (associated with hereditary haemorrhagic telangiectasia), *ENG, SMAD9, CAV1, KCNK3*
     - 1.2.3 Unknown
   - 1.3 Drug and toxin induced
   - 1.4 Associated with:
     - 1.4.1 Connective tissue disease

 1.4.2 HIV infection
 1.4.3 Portal hypertension
 1.4.4 Congenital heart diseases
 1.4.5 Schistosomiasis

1′. Pulmonary veno-occlusive disease and/or pulmonary capillary haemangiomatosis

1″. Persistent pulmonary hypertension of the newborn (PPHN)

2. Pulmonary hypertension as a result of left heart disease where treatment is best aimed at the underlying left heart disease:
 2.1 Left ventricular systolic dysfunction
 2.2 Left ventricular diastolic dysfunction
 2.3 Valvular disease
 2.4 Congenital/acquired left heart inflow/outflow tract obstruction and congenital cardiomyopathies

3. Pulmonary hypertension as a result of lung diseases and/or hypoxia:
 3.1 Chronic obstructive pulmonary disease
 3.2 Interstitial lung disease
 3.3 Other pulmonary diseases with mixed restrictive and obstructive pattern
 3.4 Sleep-disordered breathing
 3.5 Alveolar hypoventilation disorders
 3.6 Chronic exposure to high altitude
 3.7 Developmental lung diseases

4. Pulmonary hypertension as a result of chronic thrombotic or embolic disease (CTEPH)

5. Pulmonary hypertension with unclear multifactorial mechanisms:
 5.1 Haematological disorders: chronic haemolytic anaemia, myeloproliferative disorders, splenectomy
 5.2 Systemic disorders: sarcoidosis, pulmonary histiocytosis, lymphangioleiomyomatosis
 5.3 Metabolic disorders: glycogen storage disease, Gaucher's disease, thyroid disorders
 5.4 Others: tumoural obstruction, fibrosing mediastinitis, chronic renal failure, segmental pulmonary hypertension.

The type and hence the underlying cause for PAH has a major impact on prognosis. Untreated severe idiopathic pulmonary hypertension has a 5-year survival of only 27%, but this can be more than doubled with targeted treatments. Systemic sclerosis has a 5-year survival of 80% without PAH and 40% with (Stupi et al. 1986).

Pathophysiology varies between the different types of pulmonary hypertension and so right-heart catheter studies are normally carried out in specialist centres to establish where the restriction to flow or increased pressure originates from and is combined with echocardiography to establish if there are intracardiac shunts. Clinical signs in PAH would include tachycardia, increased jugular venous pressure, right ventricular heave, loud second heart sound and tricuspid regurgitation, combined with hepatomegaly and ascites and eventually ankle swelling.

Factors indicating a poor prognosis include right atrial pressure greater than 10 mm Hg, cardiac index less than 2.1, and mixed venous oxygen saturation of less than 63%. If the problem is IPAH, that is, a vasculopathy resulting from proliferation of the intima and media of the pulmonary arterial bed with narrowing and over-reactivity of the pulmonary capillaries (McLaughlin et al. 2009), then the patient may overreact to vasoconstrictor drugs and hypoxia. This is important when considering supportive therapies in the perioperative period, particularly including oxygen, CPAP, or NIV. The 6 min walking test appears to give an indication of survival at 20 months. If the walking distance is less than 332 m, survival is less than 20%.

It is important to distinguish between idiopathic pulmonary arterial hypertension (IPAH) and pulmonary hypertension secondary to left-sided heart problems, in particular left ventricular diastolic dysfunction (LVDD). In IPAH, patients are younger with fewer co-morbidities, ECG signs of right axis deviation, right ventricular hypertrophy, and ST depression inferiorly and anteriorly (Fig. 82.8). Echocardiography shows normal left atrial size and mitral flow. Magnetic resonance imaging shows increased right ventricular mass, with moderate or severe impairment of right ventricular function and the interventricular septum pushed over from right to left. Pulmonary capillary occlusion pressures are normal. Those with LVDD generally have a better prognosis and tend to be older, with hypertension, diabetes, and atrial fibrillation. ECG shows left axis deviation, left ventricular hypertrophy, and lateral ST depression. Echocardiography shows a large left atrium, and a high ratio (>15) of mitral peak velocity of early filling (E) to early diastolic mitral annular velocity (EO). There is a normal ratio of right to left ventricular mass and septal position. Right ventricular function is normal or mildly impaired, with a raised pulmonary arterial wedge pressure (Kiely et al. 2013). It is important that the two are distinguished, because pulmonary arterial/capillary dilators may allow back pressure into the pulmonary vasculature that causes pulmonary oedema in the LVDD group.

Specialized therapies for idiopathic pulmonary arterial hypertension include oral therapies such as bosentan, an endothelin receptor agonist (Rubin et al. 2002; Denton et al. 2006), which may cause reversible impairment of liver function. A small percentage of IPAH alone respond to calcium channel blockers such as diltiazem or nifedipine, but other forms of PAH do not. More recently, sildenafil, which is a phosphodiesterase inhibitor (and so should not be used with nitrates), has been shown to improve walking distance (Galie et al. 2005). Its action is via inhibition of phosphodiesterase 5, which would otherwise break down nitric oxide, which acts via cyclic GMP to relax the pulmonary vasculature and to reduce cellular proliferation. Intravenous or nebulized prostacyclin via a central or Hickman line has been shown to improve survival (Barst et al. 1996; Channick et al. 2006; McLaughlin et al. 2006). Iloprost is more stable than epoprostenol and more commonly used in the United Kingdom. Importantly, line infections often present with worsening of dyspnoea. Nitric oxide concentrations are low in the pulmonary circulation in PAH. It has been possible to inject controlled nitric oxide gas into the breathing systems in theatre and ICU in these patients to dilate the pulmonary vasculature, but metabolites are toxic and so need to be monitored. Arginine has been used as a precursor of nitric oxide in sickle cell disease. These therapies are not helpful in left-sided heart disease or pulmonary

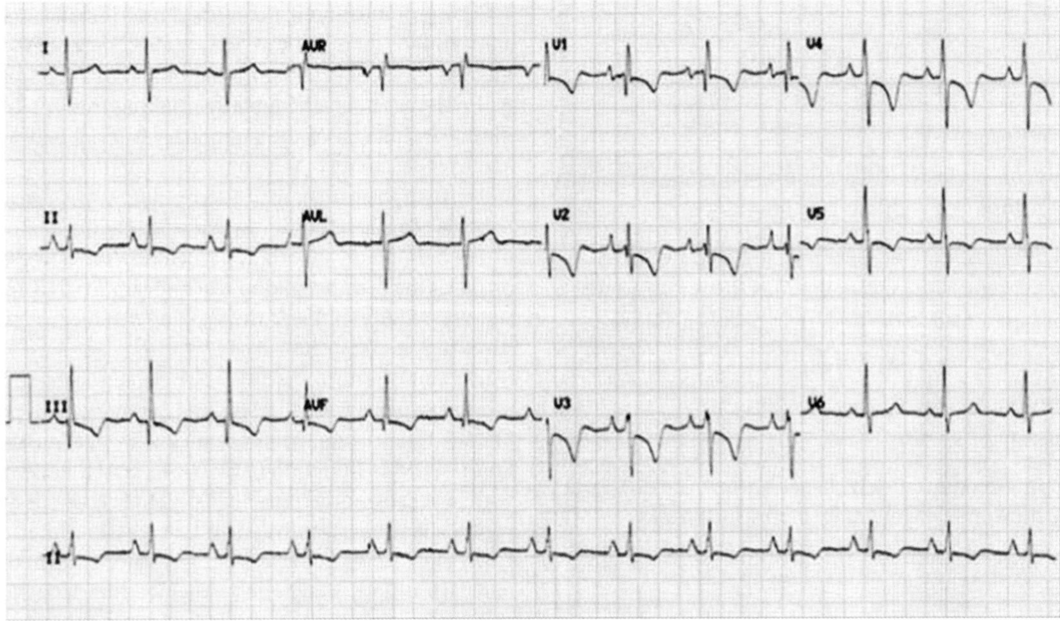

Figure 82.8 ECG with pulmonary arterial hypertension. ECG showing right heart strain with dominant R wave in V1, depressed ST and inverted T waves in the inferior and right chest leads, and right axis deviation, consistent with pulmonary hypertension.

veno-occlusive disease and may even allow back pressure to produce pulmonary oedema.

CTEPH occurs in about 4% of patients at 2 years after a symptomatic pulmonary embolus. It particularly affects those who have had a massive pulmonary embolus or ongoing breathlessness or deep vein thrombosis (Fig. 82.9). The right ventricle can produce a maximum systolic pulmonary artery pressure of 50 mm Hg in the acute situation. Higher levels suggest that there is pre-existing pulmonary artery disease and CTEPH. Treatment is with anticoagulation and consideration for pulmonary endarterectomy. If the mean pulmonary artery pressure in CTEPH exceeds 50 mm Hg, life expectancy is 10% at 5 years, compared with a 5–10% perioperative mortality for pulmonary endarterectomy.

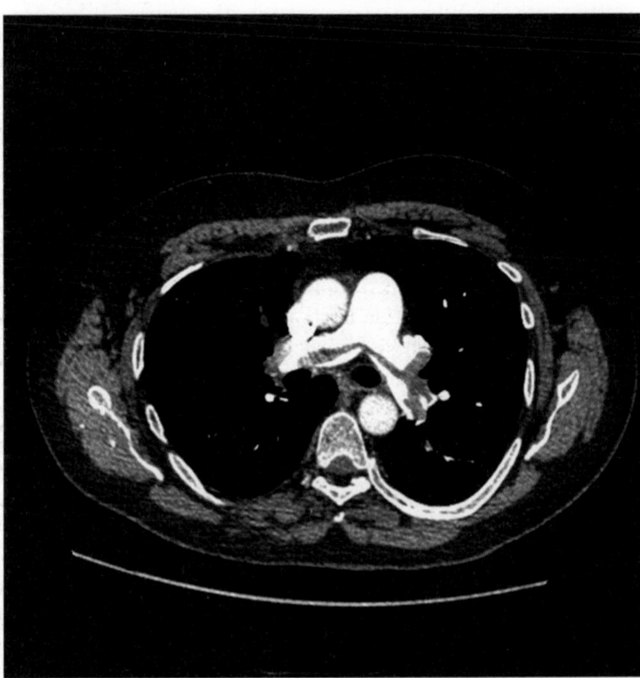

Figure 82.9 CT pulmonary angiogram showing saddle embolus across the division of the pulmonary artery into left and right main branches.

Patients often present with worsening exercise tolerance and even syncopal episodes as a result of borderline cardiac output as pulmonary vascular resistance increases. As this happens, arrhythmias may occur and right heart coronary artery flow may decrease as the pressures in the right heart and hence right heart wall tension increase. Treatment of right heart failure is therefore important in the perioperative period, which may include off-loading or avoiding fluid overload with diuretics or considering continuous veno-venous haemofiltration. Mechanical ventilation may increase pulmonary artery pressures and so regional or local techniques are important. Avoidance of hypoxia and atelectasis with CPAP or NIV can be effective especially if patients are developing pneumonia.

Increasing right heart overload may occur in PAH in pregnancy in patients who lack reserve. This used to be a major cause of mortality (30–56%) and often meant that pregnancy was avoided or terminated. However, the situation has improved with nebulized iloprost (Elliot et al. 2005). In a study of pulmonary hypertension patients scheduled for early delivery by Caesarean section, nebulized iloprost was started in 9 of 10 patients. Three patients required intravenous iloprost infusions. Nine patients delivered by Caesarean and one delivered spontaneously. Low-molecular-weight heparin was used in 9 of 10 pregnancies (five at full therapeutic dose and four at a prophylactic dose, including one woman with a suprarenal inferior vena cava filter inserted during pregnancy). All patients received epidural or combined spinal–epidural anaesthesia. The majority had radial arterial lines and central venous catheters. Cardiac output monitoring was performed with Swan–Ganz catheters in two women and LiDCO™ (LiDCO System,

London, UK) monitoring in the remainder. All 10 pregnancies produced live babies. One mother died at 4 weeks after deciding to stop her treatment. One patient went on to pulmonary endarterectomy. This survival rate was very high compared with earlier studies. Management was by a team of anaesthetists, intensivists, pulmonary vascular physicians, obstetricians, and haematologists (Kiely et al. 2010).

However, patients may present for non-obstetric surgery, either cardiothoracic or non-cardiothoracic. They are at risk of developing right heart failure, because of falling contractility, increased pulmonary vascular resistance, or fluid overload, and may initially present at many locations, not just at specialized centres. Stress, hypoxia, and tachycardia or arrhythmias may precipitate a decrease in contractility and increased pulmonary vascular resistance. Outcomes will vary greatly depending on the indication for surgery, co-morbidity, and the presence of sepsis. Studies have shown perioperative mortality rates for non-cardiac and non-obstetric surgery of 7% (Ramakrishna et al. 2005) and 14% (Minai et al. 2006). So far, most non-cardiac and non-obstetric surgical cases requiring anaesthesia have either been managed with local or regional anaesthesia, sometimes combined with sedation or by general anaesthesia, often with a regional block. If mechanical ventilation is needed, risks are higher and it should be with lung protective ventilation with tidal volumes of 6 ml^{-1} kg and moderate PEEP to avoid over-distension (Fernandez-Perez et al. 2008).

More recently, Price et al. (2010) studied 28 patients with mild to moderate pulmonary hypertension, 21 of whom were New York Heart Association functional class I-II, undergoing surgery from 2000 to 2007. Fifty per cent of surgery was under general anaesthetic combined with regional anaesthesia and 50% under regional alone. Perioperative mortality overall was 7%. Death rates were higher (50%) for emergency cases (n = 4). Perioperative complications occurred in 29% and were more common in emergency, major and prolonged surgery (average 193 *vs* 112 min).

Restrictive lung disease

Interstitial lung diseases

These are a family of diseases sometimes known as idiopathic interstitial pneumonias that pose major problems to the anaesthetist because of their physiological effects on the respiratory systems and their relationship to other diseases. Their effects range from inflammation of the connective tissue within the lung, which is particularly the case with sarcoid, to fibrosis in idiopathic pulmonary fibrosis, and airspace filling with alveolar proteinosis or desquamative interstitial pneumonitis (Wallis and Spinks 2015). A precise diagnosis is not always available, which makes planning and prognostication difficult. This lack of clarity is a major issue for anaesthesia and intensive care, because the outlook with the different diseases varies considerably. They may also be confused with infection, connective tissue diseases, vasculitis, lymphoma, and some lung cancers and complicated by pulmonary embolism. Perioperative deterioration may be as a result of an exacerbation of the disease itself, infection, or any of the complications associated with anaesthesia and surgery. Pulmonary fibrosis may be drug induced. Drugs include bleomycin, busulfan, cyclophosphamide, methotrexate, amiodarone, and nitrofurantoin. High oxygen levels are a particular issue for anaesthetists, who may be called upon to anaesthetize patients who have had bleomycin therapy for lymphoma (Donat 1999). High oxygen levels can exacerbate pulmonary toxicity of bleomycin. This is a long-term risk and therefore reduced inspired oxygen should be used to target 90% saturation.

Idiopathic pulmonary fibrosis

Idiopathic pulmonary fibrosis is caused by chronic inflammation of the alveoli, which leads to scarring and progressive fibrosis with a poor prognosis. There is repetitive epithelial lung injury and loss of alveolar capillary integrity which triggers inappropriate, progressive, widespread, and heterogeneous lung scarring. This decreases compliance, increases resistance, reduces lung volumes (Nava and Rubini 1999), and worsens gas diffusion, resulting in hypoxia and eventually hypercapnia. It is the commonest interstitial lung disease, with an incidence of 7.44:100 000 of the population in the United Kingdom (Navaratnam et al. 2011) and appears to have a higher incidence in mainland Europe and the United States. The incidence increases with age.

Clinically, patients may complain of progressively worsening shortness of breath, especially on exertion, with a dry cough. Patients are usually more than 50 years old with a gradual onset of breathlessness, usually over at least 3 months. There will be fine crackles at the bases, tachypnoea, and the fingers may be clubbed. At first, the chest X-ray may appear normal, but CT will reveal abnormal features (Fig. 82.10). Clinical signs include hypoxia, dyspnoea, finger clubbing, and fine crackles at lung bases. Chest X-rays show a reticular pattern, traction bronchiectasis, and volume loss. High-resolution CT shows bibasal reticular shadowing and honeycombing, but only minimal ground-glass opacities (Fig. 82.11).

Idiopathic pulmonary fibrosis is progressive and generally fatal, with a median survival of less than 5 years from diagnosis, with chronic inflammation of the alveolar wall. Patients with disease severe enough to require ventilation for acute respiratory failure while on the waiting list for lung transplantation often have a higher elastance than non-survivors with respiratory ARDS, which in turn is four times higher than ventilated patients with normal lungs. Chest wall elastance was 15% above normal, probably related to the increased lung recoil, which would place the chest wall into the lower flat portion of the pressure–volume curve (Nava and Rubini 1999). These patients also have increased lung resistance despite the expected increased elastic recoil. Gibson and Pride (1977) had suggested that this was as a result of the reduced lung volume causing airway narrowing. However, this was less severe than resistance changes in COPD, with all but one patient returning to baseline pressure after a 3 s expiratory hold. In patients with end-stage disease, in contrast to earlier disease, rapid shallow breathing in response to the stiffness of the lungs, leads to alveolar hypoventilation with an increase in Pa_{CO_2}. Lung and chest wall mechanics in patients who are ventilated and have severe idiopathic pulmonary fibrosis are a major problem. The poor compliance results in high airway pressures, combined with poor diffusion of oxygen and to a lesser extent carbon dioxide.

The diagnosis of idiopathic pulmonary fibrosis relies on the exclusion of known causes of interstitial lung diseases, including drugs, environmental causes, and connective tissue diseases. Essentially the aetiology is unknown, but there may be links to viruses, including Epstein–Barr, herpes simplex, hepatitis C, cytomegalovirus, parvovirus B19, torque teno, and herpes viruses 7 and 9, and sometimes a familial association. It is more common in people who smoke

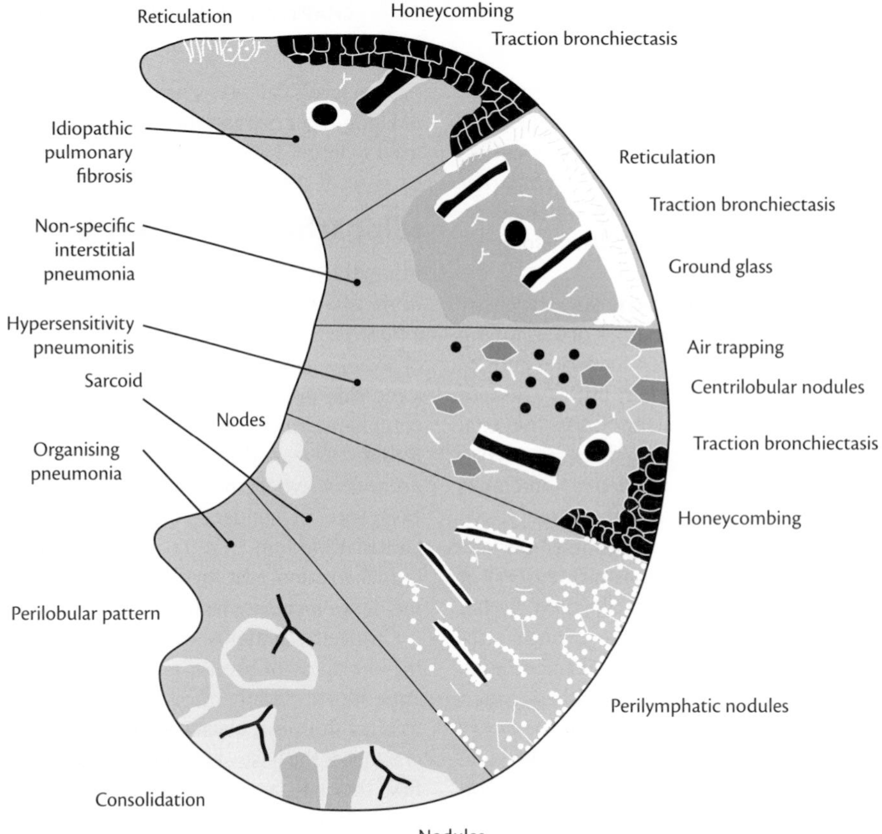

Figure 82.10 Simplified diagram of typical high-resolution computed tomography appearance of the most commonly encountered interstitial lung diseases. Idiopathic pulmonary fibrosis (usual interstitial pneumonia pattern; lower-lung predominant subpleural reticulations, traction bronchiectasis, and honeycombing with paucity of ground-glass opacification). Non-specific interstitial pneumonia (lower-lung predominant subpleural ground-glass opacification and fine reticulations, with traction bronchiectasis in the fibrotic stage and typically an absence of honeycombing). Hypersensitivity pneumonitis—acute: centrilobular or geographical ground-glass opacification and air trapping (mosaic attenuation); chronic: fibrosis with reticulation, traction bronchiectasis, and possibly honeycombing. Sarcoidosis (mediastinal and bihilar lymphadenopathy, perilymphatic nodularity; when fibrotic often perihilar, mass-like, or honeycombing). Organizing pneumonia (nodules or consolidation, often a perilobular pattern, fluctuation).

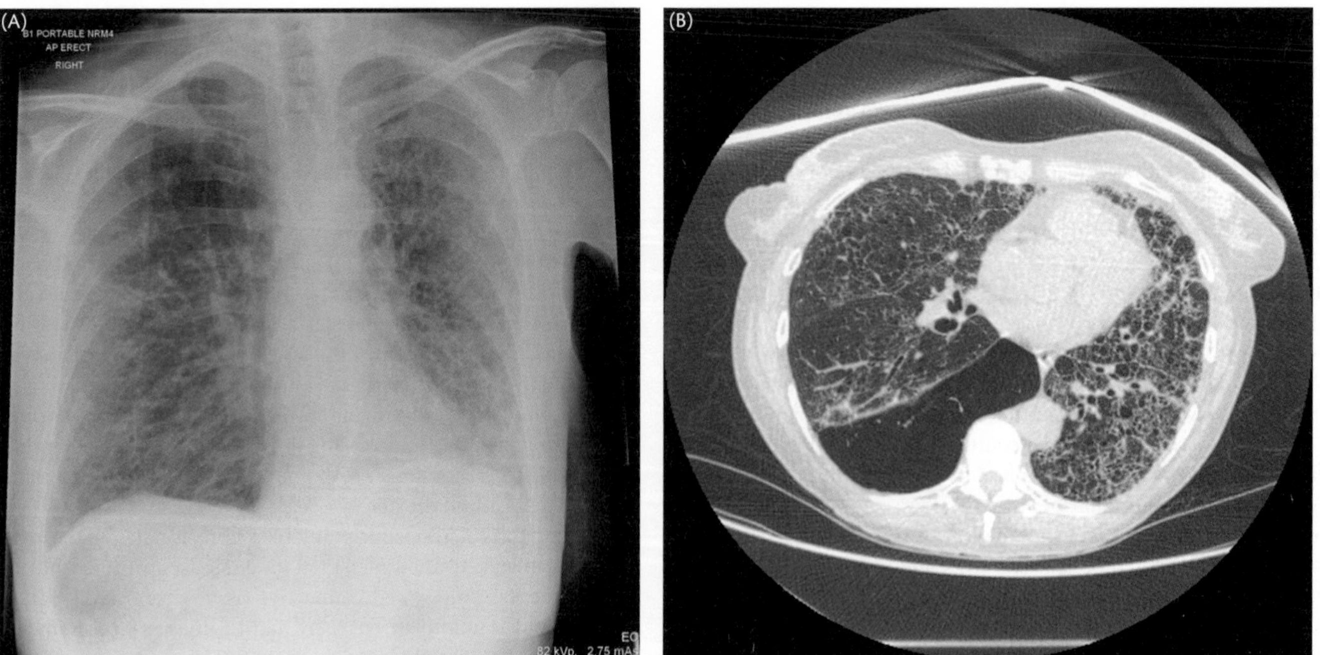

Figure 82.11 Lung fibrosis on (A) chest X-ray and (B) chest computed tomography scan showing extensive lung fibrosis, bronchiectasis, and honeycombing with large bulla.

and in people who have been exposed to dust from wood, metals, textiles, or stone, cattle or farming and there may be links to gastro-oesophageal reflux disease. Unfortunately steroids and immunosuppressive drugs show no major benefit, although steroids and cyclophosphamide are often tried. Pirfenidone, nintedanib, and acetylcysteine were postulated to reduce inflammation in the lungs, but have not yet been shown to cause major improvement. However, NICE recommends pirfenidone in patients with a forced vital capacity of 50–80% of predicted, where it may slow the rate of decline, but it does not reverse existing fibrosis (Noble et al. 2011; King et al. 2014). The only long-term treatment that can prolong survival is lung transplantation (Davies et al. 2003; Richeldi et al. 2003; Mason et al. 2007).

The main concern initially is to exclude a treatable cause. Bronchoscopy may show certain cell types, such as lymphocytosis in hypersensitivity pneumonitis or sarcoidosis (Wallis and Spinks 2015), or reveal malignant cells or infection, but may not be possible in the awake, spontaneously breathing patient. Lung biopsy may be attempted, showing diffuse alveolar damage and fibrosis, but risks pneumothorax or other complications. Video-assisted thorascopic biopsy has an overall 30-day mortality risk of 2.1%, compared with 4.3% in open lung biopsy. However, risks in individual cases may be much higher and increase with age (Nguyen and Meyer 2013).

Acute exacerbations occasionally present on a background of minimal symptoms, with unexplained worsening of dyspnoea over 30 days with new lung infiltrates. A CT pulmonary angiogram is useful to exclude pulmonary embolism. Mechanical ventilation of the lungs is often required before the diagnosis is clear, because a full work-up may not be possible in the time available. Severe acute exacerbations present major clinical and ethical challenges because of the poor outcome. Transplantation in the ICU setting is extremely difficult (Papiris et al. 2010). Patients may also require their lungs to be mechanically ventilated because another pathology is overlying the condition, such as a pneumonia. Unfortunately mechanical ventilation does not improve survival in patients presenting with a terminal exacerbation of severely progressive disease.

Idiopathic pulmonary fibrosis is a major problem for anaesthesia. The first issue is one of the risk:benefit ratio of surgery in a patient with a progressive life-limiting disease. The addition of perioperative atelectasis, mechanical ventilation, and drugs that depress the respiratory centres may produce respiratory failure in a patient who would otherwise continue to maintain adequate ventilation and gas transfer for many months (Utz et al. 2001).

Postoperative causes of exacerbation have been found to have a mortality of approximately 44% compared with 90% in the non-operative group. Other exacerbating factors such as pneumothorax, heart failure, and pulmonary embolism should be excluded.

The use of anaesthesia in the context of lung fibrosis requiring lung transplantation is well described (Della Rocca et al. 2000; Vicente et al. 2006). However, there is a major issue of how to deal with a non-transplant patient with existing lung fibrosis in the perioperative period. In lung fibrosis, the lungs are stiff and the transfer factor is reduced, so making lung recruitment difficult and the effects of PEEP unpredictable. High PEEP is associated with a worsened outcome in exacerbations of idiopathic pulmonary fibrosis (Fernandez-Perez et al. 2008). Lung fibrosis is associated with a large number of pathologies, many of which have wider systemic effects, while lung fibrosis itself will raise pulmonary artery pressures and elevate the work of the right ventricle.

Regional or local techniques are preferable, to maintain as close to normal spontaneous breathing as possible. Unfortunately some surgery requires general anaesthesia; most commonly intra-abdominal and intrathoracic procedures. There are exceptions to this where with gentle surgery, including those requiring pneumoperitoneum under low CO_2 insufflation pressures, pressure-controlled ventilation through the Supreme® (Teleflex, Inc., Wayne, PA, USA) laryngeal mask airway, has been used with the position confirmed by bronchoscopy, combining general anaesthesia with an epidural during laparoscopic cholecystectomy in a patient with severe pulmonary fibrosis (Carron et al. 2009). Epidural block from T4 to L1 was established before induction with remifentanil and propofol, plus cisatracurium. This technique, although producing smoother wakening than endotracheal intubation, could be criticized because of the increased risk of pulmonary aspiration of gastric contents (Hohlrieder et al. 2007).

Although spontaneous breathing may potentially allow a more normal pattern and distribution of ventilation, it produces three other difficulties. Hypercarbic patients may hypoventilate further as a result of the impact of anaesthetic drugs on respiratory drive and this hypoventilation may increase Pa_{CO_2} to unsustainable levels. Atelectasis may occur as a result of hypoventilation in these patients in whom lung recruitment is less effective. Conversion to tracheal intubation and mechanical ventilation in the event of a deterioration adds complexity.

Lung fibrosis has very occasionally been described after anaesthesia in patients with no previous history, underlying disease, or obvious drug cause (Kimura and Mizutani 2001); however, it is likely that this is a form of lung damage secondary to a cause inducing ARDS. Deterioration has been seen in the opposite lung in patients with idiopathic pulmonary fibrosis who are undergoing lung biopsy under general anaesthesia (Hoshikawa and Kondo 2004; Kondoh et al. 2006). This may be as a result of other indirectly related factors such as hyperoxygenation or lung distension (Mallick 2008). Mortality in this situation is higher than 50%.

There are other causes of interstitial lung disease (Chapman et al. 2014), such as non-specific interstitial pneumonia, respiratory bronchiolitis-associated interstitial disease, desquamative interstitial pneumonia, and cryptogenic organizing pneumonia. These have a better prognosis than idiopathic lung fibrosis.

Non-specific interstitial pneumonias

These may be related to connective tissue diseases, drugs, immunodeficiency, and infection. They present with breathlessness and weight loss, with basal crackles, and sometimes finger clubbing; there is a restrictive pattern of lung function and impaired gas transfer in some. Histology varies from inflammatory (NSIP1), part inflammation and some fibrosis (NSIP2), to much more fibrosis (NSIP3). The treatment is with steroids, plus bisphosphonates, proton pump inhibitors, and co-trimoxazole. Survival at 5 years is more than 50% even in NSIP3.

Cryptogenic organizing pneumonia

Alveolar and even small bronchioles become plugged with granulation tissue. This can be cryptogenic or an organizing pneumonia secondary to infection, radiotherapy, connective tissue disease, diffuse alveolar damage, inflammatory bowel disease, haematological malignancy, post-bone marrow transplant, lung malignancy, or pulmonary infarction. Frequently these patients present with a slow to resolve pneumonia and a history of increasing breathlessness of under 3 months, sometimes with crackles on examination, but no finger clubbing. CT shows areas of consolidation, with air bronchograms and ground glass. Bronchoalveolar lavage shows neutrophils, eosinophils, and lymphocytes.

Acute interstitial pneumonias

This was previously known as the Hamman–Rich syndrome and is an idiopathic form of lung disease probably related to ARDS, which comes on over a few days, usually after a viral illness with fever, arthralgia, and myalgia and crackles on examination. CT shows diffuse bilateral ground-glass appearance, consolidation, reticulation, and cysts, with traction bronchiectasis. Bronchoalveolar lavage shows increased cells of all types including red cells and haemosiderin. Treatment usually involves high-dose methylprednisolone (1 g every 3 days intravenously, followed by 1 mg kg^{-1} day^{-1} maintenance of prednisolone), but fewer than 50% survive and the disease may recur or become chronic.

Respiratory bronchiolitis associated lung disease

This is usually a disease presenting in patients of 40 years of age or more, with mixed restrictive and obstructive characteristics associated with smoking and pigmented macrophages in the bronchioles. Treatment is to stop smoking and prolonged survival is common. The disease may be desquamative interstitial pneumonia, which is a form of alveolar macrophage pneumonia.

Lymphoid interstitial pneumonia

This is a rare disease associated with connective tissue disease, immunodeficiency, infections such as pneumocystis pneumonia (PCP), autoimmune diseases, and drugs. Breathlessness advances over years and patients show lymphoid hyperplasia and lymphoid lung infiltrates progressing to fibrosis.

Eosinophilic lung diseases

Eosinophilia can be a major feature of asthma, particularly when associated with eczema or fungal infection with *Aspergillus*. Simple pulmonary eosinophilia (Loeffler's syndrome) is associated with larvae, whereas the rarer tropical pulmonary eosinophilia is associated with filaria in the blood.

Chronic eosinophilic pneumonia gradually advances over months and may be associated with asthma. Acute eosinophilic pneumonia follows a febrile illness with increasing shortness of breath. There are interstitial or alveolar infiltrates and eosinophils on bronchoalveolar lavage. Both the chronic and acute forms respond to steroids. Hypereosinophilic syndrome demonstrates very high blood eosinophilia of greater than 1.5×10^9 cells $litre^{-1}$ over many months. The disease may extend to affect the heart muscle, valves, and the pericardium and require steroids and immunosuppressant treatment. Churg–Strauss syndrome combines asthma, eosinophilia, with pulmonary infiltrates and a small- and medium-vessel vasculitis, which may affect the gastrointestinal tract and so is sometimes called eosinophilic granulomatous polyangiitis. P-ANCA and anti-MPO antibodies are usually positive. Treatment is with prednisolone, cyclophosphamide, and azathioprine.

Vasculitides

Neutrophils cause damage to small vessels in the lung, so damaging the lung itself, resulting in infiltrates, infarction, and haemorrhage into the lung.

Granulomatosis with polyangiitis affects small and medium-sized vessels in the lung accompanied by haemoptysis, breathlessness, and pleuritic chest pain. Cavitating lesions, alveolar haemorrhage, pleural effusions, and bronchiectasis are often present (Fig. 82.12). Nephritis occurs in 80%, with red cell casts on dip stick testing. Classically granulomatosis with polyangiitis causes sinusitis, nasal septal perforation, and epistaxis, in addition to a rash and muscle and joint pains. Serologically c-ANCA and anti-PR3 are positive. Treatment is with steroids and cyclophosphamide. Microscopic polyangiitis has similar symptoms and signs to granulomatosis with polyangiitis.

Goodpasture's syndrome affects the lungs and the kidneys of men more than women in the 20- to 30-year age group, although it can occur later. Immunoglobulin G is deposited on the basement membranes of alveoli and glomeruli. The resulting damage causes alveolar haemorrhage (especially in smokers) and glomerulonephritis. Anti-glomerular basement membrane antibodies are detectable. The carbon monoxide transfer coefficient is elevated because of the haemorrhage. Patients have haemoptysis and crackles in the lungs.

Polyarteritis nodosa affects middle-sized vessels and Takayasu's arteritis affects large vessels.

Sickle cell disease

Sickle cell disease produces important effects on the respiratory system and patients with sickle cell disease are more likely than most people to require surgery. Surgery typically includes cholecystectomy, or hip procedures after avascular necrosis of the femoral head. Other complications include acute splenic sequestration

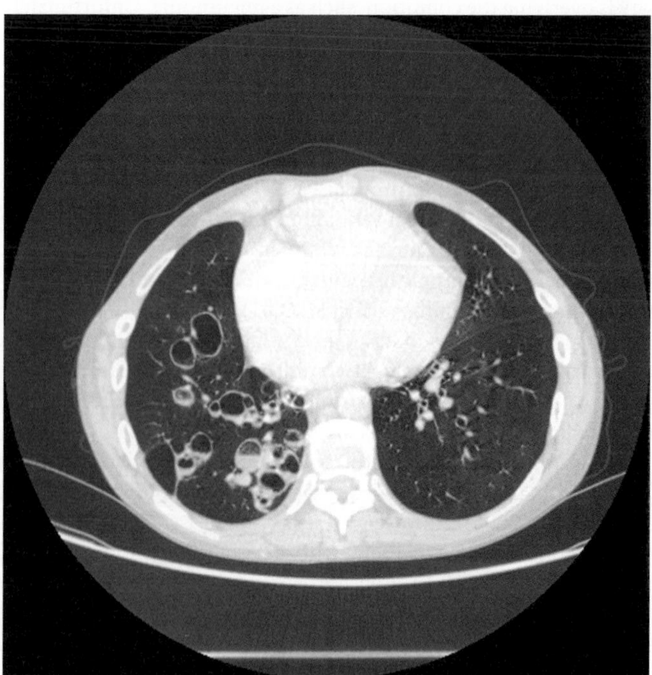

Figure 82.12 Computed tomography scan showing lung abscesses and bronchiectasis.

crises, splenic infarction or splenic abscess formation, peptic ulceration, ischaemic colitis, pancreatitis, or leg ulcers. Patients have a chronic haemolytic anaemia and vasoactive crises. Sickle cell disease is associated with increased breathlessness and occasionally pulmonary hypertension. Pneumonias occur especially as a result of *Streptococcus* pneumonia and encapsulated bacteria, viruses, and atypical pneumonias. Asthma and pulmonary emboli are common and fat emboli occur. Acute chest syndrome produces chest pain, breathlessness, and lung injury. All these problems may lead to ARDS. Treatment is to avoid sickling by giving oxygen, fluid, and analgesia. Blood transfusion or exchange transfusion may reduce sickling by reducing haemoglobin S to below 20% of the total. Hydroxycarbamide may reduce sickling by increasing fetal haemoglobin.

Immunocompromised patients and pulmonary disease

Patients who are immunocompromised may develop respiratory disease or respiratory failure as a result of either infectious or non-infectious causes. This vulnerability to infection presents problems for the anaesthetist, before, during, and after surgery. The risk of surgical complications is high, including perioperative sepsis. The non-infectious issues include the underlying disease (e.g. lymphoma, leukaemic infiltration), graft *vs* host disease, pulmonary oedema after renal transplant, drug effects (e.g. cytarabine including chemotherapy), ARDS after blood transfusion, the effect of radiotherapy, diffuse alveolar haemorrhage, idiopathic pneumonia, engraftment syndrome, post-transplant lymphoproliferative disease, bronchiolitis obliterans syndrome (BOS), and pulmonary veno-occlusive disease.

Pneumonia (PCP) is a major risk and may be present at the time of surgery. *Pneumocystis* (fungal) pneumonia is often difficult to diagnose. Features include chest X-ray showing bilateral perihilar infiltrates, alveolar shadowing and rarely pneumothorax; CD4 less than 200 μg litre^{-1}, lactate dehydrogenase (LDH) is greater than 220 U litre^{-1}.

Quantitative PCR for *Pneumocystis* helps distinguish between colonization and active infection.

β-D-glucan (BDG) is present in the cell wall of many fungi, including *Candida, Aspergillus*, and *Pneumocystis*. PCP may demonstrate extrapulmonary manifestations, affecting the central nervous system, bone marrow (may have necrosis with resultant pancytopenia), lymphadenopathy, eyes (may have retinal cotton-wool spots), thyroid swelling (may present as a rapidly enlarging thyroid mass), and the gastrointestinal tract.

PCP may be confused with ARDS, cytomegalovirus, lymphocytic interstitial pneumonia, *Mycoplasma* infections, viral pneumonia, pulmonary embolism, legionellosis, tuberculosis and *Mycobacterium avium* complex infection. Treatment can be divided into supportive, that aimed at the underlying diagnosis, and antimicrobial therapy.

Hypersensitivity pneumonitis

Hypersensitivity pneumonitis, previously known as extrinsic allergic alveolitis, is encouraged by neutropenia, impaired T-cell function, and hypogammaglobulinaemia. Infectious agents include bacteria, fungi, *Aspergillus*, parasites, and viruses.

Hypersensitivity pneumonitis occurs in farmers, or pigeon or bird keepers, or those exposed to the house dust mite. It is caused by microorganisms, animal proteins, including rat droppings, and bloom from bird feathers, and paint chemicals such as toluene. Organisms involved include *Aspergillus clavatus, Trichosporon cutaneum*, and thermophilic *Actinomyces*. This leads to fever, arthralgia, and myalgia, with crackles and wheeze in the lungs. Pulmonary function shows restrictive lung disease, sometimes with some obstruction. There is a neutrophilia, with a lymphocytosis on bronchoalveolar lavage. Blood immunoglobulin G precipitin is high. Treatment is primarily avoidance of the cause. This is followed by corticosteroids.

Exposure diseases

Pneumoconioses result from inhalation of dust particles which cause inflammation. Coal workers' pneumoconiosis is produced by coal dust causing cytokine release and then lung fibrosis. This may progress from simple pneumoconiosis to progressive massive fibrosis with opacities forming that are more than 1 cm in diameter. This can be further complicated by rheumatoid arthritis, which leads to nodules and Caplan's syndrome, which involves large nodule formation and cavitation. Other pneumoconioses include silicosis, which produces nodules and lung fibrosis. Berylliosis can occur acutely producing pulmonary oedema, which may be treated with corticosteroids to reduce subsequent inflammation and chronic berylliosis, which is a T-cell immune response causing granulomatous inflammation that is seen on chest X-ray as a reticulonodular appearance, bronchiectasis, and honeycombing. Lung function test show a restrictive defect with decreased carbon monoxide transfer coefficient.

Asbestos exposure is mainly occupational and produces pleural plaques (usually posterolaterally), diffuse pleural thickening and effusions, mesothelioma, and asbestosis. Asbestosis is chronic interstitial fibrosis as a result of asbestos exposure. Radiology shows bilateral reticulonodular patterns, which may progress to honeycombing if severe. CT shows ground-glass, subpleural opacities, septal thickening and signs of fibrosis, with traction bronchiectasis. This is a restrictive lung disease. Mesothelioma is a malignant tumour of the pleura.

Connective tissue diseases

Rheumatoid disease causes cricoarytenoid arthritis, pleuritic chest pain, an exudative effusion with low glucose, and lung fibrosis. There may be pulmonary nodules, haemoptysis, and cavitation. There is also a vasculitis. On examination, finger clubbing and basal crackles may be present. Lung function tests show a restrictive lung disease. This may progress to organizing pneumonia or even lymphocytic infiltration of terminal bronchioles, which causes obliterative bronchiolitis. Lung function tests show an obstructive picture.

Systemic lupus erythematosus

Systemic lupus erythematosus is an autoimmune disease, characterized by double-stranded DNA antibodies. There is pleuritis and exudative pleural effusions in 50% of cases, with diffuse lung fibrosis, together with a reduced carbon monoxide transfer coefficient and restrictive defect on lung function testing. Occasionally there is an acute pneumonitis, with crackles, which is treated with steroids

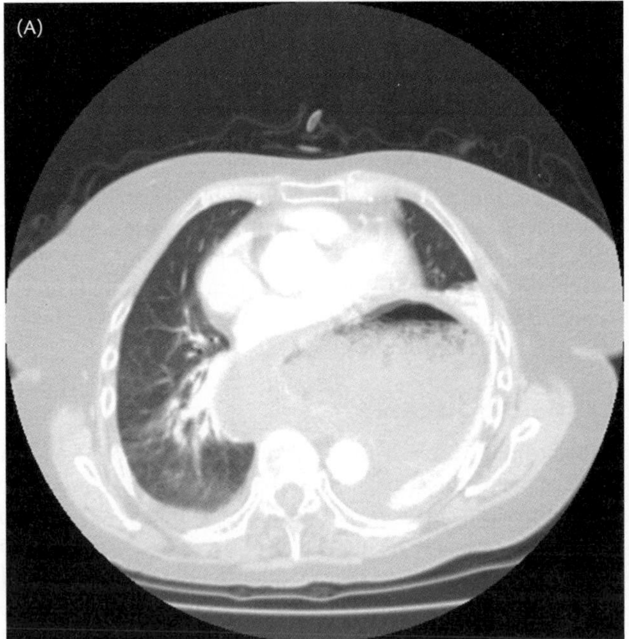

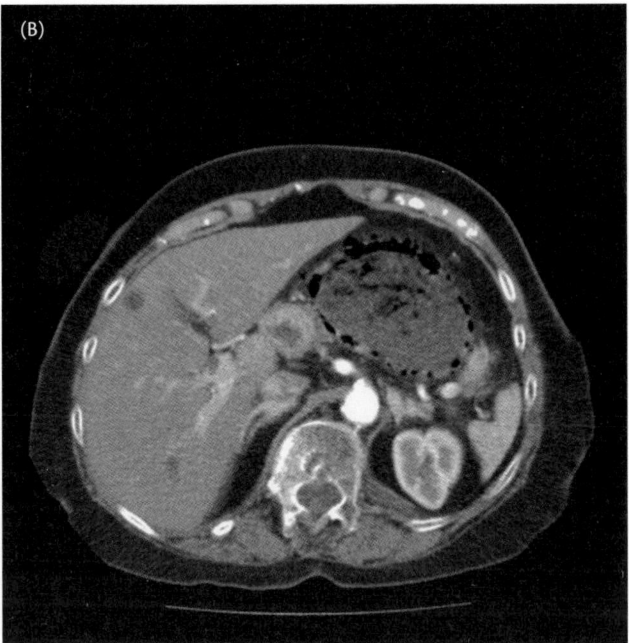

Figure 82.13 Computed tomography scans to show (A) massive strangulated hiatus hernia, presenting with chest pain, clinical signs in the chest, and sepsis, and (B) gas in infarcting stomach wall.

and cytotoxic drugs. Pulmonary hypertension as a result of vasoconstriction may occur in those with Raynaud's and pulmonary emboli may occur in those with antiphospholipid syndrome. The lungs 'shrink' although the cause is unclear and alveolar haemorrhage can occasionally occur. Drug-induced lupus can be caused by isoniazid, procainamide, hydralazine, minocycline, penicillamine, and some anticonvulsants.

Other interstitial lung diseases

Connective tissue illnesses producing interstitial lung disease also include systemic sclerosis and sarcoidosis. It may also occur associated with tuberculosis, ankylosing spondylitis, psoriasis, or histiocytosis X.

Systemic sclerosis may present as CREST syndrome (calcinosis, Raynaud's, oesophageal dysmotility in 74%, and telangiectasia). In this form, the skin becomes tight and may limit mouth opening. However, pulmonary fibrosis occurs in 26% of cases, compared with 41% in the diffuse cutaneous form. Renal disease affects 18%, cardiac disease 12%, and pulmonary hypertension occurs in 17% of patients. There is frequent gastrointestinal involvement resulting in malabsorption. Lung involvement may be exacerbated by aspiration secondary to the oesophageal disease. Steroids and cyclophosphamide may improve lung function.

Sarcoidosis is a granulomatous multisystem disease, producing lung fibrosis. Patients may have stage 1, hilar lymphadenopathy; stage 2 begins to add parenchymal infiltrate; stage 3, parenchymal infiltrate; or stage 4, lung fibrosis. Angiotensin-converting enzyme is released by macrophages and T-cell activation stimulates B cells and so serum immunoglobulins increase. Sarcoidosis also causes Sjögren's syndrome with dry eyes and mouth, laryngeal involvement, pancreatitis, hepatitis, diabetes, hypercalcaemia, that is responsive to steroids (which brings its own complications including renal stones), and myocarditis. Treatment is with steroids and methotrexate.

Drug causes include cigarette smoking, amiodarone, bleomycin, busulfan, methotrexate, and nitrofurantoin or exposure to beryllium. Other problematic treatments include radiotherapy.

Lung fibrosis may be caused or exacerbated by recurrent gastro-oesophageal reflux.

Alveolar haemorrhage

Anaesthesia may be required to allow the control of alveolar haemorrhage. There is no consensus as to what constitutes a life-threatening haemorrhage. The physiological impact on oxygenation or airways obstruction will depend on the speed of haemorrhage and location in the lung. Often it may be difficult to be certain that the bleeding is not from the nose or mouth or even haematemesis. Haemoptysis may originate from structural abnormalities such as a bronchial tumour or tuberculosis eroding through vessels, mitral stenosis, or even aortic or pseudo-aneurysm. Haemoptysis is also seen in bronchiectasis, lung abscesses, pneumonia, pulmonary embolism, or foreign bodies. It may present in rarer conditions including anti-glomerular basement membrane disease (Goodpasture's), systemic lupus erythematosus, and granulomatosis with polyangiitis (Wegener's granulomatosis) or pulmonary haemosiderosis. Fungal or parasitic infections such as *Aspergillus* mycetoma may cause major bleeds. Arteriovenous malformations, which are mostly associated with hereditary haemorrhagic telangiectasia may bleed severely. Hereditary haemorrhagic telangiectasia is a major issue, because patients are predisposed to cerebrovascular accidents and cerebral abscesses if right-sided clots or infection can pass through lung arteriovenous malformations relatively unhindered. Prophylactic antibiotics may be needed and repeated during future surgical procedures.

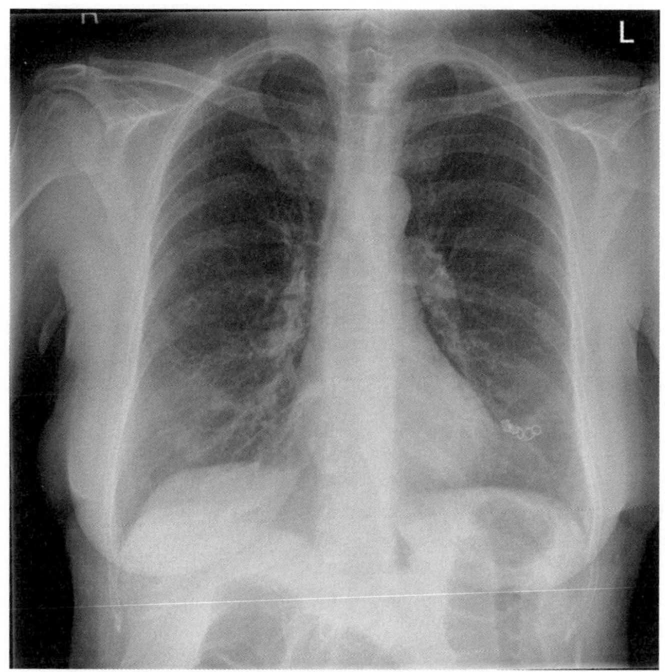

Figure 82.14 Chest X-ray to show the results of embolization of alveolar haemorrhage.

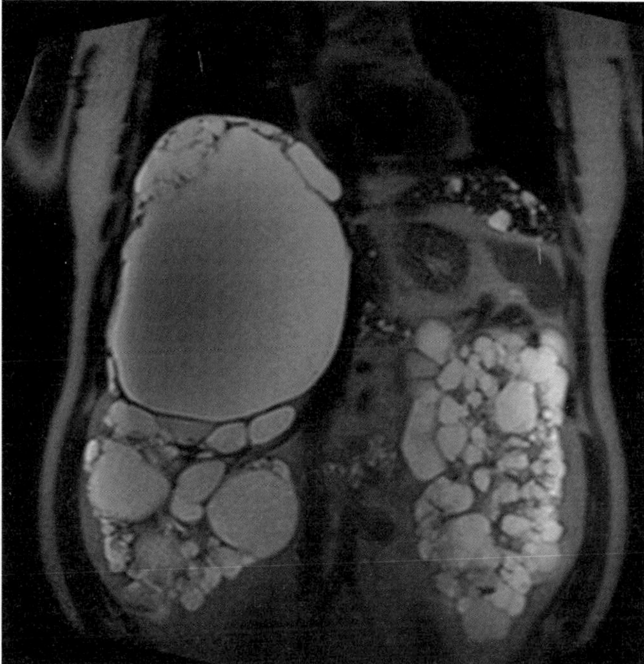

Figure 82.15 Computed tomography scan to show polycystic disease of liver and kidneys. The patient developed breathlessness because of compression of the lungs through the diaphragm. The picture shows a large cyst in the liver, which extends to the left side, along with many other cysts in the liver and kidneys. The inferior vena cava is also compressed by the large liver cysts.

Treatment is of the underlying disease or by control of the haemorrhage, or both. In some cases, airway control is needed with insertion of a double-lumen tube to isolate the good lung, while a solution is being found. Correction of clotting abnormalities and blood loss will be required. Alternative techniques will include a single-lumen tube directed into the good lung or bronchial blocker insertion. In many cases, management will be a CT scan and arteriography with embolization (Fig. 82.14). Surgical resection may be more effective in some cases. Sometimes bronchoscopy may identify the lesion and allow balloon compression, but often the view is obscured by the bleeding.

Diseases of the abdominal compartment

Hepatobiliary diseases and the lung

Chronic hepatic disease is frequently encountered in anaesthetic practice. This may impact the lung in two ways: hepatic hydrothorax and hepatopulmonary syndrome. Hepatic hydrothorax is a pleural effusion, as a result of defects in the diaphragm, that allows ascites to spread usually to the right pleura. Therefore, spontaneous bacterial peritonitis can spread to the chest and cause an empyema.

Hepatopulmonary syndrome is chronic liver disease, portal hypertension combined with arteriovenous shunting in the lungs, and arteriovenous malformations. This is as a result of increased concentrations of nitric oxide which allow shunting of blood through the lungs without the opportunity to adequately pick up oxygen. Often patients present with platypnoea because more blood flows through the lower section of the lungs when upright. Microbubbles can be seen in the left heart on echocardiography after injection on the right side. This problem will usually resolve after liver transplantation.

Multiple liver cysts, sometimes of very large size, can gradually compress the lungs from below, leading to respiratory failure (Fig. 82.15). These may belong to isolated polycystic liver disease or more commonly to autosomal dominant polycystic kidney disease. Therefore, in the latter, the illness can be combined with renal failure. Women are more susceptible to the development of massive cysts. Patients often first complain of post-prandial fullness as the cysts enlarge and as the stomach is compressed, the risks of aspiration during anaesthesia increase. The pressure effects of the cysts may cause a blockage of venous drainage from the liver leading to a pseudo-Budd–Chiari syndrome. Alternatively, cysts can impede portal blood flow causing portal hypertension. Very occasionally cystic carcinomas can develop. Patients may bleed into cysts, or cystic fluid can become infected, both of which lead to pain. Cysts can be drained radiologically, but often need deroofing surgically with an open approach, especially when they become large and prevent laparoscopic techniques. Sometimes liver resection or even transplantation is required. Massive cysts have caused respiratory failure as a result of physical compression of the lungs. Even after surgery the diaphragm may need to remodel itself before it can take up a new more efficient shape and NIV along with epidural analgesia is needed after extubation. Currently drug therapy is being developed, but at present surgery is the mainstay option.

Intra-abdominal hypertension

Raised intra-abdominal pressure (IAP) has major consequences for abdominal and pelvic organs, but also impacts the lung and other organs. Lung involvement is predominantly related to chest wall splinting, restricting and compressing the lung, through physical pressure and impaired lymphatic drainage of the lung. Standard techniques to avoid or reduce atelectasis are limited by raised IAP, including PEEP and lung recruitment. Raised IAP also makes selection of suitable PEEP pressures very difficult. The application of high ventilatory driving pressures, in an attempt to expand the lung in these patients who essentially have a very stiff wall, can damage lung tissue and impair the cardiovascular system. Intraoperatively, raised IAP will compromise oxygenation, venous return, and cardiac output and renal function. Raised IAP may acutely present on abdominal closure, when it is vital for a judgement to be made as to whether the abdominal closure should be abandoned and the abdomen left open. If abdominal pressure is too high, this may initially present with respiratory failure if extubation is attempted. Gradual weaning via a tracheostomy may be possible in borderline cases, if other abnormalities such as gut oedema can be corrected.

Raised IAP is associated with injury or disease in the abdominopelvic region including abdominal aortic surgery, pancreatitis, emergency laparotomy, or abdominal packs. Secondary raised IAP is associated with extra-abdominal pathology causing sepsis, capillary leak, or large volume resuscitation. If IAP exceeds 20 mm Hg there are respiratory consequences: raised alveolar pressure, compression atelectasis, $\dot{V}/\dot{Q}$ mismatch, hypoxaemia, hypercapnia, and acute lung injury/ARDS. Treatment may be by reducing gut oedema. However, surgery is often needed and a rapid sequence induction of anaesthesia will need to be performed. There also needs to be an awareness that venous return to the heart may decrease further and lung recruitment will be very difficult.

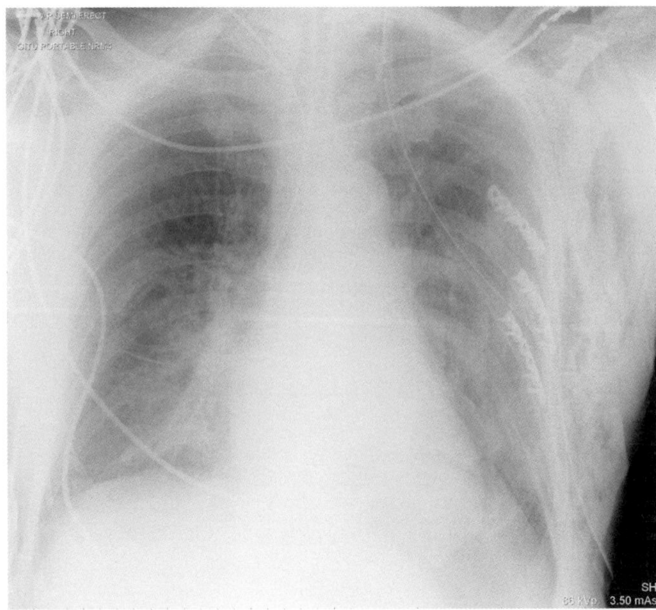

Figure 82.16 Chest X-ray showing chest trauma with rib repair of flail segment. Surgical emphysema in subcutaneous tissues. Chest drain *in situ* on left side. Tracheal tube close to carina.

Pleural effusions and pneumothoraces

Pleural effusions

Pleural effusions may contain a transudate (protein < 30 g litre^{-1}), an exudate (protein > 30 g litre^{-1} or pleural fluid protein/serum protein greater than 0.5 or pleural LDH/serum LDH > 0.6), an empyema (pH < 7.2) or blood. The cause of the effusion should be considered. If a transudate, it may commonly be related to low serum proteins, renal failure (and nephrotic syndrome), or heart failure and generally respond to treatment of the underlying cause. Exudates will depend on the cause (simple pneumonic effusions, tuberculosis, malignancy, rheumatoid (low pleural fluid glucose), post-pulmonary embolus, or oesophageal rupture. Undrained empyemas will be a constant source of sepsis and should be drained. If present at surgery they are likely to complicate postoperative recovery. Unusual causes of the effusion will also have a major impact on outcome, for example, those that occur in connective tissue diseases, chyle leak (such as after thoracic/oesophageal surgery), or secondary to sub-diaphragmatic causes such as pancreatitis (high amylase content). The size of a pleural effusion will promote atelectasis and will limit oxygenation and ventilation, and restrict the possibility of lung recruitment, so consideration should be given to preoperative drainage. However, rapid lung expansion may lead to pulmonary oedema and if the fluid is a transudate it may recur rapidly.

Pneumothoraces

Pneumothorax is a common complication of trauma (Fig. 82.16). However, spontaneous pneumothoraces occur in patients with Marfan's syndrome and homocystinuria or may have no obvious underlying cause. Rarely, they are familial. They may occur secondary to lung diseases, including emphysema, asthma, idiopathic lung fibrosis, pneumonia, including tuberculosis and pneumocystis, pulmonary infarction, and oesophageal rupture. Treatment is normally with chest drainage and treatment of the underlying cause. In some cases, small pneumothoraces can be managed conservatively. However, during anaesthesia, especially with mechanical ventilation, there is an increased risk of the pneumothorax increasing in size or becoming a tension pneumothorax. Therefore, in most cases a chest drain will be needed before anaesthesia. If a chest drain is *in situ* and bubbling, it should not be clamped and if attached to an underwater seal, this should be kept below the level of the patient. Heimlich flutter valves or similar valvular devices are useful for transporting patients and are used in some ambulant patients.

During mechanical ventilation, it is vital to ensure that the drain is functioning and to suspect a worsening pneumothorax if inflation pressures increase in patients being ventilated with volume-controlled techniques, and if tidal volumes decrease during pressure-controlled procedures. Auscultation may be unreliable in ventilated patients.

Pleurodesis for recurrent pneumothoraces or some effusions is often very painful and may cause fever and a systemic inflammatory response, which rarely leads to ARDS and respiratory failure. Adequate pain relief, which may include opiates will be required and the procedure will usually need sedation. Graded talc is the most effective sclerosant, although surgical abrasion is used where there are concerns about the long-term safety of talc. In mesothelioma effusions, radiotherapy is often needed.

Anaesthesia and chest wall disease

The chest wall effectively includes the ribs, spine, and abdomen and related musculature that surround the thoracic cavity. Diseases that affect these structures will impact lung function.

Kyphoscoliosis

Kyphoscoliosis restricts the expansion of the lungs or causes the muscles to act in an inappropriate direction, which will reduce the effectiveness of their action. There may be underlying diseases that have produced a bony abnormality, including osteomalacia or osteoporosis, or there may be neuromuscular diseases such as Von Recklinghausen's neurofibromatosis, polio, or inherited muscular dystrophies, which will also add defects of motor nerve conduction and muscle weakness, which will further impact breathing.

Ankylosing spondylitis

See also Chapter 80. The cartilages surrounding the bony structures begin to fuse and ossify. The rigid chest wall limits lung expansion and so makes lung recruitment and the application of high PEEP ineffective or even harmful.

Diseases of the central nervous system

Neuromuscular disease

See also Chapter 80.Weakness of the respiratory muscles can be produced by lesions at any level from the brain, through the spinal cord, to the anterior horn cells, through the phrenic and intercostal nerves, to the motor end-plates and neuromuscular junctions, and then within the muscle itself. At preoperative assessment it is important to assess the impact of respiratory muscle weakness, including lung function tests, which would be expected to show a restrictive defect, with low a transfer factor but normal carbon monoxide transfer coefficient. Maximal inspiratory and expiratory mouth pressures may be low, although sometimes are unreliable because of an inability to form a good seal around the mouthpiece. Sniff pressures sometimes help get round this problem. Patients may also have bulbar dysfunction, so may have difficulty in swallowing and communicating and have the complications of pulmonary aspiration. Arterial blood gases will indicate hypoventilation and give some idea of the chronicity of the ventilatory failure as indicated by an elevated bicarbonate and a pH returning from respiratory acidosis to normal pH. Peripheral oxygen saturation and Pa_{O_2} may indicate the amount of damage caused by aspiration, atelectasis, or other abnormalities. Patients may have signs of autonomic neuropathy and may also have a cardiomyopathy, with decreased contractility and arrhythmias. These may be exaggerated by electrolyte disturbances, which should be corrected. Even some peripheral neuropathies can lead to autonomic dysfunction and cardiomyopathy including Charcot–Marie–Tooth and Friedreich's ataxia. Patients likely to have cardiomyopathy or autonomic dysfunction should have an arterial line placed and arterial blood gases assessed.

Patients with neuromuscular disorders, including myopathies and established demyelination or paralysis, that is, those not in the first 24–48 h of spinal injury, may produce large numbers of acetylcholine receptors, which can be triggered by succinylcholine (suxamethonium), causing hyperkalaemia and rhabdomyolysis.

Before surgery, it is important to plan what level of care is appropriate in the case of major deterioration, so that patients fully understand the implication of surgery and its possible complications.

Spinal injury

The impact depends on the level and completeness of the cord damage. High cord damage at or above C3–5 will lead to loss of all respiratory muscle activity, other than some of the accessory muscles of respiration, which are insufficient to support ventilation. Injuries above the thoracic cord and below C3–5 will allow the diaphragm to function, but there will be a loss of thoracic expansion (Fig. 82.17). Atelectasis occurs commonly as the chest wall is drawn in by the decreasing intrathoracic pressure produced when the diaphragm contracts and descends. In addition, there will be a loss of the contraction of the abdominal muscles which normally allow the abdominal contents to act as a fulcrum as the diaphragm descends, allowing the diaphragm to expand the rib cage, which contributes to inspiration. Low thoracic cord injuries will remove the ability to produce abdominal contraction to allow powerful coughing. These varying degrees of impairment will impact particularly in the postoperative period when atelectasis is present and patients are at high risk of failure of extubation or development of subsequent respiratory failure requiring mechanical ventilation. Sometimes an abdominal binder helps overcome the effect of paralysis of the abdominal muscles.

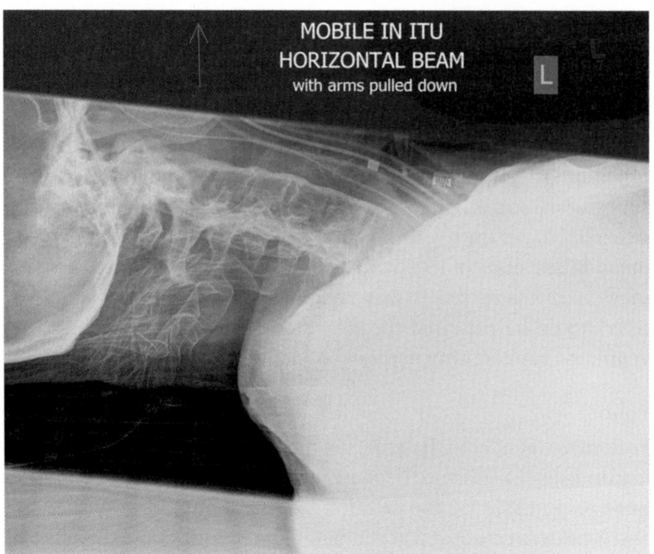

Figure 82.17 Ankylosing spondylitis. Low cervical fracture, producing respiratory failure in a patient with a stiff chest wall.

Diseases affecting the motor neurones

Unilateral and bilateral phrenic palsy

The diaphragm is innervated from the contralateral cerebral cortex. However, in some people there is a bilateral cortical distribution, which helps preserve function in strokes. The lower motor neurones originate from C3–5 nerve roots as the phrenic nerves, which pass to the surface of each hemidiaphragm, where they divide into several branches to provide muscle innervation. Diaphragm contraction causes the diaphragm to descend and also expands the lower rib cage. The nerves may be damaged during their course by trauma or malignant infiltration, neuropathies, myopathies, and neuralgic amyotrophy.

Chronic unilateral diaphragm paralysis may produce only mild symptoms on exertion, but does reduce exercise performance and respiratory muscle endurance (Hart et al. 2002). Isolated bilateral diaphragm paralysis is much more noticeable, causing severe breathlessness on lying supine with paradoxical movement of the chest and abdominal wall. Similarly, breathing when partially immersed causes severe dyspnoea as the abdominal contents push up into the thorax. Therefore, if a patient with diaphragm paralysis develops an ileus or another cause of abdominal distension, this may compress the lungs and lead to respiratory failure, because the diaphragm lacks tone.

In isolated bilateral diaphragm paralysis at rest, the Pa_{CO_2} is only slightly raised to 6 kPa. Pa_{O_2} is often between 8 and 9 kPa (Mills et al. 1997). Acute weakness causes more noticeable symptoms and if a patient is requiring ventilation, will lead to weaning difficulties, because there has not been time for any adaptation and because other lung dysfunction is likely. Therefore, during induction of anaesthesia and during tracheal extubation and in the postoperative period, patients with bilateral paralysis will need to be sitting up and the causes of increased IAP avoided. Abdominal distension may rapidly cause respiratory failure and so patients and anaesthetists should be prepared for the potential need for weaning from ventilator support after surgery.

Polio

Poliomyelitis affects the anterior horn cells, but is now relatively uncommon in Europe, because of vaccination. Polio epidemics were responsible for the creation from necessity of intensive care and long-term mechanical ventilation techniques in the late 1950s. Older patients who suffered from the effects of polio as children are still encountered. In some cases, the polio has involved the respiratory muscles. Some have borderline respiratory failure, exacerbated by kyphoscoliosis, which may have been produced by the muscle imbalances caused by polio. Constipation and abdominal distension as a result of abdominal pathology may be enough to splint the diaphragm and produce respiratory failure. Anaesthesia and surgery in this population can both lead to respiratory failure. Postoperative respiratory support may be essential, either using NIV or in more difficult cases ventilation initially via tracheal tube and later via tracheostomy if weaning is slow. The possibility of respiratory failure, tracheostomy, and prolonged weaning will need to be discussed with the patient preoperatively in appropriate cases.

Multiple sclerosis

Multiple sclerosis can affect the brain, spinal cord, and the anterior horn cells. Stressful events, including surgery and anaesthesia, may trigger exacerbations of multiple sclerosis. Weakness often affects expiratory more than inspiratory muscles and may disrupt bulbar function. About half of patients with multiple sclerosis die as a direct consequence of the disease, with pneumonia being the most common mechanism. Respiratory muscles are most affected in patients who are wheelchair bound or bedridden. In the latter case, on average, inspiratory muscle strength decreases to around 30% and expiratory muscle strength to around 20% of normal. There is also the risk of disordered control of respiration, as a result of medullary and brainstem involvement. This leads to central or OSA, and abnormal control of bulbar function and aspiration. Pyrexia also appears to exacerbate multiple sclerosis, so avoiding this is helpful.

On preoperative assessment most patients do not complain of being short of breath, unless they are experiencing an acute exacerbation or pneumonia, because they are not able to exercise (Gosselink et al. 1999). Commonly in neuromuscular disease, involvement of the respiratory system is avoided by using spinal anaesthesia where appropriate. Unfortunately, there are concerns that high concentrations of local anaesthetic might cause toxic damage to spinal nerve roots or the spinal cord. This may not be true to the same extent for epidural analgesia/anaesthesia, because the concentration around the nerve roots and the cord may be lower.

Motor neurone disease

Motor neurone disease has a generally poor prognosis with mean time from diagnosis to death of 2–3 years. Patients may present with progressive weakness. However, they may also present with bulbar abnormalities such as a spastic tongue, difficulty in swallowing, and abnormal speech. The disease paralyses the respiratory muscles, including the diaphragm, and so lying flat becomes impossible and patients develop type 2 respiratory failure. Most major surgery is often not appropriate for patients with motor neurone disease, because of the risks and overall prognosis. However, they may require minor surgery such as gastrostomy insertion. Careful consideration of how to cope with weak respiratory muscles is vital and the supine position may well be impossible without ventilatory support.

Myasthenia gravis

Myasthenia gravis is an autoimmune disease affecting the acetylcholine receptors of the neuromuscular junction. This produces fatigue in muscles and may produce chronic weakness. It is particularly associated with a history of thymoma. Acetylcholine receptor antibodies can be measured as part of the diagnosis, which can be confirmed functionally by the traditional Tensilon (edrophonium) test, where edrophonium (an anticholinesterase) is given intravenously, which will temporarily improve strength in fatigued muscles. The effect can also be measured electrophysiologically. Patients with myasthenia gravis are normally controlled on long-acting anticholinesterase drugs such as pyridostigmine. This can become complicated in the perioperative period if patients cannot take drugs orally and so miss their usual dosage. These patients are very susceptible to the action of non-depolarizing neuromuscular blocking agents and weakness can be a major feature after surgery.

Myopathies

These are an important cause of muscle weakness, including the respiratory muscles, which may also impact on cardiac muscle function and rhythm disturbance (see Chapter 80).

Conclusion

It is often possible to anticipate respiratory complications after surgery. This allows a judgement to be made with regard to the risks and potential benefits of a procedure. Patients should understand this balance of risks. Intra- and postoperative management should be tailored to the disease and preparations made for suitable support after surgery, including optimization of fluid balance and perfusion to minimize the work of the respiratory muscles and to optimize the condition of the lung. Postoperatively, this may involve HDU and ICU admission, with tracheal extubation directly onto CPAP or NIV. Optimization of the respiratory system is a balance between load and capacity. The role of the anaesthetist is to ensure that load is minimized and capacity is at a maximum for the individual patient.

Declaration of interest

None declared.

References

Abdo WF, Heunks LM. Oxygen-induced hypercapnia in COPD: myths and facts. *Crit Care* 2012; **16**: 323

Arozullah AM, Daley J, Henderson WG, Khuri SF. Multifactorial risk index for predicting postoperative respiratory failure in men after major noncardiac surgery. The National Veterans Administration Surgical Quality Improvement Program. *Ann Surg* 2000; **232**: 242–53

Arozullah AM, Khuri SF, Henderson WG, Daley J, Participants in the National Veterans Affairs Surgical Quality Improvement Program. Development and validation of a multifactorial risk index for predicting postoperative pneumonia after major noncardiac surgery. *Ann Intern Med* 2001; **135**: 847–57

Aubier M, Murciano D, Fournier M, Milic-Emili J, Pariente R, Derenne JP. Central respiratory drive in acute respiratory failure of patients with chronic obstructive pulmonary disease. *Am Rev Respir Dis* 1980a; **122**: 191–9

Aubier M, Murciano D, Milic-Emili J, Touaty E, Daghfous J, Pariente R, Derenne JP. Effects of the administration of O2 on ventilation and blood gases in patients with chronic obstructive pulmonary disease during acute respiratory failure. *Am Rev Respir Dis* 1980b; **122**: 747–54

Baloch MS, Fitzwilliams B, Mellerio J, Lakasing L, Bewley S, O'Sullivan G. Anaesthetic management of two different modes of delivery in patients with dystrophic epidermolysis bullosa. *Int J Obstet Anesth* 2008; **17**: 153–8

Barrera R, Shi W, Amar D, *et al.* Smoking and timing of cessation: impact on pulmonary complications after thoracotomy. *Chest* 2005; **127**: 1977–83

Barst RJ, Rubin LJ, Long WA, *et al.* A comparison of continuous intravenous epoprostenol (prostacyclin) with conventional therapy for primary pulmonary hypertension. *N Engl J Med* 1996; 334: **296**–301

Bateman BT, Eikermann M. Obstructive sleep apnea predicts adverse perioperative outcome: evidence for an association between obstructive sleep apnea and delirium. *Anesthesiology* 2012; **116**: 753–5

Berrisford R, Brunelli A, Rocco G, *et al.* The European Thoracic Surgery Database project: modelling the risk of in-hospital death following lung resection. *Eur J Cardiothorac Surg* 2005; **28**: 306–11

Bluman LG, Mosca L, Newman N, Simon DG. Preoperative smoking habits and postoperative pulmonary complications. *Chest* 1998; **113**: 883–9

Bokinsky G, Miller M, Ault K, Husband P, Mitchell J. Spontaneous platelet activation and aggregation during obstructive sleep apnea and its response to therapy with nasal continuous positive airway pressure. A preliminary investigation. *Chest* 1995; **108**: 625–30

Bolliger CT, Jordan P, Soler M, *et al.* Exercise capacity as a predictor of postoperative complications in lung resection candidates. *Am J Respir Crit Care Med* 1995; **151**: 1472–80

Breatnach E, Abbott GC, Fraser RG. Dimensions of the normal human trachea. *AJR Am J Roentgenol* 1984; **142**: 903–6

British Cardiac Society Guidelines, Medical Practice Committee, and approved by the British Thoracic Society and the British Society of Rheumatology. Recommendations on the management of pulmonary hypertension in clinical practice. *Heart* 2001; **86**(Suppl 1): I1–13

Canet J, Gallart L, Gomar C, *et al.* Prediction of postoperative pulmonary complications in a population-based surgical cohort. *Anesthesiology* 2010; **113**: 1338–50

Carron M, Marchet A, Ori C. Supreme laryngeal mask airway for laparoscopic cholecystectomy in patient with severe pulmonary fibrosis. *Br J Anaesth* 2009; **103**: 778–9

Channick RN, Olschewski H, Seeger W, Staub T, Voswinckel R, Rubin LJ. Safety and efficacy of inhaled treprostinil as add-on therapy to bosentan in pulmonary arterial hypertension. *J Am Coll Cardiol* 2006; **48**: 1433–7

Chapman S, Robinson G, Stradling J, West S, Wrightson J. *Oxford Handbook of Respiratory Medicine*, 3rd Edn. Oxford: Oxford University Press, 2014; 265–82

Cho MH, Boutaoui N, Klanderman BJ, *et al.* Variants in FAM13A are associated with chronic obstructive pulmonary disease. *Nat Genet* 2010; **42**: 200–2

Chung F, Subramanyam R, Liao P, Sasaki E, Shapiro C, Sun Y. High STOP-Bang score indicates a high probability of obstructive sleep apnoea. *Br J Anaesth* 2012; **108**: 768–75

Chung F, Yegneswaran B, Herrera F, Shenderey A, Shapiro CM. Patients with difficult intubation may need referral to sleep clinics. *Anesth Analg* 2008a; **107**: 915–20

Chung F, Yegneswaran B, Liao P, *et al.* STOP questionnaire: a tool to screen patients for obstructive sleep apnea. *Anesthesiology* 2008b; **108**: 812–21

Chung SA, Yuan H, Chung F. A systemic review of obstructive sleep apnea and its implications for anesthesiologists. *Anesth Analg* 2008c; **107**: 1543–63

Cook T, Woodall N, Frerk C. *NAP4: Major Complications of Airway Management in the United Kingdom*. London: Royal College of Anaesthetists, 2011

Davies Ce, Mackinnon J. Neurological effects of oxygen in chronic cor pulmonale. *Lancet* 1949; **2**: 883–5

Davies HR, Richeldi L, Walters EH. Immunomodulatory agents for idiopathic pulmonary fibrosis. *Cochrane Database Syst Rev* 2003; **3**: CD003134

Della Rocca G, Costa MG, Coccia C, *et al.* Double lung transplantation in cystic fibrosis patients: perioperative hemodynamic-volumetric monitoring. Rome Lung Transplantation Group. *Transplant Proc* 2000; **32**: 104–8

Denton CP, Humbert M, Rubin L, Black CM. Bosentan treatment for pulmonary arterial hypertension related to connective tissue disease: a subgroup analysis of the pivotal clinical trials and their open-label extensions. *Ann Rheum Dis* 2006; **65**: 1336–40

Dewachter P, Mouton-Faivre C, Emala CW, Beloucif S. Case scenario: bronchospasm during anesthetic induction. *Anesthesiology* 2011; **114**: 1200–10

Donald K. Neurological effects of oxygen. *Lancet* 1947; **16**: 1056–7

Donat SM. Peri-operative care in patients treated for testicular cancer. *Semin Surg Oncol* 1999; **17**: 282–8

Edmark L, Kostova-Aherdan K, Enlund M, Hedenstierna G. Optimal oxygen concentration during induction of general anesthesia. *Anesthesiology* 2003; **98**: 28–33

Elliot CA, Kiely DG. Pulmonary hypertension. *Contin Educ Anaesth Crit Care Pain* 2006; **6**: 17–22

Elliot CA, Stewart P, Webster VJ, *et al.* The use of iloprost in early pregnancy in patients with pulmonary arterial hypertension. *Eur Respir J* 2005; **26**: 168–73

Empey DW, Laitinen LA, Jacobs L, Gold WM, Nadel JA. Mechanisms of bronchial hyperreactivity in normal subjects after upper respiratory tract infection. *Am Rev Respir Dis* 1976; **113**: 131–9

Englbrecht JS, Langer M, Hahnenkamp K, Ellger B. Ultrasound-guided axillary plexus block in a child with dystrophic epidermolysis bullosa. *Anaesth Intensive Care* 2010; **38**: 1101–5

Escarce JJ, Shea JA, Chen W, Qian Z, Schwartz JS. Outcomes of open cholecystectomy in the elderly: a longitudinal analysis of 21,000 cases in the prelaparoscopic era. *Surgery* 1995; **117**: 156–64

Falcoz PE, Conti M, Brouchet L, *et al.* The Thoracic Surgery Scoring System (Thoracoscore): risk model for in-hospital death in 15,183 patients requiring thoracic surgery. *J Thorac Cardiovasc Surg* 2007; **133**: 325–32

Featherstone HW. Care of the lungs in anaesthesia. *Br Med J* 1932; **2**: 628–30

Fendrick AM, Monto AS, Nightengale B, Sarnes M. The economic burden of non-influenza-related viral respiratory tract infection in the United States. *Arch Intern Med* 2003; **163**: 487–94

Fernandez-Perez ER, Yilmaz M, Jenad H, *et al.* Ventilator settings and outcome of respiratory failure in chronic interstitial lung disease. *Chest* 2008; **133**: 1113–9

Fletcher C, Peto R. The natural history of chronic airflow obstruction. *Br Med J* 1977; **1**: 1645–8

Flink BJ, Rivelli SK, Cox EA, *et al.* Obstructive sleep apnea and incidence of postoperative delirium after elective knee replacement in the nondemented elderly. *Anesthesiology* 2012; **116**: 788–96

Futier E, Constantin JM, Paugam-Burtz C, *et al.* A trial of intraoperative low-tidal-volume ventilation in abdominal surgery. *N Engl J Med* 2013; **369**: 428–37

Galatz LM, Silva MJ, Rothermich SY, *et al.* Nicotine delays tendon-to-bone healing in a rat shoulder model. *J Bone Joint Surg Am* 2006; **88**: 2027–34

Galie N, Ghofrani HA, Torbicki A, *et al.* Sildenafil citrate therapy for pulmonary arterial hypertension. *N Engl J Med* 2005; **353**: 2148–57

Gan WQ, Man SF, Senthilselvan A, Sin DD. Association between chronic obstructive pulmonary disease and systemic inflammation: a systematic review and a meta-analysis. *Thorax* 2004; **59**: 574–80

Gibson GJ, Pride NB. Pulmonary mechanics in fibrosing alveolitis: the effects of lung shrinkage. *Am Rev Respir Dis* 1977; **116**: 637–47

Global Initiative for Chronic Obstructive Lung Disease (GOLD). *Global Strategy for the Diagnosis, Management, and Prevention of COPD*. 2013; Available from http://www.goldcopd.org/

Gosselink R, Kovacs L, Decramer M. Respiratory muscle involvement in multiple sclerosis. *Eur Respir J* 1999; **13**: 449–54

Greenberg H, Ye X, Wilson D, Htoo AK, Hendersen T, Liu SF. Chronic intermittent hypoxia activates nuclear factor-kappaB in cardiovascular tissues in vivo. *Biochem Biophys Res Commun* 2006; **343**: 591–6

Greenblatt DY, Kelly KJ, Rajamanickam V, *et al.* Preoperative factors predict perioperative morbidity and mortality after pancreaticoduodenectomy. *Ann Surg Oncol* 2011; **18**: 2126–35

Gupta RM, Parvizi J, Hanssen AD, Gay PC. Postoperative complications in patients with obstructive sleep apnea syndrome undergoing hip or knee replacement: a case-control study. *Mayo Clin Proc* 2001; **76**: 897–905

Hamnegard CH, Wragg S, Mills G, *et al.* The effect of lung volume on transdiaphragmatic pressure. *Eur Respir J* 1995; **8**: 1532–6

Hanson CW, 3rd, Marshall BE, Frasch HF, Marshall C. Causes of hypercarbia with oxygen therapy in patients with chronic obstructive pulmonary disease. *Crit Care Med* 1996; **24**: 23–8

Harpole DH, Jr, Decamp MM, Jr, Daley J, *et al.* Prognostic models of thirty-day mortality and morbidity after major pulmonary resection. *J Thorac Cardiovasc Surg* 1999; **117**: 969–79

Hart N, Nickol AH, Cramer D, *et al.* Effect of severe isolated unilateral and bilateral diaphragm weakness on exercise performance. *Am J Respir Crit Care Med* 2002; **165**: 1265–70

Hedenstierna G, Rothen HU. Respiratory function during anesthesia: effects on gas exchange. *Compr Physiol* 2012; **2**: 69–96

Hohlrieder M, Brimacombe J, Eschertzhuber S, Ulmer H, Keller C. A study of airway management using the ProSeal LMA laryngeal mask airway compared with the tracheal tube on postoperative analgesia requirements following gynaecological laparoscopic surgery. *Anaesthesia* 2007; **62**: 913–8

Holden DA, Rice TW, Stelmach K, Meeker DP. Exercise testing, 6-min walk, and stair climb in the evaluation of patients at high risk for pulmonary resection. *Chest* 1992; **102**: 1774–9

Hoshikawa Y, Kondo T. [Perioperative lung injury: acute exacerbation of idiopathic pulmonary fibrosis and acute interstitial pneumonia after pulmonary resection]. *Nihon Geka Gakkai Zasshi* 2004; **105**: 757–62

HUFFMYER JL, Littlewood KE, Nemergut EC. Perioperative management of the adult with cystic fibrosis. *Anesth Analg* 2009; **109**: 1949–61

Hung J, Whitford EG, Parsons RW, Hillman DR. Association of sleep apnoea with myocardial infarction in men. *Lancet* 1990; **336**: 261–4

Idvall J. Ketamine monoanaesthesia for major surgery in epidermolysis bullosa. Case report. *Acta Anaesthesiol Scand* 1987; **31**: 658–60

Imberger G, Mcilroy D, Pace NL, Wetterslev J, Brok J, Moller AM. Positive end-expiratory pressure (PEEP) during anaesthesia for the prevention of mortality and postoperative pulmonary complications. *Cochrane Database Syst Rev* 2010; **9**: CD007922

Iohom G, Lyons B. Anaesthesia for children with epidermolysis bullosa: a review of 20 years' experience. *Eur J Anaesthesiol* 2001; **18**: 745–54

Jensen JA, Goodson WH, Hopf HW, Hunt TK. Cigarette smoking decreases tissue oxygen. *Arch Surg* 1991; **126**: 1131–4

Jorgensen LN, Kallehave F, Christensen E, Siana JE, Gottrup F. Less collagen production in smokers. *Surgery* 1998; **123**: 450–5

Kaw R, Gali B, Collop NA. Perioperative care of patients with obstructive sleep apnea. *Curr Treat Options Neurol* 2011a; **13**: 496–507

Kaw R, Pasupuleti V, Thota P, Abboussouan L. Obesity hypoventilation syndrome: an emerging and unrecognized risk factor among surgical patients. *Am J Resp Crit Care Med* 2011b; **183**: A3147

Kaw R, Pasupuleti V, Walker E, Ramaswamy A, Foldvary-Schafer N. Postoperative complications in patients with obstructive sleep apnea. *Chest* 2012; **141**: 436–41

Khuri SF, Daley J, Henderson W, *et al.* National Veterans Administration Surgical Risk Study: risk adjustment for the comparative assessment of the quality of surgical care. *J Am Coll Surg* 1995; **180**: 519–31

Kiely DG, Condliffe R, Webster V, *et al.* Improved survival in pregnancy and pulmonary hypertension using a multiprofessional approach. *BJOG* 2010; **117**: 565–74

Kiely DG, Elliot CA, Sabroe I, Condliffe R. Pulmonary hypertension: diagnosis and management. *BMJ* 2013; **346**: f2028

Kimura T, Mizutani T. [Unilateral pulmonary fibrosis following ipsilateral single-lung ventilation and anesthesia]. *Masui* 2001; **50**: 651–4

King TE, Jr, Bradford WZ, Castro-Bernardini S., *et al.* A phase 3 trial of pirfenidone in patients with idiopathic pulmonary fibrosis. *N Engl J Med* 2014; **370**: 2083–92

Kinugasa S, Tachibana M, Yoshimura H, *et al.* Postoperative pulmonary complications are associated with worse short- and long-term outcomes after extended esophagectomy. *J Surg Oncol* 2004; **88**: 71–7

Kondoh Y, Taniguchi H, Kitaichi M, *et al.* Acute exacerbation of interstitial pneumonia following surgical lung biopsy. *Respir Med* 2006; **100**: 1753–9

Lawrence VA, Dhanda R, Hilsenbeck SG, Page CP. Risk of pulmonary complications after elective abdominal surgery. *Chest* 1996; **110**: 744–50

Lawrence VA, Hilsenbeck SG, NoVECK H, Poses RM, Carson JL. Medical complications and outcomes after hip fracture repair. *Arch Intern Med* 2002; **162**: 2053–7

Levine PH. An acute effect of cigarette smoking on platelet function. A possible link between smoking and arterial thrombosis. *Circulation* 1973; **48**: 619–23

Lightowler JV, Wedzicha JA, Elliott MW, Ram FS. Non-invasive positive pressure ventilation to treat respiratory failure resulting from exacerbations of chronic obstructive pulmonary disease: Cochrane systematic review and meta-analysis. *BMJ* 2003; **326**: 185

Loadsman JA, Hillman DR. Anaesthesia and sleep apnoea. *Br J Anaesth* 2001; **86**: 254–66

Magnusson L, Spahn DR. New concepts of atelectasis during general anaesthesia. *Br J Anaesth* 2003; **91**: 61–72

Makris D, Desrousseaux B, Zakynthinos E, Durocher A, Nseir S. The impact of COPD on ICU mortality in patients with ventilator-associated pneumonia. *Respir Med* 2011; **105**: 1022–9

Mallick S. Outcome of patients with idiopathic pulmonary fibrosis (IPF) ventilated in intensive care unit. *Respir Med* 2008; **102**: 1355–9

Manzano F, Fernandez-Mondejar E, Colmenero M, *et al.* Positive-end expiratory pressure reduces incidence of ventilator-associated pneumonia in nonhypoxemic patients. *Crit Care Med* 2008; **36**: 2225–31

Markos J, Mullan BP, Hillman DR, *et al.* Preoperative assessment as a predictor of mortality and morbidity after lung resection. *Am Rev Respir Dis* 1989; **139**: 902–10

Mason DP, Brizzio ME, Alster JM, *et al.* Lung transplantation for idiopathic pulmonary fibrosis. *Ann Thorac Surg* 2007; **84**: 1121–8

Mason RA, Steane PA. Anaesthesia for a patient with carcinoid syndrome. *Anaesthesia* 1976; **31**: 243–6

Mazo V, Sabate S, Canet J, *et al.* Prospective external validation of a predictive score for postoperative pulmonary complications. *Anesthesiology* 2014; **121**: 219–31

McAlister FA, Khan NA, Straus SE, *et al.* Accuracy of the preoperative assessment in predicting pulmonary risk after nonthoracic surgery. *Am J Respir Crit Care Med* 2003; **167**: 741–4

McGill WA, Coveler LA, Epstein BS. Subacute upper respiratory infection in small children. *Anesth Analg* 1979; **58**: 331–3

McLaughlin VV, Archer SL, Badesch DB, *et al.* ACCF/AHA 2009 expert consensus document on pulmonary hypertension a report of the American College of Cardiology Foundation Task Force on Expert Consensus Documents and the American Heart Association developed in collaboration with the American College of Chest Physicians; American Thoracic Society, Inc.; and the Pulmonary Hypertension Association. *J Am Coll Cardiol* 2009; **53**: 1573–619

McLaughlin VV, Oudiz RJ, Frost A, *et al.* Randomized study of adding inhaled iloprost to existing bosentan in pulmonary arterial hypertension. *Am J Respir Crit Care Med* 2006; **174**: 1257–63

Memtsoudis S, Liu SS, Ma Y, *et al.* Perioperative pulmonary outcomes in patients with sleep apnea after noncardiac surgery. *Anesth Analg* 2011; **112**: 113–21

Memtsoudis SG, Besculides MC, Gaber L, Liu S, Gonzalez Della Valle A. Risk factors for pulmonary embolism after hip and knee arthroplasty: a population-based study. *Int Orthop* 2009; **33**: 1739–45

Milic-Emili J, Aubier M. Some recent advances in the study of the control of breathing in patients with chronic obstructive lung disease. *Anesth Analg* 1980; **59**: 865–73

Mills GH, Kyroussis D, Hamnegard CH, *et al.* Cervical magnetic stimulation of the phrenic nerves in bilateral diaphragm paralysis. *Am J Resp Crit Care Med* 1997; **155**: 1565–9

Minai OA, Venkateshiah SB, Arroliga AC. Surgical intervention in patients with moderate to severe pulmonary arterial hypertension. *Conn Med* 2006; **70**: 239–43

Moppett I, Curran J. Smoking and the surgical patient. *Br J Anaesth CEPD Reviews* 2001; **1**: 122–4

Nakahara K, Monden Y, Ohno K, Miyoshi S, Maeda H, Kawashima Y. A method for predicting postoperative lung function and its relation to postoperative complications in patients with lung cancer. *Ann Thorac Surg* 1985; **39**: 260–5

Nakahara K, Ohno K, Hashimoto J, *et al.* Thymoma: results with complete resection and adjuvant postoperative irradiation in 141 consecutive patients. *J Thorac Cardiovasc Surg* 1988; **95**: 1041–7

Nava S, Rubini F. Lung and chest wall mechanics in ventilated patients with end stage idiopathic pulmonary fibrosis. *Thorax* 1999; **54**: 390–5

Navaratnam V, Fleming KM, West J, *et al.* The rising incidence of idiopathic pulmonary fibrosis in the U.K. *Thorax* 2011; **66**: 462–7

Neligan PJ, Porter S, Max B, Malhotra G, Greenblatt EP, Ochroch EA. Obstructive sleep apnea is not a risk factor for difficult intubation in morbidly obese patients. *Anesth Analg* 2009; **109**: 1182–6

Nguyen W, Meyer KC. Surgical lung biopsy for the diagnosis of interstitial lung disease: a review of the literature and recommendations for optimizing safety and efficacy. *Sarcoidosis Vasc Diffuse Lung Dis* 2013; **30**: 3–16

National Institute for Health and Care Excellence. *Chronic Obstructive Pulmonary Disease: Management of Chronic Obstructive Pulmonary Disease in Adults in Primary and Secondary Care.* Clinical Guideline CG101. 2010. Available from https://www.nice.org.uk/guidance/CG101

NOBLE PW, Albera C, Bradford WZ, *et al.* Pirfenidone in patients with idiopathic pulmonary fibrosis (CAPACITY): two randomised trials. *Lancet* 2011; **377**: 1760–9

Papiris SA, Manali ED, Kolilekas L, *et al.* Clinical review: idiopathic pulmonary fibrosis acute exacerbations--unravelling Ariadne's thread. *Crit Care* 2010; **14**: 246

Pedersen T. Complications and death following anaesthesia. A prospective study with special reference to the influence of patient-, anaesthesia-, and surgery-related risk factors. *Dan Med Bull* 1994; **41**: 319–31

Pedersen T, Eliasen K, Henriksen E. A prospective study of risk factors and cardiopulmonary complications associated with anaesthesia and surgery: risk indicators of cardiopulmonary morbidity. *Acta Anaesthesiol Scand* 1990; **34**: 144–55

Pedersen T, Viby-Mogensen J, Ringsted C. Anaesthetic practice and postoperative pulmonary complications. *Acta Anaesthesiol Scand* 1992; **36**: 812–8

Pierce RJ, Copland JM, Sharpe K, Barter CE. Preoperative risk evaluation for lung cancer resection: predicted postoperative product as a predictor of surgical mortality. *Am J Respir Crit Care Med* 1994; **150**: 947–55

Powell B, Al Mukhtar A, Mills GH. Carcinoid: the disease and its implications for anaesthesia. *Contin Educ Anaesth Crit Care Pain* 2010; **11**: 9–13

Price LC, Montani D, Jais X, *et al.* Noncardiothoracic nonobstetric surgery in mild-to-moderate pulmonary hypertension. *Eur Respir J* 2010; **35**: 1294–302

PROVE Network Investigators for the Clinical Trial Network of the European Society of Anaesthesiology, Hemmes SN, Gama de Abreu M, *et al.* High versus low positive end-expiratory pressure during general anaesthesia for open abdominal surgery (PROVHILO trial): a multicentre randomised controlled trial. *Lancet* 2014; **384**: 495–503

Ramachandran SK, Nafiu OO, Ghaferi A, Tremper KK, Shanks A, Kheterpal S. Independent predictors and outcomes of unanticipated early postoperative tracheal intubation after nonemergent, noncardiac surgery. *Anesthesiology* 2011; **115**: 44–53

Ramakrishna G, Sprung J, Ravi Bs, Chandrasekaran K, McGoon MD. Impact of pulmonary hypertension on the outcomes of noncardiac surgery: predictors of perioperative morbidity and mortality. *J Am Coll Cardiol* 2005; 45: 1691–9

Reinius H, Jonsson L, Gustafsson S, *et al.* Prevention of atelectasis in morbidly obese patients during general anesthesia and paralysis: a computerized tomography study. *Anesthesiology* 2009; 111: 979–87

Richeldi L, Davies HR, Ferrara G, Franco F. Corticosteroids for idiopathic pulmonary fibrosis. *Cochrane Database Syst Rev* 2003; **3**: CD002880

Robinson TD, Freiberg DB, Regnis JA, Young IH. The role of hypoventilation and ventilation-perfusion redistribution in oxygen-induced hypercapnia during acute exacerbations of chronic obstructive pulmonary disease. *Am J Respir Crit Care Med* 2000; **161**: 1524–9

Rosen AK, Geraci JM, Ash AS, Mcniff KJ, Moskowitz MA. Postoperative adverse events of common surgical procedures in the Medicare population. *Med Care* 1992; **30**: 753–65

Rothen HU, Sporre B, Engberg G, Wegenius G, Hedenstierna G. Reexpansion of atelectasis during general anaesthesia may have a prolonged effect. *Acta Anaesthesiol Scand* 1995; **39**: 118–25

Rubin LJ, Badesch DB, Barst RJ, *et al.* Bosentan therapy for pulmonary arterial hypertension. *N Engl J Med* 2002; **346**: 896–903

Rytila P, Rehn T, Ilumets H, *et al.* Increased oxidative stress in asymptomatic current chronic smokers and GOLD stage 0 COPD. *Respir Res* 2006; **7**: 69

Serpa Neto A, Hemmes SN, Barbas CS, *et al.* Protective versus conventional ventilation for surgery: a systematic review and individual patient data meta-analysis. *Anesthesiology* 2015; **30**: 125–34

Simonneau G, Gatzoulis MA, Adatia I, *et al.* Updated clinical classification of pulmonary hypertension. *J Am Coll Cardiol* 2013; **62**: D34–41

Singh M, Liao P, Kobah S, Wijeysundera DN, Shapiro C, Chung F. Proportion of surgical patients with undiagnosed obstructive sleep apnoea. *Br J Anaesth* 2013; **110**: 629–36

Skolnick ET, Vomvolakis MA, Buck KA, Mannino SF, Sun LS. Exposure to environmental tobacco smoke and the risk of adverse respiratory events in children receiving general anesthesia. *Anesthesiology* 1998; **88**: 1144–53

Smetana GW, Lawrence VA, Cornell JE, American College of Physicians. Preoperative pulmonary risk stratification for noncardiothoracic surgery: systematic review for the American College of Physicians. *Ann Intern Med* 2006; **144**: 581–95

Snelgrove RJ, Jackson PL, Hardison MT, *et al.* A critical role for LTA4H in limiting chronic pulmonary neutrophilic inflammation. *Science* 2010; **330**: 90–4

Soriano JB, Maier WC, Egger P, *et al.* Recent trends in physician diagnosed COPD in women and men in the UK. *Thorax* 2000; **55**: 789–94

Squadrone V, Coha M, Cerutti E, *et al.* Continuous positive airway pressure for treatment of postoperative hypoxemia: a randomized controlled trial. *JAMA* 2005; **293**: 589–95

Squadrone V, Massaia M, Bruno B, *et al.* Early CPAP prevents evolution of acute lung injury in patients with hematologic malignancy. *Intensive Care Med* 2010; **36**: 1666–74

Stupi AM, Steen VD, Owens GR, *et al.* Pulmonary hypertension in the CREST syndrome variant of systemic sclerosis. *Arthritis Rheum* 1986; **29**: 515–24

Tait AR, Knight PR. Intraoperative respiratory complications in patients with upper respiratory tract infections. *Can J Anaesth* 1987; **34**: 300–3

Tait AR, Malviya S. Anesthesia for the child with an upper respiratory tract infection: still a dilemma? *Anesth Analg* 2005; **100**: 59–65

Tait AR, Malviya S, Voepel-Lewis T, *et al.* Risk factors for perioperative adverse respiratory events in children with upper respiratory tract infections. *Anesthesiology* 2001; **95**: 299–306

Utz JP, Ryu JH, Douglas WW, *et al.* High short-term mortality following lung biopsy for usual interstitial pneumonia. *Eur Respir J* 2001; **17**: 175–9

Valipour A, Makker HK, Hardy R, *et al.* Symptomatic gastroesophageal reflux in subjects with a breathing sleep disorder. *Chest* 2002; **121**: 1748–53

Van Lier F, Van der Geest PJ, Hoeks SE, *et al.* Epidural analgesia is associated with improved health outcomes of surgical patients with chronic obstructive pulmonary disease. *Anesthesiology* 2011; **115**: 315–21

Veall GR, Peacock JE, Bax ND, Reilly CS. Review of the anaesthetic management of 21 patients undergoing laparotomy for carcinoid syndrome. *Br J Anaesth* 1994; **72**: 335–41

Vicente R, Morales P, Ramos F, Sole A, Mayo M, Villalain C. Perioperative complications of lung transplantation in patients with emphysema and fibrosis: experience from 1992-2002. *Transplant Proc* 2006; **38**: 2560–2

von Ungern-Sternberg BS, Boda K, Schwab C, Sims C, Johnson C, Habre W. Laryngeal mask airway is associated with an increased incidence of adverse respiratory events in children with recent upper respiratory tract infections. *Anesthesiology* 2007; **107**: 714–9

Wahi R, McMurtrey MJ, Decaro LF, *et al.* Determinants of perioperative morbidity and mortality after pneumonectomy. *Ann Thorac Surg* 1989; **48**: 33–7

Wallis A, Spinks K. The diagnosis and management of interstitial lung diseases. *BMJ* 2015; **350**: h2072

Walz MK, Peitgen K, Thurauf N, *et al.* Percutaneous dilatational tracheostomy--early results and long-term outcome of 326 critically ill patients. *Intensive Care Med* 1998; **24**: 685–90

Warner MA, Divertie MB, Tinker JH. Preoperative cessation of smoking and pulmonary complications in coronary artery bypass patients. *Anesthesiology* 1984; **60**: 380–3

Woehlck HJ, Connolly LA, Cinquegrani MP, Dunning MB, 3rd, Hoffmann RG. Acute smoking increases ST depression in humans during general anesthesia. *Anesth Analg*1999; **89**: 856–60

Woodhouse N, Wild JM, Paley MN, *et al.* Combined helium-3/proton magnetic resonance imaging measurement of ventilated lung volumes in smokers compared to never-smokers. *J Magn Reson Imaging* 2005; **21**: 365–9

Yonker-Sell AE, Connolly LA. Twelve hour anaesthesia in a patient with epidermolysis bullosa. *Can J Anaesth* 1995; **42**: 735–9

CHAPTER 83

Heart disease and anaesthesia

Stefan De Hert and Patrick Wouters

Introduction

Heart disease is a potential source of perioperative complications. The risk of such complications depends on the patient's condition before surgery, the prevalence of co-morbidities, and the type of the surgical procedure. Perioperative cardiac complications may specifically arise in patients with documented or asymptomatic ischaemic heart disease, left ventricular dysfunction, or valvular and congenital heart disease when the perioperative period is associated with increased cardiac stress as a result of haemodynamic disturbances. It is therefore of utmost importance that such patients are identified and adequately prepared for and carefully treated during the perioperative period.

Hypertension

Cardiovascular disease is a leading cause of mortality worldwide. Hypertension is one of the major risk factors for cardiovascular disease, including stroke, coronary artery disease, heart failure, peripheral vascular disease, and renal disease. Hypertension refers to a chronic elevation of systemic arterial pressure above a certain threshold value above which vascular damage starts to occur. This is accepted to be the case when systolic blood pressure is higher than 120 mm Hg and diastolic blood pressure higher than 80 mm Hg.

Classifications of hypertension

Classically, hypertension is subdivided according to the underlying aetiology into primary and secondary hypertension. Primary (essential, idiopathic) hypertension refers to the presence of a persistent elevated increase in blood pressure without any obvious or clearly visible reason. Secondary hypertension is present when a well-defined aetiology for the hypertension is identified, such as renovascular disease or primary aldosteronism. Hypertension is primary in about 95% of cases while secondary hypertension is present in the remaining 5% of cases.

Hypertension can be classified into different categories according to the level of the elevated blood pressure. The cardiovascular risk associated with an elevated blood pressure has been shown to increase in a linear fashion starting from a blood pressure above approximately 115/75 mm Hg (Kikuya et al. 2007). It may therefore be questionable to make a classification based on arbitrary cut-off values. Nevertheless, the use of such cut-off values simplifies diagnostic and treatment strategies in daily clinical practice. Table 83.1 summarizes the classification of blood pressure values as proposed in 2013 by the task force for the management of arterial hypertension of the European Society of Hypertension and the European Society of Cardiology (Mancia et al. 2013). The US Joint National Committee guidelines on hypertension have unified the normal and high normal blood pressure categories into a single entity that was termed 'prehypertension' (Chobanian et al. 2003). According to this approach, the presence of such pressures should be considered to constitute a higher than average risk for cardiovascular events than those with lower blood pressures. Adults with systolic blood pressures of 102–139 mm Hg and diastolic blood pressures of 80–89 mm Hg have indeed been shown to have a 3.5 times greater relative risk for myocardial infarction and a 1.7 times greater relative risk for symptomatic myocardial ischaemia than subjects with lower blood pressure values (Qureshi et al. 2005). This concept of 'prehypertension', however, gives little objective support and structure in the design of specific preventive and therapeutic strategies with regard to the different levels of elevated blood pressure. This has resulted in a new approach in the definition of hypertension in which the disease is not confined to an isolated elevated blood pressure but where blood pressure is only one component of the global cardiovascular risk (Giles et al. 2005, 2009).

Table 83.1 Classification of blood pressures according to 2013 Guidelines for the management of arterial hypertension by the Task Force for the management of Arterial Hypertension of the European Society of Hypertension and of the European Society of Cardiology

Category	Systolic BP		Diastolic BP
Optimal	<120	and	<80
Normal	120–129	and/or	80–84
High normal	130–139	and/or	85–89
Grade 1 hypertension	140–159	and/or	90–99
Grade 2 hypertension	160–179	and/or	100–109
Grade 3 hypertension	≥180	and/or	≥110
Isolated systolic hypertension	≥140	and	<90

BP, blood pressure (reported in mm Hg).

Reproduced from Giuseppe Mancia *et al.* 2013 ESH/ESC Guidelines for the management of arterial hypertension, *European Heart Journal*, 2013, 34, 28, pp. 2159–2219; www.escardio.org/guidelines, by permission of European Society of Cardiology.

Hypertension as a disease

Hypertension is a progressive cardiovascular disease that arises from complex and interrelated aetiologies. Early markers of the disease may be present before blood pressure elevation becomes sustained. Progression of the disease is characterized by functional and structural changes in the vasculature that may affect normal function of the heart, the kidney, the brain, and other organs and ultimately lead to premature morbidity and mortality. In this new definition, elevated blood pressure (as a symptom of the disease) is clearly separated from hypertension (the disease). As such, elevated blood pressure serves as a biomarker for the disease hypertension (Giles et al. 2005, 2009). It is important to note that individuals with the same levels of elevated blood pressure might have different stages of hypertension and even that some individuals may present with elevated blood pressure in the absence of the disease hypertension. Subjects are in fact diagnosed as either normal or hypertensive based on an integrated assessment of their cardiovascular status. The progression of hypertension is then characterized by a cumulative appearance of markers of hypertensive cardiovascular disease and evidence of target organ damage, irrespective of the level of blood pressure increase.

The classification of the 'disease' hypertension is summarized in Table 83.2. Individuals with optimal levels of blood pressure and no identifiable markers of cardiovascular disease are considered as normal. Resting average blood pressure levels are usually less than 120/80 mm Hg but may occasionally be elevated to 140/90 mm Hg or higher. *Stage 1 hypertension* is characterized by early signs of functional or structural changes in the heart or small arteries of various organs. Blood pressure levels are above 115/75 mm Hg and may be elevated, especially in the presence of external stress factors. These patients frequently have more than one cardiovascular risk factor (Box 83.1). This category applies only to those individuals with early markers of disease (Table 83.3) without any evidence of target organ damage (Table 83.4). In *stage 2 hypertension*, individuals frequently have blood pressure of 140/90 mm Hg or higher, with much higher levels in the presence of physiological or psychological stress. Of note, individuals with numerous markers of disease or limited evidence of early target organ damage are also included in this group regardless of blood pressure levels. Untreated patients with *stage 3 hypertension* usually have sustained resting blood pressure levels of 140/90 mm Hg or higher, and higher levels are common. All individuals with clinical evidence of overt target organ damage, cardiovascular disease, or both, and those who have already suffered cardiovascular events are included in this category, regardless of their blood pressure levels. Stage 3 hypertension therefore represents the advanced stage of the hypertensive continuum in which overt organ damage is present and cardiovascular events are to be expected or have already occurred.

Diagnostic evaluation

Diagnostic evaluation aims to establish the blood pressure levels, identify potential secondary causes of hypertension, and evaluate the overall cardiovascular risk by searching for other risk factors, target organ damage, concomitant diseases, or accompanying clinical conditions. The diagnostic procedures have been addressed in several guidelines (Chobanian et al., 2003; O'Brie et al., 2003; Mancia et al. 2013) and include repeated blood pressure measurements, medical history, physical examination, and finally laboratory and more invasive technical investigations.

As a result of the importance of subclinical organ damage in the staging of hypertensive disease, signs of target organ involvement should be carefully investigated. Investigations include electrocardiography and echocardiography, ultrasound scanning of the carotid and peripheral arteries to assess vascular involvement, estimation of kidney function, fundoscopy, and evaluation of potential cerebral damage. Availability, prognostic value, and relative cost of the different investigations to detect subclinical organ damage are summarized in Table 83.5.

Treatment

In hypertensive patients, the primary goal of treatment is to achieve a maximal reduction of the long-term total risk of cardiovascular disease. The decision to start antihypertensive treatment should therefore be based on two criteria which are the level of systolic and diastolic blood pressure and the level of total cardiovascular risk. This implies treatment of the raised blood pressure as such but also of all associated reversible risk factors. Although hard evidence is scanty, most guidelines on treatment of hypertension treatment recommend a blood pressure target of less than 130/80 mm Hg for high-risk patients (Chobanian et al., 2003; Zanchetti et al. 2009; Mancia et al. 2013). Apart from lifestyle adaptations, several classes of drugs are nowadays available including diuretics, angiotensin-converting enzyme inhibitors, angiotensin receptor antagonists, β-blockers, and calcium antagonists. Use of these different therapeutic strategies will

Table 83.2 Classification of hypertension

Classification	Definition	CV risk factors	Early disease markers	Target organ disease
Normal	Normal BP or rare BP elevations No identifiable CV disease	None or few	None	None
Stage 1 hypertension	Occasional or intermittent BP increase and early CV disease	Several	Usually present	None
Stage 2 hypertension	Sustained BP increase or progressive CV disease	Many	Overtly present	Early signs
Stage 3 hypertension	Marked and sustained BP increase or advanced CV disease	Many	Overtly present with progression	Overtly present with or without CV events

BP, blood pressure; CV, cardiovascular.

Reproduced from Giles et al., Definition and Classification of Hypertension: An Update, *Journal of Clinical Hypertension*, 11, 11, pp. 611–614, Copyright 2009, Wiley Periodicals, Inc and World Hypertension League.

Box 83.1 Cardiovascular risk factors

- Increasing age
- Elevated blood pressure
- High heart rate
- Overweight/obesity → increased body mass index
- Central obesity → increased abdominal circumference → increased waist-to-hip ratio
- Dyslipidaemia → elevated LDL or non-HDL cholesterol → Low HDL cholesterol → elevated triglycerides
- Elevated blood glucose, insulin resistance, or diabetes
- Chronic kidney disease
- Smoking
- Family history of premature CVD (age <50 years in men, <60 years in women)
- Sedentary lifestyle
- Psychosocial stress factors
- Elevated hs-CRP.

CVD, cardiovascular disease; hs-CRP, high sensitivity C-reactive protein; HDL, high-density lipoprotein; LDL, low-density lipoprotein.

Reproduced from Giles et al., Definition and Classification of Hypertension: An Update, *Journal of Clinical Hypertension*, 11, 11, pp. 611–614, Copyright 2009, Wiley Periodicals, Inc and World Hypertension League.

Table 83.3 Early markers of hypertensive cardiovascular disease

System	Physiological alteration
Blood pressure	Loss of nocturnal BP dipping
	Exaggerated BP responses to exercise or mental stress
	Salt sensitivity
	Widened pulse pressure
Heart	LV hypertrophy (mild)
	Increased atrial filling pressure
	Decreased diastolic relaxation
	Increased natriuretic peptide levels
Vascular	Increased central arterial stiffness
	Small artery stiffness
	Increased systemic vascular resistance
	Increased wave reflection
	Increased systolic pressure augmentation
	Increased carotid intimal-media thickness
	Coronary calcification or stenoses
	Endothelial dysfunction
	Capillary rarefaction
Renal	Microalbuminuria (30–300 mg/day)
	Elevated serum creatinine
	Reduced estimated GFR (60–90 mL/min)
Retinal	Hypertensive retinal changes

BP, blood pressure; GFR, glomerular filtration rate; LV, left ventricular.

Reproduced from Giles et al., Definition and Classification of Hypertension: An Update, *Journal of Clinical Hypertension*, 11, 11, pp. 611–614, Copyright 2009, Wiley Periodicals, Inc and World Hypertension League.

Table 83.4 Hypertensive target organ damage

System	Evidence of target organ damage
Heart	LV hypertrophy (moderate to severe)
	Systolic and/or diastolic cardiac dysfunction
	Symptomatic heart failure
	Myocardial infarction
	Angina pectoris
	IHD or prior revascularization
Vascular	Peripheral arterial disease
	Carotid arterial disease
	Aortic aneurysm
	Wide pulse pressure (>65 mm Hg)
Renal	Albuminuria (>300 mg/day)
	Chronic kidney disease (GFR <60 mL/min)
	End-stage renal disease
Cerebrovascular	Stroke
	Transient ischaemic attack
	Decreased cognitive function
	Dementia
	Loss of vision

Reproduced from Giles et al., Definition and Classification of Hypertension: An Update, *Journal of Clinical Hypertension*, 11, 11, pp. 611–614, Copyright 2009, Wiley Periodicals, Inc and World Hypertension League.

Table 83.5 Availability, prognostic value and cost of markers of hypertensive disease on a relative scale scoring from 0 to 4 pluses

Marker	Availability	Predictive value	Cost
Electrocardiography	++++	++	+
Echocardiography	+++	+++	++
Carotid intima–media thickness	+++	+++	++
Pulse wave velocity	+	+++	++
Ankle–brachial index	++	++	+
Coronary calcium content	+	+	++++
Cardiac/vascular tissue composition	+	?	++
Circulatory collagen markers	+	?	++
Endothelial dysfunction	+	++	+++
Cerebral lacunae white matter lesion	++	?	++++
Estimated GFR creatinine clearance	++++	+++	+
Microalbuminuria	++++	+++	+

GFR, glomerular filtration rate.

Reproduced from Giuseppe Mancia *et al.* 2013 ESH/ESC Guidelines for the management of arterial hypertension. *European Heart Journal* Jul 2013, 34 (28) 2159–2219. DOI: 10.1093/eurheartj/eht151. www.escardio.org/guidelines, Copyright © 2013, by permission of European Society of Cardiology.

depend on the severity of the disease (Table 83.6 and Table 83.7). The 2013 guidelines for the management of arterial hypertension of the European Society of Hypertension and the European Society of Cardiology have proposed a targeted therapeutic approach that is based on the assessment of both the blood pressure and the presence

Table 83.6 Recommendations for the initiation of antihypertensive treatment according to the 2013 guidelines for the management of arterial hypertension of the European Society of Hypertension and the European Society of Cardiology

	NORMAL **SBP 120–129 mm Hg** **or** **DBP 80–84 mm Hg**	**HIGH NORMAL** **SBP 130–139 mm Hg** **or** **DBP 85–89 mm Hg**	**GRADE 1 HYPERTENSION** **SBP 140–159 mm Hg** **or** **DBP 90–99 mm Hg**	**GRADE 2 HYPERTENSION** **SBP 160–179 mm Hg** **or** **DBP 100–109 mm Hg**	**GRADE 3 HYPERTENSION** **SBP ≥180mm Hg** **or** **DBP ≥110 mm Hg**
No other risk factors	NO treatment	NO treatment	Lifestyle changes for several months then drug treatment if BP uncontrolled	Lifestyle changes for several weeks then drug treatment if BP uncontrolled	Lifestyle changes AND immediate drug treatment
1–2 risk factors	Lifestyle changes	Lifestyle changes	Lifestyle changes for several weeks then drug treatment if BP uncontrolled	Lifestyle changes for several weeks then drug treatment if BP uncontrolled	Lifestyle changes AND immediate drug treatment
≥3 risk factors metabolic syndrome organ damage	Lifestyle changes	Lifestyle changes AND consider drug treatment	Lifestyle changes AND drug treatment	Lifestyle changes AND drug treatment	Lifestyle changes AND immediate drug treatment
Diabetes	Lifestyle changes	Lifestyle changes AND drug treatment	Lifestyle changes AND drug treatment	Lifestyle changes AND drug treatment	Lifestyle changes AND immediate drug treatment
Established CV or renal disease	Lifestyle changes AND immediate drug treatment	Lifestyle changes AND immediate drug treatment	Lifestyle changes AND immediate drug treatment	Lifestyle changes AND immediate drug treatment	Lifestyle changes AND immediate drug treatment

The different gradings of hypertension refer to the grading proposed by the 2013 guidelines for the management of arterial hypertension of the European Society of Hypertension and the European Society of Cardiology (Mancia et al. 2013) and shown in Table 83.1. These allow for an objective classification of the disease. The concept of hypertension as a cardiovascular disease is similar to what is proposed by the American Hypertension Working Group (Table 83.2) (Giles et al. 2005) but the use of blood pressure threshold values allow a clinically useful tool in the design of therapeutic strategies, which is lacking with the classification of the Hypertension Working Group. CV, cardiovascular; DBP, diastolic blood pressure; SBP, systolic blood pressure.

of risk factors (Table 83.6) (Mancia et al. 2013). The choice of specific drug classes will in part depend on the presence or absence of such specific risk factors (Table 83.7). In general, it is accepted that antihypertensive therapy should ideally be initiated before cardiovascular damage occurs.

Malignant hypertension and hypertensive emergencies

Malignant hypertension is a syndrome of severe elevation of arterial blood pressure with diastolic pressures usually greater than 140 mm Hg and with vascular damage that may manifest as retinal haemorrhages, with exudates or papilloedema, or both. Severe or poorly treated essential hypertension is the most common cause and its incidence has decreased substantially as a result of earlier and more effective treatment of hypertension.

The most dangerous condition associated with malignant hypertension is hypertensive encephalopathy. Other hypertensive emergencies include hypertensive left ventricular failure; hypertension with unstable angina or myocardial infarction; hypertension causing aortic dissection, subarachnoid haemorrhage, or cerebrovascular accident; crisis associated with phaeochromocytoma; hypertension after use of recreational drugs (cocaine, LSD, XTC); and severe pre-eclampsia or eclampsia. It is obvious that these conditions require prompt and aggressive treatment aiming to reduce blood pressure.

Ischaemic heart disease

Ischaemic heart disease is the leading cause of mortality in the Western world. Also in the perioperative setting, cardiac ischaemic events constitute a major source of perioperative complications. In major non-cardiac surgery, the incidence of cardiac death is estimated between 0.5% and 1.5%, and of major cardiac complications between 2.0% and 3.5% (Kristensen et al. 2014). Perioperative cardiac complications are either caused by myocardial ischaemia or by acute coronary thrombosis. Myocardial ischaemia may result from an increase in myocardial oxygen demand (tachycardia, hypertension, pain) or a decreased myocardial oxygen supply (hypotension, vasospasm, tachycardia, hypoxia, anaemia), or a combination of these. Coronary plaque rupture may be caused by any factor that increases intracoronary wall stress (Fig. 83.1) (De Hert 2009). In addition, the presence of a hypercoagulable state, leucocyte activation, and activation of the inflammatory response may greatly contribute to the pathophysiology of coronary artery occlusion.

The dramatic impact of perioperative myocardial ischaemic events on patient outcome and healthcare resources underscores the need for a thorough perioperative strategy to identify the patients at risk and prevent perioperative myocardial ischaemic events. Recently, the preoperative assessment and perioperative management of patients with coronary artery disease have been addressed both in the United States and in Europe and published guidelines are now available (Fleisher et al. 2014; Kristensen et al. 2014).

Prediction of cardiac risk

The *Revised Cardiac Risk Index* is frequently used to identify those patients with an increased cardiac risk. It assigns one point for the presence of each of the following six risk factors: high-risk

Table 83.7 Preferred antihypertensive drugs as a function of the associated subclinical organ damage and/or clinical event

Subclinical organ damage	Preferred drugs
Left ventricular hypertrophy	ACEI, CA, ARB
Asymptomatic atherosclerosis	CA, ACEI
Microalbuminuria	ACEI, ARB
Renal dysfunction	ACEI, ARB
Clinical event	**Preferred drugs**
Previous stroke	Any blood pressure lowering agent
Previous myocardial infarction	BB, ACEI, ARB
Angina pectoris	BB, CA
Heart failure	BB, CA, Anti-aldosterone agents
Atrial fibrillation: ◆ Permanent ◆ Recurrent	BB, non-dihydropyridine CA, ARB, ACEI
Renal failure	ACEI, ARB, loop diuretics
Peripheral arterial disease	CA
Specific conditions	**Preferred drugs**
Isolated systolic hypertension	Diuretics, CA
Metabolic syndrome	ACEI, ARB, CA
Diabetes mellitus	ACEI, ARB
Pregnancy	CA, methyldopa, BB

ACEI, angiotensin converting enzyme inhibitor; ARB, angiotensin receptor blocker; BB, β-blocker; CA, calcium antagonist.

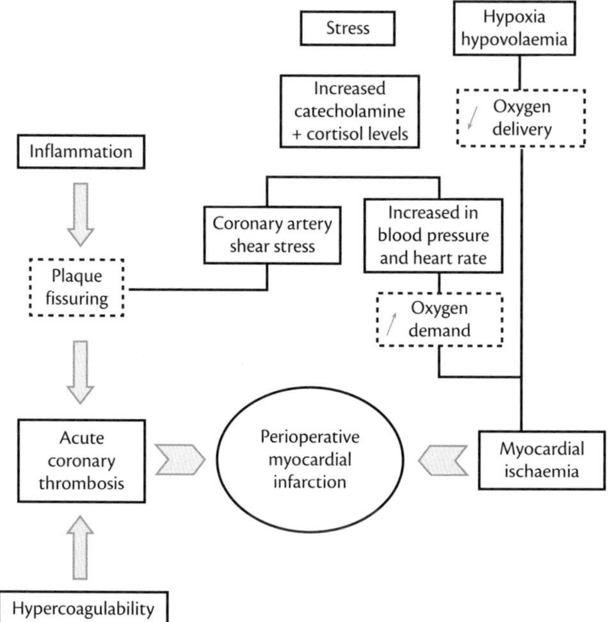

Figure 83.1 Different possible pathophysiological pathways leading to the occurrence of a perioperative myocardial infarction.

de Hert, S. G. Preoperative cardiovascular assessment in noncardiac surgery: an update. *European Journal of Anaesthesiology*, Volume 26, Issue 6, pp. 449–457, Copyright © 2009 European Society of Anaesthesiology.

surgical procedure, history of ischaemic heart disease, history of congestive heart failure, history of cerebrovascular accident, preoperative treatment with insulin, or a serum creatinine greater than 175 μmol litre^{-1} (2.0 mg dl^{-1}). The estimated risk of major cardiac complications for indices 0, 1, 2, and 3 or higher are 0.4 (0.1–0.8)%, 1.0 (0.5–1.4)%, 2.4 (1.3–3.5)% and 5.4 (2.8–7.9)%, respectively.

Preoperative assessment of the cardiac patient

Recent guidelines have proposed a stepwise approach for the perioperative cardiac assessment and management of cardiac patients scheduled for non-cardiac surgery (Fleisher et al. 2014; Kristensen et al. 2014). This approach involves first an assessment of the urgency of the surgery. In case of an elective intervention, patients are screened for the presence of active cardiac conditions (Box 83.2). If one of these conditions is present, they should be further evaluated and when necessary, treated. It should be obvious that at all times, the potential benefits of delaying surgery for further evaluation or to optimize treatment, or both, must be weighed against the risk of delaying the surgical intervention. With respect to a recent myocardial infarction, it is recommended to wait for 4–6 weeks before performing elective surgery.

If no active cardiac conditions are present, the next step is to assess the risk of surgery (Box 83.3). Many surgical procedures are associated with a low risk of perioperative complications even in high-risk patients. In such cases it is recommended to proceed with planned surgery. In the case of intermediate or high-risk surgery, further assessment of the patient's physical status is indicated.

Subsequently, the patient's functional capacity is evaluated. When a patient is capable of performing an activity equal or greater than 4 metabolic equivalents without symptoms, the recommendation is to proceed with surgery. If, however, the patient is symptomatic or the functional capacity of the patient is unknown, further assessment is indicated.

Box 83.2 Active cardiac conditions

1. Unstable coronary syndromes:
   - Unstable or severe angina
   - Recent myocardial infarction (within 30 days)
2. Decompensated heart failure
3. Significant arrhythmias:
   - High-grade atrioventricular block
   - Symptomatic ventricular arrhythmias
   - Supraventricular arrhythmias with uncontrolled ventricular rate (>100 beats min^{-1} at rest)
   - Symptomatic bradycardia
   - Newly recognized ventricular tachycardia
4. Severe valvular disease:
   - Severe aortic stenosis (mean pressure gradient > 40 mm Hg, area < 1 cm^2 or symptomatic)
   - Symptomatic mitral stenosis.

Box 83.3 Surgical risk stratification

1. High risk (cardiac risk >5%):
   - Aortic surgery
   - Major vascular surgery
   - Peripheral vascular surgery
2. Intermediate risk (cardiac risk 1–5%):
   - Intraperitoneal and intrathoracic surgery
   - Carotid endarterectomy
   - Head and neck surgery
   - Orthopaedic surgery
   - Prostate surgery
3. Low risk (cardiac risk <1%):
   - Endoscopic procedures
   - Superficial procedures
   - Cataract surgery
   - Breast surgery
   - Ambulatory surgery.

Preoperative tests

The ultimate aim of additional preoperative testing is to provide an objective measure of functional capacity, and to identify the importance of possible preoperative myocardial ischaemia and rhythm disturbances. Several non-invasive tests are available including resting 12-lead electrocardiogram, evaluation of left ventricular function by echocardiography, radionucleotide angiography, or contrast ventriculography and exercise stress testing. In patients who cannot exercise, two alternative techniques can be used to assess the significance of coronary artery disease. One technique is to increase myocardial oxygen demand mainly by increasing heart rate (by pacing or dobutamine), the other is to induce a hyperaemic response by pharmacological vasodilators such as dipyridamole or adenosine.

Preoperative treatment

The potential benefits of preoperative coronary revascularization remain a point of debate. In essence, the indications for preoperative coronary revascularization are identical to those in the non-operative setting. Percutaneous coronary revascularization necessitates postprocedural administration of antiplatelet therapy, the duration of which depends on the type of stent used. As antiplatelet therapy may increase the risk of perioperative bleeding, these drugs are usually discontinued at the time of surgery. It has been recognized that such action may have disastrous consequences for the surgical patient and therefore specific guidelines have been developed for the management of such patients (Fig. 83.2) (Fleisher et al. 2014; Kristensen et al. 2014).

Another approach is to optimize medical treatment in an attempt to minimize the perioperative stress response as much as possible. Perioperative β-blocker therapy has gained wide interest but the recent results of the POISE study, which observed an increased mortality and incidence of stroke in the β-blocker treatment group has led to questioning of the idea that perioperative β-blocker treatment improves outcome. Further studies on the subject are ongoing and currently continuation of β-blocker therapy in patients who are already on such medication is the only strong recommendation with regard to β-blockers (Fleisher et al. 2009, 2014; Kristensen et al. 2014).

Statins also seem to improve perioperative outcome. Initially used for their cholesterol-lowering properties, there is now ample evidence that their pleiotropic effects may help in decreasing the incidence of perioperative cardiac events and hence improve outcome. It is recommended that statins should be continued for all patients taking this medication who are scheduled for non-cardiac surgery.

Aspirin (acetylsalicylic acid) has a key role in the primary and secondary prevention of cardiovascular disease and it is commonly used, in association with clopidogrel, for the prevention of coronary stent thrombosis. Its potential beneficial effect in the perioperative period with non-cardiac surgery is less well established. Concerns with regard to perioperative bleeding complications have been a frequent reason to interrupt this therapy. It was suggested that aspirin should only be discontinued if it may cause bleeding risk with increased mortality or if sequelae are similar to the expected cardiovascular risks of acetylsalicylic acid withdrawal. Aspirin withdrawal was reported to be associated with a three-fold higher risk of major cardiac events.

The potential beneficial effects of perioperative α_2-agonists and calcium channel blockers remain to be definitively established. Nitrates may be considered for the prevention of myocardial ischaemia, although really strong evidence is missing about potential effects on outcome. The strategy with regard to angiotensin-converting enzymes is controversial. Severe hypotension has been described with induction of anaesthesia, especially in the presence of concomitant β-blocker use. The severity of the hypotension seems related to the dosage of the daily therapy. Therefore omission on the day of surgery may be considered when they are prescribed for hypertension, but they should be resumed after surgery as soon as the haemodynamic status is stable. In stable patients with left ventricular dysfunction, it is recommended to continue the angiotensin-converting enzyme therapy.

Perioperative myocardial infarction

A perioperative myocardial infarction has been associated with a 30–50% perioperative mortality and reduced long-term survival. Therefore accurate diagnosis and prompt treatment is essential. Perioperative myocardial infarction can be diagnosed by assessing clinical symptoms, serial electrocardiograms, cardiac-specific biomarkers, and various imaging technologies. Currently, there seem to be no clear-cut standard criteria for the diagnosis of perioperative myocardial infarction in patients undergoing non-cardiac surgery. Postoperative troponin measurement is recommended in patients with electrocardiographic changes or chest pain typical of the acute coronary syndrome. Assessment of pro-B-type natriuretic peptide is gaining interest as a predictor of adverse events and outcome after non-cardiac surgery.

Cardiac rhythm disturbances and conduction defects

The heart generates its own electrical impulse. In normal conditions, cardiac action potentials are generated in the sino-atrial node and then transmitted through Purkinje fibres in the atria to the atrioventricular node from where they spread throughout the ventricular walls in a very specific sequence such that the heart muscle contracts as efficiently as possible. The pacemaker cells of the heart spontaneously depolarize at a regular rhythm, thereby generating the normal heart rate (Park and Fishman 2011). An abnormal spontaneous depolarization will result in cardiac arrhythmias. When the activity of the primary pacemaker cells does not propagate to the rest of the heart, heart block will occur. In such cases a latent pacemaker may take over, spontaneously depolarize and create an action potential. Usually this occurs at slower rates than at the sino-atrial node.

Abnormal heart rhythms fall into two general classes: excessively slow heart rates, known as bradyarrhythmias or bradycardias, and overly rapid heart rates, known as tachyarrhythmias or tachycardias. While single isolated extra or skipped heart beats most often present in otherwise normal hearts and are usually harmless, serious heart rhythm disturbances are caused by an underlying heart disease such as coronary artery disease, valve disease, heart muscle disease, or by a direct malfunction of the electrical conduction system. Arrhythmias may originate from the atria or from the ventricles, while conduction defects can be localized anywhere in the cardiac electrical pathway.

Atrial arrhythmias

Sinus arrhythmias refer to rhythm disturbances originating from the sinus node. Occurrence of cyclic changes in the heart rate during breathing is a common and harmless phenomenon in children and in adults. *Premature atrial extrasystoles* are a common phenomenon, which usually pass unrecognized. They occur when a beat is generated early in the atria, causing the heart to beat before the next regularly expected heartbeat.

When the sinus node sends out electrical signals faster than usual, the heart rate will increase and *sinus tachycardia* will occur. This is frequently a physiological response to increased stress but may also occur as a result of an underlying anatomical or pathophysiological problem. *Atrioventricular nodal re-entrant tachycardias* are the most common form of regular supraventricular tachycardia. These occur when a re-entry circuit forms within or just next to the atrioventricular node. The circuit usually involves two anatomical pathways: a fast and a slow pathway, which are both in the right atrium. The slow pathway (which is usually targeted for ablation) is located inferiorly and slightly posterior to the atrioventricular node. The fast pathway is usually located just superior and posterior to the atrioventricular node. Most commonly, the anterograde conduction is via the slow pathway and the retrograde conduction is via the fast pathway. *Wolff–Parkinson–White syndrome* is a type of atrioventricular re-entry tachycardia. It is caused by an accessory pathway that connects the atria and the ventricles, in addition to the atrioventricular node. This accessory pathway is known as the bundle of Kent. This accessory pathway does not share the rate-slowing properties of the atrioventricular node, and may conduct electrical activity at a significantly higher rate than the atrioventricular node.

Sick sinus syndrome is an abnormality involving the generation of the action potential by the sinus node. It is characterized by an atrial rate that is inappropriate for physiological requirements. Manifestations include severe sinus bradycardia, sinus pauses or arrest, sinus node exit block, chronic atrial tachyarrhythmias, and alternating periods of atrial bradyarrhythmias and tachyarrhythmias. *Sick sinus syndrome* is a collection of conditions with multiple causes. Degenerative fibrosis may be an important cause, but there is increasing evidence that ion channels are involved in familial disease, as well as the variants related to heart failure and atrial fibrillation. They may also be important in the ageing-related syndrome. If this is the case, manipulation of the expression of the genes regulating the ion channels in the node could be a future powerful therapeutic tool. Therapy will mainly depend on the manifestation of the disease with pacemakers in the case of severe bradycardias and drug treatment in cases of tachyarrhythmias (Lévy 2000; Blomström-Lundqvist et al. 2003).

Atrial fibrillation is the most common cardiac arrhythmia. The normal electrical impulses that are generated by the sinoatrial node are overwhelmed by disorganized electrical impulses that originate in the atria and pulmonary veins. The result is conduction of irregular impulses to the ventricles leading to an irregular heartbeat. *Atrial fibrillation* may be asymptomatic but can result in palpitations, fainting, chest pain, or congestive heart failure. People with *atrial fibrillation* have an increased risk of stroke because blood may pool and form clots in the fibrillating atria and especially in the left atrial appendage.

Atrial fibrillation is classified into three categories. All patients with atrial fibrillation are initially in the category called *first-detected atrial fibrillation*. These patients may or may not have had previous undetected episodes. If a first-detected episode self-terminates in less than 7 days and then another episode begins later on, the case has moved into the category of *paroxysmal atrial fibrillation*. Although patients in this category have episodes lasting up to 7 days, in most cases of paroxysmal atrial fibrillation the episodes will self-terminate in less than 24 h. If, instead, the episode lasts for more than 7 days, it is unlikely to self-terminate, and it is called *persistent atrial fibrillation*. In this case, the episode may still be terminated by cardioversion. If cardioversion is unsuccessful or it is not attempted, and the episode is ongoing for a long time, the *atrial fibrillation* is termed *permanent* (Lévy 2000; Fuster et al. 2006, 2011; Mitchell and CCS Atrial Fibrillation Guidelines Committee 2011). In addition to these three categories, which are mainly defined by episode timing and termination, the American College of Cardiology (ACC)/American Heart Association (AHA)/ European Society of Cardiology guidelines describe additional categories in terms of other characteristics of the patients. *Lone atrial fibrillation* is diagnosed when there are no clinical or echocardiographic findings of other cardiovascular disease (including hypertension), related pulmonary disease, or cardiac abnormalities such as enlargement of the left atrium, and the patient is under 60 years of age. When there is no evidence of rheumatic mitral valve disease, a prosthetic heart valve, or mitral valve repair, the diagnosis is that of *non-valvular atrial fibrillation*. In the setting of a primary condition which may be the cause of the atrial fibrillation, such as acute myocardial infarction, cardiac surgery, pericarditis, myocarditis, hyperthyroidism, pulmonary embolism, pneumonia, or other acute pulmonary disease, the disease is called *secondary atrial fibrillation* (Fuster et al. 2011; Mitchell and CCS Atrial Fibrillation Guidelines Committee 2011).

Atrial fibrillation can be treated with medications that either slow the heart rate or revert the heart rhythm back to normal. Synchronized electrical cardioversion may be used to convert atrial fibrillation to a normal heart rhythm. Surgical and catheter-based therapies may also be used to prevent recurrence of atrial fibrillation in certain individuals. People with atrial fibrillation are often given anticoagulants or aspirin to prevent clot formation and to protect them from stroke (Lévy 2000; Fuster et al. 2006, 2011; Surawicz et al. 2009; Mitchell and CCS Atrial Fibrillation Guidelines Committee 2011).

Atrial flutter is caused by a re-entrant rhythm in either the right or left atrium. It is usually associated with tachycardia and occurs most often in association with underlying cardiovascular disease such as coronary artery disease or cardiomyopathy. Occasionally it may present spontaneously in people with otherwise normal hearts. It is present typically as an irregular rhythm and frequently degenerates into atrial fibrillation. With *atrial flutter*, the re-entrant loop circles the right atrium, passing through the cavo-tricuspid isthmus and the atrial rate is typically about 240–350 beats min^{-1}. This rate may be slowed by antiarrhythmic agents. Another variant of *atrial flutter* follows a different re-entry pathway to type I flutter, and is typically faster, usually 340–350 beats min^{-1}. Treatment is usually similar to that for atrial fibrillation.

Diagnosis of supraventricular tachyarrhythmias is initially based on a 12-lead surface electrocardiogram. This is then followed by more sophisticated electrophysiological examination. Treatment aims at restoring the normal heart rhythm or if this is not possible restoring heart rate within the physiological limits. Depending on the underlying disease, treatment may be medical or more invasive (cardioversion, ablation, pacemaker) (Lévy 2000).

Ventricular arrhythmias

Premature ventricular complexes are abnormal electrical impulses arising in the ventricles. They often produce palpitations, but generally have very few medical implications. *Ventricular tachycardia* is a rapid heart rhythm originating within the ventricles. It disrupts the normal orderly contraction of the ventricular muscle, so that the ventricle's ability to eject blood is significantly reduced. Combined with the excessive heart rate, ventricular tachycardia can substantially lower cardiac output with loss of consciousness, or even sudden death as a result. *Ventricular fibrillation* is a rapid, chaotic ventricular arrhythmia that immediately disrupts any ordered ventricular contraction. Unless cardiopulmonary resuscitation is initiated promptly, sudden death will occur.

Conduction defects

Atrioventricular block can be defined as a delay or interruption in the transmission of an impulse from the atria to the ventricles as a result of an anatomical or functional impairment in the conducting system. The conduction disturbance can be transient or permanent, and can have many causes. Conduction can be delayed, intermittent, or absent. The commonly used terminology includes first-degree (slowed conduction without missing beats), second-degree (intermittent conduction, often in a regular pattern, e.g. 2:1, 3:2, or higher degrees of block), and third-degree or complete atrioventricular block. A *first-degree atrioventricular block* is caused by a delay in conduction through the atrioventricular node which results in a P–R interval of the ECG of greater than 0.2 s. This may be caused by ageing, ischaemia, myocarditis, cardiomyopathy, aortic regurgitation, or any cause of increased vagal tone. This heart block is usually asymptomatic. The *second-degree atrioventricular block* can be subdivided into *Mobitz type I (Wenckebach)* and *Mobitz type II*. *Mobitz type I* is caused by a delay in conduction through the atrioventricular node with a progressive prolongation of the P–R interval until there is a dropped beat. This rhythm is usually asymptomatic and requires no specific therapy. *Mobitz type II* is caused by a block below the atrioventricular node (usually in the His–Purkinje fibres). A sudden block of conduction occurs without progressive elongation of the P–R interval. The failure of one or more P waves to conduct to the ventricles can ultimately lead to syncope (called Stokes–Adams attacks). A *type II block* is permanent and may progress to higher or even complete heart block.

A *right bundle branch block* is a defect in the electrical conduction through the ventricles. With a blockage in the right bundle branch, the left ventricle is excited in time, while the excitation of the right ventricle takes a detour via the left bundle branch. The left bundle branch is made up of the smaller anterior fascicle with blood supply from the septal branches of the left anterior descending artery and the larger posterior fascicle that usually has dual blood supply from the left anterior descending artery and the right coronary artery. A *left anterior fascicular block* causes delayed activation of the anterosuperior left ventricular wall. A *left posterior fascicular block* is less common then a left anterior fascicular block and results in delayed activation of the inferoposterior left ventricular wall. Both hemiblocks are associated with coronary artery disease and therefore such patients should have a thorough preoperative evaluation. Complete *left bundle branch block* presents with a QRS complex of greater than 0.12 s and notched R waves in all leads. Incomplete left bundle branch block shows a similar pattern of wide R waves in all leads, but the QRS complex is 0.10–0.12 s. These two blocks are also associated with coronary artery disease.

Bifascicular heart block is defined as a hemiblock and right bundle branch block. This is also associated with coronary artery disease and may over time progress to complete heart block. Diagnosis of these blocks is made on electrocardiographic criteria (Surawicz et al. 2009). Indications for temporary transcutaneous pacing are presented in recent guidelines of the American Heart Society (Epstein et al. 2008). During administration of general anaesthesia, first-degree atrioventricular block with bifascicular block and first-degree atrioventricular block and left bundle branch block are recommended as elective indications for temporary pacing although there is little evidence to support the need for this approach.

A *third degree (complete or trifascicular) atrioventricular block* is present when there is no conduction from the atria to the ventricles. If the block is above the atrioventricular node the rate is 45–55 beats min^{-1} and the QRS complex is normal. If the block is below the atrioventricular node the heart rate will usually not exceed 30–40 beats min^{-1} and the QRS complex will be wide in all leads. This block should always be treated with a temporary or permanent pacemaker.

The *long QT syndrome* is a disorder of myocardial repolarization characterized by a prolonged QT interval on the electrocardiogram. This syndrome is associated with an increased risk of a characteristic life-threatening cardiac arrhythmia, known as torsades de pointes. It may be congenital or acquired. Because of the high mortality, treatment is essential. β-blockers shorten the QT interval in patients with long QT syndrome and decrease mortality. Other measures include lifestyle modification, correcting underlying causes, and placement of an implantable defibrillator.

Hereditary arrhythmogenic syndromes

In recent years, it has become evident that a number of cardiac rhythm disturbances are related to genetic alterations and can be inherited. These include congenital long QT-syndrome, Brugada syndrome,

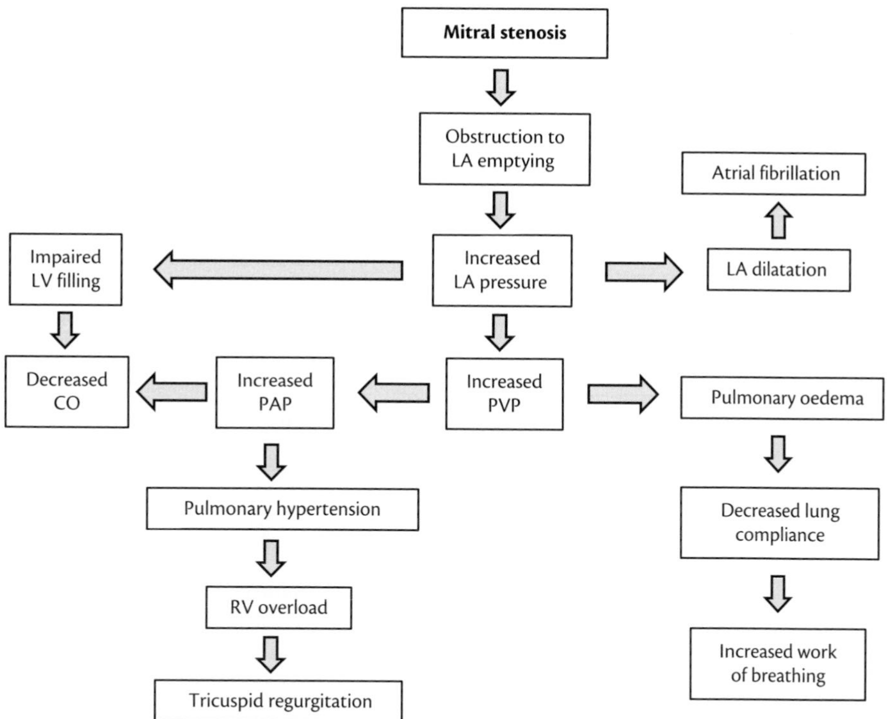

Figure 83.2 Mitral stenosis. CO, cardiac output; LA, left atrial; PAP, pulmonary arterial pressure; PVP, pulmonary venous pressure; RV, right ventricular.

congenital sick sinus syndrome, arrhythmogenic right ventricular dysplasia cardiomyopathy and catecholaminergic polymorphic ventricular tachycardia. These are life-threatening entities and a cause of sudden death which can be prevented by defibrillator implantation.

Valvular heart disease

Valvular heart disease refers to any disease process involving any valve of the heart: the mitral and aortic valve on the left side and the tricuspid and pulmonary valve on the right side of the heart. Valvular heart disease may be as a result of a stenosis or an insufficiency of the valve, or both. It is characterized by pressure or volume overload (or both) to the atria and the ventricles. It is this overload that will be responsible for the symptomatology of the disease. Valvular heart disease may be congenital or acquired. Mitral and aortic valve disease are more common than tricuspid and pulmonary valve disease because of the higher pressure ranges they experience (Maganti et al. 2010).

Mitral valve

Mitral stenosis

Worldwide, rheumatic fever still is the major cause of mitral stenosis. However, in the more developed countries, mitral valve disease mainly occurs in older patients as a result of a degenerative cause with a reported incidence between 0.02% and 0.2%.

The normal mitral valve area is 4–6 cm^2. Once the orifice decreases below 2 cm^2 the pressure gradient between left atrium and left ventricle has to increase to maintain adequate filling of the left ventricle. This pressure overload has a number of pathophysiological consequences resulting in a decreased left ventricular output and an increased right ventricular afterload and right ventricular failure (see Fig. 83.2).

Basically, the narrowed mitral orifice interferes with the filling of the left ventricle, and any additional negative influence on normal left ventricular filling will aggravate symptoms of mitral stenosis. These include tachycardia (shortening of the left ventricular diastolic filling time) and loss of the atrial contribution to the filling of the left ventricle such as with atrial fibrillation.

Mitral regurgitation

Mitral regurgitation is the most common valvular disease and occurs when normal coaptation of the mitral leaflets is lost. The prevalence of moderate to severe mitral regurgitation is estimated at 2.5%. Two major distinct entities of mitral regurgitation can be identified: *functional mitral regurgitation*, which is the consequence of a disturbance of the complex interaction of the different subunits of the mitral valve and *structural mitral regurgitation*, which is the consequence of structural changes of the valve apparatus (McCarthy et al. 2010; Ghoreishi et al. 2011; Michelena et al., 2011; Di Mauro et al. 2013).

Mitral regurgitation results in a large volume load on the left atrium. In acute mitral regurgitation such as with rupture of the chordae tendineae, this volume overload suddenly increases left atrial pressures with subsequent increases in pulmonary artery pressures and ultimately even pulmonary oedema. In chronic mitral regurgitation, the left ventricle is able to develop adaptive mechanisms for the volume overload. These include left ventricular and left atrial dilatation and eccentric left ventricular hypertrophy. Initially, left ventricular function is preserved, but with the progression of the disease, left ventricular dysfunction will develop. The ejection fraction tends to underestimate the functional consequence of the mitral valve disease as part of the ejection fraction is not pumped forward but back into the left atrium. As a result of increased left ventricular filling pressures and decreased

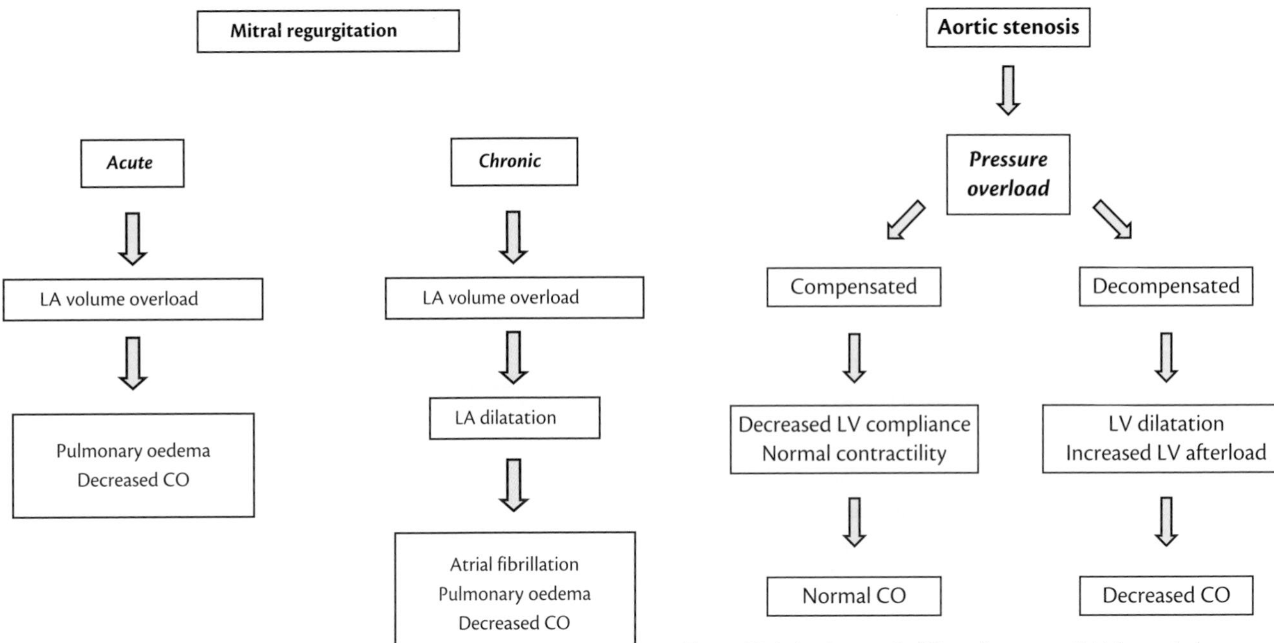

Figure 83.3 Mitral regurgitation. CO, cardiac output; LA, left atrial.

Figure 83.4 Aortic stenosis. CO, cardiac output; LV, left ventricular.

compliance of the left ventricle, diastolic dysfunction is present (McCarthy et al. 2010; Ghoreishi et al. 2011; Michelena et al., 2011; Di Mauro et al. 2013) (Fig. 83.3).

Aortic valve

Aortic stenosis

Although rheumatic disease has become a rare condition in the Western population, it remains the most common cause of aortic stenosis worldwide. In Western populations, calcific degenerative disease is the leading cause of aortic stenosis. A normal aortic valve has an orifice of 2–4 cm^2. Severe aortic stenosis is diagnosed if one or more of the following features are present: a blood flow velocity through the aortic valve greater than 4 m s^{-1}, a mean pressure gradient greater than 50 mm Hg, an aortic valve orifice less than 1 cm^2, and an aortic valve orifice *vs* left ventricular outflow tract area ratio of less than 0.25.

The narrowing of the valve orifice increases the resistance of blood flow through the valve. This results in an increased pressure gradient across the valve. The left ventricle adapts to this increased pressure gradient with a concentric hypertrophy and consequently a decreased compliance and elevated left ventricular filling pressures. Initially these compensating mechanisms allow for preservation of a normal stroke volume but with progression of the disease left atrial pressure will increase, ventricular dilation will occur and ultimately left ventricular failure will develop (Horstkotte and Loogen 1988; Torsher et al. 1998; Kertai et al. 2004) (Fig. 83.4). The atrial contribution to left ventricular filling becomes increasingly more important and may account for up to 40% of the cardiac output. Maintenance of sinus rhythm is therefore mandatory in these patients.

Aortic regurgitation

Worldwide, rheumatic fever still is the main cause of aortic regurgitation. However, this condition has become rare in the western hemisphere, where congenital or degenerative diseases constitute the main causes. Patients with aortic stenosis often also have aortic regurgitation.

Structural changes of the cusps or the aortic annulus (or both) will impair efficient closure of the aortic valve resulting in regurgitation of a part of the stroke volume back into the left ventricle during diastole. This provokes a volume load to the left ventricle resulting in an increased left ventricular end-diastolic volume and wall stress. In severe aortic regurgitation, the regurgitant fraction can amount up to 60% of the stroke volume. To maintain cardiac output, heart rate is increased. Bradycardia is poorly tolerated in aortic regurgitation, as an increased diastolic time also implies an increased regurgitation time. The combination of increased heart rate resulting in a shorter coronary perfusion time, increased end-diastolic pressure, and low diastolic aortic pressure, predispose to myocardial ischaemia which further impairs myocardial function. In chronic, slowly progressive aortic regurgitation, however, oxygen balance is maintained for a long period as a result of dilatation of the left ventricle and consequent decrease in wall tension (Dujardin et al. 1999; Goldbarg and Halperin 2008) (Fig. 83.5).

Mild to moderate aortic regurgitation is well tolerated and these patients are mostly asymptomatic. Even severe aortic regurgitation can remain unrecognized for a long period.

Symptoms differ between an acute aortic regurgitation such as occurring after trauma or aortic dissection (acute chest pain, shortness of breath, cardiogenic shock) and chronic aortic regurgitation (initially asymptomatic, later exertional dyspnoea or at rest, tachycardia, palpitations caused by arrhythmias and angina). See Figure 83.5.

Tricuspid and pulmonary valve

Tricuspid and pulmonary valve disease only rarely cause significant problems because of the low pressure systems they exist in. Tricuspid stenosis is almost always caused by rheumatic fever and is then frequently associated with mitral stenosis. Tricuspid regurgitation is in most cases caused by dilation of the right ventricle. This may result from left-sided heart disease, including mitral valve

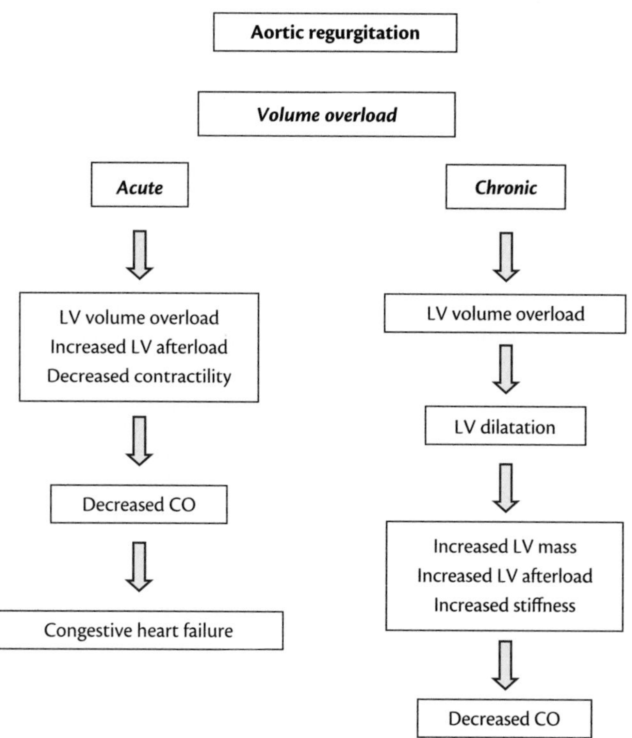

Figure 83.5 Aortic regurgitation. CO, cardiac output; LV, left ventricular.

abnormalities and cardiomyopathy and right ventricular dysfunction secondary to pulmonary disease or pulmonary hypertension (Hung 2010; Irwin 2010).

The most common cause of pulmonary valve stenosis is congenital heart disease, but it may also occur as a consequence of rheumatic heart disease. Pulmonary hypertension is the most common cause of pulmonary regurgitation. Indeed, most frequently, pulmonary regurgitation is not a primary process but secondary to, for example, pulmonary hypertension or dilated cardiomyopathy.

Heart failure

Heart failure can be subdivided into four stages based on the presence of risk factors, underlying heart disease, and symptoms. Stage A refers to the presence of risk factors for heart failure but without any structural heart disease. Stage B refers to the presence of structural heart disease but still without symptoms. Stage C is the presence of structural heart disease with symptoms of heart failure and stage D refers to the presence of refractory heart failure.

From a pathophysiological point of view, heart failure can be subdivided into systolic and diastolic ventricular dysfunction. Systolic heart failure is defined as a decrease in contractility of the ventricle such that it is not capable of providing adequate blood supply to the tissues. Usually this occurs when left ventricular ejection fraction drops below 40%. However, 30–50% of patients present with heart failure in the presence of a preserved left ventricular ejection fraction. If signs and symptoms of congestive heart failure (exercise intolerance, fatigue, dyspnoea, and pulmonary oedema) develop in a patient with normal or near-normal systolic function, then diastolic heart failure is present. The pathophysiological basis of diastolic heart failure is related to an impairment of the normal filling pattern of the ventricle and may range from impaired myocardial relaxation to restrictive filling (Pirracchio et al. 2007).

In the perioperative period, patients with chronic heart failure may develop acute decompensation as a result of the withdrawal of medication and the occurrence of perioperative haemodynamic disturbances. The primary target for the treatment of acute heart failure is to restore proper tissue perfusion and to correct the causes of the exacerbations such as acute rhythm disturbances, myocardial ischaemia, hypertensive crisis, and hypotension.

Congenital heart disease

Congenital heart disease (CHD) has a worldwide incidence of 0.8% and is the most common inborn defect, accounting for almost a third of all congenital diseases (Hoffman 1995). Between 10% and 15% of affected children have associated congenital anomalies of the skeletal, genitourinary, or gastrointestinal system. There are numerous cardiac defects, presenting in so many forms and combinations that even specialized physicians occasionally struggle over terminology and correct diagnosis.

The introduction of the 'sequential segmental analysis' technique, a diagnostic approach almost entirely based on cardiac imaging of anatomical landmarks, and less on the detailed knowledge of cardiac embryogenesis, has facilitated the interpretation of complex cardiac malformations and certainly made this field of expertise more accessible to non-specialists (Anderson et al. 1984). The basic concept of this technique, also referred to as the WYSIWYD approach ('What You See Is What You Determine'), is that any heart can be considered in three segments, that is, atrial chambers, ventricular mass, and great arteries, and categorized by a sequential description of the arrangement of the component segments and their interconnections (Fig. 83.6).

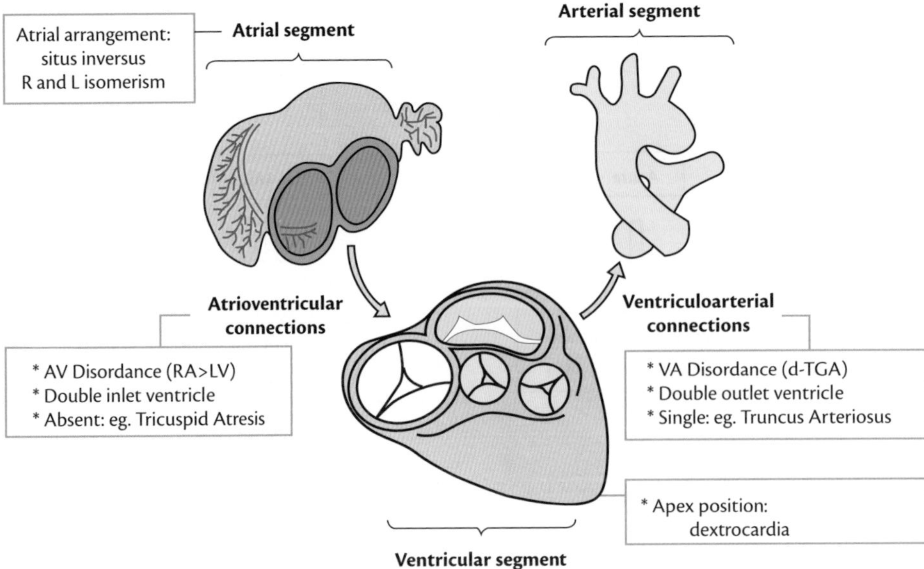

Figure 83.6 Three segments of the heart analysed sequentially. d-TGA, d-type transposition of the great arteries.
This figure was published in *Diagnosis and Management of Adult Congenital Heart Disease*. Gatzoluis, MA *et al.* Copyright © Elsevier 2003.

In children undergoing non-cardiac surgery, the presence of congenital heart disease is known to increase morbidity and mortality (Ramamoorthy et al. 2010). A large study on the incidence of perioperative cardiac arrest in children revealed that 88% of cases had CHD (Flick et al. 2007). High risk factors were age less than 1 year, premature birth, severe cyanosis, poorly compensated heart failure, pulmonary hypertension, complex cardiac lesions, multiple coexisting diseases, and invasive and emergency surgery. While the majority of arrests occurred in the setting of cardiac surgery, in non-cardiac surgery 27% of reported arrests were in CHD patients. In neonates and infants, the presence of CHD is associated with a two-fold increase in mortality from non-cardiac surgery (Baum et al. 2000). The four highest risk groups are infants with functional single ventricle, suprasystemic pulmonary hypertension, left ventricular outflow tract obstruction, and dilated cardiomyopathy (Friesen and Williams 2008; Ramamoorthy et al. 2010; Lynch et al. 2011). It is currently recommended that such patients be treated in highly specialized paediatric centres (Sumpelmann and Osthaus 2007).

As a result of significant advances in prenatal diagnosis, cardiac surgery, interventional cardiology, and perioperative medicine, about 90% of infants with CHD are expected to reach adulthood today (Hoffman et al. 2004). This success story has resulted in a growing cohort of young adults with CHD who now even outnumber the paediatric CHD population. Most of these patients with 'grown-up' congenital heart disease (GUCHD) require lifelong cardiac follow-up and deserve specific attention when they present for surgical, interventional, or obstetric procedures for which anaesthesia care is needed (Lovell 2004). Perioperative morbidity and mortality are increased in adults with repaired or palliated CHD but few guidelines exist on perioperative management of these patients (Fleisher et al. 2007).

This section will focus on anaesthesia for non-cardiac procedures in adults with congenital heart disease. For paediatric anaesthesia the reader is referred to excellent reviews on non-cardiac surgery in children with CHD (Sumpelmann and Osthaus 2007; Gottlieb and Andropoulos 2013). Still it is impossible to cover all congenital heart defects or clinical scenarios which an anaesthetist may encounter in this high-risk GUCHD population. A common approach to classify CHD is the functional distinction between non-cyanotic and cyanotic defects, or by separating simple from complex lesions. However, patients may present at various stages of their disease with untreated, palliated, or corrected lesions, and migrate from one category to another. They may or may not have residual defects or develop late-onset complications from the initial surgery. All these factors will modify an individual patient's risk and influence the perioperative management plan. For the purpose of this chapter, a pathophysiology-based approach, identifying four principal types of flow abnormality, offers the more appropriate framework to discuss any of these prevailing clinical scenarios.

Pathophysiology of congenital heart disease

The pathophysiological consequences of CHD relate primarily to the resultant type of flow abnormality as caused by (1) an obstruction, (2) a regurgitation, (3) a shunting lesion, (4) a mixing defect, and any combination of these.

The effects of a simple *obstruction* or *regurgitation* are largely comparable to those described for acquired disease. Congenital narrowing of left or right ventricular outflow can occur at the subvalvular, valvular, and supravalvular level and will produce pressure overload and ventricular hypertrophy (Rhodes et al. 2008). More distal lesions cause additional maldistribution of flow such as in coarctation of the aorta or distal pulmonary artery stenosis. Isolated regurgitant lesions rarely occur as a primary congenital defect except for Ebstein's malformation of the tricuspid valve. Because regurgitant lesions of the atrioventricular valves frequently result from an abnormal development of the endocardial cushion, these patients usually present with additional shunts at the atrial or ventricular level, or both. This particular malformation can present with variable degrees of severity and is frequently associated with trisomy 21.

Left-to-right shunts

Left-to-right shunts are the most common lesions representing more than half of CHD cases. In the absence of other lesions, blood will pass through open communications along a pressure gradient and follow the path of least resistance. In patent ductus arteriosus or isolated septal defects, shunting occurs from the high-pressure systemic to the low-pressure pulmonary circulation. The recirculation of blood in the low-pressure circuit causes volume overload of the right ventricle and pulmonary circulation, which if sufficiently large, will produce and manifest as congestive heart failure. Shunts through atrial septal defects tend to become larger with age because of loss of compliance and higher filling pressures in the left ventricle (Sommer et al. 2008). Symptoms often develop only in the fourth or fifth decade unless paradoxical emboli lead to the diagnosis. With large ventricular septal defects, direct exposure of the pulmonary arteries to the high systemic circulatory pressures in the left ventricle affects pulmonary vasomotor tone and augments vasoreactivity. If left untreated, the pulmonary circulation under systemic pressure will undergo morphological changes that ultimately result in irreversible and fixed pulmonary hypertension (Eisenmenger's syndrome). Whenever pressures in the pulmonary vascular system exceed systemic pressures, the shunt direction is reversed [right-to-left (R–L)] and cyanosis develops.

Right-to-left shunts

Right-to-left shunts do not typically produce congestive heart failure but instead cause cyanosis and an increased risk of paradoxical emboli. For R–L shunts to occur, there must be an increased resistance to flow in the pulmonary circulation forcing blood towards the systemic circulation through an open communication. In children, tetralogy of Fallot is the most common defect causing R–L shunting through a ventricular septal defect as a result of obstructions at the right ventricular infundibulum and pulmonary valve. Pulmonary hypertension at systemic pressure levels also causes R–L shunting and is the primary cause of R-L shunting in adults (Eisenmenger's syndrome).

Mixing

Mixing lesions encompass the more complex defects such as d-type transposition of the great arteries (d-TGA), truncus arteriosus, and all univentricular hearts. In d-TGA, the parallel arrangement of pulmonary and systemic flow is only compatible with life if there is a mixing chamber connecting both circuits. If not, an urgent intervention is performed to create an atrial septal defect (Rashkind procedure). In patients who only have a single functional ventricle connecting to either the systemic or pulmonary systems, patency of the ductus arteriosus is of vital importance to guarantee perfusion through both circuits. In all of these patients the obligatory mixing of desaturated and saturated blood causes cyanosis of which the degree depends on the ratio of pulmonary to systemic flow as determined by the relative resistances in systemic and pulmonary vascular beds. Surgical repair is performed as soon as possible in these neonates to convert the parallel circuitry into a serial system. Patients with univentricular hearts require a specific series of interventions to achieve this goal. The single (right or left) ventricle is connected to the systemic arterial system and the returning systemic venous blood is directed passively over the pulmonary arterial system. This transformation is performed in two separate procedures connecting the superior vena cava to the pulmonary artery first (Glenn or Hemi-Fontan procedure), followed by a second step to also connect the inferior vena cava with the pulmonary artery. Francis Fontan was the first to demonstrate that this haemodynamic configuration, in which there is no subpulmonary ventricle, is compatible with life, provided that pulmonary vascular tone remains low (Fontan and Baudet 1971).

Preoperative risk assessment and preparation

About 25% of adults with CHD survive into adulthood without surgical or interventional cardiac treatment but the vast majority have undergone a cardiac procedure at the time they present for non-cardiac surgery (Cannesson et al. 2009). Management of CHD patients requires insight into (1) the primary cardiac lesion, (2) the type of cardiac surgical or interventional procedure(s) performed, (3) the presence of residual defects or sequelae, (4) the current physical status (i.e. balanced *vs* unbalanced), (5) the effects of surgery or pregnancy on their pathophysiological condition, and (6) the presence of co-morbidity. A complete history and physical examination is always required and available technical and laboratory data should be collected and reviewed. In the ACC/AHA 2007 Guidelines on perioperative cardiovascular evaluation and care for non-cardiac surgery, a comprehensive work of 62 pages, only half a page is dedicated to the subject of congenital heart disease (Fleisher et al. 2007). Many of the general principles of risk assessment in this document also apply for CHD, with stratification according to clinical predictors and invasiveness of surgery being the primary determinants in the framework. However, it is increasingly clear that even simple congenital heart lesions can be associated with long-term complications and CHD in adults should be viewed as a systemic condition with associated multiorgan disease (Khairy and Landzberg 2008). Several factors unique to this population must be considered, such as the presence and magnitude of shunts, valvular lesions, dysrhythmias, pulmonary vascular disease, cyanosis, prosthetic material, and the consequences of an extraordinary haemodynamic condition such as a systemic right ventricle or absent subpulmonary ventricle (Fontan circulation), see Box 83.4. There are no large studies to rely on when it comes to quantifying perioperative risk associated with these specific conditions. Importantly, risk may also be increased by disease in other systems that can either be co-incident or related to the patient's congenital syndrome (metabolic, renal, pulmonary disease).

In general, *cardiac medication* should be continued throughout the perioperative period. Patients with shunts or conduits receive antiplatelet therapy while others, for example, patients with mechanical cardiac valves, are treated with vitamin K antagonists. According to the most recent guidelines, vitamin K antagonists should be stopped for 5 days before surgery and resumed between 12 and 24 h after surgery when there is adequate haemostasis (Douketis et al.

Box 83.4 Independent predictors of perioperative complications in CHD

- Pulmonary hypertension
- Dysrhythmias
- Ventricular dysfunction
- Arterial desaturation (<85%)
- Polycythaemia (haematocrit >55%).

2012). Bridging anticoagulant therapy with unfractioned or low-molecular weight heparin is recommended in patients at high risk for thromboembolism. Aspirin should not be stopped around the time of surgery for patients at high risk for thromboembolic events. *Premedication* is often indicated to control anxiety and oxygen consumption but should be used with caution in cyanotic patients and in patients with pulmonary hypertension. Longer periods of starvation should be avoided in cyanotic and in shunt-dependent patients who poorly tolerate hypovolaemia.

Patients with *cyanotic heart disease* have an increased risk for intravascular thrombosis as a result of secondary polycythaemia and high blood viscosity. Normovolaemic haemodilution should be considered when the haematocrit exceeds 60%, and phlebotomy may be useful above 65% though carefully balancing the beneficial effect on blood rheology against the reduction in blood oxygen content (Khairy et al. 2007). Iron deficiency is common and is an independent predictor of thrombosis in patients with Eisenmenger syndrome (Ammash and Warnes 1996). Paradoxically, cyanotic patients are also at increased risk for major perioperative bleeding because of abnormalities in platelet function and coagulation pathways. Of particular risk is thoracic surgery where diffuse bleeding may occur as a result of marked neovascularization and numerous collaterals between systemic and pulmonary vessels.

Pulmonary hypertension defined as a mean pulmonary artery pressure greater than 25 mm Hg is a known risk factor for perioperative morbidity and mortality (Ramakrishna et al. 2005; Lai et al. 2007). In CHD patients, pulmonary hypertension may arise from left heart disease or pulmonary venous obstruction but the primary cause in this group is a large systemic to pulmonary shunt, that is, category 1.3.2 pulmonary hypertension according to the new WHO classification (McLaughlin et al. 2009). Eisenmenger complex has become less prevalent because cardiac repair is performed early in childhood nowadays precisely to avoid this dramatic development. Still, patients who underwent surgery in the era when definitive surgery was performed late or patients born in regions where cardiac surgery for infants is not readily accessible may present with this unfavourable haemodynamic condition. It is characterized by pulmonary vascular resistance higher than 10 Wood units with a bidirectional or R–L shunt. The pulmonary vascular system has become unresponsive to vasodilators and the balance between systemic and pulmonary circulation, hence the direction and amount of shunting, is strongly dependent on changes in systemic vascular resistance. Sudden decreases in systemic vascular resistance as a result of general anaesthesia or extensive neuraxial block can augment R–L shunting. In obstetrics, the presence of pulmonary hypertension is associated with a maternal mortality of 30% and the incidence of fetal death has been reported to be as high as 50% if maternal arterial saturation is less than 85% or if haematocrit exceeds 65% (Presbitero et al. 1994).

Both left- and right-sided *heart failure* are common in CHD and add to perioperative risk. The management is similar to acquired forms of heart failure and optimization of treatment in the preoperative period is an absolute necessity. Of particular interest is failure of the systemic right ventricle in patients with congenitally corrected or atrially switched TGA and in hypoplastic left heart syndrome, which remains a poorly understood phenomenon.

Atrial and ventricular dysrhythmias are frequent in GUCHD either as a primary feature of the congenital lesion or as a consequence of surgical repair and palliation. Atrial surgery and atrial distension are associated with supraventricular dysrhythmias in 20–45% of patients. Ventricular dysrhythmias are often the result of previous ventriculotomy or develop secondary to heart failure. A considerable number of patients may present with intracardiac defibrillators.

Current guidelines on the prevention of *infective endocarditis* have become far more restrictive with regard to the use of preoperative prophylactic antibiotics. For CHD patients, only those with the highest risk, that is, (1) previous endocarditis, (2) cyanotic CHD that is unrepaired or palliated with shunts or conduits, (3) prosthetic material or devices during the first 6 months after the procedure, and (4) partially repaired CHD with residual defects close to the site of prosthetic material, should receive prophylaxis and only for procedures likely to produce bacteraemia, such as dental, oral, respiratory tract, genitourinary and gastrointestinal surgery (Wilson et al. 2007). CHD cardiologists are concerned about the scientific basis of these guidelines and question their safety (Di Filippo et al. 2012).

Anaesthesia and intraoperative management

There are no evidence-based recommendations regarding anaesthetic techniques for patients with CHD undergoing non-cardiac surgery. A pathophysiology-based approach and adherence to appropriate haemodynamic objectives is more important than the selection of a specific anaesthetic drug or technique. Lesion-specific anatomy and physiology, degree of severity, and the clinical stage (untreated, palliated, corrected) in which CHD presents, and the physical condition of the patient and the planned intervention compose the primary determinants for individual decision-making. Adults who underwent complete anatomical repair without sequelae and no functional deterioration can be managed with conventional approaches. In contrast, patients with complex CHD facing moderate to major surgery require specific and specialized management. Some excellent reviews have been written on this subject (Lovell 2004; Cannesson et al. 2009; Seal et al. 2011).

Most general *anaesthetic drugs and techniques* induce mild vasodilation in the arterial and venous compartment and cause a slight degree of myocardial depression. This is partly because they decrease sympathetic tone. Vasodilation is well tolerated in most cardiac patients because it promotes forward systemic flow. The important exceptions to this rule are defects associated with obstructions and defects associated with R–L shunts, which may rapidly deteriorate with sympatholysis and systemic vasodilation. Because etomidate has fewer direct effects on cardiac function and ketamine better preserves sympathetic tone, these drugs have been advocated as more appropriate induction agents for such patients. Alternatively, vasopressors such as phenylephrine or noradrenaline (norepinephrine) can be used to counteract the vasodilatory effects of propofol or volatile anaesthetics. When neuraxial anaesthesia is considered, excessive systemic vasodilation should be avoided in patients with R–L shunts and obstructions. Furthermore, the presence of coagulation abnormalities secondary to the disease or its treatment ought to be excluded.

The effect of positive pressure ventilation also varies with the specific pathophysiological status and can suddenly disrupt a delicate homeostatic balance in complex heart disease. Again, conditions associated with reduced systolic left ventricular function and L–R shunts in general benefit from gentle positive pressure ventilation as it reduces left ventricular afterload. The concomitant increase in pulmonary vascular resistance and the reduction in systemic venous return however is unfavourable for patients with R–L shunts and forms a particular challenge for patients with Fontan circulation.

The decision to use more *extensive (invasive) monitoring*, in addition to the obligatory standard equipment, should be based on an individual, case-specific risk:benefit analysis. Intravenous lines can be hard to establish in patients with CHD because of previous repetitive vessel access. In patients with shunts and mixing lesions it is of utmost importance to exclude air from all intravenous lines and maximize the efforts to avoid systemic air embolism.

Arterial lines are often of great value but should not be placed on the side of a previous systemic-to-pulmonary shunt or distal to an aortic coarctation. Central venous catheters are considered relatively safe, particularly when ultrasound is used for placement. Patients with CHD often have abnormal anatomical variations or underwent surgical modification of central venous return. A persistent left superior vena cava is more frequent in CHD and may drain directly into the left atrium in 10–20% of cases (Povoski et al. 2011). In patients with cava-pulmonary anastomoses, a catheter in the jugular or subclavian vein will not provide central venous pressure but pulmonary artery pressures instead. Here, the decision to insert a central line should never be taken lightly because venous thrombosis has devastating consequences for such patients.

The threshold to use pulmonary artery catheters should be high as they expose CHD patients to additional risks. If cardiac output measurements are considered an essential part of the haemodynamic management plan, transpulmonary thermodilution using central arterial catheters equipped with a thermistor may offer a valid alternative (Wouters et al. 2005). Transoesophageal echocardiography is undoubtedly the best available tool to monitor complex cases but it requires a high level of expertise and experience in CHD.

Near-infrared spectroscopy is gradually being accepted as a non-invasive means to follow trends in venous oxygen saturation and may be of particular value to monitor changes in oxygen supply/demand in the setting of complex circulatory physiology (Moerman and Wouters 2010). Dynamic preload variables such as pulse pressure variation have shown superior to static venous pressure measurements and could also be useful adjuncts here. Their precise clinical value yet needs to be confirmed in this population.

The two most challenging CHD scenarios any anaesthetist may encounter in a non-cardiac practice are Eisenmenger syndrome and single ventricle physiology after Fontan repair. Eisenmenger syndrome is an end-stage disease that is now less prevalent because of preventive surgical strategies but life expectancy of Fontan patients has steadily grown and the number of adults presenting for non-cardiac surgery or labour and delivery will continue to increase in the next few years. Circulatory homeostasis in Fontan patients depends on the maintenance of a minimum resistance to flow in the pulmonary vasculature that allows passage of systemic venous blood along a pressure gradient to the left atrium (there is no right ventricle to pump blood over the pulmonary vascular system). Factors that increase pulmonary vascular resistance will decrease flow, cause venous congestion and impair oxygenation. Strict control of metabolic homeostasis, analgesia and normothermia are a prerequisite but postural changes and positive pressure ventilation can also affect the delicate haemodynamic balance and should be closely monitored and adjusted. Communication with the surgical team about the patient-specific pathophysiology and associated risks may lead to modifications in the surgical approach. For example, while laparoscopic interventions are generally considered less invasive than open laparotomies for abdominal surgery, the installation of a pneumoperitoneum is a significant haemodynamic challenge for patients with Fontan circulation. Adherence to low insufflation pressures and avoidance of extreme Trendelenburg position are required to avoid haemodynamic collapse but such restrictions degrade the surgical conditions to the extent that only experienced surgeons can succeed.

In patients with chronic pulmonary hypertension, haemodynamic management also centres on the control of pulmonary vascular resistance. Acute exacerbations of PHT can cause right ventricular failure or enhance R–L shunting and cyanosis if shunt defects exist. Besides the well-known measures to avoid increases in pulmonary vascular resistance, pulmonary vasodilators, that is, vasodilators selectively administered via inhalation such as nitric oxide and epoprostenol, should be considered and be readily available. Systemic vasodilation however has to be avoided or treated at all cost. Indeed, the ratio of systemic to pulmonary vascular resistance determines the direction and magnitude of the shunt and is an important determinant of right ventricular perfusion. In patients with Eisenmenger syndrome, pulmonary vascular tone is not responsive to vasodilators and systemic vascular tone is the only component that can be modified pharmacologically to control systemic vascular resistance/pulmonary vascular resistance ratio. Echocardiography is the undisputed monitoring tool to assess right ventricular function. The ratio of right-to-left ventricular dimension (normal RV < 0.6 LV size) and the position and motion of interatrial and interventricular septae are reliable parameters to assess right ventricular function and monitor ventricular interdependence.

Postoperative care

Patients with severe CHD or patients requiring high-risk surgery should be admitted to a postoperative intensive care unit with experience in complex haemodynamic management. An increased incidence of major bleeding, dysrhythmias, and thromboembolic events should be anticipated in the postoperative setting. Admission should be planned well in advance for patients with significant intracardiac shunting, heart failure, pulmonary hypertension, functional single ventricle, cyanosis, coagulation abnormalities, and major arrhythmias.

Conclusion

The number of adults with CHD continues to grow and at some stage in their life a substantial proportion will need a non-cardiac surgical intervention or a procedure for which anaesthesia care is needed. This group has an increased risk for perioperative complications but there are no evidence-based guidelines on anaesthesia management. This is partly as a result of the complexity of the disease, the variety of defects and pathophysiological consequences, and the various clinical stages, ranging from untreated to palliated and repaired defects, in which patients may present. Anaesthetists should understand the pathophysiology and anaesthetic implications of the cardiac lesion. Proper risk assessment also includes knowledge of previous interventions, current functional reserve and co-morbidities. The perioperative plan, including risk reduction strategies, possible modifications of the surgical approach, and postoperative surveillance should be discussed with cardiologists, surgeons, and intensivists in order to optimize outcome in this challenging population.

Declaration of interest

None declared.

References

Ammash N, Warnes CA. Cerebrovascular events in adult patients with cyanotic congenital heart disease. *J Am Coll Cardiol* 1996; **28**: 768–72

Anderson RH, Becker AE, Freedom RM, *et al.* Sequential segmental analysis of congenital heart disease. *Pediatr Cardiol* 1984; **5**: 281–7

Baum VC, Barton DM, Gutgesell HP. Influence of congenital heart disease on mortality after noncardiac surgery in hospitalized children. *Pediatrics*, 2000; **105**: 332–5

Blomström-Lundqvist C, Scheinman MM, Aliot EM, *et al.* ACC/AHA/ESC guidelines for the management of patients with supraventricular arrhythmias–executive summary: a report of the American College of Cardiology/American Heart Association Task Force on Practice Guidelines and the European Society of Cardiology Committee for Practice Guidelines (writing committee to develop guidelines for the management of patients with supraventricular arrhythmias). *Circulation* 2003; **108**: 1871–909

Cannesson M, Earing MG, Collange V, Kersten JR. Anesthesia for noncardiac surgery in adults with congenital heart disease. *Anesthesiology* 2009; **111**: 432–40

Chobanian AV, Bakris GL, Black HR, *et al.* Joint National Committee on Prevention, Detection, Evaluation, and Treatment of High Blood Pressure. National High Blood Pressure Education Program Coordinating Committee on Prevention, Detection, Evaluation, and Treatment of High Blood Pressure. *Hypertension* 2003; **42**: 1206–52

De Hert SG. Preoperative cardiovascular assessment in noncardiac surgery: an update. *Eur J Anaesthesiol* 2009; **26**: 449–57

Di Filippo S. Prophylaxis of infective endocarditis in patients with congenital heart disease in the context of recent modified guidelines. *Arch Cardiovasc Dis* 2012; **105**: 454–60

Di Mauro M, Gallina S, D'Amico MA, *et al.* Functional mitral regurgitation From normal to pathological anatomy of mitral valve. *Int J Cardiol* 2013; **163**: 242–8

Dobrzynski H, Boyett MR, Anderson R. New insights into pacemaker activity: promoting understanding of sick sinus syndrome. *Circulation* 2007; **115**: 1921–32

Douketis JD, Spyropoulos AC, Spencer FA, *et al.* Perioperative management of antithrombotic therapy: Antithrombotic Therapy and Prevention of Thrombosis, 9th ed: American College of Chest Physicians Evidence-Based Clinical Practice Guidelines. *Chest* 2012; **141**(2 Suppl): e326S–50S

Dujardin KS, Enriquez Sarano M, Schaff HV, Bailey KR, Seward JB, Tajik AJ. Mortality and morbidity of aortic regurgitation in clinical practice: a long-term follow-up study. *Circulation* 1999; **99**: 1851–7

Epstein AE, DiMarco JP, Ellenbogen KA, *et al.* ACC/AHA/HRS 2008 Guidelines for Device-Based Therapy of Cardiac Rhythm Abnormalities: a report of the American College of Cardiology/American Heart Association Task Force on Practice Guidelines (Writing Committee to Revise the ACC/AHA/NASPE 2002 Guideline Update for Implantation of Cardiac Pacemakers and Antiarrhythmia Devices): developed in collaboration with the American Association for Thoracic Surgery and Society of Thoracic Surgeons. *Circulation* 2008; **117**: e350–408

Fleisher LA, Beckman JA, Brown KA, *et al.* ACC/AHA 2007 guidelines on perioperative cardiovascular evaluation and care for noncardiac surgery: a report of the American College of Cardiology/American Heart Association Task Force on Practice Guidelines (Writing Committee to Revise the 2002 Guidelines on Perioperative Cardiovascular Evaluation for Noncardiac Surgery): developed in collaboration with the American Society of Echocardiography, American Society of Nuclear Cardiology, Heart Rhythm Society, Society of Cardiovascular Anesthesiologists, Society for Cardiovascular Angiography and Interventions, Society for Vascular Medicine and Biology, and Society for Vascular Surgery. *Circulation* 2007; **116**: e418–99

Fleisher LA, Beckman JA, Brown KA, *et al.* 2009 ACCF/AHA focused update on perioperative beta blockade incorporated into the ACC/AHA 2007 guidelines on perioperative cardiovascular evaluation and care for noncardiac surgery. *J Am Coll Cardiol* 2009; **54**: e13–e118

Fleisher LA, Fleischmann KE, Auerbach AD, *et al.* 2014 ACC/AHA guideline on perioperative cardiovascular evaluation and management of patients undergoing noncardiac surgery: a report of the American College of Cardiology/American Heart Association Task Force on practice guidelines. *J Am Coll Cardiol* 2014; **64**: e77–137

Flick RP, Sprung J, Harrison TE, *et al.* Perioperative cardiac arrests in children between 1988 and 2005 at a tertiary referral center: a study of 92,881 patients. *Anesthesiology* 2007; **106**: 226–37

Fontan F, Baudet E. Surgical repair of tricuspid atresia. *Thorax* 1971; **26**: 240–8

Friesen RH, Williams GD. Anesthetic management of children with pulmonary arterial hypertension. *Paediatr Anaesth* 2008; **18**: 208–16

Fuster V, Rydén LE, Cannom DS, *et al.* ACC/AHA/ESC 2006 Guidelines for the Management of Patients with Atrial Fibrillation: a report of the American College of Cardiology/American Heart Association Task Force on Practice Guidelines and the European Society of Cardiology Committee for Practice Guidelines (Writing Committee to Revise the 2001 Guidelines for the Management of Patients With Atrial Fibrillation): developed in collaboration with the European Heart Rhythm Association and the Heart Rhythm Society. *Circulation* 2006; **114**: e257–354

Fuster V, Rydén LE, Cannom DS, *et al.* 2011 ACCF/AHA/HRS focused updates incorporated into the ACC/AHA/ESC 2006 guidelines for the management of patients with atrial fibrillation: a report of the American College of Cardiology Foundation/American Heart Association Task Force on practice guidelines. *Circulation* 2011; **123**: e269–367

Ghoreishi M, Dawood M, Stauffer CE, Gammie JS. Mitral regurgitation: current trends in diagnosis and management. *Hosp Pract (Minneap)* 2011; **39**: 181–92

Giles TD, Berk BC, Black HR, *et al.* Expanding the definition and classification of hypertension. *J Clin Hypertens* 2005; **7**: 505–12

Giles TD, Materson BJ, Cohn JN, Kostis JB. Definition and classification of hypertension: an update. *J Clin Hypertens* 2009; **11**: 611–4

Goldbarg SH, Halperin JL. Aortic regurgitation: disease progression and management. *Nat Clin Pract Cardiovasc Med* 2008; **5**: 269–79

Gollob MH, Blier L, Brugada R, *et al.* Recommendations for the use of genetic testing in the clinical evaluation of inherited cardiac arrhythmias associated with sudden cardiac death: Canadian Cardiovascular Society/Canadian Heart Rhythm Society Joint Position Paper. *Can J Cardiol* 2011; **27**: 232–45

Gottlieb EA, Andropoulos DB. Anesthesia for the patient with congenital heart disease presenting for noncardiac surgery. *Curr Opin Anaesthesiol* 2013; **26**: 318–26

Hermann Haugaa K, Edvardsen T, Amlie JP. Prediction of life-threatening arrhythmias – still an unresolved problem. *Cardiology* 2011; **118**: 129–37

Hoffman JI. Incidence of congenital heart disease: I. Postnatal incidence. *Pediatr Cardiol* 1995; **16**: 103–13

Hoffman JI, Kaplan S, Liberthson RR. Prevalence of congenital heart disease. *Am Heart J* 2004; **147**: 425–39

Horstkotte D, Loogen F. The natural history of aortic valve stenosis. *Eur Heart J* 1988; **9**(Suppl E): 57–64

Hung J. The pathogenesis of functional tricuspid regurgitation. *Semin Thorac Cardiovasc Surg* 2010; **22**: 76–8

Irwin RB, Luckie M, Khattar RS. Tricuspid regurgitation: contemporary management of a neglected valvular lesion. *Postgrad Med J* 2010; **86**: 648–55

Kaufman ES. Mechanisms and clinical management on inherited channelopathies: long QT syndrome, Brugada syndrome, catecholaminergic polymorphic ventricular tachycardia, and short QT syndrome. *Heart Rhythm* 2009; **6**: S51–5

Kertai MD, Bountioukos M, Boersma E, *et al.* Aortic stenosis: an underestimated risk factor for perioperative complications in patients undergoing noncardiac surgery. *Am J Med* 2004; **116**: 8–13

Khairy P, Landzberg MJ. Adult congenital heart disease: toward prospective risk assessment of a multisystemic condition. *Circulation* 2008; **117**: 2311–2

Khairy P, Poirier N, Mercier LA. Univentricular heart. *Circulation* 2007; **115**: 800–12

Kikuya M, Hansen TW, Thijs L, *et al.* International Database on Ambulatory blood pressure monitoring in relation to Cardiovascular Outcomes Investigators. Diagnostic thresholds for ambulatory blood pressure monitoring based on 10-year cardiovascular risk. *Circulation* 2007; **115**: 2145–52

Kristensen SD, Knuuti J, Saraste A, *et al.* 2014 ESC/ESA Guidelines on non-cardiac surgery: cardiovascular assessment and management: The Joint Task Force on non-cardiac surgery: cardiovascular assessment and management of the European Society of Cardiology (ESC) and the European Society of Anaesthesiology (ESA). *Eur Heart J* 2014; **35**: 2383–431

Lai HC, Lai HC, Wang KY, *et al.* Severe pulmonary hypertension complicates postoperative outcome of non-cardiac surgery. *Br J Anaesth* 2007; **99**: 184–90

Lévy S. Classification system of atrial fibrillation. *Curr Opin Cardiol* 2000; **15**: 54–7

Lovell AT. Anaesthetic implications of grown-up congenital heart disease. *Br J Anaesth* 2004; **93**: 129–39

Lynch J, Pehora C, Holtby H, Schwarz SM, Taylor K. Cardiac arrest upon induction of anesthesia in children with cardiomyopathy: an analysis of incidence and risk factors. *Paediatr Anaesth* 2011; **21**: 951–7

Maganti K, Rigolin VH, Enriquez Sarano M, Bonow RO. Valvular heart disease: diagnosis and management. *Mayo Clin Proc* 2010; **85**: 483–500

Mancia G, Fagard R, Narkiewicz K, *et al.* 2013 2013 ESH/ESC Guidelines for the management of arterial hypertension: *Eur Heart J* 2013; **34**: 2159–219

McCarthy KP, Ring L, Rana BS. Anatomy of the mitral valve: understanding the mitral valve complex in mitral regurgitation. *Eur J Echocardiogr* 2010; **11**: 3–9

McLaughlin VV, Archer SL, Badesch DB, *et al.* ACCF/AHA 2009 expert consensus document on pulmonary hypertension: a report of the American College of Cardiology Foundation Task Force on Expert Consensus Documents and the American Heart Association: developed in collaboration with the American College of Chest Physicians, American Thoracic Society, Inc., and the Pulmonary Hypertension Association. *Circulation* 2009; **119**: 2250–94

Michelena HI, Topilsky Y, Suri R, Enriquez-Sarano M. Degenerative mitral valve regurgitation: understanding basic concepts and new developments. *Postgrad Med* 2011; **123**: 56–69

Mitchell LB, CCS Atrial Fibrillation Guidelines Committee. Canadian Cardiovascular Society atrial fibrillation guidelines 2010: prevention and treatment of atrial fibrillation following cardiac surgery. *Can J Cardiol* 2011; **27**: 91–7

Moerman A, Wouters P. Near-infrared spectroscopy (NIRS) monitoring in contemporary anesthesia and critical care. *Acta Anaesthesiol Belg* 2010; **61**: 185–94

O'Brie E, Asmar R, Beilin L, *et al.* European Society of Hypertension recommendations for conventional, ambulatory and home blood pressure measurement. *J Hypertens* 2003; **21**: 821–48

Park DS, Fishman GI. The cardiac conduction system. *Circulation* 2011; **123**: 904–15

Pirracchio R, Cholley B, De Hert S, Solal AC, Mebazaa A. Diastolic heart failure in anaesthesia and critical care. *Br J Anaesth* 2007, **98**: 707–21

Povoski SP, Khabiri H. Persistent left superior vena cava: review of the literature, clinical implications, and relevance of alterations in thoracic central venous anatomy as pertaining to the general principles of central venous access device placement and venography in cancer patients. *World J Surg Oncol* 2011; **9**: 173

Presbitero P, Somerville J, Stone S, Aruta E, Spiegelhalter D, Rabajoli F. Pregnancy in cyanotic congenital heart disease. Outcome of mother and fetus. *Circulation* 1994; **89**: 2673–6

Qureshi AI, Suri MF, Kirmani JF, Divani AA, Mohammad Y. Is prehypertension a risk factor for cardiovascular disease? *Stroke* 2005; **36**: 1859–63

Ramakrishna G, Sprung J, Ravi BS, *et al.* Impact of pulmonary hypertension on the outcomes of noncardiac surgery: predictors of perioperative morbidity and mortality. *J Am Coll Cardiol* 2005; **45**: 1691–9

Ramamoorthy C, Haberkern CM, Bhananker SM, *et al.* Anesthesia-related cardiac arrest in children with heart disease: data from the Pediatric Perioperative Cardiac Arrest (POCA) registry. *Anesth Analg* 2010; **110**: 1376–82

Rhodes JF, Hijazi ZM, Sommer RJ. Pathophysiology of congenital heart disease in the adult, part II. Simple obstructive lesions. *Circulation* 2008; **117**: 1228–37

Schimpf R, Veltmann C, Wolpert C, Borggrefe M. Arrhythmogenic hereditary syndromes: Brugada syndrome, long QT syndrome, short QT syndrome and CPVT. *Minerva Cardioangiol* 2010; **58**: 623–6

Seal R. Adult congenital heart disease. *Paediatr Anaesth* 2011; **21**: 615–22

Sommer RJ, Hijazi ZM, Rhodes JF, Jr., Pathophysiology of congenital heart disease in the adult: part I: Shunt lesions. *Circulation* 2008; **117**: 1090–9

Sumpelmann R, Osthaus WA. The pediatric cardiac patient presenting for noncardiac surgery. *Curr Opin Anaesthesiol* 2007; **20**: 216–20

Surawicz B, Childers R, Deal BJ, Gettes LS. AHA/ACCF/HRS recommendations for the standardization and interpretation of the electrocardiogram. Part III; intraventricular conduction disturbances. *J Am Coll Cardiol* 2009; **53**: 976–81

Torsher LC, Shub C, Rettke SR, Brown DL. Risk of patients with severe aortic stenosis undergoing noncardiac surgery. *Am J Cardiol* 1998; **81**: 448–52

Wilson W, Taubert KA, Gewitz M, *et al.* Prevention of infective endocarditis: guidelines from the American Heart Association: a guideline from the American Heart Association Rheumatic Fever, Endocarditis, and Kawasaki Disease Committee, Council on Cardiovascular Disease in the Young, and the Council on Clinical Cardiology, Council on Cardiovascular Surgery and Anesthesia, and the Quality of Care and Outcomes Research Interdisciplinary Working Group. *Circulation* 2007; **116**: 1736–54

Wouters PF, Quaghebeur B, Sergeant P, Van Hemelrijck J, Vandermeersch E. Cardiac output monitoring using a brachial arterial catheter during off-pump coronary artery bypass grafting. *J Cardiothorac Vasc Anesth* 2005; **19**: 160–4

Zanchetti A, Grassi G, Mancia G. When should antihypertensive drug treatment be initiated and to what levels should systolic blood pressure be lowered? A critical reappraisal. *J Hypertens* 2009; **27**: 923–34

CHAPTER 84

Haematological and coagulation disorders and anaesthesia

Herman G. D. Hendriks and Joost T. M. de Wolf

Anaemia

One of the most important functions of haemoglobin (Hb) is the delivery of oxygen to the organs. Besides the amount of Hb in blood and its saturation with oxygen, oxygen delivery is determined by the oxyhaemoglobin (HbO_2) dissociation curve and oxygen tension in the tissue.

Relationship of haemoglobin and oxygen

The oxygen-binding affinity of haemoglobin is graphically represented by a sinusoidal relationship between haemoglobin oxygen saturation (So_2) and the partial pressure of oxygen (Po_2). The relationship of haemoglobin and oxygen, expressed in the HbO_2 dissociation curve, enables both efficient loading of oxygen in the lungs at high Po_2 and efficient unloading in the tissues at low Po_2.

The P_{50}, normally 26 mm Hg, defines the oxygen tension at which 50% of the haemoglobin is saturated with oxygen. A rightward shift of the curve implies a decline of the binding affinity of haemoglobin for oxygen and a higher P_{50} resulting in a faster release of oxygen by the haemoglobin molecules. A left shift of the oxyhaemoglobin curve implies the opposite (see Fig. 84.1).

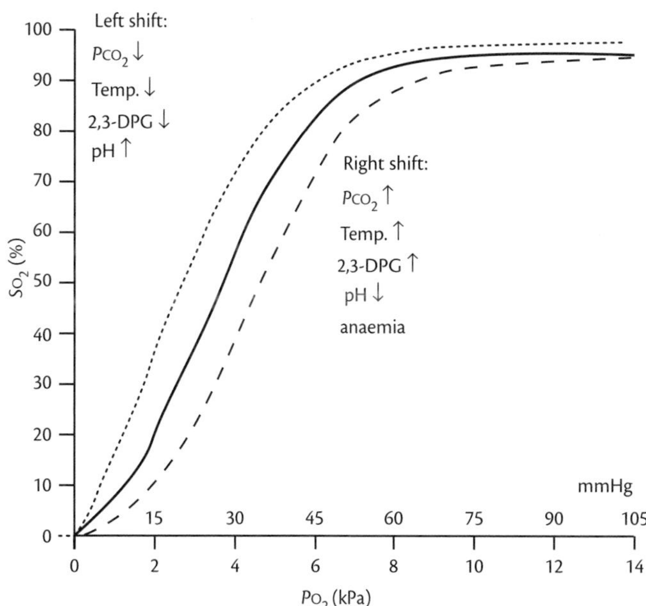

Figure 84.1 The oxygen–haemoglobin dissociation curve. A right shift implies a decline of the binding affinity of haemoglobin for oxygen and a higher P_{50} resulting in a faster release of oxygen by the haemoglobin molecules.

Energy, oxygen, and aerobic metabolism

The goal of aerobic metabolism is to generate energy by the conversion of nutrient fuels. This process consumes oxygen and produces carbon dioxide. The role of the circulatory system is to deliver oxygen and nutrient fuels to the tissues of the body and to remove carbon dioxide. The oxygen transport is characterized by four variables: (1) the oxygen concentration of the blood, (2) the delivery rate of oxygen in arterial blood, (3) the rate of oxygen uptake from the capillaries into the tissues, and (4) the fraction of oxygen in capillary blood that is taken up into the tissues.

Oxygen content of the blood

The O_2 content of the blood is the sum of O_2 bound to Hb and O_2 dissolved in plasma.

Haemoglobin-bound oxygen

The content of haemoglobin-bound O_2 (HbO_2) is determined by the following equation:

$$HbO_2(\text{ml dl}^{-1}) = 1.34 \times Hb \times So_2 \qquad (84.1)$$

Hb is the haemoglobin concentration in the blood (g dl^{-1}).
1.34 is the oxygen binding capacity of Hb (ml O_2 per gram of Hb).
So_2 is the saturation of Hb with oxygen expressed as a fraction.

This equation means that when Hb is fully saturated with O_2 ($So_2 = 1$) each gram of Hb will bind 1.34 ml of O_2.

Dissolved oxygen

The concentration amount of dissolved O_2 in blood (ml dl^{-1}) at normal body temperature is determined by the following equation:

$$\text{Dissolved } O_2(\text{ml dl}^{-1}) = 0.0225 \times Po_2(\text{kPa}) \quad (84.2)$$

From this equation it is concluded that only a minimal amount of O_2 is dissolved in the blood: if the Po_2 is 13.3 kPa only 3 ml O_2 is dissolved in 1 litre of blood.

Arterial oxygen content

The O_2 content of arterial blood (Ca_{O_2}) is the sum of HbO_2 and dissolved O_2 where So_2 and Po_2 of arterial blood are used (Sa_{O_2} and Pa_{O_2}), resulting in the following equation:

$$Ca_{O_2} = (1.34 \times \text{Hb} \times Sa_{O_2}) + (0.0225 \times Pa_{O_2}) \quad (84.3)$$

If the Hb = 15 g dl^{-1}, Sa_{O_2} = 0.98, Pa_{O_2} = 13.3 kPa, then, HbO_2 = 19.7 ml dl^{-1} (197 ml $litre^{-1}$), dissolved O_2 = 0.3 ml dl^{-1} (3 ml $litre^{-1}$), and therefore Ca_{O_2} = 200 ml $litre^{-1}$ (of which only 1.5% is dissolved in plasma). With a total blood volume of 5 litres, of which 25% is arterial, the O_2 content of the blood in the arterial circulation = (5 × 200) × 0.25 = 250 ml.

The importance of Hb becomes clear when we imagine what would happen if we depended solely on dissolved O_2 in plasma. Then a cardiac output of 93 litres min^{-1} would be necessary to deliver 250 ml min^{-1} oxygen for an adult at rest. This example clearly shows that Hb is a major determinant of the amount of O_2 in the blood.

Venous oxygen content

The O_2 content of venous blood (Cv_{O_2}) is calculated in the same way as for Ca_{O_2}, but now with venous values (Sv_{O_2} and Pv_{O_2}). These values are best measured in mixed venous blood from the pulmonary artery. Normal Sv_{O_2} = 0.73 and Pv_{O_2} = 5.33 kPa resulting in a Cv_{O_2} of approximately 150 ml $litre^{-1}$. With a total blood volume = 5 litres of which 75% is venous, the O_2 content of the blood in the venous circulation will be 3.75 × 150 = 562.5 ml.

Total oxygen content

The contribution of dissolved O_2 to the total amount of O_2 content is so small that it is usually left out of the equation. In practice, the O_2 content of blood is considered equivalent to Hb-bound O_2. Using the values derived in the previous sections on arterial and venous oxygen content we can determine that the total amount of oxygen in the blood is roughly 810 ml (250 + 560). Based on the assumption that an adult consumes 250 ml O_2 per min at rest the blood has enough oxygen for only 3–4 min of aerobic metabolism!

Oxygen delivery

$\dot{D}o_2$ is the amount of oxygen (in ml) that reaches the capillaries every minute, and is described in the following equation:

$$\dot{D}o_2 = \text{CO (litres min}^{-1}) \times Ca_{O_2}(\text{ml litre}^{-1}) \quad (84.4)$$

or

$$\dot{D}o_2 = \text{CO} \times 1.34 \times \text{Hb (g litre}^{-1}) \times So_2 \quad (84.5)$$

CO, cardiac output. For an adult at rest, $\dot{D}o_2$ = 1 litre min^{-1}.

Oxygen uptake

$\dot{V}o_2$ is the amount of O_2 (ml min^{-1}) which is taken up by the tissues every minute. As O_2 cannot be stored in the tissues, $\dot{V}o_2$ also describes the O_2 consumption, and can be calculated with the following formula:

$$\dot{V}o_2 = \text{CO (litres min}^{-1}) \times (Ca_{O_2} - Cv_{O_2}) \quad (84.6)$$

or

$$\dot{D}o_2 = \text{CO} \times 1.34 \times \text{Hb (g litre}^{-1}) \times (Sa_{O_2} - Sv_{O_2}) \quad (84.7)$$

For an adult at rest the $\dot{V}o_2$ = 250 ml min^{-1}.

Oxygen extraction ratio

The oxygen extraction ratio (O_2ER) describes the amount of oxygen taken up by the tissues relative to the amount of oxygen offered:

$$O_2ER = \dot{V}o_2 / \dot{D}o_2$$

The O_2ER is equivalent to $Sa_{O_2} - Sv_{O_2}$ when Sa_{O_2} is close to 1. Normally O_2ER is about 25% and might increase to a maximum level of about 50%.

If, as a result of bleeding and the resulting anaemia $\dot{D}o_2$ is decreasing, $\dot{V}o_2$ might remain unchanged as a result of an increase of the O_2ER. This situation is called compensated hypovolaemia. If, however, O_2ER reaches the maximum level of 50%, and $\dot{D}o_2$ is declining further, $\dot{V}o_2$ definitively decreases. This point, called critical $\dot{D}o_2$, is the start of anaerobic metabolism and the appearance of lactic acidosis, ischaemic electrocardiogram changes, neurological dysfunction, and hypovolaemic shock. An oxygen extraction of 50% [Sa_{O_2} (pulse oximeter) – Scv_{O_2} (blood from central venous catheter = 50%] can be used as an indication for transfusion of red blood cells.

Anaemia and adaptive mechanisms

There are several compensatory mechanisms to cope with anaemia.

1. With decreasing Hb, a redistribution of blood and oxygen takes place in favour of the vital tissues such as the myocardium and brain, and at the cost of mesenteric tissues, kidney, muscles, and skin. If these vital organs are affected, the patient is considered to be in hypovolaemic shock.
2. Shift of the oxyhaemoglobin dissociation curve to the right as a result of an increase in 2,3-diphosphoglycerate (2,3-DPG) in the erythrocyte, resulting in a decreased affinity of Hb for oxygen and an enhanced delivery of oxygen to the tissues. This right shift is enhanced by an increase in temperature and a decreased pH.

   These compensatory mechanisms are sufficient with a Hb concentration greater than 100 g $litre^{-1}$ (6 mmol $litre^{-1}$) and at rest; but with exertion and with a Hb concentration less than 100 g $litre^{-1}$ (6 mmol $litre^{-1}$) additional compensatory mechanisms are needed.

3. Decreased peripheral vascular resistance in order to increase cardiac output. It is associated with a decreased afterload, decreasing blood pressure, and increased preload, and results in an increased blood flow to the periphery.
4. Increased cardiac output in chronic anaemia especially by increasing cardiac stroke volume and in acute anaemia by increasing heart rate. The goal of increasing cardiac output is to enhance the amount of oxygen which can be extracted by the tissues.

Many of these adaptive responses are modified by the speed of blood loss and patient characteristics such as age, co-morbidity, pre-existing volume status, Hb concentration, and the use of medications with cardiac effects (β-blockers) or peripheral vascular effects (antihypertensives).

Blood loss triggers compensatory responses in order to maintain blood volume and tissue perfusion. The earliest response involves movement of interstitial fluid into the capillaries (transcapillary refill) resulting in haemodilution. Acute blood loss also leads to activation of the renin–angiotensin–aldosterone system in order to retain both sodium and water. This helps to replenish the interstitial fluid deficit created by transcapillary refill.

Symptoms and signs of anaemia

In addition to the Hb concentration, age and concurrent diseases affect the symptoms of anaemia. Common symptoms are fatigue, weakness, and reduced physical and mental endurance. Palpitations and a pounding pulse might be experienced with increased cardiac output, whereas postural hypotension, vertigo, and syncope are symptoms related to decreased peripheral vascular resistance. When compensatory mechanisms are insufficient to maintain organ oxygenation, dyspnoea, headache, tinnitus, sleeping disorders, lethargy, and reduced cognitive function can occur. With increasing chronic anaemia, the symptoms of cardiac failure can occur, with palpitations, oedema, and dyspnoea on exertion, or even at rest. And finally, organ damage might develop with an even further decrease of Hb concentration leading to, for instance, angina pectoris or transient cerebral ischaemia.

Management of anaemia

The standard treatment for perioperative anaemia is the administration of red blood cell (RBC) concentrates. However, in order to reduce the risk to which patients are exposed when transfused with RBCs, a restrictive transfusion strategy is used where RBCs are administered to achieve the minimum acceptable Hb.

Adverse effects of red blood cell transfusion

Due to a variety of donor screening interventions such as serological assays, nucleic acid assays, and measures to reduce the risk of infection, transfusion services have been able to considerably decrease the risk of transfusion.

In a recent guideline from the AABB (formerly, the American Association of Blood Banks) (Carson et al. 2012b) these risks were summarized and compared with the incidence of other types of risk (Table 84.1).

Table 84.1 Risk of adverse effects of RBC transfusion compared with other risks

HIV	1:1 467 000
HCV	1:1 149 000
HBV	1:312 500
Fatal haemolysis	1:1 250 000
Life-threatening reaction	1:139 908
TRALI	1:12 500
TACO	1:100
Fever	1:100
Killed on a single airline flight	1:29 400 000 to 1:588 235
Lightning fatalities	1:50 000 000 to 1:500 000
Fatal fall	1:12 195
Fatal motor vehicle accidents	1:7692
Death from medical error	1:476

HIV, human immunodeficiency virus; HCV, hepatitis C virus; HBV, hepatitis B virus; TRALI, transfusion related acute lung injury; TACO, transfusion associated circulatory overload.

Data from Carson JL, *et al.* Clinical Transfusion Medicine Committee of the AABB. Red blood cell transfusion: a clinical practice guideline from the AABB. *Annals of Internal Medicine*, Volume 157, pp. 49–58, 2012.

Strategies to further reduce allogeneic blood transfusion mortality

Transfusion-related acute lung injury

Transfusion-related acute lung injury (TRALI) is defined as a new acute lung injury occurring within 6 h after a transfusion, with a clear relationship to the transfusion, in a patient without risk factors for acute lung injury other than transfusion. This definition requires that circulatory overload be ruled out. Other risk factors for acute lung injury include sepsis, aspiration, pneumonia, toxic inhalation, lung contusion, near drowning, multiple trauma, burn injury, acute pancreatitis, cardiopulmonary bypass, and drug overdose. Clinically TRALI is characterized by dyspnoea, hypoxia, and bilateral lung infiltrates. There are several theories about the pathogenesis of transfusion-related acute lung injury. First, antibodies in the blood of the donor are directed to white blood cells in the patient. These antibodies lead to aggregates of leucocytes which causes inflammatory reactions in the microcirculation of the lung. Another explanation of TRALI is related to the accumulation of soluble biological response mediators during the storage of cellular blood components. The role of antibodies is supported by the finding that in many cases of TRALI, blood products from multiparous women are involved. Antibodies are often formed during pregnancy. Many countries including the United Kingdom, several European countries, the United States, and Canada converted to male-only fresh frozen plasma in order to reduce the incidence of TRALI. Some countries also converted to male-only platelet donors, while others use buffycoat platelets from random donors suspended in male-only plasma.

Haemolytic transfusion reactions

In haemolytic transfusion reactions, donor erythrocytes are destroyed by 'naturally occurring' or regular antibodies to ABO antigens or irregular antibodies to other red cell antigens produced after contact with donor erythrocytes through transfusion or pregnancy, or by both of these mechanisms. Fatalities as a result of haemolytic transfusion reactions are mostly caused by ABO incompatibility. The commonest cause of these fatalities is the failure to properly identify the intended recipient and most incorrect blood transfusions occur in the operating room. To prevent these ABO haemolytic transfusion reactions, proper identification of the transfusion recipient and of the pretransfusion blood specimen is essential. Nowadays, electronic identification systems using special wristbands for the identification of transfusion recipients are available.

The formation of irregular antibodies is not a random process. About 1% of the patient population receiving blood transfusion forms irregular antibodies. However, many of these patients are high responders, and 20–25% of these patients form more than one irregular antibody. Patients with haemoglobinopathies are especially prone to form these irregular antibodies. In order to prevent antibody formation these patients are transfused with blood matched for erythrocyte antigens to which antibodies were not formed yet.

Avoidance of unnecessary blood transfusions

The avoidance of unnecessary blood transfusion through the use of evidence-based transfusion guidelines is the most efficient way to reduce potentially fatal transfusion complications.

RBCs and outcome

Recently, other risks of allogeneic transfusions have been reported which are not as obviously linked to transfusions and can be attributed to other events or the recipients' co-morbidities. Observations showed that allogeneic blood transfusions are associated with negative patient outcomes. Studies comparing transfused patients with non-transfused patients show unfavourable outcomes associated with allogeneic blood transfusions such as higher mortality and morbidity rates in various patient populations. Increased rates of neurological complications such as postoperative stroke, pulmonary complications, sepsis and other infections, wound complications, cardiac complications, acute kidney injury, and thromboembolic complications are reported in patients receiving allogeneic transfusions (Shander et al. 2011). Most studies, which are often observational, demonstrate a correlation between allogeneic transfusion and unfavourable outcome which does not necessarily imply causation. Often, patients who need an allogeneic transfusion are sicker, have more co-morbidity, and have a lower Hb concentration compared with patients who do not need a transfusion. Besides, anaemia in these patients is often caused by chronic illness and the activation of the inflammatory response. All these factors alone might be responsible for the worse outcome after surgery compared with patients who do not need a blood transfusion.

Stored blood, storage lesions, and outcome

During storage of RBCs, changes are observed such as the generation of cytokines in the storage medium, changes in the RBC membrane that alter the deformability of the RBCs, the inability to scavenge nitric oxygen, and a decrease in intracellular 2,3-DPG, which is necessary for the release of oxygen by haemoglobin.

Observational studies showed that an increasing period of storage of RBC before transfusion was associated with a worse outcome as a result of an immunosuppressive effect resulting in increased rates of infection, organ failure, length of hospital stay, and mortality. The results of the ARIPI study were published (Fergusson et al. 2012). In this study, patients from the neonatal intensive care were randomly assigned to receive transfusion of RBCs stored for 7 days or less (5.1 (SD 2.0) days, median 5; $n = 188$) or standard-issue RBCs stored for 14.6 (SD 8.3) days, median 13 ($n = 189$). Pretransfusion Hb and the mean and median volumes of transfused RBCs (a mean of 2/3 of the blood volume) were similar in both groups. The use of fresh RBCs did not improve outcomes in these patients. There were no statistically significant differences in primary outcome, mortality, or major neonatal morbidities associated with acute organ dysfunction or failure. There were no significant differences in the rate of clinically suspected or confirmed infections, transfusion reactions, and length of neonatal intensive care unit stay. Two other large studies of the effects of the duration of RBC storage are finished. The ABLE study (Lacroix et al. 2015) is a large randomized study in which adult trauma or intensive care patients received RBCs stored for 8 days or less or stored for longer than 8 days with mortality at the end of hospital stay as the outcome measure. They concluded that the transfusion of red blood cell units stored for 7 days or less does not improve the outcome of critically ill adults compared to the transfusion of units stored for about 3 weeks (22.0 (SD 8.4) days). Steiner and her colleagues in the US National Heart, Lung and Blood Institutes Transfusion Medicine/Hemostasis Clinical Trials Network have designed a trial called the Red Cell Storage Age Study (Steiner et al. 2015). They included 1098 patients 12 years of age or older who were undergoing complex cardiac surgery and were likely to undergo transfusion of red cells who were randomly assigned to receive leucocyte-reduced red cells stored for 10 days or less (shorter-term storage group) or for 21 days or more (longer-term storage group) for all intraoperative and postoperative transfusions. The primary outcome was the change in Multiple Organ Dysfunction Score (MODS).

Steiner et al. found that the duration of red-cell storage was not associated with significant differences in the change in MODS. The authors concluded that the transfusion of red cells stored for 10 days or less was not superior to the transfusion of red cells stored for 21 days or more among patients 12 years of age or older who were undergoing complex cardiac surgery. Currently, however, the evidence does not support a clinically relevant relationship between the age of transfused RBCs and morbidity and mortality.

Perioperative anaemia and outcome

From studies in patients who refuse blood transfusions, for example, patients of the Jehovah's Witness faith, and patients with alloantibodies and haemolytic anaemia who cannot be transfused with allogeneic blood, and in situations where blood is not available (combat or trauma situations), it is suggested that the minimum Hb concentration compatible with life is around 25 g litre^{-1} (= 1.6 mmol litre^{-1}), and possibly higher in the presence of co-morbidity such as cardiovascular disease (Mackenzie et al. 2010). Carson et al. (1988) were among the first to demonstrate a relationship between anaemia and perioperative mortality. Mortality ranged from 7.1% in patients with a Hb concentration above 100 g litre^{-1} (6.2 mmol litre^{-1}) to 61.5% for patients with Hb concentration below 60 g litre^{-1} (3.6 mmol litre^{-1}). Mortality rates were also related to blood loss during surgery; none of the patients died with a Hb concentration above 80 g litre^{-1} (4.8 mmol litre^{-1}) and operative blood loss below 500 ml. Furthermore, in many studied populations such as the elderly, patients undergoing various types of surgery (cardiac, orthopaedic, etc), transplant recipients, critically ill patients, patients with medical conditions such as chronic renal disease, stroke, acute coronary disease, heart failure, diabetes mellitus, and dementia, anaemia is associated with several unfavourable outcomes including higher short- and long-term mortality, increased risk of fractures, renal disease, heart failure, cardiovascular events, readmissions, poorer graft outcome, worse functional status, and lower quality of life (Vamvakas et al. 2010). On the other hand, there are also studies published that failed to determine a negative effect of anaemia on mortality and morbidity in patients undergoing orthopaedic surgery (Mantilla et al. 2011). In another study in more than 6 million patients undergoing orthopaedic operations, anaemia was not associated with higher mortality (Memtsoudis et al. 2010).

Perioperative anaemia and management

Despite these discrepancies there are good reasons to evaluate preoperative patients for anaemia, especially those undergoing elective surgery. If present, the aetiology of the anaemia and deficiencies in iron, vitamin B12, and folic acid should be evaluated and corrected (Goodnough et al. 2011). Anaemia is not a diagnosis but (in most cases) the result of an underlying disease. Although there are many publications suggesting an unfavourable outcome in anaemic patients, it is not clear if this is as a result of the anaemia itself or as a result of the disease causing anaemia. There is no evidence that preoperative correction of anaemia by blood transfusion or erythropoiesis-stimulating agents such as erythropoietin without treating the cause of the anaemia improves outcome. Especially in the light of adverse events, complications and the costs of RBCs and erythropoietin, restriction in the use of these products is recommended.

Spahn (2010) performed a systemic review of the literature to determine the effects of patient blood management interventions on the unfavourable outcome in anaemic patients undergoing major orthopaedic surgery. Preoperative anaemia occurred in 24 (SD 9) % of patients undergoing total hip or knee arthroplasty and occurred in 44 (SD 9) % of hip fracture patients. Effects on outcomes of iron- or erythropoietin-based patient blood management interventions were studied in five randomized controlled trials (RCTs) and five cohort studies. Although the numerical trends were in favour of outcome improvement, solid scientific evidence based on statistically significant differences in adequately designed and powered primary end-point trials is still missing. By far the largest RCT was the study of Weber et al. (2005) (50% of the total number of patients included in the 5 RCTs. In this RCT with 704 patients undergoing orthopaedic surgery, the effect of preoperative administration of epoetin alfa was studied. In the epoetin group, patients received once-weekly 40 000 IU epoetin alfa for 3 weeks and on the day of surgery together with oral iron daily for 3 weeks. All patients received blood transfusions when needed according to a hospital transfusion protocol. In the epoetin group, 9% of the patients received allogeneic transfusions compared with 37% of the patients in the control group. Between the two groups no difference was found concerning time to ambulation or time to discharge. There were no differences in infection rate or adverse events frequency. Due to the costs of erythropoietin (per patient US$1475 = €1164) the cost to save 1 unit of RBC was US$2166 (= €1711); the price of 1 unit of RBC is $266 or €210). Although fewer allogeneic blood transfusions were administered, no improvements in outcome or health benefit were demonstrated, nor were the high costs justified.

In summary, neither the hazards of anaemia nor the hazards of RBCs can be neglected. Avoidance of unnecessary blood transfusions with a restrictive transfusion policy through the use of evidence-based transfusion guidelines is recommended. Adequately designed and powered primary end-point trials should inform us about the effect of treatment of preoperative anaemia on outcome; the same is true for the use of transfusion substitutes as erythropoietin. The introduction of transfusion substitutes as alternatives for the standard use of RBC should only be introduced after RCTs have shown that the substitute not only reduces the use of allogeneic blood transfusion as an intermediate end-point but also leads to health benefit as a primary outcome.

Thresholds for allogeneic red blood cell transfusion

Recently guidelines focused on Hb concentration thresholds, that might trigger RBC transfusion were published by the AABB (Carson et al. 2012b). A committee of 20 experts in the field of anaesthesiology, cardiology, paediatrics, internal medicine, haematology, critical care, trauma surgery, GRADE (grading of recommendations assessment, development, and evaluation) methodology, and pathology developed these guidelines based on an updated systematic review. This updated systematic review was published separately by the Cochrane Collaboration (Carson et al. 2012a).

The recommendations are:

A. In hospitalized, haemodynamically stable patients:

1. The AABB recommends adhering to a restrictive transfusion strategy
2. In adult and paediatric intensive care unit patients, transfusion should be considered at Hb concentrations of 70 g litre^{-1} (4.3 mmol litre^{-1}) or less
3. In postoperative surgical patients, transfusion should be considered at a Hb concentration of 80 g litre^{-1} (5 mmol litre^{-1}) or less or for symptoms (chest pain, orthostatic hypotension, or tachycardia unresponsive to fluid resuscitation, or congestive heart failure).

Quality of evidence: high ('high' indicates considerable confidence in the estimate of effect. The true effect probably lies close to the estimated effect, and future research is unlikely to change the estimate of the health intervention's effect).
Strength of recommendation: strong (indicating judgment that most well-informed people will make the same choice; We recommend ...).

B. In hospitalized, haemodynamically stable patients with preexisting cardiovascular disease:

1. The AABB suggest adhering to a restrictive transfusion strategy
2. Transfusion should be considered at a Hb concentration of 80 g litre^{-1} (5 mmol litre^{-1}) or less or for symptoms (chest pain, orthostatic hypotension or tachycardia unresponsive to fluid resuscitation, or congestive heart failure)

Quality of evidence: moderate ('moderate' indicates confidence that the estimate is close to the truth. Further research is likely to have an important effect on confidence in the estimate and may change the estimate of the health intervention's effect.

Strength of recommendation: weak (indicating judgment that a majority of well-informed people will make the same choice, but a substantial minority will not; 'We suggest ...').

C. In hospitalized, haemodynamically stable patients with the acute coronary syndrome:

The AABB cannot recommend for or against a liberal or restrictive RBC transfusion threshold. Further research is needed to determine the optimal threshold. In contrast, the European Society of Cardiology has recommended transfusion in patients with the acute coronary syndrome at a Hb concentration of below 80 g litre^{-1} (5 mmol litre^{-1}) (Bassand et al. 2007).

Haemoglobinopathy

Haemoglobinopathies are diseases related to abnormalities in structure or production of haemoglobin. If a patient with a haemoglobinopathy requires surgery, several questions might arise for the anaesthesiologist related to these diseases, for instance, related to the prevention of sickle cell crises and transfusion policy in the perioperative period. Sickle cell disease and thalassaemia are the most prevalent forms of haemoglobinopathy.

The Hb molecules contained within the erythrocyte are essential for life by transporting oxygen to the tissues. Other functions are the transport of carbon dioxide (CO_2) and bioavailability of nitric oxygen. A haemoglobin molecule consists of two different pairs of polypeptide globin chains. Each of these chains encloses an iron-containing haem group. In adults 95–100% of the Hb is HbA which has two α and two β chains; 2.2–3.2% is HbA_2 (two α and two δ chains) and 0–1% HbF (fetal Hb: two α and γ chains). Mutations in the globin genes might lead to synthesis of a structurally abnormal Hb as in sickle cell disease or to a reduced rate of synthesis of a qualitatively normal globin chain as in thalassaemia.

Sickle cell disease

Sickle cell disease arises as a result of a point mutation in the globin gene, by which glutamic acid in the β-chain is replaced by the amino acid valine. As a result, the Hb of sickle cell patients (HbS) can polymerize when deoxygenated and produce deleterious effects because of reduced solubility of the haemoglobin molecule. Long polymers lead to the erythrocytes becoming sickle shaped and rigid so that they block the flow of blood through capillaries. Fully oxygenated haemoglobin S is as soluble as haemoglobin A. Haemoglobin A and especially haemoglobin A_2 and haemoglobin F in a red cell are effective in retarding sickling, whereas the presence of haemoglobin C facilitates sickling. Because acidosis and an increase in temperature shift the oxygen dissociation curve to the right, they stimulate sickling. On the other hand, cold might enhance sickling by slowing flow through capillaries.

Populations originating from sub-Saharan Africa, the Middle East, and parts of the Mediterranean are predominantly affected. Because of population movements approximately 12 000 people in the United Kingdom and more than 70 000 people in the United States and 1 in 60 people in West Africa now suffer from this disease.

Clinical features

Sickle cell disease is characterized by a shortened life expectancy of 25–30 years, chronic haemolytic anaemia, extensive vascular disease, progressive organ damage, and acute exacerbations. The most common acute complications are pain crises and acute chest syndrome. Sickle cell crises can be defined as an acute illness characterized by exacerbation of the clinical features of sickle cell disease, such as pain, anaemia, or jaundice. Infection, hypoxia, exposure to cold, dehydration, physical exertion, acidosis, extensive trauma or injury, and psychological stress can bring on a crisis. Acute chest syndrome is defined as a syndrome consisting of chest pain, dyspnoea, fever, and pulmonary infiltrates on chest X-ray. The shortened life expectancy is mostly as a result of organ damage and especially acute chest syndrome.

Perioperative management

The most frequent surgical procedures in sickle cell patients are orthopaedic procedures (total and revision of total hip replacement), ENT procedures, cholecystectomy, and obstetric and gynecological procedures. The incidence of acute sickle cell exacerbations is 0% for tonsillectomy, 2.9% for hip surgery, 3.9% for myringotomy, 7.8% for intra-abdominal non-obstetric surgery, 16.9% for Caesarean section and hysterectomy, and 18.6% for dilatation and curettage. Patients with sickle cell disease are at increased risk of complications such as acute chest syndrome and pain crises in the perioperative period (Firth, 2009). There is a lot of uncertainty concerning the role of blood transfusion in the prevention of sickle cell complications in the perioperative period (Buck et al. 2005). One of the few RCTs in this area (Vichinsky et al. 1995; Hirst and Williamson 2012) was published in 1995. In this study, patients undergoing 604 operations were randomly allocated to: Group 1, receiving an aggressive transfusion regimen to reduce HbS to less than 30% and a preoperative Hb of 100 g litre^{-1} (6.2 mmol litre^{-1}) by exchange transfusions in 57% of the patients and repeated transfusions in 30% of the patients; or Group 2, treated with a conservative regimen, in which a preoperative Hb of 100 g litre^{-1} (6.2 mmol litre^{-1}) was achieved irrespective of the HbS concentration. In Group 2, in which the preoperative HbS percentage was 59%, 77% of the patients received a single transfusion. The conclusion of the study was that a conservative regimen was as effective as an aggressive regimen in preventing perioperative complications, whereas with the conservative approach only half as many transfusion-associated complications occurred. Probably, a Hb of 100 g litre^{-1} (6 mmol litre^{-1}) should be achieved, irrespective of the percentage of HbS.

Complications of transfusion

Besides the well-known transfusion reactions a rare though serious complication has been described recently in sickle cell patients (Raj et al. 2013). This complication, posterior reversible encephalopathy syndrome, includes the presence of headache, seizures, encephalopathy, and visual disturbances, in addition to specific findings on magnetic resonance imaging. Clinical management includes treatment and prevention of further seizures, monitoring and management of hypertension, and standard measures to treat increased intracranial pressure.

Alloimmunization is one of the most important complications of transfusion therapy in sickle cell disease (Yazdanbakhsh et al.

2012). Up to 50% of sickle cell patients have alloantibodies which makes the availability of red blood cell concentrates difficult. The most life-threatening consequence of alloimmunization in patients with sickle cell disease is the development of delayed haemolytic transfusion reaction (DHTR) with hyperhaemolysis. Its clinical presentation might resemble a pain crisis. DHTR usually occurs between 5 and 15 days after a transfusion and is characterized by a marked decrease in the Hb concentration with the destruction of both transfused and autologous red blood cells, and exacerbation of sickle cell symptoms. Additional transfusions exacerbate the process and result in life threatening anaemia. Management includes corticosteroids and intravenous immunoglobulin.

Coagulation disorders

Circulating blood in vessels is in a liquid state, but changes rapidly to a solid state after leaving these vessels. This blood clotting or coagulation minimizes blood loss and is essential for survival. Perfect haemostasis means control of bleeding without the occurrence of thrombotic events. There is, however, a variety of disorders which interfere with this delicate balance. A reduced coagulation increases the risk of blood loss, and the opposite, increased activation, may result in thrombosis. Disorders of coagulation are inborn or acquired. Also, many drugs interfere (mostly intended) with this balance resulting in a decreased or increased coagulation activity. Even patients with normal haemostasis can develop massive bleeding perioperatively (Levy and Azran 2010).

Coagulation management requires an understanding of this balance and the knowledge that an altered coagulation activity may result in clinically relevant bleeding or arterial or venous thrombosis. Thrombosis can be induced by excess of coagulation activation or by the absence of anticoagulants suppressing coagulation. The key is an understanding that every anticoagulant action enhances the risk of bleeding and every procoagulant action enhances the risk of thrombosis.

Haemostasis

The haemostatic system is a balanced interaction of the vascular endothelium, blood cells, and blood-coagulation proteins. Vascular injury leads immediately to vasoconstriction followed by platelet disposition at the damaged site, called *primary haemostasis*. Incorporating cross-linked fibrin to strengthen the platelet-plug is called *secondary haemostasis*. The terms primary and secondary haemostasis are used for diagnostic purposes as well as educational but the process underlying haemostasis is a far more complex interplay, yet not fully understood, than reflected in this model. Currently a cell-based model of coagulation is used to understand haemostasis (Hoffman and Monroe 2001; Tanaka et al. 2009). This model distinguishes initiation, amplification, and propagation. In the initiating phase, coagulation starts with a disrupted endothelium favouring localized coagulation. During amplification and propagation, activated platelets adhere to the endothelium generating additional thrombin.

Endothelium

Blood vessels are lined by endothelial cells providing a smooth surface for undisrupted blood flow. Intact endothelium is not just a tube conducting blood in the right direction but has multiple anticoagulant properties that actively maintain blood in the liquid state. Nitric oxide, prostacyclin (PGI_2), and adenosine diphosphatase (ADP-ase) are produced by the endothelial cell. Nitric oxide causes smooth muscle relaxation resulting in vasodilation. PGI_2 is also an active vasodilator and in addition inhibits platelet activation. Platelet activation is also inhibited by ADP-ase by clearing away the platelet activator ADP. Intact endothelium also inhibits fibrin formation by production of thrombomodulin and heparin sulphate. Fibrinolysis, the enzymatic breakdown of a clot, is also under the control of the endothelium by secretion of tissue plasminogen activator (tPA). (Sagripanti and Carpi 2000). As soon as endothelial cells are damaged, this antithrombotic activity is switched to a prothrombotic response.

Vasoconstriction is the first response to control blood loss. This vasoconstriction is a rapid process and is caused by the interaction of autonomic nerves, muscle cells, and several mediators such as serotonin and (nor)adrenaline. The second response to control blood loss is triggered as soon as blood is exposed to subendothelial proteins where *collagen* activates platelets and *tissue factor* starts the coagulation system with the result that both systems are activated simultaneously. Figure 84.2 depicts the influence of intact endothelium on haemostasis and the changes induced by vascular injury.

The endothelium is crucial for haemostasis but unfortunately, tests to evaluate this important influence on haemostasis are not available.

Platelets

Platelets are small (size range from 2–4 microns), non-nucleated, disc-shaped cells. Their production in the bone marrow is regulated by thrombopoietin. The average lifespan is approximately 10 days and the platelet count in healthy individuals is in the range of 150–400 × 10^9 cells litre^{-1}, so each day 15–40 × 10^9 new platelets litre^{-1} are produced.

These platelets circulate in an inactive state meaning they will not clump together. However, in the presence of endothelial damage, a chain of events is triggered. On vessel injury, collagen is exposed to the circulating platelets. With their surface glycoprotein (GP Ib) platelets indirectly bind to the exposed collagen: they need an intermediary, the von Willebrand factor (vWF) (Franchini and Lippi, 2007). The vWF binds firmly to the collagen and exposes a large number of platelet binding sites. When blood flow is high, as it is in arteries, it is important to slow down the speed of the platelets. The vWF is able to change its shape under pressure to a rod-like structure which is able to slow down and eventually bind the platelets. This binding is called adhesion and activates platelets (see Fig. 84.2). Activated platelets release their intracellular granules into the microenvironment around the vessel injury. These granules contain α-granules (procoagulant proteins such as factor V, fibrinogen, and vWF) and dense granules (ADP, calcium ions, and serotonin) promoting further platelet activation. This activation of platelets after adhesion can also be elicited by physiological agonists such as adenosine ADP, adrenaline, and thrombin (Furie and Furie 2008).

Activated platelets change their form from discoid to spherical with extending pseudopods and change their platelet surface (so-called flip-flop reaction) into a phospholipid surface, the ideal surface to bind and assemble activated coagulation factors in an optimal way.

The next step is *aggregation* and this is tightly inter-linked with adhesion. Glycoprotein IIb–IIIa (GPIIb/IIIa) is the most abundant glycoprotein receptor on the platelet surface and binds fibrinogen.

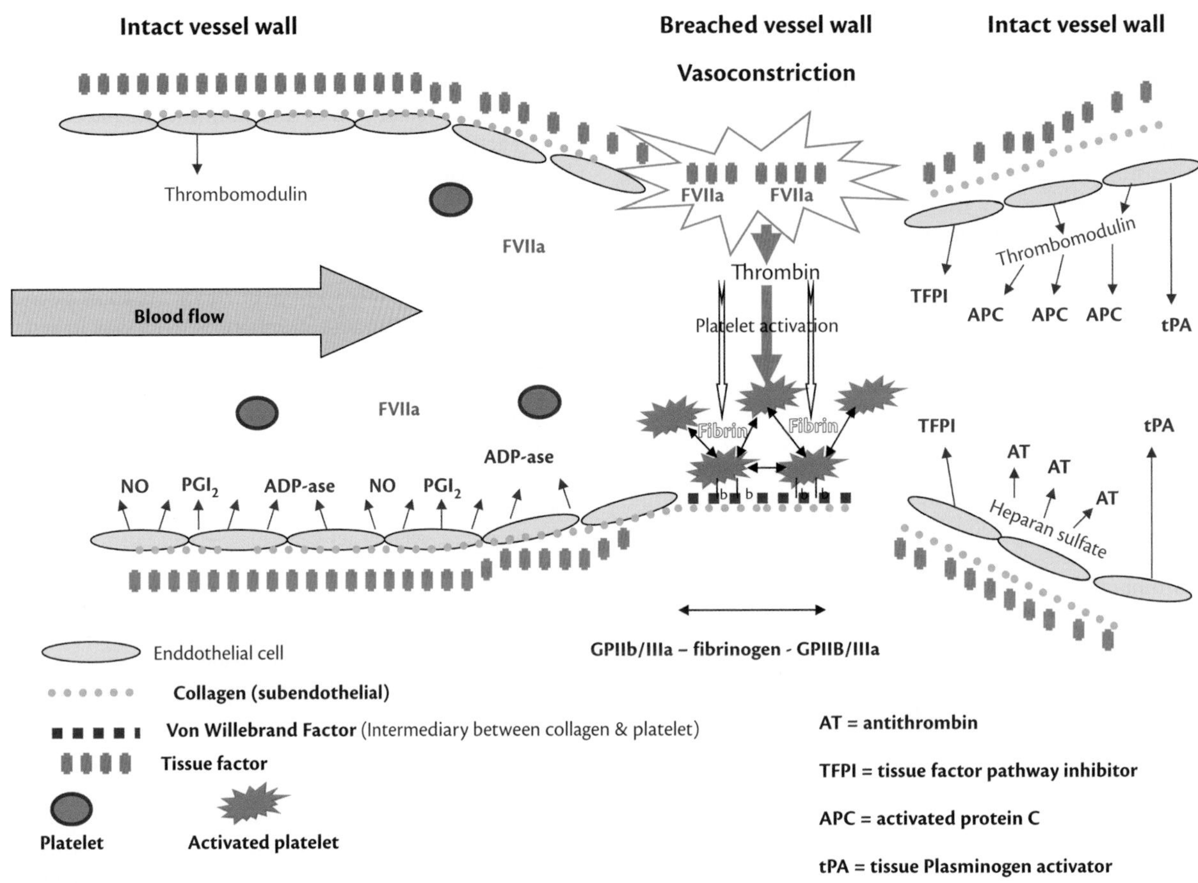

Figure 84.2 Coagulation and the endothelium. Left: the intact vessel wall provides a defence against thrombus formation by the secretion of nitric oxide (NO), prostacyclin (PGI_2), and ADP-ase. Middle: damage to the vessel wall exposes collagen and tissue factor which activates platelets and initiates fibrin formation respectively. Vasoconstriction reduces blood flow preventing a wash out of activated clotting factor and platelets. Right: intact endothelium immediately after the breached vessel wall localizes the initiation of coagulation at the site of injury. Thrombomodulin binds thrombin, which activates protein C. Together with antithrombin (AT) they inhibit activated coagulation factors. Tissue plasminogen activator (tPA) activates plasminogen (and this reaction is highly accelerated by thrombin) into plasmin. Plasmin degrades fibrin into fibrin degradation products.

This GPIIb/IIIa receptor is inactive in the resting platelet. But when the platelet is activated the conformational change exposes the GPIIb/IIIa receptor, binding fibrinogen and this pulls the platelets together, called aggregation (see Fig. 84.3). The platelet plug is formed by adhesion and aggregation and strengthened by the formation of fibrin.

The coagulation protein system

The formed platelet plug is limited in duration and strength. The next step is stabilization and strengthening by the coagulation protein system.

The many coagulation proteins circulate as inactive proenzymes in the blood, comparable to circulating inactivated platelets. Coagulation proteins are descibed by a Roman numeral and when activated a lowercase '*a*' is assigned to indicate the active form: in this chapter, the Roman numeral will be preceded by 'F' for factor. Coagulation starts with FVII. Approximately 1–2% of FVII circulates in active form but this protease is not catalytically active until it binds to tissue factor (TF). On vessel damage, activated FVII (FVIIa) binds to the subendothelial tissue factor initiating coagulation on the surface of cells that express tissue factor (Pathak et al. 2006). This initial trigger (TF–FVIIa binding) is amplified into a rapid tightly controlled sequence of interactions resulting in the formation of the end product, fibrin. The sequence of interactions is depicted in Fig. 84.3. The FVIIa–TF complex activates both FIX and FX which leads to thrombin production. The coagulation proteins and their characteristics are summarized in Table 84.2.

In the coagulation cascade, activated platelets are essential for the formation of an effective clot: they deliver several coagulation factors and the platelet phospholipid surface is vital for the speed and localization of the formed fibrin clot.

The liver synthesizes most coagulation factors, with the exception of FVIII and the vWF (Castaman et al. 2003). Vitamin K is essential for the manufacture of the coagulant factors II, VII, IX, and X (and protein C and S), enabling these factors to bind ionized calcium, which is required for their activation. This calcium and vitamin K dependency of the formation of fibrin has broad clinical applications. Coagulation is decreased in the absence of ionized calcium (as in citrated blood) and in the absence of vitamin K (as in patients treated with vitamin-K antagonists such as warfarin).

The enzyme reaction of coagulation factors is dependent on their concentration (Fig. 84.4). A concentration equal or greater than 20% (corresponding with an INR ≥1.8) is sufficient for the formation of fibrin. It is, however, important to realize that a

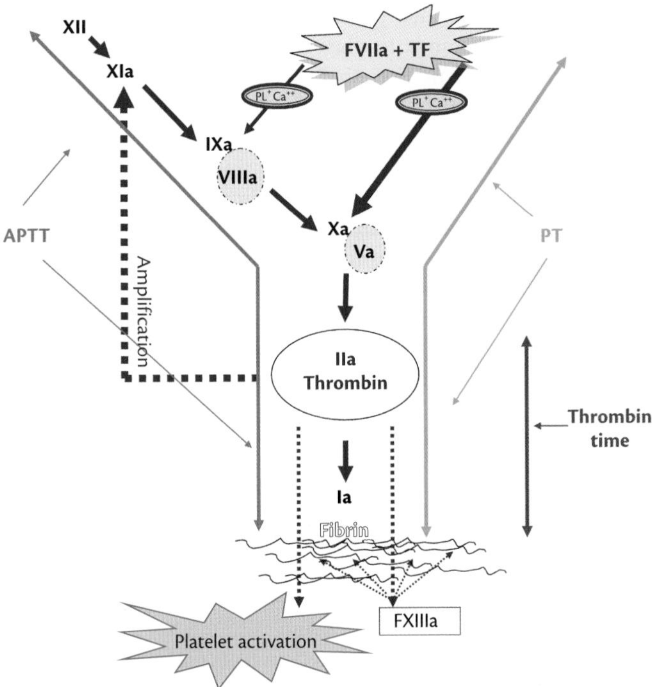

Figure 84.3 Coagulation activation starts with the TF–FVIIa complex resulting in the formation of fibrin. By disruption of the endothelium, TF is bound to the circulating FVII. This FVIIa–TF complex activates both FIX and FX [calcium ions, Ca^{2+}, and a phospholipid (PL) surface are necessary for this activation]. Activated FX (FXa) binds to the platelet membrane and cleaves prothrombin to thrombin. Thrombin is the key player: a small amount of formed thrombin activates FXI where a loop reinforces additional thrombin formation. Thrombin also activates platelets providing a surface for the coagulation reactions. Factor IXa binds with FVIIIa to the platelet surface where it activates FX. Factor Xa binds with FVa to the platelet surface where it activates FII (prothrombin) into thrombin. In addition, thrombin activates also FXIII. FXIIIa cross-links fibrin which increases the strength of the clot.

concentration of 20% is sufficient only if there are no other factors with a negative influence on coagulation, a condition seldom met in a clinical situation.

Natural anticoagulants

It is important to localize haemostatic activation to prevent thrombus formation and vascular occlusion in healthy vessels. Intact endothelium and the natural circulating anticoagulants are pivotal in localizing blood coagulation to restricted areas (i.e. vascular injury).

Intact endothelium is actively nonthrombogenic. It produces not only nitric oxide and PGI_2 but also a strong anticoagulant: tissue factor pathway inhibitor (TFPI). TFPI by itself is inactive and must first bind to FXa to become active. Activated TFPI inhibits the FVIIa/TF complex stopping coagulation activation at its very beginning (see Fig. 84.5). Coagulation factors further in the cascade have their natural inhibitors. Antithrombin, produced in the liver, is one of the most important inhibitors and inhibits not only thrombin (IIa), but also coagulation factors IXa, Xa, and XIa. The rate of antithrombin inactivation is slow but is accelerated 2000–4000-fold in the presence of heparin (Olson et al. 1992). Healthy endothelium is coated with antithrombin bound to endothelial heparan sulfate which neutralizes activated coagulation factors to localize coagulation (Evans et al. 1992). Again, another example showing that intact endothelium is non-thrombogenic. Infusion with heparin will not only inactivate clot-bound thrombin but also free circulating activated factors, making it a potent anticoagulant with broad clinical applications.

Healthy endothelial cells express thrombomodulin on their surface. Thrombomodulin binds thrombin and, as the name suggests, 'modulates' it. After this conformational change thrombin is unable to activate platelets or coagulation factors. Instead, it activates protein C and this activated protein C in conjunction with its cofactor

Table 84.2 Coagulation proteins and their characteristics

Factor	Descriptive name	Plasma concentration	T½ (h)		Available
I	Fibrinogen	300 mg dl^{-1}	48–96		Haemcompletan P*
II	Prothrombin	100 μg ml^{-1}	72–120	Vitamin K dependent	4FC
III	Tissue factor	–	–		
IV	Calcium				Calcium chloride
V	Labile factor	200 ng ml^{-1}	12–36		
VII	Proconvertin	0.5 μg ml^{-1}	4–6	Vitamin K dependent	4FC, rFVIIa
VIIIc	Antihaemophilic factor (A)	0.15 μg ml^{-1}	10–18		rFVIIIa Haemate-P*
vWF	Von Willebrand factor	8 μg ml^{-1}	10		Haemate-P*
IX	Christmas factor	5 μg ml^{-1}	18–36	Vitamin K dependent	4FC, FIX
X	Stuart–Prower factor	10 μg ml^{-1}	24–60	Vitamin K dependent	4FC
XI	Rosenthal factor	6 μg ml^{-1}	40–80		
XII	Hageman factor	30 μg ml^{-1}	60		
XIII	Fibrin-stabilizing factor	20 μg ml^{-1}	40–50		Fibrogammin

The number assigned to a coagulation factor is based on historical grounds and has unfortunately nothing to do with their place in the cascade. 4FC, four-factor concentrates (i.e. FII, FVII, FIX, and FX); rFVIIa, recombinant activated factor VII.

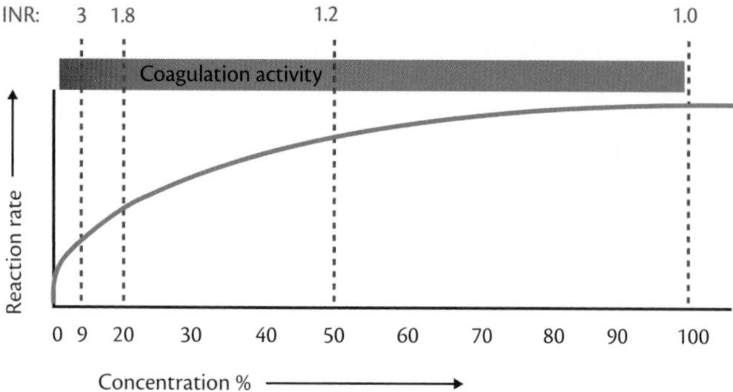

Figure 84.4 The relation between coagulation factor concentration and reaction speed. High concentrations of coagulation factors achieve a high enzyme reaction. Moderate deficiencies are usually without clinical consequences (right side of bar, green area in coagulation activity). If the concentration of coagulation factors gradually drops below 20% corresponding with an INR activity of 1.8, coagulation activity is impaired (left side of bar, red area in coagulation activity).

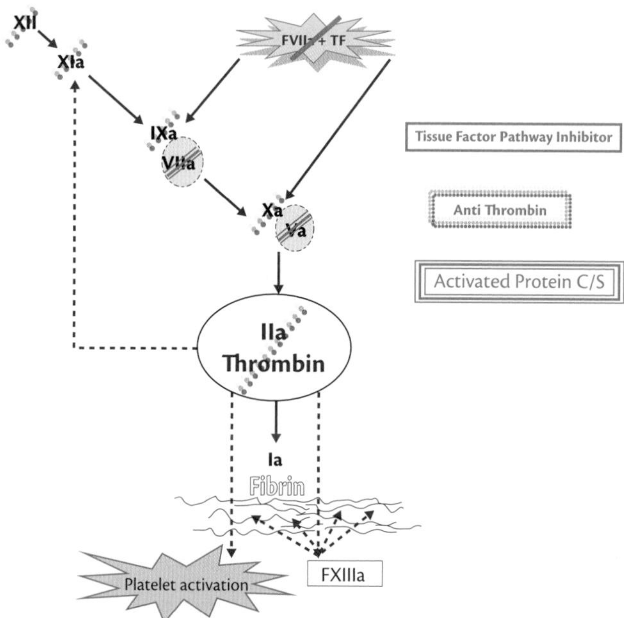

Figure 84.5 Natural coagulation inhibitors. The three main inhibitors with their targets: tissue factor pathway inhibitor (TFPI), the activated protein C/S system, and antithrombin (AT). TFPI is produced in the endothelial cells. AT and APC are produced in the liver and connected to the endothelium by heparan sulphate and thrombomodulin respectively (see Fig. 84.2).

protein S inhibits the co-factors Va and VIIIa. As a result, coagulation is blocked in the intact vessel wall and activated by vessel damage. Thrombin appears to be a 'double agent', promoting anticoagulation in an intact endothelium and promoting coagulation by endothelial damage.

The fibrinolytic system

The fibrinolytic system ensures localization of fibrin formation and removes the fibrin clot after wound healing. Fibrinolysis shares several similarities with the coagulation system: it requires activation steps of proenzymes which can be accelerated by substrates and the fibrinolytic system has its own inhibitors.

Fibrinolysis is initiated by the release of tPA produced in the endothelium. tPA binds to plasminogen and converts it to the active enzyme plasmin. Endothelial cells produce and release tPA continuously, which is cleared by the liver, unless it is bound to fibrin.

Plasmin cleaves fibrin resulting in fibrin degradation products including D-dimer. An increased concentration of D-dimer indicates fibrin formation and subsequent lysis. tPA is, however, a slow activator of plasminogen. In the presence of fibrin, the activation of plasminogen into plasmin by tPA is accelerated, leading to reinforced fibrinolysis. As soon as fibrin is cleared, plasmin production declines, making it a self-regulating system. Another, less important, activator of plasminogen is urokinase plasminogen activator.

Fibrinolysis inhibitors

There are inhibitors to limit fibrinolysis. The inhibitor of tPA (and urokinase) is plasminogen activator inhibitor 1 (PAI-1). It binds and inactivates free-floating tPA. Fibrin-bound tPA, however, is very slowly inhibited by plasminogen activator inhibitor 1. Another inhibitor is α-antiplasmin, which, as the name suggests, inhibits plasmin. Thrombin-activatable fibrinolysis inhibitor is activated by high concentrations of thrombin and protects the fibrin clot against lysis (Bouma and Mosnier 2005).

In summary, haemostasis is a harmony of procoagulant, anticoagulant, fibrinolytic, and antifibrinolytic activities. A disturbance in this delicate balance results in bleeding or thrombosis.

Coagulation monitoring

Limitations of coagulation monitoring

The monitoring of coagulation is a challenging venture: the process underlying haemostasis is not fully understood, endothelium is important but there are no methods for assessing endothelial function, and tests are time-consuming (by the time the test results are available it is often a retrospective study). In addition, most coagulation tests are static (snapshot) while coagulation is a dynamic interplay and most tests are performed on isolated plasma ignoring the interplay with platelets and other cells. With all these limitations it is obvious that there is no test that accurately predicts blood loss during and after surgery. To treat coagulopathy, interpretation of the test results is important and should be evaluated in relation to the clinical picture.

The cornerstone test of coagulation is the history of the patient, including physical signs. Platelet abnormalities will reveal skin and mucosal bleeding, petechiae, and prolonged bleeding from skin lacerations. Frequent epistaxis and abundant menorrhagia are other signs of thrombocytopaenia. Abnormalities in the coagulation proteins are associated with haemarthroses. A history of excessive bleeding after a dental extraction or after minor surgery needs further evaluation. On the other hand, deficiencies of anticoagulants (e.g. a factor C deficiency) are associated with thrombotic complications such as deep venous thrombosis or pulmonary embolism.

In patients with known coagulopathies (von Willebrand's disease, haemophilia) the anaesthesiologist can liaise with the haematologist to arrange appropriate factor replacement before surgery. For patients taking anticoagulant medication, consideration must be given on an individual patient basis, to the relative risks of continuing (bleeding) or stopping (thrombotic events) the medication.

Coagulation tests

In most hospitals, routine coagulation testing consists of the prothrombin time (PT), activated partial thromboplastin time (aPTT), thrombin time (TT), plasma fibrinogen concentration, and a platelet count.

The coagulation cascade has historically been described as having two pathways (see Fig. 84.3): the intrinsic pathway measured by the aPTT and the extrinsic pathway measured by the PT, with a final common pathway measured by the TT. These tests evaluate the coagulation proteins as they are artificially stimulated in plasma at a temperature of 37°C. The test result is the time (in seconds) it takes to form fibrin strands after artificial stimulation. The aPTT is stimulated with a contact activator (kaolin, Celite®) and tests the intrinsic route (factors XII, XI, IX, and VIII). In the PT, tissue factor is added to test the extrinsic route (FVII) (see Fig. 84.3).

Interpretation of the test results is made with reference to the patient's clinical evaluation. In liver cirrhosis, the PT is often prolonged as a result of a decreased production of coagulation factors in the liver. Therefore, PT is used in many assays (Child–Pugh score, MELD score) to evaluate liver function. However, with a prolonged PT and a platelet count of less than 100×10^9 cells litre^{-1} it is possible to perform a liver transplantation without the use of prohaemostatics and without the administration of any blood products (Boer et al. 2005). Probably as a result of a decrease in the anticoagulants produced in the liver and an increase in coagulation factors produced in the endothelium (FVIII and VWF), a new balance in haemostasis is created. This shows that PT and aPTT are screening tests for the amount of coagulation proteins, not to predict blood loss or to guide therapy. These tests provide little information about the natural coagulation process in the patient and provide no information on anticoagulation. Again the clinical situation is often by far the best guide. For instance, patients with Glanzmann thrombasthenia (severe inherited thrombocytopathy, caused by a deficiency in GPIIb/IIIa receptor) have no abnormalities in routine coagulation tests, however they bleed profoundly during invasive procedures. A prolonged PT in patients with advanced liver disease will in many cases not be associated with bleeding during a liver transplantation, but a trauma patient with a prolonged PT has a high risk of losing blood during surgery.

In general, the PT and aPTT will detect protein coagulation abnormalities. The aPTT is used for the evaluation of heparin therapy and the PT for the effect of vitamin-K antagonists. A level of 1.5 times the upper limit of the PT and aPTT is generally considered a risk for bleeding during surgery because the concentration of coagulation proteins has decreased below a critical level.

Different activators for the PT are used, producing variability in test results and making comparisons between PTs from different clinics impossible. A corrected PT for the used activator is expressed as the international normalized ratio (INR). An INR of 1 means there is a coagulation activity of 100%; a INR of 1.8 indicates a coagulation activity of 20% (see Fig. 84.4). If the INR is greater than 1.8 it is recommended not to perform a neuraxial block because of the increased risk of an epidural haematoma.

Thrombin time

The time it takes to form fibrin strands after addition of thrombin to citrated plasma. It gives an impression of the speed of the transformation of fibrinogen into fibrin.

Platelet count

A normal platelet count is between 150 and 400×10^9 cells litre^{-1}. A minimum count of 50×10^9 cells litre^{-1} is considered sufficient for most invasive procedures, but in situations where a small amount of blood loss causes serious problems (such as eye surgery and neurosurgery), a platelet count of 100×10^9 cells litre^{-1} is considered the minimum. These recommendations are based on two assumptions: all the counted platelets are properly functioning and secondly, there are no other defects in the haemostatic system. These two assumptions are not always met in a clinical situation. Counting tells us nothing about the function of the platelets and simple platelet function tests are not available. For instance, the administration of aspirin (acetylsalicylic acid) will change the function of the platelets but leave their number unaffected. Clinical judgement and the results of additional coagulation tests will ultimately define the number of required platelets.

A platelet count of greater than 450×10^9 cells litre^{-1} may increase the risk of thrombosis but this depends on the presence of other risk factors for thrombosis.

Plasma fibrin concentration

The plasma fibrin concentration is derived from the time it takes to form fibrin after thrombin is added to the plasma with a dilution technique.

Thromboelastography/thromboelastometry

Routine laboratory tests are performed on plasma and provide no information about interactions of blood cells, procoagulants and anticoagulants, and pro- and antifibrinolytic factors, all essential in the clotting process. Whole-blood clot testing, taking into account all of these interactions, has gained popularity. Two systems are used to evaluate the whole clotting process from initiation, through acceleration, and finally the stability of the formed clot: the TEG® (Haemonetics Corp., Braintree, MA, USA) or thromboelastography and the ROTEM® (Tem International GmbH, Munich, Germany) or thromboelastometry. The ROTEM® is based on thromboelastographic principles and generates a similar trace to TEG®. Figure 84.6 displays the instrument and the tracing.

The most important differences between the TEG® and ROTEM® are related to the different activators used: in TEG® no activator is used (native TEG®) or kaolin, whereas in ROTEM® either thromboplastin/phospholipid (inTEM) or thromboplastin (exTEM) is used. As a consequence, the measured variables are not interchangeable and for clinical interpretation it is important to know which activator is used. (Nielsen 2007; Venema et al. 2010).

Thromboelastography/-metry informs you how fast the clot is formed, how strong the clot is, and, last but not least, if the clot will dissolve or not. The variables giving this information are: TEG® reaction time (*r*)/ROTEM® clotting time (*CT*) represent the time from initiating the test to the initial fibrin formation (defined as a tracing amplitude of 2 mm). Prolongation indicates coagulation deficiencies or a heparin effect. TEG kinetic time (*k*)/ROTEM® clot formation time (*CFT*) represents the time from clot initiation (amplitude of 2 mm) to the time when the amplitude reaches 20 mm. TEG®/ROTEM® α angle (α) is the tangent of the curve made as the k is reached and represents the speed of clot formation. TEG® maximal amplitude (MA)/ROTEM® maximum clot formation (MCF) is the greatest amplitude of the trace. It reflects the absolute clot strength. A low MA/MCF indicates a decreased platelet number (or function)

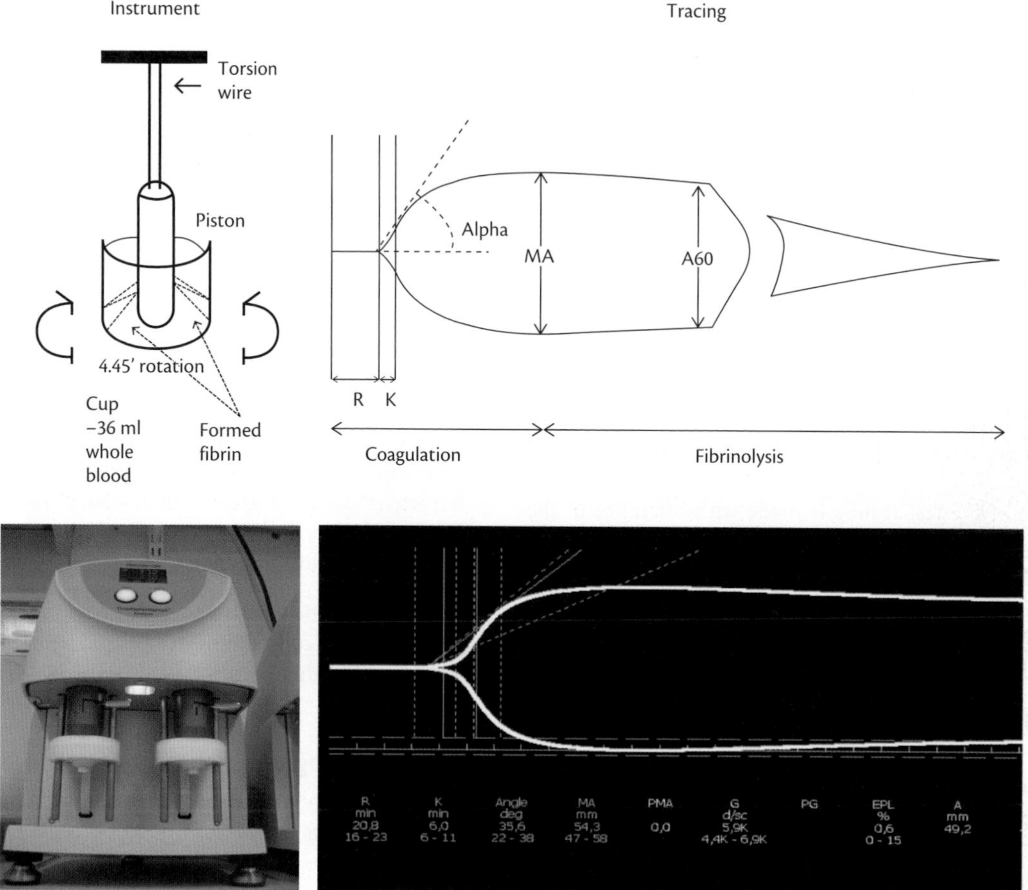

Figure 84.6 The thromboelastograph and its tracing. The cup contains whole blood (the TEG® 0.36 ml, the ROTEM® 0.34 ml) and is oscillated at an angle of 4°45′. The suspended piston in the cup monitors the motion and is converted to an electric signal. A computer translates this signal to the tracing. Liquid blood does not transmit torque from cup to piston, resulting in a straight line on the tracing. A strong clot, however, moves the piston directly in phase with the cup, producing a huge magnitude in the tracing. Lysis diminishes transfer motion with consequent reduced tracings.

or decreased plasma fibrinogen concentration (or function), or both of these. TEG® A_{60} is the extent of *fibrinolysis* measured 60 min after MA and represents the stability of the clot.

TEG® was first clinically used in 1985 in liver transplantation (Kang et al. 1985). Nowadays most departments use thromboelastography/-metry for guiding and evaluating coagulation therapy. The measurements correlate with many coagulation disturbances and their changes after treatment. Goal-directed therapy with thromboelastography/-metry represents an important step for a more rational approach to a complex matter although the evidence is still weak (Wikkelsoe et al. 2011; Ranucci et al. 2012).

Prohaemostatic therapy

If a specific defect in the haemostatic system is known, treatment is tailored to restore this defect. In haemophilia A, the cornerstone of therapy is restoration of factor VIII, and in haemophilia B, factor IX. A surgical patient, however, often starts surgery with a normal coagulation system. If, during a surgical procedure, bleeding occurs, the underlying defect in the haemostatic system is not always clear.

Administration of prohaemostatics must be guided by coagulation tests. An excellent coagulation test is the clinical field (i.e. the surgical wound). If there are abnormalities in the coagulation tests without clinical bleeding, a correction is hardly necessary. Therefore, coagulopathy treatment is patient tailored and guided by tests results *and* the clinical condition of the patient.

Treatment of bleeding patients is based on the administration of *blood products* or the administration of *pharmacological drugs* including antifibrinolytics, or both of these methods.

Prohaemostatics: blood products

Blood products such as fresh frozen plasma (FFP) and platelets are the mainstay of treatment for blood loss but these are administered mostly on an empirical basis.

Fresh frozen plasma

After donation plasma is stored at −30°C within 6 h of collection to preserve heat-labile factors such as V and VIII. For use, FFP must be thawed to 37°C and used immediately. Administration of FFP requires ABO compatibility. The volume of 1 unit of FFP is approximately 300 ml.

Indications for transfusing FFP

Guidelines for the clinical use of FFP are largely based on evidence from clinical studies and expert opinion. There are large variations in use and inappropriate use (Pinkerton and Callum 2010; Tinmouth 2012). In general, disturbance of coagulation may become clinically relevant if factors decrease below a concentration of 20% corresponding with an INR of 1.8 (see Fig. 84.4). It is important to realize that this cut-off point is situation dependent. If other factors are involved that have a negative influence on coagulation, a higher concentration of coagulation factors for optimal coagulation is probably required. Additional impairments of coagulation are caused by acidosis, hypocalcaemia, anaemia, hypothermia, and their combination (Lier et al. 2008). In Figure 84.7, the influence of acidosis and hypothermia is highlighted on TEG®-tracings from an *in vitro* study (Ramaker et al. 2009).

In the clinical setting, especially in trauma patients, a concentration of coagulation factors of 20% might be insufficient because there are several factors negatively influencing clot formation such as hypothermia and acidosis. Correction of coagulation is not only the administration of coagulation factors to at least a coagulation factor concentration of 20% but also the correction of a temperature

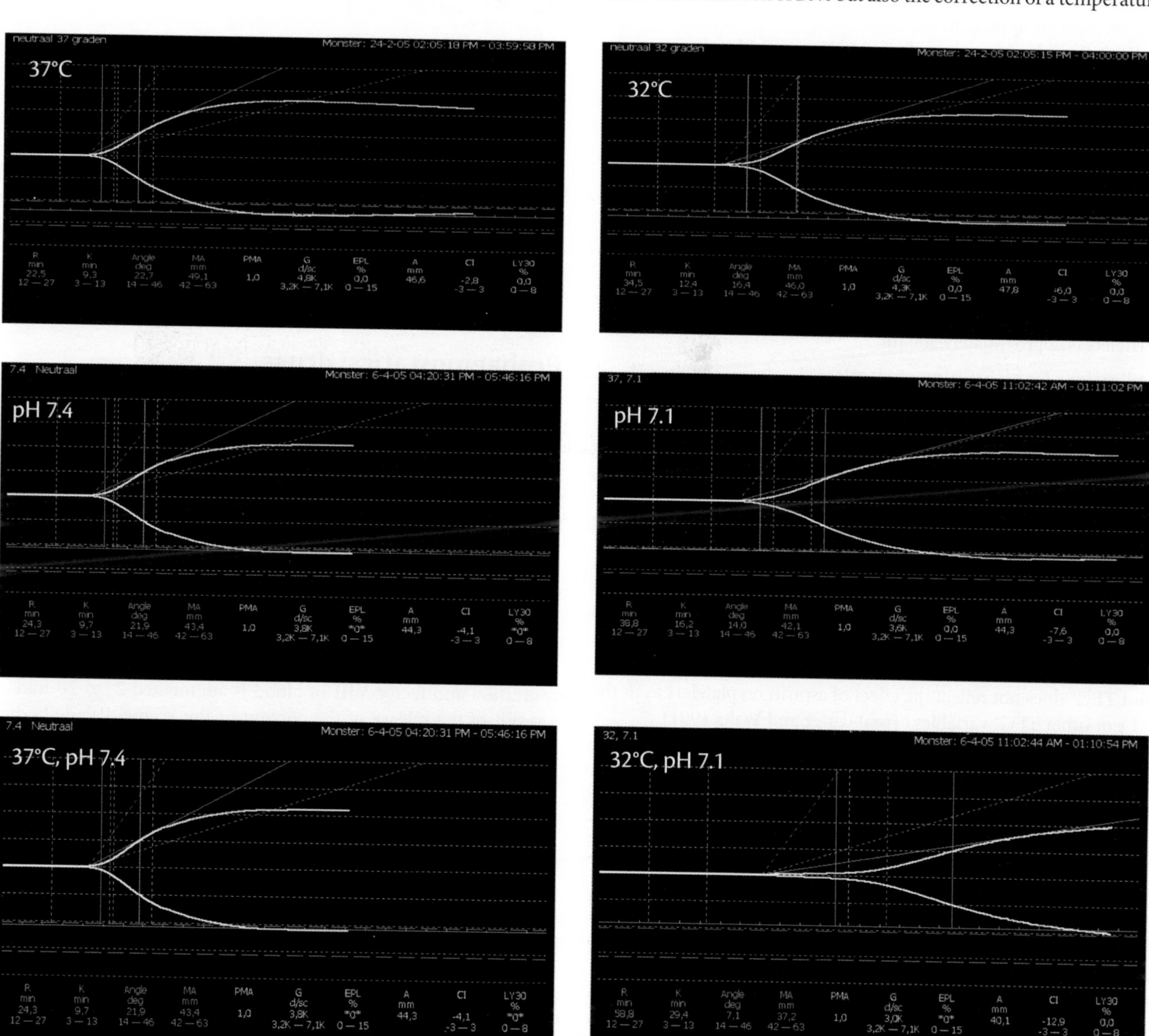

Figure 84.7 The negative effects of acidosis and hypothermia on clot formation and clot strength as shown in thromboelastographic tracings. Acidosis and hypothermia cause a significant impairment of clot formation and clot strength as shown on the thromboelastographic variables from an *in vitro* study. Left panel show the TEG® tracings at a temperature of 37°C (top), a pH of 7.4 (middle), and the combination (bottom). In the right panel. the effects of a temperature drop to 32°C (top), artificial acidification to 7.1 (middle), and the combination of temperature drop and acidification (bottom) are shown.

Reproduced with permission from Ariez Publishing: HGD Hendriks, van der Meer J: Trombo-elastografie. *Nederlands Tijdschrift voor Hematologie* 2007:4 (6):215–220. TEG® Hemostasis Analyzer tracing images used by permission of Haemonetics Corporation. TEG® is a registered trademark of Haemonetics Corporation.

decrease and acidosis. Correction of anaemia seems from a theoretical point of view plausible: the erythrocytes push the platelets to the damaged site and at a low haematocrit concentration, fewer platelets are pushed to the vessel wall. The optimal haematocrit might be higher for optimal coagulation than is required for oxygen transport. A haematocrit of 30% or higher is advised for optimal coagulation although hard evidence is lacking (Lier et al. 2008).

For the administration of FFP, coagulation tests are important to determine the concentration of coagulation factors. Prophylactic correction of an abnormal PT or INR has no rationale. In thromboelastography/-metry, *r* and *CT* are prolonged by a deficiency of coagulation factors and may be a useful guide for diagnostis and the therapeutic approach.

With the administration of large volumes of FFP there are also large volumes of citrate administered. If the capacity of the liver to metabolize this citrate is exceeded, citrate toxicity may result in hypocalcaemia. This hypocalcaemia can contribute to coagulopathy and therefore plasma calcium concentration is measured after FFP administration and corrected as necessary.

Platelets

Platelets are stored at room temperature and have a shelf life limited to 5 days. ABO matching is recommended but not always practised because platelets express antigens poorly. The volume of donated platelets is approximately 300 ml.

Indications for transfusion of platelets

There is no absolute threshold for platelet transfusion. Platelets are administered in general if the platelet count decreases below 50×10^9 cells litre^{-1}. In situations where a small volume of blood loss has serious consequences (such as neurosurgery), a platelet count of 100×10^9 cells litre^{-1} is considered the minimum. But platelet counting does not inform us about platelet function. There is no bed-side test to evaluate the platelet function. Thromboelastography/-metry is frequently used to guide platelet administration. The clot strength, expressed in MA (TEG®) or MCF (ROTEM®), is dependent on the interaction of platelets and fibrin but platelets have the greatest influence on MA (Chandler, 1995). But TEG® does not reflect the effect of aspirin on platelets as in the MA or other TEG® variables (Trentalange and Walts 1991).

Currently there is no bed-side platelet function test. Platelet count and thromboelastographaphy/-metry in combination with clinical observation should guide platelet administration. After platelet administration, it is necessary to evaluate the effect not only in the clinical field but also by counting platelets.

Fibrinogen concentration

Fibrinogen is crucial for platelet aggregation and fibrin formation. In severe blood loss, fibrinogen is the first haemostatic factor to decrease critically (Hiippala et al. 1995). Without doubt, plasma fibrinogen concentration should be measured and if necessary corrected. However, the optimal plasma fibrinogen concentration is not defined and varies from 1.0 g litre^{-1} to 2.0 g litre^{-1} (Bolliger et al. 2009). The required concentration is probably dependent on the clinical situation and on the existence of additional impairments of coagulation. The efficacy and safety of high-dose administration is unknown and may increase the risk of thrombotic events (Ozier and Hunt 2011).

Fibrinogen supplementation is through administration of plasma-derived fibrinogen concentrates or cryoprecipitate. High-dose FFP (up to 15 ml kg^{-1}) results in only a small increase in the plasma concentration and therefore is not the first-choice treatment (Chowdary et al. 2004). Of course, when high volume is necessary, FFP supplementation is an option. Again, after fibrinogen administration the fibrinogen plasma concentration and, if available, the results of thromboelastography/-metry, in combination with the effects on the clinical field will eventually define if correction has been sufficient.

Cryoprecipitate

Cryoprecipitate (CPP) is prepared from the cold-insoluble proteins removed from thawed FFP. It contains concentrated factor VIII, XIII, vWF, and fibrinogen.

Indications for cryoprecipitate

The primary indication is reversal of hypofibrinogenaemia caused by massive transfusion (Benjamin and Laughlin 2012). Haemophilia used to be treated with CPP but nowadays therapy is with factor concentrates including recombinant factor VIIa.

In contrast to CPP, fibrinogen concentrate is pasteurized, reducing the risk of pathogen transmission and immune-mediated complications. These advantages of fibrinogen and factor concentrates over CPP will probably result in decreased CPP use, although clinical studies are needed to define the future use of CPP (Sørensen and Bevan 2010).

Prohaemostatics: drugs

There are only a few drugs aimed at reducing bleeding and transfusion requirements. These drugs (see Table 84.3) aim to improve the primary haemostasis (formation of platelet plug), the secondary haemostasis (fibrin formation), or inhibit fibrinolysis. The expected benefit of prohaemostatics should be balanced with the risk of thrombosis.

Desmopressin

The vasopressin analogue D-arginine vasopressin has fewer vasoactive effects but possesses some antidiuretic effects (Mannucci et al. 1977). After desmopressin administration, the vWF concentration and factor VIII in blood is augmented 2- to 20-fold as a result of the release of the content of the Weibel Palade bodies in endothelial cells. After intravenous desmopressin administration the peak concentration in plasma is reached after 30–60 min. There is no *de novo* synthesis and the effect lasts for 12–24 h and diminishes with repeated injections (tachyphylaxis). The useful dose is 0.3 μg kg^{-1}. The effect of desmopressin varies from person to person but for the individual, the effect is reproducible. Munucci et al. (1977) published the rationale for its use in the treatment of patients with

Table 84.3 Pharmacological agents to improve haemostasis

	Prohaemostatic drug	Dose
Primary haemostasis	Desmopressin	0.3 μg kg^{-1} intravenously in 15 min
Secondary haemostasis	Recombinant factor VIIa	100 μg kg^{-1} intravenously in 10 min
Inhibition of fibrinolysis	Tranexamic acid	1–20 g intravenously over 20 min to 12 h

mild haemophilia A and type I von Willebrand's disease. Since then, the drug has been used in many clinical settings with variable success in reducing blood loss. Overall evidence does not support a beneficial effect of desmopressin in haemostatically normal patients undergoing elective surgical procedures (Porte and Leebeek 2002; Ozier and Schlumberger 2006; Levy 2008).

A meta-analysis of randomized clinical trials concluded that desmopressin slightly reduced blood loss in surgical patients without a reduction in the proportion of patients who received transfusions (Creszenzi et al. 2008).

The administration of desmopressin has some undesirable effects. Flushing, hypotension, headache, and increased heart rate are caused by vasodilation. These side-effects can be avoided if the drug is administered slowly (i.e. over 15 min). In children, there is an additional risk for water retention and hyponatraemia caused by the antidiuretic effect. In cardiac surgery, a 2.4-fold increased risk of myocardial infarction was found with the use of DDAVP (Levi et al. 1999).

Although the theoretical concept of raising vWF and FVIII in bleeding patients with platelets is attractive, current evidence does not support the routine use of desmopressin.

Factor VIIa

Recombinant activated factor VII (rFVIIa) is safely used for treatment and prevention of bleeding in haemophiliacs with circulating inhibitors to their replacement factors and for patients with Glanzmann disease not responding to platelet therapy.

FVIIa binds to tissue factor that is exposed by subendothelial tissue. This complex—as discussed earlier—leads to a 'thrombin burst', cleaving fibrinogen into fibrin. The necessity of subendothelial tissue factor should ensure a localized effect of rFVIIa, without systemic activation of coagulation. RFVIIa has been used in many other patient groups, often as a rescue therapy in bleeding patients not responding to 'conventional' therapy (i.e. off-label use). Case reports of successful rescue therapy make up the majority of the literature but have no adequate controls and are mostly without safety concerns. Published RCTs do not support the efficacy of rFVIIa to control bleeding in many clinical situations (Birchall et al. 2008), including paediatric cardiac surgery (Guzetta et al. 2012). An evaluation of thromboembolic events in all published randomized, placebo-controlled trials of rFVIIa used on an off-label basis revealed a significant increase in the risk of arterial thromboembolic events, especially among the elderly (Levi M et al. 2010).

Outside the field of haemophilia and Glanzmann disease, rFVIIa must be considered with caution. Rescue therapy for life-threatening massive bleeding refractory to conventional therapy with rFVIIa should only be considered if an optimal haemostatic environment is ensured. If one element in coagulation is missing or deficient, haemostasis will be poor, even if the other elements are abundant. Thus it is vital to ensure that not only the fibrinogen plasma concentration (≥1 g litre^{-1}) and platelet number (≥50 × 10^9 cells litre^{-1}) but also temperature, pH, haemoglobin, and plasma calcium should be optimized.

Antifibrinolytics

Antifibrinolytic drugs should ideally be used in situations with hyperfibrinolysis disturbing the balance between clot formation and clot breakdown. However, monitoring of hyperfibrinolysis is not easy: a simple test showing hyperfibrinolysis does not exist with the exception of thromboelastography/-metry.

Aprotinin, a widely used antifibrinolytic, was withdrawn in 2007 from worldwide marketing and is not discussed in this chapter.

Plasminogen binds to fibrin at the lysine-binding site and is converted to plasmin in combination with a plasminogen activator (tPA). When this lysine-binding site is blocked, the plasminogen conversion is very slow resulting in decreased fibrinolysis. There are two lysine analogues which block the lysine-site: ε-aminocaproic acid (EACA) and tranexamic acid. The focus will be on the most studied drug, tranexamic acid.

Tranexamic acid is seven times more potent than EACA and effective in reducing blood loss in cardiac surgery, orthopaedic surgery, and liver transplantation (Cid and Lozano 2005; Brown et al. 2007; Molenaar et al. 2007; Henry et al. 2011; Yang et al. 2012).

A cumulative meta-analysis showed that there is reliable evidence that tranexamic acid reduces the need for transfusion in surgical patients (Ker et al. 2012). A large randomized trial (including 20 211 patients in 40 different countries) with major trauma showed a reduction in mortality in patients receiving tranexamic acid compared with placebo (Shakur et al. 2010). Occlusive vascular events were 1.7% in the tranexamic acid group compared with 2.0% in the placebo group, indicating that tranexamic acid seems to be safe. However, there were no detectable differences in the rate of transfusion and the need for surgical (re)exploration between the two groups in this large study. In a further analysis, the authors found strong evidence that administration of tranexamic acid within 1 h was favourable compared with administration at a later stage (Roberts et al. 2011).

The many studies with tranexamic acid administration do not show major adverse events and also, in contrast to what might be expected from its mechanism, no increased thrombotic complications were found. However, patients included in RCTs are often highly selected patients and are not always representative of our clinical patients. Therefore, although the occurrence of thromboembolic complications is rare and difficult to attribute to tranexamic acid administration, it remains always a point of consideration, especially in patients with hypercoagulable states.

Dosing varies widely in the literature and clinical practice (Ngaage and Bland 2010; Koster and Schirmer 2011). Further studies are needed to find the optimal dose.

Declaration of interest

None declared.

References

Bassand JP, Hamm CW, Ardissino S, *et al.* Guidelines for the diagnosis and treatment of non-ST-segment elevation acute coronary syndromes. *Eur Heart J* 2007; **28**: 1598–660

Benjamin RJ, McLaughlin LS. Plasma components: properties, differences, and uses. *Transfusion* 2012; **52**: 9S–19S

Birchall J, Stanworth SJ, Duffy MR, Doree CJ, Hyde C. Evidence for the use of recombinant factor VIIa in the prevention and treatment of bleeding in patients without hemophilia. *Transfus Med Rev* 2008; **22**: 177–87

Boer MT, Molenaar IQ, Hendriks HGD, Slooff MJH, Porte RJ. Minimizing blood loss in liver transplantation: progress through research and evolution of techniques. *Dig Surg* 2005; **22**: 265–75

Bolliger D, Szlam F, Molinaro RJ, Rahe-Meyer N, Levy JH, Tanaka KA. Finding the optimal concentration range for fibrinogen replacement after severe haemodilution: an in vitro model. *Br J Anaesth* 2009; **102**: 793–9

Bouma BN, Mosnier LO. Thrombin activatable fibrinolysis inhibitor at the interface between coagulation and fibrinolysis. *Pathofysiol Haemost Thromb* 2005; **33**: 375–81

Brown JR, Birkmeyer NJ, O'Connor GT. Meta-analysis comparing the effectiveness and adverse outcomes of antifibrinolytic agents in cardiac surgery. *Circulation* 2007; **115**: 2801–13

Buck J, Casbard A, Llewelyn C, Johnson T, Davies S, Williamson L. Preoperative transfusion in sickle cell disease: a survery of practice in England. *Eur J Haematol* 2005; **75**: 14–21

Carson JL, Carless PA, Hebert PC. Transfusion thresholds and other strategies for guiding allogeneic red blood cell transfusion. *Cochrane Database Syst Rev* 2012a; **18**: CD002042

Carson JL, Grossman BJ, Kleinman S, *et al.* Red blood cell transfusion: a clinical practice guideline from the AABB. *Ann Intern Med* 2012b; **157**: 49–58

Carson JL, Poses RM, Spence RK, Bonavita G. Severity of anaemia and operative mortality and morbidity. *Lancet* 1988; **1**: 727–9

Castaman G, Federici AB, Rodeghiero F, Manucci PM. Von Willebrand's disease in the year 2003: towards the complete identification of gene defects for correct diagnosis and treatment. *Haematologica* 20003; **88**: 94–108

Chandler WL. The thromboelastography and the thromboelastograh technique. *Semin Thromb Hemost* 1995; **21**: 1–6

Chowdary P, Saayman AG, Paulus U, Findlay GP and Collins PW. Efficacy of standard dose and 30ml/kg fresh frozen plasma in correcting laboratory parameters of haemostasis in critically ill patients. *Br J Haematol* 2004; **125**: 69–73

Cid J and Lozano M. Tranexamic acid reduces allogeneic red cell transfusions in patients undergoing total knee arthroplasty: results of a meta-analysis of randomized controlled trials. *Transfusion* 2005; **45**: 1302–7

Creszenzi G, Landoni G, Biondi-Zoccai G, *et al.* Desmopressin reduces transfusion needs after surgery: a meta-analysis of randomized clinical trials. *Anesthesiology* 2008; **109**: 1063–76

Evans DL, Marshall CJ, Christey PB, Carreel RW. Heparin binding site, conformational change, and activation of antithrombin. *Biochemistry* 1992; **31**: 2629–42

Fergusson DA, Hebert P, Hogan DL, *et al.* Effect of fresh red blood cells transfusions on clinical outcomes in premature, very low birth weight infants. *JAMA* 2012; **308**: 1443–51

Firth PG. Anesthesia and hemoglobinopathies. *Anesthesiol Clin* 2009; **27**: 321–36

Franchini M, Lippi G. The role of von Willebrand factor in hemorrhagic and thrombotic disorders. *Crit Rev Clin Lab Sci* 2007; **44**: 115–49

Furie B, Furie BC. Mechanisms of thrombus formation. *N Engl J Med* 2008; **359**: 938–49

Goodnough LT, Maniatis A, Earnshaw P, *et al.* Detection, evaluation, and management of preoperative anaemia in the elective orthopaedic surgical patient: NATA guidelines. *Br J Anaesth* 2011; **106**: 13–22

Guzetta NA, Russell IA, Williams GD. Review of the off-label use of recombinant activated factor VII in pediatric cardiac surgery patients. *Anesth Analg* 2012; **115**: 364–78

Henry DA, Carless PA, Moxey AJ, *et al.* Anti-fibrinolytic use for minimizing perioperative allogenic blood transfusion. *Cochrane Database Syst Rev* 2011; **16**: CD001886

Hiippala ST, Myllylä GJ, Vahtera EM. Hemostatic factors and replacement of major blood loss with plasma-poor red cell concentrates. *Anesth Analg* 1995; **81**: 360–5

Hirst C, Williamson L. Preoperative blood transfusions for sickle cell disease. *Cochrane Database of Syst Rev* 2012; **18**: CD003149

Hoffman M, Monroe DM 3rd. A cell- based model of hemostasis. *Thromb Haemost* 2001; **85**: 958–65

Kang YG, Martin DJ, Marquez J, *et al.* Intraoperative changes in blood coagulation and thromboelastographic monitoring in liver transplantation. *Anest Analg* 1985; **64**: 888–96

Ker K, Edwards P, Perel P, Shakur H, Roberts I. Effect of tranexamic acid on surgical bleeding: a systematic review and cumulative meta-analysis. *BMJ* 2012; **44**: e3054.

Koster A, Schirmer U. Re-evaluation of the role of antifibrinolytic therapy with lysine analogs during cardiac surgery in the post aprotinin era. *Curr Opin Anaesthesiol* 2011; **24**: 92–7

Lacroix J, Hébert PC, Fergusson D, *et al.* [The ABLE study: A randomized controlled trial on the efficacy of fresh red cell units to improve the outcome of transfused critically ill adults]. *Transfus Clin Biol* 2015; **22**: 107–11

Levi M, Cromheecke ME, de Jonge E, *et al.* Pharmacological strategies to decrease excessive blood loss in cardiac surgery: a meta-analysis of clinically relevant endpoints *Lancet* 1999; **354**: 1940–7

Levi M, Levy JH, Anderson HF, Truloff D. Safety of recombinant activated factor VII in randomized clinical trials. *N Engl J Med* 2010; **363**: 1791–800

Levy JH. Pharmacological methods to reduce perioperatieve bleeding. *Transfusion* 2008; **48**: 31S–38S

Levy JH, Azran M. Anesthetic concerns for patients with coagulopathy. *Curr Opin Anaesthesiol* 2010; **23**: 400–5

Lier H, Krep H, Schroeder S, Stuber F. Preconditions of hemostasis in trauma: a review. The influence of acidosis, hypocalcemie, anemia, and hypothermie on functional hemostasisin trauma. *J Trauma* 2008; **65**: 951–60

Mackenzie CF, Moon-Massat PF, Shander A, Javidroozi M, Greenburg AG. When blood is not an option: factors affecting survival after the use of a hemoglobin-based oxygen carrier in 54 patients with life threatening anemia. *Anesth Analg* 2010; **110**: 685–93

Mannucci PM, Ruggeri ZM, Pareti FI, Capitanio A. 1-Deamino-8-d-argininevasopressin: a new pharmacological approach to the management of haemophilia and von Willebrand's diseases. *Lancet* 1977; **23**: 869–72

Mantilla CB, Wass CT, Goodrich KA, *et al.* Risk for perioperative myocardial infarction and mortality in patients undergoing hip or knee arthroplasty: the role of anemia. *Transfusion* 2011; **51**: 82–91

Memtsoudis SG, Della Valle AG, Besculides MC, Esposito M, Koulouvaris P, Salvati EA. Risk factors for perioperative mortality after lower extremity arthroplasty: a population based study of 6.901.324 patient discharges. *J Arthroplasty* 2010; **25**: 19–26

Molenaar IQ, Warnaar N, Groen H, Tenvergert EM, Slooff MJH, Porte RJ. Efficacy and safety of antifibrinolytic drugs in liver transplantation: a systemic review and meta-analysis. *Am J Transplant* 2007; **7**: 185–94

Ngaage DL, Bland JM. Lessons from aprotinin: is the routine use and inconsistent dosing of tranexamic acid prudent? Meta-analysis of randomized and large matched observational studies. *Eur J Cardiothorac Surg* 2010; **37**: 1375–83

Nielsen VG. A comparison of the thromboelastograph and the ROTEM. *Blood Coagul Fibrinolysis* 2007; **18**: 247–52

Olson ST, Björk I, Sheffer R, Craig PA, Shore JD, Choay J. Role of the antithrombin-binding pentasaccharide in heparin acceleration of antithrombin-proteinase reactions. Resolution of the antithrombin conformational change contribution to heparin rate enhancement. *J Biol Chem* 1992; **267**: 12528–38

Ozier Y, Hunt BJ. Against: fibrinogen concentrate for management of bleeding: against indiscriminate use. *J Thromb Haemost* 2011; **9**: 6–8

Ozier Y, Schlumberger S. Pharmacological approaches to reducing blood loss and transfusions in the surgical patient. *Can J Anaesth* 2006; **53**: S21–9

Pathak A, Zhao R, Roberts HR, Sheridan BC, Selzman CH, Stouffler GA. Thrombin generation in vascular tissue. *J Thromb Haemost* 2006; **4**: 60–7

Pinkerton PH, Callum MD. Rationalizing the clinical use of frozen plasma. *CMAJ* 2010; **182**: 1019–20

Porte RJ, Leebeek FW. Pharmacological strategies to decrease transfusion requirements in patients undergoing surgery. *Drugs* 2002; **62**: 2193–211

Raj S, Killinger J, Overby P. Blood transfusion in sickle cell disease leading to posterior reversible encephalopathy syndrome (PRES). *J Child Neurol* 2013; **28**:1284–6

Ramaker AJ, Meyer P, van der Meer J, *et al.* Effects of acidosis, alkalosis, hyperthermia and hypothermia on haemostasis: results of point-of-care testing with the thromboelastography analyser. *Blood Coagul Fibrinolysis* 2009; **20**: 436–9

Ranucci MR, Baryshnikova E, Colella D. Monitoring prohemostatic treatment in bleeding patients. *Semin Thromb Hemost* 2012; **38**: 282–91

Roberts I, Shakur H, Afolabi A, *et al.* The importance of early treatment with tranexamic acid in bleeding trauma patients: an exploratory analysis of the CRASH-2 randomised controlled trial. *Lancet* 2011; **377**: 1096–101

Sagripanti A, Carpi A. Antithrombic and prothrombic activities of the vascular endothelium. *Biomed Pharmacother* 2000; **54**: 107–11

Shakur H, Roberts I, Bautista R, et al. Effects of tranexamic acid on death, vascular occlusive agents, and blood transfusion in trauma patients with significant haemorrhage (CRASH-2): a randomized, placebo-controlled trial. *Lancet* 2010; **376**: 23–32

Shander A, Javidroozi M, Ozawa S, Hare GMT. What is really dangerous: anaemia or transfusion. *Br J Anaesth* 2011; **107**: 141–59

Sørensen B, Bevan D. A critical evaluation of cryoprecipitate for replacement of fibrinogen. *Br J Haematol* 2010; **149**: 834–43

Spahn DR. Anemia and patient blood management in hip and knee surgery. A systemic review of the literature. *Anesthesiology* 2010; **113**: 482–95

Steiner ME, Ness PM, Assmann SF, *et al.* Effects of red-cell storage duration on patients undergoing cardiac surgery. *N Engl J Med* 2015; **372**: 1419–29

Tanaka KA, Key NS, Levy JH. Blood coagulation: hemostasis and thrombin regulation. *Anesth Analg* 2009; **108**: 1433–46

Tinmouth A. Evidence for a rationale use of frozen plasma for the treatment and prevention of bleeding. *Transfus Apheresis Sci* 2012; **46**: 293–8

Trentalange MJ, Walts LF. A comparison of thromboelastogram and template bleeding time in the evaluation of platelet function after aspirin ingestion. *J Clin Anesth* 1991; **3**: 377–81

Vamvakas EC, Blajchman MA. Blood still kills: six strategies to further reduce allogeneic blood transfusion-related mortality. *Transfus Med Rev* 2010; **24**: 77–124

Venema LF, Post WJ, Hendriks HGD, *et al.* An assessment of clinical interchangeability of TEG and RoTEM thromboelastographic variables in cardiac surgical patients. *Anesth Analg* 2010; **111**: 339–44

Vichinsky EP, Haberkern CM, Neumayr L, *et al.* A comparison of conservative and aggressive transfusion regimens in the perioperative management of sickle cell disease. *N Engl J Med* 1995; **333**: 206–13

Weber EWG, Slappendel R, Hemon Y, *et al.* Effects of epoetin alfa on blood transfusions and postoperative recovery in orthopaedic surgery: the European Epoetin Alfa Surgery Trial (EEST). *Eur J Anaesth* 2005; **22**: 249–57

Wikkelsoe AJ, Afshari A, Wetterslev J, Brok J, Moeller AM. Monitoring patients at risk of massive transfusion with thrombelastography or thrombelastometry: a systematic review. *Acta Anaesthesiol Scand* 2011; **55**: 1174–89

Yang ZG, Chen WP, Wu LD. Effectiveness and safety of tranexamic acid in reducing blood loss in total knee arthroplasty: a meta-analysis. *J Bone Joint Surg Am* 2012; **94**: 1153–9

Yazdanbakhsh K, Ware RE, Noizat-Pirenne F. Red blood cell alloimmunization in sickle cell disease: pathophysiology, risk factors and transfusion management. *Blood* 2012; **120**: 528–37

CHAPTER 85

Hepatic and renal disease and anaesthesia

Komal Ray and Mark Bellamy

Anaesthesia for patients with liver disease

The liver is the largest solid organ, weighing 1–1.5 kg, whose blood flow accounts for 25–30% of cardiac output. It has important metabolic, synthetic, and detoxification functions. The liver has excellent functional reserve; up to 75–85% hepatocellular dysfunction can occur before derangement in serum liver function tests is seen.

The majority of patients presenting with liver disease, including those who subsequently undergo transplantation, have chronic liver disease. This ranges from mild dysfunction, evident only by slightly deranged liver function tests, through to the anatomical and structural changes seen in fibrosis or cirrhosis. Although cirrhosis is a histological diagnosis, its functional and structural clinical correlates are well known. A minority of patients present not with chronic liver disease, but with acute hepatocellular dysfunction or necrosis. This is generally a response to a specific insult, and has rather different implications for the patient's physiology, and thus for the anaesthetist, as compared with the changes seen in chronic liver disease. O'Grady et al. (1993) have categorized the acute liver failure group as hyperacute, acute, and subacute (Table 85.1, King's College Classification).

According to this classification, the presentation of liver failure can vary hugely, through a spectrum from 'subclinical' to life-threatening multisystem organ failure. Causes of liver failure are described in Table 85.2. In the United Kingdom, the commonest cause of acute liver failure is paracetamol (acetaminophen) toxicity (65%) (Bernal et al. 2013). This is a specific UK issue; in the rest of the world, viral hepatitis predominates.

Chronic liver disease has a number of causes, including metabolic disorders, and hereditary and autoimmune causes. However, alcohol and post-viral cirrhosis remain the most important causes in patients presenting for transplantation. The prevalence of liver disease secondary to infections and alcohol is rising in the developed world. Both hepatitis B and hepatitis C are major causes of post-viral cirrhosis (Schuppan and Afdhal 2008). In developed countries, hepatitis C is the more important. Cirrhosis after hepatitis C infection may take up to 15 years to develop. In the United Kingdom, patients with end-stage liver disease may have multiple aetiologies; for example, hepatitis C infection and alcohol use. There are approximately 7500 deaths each year in the United Kingdom related to liver failure.

Table 85.1 Categories of liver failure

Liver failure	Definition
Hyperacute	Jaundice-to-encephalopathy period less than 7 days
Acute	Encephalopathy within 8 weeks of onset of jaundice
Subacute	Encephalopathy within 2–6 months of onset of jaundice
Chronic	Gradual destruction of liver tissue resulting in impaired function

Table 85.2 Causes of liver failure

Acute	
Infection	Viral: hepatitis A, B with or without delta agent, E; cytomegalovirus, Epstein–Barr virus
Drugs	Paracetamol, isoniazid, rifampicin, Reyes syndrome, NSAID
Toxin	*Amanita phalloides* mushroom poisoning (esp. Continental Europe in season)
Others	HELLP syndrome, severe shock states (cardiogenic, septic)
Chronic	
Common	
Infection: viral hepatitis	Hepatitis B (worldwide, including delta agent infection); hepatitis C; hepatitis B, hepatitis E.
Alcohol liver disease (ALD) autoimmune	Sero-negative hepatitis (presumed autoimmune; previously termed non-A non-B hepatitis)
Less common	
Drugs	
Toxins	
Biliary obstruction	Primary biliary cirrhosis, primary sclerosing cholangitis, autoimmune overlap, secondary biliary cirrhosis (congenital, stone, surgical duct injury)
Metabolic	Wilson's disease, haemochromatosis, α1-antitrypsin deficiency

Clinical manifestations

Cardiovascular

Patients with advanced chronic liver disease often have a characteristic hyperdynamic circulation with high cardiac output and low systemic vascular resistance. This is associated with (and may be a consequence of) increased circulating pro-inflammatory autacoids. These include tumour necrosis factor (TNF) and platelet-activating factor. Clinical features may include skin manifestations such as spider naevi, or pulmonary manifestations such as small intrapulmonary shunts.

The vascular changes may be accompanied by cirrhotic cardiomyopathy. Cirrhotic cardiomyopathy is characterized by impaired cardiac contractility, diastolic dysfunction, decreased β-adrenergic receptor function, post-receptor dysfunction, and defective excitation–contraction coupling (Rahman and Mallett 2015). This leads to heart failure which can be partially masked by a vasodilated, hyperdynamic circulation.

Not all cardiac dysfunction in patients with liver disease is directly attributable to liver disease. Coronary artery disease may coexist especially where other risk factors are present. Preoperative cardiac investigations including a resting electrocardiogram (ECG), echocardiogram, and in some cases dynamic testing (stress ECG, stress echo, or cardiopulmonary exercise testing) can be useful to establish baseline function, risk stratification, and to elucidate aetiology and hence the best management strategy in the perioperative period.

Pulmonary

Restrictive lung disease pattern

This can result from many causes, including those not specifically related to liver disease. However, in patients with end-stage cirrhotic liver disease, both ascites and pleural effusions are relatively common. Either can result in compromised pulmonary expansion and excursion. The management is complex, as ascites and pleural effusions may be resistant both to diuretic therapy and to drainage. Use of spironolactone or, in some cases, loop diuretics may be helpful in controlling ascites and pleural effusions at an early stage. However, in late disease, use of these drugs may be limited by renal dysfunction or hyponatraemia. Insertion of a chest drain, or short-term tapping of an effusion, may provide a temporary, bridging solution in those patients who are particularly hypoxic, thereby facilitating anaesthesia and surgery. In those who have only minimally compromised respiratory function, it is often better to tolerate a moderate but stable pleural effusion. Alternative treatment strategies in late disease include shunting [either traditional portosystemic shunting, or much more commonly nowadays, transjugular intrahepatic portosystemic shunting (TIPSS)]. In severe cases, hepatic hydrothorax may also require treatment with a definitive surgical shunt. The use of such techniques is, however, only seen in specialist centres, and is generally palliative. Moreover, it is not without its risks: the TIPSS procedure may result in an even more hyperdynamic circulation, sometimes resulting in high-output cardiac failure and pulmonary oedema. It also allows increased translocation of gut toxins into the systemic circulation, bypassing hepatic reticuloendothelial cells. This may result in deteriorating encephalopathy. Consequently, the technique is only suitable for patients who are not already encephalopathic; in those who become encephalopathic after shunting, it may be necessary to reverse the procedure. TIPSS is generally used as a bridging technique to transplantation, or in end-stage patients as a palliative procedure. In those who suffer incapacitating encephalopathy after a shunt is performed, it may be necessary to reverse the procedure.

Intrapulmonary shunt

True hepatopulmonary syndrome comprises a triad of acute/chronic liver disease, hypoxaemia, and right-to-left shunt as a result of intrapulmonary vasodilation. Potential mediators associated with the syndrome include glucagon, vasoactive intestinal peptide, prostacyclin, and nitric oxide. Characteristically, patients are hypoxic at rest, and desaturate spectacularly on exercise. Interestingly, and perhaps paradoxically, hypoxaemia is worse in the sitting/standing position than when supine (orthodeoxia). Diagnosis may be supported by a chest computed tomography scan, or radiolabelled albumin (^{99m}TcMAA, technetium macroaggregated albumin) lung perfusion scan, but the definitive diagnostic test is bubble contrast echocardiography (Abrams et al. 1995). This involves rapid injection of an agitated fluid solution (often 10–20 ml of an agitated modified fluid gelatin) into the right side of the circulation (either through a central venous catheter or a relatively proximal peripheral cannula in a large vein), while performing continuous imaging by echocardiography. Passage of the bubble contrast medium is seen through the right heart chambers; in the normal patient, the microbubbles are dispersed by the pulmonary circulation. Subsequent visualization of the bubbles in the left heart chambers is diagnostic of a right-to-left shunt. If bubbles are seen after a few cardiac cycles (often two to three cardiac cycles), this suggests the transit of bubbles through intrapulmonary anatomical shunts, and is consistent with a diagnosis of hepatopulmonary syndrome. Immediate appearance of bubble contrast in the left heart is inconsistent with intrapulmonary shunting, but rather is a sign of an anatomical intracardiac shunt. Assessment of the anaesthetic significance of hepatopulmonary syndrome is predominantly functional. It is often a fixed (or semifixed) lesion which only resolves after liver transplantation, and even then over a period of months and only in a proportion of cases. However, further progression of disease is generally arrested by liver transplantation.

Pulmonary hypertension

This is thought to affect up to 4% of patients with cirrhosis. The diagnosis is made when the mean pulmonary artery pressure is greater than 25 mm Hg in the presence of a normal left-sided filling pressure (normal pulmonary capillary wedge pressure) (Aldenkortt et al. 2014). Although the diagnosis may be confirmed by cardiac catheterization (e.g. passing a Swan–Ganz catheter), it is generally suggested by the estimated pulmonary artery pressure on echocardiography. Echocardiography can estimate the gradient between the pressure in the right ventricle (a good surrogate for the pulmonary artery systolic pressure) and that in the right atrium, by measuring the velocity of the tricuspid regurgitant jet. However, this technique is dependent on the presence of a regurgitant jet, and adequate echocardiographic windows. Right ventricular dilatation and failure is a late sign, and suggests that anaesthetic and surgical manoeuvres could readily precipitate decompensation. Most commonly, pulmonary hypertension associated with liver disease occurs as part of the portopulmonary syndrome. In this syndrome, there is an association between portal hypertension and pulmonary hypertension. Moreover, the elevated pulmonary artery pressure is often associated with the presence of *ascites* or pleural effusions. Important considerations include the degree of reversibility. In pure early portopulmonary hypertension, the pulmonary artery pressure often falls to manageable levels with drainage of ascites. However, pulmonary hypertension may develop independently of portal hypertension. The aetiology is based on a presumed imbalance between vasomediators. Once well established, pulmonary hypertension may become severe and progressive, resulting in right ventricular failure and death.

Renal

The hepatorenal syndrome is a specific form of renal dysfunction in patients with advanced chronic liver disease (Dundar and Yilmazlar 2015). It needs to be distinguished from acute kidney injury (AKI) occurring as a result of intercurrent sepsis or multiorgan failure complicating acute hepatic failure. In hepatorenal syndrome, the histological appearances of the kidney are normal. Diagnostic criteria include a serum creatinine greater than 133 μmol litre^{-1} in a patient with cirrhosis and ascites, after all other pathologies have been excluded/treated. The aetiology of hepatorenal syndrome is related to vasodilation and an imbalance between the vascular tone of afferent and efferent arterioles, caused in part by altered hormone release in the renin–angiotensin/antidiuretic hormone/sympathetic system. This may be further exacerbated by systemic factors, including hypertension, relative hypovolaemia, and infection.

Two types of hepatorenal syndrome are described (Arroyo et al. 1996). In type 1, there is rapid, severe progressive renal failure, typically developing in under 2 weeks, and carrying a high mortality. It is commonly precipitated by spontaneous bacterial peritonitis. In patients presenting to intensive care, it is more commonly seen than chronic liver failure. Treatment includes high-dose terlipressin (Gluud et al. 2012), infusion of 20% albumin solution, antibiotics in those cases where infection is thought to be the precipitating cause, or performing a TIPSS. There may also be a role for short-term use of vasopressor agents (Velez and Nietert 2011). General supportive measures and addressing the underlying cause are important. Nevertheless, the prognosis remains poor. In type 2 hepatorenal syndrome, there is a moderate reduction in glomerular filtration rate (GFR). Treatment includes reducing portal hypertension, and secondary prevention—avoiding nephrotoxins and meticulously managing fluid balance

Neurological

Hepatic encephalopathy may range from memory difficulties, loss of concentration or confusion, through to deep unconsciousness and may present as a life-threatening complication of end-stage liver disease. Classification of encephalopathy is shown in Table 85.3. Precipitating factors include infection, bleeding (particularly gastrointestinal haemorrhage with its associated protein load), excessive dietary protein, hypoglycaemia and some drugs. It is related to accumulation of toxins such as ammonia, whose metabolism in astrocytes can give rise to glutamate, a γ-aminobutyric acid (GABA) agonist. There is additionally altered permeability of the blood–brain barrier. Management is based on treating the underlying cause where possible. There is a role for drugs such as lactulose and neomycin, which can reduce the degree of gut-driven translocation (Riordan and Williams 1997). In cases where cerebral oedema is thought to be an issue, some clinicians resort to tracheal intubation and mechanical ventilation, often additionally using mannitol. Historically, some centres have used intracranial pressure monitoring, although this needs to be carefully balanced against the risk of intracranial bleeding.

Wernicke's encephalopathy is seen with alcoholic liver disease with thiamine deficiency

Table 85.3 West Haven grades of hepatic encephalopathy

Grade	Status	Neurological signs
0	Alert, oriented	None
1	Drowsy, oriented	Tremor, apraxia, incoordination
2	Drowsy, disoriented	Asterixis, dysarthria, ataxia
3	Agitated, aggressive	Asterixis, muscle rigidity, Babinski sign, hyperreflexia
4	Unresponsive to deep painful stimuli	Decerebration

Haematological

Anaemia

As a result of chronic blood loss, hypersplenism, chronic illness, functional iron deficiency (possibly associated with abnormalities of hepcidin regulation), and malnutrition.

Coagulation

The liver is involved with synthesis of all coagulation factors except factor VIII. In addition there is deficiency of protein C, protein S and antithrombin III; this can lead to a severe coagulopathic state, but also, paradoxically, to a prothrombotic tendency. Thrombocytopenia and platelet dysfunction are also seen. Routine correction of coagulopathy is not needed unless there is active bleeding, or a high risk of bleeding; the complications of blood product administration may exceed the benefit (Ozier and Tsou 2008), and correction of coagulopathy can mask trends for prognostic markers. For example, prothrombin time is used as a key indicator in deciding on transplantation in cases of acute liver failure. Dysfibrinogenaemia and fibrinolysis are also common (Cheema et al. 1996); unpicking the various elements of liver-related coagulopathy in liver disease can be extremely challenging in the perioperative clinical environment. The use of thromboelastography has proved invaluable, and in several studies superior to the use of traditional measures of clotting in appropriately guiding blood product administration (Kang et al. 1985).

Gastrointestinal

Nutrition

Nutrition is an important concern in the patient with liver failure, which is associated with a catabolic state. Hypoglycaemia can occur easily as glycogen stores are depleted and hepatic gluconeogenesis is impaired. Feeding should be established as soon as possible.

Portal hypertension

Portal hypertension is common in liver failure as a result of increased hepatic vascular resistance and increased portal venous inflow. Once a portal venous pressure of greater than 10 mm Hg is reached, portosystemic collaterals may develop. Problems related to portal hypertension are:

Varices: this carries potential for haemorrhage which can be life-threatening. Treatment of varices includes β-blockers, octreotide/terlipressin, physical measures such as injection with glue, banding, and in extreme cases TIPSS, surgical portosystemic shunting, or oesophageal transection (Triantos and Kalafateli 2014).

Splenomegaly: spleen enlargement is commonly seen with portal hypertension but does not bear a relation with severity. Sequestration of platelets and leucocytes is common with splenomegaly. Platelet transfusion is not indicated in this situation unless an invasive procedure is required.

Ascites: is presence of fluid in the peritoneal cavity; where massive, this may give rise to respiratory embarrassment, and impaired renal function. Treatment is with diuretics, sodium-and-water restriction, and paracentesis, with concurrent protein (20% albumin) supplementation.

Delayed gastric emptying

Gastric emptying is prolonged in liver disease and is related to an unclear and complex pathophysiology. H_2 antagonists and protein pump inhibitors (these are also useful for limiting the risk of variceal bleeds) offer protection against acid aspiration syndrome.

Fluid/electrolyte

Secondary hyperaldosteronism and increased secretion of antidiuretic hormone cause water retention, hypervolaemia, and *apparent* relative hyponatraemia but actual hypernatraemia (Schrier 2011).

Assessing liver function

Liver function tests need to be considered alongside assessment of the patient's disease, and with the anaesthetic and perioperative implications. Table 85.4 gives a starting point, although a more complex clinical picture is often seen.

Table 85.4 Liver function tests and hepatic diagnostic imaging

Liver function tests		
Test	**Typical reference range**	**Clinical implication**
Bilirubin	2–17 μmol litre^{-1}	Cholestasis/ biliary obstruction
ALT (alanine transaminase)	0–45 IU litre^{-1}	Hepatocellular damage, Liver-specific
AST(aspartate transaminase)	0–35 IU litre^{-1}	Hepatocellular damage, Non- specific (liver, kidney, heart, red blood cell)
ALP (alkaline phosphatase)	30–120 IU litre^{-1}	Cholestasis/ biliary obstruction, disease, pregnancy
γ-glutamyl transferase	0–30 IU litre^{-1}	Cholestasis/ biliary obstruction, alcoholic liver disease
5′-nucleotidase	2–10 IU litre^{-1}	Cholestasis/ biliary obstruction
PT (prothombin time)	10–12 s	Synthetic function
Albumin	40–60 g litre^{-1}	Synthetic function
Imaging		
Ultrasound scan (US)		
Endoscopic retrograde cholangiopancreatography (ERCP)		
Computed tomography (CT) scan		
Magnetic resonance cholangiopancreatography (MRCP)		

Risk stratification

Risk stratification is important for establishing the likely prognosis of liver disease, and therefore prioritization for transplantation or other treatments. A number of scoring systems have been developed, and have found favour in different healthcare systems. The progenitor all of these is the Child–Turcotte–Pugh score (Table 85.5 and Table 85.6) originally developed to describe risk in alcoholic liver disease (Child and Turcotte 1964; Pugh et al. 1973); however, a number of other scores have better prognostic significance across the range of aetiology. These include the Mayo Clinic Model for End-Staged Liver Disease (MELD) score, and its UK derivation, the United Kingdom End-Stage Liver Disease Score (UKELD).

MELD score

This scoring system was originally developed in the Mayo clinic as the Mayo end-stage liver disease score (MELD score) used to predict short-term mortality after TIPSS (Kamath and Kim 2007) (Table 85.7). It is calculated using the variables: bilirubin mg dl^{-1}, INR (international normalized ratio for PT) and creatinine mg dl^{-1} by the equation:

$$(3.8 \times \ln \text{bilirubin}) + (11.2 \times \ln \text{INR}) + (9.6 \times \ln \text{creatinine})$$

where ln is the natural logarithm of the physiological variables.

Preoperative assessment

The anaesthetic preoperative assessment of patients with liver disease initially focuses on the same factors as the preoperative

Table 85.5 Child–Turcotte–Pugh score

Clinical/ biochemical variable	**1**	**2**	**3**
Encephalopathy	None	Minimal grade 1/2	Advanced grade 3/4
Ascites	Absent	Mild–moderate	Severe
Bilirubin μ mol/L	<35	35–60	>60
Albumin g/L	>35	28–35	<28
PT (seconds prolonged)	1–4	4–6	>6

Anaesthetic risk: Child–Pugh A score < 6 (low risk), Child–Pugh B score 7–9 (medium risk), Child–Pugh C score >10 (high risk).

Reproduced with permission from Pugh RN, Murray-Lyon IM, Dawson JL, Pietroni MC, Williams R, Transection of the oesophagus for bleeding oesophageal varices. *British Journal of Surgery*, Volume 60, Issue 8, pp. 646–9, Copyright © 1973 British Journal of Surgery Society Ltd.

Table 85.6 Child–Turcotte–Pugh score: morbidity/mortality

Points	**Class**	**1-year survival**	**Perioperative morbidity/ mortality**
5–6	A	100%	10%
7–9	B	81%	30%
10–15	C	45%	82%

Reproduced with permission from Pugh RN, Murray-Lyon IM, Dawson JL, Pietroni MC, Williams R, Transection of the oesophagus for bleeding oesophageal varices. *British Journal of Surgery*, Volume 60, Issue 8, pp. 646–9, Copyright © 1973 British Journal of Surgery Society Ltd.

Table 85.7 MELD 3-month mortality

MELD score	Mortality (%)
≥40	71.3
30–39	52.6
20–29	19.6
10–19	6.0
<9	1.9

assessment of any other patients, including a past medical history (with special reference to cardiovascular, respiratory, allergy status, and anaesthetic history) and full physical examination, but in addition should focus on those factors specific to the liver disease, including:

- Aetiology and severity of liver disease
- Extra-hepatic manifestations
- Risk assessment
- General condition: hydration, nutrition
- Associated co-morbid conditions.

Investigations

- Routine: full blood count, electrolytes, renal function, clotting screen
- Liver function tests (see Table 85.4)
- Chest X ray, ECG
- Other: arterial blood gases, echocardiography.

Premedication

Premeditation may not necessarily be required. However, individual patients may benefit from a mild anxiolytic drug (preferably one which will not cause undue sedation in the presence of liver disease or encephalopathy). The physiological processes giving rise to encephalopathy are believed to involve the GABAminergic pathway, and hence agents which further interact with this pathway may produce an unpredictable degree of sedation. Specific therapies may be used to target coagulation and gastric acid production (and therefore the risk of gastrointestinal haemorrhage). Commonly used agents include:

- Short-acting oral temazepam in absence of neurological impairment—avoid intramuscular injections
- H_2 receptor antagonists or proton pump inhibitors
- Preoperative vitamin K, preoperative or intraoperative tranexamic acid.

Relevant anaesthetic pharmacology

Anaesthetic induction agents

Sensitivity to the sedative and cardiorespiratory depressant effects of induction agents is increased. This may in part relate to altered protein binding and volume of distribution, in part to the reduced clearance of sedative drugs, and in part as a result of a change in the receptor population density. Moreover, baseline alterations in conscious level secondary to hepatic encephalopathy can also play a role. Reduced plasma proteins cause an increase in the unbound fraction of highly protein-bound drugs (such as thiopental).

Neuromuscular blocking drugs

Patients with liver disease may have reduced plasma cholinesterase which in theory could prolong the duration of action of succinylcholine (suxamethonium) or mivacurium. Atracurium and cisatracurium are less dependent on hepatic and renal metabolism (although not all clearance is by Hoffmann elimination). Consequently, although a prolonged duration of action may be seen with these agents, it is limited and they remain a clinically viable choice. That said, accumulation of atracurium metabolites (particularly laudanosine) has been described in critically ill patients with multiple organ failure, although the clinical relevance of this observation appears to be limited (Boyd et al. 1996). Aminosteroid non-depolarizing agents have also been used (cautiously) in patients with liver disease, with reasonable success. Vecuronium undergoes deacetylation by the liver (30–40%) and is excreted in bile and urine. Rocuronium is excreted unchanged in bile/urine. The action of both of these agents may be prolonged in severe liver disease.

Opioids

Fentanyl is safe for intraoperative use, as a result of its clean metabolic and side-effect profile. It undergoes renal excretion, and has the advantage of not having active metabolites (in contrast to morphine). Alfentanil is another popular choice, and is also given by infusion to patients in intensive care. However, in patients with advanced liver disease it exhibits a prolonged half-life and an increased volume of distribution, presumably related to its reduced protein binding. Remifentanil is an attractive option owing to its short duration of action, extra-hepatic metabolism, and predictable elimination kinetics. Although its metabolism in theory relies on the presence of plasma esterases, it remains clinically very easy to use even in advanced liver disease and liver transplantation.

Morphine undergoes glucuronidation in the liver. Elimination could in theory be delayed in severe liver disease as a result of reduced liver blood flow and a reduced extraction ratio. In clinical practice, however, this is not a major problem except in patients who have coexisting renal impairment, where there may be a clinical issue because of the accumulation of its active metabolite, morphine-6-glucuronide. Again, this is seldom a significant problem intraoperatively in real-world anaesthesia, but is an important consideration when deciding on a postoperative pain management regimen or a critical care sedation regimen.

Volatile anaesthetic agents

Isoflurane, sevoflurane, and desflurane have all been used in patients with advanced liver disease, in hepatic resection, and in liver transplantation. They are all considered to be 'safe' because of their minimal hepatic metabolism. They do, however, have varying effects on preservation of the hepatic artery buffer response. Each of them preserves this reasonably well, compared with the older volatile agents, halothane and enflurane (O'Riordan et al. 1997). It is not known whether, in liver transplantation, post-reperfusion preservation of blood flow is beneficial or leads to hepatic sinusoidal strain and injury. This could in theory represent a similar pathological process to the 'small-for-size' syndrome. In liver transplantation, isoflurane and sevoflurane may have significant advantages over total intravenous anaesthesia (propofol infusion) because of their ability to potentiate ischaemic preconditioning.

Conduct of anaesthesia

The anaesthetic technique selected will depend on the surgery to be performed and any specific patient issues. Key principles have been discussed previously; important additional considerations include the maintenance of haemodynamic stability so as not to decompensate the liver disease or precipitate further organ failure (Padmakumar and Bellamy 2012). Many patients with advanced liver disease exhibit a vasodilated, hyperdynamic circulation, associated with high basal autacoid expression. Indeed, circulating plasma concentrations of TNF-α and platelet activating factor may be a factor of several hundred times those seen in healthy controls. It is therefore important to pay attention to volume status and potentially the need for vasopressors (including vasopressin or terlipressin) (Hong et al. 2012). Associated with this, it is important to maintain appropriate renal perfusion (and monitor urine output).

Pathological changes likely to impact anaesthetic management also include the presence of ascites and pleural effusions. These can compromise respiratory function in several ways. The loss of functional residual capacity, and a range of portopulmonary and hepatopulmonary syndromes (potentially offset by orthodeoxia), may lead to unexpected intraoperative hypoxia and reduced cardiac output. Appropriate management with the addition of positive end-expiratory pressure, volume support, vasoactive agents, or drainage of fluid collections may be necessary.

Perioperative management of coagulopathy and bleeding tendency may also prove both challenging and controversial. The advice of a haematologist with a special interest in coagulation should normally be sought. Abnormal preoperative testing results do not necessarily correlate well with intraoperative and perioperative bleeding risk. However, factors such as previous abdominal surgery, in the case of an abdominal operation, and the presence of varices may be more predictive of intraoperative haemorrhage than are clotting tests. Consequently, the extent to which clotting should be corrected before surgery is controversial; there is a growing body of evidence that the complications of aggressive blood product administration may exceed the clinical benefit. Intraoperatively, near-patient monitoring (such as thromboelastography) in the management of major haemorrhage and product administration has a weak evidence base. Its main advantage rests in the quicker availability of results compared with laboratory tests. Thromboelastography also gives an overview of the 'whole clotting process', which exhibits considerable redundancy, rather than information on its individual components, which may only be relevant once redundancy of the entire system has been overwhelmed.

Postoperative pain relief

The choice of an appropriate pain relief technique is highly dependent on the nature of the surgery undertaken. In cases of mild to moderate liver disease, very little modification of standard analgesic techniques may be required. In most patients, however, avoidance of non-steroidal anti-inflammatory drugs (NSAIDs) is highly desirable. The use of continuous opioid infusions should generally be avoided, although patient-controlled analgesia is generally well tolerated. Regional techniques may also be used if clotting permits, although the decision to site an epidural catheter (particularly a thoracic epidural catheter) should also take into consideration the presence of varices, which are a systemic phenomenon and may theoretically involve the epidural space.

The use of paracetamol postoperatively must also be carefully balanced against potential disadvantages. Patients with advanced liver disease may be more susceptible to oxidant stress; however, paracetamol is used in many liver transplant centres after transplantation, but with judicious dosing (Feltracco et al. 2014). Paracetamol is not itself hepatotoxic; rather, liver damage is caused by its redox metabolite, *N*-acetyl-*p*-benzoquinone imine (NAPQI).

Postoperative monitoring in a critical care environment should generally be considered, even where the nature of the surgery would not normally mandate this. Monitoring should be continued until it can be reasonably assured that the patient shows no ongoing evidence of haemodynamic compromise and is no longer considered to be at risk for the development of perioperative organ dysfunction.

Anaesthesia and renal disease

The term 'acute renal failure' has been superseded by the syndrome-based definition, acute kidney injury (AKI). Clinically AKI is characterized by a rapid reduction in kidney function resulting in a failure to maintain fluid, electrolyte, and acid–base homoeostasis. It is a spectrum extending from less severe forms of injury to more advanced injury when acute kidney failure may require renal replacement therapy. AKI occurs in 1–5% of all hospital admissions and is associated with a high morbidity and mortality. Renal function recovers in the majority of patients; however, 5–10% require long-term renal replacement therapy.

AKI is defined when one of the following criteria is met:

- Serum creatinine increases by 26 μmol litre or more within 48 h *or*
- Serum creatinine increases by 1.5-fold or more from the reference value, which is known or presumed to have occurred within 1 week *or*
- Urine output is less than 0.5 ml kg^{-1} h for more than 6 consecutive hours.

Once the diagnosis of AKI has been established, its severity can be determined using the staging system of the international guideline group, Kidney Disease: Improving Global Outcomes (KDIGO) (KDIGO Acute Kidney Injury Work Group 2012) (Table 85.8).

Table 85.8 AKI staging (KDIGO)

Stage	Serum creatinine	Urine output
1	Increase ≥26 μmol/L within 48hrs or Increase ≥1.5 to 1.9 × reference SCr	<0.5 mL/kg/hr for >6 consecutive hrs
2	Increase ≥2 to 2.9 × reference SCr	<0.5 mL/kg/hr for >12 hrs
3	Increase ≥3 × reference SCr or Increase 354 μmol/L or Commenced on renal replacement therapy irrespective of stage	<0.3 mL/kg/hr for >24 hrs or anuria for 12 hrs

Reprinted by permission from Macmillan Publishers Ltd. *Kidney International Supplements*, Kidney Disease: Improving Global Outcomes (KDIGO) Acute Kidney Injury Work Group. KDIGO Clinical Practice Guideline for Acute Kidney Injury. Volume 2, Issue 1, pp. 19–36, Copyright © 2012 International Society of Nephrology.

Pathophysiology of acute kidney injury

The GFR is the volume of plasma filtered per unit time by all the glomeruli of the kidneys (hence, it is a global and average or summed value). This is typically 125 ml min^{-1} in adults. Renal autoregulation maintains GFR at mean arterial pressures between 70 and 170 mm Hg. Autoregulation may be compromised either by pathological processes or by drug therapies, leading to AKI.

Biomarkers of renal function

A number of biomarkers of renal and renal tubular injury are currently of interest in AKI; these include neutrophil gelatinase-associated lipocalin (NGAL), cystatin C (CyC), liver-type fatty acid binding protein (L-FABP), interleukin 18 (IL-18), and kidney injury molecule-1 (KIM-1), but none of these is in routine clinical practice as yet. These markers have, however, proved of greater value than creatinine in the research setting, particularly for quantifying and predicting early clinical AKI in a critical care setting (Charlton et al. 2014).

The NGAL protein is found in excess in blood and urine in patients with AKI up to 48 h before the observed elevation in serum creatinine concentration. It is one of the most upregulated genes in the kidney after ischaemia.

CyC is a 120-amino acid protein. It is an important extracellular cysteine protease inhibitor, preventing the breakdown of proteins outside the cell. CyC is produced by all nucleated cells. It is of interest in a number of pathological processes, including the onset of cardiovascular disease and possibly of Alzheimer's disease. Its clearance is a good descriptor of renal function. CyC is an early predictive biomarker of AKI and is of interest as an alternative to creatinine in calculating estimated GFR.

Despite its limitations, however, creatinine remains the most commonly measured bedside biomarker of renal injury. Creatinine is an end product of skeletal muscle metabolism; serum creatinine concentration is a function of, among other things, skeletal muscle mass. It is freely filtered through the kidney, not reabsorbed, and small amounts can be actively secreted. When GFR decreases by more than 50%, the creatinine load exceeds maximum filtration, and the serum creatinine concentration becomes elevated. Therefore while a rising serum creatinine may signify muscle breakdown, it is most commonly indicative of renal dysfunction. It must be remembered that the trend of serum creatinine is important, as concentration is related to body skeletal muscle mass. Therefore, where it is diminished, for example in the elderly patient, a 'normal range' laboratory creatinine may indicate AKI. Creatinine clearance is often estimated from serum creatinine and patient characteristics.

Estimated GFR can be calculated using any one of a number of formulae. The traditional version was the Cockcroft and Gault formula; more common nowadays is the better-validated four-variable Modification of Diet in Renal Disease (MDRD) equation (Delanaye and Mariat 2013):

$$\text{GFR (ml min}^{-1}\text{1.73 m}^{-2}) = 186 \times (\text{serum creatinine}/88.4)^{-1.154} \times (\text{age})^{-0.203} \times (0.742 \text{ if female}) \times (1.210 \text{ if black}) \quad (85.1)$$

where serum creatinine is in µmol $litre^{-1}$, and age is in years (SI units).

This equation, however, is only an estimate. The automated immunoassay of CyC is a promising new approach to deriving more accurate values, but to gain real rather than predicted creatinine clearance, it is necessary to perform a 24 h urine collection and formally derive creatinine clearance.

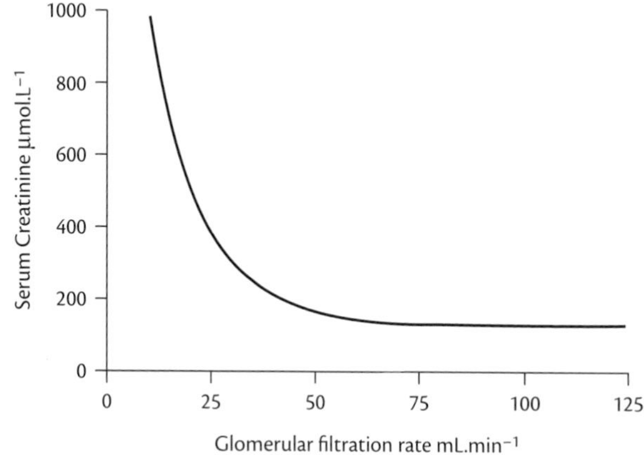

Figure 85.1 Plot of serum creatinine as a function of glomerular filtration rate.

Table 85.9 Causes of AKI

Pre-renal	Renal (intrinsic)	Post-renal
Hypovolaemia (D&V, haemorrhage)	Glomerulonephritis	Obstruction of:
	Tubular:	Pelvi-calyceal system
Low cardiac output	Ischaemia: pancreatitis, burns	Ureter
Low BP (sepsis, drugs)	Exogenous toxin: radio contrast	VUJ: bladder
Reno-vascular occlusion	Endogenous toxins: rhabdomyolysis	Bladder neck: urethra
	Vascular	
	Interstitial	

Figure 85.1 demonstrates the relationship between creatinine and GFR. Note that creatinine only begins to increase after more than 50% of renal nephron function has been lost signifying that an increase in creatinine is a late sign of renal injury and thus is critically important. Note that GFRs higher than 90 ml min^{-1} have not been plotted as these fall well within the healthy range and most laboratories do not report these other than 'greater than 90 ml min^{-1}'.

AKI is caused by pre-renal (60%), renal (20–40%) and post-renal (1–10%) factors as shown in Table 85.9. The outer medulla with its high metabolic demands (oxygen extraction ratio of 90%) is particularly vulnerable to hypoperfusion and hypoxia both in normal patients and in those with CKD.

Acute kidney injury prevention

Risk stratification

It is important to identify patients at high risk of developing AKI so as to minimize modifiable risk factors and adopt appropriate preventable measures. Risk factors could be related either to the patient or the type of surgery (Table 85.10).

Avoidance of nephrotoxins

A number of medications or classes of medication commonly used in the perioperative period have potentially adverse effects on renal

Table 85.10 Risk factors associated with development of AKI

Patient factors	Surgical factors
Age > 75 years	Duration of surgery
Chronic kidney disease	Intraperitoneal surgery
Cardiac failure	Duration of cardiopulmonary bypass
Liver disease, jaundice	Cross-clamp time
Diabetes mellitus	Use of intra-aortic balloon pump
Atherosclerotic peripheral vascular disease	
Nephrotoxic drugs	
Hypovolaemia	
Sepsis	

Box 85.1 Drugs which can potentially compromise renal function

- Analgesics: aspirin, NSAIDs
- Antibiotics: aminoglycosides, amphotericin, vancomycin
- Angiotensin-converting enzyme inhibitors, angiotensin receptor blockers
- Antineoplastic: cisplatin, methotrexate
- Immunosuppressant: ciclosporin
- Radiocontrast media.

function. Some commonly used nephrotoxic agents are listed in Box 85.1. Perhaps the best known among these are the NSAIDs. NSAIDs can impair renal autoregulation and also contribute to interstitial nephritis. The decision to use or withhold NSAIDs is a difficult one. Beneficially, they provide extremely effective perioperative analgesia, minimizing the requirement for opioid drugs. They provide (at least theoretically) a degree of potentially beneficial immunomodulation. NSAIDs may also attenuate other arachidonic acid cascade-mediated processes, such as the peritoneal traction syndrome. Detrimentally, they may exacerbate any bleeding tendency, impairing platelet function and adversely modulating vascular endothelial function. NSAIDs have several potentially undesirable effects on renal function; they are known to adversely affect autoregulation, and have been associated with perioperative and postoperative kidney injury. Hence they should generally be avoided in patients with either patient-related or procedure-related renal risk factors.

Angiotensin-converting enzyme inhibitors and angiotensin receptor blockers may also adversely affect renal autoregulation. These agents are thought to selectively reduce efferent arterial tone, thereby reducing glomerular perfusion pressure. That said, there is little evidence of benefit from discontinuing these agents before surgery.

The role of intravenous radiological contrast media as a risk factor in AKI is well recognized. Careful consideration should be given to the risk:benefit ratio of using intravenous contrast medium; discussion with the radiologist regarding alternative agents is also worthwhile, as newer iso-osmolar or low osmolar non-ionic contrast agents are thought to be less nephrotoxic. When the use of traditional contrast medium is unavoidable, the minimum dose compatible with adequate diagnostic discrimination should be used. Renal function should be rechecked up to 72 h after the procedure in high-risk patients to confirm stable renal function and facilitate early intervention in those in whom otherwise unsuspected AKI may have resulted.

Recent clinical trials data in critical care patients, although not specifically in the perioperative setting, have also suggested a potentially nephrotoxic effect of colloidal solutions, and in particular some of the high-molecular-weight starches. Consequently, these should probably be avoided for fluid resuscitation in those at risk of renal dysfunction until further evidence emerges (Hartog et al. 2011; Myburgh et al. 2012; Perner et al. 2012).

Acute kidney injury secondary to rhabdomyolysis

Rhabdomyolysis is of interest to the anaesthetist, as it occurs in a number of clinical scenarios. These include the morbidly obese patient undergoing prolonged anaesthesia and surgery (where rhabdomyolysis may result from tissue pressure points in the context of impaired perfusion or a reduced cardiac output) as well as in trauma patients, those with crush injuries, and those with compartment syndrome. Rhabdomyolysis-induced AKI results from skeletal muscle injury with the release of myoglobin, a muscle breakdown product. Myoglobin is freely filtered by the kidneys and is directly toxic to the tubular epithelial cells. Its effects may be heightened where there is coexisting hypovolaemia and acidosis. Management includes volume assessment and close monitoring with aggressive fluid resuscitation, and alkalinization of the urine.

Fluid resuscitation with sodium chloride 0.9% is preferred at a rate of 10–15ml kg^{-1} h^{-1} to achieve high urinary flow rates (>100 ml h^{-1}), with the cautious addition of sodium bicarbonate 1.4% to maintain urinary pH more alkaline than 6.51. Throughout this process, the patient's volume status must be carefully evaluated; once adequately fluid resuscitated, care must be taken not to precipitate pulmonary oedema.

Mannitol is still thought by some to have a role because of its properties as an osmotic diuretic and free radical scavenger. However, there is little clinical outcome evidence to support its use. Inappropriate use of mannitol can precipitate pulmonary oedema particularly if used with hypertonic sodium bicarbonate.

Management of acute kidney injury in the perioperative setting

Management of AKI in the perioperative period poses numerous challenges for the anaesthetist. The first priority remains management of the physiology of the patient with AKI, with special regard to any precipitating or underlying causes. Anaesthesia or support for surgical procedures may be requested in patients whose underlying cause has not been fully elucidated or treated. The role of the anaesthetist may therefore include both diagnostic and treatment elements. Almost by definition, this patient group represents a sick and haemodynamically compromised cohort. Management of 'critical care' conditions such as septic or haemorrhagic shock is likely to form a necessary part of the management. A number of additional measures may be of use in managing either incipient or established AKI:

- Haemodynamic resuscitation and optimization (following standard practice).

- Avoidance or discontinuation of known and presumed nephrotoxins.
- Renal replacement therapy: this term encompasses a range of treatments designed to support or replace kidney function. Most commonly, in the perioperative or critical care setting, continuous venovenous haemofiltration is the modality encountered. Intermittent haemodialysis and peritoneal dialysis are common alternatives.
- Consideration of pharmacological prophylactic agents: any of the traditional pharmacological agents have demonstrated false promise and few are still used in clinical practice. These include:
  - Dopamine: a non-selective dopamine receptor agonist which at low dose (0.5–3.0 $\mu g\ kg^{-1}\ min^{-1}$) was thought to be beneficial in AKI by augmenting renal blood flow. However, currently there is no evidence to support any clinical outcome benefit in patients with, or at risk of, AKI.
  - Fenoldopam: a selective dopamine D1 receptor agonist which decreases systemic vascular resistance while increasing renal blood flow to both the cortex and medullary regions in the kidney. A meta-analysis concluded that fenoldopam reduces the need for renal replacement therapy and mortality in patients with AKI.
  - Diuretics (furosemide/mannitol): there remains no evidence of an improvement in clinical outcome.
  - Atrial natriuretic peptide: some studies have suggested there may be benefit in cardiac surgery patients. As yet no study has demonstrated benefit in other surgical populations.
  - Nesiritide (recombinant human β natriuretic peptide): outcome benefit has been seen in cardiac and abdominal aneurysm surgery. Further trials of this potentially promising agent are needed.
- Tight glycaemic control: better renal outcomes have been observed when using tight glycaemic control in diabetic patients during the perioperative period. However, there have been limited studies, and further assessment as to the clinical effect and pathophysiology are needed.

Investigations

A number of investigations may be useful in elucidating the cause and likely prognosis of AKI; however, relatively few of these are relevant to the immediate perioperative management of the patient with AKI. The more common investigations are listed in Box 85.2 and Table 85.11.

Other investigations

Consideration should be given to additional investigations, which may have direct consequences for the conduct of anaesthesia. There may also be implications for the nature of any surgical or radiological intervention proposed. The following general points give a guide to these areas. Examination of the chest X-ray is of direct relevance to the conduct of anaesthesia. Special attention should be paid to heart size, pulmonary vasculature (looking for evidence of upper lobe venous diversion), and evidence of pulmonary interstitial infiltrates (pulmonary oedema, infection, autoimmune conditions). An ECG may give early warning of electrolyte disorders, in particular hyperkalaemia as evidenced by the classic 'peaked' T

Box 85.2 Standard blood tests

Blood tests

- Urea and electrolytes: urea disproportionately higher in prerenal, gastrointestinal bleeds, catabolic state
- Ca^{2+}, PO_4^{3-}: Acidaemia ↑ ionized Ca^{2+}
- Full blood count anaemia indicates chronic renal failure:
  - Platelets: liver disease, HELLP, sepsis
  - Platelets: vasculitis
  - Blood film: haemolytic uraemic syndrome, myeloma
- Coagulation
- Liver function tests
- Lactate dehydrogenase (suggestive of haemolytic uraemic syndrome)
- Creatine kinase: increased in rhabdomyolysis
- Blood culture
- Immunology: ANCA, antiglomerular basement membrane antibody, immunoglobulins, complement components C3/4, rheumatoid factor, antinuclear antibody, extractable nuclear antigen, and the double stranded DNA (suggestive of lupus), cryoglobulins, anticardiolipin, anti-β2-glycoprotein-1 antibodies
- ↑ Erythrocyte sedimentation rate: suggestive of systemic lupus erythematosus, autoimmune and inflammatory conditions
- Immunophoresis for paraproteins
- Viral article testing before dialysis (should include HIV, HBsAg, HCVAb).

Urine

- Culture and sensitivity
- Microscopy:
  - Red blood cell cast: suggestive of glomerulonephritis
  - White blood cell cast: consider acute pyelonephritis
  - Eosinophils: consider interstitial nephritis
- Bence Jones proteins: consider myeloma
- Urine electrolytes and osmolality: may be unreliable in the elderly (sub-clinical renal impairment) and those on diuretics. May help to distinguish AKI causes.

Table 85.11 Urinary electrolyte measurements in pre-renal and renal failure

Index	Pre-renal	Renal
Urinary Na (mmol $litre^{-1}$)	<20	>40
Urine osmolarity (mOsm $litre^{-1}$)	>500	<350
Urine/plasma urea	>8	<3
Specific gravity	High 1.020	Fixed 1.010–1.020

wave. Ischaemia is less readily detected on a resting ECG but evidence of ventricular hypertrophy, conduction abnormalities, or old myocardial infarction may be present. These findings are far more common in patients with chronic kidney disease (CKD) than AKI, but may exist independently as evidence of a significant underlying condition. There is also a group of patients who suffer acute on chronic kidney injury, in whom the cardiovascular consequences of CKD or diabetes may well be significant.

Renal ultrasound should be performed, looking in particular for kidney size, ureteric obstruction, and blood flow (Doppler studies). This may help inform any surgical or radiological intervention, and may be both diagnostically and prognostically significant.

Chronic kidney disease

CKD represents progressive and irreversible reduction in kidney function. Common causes for CKD are listed in Box 85.3. It can be classified into five stages based on estimated GFR (Box 85.4).

Systemic manifestations of chronic kidney disease

The patient with renal disease is of interest to the anaesthetist not just because of the biochemical abnormalities (e.g. a raised creatinine and urea, potentially raised serum potassium) associated with kidney failure, but because the wider manifestations of renal disease are truly multisystem and increase the overall level of perioperative risk dramatically. Moreover, the presence of renal disease may be indicative of an underlying causative pathology. Examples might include severe arterial hypertension, rheumatoid arthritis, vasculitis, or diabetes. Some conditions, for example, systemic arterial hypertension, can be either a cause of CKD, or a consequence of it. In either case, the patient may suffer severe associated systemic manifestations.

Cardiovascular

Cardiovascular disease is very common in patients with kidney disease, and accounts for up to 48% of deaths in this patient group. Systemic arterial hypertension is most common with an incidence of 80%. Plasma volume expansion and water retention is often a contributory cause. This is often further compounded by a derangement of the homeostatic mechanisms dependent on the renin–angiotensin system. Ischaemic heart disease is frequently seen. It may be further exacerbated by accelerated atherosclerosis, hypertension, and fluid overload resulting in left ventricular hypertrophy and failure. Uraemic pericarditis (evidenced by a classic 'pericardial rub') if untreated may progress to cardiac tamponade.

Box 85.3 Common causes of CKD

- Diabetes mellitus: 30%
- Hypertension: 24%
- Glomerulonephritis:17%
- Chronic pyelonephritis: 5%
- Polycystic kidney: 4%
- Unknown: 20%.

Box 85.4 Classification of CKD

- Stage 1: normal GFR with other evidence of renal damage
- Stage 2: GFR 60–90 ml min^{-1} with other evidence of renal damage
- Stage 3: GFR 30–60 ml min^{-1}; moderate CKD
- Stage 4: GFR 15–30 ml h^{-1}; severe CKD
- Stage 5: GFR <15 ml min^{-1}. End-stage renal failure. Dialysis dependent

Respiratory complications are common particularly in the postoperative period. Pulmonary oedema may be precipitated by a number of causes. These include myocardial ischaemia; the effects of volume overload (either as a feature of the pathology, or an iatrogenic consequence of intraoperative fluid management); and acute diastolic dysfunction potentially exacerbated by tachycardia, anaemia, or drugs. Pleural effusion may complicate the perioperative course, contributing to hypoxaemia both intraoperatively and, particularly, postoperatively. This may be associated with ventilation perfusion mismatch and restricted ventilatory excursion. Pleural effusion may potentially be associated with pericardial effusion and compromised venous return. The causes of pleural effusions are many. They may reflect poor cardiac function, hypoproteinaemia, or salt and water retention. Careful consideration should be given to draining pleural effusions in the perioperative period; this may significantly reduce postoperative respiratory embarrassment, but may occasionally predispose to re-expansion pulmonary oedema. There may additionally be a risk of technical complications associated with the drainage procedure (including pain, pneumothorax, and bleeding). In many cases, pleural effusion may be self-limiting, and respond to therapy of the underlying cause (e.g. close attention to fluid balance, nutrition, and protein status). CKD patients are predisposed to infection as a result of impaired cellular and humoral immunity, and this in combination with other factors may be a cause of postoperative chest infection.

Neurological

Neurological abnormalities can vary from mild personality changes, through asterixis, myoclonus, encephalopathy, to convulsions. Peripheral neuropathy is common, initially a distal glove and stocking sensory loss progressing to motor changes. Presence of peripheral neuropathy should alert the clinician to the potential presence of autonomic neuropathy. Important features could include delayed gastric emptying, postural hypotension, silent myocardial ischaemia, or infarction. Dialysis dementia is occasionally seen in patients who have been treated with haemodialysis for many years; it is far less commonly seen in peritoneal dialysis patients (Wolfgram et al. 2015).

Dialysis disequilibrium syndrome

Dialysis disequilibrium syndrome occurs with rapid initial reduction in plasma urea concentration. The causes of this syndrome are poorly understood (Patel et al. 2008). Its clinical presentation can be variable, from headache, through restlessness and agitation, to coma and potentially death. The mechanism includes cerebral oedema and raised intracranial pressure; however, the precise underlying causes are poorly understood. Attempts to treat the disequilibrium syndrome are centred on management of raised intracranial pressure and cerebral oedema. Because these are often only partially effective, the syndrome has a high morbidity and mortality. Avoidance is therefore key.

Gastrointestinal

Gastrointestinal problems are frequently seen. These include anorexia, nausea, and vomiting, which may contribute to malnutrition. Gastric emptying is delayed. Acid hypersecretion may also be an issue. Consequently, there is a significant risk both of acid aspiration and stress ulceration in the perioperative period. Appropriate prophylaxis should form a part of the anaesthetic technique. This could include use of proton pump inhibitors, antacids, or H_2 receptor blockers. Some anaesthetists, depending on the clinical scenario, also favour a modified rapid sequence induction.

Fluid and electrolyte disturbances

Fluid and electrolyte disturbances are common even in the 'well-dialysed' patient. These are likely to include hypocalcaemia, hyperphosphataemia, hyponatraemia, hyperkalaemia, and metabolic acidosis. The likelihood of seeing these electrolyte abnormalities depends on the severity of the renal disease, whether or not the patient is dialysed (and if so, how recently), and the dialysis technique used.

Haematological

Anaemia is common, sometimes severe but generally well tolerated. Its aetiology is multifactorial. A common feature is the duality of reduced erythropoietin production and functional iron deficiency. Some patients are treated effectively with erythropoietin replacement therapy, whereas others are resistant to this, and may suffer 'functional iron deficiency', responsive to intravenous (but not oral) iron supplementation (Cavill I, 2002). Dietary and nutritional factors may also play a part.

Platelet activity is reduced in uraemia. This is in part because of an intrinsic reduction in platelet function, associated with poor platelet factor 3 activity, and in part as a result of the interaction between platelets and the vascular endothelium. Consequently, there are both decreased adhesion and aggregation. These effects are further exacerbated by a reduced concentration of von Willebrand factor. The interaction between von Willebrand factor and factor VIII facilitates platelets binding to vessel wall collagen via the GP1B receptor. This interaction can be restored in around 50% of patients with uraemic platelet dysfunction by the administration of desmopressin (DDAVP).

Immunological

Both cell-mediated and humoral immunity are inhibited resulting in predisposition to infections. Sepsis is a major cause of death in CKD patients.

Dialysis

Haemodialysis

Treatment for end-stage renal failure is usually given three to four times per week in intensive dialysis sessions lasting several hours. During these sessions, there is, according to the patient's physiology (and whether or not there is any preservation of native renal function) significant fluid removal, fluid shifts, and correction of electrolytes and middle molecules. This can result in marked hypotension, post-dialysis hypovolaemia (predisposing to hypotension at induction of anaesthesia), and potentially the disequilibrium syndrome. Haemodialysis requires vascular access. This may be provided through an indwelling intravenous access catheter (short term), temporary fistula, or permanent (surgically created) arteriovenous shunt (long term). By definition, haemodialysis is an extracorporeal circulation, and requires systemic anticoagulation. This is usually achieved by heparinization. Surgery should be planned for 4–6 h after the most recent dialysis session. Post-dialysis electrolytes need to be checked, to confirm the effectiveness of dialysis and the starting baseline before surgery. Considerable variation in post-dialysis electrolyte concentrations may be seen. Patients who habitually have a high potassium concentration tolerate hyperkalaemia well, and in many cases may safely undergo anaesthesia with potassium concentrations above the normal range. Hypovolaemia and residual anticoagulation effects of heparin may be seen intraoperatively. Depending on the nature and magnitude of surgery, anticipated blood and fluid shifts, it may be necessary to arrange a further session of haemodialysis for the postoperative period.

Peritoneal dialysis

This is a slow and continuous process performed through a temporary or permanent catheter inserted into the peritoneum. Dialysis fluid should be drained preoperatively to avoid respiratory compromise. As with haemodialysis, electrolytes and coagulation should be rechecked before surgery. Depending on the nature of the surgical procedure, further peritoneal dialysis may not be practicable in a postoperative setting, in which case postoperative haemofiltration or haemodialysis should be planned. To facilitate this, it may be prudent to establish either temporary or permanent vascular access while the patient is under anaesthesia.

Preoperative assessment

In addition to the standard preoperative assessment appropriate to any patient, special consideration should be given to the fact that the patient with CKD is likely to be a high-risk patient with multisystem involvement. Special attention should therefore be given to a careful and thorough cardiorespiratory assessment. Features of autonomic neuropathy should also be sought, as these may predict intraoperative risk. In particular, an excessive haemodynamic response (either rate rhythm or cardiac output/blood pressure) to postural change or a Valsalva manoeuvre may give some clue. The dialysis history should also be noted. The patient's normal fluid balance and intake and output assessment (including whether there is any native urine output) may also be useful, as these will give some guide as to the prudence or otherwise of intraoperative volume loading.

There should be a full multidisciplinary discussion (surgeon, nephrologist, and anaesthetist) of the postoperative management and dialysis plan. The appropriate postoperative environment should also be discussed; a general surgical ward may not provide the best setting. A renal ward, dialysis bed, or critical care bed may be deemed more appropriate, depending on the burden of comorbidity and nature of surgery.

Perioperative care

Prior to the patient being transferred into the anaesthetic room or operating theatre, a full team brief should take place, alerting the theatre staff to the comorbidities suffered by the patient, and any special risk factors associated with these. Particular attention should be paid in this briefing to the presence of arteriovenous fistulae and the need for appropriate protection and periodic checking of these in the perioperative period. The existence of autonomic neuropathy should alert the team to the risk of delayed gastric emptying and high gastric acid production. Appropriate consideration should be given to risk of aspiration and the need for antacid prophylaxis. Sites of arteriovenous fistulae must be protected by wrapping in cotton wool or Gamgee. These sites should not be used for cannulation, whether venous or arterial, or for the positioning of non-invasive blood pressure monitoring cuffs.

Appropriate monitoring should be established before the induction of anaesthesia. Traditionally, ECG monitoring using the CM 5 configuration is used for the best detection of myocardial ischaemia. Automated ST-segment monitoring is of value, as this may detect early and often subtle degrees of ST-segment change. The role of central venous pressure monitoring to guide fluid administration is controversial; dynamic measures, including oesophageal Doppler monitoring and other forms of stroke volume monitoring, may be of greater value. That said, central venous cannulation is of value as a route of administration of vasopressors and cardiovascularly active drugs. The convenience of central venous catheterization needs to be balanced against the potential difficulty and risks involved, particularly in this patient group who may have had numerous previous central venous catheters (in particular for dialysis access) and who may therefore have very few remaining sites available for central venous cannulation. Moreover, these sites are often precious, and where possible should be reserved for future dialysis access. Neuromuscular function and temperature monitoring are beneficial, and there is little rational argument for omitting these. All patients should be kept warm using fluid warmers and forced air warmers to avoid hypothermia, which can contribute to coagulopathy and the neurohumoral stress response.

Sepsis is a common cause of death. Strict asepsis must be followed. Hepatitis B and C have an increased prevalence in the dialysis population. Universal precautions should be emphasized, for the protection of the patient, staff, and future patients.

Drugs

Drugs may either be excreted unchanged or as water-soluble metabolites. The precise modification of those processes in renal disease varies according to the individual agent, and depends on a number of factors. More often than not, derangements in patient physiology (e.g. secondary to cardiovascular disease or relative hypovolaemia) may have greater relevance for dose modification than the altered pharmacokinetics or pharmacodynamics secondary to renal failure. Both the water solubility of a drug and its distribution are important when considering modification of the loading dose. Changes in receptor pharmacology may also be important, with either increased or reduced receptor expression in disease. In practical terms, the loading doses of many anaesthetic drugs are often little changed, although slower injection and titration against effect is prudent. Alteration of dose interval or infusion rate in the maintenance phase is often more sensitive to the effects of renal disease. Hypoalbuminaemia and acidosis may result in reduced protein binding and an increased free faction of highly protein-bound drugs (e.g. many anaesthetic induction agents). Anaesthetic drugs may have a secondary effect through reduction of renal blood flow, and hence GFR, on both their own clearance and clearance of other drugs.

Induction agents

Barbiturates are excreted unchanged in the urine (24%), though the initial recovery of consciousness is related to redistribution and thus is not a function of excretion or metabolism. Increased sensitivity to barbiturate drugs is seen possibly as a result of reduced protein binding. The effects of etomidate are similarly enhanced because of decreased protein binding. The pharmacokinetics of propofol appear little changed with impaired renal function. Benzodiazepines undergo primarily hepatic metabolism, but again there is increased sensitivity related to reduced protein binding and an increased free fraction. Ketamine undergoes primarily hepatic metabolism, though its two principal metabolites then undergo renal excretion. Ketamine in critical illness shows an increased half-life because of a relatively greater increase in its volume of distribution than its clearance. Interestingly, there are several reports of ketamine abuse giving rise to renal dysfunction through precipitation of its metabolites in the ureter, causing obstruction. This resolves on discontinuation of the drug.

Analgesics

Morphine is metabolized in the liver to water-soluble metabolites which are excreted by the kidney. These metabolites (morphine-3- and morphine-6-glucuronide) possess pharmacological activity. The long-acting metabolite morphine-6-glucuronide has greater μ-receptor selectivity and is more potent than its parent compound (45–60-fold in a mouse model), so contributes significantly to the clinical effectiveness of morphine.

Pethidine similarly undergoes demethylation in the liver. Its water-soluble metabolite norpethidine is liable to accumulation in renal failure, and has the potential to cause convulsions. Its use is generally avoided in severe renal impairment where alternative analgesic strategies may be used.

Similarly, both codeine and dihydrocodeine are susceptible to an unpredictably prolonged half-life (up to five-fold) and are therefore best avoided where suitable alternatives exist. Oxycodone has active metabolites hence the dose should be reduced in renal failure, the dosing interval increased, and titrated to effect. Tramadol is a centrally acting agent that inhibits noradrenaline and serotonin reuptake by nerve cells, and acts on μ-opioid receptors. Tramadol has active metabolites excreted by the kidney; hence the dose-interval may need to be increased. Nevertheless, it has been advocated as an appropriate drug for the management of moderate pain in renal disease patients.

The short and ultra-short-acting opioids alfentanil and remifentanil undergo hepatic and plasma-based metabolism respectively. Alterations in their kinetics in renal dysfunction are clinically minimal. Their use is thus similar to that in healthy patients. Postoperatively, there is a good safety track record of patient-controlled analgesia systems using fentanyl. There is also wide experience of morphine patient-controlled analgesia systems in this setting, which can safely be used with appropriate monitoring. Paracetamol is likewise safe to use in standard doses. There is, however, little or no role for NSAIDs given their exaggerated risk:benefit profile in this patient group.

Volatile agents

Enflurane and sevoflurane are both biotransformed to inorganic fluoride, although the plasma concentrations produced are below nephrotoxic levels. Isoflurane and, in particular, desflurane are metabolized by the liver to a much lesser extent and so have virtually no direct nephrotoxic potential. The effects of vasodilation and myocardial depression remain of potential significance but should be minimized in judicious use.

Neuromuscular blocking agents

Suxamethonium (succinylcholine) is a depolarizing neuromuscular blocking agent, giving rise to muscle fasciculation and release of potassium. This is potentially problematic in the patient who already has an elevated potassium, as it may dispose to cardiac arrest. The potential for an exaggerated or sustained hyperkalaemic response generally means that the risks of using suxamethonium outweigh the benefits. Non-depolarizing neuromuscular blocking agents (atracurium, cisatracurium, vecuronium, rocuronium) are good choices as they have excretion pathways which are not absolutely reliant on the kidney (although it is now well established that atracurium, while undergoing a Hoffman degradation primarily, is in part renally excreted and has a prolonged half-life in hepatorenal failure).

The use of the aminosteroid neuromuscular blocking agent rocuronium or vecuronium is attractive, particularly as their effects may be antagonized by the new agent sugammadex. Sugammadex is a modified γ-cyclodextrin, a selective neuromuscular blocking drug-binding agent designed to encapsulate rocuronium but which is also effective at binding vecuronium. While the pharmacokinetics of rocuronium are only minimally altered in severe renal impairment, leading to little alteration in its clinical use, the pharmacokinetics of sugammadex are markedly altered. Sugammadex, and the sugammadex–rocuronium complex, are excreted in the urine. Nevertheless, even in severe renal failure, sugammadex appears effective as an agent to antagonize the clinical effects of rocuronium-induced neuromuscular block (Panhuizen et al. 2015). The aminosteroid neuromuscular blocking drug pancuronium is best avoided in severe renal impairment, as it has a long duration of action and is 80% renally excreted.

Conduct of anaesthesia

The anaesthetic technique used should be one which takes account of the alterations in patient physiology, pharmacodynamics, and pharmacokinetics. This may involve careful positioning, close monitoring, and modification of the dose, route of administration, and rate of administration of anaesthetic and analgesic agents (as categorized previously). Provided such measures are taken, most anaesthetic techniques can reasonably be applied to the patient with renal impairment. The precise choice of technique will depend on operator experience, the surgery to be undertaken, and the clinical setting, as much as on the theoretical considerations. For example, patients undergoing short-duration anaesthesia for day-case procedures, apart from appropriate airway protection, are unlikely to require a significantly different anaesthetic technique to any other patient undergoing anaesthesia for a similar procedure.

Postoperative care

The issues relating to postoperative analgesia and environment have been discussed previously. A multimodal approach to postoperative analgesia is likely to prove the safest and most effective option. However, when planning regional anaesthetic techniques or local blocks, it is important to remember that many patients with significant renal dysfunction also have derangements of clotting and platelet function and an increased susceptibility to infection. These are not absolute contraindications to the use of blocks and regional techniques, but rather factors to be taken into consideration when balancing risk against benefit. More important is a multidisciplinary team approach to the postoperative management of the patient with significant renal disease, together with appropriate monitoring and follow-up so that potential complications of surgery or anaesthesia, or deterioration in general medical state, can be spotted early and managed in a timely fashion.

Declaration of interest

None declared.

References

Abrams GA, Jaffe CC, Hoffer PB, Binder HJ, Fallon MB. Diagnostic utility of contrast echocardiography and lung perfusion scan in patients with hepatopulmonary syndrome. *Gastroenterology* 1995; **109**: 1283–8

Aldenkortt F, Aldenkortt M, Caviezel L, Waeber JL, Weber A, Schiffer E. Portopulmonary hypertension and hepatopulmonary syndrome. *World J Gastroenterol* 2014; **20**: 8072–81

Arroyo V, Ginès P, Gerbes AL, *et al.* Definition and diagnostic criteria of refractory ascites and hepatorenal syndrome in cirrhosis. International Ascites Club. *Hepatology* 1996; **23**: 164–76

Bernal W, Hyyrylainen A, Gera A, *et al.* Lessons from look-back in acute liver failure? A single centre experience of 3300 patients. *J Hepatol* 2013; **59**: 74–80

Boyd AH, Eastwood NB, Parker CJ, Hunter JM. Comparison of the pharmacodynamics and pharmacokinetics of an infusion of cis-atracurium (51W89) or atracurium in critically ill patients undergoing mechanical ventilation in an intensive therapy unit. *Br J Anaesth* 1996; **76**: 382–8

Cavill I. Iron and erythropoietin in renal disease. *Nephrol Dial Transplant* 2002; **17**(Suppl) 5: 19–23

Charlton JR, Portilla D, Okusa MD. A basic science view of acute kidney injury biomarkers. *Nephrol Dial Transplant* 2014; **29**: 1301–11

Cheema SP, Webster NR, Dunn F, Bellamy MC. Mediators of fibrinolysis in orthotopic liver transplantation. *Clin Transplant* 1996; **10**: 24–7

Child CG, Turcotte JG. Surgery and portal hypertension. In Child CG, ed. *The Liver and Portal Hypertension*. Philadelphia, PA: Saunders, 1964: 50–64

Delanaye P, Mariat C. The applicability of eGFR equations to different populations. *Nat Rev Nephrol* 2013; **9**: 513–22

Dundar HZ, Yilmazlar T. Management of hepatorenal syndrome. *World J Nephrol* 2015; **4**: 277–86

Feltracco P, Carollo C, Barbieri S, *et al.* Pain control after liver transplantation surgery. *Transplant Proc* 2014; **46**: 2300–7

Gluud LL, Christensen K, Christensen E, Krag A. Terlipressin for hepatorenal syndrome. *Cochrane Database Syst Rev* 2012; **9**: CD005162

Hartog CS, Bauer M, Reinhart K. The efficacy and safety of colloid resuscitation in the critically ill. *Anesth Analg* 2011; **112**: 156–64

Hong SH, Lee JM, Choi JH, Chung HS, Park JH, Park CS. Perioperative assessment of terlipressin infusion during living donor liver transplantation. *J Int Med Res* 2012; **40**: 225–36

Kamath PS, Kim WR. The model for end-stage liver disease (MELD). *Hepatology* 2007; **45**: 797–805

Kang YG, Martin DJ, Marquez J, *et al.* Intraoperative changes in blood coagulation and thrombelastographic monitoring in liver transplantation. *Anesth Analg* 1985; **64**: 888–96

Kidney Disease: Improving Global Outcomes (KDIGO) Acute Kidney Injury Work Group. KDIGO Clinical Practice Guideline for Acute Kidney Injury. *Kidney Int* Suppl 2012; **2**: 19–36

Myburgh JA, Finfer S, Bellomo R, *et al.* Hydroxyethyl starch or saline for fluid resuscitation in intensive care. *N Engl J Med* 2012; **367**: 1901–11

O'Grady JG, Schalm SW, Williams R. Acute liver failure: redefining the syndromes. *Lancet* 1993; **342**: 273–5

O'Riordan J, O'Beirne HA, Young Y, Bellamy MC. Effects of desflurane and isoflurane on splanchnic microcirculation during major surgery. *Br J Anaesth* 1997; **78**: 95–6

Ozier Y, Tsou MY. Changing trends in transfusion practice in liver transplantation. *Curr Opin Organ Transplant* 2008; **13**: 304–9

Padmakumar AD, Bellamy MC. Liver transplantation: haemodynamic changes, cardiac output monitoring and inotropic support.

In: Wagener G, ed. *Liver Anesthesiology and Critical Care Medicine*. New York: Springer, 2012; 139–47

Panhuizen IF, Gold SJ, Buerkle C, *et al*. Efficacy, safety and pharmacokinetics of sugammadex 4 mg kg-1 for reversal of deep neuromuscular blockade in patients with severe renal impairment. *Br J Anaesth* 2015; **114**: 777–84

Patel N, Dalal P, Panesar M. Dialysis disequilibrium syndrome: a narrative review. *Semin Dial* 2008; **21**: 493–8

Perner A, Haase N, Guttormsen AB, *et al*. Hydroxyethyl starch 130/0.42 versus Ringer's acetate in severe sepsis. *N Engl J Med* 2012; **367**: 124–34

Pugh RN, Murray-Lyon IM, Dawson JL, Pietroni MC, Williams R. Transection of the oesophagus for bleeding oesophageal varices. *Br J Surg* 1973; **60**: 646–9

Riordan SM, Williams R. Treatment of hepatic encephalopathy. *N Engl J Med* 1997; **337**: 473–9

Schrier RW. Use of diuretics in heart failure and cirrhosis. *Semin Nephrol* 2011; **31**: 503–12

Schuppan D, Afdhal NH. Liver cirrhosis. *Lancet* 2008; **371**: 838–51

Rahman S, Mallett SV. Cirrhotic cardiomyopathy: Implications for the perioperative management of liver transplant patients. *World J Hepatol* 2015; **7**: 507–20

Triantos C, Kalafateli M. Endoscopic treatment of esophageal varices in patients with liver cirrhosis. *World J Gastroenterol* 2014; **20**: 13015–26

Velez JC, Nietert PJ. Therapeutic response to vasoconstrictors in hepatorenal syndrome parallels increase in mean arterial pressure: a pooled analysis of clinical trials. *Am J Kidney Dis* 2011; **58**: 928–38

Wolfgram DF, Szabo A, Murray AM, Whittle J. Risk of dementia in peritoneal dialysis patients compared with hemodialysis patients. *Perit Dial Int* 2015; **35**: 189–98

CHAPTER 86

Anaesthesia in the elderly

Bernadette Veering and Chris Dodds

Age only matters when one is ageing, now I have arrived at a great age I might as well be 20.

Pablo Picasso 1881–1973

Introduction

It is interesting to remember that only a few decades ago, providing surgery and anaesthesia to patients more than 65 years of age was limited to surgery of minor or intermediate complexity. Now, for most clinical anaesthetists, the majority of their practice will be in providing safe anaesthesia for patients over the age of 65 and often well over 90 undergoing complex major surgery. Our understanding of the specific needs and challenges of this age group has improved but the incidence of some of the major complications has remained identical for the last 60–70 years.

This chapter covers the demographic challenges we face, specific aspects of assessing the elderly patient for anaesthesia, the basic anatomical and physiological changes that occur with ageing, the additional effects of chronic diseases, and the legacy of a lifetime of individual ailments and injuries that, all together, lead to the truly individual nature of an elderly patient. The impact that these changes have on the pharmacology of anaesthetic drugs as viewed both from the perspective of pharmacokinetics (drug disposition) and pharmacodynamics (the relationship between drug concentration and drug effect) are further elucidated The anaesthetic management, both for general and regional anaesthesia, and the associated outcomes is described. Finally, the cognitive dysfunction that occurs much more commonly in the elderly and the ethical issues of providing care are reviewed.

Demography

Demography is a statistical description of the way a population changes over time. The major influences on population change are those related to births, deaths, ageing, and migration. A stable population is one where the balance between the sex and age distribution of that population remains steady; it does not mean that the total number in that group are static.

The data used to estimate population numbers may be acquired from national registers, of births and deaths, for instance, or by intermittent census. A census process is very costly in both funding and personnel time and so is often only performed at regular but widely spaced intervals; the United Kingdom census is taken every 10 years, for instance. The number of people in a population at any given time is a balance between those born and those who migrate into the population against those who die and those who emigrate. Within a population, there are divisions into subgroups related to age, gender, or socioeconomic status.

One of the most useful descriptions of a population is through the generation of a 'population pyramid'. These graphically display age on the x-axis and numerical size on the y-axis with male groups lying to the left of midline and female groups to the right. An ideal pyramid has low birth and death rates but a high population capable of working. The majority of countries now have 'top-heavy' pyramids with a bulge of elderly people and few 'workers'.

The key to a financially robust population is related to the replacement ratio and the dependency ratio. The first is the number of children born to each female. This varies but is very close to 2.3 live births/female. The ratio across the majority of the world is less, often as low as 1.8 live births/female. The impact of this is that there are not enough people entering paid employment and therefore not enough state income generated to provide for the state's dependent population. The dependency ratio is the number of people who are too young and those too old to work compared with those old enough to be in paid employment. A variant of this, the inverse dependency ratio, describes how many people have to be in work to provide for one dependent person. While those too young will mature into independency, the elderly will increase in dependency as they age. This has clear challenges for any nation trying to deliver a state-supported social programme, including a health service.

Having identified that the state is increasingly unlikely to be able to pay for all the needs of an ageing population, it is imperative that any medical procedure does not increase dependency. This requires meticulous preoperative assessment and preparation for anaesthesia and surgery based on understanding the changes that accompany ageing. These include the organ systems, the impact these changes have on drug handling, and outcome.

Ageing

There is no clear definition of ageing but it is usually agreed to start after sexual maturity and includes intracellular changes that progressively affect cells, organ systems, and finally the whole organism. It may be seen as a collection of changes that increase the likelihood that the organism will die. Chronological age is a poor guide to outcome and biological age has been seen as an attractive alternative. The suggestion that there is also a clinical age has yet to gain wide acceptance. Specific changes occur in the major organ systems.

Central nervous system

Ageing decreases brain size because of a general reduction in neurone density in grey matter, with a loss of 30% of brain mass by the age of 80. In addition, the density of dendritic spines and the number of functional synapses decrease (Sullivan et al. 2004). The reduction in neuronal density is accompanied by a decline in cerebral blood flow and in cerebral oxygen consumption. The diameter of the myelinated fibres in the dorsal and ventral roots becomes smaller and the number of these fibres decreases with age. The connective tissue sheaths covering the nerve tissues become weakened, allowing local anaesthetics to penetrate the sheaths more rapidly. There is a steady loss of peripheral nerve fibres with a slowing of the conduction velocity, especially in motor nerves (Dorfman and Bosley 1979). These changes may all lead to functional decline. Functional magnetic resonance imaging studies have provided clear evidence of age differences in task-related brain activity in relation to the anatomical and functional decline. Consequently, the brain mechanisms that might underlie age differences in cognitive performance might be elucidated (Grady 2012). A variety of changes occur in neurotransmitter function with ageing (Dickstein et al. 2007). The number of dopamine, acetylcholine, and serotonin receptors, their binding sites, and concentrations decrease with age even in the absence of dementia.

The age-related decline in neurone quantity, quality, or both, and depletion of brain neurotransmitters, impaired glucose metabolism, and hormonal changes, particularly in the sex and growth hormones, may all be associated with changes in response to a variety of drugs. In addition, drugs may have greater penetrance into the elderly central nervous system (CNS), accounting for the altered pharmacodynamic response to drugs. These changes in the CNS are important, as it is the site of action for most anaesthetic drugs and adjuvants.

Autonomic nervous system

Normal ageing is associated with a progressive impairment of autonomic homeostasis. Elderly people respond to stresses of different degrees and types with a larger increase in noradrenaline (norepinephrine) concentrations. In addition, the β-receptor affinity for adrenergic agonists and antagonists appears to be blunted (Rooke 2000). The changes in autonomic function have been referred to as physiological β-blockade. Baroreceptor sensitivity declines progressively with age resulting in reduced compensatory blood pressure and heart rate responses when the carotid blood pressure alters (Ebert et al. 1992). This is as a result of an impaired parasympathetic component of the arterial baroreflex with advancing age, while the sympathetic component can be well maintained in healthy older individuals. Advancing age predisposes a patient to perioperative hypothermia because of a decline in thermoregulatory response (Frank 2007). Differences in sympathetic haemodynamic responses to noxious stimuli may contribute to the variability in the response to drugs between younger and older patients. The processes of the autonomic nervous system involved in the maintenance of homeostasis become less effective with increasing age enhancing hypotension during anaesthesia. The chronotropic response of the heart to atropine, which is frequently used in the reversal of neuromuscular block, is diminished in the elderly.

The cardiovascular system

With ageing, anatomical and physiological changes occur in the cardiovascular system. The hallmark of vascular ageing is stiffening caused by a loss of elasticity. As a result, advancing age is associated with an increased systolic blood pressure, widening of pulse pressure, and a generalized hypertrophy of the left ventricular wall (Lakatta 1993). The age-related increase in stiffness of the left ventricle causes cardiac function to be more dependent on ventricular filling. This compensatory increase in end-diastolic volume is associated with an increase in end-diastolic pressure in comparison to younger subjects. The elderly are unable to respond to stress by significantly increasing their left ventricular ejection fraction. During stress, the elderly increase their cardiac output by raising their left ventricular end-diastolic volume and consequently their stroke volume increases. On the other hand, during stress healthy younger individuals increase their ejection fraction by 10–25% compared with resting values by increased adrenergic stimulation (increased heart rate and contractility) (Barodka 2011). Cardiac reserve decreases with age and is further influenced by concomitant cardiac diseases. Increased vagal tone and a decreased sensibility of adrenergic receptors lead to a reduction in the heart rate response. Thus with advancing age, cardiac dilation is a compensatory response, offsetting diminished contractility and heart rate.

The respiratory system

The alveolar–arterial oxygen gradient increases with age. Decreased elastic recoil of the lungs and loss of alveolar surface area lead to increased closing volume, increased air trapping, and ventilation/perfusion mismatching. This leads to an increased physiological shunting and a gradual decline in arterial $P\text{O}_2$ as is shown in Figure 86.1 (Sprung et al. 2006). Consequently, increasing the fraction of inspired oxygen to maintain an adequate arterial $P\text{O}_2$ under anaesthesia is recommended (Gunnarson et al. 1991). Vital capacity and forced expiratory volume in 1 s decline gradually with age. On the other hand, residual volume, functional residual capacity, and closing volume increase with age, whereby the total lung capacity remains the same (Wahba 1983). In addition, elderly people show a marked reduction in the ventilatory response to imposed hypercapnia and hypoxia. Ageing is also associated with an impairment of laryngeal reflexes making the elderly patients more vulnerable to silent aspiration.

Hepatic system

By the age of 80, there is a decrease in hepatic size along with a proportional reduction in blood flow by at least 30% (Wynne et al. 1989). Age-associated changes in the hepatic system will contribute to alterations in drug metabolism (Wilkinson 2005). The hepatic clearance in elderly people is reduced both for high-extraction (flow-limited) and low-extraction (capacity-limited) drugs. For high-extraction (flow-limited) drugs there is almost a linear correlation with the age-related reduction in hepatic blood flow, which may also be the explanation for the reduction in hepatic clearance. Reduction in hepatic mass with age might be associated with a decrease in clearance of drugs with low intrinsic clearance as a result of fewer functioning cells. In addition, there is some evidence that the activity of phase I reactions (oxidation, reduction, hydrolysis) is probably decreased with advancing age (Wilkinson 2005).

Kidney

The biological ageing process includes progressive deterioration of renal structure and function. During ageing, a progressive decrease in the number and surface area of glomeruli and length and volume of the proximal tubules occurs together with an increased incidence and severity of glomerular sclerosis (Epstein 1996). There is a decrease in renal blood flow, starting around the age of 40 years resulting in an approximately 50% loss at the age

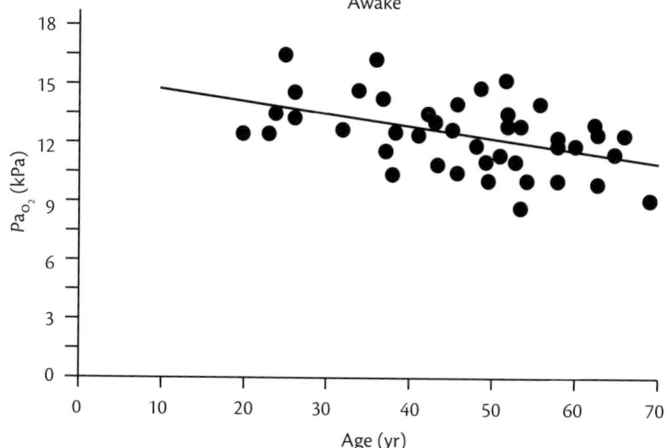

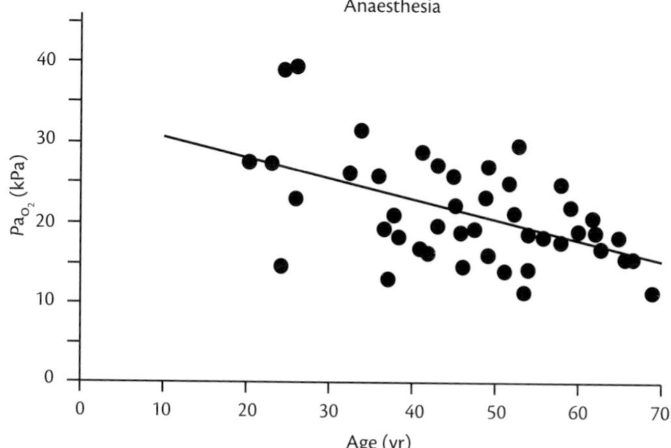

Figure 86.1 Relationship between Pa_{O_2} and age in the awake state (FI_{O_2} = 0.21) and during anaesthesia (FI_{O_2} = 0.40). Correlations: awake: $r = -0.44$, $P < 0.01$; anaesthesia: $r = -0.50$, $P < 0.001$.

Reproduced with permission from Gunnarson, L., Tokics, L., Gustavsson, H., et al. Influence of age on atelectasis formation and gas exchange impairment during general anaesthesia. *British Journal of Anaesthesia*, 1991, Volume 66, Issue 6, pp. 423–32, by permission of the Board of Management and Trustees of the British Journal of Anaesthesia.

of 80. Despite the decrease in glomerular filtration rate with age, there is no increase in serum creatinine because of a decrease in muscle mass and creatinine production. The ability to concentrate urine is decreased and the ageing kidney is less responsive to vasopressin (Faul et al. 1993). Hydrophilic drugs are predominantly eliminated by the kidney. The elimination of these drugs and their metabolites is slower in older than in younger patients resulting in prolonged elimination half-lives and longer duration of actions. Consequently, the administration of drugs in the perioperative period may be affected.

Body composition, pharmacokinetics, and pharmacodynamics

Clinical observations frequently suggest that older patients exhibit enhanced sensitivity to a variety of agents and often require smaller doses of drug to produce a given effect as compared with younger patients. Those altered dose requirements of anaesthetic agents are based either on pharmacokinetic or pharmacodynamic changes, or both (Sadean and Glass 2003; Vuyk 2003). Pharmacokinetic changes may cause modifications in the drug concentration available at receptor sites in the elderly with consequent alterations in the effect of a specific drug. The total body composition changes gradually as individuals age (Fulop et al. 1985). The intracellular water content declines as people age which may lead to a decrease in the total body water. Consequently the adipose tissue will relatively increase somewhat more in women than in men. Disposition (distribution and elimination) may be altered by these changes in body composition. In the case of hydrophilic drugs such as morphine, a reduction in the apparent distribution volume may be anticipated with higher corresponding plasma concentrations. On the other hand, the distribution volumes of lipophilic drugs would be expected to increase with lower corresponding plasma concentrations and increases in the corresponding elimination half-lives. The major plasma binding proteins for most anaesthetic drugs are albumin and α_1-acid glycoprotein (AAG). Albumin binds mainly acidic drugs, for instance, propofol and benzodiazepines, while AAG binds mainly basic drugs such as opioids and local anaesthetic agents. The concentration of serum albumin has been found to decrease whereas the concentration of AAG appeared to be unaltered with age (Veering et al. 1990).

Pharmacodynamic changes reflect differences in the intrinsic sensitivity to a given drug concentration, independently from changes in the pharmacokinetics. The changes in responsiveness may result from changes in the number of receptors, their affinity for the drug, or alterations of their characteristics. Receptors are in a dynamic state, under the influence of physiological and pathological factors mediated by hormones, neurotransmitters, and intracellular messengers (Vuyk 2003).

So far, hardly any study has observed the effect of age on the pharmacodynamics of intravenous anaesthetic agents. Clinically it is obvious that geriatric patients need less anaesthetic agent as compared with the dose requirement of younger patients. The degree of change may differ from one drug to another. PK/PD (pharmacokinetic/pharmacodynamic) modelling is a technique which integrates a pharmacokinetic and a pharmacodynamic model into one set of mathematical expressions. Such a model can describe the effect–time courses resulting from a drug dose and will predict more precisely the dose regimen of anaesthetic agents for elderly surgical patients. Recent advances in PK/PD models include using age as a covariate, making it possible to predict more adequately an optimal individual dose requirement of specific drugs (Kruijt et al. 2011).

Changes in anaesthetic and analgesic requirements

Table 86.1 summarizes how the physiological changes with increasing age affect the pharmacokinetics and pharmacodynamics of commonly used anaesthetic and analgesic drugs (White et al. 2012). The anatomical changes of the CNS and the depletion of neurotransmitters associated with ageing may have important implications for drug responses.

Inhalation agents

Elderly patients exhibit an increased responsiveness to inhalation agents. The minimum alveolar concentration (MAC) of inhalation agents gradually decreases with age and can be as much as 30%

Table 86.1 Age-related changes in organ system function and effect on pharmacokinetic (PK) and pharmacodynamic (PD) changes in the elderly and implications for anaesthetic management

PK and PD changes	Organ system changes	Implications for anaesthetic dosing	Effect on anaesthetic medications
Drug absorption	↑ gastric emptying time	Minimal as most anaesthetic drugs are given IV	None for anaesthetic drugs administered via the parenteral route
	↓ in intestinal motility		
	↓ gastric acid production	Medications given via the oral route may be poorly absorbed	↓ absorption of oral digoxin or analgesic medications
	↓ intestinal blood flow		
	↓ absorption capacity		
Drug distribution	Body composition changes: ↓ total body water	↑ peak drug concentrations after IV bolus doses	↑ initial blood concentration → ↑ potency of hydrophilic drugs after a standard IV bolus dose (e.g. propofol, opioids, midazolam)
	↑ body fat	↑ volume of distribution → prolonged effect for lipophilic drugs	Prolonged duration (↑ half-life) for lipophilic drugs (e.g. benzodiazepines, inhaled anaesthetic agents especially isoflurane)
	↓ cardiac output	↑ circulation time	↑ time to onset of hypnosis during induction of anaesthesia
Plasma protein binding	↓ plasma proteins	↓ binding of anaesthetic medications by proteins (e.g. albumin) → ↑ free (active) drug	↑ free-drug concentrations of highly protein bound drugs (e.g. propofol) → ↑ potency after a standard IV bolus dose
Drug metabolism	↓ liver function secondary to ↓ hepatic blood flow	↓ clearance of many anaesthetic medications	↑ duration of anaesthetic drugs 'cleared' as they pass through the liver (e.g. opioids, lidocaine, ketamine)
	↓ Phase 1 metabolism (e.g. drug oxidation, reduction, and hydrolysis)		Slightly ↑ duration of anaesthetic drugs metabolized by the liver (i.e. diazepam, lidocaine)
Drug elimination	↓ renal blood flow → ↓ GFR ↓ renal function	↓ clearance of drugs eliminated by the kidney	↑ duration of anaesthetic drugs primarily eliminated by the kidney (i.e. NMBAs, opioids)
CNS drug sensitivity	Cerebral atrophy → ↓ white matter and neurones in the brain	↑ sensitivity to anaesthetic drugs	↑ sensitivity to propofol → ↓ dose by 40% to 50% in patients ≥65 years
	↓ receptor sites (e.g. GABA, NMDA, β adrenergic, muscarinic)	Anaesthetic agents exert their effects at lower blood and effect-site concentrations	↑ sensitivity to sedatives and opioids, especially remifentanil
			↓ MAC for inhalational anaesthetic agents
	↓ neurones in the spinal cord and deterioration in myelin sheaths of nerves		↑ sensitivity to local anaesthetics
	Progressive closure of the intervertebral foramina ↓ volume of CSF	↓ area of the epidural space	↑ spread of local anaesthetic and ↑ levels of analgesia after spinal or epidural block → ↓ dose

GFR = glomerular filtration rate; MAC = minimal alveolar concentration; CSF = cerebral spinal fluid; CNS = central nervous system; GABA = gamma-aminobutyric acid; NMDA = *N*-methyl-D-aspartate; NMBAs = neuromuscular blocking agents.

Reproduced with permission from White, P.F., White, L.M., Monk, T, *et al.* Perioperative care for the older outpatient undergoing ambulatory surgery. *Anesthesia and Analgesia*, Volume 114, pp. 1190–215, Copyright © 2012 International Anesthesia Research Society.

lower by the age of 80 (Fig. 86.2) (Mapleson 1996). In general, the MAC of all inhalation agents decreases approximately 6% per decade of age over 40 years. For example, the MAC for sevoflurane is 2.3% in children of 1 year of age *vs* 0.9% in patients of 80 years (Nakajima et al. 1993).

Induction agents

Elderly patients exhibit a greater dose-responsiveness to induction agents, which is mainly as a result of changes in the pharmacokinetics. The induction dose of thiopental decreases linearly with age (Stanski and Maitre 1990). For thiopental, etomidate, and propofol, a decline in the initial volume of distribution appears to be the most important change (Arden et al. 1986; Stanski and Maitre 1990; Schnider et al. 1999). The EC_{50} for EEG changes for etomidate and thiopental is the same in younger and older patients, indicating that pharmacodynamic mechanisms play no role in the greater sensitivity.

Elderly patients are more sensitive to the hypnotic effects of propofol than are younger people (Schnider et al. 1999). The onset of the hypnotic effect may be slower as a result of slower blood–brain circulation times in the elderly. The decrease in blood pressure is more profound after any given dose of propofol and will be

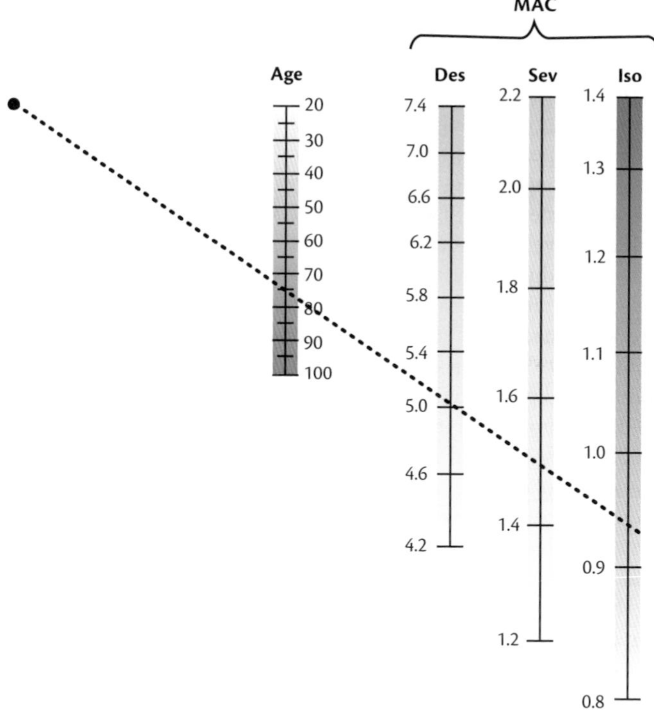

Figure 86.2 Normogram for minimum alveolar concentration (MAC) as a function of age. The MACs for desflurane (Des), sevoflurane (Sev), and isoflurane (Iso) can be determined by placing a ruler on the *dot* at left and drawing a line through the age of the patient. Where the line crosses the respective MAC normogram line yields the MAC value for that age. The *dotted line* shows an example for MAC in a 75-year-old patient.

Reproduced with permission from Rivera, R., Antognini, J.F. Perioperative drug therapy in elderly patients. *Anesthesiology*, Volume 110, Issue 5, pp. 1176–81, Copyright © 2009 American Society of Anesthesiology.

reached later in the elderly. A decline in the initial volume of distribution and metabolic clearance appears to be the most important change, leading to higher concentrations in older patients. The dose to achieve a certain effect is decreased by 30–50% in the elderly. Older patients wake up at lower concentrations. So changes in the propofol dose *vs* effect relationship appear to be as a result of age-related changes in pharmacokinetics rather than changes in the pharmacodynamics in the elderly patients. Caution is warranted when propofol is infused for sedation during spinal anaesthesia. Elderly patients wake up later compared with younger patients and for that reason the elderly should be observed for a longer period after termination of sedation with propofol (Shinozaki et al. 2002).

Opioids

Elderly patients seem to be more sensitive to opioids and require lower doses. This is explained either by pharmacokinetic or pharmacodynamic changes or by both. The pharmacokinetics of fentanyl and alfentanil were unaffected by age (Scott and Stanski 1987). However, the dose of fentanyl and alfentanil required to achieve a given level of depression of the EEG decreased by 50% from the age of 20 to 89 years. The increased sensitivity may be caused by functional changes of the opioid receptor, by a decline of the quantity of receptors, or ageing-related changes in opioid receptor binding in the CNS. Increased penetration of opioids in the CNS may play a role as well. There are very few studies that investigate the effect of age on the dose-response relationship of sufentanil (Matteo et al. 1990). The pharmacokinetics of sufentanil are unchanged in the elderly compared with younger patients and the reduction in dose requirements in elderly patients is probably as a result of a pharmacodynamic mechanism. Age affects both the pharmacokinetics and pharmacodynamics of remifentanil. The central volume and clearance of remifentanil decreased in elderly patients, resulting in higher plasma concentrations (Minto et al. 1997). In addition, the brain sensitivity is increased, with the EC_{50} for EEG suppression markedly decreased in the elderly. This important study provided information on the dosing of remifentanil in the elderly. It appeared that the bolus dose should be halved and infusion rates decreased to one-third in the elderly to achieve the same effect (Minto et al. 1997). Even though there is marked interindividual variability among the elderly in general, the emergence from anaesthesia with remifentanil will be slower in older than younger patients.

Older patients may be more sensitive to the effects of morphine. This is probably as a result of higher peak plasma concentrations, which is caused by reduced distribution volumes and by decreased clearance of active metabolites of morphine (Owen et al. 1983). Morphine is metabolized to morphine-6-glucoronide (M6G) and morphine-3-glucoronide (M3G), whose elimination is significantly reduced with renal failure (Smith 2011). M6G has analgesic properties and M3G is associated with neuroexcitatory phenomena. M6G may accumulate because of the age-related reduction in renal function or relative dehydration. It is recommended to lower the initial dose by 50% when starting therapy. Increases in dose escalation should not exceed 33–50%.

Neuromuscular blocking drugs

The initial dose of non-depolarizing neuromuscular blocking drugs is unaltered in elderly patients compared with younger ones. However, the onset time in elderly patients is increased irrespective of the study drug (Cope and Hunter 2003). The pharmacokinetics of several non-depolarizing neuromuscular blocking agents changes with increasing age. The duration of action may be extended as the clearance of these agents is decreased while the elimination half-life is increased in the elderly. The pharmacodynamics of neuromuscular blocking agents are unaltered by age. Again, the altered features of the neuromuscular blocking agents in the elderly are primarily as a result of changes in pharmacokinetics.

Sugammadex has been introduced recently to reverse profound neuromuscular block after the administration of vecuronium or rocuronium. The dose to facilitate rapid reversal from moderate neuromuscular block induced by rocuronium was the same in younger and older patients (McDonagh et al. 2011).

Benzodiazepines

Elderly patients exhibit a greater dose–drug response to benzodiazepines. The duration of the effects of benzodiazepines such as sedation, amnesia, and respiratory depression can be very prolonged in the elderly. The increased sensitivity to midazolam in elderly patients appears to be related to pharmacodynamic changes rather than to altered pharmacokinetics (Jacobs et al. 1995). The greater sensitivity to benzodiazepines in the elderly is probably based on increased receptor-binding affinity, impaired homeostatic mechanisms, and higher sensitivity of the aged CNS.

Conclusion: intravenous agents in the elderly

Physiological and pharmacological changes must be taken into account when anaesthetizing elderly patients. Based on the information from the few pharmacokinetic studies in older individuals, highly lipophilic drugs appear to show a trend towards a reduced initial volume of distribution and a slower clearance rate. Smaller induction doses should be administered much more slowly to reduce their anticipated profound haemodynamic effects. In addition, smaller or less frequent maintenance doses and slower infusion rates should be administered to avoid an increase in the plasma concentration of the various drugs. In general, drug doses should be decreased by 30–50% in the elderly. One should realize that increasing age is associated with large inter-individual variability in dose requirements. As such, it is important to titrate a dose against the desired clinical effect in an older patient. The suggested intravenous drug doses for elderly patients are summarized in Table 86.2 (Rivera and Antognini 2009).

Regional anaesthesia

Neuraxial techniques and peripheral nerve blocks are routinely performed in elderly patients. During thoracic, abdominal, pelvic, and lower extremity surgery, epidural anaesthesia is regularly added to 'light' general anaesthesia in elderly surgical patients.

Spinal anaesthesia is especially indicated in orthopaedic surgery, peripheral vascular surgery of the lower extremities, genitourological surgery, gynaecological procedures and inguinal surgery. Elderly patients appear to be more sensitive to the blocking action of local anaesthetic agents. Age-related changes in the CNS and peripheral nervous system (PNS) as described previously will all contribute to altered nerve block characteristics (dose–response relationship).

With epidural anaesthesia, higher levels of block should be anticipated both after lumbar and thoracic administration of a fixed dose of a local anaesthetic solution (Veering et al. 1987; Hirabayashi and Shimuzi 1993; Simon et al. 2002, 2004). With advancing age, anatomical and physiological changes occur in the epidural space. The epidural compliance increases, whereas its resistance decreases. In addition, the residual epidural pressure increases. In younger people, the areolar tissue around the intervertebral foramina is soft and loose, whereas in the elderly, this areolar tissue becomes dense and firm. This leads to the progressive sclerotic closure of intervertebral foramina. All these factors together with the described changes in the CNS and PNS will contribute to increases in longitudinal spread of analgesia with advancing age (Tsui et al. 2004).

As the responsiveness to β-adrenergic agonists is reduced with ageing, a small dose of adrenaline (epinephrine) added to a local anaesthetic solution does not appear to be a reliable detector of unintentional intravascular injection (Guinard et al. 1995).

The baricity of the anaesthetic solution is the main factor influencing the clinical features of spinal anaesthesia. With isobaric solutions the level of analgesia is unaltered in older compared with younger patients. On the other hand, with a hyperbaric solution, a faster onset and a higher level of analgesia are demonstrated with increasing age. The duration of both sensory and motor block is prolonged in the elderly irrespective of the baricity of the solution (Tsui et al. 2004; Veering 2012).

Peripheral nerve blocks are used in elderly patients especially as a supplementary analgesic technique for upper limb trauma, hip, and knee surgery. Atrophy of peripheral nerves together with a decrease in conduction velocity, in particular of motor nerves, and deterioration of myelin sheaths may result in an altered quality of the nerve block. Studies of the effect of age on the clinical course of peripheral nerve blocks are very limited at present. The duration of complete motor and sensory block appeared to be prolonged with age after brachial plexus block with ropivacaine (Paqueron et al. 2002) as well as after sciatic nerve block with mepivacaine (Hanks et al. 2006).

Regional anaesthesia may cause some problems in elderly patients. The techniques of spinal and epidural anaesthesia are made more difficult, so there is always a chance of a technical failure. This is often as a result of the changes in anatomical configuration of the lumbar and thoracic spine. Elderly individuals often have a dorsal kyphosis and an increased inability to flex the hips and knees because of osteoarthritic changes and chondrocalcinosis. Moreover, the intervertebral foramina are narrowed by sclerotic changes and calcification in elderly patients. Also the ligamentum flavum probably changes into a form that is easily ossified. As a consequence, it can be very difficult to place and advance the epidural or spinal needle.

In elderly patients, hypotension and bradycardia are the most frequent side-effects of central neural blockade. Hypotension is common with high levels of epidural and spinal anaesthesia as a

Table 86.2 Intravenous drug doses

Drugs	Young patient	Elderly patient
Sedative hypnotics		
Midazolam	0.05 mg/kg	0.02 mg/kg
Propofol: bolus	2–2.5 mg/kg	1–2 mg/kg
Propofol: maintenance	100–200 μg/kg/min	50–100 μg/kg/min
Ketamine	0.5–2 mg/kg	0.3–1.5 mg/kg
Etomidate	0.2–0.3 mg/kg	0.1–0.2 mg/kg
Thiopental	3–5 mg/kg	1.5–3 mg/kg
Opioids		
Fentanyl	1–2 μg/kg	0.5–1 μg/kg
Morphine	0.03–0.06 mg/kg	0.02–0.03 mg/kg
Sufentanil	0.5–10 μg/kg	0.25–5 μg/kg
Remifentanil: bolus	0.1 μg/kg	0.05 μg/kg
Remifentanil: maintenance	0.5–2 μg/kg/min	0.3–1.5 μg/kg/min
Neuromuscular blocking drugs		
Suxamethonium	0.5–1.0 mg/kg	0.5–1.0 mg/kg
Rocuronium	0.1–0.6 mg/kg	0.05–0.4 mg/kg
Vecuronium	0.02–0.06 mg/kg	0.01–0.04 mg/kg
Pancuronium	0.02–0.1 mg/kg	0.01–0.05 mg/kg
Cisatracurium	0.05–0.2 mg/kg	0.05–0.2 mg/kg
Atracurium	0.2–0.5 mg/kg	0.2–0.5 mg/kg
Doxacurium	0.01–0.03 mg/kg	0.005–0.03 mg/kg

Reproduced with permission from Rivera, R., Antognini, J.F. Perioperative drug therapy in elderly patients. *Anesthesiology*, Volume 110, pp. 1176–81, Copyright © 2009 American Society of Anesthesiology.

result of blockade of the sympathetic nerve system (Fig. 86.3) (Simon et al. 2002). Bradycardia may be partly caused by decreased sensibility of adrenergic receptors and involvement of cardiac sympathetic fibres during high levels of analgesia (Veering and Cousins 2000). Intravenous administration of a colloid solution in combination with an α-agonist given in the first 5–10 min when the block is developing appeared to be effective in counteracting the expected decline in central venous pressure and systemic vascular resistance (Critchley 1996). The incidence of hypotension is often greater in older patients with hypertension and limited cardiac reserve when compared with young healthy patients and may be harmful.

One method to try to limit these cardiovascular changes is the use of incremental injections of local anaesthetic solutions by means of a continuous spinal or epidural catheter technique or combined spinal–epidural anaesthesia in order to control the level of the block (Minville et al. 2006). Another method is to reduce the dose with the aim to avoid a high sympathetic block. The interaction with local anaesthetic agents and opioids is synergistic for both epidural and spinal anaesthesia. As a result, a lower dose of either the local anaesthetic or the opioid will be effective when they are combined and in addition the analgesia is preserved with fewer adverse effects. This technique of reduced doses of both agents was effectively illustrated in elderly patients scheduled for hip fracture surgery (Ben-David et al. 2001; Olofsson et al. 2004). A combination of only 4 mg of bupivacaine with fentanyl (20 μg) or a dose of 7.5 mg of a hyperbaric bupivacaine solution in combination with sufentanil resulted in an effective block without any cardiovascular adverse event. Elderly patients who have central neural blockade are especially at risk of hypothermia as a result of the vasodilation produced by sympathetic block leading to an increased rate of heat loss. It is important that the temperature should be monitored in these patients (Sessler 2008).

The clearances of bupivacaine, ropivacaine, and lidocaine after epidural administration decrease with age possibly resulting in increased accumulation of these agents during continuous infusion or after intermittent epidural injections (Veering et al. 1987; Simon and Veering 2010). Reducing the dose will not influence the quality of nerve block as elderly patients appeared to be more sensitive to the blocking action of local anaesthetic agents. Systemic absorption of local anaesthetics after epidural and subarachnoid administration appears to be biphasic (Veering et al. 1990; Simon et al. 2004, 2006; Tsui et al. 2004). After epidural administration, the systemic absorption was unchanged with advancing age. Therefore the observed age-related changes in the nerve block characteristics with epidural anaesthesia are probably connected to changes in the pharmacodynamics or local distribution, or both, rather than alterations in the pharmacokinetics (i.e. the rate of systemic absorption of local anaesthetic agents).

A population PK/PD model capable of linking the kinetic data to the analgesic effects of local anaesthetics (i.e. sensory neural blockade) has been developed (Olofsen et al. 2008). By fine tuning this model it may be feasible to identify factors that influence the time course of epidural anaesthesia and to develop and investigate new local anaesthetic agents for epidural use.

Intrathecal and epidural opioids are administered to surgical patients to provide prolonged postoperative analgesia. Elderly people may be more sensitive to opioids (see previous discussion) and as such have a greater probability of respiratory depression. A reduction in the requirements of epidural morphine in older patients has been reported and is thought to be related to higher cerebrospinal fluid concentrations (Ready et al. 1987). As the elderly are more sensitive to benzodiazepines, caution should be used when they are given as premedication and concomitantly in elderly patients receiving spinal opioids.

Regional *vs* general anaesthesia in the elderly

Increasing numbers of elderly patients will undergo major complex surgery. The incidence of pre-existing disease is high in older patients and as a consequence the elderly are at an increased risk of developing perioperative complications with the potential for a poorer postoperative outcome. Postoperative outcome is not only determined by pre-existing co-morbidities but also by the severity of the surgery, the anaesthetic technique, and the quality of perioperative care.

The decision whether to use regional or general anaesthesia in elderly patients should be based on outcome data. Research in this

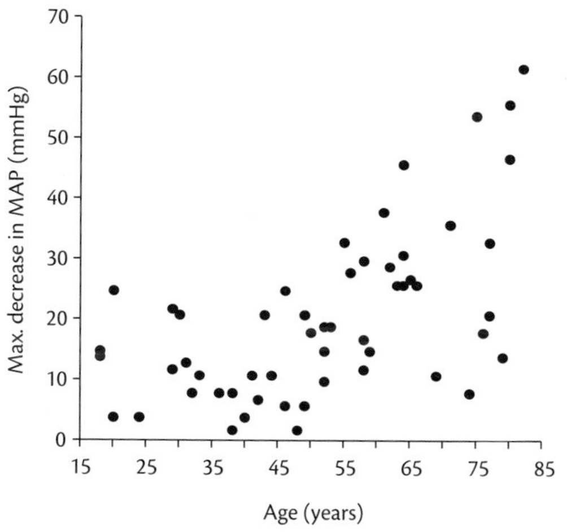

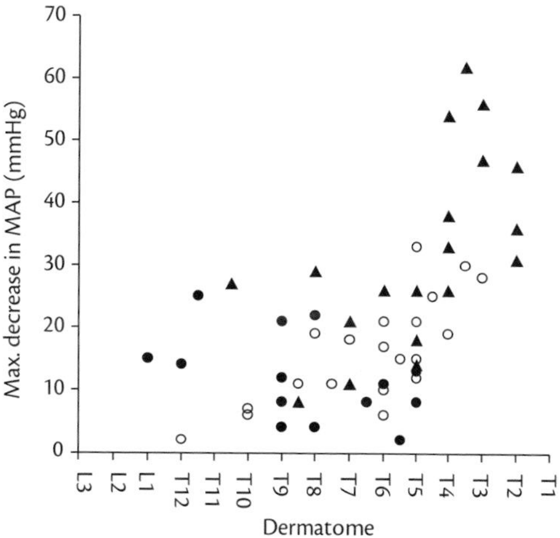

Figure 86.3 Relationship between the max decrease of mean arterial pressure (MAP) and the height of anaesthesia as a function of age.
Reproduced with permission from Simon, M.J., Veering, B.T., Stienstra, R., van Kleef, J.W., Burm, A.G., The effects of age on neural blockade and hemodynamic changes after epidural anesthesia with ropivacaine, *Anesthesia and Analgesia*, Volume 94, Issue 5, pp. 1325–30, Copyright © International Anesthesia Research Society 2002.

area has focused on elderly patients with clinically significant co-morbidities such as ischaemic heart disease, renal insufficiency, chronic obstructive pulmonary disease, and diabetes and cognitive deficits undergoing peripheral vascular surgery of the lower extremities or surgery for hip fracture repair. These surgical procedures are frequently performed in the elderly.

Cardiac and pulmonary complications remain the main causes of perioperative morbidity associated with vascular and orthopaedic procedures in the elderly population (Veering 2008). Discrepancies, however, exist between the early studies that assessed the influence of anaesthetic technique on perioperative outcome in this frail population (Veering 2008). Some investigators found a reduction in cardiac morbidity whereas others could not demonstrate any beneficial effects of regional anaesthesia on postoperative outcome. However, interpretation of these results is unclear because of a lack of data from major studies and because most studies were insufficiently powered with a lack of standardization. The only conclusion at the moment is that, in this frail population, intraoperative regional anaesthesia decreases the incidence of postoperative pulmonary complications (Ballantyne 2004).

More recently Neumann et al. (2012) demonstrated in a retrospective cohort study of 18 000 elderly patients having surgery for repair of hip fracture that regional anaesthesia markedly decreased the incidence of respiratory complications. The consensus until now is that no single anaesthetic technique has been found to be superior for older frail patients who are prone to develop postoperative complications. Optimal anaesthetic care for the frail elderly patient involves not only tailor-made anaesthesia but also adequate treatment of pre-existing medical problems. Factors other than the choice of anaesthesia may be crucial for long-term survival (Norris et al. 2001).

Once the options for managing an elderly surgical patient have been reviewed, the next stage in the surgical pathway is a detailed preoperative assessment and risk analysis for that individual patient.

Preoperative assessment of the elderly

The basic principles for safe and effective pre-assessment are the same as for any other patient but there are some areas that are more important with advancing age.

Communication

The special senses of sight, hearing, touch, and balance all deteriorate with age. By the age of 70, blindness occurs in up to 30% of patients and deafness in almost the same number. Many have both problems. Even in the United Kingdom, up to 10% of the elderly are illiterate and about 5% will have learning difficulties. It is clear that seeking an accurate history and giving advice on which to base informed consent is not an easy task. Reading a standard consent form may prove impossible for a patient.

Local dialects will also influence interpretation as the meaning of common words may vary markedly across quite small geographical areas. This variation is more preserved in the less geographically mobile elderly population.

Assessment of behavioural adaption

Once the level of communication is established an assessment of the functional capability (see 'Functional assessment') of the patient should be made. This differs from younger adults in that chronic conditions such as arthritis may impose limits on exercise that can mask deteriorating cardiovascular status. Activities of daily living should be reviewed as these do give a reliable assessment of preoperative status and may identify those who will need a high level of support to maintain independent living at home.

Almost all chronic conditions have a strong behavioural or adaptive component to them, and failing to seek this leads to underestimation of the severity of that condition. The elderly are very capable in managing their long-term conditions and adapting their lifestyle to minimize the impact that even severe chronic illness has. Examples include fluid restriction before social events or hospitalization, or limiting movement rather than increasing analgesic medication and risking constipation. This adaption can be maintained until almost all residual functional capacity has been lost.

Specific aspects

Cognition

Important information may have to be garnered from relatives or carers, but should include any previous episode of delirium possibly related to previous operations, chest infections, or other physical stress. A cognitive review using a validated tool such as the MMST (Mini-Mental State Evaluation) or the AMT (Abbreviated Mental Test) should be performed and recorded in the case notes. Any variation in cognition noted by the relatives that could be suggestive of an early dementing process should also be documented. However, non-specialist clinical staff should not make a diagnosis of dementia.

Frailty

Outcome from surgery is profoundly influenced by the physical condition of the patient (Clegg et al. 2013) and their ability to mount an appropriate stress response to the operation. Recognition that the 'bedside' appearance of frailty has major implications for outcome is now widespread, despite variations of its precise definition (Makary et al. 2010; Kim et al. 2013; Velanovich et al. 2013). The commonest descriptions include variations of the following:

- Unexplained weight loss of greater than 5 kg in 6 months
- Weak hand grip
- Slow 'get up and go'
- Slow walking pace
- Reduced physical activity.

The causes of frailty and its treatment are still being investigated but one contender is a form of immune senescence, possibly related to increased interleukin 6 concentrations. Of the research interventions aimed at improving frailty, exercise appears to be the most cost-effective (Thomas et al. 2010).

Depression

A large proportion of elderly surgical patients have clinical depression. This is an independent risk factor in poor postoperative outcome. It will only be recognized if actively sought, as the 'quiet, withdrawn' depressive patient will appear to simply lack good communication skills and possibly have loss of hearing. Seeking specialist assessment through the psychiatric team at the earliest opportunity is wise.

Advanced directives

Across the world, the legally binding views of patients in regard to their explicit and informed consent are now also being recorded to ensure that their wishes are followed if they lose the competence to express these opinions at a later stage of life. This may occur during a major illness where direct communication may be lost, for example, while being artificially ventilated in a critical care unit.

Advocacy processes are often in place to ensure that as much information on the wishes of the patient is gathered before major decisions on their healthcare are made. It is imperative that every attempt to communicate and get informed consent should be made and recorded in the case notes. However, the imperative in emergency situations is to act to support the patient while simultaneous attempts to identify their wishes are made.

Medication

The elderly are the greatest users of medication, and often take two or more drugs as long-term therapy. The combination of adverse side-effects and poor compliance often mean that a period of supervised withdrawal of drug therapy may be necessary before moving to elective surgery. Prescribed medication may form only a small part of the range of over-the-counter and herbal remedies being taken. It is not uncommon for important medication to be missed 'because it was upsetting them' with clear risks to anaesthesia and surgery.

Risk assessment

The use of rating scales to estimate the risk of any procedure to an individual patient is seldom precise. The commonest scale used is the American Society of Anesthesiologists (ASA) scale and this continues to be predictive of outcome in the elderly. Others have been developed for surgical groups and even specific operative procedures. These include the Possum (Copeland et al. 1991) and P-Possum scales (Portsmouth modification of the original Possum scale) (Prytherch et al. 1998) which use a combination of physiological variables and operative factors in estimating the outcome for an individual. Surgical speciality-specific versions exist for vascular, orthopaedic, and colon cancer.

It is important to remember that these rating scales are much better at the estimation of population outcomes (but even this is subject to variation between populations rather than simply surgical units). Individual outcome prediction is still poor with large variations between predicted and realized surgical outcome.

Functional assessment

For major surgery (and increasingly for intermediate level procedures) a global assessment of the patient's ability to mount an effective response to the surgical stress helps predict likely problems perioperatively. These assessments may include the patient's ability to perform normal activities and compare these to known metabolic equivalent (MET) demands. This assessment of METs has been used extensively and with reasonable reliability in younger patients. A figure of less than 4 METs, about the same as being able to climb two flights of stairs, is often used as a marker of likely poor outcome. Unfortunately in the elderly, factors such as arthritis may limit their performance and mask an underlying poor functional state.

Cardiopulmonary exercise testing is widely used for major surgery as a comprehensive tool for assessing aerobic delivery. It is largely risk free and can be performed on most patients. Low values for anaerobic thresholds are predictive of poor outcome.

Specific testing of organ systems such as for coronary arterial disease may be indicated and for those with limited locomotive ability; dobutamine stress echocardiography appears to hold the most value.

Where functional limitations are identified there is a need to reconsider both the surgical and the anaesthetic options. It may also be possible to improve the patient's functional reserve. This has become more common in elective surgical cases.

Preoperative optimization

The initial descriptions of optimization were on acutely ill patients scheduled for urgent surgery. They were admitted to critical care facilities and intravenous fluids and inotropes were titrated to improve oxygen delivery. Outcome was improved in these patients. However, this is not a practical reality for many surgical units and other techniques have been explored.

For elective procedures, exercise classes, dietary modification, and careful reviewing of medication (including smoking and alcohol) have all improved outcome. They need time, often measured in weeks, and this may not be appropriate in surgery for cancer for instance.

One measure that can be used rapidly is to transfuse the patient back to a 'normal' adult haemoglobin concentration. The use of transfusion triggers has clear merit but increasing the haemoglobin from 8 to 12g dl^{-1} reduces the cardiac output by 50% for the same oxygen delivery. This may prove vital in the postoperative period when catabolic stresses peak.

Postoperative challenges more common in the elderly

Delirium/postoperative cognitive dysfunction

One of the most dangerous complications in the perioperative period is that of changed cognitive state. This may be acute as delirium or more insidious and long-lasting as postoperative cognitive dysfunction (POCD). These occur in patients of all age groups but are far more commonly associated with the elderly.

Delirium may occur very rapidly after any medical event, including chest infections at home. However, it is very common after medical admission to hospital and especially after major surgery. It occurs in about 35% of postoperative elderly patients but the range is from almost 0% in minor outpatient surgery such as cataract surgery to more than 75% in open cardiac surgery. There are assessment tools such as the Confusion Assessment Method (Leslie et al. 2008) that are useful in clarifying the diagnosis. It is related to frailty and has a poor prognostic value as the risk of developing a dementia is two to three times greater over a 3-year period.

It is usually defined into three broad groups;

- Withdrawal or intoxication
- Multiple aetiology
- As a result of a general medical condition.

The last of these is the most commonly seen but alcohol withdrawal remains a possibility in all patients. The most commonly observed presentation is of an acutely distressed patient but the withdrawn and unresponsive presentation is often missed. The major features (described in the fifth edition of the *Diagnostic and Statistical Manual of Mental Disorders*) include:

- Disturbance of attention: reduced awareness of their environment with increased distractability including a reduced ability to focus, maintain, or change attention
- A change in cognition such as memory deficit or disorientation, that is not explained by a pre-existing or evolving dementia
- The disturbance develops quickly; usually within hours to days and tends to fluctuate over time
- There is often evidence from the history, physical examination, or routine investigations indicating that the disturbance may be as a result of medication, drug withdrawal, a general medical condition, or combinations of all of these.

From an anaesthetic perspective, emerging evidence suggests that a simple checklist for use in the recovery area can improve both outcome and time in hospital by triggering referral to the multispecialist cognitive management team within the geriatric or psychiatric departments (Dodds et al. 2013).

Specific precipitating factors include fluid imbalance, poor pain control, the use of centrally active anticholinergic agents, and hypoxia.

Treatment can be difficult (National Institute for Health and Care Excellence 2012). Strategies to reduce agitation such as brightly lit rooms, relatives or carers known to the patient being in attendance, visible clocks to aid time orientation, and frequent reassurance from the clinical staff are all effective to a degree but for some patients, who are a risk to themselves or others, medication may be needed. This appropriate medication should be administered under the guidance of the multidisciplinary cognitive team. Acute management consists of haloperidol, although it is an off-licence use, which should be used in an escalating dose and stopped as soon as possible.

POCD has been identified as a complication of surgery and anaesthesia since the 1950s. Unfortunately the incidence has not changed since then despite the advances in monitoring, drugs, and surgical techniques. The definition of POCD has yet to be fully agreed unlike delirium but most describe changes in cognitive function including memory, planning, organization, attention, and information processing. One of the more socially disruptive but very common problems is disinhibition. These changes present between 3 and 7 days after surgery, often after the patient has been discharged home. They may last for a few months but in about half of all cases they are permanent. Age is one of the most important independent predictors and for major abdominal surgery the incidence of POCD is nearly 25% decreasing to 10% after 3 months at age 65. At this point there is very little further recovery and the deficit is permanent. Advanced age increases the incidence and by 75 years of age the early incidence is nearer to 40% and there is a greater degree of residual dysfunction.

Many attempts to elucidate the cause have failed to find a single major factor, such as hypoxia or hypotension, and many studies were simply of too small a size to give meaningful results. However, recent work suggests that an underlying inflammatory process may be to blame, and acute stresses such as an episode of hypoxia may then trigger the onset of POCD.

Many of the pro-inflammatory factors are raised and activation of the astrocytic system would fit with this proposed model. Much more research is needed before treatment options may be considered but avoidance of known precipitating anaesthetic agents would be wise. These include ketamine and nitrous oxide. The role of xenon as a neuroprotective agent is still being explored. Certainly, at present, there is no firm evidence for choosing a regional anaesthetic technique over general anaesthesia in order to prevent POCD.

Ethical issues

The care of the elderly is fraught with many ethical issues that are similar to those in children and patients with learning difficulties. The four principles that all clinical decisions have to adhere to are:

- Beneficence: the action to do good
- Non-maleficence: the action should do no harm
- Autonomy: the action should respect the rights of the individual patient
- Justice: the action should consider the rights of an individual against those of society.

This can be daunting when faced with complex elderly patients who may have lost the capacity to make judgements on their own healthcare. It is important to get as complete a picture as possible before deciding on treatment, and if there is an urgent need for intervention, the course that is least irreversible should be chosen. An example of this would be an elderly patient with a compromised limb from poor circulation, who also has a severe infection in that limb. The delirium triggered by the infection has rendered that patient incompetent to make an informed decision themselves but, they had stated before, that amputation of the compromised limb was not acceptable to them. In this case, treating the infection with the aim of also treating the delirium would be the wisest choice. It is doing good and least harm to the patient and allowing them the chance to regain their autonomy. In this case, there is no real dilemma with 'justice' as the treatment does not compromise other patients' care.

Conclusion

As anaesthetists we are faced with an increasing number of elderly surgical patients. It is a challenge to provide optimal perioperative care. Elderly patients should be viewed from the perspective of understanding the process of ageing, how it occurs, how it affects specific organ systems, and how it may influence clinical care, when a patient is subjected to operation. The whole operative process should be reviewed, including the scope for preoperative optimization, choices of anaesthetic technique and agents, and likely postoperative complications. These should all be balanced within the ethical framework defined by that patient's express wishes. We must remember that with ageing, pharmacokinetic or pharmacodynamic changes, or both, occur that affect handling of intravenous, inhalation, and local anaesthetic agents. Consequently, elderly patients may demonstrate increased sensitivity to anaesthetic agents. All these changes with age should be viewed against the background of the large variations among older individuals. Ageing is only one of the many sources of variability in drug response. Besides internal factors such as genetics and diseases, external factors such as lifestyle variables (i.e. physical activity, smoking, alcohol use, nutritional intake, and education) may all contribute to the lowered dosage requirements. The anaesthetist should titrate a dose until the desired effect has been achieved in an older patient.

Declaration of interest

None declared.

References

American Psychiatric Association. *Diagnostic and Statistical Manual of mental Disorders*, 5th Edn. Washington, DC: American Psychiatric Association, 2013

Arden JR, Holley FO, Stanski DR. Increased sensitivity to etomidate in the elderly: initial distribution versus altered brain response. *Anesthesiology* 1986; **65**: 19–27

Ballantyne JC. Does epidural analgesia improve surgical outcome? *Br J Anaesth* 2004; **92**: 4–6

Barodka VM. Review article: implications of vascular ageing. *Anesth Analg* 2011; **112**: 1048–60

Ben-David B, Frankel R, Arzumonov T, Marchevsky Y, Volpin G. Minidose bupivacaine-fentanyl spinal anaesthesia for surgical repair of hip fracture in the aged. *Anesthesiology* 2000; **92**: 6–10

Clegg A, Young J, Iliffe S, Rikkert MO, Rockwood K. Frailty in elderly people. *Lancet* 2013; **381**: 752–62

Cope TM, Hunter JM. Selecting neuromuscular-blocking drugs for elderly patients. *Drugs Ageing* 2003; **20**: 125–40

Copeland GP, Jones D, Walters M. POSSUM: a scoring system for surgical audit. *Br J Surg* 1991; **78**: 355–60

Critchley LAH. Hypotension, subarachnoid block and the elderly patient. *Anaesthesia* 1996; **51**: 1139–43

Dickstein DL, Kabaso D, Rocher AB, Luebke JI, Wearne SL, Hof PR. Changes in the structural complexity of the aged brain. *Aging Cell* 2007; **6**: 275–84

Dodds C, Foo I, Jones K, Singh SK, Waldmann C. Peri-operative care of elderly patients – an urgent need for change: a consensus statement to provide guidance for specialist and non-specialist anaesthetists. *Perioper Med* 2013; **2**: 1–6

Dorfman LJ, Bosley TM. Age-related changes in peripheral and central nerve condition in man. *Neurology* 1979; **29**: 38–44

Ebert TJ, Morgan BJ, Barney JA, Denahan T, Smith JJ. Effects of ageing on baroreflex regulation of sympathetic activity in humans. *Am J Physiol* 1992; **263**: H798–803

Epstein M. Ageing and the kidney. *J Am Soc Nephrol* 1996; **7**: 1106–22

Faull CM, Holmes C, Baylis PH. Water balance in elderly people: is there a deficiency of vasopressin? *Age Ageing* 1993; **22**: 114–20

Frank SM. Body temperature management in the elderly surgical patient. In: Sieber FE, ed. *Geriatric Anaesthesia*. New York: McGraw-Hill, 2007; 211–21

Fulop TJ, Worum J, Csongor J, *et al.* Body composition in elderly people. *Gerontology* 1985; **31**: 6–14

Grady C. The cognitive neuroscience of ageing. *Nat Rev Neurosci* 2012; **20**: 491–505

Gunnarson L, Tokics L, Gustavsson H, *et al.* Influence of age on atelectasis formation and gas exchange impairment during general anaesthesia. *Br J Anaesth* 1991; **66**: 423–32

Guinard JP, Mulroy MF, Carpenter RL. Ageing reduces the reliability of epidural epinephrine test doses. *Reg Anesth* 1995; **20**: 193–8

Hanks RK, Pietrobon R, Steele SM. The effect of age on sciatic nerve block duration. *Anesth Analg* 2006; **102**: 588–92

Hirabayashi Y, Shimizu R. Effect of age on extradural dose requirement in thoracic extradural anaesthesia. *Br J Anaesth* 1993; **71**: 445–6

Jacobs JR, Reves JG, Marty J, White WD, Bai SA, Smith LR. Ageing increases pharmacodynamic sensitivity to the hypnotic effects of midazolam. *Anesth Analg* 1995; **80**: 143–8

Kim H, Higgins PA, Canaday DH, Burant CJ, Hornick TR. Frailty assessment in the geriatric outpatient clinic. *Geriatr Gerontol Int* 2014; **14**: 78–83

Kruijt Spanjer MR, Bakker NA, Absolaom AR. Pharmacology in the elderly and newer anaesthesia drugs. *Best Pract Res Clin Anaesthesiol* 2011; **25**: 355–65

Lakatta EG. Cardiovascular regulatory mechanism in advanced age. *Physiol Rev* 1993; **73**: 413–67

Leslie A, Wei BA, Fearing MA, Sternberg EJ, Inouye SK. The confusion assessment method: a systematic review of current usage. *J Am Geriatr Soc* 2008; **56**: 823–830

Makary MA, Segev DL, Pronovost PJ, *et al.* Frailty as a predictor of surgical outcomes in older patients. *J Am Coll Surg* 2010; **210**: 901–8

Mapleson WW. Effect of age on MAC in humans: a meta-analysis. *Br J Anaesth* 1996; **76**: 179–85

Matteo RS, Schwartz AE, Ornstein E, Young WL, Chang WJ. Pharmacokinetics of sufentanil in the elderly surgical patient. *Can J Anaesth* 1990; **37**: 852–6

McDonagh DL, Benedict PE, Kovac AL. Efficacy, safety, and pharmacokinetics of sugammadex for the reversal of rocuronium-induced neuromuscular blockade in elderly patients. *Anesthesiolgy* 2011; **114**: 318–29

Minto CF, Schnider TW, Egan T, *et al.* The influence of age and gender on the pharmacodynamics of remifentanil: I. Model development. *Anesthesiology* 1997; **86**: 10–23

Minto CF, Schnider TW, Shafer SI, *et al.* The influence of age and gender on the pharmacodynamics of remifentanil: II. Model application. *Anesthesiology* 1997; **86**: 24–33

Minville V, Fourcade O, Grousset D, et al. Spinal anaesthesia using single injection small-dose bupivacaine versus continuous catheter injection techniques for surgical repair of hip fracture in elderly patients. *Anesth Analg* 2006; **102**: 1559–63

Nakajima R, Nakajima Y, Ikeda K. Minimum alveolar concentration of sevoflurane in elderly patients. *Br J Anaesth* 1993; **70**: 273–5

Neuman MD, Silber JH, Elkassabany NM, Ludwig JM, Fleisher LA. Comparative effectiveness of regional versus general anesthesia for hip fracture surgery in adults. *Anesthesiology* 2012; **117**: 72–92

National Institute for Health and Care Excellence. *Guidance on the Treatment of Delirium*. 2012. Available from https://www.nice.org.uk/guidance/cg103

Norris EJ, Beattie C, Perler BA. Double-masked randomized trial comparing alternate combinations of intraoperative anaesthesia and postoperative analgesia in abdominal aortic surgery. *Anesthesiology* 2001; **95**: 1054–67

Olofsen E, Burm AGL, Simon M, Veering BT, van Kleef J, Dahan A. Population pharmacokinetic-pharmacodynamic modeling of epidural anesthesia. *Anesthesiology* 2008; **109**: 664–74

Olofsson C, Nygards EB, Bjersten AB, Hessling A. Low-dose bupivacaine with sufentanil prevents hypotension after spinal anaesthesia for hip repair in elderly patients. *Acta Anaesthesiol Scand* 2004; **48**: 1240–4

Owen JA, Sitar DS, Berger L. Age-related morphine kinetics. *Clin Pharmacol Ther* 1983; **34**: 364–8

Paqueron X, Boccara G, Bendahou M, Coriat P, Riou B. Brachial plexus nerve block exhibits prolonged duration in the elderly. *Anesthesiology* 2002; **97**: 1245–9

Prytherch DR, Whiteley MS, Higgins B, Weaver PC, Prout WG, Powell SJ. POSSUM and Portsmouth POSSUM for predicting mortality. Physiological and Operative Severity Score for the enUmeration of Mortality and morbidity. *Br J Surg* 1998; **85**: 1217–20

Ready LB, Chadwick HS, Ross B. Age predicts effective epidural morphine dose after abdominal hysterectomy. *Anesth Analg* 1987; **66**: 1215–8

Rivera R, Antognini JF. Perioperative drug therapy in elderly patients. *Anesthesiology* 2009; **110**: 1176–81

Rooke GA. Autonomic and cardiovascular function in the geriatric patient. *Anesthesiol Clin North America* 2000; **18**: 31–46

Sadean MR, Glass PS. Pharmacokinetics in the elderly. *Best Pract Res Clin Anesthesiol* 2003; **17**: 191–205

Schnider TW, Minto CF, Shafer SL. The influence of age on propofol pharmacodynamics. *Anesthesiology* 1999; **90**: 1502–16

Scott JC, Stanski DR. Decreased fentanyl/alfentanil dose requirement with increasing age. A pharmacodynamic basis. *J Pharmacol Exp Ther* 1987; **240**: 159–66

Sessler DI. Temperature monitoring and perioperative thermoregulation. *Anesthesiology* 2008; **109**: 318–38

Shinozaki M, Usui Y, Yamaguchi S, Okuda Y, Kitayama T. Recovery of psychomotor function after propofol sedation is prolonged in the elderly. *Can J Anaesthesiol* 2002; **49**: 927–31

Simon MJ, Veering BT. Factors affecting the pharmacokinetics and neural block characteristics after epidural administration of local anaesthetics. *Eur J Pain Suppl* 2010; **4**: 209–18

Simon MJG, Veering BT, Burm AGL, Stienstra R, Van Kleef JW. The effect of age on the the systemic absorption and disposition of ropivacaine following epidural anaesthesia. *Anesth Analg* 2006; **101**: 276–82

Simon MJ, Veering BT, Stienstra R, van Kleef JW, Burm AG. The effects of age on neural blockade and hemodynamic changes after epidural anesthesia with ropivacaine. *Anesth Analg* 2002; **94**: 1325–30

Simon MJ, Veering BT, Stienstra R, van Kleef JW, Burm AG. Effect of age on the clinical profile and systemic absorption and disposition of levobupivacaine after epidural administration. *Br J Anaesth* 2004; **93**: 512–20

Smith HS. The metabolism of opioid agents and the clinical impact of their active metabolites. *Clin J Pain* 2011; **27**: 824–38

Sprung J, Gajic O, Warner DO. Review article: Age related alterations in respiratory function - anaesthetic considerations. *Can J Anaesth* 2006; **53**: 1244–57

Stanski DR, Maitre PO. Population pharmacokinetics and pharmacodynamics of thiopental: the effect of age revisited. *Anesthesiology* 1990; **72**: 412–22

Sullivan EV, Rosenbloom M, Serventi KL, Pfefferbaum A. Effects of age and sex on volumes of the thalamus, pons, and cortex. *Neurobiol Ageing* 2004; **25**: 185–92

Thomas S, Mackintosh S, Halbert J. Does the 'Otago exercise programme' reduce mortality and falls in older adults?: a systematic review and meta-analysis. *Age Ageing* 2010; **39**: 681–7

Tsui BC, Wagner A, Finucane B. Regional anaesthesia in the elderly: a clinical guide. *Drugs Aging* 2004; **21**: 895–910

Veering BT. Are epidurals worthwhile in vascular surgery. *Curr Opin Anesthesiol* 2008; **21**: 616–8

Veering BT. Regional anaesthesia in the elderly. In McLeod GA, McCartney CJL, Wildsmith JAW, eds. *Principles and Practice of Regional Anaesthesia*, 4th Edn. Oxford: Oxford University Press, 2012; 263–8

Veering BT, Burm AGL, Souverijn JHM, Serree JMP, Spierdijk J. The effect of age on serum concentration of albumin and alpha-1-acid glycoprotein. *Br J Clin Pharmacol* 1990; **29**: 201–6

Veering BT, Burm AGL, Van Kleef JW,Hennis PJ, Spierdijk J. Epidural anaesthesia with bupivacaine: effects of age on neural blockade and pharmacokinetics. *Anesth Analg* 1987; **66**: 589–94

Veering BT, Burm AGL, Vletter AA, van den Heuvel RPM, Onkenhout W, Spierdijk J. The effect of age on the systemic absorption and systemic disposition of bupivacaine after epidural administration. *Clin Pharmacokinet* 2004; **22**: 75–84

Veering BT, Cousins MJ. Cardiovascular and pulmonary effects of epidural anaesthesia. *Anaesth Intensive Care* 2000; **28**: 620–35

Velanovich V, Antoine H, Swartz A, Peters D, Rubinfeld I. Accumulating deficits model of frailty and postoperative mortality and morbidity: its application to a national database. *J Surg Res* 2013; **183**: 104–10

Vuyk J. Pharmacodynamics in the elderly. *Best Pract Res Clin Anaesthesiol* 2003; **17**: 207–18

Wahba WM. Influence of ageing on lung function-clinical significance of changes from age twenty. *Anesth Analg* 1983; **62**: 764–76

White PF, White LM, Monk, T, et al. Perioperative care for the older outpatient undergoing ambulatory surgery *Anesth Analg* 2012; **114**: 1190–215

Wilkinson GR. Drug metabolism and variability among patients in drug response. *N Engl J Med* 2005; **352**: 2211–21

Wynne HA, Cope LH, Mutch E, Rawlins MD, Woodhouse KW, James OFW. The effect of age upon liver volume and apparent liver blood flow in healthy man. *Hepatology* 1989; **9**: 297–301

CHAPTER 87

Anaesthesia for the obese patient

Frédérique S. Servin and Valérie Billard

Introduction

Overweight and obesity are defined as abnormal or excessive fat accumulation. They are associated with increased morbidity and mortality and have specific implications for anaesthesia.

A crude measure of obesity is the body mass index (BMI), a person's weight (in kilograms) divided by the square of his or her height (in metres). A person with a BMI of 30 kg m^{-2} or more is generally considered as obese. A person with a BMI equal to or more than 25 kg m^{-2} is defined as overweight (Table 87.1). The typical patient currently proposed for bariatric surgery has a BMI around 50 kg m^{-2}, and patients with a BMI of more than 70 kg m^{-2} are not uncommon.

Other definitions of obesity have been used in the past, such as the percentage that actual body weight exceeds ideal body weight, which is calculated as a function of height and gender (Cheymol 2000). Several formulas to calculate ideal body weight have been described, but they all return similar values (Pai and Paloucek 2000).

In many countries, including developing ones, obesity is growing into an epidemic and a major health problem, so much so that the US Department of Health and Human Services issued a plan of action against this condition in 2001, 'The Surgeon General's call to action to prevent and decrease overweight and obesity' (http://www.surgeongeneral.gov/library) (Fig. 87.1).

Table 87.1 World Health Organization standard classification of obesity

	BMI (kg m^{-2})	Risk of co-morbidities
Normal	18.5–24.9	Average
Overweight		
Preobese	25.0–29.9	Slightly increased
Obesity class I	30.0–34.9	Moderate
Obesity class II	35.0–39.9	Severe
Obesity class III	≥40	Very severe

Reprinted from the WHO Database on Body Mass Index, Copyright © 2006 World Health Organization. http://apps.who.int/bmi/index.jsp?introPage=intro_3.html. Data from WHO. Physical status: the use and interpretation of anthropometry. Report of a WHO Expert Committee. WHO Technical Report Series 854. Geneva: World Health Organization, 1995; WHO. Obesity: preventing and managing the global epidemic. Report of a WHO Consultation. WHO Technical Report Series 894. Geneva: World Health Organization, 2000; and WHO expert consultation. Appropriate body-mass index for Asian populations and its implications for policy and intervention strategies. *The Lancet*, 2004; 157–163.

Thus, any anaesthetist will have to treat obese patients either for bariatric surgery, or for any other surgical condition, including emergencies. In this context, all anaesthetists should have an appropriate understanding of the physiopathological changes associated with obesity and the anaesthetic implications for such patients.

Physiopathological consequences of obesity

As stated by Haslam and James (2005), 'Hippocrates wrote "Corpulence is not only a disease itself, but the harbinger of others", recognizing that obesity is a medical disorder that also leads to many comorbidities'. Obesity significantly reduces life expectancy through a number of physiopathological changes such as metabolic syndrome, including hypertension and diabetes, cardiovascular disorders, sleep apnoea syndrome, arthritis, and even increased prevalence of cancer.

One of the rationales for bariatric surgery is that most of those changes are improved by weight loss. Given the increasing prevalence of severely obese patients, a scientific advisory board from the American Heart Association provided recommendations about the perioperative management of morbidly obese patients undergoing surgery (Poirier et al. 2009).

Metabolic syndrome

The metabolic syndrome may be defined by the presence of the following (McCullough 2011): android or central obesity (Aucouturier et al. 2009), abnormal concentrations of triglycerides, high-density lipoprotein cholesterol and fasting glucose, and hypertension. The simple measure of waist circumference has been used to recognize this syndrome (Bauduceau et al. 2007). It is a major feature of obesity not only by its prevalence (25% in the United States), but also as a promoter of the development of diabetes and cardiovascular disease. Bariatric surgery may significantly improve this syndrome, and cure diabetes mellitus (Proczko-Markuszewska et al. 2012; Yip et al. 2012). For the anaesthetist, the implications of the metabolic syndrome are mainly linked to the associated cardiovascular disorders (Tung 2010).

Cardiovascular changes

Cardiac output is increased according to the amount of fat tissue (0.1 litres min^{-1} are required to perfuse every kilogram of fat tissue) (Reisin and Frohlich 1981). As heart rate is not modified, this increase in cardiac output is mainly linked to an increase in stroke volume. This will lead to left ventricular dilatation and hypertrophy

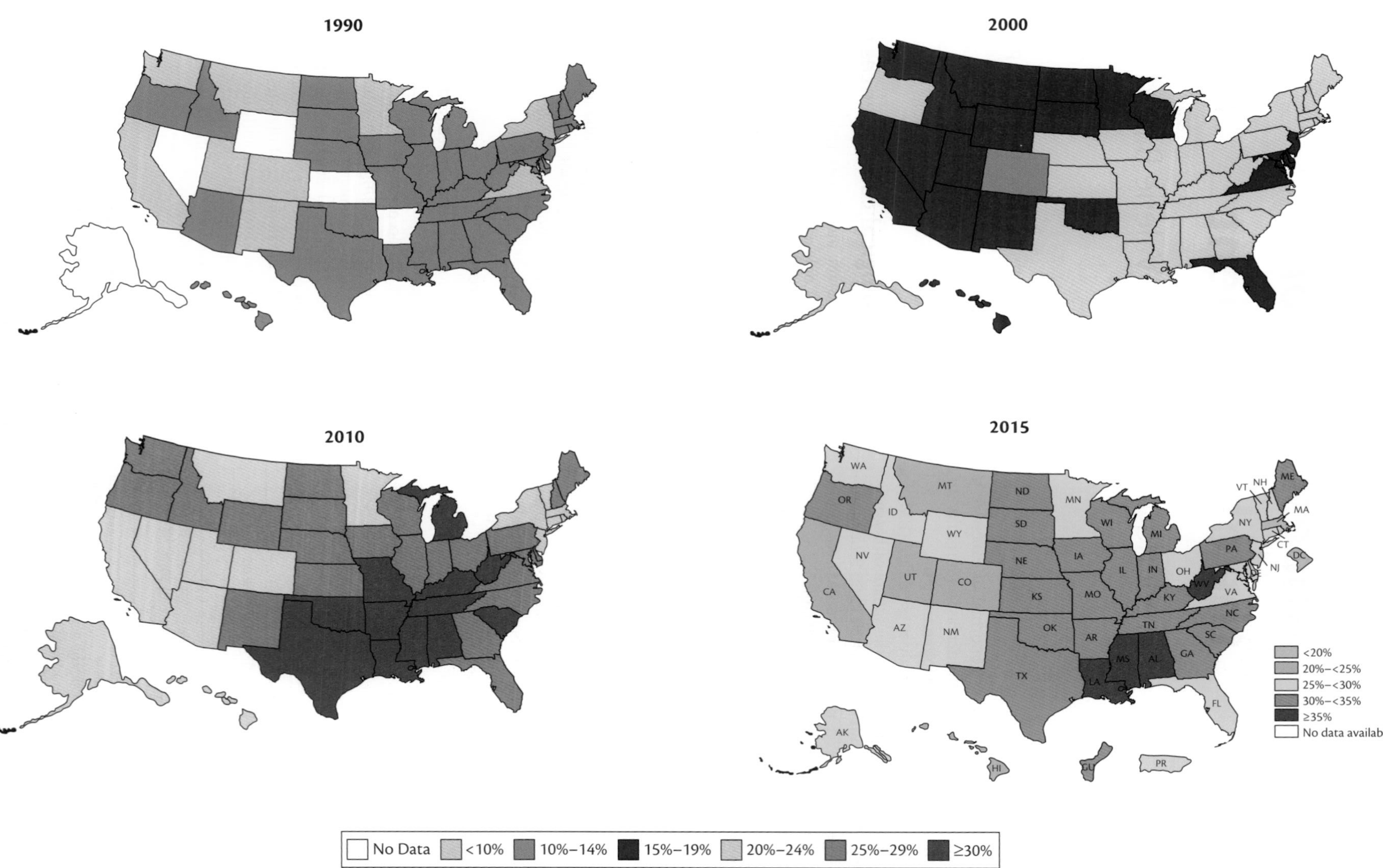

Figure 87.1 Obesity trends among adults in the United States. Behavioural Risk Factor Surveillance System [BMI ≥30, or about 30 lbs (13.6 kg) overweight for 54″ (1.65 m) person]. The legend was modified in 2015.

Source: Behavioural Risk Factor Surveillance System (BRFSS), CDC, (http://www.cdc.gov/obesity/data/prevalence-maps.html). This legend was modified in 2015.

(Alpert 2001) and reduced cardiovascular reserve. These changes, which may appear years before the overt cardiovascular complications of obesity, are corrected by weight loss. Over time, hypertension is frequent in obese patients and is associated with a significant risk of ischaemic heart disease and left ventricular failure.

An Obesity Surgery Mortality Risk Score (OS-MRS) has been validated (DeMaria et al. 2007) including five risk variables: BMI of 50 kg m^{-2} or higher, male gender, hypertension, risk of pulmonary embolism, and age 45 years or greater. Class A (low risk) includes patients with no or one risk factor; class B (intermediate risk), patients with two to three risk factors; and class C (high risk), patients with four to five risk factors. Interestingly, diabetes mellitus was not identified as an independent risk factor for mortality.

Renal function

Obese patients have larger kidneys than patients of normal weight (Naeye and Roode 1970). The glomerular filtration rate is increased as well as tubular excretion, which may be proportionally even greater (Stockholm et al. 1980). Estimation of creatinine clearance from serum creatinine using formulae such as the Cockroft–Gault equation (Cockcroft and Gault 1976) or the MDRD (Modification of Diet in Renal Disease) equation (Levey et al. 1999) overpredicts creatinine clearance when using actual body weight and underestimates it when using ideal body weight (Wilhelm and Kale-Pradhan 2011). A calculation using both serum and urine data is therefore preferable when preoperative renal failure is suspected. Moreover, an accurate calculation is the only method to be recommended for postoperative renal failure and to adjust drug dosage (e.g. antibiotics, heparin), because serum creatinine changes are delayed after acute kidney injury (6–24 h), are apparent only after massive tubular damage, and can be obscured by several factors including haemodilution.

Obstructive sleep apnoea syndrome

Obesity is an independent risk factor for obstructive sleep apnoea (OSA) (Ramachandran et al. 2010), through an increased tendency for collapse of the pharyngeal airway (Isono 2009). This condition must be recognized during the preoperative evaluation, and its severity assessed since it directly influences perioperative outcome. In elective surgery, when clinical signs and history suggest OSA, sleep studies (polysomnography) will estimate its severity. This should be done sufficiently in advance of surgery to allow preoperative preparation, including preoperative use of continuous positive airway pressure (CPAP) or mandibular advancement, and preoperative weight loss if feasible (Gross et al. 2006). After general anaesthesia, patients with OSA should be fully awake before tracheal extubation with full recovery from neuromuscular block. Tracheal extubation should be carried out in the semi-upright position and the patient maintained in this position during the recovery period. In the postoperative period, CPAP should be resumed as soon as possible but the settings may need to be modified (Brown et al. 2012). Non-opioid analgesia including regional analgesia techniques are preferred when suitable (see 'Postoperative analgesia').

Respiratory consequences of obesity

The energy expenditure required to move a larger body mass, along with the metabolic activity of increased adipose tissue, lead to an increased oxygen consumption and carbon dioxide production

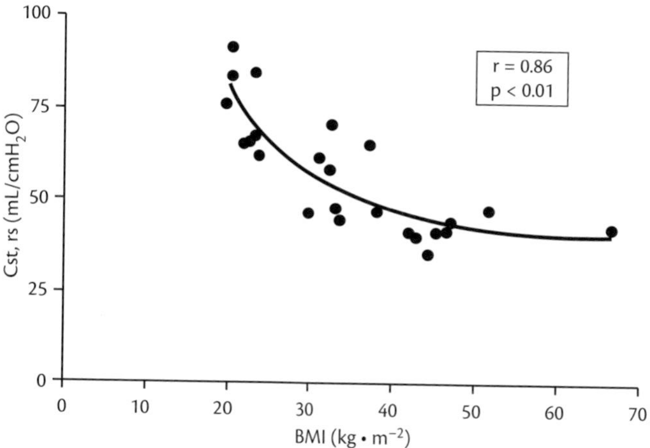

Figure 87.2 Relationships between compliance of the total respiratory system (Cst,rs) and body mass index (BMI).

Reproduced from Pelosi P, et al. The effects of body mass on lung volumes, respiratory mechanics, and gas exchange during general anesthesia. *Anesthesia and Analgesia*, Volume 87, Issue 3, pp. 654–660, Copyright © International Anesthesia Research Society 1998.

(Luce 1980). In morbidly obese patients, the respiratory rate tends to increase while tidal volume is reduced, albeit moderately, with a net increase in minute ventilation (Littleton 2012). The reasons for the higher respiratory rate remain controversial. Fatty infiltration of the chest wall reduces its compliance (Fig. 87.2), while the expiratory reserve volume decreases exponentially with increasing BMI (Littleton 2012).

Functional residual capacity is proportionally less affected, since residual volume is preserved. The changes in lung volumes seem to be mainly related to fat acting as a load, both compressing the chest wall and displacing the diaphragm. Lung compliance is also reduced, through decreased lung volumes leading to microatelectasis. These changes are more important in the supine position, which is not always well tolerated by morbidly obese patients. Obese patients have ventilation/perfusion mismatch leading to an increased alveolar–arterial oxygen gradient, which is worse in the supine position. Thus, the tolerance of obese patients to apnoea is poor, with an early onset of hypoxaemia (Lin and Lin 2012). Most of the changes associated with obesity are reversed after significant weight loss (de Souza et al. 2010).

Pharmacological changes in the obese patient

Pharmacokinetics

Absorption

Obesity by itself does not modify intestinal absorption of drugs (Cheymol 2000). Nevertheless, some bariatric surgical procedures (gastric or intestinal bypasses) may promote impaired absorption syndromes. Patients who have had gastric bypass frequently show vitamin K deficiency, and sometimes vitamin D, vitamin B12, or folate deficiency (Malone 2008).

Distribution

Obesity is associated with an inflammatory state (Wellen and Hotamisligil 2003). α1-acid glycoprotein (AAG) concentration may double in obese patients when compared with controls of normal weight (Zini et al. 1990). As a consequence, the active free fraction of drugs that are weak bases such as fentanyl and congeners may be markedly lowered, thus reducing their efficacy.

The increase in fat tissue mass is obviously a major factor affecting changes in the apparent volume of distribution in obese patients, but obesity is also associated with increases in blood volume and in the size of many organs (liver or kidneys, for example) (Kjellberg and Reizenstein 1970). Consequently, the volume of the central compartment is usually increased, as well as the volume of distribution at steady state even in drugs that do not penetrate fat. Lean body mass is also greater in obese patients (Janmahasatian et al. 2005). Thus, to reach the same concentration and therefore the same clinical effect, the dose of most drugs needs to be increased. Of course, the drugs that are readily distributed into fat need greater dosage adjustments than those that remain in the extracellular spaces, since fat body mass is much more increased than lean body mass (Cheymol 1993). One must nevertheless keep in mind that adjusting hydrophilic drug dosage on ideal body weight in morbidly obese patients may lead to under-dosing.

Elimination

Hepatic metabolism

Obesity is associated with increased cardiac output, blood volume, and organ blood flow, but functional hepatic blood flow remains mostly unchanged despite the increase in liver size, possibly as a result of fatty infiltration of the liver which may impair liver function even if standard biochemical tests of liver function remain normal (Adler and Schaffner 1979). The clearance of drugs principally metabolized by phase I processes is usually unchanged, as is that of acetylated drugs, despite an increased activity of some cytochrome P450 enzymes. Conversely, the clearance of many conjugated drugs increases in parallel with total body weight, possibly through extrahepatic conjugation pathways (Abernethy et al. 1983).

Renal elimination

Obese patients have larger kidneys than patients of normal weight (Naeye and Roode 1970). The glomerular filtration rate is increased as is tubular excretion, which may be proportionally even greater (Stockholm et al. 1980). As a consequence, the elimination of drugs excreted through the kidney is enhanced.

Pharmacodynamics

There is very little information in the literature on pharmacodynamic changes in obese patients. This condition does not seem to affect the concentration–effect relationship for hypnotic drugs (Servin et al. 1993) or neuromuscular blocking agents. Some studies on human pain thresholds have yielded contradictory results, some claiming increased and others reduced pain sensitivity in the obese (McKendall and Haier 1983; Zahorska-Markiewicz et al. 1983; Ramzan et al. 1993). Nociceptive threshold appears to be increased in obese rats (Ramzan et al. 1993). It seems that even non-diabetic obese patients display a sub-clinical conduction defect in small-diameter sensory fibres, mimicking the metabolic peripheral neuropathy such as observed in hyperinsulinaemia (Miscio et al. 2005).

Bariatric surgery

Bariatric surgery, or weight loss surgery, includes various procedures which aim to cause a significant sustained loss of weight associated with a reduction in co-morbidities such as diabetes mellitus or cardiovascular risk, and ultimately a reduction in mortality (Inabnet et al. 2012; Jimenez et al. 2012). It is mainly offered to patients younger than 60 years of age with a BMI of at least 40 kg m^{-2}. It is currently the most frequent circumstance when an anaesthetist has to manage morbidly obese patients for elective surgery.

The most frequent procedures are gastric banding and sleeve gastrectomy, which reduce the functional size of the stomach, and gastric bypass in which a part of the small intestine is resected and rerouted to a small residual gastric pouch. All those procedures can be done through a laparotomy, but nowadays most are performed laparoscopically.

Adjustable gastric banding

Adjustable gastric banding is a procedure in which the functional size of the stomach is reduced by a silicone band inserted around part of the stomach leaving only a small pouch with a narrow outlet. The silicone band is adjusted by injecting more or less saline in a port placed just under the skin. Gastric banding has been a very popular procedure considered by many surgeons and patients as minimally invasive and potentially reversible. It is more and more frequently proposed as an outpatient procedure (Elli et al. 2013). Nevertheless, over time some concerns have arisen both about the efficacy of the procedure, and its long-term complications (Romy et al. 2012). In a cohort of 442 patients matched for age, sex, and BMI having either gastric banding or Roux-en-Y gastric bypass with a follow up of 6 years, the weight loss was significantly more and lasted longer in the bypass group. More importantly perhaps, the long-term complication rate was significantly higher with gastric banding (41.6% *vs* 19%, $P < 0.001$), with most of the complications related to oesophageal dilation and food intolerance. This is an important point for the anaesthetist: many such patients are subsequently referred for plastic surgical procedures to remove excess skin after weight loss, and they should be considered at high risk of aspiration of 'gastric contents' and receive a rapid sequence induction of anaesthesia with cricoid pressure and tracheal intubation, after complete deflation of the gastric band before induction (Avriel et al. 2012).

Gastric bypass

The most common form of gastric bypass is the Roux-en-Y gastric bypass. A small stomach pouch is created with staples, and connected to the distal small intestine. The upper part of the small intestine is then reattached in a Y-shaped configuration. The gastric bypass is currently considered to be the gold standard in bariatric surgery and has been performed on hundreds of thousands of patients (Livingston 2010).

Sleeve gastrectomy

Sleeve gastrectomy is a relatively new procedure in which the stomach is reduced to about 15% of its original size, by surgical removal of a large portion of the stomach, following the major curve. It is considered to be a less 'traumatic' procedure than gastric bypass and can be used as a first step in massively obese patients to obtain a significant weight loss before a gastric bypass (Catheline et al. 2012). Its current results and complication rate are similar to those of Roux-en-Y gastric bypass (Boza et al. 2012). The most frequent complication after sleeve gastrectomy is staple line leak (Sakran et al. 2013).

General anaesthesia for the obese patient

Preoperative assessment, preparation, and premedication

The preoperative assessment of a morbidly obese patient should consider the potential technical problems: peripheral venous access, positioning on the operating table, tolerance of the supine position, landmarks for central venous access or regional anaesthesia, and tracheal intubation (see later in chapter). It should also identify causes of perioperative morbidity such as the presence of OSA (the importance of which should be quantified), or a history of venous thromboembolism (VTE).

If significant unrecognized OSA is diagnosed, the patient should be referred to a specialist to be treated by nocturnal CPAP or mandibular advancement before elective surgery.

Although obese patients are frequently anxious or depressed, sedatives in premedication should be used with caution. An antacid premedicant is often proposed, mainly to prevent acid aspiration during a difficult intubation. Measures to prevent VTE are mandatory (see 'Venous thromboembolism and its prevention in the obese patient').

Which drugs, which dosing scheme?

Hypnotic agents

Thiopental

Obese patients require a higher absolute dose (in mg) than lean patients, as a result of increased cardiac output, lean body mass, and distribution (Wada et al. 1997). Adjusting the dose to ideal body mass would result in under-dosing the obese patient. Thiopental is extensively stored in fat tissues, resulting in an increased volume of distribution and terminal half-life, which are good reasons to limit its use to a single induction bolus.

Propofol

Propofol is a lipophilic drug, but not so lipophilic that it concentrates mainly in fat. Its distribution volume, therefore, is increased proportionally to the total body weight (Servin et al. 1993). Propofol is mainly eliminated after conjugation and its metabolic clearance also increases with obesity. Thus, propofol dosage during maintenance of anaesthesia in the morbidly obese should be calculated on total body weight. If target-controlled infusion is used, the best model in this population is the Marsh model, which includes only total body weight as a covariate (La Colla et al. 2009).

The propofol dose required for induction of anaesthesia remains subject to debate (Ingrande et al. 2011; Van Kralingen et al. 2011a). It is certainly higher than normal but a calculation based on total body weight may lead to overdosage with haemodynamic consequences: careful titration against effect is recommended.

Volatile anaesthetics

Both sevoflurane and desflurane have been used extensively and satisfactorily for maintenance of anaesthesia in morbidly obese patients. However, a faster early recovery after desflurane compared with sevoflurane is consistent with the pharmacokinetics, with desflurane demonstrating absence of accumulation (De Baerdemaeker et al. 2003). Similarly, early (2 h) and late (24h) postoperative respiratory function are better after desflurane than after propofol maintenance both for volumes (vital capacity) and flows (forced expiratory volume in 1 s) and are more sensitive to BMI after propofol than after desflurane (Zoremba et al. 2011).

Nitrous oxide did not markedly increase bowel distension during laparoscopic bariatric surgery (Brodsky et al. 2005).

Opioids

Morphine

The pharmacokinetics of morphine in the obese have not been reported. One may nevertheless assume that morphine, which is metabolized by conjugation, may have an increased metabolism in obese patients, with no accumulation of the active metabolites which are eliminated through the kidney. Morphine is bound in plasma to albumin, and its unbound fraction probably remains normal. Thus, as far as analgesia is concerned, the obese patient probably requires more morphine than the lean one. Nevertheless, the main problem with morphine use in the obese is respiratory depression and hypoxaemia, even in the absence of sleep apnoea syndrome. Morphine should therefore always be part of a multimodal analgesic protocol to minimize the dosage, and titrated to effect under close monitoring in this population.

Fentanyl and congeners (alfentanil, sufentanil, remifentanil)

Fentanyl and alfentanil pharmacokinetics in the obese have not been reported in peer-reviewed research articles.

Despite its large volume of distribution, fentanyl should not be administered as a function of total body weight in obese patients, but rather proportionally to a so-called pharmacokinetic mass, linked to clearance (Shibutani et al. 2004). Nevertheless, the cumulative properties of fentanyl do not favour its use in obese patients when repeated or high doses are required.

Sufentanil has been studied in more detail: as might be expected from its high lipid solubility, the total volume of distribution of sufentanil is increased in the obese patient (Schwartz et al. 1991). This increase is moderate since the data lose statistical significance if expressed as a function of body weight. The most recent pharmacokinetic model published for sufentanil does not include body weight as a significant covariate (Gepts et al. 1995). Interestingly, it performed well when used for sufentanil target-controlled infusion in morbidly obese patients despite a slight overestimation of plasma sufentanil concentrations specifically when the BMI was greater than 40 kg m^{-2} (Slepchenko et al. 2003). The authors concluded that the pharmacokinetic parameters derived from a normal-weight population accurately predicted plasma sufentanil concentrations in morbidly obese patients.

The pharmacokinetic properties of remifentanil (small volume of distribution, high clearance, no lingering effects), renders it a relatively ideal drug for use during anaesthesia in the obese patient. Apart from the (expected) high clearance, another important feature of remifentanil pharmacokinetics is its apparent independence from body weight, with only the lean body mass appearing as a significant morphological covariate in the model (Minto et al. 1997). As a consequence, remifentanil pharmacokinetics are not markedly different in obese *vs* lean subjects. In clinical practice, remifentanil dosing regimens should be based on lean body mass and not on total body weight.

Neuromuscular blocking agents and reversal agents

Neuromuscular blocking agents are water-soluble drugs. As such, their dosage in obesity should not be based on total body weight, but rather on lean body mass, or on ideal body weight (Leykin et al.

2004a, 2004b). As it is not always easy to estimate the adequate dose to use, monitoring is mandatory. Conversely, to obtain complete neuromuscular paralysis, suxamethonium dosage should be 1 mg kg^{-1} total body weight (Lemmens and Brodsky 2006).

A complete recovery from neuromuscular block is mandatory before tracheal extubation in the obese patient. Sugammadex may be a useful agent to allow adequate rocuronium dosage and complete reversal, but the dose calculated from ideal body weight is insufficient to ensure adequate recovery (Llaurado et al. 2012). This confirms that, because of an increased lean body mass and extracellular volume in morbidly obese compared with lean patients, the doses of water-soluble drugs should be based on lean body mass and not ideal body weight in this population.

Antibiotics

Few data are available regarding disposition of antibiotics in obese patients.

For vancomycin, absolute values of both apparent volume of distribution and clearance are increased proportionally to total body weight. As efficacy is a greater concern than toxicity, the daily dose should be calculated based on total body weight, and dosing interval for intermittent boluses should take into account an estimate of renal function (Bearden and Rodvold 2000). Both should be adjusted to daily measured drug concentration.

Aminoglycosides are highly polar drugs distributing poorly in fat. The principal concern in this instance is toxicity. The initial drug dose should be based on ideal body weight plus 40% of the difference between actual and ideal body weight rather than total body weight (Bearden and Rodvold 2000) and adjusted according to plasma concentration.

For ciprofloxacin, the volume of distribution is increased but not proportionally to the body weight (i.e. volume of distribution kg^{-1} decreases) as is clearance. Thus doses should be adjusted to ideal body weight plus 45% of the difference between actual and ideal body weight.

When using cefazolin for surgical antibiotic prophylaxis, the distribution volume increases with weight, whereas clearance does not (Van Kralingen et al. 2011a). Increasing the initial dose from 1 g to 2 g in obese patients resulted in similar plasma concentrations as 1 g in non-obese patients and is therefore recommended (Bearden and Rodvold 2000).

Preparation for induction of anaesthesia

Positioning is very important in obese patients in whom pressure injuries may easily happen (Brodsky 2002). An operating table and accessories designed for obese patients should be used with the patient transferred directly from the bed as theatre trolleys usually have a maximum capacity of 140 or 160 kg. Sufficient staff to help transfer the patient should be available. The supine position is frequently poorly tolerated by obese patients and a semi-recumbent position with the head raised may greatly improve mask oxygenation and tracheal intubation. All accessories must be adapted to obese patients, for example, blood pressure cuffs.

Peripheral venous access is more likely to be difficult in obese than in lean patients. When visual or tactile localization fails, ultrasound-guided insertion may decrease both the time to place a venous line, especially in the upper arm, and the number of attempts (Gregg et al. 2010; Joing et al. 2012), provided the practitioner has already gained good experience with the technique.

Induction of anaesthesia

Oxygenation

Rapid sequence induction of anaesthesia is recommended in morbidly obese patients, not so much because of the risk of aspiration of gastric contents (see 'Is there a risk of aspiration of gastric content?'), but rather as a result of poor tolerance of apnoea leading to rapid hypoxaemia. In the supine position, the delay after preoxygenation to a Sp_{O_2} decrease to less than 90% is around 2.7–3 min but can be less than 1 min in some patients (Altermatt et al. 2005).

The first mechanism contributing to rapid development of hypoxaemia is a reduction in lung volumes observed in morbidly obese patients even when awake (see 'Respiratory consequences of obesity'). This reduction is exacerbated by anaesthesia and is compounded by a reduction in lung compliance (Pelosi et al. 1998). The second contributory mechanism is the presence of atelectasis, which is present before induction but increased by it (Eichenberger et al. 2002). Atelectasis persists longer in morbidly obese than in lean patients and can be observed up to 24 h after surgery.

As a consequence, standard preoxygenation by spontaneous breathing of pure oxygen through a face mask is not sufficient in this population, and is associated with a very short duration of apnoea before hypoxaemia ensues. Performing induction in the semi-upright position can lengthen the delay before hypoxaemia by around 1 min. The application of CPAP during preoxygenation reduces atelectasis formation and increases the time of non-hypoxaemic apnoea by 50% (Coussa et al. 2004; Gander et al. 2005). The addition of pressure support ventilation to positive end-expiratory pressure (PEEP) increases the efficacy of preoxygenation, shortens the time to reach the maximal fractional end-tidal oxygen concentration and achieves a higher fractional end-tidal oxygen value (Delay et al. 2008). However, in this study, the times to reach the maximal fractional end-tidal oxygen concentration were longer than usually published in patients of normal weight, thus stressing that in morbidly obese patients preoxygenation should be for at least 3 min.

Nevertheless, all of these interventions, while useful, are all short term, and a recent study has demonstrated the benefit of applying a recruitment manoeuvre after tracheal intubation to improve respiratory function during the initial period of maintenance of anaesthesia (Futier et al. 2011).

Rapid sequence induction

Any intravenous agent suitable for rapid sequence induction can be used in morbidly obese patients. Depth of anaesthesia monitoring may help. To ensure adequate anaesthesia during tracheal intubation, we recommend giving opioids before induction, taking into account the drug onset time.

Suxamethonium (succinylcholine) is frequently used to rapidly provide neuromuscular block and offers good intubating conditions following induction of anaesthesia. Nevertheless, suxamethonium use is not devoid of unwanted effects, and an alternative is high-dose rocuronium (Gaszynski and Szewczyk 2011), with sugammadex readily available to reverse neuromuscular block if required in an emergency (Desforges and McDonnell 2011).

Is tracheal intubation more difficult?

Considering the poor tolerance to apnoea of morbidly obese patients, a careful assessment of the airway and prediction of difficult tracheal intubation is particularly important. Morbid obesity *per se* does not seem to be an independent factor for difficult intubation (Mashour et al. 2008), and neither is OSA in obese patients (Neligan et al. 2009b). The problem is rather the poor predictive value of the preoperative tests (Juvin et al. 2003), even with a modified Mallampati test with craniocervical extension (Mashour et al. 2008). The measure of neck circumference has been proposed as a useful adjunct to airway assessment, as some authors describe a thick neck as a predictor of difficult intubation (Brodsky et al. 2002) but others did not. Finally diabetes mellitus was also a significant predictor of difficult laryngoscopy (Mashour et al. 2008). In order to optimize intubating conditions, positioning the patient in a 'ramped' (with the head placed on a pillow or folded blankets so that the external auditory meatus and the sternal notch are horizontally aligned) rather than the 'sniff' position improved intubating conditions, specifically in obese patients (Collins et al. 2004). Video-assisted laryngoscopy may be used to decrease duration of intubation and limit desaturation (Dhonneur et al. 2009).

In preparing a strategy for failed intubation, ventilation of the lungs through a facemask is more likely to be difficult in morbidly obese patients (Langeron et al. 2000). Laryngeal mask airways (LMAs) are usually easy to insert and provide efficient ventilation of the lungs and oxygenation as rescue devices (Abdi et al. 2009). The intubating LMA Fastrach™ (Teleflex Incorporated, Wayne, PA, USA) was considered even more efficient in controlling the airway in morbidly obese than non-obese patients (Combes et al. 2005). Consequently, these devices should be immediately available.

Is there a risk of aspiration of gastric contents?

In the absence of gastric banding or pregnancy, the risk of aspiration of gastric contents is not increased in obese patients, in whom both the gastric fluid volume and pH are no different from those of lean subjects (Juvin et al. 2001).

The presence of a gastric band, even if the ring is deflated, must be considered as an obstacle to gastric emptying, and conveys a high risk of aspiration (Kocian and Spahn 2005). Such patients may be selected for bariatric surgery after failure or short-lasting efficacy of gastric banding.

Pregnancy induces a triple risk during induction of anaesthesia:

- Intubation is more likely to be difficult because of anatomical changes
- Duration of non-hypoxic apnoea is reduced by an increase in cardiac output
- Gastric acidity and gastric volume are increased resulting after the first trimester in a very high risk of aspiration (Vallejo 2007).

These major risks are enhanced in morbidly obese patients and they provide a strong indication for regional anaesthesia whenever possible for delivery and for surgery: where regional anaesthesia is otherwise contraindicated, is refused by the patient, or fails because of technical difficulties, all of the precautions previously described for induction of anaesthesia should be implemented.

Maintenance of anaesthesia

Ventilation and oxygenation

General anaesthesia decreases diaphragmatic muscular tone and increases intra-abdominal pressure, especially in the supine position and during laparoscopic surgery. These changes decrease all lung volumes and compliance, and favour airway closure by external compression, inducing hypoxaemia and atelectasis (Valenza et al. 2007; Reinius et al. 2009). Alveolar–arterial PO_2 difference is increased in morbidly obese patients (Sprung et al. 2003). Consequently, standard inspired oxygen concentrations may not guarantee adequate arterial oxygen saturation.

Manoeuvres

PEEP decreases elastance of the respiratory system in obese patients, and improves oxygenation (Pelosi et al. 1999). The optimum level of PEEP may be determined by estimating compliance. Recruitment manoeuvres using sustained lung inflation followed by PEEP decrease atelectasis for a longer time than recruitment manoeuvres alone (Reinius et al. 2009) and improve oxygenation (Chalhoub et al. 2007), especially during laparoscopic bariatric surgery (Whalen et al. 2006). They also reduce the alveolar–arterial PO_2 gradient (Chalhoub et al. 2007). However, they may induce haemodynamic instability and require fluid load or vasopressors. The benefit of the manoeuvres ceases after tracheal extubation.

Posture

The beach-chair position has been reported to increase lung volumes and decrease elastance similarly to PEEP, the combination of both being necessary to correct respiratory function during pneumoperitoneum (Valenza et al. 2007). However, the effect of posture is debated and other groups found no benefit of a 30° head-up position on oxygenation or respiratory function (Casati et al. 2000; Sprung et al. 2002). When required for surgery, the prone position increases functional residual capacity, lung compliance, and oxygenation compared with the supine position (Pelosi et al. 1996).

Ventilation mode

Pressure-controlled ventilation produced no clear benefit compared with volume-controlled ventilation with similar minute volume. It reduced peak inspiratory airway pressure but did not affect plateau pressure (the most important for barotrauma), haemodynamic stability, or postoperative arterial blood gases (De Baerdemaeker et al. 2008; Hans et al. 2008). One study found improved oxygenation during anaesthesia (Cadi et al. 2008), but another did not (Hans et al. 2008).

Tidal volume

In the obese, not only are awake lung volumes not increased in proportion to total body weight but they are even smaller than those observed in non-obese patients (Jones and Nzekwu 2006). Thus, tidal volume should rather be based on ideal rather than actual body weight: a tidal volume between 8 and 10 ml kg^{-1} ideal body weight is usually selected initially. Subsequently the tidal volume is adjusted according to the end-tidal CO_2, with 30–35 cm H_2O as a maximum inspiratory pressure.

Sprung et al. (2003) investigated the effect of doubling the tidal volume on airway closure and atelectasis during laparoscopic surgery. They observed an improvement in compliance, both before and during pneumoperitoneum, but no clear benefit on oxygenation and they concluded by not recommending this intervention.

Tracheal extubation

As mentioned previously, tracheal extubation should be delayed until the patient is awake and recovery from neuromuscular block has been achieved. The patient should be in the sitting position and ideally able to demonstrate good tidal volumes before the tracheal tube is removed. After extubation, the application of CPAP improves forced expiratory volume in 1 s, forced vital capacity, and peak expiratory flow rate (Neligan et al. 2009a).

Which monitoring?

'Non-invasive' cardiac output monitoring uses algorithms that were validated in lean patients and may not be valid in the morbidly obese. Some authors suggested calibrating the oesophageal Doppler monitor for a BMI of 30 kg m^{-2}, whatever the actual value (Erlandsson et al. 2006). Extrapolation of readings from pulse contour monitors without calibration may return unreliable results. The use of a LiDCO™ (LiDCO System, London, UK) monitor with lithium calibration to maintain stroke volume variation at less than 10% has been proposed to guide intravenous fluid loading in morbidly obese patients undergoing laparoscopic bariatric surgery and resulted in the administration of approximately 2 litres of crystalloid for 3.5 h of surgery (Jain and Dutta 2010).

Bispectral Index™ (BIS™, Covidien, now Medtronic Minimally Invasive Therapies, Minneapolis, MN, USA) monitoring has been used to titrate propofol during bariatric surgery (Van Kralingen et al. 2011b). Its use resulted in a propofol infusion rate around 5 mg kg^{-1} h^{-1}, irrespective of whether propofol was combined with remifentanil or with epidural analgesia.

Fluid management during surgery

There is still a debate in the literature between 'restrictive' and 'liberal' approaches to fluid management during surgery in the morbidly obese. In the liberal approach, it is suggested to give a lot of fluids regardless of the estimated fluid loss (>10 ml kg^{-1} h^{-1}, i.e. up to 4–5 litres for 2 h of surgery) (Ogunnaike et al. 2002) in order to prevent rhabdomyolysis-induced acute kidney injury. The restrictive approach proposes a smaller baseline fluid load to compensate for estimated insensible (<1 mg kg^{-1} h^{-1} even in abdominal surgery) and urine losses, supplemented by additional 'boluses' of crystalloid or colloid to correct hypotension, tachycardia, or indices of fluid responsiveness (Chappell et al. 2008).

In comparative studies, the restrictive approach resulted in a lower volume of fluid administered and a lower urine output, but there was no effect on serum creatinine or creatine kinase (Wool et al. 2010; Matot et al. 2012). We would suggest a total hourly rate of fluid administration of less than 5 ml kg^{-1} with replacement of blood loss.

In morbidly obese patients suspected of being hypovolaemic through preoperative transthoracic echocardiography, an individualized rehydration strategy before induction of anaesthesia may improve cardiovascular stability (Pösö et al. 2014).

Postoperative fluid should also be controlled to optimize oxygenation and wound healing. Urine output is a more reliable indicator of hypovolaemia postoperatively than intraoperatively because there is no influence of raised intra-abdominal pressure. The standard target for urine output of 0.5 ml kg^{-1} h^{-1} may be insufficient in the morbidly obese because renal blood flow and glomerular filtration are higher than normal. Daily body weight measurements may reveal fluid overload.

Recovery and postoperative care

Postoperative analgesia

Postoperative analgesia has not been extensively studied in morbidly obese patients. Regional analgesia is a good choice, but should not limit ambulation. Otherwise, a multimodal analgesic regimen is useful in order to reduce morphine requirements. Morbidly obese patients are often sensitive to the respiratory depressant effects of morphine and patient-controlled analgesia may be useful with the patient monitored in an appropriate setting. Most of the following recommendations are based on the pharmacological properties of the drugs.

Weak opioids and opioid-related analgesics

Codeine, oxycodone

Codeine is a prodrug and has to be transformed into morphine by the enzyme debrisoquine hydroxylase (CYP2D6) to be effective. As a consequence, the effects of codeine are the same as morphine, with a time delay related to the biotransformation. A significant minority of individuals (about 10% of the European population) lack the ability to transform codeine into morphine (Lotsch et al. 2004). In morbidly obese patients, conjugation pathways are often enhanced, and the clearance of conjugated drugs is therefore increased. However, the variability of morphine production is increased and it is therefore more reliable, in this population sensitive to the respiratory depressant effects of the drug, to titrate morphine itself rather than a pro-drug.

Tramadol

Tramadol is a racemic mixture of two enantiomers with similar pharmacokinetics: a volume of distribution at steady state of about 3.5 litres kg^{-1}, and an intermediate elimination clearance of about 500 ml min^{-1} (Reeves and Burke 2008). Tramadol also undergoes hepatic metabolism via the cytochrome P450 iso-enzyme CYP2D6, and is *O*- and *N*-demethylated to five different metabolites. One of these, M1 (*O*-desmethyltramadol) is active, and may accumulate with repeated doses (Lehtonen et al. 2010). Tramadol has not been specifically studied in the obese patient, but we can infer from its pharmacological properties that the initial dose should be high, and the dosing interval increased as a result of its cumulative potential. In the future, pupillometry may perhaps be used to titrate tramadol to effect.

Non-opioid analgesics

Non-steroidal anti-inflammatory drug

Non-steroidal anti-inflammatory drugs (NSAIDs) may be used in morbidly obese patients with the usual precautions and contraindications, especially those related to impaired renal function. They may even help to control the metabolic syndrome (Gao et al. 2009). In the perioperative period, as part of a multimodal analgesia protocol, NSAIDs may help reduce the dose of postoperative opioids and therefore the risk of respiratory impairment. Their small volume of distribution [0.15 litres kg^{-1} for ketoprofen (Debruyne et al. 1987)] suggests that they do not penetrate the adipose tissue and therefore the effective doses are little modified by obesity.

Paracetamol (acetaminophen)

Although the pharmacokinetics of paracetamol have not been studied in obese patients, its volume of distribution (0.9 litres kg^{-1}) in patients of normal weight (Forrest et al.1982) suggests that some increase in dose may be necessary to achieve full analgesic effect.

Rhabdomyolysis

Rhabdomyolysis is a frequent postoperative complication in obese patients: its incidence has been estimated as 7% in bariatric surgery (Ettinger et al. 2008) but it can be much higher when the BMI exceeds 50 kg m^2, with a long operation, and in patients with hypertension, diabetes, hepatic steatosis, or intraoperative hypotension.

Muscle cell damage as a result of prolonged muscle compression results in fluid extravasation, which may result in hypovolaemia and vasoconstriction. Acute kidney injury can be caused by both dehydration and renal tubular obstruction from precipitation of myoglobin. Muscle cytolysis also induces hyperkalaemia, hyperphosphataemia, hyperuricaemia, and metabolic acidosis (Menezes Ettinger et al. 2005).

Prevention of rhabdomyolysis includes careful padding of all pressure points, use of pneumatic beds, avoidance of hypotension, and selection of patients and medical team in order to limit the duration of the procedure. Diagnosis is suspected when there is tea-coloured urine, decubitus erythema at pressure points (shoulders, back, buttocks, calves), or oliguria. It is confirmed by elevated serum creatine kinase (greater than five-fold) (Ettinger et al. 2007).

Treatment is based, in obese as in lean patients, on hydration and monitored by urine flow and repeated creatine kinase and creatinine assays. Bicarbonate has been proposed to maintain urinary pH higher than 6 in order to prevent precipitation of myoglobin and tubular obstruction. Mannitol may be used to stimulate urine output but if additional fluid replacement is not anticipated, dehydration and hypovolaemia may be exacerbated: any further interpretation of urine output as a marker of hydration and volume loading will be precluded. Furosemide is recommended only when fluid loading has induced pulmonary oedema.

Gentle massage of the damaged muscles can reverse the vicious circle of oedema and ischaemia that can easily develop with rhabdomyolysis with resulting compartment syndrome. If severe rhabdomyolysis affects the limbs or retroperitoneal muscles, compartment syndrome should be anticipated and, if suspected, decompressive fasciotomy performed as a matter of urgency.

Venous thromboembolism and its prevention in the obese patient

Obesity is associated with an increased risk of pulmonary embolism which is directly related to BMI (Goldhaber 2004). Other risk factors are frequently found in this population, such as hypertension, poor mobility, diabetes, and large varicose veins. The incidence of symptomatic VTE after bariatric surgery is approximately 1% with suboptimal prophylactic protocols (Hamad and Choban 2005). It is delayed after the procedure [13 days on average, with one-third (Carmody et al. 2006) to three-quarters (Steele et al. 2011) of events occurring after hospital discharge] and mortality is high (27%).

Consequently, prolonged VTE prophylaxis using low-molecular-weight heparin (LMWH) is recommended by most specialist societies for bariatric surgery and also for any major procedure, cancer surgery, after major trauma, or in patients having multiple risk factors. It should be combined with mechanical devices such as graduated compression stockings or intermittent pneumatic compression and these should be implemented before surgery (Geerts et al. 2008; Kakkos et al. 2008). Early postoperative ambulation, facilitated by appropriate anaesthetic techniques, is also strongly recommended.

Administration of LMWH every 12 h is recommended to improve the efficacy of prophylaxis, although the level of proof for this strategy is poor. When low-dose unfractionated heparin is used, it should be given three times a day (Geerts et al. 2008). There is no consensus about the dose but standard doses used in non-obese patients are definitely insufficient in the obese. Seeking therapeutic concentrations of antifactor Xa (0.18–0.44 U ml^{-1}), Rowan et al. (2008) found that after the third dose of enoxaparin 30 mg twice daily, fewer than 10% of patients had reached the lower limit of the therapeutic range. Increasing enoxaparin dose to 40 mg every 12 h increased the number of patients above the therapeutic threshold to 40% (Rowan et al. 2008) and decreased the number of venous thromboembolic events and duration of hospital stay (Scholten et al. 2002). When increasing to 60 mg $(12\ h)^{-1}$, Simone et al. (2008) found all patients were above the lower limit of the therapeutic range, but 57% were above the upper limit. Our suggestion is to give enoxaparin (or another LMWH at equipotent doses) 40 mg every 12 h up to a BMI of 60 kg m^{-2} and 60 mg twice daily when the BMI is greater.

Another option would be to adjust the dose to total body weight, based on the finding that after a fixed dose, the area under the concentration–time curve decreased linearly with body weight (Frederiksen et al. 2003) whereas after a dose adjusted for total body weight, peak concentration is independent of BMI (Sanderink et al. 2002).

Freeman et al. (2012) compared enoxaparin 0.5 mg kg^{-1} with 0.4 mg kg^{-1} or 40 mg fixed dose and concluded that 0.5 mg kg^{-1} achieved the desired peak concentration more frequently than with either alternative regimen. Similar findings were described for dalteparin suggesting that it should be dosed as a function of total body weight or ideal body weight plus 40% of the excess over ideal body weight (Hanley et al. 2010).

Pharmacological prophylaxis should be maintained for at least 10 days after discharge (12–13 days postoperatively) (Raftopoulos et al. 2008), and possibly much longer since the incidence of venous thromboembolic events was described to increase from 0.88% at discharge to 2.17% within 1 month and 2.99% within 6 months (Steele et al. 2011).

Regional anaesthesia in the obese patient

Regional anaesthesia is beneficial in obese patients, first to avoid general anaesthesia and its additional morbidity, but also to treat postoperative pain and improve rehabilitation. However, it may be difficult to manage both from the technical perspective and to determine drug dosage, especially in obstetrics.

Regional anaesthetic techniques tend to be more difficult in the obese because bony landmarks may be difficult to feel and the depth between the skin and the nerves is hard to estimate (Ingrande et al. 2009). Ultrasound guidance has been shown to be helpful for neuraxial and peripheral blocks (Brodsky and Lemmens 2007) although there are technical limitations of ultrasonography in the morbidly obese. It should therefore be anticipated that proficiency in ultrasound-guided regional anaesthesia should be obtained in non-obese patients [for spinal blocks in non-obese patients, it has been estimated that at least 30–40 cases are required to reach proficiency (Chin and Perlas 2011)] before attempting techniques in obese patients.

Neuraxial block

The distance from the skin to the epidural space is increased, but not linearly, with BMI. At the lumbar level for epidural labour analgesia, the average skin–space distance was estimated to be approximately 6.5 cm (Balki et al. 2009). In bariatric surgical patients (average BMI 48, range 36–91 kg m^{-2}), the epidural space was measured at an average of 9 cm from the skin (range 5.5–11 cm) when the needle was inserted cranially at an angle of 60–90° (Nishiyama et al. 2012). These findings suggest that a standard 8 cm epidural needle would be reasonable to use in the first instance, but a longer needle should be available (Soens et al. 2008). For spinal anaesthesia, the use of an introducer may so limit the depth of insertion of the needle that it will not reach the subarachnoid space (Corfe 2008).

The skin-to-epidural space depth also increases (by at least 1–2 cm) when moving from the sitting to the lateral position (Hamza et al. 1995). Therefore, we recommend that the catheter is advanced at least 4 cm into the epidural space when it is inserted with the patient in the sitting position to avoid migration of the catheter from the epidural space with patient repositioning. Conversely, inserting the catheter in the lateral head-down position reduces the risk of epidural vein puncture (Bahar et al. 2004). When identification of the midline is difficult it may be useful to ask the patient to help (Marroquin et al. 2011).

The cerebrospinal fluid volume may be reduced by increased abdominal pressure, and may result in extended block after neuraxial anaesthesia (Hogan et al. 1996; Ingrande et al. 2009). An increased incidence of hypotension or bradycardia in morbidly obese compared with non-obese patients has also been described during epidural analgesia for labour (Vricella et al. 2011). Combined spinal–epidural anaesthesia in the obese is associated with an increased risk of high block and adverse cardiovascular effects (Brodsky and Mariano 2011).

However, there are insufficiently consistent and robust data upon which to base epidural or spinal analgesia dosing schedules in morbidly obese patients. For labour analgesia, spinal bupivacaine doses vary widely between studies from 5 ml of 0.125% [+ fentanyl 7.5 μg + adrenaline 5 μg ml^{-1} (Vricella et al. 2011)], to 12 ml of 0.25% (Milligan et al. 1993) or 20 ml of 0.067% (Panni and Columb 2006). For Caesarean section, an ED_{50} dose of spinal bupivacaine when combined with fentanyl 10 μg and morphine 200 μg, has been estimated to be approximately 10 mg in obese patients (Carvalho et al. 2011). In the same study, the ED_{95} in obese patients was estimated to be approximately 15 mg compared with 11 mg in lean patients but these values were extrapolated using probit analysis and may be unreliable (Carvalho et al. 2011). In knee arthroplasty, the ED_{50} for successful spinal anaesthesia did not differ in obese patients, but the incidence of tourniquet pain was lower (Kim et al. 2012).

For pain management after bariatric surgery, epidural analgesia by a continuous infusion of 6–15 ml h^{-1} of bupivacaine 0.1% + fentanyl 3 μg ml^{-1} was effective and decreased the time to passing of flatus but, surprisingly, it was also associated with a greater risk of wound infection compared with patient-controlled intravenous morphine (Charghi et al. 2003). An alternative to neuraxial analgesia after laparoscopic bariatric surgery is administration of intraperitoneal bupivacaine, which has been demonstrated to decrease postoperative pain either by continuous infusion (Sherwinter et al. 2008) or aerosolization (10 ml at 0.5%) (Alkhamesi et al. 2008), but the influence on analgesic consumption is inconsistent (Cottam et al. 2007; Symons et al. 2007) while the effect on postoperative nausea and vomiting is negligible.

Peripheral nerve block

Because of anatomical and technical challenges, nerve blocks had a two to four times higher risk of failure in obese *vs* non obese patients (Nielsen et al. 2005), although this study was done at a time when ultrasound-guided techniques were not used widely and the technology was inferior to that available today. Axillary brachial plexus bock in obese patients was associated with increased requirement for supplemental nerve blocks, a higher incidence of vascular puncture (27% *vs* 9%), and fewer satisfied patients (Hanouz et al. 2010). A higher success rate of nerve block (supraclavicular brachial plexus) was found in diabetic patients and the authors assumed that the nerves of diabetic patients may be more sensitive to local anaesthetics, or the finding was related to subclinical diabetic neuropathy (Gebhard et al. 2009).

However, the potential benefits on perioperative morbidity by avoiding general anaesthesia mean that it can be worthwhile attempting regional anaesthesia even when there is an increased failure rate in the obese. For example, multilevel nerve stimulator-guided paravertebral block has been proposed for breast cancer surgery: surgical anaesthesia was achieved in 76.9% of morbidly obese patients and the failure rate (no analgesia) was 11.5% (Naja et al. 2011). Some trials, however, suggest that regional anaesthetic techniques can be less effective in obese patients; for example, transversus abdominis plane block failed to reduce post-abdominoplasty opioid requirements to the same extent in post-bariatric surgery patients compared with other patients (Gravante et al. 2011).

Conclusion

Maximizing the safety of anaesthesia for morbidly obese patients requires a good knowledge of the anatomical, physiological, and pathological effects of obesity and great care and attention to detail in planning and executing anaesthetic management from the pre-operative assessment to the postoperative period. Even in elective surgery, many cases can be technical challenges and only a step-by-step approach to the avoidance of potential adverse events will result in the optimal outcome.

Declaration of interest

None declared.

References

Abdi W, Dhonneur G, Amathieu R, *et al.* LMA supreme versus facemask ventilation performed by novices: a comparative study in morbidly obese patients showing difficult ventilation predictors. *Obes Surg* 2009; **19**: 1624–30

Abernethy DR, Divoll M, Greenblatt DJ, Ameer B. Obesity, sex, and acetaminophen disposition. *Clin Pharmacol Ther* 1982; **31**: 783–90

Abernethy DR, Greenblatt DJ, Divoll M, Shader RI. Enhanced glucuronide conjugation of drugs in obesity: studies of lorazepam, oxazepam, and acetaminophen. *J Lab Clin Med* 1983; **101**: 873–80

Adler M, Schaffner F. Fatty liver hepatitis and cirrhosis in obese patients. *Am J Med* 1979; **67**: 811–6

Alkhamesi NA, Kane JM, Guske PJ, Wallace JW, Rantis PC. Intraperitoneal aerosolization of bupivacaine is a safe and effective method in controlling postoperative pain in laparoscopic Roux-en-Y gastric bypass. *J Pain Res* 2008; **1**: 9–13

Alpert MA. Obesity cardiomyopathy: pathophysiology and evolution of the clinical syndrome. *Am J Med Sci* 2001; **321**: 225–36

Altermatt FR, Munoz HR, Delfino AE, Cortinez LI. Pre-oxygenation in the obese patient: effects of position on tolerance to apnoea. *Br J Anaesth* 2005; **95**: 706–9

Aucouturier J, Meyer M, Thivel D, Taillardat M, Duche P. Effect of android to gynoid fat ratio on insulin resistance in obese youth. *Arch Pediatr Adolesc Med* 2009; **163**: 826–31

Avriel A, Warner E, Avinoach E, *et al.* Major respiratory adverse events after laparascopic gastric banding surgery for morbid obesity. *Respir Med* 2012; **106**: 1192–8

Bahar M, Chanimov M, Cohen ML, *et al.* The lateral recumbent head-down position decreases the incidence of epidural venous puncture during catheter insertion in obese parturients. *Can J Anaesth* 2004; **51**: 577–80

Balki M, Lee Y, Halpern S, Carvalho JC. Ultrasound imaging of the lumbar spine in the transverse plane: the correlation between estimated and actual depth to the epidural space in obese parturients. *Anesth Analg* 2009; **108**: 1876–81

Bauduceau B, Vachey E, Mayaudon H, *et al.* Should we have more definitions of metabolic syndrome or simply take waist measurement?. *Diabetes Metab* 2007; **33**: 333–9

Bearden DT, Rodvold KA. Dosage adjustments for antibacterials in obese patients: applying clinical pharmacokinetics. *Clin Pharmacokinet* 2000; **38**: 415–26

Boza C, Gamboa C, Salinas J, Achurra P, Vega A, Perez G. Laparoscopic Roux-en-Y gastric bypass versus laparoscopic sleeve gastrectomy: a case-control study and 3 years of follow-up. *Surg Obes Relat Dis* 2012; **8**: 243–9

Brodsky JB. Positioning the morbidly obese patient for anesthesia. *Obes Surg* 2002; **12**: 751–8

Brodsky JB, Lemmens HJ. Regional anesthesia and obesity. *Obes Surg* 2007; **17**: 1146–9

Brodsky JB, Lemmens HJ, Brock-Utne JG, Vierra M, Saidman LJ. Morbid obesity and tracheal intubation. *Anesth Analg* 2002; **94**: 732–6

Brodsky JB, Lemmens HJ, Collins JS, Morton JM, Curet MJ, Brock-Utne JG. Nitrous oxide and laparoscopic bariatric surgery. *Obes Surg* 2005; **15**: 494–6

Brodsky JB, Mariano ER. Regional anaesthesia in the obese patient: lost landmarks and evolving ultrasound guidance. *Best Pract Res Clin Anaesthesiol* 2011; **25**: 61–72

Brown KA, Bertolizio G, Leone M, Dain SL. Home noninvasive ventilation: what does the anesthesiologist need to know? *Anesthesiology* 2012; **117**: 657–68

Cadi P, Guenoun T, Journois D, Chevallier JM, Diehl JL, Safran D. Pressure-controlled ventilation improves oxygenation during laparoscopic obesity surgery compared with volume-controlled ventilation. *Br J Anaesth* 2008; **100**: 709–16

Carmody BJ, Sugerman HJ, Kellum JM, *et al.* Pulmonary embolism complicating bariatric surgery: detailed analysis of a single institution's 24-year experience. *J Am Coll Surg* 2006; **203**: 831–7

Carvalho B, Collins J, Drover DR, Atkinson RL, Riley ET. ED(50) and ED(95) of intrathecal bupivacaine in morbidly obese patients undergoing cesarean delivery. *Anesthesiology* 2011; **114**: 529–35

Casati A, Comotti L, Tommasino C, *et al.* Effects of pneumoperitoneum and reverse Trendelenburg position on cardiopulmonary function in morbidly obese patients receiving laparoscopic gastric banding. *Eur J Anaesthesiol* 2000; **17**: 300–5

Catheline JM, Fysekidis M, Dbouk R, *et al.* Weight loss after sleeve gastrectomy in super superobesity. *J Obes* 2012; **2012**: 959260

Chalhoub V, Yazigi A, Sleilaty G, *et al.* Effect of vital capacity manoeuvres on arterial oxygenation in morbidly obese patients undergoing open bariatric surgery. *Eur J Anaesthesiol* 2007; **24**: 283–8

Chappell D, Jacob M, Hofmann-Kiefer K, Conzen P, Rehm M. A rational approach to perioperative fluid management. *Anesthesiology* 2008; **109**: 723–40

Charghi R, Backman S, Christou N, Rouah F, Schricker T. Patient controlled i.v. analgesia is an acceptable pain management strategy in morbidly obese patients undergoing gastric bypass surgery. A retrospective comparison with epidural analgesia. *Can J Anaesth* 2003; **50**: 672–8

Cheymol G. Clinical pharmacokinetics of drugs in obesity. An update. *Clin Pharmacokinet* 1993; **25**: 103–14

Cheymol G. Effects of obesity on pharmacokinetics implications for drug therapy. *Clin Pharmacokinet* 2000; **39**: 215–31

Chin KJ, Perlas A. Ultrasonography of the lumbar spine for neuraxial and lumbar plexus blocks. *Curr Opin Anaesthesiol* 2011; **24**: 567–72

Cockcroft DW, Gault MH. Prediction of creatinine clearance from serum creatinine. *Nephron* 1976; **16**: 31–41

Collins JS, Lemmens HJ, Brodsky JB, Brock-Utne JG, Levitan RM. Laryngoscopy and morbid obesity: a comparison of the 'sniff' and 'ramped' positions. *Obes Surg* 2004; **14**: 1171–5

Combes X, Sauvat S, Leroux B, *et al.* Intubating laryngeal mask airway in morbidly obese and lean patients: a comparative study. *Anesthesiology* 2005; **102**: 1106–9

Corfe J. Length of spinal needles. *Anaesthesia* 2008; **63**: 444–5

Cottam DR, Fisher B, Atkinson J, *et al.* A randomized trial of bupivicaine pain pumps to eliminate the need for patient controlled analgesia pumps in primary laparoscopic Roux-en-Y gastric bypass. *Obes Surg* 2007; **17**: 595–600

Coussa M, Proietti S, Schnyder P, *et al.* Prevention of atelectasis formation during the induction of general anesthesia in morbidly obese patients. *Anesth Analg* 2004; **98**: 1491–5

De Baerdemaeker LE, Struys MM, Jacobs S, *et al.* Optimization of desflurane administration in morbidly obese patients: a comparison with sevoflurane using an 'inhalation bolus' technique. *Br J Anaesth* 2003; **91**: 638–50

De Baerdemaeker LE, Van der Herten C, Gillardin JM, *et al.* Comparison of volume-controlled and pressure-controlled ventilation during laparoscopic gastric banding in morbidly obese patients. *Obes Surg* 2008; **18**: 680–5

de Souza SA, Faintuch J, Cecconello I. Spirometric function improves in the morbidly obese after 1-year post-surgery. *Obes Surg* 2010; **20**: 1273–7

Debruyne D, Hurault de Ligny B, Ryckelynck JP, Albessard F, Moulin M. Clinical pharmacokinetics of ketoprofen after single intravenous administration as a bolus or infusion. *Clin Pharmacokinet* 1987; **12**: 214–21

Delay JM, Sebbane M, Jung B, *et al.* The effectiveness of noninvasive positive pressure ventilation to enhance preoxygenation in morbidly obese patients: a randomized controlled study. *Anesth Analg* 2008; **107**: 1707–13

DeMaria EJ, Murr M, Byrne TK, *et al.* Validation of the obesity surgery mortality risk score in a multicenter study proves it stratifies mortality risk in patients undergoing gastric bypass for morbid obesity. *Ann Surg* 2007; **246**: 578–82

Desforges JC, McDonnell NJ. Sugammadex in the management of a failed intubation in a morbidly obese patient. *Anaesth Intensive Care* 2007; **39**: 763–4

Dhonneur G, Abdi W, Ndoko SK, *et al.* Video-assisted versus conventional tracheal intubation in morbidly obese patients. *Obes Surg* 2009; **19**: 1096–101

Eichenberger A, Proietti S, Wicky S, *et al.* Morbid obesity and postoperative pulmonary atelectasis: an underestimated problem. *Anesth Analg* 2002; **95**: 1788–92

Elli EF, Masrur MA, El Zaeedi M, *et al.* Four-year experience with outpatient laparoscopic adjustable gastric banding. *Surg Obes Relat Dis* 2013; **9**: 693–5

Erlandsson K, Odenstedt H, Lundin S, Stenqvist O. Positive end-expiratory pressure optimization using electric impedance tomography in morbidly obese patients during laparoscopic gastric bypass surgery. *Acta Anaesthesiol Scand* 2006; **50**: 833–9

Ettinger JE, de Souza CA, Santos-Filho PV, *et al.* Rhabdomyolysis: diagnosis and treatment in bariatric surgery. *Obes Surg* 2007; **17**: 525–32

Ettinger JE, Marcilio de Souza CA, Azaro E, *et al.* Clinical features of rhabdomyolysis after open and laparoscopic Roux-en-Y gastric bypass. *Obes Surg* 2008; **18**: 635–43

Forrest JA, Clements JA, Prescott LF. Clinical pharmacokinetics of paracetamol. *Clin Pharmacokinet* 1982; **7**: 93–107

Frederiksen SG, Hedenbro JL, Norgren L. Enoxaparin effect depends on body-weight and current doses may be inadequate in obese patients. *Br J Surg* 2003; **90**: 547–8

Freeman A, Horner T, Pendleton RC, Rondina MT. Prospective comparison of three enoxaparin dosing regimens to achieve target anti-factor Xa levels in hospitalized, medically ill patients with extreme obesity. *Am J Hematol* 2012; **87**: 740–3

Futier E, Constantin JM, Pelosi P, *et al.* Noninvasive ventilation and alveolar recruitment maneuver improve respiratory function during and after intubation of morbidly obese patients: a randomized controlled study. *Anesthesiology* 2011; **114**: 1354–63

Gander S, Frascarolo P, Suter M, Spahn DR, Magnusson L. Positive end-expiratory pressure during induction of general anesthesia increases duration of nonhypoxic apnea in morbidly obese patients. *Anesth Analg* 2005; **100**: 580–4

Gao XR, Adhikari CM, Peng LY, *et al.* Efficacy of different doses of aspirin in decreasing blood levels of inflammatory markers in patients with cardiovascular metabolic syndrome. *J Pharm Pharmacol* 2009; **61**: 1505–10

Gaszynski TM, Szewczyk T. Rocuronium for rapid sequence induction in morbidly obese patients: a prospective study for evaluation of intubation conditions after administration 1.2 mg kg^{-1} ideal body weight of rocuronium. *Eur J Anaesthesiol* 2011; **28**: 609–10

Gebhard RE, Nielsen KC, Pietrobon R, Missair A, Williams BA. Diabetes mellitus, independent of body mass index, is associated with a 'higher success' rate for supraclavicular brachial plexus blocks. *Reg Anesth Pain Med* 2009; **34**: 404–7

Geerts WH, Bergqvist D, Pineo GF, *et al.* Prevention of venous thromboembolism: American College of Chest Physicians Evidence-Based Clinical Practice Guidelines (8th Edition). *Chest* 2008; **133**(Suppl): 381S–453S

Gepts E, Shafer SL, Camu F, *et al.* Linearity of pharmacokinetics and model estimation of sufentanil. *Anesthesiology* 1995; **83**: 1194–204

Goldhaber SZ. Pulmonary embolism. *Lancet* 2004; **363**: 1295–305

Gravante G, Castri F, Araco F, Araco A. A comparative study of the transversus abdominis plane (TAP) block efficacy on post-bariatric vs aesthetic abdominoplasty with flank liposuction. *Obes Surg* 2011; **21**: 278–82

Gregg SC, Murthi SB, Sisley AC, Stein DM, Scalea TM. Ultrasound-guided peripheral intravenous access in the intensive care unit. *J Crit Care* 2000; **25**: 514–9

Gross JB, Bachenberg KL, Benumof JL, *et al.* Practice guidelines for the perioperative management of patients with obstructive sleep apnea: a report by the American Society of Anesthesiologists Task Force on Perioperative Management of patients with obstructive sleep apnea. *Anesthesiology* 2006; **104**: 1081–93

Hamad GG, Choban PS. Enoxaparin for thromboprophylaxis in morbidly obese patients undergoing bariatric surgery: findings of the prophylaxis against VTE outcomes in bariatric surgery patients receiving enoxaparin (PROBE) study. *Obes Surg* 2005; **15**: 1368–74

Hamza J, Smida M, Benhamou D, Cohen SE Parturient's posture during epidural puncture affects the distance from skin to epidural space. *J Clin Anesth* 1995; **7**: 1–4

Hanley MJ, Abernethy DR, Greenblatt DJ Effect of obesity on the pharmacokinetics of drugs in humans. *Clin Pharmacokinet* 2010; **49**: 71–87

Hanouz JL, Grandin W, Lesage A, Oriot G, Bonnieux D, Gerard JL Multiple injection axillary brachial plexus block: influence of obesity on failure rate and incidence of acute complications. *Anesth Analg* 2010; **111**: 230–3

Hans GA, Pregaldien AA, Kaba A, *et al.* Pressure-controlled ventilation does not improve gas exchange in morbidly obese patients undergoing abdominal surgery. *Obes Surg* 2008; **18**: 71–6

Haslam DW, James WP Obesity. *Lancet* 2005; **366**: 1197–209

Hogan QH, Prost R, Kulier A, Taylor ML, Liu S, Mark L. Magnetic resonance imaging of cerebrospinal fluid volume and the influence of body habitus and abdominal pressure. *Anesthesiology* 1996; **84**: 1341–9

Inabnet WB, III, Winegar DA, Sherif B, Sarr MG Early outcomes of bariatric surgery in patients with metabolic syndrome: an analysis of the bariatric outcomes longitudinal database. *J Am Coll Surg* 2012; **214**: 550–6

Ingrande J, Brodsky JB, Lemmens HJ Regional anesthesia and obesity. *Curr Opin Anaesthesiol* 2009; **22**: 683–6

Ingrande J, Brodsky JB, Lemmens HJ Lean body weight scalar for the anesthetic induction dose of propofol in morbidly obese subjects. *Anesth Analg* 2011; **113**: 57–62

Isono S. Obstructive sleep apnea of obese adults: pathophysiology and perioperative airway management. *Anesthesiology* 2009; **110**: 908–21

Jain AK, Dutta A. Stroke volume variation as a guide to fluid administration in morbidly obese patients undergoing laparoscopic bariatric surgery. *Obes Surg* 2010; **20**: 709–15

Janmahasatian S, Duffull SB, Ash S, Ward LC, Byrne NM, Green B. Quantification of lean bodyweight. *Clin Pharmacokinet* 2005; **44**: 1051–65

Jimenez A, Casamitjana R, Flores L, *et al.* Long-term effects of sleeve gastrectomy and Roux-en-Y gastric bypass surgery on type 2 diabetes mellitus in morbidly obese subjects. *Ann Surg* 2012; **256**: 1023–9

Joing S, Strote S, Caroon L, *et al.* Videos in clinical medicine. Ultrasound-guided peripheral i.v. placement. *N Engl J Med* 2012; **366**: e38

Jones RL, Nzekwu MM. The effects of body mass index on lung volumes. *Chest* 2006; **130**: 827–33

Juvin P, Fevre G, Merouche M, Vallot T, Desmonts JM. Gastric residue is not more copious in obese patients. *Anesth Analg* 2001; **93**: 1621–2

Juvin P, Lavaut E, Dupont H, *et al.* Difficult tracheal intubation is more common in obese than in lean patients. *Anesth Analg* 2003; **97**: 595–600

Kakkos SK, Caprini JA, Geroulakos G, *et al.* Combined intermittent pneumatic leg compression and pharmacological prophylaxis for prevention of venous thromboembolism in high-risk patients. *Cochrane Database Syst Rev* 2008; **4**: CD005258

Kim WH, Lee JH, Ko JS, *et al.* The effect of body mass index on spinal anaesthesia for total knee replacement arthroplasty: a dose-response study. *Anaesth Intensive Care* 2012; **40**: 410–6

Kjellberg J, Reizenstein P. Body composition in obesity. *Acta Med Scand* 1970; **188**: 161–9

Kocian R, Spahn DR. Bronchial aspiration in patients after weight loss due to gastric banding. *Anesth Analg* 2005; **100**: 1856–7

La Colla L, Albertin A, La Colla G, *et al.* No adjustment vs. adjustment formula as input weight for propofol target-controlled infusion in morbidly obese patients. *Eur J Anaesthesiol* 2009; **26**: 362–9

Langeron O, Masso E, Huraux C, *et al.* Prediction of difficult mask ventilation. *Anesthesiology* 2000; **92**: 1229–36

Lehtonen P, Sten T, Aitio O, *et al.* Glucuronidation of racemic O-desmethyltramadol, the active metabolite of tramadol. *Eur J Pharm Sci* 2010; **41**: 523–30

Lemmens HJ, Brodsky JB. The dose of succinylcholine in morbid obesity. *Anesth Analg* 2006; **102**: 438–42

Levey AS, Bosch JP, Lewis JB, Greene T, Rogers N, Roth D. A more accurate method to estimate glomerular filtration rate from serum creatinine: a new prediction equation. Modification of Diet in Renal Disease Study Group. *Ann Intern Med* 1999; 130: 461–70

Leykin Y, Pellis T, Lucca M, Lomangino G, Marzano B, Gullo A. The effects of cisatracurium on morbidly obese women. *Anesth Analg* 2004a; **99**: 1090–4

Leykin Y, Pellis T, Lucca M, Lomangino G, Marzano B, Gullo A. The pharmacodynamic effects of rocuronium when dosed according to real body weight or ideal body weight in morbidly obese patients. *Anesth Analg* 2004b; **99**: 1086–9

Lin CK, Lin CC. Work of breathing and respiratory drive in obesity. *Respirology* 2012; **17**: 402–11

Littleton SW. Impact of obesity on respiratory function. *Respirology* 2012; **17**: 43–9

Livingston EH. The incidence of bariatric surgery has plateaued in the U.S. *Am J Surg* 2010; **200**: 378–85

Llaurado S, Sabate A, Ferreres E, Camprubi I, Cabrera A. Sugammadex ideal body weight dose adjusted by level of neuromuscular blockade in laparoscopic bariatric surgery. *Anesthesiology* 2012; **117**: 93–8

Lotsch J, Skarke C, Liefhold J, Geisslinger G. Genetic predictors of the clinical response to opioid analgesics: clinical utility and future perspectives. *Clin Pharmacokinet* 2004; **43**: 983–1013

Luce JM. Respiratory complications of obesity. *Chest* 1980; **78**: 626–31

Malone M. Recommended nutritional supplements for bariatric surgery patients. *Ann Pharmacother* 2008; **42**: 1851–8

Marroquin BM, Fecho K, Salo-Coombs V, Spielman FJ. Can parturients identify the midline during neuraxial block placement?. *J Clin Anesth* 2011; **23**: 3–6

Mashour GA, Kheterpal S, Vanaharam V, *et al.* The extended Mallampati score and a diagnosis of diabetes mellitus are predictors of difficult laryngoscopy in the morbidly obese. *Anesth Analg* 2008; **107**: 1919–23

Matot I, Paskaleva R, Eid L, *et al.* Effect of the volume of fluids administered on intraoperative oliguria in laparoscopic bariatric surgery: a randomized controlled trial. *Arch Surg* 2012; **147**: 228–34

McCullough AJ. Epidemiology of the metabolic syndrome in the USA. *J Dig Dis* 2011; **12**: 333–40

McKendall MJ, Haier RJ. Pain sensitivity and obesity. *Psychiatry Res* 1983; **8**: 119–25

Menezes Ettinger JE, dos Santos Filho PV, Azaro E, *et al.* Prevention of rhabdomyolysis in bariatric surgery. *Obes Surg* 2005; **15**: 874–9

Milligan KR, Cramp P, Schatz L, Johnston D, Carp H. The effect of patient position and obesity on the spread of epidural analgesia. *Int J Obstet Anesth* 1993; **2**: 134–6

Minto CF, Schnider TW, Shafer SL. Pharmacokinetics and pharmacodynamics of remifentanil. II. Model application. *Anesthesiology* 1997; **86**: 24–33

Miscio G, Guastamacchia G, Brunani A, Priano L, Baudo S, Mauro A. Obesity and peripheral neuropathy risk: a dangerous liaison. *J Peripher Nerv Syst* 2005; **10**: 354–8

Naeye RL, Roode P. The sizes and numbers of cells in visceral organs in human obesity. *Am J Clin Pathol* 1970; **54**: 251–3

Naja ZM, Naccache N, Ziade F, El Rajab M, Itani T, Baraka A. Multilevel nerve stimulator-guided paravertebral block as a sole anesthetic technique for breast cancer surgery in morbidly obese patients. *J Anesth* 2011; **25**: 760–4

Neligan PJ, Malhotra G, Fraser M, *et al.* Continuous positive airway pressure via the Boussignac system immediately after extubation improves lung function in morbidly obese patients with obstructive sleep apnea undergoing laparoscopic bariatric surgery. *Anesthesiology* 2009a; **110**: 878–84

Neligan PJ, Porter S, Max B, Malhotra G, Greenblatt EP, Ochroch EA. Obstructive sleep apnea is not a risk factor for difficult intubation in morbidly obese patients. *Anesth Analg* 2009b; **109**: 1182–6

Nielsen KC, Guller U, Steele SM, Klein SM, Greengrass RA, Pietrobon R. Influence of obesity on surgical regional anesthesia in the ambulatory setting: an analysis of 9,038 blocks. *Anesthesiology* 2005; **102**: 181–7

Nishiyama T, Kohno Y, Koishi K. Anesthesia for bariatric surgery. *Obes Surg* 2012; **22**: 213–19

Ogunnaike BO, Jones SB, Jones DB, Provost D, Whitten CW. Anesthetic considerations for bariatric surgery. *Anesth Analg* 2002; **95**: 1793–805

Pai MP, Paloucek FP. The origin of the 'ideal' body weight equations. *Ann Pharmacother* 2000; **34**: 1066–9

Panni MK, Columb MO. Obese parturients have lower epidural local anaesthetic requirements for analgesia in labour. *Br J Anaesth* 2006; **96**: 106–10

Pelosi P, Croci M, Calappi E, *et al.* Prone positioning improves pulmonary function in obese patients during general anesthesia. *Anesth Analg* 1996; **83**: 578–83

Pelosi P, Croci M, Ravagnan I, *et al.* The effects of body mass on lung volumes, respiratory mechanics, and gas exchange during general anesthesia. *Anesth Analg* 1998; **87**: 654–60

Pelosi P, Ravagnan I, Giurati G, *et al.* Positive end-expiratory pressure improves respiratory function in obese but not in normal subjects during anesthesia and paralysis. *Anesthesiology* 1999; **91**: 1221–31

Poirier P, Alpert MA, Fleisher LA, *et al.* Cardiovascular evaluation and management of severely obese patients undergoing surgery: a science advisory from the American Heart Association. *Circulation* 2009; **120**: 86–95

Pösö T, Winsö O, Aroch R, *et al.* Perioperative fluid guidance with transthoracic echocardiography and pulse-contour device in morbidly obese patients. *Obes Surg* 2014; **24**: 2117

Proczko-Markuszewska M, Stefaniak T, Kaska L, Kobiela J, Sledzinski Z. Impact of Roux-en-Y gastric bypass on regulation of diabetes type 2 in morbidly obese patients. *Surg Endosc* 2012; **26**: 2202–7

Raftopoulos I, Martindale C, Cronin A, Steinberg J. The effect of extended post-discharge chemical thromboprophylaxis on venous thromboembolism rates after bariatric surgery: a prospective comparison trial. *Surg Endosc* 2008; **22**: 2384–91

Ramachandran SK, Kheterpal S, Consens F, *et al.* Derivation and validation of a simple perioperative sleep apnea prediction score. *Anesth Analg* 2010; **110**: 1007–15

Ramzan I, Wong BK, Corcoran GB. Pain sensitivity in dietary-induced obese rats. *Physiol Behav* 1993; **54**: 433–5

Reeves RR, Burke RS. Tramadol: basic pharmacology and emerging concepts. *Drugs Today (Barc)* 2008; 44: 827–36

Reinius H, Jonsson L, Gustafsson S, *et al.* Prevention of atelectasis in morbidly obese patients during general anesthesia and paralysis: a computerized tomography study. *Anesthesiology* 2009; **111**: 979–87

Reisin E, Frohlich ED. Obesity. Cardiovascular and respiratory pathophysiological alterations. *Arch Intern Med* 1981; **141**: 431–4

Romy S, Donadini A, Giusti V, Suter M. Roux-en-Y gastric bypass vs gastric banding for morbid obesity: a case-matched study of 442 patients. *Arch Surg* 2012; **147**: 460–6

Rowan BO, Kuhl DA, Lee MD, Tichansky DS, Madan AK. Anti-Xa levels in bariatric surgery patients receiving prophylactic enoxaparin. *Obes Surg* 2008; **18**: 162–6

Sakran N, Goitein D, Raziel A, *et al.* Gastric leaks after sleeve gastrectomy: a multicenter experience with 2,834 patients. *Surg Endosc* 2013; **27**: 240–5

Sanderink GJ, Le Liboux A, Jariwala N, *et al.* The pharmacokinetics and pharmacodynamics of enoxaparin in obese volunteers. *Clin Pharmacol Ther* 2002; **72**: 308–18

Scholten DJ, Hoedema RM, Scholten SE. A comparison of two different prophylactic dose regimens of low molecular weight heparin in bariatric surgery. *Obes Surg* 2002; **12**: 19–24

Schwartz AE, Matteo RS, Ornstein E, Young WL, Myers KJ. Pharmacokinetics of sufentanil in obese patients. *Anesth Analg* 1991; **73**: 790–3

Servin F, Farinotti R, Haberer JP, Desmonts JM. Propofol infusion for maintenance of anesthesia in morbidly obese patients receiving nitrous oxide. A clinical and pharmacokinetic study. *Anesthesiology* 1993; **78**: 657–65

Sherwinter DA, Ghaznavi AM, Spinner D, *et al.* Continuous infusion of intraperitoneal bupivacaine after laparoscopic surgery: a randomized controlled trial. *Obes Surg* 2008; **18**: 1581–6

Shibutani K, Inchiosa MA, Jr, Sawada K, Bairamian M. Accuracy of pharmacokinetic models for predicting plasma fentanyl concentrations in lean and obese surgical patients: derivation of dosing weight ('pharmacokinetic mass'). *Anesthesiology* 2004; **101**: 603–13

Simone EP, Madan AK, Tichansky DS, Kuhl DA, Lee MD. Comparison of two low-molecular-weight heparin dosing regimens for patients undergoing laparoscopic bariatric surgery. *Surg Endosc* 2008; **22**: 2392–5

Slepchenko G, Simon N, Goubaux B, *et al.* Performance of target-controlled sufentanil infusion in obese patients. *Anesthesiology* 2003; **98**: 65–73

Soens MA, Birnbach DJ, Ranasinghe JS, van Zundert A. Obstetric anesthesia for the obese and morbidly obese patient: an ounce of prevention is worth more than a pound of treatment. *Acta Anaesthesiol Scand* 2008; **52**: 6–19

Sprung J, Whalley DG, Falcone T, Warner DO, Hubmayr RD, Hammel J. The impact of morbid obesity, pneumoperitoneum, and posture on respiratory system mechanics and oxygenation during laparoscopy. *Anesth Analg* 2002; **94**: 1345–50

Sprung J, Whalley DG, Falcone T, Wilks W, Navratil JE, Bourke DL. The effects of tidal volume and respiratory rate on oxygenation and respiratory mechanics during laparoscopy in morbidly obese patients. *Anesth Analg* 2003; **97**: 268–74

Steele KE, Schweitzer MA, Prokopowicz G, *et al.* The long-term risk of venous thromboembolism following bariatric surgery. *Obes Surg* 2011; **21**: 1371–6

Stockholm KH, Biochner-Mortensen J, Hoilund-Carlsen PF. Increased glomerular filtration rate and adrenocortical function in obese women. *Int J Obes* 1980; **4**: 57–63

Symons JL, Kemmeter PR, Davis AT, *et al.* A double-blinded, prospective randomized controlled trial of intraperitoneal bupivacaine in laparoscopic Roux-en-Y gastric bypass. *J Am Coll Surg* 2007; **204**: 392–8

Tung A. Anaesthetic considerations with the metabolic syndrome. *Br J Anaesth* 2010; **105**(Suppl 1): i24–i33

Valenza F, Vagginelli F, Tiby A, *et al.* Effects of the beach chair position, positive end-expiratory pressure, and pneumoperitoneum on respiratory function in morbidly obese patients during anesthesia and paralysis. *Anesthesiology* 2007; **107**: 725–32

Vallejo MC. Anesthetic management of the morbidly obese parturient. *Curr Opin Anaesthesiol* 2007; **20**: 175–80

Van Kralingen S, Taks M, Diepstraten J, *et al.* Pharmacokinetics and protein binding of cefazolin in morbidly obese patients. *Eur J Clin Pharmacol* 2011a; **67**: 985–92

Van Kralingen S, van de Garde EM, van Dongen EP, *et al.* Maintenance of anesthesia in morbidly obese patients using propofol with continuous BIS-monitoring: a comparison of propofol-remifentanil and propofol-epidural anesthesia. *Acta Anaesthesiol Belg* 2011b; **62**: 73–82

Vricella LK, Louis JM, Mercer BM, Bolden N. Impact of morbid obesity on epidural anesthesia complications in labor. *Am J Obstet Gynecol* 2011; **205**: 370–6

Wada DR, Bjorkman S, Ebling WF, *et al.* Computer simulation of the effects of alterations in blood flows and body composition on thiopental pharmacokinetics in humans. *Anesthesiology* 1997; **87**: 884–99

Wellen KE, Hotamisligil GS. Obesity-induced inflammatory changes in adipose tissue. *J Clin Invest* 2003; **112**: 1785–8

Whalen FX, Gajic O, Thompson GB, *et al.* The effects of the alveolar recruitment maneuver and positive end-expiratory pressure on arterial oxygenation during laparoscopic bariatric surgery. *Anesth Analg* 2006; **102**: 298–305

Wilhelm SM, Kale-Pradhan PB. Estimating creatinine clearance: a meta-analysis. *Pharmacotherapy* 2011; **31**: 658–64

Wool DB, Lemmens HJ, Brodsky JB, *et al.* Intraoperative fluid replacement and postoperative creatine phosphokinase levels in laparoscopic bariatric patients. *Obes Surg* 2010; **20**: 698–701

Yip K, Heinberg L, Giegerich V, Schauer PR, Kashyap SR. Equivalent weight loss with marked metabolic benefit observed in a matched cohort with and without type 2 diabetes 12 months following gastric bypass surgery. *Obes Surg* 2012; **22**: 1723–9

Zahorska-Markiewicz B, Kucio C, Pyszkowska J. Obesity and pain. *Hum Nutr Clin Nutr*1983; **37**: 307–10

Zini R, Riant P, Barre J, Tillement JP. Disease-induced variations in plasma protein levels. Implications for drug dosage regimens (Part II). *Clin Pharmacokinet* 1990; **19**: 218–29

Zoremba M, Dette F, Hunecke T, Eberhart L, Braunecker S, Wulf H. A comparison of desflurane versus propofol: the effects on early postoperative lung function in overweight patients. *Anesth Analg* 2011; **113**: 63–9

PART 13

Critical care and the anaesthetist

Neil Soni and Jonathan G. Hardman

CHAPTER 88

Pre-surgical optimization of the high-risk patient

Andrew J. Clarkin and Nigel R. Webster

Introduction

There is a small group of patients undergoing surgery who comprise the majority of perioperative deaths. In order to reduce the morbidity and mortality associated with anaesthesia and surgery it is necessary to identify this high-risk group and target it with appropriate interventions. A number of studies have shown that if this group is identified and managed aggressively in the operative period using goal-directed therapy then morbidity, mortality, and length of stay can all be reduced. The optimal form of this management is called pre-optimization and involves pre-emptive admission to the intensive care unit (ICU) before surgery, although there are also beneficial effects from intra- and postoperative optimization. It requires an understanding of oxygen delivery, the use of cardiac output monitoring to guide fluid and inotrope administration, and the attainment of supranormal physiological goals.

History of pre-optimization

There is a large body of evidence demonstrating the benefits of increasing the oxygen delivery beyond normal during the perioperative period. The concept emerged in the 1980s based on observational work conducted by Bland and Shoemaker. They showed that increased cardiac output causing supranormal levels of oxygen delivery and consumption was associated with greater survival than normal oxygen delivery (Bland et al. 1985). The proposed explanation of these findings was that the elevated levels are those required to meet the increased metabolic requirements of the patient, and in a subsequent study Shoemaker et al. (1992) showed a link between increasing oxygen debt and mortality. Although these values were identified in patients who increased their cardiac output spontaneously, they postulated that those who failed to do so would benefit from pharmacological augmentation to prevent the oxygen debt and mortality.

Values seen in survivors:

- Cardiac index (CI): >4.5 litres min^{-1} m^{-2}
- Oxygen delivery index ($\dot{D}o_2I$): >600 ml min^{-1} m^{-2}
- Oxygen consumption index ($\dot{V}o_2I$): >170 ml min^{-1} m^{-2}.

In another study, Shoemaker et al. (1988) demonstrated a significant reduction in morbidity and mortality of high-risk patients when physiological goals were set and targeted in a systematic manner. They used a pulmonary artery (PA) catheter to monitor the patients and instituted goal-directed therapy preoperatively to meet elevated values of CI, $\dot{D}o_2I$, and $\dot{V}o_2I$. In order to meet these goals they used intravenous fluids and blood, inotropes (principally dobutamine), vasodilators (including glyceryl trinitrate and sodium nitroprusside), and vasoconstrictors [such as noradrenaline (norepinephrine) and dopamine]. The patients who were managed with these supranormal targets had a greatly improved mortality (4% *vs* 33%) compared with those in whom the targets were normal values for physiological parameters such as blood pressure, heart rate, $\dot{D}o_2$, and PA occlusion pressure. As a result of this landmark study, the concept of managing high-risk surgical patients by instituting goal-directed therapy to meet supranormal physiological values emerged. Further studies were then conducted which confirmed the benefits shown by Shoemaker et al.

In a randomized controlled trial, Boyd et al. (1993) admitted high-risk surgical patients to intensive care preoperatively and instituted haemodynamic monitoring including PA catheterization. They targeted normal values of arterial pressure, PA occlusion pressure, oxygen saturation, haemoglobin concentration, and urine output. In the treatment group, they also targeted a $\dot{D}o_2I$ greater than 600 ml min^{-1} m^{-2} using dopexamine as an inotrope to achieve this. This protocol was continued postoperatively until the lactate was normal for two consecutive readings. They demonstrated a 75% reduction in mortality and fewer postoperative complications.

Wilson et al. (1999) compared standard perioperative care against pre-optimization in intensive care or high dependency units using intravenous fluid and blood to achieve PA occlusion pressures greater than 12 mm Hg, haemoglobin concentrations greater than 110 g $litre^{-1}$, and using either adrenaline (epinephrine) or dopexamine to achieve a $\dot{D}o_2I$ greater than 600 ml min^{-1} m^{-2}. They demonstrated a mortality reduction of 82% in the treatment group, and a reduced incidence of complications and hospital length of stay in the dopexamine group.

These key papers confirmed the morbidity and mortality benefits of preoperative optimization of oxygen delivery in high-risk surgical patients. Since their publication, the principles of goal-directed therapy to optimize oxygen delivery have been shown to be beneficial in orthopaedic trauma patients (Sinclair et al. 1997), general surgical patients (Lobo et al. 2000), and cardiac surgical patients (Polonen et al. 2000). Further studies such as those by Donati et al. (2007) and Pearse et al. (2005) have looked at goal-directed therapy beginning intraoperatively and postoperatively. These have demonstrated reduced rates of organ dysfunction and length of stay although not a mortality benefit.

Controversy

Despite the plethora of good evidence supporting the use of pre-optimization of the high-risk surgical patient, it remains a controversial subject with limited adoption (Singh and Manji 2001) for a number of reasons:

1. Outcomes are dependent on patient selection
2. Critical care resource implications
3. Use of PA catheter
4. Outcomes are because of additional fluid.

Patient selection

As described, the studies that have shown a morbidity and mortality benefit are those which implemented goal-directed therapy for patients classed as high risk—those with a greater chance of mortality because of an inability to meet the oxygen requirements associated with surgery. There have been notable studies that have failed to demonstrate a benefit from goal-directed therapy, and these have contributed to the scepticism around this therapy. Gattinoni et al. (1995) compared supranormal CI and normal $S\bar{v}_{O_2}$ to a control group of normal CI and failed to achieve an improvement in morbidity or mortality. However, the patient population was different to previous studies in that these were patients who were already critically ill and included patients with sepsis syndrome or septic shock. Moreover, the targets in the treatment groups were only met in 44.9% and 66.7% respectively. Hayes et al. (1994) used dobutamine to achieve supranormal levels of CI and oxygen delivery in those who failed to respond to fluid therapy and low-dose dopamine in a mixed population of medical and surgical patients admitted to ICU. Despite this, there was no difference in oxygen consumption between the treatment and control groups and a higher in-hospital mortality rate in the treatment group. Again, the patients were already critically ill at the start of treatment with established organ failure and in this study, very high doses of dobutamine were used to meet the targets. These results contrast with those demonstrated by Rivers et al. (2001) who showed that in patients with severe sepsis and septic shock, early and aggressive fluid resuscitation supplemented with dobutamine administration to maintain Scv_{O_2} above 70% reduces mortality.

Rather than refuting goal-directed therapy as beneficial, these studies highlight the importance of correctly identifying patients who stand to benefit from goal-directed therapy and the dangers of extrapolating the results to other populations. The described therapies are effective if implemented before surgery and the attendant elevation of oxygen consumption and cellular hypoxia, whereas benefit has not been seen in patients who are not high risk, if supranormal $\dot{D}o_2$ targets are not used, or if organ failure or septic shock is established. When critical illness is already established, they should be avoided.

Critical care resources

Critical care resources are limited and vary widely between countries (Wunsch et al. 2008). Lack of bed availability may impact the ability to admit patients either pre- or postoperatively to implement goal-directed therapy. Preoperative optimization is not currently regarded as an essential component of perioperative care and absence of acute organ failure or need for organ support often precludes ICU admission. Critical care units are expensive resources and unnecessary admission is not economically responsible.

The perception that prophylactic ICU admission and goal-directed therapy would incur additional expense and increase the cost of patient care was questioned by Guest et al. (1997) who conducted a cost-effectiveness analysis of Boyd et al.'s (1993) earlier study into supranormal oxygen delivery. They analysed the medical care and resource utilization in the study groups and identified the unit price of each resource, allowing them to calculate the treatment cost of each patient. The cost of standard care was an average of GBP £1259 more than pre-optimization, attributable mainly to the expense of treating postoperative complications. Fenwick et al. (2002) conducted a retrospective cost-effectiveness analysis of Wilson et al.'s (1999) pre-optimization trial. They demonstrated a lower overall cost of treatment with an optimization strategy than with standard care and an average saving of EUR €5655. This saving was because of a reduction of postoperative resource consumption and of in-patient stay, which more than offset the expense incurred by implementing pre-optimization.

The reduced incidence of complications and need for critical care and the reduction in hospital length of stay which results from the implementation of goal-directed therapy in a high-risk population makes this a more fiscally efficient strategy than the current model of reacting to complications once they have developed. There is also evidence that instituting the described therapies postoperatively without preoperative intervention can reduce morbidity and hospital stay, further reducing the burden on critical care resources (Pearse et al. 2005).

Pulmonary artery catheter

The majority of studies demonstrating improved outcomes after goal-directed therapy have used oxygen delivery as the targeted index. This has been calculated using a PA catheter to measure cardiac output. However, there has been a trend away from using the PA catheter as research has called into question its utility and suggested increased mortality associated with its use (Connors et al. 1996; Sandham et al. 2003). Despite these concerns, the described benefits to morbidity and mortality when an appropriate patient group is selected and PA catheterization is used to guide therapy have been confirmed in a meta-analysis (Kern and Shoemaker 2002). Moreover, Hamilton et al. (2011) conducted a meta-analysis into goal-directed therapy and showed improved mortality rates when PA catheterization is used compared with other cardiac output monitors.

It is important to recognize that the improved outcomes result from individualized fluid and vasoactive therapy increasing the oxygen delivery, and that the PA catheter is simply used as a flow monitor to guide this. Avoidance or unavailability of a PA catheter should not preclude goal-directed therapy. Pre-optimization can be delivered using alternatives to the PA catheter: the key is that they must be monitors of blood flow to permit assessment of oxygen delivery.

Additional fluid requirements

The various optimization algorithms seek to increase cardiac output and tissue oxygenation by maximizing ventricular filling with intravenous fluid administration and patients in the treatment arm tend to receive more fluid intraoperatively (Abas and Hill 2008).

Some of the studies have demonstrated an outcome benefit without recourse to inotropic therapy (Sinclair et al. 1997; Gan et al. 2002). Fluid management is therefore an important component and prevention of both occult fluid depletion and volume overload are essential. Some suggest that the increased fluid administration observed in the treatment arms supports the hypothesis that patients simply require additional fluid and that this could be administered without the need for cardiac output monitoring or inotropic therapy. While it is appealing to administer additional volume without stroke volume guidance, this has not been shown to have the same benefits as goal-directed therapy (Cuthbertson et al. 2011). Fluid administration is only appropriate while there is recruitable cardiac output and blind administration is unlikely to position the patient optimally on the Frank–Starling curve. A patient undergoing surgery requires the correct amount of fluid and this cannot be identified without monitoring.

Optimizing the filling status improves outcomes but the addition of inotropic support has further beneficial effects (Pearse et al. 2008; Hamilton et al. 2011). The high-risk population described is at risk of tissue oxygen debt because of impaired physiological reserve combined with general anaesthesia even with optimal filling (Lobo et al. 2006). In addition, the use of inodilators such as dopexamine has been shown to improve microvascular blood flow compared with fluid alone (Jhanji et al. 2010).

Optimization of haemodynamics in the perioperative period has been confirmed as beneficial on rates of mortality and surgical outcomes in numerous studies over the past 25 years. Despite concerns regarding invasive monitoring and resource utilization, and early problems associated with the principles being extrapolated to other populations, it has repeatedly been shown in meta-analyses to improve outcomes even when compared with the improving outcomes of standard care (Kern and Shoemaker 2002; Poeze et al. 2005; Hamilton et al. 2011).

Oxygen delivery

Oxygen is required for energy production in the mitochondria by aerobic metabolism. It is transported in the blood, the majority bound to haemoglobin with a small quantity dissolved in the plasma; it is not stored in the tissues. Oxygen delivery ($\dot{D}O_2$) is therefore reliant on oxygen content of arterial blood (Ca_{O_2}) and cardiac output (CO).

$$\dot{D}o_2(\text{ml min}^{-1}) = \text{CO (litres min}^{-1}) \times Ca_{O_2}\ (\text{ml litre}^{-1}) \qquad (88.1)$$

In health, global $\dot{D}O_2$ usually far outweighs oxygen consumption ($\dot{V}O_2$), which varies between tissues depending on their metabolic activity. The extraction ratio (ER) describes the fraction of delivered oxygen which is consumed by the tissues. As oxygen delivery to the tissues reduces as a result of hypoxia or reduced cardiac output, aerobic metabolism is maintained by extracting a greater fraction of oxygen from the delivered blood. As a result, the mixed venous oxygen content drops and the extraction ratio rises. Eventually a threshold is reached and the $\dot{V}O_2$ begins to drop. This is classed as the critical $\dot{D}O_2$ and beyond this level $\dot{V}O_2$ is said to be *supply dependent*. Beyond this critical $\dot{D}O_2$ there is an inadequate oxygen supply to the cells to meet the requirement for aerobic metabolism and anaerobic metabolism will begin.

$$\dot{V}o_2(\text{ml min}) = \text{CO (litre min}^{-1}) \times (Ca_{O_2} - Cv_{O_2})(\text{ml litre}^{-1}) \qquad (88.2)$$

$$\text{ER}(\%) = \dot{V}o_2/\dot{D}o_2 \qquad (88.3)$$

Very high oxygen extraction ratios are suggestive of inadequate oxygen delivery. A clinically useful marker of oxygen extraction is the mixed venous oxygen saturation ($S\bar{v}_{O_2}$). The term mixed venous is used to denote that the sampled blood is taken from the PA after mixing of systemic venous blood from the superior and inferior vena cava, ensuring that global oxygen consumption is considered. Measurement of $S\bar{v}_{O_2}$ requires placement of a PA catheter in order to sample blood after mixing has occurred in the right heart. In the absence of a PA catheter, central venous oxygen saturation (Scv_{O_2}) measured from blood in the superior vena cava can be used as a surrogate. This method requires a central venous line but must be interpreted as a regional rather than global measure. Once a catheter is sited, intermittent measurements of oxygen saturation are made simply by aspirating a blood sample and processing in a point-of-care blood gas analyser. With modern catheters, both $S\bar{v}_{O_2}$ and (Scv_{O_2}) can also be continuously measured *in vivo* using catheters with fibreoptic oximeters.

The extraction ratio can also be calculated using the arterial and mixed venous oxygen saturations as the variable that changes between arterial and mixed venous oxygen content is the saturation.

$$\text{ER}(\%) = (Sa_{O_2} - S\bar{v}_{O_2}) / Sa_{O_2} \qquad (88.4)$$

As oxygen delivery falls, so the amount of oxygen extracted from the blood rises to maintain an adequate tissue supply. This increased extraction causes the venous blood returning to the right heart to have a reduced oxygen content and this is evident in the oxygen saturation. Falling $S\bar{v}_{O_2}$ or Scv_{O_2} can be used as a measure of increasing extraction ratio and therefore reduced oxygen delivery. If left uncorrected this reduction in $\dot{D}O_2$ will cause tissue hypoxia and a reliance on anaerobic metabolism with consequent lactate generation.

The effects of tissue hypoxia are broad (Karimova and Pinsky 2001; Davies and Wilson 2004). The endothelium becomes activated, causing inflammation, capillary leak with loss of barrier function, and vasoconstriction. Leucocytes and platelets are activated and there is a procoagulant state. Splanchnic hypoperfusion causes disruption of the enteric mucosal barrier with translocation of microorganisms and endotoxin into the circulation. These changes precipitate dysfunction of the microcirculation and eventually organ failure and death.

Implementing pre-optimization

In order to achieve the described benefits from haemodynamic optimization in the perioperative period, it is essential that a number of steps are followed (Lees et al. 2009). To improve rates of morbidity and mortality it is necessary to identify those patients at high risk of these complications. Once a patient is identified, they should be admitted to intensive care and appropriate monitoring instituted. This monitoring should allow quantification of appropriate physiological parameters and assessment of response to treatment. Once appropriate monitoring is in place, a therapeutic algorithm should be followed to target specific predefined physiological goals. This goal-directed therapy should comprise optimization of arterial oxygen content and cardiac output through the use of intravenous fluid loading and inotropic support. When the targets have been met, then the surgery should take place with continued adherence to the haemodynamic goals. The patient should return to the ICU postoperatively to continue the treatment protocol.

Identification of high-risk patients

There is a small subset of patients who account for the majority of perioperative deaths. Pearse et al. (2006) demonstrated that of over 4 million surgical procedures performed during a 70-month period, 12.5% could be classified as high risk with an expected mortality rate of greater than 5%. The mortality rate of patients undergoing high-risk surgery was 12.3%, compared with 0.42% in the standard-risk group, and accounted for more than 80% of all deaths during the study period. Therefore, if interventions are to be instituted to reduce the risk of perioperative mortality, a means of identifying the at-risk patient is required.

In general terms, increased operative risk is related to increased oxygen demand and the patient's ability to meet this demand; inability to do so is directly related to mortality (Clowes and Del Guercio 1960). Both surgical and patient factors have a bearing on this.

Surgical factors: factors which increase the stress response to the surgical insult and so the oxygen demand such as extent and duration of surgery are associated with increased rates of complications and death. For example, major intra-abdominal surgery is associated with an increased oxygen demand of 40% or more which must be met with increased oxygen delivery or extraction (Older and Hall 2004).

Patient factors: the key factor is the ability to meet the increased oxygen requirements imposed by the surgery. Patients with adequate physiological reserve are able to meet this requirement by increasing their oxygen delivery, primarily by increasing their cardiac output. Reduced cardiopulmonary reserve limits this response.

There have been numerous criteria described for identifying the high-risk surgical patient. Simple clinical criteria such as presence of one or more risk factors from a list (Pearse et al. 2005) can be used, or more complex scoring systems such as the Portsmouth Physiologic and Operative Severity Score enUmeration of Mortality (P-POSSUM) which attempts to predict mortality based on parameters such as age, cardiac and respiratory disease, conscious level, haemodynamics, laboratory investigations, and nature of surgery (Prytherch et al. 1998). Similarly there have been cardiac risk indices described by Goldman, Lee and Detsky, and the Duke Activity Status Index. The best-validated method for assessing cardiorespiratory function is cardiopulmonary exercise testing (Older and Hall 2004).

A degree of pragmatism is required—it may not be practical to subject patients requiring emergency surgery to cardiopulmonary exercise testing. However, it is essential that the high-risk patient be identified in order that they receive appropriate management in the perioperative period (Box 88.1).

A proportion of the patients identified will be at high risk of perioperative myocardial ischaemia and excessive β-stimulation as a result of inotrope administration may exacerbate this. These patients have often been excluded from studies of pre-optimization, and safety limits set to prevent undue tachycardia or ECG changes. Successful management requires optimal disease control preoperatively and perioperative β-blockade may be more appropriate than the supranormal oxygen delivery described (Pearse et al. 2004; Flynn et al. 2011). However, hypovolaemia remains a risk necessitating accurate fluid administration, and the principles of monitoring and fluid management outlined should be followed.

Box 88.1 Presence of one or more factors denotes a high risk for the surgical patient

- Severe cardiac or respiratory illness resulting in severe functional limitation
- Extensive surgery planned for carcinoma involving bowel anastomosis
- Acute massive blood loss (>2.5 litres)
- Aged over 70 years with moderate functional limitation of one or more organ systems
- Septicaemia (positive blood cultures or septic focus)
- Respiratory failure (Pa_{O_2} < 8 kPa on FI_{O_2} > 0.4, i.e. Pa_{O_2} : FI_{O_2} ratio < 20 kPa or ventilation > 48 h)
- Acute abdominal catastrophe (e.g. pancreatitis, perforated viscous, gastrointestinal bleed)
- Acute kidney injury (urea > 20 mmol l^{-1}, creatinine > 260 μ mol l^{-1})
- Surgery for abdominal aortic aneurysm.

Data from 'Early goal-directed therapy after major surgery reduces complications and duration of hospital stay. A randomised, controlled trial [ISRCTN38797445]', Rupert Pearse, Deborah Dawson, Jayne Fawcett, Andrew Rhodes, R Michael Grounds and E David Bennett, *Critical Care*, 2005 9:R687.

Monitoring

It is clear that, by identifying patients at risk of tissue hypoxia and preventing this insult, the incidence of postoperative complications can be reduced with a beneficial effect on surgical mortality. This detection and prevention is dependent on being able to make a meaningful assessment of the haemodynamic status of the patient and to use this assessment to guide therapy; no monitoring will improve outcome unless coupled to a treatment that itself improves outcome (Pinsky 2007).

Physiological monitoring is a core component of anaesthesia and intensive care. The most commonly measured parameters are heart rate, arterial pressure, and oxygen saturation; invasive arterial pressure and central venous pressure measurements are frequently added in higher-risk populations. The essential function of the cardiovascular system is delivery of oxygen to the tissues yet the parameters listed give no measure of blood flow or oxygen delivery. They give a measure of the status of the cardiovascular system with the assumption that achieving normal values equate to normal function and prevention of organ injury. The assumption fails to deal with underlying pathological mechanisms. Arterial pressure may be adequate but maintained by elevated systemic vascular resistance in the face of a reduced cardiac output. If outcomes are to be improved, therapeutic interventions must be delivered and guided by the physiological responses detected by appropriate monitoring (Table 88.1).

The principle of goal-directed therapy is to ensure adequate oxygen delivery to prevent ischaemia and an oxygen debt. This is achieved by ensuring adequate preload to optimize the position

Table 88.1 Required monitoring

Equipment	Variables to be monitored
Pulse oximeter	Arterial oxygen saturation
Electrocardiograph	Heart rate, dysrhythmias
Arterial catheter	Systolic, diastolic, and mean blood pressure; blood gas analysis; haemoglobin concentration
Central venous catheter	Central venous oxygen saturation, administration of inotropes
Cardiac output monitor—one of:	
Pulmonary artery catheter	Stroke volume, cardiac index, mixed venous oxygen saturation
Pulse contour analysis	Stroke volume, cardiac index, pulse pressure variation, stroke volume variation
Oesophageal Doppler	Stroke volume, cardiac index, corrected flow time

on the Frank–Starling curve, and then when the patient's intravascular volume status is optimal, inotropes and vasodilators are started as required to reach a predetermined $\dot{D}o_2$. Neither central venous pressure nor PA occlusion pressure is reliable in assessing fluid responsiveness (Michard and Teboul 2002; Marik et al. 2008); a measure of blood flow is required to make a meaningful assessment of response to a fluid challenge. Flow measurement is also required for quantifying the cardiac output in order to calculate the $\dot{D}o_2$. The early studies into goal-directed therapy all utilized the PA catheter to measure cardiac output and so oxygen delivery. As use of the PA catheter has declined, there have been a number of less-invasive cardiac output monitors developed for use in the operating theatre and critical care environments. These include the oesophageal Doppler monitor (Singer 2009) and a variety of arterial pressure waveform analysis systems. The pressure waveform systems can be calibrated (e.g. using transpulmonary thermodilution or lithium dilution) or uncalibrated. All of these systems give an indication of stroke volume and cardiac output and they should be used to direct therapy.

Goal-directed therapy

The aim of pre-optimization is to prevent an oxygen debt in those at risk by manipulating the factors that affect oxygen flux. The most extensively studied target is a supranormal $\dot{D}o_2I$; achievement of a $\dot{D}o_2I$ of 600 ml min^{-1} m^{-2} has been shown to confer a survival benefit (Hamilton et al. 2011). Other measures have also been studied: maintaining an oxygen extraction ratio (calculated using central rather than mixed venous oxygen saturations) below 27% (Donati et al. 2007), and targeting a corrected flow time greater than 0.35s (Abbas and Hill 2008) improved rates of complications and length of stay.

Tissue oxygenation is maintained by ensuring adequate arterial oxygen content and elevating oxygen delivery to supranormal levels by increasing the cardiac output and controlling the systemic vascular resistance if required. Goals are predefined and the haemodynamics manipulated to achieve those goals before surgery.

Oxygen content

In high-risk patients who lack the cardiorespiratory reserve to meet the increased oxygen requirements posed by surgery, there is an increased risk of complications and death. Oxygen delivery can be increased by increasing the arterial oxygen content (Ca_{O_2}) or the cardiac output.

Arterial oxygen content is dependent on the oxygen saturation and the haemoglobin concentration. There is a small amount of dissolved oxygen in the plasma but this fraction is far smaller than that bound to haemoglobin. Oxygen content can be increased then by ensuring adequate haemoglobin concentration and oxygen saturation, both standard measures in anaesthesia and intensive care.

$$Ca_{O_2}\ (\text{ml } O_2 \text{ per litre of blood}) = [1.34 \times \text{Hb (g litre}^{-1}) \times Sa_{O_2}] + [0.225 \times Pa_{O_2}\ (\text{kPa})] \quad (88.5)$$

While it is an attractive prospect to improve oxygen delivery by increasing the haemoglobin concentration, there is a trade-off between oxygen-carrying capacity and blood rheology. There are also risks associated with blood transfusion itself, such as allergy, haemolysis, and immunosuppression. Some of the studies have mandated a minimum haemoglobin concentration or haematocrit but the targets have been variable: in one of the early studies, Boyd et al. (1993) kept the haemoglobin above 120 g litre^{-1}. In a more recent study, when transfusion practices had changed, Pearse et al. (2005) had a limit of 80 g litre^{-1} and still showed a benefit in the protocol group. An optimum haemoglobin concentration that is adequate for oxygen transport but does not compromise blood flow should be the goal. A concentration of 70 g litre^{-1} or more—higher in those patients with ischaemic heart disease—is sufficient for this and may be superior to a more liberal transfusion strategy (Hebert et al. 1999). The nature of surgery and expected blood loss will have a bearing on this level and will need to be taken into account when preparing the patient for surgery.

Hypoxia should also be avoided and oxygen administered if required to keep the patient well oxygenated. Oxygen saturations of 94% would be a reasonable target to ensure adequate arterial oxygen content. Continuous positive airways pressure may be required to achieve this, particularly after surgery.

These determinants of oxygen content should be achieved before further efforts are made to elevate the oxygen delivery; otherwise, there is the risk of excessive fluid administration and associated risks.

Fluid loading

The first step in optimizing the delivery of oxygen is to increase the cardiac output through administration of intravenous fluids. Inappropriate fluid administration not only lacks benefit to the patient but also causes harm by increasing tissue oedema and impairing oxygen transfer in the lung and peripheral tissues leading to tissue hypoxia. It is therefore essential to assess whether a patient is fluid responsive—whether they have recruitable cardiac output—and to avoid unnecessary fluid therapy.

Assessing fluid responsiveness

Fluid responsiveness is the ability to increase the stroke volume and thus cardiac output in response to a fluid challenge; an increase of 10–15% is generally taken as a positive response (Marik et al. 2008). By administering a rapid intravenous fluid bolus, the venous return

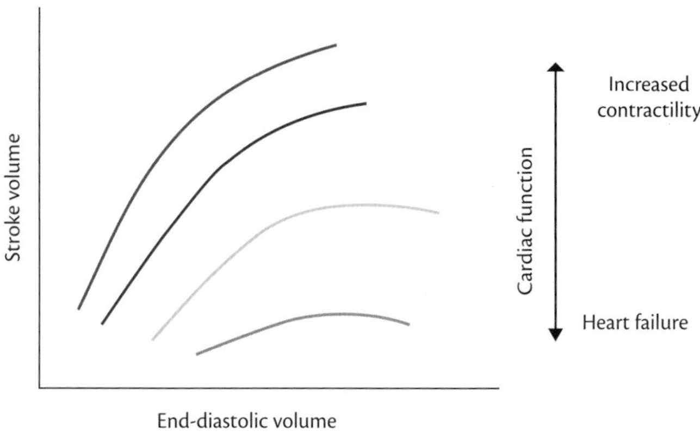

Figure 88.1 Examples of Frank–Starling curves.

is increased and so the end-diastolic volume rises. If the patient is on the ascending part of the Frank–Starling curve then the stroke volume will increase. As the flat upper portion of the curve is reached there will be little change to stroke volume in response to volume administration and the patient is no longer fluid responsive; fluid is no longer beneficial and should be stopped (Fig. 88.1).

It is important to note that a positive response to a fluid challenge does not necessarily mean that the patient is hypovolaemic. Most people will increase their stroke volume in response to an increased venous return. Under these circumstances, intravenous fluid is not being used to replenish a circulatory deficit but to augment the venous return and so the cardiac output.

Traditionally, the response of the central venous pressure or PA occlusion pressure was used as a measure of the preload response to a fluid challenge. This has been shown to be an ineffective means of quantifying response to fluid and should not be used (Michard and Teboul 2002; Marik et al. 2008). The response to a fluid challenge should be assessed using either a measure of stroke volume or cardiac output, or a surrogate dynamic variable such as pulse pressure variation (PVV) or stroke volume variation (SVV).

While fluid responsiveness can be assessed by measuring the change in stroke volume in response to a fluid challenge, the potential harm of excessive fluid administration can be avoided through the use of predictors of fluid responsiveness. If these predictors suggest that the patient will not respond, then fluid administration can be avoided altogether. There are two methods which can be utilized: passive leg raising (PLR) which acts as a reversible fluid challenge and assessing the cyclical variation in venous return associated with positive pressure ventilation:

1. Passive leg raise. Raising and holding the legs at 30–45° above the chest causes an increase in venous return equivalent to a 300 ml fluid challenge that persists for 2–3 min. The immediate haemodynamic response can be used as a measure of fluid responsiveness while avoiding the potential of fluid overload (Boulain et al. 2002; Monnet and Teboul 2008). Total body water is unchanged and excessive fluid administration is avoided in non-responders.

2. Positive pressure ventilation. When a patient with no spontaneous respiratory effort is mechanically ventilated, there will be an increase in right atrial pressure during the inspiratory phase. The pressure will oppose the venous return and cause a reduction in atrial filling. Right and thus left ventricular filling will drop and so there will be a cyclical fall in stroke volume and arterial pulse pressure. These cyclical variations can be indexed to give the stroke volume variation (SVV = $SV_{max} - SV_{min}/SV_{mean}$, averaged over 30 s) of 10% or more is predictive of fluid responsiveness (Berkenstadt et al. 2001). As the main determinant of pulse pressure is stroke volume, the PPV is also a good predictor of fluid responsiveness—a value of 13% or over is predictive of a positive response to a fluid challenge (Michard et al. 2000). PVV has the additional advantage of requiring only an arterial waveform as opposed to a flow measurement device and has been shown to have a greater diagnostic accuracy than either SVV or systolic pressure variation (Marik et al. 2009).

The changing intrathoracic pressure causes a varying venous return and thus similar effects on the cardiac output to a fluid challenge, again with the avoidance of excessive fluid administration. The absolute value of the variation characterizes the degree of responsiveness and exogenous fluid is administered only if the patient is predicted to respond. These values must be interpreted carefully—spontaneous or pressure-supported ventilation or an open chest will affect the intrathoracic pressure and the variation in venous return. It can be seen that the change in intrathoracic pressure will also be affected by the tidal volume and it is recommended that these measures are used in patients ventilated with a tidal volume of 8 ml kg^{-1} or more (Marik et al. 2009).

Fluid challenge

A fluid challenge should be administered as a rapid bolus of intravenous fluid. It should be large enough to increase the end-diastolic volume and so the stroke volume if the patient lies on the ascending side of the Frank–Starling curve, while not so large as to cause excessive volume administration as the upper portion of the curve is approached. If the infused volume is inadequate then the end-diastolic volume will not increase, risking a false-negative result. A bolus of 3 ml kg^{-1} is a safe and appropriate volume to make an assessment of response. This volume should be administered over 5–10 min in order to cause a stretch in the ventricle large enough to have detectable effects on the stroke volume (Cecconi et al. 2011). If the stroke volume increases by 10% or more then the patient is fluid responsive (Table 88.2). The stroke volume may subsequently fall as the administered fluid redistributes but the knowledge that the patient remains on the ascending limb of the curve supports further fluid challenges if required. If the stroke volume fails to increase in response to a fluid bolus then the patient is no longer fluid responsive and further administration should be avoided.

Table 88.2 Positive response to a fluid challenge

Direct measurements	
Stroke volume	Increase of 10% or greater
Cardiac index	Increases
Predictors	
Pulse pressure variation	Absolute value >13%
Stroke volume variation	Absolute value >10%

Inotropes

When the haemodynamic goals cannot be met with intravenous fluid therapy alone then inotropic support will be required. The agents which have been most studied are dobutamine, dopexamine, and adrenaline.

Dobutamine is a direct-acting β-adrenoreceptor agonist, acting primarily at β1 receptors with weak β2 activity. It increases the cardiac output via heart rate and contractility and acts as a peripheral vasodilator despite α1 stimulation. Dopexamine is a dopamine analogue that has effects at β2 and dopamine receptors. It acts as a positive inotrope and peripheral vasodilator, improving flow in the microcirculation and splanchnic vessels, and has anti-inflammatory effects. Adrenaline is an agonist of all adrenoreceptor types. It increases cardiac output and vascular tone.

When the use of fluids was compared against fluids and dobutamine to reach a target $\dot{D}o_2I$ of 600 ml min^{-1} m^{-2} in high-risk patients, worse outcomes and complication rates were found in those treated with fluids alone, while those treated with fluids and dobutamine were more likely to reach their target oxygen delivery (Lobo et al. 2006). Dopexamine has been shown to confer a benefit on both mortality and length of stay when used at doses up to 1 μg kg^{-1} min^{-1} although higher doses lack this effect (Pearse et al. 2008). Dopexamine was compared with adrenaline in another study targeting the $\dot{D}o_2I$—this showed a mortality improvement in both treatment groups compared with the control population but that only the dopexamine group had improved rates of complications and length of stay (Wilson et al. 1999).

Therefore, the use of inotropic agents confers benefits on patients receiving perioperative haemodynamic manipulation. The maximal benefits are seen with dobutamine or dopexamine rather than adrenaline. However, care is required when implementing these therapies as the increased heart rate and consequent myocardial oxygen consumption may be hazardous in patients with ischaemic heart disease or at risk of ischaemic cardiac events.

Vasoactive drugs

The aim of the described therapies is to increase the cardiac output, and it is the increase in tissue oxygen delivery that has been shown to improve outcomes. Manipulation of the cardiac output will affect the arterial pressure and the majority of studies have included this measure as a controlled variable. Anaesthesia and the vasodilating effects of inotropic agents may cause a reduction in vascular resistance and overall reduction in mean arterial pressure. Similarly, underlying elevated vascular tone coupled with an increased cardiac output may cause arterial hypertension. It is important therefore that the mean arterial pressure is controlled within an appropriate range for the patient and this might require the use of a vasoconstrictor such as noradrenaline or a vasodilator such as glyceryl trinitrate.

Timing of surgery

The key difference between the studies demonstrating an improved outcome and those that have not is the timing of the intervention. If treatment is delayed until tissue hypoxia is established, such as in patients with septic shock, then the benefits are not seen and supranormal oxygen delivery is detrimental (Hayes et al. 1994; Gattinoni et al. 1995). If oxygen debt is irreversible, then cell death and resultant organ failure will not respond to increases in oxygen delivery. It is necessary to institute these therapies pre-emptively.

The early studies showing improved mortality rates began treatment before surgery and did not operate until the oxygen delivery targets had been met. Later research has shown that intraoperative and postoperative haemodynamic manipulation also confers a benefit although this is seen on rate of complications and length of stay but not overall mortality. It is preferable therefore to admit high-risk patients to intensive care before surgery in order to begin monitoring and goal-directed therapy and operate once those goals have been met. However, if this is unachievable it is still beneficial to use goal-directed therapy intraoperatively and then continue it

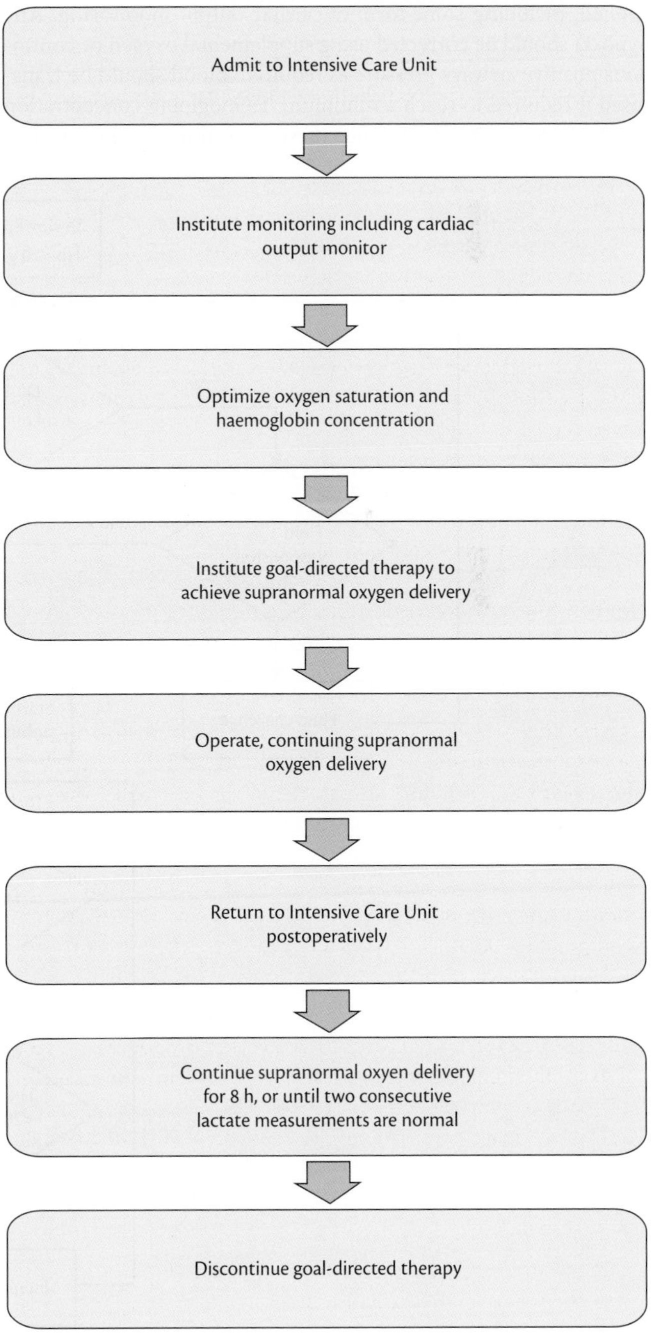

Figure 88.2 Sequence of events during perioperative optimization.

postoperatively if possible. This postoperative management should continue for 8 h or until the serum lactate is normal (Boyd et al. 1993; Pearse et al. 2005).

Algorithm

Patients who are classified as high risk according to the criteria listed should have coexisting disease treated optimally before surgery. They should then be admitted to intensive care preoperatively. In the absence of ICU beds, consideration should be given as to whether the management algorithm can be safely followed in a high-dependency unit. If not, then intraoperative optimization should be used and continued postoperatively if an appropriate critical care bed is available. Appropriate monitoring should be applied, including some form of cardiac output monitoring. Any hypoxia should be corrected using supplemental oxygen or continuous positive airways pressure as required. Blood should be transfused if required to reach a minimum haemoglobin concentration of 70 g litre^{-1} (Fig. 88.2). Once these conditions have been met, goal-directed therapy should be instituted to reach and maintain supranormal oxygen delivery (Table 88.3).

Table 88.3 Treatment goals

Condition	Measurement
Oxygen saturation	≥94%
Haemoglobin concentration	>70 g litre^{-1}
Mean arterial pressure	70–100 mm Hg
Urine output	>0.5 ml kg^{-1} h^{-1}

The cardiac output monitor should be used to assess fluid responsiveness and oxygen delivery. A $\dot{D}O_2I$ of 600 ml min^{-1} m^{-2} should be targeted. If the $\dot{D}O_2I$ is not available then a CI of 4.5 ml min^{-1} m^{-2} or an oxygen extraction ratio of less than 27% should be used. If this value is not met then intravenous fluid challenges should be

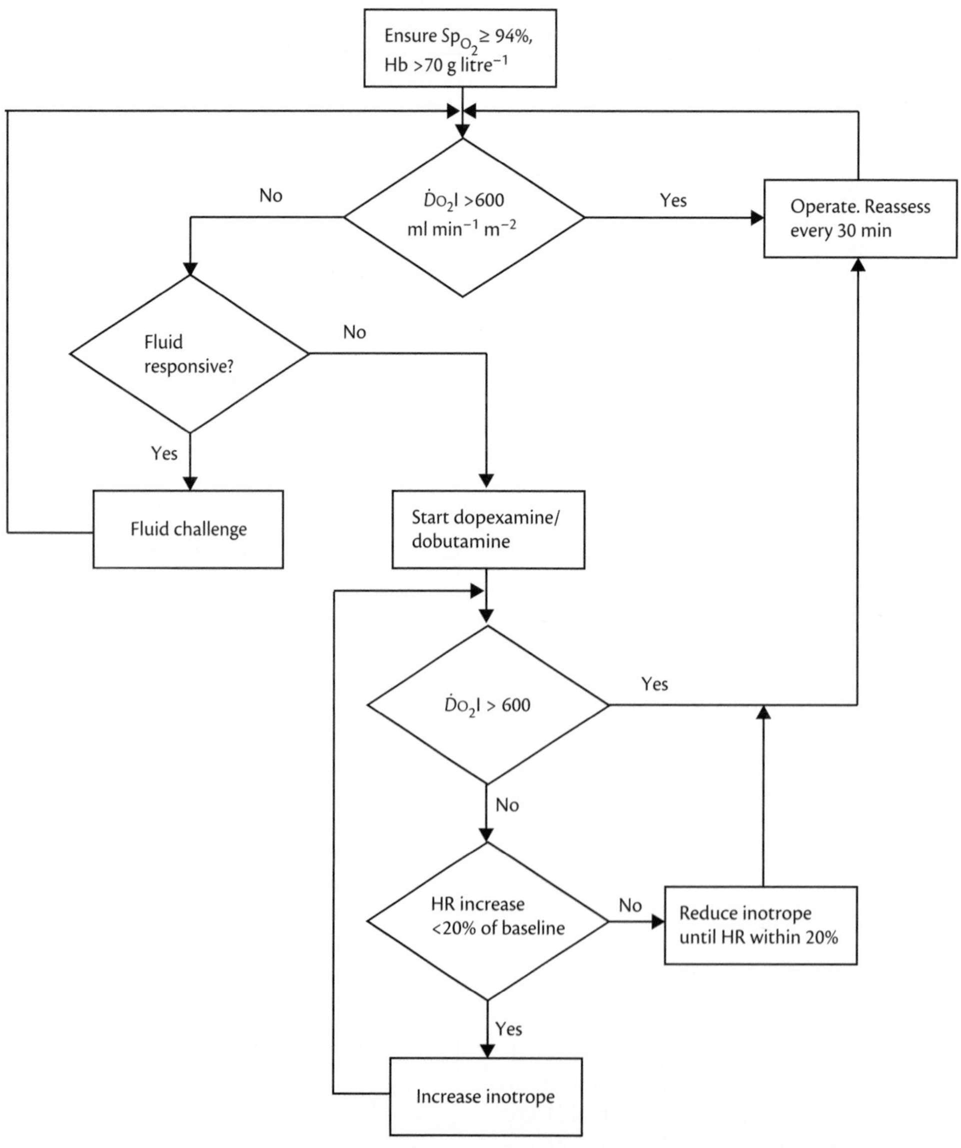

Figure 88.3 Goal-directed therapy algorithm to achieve supranormal oxygen delivery. HR, heart rate.

Table 88.4 Targets for goal-directed therapy

Condition	Measurement
Oxygen delivery index	600 ml min^{-1} m^{-2}
If oxygen delivery index unavailable:	
Cardiac index	4.5 litres min^{-1} m^{-2}
Oxygen extraction ratio	27%

administered while the patient is fluid responsive or predicted to be fluid responsive. If the $\dot{D}o_2I$ is still below target when an optimum position on the Frank–Starling curve has been reached then either dopexamine or dobutamine should be started to increase the cardiac output. This should be titrated up until the target is met, for example, by increasing the infusion rate by a standard increment every 30 min (Boyd et al. 1993) (Table 88.4 and Fig. 88.3).

If the patient develops chest pain, tachycardia (an increase is heart rate of more than 20% of baseline), or ischaemic ECG changes then further increases in inotrope should be avoided and the infusion rate may need to be reduced. A mean arterial pressure adequate for the patient should also be maintained and this may require vasopressors or vasodilators.

Once the patient is optimally filled and the oxygen delivery targets are met, the patient should be transferred to the operating theatre and the surgery performed. The supranormal oxygen delivery should continue during surgery following the same treatment algorithm.

After surgery, the patient should be returned to intensive care. The treatment protocol should continue for 8 h or until the two consecutive measurements of serum lactate are normal. It should then be discontinued and the patient discharged from the ICU.

Conclusion

Over the past three decades, a succession of studies have demonstrated that the morbidity and mortality resulting from tissue hypoxia in the perioperative period can be predicted and prevented. Patients who lack the physiological reserve to elevate their cardiac output spontaneously to supranormal levels to meet the increased oxygen requirements around the time of surgery incur an oxygen debt that is associated with adverse outcomes. These patients should be identified before surgery and managed using a treatment algorithm to attain a pre-defined goal of supranormal oxygen delivery. The use of haemodynamic monitoring which estimates stroke volume facilitates accurate assessment of cardiac filling, prevents inadequate or excessive fluid administration, and guides the inotropic therapy required to meet specified goals. There are both patient outcome and economic benefits to this management strategy that support the individualized goal-directed therapy approach to managing high-risk patients.

Declaration of interest

None declared.

References

Abbas SM, Hill AG. Systematic review of the literature for the use of oesophageal Doppler monitor for fluid replacement in major abdominal surgery. *Anaesthesia* 2008; **63**: 44–51

Berkenstadt H, Margalit N, Hadani M, *et al.* Stroke volume variation as a predictor of fluid responsiveness in patients undergoing brain surgery. *Anesth Analg* 2001; **92**: 984–9

Bland RD, Shoemaker WC, Abraham E, Cobo JC. Hemodynamic and oxygen transport patterns in surviving and nonsurviving postoperative patients. *Crit Care Med* 1985; **13**: 85–90

Boulain T, Achard JM, Teboul JL, Richard C, Perrotin D, Ginies G. Changes in BP induced by passive leg raising predict response to fluid loading in critically ill patients. *Chest* 2002; **121**: 1245–52

Boyd O, Grounds RM, Bennett ED. A randomized clinical trial of the effect of deliberate perioperative increase of oxygen delivery on mortality in high-risk surgical patients. *JAMA* 1993; **270**: 2699–707

Cecconi M, Parsons AK, Rhodes A. What is a fluid challenge? *Curr Opin Crit Care* 2011; **17**: 290–5

Clowes GH, Jr, Del Guercio LR. Circulatory response to trauma of surgical operations. *Metabolism* 1960; **9**: 67–81

Connors AF, Jr, Speroff T, Dawson NV, *et al.* The effectiveness of right heart catheterization in the initial care of critically ill patients. SUPPORT Investigators. *JAMA* 1996; **276**: 889–97

Cuthbertson BH, Campbell MK, Stott SA, *et al.* A pragmatic multi-centre randomised controlled trial of fluid loading in high-risk surgical patients undergoing major elective surgery – the FOCCUS study. *Crit Care* 2011; **15**: R296

Davies SJ, Wilson RJ. Preoperative optimization of the high-risk surgical patient. *Br J Anaesth* 2004; **93**: 121–8

Donati A, Loggi S, Preiser JC, *et al.* Goal-directed intraoperative therapy reduces morbidity and length of hospital stay in high-risk surgical patients. *Chest* 2007; **132**: 1817–24

Fenwick E, Wilson J, Sculpher M, Claxton K. Pre-operative optimisation employing dopexamine or adrenaline for patients undergoing major elective surgery: a cost-effectiveness analysis. *Intensive Care Med* 2002; **28**: 599–608

Flynn BC, Vernick WJ, Ellis JE. Beta-blockade in the perioperative management of the patient with cardiac disease undergoing non-cardiac surgery. *Br J Anaesth* 2011; **107**(Suppl 1): 3–15

Gan TJ, Soppitt A, Maroof M, *et al.* Goal-directed intraoperative fluid administration reduces length of hospital stay after major surgery. *Anesthesiology* 2002; **97**: 820–6

Gattinoni L, Brazzi L, Pelosi P, *et al.* A trial of goal-oriented hemodynamic therapy in critically ill patients. SvO2 Collaborative Group. *N Engl J Med* 1995; **333**: 1025–32

Guest JF, Boyd O, Hart WM, Grounds RM, Bennett ED. A cost analysis of a treatment policy of a deliberate perioperative increase in oxygen delivery in high risk surgical patients. *Intensive Care Med* 1997; **23**: 85–90

Hamilton MA, Cecconi M, Rhodes A. A systematic review and meta-analysis on the use of preemptive hemodynamic intervention to improve postoperative outcomes in moderate and high-risk surgical patients. *Anesth Analg* 2011; **112**: 1392–402

Hayes MA, Timmins AC, Yau EH, Palazzo M, Hinds CJ, Watson D. Elevation of systemic oxygen delivery in the treatment of critically ill patients. *N Engl J Med* 1994; **330**: 1717–22

Hebert PC, Wells G, Blajchman MA, *et al.* A multicenter, randomized, controlled clinical trial of transfusion requirements in critical care. Transfusion Requirements in Critical Care Investigators, Canadian Critical Care Trials Group. *N Engl J Med* 1999; **340**: 409–17

Jhanji S, Vivian-Smith A, Lucena-Amaro S, Watson D, Hinds CJ, Pearse RM. Haemodynamic optimisation improves tissue microvascular flow and oxygenation after major surgery: a randomised controlled trial. *Crit Care* 2010; **14**: R151

Karimova A, Pinsky DJ. The endothelial response to oxygen deprivation: biology and clinical implications. *Intensive Care Med* 2001; **27**: 19–31

Kern JW, Shoemaker WC. Meta-analysis of hemodynamic optimization in high-risk patients. *Crit Care Med* 2002; **30**: 1686–92

Lees N Hamilton M, Rhodes A. Clinical review: goal-directed therapy in high risk surgical patients. *Crit Care* 2009; **13**: R231

Lobo SM, Salgado PF, Castillo VG, *et al.* Effects of maximizing oxygen delivery on morbidity and mortality in high-risk surgical patients. *Crit Care Med* 2000; **28**: 3396–404

Lobo SM, Lobo FR, Polachini CA, *et al.* Prospective, randomized trial comparing fluids and dobutamine optimization of oxygen delivery in high-risk surgical patients [ISRCTN42445141]. *Crit Care* 2006; **10**: R72

Marik PE, Baram M, Vahid B. Does central venous pressure predict fluid responsiveness? A systematic review of the literature and the tale of seven mares. *Chest* 2008; **134**: 172–8

Marik PE, Cavallazzi R, Vasu T, Hirani A. Dynamic changes in arterial waveform derived variables and fluid responsiveness in mechanically ventilated patients: a systematic review of the literature. *Crit Care Med* 2009; **37**: 2642–7

Michard F, Boussat S, Chemla D, *et al.* Relation between respiratory changes in arterial pulse pressure and fluid responsiveness in septic patients with acute circulatory failure. *Am J Respir Crit Care Med* 2000; **162**: 134–8

Michard F, Teboul JL. Predicting fluid responsiveness in ICU patients: a critical analysis of the evidence. *Chest* 2002; **121**: 2000–8

Monnet X, Teboul JL. Passive leg raising. *Intensive Care Med* 2008; **34**: 659–63

Older P, Hall A. Clinical review: how to identify high-risk surgical patients. *Crit Care* 2004; **8**: 369–72

Pearse RM, Rhodes A, Grounds RM. Clinical review: how to optimize management of high-risk surgical patients. *Crit Care* 2004; **8**: 503–7

Pearse R, Dawson D, Fawcett J, Rhodes A, Grounds RM, Bennett ED. Early goal-directed therapy after major surgery reduces complications and duration of hospital stay. A randomised, controlled trial [ISRCTN38797445]. *Crit Care* 2005; **9**: R687–93

Pearse RM, Harrison DA, James P, *et al.* Identification and characterisation of the high-risk surgical population in the United Kingdom. *Crit Care* 2006; **10**: R81

Pearse RM, Belsey JD, Cole JN, Bennett ED. Effect of dopexamine infusion on mortality following major surgery: individual patient data meta-regression analysis of published clinical trials. *Crit Care Med* 2008; **36**: 1323–9

Pinsky MR. Hemodynamic evaluation and monitoring in the ICU. *Chest* 2007; **132**: 2020–9

Poeze M, Greve JW, Ramsay G. Meta-analysis of hemodynamic optimization: relationship to methodological quality. *Crit Care* 2005; **9**: R771–9

Polonen P, Ruokonen E, Hippelainen M, Poyhonen M, Takala J. A prospective, randomized study of goal-oriented hemodynamic therapy in cardiac surgical patients. *Anesth Analg* 2000; **90**: 1052–9

Prytherch DR, Whiteley MS, Higgins B, Weaver PC, Prout WG, Powell SJ. POSSUM and Portsmouth POSSUM for predicting mortality. Physiological and Operative Severity Score for the enUmeration of Mortality and morbidity. *Br J Surg* 1998; **85**: 1217–20

Rivers E, Nguyen B, Havstad S, *et al.* Early goal-directed therapy in the treatment of severe sepsis and septic shock. *N Engl J Med* 2001; **345**: 1368–77

Sandham JD, Hull RD, Brant RF, *et al.* A randomized, controlled trial of the use of pulmonary-artery catheters in high-risk surgical patients. *N Engl J Med* 2003; **348**: 5–14

Shoemaker WC, Appel PL, Kram HB. Role of oxygen debt in the development of organ failure sepsis, and death in high-risk surgical patients. *Chest* 1992; **102**: 208–15

Shoemaker WC, Appel PL, Kram HB, Waxman K, Lee TS. Prospective trial of supranormal values of survivors as therapeutic goals in high-risk surgical patients. *Chest* 1988; **94**: 1176–86

Sinclair S, James S, Singer M. Intraoperative intravascular volume optimisation and length of hospital stay after repair of proximal femoral fracture: randomised controlled trial. *Br Med J* 1997; **315**: 909–12

Singer M. Oesophageal Doppler. *Curr Opin Crit Care* 2009; **15**: 244–8

Singh S, Manji M. A survey of pre-operative optimisation of high-risk surgical patients undergoing major elective surgery. *Anaesthesia* 2001; **56**: 988–90

Wilson J, Woods I, Fawcett J, *et al.* Reducing the risk of major elective surgery: randomised controlled trial of preoperative optimisation of oxygen delivery. *Br Med J* 1999; **318**: 1099–103

Wunsch H, Angus DC, Harrison DA, *et al.* Variation in critical care services across North America and Western Europe. *Crit Care Med* 2008; **36**: 2787–93

CHAPTER 89

Acute illness in the postoperative period

Gernot Marx and Michael Fries

Introduction

Healthcare systems in the United States and Europe will face profound changes in the next decade. Despite resources becoming more limited, the numbers of patients requiring surgery including invasive and complex operations in a range of disciplines including cardiac and vascular surgery, neurosurgery, abdominal surgery, orthopaedic surgery, gynaecology, and urology are steadily increasing (http://ec.europa.eu/eurostat/web/products-datasets/-/hlth_co_proc2).

Table 89.1 lists the number of patients undergoing major surgery in selected European countries in 2005 and 2009.

The average age of patients is also increasing. For example, the average age for isolated coronary artery bypass grafting has risen from 64 years in 1999 to 67 years in 2009, with more than 20% of patients undergoing a coronary artery bypass graft, in most of Europe, being older than 75 years. Octogenarians represent more than 5% of patients (Bridgewater et al. 2010). There is a strong association between age and postoperative mortality, which increases from less than 1% in patients younger than 56 years to 7% in those aged 80 years or older. Factors contributing to prolonged hospitalization and increased postoperative morbidity and mortality are well recongized in cardiac surgery and include obesity, diabetes, structural lung disease, arteriopathy, and preoperative renal failure (Bridgewater et al. 2010). Similar risk factors have been described in vascular surgery, total hip replacement, and transurethral resection of the prostate (Armitage et al. 2010; Gupta et al. 2012).

Table 89.1 Total number of complex surgical procedures performed in selective European countries for 2005 and 2009 (Austria, Denmark, France, Germany, Italy, Luxemburg, Netherlands, Spain, Sweden, Switzerland, United Kingdom)

Surgical discipline	Procedure	2005	2009
Cardiovascular	Coronary artery bypass grafting	219 865	175 993
	Aneurysm repair	25 422	20 528
	Femoro-popliteal bypass	52 730	46 887
	Carotid endarterectomy	83 682	88 786
Neurosurgery	Intracranial bleeding	32 045	33 748
	Tumour resection	47 258	48 776
Abdominal surgery	Colectomy	300 853	298 675
Orthopaedic surgery	Hip-/knee endoprosthesis	1 040 128	1 206 456
Urology	Prostatectomy	243 261	226 739
Gynaecology	Hysterectomy	419 956	375 039
	Mastectomy	114 612	119 601

While there is considerable variation in the intensity of surgical procedures performed within the last year of life, it is well documented that up to 20% of elderly people in industrialized countries die in the intensive care unit (ICU) and of these, half undergo mechanical ventilation and a quarter undergo cardiopulmonary resuscitation (The SUPPORT Principal Investigators 1995; Prendergast et al. 1998; Angus et al. 2004; Kwok et al. 2011).

Despite recent advances, the perioperative period still predisposes to a disproportionately large number of problems and complications, especially in the early postoperative phase. Many risk factors are not modifiable, but some critical conditions arising during or after surgical procedures may be preventable or, if anticipated, need both recognition and intervention to mitigate risk. Acute illness in the immediate postoperative period differs from the frequently observed and mostly benign problems that are encountered in recovery rooms although these complications may require intervention in 25% of cases (Hines et al. 1992). See Box 89.1 for typical complications in post-anaesthesia care units (i.e. recovery rooms). These complications generally have little impact on length of hospital stay or the clinical course. There are far more serious complications that may necessitate admission to the ICU. These include *sepsis, cardiovascular complications* (*myocardial infarction, pulmonary embolism,*

Box 89.1 Typical complications in the recovery room

- Nausea and vomiting
- Upper airway obstruction
- Hypotension
- Rhythm disturbances
- Neurological compromise

and *stroke*), and *massive bleeding*. These acute complications may not be preventable but are associated with increased mortality in comparison to those patients with planned admission to the ICU (Vlayen et al. 2012).

This chapter provides an overview of those aspects of critical care that are pertinent to the immediate postoperative phase.

Sepsis

The term sepsis characterizes the complex systemic inflammatory response of a human to the invasion of microorganisms (e.g. bacteria, viruses, and fungi). It incorporates the sub-definitions sepsis, severe sepsis, and septic shock. Sepsis and persistent shock is associated with a mortality of up to 55% (Engel et al. 2007). The incidence of sepsis is not only high but a continuous increase has been observed over recent years (Dombrovskiy et al. 2003; Linde-Zwirble and Angus 2004).

Anaesthetists, either in the operating theatre or as part of a medical emergency team, are often involved in the early diagnosis and management of septic patients. Explicit knowledge about early detection and the appropriate treatment is mandatory. The mortality rate of septic patients, especially those with shock, is high and progresses by 10% for each hour of treatment delay (Kumar et al. 2006). To increase awareness and hence decrease mortality from sepsis, the 'Surviving Sepsis Campaign' (http://www.survivingsepsis.org) was initiated in 2002 by the Society of Critical Care Medicine, the European Society of Intensive Care Medicine, and the International Sepsis Forum. This culminated in the release of international guidelines in 2004, which advocated the use of resuscitation bundles (Dellinger et al. 2004). Implementation of specific sepsis bundles have been shown to improve outcome in septic patients (Castellanos-Ortega et al. 2010; Nguyen et al. 2011). These guidelines have been updated (Dellinger et al. 2012).

Common foci for sepsis in adults are the respiratory tract, urogenitary system, and device-related infections (i.e. line-associated infections), while in surgical patients there may be wound infections or peritonitis after abdominal operations. Diagnosis of sepsis is difficult and a range of criteria need to be considered which might indicate an inflammatory response, inherent organ dysfunction, and signs including those of reduced tissue perfusion, arterial hypoxaemia, encephalopathy, decreased urine output, and coagulation abnormalities (Box 89.2). Many of these alterations may also present in other acute illnesses such as pulmonary embolism or myocardial infarction. Accurate diagnosis of sepsis can be improved using laboratory variables, of which C-reactive protein is probably the most widely used. Procalcitonin is considered superior to C-reactive protein and concentrations greater than 2 ng ml^{-1} are highly indicative of a bacterial infection; however, major trauma and highly invasive surgical procedures may also induce an increase in serum procalcitonin (Meisner et al. 1998; Harbarth et al. 2001; Clech et al. 2004). If the focus cannot be clearly identified then imaging studies will be necessary, including the use of computed tomography, but if the patient is deemed unstable then ultrasound may be useful.

The microorganisms inducing sepsis may be either Gram-negative (e.g. *Escherichia coli, Pseudomonas aeruginosa*, Enterobacteriaceae, and *Serratia marcescens*) or Gram-positive bacteria (*Staphylococcus aureus*, coagulase-negative staphylococci, and enterococci). Identification of microorganisms in body fluids is culture dependent and usually takes more than 24 h before results are available. Even when infection is highly likely, cultures will be positive in only about 30% of cases (Vincent et al. 1995; Alberti et al. 2002). Newer, faster, and more reliable test methods, including the polymerase chain reaction, are currently under investigation and—if positively evaluated—may dramatically impact the time and accuracy of detection of microorganisms (Tissari et al. 2010).

Box 89.2 Diagnostic criteria for sepsis

Infection, documented or suspected, and some of the following:

General variables

- Fever (>38.3°C)
- Hypothermia (core temperature < 36°C)
- Heart rate > 90 min^{-1} or > 2 SD above the normal value for age
- Tachypnoea
- Altered mental status
- Significant oedema or positive fluid balance (>20 ml kg^{-1} over 24 h)
- Hyperglycaemia (plasma glucose > 140 mg dl^{-1} or 7.7 mmol litre^{-1}) in the absence of diabetes.

Inflammatory variables

- Leucocytosis (WBC count > 12 000 µl^{-1})
- Leucopenia (WBC count < 4000 µl^{-1})
- Normal WBC count with > 10% immature forms
- Plasma C-reactive protein > 2 SD above the normal value
- Plasma procalcitonin > 2 SD above the normal value.

Haemodynamic variables

- Arterial hypotension (systolic blood pressure < 90 mm Hg; MAP < 70 mm Hg; or a systolic blood pressure decrease > 40 mm Hg in adults or > 2 SD below normal for age).

Organ dysfunction variables

- Arterial hypoxaemia (Pa_{O_2}/FI_{O_2} < 300)
- Acute oliguria (urine output < 0.5 ml kg^{-1} h^{-1} or 45 mmol litre^{-1} for at least 2 h, despite adequate fluid resuscitation)
- Creatinine increase greater than 0.5 mg dl^{-1} or 44.2 µmol litre^{-1}
- Coagulation abnormalities (INR > 1.5 or a PTT > 60 s)
- Ileus (absent bowel sounds)
- Thrombocytopenia (platelet count, <100 000 µl^{-1})
- Hyperbilirubinaemia (plasma total bilirubin > 4 mg dl^{-1} or 70 µmol litre^{-1})
- Encephalopathy.

Tissue perfusion variables

- Hyperlactatemia (> upper limit of lab normal)
- Decreased capillary refill or mottling.

Until then, if sepsis is suspected it is recommended that blood samples (10 ml each) are taken under sterile conditions from at least two different locations and incubated in anaerobic and aerobic blood culture bottles (Dellinger et al. 2004). It is also recommended that a bronchoalveolar lavage, urine samples, and, whenever possible, suspected tissue samples be taken for microbiological analyses.

Prompt and accurate treatment of septic patients is vital in order to improve the otherwise grave prognosis. Of the therapeutic approaches, causative, supportive, and adjunctive, early eradication of the septic focus has the highest priority. Source control with complete surgical removal of infected tissue is a key element for effective treatment (Koperna and Schulz 2000). Surgical approaches may include image-guided drainage of abscesses, explantation of implanted devices (pacemakers, endoprotheses, artificial valves, etc.), or more radical approaches such as laparotomy, fasciotomy, or amputation (Sia et al. 2005; Mehendiratta et al. 2007; van Ruler et al. 2007). In conjunction with surgical eradication of septic foci, early initiation of antimicrobial therapy is equally important and should not be delayed after the diagnosis of sepsis is made (Garnacho-Montero et al. 2003; Leone et al. 2003). The empirical therapy is based on the type of infection with consideration of the individual patient (age, referred from a healthcare facility, risk factor for multidrug resistance, previous antibiotics exposure, etc.) and local ecology including the local resistance of microorganisms (Bodi et al. 2001). In the sicker patients presenting with septic shock, a combination therapy might be considered to cover nosocomial infections with organisms such as meticillin-resistant *Staphylococcus aureus* or *Pseudomonas aeruginosa*, although this approach has only been proved effective in patients with community-acquired pneumonia (Martin-Loeches et al. 2010). Re-evaluation of the antibiotics as soon as microbiological results with susceptibility are available should focus treatment, increase efficacy, reduce costs, and prevent multidrug resistance. With some exceptions, treatment duration is not required for more than 7–10 days (Chastre et al. 2003; Nobre et al. 2008).

Septic shock has a characteristic haemodynamic profile: massively decreased systemic vascular resistance, which, after volume repletion, is associated with supranormal cardiac output but in conjunction with signs of tissue hypoperfusion, that is, skin mottling or elevated serum lactate, or both, although these are not always observed. Initially, patients with septic shock usually present with arterial hypotension and it is recommended to target mean arterial pressure (MAP) greater than 65 mm Hg by administration of adequate volume that may initially require up to 25 ml kg^{-1}. However, to avoid pulmonary oedema or excessively high cardiac filling pressures, it is recommended that cardiac preload using volumetric parameters (transpulmonary indicator dilution, echocardiography) is used rather than filling pressures (central venous pressure, pulmonary capillary wedge pressure) (Buhre et al. 2001; Kumar et al. 2004). The choice of fluid is contentious but it seems reasonable to avoid starches because of the alleged association with negative effects on renal function (Brunkhorst et al. 2008). It has also been suggested that gelatine-containing solutions might also impair renal function and the maximum permissible dose is around 50 ml kg^{-1} body weight (Dart et al. 2010).

Both stabilization of MAP and an adequate urine output (>0.5 ml kg^{-1} body weight h^{-1}) should be targets of haemodynamic management. If in the initial phase of fluid repletion or after adequate volume administration a MAP less than 65 mm Hg persists, then vasopressors should be used to maintain sufficient organ blood flow. This is contentious but noradrenaline (norepinephrine) is probably the most widely used drug with, apparently, fewer side-effects than dopamine (De Backer et al. 2010). Although a so-called relative vasopressin deficiency has been reported in septic shock patients, the combination of noradrenaline with vasopressin was not superior to noradrenaline alone in a randomized controlled trial (Sharshar et al. 2003; Russell et al. 2008). Myocardial dysfunction has been described in patients with septic shock and is contributory to the situations where low cardiac output persists despite adequate cardiac filling pressures (Zanotti-Cavazzoni et al. 2009). Here, the use of inotropic agents such as dobutamine can be considered. Titrating cardiac output and oxygen delivery to predefined supranormal concentrations has not been found to improve outcome in septic shock patients (Hayes et al. 1994; Gattinoni et al. 1995).

Even with correction of macrocirculatory variables, signs of tissue hypoperfusion and inadequate cellular metabolism may persist as consequences of microcirculatory and mitochondrial dysfunction (Balestra et al. 2009). It is therefore reasonable to use goals for resuscitation which more reliably reflect adequate cellular oxygen delivery; for example, an increase in central venous oxygen saturation (Scv_{O_2}) to concentrations above 70% (Rivers et al. 2001). Of note, low Scv_{O_2} is observed in under-resuscitated patients seen in emergency departments but in contrast, ICU patients may present with high Scv_{O_2} values that may reflect inadequate tissue oxygen extraction rather than limited oxygen delivery, and extremely high Scv_{O_2} values are predictive of dismal outcomes (van Beest et al. 2008; Pope et al. 2010). Recently, the concept of Scv_{O_2}-guided treatment for severe sepsis and septic shock has found no improvement in survival in a large multicentre study (ProCESS Investigators 2014). In this context, lactate clearance has emerged as an additional end-point of resuscitation and treatment protocols aimed to decrease high initial lactate concentrations have been associated with improved outcomes (Jansen et al. 2010). Measurements always need to be interpreted in the clinical context.

Optimal haemoglobin concentrations in septic shock are uncertain. Values of 10–12 g dl^{-1} were not found to be superior to values of 7–9 g dl^{-1} (Hebert et al. 1999) in patients where shock had resolved, but at least in the initial phase of resuscitation, when Scv_{O_2} was less than 70%, raising haemoglobin concentrations to 10 g dl^{-1} improved survival (Rivers et al. 2001). In general, the use of other blood products such as fresh frozen plasma or platelets with the aim to correct laboratory variables is not recommended unless bleeding is obvious.

Adjunctive therapy of sepsis comprises the administration of low-dose corticosteroids, insulin, and, until recently, recombinant activated human protein C. Relative adrenal insufficiency, in sepsis, may render the patient susceptible to typical side-effects of this condition such as hypoglycaemia and low blood pressure. The rationale to administer exogenous hydrocortisone appears sound and a study in septic patients with shock demonstrated both a reduction in mortality and earlier resolution of shock (Annane et al. 2002). In this study, fludrocortisone was also administered. More recently published trials could not repeat these positive findings (Sprung et al. 2008; COIITSS Study Investigators 2010). Current recommendations are that hydrocortisone should only be given to patients in septic shock whose blood pressure responds poorly to vasopressor and fluid therapy (Dellinger et al. 2008).

Activated protein C regulates various pivotal functions in blood clotting, inflammation, and permeability of blood vessels (Mosnier et al. 2007). The use of activated protein C was primarily based on two large randomized trials. The PROWESS trial, with 1690 patients with Acute Physiology and Chronic Health Evaluation II scores greater than 25, documented a 6.1% reduction in absolute total mortality with a relative risk reduction of 19.4% and number needed to treat of 16 (Bernard et al. 2001). This effect was less pronounced in patients with recent surgery (Dellinger et al. 2008). The ADDRESS trial focused on less severely sick patients, and was stopped early (Abraham et al. 2005). Activated protein C also carried a significant risk of bleeding so that the European Medicines Agency mandated the PROWESS-SHOCK trial where no survival benefit was seen. The drug was withdrawn in October 2011 (http://www.fda.gov/Drugs/DrugSafety/ucm277114.htm).

Blood glucose control at concentrations around 100 mg dl^{-1} seemed promising (van den Berghe et al. 2001). Two multicentre trials could not corroborate these findings but reported increased mortality and higher incidence of hypoglycaemia when the so-called intensive insulin therapy approach was used (Brunkhorst et al. 2008; NICE-SUGAR Study Investigators 2009). The use of intensive insulin therapy, previously advocated in the Surviving Sepsis Campaign guidelines, has been rejected in newer national guidelines (Reinhart et al. 2010).

The complexity of sepsis associated with delayed recognition is responsible for the high mortality rates so early treatment is crucial to improve outcome. Anaesthetists are frequently the first physicians to intervene either during surgical procedures as part of source control or as part of a medical outreach team.

Cardiovascular complications

Myocardial infarction

The perioperative period carries a significant risk for acute cardiovascular complications such as myocardial infarction, pulmonary embolism, and stroke. A study from Spain found that in 4.3% of patients undergoing elective surgery with an intermediate to high surgery-specific risk, at least one of the following occurred: cardiac death, cerebrovascular death, non-fatal cardiac arrest, acute myocardial infarction, congestive heart failure, new cardiac arrhythmia, angina, or stroke (Sabate et al. 2011). This agrees with previously published data from other industrialized countries reporting a risk between 1% and 7% (Boersma et al. 2005; Devereaux et al. 2008). Devereaux et al. (2011) found an incidence for myocardial infarction alone of 5%. Given that more than 200 million major surgeries are performed annually (Weiser et al. 2008), this would suggest that approximately 10 million people suffer from perioperative myocardial infarction each year. The likelihood of developing a major perioperative cardiovascular adverse event is associated with a number of predictive factors including age, gender, type and length of surgery, and pre-existing medical conditions as listed in Box 89.3. Therefore, extensive knowledge and a detailed preoperative evaluation are required to identify specific risks and to react in a timely and appropriate way if one of these life-threatening events occurs.

As incidence of coronary artery disease in the industrialized world is high and a simple inconspicuous physical examination does not exclude the risk of a cardiovascular event, especially in asymptomatic patients older than 50 years of age, there should be a special focus on the preoperative evaluation (Lee et al. 1999). The assessment of asymptomatic patients and those with a known history of coronary heart disease should be tailored to both the individual patient and the planned procedure. Depending on the urgency of the surgical illness, the anaesthetist has to determine whether the patient requires further assessment that might decrease the risk of cardiovascular complications. A careful evaluation may result in changes in medication or of the scheduled procedure, including cancellation of the operation, so discussion not only with the patient but also all the involved parties is important. This includes planning of the monitoring during and after the procedure.

The first step typically includes a careful history to identify serious cardiac conditions such as prior angina or myocardial infarction but also significant dysrhythmias or valvular disease. The functional capacity of the patient is important. This is often reported in metabolic equivalents that show good correlation with other commonly used markers of exercise capacity such as treadmill testing. A metabolic equivalent of less than four is considered to be associated with a higher risk of cardiovascular complications. Physical examination and routine laboratory tests are also recommended and include assessment of vital signs such as heart rate, blood pressure, and pulse oximetry. Special attention should be paid to preoperative anaemia as a low haematocrit of less than 28% is associated with an increased rate of postoperative complications

Box 89.3 Predictors of major cardiovascular events in the perioperative period

- Age > 70 years
- Male gender
- High surgical risk
- History of coronary artery disease
- History of congestive heart failure
- History of previous cerebrovascular event
- History of chronic kidney disease
- History of arterial hypertension
- History of diabetes mellitus
- Heart rhythm other than sinus rhythm
- Functional capacity less than 4 metabolic equivalents
- Duration of surgery greater than 3 h
- Intraoperative tachycardia, bradycardia, or arterial hypotension.

Table 89.2 Procedure-related risk for myocardial ischaemia depending on the type of surgery

High (>5%)	Intermediate (1–5%)	Low (<1%)
Cardiothoracic surgery	Abdominal surgery	Breast/gynaecological surgery
Major vascular surgery	Endovascular aneurysm repair	Ophthalmologic surgery
	Head and neck surgery	Endocrine surgery
	Major urological surgery	Dental surgery

including myocardial ischaemia (Hogue et al. 1998). The type of surgery also influences the risk of myocardial ischaemia with the highest risk seen for major vascular surgery (Table 89.2).

A disease-specific approach to the evaluation of known or occult coronary artery disease, arterial hypertension, or valvular heart disease is extensively reviewed in the guidelines on perioperative cardiovascular evaluation and care for non-cardiac surgery (Fleisher et al. 2007) and in Chapters 41 and 42. Newer guidelines, which include cardiac assessment of the preoperative patient, have been published by the European Society of Anaesthesiology (De Hert et al. 2011). Both guidelines specifically address the administration or discontinuation of cardiovascular medications including statins and β-blockers and are outside the scope of this chapter.

While anaesthetic regimens and the drugs used clearly influence numerous physiological variables, to date, no single study shows superiority of one drug or technique over another with regard to overall outcome. In cardiac surgery, volatile anaesthetics have been shown to decrease the release of cardiac troponin and to improve left ventricular function when compared with intravenously administered agents such as propofol or midazolam (De Hert et al. 2004; Forlani et al. 2004). Whether these findings can be generalized to non-cardiac surgery patients remains elusive. The use of epidural anaesthesia techniques has been considered of benefit in abdominal surgery for early postoperative mobilization with studies suggesting improved perioperative outcomes in this group of patients; however, the benefit is offset by (dependent on the extent of the block) significant haemodynamic effects including arterial hypotension and blockade of cardioaccelerators. Despite these physiological considerations, randomized controlled trials in cardiac surgery patients did not show a higher incidence of myocardial infarction when thoracic epidural block was used (Liu et al. 2004). Similar findings were confirmed in several large trials in patients with other types of surgery including gastric, biliary, or colon surgery (Rigg et al. 2002; Park et al. 2011).

The prophylactic use of glyceryl trinitrate in patients at high cardiac risk cannot be recommended as the combination of a venodilator and anaesthetic agents may result in dramatic hypotension. Indeed, no study has documented improved outcomes with the prophylactic use of intravenous glyceryl trinitrate (Coriat et al. 1984; Dodds et al. 1993). However, maintenance of body temperature within a normothermic range does play a crucial role in preventing myocardial ischaemia. Temperatures below 35°C are associated with an increased risk of cardiac morbidity. Active warming with forced air results in a significantly reduced rate of cardiac events such as cardiac arrest, severe arrhythmias, and myocardial infarction (Frank et al. 1997). Other methods of maintaining normal body temperature may also include heating blankets, pre-warmed infusions, or intravascular approaches.

Hyperglycaemia is an independent risk factor for cardiovascular events and in patients with acute myocardial infarction, glucose concentrations exceeding 200 mg dl^{-1} are correlated with increased mortality. In contrast, strategies to tightly control blood glucose concentrations around 100 mg dl^{-1} had initially been promising in medical ICU patients (van den Berghe et al. 2001) but a multicentre trial reported increased mortality and incidence of hypoglycaemia when the so-called intensive insulin therapy approach was used (NICE-SUGAR Study Investigators 2009). No specific data with regard to the optimal glucose concentrations exist during the perioperative period. Most authorities engaged in the treatment of intensive care patients recommend concentrations between 140 and 180 mg dl^{-1} (Maerz and Akhtar 2011).

Definitive diagnosis of myocardial infarction has been problematic in the perioperative setting as there may be no clinical symptoms; subtle, if any, ECG changes that may be transient; and a creatine kinase-MB isoenzyme with limited value as a result of coexisting skeletal muscle injury (Adams et al. 1994). With the introduction of highly specific cardiac enzymes (i.e. cardiac troponins), the definition of myocardial infarction has dramatically changed (Thygesen et al. 2007). During general anaesthesia, sedation, or in combination with regional anaesthesia, myocardial ischaemia may be underdiagnosed as classical angina-like symptoms are hardly reported. More aggressive or invasive monitoring of cardiac function under general anaesthesia might therefore be helpful to identify myocardial dysfunction as a consequence of ischaemia. Most of these monitoring devices are either invasive (pulmonary artery catheter) or do not allow for continuous assessment (transoesophageal echocardiography). Pulmonary artery catheters may provide crucial knowledge about the haemodynamic status of an individual patient but their use is associated with potential life-threatening risks. Routine use of pulmonary artery catheters in patients who are unlikely to develop haemodynamic instability is therefore not recommended although its use may be reasonable in patients at risk for major haemodynamic disturbances. The decision should be based on three parameters: patient disease, surgical procedure (i.e. intraoperative and postoperative fluid shifts), and practice setting (experience in use and interpretation of results), because incorrect interpretation of the data from a pulmonary artery catheter may also cause harm (Jain et al. 2003). Intraoperative ST-segment monitoring is recognized as a tool to detect myocardial ischaemia, but the sensitivity and specificity of ST-segment changes vary widely in different reports. Nevertheless, occurrence of such changes is—depending on the magnitude and duration of the alteration—associated with cardiac morbidity and mortality (Landesberg 2005). Different patient monitors use differing algorithms and most available data have been extracted with regular Holter monitors. It appears appropriate in patients with long-lasting ST-segment changes to perform further investigations such as laboratory testing of cardiac troponin and a 12-lead electrocardiogram. Apart from ST-segment changes, perioperative myocardial infarction may become apparent as severe haemodynamic instability (i.e. arterial hypotension) with or without concomitant dysrhythmias. In this context, transoesophageal echocardiography to examine cardiac function in patients who do not respond to corrective therapy is strongly recommended (American Society of Anesthesiologists 2010). Use of transoesophageal echocardiography can identify wall motion abnormalities that are indicative of myocardial ischaemia and link these alterations to the corresponding coronary artery (Fig. 89.1).

The most severe complication of myocardial infarction is cardiogenic shock, which develops in approximately 5–10% of patients. This carries a bad prognosis with mortality rates as high as 70% (Reynolds and Hochman 2008). The pathophysiology of cardiogenic shock is dependent on the extent of myocardial injury, which causes both systolic and diastolic dysfunction, with a concurrent decrease in cardiac output. This, in turn, aggravates coronary and systemic perfusion deficits resulting in cell death in the border zone of the infarct region and peripheral arterial vasoconstriction. Interestingly, cardiac output and left ventricular ejection fraction

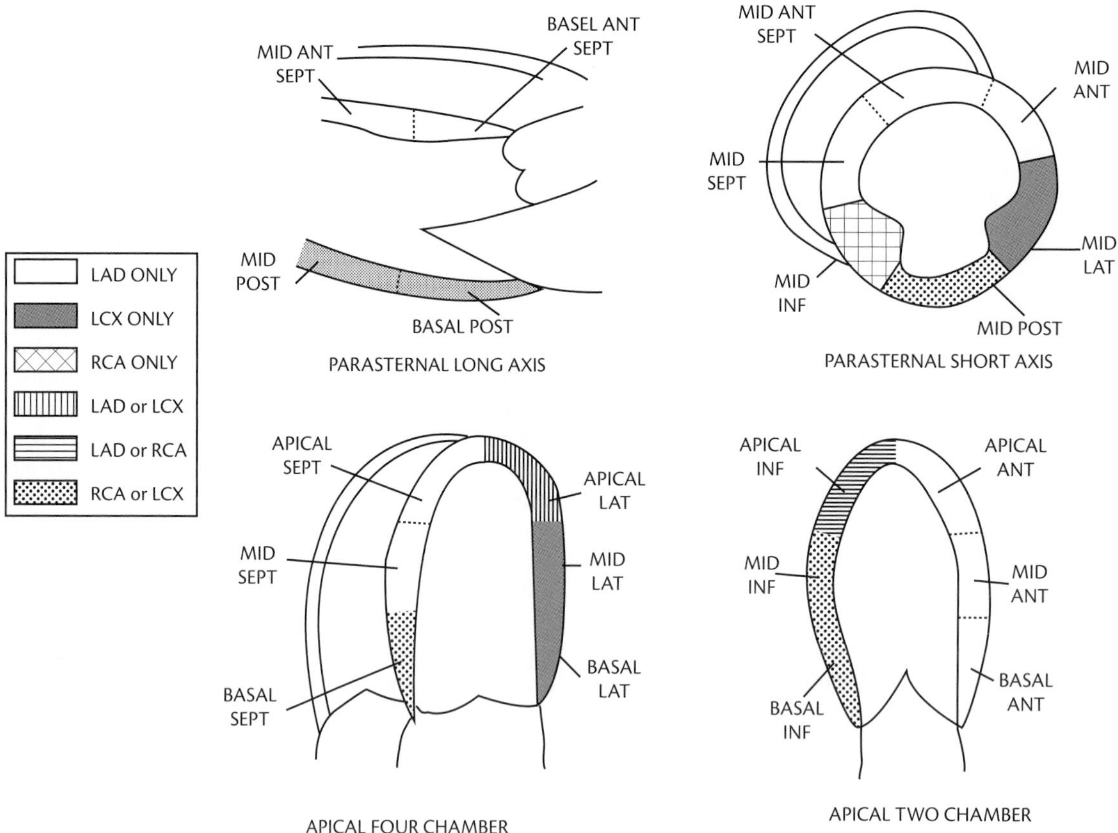

Figure 89.1 Distribution areas of the three main coronary vessels.
Reproduced from Winter R et al., 'Real-time perfusion adenosine stress echocardiography in the coronary care unit: a feasible bedside tool for predicting coronary artery stenosis in patients with acute coronary syndrome', *European Journal of Echocardiography*, 2005, 6, 1, pp. 31–40, by permission of European Society of Cardiology.

are not the only determinants of the development of cardiogenic shock, as many patients with severely impaired heart function do not show these typical haemodynamic derangements (Ramanathan et al. 2004). Some data indicate that the use of certain cardiovascular drugs such as angiotensin-converting enzyme inhibitors and β-blockers may trigger cardiogenic shock and this is true for intravenous opioids such as morphine, particularly during the perioperative period (Meine et al. 2005). Diagnosis of cardiogenic shock with a pulmonary artery catheter shows signs of elevated left-sided filling pressures (left ventricular end-diastolic pressure >18 mm Hg) and decreased cardiac index (<1.8 litres min^{-1} m^{-2} without support or <2.0–2.2 litres min^{-1} m^{-2} with support). The clinical reality would probably be more accurately reflected by the following scenario: unexplained and sudden hypotension, which does not respond to fluid challenge, together with clinical signs of tissue hypoperfusion should prompt either transoesophageal or transthoracic echocardiography, which will identify a severely depressed left ventricle with surrogate parameters of elevated cardiac filling pressures.

On diagnosis, treatment needs to be initiated. General measures include maintenance of arterial oxygenation and pH values at near normal concentrations. Inspired oxygen fraction should be titrated to target a peripheral oxygen saturation between 95% and 98%. The threshold to initiate mechanical ventilation in a spontaneously breathing patient should be low. Haemodynamic support with inotropes to titrate arterial pressures to values of around 65–70 mm Hg is usually achieved with noradrenaline, which besides its potent vasoconstrictor effects, also shows inotropic actions. Dobutamine can be added to increase the cardiac index. A downside of catecholamines is that they increase myocardial oxygen consumption and may further harm an already failing ventricle. Newer studies in heart failure patients and using alternative drugs such as vasopressin or levosimendan have failed to show favourable results although many centres are using these agents (Mebazaa et al. 2007). Intensive insulin therapy is recommended as it has been shown to improve survival in patients with cardiogenic shock (Antmann et al. 2004).

A mainstay for haemodynamic support in cardiogenic shock has been the use of intra-aortic balloon counter-pulsation (Fig. 89.2). These mechanical devices use helium-driven balloons to reduce afterload while concurrently increasing coronary perfusion. Use of intra-aortic balloon counter-pulsation is independently associated with higher survival rates regardless whether percutaneous coronary intervention, fibrinolytic therapy, or no reperfusion has been used (Chen et al. 2003). However, a multicentre trial has not consistently found improved outcomes for the use of intra-aortic balloon counter-pulsation (Thiele et al. 2012). Complications include a significant risk of bleeding, limb ischaemia, and renal failure, but the incidence of these has consistently decreased over the last decade. An alternative is the miniaturized rotary blood pump which can not only augment a failing left ventricle with flows between 2.5 and 5 litres min^{-1} (Fig. 89.2), but also unload the left ventricle from volume issues. Direct comparison between percutaneous

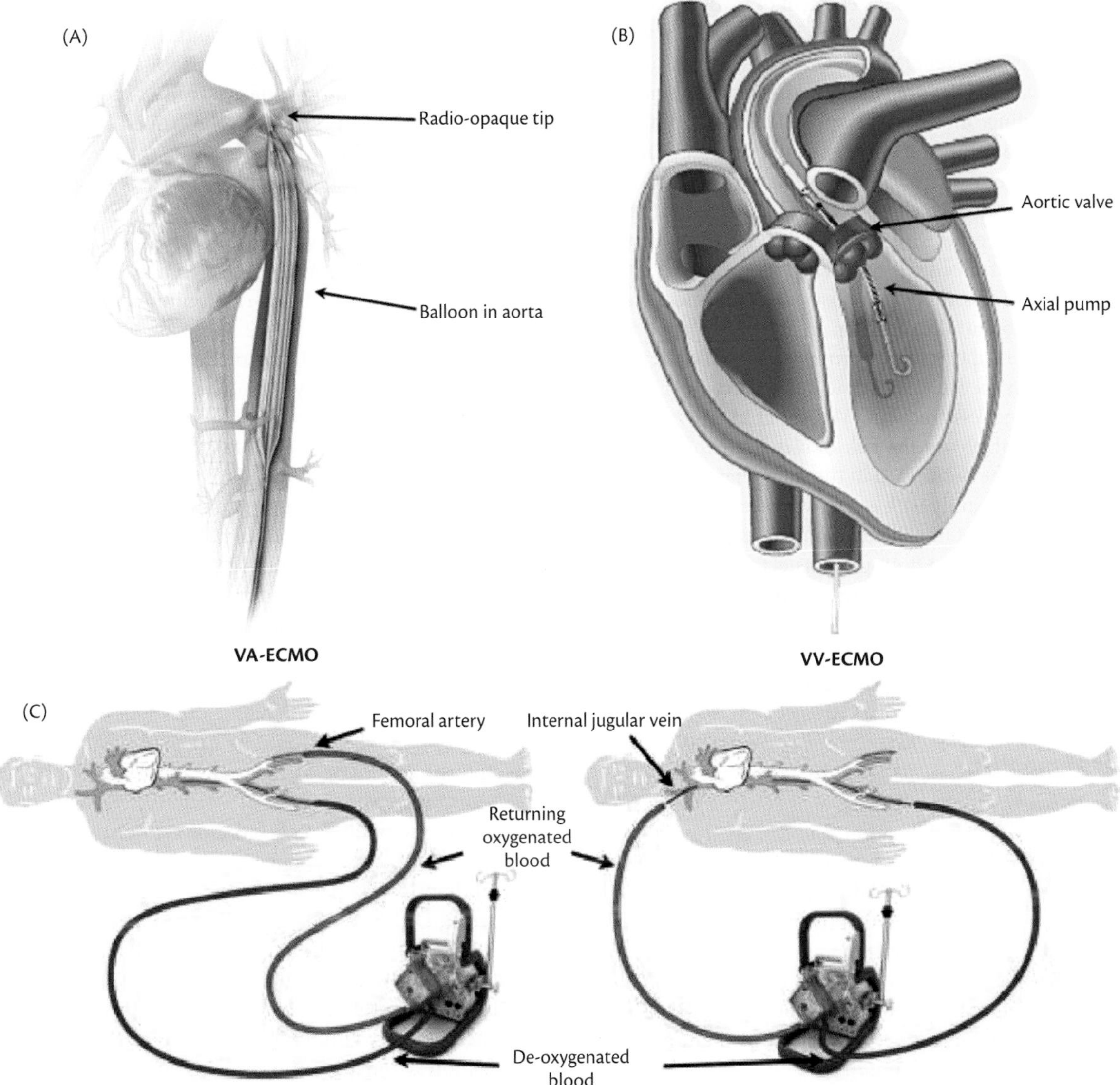

Figure 89.2 Illustration of commercially available systems for mechanical circulatory support. (A) Intra-aortic balloon pump; (B) microaxial rotary blood pump (Impella® 2.5); and (C) centrifugal blood pump with extracorporeal membrane oxygenation.

(A) Reproduced with permission from Maquet GmbH & Co. KG, Rastatt, Germany.

(B) Reproduced with permission from Abiomed.

(C) Reproduced with permission from Maquet GmbH & Co. KG, Rastatt, Germany.

support with Impella® pumps (Abiomed, Danvers, MA, USA) and intra-aortic balloon pumps has not shown clear benefit (Cheng et al. 2009).

Persisting shock may require treatment that is even more aggressive, with extracorporeal life support including veno-arterial extracorporeal membrane oxygenation or ventricular assist devices (Fig. 89.2). Use of such a device offers the advantage to augment both ventricles and to bridge the patient to a condition in which a definite treatment option can be evaluated. This approach is highly invasive and needs a dedicated interdisciplinary team that is properly skilled. Single-centre experiences consistently report survival rates ranging from 25% to 39%. The decision to initiate extracorporeal life support in patients not responding to conventional therapy including the use of an intra-aortic balloon pump will always be dependent on local experience and several individual factors. These individual factors include patient-related data such as prolonged cardiopulmonary resuscitation with inadequate perfusion, advanced age, advanced malignancy, and existing organ dysfunction (advanced chronic obstructive pulmonary disease, interstitial lung disease, liver cirrhosis, previous stroke with significant disability, dementia, and end-stage renal failure), but also local circumstances (availability of a 24/7 team, availability of appropriate equipment, and distance to a centre providing extracorporeal support). Notwithstanding these limitations, management of patients with refractory cardiogenic shock should include consideration of early access to extracorporeal life support until the benefits of revascularization are realized. The devices serve as a bridge to decision or transplantation but if the latter is not possible, then implantable ventricular assist devices hold the promise of a viable destination therapy (Cove and MacLaren 2010).

The cornerstone and only causal treatment of myocardial infarction is to re-establish blood flow to the clogged coronary artery. This requires the use of agents with a dramatic impact on blood coagulation and will predispose patients with recent surgery to a higher risk of bleeding. International guidelines deal with indication, timing, and procedures of coronary interventions. However, few data are available in the perioperative setting, as historically patients with recent surgery have been excluded in trials of fibrinolytic agents, which are otherwise impressive in terms of improved outcomes. The risk of bleeding, however, has to be put in relation to the very high mortality rate observed in surgical patients who develop symptomatic myocardial infarction (Mangano and Goldman 1995). The superiority of primary coronary angioplasty was demonstrated in the late 1990s, and since then, worries about bleeding have become less frequent (Weaver et al. 1997). No prospective data are available on the risk of bleeding when coronary interventions have to be performed in the immediate perioperative period. Only one small study with a retrospective design evaluated the safety and feasibility of immediate coronary angiography in the acute perioperative setting. Of 48 patients, 41 underwent angioplasty, 3 were referred for bypass surgery, and 1 was treated with intracoronary therapy after unsuccessful angioplasty. The overall survival of 65% in this series (31 of 48 patients) suggests that an immediate invasive strategy may reduce mortality among postoperative myocardial infarction patients (Berger et al. 2001).

Pulmonary embolism

Pulmonary embolism is defined as partial or complete occlusion of a branch of the pulmonary circulation, and usually this will be the result of venous thromboembolism from large veins of the lower limbs and pelvic region (Tapson 2008). Factors partially related to the perioperative period, which predispose patients to an increased risk of pulmonary embolism, are shown in Table 89.3 (Anderson and Spencer 2003). Several operations also carry a high risk of periprocedural pulmonary embolism not from venous thromboembolism but as a result of air, foreign bodies, bone marrow, or amniotic fluid entering the pulmonary circulation. Regardless of the source of the embolus, the haemodynamic alterations are related to the degree to which the pulmonary circulation is occluded. Clinical symptoms and signs may be minimal with a small distal thrombus or result in sudden death when a main branch of the pulmonary artery is suddenly clogged. The clinical manifestations such as sudden dyspnoea, tachypnoea, tachycardia, and chest pain are non-specific and can be caused by other acute illnesses, and under general anaesthesia or in sedated patients most of these symptoms and signs are not seen. As with perioperative myocardial infarction, suspicion of pulmonary embolism may derive from a sudden and unexpected decrease in arterial pressure, accompanied by a decrease in end-tidal carbon dioxide, which does not or only temporarily responds to volume administration. This may be accompanied by other disturbances in gas exchange.

Table 89.3 Predisposing factors for pulmonary embolism

High risk	Moderate risk	Low risk
Fractures of the leg or hip Joint surgery Major trauma Spinal cord injury	Malignancy Chemotherapy Central venous line Oral contraceptive therapy Hormone replacement History of venous thromboembolism Genetic risk factors (including antithromin 111 deficiency and factor V Leiden)	Increasing age Obesity Laparoscopic surgery Bed rest >3 days Pregnancy

The European Society of Cardiology guideline uses a haemodynamic profile to discriminate between high-risk and non-high-risk pulmonary embolism. High-risk pulmonary embolism is classified as systolic blood pressure less than 90 mm Hg or a decrease of greater than 40 mm Hg for more than 15 min that was not triggered by new-onset arrhythmia, hypovolaemia, or sepsis (Torbicki et al. 2008). This stratification allows a risk-adapted management in which patients who are in shock but haemodynamically stable need to undergo immediate computed tomography. If the patient is deemed too unstable then echocardiography should be carried out. Abnormal right ventricular wall motion, right ventricular dilatation, paradoxical septal motion, tricuspid valve insufficiency, increased pulmonary artery pressure, inferior vena cava congestion, and a dilated pulmonary artery are typical echocardiographic signs and highly indicative of pulmonary embolism. Sometimes thrombi can be directly visualized in the pulmonary artery. In patients who are haemodynamically stable, the probability of a pulmonary embolism should be calculated before laboratory and imaging studies are performed. The most widely accepted score is the Wells score which is based on clinical variables that are each graded between 1 and 3. A score of greater than 6 carries a high risk while a score lesser than 2 signifies a low risk of having pulmonary embolism (Wells et al. 2000). Further diagnostic steps include measuring D-dimers, a degradation product of fibrin in the presence of plasmin. The negative predictive value is extremely high so that further testing in patients with low and intermediate risk can then be omitted. Unfortunately, in the perioperative setting, D-dimer testing is limited by the fact that recent surgery induces coagulation system activation and hence elevated concentrations of D-dimers, so the test is non-specific (Kabrhel et al. 2010). If clinical signs of pulmonary embolism have been found, the Wells score is high, and the D-dimer testing is positive, imaging studies should be performed. There are no specific chest radiography changes in pulmonary embolism but it may reveal other pathologies to explain the deterioration of the patient. Multidetector computed tomography with intravenous contrast is mandated (Stein et al. 2006), and if the scan suggests emboli in the pulmonary arteries it should be extended to check the pelvic and femoral region for deep vein thrombosis.

In patients who are haemodynamically stable, treatment of pulmonary embolism is by the administration of heparin or fondaparinux. Low-molecular-weight heparin, although equally effective in resolution of the clot, has advantages over unfractionated heparin as it has greater bioavailability and a lower incidence of heparin-induced thrombocytopenia. In addition, monitoring is usually not necessary. Patients with severe renal insufficiency and a higher risk of bleeding are preferably treated with unfractionated heparin targeting an activated partial thromboplastin time (aPTT) of 1.5–2.5 times of the normal value. If heparin-induced thrombocytopenia has been diagnosed or is suspected, the use of a direct thrombin inhibitor such as argatroban or lepirudin should be considered. The role of oral direct thrombin inhibitors (dabigatran), or oral anti-factor Xa inhibitors (rivaroxaban; apixaban), has not been established but several phase three clinical trials are underway. The use of idraparinux would seem very attractive, as it requires dosing only once a week (Equinox Investigators 2011).

Patients who are haemodynamically unstable with high-risk pulmonary embolism require immediate thrombolysis to reduce right ventricular afterload and normalize right ventricular function. In non-surgical settings, approximately 92% of patients respond to thrombolysis within the first 36 h (Meneveau et al. 2006). The currently approved thrombolytic regimens that are endorsed by the European Society of Cardiology are shown in Table 89.4. The inherent risk of bleeding when thrombolysis is applied is significant, summing up to a cumulative rate of major bleeding of 13% and fatal or intracranial haemorrhage in 1.8% of patients (Torbicki et al. 2008). While the benefits of thrombolysis are well documented with regard to resolving thromboembolic obstruction with resultant beneficial effects on haemodynamic parameters, its use, in terms of clinical outcomes, has not yet been confirmed (Goldhaber et al. 1993).

In the perioperative period, the risk of bleeding has to be carefully weighed against the mortality rate of up to 52% in patients with shock as a result of pulmonary embolism (Goldhaber et al. 1999). In this context, otherwise absolute contraindications (haemorrhagic stroke, gastrointestinal bleeding, or recent major surgery/trauma) for the use of thrombolytic agents might become relative. Findings from a registry suggest that even in these settings, thrombolysis can be safely used although large-scale data, as in perioperative myocardial infarction, is lacking (Kasper et al. 1997). The decision to initiate thrombolytic therapy in a patient with recent surgery or even during surgery will remain an individual one after carefully evaluating the risks and benefits of such an approach. In centres with cardiothoracic surgery capabilities, pulmonary embolectomy might be a rescue option if thrombolysis is deemed too risky or a patient does not respond to lysis (Leacche et al. 2005). Other techniques occasionally used are percutaneous catheter embolectomy and fragmentation although data are limited to case reports or small series (Kucher et al. 2005).

Right ventricular failure with consecutive cardiogenic shock is the most common cause of death in pulmonary embolism, so especially if thrombolysis has been deemed too risky, a strategy for supportive treatment is required. Fluid administration has to be carefully titrated to avoid further mechanical overstretch. Noradrenaline is recommended to maintain arterial pressures around 65–70 mm Hg while dobutamine should be added to improve the cardiac index

Table 89.4 Thrombolytic regimens for pulmonary embolism

Streptokinase	250 000 IU as a loading dose over 30 min, followed by 100 000 IU h^{-1} over 12–24 h
	Accelerated regimen: 1.5 million IU over 2 h
Urokinase	4400 IU kg^{-1} as a loading dose over 10 min, followed by 4400 IU kg^{-1} h^{-1} over 12–24 h
	Accelerated regimen: 3 million IU over 2 h
Recombinant tissue plasminogen activator	100 mg over 2 h *or*
	0.6 mg kg^{-1} over 15 min (maximum dose 50 mg)

only in normotensive patients (Jardin et al. 1985). As the majority of patients with cardiogenic shock as a result of right ventricular failure will present with arterial hypotension, adrenaline might be superior in this setting (Layish and Tapson 1997). The calcium-sensitizer levosimendan may restore right ventricular to pulmonary arterial coupling in acute pulmonary embolism as a result of combined pulmonary vasodilation and increased right ventricular contractility (Kerbaul et al. 2007). Reducing right ventricular afterload as a consequence of pulmonary embolism can be achieved by the administration of agents that selectively dilate the pulmonary circulation (Zamanian et al. 2007). These drugs might be delivered via inhalation (nitric oxide, epoprostenol) or as enteral medication (sildenafil, endothelin antagonists). It is not known if these approaches are associated with improved outcomes, but they are frequently used in modern intensive care medicine despite the enormous costs.

Perioperative stroke

Stroke is a major contributor to morbidity and mortality. Moreover, it is the most frequent cause of long-term disability and is associated with an enormous burden for both society and the individual (American Heart Association 2012). Data from the American College of Surgeons National Surgical Quality Improvement Program found that the overall incidence of perioperative stroke in non-cardiac and non-neurological surgery is only around 0.1% (Mashour et al. 2011). However, in selected procedures such as explorative laparotomy, amputation, and colectomy in patients over the age of 65 years, the rate increases up to 1.1%. Besides age, other risk factors include recent myocardial infarction, acute kidney injury, dialysis, and hypertension (Mashour et al. 2011). In cardiac surgery, the rate of perioperative stroke is, depending on the procedure, much higher with rates reported to be as high as 12% (Naylor and Bown 2011).

Although the overall incidence in the perioperative period is much lower than that of myocardial infarction or pulmonary embolism, the consequences of perioperative stroke are usually catastrophic. This is reflected in the mortality rate for perioperative stroke, which is reported to be between 26% and 87% (Bateman et al. 2009). This is in stark contrast to the mortality rate reported in stroke victims in non-surgical settings, which has been found to be around 16% (El Saed et al. 2006). Reasons for this might include a delay in recognition because of anaesthesia. Therefore, anaesthetists should be aware of risk factors, rapid identification, and possible treatment strategies to reduce morbidity and mortality as a consequence of perioperative stroke.

It is now commonly believed that an inflammatory response even from outside the brain displays a major contributor for both stroke susceptibility and severity (Elkind 2010). As the perioperative period is associated with a dramatic increase in various inflammatory cascades that include the release of cytokines such as interleukin-1 and interleukin-6, this might also explain the increased mortality observed in perioperative stroke. A minority of patients develop immediate intraoperative stroke but rather it is diagnosed after the first postoperative day and this may be attributable to delayed recognition in patients recovering from anaesthesia. As in non-surgical settings, the vast majority of strokes are as a result of thrombosis and there are several predisposing factors in the perioperative period which include the previously mentioned inflammatory state. Hypercoagulability and dysfunction of the endothelium are common during and after surgical procedures and vessels are prone to plaque rupture, vasospasms, and thrombus formation. An increase in stroke incidence was reported in large trials of perioperative β-blockade, which was associated with arterial hypotension although the temporal relationship has not been fully elucidated (Devereuax et al. 2008). Perioperative stroke is therefore probably more complex in its aetiology and the term watershed stroke is often used to describe the fact that ischaemia occurs in regions that are localized in the border zones between the territories of two major arteries in the brain (Bamford et al. 1991).

After a recent stroke, prevention of perioperative stroke can be achieved by optimal timing if elective surgery is planned. Postponing the case for a longer period seems reasonable as it has been shown that cerebral autoregulation and the vasomotor response to carbon dioxide is impaired for up to 6 months after a recent stroke (Aries et al. 2010). Patients with high-grade (>70%) symptomatic carotid artery stenosis should be informed about their high risk of perioperative stroke and carotid endarterectomy should be offered, but if the stenosis is less than 50% then endarterectomy is contraindicated. Re-vascularization for patients with high-grade stenosis but who are asymptomatic remains controversial (Liapis et al. 2009). Intraoperative blood pressure management is important given the fact that the majority of perioperative strokes are pathophysiologically watershed infarctions. Maintenance of adequate cerebral perfusion is also mandatory in case of a cerebral embolic event. It remains difficult to define optimal blood pressure targets because of a great inter-individual range observed for the lower limit of autoregulation (Larsen et al. 1994). Common practice is to maintain mean or systolic blood pressure within 20% of the baseline blood pressure, which is defined as the first arterial pressure recorded in a patient entering the operating theatre.

Treatment of perioperative stroke is dependent on timely recognition. This is hampered in the early postoperative period because of a lack of classification of signs or scoring systems that might allow earlier identification of stroke symptoms (Whiteley et al. 2011). Some hospitals have successfully introduced acute stroke teams which aim to bring suspected stroke patients to appropriate imaging (computed tomography) within 25 min after the onset of symptoms (Nazir et al. 2009). The only proved treatment for ischaemic stroke is the intravenous administration of recombinant tissue plasminogen activator but this is not advocated by international guidelines, within 14 days after major surgery (Adams et al. 2007). It remains to be seen if more tailored therapy including endovascular approaches may be useful in the surgical setting (Hopkins and Ecker 2008).

Massive bleeding

Trauma and consequences thereof are the leading cause of death in patients under the age of 45 in Europe and the United States (Soreide et al. 2009). Anaesthetists are involved in every aspect of the treatment of patients with severe trauma: from the initial resuscitation on the scene, the transport to the hospital, and the evaluation process in the emergency department. Anaesthetists are also an integral part of the team initially performing damage control surgery. A detailed guideline concerning the treatment of bleeding patients after major trauma has been published to guide the resuscitation process (Rossaint et al. 2010).

Uncontrolled, massive bleeding accounts for the majority of early deaths in traumatized patients (Hoyt 2004). Massive bleeding is defined as loss of the total circulating blood volume within 24 h or loss of 50% of the total circulating blood volume within 3 h or continuing blood loss of more than 150 ml min^{-1} (Stainsby et al. 2000). Continuing exsanguination results in hypovolaemic shock with concomitant acidosis and heat loss, both of which culminate in coagulopathy, which further aggravates bleeding, acidosis, and hypothermia. This vicious circle has been coined the 'lethal triad'. The presence of this clinical entity is associated with a fourfold increase in mortality (MacLeod et al. 2003). To avoid ongoing bleeding in a period where definitive surgery is not possible to stop haemorrhage, damage control resuscitation is advocated. This comprises the correction of acidosis, the administration of calcium, and the preservation of normothermia to combat the lethal triad. Furthermore, the concept also consists of permissive hypotension, which allows for systolic blood pressures of around 90 mm Hg in an attempt to improve clot formation and to minimize excessive volume administration, which will further aggravate coagulopathy. Although the scientific evidence for such an approach is low (Bickell et al. 1994; Turner et al. 2000), some professional societies advocate permissive hypotension if there is no suspicion of traumatic brain injury which would require higher perfusion thresholds.

The time interval between initial trauma and ultimate surgical control should be kept as short as possible, and measures taken on the scene (or at best while already on the transport) should only include those necessary to stabilize vital parameters (Cothren et al. 2007). This changing paradigm represents a compromise between the 'scoop and run' and 'stay and play' approach and is coined 'treat and go'. However, common practice and acknowledgement of the mentioned pathophysiological changes should also include a stepwise approach for the necessary surgical procedures in the case of severe haemorrhagic shock and coagulopathy. This avoids further aggravation of the lethal triad and includes stabilization of fractures by external fixation and packing for abdominal organ injury. Using this so-called damage control surgery strategy results in shorter operation durations and increased survival (Rotondo et al. 1993). This also applies to the use of external stabilization of pelvic fractures, which can result in dramatic bleeding, and are best managed by external fixation. Only where haemodynamic stabilization cannot be achieved with this approach, should more aggressive treatment including laparotomy and tamponade of the inner pelvis be performed. The use of angiographic embolization should always be considered early and might be an alternative to a surgical strategy (Tai et al. 2011; Thorson et al. 2012).

Invasive ventilation is used in many severely injured patients to ensure adequate oxygenation and airway patency in neurologically compromised trauma victims. Special attention should be paid to the prevention of excessive hyperventilation, which seems common in trauma and cardiac arrest victims and is associated with dismal outcomes (Davis et al. 2003; Aufderheide et al. 2004). Coagulopathy is present already in up to 30% of patients after severe trauma at the time of reaching the emergency department (Maegele et al. 2007). Recognition of coagulopathy is based on laboratory findings, which should be performed as early as possible including determination of prothrombin time, aPTT, thrombocyte count, and fibrinogen concentration. Given the fact that many of these measurements are time-consuming, newly available point-of-care testing methods including thromboelastography might be an attractive alternative (Ganter and Hofer 2008).

Initial resuscitation of patients with massive bleeding includes the use of intravenous fluids to maintain adequate organ perfusion. However, there is still ongoing debate about the fluid of choice. Trials comparing crystalloids and colloids differ substantially with regard to study design, patient selection, and outcome. Some data have suggested that, in settings other than trauma, colloids are associated with increased mortality (Schierhout and Roberts 1998). Therefore, the use of crystalloid fluids is advocated as first-line therapy. Hyperoncotic solutions can be considered (Rossaint et al. 2010). Coagulopathy will require blood products including the use of fresh frozen plasma, packed red blood cells, thrombocytes, and the administration of haemostatic therapies. Bleeding-associated anaemia, changes in the rheology of circulating blood, and a deficiency in adenosine diphosphate will affect thrombocyte adhesion. Packed red blood cells should therefore be administered, targeting haemoglobin concentrations of 7–9 g dl^{-1}. Higher haemoglobin concentrations of around 9–10 g dl^{-1} are associated with better cerebral oxygenation in patients with traumatic brain injury in some studies (Smith et al. 2005) but there are also robust data showing no effects (Zygun et al. 2009) and one study that linked increased use of packed red blood cells to increased mortality (Salim et al. 2008). Thus, this recommendation also applies for patients with traumatic brain injury (Rossaint et al. 2010). Fresh frozen plasma contains several coagulation factors and is widely used in patients requiring massive transfusion. It is recommended to substitute plasma early with amounts of 10–15 ml kg^{-1} body weight in a ratio of 1:1 with packed red blood cells (Holcomb et al. 2008; Spinella et al. 2008; Rossaint et al. 2010). Thrombocytes are essential for clot formation, although normal ranges are above 150 000 μl^{-1}, spontaneous bleeding is rarely seen in patients with counts greater than 50 000 μl^{-1} (Hunt et al. 1998). Substitution of thrombocytes/ platelets is therefore recommended below this threshold (Rossaint et al. 2010). It is noteworthy that volume overload as a consequence of massive transfusion may be associated with compromise of the cardiopulmonary system albeit a causal relationship has not yet been proved (Nathens 2006).

Fibrinogen is a glycoprotein that is synthesized in the liver. During massive bleeding, critical concentrations below 2 g $litre^{-1}$ are often found. Early substitution of fibrinogen is associated with decreased blood loss (Stinger et al. 2008; Solomon et al. 2010) and it is therefore recommended to administer fibrinogen when plasma concentrations are below 1.5–2 g $litre^{-1}$ (Rossaint et al. 2010). Use of prothrombin complex concentrates are mandated only in patients with a known deficiency in vitamin K-dependent coagulation factors, mostly because of liver insufficiency or because of a treatment with coumarin derivatives (Bruce and Nokes 2008). In recent years, numerous case reports have been published on the use of recombinant activated coagulation factor VII (rFVIIa). While its use is undoubtedly indicated in patients with congenital or inherited deficiency of FVIIa, its use in patients with massive bleeding is less clear. Only one randomized controlled trial demonstrated reduced transfusion requirements and a lesser incidence of acute lung injury in patients with blunt abdominal trauma (Boffard et al. 2005). Use of rFVIIa is recommended only when conventional treatment including surgical control does not terminate continuing bleeding (Rossaint et al. 2010). Another detrimental side-effect of massive bleeding and the activation of the coagulation system is hyperfibrinolysis. As aprotinin has been taken off the market following concerns about its safety in cardiac surgery patients, tranexamic acid is currently widely used. Tranexamic acid has been shown to reduce mortality in trauma patients with massive bleeding in a recent large randomized controlled trial (CRASH-2 Trial Collaborators 2010). The use of tranexamic acid in trauma patients with massive bleeding is therefore recommended, using a bolus of 10–15 mg kg^{-1} body weight followed by a continuous infusion of 1–5 mg kg^{-1} body weight h^{-1}. Desmopressin is a synthesized analogue of the antidiuretic hormone, which increases the plasma concentrations of factor VIII and von Willebrand factor. Two meta-analyses have shown reduced transfusion requirements but no impact on mortality when desmopressin was administered in settings other than

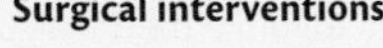

Figure 89.3 Initial management of massive bleeding in trauma patients.

trauma (Creszenzi et al. 2008). Routine use is therefore not recommended but may be considered in patients receiving antiplatelet therapy (Rossaint et al. 2010).

Management of traumatized patients with massive bleeding is one of the major challenges in modern medicine as it requires not only detailed knowledge of the pathophysiological changes but is also dependent on highly motivated and skilled teams with the ability to communicate and to plan the best approach for the treatment of the patient. The current guideline on massive bleeding in traumatized patients marks a big step forward in this process and an algorithm combining surgical interventions and coagulation management, together with stabilization of vital parameters is displayed in Figure 89.3.

Conclusion

The number of patients of increasing age undergoing more complex surgical procedures is steadily increasing. Operations that would not have been considered 10 years ago are now commonly performed. With increasing age and comorbidities, the probability of developing severe complications increases concurrently. Anaesthetists are crucial in the early management of patients developing or presenting with acute illness in the peri- and postoperative period. Accurate and timely recognition of life-threatening conditions such as sepsis, myocardial infarction, pulmonary embolism, and massive bleeding require in-depth knowledge of physiological and pathophysiological processes. Only early and prompt interventions hold promise for improved patient outcome and reduced morbidity.

Declaration of interest

Dr Marx has received research grants and honoraria for lecturing from Edwards Life Sciences and consulting, research grants and honoraria for lecturing from B. Braun Melsungen AG.

References

Abraham E, Laterre PF, Garg R, *et al.* Drotrecogin alfa (activated) for adults with severe sepsis and a low risk of death. *N Engl J Med* 2005; **353**: 1332–41

Adams HP, Jr, del Zoppo G, Alberts MJ, *et al.* Guidelines for the early management of adults with ischemic stroke: a guideline from the American Heart Association/American Stroke Association Stroke Council, Clinical Cardiology Council, Cardiovascular Radiology and Intervention Council, and the Atherosclerotic Peripheral Vascular Disease and Quality of Care Outcomes in Research Interdisciplinary Working Groups: The American Academy of Neurology affirms the value of this guideline as an educational tool for neurologists. *Stroke* 2007; **38**: 1655–711

Adams JE 3rd, Sicard GA, Allen BT, *et al.* Diagnosis of perioperative myocardial infarction with measurement of cardiac troponin I. *N Engl J Med* 1994; **330**: 670–4

Alberti C, Brun-Buisson C, Burchardi H, *et al.* Epidemiology of sepsis and infection in ICU patients from an international multicentre cohort study. *Intensive Care Med* 2002; **28**: 108–21

American Heart Association. Heart disease and stroke statistics—2012 update. A report from the American Heart Association. *Circulation* 2012; **125**: e2–e220

American Society of Anesthesiologists and Society of Cardiovascular Anesthesiologists Task Force on Transesophageal Echocardiography. Practice guidelines for perioperative transesophageal echocardiography. An updated report by the American Society of Anesthesiologists and the Society of Cardiovascular Anesthesiologists Task Force on Transesophageal Echocardiography. *Anesthesiology* 2010; **112**: 1084–96

Anderson FA Jr, Spencer FA. Risk factors for venous thromboembolism. *Circulation* 2003; **107**: 9–16

Angus DC, Barnato AE, Linde-Zwirble WT, *et al.* Use of intensive care at the end of life in the United States: an epidemiologic study. *Crit Care Med* 2004; **32**: 638–43

Annane D, Sébille V, Charpentier C, *et al.* Effect of treatment with low doses of hydrocortisone and fludrocortisone on mortality in patients with septic shock. *JAMA* 2002; **288**: 862–71

Antman EM, Anbe DT, Armstrong PW, *et al.* ACC/AHA guidelines for the management of patients with ST-elevation myocardial infarction: executive summary: a report of the American College of Cardiology/American Heart Association Task Force on Practice Guidelines (Writing Committee to Revise the 1999 Guidelines for the Management of Patients With Acute Myocardial Infarction). *Circulation* 2004; **110**: 588–636

Aries MJ, Elting JW, De Keyser J, Kremer BP, Vroomen PC. Cerebral autoregulation in stroke: a review of transcranial Doppler studies. *Stroke* 2010; **41**: 2697–704

Armitage JN, van der Meulen JH; Royal College of Surgeons Co-morbidity Consensus Group. Identifying co-morbidity in surgical patients using administrative data with the Royal College of Surgeons Charlson Score. *Br J Surg* 2010; **97**: 772–81

Aufderheide TP, Sigurdsson G, Pirrallo RG, *et al.* Hyperventilation-induced hypotension during cardiopulmonary resuscitation. *Circulation* 2004; **109**: 1960–5

Balestra GM, Legrand M, Ince C. Microcirculation and mitochondria in sepsis: getting out of breath. *Curr Opin Anaesthesiol* 2009; **22**: 184–90

Bamford J, Sandercock P, Dennis M, Burn J, Warlow C. Classification and natural history of clinically identifiable subtypes of cerebral infarction. *Lancet* 1991; **337**: 1521–6

Bateman BT, Schumacher HC, Wang S, Shaefi S, Berman MF. Perioperative acute ischemic stroke in noncardiac and nonvascular surgery: incidence, risk factors, and outcomes. *Anesthesiology* 2009; **110**: 231–8

Berger PB, Bellot V, Malcolm R, *et al.* An immediate invasive strategy for the treatment of acute myocardial infarction early after noncardiac surgery. *Am J Cardiol* 2001; **87**: 1100–2

Bernard GR, Vincent JL, Laterre PF, *et al.* Efficacy and safety of recombinant human activated protein c for severe sepsis. *N Engl J Med* 2001; **344**: 699–709

Bickell WH, Wall MJ, Jr, Pepe PE, *et al.* Immediate versus delayed fluid resuscitation for hypotensive patients with penetrating torso injuries. *N Engl J Med* 1994; **331**: 1105–9

Bodí M, Ardanuy C, Olona M, Castander D, Diaz E, Rello J. Therapy of ventilator-associated pneumonia: the Tarragona strategy. *Clin Microbiol Infect* 2001; **7**: 32–3

Boersma E, Kertai MD, Schouten O, *et al.* Perioperative cardiovascular mortality in noncardiac surgery: validation of the Lee cardiac risk index. *Am J Med* 2005; **118**: 1134–41

Boffard KD, Riou B, Warren B, *et al.* NovoSeven Trauma Study Group. Recombinant factor VIIa as adjunctive therapy for bleeding control in severely injured trauma patients: two parallel randomized, placebo-controlled, double-blind clinical trials. *J Trauma* 2005; **5**: 8–15

Bridgewater B, Gummert J, Kinsman R, Walton P. *Towards Global Benchmarking: the 4th EACTS Adult Cardiac Surgical Database Report 2010.* Henley-on-Thames: Dendrite Clinical Systems; 2010

Bruce D, Nokes TJ. Prothrombin complex concentrate (Beriplex P/N) in severe bleeding: experience in a large tertiary hospital. *Crit Care* 2008; **12**: R105

Brunkhorst FM, Engel C, Bloos F, *et al.* Intensive insulin therapy and pentastarch resuscitation in severe sepsis. *N Engl J Med* 2008; **358**: 125–39

Buhre W, Buhre K, Kazmaier S, Sonntag H, Weyland A. Assessment of cardiac preload by indicator dilution and transoesophageal echocardiography. *Eur J Anaesthesiol* 2001; **18**: 662–7

Castellanos-Ortega A, Suberviola B, García-Astudillo LA, *et al.* Impact of the Surviving Sepsis Campaign protocols on hospital length of stay and mortality in septic shock patients: results of a three-year follow-up quasi-experimental study. *Crit Care Med* 2010; **38**: 1036–43

Chastre J, Wolff M, Fagon JY, *et al.* Comparison of 8 vs 15 days of antibiotic therapy for ventilator-associated pneumonia in adults: a randomized trial. *JAMA* 2003; **290**: 2588–98

Chen EW, Canto JG, Parsons LS, *et al.* Relation between hospital intra-aortic balloon counterpulsation volume and mortality in acute myocardial infarction complicated by cardiogenic shock. *Circulation* 2003; **108**: 951–7

Cheng JM, den Uil CA, Hoeks SE, *et al.* Percutaneous left ventricular assist devices vs. intra-aortic balloon pump counterpulsation for treatment of cardiogenic shock: a meta-analysis of controlled trials. *Eur Heart J* 2009; **30**: 2102–8

Clec'h C, Ferriere F, Karoubi P, *et al.* Diagnostic and prognostic value of procalcitonin in patients with septic shock. *Crit Care Med* 2004; **32**: 1166–9

COIITSS Study Investigators, Annane D, Cariou A, *et al.* Corticosteroid treatment and intensive insulin therapy for septic shock in adults: a randomized controlled trial. *JAMA* 2010; **303**: 341–8

Coriat P, Daloz M, Bousseau D, Fusciardi J, Echter E, Viars P. Prevention of intraoperative myocardial ischemia during noncardiac surgery with intravenous nitroglycerin. *Anesthesiology* 1984; **61**: 193–6

Cothren CC, Moore EE, Hedegaard HB, Meng K. Epidemiology of urban trauma deaths: a comprehensive reassessment 10 years later. *World J Surg* 2007; **31**: 1507–11

Cove ME, MacLaren G. Clinical review: mechanical circulatory support for cardiogenic shock complicating acute myocardial infarction. *Crit Care* 2010; **14**: 235

CRASH-2 trial collaborators, Shakur H, Roberts I, Bautista R, *et al.* Effects of tranexamic acid on death, vascular occlusive events, and blood transfusion in trauma patients with significant haemorrhage (CRASH-2): a randomised, placebo-controlled trial. *Lancet* 2010; **376**: 23–32

Crescenzi G, Landoni G, Biondi-Zoccai G *et al.* Desmopressin reduces transfusion needs after surgery: a meta-analysis of randomized clinical trials. *Anesthesiology* 2008; **109**: 1063–76

Dart AB, Mutter TC, Ruth CA, Taback SP. Hydroxyethyl starch (HES) versus other fluid therapies: effects on kidney function. *Cochrane Database Syst Rev* 2010; **20**: CD007594

Davis DP, Hoyt DB, Ochs M, *et al.* The effect of paramedic rapid sequence intubation on outcome in patients with severe traumatic brain injury. *J Trauma* 2003; **54**: 444–53

De Backer D, Biston P, Devriendt J, *et al.* Comparison of dopamine and norepinephrine in the treatment of shock. *N Engl J Med* 2010; **362**: 779–89

De Hert S, Imberger G, Carlisle J, *et al.* Preoperative evaluation of the adult patient undergoing non-cardiac surgery: guidelines from the European Society of Anaesthesiology. *Eur J Anaesthesiol* 2011; **28**: 684–722

De Hert SG, Van Der Linden PJ, Cromheecke S, *et al.* Choice of primary anesthetic regimen can influence intensive care unit length of stay after coronary surgery with cardiopulmonary bypass. *Anesthesiology* 2004; **101**: 9–20

Dellinger RP, Carlet JM, Masur H, *et al.* Surviving Sepsis Campaign guidelines for management of severe sepsis and septic shock. *Crit Care Med* 2004; **32**: 858–73

Dellinger RP, Levy MM, Rhodes A, *et al.* Surviving sepsis campaign: international guidelines for management of severe sepsis and septic shock: 2012. *Crit Care Med* 2013; **41**: 580–637

Devereaux PJ, Xavier D, Pogue J, *et al.* Characteristics and short-term prognosis of perioperative myocardial infarction in patients undergoing noncardiac surgery: a cohort study. *Ann Internal Med* 2011; **154**: 523–8

Devereaux PJ, Yang H, Yusuf S, *et al.* Effects of extended-release metoprolol succinate in patients undergoing non-cardiac surgery (POISE trial): a randomised controlled trial. *Lancet* 2008; **371**: 1839–47

Devereaux PJ, Yang H, Yusuf S, *et al.* Effects of extended-release metoprolol succinate in patients undergoing non-cardiac surgery (POISE trial): a randomised controlled trial. *Lancet* 2008; **371**: 1839–7

Dodds TM, Stone JG, Coromilas J, Weinberger M, Levy DG. Prophylactic nitroglycerin infusion during noncardiac surgery does not reduce perioperative ischemia. *Anesth Analg* 1993; **76**: 705–13

Dombrovskiy VY, Martin AA, Sunderram J, *et al.* Rapid increase in hospitalization and mortality rates for severe sepsis in the United States: a trend analysis from 1993 to 2003. *Crit Care Med* 2007; **35**: 1414–5

Elkind MS. Inflammatory mechanisms of stroke. *Stroke* 2010; **41**: S3–8

El-Saed A, Kuller LH, Newman AB, *et al.* Geographic variations in stroke incidence and mortality among older populations in four US communities. *Stroke* 2006; **37**: 1975–9

Engel C, Brunkhorst FM, Bone HG, *et al.* Epidemiology of sepsis in Germany: results from a national prospective multicenter study. *Intensive Care Med* 2007; **33**: 606–18

Equinox Investigators. Efficacy and safety of once weekly subcutaneous idrabiotaparinux in the treatment of patients with symptomatic deep venous thrombosis. *J Thromb Haemost* 2011; **9**: 92–9

Fleisher LA, Beckman JA, Brown KA, *et al.* ACC/AHA 2007 Guidelines on perioperative cardiovascular evaluation and care for noncardiac surgery: executive summary: a report of the American College of Cardiology/American Heart Association Task Force on Practice Guidelines. *Circulation* 2007; **116**: 1971–96

Forlani S, Tomai F, De Paulis R, *et al.* Preoperative shift from glibenclamide to insulin is cardioprotective in diabetic patients undergoing coronary artery bypass surgery. *J Cardiovasc Surg (Torino)* 2004; **45**: 117–22

Frank SM, Fleisher LA, Breslow MJ, *et al.* Perioperative maintenance of normothermia reduces the incidence of morbid cardiac events: a randomized clinical trial. *JAMA* 1997; **277**: 1127–34

Ganter MT, Hofer CK. Coagulation monitoring: current techniques and clinical use of viscoelastic point-of-care coagulation devices. *Anesth Analg* 2008; **106**: 1366–75

Garnacho-Montero J, Garcia-Garmendia JL, Barrero-Almodovar A, *et al.* Impact of adequate empirical antibiotic therapy on the outcome of patients admitted to the intensive care unit with sepsis. *Crit Care Med* 2003; 31: 2742–51

Gattinoni L, Brazzi L, Pelosi P, *et al.* A trial of goal-oriented hemodynamic therapy in critically ill patients. *N Engl J Med* 1995; **333**: 1025–32

Goldhaber SZ, Haire WD, Feldstein ML, *et al.* Alteplase versus heparin in acute pulmonary embolism: randomised trial assessing right-ventricular function and pulmonary perfusion. *Lancet* 1993; **341**: 507–11

Goldhaber SZ, Visani L, De Rosa M. Acute pulmonary embolism: clinical outcomes in the International Cooperative Pulmonary Embolism Registry (ICOPER). *Lancet* 1999; **353**: 1386–9

Gupta PK, Mactaggart JN, Natarajan B, *et al.* Predictive factors for mortality after open repair of paravisceral abdominal aortic aneurysm. *J Vasc Surg* 2012; **55**: 666–73

Harbarth S, Holeckova K, Froidevaux C, *et al.* Diagnostic value of procalcitonin, interleukin-6, and interleukin-8 in critically ill patients admitted with suspected sepsis. *Am J Respir Crit Care Med* 2001; **164**: 396–402

Hayes MA, Timmins AC, Yau EHS, *et al.* Elevation of systemic oxygen delivery in the treatment of critically ill patients. *N Engl J Med* 1994; **330**: 1717–22

Hébert PC, Wells G, Blajchman MA, *et al.* A multicenter, randomized, controlled clinical trial of transfusion in critical care. *N Engl J Med* 1999; **340**: 409–17

Hines R, Barash PG, Watrous G, O'Connor T. Complications occurring in the postanesthesia care unit: a survey. *Anesth Analg* 1992; **74**: 503–9

Hogue CW Jr, Goodnough LT, Monk TG. Perioperative myocardial ischemic episodes are related to hematocrit level in patients undergoing radical prostatectomy. *Transfusion* 1998; **38**: 924–31

Holcomb JB, Wade CE, Michalek JE *et al.* Increased plasma and platelet to red blood cell ratios improves outcome in 466 massively transfused civilian trauma patients. *Ann Surg* 2008; **248**: 447–58

Hopkins LN, Ecker RD. Cerebral endovascular neurosurgery. *Neurosurgery* 2008; **62**: 1483–501

Hoyt DB. A clinical review of bleeding dilemmas in trauma. *Semin Hematol* 2004; **41**: 40–3

Hunt BJ. Indications for therapeutic platelet transfusions. *Blood Rev* 1998; **12**: 227–33

Jain M, Canham M, Upadhyay D, Corbridge T. Variability in interventions with pulmonary artery catheter data. *Intensive Care Med* 2003; **29**: 2059–62

Jansen TC, van Bommel J, Schoonderbeek FJ, *et al.* Early lactate-guided therapy in intensive care unit patients: a multicenter, open-label, randomized controlled trial. *Am J Respir Crit Care Med* 2010; **182**: 752–61

Jardin F, Genevray B, Brun-Ney D, Margairaz A. Dobutamine: a hemodynamic evaluation in pulmonary embolism shock. *Crit Care Med* 1985; **13**: 1009–12

Kabrhel C, Mark Courtney D, Camargo CA Jr, *et al.* Factors associated with positive D-dimer results in patients evaluated for pulmonary embolism. *Acad Emerg Med* 2010; **17**: 589–97

Kasper W, Konstantinides S, Geibel A, *et al.* Management strategies and determinants of outcome in acute major pulmonary embolism: results of a multicenter registry. *J Am Coll Cardiol* 1997; **30**: 1165–71

Kerbaul F, Gariboldi V, Giorgi R, *et al.* Effects of levosimendan on acute pulmonary embolism-induced right ventricular failure. *Crit Care Med* 2007; **35**: 1948–54

Koperna T, Schulz F. Relaparotomy in peritonitis: prognosis and treatment of patients with persisting intraabdominal infection. *World J Surg* 2000; **24**: 32–7

Kucher N, Windecker S, Banz Y, *et al.* Percutaneous catheter thrombectomy device for acute pulmonary embolism: in vitro and in vivo testing. *Radiology* 2005; **236**: 852–8

Kumar A, Anel R, Bunnell E, *et al.* Pulmonary artery occlusion pressure and central venous pressure fail to predict ventricular filling volume, cardiac performance, or the response to volume infusion in normal subjects. *Crit Care Med* 2004; **32**: 691–9

Kumar A, Roberts D, Wood KE, *et al.* Duration of hypotension before initiation of effective antimicrobial therapy is the critical determinant of survival in human septic shock. *Crit Care Med* 2006; **34**: 1589–96

Kwok AC, Semel ME, Lipsitz SR, *et al.* The intensity and variation of surgical care at the end of life: a retrospective cohort study. *Lancet* 2011; **378**: 1408–13

Landesberg G. Monitoring for myocardial ischemia. *Best Pract Res Clin Anaesthesiol.* 2005; **19**: 77–95

Larsen FS, Olsen KS, Hansen BA, Paulson OB, Knudsen GM. Transcranial Doppler is valid for determination of the lower limit of cerebral blood flow autoregulation. *Stroke* 1994; **25**: 1985–8

Layish DT, Tapson VF. Pharmacologic hemodynamic support in massive pulmonary embolism. *Chest* 1997; **111**: 218–24

Leacche M, Unic D, Goldhaber SZ, *et al.* Modern surgical treatment of massive pulmonary embolism: results in 47 consecutive patients after rapid diagnosis and aggressive surgical approach. *J Thorac Cardiovasc Surg* 2005; **129**: 1018–23

Lee TH, Marcantonio ER, Mangione CM, *et al.* Derivation and prospective validation of a simple index for prediction of cardiac risk of major noncardiac surgery. *Circulation* 1999; **100**: 1043–9

Leone M, Bourgoin A, Cambon S, Dubuc M, Albanèse J, Martin C. Empirical antimicrobial therapy of septic shock patients: adequacy and impact on the outcome. *Crit Care Med* 2003; **31**: 462–7

Liapis CD, Bell PR, Mikhailidis D, *et al.* ESVS guidelines. Invasive treatment for carotid stenosis: indications, techniques. *Eur J Vasc Endovasc Surg* 2009; **37**: 1–19

Linde-Zwirble WT, Angus DC. Severe sepsis epidemiology: sampling, selection, and society. *Crit Care* 2004; **8**: 2226

Liu SS, Block BM, Wu CL. Effects of perioperative central neuraxial analgesia on outcome after coronary artery bypass surgery: a meta-analysis. *Anesthesiology* 2004; **101**: 153–61

MacLeod JB, Lynn M, McKenney MG, *et al.* Early coagulopathy predicts mortality in trauma. *J Trauma* 2003; **55**: 39–44

Maegele M, Lefering R, Yucel N, *et al.* Early coagulopathy in multiple injury: an analysis from the German Trauma Registry on 8724 patients. *Injury* 2007; **38**: 298–304

Maerz LL, Akhtar S. Perioperative glycemic management in 2011: paradigm shifts. *Curr Opin Crit Care* 2011; **17**: 370–5

Mangano DT, Goldman L. Preoperative assessment of patients with known or suspected coronary disease. *N Engl J Med* 1995; **333**: 1750–6

Martin-Loeches I, Lisboa T, Rodriguez A, *et al.* Combination antibiotic therapy with macrolides improves survival in intubated patients with community-acquired pneumonia. *Intensive Care Med* 2010; **36**: 612–20

Mashour GA, Shanks AM, Kheterpal S. Perioperative stroke and associated mortality after noncardiac, nonneurologic surgery. *Anesthesiology* 2011; **114**: 1289–96

Mebazaa A, Nieminen MS, Packer M, *et al.* Levosimendan vs dobutamine for patients with acute decompensated heart failure: the SURVIVE randomized trial. *JAMA* 2007; **297**: 1883–91

Mehendiratta V, McCarty BC, Gomez L, Graviss EA, Musher DM. Computerized tomography (CT)-guided aspiration of abscesses: outcome of therapy at a tertiary care hospital. *J Infect* 2007; **54**: 122–8

Meine TJ, Roe MT, Chen AY, *et al.* Association of intravenous morphine use and outcomes in acute coronary syndromes: results from the CRUSADE Quality Improvement Initiative. *Am Heart J* 2005; **149**: 1043–9

Meisner M, Tschaikowsky K, Hutzler A, Schick C, Schuttler J. Postoperative plasma concentrations of procalcitonin after different types of surgery. *Intensive Care Med* 1998; **24**: 680–4

Meneveau N, Seronde MF, Blonde MC, *et al.* Management of unsuccessful thrombolysis in acute massive pulmonary embolism. *Chest* 2006; **129**: 1043–50

Mosnier LO, Zlokovic BV, Griffin JH. The cytoprotective protein C pathway. *Blood* 2007; **109**: 3161–72

Nathens AB. Massive transfusion as a risk factor for acute lung injury: association or causation? *Crit Care Med* 2006; **34**(5 Suppl): S144–50

Naylor AR, Bown MJ. Stroke after cardiac surgery and its association with asymptomatic carotid disease: an updated systematic review and meta-analysis. *Eur J Vasc Endovasc Surg* 2011; **41**: 607–24

Nazir FS, Petre I, Dewey HM. Introduction of an acute stroke team: an effective approach to hasten assessment and management of stroke in the emergency department. *J Clin Neurosci* 2009; **16**: 21–5

Nguyen HB, Kuan WS, Batech M, *et al.* Outcome effectiveness of the severe sepsis resuscitation bundle with addition of lactate clearance as a bundle item: a multi-national evaluation. *Crit Care* 2011; **15**: R229

NICE-SUGAR Study Investigators. Intensive versus conventional glucose control in critically ill patients. *N Engl J Med* 2009; **360**: 1283–97

Nobre V, Harbarth S, Graf JD, Rohner P, Pugin J. Use of procalcitonin to shorten antibiotic treatment duration in septic patients: a randomized trial. *Am J Respir Crit Care Med* 2008; **177**: 498–505

Park WY, Thompson JS, Lee KK. Effect of epidural anesthesia and analgesia on perioperative outcome: a randomized, controlled Veterans Affairs cooperative study. *Ann Surg* 2001; **234**: 560–9

Pope JV, Jones AE, Gaieski DF, *et al.* Multicenter study of central venous oxygen saturation (ScvO(2)) as a predictor of mortality in patients with sepsis. *Ann Emerg Med* 2010; **55**: 40–6.e1

Prendergast TJ, Claessens MT, Luce JM. A national survey of end-of-life care for critically ill patients. *Am J Respir Crit Care Med* 1998; **158**: 1163–7

ProCESS Investigators, Yealy DM, Kellum JA, *et al.* A randomized trial of protocol-based care for early septic shock. *N Engl J Med* 2014; **370**: 1683–93

Ramanathan K, Harkness SM, Nayar AC, *et al.* Cardiogenic shock in patients with preserved left ventricular systolic function: characteristics and insight into mechanisms. *J Am Coll Cardiol* 2004; **43**: 241A

Reinhart K, Brunkhorst FM, Bone HG, *et al.* Prevention, diagnosis, therapy and follow-up care of sepsis: 1st revision of S-2k guidelines of the German Sepsis Society and the German Interdisciplinary Association of Intensive Care and Emergency Medicine. *Ger Med Sci* 2010; **28**; 8

Reynolds HR, Hochman JS. Cardiogenic shock: current concepts and improving outcomes. *Circulation* 2008; **117**: 686–97

Rigg JR, Jamrozik K, Myles PS, *et al.* Epidural anaesthesia and analgesia and outcome of major surgery: a randomised trial. *Lancet* 2002; **359**: 1276–82

Rivers E, Nguyen B, Havstad S, *et al.* Early goal-directed therapy in the treatment of severe sepsis and septic shock. *N Engl J Med* 2001; **345**: 1368–77

Rossaint R, Bouillon B, Cerny V, *et al.* Management of bleeding following major trauma: an updated European guideline. *Crit Care* 2010; **14**: R52

Rotondo MF, Schwab CW, McGonigal MD, *et al.* "Damage control": an approach for improved survival in exsanguinating penetrating abdominal injury. *J Trauma* 1993; **35**: 375–82

Russell JA, Walley KR, Singer J, *et al.* Vasopressin versus norepinephrine infusion in patients with septic shock. *N Engl J Med* 2008; **358**: 877–87

Sabaté S, Mases A, Guilera N, *et al.* Incidence and predictors of major perioperative adverse cardiac and cerebrovascular events in non-cardiac surgery. *Br J Anaesth* 2011; **107**: 879–90

Salim A, Hadjizacharia P, DuBose J, *et al.* Role of anemia in traumatic brain injury. *J Am Coll Surg* 2008; **207**: 398–406

Schierhout G, Roberts I. Fluid resuscitation with colloid or crystalloid solutions in critically ill patients: a systematic review of randomised trials. *BMJ* 1998; **316**: 961–4

Sharshar T, Blanchard A, Paillard M, *et al.* Circulating vasopressin levels in septic shock. *Crit Care Med* 2003; **31**: 1752–8

Sia IG, Berbari EF, Karchmer AW. Prosthetic joint infections. *Infect Dis Clin North Am* 2005; **19**: 885–914

Solomon C, Pichlmaier U, Schoechl H, *et al.* Recovery of fibrinogen after administration of fibrinogen concentrate to patients with severe bleeding after cardiopulmonary bypass surgery. *Br J Anaesth* 2010; **104**: 555–62

Soreide K. Epidemiology of major trauma. *Br J Surg* 2009; **96**: 697–8

Spinella PC, Perkins JG, Grathwohl KW, *et al.* Effect of plasma and red blood cell transfusions on survival in patients with combat related traumatic injuries. *J Trauma* 2008; **64**: 69–77

Sprung CL, Annane D, Keh D, *et al.* Hydrocortisone therapy for patients with septic shock. *N Engl J Med* 2008; **358**: 111–24

Stainsby D, MacLennan S, Hamilton PJ. Management of massive blood loss: a template guideline. *Br J Anaesth* 2000; **85**: 487–91

Stein PD, Fowler SE, Goodman LR, *et al.* Multidetector computed tomography for acute pulmonary embolism. *N Engl J Med* 2006; **354**: 2317–27

Stinger HK, Spinella PC, Perkins JG, *et al.* The ratio of fibrinogen to red cells transfused affects survival in casualties receiving massive transfusions at an army combat support hospital. *J Trauma* 2008; **64**: 79–85

Tai DK, Li WH, Lee KY, *et al.* Retroperitoneal pelvic packing in the management of hemodynamically unstable pelvic fractures: a level I trauma center experience. *J Trauma* 2011; **71**: E79–86

Tapson VF. Acute pulmonary embolism. *N Engl J Med* 2008; **358**: 1037–52

The SUPPORT Principal Investigators. A controlled trial to improve care for seriously ill hospitalized patients. *JAMA* 1995; **274**: 1591–8. [Erratum in *JAMA* 1996; **275**: 1232]

Thiele H, Zeymer U, Neumann FJ, *et al.* Intraaortic balloon support for myocardial infarction with cardiogenic shock. *N Engl J Med* 2012; **367**: 1287–96

Thorson CM, Ryan ML, Otero CA, *et al.* Operating room or angiography suite for hemodynamically unstable pelvic fractures? *J Trauma Acute Care Surg* 2012; **72**: 364–72

Thygesen K, Alpert JS, White HD, for the Joint ESC/ACCF/AHA/WHF Task Force for the Redefinition of Myocardial Infarction. Universal definition of myocardial infarction. *J Am Coll Cardiol* 2007; **50**: 2173–95

Tissari P, Zumla A, Tarkka E, *et al.* Accurate and rapid identification of bacterial species from positive blood cultures with a DNA-based microarray platform: an observational study. *Lancet* 2010; **375**: 224–30

Torbicki A, Perrier A, Konstantinides S, *et al.* Guidelines on the diagnosis and management of acute pulmonary embolism: the Task Force for the Diagnosis and Management of Acute Pulmonary Embolism of the European Society of Cardiology (ESC). *Eur Heart J* 2008; **29**: 2276–31

Turner J, Nicholl J, Webber L, *et al.* A randomised controlled trial of prehospital intravenous fluid replacement therapy in serious trauma. *Health Technol Assess* 2000; **4**: 1–57

van Beest PA, Hofstra JJ, Schultz MJ, Boerma EC, Spronk PE, Kuiper MA. The incidence of low venous oxygen saturation on admission to the intensive care unit: a multi-center observational study in The Netherlands. *Crit Care* 2008; **12**: R33

Van den Berghe G, Wouters P, Weekers F, *et al.* Intensive insulin therapy in critically ill patients. *N Engl J Med* 2001; **345**: 1359–67

van Ruler O, Lamme B, Gouma DJ, Reitsma JB, Boermeester MA. Variables associated with positive findings at relaparotomy in patients with secondary peritonitis. *Crit Care Med* 2007; **35**: 468–76

Vincent JL, Bihari DJ, Suter PM, *et al.* The prevalence of nosocomial infection in intensive care units in Europe. Results of the European Prevalence of Infection in Intensive Care (EPIC) Study. EPIC International Advisory Committee. *JAMA* 1995; **274**: 639–44

Vlayen A, Verelst S, Bekkering GE, Schrooten W, Hellings J, Claes N. Incidence and preventability of adverse events requiring intensive care admission: a systematic review. *J Eval Clin Pract* 2012; **18**: 485–97

Weaver WD, Simes RJ, Betriu A, *et al.* Comparison of primary coronary angioplasty and intravenous thrombolytic therapy for acute myocardial infarction: a quantitative review *JAMA* 1997; **278**: 2093–8

Weiser TG, Regenbogen SE, Thompson KD, *et al.* An estimation of the global volume of surgery: a modelling strategy based on available data. *Lancet* 2008; **372**: 139–44

Wells PS, Anderson DR, Rodger M, *et al.* Derivation of a simple clinical model to categorize patients probability of pulmonary embolism: increasing the models utility with the SimpliRED D-dimer. *Thromb Haemost* 2000; **83**: 416–20

Whiteley WN, Wardlaw JM, Dennis MS, Sandercock PA. Clinical scores for the identification of stroke and transient ischaemic attack in the emergency department: a crosssectional study. *J Neurol Neurosurg Psychiatry* 2011; **82**: 1006–10

Zamanian RT, Haddad F, Doyle RL, Weinacker AB. Management strategies for patients with pulmonary hypertension in the intensive care unit. *Crit Care Med* 2007; **35**: 2037–50

Zanotti-Cavazzoni SL, Hollenberg SM. Cardiac dysfunction in severe sepsis and septic shock. *Curr Opin Crit Care* 2009; **15**: 392–7

Zygun DA, Nortje J, Hutchinson PJ, *et al.* The effect of red blood cell transfusion on cerebral oxygenation and metabolism after severe traumatic brain injury. *Crit Care Med* 2009; **37**: 1074–8

CHAPTER 90

Transport of the critically ill patient

Laura Flutter, Christoph Melzer-Gartzke, Claudia Spies, and Julian Bion

Introduction

Transporting critically ill patients started in the Napoleonic Wars with Baron Dominique Larrey's *ambulances volantes* providing rapid evacuation of injured soldiers from the battlefield to a place of safety where they could receive prompt surgery. Greater technical sophistication emerged during World War II, and subsequently with the American involvement in Vietnam. It is now possible to repatriate critically injured soldiers thousands of miles by air while continuing to deliver full organ system support during transfer. The same principles, techniques, and skills apply to civilian transfers, whether primary or secondary, inter-hospital or intra-hospital. Transport medicine is now seen as a specific set of competencies shared between emergency medicine, intensive care medicine, and anaesthesia, in which the attending physician must be able to manage a team capable of preparing for a transfer of a few minutes to many hours with a patient requiring complex organ support. Familiarity with the process of transfer and its inherent dangers is now recognized as an essential component of a comprehensive anaesthesia training programme. In the United Kingdom, the Royal College of Anaesthetists (RCoA) requires trainees to demonstrate evidence of training in this rapidly expanding field at both basic and advanced levels. The German Association for Intensive Care and Emergency Medicine [Deutsche Interdisziplinare Vereiningung fur Intensive und Notfalimedezin (DIVI)] developed an interdisciplinary curriculum for the training of special skills in intensive care transport (DIVI 2008).

There are substantial international variations between healthcare systems in the coordination and support provided for primary and secondary transport, from the unified system in France, the Service Aero-Medicale d'Urgence (SAMU), through to approaches based on national standards but using *ad hoc* local provision, such as the United Kingdom. The latter approach is most likely to depend on trainee anaesthetists as the attending physician, with transfers performed outside normal working hours (Jameson and Lawler 2000; Gray et al. 2003; Spencer et al. 2004). In Germany, where healthcare organization is the responsibility of the federal states, 16 legal principles describe the organization of the emergency services, including the structures and responsibilities for intensive care and inter-hospital transport. Some federal states have developed specific coordinating centres and operating procedures for inter-hospital and intensive care transfers (Hennes 2005).

In 1997, an estimated 11 000 transfers took place between critical care units in the United Kingdom (Mackenzie et al. 1997). This number is likely to have increased as a consequence of centralization, continuing critical care bed shortages, and the much larger number of intra-hospital transfers for diagnostic testing or interventions which are unable to be performed at the bedside (Fromm and Dellinger 1992). Despite the creation of critical care networks, designed to facilitate the safe and efficient transfer of patients between hospitals with varying critical care capacity, secondary transport is still often poorly organized and executed (Lovell et al. 2001; Damm et al. 2005; Gillman et al. 2006; Papson et al. 2007).

In this chapter, we focus on secondary transfers, and review the indications, complications, and processes of care required to maximize patient safety through meticulous planning and training.

The literature

A literature search was conducted using the databases PubMed, Medline, CINAHL, Web of Science, Cochrane database, Ovid, and Google scholar using the search terms transport, transfer, transportation, inter-hospital, intra-hospital, ambulance, helicopter, aircraft, and critical care. There were 225 publications of which 12 were systematic reviews, 2 randomized controlled trial, and 54 were cohort or observational studies. The remainder were expert statements or opinion-based reviews.

Indications for and types of transport

The terminology is now well established.

A primary transfer relates to the carriage by ambulance from scene to the emergency department.

Secondary transfer describes the continuation of the patient to either another department within the hospital or to another hospital entirely.

Tertiary transfer occurs between hospitals for non-clinical reasons, such as repatriation, to be closer to family or for insurance purposes.

The transfer of critically ill patients within the hospital for diagnostic testing or procedures will often be the responsibility of the anaesthesia team. Using the intensive care unit (ICU) team, which is more familiar with the specific therapy and history of the patient and does not necessitate handover, must be pragmatically balanced against staff availability. The most common destinations for unwell patients are either the computed tomography scanner (Waydhas et al. 1995; Bercault et al. 2005; Voigt et al. 2009) or the operating theatre (Szem et al. 1995; Waydhas et al. 1995). Although intra-hospital transfers may be comparatively shorter than for those travelling to another hospital, the risks are just as prevalent and well documented (Beckmann et al. 2004; Warren et al. 2004).

Modes of transport and special considerations

There are a number of different modes of transport available and choice of an appropriate vehicle will depend on a number of factors including (Gray et al. 2004):

1. Distance to be travelled
2. Stability and organ support of the patient
3. The urgency of the transfer
4. Weather
5. Time of day
6. Availability of vehicle.

All modes of transport will expose the patient to physiological changes. The principal forces are acceleration and deceleration but this may be exacerbated by vibration, temperature changes, motion sickness, and noise that may contribute to patient instability and anxiety (Gillman et al. 2006; Flutter et al. 2009), and to discomfort for the attendants.

Land

For the transfer of patients between hospitals, road vehicles are often suitable. They are more cost-effective than air transportation, provide a better environment for monitoring, and are less influenced by meteorological disturbance (Wallace and Ridley 1999). It is also possible to stop the vehicle, facilitating emergency management.

Rotary

Air transfer is primarily reserved for distances greater than 50 miles (80 km), with helicopters the most useful for distances of 50–150 miles (80–240 km). While the fastest method of covering this distance, transfer times from aircraft to land vehicle before arrival at the receiving unit may negate the benefit of increased speed of transit (Wallace and Ridley 1999). Furthermore, the complexity of arranging a helicopter transfer may also result in an increased transfer time from decision to transfer (Karanicolas et al. 2008). Weather, issues with night flying, excessive noise, and vibration are all negative aspects of helicopter transfer (de Melio and Thompson 1990). There is an increased risk of physiological disturbance on longer flights and for patients who require inotropic support (Seymour et al. 2008).

Fixed wing

Fixed-wing aircraft are better for distances greater than 150 miles (240 km) and it is possible to move patients between continents if required with a service that is usually provided by either private medical companies or the military (Valenzuela et al. 1990; Turner et al. 2009; Sand et al. 2010). Standards of operation for air ambulances have been developed by regulatory bodies such as the Federal Aviation Authority (United States), Civil Aviation Authority (United Kingdom) and Joint Aviation Authority (Europe).

Air travel at altitude is primarily complicated by changes to relative humidity, partial pressure of oxygen, and atmospheric pressure (Rice et al. 2008). All aircraft deemed suitable for this type of transfer have pressurized cabins. However, the typical pressure created is equivalent to 5000–8000 feet atmospheric (1500–2400 m), with a resultant decrease in the partial pressure of oxygen to 8.7 kPa (65 mm Hg) (Seymour et al. 2008). This has been shown to cause a reduction in oxygen saturation of 5% in patients with ischaemic heart disease (Essebag et al. 2003). While this can of course be successfully corrected with oxygen supplementation, it may be an important factor for long transfers when supplies may be limited. For non-intubated patients with borderline oxygenation, it is wise to consider intubation before starting the transport.

An additional concern with air travel at altitude is gas expansion. As dictated by Boyle's law ($P \times V$ = constant or $V_1 \times P_1 = P_2 \times V_2$), any trapped gas will expand as the ambient pressure decreases. Consequently, at 8000 feet, any air-filled space, such as the middle ear, sinuses and bowel, will expand by 35%, potentially causing pain or barotrauma. In the case of air in the pleural cavity, this may result in a tension pneumothorax. If a pneumothorax is diagnosed or suspected before transfer, it is vital that chest drains are inserted and left unclamped. The same is true for gas trapped in the stomach, necessitating the insertion of a nasogastric tube, and for air in equipment such as tracheal tube cuffs and intravenous infusion lines (Essebag et al. 2003). It is possible to pressurize the cabin to sea level in some aircraft although this will reduce speed and increase fuel consumption.

Whichever method of transport is chosen, it must be fully equipped for the transport of critical care patients and medical personnel. Importantly this incorporates the provision of adequate lighting, heating, and air conditioning (Intensive Care Society 2011).

Complications and risks associated with transport

The transfer of critically ill patients is an inherently risky procedure, with workload implications for the transferring ICU. A North American cancer centre study (Voigt et al. 2009) demonstrated that patients undergoing transfer within the first 24 h of ICU admission were more severely ill, had a longer length of stay in critical care, and a higher hospital mortality rate. Of 948 admissions, 413 (44%) underwent 800 transfers, most commonly for diagnostic and interventional imaging. This level of workload and patient complexity requires a systematic approach to minimize risk not just to the transported patient, but also to other patients in the ICU in terms of opportunity cost if staffing is limited.

The main determinants of risk common to all patient movements are dependence on organ system support, physiological instability and limited reserve, and separation from complex diagnostic and therapeutic interventions. Attention was drawn to the risks in 1970 when it was found that during the transfer of cardiac patients, 84% experienced arrhythmias, with 44% requiring emergency treatment (Taylor et al. 1970). Further evidence was published in 1975 of the risks of transfer from the operating theatre to critical care, with 21% of patients experiencing a significant event on this relatively short transfer (Waddell 1975). The authors called for increased recognition of the potential pitfalls of transfer with improved planning and vigilance. In 2007, complications were still common (Handy and Zwanenberg 2007).

Over the last three decades, the risks of adverse events during transfer have been emphasized both by epidemiological data (Lovell et al. 2001; Shirley and Stott 2001; Beckmann 2004; Damm et al. 2005; Gillman et al. 2006; Lahner et al. 2007; Papson et al. 2007) and professional critical care society reports and standards [Ferdinande 1999; Australasian College for Emergency Medicine et al. 2003; Warren et al. 2004; SIAARTI Study Group for Safety in Anesthesia and Intensive Care 2006; Intensive Care Society 2002 (updated 2011)]. These were summarized by Fanara et al. (2010) where six core categories of adverse events were identified: respiratory, cardiovascular, neurological, hypothermia, equipment malfunction, and human error. The incidence of adverse events is unclear because of the lack of standard definitions. The most consistent estimate for major adverse events requiring therapeutic intervention or with serious threat to life is approximately 8% (Smith et al. 1990; Szem et al. 1995; Wallen et al. 1995; Stearley 1998).

This is an unacceptable additional level of risk in what is an already high-risk group of patients. In 2006, an Australian study showed that 91% of documented adverse events (n = 272) were preventable (Flabouris et al. 2006). In the United Kingdom, there has been a move towards providing a dedicated transfer service. University College Hospital London reported a reduction in the number of adverse events and in 12 h mortality associated with transfer by a dedicated retrieval team as compared with a standard ambulance with medical escort combination (Bellingan et al. 2000). Similarly, a Dutch study used measured changes in vital signs to demonstrate the safety of a specialist retrieval team using a mobile ICU according to national guidelines (Wiegersma et al. 2011).

Various factors contribute to the potential for serious adverse events during transfer. The duration, which ranges from minutes to many hours, is a period in which the underlying clinical condition may worsen independent of the movement of the patient. The physical disturbance caused by the transfer as a result of vibration and acceleration or deceleration forces, and the change from ICU to transport equipment, may have adverse effects on physiology and potentially exacerbate the patient's condition (Ferdinande 1999; Stevenson et al. 2002; Gillman et al. 2006). During transfer, access to the patient is often limited, and changes in the patient's condition may not be observed or may be difficult to manage.

Equipment failure is common. In 2005, a French study found that there were adverse events involving portable ventilators, predominantly untimely alarms and gas or electrical failures, in 22% of intra-hospital transfers (Damm et al. 2005). Papson (2007) found equipment failures in almost half of the adverse events analysed involving ventilators and airway devices in addition to monitoring failure. The number of infusions and pumps has been linked to equipment-related adverse events (Doring et al. 1999). As the number and variety of devices and drugs which can be transported with the patient during transfer is limited, this may also result in suboptimal management of the patient's condition.

For practical purposes, it is useful to consider the risks of transfer by organ system in order to categorize and pre-empt their potential for harm.

Airway

Emergency management of airway complications is difficult in transit. The airway must be secured before transfer. In 1981, the most common secondary injury to comatose head injury patients on transfer to a neurosurgical unit was airway obstruction (Gentleman and Jennett 1981). Other causes of deterioration include:

1. Deterioration of underlying condition:
   - Reduced conscious level
   - Swelling of the airway as a result of burns or anaphylaxis
   - Spinal injury incompletely immobilized resulting in extension of clinical syndrome
2. Compromise to an established airway:
   - Tracheal tubes can easily become dislodged, disconnected, or kinked if not secured adequately and monitored vigilantly.

Breathing

Intra-hospital transfer of ventilated patients can lead to a significant deterioration in long-term respiratory function (Waydhas et al. 1995). This may be because of a number of factors:

1. Worsening lung pathology:
   - The inadvertent physiotherapy provided by the vibrational forces and physical movement of the patient can be both beneficial and detrimental. Mucous plugs can become lodged within major airways
   - Lung contusions and oedema may worsen
   - Expansion of haemothorax
2. Ventilation/perfusion mismatch:
   - It is unlikely that the optimal position of the patient will be maintained for the duration of transfer
   - Failure to maintain alveolar recruitment when changing to a transport ventilator or if using open tracheal suction systems
3. Pneumothoraces:
   - Chest drains may become blocked, kinked, or dislodged
   - The optimal position of the drain below the patient may be compromised
4. Ventilator failure: this may be as a result of disconnection, gas supply, or power failure
5. Monitoring: pulse oximetry and capnography inaccuracies.

Circulation

Circulatory compromise may occur because of a variety of reasons and can easily go unnoticed in the patient prepared for transfer:

1. Haemorrhage: caused by or worsened by the movement of the patient and may be concealed by the positioning of the patient and equipment for transfer
2. Volume replacement:
   - Central and peripheral lines may become dislodged or kinked
   - Volume replacement may be infused at a reduced flow rate because of patient positioning
3. Drugs: vasopressor and inotrope infusion rates may be interrupted by displacement of central venous catheters of equipment failure
4. Monitoring: arterial and venous monitoring may become disconnected or provide inaccurate readings as a result of artifact or poor positioning.

Renal

Renal function may deteriorate, particularly during longer transfers, as a consequence of the following:

- Unobserved hypovolaemia causing oliguria
- Displacement, blockage, or kinking of urinary catheter causing acute urinary retention
- In renal failure, inability to continue haemofiltration in transit may result in acidosis, hyperkalaemia, and hyperhydration.

Metabolic

The stress response, and less meticulous monitoring, may adversely influence glycaemic control.

Neurology

The movement of patients with head injuries is particularly hazardous, but also extremely common. The risks to the nervous system associated with transfer are:

1. Changes to intracranial pressure (ICP):
    - Movement alone with the additional forces of transfer may cause a detrimental increase in ICP
    - ICP may increase if cardiovascular compromise or ventilatory issues are not managed appropriately
    - Patient position is also unlikely to be optimal for ICP protection
2. Pain: it is important to remember that movement is a potentially painful experience for patients. Untreated, this can be damaging to all organ systems
3. Sedation: inadequate sedation, both over- and under-sedation, is a common complication resulting in worsening of neurological parameters and cardiovascular compromise with potential respiratory, renal and metabolic involvement
4. Monitoring:
    - ICP monitoring devices may become dislodged or disconnected or provide false readings due to movement artifact
    - Alarms for all monitors (vital signs and respiratory) must be set to appropriate limits. Otherwise, repeated false alarms will diminish the alertness to the important alarm indicating relevant deterioration of the patient's condition.

Host defence

- Timely administration of antimicrobials may be compromised
- Temperature control: abnormalities may not be detected and treated; patients are particularly at risk of developing hypothermia
- Wound sites: movement may displace dressings and devices leading to contamination of wound and device insertion sites
- Poor aseptic technique in managing central venous catheters and connections
- Neutropenic patients and patients under immunosuppressive therapy after organ transplantation need special adherence to hygienic rules.

Equipment

Equipment malfunctions are commonly a result of battery failure and this includes infusion pumps, ventilators, and cardiovascular or respiratory monitoring (Beckmann, 2004; Damm et al. 2005; Papson et al. 2007).

Transfer equipment

National guidelines for the provision of transfer equipment (Ferdinande 1999; Intensive Care Society 2011) emphasize the need to maintain a level of care during transfer comparable to that provided in the ICU. Clearly, a balance must be struck between comprehensive provision and parsimony demanded by lack of space. The equipment must be capable of maintaining continuity and standards of care from stabilization to transfer. The equipment used should be dedicated to the purpose of transfer and checked routinely. Daily review and pre-and post-transport checklists should be used to ensure that no items are missing, those used are replaced, and that equipment is functioning. Electrical equipment must be fully charged during storage while drugs are maintained at the correct storage temperatures and within use-by date.

All departments should follow local guidelines when finalizing transfer equipment protocols. However, in general, the minimum equipment requirements are as follows [Association of Anaesthetists of Great Britain and Ireland (AAGBI) 2006]:

1. Airway equipment, including suction device
2. Adequate oxygen supply
3. Portable ventilator
4. Self-inflating bag/valve and mask
5. Chest decompression equipment
6. Portable multifunction monitor, to include:
    - ECG
    - Invasive/non-invasive blood pressure
    - Central venous pressure
    - Pulse oximetry
    - Capnography for the ventilated patient
    - Temperature
7. Defibrillator
8. Battery-powered syringe and volumetric pumps
9. Spare batteries
10. Warming blanket.

In addition, a minimum number of emergency drugs must also be included:

1. Hypnotics
2. Neuromuscular blocking agent
3. Analgesics
4. Anticonvulsants
5. Vasoactive drugs
6. Resuscitation drugs
7. Intravenous fluids
8. Mannitol 20%.

The Intensive Care Society (2011) also stipulates a number of other equipment requirements for transfer staff; these include the following:

1. Mobile telephone
2. High visibility, protective, and warm clothing
3. Money for return transfer
4. Antiemetic if known to suffer from motion sickness.

It is important to include equipment specific to paediatric patients and to ensure staff are adequately trained in its use.

Equipment under-provision is common. In 2008, a survey in the United Kingdom revealed that 29.3%, 13.5%, 19.2%, 1.6%, 25%, and 29% of hospitals provide a dedicated transfer trolley, protective clothing, fluorescent jacket, boots, mobile telephone, and insurance cover, respectively (Ahmed and Majeed 2008).

Carriage and storage

Compartmentalized transfer packs provide organized equipment carriage. These are best suited to the carriage of non-electrical equipment and often have smaller pouches within the sack to organize kit into logical divisions such as venous access or airway adjuncts.

There are dangers inherent in carrying larger electrical apparatus on top of the patient so that equipment must be stowed carefully either on the floor or secured to the patient trolley. In the event of an accident, unsecured equipment can become hazardous projectiles with potential to cause significant injury.

A suitable trolley to which large pieces of equipment can be secured facilitates safe transfer. In Europe, the transfer trolley must comply with the European Committee for Standardization (1999) and must be able to withstand 10 G deceleration in five directions when secured. The trolley must also:

1. Be robust and lightweight
2. Have facilities to attach ventilator, infusion pumps, suction, and monitoring
3. Have a low centre of gravity when loaded
4. Be suitable for actual or potential spinal injury patients
5. Be able to withstand CPR
6. Have cot sides
7. Have a head-down function for vomiting patients
8. Be compatible with the fixation system of the vehicle or the helicopter.

Electrical equipment

It is essential that the equipment used for transfer is lightweight, robust, and able to be powered by battery (Wallace and Ridley 1999).

As discussed previously, many adverse events are due to equipment failure. It is imperative that equipment is re-charged during storage; during transit, an external power supply must be used wherever possible. In addition, it is recommended that long-lasting lithium batteries and low-battery alarm systems are available (Warren 2004; Intensive Care Society 2011).

There has been considerable interest in the development of Bluetooth technology to minimize the cables required for patient monitoring. Although this has been shown to be compatible with other medical devices (Wallin and Wajntraub 2004), an accurate system is not yet available.

Ventilation

The choice of ventilatory support should be determined by the patient's clinical condition and requirements (Stevenson et al. 2002). Mechanical ventilation has been shown to provide better quality respiratory support during transfer than manual ventilation, in terms of consistent tidal volumes, respiratory cycles, and oxygenation. Manual ventilation results in significantly greater variation in tidal volume and positive end expiratory pressure than in the mechanical group, as was shown in 2003 when a mechanical ventilator with no air mix and patient triggering function (LTV™ 1000 transport ventilator; Pulmonetic Systems; Colton, CA, USA) was compared with manual ventilation with a Jackson-Rees circuit with oxygen flow of 10 litres min^{-1} although patient numbers were small (22 transports, 16 patients) (Nakamura et al. 2003). Both of these variables are important in the unwell, ventilated patient (Richard et al. 2001).

An important consideration is that portable ventilators are inferior in capability to standard critical care ventilators. Portable ventilators provided less accurate tidal volumes and less effective triggering (Zanetta et al. 2002). Chipman et al. (2007) tested 15 transport ventilators using bench and animal models and stated that only two ventilators met all the trial targets.

It may be possible to use an ICU ventilator during the transfer if there are sufficient battery packs and an adequate gas supply on a special stretcher. This is increasingly available for intra-hospital transport and may be particularly suitable in situations such as the transfer of critical care patients with acute respiratory distress syndrome (Barton et al. 1997).

Oxygen

The amount of oxygen required will depend of the needs of the patient and journey time and must be calculated. The total oxygen transported should be twice the estimated requirement. For shorter intra-hospital transfers it is adequate to provide sufficient oxygen for 1 h.

The calculation for oxygen requirements is as follows: minute volume × FI_{O_2} + ventilator requirement.

Nomograms are available which determine duration of supply for a given cylinder capacity related to flowmeter rate (Lutman and Petros 2006).

The capacity of oxygen cylinders is shown in Table 90.1.

All cylinders and connectors must be checked before transfer and should be full. In the event of ventilator failure it may be necessary to use a resuscitation circuit; it is therefore imperative that a spare cylinder is available to which this circuit can be attached. A central gas supply should be used wherever available to spare the oxygen of the transport unit.

Extracorporeal membrane oxygenation

Extracorporeal membrane oxygenation (ECMO) is now recognized as a treatment for adult patients with severe but reversible respiratory failure. This is a service currently restricted to specialized referral centres, thus often necessitating transfer for treatment. The CESAR study showed improved 6-month survival without disability after transfer of patients with severe respiratory failure to an ECMO-capable centre. Of note, two patients in the referral group

Table 90.1 The capacity of oxygen cylinders

Oxygen cylinder size						
Order code	C	D	E	F	G	J
Volume (litres)	1.2	2.3	4.7	9.4	23.6	47.2
Capacity (litres)	170	340	680	1360	3400	6800
Time to empty from full when using 10 litres min^{-1}	15 min	30 min	1 h	2¼ h	5½ h	11¼ h

died during transfer (Peek et al. 2009). Further evidence from a joint Australian and New Zealand team demonstrated improved survival for patients with acute respiratory distress syndrome secondary to H1N1 influenza, with ECMO (Noah et al. 2011). An ECMO retrieval service for patients with severe cardiac or respiratory failure who are unsuitable for transfer using conventional ventilation was developed in Australia, and of 40 patient retrievals using ECMO, 85% survived to hospital discharge with no deaths or major morbidity associated with transfer (Forrest et al. 2011). A military team based in Germany has also successfully used pump-less extracorporeal lung assistance to transport military casualties with severe lung injury (Fang et al. 2011). These advanced technologies require special expertise in the transfer team to minimize risk to the patient.

Inhaled nitric oxide

Inhaled nitric oxide (iNO) potentially improves oxygenation, reduces pulmonary artery pressures, and may help avoid the need for ECMO. Hence the use of iNO is another rescue medication which may facilitate transfer (Gerlach et al. 2003; Rossaint et al. 1993; Westrope et al. 2004). Delivery systems can be adapted to all respiratory circuits.

Transfer staff: competencies and training

The composition of the transfer team is determined by the needs of the patient but has a minimum of two trained escorts (Guidelines Committee of the American College of Critical Care Medicine 1993; Warren et al. 2004). A designated team leader is vital and in 1169 transfers in North America there was no difference in clinical outcome between nurse- or doctor-led teams (Burney et al. 1995). However, this is dependent on the quality assurance of the countries and the legal prerequisites and requires evaluation by the responsible parties of each country.

Not all patients will require anaesthetic support for transfer. In the United Kingdom, the AAGBI (2006) has published guidelines on the levels of support that may be required. The patients who do not need anaesthetic input include:

- Patients who are not likely to need airway or ventilatory support
- Patients for whom attempting cardiopulmonary resuscitation would be inappropriate
- Patients being transferred for acute definitive management for whom anaesthesia support will not affect their outcome.

For patients requiring cardiovascular or respiratory support, it is imperative to include an appropriately trained doctor for transfer (Kaplan et al. 1987), with experience in advanced airway management and training in anaesthesia or critical care (Girotti et al. 1988). The level of experience of the doctor has been shown to be negatively correlated with the number of adverse events during transfer (Papson et al. 2007), although this may be mitigated by appropriate training of more junior staff (SIAARTI Study Group for Safety in Anesthesia and Intensive Care 2006).

In recognition of the risks of transfer, the need for structured and standardized training in transport medicine is now recognized. In the United Kingdom, in 1997, the Intensive Care Society published their first guidelines, *Guidelines for the Transport of the Critically Ill Adult*, subsequently revised and updated in 2002, and then in 2011. Further guidance was produced and published by a North American team in 2004 (Warren et al. 2004) with the aim of improving patient safety with a standardized approach. In Germany, the DIVI published curricula for training nurses and doctors in inter-hospital transport and standard operating procedures. A national training course has been developed in the United Kingdom, the Safe Transfer and Retrieval (StaR) course, which is designed to incorporate the key elements of transfer. In addition, a number of regional centres now provide their own variation, in order to satisfy the increased requirement for trainees to demonstrate objectively their capabilities in transfer medicine. Certainly, in the United Kingdom the need to complete a course in order to fulfil training requirements for successful progression to consultant level has stimulated interest in the area, although evidence to suggest that this results in improved transfer services is still lacking. A Dutch study found that implementing simulator-based training could help to identify the failure to anticipate problems in advance, suggesting that this will be a useful teaching tool for mobile ICU teams (Droogh et al. 2012).

Organizing a transfer

Key considerations include indications, contraindications, establishing the team, patient and family preparation, and communication with, and expectations of, receiving site/hospital.

At a senior management level, there are a number of factors that must be considered in order to organize an effective transport team within a hospital. These include a multidisciplinary team consisting of nurses, physicians, hospital administration, and emergency services transport coordinators for out-of-hospital transfer (Warren et al. 2004). This team is then able to assess the requirements for a transfer service on-demand, and establish local guidelines for inter-hospital co-operation. In the United Kingdom and across much of Europe and North America, transfer networks have been created to facilitate the transfer of patients for both therapeutic intervention and to accommodate bed shortages within regions (Iwashyna et al. 2009; Intensive Care Society 2011).

In order to complete a successful transfer of a critically ill patient there must be meticulous planning. The risks of transfer must be measured against the potential benefits (Durairaj et al. 2003). The availability of patient testing or simple procedures at the bedside should be considered (Porter et al. 1999; McCunn et al. 2000). The choice of patient for transfer must be taken by a senior clinician, and involves the evaluation of a number of important factors, including the characteristics of the patient, the indications for transfer, and the level of transfer personnel and equipment available (Lee et al. 1996). Although clinicians may feel that the condition of the patient must be the principal determinant for transfer suitability, this was not found to be the case in a study conducted in the Netherlands. A survey of 95 lead critical care clinicians found that even the most critically ill patients were considered suitable for transfer providing adequately trained personnel and equipment could be available (Lieshout et al. 2008). Interestingly, neither the age of the patient nor severity of respiratory support, as indicated by positive end-expiratory pressure, were considered barriers to transfer.

There must be thorough discussion between transferring units (Venkataraman and Orr 1992), while the availability of adequately trained personnel (Wiegersma et al. 2011) and suitable equipment should be ascertained with adequate notice. An analysis of transfers by Voigt et al. (2009) in a North American critical care unit found that the majority of transfers within the hospital were performed during weekday afternoons and evenings, after decisions made on the morning round—a useful insight for staff allocations.

An Australian study found that teams that had prior experience of transfer, and those who re-checked their equipment before movement were less likely to suffer an adverse event in transit (Beckmann et al. 2004).

Communication is a vital element to a successful transfer. It is the responsibility of the team leader to ensure all aspects of communication have been considered before departure:

1. Patient and relatives: where possible, consent for transfer should be obtained from the patient with the indications and risks clearly explained (Intensive Care Society 2011). The same information must be relayed to the relatives. This informed consent can be supported via standard information displayed on a website especially if highly sophisticated treatment is intended (ARDS Zentrum Berlin 2007).
2. Transferring specialist: the consultant with clinical responsibility must make the final decision for transfer and discuss this with the receiving hospital unit. Other teams involved in the patient's care must also be informed. The transferring specialist must also discuss the needs of the transfer with the appropriate transfer team. This will involve briefing the team leader.
3. Team leader: the team leader must clearly discuss the needs of the patient with the team before departure; in addition, they must inform the receiving unit on departure from the referring unit and provide an estimation of arrival time.
4. During transfer: it is important to maintain communication with the receiving unit during transfer.
5. Handover: the team leader must complete a clear and thorough handover to the receiving team (see 'Handover and documentation').
6. Debrief: a team discussion after completion of the transfer is a useful exercise to highlight any areas for improvement.

The receiving unit must be given the following information:

1. Name and role of transferring specialist
2. Patient's name, age, and sex
3. Reason for transfer
4. Medical history: relevant details only, full written history available in notes
5. Details of current clinical condition
6. Details of current therapy
7. Change in therapy to be undertaken for transfer
8. Infection risk
9. State of family communication
10. Mode of transfer
11. Time frame of transfer
12. Contact details for referring team.

The details of this communication must be clearly documented in the medical records.

Patient preparation

As a general principle, it is vital for the patient to be fully stabilized and resuscitated before transfer (Andrews et al. 1990). In exceptional circumstances, this may be impractical, such as a ruptured aortic aneurysm. Patients with unstable cardiovascular or respiratory physiology have an understandably higher risk of mortality (Schiff et al. 1986). The same level of care must be taken for both intra- and inter-hospital transfers, as the risks are comparable (Gray et al. 2004).

Preparation before transfer is vital to ensure patient safety. It is helpful to refer to national or local guidelines, which often provide a checklist (Intensive Care Society 2011).

The key elements to consider are:

1. Patient physiology, medication, and equipment
2. Transfer team
3. Transport.

A thorough review by body system is essential to optimize physiological stability before movement. It may be helpful to use the ABCDE acronym to minimize the potential for neglecting any element of the patients care.

- A: a definitive airway is imperative before transfer. This may necessitate elective intubation in a spontaneously ventilating patient if the potential for compromise during transfer is considered (e.g. head injury patient with fluctuating conscious level). As a rule, a Glasgow Coma Scale (GCS) score of less than 8 is considered a suitable level for intubation. The airway, whether tracheal tube or tracheostomy, must be firmly secured without compromising cerebral blood flow and drainage. Indications for elective intubation before transfer (Greaves et al. 2009):
    1. Glasgow coma score of 8 or lower
    2. Significantly deteriorating conscious level—motor score decrease greater than 2 points
    3. No protective laryngeal reflex
    4. Hypoxaemia Pa_{O_2} less than 13 kPa on oxygen
    5. Hypercarbia Pa_{CO_2} greater than 6 kPa
    6. Spontaneous hyperventilation causing Pa_{CO_2} less than 4 kPa
    7. Bilateral fractured mandible
    8. Copious bleeding into mouth (e.g. base of skull fracture)
    9. Seizures
    10. Burns with risk of airway obstruction.

11. C-spine: a hard collar and blocks is the most effective method of c-spine immobilization for patients with known or suspected cervical spine injury.

- B: for those patients spontaneously ventilating, a non-rebreathing mask with high-flow oxygen is recommended while the patient should ideally be sitting upright. Chest drains should be checked and one-way valve drainage fitted if possible. Invasively ventilated patients should be stabilized on the chosen transport ventilator with adequate gas exchange demonstrated on arterial blood gas analysis. Pre-emptive suction should be used where deemed necessary.
- C: heart rate and blood pressure should be stabilized with intravascular volume replacement and a minimum of two reliable sites of intravenous access. Central venous access may need to be considered if peripheral access is difficult or there is cardiovascular instability. For longer journeys, at least one access should be connected to fluid replacement and must be accessible. Syringe drivers and volumetric infusion pumps are recommended to provide reliable administration. Adequate organ perfusion and haemoglobin must be established before transfer. Arterial access may also be needed, although the limitations due to movement artifact and inaccurate transducer placement must not be overlooked.
- D: sedation must be assessed before beginning the transfer and modifications made as necessary. The additional stimulation of physical movement may necessitate increased administration of sedative medication to facilitate safe transfer, for example, in head injury patients with the potential for increasing intracerebral pressure. A bolus of neuromuscular blocking agent is often necessary. Blood glucose must be checked routinely. ICP monitoring should be considered and antiseizure medication optimized where appropriate.
- E: the patient must be thoroughly examined before transfer, because access will be limited during transit. It is important to document findings for the receiving unit. Hypothermia is common during transfer. Provision for additional warming facilities should be considered. All long bone and pelvic fractures should be immobilized where possible.

Monitoring and equipment

The minimum standards as recommended by the Intensive Care Society (2011) in the United Kingdom are:

1. ECG
2. Blood pressure
3. Oxygen saturation
4. End-tidal carbon dioxide in ventilated patients
5. Temperature.

Once the patient is stabilized, they can be prepared for transfer. With the volume of equipment needed for many critically ill patients it is worth remembering the limitations of the mode of transport chosen. As mentioned previously, access will be limited regardless of vehicle, indeed intra-hospital transfers are also complicated by poor access to the patient. For transfers within the hospital it is useful to attach equipment to the inside of the bed space to minimize the potential for damage in enclosed space such as lifts. For transfers involving a vehicle, at least one side of the trolley is likely to be against the sidewall. For British ambulance transfers this is typically the left side. Positioning equipment on the right of the trolley will avoid unnecessary adjustments. In addition, the clinician will be seated on the right of the patient; therefore, it is useful to position arterial and venous access on this side.

Intra-transport management and monitoring

If patient stabilization has been achieved and all suitable planning is undertaken, the transfer should be safe and uneventful (Gray et al. 2004).

Monitoring

This should be the same monitoring used during the stabilization of the patient. During this period, it is important to note the capnography reading. Continuous end-tidal carbon dioxide monitoring has been recommended for all patients with tracheal tubes and tracheostomies who are intubated and ventilator dependent (Cook et al. 2011). However, the end-tidal carbon dioxide concentrations should be expected to be different to arterial carbon dioxide. For those patients in whom careful arterial carbon dioxide monitoring is required, such as traumatic brain injury, it may be helpful to ascertain a direct comparison with arterial samples before departure. For patients with a high end-tidal carbon dioxide reading, the arterial value is likely to be considerably higher. In addition, there are important reasons for an unexpectedly low end-tidal carbon dioxide reading such as low cardiac output or hyperventilation.

The monitor must be clearly visible with suitable alarms in place to detect any physiological derangement. Ensuring that monitoring of vital functions throughout transfer will reduce the risk of complications (Warren et al. 2004).

Management

It is useful to have pre-planned patient assessment at critical points during the transfer. Clearly, the patient will be fully assessed before departure. Subsequent checks could be performed once positioned in the vehicle, before leaving the vehicle, on arrival at the receiving unit with the receiving team, and at any time should physiological disturbance be noted.

A thorough method for assessing the patient is with the ABCDE system. This will ensure that all aspects of patient physiology are reviewed, providing the most robust method for determining the cause of any problems encountered.

The responsibility of the patient remains with the referring clinician until a full handover has been given to the receiving unit. Consequently, advice should be considered and sought from the referring unit if necessary.

Handover and documentation

Documentation

A clear and concise record must be maintained at all stages of the transfer. This will commence before departure with documentation of the patient's condition, the reason for the transfer, and the details of the referring and receiving consultants. Immediately before starting the transfer, an assessment of the patient's physiology must be completed and recorded. During the transfer, vital signs should be recorded regularly in addition to any clinical events and therapies administered (Intensive Care Society 2011).

The Intensive Care Society in the United Kingdom recommends the development of standardized documentation for inter- and intra-hospital transfers across critical care networks. This should facilitate the generation of data through duplication documentation for audit purposes.

Handover

In the United Kingdom the Intensive Care Society guidelines (2011) recommend both verbal and written handovers of all elements of patient care at the receiving unit, including vital signs, clinical events, and therapies during transfer. The transferring team leader must provide a clear and concise handover to the receiving clinician. This is no less important for the intra-hospital transfer, with this important stage of patient care often being informal, unstructured, and inconsistent (Nagpal et al. 2010). Indeed a study published in 2007 suggested that the healthcare profession could learn useful lessons from Formula One and aviation models (Catchpole et al. 2007) for handover. Catchpole et al. consulted specialists in aviation and Formula One to produce a structured handover for patients transferred between theatre and intensive care, focusing on leadership, task allocation, standardized processes, checklists, and communication. Although the study group was too small to demonstrate evidence of a reduction in mortality, they were able to show a significant reduction in technical errors and information omissions.

Receiving team

It is vital that the new team performs a thorough assessment of the patient on arrival preferably by a consensus-based checklist. At this point, it is also possible to change the transfer equipment to the monitors, ventilators, and infusion devices of the new unit. The transfer equipment can then be taken back to the referring unit.

It is considered courteous to provide the transfer team with refreshments before their departure.

Quality management

The success of the transport of critical ill patients depends on the way the transporting team can manage the complex processes and especially at the interfaces. The quality requirements are high and therefore it is not only for legal requirements that it is recommended to implement a quality management system, which helps to establish a continuous improving process. All the above-cited requirements, staff training, vehicles, equipment, guidelines, and checklists must be adopted to the local situation and can be described according to Donabedian's framework of quality: structure, process, and results. A critical incident reporting system serves to identify the most important points to be discussed in quality circles and to start improvement. Additional research is needed to identify relevant measurable quality indicators.

Professional indemnity

Many personnel are unclear of the level of personal insurance required for inter-hospital transfers. The AAGBI recommended in their transfer guidance issued in 2006 that all staff must have suitable medical indemnity and personal accident insurance. The issue was highlighted in a recent postal survey published in *Anaesthesia*. A total of 269 RCoA college tutors answered a questionnaire regarding transfer arrangements within their hospitals. More than 30% indicated that they were unsure on the amount of cover provided by the hospital and just 9% documented that additional personal insurance was required for anaesthesia staff of any grade involved in transfer (Knowles et al. 1999).

Data from North America for both primary and secondary transfers reveal a collision rate of 5:10 000 responses with a death rate of 12.7:100 000 emergency medical personnel (Maguier et al. 2002). The highest rate of collisions occurs with road transport using 'lights and sirens' (Biggers et al. 1996). A study published by Lutman et al. (2008) documented the number of accidents of both air and land transfer in the United Kingdom between 1999 and 2004. For road vehicles, the number of accidents ranged from 306 to 369 per year with an average of 579 casualties per year and a total of 40 fatalities for the whole period. The data they provide is unable to estimate the rate of accidents as the total number of driving hours is unknown. For helicopter transport, no fatalities were documented, while a total of five medical personnel were killed in a single fixed-wing accident in the same time period.

These studies demonstrate that undertaking a transfer (particularly a fast *road* transfer) can be dangerous for both medical personnel and the general public. All members of the transfer team must have adequate insurance before departure.

Anaesthesia in the intensive care unit patient

Patients receiving care on the ICU occasionally require surgery; this might be for ongoing treatment of their primary pathology, or may represent investigative or resuscitative treatment. The subject is included in this chapter because it may be considered as requiring the generic skills of the anaesthetist *plus* the skills required in transfer of the critically ill patient. Specific issues may arise when dealing with the patient from the ICU, and in this section, we will deal briefly with the following:

- The transition between sedation and anaesthesia
- Organ protection (lung, kidney, and brain)
- Infection control
- Gastric contents
- Drugs (ongoing infusions, impact of in-theatre drugs)
- Invasive monitoring
- Physical protection.

Risk assessment

Any anaesthesia or surgery in the critically ill patient carries significant risk. There should be careful assessment and discussion between the teams involved as to the necessity of any such procedure in the context of their medical condition. The critical care team will usually be fully aware of all aspects of management, but often the anaesthetist will meet the patient immediately before anaesthesia. It is essential there is adequate discussion and handover of all aspects of the case including a risk assessment.

The transition between sedation and anaesthesia

An unresponsive patient on the ICU is not necessarily unaware of their surroundings, and sedation should almost always be deepened when surgery is anticipated. Short-acting drugs (e.g. propofol and modern inhalation anaesthetics) are preferable to long-acting sedatives (e.g. midazolam and morphine) in that they may be rapidly reversed in the event of cardiovascular instability and in that they are likely to interfere less with ventilatory management and weaning after return to the ICU.

Induction of anaesthesia should be titrated carefully, and with regard to arterial pressure. Critically ill patients who have been receiving infusion(s) of sedative drugs can be very sensitive to anaesthetic agents with respect to cardiac depression and vasodilation.

After surgery, it is very common to transfer patients back to the ICU while still under the effects of the general anaesthetic. Care should be taken not to allow anaesthesia to wear off while deep neuromuscular block persists.

Neuromuscular block is often used even when not strictly necessary in order to minimize the risk of patient–ventilator asynchrony during transfer, and there is some merit in this approach. However, it must be borne in mind that neuromuscular blocking agents will often have prolonged effects in critically ill patients (due to muscle and electrolyte changes) and that this might interfere with the reinstitution of spontaneous breathing and weaning after surgery. Neuromuscular blocking agents may also accumulate in patients with impaired liver and kidney function, and the dose should be minimized, when possible. Of particular importance is the risk of using suxamethonium (succinylcholine) in the long-term, bed-bound patient, where dangerous hyperkalaemia (risking dysrhythmia) may be triggered (Blanié et al. 2012).

Organ protection

Systemic inflammation, hypoxaemia, hypoalbuminaemia, acidaemia, and pathological disturbance in organ perfusion (due to vasodilation and impaired cardiac function) often combine to place end-organs at risk. Meticulous care should be taken in assuring adequate organ perfusion pressure and arterial oxygenation.

Patients' lungs will be at risk of ventilator-associated lung injury, and a continued lung-protective ventilation strategy is vital if lung injury is to be avoided (Severgnini et al. 2013). Large tidal volumes should be avoided and positive end-expiratory pressure should be maintained at the level used before surgery; indeed, in general, it is wise to mirror the ventilator strategy used in the ICU as far as possible. Lung protection is reliant upon avoiding excessive distension and collapse–reopening of alveoli, and it is usually better to tolerate moderate hypercapnia or mild hypoxaemia during surgery than to expose the patient's lungs to excessive ventilatory forces. Consideration should also be given to sputum clearance: patients on the ICU often have increased sputum production, and hypoxaemia due to sputum plugging may occur.

Brain perfusion should be maintained (in susceptible patients) through appropriate positioning, avoidance of neck compression, and assurance of appropriate cerebral perfusion pressure. The liver and kidneys should be protected through assuring adequate organ oxygen delivery (cardiac output, mean arterial pressure, haemoglobin and Pa_{O_2}) and avoidance of organotoxic drugs (e.g. halothane and non-steroidal anti-inflammatory drugs). In patients with impaired liver or kidney function, drugs that are critically dependent upon those organs for drug elimination should be avoided, where possible; in this context, spontaneously degrading neuromuscular blocking agents (e.g. atracurium) are preferable to those requiring hepatic excretion (e.g. vecuronium).

Infection control

Critically ill patients are often immunocompromised and are often undergoing complex antimicrobial regimens. It is important that the anaesthetist avoids placing the patient at risk of new infection, and that ongoing antimicrobial regimens are adhered to (i.e. that scheduled doses are not missed during prolonged surgery).

Gastric contents

The critically ill patient will often have delayed gastric emptying, and may be receiving gastric feeding. The anaesthetist should treat all such patients as being at risk of aspiration of gastric contents.

Coagulopathy

This is extremely common in the critically ill and may be pertinent in terms of the surgery undertaken or interventions planned, such as replacing lines. Checking and correcting coagulation status (or making provision to do so) is essential.

Biochemistry

These patients often have renal and liver impairment but in particular may be undergoing dialysis or other interventions. Discussion with the intensive care team as to the current biochemical position may influence the timing of surgery in semi-elective situations where optimization is possible. This may not always be possible in an emergency.

Drugs

Patients on the ICU often present to the anaesthetist a bewildering array of infusions, and while there is some sense in simplifying the immediate patient environment for safe transfer, there is also the argument that finely balanced intensive therapy should be disturbed as little as possible during surgery.

All vasoactive and inotropic infusion should be maintained, and the anaesthetist should assure themselves of familiarity with the identities, concentrations, and associated venous access for each infusion.

Insulin infusions should be maintained, and blood glucose monitored regularly during surgery. Other short-duration infusions (e.g. antibiotics) should be completed before transfer, ideally.

As mentioned previously, careful consideration should be given to whether neuromuscular blocking agents are necessary during transfer and surgery, and to the anticipated duration of residual sedative drugs after surgery. The aim should be to complete surgery safely, while minimizing the effect on the patient's subsequent recovery on the ICU.

Invasive monitoring

Patients typically have the benefit of central venous and arterial pressure monitoring on the ICU. These should be utilized in the operating theatre, and values should be titrated to those previously achieved on the ICU. Of particular importance is the need to maintain the sterility of indwelling vascular access during visits to the operating theatre; co-infection is common and dangerous in critically ill patient and is often related to line sepsis.

Attention must be paid to ongoing infusions into such lines, and drug infusions should not be accidentally flushed into the patient by inappropriate use of injection ports. The anaesthetist must ensure familiarity with which drug is being infused (and where) before using the patient's existing vascular access.

Visits to the operating theatre present the opportunity for the re-siting of time-expired vascular catheters, and it is worth checking before surgery (with the ICU nurses, doctors, or both) whether any such catheters need replacing. If such replacement is performed in theatre, meticulous attention should be paid to asepsis and to documentation of the re-siting.

Physical protection

Critically ill patients are at increased risk of physical injury. Their skin is often thinned and delicate, their muscles are wasted, and they have impaired immunity. Transfer between bed and operating table, and positioning on the operating table present to the patient significant risks of cutaneous, muscular, and bony injury; the effect of such apparently minor injuries can be catastrophic in the already-unwell patient. Meticulous attention to detail, adequate staffing, appropriate use of lifting/transfer adjuncts, and excellent communication are key.

The patient and their family

For both patient and their family, critical illness is extremely stressful. An anaesthetic, almost invariably, is perceived as an additional risk. Discussion with the patient is essential where possible and with the family where relevant. The critical care team usually lead on this but it is wise for the anaesthetist also to discuss their role with the patient and relatives where possible.

Declaration of interest

None declared.

References

Ahmed I, Majeed A. Risk management during inter-hospital transfer of critically ill patients: making the journey safe. *Emerg Med J* 2008; **25**: 502–5

ARDS Zentrum Berlin. 2007. ARDS Center. Available from http://www.ards.charite.de/patientenuebernahme_ards.htm

Andrews P, Piper I, Dearden N, Miller J. Secondary insults during intrahospital transport of head-injured patients. *Lancet* 1990; **335**: 327–30

Association of Anaesthetists of Great Britain and Ireland. *Recommendations for the Safe Transfer of Patients with Brain Injury*. London: AAGBI, 2006 Available from http://www.aagbi.org/sites/default/files/braininjury.pdf

Australasian College for Emergency Medicine, Australian and New Zealand College of Anaesthetists and Joint Faculty of Intensive Care Medicine. Minimum standards for intrahospital transport of critically ill patients. *Emerg Med (Fremantle)* 2003; **15**: 202–4

Barton A, Tuttle-Newhall J, Szalados J. Portable power supply for continuous mechanical ventilation during intra-hospital transport of critically ill patients with ARDS. *Chest* 1997; **112**: 560–3

Beckmann U, Gillies DM, Berenholtz SM, Wu AW, Pronovost P. Incidents relating to the intra-hospital transfer of critically ill patients. An analysis of the reports submitted to the Australian Incident Monitoring Study in Intensive Care. *Intensive Care Med* 2004; **30**: 1579–85

Bellingan G, Olivier T, Batson S, Webb A. Comparison of a specialist retrieval team with current United Kingdom practice for the transport of critically ill patients. *Intensive Care Med* 2000; **26**: 740–4

Bercault N, Wolf M, Runge I, Fleury J, Boulain T. Intrahospital transport of critically ill ventilated patients: a risk factor for ventilator-associated pneumonia-a matched cohort study. *Crit Care Med* 2005; **33**: 2471–8

Biggers WA Jr, Zachariah BS, Pepe PE. Emergency medical vehicle collisions in an urban system. *Prehosp Disaster Med* 1996; **11**: 195–201

Blanié A, Ract C, Leblanc P-E, *et al.* The limits of succinylcholine for critically ill patients. *Anesth Analg* 2012; **115**: 873–9

Burney RE, Hubert D, Passini L, Maio R. Variation in air medical outcomes by crew composition: a two-year follow-up. *Ann Emerg Med* 1995; **25**: 187–92

Catchpole KR, de Leval MR, McEwan A, *et al.* Patient handover from surgery to intensive care: using Formula 1 pit-stop and aviation models to improve safety and quality. *Pediatr Anesth* 2007; **17**: 470–8

Cook T, Woodall N, Harper J, Benger J. Major complications of airway management in the UK: results of the Fourth National Audit Project of the Royal College of Anaesthetists and the Difficult Airway Society. Part 2: intensive care and emergency departments. *Br J Anaesth* 2011; **106**: 632–42

Chipman D, Caramez M, Miyoshi E, Kratohvil J, Kacmarek R. Performance comparison of 15 transport ventilators. *Respir Care* 2007; **52**: 740–51

Damm C, Vandelet P, Petit J, Richard JC, Veber B, Bonmarchand G, Dureuil B. Complications during the intrahospital transport in critically ill patients. *Ann Fr Anesth Reanim* 2005; **24**: 24–30

de Mello W, Thompson M. The disadvantages of helicopter transfer. *Br J Hosp Med* 1990; **43**: 328

Deutsche Interdisziplinare Vereiningung fur Intensive und Notfalimedezin (DIVI). DIVI, 2008. Available from http://www.divi-org.de

Doring BL, Kerr ME, Lovasik DA, Thayer T. Factors that contribute to complications during intrahospital transport of the critically ill. *J Neurosci Nurs* 1999; **31**: 80–6

Durairaj L, Will JG, Torner JC, Doebbeling BN. Prognostic factors for mortality following interhospital transfers to the medical intensive care unit of a tertiary referral center. *Crit Care Med* 2003; **31**: 1981–6

Essebag V, Halabi A, Churhill-Smith M, Lutchmedial S. Air medical transport in cardiac patients. *Chest* 2003; **124**: 1937–45

European Committee for Standardization. Medical Vehicles and their Equipment - Road Ambulances. EN 1789, 1999. Available from http://www.cenorm.be

Fanara B, Manzon C, Barbot O, Desmettre T, Capellier G. Recommendations for the intra-hospital transport of critically ill patients. *Crit Care* 2010; **14**: 87

Fang R, Allan PF, Womble SG, *et al.* Closing the 'care in the air' capability gap for severe lung injury: the Landstuhl Acute Lung Rescue Team and extracorporeal lung support. *J Trauma* 2011; **71**: 591–7

Ferdinande P. Recommendations for intra-hospital transport of the severely head injured patient. Working Group on Neurosurgical Intensive Care of the European Society of Intensive Care Medicine. *Intensive Care Med* 1999; **25**: 1441–3

Flabouris A, Runciman WB, Levings B. Incidents during out-of-hospital patient transportation. *Anaesth Intensive Care* 2006; **34**: 228–36

Flutter C, Ruth M, Aldington D. Pain management during Royal Air Force strategic aeromedical evacuations. *J R Army Med Corps* 2009; **155**: 61–3

Forrest P, Ratchford J, Burns B, *et al.* Retrieval of critically ill adults using extracorporeal membrane oxygenation: an Australian experience. *Intensive Care Med* 2011; **37**: 824–30

Fromm R, Jr, Dellinger R. Transport of critically ill patients. *J Intensive Care Med* 1992; **7**: 223–33

Gentleman D, Jennett B. Hazards of inter-hospital transfer of comatose head-injured patients. *Lancet* 1981; **318**: 853–5

Gerlach H, Keh D, Semmerow A, *et al.* Dose–response characteristics during long-term inhalation of nitric oxide in patients with severe acute respiratory distress syndrome. *Am J Respir Crit Care Med* 2003; **167**: 1008–15

Gillman L, Leslie G, Williams T, Fawcett K, Bell R, McGibbon V. Adverse events experienced while transferring the critically ill patient from the emergency department to the intensive care unit. *Emerg Med J* 2006; **23**: 858–61

Girotti MJ, Pagliarello G, Todd TR, *et al.* Physician-accompanied transport of surgical intensive care patients. *Can J Anaesth* 1988; **35**: 303–8

Gray A, Gill S, Airey M, Williams R. Descriptive epidemiology of adult critical care transfers from the emergency department. *Emerg Med J* 2003; **20**: 242–6

Gray A, Bush S, Whiteley S. Secondary transport of the critically ill and injured adult. *Emerg Med J* 2004; **21**: 281–5

Greaves I, Porter K, Garner, J. *Trauma Care Manual.* London: Edward Arnold, 2009

Guidelines Committee of the American College of Critical Care Medicine; Society of Critical Care Medicine and American Association of Critical-Care Nurses Transfer Guidelines Task Force. Guidelines for the transfer of critically ill patients. *Crit Care Med* 1993; **21**: 931–7

Handy JM, Van Zwanenberg G. Secondary transfer of the critically ill patient. *Curr Anaesth Crit Care* 2007; **18**: 303–10

Hennes P. Intensive care transport. In: Huf R, Sefrin P, Weinlich M, eds. *Intensive Care Transport*, 2nd Edn. Osttirol: Matrei, 2005; A-9971

Intensive Care Society. *Guidelines for the Transport of the Critically Ill Adult.* London: Intensive Care Society, 2011. Available from http://members.ics.ac.uk/ICS/guidelines-and-standards.aspx

Iwashyna T, Christie J, Kahn J, Asch D. Uncharted paths hospital networks in critical care. *Chest* 2009; **135**: 827–33

Jameson PP, Lawler PG. Transfer of critically ill patients in the Northern region. *Anaesthesia* 2000; **55**: 489

Kaplan L, Walsh D, Burney RE. Emergency aeromedical transport of patients with acute myocardial infarction. *Ann Emerg Med* 1987; **16**: 55–7

Karanicolas P, Bhatia P, Williamson J, Malthaner R, Parry N, Girotti M, Gray D. The fastest route between two points is not always a straight line. An analysis of air and land transfer of non penetrating trauma patients. *J Trauma* 2008; **61**: 396–403

Knowles P, Bryden D, Kishen R, Gwinnutt C. Meeting the standards for interhospital transfer of adults with severe head injury in the United Kingdom. *Anaesthesia* 1999; **54**: 280–3

Lahner D, Nikolic A, Marhofer P, *et al.* Incidence of complications in intrahospital transport of critically ill patients – experience in an Austrian university hospital. *Wien Klin Wochenschr* 2007; **11**: 412–6

Lee A, Lum ME, Beehan SJ, Hillman KM. Interhospital transfers: decision-making in critical care areas. *Crit Care Med* 1996; **24**: 618–22

Lieshout E, Vos R, Binnekade J, Haan R, Schultz M, Vroom M. Decision making in interhospital transport of critically ill patients: national questionnaire survey among critical care physicians. *Intensive Care Med* 2008; **34**: 1269–73

Lovell MA, Mudaliar MY, Klineberg PL. Intrahospital transport of critically ill patients: complications and difficulties. *Anaesth Intensive Care* 2001; **29**: 400–5

Lutman D, Petros AJ. How many oxygen cylinders do you need to take on transport? A nomogram for cylinder size and duration. *Emerg Med J* 2006; **23**: 703–4

Lutman D, Montgomery M, Ramnarayan P, Petros A. Ambulance and aeromedical accident rates during emergency retrieval in Great Britain. *Emerg Med J* 2008; **25**: 301–2

Mackenzie PA, Smith EA, Wallace PG. Transfer of adults between intensive care units in the United Kingdom: postal survey. *Br Med J* 1997; **314**: 1455–6

Maguire BJ, Hunting KL, Smith GS, *et al.* Occupational fatalities in emergency medical services: a hidden crisis. *Ann Emerg Med* 2002; **40**: 625–32

McCunn M, Mirvis S, Reynolds N, *et al.* Physician utilization of a portable computed tomography scanner in the intensive care unit. *Crit Care Med* 2000; **28**: 3808–13

Nagpal K, Arora S, Abboudi M, *et al.* Postoperative handover: problems, pitfalls, and prevention of error. *Ann Surg* 2010; **252**: 171–6

Nakamura T, Fujino Y, Uchiyama A, Mashimo T, Nishimura M. Intrahospital transport of critically ill patients using ventilator with patient-triggering function. *Chest* 2003; **123**: 159–64

Noah M, Peek GJ, Finney SJ, *et al.* Referral to an extracorporeal membrane oxygenation center and mortality among patients with severe 2009 influenza A(H1N1). *JAMA* 2011; **306**: 1659–68

Papson JP, Russell KL, Taylor DM. Unexpected events during the intrahospital transport of critically ill patients. *Acad Emerg Med* 2007; **14**: 574–7

Peek GJ, Mugford M, Tiruvoipati R, *et al.* Efficacy and economic assessment of conventional ventilatory support versus extracorporeal membrane oxygenation for severe adult respiratory failure (CESAR): a multicentre randomised controlled trial. *Lancet* 2009; **374**: 1351–63

Porter JM, Ivatury RR, Kavarana M, *et al.* The surgical intensive care unit as a cost-efficient substitute for an operating room at a Level I trauma center. *Am Surg* 1999; **65**: 328–30

Rice DH, Kotti G, Beninati W. Clinical review: critical care transport and austere critical care. *Crit Care* 2008; **12**: 207

Richard J, Maggiore S, Jonson B, Mancebo J, Lemaire F, Brochard L. Influence of tidal volume on alveolar recruitment respective role of PEEP and a recruitment maneuver. *Am J Respir Crit Care Med* 2001; **163**: 1609–13

Rossaint R, Falke K, Lopez F, Slama K, Pison U, Zapol W. Inhaled nitric oxide for the adult respiratory distress syndrome. *N Engl J Med* 1993; **328**: 399–405

Sand M, Bollenbach M, Sand D, *et al.* Epidemiology of aeromedical evacuation: an analysis of 504 cases. *J Travel Med* 2010; **17**: 405–9

Schiff RL, Ansell DA, Schlosser JE, Idris AH, Morrison A, Whitman S. Transfers to a public hospital. A prospective study of 467 patients. *N Engl J Med* 1986; **314**: 552–7

Severgnini P, Selmo G, Lanza C, *et al.* Protective mechanical ventilation during general anesthesia for open abdominal surgery improves postoperative pulmonary function. *Anesthesiology* 2013; **118**: 1307–21

Seymour CW, Kahn JM, Schwab CW, Fuchs BD. Adverse events during rotary-wing transport of mechanically ventilated patients: a retrospective cohort study. *Crit Care* 2008; **12**: 71

Shirley PJ, Stott SA. Clinical and organisational problems in patients transferred from the intensive care unit to other areas within the hospital for diagnostic procedures. *Br J Anaesth* 2001; **87**: 346–7

SIAARTI Study Group for Safety in Anesthesia and Intensive Care. Recommendations on the transport of critically ill patient. *Minerva Anestesiol* 2006; **72**: XXXVII–LVII

Smith I, Fleming S, Cernaianu A. Mishaps during transport from the intensive care unit. *Crit Care Med* 1990; **18**: 278–81

Spencer C, Watkinson P, McCluskey A. Training and assessment of competency of trainees in the transfer of critically ill patients. *Anaesthesia* 2004; **59**: 1248–9

Stearley HE. Patients' outcomes: intrahospital transportation and monitoring of critically ill patients by a specially trained ICU nursing staff. *Am J Crit Care* 1998; **7**: 282–7

Stevenson V, Haas C, Wahl W. Intrahospital transport of the adult mechanically ventilated patient. *Respir Care Clin N Am* 2002; **8**: 1–35

Szem J, Hydo L, Fischer E, *et al.* High-risk intrahospital transport of critically ill patients: safety and outcome of the necessary 'road trip'. *Crit Care Med* 1995; **23**: 1660–6

Taylor J, Landers C, Chulay J, Hood W, Abelmann W. Monitoring high-risk cardiac patients during transportation in hospital. *Lancet* 1970; **ii**: 1205–8

Turner S, Ruth M, Tipping R. Critical Care Air Support Teams and deployed intensive care. *J R Army Med Corps* 2009; **155**: 171–4

Valenzuela TD, Criss EA, Copass MK, Luna GK, Rice CL. Critical care air transportation of the severely injured: does long distance transport adversely affect survival? *Ann Emerg Med* 1990; **19**: 169–72

Venkataraman ST, Orr RA. Intrahospital transport of critically ill patients. *Crit Care Clin*, 1992; **8**: 525–31

Voigt L, Pastores S, Raoof N, Thaler H, Halpern N. Review of a large clinical series: intrahospital transport of critically ill patients: outcomes, timing, and patterns. *J Intensive Care Med* 2009; **24**: 108

Waddell G. Movement of critically ill patients within hospital. *BMJ* 1975; **2**: 417–9

Wallace P, Ridley S. Transport of critically ill patients. *BMJ* 1999; **319**: 368–71

Wallen E, Venkataraman S, Grosso MJ, Kiene K, Orr RA. Intrahospital transport of critically ill pediatric patients. *Crit Care Med* 1995; **23**: 1588–95

Wallin, M, Wajntraub S. Evaluation of bluetooth as a replacement for cables in intensive care and surgery. *Anesth Analg* 2004; **98**: 763–7

Warren J, Fromm R Jr, Orr R, Rotello L, Horst H. Guidelines for the inter- and intrahospital transport of critically ill patients. *Crit Care Med* 2004; **32**: 256–62

Waydhas C, Schneck G, Duswald KH. Deterioration of respiratory function after intra-hospitaltransport of critically ill surgical patients. *Intensive Care Med* 1995; **21**: 784–9

Westrope C, Roberts N, Nichani S, Hunt C, Peek G, Firmin R. Experience with mobile inhaled nitric oxide during transport of neonates and children with respiratory insufficiency to an extracorporeal membrane oxygenation center. *Pediatr Crit Care Med* 2004; **5**: 542–6

Wiegersma J, Droogh J, Zijlstra J, Fokkema J, Ligtenberg J. Quality of interhospital transport of the critically ill: impact of a Mobile Intensive Care Unit with a specialized retrieval team. *Crit Care* 2011; **15**: 75

Zanetta G, Robert D, Guerin C. Evaluation of ventilators used during transport of ICU patients—a bench study. *Intensive Care Med* 2002; **28**: 443–51

CHAPTER 91

Advanced life support

Jerry P. Nolan

Introduction

Anaesthetists have always played a central role in advanced life support (ALS) and were responsible for establishing the earliest hospital-based cardiopulmonary resuscitation (CPR) teams (Sykes 1964; Sykes and Orr 1966). The ultimate medical emergency is cardiac arrest which requires immediate, effective treatment if the patient is to have any chance of a good-quality survival. The cardiovascular and respiratory interventions that form the basis of ALS are fundamental skills for every anaesthetist and intensivist—the medical profession and the public would expect us to deliver these interventions to the highest standard.

Epidemiology and outcome of cardiac arrest

In 2006, coronary heart disease accounted for one of every six deaths (a total of 425 425) in the United States and one-third of these deaths occurred within 1 h of symptom onset (Lloyd-Jones et al. 2010). Approximately 80% of all sudden cardiac deaths are caused by coronary heart disease (Myerburg and Junttila 2012). In Europe, the annual incidence of emergency medical system (EMS)-treated out-of-hospital cardiopulmonary arrest (OHCA) for all rhythms is 40 per 100 000 population (Berdowski et al. 2010) with ventricular fibrillation (VF) arrest accounting for about one-third of these. However, the incidence of VF is declining: most recently reported as 23.7% among EMS-treated arrests of cardiac aetiology (McNally et al. 2011). Survival to hospital discharge is 8–10% for all-rhythm and around 21–27% for VF cardiac arrest (Nichol et al. 2008; McNally et al. 2011).

The incidence of in-hospital cardiac arrest (IHCA) is difficult to assess because it is heavily influenced by factors such as the criteria for hospital admission and implementation of a do not attempt cardiopulmonary resuscitation (DNACPR) policy. The reported incidence of IHCA is in the range of 1–5 per 1000 admissions. There is some evidence that survival rates after IHCA are slowly increasing (Girotra et al. 2012). Data from the UK National Cardiac Arrest Audit (NCAA) indicate that survival to hospital discharge after IHCA is 18.4% (all rhythms) (Nolan et al. 2014). The initial rhythm is VF or pulseless ventricular tachycardia (pVT) in 16.9% of cases and, of these, 49% survive to leave hospital; after pulseless electrical activity (PEA) or asystole, 10.5% survive to hospital discharge. These NCAA data are based on 22 628 adults (aged ≥16 years) in 144 hospitals participating in NCAA (increasing numbers of hospitals during April 2011 to March 2013) with known presenting/first documented rhythm and complete data for return of spontaneous circulation (ROSC) and survival to hospital discharge. All these individuals received chest compressions, defibrillation, or both, and attendance by a resuscitation team in response to a 2222 call. Many patients sustaining an IHCA have significant comorbidity, which influences the initial rhythm and, in these cases, strategies to prevent cardiac arrest are particularly important.

The published incidence of perioperative cardiac arrest ranges from 2.4 to 34.6 per 10 000. This wide range reflects differences in case-mix (some studies include neonates, cardiac surgery, or both) and in the definition of 'perioperative' (see 'Perioperative cardiac arrest').

Prevention of unexpected cardiac arrest

Most adults who survive an IHCA have a witnessed and monitored VF arrest and are defibrillated immediately (Meaney et al. 2010). The underlying cause of arrest in this group is usually primary myocardial ischaemia. In contrast, cardiac arrest in patients in unmonitored ward areas (accounting for the majority of IHCAs in the United Kingdom) is usually a predictable event not caused by primary cardiac disease (National Confidential Enquiry into Patient Outcome and Death 2005). In this group, cardiac arrest often follows a period of physiological deterioration involving unrecognized or inadequately treated hypoxaemia and hypotension (Kause et al. 2004). The underlying cardiac arrest rhythm is usually asystole or PEA, and the chance of survival to hospital discharge is extremely poor (6–7%).

Identifying the deteriorating patient

Many of these IHCAs could be prevented by implementing a rapid response system (RRS) (Jones et al. 2011).

The RRS comprises (a) an afferent limb (Devita et al. 2010): staff education, monitoring of patients, recognition of patient deterioration, and a system to call for help; and (b) an efferent limb: an effective response (Smith 2010). Early warning scores (EWS), or calling criteria have been adopted by many hospitals to assist in the early detection of critical illness. EWS systems allocate points to routine vital sign measurements on the basis of their deviation from the normal range. The weighted score of one or more vital sign observations, or more often the total EWS, is used to alert ward staff or critical care outreach teams to the deteriorating condition of the patient. A National Health Service (NHS) Early Warning Score (NEWS) has been developed and is being implemented in all NHS hospitals.

The response to the deteriorating patient

Having established a system to identify the patient at risk of cardiac arrest, the response must be rapid and effective if cardiac arrest is to be prevented. This could take the form of a resuscitation team that responds not just to cardiac arrest calls but also to medical emergencies, frequently termed the medical emergency team or rapid response team. A systematic review failed to show that RRS reduce the incidence of unexpected cardiac arrest (Chan et al. 2010) but implementation of a RRS in Sydney, Australia, was associated with a reduced incidence of IHCA and mortality (Chen et al. 2014). Some studies with historical control groups show a reduction in cardiac arrests, deaths, and unanticipated intensive care unit (ICU) admissions, improved detection of medical errors, treatment-limitation decisions, and reduced postoperative ward deaths; however, a cluster-randomized controlled trial of the medical emergency team system failed to show improvements in these end-points (Hillman et al. 2005). In the United Kingdom, a system of pre-emptive ward care, based predominantly on individual or teams of nurses, known as critical care outreach, has developed (McDonnell et al. 2007). There are also no high-quality data to show benefit for outreach systems (Gao et al. 2007).

Resuscitation decisions

Cardiopulmonary resuscitation is not going to be successful if cardiac arrest occurs as the final stage of a progressive and irreversible decline in the patient's health. Unfortunately, an intervention that was intended to restore a spontaneous circulation and enable a reversible condition to be treated is now being used in large numbers of patients with multiple and irreversible comorbidities. Under these circumstances, it is hardly surprisingly that long-term survival rates are so poor. Patients for whom CPR will not prolong life, but will, at best, merely prolong the dying process, should be identified early. In these cases, a DNACPR decision should be made in advance of cardiac arrest. In this way, terminally ill patients will be allowed to die with dignity and the resources of the resuscitation team can be available for those with acute, reversible illness. If a DNACPR decision is made because the patient has no chance of surviving a CPR attempt, it is generally inappropriate to discuss it with the patient or relatives—this is no different to any other highly invasive medical intervention; however, the patient, the relatives, or both, should be informed of the decision. It is quite different if a DNACPR decision is being considered because of concerns about the patient's quality of life should they survive. In these cases, every effort should be made to discuss the decision with the patients, the relatives, or both. The decision-making process is based on current guidance from the British Medical Association, Resuscitation Council (UK), and Royal College of Nursing. A standardized form is used to record and communicate DNAR decisions (http://www.resus.org.uk/pages/DNARrstd.htm). A DNACPR decision refers specifically to CPR and not to other treatment. Increasingly, DNACPR decisions are being incorporated into wider treatment plans such as the Recommended Summary Plan for Emergency Care and Treatment (ReSPECT)—also known in the United States as Physician Orders for Life-Sustaining Treatment—that focus more on what will be done for the patient rather than what will be withheld (Fromme et al. 2012).

In theory, full implementation of a DNACPR policy and a RRS should eliminate unexpected cardiac arrest. This ideal is highly unlikely to be achieved but this is the rationale for making unexpected cardiac arrest a primary quality indicator.

Advanced life support

The precise sequence of actions after cardiac arrest in hospital depends on several factors, including the location (clinical/non-clinical area, monitored/unmonitored area), the skills of the first responders, the available equipment, and the hospital response system to cardiac arrest. Guidelines for CPR are published by the Resuscitation Council (UK) (Nolan and Soar 2015) and the European Resuscitation Council (Monsieurs et al. 2015); they are based on a comprehensive review of resuscitation science that is published every 5 years by the International Liaison Committee on Resuscitation (Nolan et al. 2015a).

The advanced life support algorithm

The ALS algorithm (Fig. 91.1) is a standardized approach to cardiac arrest management. It enables treatment to be delivered expediently, without protracted discussion; each member of the resuscitation team can predict and prepare for the next stage in the patient's treatment, further enhancing efficiency of the team.

The interventions that unquestionably improve survival after cardiac arrest are prompt and effective bystander basic life support, uninterrupted, high-quality chest compressions, and early defibrillation for VF/pVT. The use of adrenaline (epinephrine) increases rates of ROSC (Jacobs et al. 2011) but no resuscitation drugs or advanced airway interventions have been shown to increase survival to hospital discharge after cardiac arrest. A large observational study from Japan documented increased ROSC but reduced 1-month survival rates (adjusted for covariates) in patients receiving adrenaline after OHCA (Hagihara et al. 2012). In comparison with placebo, amiodarone increases the rate of ROSC after VF out-of-hospital cardiac arrest (Kudenchuk et al. 2016). The results of adequately powered, ongoing randomized controlled trials will help define the role of adrenaline in ALS.

Although drugs and advanced airways are still included among ALS interventions, they are of secondary importance to high-quality, uninterrupted chest compressions and early defibrillation.

Shockable rhythms

The first monitored rhythm after either in- or out-of-hospital cardiac arrest is VF/pVT in 25% of cases. In a further 25% of cardiac arrests, VF/pVT will also occur at some stage during resuscitation after an initial documented rhythm of asystole or PEA (Meaney et al. 2010).

Treatment of shockable rhythms

1. Confirm cardiac arrest—check for signs of life, breathing, and pulse simultaneously.
2. Call the resuscitation team.
3. Perform uninterrupted chest compressions while applying self-adhesive defibrillation pads.
4. Plan actions before pausing CPR for rhythm analysis and communicate these to the team.
5. Stop chest compressions; confirm VF/pVT from the ECG. This pause in chest compressions should be brief and no longer than 5 s.
6. Resume chest compressions immediately; warn all rescuers *other than the individual performing the chest compressions* to 'stand clear' and remove any oxygen delivery device as appropriate.
7. The designated person selects the appropriate energy setting on the defibrillator and presses the charge button. Choose an

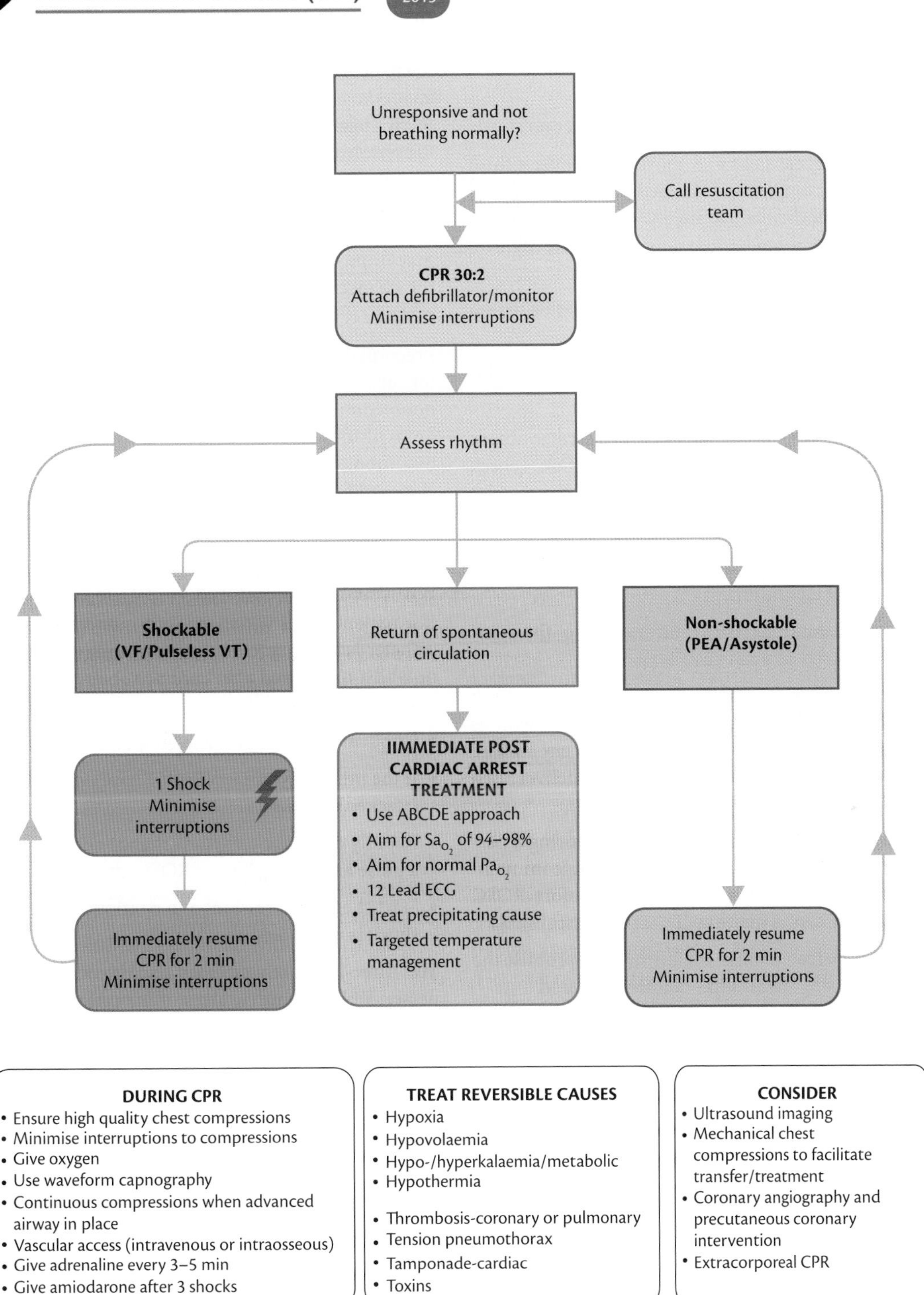

Figure 91.1 The Advanced Life Support algorithm.
Reproduced with the kind permission of the Resuscitation Council (UK).

energy setting of at least 150 J for the first shock, the same or a higher energy for subsequent shocks, or follow the manufacturer's guidance for the particular defibrillator.

8. Ensure that the rescuer giving the compressions is the only person touching the patient.
9. Once the defibrillator is charged and the safety check is complete, tell the rescuer doing the chest compressions to 'stand clear'; when clear, give the shock.
10. After shock delivery immediately restart CPR using a ratio of 30:2, starting with chest compressions. Do not pause to reassess

the rhythm or feel for a pulse. This pause in chest compressions should be brief and no longer than 5 s.

11. Continue CPR for 2 min; the team leader prepares the team for the next pause in CPR.
12. Pause briefly to check the monitor.
13. If VF/pVT, repeat steps 6–12 above and deliver a second shock.
14. If VF/pVT persists, repeat steps 6–8 above and deliver a third shock. Resume chest compressions immediately. Give adrenaline 1 mg i.v. and amiodarone 300 mg i.v. while performing a further 2 min CPR. Withhold adrenaline if there are signs of ROSC during CPR.
15. Repeat this 2 min CPR—rhythm/pulse check—defibrillation sequence if VF/pVT persists.
16. Give further adrenaline 1 mg i.v. after alternate shocks (i.e. approximately every 3–5 min).
17. If organized electrical activity compatible with a cardiac output is seen during a rhythm check, seek evidence of ROSC (check for signs of life, a central pulse, and end-tidal CO_2 if available)
    a. If there is ROSC, start post-resuscitation care.
    b. If there are no signs of ROSC, continue CPR and switch to the non-shockable algorithm.
18. If asystole is seen, continue CPR and switch to the non-shockable algorithm.[1]

The interval between stopping compressions and delivering a shock must be minimized. Longer interruptions to chest compressions reduce the chance of a shock restoring a spontaneous circulation. Chest compressions are resumed immediately after delivering a shock (without checking the rhythm or a pulse) because:

- Even if the defibrillation attempt is successful in restoring a perfusing rhythm, it is very rare for a pulse to be palpable immediately after defibrillation. The duration of asystole before ROSC can be longer than 2 min in as many as 25% of successful shocks.
- The delay in trying to palpate a pulse will further compromise the myocardium if a perfusing rhythm has not been restored.
- If a perfusing rhythm has been restored, giving chest compressions does not increase the chance of VF recurring.
- In the presence of post-shock asystole, chest compressions may usefully induce VF.

The first dose of adrenaline is given during the 2 min period of CPR after delivery of the third shock. Give amiodarone 300 mg after three defibrillation attempts. Do not stop CPR to check the rhythm before giving drugs unless there are clear signs of ROSC. Subsequent doses of adrenaline are given after alternate 2 min loops of CPR (which equates to every 3–5 min) for as long as cardiac arrest persists. If VF/pVT persists, or recurs, a further dose of 150 mg amiodarone may be given after five defibrillation attempts.

When the rhythm is checked 2 min after giving a shock, if a non-shockable rhythm is present, and the rhythm is one that could be compatible with a pulse, try to palpate a central pulse and look for other evidence of ROSC (e.g. sudden increase in end-tidal CO_2 or evidence of cardiac output on any invasive monitoring equipment). Rhythm checks must be brief, and pulse checks undertaken only if a rhythm that could be compatible with a pulse is observed. If a rhythm compatible with a pulse is seen during a 2 min period of CPR, do not interrupt chest compressions to palpate a pulse unless the patient shows signs of life suggesting ROSC. If there is any doubt about the presence of a palpable pulse, resume CPR. If the patient has ROSC, begin post-resuscitation care. If the patient's rhythm changes to asystole or PEA, see 'Non-shockable rhythms (PEA and asystole)'.

If there is doubt about whether the rhythm is asystole or extremely fine VF, do not attempt defibrillation; instead, continue chest compressions and ventilation as continuing high-quality CPR may improve the amplitude and frequency of the VF and improve the chance of subsequent successful defibrillation to a perfusing rhythm. If the rhythm is clearly VF, attempt defibrillation.

[1] Adapted with kind permission of the Resuscitation Council (UK): Advanced Life Support 7th Edition.

Precordial thump—A precordial thump has a very low success rate for cardioversion of a shockable rhythm. Its routine use is therefore not recommended. Consider a precordial thump only when it can be used immediately, while awaiting the arrival of a defibrillator in a monitored VF/pVT arrest. Using the ulnar edge of a tightly clenched fist, deliver a sharp impact to the lower half of the sternum from a height of about 20 cm, then retract the fist immediately to create an impulse-like stimulus.

Witnessed and monitored VF/pVT in the cardiac arrest

If a patient has a witnessed and monitored cardiac arrest in the catheter laboratory, coronary care unit (CCU), a critical care area, or whilst monitored after cardiac surgery, and a manual defibrillator is rapidly available:

- Confirm cardiac arrest and shout for help
- If the initial rhythm is VF/pVT, give up to three quick successive (stacked) shocks
- Rapidly check for a rhythm change and, if appropriate check for a pulse and other signs of ROSC after each defibrillation attempt
- Start chest compressions and continue CPR for 2 min if the third shock is unsuccessful.

This three-shock strategy may also be considered for an initial, witnessed VF/pVT cardiac arrest if the patient is already connected to a manual defibrillator—an intraoperative cardiac arrest where defibrillation pads had been applied before the operation is an example.

Non-shockable rhythms (PEA and asystole)

Pulseless electrical activity (PEA) is organized cardiac electrical activity in the absence of any palpable pulses. These patients often have some mechanical myocardial contractions but they are too weak to produce a detectable pulse or blood pressure (a condition sometimes described as pseudo-PEA). PEA may be caused by reversible conditions that can be treated—this is particularly true in the case of perioperative cardiac arrest.

Asystole is the absence of electrical activity on the ECG trace. During CPR, ensure the ECG pads are attached to the chest and the correct monitoring mode is selected.

Treatment for PEA and asystole

- Start CPR 30:2
- Give adrenaline 1 mg i.v./i.o. as soon as intravascular access is achieved
- Continue CPR 30:2 until the airway is secured—then continue chest compressions without pausing during ventilation

- Recheck the rhythm after 2 min:
  - If electrical activity compatible with a pulse is seen, check for a pulse and/or signs of life:
    - If a pulse and/or signs of life are present, start post-resuscitation care
    - If no pulse and/or no signs of life are present (PEA or asystole):
      - Continue CPR
      - Recheck the rhythm after 2 min and proceed accordingly
      - Give further adrenaline 1 mg i.v. every 3–5 min (during alternate 2 min loops of CPR)
    - If VF/pVT at rhythm check, change to shockable side of algorithm.[2]

During CPR

During the treatment of cardiac arrest, emphasis is placed on good quality chest compressions between defibrillation attempts, recognizing and treating reversible causes (4 Hs and 4 Ts), obtaining a secure airway, and vascular access.

During CPR with a 30:2 ratio, the underlying rhythm may be seen clearly on the monitor as compressions are paused to enable ventilation. If VF is seen during this brief pause (whether on the shockable or non-shockable side of the algorithm), do not attempt defibrillation at this stage; instead, continue with CPR until the 2 min period is completed. Knowing that the rhythm is VF, the team should be fully prepared to deliver a shock with minimal delay at the end of the 2-min period of CPR.

Maintain high-quality, uninterrupted chest compressions

The quality of chest compressions and ventilations are important determinants of outcome (Meaney et al. 2013), yet are frequently performed poorly by healthcare professionals. A recent study of more than 1000 out-of-hospital cardiac arrests documented chest compressions with a median depth of less than 4 cm in more than half of cases and there was a strong association between survival and compression depth (Stiell et al. 2012). Compressions should be of adequate depth (5–6 cm) and rate (100–120 min^{-1}), and pressure released completely from the chest between compressions—leaning on the chest between compressions will impair cardiac output (Zuercher et al. 2010). As soon as the airway is secured, continue chest compressions without pausing during ventilation. To reduce fatigue, change the individual undertaking compressions every 2 min or earlier if necessary.

Optimizing the quality of cardiopulmonary resuscitation

There are now several defibrillator models that incorporate CPR feedback systems. These comprise either a puck that is placed on the sternum, or modified defibrillator patches, both of which incorporate an accelerometer that enables measurement of chest compression rate and depth. Measurement of the changes in chest impedance enable ventilation rate to be recorded. These modified defibrillators can provide audio feedback in real-time (e.g. 'push faster', 'push harder') and downloaded data can be used for team debriefing after the event. Use of a CPR feedback device results in CPR performance that is closer to that specified in the guidelines but, as yet, their use has not been shown to improve survival (Yeung et al. 2009; Hostler et al. 2011). These devices may fail to compensate for compression of the underlying mattress during CPR on a bed when providing feedback.

Mechanical cardiopulmonary resuscitation devices

It is difficult to maintain high-quality chest compressions if CPR is prolonged or during transport to hospital. Under these circumstances, mechanical chest-compression devices can provide high-quality CPR for long periods. There are two mechanical chest compressions devices in clinical use: the AutoPulse® (ZOLL Medical Corporation, Chelmsford, MA, USA), which comprises a backboard and battery-powered band that tightens around the patient's chest at 80 min^{-1}, and the LUCAS™ (Physio-Control Inc./Jolife AB, Lund, Sweden) comprising a battery-powered suction cup that pushes down and pulls up (active compression-decompression) on the patient's sternum. Although both of these devices improve haemodynamics during cardiac arrest in animals, a comparison of the AutoPulse® with high-quality conventional CPR in OHCA, the Circulation Improving Resuscitation Care (CIRC) trial, showed no improvement in outcome (Wik et al. 2014) and two large, multicentre, randomized trials of the LUCAS™ have similarly shown no improvement in outcome (Rubertsson et al. 2014; Perkins et al. 2015).

Occasionally, an acute coronary occlusion will result in intractable VF, which is unresponsive despite repeated attempts at defibrillation. Under these circumstances, these mechanical devices have been used to provide CPR to enable patients in cardiac arrest to undergo percutaneous coronary intervention (PCI), revascularization, followed by successful defibrillation (Wagner et al. 2010). The mechanical CPR devices are also likely to be of value whenever prolonged CPR is required and when patients require CPR during transport.

The impedance threshold device (ITD) is a valve that can be placed between a self-inflating bag and a facemask, tracheal tube, or supraglottic airway device. When the chest wall recoils during CPR, the valve prevents passive inflow of air into the lungs but still allows positive pressure ventilation. This increases the extent of the negative intrathoracic pressure during the decompression phase of CPR, thereby enhancing venous return and increasing cerebral and cardiac perfusion. In a randomized trial comparing conventional CPR with active compression–decompression CPR combined with an ITD (ACD-ITD) after OHCA, there was improved survival to hospital discharge with good neurological function in the ACD-ITD group (Aufderheide et al. 2011a). However, in this study it was impossible to blind the intervention and the relative contributions of ACD and the ITD are unknown. In contrast, a study of the active ITD compared with a sham valve when used during conventional CPR showed no benefit with the ITD (Aufderheide et al. 2011b). The ITD is rarely used in the United Kingdom.

Airway and ventilation

In the hands of skilled intubators, such as anaesthetists, tracheal intubation is the optimal method for securing the airway during CPR. The advantages of tracheal intubation over bag–mask ventilation include maintenance of a patent airway that is protected from aspiration of gastric contents, ability to provide an adequate tidal volume reliably even when chest compressions are uninterrupted, the potential to free the rescuer's hands for other tasks, and the ability to suck-out airway secretions. Use of a bag–mask is more likely to cause gastric distension, regurgitation, and the risk of aspiration. Those skilled in tracheal intubation should be able to undertake

[2] Adapted with kind permission of the Resuscitation Council (UK): Advanced Life Support 7th Edition.

laryngoscopy without stopping chest compressions; a brief pause (<5 s) in chest compressions may be required only as the tube is passed through the vocal cords. After intubation, correct tube position is confirmed using waveform capnography (this must be available whenever intubation is attempted regardless of location) and clinical examination, and then secured carefully. Once the patient's trachea has been intubated, chest compressions are continued at a rate of 100–120 min^{-1} without pausing during ventilation.

In the hands of other healthcare professionals, the role of tracheal intubation during CPR is much less certain. No studies have shown that tracheal intubation increases survival after cardiac arrest. Incorrect placement of the tracheal tube can be catastrophic and is common in cardiac arrest if unskilled personnel attempt intubation. Rates of unrecognized oesophageal intubation in some paramedic systems are as high as 17%; the Scottish Ambulance Service reported 2.5% of tracheal tubes to be in the oesophagus when emergency physicians assessed the patient on admission to hospital (Lyon et al. 2010). Attempted intubation by the relatively unskilled can cause prolonged interruptions in chest compressions: in a study of 100 OHCAs, the median duration of the interruption in chest compressions associated with the first intubation attempt was 47 s and in one-third of cases this interruption exceeded 1 min (Wang et al. 2009). Tracheal intubation would have to show substantial advantages over other airway techniques if these are to compensate for such prolonged interruptions in chest compressions.

A bag–mask, or preferably, a supraglottic airway device should be used in the absence of personnel skilled in tracheal intubation. Both the i-gel® (Intersurgical Ltd., Workingham, UK) and the LMA Supreme® (Teleflex, Inc., Wayne, PA, USA) have characteristics (ease of insertion and relatively high laryngeal seal pressures) that might make them suitable for use during CPR. After a cluster-randomized feasibility study of these two devices in out-of-hospital cardiac arrest (Benger et al. 2016), the i-gel® is now being compared with tracheal intubation in a large cluster-randomized trial as part of a step-wise approach to airway management. Once a supraglottic airway device has been inserted, attempt to deliver continuous chest compressions, uninterrupted during ventilation. Ventilate the lungs at 10 breaths min^{-1}; do not hyperventilate the lungs. If excessive gas leakage causes inadequate ventilation of the patient's lungs, chest compressions will have to be interrupted to enable ventilation (using a compression–ventilation ratio of 30:2).

Capnography

The risk of unrecognized oesophageal intubation can be minimized by using a reliable technique for detecting oesophageal placement of the tracheal tube (Cook et al. 2011). When tracheal intubation is undertaken less than 30 min after onset of cardiac arrest, waveform capnography has 100% sensitivity and 100% specificity for verifying placement of the tube in a major airway (Grmec 2002; Soar et al. 2015). If tracheal intubation is delayed by more than 30 min, pulmonary blood flow may be so low during CPR that carbon dioxide (CO_2) is undetectable despite a correctly placed tracheal tube (Soar et al. 2015). During CPR, capnography also provides feedback on quality of chest compressions (better chest compressions will generate higher end-tidal CO_2 values) (Sheak et al. 2015), enables prediction of those more likely to achieve ROSC (an end-tidal CO_2 value >10 mm Hg predicts ROSC) (Grmec and Kupnik 2003), and provides an early indication of ROSC (the end-tidal CO_2 increases suddenly) (Pokorna et al. 2010).

Vascular access

Although peak drug concentrations are higher and circulation times are shorter when drugs are injected into a central venous catheter compared with a peripheral cannula, insertion of a central venous catheter interrupts CPR and is associated with several potential complications. Peripheral venous cannulation is quicker, easier, and safer. Drugs injected peripherally must be followed by a flush of at least 20 ml of fluid and elevation of the extremity for 10–20 s to facilitate drug delivery to the central circulation. If i.v. access cannot be established within the first 2 min of resuscitation, insert an intraosseous (i.o.) device into either the tibia or the humerus (Fig. 91.2). Drugs injected via the i.o. route will achieve adequate plasma concentrations (Buck et al. 2007). Effective fluid resuscitation can also be achieved via an i.o. device.

Reversible causes

The potentially reversible causes of cardiac arrest are divided into two groups of four based upon their initial letter—either H or T [Resuscitation Council (UK) 2015]:

- Hypoxia
- Hypovolaemia
- Hyperkalaemia, hypokalaemia, hypoglycaemia, hypocalcaemia, acidaemia and other metabolic disorders
- Hypothermia
- Tension pneumothorax
- Tamponade

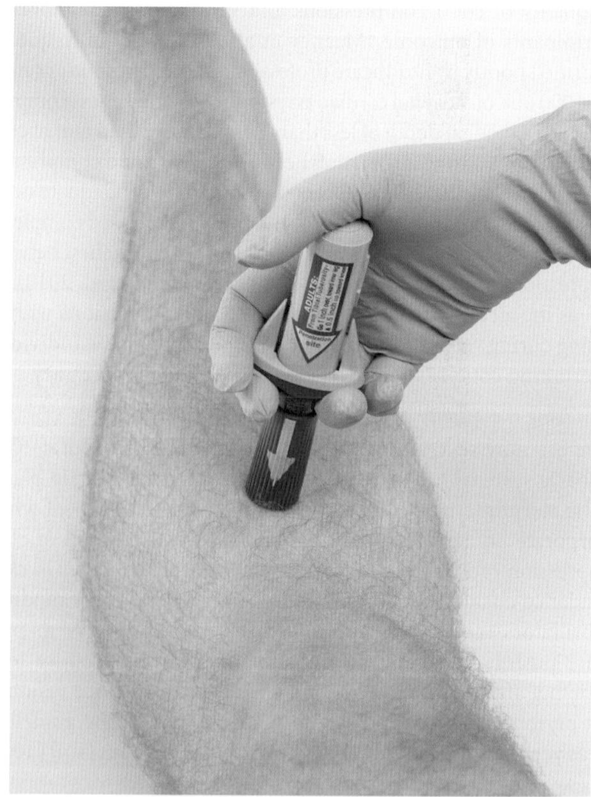

Figure 91.2 An intraosseous device inserted into the tibia.
Reproduced with the kind permission of the Resuscitation Council (UK).

- Toxins
- Thrombosis (pulmonary embolism or coronary thrombosis).

The four Hs

- During CPR the risk of *hypoxaemia* is minimized by ventilating the patient's lungs with 100% oxygen.
- PEA caused by *hypovolaemia* is usually secondary to severe haemorrhage—stop the bleeding (with surgery if appropriate) and restore intravascular volume rapidly with fluid and blood products.
- *Hyperkalaemia*, hypokalaemia, hypoglycaemia, hypocalcaemia, acidaemia and other metabolic disorders are detected by biochemical tests or suggested by the patient's medical history (e.g. renal failure). A 12-lead ECG may show suggestive features. Calcium chloride 10 ml 10% (6.8 mmol) is given as an i.v. bolus if there is hyperkalaemia, hypocalcaemia, or calcium channel-blocker overdose.
- Suspect *hypothermia* after OHCA in a cold environment (e.g. drowning).

The four Ts

- A *tension pneumothorax* may be the primary cause of PEA. It may follow attempts at central venous catheter insertion. The diagnosis is made clinically. Decompress rapidly by thoracostomy or needle thoracocentesis and then insert a chest drain.
- Cardiac *tamponade* is difficult to diagnose because the typical signs of distended neck veins and hypotension cannot be assessed during cardiac arrest. Cardiac arrest after penetrating chest trauma or after cardiac surgery should raise strong suspicion of tamponade—consider a resuscitative thoracotomy in this situation.
- In the absence of a specific history of accidental or deliberate ingestion, poisoning by therapeutic or *toxic* substances may be difficult to detect. Where available, the appropriate antidotes should be used but most often the required treatment is supportive.
- *Thromboembolism*—if massive pulmonary embolism is thought to be the cause of cardiac arrest, consider giving a thrombolytic drug immediately. After fibrinolysis during CPR for acute pulmonary embolism, survival and good neurological outcome have been reported in cases requiring in excess of 60 min of CPR. If a fibrinolytic drug is given in these circumstances, consider performing CPR for at least 60–90 min before termination of resuscitation attempts.

Use of ultrasound during advanced life support

In the presence of PEA, in skilled hands, ultrasound can be useful for the detection of potentially reversible causes of cardiac arrest [e.g. cardiac tamponade, pulmonary embolism, ischaemia (regional wall motion abnormality), aortic dissection, hypovolaemia, and pneumothorax] (Price et al. 2010). The Focused Echocardiography Extended Life Support Course (FEEL-UK) teaches the main principles in using echocardiography in cardiac arrest. Ultrasound examination must not cause prolonged interruptions to chest compressions and a sub-xiphoid probe position is recommended (Fig. 91.3). By placing the probe just before chest compressions are paused for a planned rhythm assessment, a well-trained operator can obtain views within 10 s. Pseudo-PEA describes the echocardiographic detection of cardiac motion in the presence of a clinical diagnosis of PEA. The diagnosis of pseudo-PEA is important because it carries a better prognosis than true PEA and will influence treatment (Prosen et al. 2010). In a prospective study of 100 out-of-hospital cardiac arrests,

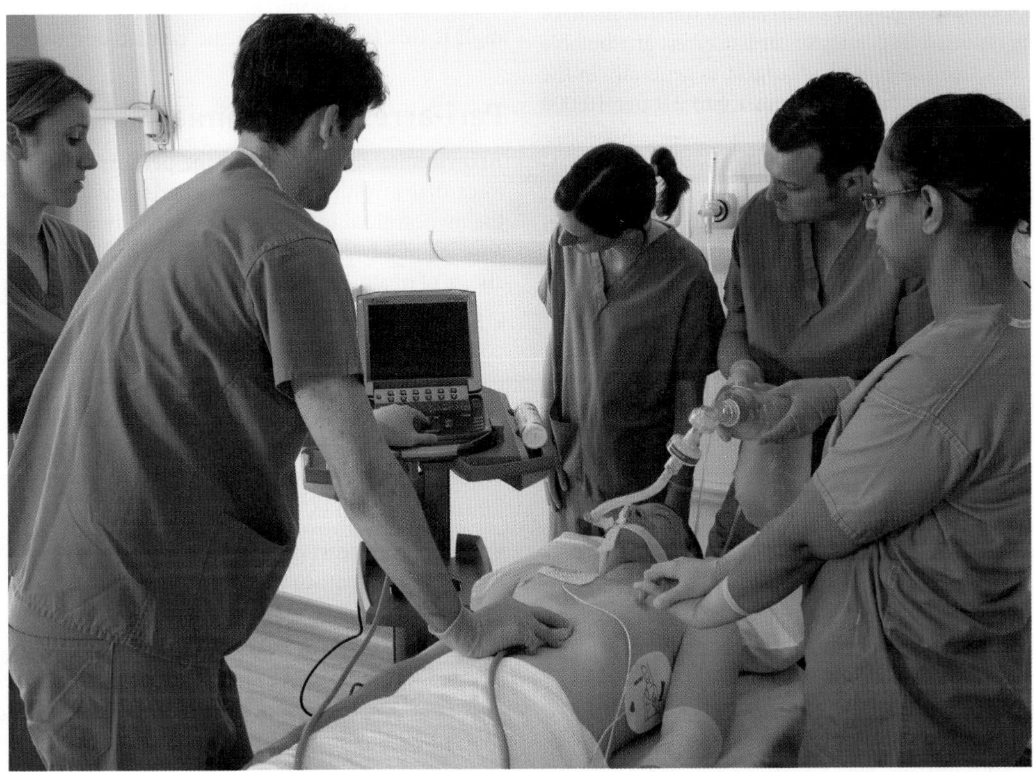

Figure 91.3 Sub-xiphoid position for ultrasound probe during cardiopulmonary resuscitation.

use of FEEL enabled detection of cardiac motion in 36 (70%) of 51 patients with suspected PEA (Breitkreutz et al. 2010).

Extracorporeal life support

Several observational studies document the successful use of extracorporeal life support (ECLS) in selected cases of cardiac arrest refractory to standard ALS techniques (Chen et al. 2008; Shin et al. 2011). Several centres in the world have reported using ECLS, including those in Japan, Taiwan, Korea, France, and the United States. It has been generally used for IHCA or for patients admitted in refractory cardiac arrest after OHCA. There have been case reports describing implementation of ECLS in the out-of-hospital setting. Patients are selected for ECLS on the basis of having a potentially reversible cause of cardiac arrest, for example, an occluded coronary artery. The technique involves arteriovenous cannulation during CPR and rapid establishment of the patient on extracorporeal membrane oxygenation. The patient can also be rapidly cooled using the extracorporeal circuit, which will provide some neuroprotection (see 'Targeted temperature management') (Nagao et al. 2010). After ECLS, investigators have reported survival rates with good neurological outcome as high as 23% for IHCA (Shin et al. 2011) and 12% for out-of-hospital cardiac arrest (Nagao et al. 2010).

Perioperative cardiac arrest

Epidemiology and outcome from perioperative cardiac arrest

The published incidence of perioperative cardiac arrest ranges from 2.4 to 34.6 per 10 000; a very recent large study from the United States reported an incidence of 5.6 per 10 000 cases (Nunnally et al. 2015). This wide range reflects differences in case-mix (some include neonates, cardiac surgery, or both) and in the definition of perioperative. The reported frequency of cardiac arrest attributable primarily to anaesthesia in non-cardiac surgery is generally in the range 0.2 to 1.1 per 10 000 adults and from 1.4 to 2.9 per 10 000 children (Zuercher and Ummenhofer 2008).

In one large series from the Mayo Clinic, Rochester, MN, USA, 34.5% of 223 patients sustaining perioperative cardiac arrest survived to hospital discharge. The primary arrest rhythms recorded in the Mayo Clinic series were asystole in 41.7%, VF in 35.4%, PEA in 14.4%, and unknown in 8.5%. Causes of cardiac arrest were divided into bleeding, cardiac, and other (mainly drug-induced cardiac arrest and hypoxia). Cardiac arrest caused by bleeding had the highest mortality, with only 10.3% of these patients surviving to hospital discharge. This very high mortality associated with preoperative cardiac arrest caused by bleeding is consistent with several other studies. Of the 24 (10.8%) perioperative cardiac arrests attributable to anaesthesia, 13 were medication related and 11 were caused by hypoxia. Nine of the cardiac arrests were related to the use of neuromuscular blocking agents. Among a large series of 2524 perioperative cardiac arrests, the overall survival to hospital discharge rate was 31.7% (Krishna Ramachandran et al. 2013).

Treatment of intraoperative cardiac arrest

As patients in the operating room are normally fully monitored, there should be little delay in diagnosing cardiac arrest. High-risk patients will often have invasive blood pressure monitoring, which is invaluable in the event of cardiac arrest. If the patient is considered high risk for cardiac arrest, self-adhesive defibrillation patches can be applied before induction of anaesthesia. Asystole VF will be detected immediately but PEA might not be immediately obvious: immediately feel for a pulse if there is loss of the pulse oximeter signal and end-tidal CO_2 waveform. Some modification to the standard ALS algorithm is appropriate for the treatment of intraoperative cardiac arrest. Regardless of the rhythm, look for reversible causes immediately—hypoxaemia and hypovolaemia will be the most common in this setting.

Treatment of intraoperative ventricular fibrillation

Given that this will be a monitored and witnessed episode of VF, it is appropriate to apply an immediate precordial thump while waiting for a defibrillator to arrive. Assuming that the precordial thump is ineffective, give chest compressions and provide ventilation until the defibrillator arrives. Attempt defibrillation and follow the standard ALS algorithm. If the patient is already attached to a defibrillator (via self-adhesive patches) at the time of VF cardiac arrest, give up to three stacked shocks before starting chest compressions (as discussed previously).

Treatment of intraoperative asystole

Stop any surgical activity likely to be causing excessive vagal activity—if this is the likely cause give 0.5 mg atropine (not the 3 mg described in the 2005 guidelines). Start CPR and immediately look for other reversible causes.

Treatment of intraoperative pulseless electrical activity

Start CPR while looking quickly for reversible causes. Give fluid unless you are certain the intravascular volume is adequate. Stop giving the anaesthetic. While a vasopressor will be required, in these circumstances 1 mg of adrenaline (described in the standard ALS algorithm) may be excessive. Give a much smaller dose of adrenaline or another vasopressor initially (e.g. 1 ml of 1 in 10 000 adrenaline = 0.1 mg); if this fails to restore the cardiac output, increase the dose.

Peri-arrest arrhythmias

Arrhythmias are common in the peri-arrest period: they may lead to cardiac arrest or they may occur soon after ROSC, a time when the myocardium is frequently 'electrically unstable'. The presence or absence of adverse symptoms or signs will dictate the urgency and choice of treatment for most arrhythmias. Adverse features comprise:

- Shock: hypotension (systolic blood pressure < 90 mm Hg), pallor, sweating, cold, extremities, confusion or impaired consciousness
- Syncope
- Heart failure
- Myocardial ischaemia: chest pain, evidence of myocardial ischaemia on 12-lead ECG, or both
- Extremes of heart rate: tachycardia greater than 150 min^{-1}; bradycardia less than 40 min^{-1}.

In general, the presence of adverse features implies the need for more rapid treatment (electrical cardioversion for tachyarrhythmia or pacing for bradyarrhythmia). In the absence of adverse features, the use of drugs (pharmacological/chemical cardioversion) is usually appropriate.

Tachyarrhythmia

The adult tachycardia algorithm is shown in Figure 91.4.

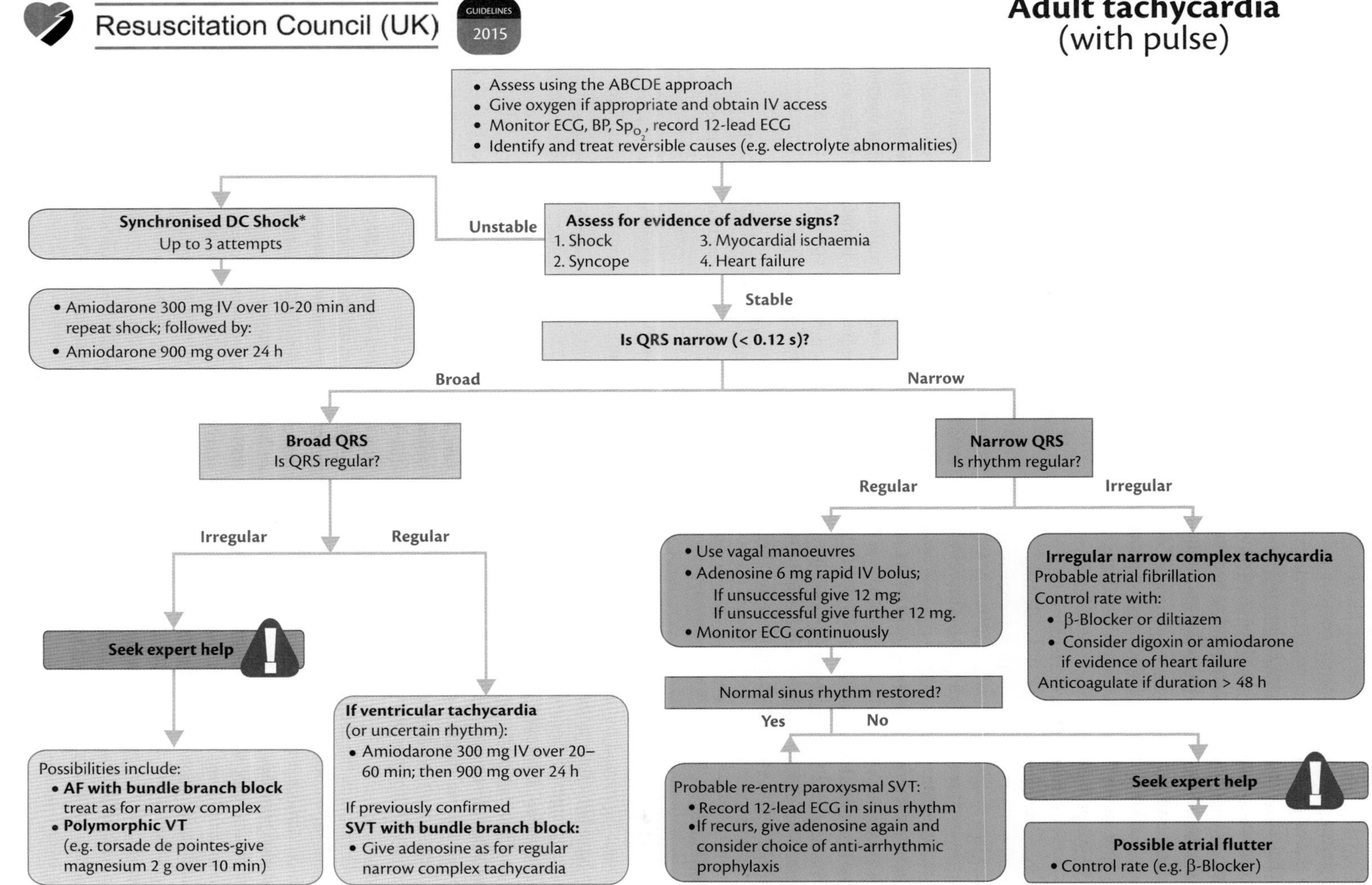

Figure 91.4 The tachycardia algorithm.

Reproduced with the kind permission of the Resuscitation Council (UK).

Synchronized cardioversion

Before cardioversion is attempted, the patient will require anaesthesia or sedation. This can be challenging because, by definition, these patients are cardiovascularly unstable. Patients who are not fasted will require a rapid sequence induction (RSI) and tracheal intubation but in these haemodynamically unstable patients, the RSI can be modified: the induction drug is injected slowly and, once cricoid pressure is applied, the lungs are inflated gently until the onset of full muscle paralysis enables intubation to be achieved. The risks of aspiration associated with this 'modified RSI' must be weighed against the risks of profound cardiovascular collapse caused by rapid injection of an excessive dose of induction drug. Have a vasopressor, such as metaraminol, ready to inject. Ketamine is less likely to cause hypotension than other induction drugs. Its emergence phenomena have probably been overstated but its sympathomimetic properties may exacerbate tachyarrhythmias.

Set the defibrillator to deliver a synchronized shock; this delivers the shock to coincide with the R wave. An unsynchronized shock could coincide with a T wave and cause VF. For a broad-complex tachycardia or atrial fibrillation (AF), start with 120–150 J and increase in increments if this fails. Atrial flutter and regular narrow-complex tachycardia will often be terminated by lower-energy shocks; therefore, start with 70–120 J. If cardioversion fails to terminate the arrhythmia, and adverse features persist, give amiodarone 300 mg i.v. over 10–20 min and attempt further synchronized cardioversion. The loading dose of amiodarone can be followed by an infusion of 900 mg over 24 h given preferably via a central vein.

Treatment of atrial fibrillation

This is the commonest perioperative arrhythmia. Patients who have been in AF for more than 48 h may have developed atrial thrombus and, in general, should not be treated by cardioversion (electrical or chemical) until they have been fully anticoagulated for at least 3 weeks, or unless transoesophageal echocardiography has detected no evidence of atrial thrombus. However, if the AF is associated with adverse features and the patient is deteriorating, immediate electrical cardioversion may be required. In this case, if not contraindicated by recent or ongoing surgery, give an i.v. bolus injection of unfractionated heparin followed by a continuous infusion to maintain the activated partial thromboplastin time at 1.5–2 times the reference control value.

If the aim is to control heart rate, the drug of choice is a β-blocker (e.g. metoprolol, atenolol, or esmolol). Digoxin may be used in patients with heart failure. Amiodarone is most useful in maintaining rhythm control but also provides rate control and is often used in the perioperative or critical care setting, or both. Amiodarone, 300 mg i.v. over 20–60 min followed by 900 mg over 24 h, can be used to attempt chemical cardioversion. Flecainide is usually more successful but few anaesthetists are familiar with its use and it is contraindicated in the presence of heart failure, known left ventricular impairment or ischaemic heart disease, or a prolonged QT interval. Magnesium is also used (e.g. 2 g injected over 10 min followed by a further 3 g over 3 h) but the data supporting this are limited.

Bradyarrhythmia

The bradycardia algorithm is shown in Figure 91.5. If adverse features are present, initial treatment is usually pharmacological (atropine 500 mcg i.v., repeat every 3–5 min, as required, to a total of 3 mg); pacing is used for patients in whom initial pharmacological treatment is ineffective or inadequate and those with risk factors for asystole. In the perioperative setting, transcutaneous pacing is likely to be the most rapidly achievable, and will buy time until a temporary transvenous wire can be inserted. Transcutaneous pacing can be painful and may fail to achieve effective electrical 'capture' (i.e. a QRS complex after the pacing stimulus) or fail to achieve a mechanical response (i.e. palpable pulse). Verify electrical capture on the monitor or ECG and check that it is producing a pulse. Reassess the patient's condition. If the patient is not anaesthetized, give analgesia and sedation as necessary to control pain and attempt to identify the cause of the bradyarrhythmia.

Post-resuscitation care

Return of a spontaneous circulation is a critical step in the continuum of resuscitation, but the quality of the patient's ultimate survival depends on interventions applied in the post-resuscitation phase, which is the final link in the chain of survival (Nolan et al. 2015b). Post-resuscitation treatment starts at the location where ROSC is achieved (this may include the operating room) but, once stabilized, the patient is transferred to the most appropriate high-care area (e.g. ICU or, if conscious, CCU) for continued monitoring and treatment.

The post-cardiac arrest syndrome

The post-cardiac arrest syndrome comprises (Nolan et al. 2008) the following:

- Post-cardiac arrest brain injury
- Post-cardiac arrest myocardial dysfunction
- Systemic ischaemia/reperfusion response
- Persisting precipitating pathology.

The severity of the post-cardiac arrest syndrome varies with the duration and cause of cardiac arrest; it may be absent if the cardiac arrest is brief. Post-cardiac arrest brain injury manifests as coma, seizures, myoclonus, varying degrees of neurological dysfunction, and brain death. Post-cardiac arrest brain injury may be exacerbated by microcirculatory failure, impaired autoregulation, hypercarbia, hypoxaemia and hyperoxaemia, pyrexia, hyperglycaemia, and seizures. Significant myocardial dysfunction is common after cardiac arrest but typically recovers by 2–3 days (Laurent et al. 2002). The whole-body ischaemia/reperfusion that occurs with resuscitation from cardiac arrest activates immunological and coagulation pathways contributing to multiple organ failure and increasing the risk of infection. Thus, the post-cardiac arrest syndrome has many features in common with sepsis, including intravascular volume depletion and vasodilation (Adrie et al. 2002). About 60% of patients initially comatose after OHCA will develop pneumonia (Perbet et al. 2011).

Optimizing organ function

Airway and breathing

Patients who have had a brief period of cardiac arrest may recover consciousness, maintain their airway safely, and breathe adequately

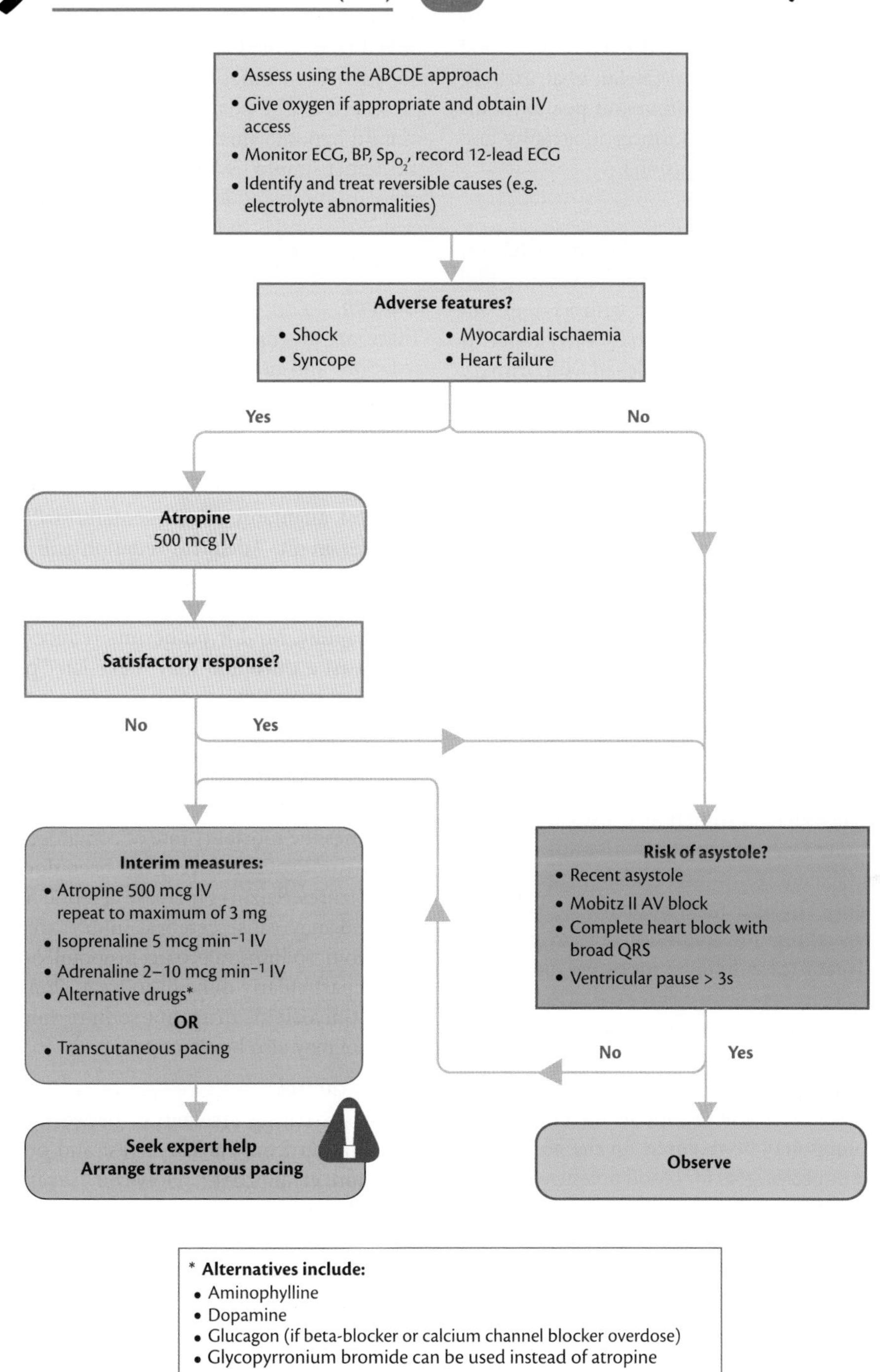

Figure 91.5 The bradycardia algorithm.

Reproduced with the kind permission of the Resuscitation Council (UK).

without the need for tracheal intubation. These patients may then be treated on a CCU. Patients remaining comatose and those with inadequate ventilation will need support with mechanical ventilation via a tracheal tube.

Several animal studies have demonstrated that hyperoxaemia causes oxidative stress and harms post-ischaemic neurones (Pilcher et al. 2012). The clinical studies investigating this phenomenon comprise analyses of large ICU databases (Kilgannon et al. 2010; Bellomo et al. 2011). Unfortunately, these clinical data are inconsistent probably because they lack the sensitivity to detect the impact of hyperoxaemia during the first 1 h after ROSC, which is the period that has been investigated in the animal studies. Although the lack of robust data is acknowledged, current recommendations are to titrate the inspired oxygen concentration to maintain the arterial blood oxygen saturation in the range of 94–98% as soon as arterial blood oxygen saturation can be monitored reliably [by blood gas analysis, pulse oximetry (Sp_{O_2}), or both] (Nolan et al. 2015b). Ventilation is adjusted to achieve normocarbia and this is monitored using the end-tidal CO_2 with waveform capnography and arterial blood gas values (see 'Cerebral perfusion').

Circulation

Coronary artery disease is the most common cause of OHCA: it accounts for about 80% of sudden cardiac deaths (Myerburg and Junttila 2012). Many of these will be associated with ST-segment elevation myocardial infarction (STEMI) for which early reperfusion therapy is required. Reperfusion can be achieved with primary PCI, fibrinolysis, or both. Primary PCI is the preferred treatment if a first medical contact-to-balloon time of less than 90 min can be achieved because it is much more likely than fibrinolytic therapy to establish full reperfusion. The early post-resuscitation 12-lead ECG is less reliable for predicting acute coronary occlusion than it is in those who have not had a cardiac arrest (Sideris et al. 2011; Staer-Jensen et al. 2015). Recent evidence suggests that about 25% of patients with no obvious extra cardiac cause for their cardiac arrest but who do not have evidence of STEMI on their initial 12-lead ECG will have a coronary lesion on angiography that is amenable to stenting (Dumas et al. 2010; Radsel et al. 2011; Dumas et al. 2016). The trend is to consider immediate coronary artery angiography in all OHCA patients with no obvious, non-cardiac cause of arrest.

Post-cardiac arrest myocardial dysfunction causes haemodynamic instability, which manifests as hypotension, a low cardiac output, and arrhythmias (Zia and Kern 2011). Early echocardiography will enable the extent of myocardial dysfunction to be quantified. In the ICU, an arterial line for continuous blood pressure monitoring is essential. Treatment with fluid, inotropes, and vasopressors may be guided by blood pressure, heart rate, urine output, and rate of plasma lactate clearance and central venous oxygen saturations. Non-invasive cardiac output monitors may help to guide treatment (Tagami et al. 2012). If treatment with fluid resuscitation and vasoactive drugs is insufficient to support the circulation, an intra-aortic balloon pump may be required. In the absence of definitive data supporting a specific goal for blood pressure, aim for a mean arterial blood pressure to achieve an adequate urine output (1 ml kg^{-1} h^{-1}) and normal or decreasing plasma lactate values, taking into consideration the patient's normal blood pressure, the cause of the arrest, and the severity of any myocardial dysfunction (Nolan et al. 2015b).

Brain

In patients surviving to ICU admission but subsequently dying in hospital, brain injury is the cause of death in approximately two-thirds after OHCA and in about a quarter after IHCA (Laver et al. 2004, Lemiale et al. 2013).

Cerebral perfusion

Immediately after ROSC there is a period of cerebral hyperaemia. After asphyxial cardiac arrest, brain oedema may occur transiently after ROSC but it is associated only rarely with clinically relevant increases in intracranial pressure (Nolan et al. 2008). Autoregulation of cerebral blood flow is impaired after cardiac arrest; thus, cerebral perfusion varies with cerebral perfusion pressure instead of being linked to neuronal activity. Maintain mean arterial pressure near the patient's normal level. Cerebral vascular reactivity to CO_2 is preserved in the post-cardiac arrest period, even in the presence of mild hypothermia (Bisschops et al. 2010). For this reason, normocapnia should be the aim; in post-cardiac arrest patients, overventilation causing hypocapnia causes cerebral ischaemia (Bouzat et al. 2013) and is independently associated with poor neurological outcome (Roberts et al. 2013).

Sedation

There are no data to support a defined period of ventilation, sedation, and neuromuscular block after cardiac arrest; however, patients need to be well sedated during treatment with therapeutic hypothermia, and the duration of sedation and ventilation is influenced by this treatment. Sedation is achieved typically with a combination of opioids and hypnotics. Short-acting drugs (e.g. propofol, alfentanil, or remifentanil) will enable earlier neurological assessment. Adequate sedation will reduce oxygen consumption. During hypothermia, optimal sedation can reduce or prevent shivering, which enables the target temperature to be achieved more rapidly. Mild hypothermia reduces clearance of many drugs by at least a third and may make later prognostication unreliable (Tortorici et al. 2007).

Control of seizures

Seizures occur in 25% of those who remain comatose after cardiac arrest (Nielsen et al. 2011). Although patients with seizures have four times the mortality rate of comatose patients without seizures, good neurological recovery has been documented in 17% of those with seizures. Seizures increase cerebral metabolism by up to threefold and may cause cerebral injury: treat with benzodiazepines, phenytoin, sodium valproate, propofol, or a barbiturate. Myoclonus can be particularly difficult to treat; clonazepam is the most effective antimyoclonic drug, but sodium valproate, levetiracetam, and propofol may also be effective.

Glucose control

There is a strong association between high blood glucose after resuscitation from cardiac arrest and poor neurological outcome (Daviaud et al. 2014). However, severe hypoglycaemia is also associated with increased mortality in critically ill patients and comatose patients are at particular risk from unrecognized hypoglycaemia. Increased glucose variability may be more harmful than the absolute values of glucose (Cueni-Villoz et al. 2011). Based on the available data and expert consensus, after ROSC, blood glucose should be maintained at 10 mmol $litre^{-1}$ or lower. Avoid hypoglycaemia (<4.0 mmol $litre^{-1}$).

Targeted temperature management

Pyrexia is common in the first 48 h after cardiac arrest and is associated with poor outcome; therefore, treat any hyperthermia occurring after cardiac arrest with antipyretics or active cooling.

Mild hypothermia is neuroprotective and improves outcome after a period of global cerebral hypoxia-ischaemia. Cooling suppresses many of the pathways leading to delayed cell death, including apoptosis (programmed cell death) (Polderman 2009). Hypothermia decreases the cerebral metabolic rate for oxygen by about 6% for each 1°C reduction in temperature and this may reduce the release of excitatory amino acids and free radicals.

All studies of post-cardiac arrest therapeutic hypothermia have included only patients in coma. There is good evidence supporting the use of induced hypothermia in comatose survivors of out-of-hospital cardiac arrest caused by VF (Holzer 2010, Nolan et al. 2003). Two randomized trials demonstrated improved neurological outcome at hospital discharge or at 6 months in comatose patients after out-of-hospital VF cardiac arrest (Bernard et al. 2002; Hypothermia after Cardiac Arrest Study Group 2002). Cooling was initiated within minutes to hours after ROSC and a temperature range of 32–34°C was maintained for 12–24 h. The use of hypothermia for non-shockable rhythms and after IHCA is supported mainly by observational data, which have a substantial risk of bias. Despite this, many centres use hypothermia irrespective of the initial cardiac arrest rhythm or location. In the Targeted Temperature Management trial, 950 all-rhythm OHCA patients were randomized to 24 h of temperature control at either 33°C or 36°C (Nielsen et al. 2012). Strict protocols were followed for assessing prognosis and for withdrawal of life-sustaining treatment. There was no difference in the primary outcome—all-cause mortality, and neurological outcome at 180 days was also similar. Importantly, patients in both arms of this trial had their temperature well controlled so that fever was prevented even in the 36°C group. After a review of all the available science, an international consensus group recommended that temperature control is continued for at least 24 h in comatose post-cardiac arrest patients (Donnino et al. 2016); a constant temperature somewhere in the range 32–36°C but there was no consensus for any specific temperature within this range. Clinicians will need to decide locally which target temperature to adopt in their post resuscitation protocol but in the absence of clear benefit for 33°C compared with 36°C, many ICUs in the United Kingdom have adopted a target of 36°C.

Cooling techniques The practical application of targeted temperature management (TTM) comprises induction of cooling (unless the patient is already at target temperature), maintenance, and rewarming. Earlier cooling after ROSC probably produces better outcome. External or internal cooling techniques, or both, can be used to initiate cooling. Infusion of 30 ml kg^{-1} of 4°C 0.9% sodium chloride or Hartmann's solution decreases core temperature by approximately 1.5°C and, until recently, was thought to be well tolerated even in patients with post-cardiac arrest myocardial dysfunction (Holzer 2010). A recent randomized controlled trial in which post-cardiac arrest patients were assigned to either 2 litres of 4°C normal saline prehospital or standard care, showed no difference in survival to hospital discharge (Kim et al. 2014). Patients who received prehospital cold i.v. fluid were more likely than the control group to re-arrest during transport and to have pulmonary oedema on their initial chest X-ray. Thus, the use of prehospital i.v. cold fluid is not recommended (Donnino et al. 2016) but careful use (with close monitoring) in hospital is reasonable. Other methods of temperature control are listed in Box 91.1.

In most cases, it is easy to cool patients initially after ROSC because the temperature usually decreases spontaneously within this first hour. A confounder in many observational studies of TTM is that patients with the worse outcome tend to be faster to cool spontaneously (Benz-Woerner et al. 2012). Shivering is prevented with sedation and bolus doses of neuromuscular blocking drug. Magnesium sulfate (e.g. 5 g infused over 5 h) will reduce the shivering threshold.

Box 91.1 Methods for targeted temperature management

- Simple ice packs, wet towels, or both (inexpensive but may be more time-consuming for nursing staff, may result in greater temperature fluctuations, and do not enable controlled rewarming)
- Ice-cold fluids alone cannot be used to maintain hypothermia, but even the addition of simple ice packs may control the temperature adequately
- Cooling blankets or pads (Fig. 91.6)
- Water or air circulating blankets
- Water circulating gel-coated pads
- Intravascular heat exchanger, placed usually in the femoral or subclavian veins (Fig. 91.7)
- Cardiopulmonary bypass.

Maintenance of target temperature is best achieved with external (Fig. 91.6) or internal (Fig. 91.7) cooling devices that include continuous temperature feedback to achieve a set target temperature. The temperature is typically monitored from a thermistor placed in the bladder, oesophagus, or both. There are no data indicating that any specific cooling technique increases survival when compared with any other cooling technique; however, internal devices enable more precise temperature control compared with external techniques (Deye et al. 2015). The temperature is maintained in the target range (32–36°C) for 24 h followed by controlled rewarming at 0.25–0.5°C h^{-1} and strict avoidance of hyperthermia. Plasma electrolyte concentrations can change rapidly during cooling and rewarming—frequent measurement and careful electrolyte replacement is essential.

Physiological effects and complications of targeted temperature management The well-recognized physiological effects of TTM (Box 91.2) need to be managed carefully (Polderman 2004).

Contraindications to targeted temperature management Generally recognized contraindications to therapeutic hypothermia, but which are not applied universally, include severe systemic infection, established multiple organ failure, and pre-existing medical coagulopathy (fibrinolytic therapy is not a contraindication to therapeutic hypothermia).

Prognostication

Predicting the eventual outcome of those remaining comatose after initial resuscitation from cardiac arrest is difficult and there are many pitfalls. Clinicians would not wish to withdraw treatment if there is a realistic chance that the patient could eventually make a good neurological recovery; however, continued treatment of a patient who is not going to make a good recovery is potentially distressing for relatives and is expensive. Guidelines from the American Academy of Neurology published in 2006 indicated that 3 days after cardiac arrest and in the absence of sedation, a motor response to

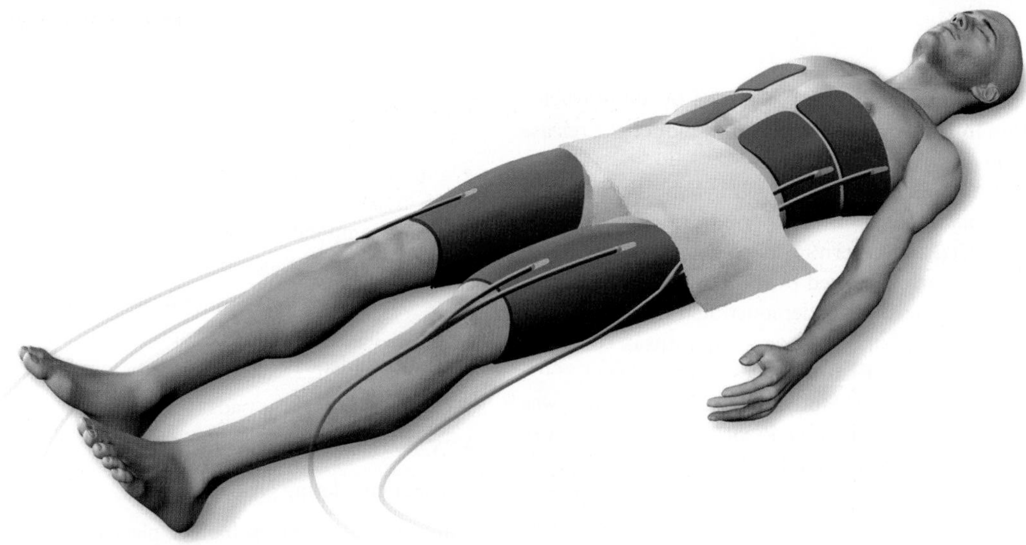

Figure 91.6 External temperature management system for inducing mild hypothermia in the post-cardiac arrest phase.
© 2016 C. R. Bard, Inc. Used with permission.

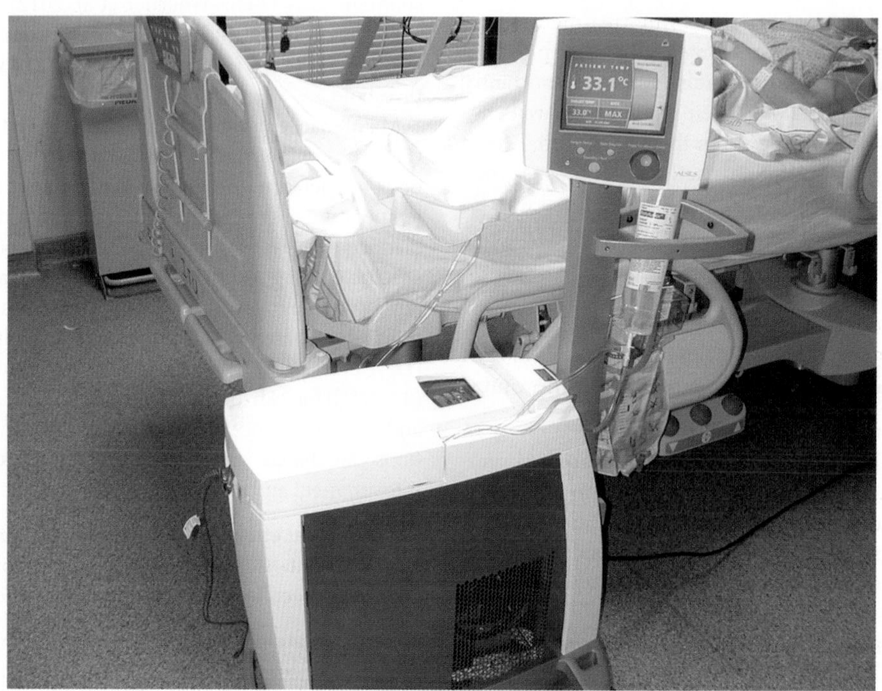

Figure 91.7 Intravascular temperature management system.
Reproduced with permission of Jerry Nolan. © 2013.

Box 91.2 Physiological effects and complications of mild hypothermia

- Shivering: increases metabolic and heat production, and reduces cooling rates
- Increased systemic vascular resistance, arrhythmias (usually bradycardia)
- Diuresis and electrolyte abnormalities such as hypophosphataemia, hypokalaemia, hypomagnesaemia, and hypocalcaemia
- Decreased insulin sensitivity and insulin secretion causing hyperglycaemia
- Impaired coagulation and increased bleeding
- Impaired immune response and increased infection, especially pneumonia
- Increased serum amylase
- Clearance of sedative drugs and neuromuscular blocking agents reduced by up to 30% at a core temperature of 34°C.

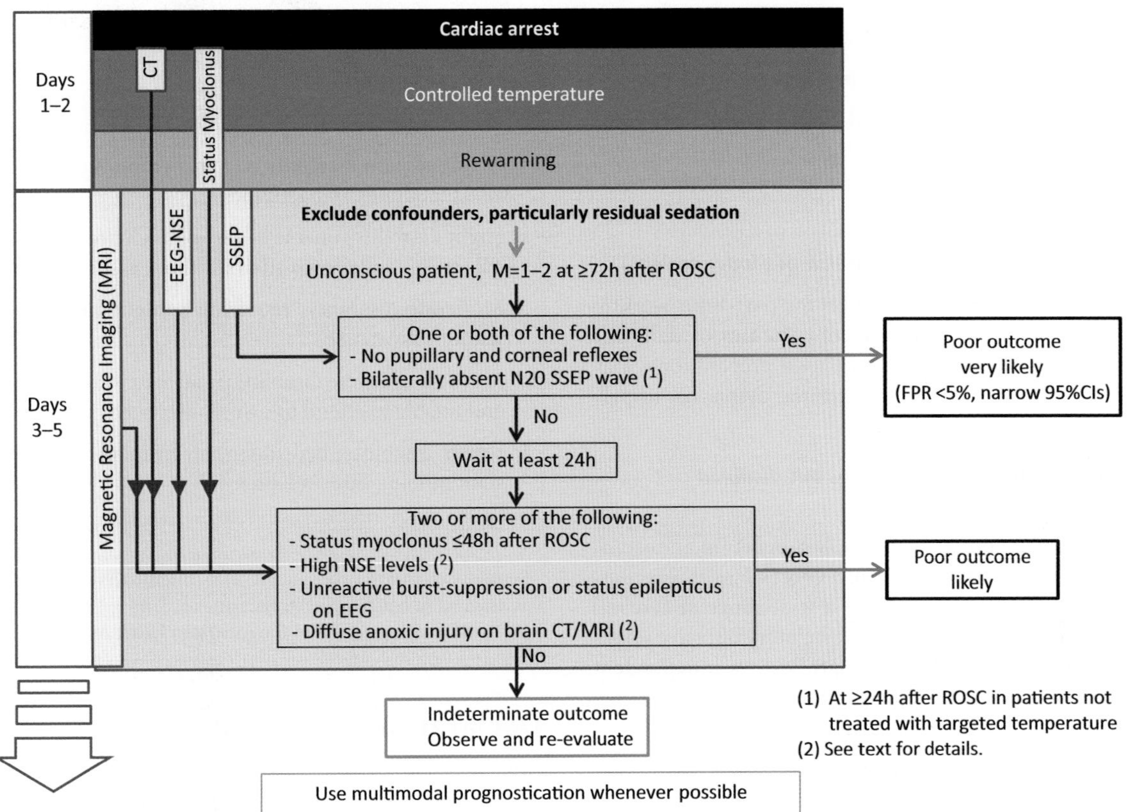

Figure 91.8 Prognostication algorithm. The algorithm is entered 72 h after ROSC if, after the exclusion of confounders (particularly residual sedation), the patient remains unconscious with a Glasgow Motor Score of 1 or 2. The absence of pupillary and corneal reflexes and/or bilaterally absent N20 SSEP wave indicate a poor outcome is very likely. If neither of the features is present, wait at least 24 h before reassessing. At this stage, two or more of the following indicate that a poor outcome is likely: status myoclonus ≤48 h; high neuron-specific enolase values; unreactive burst suppression or status epilepticus on EEG; diffuse anoxic injury on brain CT and/or MRI. If none of these criteria is met, consider continuing to observe and re-evaluate.

pain comprising extension or nothing, or fixed dilated pupils, or absent corneal reflexes, were reliable indications of a poor outcome (Wijdicks et al. 2006). However, these guidelines were based on data collected before the widespread implementation of therapeutic hypothermia. The use of hypothermia, and the increased sedation often given with this therapy, can delay recovery of motor response for 5–6 days after cardiac arrest (Oddo and Rossetti 2011; Bouwes et al. 2012; Sandroni et al. 2013; Kamps et al. 2013). Based on recent data, after use of therapeutic hypothermia, reliable prognostication cannot be achieved until at least 3 days after return to normothermia (Sandroni et al. 2013). European guidelines on prognostication after cardiac arrest recommend a multimodal approach (Sandroni et al. 2014; Oddo and Rossetti 2014; Nolan et al. 2015b) (Fig. 91.8). Full details are given in the European Guidelines document but in principle, a combination of the following modes is used to predict a poor outcome at least 3 days after cardiac arrest:

- Clinical examination: Glasgow Coma Scale score, pupillary response to light, corneal reflex, presence of seizures
- Neurophysiological studies: somatosensory evoked potentials and electroencephalography
- Biochemical markers: neuron-specific enolase is the most commonly used
- Imaging studies: brain CT and magnetic resonance imaging.

Organ donation

Up to 16% of patients who achieve sustained ROSC after cardiac arrest develop clinical brain death and can be considered for organ donation (Adrie et al. 2008). Transplant outcomes from the use of these organs are similar to those achieved with organs from other brain-dead donors (Sandroni et al. 2010). In Spain, in particular, highly proactive, controversial strategies are used to maximize the number of organs that can be donated after cardiac arrest. After OHCA, if ROSC is not achieved after 30 min of CPR by the EMS patients are transported to hospital with continuous CPR delivered by a mechanical device (Rodriguez-Arias and Deballon 2012). After death is declared in hospital, extracorporeal membrane oxygenation is started so that organs are preserved until consent for donation is given by the family. An aortic blocker is used to prevent blood flow to the potential donor's brain.

Long-term outcomes

In a systematic review of studies of quality of life among cardiac arrest survivors, 46 of 70 studies concluded that quality of life was good, 17 of the studies were neutral, and 7 studies concluded that quality of life was poor (Elliott et al. 2011). The difficulty is that the studies used a wide variety of assessment tools. Although some

Box 91.3 The Cerebral Performance Category Scale

1. Good cerebral performance (*normal life*)

Conscious, alert, able to work, and lead a normal life. May have minor psychological or neurological deficits (mild dysphasia, non-incapacitating hemiparesis, or minor cranial nerve abnormalities).

2. Moderate cerebral disability (*disabled but independent*)

Conscious. Sufficient cerebral function for part-time work in sheltered environment or independent activities of daily life (dress, travel by public transportation, food preparation). May have hemiplegia, seizures, ataxia, dysarthria, dysphasia, or permanent memory or mental changes.

3. Severe cerebral disability (*conscious but disabled and dependent*)

Conscious; dependent on others for daily support (in an institution or at home with exceptional family effort). Has at least limited cognition. This category includes a wide range of cerebral abnormalities, from patients who are ambulatory but have severe memory disturbances or dementia precluding independent existence to those who are paralysed and can communicate only with their eyes, as in the locked-in syndrome.

4. Coma/vegetative state (*unconscious*)

Unconscious, unaware of surroundings, no cognition. No verbal or psychological interaction with environment.

5. Brain death (*certified brain dead or dead by traditional criteria*)

Adapted with permission from *Annals of Emergency Medicine*, Volume 53, Issue 2, Stilel *et al.* Comparison of the Cerebral Performance Category Score and the Health Utilities Index for Survivors of Cardiac Arrest, pp. 241–248. Copyright © 2009 American College of Emergency Physicians.

investigators have concluded that cerebral performance category (CPC; Box 91.3), the most commonly used scale for indicating neurological outcome, provides a good indication of quality of life after cardiac arrest (Stiell et al. 2009), others have concluded that it is relatively insensitive (Elliott et al. 2011). Many cardiac arrest survivors have long-term memory problems (Mateen et al. 2011; Orbo et al. 2015; Sulzgruber et al. 2015) but would still be classified as CPC 1. Another weakness of the CPC scale is that it does not take into account the patient's pre-arrest neurological status—many of these patients may been CPC 2 or even CPC 3 before their cardiac arrest. For this reason, investigators of several recent, large CPR trials have used the modified Rankin scale (Bonita and Beaglehole 1988) (Box 91.4) to assess long-term neurological outcome. A modified Rankin score of 3 or lower is generally considered to represent a good outcome. In a recent large study that recruited more than 8000 OHCA patients in North America, 72% of survivors had a modified Rankin score of 3 or lower at the time of hospital discharge (Aufderheide et al. 2011b). Rehabilitation programmes may improve long-term cognitive function of cardiac arrest survivors (Moulaert et al. 2015).

Box 91.4 Modified Rankin Scale

Score	Description
0	No symptoms at all
1	No significant disability despite symptoms; able to carry out all usual duties and activities
2	Slight disability; unable to carry out all previous activities, but able to look after own affairs without assistance
3	Moderate disability; requiring some help, but able to walk without assistance
4	Moderately severe disability; unable to walk without assistance and unable to attend to own bodily needs without assistance
5	Severe disability; bedridden, incontinent and requiring constant nursing care and attention
6	Dead.

Reproduced from van Swieten JC et al. Interobserver agreement for the assessment of handicap in stroke patients. *Stroke*, 19: 604–607, Copyright 1988, with permission from the American Heart Association.

Declaration of interest

None declared.

References

Adrie C, Adib-Conquy M, Laurent I, *et al.* Successful cardiopulmonary resuscitation after cardiac arrest as a "sepsis-like" syndrome. *Circulation* 2002; **106**: 562–8

Adrie C, Haouache H, Saleh M, *et al.* An underrecognized source of organ donors: patients with brain death after successfully resuscitated cardiac arrest. *Intensive Care Med* 2008; **34**: 132–7

Aufderheide TP, Frascone RJ, Wayne MA, *et al.* Standard cardiopulmonary resuscitation versus active compression-decompression cardiopulmonary resuscitation with augmentation of negative intrathoracic pressure for out-of-hospital cardiac arrest: a randomised trial. *Lancet* 2011a; **377**: 301–11

Aufderheide TP, Nichol G, Rea TD, *et al.* A trial of an impedance threshold device in out-of-hospital cardiac arrest. *N Engl J Med* 2011b; **365**: 798–806

Bellomo R, Bailey M, Eastwood GM, *et al.* Arterial hyperoxia and in-hospital mortality after resuscitation from cardiac arrest. *Crit Care* 2011; **15**: R90

Benger J, Coates D, Greenwood R, *et al.* Randomised comparison of the effectiveness of the laryngeal mask airway supreme, i-gel and current practice in the initial airway management of out of hospital cardiac arrest: a feasibility study. *Br J Anaesth* 2016; **116**: 262--8

Benz-Woerner J, Delodder F, Benz R, *et al.* Body temperature regulation and outcome after cardiac arrest and therapeutic hypothermia. *Resuscitation* 2012; **83**: 338–42

Berdowski J, Berg RA, Tijssen JG, Koster RW. Global incidences of out-of-hospital cardiac arrest and survival rates: systematic review of 67 prospective studies. *Resuscitation* 2010; **81**: 1479–87

Bernard SA, Gray TW, Buist MD, *et al.* Treatment of comatose survivors of out-of-hospital cardiac arrest with induced hypothermia. *N Engl J Med* 2002; **346**: 557–63

Bisschops LL, Hoedemaekers CW, Simons KS, Van Der Hoeven JG. Preserved metabolic coupling and cerebrovascular reactivity during mild hypothermia after cardiac arrest. *Crit Care Med* 2010; **38**: 1542–7

Bonita R, Beaglehole R. Recovery of motor function after stroke. *Stroke* 1988; **19**: 1497–500

Bouwes A, Binnekade JM, Kuiper MA, *et al.* Prognosis of coma after therapeutic hypothermia: a prospective cohort study. *Ann Neurol* 2012; **71**: 206–12

Bouzat P, Suys T, Sala N, Oddo M. Effect of moderate hyperventilation and induced hypertension on cerebral tissue oxygenation after cardiac arrest and therapeutic hypothermia. *Resuscitation* 2013; **84**: 1540–5

Breitkreutz R, Price S, Steiger HV, *et al.* Focused echocardiographic evaluation in life support and peri-resuscitation of emergency patients: a prospective trial. *Resuscitation* 2010; **81**: 1527–33

Buck ML, Wiggins BS, Sesler JM. Intraosseous drug administration in children and adults during cardiopulmonary resuscitation. *Ann Pharmacother* 2007; **41**: 1679–86

Chan PS, Jain R, Nallmothu BK, Berg RA, Sasson C. Rapid response teams: a systematic review and meta-analysis. *Arch Intern Med* 2010; **170**: 18–26

Chen J, Ou L, Hillman K, *et al.* The impact of implementing a rapid response system: a comparison of cardiopulmonary arrests and mortality among four teaching hospitals in Australia. *Resuscitation* 2014; **85**: 1275–81

Chen YS, Lin JW, Yu HY, *et al.* Cardiopulmonary resuscitation with assisted extracorporeal life-support versus conventional cardiopulmonary resuscitation in adults with in-hospital cardiac arrest: an observational study and propensity analysis. *Lancet* 2008; **372**: 554–61

Cook TM, Woodall N, Harper J, Benger J, Fourth National Audit, Project. Major complications of airway management in the UK: results of the Fourth National Audit Project of the Royal College of Anaesthetists and the Difficult Airway Society. Part 2: intensive care and emergency departments. *Br J Anaesth* 2011; **106**: 632–42

Cueni-Villoz N, Devigili A, Delodder F, *et al.* Increased blood glucose variability during therapeutic hypothermia and outcome after cardiac arrest. *Crit Care Med* 2011; **39**: 2225–31

Daviaud F, Dumas F, Demars N, *et al.* Blood glucose level and outcome after cardiac arrest: insights from a large registry in the hypothermia era. *Intensive Care Med* 2014; **40**: 855–62

Devita MA, Smith GB, Adam SK, *et al.* "Identifying the hospitalised patient in crisis" – a consensus conference on the afferent limb of rapid response systems. *Resuscitation* 2010; **81**: 375–82

Deye N, Cariou A, Girardie P, *et al.* Endovascular versus external targeted temperature management for patients with out-of-hospital cardiac arrest: a randomized, controlled study. *Circulation* 2015; **132**: 182–93

Donnino M, Andersen LW, Berg KM, *et al.* Temperature management after cardiac arrest. An advisory statement by the Advanced Life Support Task Force of the International Liaison Committee on Resuscitation and the American Heart Association Emergency Cardiovascular Care Committee. *Resuscitation* 2016; **98**: 97–104

Dumas F, Cariou A, Manzo-Silberman S, *et al.* Immediate percutaneous coronary intervention is associated with better survival after out-of-hospital cardiac arrest: insights from the PROCAT (Parisian Region Out of hospital Cardiac ArresT) registry. *Circ Cardiovasc Interv* 2010; **3**: 200–7

Dumas F, Bougouin W, Geri G, *et al.* Emergency percutaneous coronary intervention in post-cardiac arrest patients without ST-segment elevation pattern. *Am Coll Cardiol Interv* 2016; **9**: 1011–8

Elliott VJ, Rodgers DL, Brett SJ. Systematic review of quality of life and other patient-centred outcomes after cardiac arrest survival. *Resuscitation* 2011; **82**: 247–56

Fromme EK, Zive D, Schmidt TA, Olszewski E, Tolle SW. POLST Registry do-not-resuscitate orders and other patient treatment preferences. *JAMA* 2012; **307**: 34–5

Gao H, Harrison DA, Parry GJ, Daly K, Subbe CP, Rowan K. The impact of the introduction of critical care outreach services in England: a multicentre interrupted time-series analysis. *Crit Care* 2007; **11**: R113

Girotra S, Nallamothu BK, Spertus JA, *et al.* Trends in survival after in-hospital cardiac arrest. *N Engl J Med* 2012; **367**: 1912–20

Grmec S. Comparison of three different methods to confirm tracheal tube placement in emergency intubation. *Intensive Care Med* 2002; **28**: 701–4

Grmec S, Kupnik D. Does the Mainz Emergency Evaluation Scoring (MEES) in combination with capnometry (MEESc) help in the prognosis of outcome from cardiopulmonary resuscitation in a prehospital setting? *Resuscitation* 2003; **58**: 89–96

Hagihara A, Hasegawa M, Abe T, Nagata T, Wakata Y, Miyazaki S. Prehospital epinephrine use and survival among patients with out-of-hospital cardiac arrest. *JAMA* 2012; **307**: 1161–8

Hillman K, Chen J, Cretikos M, *et al.* Introduction of the medical emergency team (MET) system: a cluster-randomised controlled trial. *Lancet* 2005; **365**: 2091–7

Holzer M. Targeted temperature management for comatose survivors of cardiac arrest. *N Engl J Med* 2010; **363**: 1256–64

Hostler D, Everson-Stewart S, Rea TD, *et al.* Effect of real-time feedback during cardiopulmonary resuscitation outside hospital: prospective, cluster-randomised trial. *BMJ* 2011; **342**: d512

Hypothermia after Cardiac Arrest Study Group. Mild therapeutic hypothermia to improve the neurologic outcome after cardiac arrest. *N Engl J Med* **346**: 549–56

Jacobs IG, Finn JC, Jelinek GA, Oxer HF, Thompson PL. Effect of adrenaline on survival in out-of-hospital cardiac arrest: a randomised double-blind placebo-controlled trial. *Resuscitation* 2011; **82**: 1138–43

Jones DA, Devita MA, Bellomo R. Rapid-response teams. *N Engl J Med* 2011; **365**: 139–46

Kamps MJ, Horn J, Oddo M, *et al.* Prognostication of neurologic outcome in cardiac arrest patients after mild therapeutic hypothermia: a meta-analysis of the current literature. *Intensive Care Med* 2013; **39**: 1671–82

Kause J, Smith G, Prytherch D, Parr M, Flabouris A, Hillman K. A comparison of antecedents to cardiac arrests, deaths and emergency intensive care admissions in Australia and New Zealand, and the United Kingdom – the ACADEMIA study. *Resuscitation* 2004; **62**: 275–82

Kilgannon JH, Jones AE, Shapiro NI, *et al.* Association between arterial hyperoxia following resuscitation from cardiac arrest and in-hospital mortality. *JAMA* 2010; **303**: 2165–71

Kim F, Nichol G, Maynard C, *et al.* Effect of prehospital induction of mild hypothermia on survival and neurological status among adults with cardiac arrest: a randomized clinical trial. *JAMA* 2014; **311**: 45–52

Krishna Ramachandran S, Mhyre J, Kheterpal S, *et al.* Predictors of survival from perioperative cardiopulmonary arrests: a retrospective analysis of 2,524 events from the Get With The Guidelines-Resuscitation registry. *Anesthesiology* 2013; **119**: 1322–39

Kudenchuk PJ, Brown SP, Daya M, *et al.* Amiodarone, Lidocaine, or Placebo in Out-of-Hospital Cardiac Arrest. *N Engl J Med* 2016; **374**: 1711–22

Laurent I, Monchi M, Chiche JD, *et al.* Reversible myocardial dysfunction in survivors of out-of-hospital cardiac arrest. *J Am Coll Cardiol* 2002; **40**: 2110–6

Laver S, Farrow C, Turner D, Nolan J. Mode of death after admission to an intensive care unit following cardiac arrest. *Intensive Care Med* 2004; **30**: 2126–8

Lemiale V, Dumas F, Mongardon N, *et al.* Intensive care unit mortality after cardiac arrest: the relative contribution of shock and brain injury in a large cohort. *Intensive Care Med* 2013; **39**: 1972–80

Lloyd-Jones D, Adams RJ, Brown TM, *et al.* Heart Disease and Stroke Statistics – 2010 Update: a report from the American Heart Association. *Circulation* 2010; **121**: e46–215

Lyon RM, Ferris JD, Young DM, McKeown DW, Oglesby AJ, Robertson C. Field intubation of cardiac arrest patients: a dying art? *Emerg Med J* 2010; **27**: 321–3

Mateen FJ, Josephs KA, Trenerry MR, *et al.* Long-term cognitive outcomes following out-of-hospital cardiac arrest: a population-based study. *Neurology* 2011; **77**: 1438–45

McDonnell A, Esmonde L, Morgan R, *et al.* The provision of critical care outreach services in England: findings from a national survey. *J Crit Care* 2007; **22**: 212–8

McNally B, Robb R, Mehta M, *et al.* Out-of-Hospital Cardiac Arrest Surveillance—Cardiac Arrest Registry to Enhance Survival (CARES), United States, October 1, 2005–December 31, 2010. *MMWR Surveill Summ* 2011; **60**: 1–19

Meaney PA, Bobrow BJ, Mancini ME, *et al.* Cardiopulmonary resuscitation quality: improving cardiac resuscitation outcomes both inside and outside the hospital: a consensus statement from the American Heart Association. *Circulation* 2013; **128**: 417–35

Meaney PA, Nadkarni VM, Kern KB, Indik JH, Halperin HR, Berg RA. Rhythms and outcomes of adult in-hospital cardiac arrest. *Crit Care Med* 2010; **38**: 101–8

Monsieurs K, Nolan JP, Bossaert LL, *et al.* European Resuscitation Council Guidelines for Resuscitation 2015 Section 1 Executive Summary. *Resuscitation* 2015; **95**: 1–80

Moulaert VR, Van Heugten CM, Winkens B, *et al.* Early neurologically-focused follow-up after cardiac arrest improves quality of life at one year: a randomised controlled trial. *Int J Cardiol* 2015; **193**: 8–16

Myerburg RJ, Junttila MJ. Sudden cardiac death caused by coronary heart disease. *Circulation* 2012; **125**: 1043–52

Nagao K, Kikushima K, Watanabe K, *et al.* Early induction of hypothermia during cardiac arrest improves neurological outcomes in patients with out-of-hospital cardiac arrest who undergo emergency cardiopulmonary bypass and percutaneous coronary intervention. *Circ J* 2010; **74**: 77–85

National Confidential Enquiry into Patient Outcome and Death. *An Acute Problem?* London: NCEPOD, 2005

Nichol G, Thomas E, Callaway CW, *et al.* Regional variation in out-of-hospital cardiac arrest incidence and outcome. *JAMA* 2008; **300**: 1423–31

Nielsen N, Sunde K, Hovdenes J, *et al.* Adverse events and their relation to mortality in out-of-hospital cardiac arrest patients treated with therapeutic hypothermia. *Crit Care Med* 2011; **39**: 57–64

Nielsen N, Wetterslev J, Al-Subaie N, *et al.* Target Temperature Management after out-of-hospital cardiac arrest--a randomized, parallel-group, assessor-blinded clinical trial--rationale and design. *Am Heart J* 2012; **163**: 541–8

Nolan JP, Hazinski MF, Aicken R, *et al.* Part I. Executive Summary: 2015 International Consensus on cardiopulmonary Resuscitation and Emergency Cardiovascular Care Science with Treatment Recommendations. *Resuscitation* 2015a; **95**: e1–e32

Nolan JP, Morley PT, Vanden Hoek TL, Hickey RW. Therapeutic hypothermia after cardiac arrest. An advisory statement by the Advancement Life support Task Force of the International Liaison committee on Resuscitation. *Resuscitation* 2003; **57**: 231–5

Nolan JP, Neumar RW, Adrie C, *et al.* Post-cardiac arrest syndrome: epidemiology, pathophysiology, treatment, and prognostication. A Scientific Statement from the International Liaison Committee on Resuscitation; the American Heart Association Emergency Cardiovascular Care Committee; the Council on Cardiovascular Surgery and Anesthesia; the Council on Cardiopulmonary, Perioperative, and Critical Care; the Council on Clinical Cardiology; the Council on Stroke. *Resuscitation* 2008; **79**: 350–79

Nolan JP, Soar J, Cariou A, *et al.* European Resuscitation Council and European Society of Intensive Care Medicine 2015 guidelines for post-resuscitation care. *Intensive Care Medicine* 2015b; **41**: 2039–56

Nolan JP, Soar J, Smith GB, *et al.* Incidence and outcome of in-hospital cardiac arrest in the United Kingdom National Cardiac Arrest Audit. *Resuscitation* 2014; **85**: 987–92

Nolan J, Soar J. *Resuscitation Guidelines 2015.* London: Resuscitation Council (UK), 2015. Available from https://www.resus.org.uk/resuscitation-guidelines/

Nunnally ME, O'Connor MF, Kordylewski H, Westlake B, Dutton RP. The incidence and risk factors for perioperative cardiac arrest observed in the national anesthesia clinical outcomes registry. *Anesth Analg* 2015; **120**: 364–70

Oddo M, Rossetti AO. Predicting neurological outcome after cardiac arrest. *Curr Opin Crit Care* 2011; **17**: 254–9

Oddo M, Rossetti AO. Early multimodal outcome prediction after cardiac arrest in patients treated with hypothermia. *Crit Care Med* 2014; **42**: 1340–7

Orbo M, Aslaksen PM, Larsby K, *et al.* Relevance of cognition to health-related quality of life in good-outcome survivors of out-of-hospital cardiac arrest. *J Rehabil Med* 2015; **47**: 860–6

Perbet S, Mongardon N, Dumas F, *et al.* Early-onset pneumonia after cardiac arrest: characteristics, risk factors and influence on prognosis. *Am J Respir Crit Care Med* 2011; **184**: 1048–54

Perkins GD, Lall R, Quinn T, *et al.* Mechanical versus manual chest compression for out-of-hospital cardiac arrest (PARAMEDIC): a pragmatic, cluster randomised controlled trial. *Lancet* 2015; **385**: 947–55

Pilcher J, Weatherall M, Shirtcliffe P, Bellomo R, Young P, Beasley R. The effect of hyperoxia following cardiac arrest—a systematic review and meta-analysis of animal trials. *Resuscitation* 2012; **83**: 417–22

Pokorna M, Necas E, Kratochvil J, Skripsky R, Andrlik M, Franek O. A sudden increase in partial pressure end-tidal carbon dioxide (P(ET)CO(2)) at the moment of return of spontaneous circulation. *J Emerg Med* 2010; **38**: 614–21

Polderman KH. Application of therapeutic hypothermia in the intensive care unit. Opportunities and pitfalls of a promising treatment modality - Part 2: Practical aspects and side effects. *Intensive Care Med* 2004; **30**: 757–69

Polderman KH. Mechanisms of action, physiological effects, and complications of hypothermia. *Crit Care Med* 2009; **37**: S186–202

Price S, Uddin S, Quinn T. Echocardiography in cardiac arrest. *Curr Opin Crit Care* 2010; **16**: 211–5

Prosen G, Krizmaric M, Zavrsnik J, Grmec S. Impact of modified treatment in echocardiographically confirmed pseudo-pulseless electrical activity in out-of-hospital cardiac arrest patients with constant end-tidal carbon dioxide pressure during compression pauses. *J Int Med Res* 2010; **38**: 1458–67

Radsel P, Knafelj R, Kocjancic S, Noc M. Angiographic characteristics of coronary disease and postresuscitation electrocardiograms in patients with aborted cardiac arrest outside a hospital. *Am J Cardiol* 2011; **108**: 634–8

Resuscitation Council (UK). Adult advanced life support. 2015. Available from https://www.resus.org.uk/resuscitation-guidelines/adult-advanced-life-support

Roberts BW, Kilgannon JH, Chansky ME, Mittal N, Wooden J, Trzeciak S. Association between postresuscitation partial pressure of arterial carbon dioxide and neurological outcome in patients with post-cardiac arrest syndrome. *Circulation* 2013; **127**: 2107–13

Rodriguez-Arias D, Deballon IO. Protocols for uncontrolled donation after circulatory death. *Lancet* 2012; **379**: 1275–6

Rubertsson S, Lindgren E, Smekal D, *et al.* Mechanical chest compressions and simultaneous defibrillation vs conventional cardiopulmonary resuscitation in out-of-hospital cardiac arrest: the LINC randomized trial. *JAMA* 2014; **311**: 53–61

Sandroni C, Adrie C, Cavallaro F, *et al.* Are patients brain-dead after successful resuscitation from cardiac arrest suitable as organ donors? A systematic review. *Resuscitation* 2010; **81**: 1609–14

Sandroni C, Cariou A, Cavallaro F, *et al.* Prognostication in comatose survivors of cardiac arrest: An advisory statement from the European Resuscitation Council and the European Society of Intensive Care Medicine. *Intensive Care Med* 2014; **40**: 1816–31

Sandroni C, Cavallaro F, Callaway CW, *et al.* Predictors of poor neurological outcome in adult comatose survivors of cardiac arrest: a systematic review and meta-analysis. Part 2: Patients treated with therapeutic hypothermia. *Resuscitation* 2013; **84**: 1324–38

Sheak KR, Wiebe DJ, Leary M, *et al.* Quantitative relationship between end-tidal carbon dioxide and CPR quality during both in-hospital and out-of-hospital cardiac arrest. *Resuscitation* 2015; **89**: 149–54

Shin TG, Choi JH, Jo IJ, *et al.* Extracorporeal cardiopulmonary resuscitation in patients with inhospital cardiac arrest: A comparison with conventional cardiopulmonary resuscitation. *Crit Care Med* 2011; **39**: 1–7

Sideris G, Voicu S, Dillinger JG, *et al.* Value of post-resuscitation electrocardiogram in the diagnosis of acute myocardial infarction in out-of-hospital cardiac arrest patients. *Resuscitation* 2011; **82**: 1148–53

Smith GB. In-hospital cardiac arrest: is it time for an in-hospital 'chain of prevention'? *Resuscitation* 2010; **81**: 1209–11

Soar J, Nolan JP, Bottiger BW, *et al.* European Resuscitation Council Guidelines for Resuscitation 2015 Section 3 Adult Advanced Life Support. *Resuscitation* 2015; **95**: 99–146

Staer-Jensen H, Nakstad ER, Fossum E, *et al.* Post-resuscitation ECG for selection of patients for immediate coronary angiography in out-of-hospital cardiac arrest. *Circ Cardiovasc Interv* 2015; **8**: e002784

Stiell IG, Brown SP, Christenson J, *et al.* What is the role of chest compression depth during out-of-hospital cardiac arrest resuscitation? *Crit Care Med* 2012; **40**: 1192–8

Stiell IG, Nesbitt LP, Nichol G, *et al.* Comparison of the Cerebral Performance Category score and the Health Utilities Index for survivors of cardiac arrest. *Ann Emerg Med* 2009; **53**: 241–8

Sulzgruber P, Kliegel A, Wandaller C, *et al.* Survivors of cardiac arrest with good neurological outcome show considerable impairments of memory functioning. *Resuscitation* 2015; **88**: 120–5

Sykes MK. Organization of a resuscitation service and results of treatment. *Proc R Soc Med* 1964; **57**: 372–5

Sykes MK, Orr DS. Cardio-pulmonary resuscitation. A report on two years' experience. *Anaesthesia* 1966; **21**: 363–371

Tagami T, Kushimoto S, Tosa R, *et al.* The precision of PiCCO(R) measurements in hypothermic post-cardiac arrest patients. *Anaesthesia* 2012; **67**: 236–43

Tortorici MA, Kochanek PM, Poloyac SM. Effects of hypothermia on drug disposition, metabolism, and response: a focus of hypothermia-mediated alterations on the cytochrome P450 enzyme system. *Crit Care Med* 2007; **35**: 2196–204

Wagner H, Terkelsen CJ, Friberg H, *et al.* Cardiac arrest in the catheterisation laboratory: a 5-year experience of using mechanical chest compressions to facilitate PCI during prolonged resuscitation efforts. *Resuscitation* 2010; **81**: 383–7

Wang HE, Simeone SJ, Weaver MD, Callaway CW. Interruptions in cardiopulmonary resuscitation from paramedic endotracheal intubation. *Ann Emerg Med* 2009; **54**: 645–52.e1

Wijdicks EF, Hijdra A, Young GB, Bassetti CL, Wiebe S. Practice parameter: prediction of outcome in comatose survivors after cardiopulmonary resuscitation (an evidence-based review): report of the Quality Standards Subcommittee of the American Academy of Neurology. *Neurology* 2006; **67**: 203–10

Wik L, Olsen JA, Persse D, *et al.* Manual vs. integrated automatic load-distributing band CPR with equal survival after out of hospital cardiac arrest. The randomized CIRC trial. *Resuscitation* 2014; **85**: 741–8

Yeung J, Meeks R, Edelson D, Gao F, Soar J, Perkins GD. The use of CPR feedback/prompt devices during training and CPR performance: a systematic review. *Resuscitation* 2009; **80**: 743–51

Zia A, Kern KB. Management of postcardiac arrest myocardial dysfunction. *Curr Opin Crit Care* 2011; **17**: 241–6

Zuercher M, Hilwig RW, Ranger-Moore J, *et al.* Leaning during chest compressions impairs cardiac output and left ventricular myocardial blood flow in piglet cardiac arrest. *Crit Care Med* 2010; **38**: 1141–6

Zuercher M, Ummenhofer W. Cardiac arrest during anesthesia. *Curr Opin Crit Care* 2008; **14**: 269–74

Index

Tables, figures, and boxes are indicated by an italic *t*, *f*, and *b* following the page number